BASEBALL PROSPECTUS 2022

The Essential Guide to the 2022 Season

Edited by Patrick Dubuque, Craig Goldstein and Robert O'Connell

Darius Austin, Emma Baccellieri, Demetrius Bell, Sydney Bergman, Daniel Brim, Grant Brisbee, Russell A. Carleton, Ben Carsley, Alex Chamberlain, Michael Clair, Alex Coffey, Zach Crizer, Patrick Dubuque, Mike Duncan, Daniel R. Epstein, Drew Fairservice, Connor Farrell, James Fegan, Chad Finn, Noah Frank, Bailey Freeman, Ken Funck, Brendan Gawlowski, Mike Gianella, Steven Goldman, Bryan Grosnick, Jon Hegglund, Justin Klugh, Patrick Lackey, Rob Mains, Kelsey McKinney, Dan McQuade, Brian Menéndez, Steve Neuman, Joan Niesen, Alva Noë, Marc Normandin, Dustin Nosler, Robert O'Connell, Jeffrey Paternostro, Gary Phillips, Mike Piellucci, Kate Preusser, Tommy Rancel, Matthew Ritchie, David Roth, Shaker Samman, Janice Scurio, Ginny Searle, Jarrett Seidler, Jordan Shusterman, Susan Slusser, Ben Spanier, Matt Sussman, Michael Tae Sweeney, Jon Tayler, Shakeia Taylor, Lauren Theisen, John Trupin, Levi Weaver, Collin Whitchurch, Tony Wolfe, Alex Wong

Cliff Corcoran and Bret Sayre, Associate Editors
Robert Au, Harry Pavlidis and Amy Pircher, Statistics Editors

Library of Congress Cataloging-in-Publication Data:
paperback
ISBN-10: 1950716902
ISBN-13: 978-1950716906

Project Credits
Cover Design: Ginny Searle
Interior Design and Production: Amy Pircher, Robert Au
Layout: Amy Pircher, Robert Au

Cover Photos
Front Cover: Juan Soto. © Orlando Ramirez-USA TODAY Sports

Baseball icon courtesy of Uberux, from https://www.shareicon.net/author/uberux

Manufactured in the United States of America
10 9 8 7 6 5 4 3 2 1

This book is dedicated to our friend Rob McQuown.

Thanks for the research, and for everything else.

Table of Contents

NL West

AL West

Foreword

by Doug Glanville

When you play professionally for a long time, you hope that people will see value in your game that is impossible to measure. That your game has soul—intangibles that capture the magic you create. Yet, those of us who love baseball also have a love affair with numbers that demands that we count and keep on counting.

During my year-plus in Double-A, the Cubs had an initiative that measured "winning baseball." It was a chart with all of these columns where you could earn points or lose points (they called the latter demerits). The columns were not full of traditional statistics. Instead, they had "move the runner over with two outs" or "get down the sacrifice bunt" or "hit the cutoff man."

I was consistently a points leader, but when it came down to it, when the higher-ups checked in, the questions naturally went right back to "well, why is he only hitting .246?" I was not exactly putting up earth-shattering, first-round-pick production, but I was playing "winning baseball." I recall having shared frustration with my hitting coach, Ernie Rosseau, who noted I was embracing these new metrics while relegating the traditional ones. It was an early lesson in what ethicist Tom Murray would say quite often: "You reward what you value." And if you truly believed these data points were valuable (aka winning), then it was important to stand behind them.

Unless we fight for it, we will continue to measure the same values that become so entrenched that they are indistinguishable from measuring 90 feet from home to first.

Why measure a constant?

Baseball has always had an obsession with contextualizing numbers to understand its past (potential), to frame its present (performance) and to anticipate its future (prediction)—three distinct career time zones that constantly change, circling a debate that will remain eternal.

That eternity is a result of an unsolvable equation that contains multiple variables that torment us at times and exhilarate us at others. But just as in our everyday life, we will never outrun time; it remains a variable that creeps in the shadows, making context a moving target.

As a big-league player, I was mostly known as a contact hitter with speed and defense. But I played at a time of deep stat inflation. The numbers were artificially enhanced by performance-enhancing drugs, beginning a significant run of annual record-setting league home-run totals and the doubt that comes when every performer is viewed with skepticism. This has left the Baseball Hall of Fame induction process in shambles, as voters and fans alike struggle to identify authenticity.

However, in my career, it started right from the day I was drafted.

I was drafted one pick ahead of Manny Ramirez. So with the benefit of hindsight, that would be a laughable mistake by the Cubs' scouting department (and the other 11 teams that picked before the Cubs.) Yet, the numbers fail us because they cannot reconsider measures of enhanced performance on their own, nor decide how to weigh what it means to play clean versus not to. Is there a world where I was a better selection than Ramirez? Maybe, but we would have to create it—and enforce it.

Our metrics need guidance, a sense of value, a moral code of sorts to help produce an outcome that has meaning to us all. Yet, this collision of the quantitative and the qualitative will always be a seesaw that remains in motion, one that will never allow us to remain in equilibrium for long.

In response, we cannot simply choose to play in our own world for the sake of control. We are responsible for the relativity that lies are at the heart of competition; at its best, competition that is fair. An effort that requires constant vigilance. We learned that numbers do lie because we lie to ourselves, telling the numbers where to go and what to find. That is, unless we yield to time so it can do its work and leave us with the fossils of hard truths, no matter how much dirt the beneficiaries of inflation may have poured on them.

I interviewed with the Tampa Bay Rays in 2014, and I was pleasantly surprised that hardly any of their questions related to tactical decisions in response to in-game scenarios. They cared about how I would deal with a disgruntled aging starting pitcher, how I would manage pre-game stretch, or when I would call a team meeting.

I did not get that job, but not long afterwards, when I was interviewing Rays center fielder Kevin Kiermaier before a game, I ran into Rays President of Baseball Operations Erik Neander, who was part of my interview process. I asked him about Kiermaier, his contract and his defense. Neander's response was, "never will someone like Kevin Kiermaier be underappreciated again."

Selfishly, as a glove man, that was music to my ears. Somehow, the data had taken us to a future that would shine brighter on my past as a defender (although it probably does not help me when it comes to walk-rate and on-base percentage). The fact that I played extremely shallow or backed up on every single ball never played much into what was being measured. Shallow play may not translate to defensive runs saved as a way to win a Gold Glove today, but at least someone was in tune with these aspects of defense to assess defensive performance, and thus defensive value, in a more granular way. Feedback by which I could have made adjustments, just as when my coach, the late John Vukovich, set me on a path to playing shallower by telling me directly, "You need to play shallower. You like going back on balls."

That is how we change the past, by letting the future inform our understanding of it. Today, I look at the conversation with "Vuk" as if he was predicting the future.

When my kids were at that stage when they all could get into the minivan but could barely buckle themselves in, I became inspired to measure this new world—one with constant snacks, unexpected meltdowns and sheer chaos. Quantifying it became a therapeutic way to survive the unfamiliar mayhem, a big departure from my final major-league days spent living in a non-kid-friendly environment; the one I settled into after the 2003 NLCS, when I was single, driving a Range Rover and willing to pay $100 to fill up a gas tank.

So I started writing *The Daddy Games*, a parenting blog to capture the insanity of it all. I talked about everything from the time my son mysteriously managed to get a knot on his head during a piano lesson, to the alien dance we call "dinner" with four kids under 10.

The blog featured my own statistical creations—Cheerios per Hour, Tooth Decay Decay (yes, "Decay" is twice) Rate, Misaligned Reason Zone, or even Re-Backing Retrofit Excuse Rate—metrics that made sense of the world we lived in as parents. The kids did not care about much that was quantifiable; in fact, many could barely count at that point in time, but they expanded my sensibilities in two directions. One direction made me try to measure an experience that is like no other, a seemingly impossible task, but an effort that reminds me so much of what I enjoy about baseball. The other was to teach me why it is important not to always measure.

I brought that to my love of baseball. That no matter how far we drill down, we will not be all-knowing. In fact, when we capture an elegant measure of performance, we also change the past and how we see it. It is a beautiful equilibrium and part of why we will never know how to fully compare the 1927 Yankees to the 2027 Yankees. But we have to do it anyway, because we will learn a lot by trying.

Baseball Prospectus is chock full of data that has made me a better analyst of the game that I have covered for more than a decade now. What I appreciate about what it has done in these pages is elevate the humanity of the game. The writers of the scouting reports do not just analyze, they express hope, they makes us laugh, they tell the story of these players. That's something that I deeply value because I was one of those guys—a player that wanted people to understand that my Triple-A manager made my life a nightmare, and that I played between 2000 and 2002 with my father constantly in and out of a hospital until he passed the day I notched my 1000th hit in the final game of the 2002 season.

Sure, empathy is not a reason to draft me, or trade me for Chipper Jones. It is not a reason to put me in the starting lineup, or vote for me for the Hall of Fame. As a player, I fully understand that.

But I also understand that, without knowing who these players are, and what their stories tell, we will never embrace the full meaning of how they perform. Or why they perform. And when we find meaning in others' journeys, we tend to look for it in our own.

I want to thank Baseball Prospectus for this opportunity to write freely about the game I have loved since I could pick up a bat. In the following pages, you will learn about teams and players to a depth that will make you a much more informed keeper of the game. You will also pick up expressions, like I did one year when I found a term that perfectly described my offensive approach: "hacktastic."

Still, we must remember, behind every data point is a story, and behind every story is a baseball. ■

—Doug Glanville is a baseball analyst and multi-media journalist for ESPN and for the Chicago Cubs on Marquee Sports Network, an Emmy-winning writer and television show host, a professor at the University of Connecticut, the author of The Game from Where I Stand *and a retired MLB player.*

Statistical Introduction

by Bryan Grosnick

The history of baseball is a history of numbers. What started on the scoreboard moved through the advent of the box score, to the backs of baseball cards, to *Moneyball* and well beyond. Statistics have long helped so many people better understand the history, the personalities and the stories of baseball in so many ways. While the study of statistics is not the only way to enjoy America's pastime, it is one of the ways that we here at Baseball Prospectus have engaged with baseball and shared our love of the game over 26 editions of this very Annual and nearly 30 years online.

What this section of the book is designed to do is help you get familiar with some of the metrics that we think help tell the story of baseball. Our hope is that these give you a new way to engage with the game we all care so much about, or at least give you something else to think about or discuss during your next conversation. *"Who's better, Carlos Correa or Corey Seager?" "How many games do you think the Rays will win next season?" "Why is Jacob deGrom so good?"* Our statistics might help you think differently about these questions, or a million others.

As always, if you have any questions about how a metric is developed, what it's trying to measure, or what an acronym stands for, stop by the Baseball Prospectus website and check out our Glossary, search for an article, or engage directly with our team. Our goal is to share our love of the game—and its statistics—with you.

Offense

If you're interested in learning how *good* a hitter was in a given year, or over their career, start with our proprietary metric Deserved Runs Created Plus (**DRC+**). Built by Jonathan Judge in concert with our stats team, this metric measures everything that a hitter can do at the dish. Not only does this measure whether the player got a hit, reached base via some other means, or made an out, it also integrates hitting for power and moving runners over. It's also scaled so that **a DRC+ of 100 is roughly equivalent to league-average performance**. In short, a DRC+ of 150 is outstanding, a DRC+ of 100 is average, and a DRC+ of 75 means that you're probably not an everyday player, no matter how fantastic your defense is.

What makes DRC+ special is how it accounts not just for the events that take place (hits, strikeouts, homers, etc.), but how it takes *context* into account. The model behind DRC+ adjusts for how the ballpark affects play, the talent of the opposing pitcher, league, temperature, and other factors. Not only does it tell us how successful a player was, it also does a better job of predicting how that same player *will do in the future* than any other statistic we've found over the years. (We'll talk more about predicting the future later.)

DRC+ does not account for baserunning, so we use Baserunning Runs (**BRR**) to give runners credit for what they do between the bags. That certainly includes the value gained or lost during an attempted stolen base, but also includes things like going first to third on a single or advancing on an outfield fly.

Defense

Our key defensive metric is Fielding Runs Above Average (**FRAA**), which represents the positive or negative value offered by a player's actions in run prevention. Defining defensive value is trickier than offensive value; instead of the relatively straightforward, one-on-one, batter-versus-pitcher dynamic, fielding can involve a lot more subjectivity depending on how balls are hit, fielder positioning and plenty of other factors. Most "advanced" defensive metrics are based on "zone" data: statisticians record batted-ball type and estimated landing location, and feed this data into models that generate expected outs compared to actual outs.

FRAA does *not* use zone data for two primary reasons: the noise and unintentional bias in zone-based fielding analysis, and the fact that most zone data is private, instead of public. Instead, FRAA (for all positions other than catcher) is built from play-by-play data: we count the number of fielding plays made by each player, then compare that to expected plays for an average fielder at their position, based on the ground-ball tendencies of the pitchers they played behind and the handedness of the batters those pitchers faced. After that, we adjust for park and base-out situations to get our FRAA number. By doing this, we avoid the subjectivity that's found in other fielding metrics.

The toughest and most-critical defensive position on the field requires a different methodology than the one we've just outlined. Catchers not only have to "field their position" like everyone else on the diamond, they also have to prevent pitches from sailing through to the backstop, prevent baserunners from stealing, and "frame" pitches to make them more (or less) likely to be called strikes.

This last part, typically called "pitch framing" or "presentation," is the trickiest to quantify and one of the major sabermetric innovations of the last dozen years. Our mixed-model approach takes pitch-tracking data (for the seasons that data exists) and adjusts for factors including pitcher, umpire, batter and home-field advantage. That gives us a number of strikes that the catcher is adding to a pitcher's performance, which we convert to runs added or lost using linear weights.

These framing runs have a significant effect on a catcher's overall defensive value (though a bit less this year than in some previous years, as framing skill appears to have improved across the game). When they are combined with the runs added or lost from pitch blocking, stolen base prevention, and fielding balls in play, we get our final FRAA number for catchers.

Pitching

Here at Baseball Prospectus, we do our best to separate the effects of pitching from the effects of fielding, in order to better isolate each pitcher's contribution to run prevention. As a community, we've come a long way from the initial sabermetric theory that pitchers have little control over balls in play, and we've created a detailed "defense-independent" pitching metric that also includes some measure of how pitchers influence balls in play.

Deserved Run Average (**DRA**) is our core pitching metric that evaluates a pitcher's performance in a way that *looks a lot like earned run average (ERA), but is actually very different under the hood*. For starters, DRA is set to the scale of runs allowed per nine innings (RA9), instead of *earned* runs, so DRA numbers tend to be a touch higher than what you'd normally expect from ERA.

When creating DRA, we start with an event-by-event look at everything the pitcher does on the mound, and then we adjust the value of each event based on environmental factors including park, batter, catcher, umpire, base-out situation, run differential, inning, home-field advantage, pitcher role, temperature and (most recently) plate difference—this accounts for pitchers who "tunnel," or throw consecutive pitches that look similar to the hitter but ultimately behave differently. We use a mixed-model approach including all these factors that is similar to our DRC+ and FRAA model (which also includes the pitcher's effect on stolen bases and passed balls/wild pitches) in order to get our final DRA number.

In addition to the DRA number (that looks a lot like ERA), we also share **DRA–**, which is very similar to our DRC+ number for hitters. It is a simple way to compare performance to "average," with a DRA– of 100 indicating middle-of-the-road performance. Since we're used to pitcher statistics like ERA for which lower numbers are better, good performance is represented as lower than 100; a DRA– of 75 tells you that a pitcher is about 25% better than league average. On the other side, a DRA– of 150 tells you that things are going very, very poorly for the pitcher in question.

Projections

For those of you who wish to go beyond what a player *did* and want to discover what they *will do*, we have our **PECOTA** projections. These days, PECOTA bears very little resemblance to the original product created by Nate Silver in the early 2000s, and uses none of Silver's spreadsheets or code. Today, PECOTA builds a 10-year forecast of a player's projected future performance based on that player's past, the tendencies of professional ballplayers in the major, minor, and overseas leagues, and factors including the effects of age and the locations where players take the field.

What makes PECOTA unique among public projection systems is that it doesn't just provide a point estimate, but also a *probability distribution* for each player. The point estimate you see in this book is the median forecast, but, on our website, you can find further information as to how much better or worse a player might be if that median forecast doesn't pan out. Please keep in mind that all forecasts have uncertainty, and our goal with PECOTA, beyond simple accuracy, is to make clear both how uncertain our forecasts are, as well as what the rest of that probability distribution can look like.

Now that the basics are out of the way, it's time to break down everything we're including in the book this year.

Team Prospectus

The heart of this book is the team chapter; you'll find one for each of the 30 major-league franchises . . . rest assured that we did not forget the Cardinals this year. The first page of each chapter includes a box that includes a stadium diagram as well as key statistics for the team in question. (On this page, you can see an example for the Baltimore Orioles.)

Beneath the team name, you'll find the team's un-adjusted 2021 win-loss record and its ranking within its division. Then it's on to 12 important statistics that give you a picture of how the team performed, holistically, over the course of the previous season. Each of those statistics gives you the value for the team, as well as the ordinal ranking among the 30 MLB teams (with 1st always "best" and 30th the "worst").

Pythag (short for "Pythagenpat") is an adjusted version of the team's 2021 winning percentage calculated based on runs scored per game (**RS/G**) and runs allowed per game (**RA/G**). Those numbers are run through a version of Bill James' Pythagorean formula that has been refined and improved by David Smyth and Brandon Heipp. We also include Deserved Winning Percentage (**dWin%**), which uses the frameworks that underpin DRC+ and DRA (along with depth charts) to estimate team runs scored and allowed in 2021 as the inputs for the same Pythagenpat formula used above. Then we have **Payroll**, which is the combined salary of all of the team's on-field players, as well as Marginal Dollars per Marginal Win (**M$/MW**). The latter metric, developed by Doug Pappas, tells us how much money the team spent for each win above the replacement level.

In the right-hand column, we start with Defensive Efficiency Rating (**DER**), which indicates the percentage of balls in play converted to outs for the team and serves as a quick shorthand for team-fielding skill. Then there's **DRC+** to indicate the overall offensive ability of the team as compared to league average, and **DRA–** to indicate the overall pitching ability of the team, as well. Beneath DRA– is another pitching metric: Fielding Independent Pitching (**FIP**), which resembles ERA but is based only on strikeouts, walks and home runs recorded by the team's pitchers. Finally, we have **B-Age** to tell us the average age of a team's batters (weighted by plate appearances), and **P-Age** to do the same for the team's pitchers (weighted by innings pitched), with the corresponding rankings going from youngest (1st) to oldest (30th).

After the stats, we focus on the home ballpark for each franchise. First, there's a lovely diagram of the park's dimensions including distances to the outfield wall. After a couple of bullet points about the playing surface and history of the park, there's a graphic that indicates the height of the wall from left-field pole to right-field pole. Then we offer a table with the single-season park factors for the stadium. Like DRC+ and DRA–, these factors are displayed as indexes: 100 is average, 110 means that the park inflates the relevant statistic by 10 percent, and 90 means that the park deflates the relevant statistic by 10 percent. On this table, we show **Runs** (runs scored), **Runs/RH** (runs produced by right-handed hitters), **Runs/LH** (runs produced by left-handed hitters), **HR/RH** (home runs by right-handed hitters) and **HR/LH** (home runs by left-handed hitters).

Lastly, we indicate the team's top hitter and pitcher by our Wins Above Replacement Player (**WARP**) metric (which we'll explain a little later in this section), as well as the player we've identified as the team's top prospect.

The second page of each team chapter features three graphs. **Payroll History** compares the team payroll to MLB average and the average for the team's division over time.

Graph number two is **Future Commitments** and displays the team's future payroll outlays, if any exist. Due in part to the labor stoppage and time of printing of this book, these figures (current as of January 1, 2022) will ultimately change before Opening Day. (Check Baseball Prospectus' Cot's Baseball Contracts page for the most current data.)

Farm System Ranking, the third and final graph, shows how the Baseball Prospectus prospect team has ranked this organization's farm system each year, going back 10 years.

After that, we have a **Personnel** section that lists some of the important decision-makers and upper-level field- or operations-staff members for the franchise. We also like to share the names of any former Baseball Prospectus staff members who are currently part of the organization, and occasionally someone shows up on both of those lists!

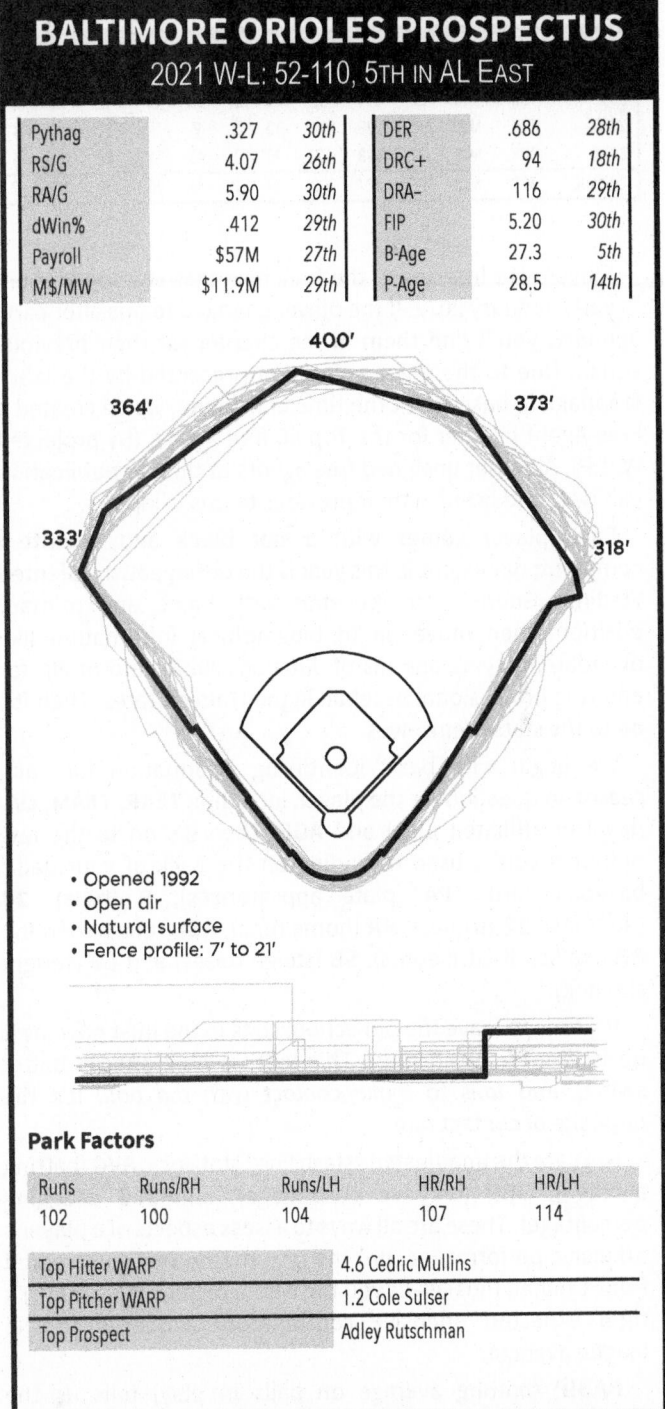

BALTIMORE ORIOLES PROSPECTUS

2021 W-L: 52-110, 5TH IN AL EAST

Pythag	.327	*30th*	DER	.686	*28th*
RS/G	4.07	*26th*	DRC+	94	*18th*
RA/G	5.90	*30th*	DRA–	116	*29th*
dWin%	.412	*29th*	FIP	5.20	*30th*
Payroll	$57M	*27th*	B-Age	27.3	*5th*
M$/MW	$11.9M	*29th*	P-Age	28.5	*14th*

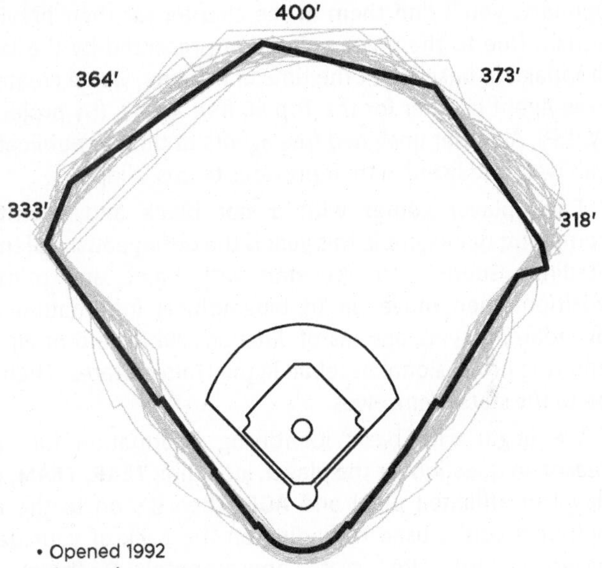

- Opened 1992
- Open air
- Natural surface
- Fence profile: 7′ to 21′

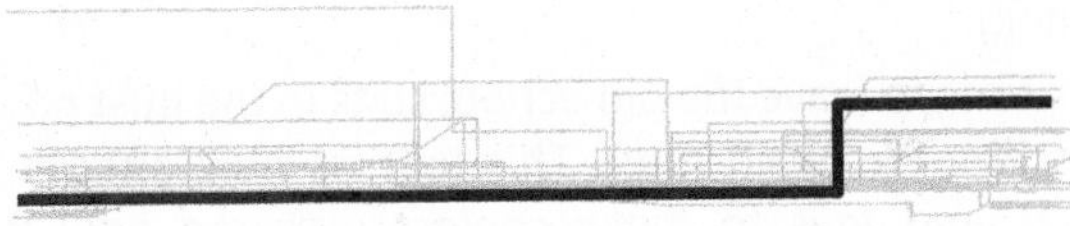

Park Factors

Runs	Runs/RH	Runs/LH	HR/RH	HR/LH
102	100	104	107	114

Top Hitter WARP	4.6 Cedric Mullins
Top Pitcher WARP	1.2 Cole Sulser
Top Prospect	Adley Rutschman

Position Players

After all the franchise-centric information and a carefully-crafted essay on the team, it's time for the player comments. (The player comments come with a byline or two, but that's a rough guide; due to player movement, each comment is not guaranteed to match the franchise byline.)

Vladimir Guerrero Jr. 1B Born: 03/16/99 Age: 23 Bats: R Throws: R Height: 6'2" Weight: 250 lb. Origin: International Free Agent, 2015

YEAR	TEAM	LVL	AGE	PA	R	2B	3B	HR	RBI	BB	K	SB	CS	Whiff%	AVG/OBP/SLG	DRC+	BABIP	BRR	FRAA	WARP
2019	BUF	AAA	20	34	7	1	0	3	8	4	2	1	0		.367/.441/.700	138	.320	-0.1	3B(7): 0.1	0.2
2019	TOR	MLB	20	514	52	26	2	15	69	46	91	0	1	24.5%	.272/.339/.433	104	.308	-3.1	3B(96): -4.5	0.8
2020	TOR	MLB	21	243	34	13	2	9	33	20	38	1	0	24.7%	.262/.329/.462	116	.282	-0.8	1B(34): 1.8	1.1
2021	TOR	MLB	22	698	123	29	1	48	111	86	110	4	1	27.8%	.311/.401/.601	158	.313	-2.4	1B(133): -6.4, 3B(1): -0.0	5.7
2022 DC	*TOR*	*MLB*	*23*	*621*	*112*	*27*	*2*	*33*	*109*	*70*	*109*	*2*	*2*	*27.0%*	*.299/.386/.540*	*148*	*.323*	*-0.6*	*1B -2*	*5.0*

Comparables: Rafael Devers, Mike Trout, Jason Heyward

Players are listed with the franchise that employed them in early January 2022. If the player changed teams after early January, you'll find them in the chapter for their previous squad. Due to the unique situation presented by the labor stoppage in baseball at the time of printing, we've created a Free Agent chapter for the Top-50 free agents (by projected WARP). All other unsigned free agents at time of publication can be found listed in their previous teams' chapters.

Each player comes with a stat block and a written comment: our example this year is the outrageously talented Vladimir Guerrero Jr. We start with name and primary position, then move on to biographical information like birthdate, playing age (as of June 30, 2022), and origin for entering professional baseball in the United States. Then it's on to the stats themselves.

We begin with basic identifying information for each season in question for the player, including **YEAR**, **TEAM**, **LVL** (level of affiliated play) and **AGE**. Then it's on to the raw numbers you're used to finding on the back of your dad's baseball cards: **PA** (plate appearances), **R** (runs), **2B** (doubles), **3B** (triples), **HR** (home runs), **RBI** (runs batted in), **BB** (walks), **K** (strikeouts), **SB** (stolen bases) and **CS** (caught stealing).

It's time to leave the old-school stats in the dust now: next up is **Whiff%** (whiff rate). This tells us how often a batter swings and *fails to make contact with the ball*. It's the opposite of contact rate.

Next are the unadjusted "slash line" statistics: **AVG** (batting average), **OBP** (on-base percentage), and **SLG** (slugging percentage). These are all ways to assess aspects of a player's offensive performance, but the next metric **DRC+** (Deserved Runs Created Plus) gives you the whole picture. It's a player's total expected offensive contribution compared to the league average.

BABIP (batting average on balls in play) tells us the percentage of times that a ball the batter hit into the field of play ended up as a hit. This stat sometimes helps us identify if a batter is lucky or not; high BABIPs sometimes mean better luck than average. Just keep in mind that the great hitters also tend to post high BABIPs, and so do hitters who are fast on their feet and hit ground balls.

Next up are two metrics introduced earlier in this section. **BRR** (Baserunning Runs) accounts for all baserunning events, including swiped bags and failed attempts, as well as other things. **FRAA** (Fielding Runs Above Average) is a defensive metric that not only has the player's positive or negative value at each of the three positions they played most frequently, but also the number of games they appeared at those positions in parentheses.

The final column is **WARP** (Wins Above Replacement Player), a holistic metric for total player value. For our position players, this means that it takes into account hitting runs above average (an input used in DRC+), BRR, and FRAA, then adjusts for positions played. WARP is a cumulative statistic that credits a player for their value above "replacement level"—think the quality of players that are freely available after the start of the season.

Just below the player's most recent season, you'll find future data: that's the PECOTA projection and comparables. We'll talk about those a bit more in an upcoming section.

Will Smith

YEAR	TEAM	P. COUNT	FRM RUNS	BLK RUNS	THRW RUNS	TOT RUNS
2019	LAD	6644	3.2	0.1	0.7	4.0
2019	OKC	7760	-2.0	0.0	1.0	-1.0
2020	LAD	4351	-3.0	0.1	0.1	-2.8
2021	LAD	16176	8.8	-0.3	0.4	8.9
2022	*LAD*	*16835*	*4.7*	*0.1*	*0.1*	*4.9*

Catchers

As mentioned earlier in this introduction, catchers have defensive responsibilities that exceed those of fielders at other positions. For that reason, we create a special, separate box just for their unique catching stats. Let's check out Dodgers catcher Will Smith as an example.

You should be familiar with the **YEAR** and **TEAM** columns by now; they match the stat boxes for position players and pitchers. **P. COUNT** (pitch count) tells us the number of pitches thrown that the catcher was behind the plate for. (This includes swinging strikes, fouls and balls in play.) **FRM RUNS** (framing runs) is the total value in runs that the catcher provided or lost by receiving the pitch in a way that influenced the umpire to call a strike. **BLK RUNS** (blocking runs) is the total value in runs above or below average for the catcher's ability to prevent wild pitches and passed balls. **THRW RUNS** (throwing runs) is the total value in runs that the catcher provided or lost from throwing out base stealers *and* preventing them from attempting to steal, as well. (Don't worry, this takes into account factors such as pitcher delivery and speed of the baserunner.) **TOT RUNS** (total runs) is the sum of the previous three statistics, a total run value for the catcher's framing, blocking and throwing.

Pitchers

Corbin Burnes, the 2021 National League Cy Young winner, is our example for the pitcher stat block. Much like the position player version, this block includes biographical information up at the top, followed by the same **YEAR**, **TEAM**, **LVL**, and **AGE** columns found for the position players.

Next are the pitcher versions of those "baseball card" statistics by season: **W** (wins), **L** (losses), **SV** (saves), **G** (games pitched), **GS** (games started), **IP** (innings pitched), **H** (hits allowed) and **HR** (home runs allowed). Then we feature two rate statistics, **BB/9** (walks per nine innings) and **K/9** (strikeouts per nine innings), before offering the unadjusted total **K** (strikeouts).

GB% (ground ball percentage) is, as you might guess, the percentage of all batted balls in play hit on the ground, including both outs and hits. Please note that, since this is based on the same observational data we talked about in the fielding section, it is subject to occasional human error and bias but still pretty useful.

BABIP (batting average on balls in play) is created the same way that it is for hitters, but it is a bit more useful a metric when trying to predict future performance in pitchers. League-average BABIP for pitchers is typically in the .290–.300 range; BABIP higher than that in pitchers can often be attributed to a leaky defense or bad luck (but not always!) and can indicate potential improved performance in the future. Of course, low BABIP may mean that future performance might not be as sharp as the season that BABIP was posted.

Most long-time baseball fans will recognize **WHIP** (walks plus hits per inning pitched) and especially **ERA** (earned run average), as these are common metrics to measure pitching skill. ERA measures earned runs—*not total runs*—allowed per nine innings of pitching. **DRA–** (Deserved Run Average Minus) was explained earlier; it's a measure of how effective a pitcher's performance was compared to league average.

WARP (Wins Above Replacement Player) is on the same scale as it is for hitters, though it is calculated specifically for pitching performance, with DRA as the primary input. You might see that relief pitchers have a lower WARP than you might expect; this is due to their limited innings and the fact that WARP does not take leverage into account. For this reason, you may choose to judge high-leverage relievers differently than WARP does.

A pitcher's median fastball velocity (50th percentile) is listed as **MPH**, in order to give you an example of what their typical fastball looks like. Note that this is only available for major-league pitchers, as the data for minor-league pitchers is not publicly available.

The last metrics for each pitcher are additional rates that help describe how they pitch. **FB%** (fastball percentage) is the percentage of fastballs thrown out of all pitches. **Whiff%** (whiff rate) is the percentage of swinging strikes by hitters on all pitches. Finally, **CSP** (called strike probability) shows the likelihood of any pitch by the hurler resulting in a called strike. This metric is adjusted and controls for factors including handedness, umpire, pitch type, count and location.

PECOTA

We're finally to the point in this intro where we get to talk in depth about PECOTA, Baseball Prospectus' signature projection system. Each player comment includes a PECOTA projection, and all projections for 2022 are for the player as of the date we went to press in early January. They are projected into the park context indicated by the team abbreviation; all PECOTA-projected statistics represent a player's projected major-league performance.

Our PECOTA projections have two major inputs into that final stat line you see: how the player is expected to perform, and how much playing time they'll have available to record that performance. We work to estimate playing time for each player based on team rosters and depth charts, and any projections based on that are noted as **2022 DC**. However, many players aren't projected to receive major-league playing time. Maybe the player in question is a prospect or a minor-league depth option. These players will get a different projection, labeled **2022 non-DC**. This is what we would project the player to provide in 251 plate appearances or 50 innings pitched.

The final piece of the puzzle is the comparables. At the bottom of the stat box, you'll see three names after the word "Comparables." These are the player's three highest-scoring comparable players as determined by PECOTA. Essentially, these players are examples of what PECOTA expects the shape of that player's performance to look like for 2022. Keep in mind that these comparables are meant to match the age of the player in question; if a 23-year-old hitter like Vladimir

Corbin Burnes RHP Born: 10/22/94 Age: 27 Bats: R Throws: R Height: 6'3" Weight: 225 lb. Origin: Round 4, 2016 Draft (#111 overall)

YEAR	TEAM	LVL	AGE	W	L	SV	G	GS	IP	H	HR	BB/9	K/9	K	GB%	BABIP	WHIP	ERA	DRA-	WARP	MPH	FB%	Whiff%	CSP
2019	SA	AAA	24	0	1	0	8	7	22^1	29	2	3.6	10.1	25	48.5%	.409	1.70	8.46	79	0.4				
2019	MIL	MLB	24	1	5	1	32	4	49	70	17	3.7	12.9	70	44.1%	.424	1.84	8.82	70	1.3	95.4	56.7%	36.7%	46.6%
2020	MIL	MLB	25	4	1	0	12	9	59^2	37	2	3.6	13.3	88	47.2%	.285	1.02	2.11	61	1.9	95.1	67.7%	34.8%	41.0%
2021	MIL	MLB	26	11	5	0	28	28	167	123	7	1.8	12.6	234	49.3%	.309	0.94	2.43	58	5.3	95.5	63.0%	37.0%	52.2%
2022 DC	*MIL*	*MLB*	*27*	*12*	*7*	*0*	*29*	*29*	*174.7*	*133*	*18*	*2.4*	*11.9*	*231*	*47.9%*	*.292*	*1.04*	*2.38*	*61*	*4.8*	*95.4*	*63.4%*	*36.6%*	*49.6%*

Comparables: Miles Mikolas, Tyson Ross, Max Scherzer

Guerrero Jr. lists Adrián Beltré as a comparable, he's being compared to the 23-year-old Beltré, not the late-career Rangers version or his career as a whole.

Managers

Near the back of the book, you'll find a chapter containing statistics for each major-league manager. For each manager, you'll find a block including a number of statistics pulled from their last five years on the bench. For more information on the statistics back there and what they mean, please visit the Glossary at www.baseballprospectus.com.

The managers are organized by the metric you'll find next to each manager's name: **wRM+** (weighted reliever management plus). Developed by Rob Arthur and Rian Watt, this statistic measures how well a manager aligns their best relievers to the moments of highest leverage. To do this, we use both our DRA metric and a scale called Leverage Index. Like DRC+ and DRA–, wRM+ is scaled to league average; a wRM+ of 105 indicates that the manager used his relievers about five percent "better" than average. Conversely, a wRM+ of 95 indicates that the relievers were used about five percent "worse" than average.

The wRM+ stat does not have a strong correlation with each manager, but it is statistically significant. In other words, a manager isn't *entirely* responsible for their team's wRM+, but he or she does have an effect on that number.

What Labor War Is Good For

by Marc Normandin

For the first time since the winter leading into the 1994 season, Major League Baseball and the MLB Players Association failed to come to terms on a new Collective Bargaining Agreement before the previous one expired. If you couldn't tell just by looking at the dates involved, this is an abnormal occurrence. It didn't used to be, though. No, prior to the mid-1990s, the two sides would pretty regularly fail to agree, not just before early December rolled around, but even into spring training (hello to the three previous spring lockouts), and sometimes—such as in '94—into the start of the actual campaign.

You often see a certain sentiment expressed, to the great ire of the union, in the articles and tweets and soundbites of mainstream baseball journalists and reporters, even the ones who understand that the owners have more than overreached again and again. And it is this: "No one wants a work stoppage." There is always a "but" or a "however" following that phrase, as maybe the journalist in question is about to explain or give some context as to why there is going to be a lockout or a strike and doesn't want to come off as blaming the players for the actions of the owners, but still, those six words are irksome when they're arranged just so. A work stoppage is not, in itself, a losing state.

Unions can't get anything actually useful done in negotiations without the threat of a work stoppage from their side or the ability to withstand one from the other. If striking is what it takes to get a fair deal, then a work stoppage should be a positive, or, at the very least, a systemic necessity, not a tragedy for everyone. The same goes for refusing ridiculous overtures from management with said refusal resulting in a lockout. The players shouldn't abandon their proposals simply because fans don't get to watch baseball games. If waiting for the teams to come to their senses comes at the cost of 2022 regular season games, that should also be viewed as a positive.

"But Marc," you think, as you consider skipping this essay by a clearly biased individual, "why should I care about millionaires fighting against billionaires?" This is more generally speaking, but the difference between a million and a billion is more than just a few zeroes. I'm not even talking about who has possession of actual, world-directing capital, or the business practices that map onto other industries, or how many generations out the families of each wouldn't have to worry about money because of their earnings. Just think about one million vs. one billion. It's difficult to comprehend the actual meaning behind the difference! One million miles is the equivalent distance to driving around Earth 40 times. One billion miles is *40,000 trips* around the same Earth. Alex Rodriguez has been paid more than any player in MLB history to this point, and, if you adjust for inflation, those 22 years of earnings come in just shy of $500 million. The Dodgers made more revenue than that in 2019—the last full season for which such data was available at the time of publication[1]—alone, and they weren't even first among the league's 30 clubs in revenues that year.

Obviously, Alex Rodriguez's family isn't going hungry, and neither is Mike Trout's, or Bryce Harper's, or Mookie Betts'. Those players are just the biggest benefactors of the previous arrangements between the league and the PA, however. The vast majority of MLB's players are not set for life like those guys. No, most of the players you see in the league are being paid close to the league minimum, often prorated between shuttles to Triple-A. The league-average salary keeps dropping because of this, but even that $4.17-million figure doesn't tell the whole tale. You need to look at the median salary for that: it's just $1.1 million. That, too, is even a little high compared to the reality of things.

Travis Sawchik provided important details at *The Score*[2] following the league's December lockout of the players. The aforementioned guys at the top get paid, and the people who still think that ticket prices are tied to player salaries—despite examples such as the Red Sox boldly raising ticket prices after salary-dumping Betts and David Price—get to gnash their teeth and blame the players' income for teams deciding that, I don't know, they should start charging fans for catching foul balls, which are MLB property. The rest of the league, though? Not even close. Per Sawchik, in 2019, 63.2% of the players who took the field were not yet arbitration eligible, and they accounted for 53.6% of the accrued service time. Their pay? That was just 9.8% of what MLB paid out. No other league is like this, just MLB. The league might not have an actual salary cap, and the stars certainly get their share, but what about everyone else? And that, given the numbers, is meant almost literally: it can't really be a fight between millionaires and billionaires when most of the people in said fight don't qualify as either.

Once you realize that, it becomes that much easier to think of most professional baseball players as workers rather than rich folks trying to get even richer at your expense. Obviously, they're already compensated better than the fall's (successful) striking John Deere employees and (successful) strike-threatening concessioners of San Francisco's Oracle Park, but they are workers all the same; they are the generators of profit for capitalists who take the bulk of that profit. The professional-sports industry creates, unfairly or not, far more profit than most. Until the pandemic-shortened 2020 interfered, MLB saw *17 consecutive seasons* of record revenues, culminating in 2019's $10.7 billion. And that's just the profits the league bothered to report: it doesn't include whatever they're hiding in the books they refuse to open, it doesn't include the near-endless line of low-to-no interest credit[3] they have open thanks to ever-increasing franchise values, it doesn't include the dollars the baseball side invested into side projects like real estate and profited from further, and it certainly doesn't include any of the skillful tax-dodging[4] that billionaire sports owners across the various major leagues are so fond of. MLB generates significant profit, and the players are simply asking for more of that, which they created, to go into the pockets of their lower-paid members, for the exploitation of that particular class of players to end. In response, MLB locked them all out.

Remember all of this—teams' very clear preference for cheaper players; that only the very best truly make it, financially speaking; that the average career length in MLB doesn't even get you to free agency, where the real money is—and factor in few additional items, like MLB's scaling back of the draft and hard-capping international bonus pools, that teams pay all but the minor leaguers repeating Triple-A a sub-poverty-level wage, and so on.

And consider, too, how we started, with a reminder that the threat of a work stoppage is a powerful tool for a union. It becomes pretty clear, in a hurry, that the only ones who shouldn't want a work stoppage are the owners. And yet, they enacted one. Most of the reason there even is a 2021–22 lockout on the record is because the owners threw a tantrum over the union asking to raise the minimum salary, speed up the arbitration process, and let players get to free agency a year sooner. These are not unreasonable requests, and they are certainly not ones that should have led to a lockout, especially not when things the owners want—the expanded postseason that will generate hundreds of millions of dollars in revenue annually, for one—require union approval. The thing is, though, that the owners love that they've had an easy go of it for years now, dealing with a union that fell for the lie of labor peace and avoided potential work stoppages at great cost to its members, past, present and future. That behavior peaked with the horrendous 2016 agreement that allowed the owners to really go masks-off on service-time manipulation and non-competitive team-building cycles. Now, the players have woken up and had enough. So, they were essentially locked out for daring to come to their senses.

The only way the owners will similarly come to their senses and recognize the reality of things is for the potential for work stoppages to become normal once again. The version of the MLBPA led by Marvin Miller stood firm, enacted strikes and withstood lockouts; Donald Fehr's, at least before the steroid scandals gave Bud Selig Congressional and public support, worked similarly, in that it was willing to declare war rather than preserve the peace, if war was what was needed.

Sometime during the later years of Fehr's tenure as executive director, though, the priorities of the union changed, opening the door for Selig and company to begin to claw back at the players' gains: putting caps on draft spending; ramping up free-agent compensation; relying on inexpensive, pre-arbitration players at the expense of veteran free agents in a way that had not been seen since the three years of collusion in the 1980s. MLB had the union where they wanted it, and the players were still comfortable enough to not realize they were signing into existence a worse world for future members. That's exactly the kind of thing Miller would have seen coming; in fact, Fehr had him come back to the PA in 1990 to tell them that very thing, when disagreements between the veterans and the arbitration-eligible players came to a head and threatened to split solidarity.

Miller, according to John Helyar's *Lords of the Realm*, told the assembled players that, "Failing to support the democratically arrived-at decisions of your negotiating committee, your executive director, and your staff can only have one result: a permanent loss of credibility. If you waver, you can count on one thing: the owners will never again take the player reps seriously. The issue here is no longer salary arbitration. It's the future effectiveness of the union."[5]

It was a lesson the union forgot for too long in this century, but it is one they seem to grasp once more. And the internalizing of that message—that the union's job in the present is to ensure the future effectiveness of the union—is what allowed the players to beat back MLB's very public attacks on them prior to the 2020 season, and is also what resulted in the first lockout in the league since 1990. And that's good: Look what labor peace wrought compared to the gains from decades of being willing to strike or force the issue—whatever issue—with the owners until they became so angry that they decided to lock the players out. Historically, lockouts and strikes are where the union has made its most significant and landscape-altering gains.

No one wants a work stoppage, in the sense that it would be just swell if everyone involved acted like adults and actively worked to ensure a fair agreement was reached. Peace is good, after all. Conflict . . . is bad! That's not the reality of the situation, though. There is no such thing as labor peace, not now, not ever, because if the owners are so thrilled with a deal that they aren't fighting it, then the deal is not a good one for the players and is likely straight-up unfair to them. The same goes for UPS drivers, Kellogg's factory employees, John Deere workers, Starbucks baristas, or the ever-growing online-media-union membership: it is a rare thing, indeed, that the bosses aren't trying to squeeze labor for everything it is worth and then some. Squeezing is the game itself.

If it all seems too easy, you aren't asking for enough, you are not pushing hard enough. Labor peace is simply the owners getting what they want, and with little effort. There is a reason that the league offered to (illegally) pay Robert Cannon's salary and office expenses when he was nearly the PA's first executive director back in 1966, and it's because his message to the players was to "make no demands, no public statements."[6] And it's because having a guy like that working for the other side would be worth just about any salary. There's a reason Miller didn't get the same offer, and it's not because he pointed out the illegality of it, either.

Peace gets you to the place where the 2016 CBA happens, with its thousand paper cuts the league and players are still feeling. Conflict gets you a pension, and one with a cost-of-living adjustment. Conflict gets you arbitration, it gets you free agency, it wins you a tripling of the league-minimum salary over the course of a single CBA, it brings a federal district judge in to tell the owners they've overstepped their bounds and need to recognize that all of these gains are collectively bargained and can't be unilaterally disposed of. Conflict keeps you from agreeing to a salary cap, and it keeps you from allowing the league to turn the competitive-balance-tax threshold into a de facto cap.

Conflict gets you everywhere; peace gets you what the bosses feel like offering. Conflict, and more of it, is what the union needs to brace for in order to fully reverse the damage of the last 20 years of collective bargaining agreements; a single CBA, a single lockout, is not enough. The players relaxing too much after winning so much is what allowed the owners to find new ways to claw back what had been won in the first place. More conflict is needed, or else this is going to be cyclical, and we'll be right back in 2016, only with new faces in the starring roles, new faces that inherited a weaker position than their predecessors thanks to those very predecessors.

—Marc Normandin writes on baseball's labor issues at marcnormandin.com.

---

1. https://www.forbes.com/sites/mikeozanian/2019/04/10/baseball-team-values-2019-yankees-lead-league-at-46-billion
2. https://www.thescore.com/mlb/news/2241177/manfreds-letter-ought-to-be-a-call-for-players-to-dig-in
3. https://www.baseballprospectus.com/news/article/58941/veteran-presence-mlbs-presentation-to-mlbpa-impugns-trust/
4. https://www.marcnormandin.com/2021/07/09/taxes-are-one-more-reason-you-cant-trust-mlb-owners-crying-poor/
5. Heylar, p. 451
6. https://sabr.org/bioproj/person/robert-cannon/

ATLANTA BRAVES

Essay by Bailey Freeman

Player comments by Demetrius Bell and BP staff

It was one of the shortest interviews recorded during the World Series media blitz. Paul Byrd approached Braves outfielder Guillermo Heredia with a simple question, one that had been asked of him several times before. "Is this a time to be cocky or humble?" Heredia turned to the Bally Sports camera and repeated his mantra. "Cocky. All the time. It's no question for me."

The 30-year-old Heredia was waived by the Mets and scooped up by the Braves at the dawn of spring training. In 2021, he appeared in 120 games for Atlanta but made some of his biggest contributions when he wasn't in the lineup. The Braves celebrated the 4th of July with a pinch-hit, walk-off single from Max Fried, prompting Heredia to explode from the dugout brandishing two pink plastic swords, nearly steamrolling the ace pitcher in the process. In the grand scheme of the season, the Braves were still in a rough spot. Fried's heroics had brought their record up to just 41-42. Righty Mike Soroka had already suffered a complete re-tear of his Achilles, and left fielder Marcell Ozuna had landed on the 60-day injured list, only to be promptly arrested for domestic violence. Right fielder Ronald Acuña Jr. tore the anterior cruciate ligament in his right knee just two weeks later, an injury which ended the season of Atlanta's best player, a prodigious superstar who almost single-handedly powered their offense in the first half of the season. Yet, even in their worst stretches, the Braves remained confident in their ability to turn things around.

The Atlanta Braves won the World Series in 2021. That feels equally weird and wonderful to say. As a lifelong fan, this wasn't technically my first rodeo. My mother assures me that I was cradled in her arms as Marquis Grissom caught 1995's final out in Atlanta-Fulton County Stadium, but I was only two months old at the time. Not only was this my first championship with object permanence, it came in what was serendipitously my first year as an Atlanta resident. I was privileged enough to spend a month's rent on a ticket to Game 4 and to attend the Truist Park watch party for the Game 6 clincher in Houston. As Dansby Swanson fielded the final groundball of the season, I observed a collective spiritual crisis permeating a sea of ecstatic Braves fans. The proverbial dog had finally caught the car. It seems that witnessing your team become champions irreversibly alters

ATLANTA BRAVES PROSPECTUS

2021 W-L: 88-73, 1st in NL East

Pythag	.586	*7th*	DER	.713	*4th*
RS/G	4.91	*8th*	DRC+	99	*11th*
RA/G	4.07	*7th*	DRA-	92	*8th*
dWin%	.557	*8th*	FIP	4.01	*10th*
Payroll	$131M	*14th*	B-Age	28.4	*8th*
M$/MW	$2.9M	*13th*	P-Age	29.8	*15th*

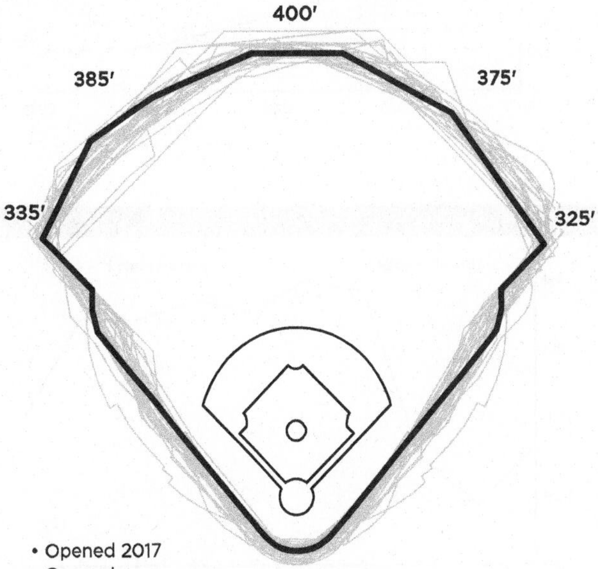

- Opened 2017
- Open air
- Natural surface
- Fence profile: 6′ to 16′

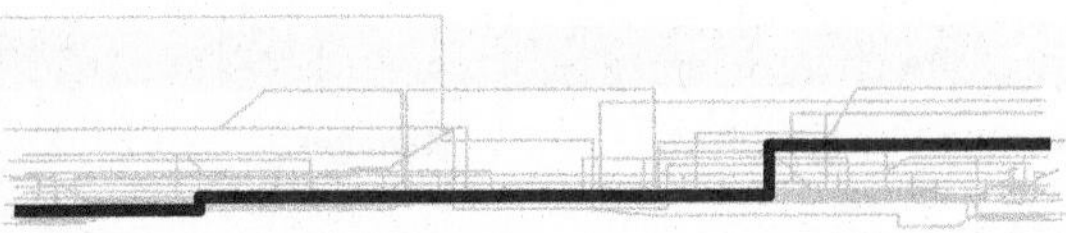

Park Factors

Runs	Runs/RH	Runs/LH	HR/RH	HR/LH
98	98	97	96	95

Top Hitter WARP	4.5 Ozzie Albies
Top Pitcher WARP	4.5 Charlie Morton
Top Prospect	Kyle Muller

Payroll History (in millions)

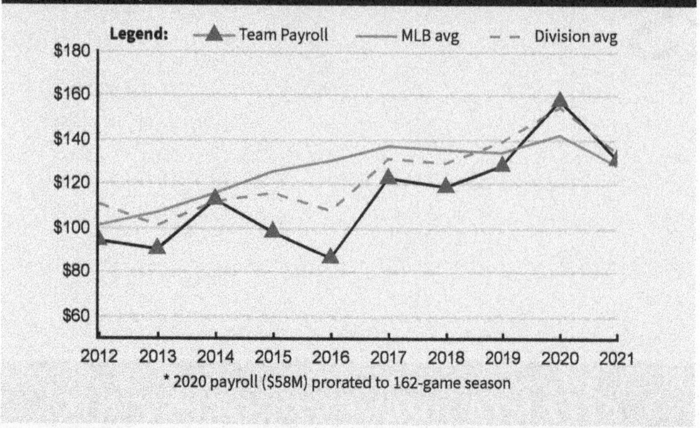

Future Commitments (in millions)

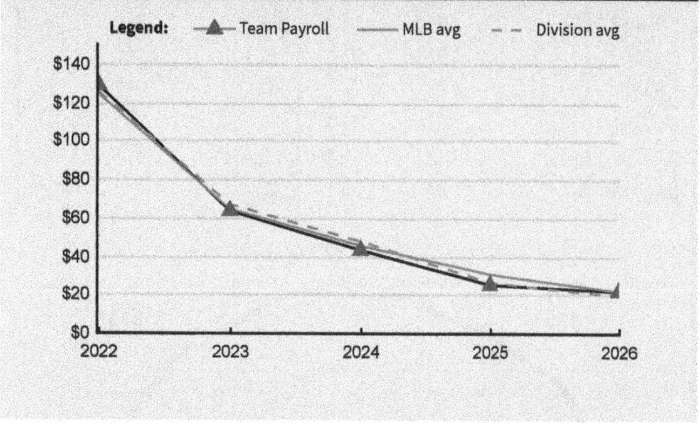

Farm System Ranking

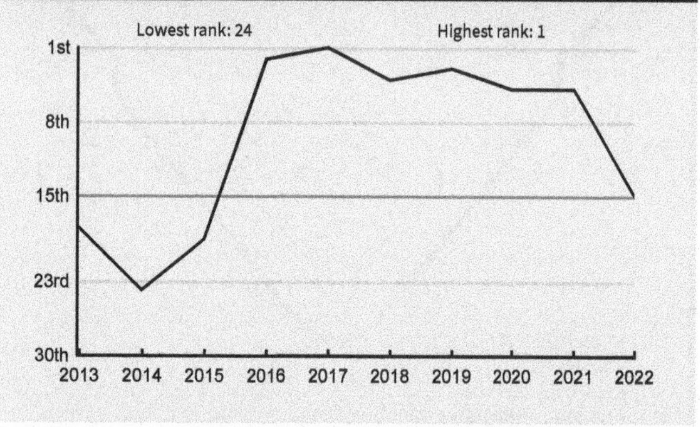

Personnel

Executive Vice President, General Manager
Alex Anthopoulos

Vice President, Baseball Operations
Mike Fast

Assistant General Manager, Research and Development
Jason Paré

Assistant General Manager, Player Development
Ben Sestanovich

Manager
Brian Snitker

BP Alumni
Trevor Andresen
Mike Fast
Jason Paré
Ronit Shah
Will Siskel
Noah Woodward
Colin Wyers

the fan experience. Getting the Commissioner's Trophy in Freddie Freeman's hands might as well be the logical conclusion of baseball fandom itself. What more is there to do? Sure, they could try to win it all again, but will it ever be the same?

The experience of winning it all is something Atlantans are still coming to terms with. Since 1995, the state of Georgia hadn't won a Big Four pro-sports-league title, nor the NCAA Division I equivalents. The proud Atlanta United faithful will happily point to their MLS Cup triumph in 2018, but the Atlanta Dream have been swept all three times they reached the WNBA Finals. It's safe to say that playoff success is uncommon in the Peach State, where numbers like 28–3, 3–1, and 2nd-and-26 give proud Georgians the vapors. The Braves made their most-recent contribution in 2020, losing the NLCS to the Dodgers in classic fashion. Like many other atomized young professionals in that year of widespread human suffering, I watched alone, living and dying by every pitch from the comfort of a starter apartment. But, as the unlikely Braves marched onward in 2021, the constant sense of dread we all have for our beloved teams began to fade. By the time they reached the World Series, hope did indeed spring eternal. I knew they could win, yet I also didn't know what to do with myself when it happened.

The most successful form of therapy was watching Jorge Soler's majestic Game 6 blast approximately 1,000 times. That repetition was necessary to reinforce reality. As the clip looped on my computer screen, I kept expecting the 6-foot-4 slugger to eventually swing and miss at Luis Garcia's 3-2 offering. Yet, the ball sailed over Minute Maid Park's train tracks on every loop through. The acquisition of Soler—alongside fellow outfielders Joc Pederson, Adam Duvall and Eddie Rosario—took some presumption. When the trading deadline arrived, the Braves hadn't been above .500 all season and had just lost their best player. When it came to rebuilding their outfield on the fly, Atlanta certainly had a type. They were willing to bet on the bounce-back potential of struggling trade targets just as they bet on the bounce-back potential of their struggling team. In 2019, the last full MLB season, Soler hit 48 homers, Rosario received down-ballot MVP votes, and Pederson put up a 122 DRC+. Their credentials portended productivity down the stretch. It helped that their trade values had completely bottomed out, as the Braves didn't have a large pool of prospects to trade from, a long-term consequence of international-signing improprieties under banished former general manager John Coppollela.

While it was somewhat cocky for a losing team to be active buyers at the trade deadline, their confidence wasn't unfounded. The Braves appeared due for what some consider to be an oxymoron: positive regression. It was there at the individual level, when reigning MVP Freddie Freeman hit an uncharacteristic .228 through his first 60 games but had a .305 expected batting average according to Statcast. It was there at the unit level, as Atlanta's bullpen misfortunes reversed in the second half with the magic of fielding-independent-pitching regression. And it was there at the team level. When their playoff chances dipped below 10 percent in late July, the Braves still had the best run differential in their division. That underlying true talent allowed them to keep pace with the Phillies and Mets despite their rivals' acquisitions of, respectively, All-Star righty Kyle Gibson and human lightning bolt Javier Báez. Yet, the Braves' most telling in-season adjustment came in mid-May, when the formerly shift-averse Braves started moving infielders around like they were trapped in a game of bullet chess. The 2021 Braves are a reminder that confidence and introspection aren't mutually exclusive. The personnel and strategy changed, but the chutzpah was unwavering.

One luxury the 2021 Atlanta Braves had was time. MLB's return to a 162-game schedule stood in stark contrast to the hectic sprint of 2020. This was a season of attrition. Every team was going to struggle at some point, but there would be ample opportunities to retool. As the Braves marched forward into division contention, their rivals rolled over and exposed their soft underbellies. A late-September sweep of the Phillies secured Atlanta's fourth-straight NL East title in almost anticlimactic fashion. Despite winning just 88 games, fewer than the Blue Jays and Mariners, both of whom missed the playoffs, the Braves punched their ticket to October. A relentless commitment to simply making the playoffs is perhaps the best a franchise can hope for. The 2020 Dodgers broke through after coming up short the previous seven seasons. The 2019 Nationals got it done as a wild card after being unceremoniously ousted from four Division Series in the previous seven years. It wasn't supposed to be this Braves team. The Hollywood script would've ended with a gem from Soroka and a pivotal home run from Acuña. But if October baseball really is a lottery, teams should scrounge up as many tickets as they can. The Braves weren't going to punt a season within their competitive window, so GM Alex Anthopoulos brought in whatever reinforcements he could to complement Freeman, third baseman Austin Riley, second baseman Ozzie Albies, veteran righty Charlie Morton and Fried. They didn't have to be the best. They just had to be good enough.

At the center of it all was manager Brian Snitker, Atlanta's captain through choppy waters. The 2021 season was his 45th in the Braves' organization. He received his first coaching offer from none other than Henry Aaron. In an industry of entropy, in which players, coaches and executives hop from franchise to franchise, Snitker has been a constant. As Ozuna's mix-it-ups turned to Pablo Sandoval's hugs turned to Heredia's sword slashes, Snitker acted as steward for an upbeat, eccentric locker room, resting curmudgeon face and all. I mean, Joc Pederson was wearing grandma's pearls, for crying out loud! Nobody has ever worn grandma's pearls and not believed in themselves.

Snitker knew when to believe in his ballclub, too. Game 4 of the World Series felt, for all the world, like a passing move, as the Braves, up 2–1 but strapped for pitching, turned to Dylan Lee, Kyle Wright and Chris Martin to handle the early innings. When Riley cut the Astros' lead to a run with an RBI single in the bottom of the sixth, Snitker called upon his bullpen ace, Tyler Matzek. It was an aggressive move to burn one of the team's best relievers while still trailing, especially given Atlanta's lack of playoff pitching depth, but the gambit succeeded. The Braves' offense piggybacked off Matzek's scoreless inning with back-to-back home runs from Dansby Swanson and Jorge Soler, allowing Snitker to close out the game with Luke Jackson and Will Smith. Using Matzek was hardly a mind-blowing piece of strategy, but it was emblematic of Snitker's quiet certainty. It also helped secure the most pivotal game of the Series.

That confidence had conditions, though. It never devolved into blind faith. This was best illustrated in Game 5, a game that would've surely been started by Morton if not for the fractured fibula he suffered in Game 1. When a rough outing from A.J. Minter gave Houston a 7–5 lead in the fifth, Snitker rode out the loss with Chris Martin and Drew Smyly. This set Atlanta up nicely for the Game 6 clincher. Max Fried avoided the baseball gods' last gasp by escaping an ankle stamping unscathed and pitching six scoreless innings. The game then turned over to a rested Matzek and Smith, who easily closed out the season, dispatching the Astros 7–0 in Houston. Not only did the Braves win the World Series, they never even faced an elimination game throughout the playoffs, something that could be said about only the 2013 and '18 Red Sox in the last decade.

So, were the Braves great because they believed in themselves? No. They believed in themselves because they were great. They certainly had the credentials of a championship team, having won the NL East the previous three seasons. Even with some key players missing, they still had a sneaky-good rotation fronted by Morton, Fried and Ian Anderson, a rocksteady infield anchored by reigning NL MVP Freeman and an outfield full of power potential. What some characterize as confidence might just have been self-awareness. At all levels, the Braves were hyperaware of how much better they could be, even though they didn't have a winning record until August 6.

Baseball is a humbling pursuit. The best pitchers still frequently miss their fastball spots, and the most prolific hitters make outs more than half the time. The cockiness preached by Guillermo Heredia is a defense mechanism against this condition. His Spanglish rallying cry of "nada humble" is as appropriate as it gets for a team at this juncture. The Braves are World Series champions, but they'll be humbled again soon. But now? Now is the time to be cocky.

—Bailey Freeman is the creator of the YouTube channel Foolish Baseball.

HITTERS

Ronald Acuña Jr. RF

Born: 12/18/97 Age: 24 Bats: R Throws: R Height: 6'0" Weight: 205 lb. Origin: International Free Agent, 2014

YEAR	TEAM	LVL	AGE	PA	R	2B	3B	HR	RBI	BB	K	SB	CS	Whiff%	AVG/OBP/SLG	DRC+	BABIP	BRR	FRAA	WARP
2019	ATL	MLB	21	715	127	22	2	41	101	76	188	37	9	27.7%	.280/.365/.518	120	.337	7.9	CF(100): -2.8, LF(46): 5.0, RF(35): -0.6	5.6
2020	ATL	MLB	22	202	46	11	0	14	29	38	60	8	1	29.9%	.250/.406/.581	128	.302	2.5	CF(34): 0.3, RF(28): 0.3	1.6
2021	ATL	MLB	23	360	72	19	1	24	52	49	85	17	6	27.6%	.283/.394/.596	137	.311	3.4	RF(80): -5.2, CF(2): 0.2	2.6
2022 DC	*ATL*	*MLB*	*24*	*588*	*121*	*25*	*2*	*36*	*88*	*81*	*147*	*27*	*10*	*27.5%*	*.277/.389/.559*	*148*	*.323*	*1.8*	*RF -3, CF 0*	*5.3*

Comparables: Mike Trout, Justin Upton, Giancarlo Stanton

A wise ATLien once wrote "you can plan a pretty picnic, but you can't predict the weather." That might be truer on a July day in Miami than anywhere else, where misfortune struck like lightning amidst the Most Valuable Picnic-level season that Acuña Jr. was having. Atlanta was 44-44 on the day that Acuña was injured, and his absence from the roster for the rest of the season was the butterfly flapping its wings, resulting in an unpredicted tidal wave of production from the quartet of replacements that Alex Anthopoulos called on in his stead—you might say it happened for a reason, one can't be mad. The replacements' success aside, Acuña's health is paramount to the future of the organization. He was threatening for a 40-40 season prior to his injury, and health of his knee pending, it's easy to see him taking another, ahem, run at it in the future. Only 24 years old heading into the 2022 season, no one would fault you for planning on a smooth recovery and a few more MVP-type campaigns going forward. Let's hope that's exactly the case, as already three years into his (up to) 10-year contract, Atlanta fans might be realizing that what once looked like forever doesn't seem so long anymore.

Ozzie Albies 2B

Born: 01/07/97 Age: 25 Bats: S Throws: R Height: 5'8" Weight: 165 lb. Origin: International Free Agent, 2013

YEAR	TEAM	LVL	AGE	PA	R	2B	3B	HR	RBI	BB	K	SB	CS	Whiff%	AVG/OBP/SLG	DRC+	BABIP	BRR	FRAA	WARP
2019	ATL	MLB	22	702	102	43	8	24	86	54	112	15	4	23.0%	.295/.352/.500	112	.325	5.0	2B(158): -0.6	4.3
2020	ATL	MLB	23	124	21	5	0	6	19	5	30	3	1	24.8%	.271/.306/.466	97	.317	0.1	2B(29): 0.7	0.5
2021	ATL	MLB	24	686	103	40	7	30	106	47	128	20	4	25.0%	.259/.310/.488	107	.278	3.0	2B(156): 10.8	4.5
2022 DC	*ATL*	*MLB*	*25*	*577*	*87*	*28*	*5*	*19*	*78*	*42*	*109*	*13*	*4*	*24.4%*	*.265/.324/.453*	*107*	*.300*	*1.1*	*2B 1*	*2.9*

Comparables: Roberto Alomar, Bill Mazeroski, Rennie Stennett

Albies feels straight out of MLB: The Show's create-a-player mode thanks to his diminutive build generating potent power at the plate. It's frankly a combination of stature and power that shouldn't exist in real life and yet reality has delivered the joys of seeing mini-sluggers like Jose Altuve and Albies crushing baseball alongside the relative titans of the sport. While it might not have been unreasonable for scouts to question the legitimacy of Albies' pop, the native of Curaçao is now at four consecutive seasons topping a .190 Isolated Power, including two seasons over the .200 mark. With his power in tow and his glove (back to) living up to expectations, there are few better second baseman across baseball—real or created.

William Contreras C

Born: 12/24/97 Age: 24 Bats: R Throws: R Height: 6'0" Weight: 180 lb. Origin: International Free Agent, 2015

YEAR	TEAM	LVL	AGE	PA	R	2B	3B	HR	RBI	BB	K	SB	CS	Whiff%	AVG/OBP/SLG	DRC+	BABIP	BRR	FRAA	WARP
2019	FLO	A+	21	207	26	11	0	3	22	14	44	0	0		.263/.324/.368	105	.329	-0.5	C(43): -5.0	0.1
2019	MIS	AA	21	209	24	9	0	3	17	15	40	0	0		.246/.306/.340	103	.295	0.5	C(53): -0.3	0.9
2020	ATL	MLB	22	10	0	1	0	0	1	0	4	0	0	40.9%	.400/.400/.500	79	.667	-0.3	C(4): 0.1	0.0
2021	LAR	WIN	23	74	9	2	0	2	13	8	14	0	0		.215/.311/.338		.245			
2021	GWN	AAA	23	171	26	8	0	9	29	13	36	0	0		.290/.357/.516	112	.327	0.0	C(34): -1.1	0.7
2021	ATL	MLB	23	185	19	4	1	8	23	19	54	0	0	36.4%	.215/.303/.399	94	.265	0.4	C(49): -4.4	0.2
2022 DC	*ATL*	*MLB*	*24*	*58*	*7*	*2*	*0*	*1*	*8*	*4*	*16*	*0*	*0*	*34.2%*	*.234/.303/.394*	*86*	*.305*	*-0.1*	*C -1*	*0.1*

Comparables: Christian Vázquez, Héctor Sánchez, Salvador Perez

YEAR	TEAM	P. COUNT	FRM RUNS	BLK RUNS	THRW RUNS	TOT RUNS
2019	MIS	6458	1.0	0.0	-0.5	0.5
2019	FLO	5730	-4.1	-0.6	0.7	-4.0
2020	ATL	404	0.1	0.0	0.0	0.1
2021	ATL	6935	-4.0	-0.5	0.0	-4.5
2021	GWN	4102	-0.7	-0.1	0.3	-0.6
2021	LAR	1492			0.0	0.0
2022	*ATL*	*2405*	*0.3*	*-0.1*	*0.0*	*0.2*

Novice cooks get better via trial and error. No one comes up with their signature menu item by nailing it on the first go-around. Even Michelin-starred chefs make mistakes on their way to creating their dazzling dishes, taking little tastes along the way to determine what needs to be added, and just as relevantly, what needs to be subtracted. That's what these past two seasons in the majors have been for Contreras: tastes along the way, learning what refinements are necessary, then back to cook a little more. His 2020 was brief and unrefined, but had a bright finish and it was easy to dream of what could be. Last season exposed some bitter notes both at and behind the plate, but it's nothing that a little more seasoning can't address. Contreras' time in Triple-A might have overstated what he can do in terms of batting average, but the power is legitimate and he shouldn't have trouble sticking behind the plate, where the offensive bar is pretty low. He showed in 2021 that he could break a few eggs; the future will determine whether he can make an omelette.

Travis d'Arnaud C

Born: 02/10/89 Age: 33 Bats: R Throws: R Height: 6'2" Weight: 210 lb. Origin: Round 1, 2007 Draft (#37 overall)

YEAR	TEAM	LVL	AGE	PA	R	2B	3B	HR	RBI	BB	K	SB	CS	Whiff%	AVG/OBP/SLG	DRC+	BABIP	BRR	FRAA	WARP
2019	NYM	MLB	30	25	2	0	0	0	2	2	5	0	0	30.8%	.087/.160/.087	86	.111	0.2	C(9): -0.2	0.1
2019	TB	MLB	30	365	50	16	0	16	67	30	80	0	1	26.1%	.263/.323/.459	101	.295	0.5	C(76): -2.1, 1B(21): -1.7	1.2
2019	LAD	MLB	30	1	0	0	0	0	0	0	0	0	0	0.0%	.000/.000/.000	105				0.0
2020	ATL	MLB	31	184	19	8	0	9	34	16	50	1	0	30.9%	.321/.386/.533	109	.411	-0.8	C(35): 4.4	1.2
2021	ATL	MLB	32	229	21	14	0	7	26	17	53	0	0	24.4%	.220/.284/.388	89	.260	-0.3	C(57): 6.4	1.3
2022 DC	*ATL*	*MLB*	*33*	*504*	*62*	*22*	*0*	*13*	*62*	*42*	*110*	*0*	*1*	*25.9%*	*.232/.304/.375*	*83*	*.277*	*-0.8*	*C 6, 1B -1*	*1.4*

Comparables: Sherm Lollar, Benito Santiago, Terry Steinbach

YEAR	TEAM	P. COUNT	FRM RUNS	BLK RUNS	THRW RUNS	TOT RUNS
2019	TB	9708	-0.5	-0.2	0.3	-0.5
2019	NYM	899	-0.1	0.0	0.0	-0.1
2019	LAD		0.0	0.0	-0.2	-0.2
2020	ATL	5251	4.8	0.0	0.7	5.4
2021	ATL	7703	5.0	0.2	0.0	5.2
2022	*ATL*	*14430*	*7.6*	*-0.3*	*0.0*	*7.3*

You don't know what you've got until they're gone, and d'Arnaud is living proof. Even though the veteran catcher wasn't exactly lighting the world on fire with his bat during the early stages of the 2021 season, his serious thumb injury made it abundantly clear just how much even an average bat at catcher can mean to any lineup at the major-league level. While his WARP won't jump off the page, everyday looks at replacement-level catchers let you know how valuable that figure can be. d'Arnaud showed improved offensive production following his return from a serious thumb injury in August, with a boosted walk rate and slugging percentage compared to his pre-injury performance. So while it was a down season in aggregate, it's reasonable to anticipate something close to a league-average bat to go with above-average defense in 2022, despite the offensive stumble this year.

Adam Duvall OF

Born: 09/04/88 Age: 33 Bats: R Throws: R Height: 6'1" Weight: 215 lb. Origin: Round 11, 2010 Draft (#348 overall)

YEAR	TEAM	LVL	AGE	PA	R	2B	3B	HR	RBI	BB	K	SB	CS	Whiff%	AVG/OBP/SLG	DRC+	BABIP	BRR	FRAA	WARP
2019	GWN	AAA	30	429	74	20	4	32	93	48	86	1	0		.266/.364/.602	144	.261	0.0	LF(51): 3.5, RF(26): 1.3	3.8
2019	ATL	MLB	30	130	17	4	1	10	19	7	39	0	0	28.3%	.267/.315/.567	101	.306	0.6	LF(31): 1.5, RF(2): -0.5	0.6
2020	ATL	MLB	31	209	34	8	0	16	33	15	54	0	0	27.1%	.237/.301/.532	117	.240	0.3	LF(45): -1.0, RF(17): -2.7, CF(1): -0.0	0.7
2021	MIA	MLB	32	339	41	10	1	22	68	21	105	5	0	28.8%	.229/.277/.478	98	.263	-1.2	RF(66): 7.2, LF(16): -1.9, CF(8): -0.2	1.4
2021	ATL	MLB	32	216	26	7	1	16	45	14	69	0	0	29.9%	.226/.287/.513	104	.254	-0.1	LF(35): 5.2, CF(22): -0.3, RF(11): -0.5	1.4
2022 DC	*ATL*	*MLB*	*33*	*565*	*80*	*22*	*1*	*31*	*93*	*42*	*162*	*2*	*2*	*28.7%*	*.222/.290/.455*	*93*	*.258*	*-0.4*	*1B 0, LF 0*	*0.8*

Comparables: Gary Redus, Roy Sievers, Dave Kingman

In 2020 at Truist Park, Duvall hit .287/.364/.575 with a .938 OPS and .287 in Isolated Power. Duvall enjoyed Cobb County so much that when he went back to the stadium as a visitor during the first half of 2021, he racked up 10 hits over 25 plate appearances, with four home runs and 13 RBI, to boot. Perhaps realizing he'd ended their relationship too soon back when he non-tendered Duvall in the offseason, Alex Anthopoulos wooed Duvall once more, ultimately rekindling things in late July as part of a full outfield revamp in Atlanta. Duvall responded by boosting his slugging 35 points for his new-old home park, and helped power the team to a World Series victory in the fall. Who says you can't go home again?

Vaughn Grissom IF

Born: 01/05/01 Age: 21 Bats: R Throws: R Height: 6'3" Weight: 180 lb. Origin: Round 11, 2019 Draft (#337 overall)

YEAR	TEAM	LVL	AGE	PA	R	2B	3B	HR	RBI	BB	K	SB	CS	Whiff%	AVG/OBP/SLG	DRC+	BABIP	BRR	FRAA	WARP
2019	BRA	ROK	18	184	22	7	1	3	23	16	27	3	0		.288/.361/.400		.323			
2021	AUG	A	20	328	52	15	4	5	33	34	49	13	3		.311/.402/.446	127	.360	1.6	SS(35): -3.2, 3B(23): 1.8, 2B(10): 3.0	2.3
2021	ROM	A+	20	52	12	2	0	2	10	11	5	3	0		.378/.519/.595	139	.375	0.9	SS(8): -0.8, 2B(2): 0.1	0.4
2022 non-DC	*ATL*	*MLB*	*21*	*251*	*23*	*10*	*1*	*3*	*23*	*19*	*47*	*4*	*1*	*23.8%*	*.249/.320/.361*	*89*	*.300*	*0.2*	*SS -1, 3B 1*	*0.5*

Comparables: Yairo Muñoz, Johan Camargo, Yamaico Navarro

It was a doozy of a season for Grissom, as he took himself from a 2019 11th-rounder to a Top-10 prospect in the system. The former prep product from Oviedo, FL oozes with upside. He makes tons of contact because his relatively flat swing allows him to cover most of the plate. Pair that with impressive discipline and you've got a recipe for high averages and on-base rates but fairly modest power output. Grissom has the type of frame and bat speed to generate pop, but it would require tweaking his swing plane to incorporate some loft. He might not be a shortstop when it's all said and done, but center field could be an option. Grissom will make his bones at the plate, though, and how much power he's able to harness will determine how high his ceiling will be. There's a lot of variance in the profile at present, but much of it is positive.

★ ★ ★ *2022 Top 101 Prospect* **#58** ★ ★ ★

Michael Harris II OF

Born: 03/07/01 Age: 21 Bats: L Throws: L Height: 6'0" Weight: 195 lb. Origin: Round 3, 2019 Draft (#98 overall)

YEAR	TEAM	LVL	AGE	PA	R	2B	3B	HR	RBI	BB	K	SB	CS	Whiff%	AVG/OBP/SLG	DRC+	BABIP	BRR	FRAA	WARP
2019	BRA	ROK	18	119	15	6	3	2	16	9	20	5	2		.349/.403/.514		.414			
2019	ROM	A	18	93	11	2	1	0	11	9	22	3	0		.183/.269/.232	84	.246	-0.5	RF(18): 5.3, CF(4): 0.8	0.7
2021	ROM	A+	20	420	55	26	3	7	64	35	76	27	4		.294/.362/.436	116	.349	1.9	CF(76): 5.5, RF(9): -0.3, LF(7): 6.2	3.5
2022 non-DC	*ATL*	*MLB*	*21*	*251*	*21*	*11*	*1*	*2*	*21*	*17*	*55*	*8*	*2*	*25.0%*	*.239/.299/.338*	*72*	*.304*	*0.6*	*CF 2, RF 0*	*0.3*

Comparables: Christian Yelich, Albert Almora Jr., Austin Meadows

Spring training is the land of opportunity for some and also the land of wild-eyed speculation for others. So when Harris took full advantage of the chance as a non-roster invitee, Braves fans were busy penciling in the outfield of the future. He kept the momentum going into his High-A season, as he played well enough to earn an invite to the 2021 Futures Game. While Harris didn't hit for a ton of power during his time in Rome, he continued to show that his hit tool is something to be excited about in addition to his ability to swipe bases and cover his portion of the outfield. He's still pretty far from reaching the big leagues, but it's pretty clear that it's "when" and not "if" he will be doing his thing in a major-league ballpark near you.

Guillermo Heredia CF

Born: 01/31/91 Age: 31 Bats: R Throws: L Height: 5'10" Weight: 195 lb. Origin: International Free Agent, 2016

YEAR	TEAM	LVL	AGE	PA	R	2B	3B	HR	RBI	BB	K	SB	CS	Whiff%	AVG/OBP/SLG	DRC+	BABIP	BRR	FRAA	WARP
2019	DUR	AAA	28	30	3	1	0	1	4	1	10	0	1		.214/.267/.357	78	.294	0.0	CF(8): -0.2	0.0
2019	TB	MLB	28	231	31	13	0	5	20	18	60	2	2	27.4%	.225/.306/.363	81	.293	2.0	CF(41): 0.7, RF(28): 0.7, LF(14): 0.1	0.7
2020	PIT	MLB	29	18	2	0	0	0	2	2	4	1	0	18.8%	.188/.278/.188	93	.250	-0.2	RF(5): 0.1, CF(2): 2.4	0.3
2020	NYM	MLB	29	18	4	0	0	2	3	1	5	0	0	21.4%	.235/.278/.588	109	.200	-0.1	CF(7): -0.6	0.0
2021	ATL	MLB	30	347	46	26	0	5	26	32	81	0	0	27.5%	.220/.311/.354	85	.282	2.2	CF(108): 1.5, LF(21): -0.8	1.1
2022 DC	*ATL*	*MLB*	*31*	*343*	*39*	*16*	*0*	*6*	*35*	*31*	*81*	*2*	*2*	*26.5%*	*.224/.313/.348*	*85*	*.285*	*-0.3*	*CF 1, LF 1*	*0.7*

Comparables: Rajai Davis, Jarrod Dyson, Dexter Fowler

Heredia is your typical fourth outfielder. He got a chance to play far more regularly than anybody expected this year and during that period, showed exactly why he's a fourth outfielder. He is, however, an absolute delight and few players in baseball take more joy and glee in showing up to the ballpark everyday. This is a guy who celebrated a walk-off victory by hopping the dugout rail and sprinting to the celebration pile—reaching first base quicker than the guy who actually hit the walk-off. He also did this while holding two plastic swords in hand. Anybody who brings plastic swords to work is someone who loves their job with a passion, and Heredia loves this sport with everything he's got.

★ ★ ★ *2022 Top 101 Prospect* **#75** ★ ★ ★

Shea Langeliers C

Born: 11/18/97 Age: 24 Bats: R Throws: R Height: 6'0" Weight: 205 lb. Origin: Round 1, 2019 Draft (#9 overall)

YEAR	TEAM	LVL	AGE	PA	R	2B	3B	HR	RBI	BB	K	SB	CS	Whiff%	AVG/OBP/SLG	DRC+	BABIP	BRR	FRAA	WARP
2019	ROM	A	21	239	27	13	0	2	34	17	55	0	0		.255/.310/.343	89	.325	-1.0	C(42): 2.6	0.6
2021	MIS	AA	23	370	56	13	0	22	52	36	97	1	0		.258/.338/.498	136	.299	0.3	C(79): -12.9	1.6
2022 non-DC	*ATL*	*MLB*	*24*	*251*	*25*	*10*	*0*	*7*	*27*	*19*	*75*	*0*	*0*	*32.8%*	*.223/.289/.375*	*77*	*.298*	*-0.4*	*C -3*	*0.1*

Comparables: José Briceño, Elias Díaz, Will Smith

YEAR	TEAM	P. COUNT	FRM RUNS	BLK RUNS	THRW RUNS	TOT RUNS
2019	ROM	5708	2.0		0.4	2.4
2021	MIS	11234	-13.8	0.4	0.5	-13.0
2022	*ATL*	*6956*	*-2.3*	*-0.1*	*0.0*	*-2.4*

While the replacement-level catchers that the Braves used for the majority of the 2021 season were busy languishing in the DRC+ doldrums, all fans could do was recreate that one meme taken from the old animated X-Men show. It's the one where a restless Wolverine is lying on a bed in one frame and longingly caressing a photo in another frame. If the clawed mutant represented Braves fans, then the figure in the photo was Langeliers, who was in Double-A tearing it up with a DRC+ of 136. You won't have to wait too much longer to see Langeliers; he took a leap at the plate to go with a strong reputation behind it. Just put the photo back on the shelf and sleep tight, he'll be on his way to the majors pretty soon.

Marcell Ozuna LF

Born: 11/12/90 Age: 31 Bats: R Throws: R Height: 6'1" Weight: 225 lb. Origin: International Free Agent, 2008

YEAR	TEAM	LVL	AGE	PA	R	2B	3B	HR	RBI	BB	K	SB	CS	Whiff%	AVG/OBP/SLG	DRC+	BABIP	BRR	FRAA	WARP
2019	STL	MLB	28	549	80	23	1	29	89	62	114	12	2	27.7%	.241/.328/.472	119	.257	3.3	LF(129): -11.2	2.5
2020	ATL	MLB	29	267	38	14	0	18	56	38	60	0	0	31.4%	.338/.431/.636	149	.391	-0.8	LF(19): 2.3, RF(2): -0.5	2.4
2021	GIG	WIN	30	90	10	4	0	4	13	10	13	0	0		.316/.389/.519		.333			
2021	ATL	MLB	30	208	21	6	0	7	26	19	46	0	0	27.5%	.213/.288/.356	95	.244	0.3	LF(48): 3.2	1.0
2022 DC	*ATL*	*MLB*	*31*	*209*	*35*	*8*	*0*	*10*	*31*	*23*	*44*	*1*	*1*	*28.1%*	*.262/.347/.478*	*118*	*.294*	*-0.2*	*LF 0*	*0.4*

Comparables: Rondell White, Ellis Burks, Tim Raines

www.menstoppingviolence.org | Men Stopping Violence is a community-based activist organization in Atlanta that works to involve men in combatting male violence against women.

The National Domestic Violence Hotline is 1-800-799-7233 and thehotline.org is a helpful starting point to find resources and information as to how to get help.

★ ★ ★ *2022 Top 101 Prospect* **#71** ★ ★ ★

Cristian Pache OF

Born: 11/19/98 Age: 23 Bats: R Throws: R Height: 6'2" Weight: 215 lb. Origin: International Free Agent, 2015

YEAR	TEAM	LVL	AGE	PA	R	2B	3B	HR	RBI	BB	K	SB	CS	Whiff%	AVG/OBP/SLG	DRC+	BABIP	BRR	FRAA	WARP
2019	MIS	AA	20	433	50	28	8	11	53	34	104	8	11		.278/.340/.474	119	.351	-2.0	CF(58): 1.1, RF(23): 3.0, LF(22): 0.1	2.8
2019	GWN	AAA	20	105	13	8	1	1	8	9	18	0	0		.274/.337/.411	96	.329	-1.4	CF(23): -3.2, RF(3): 3.5	0.2
2020	ATL	MLB	21	4	0	0	0	0	0	0	2	0	0	33.3%	.250/.250/.250	96	.500		LF(2): 0.2	0.0
2021	GWN	AAA	22	353	50	15	0	11	44	30	97	9	7		.265/.330/.414	89	.347	0.6	CF(79): -3.9, RF(4): 0.1	0.5
2021	ATL	MLB	22	68	6	3	0	1	4	2	25	0	0	36.9%	.111/.152/.206	65	.162	1.2	CF(22): -1.8	-0.1
2022 DC	*ATL*	*MLB*	*23*	*336*	*37*	*15*	*2*	*6*	*36*	*21*	*99*	*6*	*4*	*32.1%*	*.225/.279/.356*	*69*	*.308*	*0.5*	*CF -1*	*-0.2*

Comparables: Manuel Margot, Anthony Gose, Melky Cabrera

If you ever need a reminder that prospect development is rarely ever linear, Pache is a living and breathing example. After his appearance in the 2020 postseason, it felt safe to assume that the time was now for Pache to assume control of center field for the Braves. He played a grand total of 22 games in the big leagues for Atlanta before an injury helped put him back on the farm for the rest of the 2021 season (outside of a cameo in the playoffs when Jorge Soler hit the COVID-19 IL). While it may have been unfair for minor-league hitters to have to deal with an outfielder who was quite clearly major-league ready defensively, it was clear that he still needed some time in a low-pressure situation to bring his bat up to snuff. If that happens, Pache's glove will make him an above-average player in aggregate, but there's never been more reason for doubt.

Manny Piña C

Born: 06/05/87 Age: 35 Bats: R Throws: R Height: 6'0" Weight: 222 lb. Origin: International Free Agent, 2004

YEAR	TEAM	LVL	AGE	PA	R	2B	3B	HR	RBI	BB	K	SB	CS	Whiff%	AVG/OBP/SLG	DRC+	BABIP	BRR	FRAA	WARP
2019	MIL	MLB	32	179	10	8	0	7	25	16	50	0	0	27.1%	.228/.313/.411	86	.284	-0.5	C(53): 8.7	1.2
2020	MIL	MLB	33	45	4	1	0	2	5	3	11	0	0	27.6%	.231/.333/.410	100	.269	-0.2	C(13): 2.0	0.4
2021	MIL	MLB	34	208	27	6	0	13	33	22	38	0	0	23.8%	.189/.293/.439	111	.162	0.4	C(65): 7.2	2.0
2022 DC	*ATL*	*MLB*	*35*	*189*	*22*	*7*	*0*	*5*	*22*	*17*	*40*	*0*	*0*	*24.4%*	*.225/.313/.370*	*86*	*.267*	*-0.3*	*C 5*	*1.0*

Comparables: Martín Maldonado, René Rivera, Francisco Cervelli

YEAR	TEAM	P. COUNT	FRM RUNS	BLK RUNS	THRW RUNS	TOT RUNS
2019	MIL	6204	8.1	0.2	0.4	8.7
2020	MIL	1750	1.7	0.0	0.0	1.7
2021	MIL	7534	4.4	0.6	0.4	5.3
2022	*ATL*	*7215*	*4.9*	*0.9*	*0.5*	*6.3*

The life of a backup catcher is thankless. Catchers already have a lot more on their plate than the average position player—learning the tendencies for and developing a rapport with every pitcher on your staff, controlling the running game, receiving pitches, acting as a conveniently placed end table for umpires, the list goes on. Backups have to do the same thing, all while knowing they're only going to need to use that knowledge and preparation once or twice a week. That's even more extreme when you're a backup for an All-Star-caliber catcher [every Cardinals and Royals backup catcher from the last decade nods knowingly]. Oh, and you've got to be able to hit a little bit, too, even though you've never been able to hit all that well to begin with. Otherwise you'd be a starter, and not a backup. This has been Piña's life for the better part of the last decade, and he's played the part well. He won't hit for average, but walks and hits for just enough pop to settle in right around league-average offensively. He also gets good marks for his defense and framing, and the Brewers have clearly liked the way he handles the pitching staff enough to employ him for the last six years. The one positive of being a backup catcher? A longer shelf life thanks to less wear-and-tear on the knees. Piña is in his mid-30s now, and will continue to ply his trade, professionally yet thanklessly, for at least another two seasons thanks to Atlanta picking him up before the lockout.

Austin Riley 3B

Born: 04/02/97 Age: 25 Bats: R Throws: R Height: 6'3" Weight: 240 lb. Origin: Round 1, 2015 Draft (#41 overall)

YEAR	TEAM	LVL	AGE	PA	R	2B	3B	HR	RBI	BB	K	SB	CS	Whiff%	AVG/OBP/SLG	DRC+	BABIP	BRR	FRAA	WARP
2019	GWN	AAA	22	194	39	13	0	15	41	20	39	0	0		.293/.366/.626	145	.300	0.2	3B(30): -1.2, LF(7): -0.9, 1B(4): 0.3	1.4
2019	ATL	MLB	22	297	41	11	1	18	49	16	108	0	2	38.6%	.226/.279/.471	84	.293	-0.5	LF(58): 1.4, 1B(6): -0.7, 3B(5): -0.3	0.4
2020	ATL	MLB	23	206	24	7	1	8	27	16	49	0	0	30.1%	.239/.301/.415	94	.280	0.5	3B(46): 2.5, 1B(4): 0.6, LF(4): -0.2	0.7
2021	ATL	MLB	24	662	91	33	1	33	107	52	168	0	1	28.1%	.303/.367/.531	121	.368	-0.3	3B(156): -0.7, 1B(10): -0.3, RF(1): 0.1	3.9
2022 DC	*ATL*	*MLB*	*25*	*549*	*85*	*25*	*1*	*27*	*91*	*42*	*136*	*0*	*1*	*28.2%*	*.271/.338/.498*	*121*	*.321*	*-0.8*	*3B 0, 1B 0*	*3.0*

Comparables: Mike Moustakas, Nolan Arenado, Maikel Franco

In June of 1996, Stone Cold Steve Austin took part in the latter stages of WWE's King of the Ring tournament in Milwaukee. He defeated Marc Mero in the semis and then squared off against Jake "The Snake" Roberts in the finals. Roberts had recently returned to the company with a preacher gimmick (he had become a born-again Christian and real-life preacher) that involved him frequently quoting the Bible. Austin dispatched Roberts in under five minutes and gave a post-victory speech, telling the preacher and the listening world that while he could invoke John 3:16 all he wanted, "Austin 3:16 says I just whipped your ass!"

Riley fell three total bases shy of 316 in 2021, but he lived the tenets of Austin 3:16 to the fullest anyway; just ask any National League pitcher. The third baseman put together a dominant season, showing that he could reliably access the light-tower power he flashed in the immediate aftermath of his big-league debut, but which had since gone cold. While there's plenty of swing-and-miss tendency remaining in his game, Riley showed the ability to cut down on whiffs against breaking balls and off-speed pitches, and good things happen whenever he makes contact. No one thought Riley was going to be a bust because of his disappointing 2020 campaign, but putting together a down-ballot MVP season was something of a Stone Cold Stunner.

Braden Shewmake SS
Born: 11/19/97 Age: 24 Bats: L Throws: R Height: 6'4" Weight: 190 lb. Origin: Round 1, 2019 Draft (#21 overall)

YEAR	TEAM	LVL	AGE	PA	R	2B	3B	HR	RBI	BB	K	SB	CS	Whiff%	AVG/OBP/SLG	DRC+	BABIP	BRR	FRAA	WARP
2019	ROM	A	21	226	37	18	2	3	39	21	29	11	3		.318/.389/.473	128	.359	2.8	SS(39): -0.2	1.7
2019	MIS	AA	21	52	7	0	0	0	1	4	11	2	0		.217/.288/.217	90	.278	-0.1	SS(14): 2.0	0.3
2021	MIS	AA	23	344	40	14	3	12	40	17	75	4	2		.228/.271/.401	100	.262	-0.4	SS(79): 5.3	1.5
2022 non-DC	*ATL*	*MLB*	*24*	*251*	*22*	*11*	*1*	*5*	*25*	*13*	*57*	*3*	*2*	*27.2%*	*.236/.284/.362*	*74*	*.292*	*0.2*	*SS 2*	*0.3*

Comparables: Niko Goodrum, Brad Miller, Asdrúbal Cabrera

The Braves have been known to be aggressive when it comes to promoting intriguing prospects, and Shewmake is a prime example of that philosophy. After spending his initial time in Double-A struggling, Shewmake finally got around to looking more and more like the hitter who tore up High-A. This was especially true as he started developing power to complement his already-good hit tool and was putting plenty of good contact on the ball once he started getting used to the level of play at Mississippi. Defensively, he's continued to field his position in a consistent manner while using his arm to steal a few tough outs. That arm may end up being the reason why he continues moving up the organizational ladder and finding himself in a utility role once he arrives in the bigs.

Dansby Swanson SS
Born: 02/11/94 Age: 28 Bats: R Throws: R Height: 6'1" Weight: 190 lb. Origin: Round 1, 2015 Draft (#1 overall)

YEAR	TEAM	LVL	AGE	PA	R	2B	3B	HR	RBI	BB	K	SB	CS	Whiff%	AVG/OBP/SLG	DRC+	BABIP	BRR	FRAA	WARP
2019	ATL	MLB	25	545	77	26	3	17	65	51	124	10	5	27.5%	.251/.325/.422	95	.300	1.7	SS(126): 0.0	1.8
2020	ATL	MLB	26	264	49	15	0	10	35	22	71	5	0	31.6%	.274/.345/.464	99	.350	2.2	SS(60): -0.2	0.9
2021	ATL	MLB	27	653	78	33	2	27	88	52	167	9	3	30.5%	.248/.311/.449	98	.297	0.3	SS(159): -6.2	1.6
2022 DC	*ATL*	*MLB*	*28*	*571*	*76*	*26*	*2*	*18*	*73*	*48*	*146*	*7*	*4*	*30.1%*	*.239/.309/.403*	*91*	*.299*	*0.1*	*SS -1*	*1.4*

Comparables: Shawon Dunston, Dave Concepcion, Alan Trammell

There are two versions of this guy that you're liable to see at a ballpark during any given season. Sometimes, it'll be a lovely couple of weeks where Swanson is coming up to the plate and crushing the baseball on a regular basis. The other version stays around for a fortnight or so, and spends his time scuffling mightily at the plate. Which one is the real Swanson? It's possible that the two Swansons that we see on the diamond are both interlopers and the genuine article is trapped in some alternate dimension that us mere mortals and earthlings currently have no access to. Either way, it's about time we see the real Swanson make his presence known. The boom-or-bust periods are fairly jarring to witness at this point, but that's the Duality of Dansby. One way or another, though, one of these Swansons showed up every day, playing in 160 of 162 games after playing in all 60 in 2020. While they might average out to an, um, average player, there's real value in simply being present.

Stephen Vogt C
Born: 11/01/84 Age: 37 Bats: L Throws: R Height: 6'0" Weight: 216 lb. Origin: Round 12, 2007 Draft (#365 overall)

YEAR	TEAM	LVL	AGE	PA	R	2B	3B	HR	RBI	BB	K	SB	CS	Whiff%	AVG/OBP/SLG	DRC+	BABIP	BRR	FRAA	WARP
2019	SAC	AAA	34	72	9	3	0	4	7	14	11	0	0		.241/.389/.500	123	.233	-1.1	C(9): 0.7, 1B(6): -0.3, LF(1): -0.1	0.4
2019	SF	MLB	34	280	30	24	2	10	40	20	66	3	1	26.8%	.263/.314/.490	94	.311	0.2	C(60): 2.6, LF(7): -0.2, 1B(1): 0.0	1.2
2020	ARI	MLB	35	81	6	5	0	1	7	8	18	0	0	19.6%	.167/.247/.278	81	.204	-0.4	C(23): 1.4, 1B(1): 0.1	0.2
2021	ATL	MLB	36	87	7	0	0	2	8	8	20	0	0	24.9%	.167/.241/.244	81	.193	0.4	C(23): 0.2	0.2
2021	ARI	MLB	36	151	17	6	1	5	17	18	36	0	0	27.2%	.212/.307/.386	94	.253	-1.2	C(40): 2.1, 1B(2): -0.0	0.6
2022 non-DC	*ATL*	*MLB*	*37*	*251*	*25*	*11*	*0*	*7*	*27*	*25*	*59*	*0*	*1*	*25.8%*	*.215/.298/.368*	*78*	*.261*	*-0.3*	*C 1, 1B 0*	*0.5*

Comparables: Johnny Edwards, Gregg Zaun, Ramon Hernandez

YEAR	TEAM	P. COUNT	FRM RUNS	BLK RUNS	THRW RUNS	TOT RUNS
2019	SF	7706	0.2	-0.2	0.8	0.8
2019	SAC	1375	0.2	-0.1	0.1	0.2
2020	ARI	2961	1.7	0.0	0.1	1.7
2021	ARI	5282	0.9	0.0	0.2	1.1
2021	ATL	3089	0.5	-0.1	0.0	0.4
2022	*ATL*	*6956*	*0.6*	*0.1*	*0.0*	*0.6*

Vogt's best game of the season was on September 9, when he had his first multi-homer game since 2017. He didn't even get to finish that game because he injured his hip. That one night of dizzying peaks and cavernous valleys belies what was otherwise a pedestrian season for the veteran catcher. If that's the end for Vogt, who played a big role in reshaping Atlanta's clubhouse after his mid-season acquisition, then he went out in a shining blaze of glory.

Drew Waters OF
Born: 12/30/98 Age: 23 Bats: S Throws: R Height: 6'2" Weight: 185 lb. Origin: Round 2, 2017 Draft (#41 overall)

YEAR	TEAM	LVL	AGE	PA	R	2B	3B	HR	RBI	BB	K	SB	CS	Whiff%	AVG/OBP/SLG	DRC+	BABIP	BRR	FRAA	WARP
2019	MIS	AA	20	454	63	35	9	5	41	28	121	13	6		.319/.366/.481	108	.436	-2.1	LF(55): 8.1, CF(38): 6.7, RF(18): -1.0	3.3
2019	GWN	AAA	20	119	17	5	0	2	11	11	43	3	0		.271/.336/.374	66	.429	0.7	RF(16): 2.4, LF(7): 0.4, CF(3): 0.7	0.3
2021	GWN	AAA	22	459	70	22	1	11	37	47	142	28	9		.240/.329/.381	85	.341	2.1	LF(44): 4.3, CF(38): 6.2, RF(25): 2.8	2.2
2022 DC	*ATL*	*MLB*	*23*	*298*	*35*	*15*	*2*	*5*	*30*	*24*	*94*	*7*	*3*	*32.8%*	*.224/.295/.354*	*74*	*.324*	*0.6*	*LF 3, RF 2*	*0.4*

Comparables: Colby Rasmus, Byron Buxton, Alex Verdugo

Any delusions of grandeur that involved Waters making his Braves debut during 2021 dissolved once he got around to playing in Triple-A for a full season. Long-known for his skills at the plate, Waters' production evaporated with prolonged exposure to Triple-A arms. There were always questions as to whether Waters' hacking tendencies would dilute his overall talent but until this year, he'd made it work. Sometimes, the moves an organization *doesn't* make speaks the loudest, and when Atlanta was in dire need of outfielders, they opted not to turn to their touted prospects in Triple-A. The offensive drought doesn't mean that he's out of the organizational plans for the future, but it does mean that stark adjustments are in order. A little more patience is step one, but so is harder contact and a bit more loft when he does make the choice to offer at a pitch. He's still solid in center or a corner outfield spot, so if he can start to make some changes at the plate, a rising tide could lift the whole profile.

PITCHERS

Ian Anderson RHP Born: 05/02/98 Age: 24 Bats: R Throws: R Height: 6'3" Weight: 170 lb. Origin: Round 1, 2016 Draft (#3 overall)

YEAR	TEAM	LVL	AGE	W	L	SV	G	GS	IP	H	HR	BB/9	K/9	K	GB%	BABIP	WHIP	ERA	DRA-	WARP	MPH	FB%	Whiff%	CSP
2019	MIS	AA	21	7	5	0	21	21	111	82	8	3.8	11.9	147	44.4%	.290	1.16	2.68	71	2.4				
2019	GWN	AAA	21	1	2	0	5	5	24^2	23	5	6.6	9.1	25	37.1%	.277	1.66	6.57	101	0.3				
2020	ATL	MLB	22	3	2	0	6	6	32^1	21	1	3.9	11.4	41	53.1%	.250	1.08	1.95	68	0.9	94.3	48.5%	29.0%	46.6%
2021	GWN	AAA	23	0	0	0	4	4	14^2	12	0	5.5	12.3	20	51.4%	.343	1.43	3.68	84	0.3				
2021	ATL	MLB	23	9	5	0	24	24	128^1	105	16	3.7	8.7	124	48.2%	.265	1.23	3.58	88	1.9	94.7	47.4%	28.9%	55.1%
2022 DC	*ATL*	*MLB*	*24*	*8*	*7*	*0*	*24*	*24*	*126.3*	*113*	*13*	*4.3*	*9.3*	*130*	*48.0%*	*.294*	*1.38*	*3.93*	*95*	*1.4*	*94.6*	*47.6%*	*28.9%*	*53.8%*

Comparables: Johnny Cueto, Eduardo Rodriguez, Daniel Hudson

After appearing to cruise through the minors on "easy" mode, Anderson was dropped into the 2020 campaign with the level ratcheted up to "hard," as he was tasked with joining a depleted rotation mid-pennant race, and then help carry the team through the playoffs on the back of an upgraded changeup. He managed to complete the level without losing a life, only to learn that 2020 was the prologue and 2021 was the real game, so to speak. Armed with that nasty changeup, a sharp fastball and a refined curveball, Anderson embarked on the adventure that was a full regular season at the major-league level. It was complete with its ups and downs, as he'd display dominant stretches at times, while at others, he hit a difficulty spike. The important thing is that the increased difficulty didn't seem to throw him off his trajectory towards the top of the rotation, and having helped pitch Atlanta to the World Series, Anderson is on the cusp of unlocking "legendary" mode.

Ryan Cusick RHP Born: 11/12/99 Age: 22 Bats: R Throws: R Height: 6'6" Weight: 235 lb. Origin: Round 1, 2021 Draft (#24 overall)

YEAR	TEAM	LVL	AGE	W	L	SV	G	GS	IP	H	HR	BB/9	K/9	K	GB%	BABIP	WHIP	ERA	DRA-	WARP	MPH	FB%	Whiff%	CSP
2021	AUG	A	21	0	1	0	6	6	16^1	15	1	2.2	18.7	34	57.1%	.519	1.16	2.76	57	0.5				
2022 non-DC	*ATL*	*MLB*	*22*	*2*	*2*	*0*	*57*	*0*	*50*	*44*	*7*	*4.1*	*10.4*	*58*	*43.1%*	*.300*	*1.35*	*4.19*	*101*	*0.2*				

Comparables: Taylor Widener, Steven Jennings, John Carver

Atlanta used their 2021 first-round pick on the tall right-handed Cusick from Wake Forest. The former Demon Deacon went from baptizing the ACC to being hell on hitters in Low-A—albeit in small doses, averaging 2 ⅔ innings per start. He attacks hitters with fire, a fastball that can clock 100 on the radar gun, and his complementary brimstone is a power curve that can bring batters to their knees. Speaking of which, it's time to confess: the curve is lacking in consistency, and his third pitch is a rarely used firm changeup. Pair those sins with command and control issues, and more than a couple scouts will testify that his long-term residence will be in the bullpen. His professional debut gives hope to the faithful that he can avoid such condemnations, and the implementation of a slider after he signed could be a positive development for either role going forward. May he begin to answer those questions as soon as next year, amen.

Dylan Dodd LHP Born: 06/06/98 Age: 24 Bats: L Throws: L Height: 6'3" Weight: 210 lb. Origin: Round 3, 2021 Draft (#96 overall)

YEAR	TEAM	LVL	AGE	W	L	SV	G	GS	IP	H	HR	BB/9	K/9	K	GB%	BABIP	WHIP	ERA	DRA-	WARP	MPH	FB%	Whiff%	CSP
2021	AUG	A	23	0	1	0	3	3	11	10	0	2.5	11.5	14	38.5%	.385	1.18	4.91	92	0.1				
2022 non-DC	*ATL*	*MLB*	*24*	*2*	*3*	*0*	*57*	*0*	*50*	*50*	*8*	*3.8*	*7.3*	*40*	*34.4%*	*.287*	*1.43*	*5.05*	*119*	*-0.3*				

Comparables: Lucas Gilbreath, Jack Dashwood, Thomas Szapucki

Even going back to his days at Southeast Missouri State, Dodd has shown the ability to improve pretty quickly. The Braves got to see this for themselves, as Dodd needed only 11 innings in Low-A before making it to High-A to end the season. While it would be unreasonable to think that he's going to ride a turbo-fueled rocket ship to the majors, it would make sense that Dodd—with 2022 being his age-24 season—will be fast-tracked. He's already got solid command of both his nifty changeup and fastball, with the latter pitch hitting the mid-90s while in college. His curveball and slider are solid pitches on their own merits, and the four-pitch mix gives him a good chance to remain a starter, if a likely back-end one. There's very little flashy here, but Dodd is a probable major-leaguer. If he gets there, he'll join Shae Simmons as the only other Redhawk to wear a Braves uniform and Joey Lucchesi as the only other active player from Southeast Missouri State in the majors.

Bryce Elder RHP Born: 05/19/99 Age: 23 Bats: R Throws: R Height: 6'2" Weight: 220 lb. Origin: Round 5, 2020 Draft (#156 overall)

YEAR	TEAM	LVL	AGE	W	L	SV	G	GS	IP	H	HR	BB/9	K/9	K	GB%	BABIP	WHIP	ERA	DRA-	WARP	MPH	FB%	Whiff%	CSP
2021	ROM	A+	22	2	1	0	9	9	45	38	2	4.0	11.0	55	58.6%	.316	1.29	2.60	79	0.9				
2021	MIS	AA	22	7	1	0	9	9	56	39	7	2.7	9.6	60	58.7%	.244	1.00	3.21	86	1.0				
2021	GWN	AAA	22	2	3	0	7	7	36^2	18	1	4.9	9.8	40	53.5%	.200	1.04	2.21	81	0.9				
2022 non-DC	*ATL*	*MLB*	*23*	*2*	*2*	*0*	*57*	*0*	*50*	*47*	*5*	*4.6*	*9.2*	*50*	*52.3%*	*.306*	*1.46*	*4.44*	*105*	*0.0*				

Comparables: Chad Kuhl, Scott Baker, Robert Gsellman

You hear a lot about multi-sport athletes who ultimately end up in the baseball pipeline, but it's not as common to hear about it when the other sport is golf. While Elder played baseball early in his life, he gravitated to the links before returning to split duty between baseball and golf as a sophomore in high school. His time away didn't seem to show much of an impact, as Elder showed the strike-throwing prowess and clean delivery of a, well, *more mature* pitcher. He landed at the University of Texas, eventually becoming their Friday night starter thanks to a deep repertoire he could land for strikes. Elder cut a swath through the minors thanks to his sinker/slider heavy approach, pitching at three levels and ending the season knocking on the door to the majors. He hasn't had as much success with the minor-league strike zone compared to what he did in college, but he made up for it with his ability to induce ground balls and seems like a lock to remain a starter. The fifth-round pick hasn't generated as much buzz among fans as his fellow prospect, Spencer Strider, but he's earned his place among Atlanta's bevy of pitching prospects, and in due time they'll be sure to respect their Elder.

Max Fried LHP

Born: 01/18/94 Age: 28 Bats: L Throws: L Height: 6'4" Weight: 190 lb. Origin: Round 1, 2012 Draft (#7 overall)

YEAR	TEAM	LVL	AGE	W	L	SV	G	GS	IP	H	HR	BB/9	K/9	K	GB%	BABIP	WHIP	ERA	DRA-	WARP	MPH	FB%	Whiff%	CSP
2019	ATL	MLB	25	17	6	0	33	30	165^2	174	21	2.6	9.4	173	52.8%	.338	1.33	4.02	89	2.7	93.9	57.0%	26.0%	47.8%
2020	ATL	MLB	26	7	0	0	11	11	56	42	2	3.1	8.0	50	52.3%	.268	1.09	2.25	85	1.1	93.2	51.9%	25.6%	46.7%
2021	ATL	MLB	27	14	7	0	28	28	165^2	139	15	2.2	8.6	158	51.0%	.281	1.09	3.04	81	3.1	94.0	50.4%	24.7%	57.2%
2022 DC	*ATL*	*MLB*	*28*	*10*	*8*	*0*	*27*	*27*	*156.7*	*147*	*16*	*2.7*	*8.6*	*149*	*51.3%*	*.298*	*1.24*	*3.51*	*89*	*2.1*	*93.9*	*52.1%*	*25.1%*	*53.6%*

Comparables: Tom Glavine, Andy Pettitte, Johan Santana

After a 2020 season that saw Fried's outstanding surface stats outpace his still-very-good peripherals, it wasn't unreasonable to anticipate a (small) step back. That didn't happen. Instead, Fried improved his underlying qualities, upping his strikeout rate, slashing his walk rate and maintaining a groundball percentage over 50. His ERA backslid a touch, but make no mistake: Fried authored a top-tier season, culminating in a Game 6 World Series clincher. One thing that did carry over from 2020 for the gangly Californian? A decreased reliance on his four-seamer in favor of mixing in a sinker around 11% of the time. The increased diversity in pitches helped keep batters guessing at the dish, rather than sitting on his bodacious breakers. The curveball in particular continues to buckle knees, as it arcs high out of his hand before seeming to pause, then comes crashing down harder than a bass drop in an EDM banger. At this point it's hard to see anything Fried could do better, beyond shouldering a larger workload—he's capped out under 170 innings in each of his last two seasons. Entering his age-28 season with an expanding repertoire to turn lineups over with, it shouldn't surprise if he conquers that hill next.

Jay Jackson RHP

Born: 10/27/87 Age: 34 Bats: R Throws: R Height: 6'1" Weight: 195 lb. Origin: Round 9, 2008 Draft (#281 overall)

YEAR	TEAM	LVL	AGE	W	L	SV	G	GS	IP	H	HR	BB/9	K/9	K	GB%	BABIP	WHIP	ERA	DRA-	WARP	MPH	FB%	Whiff%	CSP
2019	SA	AAA	31	5	2	8	34	0	40^2	28	1	2.2	12.0	54	35.8%	.300	0.93	1.33	70	1.0				
2019	MIL	MLB	31	1	0	0	28	0	30^1	22	6	5.3	13.9	47	36.9%	.276	1.32	4.45	78	0.7	94.6	41.5%	39.3%	41.3%
2021	SAC	AAA	33	1	0	0	10	0	14	5	1	0.6	15.4	24	65.2%	.182	0.43	1.29	67	0.3				
2021	SF	MLB	33	2	1	0	23	1	21^2	15	3	5.0	11.6	28	28.0%	.261	1.25	3.74	89	0.3	94.8	34.8%	29.9%	50.7%
2022 DC	*ATL*	*MLB*	*34*	*3*	*2*	*0*	*59*	*0*	*51.7*	*39*	*7*	*3.5*	*11.5*	*66*	*38.0%*	*.272*	*1.15*	*3.13*	*81*	*0.7*	*94.7*	*37.0%*	*32.9%*	*47.7%*

Comparables: Anthony Swarzak, Bob Howry, Al Reyes

Jackson's write-ups in the present publication stretch from 2009 to 2012, with a seven-year hiatus before a lineout in the 2020 annual. He has pitched in 56 major-league innings across three non-consecutive seasons. He has been in seven major-league organizations (Atlanta will be his eighth), along with a year pitching for the Chiba Lotte Marines and three with the Hiroshima Carp in NPB. As a 34-year-old reliever, he brings the requisite fastball-slider combination, though he uses the slider as his primary pitch, playing the fastball off of the breaker. He was a key relief arm during the Giants' dominant stretch run. From this profile alone, you'd deduce that Jackson was a deeply driven and determined person, someone who has given most of his life to baseball, even when its love for him was sometimes fleeting and fickle. Which makes it all the more infuriating that, as a Black baseball player, Jackson was subject to violent racist abuse on social media after a three-run outing against the Diamondbacks in early August. Jackson shared these messages with the world, revealing more depressing examples of the depths of racist hate that permeate a segment of baseball's fan base. Jackson forged a long, grinding career in baseball, mostly out of the spotlight, only to be served up threats and insults when he momentarily entered it for the wrong reasons. Jackson reflected a mirror on some fans' virulent racism, and then, later in the series, got back to work, throwing shutout innings on consecutive days, striking out the side each time.

Luke Jackson RHP

Born: 08/24/91 Age: 30 Bats: R Throws: R Height: 6'2" Weight: 210 lb. Origin: Round 1, 2010 Draft (#45 overall)

YEAR	TEAM	LVL	AGE	W	L	SV	G	GS	IP	H	HR	BB/9	K/9	K	GB%	BABIP	WHIP	ERA	DRA-	WARP	MPH	FB%	Whiff%	CSP
2019	ATL	MLB	27	9	2	18	70	0	72^2	76	10	3.2	13.1	106	59.1%	.388	1.40	3.84	67	2.0	96.3	37.9%	36.8%	42.5%
2020	ATL	MLB	28	2	0	0	19	0	26^1	39	2	4.4	6.8	20	61.9%	.389	1.97	6.84	102	0.3	94.5	37.4%	23.2%	43.0%
2021	ATL	MLB	29	2	2	0	71	0	63^2	45	6	4.1	9.9	70	52.5%	.255	1.16	1.98	86	1.0	95.9	35.7%	30.7%	54.0%
2022 DC	*ATL*	*MLB*	*30*	*3*	*3*	*5*	*67*	*0*	*58*	*54*	*6*	*4.0*	*9.6*	*62*	*52.1%*	*.306*	*1.37*	*3.96*	*96*	*0.3*	*95.7*	*36.5%*	*30.8%*	*49.3%*

Comparables: Jeremy Jeffress, Zach McAllister, Ryan Webb

The motto for the City of Atlanta is simply one word: "Resurgens," Latin for "Rising Again." While Truist Park is a few miles away from the actual city itself, it appears that Jackson has taken this motto to heart. After a bit of a letdown in 2020 following a solid 2019 campaign, Jackson returned to form in 2021 and did so by doing what brought him to the 1.0 WARP club two seasons ago: His fastball whiff percentage in 2021 landed at 22.2%, more than double his 2020 figure. He also induced more swings-and-misses with his curveball and his signature slider, which he used as an out-pitch with impressive effect. Perhaps most refreshingly, Jackson finally endured a season that didn't see him fall prey to the types of dinks and dunks that can unravel a reliever: While his BABIP had run in the high .380s the last two seasons, it settled in at .255 in 2021. Jackson has the occasional blowup or series where his stuff leaves him (think the NLCS), but he's shown the resiliency required for high-leverage arms. Relievers are prone to more variance than most other positions, so it remains to be seen if Jackson's resurgens will last or give way to regression, at which point he may or may not resurgens again. If you think about it, we all resurgens until we don't. Who knew the Braves had such an existential pitcher?

Tyler Matzek LHP Born: 10/19/90 Age: 31 Bats: L Throws: L Height: 6'3" Weight: 230 lb. Origin: Round 1, 2009 Draft (#11 overall)

YEAR	TEAM	LVL	AGE	W	L	SV	G	GS	IP	H	HR	BB/9	K/9	K	GB%	BABIP	WHIP	ERA	DRA-	WARP	MPH	FB%	Whiff%	CSP
2019	GWN	AAA	28	0	0	0	5	0	10	10	1	4.5	11.7	13	48.1%	.360	1.50	9.00	85	0.2				
2020	ATL	MLB	29	4	3	0	21	0	29	23	1	3.1	13.3	43	45.5%	.338	1.14	2.79	65	0.9	94.3	70.8%	27.6%	47.8%
2021	ATL	MLB	30	0	4	0	69	0	63	40	3	5.3	11.0	77	37.8%	.262	1.22	2.57	85	1.1	96.1	70.6%	30.0%	54.4%
2022 DC	*ATL*	*MLB*	*31*	*3*	*3*	*0*	*67*	*0*	*58*	*47*	*8*	*4.6*	*10.8*	*70*	*40.4%*	*.277*	*1.32*	*3.94*	*95*	*0.4*	*95.7*	*70.7%*	*29.5%*	*52.8%*

Comparables: Andrew Miller, Arthur Rhodes, Steve Karsay

In case you figured that Matzek's miracle comeback during the 2020 season was just a result of the 60-game sprint injecting some enjoyable but short-lived variance, Matzek removed all doubt by going out and delivering an encore performance over a full season. It wasn't completely smooth sailing for Matzek, but if anybody has the fortitude to rebound from a down period, it's this guy. Matzek's walk rate did go up a little bit, but oftentimes the option batters had against him was either find a way to take a walk or put some weak contact on his elusive slider. By the time the postseason rolled around, weak contact was basically a victory when Matzek was on the mound. His performance (along with the rest of the Night Shift) in the NLCS against the Dodgers will go down in Atlanta lore. The only thing more gratifying than Matzek's return from the yips and independent ball is his sustained success being parlayed into a World Series championship.

A.J. Minter LHP Born: 09/02/93 Age: 28 Bats: L Throws: L Height: 6'0" Weight: 215 lb. Origin: Round 2, 2015 Draft (#75 overall)

YEAR	TEAM	LVL	AGE	W	L	SV	G	GS	IP	H	HR	BB/9	K/9	K	GB%	BABIP	WHIP	ERA	DRA-	WARP	MPH	FB%	Whiff%	CSP
2019	GWN	AAA	25	2	2	5	20	0	22^2	24	4	1.2	11.9	30	37.7%	.351	1.19	3.57	74	0.6				
2019	ATL	MLB	25	3	4	5	36	0	29^1	36	3	7.1	10.7	35	38.6%	.393	2.01	7.06	115	0.1	93.4	81.6%	30.5%	45.4%
2020	ATL	MLB	26	1	1	0	22	0	21^2	15	1	3.7	10.0	24	48.1%	.280	1.11	0.83	86	0.4	90.9	81.4%	29.1%	47.1%
2021	GWN	AAA	27	0	0	6	7	0	7^1	0	0	3.7	12.3	10	41.7%	.000	0.41	0.00	90	0.1				
2021	ATL	MLB	27	3	6	0	61	0	52^1	44	2	3.4	9.8	57	46.5%	.300	1.22	3.78	80	1.0	91.2	86.6%	31.5%	53.5%
2022 DC	*ATL*	*MLB*	*28*	*3*	*3*	*0*	*67*	*0*	*58*	*50*	*7*	*3.6*	*10.9*	*70*	*43.7%*	*.299*	*1.26*	*3.54*	*88*	*0.6*	*91.4*	*84.9%*	*30.9%*	*51.0%*

Comparables: B.J. Ryan, Antonio Osuna, Joe Smith

Minter may not be wearing black, but it's pretty clear that he's back. He showed glimpses of it in 2020, when he made a minor rebound from what was a disastrous 2019 for the lefty. Minter posted career-lows in cFIP, DRA and DRA–, and did so by continuing to find ways to use his cutter to induce some really weak contact. Things really solidified for him after he spent a few weeks in the minors: recalled on August 12, Minter dominated from that point forward. In 19 late-season innings, he recorded a 1.89 ERA (2.01 FIP), with 20 strikeouts against just six walks. Opponents batted .182/.219/.212 in that time period, and Minter saw that success and confidence carry over into a successful postseason run. The lofty comparisons to dominant relievers of the recent past are gone, but that's only allowed Minter to settle in as himself.

Charlie Morton RHP Born: 11/12/83 Age: 38 Bats: R Throws: R Height: 6'5" Weight: 215 lb. Origin: Round 3, 2002 Draft (#95 overall)

YEAR	TEAM	LVL	AGE	W	L	SV	G	GS	IP	H	HR	BB/9	K/9	K	GB%	BABIP	WHIP	ERA	DRA-	WARP	MPH	FB%	Whiff%	CSP
2019	TB	MLB	35	16	6	0	33	33	194^2	154	15	2.6	11.1	240	47.8%	.299	1.08	3.05	72	4.9	94.5	49.0%	29.6%	50.0%
2020	TB	MLB	36	2	2	0	9	9	38	43	4	2.4	9.9	42	42.1%	.355	1.39	4.74	83	0.8	93.6	56.4%	25.0%	52.4%
2021	ATL	MLB	37	14	6	0	33	33	185^2	136	16	2.8	10.5	216	47.5%	.271	1.04	3.34	72	4.5	95.4	49.5%	29.1%	54.0%
2022 DC	*ATL*	*MLB*	*38*	*10*	*7*	*0*	*25*	*25*	*152.7*	*127*	*18*	*2.9*	*9.7*	*165*	*45.7%*	*.278*	*1.15*	*3.23*	*83*	*2.6*	*95.0*	*50.0%*	*28.8%*	*52.9%*

Comparables: Dennis Martinez, Tom Candiotti, Orlando Pena

In a now-infamous WWE segment from 2013, Mark Henry went to the ring and announced his retirement. In a moment that felt authentic, John Cena came out and congratulated him on his career. This turned out to be a trap, as Henry suddenly body slammed Cena. Afterwards, Henry screamed "I got a lot left in the tank," and proceeded to wrestle for a few more years before actually retiring. Morton similarly body slammed every opposing hitter he could reach, posting one of the best seasons he's had since his initial career resurgence in 2017. Despite reaching age 37, Morton was able to get through 2021 without the shoulder issues that had previously plagued him. This resulted in the velocity on all of his pitches going up a tick, which means that there were moments where his curveball literally brought some batters to their knees as they whiffed. Morton truly solidified his face turn in Atlanta by pitching on a broken leg in Game 1 of the World Series, striking out Jose Altuve before needing to leave the game. He re-upped with the team for another run next year.

★ ★ ★ *2022 Top 101 Prospect* **#56** ★ ★ ★

Kyle Muller LHP Born: 10/07/97 Age: 24 Bats: R Throws: L Height: 6'7" Weight: 250 lb. Origin: Round 2, 2016 Draft (#44 overall)

YEAR	TEAM	LVL	AGE	W	L	SV	G	GS	IP	H	HR	BB/9	K/9	K	GB%	BABIP	WHIP	ERA	DRA-	WARP	MPH	FB%	Whiff%	CSP
2019	MIS	AA	21	7	6	0	22	22	111^2	81	5	5.5	9.7	120	39.2%	.286	1.33	3.14	108	0.2				
2021	GWN	AAA	23	5	4	0	17	17	79^2	66	9	4.7	10.5	93	41.6%	.286	1.36	3.39	78	2.0				
2021	ATL	MLB	23	2	4	0	9	8	36^2	26	2	4.9	9.1	37	37.5%	.261	1.25	4.17	106	0.2	93.4	42.4%	31.4%	54.2%
2022 DC	*ATL*	*MLB*	*24*	*4*	*3*	*0*	*33*	*4*	*46.7*	*41*	*6*	*5.1*	*9.4*	*49*	*39.4%*	*.288*	*1.46*	*4.59*	*107*	*0.2*	*93.4*	*42.4%*	*31.4%*	*54.2%*

Comparables: Robbie Erlin, Eduardo Rodriguez, Jake Thompson

When Muller made his major-league debut in June, it felt like the sky was the limit. He came up tossing the high heater that the fans had been waiting for, he was keeping the runs to a minimum and was giving Atlanta enough innings to justify as long of a look as possible. His first six starts were very encouraging, but then August rolled around. That's when his latent command issues popped up again and after two poor starts, Muller's first adventure in the majors came to a close. It was an unfortunate end to a promising major-league stint but at least Muller has an idea of what needs to be fixed. Whether he can fix it is another matter altogether, as his command and control woes have dogged him for a while yet.

Darren O'Day RHP Born: 10/22/82 Age: 39 Bats: R Throws: R Height: 6'4" Weight: 220 lb. Origin: Undrafted Free Agent, 2006

YEAR	TEAM	LVL	AGE	W	L	SV	G	GS	IP	H	HR	BB/9	K/9	K	GB%	BABIP	WHIP	ERA	DRA-	WARP	MPH	FB%	Whiff%	CSP
2019	ATL	MLB	36	0	0	0	8	0	5^1	3	0	1.7	10.1	6	23.1%	.231	0.75	1.69	102	0.0	86.9	55.1%	35.0%	47.5%
2020	ATL	MLB	37	4	0	0	19	0	16^1	8	1	2.8	12.1	22	27.0%	.194	0.80	1.10	92	0.2	86.1	57.1%	31.9%	44.8%
2021	NYY	MLB	38	0	0	0	12	0	10^2	9	2	3.4	9.3	11	26.7%	.250	1.22	3.38	101	0.1	85.7	51.3%	28.1%	46.9%
2022 non-DC	*NYY*	*MLB*	*39*	*2*	*2*	*0*	*57*	*0*	*50*	*42*	*9*	*2.7*	*10.5*	*58*	*32.6%*	*.276*	*1.15*	*3.80*	*94*	*0.3*	*85.9*	*54.2%*	*30.3%*	*46.0%*

Comparables: Jason Frasor, Todd Jones, Mike Marshall

Did you realize O'Day is 39 years old already? Weirdo journeyman relievers don't age; they just exist in stasis at the periphery of your awareness until they eventually fade away. Nevertheless, this is his 12th *Annual* comment, most of which fit into three tidy categories: 1) submarine delivery, 2) low velocity and 3) premature demise. All three still hold true. His release point could win a limbo contest against kindergarteners and his fastball is a few ticks too slow to time travel in a DeLorean. He threw only 52 ⅓ innings over the last four years and spent the second half of 2021 on the IL, so it's fair to wonder if this is the end of the line for real this time. Based on his resiliency over the course of a long, impressive career, and the wisdom of actuaries, it probably isn't. Atlanta, at least, was willing to bet $1 million in guaranteed money on the actuaries.

Richard Rodríguez RHP Born: 03/04/90 Age: 32 Bats: R Throws: R Height: 6'4" Weight: 220 lb. Origin: International Free Agent, 2010

YEAR	TEAM	LVL	AGE	W	L	SV	G	GS	IP	H	HR	BB/9	K/9	K	GB%	BABIP	WHIP	ERA	DRA-	WARP	MPH	FB%	Whiff%	CSP
2019	PIT	MLB	29	4	5	1	72	0	65^1	65	14	3.2	8.7	63	43.7%	.280	1.35	3.72	97	0.8	93.3	85.2%	23.9%	48.6%
2020	PIT	MLB	30	3	2	4	24	0	23^1	15	3	1.9	13.1	34	38.5%	.250	0.86	2.70	74	0.6	93.2	72.4%	36.0%	46.4%
2021	ATL	MLB	31	1	2	0	27	0	26	23	6	1.7	3.1	9	31.9%	.200	1.08	3.12	150	-0.4	93.2	84.9%	16.3%	54.7%
2021	PIT	MLB	31	4	2	14	37	0	38^1	27	2	1.2	7.7	33	29.2%	.240	0.83	2.82	110	0.1	93.3	87.0%	23.3%	58.8%
2022 DC	*FA*	*MLB*	*32*	*3*	*3*	*0*	*71*	*0*	*61.7*	*63*	*10*	*2.3*	*7.6*	*52*	*34.7%*	*.294*	*1.27*	*4.39*	*108*	*0.0*	*93.3*	*83.6%*	*23.8%*	*53.3%*

Comparables: Nick Vincent, Anthony Varvaro, Darren O'Day

In 2020, Rodríguez made the All-"Should Have Been Traded At The Deadline" team as a high-leverage reliever who stayed put on a team going nowhere. He did get traded from Pittsburgh this time around, but only after the sticky stuff crackdown appeared to rob him of his best stuff. His previously lofty strikeout rate nosedived just as his home run rate did the opposite. That, friends, is officially Not What You Want. It also wasn't what Atlanta wanted, as Rodríguez found himself increasingly on the margins and was ultimately left off the playoff roster. Rodríguez managed to record solid ERAs even as his peripherals crumbled, but that's not going to hold much longer unless he can find a way to recover some spin.

Spencer Schwellenbach RHP Born: 05/31/00 Age: 22 Bats: R Throws: R Height: 6'1" Weight: 200 lb. Origin: Round 2, 2021 Draft (#59 overall)

Everybody loves a good two-way player in baseball. Baseball Prospectus definitely loves two-way players, seeing as how we dedicated an entire week of 2021 coverage to Shohei Ohtani. You're probably going to read tons of glowing words about Ohtani later on in this book, and one person who currently has dreams of having similar words written about him is Schwellenbach. Atlanta's second-round pick in 2021 is coming off of a college swan song that saw him win the John Olerud Award as the best two-way player in college baseball. He would've been drafted high as either a righty with three lovely pitches in his arsenal or a shortstop with a good hit tool and fine defensive ability. Atlanta took him and announced him as a pitcher, so that is likely going to be the path he takes. Tommy John surgery has ensured that he won't be seen on a mound for a while, but Schwellenbach will surely be one of the more intriguing prospects out there once he begins his journey to the Show.

Jared Shuster LHP Born: 08/03/98 Age: 23 Bats: L Throws: L Height: 6'3" Weight: 210 lb. Origin: Round 1, 2020 Draft (#25 overall)

YEAR	TEAM	LVL	AGE	W	L	SV	G	GS	IP	H	HR	BB/9	K/9	K	GB%	BABIP	WHIP	ERA	DRA-	WARP	MPH	FB%	Whiff%	CSP
2021	ROM	A+	22	2	0	0	15	14	58^1	47	10	2.3	11.3	73	34.7%	.272	1.06	3.70	95	0.6				
2021	MIS	AA	22	0	0	0	3	3	14^2	19	5	3.1	10.4	17	36.2%	.341	1.64	7.36	90	0.2				
2022 non-DC	*ATL*	*MLB*	*23*	*2*	*3*	*0*	*57*	*0*	*50*	*51*	*8*	*3.5*	*8.6*	*47*	*34.3%*	*.305*	*1.43*	*5.01*	*120*	*-0.3*				

Comparables: Danny Duffy, Jeanmar Gómez, Zach Jackson

Landing in Double-A two years after being drafted isn't particularly aggressive development for a polished college pitcher, but it wasn't necessarily the plan for Shuster. The 25th-overall selection in 2020 spent the majority of the season in High-A, missing copious bats thanks to a fall-off-the-table changeup. He was likely to spend the whole year at that level but for a COVID outbreak hitting Double-A Mississippi, leaving them in need of players. He garnered three starts in September and found out the difference between lower- and upper-minors hitters. His fastball has settled in at 90-92, touching 94 after flashing higher in his COVID-shortened draft year at Wake Forest, with that changeup serving as his go-to secondary. It's not uncommon for changeup-first pitchers to struggle in Double-A after strong performances in A-ball, but it does place emphasis on Shuster further developing his breaking ball—which has gone from sweepy and slurvy to tighter 10-4 action—and refining his command. He's likely to return to Double-A to open 2022.

Will Smith LHP Born: 07/10/89 Age: 32 Bats: R Throws: L Height: 6'5" Weight: 255 lb. Origin: Round 7, 2008 Draft (#229 overall)

YEAR	TEAM	LVL	AGE	W	L	SV	G	GS	IP	H	HR	BB/9	K/9	K	GB%	BABIP	WHIP	ERA	DRA-	WARP	MPH	FB%	Whiff%	CSP
2019	SF	MLB	29	6	0	34	63	0	65^1	46	10	2.9	13.2	96	42.1%	.277	1.03	2.76	73	1.6	92.8	46.8%	34.3%	44.8%
2020	ATL	MLB	30	2	2	0	18	0	16	11	7	2.3	10.1	18	30.0%	.121	0.94	4.50	112	0.1	92.7	45.2%	36.7%	43.5%
2021	ATL	MLB	31	3	7	37	71	0	68	49	11	3.7	11.5	87	31.3%	.250	1.13	3.44	93	0.9	92.9	47.3%	33.1%	51.5%
2022 DC	*ATL*	*MLB*	*32*	*3*	*3*	*32*	*67*	*0*	*58*	*47*	*9*	*3.2*	*12.0*	*77*	*34.9%*	*.289*	*1.16*	*3.40*	*85*	*0.7*	*92.9*	*47.0%*	*33.7%*	*49.2%*

Comparables: Tyler Clippard, Antonio Bastardo, Brett Cecil

Up until August, Smith seemed like a pretty normal closer. The bullpen was where he spent all of his days; Chillin' out, maxin' and relaxin' before it was his turn to toss the baseball at the end of the game. Then August rolled around and he started making trouble in the neighborhood. It wasn't just one little fight, either, as the southpaw allowed over 30% of his earned runs on this season in that month alone. It's a good thing Brian Snitker has the patience of Uncle Phil, though, as Smith locked his game down once the calendar flipped to September, allowing only two earned runs to close out the season, followed by 11 brilliant, scoreless innings in October. After a rough 2020 and some inconsistency in 2021, many Atlanta fans were ready to try someone else in the closer role, but Smith's dominance during a magical postseason run has left him the Prince of Cobb County.

Mike Soroka RHP

Born: 08/04/97 Age: 24 Bats: R Throws: R Height: 6'5" Weight: 225 lb. Origin: Round 1, 2015 Draft (#28 overall)

YEAR	TEAM	LVL	AGE	W	L	SV	G	GS	IP	H	HR	BB/9	K/9	K	GB%	BABIP	WHIP	ERA	DRA-	WARP	MPH	FB%	Whiff%	CSP
2019	GWN	AAA	21	1	0	0	2	2	9^1	5	1	1.0	9.6	10	72.7%	.190	0.64	3.86	92	0.2				
2019	ATL	MLB	21	13	4	0	29	29	174^2	153	14	2.1	7.3	142	50.6%	.282	1.11	2.68	90	2.7	92.4	63.5%	22.7%	47.9%
2020	ATL	MLB	22	0	1	0	3	3	13^2	11	0	4.6	5.3	8	61.0%	.268	1.32	3.95	93	0.2	92.4	59.3%	22.6%	46.9%
2022 DC	*ATL*	*MLB*	*24*	*5*	*5*	*0*	*17*	*17*	*89*	*89*	*9*	*3.1*	*8.1*	*80*	*51.1%*	*.307*	*1.35*	*4.09*	*101*	*0.7*	*92.4*	*62.9%*	*22.7%*	*47.7%*

Comparables: Julio Teheran, Ramon Martinez, Félix Hernández

It's commonly said that lightning doesn't strike twice, but there are some clear exceptions. For example, lightning strikes the Empire State Building 23 times per year on average. Soroka, for his part, is averaging one strike per year over the last couple seasons, none of them coming from the pitching mound. He originally tore his Achilles tendon three starts into the 2020 season, and he suffered a complete re-tear while walking to the clubhouse in June of 2021. When healthy in 2019, he deployed a power sinker and a bat-missing slider to earn All-Star honors and land down-ballot Cy Young votes. We don't know what the current iteration of Soroka will look like, though, as he won't have thrown a competitive pitch in upwards of two seasons, and will be working from a twice-repaired Achilles on his drive leg. Given the simple and non-strenuous way he tore his tendon for a second time, it might be tempting to think the only way to avoid additional lightning strikes to his health is to limit his movement as much as possible. Of course, the Empire State Building doesn't move at all, and look at where that gets it.

★ ★ ★ *2022 Top 101 Prospect* **#85** ★ ★ ★

Spencer Strider RHP

Born: 10/28/98 Age: 23 Bats: R Throws: R Height: 6'0" Weight: 195 lb. Origin: Round 4, 2020 Draft (#126 overall)

YEAR	TEAM	LVL	AGE	W	L	SV	G	GS	IP	H	HR	BB/9	K/9	K	GB%	BABIP	WHIP	ERA	DRA-	WARP	MPH	FB%	Whiff%	CSP
2021	AUG	A	22	0	0	0	4	4	15^1	6	0	2.9	18.8	32	25.0%	.300	0.72	0.59	53	0.5				
2021	ROM	A+	22	0	0	0	3	3	14^2	9	1	3.7	14.7	24	43.3%	.276	1.02	2.45	82	0.3				
2021	MIS	AA	22	3	7	0	14	14	63	48	6	4.1	13.4	94	30.7%	.321	1.22	4.71	80	1.3				
2021	ATL	MLB	22	1	0	0	2	0	2^1	2	1	3.9	0.0	0	25.0%	.143	1.29	3.86	145	0.0	97.8	78.9%	18.2%	55.0%
2022 DC	*ATL*	*MLB*	*23*	*7*	*3*	*0*	*55*	*3*	*58*	*50*	*9*	*4.7*	*11.9*	*77*	*33.0%*	*.303*	*1.39*	*4.57*	*106*	*0.1*	*97.8*	*78.9%*	*18.2%*	*55.0%*

Comparables: Tyler Thornburg, Joe Ryan, Armando Galarraga

Strider suddenly and startlingly exploded onto the professional baseball scene. The former Clemson Tiger took the lemons of being drafted in one of the worst possible years and made lemonade by slicing and dicing his way through each fruitful level of the minors. Strider bombarded minor-league hitters with eye-popping velocity, tearing through all four full-season levels (mostly at Double-A) before earning a cup of coffee in the majors. In his first inning as a big-leaguer, his fastball topped out at 100 and it became immediately clear why the Braves decided that he could potentially help them out in October. He didn't end up pitching in the playoffs at any point, and is likely to resume a role in the starting rotation come 2022. Aside from the blazing fastball, Strider offers a plus breaking ball with sharp, downward tilt and slurvy break. He hasn't had to use a third pitch (changeup) much, and while two-pitch starters are more and more common these days, Strider might be well suited for relief dominance when it is all said and done.

Freddy Tarnok RHP

Born: 11/24/98 Age: 23 Bats: R Throws: R Height: 6'3" Weight: 185 lb. Origin: Round 3, 2017 Draft (#80 overall)

YEAR	TEAM	LVL	AGE	W	L	SV	G	GS	IP	H	HR	BB/9	K/9	K	GB%	BABIP	WHIP	ERA	DRA-	WARP	MPH	FB%	Whiff%	CSP
2019	BRA	ROK	20	0	1	0	3	3	8	3	1	1.1	10.1	9	50.0%	.118	0.50	3.38						
2019	FLO	A+	20	3	7	0	19	19	98	105	6	3.3	7.5	82	36.5%	.330	1.44	4.87	106	0.9				
2021	ROM	A+	22	3	2	0	7	5	28^1	21	6	4.1	15.2	48	34.5%	.306	1.20	4.76	74	0.6				
2021	MIS	AA	22	3	2	0	9	9	45	35	2	3.0	12.2	61	33.3%	.324	1.11	2.60	81	0.9				
2022 DC	*ATL*	*MLB*	*23*	*3*	*2*	*0*	*25*	*3*	*32.3*	*28*	*4*	*4.4*	*9.7*	*35*	*34.1%*	*.284*	*1.37*	*4.38*	*105*	*0.1*				

Comparables: Michael Fulmer, Michael Bowden, Nathan Eovaldi

If there is ever an example of the eye test still being valuable in today's analytic age, Tarnok is living proof of it. At the High-A level, Tarnok wasn't exactly doing anything to pop his numbers off the pages. However, watching him revealed that Tarnok was a project that was slowly-but-surely coming together. He got a promotion to Double-A off the strength of those visual flashes of brilliance alone, and he paid that confidence off by putting it together at the next level. Missing bats has never been Tarnok's issue, but his high-effort delivery and inconsistent secondaries mean he'll walk more than his fair share of batters. He was cutting down on the free passes in Double-A, and while his breaking ball will flash above-average, it all adds up to a profile that might flourish in relief. If Atlanta pursues that option, he could see the majors as soon as next year. Otherwise he should return to Double-A as a starter, and continue to build upon the adjustments he's already making.

Touki Toussaint RHP Born: 06/20/96 Age: 26 Bats: R Throws: R Height: 6'3" Weight: 215 lb. Origin: Round 1, 2014 Draft (#16 overall)

YEAR	TEAM	LVL	AGE	W	L	SV	G	GS	IP	H	HR	BB/9	K/9	K	GB%	BABIP	WHIP	ERA	DRA-	WARP	MPH	FB%	Whiff%	CSP
2019	GWN	AAA	23	1	6	0	10	10	39^{2}	51	5	6.4	10.0	44	41.8%	.393	1.99	7.49	116	0.2				
2019	ATL	MLB	23	4	0	0	24	1	41^{2}	44	5	5.6	9.7	45	42.5%	.345	1.68	5.62	99	0.4	93.7	49.4%	29.7%	41.3%
2020	ATL	MLB	24	0	2	0	7	5	24^{1}	27	7	5.9	11.1	30	37.7%	.328	1.77	8.88	100	0.3	94.2	41.1%	31.9%	42.2%
2021	GWN	AAA	25	2	1	0	7	4	20^{2}	12	1	5.2	12.2	28	61.0%	.275	1.16	3.48	83	0.5				
2021	ATL	MLB	25	3	3	0	11	10	50	43	11	4.0	8.6	48	46.4%	.252	1.30	4.50	100	0.5	92.8	51.6%	25.6%	55.8%
2022 DC	*ATL*	*MLB*	*26*	*7*	*3*	*0*	*55*	*3*	*60.7*	*55*	*7*	*4.9*	*10.0*	*67*	*46.3%*	*.299*	*1.45*	*4.77*	*110*	*0.0*	*93.3*	*48.7%*	*27.8%*	*50.0%*

Comparables: Travis Wood, Robinson Tejeda, Fernando Nieve

If Toussaint was the pitcher that everybody wanted him to be, then we got a glimpse of it on July 25, 2021. He struck out 10 with a curveball that made batters look like they were swinging at ghosts. His command was also as good as it's ever been and he kept the baserunners to a minimum. That version of Toussaint has been all too rare, though. Far more often, the Toussaint that shows up in major-league games has iffy—if any—command, an elevated walk rate, and a fastball so flat it routinely goes for home runs. At this point, his strikeout rate barely touches league-average, and the traffic on the basepaths too often ends up cleared via the longball, rather than a double play (despite decent ground-ball tendencies). Of his 11 major-league appearances last year, 10 came as a starter, but at this point Toussaint's future lies in the bullpen if it lies in the major leagues at all. The hope is that his stuff will play up in shorter bursts, and his tendency to put men on base can be mitigated by not needing to turn the lineup over.

Jacob Webb RHP Born: 08/15/93 Age: 28 Bats: R Throws: R Height: 6'2" Weight: 210 lb. Origin: Round 18, 2014 Draft (#553 overall)

YEAR	TEAM	LVL	AGE	W	L	SV	G	GS	IP	H	HR	BB/9	K/9	K	GB%	BABIP	WHIP	ERA	DRA-	WARP	MPH	FB%	Whiff%	CSP
2019	GWN	AAA	25	0	1	1	10	0	10^{1}	9	1	7.8	10.5	12	50.0%	.296	1.74	6.97	90	0.2				
2019	ATL	MLB	25	4	0	2	36	0	32^{1}	24	4	3.3	7.8	28	38.9%	.235	1.11	1.39	108	0.2	95.2	54.1%	26.2%	47.5%
2020	ATL	MLB	26	0	0	0	8	0	10	7	0	4.5	9.0	10	60.0%	.280	1.20	0.00	91	0.2	93.8	52.4%	32.9%	47.4%
2021	GWN	AAA	27	1	2	6	24	0	24	17	2	2.6	12.7	34	42.1%	.278	1.00	3.00	76	0.6				
2021	ATL	MLB	27	5	4	1	34	0	34^{1}	38	4	3.7	8.7	33	34.3%	.340	1.51	4.19	108	0.2	94.2	44.5%	31.1%	53.5%
2022 DC	*ATL*	*MLB*	*28*	*2*	*3*	*0*	*59*	*0*	*51.7*	*49*	*7*	*3.7*	*9.6*	*55*	*39.8%*	*.302*	*1.36*	*4.27*	*103*	*0.1*	*94.4*	*47.6%*	*30.4%*	*51.5%*

Comparables: Derek Law, Wander Suero, Fernando Abad

There's something to be said about giving someone exactly what they expect while also doing nothing less and nothing more. Being the person in the friend group who is known for being consistently consistent is a nice role to have. After delivering 0.2 WARP for three straight seasons, you know exactly what to expect of Webb. If you compare his 2021 campaign to his 2019 season, his numbers are eerily similar. Even looking past the identical WARP numbers, it is fascinating to see a pitcher basically deliver an encore performance. Webb *did* make some actual alterations, slinging his changeup a plurality of the time—a career-high rate. That didn't change the results though, and it's unlikely to have a substantive impact on Webb's profile going forward. It might not be exciting, but it's fair to expect more of the same.

Kyle Wright RHP Born: 10/02/95 Age: 26 Bats: R Throws: R Height: 6'4" Weight: 215 lb. Origin: Round 1, 2017 Draft (#5 overall)

YEAR	TEAM	LVL	AGE	W	L	SV	G	GS	IP	H	HR	BB/9	K/9	K	GB%	BABIP	WHIP	ERA	DRA-	WARP	MPH	FB%	Whiff%	CSP
2019	GWN	AAA	23	11	4	0	21	21	112^{1}	107	13	2.8	9.3	116	47.3%	.314	1.26	4.17	83	2.4				
2019	ATL	MLB	23	0	3	0	7	4	19^{2}	24	4	5.9	8.2	18	41.0%	.351	1.88	8.69	109	0.1	94.7	54.4%	23.8%	43.7%
2020	ATL	MLB	24	2	4	0	8	8	38	35	7	5.7	7.1	30	44.7%	.262	1.55	5.21	123	-0.1	94.4	48.4%	24.0%	43.5%
2021	GWN	AAA	25	10	5	0	24	24	137	117	9	3.0	9.0	137	51.6%	.293	1.18	3.02	88	2.7				
2021	ATL	MLB	25	0	1	0	2	2	6^{1}	7	2	7.1	8.5	6	40.0%	.294	1.89	9.95	120	0.0	93.4	51.1%	29.4%	55.5%
2022 DC	*ATL*	*MLB*	*26*	*7*	*6*	*0*	*48*	*11*	*85.7*	*83*	*10*	*4.1*	*8.6*	*81*	*47.4%*	*.304*	*1.43*	*4.50*	*107*	*0.3*	*94.3*	*50.0%*	*25.0%*	*45.9%*

Comparables: Edinson Vólquez, Anthony Banda, Daniel Mengden

It must have felt like everything had gone wrong for Mr. Wright, at least at the major-league level. After starting eight games in the shortened 2020 season, Wright barely sniffed the big leagues in 2021 and left a bit of a stench in both his brief starts. So it was something of a record-scratch moment when he ended up on the hill in Games 2 and 4 of the World Series delivering 5 ⅔ innings of much-needed relief for a beleaguered Atlanta pitching staff. He only made it there as an injury replacement, but it's less about how one gets an opportunity than what they do with it. Wright continues to straddle the Quad-A line, finding success in Triple-A, while struggling in the majors, and we might be approaching the point where it is best to see what he can do over a full season in relief—because we know how it worked in the World Series.

Kirby Yates RHP Born: 03/25/87 Age: 35 Bats: L Throws: R Height: 5'10" Weight: 205 lb. Origin: Round 26, 2005 Draft (#798 overall)

YEAR	TEAM	LVL	AGE	W	L	SV	G	GS	IP	H	HR	BB/9	K/9	K	GB%	BABIP	WHIP	ERA	DRA-	WARP	MPH	FB%	Whiff%	CSP
2019	SD	MLB	32	0	5	41	60	0	60^{2}	41	2	1.9	15.0	101	47.5%	.328	0.89	1.19	59	1.9	93.5	57.1%	34.6%	45.3%
2020	SD	MLB	33	0	1	2	6	0	4^{1}	7	1	8.3	16.6	8	38.5%	.500	2.54	12.46	83	0.1	93.6	64.4%	41.3%	46.0%
2022 DC	*ATL*	*MLB*	*35*	*2*	*2*	*0*	*52*	*0*	*45.3*	*35*	*6*	*2.9*	*12.3*	*62*	*41.3%*	*.289*	*1.10*	*3.11*	*79*	*0.7*	*93.6*	*58.3%*	*35.7%*	*45.4%*

Comparables: Justin Miller, Brad Brach, Mike Timlin

A near-contention club in need of veteran bullpen reinforcements signing a recently elite reliever to a pillow contract laden with appearance incentives? What's not to love? Yates' deal with the Blue Jays was an ideal arrangement for both sides that went south almost immediately. Rather than a return to form, Yates threw just 25 pitches over two spring training appearances before a flexor-pronator strain foreshadowed his second Tommy John procedure.

Without Yates, bullpen woes plagued the Blue Jays during the season's opening months as they searched for stability around newly-minted closer Jordan Romano. While Blue Jays fans wonder what a full season of healthy Yates production would've meant for the club's playoff chase, general manager Ross Atkins will spend the winter chasing another near miss: becoming the first big-league team to ever roster two guys named "Kirby" at the same time.

Huascar Ynoa RHP Born: 05/28/98 Age: 24 Bats: R Throws: R Height: 6'2" Weight: 220 lb. Origin: International Free Agent, 2014

YEAR	TEAM	LVL	AGE	W	L	SV	G	GS	IP	H	HR	BB/9	K/9	K	GB%	BABIP	WHIP	ERA	DRA-	WARP	MPH	FB%	Whiff%	CSP
2019	FLO	A+	21	0	1	0	3	3	11	10	0	4.9	13.1	16	59.3%	.370	1.45	3.27	98	0.1				
2019	MIS	AA	21	1	2	1	6	0	13^{2}	17	2	3.3	9.9	15	65.1%	.375	1.61	5.27	75	0.3				
2019	GWN	AAA	21	3	5	0	17	14	72^{2}	80	14	4.2	9.8	79	42.7%	.332	1.57	5.33	96	1.1				
2019	ATL	MLB	21	0	0	0	2	0	3	6	1	3.0	9.0	3	41.7%	.455	2.33	18.00	114	0.0	97.7	60.6%	24.1%	41.3%
2020	ATL	MLB	22	0	0	0	9	5	21^{2}	23	2	5.4	7.1	17	55.9%	.318	1.66	5.82	99	0.3	95.0	44.3%	25.5%	45.9%
2021	GWN	AAA	23	0	0	0	2	2	8^{1}	8	1	4.3	11.9	11	45.5%	.333	1.44	4.32	102	0.1				
2021	ATL	MLB	23	4	6	0	18	17	91	76	14	2.5	9.9	100	47.3%	.272	1.11	4.05	79	1.8	96.8	44.9%	28.3%	54.3%
2022 DC	*ATL*	*MLB*	*24*	*8*	*7*	*0*	*24*	*24*	*123.7*	*117*	*15*	*3.6*	*9.0*	*124*	*47.8%*	*.299*	*1.35*	*4.14*	*101*	*0.7*	*96.5*	*45.0%*	*27.8%*	*52.9%*

Comparables: Ubaldo Jiménez, Homer Bailey, Matt Wisler

How do you go from being considered a spot starter at best to maybe turning into a decent starter going forward? There's not much to it! All you need to do is follow two easy steps: First, start throwing your fastball a lot harder. Adding nearly two miles-per-hour to your fastball may not seem like a lot, but tell that to the batters who will suddenly be whiffing on a much higher percentage of your heaters! The second step is to do a better job of locating your slider. That's *much* easier said than done and it's not going to happen for you every game, but when it does happen, the opposing hitter better watch out! Pepper in an occasional changeup to pick up outs every now and then and there you have it! You too can go from having a minuscule K-BB percentage to making massive gains in that department! The Ynoa Method is not a guarantee, results may vary, void where prohibited, punching a bench may result in broken hands and is not endorsed, all federal, state and local regulations apply.

Lineouts

Hitters

HITTER	POS	TEAM	LVL	AGE	PA	R	2B	3B	HR	RBI	BB	K	SB	CS	AVG/OBP/SLG	DRC+	BABIP	BRR	FRAA	WARP
Ehire Adrianza	3B	ATL	MLB	31	209	32	9	2	5	28	21	42	0	0	.247/.327/.401	98	.290	-0.4	3B(16): -0.8, RF(14): -2.0, 2B(7): 0.2	0.4
Abraham Almonte	LF	TOR	WIN	32	105	8	2	0	0	6	22	26	5	1	.183/.362/.207		.268			
	LF	GWN	AAA	32	83	16	4	0	3	19	21	14	3	3	.403/.554/.613	140	.489	-0.4	LF(9): -2.3, RF(8): -0.4	0.4
	LF	ATL	MLB	32	175	20	12	0	5	19	26	38	1	1	.216/.331/.399	100	.255	-0.9	LF(40): -2.0, RF(4): -0.2	0.3
Orlando Arcia	UT	GWN	AAA	26	322	54	16	0	17	37	31	38	5	3	.282/.351/.516	133	.272	1.2	SS(65): 4.2, LF(4): -0.2, 3B(3): 0.3	2.7
	UT	ATL	MLB	26	78	9	3	0	2	13	7	16	1	0	.214/.282/.343	93	.245	0.3	LF(14): 0.4, SS(3): 0.2, 2B(1): -0.0	0.3
	UT	MIL	MLB	26	11	0	0	0	0	1	0	3	0	0	.091/.091/.091	84	.125		3B(3): -0.1, SS(2): 0.0	0.0
Mahki Backstrom	1B	BRA	ROK	19	146	19	5	2	3	12	22	56	1	0	.172/.301/.320		.281			
Sean Kazmar Jr.	IF	GWN	AAA	36	276	29	9	0	9	26	17	44	3	0	.215/.264/.355	94	.224	0.7	3B(40): 7.3, 2B(24): 1.4, 1B(11): 0.6	1.6
	IF	ATL	MLB	36	2	0	0	0	0	0	0	0	0	0	.000/.000/.000	95		0.0		0.0
Jason Kipnis	2B	GWN	AAA	34	228	36	10	2	10	32	27	50	1	0	.290/.390/.518	123	.341	0.4	2B(48): -1.6, LF(6): 0.1	1.2
Jeff Mathis	C	ATL	MLB	38	9	0	0	0	0	0	0	5	0	0	.000/.000/.000	77			C(3): 0.1	0.0
Chadwick Tromp	C	SAC	AAA	26	204	23	12	0	6	24	10	47	0	0	.224/.265/.380	81	.264	-0.1	C(43): 1.1	0.3
	C	SF	MLB	26	18	1	0	0	1	2	0	4	0	0	.222/.222/.389	96	.231	-0.4	C(8): 0.1	0.0
Luke Waddell	IF	PEJ	WIN	22	71	11	5	0	0	9	9	8	3	0	.311/.394/.393		.352			
	IF	ROM	A+	22	78	15	1	0	6	13	7	13	1	1	.304/.372/.580	134	.294	-0.1	SS(8): -0.5, 3B(5): 1.1, 2B(4): 0.2	0.6
	IF	MIS	AA	22	33	3	0	0	0	2	2	4	1	1	.161/.212/.161	98	.185	0.2	2B(5): 0.0, SS(2): 0.1, 3B(1): -0.1	0.1

Ehire Adrianza is something close to the platonic ideal of a replacement level player, accruing a mere 2.5 WARP while playing 20-plus games at seven different in his nine-year career. None of that mattered when he stroked a timely broken-bat double in the NLCS. ⚾ In order for Atlanta to overhaul their entire outfield and create their storybook season, they needed an outfield in need of overhauling. Thank **Abraham Almonte**, who held his own for a couple months but also made it obvious that Alex Anthopoulos should maybe get a couple of bodies. ⚾ **Orlando Arcia** shares a name with the Florida city that served as the fill-in host for the 2021-22 winter meetings. We couldn't confirm this as a fact, but it sure feels like the universal meaning of "Orlando" is "dismal replacement." ⚾ It was a down year at the plate for **Makhi Backstrom** but those types of seasons could be few and far between for the young first baseman. The pop in his bat is how he went from being an 18th-round pick to an intriguing prospect and it'll also be the reason why he makes any future waves. ⚾ **Tyler Flowers** once said his goal was to stick around until his first year of arbitration to prove he was worth more than minimum wage. Instead, he lasted 12 seasons and put up nearly 20 WARP before the spinal cord could take no more. ⚾ **Sean Kazmar Jr.** last played in the bigs in 2008, and was last seen in this annual in 2012. Thirteen years later, he made it back to the show and received a well-deserved standing ovation from his dugout upon his first plate appearance. He retired at season's end, his own Odyssey complete. Never give up, folks. ⚾ The good news: **Jason Kipnis** got plenty of playing time last season and put up some of the best numbers he's had in a while. The bad news: It all happened at Triple-A. ⚾ **Jeff Mathis** spent the majority of the 2021 season in Triple-A Gwinnett, breaking ground as the first player-coach in history to neither play nor, technically, coach. It's incredible to think that the man who once invited the scorn of every 2005 sabermetrician is now, 16 years later, the baseball equivalent of Mr. Chips. ⚾ **Ambioris Tavarez**'s name may not immediately ring a bell, but the tall shortstop is the first significant international prospect that the Braves have signed since being sanctioned for a slew of infractions in 2017. ⚾ "Tromper" is a French verb meaning "to fool" or "to trick," e.g. the *trompe-l'oeil* ("fool the eye") painting style, or the underrated Pixies album *Trompe le Monde* ("Fool the World"). Aruban **Chadwick Tromp** is a third-string catcher who, in 82 major-league plate appearances, has taken precisely one walk. Even with capable defense, it's unlikely Tromp will fool anyone into giving him significant playing time with a batting eye as gullible as his. ⚾ Fifth-rounder **Luke Waddell** has a broad-based skill set but lacks a standout tool. The likely utility man can spot up at shortstop, which paired with his bat-to-ball ability could propel him to the majors.

Pitchers

PITCHER	TEAM	LVL	AGE	W	L	SV	G	GS	IP	H	HR	BB/9	K/9	K	GB%	BABIP	WHIP	ERA	DRA-	WARP	MPH	FB%	WHF	CSP
Thomas Burrows	GWN	AAA	26	3	1	0	35	1	47^2	29	4	6.4	12.7	67	36.6%	.266	1.32	2.64	84	1.0				
Jesse Chavez	GWN	AAA	37	1	0	2	13	0	20	12	1	3.6	12.2	27	57.1%	.275	1.00	2.25	84	0.4				
	ATL	MLB	37	3	2	0	30	4	33^2	22	0	2.9	9.6	36	43.0%	.256	0.98	2.14	92	0.4	90.1	79.9%	17.7%	55.3%
Tucker Davidson	GWN	AAA	25	2	2	0	4	4	23	11	2	2.0	11.0	28	54.9%	.184	0.70	1.17	85	0.5				
	ATL	MLB	25	0	0	0	4	4	20	15	3	3.6	8.1	18	42.1%	.226	1.15	3.60	100	0.2	93.3	49.8%	27.5%	56.0%
Grant Dayton	ATL	MLB	33	0	0	0	13	0	13	15	2	4.2	9.7	14	24.4%	.333	1.62	6.23	104	0.1	91.6	65.2%	27.8%	49.9%
Jasseel De La Cruz	GWN	AAA	24	1	3	0	20	15	56^1	63	8	5.3	8.8	55	42.2%	.333	1.70	7.03	108	0.5				
Joey Estes	AUG	A	19	3	6	0	20	20	99	66	7	2.6	11.5	127	34.2%	.259	0.96	2.91	100	0.9				
Daysbel Hernández	MOC	WIN	24	0	1	10	25	0	27	21	2	2.3	12.3	37	59.5%	.322	1.04	2.67						
	MIS	AA	24	3	1	3	26	0	32^2	23	3	4.4	12.7	46	55.6%	.299	1.19	2.76	76	0.7				
	GWN	AAA	24	0	1	0	10	0	9^2	8	1	6.5	11.2	12	37.5%	.304	1.55	7.45	91	0.2				
Jake Higginbotham	ROM	A+	25	0	0	0	6	0	7^1	1	0	1.2	13.5	11	63.6%	.091	0.27	0.00	91	0.1				
Dylan Lee	GWN	AAA	26	5	1	1	35	0	46^2	29	4	1.2	10.4	54	35.1%	.231	0.75	1.54	77	1.2				
	ATL	MLB	26	0	0	0	2	0	2	3	1	0.0	13.5	3	33.3%	.400	1.50	9.00	103	0.0	93.0	41.4%	27.8%	63.7%
Sean Newcomb	GWN	AAA	28	3	0	4	15	0	16^2	9	1	2.2	15.1	28	41.9%	.267	0.78	1.62	73	0.5				
	ATL	MLB	28	2	0	1	32	0	32^1	28	1	7.5	12.0	43	37.2%	.355	1.70	4.73	96	0.4	95.6	57.4%	25.6%	51.7%
Tanner Roark	GWN	AAA	34	4	1	3	24	3	46^1	38	2	3.1	8.5	44	55.2%	.295	1.17	2.14	90	0.9				
	TOR	MLB	34	0	1	0	3	1	7	7	3	2.6	6.4	5	37.5%	.190	1.29	6.43	119	0.0	90.6	40.5%	15.3%	54.1%
Edgar Santana	ATL	MLB	29	3	0	0	41	0	42^2	37	7	2.5	7.0	33	48.5%	.246	1.15	3.59	95	0.5	94.4	65.0%	26.5%	57.8%
Josh Tomlin	ATL	MLB	36	4	0	0	35	0	49^1	69	10	0.9	6.8	37	34.3%	.358	1.50	6.57	114	0.1	86.8	69.7%	23.6%	54.1%
Darius Vines	AUG	A	23	2	0	0	8	8	36	24	3	2.5	12.0	48	51.8%	.256	0.94	2.25	66	1.0				
	ROM	A+	23	4	4	0	14	14	75	60	12	2.3	9.7	81	43.5%	.255	1.05	3.24	93	0.9				

Thomas Burrows is entering his age-27 season without having reached the majors. His fastball, slider and strikeout rate belong in a big-league bullpen while his control issues belong in a therapist's office. The Braves are the fourth club that **Jesse Chavez** has recorded a second stint with—Blue Jays (2012, 2016), Rangers (2018, 2019), Angels (2017, spring training 2021), and Atlanta (2010, 2021)—and it was the most successful reunion yet. He posted the best season of his career by ERA and FIP and, oh yeah, brought home a World Series ring. "You win some, you lose some" the saying goes, though **Tucker Davidson** did neither in his four major-league starts and one World Series appearance. He did show why the club holds him in high regard in that time, though. He lost a significant chunk of the season to a forearm strain, but gained a big following on TikTok. What was that saying again? **Grant Dayton** hasn't thrown more than 40 innings in a single season, across all levels, since 2016 due to injury and ineffectiveness. Perhaps he should change his name to Grant Health. **Jasseel De La Cruz** made the major leagues in 2020, only he didn't actually make a big-league appearance, getting optioned back down before getting into a game. Last year didn't even afford him the privilege of a day or two of service time, as the fireballing righty with the bat-missing slider missed the zone far too often. With each passing year, a relief role is looking more likely. Let's hope it's in the majors. **Joey Estes** has come along quickly for a prep product, flashing three average to slightly above pitches in his fastball, changeup and slider. He's reluctant to issue free passes, too, attacking hitters with aplomb, evidenced by his 14-strikeout, no-walk complete game in August. **Daysbel Hernandez** offers up a high-90s fastball, an electric slider and control that is inversely proportional to the quality of his stuff. He's got late-innings potential if he can rein in the walks. Unfortunately for **Jake Higginbotham**, he lost a ton of the 2021 season due to injury, he's suffered serious injuries before and he's already 25. Fortunately for him, he's a lefty with enough athleticism and stuff to give him a shot out of the bullpen. **Dylan Lee** got into more playoff games than he made regular-season big-league appearances. The 27-year-old southpaw can likely hang around as LOOGY depth, but his grand stage appearances were more representative of pitching staff distress than anything else. **Sean Newcomb** should look into a career in marketing and promotions because he excels at handing out free passes. We're guessing **Tanner Roark** wasn't very good at the Donkey Kong video games either, since he has so much trouble missing barrels. After losing the 2019 and 2020 seasons due to Tommy John surgery and a PED suspension, respectively, **Edgar Santana** deployed his mid-90s fastball and reliable slider to put together a useful, if anonymous, season in relief for Atlanta. **Josh Tomlin** still pitches as if giving up a walk means that the world as we know it will come to a horrible and agonizing end. If he keeps throwing 88 mph in the zone, his major-league career might come to a horrible and agonizing end. **Darius Vines** has a well-rounded four-pitch mix that helped him tear up the lower minors. He looks even better in looped, six-second clips.

MIAMI MARLINS

Essay by Jarrett Seidler

Player comments by Michael Clair and BP staff

If Jeffrey Loria had his way, Trevor Rogers may never have been a Marlin.

Notorious for interfering in baseball matters that few other owners would dare touch, Loria had been persuaded by members of the Marlins' front office that the team should draft University of Kentucky first baseman Evan White over Rogers with the number-13 pick in the 2017 amateur draft, per longtime Miami reporters Barry Jackson and Craig Mish.

On the surface, Loria's men had some valid points: prep arms are the lowest-probability players you can draft in the first round. Rogers was not only a high-school pitcher, but one who was nearly all projection, a tall, skinny kid who could touch the mid-90s but couldn't sit there and had no clear plus secondary offering. Age and level of competition are extremely important modeling factors when dealing with high-school draft prospects, and Rogers was very old for his class (19 years and 6 months at the time of the draft) and from the middle of nowhere in southeast New Mexico. He was exactly the type of draftee smart teams are never supposed to take in the top half of the first round, especially with a solid Southeastern Conference bat on the board.

Michael Hill and Stan Meek ran Miami's draft room that year as the team's president of baseball operations and amateur scouting director, respectively. Eventually, they were able to convince Loria to step aside and let them draft the player they thought was the best man: the overaged prep lefty without an obvious out-pitch. It was a huge swing into a stiff headwind.

Four years later, Rogers was the runner up for the 2021 National League Rookie of the Year, while White, drafted four picks later by Seattle, has yet to produce a positive WARP season. Two months after the Rogers pick, Loria sold the team to a group led by money manager Bruce Sherman and Hall of Famer Derek Jeter.

⚾ ⚾ ⚾

The Marlins have become one of the best franchises in baseball at developing pitchers.

MIAMI MARLINS PROSPECTUS

2021 W-L: 67-95, 4TH IN NL EAST

Pythag	.446	22nd	DER	.692	22nd
RS/G	3.85	29th	DRC+	81	30th
RA/G	4.33	13th	DRA-	94	10th
dWin%	.439	24th	FIP	3.94	6th
Payroll	$57M	28th	B-Age	28.5	6th
M$/MW	$2.2M	6th	P-Age	27.2	2nd

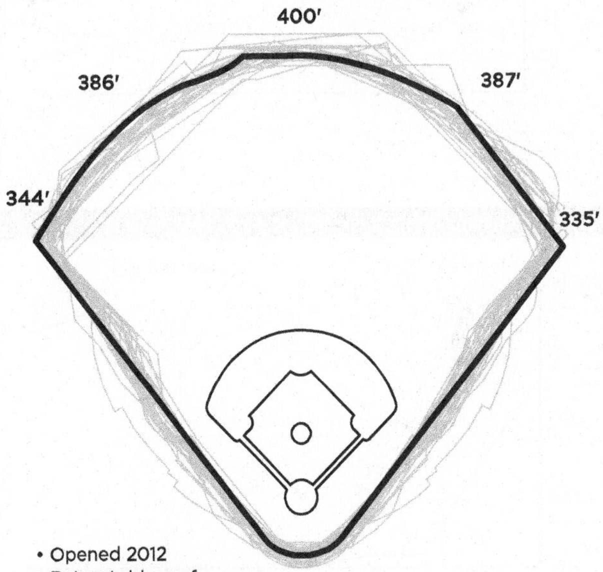

- Opened 2012
- Retractable roof
- Synthetic surface
- Fence profile: 7′ to 11′6″

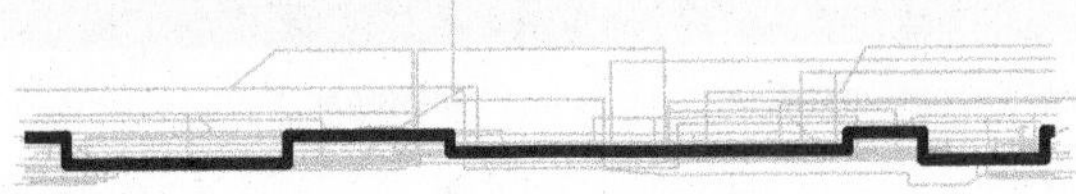

Park Factors

Runs	Runs/RH	Runs/LH	HR/RH	HR/LH
98	97	98	92	94

Top Hitter WARP	2.6 Jesús Aguilar
Top Pitcher WARP	4.0 Sandy Alcantara
Top Prospect	Max Meyer

Payroll History (in millions)

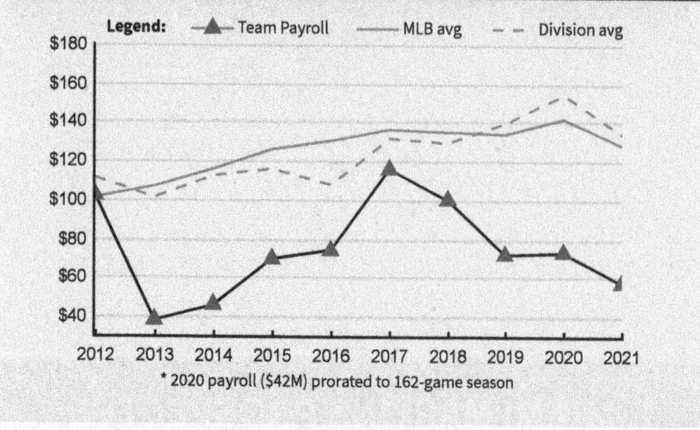

Future Commitments (in millions)

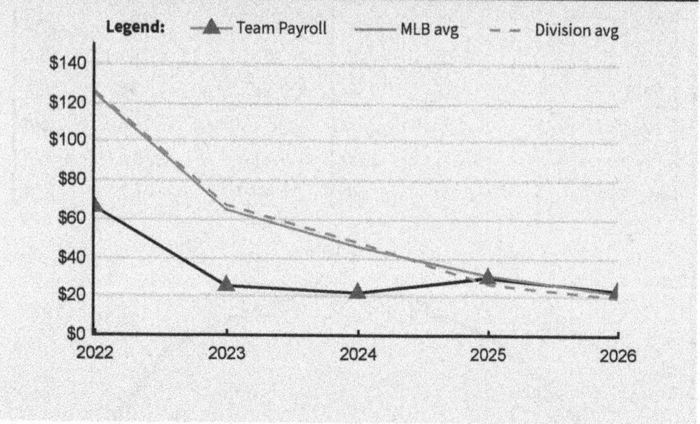

Farm System Ranking

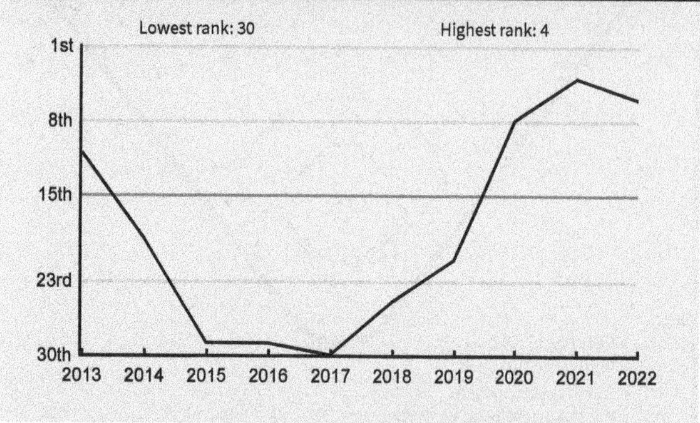

Personnel

Chief Executive Officer
Derek Jeter

General Manager
Kim Ng

Assistant General Manager
Daniel Greenlee

Assistant General Manager
Brian Chattin

Vice President, Player Development and Scouting
Gary Denbo

Manager
Don Mattingly

BP Alumni
John Eshleman

I know what you're thinking: this team hasn't been good at much of anything for a long time. Loria was more interested in art and revenue-sharing money than winning. His administration left scant infrastructure for his successors, and Sherman's group has yet to truly make the financial investments needed to build a consistent winner. They started yet another rebuild right after buying the team, immediately shipping off the entire starting outfield—including defending NL MVP Giancarlo Stanton and the player who would win the award the following year, Christian Yelich—to cut payroll; a year after that, they sent All-Stat catcher J.T. Realmuto to Philadelphia.

But the new regime has invested in the process in a way Loria did not. Jeter became CEO, and while his key hires, including general manager Kim Ng and vice president of player development and scouting Gary Denbo, have had a distinct Bronx flavor, there are far worse organizations than the Yankees to emulate. New York never drafts high due to its perpetual major-league success, yet it cranks out well more than its share of good prospects, most notably low-investment pitching prospects who become integral pieces of major-league pitching staffs (most recently, Jonathan Loáisiga and Garrett Whitlock). Every year, without fail, an unheralded pitcher or two—often a recent mid-round pick out of a southeastern college—shows up in the Yankees' system throwing harder with a new plus slider and becomes a notable prospect.

Since Denbo took over player development, this has started happening in the Marlins' system, too, but with a new twist: all of a sudden, the Marlins are turning into a changeup finishing school for young pitchers.

If developing fastballs and breaking balls is the science of pitch design, developing changeups is the art. The keys to a good fastball are mostly quantifiable and known. Every team is trying to maximize velocity and spin rate in 2022, and almost all of them are good at it. Most have started looking towards developing newer concepts, like spin axis and vertical approach angles—it unsurprisingly turns out that outlier vertical movements (or what the hitter perceives as outlier movements) induce more whiffs. Conversely, while many pitchers learn or improve a hard slider in the minors—to the point that evaluators almost expect it if you have good arm speed—few truly improve their curveballs much. The old scouting maxim that "you can't teach spin" seems to apply to most pitchers on their breaking balls, absent the use of foreign substances like Spider Tack.

But the changeup is not a pitch of immutable characteristics. You can typically figure out which pitchers have the best fastballs and breaking balls by going on Baseball Savant or Brooks Baseball and looking at tables and charts of velocity, movement and spin. You would not even come close to picking out the best changeups by doing that.

The changeup fools hitters by looking like one pitch at the decision point and then coming in at a different speed and shape than expected. Movement is a huge key to a great changeup, but it does not have to be a certain movement in a certain way. All of the deceptive arts of pitching go into it. It must tunnel well off your fastball (if it also does so off your breaking ball, that's even better). You have to maintain the same arm speed and release point as the heater to avoid tipping or casting the pitch.

It is the easiest pitch to teach and the hardest to master.

Rogers had a bumpy path as a prospect after the Marlins put so much faith in his development. He got throttled in his 2018 professional debut in Low-A, posting a 5.82 ERA in 72 2/3 innings. His underlying peripherals were better than his results, and he threw strikes, but that was about all he had going. He could not hold his peak velocity pitching on a regular turn, and nothing other than his fastball was capable of making hitters miss. A High-A run in 2019 went better; he threw more consistently in the low 90s, and both his slider and changeup improved, now projecting as average and even flashing plus in some outings. He made it to Double-A to finish that season and at least looked to be on a major-league path, if not a particularly exciting one.

Still, he was not considered a top prospect. We evaluated 206 players for the 2020 Top 101 Prospects. Rogers was not on that list. He ranked ninth within Miami's system. He was, at that moment, a pitcher who still needed a few things to come together to become a fourth starter in a couple years' time.

Rogers got the call to the majors in late August 2020, as the Marlins unexpectedly contended in a wild, wacky short season. He threw harder than he ever had before, averaging 93.7 miles per hour on the fastball, and he was slinging them in with high spin. The slider and changeup that needed work to get to average were suddenly above-average or plus. His 6.11 ERA in that major-league opportunity was ugly, but it was mostly caused by a ghoulish outing in Philadelphia, after which pitching coach Mel Stottlemyre Jr. told Rogers that he was tipping pitches. Rogers posted a 73 DRA–, and his 2021 PECOTA already posited that he was an above-average major-league pitcher.

The lean lefty made some more noticeable improvements in his full rookie season in 2021. His fastball velocity continued the year-over-year gains; he jumped nearly another full tick to average 94.6 mph. After exceptional small-sample results with the changeup in 2020, he maintained above-average effectiveness with the pitch while ratcheting up its usage, especially against righties. He now had two offspeed pitches of similar velocity that he could dot either corner with. In short, he was the best rookie pitcher in baseball.

Trevor Rogers, Changeup Usage/Effectiveness by Year

Season	Usage	CSW
2020	18.7%	30.2%
2021	27.5%	26.1%

2021 league average CSW (called strikes plus whiffs) rate on changeups: 25.0%

A few weeks after drafting Rogers, the Marlins traded reliever David Phelps to the Mariners for four unheralded prospects. One of them was another A-ball pitcher who threw a whole lot of strikes and didn't have an obvious plus pitch. Shortly after the trade, that pitcher, Pablo López, started developing more velocity and better secondary offerings. A year later, he was in Miami's rotation, and his fastball kept ticking up; he's been sitting around 94 mph for the past two seasons. His changeup has become increasingly nasty and tunnels well with his fastball and sinker. He has thrown it more and more in the majors, jumping from 18.9 percent in 2018 to 32.4 percent in 2021.

Pablo López, Changeup Usage/Effectiveness by Year

Season	Usage	CSW
2018	18.9%	29.5%
2019	21.9%	26.8%
2020	29.9%	26.7%
2021	32.4%	27.7%

During the 2017–18 winter firesale, the Marlins picked up a boatload of hitting prospects who turned out not to be able to hit, but also some interesting pitching prospects from St. Louis. At the time, Sandy Alcantara hit triple digits on the radar gun regularly but with middling command and a surprisingly low strikeout rate. Those are common prospect–Mad Libs entries for "future reliever." We thought he was the fourth-best prospect the Marlins acquired that offseason and would probably be a closer sooner rather than later.

A strange thing happened when Alcantara got into the Miami system: he started pounding the strike zone. He still wasn't really missing many bats, but even so, he established himself as a rotation stalwart in 2019, recording nearly 200 league-average innings while leaning heavily on a fastball/sinker/slider mix. His changeup was still mostly an afterthought through 2020, but he had good success with it in sparing use. Like Rogers, he started throwing it a lot more in 2021, nearly twice as often as he ever had before. It continued to make batters miss, because it tunneled well with the other key parts of his arsenal, and it was a major component of Alcantara's breakout from a guy fronting a bad rotation to a bona fide front-of-the-rotation starting pitcher. Right before the lockout, he signed a five-year, $56 million contract extension, the largest deal ever for a pitcher in his first year of arbitration eligibility.

Sandy Alcantara, Changeup Usage/Effectiveness by Year

Season	Usage	CSW
2018	13.1%	34.7%
2019	12.8%	24.2%
2020	10.0%	28.4%
2021	23.3%	30.2%

The 2021 season was a step back for the Marlins. After an unexpected playoff appearance in 2020 that was more an expanded-playoff mirage than truly reflective of the team's underlying talent, Miami was once again one of the worst clubs in the National League, even with all the improvements on the mound.

More pitching help is on the horizon. Sixto Sánchez ranked as the fourth-best prospect in baseball heading into 2021, coming off his own huge changeup development. He missed all of last season with shoulder injuries, but, if he's healthy, he'll be a star. Edward Cabrera debuted last year. While he has had his own troubles staying on the mound, when he's right, he can sit in the high 90s with a great changeup. Max Meyer, the number-three pick in the 2020 Draft, has premium velocity and his slider is the best breaking pitch in the entire minor leagues; if he has the same late changeup development that his organizational forerunners did, he'll be an ace. Eury Perez and Dax Fulton both jumped into this year's Top 101 Prospects list off huge showings as teenagers in A-ball; their firm changes are already improving, too. The Marlins' 2020 fourth-rounder, Jake Eder, went straight to Double-A after an underwhelming career at Vanderbilt and started throwing good strikes all of a sudden. The only thing preventing him from joining Meyer, Cabrera, Perez and Fulton in the Top 101 is a poorly-timed, late-summer Tommy John surgery, and he still didn't miss by much.

Way back in 2003, the Florida Marlins won a World Series behind a sensational crop of young pitchers—led by phenoms Dontrelle Willis and Josh Beckett—and timely acquisitions like Hall of Fame catcher Iván Rodríguez. Throughout the remainder of Loria's ownership, the C-suite never invested enough in the team to give it another run, even when the future seemed promising. The early days of Sherman's ownership have provided at least one reason for optimism: Sitting on the edge of contention at the 2020 deadline, they pushed their chips to the middle and went for it, picking up center fielder Starling Marte in trade. As the sun rises on Miami's contention window, they'll need to supplement all their young pitching with some bats to reach the true goal of player development: win.

—Jarrett Seidler is an author for Baseball Prospectus.

HITTERS

Jesús Aguilar 1B

Born: 06/30/90 Age: 32 Bats: R Throws: R Height: 6'3" Weight: 277 lb. Origin: International Free Agent, 2007

YEAR	TEAM	LVL	AGE	PA	R	2B	3B	HR	RBI	BB	K	SB	CS	Whiff%	AVG/OBP/SLG	DRC+	BABIP	BRR	FRAA	WARP
2019	MIL	MLB	29	262	26	9	0	8	34	31	59	0	0	27.3%	.225/.320/.374	96	.264	-1.3	1B(60): -0.1, 3B(2): -0.0	0.5
2019	TB	MLB	29	107	13	3	0	4	16	12	22	0	0	23.2%	.261/.336/.424	101	.290	-1.3	1B(15): -0.2	0.2
2020	MIA	MLB	30	216	31	10	0	8	34	23	40	0	1	22.3%	.277/.352/.457	116	.306	-0.5	1B(31): 0.7, 3B(1): -0.0	0.9
2021	MIA	MLB	31	510	49	23	0	22	93	46	93	0	0	25.8%	.261/.329/.459	111	.279	0.6	1B(113): 6.3, 3B(2): 0.0	2.6
2022 DC	*MIA*	*MLB*	*32*	*568*	*87*	*23*	*1*	*24*	*76*	*59*	*114*	*0*	*0*	*25.3%*	*.263/.344/.462*	*115*	*.294*	*-1.0*	*1B 2*	*2.1*

Comparables: Andres Galarraga, Paul Konerko, Orlando Cepeda

Woe be a right-handed first baseman, the paralegal of the baseball world (at least according to one website that listed paralegals as the most underappreciated job). Since being claimed off waivers from the Rays, Aguilar has been one of Miami's most productive and consistent bats, but teams weren't knocking down the door to acquire his services around the deadline. He underwent knee surgery in September and is expected to be healthy for next season, but as he's entering his final year of arbitration, there are no guarantees he'll be suiting up in a Marlins uniform long term. Some team will surely want a player who has hit 30 HRs in about a full season's worth of at-bats over the last two years, so he won't have to go and do ... whatever it is paralegals do.

Brian Anderson 3B

Born: 05/19/93 Age: 29 Bats: R Throws: R Height: 6'3" Weight: 208 lb. Origin: Round 3, 2014 Draft (#76 overall)

YEAR	TEAM	LVL	AGE	PA	R	2B	3B	HR	RBI	BB	K	SB	CS	Whiff%	AVG/OBP/SLG	DRC+	BABIP	BRR	FRAA	WARP
2019	MIA	MLB	26	520	57	33	1	20	66	44	114	5	1	27.4%	.261/.342/.468	108	.305	2.2	3B(67): -0.1, RF(55): 6.5	2.8
2020	MIA	MLB	27	229	27	7	1	11	38	22	66	0	0	34.5%	.255/.345/.465	108	.323	-0.2	3B(56): 7.7, 1B(1): -0.1, 2B(1): -0.0	1.5
2021	MIA	MLB	28	264	24	9	0	7	28	26	65	5	0	28.2%	.249/.337/.378	93	.317	0.4	3B(65): 6.2, SS(1): 0.1	1.3
2022 DC	*MIA*	*MLB*	*29*	*500*	*61*	*21*	*1*	*15*	*65*	*47*	*121*	*2*	*2*	*29.3%*	*.237/.327/.402*	*100*	*.291*	*-0.5*	*3B 4*	*1.7*

Comparables: Danny Valencia, Chase Headley, Chris Johnson

We've all felt unfairly left out, ignored, our life's greatest accomplishments not given the respect they deserve. "Yes, Mom, the $600 LEGO Ghostbusters HQ I built *does* make me a success." That's Anderson. An above-average hitter with solid defense at third base made him arguably the Marlins best player from 2017-20, even as his name and his home ballpark made people ask, "Who?" when his name was brought up. Unfortunately, 2021 was the year Anderson stepped on all those LEGOs, metaphorically speaking, as multiple left shoulder subluxations kept him on the IL for most of the season before surgery shut him down for good in September. He's expected to be healthy next season and ready to return to his place in the heart of the Marlins lineup. Appreciate him now, so you can remember him as some guy later.

Jon Berti IF Born: 01/22/90 Age: 32 Bats: R Throws: R Height: 5'10" Weight: 190 lb. Origin: Round 18, 2011 Draft (#559 overall)

YEAR	TEAM	LVL	AGE	PA	R	2B	3B	HR	RBI	BB	K	SB	CS	Whiff%	AVG/OBP/SLG	DRC+	BABIP	BRR	FRAA	WARP
2019	NO	AAA	29	79	14	1	0	4	8	15	11	5	0		.290/.430/.500	118	.292	1.0	3B(9): -0.6, CF(6): 0.9, SS(5): 0.4	0.6
2019	MIA	MLB	29	287	52	14	1	6	24	24	73	17	3	24.6%	.273/.348/.406	86	.360	5.4	SS(32): -1.3, CF(21): -0.8, 3B(20): 1.2	0.9
2020	MIA	MLB	30	149	21	5	0	2	14	23	37	9	2	19.6%	.258/.388/.350	97	.354	1.5	2B(21): 0.5, CF(9): -1.5, RF(7): 0.8	0.5
2021	MIA	MLB	31	271	35	10	1	4	19	32	61	8	4	21.7%	.210/.311/.313	84	.265	2.9	3B(46): 1.4, 2B(27): -1.5, LF(7): -0.2	0.6
2022 DC	*MIA*	*MLB*	*32*	*225*	*27*	*8*	*1*	*4*	*20*	*26*	*47*	*11*	*4*	*22.0%*	*.226/.331/.346*	*92*	*.280*	*0.9*	*CF -1, LF 0*	*0.6*

Comparables: Ryan Goins, Ryan Roberts, Phil Gosselin

Berti is the quintessential cult player: At his best, he draws walks, rarely takes ugly hacks, steals bases and pushes for the extra base at every opportunity, all while playing every position under the sun. Heck, he even helped save Bowling Green's baseball program after the school threatened to cut the program due to COVID-related budget issues. He does it all! After a rough first two months in '21, Berti was just getting hot when he was hit by a pitch against the Padres and suffered a concussion that ended his season. Kim Ng has talked publicly about valuing position flexibility, so assuming Berti is healthy, he should have a shot at the speedy supersub role again in 2022.

JJ Bleday OF Born: 11/10/97 Age: 24 Bats: L Throws: L Height: 6'3" Weight: 205 lb. Origin: Round 1, 2019 Draft (#4 overall)

YEAR	TEAM	LVL	AGE	PA	R	2B	3B	HR	RBI	BB	K	SB	CS	Whiff%	AVG/OBP/SLG	DRC+	BABIP	BRR	FRAA	WARP
2019	JUP	A+	21	151	13	8	0	3	19	11	29	0	0		.257/.311/.379	108	.306	-1.2	RF(32): -0.8	0.4
2021	MSS	WIN	23	115	20	8	2	5	24	20	23	2	0		.316/.435/.600		.373			
2021	PNS	AA	23	468	52	22	3	12	54	64	101	5	3		.212/.323/.373	103	.250	0.0	RF(38): 5.8, LF(28): 5.2, CF(23): 1.1	2.8
2022 non-DC	*MIA*	*MLB*	*24*	*251*	*23*	*11*	*1*	*5*	*24*	*24*	*61*	*0*	*1*	*26.9%*	*.216/.298/.343*	*74*	*.275*	*-0.2*	*RF 1, CF 0*	*0.2*

Comparables: Abraham Almonte, Zoilo Almonte, Carlos Peguero

What will a missed year of minor league baseball mean for players? For Bleday, the Marlins hope it just means a lot of rust that he struggled to shake off. The fourth overall pick in 2019, some fans were hoping the former NCAA home run champ might reach the Marlins roster by midseason. Instead, it took a hot streak at the end of the year to get his average over .200, while the three players taken ahead of him (Adley Rutschman, Bobby Witt Jr and Andrew Vaughn) all elevated their games. Bleday will take a walk and has a good arm, but he lacks the footspeed to play anywhere but a corner. The good news: In the Arizona Fall League, he looked exactly (1.035 OPS) like the player the Marlins picked.

Lewis Brinson OF Born: 05/08/94 Age: 28 Bats: R Throws: R Height: 6'5" Weight: 212 lb. Origin: Round 1, 2012 Draft (#29 overall)

YEAR	TEAM	LVL	AGE	PA	R	2B	3B	HR	RBI	BB	K	SB	CS	Whiff%	AVG/OBP/SLG	DRC+	BABIP	BRR	FRAA	WARP
2019	NO	AAA	25	339	56	15	4	16	56	32	100	16	5		.270/.361/.510	94	.356	3.0	CF(50): 5.2, RF(27): 5.2, LF(6): -0.5	2.1
2019	MIA	MLB	25	248	15	9	1	0	15	13	74	1	1	32.9%	.173/.236/.221	57	.255	1.4	CF(60): 6.0, RF(11): 1.0	0.5
2020	MIA	MLB	26	112	14	6	0	3	12	6	30	4	0	30.8%	.226/.268/.368	91	.288	1.5	RF(31): -2.5, LF(21): -0.0, CF(7): -0.2	0.1
2021	JAX	AAA	27	48	3	1	1	1	3	2	11	2	0		.283/.313/.413	96	.353	0.1	CF(6): -0.6, RF(2): 0.1, LF(1): 0.2	0.1
2021	MIA	MLB	27	290	24	14	0	9	33	13	72	1	1	31.2%	.226/.263/.376	84	.273	1.1	LF(51): 1.8, CF(33): -2.6, RF(4): 0.1	0.6
2022 non-DC	*MIA*	*MLB*	*28*	*251*	*25*	*10*	*1*	*7*	*28*	*14*	*63*	*2*	*2*	*31.0%*	*.231/.283/.390*	*77*	*.284*	*0.2*	*CF 1, RF 0*	*0.2*

Comparables: Aaron Hicks, Jake Marisnick, Jordan Schafer

If there were a song like Billy Joel's "We Didn't Start the Fire," but instead it ran off the names like Brien Taylor, Brandon Wood, Tim Beckham, Bryan Bullington and the like, it would probably be time to remix the song and add Brinson's name to the list. The rare four-time BP top 100 prospect actually enjoyed a couple of hot streaks in 2021, but the law of averages came for him every time. Despite making some slight improvements over the years, there is only one active player with a lower OPS and more than 1,000 plate appearances. That's Drew Butera, who received all of 32 big-league PA in 2021. Dropped from the Miami's 40-man after the World Series, Brinson is on his way to new pastures.

Peyton Burdick OF Born: 02/26/97 Age: 25 Bats: R Throws: R Height: 6'0" Weight: 205 lb. Origin: Round 3, 2019 Draft (#82 overall)

YEAR	TEAM	LVL	AGE	PA	R	2B	3B	HR	RBI	BB	K	SB	CS	Whiff%	AVG/OBP/SLG	DRC+	BABIP	BRR	FRAA	WARP
2019	BAT	SS	22	25	3	0	1	1	5	2	5	1	1		.318/.400/.545		.375			
2019	CLI	A	22	288	57	20	3	10	59	32	67	6	6		.307/.408/.542	132	.380	-0.4	LF(59): 11.2, RF(2): 0.4	3.1
2021	PNS	AA	24	460	71	17	2	23	52	76	135	9	5		.231/.376/.472	133	.293	0.3	CF(50): -5.1, LF(25): 0.9, RF(15): -1.2	2.7
2021	JAX	AAA	24	31	5	3	0	0	1	3	11	0	0		.143/.226/.250	77	.235	0.1	LF(3): -0.5, CF(3): -0.8, RF(1): -0.1	-0.1
2022 non-DC	*MIA*	*MLB*	*25*	*251*	*27*	*11*	*1*	*8*	*29*	*28*	*81*	*2*	*2*	*35.1%*	*.215/.318/.390*	*91*	*.302*	*0.0*	*LF 2, CF 0*	*0.7*

Comparables: Chris Heisey, Adam Engel, Jaycob Brugman

The Marlins' minor league player of the year, Burdick is a big ol' slugger who is expected to add even more power to his game as he progresses. He can take a walk and he can even hack it in center, so he's not quite an Adam Dunn type (so far), though there is a frightening amount of whiff in his game. If this were a decade ago, he'd be every internet baseball writer's favorite prospect and we'd have FREE BURDICK T-shirts hanging around. Heck, maybe we should do that anyway. Have you seen what the kids are wearing these days? They love nostalgia, poorly fitting graphic tees and being disappointed by the future.

Jazz Chisholm Jr. 2B Born: 02/01/98 Age: 24 Bats: L Throws: R Height: 5'11" Weight: 184 lb. Origin: International Free Agent, 2015

YEAR	TEAM	LVL	AGE	PA	R	2B	3B	HR	RBI	BB	K	SB	CS	Whiff%	AVG/OBP/SLG	DRC+	BABIP	BRR	FRAA	WARP
2019	JXN	AA	21	364	51	6	5	18	44	41	123	13	4		.204/.305/.427	104	.261	2.6	SS(88): -5.7	1.1
2019	JAX	AA	21	94	6	4	2	3	10	11	24	3	0		.284/.383/.494	104	.370	-0.5	SS(22): -2.4	0.0
2020	MIA	MLB	22	62	8	1	1	2	6	5	19	2	2	25.7%	.161/.242/.321	82	.200	-0.1	2B(13): -1.4, SS(9): -0.1	-0.1
2021	MIA	MLB	23	507	70	20	4	18	53	34	145	23	8	30.1%	.248/.303/.425	86	.319	2.1	2B(91): 2.3, SS(37): -4.9	0.9
2022 DC	*MIA*	*MLB*	*24*	*566*	*77*	*21*	*6*	*24*	*73*	*42*	*157*	*16*	*5*	*29.9%*	*.241/.305/.446*	*97*	*.299*	*1.9*	*2B 0, SS 0*	*2.0*

Comparables: Nick Franklin, Jonathan Villar, Eugenio Suárez

With bright blue locks and an OPS over 1.000 a few weeks into the season, it looked like we found baseball's newest superstar. But young, electric, big-swinging middle infielders tend to not have the most direct development path, so of course Chisholm slumped, especially as he battled multiple injuries. He showed off the power and speed you'd want from a top prospect—a particular rubber band-snap swing on a letter-high 100-mph fastball from Jacob deGrom practically burned itself into screens showing highlights—while also whiffing and committing errors more often than anyone would like. He has more charisma than perhaps anyone in the game; he wears a chain of his initials, with the "J" in the shape of his silhouette during a leaping catch. "My first SportsCenter Top 10," he said. So yeah, he'll be A-OK.

Garrett Cooper RF/1B Born: 12/25/90 Age: 31 Bats: R Throws: R Height: 6'5" Weight: 235 lb. Origin: Round 6, 2013 Draft (#182 overall)

YEAR	TEAM	LVL	AGE	PA	R	2B	3B	HR	RBI	BB	K	SB	CS	Whiff%	AVG/OBP/SLG	DRC+	BABIP	BRR	FRAA	WARP
2019	MIA	MLB	28	421	52	16	1	15	50	33	110	0	0	23.4%	.281/.344/.446	99	.357	-1.4	1B(73): -0.8, RF(31): 5.3	1.4
2020	MIA	MLB	29	133	20	8	0	6	20	11	31	0	0	22.2%	.283/.353/.500	114	.337	-0.9	1B(15): 0.4	0.5
2021	MIA	MLB	30	250	30	10	1	9	33	30	68	1	1	27.2%	.284/.380/.465	104	.374	-2.1	RF(41): -2.4, 1B(19): -0.2	0.3
2022 DC	*MIA*	*MLB*	*31*	*118*	*15*	*5*	*0*	*3*	*15*	*12*	*28*	*0*	*0*	*25.6%*	*.245/.333/.410*	*103*	*.303*	*-0.2*	*RF 0, 1B 0*	*-0.1*

Comparables: Steve Pearce, Darin Ruf, Nelson Cruz

Cooper is a man of constants: He hits, he moves all over the field in search of regular playing time and, unfortunately, he gets hurt. In four years with the Marlins, Cooper has been on the IL eight separate times. This time, Cooper's season ended on July 19 with a left elbow sprain which eventually required Tommy John surgery. It's the same procedure Rhys Hoskins had in October 2020, so while we can't assume every player will respond the same way, Cooper is expected to return to his steady work of lashing hard-hit balls all over the park in the spring, and parts of the summer. It would just be nice if he could do all that while staying at first base or DH.

Bryan De La Cruz OF Born: 12/16/96 Age: 25 Bats: R Throws: R Height: 6'2" Weight: 175 lb. Origin: International Free Agent, 2013

YEAR	TEAM	LVL	AGE	PA	R	2B	3B	HR	RBI	BB	K	SB	CS	Whiff%	AVG/OBP/SLG	DRC+	BABIP	BRR	FRAA	WARP
2019	FAY	A+	22	183	29	14	2	4	19	16	33	5	1		.276/.339/.460	116	.318	0.3	RF(32): 0.2, LF(6): -0.5, CF(2): -0.1	0.9
2019	CC	AA	22	300	45	14	4	4	24	24	60	7	5		.283/.340/.409	99	.343	4.7	LF(30): 2.6, RF(29): 0.2, CF(5): -0.6	1.7
2021	TOR	WIN	24	69	6	4	0	1	12	5	12	0	0		.226/.290/.339		.260			
2021	SUG	AAA	24	293	48	17	0	12	50	17	59	2	4		.324/.362/.518	111	.373	1.9	RF(22): -1.3, LF(19): -0.3, CF(16): -1.5	1.3
2021	MIA	MLB	24	219	17	7	2	5	19	18	53	1	1	25.3%	.296/.356/.427	99	.380	0.2	CF(24): 2.1, RF(23): 1.7, LF(16): -0.8	1.1
2022 DC	*MIA*	*MLB*	*25*	*421*	*48*	*18*	*2*	*8*	*45*	*29*	*98*	*4*	*3*	*24.9%*	*.255/.311/.380*	*86*	*.321*	*0.1*	*CF 1*	*0.9*

Comparables: Marcell Ozuna, Juan Lagares, Lorenzo Cain

The problem with de la Cruz has almost nothing to do with him as a player. The problem is that de la Cruz is the type of player the Marlins hope for with every trade they make: Swap out one reliever on an expiring deal (in this case, Yimi García) and get back an undervalued hitter (see above). Unfortunately for all parties, de la Cruz almost certainly will not continue posting an Austin Jacksonian BABIP. Even if he *did untap* some magical ability to avoid gloves and play above what many consider to be his fourth outfielder future, Miami would need to pull off the same trick another three or four more times.

José Devers MI Born: 12/07/99 Age: 22 Bats: L Throws: R Height: 6'0" Weight: 174 lb. Origin: International Free Agent, 2016

YEAR	TEAM	LVL	AGE	PA	R	2B	3B	HR	RBI	BB	K	SB	CS	Whiff%	AVG/OBP/SLG	DRC+	BABIP	BRR	FRAA	WARP
2019	MRL	ROK	19	46	7	3	1	0	2	4	4	3	1		.275/.370/.400		.306			
2019	JUP	A+	19	138	13	3	1	0	3	8	20	5	0		.325/.384/.365	114	.387	-1.4	SS(32): -1.8	0.2
2021	JAX	AAA	21	41	4	1	1	0	3	1	5	0	0		.231/.250/.308	102	.265	1.2	SS(8): -0.7, 2B(3): 0.2	0.2
2021	MIA	MLB	21	46	7	3	0	0	5	3	11	0	0	24.0%	.244/.304/.317	79	.323	0.3	2B(13): 0.2, SS(5): -0.8	0.0
2022 DC	*MIA*	*MLB*	*22*	*32*	*3*	*1*	*0*	*0*	*2*	*1*	*5*	*0*	*1*	*22.8%*	*.242/.292/.328*	*68*	*.295*	*0.1*	*2B 0*	*0.0*

Comparables: Ketel Marte, Luis García, Wilmer Flores

The younger cousin of Red Sox star Rafael played against his kin on May 28, with the elder Devers blowing a kiss when José stepped into the box. But other than the name and their boyish demeanors, the two are almost inverse versions of each other. The Marlins' Devers is lightning fast and has a smooth glove up the middle, but he's a contact hitter with only one home run in 220 professional games. This Devers also flew up the org chart like his cousin, playing only 35 games in High-A before going to Triple-A and the Majors at the age of 21. So he has lots of time to muscle up even as shoulder surgery cut his season short in mid-June. The team is clearly high on him, so a future as a utility infielder looks to be his absolute floor.

Isan Díaz 3B/2B Born: 05/27/96 Age: 26 Bats: L Throws: R Height: 5'11" Weight: 201 lb. Origin: Round 2, 2014 Draft (#70 overall)

YEAR	TEAM	LVL	AGE	PA	R	2B	3B	HR	RBI	BB	K	SB	CS	Whiff%	AVG/OBP/SLG	DRC+	BABIP	BRR	FRAA	WARP
2019	NO	AAA	23	435	89	21	2	26	70	49	96	5	4		.305/.395/.578	115	.349	0.3	2B(99): -0.7	2.8
2019	MIA	MLB	23	201	17	5	2	5	23	19	59	0	3	28.2%	.173/.259/.307	69	.224	0.1	2B(48): -0.2	0.0
2020	MIA	MLB	24	22	3	0	0	0	1	0	7	0	0	32.4%	.182/.182/.182	74	.267	0.0	2B(7): 1.0	0.1
2021	JAX	AAA	25	116	16	8	1	5	15	11	30	0	2		.243/.328/.485	108	.294	-2.0	3B(20): 2.2, 2B(8): -1.3	0.4
2021	MIA	MLB	25	278	25	9	0	4	17	34	73	1	1	31.8%	.193/.293/.282	71	.256	-1.2	3B(37): 2.9, 2B(35): -2.0	-0.1
2022 DC	*MIA*	*MLB*	*26*	*61*	*7*	*2*	*0*	*2*	*7*	*6*	*17*	*0*	*0*	*31.0%*	*.224/.311/.398*	*89*	*.294*	*0.0*	*3B 0, 2B 0*	*0.1*

Comparables: Hernán Pérez, Eduardo Escobar, César Hernández

Spring training is never predictive, but if you go 0-for-your three last weeks, there might be something there. Yet for more than half the Marlins games this season, Díaz was number 1 in your scorecard, which is fitting because it's also the number that his batting average begins with. After a dominant 2019 in the minors, and a homer against Jacob deGrom in his first big-league game, Díaz's .562 OPS since his bdebut is the second-lowest in the majors among players with at least 500 PA in that time—and Austin Hedges has the benefit of being a catcher.

Lewin Díaz 1B Born: 11/19/96 Age: 25 Bats: L Throws: L Height: 6'4" Weight: 217 lb. Origin: International Free Agent, 2013

YEAR	TEAM	LVL	AGE	PA	R	2B	3B	HR	RBI	BB	K	SB	CS	Whiff%	AVG/OBP/SLG	DRC+	BABIP	BRR	FRAA	WARP
2019	EST	WIN	22	127	11	6	1	3	20	9	22	0	0		.276/.331/.422		.315			
2019	FTM	A+	22	234	34	11	1	13	36	14	40	0	0		.290/.333/.533	149	.297	-1.1	1B(52): 5.9	2.4
2019	PNS	AA	22	138	12	16	1	6	26	8	23	0	0		.302/.341/.587	120	.320	-0.8	1B(31): -0.2	0.6
2019	JAX	AA	22	129	16	6	0	8	14	11	28	0	1		.200/.279/.461	120	.188	-0.3	1B(30): -2.4	0.4
2020	EST	WIN	23	93	10	1	1	3	12	10	16	1	0		.207/.301/.354		.222			
2020	MIA	MLB	23	41	2	2	0	0	3	2	12	0	0	23.4%	.154/.195/.205	73	.222	0.0	1B(11): 2.2	0.2
2021	JAX	AAA	24	312	52	15	0	20	51	26	60	2	0		.248/.327/.518	134	.246	-1.5	1B(63): 7.5, LF(4): -0.1	2.4
2021	MIA	MLB	24	128	16	4	1	8	13	6	33	0	0	28.1%	.205/.242/.451	87	.210	-0.6	1B(32): 6.0	0.6
2022 DC	*MIA*	*MLB*	*25*	*102*	*12*	*4*	*0*	*4*	*14*	*5*	*23*	*0*	*0*	*25.7%*	*.233/.286/.433*	*89*	*.262*	*-0.1*	*1B 0*	*-0.1*

Comparables: Chris Parmelee, Kendrys Morales, Mark Trumbo

Inside Llewyn Davis is a film about a struggling folk singer who travels the country in hopes of making it big, finding cats all along the way. *Inside Lewin Díaz* is about a smooth-fielding first baseman who is struggling to make enough contact to hold down the position that demands the most offensive output. The Marlins were incredibly high on Díaz entering the 2020 season, so he might still be making up for lost development time from the lack of a minor-league campaign that year. Which is unfortunate, because his approach falls apart at the major-league level: He swung at almost everything, and wound up with two strikes on him in two-thirds of his at-bats (and 0-2 in a third, which is no way to live). Given full-time at-bats the final month of the season, Díaz cracked five home runs and got his average up nearly 100 points…even if that just got him over the Mendoza line. Probably needs a cat.

Avisaíl García RF Born: 06/12/91 Age: 31 Bats: R Throws: R Height: 6'4" Weight: 250 lb. Origin: International Free Agent, 2007

YEAR	TEAM	LVL	AGE	PA	R	2B	3B	HR	RBI	BB	K	SB	CS	Whiff%	AVG/OBP/SLG	DRC+	BABIP	BRR	FRAA	WARP
2019	TB	MLB	28	530	61	25	2	20	72	31	125	10	4	32.0%	.282/.332/.464	99	.340	-3.4	RF(92): -5.1, CF(12): 1.9	0.8
2020	MIL	MLB	29	207	20	10	0	2	15	20	49	1	3	34.7%	.238/.333/.326	91	.315	-1.2	CF(44): -5.7	-0.3
2021	MIL	MLB	30	515	68	18	0	29	86	38	121	8	4	33.6%	.262/.330/.490	114	.291	0.0	RF(121): 2.0, CF(1): 0.0	2.6
2022 DC	*MIA*	*MLB*	*31*	*557*	*77*	*22*	*1*	*20*	*71*	*42*	*135*	*7*	*3*	*33.2%*	*.256/.326/.430*	*103*	*.311*	*0.0*	*RF -1*	*1.5*

Comparables: Roberto Clemente, Jermaine Dye, Ollie Brown

Boomers love a good network sitcom, and *Last Man Standing*, a Tim Allen vehicle in which the *Home Improvement* star blusters around as the only man in a house full of women, is right up their alley. That's the only way one can explain the show lasting for a whopping nine seasons before coming to a merciful end in 2021. Fans of that show undoubtedly enjoyed watching García in 2021. He was essentially the last man standing in an outfield that battled injuries and inconsistent performance throughout the season. García paced an otherwise moribund Brewers lineup in DRC+, posted career-best numbers in the power department, mostly avoided stepping in any of the outfield holes swallowing up his teammates, and bounced back from some poor defensive numbers in 2020 to boot. If that wasn't reason enough for boomers to love García, he also hustles down the line on every grounder as if it were Game 7 of the World Series. Like *Last Man Standing*, García's staying power has been surprising given how long it took his career to get started. Unlike the show, however, he seems to still have a lot left in the tank. The Marlins certainly think so, signing him to a four-year deal for a guaranteed $53 million with an option for a fifth year.

Monte Harrison OF Born: 08/10/95 Age: 26 Bats: R Throws: R Height: 6'3" Weight: 225 lb. Origin: Round 2, 2014 Draft (#50 overall)

YEAR	TEAM	LVL	AGE	PA	R	2B	3B	HR	RBI	BB	K	SB	CS	Whiff%	AVG/OBP/SLG	DRC+	BABIP	BRR	FRAA	WARP
2019	NO	AAA	23	244	41	7	2	9	24	25	73	20	2		.274/.357/.451	86	.373	3.5	CF(32): 2.9, RF(19): -2.1, LF(3): 0.8	0.9
2020	MIA	MLB	24	51	8	1	0	1	3	4	26	6	0	42.5%	.170/.235/.255	59	.350	1.3	CF(16): 1.4, RF(13): -0.0	0.2
2021	JAX	AAA	25	308	47	8	1	15	52	31	121	24	3		.242/.331/.446	81	.370	4.0	CF(43): 13.2, RF(11): -0.5, LF(10): 0.3	2.0
2021	MIA	MLB	25	11	0	1	0	0	0	0	3	0	1	26.3%	.200/.200/.300	89	.286	-0.1	CF(4): 0.1, RF(3): -0.0	0.0
2022 DC	*MIA*	*MLB*	*26*	*153*	*16*	*5*	*0*	*4*	*16*	*11*	*59*	*5*	*2*	*40.1%*	*.201/.277/.356*	*70*	*.310*	*0.5*	*CF 1, LF 0*	*0.1*

Comparables: Aaron Hicks, Peter Bourjos, Jake Marisnick

Swing for the moon, they say, and if you miss, you'll still wind up among the stars. Unfortunately in baseball, if you swing for the moon and end up striking out 39% of the time, those stars will be the street lamps outside the window, shuttling between Triple-A and the bigs. Harrison did offer one magical moment in 2021, an incredible catch for Jacksonville in which he scaled the wall, realized the ball was going to die at the warning track, then used his feet to push off and dive forward for the catch. It was an apt metaphor for the prep star's professional career, except the catch part. Harrison still tantalizes with his combination of power and speed, but at 26, the window is closing.

Alex Jackson C Born: 12/25/95 Age: 26 Bats: R Throws: R Height: 6'2" Weight: 215 lb. Origin: Round 1, 2014 Draft (#6 overall)

YEAR	TEAM	LVL	AGE	PA	R	2B	3B	HR	RBI	BB	K	SB	CS	Whiff%	AVG/OBP/SLG	DRC+	BABIP	BRR	FRAA	WARP
2019	GWN	AAA	23	345	52	9	0	28	65	20	118	1	0		.229/.313/.533	108	.261	-3.3	C(78): 15.8	2.9
2019	ATL	MLB	23	15	0	0	0	0	0	1	5	0	0	45.5%	.000/.133/.000	84			C(4): 0.3	0.1
2020	ATL	MLB	24	7	0	1	0	0	0	0	4	0	0	61.5%	.286/.286/.429	74	.667	-0.6	C(4): -0.1	-0.1
2021	GWN	AAA	25	123	21	9	1	11	36	11	35	1	0		.287/.366/.694	120	.317	-1.4		0.6
2021	MIA	MLB	25	123	11	4	0	3	12	11	60	0	0	50.5%	.157/.260/.278	43	.311	0.1	C(34): -0.9, RF(1): -0.0	-0.5
2021	ATL	MLB	25	28	2	0	0	0	0	2	13	0	0	55.8%	.043/.214/.043	63	.100	0.9	C(9): -0.3	0.0
2022 DC	*MIA*	*MLB*	*26*	*59*	*7*	*2*	*0*	*2*	*7*	*4*	*26*	*0*	*0*	*45.4%*	*.200/.289/.423*	*86*	*.325*	*-0.1*	*C 0*	*0.1*

Comparables: John Ryan Murphy, Welington Castillo, Christian Vázquez

YEAR	TEAM	P. COUNT	FRM RUNS	BLK RUNS	THRW RUNS	TOT RUNS
2019	ATL	534	0.3	0.0	0.0	0.3
2019	GWN	11041	16.1	0.0	0.8	16.9
2020	ATL	332	-0.1	0.0	0.0	0.0
2021	ATL	1113	-0.2	0.0	0.0	-0.2
2021	MIA	4249	-0.6	0.1	-0.5	-1.0
2021	GWN	3024	0.4	0.0	0.4	0.8
2022	*MIA*	*2405*	*-0.2*	*0.0*	*0.0*	*-0.2*

Even in these enlightened, strikeout-friendly times, there's still a limit to how often a player can whiff and get away with it. And at that periphery, you need to be able to crush the ball when you make contact. Jackson is struggling with both: Not only did he whiff on nearly 50% of fastballs and 56% of breaking balls, but he slugged under .200 against those pitches, too. Making it all the worse, the Marlins acquired Jackson by giving up Adam Duvall—a popular clubhouse presence and productive slugger—to a division rival. Still, Jackson has hit 39 home runs across fewer than 500 plate appearances in Triple-A in 2019 and '21, and has nothing left to prove at the level, or at least nothing insurmountable. A catcher with decent defense and power, Jackson will get a few more chances to figure it out, even if it's not in Miami.

Joe Mack C/DH Born: 12/27/02 Age: 19 Bats: L Throws: R Height: 6'1" Weight: 210 lb. Origin: Round 1, 2021 Draft (#31 overall)

YEAR	TEAM	LVL	AGE	PA	R	2B	3B	HR	RBI	BB	K	SB	CS	Whiff%	AVG/OBP/SLG	DRC+	BABIP	BRR	FRAA	WARP
2021	MRL	ROK	18	75	9	1	0	1	2	20	22	0	1		.132/.373/.208		.194			
2022															*No projection*					

Comparables: Alberto Mineo, Bryant Aragon, Carlos Rodriguez

The Marlins haven't had much luck drafting first-round catchers. Kyle Skipworth, their top pick in 2008, played all of four major-league games. Blake Anderson never made the Majors and made "Workaholics" instead. (Wait, different Blake Anderson.) To be fair to Miami, all high school catchers are riskier than indoor dining in Fort Lauderdale, but Mack is also that ultra-seductive left-handed hitting catcher.

Joe Panik IF Born: 10/30/90 Age: 31 Bats: L Throws: R Height: 6'1" Weight: 205 lb. Origin: Round 1, 2011 Draft (#29 overall)

YEAR	TEAM	LVL	AGE	PA	R	2B	3B	HR	RBI	BB	K	SB	CS	Whiff%	AVG/OBP/SLG	DRC+	BABIP	BRR	FRAA	WARP
2019	NYM	MLB	28	103	17	4	1	2	12	7	9	0	0	9.4%	.277/.333/.404	102	.289	-0.4	2B(28): -1.2	0.3
2019	SF	MLB	28	388	33	17	1	3	27	36	38	4	2	10.8%	.235/.310/.317	90	.254	0.2	2B(90): 5.7	1.6
2020	TOR	MLB	29	141	18	6	0	1	7	20	27	0	0	18.3%	.225/.340/.300	91	.283	0.3	2B(18): -3.4, SS(14): 0.3, 3B(12): -2.2	-0.2
2021	MIA	MLB	30	134	8	3	0	1	7	9	20	2	0	14.2%	.172/.241/.221	84	.198	0.0	2B(17): -2.1, 3B(11): -0.0, 1B(6): -0.6	-0.1
2021	TOR	MLB	30	123	9	6	0	2	11	8	14	0	0	14.8%	.246/.293/.351	98	.263	-0.7	3B(21): 1.1, 2B(10): 0.6, 1B(3): 0.1	0.5
2022 DC	*FA*	*MLB*	*31*	*276*	*25*	*11*	*0*	*4*	*25*	*24*	*33*	*2*	*1*	*14.6%*	*.236/.310/.341*	*79*	*.257*	*-0.2*	*2B 0, 3B -1*	*0.1*

Comparables: Adam Kennedy, Nellie Fox, Ray Durham

The good news is that teams will always value a player like Panik, who can wear a bunch of gloves and can get on base at a decent clip. The bad news is that Panik's defense suffered last year and his bat is losing the little punch it had, while his whiffs have gone up. It's a bad combo, and the league noticed, throwing him tons of strikes and daring him to hit them. If this is the last time Panik is written about in this book, then we'll always remember him for being the 4 in San Francisco's crucial 4-6-3 double play in the 2014 World Series, the first overturned call in postseason history.

Miguel Rojas SS Born: 02/24/89 Age: 33 Bats: R Throws: R Height: 6'0" Weight: 188 lb. Origin: International Free Agent, 2005

YEAR	TEAM	LVL	AGE	PA	R	2B	3B	HR	RBI	BB	K	SB	CS	Whiff%	AVG/OBP/SLG	DRC+	BABIP	BRR	FRAA	WARP
2019	MIA	MLB	30	526	52	29	1	5	46	32	62	9	5	16.5%	.284/.331/.379	96	.314	-2.2	SS(125): -5.9, 1B(6): -0.2, 2B(3): -0.1	0.8
2020	MIA	MLB	31	143	20	10	1	4	20	16	18	5	1	17.3%	.304/.392/.496	121	.330	-0.4	SS(39): 6.6, 1B(1): -0.0, 3B(1): 0.0	1.4
2021	MIA	MLB	32	539	66	30	3	9	48	37	74	13	3	19.3%	.265/.322/.392	97	.295	0.4	SS(128): -16.7	0.0
2022 DC	*MIA*	*MLB*	*33*	*566*	*69*	*27*	*2*	*10*	*58*	*41*	*79*	*8*	*4*	*18.7%*	*.263/.324/.386*	*94*	*.292*	*0.0*	*SS -2*	*1.5*

Comparables: Luis Aparicio, Omar Vizquel, Rich Aurilia

There's something that is so soothing, so calming and so peaceful about a player like Rojas posting what are essentially his career averages in 2021. It means that the world works as designed. You don't need fancy tools like PECOTA to attempt to predict it and you don't need philosophers to imagine the shape and scope of the universe: Sometimes it simply is. And that's Rojas: a light-hitting infielder who can show off some serious glovework, even if most of the numbers agree that he lost a little bit in his age-32 season. After reaching 500 plate appearances his 2022 option vested and he'll be back to take his place as beloved Marlins leader, community member and shortstop with some truly amazing kicks who gives you exactly what you expect. There are worse things in life.

Jesús Sánchez OF Born: 10/07/97 Age: 24 Bats: L Throws: R Height: 6'3" Weight: 222 lb. Origin: International Free Agent, 2014

YEAR	TEAM	LVL	AGE	PA	R	2B	3B	HR	RBI	BB	K	SB	CS	Whiff%	AVG/OBP/SLG	DRC+	BABIP	BRR	FRAA	WARP
2019	MTG	AA	21	316	32	11	1	8	49	24	65	5	4		.275/.332/.404	107	.327	-0.1	RF(72): 0.2	1.3
2019	DUR	AAA	21	71	6	2	1	1	5	6	20	0	0		.206/.282/.317	78	.279	-0.6	RF(15): 0.9	0.1
2019	NO	AAA	21	78	11	1	0	4	9	9	15	0	0		.246/.338/.446	100	.250	0.1	CF(8): -1.6, RF(8): 4.5	0.5
2020	MIA	MLB	22	29	1	1	0	0	2	4	11	0	0	25.0%	.040/.172/.080	68	.071	0.0	RF(10): -0.1	0.0
2021	TOR	WIN	23	84	11	10	0	0	8	12	15	1	0		.324/.429/.465		.411			
2021	JAX	AAA	23	155	23	5	4	10	31	12	29	1	0		.348/.406/.652	140	.382	0.6	RF(21): 6.7, LF(11): -0.7	1.8
2021	MIA	MLB	23	251	27	8	2	14	36	20	78	0	1	29.4%	.251/.319/.489	94	.316	-2.5	RF(41): 0.3, LF(21): 1.2	0.5
2022 DC	*MIA*	*MLB*	*24*	*428*	*51*	*17*	*3*	*14*	*55*	*32*	*107*	*2*	*1*	*27.8%*	*.234/.297/.406*	*87*	*.284*	*0.0*	*LF 5, RF 0*	*1.2*

Comparables: Carlos González, Moisés Sierra, Jesse Winker

If Jesús saves, then the 2021 Marlins should have been in better shape considering that they had *three:* Aguilar, Luzardo and Sánchez. Though Sánchez dropped out of the prospect rankings before this season, he showed off all the skills that had scouts drooling over him and inspired the Marlins to pry him away from the Rays along with Ryne Stanek in 2019. Though he still struggles with plate discipline—what exciting young slugger other than Juan Soto doesn't?—Sánchez displayed better-than-expected reads in the outfield and cut down on the times he chopped the ball into the infield dirt, allowing him to show off his immense exit velocity. He hammered 11 home runs in August and September and could honestly be the Marlins' best outfielder since some schmoes named Christian Yelich and Giancarlo Stanton.

Magneuris Sierra OF Born: 04/07/96 Age: 26 Bats: L Throws: L Height: 5'11" Weight: 178 lb. Origin: International Free Agent, 2012

YEAR	TEAM	LVL	AGE	PA	R	2B	3B	HR	RBI	BB	K	SB	CS	Whiff%	AVG/OBP/SLG	DRC+	BABIP	BRR	FRAA	WARP
2019	JAX	AA	23	197	21	8	2	1	7	13	32	7	1		.282/.337/.365	103	.338	2.1	CF(21): 0.6, RF(15): 4.2, LF(4): 1.7	1.7
2019	NO	AAA	23	352	56	11	7	6	21	15	58	26	10		.271/.304/.399	85	.313	3.7	CF(32): -0.6, LF(24): -2.0, RF(23): 1.3	0.7
2019	MIA	MLB	23	42	5	1	1	0	1	2	7	3	3	10.7%	.350/.381/.425	91	.424	-0.6	CF(9): 3.4, RF(5): 0.3	0.4
2020	MIA	MLB	24	53	8	3	1	0	7	5	9	4	1	17.1%	.250/.333/.364	91	.306	-0.1	CF(11): 3.9, LF(5): 0.7, RF(4): -0.0	0.6
2021	MIA	MLB	25	225	27	6	1	0	5	15	50	11	0	22.5%	.230/.281/.268	71	.302	2.9	CF(54): 2.6, LF(16): -0.3, RF(8): -0.7	0.6
2022 non-DC	*MIA*	*MLB*	*26*	*251*	*8*	*9*	*1*	*2*	*8*	*15*	*44*	*8*	*4*	*21.7%*	*.235/.287/.323*	*66*	*.282*	*0.9*	*CF 0, RF 0*	*-0.1*

Comparables: Raimel Tapia, Alexi Amarista, Ender Inciarte

Keep Sierra's name handy the next time you're at bar trivia because his name could come up:

Who holds the record with 65 consecutive games with at least one plate appearance to start a season without recording an RBI? Sierra.

Which active player (not a pitcher) has the most plate appearances without a home run? Sierra.

And finally, for the victory and $25 towards well drinks at Dr. Chug's Glug-Glug Bar, who was the first automatic runner to be picked off *second base* in extra innings? If you guessed Sierra again, you'd be right.

Jacob Stallings C Born: 12/22/89 Age: 32 Bats: R Throws: R Height: 6'5" Weight: 225 lb. Origin: Round 7, 2012 Draft (#226 overall)

YEAR	TEAM	LVL	AGE	PA	R	2B	3B	HR	RBI	BB	K	SB	CS	Whiff%	AVG/OBP/SLG	DRC+	BABIP	BRR	FRAA	WARP
2019	IND	AAA	29	61	11	9	0	2	7	4	9	0	0		.275/.361/.569	112	.286	-3.4	C(15): 1.1	0.1
2019	PIT	MLB	29	210	26	5	0	6	13	16	40	0	0	24.7%	.262/.325/.382	93	.303	0.8	C(61): 10.0, P(1): -0.0	1.8
2020	PIT	MLB	30	143	13	7	0	3	18	15	40	0	0	26.1%	.248/.326/.376	91	.337	-0.6	C(42): 6.0	0.9
2021	PIT	MLB	31	427	38	20	1	8	53	49	85	0	0	23.4%	.246/.335/.369	97	.297	-2.5	C(104): 9.1, 1B(1): -0.0	2.3
2022 DC	*MIA*	*MLB*	*32*	*408*	*44*	*18*	*0*	*7*	*44*	*41*	*81*	*0*	*1*	*23.7%*	*.236/.321/.358*	*88*	*.284*	*-0.6*	*C 4*	*1.6*

Comparables: Dustin Garneau, Curt Casali, Ryan Hanigan

YEAR	TEAM	P. COUNT	FRM RUNS	BLK RUNS	THRW RUNS	TOT RUNS
2019	PIT	7741	7.3	0.5	1.2	9.0
2019	IND	2150	0.9	0.0	0.5	1.4
2020	PIT	6186	4.2	0.0	0.5	4.7
2021	PIT	15291	4.8	1.4	0.3	6.5
2022	*MIA*	*15632*	*3.8*	*2.9*	*0.3*	*7.0*

Pirates fans with concerns that Oneil Cruz is just plain too tall to play shortstop can take some solace in the development of Stallings, who has worked tirelessly to provide Gold Glove-caliber defense despite his height. A stereotypical gym rat and coach's son who made his Pirates debut while his father was coaching the Pitt basketball team, Stallings is a late bloomer who has made himself into a rock behind the dish with a strong arm, surprising agility and a reputation for plus game-calling skills. At the plate he has fringe power but displays a patient approach and makes enough contact to keep from being an easy out—last year DRC+ pegged him as a league average hitter. Already 32, Stallings isn't about to spend the next decade as a first division starter, but his skill-set should age gracefully and earn him paychecks for years to come. He'll earn his next ones in Miami, working with the club's talented pitchers.

★ ★ ★ *2022 Top 101 Prospect* **#45** ★ ★ ★

Kahlil Watson SS

Born: 04/16/03 Age: 19 Bats: L Throws: R Height: 5'9" Weight: 178 lb. Origin: Round 1, 2021 Draft (#16 overall)

YEAR	TEAM	LVL	AGE	PA	R	2B	3B	HR	RBI	BB	K	SB	CS	Whiff%	AVG/OBP/SLG	DRC+	BABIP	BRR	FRAA	WARP
2021	MRL	ROK	18	42	13	3	2	0	5	8	7	4	1		.394/.524/.606		.500			
2022															*No projection*					

"I would have said you're crazy."

That's DJ Svihlik, the Marlins' director of amateur scouting on the chances that Watson would fall to them at 16th overall.

ESPN's Kiley McDaniel called it a case of "personnel malpractice" for Watson to fall to 16.

So, if you're wondering why Watson earned a $4,540,790 signing bonus, it's not because he has a love for that particularly specific number. That was the absolute maximum amount the Marlins could offer the once-potential top overall selection without losing future draft picks. The undersized but hardly underpowered shortstop quickly inserts near the top of the Marlins' prospect list. He'll be worth it.

Joey Wendle 3B

Born: 04/26/90 Age: 32 Bats: L Throws: R Height: 6'1" Weight: 195 lb. Origin: Round 6, 2012 Draft (#203 overall)

YEAR	TEAM	LVL	AGE	PA	R	2B	3B	HR	RBI	BB	K	SB	CS	Whiff%	AVG/OBP/SLG	DRC+	BABIP	BRR	FRAA	WARP
2019	TB	MLB	29	263	32	13	2	3	19	14	47	8	3	20.3%	.231/.293/.340	82	.272	-0.3	2B(48): 4.2, 3B(27): -1.4, SS(10): 0.0	0.6
2020	TB	MLB	30	184	24	9	2	4	17	10	35	8	2	18.9%	.286/.342/.435	92	.338	-1.3	3B(28): 2.9, 2B(20): 0.5, SS(10): 1.9	0.8
2021	TB	MLB	31	501	73	31	4	11	54	28	113	8	6	25.1%	.265/.319/.422	90	.327	1.1	3B(107): 0.0, SS(25): 4.0, 2B(16): 0.5	1.7
2022 DC	*MIA*	*MLB*	*32*	*353*	*39*	*18*	*3*	*6*	*39*	*22*	*76*	*7*	*3*	*23.7%*	*.251/.315/.384*	*88*	*.312*	*0.5*	*LF 0, 3B 0*	*0.7*

Comparables: Tommy La Stella, Brock Holt, Justin Turner

Like many 31-year-olds, Wendle finally settled down and found a home. Instead of a nice place in the suburbs or a fancy condo downtown, he settled in at third base where he made 107 overall appearances including 82 starts. He did take some out-of-town trips to the six and spent some time at the keystone, but most nights he manned the hot corner. At the plate, he went on fishing expeditions out of the zone quite a bit, but his contact levels remained better than most, even if he did punch out more than expected. DRC+ doesn't much care for his offense, but the league recognized it via an All-Star appearance in July. Tampa recognized what that meant for a second-year arbitration eligible player and shipped him to Miami in November. We'll see whether his OPS+ finds more harmony with DRC+ now that he's out of Tampa.

PITCHERS

Sandy Alcantara RHP

Born: 09/07/95 Age: 26 Bats: R Throws: R Height: 6'5" Weight: 200 lb. Origin: International Free Agent, 2013

YEAR	TEAM	LVL	AGE	W	L	SV	G	GS	IP	H	HR	BB/9	K/9	K	GB%	BABIP	WHIP	ERA	DRA-	WARP	MPH	FB%	Whiff%	CSP
2019	MIA	MLB	23	6	14	0	32	32	197^{1}	179	23	3.7	6.9	151	44.1%	.274	1.32	3.88	103	1.7	95.6	57.0%	23.8%	47.9%
2020	MIA	MLB	24	3	2	0	7	7	42	35	4	3.2	8.4	39	49.6%	.277	1.19	3.00	86	0.8	96.7	60.0%	24.1%	51.1%
2021	MIA	MLB	25	9	15	0	33	33	205^{2}	171	21	2.2	8.8	201	52.8%	.273	1.07	3.19	81	4.0	98.0	50.1%	27.5%	54.6%
2022 DC	*MIA*	*MLB*	*26*	*12*	*8*	*0*	*29*	*29*	*180.7*	*163*	*18*	*2.8*	*8.0*	*160*	*50.6%*	*.284*	*1.21*	*3.38*	*87*	*2.7*	*97.3*	*52.6%*	*26.3%*	*52.7%*

Comparables: A.J. Burnett, Dave Stieb, Mike Mussina

Say hello to the Marlins' newest ace. Alcantara further cut down on his walks, induced batters to chase more often and broke the vaunted 200 inning *and* 200 strikeout plateau. The limitation in his game used to be that he couldn't throw breaking pitches for strikes; he still doesn't, but now he knows how to throw breaking pitches that *look* like strikes. Alcantara throws five pitches, though he's mostly junked his curveball, and batters appear helpless against a mix of his 98-mph fastball and a slider that batters whiffed on 38% of the time. After getting pasted with a 10-spot August 6 at Coors, Alcantara posted a 2.21 ERA the rest of the way—including a 14 K complete game against the Mets, topping 100+ mph in the eighth and ninth innings. You don't want to jinx anyone, but if Jacob deGrom slips at all, Alcantara just might be the best starter in the NL East.

Anthony Bass RHP Born: 11/01/87 Age: 34 Bats: R Throws: R Height: 6'2" Weight: 200 lb. Origin: Round 5, 2008 Draft (#165 overall)

YEAR	TEAM	LVL	AGE	W	L	SV	G	GS	IP	H	HR	BB/9	K/9	K	GB%	BABIP	WHIP	ERA	DRA-	WARP	MPH	FB%	Whiff%	CSP
2019	LOU	AAA	31	1	1	9	19	0	20^1	13	1	2.7	8.4	19	52.7%	.222	0.93	2.21	89	0.4				
2019	SEA	MLB	31	2	4	5	44	0	48	30	5	3.2	8.1	43	53.1%	.207	0.98	3.56	93	0.7	95.4	52.7%	27.9%	44.5%
2020	TOR	MLB	32	2	3	7	26	0	25^2	17	2	3.2	7.4	21	61.4%	.224	1.01	3.51	87	0.5	94.8	54.2%	28.0%	44.3%
2021	MIA	MLB	33	3	9	0	70	1	61^1	55	11	3.5	8.5	58	44.0%	.272	1.29	3.82	96	0.7	95.4	49.3%	26.9%	55.8%
2022 DC	*MIA*	*MLB*	*34*	*3*	*3*	*0*	*67*	*0*	*58*	*55*	*7*	*3.3*	*8.7*	*56*	*47.3%*	*.298*	*1.31*	*3.91*	*97*	*0.3*	*95.3*	*50.7%*	*27.3%*	*51.9%*

Comparables: Matt Albers, Jason Grimsley, Tommy Hunter

Every fanbase has that one player who they blame for everything, the guy they treat like he's Paul Sheldon and they're Annie Wilkes. Bass is that player for the Marlins. After becoming the Blue Jays closer in 2020, Bass was given a two-year, $5 million contract with the Marlins. While his slider still moves like it's soaring on the wings of angels, Bass gave up barreled balls nearly 10% of the time and watched as they soared out of the park with frightening regularity. Wins and losses may not say a whole lot, but Bass found himself on the bad end of too many L's for fans to have much excitement for the second year of his deal.

Anthony Bender RHP Born: 02/03/95 Age: 27 Bats: R Throws: R Height: 6'4" Weight: 205 lb. Origin: Round 20, 2016 Draft (#613 overall)

YEAR	TEAM	LVL	AGE	W	L	SV	G	GS	IP	H	HR	BB/9	K/9	K	GB%	BABIP	WHIP	ERA	DRA-	WARP	MPH	FB%	Whiff%	CSP
2019	WIS	A	24	0	1	5	10	0	13^2	10	1	1.3	9.9	15	58.6%	.321	0.88	1.32	89	0.2				
2019	CAR	A+	24	2	1	4	15	0	17	13	1	3.2	8.5	16	45.8%	.261	1.12	1.59	91	0.2				
2019	BLX	AA	24	0	1	0	4	0	5^2	8	1	1.6	6.4	4	45.0%	.389	1.59	1.59	97	0.0				
2021	MIA	MLB	26	3	2	3	60	1	61^1	45	5	2.9	10.4	71	49.3%	.276	1.06	2.79	81	1.2	97.0	53.0%	30.2%	55.1%
2022 DC	*MIA*	*MLB*	*27*	*3*	*3*	*4*	*67*	*0*	*58*	*49*	*7*	*3.5*	*9.3*	*60*	*46.1%*	*.277*	*1.24*	*3.66*	*91*	*0.5*	*97.0*	*53.0%*	*30.2%*	*55.1%*

Comparables: Pete Fairbanks, Wander Suero, Mike Timlin

With apologies to Devin Williams, *this* is the real Airbender. A total steal by the Marlins organization, Bender is a former 20th-round pick who had multiple stints in Indy ball—even winning the 2020 American Association championship with the perfectly named Milwaukee Milkmen—before signing with the Fish for 2021. Bender mixes a high-90s fastball with a darting slider that generates whiffs 47% of the time. You just might be looking at the Marlins' closer of the future, a testament to never giving up, and a hint that it's time for milk-people to become a more crucial element of society again.

Richard Bleier LHP Born: 04/16/87 Age: 35 Bats: L Throws: L Height: 6'3" Weight: 215 lb. Origin: Round 6, 2008 Draft (#183 overall)

YEAR	TEAM	LVL	AGE	W	L	SV	G	GS	IP	H	HR	BB/9	K/9	K	GB%	BABIP	WHIP	ERA	DRA-	WARP	MPH	FB%	Whiff%	CSP
2019	BAL	MLB	32	3	0	4	53	1	55^1	65	6	1.3	4.9	30	59.6%	.317	1.32	5.37	110	0.3	89.1	64.7%	17.1%	53.1%
2020	BAL	MLB	33	0	0	0	2	0	3	1	0	0.0	12.0	4	83.3%	.167	0.33	0.00	69	0.1	89.5	43.6%	42.1%	46.4%
2020	MIA	MLB	33	1	1	0	19	0	13^2	13	0	2.6	4.6	7	68.9%	.289	1.24	2.63	88	0.2	89.0	55.3%	11.5%	48.9%
2021	MIA	MLB	34	3	2	0	68	0	58	51	4	0.9	6.8	44	65.7%	.281	0.98	2.95	91	0.8	90.2	62.8%	19.9%	62.3%
2022 DC	*MIA*	*MLB*	*35*	*3*	*3*	*0*	*67*	*0*	*58*	*61*	*4*	*1.7*	*5.5*	*35*	*61.0%*	*.295*	*1.24*	*3.50*	*93*	*0.4*	*89.8*	*62.0%*	*18.9%*	*58.3%*

Comparables: Craig Stammen, Blaine Boyer, Matt Whiteside

Tired of strikeouts and velocity dominating the baseball conversation the way the stock market dominates discussion of economic health? Then, buddy, have we got a player for you. Bleier's fastball barely touches 90; he relies instead on excellent command and the ability to induce weak grounders seemingly at will. Among active relievers with at least 200 games, his career ERA is 15th … while his K/9 is the worst, .32 lower than T.J. McFarland's. Long live baseball's glorious outliers.

★ ★ ★ *2022 Top 101 Prospect* **#69** ★ ★ ★

Edward Cabrera RHP Born: 04/13/98 Age: 24 Bats: R Throws: R Height: 6'5" Weight: 217 lb. Origin: International Free Agent, 2015

YEAR	TEAM	LVL	AGE	W	L	SV	G	GS	IP	H	HR	BB/9	K/9	K	GB%	BABIP	WHIP	ERA	DRA-	WARP	MPH	FB%	Whiff%	CSP
2019	JUP	A+	21	5	3	0	11	11	58	37	1	2.8	11.3	73	47.3%	.281	0.95	2.02	76	1.4				
2019	JAX	AA	21	4	1	0	8	8	38^2	28	6	3.0	10.0	43	48.5%	.242	1.06	2.56	86	0.5				
2021	JUP	A	23	0	0	0	2	2	6	4	0	0.0	16.5	11	36.4%	.364	0.67	0.00	89	0.1				
2021	PNS	AA	23	2	1	0	5	5	26	19	3	2.1	11.4	33	48.3%	.296	0.96	2.77	85	0.5				
2021	JAX	AAA	23	1	3	0	6	6	29^1	22	4	5.8	14.7	48	37.7%	.316	1.40	3.68	77	0.7				
2021	MIA	MLB	23	0	3	0	7	7	26^1	24	6	6.5	9.6	28	40.6%	.286	1.63	5.81	107	0.1	96.8	38.5%	28.1%	52.7%
2022 DC	*MIA*	*MLB*	*24*	*7*	*5*	*0*	*52*	*8*	*72.7*	*59*	*10*	*4.7*	*11.0*	*89*	*41.6%*	*.282*	*1.33*	*4.08*	*97*	*0.7*	*96.8*	*38.5%*	*28.1%*	*52.7%*

Comparables: Alex Cobb, Jake Odorizzi, Tyler Mahle

Cabrera was skipped over when he was first eligible to sign in 2014. He joined up with the Marlins for $100,000 the next year, and he's been flying up prospect lists ever since. His fastball and sinker flirt with triple digits and his slider and changeup both grade above-average. After dominating in the minors, Cabrera had the training wheels kept on as he wasn't allowed to throw more than 80 pitches in any start after his promotion. The walks look troublesome and the K's are down, but the Fish were clearly worried more about continuing his development than unleashing him on major-league batters—especially after no 2020 season—so don't put much stock into his big-league audition. Honestly, the Marlins have so many good arms right now, they might be better off just going with a 10-man rotation in the future and figuring out how to score runs later.

Paul Campbell RHP
Born: 07/26/95 Age: 26 Bats: L Throws: R Height: 6'0" Weight: 210 lb. Origin: Round 21, 2017 Draft (#619 overall)

YEAR	TEAM	LVL	AGE	W	L	SV	G	GS	IP	H	HR	BB/9	K/9	K	GB%	BABIP	WHIP	ERA	DRA-	WARP	MPH	FB%	Whiff%	CSP
2019	CHA	A+	23	5	4	0	11	9	59	52	3	2.6	7.5	49	47.4%	.293	1.17	4.12	99	0.7				
2019	MTG	AA	23	8	4	0	16	11	85^{2}	74	6	2.1	6.6	63	35.3%	.275	1.10	3.36	113	-0.1				
2021	JAX	AAA	25	0	0	0	3	3	10^{2}	3	1	5.1	7.6	9	30.8%	.080	0.84	0.84	104	0.1				
2021	MIA	MLB	25	2	3	0	16	1	26^{2}	32	5	3.4	8.8	26	41.9%	.338	1.58	6.41	97	0.3	92.6	59.2%	24.7%	54.1%
2022 DC	*MIA*	*MLB*	*26*	*2*	*2*	*0*	*44*	*0*	*38.7*	*39*	*5*	*3.6*	*7.5*	*32*	*39.2%*	*.294*	*1.41*	*4.70*	*113*	*-0.1*	*92.6*	*59.2%*	*24.7%*	*54.1%*

Comparables: Austin Voth, Wandy Peralta, Adam Warren

A Rule 5 pick from the Rays, Campbell had an unsightly 8.74 ERA through his first five appearances before getting popped for a PED suspension in early May. The beating wasn't a total surprise: The former 21st-round pick is the prototypical low-strikeout, low-walk "control artist" who errs toward the middle of the plate rather than off the edge, leading to a lot of well-hit line drives. In the majors, that behavior got punished. To make matters worse, he was known more for his high spin rates than his pure stuff, something that was surely a worry after the baseball's crackdown on foreign substances. Activated in early August, he still ranked among baseball's elite in spin—and the results looked a lot better. An impressive showing in three rehab appearances gave some hope for the future, though expect Campbell to get some more MiLB seasoning next year.

Jake Eder LHP
Born: 10/09/98 Age: 23 Bats: L Throws: L Height: 6'4" Weight: 215 lb. Origin: Round 4, 2020 Draft (#104 overall)

YEAR	TEAM	LVL	AGE	W	L	SV	G	GS	IP	H	HR	BB/9	K/9	K	GB%	BABIP	WHIP	ERA	DRA-	WARP	MPH	FB%	Whiff%	CSP
2021	PNS	AA	22	3	5	0	15	15	71^{1}	43	3	3.4	12.5	99	50.3%	.261	0.98	1.77	82	1.4				
2022 non-DC	*MIA*	*MLB*	*23*	*2*	*2*	*0*	*57*	*0*	*50*	*43*	*6*	*4.2*	*9.9*	*55*	*46.8%*	*.293*	*1.35*	*4.05*	*98*	*0.2*				

Comparables: Génesis Cabrera, Francisco Liriano, Fernando Nieve

Another testament to the existential terror of our flesh prisons: Eder flashed first-round stuff at Vanderbilt, but a lack of consistency and control kept him out of the weekend rotation for most of undergrad. A strong showing in the Cape Cod League caught the Marlins' eye, with Miami's minor-league pitching coach Scott Aldred calling him "The steal of the draft." That proved true, as an improved slider and mid-90s fastball had him absolutely dominating Double-A hitters in his pro debut. Unfortunately, after 15 starts—two more than he made for Vanderbilt in his career—Eder succumbed to Tommy John surgery and is expected to miss the 2022 season. It's further proof that if you want body horror, don't watch a David Cronenberg film: Just watch sports.

Dylan Floro RHP
Born: 12/27/90 Age: 31 Bats: L Throws: R Height: 6'2" Weight: 203 lb. Origin: Round 13, 2012 Draft (#422 overall)

YEAR	TEAM	LVL	AGE	W	L	SV	G	GS	IP	H	HR	BB/9	K/9	K	GB%	BABIP	WHIP	ERA	DRA-	WARP	MPH	FB%	Whiff%	CSP
2019	LAD	MLB	28	5	3	0	50	0	46^{2}	46	4	2.7	8.1	42	48.3%	.307	1.29	4.24	95	0.6	93.9	67.5%	26.3%	51.4%
2020	LAD	MLB	29	3	0	0	25	0	24^{1}	23	1	1.5	7.0	19	57.3%	.297	1.11	2.59	88	0.4	93.5	46.9%	23.3%	45.7%
2021	MIA	MLB	30	6	6	15	68	0	64	53	2	3.5	8.7	62	49.2%	.282	1.22	2.81	93	0.8	93.8	62.8%	23.0%	51.8%
2022 DC	*MIA*	*MLB*	*31*	*3*	*3*	*26*	*67*	*0*	*58*	*56*	*6*	*3.1*	*7.8*	*50*	*49.8%*	*.294*	*1.31*	*3.89*	*98*	*0.3*	*93.8*	*61.1%*	*23.5%*	*50.8%*

Comparables: Juan Gutierrez, Joe Smith, Jim Johnson

Modern baseball is all about maximizing what you're good at and getting rid of what you're not. So, when Floro was with the Dodgers, a team that seems to have unlocked the secrets to the universe, they phased out his four-seamer. But after watching his slider get hit to a .348 tune last year, Floro cut that pitch and brought the heater back. It led to him having similar numbers to 2020—plenty of success, though more with weak contact than Pitching Ninja-ready GIFs. Which means either a) there's more than one correct way to do things or b) free will is a lie. You can choose which you prefer.

★ ★ ★ *2022 Top 101 Prospect* **#76** ★ ★ ★

Dax Fulton LHP
Born: 10/16/01 Age: 20 Bats: L Throws: L Height: 6'7" Weight: 225 lb. Origin: Round 2, 2020 Draft (#40 overall)

YEAR	TEAM	LVL	AGE	W	L	SV	G	GS	IP	H	HR	BB/9	K/9	K	GB%	BABIP	WHIP	ERA	DRA-	WARP	MPH	FB%	Whiff%	CSP
2021	JUP	A	19	2	4	0	15	14	58^{2}	50	3	4.6	10.1	66	51.6%	.313	1.36	4.30	109	0.3				
2021	BEL	A+	19	0	1	0	5	5	19^{2}	21	3	3.7	8.2	18	56.9%	.327	1.47	5.49	103	0.2				
2022 non-DC	*MIA*	*MLB*	*20*	*2*	*3*	*0*	*57*	*0*	*50*	*54*	*6*	*5.4*	*6.9*	*38*	*45.6%*	*.309*	*1.68*	*5.79*	*129*	*-0.6*				

Comparables: Luis Patiño, Jacob Turner, Vin Mazzaro

Just 19 years old, Fulton was a long-term gamble from the Marlins. He had the talent to go early in the first round, but Tommy John surgery cost him his senior year of high school and allowed the Marlins to snag him with an above-slot bonus at 40th overall. Between him and Max Mayer, the Marlins could wind up with the greatest haul from the 2020 Draft. Fulton combines a good curveball and power change to the ol' Chris R. Young extension/deception fastball that gets to the plate faster than it has any right to. In his final two starts with Jupiter, Fulton struck out 18 batters in 10 innings, walked none and gave up two hits to earn a promotion to Beloit. The kid's got the goods.

Braxton Garrett LHP Born: 08/05/97 Age: 24 Bats: R Throws: L Height: 6'2" Weight: 202 lb. Origin: Round 1, 2016 Draft (#7 overall)

YEAR	TEAM	LVL	AGE	W	L	SV	G	GS	IP	H	HR	BB/9	K/9	K	GB%	BABIP	WHIP	ERA	DRA-	WARP	MPH	FB%	Whiff%	CSP
2019	JUP	A+	21	6	6	0	20	20	105	92	13	3.2	10.1	118	53.9%	.294	1.23	3.34	89	1.8				
2019	JAX	AA	21	0	1	0	1	1	1^{2}	4	0	16.2	5.4	1	55.6%	.444	4.20	16.20	138	0.0				
2020	MIA	MLB	22	1	1	0	2	2	7^{2}	8	3	5.9	9.4	8	61.9%	.278	1.70	5.87	104	0.1	90.0	48.9%	23.1%	38.3%
2021	JAX	AAA	23	5	4	0	18	18	85^{2}	73	10	3.4	9.0	86	45.3%	.281	1.23	3.89	112	0.6				
2021	MIA	MLB	23	1	2	0	8	7	34	42	3	5.3	8.5	32	36.2%	.398	1.82	5.03	118	0.0	90.1	49.2%	21.8%	53.2%
2022 DC	*MIA*	*MLB*	*24*	*6*	*4*	*0*	*48*	*4*	*62*	*60*	*8*	*4.3*	*8.2*	*56*	*43.5%*	*.293*	*1.45*	*4.69*	*112*	*0.1*	*90.1*	*49.1%*	*22.0%*	*51.2%*

Comparables: Daniel Norris, Ross Detwiler, Jake Odorizzi

Hopefully Garrett had one of those credit cards that gives you double points for travel, because he did a *lot* of it. The no. 7 overall pick in 2016 was recalled from Jacksonville *six* separate times in 2021, somehow appearing in only eight big-league games despite the constant shuttling. Unfortunately, Garrett's fastball barely scrapes 90 mph, which makes his curveball all the more important. While scouts drool over the movement of the spinner, the destination hasn't lived up to the journey. Too often, the left-hander left it over the middle third of the plate, and major-league hitters spanked it to the tune of a .444 average.

Louis Head RHP Born: 04/23/90 Age: 32 Bats: R Throws: R Height: 6'1" Weight: 180 lb. Origin: Round 18, 2012 Draft (#563 overall)

YEAR	TEAM	LVL	AGE	W	L	SV	G	GS	IP	H	HR	BB/9	K/9	K	GB%	BABIP	WHIP	ERA	DRA-	WARP	MPH	FB%	Whiff%	CSP
2019	DODL	ROK	29	0	1	0	5	2	7^{1}	13	1	3.7	9.8	8	45.8%	.545	2.18	9.82						
2019	TUL	AA	29	2	1	1	6	0	10^{2}	9	1	2.5	13.5	16	43.5%	.364	1.13	3.38	91	0.1				
2019	OKC	AAA	29	1	0	0	9	0	12	20	2	5.3	10.5	14	45.9%	.514	2.25	8.25	77	0.2				
2021	DUR	AAA	31	0	0	5	26	0	28^{2}	20	2	3.1	11.6	37	47.0%	.281	1.05	2.20	84	0.6				
2021	TB	MLB	31	2	0	0	27	2	35	21	2	2.3	8.2	32	31.1%	.216	0.86	2.31	108	0.2	94.0	52.4%	25.5%	53.5%
2022 DC	*MIA*	*MLB*	*32*	*2*	*2*	*0*	*52*	*0*	*45.3*	*41*	*6*	*3.4*	*9.0*	*45*	*38.2%*	*.284*	*1.28*	*4.11*	*101*	*0.1*	*94.0*	*52.4%*	*25.5%*	*53.5%*

Comparables: Jim Miller, Tyler Sturdevant, Javy Guerra

Did you know you can save an estimated $10,000 to $30,000 on energy costs over the life of a solar panel system? If you didn't, you can bet Head did. With the minor-league season canceled in 2020, he spent the time he would be pitching selling solar panels in Arizona. A year later, he was a surprisingly key member of a playoff bullpen. The Rays racked up a ton of airline points sending Head between Tampa Bay and Durham about a dozen times throughout the year. Despite the ups and downs, the results were promising. He worked off a traditional fastball-slider combination. He controlled the low-90s heater well and the slider racked up positive pitch values. No stranger to the road, Head was traded to Miami this winter.

Elieser Hernandez RHP Born: 05/03/95 Age: 27 Bats: R Throws: R Height: 6'0" Weight: 214 lb. Origin: International Free Agent, 2011

YEAR	TEAM	LVL	AGE	W	L	SV	G	GS	IP	H	HR	BB/9	K/9	K	GB%	BABIP	WHIP	ERA	DRA-	WARP	MPH	FB%	Whiff%	CSP
2019	NO	AAA	24	3	1	0	9	9	48	35	0	2.6	12.9	69	32.4%	.315	1.02	1.13	81	0.7				
2019	MIA	MLB	24	3	5	0	21	15	82^{1}	76	20	2.8	9.3	85	33.5%	.267	1.24	5.03	92	1.2	90.6	55.3%	25.3%	50.1%
2020	MIA	MLB	25	1	0	0	6	6	25^{2}	21	5	1.8	11.9	34	33.8%	.267	1.01	3.16	82	0.5	91.4	58.9%	29.2%	56.7%
2021	JAX	AAA	26	0	1	0	5	5	21^{1}	11	3	1.3	13.5	32	35.7%	.205	0.66	2.95	89	0.4				
2021	MIA	MLB	26	1	3	0	11	11	51^{2}	54	13	2.4	9.2	53	38.1%	.293	1.32	4.18	94	0.6	90.9	54.2%	24.1%	60.8%
2022 DC	*MIA*	*MLB*	*27*	*6*	*5*	*0*	*19*	*19*	*97*	*90*	*15*	*2.6*	*8.9*	*96*	*35.5%*	*.286*	*1.23*	*4.07*	*100*	*0.8*	*90.9*	*55.4%*	*25.4%*	*56.8%*

Comparables: Shawn Chacon, Frankie Montas, Justin Grimm

Meet Hernandez, or, as he now could be called, My Body After One Time in the Gym. A solid mid-rotation option, Hernandez made it through just two starts before right biceps inflammation put him on the IL. Then, in his first game back, he got hurt again—this time straining his quad on the basepaths. "[T]o see him get injured running the bases leaves a bad taste in your mouth," Garrett Cooper said about watching a pitcher run the bases. Though in reality he's 26, Hernandez has an old man's skillset, too, relying on good command of a low-90s fastball that he likes to use up in the zone to garner weak fly balls. And occasionally less weak ones. As long as he keeps up the approach, our fragile friend is always going to give up his share of home runs; it's whether they're solo or not that will determine his success in a given year.

Jordan Holloway RHP Born: 06/13/96 Age: 26 Bats: R Throws: R Height: 6'6" Weight: 230 lb. Origin: Round 20, 2014 Draft (#587 overall)

YEAR	TEAM	LVL	AGE	W	L	SV	G	GS	IP	H	HR	BB/9	K/9	K	GB%	BABIP	WHIP	ERA	DRA-	WARP	MPH	FB%	Whiff%	CSP
2019	JUP	A+	23	4	11	0	21	21	95	77	6	6.3	8.8	93	51.4%	.281	1.51	4.45	104	0.9				
2020	MIA	MLB	24	0	0	0	1	0	0^{1}	2	0	27.0	0.0	0	66.7%	.667	9.00	0.00	146	0.0	96.8	62.5%	0.0%	46.9%
2021	JAX	AAA	25	0	5	0	8	6	31^{1}	29	5	4.0	8.3	29	47.2%	.286	1.37	4.88	111	0.2				
2021	MIA	MLB	25	2	3	0	13	4	36	23	3	6.5	9.0	36	42.7%	.215	1.36	4.00	103	0.3	95.7	45.0%	27.2%	55.9%
2022 DC	*MIA*	*MLB*	*26*	*2*	*2*	*0*	*44*	*0*	*38.7*	*38*	*6*	*6.0*	*8.7*	*37*	*44.8%*	*.296*	*1.65*	*5.65*	*128*	*-0.4*	*95.8*	*45.3%*	*26.8%*	*55.8%*

Comparables: Tyler Thornburg, Armando Galarraga, Casey Janssen

You know the action movies where our hero disappears for years on end, is presumed dead, and then returns to take down the bad guys? That's essentially what Holloway's career has been. Heck, it's been so long since he's been drafted, he could be a doctor by now. Instead, after finally reaching the big leagues for all of four batters in 2020, he got a chance to actually show off his skills in 2021. His mechanics and command suffered when starting, but his fastball and slider played up out of the bullpen. Meanwhile, his repertoire was a study in madness: He swapped out a sinker for his four-seam in the middle of the summer, then switched back, then worked in a changeup for no real reason; none of this even aligned with his relief appearances compared to his starts. If anything, he's hard to write up a book against. His control has never been great, but the sequel, *Holloway 2: Jordan's Revenge,* could be even better.

Pablo López RHP Born: 03/07/96 Age: 26 Bats: L Throws: R Height: 6'4" Weight: 225 lb. Origin: International Free Agent, 2012

YEAR	TEAM	LVL	AGE	W	L	SV	G	GS	IP	H	HR	BB/9	K/9	K	GB%	BABIP	WHIP	ERA	DRA-	WARP	MPH	FB%	Whiff%	CSP
2019	NO	AAA	23	0	0	0	2	2	9^1	10	0	2.9	9.6	10	61.5%	.385	1.39	1.93	89	0.1				
2019	MIA	MLB	23	5	8	0	21	21	111^1	111	15	2.2	7.7	95	47.3%	.303	1.24	5.09	90	1.7	93.7	58.7%	23.6%	48.5%
2020	MIA	MLB	24	6	4	0	11	11	57^1	50	4	2.8	9.3	59	52.8%	.293	1.19	3.61	70	1.6	93.7	63.1%	26.5%	47.2%
2021	MIA	MLB	25	5	5	0	20	20	102^2	89	11	2.3	10.1	115	46.3%	.302	1.12	3.07	74	2.3	93.7	58.0%	25.8%	52.4%
2022 DC	*MIA*	*MLB*	*26*	*8*	*6*	*0*	*24*	*24*	*121.3*	*104*	*13*	*2.5*	*9.2*	*124*	*47.8%*	*.282*	*1.14*	*3.16*	*82*	*2.1*	*93.7*	*59.2%*	*25.5%*	*50.5%*

Comparables: Chris Archer, Pedro Astacio, Johnny Cueto

The *Deep Impact* to Sandy Alcantara's *Armageddon*, the *Antz* to his *A Bug's Life*, the *Olympus Has Fallen* to his *White House Down*, López may lack the name recognition of his teammate, but he's been nearly as good. Armed with a true five-pitch mix led by a nasty changeup, López limits hard contact and free passes—perhaps the most satisfying thing to watch as a fan. The metrics are impressed as well. López was the 13th best pitcher in all of baseball (100 IP min.) in terms of DRA–, after finishing 14th in 2020. He missed half the 2021 season with a right rotator cuff strain, but returned to pitch 1 ⅔ innings and strike out four batters on the season's final day.

Jesús Luzardo LHP Born: 09/30/97 Age: 24 Bats: L Throws: L Height: 6'0" Weight: 218 lb. Origin: Round 3, 2016 Draft (#94 overall)

YEAR	TEAM	LVL	AGE	W	L	SV	G	GS	IP	H	HR	BB/9	K/9	K	GB%	BABIP	WHIP	ERA	DRA-	WARP	MPH	FB%	Whiff%	CSP
2019	ASGR	ROK	21	0	0	0	1	1	2	1	0	0.0	22.5	5	100.0%	.500	0.50	0.00						
2019	STK	A+	21	1	0	0	3	1	10	6	1	0.0	16.2	18	44.4%	.313	0.60	0.90	68	0.2				
2019	LV	AAA	21	1	1	0	7	7	31	29	3	2.3	9.9	34	55.1%	.306	1.19	3.19	84	0.5				
2019	OAK	MLB	21	0	0	2	6	0	12	5	1	2.3	12.0	16	42.3%	.160	0.67	1.50	89	0.2	96.4	48.5%	37.7%	44.7%
2020	OAK	MLB	22	3	2	0	12	9	59	58	9	2.6	9.0	59	46.2%	.308	1.27	4.12	89	1.0	95.8	53.3%	29.7%	46.2%
2021	LV	AAA	23	2	2	0	8	8	29	33	3	4.7	8.1	26	47.2%	.349	1.66	6.52	99	0.1				
2021	MIA	MLB	23	4	5	0	12	12	57^1	60	9	5.0	9.1	58	36.5%	.319	1.60	6.44	120	-0.1	95.6	46.4%	30.2%	49.8%
2021	OAK	MLB	23	2	4	0	13	6	38	46	11	3.8	9.5	40	38.5%	.333	1.63	6.87	110	0.1	95.9	59.2%	28.6%	54.5%
2022 DC	*MIA*	*MLB*	*24*	*8*	*7*	*0*	*36*	*22*	*124*	*116*	*16*	*3.7*	*9.5*	*130*	*41.9%*	*.303*	*1.35*	*4.25*	*102*	*0.7*	*95.7*	*51.8%*	*29.8%*	*50.1%*

Comparables: Sean Burnett, Jaime García, Will Smith

Throw this season away. Dump it in the trash. Use one of those "Men in Black" memory scramblers on yourself and hope too much of your own life doesn't get caught up in its light ray. Luzardo went from top prospect to future ace before it all fell apart in 2021, eventually getting swapped for center fielder Starling Marte at the deadline. The Fish changed his pitch mix, and Luzardo ditched the hard stuff for more of his off-speed offerings, though that mostly rearranged deck chairs. The real issue is Luzardo walked too many batters and left too many pitches over the heart of the plate. There's more tinkering left to do, as he also demonstrates some pretty clear differences in release point between his fastball and his changeup, allowing batters to gear up for the hard stuff. Young pitchers are more fickle than young love, though, and he finished with 11 Ks in 5 ⅓ IP against the Phillies.

★ ★ ★ *2022 Top 101 Prospect* **#24** ★ ★ ★

Max Meyer RHP Born: 03/12/99 Age: 23 Bats: L Throws: R Height: 6'0" Weight: 196 lb. Origin: Round 1, 2020 Draft (#3 overall)

YEAR	TEAM	LVL	AGE	W	L	SV	G	GS	IP	H	HR	BB/9	K/9	K	GB%	BABIP	WHIP	ERA	DRA-	WARP	MPH	FB%	Whiff%	CSP
2021	PNS	AA	22	6	3	0	20	20	101	84	7	3.6	10.1	113	52.7%	.304	1.23	2.41	91	1.5				
2021	JAX	AAA	22	0	1	0	2	2	10	6	1	1.8	15.3	17	47.4%	.278	0.80	0.90	72	0.3				
2022 non-DC	*MIA*	*MLB*	*23*	*2*	*2*	*0*	*57*	*0*	*50*	*48*	*6*	*4.2*	*8.9*	*49*	*48.4%*	*.303*	*1.43*	*4.43*	*105*	*0.1*				

Comparables: Trevor Bauer, Kevin Gausman, Chad Kuhl

If you opened this expecting to read about the German national team soccer player, apologies, but also we have no idea how you made it this far into the book without realizing this is not about association football. If you're here for the Marlins pitcher, you're in luck, because the news is *good.* The third-overall pick made his pro debute at Double-A and basically mirrored his college performance thanks to a fastball that can remain in the upper-90s deep into starts. His slider somehow transforms pro hitters into college sophomores, to the point that it's confusing to see them flail with wood bats. His string of success even earned him two end-of-season starts in Triple-A where, somehow, he was even better. Honestly, maybe the German national team should call him up and see what he can do.

Nick Neidert RHP Born: 11/20/96 Age: 25 Bats: R Throws: R Height: 6'1" Weight: 202 lb. Origin: Round 2, 2015 Draft (#60 overall)

YEAR	TEAM	LVL	AGE	W	L	SV	G	GS	IP	H	HR	BB/9	K/9	K	GB%	BABIP	WHIP	ERA	DRA-	WARP	MPH	FB%	Whiff%	CSP
2019	JUP	A+	22	0	1	0	2	2	9^1	10	1	3.9	5.8	6	29.0%	.300	1.50	4.82	98	0.1				
2019	NO	AAA	22	3	4	0	9	9	41	45	4	4.8	8.1	37	23.8%	.339	1.63	5.05	123	-0.6				
2020	MIA	MLB	23	0	0	0	4	0	8^1	10	1	2.2	4.3	4	60.7%	.333	1.44	5.40	105	0.1	91.8	59.8%	12.9%	52.5%
2021	JAX	AAA	24	6	4	0	14	13	68^2	71	8	2.8	6.8	52	43.0%	.296	1.34	3.67	121	0.2				
2021	MIA	MLB	24	1	2	0	8	7	35^2	31	4	5.8	5.3	21	35.2%	.262	1.51	4.54	145	-0.5	91.8	47.0%	18.5%	57.4%
2022 DC	*MIA*	*MLB*	*25*	*4*	*3*	*0*	*40*	*3*	*45.3*	*50*	*6*	*4.0*	*6.9*	*34*	*39.9%*	*.307*	*1.55*	*5.63*	*128*	*-0.4*	*91.8*	*48.6%*	*17.8%*	*56.8%*

Comparables: Kyle Davies, Drew Hutchison, Robbie Erlin

If you've been an annual reader of this here annual, then you might already know that Neidert has drawn constant comparisons to Kyle Hendricks the way every stout man with a white beard gets comped to Santa Claus. But that's what happens when you have a below-average fastball, a changeup that batters can't hit and two decent off-speed offerings. Neidert's never going to strike out many, which means he really needs to limit the walks, something he didn't do in 2021. He does have better command than he showed, regularly burying changeups and sliders right on the edge of the bottom of the strike zone while, in a twist of modern pitching, throwing his curveball almost exclusively in the upper corner. He may be no team's first choice, but he's better than many clubs' sixth or seventh.

Kyle Nicolas RHP Born: 02/22/99 Age: 23 Bats: R Throws: R Height: 6'4" Weight: 223 lb. Origin: Round 2, 2020 Draft (#61 overall)

YEAR	TEAM	LVL	AGE	W	L	SV	G	GS	IP	H	HR	BB/9	K/9	K	GB%	BABIP	WHIP	ERA	DRA-	WARP	MPH	FB%	Whiff%	CSP
2021	BEL	A+	22	3	2	0	13	12	59^2	57	13	3.6	13.0	86	33.3%	.328	1.36	5.28	81	1.2				
2021	PNS	AA	22	3	2	0	8	8	39^1	23	3	5.7	11.4	50	29.2%	.235	1.22	2.52	110	0.2				
2022 non-DC	*PIT*	*MLB*	*23*	*2*	*3*	*0*	*57*	*0*	*50*	*49*	*9*	*5.4*	*10.1*	*56*	*31.9%*	*.307*	*1.59*	*5.73*	*127*	*-0.5*				

Comparables: Rocky Coppinger, Jeff Karstens, Jordan Yamamoto

The Marlins have such a wealth of pitching in their system they may as well start a baseball-themed space tourism business. (Only one Q: Which pitcher will wear a Bezos-esque cowboy hat for the initial launch?) Grabbed with the 61st overall pick in the 2020 draft, Nicolas used a fastball that can flash triple digits and a hard slider to dominate in his very first professional game, pitching five innings of one-hit ball with eight K's. Called up to Double-A later in the season, he nearly did the same, this time pitching five innings of no-hit baseball with six K's. Like a lot of young hard-throwers, his control can be messy at times, but hey, what's life if not a constant battle for self improvement out there among the stars?

Steven Okert LHP Born: 07/09/91 Age: 30 Bats: L Throws: L Height: 6'2" Weight: 202 lb. Origin: Round 4, 2012 Draft (#148 overall)

YEAR	TEAM	LVL	AGE	W	L	SV	G	GS	IP	H	HR	BB/9	K/9	K	GB%	BABIP	WHIP	ERA	DRA-	WARP	MPH	FB%	Whiff%	CSP
2019	SAC	AAA	27	8	2	0	50	4	57^2	64	14	2.8	11.7	75	26.7%	.340	1.42	5.31	93	0.6				
2021	JAX	AAA	29	2	0	4	15	0	20	13	1	1.8	13.1	29	24.4%	.308	0.85	1.80	81	0.5				
2021	MIA	MLB	29	3	1	0	34	0	36	22	5	3.8	10.0	40	32.5%	.221	1.03	2.75	88	0.5	92.4	40.4%	30.4%	51.2%
2022 DC	*MIA*	*MLB*	*30*	*2*	*2*	*0*	*52*	*0*	*45.3*	*39*	*7*	*3.1*	*10.5*	*52*	*31.6%*	*.284*	*1.22*	*4.05*	*99*	*0.2*	*92.4*	*40.4%*	*30.4%*	*51.2%*

Comparables: Evan Marshall, Xavier Cedeño, Jared Hughes

Signed to a minor-league deal before the season, Okert went 1,004 days between big-league appearances before getting called back up to the majors. Once there, Okert's slider became the kind of creature that left-handed batters cowered in fear from. Lefties hit only .108 against the pitch (.140 overall) and whiffed on the pitch over 40% of the time. These are the kind of gems the Marlins are hoping to hit upon as they remake the roster. The only problem is you usually find them in the back of the bullpen...and not in the middle of the lineup.

★ ★ ★ *2022 Top 101 Prospect* **#54** ★ ★ ★

Eury Perez RHP Born: 04/15/03 Age: 19 Bats: R Throws: R Height: 6'8" Weight: 200 lb. Origin: International Free Agent, 2019

YEAR	TEAM	LVL	AGE	W	L	SV	G	GS	IP	H	HR	BB/9	K/9	K	GB%	BABIP	WHIP	ERA	DRA-	WARP	MPH	FB%	Whiff%	CSP
2021	JUP	A	18	2	3	0	15	15	56	32	2	3.4	13.2	82	36.0%	.268	0.95	1.61	78	1.2				
2021	BEL	A+	18	1	2	0	5	5	22	11	5	2.0	10.6	26	37.7%	.133	0.73	2.86	92	0.3				
2022 non-DC	*MIA*	*MLB*	*19*	*2*	*3*	*0*	*57*	*0*	*50*	*49*	*8*	*4.3*	*9.0*	*50*	*34.1%*	*.298*	*1.46*	*5.23*	*121*	*-0.4*				

Comparables: Luis Patiño, Jacob Turner, Julio Teheran

Chalk this one up to a victory for all the scouts who love to talk about "projection." Signed for $200,000 in 2019, Perez grew four inches, gained more than 50 pounds (hey! Baseball players: They're just like us ... except his is mostly muscle), and took his fastball from the mid-80s to the mid-90s. Forget the strikeouts and sub-2.00 ERA, perhaps most impressive is that despite missing the 2020 season and growing to 6-foot-8, he still managed to have great control, something many tall hurlers struggle with early in their careers. Perez has said he wants to be in the majors within two years and, assuming he keeps up at this rate, will stand 7-foot-4, weigh 300 pounds and throw a 120-mph fastball. For the sake of his mechanics (and his comfort flying on the team jet), let's hope he's done growing.

Zach Pop RHP Born: 09/20/96 Age: 25 Bats: R Throws: R Height: 6'4" Weight: 220 lb. Origin: Round 7, 2017 Draft (#220 overall)

YEAR	TEAM	LVL	AGE	W	L	SV	G	GS	IP	H	HR	BB/9	K/9	K	GB%	BABIP	WHIP	ERA	DRA-	WARP	MPH	FB%	Whiff%	CSP
2019	BOW	AA	22	1	0	0	8	0	10^2	7	0	3.4	9.3	11	63.0%	.259	1.03	0.84	101	0.1				
2021	MIA	MLB	24	1	0	0	50	0	54^2	54	3	4.0	8.4	51	55.8%	.321	1.43	4.12	101	0.5	95.5	67.7%	25.9%	47.8%
2022 DC	*MIA*	*MLB*	*25*	*2*	*2*	*0*	*52*	*0*	*45.3*	*43*	*4*	*4.0*	*8.8*	*44*	*55.6%*	*.308*	*1.40*	*4.33*	*102*	*0.1*	*95.5*	*67.7%*	*25.9%*	*47.8%*

Comparables: Jacob Webb, Ben Taylor, Wyatt Mills

Despite being armed with some truly elite stuff, Pop has been through more teams than copies of U2's 1997 "Pop" passed through used CD stores. Sure, his stuff isn't *of the moment* (also like the U2 record), as Pop is an east-west pitcher relying on a heavy mid-90s sinker and a biting slider. Pop got better with repeated listens—sorry, appearances—especially after he started throwing his slider harder, adding about 4 mph over the final months compared to the start of the year. He also went his final 34 appearances without giving up a home run, which will make the occasional free pass easier to swallow. This season will likely be forgotten—also like the U2 record—though hopefully Pop is unlike the band in that his best days are in the future.

Cody Poteet RHP Born: 07/30/94 Age: 27 Bats: R Throws: R Height: 6'1" Weight: 190 lb. Origin: Round 4, 2015 Draft (#116 overall)

YEAR	TEAM	LVL	AGE	W	L	SV	G	GS	IP	H	HR	BB/9	K/9	K	GB%	BABIP	WHIP	ERA	DRA-	WARP	MPH	FB%	Whiff%	CSP
2019	JAX	AA	24	5	3	0	13	13	84	63	3	2.0	6.2	58	49.4%	.252	0.98	2.25	97	0.7				
2019	NO	AAA	24	2	3	0	10	10	52^1	65	13	3.3	5.8	34	37.7%	.327	1.61	5.68	112	-0.3				
2021	JAX	AAA	26	1	0	0	2	2	8	6	1	3.4	13.5	12	29.4%	.313	1.13	3.38	102	0.1				
2021	MIA	MLB	26	2	3	0	7	7	30^2	25	7	4.7	9.4	32	33.3%	.234	1.34	4.99	106	0.2	93.8	48.7%	24.1%	57.8%
2022 DC	*MIA*	*MLB*	*27*	*3*	*2*	*0*	*25*	*3*	*34*	*32*	*5*	*3.8*	*8.2*	*30*	*38.4%*	*.286*	*1.38*	*4.66*	*111*	*0.0*	*93.8*	*48.7%*	*24.1%*	*57.8%*

Comparables: Erick Fedde, Wil Crowe, Colin Rea

A darling of the spin-rate fetishists, Poteet looked great through his first three starts before teams got a look at his stuff and he hit the rookie wall. Of the 251 pitchers who threw at least 100 changeups, only one elicited a lower batting average on them (0.083). Unfortunately, there are two reasons to worry: 1. Poteet hurt his knee in his seventh and final big-league start, suffered a setback during a rehab assignment and didn't appear again. 2. His final start came in the first week of baseball's crackdown on sticky stuff and his spin rates took a nosedive. Though the league in general built those numbers back up in his absence, he'll need to answer some questions and see if the dramatic spike in his strikeout rate continues next season.

Trevor Rogers LHP Born: 11/13/97 Age: 24 Bats: L Throws: L Height: 6'5" Weight: 217 lb. Origin: Round 1, 2017 Draft (#13 overall)

YEAR	TEAM	LVL	AGE	W	L	SV	G	GS	IP	H	HR	BB/9	K/9	K	GB%	BABIP	WHIP	ERA	DRA-	WARP	MPH	FB%	Whiff%	CSP
2019	JUP	A+	21	5	8	0	18	18	110^1	97	7	2.0	10.0	122	40.8%	.307	1.10	2.53	95	1.6				
2019	JAX	AA	21	1	2	0	5	5	26	25	3	3.1	9.7	28	28.8%	.319	1.31	4.50	107	0.1				
2020	MIA	MLB	22	1	2	0	7	7	28	32	5	4.2	12.5	39	46.1%	.380	1.61	6.11	73	0.7	93.8	60.0%	30.1%	47.8%
2021	JUP	A	23	1	0	0	2	2	8^1	4	0	3.2	13.0	12	64.7%	.235	0.84	0.00	89	0.1				
2021	MIA	MLB	23	7	8	0	25	25	133	107	6	3.1	10.6	157	39.6%	.307	1.15	2.64	76	2.9	94.8	57.7%	31.0%	54.2%
2022 DC	*MIA*	*MLB*	*24*	*9*	*7*	*0*	*25*	*25*	*137.3*	*120*	*18*	*3.4*	*10.4*	*158*	*41.1%*	*.293*	*1.25*	*3.72*	*92*	*1.7*	*94.6*	*58.1%*	*30.8%*	*53.3%*

Comparables: Zack Britton, Jordan Zimmermann, Blake Snell

DRA was already sold on Rogers despite poor surface-level results in 2020, and after a true breakout campaign for the 23-year-old, the Marlins now have three pitchers who legitimately could be another team's ace. That's hard to fathom on a team that won just 67 games. Rogers' season is even more impressive when you learn the sobering facts that he missed more than a month of the season with COVID-19, lost both of his grandfathers to the virus, then saw his mother hospitalized with the disease for three weeks before she was able to return home. In his first start back, Rogers wrote "Mom" and his grandfathers' initials on the mound: a reminder of the human side of this sport and the fact that, for as much as we'd all like it to be done, the pandemic is not over.

★ ★ ★ *2022 Top 101 Prospect* **#74** ★ ★ ★

Sixto Sánchez RHP Born: 07/29/98 Age: 23 Bats: R Throws: R Height: 6'0" Weight: 234 lb. Origin: International Free Agent, 2015

YEAR	TEAM	LVL	AGE	W	L	SV	G	GS	IP	H	HR	BB/9	K/9	K	GB%	BABIP	WHIP	ERA	DRA-	WARP	MPH	FB%	Whiff%	CSP
2019	JUP	A+	20	0	2	0	2	2	11	14	1	1.6	4.9	6	60.5%	.351	1.45	4.91	114	0.1				
2019	JAX	AA	20	8	4	0	18	18	103	87	5	1.7	8.5	97	47.3%	.288	1.03	2.53	79	1.8				
2020	MIA	MLB	21	3	2	0	7	7	39	36	3	2.5	7.6	33	58.0%	.303	1.21	3.46	78	0.9	98.2	47.0%	24.9%	50.5%
2022 DC	*MIA*	*MLB*	*23*	*5*	*4*	*0*	*17*	*17*	*83.7*	*82*	*8*	*2.9*	*8.1*	*75*	*50.4%*	*.304*	*1.31*	*3.89*	*96*	*0.9*	*98.2*	*47.0%*	*24.9%*	*50.5%*

Comparables: CC Sabathia, Randall Delgado, Julio Teheran

After showing off the tantalizing talent that has made him a prospect hound's dream for years, Sánchez ended up not throwing a single pitch outside of spring training last year. After cutting a workout short in early April because of shoulder pain, the rookie took some time to rest and build back up to playing shape, but the building never happened. Finally, in July, Sánchez had surgery in his shoulder for a small tear in the posterior capsule. The hope is he'll be back with the team for spring training and, somehow, still only be 23.

LINEOUTS

Hitters

HITTER	POS	TEAM	LVL	AGE	PA	R	2B	3B	HR	RBI	BB	K	SB	CS	AVG/OBP/SLG	DRC+	BABIP	BRR	FRAA	WARP
Yiddi Cappe	SS	DSL MIA	ROK	18	216	31	17	1	2	27	19	35	9	8	.270/.329/.402		.308			
Griffin Conine	OF	BEL	A+	23	288	45	7	2	23	59	46	103	3	0	.247/.382/.587	123	.318	-0.1	RF(46): 6.3, LF(9): 1.0	2.4
	OF	PNS	AA	23	173	18	4	0	13	25	12	82	0	1	.176/.243/.447	61	.234	0.0	RF(20): 1.6, LF(14): 0.9	0.0
Jerar Encarnación	RF	PNS	AA	23	260	24	12	1	9	28	24	99	5	5	.222/.308/.400	78	.341	-1.4	RF(27): 1.2, 1B(16): 0.5, LF(12): -0.4	0.1
Erik González	IF	ESC	WIN	29	118	14	2	1	0	9	8	29	4	3	.266/.322/.303		.363			
	IF	IND	AAA	29	50	6	2	1	0	4	4	10	0	0	.140/.240/.233	89	.176	0.0	3B(5): 0.4, SS(5): 1.0, 1B(3): -0.2	0.2
	IF	PIT	MLB	29	229	17	7	1	2	21	8	40	2	2	.232/.258/.300	79	.274	-1.7	3B(38): 4.0, SS(17): 0.7, 1B(13): 0.3	0.5
Victor Mesa Jr.	CF	JUP	A	19	474	66	21	11	5	71	33	102	12	5	.266/.316/.402	98	.329	2.3	CF(85): 11.2, LF(16): 1.9, RF(5): -0.7	2.9
Víctor Víctor Mesa	CF	BEL	A+	24	225	31	12	1	4	25	16	37	11	1	.306/.357/.432	114	.355	-1.3	CF(42): 8.7, LF(5): 0.1	1.8
	CF	PNS	AA	24	91	8	1	0	0	2	12	19	0	1	.093/.231/.107	96	.121	-0.7	CF(16): 0.8, LF(3): -0.3, RF(1): 0.4	0.3
Brian Miller	OF	JAX	AAA	25	443	53	16	3	2	34	34	88	36	8	.268/.326/.338	87	.335	2.1	CF(53): -2.5, RF(31): 2.6, LF(28): 2.8	1.3
	OF	MIA	MLB	25	11	1	0	0	0	0	0	3	0	0	.273/.273/.273	87	.375	0.0	LF(2): 0.4, CF(2): -0.1, RF(1): -0.0	0.0
Cody Morissette	2B/3B	JUP	A	21	159	22	8	1	1	10	20	38	0	2	.204/.308/.299	94	.273	-0.4	2B(16): -1.2, 3B(14): 2.2, SS(2): -0.3	0.4
Nasim Nunez	SS	JUP	A	20	228	33	2	1	0	10	35	46	33	10	.243/.366/.265	105	.319	2.2	SS(48): 2.7	1.3
Lorenzo Quintana	1B	JAX	AAA	32	226	28	14	3	9	34	14	45	0	0	.294/.354/.525	119	.336	-0.3	1B(34): -1.6, C(10): 0.7, 3B(1): -0.3	0.9
	1B	SUG	AAA	32	113	11	3	0	0	4	9	19	2	0	.311/.372/.340	99	.381	0.5	1B(13): -2.1, C(10): -0.2	0.1
Jose Salas	SS	MRL	ROK	18	107	14	10	0	1	11	11	23	8	5	.370/.458/.511		.485			
	SS	JUP	A	18	123	12	4	0	1	8	11	28	6	0	.250/.333/.315	99	.325	2.1	SS(25): -2.6	0.3
Connor Scott	OF	BEL	A+	21	435	80	25	6	10	46	31	92	14	6	.276/.333/.446	101	.336	0.2	RF(41): 5.5, CF(22): -1.7, LF(17): -0.3	1.7

After electing not to sign at the end of 2019 when every team's bonus pools were depleted, then having to wait through 2020 because of, you know, a global pandemic, **Yiddi Cappe** finally signed with the Marlins in January for $3.5 million. The lithe shortstop has drawn optimistic comparisons to Carlos Correa, and fans will have years to compare their height, their tools, and possibly their love of fedoras.

Just like the royal courts of olde, as long as there are Marlins and Conines, the two should be united. **Griffin Conine** led the system with 36 home runs, but a 47% K rate in Double-A is not the stuff Mr. Marlins are made of.

After an explosive 2019 season that saw **Jerar Encarnación** stay on the field and demonstrate his raw power, he's lost two seasons: one to the alternate training site, and the other to a host of nagging injuries. He's still a bit of an adventure in the outfield and he struck out in more than 40% of his at-bats in Double-A, so the gulf between himself and the Marlins outfield is only growing larger.

Erik González continues to find big-league jobs—including his 71-game stint last year with the Pirates—based on his well-deserved reputation for quality glovework, especially on the left side of the infield. It's a good thing he has that going for him, as his free-swinging ways and lack of pop have made him one of the most consistently unproductive hitters in baseball.

You know that family get-togethers have to be a little more fraught now that **Victor Mesa Jr.** has flown past his brother Victor^2 in the the Marlins organization. Their parents say they're both great baseball players, but Jr. can't help but point out that he picked up more extra-base hits in 2021 than his brother has in his entire minor-league career.

The player the "Airplane" writers would have had a field day with. Originally signed by the Marlins for $5 million, **Victor Victor Mesa's** not just repeating his name anymore. He's now repeating levels of the minors—and that's not as fun to write.

Brian Miller made his big-league debut July 30th and quickly rapped his first big-league hit in the fifth inning. He even got two more. He probably doesn't have the bat for a backup outfield job, and fifth outfielders are as rare in this economy as a fully functional supply chain.

Cody Morrissette is getting an early jump on life by moving to Miami about 40 years before the rest of his friends. The New Hampshire native and Boston College infielder impressed with the bat in his first two seasons before having a down year in 2021. The Marlins snagged him in the second round anyway, on the premise that 2021 shouldn't count against anyone.

Do you mourn the days when a middle infielder didn't need to do anything on offense? Do you dream of a day when a "power-hitting shortstop" finishes with about eight dingers? Does the name "Rey Ordóñez" make you rush to the nearest confession booth for dirty thoughts? Then **Nasim Nunez** is your man.

Originally signed by the Astros after starring in the Cuban leagues, **Lorenzo Quintana** is one of the few over-30 players yet to reach the major leagues. Sadly, there will be no Forbes 30 over 30 list. While he certainly has the bat, his glove necessitated a move from behind the dish, making it a much steeper climb to the Show.

Shockingly, for a team in existence in the '90s and this "every position is a slugger" world, only one shortstop has ever cracked 25-plus dingers for the Marlins: Hanley Ramirez. Unless Miguel Rojas just goes off in 2022, **Jose Salas** is lined up for a chance to be the second.

It's been four years since **Connor Scott** was picked 13th overall in the 2018 draft. The good: He's made slow yet steady improvement every season, displaying the possibility of a future 20-20 season. The bad: He's yet to advance beyond High-A. Just remember: If he had just been selected out of college and posted a .779 OPS, folks would be a lot more enthusiastic. Prospects, like chilis, take time.

Pitchers

PITCHER	TEAM	LVL	AGE	W	L	SV	G	GS	IP	H	HR	BB/9	K/9	K	GB%	BABIP	WHIP	ERA	DRA-	WARP	MPH	FB%	WHF	CSP
Parker Bugg	JAX	AAA	26	6	2	0	32	4	66^{2}	49	10	6.1	11.5	85	25.8%	.255	1.41	4.46	90	1.2				
Daniel Castano	JAX	AAA	26	7	2	0	14	14	78^{1}	69	16	1.8	6.2	54	48.3%	.237	1.09	3.91	110	0.7				
	MIA	MLB	26	0	2	0	5	4	20^{1}	22	3	3.5	5.8	13	37.1%	.288	1.48	4.87	114	0.0	90.4	51.7%	17.1%	60.4%
Ross Detwiler	SD	MLB	35	1	0	0	7	0	7	3	2	6.4	7.7	6	41.2%	.067	1.14	2.57	101	0.1	90.1	51.7%	20.4%	53.6%
	MIA	MLB	35	2	1	0	46	5	45^{1}	41	8	3.0	11.1	56	39.3%	.289	1.24	4.96	84	0.8	92.0	51.0%	24.6%	52.8%
Tommy Eveld	JAX	AAA	27	5	3	6	36	0	44^{2}	38	8	3.2	10.9	54	31.6%	.286	1.21	3.63	92	0.8				
Jake Fishman	JAX	AAA	26	5	1	1	34	2	56^{1}	44	7	2.7	8.1	51	46.2%	.248	1.08	3.67	106	0.6				
Sean Guenther	PNS	AA	25	1	0	0	11	0	17^{2}	11	1	1.5	13.2	26	47.2%	.286	0.79	1.02	81	0.4				
	JAX	AAA	25	3	1	1	15	1	22^{2}	21	2	1.6	11.1	28	39.0%	.333	1.10	4.76	94	0.4				
	MIA	MLB	25	0	1	0	14	0	20^{1}	31	1	4.4	6.6	15	44.7%	.411	2.02	9.30	113	0.0	93.2	56.9%	21.3%	55.5%
Jorge Guzman	JAX	AAA	25	0	1	4	9	0	15^{1}	14	1	5.3	11.7	20	31.7%	.325	1.50	3.52	84	0.3				
	MIA	MLB	25	0	0	0	2	0	1^{2}	4	0	32.4	16.2	3	33.3%	.667	6.00	32.40	91	0.0	96.0	63.9%	43.5%	38.4%
Zach McCambley	BEL	A+	22	2	4	0	11	11	57	52	10	0.9	11.5	73	38.3%	.302	1.02	3.79	76	1.3				
	PNS	AA	22	1	6	0	9	9	40	41	11	4.5	10.6	47	39.0%	.319	1.53	5.18	105	0.3				

No, it's not a nickname that Flash Thompson had for Spider-Man: "That gosh darn **Parker Bugg**!" Instead, Bugg is a big, tall reliever who can whiff batters by the dozen while having a somewhat vague idea of the strike zone. But Spidey probably had issues aiming his webshooters when he first built them, too. A real throwback pitcher, **Daniel Castano** struggles to break 90 with his fastball, doesn't strike out batters and still makes it work as a depth option at the back of the bullpen. His flashiest stuff actually comes off the mound, when "The Italian Stallion" rocks a cowboy hat, mustache and—best of all—a vintage teal Marlins logo belt buckle. Tired of being a ground-ball pitcher, **Ross Detwiler** reinvented himself like the nerdy kid hoping to land a prom date. He got rid of the glasses, bought a whole new wardrobe and transformed into a strikeout-getting cutter/fastball popular kid. And like every pop-culture teenager who reworks their image, the makeover worked like a charm. With his long hair, an anti-hero's mustache, a cap curved like every Little Leaguer from 20 years ago and a save celebration where he raises his arms like he just threw a TD, "Touchdown" **Tommy Eveld** is the next cult favorite…once he makes the big leagues. Part of the Marlins taxi squad last year, Eveld's knocking on that door. It should be a law that anyone named "Fishman" is required to play for the Marlins at least once in their life. **Jake Fishman**, it's your turn now. Blame your parents. Armed with a 93-mph fastball, **Sean Guenther** sat down minor leaguers in bunches by displaying excellent command, traits that deserted him in the big leagues. A candidate to be dropped off the 40-man roster, some team will hope he can repeat his MiLB performance at a higher level. Originally acquired as part of the Giancarlo Stanton trade, **Jorge Guzman** missed the first half of the season rehabbing from an elbow injury, made his second and third major-league appearances of his career, and returned to the IL with another elbow injury. Nothing—a young child's hopeful smile or even a writer's ego—is more fragile than a pitcher's arm. The second-highest drafted player from the Coastal Carolina Chanticleers—the only team named after an animal from Chaucer's *The Canterbury Tales*—**Zach McCambley** struggled after a promotion to Double-A. His curveball is already a plus-plus pitch, so his future as a starter all depends on how well he can develop a third offering. Otherwise, get ready for the first closer in history to enter to a dramatic reading of "The Knight's Tale."

NEW YORK METS

Essay by Alva Noë

Player comments by Jon Tayler and BP staff

The Mets are a hard team to love. This may be their distinctive charm. Just when you think things couldn't get any worse, they find a way, some ingenious new form of dysfunction you hadn't even thought was possible. To be a Mets fan is to be caught up in an intoxicating co-dependence. They knock you down. They pull you back up. They knock you down again.

They were at it again in 2021. I recall watching Jacob deGrom throw long toss at Citi Field before his daytime start against the Diamondbacks on May 9, when the Mets were in first place. As if by stage direction, the sundry cast of characters who had been scattered around the field, stretching and sprinting, wandered away, stage right or stage left, until deGrom was alone in shallow center field, center stage. He turned to face home plate. He stared. He meditated. A model of focus, the slender ace was the focus of our attention. Together, we marked what seemed like his inevitable path to super-dominance.

We all know what happened next. Jacob deGrom struck out eight of the first nine batters he faced that day. He did not face a tenth, leaving the game with arm soreness. The Mets went on to win, but that was, we now know, a sign of things to come. By early July, Mets fans were starting to realize that the end of their team's season was arriving earlier than scheduled. The team went 29-45 after the All-Star break, and deGrom never even pitched in the second half of the season, his ERA frozen at an impossible 1.08 (with 146 strikeouts over 15 games and 92 innings pitched).

Backed by a rotation of deGrom, Noah Syndergaard, Carlos Carrasco and Taijuan Walker, as well as major additions to the offense, the Mets had won the preseason's paper championships; they were widely touted to be the team to beat in the NL East. And, oh, were they beaten.

⚾ ⚾ ⚾

As miserable as the 2021 season was, things looked even more grim as the offseason got underway. Noah Syndergaard and right fielder Michael Conforto, both young and still not fully actualized stars on whom Mets fans had long pinned their hopes, decided to turn down qualifying offers and explore free agency. Syndergaard signed with the Angels,

NEW YORK METS PROSPECTUS

2021 W-L: 77-85, 3RD IN NL EAST

Pythag	.478	*17th*	DER	.703	*13th*
RS/G	3.93	*27th*	DRC+	90	*25th*
RA/G	4.12	*9th*	DRA-	90	*4th*
dWin%	.520	*14th*	FIP	3.96	*8th*
Payroll	$195M	*3rd*	B-Age	28.5	*15th*
M$/MW	$6.3M	*26th*	P-Age	30.0	*17th*

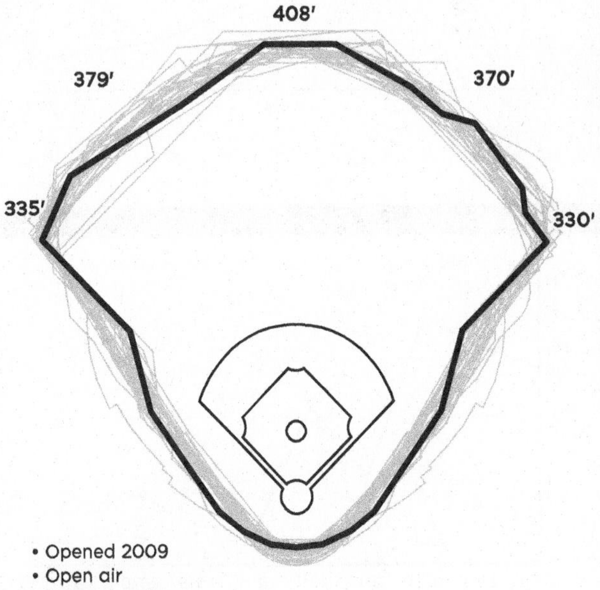

- Opened 2009
- Open air
- Natural surface
- Fence profile: 8'

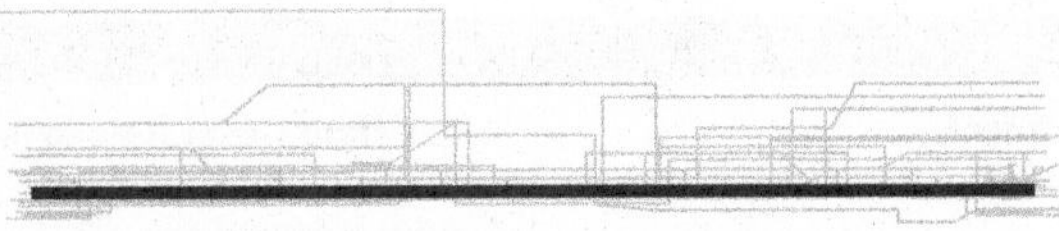

Park Factors

Runs	Runs/RH	Runs/LH	HR/RH	HR/LH
103	103	102	100	101

Top Hitter WARP	3.0 Pete Alonso
Top Pitcher WARP	3.2 Jacob deGrom
Top Prospect	Francisco Alvarez

Payroll History (in millions)

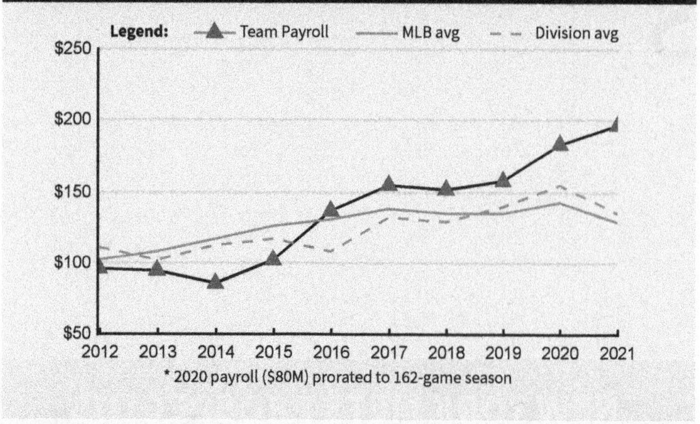

Future Commitments (in millions)

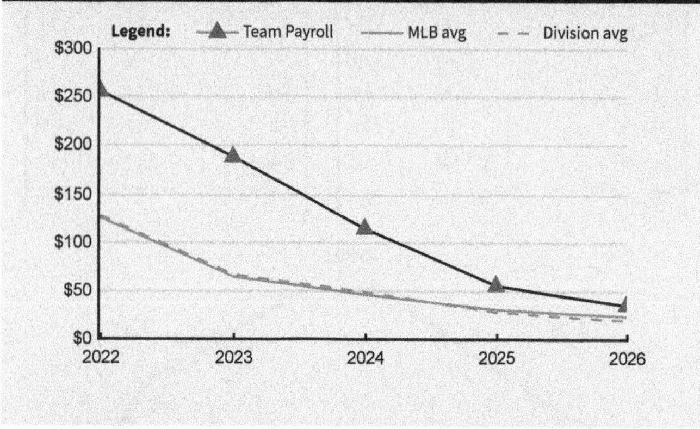

Farm System Ranking

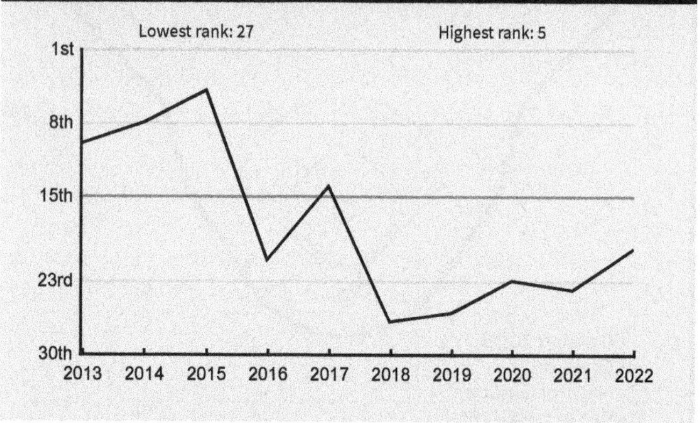

Personnel

President
Sandy Alderson

General Manager
Billy Eppler

Vice President, International & Amateur Scouting
Tommy Tanous

Assistant General Manager, Baseball Operations
Ian Levin

Assistant General Manager, Professional Scouting
Bryn Alderson

Manager
Buck Showalter

BP Alumni
Tatiana DeRouen

and it was pretty clear by the start of the lockout that Conforto wasn't coming back. An effort to sign lefty Steven Matz faltered when the former Met accepted an offer from the Cardinals without giving the Mets a chance to counter. That was surprising given that Matz, a Long Island native and lifelong Mets fan whom the Mets had first drafted out of high school, shone so memorably with the New York when he first hit the majors in 2015. The perceived betrayal prompted Mets owner Steve Cohen to whine publicly on Twitter.

As Thanksgiving approached, the Mets were without a manager or general manager. On top of that, the whole front office seemed uncertain and in disarray. It was, for many, a familiar place. Team president Sandy Alderson's stated plan to hand over his baseball responsibilities to a general manager and a president for baseball operations was scuttled, as he and Cohen struggled to find candidates who were both qualified and interested in the positions. The recent history there was not good. The last GM was let go two months after he was arrested for drunk driving (he was later acquitted), but not before he publicly lambasted his own stars for lack of discipline in their personal training regimens. The GM before that was fired for sexually harassing a journalist.

Mets fans had been delighted in late 2020 when hedge-fund billionaire Cohen, another Long Island local boy made good, bought the Mets from the cash-strapped and disgraced Wilpon family. But the new ownership had gotten off to a slow start. Shortstop Francisco Lindor arrived in a blockbuster trade with Cleveland and, thanks to the new Cohen regime, signed a historically large contract extension. The establishment opined that Lindor was a difference maker, one of the best shortstops in the game, a man of smiles, a sure-fire leader in the clubhouse. But he failed to perform, at the start anyway. In high pressure spots, he was a reliable out. His leadership also came under fire as tensions between Lindor and second baseman Jeff McNeil reportedly led the two to come to blows in the tunnel mid-game in early May. The other new guy in town, catcher James McCann, was equally lackluster.

But it wasn't only the new New Yorkers who were falling short of expectations. McNeil, Conforto and left fielder Dominic Smith all suffered year-long slumps. The pitching situation was, if anything, worse; at least the hitters were able to show up to work. Hopes that Syndergaard, who had undergone Tommy John surgery in March 2020, might rejoin the rotation were dashed when he experienced a setback in May, and the new right-handed starter Cookie Carrasco, who had been brought in to bolster the middle of the rotation as part of the Lindor trade, pulled his hamstring in spring training and was slow to return. By summer, the Mets' rotation looked like an amateur hour.

The 2021 season was not without some bright spots. Marcus Stroman had a strong season on the mound, and Javier Báez—came over from the Cubs at the trade deadline—was intermittently incandescent. Center fielder Brandon Nimmo, sprinting to first base after yet another walk, and first baseman Pete Alonso, eyes shut visualizing home runs before each at bat, modeled dedication and a commitment to achievement. There were also a few amusing, even uplifting side stories, foremost among them the better-than-expected performance of a small legion of substitutes—outfielder Kevin Pillar, infielder Jonathan Villar, catcher Tomás Nido, as well as rookie Patrick Mazeika—who became known collectively as "the bench mob."

And then there was the ace, deGrom. The best pitcher in baseball. A man who rivaled Dwight Gooden and, yes, even Tom Seaver in the pantheon of Mets pitching greats (a pantheon that includes, in no particular order, Pedro Martínez, Jerry Koosman, Johan Santana, R.A. Dickey, Tom Glavine, Tug McGraw, Ron Darling and, my particular favorite, the briefly stratospheric Matt Harvey). But, of course, it was deGrom's season-ending injury, more than anything else, that brought the Mets' campaign to an ignominious conclusion. All that work, all those hopes, undone by a single tendon.

So, yeah, it was hard, very hard, to be a Mets fan in 2021.

Everything took a dramatic turn in the last two weeks before the lockout. The Mets hired Billy Eppler as GM. He and Cohen went on a free-agent shopping spree, signing not only A-list center fielder Starling Marte, infielder Eduardo Escobar, and outfielder Mark Canha, but also, *very* remarkably, superstar pitcher Max Scherzer. By year's end, the Mets had landed a new skipper, the tried and true and well-respected Buck Showalter. And they may not be done yet. There are certainly still needs at third base and in the middle of the rotation.

As a result of Eppler's ambition and Cohen's largesse, the Mets are once again poised to win the preseason speculative championships. But to judge by the mood on Mets Twitter, and the unending snark and cynicism of at least a good portion of the Mets podcast universe, Mets fans are, at best, only cautiously optimistic. There are two different whys that need answering here. The first is straightforward: why the *caution*, or even, why the pessimism? And here, the answer is also pretty straightforward. Past performance does not a winner make. Clubhouse chemistry, keeping key players healthy, managing players effectively—these are the sometimes-imponderable challenges that every team faces, and that have tended, historically, to unman the Mets. Smart money ought to sit back and adopt a watch-and-wait attitude, especially since the Mets are an increasingly rare animal in today's contention-cycle-focused sport: a team from which you never really know what you'll get from year to year.

But why the *cynicism*? Why are so many online voices so sour about a team they ostensibly love?

What does it mean to love a baseball team in 2022?

When a sports-fan friend of mine moved to New York from the UK a few years back, I was alarmed to learn that his first baseball contact took place at Yankee Stadium. I realized that, as a stranger to our game, he was helpless to appreciate the different meanings of the Mets and the Yankees. I had to intervene. Before nostalgia could take root, and without in any way overstating matters, I tried to help him see that the choice was something like one between good and evil, between progress and establishment, between the people and the bosses. He saw the light, and I'm glad to have saved him (again, not wishing to put too fine a point on it).

But now, I'm not so sure.

When I was a kid, it was common knowledge that the Mets, well, they sucked. Even when they excelled, they somehow did it as outsiders. That was the Miracle Mets spirit of '69, and it was the energy behind Tug McGraw's 1973 war cry, as he stomped victorious from the mound, slapping his thighs with his mitt, "You gotta believe!" Even when the Mets achieved greatness thanks to the importation of talents groomed elsewhere (Gary Carter, Keith Hernandez, Mike Piazza), the team's real charm had less to do with mere winning and more to do with its struggles and personality. Think Gooden and Darryl Strawberry trying to cope with the pressures of stardom; think Keith smoking between innings and hamming it up on *Seinfeld*. The Mets may be a hard team to love, especially in the moment, but they are so easy to forgive.

The thing is, of course, that most of the time, the Mets, like every other team, did not excel. But that was no impediment to our devotion. That is proof positive that winning isn't everything. You aren't playing if you aren't playing to win, yes. But you don't need to win to play. The *point* isn't victory; the point, the source of value, for fans no less than players, is something less tangible; it's the aspiration, the process, the work.

In my judgment, baseball has tended to lose sight of this. Modern statistical overload has led people to reduce the game to the uninteresting quanta on which it depends. I have no argument with knowledge, but you can't squeeze *judgment* out of numbers, and value itself is of no derivable magnitude. In baseball, as in business, indeed, as in life, numbers tell the story, but never the whole story. Numbers are not, and never will be, the source of a baseball story's interest or value. It isn't the numbers—velocity, spin rate, etc.—that tell us what we need to understand when deGrom leaves a batter paralyzed by a backdoor slider at the knees. It's the look on deGrom's face and that of the hapless hitter.

Which brings us back to the question of what to make of these new New York Mets as we face 2022, and how to explain the cynicism on display in the fan base. Many Mets fans, to be sure, will applaud the hiring of Eppler and his signings of Marte and Scherzer. These seem like smart baseball moves for a team bent on winning. But the jury is out, not only on whether this will make the Mets winners, but also, and more importantly, on what the new Mets narrative is going to be. The splashy moves made by the Mets this offseason may mark a new commitment on the part of management to an ethos of aspiration, achievement and excellence. This might be reflected in the hiring of Buck Showalter as manager; Showalter has, after all, demonstrated an ability over his long career to make change at the level of team culture. Were he to do the same in New York, it would be a beautiful thing and a joy to witness, regardless of how many games the Mets win in 2022.

Or it might be that Cohen's takeover, and makeover, represent something less positive, a shifting of the team in the direction of the reductionism now endemic in baseball. Win or lose, these new Mets of Cohen would be more quantized, more analytical, less passionate and, thus, less lovable. And that would be a loss, regardless of how many games they win in 2022. ■

—Alva Noë is a professor at the University of California, Berkeley.

HITTERS

Pete Alonso 1B Born: 12/07/94 Age: 27 Bats: R Throws: R Height: 6'3" Weight: 245 lb. Origin: Round 2, 2016 Draft (#64 overall)

YEAR	TEAM	LVL	AGE	PA	R	2B	3B	HR	RBI	BB	K	SB	CS	Whiff%	AVG/OBP/SLG	DRC+	BABIP	BRR	FRAA	WARP
2019	NYM	MLB	24	693	103	30	2	53	120	72	183	1	0	28.2%	.260/.358/.583	136	.280	0.0	1B(156): 6.2	5.7
2020	NYM	MLB	25	239	31	6	0	16	35	24	61	1	0	30.4%	.231/.326/.490	119	.242	-2.5	1B(39): -5.0	0.3
2021	NYM	MLB	26	637	81	27	3	37	94	60	127	3	0	24.9%	.262/.344/.519	128	.274	-1.1	1B(148): -4.6	3.0
2022 DC	*NYM*	*MLB*	*27*	*564*	*102*	*26*	*1*	*33*	*111*	*54*	*120*	*1*	*1*	*25.3%*	*.266/.354/.523*	*133*	*.291*	*-0.8*	*1B 0*	*3.5*

Comparables: Kendrys Morales, Mark Trumbo, José Osuna

The 2020 slump that followed Alonso's breathtaking debut now looks more like just that: a slump. The burly first baseman got off to a relatively slow start in 2021, with just seven homers and a .786 OPS over the first two months, but roared back to life after that, posting a .540 slugging percentage and going deep roughly once every three games. The power that receded during the pandemic season came back, albeit not to the same historic levels, but the juiced ball puts a sizable asterisk on everyone's 2019 stats, and it's not as if this version of Alonso is a bad one. He's still a hard-hit rate and exit velocity champion, and he finished top 10 among first basemen in slugging percentage, DRC+, wOBA and ISO, with only Vladimir Guerrero Jr. and Matt Olson hitting more home runs at the position. He even managed to cut down on his strikeouts, too. He remains a locked-in piece of the team's core.

★ ★ ★ *2022 Top 101 Prospect* **#10** ★ ★ ★

Francisco Álvarez C Born: 11/19/01 Age: 20 Bats: R Throws: R Height: 5'10" Weight: 233 lb. Origin: International Free Agent, 2018

YEAR	TEAM	LVL	AGE	PA	R	2B	3B	HR	RBI	BB	K	SB	CS	Whiff%	AVG/OBP/SLG	DRC+	BABIP	BRR	FRAA	WARP
2019	MTS	ROK	17	31	8	4	0	2	10	4	4	0	1		.462/.548/.846		.500			
2019	KNG	ROA	17	151	24	6	0	5	16	17	33	1	1		.282/.377/.443		.344			
2021	SLU	A	19	67	12	5	0	2	12	15	7	2	2		.417/.567/.646	143	.450	0.1	C(10): -1.5	0.4
2021	BRK	A+	19	333	55	13	1	22	58	40	82	6	3		.247/.351/.538	154	.260	0.8	C(49): -7.6	2.5
2022 non-DC	*NYM*	*MLB*	*20*	*251*	*27*	*10*	*0*	*8*	*29*	*23*	*66*	*1*	*2*	*30.6%*	*.232/.316/.401*	*94*	*.292*	*-0.1*	*C -6*	*0.3*

Comparables: Gary Sánchez, Christian Bethancourt, Giancarlo Stanton

YEAR	TEAM	P. COUNT	FRM RUNS	BLK RUNS	THRW RUNS	TOT RUNS
2019	KNG	3392			0.7	0.7
2021	SLU	1391	-1.3	-0.2	-0.2	-1.7
2021	BRK	6975	-6.7	-1.2	0.9	-6.9
2022	*NYM*	*6956*	*-4.2*	*-1.1*	*0.0*	*-5.3*

The Mets' catcher of the future can't get there fast enough. New York's backstops posted a grisly .568 OPS on the season, 29th in the majors, and ranked in the bottom quartile by WARP. Álvarez, meanwhile, didn't miss a beat despite the skipped 2020 season, holding his own in High-A despite being four years young for the level. His enormous power showed up plenty, he displayed good patience at the plate, and his defense, while still a work in progress, continues to improve, and he only just turned 20 in November. Everything here continues to point toward the franchise finally filling the Mike Piazza-shaped hole behind home plate—ideally, for both the Mets and their fans, sooner rather than later.

★ ★ ★ *2022 Top 101 Prospect* **#13** ★ ★ ★

Brett Baty 3B Born: 11/13/99 Age: 22 Bats: L Throws: R Height: 6'3" Weight: 210 lb. Origin: Round 1, 2019 Draft (#12 overall)

YEAR	TEAM	LVL	AGE	PA	R	2B	3B	HR	RBI	BB	K	SB	CS	Whiff%	AVG/OBP/SLG	DRC+	BABIP	BRR	FRAA	WARP
2019	MTS	ROK	19	25	5	3	0	1	8	5	6	0	0		.350/.480/.650		.462			
2019	KNG	ROA	19	186	30	12	2	6	22	24	56	0	0		.222/.339/.437		.302			
2019	BRK	SS	19	17	2	1	0	0	3	6	3	0	0		.200/.529/.300		.286			
2021	SRR	WIN	21	102	16	5	1	1	15	11	31	1	0		.292/.373/.404		.431			
2021	BRK	A+	21	209	27	14	1	7	34	24	53	4	3		.309/.397/.514	118	.402	-0.3	3B(41): 6.7, LF(3): -0.4	1.6
2021	BNG	AA	21	176	16	8	0	5	22	22	45	2	0		.272/.364/.424	91	.350	0.0	3B(24): -0.8, LF(15): 1.4	0.4
2022 non-DC	*NYM*	*MLB*	*22*	*251*	*23*	*11*	*1*	*4*	*24*	*22*	*71*	*0*	*1*	*29.3%*	*.230/.306/.351*	*79*	*.315*	*-0.2*	*3B 1, LF 1*	*0.2*

Comparables: Jeimer Candelario, Abraham Toro, Eugenio Suárez

Nominative determinism demanded that Baty hit, and hit he has. His lost 2020 didn't translate into further struggles in '21: He easily handled his first trip to High-A, then put up a good showing in the cauldron that is Double-A, even cutting down on his strikeouts while there. His big raw power has yet to translate to live action, but what has to encourage the Mets is more contact for a player who looked like his MLB future was going to be Three True

Outcomes-dependent. That's likely still the case, and a probable eventual move off third base won't help that overall value, nor does his relatively advanced age compared to other high school prospects. How he does with another taste of Double-A in 2022 will go a long way toward establishing Baty as a legitimate top prospect, or something closer to the Mets' version of Bobby Dalbec.

Mark Canha OF Born: 02/15/89 Age: 33 Bats: R Throws: R Height: 6'2" Weight: 209 lb. Origin: Round 7, 2010 Draft (#227 overall)

YEAR	TEAM	LVL	AGE	PA	R	2B	3B	HR	RBI	BB	K	SB	CS	Whiff%	AVG/OBP/SLG	DRC+	BABIP	BRR	FRAA	WARP
2019	OAK	MLB	30	497	80	16	3	26	58	67	107	3	2	23.0%	.273/.396/.517	128	.308	1.4	CF(56): -3.2, RF(27): 1.9, 1B(15): -1.4	3.5
2020	OAK	MLB	31	243	32	12	2	5	33	37	54	4	0	24.1%	.246/.387/.408	110	.307	-0.8	RF(17): 0.6, LF(15): 1.7, CF(9): 0.1	1.1
2021	OAK	MLB	32	625	93	22	4	17	61	77	128	12	2	21.5%	.231/.358/.387	114	.274	2.7	LF(106): -15.9, RF(27): -0.3, CF(23): 0.6	2.1
2022 DC	*NYM*	*MLB*	*33*	*539*	*90*	*22*	*2*	*18*	*74*	*70*	*108*	*5*	*2*	*21.8%*	*.241/.370/.422*	*117*	*.281*	*-0.2*	*RF 4, LF -1*	*3.1*

Comparables: Orlando Merced, Michael Cuddyer, Dexter Fowler

For the last three seasons, Canha was the platonic ideal of an Oakland A's player: cheap, highly underrated, shaped like a refrigerator box, looks like he could be named Brad. And over those last three seasons, he produced a higher wOBA (.355) than, among others, Jose Altuve, Joey Gallo and, the man he's replacing in New York, Michael Conforto. Was that the right call for the Mets? Canha's wOBA, ISO, hard-hit and barrel rates have been going in the wrong direction since 2019, and when you look at the batted-ball numbers, it's that season—you know, the goofy one full of juiced baseballs—that feels like the outlier. What has been steady, though, is his terrific patience; even if the power doesn't return to his previous highs, his excellent walk rate, which has barely budged from season to season, and aversion to whiffs keep him afloat offensively. That stability and selectivity should help him adjust to and thrive in his new home, too.

J.D. Davis 3B Born: 04/27/93 Age: 29 Bats: R Throws: R Height: 6'3" Weight: 218 lb. Origin: Round 3, 2014 Draft (#75 overall)

YEAR	TEAM	LVL	AGE	PA	R	2B	3B	HR	RBI	BB	K	SB	CS	Whiff%	AVG/OBP/SLG	DRC+	BABIP	BRR	FRAA	WARP
2019	NYM	MLB	26	453	65	22	1	22	57	38	97	3	0	28.1%	.307/.369/.527	118	.355	0.7	LF(79): -5.5, 3B(31): -0.4	2.0
2020	NYM	MLB	27	229	26	9	0	6	19	31	56	0	0	29.3%	.247/.371/.389	107	.318	-1.4	3B(34): -0.4, LF(8): -0.3	0.6
2021	SYR	AAA	28	49	8	4	0	4	7	10	14	0	0		.316/.469/.737	112	.400	0.3	3B(10): -0.2, 1B(3): 0.1	0.2
2021	NYM	MLB	28	211	18	12	0	5	23	24	68	1	0	41.0%	.285/.384/.436	85	.426	-2.1	3B(50): -5.3	-0.4
2022 DC	*NYM*	*MLB*	*29*	*110*	*17*	*5*	*0*	*4*	*16*	*12*	*33*	*0*	*0*	*36.4%*	*.242/.342/.435*	*106*	*.331*	*-0.1*	*3B -1*	*0.1*

Comparables: Danny Valencia, Brian Anderson, Chris Johnson

Davis is the free frogurt that comes with the cursed Krusty doll in Treehouse of Horror III: an ostensibly good thing, endlessly compromised. For example: After a 2020 in which he smashed the ball into the ground relentlessly, he added a whopping 10 degrees to his launch angle, slashed his ground-ball rate by nearly 20 points, and went from a 20% line-drive rate to a 31% mark. That's good. He also hit more infield pop-ups, saw his hard-hit rate fall for a third straight year, and went deep just five times in 73 games. That's bad. Another one: He kept the one good development from his bad '20, an improved walk rate, en route to posting a higher wOBA than José Abreu, Manny Machado and Randy Arozarena. That's good. He also saw his strikeout rate balloon to 32.2%, had the third-highest swinging-strike rate among hitters with 200 or more plate appearances, and made less contact in the strike zone despite swinging there more often. That's bad. So it goes with Davis, whose inflated BABIP masked a bad year at the plate, and whose defense doesn't play at either the hot corner or in the outfield. And he also contains potassium benzoate. (That's bad.)

Eduardo Escobar 3B/2B Born: 01/05/89 Age: 33 Bats: S Throws: R Height: 5'10" Weight: 193 lb. Origin: International Free Agent, 2006

YEAR	TEAM	LVL	AGE	PA	R	2B	3B	HR	RBI	BB	K	SB	CS	Whiff%	AVG/OBP/SLG	DRC+	BABIP	BRR	FRAA	WARP
2019	ARI	MLB	30	699	94	29	10	35	118	50	130	5	1	24.8%	.269/.320/.511	113	.283	-0.7	3B(144): -7.9, 2B(33): 1.5	2.5
2020	ARI	MLB	31	222	22	7	3	4	20	15	41	1	0	21.6%	.212/.270/.335	84	.244	1.0	3B(47): 0.2, 2B(3): -0.1	0.2
2021	MIL	MLB	32	199	27	12	2	6	25	19	39	0	0	22.7%	.268/.342/.458	99	.313	-0.6	3B(34): -7.3, 1B(18): -0.4	-0.3
2021	ARI	MLB	32	400	50	14	3	22	65	29	85	1	0	24.3%	.246/.300/.478	107	.261	0.9	3B(65): -2.0, 2B(42): -2.9, SS(1): -0.0	1.4
2022 DC	*NYM*	*MLB*	*33*	*519*	*71*	*23*	*3*	*17*	*81*	*42*	*101*	*2*	*2*	*23.6%*	*.244/.312/.417*	*92*	*.278*	*-0.2*	*3B -3, 2B 0*	*0.6*

Comparables: Toby Harrah, Rico Petrocelli, Clete Boyer

While earning his first All-Star appearance in his age-32 season may have been the most noteworthy aspect of Escobar's 2021 season, moving from the sad-sack Diamondbacks to the contending Brewers for the stretch run was probably a close second. Excluding the wonkiness of the pandemic-shortened 2020 season, Escobar has now been a solidly above-average hitter for the better part of the last five years, and Milwaukee wisely recognizing that he's not a multi-positional option anymore actually added to his value, as splitting time between third and first made him less of a defensive sieve than when Arizona was throwing him up the middle more often than he should be. Escobar's warts—the aforementioned defense, average baserunning and a propensity to swing and miss—make him overextended in a starring role; his inclusion on the NL team was more a byproduct of the "every team gets a rep" rule than anything else. But he's a solid complementary piece. The Mets signed him to a two-year deal in the offseason, where he'll continue to stand on the infield dirt and mash left-handed pitching.

Luis Guillorme IF Born: 09/27/94 Age: 27 Bats: L Throws: R Height: 5'10" Weight: 190 lb. Origin: Round 10, 2013 Draft (#296 overall)

YEAR	TEAM	LVL	AGE	PA	R	2B	3B	HR	RBI	BB	K	SB	CS	Whiff%	AVG/OBP/SLG	DRC+	BABIP	BRR	FRAA	WARP
2019	SYR	AAA	24	278	33	12	0	7	32	39	42	4	4		.307/.412/.452	117	.346	0.7	2B(30): -0.7, SS(26): -2.2, 3B(13): 0.5	1.5
2019	NYM	MLB	24	70	8	4	0	1	3	7	14	0	0	19.7%	.246/.324/.361	88	.304	0.4	2B(8): -0.0, SS(8): -0.4, 3B(5): -0.0	0.2
2020	NYM	MLB	25	68	6	6	0	0	9	10	17	2	0	20.7%	.333/.426/.439	90	.463	0.1	3B(4): -0.6, SS(3): 0.0, P(1): -0.0	0.1
2021	SYR	AAA	26	28	4	0	0	0	1	3	2	0	0		.304/.393/.304	112	.318	0.1	2B(3): 0.1, 3B(3): -0.3, SS(3): 0.4	0.2
2021	NYM	MLB	26	156	13	3	0	1	5	23	23	0	2	14.9%	.265/.374/.311	101	.315	-0.1	3B(27): -2.3, 2B(18): 1.2, SS(11): -0.9	0.4
2022 DC	*NYM*	*MLB*	*27*	*184*	*23*	*7*	*0*	*1*	*19*	*22*	*26*	*0*	*1*	*16.0%*	*.248/.347/.334*	*90*	*.289*	*-0.2*	*2B 0, SS 0*	*0.4*

Comparables: Eduardo Escobar, Danny Santana, Didi Gregorius

Are we sure that Luis Guillorme isn't Luis Arraez in disguise? They've got the same contact-heavy approach with little to no power and miniscule swinging-strike rate, and both can play multiple positions, some of them well and some of them in ways that'll make you cry. Minnesota Luis is a starter, though, while New York Luis cracks the lineup mostly when injuries open the door; otherwise, he's a defensive replacement or pinch-hitter. But is there more here? He kept the plate discipline gains he made in 2020, which helped make him a league-average hitter by DRC+. If he can nudge his launch angle back up to double digits and turn more of his ground balls into line drives, that could be the ticket to more production, and to more regular at-bats.

Khalil Lee OF

Born: 06/26/98 Age: 24 Bats: L Throws: L Height: 5'10" Weight: 170 lb. Origin: Round 3, 2016 Draft (#103 overall)

YEAR	TEAM	LVL	AGE	PA	R	2B	3B	HR	RBI	BB	K	SB	CS	Whiff%	AVG/OBP/SLG	DRC+	BABIP	BRR	FRAA	WARP
2019	NWA	AA	21	546	74	21	3	8	51	65	154	53	12		.264/.363/.372	90	.374	2.7	RF(55): -5.4, CF(45): -6.1, LF(8): -0.1	0.1
2021	SYR	AAA	23	388	67	20	2	14	37	71	115	8	10		.274/.451/.500	122	.402	-0.3	RF(61): -7.7, CF(26): 6.7, LF(11): -1.0	2.0
2021	NYM	MLB	23	18	2	1	0	0	1	0	13	0	0	55.6%	.056/.056/.111	41	.200		RF(11): -0.4	-0.1
2022 DC	*NYM*	*MLB*	*24*	*60*	*8*	*2*	*0*	*1*	*7*	*7*	*20*	*2*	*1*	*34.0%*	*.208/.333/.362*	*92*	*.319*	*0.2*	*RF 0, LF 0*	*0.1*

Comparables: Michael Saunders, Nick Williams, Rey Fuentes

Lee's short MLB stint produced a lot of wind but not much else: Over two weeks in May, he struck out 13 times and reached base just once. It was a different story in Triple-A, where he nearly tied his season high in homers and walked in nearly a fifth of his trips to the plate, but he also was caught on 10 of his 18 stolen base attempts. For his career, he's swiped bags at a mere 69% success rate, which won't have anyone in the Mets' front office thinking nice thoughts. If the speed won't save him, then the bat will have to, and while the power is starting to show a bit more, he won't get anywhere near a regular major-league role without a major improvement in contact and pitch selection.

Francisco Lindor SS

Born: 11/14/93 Age: 28 Bats: S Throws: R Height: 5'11" Weight: 190 lb. Origin: Round 1, 2011 Draft (#8 overall)

YEAR	TEAM	LVL	AGE	PA	R	2B	3B	HR	RBI	BB	K	SB	CS	Whiff%	AVG/OBP/SLG	DRC+	BABIP	BRR	FRAA	WARP
2019	CLE	MLB	25	654	101	40	2	32	74	46	98	22	5	16.9%	.284/.335/.518	115	.291	-1.7	SS(137): -5.4	2.9
2020	CLE	MLB	26	266	30	13	0	8	27	24	41	6	2	20.4%	.258/.335/.415	106	.280	0.0	SS(58): 0.5	1.0
2021	NYM	MLB	27	524	73	16	3	20	63	58	96	10	4	23.3%	.230/.322/.412	105	.248	0.9	SS(124): -0.2	2.3
2022 DC	*NYM*	*MLB*	*28*	*594*	*99*	*26*	*2*	*22*	*90*	*59*	*109*	*15*	*6*	*22.3%*	*.250/.333/.438*	*105*	*.276*	*0.8*	*SS -1*	*2.7*

Comparables: Cal Ripken Jr., Alex Rodriguez, Tony Fernandez

The worst and most vicious slump of Lindor's career was also probably the most poorly timed. Brought over from Cleveland and signed to a 10-year, $340 million deal, he hit .194/.294/.294 over his first two months in New York, homering just four times in 200 plate appearances as he consistently rolled over fastballs in the strike zone and swung through off-speed pitches. A famously serene and stable fan base handled this bumpy debut about as well as you'd expect, with the first but not last "Lindor talks about being booed" news story appearing before April ended. A summer hot streak was cut short by a strained oblique that left him sidelined until late August, and when he returned to more booing, he and others responded with a thumbs down celebration gesture that resulted in...more booing. As far as introductions go, it wasn't the best.

If you'd like to line that cloud with some silver, Lindor hit the ball hard overall and drew more walks, and from June onward, he slashed .252/.340/.482. Here to blot the sun back out are career-worst marks in whiff and contact rate, and you can't entirely blame the early slump for those. Panic if that frightens you, but patience is a virtue for a reason and practically a necessity when talking about a 28-year-old defensive wizard with two 6+ WARP seasons to his name. A homer on Opening Day wouldn't hurt, though.

Starling Marte CF

Born: 10/09/88 Age: 33 Bats: R Throws: R Height: 6'1" Weight: 195 lb. Origin: International Free Agent, 2007

YEAR	TEAM	LVL	AGE	PA	R	2B	3B	HR	RBI	BB	K	SB	CS	Whiff%	AVG/OBP/SLG	DRC+	BABIP	BRR	FRAA	WARP
2019	PIT	MLB	30	586	97	31	6	23	82	25	94	25	6	25.1%	.295/.342/.503	115	.319	3.6	CF(130): 0.6	4.0
2020	MIA	MLB	31	112	13	6	0	4	13	2	22	5	0	23.5%	.245/.286/.415	108	.275	0.4	CF(28): -1.4	0.4
2020	ARI	MLB	31	138	23	8	1	2	14	10	19	5	2	27.1%	.311/.384/.443	112	.353	0.2	CF(33): -1.9	0.5
2021	MIA	MLB	32	275	52	11	1	7	25	32	57	22	3	24.6%	.305/.405/.451	114	.376	2.4	CF(63): 3.4	2.2
2021	OAK	MLB	32	251	37	16	2	5	30	11	42	25	2	24.9%	.312/.355/.462	109	.362	3.7	CF(56): -1.2	1.6
2022 DC	*NYM*	*MLB*	*33*	*585*	*91*	*29*	*2*	*15*	*86*	*41*	*104*	*32*	*10*	*24.6%*	*.274/.345/.425*	*109*	*.319*	*2.2*	*CF 0, LF 0*	*3.1*

Comparables: Shannon Stewart, Carlos Lee, Tommy Davis

Ordinarily, a 33-year-old outfielder joining his fourth team in the last three years would earn a lineout in these pages, but even as Marte's odometer keeps racking up miles, he refuses to slow down. The veteran put up his third 3+ WARP campaign in as many full seasons—this one split between Miami and Oakland, who acquired him at the trade deadline—and parlayed that into a three-year deal with the Mets. Again, ordinarily, a player past 30 signing a long-term deal with the Mets is a recipe for all kinds of sadness, and there are reasons for concern. Marte's game is still built on legging out ground balls as opposed to patience or power; a brief spike in walk rate with the Marlins proved to be just that, and he's middle of the road when it comes to hard-hit and barrel rate. Speed is the key, and his has held, keeping him defensively viable in center field and one of the league's best threats on the bases. It might be getting late, but no one is calling off the Marte Party quite yet.

★ ★ ★ *2022 Top 101 Prospect* **#51** ★ ★ ★

Ronny Mauricio SS
Born: 04/04/01 Age: 21 Bats: S Throws: R Height: 6'3" Weight: 166 lb. Origin: International Free Agent, 2017

YEAR	TEAM	LVL	AGE	PA	R	2B	3B	HR	RBI	BB	K	SB	CS	Whiff%	AVG/OBP/SLG	DRC+	BABIP	BRR	FRAA	WARP
2019	COL	A	18	504	62	20	5	4	37	23	99	6	10		.268/.307/.357	97	.330	2.0	SS(106): -0.2	1.6
2021	LIC	WIN	20	94	8	5	0	2	8	3	21	1	0		.244/.277/.367		.299			
2021	BRK	A+	20	420	55	14	5	19	63	24	101	9	7		.242/.290/.449	115	.278	0.1	SS(87): 10.9	3.0
2021	BNG	AA	20	33	3	1	0	1	1	2	11	2	0		.323/.364/.452	89	.474	-0.3	SS(8): -0.4	0.0
2022 non-DC	*NYM*	*MLB*	*21*	*251*	*21*	*9*	*1*	*4*	*24*	*11*	*66*	*2*	*3*	*28.6%*	*.226/.268/.344*	*60*	*.294*	*0.3*	*SS 1*	*-0.2*

Comparables: Chris Owings, Addison Russell, Alcides Escobar

At the same time that the Mets theoretically cleared the deck for Mauricio in Queens by dealing away both Amed Rosario and Andrés Giménez, they simultaneously locked him out of the shortstop position for the next decade by locking up the player they got back in that trade—Francisco Lindor—to a long-term extension. Nonetheless, he remains at short. Not that New York needs to move him anywhere else at the moment: The tall but lanky Mauricio is still very much a project, and while his power has begun to blossom, his plate discipline lags behind, as much as any 20-year-old's progress can be considered sluggish. Still, he's a switch-hitter with plus tools, pending the ever-elusive hit tool, including a powerful arm that would translate easily to a move to third base. The upside remains immense, even if the future is murky.

James McCann C
Born: 06/13/90 Age: 32 Bats: R Throws: R Height: 6'3" Weight: 220 lb. Origin: Round 2, 2011 Draft (#76 overall)

YEAR	TEAM	LVL	AGE	PA	R	2B	3B	HR	RBI	BB	K	SB	CS	Whiff%	AVG/OBP/SLG	DRC+	BABIP	BRR	FRAA	WARP
2019	CHW	MLB	29	476	62	26	1	18	60	30	137	4	1	28.7%	.273/.328/.460	90	.359	0.1	C(106): -15.1	-0.1
2020	CHW	MLB	30	111	20	3	0	7	15	8	30	1	1	29.2%	.289/.360/.536	111	.339	-0.4	C(30): 3.6	0.9
2021	NYM	MLB	31	412	29	12	1	10	46	32	115	1	2	27.1%	.232/.294/.349	80	.304	-1.7	C(107): -0.9, 1B(6): -0.0	0.4
2022 DC	*NYM*	*MLB*	*32*	*376*	*48*	*15*	*0*	*11*	*51*	*29*	*97*	*1*	*1*	*27.0%*	*.232/.302/.378*	*80*	*.295*	*-0.5*	*C -7*	*0.0*

Comparables: Terry Steinbach, Mike Stanley, Kurt Suzuki

YEAR	TEAM	P. COUNT	FRM RUNS	BLK RUNS	THRW RUNS	TOT RUNS
2019	CHW	15359	-13.4	-0.1	0.6	-13.0
2020	CHW	4053	3.3	0.0	0.0	3.3
2021	NYM	13585	0.0	-0.1	0.5	0.4
2022	*NYM*	*14430*	*-7.7*	*-0.9*	*-0.1*	*-8.7*

Who is the real James McCann? The gamble the Mets took when they signed him was that his two seasons with the White Sox, when he went from anonymous backup to slugging All-Star, represented his true talent level. Unfortunately for them, his first season in New York was a repeat of his early years in Detroit: no power and below-average offense. Not only that, but he backslid defensively, ranking 54th out of 60 qualified catchers in FRAA a year after finishing 10th league-wide. And while he kept the plate patience gains he made in Chicago, posting the highest walk rate of his career, that didn't mitigate all the balls he smashed into the dirt; his ground-ball rate was a career high, too. Add to that a big drop in hard-hit rate, a BABIP that went from Ichiro-esque to something more catcher-appropriate and persistent struggles against right-handers (a .599 OPS against them in 2021 and a .633 career mark), and the answer to the question of who McCann is becomes that much clearer: someone who is miscast as a starter and should be the weak side of a platoon.

Jeff McNeil 2B
Born: 04/08/92 Age: 30 Bats: L Throws: R Height: 6'1" Weight: 195 lb. Origin: Round 12, 2013 Draft (#356 overall)

YEAR	TEAM	LVL	AGE	PA	R	2B	3B	HR	RBI	BB	K	SB	CS	Whiff%	AVG/OBP/SLG	DRC+	BABIP	BRR	FRAA	WARP
2019	NYM	MLB	27	567	83	38	1	23	75	35	75	5	6	20.0%	.318/.384/.531	123	.337	-3.0	LF(71): -5.8, RF(42): -1.4, 2B(37): -3.0	2.3
2020	NYM	MLB	28	209	19	14	0	4	23	20	24	0	2	17.5%	.311/.383/.454	109	.335	-1.9	LF(28): -1.6, 2B(12): 1.1, 3B(9): 1.6	1.0
2021	NYM	MLB	29	426	48	19	1	7	35	29	58	3	0	18.2%	.249/.317/.358	94	.276	1.8	2B(79): -1.6, 3B(2): 0.0	1.2
2022 DC	*NYM*	*MLB*	*30*	*328*	*51*	*17*	*1*	*8*	*49*	*23*	*42*	*3*	*2*	*18.2%*	*.281/.351/.440*	*114*	*.305*	*-0.1*	*RF -1, 2B 0*	*1.5*

Comparables: Justin Turner, Tommy La Stella, Yangervis Solarte

The power that McNeil showed in 2018 in the minors and in '19 with the Mets has since vanished, with his slugging percentage slipping into Ozzie Smith territory, and without the glove to match. While he battered fastballs in his first full season with New York, hitting .339 with a .545 slugging percentage against them, those numbers fell to .253 and .349, respectively, leaving him exposed as well against breaking balls (a .318 wOBA on those) and off-speed stuff (.286). With most balls smacked into the ground or popped up, McNeil has no margin for error, and until he can prove to opposing pitchers that he can handle hard stuff in the strike zone, he'll continue living on the razor's edge at the plate. The good news is that his struggles didn't cause him to abandon his good plate discipline, as he neither whiffed more nor expanded the zone on the regular. He's still a contact machine; he just has to make it count again.

Tomás Nido C
Born: 04/12/94 Age: 28 Bats: R Throws: R Height: 6'0" Weight: 211 lb. Origin: Round 8, 2012 Draft (#260 overall)

YEAR	TEAM	LVL	AGE	PA	R	2B	3B	HR	RBI	BB	K	SB	CS	Whiff%	AVG/OBP/SLG	DRC+	BABIP	BRR	FRAA	WARP
2019	SYR	AAA	25	40	3	1	0	0	4	1	13	0	0		.289/.300/.316	76	.423	-0.9	C(11): 0.7	0.0
2019	NYM	MLB	25	144	9	5	0	4	14	7	37	0	0	37.1%	.191/.231/.316	76	.232	-1.3	C(48): 8.0	0.8
2020	NYM	MLB	26	26	4	1	0	2	6	2	6	0	0	32.7%	.292/.346/.583	104	.313	0.0	C(7): 0.4	0.1
2021	NYM	MLB	27	161	16	5	1	3	13	5	44	1	0	38.0%	.222/.261/.327	75	.292	-1.8	C(52): 9.1, 3B(1): -0.0	0.9
2022 DC	*NYM*	*MLB*	*28*	*180*	*20*	*8*	*0*	*3*	*25*	*8*	*50*	*0*	*0*	*36.0%*	*.220/.265/.341*	*58*	*.293*	*-0.3*	*C 8*	*0.7*

Comparables: Sandy León, Roberto Pérez, Jesús Sucre

Nido's brief flirtation with actual hitting in 2020 was a mere one-night stand, with the harsh light of day showing him to be the same glove-first backstop he's been in his short Mets career. Not that there's anything wrong with that: Every MLB team is, after all, required by law to have a Jeff Mathis-type somewhere in the organization, and in New York, that's Nido, who finished eighth in the league in CDA. Even so, his offense reached the level of barely tolerable, keyed by too many strikeouts and not enough walks. An automatic out at the plate, he needs to keep stealing them behind it to justify a roster spot—that, or he'll have to go full Sarah Connor in *Terminator 2* to try to stop the Skynet for backup catchers that is the automatic strike zone.

YEAR	TEAM	P. COUNT	FRM RUNS	BLK RUNS	THRW RUNS	TOT RUNS
2019	SYR	1379	0.6	0.1	0.0	0.7
2019	NYM	5589	6.6	0.1	1.3	8.0
2020	NYM	1049	0.8	0.0	0.0	0.9
2021	NYM	5964	8.4	0.1	0.3	8.9
2022	*NYM*	*7215*	*7.2*	*0.9*	*0.6*	*8.7*

Brandon Nimmo RF
Born: 03/27/93 Age: 29 Bats: L Throws: R Height: 6'3" Weight: 206 lb. Origin: Round 1, 2011 Draft (#13 overall)

YEAR	TEAM	LVL	AGE	PA	R	2B	3B	HR	RBI	BB	K	SB	CS	Whiff%	AVG/OBP/SLG	DRC+	BABIP	BRR	FRAA	WARP
2019	SYR	AAA	26	44	10	2	0	1	6	8	8	3	0		.200/.364/.343	102	.231	0.0	CF(8): 0.3, LF(2): -0.2	0.2
2019	NYM	MLB	26	254	34	11	1	8	29	46	71	3	0	27.6%	.221/.375/.407	97	.293	1.0	CF(43): -0.4, LF(38): -0.3, RF(6): 0.7	1.0
2020	NYM	MLB	27	225	33	8	3	8	18	33	43	1	2	21.8%	.280/.404/.484	114	.326	-2.9	CF(44): -0.3, LF(22): -2.1, RF(10): 0.8	0.7
2021	SYR	AAA	28	36	5	1	0	0	0	5	3	0	0		.172/.333/.207	116	.192	-0.1	CF(9): -1.2	0.1
2021	NYM	MLB	28	386	51	17	3	8	28	54	79	5	4	22.7%	.292/.401/.437	111	.366	0.1	CF(84): 5.8, LF(10): -0.1	2.7
2022 DC	*NYM*	*MLB*	*29*	*497*	*92*	*21*	*3*	*12*	*56*	*69*	*100*	*6*	*3*	*22.0%*	*.262/.380/.421*	*121*	*.318*	*0.1*	*LF 0, RF 6*	*3.7*

Comparables: Josh Reddick, Dexter Fowler, Jake Marisnick

Boring consistency is as much Nimmo's hallmark as his ever-present smile and full-speed jog to first base after a walk. When healthy, he's a superb presence atop the lineup, the kind of guy who's always on first when you look up, but you never remember how he got there. At this point, expecting him to hit for more than moderate power is probably a mistake, though it's not as if he totes a noodle bat; he's just not someone who's going to reign atop the exit velocity rankings. That can't help but feel like nitpicking given that 2021 was his third season out of the last four with a .400 OBP or better. Complaining about Nimmo's production is like whining that your BMW doesn't also have wings. Another season of results like that (and ideally without another long injury absence), and he'll be one of the better—and probably more underrated—free agents next winter, if he still is one by then.

Jaylen Palmer CF
Born: 07/31/00 Age: 21 Bats: R Throws: R Height: 6'4" Weight: 208 lb. Origin: Round 22, 2018 Draft (#650 overall)

YEAR	TEAM	LVL	AGE	PA	R	2B	3B	HR	RBI	BB	K	SB	CS	Whiff%	AVG/OBP/SLG	DRC+	BABIP	BRR	FRAA	WARP
2019	KNG	ROA	18	276	41	12	2	7	28	31	108	1	3		.260/.344/.413		.434			
2021	SLU	A	20	291	51	13	4	2	24	39	81	23	5		.276/.378/.386	97	.398	0.9	3B(27): -1.2, CF(17): -0.4, 2B(11): 1.6	0.9
2021	BRK	A+	20	169	28	5	2	4	15	25	65	7	1		.189/.314/.336	79	.311	1.6	CF(27): -1.8, RF(8): -0.6, 3B(4): -0.3	0.0
2022 non-DC	*NYM*	*MLB*	*21*	*251*	*19*	*9*	*1*	*2*	*19*	*23*	*92*	*5*	*3*	*37.0%*	*.195/.275/.289*	*56*	*.317*	*0.6*	*CF 1, 3B -1*	*-0.6*

Comparables: Jeimer Candelario, Rymer Liriano, Jordan Schafer

It's fun to imagine the kind of rules changes necessary to make certain prospects into stars. What if baseball made every player rotate defensive positions each inning, home runs were worth 10 and you got to keep swinging until you put the ball in play? Palmer's jerseys would be selling out. In this universe with these sad, boring rules, Palmer remains all projection. There's thunder in his bat to go with a strong arm and plus speed on a tall, big frame, and a good feel for pitch recognition, even as he was otherwise flailing in High-A in the back half of the year. Contact is the big question offensively, and his future defensive position is up in the air, with the Mets trying him mostly at third base or in the outfield on account of his above-average arm and nearly fleet feet. The good news is there's a lot of time left for Palmer to shake out, or for the sport to transform.

Kevin Pillar OF
Born: 01/04/89 Age: 33 Bats: R Throws: R Height: 6'0" Weight: 200 lb. Origin: Round 32, 2011 Draft (#979 overall)

YEAR	TEAM	LVL	AGE	PA	R	2B	3B	HR	RBI	BB	K	SB	CS	Whiff%	AVG/OBP/SLG	DRC+	BABIP	BRR	FRAA	WARP
2019	SF	MLB	30	628	82	37	3	21	87	18	86	14	5	18.0%	.264/.293/.442	100	.275	3.9	CF(129): -11.8, RF(27): -0.0	1.7
2019	TOR	MLB	30	17	1	0	0	0	1	0	3	0	0	12.9%	.063/.059/.063	91	.071	0.0	CF(4): 0.2	0.1
2020	COL	MLB	31	97	14	5	1	2	13	5	18	4	1	24.9%	.308/.351/.451	103	.366	1.7	CF(21): -3.1, RF(1): 1.2	0.3
2020	BOS	MLB	31	126	20	7	2	4	13	8	23	1	1	25.7%	.274/.325/.470	106	.311	1.5	RF(24): 0.3, CF(6): 0.3, LF(2): 0.6	0.7
2021	NYM	MLB	32	347	40	11	2	15	47	11	81	4	3	24.7%	.231/.277/.415	94	.261	0.6	CF(57): -4.2, LF(52): -0.1, RF(22): 0.5	0.8
2022 DC	*FA*	*MLB*	*33*	*449*	*41*	*21*	*1*	*11*	*47*	*20*	*92*	*9*	*4*	*24.0%*	*.232/.280/.370*	*74*	*.273*	*0.5*	*CF -2, RF 0*	*-0.2*

Comparables: Coco Crisp, Jim Piersall, Juan Beniquez

Once a mainstay in Toronto, Pillar has spent his early-30s as the go-to backup center fielder for contenders who don't like spending too much. The problem is that Pillar at this stage is stretched in center, as his speed continues to decline with age, dragging his defensive numbers down with it. He's better suited to hold down left or right, but that creates a whole new issue: His bat is far better suited to the middle pasture than the corners. His walk-to-strikeout ratio was one of the worst in the league among players with 300 or more plate appearances, and his all-or-nothing approach didn't supply a lot of all. It's not like there's good news hiding in the peripherals, either; if anything, the batted-ball metrics think he and his .297 wOBA got off light. Like an imploded building turning to dust in a flash, collapse here seems imminent.

Alex Ramirez OF
Born: 01/13/03 Age: 19 Bats: R Throws: R Height: 6'3" Weight: 170 lb. Origin: International Free Agent, 2019

YEAR	TEAM	LVL	AGE	PA	R	2B	3B	HR	RBI	BB	K	SB	CS	Whiff%	AVG/OBP/SLG	DRC+	BABIP	BRR	FRAA	WARP
2021	SLU	A	18	334	41	15	4	5	35	23	104	16	7		.258/.326/.384	84	.376	-3.4	CF(46): 1.7, RF(22): 5.1, LF(5): -0.8	0.8
2022 non-DC	*NYM*	*MLB*	*19*	*251*	*19*	*10*	*2*	*2*	*20*	*13*	*88*	*7*	*4*	*36.8%*	*.210/.262/.309*	*51*	*.325*	*0.9*	*CF 3, RF 3*	*0.0*

Comparables: Jasson Dominguez, Carlos Tocci, Luigi Rodriguez

One thing you won't hear a lot from scouts is when a guy swings fast. It's always hard: throws hard, swings hard, tries hard. Scouts like the word hard. Ramirez, meanwhile, really whips that bat head around, though the effect is heightened by the way he coils up in his stride, pulling his front knee inward before stepping forward, his hands and even fingers busy moving until the point of contact. If all that sounds like maybe a bit too much, you're right; all those moving parts make it difficult to repeat a swing, and helps lead to Ramirez's inconsistency at the plate. Add that to the fact that he's young for his level and that his power remains theoretical, and you might be surprised to find that the result is a kid absolutely holding his own in Low-A despite it all. Ramirez will need to do some refining, but the raw material here is unquestionable. The Mets will be happy if he learns fast.

Hayden Senger C

Born: 04/03/97 Age: 25 Bats: R Throws: R Height: 6'1" Weight: 210 lb. Origin: Round 24, 2018 Draft (#710 overall)

YEAR	TEAM	LVL	AGE	PA	R	2B	3B	HR	RBI	BB	K	SB	CS	Whiff%	AVG/OBP/SLG	DRC+	BABIP	BRR	FRAA	WARP
2019	COL	A	22	353	27	21	1	4	36	25	64	0	0		.230/.324/.345	116	.275	-2.7	C(69): 5.6	2.1
2021	BRK	A+	24	47	10	5	1	2	4	3	16	0	0		.302/.362/.605	90	.440	0.1	C(9): 1.4	0.2
2021	BNG	AA	24	205	23	13	1	3	10	16	62	0	0		.254/.337/.387	82	.368	-0.5	C(44): 3.9, 1B(1): 0.2	0.7
2022 non-DC	*NYM*	*MLB*	*25*	*251*	*20*	*12*	*1*	*3*	*21*	*15*	*75*	*0*	*0*	*32.3%*	*.204/.275/.313*	*60*	*.288*	*-0.3*	*C 1, 1B 0*	*-0.1*

Comparables: Aramis Garcia, Michael McKenry, Cameron Rupp

YEAR	TEAM	P. COUNT	FRM RUNS	BLK RUNS	THRW RUNS	TOT RUNS
2019	COL	9632	4.2		1.2	5.4
2021	BNG	6397	4.2	0.0	0.1	4.3
2021	BRK	1362	0.8	-0.1	0.6	1.2
2022	*NYM*	*6956*	*1.5*	*-0.5*	*0.0*	*1.1*

Everything about Senger's profile screams "backup catcher:" He's a good defender with a strong arm, but aside from a short hot stretch in rookie ball three years ago, he's been an average-at-best hitter. He did his best to shed that label in 2021 by battering High-A, and while his Double-A stats don't stand out, he managed to draw some walks and showed a little more power than seasons previous. The glove and arm are the top tools here, though, and represent his best hope to achieve the escape velocity needed to reach the majors. And in case any grain of excitement survived reading this comment, the Mets thought so highly of him that they left him unprotected in the Rule 5 draft.

Dominic Smith LF

Born: 06/15/95 Age: 27 Bats: L Throws: L Height: 6'0" Weight: 239 lb. Origin: Round 1, 2013 Draft (#11 overall)

YEAR	TEAM	LVL	AGE	PA	R	2B	3B	HR	RBI	BB	K	SB	CS	Whiff%	AVG/OBP/SLG	DRC+	BABIP	BRR	FRAA	WARP
2019	NYM	MLB	24	197	35	10	0	11	25	19	44	1	2	26.2%	.282/.355/.525	111	.320	2.6	1B(36): -0.4, LF(32): -0.5, RF(1): -0.1	1.1
2020	NYM	MLB	25	199	27	21	1	10	42	14	45	0	0	26.0%	.316/.377/.616	111	.368	0.1	1B(25): -0.9, LF(23): -4.5	0.2
2021	NYM	MLB	26	493	43	20	0	11	58	32	112	2	1	27.7%	.244/.304/.363	81	.298	-1.1	LF(114): -6.1, 1B(15): -0.1	-0.1
2022 DC	*NYM*	*MLB*	*27*	*213*	*29*	*10*	*0*	*6*	*32*	*15*	*49*	*0*	*0*	*27.1%*	*.250/.315/.411*	*92*	*.305*	*-0.3*	*LF 0, 1B 0*	*-0.2*

Comparables: Matt Olson, Logan Morrison, Ronald Guzmán

Finally healthy enough to play a full season and entrenched as the starter in left field after two breakout half-seasons, Smith promptly went to pieces. No regular player lost more ISO than he did from 2020 to '21, with a drop of close to 200 points. His BABIP declined precipitously, too, with his batted-ball metrics all going backwards. Even his defense and baserunning, already abysmal, grew worse. And for as easy as it is to find the problems, identifying solutions is tougher. One place to start: Smith slugged a mere .381 on fastballs after slugging .593 and .577 on them in 2020 and '19, respectively. He also finished with a -31 run value—fifth-worst in the majors among qualified hitters—on pitches in the shadow part of the strike zone, aka high and low, as he was undone by an over-aggressive approach against heaters that he couldn't damage and breaking balls that he couldn't handle. Finding a way to beat the shift, which he now sees more than ever and which he posted a .265 wOBA against, wouldn't hurt either. Closing those holes would go a long way toward reestablishing him as a franchise building block; so would the NL adopting the DH, as he's borderline unplayable in left. He's got a lot of work to do.

Mark Vientos 3B

Born: 12/11/99 Age: 22 Bats: R Throws: R Height: 6'4" Weight: 185 lb. Origin: Round 2, 2017 Draft (#59 overall)

YEAR	TEAM	LVL	AGE	PA	R	2B	3B	HR	RBI	BB	K	SB	CS	Whiff%	AVG/OBP/SLG	DRC+	BABIP	BRR	FRAA	WARP
2019	COL	A	19	454	48	27	1	12	62	22	110	1	4		.255/.300/.411	111	.311	-4.9	3B(100): -2.7	1.2
2021	BNG	AA	21	306	43	16	0	22	59	26	87	0	1		.281/.346/.580	123	.327	-1.9	3B(41): -4.4, LF(12): -0.2, 1B(11): -0.1	1.1
2021	SYR	AAA	21	43	9	2	0	3	4	7	13	0	1		.278/.395/.583	110	.350	-0.1	3B(9): 1.2, LF(1): -0.1	0.3
2022 DC	*NYM*	*MLB*	*22*	*60*	*8*	*2*	*0*	*2*	*9*	*3*	*19*	*0*	*0*	*35.4%*	*.234/.294/.426*	*87*	*.313*	*-0.1*	*SS 0, 3B 0*	*0.1*

Comparables: Miguel Andújar, Austin Riley, Brandon Drury

Vientos creates a mighty wind when he swings and misses, but when he connects, the ball has a tendency to soar. That happened plenty in 2021, as he doubled his full-season high in home runs while battering Double-A pitching, and while that came with a strikeout rate hovering near 30%, it also featured his highest walk rate as a pro and more contact than previous stops. The oldest and least experienced of New York's infield prospects, Vientos is making constant adjustments to his stride and his swing, and despite his profile, he's not the kind of hitter to shut his eyes and pull. There's a real chance he reaches the majors by late 2022, though the current third baseman is more likely to debut as an outfielder and, if he's lucky, make another debut soon after as one of the National League's new designated hitters.

PITCHERS

Dellin Betances RHP

Born: 03/23/88 Age: 34 Bats: R Throws: R Height: 6'8" Weight: 265 lb. Origin: Round 8, 2006 Draft (#254 overall)

YEAR	TEAM	LVL	AGE	W	L	SV	G	GS	IP	H	HR	BB/9	K/9	K	GB%	BABIP	WHIP	ERA	DRA-	WARP	MPH	FB%	Whiff%	CSP
2019	NYY	MLB	31	0	0	0	1	0	0^{2}	0	0	0.0	27.0	2			0.00	0.00	100	0.0	94.8	62.5%	0.0%	60.2%
2020	NYM	MLB	32	0	1	0	15	0	11^{2}	12	0	9.3	8.5	11	41.2%	.353	2.06	7.71	124	0.0	93.7	45.6%	21.4%	45.8%
2021	NYM	MLB	33	0	0	0	1	0	1	0	0	9.0	9.0	1	100.0%	.000	1.00	9.00	110	0.0	92.5	57.1%	16.7%	47.2%
2022 DC	*FA*	*MLB*	*34*	*1*	*1*	*0*	*35*	*0*	*30.7*	*24*	*4*	*5.3*	*12.0*	*41*	*43.6%*	*.296*	*1.38*	*4.34*	*99*	*0.1*	*93.5*	*47.2%*	*20.6%*	*46.2%*

Comparables: John Wetteland, Craig Kimbrel, Roberto Hernandez

The five seasons that turned Betances from failed starter prospect into dominant relief ace nuked his arm in the process. After compiling 373 ⅓ innings from 2014 to '17 (the most of any reliever in that span), he's thrown a grand total of 13 ⅓ since, with a 7.43 ERA, 13 walks and a fastball that went from 98.3 mph at his peak to a thoroughly depressing 91.6 last season. Unsurprisingly, that season consisted of a single appearance in early April, followed by a trip to the IL with a right shoulder injury that turned into surgery in late June, the second time said shoulder has sidelined him in the last three years. Whatever is left of Betances—if anything is left—will be up to some enterprising and experienced training staff to resurrect.

Carlos Carrasco RHP Born: 03/21/87 Age: 35 Bats: R Throws: R Height: 6'4" Weight: 224 lb. Origin: International Free Agent, 2003

YEAR	TEAM	LVL	AGE	W	L	SV	G	GS	IP	H	HR	BB/9	K/9	K	GB%	BABIP	WHIP	ERA	DRA-	WARP	MPH	FB%	Whiff%	CSP
2019	CLE	MLB	32	6	7	1	23	12	80	92	18	1.8	10.8	96	41.0%	.357	1.35	5.29	85	1.4	93.7	46.0%	31.2%	47.6%
2020	CLE	MLB	33	3	4	0	12	12	68	55	8	3.6	10.9	82	46.2%	.294	1.21	2.91	76	1.6	93.8	39.3%	32.7%	45.3%
2021	NYM	MLB	34	1	5	0	12	12	53^{2}	59	12	3.0	8.4	50	43.2%	.299	1.43	6.04	107	0.3	93.3	50.6%	27.4%	52.2%
2022 DC	*NYM*	*MLB*	*35*	*7*	*7*	*0*	*25*	*25*	*116.3*	*114*	*17*	*2.9*	*9.2*	*119*	*43.0%*	*.308*	*1.30*	*4.22*	*101*	*0.8*	*93.6*	*45.6%*	*30.1%*	*48.8%*

Comparables: Andy Ashby, Chris Carpenter, Darryl Kile

This most recent winner of the "Met Whose Spring Training Injury Ruined His Season" award, Carrasco was delayed first by elbow soreness, then by a torn hamstring in late March that went from "he'll be back in early May" in April to "no timetable at all" in June, as is standard procedure in Queens. It took until the end of July for the veteran righty to appear in a Mets uniform, though he would've been better off going home instead, with a plunge in strikeouts and a spike in homers turning him into fifth starter flotsam. Nor was he fully healthy anyway, undergoing surgery in October to remove bone chips from that troublesome elbow. Interestingly, his velocity was pretty much the same from '20 to '21, though his spin rates took precipitous tumbles from the year prior and never bounced back. It's tempting to give Carrasco a mulligan and assume that better health will bring him back to the mid-rotation starter he was in Cleveland. It would have been a safer bet if his deal had been of the one-year variety.

Miguel Castro RHP Born: 12/24/94 Age: 27 Bats: R Throws: R Height: 6'7" Weight: 205 lb. Origin: International Free Agent, 2012

YEAR	TEAM	LVL	AGE	W	L	SV	G	GS	IP	H	HR	BB/9	K/9	K	GB%	BABIP	WHIP	ERA	DRA-	WARP	MPH	FB%	Whiff%	CSP
2019	BAL	MLB	24	1	3	2	65	0	73^{1}	63	10	5.0	8.7	71	48.3%	.269	1.42	4.66	101	0.7	97.6	49.0%	27.8%	45.0%
2020	NYM	MLB	25	1	2	0	10	0	9	11	1	8.0	14.0	14	43.5%	.455	2.11	4.00	86	0.2	98.8	55.2%	37.1%	44.5%
2020	BAL	MLB	25	1	0	1	16	0	15^{2}	17	3	2.9	13.8	24	57.5%	.378	1.40	4.02	65	0.5	98.0	47.4%	26.7%	48.8%
2021	NYM	MLB	26	3	4	0	69	2	70^{1}	48	7	5.5	9.9	77	51.4%	.241	1.29	3.45	94	0.9	98.2	43.5%	32.5%	50.3%
2022 DC	*NYM*	*MLB*	*27*	*3*	*3*	*0*	*67*	*0*	*58*	*49*	*6*	*5.0*	*10.1*	*65*	*50.1%*	*.291*	*1.40*	*4.12*	*95*	*0.4*	*98.1*	*45.8%*	*31.2%*	*48.7%*

Comparables: Arodys Vizcaíno, Jordan Lyles, Brandon League

Despite the triple-digit velocity he's capable of reaching with his four-seamer, Castro's fastball remains too hittable, and his changeup, while boasting good numbers, is reserved mostly for left-handed hitters. The slider was about the only thing that worked, with a .131 batting average against, .205 wOBA and 41.5% strikeout rate, though even that last figure was a drop from his 2020 results. Equally troubling is that the tall righty still struggles badly to throw strikes, with an ugly 14.2% walk rate, ninth-highest among qualified relievers. The heat keeps hitters from squaring him up, but it's easier and just as productive to wait Castro out and let him beat himself with his poor control or make him throw strikes. Still, that you can say all these negative things about a guy who still posted an above-average DRA– shows how valuable it can be to just not allow balls in play, unrepeatable BABIP or no. A walk every other inning is easier to swallow when you're only giving up hits two out of every three.

Jacob deGrom RHP Born: 06/19/88 Age: 34 Bats: L Throws: R Height: 6'4" Weight: 180 lb. Origin: Round 9, 2010 Draft (#272 overall)

YEAR	TEAM	LVL	AGE	W	L	SV	G	GS	IP	H	HR	BB/9	K/9	K	GB%	BABIP	WHIP	ERA	DRA-	WARP	MPH	FB%	Whiff%	CSP
2019	NYM	MLB	31	11	8	0	32	32	204	154	19	1.9	11.3	255	43.6%	.285	0.97	2.43	67	5.6	97.2	49.2%	31.9%	46.0%
2020	NYM	MLB	32	4	2	0	12	12	68	47	7	2.4	13.8	104	42.5%	.288	0.96	2.38	55	2.4	98.8	44.9%	41.0%	44.2%
2021	NYM	MLB	33	7	2	0	15	15	92	40	6	1.1	14.3	146	44.6%	.213	0.55	1.08	52	3.2	99.5	57.6%	41.7%	47.1%
2022 DC	*NYM*	*MLB*	*34*	*10*	*4*	*0*	*24*	*24*	*126.3*	*82*	*13*	*1.8*	*13.6*	*191*	*43.7%*	*.281*	*0.85*	*1.41*	*37*	*5.2*	*98.5*	*51.5%*	*38.0%*	*46.0%*

Comparables: Max Scherzer, Justin Verlander, Bob Gibson

Like Prometheus, deGrom dared steal the fire of the gods for himself, and like Prometheus, he was punished for his insolence, only instead of having his liver pecked out every day by an eagle, he had to endure the back-and-forth proclamations of "he's fine, he's not fine, no wait he's fine, no wait he's really not fine" that is the Mets' specialty. Forearm tightness and elbow discomfort cut short the two-time Cy Young winner's season and one of the most dominant stretches in MLB history. He posted a higher whiff rate than Aroldis Chapman and a strikeout rate equal to Josh Hader's in twice as many innings. Batters hit .096 with a 58.1% whiff rate on his slider, and their .160 OBP against him was only 10 points better than what pitchers put up league-wide. He averaged—*averaged*—99.1 mph on his fastball, a whopping 1.5 mph ahead of second-place Sandy Alcantara; only eight other pitchers averaged 99 or better, and they were all relievers. Few if any have slipped the surly bonds of earth to touch the face of Koufax like this, but hopefully deGrom's quest for pitcher immortality doesn't have the same grisly ending.

Edwin Díaz RHP Born: 03/22/94 Age: 28 Bats: R Throws: R Height: 6'3" Weight: 165 lb. Origin: Round 3, 2012 Draft (#98 overall)

YEAR	TEAM	LVL	AGE	W	L	SV	G	GS	IP	H	HR	BB/9	K/9	K	GB%	BABIP	WHIP	ERA	DRA-	WARP	MPH	FB%	Whiff%	CSP
2019	NYM	MLB	25	2	7	26	66	0	58	58	15	3.4	15.4	99	36.4%	.381	1.38	5.59	62	1.8	97.6	66.2%	37.9%	46.0%
2020	NYM	MLB	26	2	1	6	26	0	25^{2}	18	2	4.9	17.5	50	45.5%	.381	1.25	1.75	49	1.0	97.9	61.9%	48.2%	43.6%
2021	NYM	MLB	27	5	6	32	63	0	62^{2}	43	3	3.3	12.8	89	32.4%	.308	1.05	3.45	74	1.4	98.9	62.2%	35.1%	51.0%
2022 DC	*NYM*	*MLB*	*28*	*3*	*3*	*33*	*67*	*0*	*58*	*41*	*7*	*3.2*	*13.9*	*89*	*38.2%*	*.296*	*1.08*	*2.97*	*71*	*1.1*	*98.5*	*63.0%*	*38.2%*	*48.5%*

Comparables: Kenley Jansen, Craig Kimbrel, Gregg Olson

Of Díaz's three seasons in New York so far, one was an abject disaster, one was two months of dominant relief work and one was fine. What will the fourth be? If you're an optimistic sort, you can point to the fact that the majority of his bad numbers in 2021 came from a July in which he gave up nine runs and eight walks in 11 innings. If you're a less charitable sort, you'll point to the pedestrian (for him, anyway) 34.6% strikeout rate, 10 points off both his breakout 2018 and excellent '20. Those missing whiffs didn't turn into any extra damage, nor did they come with a drop in velocity; in fact, Díaz actually added heat to his fastball, which clocked in at 98.8 mph on average, his fastest ever. Instead, he just gave up more contact in the strike zone and got fewer swings-and-misses, particularly on his four-seamer. As is, he'll continue handling the ninth for the Mets with an eye toward breaking the bank next winter.

J.T. Ginn RHP
Born: 05/20/99 Age: 23 Bats: R Throws: R Height: 6'2" Weight: 200 lb. Origin: Round 2, 2020 Draft (#52 overall)

YEAR	TEAM	LVL	AGE	W	L	SV	G	GS	IP	H	HR	BB/9	K/9	K	GB%	BABIP	WHIP	ERA	DRA-	WARP	MPH	FB%	Whiff%	CSP
2021	SLU	A	22	2	1	0	8	8	38^{2}	26	3	2.3	8.1	35	57.4%	.237	0.93	2.56	78	0.9				
2021	BRK	A+	22	3	4	0	10	10	53^{1}	49	0	2.0	7.8	46	64.2%	.308	1.14	3.38	96	0.6				
2022 non-DC	*NYM*	*MLB*	*23*	*2*	*2*	*0*	*57*	*0*	*50*	*53*	*4*	*3.4*	*6.3*	*34*	*53.8%*	*.303*	*1.44*	*4.55*	*109*	*0.0*				

Comparables: Spencer Howard, Kyle Kendrick, Brad Bergesen

After a torn UCL suffered the spring before the 2020 Draft robbed Ginn of his first year with the Mets, the ex-Mississippi State product finally made it to a mound last season and appeared intact, showing good control in two stops of A ball. Most importantly, his fastball velocity was in the 91–95 mph range he displayed in college. Still, the lingering command issues of TJS rehab blurred an already blurry set of secondaries, as his cutter, slider and curve had a habit of blending in with each other. The key now will be as many innings as he can handle in '22 to allow him to continue to sharpen those pitches and stretch himself out as a starter—one with mid-rotation upside if all goes to plan.

Robert Gsellman RHP
Born: 07/18/93 Age: 28 Bats: R Throws: R Height: 6'4" Weight: 200 lb. Origin: Round 13, 2011 Draft (#402 overall)

YEAR	TEAM	LVL	AGE	W	L	SV	G	GS	IP	H	HR	BB/9	K/9	K	GB%	BABIP	WHIP	ERA	DRA-	WARP	MPH	FB%	Whiff%	CSP
2019	NYM	MLB	25	2	3	1	52	0	63^{2}	64	7	3.3	8.5	60	43.6%	.317	1.37	4.66	95	0.8	95.4	51.7%	26.4%	46.9%
2020	NYM	MLB	26	0	0	0	6	4	14	22	4	5.1	5.8	9	41.5%	.367	2.14	9.64	128	-0.1	93.8	64.0%	16.9%	44.9%
2021	NYM	MLB	27	0	1	0	17	1	28^{2}	27	3	2.2	5.3	17	47.8%	.270	1.19	3.77	107	0.2	94.1	62.8%	21.7%	52.9%
2022 DC	*FA*	*MLB*	*28*	*2*	*3*	*0*	*57*	*0*	*49.3*	*52*	*5*	*3.2*	*7.1*	*39*	*46.9%*	*.312*	*1.42*	*4.75*	*112*	*-0.1*	*94.5*	*58.9%*	*22.5%*	*49.2%*

Comparables: Randall Delgado, David Pauley, Chad Kuhl

The Mets have used Gsellman in just about every pitching role possible—starter, closer, opener, multi-inning swingman—all with the same result: not much. That continued to be the case in 2021, as did his unfortunate run of injuries; this time, he was knocked out for three months by a mid-June lat strain. That makes it three straight years in which he's spent a significant chunk of the season on the injured list, but when he has been available, he hasn't been of much use anyway, with a 5.08 ERA and meager 18.4% strikeout rate over that span. It's safe to assume Gsellman rejected the organization's latest bid to make him a third baseman or bench coach or public address announcer in 2022, after which they non-tendered him early in the offseason.

Brad Hand LHP
Born: 03/20/90 Age: 32 Bats: L Throws: L Height: 6'3" Weight: 224 lb. Origin: Round 2, 2008 Draft (#52 overall)

YEAR	TEAM	LVL	AGE	W	L	SV	G	GS	IP	H	HR	BB/9	K/9	K	GB%	BABIP	WHIP	ERA	DRA-	WARP	MPH	FB%	Whiff%	CSP
2019	CLE	MLB	29	6	4	34	60	0	57^{1}	53	6	2.8	13.2	84	27.2%	.364	1.24	3.30	85	1.1	92.7	46.0%	30.7%	50.5%
2020	CLE	MLB	30	2	1	16	23	0	22	13	0	1.6	11.9	29	26.5%	.265	0.77	2.05	101	0.2	91.6	48.1%	24.8%	51.9%
2021	NYM	MLB	31	1	0	0	16	0	13^{1}	12	1	3.4	9.4	14	48.6%	.324	1.28	2.70	90	0.2	92.7	62.0%	22.8%	53.3%
2021	WAS	MLB	31	5	5	21	41	0	42^{2}	31	5	3.8	8.9	42	40.2%	.239	1.15	3.59	103	0.3	93.2	56.1%	19.8%	56.6%
2021	TOR	MLB	31	0	2	0	11	0	8^{2}	13	3	3.1	5.2	5	30.3%	.333	1.85	7.27	119	0.0	93.1	56.7%	22.2%	57.1%
2022 DC	*FA*	*MLB*	*32*	*3*	*3*	*0*	*71*	*0*	*61.7*	*56*	*9*	*3.2*	*9.3*	*63*	*38.2%*	*.292*	*1.27*	*4.23*	*101*	*0.2*	*92.8*	*53.8%*	*23.3%*	*54.3%*

Comparables: Tyler Clippard, Jon Rauch, Jeremy Affeldt

It's not unfair to suggest that Hand was 2021's single most impactful player. But how?

The veteran lefty cruises through the first three months of the season, including nine scoreless innings in April. He unintentionally walks a mere nine hitters of 143 faced. He posts 18 saves. ... In July, he wobbles. He takes a loss in his final outing ahead of the All-Star break. The week after the break is worse. Hand only gets two outs combined in his next two outings, blowing two saves and pushing the Nationals out of the playoff race completely. The Nats blow it up, trading Trea Turner and Max Scherzer. End of an era. ... Hand is dealt to the Toronto Blue Jays. He pitches 11 times for Toronto. He allows 10 runs. He is tagged with two losses and one blown save. He is designated for assignment. The Blue Jays miss the playoffs by one game. End of a dream. ... Hand finishes his year with the Mets. He acquits himself nicely, pitching to a 2.70 ERA in 16 games. The Mets go 5-11 in those games. They sit within shouting distance when he joins the team, just three games out of first. They finish a distant 11 ½ games behind eventual champs Atlanta. The Mets later, in a cosmic realignment rarely seen in professional sports, sign Scherzer to one of the most lucrative free agent deals ever awarded on a per year basis. Beginning of the end.

And here you were thinking Hand was just an aging lefty reliever with declining swing and miss rates.

Joey Lucchesi LHP
Born: 06/06/93 Age: 29 Bats: L Throws: L Height: 6'5" Weight: 225 lb. Origin: Round 4, 2016 Draft (#114 overall)

YEAR	TEAM	LVL	AGE	W	L	SV	G	GS	IP	H	HR	BB/9	K/9	K	GB%	BABIP	WHIP	ERA	DRA-	WARP	MPH	FB%	Whiff%	CSP
2019	SD	MLB	26	10	10	0	30	30	163^{2}	144	23	3.1	8.7	158	46.6%	.274	1.22	4.18	102	1.5	90.4	64.7%	25.6%	46.0%
2020	SD	MLB	27	0	1	0	3	2	5^{2}	13	0	3.2	7.9	5	37.5%	.542	2.65	7.94	103	0.1	89.9	65.0%	31.6%	47.7%
2021	NYM	MLB	28	1	4	0	11	8	38^{1}	34	4	2.6	9.6	41	38.2%	.313	1.17	4.46	96	0.4	91.3	63.3%	23.8%	57.7%
2022 DC	*NYM*	*MLB*	*29*	*2*	*2*	*0*	*44*	*0*	*38.7*	*36*	*5*	*2.9*	*9.3*	*40*	*42.2%*	*.300*	*1.27*	*4.06*	*98*	*0.3*	*90.7*	*64.2%*	*25.2%*	*50.8%*

Comparables: Josh Collmenter, Alex Wood, Francisco Liriano

Sometimes the universe is in on the joke, and putting a guy named "Joey Lucchesi" on a New York team is the universe leaning fully into the punchline. It's fun to imagine a season where he broke out as a star with the Mets; imagine a dugout celebration of pinched Italian chef fingers and kisses and Gary Cohen exclaiming "Mamma mia!" after every strikeout. But to the dismay of every Rocco, Tony and Sal in the tri-state area, such feats from a paisan didn't come to pass: on the way to his best season so far, the lefty blew out his elbow in mid-June. That'll keep him sidelined likely through 2022, which is unfortunate timing both for a team that could use him as rotation depth and for a player who is just entering the arbitration phase of his career. To quote Silvio Dante, it's anti-Italian discrimination.

Seth Lugo RHP Born: 11/17/89 Age: 32 Bats: R Throws: R Height: 6'4" Weight: 225 lb. Origin: Round 34, 2011 Draft (#1032 overall)

YEAR	TEAM	LVL	AGE	W	L	SV	G	GS	IP	H	HR	BB/9	K/9	K	GB%	BABIP	WHIP	ERA	DRA-	WARP	MPH	FB%	Whiff%	CSP
2019	NYM	MLB	29	7	4	6	61	0	80	56	8	1.8	11.7	104	43.4%	.267	0.90	2.70	71	2.1	94.4	56.8%	26.6%	52.1%
2020	NYM	MLB	30	3	4	3	16	7	36^2	40	8	2.5	11.5	47	50.5%	.344	1.36	5.15	71	1.0	93.4	55.4%	30.1%	48.1%
2021	NYM	MLB	31	4	3	1	46	0	46^1	41	6	3.7	10.7	55	41.7%	.307	1.29	3.50	87	0.7	94.0	54.1%	31.0%	56.3%
2022 DC	*NYM*	*MLB*	*32*	*3*	*3*	*4*	*74*	*0*	*64.7*	*55*	*8*	*3.1*	*10.1*	*72*	*44.4%*	*.288*	*1.19*	*3.39*	*85*	*0.8*	*94.0*	*55.2%*	*29.6%*	*53.0%*

Comparables: Tim Worrell, Stan Williams, David Phelps

It seems as if the Mets have made up their mind on Lugo; once he returned from elbow surgery in June, the Mets installed him into the bullpen and left him there despite the rotation's midsummer collapse. That's been his home for most of his career, and he settled back in like he never left, though as more of a short-outing traditional reliever than the multi-inning swingman he's been in the past. Part and parcel of that success was more of his signature high-spin curveball, which he tossed at its highest rate since 2018. Coupled with fastball velocity that remains steady in the 93–95 mph range, that was enough for Lugo to be one of New York's more efficient relievers; take out a five-run disaster against Pittsburgh in July, which couldn't have been real, and his ERA would've been a sparkling 2.56. The batted ball peripherals are less rosy about his season, and a reliable third pitch remains frustratingly out of reach, with neither his sinker nor slider functioning as anything other than a weak change of pace. Those problems stand out less in short bursts, and with free agency on the horizon, it's unlikely that he'll chafe at the newfound stability.

Trevor May RHP Born: 09/23/89 Age: 32 Bats: R Throws: R Height: 6'5" Weight: 240 lb. Origin: Round 4, 2008 Draft (#136 overall)

YEAR	TEAM	LVL	AGE	W	L	SV	G	GS	IP	H	HR	BB/9	K/9	K	GB%	BABIP	WHIP	ERA	DRA-	WARP	MPH	FB%	Whiff%	CSP
2019	MIN	MLB	29	5	3	2	65	0	64^1	43	8	3.6	11.1	79	34.2%	.233	1.07	2.94	91	1.0	95.7	62.9%	30.1%	47.3%
2020	MIN	MLB	30	1	0	2	24	0	23^1	20	5	2.7	14.7	38	25.5%	.326	1.16	3.86	86	0.4	96.6	51.7%	43.0%	45.3%
2021	NYM	MLB	31	7	3	4	68	0	62^2	55	10	3.4	11.9	83	35.8%	.302	1.26	3.59	80	1.2	96.7	60.3%	32.7%	54.3%
2022 DC	*NYM*	*MLB*	*32*	*3*	*3*	*4*	*67*	*0*	*58*	*48*	*9*	*3.4*	*11.7*	*75*	*35.4%*	*.296*	*1.22*	*3.71*	*89*	*0.5*	*96.5*	*59.5%*	*33.7%*	*51.4%*

Comparables: Liam Hendriks, Jeremy Jeffress, Matt Wise

In 2020, May's fastball did one of two things: get swung on and missed, or get blasted to hell. His four-seamer had an ugly .575 slugging percentage against despite a whiff rate of 46.9%—the fourth-highest rate among all pitchers that year. In 2021, he pulled off an even weirder trick: He threw his fastball 10% more and lost nearly 15 points of whiff rate but also shed 200 points of slugging. Location played a big role in that, with May working the upper half of the strike zone more often, allowing his fastball's high spin and velocity—96.5 mph on average—to produce pop flies and whiffs and better set up his slider. Even with a loss of strikeouts, it's a recipe for success, or at least for another season of good results in the late innings.

Tylor Megill RHP Born: 07/28/95 Age: 26 Bats: R Throws: R Height: 6'7" Weight: 230 lb. Origin: Round 8, 2018 Draft (#230 overall)

YEAR	TEAM	LVL	AGE	W	L	SV	G	GS	IP	H	HR	BB/9	K/9	K	GB%	BABIP	WHIP	ERA	DRA-	WARP	MPH	FB%	Whiff%	CSP
2019	COL	A	23	3	2	2	14	3	31	23	1	4.4	11.9	41	33.3%	.314	1.23	2.61	85	0.5				
2019	STL	A+	23	3	4	0	7	7	35^2	36	1	2.5	10.6	42	52.5%	.350	1.29	4.04	92	0.6				
2021	BNG	AA	25	2	1	0	5	5	26	21	1	2.4	14.5	42	58.2%	.370	1.08	3.12	73	0.6				
2021	SYR	AAA	25	0	0	0	3	3	14^1	11	2	3.1	10.7	17	48.6%	.257	1.12	3.77	101	0.2				
2021	NYM	MLB	25	4	6	0	18	18	89^2	88	19	2.7	9.9	99	42.8%	.301	1.28	4.52	81	1.7	94.7	57.6%	26.0%	56.3%
2022 DC	*NYM*	*MLB*	*26*	*8*	*6*	*0*	*22*	*22*	*117.7*	*105*	*14*	*3.1*	*9.5*	*125*	*44.3%*	*.297*	*1.24*	*3.59*	*89*	*1.6*	*94.7*	*57.6%*	*26.0%*	*56.3%*

Comparables: A.J. Griffin, JT Brubaker, Chris Stratton

A reliever in college, Megill was flipped to the rotation in 2019 in High-A and has stuck as a starter since. The whiffs made the trip with him to the majors, though he also discovered a new nemesis: the dinger. It took nine MLB starts to match the nine he gave up over his entire minor-league career. Still, there's a lot to like here: a fastball that zips in at 95 mph, two useful secondaries and better command than he showed in the minors. If anything, he could stand to work on the edges and outside a little bit more, and adding either more bite or sweep to his slider, or more run or sink to his changeup, would help there. There's room for him to grow, and a pitching-starved Mets team can definitely use him as a plug-and-play fifth starter as he develops. Like Megilla Gorilla, he'll try again next week.

Eric Orze RHP Born: 08/21/97 Age: 24 Bats: R Throws: R Height: 6'4" Weight: 195 lb. Origin: Round 5, 2020 Draft (#150 overall)

YEAR	TEAM	LVL	AGE	W	L	SV	G	GS	IP	H	HR	BB/9	K/9	K	GB%	BABIP	WHIP	ERA	DRA-	WARP	MPH	FB%	Whiff%	CSP
2021	BRK	A+	23	1	2	1	13	0	20	19	2	2.7	11.7	26	41.5%	.333	1.25	4.05	76	0.4				
2021	BNG	AA	23	2	0	4	11	0	17^1	12	2	0.5	13.0	25	52.6%	.278	0.75	2.60	83	0.3				
2021	SYR	AAA	23	1	0	0	10	0	12^1	7	1	5.1	11.7	16	29.6%	.240	1.14	2.19	88	0.2				
2022 non-DC	*NYM*	*MLB*	*24*	*2*	*2*	*0*	*57*	*0*	*50*	*45*	*7*	*3.5*	*9.9*	*55*	*40.6%*	*.298*	*1.31*	*4.17*	*100*	*0.2*				

Comparables: Shawn Armstrong, Kyle McGrath, Jason Bergmann

Orze is the kind of story you love to see. Two separate cancer diagnoses kept him off the field sporadically throughout his college career, but he showed enough in his senior year to get tabbed in the fifth round of the truncated 2020 draft by the Mets, who turned him into a full-time reliever. Armed with a 94-95 mph fastball and a plus splitter, he blazed his way up the minor-league ladder, posting excellent strikeout numbers coupled with exceptional command. His profile is a one-inning reliever with big swing-and-miss potential, armed with an earned sense of toughness and perspective to which no pressure situation on the mound could compare.

David Peterson LHP Born: 09/03/95 Age: 26 Bats: L Throws: L Height: 6'6" Weight: 240 lb. Origin: Round 1, 2017 Draft (#20 overall)

YEAR	TEAM	LVL	AGE	W	L	SV	G	GS	IP	H	HR	BB/9	K/9	K	GB%	BABIP	WHIP	ERA	DRA-	WARP	MPH	FB%	Whiff%	CSP
2019	BNG	AA	23	3	6	0	24	24	116	119	9	2.9	9.5	122	52.0%	.342	1.34	4.19	88	1.6				
2020	NYM	MLB	24	6	2	0	10	9	49^{2}	36	5	4.3	7.2	40	44.2%	.233	1.21	3.44	113	0.2	92.3	53.2%	26.2%	44.5%
2021	NYM	MLB	25	2	6	0	15	15	66^{2}	64	11	3.9	9.3	69	47.3%	.310	1.40	5.54	100	0.6	92.8	58.6%	25.5%	52.7%
2022 DC	*NYM*	*MLB*	*26*	*6*	*5*	*0*	*40*	*11*	*71*	*65*	*8*	*3.8*	*9.0*	*71*	*47.9%*	*.297*	*1.34*	*4.15*	*98*	*0.6*	*92.6*	*56.9%*	*25.7%*	*50.0%*

Comparables: Framber Valdez, Jordan Montgomery, Adam Conley

Inside every lefty with middling velocity but good command and control are two wolves. One is 2020 David Peterson, who sprang out of the Mets' farm system as a fully-formed fifth starter, generating lots of weak contact with a fastball that averaged just 92.1 mph. The other is 2021 David Peterson, who was battered non-stop before a broken toe put an end to his season in July. Part of the problem was his decision to showcase his sinker, nearly doubling its usage rate. That was a mistake: Batters annihilated that pitch, with a .507 slugging percentage and .390 wOBA. The margin for error when you throw 92 is perilously thin, and it becomes practically nonexistent when you keep serving up sinkers that don't drop. For Peterson to straddle successfully the divide between a useful back-end starter and a poor man's J.A. Happ, he'll need to take a lesson from his summer replacement, Trevor Williams, or at least the one wolf of his.

Jake Reed RHP Born: 09/29/92 Age: 29 Bats: R Throws: R Height: 6'2" Weight: 195 lb. Origin: Round 5, 2014 Draft (#140 overall)

YEAR	TEAM	LVL	AGE	W	L	SV	G	GS	IP	H	HR	BB/9	K/9	K	GB%	BABIP	WHIP	ERA	DRA-	WARP	MPH	FB%	Whiff%	CSP
2019	ROC	AAA	26	5	3	0	45	1	75	75	7	4.2	11.0	92	42.8%	.366	1.47	5.76	84	1.6				
2021	SL	AAA	28	0	0	1	8	0	10^{2}	13	1	5.1	14.3	17	48.1%	.480	1.78	8.44	84	0.1				
2021	SYR	AAA	28	0	1	0	8	0	8	7	1	2.3	9.0	8	40.9%	.286	1.13	4.50	97	0.1				
2021	OKC	AAA	28	0	0	0	9	0	10^{1}	12	1	0.9	9.6	11	33.3%	.393	1.26	2.61	90	0.1				
2021	LAD	MLB	28	0	0	0	6	1	5^{1}	5	1	3.4	8.4	5	35.3%	.267	1.31	3.38	95	0.1	87.2	31.0%	27.5%	51.9%
2021	NYM	MLB	28	0	1	0	4	0	4^{2}	5	0	0.0	9.6	5	42.9%	.357	1.07	3.86	78	0.1	88.0	43.4%	26.5%	59.6%
2022 DC	*NYM*	*MLB*	*29*	*2*	*2*	*0*	*52*	*0*	*45.3*	*44*	*6*	*3.4*	*8.9*	*44*	*39.1%*	*.304*	*1.34*	*4.50*	*106*	*0.0*	*87.8*	*36.9%*	*27.0%*	*55.5%*

Comparables: Jimmy Cordero, Cory Gearrin, Steven Okert

Reed's arsenal and approach are interesting enough that both the Dodgers and Rays took a shot on him when he hit waivers during the season, only for each to cough him back up due to roster crunches; that feat alone is almost worthy of a certificate, albeit an awkward-looking one. His stint with the Mets—his fourth organization in 2021—was equally short, owing to a strained forearm, but what he showed is plenty intriguing. His sinker floats in at 88 mph, but his drop-down sidearm delivery makes it tough for batters to pick up as it dives and burrows inside. His slider, meanwhile, mirrors that sinker before swerving outside at the last second, à la Darren O'Day's breaker. The total package is hell on righties, and gives Reed a ceiling far higher than you'd expect from a late-summer waiver wire claim.

Sean Reid-Foley RHP Born: 08/30/95 Age: 26 Bats: R Throws: R Height: 6'3" Weight: 230 lb. Origin: Round 2, 2014 Draft (#49 overall)

YEAR	TEAM	LVL	AGE	W	L	SV	G	GS	IP	H	HR	BB/9	K/9	K	GB%	BABIP	WHIP	ERA	DRA-	WARP	MPH	FB%	Whiff%	CSP
2019	BUF	AAA	23	3	5	0	20	19	89	78	13	6.6	10.6	105	43.0%	.294	1.61	6.47	104	0.9				
2019	TOR	MLB	23	2	4	0	9	6	31^{2}	33	5	6.0	8.0	28	42.4%	.298	1.71	4.26	127	-0.1	92.7	50.2%	23.9%	46.3%
2020	TOR	MLB	24	1	0	0	5	0	6^{2}	3	0	8.1	8.1	6	61.1%	.167	1.35	1.35	92	0.1	94.5	61.7%	30.0%	35.7%
2021	SYR	AAA	25	0	0	0	10	0	11^{1}	5	1	4.0	15.1	19	35.0%	.211	0.88	2.38	79	0.3				
2021	NYM	MLB	25	2	1	0	12	0	20^{2}	22	3	3.9	11.3	26	36.8%	.352	1.50	5.23	91	0.3	93.9	62.8%	28.9%	55.6%
2022 DC	*NYM*	*MLB*	*26*	*2*	*2*	*0*	*52*	*0*	*45.3*	*40*	*7*	*5.2*	*10.4*	*52*	*40.6%*	*.295*	*1.46*	*4.84*	*108*	*0.0*	*93.6*	*58.8%*	*27.5%*	*50.1%*

Comparables: Randall Delgado, Robert Gsellman, Lucas Sims

Some words in the English language are pretty dumb: cleave, for example, means both to join two things and split them, which is just a terrible idea. For pitchers, the same is true with the word "predictable." Case in point: Reid-Foley's season was a tale of two call-ups. From April 22 to May 29, he pitched 13.1 innings out of the Mets' bullpen and was untouchable, striking out 20 against four walks with a .558 OPS against. Sent down to Triple-A for two weeks, he came back in mid-June and was shelled, surrendering 12 runs and five walks in seven innings with just six whiffs. A right elbow strain brought an early end to the year and was probably partially behind that stumble, but those results are fitting for a pitcher with good stuff but who is allergic to the very idea of consistency. Nobody really sets out to be a predictable person, but bosses and managers very much appreciate it.

Antonio Santos RHP Born: 10/06/96 Age: 25 Bats: R Throws: R Height: 6'3" Weight: 223 lb. Origin: International Free Agent, 2015

YEAR	TEAM	LVL	AGE	W	L	SV	G	GS	IP	H	HR	BB/9	K/9	K	GB%	BABIP	WHIP	ERA	DRA-	WARP	MPH	FB%	Whiff%	CSP
2019	LAN	A+	22	3	6	0	18	18	99^{1}	116	11	1.6	8.7	96	39.3%	.349	1.35	4.35	104	0.1				
2019	HFD	AA	22	3	3	0	8	8	45^{2}	47	3	2.0	8.7	44	38.2%	.338	1.25	4.93	100	0.4				
2020	COL	MLB	23	0	1	0	3	1	6	14	1	6.0	6.0	4	36.0%	.542	3.00	16.50	147	-0.1	93.2	59.4%	11.7%	46.1%
2021	ABQ	AAA	24	0	5	0	34	2	45^{1}	54	10	5.4	6.4	32	41.3%	.314	1.79	7.94	112	-0.2				
2021	COL	MLB	24	0	1	0	7	0	11^{1}	9	1	4.0	7.9	10	41.9%	.267	1.24	4.76	100	0.1	95.7	63.1%	18.3%	53.4%
2022 DC	*NYM*	*MLB*	*25*	*1*	*1*	*0*	*29*	*0*	*25.7*	*29*	*4*	*4.0*	*6.8*	*19*	*40.5%*	*.308*	*1.57*	*5.86*	*131*	*-0.3*	*94.9*	*61.8%*	*16.1%*	*51.0%*

Comparables: Jesus Tinoco, Zeke Spruill, Ryan Webb

Santos never quite fought his way through the thin air of Colorado's prospect echelon, getting passed on the mountain route by other, younger arms. After what can only be assumed was a lengthy and smoke-filled ceremony performed in a dead language, Santos was formally reclassified from a starter to a reliever. A late-inning guy at Triple-A for most of 2021, he was also a frequent leave-with-head-bowed-after-allowing-runs guy. The Rockies removed him from the 40-man in November, leading the Mets to look at his 96-mph fastball (or perhaps his one remaining major league option) and pounce.

Junior Santos RHP Born: 08/16/01 Age: 20 Bats: R Throws: R Height: 6'7" Weight: 244 lb. Origin: International Free Agent, 2018

YEAR	TEAM	LVL	AGE	W	L	SV	G	GS	IP	H	HR	BB/9	K/9	K	GB%	BABIP	WHIP	ERA	DRA-	WARP	MPH	FB%	Whiff%	CSP
2019	KNG	ROA	17	0	5	0	14	14	40^2	46	4	5.5	8.0	36	30.8%	.333	1.75	5.09						
2021	SLU	A	19	6	6	0	21	16	96	108	8	3.6	7.4	79	50.0%	.339	1.52	4.59	109	0.5				
2022 non-DC	*NYM*	*MLB*	*20*	*2*	*3*	*0*	*57*	*0*	*50*	*60*	*7*	*4.7*	*5.4*	*30*	*43.3%*	*.314*	*1.73*	*6.51*	*141*	*-0.9*				

Comparables: Jeff D'Amico, Blake Beavan, Nate Cornejo

Apparently in a bid to turn him into Senior Santos, the Mets have been aggressive with Junior from the get-go, allowing him to pitch in the Gulf Coast League at 16 years old and then pushing him to the Appalachian League the next year to face college-age hitters. The absence of a 2020 season didn't slow New York's roll, with Santos, now 19, sent to Low-A, where the average hitter had three or four years on him. A giant who still isn't old enough to buy himself a beer, he needs to continue working on his command, control and secondaries; his hard fastball isn't enough to conquer leagues on its own. He might also benefit from the Mets taking the foot off the gas and letting him taste some sustained success before moving up a level.

Max Scherzer RHP Born: 07/27/84 Age: 37 Bats: R Throws: R Height: 6'3" Weight: 208 lb. Origin: Round 1, 2006 Draft (#11 overall)

YEAR	TEAM	LVL	AGE	W	L	SV	G	GS	IP	H	HR	BB/9	K/9	K	GB%	BABIP	WHIP	ERA	DRA-	WARP	MPH	FB%	Whiff%	CSP
2019	WAS	MLB	34	11	7	0	27	27	172^1	144	18	1.7	12.7	243	40.8%	.322	1.03	2.92	66	4.9	95.0	48.2%	33.9%	48.3%
2020	WAS	MLB	35	5	4	0	12	12	67^1	70	10	3.1	12.3	92	33.0%	.355	1.38	3.74	79	1.5	94.9	46.0%	32.6%	48.0%
2021	WAS	MLB	36	8	4	0	19	19	111	71	18	2.3	11.9	147	33.1%	.235	0.89	2.76	71	2.7	94.3	48.3%	35.6%	52.8%
2021	LAD	MLB	36	7	0	0	11	11	68^1	48	5	1.1	11.7	89	34.9%	.269	0.82	1.98	71	1.7	94.6	44.1%	32.3%	54.2%
2022 DC	*NYM*	*MLB*	*37*	*12*	*7*	*0*	*29*	*29*	*177.7*	*136*	*25*	*2.1*	*11.4*	*225*	*34.3%*	*.277*	*1.00*	*2.65*	*68*	*4.4*	*94.6*	*46.9%*	*34.0%*	*51.3%*

Comparables: Bob Gibson, Gaylord Perry, Don Sutton

In 2021, Scherzer set a record that he very much did not want. In 63 trips to the plate, he did not reach base, breaking Wei-Yin Chen's prior record of 49 plate appearances in 2016. Scherzer was fairly good among pitchers at putting the ball in play this year - his 44% strikeout rate was better than average - but he never hit the ball with authority, posting a .077 xwOBA. Given that those were likely the last days of pitchers stepping up to the plate, it seems probable that this record will never be broken. Oh, and Scherzer also posted his career-best ERA, went on one of the best post-trade hot streaks in modern history, recorded his first professional save in the closing innings of a winner-take-all NLDS Game 5 and added yet another Hall of Fame-quality bullet point to his Hall of Fame-quality resume. Just don't count on his bat being on that plaque.

Drew Smith RHP Born: 09/24/93 Age: 28 Bats: R Throws: R Height: 6'2" Weight: 190 lb. Origin: Round 3, 2015 Draft (#99 overall)

YEAR	TEAM	LVL	AGE	W	L	SV	G	GS	IP	H	HR	BB/9	K/9	K	GB%	BABIP	WHIP	ERA	DRA-	WARP	MPH	FB%	Whiff%	CSP
2020	NYM	MLB	26	0	1	0	8	0	7	6	2	2.6	9.0	7	35.0%	.222	1.14	6.43	103	0.1	95.4	46.8%	39.3%	42.1%
2021	NYM	MLB	27	3	1	0	31	1	41^1	28	7	3.5	8.9	41	34.0%	.212	1.06	2.40	102	0.3	95.1	56.2%	29.1%	55.3%
2022 DC	*NYM*	*MLB*	*28*	*3*	*3*	*0*	*67*	*0*	*58*	*54*	*8*	*3.3*	*9.3*	*60*	*36.9%*	*.298*	*1.30*	*4.31*	*103*	*0.1*	*95.1*	*55.2%*	*30.2%*	*53.9%*

Comparables: Bryan Morris, Justin Berg, Nick Goody

Here's a fun fact: Among the 40 relievers with a strikeout rate under 25% and at least 40 innings thrown in 2021, Smith's BABIP is the lowest of the bunch. That makes his success feel fluky, and the peripherals mostly agree. What keeps him afloat is the 95-mph fastball he spins at the top of the zone, with an 88-mph cutter as a change of pace. The latter leaks into the heart of the plate too often, though, and the search for a viable third pitch remains ongoing. The ingredients are here for a middle-inning reliever who you can't fully trust, especially since he's already sucked you in with the good season.

Taijuan Walker RHP Born: 08/13/92 Age: 29 Bats: R Throws: R Height: 6'4" Weight: 235 lb. Origin: Round 1, 2010 Draft (#43 overall)

YEAR	TEAM	LVL	AGE	W	L	SV	G	GS	IP	H	HR	BB/9	K/9	K	GB%	BABIP	WHIP	ERA	DRA-	WARP	MPH	FB%	Whiff%	CSP
2019	ARI	MLB	26	0	0	0	1	1	1	1	0	0.0	9.0	1	33.3%	.333	1.00	0.00			93.3	66.7%	20.0%	43.3%
2020	TOR	MLB	27	2	1	0	6	6	26^1	22	3	3.8	8.5	25	39.5%	.260	1.25	1.37	108	0.2	93.3	54.1%	21.0%	46.7%
2020	SEA	MLB	27	2	2	0	5	5	27	21	5	2.7	8.3	25	36.8%	.225	1.07	4.00	103	0.3	93.2	46.1%	20.0%	51.3%
2021	NYM	MLB	28	7	11	0	30	29	159	133	26	3.1	8.3	146	41.9%	.254	1.18	4.47	96	1.7	94.4	57.1%	23.6%	56.7%
2022 DC	*NYM*	*MLB*	*29*	*8*	*7*	*0*	*25*	*25*	*129.3*	*124*	*19*	*3.2*	*8.2*	*117*	*41.8%*	*.292*	*1.32*	*4.30*	*103*	*0.9*	*94.2*	*55.8%*	*23.0%*	*55.2%*

Comparables: Edwin Jackson, Dan Petry, Brett Myers

In the first half of 2021, Walker was arguably the best Mets pitcher not named deGrom or Stroman, putting up a 2.66 ERA with 95 strikeouts in 94 ⅔ innings and making the team look brilliant for scooping him up on a two-year deal for just $20 million with a player option. In the second half, he was arguably the worst pitcher in the entire world, with a 7.13 ERA in 64 ⅓ innings, just 51 strikeouts and 20 homers allowed. Most of that was the fault of a truly awful July in which opposing batters slashed a ridiculous .293/.396/.573, or just about what Fernando Tatis Jr. hit on the season as a whole. Perhaps some of that was fatigue, as Walker threw more innings in the first half alone than he had since 2017 (and since Tommy John surgery cratered his '18 and '19), and his spin rates continued to plummet long after the crackdown. The Mets believed the issue was his fastball command, and too many heaters in the middle of the plate. Whatever the problem, neither he nor the team can afford another crash like that.

Trevor Williams RHP Born: 04/25/92 Age: 30 Bats: R Throws: R Height: 6'3" Weight: 235 lb. Origin: Round 2, 2013 Draft (#44 overall)

YEAR	TEAM	LVL	AGE	W	L	SV	G	GS	IP	H	HR	BB/9	K/9	K	GB%	BABIP	WHIP	ERA	DRA-	WARP	MPH	FB%	Whiff%	CSP
2019	PIT	MLB	27	7	9	0	26	26	145^2	162	27	2.7	7.0	113	36.9%	.308	1.41	5.38	114	0.4	91.5	66.7%	22.3%	47.8%
2020	PIT	MLB	28	2	8	0	11	11	55^1	66	15	3.4	8.0	49	43.3%	.315	1.57	6.18	116	0.1	91.5	51.1%	24.3%	42.6%
2021	IOW	AAA	29	1	0	0	2	2	7	2	0	1.3	6.4	5	60.0%	.111	0.43	0.00	99	0.1				
2021	SYR	AAA	29	1	0	0	2	2	12	9	1	1.5	7.5	10	38.2%	.242	0.92	2.25	101	0.2				
2021	NYM	MLB	29	0	0	0	10	3	32^1	37	1	2.5	8.1	29	42.2%	.367	1.42	3.06	91	0.4	91.2	62.9%	25.3%	49.9%
2021	CHC	MLB	29	4	2	0	13	12	58^2	68	10	3.4	9.4	61	46.6%	.345	1.53	5.06	90	0.8	91.4	56.0%	23.6%	54.2%
2022 DC	*NYM*	*MLB*	*30*	*8*	*5*	*0*	*65*	*6*	*79.7*	*80*	*11*	*2.8*	*7.7*	*68*	*43.4%*	*.302*	*1.32*	*4.34*	*104*	*0.4*	*91.4*	*58.8%*	*23.7%*	*49.2%*

Comparables: Dick Drago, James Baldwin, Brandon McCarthy

In flagrant violation of the law that states that all soft-tossing pitchers with a dry sense of humor and knowledge of dank memes must be lefties, Williams goes against god and nature by throwing with his right hand. Still, he maintains the traditional orthodoxy of his ancestors, painting corners and getting lit up when he fails to paint corners, and he enjoyed at least on a rate basis his finest season, though the basic numbers only caught up after his midseason trade. Right or left, New York or Chicago, Williams is consistent: Either he's throwing five scoreless innings while you spend the whole time wondering, "How the hell is he getting away with this," or he's getting lit up for seven runs in three innings as you say to yourself, "That's more like it."

Calvin Ziegler RHP Born: 10/03/02 Age: 19 Bats: R Throws: R Height: 6'0" Weight: 205 lb. Origin: Round 2, 2021 Draft (#46 overall)

Passed over in the 2020 draft despite being Canada's best amateur pitcher, Ziegler followed the path of his nation's elders and moved to Florida, where he was snatched up as a second-rounder last summer. Right now, his claim to fame is being the underslot sign that allowed the Mets room to pay Kumar Rocker, which...well. He throws a hard mid-90s fastball that touches 97, but everything else is under construction, including a breaker that's neither slider nor curveball, a touch-and-go changeup and his control. Pardon his dust as he develops.

LINEOUTS

Hitters

HITTER	POS	TEAM	LVL	AGE	PA	R	2B	3B	HR	RBI	BB	K	SB	CS	AVG/OBP/SLG	DRC+	BABIP	BRR	FRAA	WARP
Albert Almora Jr.	CF	SYR	AAA	27	169	24	6	0	6	18	13	18	2	5	.270/.331/.428	116	.269	-1.7	CF(35): 5.2, LF(3): 0.3, RF(2): -0.1	1.3
	CF	NYM	MLB	27	54	3	3	0	0	0	2	17	0	0	.115/.148/.173	69	.171	0.2	CF(32): 1.3, LF(3): -0.1, RF(1): -0.0	0.2
Travis Blankenhorn	UT	SYR	AAA	24	193	22	10	0	9	30	29	53	3	2	.255/.373/.484	106	.320	-2.9	2B(29): 1.2, LF(17): -1.1, 1B(5): 0.4	0.5
	UT	NYM	MLB	24	24	3	2	0	1	4	1	8	0	0	.174/.208/.391	84	.214	0.2	2B(5): -0.3, LF(1): -0.0, RF(1): -0.0	0.0
	UT	MIN	MLB	24	0	1	0	0	0	0	0	0	0	0	.000/.000/.000				2B(1): -0.0	0.0
Carlos Cortes	OF	SRR	WIN	24	67	7	2	1	0	5	10	18	0	1	.236/.358/.309		.342			
	OF	BNG	AA	24	346	50	26	1	14	57	35	85	1	2	.257/.332/.487	110	.305	-1.6	LF(47): 11.1, RF(17): 0.1	2.4
Brandon Drury	3B	SYR	AAA	28	236	28	14	0	9	32	19	49	0	0	.257/.318/.449	107	.291	-1.9	3B(23): -1.4, 1B(17): 0.5, 2B(10): -1.0	0.5
	3B	NYM	MLB	28	88	7	5	0	4	14	3	22	0	0	.274/.307/.476	96	.328	-0.4	3B(7): -0.2, LF(6): -0.2, RF(6): -0.5	0.1
José Martínez	RF	LAG	WIN	32	78	9	2	0	0	4	6	11	0	0	.300/.359/.329		.350			
	RF	SYR	AAA	32	42	6	2	0	3	6	4	8	0	0	.263/.333/.553	112	.259	-0.9	RF(10): 5.8	0.6
Cameron Maybin	CF	SYR	AAA	34	49	5	2	0	0	5	5	14	0	0	.182/.265/.227	86	.267	0.2	LF(8): -0.4	0.1
	CF	IOW	AAA	34	43	5	1	0	1	3	4	14	1	0	.103/.186/.205	92	.125	0.7	LF(9): -1.2	0.1
	CF	NYM	MLB	34	33	2	0	0	0	0	3	12	1	0	.036/.182/.036	75	.063	0.1	CF(6): -0.6, LF(4): -0.1, RF(3): 0.1	0.0
Patrick Mazeika	C	SYR	AAA	27	180	22	9	0	7	33	17	19	0	0	.280/.356/.471	123	.276	-1.2	C(22): -0.2, 1B(14): -0.5	0.9
	C	NYM	MLB	27	87	6	3	0	1	6	4	18	0	0	.190/.253/.266	78	.230	0.1	C(24): 2.7, 1B(1): -0.0	0.4
José Peraza	2B	SYR	AAA	27	39	5	2	0	0	4	2	2	1	0	.270/.308/.324	106	.286	0.3	2B(4): 0.7, CF(4): 0.1, 3B(2): 0.2	0.3
	2B	NYM	MLB	27	154	21	7	0	6	20	9	26	1	0	.204/.266/.380	102	.209	-0.1	2B(36): 0.6, 3B(9): -0.2, LF(1): -0.0	0.6
Nick Plummer	OF	SPR	AA	24	376	52	17	4	13	46	53	108	9	8	.283/.404/.489	110	.393	-0.1	LF(33): -5.0, CF(33): -2.5, RF(17): -0.4	0.8
	OF	MEM	AAA	24	102	19	3	2	2	8	20	18	4	1	.267/.455/.440	126	.327	1.1	LF(20): -0.8, CF(4): -0.4, RF(1): -0.2	0.6
JT Schwartz	1B	SLU	A	21	100	9	5	0	0	8	13	12	2	0	.195/.320/.256	118	.222	0.7	1B(24): 2.0	0.7

The average pitcher hit .110/.150/.142 last season; you could argue that the Mets would've been better off sending Jacob deGrom to the plate any time **Albert Almora Jr.** was due to step in. The former no. 6 pick has hit rock bottom offensively, and his glove, while solid, would have to be prime Willie Mays to carry his bat. He's a fifth outfielder at best at this point. ⚾ In late April, **Travis Blankenhorn**, freshly called up from the minors, appeared in a game against the A's as a pinch-runner, scored the go-ahead run, stayed in to play defense, and botched a double play, helping to turn a win into a loss. Two days later, he was sent down to Triple-A, then designated for assignment, then claimed by the Dodgers, then DFA'd again, then claimed by the Mariners, then DFA'd a third time before ending up with the Mets, where he contributed zero before being demoted a final time in late July. Ironically, that last flight is what brought him home; the Syracuse Mets are a three-hour drive from Blankenhorn's hometown of Pottsville, PA. ⚾ In his move up to Double-A (and out of the pitcher-friendly Florida State League), **Carlos Cortes** traded some contact for power, and his second base glove for an outfielder's version. Both adaptations will serve him well, as he looks to establish himself as a bat-first utility player; 30 years ago, when men were men and benches were spacious, his ambidextrous sparkplug profile would have made him a good bet for a ten-year career. ⚾ Every summer, a deep and long run of injuries turns the Mets into a combination of itinerant trauma ward and random 2010s baseball card generator. That's how you end up with **Brandon Drury**, who resurfaced in New York and put up superficially strong numbers that, in actuality, were built on a BABIP wave, some home run luck, and a short hot stretch in late July. ⚾ "**José Martínez**, Rays designated hitter" felt like it was written in the stars long ago, but that dream pairing ended after a month's worth of mediocre plate appearances. Robbed of his destiny, he signed with New York, only to suffer the fate the Mets bestow on their players: a season-ending injury in spring training. ⚾ Bought off the Cubs in May for literally a dollar, it took **Cameron Maybin** 33 plate appearances to notch his first hit for his eighth team in the last four years. He never got another one: another hit, or even another major-league at-bat. At least the Mets let him go out on top. ⚾ Heroes and third catchers grow from arid fields. So it was for **Patrick Mazeika**: Within a week of being called up, he had two walk-offs on zero hits—a pair of grounders that turned into RBI fielder's choices. He'll always have those back-to-back nights of being stripped to the waist and doused with water and rosin powder. ⚾

José Peraza would be a perfectly fine baseball player if hitting were outlawed. Now in the itinerant backup infielder phase of his career, he proved yet again with the Mets that his bat might as well be a pool skimmer, but at least he's stopped waving it around quite so often, to the benefit of his OBP. ⚾ Late-blooming outfielder **Nick Plummer** hit his share of pipe shots at the top two levels of the minors last year after making a swing adjustment to keep his bat in the zone longer. Appropriately, a team playing in Flushing gave him a big-league contract to see if the power and patience will flow in Citi Field, a surprisingly aggressive move on a 25-year-old who's yet to make his MLB debut. ⚾ Up until the moment he swings, **JT Schwartz** looks like a prototypical hitter. He shows an excellent eye at the plate, drawing more walks than strikeouts in both his redshirt sophomore season at UCLA and his minor-league debut. And so far, that's pretty much it.

Pitchers

PITCHER	TEAM	LVL	AGE	W	L	SV	G	GS	IP	H	HR	BB/9	K/9	K	GB%	BABIP	WHIP	ERA	DRA-	WARP	MPH	FB%	WHF	CSP
Jose Butto	BRK	A+	23	1	4	0	12	12	58^1	51	11	2.3	9.3	60	44.1%	.267	1.13	4.32	90	0.8				
	BNG	AA	23	3	2	0	8	8	40^1	33	6	2.0	11.2	50	42.7%	.284	1.04	3.12	86	0.6				
Yennsy Díaz	SYR	AAA	24	0	3	1	15	0	17^1	14	5	4.7	9.9	19	23.5%	.209	1.33	6.75	98	0.3				
	NYM	MLB	24	0	2	0	20	0	25	25	5	4.3	7.6	21	32.1%	.274	1.48	5.40	115	0.0	95.6	64.2%	23.1%	53.5%
Jerad Eickhoff	SYR	AAA	30	9	2	0	16	16	79^2	80	17	2.3	8.9	79	41.2%	.299	1.26	4.86	96	1.2				
	NYM	MLB	30	0	2	0	5	4	19^2	30	9	4.6	5.9	13	29.5%	.304	2.03	8.69	138	-0.2	90.2	48.7%	17.7%	53.2%
Heath Hembree	NYM	MLB	32	0	0	1	15	0	15^2	13	2	2.9	8.6	15	36.4%	.262	1.15	3.45	105	0.1	95.4	55.6%	27.1%	54.4%
	CIN	MLB	32	2	7	8	45	0	42^1	32	10	4.0	14.5	68	23.3%	.275	1.20	6.38	77	0.9	95.5	51.3%	28.1%	52.6%
Franklyn Kilome	SYR	AAA	26	3	3	1	21	5	46	34	5	5.7	7.8	40	34.1%	.242	1.37	3.91	117	0.2				
Stephen Nogosek	SYR	AAA	26	1	5	6	27	0	35	35	2	4.1	13.4	52	28.1%	.379	1.46	5.14	81	0.8				
	NYM	MLB	26	0	1	0	1	0	3	3	2	0.0	15.0	5	28.6%	.200	1.00	6.00	76	0.1	93.9	62.5%	29.2%	57.0%
Adam Oller	BNG	AA	26	5	3	0	15	15	76	66	8	3.4	11.3	95	47.2%	.310	1.25	4.03	84	1.3				
	SYR	AAA	26	4	1	0	8	8	44	27	1	3.7	8.8	43	34.2%	.241	1.02	2.45	95	0.7				
Corey Oswalt	SYR	AAA	27	1	1	2	6	2	13	12	4	2.1	10.4	15	31.4%	.258	1.15	4.15	97	0.2				
	NYM	MLB	27	1	1	0	3	1	10^1	12	1	1.7	8.7	10	20.0%	.379	1.35	3.48	107	0.1	92.3	55.8%	32.2%	51.4%
Robert Stock	IOW	AAA	31	0	3	0	9	2	19^2	17	4	1.8	11.4	25	25.5%	.277	1.07	4.12	97	0.3				
	SYR	AAA	31	1	0	0	4	4	15^2	16	1	4.6	8.0	14	46.7%	.341	1.53	2.87	111	0.1				
	NYM	MLB	31	0	1	0	2	2	5	6	2	5.4	10.8	6	42.9%	.333	1.80	5.40	103	0.0	96.0	56.2%	32.5%	52.1%
	CHC	MLB	31	0	1	0	1	1	4	4	1	13.5	6.8	3	41.7%	.273	2.50	11.25	123	0.0	95.6	92.4%	18.5%	40.1%
Thomas Szapucki	SYR	AAA	25	0	4	0	10	9	41^2	42	5	6.0	8.9	41	36.1%	.322	1.68	4.10	114	0.3				
	NYM	MLB	25	0	0	0	1	0	3^2	7	2	7.4	9.8	4	38.5%	.455	2.73	14.73	120	0.0	91.0	68.3%	29.0%	50.4%
Josh Walker	BRK	A+	26	3	0	0	4	4	21	14	1	1.7	9.9	23	36.5%	.255	0.86	2.57	105	0.1				
	BNG	AA	26	5	1	0	8	7	44^1	32	3	1.4	8.5	42	41.3%	.246	0.88	2.64	106	0.2				
	SYR	AAA	26	1	3	0	9	9	50^1	43	5	3.2	5.9	33	40.6%	.255	1.21	5.19	116	0.3				
Jordan Yamamoto	SLU	A	25	0	0	0	3	3	9	4	0	1.0	8.0	8	52.2%	.174	0.56	1.00	95	0.1				
	SYR	AAA	25	0	3	0	7	6	22^2	27	7	2.8	7.9	20	34.7%	.308	1.50	5.96	111	0.2				
	NYM	MLB	25	1	1	0	2	1	6^2	10	0	2.7	4.1	3	26.9%	.385	1.80	4.05	114	0.0	88.7	63.1%	14.8%	59.5%

The next professional game that **Matt Allan** appears in will be his first in three years; the pandemic wiped out his 2020, and Tommy John surgery cost him all of '21. We'll see if he manages to pitch next year, or if the writers start getting desperate for new ideas and throw a typhoon at him. ⚾ A bit of a surprise 40-man addition ahead of the 2021 Rule 5 draft, **Jose Butto** has a minor-league track record of throwing strikes, turning over lineups with relative ease despite the lack of a reliable third offering. That he pulled it off in Double-A means they might even be good strikes. ⚾ Bad control has plagued **Yennsy Díaz** throughout his minor-league career with Toronto, and nothing about that changed when he was shipped to New York in exchange for Steven Matz. His 95-mph fastball will play, but only if he knows where it's going. ⚾ Like a visibly cursed Egyptian sarcophagus filled with a distressing brown goop, **Jerad Eickhoff** should never have been unearthed from whatever grave the Mets found him in. (The Rangers' alternate site, to be exact.) After he put up maybe the worst multi-inning stretch of any pitcher in the majors in 2021, odds are that other teams will let his rest be eternal. ⚾ Last summer's third-round pick, **Dominic Hamel** boasts the standard profile of a back-end starter or late-inning reliever. ⚾ **Heath Hembree** gave up more home runs in 2021 than Corbin Burnes, in a quarter of the innings. The veteran righthand actually didn't allow many baserunners, but that's cold comfort when practically every one of them ended up scoring. ⚾ Even when the Mets were so desperate for pitchers during the summer that they signed the likes of Jerad Eickhoff and Anthony Banda, **Franklyn Kilome** could only watch from Triple-A, where he spent the entire season. That's what happens when your strikeout and walk rates are nearly identical. ⚾ Pity **Stephen Nogosek**: bombed in '19 and a ghost at the alternate site in '20, he suddenly racked up tons of strikeouts in Triple-A to start the year and earned another shot in the majors. He struck out five in three innings…and then went on the injured list the next day with a shoulder strain that took too long to heal. ⚾ **Adam Oller** can sling it up to 95 mph early in starts, but usually sits below that, with an average slider, serviceable changeup and fringe cutter. He's entering his late 20s, but could emerge as a viable eighth or ninth starter on the depth chart. ⚾ **Corey Oswalt** is a good barometer of how a Mets season is going: if he's up, that means the pitching staff is in absolute shambles. True to form, he popped up in late June and did his usual thing, tossing a dozen or innings and breaking a mirror while trying to catch his pet black cat as it chased a flock of ravens. ⚾ **Robert Stock** is a reliably funny and self-deprecating presence on Twitter, who signed with the Doosan Bears of the KBO. ⚾ Despite the rough year, **Thomas Szapucki** is still a potential middle reliever. But then, we're all potential middle relievers; it's just a matter of finding out for which level. ⚾ **Josh Walker** is a 37th-rounder out of a Division II school who suffered nerve damage in his throwing arm in a 2019 car accident, making him one of the unlikeliest potential big-leaguers in a while. He also threw strikes in Triple-A, so he's got a shot of making it. ⚾ **Jordan Yamamoto** has now had two straight seasons ruined by arm troubles. Already with his third organization, he can't afford another.

PHILADELPHIA PHILLIES

Essay by Dan McQuade

Player comments by Brian Menéndez and BP staff

You sometimes see delayed steals. You rarely witness a delayed stop. In the ninth inning of a one-run game, Nationals catcher Alex Avila pulled out of his crouch. Phillies pinch-runner Travis Jankowski froze. Avila sprinted at him. As Avila advanced, ball raised, Jankowski feinted left. He feinted right. But he was stuck to the spot, as if fastened to the ground. One may as well accept one's destiny. Avila marched forward in a straight path, finally tagging the hapless Jankowski himself, 120 feet away from the plate. 2-unassisted. Avila was pretty confused by the whole situation: "You don't see it too much here, because, typically, the runner will take off one way or the other, and you get rid of the ball."

But the Phillies cannot not be weird. It is baked into their essence, imbued into the ligaments, in the space between their atoms. They are not without talent. They are not without heroes. But if baseball is an endless weave of narratives, crisscrossing and colliding, the Phillies are a found poem made out of sunflower seeds, musical intros to 1970s TV cop shows and discarded bits of software code. They're like trying to read words in a dream. They're a handful of magnesium thrown on an open flame. That we even have a proper name to describe them feels unholy; it should just be a sound outside the range that humans can hear.

Sometimes, the Phillies win baseball games. Sometimes, they lose them. These days, at the ends of seasons, they usually seem to have done about the same number of each, no matter how magisterial the individual performances. It's getting harder to remember that it wasn't always like this, that the stars used to result in a team that did star stuff.

⚾ ⚾ ⚾

Alec Bohm hit it square and lined a hanging slider into center field. Rhys Hoskins rounded third and beat the throw easily to give the Phillies the lead. In the top of the ninth, erratic Phillies closer Héctor Neris came onstage to play the hits, walking two, but got Travis d'Arnaud to fly out to right fielder Bryce Harper to end it. The Phillies beat the Braves, 2-1 and swept their season-opening three-game series.

PHILADELPHIA PHILLIES PROSPECTUS

2021 W-L: 82-80, 2ND IN NL EAST

Pythag	.493	16th	DER	.690	23rd
RS/G	4.53	13th	DRC+	94	20th
RA/G	4.60	16th	DRA-	91	6th
dWin%	.534	12th	FIP	4.08	11th
Payroll	$191M	4th	B-Age	29.7	26th
M$/MW	$5.2M	23rd	P-Age	29.2	24th

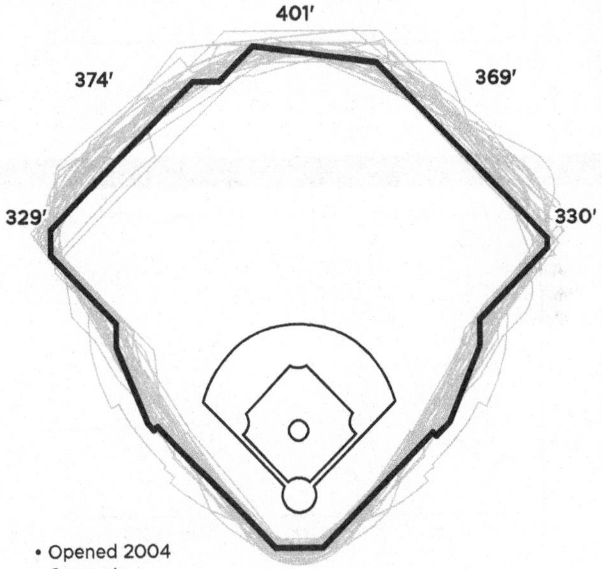

- Opened 2004
- Open air
- Natural surface
- Fence profile: 6' to 19'

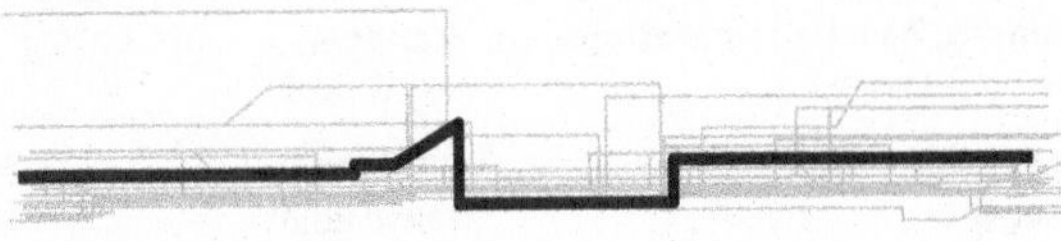

Park Factors

Runs	Runs/RH	Runs/LH	HR/RH	HR/LH
101	102	100	109	101

Top Hitter WARP	5.4 Bryce Harper
Top Pitcher WARP	5.5 Zack Wheeler
Top Prospect	Mick Abel

Payroll History (in millions)

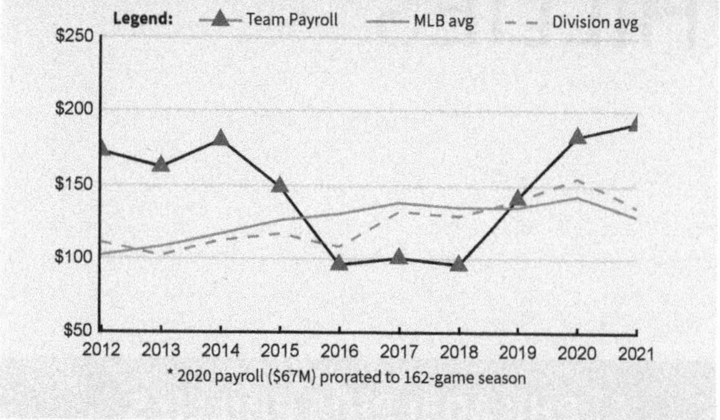

Future Commitments (in millions)

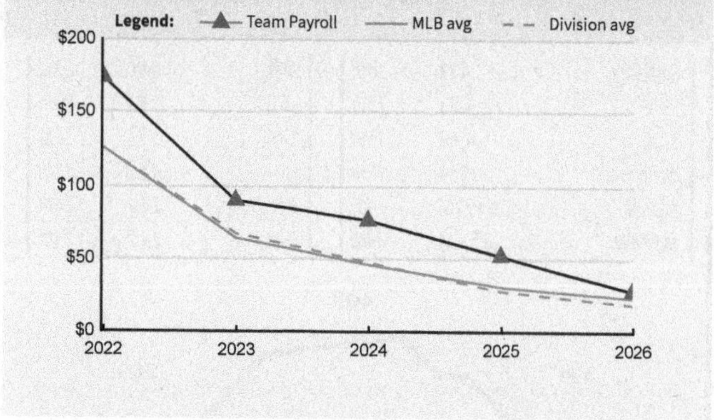

Farm System Ranking

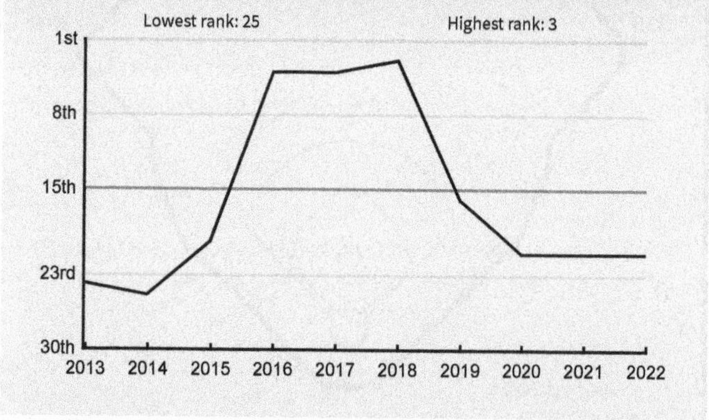

Personnel

President, Baseball Operations
Dave Dombrowski

Vice President, General Manager
Sam Fuld

Assistant General Manager
Ned Rice

Assistant General Manager
Jorge Velandia

Assistant General Manager
Anirudh Kilambi

Manager
Joe Girardi

BP Alumni
Lewie Pollis
Alex Rosen

Over the course of that series, Phillies starters Aaron Nola, Zack Wheeler and Zach Eflin combined for 20 ⅔ innings, struck out 24 and walked one. The year before, the Phillies had the worst bullpen ERA by any team since 1930; over those three days, Philadelphia's relievers pitched 7 ⅓ scoreless innings.

"Last year, we struggled in these type of games," manager Joe Girardi said postgame. "It gives us confidence moving forward. But there's a long way to go, but it's better than the alternative. Every game counts. April is just as important as any other month."

The 2021 Phillies would actually start 4-0. In their fourth game, they were stymied by Mets ace Jacob deGrom. In 2020, that would've been all she wrote, but, on this occasion, they scored five runs after he was pulled. They did all this without Bryce Harper registering an extra-base hit. Logic, a fraught deal with the Phillies, promised that he'd get going.

Things changed quite a bit after early-April. As expected, Harper went on a tear. After getting hurt and slumping in May, he had one of the best offensive stretches in Phillies history over the summer. His OPS in July was 1.023. In August, it was 1.231. In September, 1.157. Harper started the year so slow that he wasn't even an All-Star. But he finished with the best slugging percentage (.615) and OPS (1.044) in the majors. He led MLB in doubles with 42. He hit 35 homers and walked 100 times. He won NL MVP.

Wheeler, too, ascended. He was second in the Cy Young voting, getting as many first-place votes as winner Corbin Burnes of the Brewers. Wheeler went 14-10 with a 2.78 ERA. His 213 ⅓ innings pitched, 247 strikeouts, three complete games and two shutouts all led the league. No pitcher (who only pitched) had more WARP, and the only players who did were a trio of MVP candidates (Vladdy, Soto, Shohei).

And yet, the Phillies did not have a great season. The team the Phillies swept to open the season swept them back on September 30 to clinch the National League East. The Braves, completely remade by trades after injuries decimated their outfield, won the World Series in six games. Travis d'Arnaud, the guy who lined out to end the opening-season sweep, caught every inning of the postseason for Atlanta. Those Braves series were a frame befitting the Phillies' 10th consecutive season without a playoff appearance, a decade during which their status has dropped off steeply from that of a 100-win, star-studded, annually championship-contending club. The broad shapes of stars are there—an MVP outfielder, a Cy Young runner-up ace—but how it comes together is all wrong.

Ten years ago, *Sports Illustrated* sent Gary Smith, dean of the longform sportswriters, to Philadelphia several times to chronicle the Phillies' season. Smith filed multiple dispatches about how incredible it was that the Phillies were ruling Philadelphia. Here he is following around Cliff Lee:

"Cliff blinks. Is he at work already? Scores of them are dressed like his workmates, down to the very names on the backs of their shirts—why, there's HALLADAY and ROLLINS and HOWARD and UTLEY and look, even two of him, two LEEs. There's a young woman from Russia entering Barnes & Noble with his company's logo tattooed on her neck . . . and a white-haired lawyer hurrying his briefcase and deposition back to an office whose desk, shelves and walls have vanished under Phillies keepsakes . . . and that old man in a Phillies hat with a Phillies key-chain necklace who comes here every afternoon to feed the birds on his way to whisper his prayers at St. Patrick's . . . and that beefy guy in a Phillies cap who sets up his chessboard behind the Lion Crushing a Serpent sculpture every day and challenges passersby to play for cash, which Cliff would love to do because he loves playing anything for cash and playing chess till his opponents whimper—but he can't. Cliff Lee's going to work."

A good paragraph. But also a time capsule of just how wild the city was for the Phillies when they won five division titles, two pennants and a World Series over five seasons from 2007—11. Was it a dynasty? Not quite, as much as Philadelphia would like to believe. But it was an incredible run. They better build statues of Jimmy Rollins and Ryan Howard and Chase Utley and Cole Hamels. Hell, throw in Matt Stairs. Prior to that run, the Phillies were losers of 10,000-plus games, the team whose management stars Curt Schilling and Scott Rolen pretty much rightly trashed when leaving town, a team with faceless owners, one of whom bought into the team in part to get good parking spaces for Eagles games. *Sports Illustrated* once named Philadelphia the most overrated sports city, in part because nobody went to Phillies games. Then came that run, and *SI* was running multi-part features about how devout Phillies fans were.

"Go ahead, ask all the Brotherly Lovers, every last one, and they'll tell you they'll always remember exactly where and how they found out about two events in their lives that stirred totally opposite emotions," Smith wrote. "The two airplanes striking the World Trade Center . . . and Cliff Lee choosing them."

Look, even the best sportswriter can go a little over the top sometimes. But the return of Cliff Lee to Philadelphia did seem like a monumental event at the time. There was a stretch when the Phillies got a *ton* of big-name players. Lee came in a trade and returned in free agency. Roy Halladay, Roy Oswalt, Brad Lidge and Hunter Pence all came in trades. Only Lidge was part of a World Series win, but the team was perennially *right there*: aspirant in spring, rolling all summer, dangerous in the fall. Lee caught World Series pop-ups like prime Eastwood; Halladay fired a playoff no-no. If they never did quite get dynastic, they nevertheless felt like one of the two most powerful teams in baseball.

Now . . . do people even remember where they were when the Phillies signed Cliff Lee? Does anyone even care? The 2011 season, after Lee's return, was truly magical, until the Phillies lost in the first round of the playoffs. Ryan Howard's torn Achilles on the final play of the Division Series was a very literal break from one era of Phillies baseball to the next. The Phillies still make big moves—J.T. Realmuto, Wheeler, Harper—and those moves have paid off handsomely, on the individual level. But the team's pattern has shifted: aspirant in the spring, puzzling in the summer, glum by fall.

The Phillies' 82-80 record in 2021 was their first winning mark since they won 102 games 10 years prior. Harper has boosted attendance back above the 30,000-fan level. But that's still 10,000 short of the franchise's high-water mark and good for only ninth out of 15 NL teams in 2021. Philadelphians have the ballclub on a prove-it deal—show us you're more than a couple gaudy names—and the team, as yet, hasn't.

A sampling of things that happened to the 2021 Phillies: A year after having the worst bullpen since Herbert Hoover was president, the team flirted with the record for blown saves . . . and couldn't even get it! (The Nationals broke it, instead, with 36.) Aaron Nola struck out 10-straight batters in late June, tying the record, then pitched to a 5.30 ERA the rest of the way. Rhys Hoskins opened the season coming off UCL-brace surgery and suffered a season-ending abdominal tear in August. Vince Velasquez had a 6.05 ERA in 18 starts, argued with a fan while getting onto the team bus and, eventually, got cut. (He had a 8.53 ERA in four starts for the Padres afterward.) Bohm, who knocked in the winning run to complete the series-opening sweep, got demoted to the minors. With their playoff life on the line in September, the Phillies went 15 innings before notching a single run against the Baltimore Orioles. They did end up winning that series, at least. Woohoo!

Before the lockout, the Phillies did manage one small step back in the direction of legitimacy. For two seasons, the team had been using a fake Phillie Phanatic. In 2019, the Phillies sued Wayde Harrison and Bonnie Erickson, the Phanatic's creators, alleging the pair was looking to reclaim the Phanatic's rights due to a provision in copyright law, and the pair countersued. To dance around the copyright issue, the Phillies mangled their mascot: He had a reshaped nose, tassel-ier hair and stars behind his eyes. He sported a blue tail and some sort of scales on his arms.

Derivative Works Exception Phanatic was around in 2020, but, without fans, it didn't really matter. But once they returned to the park, fans let it be known that they phreaking hated this phugazi Phanatic. At one game, I actually heard him get booed. The Phillie Phanatic got booed! Fortunately, the Phillies opened their wallet for the cause and settled with Harrison and Erickson in December. The true Phanatic is back. Whether he's a harbinger of a decade-old golden era or the dour years that followed, that remains to be seen. Armed with basic pattern-recognition, and buoyed less than I used to be by hope, I have my guess.

—Dan McQuade is a co-founder of Defector, *and the site's video and multimedia editor.*

Hitters

Alec Bohm 3B Born: 08/03/96 Age: 25 Bats: R Throws: R Height: 6'5" Weight: 218 lb. Origin: Round 1, 2018 Draft (#3 overall)

YEAR	TEAM	LVL	AGE	PA	R	2B	3B	HR	RBI	BB	K	SB	CS	Whiff%	AVG/OBP/SLG	DRC+	BABIP	BRR	FRAA	WARP
2019	SCO	WIN	22	78	6	6	0	2	9	5	16	0	1		.361/.397/.528		.436			
2019	LWD	A	22	93	13	9	0	3	11	12	14	3	0		.367/.441/.595	153	.406	-0.8	3B(14): -0.6, 1B(5): -0.1	0.7
2019	CLR	A+	22	177	25	10	3	4	27	17	21	1	2		.329/.395/.506	141	.358	0.5	3B(25): 1.2, 1B(7): 0.6	1.6
2019	REA	AA	22	270	38	11	1	14	42	28	38	2	2		.269/.344/.500	138	.265	-0.9	3B(44): 0.1, 1B(12): -0.7	1.7
2020	PHI	MLB	23	180	24	11	0	4	23	16	36	1	1	25.2%	.338/.400/.481	111	.410	-0.3	3B(38): 1.2, 1B(7): -1.0	0.6
2021	LHV	AAA	24	68	8	5	0	1	6	7	15	3	1		.271/.353/.407	99	.341	0.2	3B(12): 0.1, 1B(3): -0.5	0.2
2021	PHI	MLB	24	417	46	15	0	7	47	31	111	4	0	26.5%	.247/.305/.342	81	.327	-0.3	3B(103): -6.3, 1B(7): 0.2	-0.2
2022 DC	*PHI*	*MLB*	*25*	*493*	*68*	*21*	*1*	*14*	*71*	*40*	*113*	*3*	*2*	*25.1%*	*.251/.318/.401*	*93*	*.308*	*-0.4*	*3B -1, 1B 0*	*0.8*

Comparables: Ryan Braun, Cody Asche, Chris Johnson

We'll avoid the temptation to say that the Phillies' second-year man Bohmed—it's a bit tautological, anyway—but suffice it to say last season was a bit of a shocker for the Wichita State alum. His explosive debut from 2020 was built upon an unsustainable .410 BABIP, and while Bohm still hits the ball quite hard—he was in the 89th percentile for average exit velocity and 90th percentile in hard-hit rate—he fires them straight into the ground. His launch angle last year was an unhelpful 5.6 degrees, which itself was a bump up from 2020's 4.8 figure. Bohm's BABIP was still .327, a healthy 35 points above the league average, but his slash line cratered in response to the dip. Entering the season the questions were much more about whether his bat could make up for his glove, so watching his stick detonate like this is an ominous sign to say the least, and it even earned him a month-long demotion at the end of August. His glovework didn't balance out the step-back on offense, either, and it's possible that a move down the defensive spectrum is in his near future. For now, the Phillies seem likely to give Bohm another shot both at third base and in the lineup for lack of better options. Encouraging aspects of his profile remain intact, but he should add an uppercut if he doesn't want to undercut his chances of sticking long term.

Luis García MI Born: 10/01/00 Age: 21 Bats: S Throws: R Height: 5'11" Weight: 170 lb. Origin: International Free Agent, 2017

YEAR	TEAM	LVL	AGE	PA	R	2B	3B	HR	RBI	BB	K	SB	CS	Whiff%	AVG/OBP/SLG	DRC+	BABIP	BRR	FRAA	WARP
2019	LWD	A	18	524	36	14	3	4	36	44	132	9	8		.186/.261/.255	76	.247	-4.1	SS(72): -0.5, 2B(55): -5.6	-1.0
2021	CLR	A	20	395	57	16	5	11	42	54	93	11	6		.246/.356/.423	113	.307	-0.8	SS(57): -0.9, 2B(30): -1.8	1.4
2021	JS	A+	20	70	6	2	0	2	8	10	19	4	0		.224/.333/.362	105	.289	0.6	SS(11): -0.7, 2B(4): -0.4	0.2
2022 non-DC	*PHI*	*MLB*	*21*	*251*	*20*	*9*	*1*	*3*	*21*	*21*	*70*	*5*	*3*	*26.6%*	*.202/.276/.308*	*57*	*.275*	*0.5*	*SS 0, 2B -1*	*-0.6*

Comparables: Dawel Lugo, Cole Tucker, Chris Owings

Garcia's calling cards are a solid glove and plus arm that are both good enough to keep him at shortstop in the long term. He wasn't supposed to hit for a lot of power, but the 20-year-old broke out for 13 homers in 2021 in 465 A-ball plate appearances. He appeared to get stronger as the year went on, stroking as many hard-hit balls in August as he did in June and July combined. Coming off a .516 OPS in 2019, the 250 point boost certainly restored some luster to his prospect status.

Didi Gregorius SS Born: 02/18/90 Age: 32 Bats: L Throws: R Height: 6'3" Weight: 205 lb. Origin: International Free Agent, 2007

YEAR	TEAM	LVL	AGE	PA	R	2B	3B	HR	RBI	BB	K	SB	CS	Whiff%	AVG/OBP/SLG	DRC+	BABIP	BRR	FRAA	WARP
2019	NYY	MLB	29	344	47	14	2	16	61	17	53	2	1	22.9%	.238/.276/.441	95	.237	0.9	SS(80): -7.2	0.4
2020	PHI	MLB	30	237	34	10	2	10	40	15	28	3	2	19.0%	.284/.339/.488	108	.285	1.0	SS(59): -4.5	0.6
2021	PHI	MLB	31	408	35	16	2	13	54	25	67	3	0	24.6%	.209/.270/.370	85	.217	-1.1	SS(101): -3.0	0.3
2022 DC	*PHI*	*MLB*	*32*	*525*	*71*	*21*	*2*	*17*	*84*	*37*	*84*	*5*	*2*	*23.5%*	*.242/.307/.407*	*92*	*.261*	*0.0*	*SS -2*	*1.3*

Comparables: Jimmy Rollins, Tony Fernandez, Alan Trammell

In 1997 Bad Boy Records released *Mo Money Mo Problems* by Notorious B.I.G. The problems for Gregorius D.I.D.(I) might be years more than money, though: Signed to a multi-year contract for the first time in his big-league career, the shortstop lost his touch at the plate, dropping from solidly above league-average offensive production in 2020 to well-below in 2021. One factor: He fought through a nagging injury to his throwing elbow, limiting him to 103 games and putting all sides of his game underwater. Gregorius was always at risk of aging badly thanks to a meager walk rate and exit velocities that stayed humble, low. Whether it was mostly the elbow injury, an age-related decline, or a combination of the two, Gregorius and the Phillies are both hoping that there is Life After Death.

Bryce Harper RF Born: 10/16/92 Age: 29 Bats: L Throws: R Height: 6'3" Weight: 210 lb. Origin: Round 1, 2010 Draft (#1 overall)

YEAR	TEAM	LVL	AGE	PA	R	2B	3B	HR	RBI	BB	K	SB	CS	Whiff%	AVG/OBP/SLG	DRC+	BABIP	BRR	FRAA	WARP
2019	PHI	MLB	26	682	98	36	1	35	114	99	178	15	3	34.0%	.260/.372/.510	118	.313	-1.7	RF(152): 4.1	3.7
2020	PHI	MLB	27	244	41	9	2	13	33	49	43	8	2	28.7%	.268/.420/.542	134	.279	0.2	RF(48): -5.5, CF(3): -0.2	1.2
2021	PHI	MLB	28	599	101	42	1	35	84	100	134	13	3	32.1%	.309/.429/.615	146	.359	-2.0	RF(139): 4.2	5.4
2022 DC	*PHI*	*MLB*	*29*	*604*	*125*	*30*	*1*	*30*	*104*	*101*	*140*	*10*	*4*	*31.4%*	*.269/.397/.524*	*145*	*.315*	*-0.1*	*RF -2*	*4.9*

Comparables: Ruben Sierra, Jack Clark, Johnny Callison

Consider the mom and dad from Calvin and Hobbes. If you're well into adulthood, chances are that either you or someone you know looks that way: the bob cut, the bald spot, their impossible height as seen from the child's vantage. You probably knew this person when they were younger, and looked like a normal college student. Then one day, WHAM: They *look* like a parent.

Baseball players are like this too. We spend so much time imagining their potential as prospects, then lose track of most of them after college, like people do in real life. But the ones that stay just kind of grow old behind your back. After Harper joined Philly, it was almost as if there was nothing left for him to do, from a narrative standpoint: He'd won his MVP, lived up to his billing. It wasn't like he was going to win a championship with the Phillies. The result was one of the quietest MVP seasons in memory, edging his spiritual replacement in Juan Soto and posting the second-highest DRC+ of his career, all while wearing that Judd Apatow-character beard. This is just what Harper is now: capable, reliable and a little boring. Kind of like an adult.

Adam Haseley OF Born: 04/12/96 Age: 26 Bats: L Throws: L Height: 6'1" Weight: 190 lb. Origin: Round 1, 2017 Draft (#8 overall)

YEAR	TEAM	LVL	AGE	PA	R	2B	3B	HR	RBI	BB	K	SB	CS	Whiff%	AVG/OBP/SLG	DRC+	BABIP	BRR	FRAA	WARP
2019	REA	AA	23	190	30	8	2	8	21	21	35	4	2		.267/.353/.485	130	.290	2.3	RF(23): 2.3, CF(19): -1.7, LF(2): -0.0	1.7
2019	LHV	AAA	23	78	8	6	0	2	9	8	14	1	1		.294/.377/.471	106	.346	-0.7	CF(12): -0.8, LF(5): -0.0, RF(1): -0.1	0.2
2019	PHI	MLB	23	242	30	14	0	5	26	14	60	4	0	28.9%	.266/.324/.396	79	.344	0.8	CF(40): -3.9, LF(22): 2.3, RF(10): 0.8	0.3
2020	PHI	MLB	24	92	7	5	0	0	13	7	17	0	0	15.2%	.278/.348/.342	91	.349	0.0	CF(24): -2.5, LF(11): -1.0, RF(9): -1.2	-0.3
2021	JS	A+	25	38	7	1	0	1	4	5	5	0	0		.281/.368/.406	112	.296	-0.1	CF(7): 0.5	0.2
2021	LHV	AAA	25	170	18	2	0	3	14	12	33	7	2		.224/.282/.295	90	.264	0.6	CF(18): -1.7, LF(11): -0.1, RF(9): -0.7	0.2
2021	PHI	MLB	25	21	2	1	0	0	0	0	4	0	0	26.7%	.190/.190/.238	86	.235	0.5	CF(8): -0.0, LF(2): -0.1	0.1
2022 DC	*PHI*	*MLB*	*26*	*406*	*51*	*15*	*2*	*8*	*50*	*28*	*72*	*4*	*2*	*20.9%*	*.245/.305/.364*	*83*	*.284*	*0.0*	*CF 0, LF 1*	*0.6*

Comparables: Julio Borbon, Andrew Stevenson, Jacoby Ellsbury

If the Phillies have done one thing well over the past few years, it's develop position-player prospects who feel like long-term bench pieces. That's not high praise, and Haseley fits the mold. He got his start with the Phillies in 2019 when Andrew McCutchen went down for the season, playing 67 games with the major league club; by '21, he'd cracked the opening-day roster as the starting center fielder. His stint as an everyday player didn't last long, though, as he went on the restricted list after just nine games for what was cited as personal reasons. Upon his return, Haseley was permanently demoted back to Vegas. Being that Haseley is still only 25 and a former top-10 draft pick, it wouldn't be prudent to write him off, but he needs to pick it up to avoid being another mote in the Phils' dustbin.

Rhys Hoskins 1B Born: 03/17/93 Age: 29 Bats: R Throws: R Height: 6'4" Weight: 245 lb. Origin: Round 5, 2014 Draft (#142 overall)

YEAR	TEAM	LVL	AGE	PA	R	2B	3B	HR	RBI	BB	K	SB	CS	Whiff%	AVG/OBP/SLG	DRC+	BABIP	BRR	FRAA	WARP
2019	PHI	MLB	26	705	86	33	5	29	85	116	173	2	2	23.2%	.226/.364/.454	113	.267	-1.9	1B(158): 1.8	3.0
2020	PHI	MLB	27	185	35	9	0	10	26	29	43	1	0	26.6%	.245/.384/.503	122	.276	1.0	1B(40): -4.9	0.5
2021	PHI	MLB	28	443	64	29	0	27	71	47	108	3	2	26.3%	.247/.334/.530	117	.270	-2.3	1B(103): -0.7	1.6
2022 DC	*PHI*	*MLB*	*29*	*576*	*108*	*28*	*1*	*30*	*93*	*72*	*143*	*3*	*2*	*25.8%*	*.244/.351/.489*	*121*	*.284*	*-0.7*	*1B 0*	*2.3*

Comparables: Mark McGwire, Joe Adcock, Willie McCovey

Hoskins isn't as good as you remember, but he's better than you think. He hasn't lived up to the promise he showed when he lit the National League on fire in a 50-game sample in 2017, but has been solid enough where he's since settled in. Injuries limited him to fewer than 450 plate appearances in 2021, and his dip in walk rate may be something to monitor, but what Hoskins lost in patience he made up for with power. His slugging percentage has climbed the last three seasons; the .530 mark in '21 was his highest since '17 and he set a career-high in barrel rate. He's turned himself into a consistently above-average bat and with the outfield experiments over, should slot in as a steady two-plus win player. That might not be the stardom that his debut implied, but it's exactly the type of player the Phillies could use more of to buttress their hardware-chasing stars.

Scott Kingery UT Born: 04/29/94 Age: 28 Bats: R Throws: R Height: 5'10" Weight: 180 lb. Origin: Round 2, 2015 Draft (#48 overall)

YEAR	TEAM	LVL	AGE	PA	R	2B	3B	HR	RBI	BB	K	SB	CS	Whiff%	AVG/OBP/SLG	DRC+	BABIP	BRR	FRAA	WARP
2019	PHI	MLB	25	500	64	34	4	19	55	34	147	15	4	31.9%	.258/.315/.474	88	.337	3.1	CF(65): -2.3, 3B(41): 0.9, SS(18): 2.0	1.4
2020	PHI	MLB	26	124	12	5	0	3	6	9	35	0	0	31.5%	.159/.228/.283	78	.200	-1.4	2B(29): -2.0, CF(9): -1.9	-0.4
2021	LHV	AAA	27	88	11	4	2	0	5	13	27	3	0		.181/.307/.292	79	.277	-0.1	2B(10): 1.4, SS(4): 0.2, LF(4): 0.6	0.3
2021	PHI	MLB	27	19	1	0	0	0	0	0	12	0	0	60.5%	.053/.053/.053	61	.143	0.0	RF(5): 2.4, 2B(4): -0.0, 3B(1): -0.1	0.2
2022 DC	*PHI*	*MLB*	*28*	*61*	*7*	*2*	*0*	*1*	*7*	*4*	*21*	*0*	*1*	*37.7%*	*.202/.274/.353*	*64*	*.299*	*0.1*	*CF 0*	*-0.1*

Comparables: Jemile Weeks, Erik González, Darwin Barney

Shoulder surgery ended Kingery's season in mid-July, but he wasn't much of a factor for the Phillies organization when he was on the field, either with the big-league club or in Triple-A, where he appeared in just 15 and 23 games respectively. Kingery famously signed an extension before playing a single major-league game, but it's been a tough go for him at the game's highest level. There is still time for him to reestablish himself as a quality major leaguer, but he will have to fight a steep uphill battle to get there. He was outrighted off of the 40-man roster a month before he underwent his surgery; where and how much he plays in 2022 is anyone's guess. The extension was a prudent play. If only a few of those in the field followed.

Rafael Marchan C Born: 02/25/99 Age: 23 Bats: S Throws: R Height: 5'9" Weight: 170 lb. Origin: International Free Agent, 2015

YEAR	TEAM	LVL	AGE	PA	R	2B	3B	HR	RBI	BB	K	SB	CS	Whiff%	AVG/OBP/SLG	DRC+	BABIP	BRR	FRAA	WARP
2019	LWD	A	20	265	21	16	0	0	20	24	31	1	3		.271/.347/.339	122	.311	0.9	C(48): 1.1	1.7
2019	CLR	A+	20	86	6	4	0	0	3	6	8	1	2		.231/.291/.282	112	.254	-0.3	C(22): -1.0	0.2
2020	PHI	MLB	21	9	3	0	0	1	3	1	2	0	0	33.3%	.500/.556/.875	107	.600	-0.2	C(3): -0.1	0.0
2021	LHV	AAA	22	265	28	7	0	0	19	23	45	1	0		.203/.283/.232	86	.249	3.4	C(58): -4.6	0.5
2021	PHI	MLB	22	56	7	1	1	1	4	4	10	0	0	15.9%	.231/.286/.346	97	.268	0.0	C(17): -1.4	0.1
2022 DC	*PHI*	*MLB*	*23*	*59*	*6*	*2*	*0*	*0*	*7*	*4*	*10*	*0*	*1*	*20.5%*	*.227/.292/.302*	*63*	*.272*	*0.0*	*C -1*	*-0.1*

Comparables: Francisco Mejía, Christian Vázquez, Héctor Sánchez

Here is a fun fact about Marchan: He has hit just two home runs in his professional baseball career, and both have been at the major-league level. He refusal to hit homers in the minors continued again this year across 265 plate appearances in Triple-A. Marchan could benefit from extending that streak in 2022, but the Phillies' catching corps lacks depth at the top, and right now he is the backup to incumbent starter J.T. Realmuto, who is entering his age-31 season. He appears more than capable of big-leaguing on the defensive side of the ball, and scouts think that he will hit eventually. Just don't expect pop on more than the odd occasion.

YEAR	TEAM	P. COUNT	FRM RUNS	BLK RUNS	THRW RUNS	TOT RUNS
2019	CLR	2943	-0.7	0.1	0.1	-0.5
2019	LWD	6982	0.1		0.4	0.4
2020	PHI	432	-0.1	0.0	-0.2	-0.3
2021	PHI	2072	-1.7	0.0	0.4	-1.3
2021	LHV	8561	-3.6	0.0	-0.2	-3.8
2022	*PHI*	*2405*	*-1.2*	*0.1*	*0.0*	*-1.0*

Nick Maton MI

Born: 02/18/97 Age: 25 Bats: L Throws: R Height: 6'2" Weight: 178 lb. Origin: Round 7, 2017 Draft (#203 overall)

YEAR	TEAM	LVL	AGE	PA	R	2B	3B	HR	RBI	BB	K	SB	CS	Whiff%	AVG/OBP/SLG	DRC+	BABIP	BRR	FRAA	WARP
2019	CLR	A+	22	384	35	14	3	5	45	41	71	11	8		.276/.358/.380	117	.335	-5.0	SS(65): -2.1, 2B(15): -0.1, 3B(8): -0.2	0.9
2019	REA	AA	22	72	6	3	0	2	6	9	14	1	1		.210/.306/.355	111	.234	-0.1	2B(11): -0.1, SS(8): 0.0	0.3
2021	LHV	AAA	24	252	29	11	2	5	27	38	60	3	2		.199/.332/.345	97	.252	-1.4	SS(38): -3.6, 2B(15): 0.3, 3B(13): 0.2	0.3
2021	PHI	MLB	24	131	16	7	1	2	14	10	39	2	0	31.3%	.256/.323/.385	70	.364	1.8	2B(21): -0.7, SS(20): 0.2	0.1
2022 DC	*PHI*	*MLB*	*25*	*125*	*14*	*5*	*0*	*2*	*14*	*12*	*34*	*1*	*1*	*29.4%*	*.214/.300/.340*	*71*	*.289*	*0.1*	*3B -1, SS 0*	*-0.2*

Comparables: Derek Dietrich, Cory Spangenberg, Jemile Weeks

Getting his first taste of major-league action in 2021, Maton split time equally across both middle-infield spots, and has been taking reps in the outfield in the minors to boost his defensive versatility. The outfield is the most obvious path to major-league playing time in 2022, as Maton is effectively blocked at all infield positions, but the declining play of Didi Gregorius may give him the chance to stick at shortstop. Maton comes from a baseball family; one brother, Phil, is a budding high-leverage reliever for the Astros, and the other, Jacob, is a pitching standout at Coastal Carolina University. Maton projects to be a below-average to average bat with a plus glove that plays at multiple positions—bringing more versatility to a club more in the market for specific excellence.

Mickey Moniak OF

Born: 05/13/98 Age: 24 Bats: L Throws: R Height: 6'2" Weight: 195 lb. Origin: Round 1, 2016 Draft (#1 overall)

YEAR	TEAM	LVL	AGE	PA	R	2B	3B	HR	RBI	BB	K	SB	CS	Whiff%	AVG/OBP/SLG	DRC+	BABIP	BRR	FRAA	WARP
2019	SCO	WIN	21	74	5	4	2	0	5	4	17	3	0		.186/.230/.300		.245			
2019	REA	AA	21	504	63	28	13	11	67	33	111	15	3		.252/.303/.439	103	.307	0.9	CF(94): -0.8, RF(24): 0.5	2.0
2020	PHI	MLB	22	18	3	0	0	0	0	4	6	0	0	50.0%	.214/.389/.214	86	.375	0.1	LF(5): 0.4, RF(1): 0.0	0.1
2021	LHV	AAA	23	409	42	15	8	15	65	31	101	5	2		.238/.299/.447	97	.280	-1.7	CF(59): -6.0, LF(25): 0.1, RF(10): -0.0	0.6
2021	PHI	MLB	23	37	3	0	0	1	3	3	16	0	0	41.7%	.091/.167/.182	65	.125	0.5	LF(6): -0.3, RF(3): -0.1	0.0
2022 DC	*PHI*	*MLB*	*24*	*360*	*45*	*15*	*5*	*8*	*50*	*25*	*109*	*4*	*2*	*32.5%*	*.217/.278/.368*	*68*	*.298*	*0.8*	*CF 0, LF 1*	*-0.1*

Comparables: Rey Fuentes, Clint Frazier, Michael Saunders

Like many other Phillies prospects, Moniak had a tough 2021. Coming into the season, the 2016 top overall pick looked more like a fourth outfielder than a budding star; after it, it's no sure thing that he can even be that. "I'm not, per se, counting on either one of [Moaniak and Haseley] to be on our club next year to start off," president Dave Dombrowski told reporters in November, with the same a dad might tell his kid whether he's getting a PS5 for Christmas. He hit the ball fairly well when he did connect but struck out way too much to have any sustainable offensive production. As for time, that's a matter of perspective. The fact that he'll be 23 years old on Opening Day 2022 suggests he's got more of it left; the half-decade of slow gains means it might run out faster than he thinks.

Logan O'Hoppe C

Born: 02/09/00 Age: 22 Bats: R Throws: R Height: 6'2" Weight: 185 lb. Origin: Round 23, 2018 Draft (#677 overall)

YEAR	TEAM	LVL	AGE	PA	R	2B	3B	HR	RBI	BB	K	SB	CS	Whiff%	AVG/OBP/SLG	DRC+	BABIP	BRR	FRAA	WARP
2019	ADE	WIN	19	109	17	5	0	5	18	18	23	1	1		.258/.389/.483		.295			
2019	WIL	SS	19	177	20	12	2	5	26	12	49	3	0		.216/.266/.407		.270			
2021	PEJ	WIN	21	100	19	8	0	3	17	21	15	3	1		.299/.440/.519		.328			
2021	JS	A+	21	358	43	17	2	13	48	30	63	6	3		.270/.335/.459	124	.294	0.2	C(60): 3.2	2.4
2021	REA	AA	21	57	6	1	0	3	7	1	9	0	0		.296/.333/.481	109	.310	-0.3	C(11): -0.5	0.2
2022 non-DC	*PHI*	*MLB*	*22*	*251*	*23*	*10*	*1*	*5*	*26*	*14*	*52*	*2*	*1*	*24.5%*	*.243/.295/.373*	*81*	*.290*	*0.0*	*C -2*	*0.3*

Comparables: Pablo Sandoval, Wilson Ramos, Salvador Perez

O'Hoppe broke out in 2021 and earned not one but two promotions this year, ending his season in Triple-A as a 21-year-old. He has all the makings of an everyday major-league catcher, with good power to the right side as well as positive marks for his defensive ability and makeup. The gripe right now is a just-average arm; in a sport with fewer stolen bases than in decades past, it's not the worst problem to have. And it leaves him o'hoppe, skippe and a jumppe from the majors.

YEAR	TEAM	P. COUNT	FRM RUNS	BLK RUNS	THRW RUNS	TOT RUNS
2019	WIL	4777		0.4	0.1	0.5
2019	ADE	1684		0.1	0.7	0.7
2021	REA	1517	-0.6	-0.1	0.2	-0.4
2021	JS	8805	4.1	-0.1	0.0	4.0
2021	PEJ	1520			0.0	0.0
2022	*PHI*	*6956*	*-1.1*	*-0.2*	*0.0*	*-1.4*

Roman Quinn CF Born: 05/14/93 Age: 29 Bats: S Throws: R Height: 5'10" Weight: 175 lb. Origin: Round 2, 2011 Draft (#66 overall)

YEAR	TEAM	LVL	AGE	PA	R	2B	3B	HR	RBI	BB	K	SB	CS	Whiff%	AVG/OBP/SLG	DRC+	BABIP	BRR	FRAA	WARP
2019	CLR	A+	26	25	6	3	0	1	1	3	6	2	0		.500/.565/.800	111	.692	0.3	CF(5): 0.2	0.2
2019	PHI	MLB	26	122	18	3	1	4	11	12	34	8	0	31.6%	.213/.298/.370	84	.271	0.5	CF(34): -0.6, P(2): -0.1	0.3
2020	PHI	MLB	27	116	14	3	1	2	7	5	39	12	0	30.0%	.213/.261/.315	64	.313	2.4	CF(37): -1.3, RF(2): -0.2	-0.1
2021	PHI	MLB	28	62	8	2	2	0	2	6	19	4	3	32.3%	.173/.306/.288	79	.273	0.4	CF(21): 2.4, RF(4): -0.2, LF(2): -0.2	0.3
2022 non-DC	*PHI*	*MLB*	*29*	*251*	*22*	*9*	*2*	*4*	*23*	*19*	*72*	*11*	*4*	*30.9%*	*.216/.290/.343*	*69*	*.297*	*1.3*	*CF 0, RF 0*	*0.0*

Comparables: Brandon Nimmo, Aaron Hicks, Jake Marisnick

A ruptured Achilles tendon ended Quinn's season in late May. At the time, he was playing an above-average outfield and hitting to the tune of a decidedly below-average .595 OPS. One of the league's fastest runners for more than half a decade, there was always the chance that Quinn could provide some spark in the outfield and on the basepaths, but the injury calls even his most reliable tool into question. Speed makes up for less than it used to, on big-league rosters, and if that goes as well there's not much else. On the bright side, "not much else" also describes Quinn's competition in center field, heading into the lockout.

J.T. Realmuto C Born: 03/18/91 Age: 31 Bats: R Throws: R Height: 6'1" Weight: 212 lb. Origin: Round 3, 2010 Draft (#104 overall)

YEAR	TEAM	LVL	AGE	PA	R	2B	3B	HR	RBI	BB	K	SB	CS	Whiff%	AVG/OBP/SLG	DRC+	BABIP	BRR	FRAA	WARP
2019	PHI	MLB	28	593	92	36	3	25	83	41	123	9	1	23.8%	.275/.328/.493	106	.309	2.5	C(133): 8.5, 1B(4): 0.1	4.1
2020	PHI	MLB	29	195	33	6	0	11	32	16	48	4	1	29.8%	.266/.349/.491	109	.307	0.3	C(36): 2.7, 1B(6): -0.2	1.1
2021	PHI	MLB	30	537	64	25	4	17	73	48	129	13	3	27.0%	.263/.343/.439	100	.325	3.5	C(118): 17.2, 1B(16): 0.0	4.3
2022 DC	*PHI*	*MLB*	*31*	*533*	*86*	*24*	*1*	*19*	*82*	*47*	*127*	*7*	*3*	*26.7%*	*.251/.333/.436*	*105*	*.305*	*0.0*	*C 7, 1B 0*	*3.0*

Comparables: Don Slaught, Javy Lopez, Victor Martinez

YEAR	TEAM	P. COUNT	FRM RUNS	BLK RUNS	THRW RUNS	TOT RUNS
2019	PHI	19208	7.3	1.0	0.8	9.1
2020	PHI	5047	3.1	0.0	0.2	3.3
2021	PHI	16465	15.4	0.8	0.3	16.6
2022	*PHI*	*15632*	*4.9*	*1.8*	*0.6*	*7.3*

Realmuto's third year as a Phillie was his first under his record-setting contract and he looks off to a good start. One of only six backstops to surpass three WARP, Realmuto largely held his performance from prior seasons but for a dropoff in slugging that tamped down his offensive numbers. It can be tempting to read that as an ominous sign in year one of a five-year pact, but Realmuto's plate discipline, strikeout rate, exit velocity and launch angle were all in line with his usual output. He did see a shift in batted-ball data, with an increase in balls in play to opposite field at the expense of pulled balls, possibly explaining the muted power. This could be an indicator that his bat speed is slipping, which would be worrisome indeed, and is something to keep an eye on in the coming season. What hasn't slipped at all is Realmuto's defense behind the plate, as he led all catchers in CDA, largely thanks to a league-best ability to frame pitches. He's still plenty spry on the basepaths, too, posting a career-high 13 stolen bases in his age-30 season. Realmuto might have been usurped by Will Smith as the best all-around catcher in baseball, but he remains the best behind the dish and competent at it.

Jean Segura 2B Born: 03/17/90 Age: 32 Bats: R Throws: R Height: 5'10" Weight: 220 lb. Origin: International Free Agent, 2007

YEAR	TEAM	LVL	AGE	PA	R	2B	3B	HR	RBI	BB	K	SB	CS	Whiff%	AVG/OBP/SLG	DRC+	BABIP	BRR	FRAA	WARP
2019	PHI	MLB	29	618	79	37	4	12	60	30	73	10	2	14.7%	.280/.323/.420	97	.302	1.9	SS(142): -6.3	1.6
2020	PHI	MLB	30	217	28	5	2	7	25	23	45	2	2	22.4%	.266/.347/.422	107	.314	1.3	2B(32): 4.3, 3B(24): 0.1, SS(4): -0.4	1.4
2021	PHI	MLB	31	567	76	27	3	14	58	39	78	9	3	17.3%	.290/.348/.436	110	.317	1.7	2B(128): 2.9, SS(1): -0.0	3.2
2022 DC	*PHI*	*MLB*	*32*	*581*	*88*	*26*	*2*	*13*	*80*	*42*	*83*	*14*	*6*	*17.5%*	*.276/.339/.413*	*104*	*.307*	*0.6*	*2B 5*	*3.0*

Comparables: Shawon Dunston, Tony Fernandez, Orlando Cabrera

They don't call him "Jean Jean the Hit Machine" because of his sub-7% walk rate, that's for sure. Segura seems like he is always good for a .290/.340/.430 type of line. With the arrival of Gregorius to play short, Segura became a second baseman full-time in 2020, and the move has since put him back on the better side of many defensive metrics. Overall, it's really hard to say anything bad about Segura, statistically or stylistically: he's a barrel-shaped middle-infield contact dude, a living embodiment of the Platonic ideal of "NL second baseman." But he will be entering his age-32 season in 2022, and his offensive production did slide considerably in the second half of 2021. Philly is banking on the moniker winning out over the math.

★ ★ ★ *2022 Top 101 Prospect* **#93** ★ ★ ★

Bryson Stott IF Born: 10/06/97 Age: 24 Bats: L Throws: R Height: 6'3" Weight: 200 lb. Origin: Round 1, 2019 Draft (#14 overall)

YEAR	TEAM	LVL	AGE	PA	R	2B	3B	HR	RBI	BB	K	SB	CS	Whiff%	AVG/OBP/SLG	DRC+	BABIP	BRR	FRAA	WARP
2019	PHE	ROK	21	11	3	1	1	1	3	2	0	0	0		.667/.727/1.333		.625			
2019	WIL	SS	21	182	27	8	2	5	24	22	39	5	3		.274/.370/.446		.336			
2021	PEJ	WIN	23	119	20	7	1	2	31	24	14	5	3		.318/.445/.489		.333			
2021	JS	A+	23	95	18	4	0	5	10	22	22	3	2		.288/.453/.548	134	.348	1.5	SS(16): -0.0, 2B(6): 0.1	0.8
2021	REA	AA	23	351	49	22	2	10	36	35	78	6	2		.301/.368/.481	109	.368	1.9	SS(71): -3.5, 3B(5): 1.5, 2B(4): 1.0	1.6
2021	LHV	AAA	23	41	4	0	0	1	3	8	8	1	0		.303/.439/.394	111	.375	1.4	SS(10): -2.4	0.1
2022 DC	*PHI*	*MLB*	*24*	*97*	*13*	*4*	*0*	*1*	*11*	*9*	*23*	*0*	*1*	*26.7%*	*.239/.318/.360*	*87*	*.311*	*0.0*	*SS -1*	*0.1*

Comparables: JT Riddle, Jed Lowrie, Danny Espinosa

This year will be a pivotal one for Stott. The left-handed-hitting shortstop got his first taste of Triple-A action in 2021 and should start there in 2022. He has hit will at every level of the minors so far, but the game power hasn't flashed yet. His value hinges on which traits stick: a left-handed power-hitting shortstop is extremely valuable, a contact-dependent second baseman far less so. Stott is likely to see the majors this season, but it's the long-term outlook that's the most important part of the upcoming campaign. The Phillies would take a shot at an everyday staple in '23 over someone who can field a few grounders right away.

Garrett Stubbs C Born: 05/26/93 Age: 29 Bats: L Throws: R Height: 5'10" Weight: 170 lb. Origin: Round 8, 2015 Draft (#229 overall)

YEAR	TEAM	LVL	AGE	PA	R	2B	3B	HR	RBI	BB	K	SB	CS	Whiff%	AVG/OBP/SLG	DRC+	BABIP	BRR	FRAA	WARP
2019	RR	AAA	26	235	33	11	0	7	23	24	38	12	2		.240/.332/.397	100	.261	1.1	C(54): 8.3, 2B(5): -0.8, LF(1): -0.1	1.8
2019	HOU	MLB	26	39	8	3	0	0	2	4	7	1	0	22.4%	.200/.282/.286	87	.250	0.3	C(11): -1.2, LF(7): -0.1, RF(1): -0.1	0.0
2020	HOU	MLB	27	10	1	0	0	0	1	0	0	0	1	26.7%	.125/.111/.125	98	.111	-0.5	C(8): 0.2, LF(3): 0.0	0.0
2021	SUG	AAA	28	146	25	5	0	2	15	30	29	4	0		.265/.418/.363	106	.333	2.1	C(28): -0.1, 2B(6): 0.2	0.9
2021	HOU	MLB	28	38	2	2	0	0	3	2	7	0	0	23.2%	.176/.222/.235	84	.222	0.0	C(14): -0.4, LF(2): -0.1	0.0
2022 DC	*PHI*	*MLB*	*29*	*121*	*15*	*4*	*0*	*1*	*13*	*12*	*23*	*1*	*1*	*23.1%*	*.220/.312/.328*	*77*	*.264*	*0.0*	*C-2*	*0.0*

Comparables: Carlos Corporán, Brett Hayes, Chris Herrmann

YEAR	TEAM	P. COUNT	FRM RUNS	BLK RUNS	THRW RUNS	TOT RUNS
2019	HOU	1145	-1.1	0.0	0.0	-1.1
2019	RR	7791	8.0	0.0	0.0	8.0
2020	HOU	400	0.2	0.0	0.0	0.2
2021	HOU	1256	-0.3	0.0	0.0	-0.3
2021	SUG	3981	0.3	-0.1	0.0	0.2
2022	*PHI*	*4810*	*-2.4*	*-1.7*	*0.0*	*-4.0*

Stubbs never got out of the box for Houston, another tiny sample in which he didn't cross .300 in any of batting average, on-base percentage, or slugging proving to be the final nail as the Astros continue to make Martín Maldonado the plate warmer for top prospect Korey Lee. The stubs of playing time were marred by a low BABIP and DRC+ perceives a middling-for-a-catcher bat in truth, but if Stubbs is to prove it he'll do so for Philadelphia, where the Astros traded him in November for Logan Cerny.

Matt Vierling 1B Born: 09/16/96 Age: 25 Bats: R Throws: R Height: 6'3" Weight: 205 lb. Origin: Round 5, 2018 Draft (#137 overall)

YEAR	TEAM	LVL	AGE	PA	R	2B	3B	HR	RBI	BB	K	SB	CS	Whiff%	AVG/OBP/SLG	DRC+	BABIP	BRR	FRAA	WARP
2019	CLR	A+	22	483	41	23	2	5	41	34	94	22	5		.232/.297/.329	95	.279	-2.0	LF(53): 0.5, CF(24): 0.5, RF(22): -2.2	0.9
2021	REA	AA	24	102	16	6	1	6	16	12	18	5	1		.345/.422/.644	136	.369	-0.1	CF(15): -1.0, RF(10): 4.5	1.1
2021	LHV	AAA	24	236	25	6	1	5	31	24	46	5	1		.248/.331/.359	99	.291	-0.8	LF(20): 2.5, RF(17): -1.6, 3B(11): 1.8	1.0
2021	PHI	MLB	24	77	11	3	1	2	6	4	20	2	0	24.2%	.324/.364/.479	92	.420	-0.4	1B(9): 0.5, CF(8): -0.6, LF(7): 0.1	0.1
2022 DC	*PHI*	*MLB*	*25*	*395*	*50*	*16*	*1*	*8*	*48*	*27*	*87*	*9*	*3*	*23.7%*	*.234/.298/.357*	*77*	*.288*	*0.5*	*LF 1, CF 0*	*0.2*

Comparables: Brian Anderson, Gaby Sanchez, Pablo Reyes

Vierling was a bright spot for the Phillies last year despite the meager number of plate appearances. He blossomed in the upper minors, showing a sense of plate discipline that had heretofore been unseen. That approach evaporated in the majors, and it's a bit hard to blame him when everything he swung at landed for a hit. Still, the topline stats aren't supported by his peripherals, resulting in the sub-par DRC+. His BABIP was overinflated and the slugging on display in the majors doesn't align with a relatively flat swing plane. Vierling makes hard contact when he does connect, but too often it's going into the ground. He should see a fair bit of run as a fill-in corner outfielder and first baseman, but the offensive profile is unlikely to meet the bar for those positions in anything more than a backup capacity.

Luke Williams UT Born: 08/09/96 Age: 25 Bats: R Throws: R Height: 6'1" Weight: 186 lb. Origin: Round 3, 2015 Draft (#83 overall)

YEAR	TEAM	LVL	AGE	PA	R	2B	3B	HR	RBI	BB	K	SB	CS	Whiff%	AVG/OBP/SLG	DRC+	BABIP	BRR	FRAA	WARP
2019	REA	AA	22	504	77	30	3	11	51	49	113	30	9		.238/.319/.395	101	.292	7.5	2B(40): 0.3, 3B(31): 1.8, RF(26): -1.5	2.6
2020	ADE	WIN	23	77	12	2	0	1	9	2	16	3	0		.292/.299/.361		.345			
2021	LHV	AAA	24	143	21	5	2	0	15	12	29	7	3		.270/.329/.341	89	.337	1.7	2B(14): 0.7, 3B(9): -0.2, LF(6): 2.7	0.7
2021	PHI	MLB	24	108	8	4	0	1	6	10	23	2	2	19.8%	.245/.315/.316	93	.311	-0.4	CF(15): -0.9, 2B(8): -0.1, 3B(8): -0.4	0.1
2022 DC	*PHI*	*MLB*	*25*	*351*	*40*	*14*	*1*	*5*	*38*	*27*	*71*	*12*	*4*	*22.6%*	*.222/.291/.325*	*68*	*.270*	*0.9*	*3B 1, 2B 0*	*0.0*

Comparables: Marwin Gonzalez, Johan Camargo, Charlie Culberson

Williams' hot start in Triple-A earned him his first call-up to the major-league club, which caused him to happily forfeit his spot on the US Olympic team. A swing adjustment is what catapulted Williams to success in the farm system, but the benefits haven't yet shown up in the bigs. Even with the defensive versatility he brings to the field, it's hard to imagine him sticking at the major-league level with a mark that low. The next Olympics come around in 2024, and Williams will have to do better than a .316 slugging mark to avoid having that be his next best shot at big games.

PITCHERS

★ ★ ★ *2022 Top 101 Prospect* **#41** ★ ★ ★

Mick Abel RHP Born: 08/18/01 Age: 20 Bats: R Throws: R Height: 6'5" Weight: 190 lb. Origin: Round 1, 2020 Draft (#15 overall)

YEAR	TEAM	LVL	AGE	W	L	SV	G	GS	IP	H	HR	BB/9	K/9	K	GB%	BABIP	WHIP	ERA	DRA-	WARP	MPH	FB%	Whiff%	CSP
2021	CLR	A	19	1	3	0	14	14	44^2	27	5	5.4	13.3	66	40.0%	.259	1.21	4.43	78	1.0				
2022 non-DC	*PHI*	*MLB*	*20*	*2*	*3*	*0*	*57*	*0*	*50*	*47*	*8*	*6.3*	*9.8*	*54*	*36.7%*	*.299*	*1.65*	*5.90*	*129*	*-0.6*				

Comparables: Luis Ortiz, Todd Van Poppel, Scott Kazmir

The 15th-overall pick in the 2020 draft had a promising, but abbreviated, debut. The classically framed hurler boases a high-90s, high-spin heater that frequently elicits whiffs thanks to impressive vertical break. He'll flash a plus slider and the changeup and curve are works in progress. That work was halted in late July due a confluence of COVID-19 and minor shoulder soreness, but neither are long-term concerns are present. Abel is one of the most promising arms in the minor leagues, and could move quickly should any of his secondaries or command make a jump.

José Alvarado LHP
Born: 05/21/95 Age: 27 Bats: L Throws: L Height: 6'2" Weight: 245 lb. Origin: International Free Agent, 2012

YEAR	TEAM	LVL	AGE	W	L	SV	G	GS	IP	H	HR	BB/9	K/9	K	GB%	BABIP	WHIP	ERA	DRA-	WARP	MPH	FB%	Whiff%	CSP
2019	TB	MLB	24	1	6	7	35	1	30	29	2	8.1	11.7	39	46.2%	.360	1.87	4.80	112	0.1	98.4	79.5%	31.1%	40.8%
2020	TB	MLB	25	0	0	0	9	0	9	9	2	6.0	13.0	13	41.7%	.318	1.67	6.00	98	0.1	97.1	76.8%	28.0%	42.1%
2021	PHI	MLB	26	7	1	5	64	0	55^2	42	5	7.6	11.0	68	55.8%	.298	1.60	4.20	102	0.4	99.5	80.6%	33.3%	52.5%
2022 DC	*PHI*	*MLB*	*27*	*3*	*3*	*26*	*67*	*0*	*58*	*43*	*6*	*6.3*	*11.4*	*74*	*51.7%*	*.275*	*1.44*	*4.01*	*91*	*0.5*	*99.1*	*80.1%*	*32.5%*	*49.9%*

Comparables: Rex Brothers, Bryan Shaw, David Robertson

Alvarado remains an enigma. When he's right, he's as lights-out a reliever as anyone in the game, with a video game sinker and a wipeout slider that makes for consistent GIF fodder. When he's off, he's painful to watch. Alvarado hasn't been a reliable bullpen arm since 2018 with the Rays, and even then, he did it with an alarmingly high 11% walk rate, so the regression may have been in the making. In the three years since, that walk rate has ballooned to an unsightly 18.1%. The only thing that is keeping Alvarado from being an elite bullpen arm is throwing strikes, that's no small task. Still, he will be just 26 on Opening Day, suggesting that he has plenty of chances (and full counts) ahead of him.

Cam Bedrosian RHP
Born: 10/02/91 Age: 30 Bats: R Throws: R Height: 6'1" Weight: 225 lb. Origin: Round 1, 2010 Draft (#29 overall)

YEAR	TEAM	LVL	AGE	W	L	SV	G	GS	IP	H	HR	BB/9	K/9	K	GB%	BABIP	WHIP	ERA	DRA-	WARP	MPH	FB%	Whiff%	CSP
2019	LAA	MLB	27	3	3	1	59	7	61^1	48	7	3.2	9.4	64	48.5%	.253	1.14	3.23	91	0.9	93.1	47.8%	30.3%	46.1%
2020	LAA	MLB	28	0	0	0	11	0	14^2	10	0	3.7	6.8	11	31.7%	.244	1.09	2.45	121	0.0	92.4	52.7%	22.9%	47.3%
2021	LV	AAA	29	0	0	1	4	0	5	2	0	1.8	9.0	5	41.7%	.167	0.60	0.00	100	0.0				
2021	LHV	AAA	29	2	2	2	16	0	20	18	1	3.2	9.0	20	30.4%	.315	1.25	2.25	98	0.3				
2021	OAK	MLB	29	0	0	0	9	0	9	9	2	4.0	8.0	8	34.6%	.292	1.44	2.00	109	0.0	93.2	52.0%	21.5%	56.5%
2021	PHI	MLB	29	0	0	0	11	1	10^1	8	2	6.1	7.0	8	36.7%	.214	1.45	4.35	122	0.0	93.2	49.8%	20.4%	49.8%
2021	CIN	MLB	29	0	0	0	6	0	5^2	10	2	9.5	11.1	7	40.0%	.444	2.82	11.12	101	0.0	93.0	52.1%	36.0%	54.8%
2022 DC	*FA*	*MLB*	*30*	*2*	*3*	*0*	*57*	*0*	*49.3*	*48*	*8*	*4.0*	*9.0*	*49*	*40.0%*	*.300*	*1.42*	*4.76*	*111*	*-0.1*	*93.0*	*50.2%*	*26.2%*	*49.7%*

Comparables: Dominic Leone, Edward Mujica, Chad Harville

After seven seasons as a somewhat reliable bullpen arm for the Angels, Bedrosian began the "wandering ronin" phase of his career, signing a string of minor-league contracts and declining the inevitable minor-league reassignments. He added a splitter to his repertoire in 2021 and had some success with it, generating a 33% whiff rate on the pitch, but his fastball is no longer anything special and the swing and contact rates are both creeping up ominously. Still, as one of those pitchers who's just barely too good for Triple-A and not good enough for the majors, he can expect to find himself in a lot of airports in the near future.

Archie Bradley RHP
Born: 08/10/92 Age: 29 Bats: R Throws: R Height: 6'4" Weight: 215 lb. Origin: Round 1, 2011 Draft (#7 overall)

YEAR	TEAM	LVL	AGE	W	L	SV	G	GS	IP	H	HR	BB/9	K/9	K	GB%	BABIP	WHIP	ERA	DRA-	WARP	MPH	FB%	Whiff%	CSP
2019	ARI	MLB	26	4	5	18	66	1	71^2	67	5	4.5	10.9	87	45.5%	.341	1.44	3.52	92	1.0	95.7	69.6%	23.9%	46.9%
2020	CIN	MLB	27	1	0	0	6	0	7^2	4	1	0.0	7.0	6	50.0%	.143	0.52	1.17	110	0.0	94.3	65.3%	21.3%	50.4%
2020	ARI	MLB	27	1	0	6	10	0	10^2	13	0	2.5	10.1	12	31.0%	.448	1.50	4.22	97	0.1	94.1	66.5%	24.6%	48.3%
2021	PHI	MLB	28	7	3	2	53	0	51	51	5	3.9	7.1	40	56.0%	.299	1.43	3.71	107	0.3	94.2	70.5%	17.6%	52.8%
2022 DC	*FA*	*MLB*	*29*	*3*	*3*	*0*	*71*	*0*	*61.7*	*61*	*7*	*3.5*	*8.0*	*54*	*49.4%*	*.301*	*1.39*	*4.35*	*104*	*0.1*	*94.6*	*69.7%*	*20.0%*	*50.7%*

Comparables: Collin Balester, Jeremy Jeffress, Randall Delgado

The Phillies signed Bradley to a one year, $6 million deal as part of their grand bullpen rebuilding experiment. By ERA, Bradley was slightly better in the first half than in the second half, but under the hood, he was actually much better in the latter—nearly two and a half runs better by FIP. (He stopped walking more batters than he struck out, for starters.) He'll be entering his age-29 season, so there's a good chance that he will be a useful piece for a major-league team next year. The declining fastball velo is certainly something to monitor, though.

Connor Brogdon RHP
Born: 01/29/95 Age: 27 Bats: R Throws: R Height: 6'6" Weight: 205 lb. Origin: Round 10, 2017 Draft (#293 overall)

YEAR	TEAM	LVL	AGE	W	L	SV	G	GS	IP	H	HR	BB/9	K/9	K	GB%	BABIP	WHIP	ERA	DRA-	WARP	MPH	FB%	Whiff%	CSP
2019	CLR	A+	24	2	0	0	10	0	20	11	1	2.3	10.4	23	32.6%	.222	0.80	1.80	84	0.4				
2019	REA	AA	24	1	1	2	15	0	23^2	12	4	2.7	14.8	39	28.6%	.216	0.80	2.66	70	0.6				
2019	LHV	AAA	24	3	1	2	26	0	32^1	23	4	3.3	12.2	44	38.2%	.268	1.08	3.06	68	1.0				
2020	PHI	MLB	25	1	0	0	9	0	11^1	5	3	4.0	13.5	17	36.4%	.105	0.88	3.97	83	0.2	95.0	64.7%	32.6%	41.6%
2021	PHI	MLB	26	5	4	1	56	1	57^2	47	6	2.8	7.8	50	46.4%	.258	1.13	3.43	96	0.6	95.5	64.4%	29.0%	53.8%
2022 DC	*PHI*	*MLB*	*27*	*3*	*3*	*2*	*67*	*0*	*58*	*54*	*8*	*3.3*	*9.7*	*63*	*41.3%*	*.300*	*1.29*	*4.01*	*96*	*0.3*	*95.5*	*64.5%*	*29.4%*	*52.4%*

Comparables: Juan Minaya, Chris Leroux, Ryan Garton

The first thing you notice about Brogdon is his tall, wiry frame. Standing 6 feet, 6 inches tall and weighing in at 205 pounds, he brings to mind a teenager on the tail end of a summer-long growth spurt. That tall build gets Brogdon great extension on his fastball, and he played an important role in the Phillies' bullpen in 2021, tallying 57 ⅔ innings and putting up a 3.43 ERA. He's halfway to where you want to be, coaxing swings and misses but not yet all that many strikeouts. The changeup, his best offering, isn't really an out pitch but he keeps it down and it's hard to square up, resulting in a ton of groundballs. If he can get the Ks up to where his Ichabod resemblance suggests they should be, and preserve the soft contact, he'll be in good shape.

Sam Coonrod RHP

Born: 09/22/92 Age: 29 Bats: R Throws: R Height: 6'1" Weight: 225 lb. Origin: Round 5, 2014 Draft (#148 overall)

YEAR	TEAM	LVL	AGE	W	L	SV	G	GS	IP	H	HR	BB/9	K/9	K	GB%	BABIP	WHIP	ERA	DRA-	WARP	MPH	FB%	Whiff%	CSP
2019	SAC	AAA	26	2	4	3	33	1	32^1	41	4	5.0	12.0	43	45.2%	.420	1.82	6.96	80	0.6				
2019	SF	MLB	26	5	1	0	33	0	27^2	19	3	4.9	6.5	20	49.3%	.225	1.23	3.58	107	0.2	96.4	65.3%	22.7%	47.1%
2020	SF	MLB	27	0	2	3	18	0	14^2	17	2	4.3	9.2	15	45.7%	.341	1.64	9.82	99	0.2	98.0	58.9%	29.1%	48.8%
2021	LHV	AAA	28	0	0	0	5	0	5^1	2	1	3.4	6.8	4	46.2%	.083	0.75	1.69	99	0.1				
2021	PHI	MLB	28	2	2	2	42	2	42^1	41	5	3.2	10.2	48	56.3%	.316	1.32	4.04	84	0.7	98.1	73.0%	24.9%	54.1%
2022 DC	*PHI*	*MLB*	*29*	*3*	*3*	*2*	*67*	*0*	*58*	*52*	*6*	*3.7*	*8.8*	*57*	*49.0%*	*.290*	*1.31*	*3.92*	*95*	*0.4*	*97.8*	*69.3%*	*25.4%*	*52.1%*

Comparables: Xavier Cedeño, Anthony Bass, Ryan Cook

The Phillies took a chance on Coonrod, acquiring him from the Giants after he posted a 9.82 ERA in 2020. To be fair, he'd run into a lot of bad luck, including a very flukey 43.1% strand rate. Coonrod features two different fastballs that average just south of 99 mph—a sinker that he throws more than half the time, and a four-seamer that garners a whopping 44.2% whiff rate. It's time for him to make his own luck: lean into that four-seamer, and take on meaningful innings for a deep Phillies pen.

Hans Crouse RHP

Born: 09/15/98 Age: 23 Bats: L Throws: R Height: 6'4" Weight: 180 lb. Origin: Round 2, 2017 Draft (#66 overall)

YEAR	TEAM	LVL	AGE	W	L	SV	G	GS	IP	H	HR	BB/9	K/9	K	GB%	BABIP	WHIP	ERA	DRA-	WARP	MPH	FB%	Whiff%	CSP
2019	HIC	A	20	6	1	0	19	19	87^2	86	12	2.0	7.8	76	31.3%	.296	1.20	4.41	109	0.3				
2021	FRI	AA	22	3	2	0	13	13	51	27	5	3.4	9.5	54	35.0%	.191	0.90	3.35	94	0.5				
2021	REA	AA	22	2	2	0	6	6	29^2	24	3	3.6	11.5	38	28.6%	.313	1.21	2.73	89	0.4				
2021	PHI	MLB	22	0	2	0	2	2	7	4	2	9.0	2.6	2	17.4%	.100	1.57	5.14	156	-0.1	92.8	46.6%	22.2%	48.2%
2022 DC	*PHI*	*MLB*	*23*	*5*	*6*	*0*	*36*	*14*	*77.7*	*77*	*14*	*4.6*	*9.1*	*78*	*31.2%*	*.299*	*1.51*	*5.54*	*126*	*-0.4*	*92.8*	*46.6%*	*22.2%*	*48.2%*

Comparables: Aaron Sanchez, Doug Waechter, Chase De Jong

Crouse is one of the quirkier pitchers in baseball, as he likes to incorporate a Johnny Cueto-esque shimmy into his delivery on occasion. A former second-round draft pick by the Rangers, he made his major-league debut as a Phillie in late September of 2021. His heavy dose of funk—a ton of moving parts, an unorthodox release point, a 6-foot-4 frame accordioned into just 5 ½ feet of extension on the release—may have contributed to the slew of injuries hes battled in his career. Nonetheless, he figures to be in the fold for a spot in the starting rotation in 2022. Crouse features a fastball that can reach 95, a slider that gets a lot of swings and misses and a changeup that he should throw a lot more.

Seranthony Domínguez RHP

Born: 11/25/94 Age: 27 Bats: R Throws: R Height: 6'1" Weight: 225 lb. Origin: International Free Agent, 2011

YEAR	TEAM	LVL	AGE	W	L	SV	G	GS	IP	H	HR	BB/9	K/9	K	GB%	BABIP	WHIP	ERA	DRA-	WARP	MPH	FB%	Whiff%	CSP
2019	PHI	MLB	24	3	0	0	27	0	24^2	24	3	4.4	10.6	29	52.9%	.328	1.46	4.01	93	0.3	97.5	61.2%	30.7%	46.4%
2021	REA	AA	26	1	0	0	4	0	5	8	4	5.4	5.4	3	38.1%	.235	2.20	14.40	106	0.0				
2021	LHV	AAA	26	0	1	0	12	0	12^1	13	1	5.8	11.7	16	50.0%	.343	1.70	7.30	81	0.3				
2021	PHI	MLB	26	0	0	0	1	0	1	0	0	0.0	9.0	1	50.0%	.000	0.00	0.00			95.0	71.4%	25.0%	63.1%
2022 DC	*PHI*	*MLB*	*27*	*3*	*3*	*2*	*67*	*0*	*58*	*54*	*7*	*4.2*	*9.6*	*62*	*48.5%*	*.303*	*1.40*	*4.45*	*104*	*0.1*	*97.3*	*62.1%*	*30.3%*	*47.8%*

Comparables: Joe Smith, David Robertson, Taylor Tankersley

Domínguez was very good for the Phillies in 2018, when he pitched to a sub-three ERA with 16 saves and averaged over 98 mph on his fastball. In 2019, he was downgraded to just good. Either way, when Domínguez got Tommy John surgery in late June of 2020, it was a huge blow to the Phillies pitching staff. While he was expected to miss all of 2021, he did manage to carve his way back to the bigs for a scoreless frame with one strikeout against the Marlins. The velocity was down considerably, but it's reasonable to think he can get some of that back in the offseason. Which form he returns to—the '18 high-leverage fireballer or the '19 low-res Xerox of that guy—is the question.

Zach Eflin RHP

Born: 04/08/94 Age: 28 Bats: R Throws: R Height: 6'6" Weight: 220 lb. Origin: Round 1, 2012 Draft (#33 overall)

YEAR	TEAM	LVL	AGE	W	L	SV	G	GS	IP	H	HR	BB/9	K/9	K	GB%	BABIP	WHIP	ERA	DRA-	WARP	MPH	FB%	Whiff%	CSP
2019	PHI	MLB	25	10	13	0	32	28	163^1	172	28	2.6	7.1	129	43.3%	.295	1.35	4.13	104	1.4	93.8	55.5%	20.3%	49.3%
2020	PHI	MLB	26	4	2	0	11	10	59	60	8	2.3	10.7	70	46.5%	.347	1.27	3.97	70	1.6	94.1	61.1%	24.0%	48.3%
2021	PHI	MLB	27	4	7	0	18	18	105^2	116	15	1.4	8.4	99	43.2%	.328	1.25	4.17	94	1.3	92.8	54.4%	23.0%	54.8%
2022 DC	*PHI*	*MLB*	*28*	*7*	*6*	*0*	*22*	*22*	*106.3*	*103*	*14*	*2.0*	*7.7*	*91*	*44.0%*	*.292*	*1.20*	*3.60*	*91*	*1.4*	*93.3*	*56.0%*	*22.5%*	*52.0%*

Comparables: Danny Cox, Aníbal Sánchez, John Lackey

Knee issues have plagued Eflin's major-league career, and 2021 was no different. He got off to a great start, itself in many ways a continuation of a solid 2020 season, but it was ultimately cut short when he underwent knee surgery in early September. If you combine Eflin's 2020 and 2021, you get a full season's worth of starts, and what would be his best one, with Eflin pitching to a 4.10 ERA and 3.58 FIP with just over a strikeout per inning. The key to Eflin's recent success has been his transition to being a sinkerballer. Since the 2018 season, his four-seamer and sinker usage have essentially swapped places. The Phillies hope that he'll be ready by opening day, but it'll be a coin flip; when it hits the ground, someone else should make sure to stoop down and pick it up.

Kent Emanuel LHP Born: 06/04/92 Age: 30 Bats: L Throws: L Height: 6'4" Weight: 225 lb. Origin: Round 3, 2013 Draft (#74 overall)

YEAR	TEAM	LVL	AGE	W	L	SV	G	GS	IP	H	HR	BB/9	K/9	K	GB%	BABIP	WHIP	ERA	DRA-	WARP	MPH	FB%	Whiff%	CSP
2019	RR	AAA	27	8	2	1	28	7	101^{2}	98	9	2.0	7.2	81	55.7%	.299	1.19	3.90	86	1.5				
2021	HOU	MLB	29	1	0	0	10	0	17^{2}	12	4	2.0	6.6	13	50.0%	.174	0.91	2.55	102	0.1	91.7	52.5%	13.7%	55.6%
2022 DC	*PHI*	*MLB*	*30*	*1*	*1*	*0*	*22*	*0*	*19.3*	*20*	*2*	*2.7*	*6.7*	*14*	*48.6%*	*.299*	*1.35*	*4.36*	*107*	*0.0*	*91.7*	*52.5%*	*13.7%*	*55.6%*

Comparables: Barret Browning, R.J. Alaniz, Alfredo Figaro

Emanuel is perhaps most notable for enlarging the window fans have into the process of testing and (if necessary) punishment for the detection of performance enhancing drugs. Suspended for 80 games in 2020 after 10 picograms of Dehydrochlormethyltestosterone were found in his system, Emanuel became the latest affiliated ballplayer to argue athletes are being suspended based on junk science (some reports have the sum of players suspended for the drug also known as CHCMT up to 21), entreating the league to raise the minimum allowable threshold as UFC and NASCAR have done. Making his major-league debut with 8 ⅔ innings of relief outings after his suspension expired, Emanuel wore number zero to symbolize the number of days he felt he should have been suspended. Welcome to Houston, kid, you'll fit right in. Or get picked up by Philadelphia after an arm injury limits your season to three weeks and the Astros cut you. Nevertheless.

Bailey Falter LHP Born: 04/24/97 Age: 25 Bats: R Throws: L Height: 6'4" Weight: 175 lb. Origin: Round 5, 2015 Draft (#144 overall)

YEAR	TEAM	LVL	AGE	W	L	SV	G	GS	IP	H	HR	BB/9	K/9	K	GB%	BABIP	WHIP	ERA	DRA-	WARP	MPH	FB%	Whiff%	CSP
2019	REA	AA	22	6	5	0	14	14	77^{1}	82	9	1.7	7.2	62	43.0%	.315	1.25	3.84	113	0.1				
2021	LHV	AAA	24	2	0	0	8	6	30^{2}	23	3	2.3	12.9	44	44.1%	.308	1.01	1.76	86	0.6				
2021	PHI	MLB	24	2	1	0	22	1	33^{2}	34	5	1.6	9.1	34	37.1%	.315	1.19	5.61	94	0.4	91.9	68.1%	23.3%	55.7%
2022 DC	*PHI*	*MLB*	*25*	*2*	*2*	*0*	*44*	*0*	*38.7*	*36*	*5*	*2.4*	*9.1*	*39*	*40.4%*	*.294*	*1.21*	*3.72*	*92*	*0.3*	*91.9*	*68.1%*	*23.3%*	*55.7%*

Comparables: Jarlín García, José Álvarez, Clay Holmes

Falter stands six-foot-four—not short by any means—but what is impressive is that he manages to get 7 ½ feet of extension on his pitches, which grades out as the best in baseball. For him, this means that his low-90's fastball plays more like it's in the mid-90's, with an eye-scrambling approach angle. Falter was used mostly out of the bullpen for the Phillies in 2021, but was a starter in the minors. He doesn't lead the league in any measurable category, but he might lead it in deception.

Kyle Gibson RHP Born: 10/23/87 Age: 34 Bats: R Throws: R Height: 6'6" Weight: 215 lb. Origin: Round 1, 2009 Draft (#22 overall)

YEAR	TEAM	LVL	AGE	W	L	SV	G	GS	IP	H	HR	BB/9	K/9	K	GB%	BABIP	WHIP	ERA	DRA-	WARP	MPH	FB%	Whiff%	CSP
2019	MIN	MLB	31	13	7	0	34	29	160	175	23	3.2	9.0	160	51.1%	.333	1.44	4.84	103	1.4	93.5	50.3%	29.5%	39.4%
2020	TEX	MLB	32	2	6	0	12	12	67^{1}	73	12	4.0	7.8	58	51.2%	.313	1.53	5.35	103	0.6	92.4	49.4%	23.4%	41.7%
2021	TEX	MLB	33	6	3	0	19	19	113	92	9	3.3	7.5	94	50.9%	.267	1.18	2.87	102	0.9	92.3	59.5%	26.2%	47.7%
2021	PHI	MLB	33	4	6	0	12	11	69	66	8	3.0	8.0	61	53.1%	.294	1.29	5.09	99	0.7	91.8	64.8%	23.3%	47.6%
2022 DC	*PHI*	*MLB*	*34*	*9*	*9*	*0*	*29*	*29*	*151.3*	*155*	*18*	*3.5*	*7.5*	*126*	*50.6%*	*.303*	*1.41*	*4.45*	*107*	*0.7*	*92.4*	*57.3%*	*25.7%*	*45.0%*

Comparables: Mike Hampton, Aaron Sele, Kyle Lohse

Terminal velocity is defined as the maximum possible velocity for an object as it falls through a fluid—most commonly air. Another definition is whatever number comes up when an opposing hitter makes contact off any Phillie not named Zack Wheeler. This extends to in-season acquisitions who were otherwise getting along just fine, like Gibson. He was stellar as a Ranger, recording a 2.87 ERA in 19 starts, thanks to the introduction of a cutter to his already-deep arsenal. He was actually better at the things he could control in Philadelphia, upping his ground-ball rate, maintaining his K% and lowering his walk rate, but suffered a worse fate on balls in play thanks to a shakier infield defense behind all those wormburners. It's safe to assume Gibson was neither as good as his numbers said in Texas nor as bad as they said in Philly.

Ian Kennedy RHP Born: 12/19/84 Age: 37 Bats: R Throws: R Height: 6'0" Weight: 210 lb. Origin: Round 1, 2006 Draft (#21 overall)

YEAR	TEAM	LVL	AGE	W	L	SV	G	GS	IP	H	HR	BB/9	K/9	K	GB%	BABIP	WHIP	ERA	DRA-	WARP	MPH	FB%	Whiff%	CSP
2019	KC	MLB	34	3	2	30	63	0	63^{1}	64	6	2.4	10.4	73	43.4%	.349	1.28	3.41	86	1.1	94.6	67.5%	24.3%	51.4%
2020	KC	MLB	35	0	2	0	15	1	14	20	7	3.2	9.6	15	37.5%	.325	1.79	9.00	120	0.0	93.9	49.8%	21.5%	51.2%
2021	PHI	MLB	36	3	1	10	23	0	24	18	7	3.8	10.1	27	19.0%	.200	1.17	4.12	119	0.0	94.0	82.4%	26.3%	52.0%
2021	TEX	MLB	36	0	0	16	32	0	32^{1}	27	5	1.9	9.7	35	28.6%	.278	1.05	2.51	100	0.3	94.5	82.6%	29.0%	61.0%
2022 DC	*FA*	*MLB*	*37*	*3*	*3*	*0*	*71*	*0*	*61.7*	*58*	*12*	*2.8*	*8.9*	*61*	*31.2%*	*.283*	*1.27*	*4.39*	*108*	*0.0*	*94.3*	*74.8%*	*26.1%*	*54.6%*

Comparables: John Lackey, Cal Eldred, Rick Rhoden

Kennedy started 2021 in Texas and ended up in Philadelphia, and the trip back east brought hard time. He got off to a fantastic start with the Rangers as their primary closer, but then struggled as a Philly as his walk rate, ground-ball rate and home run to fly-ball rate regressed mightily. One of the modern era's most unique transformative acts, Kennedy completed his transition from four-pitch starter with a 90-mph, behind-in-the-count fastball to a one-pitch reliever, throwing his 94-mph fastball 82.5% of the time. And for the most part it's worked! Baseball is crazy.

Corey Knebel RHP Born: 11/26/91 Age: 30 Bats: R Throws: R Height: 6'3" Weight: 224 lb. Origin: Round 1, 2013 Draft (#39 overall)

YEAR	TEAM	LVL	AGE	W	L	SV	G	GS	IP	H	HR	BB/9	K/9	K	GB%	BABIP	WHIP	ERA	DRA-	WARP	MPH	FB%	Whiff%	CSP
2020	MIL	MLB	28	0	0	0	15	0	13^{1}	15	4	5.4	10.1	15	33.3%	.314	1.73	6.07	116	0.0	94.6	62.7%	21.8%	45.9%
2021	LAD	MLB	29	4	0	3	27	4	25^{2}	16	2	3.2	10.5	30	45.9%	.233	0.97	2.45	89	0.4	96.4	58.1%	31.1%	56.1%
2022 DC	*PHI*	*MLB*	*30*	*3*	*2*	*8*	*59*	*0*	*51.7*	*40*	*7*	*3.5*	*11.8*	*67*	*41.9%*	*.284*	*1.17*	*3.19*	*78*	*0.8*	*95.9*	*59.5%*	*28.3%*	*53.0%*

Comparables: David Robertson, Jeremy Jeffress, Rod Beck

Knebel played the 2017 Brandon Morrow role for the Dodgers this season, when he was available. He wasn't as dominant as Morrow as in 2017, but he fit a middle-relief/setup role well. Coming off an injury-riddled 2019 and 2020, Knebel was nearly designated for assignment by the Brewers before the Dodgers swung a trade with Milwaukee and netted themselves a boom-or-bust bullpen arm. When he was in there, he boomed and was even called on to be the opener a few times—including the deciding game of the NLDS against the 107-win Giants and Game 1 of the NLCS against eventual World Series champion Braves. Dave Roberts trusted Knebel to pitch in big spots, even if it wasn't the end of the game. Injury risk is always going to be a thing with him, but if he can stay healthy, he figures to be a nice late-inning option for any team.

Jake Newberry RHP Born: 11/20/94 Age: 27 Bats: R Throws: R Height: 6'2" Weight: 200 lb. Origin: Round 37, 2012 Draft (#1123 overall)

YEAR	TEAM	LVL	AGE	W	L	SV	G	GS	IP	H	HR	BB/9	K/9	K	GB%	BABIP	WHIP	ERA	DRA-	WARP	MPH	FB%	Whiff%	CSP
2019	OMA	AAA	24	2	2	0	22	0	28	29	3	4.5	9.6	30	37.0%	.342	1.54	3.86	89	0.4				
2019	KC	MLB	24	1	0	0	27	0	31	29	7	4.6	8.4	29	34.1%	.262	1.45	3.77	127	-0.1	93.9	52.5%	27.5%	43.5%
2020	KC	MLB	25	1	0	1	20	0	22	20	3	4.9	9.8	24	37.5%	.321	1.45	4.09	121	0.0	93.7	45.2%	36.2%	41.2%
2021	OMA	AAA	26	3	5	2	44	0	60^1	69	6	3.1	11.2	75	42.9%	.399	1.49	5.07	78	1.5				
2021	KC	MLB	26	0	0	0	4	0	4^1	10	2	6.2	10.4	5	37.5%	.571	3.00	16.62	104	0.0	93.4	44.0%	27.3%	53.3%
2022 non-DC	*KC*	*MLB*	*27*	*2*	*2*	*0*	*57*	*0*	*50*	*49*	*6*	*4.0*	*10.3*	*57*	*38.4%*	*.322*	*1.43*	*4.67*	*109*	*-0.1*	*93.7*	*47.4%*	*31.6%*	*44.2%*

Comparables: Roman Mendez, Evan Phillips, Johnny Barbato

Unlike love, baseball is neither patient nor kind. Newberry was a longshot who made good, a 37th round pick way back in 2012 who finally found his way to the majors in 2018 and posted a decent 4.07 ERA across three major-league seasons. Last year, Newberry failed spectacularly in four April outings and was demoted to the alternate site and then the minors in early May. If he never makes it back, he'll still get to tell his grandkids he struck out Tim Anderson three of the four times he faced him.

Aaron Nola RHP Born: 06/04/93 Age: 29 Bats: R Throws: R Height: 6'2" Weight: 200 lb. Origin: Round 1, 2014 Draft (#7 overall)

YEAR	TEAM	LVL	AGE	W	L	SV	G	GS	IP	H	HR	BB/9	K/9	K	GB%	BABIP	WHIP	ERA	DRA-	WARP	MPH	FB%	Whiff%	CSP
2019	PHI	MLB	26	12	7	0	34	34	202^1	176	27	3.6	10.2	229	49.6%	.297	1.27	3.87	80	4.2	93.2	46.2%	26.7%	46.3%
2020	PHI	MLB	27	5	5	0	12	12	71^1	54	9	2.9	12.1	96	48.8%	.283	1.08	3.28	57	2.5	92.6	46.0%	31.3%	43.5%
2021	PHI	MLB	28	9	9	0	32	32	180^2	165	26	1.9	11.1	223	40.8%	.310	1.13	4.63	74	4.1	92.8	53.2%	28.0%	53.0%
2022 DC	*PHI*	*MLB*	*29*	*11*	*7*	*0*	*29*	*29*	*166*	*139*	*22*	*2.4*	*10.3*	*190*	*44.0%*	*.284*	*1.10*	*3.03*	*77*	*3.4*	*92.9*	*50.4%*	*28.2%*	*50.0%*

Comparables: Jim Palmer, Andy Benes, Steve Carlton

We don't want to declare 2021 an out and out False Alarm, but his 4.63 ERA belies what was otherwise a high-quality season that saw Nola advance in certain key metrics. His 4.3 WARP was ninth-best among all pitchers, reflecting his continued ability to miss bats and rack up strikeouts. By DRA–, Nola's figure of 75 was right in line with his career average, suggesting that there's likely to be positive regression on the way in 2022. The disconnect between his ERA and advanced metrics can in part be laid at the feet of a defense that seemed to play a game of Pass The Hatchet, resulting in plenty of Damage to topline stats. An altered pitch mix (more four-seamers and fewer sinkers) suggests Nola hasn't fallen prey to Stockholm Syndrome when it comes to relying on the defense behind him. The increased reliance on his four-seamer resulted in a career-high full-season strikeout rate of almost 30%, though that was Nowhere Near Nola's pandemic-shortened peak of 33% in 2020. Before We Run, it's worth noting that should the Phillies somehow give their stars a chance to wear their Autumn Sweaters, Nola and Zack Wheeler could combine to end a series before it starts—the thought is enough to put Tears In Your Eyes. Phillies fans haven't been given much to hold on to over these last few seasons of wheel-spinning, but at least they can proudly say "Nola Tengo."

★ ★ ★ *2022 Top 101 Prospect* **#82** ★ ★ ★

Andrew Painter RHP Born: 04/10/03 Age: 19 Bats: R Throws: R Height: 6'7" Weight: 215 lb. Origin: Round 1, 2021 Draft (#13 overall)

YEAR	TEAM	LVL	AGE	W	L	SV	G	GS	IP	H	HR	BB/9	K/9	K	GB%	BABIP	WHIP	ERA	DRA-	WARP	MPH	FB%	Whiff%	CSP
2021	PHI	ROK	18	0	0	0	4	4	6	4	0	0.0	18.0	12	88.9%	.444	0.67	0.00						
2022	*No projection*																							

The Phillies took a risk when they drafted Painter in the first round of the 2021 draft. The organization has shown little flair for developing top arms, save for Aaron Nola, and using a top asset on a hurler might be seen as trying to retrofit self-driving capabilities to a Pinto. Still, Painter was arguably the best high-school arm available, and for those who are of the "draft the best player available" persuasion, Philadelphia followed the protocol. High-school pitchers taken in the first round are notorious for not working out, but Painter's stuff is mature; he already spins his breaking stuff like a big-leaguer, and the fastball tickles the high 90s. In his first taste of pro ball this year, Painter struck out 12 in six innings and didn't allow a run. Maybe it'll work out; there's a first time for everything.

JoJo Romero LHP Born: 09/09/96 Age: 25 Bats: L Throws: L Height: 5'11" Weight: 200 lb. Origin: Round 4, 2016 Draft (#107 overall)

YEAR	TEAM	LVL	AGE	W	L	SV	G	GS	IP	H	HR	BB/9	K/9	K	GB%	BABIP	WHIP	ERA	DRA-	WARP	MPH	FB%	Whiff%	CSP
2019	REA	AA	22	4	4	0	11	11	57^2	58	4	1.9	8.1	52	47.7%	.325	1.21	4.84	89	0.8				
2019	LHV	AAA	22	3	5	0	13	13	53^2	68	8	5.9	6.7	40	49.5%	.347	1.92	6.88	148	-0.7				
2020	PHI	MLB	23	0	0	0	12	0	10^2	13	1	1.7	8.4	10	48.5%	.387	1.41	7.59	80	0.2	95.1	56.5%	28.6%	48.3%
2021	PHI	MLB	24	0	0	0	11	0	9	12	4	4.0	8.0	8	54.8%	.296	1.78	7.00	86	0.1	94.7	62.8%	20.2%	56.8%
2022 DC	*PHI*	*MLB*	*25*	*2*	*2*	*0*	*44*	*0*	*38.7*	*40*	*5*	*3.9*	*7.6*	*32*	*49.4%*	*.307*	*1.48*	*4.90*	*114*	*-0.2*	*94.9*	*60.3%*	*23.6%*	*53.4%*

Comparables: Renyel Pinto, Andy Pettitte, Brad Hand

Romero gained notoriety for crushing cans of Red Bull on his forearm in the bullpen before running out to the mound, and looked to be a promising relief arm before undergoing Tommy John surgery in May of 2021. If and when he's able to pitch for the Phillies in late 2022, he'll flash a mid 90's fastball, a plus changeup and a slider that he mostly throws to left-handed hitters. Romero is better than your average LOOGY, and at his best, he could be a multi-inning reliever or even back of the rotation starter once he is healthy again. Here's hoping that, if he makes the jump to the rotation, he keeps the can thing. Every time a stuff-heavy reliever loses his gimmick, a balance-necklaced and flavor-saver'ed angel loses its wings.

Cristopher Sánchez LHP Born: 12/12/96 Age: 25 Bats: L Throws: L Height: 6'1" Weight: 165 lb. Origin: International Free Agent, 2013

YEAR	TEAM	LVL	AGE	W	L	SV	G	GS	IP	H	HR	BB/9	K/9	K	GB%	BABIP	WHIP	ERA	DRA-	WARP	MPH	FB%	Whiff%	CSP
2019	BG	A	22	3	1	2	11	4	40^{1}	28	3	2.5	8.3	37	54.1%	.231	0.97	2.01	89	0.5				
2019	CHA	A+	22	1	0	0	12	6	34	28	0	3.4	9.5	36	52.9%	.326	1.21	1.85	94	0.5				
2021	LHV	AAA	24	5	6	0	19	17	73	58	4	5.9	11.0	89	59.4%	.297	1.45	4.68	97	1.1				
2021	PHI	MLB	24	1	0	0	7	1	12^{2}	16	1	5.0	9.2	13	59.0%	.417	1.82	4.97	93	0.2	93.9	63.0%	23.8%	54.4%
2022 DC	*PHI*	*MLB*	*25*	*2*	*2*	*0*	*44*	*0*	*38.7*	*36*	*3*	*5.3*	*9.1*	*39*	*53.8%*	*.305*	*1.53*	*4.62*	*107*	*0.0*	*93.9*	*63.0%*	*23.8%*	*54.4%*

Comparables: Justin Grimm, Daniel Ponce de Leon, César Ramos

In a small major-league sample, Sánchez pitched better than his line indicates. He struck out just over a batter an inning and got dinged by an obscene .417 BABIP. He features a sinker that sits in the mid-nineties with good movement, and he buttressed it with the needed complement: a changeup that got swings and misses at a 54% clip. Sánchez is listed at 6-foot-1, but he gets seven feet of release extension on his pitches, and his slider—clearly his third-best offering—could get better with some more horizontal break. The Phillies have the verve needed at the top of the rotation; what they could use is the kind of depth sinkerballers are born to provide. Sánchez will have every opportunity to give it.

Ranger Suárez LHP Born: 08/26/95 Age: 26 Bats: L Throws: L Height: 6'1" Weight: 217 lb. Origin: International Free Agent, 2012

YEAR	TEAM	LVL	AGE	W	L	SV	G	GS	IP	H	HR	BB/9	K/9	K	GB%	BABIP	WHIP	ERA	DRA-	WARP	MPH	FB%	Whiff%	CSP
2019	LHV	AAA	23	2	2	0	7	7	38	41	8	2.4	7.6	32	54.3%	.306	1.34	5.68	113	0.2				
2019	PHI	MLB	23	6	1	0	37	0	48^{2}	52	6	2.2	7.8	42	54.7%	.326	1.32	3.14	97	0.6	92.5	52.7%	22.5%	44.3%
2020	PHI	MLB	24	0	1	0	3	0	4	10	1	9.0	2.3	1	45.0%	.474	3.50	20.25	160	-0.1	91.4	60.6%	21.4%	38.8%
2021	PHI	MLB	25	8	5	4	39	12	106	73	4	2.8	9.1	107	58.2%	.259	1.00	1.36	85	1.8	93.3	68.2%	27.0%	50.8%
2022 DC	*PHI*	*MLB*	*26*	*9*	*7*	*0*	*27*	*27*	*132*	*121*	*13*	*3.1*	*8.4*	*123*	*54.5%*	*.293*	*1.26*	*3.48*	*87*	*1.6*	*93.2*	*65.9%*	*26.2%*	*49.6%*

Comparables: John Gant, Andy Pettitte, Fernando Nieve

If you were asked who you thought was the Phillies' third-best pitcher by WARP in 2021 (after Wheeler and Nola), how many would it take before you got to Suárez? Pitching exclusively out of the bullpen from his call-up in early May, Suárez finally got his chance to settle into a spot in the starting rotation in early August. Once he did, he pitched spectacularly, netting a 1.51 ERA in 65 ⅔ innings of work. There's plenty of room for regression here, as a .247 BABIP and an 86.3% strand rate almost certainly won't hold, but Suárez misses enough bats and induces more than enough weak contact to be a plenty capable fourth starter, which is exactly where he'll project to be on Opening Day 2022.

Zack Wheeler RHP Born: 05/30/90 Age: 32 Bats: L Throws: R Height: 6'4" Weight: 195 lb. Origin: Round 1, 2009 Draft (#6 overall)

YEAR	TEAM	LVL	AGE	W	L	SV	G	GS	IP	H	HR	BB/9	K/9	K	GB%	BABIP	WHIP	ERA	DRA-	WARP	MPH	FB%	Whiff%	CSP
2019	NYM	MLB	29	11	8	0	31	31	195^{1}	196	22	2.3	9.0	195	42.9%	.316	1.26	3.96	85	3.5	96.9	59.1%	23.0%	50.8%
2020	PHI	MLB	30	4	2	0	11	11	71	67	3	2.0	6.7	53	56.1%	.308	1.17	2.92	81	1.5	97.0	65.7%	22.7%	49.0%
2021	PHI	MLB	31	14	10	0	32	32	213^{1}	169	16	1.9	10.4	247	49.1%	.291	1.01	2.78	68	5.5	97.2	60.8%	26.7%	53.7%
2022 DC	*PHI*	*MLB*	*32*	*12*	*8*	*0*	*29*	*29*	*183.7*	*165*	*19*	*2.2*	*9.1*	*185*	*48.5%*	*.294*	*1.14*	*3.05*	*79*	*3.5*	*97.1*	*61.1%*	*25.4%*	*52.4%*

Comparables: Johnny Cueto, David Price, Ervin Santana

Formed in 1972, the Scottish rock band Stealers Wheel's biggest hit came with *Stuck in the Middle with You*, reaching as high as no. 6 on the Billboard Hot 100 in the US and no. 8 on the UK Singles chart. Wheeler's been a steal for the Phillies over the first two seasons of his five-year pact, recording sub-3.00 ERAs in both years and earning a second-place finish in last year's NL Cy Young race. He's done it in a variety of ways, too, abandoning his strikeout-heavy attack in 2020 for a ground-ball centric approach, then marrying the best of both worlds to dominate in 2021. The tall right-hander found success by busting hitters with arm-side fastballs then coaxing weak contact and whiffs with a slider he leaned on more than ever, throwing it about a quarter of the time. That resulted in black ink for innings thrown, shutouts and strikeouts. The Phillies should be hoping that Stealers Wheel isn't just a fit in terms of spoonerisms, though, rather that their catalog serve as some sort of guide for the organization. They already got the *Star* part down, now they just need *Everyone's Agreed That Everything Will Turn Out Fine* to come to fruition. If it doesn't, all the individual accolades Wheeler earns won't prevent the Phillies from remaining stuck in the middle of the division.

Lineouts

Hitters

HITTER	POS	TEAM	LVL	AGE	PA	R	2B	3B	HR	RBI	BB	K	SB	CS	AVG/OBP/SLG	DRC+	BABIP	BRR	FRAA	WARP
Jorge Bonifacio	RF	REA	AA	28	198	31	13	0	12	41	24	41	1	0	.251/.343/.538	131	.258	0.0	RF(31): 2.2, CF(10): -0.9, LF(4): 0.3	1.5
	RF	LHV	AAA	28	183	28	13	2	5	19	28	41	4	2	.261/.377/.471	112	.324	0.7	RF(23): 3.6, LF(8): -0.2, CF(2): -0.7	1.1
	RF	PHI	MLB	28	12	0	0	0	0	2	1	6	0	0	.091/.167/.091	83	.200		LF(2): -0.0	0.0
Johan Camargo	IF	GWN	AAA	27	436	70	24	4	19	67	47	72	0	1	.326/.401/.557	136	.361	-0.7	1B(59): -4.0, 3B(47): -1.1, RF(1): 0.0	2.3
	IF	ATL	MLB	27	18	1	0	0	0	0	2	6	0	0	.000/.111/.000	87			1B(1): -0.0, 2B(1): 0.0, 3B(1): -0.0	0.0
C.J. Chatham	MI	LHV	AAA	26	176	20	6	1	3	23	13	27	0	1	.271/.347/.381	108	.307	0.5	SS(26): -1.1, 2B(21): 0.9	0.7
Rodolfo Durán	C	REA	AA	23	119	10	7	0	5	10	5	24	0	0	.193/.227/.386	110	.200	0.2	C(28): -2.5	0.3
Freddy Galvis	SS	PHI	MLB	31	120	17	3	0	5	14	9	19	0	0	.224/.292/.393	105	.224	0.8	3B(19): -0.1, SS(10): -1.1, 2B(2): -0.1	0.4
	SS	BAL	MLB	31	274	36	12	1	9	26	18	58	1	0	.249/.306/.414	96	.290	1.7	SS(72): 7.1	1.8
Yhoswar Garcia	OF	CLR	A	19	77	7	1	1	0	8	6	23	11	2	.229/.299/.271	85	.340	1.1	RF(10): 2.4, CF(8): -0.3	0.4
Darick Hall	1B	LHV	AAA	25	471	46	27	0	14	60	55	100	0	2	.230/.338/.403	108	.270	-3.3	1B(114): 4.6	1.5
Odúbel Herrera	CF	PHI	MLB	29	492	59	27	2	13	51	29	77	6	1	.260/.310/.416	95	.285	-1.7	CF(104): 1.4, LF(23): -0.3, RF(1): -0.1	1.7
Travis Jankowski	CF	LHV	AAA	30	72	16	4	0	0	6	15	9	4	3	.304/.451/.375	125	.362	0.5	LF(9): 0.1, CF(5): -0.5, RF(3): -0.2	0.4
	CF	PHI	MLB	30	157	24	6	2	1	10	22	29	5	0	.252/.364/.351	94	.317	-0.2	CF(45): -3.8, RF(8): -0.3, LF(6): -0.1	0.1
Matt Joyce	OF	PHI	MLB	36	69	6	1	0	2	7	12	16	0	0	.091/.261/.218	93	.079	-0.7	LF(9): -0.1, RF(9): -0.0	0.1
Casey Martin	MI	CLR	A	22	301	33	17	0	6	35	28	68	15	3	.223/.316/.356	101	.277	-2.0	SS(43): 3.7, 2B(25): 0.3	1.1
	MI	JS	A+	22	126	15	4	0	1	7	13	52	2	4	.136/.232/.200	57	.241	-1.2	SS(19): 3.6, 2B(10): 0.1	0.0
Símon Muzziotti	OF	PEJ	WIN	22	83	10	1	0	0	13	15	13	3	3	.254/.398/.269		.315			
	OF	LHV	AAA	22	32	2	0	0	0	2	5	4	2	0	.200/.333/.200	110	.238	0.9	LF(5): 0.4, CF(3): -0.1	0.3
Jhailyn Ortiz	OF	JS	A+	22	303	52	11	0	19	48	29	86	4	1	.262/.358/.521	130	.316	0.5	RF(43): 1.3, CF(22): -4.6, LF(5): -0.2	1.8
	OF	REA	AA	22	88	7	1	0	4	6	9	27	0	0	.208/.307/.377	92	.261	-0.4	CF(14): 2.1, RF(6): -0.2	0.4
Rickardo Perez	C	DSL PHR	ROK	17	146	15	3	0	0	9	22	15	3	1	.256/.370/.281		.287			
Johan Rojas	CF	CLR	A	20	351	51	15	3	7	38	26	69	25	6	.240/.305/.374	100	.283	3.4	CF(66): 11.1, RF(10): -0.7, LF(1): 0.5	2.6
	CF	JS	A+	20	74	16	3	1	3	11	7	8	8	3	.344/.419/.563	139	.352	2.5	CF(14): 2.8, LF(2): -0.3, RF(1): -0.0	1.1
Ronald Torreyes	3B/SS	LHV	AAA	28	36	3	4	0	0	4	6	6	0	0	.276/.417/.414	113	.348	0.0	SS(3): 0.3, CF(3): -0.0, 2B(1): -0.0	0.2
	3B/SS	PHI	MLB	28	344	30	10	1	7	41	19	41	2	1	.242/.286/.346	92	.258	1.0	3B(50): -2.3, SS(44): -1.5, 2B(11): 1.1	0.7
Jordan Viars	LF/1B	PHI	ROK	17	64	13	1	0	3	18	11	12	2	0	.255/.406/.468		.257			
Ethan Wilson	RF	CLR	A	21	117	15	4	2	3	17	10	25	2	2	.215/.282/.374	101	.253	0.5	RF(9): -0.4, LF(7): -0.4, CF(6): -1.1	0.3

Jorge Bonifacio feels like he's been around forever despite being just 28 years old ,and has failed to establish himself as anything more than a Quad-A slugger.

Johan Camargo's 2018 doesn't feel *that* long ago, when he was an above-average contributor to a division winner. That season was buoyed by a BABIP that he's not since replicated, proving the luck dragons will get you coming or going.

Known for his defensive versatility and contact-oriented approach at the plate, **C.J. Chatham** could well end up seeing some major-league time this year. Just don't expect too much power to come out of his bat.

Rodolfo Duran brings a plus arm behind the dish, good blocking ability and a knack for calling games—all of which should transfer at the major-league level. His bat and receiving skills may keep him from becoming an everyday catcher, but as he is now, he should make a perfectly fine backup.

Freddy Galvis is the type of player who always has a gig. His bat doesn't stop traffic, but it plays, and he still brings positive defensive value at a premium spot. A permanent move to second base may be inevitable at some point, but a lot of teams can do a lot worse than Galvis at shortstop (and will, since he's headed to Japan).

Yhoswar Garcia received a cool $2.5 million signing bonus as an international prospect in March of 2020. He turned 20 in September, so he still has plenty of time to grow into his potential. At the moment, his speed is the thing that sets him apart, but there is reason to believe that he can develop some serious power as he fills out his frame, thanks to hands as fast as his feet.

Darick Hall has shown big power throughout the lower levels of the minors but only hit 14 homers in his first go in Triple-A in 2021. Even so, Hall's walks-and-strikeout skillset is trending in the right direction, and as a left-handed hitter, he is on the long side of the platoon. If he plans to wear a major-league uniform in 2021 and stick there, the power will need to keep up with the promotions.

Odúbel Herrera rejoined the Phillies after sitting out the 2020 season under suspension for violating MLB's domestic violence policy, and got the lion's share of center-field duty for want of alternatives. Philadelphia still lacks the alternatives, but declined his option anyway; it's hard to imagine him getting much playing time elsewhere.

Travis Jankowski is more of a late-inning defensive replacement than everyday player, but his career-high .364 OBP means that if his turn does come around, it won't kill you. He may not get a ton of extra-base hits, but getting on base and playing a competent center are rare enough talents you really don't need a third.

Pitchers rejoiced when they saw **Matt Joyce** at the plate, as the platoon lefty fell apart at the dish. He can probably find an NRI somewhere but, at 37, may be nearing the end of the line.

Casey Martin's ceiling remains extremely high, but his approach at the plate may keep him from reaching it. One of the most athletic players in the Phillies' system, with top-of-the-line speed and plenty of raw power, he brings oodles of swing-and-miss along with those traits. With a little more refinement, he can stay at short, but second, third or even center field may be more likely for his future.

Simon Muzziotti moved through five different levels in 2021, and many believe the glove is ready to play an above-average center today. The hit tool is decent enough, but the power might charitably be called well below-average and might accurately be called "what power?"

Throughout his professional career, one thing that **Jhailyn Ortiz** had delivered on is his power potential; he's simply got some of the best raw pop anywhere in the Phillies' system. He got some reps in center field, but in reality the best-case scenario is sneaking his plus arm into right. Even that won't matter unless he improves what players of his ilk always need to work on: trimming the swing-and-miss.

Rickardo Perez is only 17 years old, so who can tell, but his bat-to-ball skills mean that the evolution into whatever the catcher becomes should go pretty smoothly.

Johan Rojas has one of the more exciting power/speed combos in the system. Still raw, he has shown the ability to adjust at the plate and make consistent hard contact. If he fills out, the game power will begin to meet the raw power, which will be necessary if he has to move out of center.

For the first time since 2018, **Ronald Torreyes** played over 100 games at the major-league level. He had a below-average DRC+, again, but chances are he'll find his way to one roster or another in 2022. Nobody wants him, everybody needs him—the credo of the utility guy.

A third-round draft pick in 2021, **Jordan Viars** made his pro ball debut just one day after his 18th birthday, and had a really good showing in the Florida Complex League, posting an .874 OPS in 64 plate appearances. He has raw power to spare, above-average plate discipline and he's athletic enough to stick in a corner outfield spot.

A second-rounder in 2021, **Ethan Wilson** possessed one of the better bat-to-ball skill sets in his class, and above-average raw power. Neither quality showed up in his first year of pro ball, but the template is strong; he projects to have enough thump to play every day.

Pitchers

PITCHER	TEAM	LVL	AGE	W	L	SV	G	GS	IP	H	HR	BB/9	K/9	K	GB%	BABIP	WHIP	ERA	DRA-	WARP	MPH	FB%	WHF	CSP
Mark Appel	REA	AA	29	0	1	0	8	6	24^{2}	28	4	5.5	8.8	24	25.0%	.353	1.74	5.84	116	0.0				
	LHV	AAA	29	3	5	0	15	9	46^{2}	38	8	6.6	6.9	36	41.0%	.242	1.54	6.17	120	0.2				
Kyle Dohy	REA	AA	24	4	0	2	26	0	37^{1}	17	2	3.9	13.5	56	45.2%	.214	0.88	2.17	78	0.7				
	LHV	AAA	24	0	0	0	6	0	5^{1}	4	1	20.3	15.2	9	18.2%	.300	3.00	8.44	111	0.0				
	PHI	MLB	24	0	0	0	1	0	1	1	0	9.0	9.0	1	66.7%	.333	2.00	0.00	121	0.0	90.0	90.0%		
David Hale	PHI	MLB	33	0	2	0	17	1	26^{2}	30	5	3.0	7.1	21	40.0%	.313	1.46	6.41	112	0.1	93.0	55.5%	20.0%	51.4%
Damon Jones	LHV	AAA	26	1	5	1	34	0	41^{1}	39	3	7.8	12.4	57	51.0%	.371	1.81	5.44	101	0.5				
	PHI	MLB	26	0	0	0	1	0	0^{1}	1	0	54.0	0.0	0	50.0%	.500	9.00	0.00	94	0.0	94.0	81.8%	0.0%	33.4%
Brandon Kintzler	PHI	MLB	36	2	1	0	29	1	29^{2}	45	7	2.4	6.7	22	58.2%	.369	1.79	6.37	105	0.2	92.3	74.2%	15.9%	54.4%
Brady Lail	LHV	AAA	27	1	0	1	31	1	40	38	9	5.6	9.7	43	41.7%	.293	1.58	6.08	102	0.5				
	TAC	AAA	27	0	1	1	4	1	6	3	0	3.0	10.5	7	20.0%	.200	0.83	1.50	115	0.0				
	SEA	MLB	27	0	0	0	2	0	2	4	1	0.0	4.5	1	44.4%	.375	2.00	13.50	98	0.0	90.3	57.1%	26.7%	65.6%
Ethan Lindow	JS	A+	22	3	6	0	12	10	67^{1}	65	11	1.5	7.9	59	34.2%	.298	1.13	3.21	134	-0.8				
	REA	AA	22	0	2	0	6	5	17^{2}	19	5	5.6	11.7	23	35.4%	.326	1.70	6.11	97	0.2				
Yoan López	GWN	AAA	28	3	2	2	32	0	32^{2}	30	3	3.0	9.6	35	52.9%	.329	1.26	3.03	82	0.7				
	ARI	MLB	28	0	0	0	13	0	12^{1}	18	3	4.4	9.5	13	45.2%	.385	1.95	6.57	110	0.1	95.9	51.6%	28.6%	55.7%
Adonis Medina	LHV	AAA	24	4	5	0	17	17	67^{2}	71	10	3.5	7.3	55	46.8%	.298	1.43	5.05	114	0.4				
	PHI	MLB	24	0	0	0	4	1	7^{2}	9	0	4.7	7.0	6	47.8%	.391	1.70	3.52	120	0.0	92.5	65.0%	26.4%	51.1%
Matt Moore	LHV	AAA	32	0	2	0	5	5	19^{1}	20	5	5.1	10.2	22	20.8%	.313	1.60	4.66	124	0.0				
	PHI	MLB	32	2	4	0	24	13	73	78	15	4.7	7.8	63	37.7%	.303	1.59	6.29	120	-0.1	92.6	56.7%	22.0%	51.9%
Francisco Morales	REA	AA	21	4	13	0	22	20	83	76	11	6.5	11.9	110	40.8%	.323	1.64	6.94	84	1.4				
	LHV	AAA	21	0	1	0	2	2	8^{2}	6	0	7.3	7.3	7	44.0%	.240	1.50	0.00	114	0.1				
Scott Moss	COL	AAA	26	1	5	0	9	7	20^{1}	20	2	6.6	12.8	29	26.9%	.360	1.72	7.08	93	0.3				
Nick Nelson	SWB	AAA	25	3	4	1	29	5	52	50	6	5.0	10.7	62	54.5%	.324	1.52	3.81	84	1.1				
	NYY	MLB	25	0	2	0	11	2	14^{1}	15	0	10.0	13.8	22	35.1%	.405	2.16	8.79	106	0.1	96.6	53.8%	30.7%	52.9%
Ramón Rosso	AGU	WIN	25	0	2	0	10	6	27^{2}	30	3	3.3	7.2	22	45.9%	.307	1.45	5.53						
	LHV	AAA	25	0	2	0	21	3	29^{1}	28	2	5.8	8.6	28	41.7%	.317	1.60	4.60	102	0.4				
	PHI	MLB	25	0	0	0	7	0	8	10	2	3.4	7.9	7	44.0%	.348	1.63	5.62	93	0.1	94.9	59.0%	17.8%	54.6%

Mark Appel made his grand comeback to professional baseball after a three-year absence, demonstrating equal parts life and rust. The former first-overall pick has been admirably transparent about the struggles he faced during and after his time in the Astros' organization, promoting mental health care inside and outside of sports. **Kyle Dohy's** big strikeout numbers come with the usual flaw: free passes. Dohy had a one-inning cup of coffee in 2021, and it went how it had to: a strikeout, a walk, a universe balanced. The nearly seven feet of extension he gets off the rubber suits him; if he's doing something, he's doing it all the way. It was a rough 2021 for the journeyman **David Hale**. After posting two seasons in a row with sub-4 ERA's, he turned an opportunity for a would-be uptick into an even worse stretch, posting an unsightly 6.41 mark in 33 games with the Phillies. **Damon Jones** is a hard-throwing lefty who can get swings and misses in bulk, but his command is too suspect to make him a reliable bullpen piece at the major-league level. On the off chance that he can find the strike zone in 2022, the stuff will definitely play, especially a sweeping slider that looks like a legitimate out pitch. **Brandon Kintzler** is a few years removed from his stretch as a medium- to high-leverage pitcher, but he was a useful bullpen arm as recently as 2020 with Miami. As much as Kintzler rode luck to a good 2020 season, he was unlucky in 2021; his DRA– was actually better in the latter season than in the former. At this point, Kintzler is a replacement-level pitcher who will find his way onto a club. **Brady Lail** has played a lot of places, but one of them is not Philadelphia, despite being claimed by the Phillies in late May. He did pitch 40 innings with good enough peripheral numbers to lead you to believe there's something more there, however slight. After he didn't pitch at the alternate site in 2020, it was hard to know what to expect from **Ethan Lindow**. He pitched well enough to earn a promotion to Double-A, but the results were not great across a small sample. Lindow features a deep arsenal of average pitches that play up because of one key virtue: he throws tons of strikes. In the ultimate change of scenery, **Yoan López** found himself leaving the desert in exchange for the lush greenery of summer in the south. Unfortunately for him, that greenery was observed in Gwinnett rather than Atlanta. **Adonis Medina** is a tough pitcher to pin down: He has good stuff, good command and at least three plus pitches, but the results in the high minors don't line up with the eye test. The culprit is command causing the stuff to play down. He might work best as a reliever. **Erik Miller** fits the Phillies theme: arm of a starter, command of a reliever. His bat-missing fastball has waxed velocity over the year, but his control waned in response. He'll also spin a 12-to-6 curve that plays against righties, which gives him a shot to stick in the rotation. Once regarded among the best prospects in the game, **Matt Moore** has a journeyman's resume thanks to an affinity for handing out free passes. After a strong stint in the NPB, Philadelphia picked him up as a back-end starter, but unfortunately for all involved, Moore was less. **Francisco Morales** has a powerful fastball-slider profile that could play at the major-league level sooner rather than later. The former can reach as high as 98 mph, and the latter gets swings and misses in bulk. The walks are a concern, but the fact that so many other Phillies farmhands have it worse helps paint over them. If turned into a reliever full-time, he could pitch important innings as soon as this year. To conclude last season, **Scott Moss** made a long-awaited and much-needed transition to the bullpen, where he should remain. There, he can harness his fastball and, ideally, mask his poor control, making him a useful if unspectacular middle relief option. Last year, **Nick Nelson** pitched like a blindfolded six-year-old on a sugar high playing Pin the Tail on the Donkey, except the tail was a 98-mph fastball and the donkey was the screen behind home plate. But hey! He has **GreatStuff™!** **Ramón Rosso** has the raw ingredients to be a useful big-league reliever in an upper-90s fastball and a slider with good horizontal movement, but thus far the results have been grosso.

WASHINGTON NATIONALS

Essay by Noah Frank

Player comments by Sydney Bergman, Jarrett Seidler and BP staff

Perhaps you've spent some time recently wondering what it all means.

Major world events will have a way of doing that, especially ones that leave you without your usual distractions, stuck at home for the better part of two years. So will the furiously swift end to a competitive cycle of baseball, one that left no room to truly celebrate a championship. One moment, your team exorcising every playoff demon on its way to the top of the mountain across an unbelievable fever dream of a month of October. Then, before you know it, you're sorting through the returns from the trades of the stars that got you to the top of that mountain, squinting at MLB ETA dates and prospect comps.

Why you believe this all went down this way, and how you think it'll go from here, depend on the particular combination of foreordination and free will you ascribe to the way things work. There is something approaching scientific consensus that the universe is expanding from its point of origin, but there are some competing theories about just how existence will ultimately resolve. Two somewhat complementary theories are The Big Crunch and The Big Bounce. The former hypothesizes that gravity and matter will eventually conspire to essentially reverse the expansion of The Big Bang, contracting the universe back to its point of origin. The latter suggests the same collapse, followed by another expansion (another Big Bang), and another collapse, on and on, ad infinitum. The universe's own cycling of competitive windows, as it were.

(Nationals fans may find some humor, if not a sense of cosmic predestination, in the fact that the scientists who discovered that the universe is actually continuing to expand more quickly won the Nobel Prize in 2011, the last year of the franchise's first incarnation.)

After years of postseason appearances dictated by Murphy's Law, the 2019 run came together in a way that felt like general manager Mike Rizzo had surrendered the Time Stone (personified, perhaps, by World Series Game 5 starter Joe Ross) to the baseball gods in order to summon the single sliver of the multiverse in which the Nationals would win the title. What else explains the deflection off Brewers right

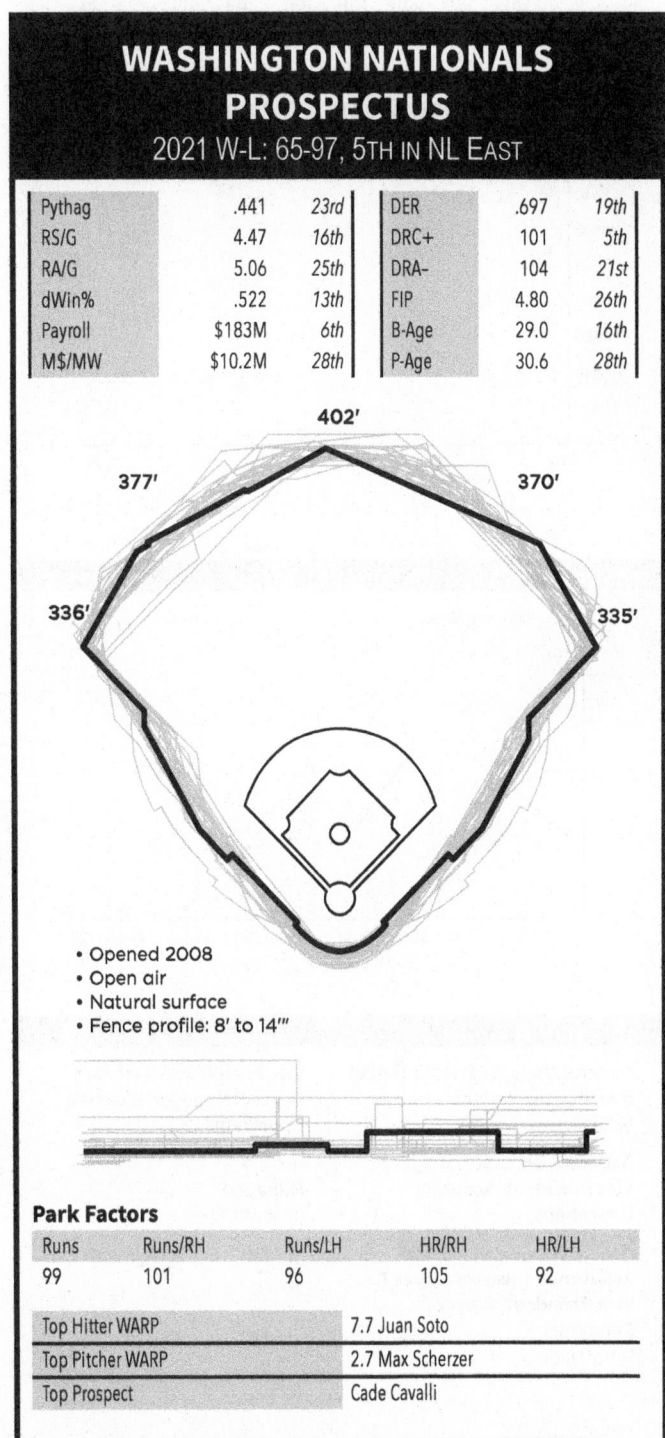

WASHINGTON NATIONALS PROSPECTUS

2021 W-L: 65-97, 5TH IN NL EAST

Pythag	.441	*23rd*	DER	.697	*19th*
RS/G	4.47	*16th*	DRC+	101	*5th*
RA/G	5.06	*25th*	DRA-	104	*21st*
dWin%	.522	*13th*	FIP	4.80	*26th*
Payroll	$183M	*6th*	B-Age	29.0	*16th*
M$/MW	$10.2M	*28th*	P-Age	30.6	*28th*

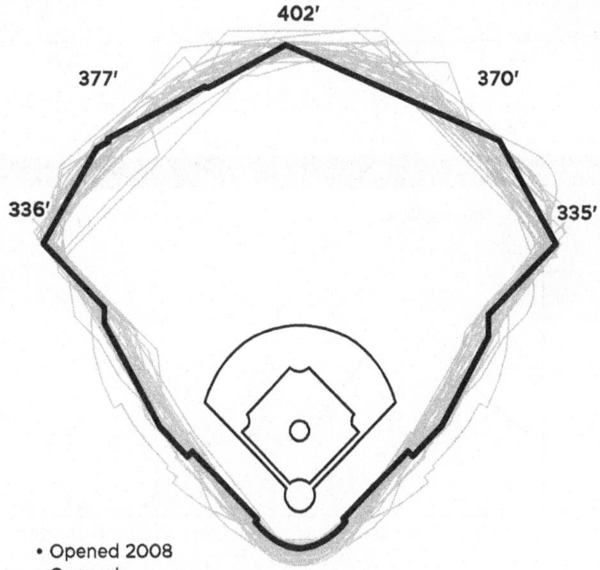

- Opened 2008
- Open air
- Natural surface
- Fence profile: 8' to 14'"

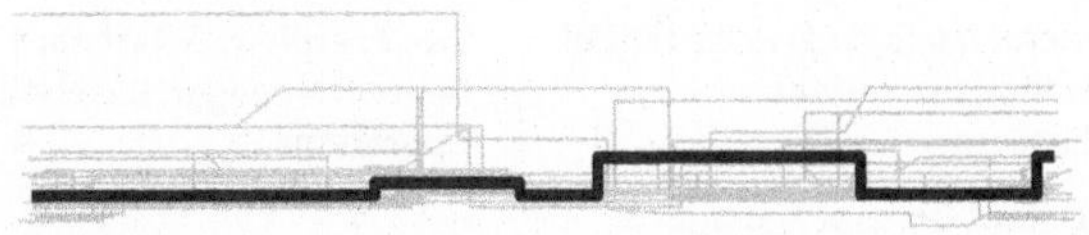

Park Factors

Runs	Runs/RH	Runs/LH	HR/RH	HR/LH
99	101	96	105	92

Top Hitter WARP	7.7 Juan Soto
Top Pitcher WARP	2.7 Max Scherzer
Top Prospect	Cade Cavalli

Payroll History (in millions)

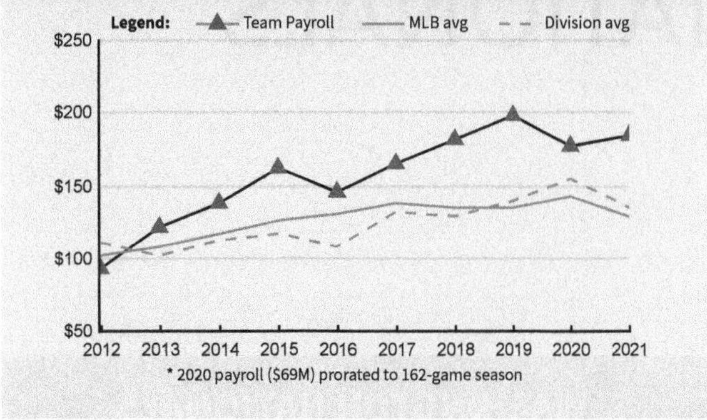

Future Commitments (in millions)

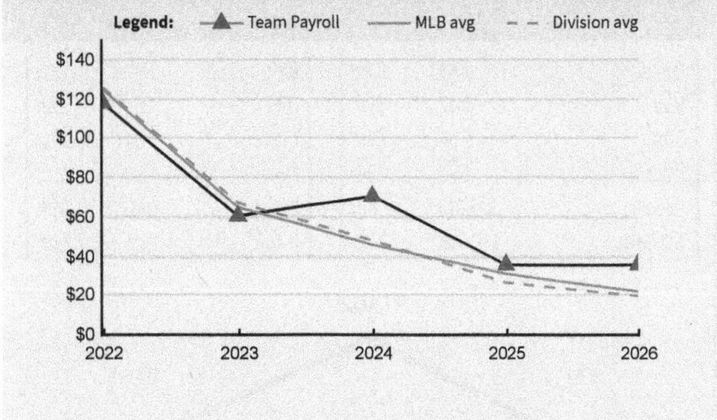

Farm System Ranking

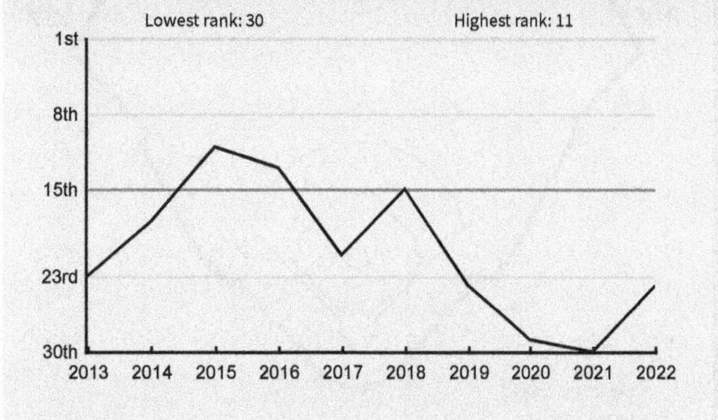

Personnel

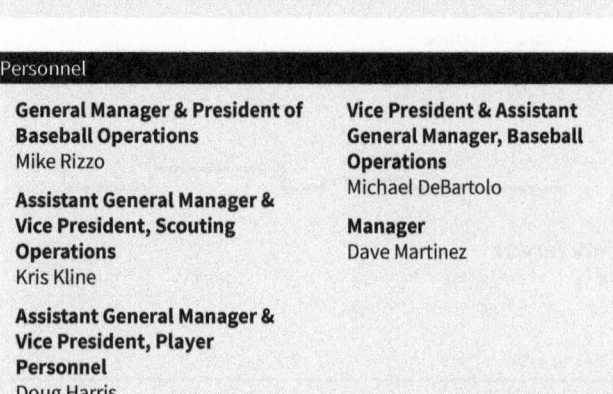

General Manager & President of Baseball Operations
Mike Rizzo

Assistant General Manager & Vice President, Scouting Operations
Kris Kline

Assistant General Manager & Vice President, Player Personnel
Doug Harris

Vice President & Assistant General Manager, Baseball Operations
Michael DeBartolo

Manager
Dave Martinez

fielder Trent Grisham's glove, the cough of wind from beyond knocking down Dodgers catcher Will Smith's would-be walk-off home run, the doink drawing iron instead of curling foul inside the pole? This was the year after the window was supposed to have closed, after all, with former and future NL MVP Bryce Harper leaving the prior offseason to join the Nationals' closest geographical division rival.

The Nats have long tempted the fates of time, mainly through the draft. There're the Zimmermen(n), sure, but also Anthony Rendon and Tony Renda, the latter another infielder selected the following year. The year that the Padres drafted Trea Turner, the Nats selected Jake Cousins, erstwhile Washington quarterback Kirk Cousins' cousin. Naturally, the Nationals drafted Darren Baker just months before firing his dad, Dusty. And don't forget that, due to a game resumed following a rain suspension, Juan Soto's first career home run—in the record books, anyway—officially came before his major-league debut.

But it was the Nationals winning it all that seemed finally to upend the natural order of the universe. For all the release of seven years of angst, the Nats got their ring, and their parade . . . and that was it. By the time Opening Day finally brought baseball back to Washington in an empty stadium the next July—a Max Scherzer loss in front of 40,000 empty seats—things had changed on some elemental level. The team wouldn't sniff a record above .500 again until the following season, shortly before their utter collapse, as they closed the 2021 season by going 25-59 from July 1 on.

Rizzo's teardown was swift and fierce. Anything not bolted to the ship was swept up in the vortex of a 36-hour tornado that leveled the big-league roster, leaving it absolutely unrecognizable on the other side of the trade deadline. Only first baseman Josh Bell was left surveying and inventorying the wreckage. But the contraction of the Nats had really begun immediately after the 2019 World Series, even if they didn't realize it at the time.

As magical as that October was, by the next month, it had all gone wrong. November began with a parade and that cringe-inducing White House visit, and ended with the first human infections from a virus that would change all of our lives immeasurably. While a good many of us now separate our lives into pre- and post- the dawn of the pandemic, Nats fans might as well draw that same temporal demarcation line.

Marking the transition was the sudden reemergence of NATITUDE, the team's slogan and self-adorned identity from the beginning of its ascendant years, which had been dormant since early 2014.

NATITUDE reappeared on February 2, 2020—yes, Groundhog Day, for those keen observers who've noticed a time-loop theme, here—attached to a tweeted pre-spring-training video of manager Dave Martinez strutting through the bowels of Nationals Park, the echoing broadcasts of the end of Game 7 following him into his office. In the clip, Martinez sits down at his desk, fields a phone call from Rizzo and says, "Hey, what's going on Riz? What's next?"

The tweet itself reads: "OK . . . what's next? #NATITUDE"

Reviving NATITUDE—all caps, always—was a bizarre decision. Not because there's anything wrong or foolhardy about trying to recapture a past bit of magic, but because of what that particular bit of verbal gymnastics referenced.

In its original incarnation, NATITUDE was inseparable from the anticipation of Harper's ascendance to the big leagues. It was the expression of a team that was about to be good, and then about to be even better, once its impossibly hyped second young star joined forces with fellow top-overall draft pick Stephen Strasburg, coming back from injury for his own first (almost) full season in the bigs. The spirit worked for a team and a fan base that had never tasted success, one for whom the only stated goal was to "play meaningful games in September," as Rizzo repeatedly said back then.

From the top of the mountain, NATITUDE didn't make much sense, especially considering that Harper had left town before the title run. The Nats had managed, incredibly, to find a player perhaps even better than Harper to fill the Bryce-sized void in right field, but for everything great that Juan Soto is as both a player and a personality, he is not an avatar of the same hashtag. Soto's emergence helped the team to a title, but heading into 2020, he was not guiding some plucky band of upstarts—he was just the young guy on the oldest team in baseball, a squad desperately trying and failing to keep the wheels on for one more shot at glory.

Obviously, that didn't work out. But it was especially strange considering the timing. If there was any player this misguided second effort at NATITUDE best represented, it was the free agent upon whom Washington spent a chunk of the money they might have otherwise spent keeping Harper: lefty starter Patrick Corbin.

Corbin's arrival in DC the winter before the title was followed by a couple other very strange tweets, presumably directed at the haters—"cAnT gIvE pAtRiCk CoRbIn SiX yEaRs ThO"—that were representative of a team used to being near the top and also getting a bit defensive about its inability to actually reach the peak. NATITUDE, though, was the innocent celebration of first-time success, not the ability to dish out sick burns. If it never made sense to bring back once Harper was gone, the misstep has seemed even more obvious in the wake of what Strasburg and Corbin have done the last two seasons.

Of the 49 pitchers who threw at least 200 combined innings between the pandemic-shortened 2020 campaign and 2021, only one surrendered a slugging percentage above .500: Corbin. His .292 batting average against was also (easily) the highest among that group, as was his 134 OPS+ against (roughly what Brandon Crawford has done at the plate over the same time). To rub more salt in the wound, a hurler that shares his name—newly-minted Cy Young winner Corbin Burnes—was the very best pitcher in baseball in many of the same categories. How's that for some sick burns?

Even with a shortened 2020 campaign that paid players just 37 percent of their salaries, the Nats have paid Strasburg and Corbin nearly $80 million combined since their title year to produce a combined 0.9 WARP. They've posted a combined 5.52 ERA in 264 total innings over the last two seasons, and they're owed a combined $188.25 million over the next three, with Strasburg due an additional $70 million over the two seasons after that.

In all, the Nats are spending $385 million for 13 total years from that duo. The Phillies gave Harper, who just won his second MVP, $330 million for the same amount of years.

Only hindsight is 20/20, and the decision to retain Strasburg, especially, after his magical performance en route to the franchise's first title (and after Harper had already left) was certainly understandable. It was even moreso when you consider this astounding fact: Strasburg is the last pitcher the Nats have drafted and developed to net them as much as a single win above replacement in the big leagues.

Take a deep breath and really let that soak in. For every Lucas Giolito or Nick Pivetta or Robbie Ray—oh, look, another award winner—they've traded away, there is an equal or greater bust, like A.J. Cole or Jake Johansen or Andrew Suarez, who hasn't worked out for any number of reasons.

But enough about the past. We're here to look at the future, to wonder when this club will once again play meaningful games in September.

Through that prism, then, how does NATITUDE's revival fit into your view of life, the universe and everything? If you're a Big Cruncher, it might feel like a harbinger of a decade of discontented winters before the team's inevitable move back to Montréal. To the more optimistic of the Big Bouncers, perhaps the universe has already collapsed and sprung anew—metaphorically, if not astrophysically—on a 13-year echo.

Trying to draw a perfect parallel is a fool's errand, but we're all fools anyway, staring out the window and waiting for spring. Maybe 6-foot-4 country hardballer Cade Cavalli—drafted in 2020—is this cycle's 6-foot-4 country hardballer Jordan Zimmermann, who made his MLB debut in 2009, after being selected in 2007. There's a good chance Cavalli makes the big leagues in 2022, and, depending on a great many off-the-field issues, there is a reasonable case to be made that the Nats could be headed for a 59-103-ish kind of season, like the one they had during Zimmermann's rookie campaign.

Viewed through this cyclical lens, Soto's analog becomes not Harper but the actual face of the franchise, Ryan Zimmerman. By 2007, Zimmerman was the best player on a bad team, leading the club in WARP three times in four years, over which the Nats averaged nearly 97 losses. The first year of promise for that club was 2011, after which Zimmerman was signed to a major extension, which would keep him in Washington for the rest of his career. On that same projected cycle, Soto's own extension would come after 2024, his final arbitration year and the true beginning of the Nats' next competitive cycle.

This Nats rebuild shares echoes with the original build, with the obvious difference of Strasburg and Corbin. There is certainly the chance that at least one will rebound going forward; Corbin's arm may be cooked, but Strasburg has a rosier prognosis. For better or worse, they'll be tied to Washington—and command a significant chunk of payroll—for the next several years. Knowing that, looking at this next Big Bounce, the question becomes this: After a long cycle of being bad, followed by a long one of being good, what is this franchise moving forward?

Despite being the newest franchise in the majors (if you choose to ignore its Montréal roots, as the organization is mostly happy to do), the Nats have had the ambition to be regarded as something greater than a quasi-expansion club, placing themselves in the same echelon as the generational giants of the sport. They were able to ride the wave of goodwill from their relocation and new ballpark until the start of their initial competitive cycle, and then were able to lean on their on-field success. But to be one of the big boys, you have to aim to compete just about every year.

For a team that has run its outward presence on bravado for the better part of the last decade, the Nationals are likely to remain bad for a while, in spite of whatever Soto does. Will the bloat from what could turn out to be two of the worst pitching contracts in modern history push the beginning of their next competitive window to some undefined, murky end point, like that of their MASN-adjoined neighbors to the north? Or will ownership actually act like one of the big legacy teams and buy the dip, spending their way through the downturn?

There is some parallel universe in which NATITUDE never left; in which Harper led the club to its first title and was locked up by Washington for the rest of his career; in which any number of other events may have sent the world spinning in an entirely different direction. But we don't live in that slice of reality. We live in this one, and the Nats have to decide what to make of it.

—Noah Frank is a freelance writer and editor in Washington, DC, and a contributing writer for Baseball Prospectus.

Hitters

Riley Adams C

Born: 06/26/96 Age: 26 Bats: R Throws: R Height: 6'4" Weight: 246 lb. Origin: Round 3, 2017 Draft (#99 overall)

YEAR	TEAM	LVL	AGE	PA	R	2B	3B	HR	RBI	BB	K	SB	CS	Whiff%	AVG/OBP/SLG	DRC+	BABIP	BRR	FRAA	WARP
2019	DUN	A+	23	83	12	3	0	3	12	14	18	1	0		.277/.434/.462	122	.341	0.2	C(19): 2.9	0.8
2019	NH	AA	23	332	46	15	2	11	39	32	105	3	1		.258/.349/.439	97	.362	1.1	C(57): -1.6	1.0
2021	BUF	AAA	25	143	20	6	1	7	17	16	46	0	0		.239/.371/.487	101	.323	-0.6	C(25): -0.8	0.4
2021	WAS	MLB	25	90	11	6	1	2	10	13	28	0	0	25.7%	.268/.422/.465	90	.415	1.5	C(23): -4.5	0.0
2021	TOR	MLB	25	30	2	2	0	0	0	2	12	0	0	40.4%	.107/.167/.179	70	.188	0.0	C(11): -0.6	-0.1
2022 DC	*WAS*	*MLB*	*26*	*219*	*28*	*9*	*0*	*6*	*28*	*23*	*70*	*0*	*0*	*31.0%*	*.207/.320/.374*	*88*	*.290*	*-0.3*	*C -10*	*-0.4*

Comparables: Nick Hundley, Brett Hayes, Yan Gomes

The Toronto Blue Jays should probably stop taking Mike Rizzo's calls. Two years ago, they traded Daniel Hudson for Kyle Johnston (who did have a good 2021... in Double-A). This year, they gave up Adams for Brad Hand. Hand dealt them a ERA above 7.00 and a swift DFA to the Mets, while Adams went from Mathis to masher, posting a Sotonian slashline and, well, not being flushed to Flushing. Adams' framing remains un-Mathisian, but he's got a while to grow into the position with a rebuilding franchise. Which seems like a pretty good deal all around.

YEAR	TEAM	P. COUNT	FRM RUNS	BLK RUNS	THRW RUNS	TOT RUNS
2019	NH	7812	-1.2	-0.6	0.3	-1.5
2019	DUN	2515	2.7	-0.1	0.0	2.6
2021	TOR	1110	-0.5	-0.1	0.0	-0.5
2021	WAS	3100	-4.5	-0.1	0.0	-4.5
2021	BUF	3568	-1.1	-0.1	0.1	-1.1
2022	*WAS*	*8418*	*-9.0*	*0.0*	*-0.1*	*-9.1*

Alex Avila C

Born: 01/29/87 Age: 35 Bats: L Throws: R Height: 5'11" Weight: 228 lb. Origin: Round 5, 2008 Draft (#163 overall)

YEAR	TEAM	LVL	AGE	PA	R	2B	3B	HR	RBI	BB	K	SB	CS	Whiff%	AVG/OBP/SLG	DRC+	BABIP	BRR	FRAA	WARP
2019	ARI	MLB	32	201	22	8	0	9	24	36	68	1	0	37.4%	.207/.353/.421	95	.287	-0.8	C(54): 3.8, P(2): -0.0	1.0
2020	MIN	MLB	33	62	6	2	0	1	2	11	22	0	0	35.1%	.184/.355/.286	79	.308	1.0	C(22): -1.2	0.0
2021	WAS	MLB	34	111	5	9	1	1	9	19	37	0	0	39.9%	.191/.345/.348	73	.314	-0.9	C(27): -1.8, 2B(1): -0.0	-0.2
2022 non-DC	*WAS*	*MLB*	*35*	*251*	*27*	*10*	*0*	*6*	*26*	*42*	*87*	*0*	*0*	*37.8%*	*.195/.338/.348*	*89*	*.299*	*-0.4*	*C -3, 2B 0*	*0.5*

Comparables: Miguel Montero, Darrell Porter, Brent Mayne

YEAR	TEAM	P. COUNT	FRM RUNS	BLK RUNS	THRW RUNS	TOT RUNS
2019	ARI	7141	4.2	0.4	0.0	4.6
2020	MIN	2454	-1.4	0.0	0.0	-1.4
2021	WAS	3754	-1.7	0.1	0.0	-1.6
2022	*WAS*	*6956*	*-0.4*	*0.7*	*0.2*	*0.5*

The Nationals signed Avila as a pitcher whisperer, largely on the basis of his having worked with three of their five opening-day starters. He did, in fact, produce good numbers working with Max Scherzer—which is more credit to Scherzer's season than Avila's influence, given that Scherzer posted similar ERA splits with every other catcher. And he proved mildly disastrous in working with Corbin, again more attributable to Corbin's faulty command than his own skills. (He only worked two games with Lester.) However, nothing is more emblematic of the Nationals' season overall than Avila experiencing bilateral calf strains after playing (a fairly competent) second base. It's for the best that his contributions during his final season involved slowly strolling to first.

Tres Barrera C

Born: 09/15/94 Age: 27 Bats: R Throws: R Height: 6'0" Weight: 206 lb. Origin: Round 6, 2016 Draft (#184 overall)

YEAR	TEAM	LVL	AGE	PA	R	2B	3B	HR	RBI	BB	K	SB	CS	Whiff%	AVG/OBP/SLG	DRC+	BABIP	BRR	FRAA	WARP
2019	HBG	AA	24	403	42	23	0	8	46	36	69	1	2		.249/.323/.381	113	.285	-2.6	C(93): 4.4	2.3
2019	WAS	MLB	24	2	0	0	0	0	0	0	0	0	0	0.0%	.000/.000/.000	89				0.0
2021	ROC	AAA	26	201	14	5	0	3	18	24	43	0	0		.201/.302/.284	96	.244	-0.9	C(54): -0.8	0.5
2021	WAS	MLB	26	107	8	3	1	2	10	12	22	0	0	22.7%	.264/.374/.385	101	.328	0.2	C(29): 3.8	0.9
2022 DC	*WAS*	*MLB*	*27*	*61*	*7*	*2*	*0*	*1*	*7*	*5*	*13*	*0*	*0*	*26.6%*	*.223/.304/.347*	*77*	*.272*	*-0.1*	*C 2*	*0.3*

Comparables: Michael McKenry, Omar Narváez, Brett Hayes

YEAR	TEAM	P. COUNT	FRM RUNS	BLK RUNS	THRW RUNS	TOT RUNS
2019	WAS	24	0.0	0.0	0.0	0.0
2019	HBG	12337	2.6	0.1	1.7	4.4
2021	WAS	3915	3.1	0.0	0.1	3.2
2021	ROC	7666	-1.1	0.2	0.5	-0.4
2022	*WAS*	*2405*	*1.3*	*0.1*	*0.0*	*1.3*

Barrera began the season as, fittingly, a third catcher. A prospect only by the loosest of definitions—and because of the Nationals' threadbare farm system—he put up perfectly cromulent offensive numbers in addition to his decent framing and game calling. His most notable contributions may have come off the field, as he has been outspoken about league policies over DHCMT, a banned performance-enhancing substance for which he tested positive for in 2020 and served a 60-game suspension. With the Nationals having made catching a priority at the trade deadline, he'll end up as he started: third on the depth chart.

Josh Bell 1B

Born: 08/14/92 Age: 29 Bats: S Throws: R Height: 6'4" Weight: 255 lb. Origin: Round 2, 2011 Draft (#61 overall)

YEAR	TEAM	LVL	AGE	PA	R	2B	3B	HR	RBI	BB	K	SB	CS	Whiff%	AVG/OBP/SLG	DRC+	BABIP	BRR	FRAA	WARP
2019	PIT	MLB	26	613	94	37	3	37	116	74	118	0	1	25.5%	.277/.367/.569	132	.288	-3.2	1B(134): -12.2	2.6
2020	PIT	MLB	27	223	22	3	0	8	22	22	59	0	0	33.6%	.226/.305/.364	94	.273	-0.6	1B(35): -1.3	0.2
2021	WAS	MLB	28	568	75	24	1	27	88	65	101	0	0	24.1%	.261/.347/.476	127	.276	-3.3	1B(119): -6.9, LF(9): -0.6, RF(1): -0.4	2.1
2022 DC	*WAS*	*MLB*	*29*	*565*	*83*	*22*	*1*	*21*	*93*	*63*	*106*	*1*	*2*	*25.2%*	*.246/.333/.427*	*107*	*.273*	*-0.7*	*1B -2*	*0.8*

Comparables: Paul Konerko, Greg Colbrunn, Sean Casey

BABIP is, in part, a luck stat. Maybe the ball takes a funny bounce off a rock in the outfield. Maybe a shortstop gets distracted by a passing butterfly. But if you put the ball in play, you never know what's gonna happen. BABIP bad luck was likely responsible for Bell's extremely chilly start to the season. Taken together with his cool 2020, and it looked like maybe the Nuttings actually won a trade for once. But sometimes luck puts the ball in play and sometimes it gets you the hell out of Pittsburgh. Bell's post-April numbers were a return to his 2019 form. Underappreciated are his low chase/waste rate which, combined with ability to hit the ball quite hard, make him perfect as the 1B/LF/DH type. His role on the Nationals as the guy not named Soto who can mash seems secure.

Starlin Castro 3B

Born: 03/24/90 Age: 32 Bats: R Throws: R Height: 6'2" Weight: 218 lb. Origin: International Free Agent, 2006

YEAR	TEAM	LVL	AGE	PA	R	2B	3B	HR	RBI	BB	K	SB	CS	Whiff%	AVG/OBP/SLG	DRC+	BABIP	BRR	FRAA	WARP
2019	MIA	MLB	29	676	68	31	4	22	86	28	111	2	2	19.2%	.270/.300/.436	99	.293	-2.3	2B(117): -8.6, 3B(45): -0.4, SS(3): -0.3	1.2
2020	WAS	MLB	30	63	9	3	1	2	4	3	13	0	0	22.0%	.267/.302/.450	99	.311	-0.2	2B(16): 0.1	0.2
2021	WAS	MLB	31	346	25	20	0	3	38	26	62	0	1	22.2%	.283/.333/.375	92	.339	-4.4	3B(85): 5.5, SS(1): -0.1	1.0
2022 non-DC	*FA*	*MLB*	*32*	*251*	*26*	*11*	*0*	*6*	*28*	*17*	*44*	*1*	*1*	*21.6%*	*.267/.322/.413*	*96*	*.305*	*-0.3*	*2B -1, 3B 1*	*0.6*

Comparables: Bill Mazeroski, Jim Fregosi, Roberto Alomar

www.acalltomen.org | A Call to Men is a multicultural organization that is reaching out across class and race lines to encourage men to stand up and be heard in opposition to violence against women.

The National Domestic Violence Hotline is 1-800-799-7233. It is confidential and available 24/7/365.

Alcides Escobar SS

Born: 12/16/86 Age: 35 Bats: R Throws: R Height: 6'1" Weight: 205 lb. Origin: International Free Agent, 2003

YEAR	TEAM	LVL	AGE	PA	R	2B	3B	HR	RBI	BB	K	SB	CS	Whiff%	AVG/OBP/SLG	DRC+	BABIP	BRR	FRAA	WARP
2019	CHA	AAA	32	405	52	28	0	10	70	32	64	6	2		.286/.343/.444	100	.320	-0.8	SS(49): 2.0, 3B(41): 0.6	1.5
2021	OMA	AAA	34	133	23	7	0	5	16	6	29	2	0		.274/.311/.452	100	.319	1.0	SS(24): 3.9, 2B(8): -0.8, 3B(2): -0.0	0.8
2021	WAS	MLB	34	349	53	21	2	4	28	17	56	3	0	22.0%	.288/.340/.404	96	.337	-0.2	SS(61): -5.2, 2B(18): 0.3	0.5
2022 DC	*WAS*	*MLB*	*35*	*531*	*72*	*26*	*1*	*8*	*55*	*29*	*94*	*5*	*2*	*23.9%*	*.248/.299/.358*	*77*	*.292*	*-0.3*	*SS 0, 3B 0*	*0.3*

Comparables: Luis Aparicio, Jose Vizcaino, Don Kessinger

A strange market inefficiency the Nationals seem to have discovered is identifying and rehabilitating otherwise washed middle infielders. Howie Kendrick never really lost his swing, but lost his love for the game (and then made history). Josh Harrison transitioned from marginal to tradeable. Escobar went from magic to mundane with the Royals, then dropped out of the Big Show altogether before being summoned to Washington. Underlying problems persist: He walks rarely and hits for modest power. Still, there's treasure to be found in the scrap heap—especially when it has the glint of a World Series ring—and Escobar could be the Nationals' everyday shortstop next year as the club tries to do a similar rehabilitation on itself.

Lucius Fox IF Born: 07/02/97 Age: 25 Bats: S Throws: R Height: 6'1" Weight: 185 lb. Origin: International Free Agent, 2015

YEAR	TEAM	LVL	AGE	PA	R	2B	3B	HR	RBI	BB	K	SB	CS	Whiff%	AVG/OBP/SLG	DRC+	BABIP	BRR	FRAA	WARP
2019	MTG	AA	21	431	60	16	8	3	33	53	89	37	11		.230/.340/.342	102	.293	-0.6	SS(79): -4.4, 2B(12): 1.5, 3B(9): 1.5	1.4
2019	DUR	AAA	21	49	6	0	1	0	1	6	15	2	0		.143/.250/.190	82	.222	0.5	SS(12): 0.4, 2B(1): -0.1	0.2
2021	OMA	AAA	23	252	41	14	0	4	21	33	61	19	2		.242/.347/.363	91	.318	4.0	2B(33): -2.5, SS(16): -0.7, CF(8): 1.9	0.8
2022 DC	*WAS*	*MLB*	*24*	*95*	*10*	*3*	*0*	*0*	*9*	*9*	*28*	*3*	*2*	*29.4%*	*.213/.301/.299*	*66*	*.312*	*0.4*	*SS 0, 3B 0*	*-0.1*

Comparables: J.P. Crawford, Tyler Wade, Nick Franklin

Turn the clock back to 1977, and Fox could be a starter, with his defense, speed and athleticism more than making up for his lack of offensive acumen. Put a little less plutonium in your time machine and Fox could still be a major leaguer, a back-up middle infielder and deadly pinch running weapon on several circa-'96 clubs. Alas, the calendar says 2022, and the combination of developmental focus on power and rosters that emphasize pitching depth over offensive utility mean that Fox's fun set of skills are unlikely to grace a major league roster for more than a moment here or there. If there's a team that might give his throwback set of skills a chance, it's the one that also employs Alcides Escobar, but even in Washington, it's likely that this Fox won't hunt.

Luis García 2B Born: 05/16/00 Age: 22 Bats: L Throws: R Height: 6'2" Weight: 224 lb. Origin: International Free Agent, 2016

YEAR	TEAM	LVL	AGE	PA	R	2B	3B	HR	RBI	BB	K	SB	CS	Whiff%	AVG/OBP/SLG	DRC+	BABIP	BRR	FRAA	WARP
2019	SUR	WIN	19	87	6	4	2	0	6	8	13	2	2		.276/.345/.382		.323			
2019	HBG	AA	19	553	66	22	4	4	30	17	86	11	5		.257/.280/.337	92	.299	2.7	SS(93): -2.8, 2B(38): 0.2	1.5
2020	WAS	MLB	20	139	18	6	0	2	16	5	29	1	1	29.1%	.276/.302/.366	82	.340	0.0	2B(37): -11.2, SS(3): -0.0	-1.0
2021	ROC	AAA	21	159	26	3	0	13	25	15	26	1	1		.303/.371/.599	147	.288	0.8	SS(28): -0.6, 2B(9): -0.2	1.3
2021	WAS	MLB	21	247	29	18	2	6	22	11	43	0	2	24.5%	.242/.275/.411	86	.273	-1.9	2B(59): -0.8, SS(8): -0.5	0.1
2022 DC	*WAS*	*MLB*	*22*	*350*	*42*	*14*	*2*	*8*	*49*	*18*	*66*	*4*	*3*	*25.5%*	*.258/.299/.390*	*86*	*.300*	*0.2*	*2B -1, SS 0*	*0.5*

Comparables: Rubén Tejada, Rougned Odor, Adalberto Mondesi

The Nationals are the most aggressive organization around on position player assignments. If they think you can handle a promotion, you're getting promoted. Washington pushed a teenaged Juan Soto from Low-A to the majors in six weeks, and he was more than ready for it. García was sent to full-season ball at 17 and Double-A at 18, and then he was launched into the majors—as a starting second baseman—just a few months after his 20th birthday in 2020. On paper, he didn't really deserve any of these promotions, and he's struggled pretty mightily so far in The Show. He spent a good chunk of the first half in Triple-A, and for the first time as a professional he absolutely smoked the ball when he was down, some of that before he could legally drink. He was brought up for good in late-July, and while the performance wasn't there, there are obvious improvements lurking in his batted ball profile: his average exit velocity shot up from 83.5 mph to 86.8 mph and his Z-Contact rate spiked from 80.1% to 89.3%. García hasn't been prospect-eligible for two offseasons now, but he's still younger than many of our Top 101 Prospects, and as talented as all but the top names on that list.

César Hernández 2B Born: 05/23/90 Age: 32 Bats: S Throws: R Height: 5'10" Weight: 195 lb. Origin: International Free Agent, 2006

YEAR	TEAM	LVL	AGE	PA	R	2B	3B	HR	RBI	BB	K	SB	CS	Whiff%	AVG/OBP/SLG	DRC+	BABIP	BRR	FRAA	WARP
2019	PHI	MLB	29	667	77	31	3	14	71	45	100	9	2	17.2%	.279/.333/.408	96	.313	-1.3	2B(157): -6.7	1.5
2020	CLE	MLB	30	261	35	20	0	3	20	24	57	0	0	20.1%	.283/.355/.408	92	.364	0.2	2B(58): 5.4	1.2
2021	CHW	MLB	31	217	24	4	0	3	15	21	45	1	1	19.8%	.232/.309/.299	88	.286	-1.1	2B(53): 1.6, SS(1): -0.0	0.5
2021	CLE	MLB	31	420	60	17	2	18	47	38	90	0	0	23.6%	.231/.307/.431	104	.256	-1.1	2B(89): -6.2	1.0
2022 DC	*WAS*	*MLB*	*32*	*422*	*63*	*15*	*1*	*8*	*45*	*40*	*85*	*5*	*3*	*21.4%*	*.248/.326/.370*	*91*	*.298*	*0.1*	*2B 0*	*1.0*

Comparables: Tony Taylor, Ray Durham, Frank White

All the César/Caesar name puns that team social media accounts tend to fall back on with Hernández work, if we equate being functionally league average on both sides of the ball with brutally conquering most of Europe. And maybe we should. Baseball is extremely hard. And Caesar killed a lot of people but never squared up 95 mph at the letters, nor lifted 20 bombs in a season like César somehow managed to accomplish in 2021. They didn't even *have* bombs in Caesar's time. But if we're keeping the comparison going, the end of Hernández's season was something akin to Caesar's landing at Kent. He arrived at a new location, accomplished exceedingly little while he was actually there, and it will look like a brief and irrelevant blip if everything returns to career norms afterward. Luckily for Caesar, he didn't have to sweat out a decision on a club option after his career low point.

★ ★ ★ *2022 Top 101 Prospect* **#66** ★ ★ ★

Brady House SS Born: 06/04/03 Age: 19 Bats: R Throws: R Height: 6'4" Weight: 215 lb. Origin: Round 1, 2021 Draft (#11 overall)

YEAR	TEAM	LVL	AGE	PA	R	2B	3B	HR	RBI	BB	K	SB	CS	Whiff%	AVG/OBP/SLG	DRC+	BABIP	BRR	FRAA	WARP
2021	NAT	ROK	18	66	14	3	0	4	12	7	13	0	0		.322/.394/.576		.357			
2022															*No projection*					

Comparables: Pedro Guerrero, Daniel Bravo, Yairo Muñoz

Washington has a long history as a draft slide backstop, owing to their willingness to get really aggressive on talent and bonuses in the first round. House was not expected to last much past the first half-dozen picks as one of the draft's highest-ceiling prep hitters. Once again, teams in front of the Nats cut deals with perceived lesser talents to spread their bonus pool around in later rounds, and once again, the Nats jumped on it, signing House for an above-slot $5 million. There's near-universal agreement that House has the potential for tremendous power. There's less agreement about his hit tool, which could be hampered by swing length and path, and he might end up sliding from shortstop to a corner. The upside here is immense, even if Nats fans reading this are already shuddering remembering how recently all of this was said about Carter Kieboom.

Carter Kieboom 3B

Born: 09/03/97 Age: 24 Bats: R Throws: R Height: 6'2" Weight: 215 lb. Origin: Round 1, 2016 Draft (#28 overall)

YEAR	TEAM	LVL	AGE	PA	R	2B	3B	HR	RBI	BB	K	SB	CS	Whiff%	AVG/OBP/SLG	DRC+	BABIP	BRR	FRAA	WARP
2019	FRE	AAA	21	494	79	24	3	16	79	68	100	5	2		.303/.409/.493	108	.362	0.9	SS(62): -5.1, 2B(41): 2.8, 3B(10): -0.3	2.5
2019	WAS	MLB	21	43	4	0	0	2	2	4	16	0	0	26.7%	.128/.209/.282	79	.143	0.1	SS(10): -1.0	0.0
2020	WAS	MLB	22	122	15	1	0	0	9	17	33	0	1	25.6%	.202/.344/.212	86	.299	0.7	3B(31): 2.6	0.4
2021	ROC	AAA	23	181	26	7	0	5	23	26	31	1	1		.236/.376/.385	123	.268	0.7	3B(40): 3.1	1.4
2021	WAS	MLB	23	249	26	6	0	6	20	25	62	0	0	29.5%	.207/.301/.318	89	.258	-1.1	3B(60): -4.3	-0.1
2022 DC	*WAS*	*MLB*	*24*	*503*	*64*	*18*	*1*	*13*	*65*	*56*	*123*	*2*	*1*	*28.4%*	*.230/.332/.370*	*91*	*.291*	*-0.6*	*3B 0*	*0.7*

Comparables: J.P. Crawford, Luis Sardinas, Yolmer Sánchez

Three is the smallest number of elements one needs to form a pattern. Anthony Rendon, an MVP-caliber left-side infielder for the Nationals, wore number 6. Trea Turner, an MVP-caliber left-side infielder for the Nationals, wore number 7. Kieboom, a left-side infielder for the Nationals, certainly wears number 8, but that's about where the comparisons with his former teammates end. Kieboom lacks Rendon's production at the plate as well as Turner's sparkling defense. He made modest improvements in hitting for power in 2021, though anything above his 2020 ISO (.010!) would be. He profiles most similarly to another previous Nationals player: Tyler Moore. Which is a big nein.

Victor Robles CF

Born: 05/19/97 Age: 25 Bats: R Throws: R Height: 6'0" Weight: 205 lb. Origin: International Free Agent, 2013

YEAR	TEAM	LVL	AGE	PA	R	2B	3B	HR	RBI	BB	K	SB	CS	Whiff%	AVG/OBP/SLG	DRC+	BABIP	BRR	FRAA	WARP
2019	WAS	MLB	22	617	86	33	3	17	65	35	140	28	9	23.5%	.255/.326/.419	88	.310	4.7	CF(141): 8.8, RF(15): 1.3	3.1
2020	WAS	MLB	23	189	20	5	1	3	15	9	53	4	1	27.8%	.220/.293/.315	78	.298	3.5	CF(52): 0.9	0.5
2021	ROC	AAA	24	93	14	8	1	4	8	7	26	6	1		.301/.370/.566	100	.396	0.5	CF(22): 2.5	0.6
2021	WAS	MLB	24	369	37	21	1	2	19	33	85	8	6	25.6%	.203/.310/.295	78	.271	-0.5	CF(104): -0.5	0.4
2022 DC	*WAS*	*MLB*	*25*	*222*	*31*	*10*	*1*	*5*	*27*	*17*	*53*	*8*	*4*	*25.8%*	*.234/.326/.389*	*94*	*.294*	*0.7*	*CF 0*	*0.8*

Comparables: Manuel Margot, Carlos Gómez, Byron Buxton

There's nothing nice about a 69 OPS+ for a fifth outfielder on a team desperate for warm bodies. Robles has attempted to remake himself twice: bulking up for 2020, which tarnished his usually sparkling outfield defense, then slimming down for 2021, which deadened his ability to hit. There are a few flickers of hope for a once-highly-touted prospect: He earned a career-high walk rate, struck out less frequently than in 2020 and chased/wasted at approximately league-average rates. But there's something clearly amiss. He's bottom-five percent in almost every hitting stat and his contact-oriented approach at the plate is mainly his elbow colliding frequently with the ball. It's just too bad that his bat doesn't.

★ ★ ★ *2022 Top 101 Prospect* **#39** ★ ★ ★

Keibert Ruiz C

Born: 07/20/98 Age: 23 Bats: S Throws: R Height: 6'0" Weight: 225 lb. Origin: International Free Agent, 2015

YEAR	TEAM	LVL	AGE	PA	R	2B	3B	HR	RBI	BB	K	SB	CS	Whiff%	AVG/OBP/SLG	DRC+	BABIP	BRR	FRAA	WARP
2019	TUL	AA	20	310	33	9	0	4	25	28	21	0	0		.254/.329/.330	127	.261	-4.0	C(61): 4.5	2.2
2019	OKC	AAA	20	40	6	0	0	2	9	2	1	0	0		.316/.350/.474	118	.286	0.6	C(9): -1.4	0.2
2020	LAD	MLB	21	8	1	0	0	1	1	0	3	0	0	21.4%	.250/.250/.625	86	.250		C(2): 0.3	0.0
2021	ROC	AAA	22	85	11	6	0	5	14	7	6	0	0		.308/.365/.577	135	.284	-1.3	C(19): 0.5	0.6
2021	OKC	AAA	22	231	39	18	0	16	45	23	27	0	0		.311/.381/.631	140	.293	-1.0	C(44): 2.6	2.2
2021	WAS	MLB	22	89	9	3	0	2	14	6	4	0	0	9.5%	.284/.348/.395	119	.280	-0.6	C(21): 0.5	0.6
2021	LAD	MLB	22	7	1	0	0	1	1	0	5	0	0	54.5%	.143/.143/.571	83			C(2): 0.0	0.0
2022 DC	*WAS*	*MLB*	*23*	*344*	*47*	*14*	*0*	*10*	*52*	*25*	*37*	*0*	*0*	*14.4%*	*.267/.329/.419*	*103*	*.275*	*-0.6*	*C 0*	*1.7*

Comparables: Christian Bethancourt, Ketel Marte, Freddie Freeman

YEAR	TEAM	P. COUNT	FRM RUNS	BLK RUNS	THRW RUNS	TOT RUNS
2019	OKC	1470	-0.9	0.0	-0.3	-1.2
2019	TUL	8965	3.8	0.0	1.1	4.9
2020	LAD	315	-0.1	0.0	0.4	0.3
2021	WAS	3216	0.7	0.1	-0.3	0.5
2021	LAD	67	0.0	0.0	0.0	0.0
2021	OKC	6748	3.7	-0.2	0.2	3.7
2021	ROC	2573	1.1	0.1	0.0	1.1
2022	*WAS*	*13228*	*-0.4*	*0.0*	*0.0*	*-0.4*

The concept of "prospect fatigue"—where a top farmhand hangs around so long that everyone gets sick of hearing about their potential if not realized—hit Ruiz a while back. If you run back to his teenage years in A-ball, his potential was boundless on both sides of the plate; he then stagnated for two years in Double-A, but they were his age-19/20 seasons. While Ruiz was struggling to actualize his power potential in the minors, Will Smith not only beat him to the majors but rapidly established himself as one of the league's top catchers. That made Ruiz superfluous to future plans in Dodger blue, and thus one of the more obvious trade chips-in-waiting. Los Angeles held on until he started hitting for power when the minors resumed last May, and were richly rewarded with Trea Turner and Max Scherzer by the Nationals. Ruiz should finally get a clean shot at establishing himself as a solid major-league option...although Riley Adams sure did make his own good impression in Washington.

Juan Soto RF

Born: 10/25/98 Age: 23 Bats: L Throws: L Height: 6'2" Weight: 224 lb. Origin: International Free Agent, 2015

YEAR	TEAM	LVL	AGE	PA	R	2B	3B	HR	RBI	BB	K	SB	CS	Whiff%	AVG/OBP/SLG	DRC+	BABIP	BRR	FRAA	WARP
2019	WAS	MLB	20	659	110	32	5	34	110	108	132	12	1	24.0%	.282/.401/.548	133	.312	1.6	LF(150): 1.4	5.4
2020	WAS	MLB	21	196	39	14	0	13	37	41	28	6	2	21.5%	.351/.490/.695	163	.363	-0.3	LF(36): -3.9, RF(6): -1.1	1.6
2021	WAS	MLB	22	654	111	20	2	29	95	145	93	9	7	20.0%	.313/.465/.534	164	.332	-1.3	RF(144): 6.9	7.7
2022 DC	*WAS*	*MLB*	*23*	*599*	*122*	*23*	*2*	*27*	*105*	*126*	*91*	*9*	*4*	*20.2%*	*.297/.448/.536*	*171*	*.317*	*0.0*	*RF 4*	*7.6*

Comparables: Boog Powell, Johnny Callison, Bryce Harper

What does value mean? Soto is undoubtedly the most valuable player on the Nationals and possibly in the National League. Finding deficiencies in his game is like looking for an A- on a valedictorian's report card. His slashlines speak for themselves. He missed another batting title by a breath, led the league in walks (somewhat inflated by teams pitching around him, sure) and got his swing right after besting Ohtani in the most compelling (and adorable) round of the Home Run Derby. He's 23 and is, by all accounts, exactly who he appears. The issue—a Troutonian one—is what a franchise values. What organized baseball values. The Nationals let Harper and Rendon walk, and offloaded Turner in a trade that signaled a full rebuild. Soto will likely command a significant fraction of a billion dollars once he hits free agency. As he should. He's proven his value. Unless of course what the Nationals value is, ugh, "financial flexibility."

Lane Thomas OF

Born: 08/23/95 Age: 26 Bats: R Throws: R Height: 6'0" Weight: 185 lb. Origin: Round 5, 2014 Draft (#144 overall)

YEAR	TEAM	LVL	AGE	PA	R	2B	3B	HR	RBI	BB	K	SB	CS	Whiff%	AVG/OBP/SLG	DRC+	BABIP	BRR	FRAA	WARP
2019	MEM	AAA	23	304	42	17	2	10	44	32	80	11	6		.268/.352/.460	92	.343	0.6	CF(37): 4.8, LF(32): -2.9, RF(3): -0.3	1.0
2019	STL	MLB	23	44	6	0	1	4	12	4	8	1	1	21.1%	.316/.409/.684	115	.308	0.3	CF(19): 2.2, RF(5): 0.3, LF(2): -0.1	0.5
2020	STL	MLB	24	40	5	2	0	1	2	4	13	0	0	28.1%	.111/.200/.250	87	.136	-0.1	RF(14): 1.3, CF(7): -0.6	0.1
2021	MEM	AAA	25	127	18	5	2	4	20	12	35	3	2		.265/.339/.451	98	.347	-0.3	CF(18): 0.3, RF(4): -0.1, LF(3): 1.5	0.5
2021	STL	MLB	25	58	2	1	0	0	1	10	17	2	1	27.3%	.104/.259/.125	84	.161	-0.6	RF(10): -0.4, LF(6): 0.3, CF(3): 0.0	0.0
2021	WAS	MLB	25	206	33	14	2	7	27	27	46	4	2	19.6%	.270/.364/.489	111	.325	-1.6	CF(39): -1.0, LF(6): -0.6, 2B(1): 0.0	0.8
2022 DC	*WAS*	*MLB*	*26*	*459*	*69*	*19*	*3*	*14*	*59*	*48*	*113*	*9*	*6*	*22.0%*	*.235/.323/.407*	*97*	*.291*	*0.8*	*CF 0, LF -1*	*1.5*

Comparables: Aaron Hicks, Starling Marte, Desmond Jennings

Aging can be tough to talk about. Fortunately, Rizzo is here to listen. If you're experiencing the signs of having signed a struggling Jon Lester to round out your ailing pitching staff, Rizzo can help. He'll ship Lane Thomas directly to your door in a discrete trade package. Once in Washington, Thomas will increase the vigor of your outfield bats, put some pep in your center-fielding step with an elite sprint speed, and post a chase/waste rate that would suggest long endurance in a career as a major leaguer. So what are you waiting for? Get Rizzo.

Ryan Zimmerman 1B

Born: 09/28/84 Age: 37 Bats: R Throws: R Height: 6'3" Weight: 215 lb. Origin: Round 1, 2005 Draft (#4 overall)

YEAR	TEAM	LVL	AGE	PA	R	2B	3B	HR	RBI	BB	K	SB	CS	Whiff%	AVG/OBP/SLG	DRC+	BABIP	BRR	FRAA	WARP
2019	WAS	MLB	34	190	20	9	0	6	27	17	39	0	0	26.6%	.257/.321/.415	98	.297	-1.1	1B(44): 1.0	0.5
2021	WAS	MLB	36	273	27	16	0	14	46	16	77	0	0	28.4%	.243/.286/.471	99	.289	-1.5	1B(54): -1.4	0.4
2022 DC	*FA*	*MLB*	*37*	*207*	*22*	*9*	*0*	*7*	*25*	*15*	*53*	*0*	*0*	*28.8%*	*.235/.298/.414*	*90*	*.285*	*-0.3*	*1B 0*	*0.1*

Comparables: Adrián Beltré, Brooks Robinson, Aramis Ramirez

Zimmerman took what was likely his last at-bat in a Nationals uniform for a bottom-scraping team on an inauspicious day in early October. His career—as the first of the franchise, the face of the franchise—might be defined similarly. Not as what was, but what could have been. The team floundered during his best years, surrounding him with a cast of remember-that-guys, gambling that his future would be brighter than his present. A bet stymied by the kind of injuries that inevitably come with age. He survived, though: the Josh Willingham Era, the Bryce Harper Era and now the Juan Soto Era.

Perhaps there's a special kind of value to that survival, from the offensive fire of his youth to, in his later years, the pretty-good-for-a-first-baseman defense. Always, a tendency to get big hits at memorable moments, none more exciting than the Nats' first ever World Series home run—off Gerrit Cole, no less. But all careers end. So Zimmerman took what was likely his final at-bat in a Nationals uniform, to cheering, to tears, to a city that knows the bad times only makes the good ones sweeter, a fitting fanfare as Mr. Walkoff walked off the field for one last time.

PITCHERS

Joan Adon RHP

Born: 08/12/98 Age: 23 Bats: R Throws: R Height: 6'2" Weight: 242 lb. Origin: International Free Agent, 2016

YEAR	TEAM	LVL	AGE	W	L	SV	G	GS	IP	H	HR	BB/9	K/9	K	GB%	BABIP	WHIP	ERA	DRA-	WARP	MPH	FB%	Whiff%	CSP
2019	HAG	A	20	11	3	0	22	21	105	93	8	3.8	7.7	90	45.6%	.286	1.30	3.86	120	-0.2				
2021	WIL	A+	22	6	4	0	17	17	87	77	7	3.3	9.4	91	46.1%	.299	1.25	4.97	87	1.3				
2021	HBG	AA	22	1	2	0	3	3	14	15	1	3.2	15.4	24	37.1%	.412	1.43	6.43	79	0.3				
2021	WAS	MLB	22	0	0	0	1	1	5^1	6	1	5.1	15.2	9	72.7%	.500	1.69	3.38			95.3	54.3%	33.3%	60.0%
2022 DC	*WAS*	*MLB*	*23*	*2*	*1*	*0*	*17*	*3*	*25.7*	*24*	*3*	*4.5*	*9.2*	*26*	*43.7%*	*.297*	*1.44*	*4.77*	*109*	*0.1*	*95.3*	*54.3%*	*33.3%*	*60.0%*

Comparables: Michael Fulmer, Alex Cobb, Joe Ross

The Nationals called on Adon to make his major-league debut in Game 162 against Boston, with only four starts spread across six weeks in the high-minors. It was a meaningless game for Washington, merely a chance to celebrate Ryan Zimmerman and then pack up and go home for a long winter, so they took a look at a promising prospect already on the 40-man. Yet it meant *everything* to the Red Sox, who needed a win to clinch a Wild Card spot. For five innings-plus, Adon baffled Boston batters by spotting mid-90s heat and getting chases with his plus slider. For a hot minute, it looked like his effort might buy the Toronto Blue Jays a Game 163, before the Nats bullpen did Nats bullpen things behind him. Adon's final day heroics capped off a strong conclusion to his season as his command and secondary offerings improved. He's been pegged with a reliever projection for years—and usual developmental caveats like changeup improvement and effort in the delivery do still apply—but the Adon that showed up in October has every chance to start.

Gerardo Carrillo RHP Born: 09/13/98 Age: 23 Bats: R Throws: R Height: 5'10" Weight: 170 lb. Origin: International Free Agent, 2016

YEAR	TEAM	LVL	AGE	W	L	SV	G	GS	IP	H	HR	BB/9	K/9	K	GB%	BABIP	WHIP	ERA	DRA-	WARP	MPH	FB%	Whiff%	CSP
2019	RC	A+	20	5	9	0	23	21	86	87	3	5.3	9.0	86	54.2%	.339	1.60	5.44	125	-1.0				
2021	TUL	AA	22	3	2	0	15	14	59^1	49	9	4.4	10.6	70	48.7%	.280	1.31	4.25	83	0.9				
2021	HBG	AA	22	0	5	0	8	8	37	40	5	5.1	9.2	38	49.1%	.330	1.65	5.59	108	0.1				
2022 DC	*WAS*	*MLB*	*23*	*2*	*2*	*0*	*17*	*3*	*25.7*	*26*	*3*	*5.4*	*8.2*	*23*	*47.7%*	*.310*	*1.64*	*6.09*	*131*	*-0.3*				

Comparables: Aaron Sanchez, Blake Beavan, Jimmy Haynes

Third wheels don't *have* to be bad. Sure, we've all had that friend who hung around a little too long on a date that wasn't actually *their* date (or worse yet, perhaps been that friend ourselves). But sometimes, it's all just fine; think about how well Ted Mosby worked as Marshall and Lily's chronic third wheel in *How I Met Your Mother*. Carrillo was the clear third wheel coming back to the Nats in the Turner/Scherzer deal, well behind the two Top 101 prospects fronting the return. Yet he's a pretty decent prospect in his own right, a hard-throwing live arm with developing feel for spin who has already pitched decently in Double-A. He's going to have to cut his walk rate and develop a better change of pace pitch to not just be tagging along in the rotation, but even a reliever is a better outcome than the end of *HIMYM*.

★ ★ ★ *2022 Top 101 Prospect* **#19** ★ ★ ★

Cade Cavalli RHP Born: 08/14/98 Age: 23 Bats: R Throws: R Height: 6'4" Weight: 230 lb. Origin: Round 1, 2020 Draft (#22 overall)

YEAR	TEAM	LVL	AGE	W	L	SV	G	GS	IP	H	HR	BB/9	K/9	K	GB%	BABIP	WHIP	ERA	DRA-	WARP	MPH	FB%	Whiff%	CSP
2021	WIL	A+	22	3	1	0	7	7	40^2	24	1	2.7	15.7	71	49.3%	.329	0.89	1.77	63	1.2				
2021	HBG	AA	22	3	3	0	11	11	58	39	2	5.4	12.4	80	38.3%	.296	1.28	2.79	80	1.1				
2021	ROC	AAA	22	1	5	0	6	6	24^2	33	2	4.7	8.8	24	52.5%	.397	1.86	7.30	109	0.2				
2022 non-DC	*WAS*	*MLB*	*23*	*2*	*2*	*0*	*57*	*0*	*50*	*45*	*6*	*5.0*	*10.6*	*58*	*42.9%*	*.309*	*1.47*	*4.71*	*106*	*0.0*				

Comparables: Clay Buchholz, John Gant, Jason Hammel

"Cavalli" is Italian for "horses," so you can expect to hear equine-related puns forever if Cade becomes as good as we think he'll be. Cavalli came to Oklahoma as a two-way player and battled injuries and command woes on the mound for his first two years. He started pulling it together as a full-time pitcher for the collegiate national team in the summer between his sophomore and junior years, and was one of the hottest pitchers in college baseball early in 2020 when the world shut down. The always-gambling Nationals threw a big bet that his command improvements were real, and the chips are starting to stack up on their side of the table. Cavalli quickly blew through much of the minors, stopping off to repeatedly hit 100 mph at the Futures Game. The strike-throwing issues aren't totally resolved, but his fastball/breaking ball/changeup mix is electric and the likelihood he sticks as a starter long-term is rising. He's one of the top pitching prospects in the minors now and he'll be jockeying for a rotation spot as soon as this year.

Patrick Corbin LHP Born: 07/19/89 Age: 32 Bats: L Throws: L Height: 6'4" Weight: 220 lb. Origin: Round 2, 2009 Draft (#80 overall)

YEAR	TEAM	LVL	AGE	W	L	SV	G	GS	IP	H	HR	BB/9	K/9	K	GB%	BABIP	WHIP	ERA	DRA-	WARP	MPH	FB%	Whiff%	CSP
2019	WAS	MLB	29	14	7	0	33	33	202	169	24	3.1	10.6	238	48.7%	.295	1.18	3.25	79	4.3	92.1	53.7%	31.8%	41.6%
2020	WAS	MLB	30	2	7	0	11	11	65^2	85	10	2.5	8.2	60	45.2%	.362	1.57	4.66	104	0.6	90.5	52.2%	23.7%	46.2%
2021	WAS	MLB	31	9	16	0	31	31	171^2	192	37	3.1	7.5	143	46.0%	.312	1.47	5.82	117	0.0	92.6	56.4%	25.1%	53.9%
2022 DC	*WAS*	*MLB*	*32*	*9*	*8*	*0*	*25*	*25*	*145*	*151*	*22*	*3.0*	*8.1*	*129*	*45.7%*	*.306*	*1.37*	*4.63*	*109*	*0.5*	*92.1*	*55.1%*	*26.5%*	*49.7%*

Comparables: Jim Kaat, Donovan Osborne, Jason Marquis

The main advantage Washington got from having Corbin pitch in 2021 was draft position for 2022. Corbin went from World Series Game 7 winner to a marginal starter in everything but his contract amount. His four-seamer declined from potent to potable; he lost precipitous spin off his curveball before it was cool. His slider is his only effective weapon, though it too has diminished bite. He is, in his peripherals and in sum, real bad. Whether the issue is mechanical, psychological, or metaphysical, the answer may be geographical: a rehab stint to figure himself out.

Paolo Espino RHP Born: 01/10/87 Age: 35 Bats: R Throws: R Height: 5'10" Weight: 215 lb. Origin: Round 10, 2006 Draft (#311 overall)

YEAR	TEAM	LVL	AGE	W	L	SV	G	GS	IP	H	HR	BB/9	K/9	K	GB%	BABIP	WHIP	ERA	DRA-	WARP	MPH	FB%	Whiff%	CSP
2019	TOR	WIN	32	3	1	1	6	4	26^2	21	0	2.0	8.1	24	36.4%	.276	1.01	1.69						
2019	FRE	AAA	32	8	4	0	17	17	92^1	97	15	2.3	9.1	93	38.0%	.317	1.31	5.65	100	0.5				
2020	TOR	WIN	33	2	3	0	6	6	29	22	2	1.9	6.5	21	34.9%	.238	0.97	3.72						
2020	WAS	MLB	33	0	0	0	2	1	6	8	1	3.0	10.5	7	44.4%	.412	1.67	4.50	78	0.1	90.2	54.5%	28.0%	47.7%
2021	WAS	MLB	34	5	5	1	35	19	109^2	108	19	2.1	7.6	92	35.9%	.283	1.21	4.27	103	0.8	89.1	55.3%	20.2%	58.5%
2022 DC	*WAS*	*MLB*	*35*	*9*	*9*	*0*	*58*	*21*	*133.3*	*138*	*23*	*2.5*	*7.1*	*104*	*36.5%*	*.288*	*1.32*	*4.72*	*114*	*0.0*	*89.1*	*55.3%*	*20.5%*	*58.0%*

Comparables: Jared Hughes, Wade LeBlanc, Austin Bibens-Dirkx

"Irreplaceable" was the number one hit in 2007 when Espino first signed with Cleveland. Over the next 14 years, he proved eminently replaceable, with a Homeric transaction page and permanent status as the fringiest of fringe players. The Nationals signed him as a stopgap starter in late 2020, then to a minor-league deal in 2021. He shone in the first half, with a K/BB ratio driven by a low occurrence of free passes—he gave up four walks in 18 games from April through June, which is particularly impressive given his junkballer arsenal. Still, regression stepped in in July and August, dropping him from elite(ish) to merely serviceable. But anything above replacement was a win, and Espino is likely to find placement on a major-league roster in the coming season.

Erick Fedde RHP Born: 02/25/93 Age: 29 Bats: R Throws: R Height: 6'4" Weight: 200 lb. Origin: Round 1, 2014 Draft (#18 overall)

YEAR	TEAM	LVL	AGE	W	L	SV	G	GS	IP	H	HR	BB/9	K/9	K	GB%	BABIP	WHIP	ERA	DRA-	WARP	MPH	FB%	Whiff%	CSP
2019	HBG	AA	26	2	0	0	5	4	24^{2}	18	2	1.8	9.9	27	50.8%	.262	0.93	2.55	92	0.3				
2019	FRE	AAA	26	1	1	0	2	2	10	19	5	3.6	9.0	10	36.1%	.452	2.30	12.60	114	0.0				
2019	WAS	MLB	26	4	2	0	21	12	78	81	11	3.8	4.7	41	48.8%	.288	1.46	4.50	122	-0.1	92.5	55.2%	16.8%	46.4%
2020	WAS	MLB	27	2	4	0	11	8	50^{1}	47	10	3.9	5.0	28	55.0%	.234	1.37	4.29	104	0.5	93.7	55.5%	15.3%	46.2%
2021	WAS	MLB	28	7	9	0	29	27	133^{1}	144	23	3.2	8.6	128	48.4%	.320	1.44	5.47	94	1.7	93.9	43.5%	22.3%	51.7%
2022 DC	*WAS*	*MLB*	*29*	*6*	*7*	*0*	*22*	*22*	*106.3*	*111*	*14*	*3.3*	*7.3*	*86*	*48.4%*	*.301*	*1.41*	*4.67*	*110*	*0.2*	*93.7*	*47.0%*	*20.4%*	*50.1%*

Comparables: Chad Bettis, Doug Fister, Garrett Stephenson

You awake to the sound of your captors returning. It's cold where you are, damp, the stench of the cell where Gul Madred has been keeping you pungent. The lamps blink on above you. "How many?" they ask.

The Federation trained you for this. You don't get to be Jean-Luc Picard by shrinking from danger. "Four," you say.

Because there are four pitch types, only four. A cutter, a sinker, a change and a slider. Four. You're sure of it. But doubt surges. Could it be five? Six? Three? You begin to waver in your convictions, in your sense of self, a shimmering uncertainty about their number. Below that, the fundamental truth of their efficacy: Poor. Their outcomes: Worse.

Gul Madred smiles a Cardassian sort of smile at you. "Fetch it again."

You groan, exhausted, as they wheel in a monitor. It plays what it always plays: a four-hour slog of a Washington-Philadelphia game from June 2021. You could recite it by now, each repetition somehow worse than the previous. Seven total bases for Travis Jankowski. A netting-related delay. A Fedde of a start, with five runs on six hits in four innings, a game score of 28. You'll do anything—almost anything—not to see it again.

"How many?" your inquisitor asks, as if sensing your will beginning to dissolve.

"Four," you gasp. "There are four." And they, smiling, cue the video.

Kyle Finnegan RHP Born: 09/04/91 Age: 30 Bats: R Throws: R Height: 6'2" Weight: 200 lb. Origin: Round 6, 2013 Draft (#191 overall)

YEAR	TEAM	LVL	AGE	W	L	SV	G	GS	IP	H	HR	BB/9	K/9	K	GB%	BABIP	WHIP	ERA	DRA-	WARP	MPH	FB%	Whiff%	CSP
2019	MID	AA	27	0	1	9	21	0	22^{2}	16	0	2.8	14.3	36	54.2%	.333	1.01	1.59	72	0.4				
2019	LV	AAA	27	3	1	5	21	0	28	23	3	3.9	11.6	36	40.9%	.323	1.25	2.89	78	0.5				
2020	WAS	MLB	28	1	0	0	25	0	24^{2}	21	2	4.7	9.9	27	50.0%	.297	1.38	2.92	86	0.5	95.2	70.4%	28.3%	51.0%
2021	WAS	MLB	29	5	9	11	68	0	66	64	9	4.6	9.3	68	47.6%	.309	1.48	3.55	96	0.7	95.7	68.4%	25.1%	55.6%
2022 DC	*WAS*	*MLB*	*30*	*3*	*3*	*33*	*67*	*0*	*58*	*54*	*7*	*4.3*	*9.5*	*61*	*47.7%*	*.300*	*1.41*	*4.36*	*101*	*0.2*	*95.6*	*68.8%*	*25.7%*	*54.7%*

Comparables: Eric Yardley, Kirby Yates, Rob Wooten

Sometimes pressure makes diamonds; sometimes it just makes dust. Finnegan received a promotion to being the club's de facto closer following the trade deadline fire sale. He certainly earned the title of closer by being rock solid in August, then the title of *Nationals'* closer when he crumbled in September. His late-summer success hinged on increased usage of his slider that, counterintuitively, drew fewer whiffs (exactly zero in August) though deadened contact, a pitch used to limited efficacy in September. Still, he's got a blazing sinker, a decent splitter and the (for a very limited value of the word) swagger, so he's likely to get used as a good-but-not-great bullpen guy in 2022.

Josiah Gray RHP Born: 12/21/97 Age: 24 Bats: R Throws: R Height: 6'1" Weight: 190 lb. Origin: Round 2, 2018 Draft (#72 overall)

YEAR	TEAM	LVL	AGE	W	L	SV	G	GS	IP	H	HR	BB/9	K/9	K	GB%	BABIP	WHIP	ERA	DRA-	WARP	MPH	FB%	Whiff%	CSP
2019	GL	A	21	1	0	0	5	5	23^{1}	13	0	2.7	10.0	26	37.0%	.241	0.86	1.93	94	0.3				
2019	RC	A+	21	7	0	0	12	12	67^{1}	52	3	1.7	10.7	80	36.3%	.293	0.97	2.14	75	1.2				
2019	TUL	AA	21	3	2	0	9	8	39^{1}	33	0	2.5	9.4	41	34.3%	.317	1.12	2.75	77	0.6				
2021	OKC	AAA	23	1	1	0	4	3	15^{2}	8	3	1.1	12.6	22	36.4%	.167	0.64	2.87	85	0.2				
2021	WAS	MLB	23	2	2	0	12	12	62^{2}	56	15	4.0	9.0	63	29.6%	.258	1.34	5.31	116	0.0	94.6	51.9%	28.3%	51.9%
2021	LAD	MLB	23	0	0	0	2	1	8	7	4	5.6	14.6	13	29.4%	.231	1.50	6.75	86	0.1	94.8	50.0%	44.7%	47.7%
2022 DC	*WAS*	*MLB*	*24*	*8*	*7*	*0*	*25*	*25*	*134.7*	*120*	*21*	*3.5*	*9.7*	*145*	*33.0%*	*.287*	*1.29*	*4.21*	*100*	*1.1*	*94.6*	*51.7%*	*30.4%*	*51.4%*

Comparables: Trevor Bauer, Daniel Hudson, Johnny Cueto

Historically, a pitcher with Gray's 2021 pitch selection would be quickly bound for bullpen work. He largely shelved his changeup, so over 96% of his pitches were four-seam fastballs and breaking balls. While he throws two breaking balls, they have very similar velocity and horizontal movement profiles, such that they were at times difficult to distinguish when he was a prospect. Just a few years ago, the industry would've shunted him off into a future closer bucket as a fastball/slurve guy and thought no more of it. We look a little deeper into these things now, and it turns out that Gray's fastball and breaking balls all tunnel well off of each other; the curveball now drops and spins substantially more than the slider, enough that batters are now the ones who have a hard time distinguishing between them—until it's too late. The Nationals picked him up from the Dodgers in the Scherzer/Turner trade and immediately inserted him in the rotation. He subsequently posted huge whiff rates on both breaking balls, buoying hope that he'll be a solid major-league starting pitcher sooner rather than later.

Will Harris RHP

Born: 08/28/84 Age: 37 Bats: R Throws: R Height: 6'4" Weight: 236 lb. Origin: Round 9, 2006 Draft (#258 overall)

YEAR	TEAM	LVL	AGE	W	L	SV	G	GS	IP	H	HR	BB/9	K/9	K	GB%	BABIP	WHIP	ERA	DRA-	WARP	MPH	FB%	Whiff%	CSP
2019	HOU	MLB	34	4	1	4	68	0	60	42	6	2.1	9.3	62	52.9%	.247	0.93	1.50	86	1.0	91.3	58.0%	29.8%	46.4%
2020	WAS	MLB	35	0	1	1	20	0	17^{2}	21	3	4.6	10.7	21	42.6%	.353	1.70	3.06	89	0.3	90.7	77.7%	28.9%	42.6%
2021	WAS	MLB	36	0	1	0	8	0	6	7	1	4.5	13.5	9	33.3%	.353	1.67	9.00	86	0.1	90.2	80.7%	26.5%	55.8%
2022 DC	*WAS*	*MLB*	*37*	*2*	*2*	*0*	*59*	*0*	*51.7*	*48*	*7*	*3.1*	*9.8*	*56*	*45.4%*	*.301*	*1.27*	*3.89*	*94*	*0.3*	*90.9*	*69.3%*	*28.8%*	*47.0%*

Comparables: Fernando Rodney, Darren O'Day, Mike Timlin

Thoracic outlet syndrome is a career-altering diagnosis. It's what turned Matt Harvey from The Dark Knight of Gotham into a guy wearing a generic Spirit Halloween black caped crime fighter costume. Chris Carpenter only made it back for six starts before he just couldn't go anymore. It's been the end of the line for some pitchers, and many others have come back with diminished stuff and results. (Unfortunately for Washington, this isn't the only comment in this chapter where thoracic outlet surgery will come up.) Harris started dealing with numbness and swelling in his pitching hand in March. An initial diagnostic procedure ruled out blood clots or TOS, and he actually came back to the majors for a handful of appearances before being shut down again with the same symptoms. A second opinion brought along the dreaded thoracic outlet diagnosis, and Harris had surgery in early-June. It's going to be a tough road back at his age, but he already went from pinging around on waivers in his late-20s to a half-decade run as one of the best relievers in the game, so perhaps there's a bit more magic left somewhere in there.

Cole Henry RHP

Born: 07/15/99 Age: 22 Bats: R Throws: R Height: 6'4" Weight: 215 lb. Origin: Round 2, 2020 Draft (#55 overall)

YEAR	TEAM	LVL	AGE	W	L	SV	G	GS	IP	H	HR	BB/9	K/9	K	GB%	BABIP	WHIP	ERA	DRA-	WARP	MPH	FB%	Whiff%	CSP
2021	WIL	A+	21	3	3	0	9	8	43	23	3	2.3	13.2	63	46.4%	.247	0.79	1.88	74	1.0				
2022 non-DC	*WAS*	*MLB*	*22*	*2*	*2*	*0*	*57*	*0*	*50*	*42*	*6*	*3.7*	*9.8*	*54*	*41.6%*	*.283*	*1.27*	*3.87*	*95*	*0.3*				

Comparables: Johnny Cueto, Daniel Hudson, Justin Masterson

If the Nationals are going to build a viable homegrown core anytime soon, they're going to have to hit big on some higher-upside gambles like Henry. He got a well-overslot $2 million bonus in the second round in 2020 despite just 77 ⅓ innings at LSU; the bonus was partially because of his draft-eligible sophomore status and partially because he flashed a big performance and profile jump to a viable three-pitch starting prospect before the pandemic shut college baseball down that year. The performance jump carried over into 2021, and he pitched splendidly when on the mound. Unfortunately, his history of elbow issues from college also carried over, and he missed almost three months with soreness. Combine that with a higher-effort delivery and some inconsistency with his changeup, and we're edging close to relief risk bingo here. Better hope they don't call O-69 on his command!

Andry Lara RHP

Born: 01/06/03 Age: 19 Bats: R Throws: R Height: 6'4" Weight: 180 lb. Origin: International Free Agent, 2019

YEAR	TEAM	LVL	AGE	W	L	SV	G	GS	IP	H	HR	BB/9	K/9	K	GB%	BABIP	WHIP	ERA	DRA-	WARP	MPH	FB%	Whiff%	CSP
2021	NAT	ROK	18	3	2	0	9	7	39^{2}	35	5	2.9	10.7	47	46.7%	.300	1.21	4.54						
2021	FBG	A	18	0	1	0	2	2	8^{2}	6	2	8.3	5.2	5	20.0%	.174	1.62	5.19	162	-0.2				
2022 non-DC	*WAS*	*MLB*	*19*	*2*	*3*	*0*	*57*	*0*	*50*	*62*	*10*	*8.1*	*6.3*	*35*	*31.3%*	*.323*	*2.16*	*8.91*	*173*	*-1.7*				

Comparables: Brailin Rodriguez, Rainiery Rodriguez, Edgar Sanchez

Lara has been hyped as one of the most interesting prospects in the Washington system since he signed for over a million bucks in July 2019. That was partially due to how good he looked on complex backfields, and partially because there's hardly anything else to talk about on the Nats farm. He finally got on a professional field in 2021 and he's as precocious and projectable as advertised, although for now he's merely throwing in the low-90s. The curve and slider are interesting but run together, and there's not much command or changeup at present. For now, he's an interesting live arm to watch in a system that lacks interesting prospects to watch; check back again in a few years to see if he made a big jump.

Kyle McGowin RHP

Born: 11/27/91 Age: 30 Bats: R Throws: R Height: 6'3" Weight: 202 lb. Origin: Round 5, 2013 Draft (#157 overall)

YEAR	TEAM	LVL	AGE	W	L	SV	G	GS	IP	H	HR	BB/9	K/9	K	GB%	BABIP	WHIP	ERA	DRA-	WARP	MPH	FB%	Whiff%	CSP
2019	HBG	AA	27	1	1	0	6	6	32^{1}	22	2	2.5	10.0	36	38.5%	.263	0.96	2.51	87	0.5				
2019	FRE	AAA	27	7	2	0	11	11	60^{2}	59	8	2.5	10.1	68	46.1%	.323	1.25	3.86	82	1.0				
2019	WAS	MLB	27	0	0	1	7	1	16	22	7	2.3	10.1	18	43.4%	.333	1.63	10.12	89	0.3	91.0	52.3%	30.5%	43.3%
2020	WAS	MLB	28	1	0	1	9	0	11	9	2	4.1	13.1	16	38.5%	.292	1.27	4.91	87	0.2	91.5	28.1%	38.5%	45.6%
2021	ROC	AAA	29	1	0	0	9	0	9^{2}	3	0	2.8	9.3	10	43.5%	.136	0.62	0.93	93	0.2				
2021	WAS	MLB	29	0	0	0	27	0	30	21	5	4.2	10.5	35	35.1%	.222	1.17	4.20	94	0.4	91.2	31.4%	28.3%	53.7%
2022 non-DC	*WAS*	*MLB*	*30*	*2*	*2*	*0*	*57*	*0*	*50*	*43*	*8*	*3.3*	*10.1*	*56*	*39.5%*	*.281*	*1.24*	*4.03*	*96*	*0.3*	*91.2*	*33.6%*	*30.4%*	*50.9%*

Comparables: Pedro Villarreal, Brandon Workman, Deck McGuire

Do you have a game you're definitely going to lose?
Do you not want to use a good pitcher just in case something happens to them?
Do you not care if the game gets really out of hand?

Enter McGowin.

The right-hander remade himself as a slider specialist following a move to the bullpen to fairly good effect. His slider boasts a 40% whiff/swing rate, while limiting on-base traffic. His fastballs, however, remain a work in progress and his usage in the "you lose some" side of "you win some, you lose some, and that's baseball" won't change until they do.

Patrick Murphy RHP

Born: 06/10/95 Age: 27 Bats: R Throws: R Height: 6'5" Weight: 235 lb. Origin: Round 3, 2013 Draft (#83 overall)

YEAR	TEAM	LVL	AGE	W	L	SV	G	GS	IP	H	HR	BB/9	K/9	K	GB%	BABIP	WHIP	ERA	DRA-	WARP	MPH	FB%	Whiff%	CSP
2019	NH	AA	24	4	7	0	18	18	84	75	7	2.9	9.2	86	51.6%	.286	1.21	4.71	103	0.5				
2020	TOR	MLB	25	0	0	0	4	0	6	6	0	3.0	7.5	5	50.0%	.333	1.33	1.50	92	0.1	96.8	59.6%	20.8%	50.0%
2021	BUF	AAA	26	1	1	0	10	0	14^{2}	8	0	4.9	10.4	17	66.7%	.242	1.09	0.00	89	0.3				
2021	WAS	MLB	26	0	2	0	17	0	18^{2}	19	2	2.9	11.1	23	47.2%	.333	1.34	5.30	86	0.3	96.8	68.2%	26.0%	55.6%
2021	TOR	MLB	26	0	1	0	8	0	9^{1}	12	1	3.9	5.8	6	43.8%	.355	1.71	4.82	118	0.0	96.1	60.7%	15.5%	55.6%
2022 DC	*WAS*	*MLB*	*27*	*2*	*2*	*0*	*52*	*0*	*45.3*	*42*	*5*	*3.8*	*7.9*	*40*	*48.8%*	*.289*	*1.37*	*4.21*	*99*	*0.2*	*96.6*	*64.9%*	*22.4%*	*54.9%*

Comparables: Juan Minaya, Austin Brice, Lou Trivino

Not to be confused with Patrick Murphy, the former Blue Dog House Democrat from Pennsylvania (more recently President Obama's final Secretary of the Army), or Patrick Murphy, the former No Labels House Democrat from Florida (who later lost a Senate election to Marco Rubio), this Patrick Murphy is a hard-throwing, oft-injured reliever who got claimed off waivers from the Blue Jays in August. We apologize if you're also named Patrick Murphy, but two centrist politicians and a hurler who spins it right down the middle all the time is enough mediocrity for one comment.

Sean Nolin LHP

Born: 12/26/89 Age: 32 Bats: L Throws: L Height: 6'4" Weight: 250 lb. Origin: Round 6, 2010 Draft (#186 overall)

YEAR	TEAM	LVL	AGE	W	L	SV	G	GS	IP	H	HR	BB/9	K/9	K	GB%	BABIP	WHIP	ERA	DRA-	WARP	MPH	FB%	Whiff%	CSP
2019	BIR	AA	29	1	1	0	4	4	16^{2}	26	5	3.2	8.6	16	27.6%	.396	1.92	8.10	133	-0.2				
2019	TAC	AAA	29	6	4	0	15	14	79^{1}	78	13	2.9	8.4	74	38.2%	.295	1.31	4.76	119	-0.4				
2021	ROC	AAA	31	3	3	0	11	9	47^{1}	46	7	2.9	9.9	52	47.3%	.315	1.29	3.80	105	0.5				
2021	WAS	MLB	31	0	2	0	10	5	26^{2}	32	4	4.4	6.7	20	35.2%	.337	1.69	4.39	122	-0.1	90.7	46.7%	20.8%	56.6%
2022 DC	*FA*	*MLB*	*32*	*2*	*2*	*0*	*17*	*3*	*24.3*	*25*	*4*	*3.5*	*7.4*	*20*	*38.4%*	*.298*	*1.44*	*5.11*	*119*	*-0.1*	*90.7*	*46.7%*	*20.8%*	*56.6%*

Comparables: Hector Noesí, Wade LeBlanc, Ross Detwiler

Nine years ago, we ranked Nolin as the no. 97 prospect in baseball, citing his four-pitch repertoire and advanced pitchability. Then things slowly started unraveling. He got shelled in his major-league debut in May 2013. He stagnated in the upper-minors in 2014, with reports softening on his fastball and both breaking pitches. He was shipped to Oakland in the Josh Donaldson trade after that season, by which time he'd fallen to a potential back-of-the-rotation type, then went on waivers to Milwaukee after six mediocre starts. Tommy John surgery wiped out his next two seasons. From there, his career started wandering so aimlessly you might've thought it was lost entirely: a year in a Double-A bullpen, a stint in the Atlantic League, a not-particularly-successful season in NPB. He came back from Japan on a minor-league pact with Washington before the 2021 season, and the transaction was so under-the-radar that it doesn't even appear in his own MLB transaction log. He was mere organizational depth for a team that did not rate to need it...right up until they just needed fresh arms after the trade deadline. For the first time in almost six years, Nolin was a major leaguer. Sure, he wasn't particularly good, and the only thing anyone will remember is when he threw at Freddie Freeman. But he made it all the way back from the brink, and that shouldn't go without notice.

Tanner Rainey RHP

Born: 12/25/92 Age: 29 Bats: R Throws: R Height: 6'2" Weight: 247 lb. Origin: Round 2, 2015 Draft (#71 overall)

YEAR	TEAM	LVL	AGE	W	L	SV	G	GS	IP	H	HR	BB/9	K/9	K	GB%	BABIP	WHIP	ERA	DRA-	WARP	MPH	FB%	Whiff%	CSP
2019	FRE	AAA	26	2	2	2	16	0	18	16	1	6.0	16.0	32	56.8%	.417	1.56	4.00	68	0.4				
2019	WAS	MLB	26	2	3	0	52	0	48^{1}	32	6	7.1	13.8	74	51.0%	.289	1.45	3.91	76	1.1	97.9	70.8%	40.7%	43.3%
2020	WAS	MLB	27	1	1	0	20	0	20^{1}	8	4	3.1	14.2	32	34.3%	.129	0.74	2.66	73	0.5	97.1	60.9%	47.3%	44.4%
2021	ROC	AAA	28	1	0	0	8	1	7^{2}	3	1	5.9	17.6	15	18.2%	.200	1.04	2.35	77	0.2				
2021	WAS	MLB	28	1	3	3	38	0	31^{2}	29	6	7.1	11.9	42	24.7%	.307	1.71	7.39	105	0.2	96.4	64.5%	35.6%	53.6%
2022 DC	*WAS*	*MLB*	*29*	*3*	*3*	*3*	*67*	*0*	*58*	*44*	*10*	*5.9*	*13.3*	*86*	*36.1%*	*.290*	*1.43*	*4.69*	*104*	*0.1*	*96.9*	*65.5%*	*38.9%*	*49.4%*

Comparables: Vinnie Pestano, Danny Coulombe, Nick Vincent

The National Hockey League once made a fantastic playoff commercial—you can find it on YouTube—titled "Name." It's narrated by Liev Schreiber as part of his deeply-intoning second career talking over Important Sports Videos, so you know it has gravitas. The commercial goes through how a name is the first thing you're given as a newborn and becomes how you're remembered, the stuff of stories and legends, on the way to being engraved on Lord Stanley's Cup if you're good and lucky enough. One of the clips flashing quickly past your eyes is of "Mario," which to a hockey fan means Lemieux and only Lemieux, no different than how Babe or Mickey or Junior or Jackie mean just one thing to a baseball fan. The first name Tanner has been carried by five major-league players. All of the Tanners are currently-active pitchers, perfectly syncing up with the name's 1993-2000 run as one of the hundred most popular names for baby boys. And unless he stops walking the world, it will never be mononymous with Rainey, except perhaps with an expletive right before it after another excruciating outing.

Joe Ross RHP

Born: 05/21/93 Age: 29 Bats: R Throws: R Height: 6'4" Weight: 223 lb. Origin: Round 1, 2011 Draft (#25 overall)

YEAR	TEAM	LVL	AGE	W	L	SV	G	GS	IP	H	HR	BB/9	K/9	K	GB%	BABIP	WHIP	ERA	DRA-	WARP	MPH	FB%	Whiff%	CSP
2019	FRE	AAA	26	2	3	0	8	8	40	48	2	1.8	7.2	32	45.7%	.380	1.40	4.28	101	0.2				
2019	WAS	MLB	26	4	4	0	27	9	64	74	7	4.6	8.0	57	43.8%	.351	1.67	5.48	106	0.5	94.2	62.8%	23.6%	44.8%
2021	WAS	MLB	28	5	9	0	20	19	108	98	17	2.8	9.1	109	42.7%	.280	1.22	4.17	90	1.6	93.6	63.5%	25.3%	55.3%
2022 DC	*WAS*	*MLB*	*29*	*3*	*3*	*0*	*12*	*12*	*45.3*	*42*	*6*	*3.0*	*8.4*	*42*	*42.7%*	*.290*	*1.28*	*4.11*	*99*	*0.4*	*93.7*	*63.4%*	*25.0%*	*53.4%*

Comparables: Miles Mikolas, Jhoulys Chacín, Jason Hammel

Someone should tell Ross to stop chanting "elbow discomfort" in front of a bathroom mirror lest it should appear. This year, Ross tossed more than a hundred innings for the first time since 2016, following Tommy John and a COVID-opt out. A few bad outings obfuscated some real gems, including an eight-inning, no-walk shutout of the Giants in June and double-digit strikeouts against the Dodgers in July. His reworked slider—a product of his reworked elbow—shone as a putaway pitch with a sub-.200 BAA. But his success may remain anecdata depending on if, and how, his arm recovers.

Jackson Rutledge RHP Born: 04/01/99 Age: 23 Bats: R Throws: R Height: 6'8" Weight: 245 lb. Origin: Round 1, 2019 Draft (#17 overall)

YEAR	TEAM	LVL	AGE	W	L	SV	G	GS	IP	H	HR	BB/9	K/9	K	GB%	BABIP	WHIP	ERA	DRA-	WARP	MPH	FB%	Whiff%	CSP
2019	NAT	ROK	20	0	0	0	1	1	1	4	0	9.0	18.0	2	80.0%	.800	5.00	27.00						
2019	AUB	SS	20	0	0	0	3	3	9	4	2	3.0	6.0	6	41.7%	.091	0.78	3.00						
2019	HAG	A	20	2	0	0	6	6	27^{1}	14	0	3.6	10.2	31	44.4%	.222	0.91	2.30	95	0.3				
2021	FBG	A	22	1	2	0	7	7	22	20	1	3.7	10.6	26	49.2%	.317	1.32	5.32	84	0.4				
2021	WIL	A+	22	0	3	0	4	4	10^{2}	17	0	7.6	8.4	10	39.5%	.447	2.44	12.66	107	0.0				
2022 non-DC	*WAS*	*MLB*	*23*	*2*	*3*	*0*	*57*	*0*	*50*	*55*	*7*	*5.7*	*7.6*	*42*	*40.9%*	*.319*	*1.75*	*6.37*	*137*	*-0.8*				

Comparables: Raúl Alcántara, Elieser Hernandez, Jo-Jo Reyes

Entering the 2021 season, Rutledge was neck-and-neck with fellow first-rounder Cade Cavalli as the top prospect on Washington's farm, with similar strengths (stuff) and questions (command and durability). While Cavalli stayed healthy and pushed his way up to Triple-A, Rutledge missed much of the season with shoulder and blister problems. On the occasions he toed the rubber, Rutledge was ghastly, fighting his mechanics and command while bouncing between the A-ball and complex levels on various rehab assignments. He's still an enormous man who can get it up into the high-90s with a wipeout slider, so there remains plenty of runway for him to figure it all out, and he'll certainly get many more chances to try. Longtime readers of this tome will already know that the majority of huge pitchers with big cheddar who don't consistently locate or stay healthy figure it out in relief—if they figure it out at all.

Stephen Strasburg RHP Born: 07/20/88 Age: 33 Bats: R Throws: R Height: 6'5" Weight: 240 lb. Origin: Round 1, 2009 Draft (#1 overall)

YEAR	TEAM	LVL	AGE	W	L	SV	G	GS	IP	H	HR	BB/9	K/9	K	GB%	BABIP	WHIP	ERA	DRA-	WARP	MPH	FB%	Whiff%	CSP
2019	WAS	MLB	30	18	6	0	33	33	209	161	24	2.4	10.8	251	50.4%	.276	1.04	3.32	69	5.6	94.1	48.3%	30.7%	44.5%
2020	WAS	MLB	31	0	1	0	2	2	5	8	1	1.8	3.6	2	35.0%	.368	1.80	10.80	108	0.0	92.0	45.8%	26.3%	42.1%
2021	WAS	MLB	32	1	2	0	5	5	21^{2}	16	4	5.8	8.7	21	37.3%	.218	1.38	4.57	104	0.1	91.5	54.9%	25.0%	52.5%
2022 DC	*WAS*	*MLB*	*33*	*9*	*8*	*0*	*27*	*27*	*145.7*	*131*	*20*	*3.5*	*10.8*	*174*	*43.1%*	*.304*	*1.29*	*4.03*	*95*	*1.5*	*93.4*	*49.7%*	*29.2%*	*46.3%*

Comparables: Don Sutton, Mickey Lolich, Luis Tiant

Back in 2019, when we had technologies like hope, it seemed like Strasburg had finally shed his perpetual branding as "Great, if he can only stay healthy, and he's never healthy." Strasburg pitched 36 innings in the 2019 postseason, and has thrown fewer than 27 since, undergoing season-ending carpal-tunnel surgery in 2020 and season-ending thoracic outlet surgery in 2021. So he'll be great, if he can stay healthy.

Mason Thompson RHP Born: 02/20/98 Age: 24 Bats: R Throws: R Height: 6'7" Weight: 223 lb. Origin: Round 3, 2016 Draft (#85 overall)

YEAR	TEAM	LVL	AGE	W	L	SV	G	GS	IP	H	HR	BB/9	K/9	K	GB%	BABIP	WHIP	ERA	DRA-	WARP	MPH	FB%	Whiff%	CSP
2019	LE	A+	21	0	5	0	7	6	22^{1}	22	3	7.7	8.9	22	38.5%	.306	1.84	7.66	141	-0.5				
2021	ELP	AAA	23	3	2	7	23	0	26^{2}	25	4	2.7	8.1	24	69.2%	.284	1.24	5.74	86	0.3				
2021	WAS	MLB	23	1	3	0	27	0	21^{2}	28	4	5.8	8.7	21	50.0%	.364	1.94	4.15	109	0.1	96.0	83.7%	20.1%	52.0%
2021	SD	MLB	23	0	0	0	4	0	3	4	0	3.0	6.0	2	50.0%	.400	1.67	3.00	95	0.0	98.1	97.7%	28.6%	54.5%
2022 DC	*WAS*	*MLB*	*24*	*2*	*2*	*0*	*52*	*0*	*45.3*	*46*	*5*	*4.8*	*7.4*	*37*	*49.2%*	*.301*	*1.56*	*5.26*	*118*	*-0.3*	*96.2*	*85.1%*	*21.1%*	*52.3%*

Comparables: Alex Burnett, Keynan Middleton, Trevor Gott

Even Washington's lesser trade deadline pieces returned some interesting prospects. 2019 playoff hero Daniel Hudson was one of the better rental relievers on the market, and he fetched Thompson and young infielder Jordy Barley from the Padres. Thompson wasn't throwing enough strikes or good off-speed pitches as a starter in San Diego's system, but the ugly pre-trade ERA at Triple-A launching pad El Paso obscured some real strides after sliding to the bullpen. He's got a bowling ball sinker which he can run up into the high 90s, and he's largely junked his previously ineffective change and curve for a new slider which posted elite whiff rates in limited usage. He's only ("only") another grade of command-and-control away from being a long-term relief weapon.

Austin Voth RHP Born: 06/26/92 Age: 30 Bats: R Throws: R Height: 6'2" Weight: 211 lb. Origin: Round 5, 2013 Draft (#166 overall)

YEAR	TEAM	LVL	AGE	W	L	SV	G	GS	IP	H	HR	BB/9	K/9	K	GB%	BABIP	WHIP	ERA	DRA-	WARP	MPH	FB%	Whiff%	CSP
2019	HBG	AA	27	1	1	0	3	3	11^{1}	11	1	1.6	8.7	11	36.7%	.345	1.15	4.76	96	0.1				
2019	FRE	AAA	27	3	5	0	12	12	61^{1}	68	7	2.2	10.0	68	40.8%	.345	1.35	4.40	88	0.8				
2019	WAS	MLB	27	2	1	0	9	8	43^{2}	33	5	2.7	9.1	44	36.8%	.259	1.05	3.30	96	0.5	92.9	60.5%	28.8%	49.9%
2020	WAS	MLB	28	2	5	0	11	11	49^{2}	57	14	3.3	8.0	44	29.6%	.297	1.51	6.34	156	-1.0	92.3	60.8%	22.2%	49.0%
2021	WAS	MLB	29	4	1	0	49	1	57^{1}	57	10	4.4	9.3	59	38.8%	.320	1.48	5.34	106	0.3	94.2	59.5%	25.2%	52.1%
2022 DC	*WAS*	*MLB*	*30*	*3*	*3*	*0*	*67*	*0*	*58*	*55*	*9*	*3.4*	*9.1*	*58*	*37.4%*	*.293*	*1.33*	*4.48*	*105*	*0.2*	*93.4*	*60.1%*	*24.6%*	*50.8%*

Comparables: Daniel Ponce de Leon, Chris Stratton, Casey Kelly

It looks like Voth took the whole "duality of the franchise" thing a little too seriously. Voth's electric first half doesn't much resemble his fizzled second. The good: He's added serious velo to his once-pokey fastball and developed a ground-ball-inducing curve whose spin spiked after June. The bad: Neither of those things actually helped with efficacy once summer set in. With the Nationals rotation looking likes Josiah Gray and a set of tumbleweeds and question marks, Voth may once again be asked to play a dual role—as a long man or fifth starter.

Lineouts

Hitters

HITTER	POS	TEAM	LVL	AGE	PA	R	2B	3B	HR	RBI	BB	K	SB	CS	AVG/OBP/SLG	DRC+	BABIP	BRR	FRAA	WARP
Yasel Antuna	SS	WIL	A+	21	457	55	26	1	12	65	46	100	4	4	.227/.307/.385	100	.270	-2.5	SS(96): -16.1	-0.4
Jeremy De La Rosa	CF	FBG	A	19	358	34	12	4	5	22	30	122	7	8	.209/.279/.316	75	.317	-1.3	CF(76): 1.1, LF(5): -0.7, RF(4): -0.2	0.1
Derek Dietrich	UT	SWB	AAA	31	143	19	4	0	5	22	27	46	0	0	.215/.413/.393	103	.321	0.5	2B(17): 2.0, 1B(11): -0.6, 3B(9): 1.2	0.7
	UT	ROC	AAA	31	160	13	3	0	3	13	13	51	0	0	.121/.270/.212	76	.167	-0.2	3B(16): -1.4, 1B(12): 0.6, 2B(9): 0.4	-0.1
Mike Ford	1B	SWB	AAA	28	29	3	0	0	0	1	3	8	0	0	.083/.207/.083	92	.118	-0.2	1B(6): -0.1	0.0
	1B	ROC	AAA	28	116	10	5	0	3	12	11	32	0	0	.202/.284/.337	91	.261	0.3	1B(21): -0.8	0.1
	1B	DUR	AAA	28	162	22	5	1	11	31	21	41	1	0	.243/.346/.529	120	.261	-0.2	1B(19): -0.5, 3B(6): 0.3	0.7
	1B	NYY	MLB	28	72	6	0	0	3	5	11	23	0	0	.133/.278/.283	89	.147	-0.9	1B(21): 0.6	0.0
Maikel Franco	3B	GWN	AAA	28	35	4	0	0	0	0	5	6	0	0	.167/.286/.167	104	.208	-0.2	1B(8): -0.6	0.0
	3B	BAL	MLB	28	403	31	22	0	11	47	20	67	0	0	.210/.253/.355	87	.225	-1.7	3B(99): -7.5, 1B(2): -0.1	-0.3
Yadiel Hernandez	LF	ROC	AAA	33	64	9	2	0	5	12	5	11	0	1	.288/.344/.576	130	.279	-0.2	LF(7): -0.5, RF(4): 0.1, CF(1): -0.0	0.4
	LF	WAS	MLB	33	289	33	8	1	9	32	22	59	3	0	.273/.329/.413	101	.318	-2.7	LF(48): 2.2, RF(13): 0.1	1.1
Sammy Infante	MI	NAT	ROK	20	143	19	5	2	3	15	17	43	3	4	.215/.329/.364		.303			
Daylen Lile	DH	NAT	ROK	18	80	16	2	0	0	10	15	20	2	1	.219/.363/.250		.311			
Jordy Mercer	IF	WAS	MLB	34	127	13	7	0	2	9	9	34	0	0	.254/.307/.364	85	.341	-0.1	2B(21): 0.4, 3B(14): -0.3, SS(6): 0.8	0.3
Drew Millas	C	SUR	WIN	23	64	8	1	0	1	5	13	4	3	1	.196/.359/.275		.196			
	C	WIL	A+	23	118	15	4	0	0	20	13	14	5	1	.284/.373/.324	119	.326	0.4	C(20): -0.4	0.6
	C	LAN	A+	23	266	34	12	1	3	28	41	39	10	2	.255/.372/.359	125	.293	0.0	C(50): 2.7	1.8
Gerardo Parra	OF	ROC	AAA	34	91	10	3	1	1	12	19	17	1	2	.222/.385/.333	117	.278	0.0	RF(12): -2.4, LF(7): -0.2	0.2
	OF	WAS	MLB	34	107	13	5	0	2	10	6	30	1	1	.237/.292/.351	75	.318	-1.7	LF(19): -0.7, CF(8): -0.4, RF(3): -0.1	-0.2
Raudy Read	1B	ROC	AAA	27	86	13	5	0	6	15	3	26	0	0	.288/.326/.575	108	.347	-0.3	1B(13): -1.9, C(1): -0.1	0.1
Adrián Sanchez	IF	ROC	AAA	30	174	21	9	0	4	20	11	28	5	2	.314/.363/.447	110	.362	1.2	2B(17): -0.2, SS(17): -0.3, 3B(12): 2.7	1.1
	IF	WAS	MLB	30	38	5	2	0	0	1	3	4	0	0	.257/.316/.314	102	.290	-0.8	2B(9): -0.2, 3B(2): -0.1, RF(1): -0.0	0.0
Andrew Stevenson	OF	ROC	AAA	27	58	11	4	0	2	8	3	11	2	0	.436/.466/.618	101	.524	0.0	CF(9): -0.1, LF(4): -0.1	0.2
	OF	WAS	MLB	27	213	22	6	0	5	23	13	61	1	1	.229/.294/.339	77	.307	-0.6	CF(31): -2.3, LF(24): 1.1, RF(11): -0.4	0.0
Blake Swihart	C	ROC	AAA	29	204	26	6	2	5	17	26	51	2	2	.198/.299/.339	87	.246	0.4	C(14): -0.4, LF(13): 2.9, RF(12): 2.7	1.0
Yasmany Tomás	OF	ROC	AAA	30	96	14	6	0	3	12	13	28	0	1	.185/.292/.370	98	.231	-0.7	1B(17): 0.2, RF(3): 1.9, 3B(1): -0.1	0.3

Yasel Antuna has been a fixture of Washington Top 10 prospect lists for around a half-decade now, partially because he got a huge bonus and partially because the farm has been so thin. He's 22 now and still hasn't made it out of A-ball or hit for either average or power or shown much defensive ability. And he's still a borderline top 10 prospect in the system, somehow. The Nationals, everybody! The Nationals keep challenging outfielder **Jeremy De La Rosa** with Darwinian assignments—stateside complex ball at 17, full-season ball at 19—and his overall offensive game has yet to catch up to his impressive bat speed. **Derek Dietrich** had already survived the collapse of his hit tool by continuing to walk and hit for power. He didn't make the Yankees out of spring training and then his power collapsed at Triple-A to the point that even the Nats didn't call him up. That's not gonna do die trich. **Mike Ford** has a history degree from Princeton and hits the ball very hard when he makes contact, but if he doesn't figure out how to make consistent contact with major-league off-speed stuff it's his playing career that's going to be history. It's hard to imagine in today's era of 24-hour news cycles and rumors being leaked left-and-right that a player of **Maikel Franco**'s caliber could sign a contract with a new team and nobody knew anything about it until a few days later. That it happened with Franco back in August (with Atlanta) tells you exactly how far his star has fallen. The Nationals picked him up on an NRI in December. It's not quite the stuff of movies. **Yadiel Hernández** spent his age-33 year as a technical rookie—having defected from Cuba after five years in the Cuban National Series, then toiling for another three in the Nationals farm system—posting slightly above replacement-level numbers. But what's a damning assessment to some is a dream to others, and there will likely be a place for him as a fourth/fifth outfielder as the Nationals rebuild. **Sammy Infante** was taken with the compensatory pick Washington got for Anthony Rendon, one of the franchise's greatest players. They had similar 2021 slash lines, which really sucks for both the Angels and Nationals. Washington gave hit-first prep outfielder **Daylen Lile** $1.75 million to eschew his Louisville commitment. He didn't actually hit much in the complex league after signing, which doesn't exactly eliminate him from contention as a top hitting prospect in this org. If the Nationals 2021 season is Teen Girl Squad, **Jordy Mercer** was firmly "What's Her Face," as an infield replacement with a league average OBP and meh power. Fortunately for Mercer, plenty of other teams are setting fire to their playoff chances, so he's likely to find employment next season in yet another burninated village. One of the approximately 274 catching prospects the Nats acquired at the trade deadline (from Oakland in the Yan Gomes/Josh Harrison deal), **Drew Millas** gets rave reviews for his defensive prowess, which is scout code for both "he's going to play in the majors forever" and "he can't really hit." Strangely, **Gerardo Parra** is exactly 40 days younger than another GP—Buster Posey—and has exactly 40 fewer career WARP. Their other similarities are, er, somewhat limited, but their careers might end in similar fashion: Retirement after 2021 wearing a World Series ring and the ire of most Dodgers fans. With all the injuries and trades, **Raudy Read** should've had a chance to claim a slice of catching time for the Nats over the course of the season, perhaps to even plant his flag as an established backup catcher. In reality, he landed on the IL a week into the minor-league season and rarely donned the tools of ignorance after his August return. Being a replacement-level player is a statistical construct meant to indicate a player's value beyond a hypothetical. [Touches ear piece] Sorry, we are being told it's actually **Adrián Sanchez**. With more than 1,200 games in a Nationals' organization uniform, Sanchez's key skills appear to comprise a pulse and an unwillingness to quit. **Andrew Stevenson** is the mullet of fourth outfielders: He can't handle his business as a starter but brings the party as a pinch-hitter in the back half of games. **Blake Swihart** got released from Triple-A by the post-deadline Remembering Some Guys Nats, which is about as bleak as it gets for a career arc. The former top 25 prospect never quite hit enough to stomach his lousy defense behind the dish, and even his mediocre hitting prowess is going out like Stan Chera. After several years with his hefty contract mostly buried in Arizona's minors, **Yasmany Tomás** came to the Nats, didn't make the team out of camp, didn't hit at all in Triple-A, and landed on the restricted list for the bulk of the season.

Pitchers

PITCHER	TEAM	LVL	AGE	W	L	SV	G	GS	IP	H	HR	BB/9	K/9	K	GB%	BABIP	WHIP	ERA	DRA-	WARP	MPH	FB%	WHF	CSP
Luis Avilán	WAS	MLB	31	0	1	0	4	0	5	7	1	5.4	7.2	4	31.6%	.333	2.00	12.60	122	0.0	89.4	42.6%	22.0%	52.9%
Ben Braymer	ROC	AAA	27	7	8	0	25	21	99^{2}	93	19	5.4	7.1	79	34.2%	.268	1.54	5.78	115	0.6				
Sam Clay	ROC	AAA	28	0	0	1	6	0	6^{1}	2	0	2.8	9.9	7	76.9%	.154	0.63	1.42	92	0.1				
	WAS	MLB	28	0	5	0	58	0	45	55	4	4.4	6.8	34	60.1%	.342	1.71	5.60	114	0.1	92.5	67.9%	21.1%	53.5%
Matt Cronin	WIL	A+	23	2	0	4	10	0	14^{2}	8	0	3.1	17.2	28	28.6%	.381	0.89	1.23	79	0.3				
	HBG	AA	23	0	1	0	10	0	11^{1}	9	2	7.9	14.3	18	21.7%	.333	1.68	5.56	84	0.2				
Steven Fuentes	WIL	A+	24	0	0	0	2	2	9	12	1	1.0	9.0	9	62.1%	.407	1.44	5.00	88	0.1				
	HBG	AA	24	0	1	0	2	2	10^{1}	13	4	1.7	9.6	11	36.4%	.310	1.45	6.97	105	0.1				
	ROC	AAA	24	0	5	0	7	5	15^{1}	37	4	8.2	5.3	9	49.3%	.478	3.33	19.96	144	-0.1				
Javy Guerra	WAS	MLB	35	0	1	0	6	0	6	12	3	4.5	6.0	4	30.8%	.409	2.50	16.50	129	0.0	91.6	57.4%	14.9%	59.5%
Ryne Harper	ROC	AAA	32	1	1	0	13	0	19^{2}	16	2	3.7	10.5	23	46.0%	.292	1.22	3.66	96	0.3				
	WAS	MLB	32	0	2	0	34	0	35^{2}	28	6	3.5	7.8	31	42.6%	.232	1.18	4.04	103	0.3	85.5	37.4%	22.6%	60.1%
Gabe Klobosits	HBG	AA	26	2	1	3	15	0	20	13	1	3.6	11.7	26	42.2%	.273	1.05	0.90	89	0.3				
	ROC	AAA	26	1	2	3	16	0	18^{1}	15	0	2.9	9.8	20	30.8%	.294	1.15	2.45	90	0.3				
	WAS	MLB	26	0	1	0	11	0	11^{1}	13	0	4.0	4.0	5	41.5%	.317	1.59	5.56	133	-0.1	94.7	66.0%	18.8%	54.1%
Andres Machado	ROC	AAA	28	0	0	0	11	0	14^{2}	17	1	2.5	11.7	19	53.5%	.381	1.43	3.68	88	0.3				
	WAS	MLB	28	1	2	0	40	0	35^{2}	30	4	3.8	7.6	30	44.2%	.260	1.26	3.53	109	0.2	94.8	70.8%	22.9%	55.0%
Francisco Perez	AKR	AA	23	3	0	2	11	0	27	8	0	3.0	15.3	46	39.5%	.186	0.63	0.67	78	0.5				
	COL	AAA	23	1	0	1	19	0	26	20	2	6.9	12.5	36	30.5%	.316	1.54	3.12	93	0.4				
	CLE	MLB	23	0	0	0	4	0	6^{2}	6	0	4.1	6.8	5	35.0%	.300	1.35	4.05	106	0.0	93.3	54.9%	21.6%	57.6%
Aldo Ramirez	NAT	ROK	20	1	1	0	4	2	7^{2}	9	0	4.7	3.5	3	51.9%	.333	1.70	8.22						
	SAL	A	20	1	1	0	8	8	31	27	1	2.3	9.3	32	54.4%	.292	1.13	2.03	90	0.4				
Jefry Rodriguez	ROC	AAA	27	2	1	0	12	11	46^{1}	41	4	4.7	8.9	46	47.7%	.303	1.40	4.86	100	0.6				
	WAS	MLB	27	0	0	0	14	1	24^{1}	25	6	6.3	7.4	20	31.1%	.279	1.73	5.92	135	-0.2	94.6	74.9%	20.2%	57.3%
Josh Rogers	NOR	AAA	26	0	3	0	4	2	17^{1}	24	6	1.6	7.3	14	35.0%	.333	1.56	7.79	118	0.1				
	ROC	AAA	26	7	3	0	14	13	73	75	8	2.6	6.0	49	41.2%	.289	1.32	3.70	123	0.1				
	WAS	MLB	26	2	2	0	6	6	35^{2}	32	7	3.5	5.6	22	30.1%	.238	1.29	3.28	145	-0.5	90.5	51.6%	18.4%	54.2%
Seth Romero	FBG	A	25	0	0	0	3	3	9^{2}	15	0	1.9	13.0	14	56.7%	.517	1.76	2.79	75	0.2				
	HBG	AA	25	0	2	0	6	6	20^{1}	21	2	4.0	15.0	34	30.6%	.404	1.48	5.31	77	0.4				
Sterling Sharp	HBG	AA	26	0	2	0	3	3	14^{2}	11	3	3.7	7.4	12	68.9%	.190	1.16	1.84	103	0.1				
	ROC	AAA	26	4	4	0	16	14	70^{2}	73	9	5.0	6.0	47	58.4%	.288	1.58	4.97	113	0.5				
Wander Suero	ROC	AAA	29	2	1	0	12	1	12^{2}	12	0	2.1	11.4	16	30.3%	.364	1.18	6.39	84	0.3				
	WAS	MLB	29	2	3	0	45	0	42^{2}	45	11	3.2	9.3	44	33.1%	.293	1.41	6.33	106	0.2	92.1	76.0%	25.5%	56.1%

Luis Avilán was already on his seventh stop on the peripatetic LOOGY voyage when his elbow went early on. The three-batter rule sucked pretty badly for Avilán, the rare changeup-reliant lefty nerfer who gets crushed by righties, but even still he should have another decade or so of NRIs in his future if his Tommy John rehab goes well. If you're a soft-tossing crafty lefty type, you better throw a heck of a lot more strikes in the high minors than **Ben Braymer** has. And if you want to win baseball games in the future, you better have better prospects for us to put in this book. Every year, Dave Martinez has one reliever he likes to grind to a fine powder through overuse, and just as **Sam Clay** didn't miss many games, his sinker didn't cool many bats. All **Matt Cronin** has done as a professional is make batters look silly with his high-spin fastball/curveball combination. Command and health willing, he should be showing up as a high-leverage major-league reliever shortly. There's plenty of space for him whenever he's ready. **Steven Fuentes** made the major-league roster twice without seeing game action, once as an emergency depth call-up and once on a phantom move to immediately be placed on the 60-day IL to open up a 40-man spot. He missed most of the season with shoulder issues; if healthy, he has a shot to contribute, most likely as a sinker/slider reliever. There are two **Javy Guerra**s in the majors and, despite their last names, neither managed to achieve a positive WAR. **Ryne Harper**'s generic top-line results belie some truly weird inner workings: He didn't crack 90 mph with a single fastball, and his bread-and-butter is three distinct flavors of breaking balls: slow, slower and slowest. In total, over three-quarters of what he throws is in the 67-79 velocity band, but he's made it work two out of the last three seasons. **Gabe Klobosits** boasts a power-limiting fastball, a ground-ball-inducing splitter and a WHIP (and mustache) he should consider shaving if he's going to stick in the bigs. Once a fireballing starting prospect in the Royals system, **Andres Machado** stalled out in as upper-minors relief depth, with just a handful of 2017 innings in the majors. Washington picked him up in minor-league free agency and he provided some perfectly mediocre middle relief. After floundering in the low minors for half a decade, **Francisco Perez** moved to the bullpen and rapidly ascended the ladder to the majors. He's mostly fastball-slider. The latter piles up Ks, the former arrested his development as a failed starter and could keep him on the bus between the majors and Triple-A. The Nationals picked up injured prospect **Aldo Ramirez** in exchange for injured slugger Kyle Schwarber at the deadline. While Schwarber hit baseballs to Mars once he got healthy, Ramirez merely made a few appearances down in the complex after his elbow healed. When healthy, he profiles as a future fourth starter. **Jefry Rodriguez** made his triumphant return to the Washington system two years after being traded for Yan Gomes. After finally making his long-awaited move to the bullpen in the majors, he still stunk. **Josh Rogers** got away with it last year, but if he wants to find consistent success with his pitch-to-contact, flyball-generating 90-mph fastball, he'd better find himself a time machine and set the dial to 1968. **Seth Romero** has only pitched a total of 85 ⅔ innings since he was a first-round pick in 2017, between myriad injuries and disciplinary issues (and also a global pandemic mixed in for fun). Tommy John surgery in 2019 took away his best stuff and it hasn't quite returned yet, although he's still capable of getting whiffs on the rare occasions he toes the rubber. **Sterling Sharp** was ceded then returned in the Rule 5 draft after looking not so, well, like himself in a few outings with Miami in 2020. His struggles continued with the Nats Triple-A club in 2021. **Wander Suero** has a three-C pitch arsenal—cutter, curveball and changeup—but what he really needs is an S: simplify. He found modest success as a one-pitch cutter specialist in 2020, only to abandon that approach in 2021, leaving him with the letters he most needs to worry about: Triple-A.

BALTIMORE ORIOLES

Essay by Matthew Ritchie

Player comments by Darius Austin and BP staff

Late into the 2018 season, the Baltimore Orioles were in the middle of their preparations for a new era. By the trade deadline, it was clear that the halcyon days of 2012–16 were in the past, and their competitive window had slammed shut. The Birds were sitting at 32-75, well on their way to the worst season in franchise history. The front office shipped off Manny Machado, Jonathan Schoop, Kevin Gausman and Zack Britton for prospect scrap metal, hoping to recoup any sort of value from the team's plummet from the upper echelon of the league. By August's arrival, all that was left from this millennium's Orioles' golden years was center fielder Adam Jones, first baseman Chris Davis and designated hitter Mark Trumbo.

Plans to introduce the next wave of Orioles players were put into motion. No moment was more indicative of this paradigm shift than August 10, 2018, when outfielder Cedric Mullins made his big-league debut. Jones had been synonymous with center field in Baltimore since he was brought over from Seattle, in 2008, in one of the few positive trades in Baltimore history. His standing as the de facto captain and champion for the city made his presence in the outfield symbolically important. In Mullins' debut, Jones departed from his post in center to play right field and allow Mullins to usher in the next era.

The inaugural moment for Cedric's reign felt like a seamless passing of the baton for Orioles fans, as Mullins went 3-for-4 with two doubles, two RBI and three runs scored. Even in the shadow of a hilariously wild loss to the Boston Red Sox, a football score of 19–12, the moment for Mullins' ascension to the position felt like a watershed occasion. He looked like he had it all—a short, compact swing from both sides of the plate, fast-twitch muscles to go with elite speed and a glove to match. Manager Buck Showalter summarized it succinctly in the post-game interview, saying, "It had to be the right guy. We think Cedric might be the right guy."

But the sheen of the Orioles' new center fielder quickly wore off in his first extended stint in the starting role. Mullins was handed the keys, placed in the leadoff spot to start the 2019 season, with the full confidence of new manager Brandon Hyde behind him. But at that moment, Mullins struggled mightily. Scratch that—he bottomed out. In 64 at-

BALTIMORE ORIOLES PROSPECTUS

2021 W-L: 52-110, 5TH IN AL EAST

Pythag	.327	30th	DER	.686	28th
RS/G	4.07	26th	DRC+	94	18th
RA/G	5.90	30th	DRA-	116	29th
dWin%	.412	29th	FIP	5.20	30th
Payroll	$57M	27th	B-Age	27.3	5th
M$/MW	$11.9M	29th	P-Age	28.5	14th

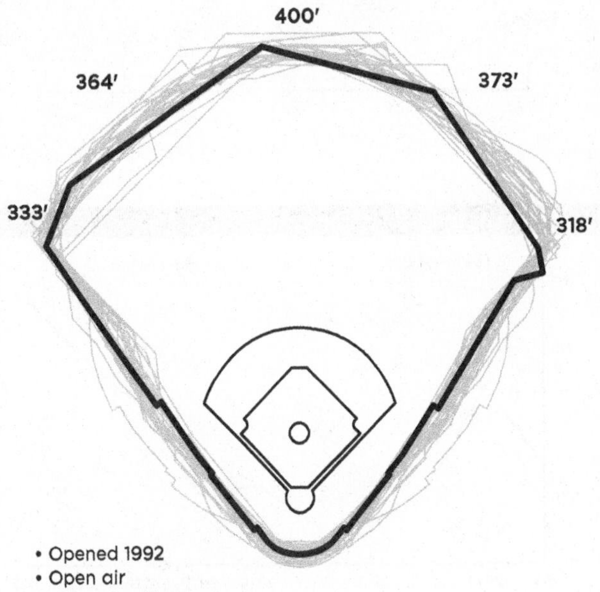

- Opened 1992
- Open air
- Natural surface
- Fence profile: 7′ to 21′

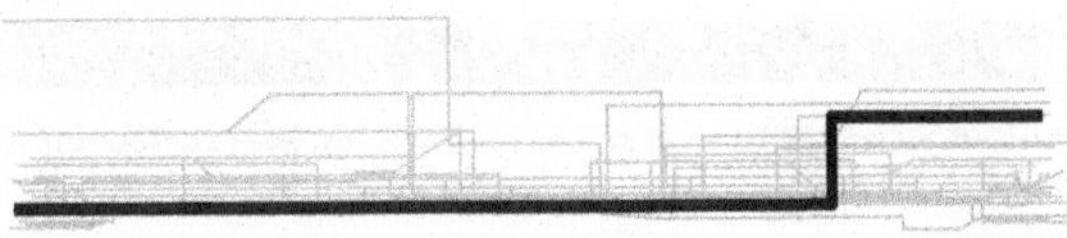

Park Factors

Runs	Runs/RH	Runs/LH	HR/RH	HR/LH
102	100	104	107	114

Top Hitter WARP	4.6 Cedric Mullins
Top Pitcher WARP	1.2 Cole Sulser
Top Prospect	Adley Rutschman

Payroll History (in millions)

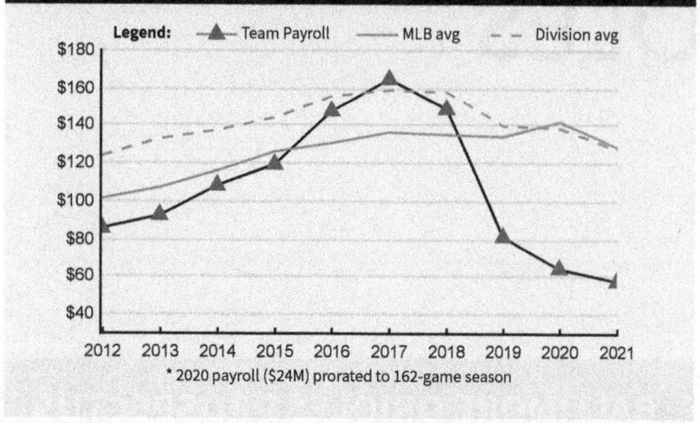

Future Commitments (in millions)

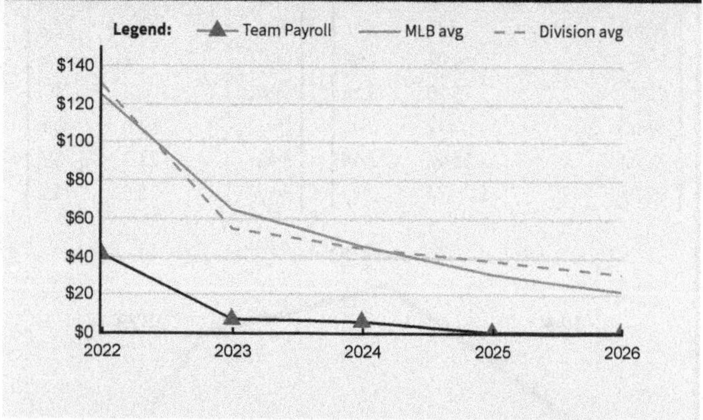

Farm System Ranking

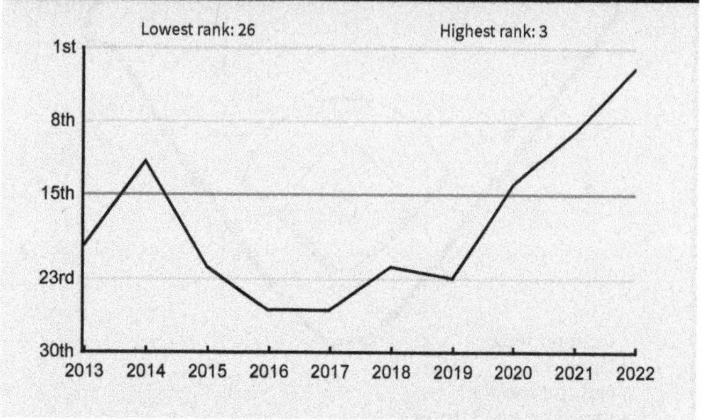

Personnel

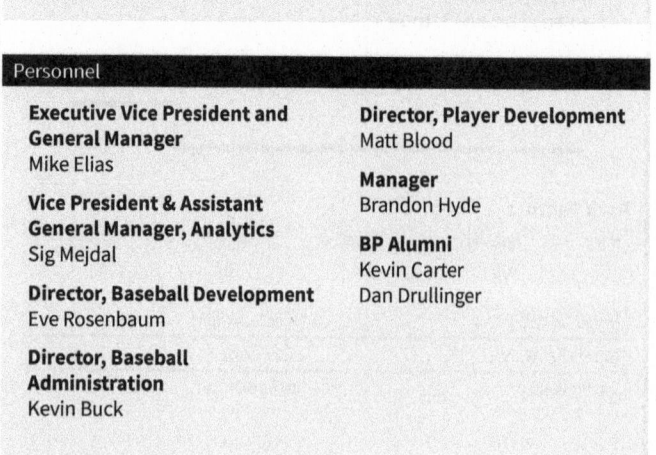

Executive Vice President and General Manager
Mike Elias

Vice President & Assistant General Manager, Analytics
Sig Mejdal

Director, Baseball Development
Eve Rosenbaum

Director, Baseball Administration
Kevin Buck

Director, Player Development
Matt Blood

Manager
Brandon Hyde

BP Alumni
Kevin Carter
Dan Drullinger

bats, Mullins totaled just six hits and just looked lost in the batter's box. The leash for that sort of production was understandably short, even for a rebuilding team, and Mullins was demoted to Triple-A Norfolk after 22 games. It wasn't meant to be an indictment of Mullins, just that he needed more time to get his confidence back. But his time at Norfolk was rife with the same issues, as he slashed an unimpressive .205/.272/.305 in 66 games. Then, on July 10, Mullins was demoted once again, to Double-A Bowie, where he'd remain for the rest of 2019. In just four months, Mullins went from the ideal centerpiece of Baltimore's long-term future to a project of a player who needed to figure it all out again. His initial failure to establish a foothold at the major-league level seemed to be just the latest in a long line of developmental failures at the hands of the Orioles. Baltimore has built an infamous reputation that insinuates that they're unable to foster legitimate, homegrown talent. There's a cruel running joke (supported by facts) that players wait until they've left the Orioles to blossom into full-fledged All-Stars, MVPs and Cy Young winners.

Reinventing a hitting philosophy is one of the most difficult processes in all sports. Day in and day out, players entrench themselves in their routines and superstitions to produce any semblance of consistency in a sport full of natural ups and downs. It's hard enough with the average starter's fastball velocity continually on the rise and every bullpen stocked with demigods that possess two knockout pitches that move in different directions. So, when it was announced before the 2021 season that Mullins would be abandoning switch-hitting to hit left-handed full time, it was impossible not to be skeptical. The move stunk of desperation. Even though Mullins approached the team with the idea during spring training in 2019, it still sounded insane. Switch-hitting is meant to be the great equalizer at the plate, erasing the advantage that pitchers have when facing same-handed batters. Switch-hitters are unicorns, with their versatility, as valuable as liquid gold, allowing managers to save an extra roster spot for a would-be platoon player.

But Mullins was at a crossroads: After clawing his way back to Baltimore in 2020 and posting a decent slash line of .271/.315/.407 in 48 games, it was clear that one side of the plate was the culprit of his inconsistency. Usually, when it's suggested that a player give up switch-hitting, it registers as a direct insult to their ability. As a right-handed batter, Mullins totaled 14 hits in 95 at-bats, with just two extra-base hits. When a lefty was on the mound, Cedric was virtually unplayable. It's a sobering reality to abandon an aspect of your game that once made you unique and special.

Cautious optimism was the tone surrounding this new version of Mullins at the dish. There were zero concerns about his ability to patrol center field; his exceptional speed and glove positioned him as a future Gold Glove candidate.

The singular focus on the left side of the plate made sense—Mullins would no longer have to dedicate half of his effort to maintaining his right-handed swing. His natural side was clearly where he was more comfortable. The key would be how he would adjust to the dreaded lefty-on-lefty matchup that haunts the splits of average hitters. Seeing a slider aimed at your front hip that breaks back over the plate takes some getting used to.

The first series of 2021, against Boston, unimportant in the grand scheme of the 162-game season, was paramount for Mullins' confidence. Repeating the disastrous beginning of 2019 after making a drastic change to his hitting approach could have shattered his confidence, but it was clear from the outset that Mullins had made the correct decision. Against Nathan Eovaldi, in his first at-bat, Mullins slapped a ball through the left side, displaying the easy bat control that endeared him to the Orioles in the first place. He finished Opening Day with two hits and a run. The next day, he led off with another single, finishing with two hits again. The third game was a true "I have arrived" moment for Mullins. In an 11–3, sweep-clinching drubbing of the Red Sox, Mullins went 5-for-5 with three doubles and reached base six times, giving the Red Sox' pitching staff nightmares. After the first at-bat, fellow believer Jake Mintz of Céspedes Family BBQ tweeted that tickets were now being sold for the "Cedric Mullins hype train."

For the first month of the season, Mullins became a beacon of hope for an Orioles team that did not have much to be excited about. He racked up 34 hits, slashing .337/.387/.545 from the lead-off spot. It was very strange to feel as if it was necessary to tune in to the start of an Orioles game, which hadn't been the case for years. There's a fundamental distrust of hot streaks that occur in Orioles uniforms. In the last few seasons, the fanbase's optimism has dissipated to such a degree that any moments of brightness are met with lukewarm enthusiasm. But it looked like Mullins was shaping up to be the real deal, hitting all the marks against left-handed pitchers. On April 29, he led all left-handed hitters in batting average (.441), OPS (1.090) and wRC+ (213). Even in a brief run of successful play, Mullins quickly helped to restore the feeling around Camden Yards.

As the season progressed, and the Orioles' record continued to plummet, Mullins' stardom was in full ascension. By mid-June, he was clearly deserving of an All-Star nod. The way he operated at the plate displayed an interesting duality: He could embody scrappiness and pluck, spraying line drives all over the field with a short, clean swing. Then, in the next at-bat, he'd unleash a no-doubt home run worthy of a much bigger player. Even with his 5-foot-8, 170-pound frame, he lived up to the nickname he earned in minors, "Parking Lot Ced." On June 5 against Cleveland, he notched another 5-for-5 performance, this time adding two home runs to his season tally. It felt like there was no limit to what he was capable of, wielding tools upon tools in every game he played.

Cedric Mullins T-Shirt Night fell smack-dab in the middle of an eight-game losing streak for the O's. It wasn't the first significant stretch of losses and certainly wasn't the last. Even though it was only June 18, it had already become abundantly clear that the 2021 Orioles were built to lose, similar to the preceding versions of the team. When Baseball Prospectus published its postseason odds for each team at the start of the season, Baltimore ranked 30th with a mere 0.3 percent chance to make the playoffs. Going into that night's matchup against the Toronto Blue Jays, Baltimore was already 23 games under .500.

Since 2016, games against the Blue Jays always remind Orioles fans of the most violent and abrupt ending to a competitive window since Tony Fernández's 11th-hour (and -inning) theatrics back in 1997. They're a reminder of what could have been, and what can be. Toronto represents the peak of developmental prowess, with Vladimir Guerrero Jr. and Bo Bichette blossoming into elite offensive talents. They went out and spent on free-agent acquisitions, actively attempting to sustain their success through pickups Robbie Ray, Marcus Semien and George Springer. Meanwhile, we could wax poetic on the horrendous choices and unfortunate outcomes that have plagued the Orioles. Chris Davis and his seven-year, $161-million behemoth infamously turned into a nightmare as the Orioles legend fell off a cliff. It has been difficult to count up even replacement-level Orioles that have stuck around for more than two years at a time since their last playoff appearance.

But on Cedric Mullins T-Shirt Night, the intense shame that leaves Oriole Park empty most games was noticeably missing. On a night with their ideological tether in town, a sparse crowd filled Camden Yards with a buzz that almost felt foreign. The draw of free bright-orange shirseys was enough to put butts in seats, as fans excitedly switched their attire to adorn their "Mullins 31" before the first pitch. The Orioles were decked out in their flawless black uniforms—it was all set up perfectly. The only hitch in the plan was that, since it was a home game, Baltimore had to survive the top of the first without losing the rare buzz that was emanating from the ballpark—no small feat for Orioles pitchers in 2021. The crowd was granted a rare reprieve, as starter Tom Eshelman delivered a rare 1-2-3 inning to start the game, dodging the 6.11 first-inning ERA that hung over each starter like the sword of Damocles. Mullins rewarded the faithful to open the bottom of the frame, depositing a 1-2 pitch from eventual Cy Young winner Robbie Ray six-rows deep into the right-field bleachers.

The bottom of the eighth inning was the pièce de résistance. The Birds strung together five runs on five hits, bookended by another home run off the bat of Mullins, this time a towering no-doubter that effectively ended any chance of a Blue Jays comeback. The home run whipped the crowd into a frenzy, with all 13,000 fans waving their orange shirts above their heads. M-V-P chants filled the night sky, as the rejuvenated Orioles faithful beckoned Mullins out of the dugout. The mild-mannered center fielder, who just two years ago was in a tailspin and teetering on the edge of failing, popped out of the dugout to take the first curtain call of his career. For a brief moment, Oriole Park felt like the setting of something significant in the baseball world, not just a beautiful shell that held the lost dreams of a storied franchise.

Mullins' coronation defied physics last year, as the brightest star in Baltimore miraculously escaped the black hole of the team's overall lack of success. His 2021 proved to be one of the greatest Orioles seasons of all time. Mullins started the All-Star Game in center field, earning a premier spot amongst the league's best. He achieved the first 30–30 season in franchise history and was the only player in 2021 to reach that plateau, standing alone as a statistical anomaly. He finished ninth in the AL MVP voting, the highest rank ever for a player on a 100-loss team. Now, Orioles fans have someone to be fiercely defensive of, which is clearly different from the mindset from 2018–2020, when supporters were willing to ship out any player to recoup some semblance of value through prospects. He's the team's talisman, with a chance to occupy a role that Baltimore has been hungry to have filled.

So when reports surfaced this winter that the Orioles were "listening" to calls regarding offers for Mullins, it was a harsh reminder of the slow, painful burn of the rebuild they find themselves in. If the 27-year-old coming off the best season of his career is not considered off-limits three years into the Mike Elias era, then it's a clear indictment of the status of the franchise. When you possess a golden goose, you don't ship it off in hopes that there's a slew of magic beans waiting to sprout out of nowhere. The pessimistic reading of this situation is that the Baltimore brass believes that the ballclub is well removed from the light at the end of the tunnel, meaning that any burst of stardom akin to Mullins' performance may be doomed to toil in mediocrity. Whether the rumors held any weight or not, it was hard to feel optimistic about the Orioles' path while they floated around. All Orioles fans can do is hold out hope that Mullins will be a star for the Next Competitive Orioles Team, and that he and other future stars aren't trapped in the black hole of a forever rebuild.

—Matthew Ritchie is a graduate student at Northwestern and a contributor at HipHopDX *and* Pitchfork.

HITTERS

★ ★ ★ *2022 Top 101 Prospect* **#46** ★ ★ ★

Colton Cowser OF Born: 03/20/00 Age: 22 Bats: L Throws: R Height: 6'3" Weight: 195 lb. Origin: Round 1, 2021 Draft (#5 overall)

YEAR	TEAM	LVL	AGE	PA	R	2B	3B	HR	RBI	BB	K	SB	CS	Whiff%	AVG/OBP/SLG	DRC+	BABIP	BRR	FRAA	WARP
2021	ORIO	ROK	21	25	8	3	0	1	8	3	4	3	2		.500/.560/.773		.588			
2021	DEL	A	21	124	22	5	0	1	26	22	19	4	2		.347/.476/.429	124	.418	-1.1	CF(16): -2.8, RF(4): 3.0	0.7
2022 non-DC	*BAL*	*MLB*	*22*	*251*	*22*	*10*	*0*	*2*	*20*	*25*	*46*	*3*	*2*	*21.3%*	*.229/.316/.317*	*76*	*.279*	*0.1*	*CF -2, RF 1*	*0.0*

Comparables: Andrew Stevenson, Adam Haseley, Mallex Smith

Sam Houston State University might not be a hotbed of major-league talent, but there's some major-league heritage there that includes Steve Sparks, Ken Boswell and Ryan Tepera. Only one player had been taken in the first round before Cowser, however: The Tigers' 1980 first-rounder Glenn Wilson, who also had the best major-league career. The aplomb with which Cowser handled his first pro assignments indicates he can top Wilson's 10.5 career WARP, as the fifth overall pick possesses an advanced approach, the ability to play center and room to develop more power.

Chris Davis 1B Born: 03/17/86 Age: 36 Bats: L Throws: R Height: 6'4" Weight: 255 lb. Origin: Round 5, 2006 Draft (#148 overall)

YEAR	TEAM	LVL	AGE	PA	R	2B	3B	HR	RBI	BB	K	SB	CS	Whiff%	AVG/OBP/SLG	DRC+	BABIP	BRR	FRAA	WARP
2019	BAL	MLB	33	352	26	9	0	12	36	39	139	0	0	38.0%	.179/.276/.326	63	.270	1.3	1B(97): -5.2, RF(1): -0.5	-1.1
2020	BAL	MLB	34	55	3	3	0	0	1	3	17	0	0	36.8%	.115/.164/.173	63	.171	-0.2	1B(15): 1.2	0.0
2022 non-DC	*BAL*	*MLB*	*36*	*251*	*25*	*8*	*0*	*8*	*28*	*24*	*89*	*0*	*0*	*36.3%*	*.191/.277/.351*	*65*	*.271*	*-0.4*	*1B -1, RF 0*	*-0.8*

Comparables: Carlos Pena, Mike Jorgensen, Tony Clark

When the end came, we didn't have to watch it. Davis announced his retirement in August, three months after he had been ruled out for the season following hip surgery and five months since he suffered a back strain in his first spring training game—his last in an Orioles uniform. Then again, perhaps we had just been watching the end for years. If it hadn't arrived when he slipped to replacement-level in his age-31 season, it surely felt like it had the following year, when he cost his team three wins. By the time he mercifully ended his record-breaking hitless streak in 2019, you'd have been hard-pressed to find an O's fan who thought they weren't watching the most painfully-protracted conclusion of a career in living memory. Baltimore will pay Davis for another 15 years, so this undoubtedly isn't the last we've heard of this disaster stretch. Let's instead try to remember him as the truly fearsome power hitter of his prime. We've spent quite enough time on his downfall.

Yusniel Diaz RF

Born: 10/07/96 Age: 25 Bats: R Throws: R Height: 6'1" Weight: 215 lb. Origin: International Free Agent, 2015

YEAR	TEAM	LVL	AGE	PA	R	2B	3B	HR	RBI	BB	K	SB	CS	Whiff%	AVG/OBP/SLG	DRC+	BABIP	BRR	FRAA	WARP
2019	FRE	A+	22	25	0	0	0	0	2	3	7	0	0		.273/.360/.273	87	.400	-0.6	CF(5): -0.3	0.0
2019	BOW	AA	22	322	45	19	4	11	53	32	67	0	3		.262/.335/.472	120	.303	0.7	RF(53): 1.5, CF(5): 0.2, LF(2): 0.2	2.1
2021	BOW	AA	24	44	3	3	0	1	6	4	13	1	0		.179/.273/.333	90	.240	0.2	LF(3): -0.2, RF(3): -0.3	0.0
2021	NOR	AAA	24	209	19	4	1	4	16	14	69	1	2		.157/.225/.251	64	.218	0.0	RF(30): 1.5, CF(10): -2.1, LF(7): 0.7	-0.2
2022 DC	*BAL*	*MLB*	*25*	*32*	*3*	*1*	*0*	*0*	*3*	*2*	*8*	*0*	*0*	*29.7%*	*.204/.270/.328*	*62*	*.265*	*0.0*	*LF 0*	*0.0*

Comparables: Jorge Bonifacio, Billy McKinney, Moisés Sierra

In the age of on-demand, Diaz has become the prospect embodiment of development hell. It has been four years since this very book raved about his Double-A debut and hinted at a September call-up. For much of the intervening period, his stalled progress could be put down to a team that had little interest in starting service time clocks and Diaz's slightly-too-common injury niggles. As recently as 2019, he still looked like a well above-average hitter for the level but remained mired at Double-A. The past couple of years have been the equivalent of Sonic the Hedgehog's unnerving teeth: an unsettling combination of wasted development time and a long-awaited Triple-A showcase which horrified rather than thrilled. More injuries (quad, toe) hampered his efforts, and a sore shoulder spoiled a slightly more promising AFL stint. Whether a swing overhaul or merely some better health is needed to help him return to his former performance levels, it's still not clear he can muster the power to earn a major-league premiere.

Kelvin Gutierrez 3B

Born: 08/28/94 Age: 27 Bats: R Throws: R Height: 6'2" Weight: 215 lb. Origin: International Free Agent, 2013

YEAR	TEAM	LVL	AGE	PA	R	2B	3B	HR	RBI	BB	K	SB	CS	Whiff%	AVG/OBP/SLG	DRC+	BABIP	BRR	FRAA	WARP
2019	OMA	AAA	24	327	41	9	2	9	43	35	71	12	1		.287/.367/.427	95	.349	2.1	3B(63): -4.5, 1B(7): -0.8, SS(1): -0.0	0.4
2019	KC	MLB	24	79	4	2	1	1	11	5	24	1	0	32.0%	.260/.304/.356	77	.367	-0.6	3B(18): -0.1	-0.1
2020	GIG	WIN	25	63	11	5	0	2	11	10	15	0	0		.396/.492/.604		.528			
2020	KC	MLB	25	12	0	0	0	0	0	3	6	0	0	45.0%	.111/.333/.111	85	.333	0.0	3B(3): -0.0	0.0
2021	GIG	WIN	26	71	15	3	0	2	12	10	11	2	1		.417/.493/.567		.479			
2021	OMA	AAA	26	38	1	3	1	0	4	2	7	0	1		.306/.342/.444	99	.379	-1.0	3B(3): -0.3	0.0
2021	NOR	AAA	26	94	10	4	0	4	13	4	21	1	1		.233/.266/.411	99	.262	0.8	3B(16): 1.1, SS(2): 0.0, LF(1): 0.1	0.5
2021	BAL	MLB	26	153	14	4	1	2	12	13	45	0	0	34.1%	.248/.327/.336	82	.356	-0.6	3B(47): 0.5	0.2
2021	KC	MLB	26	142	9	4	2	1	8	6	31	0	1	27.9%	.215/.254/.296	80	.272	-1.0		0.0
2022 DC	*BAL*	*MLB*	*27*	*510*	*53*	*17*	*3*	*9*	*54*	*34*	*125*	*6*	*2*	*30.1%*	*.235/.293/.348*	*74*	*.301*	*0.4*	*3B 0*	*-0.3*

Comparables: Chris Johnson, Erik González, Pablo Reyes

Gutierrez has power. For how often he gets to it, he just might as well be Superman with a kryptonite bat. Even that's not entirely fair. Gutierrez fires off powerful blasts, it's the angle that's the problem, like a young Scott Summers incapable of directing his optic energy. His hardest-hit ball matched Rafael Devers, for instance, who posted an ISO 174 points higher and hit home runs almost six times as often when he came to the plate. It may be unfair to compare Gutierrez to one of the finest young hitters in baseball, but it's indicative of his predicament. His 114.4-mph maximum exit velocity ranked within the top 10% of the league, while his barrels per plate appearance sat in the bottom quarter. When those batted balls aren't threatening worms everywhere, they often don't exist at all since he makes contact in under 70% of his plate appearances. Maybe there's a Professor X out there who can turn him from zero to hero.

Austin Hays OF

Born: 07/05/95 Age: 27 Bats: R Throws: R Height: 6'0" Weight: 205 lb. Origin: Round 3, 2016 Draft (#91 overall)

YEAR	TEAM	LVL	AGE	PA	R	2B	3B	HR	RBI	BB	K	SB	CS	Whiff%	AVG/OBP/SLG	DRC+	BABIP	BRR	FRAA	WARP
2019	FRE	A+	23	40	3	0	0	2	6	1	11	0	0		.162/.200/.324	102	.160	0.3	CF(7): -0.7	0.1
2019	BOW	AA	23	61	9	5	0	3	11	5	11	3	1		.268/.328/.518	113	.286	-1.0	RF(7): 1.1, CF(4): 0.1	0.3
2019	NOR	AAA	23	257	43	16	1	10	27	11	61	6	4		.254/.304/.454	93	.302	3.6	CF(39): 5.2, RF(16): -0.2, LF(1): -0.1	1.4
2019	BAL	MLB	23	75	12	6	0	4	13	7	13	2	0	25.9%	.309/.373/.574	111	.333	0.7	CF(20): 2.3	0.7
2020	BAL	MLB	24	134	20	2	0	4	9	8	25	2	3	20.2%	.279/.328/.393	104	.316	-0.7	CF(23): -1.0, LF(10): 1.5, RF(3): -0.9	0.4
2021	BAL	MLB	25	529	73	26	4	22	71	28	107	4	3	24.7%	.256/.308/.461	104	.286	3.3	LF(88): 2.6, RF(54): 3.8, CF(6): -0.2	3.1
2022 DC	*BAL*	*MLB*	*26*	*582*	*77*	*24*	*2*	*21*	*75*	*32*	*110*	*6*	*3*	*24.2%*	*.248/.299/.423*	*94*	*.275*	*0.2*	*LF 1, RF 0*	*1.5*

Comparables: Starling Marte, Avisaíl García, Teoscar Hernández

When he wasn't sidelined by his troublesome hamstrings, Hays was finally able to do what he'd never done before: be a major-league regular. That might be more than just a comment on his playing time, extending to his performance with both bat and glove. Overshadowed by the breakout taking place next to him in center field, Hays was nonetheless a good outfielder in both corners and a league-average bat, turning in the kind of display that would make him a useful complementary starter on a team with a few stars. As it happened, he was also Baltimore's second-best position player. There may be more to come from the talented athlete, but this will be more than enough to earn him a spot on the next good Orioles team, albeit one lower in the hierarchy.

★ ★ ★ *2022 Top 101 Prospect* **#88** ★ ★ ★

Gunnar Henderson SS
Born: 06/29/01 Age: 21 Bats: L Throws: R Height: 6'2" Weight: 210 lb. Origin: Round 2, 2019 Draft (#42 overall)

YEAR	TEAM	LVL	AGE	PA	R	2B	3B	HR	RBI	BB	K	SB	CS	Whiff%	AVG/OBP/SLG	DRC+	BABIP	BRR	FRAA	WARP
2019	ORI	ROK	18	121	21	5	2	1	11	11	28	2	2		.259/.331/.370		.338			
2021	DEL	A	20	157	30	11	1	8	39	14	46	5	1		.312/.369/.574	108	.404	0.8	SS(20): 3.2, 3B(11): 0.2	1.0
2021	ABD	A+	20	289	34	16	3	9	35	40	87	11	1		.230/.343/.432	98	.313	-1.9	SS(40): 4.2, 3B(23): -0.7	0.9
2022 non-DC	*BAL*	*MLB*	*21*	*251*	*22*	*11*	*1*	*5*	*25*	*20*	*81*	*3*	*2*	*29.7%*	*.209/.280/.350*	*67*	*.297*	*0.2*	*SS 1, 3B 0*	*-0.1*

Comparables: Jazz Chisholm Jr., Didi Gregorius, Gavin Cecchini

Henderson blasted his way up three levels of the minors, making the Orioles pull the trigger on a Double-A promotion less than three months after his 20th birthday. He showcased plenty of weapons along the way, including explosive pop and his cannon of an arm. The strikeout rate climbed at every step and that could be what prevents Henderson from hitting his target. Nonetheless, he is blazing his way towards the majors faster than most expected, with a real shot at becoming an impact regular.

Jahmai Jones 2B
Born: 08/04/97 Age: 24 Bats: R Throws: R Height: 6'0" Weight: 210 lb. Origin: Round 2, 2015 Draft (#70 overall)

YEAR	TEAM	LVL	AGE	PA	R	2B	3B	HR	RBI	BB	K	SB	CS	Whiff%	AVG/OBP/SLG	DRC+	BABIP	BRR	FRAA	WARP
2019	MSS	WIN	21	61	9	5	0	2	10	6	16	7	3		.302/.377/.509		.389			
2019	MOB	AA	21	544	66	22	3	5	50	50	109	9	11		.234/.308/.324	92	.288	2.6	2B(110): 13.8, CF(7): 0.4, LF(4): -0.6	3.3
2020	LAA	MLB	22	7	2	0	0	0	1	0	2	0	0	28.6%	.429/.429/.429	88	.600	-0.1	2B(2): -0.1	0.0
2021	NOR	AAA	23	295	34	9	3	11	37	35	68	11	3		.243/.337/.431	111	.287	-0.3	2B(53): -2.9, LF(11): -0.5, CF(1): -0.1	1.0
2021	BAL	MLB	23	72	5	3	0	0	3	4	26	1	0	25.4%	.149/.208/.194	67	.244	0.6	2B(23): 0.8	0.1
2022 DC	*BAL*	*MLB*	*24*	*92*	*10*	*3*	*0*	*2*	*9*	*7*	*20*	*2*	*1*	*26.0%*	*.215/.290/.351*	*75*	*.256*	*0.2*	*2B 0*	*0.1*

Comparables: Enrique Hernández, Jonathan Villar, Yolmer Sánchez

The bar was as low as it could be. The Orioles ditched presumptive second baseman Yolmer Sánchez immediately prior to the season and then watched their second basemen hit .192/.245/.282 as a unit. Within the league context, that 45 OPS+ was tied for the third-worst team performance at the keystone of all time. A very promising run from Jones at Triple-A gave him an OPS north of .900 by the end of June, making him look like the only plausible way for Baltimore to salvage some production at second since they weren't about to invest in upgrades. Instead, Jones was arguably the biggest culprit in their dubious place in history. He had already begun to slump before he was called up in mid-August and a trip to the bigs hastened that decline, leaving him looking tentative and overmatched no matter what he was thrown. If the line at Norfolk revived some hope that his athletic talent could yet make him a big-league regular, forcing the team to return to Pat Valaika did the exact opposite. The good news? The only way is up, both for Orioles second basemen and Jones. Probably.

Heston Kjerstad OF
Born: 02/12/99 Age: 23 Bats: L Throws: R Height: 6'3" Weight: 205 lb. Origin: Round 1, 2020 Draft (#2 overall)

While there was debate about the wisdom of the Orioles taking Kjerstad second overall with an underslot deal, there was far less disagreement over one thing: his ability to hit. A year and a half after he was drafted, we still haven't seen him take any reps in a professional game, both due to the pandemic and a troubling myocarditis diagnosis. At the time of writing, the outlook was improving, with Kjerstad participating in instructional camp in November. It would be nice if all we had to worry about this year is whether people were right about the hit tool.

Trey Mancini 1B/DH
Born: 03/18/92 Age: 30 Bats: R Throws: R Height: 6'3" Weight: 230 lb. Origin: Round 8, 2013 Draft (#249 overall)

YEAR	TEAM	LVL	AGE	PA	R	2B	3B	HR	RBI	BB	K	SB	CS	Whiff%	AVG/OBP/SLG	DRC+	BABIP	BRR	FRAA	WARP
2019	BAL	MLB	27	679	106	38	2	35	97	63	143	1	0	26.9%	.291/.364/.535	122	.326	-2.1	RF(87): -2.9, 1B(56): 1.4, LF(6): -0.2	3.4
2021	BAL	MLB	29	616	77	33	1	21	71	51	143	0	0	29.5%	.255/.326/.432	103	.308	-1.5	1B(77): 0.4	1.4
2022 DC	*BAL*	*MLB*	*30*	*565*	*80*	*25*	*1*	*20*	*73*	*47*	*133*	*0*	*1*	*28.9%*	*.250/.322/.428*	*101*	*.300*	*-0.8*	*1B 0*	*1.2*

Comparables: Bob Watson, J.D. Martinez, Billy Williams

Mancini was destined to be Comeback Player of the Year almost regardless of what happened in 2021, since stepping back onto a major-league field following his cancer diagnosis was such a monumental victory in itself. He didn't settle for merely appearing, soon rediscovering his 2019 form and looking like one of the league's better hitters through the end of May. Extended slumps in June and August bookended a memorable second-place finish in the Home Run Derby and perhaps spoke to the difficulty of competing over a full 162-game season under the circumstances. Of course, Mancini fought through both of those slumps and emerged at the end of the season as one of Baltimore's best hitters. Whether he's on the next good Orioles team, or even invited to be, no one will forget this comeback.

Richie Martin SS Born: 12/22/94 Age: 27 Bats: R Throws: R Height: 6'0" Weight: 190 lb. Origin: Round 1, 2015 Draft (#20 overall)

YEAR	TEAM	LVL	AGE	PA	R	2B	3B	HR	RBI	BB	K	SB	CS	Whiff%	AVG/OBP/SLG	DRC+	BABIP	BRR	FRAA	WARP
2019	BAL	MLB	24	309	29	8	3	6	23	14	83	10	1	28.5%	.208/.260/.322	66	.272	-0.6	SS(117): -1.4	-0.4
2020	CAG	WIN	25	62	9	6	0	2	6	6	13	2	1		.236/.323/.455		.275			
2021	NOR	AAA	26	112	12	4	2	1	5	14	25	5	3		.208/.321/.323	95	.271	-0.2	SS(24): 0.1, CF(2): -0.1	0.3
2021	BAL	MLB	26	105	9	2	0	1	8	4	28	0	2	28.2%	.235/.269/.286	77	.314	-0.4	SS(37): -1.3	-0.1
2022 DC	*BAL*	*MLB*	*27*	*243*	*25*	*8*	*1*	*3*	*29*	*15*	*60*	*5*	*3*	*28.3%*	*.215/.280/.317*	*62*	*.279*	*0.6*	*SS -1*	*-0.3*

Comparables: Miguel Rojas, Erik González, Chase d'Arnaud

Attempting to move beyond the dual disappointments of a poor debut and a fractured wrist that kept him out of the 2020 campaign altogether, Martin instead managed to reproduce both seasons in one. Before producing a slash line that yet again indicated that his bat isn't up to standard, he fractured his left wrist less than a year after he broke his right one. That came after he broke his hamate bone in January, limiting him to just seven at-bats in the spring. When he finally arrived back in the majors in August, he did little to showcase the glove which was supposed to be his calling card in the first place. If Baltimore's patience extends to one more trial, he can't afford another repeat—for the sake of his bones if nothing else.

Jorge Mateo UT Born: 06/23/95 Age: 27 Bats: R Throws: R Height: 6'0" Weight: 182 lb. Origin: International Free Agent, 2012

YEAR	TEAM	LVL	AGE	PA	R	2B	3B	HR	RBI	BB	K	SB	CS	Whiff%	AVG/OBP/SLG	DRC+	BABIP	BRR	FRAA	WARP
2019	TOR	WIN	24	152	16	3	1	0	10	18	31	6	1		.197/.289/.235		.252			
2019	LV	AAA	24	566	95	29	14	19	78	29	145	24	11		.289/.330/.504	82	.366	2.9	SS(100): 17.4, 2B(14): 0.1	2.9
2020	TOR	WIN	25	75	11	3	1	2	5	6	15	4	2		.309/.373/.471		.373			
2020	SD	MLB	25	28	4	3	0	0	2	1	11	1	0	35.1%	.154/.185/.269	77	.267	-0.7	2B(5): -0.0, LF(3): -0.3, RF(3): -0.2	-0.1
2021	SD	MLB	26	93	10	4	0	2	6	2	27	5	0	31.8%	.207/.250/.322	74	.276	0.8	CF(11): 0.1, 3B(8): 0.9, RF(6): -0.1	0.2
2021	BAL	MLB	26	116	9	7	1	2	8	7	28	5	3	30.6%	.280/.328/.421	91	.359	0.6	2B(18): 1.9, SS(17): -1.9, 3B(1): -0.2	0.3
2022 DC	*BAL*	*MLB*	*27*	*346*	*36*	*14*	*3*	*7*	*41*	*17*	*97*	*14*	*6*	*31.0%*	*.226/.273/.361*	*68*	*.298*	*1.9*	*2B 3, SS 1*	*0.3*

Comparables: Erik González, Eduardo Escobar, Jonathan Villar

It's nice to be wanted. Optionless on a Padres team that rarely required him for more than a pinch-something moment, Mateo went through the first four months of the season lucky to get a start per week. By June he was down to a single start in the entire month; in July he exclusively came off the bench. Where, oh where could Mateo find a major-league team who would give him an opportunity to show he could handle more than one at-bat a game? San Diego, tired of carrying a player they wouldn't start and couldn't option, cut ties in early August. Baltimore, desperate to keep their infield door revolving, eagerly snapped him up. Finally, at 26, Mateo had a chance to play every day. He started nearly every day as a utility man, playing second, third, short and both outfield corners until back inflammation ended his year. A touch of batted-ball fortune aside, it did not shake off the notion that Mateo is simply a ludicrously fast bench piece. It's still nice that someone let him try.

Ryan McKenna OF Born: 02/14/97 Age: 25 Bats: R Throws: R Height: 5'11" Weight: 195 lb. Origin: Round 4, 2015 Draft (#133 overall)

YEAR	TEAM	LVL	AGE	PA	R	2B	3B	HR	RBI	BB	K	SB	CS	Whiff%	AVG/OBP/SLG	DRC+	BABIP	BRR	FRAA	WARP
2019	BOW	AA	22	567	78	26	6	9	54	59	121	25	11		.232/.321/.365	99	.287	0.9	CF(98): -3.9, LF(19): 0.5, RF(11): 0.8	1.7
2021	NOR	AAA	24	123	25	3	1	11	23	21	33	7	3		.307/.423/.683	145	.345	-0.7	CF(22): 1.3, RF(2): -0.3, LF(1): -0.1	1.1
2021	BAL	MLB	24	197	20	6	1	2	14	24	74	1	0	34.8%	.183/.292/.266	63	.312	1.2	LF(50): 3.5, CF(18): -0.3, RF(18): -2.1	0.0
2022 DC	*BAL*	*MLB*	*25*	*159*	*18*	*6*	*0*	*4*	*17*	*18*	*48*	*2*	*2*	*32.5%*	*.204/.305/.350*	*79*	*.281*	*0.2*	*CF 0, RF 0*	*0.2*

Comparables: Daz Cameron, Brandon Nimmo, Lewis Brinson

Last year's *Annual* comment for McKenna suggested his opportunity would depend on the development of Cedric Mullins and Austin Hays. It's little surprise, then, that he went back and forth so often between Norfolk and the majors, called up nine times in total in his debut season. The contrast between his performance at the two levels has more than a whiff of Quad-A about it. The sixth-best hitter at Triple-A by DRC+, he was only the sixth-best hitter in the Baltimore outfield—a dubious distinction to say the least, and only made worse by the fact that he'd rank lower had a few other guys received a bit more playing time on the grass . McKenna must figure out how to get that Triple-A power to the majors so he can make a case for a corner spot since he's not getting regular reps in center any time soon.

Ryan Mountcastle 1B/DH Born: 02/18/97 Age: 25 Bats: R Throws: R Height: 6'4" Weight: 230 lb. Origin: Round 1, 2015 Draft (#36 overall)

YEAR	TEAM	LVL	AGE	PA	R	2B	3B	HR	RBI	BB	K	SB	CS	Whiff%	AVG/OBP/SLG	DRC+	BABIP	BRR	FRAA	WARP
2019	NOR	AAA	22	553	81	35	1	25	83	24	130	2	1		.312/.344/.527	105	.370	-1.9	1B(84): -5.5, LF(26): 2.6, 3B(9): -0.0	1.1
2020	BAL	MLB	23	140	12	5	0	5	23	11	30	0	1	29.2%	.333/.386/.492	111	.398	-0.8	LF(25): -2.9, 1B(10): 0.1	0.2
2021	BAL	MLB	24	586	77	23	1	33	89	41	161	4	3	31.6%	.255/.309/.487	108	.297	0.3	1B(84): -3.2, LF(21): -1.8	1.5
2022 DC	*BAL*	*MLB*	*25*	*614*	*80*	*26*	*1*	*24*	*84*	*42*	*160*	*2*	*2*	*30.9%*	*.247/.304/.430*	*92*	*.302*	*-0.6*	*1B -2*	*0.3*

Comparables: Jonathan Villar, Jorge Polanco, Nolan Arenado

Once you factor in the inevitable decline from a .398 BABIP, Mountcastle more or less maintained his debut performance over a much larger sample. Still barely eligible, he led all rookies in homers with 33 and showed he can walk a little more often than might have been expected in his prospect days. At the same time, the pressure intensified on his bat, as a second look at his work in left field resulted in almost exclusive usage at first or DH over the final three months. He's not king—or even prince—of the castle. He's inside the walls, however, and the royalty is on its way.

Cedric Mullins CF Born: 10/01/94 Age: 27 Bats: L Throws: L Height: 5'8" Weight: 175 lb. Origin: Round 13, 2015 Draft (#403 overall)

YEAR	TEAM	LVL	AGE	PA	R	2B	3B	HR	RBI	BB	K	SB	CS	Whiff%	AVG/OBP/SLG	DRC+	BABIP	BRR	FRAA	WARP
2019	BOW	AA	24	226	35	11	0	5	18	22	31	20	3		.271/.341/.402	121	.293	2.7	CF(31): 0.8, LF(19): 0.3	1.8
2019	NOR	AAA	24	306	40	8	2	5	24	25	51	13	4		.205/.272/.306	86	.231	1.2	CF(56): 4.2, LF(6): -0.7	1.0
2019	BAL	MLB	24	74	7	0	2	0	4	4	14	1	0	28.4%	.094/.181/.156	82	.118	0.7	CF(22): 2.0	0.4
2020	BAL	MLB	25	153	16	4	3	3	12	8	37	7	2	22.8%	.271/.315/.407	85	.350	2.1	CF(41): 3.4, LF(4): 1.4, RF(4): -0.4	0.9
2021	BAL	MLB	26	675	91	37	5	30	59	59	125	30	8	21.0%	.291/.360/.518	117	.322	1.1	CF(153): 1.1	4.6
2022 DC	*BAL*	*MLB*	*27*	*599*	*85*	*28*	*4*	*17*	*67*	*48*	*112*	*19*	*6*	*20.7%*	*.246/.314/.408*	*91*	*.283*	*1.6*	*CF 4*	*2.1*

Comparables: Mallex Smith, Aaron Hicks, Ender Inciarte

It might draw about as much respect as the Oscars these days, but in Mullins' case for Most Valuable Oriole is not an award to be scoffed at. The speedy center fielder became the first Oriole in history to go 30-30, dazzling from start to finish whether at the plate (where he gave up switch-hitting), on the basepaths or in the outfield. This was the dynamic, thrilling Mullins who raised hopes so high coming into his disastrous 2019, with a healthy helping of power on top. That season feels a distant memory now. Even if the power was a little more than we might realistically expect going forward, the Entertainer will be the center fielder in Baltimore for the foreseeable future.

Tyler Nevin 1B Born: 05/29/97 Age: 25 Bats: R Throws: R Height: 6'4" Weight: 225 lb. Origin: Round 1, 2015 Draft (#38 overall)

YEAR	TEAM	LVL	AGE	PA	R	2B	3B	HR	RBI	BB	K	SB	CS	Whiff%	AVG/OBP/SLG	DRC+	BABIP	BRR	FRAA	WARP
2019	HFD	AA	22	540	60	26	2	13	61	65	90	6	2		.251/.345/.399	118	.283	1.4	1B(98): 3.4, 3B(12): -0.3, LF(7): 0.5	3.3
2021	NOR	AAA	24	453	45	18	0	16	52	42	91	1	1		.227/.305/.392	106	.251	0.0	1B(40): 0.3, 3B(37): -3.9, LF(20): 0.4	1.4
2021	BAL	MLB	24	18	3	2	0	1	3	4	5	0	0	30.0%	.286/.444/.643	98	.375	-0.1	LF(4): 0.6, 1B(2): 0.0	0.1
2022 DC	*BAL*	*MLB*	*25*	*126*	*14*	*5*	*0*	*3*	*13*	*11*	*26*	*0*	*1*	*24.2%*	*.233/.308/.369*	*84*	*.277*	*-0.1*	*3B -1, 1B 0*	*0.0*

Comparables: Brandon Snyder, Nick Evans, Daniel Vogelbach

The Orioles made a significant effort to reintroduce some defensive versatility to Nevin's game. The former Rockies prospect had become largely confined to first base in his last season in the Colorado org, but Baltimore ensured that he expanded his experience at all four corners, including spending most of his time at third in September. There were suggestions that the focus on defense negatively affected his offense, with Nevin's average slumping while he only sporadically tapped into his raw power. The versatility will certainly reduce some of the pressure on his bat, but not to the extent of a sub-par slash line. He did take advantage of a late-season recall to make one major impression at the plate in the very last game, blasting a third-deck homer at the Rogers Centre against Hyun-Jin Ryu.

Rougned Odor 2B/3B Born: 02/03/94 Age: 28 Bats: L Throws: R Height: 5'11" Weight: 200 lb. Origin: International Free Agent, 2011

YEAR	TEAM	LVL	AGE	PA	R	2B	3B	HR	RBI	BB	K	SB	CS	Whiff%	AVG/OBP/SLG	DRC+	BABIP	BRR	FRAA	WARP
2019	TEX	MLB	25	581	77	30	1	30	93	52	178	11	9	29.4%	.205/.283/.439	85	.244	-2.5	2B(137): -13.4	-0.4
2020	TEX	MLB	26	148	15	4	0	10	30	7	47	0	1	26.0%	.167/.209/.413	78	.157	-0.2	2B(37): -0.1	0.1
2021	NYY	MLB	27	361	42	12	0	15	39	27	100	0	1	28.7%	.202/.286/.379	82	.242	0.7	2B(74): 4.7, 3B(33): 2.8	1.3
2022 non-DC	*BAL*	*MLB*	*28*	*251*	*27*	*10*	*0*	*10*	*31*	*19*	*70*	*4*	*3*	*28.3%*	*.212/.288/.399*	*83*	*.258*	*0.3*	*2B 0, 3B 0*	*0.3*

Comparables: Roberto Alomar, Bill Mazeroski, Luis Castillo

At the beginning of the season, Odor was released by the Rangers—who would lose 102 games—even though they owed him more than $24 million. He was *that* bad. After latching on with the Yankees, he played to the back of his baseball card. Odor saw the short porch in right and fell in love, trying to clear it with every swing, producing his second-highest fly-ball rate, highest pull rate and highest whiff rate of his career. Why would a contending team keep a player that a last-place club jettisoned? Mound visits*:* no one does them better! He partook in nearly every mound meeting while he was on the field, often doing most of the talking, and even initiated a few on his own. The pitching staff carried the team in 2021 and clearly, Rougie deserves most of the credit. Also, with Texas paying his full salary, he counted for $0 against the luxury tax, whereas any other player would've put at least the MLB minimum salary on the books. Of course, pinching pennies matters little compared to the boon of an 80-grade mound visitor—regardless of his on-base percentage.

★ ★ ★ *2022 Top 101 Prospect* **#2** ★ ★ ★

Adley Rutschman C
Born: 02/06/98 Age: 24 Bats: S Throws: R Height: 6'2" Weight: 220 lb. Origin: Round 1, 2019 Draft (#1 overall)

YEAR	TEAM	LVL	AGE	PA	R	2B	3B	HR	RBI	BB	K	SB	CS	Whiff%	AVG/OBP/SLG	DRC+	BABIP	BRR	FRAA	WARP
2019	ORI	ROK	21	16	3	0	0	1	3	2	2	1	0		.143/.250/.357		.091			
2019	ABD	SS	21	92	11	7	1	1	15	12	16	0	0		.325/.413/.481		.387			
2019	DEL	A	21	47	5	1	0	2	8	6	9	0	0		.154/.261/.333	104	.138	0.1	C(6): 0.1	0.2
2021	BOW	AA	23	358	61	16	0	18	55	55	57	1	2		.271/.392/.508	141	.279	0.3	C(53): 13.8, 1B(20): 0.1	4.4
2021	NOR	AAA	23	185	25	9	2	5	20	24	33	2	2		.312/.405/.490	123	.364	-0.6	C(29): 4.8, 1B(8): -1.3	1.4
2022 DC	*BAL*	*MLB*	*24*	*370*	*47*	*15*	*1*	*10*	*43*	*40*	*66*	*1*	*1*	*20.0%*	*.243/.333/.398*	*97*	*.277*	*-0.4*	*C 6*	*2.3*

Comparables: Will Smith, Yan Gomes, Sean Murphy

YEAR	TEAM	P. COUNT	FRM RUNS	BLK RUNS	THRW RUNS	TOT RUNS
2019	DEL	769	0.0		0.0	0.0
2019	ABD	1079		0.0	0.0	0.0
2021	BOW	7738	12.8	0.6	0.8	14.2
2021	NOR	4199	3.2	0.1	0.0	3.3
2022	*BAL*	*13228*	*1.9*	*0.0*	*-0.1*	*1.8*

When the "Play badly for Adley" refrain circulated among Orioles fans the year prior to Rutschman's selection in the 2019 draft, they were probably hoping that it wouldn't extend another three seasons into the future. It was at least some comfort that their 115-loss season could lead to a truly generational talent. Baltimore's great hope did nothing but reinforce that potential stardom on the farm, demolishing Double-A pitching in his delayed debut in the upper minors before repeating the trick at Triple-A Norfolk. The major-league team, meanwhile, has more than doubled those 115 losses in the intervening period. It's an unfair amount of pressure to put on any player, but the fans have sat through quite enough of the playing badly; now they need Adley to justify it.

Anthony Santander RF
Born: 10/19/94 Age: 27 Bats: S Throws: R Height: 6'2" Weight: 235 lb. Origin: International Free Agent, 2011

YEAR	TEAM	LVL	AGE	PA	R	2B	3B	HR	RBI	BB	K	SB	CS	Whiff%	AVG/OBP/SLG	DRC+	BABIP	BRR	FRAA	WARP
2019	NOR	AAA	24	209	30	15	0	5	28	13	38	3	2		.259/.311/.415	99	.298	0.9	RF(35): 2.5, LF(8): -0.1	0.9
2019	BAL	MLB	24	405	46	20	1	20	59	19	86	1	2	21.2%	.261/.297/.476	97	.285	-0.3	RF(50): -4.7, LF(40): 8.4, CF(24): 4.0	2.0
2020	BAL	MLB	25	165	24	13	1	11	32	10	25	0	1	25.6%	.261/.315/.575	118	.248	-0.2	RF(35): 0.2, LF(2): -0.1	0.9
2021	BAL	MLB	26	438	54	24	0	18	50	23	101	1	1	25.2%	.241/.286/.433	94	.275	-0.5	RF(81): -3.5, LF(4): -0.2	0.5
2022 DC	*BAL*	*MLB*	*27*	*598*	*80*	*30*	*1*	*23*	*79*	*34*	*131*	*2*	*2*	*24.3%*	*.246/.297/.434*	*89*	*.283*	*-0.6*	*RF 0, LF 0*	*0.6*

Comparables: Max Kepler, Moisés Sierra, Josh Reddick

Injuries were the blemish on an otherwise-promising 2019 campaign for Santander, whose line suffered in September when he tried to play through multiple minor issues. An oblique strain then curtailed his blistering 2020 season. The third time didn't prove to be the charm as Santander spent a decent chunk of 2021 on the IL with ankle and knee sprains as well as a COVID stint. Those ailments allow us to discount his underwhelming production, while simultaneously calling into question his ability to either stay on the field or recognize when he's not healthy enough to compete. The Orioles will happily insert peak Santander into their lineup as they move into contention; the questions of when or how often that form might resurface threaten his role in that transition.

DJ Stewart OF
Born: 11/30/93 Age: 28 Bats: L Throws: R Height: 6'0" Weight: 210 lb. Origin: Round 1, 2015 Draft (#25 overall)

YEAR	TEAM	LVL	AGE	PA	R	2B	3B	HR	RBI	BB	K	SB	CS	Whiff%	AVG/OBP/SLG	DRC+	BABIP	BRR	FRAA	WARP
2019	NOR	AAA	25	277	42	19	2	12	47	38	51	5	4		.291/.396/.548	126	.324	-1.9	LF(30): -1.7, RF(22): 1.5	1.4
2019	BAL	MLB	25	142	15	6	0	4	15	14	26	1	2	26.4%	.238/.317/.381	94	.268	-0.3	RF(26): -1.5, LF(11): -0.5	0.1
2020	BAL	MLB	26	112	13	2	0	7	15	20	38	0	0	36.0%	.193/.355/.455	101	.233	0.3	RF(21): 2.8, LF(10): 0.6	0.7
2021	BAL	MLB	27	318	39	10	0	12	33	44	89	0	0	31.7%	.204/.324/.374	93	.254	-0.4	LF(39): -0.2, RF(33): -1.3	0.6
2022 DC	*BAL*	*MLB*	*28*	*132*	*16*	*5*	*0*	*4*	*15*	*17*	*33*	*1*	*1*	*31.4%*	*.210/.326/.384*	*91*	*.260*	*0.0*	*RF 0, LF 0*	*0.2*

Comparables: Tyler Collins, Carlos Peguero, Scott Schebler

On walk rate alone, Stewart looks like a major-league regular. He would have ranked among the league's top 20 if he accumulated enough time to qualify, and that's not a fluke based on his track record in pro ball and willingness to wait out long plate appearances. It also might be the only characteristic that indicates Stewart could be a regular. Sure, he runs into a homer every now and then, but he also gets overwhelmed up in the zone and remains toothless against southpaws—who, to be fair, he is rarely allowed to see. The glove isn't going to make up for those shortcomings, nor is his performance against opposite-handed pitching. The patience also puts him in strikeout-friendly counts, which is a poor combination with an easily-exploitable swing. The best outcome as Stewart's approach stands might be some sort of Joey Gallo-lite, but when was the last time a team said "Yes, give me platoon Joey Gallo with less power and no defensive value?"

Ramón Urías MI Born: 06/03/94 Age: 28 Bats: R Throws: R Height: 6'0" Weight: 190 lb. Origin: International Free Agent, 2010

YEAR	TEAM	LVL	AGE	PA	R	2B	3B	HR	RBI	BB	K	SB	CS	Whiff%	AVG/OBP/SLG	DRC+	BABIP	BRR	FRAA	WARP
2019	MOC	WIN	25	123	14	2	0	4	11	7	23	0	0		.204/.264/.333		.214			
2019	MEM	AAA	25	375	51	24	0	9	52	44	71	4	1		.263/.369/.424	102	.310	-3.7	2B(64): -0.3, 3B(20): -1.1, SS(5): 0.4	1.2
2020	BAL	MLB	26	27	3	2	0	1	3	2	6	0	0	28.3%	.360/.407/.560	100	.444	-1.0	SS(5): -0.5, 2B(4): -0.0	-0.1
2021	NOR	AAA	27	101	14	6	1	4	12	9	25	1	1		.258/.340/.483	105	.317	0.2	2B(11): -0.6, SS(9): -0.6, 3B(4): 1.1	0.4
2021	BAL	MLB	27	296	33	14	0	7	38	28	76	1	2	26.0%	.279/.361/.412	99	.369	0.6	SS(48): 0.6, 2B(32): -0.4, 3B(10): -0.8	1.0
2022 DC	*BAL*	*MLB*	*28*	*504*	*59*	*24*	*1*	*11*	*59*	*42*	*116*	*3*	*2*	*25.8%*	*.231/.310/.366*	*85*	*.286*	*-0.5*	*SS -1, 2B 0*	*0.6*

Comparables: Tony Abreu, Jonathan Villar, Eduardo Escobar

At the risk of sounding like an old-school announcer, this guy can hit. That's not to say the Orioles have uncovered another gem for their next contender, but Urías was closer to fitting that bill than any other flier they took. Put him in the box and he'll look like he belongs, whether it's in Mexico City, Norfolk, VA, or Camden Yards. He has solid awareness of the strike zone and the patience to take a walk; his pitches per plate appearance would have ranked among the top 10 in baseball if he'd qualified. Although he hits a few too many balls on the ground to be a big power threat, he's not incapable of making loud contact. His defense was respectable enough that, while he might not be an ideal everyday shortstop, he's a valuable utility infielder. He's a good, solid ballplayer. The Orioles need some of those.

PITCHERS

Keegan Akin LHP Born: 04/01/95 Age: 27 Bats: L Throws: L Height: 5'11" Weight: 235 lb. Origin: Round 2, 2016 Draft (#54 overall)

YEAR	TEAM	LVL	AGE	W	L	SV	G	GS	IP	H	HR	BB/9	K/9	K	GB%	BABIP	WHIP	ERA	DRA-	WARP	MPH	FB%	Whiff%	CSP
2019	NOR	AAA	24	6	7	0	25	24	112^1	109	10	4.9	10.5	131	32.4%	.333	1.51	4.73	107	1.0				
2020	BAL	MLB	25	1	2	0	8	6	25^2	27	3	3.5	12.3	35	34.3%	.358	1.44	4.56	94	0.4	92.0	62.0%	28.5%	51.9%
2021	BAL	MLB	26	2	10	0	24	17	95	110	17	3.8	7.8	82	36.6%	.326	1.58	6.63	128	-0.6	92.1	57.2%	21.8%	56.9%
2022 DC	*BAL*	*MLB*	*27*	*6*	*7*	*0*	*22*	*22*	*104*	*107*	*17*	*3.9*	*8.3*	*95*	*35.7%*	*.303*	*1.46*	*5.06*	*118*	*-0.2*	*92.1*	*57.9%*	*22.9%*	*56.1%*

Comparables: Shawn Boskie, Bryan Rekar, Chris Rusin

A real magician never reveals his secrets. Akin's spread around the league fairly quickly following his debut, though: a high-spin fastball from the left side that had hitters looking in the wrong place, like any good piece of misdirection. The problem is that once people know where to look, they aren't fooled by the trick any more. Akin was no exception, watching his fastball advantage vanish and his whole act bomb as a result. If he can learn to keep people guessing more often with his other tricks, perhaps he can still recapture the mystery of the fastball. They were never the highlight of this show, but the changeup and slider need to be more consistently located to form an effective side act that helps the heater dazzle. As things stand, Akin doesn't have any secrets left up his sleeve.

Mike Baumann RHP Born: 09/10/95 Age: 26 Bats: R Throws: R Height: 6'4" Weight: 235 lb. Origin: Round 3, 2017 Draft (#98 overall)

YEAR	TEAM	LVL	AGE	W	L	SV	G	GS	IP	H	HR	BB/9	K/9	K	GB%	BABIP	WHIP	ERA	DRA-	WARP	MPH	FB%	Whiff%	CSP
2019	FRE	A+	23	1	4	0	11	11	54	40	2	4.0	12.8	77	43.1%	.317	1.19	3.83	77	1.1				
2019	BOW	AA	23	6	2	1	13	11	70	45	2	2.7	8.4	65	41.4%	.242	0.94	2.31	93	0.8				
2021	BOW	AA	25	3	2	0	10	10	38^2	29	6	4.2	9.1	39	44.2%	.237	1.22	4.89	96	0.4				
2021	NOR	AAA	25	1	1	0	6	6	27	18	0	4.3	8.7	26	37.7%	.261	1.15	2.00	97	0.4				
2021	BAL	MLB	25	1	1	0	4	0	10	13	2	5.4	4.5	5	36.8%	.306	1.90	9.90	133	-0.1	93.7	56.0%	19.8%	58.0%
2022 DC	*BAL*	*MLB*	*26*	*7*	*6*	*0*	*65*	*6*	*77.7*	*77*	*11*	*4.8*	*8.1*	*70*	*39.2%*	*.297*	*1.52*	*5.09*	*116*	*-0.3*	*93.7*	*56.0%*	*19.8%*	*58.0%*

Comparables: Austin Voth, Travis Harper, Justin Haley

It's hard to know whether the flexor strain that caused Baltimore to shut Baumann down in 2020 was the primary cause of his command woes. It's not as though the big right-hander had ever displayed pinpoint accuracy, frequently hitting double-digit walk rates at prior minor-league stops. This past year was particularly bad, however, as he issued 40 free passes in a touch over 80 frames across all levels. To make matters worse, major-league hitters treated his offerings with utter disdain, hammering almost anything he did throw in the zone. The Orioles plan to keep stretching Baumann out as a starter, so we can only hope this was all just rust and not a preview of how his arsenal will play in a larger sample.

Marcos Diplán RHP Born: 09/18/96 Age: 25 Bats: R Throws: R Height: 6'0" Weight: 200 lb. Origin: International Free Agent, 2013

YEAR	TEAM	LVL	AGE	W	L	SV	G	GS	IP	H	HR	BB/9	K/9	K	GB%	BABIP	WHIP	ERA	DRA-	WARP	MPH	FB%	Whiff%	CSP
2019	PNS	AA	22	0	1	0	8	2	11	10	1	5.7	8.2	10	16.7%	.310	1.55	4.09	124	-0.1				
2019	BLX	AA	22	3	4	3	30	5	57^2	47	6	5.8	9.8	63	43.1%	.279	1.46	4.99	112	0.0				
2021	NOR	AAA	24	3	1	0	17	0	19^2	23	1	4.1	11.9	26	30.9%	.415	1.63	4.12	93	0.3				
2021	BAL	MLB	24	2	0	0	23	0	30	22	6	4.5	7.2	24	41.7%	.205	1.23	4.50	111	0.1	93.9	62.3%	25.1%	57.4%
2022 DC	*FA*	*MLB*	*25*	*1*	*1*	*0*	*28*	*0*	*24.7*	*25*	*4*	*5.4*	*7.9*	*21*	*38.7%*	*.296*	*1.62*	*5.69*	*126*	*-0.2*	*93.9*	*62.3%*	*25.1%*	*57.4%*

Comparables: Todd Erdos, JC Ramírez, Travis Lakins Sr.

Several years removed from the peak of his prospect value, Diplán made his debut to little fanfare. He was leaned on heavily by a team that limped to a combined 5.70 bullpen ERA; despite not making his debut until August 6th, the Orioles still squeezed 30 innings out of his arm. When he came in to mop up Bruce Zimmermann's mess on the final day of the season, he also ensured that he faced a batter in all nine innings of a game in that brief 23-game relief stint. He flashed some intriguing traits, including a variably-tight low-80s curve that doesn't quite seem to make the most of its high spin rate and a Johnny Cueto-esque tendency to vary the timing of his delivery, occasionally pausing completely with his leg suspended halfway through his motion. While the production itself was mediocre at best, it was welcome relief for Baltimore.

Chris Ellis RHP Born: 09/22/92 Age: 29 Bats: L Throws: R Height: 6'5" Weight: 205 lb. Origin: Round 3, 2014 Draft (#88 overall)

YEAR	TEAM	LVL	AGE	W	L	SV	G	GS	IP	H	HR	BB/9	K/9	K	GB%	BABIP	WHIP	ERA	DRA-	WARP	MPH	FB%	Whiff%	CSP
2019	MEM	AAA	26	5	5	1	40	7	79	98	13	5.4	9.3	82	42.3%	.363	1.84	7.18	105	0.2				
2019	KC	MLB	26	0	0	0	1	0	1	1	0	9.0	0.0	0	25.0%	.250	2.00	0.00	118	0.0	93.6	35.3%	0.0%	44.7%
2021	DUR	AAA	28	1	5	0	15	13	57	61	14	4.4	9.2	58	40.2%	.303	1.56	6.32	111	0.4				
2021	TB	MLB	28	1	0	0	1	0	4	3	0	2.3	15.8	7	25.0%	.375	1.00	0.00	89	0.1	94.4	43.5%	44.4%	56.9%
2021	BAL	MLB	28	0	0	0	6	6	25^{1}	18	3	4.6	5.7	16	29.3%	.211	1.22	2.49	137	-0.3	94.0	48.8%	22.3%	54.1%
2022 DC	*FA*	*MLB*	*29*	*4*	*4*	*0*	*34*	*6*	*50.7*	*52*	*8*	*4.4*	*8.3*	*46*	*36.4%*	*.302*	*1.51*	*5.40*	*122*	*-0.3*	*94.0*	*48.0%*	*25.6%*	*54.3%*

Comparables: Nick Blackburn, Dillon Peters, Bryan Mitchell

Ellis must have felt like he got particularly short shrift after his first major-league appearance, in which the Rule 5 pick pitched a scoreless inning for the Royals in the first week of the 2019 season before being promptly returned to the Cardinals. His second appearance, almost two-and-a-half years later for the Rays, won't have made him feel much better. Ellis once again held the opposition scoreless, this time over four frames, while punching out seven, before immediately getting designated for assignment again. It's heartening that he only had to wait a week for his third appearance, as the Orioles picked him up and gave him a month-long audition in their rotation. He was fortunate to allow as few runs as he did but he also showcased his pretty curveball and velocity that will play if he can refine his command. He shouldn't have to wait another two-and-a-half years for his next shot.

Paul Fry LHP Born: 07/26/92 Age: 29 Bats: L Throws: L Height: 6'0" Weight: 205 lb. Origin: Round 17, 2013 Draft (#507 overall)

YEAR	TEAM	LVL	AGE	W	L	SV	G	GS	IP	H	HR	BB/9	K/9	K	GB%	BABIP	WHIP	ERA	DRA-	WARP	MPH	FB%	Whiff%	CSP
2019	BAL	MLB	26	1	9	3	66	0	57^{1}	54	7	4.6	8.6	55	57.0%	.299	1.45	5.34	101	0.5	90.8	52.2%	25.9%	46.2%
2020	BAL	MLB	27	1	0	0	22	0	22	22	3	3.7	11.9	29	57.6%	.339	1.41	2.45	65	0.7	92.9	53.5%	29.2%	47.1%
2021	NOR	AAA	28	0	0	0	11	0	8	5	0	10.1	7.9	7	72.7%	.227	1.75	7.87	110	0.1				
2021	BAL	MLB	28	4	5	2	52	0	47^{1}	37	3	6.7	11.4	60	47.4%	.304	1.52	6.08	90	0.7	92.9	54.6%	25.6%	51.0%
2022 DC	*BAL*	*MLB*	*29*	*3*	*3*	*0*	*67*	*0*	*58*	*48*	*6*	*5.2*	*10.5*	*68*	*52.6%*	*.288*	*1.40*	*4.15*	*97*	*0.3*	*92.4*	*53.8%*	*26.3%*	*49.2%*

Comparables: Sam Freeman, Heath Hembree, Scott Alexander

Unscored upon in 75% of his appearances, on any given day Fry was more likely to look like the reliable high-leverage option Baltimore expected after his 2020 breakout. Unfortunately, he also served up a stunning number of duds, tying for the league lead in relief appearances of three or more runs allowed with eight. When things started to go wrong, he rarely put out the fire, getting repeatedly burned by walks on those occasions. There were whispers the foreign substance crackdown robbed Fry of a key ingredient, a rumor supported by his 25 walks in 24 ⅔ frames from June 11 onwards. When he crammed five of his disaster outings into nine August appearances, even the Orioles were done—he was sent to Norfolk, where he continued to search in vain for the right recipe.

Conner Greene RHP Born: 04/04/95 Age: 27 Bats: R Throws: R Height: 6'4" Weight: 195 lb. Origin: Round 7, 2013 Draft (#205 overall)

YEAR	TEAM	LVL	AGE	W	L	SV	G	GS	IP	H	HR	BB/9	K/9	K	GB%	BABIP	WHIP	ERA	DRA-	WARP	MPH	FB%	Whiff%	CSP
2019	NWA	AA	24	3	9	1	21	16	97	101	11	3.5	7.9	85	45.0%	.313	1.43	5.29	121	-1.0				
2019	OMA	AAA	24	1	0	0	8	0	15^{1}	14	2	9.4	5.9	10	51.1%	.286	1.96	4.11	115	0.0				
2021	NOR	AAA	26	1	3	0	9	3	28	38	7	5.5	9.0	28	43.5%	.365	1.96	7.39	114	0.2				
2021	BAL	MLB	26	1	3	0	22	1	23^{1}	30	1	4.6	9.3	24	37.8%	.397	1.80	7.71	107	0.1	96.0	47.0%	29.5%	53.9%
2021	LAD	MLB	26	0	0	0	2	0	2	2	0	0.0	9.0	2	33.3%	.333	1.00	0.00	116	0.0	95.7	64.3%	33.3%	56.8%
2022 DC	*FA*	*MLB*	*27*	*1*	*1*	*0*	*28*	*0*	*24.7*	*26*	*3*	*4.9*	*7.9*	*21*	*42.0%*	*.308*	*1.60*	*5.59*	*124*	*-0.2*	*96.0*	*48.1%*	*29.8%*	*54.1%*

Comparables: Luke Jackson, Jake Thompson, Hunter Wood

Demand for Greene's services was wildly unpredictable. After promoting him for his major-league debut, the Orioles saw him give up six runs in his first three appearances then waived him, watching almost every other team pass until the Dodgers stepped in. Two scoreless outings later, Los Angeles dropped him too, allowing Baltimore to immediately pounce and bring him back into their bullpen, where he remained the rest of the way. It was a debut appropriate for a player who, despite his velocity, toiled in the minors for eight seasons before getting the call. Wildly unpredictable fits Greene's performance all too well. While there's bat-missing stuff, it misses its intended target far too often for a dependable bullpen arm.

★ ★ ★ *2022 Top 101 Prospect* **#80** ★ ★ ★

D.L. Hall LHP Born: 09/19/98 Age: 23 Bats: L Throws: L Height: 6'2" Weight: 195 lb. Origin: Round 1, 2017 Draft (#21 overall)

YEAR	TEAM	LVL	AGE	W	L	SV	G	GS	IP	H	HR	BB/9	K/9	K	GB%	BABIP	WHIP	ERA	DRA-	WARP	MPH	FB%	Whiff%	CSP
2019	FRE	A+	20	4	5	1	19	17	80^{2}	53	3	6.0	12.9	116	34.1%	.301	1.33	3.46	79	1.6				
2021	BOW	AA	22	2	0	0	7	7	31^{2}	16	4	4.5	15.9	56	59.3%	.240	1.01	3.13	80	0.6				
2022 DC	*BAL*	*MLB*	*23*	*0*	*0*	*0*	*3*	*3*	*14.3*	*11*	*2*	*6.0*	*12.3*	*19*	*42.6%*	*.290*	*1.45*	*4.40*	*100*	*0.1*				

Comparables: Josh Hader, Jason Schmidt, Franklin Morales

There was little doubt that Hall's stuff was going to play at any level if he could refine his command. What the Orioles wanted was a full season for the electric left-hander to do just that and prove that any concerns over a move to the bullpen were unfounded. What they got was the opposite: total validation of his devastating arsenal—almost 44% of the batters he faced struck out—and an extremely abbreviated campaign that saw Hall make just seven turns, only three lasting five innings or more, before a stress reaction in his elbow ended his season in mid-June. Baltimore will want to keep him starting as long as they can since Hall might have four plus pitches. But without the reps to hone his consistency, he might end up as a bullpen arm who walks a few more than you'd like but strikes out more than enough to make it work. It's a decent fallback option.

Matt Harvey RHP Born: 03/27/89 Age: 33 Bats: R Throws: R Height: 6'4" Weight: 220 lb. Origin: Round 1, 2010 Draft (#7 overall)

YEAR	TEAM	LVL	AGE	W	L	SV	G	GS	IP	H	HR	BB/9	K/9	K	GB%	BABIP	WHIP	ERA	DRA-	WARP	MPH	FB%	Whiff%	CSP
2019	LAA	MLB	30	3	5	0	12	12	59^2	63	13	4.4	5.9	39	43.1%	.276	1.54	7.09	131	-0.4	93.3	47.5%	22.1%	48.9%
2020	KC	MLB	31	0	3	0	7	4	11^2	27	6	3.9	7.7	10	42.0%	.477	2.74	11.57	116	0.0	94.3	53.5%	17.5%	50.1%
2021	BAL	MLB	32	6	14	0	28	28	127^2	160	19	2.6	6.7	95	43.1%	.333	1.54	6.27	119	-0.1	93.3	54.7%	18.9%	55.3%
2022 DC	*FA*	*MLB*	*33*	*5*	*6*	*0*	*19*	*19*	*87.3*	*98*	*13*	*2.8*	*6.2*	*60*	*42.4%*	*.303*	*1.43*	*5.05*	*120*	*-0.2*	*93.4*	*53.8%*	*19.3%*	*54.2%*

Comparables: Tim Lincecum, Andy Benes, Matt Cain

It's sometimes difficult to believe that Harvey's tumultuous career has led here. He was, in one regard, clearly Baltimore's most reliable starter, churning out 28 starts so utterly unremarkable you'd never recognize the bright star of his mid-20s. Oh, there were highs and lows in 2021 too, of course. From mid-May to mid-June he embarked on a rotten stretch where he allowed at least five earned runs in six of seven starts. In July he reeled off three straight scoreless turns that could almost offer hope he was turning things around if we weren't so acutely aware of his career trajectory. Ultimately, Harvey was the antithesis of his youthful self, the ups and downs rendered irrelevant by his employer's indifference, merely a place-holder for something younger and brighter to come.

Mickey Jannis RHP Born: 12/16/87 Age: 34 Bats: R Throws: R Height: 5'9" Weight: 195 lb. Origin: Round 44, 2010 Draft (#1331 overall)

YEAR	TEAM	LVL	AGE	W	L	SV	G	GS	IP	H	HR	BB/9	K/9	K	GB%	BABIP	WHIP	ERA	DRA-	WARP	MPH	FB%	Whiff%	CSP
2019	BNG	AA	31	7	5	0	20	18	119	123	2	2.3	7.8	103	49.0%	.336	1.29	3.10	117	-0.1				
2019	SYR	AAA	31	0	2	0	2	2	6^2	19	5	5.4	6.8	5	32.4%	.438	3.45	22.95	141	-0.1				
2021	BOW	AA	33	0	2	0	6	6	29	42	7	4.0	6.2	20	42.3%	.361	1.90	8.07	132	-0.3				
2021	NOR	AAA	33	0	5	1	13	5	47	45	6	4.8	5.6	29	36.9%	.275	1.49	4.98	136	-0.2				
2021	BAL	MLB	33	0	0	0	1	0	3^1	8	3	10.8	2.7	1	18.8%	.385	3.60	18.90	137	0.0	87.5	12.7%	0.0%	58.7%
2022 non-DC	*BAL*	*MLB*	*34*	*2*	*3*	*0*	*57*	*0*	*50*	*60*	*9*	*4.5*	*5.5*	*30*	*38.6%*	*.310*	*1.70*	*6.56*	*143*	*-1.0*	*87.5*	*12.7%*	*0.0%*	*58.7%*

Comparables: Austin Bibens-Dirkx, Jarrett Grube, Nerio Rodriguez

The knuckleball is lifeless at the best of times. It floats, devoid of the fizzing, energetic spin of a four-seam fastball or a plunging curve. It is destined to do nothing, sailing helplessly into the barrel of the bat to be returned unceremoniously at much higher speed. And then... then it flutters or swoops, sometimes almost imperceptibly, sometimes deviating so implausibly from its path that magic appears to be at work. That felt like the same kind of magic that brought Jannis to the majors at last. Excluding position players, he was the only true knuckleballer to pitch during the 2021 season. For a pitch that appears to be on life support, it's fitting that its only practitioner was a 33-year-old debutante whose own particular offering barely had a heartbeat on the day. The Astros care not for your romantic narratives. They didn't swing and miss once at Jannis' knuckler, returning the veteran of 11 pro seasons to the minors after recording seven runs, including three homers, across 71 ineffective pitches. The death of the knuckleball has been proclaimed many times before. Can you still hear a little flutter?

Dean Kremer RHP Born: 01/07/96 Age: 26 Bats: R Throws: R Height: 6'2" Weight: 200 lb. Origin: Round 14, 2016 Draft (#431 overall)

YEAR	TEAM	LVL	AGE	W	L	SV	G	GS	IP	H	HR	BB/9	K/9	K	GB%	BABIP	WHIP	ERA	DRA-	WARP	MPH	FB%	Whiff%	CSP
2019	FRE	A+	23	0	0	0	2	2	9^2	6	0	3.7	13.0	14	20.0%	.300	1.03	0.00	100	0.1				
2019	BOW	AA	23	9	4	0	15	15	84^2	75	9	3.1	9.2	87	41.1%	.299	1.23	2.98	97	0.8				
2019	NOR	AAA	23	0	2	0	4	4	19^1	30	2	1.9	9.8	21	36.5%	.467	1.76	8.84	92	0.3				
2020	BAL	MLB	24	1	1	0	4	4	18^2	15	0	5.8	10.6	22	30.6%	.306	1.45	4.82	101	0.2	92.9	51.2%	26.4%	52.1%
2021	NOR	AAA	25	1	5	0	17	13	62^1	61	9	2.9	10.0	69	46.6%	.313	1.30	4.91	87	1.2				
2021	BAL	MLB	25	0	7	0	13	13	53^2	63	17	4.2	7.9	47	30.2%	.297	1.64	7.55	140	-0.7	92.6	55.7%	20.4%	57.5%
2022 DC	*BAL*	*MLB*	*26*	*3*	*3*	*0*	*12*	*12*	*55.7*	*56*	*9*	*3.8*	*8.2*	*50*	*36.4%*	*.299*	*1.44*	*4.94*	*114*	*0.0*	*92.6*	*54.9%*	*21.5%*	*56.4%*

Comparables: Jake Faria, Kyle Wright, Mitch Keller

No matter how often he was ejected from the rotation, Kremer kept bursting back through the door from Triple-A for more. For all his persistence, however, none of his schemes seemed to work. Throw the curve less often? Tried that. Incorporate a slider more regularly? Didn't pay off. Cut back on the four-seamer? Not helping. When none of your ideas are particularly good, it doesn't really matter what you do. To Kremer's credit, the kernel of something more exists. His offerings possess above-average movement and often look like they should produce something better. At the end of the day though, he might as well have been trying to sell some moth-infested coats.

Travis Lakins Sr. RHP

Born: 06/29/94 Age: 28 Bats: R Throws: R Height: 6'1" Weight: 220 lb. Origin: Round 6, 2015 Draft (#171 overall)

YEAR	TEAM	LVL	AGE	W	L	SV	G	GS	IP	H	HR	BB/9	K/9	K	GB%	BABIP	WHIP	ERA	DRA-	WARP	MPH	FB%	Whiff%	CSP
2019	PAW	AAA	25	3	4	6	40	1	45	46	4	4.6	8.4	42	39.6%	.328	1.53	4.60	104	0.5				
2019	BOS	MLB	25	0	1	0	16	3	23^1	23	1	3.9	6.9	18	46.6%	.306	1.41	3.86	114	0.1	92.6	71.4%	25.3%	44.2%
2020	BAL	MLB	26	3	2	1	22	0	25^2	25	2	4.6	8.8	25	38.2%	.311	1.48	2.81	102	0.3	92.0	73.6%	22.5%	48.1%
2021	BAL	MLB	27	1	4	0	24	1	28	23	4	5.5	7.7	24	39.5%	.247	1.43	5.79	120	0.0	92.4	75.2%	25.7%	57.1%
2022 non-DC	*BAL*	*MLB*	*28*	*2*	*3*	*0*	*57*	*0*	*50*	*49*	*7*	*4.6*	*8.5*	*47*	*41.4%*	*.300*	*1.51*	*5.20*	*118*	*-0.3*	*92.3*	*74.2%*	*24.6%*	*52.3%*

Comparables: Kevin McCarthy, Justin Berg, Mike McClendon

Lakins was far from the only member of the 2020 Orioles bullpen who severely regressed from some small-sample success. He was both the most likely regression candidate based on his peripherals and the person with the most obvious excuse. Surgery to repair a recurrent olecranon stress fracture in his throwing elbow ended his season in early July and subsequently saw him removed from the roster upon his reinstatement from the 60-day IL. Pitching without a broken bone in his arm might at least help him get back to league-average.

Jorge López RHP

Born: 02/10/93 Age: 29 Bats: R Throws: R Height: 6'3" Weight: 200 lb. Origin: Round 2, 2011 Draft (#70 overall)

YEAR	TEAM	LVL	AGE	W	L	SV	G	GS	IP	H	HR	BB/9	K/9	K	GB%	BABIP	WHIP	ERA	DRA-	WARP	MPH	FB%	Whiff%	CSP
2019	KC	MLB	26	4	9	1	39	18	123^2	140	27	3.1	7.9	109	47.0%	.314	1.47	6.33	115	0.3	94.3	54.3%	21.3%	48.1%
2020	KC	MLB	27	0	0	0	1	0	0^2	3	0	0.0	0.0	0	40.0%	.600	4.50	27.00	172	0.0	94.1	55.0%	0.0%	58.2%
2020	BAL	MLB	27	2	2	0	9	6	38^1	43	7	2.8	6.6	28	50.0%	.305	1.43	6.34	99	0.4	93.8	60.2%	22.0%	50.1%
2021	BAL	MLB	28	3	14	0	33	25	121^2	142	21	4.1	8.3	112	50.4%	.341	1.63	6.07	111	0.4	95.4	57.9%	20.6%	55.9%
2022 DC	*BAL*	*MLB*	*29*	*8*	*3*	*0*	*62*	*3*	*64.7*	*66*	*8*	*3.5*	*7.9*	*56*	*48.9%*	*.304*	*1.41*	*4.62*	*109*	*0.1*	*94.9*	*57.4%*	*20.8%*	*53.5%*

Comparables: Hector Noesí, Anthony Lerew, JC Ramírez

Entering the season with no options and a career ERA beginning with a six, López had one purpose: to eat some innings. To the journeyman's credit, he did just that, making each of the first 25 turns through the rotation and reliably giving up runs in every single one. With an ERA of 6.35 on August 22, the Orioles finally shifted him to the bullpen, where he pitched marginally better...just not quite good enough to bring that ERA below six. It's hard to fault his consistency.

Zac Lowther LHP

Born: 04/30/96 Age: 26 Bats: L Throws: L Height: 6'2" Weight: 235 lb. Origin: Round 2, 2017 Draft (#74 overall)

YEAR	TEAM	LVL	AGE	W	L	SV	G	GS	IP	H	HR	BB/9	K/9	K	GB%	BABIP	WHIP	ERA	DRA-	WARP	MPH	FB%	Whiff%	CSP
2019	BOW	AA	23	13	7	0	26	26	148	102	8	3.8	9.4	154	39.4%	.260	1.11	2.55	91	1.8				
2021	NOR	AAA	25	0	5	0	8	8	30^1	33	4	4.7	9.8	33	48.9%	.333	1.62	6.53	110	0.3				
2021	BAL	MLB	25	1	3	0	10	6	29^2	36	6	3.9	9.1	30	44.0%	.353	1.65	6.67	114	0.0	90.9	54.1%	25.0%	56.2%
2022 DC	*BAL*	*MLB*	*26*	*3*	*3*	*0*	*12*	*12*	*54.3*	*53*	*7*	*4.2*	*9.2*	*55*	*43.0%*	*.306*	*1.45*	*4.83*	*112*	*0.1*	*90.9*	*54.1%*	*25.0%*	*56.2%*

Comparables: Matt Perisho, Dillon Peters, Hector Noesí

Lowther continued to strike opponents out at a higher rate than his 90-mph fastball portends thanks to a four-pitch mix that keeps hitters on their toes. Nonetheless, his first efforts at Triple-A and the majors demonstrated why he has never been a great prospect despite some previously excellent results. He looks destined to be mopping up innings wherever the Orioles need him which, at least in the short term, ensures that his performance, like his fastball, has little bearing on his job security.

Jordan Lyles RHP

Born: 10/19/90 Age: 31 Bats: R Throws: R Height: 6'5" Weight: 230 lb. Origin: Round 1, 2008 Draft (#38 overall)

YEAR	TEAM	LVL	AGE	W	L	SV	G	GS	IP	H	HR	BB/9	K/9	K	GB%	BABIP	WHIP	ERA	DRA-	WARP	MPH	FB%	Whiff%	CSP
2019	MIL	MLB	28	7	1	0	11	11	58^2	43	9	3.4	8.6	56	38.8%	.227	1.11	2.45	96	0.7	92.7	50.6%	21.5%	45.6%
2019	PIT	MLB	28	5	7	0	17	17	82^1	88	16	3.6	9.8	90	41.4%	.327	1.47	5.36	91	1.2	92.9	52.9%	24.6%	46.8%
2020	TEX	MLB	29	1	6	0	12	9	57^2	67	12	3.6	5.6	36	40.5%	.286	1.56	7.02	143	-0.7	92.4	48.1%	16.9%	48.6%
2021	TEX	MLB	30	10	13	0	32	30	180	194	38	2.8	7.3	146	36.8%	.300	1.39	5.15	134	-1.6	93.0	48.5%	23.7%	55.0%
2022 DC	*BAL*	*MLB*	*31*	*8*	*9*	*0*	*27*	*27*	*145.7*	*157*	*26*	*3.0*	*7.3*	*118*	*38.5%*	*.302*	*1.42*	*5.08*	*118*	*-0.3*	*92.9*	*49.1%*	*22.6%*	*52.4%*

Comparables: Jeff Suppan, Doyle Alexander, Edwin Jackson

With the team never really planning to contend in 2021 and a number of young pitchers coming off abbreviated innings counts in 2020, manager Chris Woodward basically gave Lyles the same instructions our moms used to give us when we got home from school: Do your homework, and then go play, and uhhh, just stay out there as long as you can. "Mom, I'm leading the league in home runs allowed!" [trying to get five minutes of gosh dang peace and quiet] "Mm-hmm." "Mom, I've allowed more runs than any other pitcher in the American League!" "Okay." "For the second year in a row!" [slamming down magazine] "JORDAN. Have you gotten to 180 innings yet?" "Yes!" [deep sigh] "Okay, good job, you can go play Minecraft."

John Means LHP Born: 04/24/93 Age: 29 Bats: L Throws: L Height: 6'3" Weight: 235 lb. Origin: Round 11, 2014 Draft (#331 overall)

YEAR	TEAM	LVL	AGE	W	L	SV	G	GS	IP	H	HR	BB/9	K/9	K	GB%	BABIP	WHIP	ERA	DRA-	WARP	MPH	FB%	Whiff%	CSP
2019	BAL	MLB	26	12	11	0	31	27	155	138	23	2.2	7.0	121	30.7%	.256	1.14	3.60	126	-0.5	91.9	50.7%	22.2%	46.3%
2020	BAL	MLB	27	2	4	0	10	10	43^2	36	12	1.4	8.7	42	43.9%	.216	0.98	4.53	91	0.7	93.9	52.3%	26.3%	49.8%
2021	BAL	MLB	28	6	9	0	26	26	146^2	125	30	1.6	8.2	134	32.6%	.241	1.03	3.62	109	0.7	93.0	47.9%	25.5%	54.6%
2022 DC	*BAL*	*MLB*	*29*	*9*	*8*	*0*	*27*	*27*	*148.7*	*144*	*24*	*1.9*	*7.8*	*128*	*34.7%*	*.283*	*1.18*	*3.83*	*96*	*1.5*	*92.8*	*49.2%*	*24.8%*	*52.0%*

Comparables: Bud Norris, Dillon Gee, Drew Smyly

When Means retired J.P. Crawford to complete his no-hitter on May 5, his ERA stood at 1.37 and the Orioles appeared to have a genuine Cy Young contender on their hands. Cracks started to appear as the month wore on and by early June he was on the IL with a shoulder strain. His return six weeks later offered little consolation as both his changeup and slider lost effectiveness and a worrying home run trend continued. The lefty still looked like the only reliable building block in a major-league rotation that posted an ERA north of 6.00, but it's not at all clear what his second half slump...well, means for the future.

★ ★ ★ *2022 Top 101 Prospect* **#5** ★ ★ ★

Grayson Rodriguez RHP Born: 11/16/99 Age: 22 Bats: L Throws: R Height: 6'5" Weight: 220 lb. Origin: Round 1, 2018 Draft (#11 overall)

YEAR	TEAM	LVL	AGE	W	L	SV	G	GS	IP	H	HR	BB/9	K/9	K	GB%	BABIP	WHIP	ERA	DRA-	WARP	MPH	FB%	Whiff%	CSP
2019	DEL	A	19	10	4	0	20	20	94	57	4	3.4	12.4	129	44.2%	.262	0.99	2.68	76	2.0				
2021	ABD	A+	21	3	0	0	5	5	23^1	11	2	1.9	15.4	40	42.5%	.237	0.69	1.54	69	0.6				
2021	BOW	AA	21	6	1	0	18	18	79^2	47	8	2.5	13.7	121	37.8%	.252	0.87	2.60	83	1.4				
2022 DC	*BAL*	*MLB*	*22*	*4*	*3*	*0*	*12*	*12*	*64.7*	*52*	*9*	*3.6*	*11.5*	*82*	*39.2%*	*.287*	*1.22*	*3.65*	*88*	*0.9*				

Comparables: Carlos Villanueva, Danny Salazar, Chris Archer

By the power of Gray-Rod...Rodriguez has the power—fastball, that is. He also appears to have the power to strike out anyone he faces, utterly decimating the competition over a handful of turns at High-A before dispatching his adversaries with similar ease at Double-A. Rodriguez looks more and more like the superhero the Orioles rotation desperately needs to save them. His heater might be the highlight but the rest of his weapons are developing to the point that opponents won't know where or what to look for. He's the best pitching prospect in baseball. The challenge of mastering the majors isn't far away, followed by the inevitable renaming of OPACY to Castle Gray-Rod. Master of the Universe? That could be a touch over the top...then again, he'd definitely strike out Skeletor.

Tanner Scott LHP Born: 07/22/94 Age: 27 Bats: R Throws: L Height: 6'0" Weight: 235 lb. Origin: Round 6, 2014 Draft (#181 overall)

YEAR	TEAM	LVL	AGE	W	L	SV	G	GS	IP	H	HR	BB/9	K/9	K	GB%	BABIP	WHIP	ERA	DRA-	WARP	MPH	FB%	Whiff%	CSP
2019	NOR	AAA	24	3	4	7	30	0	45^1	35	2	3.0	11.3	57	55.9%	.303	1.10	2.98	74	1.2				
2019	BAL	MLB	24	1	1	0	28	0	26^1	28	4	6.5	12.6	37	51.6%	.400	1.78	4.78	85	0.5	96.0	58.7%	34.1%	41.6%
2020	BAL	MLB	25	0	0	1	25	0	20^2	12	1	4.4	10.0	23	58.0%	.224	1.06	1.31	71	0.6	96.6	61.5%	35.9%	49.4%
2021	BAL	MLB	26	5	4	0	62	0	54	48	6	6.2	11.7	70	52.9%	.318	1.57	5.17	94	0.7	96.8	48.4%	37.2%	51.5%
2022 DC	*BAL*	*MLB*	*27*	*3*	*3*	*6*	*74*	*0*	*64.7*	*49*	*6*	*5.0*	*11.9*	*85*	*51.8%*	*.290*	*1.32*	*3.55*	*84*	*0.8*	*96.7*	*51.7%*	*36.6%*	*50.1%*

Comparables: Bruce Rondón, Scott Elbert, A.J. Minter

You can have too much of a good thing. Take Scott's slider, a pitch that opponents saw 132 times in 2020 and produced a total of three singles against. Emboldened by its continued dominance early in the season, he bumped the breaker to the top of his repertoire by June, tossing it two-thirds of the time in August. Diminishing returns kicked in, hard. Scott had never given up more than two homers on the pitch in a season before; he gave up two in both August and September as he slumped to a 9.82 second-half ERA and lost more than 10 percentage points from his strikeout rate. We could blame some of the issues on the knee sprain that twice landed him on the IL during those months, which certainly coincided with a huge drop in whiff rate. The movement remained more or less identical, but hitters don't find it too hard to make contact when the slider's in the zone. Scott needs to find the point where he can throw it often enough to maintain his absurd whiff rate, without either ballooning those walks further or being forced to throw it in the zone.

Cole Sulser RHP

Born: 03/12/90 Age: 32 Bats: R Throws: R Height: 6'1" Weight: 190 lb. Origin: Round 25, 2013 Draft (#741 overall)

YEAR	TEAM	LVL	AGE	W	L	SV	G	GS	IP	H	HR	BB/9	K/9	K	GB%	BABIP	WHIP	ERA	DRA-	WARP	MPH	FB%	Whiff%	CSP
2019	DUR	AAA	29	6	3	2	49	4	66	51	4	3.3	12.1	89	31.8%	.309	1.14	3.27	72	1.8				
2019	TB	MLB	29	0	0	0	7	0	7^1	5	0	3.7	11.0	9	35.3%	.294	1.09	0.00	92	0.1	93.5	63.8%	25.8%	44.1%
2020	BAL	MLB	30	1	5	5	19	0	22^2	17	2	6.8	7.5	19	37.5%	.250	1.50	5.56	119	0.0	93.9	57.5%	30.2%	45.0%
2021	BAL	MLB	31	5	4	8	60	0	63^1	48	5	3.3	10.4	73	40.4%	.277	1.12	2.70	82	1.2	93.3	51.1%	30.4%	56.1%
2022 DC	*BAL*	*MLB*	*32*	*3*	*3*	*13*	*74*	*0*	*64.7*	*56*	*9*	*3.7*	*10.2*	*73*	*38.4%*	*.288*	*1.28*	*3.85*	*93*	*0.5*	*93.4*	*52.8%*	*30.2%*	*53.5%*

Comparables: Brad Brach, Oliver Drake, Jared Burton

Here are some facts about Sulser's role in the 2021 Orioles season: he recorded his first save on June 1, his last on September 28, and now leads the team in saves under Brandon Hyde's management. If you didn't look too closely at that stats box above or pay attention to Baltimore's other key protagonists in the ninth, you might have slid right past the number of saves (8) and the fact that César Valdez tied Sulser's total. It's not a knock on Sulser himself, who had a rather excellent year, dominating hitters with his changeup and reining in the control issues that cost him the role in 2020. It was more of a reflection of Baltimore's opportunities—they only won 35 games across the final four months—and Hyde's extreme aversion to utilizing a single name in the ninth. Hyde has skippered the Orioles for three seasons at this point. Sulser's team-leading total in that span? 13. He thus remains the most likely player on the roster to lead the team again at the time of writing. If he's lucky, he might reach double digits next year.

Dillon Tate RHP

Born: 05/01/94 Age: 28 Bats: R Throws: R Height: 6'2" Weight: 195 lb. Origin: Round 1, 2015 Draft (#4 overall)

YEAR	TEAM	LVL	AGE	W	L	SV	G	GS	IP	H	HR	BB/9	K/9	K	GB%	BABIP	WHIP	ERA	DRA-	WARP	MPH	FB%	Whiff%	CSP
2019	BOW	AA	25	2	3	5	17	2	33^2	28	4	2.4	8.0	30	49.0%	.264	1.10	3.48	106	0.2				
2019	NOR	AAA	25	2	0	2	4	0	9	7	1	1.0	7.0	7	65.4%	.240	0.89	2.00	86	0.2				
2019	BAL	MLB	25	0	2	0	16	0	21	18	3	3.9	8.6	20	61.0%	.268	1.29	6.43	101	0.2	93.9	56.6%	21.6%	49.7%
2020	BAL	MLB	26	1	1	0	12	0	16^2	9	1	2.7	7.6	14	51.2%	.190	0.84	3.24	90	0.3	94.4	57.9%	25.0%	44.6%
2021	BAL	MLB	27	0	6	3	62	0	67^2	61	7	3.1	6.5	49	60.1%	.271	1.24	4.39	102	0.5	95.6	60.6%	22.2%	55.9%
2022 DC	*BAL*	*MLB*	*28*	*3*	*3*	*0*	*74*	*0*	*64.7*	*65*	*7*	*3.1*	*7.0*	*50*	*56.1%*	*.297*	*1.36*	*4.40*	*106*	*0.0*	*95.3*	*59.8%*	*22.5%*	*53.8%*

Comparables: Matt Bowman, Bryan Morris, Adam Russell

Tate leaned even more heavily on his hard, late-breaking sinker, which made up almost 60% of his pitches. That was also his groundball rate, a fact which ensured that the former first-rounder now has a somewhat reliable method of getting outs, even if he can't do so via the whiff. The extent of that reliability will naturally depend on the quality of Baltimore's infield defense, a unit that in itself remains loosely-defined: the O's utilized nine different second basemen and eight names at the hot corner. Regardless of who's scooping those grounders off the dirt, Tate pitched a full, league-average season out of the 'pen on the strength of his ability to avoid the barrel. His peripherals may blend in perfectly with those who pitched in relief for the last title-winning Baltimore team, but he should remain a central part of the contemporary unit for the foreseeable future.

César Valdez RHP

Born: 03/17/85 Age: 37 Bats: R Throws: R Height: 6'2" Weight: 225 lb. Origin: International Free Agent, 2005

YEAR	TEAM	LVL	AGE	W	L	SV	G	GS	IP	H	HR	BB/9	K/9	K	GB%	BABIP	WHIP	ERA	DRA-	WARP	MPH	FB%	Whiff%	CSP
2019	LIC	WIN	34	4	1	0	7	6	40^2	31	1	0.9	8.9	40	56.2%	.270	0.86	1.11						
2019	YUC	AAA	34	15	2	0	23	23	147^2	140	6	1.0	7.4	122	56.6%	.311	1.06	2.26	66	3.6				
2020	BAL	MLB	35	1	1	3	9	0	14^1	7	0	1.9	7.5	12	52.6%	.184	0.70	1.26	91	0.2	85.5	15.7%	30.3%	48.6%
2021	LIC	WIN	36	5	1	0	8	8	45^2	36	1	1.2	9.1	46	61.1%	.282	0.92	1.77						
2021	NOR	AAA	36	0	1	0	9	0	12^2	10	0	2.1	8.5	12	64.7%	.294	1.03	1.42	90	0.2				
2021	BAL	MLB	36	2	2	8	39	0	46	62	8	2.7	8.8	45	47.3%	.380	1.65	5.87	95	0.5	85.2	19.9%	28.6%	53.9%
2022 DC	*FA*	*MLB*	*37*	*0*	*0*	*0*	*14*	*0*	*12.3*	*12*	*1*	*2.7*	*7.9*	*10*	*48.2%*	*.307*	*1.34*	*4.30*	*104*	*0.0*	*85.3*	*19.3%*	*28.8%*	*53.1%*

Comparables: Matt Albers, Craig Stammen, Nelson Figueroa

Just when hitters thought it was safe to get back in the water, Valdez returned with his dead fish changeup. It seemed very much alive, helping him post a 1.23 ERA over his first 13 appearances that echoed his 2020 efforts, recording eight saves in the process. Considering he was still using it over 80% of the time, it's remarkable how long it took hitters to adjust—but adjust they did. The high-70s offering was less *Jaws* and more goldfish-in-a-bag the rest of the way. Valdez's stint in the majors lasted a little longer than those unfortunate creatures, although he might have wished it hadn't by the time he got demoted. We'd say he's gonna need a bigger fastball, but at 37, that's even less plausible than his success was in the first place.

Spenser Watkins RHP Born: 08/27/92 Age: 29 Bats: R Throws: R Height: 6'2" Weight: 185 lb. Origin: Round 30, 2014 Draft (#910 overall)

YEAR	TEAM	LVL	AGE	W	L	SV	G	GS	IP	H	HR	BB/9	K/9	K	GB%	BABIP	WHIP	ERA	DRA-	WARP	MPH	FB%	Whiff%	CSP
2019	LAK	A+	26	1	0	0	3	3	19	13	1	2.8	6.6	14	44.4%	.226	1.00	2.37	113	0.1				
2019	ERI	AA	26	3	1	0	8	7	42^1	41	3	2.1	6.8	32	37.7%	.299	1.20	4.25	115	0.0				
2019	TOL	AAA	26	5	6	0	16	14	76^2	105	22	3.3	8.8	75	32.7%	.359	1.73	7.98	123	0.0				
2021	NOR	AAA	28	1	2	0	8	6	35^2	28	6	2.8	7.6	30	35.8%	.224	1.09	3.53	112	0.3				
2021	BAL	MLB	28	2	7	0	16	10	54^2	74	14	3.1	5.8	35	33.2%	.326	1.70	8.07	150	-0.9	91.0	46.7%	18.0%	53.7%
2022 non-DC	*BAL*	*MLB*	*29*	*2*	*3*	*0*	*57*	*0*	*50*	*57*	*9*	*3.1*	*5.8*	*32*	*35.2%*	*.297*	*1.49*	*5.61*	*130*	*-0.6*	*91.0*	*46.7%*	*18.0%*	*53.7%*

Comparables: Dereck Rodríguez, Graham Godfrey, Ryan Carpenter

Paradise Valley is not a telenovela, but the Phoenix high school where Watkins was going to coach baseball before he signed a minor-league deal with the Orioles. Up to that point, the 28-year-old's six years in the Tigers organization looked largely fruitless as far as his major-league ambitions went. Turns out that Norfolk, VA and not Paradise Valley is where dreams are made, as he pitched well enough to get the call in early July and subsequently allowed no more than a run in each of his first four appearances. While the rest of his debut season was less successful, how can we be sure that Spenser's evil twin brother Spencer, consumed with jealousy at his success, didn't kidnap him and take his place in the rotation?

Alexander Wells LHP Born: 02/27/97 Age: 25 Bats: L Throws: L Height: 6'1" Weight: 195 lb. Origin: International Free Agent, 2015

YEAR	TEAM	LVL	AGE	W	L	SV	G	GS	IP	H	HR	BB/9	K/9	K	GB%	BABIP	WHIP	ERA	DRA-	WARP	MPH	FB%	Whiff%	CSP
2019	BOW	AA	22	8	6	0	24	24	137^1	123	10	1.6	6.9	105	40.8%	.276	1.07	2.95	109	0.4				
2021	NOR	AAA	24	6	3	0	13	10	54^2	49	6	1.2	7.9	48	39.3%	.274	1.02	3.29	114	0.3				
2021	BAL	MLB	24	2	3	0	11	8	42^2	53	10	3.4	5.5	26	31.6%	.303	1.62	6.75	166	-1.1	88.8	50.8%	16.4%	55.6%
2022 DC	*BAL*	*MLB*	*25*	*0*	*1*	*0*	*3*	*3*	*12.7*	*14*	*2*	*2.5*	*6.7*	*9*	*36.0%*	*.304*	*1.42*	*5.27*	*125*	*-0.1*	*88.8*	*50.8%*	*16.4%*	*55.6%*

Comparables: Kyle Lobstein, Jayson Aquino, Paul Blackburn

Wells maintained his defiance of both his peripherals and his velocity yet again upon reaching the highest level of the minors. The major leagues are always where the true test comes, and major-league hitters treated Wells like you'd expect them to treat a pitcher with a high-80s fastball and unremarkable secondaries. The Australian hurler's velocity isn't the only thing that seems like a throwback to another era—he works very quickly on the mound—although when this many batters reach base he's probably not saving all that much time.

Tyler Wells RHP Born: 08/26/94 Age: 27 Bats: R Throws: R Height: 6'8" Weight: 255 lb. Origin: Round 15, 2016 Draft (#453 overall)

YEAR	TEAM	LVL	AGE	W	L	SV	G	GS	IP	H	HR	BB/9	K/9	K	GB%	BABIP	WHIP	ERA	DRA-	WARP	MPH	FB%	Whiff%	CSP
2021	BAL	MLB	26	2	3	4	44	0	57	40	9	1.9	10.3	65	21.2%	.228	0.91	4.11	93	0.7	95.2	58.7%	28.3%	56.3%
2022 DC	*BAL*	*MLB*	*27*	*3*	*3*	*13*	*74*	*0*	*64.7*	*58*	*11*	*2.6*	*9.4*	*67*	*27.3%*	*.278*	*1.19*	*3.90*	*97*	*0.3*	*95.2*	*58.7%*	*28.3%*	*56.3%*

Comparables: Justin Grimm, Scott Barlow, Mike Ekstrom

Wells has rarely been anyone's top choice. Undrafted out of high school, a 15th-rounder in the 2016 draft out of a Division II college, ranked at the very bottom of prospect lists if at all—it's even the first time he's garnered a mention in this book. The Twins neglected to protect him in the 2020 Rule 5 draft since he'd had Tommy John surgery following the 2018 season and thus not pitched in two years. Even then he wasn't anyone's priority—16 choices had been made and the other 14 teams had passed before Baltimore made him their second selection. Their first, Mac Sceroler, was returned to the Reds after five appearances. Wells, slinging mid-90s fastballs plus a hard slider and change from his huge 6-foot-8 frame, not only stuck on the team all year but posted an above-average performance with a near-30% strikeout rate. By the end of the season, he was a top choice at last, a go-to weapon for Brandon Hyde in the late innings, even recording four saves. You know what they say: All's well when Wells ends.

Bruce Zimmermann LHP Born: 02/09/95 Age: 27 Bats: L Throws: L Height: 6'1" Weight: 215 lb. Origin: Round 5, 2017 Draft (#140 overall)

YEAR	TEAM	LVL	AGE	W	L	SV	G	GS	IP	H	HR	BB/9	K/9	K	GB%	BABIP	WHIP	ERA	DRA-	WARP	MPH	FB%	Whiff%	CSP
2019	BOW	AA	24	5	3	0	18	17	101^1	88	9	3.0	9.0	101	39.6%	.283	1.20	2.58	86	1.5				
2019	NOR	AAA	24	2	3	0	7	7	38^2	44	3	4.2	7.7	33	44.7%	.345	1.60	4.89	110	0.3				
2020	BAL	MLB	25	0	0	0	2	1	7	6	2	2.6	9.0	7	50.0%	.222	1.14	7.71	110	0.0	91.7	51.4%	19.2%	52.8%
2021	NOR	AAA	26	1	0	0	4	4	15	9	2	3.6	9.0	15	51.4%	.200	1.00	2.40	99	0.2				
2021	BAL	MLB	26	4	5	0	14	13	64^1	75	14	3.1	7.8	56	40.0%	.321	1.51	5.04	123	-0.2	91.6	42.2%	25.6%	53.9%
2022 DC	*BAL*	*MLB*	*27*	*6*	*7*	*0*	*22*	*22*	*104*	*108*	*15*	*3.4*	*8.1*	*93*	*41.5%*	*.307*	*1.42*	*4.74*	*111*	*0.1*	*91.6*	*42.7%*	*25.2%*	*53.8%*

Comparables: Matthew Boyd, John Means, David Buchanan

Select details of Zimmermann's season can be construed quite positively, if one bears in mind that his likely role has always been as a fifth starter. In over half of his appearances, he made it through five frames without giving up more than three runs, which means he kept his team in the game more often than not. His curveball and slider were both effective, with the curve drawing whiffs on over 40% of swings. And if we're focusing on the positives, his last strikeout of the season came at the expense of Vladimir Guerrero Jr., an achievement that sounds more impressive if you disregard Zimmermann's inability to escape the first inning. That's where we're at with the Baltimore native at the moment; don't look too closely at the full picture, and you might just think he's ready to stick at the back of a rotation.

LINEOUTS

Hitters

HITTER	POS	TEAM	LVL	AGE	PA	R	2B	3B	HR	RBI	BB	K	SB	CS	AVG/OBP/SLG	DRC+	BABIP	BRR	FRAA	WARP
Rylan Bannon	3B/2B	NOR	AAA	25	340	43	11	0	15	36	47	71	9	1	.176/.297/.370	111	.176	-0.2	3B(49): -1.1, 2B(29): 1.5	1.5
Samuel Basallo	C/1B	DSL OR1	ROK	16	154	18	8	0	5	19	19	32	1	0	.239/.338/.410		.278			
Adam Hall	2B	ABD	A+	22	338	40	13	2	3	27	24	100	26	1	.248/.335/.337	88	.361	2.1	2B(47): 2.7, CF(13): -0.9, SS(12): 1.5	1.0
Hudson Haskin	CF	DEL	A	22	254	44	13	1	5	33	22	60	17	5	.276/.377/.415	108	.362	-0.8	CF(39): -1.7, LF(11): -1.5, RF(3): 1.2	0.9
	CF	ABD	A+	22	109	15	6	2	0	9	10	18	5	2	.275/.389/.385	114	.342	0.5	CF(23): 2.7, RF(2): -0.4, LF(1): -0.2	0.8
Maikol Hernandez	SS	DSL OR1	ROK	17	156	20	8	1	0	15	20	33	4	3	.231/.340/.308		.300			
Coby Mayo	3B	ORIB	ROK	19	84	17	6	0	3	13	11	13	6	0	.324/.429/.535		.364			
	3B	DEL	A	19	125	27	8	1	5	26	16	26	5	0	.311/.416/.547	118	.373	1.3	3B(27): -3.3	0.4
Mason McCoy	SS	NOR	AAA	26	455	49	21	6	9	43	40	133	13	3	.221/.288/.368	79	.300	0.9	SS(80): 4.6, 2B(14): -1.4, 3B(7): -0.1	0.9
Robert Neustrom	OF	BOW	AA	24	261	30	15	3	7	50	28	44	7	2	.284/.364/.467	117	.322	-3.0	LF(34): -1.4, RF(20): -2.4	0.7
	OF	NOR	AAA	24	257	32	16	0	9	33	29	63	5	1	.232/.324/.424	104	.281	0.2	RF(33): 3.7, LF(31): 1.5	1.4
Connor Norby	2B	DEL	A	21	126	17	4	1	3	17	21	28	5	3	.283/.413/.434	113	.352	0.3	2B(26): -0.1	0.6
Anthony Servideo	IF	DEL	A	22	92	24	4	0	0	7	28	26	4	0	.246/.489/.311	116	.417	0.1	2B(13): -1.2, SS(4): 0.6	0.4
Kyle Stowers	OF	ABD	A+	23	161	25	6	1	7	32	27	55	3	3	.275/.404/.496	101	.414	-0.2	RF(18): -0.6, LF(10): 0.3, CF(5): -0.1	0.5
	OF	BOW	AA	23	276	38	15	0	17	42	34	84	4	1	.283/.377/.561	110	.362	-0.8	RF(48): -2.5, LF(9): 0.1	0.9
	OF	NOR	AAA	23	93	10	2	0	3	11	12	32	1	0	.272/.366/.407	82	.413	0.1	RF(19): -0.2, LF(2): -0.2	0.1
Reed Trimble	OF	DEL	A	21	76	11	1	0	0	6	9	21	1	0	.169/.276/.185	91	.244	0.1	CF(9): -3.0, LF(4): 0.2	-0.1
Pat Valaika	2B	NOR	AAA	28	82	9	1	0	2	7	2	22	0	0	.225/.244/.313	80	.286	0.6	2B(9): 0.7, LF(1): -0.2	0.2
	2B	BAL	MLB	28	281	17	8	0	5	25	16	76	1	1	.201/.250/.290	73	.260	-0.3	2B(72): -0.9, SS(17): -0.4, 1B(6): 0.2	-0.2
Terrin Vavra	2B/CF	BOW	AA	24	184	28	10	1	5	20	29	42	6	1	.248/.388/.430	115	.314	-1.0	2B(27): -1.7, CF(9): -1.0, SS(2): 0.3	0.6
Jordan Westburg	SS/3B	DEL	A	22	91	18	5	1	3	24	12	24	5	1	.366/.484/.592	114	.500	0.8	3B(11): -1.3, SS(8): -0.8	0.3
	SS/3B	ABD	A+	22	285	41	16	2	8	41	35	71	9	4	.286/.389/.469	114	.372	0.5	SS(40): 4.4, 3B(20): -2.1	1.6
	SS/3B	BOW	AA	22	130	15	6	2	4	14	14	32	3	0	.232/.323/.429	96	.282	0.3	SS(21): 1.7, 3B(5): 0.0	0.5
Stevie Wilkerson	2B	NOR	AAA	29	146	17	6	0	2	7	21	39	0	0	.244/.352/.341	96	.337	0.4	CF(14): -1.1, LF(9): -0.3, RF(3): -0.2	0.3
	2B	BAL	MLB	29	76	5	3	0	0	2	3	30	2	0	.167/.211/.208	58	.286	0.4	2B(26): 1.1, LF(3): -0.5, RF(1): -0.0	0.0
Austin Wynns	C	NOR	AAA	30	59	7	2	0	3	9	7	11	0	0	.333/.448/.563	125	.382	-0.1	C(12): -0.3	0.3
	C	BAL	MLB	30	139	14	4	0	4	14	8	31	1	0	.185/.232/.308	87	.211	-0.6	C(44): -8.3	-0.5

The supporting argument for defensively limited **Rylan Bannon** was always that he had hit at every level. He failed to perform at Triple-A when proximity and roster status were on his side, kicking away that crutch and leaving him tottering on the brink of the 40-man roster. ⚾ Originally too young to be eligible for the 2020 signing period, **Samuel Basallo** crept in with the delay to January 2021 and underscored the stark changes in the Orioles front office. Of the $5.75 million spent, $1.3 million went to the powerful catcher, the most Baltimore has ever given to an international amateur. He didn't look overmatched despite his youth. ⚾ **Adam Hall**'s invitation to the alternate site tellingly never arrived, forcing him to shelve his party trick—his blistering speed—for a full year. He once again demonstrated that he's quick enough to dazzle in any situation, but his absence of power means he'll be one of the last names on the big-league guest list. ⚾ **Hudson Haskin** receives Hunter Pence comparisons thanks to his funky swing mechanics and second-round pedigree, but the Tulane grad has work to do to earn the comp statistically: Pence belted 31 home runs with a .999 OPS in his first full professional season. ⚾ The other recipient of a seven-figure bonus in Baltimore's record-breaking international class, toolsy shortstop **Maikol Hernandez** has plenty of athleticism and enough projection left to indicate a very bright future. ⚾ We don't want to lay it on too thick, but the considerably over-slot selection of **Coby Mayo** might just be paying off. The big third baseman backed up his exit velocity numbers with a huge dollop of in-game power in his first pro experience, spread across the complex leagues and Low-A. ⚾ There was a moment when light-hitting utility infielder **Mason McCoy** looked as though he might force his way onto the big-league roster. That moment was when he had an .830 OPS after a month, before his .611 mark the rest of the way indicated he might not be the real McCoy after all. ⚾ A swing tweak after a slow start helped **Robert Neustrom** tap into more of his power and graduate to Triple-A. The pop is still not quite where it needs to be to support a corner outfield profile, which is probably why he was still left unprotected in the Rule 5 draft. ⚾ **Connor Norby** doesn't possess the flashiest tools and, notwithstanding a power outbreak in his final year of college, doesn't look likely to hit a ton of homers. He's already relegated to the keystone defensively so he's going to need to hit; fortunately, that's what he does best. ⚾ If you're in the market for a weird slash line, enter **Anthony Servideo**. Unfortunately, there was no opportunity to test how long the promising middle infielder could maintain a drastically above-average offensive performance with no power, as a sports hernia ended his season less than a month after it began. ⚾ There's nothing light about **Kyle Stowers**' power. Although it's not universally encouraging that he already has all the components of a three-true-outcomes profile, a hard hat may be required to take a stroll down Eutaw Street if he gets the pop to the majors. ⚾ Just saying **Reed Trimble** conjures up images of a thin, wiry hurler who might get blown off the mound, or possibly an otherwise-indescribable creature from the mind of Lewis Carroll. He's actually a switch-hitting outfielder who showed plenty of power and speed in college, even if it didn't immediately translate in his pro debut. ⚾ **Pat Valaika** made not one, but two pitching appearances and delivered one of the most efficient performances of the year, facing four hitters and retiring three on five pitches. His effectiveness on the mound paired with his ineptitude at the plate to make him a one-man wrecking crew when it came to ending games quickly. ⚾ The theory is that at some point, **Terrin Vavra** will stop walking quite so often when he faces more advanced pitching. That didn't happen in an injury-interrupted debut at Double-A, and he's not all that far away from testing the theory in the majors. ⚾ Given the number of Orioles prospects who played at three levels in 2021, you'd almost think they were hurrying to make up for something. **Jordan Westburg** didn't look rushed at any of his stops, holding his own even at Double-A while growing into some of his projected power. ⚾ For most pitchers, giving up more home runs than they hit is an inevitable fact of life. For occasional hurler **Stevie Wilkerson**, it might spell the end of his position playing. ⚾ **Austin Wynns**...extraordinarily rarely, it turns out. The Orioles went 10-35 in games the backup catcher appeared in, taking his career record to 28-87. It's unlikely Baltimore's fortunes would have changed if he became Austin Loses, but at this point, you'd think they'd have given it a shot.

Pitchers

PITCHER	TEAM	LVL	AGE	W	L	SV	G	GS	IP	H	HR	BB/9	K/9	K
Fernando Abad	NOR	AAA	35	2	1	3	26	0	25^1	30	5	2.1	9.6	27
	BAL	MLB	35	0	0	0	16	0	17^2	23	1	3.6	5.1	10
Bryan Baker	BUF	AAA	26	6	1	11	39	0	41^1	18	1	3.7	10.5	48
	TOR	MLB	26	0	0	0	1	0	1	1	0	0.0	9.0	1
Manny Barreda	CUL	WIN	32	3	2	0	6	6	36	23	5	3.3	8.0	32
	NOR	AAA	32	2	3	1	27	2	40^1	47	3	2.7	8.9	40
	BAL	MLB	32	1	0	0	3	0	2^2	4	2	6.7	6.7	2
Kyle Bradish	BOW	AA	24	1	0	0	3	3	13^2	7	0	3.3	17.1	26
	NOR	AAA	24	5	5	0	21	19	86^2	85	10	4.1	10.9	105
Kyle Brnovich	ABD	A+	23	4	1	0	8	8	34^1	18	4	2.9	12.6	48
	BOW	AA	23	2	1	0	15	11	60^2	54	10	2.2	11.1	75
Dusten Knight	NOR	AAA	30	2	2	7	35	0	38^1	29	6	3.1	9.2	39
	BAL	MLB	30	0	0	0	7	0	8^2	11	1	5.2	11.4	11
Isaac Mattson	NOR	AAA	25	0	2	2	18	0	17^1	24	3	3.1	12.5	24
	BAL	MLB	25	0	0	0	4	0	4^1	5	0	10.4	6.2	3
Cionel Pérez	LOU	AAA	25	1	2	2	31	0	30^1	26	1	3.9	12.2	41
	CIN	MLB	25	1	2	0	25	0	24	21	5	7.5	9.4	25
Drew Rom	ABD	A+	21	8	0	0	14	13	67^2	60	6	2.3	9.7	73
	BOW	AA	21	3	1	0	9	7	40	35	6	2.0	10.6	47
Kevin Smith	BOW	AA	24	0	1	1	6	5	26	18	1	3.5	12.8	37
	NOR	AAA	24	3	6	0	16	15	56^1	56	14	7.8	10.9	68
Konner Wade	NOR	AAA	29	4	2	0	20	6	73	57	11	2.2	6.2	50
	BAL	MLB	29	0	0	0	7	0	12^1	23	3	3.6	8.0	11

PITCHER	TEAM	LVL	GB%	BABIP	WHIP	ERA	DRA-	WARP	MPH	FB%	WHF	CSP
Fernando Abad	NOR	AAA	40.3%	.347	1.42	4.26	98	0.4				
	BAL	MLB	47.7%	.344	1.70	5.60	115	0.0	92.8	52.5%	13.7%	55.3%
Bryan Baker	BUF	AAA	41.8%	.175	0.85	1.31	86	0.9				
	TOR	MLB	0.0%	.333	1.00	0.00	93	0.0	94.8	73.7%	40.0%	47.8%
Manny Barreda	CUL	WIN	34.1%	.207	1.00	3.50						
	NOR	AAA	41.8%	.370	1.46	3.79	96	0.6				
	BAL	MLB	20.0%	.250	2.25	13.50	115	0.0	94.4	66.7%	21.7%	61.8%
Kyle Bradish	BOW	AA	47.6%	.333	0.88	0.00	84	0.2				
	NOR	AAA	43.2%	.336	1.43	4.26	93	1.5				
Kyle Brnovich	ABD	A+	44.2%	.192	0.84	2.36	81	0.6				
	BOW	AA	43.0%	.297	1.14	3.86	95	0.7				
Dusten Knight	NOR	AAA	46.4%	.253	1.10	3.05	98	0.6				
	BAL	MLB	46.4%	.370	1.85	9.35	94	0.1	90.8	38.7%	29.1%	58.6%
Isaac Mattson	NOR	AAA	30.0%	.457	1.73	6.23	86	0.4				
	BAL	MLB	33.3%	.333	2.31	6.23	124	0.0	92.7	65.9%	24.4%	54.8%
Cionel Pérez	LOU	AAA	49.3%	.342	1.29	3.26	79	0.7				
	CIN	MLB	51.5%	.262	1.71	6.37	100	0.2	96.2	64.3%	30.3%	53.8%
Drew Rom	ABD	A+	56.0%	.307	1.14	2.79	103	0.4				
	BOW	AA	53.3%	.293	1.10	3.83	88	0.6				
Kevin Smith	BOW	AA	50.0%	.315	1.08	1.04	85	0.4				
	NOR	AAA	35.8%	.307	1.86	6.23	103	0.7				
Konner Wade	NOR	AAA	40.8%	.218	1.03	2.96	108	0.7				
	BAL	MLB	39.6%	.444	2.27	11.68	119	0.0	89.1	63.7%	22.0%	55.1%

In the sixth inning of a mid-September contest with the Blue Jays, **Fernando Abad** made his best effort to define the 2021 Orioles in a single action: he abandoned the pretense of playing baseball entirely and body-checked the Blue Jays' baserunner as he attempted to score. How does a four-seam fastball/cutter pitcher like **Bryan Baker** distinguish himself during a quiet, efficient big-league debut in mop-up duty that sees him allow one hit and record one strikeout? Throwing two pitches to the backstop is never a bad idea! Stride confidently to the front of the "wild pitches per inning pitched" pack like you meant to do it. Lean in, as they say. Over 5,175 days after he was selected in the 12th round of the 2007 draft, **Manny Barreda** made his major-league debut and earned his first win at the same time. He lost his roster spot considerably faster than it arrived, but we know he has the patience to wait for another opportunity. **Kyle Bradish** appeared to confirm his status as the Orioles' Alternate Site breakout star when he dominated Double-A through three scoreless turns. Norfolk was a different story, but Bradish still showed enough swing-and-miss that he should be able to find a role in a rotation where even a back-end starter is a prized commodity. Part of the return for Dylan Bundy, **Kyle Brnovich** is part of the growing prospect depth that makes the front office look like it might know what it's doing. He carved up a couple of levels with his sharp curve to rank third in the system in strikeouts in his first pro season. Although Brandon Hyde indicated that he would not object to minor-league veteran **Dusten Knight** bringing his backflip save celebration to the majors, the Orioles manager never gave him an opportunity to perform one. Hyde probably wasn't doing backflips about Knight's results either, since he was scored on in five of his seven big-league appearances. **Isaac Mattson** punched out the player with the lowest strikeout rate in the AL—David Fletcher—to record his first big-league K. Unfortunately, he's got some work to do to fully translate his heady minor-league whiff rates, as his wandering fastball frequently missed his preferred location, rather than bats, up in the zone. **Cionel Pérez** was one of the players who got a fourth option year after the shortened 2020 season, and the Reds certainly needed it when he walked 20 batters in 24 innings. Things went better for him at Triple-A, and he's still just 25, but there's little more evidence he can be a stable bullpen contributor than there was when he debuted back in 2018. **Drew Rom** continued to make his four-pitch mix play up with fine command, earning himself a promotion to Double-A mid-season and closing out the year by spinning 14 scoreless frames, including five no-hit innings in his final start. At this rate, it won't be long until we see D. Rom. **Kevin Smith** doesn't have impressive stuff but he cruised through lineups on his deception and extension at Double-A. The less said about his Triple-A experience, the better. As initials go, K.W. seem ideal for a pitcher. They're particularly helpful for minor-league journeyman **Konner Wade**, whose big-league debut reinforced the notion that he won't get many of either on the mound.

BOSTON RED SOX

Essay by Chad Finn

Player comments by Ben Carsley and BP staff

Satisfying plot twists arrived by the inning for the Red Sox in 2021, the second season of Chaim Bloom's tenure as the team's chief baseball officer, to the point that rattling off all of them here would prevent us from, well, actually getting to the point.

So, just a smattering of notable satisfactions: Alex Cora returned from his one-year banishment for his prominent role in the 2017 Astros' bang-the-can-loudly cheating scandal and proved equally adept at managing personalities and managing tactically. Nathan Eovaldi seized the role of reliable workhorse, pitching 182 2/3 innings and finishing fourth in the American League Cy Young voting. Garrett Whitlock, pilfered in the Rule 5 draft from the Yankees while the scar from Tommy John surgery was still fresh on his right elbow, emerged as a most improbable relief ace. Xander Bogaerts and Rafael Devers mashed often, J.D. Martinez mashed often enough.

The Red Sox won 92 games—roughly a dozen more than the rare optimistic Bay State prognosticators projected, and 68 more than they did in the 60-game 2020 season—and wiped out the Yankees and Rays in the playoffs.

Boston fans' concept of a successful season has been warped by the dozen major professional-sports championships hoarded by the city between 2001 and '18. *It's all about the ringzzzz!* is a myopic and unfulfilling way to consume sports, but it has become a prevalent one in New England. Still, by any rational measure, the 2021 Red Sox delivered a season worth appreciating.

But Bloom's greatest feat in his sophomore season might have been his challenge to Boston's collective sports disposition of proud generational cynicism: Many, if not most, of his transactions forced Red Sox fans to temper their instinctive and learned skepticism about the unfamiliar, and just about everything else, too.

I've been writing about the Red Sox since 1998, and while so much has changed—rosters churn constantly, of course, but changes in seasons have brought changes in ownership, general managers, managers and organizational philosophies through the years—one force has remained constant. When the Red Sox sign a player who is obscure, unproductive, or both, a theme tends to permeate the ol'

BOSTON RED SOX PROSPECTUS

2021 W-L: 92-70, 2ND IN AL EAST

Pythag	.549	*9th*	DER	.665	*30th*
RS/G	5.12	*5th*	DRC+	104	*3rd*
RA/G	4.62	*18th*	DRA-	97	*12th*
dWin%	.559	*6th*	FIP	4.00	*9th*
Payroll	$180M	*8th*	B-Age	28.6	*18th*
M$/MW	$3.8M	*18th*	P-Age	29.9	*22nd*

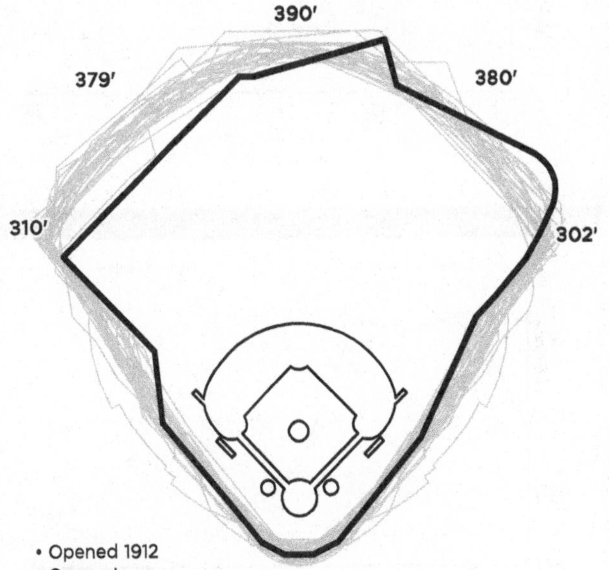

- Opened 1912
- Open air
- Natural surface
- Fence profile: 3′ to 37′

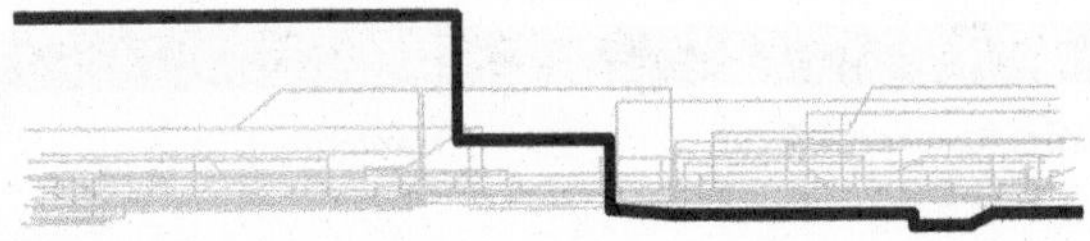

Park Factors

Runs	Runs/RH	Runs/LH	HR/RH	HR/LH
104	106	102	94	82

Top Hitter WARP	5.2 Xander Bogaerts
Top Pitcher WARP	3.1 Nathan Eovaldi
Top Prospect	Marcelo Mayer

Payroll History (in millions)

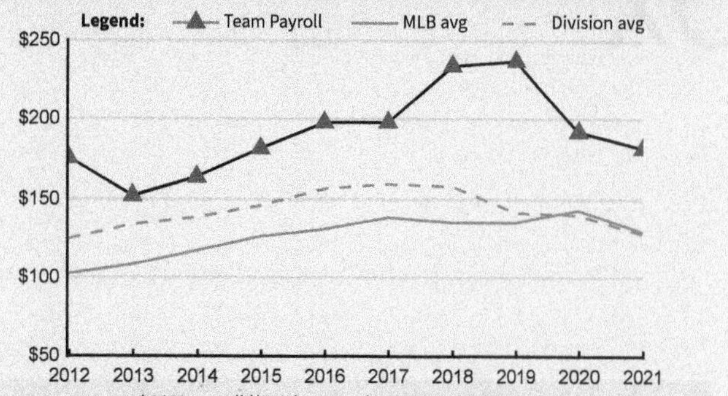

* 2020 payroll ($74M) prorated to 162-game season

Future Commitments (in millions)

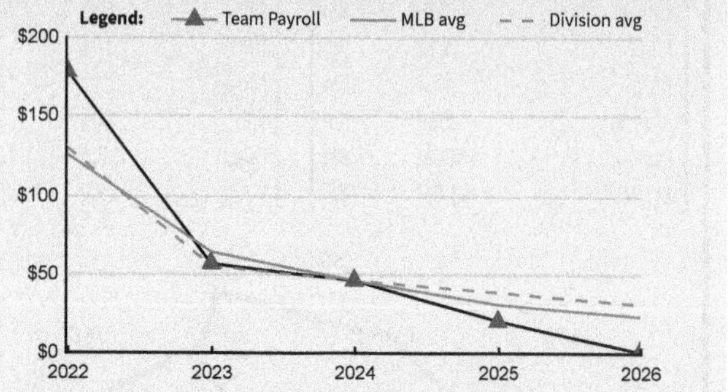

Farm System Ranking

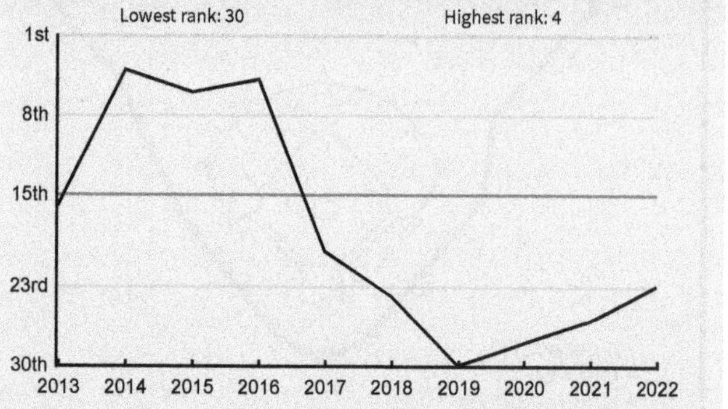

Personnel

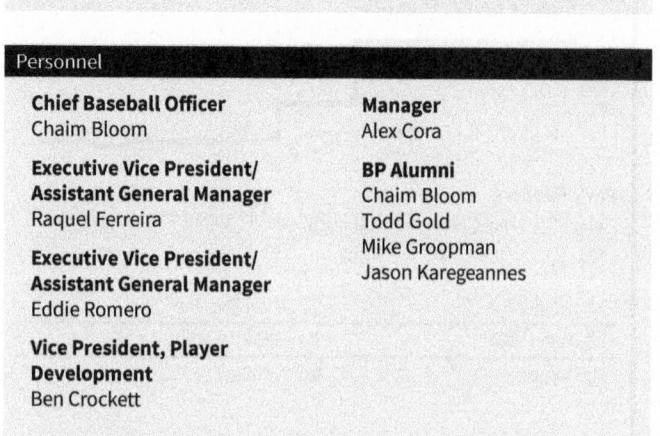

Chief Baseball Officer
Chaim Bloom

Executive Vice President/ Assistant General Manager
Raquel Ferreira

Executive Vice President/ Assistant General Manager
Eddie Romero

Vice President, Player Development
Ben Crockett

Manager
Alex Cora

BP Alumni
Chaim Bloom
Todd Gold
Mike Groopman
Jason Karegeannes

email inbox: *This guy's a bum! He hit .198 for Cleveland last year! What is [GM at the moment] doing?!?! Never thought I'd say it, but I miss [previous GM]!*

Such a mindset was emboldened in Bloom's first season, when the 2020 Red Sox paraded out 47 players, including 28 pitchers, in 60 games. The intent was obvious—he was looking to improve the talent level anywhere he could, at least incrementally, whether in the big-league bullpen, on the last spot on the bench, or at the alternate training site. But folks got wistful fast.

That season was essentially one long *So You Think You're A Big Leaguer?* tryout camp, and fans were subjected to too many pitchers (Mike Kickham, Robinson Leyer, Matt Hall, etc., etc., gag, etc.) they won't remember well, if they remember them at all. There were occasional finds; Christian Arroyo proved he could play a silky second base and, in '21, revealed a knack for being at his best in the biggest moments. But overall, the '20 Red Sox were no fun at all, and the gripes were warranted, especially when all of this occurred as a postscript to the soul-crushing, bleep-this-franchise Mookie Betts trade to the Dodgers.

If, with the Betts salary dump, Bloom was wittingly set up to be the villain, then 2021 was a remarkable lesson in how quickly redemption can come. Sure, Bloom and the talent-procurement folks in the front office had their misses in '21: Garrett Richards was erratic before the Spider Tack ban turned him into a sporadically adequate $10-million reliever; Alex Cora favorite Marwin González slashed .202/.281/.285 in an absurd 275 plate appearances before his mid-August release; and outfielder Franchy Cordero, acquired in a three-team deal that sent mediocre fan-favorite Andrew Benintendi to Kansas City and brought four prospects to Boston, had a .497 OPS, struck out 51 times in 127 at-bats and was diagnosed by late, great Red Sox broadcaster Jerry Remy as having not one but two massive holes in his swing before April was complete.

But the successes, plural, were essential and often spectacular. Enrique Hernández (signed for two years and $14 million) played a superlative center field, a very good second base on other occasions, jump-started the top of the lineup with his permanently caffeinated approach, and morphed into vintage Manny Ramirez at the plate in the postseason. Right fielder Hunter Renfroe provided 31 homers and 3.2 WARP for a mere $3.1 million. Righty Hirokazu Sawamura stabilized the bullpen in the first half (2.45 ERA, 10.6 K/9 before the break). And did we mention stealing Whitlock *from the Yankees?* We did? Well, it can't be mentioned enough.

The acquisition of Kyle Schwarber also warrants mention in this context, even though he was picked up deep into the season, on July 29. Schwarber was still recovering from a hamstring injury when Bloom acquired him from the Nationals for minor-league right-hander Aldo Ramírez, and Schwarber didn't make his Boston debut until August 13. The two weeks between his arrival and debut left plenty of time for Red Sox fans to caterwaul on their sports-radio program of choice that Bloom did nothing at the deadline while the Yankees loaded up with Anthony Rizzo and Joey Gallo. Those caterwauls had long since turned to cheers by the time October rolled around: Schwarber brought pop (.522 slugging percentage) and much-needed patience (.435 on-base percentage) to the Red Sox' lineup and was on the short list of the best pickups any team made near the deadline.

By season's end, Bloom's myriad savvy moves didn't just change the early perception of him and mute the rampant natural skepticism of Red Sox fans. It did something even more impressive: It sparked curiosity. Now, when Bloom acquires a player who may be coming off a season of modest conventional statistics or one who has very little name recognition at all, the collective initial reaction no longer defaults to *This guy is a bum! Good thing the Orioles are in the division. Fourth place here we come*, or some more vulgar version thereof.

Instead, the success and popularity of unheralded players like Renfroe (who hit .156 for the Rays in '20) or Hernández (perceived as a utility player) has resulted in a very specific question—*why are we signing this guy?*—being asked just as often, but with a much different tone. It no longer suggests a blunder has been made, sight unseen; it's now an acknowledgement that Bloom recognizes something in the player that we don't, and we're intrigued to discover what that is. It even applied to players already familiar.

The late November signing of right-hander Michael Wacha, who has posted a 5.11 ERA and 5.07 FIP for three teams since the start of the 2018 season, would have been a lightning rod for criticism. Beyond a 4.16 strikeout-to-walk ratio over the past two seasons, which suggests quality stuff, there isn't much indicating that he will prove a savvy acquisition. But it cannot be dismissed, even by the fans and media who delight in dismissing whatever they can. The 2021 results bought Bloom a rare and remarkable thing: the benefit of the doubt.

The rule was proved in a December stunner that sent Renfroe to the Brewers for old friend Jackie Bradley Jr. and a pair of intriguing infield prospects, David Hamilton and Alex Binelas. During his eight seasons with the Red Sox, Bradley was a source of division among Red Sox fans. Some loved him for his habitual spectacular catches in center field. Others loathed him for his streaky bat. Reacquiring him after a .497 OPS season might have seemed curious, except a majority of Red Sox fans seemed to recognize Bloom's tactics. He'd sold high on Renfroe. Bradley was an afterthought in the deal. It was about the two prospects, who could be used down the road in a deal to enhance the pitching staff. Let me tell you, seeing fans recognize the underpinnings of such a move was enough to make an old sportswriter's heart grow three sizes that day.

Speaking of abandoned presumptions, when Bloom came to the Red Sox after more than 14 years in the Rays' front office, the perception that he had a mandate to turn the franchise into Tampa Bay North—*here are the massive payroll restrictions, now go win 87 games, Bud*—shadowed his early months. It did not help that that the first order of business appeared to be finding a new home for Betts, a beloved five-tool talent who did everything right off the field and on and could have been his generation's Yaz or Teddy Ballgame as an adored franchise lifer but had the zany idea that he should maximize his earnings while he can. When Betts was traded to the Dodgers in February 2020 for outfielder Alex Verdugo and prospects Jeter Downs and Connor Wong, it did nothing to thwart the perception that the new boss was nothing more than an analytically driven, emotionless slave to the bottom line. After all, no Red Sox executive with a sense of history or a soul would trade for a player named Jeter. Seriously, he couldn't find a Nomar?

Two seasons later, the sting of the Betts trade has worn off somewhat, in part because he endured an injury-altered 2021 season in Hollywood, but mostly because Bloom has proven he's dastardly only when pilfering the untapped depths of other team's rosters. But Bloom has also proven upbeat, flexible and attuned to the passion fans hold for the franchise. He's reasonably accessible and always accountable (particularly in the moments when all is not going right). And for someone regarded as a member of a very specific genre of executive when he was hired—Buttoned-Down, Ivy-League Analytics Guy—it is uncanny how he has at least one classical attribute in common with two of his recent predecessors: Dan Duquette and Theo Epstein.

Duquette was the Red Sox' general manager from 1994 until March 2002, when the new ownership group led by John Henry fired him roughly 16 hours after closing their purchase. Those who remember him well will note that he pulled off a couple of all-time trade heists, acquiring future cornerstones Jason Varitek and Derek Lowe from the Mariners near the 1997 trading deadline for flammable closer Heathcliff Slocumb, then acquiring the nonpareil pitcher Pedro Martínez from the Expos following that '97 season for pitchers Carl Pavano and Brian Rose (after Cleveland refused the Expos' request to part with Jaret Wright). Duquette's detractors will note that his awkward personality put the "oof" in "aloof"—oh, and that Roger Clemens won another four Cy Young Awards after Duquette declared him to be in the "twilight of his career" in 1996.

There's a lot to sort through with Duquette's legacy. On his watch, the Red Sox' roster became a true melting pot for the first time. He recognized the value of sabermetrics but struggled to articulate the benefits, his words often ending up as sports-radio punchlines (such as when he signed Jose Offerman after Mo Vaughn's free-agent departure after the 1998 season and noted that Offerman had a better on-base percentage). He was mocked in 1997 for relying on an eccentric, 52-year-old, would-be sabermetrician named Mike

Gimbel, who kept alligators in his Brooklyn apartment, worked for the City of New York Bureau of Water Supply and was referred to as a "math wizard" by Duquette.

Duquette's greatest commonality with Bloom was his ability to find overlooked talent. The Red Sox' improbable 1995 American League East championship team—the second one Duquette oversaw—used 53 players, a franchise record to that point. Last year, Bloom's second Red Sox team used 56 players. Duquette's yard-sale finds—outfielder Troy O'Leary, knuckleballer Tim Wakefield, rotund righty Rich Garces—were not unlike Bloom unearthing Renfroe, Whitlock and Christian Arroyo. O'Leary, a Brewers discard, was one of the players Gimbel recommended.

Duquette was masterful at acquiring the right superstars and finding helpful discards, but he neglected the upper-middle class of the roster; the number-two starter behind Pedro was usually an accomplished pitcher with miles and scars on his arm (Bret Saberhagen, Ramón Martínez). Epstein remedied that immediately after taking over for interim general manager Mike Port in November 2002. Mike Timlin, a strike-throwing veteran setup man, was his first signing. That same offseason, he added corner infielders Kevin Millar and Bill Mueller, and a Twins discard named David Ortiz, who became the player that delivered in the moments that, in the past, had ended in predictable sorrow. Hernández, who delivered some Ortizian moments in the 2021 postseason and finished second to Xander Bogaerts on the Red Sox in WARP (4.5) is the flashing-neon-sign example of Bloom recognizing something special in a player perceived as a middle-class big leaguer.

Bloom's greatest commonality with Epstein—beyond the Yale roots—is his dedication to player development. At his introductory press conference, Epstein vowed to build "a player develop machine," and the 2007 World Series championship was a testament to his success in doing so, with second baseman Dustin Pedroia, closer Jonathan Papelbon, center fielder Jacoby Ellsbury and lefty starter Jon Lester all having arrived from the farm system to play significant roles. In 2020, Bloom's first full season in Boston, *Baseball America* ranked the Red Sox' farm system 20th out of 30 teams. He has since done a remarkable job of adding high-end prospects, including 2020 first-rounder Nick Yorke (a controversial pick who has thrived, posting a .928 OPS at two levels in his pro debut) and 2021 fourth-overall pick Marcelo Mayer, a five-tool shortstop.

Of course, it's not the nature of fans—particularly those who have packed generations' worth of sports championships into 20 years—to be patient. Even through the four World Series titles and all of the team's success this century, Red Sox fans have endured a unique kind of recurring identity whiplash.

Twenty seasons ago, it wasn't safe to turn on a Fox broadcast of a Red Sox–Yankees game for fear of being inundated with "Curse of the Bambino" narratives. Then, in 2004, the Red Sox prevailed in an almost unfathomably satisfying way . . . and won it all again three seasons later, then hoarded two more distinctive championships in 2013 (a tight-knit, beloved group that bonded with the city in the wake of the Boston Marathon bombing) and '18 (a franchise-record 119 wins, playoffs included). Yet, there have been strikingly lousy seasons (2012, '14, '20) mixed in, and resets both necessary and unwelcome. If you know, you know.

Bloom's first two seasons—the abbreviated, grim 2020, and the unexpected joy of '21—hit both ends of the spectrum. His willingness to constantly tweak the roster suggests stability will not come for most of the players, but that might just be what allows the Red Sox to find that stable kind of excellence from year to year. It won't be as easy for Boston fans to miss the old guy; after all, there's pieces of the old guys all over the place.

—Chad Finn is a columnist at The Boston Globe.

HITTERS

Jonathan Araúz IF

Born: 08/03/98 Age: 23 Bats: S Throws: R Height: 6'0" Weight: 195 lb. Origin: International Free Agent, 2014

YEAR	TEAM	LVL	AGE	PA	R	2B	3B	HR	RBI	BB	K	SB	CS	Whiff%	AVG/OBP/SLG	DRC+	BABIP	BRR	FRAA	WARP
2019	FAY	A+	20	354	41	19	0	8	42	30	69	5	4		.252/.322/.388	106	.296	-1.0	SS(62): -2.4, 3B(18): 1.0, 2B(6): 0.1	0.9
2019	CC	AA	20	119	12	3	2	3	13	10	19	1	1		.241/.311/.389	109	.267	-0.4	2B(15): -1.7, SS(7): 0.3, 3B(6): 0.2	0.3
2020	BOS	MLB	21	80	8	2	0	1	9	8	21	0	0	22.0%	.250/.325/.319	85	.340	0.2	2B(16): -2.0, 3B(6): -0.3, SS(4): 0.6	0.0
2021	WOR	AAA	22	267	32	8	1	6	30	30	45	2	0		.245/.326/.365	103	.274	-2.3	2B(41): 6.2, SS(13): 2.3, 3B(12): -0.8	1.4
2021	BOS	MLB	22	75	9	3	0	3	8	8	15	0	0	21.1%	.185/.274/.369	101	.191	0.0	SS(13): -0.5, 2B(12): 0.6, P(1): -0.0	0.3
2022 DC	*BOS*	*MLB*	*23*	*120*	*13*	*5*	*0*	*2*	*16*	*11*	*23*	*0*	*1*	*21.8%*	*.225/.303/.346*	*74*	*.270*	*0.0*	*SS 0, 2B 0*	*0.1*

Comparables: Jonathan Villar, Ketel Marte, Cole Tucker

We may be living through the Era of the Bat-First Backup, but Araúz is a throwback to a simpler time when the prime directives for utility infielders were to field well and make contact. The 2020 Rule 5 pick wore out his Zone 8 Commuter Rail Pass, shuttling between Worcester and Boston as the under-vaccinated Sox lost player after player to the COVID IL. He did not impress with the bat in either spot, though he did his best to get with the times on August 27, when he followed up a failed bunt attempt by smashing an inexplicable three-run homer to help the Sox beat Cleveland at a challenging moment in the season. Still just 23 years old, there's a chance the switch-hitting Araúz has some untapped potential in his lumber. It's more likely he is who he is: a fine-ish backup infielder who's only as valuable as the number of options he has remaining.

Christian Arroyo 2B

Born: 05/30/95 Age: 27 Bats: R Throws: R Height: 6'1" Weight: 210 lb. Origin: Round 1, 2013 Draft (#25 overall)

YEAR	TEAM	LVL	AGE	PA	R	2B	3B	HR	RBI	BB	K	SB	CS	Whiff%	AVG/OBP/SLG	DRC+	BABIP	BRR	FRAA	WARP
2019	DUR	AAA	24	134	21	9	1	8	29	12	26	1	0		.314/.381/.603	127	.345	1.3	3B(20): -0.5, SS(9): -0.2, 2B(1): -0.0	0.9
2019	TB	MLB	24	57	8	2	0	2	7	5	18	0	0	31.7%	.220/.304/.380	83	.300	0.0	3B(13): -0.5, 2B(1): 0.0	0.0
2020	BOS	MLB	25	54	7	1	0	3	8	4	11	0	0	25.7%	.240/.296/.440	111	.250	0.7	2B(13): 3.7, SS(2): -0.4	0.7
2020	CLE	MLB	25	0	0	0	0	0	0	0	0	0	0		.000/.000/.000				3B(1): -0.0	0.0
2021	WOR	AAA	26	38	4	1	0	0	2	2	12	1	0		.091/.184/.121	83	.136	0.3	2B(8): -0.6	0.0
2021	BOS	MLB	26	181	22	12	0	6	25	8	44	1	0	26.7%	.262/.324/.445	98	.325	-0.4	2B(51): 1.3, SS(2): -0.2	0.7
2022 DC	*BOS*	*MLB*	*27*	*189*	*21*	*9*	*0*	*4*	*22*	*11*	*46*	*0*	*1*	*27.0%*	*.222/.289/.355*	*70*	*.283*	*-0.2*	*2B 1, 3B 0*	*-0.1*

Comparables: Marwin Gonzalez, Jonathan Villar, Eduardo Escobar

Thanks to a spate of injuries and the Red Sox's mid-season COVID outbreak, Arroyo was gifted clear paths to playing time at various points throughout the year. The problem? He was all too rarely available himself. Arroyo racked up 67 days on the 10-day IL via three separate trips for a bruised hand, a bruised knee and a strained hamstring. The unvaccinated infielder then spent 25 days on the COVID-19 IL only to watch a late career José Iglesias outperform him in his absence. When healthy, Arroyo looked the same as ever: just promising enough with the bat and glove to tease everyday upside at the keystone, but too impatient and lacking in versatility to earn a long leash. He provides some value as a lefty-killing bench bat who can handle starting duties in a pinch, but it's tough to be a reliable backup when you so often need a backup yourself.

Xander Bogaerts SS

Born: 10/01/92 Age: 29 Bats: R Throws: R Height: 6'2" Weight: 218 lb. Origin: International Free Agent, 2009

YEAR	TEAM	LVL	AGE	PA	R	2B	3B	HR	RBI	BB	K	SB	CS	Whiff%	AVG/OBP/SLG	DRC+	BABIP	BRR	FRAA	WARP
2019	BOS	MLB	26	698	110	52	0	33	117	76	122	4	2	20.9%	.309/.384/.555	129	.338	-0.5	SS(153): -20.5	3.1
2020	BOS	MLB	27	225	36	8	0	11	28	21	41	8	0	23.0%	.300/.364/.502	123	.329	1.6	SS(53): -2.9	1.2
2021	BOS	MLB	28	603	90	34	1	23	79	62	113	5	1	22.0%	.295/.370/.493	126	.333	0.0	SS(138): 10.0	5.2
2022 DC	*BOS*	*MLB*	*29*	*590*	*82*	*32*	*1*	*20*	*83*	*60*	*106*	*7*	*2*	*22.1%*	*.274/.358/.456*	*117*	*.316*	*-0.3*	*SS -2*	*3.4*

Comparables: Alan Trammell, Robin Yount, Cal Ripken Jr.

For several years it felt like Bogaerts didn't get his due as one of the best overall players in the game. Perhaps it's because he was surrounded by so much talent, or because the Red Sox have been so mercurial, or because he makes everything on the diamond look so damn easy. Regardless of why it took so long, the national media finally seemed hip to Bogey's greatness last season, as he was repeatedly celebrated in print and on broadcasts. Bogaerts lived up to the praise, filling up the stat sheet and collecting myriad accolades: he was once again an All-Star, earned his fourth Silver Slugger, paced both the Red Sox and full-time shortstops in WARP and, per FRAA, had the best defensive season of his career. Though he may not swagger out of the box or give great soundbites, Bogaerts is everything a team could want in a franchise player: talented, consistent, homegrown and a proven winner. That said, a potential crisis point looms: Bogaerts can opt out of his extremely team-friendly extension after his upcoming age-29 season. He's professed a desire to stay in Boston, but once he sees the contract that Carlos Correa gets—likely topping Corey Seager's gargantuan deal—he might be more willing to test the waters. Chaim Bloom and co. need to prioritize a Rafael Devers deal, but a reworked Bogaerts extension should be next on the list as he builds on his borderline Hall of Fame trajectory.

Jackie Bradley Jr. CF

Born: 04/19/90 Age: 32 Bats: L Throws: R Height: 5'10" Weight: 196 lb. Origin: Round 1, 2011 Draft (#40 overall)

YEAR	TEAM	LVL	AGE	PA	R	2B	3B	HR	RBI	BB	K	SB	CS	Whiff%	AVG/OBP/SLG	DRC+	BABIP	BRR	FRAA	WARP
2019	BOS	MLB	29	567	69	28	3	21	62	56	155	8	6	33.0%	.225/.317/.421	86	.281	0.8	CF(144): -0.3, RF(3): 0.3	1.5
2020	BOS	MLB	30	217	32	11	0	7	22	23	48	5	2	26.1%	.283/.364/.450	98	.343	1.4	CF(55): -2.8	0.5
2021	MIL	MLB	31	428	39	14	3	6	29	28	132	7	1	34.4%	.163/.236/.261	53	.226	1.2	CF(89): 2.6, RF(17): 0.4, LF(14): 0.5	-0.3
2022 DC	*BOS*	*MLB*	*32*	*477*	*54*	*21*	*2*	*11*	*49*	*40*	*134*	*8*	*3*	*32.8%*	*.210/.294/.354*	*73*	*.280*	*0.4*	*CF -1*	*0.0*

Comparables: Dexter Fowler, Dwayne Murphy, Del Unser

Top prospect. Potential trade chip. Gold Glover. Postseason hero. Disappointment. These are just a few of the things Bradley has been during his topsy-turvy career. A new one from 2021? Afterthought. Bradley joined the Brewers late in the offseason and seemed the perfect acquisition for a team looking for some low-cost upside at center field. Instead, his offense cratered to depths never before seen in Bradley's tumultuous career, his baserunning regressed and his defense—no longer award-worthy—was merely passable. By the end of the year, he was merely a part-time player for a team that entered October with World Series aspirations and by the beginning of December he was shipped back to Boston, who got two prospects tacked on from Milwaukee for their trouble. He'll look to add another twist in '22.

★ ★ ★ *2022 Top 101 Prospect* **#44** ★ ★ ★

Triston Casas 1B
Born: 01/15/00 Age: 22 Bats: L Throws: R Height: 6'4" Weight: 252 lb. Origin: Round 1, 2018 Draft (#26 overall)

YEAR	TEAM	LVL	AGE	PA	R	2B	3B	HR	RBI	BB	K	SB	CS	Whiff%	AVG/OBP/SLG	DRC+	BABIP	BRR	FRAA	WARP
2019	GVL	A	19	493	64	25	5	19	78	58	116	3	2		.254/.349/.472	134	.300	-0.6	1B(94): -4.7, 3B(8): -1.1	2.5
2019	SAL	A+	19	7	2	1	0	1	3	0	2	0	0		.429/.429/1.000	94	.500	0.1	1B(2): -0.1	0.0
2021	SCO	WIN	21	97	19	6	0	1	11	17	18	0	1		.372/.495/.487		.475			
2021	POR	AA	21	329	57	12	2	13	52	49	63	6	3		.284/.395/.484	128	.323	-0.8	1B(73): -6.2	1.4
2021	WOR	AAA	21	42	6	3	1	1	7	8	8	1	0		.242/.381/.485	107	.280	-0.4	1B(7): 0.0	0.1
2022 DC	*BOS*	*MLB*	*22*	*333*	*43*	*15*	*2*	*9*	*40*	*36*	*77*	*1*	*1*	*27.2%*	*.239/.330/.403*	*96*	*.297*	*-0.1*	*1B -1*	*0.3*

Comparables: Ronald Guzmán, Josh Naylor, Rowdy Tellez

Casas showed out in two spots last year as he continued his ascension. The first was in Portland, where Boston's 2018 first-rounder posted a gaudy triple-slash line and displayed an advanced, patient approach for a young power hitter. The second was, more impressively, in Japan, where the then-21-year-old hit three homers for the silver medal-winning US Olympic Baseball Team en route to earning All-Olympic Team honors. The hype train has now officially left the T station for Casas, who our scouting team called the best first base prospect in the game as recently as September—right before he was promoted for a cup of coffee in Triple-A. He's got little left to prove in terms of power, approach or glovework: only the pure quality of his hit tool remains in question. If his bat can fight its way to average, Casas should be a major-league regular for a long time. If it ticks up from there we could be looking at a special player.

Franchy Cordero LF
Born: 09/02/94 Age: 27 Bats: L Throws: R Height: 6'3" Weight: 226 lb. Origin: International Free Agent, 2011

YEAR	TEAM	LVL	AGE	PA	R	2B	3B	HR	RBI	BB	K	SB	CS	Whiff%	AVG/OBP/SLG	DRC+	BABIP	BRR	FRAA	WARP
2019	ELP	AAA	24	51	7	2	1	3	8	4	19	0	0		.217/.294/.500	84	.292	0.6	CF(9): 0.5	0.2
2019	SD	MLB	24	20	2	1	0	0	1	4	7	1	0	37.8%	.333/.450/.400	83	.556	0.5	CF(5): -0.3, RF(4): -0.3	0.0
2020	ESC	WIN	25	76	9	2	0	2	10	9	21	0	0		.227/.316/.348		.295			
2020	KC	MLB	25	42	7	3	0	2	7	4	4	1	0	20.2%	.211/.286/.447	106	.188	0.5	RF(8): -0.9, CF(5): -1.0, LF(1): 0.1	0.0
2021	ESC	WIN	26	97	15	5	1	2	10	8	20	1	0		.253/.313/.402		.303			
2021	WOR	AAA	26	335	53	24	2	13	56	42	94	12	1		.300/.398/.533	103	.406	1.0	LF(54): -1.8, 1B(7): -0.6, RF(6): -0.1	1.0
2021	BOS	MLB	26	136	12	6	0	1	9	8	51	1	1	41.9%	.189/.237/.260	48	.307	-0.9	LF(33): 1.3, 1B(11): -0.3, RF(2): -0.1	-0.5
2022 DC	*BOS*	*MLB*	*27*	*154*	*19*	*8*	*1*	*4*	*19*	*13*	*50*	*2*	*1*	*36.9%*	*.234/.313/.404*	*89*	*.339*	*0.2*	*RF 0, LF 0*	*0.2*

Comparables: Brandon Nimmo, Raimel Tapia, Michael Saunders

The world would be a kinder place if we adhered to the ol' adage "if you can't say anything nice, don't say anything at all," so let's talk about Cordero's season in Triple-A. It was so good! The 27-year-old lit the East on fire, ranking 19th in OPS, 27th in SLG and 27th in RBI despite only logging about a half-season's worth of plate appearances. Of course Cordero also spent about a third of the year in Boston, where he looked more lost than a tourist mid-Big Dig. Whether he appeared in the outfield, at first base or as a pinch-hitter, Cordero was more like the type of "centerpiece" you'd find during Allston Christmas than the one you'd want in return for Andrew Benintendi. Let's leave it at this: even if you're "just" a Quad-A player, that means you're one of the thousand-or-so best baseballers on the planet. After he was DFA'd mid-ALCS, Cordero went unclaimed on waivers, meaning teams may have finally learned to stop falling for his siren's song-esque tools.

Bobby Dalbec 1B
Born: 06/29/95 Age: 27 Bats: R Throws: R Height: 6'4" Weight: 227 lb. Origin: Round 4, 2016 Draft (#118 overall)

YEAR	TEAM	LVL	AGE	PA	R	2B	3B	HR	RBI	BB	K	SB	CS	Whiff%	AVG/OBP/SLG	DRC+	BABIP	BRR	FRAA	WARP
2019	POR	AA	24	439	57	15	2	20	57	68	110	6	4		.234/.371/.454	139	.278	-2.4	3B(90): 6.8, 1B(13): 0.8	3.8
2019	PAW	AAA	24	123	12	4	0	7	16	5	29	0	2		.257/.301/.478	97	.278	-0.1	3B(17): 1.9, 1B(11): -1.3	0.3
2020	BOS	MLB	25	92	13	3	0	8	16	10	39	0	0	46.2%	.263/.359/.600	92	.394	-0.6	1B(21): 1.8, 3B(2): -0.2	0.2
2021	BOS	MLB	26	453	50	21	5	25	78	28	156	2	0	38.2%	.240/.298/.494	90	.316	1.2	1B(123): -3.9, 3B(14): -0.5, SS(2): -0.1	0.1
2022 DC	*BOS*	*MLB*	*27*	*478*	*66*	*21*	*2*	*25*	*77*	*38*	*169*	*1*	*2*	*38.3%*	*.233/.309/.469*	*101*	*.320*	*-0.4*	*1B -1, 3B 0*	*0.9*

Comparables: Danny Valencia, Brian Anderson, Ryan Rua

Inside every prototypical power-hitting first base prospect live two wolves. One wolf is first-half Dalbec: the one who hit .219/.264/.409 with an astonishing 36.8 K%. This wolf is darkness and despair, and frankly, quite unplayable. The other wolf is second-half Dalbec: he hit .269/.344/.611, earning August AL Rookie of the Month honors and playing a better first base. This handsome-ass wolf is light and hope and did enough to secure a long-term roster spot, at least. So which wolf will win long-term? That depends what opposing pitchers feed them. If Dalbec is getting a steady stream of high fastballs and low-and-away sliders from righties, the Bad Wolf rears his mangey head. But if a southpaw serves up anything over the plate? That's when the Good Wolf can truly feast. Now entering his age-27 season, Dalbec can't be trusted as more than a short-side platoon bat with prodigious power, but there's a chance he can be somewhat exceptional in that role. He'll have to fight hard to keep the Bad Wolf at bay, but at the end of the day don't we all?

Rafael Devers 3B
Born: 10/24/96 Age: 25 Bats: L Throws: R Height: 6'0" Weight: 240 lb. Origin: International Free Agent, 2013

YEAR	TEAM	LVL	AGE	PA	R	2B	3B	HR	RBI	BB	K	SB	CS	Whiff%	AVG/OBP/SLG	DRC+	BABIP	BRR	FRAA	WARP
2019	BOS	MLB	22	702	129	54	4	32	115	48	119	8	8	24.3%	.311/.361/.555	120	.339	-0.5	3B(152): 7.3, SS(1): -0.0	4.2
2020	BOS	MLB	23	248	32	16	1	11	43	13	67	0	0	31.8%	.263/.310/.483	84	.325	1.6	3B(57): -8.3	-0.5
2021	BOS	MLB	24	664	101	37	1	38	113	62	143	5	5	27.8%	.279/.352/.538	126	.307	2.8	3B(151): -8.4	3.9
2022 DC	*BOS*	*MLB*	*25*	*596*	*91*	*33*	*2*	*26*	*88*	*50*	*131*	*5*	*4*	*27.5%*	*.266/.334/.482*	*116*	*.308*	*-0.2*	*3B -1*	*2.8*

Comparables: Jim Thome, Eddie Mathews, George Brett

If asked to list the best young players in the game, most would cite Juan Soto, or the juniors Acuña, Guerrero and Tatis. That's all well and good, but Devers belongs in the conversation. At the ripe old age of 24, *Carita* enjoyed his best offensive season, pacing the Red Sox in homers and slugging. He tied for 20th overall in DRC+, trailing only José Ramírez among primary third baseman and Xander Bogaerts among teammates. When both he and big brother Bogey earned Silver Slugger awards, they became just the fourth shortstop/third baseman tandem to earn that distinction in the same year in the AL. Yet as good as Devers was, it's easy to imagine a few tweaks making him that much better. He struggled mightily with fastballs for one inexplicable stretch, and it took him longer to adjust than one might expect. His third base defense remained erratic, with Devers making a spectacular play or two for every booted ball or airmailed throw. He also dealt with right elbow inflammation down the stretch and in the postseason that had him falling to his knees in pain after big cuts. All that is to say that, while we've borne witness to some great Devers seasons, we've arguably yet to see him at his very best. With rumors of extension talks swirling as he enters his final two years of team control, two questions remain: can Devers play the hot corner through his 20s, and will John Henry pony up this time for his team's next generational talent? If the answer to the latter is "no," Red Sox fans very well may riot.

Jeter Downs SS

Born: 07/27/98 Age: 23 Bats: R Throws: R Height: 5'11" Weight: 195 lb. Origin: Round 1, 2017 Draft (#32 overall)

YEAR	TEAM	LVL	AGE	PA	R	2B	3B	HR	RBI	BB	K	SB	CS	Whiff%	AVG/OBP/SLG	DRC+	BABIP	BRR	FRAA	WARP
2019	RC	A+	20	479	78	33	4	19	75	54	97	23	8		.269/.354/.507	126	.304	2.2	SS(91): -6.0, 2B(10): -1.1	2.1
2019	TUL	AA	20	56	14	2	0	5	11	6	10	1	0		.333/.429/.688	114	.333	0.8	SS(11): -0.9, 2B(1): -0.0	0.3
2021	SCO	WIN	22	72	9	0	0	5	14	14	18	4	2		.228/.389/.491		.235			
2021	WOR	AAA	22	405	39	9	0	14	39	38	131	18	3		.190/.272/.333	73	.249	2.7	SS(79): -9.3, 2B(21): -1.1	-0.7
2022 non-DC	*BOS*	*MLB*	*23*	*251*	*24*	*9*	*0*	*7*	*26*	*20*	*76*	*7*	*3*	*32.6%*	*.203/.277/.349*	*68*	*.271*	*0.6*	*SS -2, 2B 0*	*-0.3*

Comparables: Jonathan Villar, Javier Báez, Jorge Polanco

The Sox farm system had a strong showing for the most part last season, but Jeter was Downs bad. He struggled mightily for the first time in his pro career, nearly doubling his strikeout rate from his 2019 stint in Portland. There's no real way of knowing if it was the prolonged down-time that felled the 23-year-old, or the jump to Triple-A, or the small injuries he suffered throughout the season. What we do know is that Downs was unable to adjust: he never hit better than .247 in any month, and his August and September stats were especially gruesome. There's still plenty of time for Downs to emerge as a RE2PECTable major-league contributor, and he appeared to turn a corner in the AFL. But when your team turns to Christian Arroyo, Jonathan Araúz and José Iglesias before giving you a shot, you're so far in the hole you can't even attempt a jump throw.

★ ★ ★ *2022 Top 101 Prospect* **#81** ★ ★ ★

Jarren Duran OF

Born: 09/05/96 Age: 25 Bats: L Throws: R Height: 6'2" Weight: 212 lb. Origin: Round 7, 2018 Draft (#220 overall)

YEAR	TEAM	LVL	AGE	PA	R	2B	3B	HR	RBI	BB	K	SB	CS	Whiff%	AVG/OBP/SLG	DRC+	BABIP	BRR	FRAA	WARP
2019	PEJ	WIN	22	101	15	5	2	1	9	10	20	7	2		.267/.337/.400		.329			
2019	SAL	A+	22	226	49	13	3	4	19	23	44	18	5		.387/.456/.543	140	.480	3.9	CF(50): 0.9	2.3
2019	POR	AA	22	352	41	11	5	1	19	23	84	28	8		.250/.309/.325	83	.335	6.2	CF(80): -3.6	0.9
2020	CAG	WIN	23	70	14	2	0	0	10	12	14	6	0		.236/.386/.273		.310			
2021	WOR	AAA	24	283	46	11	2	16	36	30	66	16	3		.258/.357/.516	117	.288	1.8	CF(49): -3.3, RF(7): -1.0, LF(2): 0.4	1.3
2021	BOS	MLB	24	112	17	3	2	2	10	4	40	2	1	34.7%	.215/.241/.336	58	.318	0.5	CF(28): -2.9, LF(1): -0.0	-0.4
2022 DC	*BOS*	*MLB*	*25*	*472*	*57*	*20*	*4*	*10*	*50*	*31*	*140*	*22*	*8*	*33.4%*	*.236/.300/.374*	*78*	*.328*	*2.3*	*LF 4, CF 0*	*0.7*

Comparables: Brett Gardner, Tyler Naquin, Lorenzo Cain

The major leagues may technically only be one level up from Triple-A, but as Duran proved in 2021 there's a world of difference between them. Boston's toolsy outfield prospect dazzled in Worcester, displaying more power and a more patient approach to go with his plus-plus speed. Once summoned to Boston, he looked badly overmatched as MLB-quality arms exploited his still-developing hit tool, coaxing him into striking out more than a third of the time. Of course, Duran *also* looked like a young Christian Bale starring in a Jacoby Ellsbury biopic, which has only added to the hype despite the results. A consensus top-100 prospect, Duran just turned 25 in September but his early returns have put the Red Sox in a difficult spot: he can't yet be trusted with an everyday role, but leaving him to languish as a fourth outfielder may not be best for his development. As such, expect Duran to start 2022 as a WooSox before fighting his way back to Fenway mid-season.

Enrique Hernández CF/2B

Born: 08/24/91 Age: 30 Bats: R Throws: R Height: 5'11" Weight: 190 lb. Origin: Round 6, 2009 Draft (#191 overall)

YEAR	TEAM	LVL	AGE	PA	R	2B	3B	HR	RBI	BB	K	SB	CS	Whiff%	AVG/OBP/SLG	DRC+	BABIP	BRR	FRAA	WARP
2019	LAD	MLB	27	460	57	19	1	17	64	36	97	4	0	26.7%	.237/.304/.411	93	.266	2.2	2B(85): 1.1, CF(20): -1.5, RF(17): 0.5	1.6
2020	LAD	MLB	28	148	20	8	1	5	20	6	31	0	1	24.5%	.230/.270/.410	93	.260	0.5	2B(30): 4.3, RF(9): -1.1, LF(5): 0.6	0.8
2021	BOS	MLB	29	585	84	35	3	20	60	61	110	1	0	23.6%	.250/.337/.449	109	.278	2.6	CF(93): 9.9, 2B(47): -0.4, SS(8): 0.2	4.3
2022 DC	*BOS*	*MLB*	*30*	*573*	*81*	*28*	*2*	*20*	*68*	*55*	*109*	*2*	*1*	*23.9%*	*.239/.324/.418*	*97*	*.271*	*-0.6*	*2B 2, CF 0*	*2.1*

Comparables: Carlos Beltrán, Mickey Stanley, Ellis Burks

Long an understudy, Hernández wanted a starring role. After years of serving as an oft-played utility man with the Dodgers, Hernández said the chance to play everyday was his priority upon reaching free agency. Lacking an established center fielder or second baseman, the Red Sox offered Hernández a clear path to at-bats and a modest two-year deal. He repaid them ten-fold. Hernández wasn't just one of the best free-agent signings of the year: he was one of the best players in the game period. He ranked 16th among all position players in WARP thanks in part to the second-best DRC+ of his career, but also due to his surprisingly elite defense in center field, where he made 93 of his 134 appearances. Because this is Enrique Hernández we're talking about, he put an exclamation point on his stellar season by hitting .408/.423/.837 with five homers in the playoffs, solidifying his reputation as a player who shines on the biggest stage. Hernández still did all the goofy little things that made him a fan- and clubhouse-favorite in L.A., but proved he was much more than a "glue guy" or, respectfully, just the next Brock Holt. A repeat performance in his age-30 season should have him in line for a much larger payday next winter.

Gilberto Jimenez OF Born: 07/08/00 Age: 21 Bats: S Throws: R Height: 5'11" Weight: 212 lb. Origin: International Free Agent, 2017

YEAR	TEAM	LVL	AGE	PA	R	2B	3B	HR	RBI	BB	K	SB	CS	Whiff%	AVG/OBP/SLG	DRC+	BABIP	BRR	FRAA	WARP
2019	LOW	SS	18	254	35	11	3	3	19	13	38	14	6		.359/.393/.470		.413			
2021	SAL	A	20	408	64	16	6	3	56	19	86	13	8		.306/.346/.405	102	.381	-1.0	CF(46): -3.8, RF(30): 3.6, LF(14): 0.8	1.5
2022 non-DC	*BOS*	*MLB*	*21*	*251*	*19*	*9*	*1*	*2*	*20*	*10*	*61*	*6*	*5*	*25.9%*	*.242/.282/.327*	*66*	*.318*	*0.8*	*CF -2, RF 1*	*-0.2*

Comparables: Victor Robles, Manuel Margot, Ender Inciarte

It's hard for any Red Sox prospect to be underrated given the baseball-crazed market in which they may someday play, but Jimenez just might fit the bill. The speedy outfielder put together another solid campaign, ranking fourth in the Low-A East in batting average in his age-20 season while earning good reviews for his defensive prowess and makeup. Jimenez has more tools working for him than against him, so why doesn't he rank higher on national prospect lists? For one, he's a switch-hitter in name only: he hit a paltry .211/.222/.316 from the left side of the plate. More glaringly, he has less functional power than ERCOT: he's now notched just 60 total extra-base hits across nearly 1,000 career PA. Unless the bat gets knocked out of his hands as he climbs the ladder, Jimenez is on a clear path toward carving out a major-league career. Whether he grows into any pop at all will likely determine if that's in a starting or reserve capacity.

Blaze Jordan CI Born: 12/19/02 Age: 19 Bats: R Throws: R Height: 6'2" Weight: 220 lb. Origin: Round 3, 2020 Draft (#89 overall)

YEAR	TEAM	LVL	AGE	PA	R	2B	3B	HR	RBI	BB	K	SB	CS	Whiff%	AVG/OBP/SLG	DRC+	BABIP	BRR	FRAA	WARP
2021	RSX	ROK	18	76	12	7	1	4	19	6	13	1	0		.362/.408/.667		.396			
2021	SAL	A	18	38	7	1	0	2	7	2	8	0	0		.250/.289/.444	113	.269	0.3	3B(5): -1.3, 1B(2): 0.2	0.1
2022 non-DC	*BOS*	*MLB*	*19*	*251*	*20*	*10*	*1*	*3*	*22*	*14*	*83*	*0*	*1*	*34.8%*	*.217/.267/.319*	*59*	*.319*	*-0.2*	*3B -1, 1B 0*	*-0.8*

Comparables: Luis García, Vladimir Guerrero Jr., Darling Florentino

The internet was by and large a mistake, but it did allow Jordan to earn a modicum of fame as a high schooler thanks to some fancy footage showcasing his massive raw power. We'd eventually learn that Jordan's niche celebrity wasn't indicative of how he was viewed within the industry—as a right-handed power hitter likely destined for first base, he fell to 89th overall in the 2020 draft. But the Sox liked him enough to ink him to a well-over-slot deal, and the early returns suggest that Jordan took his slide personally: he crushed the ball at the complex league before a late-season promotion to Salem. Jordan is not a premium athlete nor a lock to hit, but no one can question his power, bat speed, age relative to competition or early results. Low-A should prove a fitting test for the exquisitely named slugger as he reaches the ripe old age of 19.

J.D. Martinez DH Born: 08/21/87 Age: 34 Bats: R Throws: R Height: 6'3" Weight: 230 lb. Origin: Round 20, 2009 Draft (#611 overall)

YEAR	TEAM	LVL	AGE	PA	R	2B	3B	HR	RBI	BB	K	SB	CS	Whiff%	AVG/OBP/SLG	DRC+	BABIP	BRR	FRAA	WARP
2019	BOS	MLB	31	657	98	33	2	36	105	72	138	2	0	26.8%	.304/.383/.557	131	.342	-5.0	RF(24): 3.9, LF(15): 0.1	4.2
2020	BOS	MLB	32	237	22	16	0	7	27	22	59	1	0	28.1%	.213/.291/.389	90	.259	-2.0	RF(4): -1.3, LF(3): 0.0	0.0
2021	BOS	MLB	33	634	92	42	3	28	99	55	150	0	0	29.3%	.286/.349/.518	117	.340	-2.6	LF(30): 5.8, RF(8): 0.6	3.3
2022 DC	*BOS*	*MLB*	*34*	*593*	*91*	*33*	*1*	*28*	*91*	*56*	*139*	*2*	*1*	*28.8%*	*.272/.349/.499*	*121*	*.325*	*-0.8*	*LF 1*	*3.1*

Comparables: Bob Watson, Joe Adcock, Felipe Alou

The good news is we can safely declare Martinez's abysmal 2020 an aberration rather than a drop off a cliff. The bad news? Martinez is unquestionably in decline. Once among the most-feared sluggers in the game, Martinez is settling in as a merely above-average bat. Save for 2020, he posted his lowest slash line and WARP since 2015 ... yet was still one of the best 70 hitters in the game, per DRC+. That speaks to just how damn good JDM was in his prime. It also speaks to how wise he was *not* to opt out of his $19-plus million option for 2022, as the market is generally unkind to aging, one-dimensional sluggers. While management must feel they could get more bang-for-the-buck with the chunk of change headed Martinez's way, there are worse fates than needing to plug one of the best hitters of the past decade into the five-spot in your lineup every night. Odds are he can provide the Sox with one more solid year, but even if he can't he's proven to be well worth the investment.

★ ★ ★ *2022 Top 101 Prospect* **#17** ★ ★ ★

Marcelo Mayer SS Born: 12/12/02 Age: 19 Bats: L Throws: R Height: 6'3" Weight: 188 lb. Origin: Round 1, 2021 Draft (#4 overall)

YEAR	TEAM	LVL	AGE	PA	R	2B	3B	HR	RBI	BB	K	SB	CS	Whiff%	AVG/OBP/SLG	DRC+	BABIP	BRR	FRAA	WARP
2021	RSX	ROK	18	107	25	4	1	3	17	15	27	7	1		.275/.377/.440		.361			
2022															*No projection*					

Comparables: Luis Guillorme, Adrian Valerio, Nelson Molina

When the Red Sox picked fourth overall in the 2021 draft it represented their highest selection since 1967. It's no stretch, then, to suggest that landing Mayer was a once-in-a-lifetime opportunity for an organization that aims to be a perennial contender. Drafted from the same California high school that produced former Sox slugger Adrián González, Mayer belongs to that most seductive archetype of prospect: a toolsy shortstop who should remain at the six. At present his strongest assets are his glove and his arm, but Mayer also brings a potential plus bat to the table as evidenced by his strong showing as an 18-year-old in the Florida Complex League. Thanks to his lithe, athletic body, Mayer also projects to grow into above-average power, which gives him franchise cornerstone upside. Given that profile, it's no surprise that many viewed Mayer as the best overall prospect in the draft, though it *was* surprising that Mayer was still there for the taking at four, and that a slot deal was enough to sway the USC commit to turn pro. All in all, it was a fortuitous turn of events for an improving farm system that can now list Mayer as its top prospect.

Taylor Motter UT Born: 09/18/89 Age: 32 Bats: R Throws: R Height: 6'1" Weight: 195 lb. Origin: Round 17, 2011 Draft (#540 overall)

YEAR	TEAM	LVL	AGE	PA	R	2B	3B	HR	RBI	BB	K	SB	CS	Whiff%	AVG/OBP/SLG	DRC+	BABIP	BRR	FRAA	WARP
2019	ERI	AA	29	35	3	0	1	0	2	5	8	1	0		.148/.286/.222	97	.190	0.0	1B(4): -0.3, 3B(1): -0.1, LF(1): -0.1	0.0
2019	MID	AA	29	250	30	8	0	8	26	26	58	3	2		.213/.300/.357	100	.250	1.0	3B(20): -0.3, RF(17): 1.6, 1B(5): -0.2	0.9
2021	WOR	AAA	31	52	5	2	0	0	6	7	13	0	0		.222/.327/.267	83	.313	-1.2	3B(8): -1.2, 2B(3): -0.2, RF(1): -0.1	-0.2
2021	ABQ	AAA	31	267	54	16	1	24	57	49	50	0	0		.332/.457/.752	155	.331	-0.8	3B(23): -2.4, 2B(16): -1.4, LF(11): -1.1	2.2
2021	COL	MLB	31	22	2	0	0	0	0	2	6	0	0	23.9%	.150/.227/.150	85	.214	0.5	3B(3): 0.1, RF(1): 0.5	0.1
2021	BOS	MLB	31	7	3	1	1	0	1	1	2	0	0	40.9%	.333/.429/.833	96	.500	0.3	2B(2): -0.1	0.0
2022 non-DC	*BOS*	*MLB*	*32*	*251*	*23*	*8*	*0*	*5*	*22*	*28*	*59*	*3*	*2*	*25.3%*	*.185/.284/.302*	*60*	*.227*	*0.1*	*3B -1, 2B 0*	*-0.7*

Comparables: Ryan Goins, Adam Rosales, Steve Tolleson

A 31-year-old utility journeyman goes where he's needed and nowhere else. You'd be forgiven for thinking Motter had run out of chances, getting exiled from the KBO and hanging out in the independent leagues, and yet. Signed by the Rockies on a minor-league deal, Motter was down in Triple-A most of the year, a level at which he'd hit 44 home runs in his whole 338-game career. He then proceeded to hit 24 of them in just 68. The Rockies needed him to take Raimel Tapia's spot on the roster after their left fielder strained his big toe, but then they designated Motter for assignment after 22 plate appearances (his first hacks in the majors since 2018). So Motter took his long hair and wonky throws and his unshaven face where it belongs: Boston, where a rash of COVID-related absences had created a need for infield depth. Who knows where the road will lead this mysterious role player next? Stay tuned for this year's episode of *A Motter of Time*.

Kevin Plawecki C Born: 02/26/91 Age: 31 Bats: R Throws: R Height: 6'2" Weight: 208 lb. Origin: Round 1, 2012 Draft (#35 overall)

YEAR	TEAM	LVL	AGE	PA	R	2B	3B	HR	RBI	BB	K	SB	CS	Whiff%	AVG/OBP/SLG	DRC+	BABIP	BRR	FRAA	WARP
2019	CLE	MLB	28	174	13	10	0	3	17	12	31	0	1	19.1%	.222/.287/.342	86	.256	-1.0	C(57): 3.1, P(2): -0.0, 1B(1): 0.0	0.6
2020	BOS	MLB	29	89	8	5	1	1	17	5	14	1	0	15.9%	.341/.393/.463	108	.403	-2.1	C(20): -3.7, 1B(2): -0.0	-0.2
2021	BOS	MLB	30	173	15	7	0	3	15	12	26	0	0	16.3%	.287/.349/.389	106	.328	-1.0	C(53): 3.0	1.0
2022 DC	*BOS*	*MLB*	*31*	*189*	*22*	*8*	*0*	*4*	*23*	*15*	*28*	*0*	*0*	*17.9%*	*.260/.336/.398*	*98*	*.292*	*-0.3*	*C -2*	*0.5*

Comparables: Yan Gomes, Nick Hundley, Tyler Flowers

YEAR	TEAM	P. COUNT	FRM RUNS	BLK RUNS	THRW RUNS	TOT RUNS
2019	CLE	6790	3.4	0.2	0.3	3.9
2020	BOS	2969	-3.8	-0.1	0.5	-3.3
2021	BOS	5706	2.7	-0.3	0.5	2.9
2022	*BOS*	*6012*	*-2.1*	*0.6*	*-0.3*	*-1.7*

Thanks in part to the paucity of catching talent throughout the league, Plawecki is the type of backstop who straddles the line between below-average starter or excellent backup. It may only be a 262 PA-sample, but Plawecki has hit quite well during his Red Sox career, trading power for a low-strikeout approach that helped him earn five starts at DH last year. He remains a solid-to-good-defender, emerging as Nathan Eovaldi's quasi-personal catcher. Most importantly, *The New York Times*' Joe Lemire reported that Plawecki is the reason the Red Sox became obsessed with Robyn's "Dancing On My Own," the esoteric anthem that would've earned a place in franchise history had they ultimately won six more games. Factor in the founding role he played in Boston's post-homer laundry cart celebrations, and Plawecki brings the bat-to-ball skills, glove and goofy intangibles you want in a backup backstop. He'll reprise his role as understudy after the Sox picked up Christian Vázquez's 2022 option.

Christian Vázquez C Born: 08/21/90 Age: 31 Bats: R Throws: R Height: 5'9" Weight: 205 lb. Origin: Round 9, 2008 Draft (#292 overall)

YEAR	TEAM	LVL	AGE	PA	R	2B	3B	HR	RBI	BB	K	SB	CS	Whiff%	AVG/OBP/SLG	DRC+	BABIP	BRR	FRAA	WARP
2019	BOS	MLB	28	521	66	26	1	23	72	33	101	4	2	20.7%	.276/.320/.477	106	.305	0.0	C(119): 8.1, 1B(10): 0.8, 3B(4): 0.1	3.4
2020	BOS	MLB	29	189	22	9	0	7	23	16	43	4	3	22.9%	.283/.344/.457	104	.341	-1.4	C(42): 5.3, 2B(1): -0.0	1.1
2021	BOS	MLB	30	498	51	23	1	6	49	33	84	8	4	17.6%	.258/.308/.352	89	.301	0.9	C(132): 6.3, 2B(2): 0.0, 3B(2): -0.0	2.2
2022 DC	*BOS*	*MLB*	*31*	*425*	*48*	*19*	*0*	*10*	*48*	*30*	*73*	*5*	*3*	*18.4%*	*.255/.316/.385*	*86*	*.296*	*-0.1*	*C 9*	*2.2*

Comparables: Yadier Molina, Mike Heath, Jerry Grote

YEAR	TEAM	P. COUNT	FRM RUNS	BLK RUNS	THRW RUNS	TOT RUNS
2019	BOS	16486	8.8	-1.2	1.6	9.2
2020	BOS	6333	4.9	-0.1	-0.2	4.6
2021	BOS	18097	3.9	0.5	0.7	5.1
2022	*BOS*	*15632*	*5.5*	*-0.5*	*0.6*	*5.6*

For years Vázquez has been one of the game's more underrated backstops, providing good-to-great defensive metrics and a livelier bat than your average catcher. But in 2021 he took a step back across the board, playing more like he did in 2018 than his three strong campaigns since 2017. Age and injury have conspired to rob Vázquez of his once-legendary cannon, and he finished outside the top-20 in CDA. He also failed to crack the top-20 in DRC+ among backstops with at least 300 PA, though his workload—he led the league in innings caught at 1051.1—may be partially to blame. Vázquez's track record and the overall paucity of catching talent in the league led to the Sox exercising his $7 million option, extending his status as the organization's longest-tenured player for at least one more year. There may yet be more to come, but with free agency on the horizon and Plawecki, Connor Wong and Ronaldo Hernández all showing some promise behind him, Vázquez's stranglehold over the primary catcher spot in Boston is starting to loosen.

Alex Verdugo OF Born: 05/15/96 Age: 26 Bats: L Throws: L Height: 6'0" Weight: 192 lb. Origin: Round 2, 2014 Draft (#62 overall)

YEAR	TEAM	LVL	AGE	PA	R	2B	3B	HR	RBI	BB	K	SB	CS	Whiff%	AVG/OBP/SLG	DRC+	BABIP	BRR	FRAA	WARP
2019	LAD	MLB	23	377	43	22	2	12	44	26	49	4	1	16.2%	.294/.342/.475	105	.309	1.3	CF(61): -1.6, RF(25): 1.5, LF(22): 2.0	2.0
2020	BOS	MLB	24	221	36	16	0	6	15	17	45	4	0	18.8%	.308/.367/.478	97	.371	1.0	RF(31): -0.9, LF(22): 5.9, CF(1): -0.1	1.2
2021	BOS	MLB	25	604	88	32	2	13	63	51	96	6	2	17.7%	.289/.351/.426	105	.327	-0.7	LF(90): -1.4, CF(42): -2.2, RF(24): -1.6	2.0
2022 DC	*BOS*	*MLB*	*26*	*597*	*83*	*31*	*2*	*14*	*63*	*50*	*92*	*5*	*2*	*17.6%*	*.273/.343/.415*	*104*	*.311*	*-0.4*	*RF -1, LF 0*	*1.8*

Comparables: Carlos González, Andrew McCutchen, Byron Buxton

Verdugo plays baseball like a sentient Mountain Dew Energy Drink. He hoots and hollers from the dugout during every rally and celebrates big strikeouts from the field. He thinks each single he hits should be a double, and each double a triple. Many of his accessories are neon. At his best, Verdugo is an instant shot of adrenaline, a hype man who wants to turn every dog day of summer into a feel-good rave. But while Verdugo's bursts of energy often manifest in harmless ways, there are far too many times when he channels original-recipe 4Loko instead. He's never met a cutoff man he won't overthrow or a southpaw slider he won't chase. His Player's Weekend jersey should read TOOTBLAN. He gets antsy in big moments, often selling out for power when a single would suffice. Even with these jitters, Verdugo is a fine everyday player whose well-rounded skill set offsets his knuckleheaded tendencies. But it's hard to shake the feeling that if he became a little less Red Bull and a little more espresso he'd be all the better for it.

Connor Wong C Born: 05/19/96 Age: 26 Bats: R Throws: R Height: 6'1" Weight: 181 lb. Origin: Round 3, 2017 Draft (#100 overall)

YEAR	TEAM	LVL	AGE	PA	R	2B	3B	HR	RBI	BB	K	SB	CS	Whiff%	AVG/OBP/SLG	DRC+	BABIP	BRR	FRAA	WARP
2019	RC	A+	23	302	39	15	6	15	51	21	93	9	2		.245/.306/.507	104	.310	1.4	C(59): -5.4, 2B(10): 1.1, 3B(2): -0.0	0.8
2019	TUL	AA	23	163	17	9	1	9	31	11	50	2	1		.349/.393/.604	91	.467	0.2	C(24): -1.6, 3B(10): -0.7, 2B(4): -0.2	0.1
2021	WOR	AAA	25	208	22	13	0	8	26	9	58	7	1		.256/.288/.442	87	.323	0.7	C(44): 0.0, 2B(1): -0.4	0.5
2021	BOS	MLB	25	14	3	1	1	0	1	1	7	0	0	46.2%	.308/.357/.538	71	.667	0.6	C(5): -0.1	0.1
2022 DC	*BOS*	*MLB*	*26*	*60*	*7*	*3*	*0*	*2*	*10*	*3*	*19*	*0*	*0*	*33.2%*	*.242/.295/.414*	*81*	*.336*	*0.0*	*C 0*	*0.1*

Comparables: Grayson Greiner, Nick Hundley, Michael Perez

YEAR	TEAM	P. COUNT	FRM RUNS	BLK RUNS	THRW RUNS	TOT RUNS
2019	TUL	3381	-0.8	0.0	-0.3	-1.1
2019	RC	8610	-5.2		0.0	-5.3
2021	BOS	499	0.0	0.0	0.0	0.0
2021	WOR	6627	0.3	0.0	0.0	0.3
2022	*BOS*	*2405*	*0.0*	*0.0*	*0.3*	*0.3*

Once viewed as the least-consequential part of the return Boston secured for Mookie Betts, Wong beat fellow prospect Jeter Downs to the majors and may have a leg up on him for 2022 playing time, too. A unique entity as a catcher who offers positional versatility, Wong seems well suited to the type of super-sub role that teams increasingly value as they look to dedicate more and more roster spots to pitchers. He swings and misses too much for a player who lacks prodigious power, but is uber-athletic for a backstop and barrels enough balls that he could eventually fight his way to an everyday role. It's more likely that Wong emerges as a fun and versatile backup backstop, which is not only a great outcome but may also be the universe's way of apologizing for Blake Swihart.

★ ★ ★ *2022 Top 101 Prospect* **#40** ★ ★ ★

Nick Yorke 2B Born: 04/02/02 Age: 20 Bats: R Throws: R Height: 6'0" Weight: 200 lb. Origin: Round 1, 2020 Draft (#17 overall)

YEAR	TEAM	LVL	AGE	PA	R	2B	3B	HR	RBI	BB	K	SB	CS	Whiff%	AVG/OBP/SLG	DRC+	BABIP	BRR	FRAA	WARP
2021	SAL	A	19	346	59	14	4	10	47	41	47	11	8		.323/.413/.500	144	.353	-4.9	2B(66): 7.0	3.0
2021	GVL	A+	19	96	17	6	1	4	15	11	22	2	1		.333/.406/.571	116	.407	0.3	2B(19): -1.0	0.4
2022 non-DC	*BOS*	*MLB*	*20*	*251*	*24*	*10*	*1*	*5*	*25*	*19*	*51*	*4*	*3*	*25.5%*	*.251/.316/.378*	*89*	*.304*	*0.3*	*2B 2*	*0.7*

Comparables: Delino DeShields, Jonathan Schoop, Xavier Edwards

When the Sox popped Yorke with the 17th pick in 2020, the prevailing theory was that the Red Sox wanted to play games with their pool of draft money. That may have been true to an extent—Yorke signed for nearly a million less than his slot suggests he should've—but it elides the biggest reason why Yorke ended up a first-rounder: he can really hit. The Sox named Yorke their minor league offensive player of the year after a wildly impressive campaign spent mostly at Low-A Salem. He walked nearly as often as he struck out en route to posting a gaudy stat line, and despite starting the season slowly, hit well enough to earn an August promotion to High-A Greenville, where he also raked. Bat-first second basemen have fewer paths to value than most prospects, but when the bat is *this* good—Yorke reached base safely in a nice 68 of his final 69 contests—not much else matters. Don't be surprised if you see Yorke pop up on the top half of some top prospect lists this winter, like ours, for example.

PITCHERS

Matt Barnes RHP Born: 06/17/90 Age: 32 Bats: R Throws: R Height: 6'4" Weight: 208 lb. Origin: Round 1, 2011 Draft (#19 overall)

YEAR	TEAM	LVL	AGE	W	L	SV	G	GS	IP	H	HR	BB/9	K/9	K	GB%	BABIP	WHIP	ERA	DRA-	WARP	MPH	FB%	Whiff%	CSP
2019	BOS	MLB	29	5	4	4	70	0	64^{1}	51	8	5.3	15.4	110	47.8%	.341	1.38	3.78	70	1.7	96.8	47.2%	36.3%	39.7%
2020	BOS	MLB	30	1	3	9	24	0	23	18	4	5.5	12.1	31	45.5%	.280	1.39	4.30	80	0.5	95.7	54.1%	28.6%	44.9%
2021	BOS	MLB	31	6	5	24	60	0	54^{2}	41	8	3.3	13.8	84	42.2%	.306	1.12	3.79	66	1.5	96.1	49.8%	33.6%	57.3%
2022 DC	*BOS*	*MLB*	*32*	*3*	*3*	*18*	*74*	*0*	*64.7*	*46*	*7*	*3.8*	*12.3*	*88*	*44.6%*	*.278*	*1.14*	*2.86*	*71*	*1.2*	*96.2*	*49.9%*	*33.4%*	*50.4%*

Comparables: Jason Isringhausen, David Robertson, Francisco Cordero

Meme stocks had a less volatile 2021 than Barnes. For the better part of the season, the big righty was among the game's best relievers, maintaining a prodigious strikeout rate while displaying improved command. As of July 11—the day Barnes signed a 2-year, $18.5 million extension with a third-year option—he boasted a 2.61 ERA, was 19-for-23 in save chances and had held batters to a .174/.238/.280 line. He'd go on to have a few more strong appearances, but in August disaster struck: Barnes' velocity declined, his command and confidence wavered, and he coughed up a 9.26 ERA in 17 games the rest of the way. Though the suddenness with which Barnes went from "newly extended All-Star closer" to "left off the ALCS roster for Martín Pérez" was jarring, the overall theme shouldn't surprise: the former first-rounder has always served as a case study in reliever volatility. The Good Barnes still offers enough upside to justify his new, higher price tag, but VIX says The Bad Barnes is present enough to preclude him from joining the game's true upper echelon of firemen.

Brayan Bello RHP Born: 05/17/99 Age: 23 Bats: R Throws: R Height: 6'1" Weight: 170 lb. Origin: International Free Agent, 2017

YEAR	TEAM	LVL	AGE	W	L	SV	G	GS	IP	H	HR	BB/9	K/9	K	GB%	BABIP	WHIP	ERA	DRA-	WARP	MPH	FB%	Whiff%	CSP
2019	GVL	A	20	5	10	0	25	25	117^{2}	135	9	2.9	9.1	119	46.7%	.362	1.47	5.43	106	0.6				
2021	GVL	A+	22	5	0	0	6	6	31^{2}	25	3	2.0	12.8	45	52.9%	.328	1.01	2.27	69	0.8				
2021	POR	AA	22	2	3	0	15	15	63^{2}	66	5	3.4	12.3	87	44.8%	.381	1.41	4.66	83	1.1				
2022 DC	*BOS*	*MLB*	*23*	*0*	*0*	*0*	*14*	*0*	*12.7*	*12*	*1*	*3.7*	*9.1*	*13*	*44.5%*	*.317*	*1.40*	*4.47*	*104*	*0.0*				

Comparables: Yordano Ventura, Tommy Hanson, Alex Cobb

For a few years, calling someone "Boston's top pitching prospect" was damning with faint praise: all you really needed was one plus pitch, a working arm and a pulse. But Bello isn't just clearing a low bar: he's a legitimate talent. The 22-year-old burst onto the scene en route to a Futures Game appearance and organizational minor league pitcher of the year honors. A skinny right-hander, Bello has a plus to double-plus heater that can reach the triple-digits, a slider that shows promise and an occasionally devastating changeup that caused Peter Gammons of all people to drop a dreaded P**** M******** comp from a scout. In ancient times we might've wondered whether Bello is best suited to start or relieve long-term, but as the line between those two roles become blurrier than ever, here's all that really matters: he should be able to help the Sox in some capacity as soon as the second half of this season.

Ryan Brasier RHP Born: 08/26/87 Age: 34 Bats: R Throws: R Height: 6'0" Weight: 227 lb. Origin: Round 6, 2007 Draft (#208 overall)

YEAR	TEAM	LVL	AGE	W	L	SV	G	GS	IP	H	HR	BB/9	K/9	K	GB%	BABIP	WHIP	ERA	DRA-	WARP	MPH	FB%	Whiff%	CSP
2019	PAW	AAA	31	2	0	0	10	0	9^{1}	6	1	1.0	12.5	13	45.0%	.263	0.75	0.96	75	0.2				
2019	BOS	MLB	31	2	4	7	62	0	55^{2}	51	9	3.4	9.9	61	32.1%	.286	1.29	4.85	106	0.4	96.2	59.3%	31.2%	45.2%
2020	BOS	MLB	32	1	0	0	25	1	25	24	2	4.0	10.8	30	37.7%	.328	1.40	3.96	92	0.4	96.3	62.0%	34.1%	48.0%
2021	BOS	MLB	33	1	1	0	13	0	12	12	2	3.0	6.8	9	56.8%	.286	1.33	1.50	111	0.0	95.2	68.5%	26.0%	59.4%
2022 DC	*BOS*	*MLB*	*34*	*3*	*3*	*4*	*67*	*0*	*58*	*60*	*8*	*3.2*	*8.2*	*53*	*39.9%*	*.314*	*1.39*	*4.68*	*111*	*-0.1*	*96.0*	*62.5%*	*30.9%*	*49.7%*

Comparables: Logan Kensing, Jesus Colome, Chaz Roe

Sidelined for most of the season with a lingering left calf strain, Brasier did not join Boston's bullpen until September 3rd. He was a cromulent middle relief option in his 13 regular-season appearances, but Alex Cora had visions of 2018 dancing in his head come October, when he began to rely on Brasier for higher-leverage work. The results were not good: Brasier coughed up four runs in four postseason innings thanks in large part to a fastball that appears to have lost some of its previous zip. WYSIWYG with Brasier at this point. He's fine as the fourth or fifth right-handed option out of your 'pen, but if you're using him as a set-up man you're setting yourself up for failure.

Austin Davis LHP Born: 02/03/93 Age: 29 Bats: L Throws: L Height: 6'4" Weight: 235 lb. Origin: Round 12, 2014 Draft (#352 overall)

YEAR	TEAM	LVL	AGE	W	L	SV	G	GS	IP	H	HR	BB/9	K/9	K	GB%	BABIP	WHIP	ERA	DRA-	WARP	MPH	FB%	Whiff%	CSP
2019	LHV	AAA	26	4	1	3	37	0	52^{1}	43	2	4.1	11.0	64	37.6%	.318	1.28	2.75	86	1.1				
2019	PHI	MLB	26	0	0	0	14	0	20^{2}	22	6	6.1	10.5	24	40.4%	.314	1.74	6.53	107	0.1	93.9	58.0%	25.1%	51.0%
2020	PIT	MLB	27	0	0	0	5	0	3^{2}	1	0	2.5	7.4	3	75.0%	.125	0.55	2.45	93	0.1	93.1	58.5%	36.8%	46.8%
2020	PHI	MLB	27	0	0	0	4	0	3	10	1	3.0	6.0	2	58.8%	.563	3.67	21.00	88	0.1	94.1	50.0%	30.2%	48.9%
2021	IND	AAA	28	0	1	0	11	0	14	6	0	3.2	11.6	18	34.6%	.231	0.79	2.57	93	0.2				
2021	PIT	MLB	28	0	1	0	10	0	9^{2}	6	2	4.7	10.2	11	40.0%	.174	1.14	5.59	87	0.2	93.8	62.3%	27.9%	51.6%
2021	BOS	MLB	28	1	1	0	19	0	16^{2}	18	2	3.8	9.2	17	49.0%	.327	1.50	4.86	103	0.1	93.6	46.4%	25.9%	50.8%
2022 DC	*BOS*	*MLB*	*29*	*3*	*3*	*0*	*67*	*0*	*58*	*51*	*7*	*3.7*	*10.6*	*68*	*43.2%*	*.308*	*1.30*	*3.82*	*90*	*0.5*	*93.7*	*53.3%*	*27.0%*	*50.7%*

Comparables: Dan Jennings, Stephen Tarpley, Matt Grace

Being a reliever acquired by Chaim Bloom is like being the son of a famous broadcaster, or a football coach who knows Sean McVay: the tangential affiliation can get you farther than your own actions or results. Such is the case with Davis, a relatively anonymous lefty reliever Bloom acquired from the Pirates in July in exchange for fan-favorite post-prospect Michael Chavis. The owner of a career pre-Boston ERA close to 6.00, Davis' primary draws on paper are that he misses a lot of bats and has the theoretical ability to neutralize lefties. In reality, he walks too many batters to be effective, and he's actually coughed up a worse triple-slash line to southpaws than righties to date. Serviceable as he was with the Sox, Davis would seem to have 50/50 odds at best of surviving the offseason on the 40-man. And because we know you're wondering: Chavis hit .357 in 12 games with the Bucs.

Nathan Eovaldi RHP Born: 02/13/90 Age: 32 Bats: R Throws: R Height: 6'2" Weight: 217 lb. Origin: Round 11, 2008 Draft (#337 overall)

YEAR	TEAM	LVL	AGE	W	L	SV	G	GS	IP	H	HR	BB/9	K/9	K	GB%	BABIP	WHIP	ERA	DRA-	WARP	MPH	FB%	Whiff%	CSP
2019	BOS	MLB	29	2	1	0	23	12	67^{2}	72	16	4.7	9.3	70	44.3%	.316	1.58	5.99	107	0.4	97.6	43.7%	26.3%	47.6%
2020	BOS	MLB	30	4	2	0	9	9	48^{1}	51	8	1.3	9.7	52	49.3%	.339	1.20	3.72	74	1.2	97.6	37.7%	28.1%	49.9%
2021	BOS	MLB	31	11	9	0	32	32	182^{1}	182	15	1.7	9.6	195	42.1%	.327	1.19	3.75	85	3.1	97.0	42.3%	26.0%	58.0%
2022 DC	*BOS*	*MLB*	*32*	*10*	*8*	*0*	*27*	*27*	*156.7*	*149*	*20*	*2.0*	*8.8*	*154*	*43.5%*	*.304*	*1.17*	*3.53*	*89*	*2.2*	*97.2*	*41.9%*	*26.3%*	*55.8%*

Comparables: Chris Carpenter, Rick Rhoden, Alex Cobb

In last year's Annual, we lamented that Eovaldi "picked a bad time to have a good year" given the listlessness of his 2020 squad. In 2021 his heroics went to better use, as he ranked first on the Red Sox and 22nd overall in WARP among pitchers in what turned out to be a career year. Once known for his high-octane fastball and little else, Eovaldi has evolved, throwing a five-pitch mix in which each of his offerings—a four-seamer, splitter, slider, curveball and split-finger—is featured at least 10% of the time. Despite all the miles on his twice-repaired UCL, Eovaldi added to his postseason legacy, too, logging four solid-to-great starts and one relief appearance in which he deserved a far better fate than what Laz Díaz, Alex Cora and Martín Pérez conspired to give him. Eovaldi's final act—striking out Carlos Correa, Kyle Tucker and Chas McCormick with runners on second and third and no one out in the fourth inning of Game 6 of the ALCS—was especially impressive, if ultimately futile. Now entering the final year of his once-maligned four-year pact, Eovaldi has emerged as a bona fide no. 2 starter and October hero. If his arm holds up he should be in line for another sizable contract next winter.

Wilkelman Gonzalez RHP Born: 03/25/02 Age: 20 Bats: R Throws: R Height: 6'0" Weight: 167 lb. Origin: International Free Agent, 2018

YEAR	TEAM	LVL	AGE	W	L	SV	G	GS	IP	H	HR	BB/9	K/9	K	GB%	BABIP	WHIP	ERA	DRA-	WARP	MPH	FB%	Whiff%	CSP
2019	DSL RS1	ROK	17	0	3	0	14	14	46^1	34	3	4.7	8.5	44	39.2%	.267	1.25	3.30						
2021	RSX	ROK	19	4	2	0	8	7	35	29	1	2.1	11.8	46	40.5%	.337	1.06	3.60						
2021	SAL	A	19	0	0	0	4	4	17^2	13	1	4.1	10.2	20	34.8%	.279	1.19	1.53	106	0.1				
2022 non-DC	*BOS*	*MLB*	*20*	*2*	*3*	*0*	*57*	*0*	*50*	*54*	*8*	*5.3*	*7.5*	*41*	*34.7%*	*.307*	*1.69*	*6.28*	*138*	*-0.8*				

Comparables: Kyle Drabek, Chris Flexen, Jordan Lyles

The Red Sox had several arms in their low minors break out in 2021, but perhaps none took quite as big a step forward as Gonzalez. A slender right-hander signed out of Venezuela in 2018, Gonzalez toyed with younger hitters in the complex league before impressing against more age-appropriate competition in Salem. He features a mid-90s fastball that he can manipulate in the zone, a changeup that flashes plus and, per the ever-reliable folks at SoxProspects.com, a slider that shows far more promise than his since-abandoned curveball. Gonzalez's slight build and moderately high-effort delivery portend some reliever risk, and he's got a long developmental road ahead as he enters his age-20 season. There's mid-rotation potential here as well, though, and another strong showing from Gonzalez should put him on the national prospect map.

Jay Groome LHP Born: 08/23/98 Age: 23 Bats: L Throws: L Height: 6'6" Weight: 262 lb. Origin: Round 1, 2016 Draft (#12 overall)

YEAR	TEAM	LVL	AGE	W	L	SV	G	GS	IP	H	HR	BB/9	K/9	K	GB%	BABIP	WHIP	ERA	DRA-	WARP	MPH	FB%	Whiff%	CSP
2019	RSX	ROK	20	0	0	0	2	2	2	2	0	0.0	13.5	3	80.0%	.400	1.00	0.00						
2019	LOW	SS	20	0	0	0	1	1	2	3	0	4.5	13.5	3	28.6%	.429	2.00	4.50						
2021	GVL	A+	22	3	8	0	18	18	81^2	76	12	3.5	11.9	108	47.6%	.330	1.32	5.29	87	1.2				
2021	POR	AA	22	2	0	0	3	3	15^2	12	0	2.3	14.9	26	27.3%	.375	1.02	2.30	87	0.2				
2022 non-DC	*BOS*	*MLB*	*23*	*2*	*2*	*0*	*57*	*0*	*50*	*48*	*7*	*4.2*	*9.0*	*49*	*41.9%*	*.304*	*1.42*	*4.70*	*108*	*0.0*				

Comparables: Blake Snell, Matt Moore, Robbie Ray

In some ways Groome's 2021 was a success: he stayed mostly healthy, he missed a lot of bats and he became a father. But it wasn't all rosy for Boston's much-ballyhooed 2016 first-rounder. Despite the Ks, Groome got hit hard in Greenville, and reports suggest that his stuff still isn't all the way back more than two years removed from Tommy John surgery. The southpaw can still run his fastball up to the mid-90s when he really needs to, but he now relies on a four-pitch mix that includes an emerging slider rather than the heater/curveball combo that originally got him drafted. Time may run more slowly for talented left-handers than for the rest of us, but Groome's is likely almost up nonetheless: he'll need to show more soon to justify his spot on the 40-man roster.

Darwinzon Hernandez LHP Born: 12/17/96 Age: 25 Bats: L Throws: L Height: 6'2" Weight: 255 lb. Origin: International Free Agent, 2013

YEAR	TEAM	LVL	AGE	W	L	SV	G	GS	IP	H	HR	BB/9	K/9	K	GB%	BABIP	WHIP	ERA	DRA-	WARP	MPH	FB%	Whiff%	CSP
2019	POR	AA	22	1	4	0	10	9	40^1	33	2	7.1	13.2	59	36.2%	.341	1.61	5.13	75	0.8				
2019	PAW	AAA	22	1	2	0	7	3	17	10	2	8.5	10.6	20	35.1%	.229	1.53	4.76	116	0.1				
2019	BOS	MLB	22	0	1	0	29	1	30^1	27	1	7.7	16.9	57	42.6%	.441	1.75	4.45	77	0.7	95.7	74.3%	35.5%	45.6%
2020	BOS	MLB	23	1	0	0	7	0	8^1	5	0	8.6	14.0	13	50.0%	.278	1.56	2.16	92	0.1	94.4	72.7%	27.5%	48.7%
2021	BOS	MLB	24	2	2	0	48	0	40	29	5	7.0	12.2	54	44.6%	.279	1.50	3.38	93	0.5	95.0	74.0%	31.9%	54.5%
2022 DC	*BOS*	*MLB*	*25*	*3*	*3*	*0*	*67*	*0*	*58*	*43*	*7*	*7.0*	*12.3*	*80*	*42.3%*	*.285*	*1.51*	*4.74*	*102*	*0.1*	*95.0*	*73.9%*	*32.2%*	*52.0%*

Comparables: Jeremy Jeffress, Eric O'Flaherty, Renyel Pinto

Hernandez is the type of filthy, wild and only sporadically effective reliever who can undermine clubhouse/front office relations with a single outing. If you're the architect of a team, it must be tempting to look at Hernandez's mid-90s fastball, sweeping slider and imposing build and see a potentially devastating reliever. But if you were a manager, how could you put the young southpaw in a close game without antacids nearby? Hernandez remains an enigma, boasting the type of wipeout stuff that can make the game's best hitters look silly but such inconsistent control that he's impossible to trust. Pure talent dictates that he belongs in a major-league 'pen, but if he's going to keep posting some of the worst walk rates in the game—he issued the fifth-highest percentage of free passes among pitchers with 30 IP—he won't evolve past low-leverage work.

Rich Hill LHP Born: 03/11/80 Age: 42 Bats: L Throws: L Height: 6'5" Weight: 221 lb. Origin: Round 4, 2002 Draft (#112 overall)

YEAR	TEAM	LVL	AGE	W	L	SV	G	GS	IP	H	HR	BB/9	K/9	K	GB%	BABIP	WHIP	ERA	DRA-	WARP	MPH	FB%	Whiff%	CSP
2019	LAD	MLB	39	4	1	0	13	13	58^2	48	10	2.8	11.0	72	47.3%	.284	1.13	2.45	78	1.3	90.5	52.6%	26.0%	55.9%
2020	MIN	MLB	40	2	2	0	8	8	38^2	28	3	4.0	7.2	31	41.1%	.240	1.16	3.03	115	0.1	87.9	46.8%	16.0%	50.6%
2021	NYM	MLB	41	1	4	0	13	12	63^1	62	7	2.7	8.4	59	27.4%	.311	1.28	3.84	103	0.5	87.9	50.4%	22.5%	57.4%
2021	TB	MLB	41	6	4	0	19	19	95^1	75	14	3.4	8.6	91	39.8%	.255	1.16	3.87	109	0.4	88.5	49.4%	24.0%	56.3%
2022 DC	*BOS*	*MLB*	*42*	*7*	*7*	*0*	*22*	*22*	*113.3*	*107*	*18*	*3.2*	*8.6*	*108*	*35.9%*	*.292*	*1.31*	*4.55*	*108*	*0.4*	*88.4*	*49.7%*	*22.7%*	*55.9%*

Comparables: Chuck Finley, Jerry Koosman, Tom Candiotti

Hill continues to fight against the dying of the light, grinding out five-and-fly starts for the 10th and 11th teams of his career. He showed unexpected durability at the tender age of 41, avoiding the injured list for the first time since 2015, and the last time he threw this many innings and made this many starts in a season was literally 2007. He couldn't turn back the clock on his fastball, which rarely cracks 90 mph now; worse, he lost nearly 300 rpm off his big curveball in the immediate wake of MLB's sticky stuff crackdown. A good chunk of that spin came back by year's end, but can Hill get by on gumption instead of with gunk at his advanced age? Well, this is a man who's been left for dead over and over again and keeps springing back to life. Like Huck Finn and Tom Sawyer, he seems to get a kick out of watching people throw him a funeral, only to waltz in through a side door, alive and well.

Tanner Houck RHP Born: 06/29/96 Age: 26 Bats: R Throws: R Height: 6'5" Weight: 230 lb. Origin: Round 1, 2017 Draft (#24 overall)

YEAR	TEAM	LVL	AGE	W	L	SV	G	GS	IP	H	HR	BB/9	K/9	K	GB%	BABIP	WHIP	ERA	DRA-	WARP	MPH	FB%	Whiff%	CSP
2019	POR	AA	23	8	6	0	17	15	82^{2}	86	4	3.5	8.7	80	48.5%	.346	1.43	4.25	110	0.2				
2019	PAW	AAA	23	0	0	1	16	2	25	19	3	5.0	9.7	27	43.3%	.258	1.32	3.24	80	0.6				
2020	BOS	MLB	24	3	0	0	3	3	17	6	1	4.8	11.1	21	46.9%	.161	0.88	0.53	88	0.3	92.5	62.3%	27.1%	42.6%
2021	WOR	AAA	25	0	2	0	6	6	21	19	1	3.0	11.1	26	53.7%	.340	1.24	5.14	90	0.4				
2021	BOS	MLB	25	1	5	1	18	13	69	57	4	2.7	11.3	87	48.5%	.319	1.13	3.52	78	1.4	94.3	55.7%	30.9%	49.7%
2022 DC	*BOS*	*MLB*	*26*	*8*	*6*	*0*	*45*	*16*	*102*	*85*	*11*	*3.6*	*9.8*	*110*	*48.0%*	*.288*	*1.24*	*3.61*	*88*	*1.4*	*94.0*	*56.6%*	*30.4%*	*48.7%*

Comparables: Tyson Ross, Johnny Cueto, Adam Morgan

It's been a long, long while since the Red Sox developed a *truly* homegrown starting pitcher: those about to cite Eduardo Rodríguez should recall he had already reached Double-A when acquired from the Orioles. That organizational failure has placed quite the spotlight on Houck, a 2017 first-rounder who's doing his part to live up to the hype. Armed with a whippy delivery that helps his lively fastball and devastating slider play up, Houck dominated in his first sustained run in the majors. Among pitchers who threw as many innings as he did, Houck ranked 31st in DRA– and was one of only four rookies in that group, joining Michael Kopech, Trevor Rogers and teammate Garrett Whitlock. He also ranked 21st in K% and 31st in whiff rate, making it abundantly clear that he can miss major-league bats with the best of them. While Houck was absolute death on righties, he more than held his own against southpaws, which means there's really only one question left for Houck to answer: how many innings can he throw a year? His height, demeanor and broad shoulders suggest 150-plus, but his high-stress delivery, Sale-ian build and overall track record portend lesser workloads. In ancient times that may have called Houck's ultimate role into question, but in the modern era it doesn't really matter. Houck's floor is as a dominant multi-inning arm who can make any righty in the game look silly. That he still teases a higher ceiling makes him the most exciting young Red Sox pitcher in recent memory.

Adam Ottavino RHP Born: 11/22/85 Age: 36 Bats: S Throws: R Height: 6'5" Weight: 246 lb. Origin: Round 1, 2006 Draft (#30 overall)

YEAR	TEAM	LVL	AGE	W	L	SV	G	GS	IP	H	HR	BB/9	K/9	K	GB%	BABIP	WHIP	ERA	DRA-	WARP	MPH	FB%	Whiff%	CSP
2019	NYY	MLB	33	6	5	2	73	0	66^{1}	47	5	5.4	11.9	88	40.1%	.286	1.31	1.90	87	1.1	94.0	41.4%	29.8%	48.4%
2020	NYY	MLB	34	2	3	0	24	0	18^{1}	20	2	4.4	12.3	25	52.0%	.375	1.58	5.89	83	0.4	93.5	44.8%	26.5%	53.2%
2021	BOS	MLB	35	7	3	11	69	0	62	55	5	5.1	10.3	71	39.9%	.321	1.45	4.21	101	0.5	95.1	48.6%	27.9%	53.0%
2022 DC	*FA*	*MLB*	*36*	*2*	*2*	*0*	*57*	*0*	*49.3*	*43*	*7*	*4.8*	*10.7*	*58*	*41.2%*	*.301*	*1.41*	*4.53*	*105*	*0.0*	*94.7*	*46.5%*	*28.2%*	*52.0%*

Comparables: Heath Bell, Ryan Madson, Sergio Romo

You've got to respect Chaim Bloom for having the gall to ask "what if we built the whole bullpen out of Yankees?" Though Rule 5 pick Garrett Whitlock earned the most headlines, Bloom's decision to acquire Ottavino in the ever-rare New York salary dump paid dividends, too. Not as dominant as in his halcyon days, Ottavino was nonetheless decent for the Red Sox, finishing fifth on the club in reliever WARP. Though his strikeout rate dipped some as his walk rate increased, he was effective enough to serve as Boston's on-again off-again closer, picking up some of the slack that Matt Barnes let loose in the second half. The Northeastern alumnus earned praise for bringing veteran leadership to a 'pen with lots of fresh faces, and put his horrific 2020 postseason behind him by pitching four scoreless October innings. Now entering his age-36 season, Ottavino is no longer the force he once was, despite what the occasional .gif of his slider would lead you to believe. That said, he still deserves a spot in a contender's bullpen, and a modest two-year deal isn't out of the question.

James Paxton LHP Born: 11/06/88 Age: 33 Bats: L Throws: L Height: 6'4" Weight: 227 lb. Origin: Round 4, 2010 Draft (#132 overall)

YEAR	TEAM	LVL	AGE	W	L	SV	G	GS	IP	H	HR	BB/9	K/9	K	GB%	BABIP	WHIP	ERA	DRA-	WARP	MPH	FB%	Whiff%	CSP
2019	NYY	MLB	30	15	6	0	29	29	150^{2}	138	23	3.3	11.1	186	39.0%	.315	1.28	3.82	88	2.5	95.6	59.9%	30.7%	45.6%
2020	NYY	MLB	31	1	1	0	5	5	20^{1}	23	4	3.1	11.5	26	32.1%	.365	1.48	6.64	103	0.2	92.5	56.7%	28.4%	47.3%
2021	SEA	MLB	32	0	0	0	1	1	1^{1}	0	0	6.7	13.5	2	50.0%	.000	0.75	6.75	114	0.0	94.7	71.4%	27.3%	46.0%
2022 DC	*BOS*	*MLB*	*33*	*3*	*3*	*0*	*11*	*11*	*55.3*	*49*	*8*	*3.1*	*10.3*	*63*	*39.0%*	*.297*	*1.23*	*3.68*	*90*	*0.7*	*94.9*	*59.5%*	*30.2%*	*45.9%*

Comparables: Kevin Appier, Dan Haren, Gary Peters

In a Mariner off-season marked by frustrating passivity in the eyes of many fans, the Paxton reunion represented a salve of sorts, a pleasant surprise yielding nothing but good vibes. Even knowing his injury track record, it felt like a worthy gamble to bring back a familiar face that also came with familiar upside. Then, a dazzling spring training debut in which he struck out eight and touched 97 MPH shifted the tone of his return. Did the Mariners get a steal? Was this going to be a whole lot more than just a feel-good story? Twenty-one pitches into his season debut, the dream was already dead. A visibly distraught Paxton walked off the mound knowing something was wrong. Tommy John surgery—a box that had somehow gone unchecked in his lengthy injury history—followed shortly thereafter. Baseball lost a lot of stars to injury in 2021, but few players' untimely exits were as big a bummer, considering the circumstances.

Nick Pivetta RHP Born: 02/14/93 Age: 29 Bats: R Throws: R Height: 6'5" Weight: 214 lb. Origin: Round 4, 2013 Draft (#136 overall)

YEAR	TEAM	LVL	AGE	W	L	SV	G	GS	IP	H	HR	BB/9	K/9	K	GB%	BABIP	WHIP	ERA	DRA-	WARP	MPH	FB%	Whiff%	CSP
2019	LHV	AAA	26	5	1	0	9	6	41	23	2	4.8	12.7	58	50.6%	.256	1.10	3.07	74	1.1				
2019	PHI	MLB	26	4	6	1	30	13	93^{2}	103	20	3.7	8.6	89	42.6%	.313	1.52	5.38	96	1.2	94.8	51.1%	24.7%	48.7%
2020	PHI	MLB	27	0	0	0	3	0	5^{2}	10	3	1.6	6.4	4	26.1%	.350	1.94	15.88	128	0.0	93.6	51.0%	22.9%	52.7%
2020	BOS	MLB	27	2	0	0	2	2	10	8	1	4.5	11.7	13	29.2%	.304	1.30	1.80	123	0.0	92.6	48.4%	25.0%	45.0%
2021	BOS	MLB	28	9	8	1	31	30	155	137	24	3.8	10.2	175	38.2%	.290	1.30	4.53	96	1.7	95.0	51.9%	24.6%	56.8%
2022 DC	*BOS*	*MLB*	*29*	*8*	*7*	*0*	*25*	*25*	*129.3*	*114*	*17*	*3.5*	*9.3*	*134*	*40.0%*	*.288*	*1.27*	*3.88*	*93*	*1.5*	*94.9*	*51.6%*	*24.6%*	*55.0%*

Comparables: Pascual Perez, Lance Lynn, Brandon Morrow

Pivetta came to perfectly embody the 2021 Red Sox: occasionally magnificent, sporadically atrocious, better than anyone expected and resilient as hell. After a rough 2020 that had visions of Joe Kelly dancing in Sox's fans heads, Pivetta earned a rotation spot in spring training and held it wire-to-wire. He was downright good at first, sporting a 3.16 ERA through his first eight starts while striking out a batter per inning. But Pivetta seemed to tire as the season and his appearances went on, becoming a poster child for the "times through the order" penalty: his ERA jumped from 3.14 to 4.20 to a whopping 9.24 if batters got a third crack at him. A true workhorse he may never be, but Pivetta came up big for the Sox in several key spots late, icing Juan Soto with a vicious curveball to close out Game 162 and send his squad to the playoffs, then allowing just four runs in 13 ⅔ postseason innings. As such, he's come to perfectly embody something else, too: a modern mid-to-backend starter who'll compete for five-or-so frames, but who then needs the hook. That's not a thrilling profile, but it's not a bad get for a few sad innings from Heath Hembree and Brandon Workman, either.

Garrett Richards RHP

Born: 05/27/88 Age: 34 Bats: R Throws: R Height: 6'2" Weight: 210 lb. Origin: Round 1, 2009 Draft (#42 overall)

YEAR	TEAM	LVL	AGE	W	L	SV	G	GS	IP	H	HR	BB/9	K/9	K	GB%	BABIP	WHIP	ERA	DRA-	WARP	MPH	FB%	Whiff%	CSP
2019	LE	A+	31	0	1	0	3	3	6^{2}	8	1	10.8	10.8	8	47.4%	.389	2.40	8.10	146	-0.2				
2019	SD	MLB	31	0	1	0	3	3	8^{2}	10	2	6.2	11.4	11	41.7%	.381	1.85	8.31	89	0.1	95.0	58.0%	30.5%	46.8%
2020	SD	MLB	32	2	2	0	14	10	51^{1}	47	7	3.0	8.1	46	40.5%	.284	1.25	4.03	106	0.4	95.2	54.7%	25.9%	46.6%
2021	BOS	MLB	33	7	8	3	40	22	136^{2}	158	19	4.0	7.6	115	47.3%	.333	1.60	4.87	121	-0.3	94.4	53.5%	22.4%	57.4%
2022 DC	*FA*	*MLB*	*34*	*7*	*5*	*0*	*63*	*6*	*78.7*	*84*	*11*	*3.9*	*8.0*	*70*	*45.6%*	*.322*	*1.51*	*5.16*	*118*	*-0.3*	*94.6*	*53.8%*	*23.2%*	*55.3%*

Comparables: Francisco Liriano, Joaquin Andujar, Danny Jackson

Inked to a one-year deal with a team option, Richards seemed a worthwhile gamble for a Red Sox rotation badly in need of established arms. Through June 1, it worked: Richards boasted a 3.75 ERA over 11 starts. But then MLB cracked down on foreign substance usage, and almost overnight Richards became one of the faces of baseball's inelegant policing. Without any grip enhancers, Richards' spin rates plummeted. The consequences were dire: he coughed up an ERA close to 7.00 over his final 11 starts, spoke openly about his struggles in a sticky stuff-less world, and generally looked like he was filming a Snickers "wanna get away?" ad each time he took the mound. The veteran right-hander took his subsequent banishment to the bullpen in stride and emerged a decent reliever, posting a 3.42 ERA across 18 appearances. In fact, Richards had begun to work himself into high-leverage spots before a hamstring injury knocked him out midway through the ALDS. Chaim Bloom and co. rightfully declined Richards' $10 million option, but he showed enough in relief that he should be given the chance to, uhh, stick in some team's bullpen this season.

Chris Sale LHP

Born: 03/30/89 Age: 33 Bats: L Throws: L Height: 6'6" Weight: 183 lb. Origin: Round 1, 2010 Draft (#13 overall)

YEAR	TEAM	LVL	AGE	W	L	SV	G	GS	IP	H	HR	BB/9	K/9	K	GB%	BABIP	WHIP	ERA	DRA-	WARP	MPH	FB%	Whiff%	CSP
2019	BOS	MLB	30	6	11	0	25	25	147^{1}	123	24	2.3	13.3	218	43.0%	.311	1.09	4.40	70	3.8	93.2	46.3%	32.0%	48.4%
2021	POR	AA	32	0	0	0	2	2	7^{1}	6	1	1.2	18.4	15	38.5%	.417	0.95	2.45	74	0.2				
2021	WOR	AAA	32	1	0	0	2	2	9^{2}	7	0	3.7	14.0	15	28.6%	.333	1.14	0.93	96	0.1				
2021	BOS	MLB	32	5	1	0	9	9	42^{2}	45	6	2.5	11.0	52	47.0%	.358	1.34	3.16	96	0.5	93.8	49.3%	27.7%	52.0%
2022 DC	*BOS*	*MLB*	*33*	*10*	*6*	*0*	*25*	*25*	*150.3*	*123*	*18*	*2.4*	*11.8*	*197*	*42.5%*	*.306*	*1.09*	*3.07*	*76*	*3.1*	*93.5*	*47.7%*	*30.0%*	*50.1%*

Comparables: Steve Carlton, Fergie Jenkins, Whitey Ford

A thin and fiery lefty donning a red "Sale 41" on his back once more climbed the mound for the Red Sox last season, but it remains to be seen when *Chris Sale* will reappear. About 18 months removed from Tommy John surgery, Sale returned to the majors on August 14. He was *fine* upon his return—DRA– tells us he was average or a touch better—but certainly not the ace of yore. Sale posted his lowest strikeout rate since 2013 and his highest walk rate since 2011. Though his velocity returned to pre-surgery levels, his command was clearly off as too many of his sweeping sliders found the middle of the plate. It speaks to Peak Sale's primacy that a diminished version could still be relatively effective. That didn't make it any easier to watch him get rag-dolled down the stretch and in the playoffs save for a gutsy Game 5 ALCS bounceback. We all know that precision can be one of the last tools to return to a pitcher post-TJ, so there's reason for optimism that the vintage Sale can resurface. His resurgence carries massive short- and long-term ramifications for the Sox, because while Sale proved that a lesser version of himself can still get hitters out, he did not do so at a rate commensurate with a pitcher owed *at least* another $85 million.

Hirokazu Sawamura RHP Born: 04/03/88 Age: 34 Bats: R Throws: R Height: 6'0" Weight: 212 lb. Origin: International Free Agent, 2021

YEAR	TEAM	LVL	AGE	W	L	SV	G	GS	IP	H	HR	BB/9	K/9	K	GB%	BABIP	WHIP	ERA	DRA-	WARP	MPH	FB%	Whiff%	CSP
2021	BOS	MLB	33	5	1	0	55	0	53	45	9	5.4	10.4	61	51.4%	.279	1.45	3.06	94	0.6	96.2	45.5%	35.0%	46.9%
2022 DC	*BOS*	*MLB*	*34*	*3*	*3*	*0*	*74*	*0*	*64.7*	*57*	*8*	*4.5*	*10.5*	*75*	*48.2%*	*.309*	*1.40*	*4.27*	*100*	*0.3*	*96.2*	*45.5%*	*35.0%*	*46.9%*

Comparables: Brandon Morrow, Brendan Donnelly, Jeff Tabaka

It looks like the front office found another bullpen bargain in Sawamura. The long-time Yomiuri Giant was aces from the start, beginning his MLB career with five scoreless appearances. As of July 19th, Swamura sported a 2.87 ERA and had held opposing batters to a .210/.309/.462 line. Unfortunately, he hit the IL with a right triceps strain on July 20 and was never quite the same upon his return. He was still serviceable, eking out a 3.52 ERA in 17 appearances, but the .276/.425/.326 line he allowed suggests Sawamura was fortunate his second half wasn't downright Barnes-ian. It was still a strong stateside debut for the split-finger specialist who'll earn just north of $1 million to return to the Sox's pen. He might be a fit for high-leverage work if he could just cut down his walks, but even as is Sawamura looks like quite the steal.

Connor Seabold RHP Born: 01/24/96 Age: 26 Bats: R Throws: R Height: 6'2" Weight: 190 lb. Origin: Round 3, 2017 Draft (#83 overall)

YEAR	TEAM	LVL	AGE	W	L	SV	G	GS	IP	H	HR	BB/9	K/9	K	GB%	BABIP	WHIP	ERA	DRA-	WARP	MPH	FB%	Whiff%	CSP
2019	PHE	ROK	23	0	1	0	1	1	2^1	6	0	0.0	7.7	2	54.5%	.545	2.57	11.57						
2019	PHW	ROK	23	0	0	0	2	2	5	1	0	0.0	18.0	10	83.3%	.167	0.20	0.00						
2019	CLR	A+	23	1	0	0	2	1	9	4	1	1.0	10.0	10	50.0%	.158	0.56	1.00	99	0.1				
2019	REA	AA	23	3	1	0	7	7	40	35	2	2.3	8.1	36	45.5%	.303	1.13	2.25	102	0.3				
2021	WOR	AAA	25	4	3	0	11	11	54	43	6	3.2	8.7	52	30.9%	.261	1.15	3.50	109	0.5				
2021	BOS	MLB	25	0	0	0	1	1	3	3	1	6.0	0.0	0	40.0%	.222	1.67	6.00	137	0.0	90.7	62.8%	10.5%	52.1%
2022 DC	*BOS*	*MLB*	*26*	*3*	*3*	*0*	*20*	*6*	*42*	*44*	*6*	*3.5*	*7.7*	*35*	*36.6%*	*.307*	*1.44*	*5.18*	*118*	*-0.1*	*90.7*	*62.8%*	*10.5%*	*52.1%*

Comparables: Anthony Ranaudo, Ryan Vogelsong, Ben Lively

When the Red Sox hired Chaim Bloom, one assumes it was in part because of his track record of finding major league-caliber arms underneath the surface. He's got a ways to go before Boston's next wave of pitchers looks anything like Tampa Bay's, but Bloom's decision to ship Brandon Workman and Heath Hembree to the Phillies in exchange for Nick Pivetta and Seabold sure looks like a Rays-ian masterstroke. Despite running aground early in the season with right elbow inflammation, Seabold impressed in Worcester with his deep mix of average pitches and his above-average command. None of Seabold's mid-90s fastball, reliable changeup or developing slider features as a wipeout offering, but he uses each to great effect, mixing in a hit-or-miss curveball to give hitters *mal de debarquement* on the way back to the dugout. His arsenal proved more than enough to keep Triple-A hitters at bay, and earned Seabold a cup-of-coffee start in the majors in September. His ceiling may be as a no. 4/5 starter rather than a true rotation anchor, but his floor—a cost-controlled innings-eater who can turn over a lineup twice—makes him the type of player the Sox simply could not develop under previous regimes. Expect Seabold to help shore up the rotation at some point this season.

Josh Taylor LHP Born: 03/02/93 Age: 29 Bats: L Throws: L Height: 6'5" Weight: 245 lb. Origin: Undrafted Free Agent, 2014

YEAR	TEAM	LVL	AGE	W	L	SV	G	GS	IP	H	HR	BB/9	K/9	K	GB%	BABIP	WHIP	ERA	DRA-	WARP	MPH	FB%	Whiff%	CSP
2019	PAW	AAA	26	1	1	3	20	0	23^1	18	2	4.2	12.3	32	47.2%	.320	1.24	2.70	81	0.5				
2019	BOS	MLB	26	2	2	0	52	1	47^1	40	5	3.0	11.8	62	44.7%	.321	1.18	3.04	86	0.8	94.9	60.2%	33.7%	41.0%
2020	BOS	MLB	27	1	1	0	8	0	7^1	7	2	6.1	8.6	7	43.5%	.238	1.64	9.82	98	0.1	93.8	52.1%	28.4%	45.9%
2021	BOS	MLB	28	1	0	1	61	0	47^2	45	2	4.3	11.3	60	43.9%	.355	1.43	3.40	85	0.8	94.7	48.8%	34.0%	55.2%
2022 DC	*BOS*	*MLB*	*29*	*3*	*3*	*0*	*67*	*0*	*58*	*51*	*7*	*4.0*	*11.4*	*74*	*44.6%*	*.317*	*1.32*	*3.98*	*92*	*0.4*	*94.7*	*51.8%*	*33.5%*	*51.1%*

Comparables: Darren O'Day, Sam Freeman, Joely Rodríguez

Standard caveats about reliever volatility aside, the Sox now have a big enough sample of Taylor pitching well that he can be their Plan A among lefties in the ol' arm barn. The big southpaw reverted to his breakout 2019 form, missing enough bats to survive his high walk rate and proving to be absolute death on lefties: they just hit .143/.222/.159 against Taylor in 24 ⅓ innings. Despite missing time with a lower back strain and as a COVID close contact, Taylor finished as Boston's third-best reliever, trailing only Garrett Whitlock and first-half Matt Barnes in WARP. He's now entering his age-29 season so there might not be more upside here, but Taylor already provides plenty of value as an arm who can pitch in medium-to-high-leverage spots and neutralize left-handed bats. He should eventually be shipped to Cooperstown as the lone example of Dave Dombrowski winning a trade for a reliever.

Michael Wacha RHP Born: 07/01/91 Age: 31 Bats: R Throws: R Height: 6'6" Weight: 215 lb. Origin: Round 1, 2012 Draft (#19 overall)

YEAR	TEAM	LVL	AGE	W	L	SV	G	GS	IP	H	HR	BB/9	K/9	K	GB%	BABIP	WHIP	ERA	DRA-	WARP	MPH	FB%	Whiff%	CSP
2019	STL	MLB	27	6	7	0	29	24	126^2	143	26	3.9	7.4	104	48.0%	.318	1.56	4.76	108	0.8	93.2	50.7%	21.3%	47.0%
2020	NYM	MLB	28	1	4	0	8	7	34	46	9	1.9	9.8	37	36.4%	.366	1.56	6.62	104	0.3	93.8	42.5%	24.6%	49.4%
2021	TB	MLB	29	3	5	0	29	23	124^2	132	23	2.2	8.7	121	41.9%	.313	1.31	5.05	99	1.2	94.1	39.7%	23.1%	56.6%
2022 DC	*BOS*	*MLB*	*30*	*7*	*7*	*0*	*22*	*22*	*115.7*	*119*	*15*	*2.6*	*7.8*	*100*	*42.4%*	*.311*	*1.33*	*4.31*	*104*	*0.6*	*93.8*	*42.7%*	*22.9%*	*53.4%*

Comparables: Jhoulys Chacín, Kyle Lohse, Frank Castillo

Consistency is not a problem for Wacha: He is going to get you nearly a strikeout per inning, he will limit the amount of walks and once a game the opposition is going to take him deep. What you get is a back-end starter/bulk guy who looks great at times and like burnt toast at others. Take for example the last two months of the year: In August, he allowed 22 runs on 41 hits in 23 ⅓ innings. In September, he gave up just 10 earned runs and only 17 hits in 30 innings. It's the September performance that interested Boston. The pitch mix also remains consistent with a low-90s fastball, a cutter a few ticks below that and a changeup, which continues to be his best offering. The changeup is so effective that opposing managers should be loading up lineups with righties to take away his best offering.

Garrett Whitlock RHP

Born: 06/11/96 Age: 26 Bats: R Throws: R Height: 6'5" Weight: 225 lb. Origin: Round 18, 2017 Draft (#542 overall)

YEAR	TEAM	LVL	AGE	W	L	SV	G	GS	IP	H	HR	BB/9	K/9	K	GB%	BABIP	WHIP	ERA	DRA-	WARP	MPH	FB%	Whiff%	CSP
2019	TRN	AA	23	3	3	0	14	14	70^1	73	4	2.3	7.3	57	55.5%	.322	1.29	3.07	116	0.0				
2021	BOS	MLB	25	8	4	2	46	0	73^1	64	6	2.1	9.9	81	49.7%	.304	1.10	1.96	76	1.6	96.1	62.9%	27.6%	56.0%
2022 DC	*BOS*	*MLB*	*26*	*4*	*4*	*18*	*82*	*0*	*71*	*66*	*7*	*2.9*	*8.8*	*69*	*49.6%*	*.304*	*1.25*	*3.59*	*88*	*0.7*	*96.1*	*62.9%*	*27.6%*	*56.0%*

Comparables: Bob Wickman, Junichi Tazawa, Scott Barlow

There are certain facts about the players in our sport that no fan will ever be allowed to forget, as they are repeated ad nauseum in every relevant national broadcast. Randal Grichuk was drafted one spot ahead of Mike Trout. Rougned Odor's brother is named Rougned Odor. And now: Whitlock was a Rule 5 selection whom the Red Sox swiped from their archrival Yankees. It makes for a good story, but what's most important about Whitlock isn't where the Sox got him from: it's that he was damn good for Boston in his rookie season.

A 2017 18th-rounder who the Yankees signed to an overslot deal as a sophomore-eligible draftee, Whitlock earned a modicum of buzz early in his career as another potential product of New York's Live Arm Factory. Unfortunately, Whitlock's ascension was stayed in July of 2019 when he required Tommy John surgery. That injury is likely the only reason he was left unprotected in the Rule 5 draft, where Chaim Bloom pounced. It didn't take long for Whitlock to wow with his mid-to-high 90s fastball and bowling ball of a sinker. But it's the changeup he learned from (squints) Matt Andriese in spring training that seemed to really allow Whitlock to take the next step.

Armed with his new third pitch, Whitlock finished second on the Sox in DRA and fourth in PWARP. In fact, he placed 17th in the majors in DRA– among arms who logged as many innings as he did, and he ended the season as Alex Cora's most trusted arm out of the 'pen. The big question now is will the Sox leave Whitlock to dominate in relief, or will they try to stretch him out as a starter? Cora seemed to hint at the latter at several points throughout the season, but while Whitlock has the frame and arsenal to succeed as such, his platoon splits may give Sox brass some pause. Regardless of his future role, Whitlock only has 86.3 WARP to go to catch Babe Ruth and make the Sox and Yankees even in terms of lopsided transactions. He's on pace to get there by 2072.

Josh Winckowski RHP

Born: 06/28/98 Age: 24 Bats: R Throws: R Height: 6'4" Weight: 202 lb. Origin: Round 15, 2016 Draft (#462 overall)

YEAR	TEAM	LVL	AGE	W	L	SV	G	GS	IP	H	HR	BB/9	K/9	K	GB%	BABIP	WHIP	ERA	DRA-	WARP	MPH	FB%	Whiff%	CSP
2019	LAN	A	21	6	3	0	13	13	73^2	62	3	3.2	8.7	71	54.5%	.299	1.19	2.32	99	0.6				
2019	DUN	A+	21	4	5	1	11	10	53^2	48	5	2.9	6.2	37	49.1%	.261	1.21	3.19	107	0.4				
2021	POR	AA	23	8	3	0	21	20	100	100	10	2.7	7.9	88	50.3%	.300	1.30	4.14	100	0.8				
2021	WOR	AAA	23	1	1	0	2	2	12	5	1	2.3	9.8	13	50.0%	.148	0.67	2.25	94	0.2				
2022 DC	*BOS*	*MLB*	*24*	*0*	*0*	*0*	*14*	*0*	*12.7*	*13*	*1*	*3.6*	*6.8*	*9*	*47.9%*	*.311*	*1.47*	*4.87*	*114*	*0.0*				

Comparables: Corey Oswalt, Taylor Clarke, Luis Cessa

Franchy Cordero may have been the most famous player the Red Sox received in the Andrew Benintendi trade (side note: yikes!) but Winckowski produced the best immediate returns. Acquired via the Mets in that seemingly ill-fated three-team deal, Winckowski continued his steady ascension, logging 100-plus innings in Portland on the back of a good fastball and decent command. The righty also features a slider that flashes plus and an inconsistent change that's nonetheless a viable third option. Winckowski didn't miss a ton of bats in Double-A, but he was durable, suppressed homers and induced ground balls at a 51% clip, hinting at a future as a backend starter or multi-inning reliever who could reach Boston as soon as midway through this summer. Side note: Winckowski has also been traded for Steven Matz, which means he's been swapped for so many once-promising lefties it's a wonder he wasn't on the Biden ticket. Folks...

Lineouts

Hitters

HITTER	POS	TEAM	LVL	AGE	PA	R	2B	3B	HR	RBI	BB	K	SB	CS	AVG/OBP/SLG	DRC+	BABIP	BRR	FRAA	WARP
Miguel Bleis	CF	DSL RSR	ROK	17	136	17	6	1	4	17	12	25	7	4	.252/.331/.420		.283			
Brainer Bonaci	MI	RSX	ROK	18	162	27	13	1	2	17	21	37	12	0	.252/.358/.403		.330			
	MI	SAL	A	18	52	5	3	1	0	8	3	8	0	0	.224/.269/.327	113	.268	-1.4	SS(8): 0.4, 2B(5): 0.6	0.2
Cameron Cannon	2B	GVL	A+	23	336	46	24	0	8	39	17	34	9	4	.302/.351/.457	119	.319	-0.8	2B(50): -3.1, SS(15): 0.3	1.4
	2B	POR	AA	23	99	15	6	0	3	14	5	18	0	2	.223/.263/.383	104	.247	-0.2	2B(19): 3.3, SS(4): -0.5	0.6
Delino DeShields	CF	WOR	AAA	28	76	10	4	1	1	4	13	24	5	1	.210/.355/.355	81	.324	0.6	CF(11): -1.6, LF(7): -0.0	0.0
	CF	RR	AAA	28	305	46	9	1	5	18	50	62	16	2	.263/.392/.368	98	.331	2.1	LF(43): 1.9, CF(10): -0.9, 2B(7): -1.1	1.1
	CF	CIN	MLB	28	58	4	5	0	1	6	9	11	2	1	.255/.375/.426	106	.314	0.4	CF(18): 0.2, LF(3): 0.1	0.4
Michael Gettys	RF	WOR	AAA	25	166	24	7	0	5	14	12	60	7	1	.201/.271/.349	71	.291	0.2	RF(16): 3.0, CF(15): 2.8, LF(2): 0.2	0.5
Ronaldo Hernández	C/DH	POR	AA	23	357	44	26	1	16	53	11	70	0	2	.280/.319/.506	113	.311	-1.3	C(61): 7.1, 1B(1): 0.3	2.4
	C/DH	WOR	AAA	23	30	1	3	0	0	5	1	7	0	0	.333/.400/.444	86	.450	-0.8	C(5): -0.1	0.0
Nathan Hickey	DH/C	RSX	ROK	21	28	4	2	0	0	1	6	8	0	0	.250/.429/.350		.385			
Niko Kavadas	1B	RSX	ROK	22	29	4	2	0	1	2	7	6	0	0	.227/.414/.455		.267			
	1B	SAL	A	22	29	6	2	0	1	4	8	7	0	0	.286/.483/.524	120	.385	0.0	1B(7): 0.7	0.2
Tim Locastro	OF	ARI	MLB	28	133	11	2	0	1	5	6	26	5	3	.178/.271/.220	86	.220	-1.0	CF(27): 1.3, RF(9): -0.2, LF(6): -0.2	0.3
	OF	NYY	MLB	28	23	4	2	0	1	2	1	7	0	0	.190/.217/.429	90	.214	0.2	LF(8): -0.3, CF(1): -0.1	0.0
Jack López	IF	SAN	WIN	28	130	14	2	1	3	10	12	26	6	0	.165/.262/.278		.186			
	IF	WOR	AAA	28	252	29	14	1	3	33	19	54	15	2	.274/.345/.386	92	.343	2.2	2B(26): 2.3, SS(18): -2.3, 3B(16): 0.3	1.0
	IF	BOS	MLB	28	16	2	2	0	0	0	1	6	0	0	.154/.214/.308	79	.286	0.1	2B(6): 1.0	0.1
Matthew Lugo	SS	SAL	A	20	469	61	21	3	4	50	38	94	15	4	.270/.338/.364	104	.335	0.5	SS(93): 4.0, 2B(6): 0.9	2.2
Tyler McDonough	CF/2B	SAL	A	22	126	23	4	4	3	14	17	24	3	1	.296/.397/.491	126	.358	0.9	CF(17): -1.2, 2B(8): -0.7	0.7
Yairo Muñoz	UT	WOR	AAA	26	374	45	16	4	8	36	17	53	18	5	.308/.340/.444	106	.341	1.4	3B(54): 7.3, SS(11): 0.7, 1B(9): 1.3	2.2
	UT	BOS	MLB	26	11	0	0	0	0	0	0	2	0	0	.091/.091/.091	94	.111	0.0	2B(3): -0.1, LF(1): -0.1	0.0
Hudson Potts	3B	POR	AA	22	307	33	18	0	11	47	16	100	0	0	.217/.264/.399	75	.284	-1.3	3B(74): -1.6	-0.3
Rob Refsnyder	OF	STP	AAA	30	80	13	5	0	5	14	12	13	0	0	.318/.425/.621	133	.327	0.9	RF(8): 1.9, LF(3): -0.3	0.8
	OF	MIN	MLB	30	157	21	7	0	2	12	17	40	1	0	.245/.325/.338	89	.327	-0.5	CF(22): -0.4, LF(20): -1.1, RF(9): -0.4	0.1
Jeisson Rosario	CF	POR	AA	21	405	48	15	1	3	36	50	113	11	7	.232/.335/.307	79	.332	-1.5	CF(79): -10.6, RF(22): 0.2	-0.9
Travis Shaw	CI	NAS	AAA	31	41	6	1	0	2	8	7	8	0	0	.273/.415/.485	113	.304	-0.2	3B(9): 0.1	0.2
	CI	BOS	MLB	31	48	6	3	0	3	11	5	17	0	0	.238/.319/.524	94	.318	-0.4	1B(11): -0.1	0.0
	CI	MIL	MLB	31	202	14	8	0	6	28	19	51	0	0	.191/.279/.337	81	.230	-0.8	3B(48): 3.6, 1B(20): -0.2	0.4

The Red Sox made toolsy Dominican **Miguel Bleis** the crown jewel of their 2021 IFA class, inking him to a $1.5 million bonus. The center fielder could be a fast-mover thanks to his mature frame, or he could spend the next two years in complex ball and it'd be fine: he only just turned 18 in January. Athletic teenage shortstop prospect **Brainer Bonaci** fared reasonably well in complex league action before hitting a wall in Salem. As such, starting him back at Low-A seems like a no-Brainer. Bat-first infielder **Cameron Cannon** crushed it in Greenville before getting crushed in Portland, where he faced more age-appropriate competition. His upside remains so low it can't be Storrowed. **Delino DeShields Jr.** racked up more transactions (three) than steals (two) last season, suggesting he's entered the fifth outfielder stage of his career. None of the Rangers, Red Sox or Reds thought he could stick, but he hit well enough in Triple-A that another team should come calling. Quad-A slugger **Michael Gettys** struggled with the bat in Worcester before giving pitching a try in Complex League ball. If he proves as adept at missing bats on the mound as he is at the plate, he's got a real chance to make it. Acquired from the Rays for the low, low cost of Chris Mazza and Jeffrey Springs, **Ronaldo Hernández** hit well in Portland and Worcester after spending most of 2020 on Tampa's taxi squad. He profiles as a potential bat-first backup backstop whose arm is MLB-ready. Fifth-round pick **Nathan Hickey** was drafted as a catcher, but early reports suggest he's more likely to leave a mark at the plate than behind it. Notre Dame product **Niko Kavadas** features double-plus raw power, plenty of swing-and-miss and an athletic profile that limits him to first base. He and Bobby Dalbec may one day combine to serve both as an effective platoon and source of renewable energy. **Tim Locastro's** 30.7 ft/s sprint speed made him the fastest man in MLB. Then he mangled his knee chasing a foul ball and became tied for the slowest at 0.0 ft/s. Is it unfortunate that it took a mass COVID outbreak for light-hitting infielder **Jack López** to finally reach the majors? Sure. Is it still a good story that he got there after 883 minor-league games? You betcha. Slick-fielding shortstop prospect **Matthew Lugo** hit reasonably well in Salem in his age-20 campaign, which means he should spend plenty of time in Greenville this year. If you've ever watched Jonathan Araúz play and thought "I wish he was less polished," buy your Drive tickets now. The Red Sox's most recent third-round pick, **Tyler McDonough** is a bat-first utility-type out of NC State who feasted on younger competition in Salem. His presence in the system further confirms that Chaim Bloom is prioritizing versatile, contact-oriented players who sound like *Ray Donovan* extras. The good news is that **Yairo Muñoz** was again successful in avoiding playing for the St. Louis Cardinals. The bad news? Despite raking in Worcester he didn't play much for the Red Sox, either, likely due to his subpar glovework. Third baseman **Hudson Potts** belongs in an MCU Origin Story because he's got massive power and no idea how to use it. He's taking Maine's status as a swing state all too literally. At the time, it seemed like a damning indictment of the 2021 Twins: They really missed **Rob Refsnyder** when he was concussed in June. He was adequate, versatile and healthy at a time when the Twins were in desperate need of all three qualities, but he was still a 30-year-old journeyman. Over the course of a summer spent between Target Field and St. Paul, it became apparent that he was a little better than that, playing all over the field and hitting with some pop. He likely played himself into the 2022 roster conversation. Outfield prospect **Jeisson Rosario** either really can't hit or really loves Portland, Maine. His bat suggests he needs to spend a lot more time up north despite a glove and arm that are Fenway-ready. **Travis Shaw**'s preferred nickname may be "Mayor of Ding Dong City," but it really ought to be "any Southwest flight" because he just can't seem to get his timing right in Boston.

Pitchers

PITCHER	TEAM	LVL	AGE	W	L	SV	G	GS	IP	H	HR	BB/9	K/9	K	GB%	BABIP	WHIP	ERA	DRA-	WARP	MPH	FB%	WHF	CSP
Eduard Bazardo	WOR	AAA	25	1	1	3	11	0	11^1	16	3	4.0	9.5	12	28.9%	.371	1.85	8.74	98	0.2				
	BOS	MLB	25	0	0	0	2	0	3	1	0	6.0	9.0	3	28.6%	.143	1.00	0.00	110	0.0	94.4	34.6%	25.0%	45.4%
Austin Brice	WOR	AAA	29	3	0	2	26	2	33	25	4	3.8	9.3	34	31.8%	.259	1.18	3.27	105	0.4				
	BOS	MLB	29	0	0	0	13	0	13^2	14	2	4.6	7.9	12	41.5%	.308	1.54	6.59	110	0.0	92.9	58.8%	20.7%	54.9%
Alex Claudio	WOR	AAA	29	0	0	1	8	2	11^2	15	0	2.3	10.0	13	47.2%	.417	1.54	6.17	93	0.2				
	LAA	MLB	29	1	2	1	41	0	32^2	37	6	4.1	8.3	30	50.5%	.320	1.59	5.51	99	0.3	85.6	48.2%	26.0%	47.2%
Kutter Crawford	POR	AA	25	3	2	0	10	10	46^1	33	7	1.0	12.4	64	39.8%	.271	0.82	3.30	84	0.8				
	WOR	AAA	25	3	4	0	10	9	48^1	49	5	2.8	12.5	67	33.1%	.370	1.32	5.21	88	0.9				
	BOS	MLB	25	0	1	0	1	1	2	5	1	9.0	9.0	2	11.1%	.500	3.50	22.50	120	0.0	93.4	75.4%	28.1%	49.7%
Raynel Espinal	WOR	AAA	29	11	4	0	23	21	117^2	86	12	3.3	8.8	115	32.4%	.243	1.10	3.44	90	2.2				
	BOS	MLB	29	0	0	0	1	0	2	2	0	4.5	0.0	0	42.9%	.286	1.50	9.00	127	0.0	93.4	75.0%	21.1%	52.8%
Durbin Feltman	POR	AA	24	6	0	1	22	0	27^1	23	5	3.3	12.2	37	40.9%	.295	1.21	3.29	82	0.5				
	WOR	AAA	24	2	1	1	17	0	24^1	18	3	1.5	9.2	25	32.3%	.242	0.90	2.59	90	0.5				
Joan Martinez	POR	AA	24	0	1	5	33	0	36^1	23	0	5.0	12.6	51	48.7%	.295	1.18	2.48	84	0.6				
Chris Murphy	GVL	A+	23	5	3	0	14	14	68^1	62	17	3.0	10.7	81	38.8%	.281	1.24	4.21	103	0.4				
	POR	AA	23	3	2	0	7	6	33	30	4	3.5	12.8	47	33.8%	.356	1.30	5.45	96	0.3				
Brad Peacock	COL	AAA	33	0	4	0	11	10	34	39	6	3.7	10.1	38	34.0%	.340	1.56	7.68	115	0.2				
	BOS	MLB	33	0	1	0	2	1	5^1	6	2	5.1	5.1	3	26.3%	.235	1.69	15.19	130	0.0	90.7	44.2%	17.1%	51.6%
Yacksel Ríos	DUR	AAA	28	2	0	2	12	0	13^2	8	1	1.3	11.2	17	56.7%	.241	0.73	0.66	87	0.3				
	WOR	AAA	28	0	0	1	5	0	6	10	0	4.5	12.0	8	30.0%	.500	2.17	7.50	84	0.1				
	BOS	MLB	28	3	0	0	20	0	24^1	13	3	5.2	7.8	21	43.5%	.169	1.11	3.70	113	0.1	97.2	58.8%	27.3%	50.0%
	SEA	MLB	28	0	0	0	3	0	3	5	0	6.0	6.0	2	27.3%	.455	2.33	9.00	136	0.0	97.4	74.2%	14.3%	54.9%
Phillips Valdez	WOR	AAA	29	1	0	1	17	0	16	13	2	7.9	11.2	20	63.2%	.306	1.69	3.94	91	0.3				
	BOS	MLB	29	2	0	1	28	0	40	35	4	4.3	7.9	35	57.8%	.279	1.35	5.85	108	0.2	92.8	40.4%	23.1%	51.5%
Brandon Walter	SAL	A	24	1	1	2	13	2	31	21	0	1.7	13.4	46	67.1%	.288	0.87	1.45	67	0.8				
	GVL	A+	24	4	3	0	12	12	58^1	46	6	2.2	13.3	86	58.3%	.317	1.03	3.70	73	1.4				
Thaddeus Ward	POR	AA	24	0	0	0	2	2	8	11	0	5.6	12.4	11	60.9%	.478	2.00	5.62	96	0.1				
Brandon Workman	WOR	AAA	32	0	0	1	7	0	7	3	0	5.1	12.9	10	69.2%	.231	1.00	1.29	87	0.1				
	CHC	MLB	32	0	2	0	10	0	8	12	2	7.9	12.4	11	52.0%	.435	2.38	6.75	86	0.1	91.7	44.6%	26.4%	57.0%
	BOS	MLB	32	1	0	0	19	0	20	24	2	6.3	6.3	14	40.0%	.349	1.90	4.95	122	-0.1	90.9	30.9%	23.0%	56.5%

Right-handed reliever prospect **Eduard Bazardo** is an o away from having an elite name and a breaking ball away from having two great pitches. A strained lat forced him to spend more time on the IL than in either Worcestor's or Boston's bullpens. The Red Sox used a franchise-record 56 players in 2021, which helps to explain how Quad-A right-hander **Austin Brice** notched 13 mediocre relief appearances. It's been a few seasons since the formerly formidable **Alex Claudio** could be called upon as an effective LOOGY. That he was bounced from the Angels' beleaguered bullpen does not portend a late-career resurgence. Potential swingman **Kutter Crawford** missed plenty of bats in Portland and Worcester, thanks in part to his namesake offering. Still, his rough major-league debut proves that nominative determinism will only get him so far. The Sox swiped righty reliever **Raynel Espinal** from the Yankees in the minor-league Rule 5 draft. He earned pitcher of the year honors in Worcester, essentially making him the off-Broadway version of Garrett Whitlock. **Durbin Feltman**'s nickname should be "Sunday Morning Green Line" because it's taking him *forever* to reach Fenway. The righty reliever prospect should soon finally reach his destination after a career-best campaign ending with a dominant run in Worcester. Righty reliever prospect **Joan Martinez** has always had better stuff than his results suggest. That started to change in Portland, giving him an outside shot of filling the Joe Kelly role in Boston's bullpen. The electric, eclectic **Bryan Mata**'s steady climb through the system was stayed when he required Tommy John surgery last April. A 2023 MLB ETA now looks most likely for the effectively wild right-hander, as does a future in the bullpen. Southpaw **Chris Murphy** missed more bats but allowed more walks and contact in both Greenville and Portland, reigniting some of the concerns that made him drop to the sixth round of the 2019 draft. His ceiling remains a backend starter, while his floor remains in line at Bissell Brothers. Veteran right-hander **Brad Peacock** made two late-season appearances for Boston, got shelled and was promptly returned to Triple-A, making the Red Sox the latest entity to figure out that Peacock simply does not provide a worthwhile streaming service. The Sox shipped some cash to Seattle for right-hander **Yacksel Ríos** in June, subsequently deploying him in nearly two-dozen underwhelming relief appearances. He provides nominal depth but mostly exists so Jerry Dipoto-types can get their transactional fixes. Promising right-hander **Noah Song** continues to serve his military commitment, attending Naval flight school instead of Greenville's High-A school. It remains to be seen if he'll reclaim his mantle as Boston's truly sea-bold pitching prospect. Up-and-down right-hander **Phillips Valdez** spent nearly equal amounts of time in Boston, Worcester and on the COVID IL. Thankfully he recovered from the latter, though his ERA did not follow suit. Unheralded southpaw prospect **Brandon Walter** missed a ton of bats in Salem and Greenville, teasing a future as a back-end starter or multi-inning reliever. Fenway might not be too far off if his now-actually-fastball plays against more age-appropriate competition. Like many pitchers these days, right-hander **Thad Ward** was unable to ward off Tommy John surgery, which means he spent more time in a hospital ward than serving as a ward in Portland or Pawtucket's rotations. Count **Brandon Workman** among the millions of Americans who looked at their job last year and said "ya know what? eff this." After DFAs from both the Cubs and Red Sox he elected free agency, but the second time no one bit.

NEW YORK YANKEES

Essay by Gary Phillips

Player comments by Daniel R. Epstein and BP staff

Shortly after the Yankees' hectic 2021 season came to a whimpering, wild-card end in Boston, Brian Cashman staunchly defended his boss.

"I hate to say it," the Yankees' general manager said when asked about Hal Steinbrenner's financial dedication, "but how dare anybody question when somebody commits that amount of dollars."

But Cashman's current boss is not like his old boss—*The* Boss—and, by treating Major League Baseball's $210-million competitive-balance-tax threshold as a self-imposed salary cap in certain years, *this* Steinbrenner has led fans and reporters to criticize his devotion to the company catchphrase. Even though the Yankees routinely finish among the league's leaders in payroll and recently shelled out a record-breaking deal to ace Gerrit Cole, it's hard to believe Steinbrenner and his team are always all in on their annual championship-or-bust mantra when so much time is spent fretting over the CBT.

This Steinbrenner has made it clear that this is how *his* Yankees do things, if only from time to time. The question posed to Cashman was really, for all practical purposes, a statement: New York doesn't operate like it used to. Cashman has repeatedly insisted that that's not necessarily a bad thing—money does not buy World Series wins—but his defensiveness highlights an organizational disconnect between what the Yankees have become and what they've always marketed themselves to be.

That gap left its mark throughout the franchise in 2021. Sure, New York won 92 games, but a noticeably flawed roster fluctuated between both ends of the competitive spectrum, and another early playoff exit fell far short of the standards that are preached. Cashman said that the Yankees "went backwards in categories we didn't see coming or expect" last year, but he probably should have seen it coming, in some cases. Others outside the organization certainly did.

Denial, however, can be blinding, and the Yankees have clearly had trouble seeing what's in front of them, or what they could be capable of.

⚾ ⚾ ⚾

NEW YORK YANKEES PROSPECTUS

2021 W-L: 92-70, 3RD IN AL EAST

Pythag	.528	*11th*	DER	.705	*9th*
RS/G	4.39	*19th*	DRC+	101	*6th*
RA/G	4.13	*10th*	DRA-	94	*9th*
dWin%	.556	*9th*	FIP	3.95	*7th*
Payroll	$198M	*2nd*	B-Age	29.9	*27th*
M$/MW	$4.2M	*20th*	P-Age	29.6	*25th*

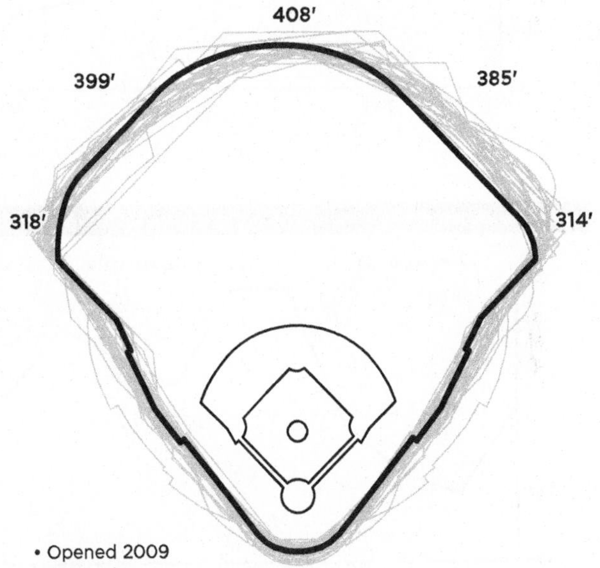

- Opened 2009
- Open air
- Natural surface
- Fence profile: 8'

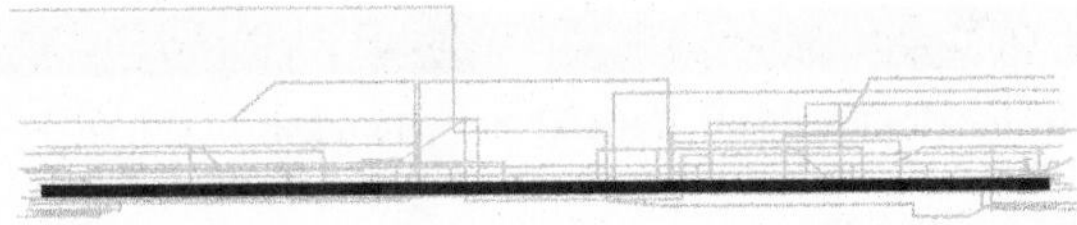

Park Factors

Runs	Runs/RH	Runs/LH	HR/RH	HR/LH
100	97	104	102	120

Top Hitter WARP	5.0 Aaron Judge
Top Pitcher WARP	4.5 Gerrit Cole
Top Prospect	Anthony Volpe

Payroll History (in millions)

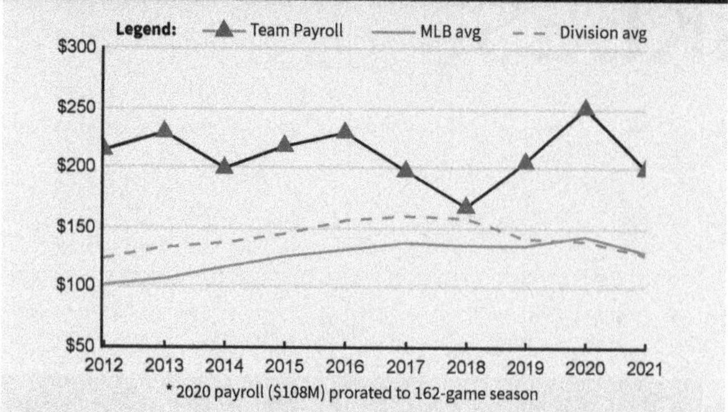

Future Commitments (in millions)

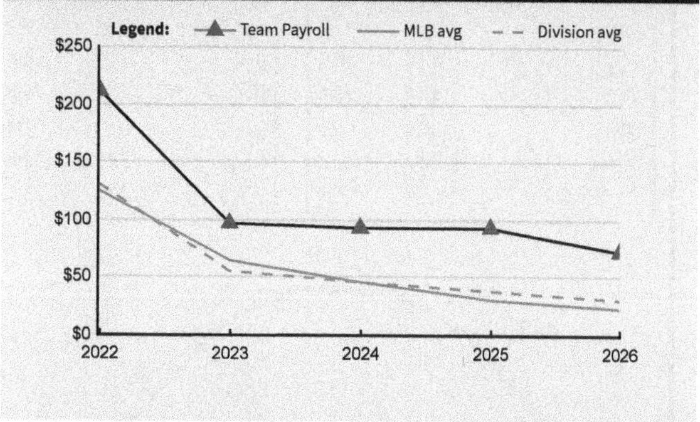

Farm System Ranking

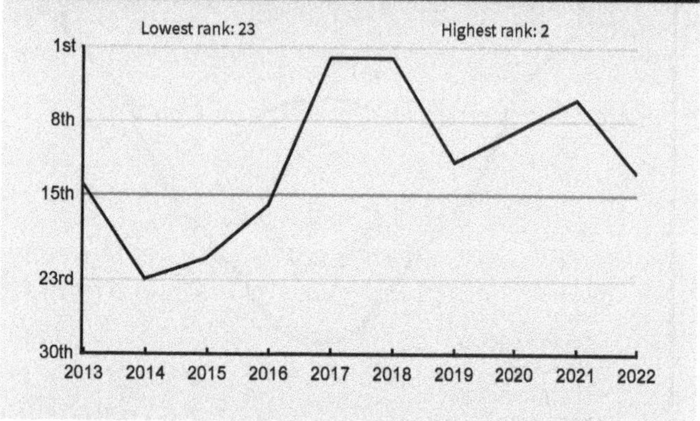

Personnel

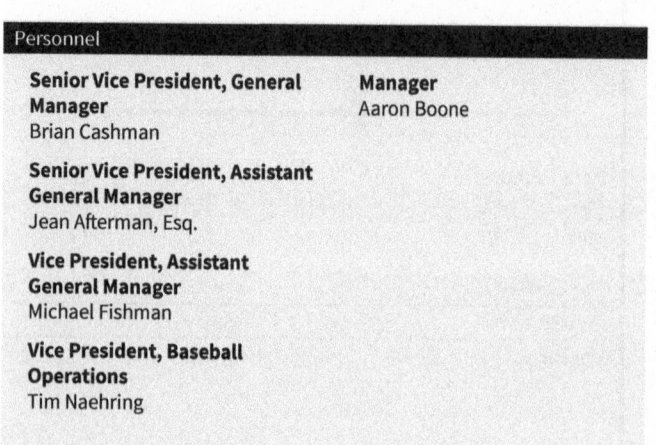

Senior Vice President, General Manager
Brian Cashman

Senior Vice President, Assistant General Manager
Jean Afterman, Esq.

Vice President, Assistant General Manager
Michael Fishman

Vice President, Baseball Operations
Tim Naehring

Manager
Aaron Boone

As much as Cashman might want to talk about unexpected backslides, the 2021 Yankees benefited from some unanticipated boons, too. If someone told you that Aaron Judge and Giancarlo Stanton would be among the top four Yankees in games played, you might have presumed this was a championship season in waiting. In this sense, then, it stands to reason that the flaws of the Yankee lineup might be deeper than a cursory look would show, as neither Judge nor Stanton can be safely assumed to put forth such a combination of health and production in the future.

The two other guys who accrued the most plate appearances, infielders DJ LeMahieu and Gleyber Torres, regressed at the plate. While the clockwork-like LeMahieu's step back neatly fits into Cashman's narrative, Torres' struggles on both sides of the ball were an area of concern well before the season started. The same can be said for catcher Gary Sánchez, who rebounded from a brutal 2020 to post something close to a league-average batting line but wasn't nearly consistent enough with that production to offset his defensive woes.

While players need to perform—a notion Steinbrenner was quick to harp on mid-season—there is also something to be said about the way New York's offense was built. The Yankees entered the season without any semblance of left-handed power despite playing in the equivalent of a port-side masher's candy store. The roster was largely, by the standard of professional athletes, unathletic; the lumbering Yankees also lacked speed (and smarts) on the bases, aside from some mid-season COVID-19 replacements.

While the concerns over the lack of athleticism and the strikeout-heavy lineup were addressed at the deadline by acquiring, respectively, the uber-athletic Joey Gallo (though he can be a windmill at the dish) and the post-stardom, contact-oriented Anthony Rizzo, getting a whole two months of a more-ideal Yankee team was a failure through and through when there was good reason to anticipate the unbalanced nature of the offense. The 2020 iteration of this team was made in a very similar, if not exact, mold. As was the 2019 squad. What's that quote about the definition of insanity again?

Speaking of which, the fielding in the Bronx was enough to drive one to the brink. The Yankees returned roughly the same contingent of fielders after leading the majors in errors in 2020; they improved to fifth-worst in 2021. They also ranked in the bottom third in defensive efficiency on ground balls and fly balls—the only other playoff team for which that was true was their wild-card counterparts in Boston. However, it didn't take a trained eye or a sabermetrician to figure out that the Yankees were losing games in the field.

To Cashman's credit, the Gallo and Rizzo trades improved the team's defense in the outfield and at first, but first base was a known defensive weakness prior to the season, and it wasn't the only one. Torres and Sánchez were the faces of the Yankees' glovework woes the last two years, though they were hardly the only perpetrators. In Sánchez's defense—no pun intended—the Yankees spent the last two seasons tinkering with his stance and prioritizing framing, which is less noticeable to the casual fan than the barrage of pitches that often get by the catcher. But Sánchez's framing skills didn't impress, either, and he was less effective than ever when it came to throwing runners out. The Yankees have been adamant that Sánchez works hard at what they ask him to practice; the results just haven't reflected that.

While many have been sick of hearing about Sánchez's work behind the plate without seeing it pay off, it is at least understandable, from the organization's perspective, why the Yankees were interested in letting it play out. Less comprehensible was the decision to install Torres at shortstop after a disastrous 2020 in the field made it clear he was stretched at the position. There was an apparent toll on his bat, to boot: Torres produced a solid .815 OPS in 19 games at second base in 2021, compared to a .671 mark in 107 games at shortstop. When his defense finally, *mercifully*, became untenable for Boone and the front office, he was banished from short in favor of Gio Urshela. Cashman conceded that Torres was "best served at second base."

The Yankees finally saw the light on Torres, but far too late—his first game at second base didn't come until September 13—and Cashman's mea culpa didn't occur until the year's postmortem. The evidence was in front of them before that and all throughout the season, but the organization was in denial about what it was seeing, though it was clear to anyone else watching. What's unclear is whether anyone has learned a lesson from this beyond not playing Torres at short—as of publication, the Yankees lacked a solution at the position, with only two members of the elite free-agent shortstop class remaining available in Carlos Correa and Trevor Story.

If and when the lockout does end, it's not certain that Steinbrenner will be willing to spend enough to reel them in. Before the lockout, rumors of the Yankees' interest in players like Andrelton Simmons and the Rangers' suddenly superfluous Isiah Kiner-Falefa floated about. Such defense-only stopgaps would be holdovers until talented shortstop prospects Oswald Peraza and Anthony Volpe arrive, but they would more accurately function as a means to avoid spending to the degree that the club can and should.

The Yankees' pitching was quite reliable in 2021. Gerrit Cole, inconsistent by his own standards, fought through the sticky-stuff ban and a late-season hamstring strain and finished second in Cy Young voting. Despite throwing a paltry number of innings over the previous few seasons, Corey Kluber and Jameson Taillon performed reasonably well when healthy, and they were backstopped by career years from Jordan Montgomery and Nestor Cortes. The bullpen faltered at the back with some missteps by Aroldis Chapman, but was lifted by a stellar season from Jonathan Loáisiga. Mid-season pickup Clay Holmes performed admirably, as well.

For all the uncovered gems and successful seasons, however, the Yankees still made several questionable choices when it came to their staff, most notably not protecting minor-league righty Garrett Whitlock in the Rule 5 Draft. He ended up becoming a relief revelation for the rival Red Sox. In and of itself, not a big deal—Rule 5 breakouts happen all the time, and teams can't hit on every single decision—but the choice to leave Whitlock unprotected didn't happen in a vacuum. Some of the pitchers the Yankees *did* protect—most notably Nick Nelson, Brooks Kriske and Albert Abreu—were unreliable at best. Yet, the Yankees repeatedly relied on those pitchers, and often in ill-suited situations. For example, Nelson had the third-highest game-entering leverage index on the team. He finished the year with an 8.79 ERA.

Inexcusable usage wasn't limited to just a few young, in-over-their-head relievers, either. The Andrew Heaney Experiment—*Can a fly-ball/home-run pitcher turn his career around in a band box? Let's find out at the most crucial point in the season!*—was doomed from the start. Chad Green was overused so much at times due to a lack of depth that Aaron Boone made note of it . . . and kept calling on the righty anyway, despite his visible ineffectiveness. There were instances of denial throughout the season, when Boone would insist something along the lines of, "He's throwing the ball really well right now," while one of his pitchers was amidst a stretch of shellings.

While pitching was one of New York's strengths in 2021, there was room for improvement, largely due to a lack of depth and poor evaluations. When the lockout ends, the Yankees will be staring at a dried-up pitching market, and they're down a starter after Kluber signed with the rival Rays. Given the pre-lockout flurry, there are few starting pitchers who can reliably step into the rotation and carry some upside, with Carlos Rodón and Clayton Kershaw, each of whom carry significant health risks, the top remaining names on the free-agent market.

The Yankees chose not to spend at all prior to the expiration of the Collective Bargaining Agreement, once again failing to patch-up their holes in a timely manner. One has to ask whether they have denied themselves the opportunity to make the necessary improvements already, whether the remaining options can rectify the handful of concerns that remain heading into 2022.

A lot of these problems, you'll notice, pertain to roster construction. For all the flak Boone takes—and he has deserved plenty—he has not been responsible for assembling baseball's not-so-mightiest heroes over the last few years.

That task falls on Cashman and a front office that heavily relies on numbers despite an analytics department that clearly isn't keeping up with the competition. The Yankees would probably deny the last two parts of that sentence, but it's no secret that the organization takes a, let's call it, collaborative approach, and that the results haven't been satisfactory.

Cashman and Boone, speaking at the press conference announcing the latter's new three-year contract, pushed back against the public perception that the Yankees' analytics department is overinvolved or even overruling in the team's decision making. The manager used words like "strawman" and "boogeyman" to describe the notion, but you would, too, if your authority on day-to-day decisions was constantly being disputed. There have also been reports[1] of scouts being pushed to the side despite Cashman comparing the organization's variety of information to a "buffet table."

In the modern era, when loads of data is used by every team, these storylines are hardly limited to the Yankees. But, with the franchise enduring its third-longest World Series drought, fans are understandably skeptical of New York's shot-callers, and spectators are asking valid questions about a process that hasn't yielded anything of note.

All these problems, of course, could easily be masked by a $5.25 billion organization.

⚾ ⚾ ⚾

There are multiple ways to win.

The thrifty-but-methodical Rays are the most obvious example, but the uber-rich Yankees don't have to fight on their turf if they don't want to. The Yankees are financial behemoths with the resources to fill holes of any size when needed. They just haven't always done that sufficiently in recent memory, discarding their Evil Empire branding in favor of bargain hunting in many cases. Even the significant upgrades New York made at last summer's trade deadline were careful to keep the team below the dreaded $210-million CBT threshold.

At November's general-manager meetings, Cashman said he expects New York's payroll to increase in 2022, but that was always going to happen due to arbitration raises. New York's pre-lockout activity didn't inspire much confidence, and Cashman also said "mission accomplished" when discussing New York's successful attempt to stay under the CBT threshold in 2021, and thus reset its penalties.

Some years the CBT threshold is a cap, others it's not. But these are the Yankee$. It doesn't ever have to be a mandate if Steinbrenner doesn't want it to be. The Yankees of the past—when George was alive—only had one mission, and it certainly didn't have anything to do with a budget. Those Yankees never worried about financial constraints or keeping title windows open. They simply propped the frame open with a big bag of money. Instead, the 2021 edition had a payroll that, without adjusting for inflation, was very similar to what it was in 2005.

The Dodgers, meanwhile, spent as if they had no idea the CBT even existed last year. While they came up short of another World Series, they went further than the Yankees and had a more-talented roster from the get-go. They happily added to it as the season went on, money be damned. Cashman called the Dodgers "a unicorn" at season's end, but the Rangers spent half a billion on their middle infield before the lockout. The Mets, with Steve Cohen doing his best impression yet of Steinbrenner's father, spent more than $250 million. The Blue Jays spent more than $240 million on their rotation, and the Tigers, Mariners and Twins each handed out one contract worth at least $100 million.

Rather than grow horns, piddle rainbows—or whatever it is unicorns do—and join the wealthy herd, the Yankees re-signed Joely Rodríguez for $2 million. Oh, and Steinbrenner lent his support to lowering the tax threshold.

It used to be, *How will the rest of the league keep up with the Yankees?*—at least financially—but now they're the ones trying to catch up. They haven't been as smart as some of their top competition, and they've let teams that typically have lower budgets outspend them. Choosing to do the latter has only amplified the former; many of the problems addressed in this essay can be fixed, or at least glossed over, with money.

While they'll presumably be back over the luxury tax threshold in 2022, the Yankees denying themselves their superpower in some years has indisputably hurt them—not only on the field, but with their reputation, too. The Yankees simply aren't what they used to be, and it's possible they never will be again as a new baseball landscape takes shape. ■

—Gary Phillips is a writer/editor at New Jersey Monthly *and a contributor to* The New York Times *and* Baseball Prospectus.

1. Erik Boland, "A look at the scouting vs. analytics debate surrounding the Yankees," *Newsday*, July 14, 2021.

HITTERS

Miguel Andújar LF Born: 03/02/95 Age: 27 Bats: R Throws: R Height: 6'0" Weight: 211 lb. Origin: International Free Agent, 2011

YEAR	TEAM	LVL	AGE	PA	R	2B	3B	HR	RBI	BB	K	SB	CS	Whiff%	AVG/OBP/SLG	DRC+	BABIP	BRR	FRAA	WARP
2019	NYY	MLB	24	49	1	0	0	0	1	1	11	0	0	30.9%	.128/.143/.128	78	.162	0.2	3B(4): -0.9	-0.1
2020	NYY	MLB	25	65	5	2	1	1	5	3	9	0	0	22.1%	.242/.277/.355	103	.269	0.5	LF(7): -1.5, 3B(6): -0.4	0.0
2021	SWB	AAA	26	63	13	1	0	5	13	7	6	0	0		.333/.397/.630	138	.289	-0.2	LF(11): -1.1, 1B(3): -0.1, 3B(1): -0.0	0.3
2021	NYY	MLB	26	162	19	2	0	6	12	7	28	0	1	19.3%	.253/.284/.383	103	.273	-0.6	LF(37): 0.3, 3B(4): -0.1	0.6
2022 DC	*NYY*	*MLB*	*27*	*339*	*47*	*13*	*1*	*11*	*55*	*18*	*53*	*1*	*1*	*20.9%*	*.265/.311/.422*	*99*	*.288*	*-0.3*	*1B -1, LF 0*	*0.6*

Comparables: Jeimer Candelario, Brandon Drury, Gio Urshela

If the 2018 Yankees were a sitcom, Andújar was the starring child actor. Long gone are the days when he dazzled audiences enough to steal a handful of first-place Rookie of the Year votes from Shohei Ohtani. In the three years since the show ended, he played just 78 games, and while DRC+ likes his production more than other metrics, eventually the league will realize he can only hit fastballs. That might be manageable if he was a defensive wiz at an up-the-middle position rather than a disaster at third base and left field. His outfield routes cost him 1.3 feet compared to MLB average—tied for 186th out of 193 outfielders. With a slumbering bat, lumbering glove and encumbering injuries, he must answer the question so many child actors cannot: *Now what?*

Jay Bruce RF

Born: 04/03/87 Age: 35 Bats: L Throws: L Height: 6'3" Weight: 230 lb. Origin: Round 1, 2005 Draft (#12 overall)

YEAR	TEAM	LVL	AGE	PA	R	2B	3B	HR	RBI	BB	K	SB	CS	Whiff%	AVG/OBP/SLG	DRC+	BABIP	BRR	FRAA	WARP
2019	SEA	MLB	32	184	27	11	0	14	28	16	53	1	0	31.5%	.212/.283/.533	103	.210	0.9	RF(24): -1.5, 1B(16): 0.5, LF(6): 2.7	0.9
2019	PHI	MLB	32	149	16	6	0	12	31	3	29	0	0	29.6%	.221/.235/.510	107	.190	0.1	LF(31): 4.1	1.1
2020	PHI	MLB	33	103	11	4	2	6	14	7	24	0	0	29.1%	.198/.252/.469	92	.197	-1.0	LF(11): 1.0, RF(6): 1.1, 1B(2): -0.2	0.3
2021	NYY	MLB	34	39	3	1	0	1	3	5	13	0	0	36.2%	.118/.231/.235	75	.150	0.0	1B(10): 0.9	0.1
2022 non-DC	*NYY*	*MLB*	*35*	*251*	*28*	*10*	*0*	*10*	*32*	*22*	*66*	*0*	*1*	*31.8%*	*.218/.292/.413*	*85*	*.259*	*-0.2*	*LF 1, RF -1*	*0.2*

Comparables: Darryl Strawberry, Dwight Evans, Bobby Abreu

It became clear that Bruce was Dancing in the Dark as a first baseman when his failed scoop of a Gleyber Torres throw cost the Yankees a game against Baltimore on April 7. His bat speed was on a Downbound Train and he seemed Blinded by the Light against breaking balls. He may have been Born to Run when he was younger, but years of injuries made his legs scream, "I'm On Fire." By the middle of April, it was evident he could no longer Prove It All Night. Glory Days—they'll pass you by.

Jasson Dominguez CF

Born: 02/07/03 Age: 19 Bats: S Throws: R Height: 5'10" Weight: 190 lb. Origin: International Free Agent, 2019

YEAR	TEAM	LVL	AGE	PA	R	2B	3B	HR	RBI	BB	K	SB	CS	Whiff%	AVG/OBP/SLG	DRC+	BABIP	BRR	FRAA	WARP
2021	YNK	ROK	18	27	5	0	0	0	1	6	6	2	0		.200/.407/.200		.286			
2021	TAM	A	18	214	26	9	1	5	18	21	67	7	3		.258/.346/.398	88	.371	0.2	CF(38): -4.4	0.1
2022 non-DC	*NYY*	*MLB*	*19*	*251*	*19*	*10*	*1*	*3*	*20*	*16*	*89*	*4*	*2*	*36.6%*	*.201/.261/.297*	*50*	*.313*	*0.3*	*CF -2*	*-0.9*

Comparables: Luigi Rodriguez, Connor Scott, Jahmai Jones

The best part of a roller coaster ride is the slow climb: The butterflies in your stomach fluttering with increasing fervor at each click of the track. Excitement crescendos as you approach the top, swelling with anticipation like a water balloon until all at once gravity takes hold and...

That's the point at which all roller coasters vary. Sometimes, the loops and twists thrill you; other times, they just roll around for a while and the ride ends sooner than you would like. The biggest challenge of any ride is to match the cacophony of emotion it builds on the way to the top.

Dominguez's coaster ascended higher than any other in the park. His thunderously loud tools and inflated baseball card prices earned lofty comparisons to Mike Trout and Mickey Mantle before he ever played a professional game. Now, his ride has begun in earnest and the first turn was...well, it didn't exactly make anyone throw his hands in the air. He's only 19 with plenty of loops ahead, but he has a lot of work to do to justify the buildup.

Joey Gallo OF

Born: 11/19/93 Age: 28 Bats: L Throws: R Height: 6'5" Weight: 250 lb. Origin: Round 1, 2012 Draft (#39 overall)

YEAR	TEAM	LVL	AGE	PA	R	2B	3B	HR	RBI	BB	K	SB	CS	Whiff%	AVG/OBP/SLG	DRC+	BABIP	BRR	FRAA	WARP
2019	TEX	MLB	25	297	54	15	1	22	49	52	114	4	2	41.4%	.253/.389/.598	114	.368	1.6	CF(38): 0.9, LF(34): 4.4	2.3
2020	TEX	MLB	26	226	23	8	0	10	26	29	79	2	0	37.5%	.181/.301/.378	77	.240	2.3	RF(53): 6.6, CF(1): -0.0	0.9
2021	TEX	MLB	27	388	57	6	1	25	55	74	125	6	0	39.3%	.223/.379/.490	122	.275	-0.3	RF(83): 13.1	3.5
2021	NYY	MLB	27	228	33	7	0	13	22	37	88	0	0	38.8%	.160/.303/.404	81	.193	1.0	LF(51): 1.6, RF(9): -0.5	0.5
2022 DC	*NYY*	*MLB*	*28*	*581*	*96*	*20*	*1*	*35*	*96*	*96*	*195*	*6*	*2*	*38.2%*	*.209/.351/.477*	*113*	*.264*	*-0.2*	*LF 6*	*3.6*

Comparables: Reggie Jackson, Adam Dunn, Billy Williams

In the culminating battle of *Avengers: Endgame*, Thor had to choose between his new monstrous ax and his customary hammer. He told Captain America to take "the little one," as he tossed him Mjölnir. Gallo became "the little one" in the same sense when he joined Aaron Judge and Giancarlo Stanton in the Yankee outfield, yet he remains just as powerful of a weapon. He finally led the league in two of the Three True Outcomes—which was more inevitable than Thanos—and finished ninth in the third category (home runs). His production lagged after the trade from Texas, but as the lone lefty in the Gallo/Judge/LeMahieu/Sánchez/Stanton gauntlet, he remains a crucial Infinity Stone heading into 2022.

Aaron Hicks CF

Born: 10/02/89 Age: 32 Bats: S Throws: R Height: 6'1" Weight: 205 lb. Origin: Round 1, 2008 Draft (#14 overall)

YEAR	TEAM	LVL	AGE	PA	R	2B	3B	HR	RBI	BB	K	SB	CS	Whiff%	AVG/OBP/SLG	DRC+	BABIP	BRR	FRAA	WARP
2019	NYY	MLB	29	255	41	10	0	12	36	31	72	1	2	31.7%	.235/.325/.443	96	.286	0.1	CF(58): -6.7	0.3
2020	NYY	MLB	30	211	28	10	2	6	21	41	38	4	1	27.9%	.225/.379/.414	118	.256	0.8	CF(50): 0.4	1.3
2021	NYY	MLB	31	126	13	3	0	4	14	14	30	0	0	29.6%	.194/.294/.333	92	.224	0.7	CF(32): -1.6	0.3
2022 DC	*NYY*	*MLB*	*32*	*437*	*65*	*17*	*1*	*16*	*58*	*64*	*100*	*7*	*3*	*28.5%*	*.229/.348/.413*	*106*	*.272*	*0.1*	*CF -2*	*1.8*

Comparables: Jim Landis, Dexter Fowler, Dwayne Murphy

Joseph Hicks reached Double-A before an errant pitch shattered his left orbital, derailing his career. He never wanted his son to follow in his footsteps, encouraging him to pursue golf instead. Naturally, telling your children not to do something is the most sure-fire way to get them to do it. Baseball worked out much better for Aaron than Joseph, but since signing a seven-year extension prior to the 2019 season, he's suffered two season-ending injuries in three years: a right flexor strain in 2019 and a torn tendon sheath in his left wrist in 2021, both requiring surgery. This begs two questions: 1) Do golfers ever tear their tendon sheaths? 2) Is there an expiration date on a parental "I told you so?"

Kyle Higashioka C Born: 04/20/90 Age: 32 Bats: R Throws: R Height: 6'1" Weight: 202 lb. Origin: Round 7, 2008 Draft (#230 overall)

YEAR	TEAM	LVL	AGE	PA	R	2B	3B	HR	RBI	BB	K	SB	CS	Whiff%	AVG/OBP/SLG	DRC+	BABIP	BRR	FRAA	WARP
2019	SWB	AAA	29	270	42	13	0	20	56	24	53	0	0		.278/.348/.581	127	.276	-3.3	C(64): 15.3	3.1
2019	NYY	MLB	29	57	8	5	0	3	11	0	26	0	0	28.5%	.214/.211/.464	55	.321	0.5	C(18): 3.0	0.3
2020	NYY	MLB	30	48	7	1	0	4	10	0	11	0	0	23.2%	.250/.250/.521	106	.242	-0.1	C(14): 2.0	0.4
2021	NYY	MLB	31	211	20	10	0	10	29	17	59	0	0	31.0%	.181/.246/.389	87	.200	-1.1	C(66): 8.1	1.3
2022 DC	*NYY*	*MLB*	*32*	*180*	*24*	*7*	*0*	*7*	*34*	*13*	*49*	*0*	*0*	*29.6%*	*.211/.273/.392*	*74*	*.253*	*-0.3*	*C 8*	*1.0*

Comparables: Carlos Corporán, Robinson Chirinos, Sandy León

YEAR	TEAM	P. COUNT	FRM RUNS	BLK RUNS	THRW RUNS	TOT RUNS
2019	SWB	9097	15.2	0.0	0.1	15.2
2019	NYY	2271	2.4	0.0	0.4	2.8
2020	NYY	1794	2.0	0.0	0.0	2.0
2021	NYY	8429	7.7	0.2	0.1	8.1
2022	*NYY*	*7215*	*6.4*	*0.3*	*-0.1*	*6.7*

The Higashioka Method can transform anyone into a beloved backup catcher in four steps:

1. *Play better defense than the starter.* Higgy's 7.0 CDA was ninth-best in MLB in 2021.
2. *Hit a home run every now and then, sometimes more than once in a game.* He only collects about six hits per month, but 10 of them cleared the fence in 2021. He doesn't make contact often, so when he does it has to be memorable.
3. *Become someone's personal catcher.* Gerrit Cole is loath to throw to anyone else.
4. *Don't play well enough to supplant the starter.* His .234 career OBP ensures he plays sparingly. There's a thin line between "beloved backup" and "reviled starter," and too much exposure would push him across it.

Ender Inciarte CF Born: 10/29/90 Age: 31 Bats: L Throws: L Height: 5'11" Weight: 190 lb. Origin: International Free Agent, 2008

YEAR	TEAM	LVL	AGE	PA	R	2B	3B	HR	RBI	BB	K	SB	CS	Whiff%	AVG/OBP/SLG	DRC+	BABIP	BRR	FRAA	WARP
2019	GWN	AAA	28	30	5	1	0	0	1	4	3	0	1		.231/.333/.269	104	.261	0.4	CF(5): 0.1	0.2
2019	ATL	MLB	28	230	30	11	2	5	24	26	41	7	1	20.6%	.246/.343/.397	99	.286	0.4	CF(63): 5.0	1.5
2020	ATL	MLB	29	131	17	2	1	1	10	12	25	4	1	23.9%	.190/.262/.250	78	.228	-1.7	CF(46): -5.5	-0.7
2021	LOU	AAA	30	65	7	3	0	0	7	6	10	0	1		.288/.354/.339	102	.347	0.9	CF(11): 2.6, RF(3): -0.5, LF(1): -0.3	0.5
2021	ATL	MLB	30	89	11	2	0	2	10	7	22	1	0	19.7%	.215/.276/.316	83	.268	0.1	CF(37): 2.0, LF(4): -0.3	0.4
2022 DC	*FA*	*MLB*	*31*	*207*	*17*	*7*	*1*	*2*	*17*	*18*	*37*	*5*	*3*	*19.9%*	*.228/.303/.316*	*70*	*.275*	*0.4*	*CF 1, RF 0*	*0.1*

Comparables: Mark Kotsay, Omar Moreno, Richie Ashburn

You can't help but feel bad for a player like Inciarte, who served six seasons in Atlanta before getting unceremoniously released in July, just three months ahead of the team's first World Series victory in 26 years. The Braves' summer outfield shuffle ensured there wouldn't be any room left for Inciarte, whose anemic bat and fading defensive prowess had already been eating into his playing time for a couple years. He then signed with the Reds, hung out for a couple weeks in Louisville and was released again by the end of August. Inciarte may have missed out on the on-field championship celebration with his old teammates, but he will get a ring, and a chance to rest his tattered hamstrings. The Yankees signed him to a minor-league deal in December.

Aaron Judge RF Born: 04/26/92 Age: 30 Bats: R Throws: R Height: 6'7" Weight: 282 lb. Origin: Round 1, 2013 Draft (#32 overall)

YEAR	TEAM	LVL	AGE	PA	R	2B	3B	HR	RBI	BB	K	SB	CS	Whiff%	AVG/OBP/SLG	DRC+	BABIP	BRR	FRAA	WARP
2019	NYY	MLB	27	447	75	18	1	27	55	64	141	3	2	36.7%	.272/.381/.540	114	.360	-0.1	RF(92): 7.7	2.8
2020	NYY	MLB	28	114	23	3	0	9	22	10	32	0	1	33.5%	.257/.336/.554	112	.283	0.3	RF(25): 2.7	0.8
2021	NYY	MLB	29	633	89	24	0	39	98	75	158	6	1	29.2%	.287/.373/.544	135	.332	-3.6	RF(114): 8.2, CF(23): -0.9	5.0
2022 DC	*NYY*	*MLB*	*30*	*574*	*109*	*21*	*1*	*31*	*94*	*69*	*139*	*5*	*3*	*29.8%*	*.272/.365/.508*	*133*	*.316*	*-0.4*	*RF 1, CF -2*	*4.1*

Comparables: Roberto Clemente, Dwight Evans, Sammy Sosa

There have only been six Yankee captains in the past 50 years, and they waited an average of 10.2 seasons before earning that title. It takes about a decade to establish oneself as the undisputed leader on and off the field—including consistent greatness over the course of several years, individual clutch moments, leadership in the locker room, overwhelming fan appeal and general charisma both in front of and away from the cameras. They uphold the legacy of solemn, stoic professionalism passed down from Lou Gehrig.

2022 will be Judge's seventh season. He's inarguably the best position player on the roster as well as a fan favorite. In 2021, to add to his progression at the plate, he took on more of a leadership role than ever before, calling a players-only meeting to snap a losing streak and counseling a teammate who failed to run out a groundball. He ended the regular season with a ninth-inning, walk-off single to defeat Tampa Bay 1-0, clinching a Wild Card berth.

Judge is not the captain of the Yankees—at least not officially—but we all know better.

DJ LeMahieu IF Born: 07/13/88 Age: 33 Bats: R Throws: R Height: 6'4" Weight: 220 lb. Origin: Round 2, 2009 Draft (#79 overall)

YEAR	TEAM	LVL	AGE	PA	R	2B	3B	HR	RBI	BB	K	SB	CS	Whiff%	AVG/OBP/SLG	DRC+	BABIP	BRR	FRAA	WARP
2019	NYY	MLB	30	655	109	33	2	26	102	46	90	5	2	16.0%	.327/.375/.518	122	.349	-2.3	2B(75): 4.2, 3B(52): 0.8, 1B(40): 1.4	4.4
2020	NYY	MLB	31	216	41	10	2	10	27	18	21	3	0	11.2%	.364/.421/.590	146	.370	-0.1	2B(37): 4.8, 1B(11): -0.3, 3B(11): -0.2	2.3
2021	NYY	MLB	32	679	84	24	1	10	57	73	94	4	2	14.3%	.268/.349/.362	106	.301	-1.4	2B(83): 1.7, 1B(55): 1.0, 3B(39): 0.5	2.8
2022 DC	*NYY*	*MLB*	*33*	*663*	*113*	*26*	*1*	*14*	*69*	*65*	*86*	*6*	*3*	*14.2%*	*.281/.356/.406*	*109*	*.307*	*-0.5*	*3B 1, 2B 0*	*2.9*

Comparables: Dustin Pedroia, Roberto Alomar, Steve Sax

There's a huge difference between hitting 'em where they ain't, and simply making contact. The 2021 version of LeMahieu could merely put the bat on the ball. His contact rate remained superb, only dropping from 89.9% to 87.6%, and his hard-hit rate of 43.5% was still eight points above MLB average. Nevertheless, pitches he regularly used to deposit onto the right-field lawn—or into the seats—became easy putouts. Some of that can be attributed to bad luck, good defense and the dejuiced baseball, but his 40-point drop in DRC+ from 2020 to 2021 was the most in MLB by any player who qualified for the batting title in both seasons (which he won in 2020). He saw 264 called strikes on pitches in the heart of the strike zone as defined by Statcast, tied for the most in MLB. It all combined to make him a solid overall player with versatile defense, but the Yankees didn't sign him through 2026 to be just solid. It may be time for LeMahieu to take a more aggressive approach at the plate, and use an adjustment to force his opponents into making an adjustment.

★ ★ ★ *2022 Top 101 Prospect* **#61** ★ ★ ★

Oswald Peraza SS

Born: 06/15/00 Age: 22 Bats: R Throws: R Height: 6'0" Weight: 165 lb. Origin: International Free Agent, 2016

YEAR	TEAM	LVL	AGE	PA	R	2B	3B	HR	RBI	BB	K	SB	CS	Whiff%	AVG/OBP/SLG	DRC+	BABIP	BRR	FRAA	WARP
2019	SI	SS	19	85	7	1	1	2	7	5	9	5	2		.241/.294/.354		.250			
2019	CSC	A	19	208	31	5	0	2	13	16	28	18	5		.273/.348/.333	108	.310	1.5	SS(44): 0.3	1.0
2021	HV	A+	21	127	20	10	0	5	16	12	24	16	1		.306/.386/.532	127	.349	1.0	SS(25): 4.9	1.4
2021	SOM	AA	21	353	51	16	2	12	40	23	82	20	8		.294/.348/.466	102	.362	-2.2	SS(69): -2.7	0.7
2021	SWB	AAA	21	31	5	0	0	1	2	2	5	2	1		.286/.323/.393	98	.304	-0.3	SS(7): 1.5	0.2
2022 DC	*NYY*	*MLB*	*22*	*195*	*24*	*7*	*0*	*3*	*24*	*12*	*46*	*8*	*3*	*28.6%*	*.248/.302/.358*	*80*	*.312*	*0.6*	*SS 0, 2B 0*	*0.3*

Comparables: Eugenio Suárez, Junior Lake, Willi Castro

Peraza is the person in your friend group who stays a few steps ahead of everyone else: Two minutes after someone in the group chat proposes a weekend getaway, he's already got the meal itinerary planned out. In 2021, he rocketed through the highest three minor-league levels and was the youngest player on both Double-A Somerset and Triple-A Scranton/Wilkes-Barre. He added the fifth tool (power) to the other four he already possessed, even if it and the hit tool are really just duct tape. He's always been an above-average defensive shortstop, but now he might not hit ninth when he makes the majors. Peraza's one of the most well-rounded prospects in baseball, and there's a good chance he'll shed that "prospect" label ahead of schedule too.

Gary Sánchez C

Born: 12/02/92 Age: 29 Bats: R Throws: R Height: 6'2" Weight: 230 lb. Origin: International Free Agent, 2009

YEAR	TEAM	LVL	AGE	PA	R	2B	3B	HR	RBI	BB	K	SB	CS	Whiff%	AVG/OBP/SLG	DRC+	BABIP	BRR	FRAA	WARP
2019	NYY	MLB	26	446	62	12	1	34	77	40	125	0	1	32.0%	.232/.316/.525	115	.244	-2.2	C(90): -6.8	1.8
2020	TOR	WIN	27	62	5	4	0	2	10	6	19	0	0		.245/.355/.434		.344			
2020	NYY	MLB	27	178	19	4	0	10	24	18	64	0	0	34.0%	.147/.253/.365	88	.159	-0.8	C(41): -1.3	0.1
2021	NYY	MLB	28	440	54	13	1	23	54	52	121	0	0	29.4%	.204/.307/.423	108	.230	-1.0	C(110): -2.9	1.9
2022 DC	*NYY*	*MLB*	*29*	*475*	*73*	*15*	*0*	*24*	*79*	*51*	*124*	*0*	*1*	*30.0%*	*.214/.310/.435*	*100*	*.239*	*-0.7*	*C -1*	*2.0*

Comparables: Jim Pagliaroni, Bill Freehan, Matt Wieters

YEAR	TEAM	P. COUNT	FRM RUNS	BLK RUNS	THRW RUNS	TOT RUNS
2019	NYY	12715	-7.7	-0.2	1.5	-6.4
2020	NYY	5546	-0.3	-0.1	-0.2	-0.7
2021	NYY	14761	-1.7	-1.6	0.2	-3.1
2022	*NYY*	*16835*	*-3.6*	*-2.6*	*-0.2*	*-6.3*

It's the oldest trick in the *Manual of Twin Hijinks,* and we bought it hook, line and sinker. Ever since they signed with the Yankees as teenagers back in 2009, the Sánchez brothers have been baseball's Mary Kate and Ashley: two twins taking turns pretending to be the same person. Once we learned their secret, telling them apart was obvious. The Good Gary went 29-for-107 with 14 walks and nine home runs from May 27-June 30. The Bad Gary was worth -23 runs on pitches over the heart and shadow of the strike zone (according to Statcast's swing-take profile) and continued to suffer inexplicable defensive lapses, which his framing no longer negates. Unfortunately, the Yankees aren't a 90s sitcom dad, and they're getting tired of not being able to rely on Good Gary to show up when they need him. Even though the wrong brother played more often in 2021, the Garys' combined WARP was tied for 11th in MLB among catchers. The club has little choice but to put up with the shenanigans; there aren't many better options around.

Giancarlo Stanton DH

Born: 11/08/89 Age: 32 Bats: R Throws: R Height: 6'6" Weight: 245 lb. Origin: Round 2, 2007 Draft (#76 overall)

YEAR	TEAM	LVL	AGE	PA	R	2B	3B	HR	RBI	BB	K	SB	CS	Whiff%	AVG/OBP/SLG	DRC+	BABIP	BRR	FRAA	WARP
2019	NYY	MLB	29	72	8	3	0	3	13	12	24	0	0	34.1%	.288/.403/.492	89	.424	-0.4	LF(10): -1.2, RF(3): -0.2	-0.1
2020	NYY	MLB	30	94	12	7	0	4	11	15	27	1	1	32.7%	.250/.387/.500	100	.333	-0.1		0.2
2021	NYY	MLB	31	579	64	19	0	35	97	63	157	0	0	32.8%	.273/.354/.516	131	.324	-0.9	RF(16): -0.8, LF(10): 0.9	3.6
2022 DC	*NYY*	*MLB*	*32*	*542*	*94*	*20*	*0*	*32*	*100*	*62*	*145*	*1*	*1*	*32.4%*	*.258/.349/.513*	*128*	*.301*	*-0.8*	*RF -1*	*3.1*

Comparables: Dwight Evans, Jack Clark, Hank Aaron

In a sense, Stanton possesses the best bat control in baseball. Other players may be more adept at merely making contact—if you're into that kind of thing—but no one else can unleash such fearsome might in every swing and still connect at all. Since 2019, only two players in MLB have achieved greater than 119-mph exit velocity on a batted ball. He's done it 12 times—despite missing most of 2019 and 2020 with injuries—while only Manny Machado could accomplish it even once. Controlling the unbridled ferocity of his swing requires the utmost precision, which is why he's prone to ugly slumps when he gets slightly out of sync. This is magnified by his net-negative baserunning and defense (when he plays the field at all), but when he's rolling, he can power the Yankees single handedly for weeks at a time.

Trey Sweeney SS Born: 04/24/00 Age: 22 Bats: L Throws: R Height: 6'4" Weight: 200 lb. Origin: Round 1, 2021 Draft (#20 overall)

YEAR	TEAM	LVL	AGE	PA	R	2B	3B	HR	RBI	BB	K	SB	CS	Whiff%	AVG/OBP/SLG	DRC+	BABIP	BRR	FRAA	WARP
2021	TAM	A	21	129	26	4	4	6	13	18	29	3	1		.245/.357/.518	119	.280	1.3	SS(25): 0.3	0.8
2022 non-DC	*NYY*	*MLB*	*22*	*251*	*22*	*10*	*2*	*4*	*24*	*20*	*58*	*2*	*2*	*24.3%*	*.219/.290/.352*	*75*	*.273*	*0.4*	*SS 1*	*0.3*

Comparables: Brandon Hicks, Jeremiah Jackson, Darnell Sweeney

As a small school, cold weather shortstop who would never stick at the position, with a chaotic swing approach, you could understand why the scouts were all over the map with Sweeney. Has he ever seen a real fastball? Has he ever faced a lefty who could throw a slider that hit the dodge button halfway to the plate? Reports of superlative exit velocities at Eastern Illinois, and a mere 13% whiff rate, told a different tale. The Yankees were comfortable enough to take him with the 20th pick, and so far, he's done nothing to betray that trust. He has the arm strength and power (and footspeed) to make him a good third baseman, if and when the time comes.

Gleyber Torres SS Born: 12/13/96 Age: 25 Bats: R Throws: R Height: 6'1" Weight: 205 lb. Origin: International Free Agent, 2013

YEAR	TEAM	LVL	AGE	PA	R	2B	3B	HR	RBI	BB	K	SB	CS	Whiff%	AVG/OBP/SLG	DRC+	BABIP	BRR	FRAA	WARP
2019	NYY	MLB	22	604	96	26	0	38	90	48	129	5	2	27.9%	.278/.337/.535	118	.296	-0.9	SS(77): -2.0, 2B(65): -0.7	3.3
2020	NYY	MLB	23	160	17	8	0	3	16	22	28	1	0	28.0%	.243/.356/.368	108	.286	0.2	SS(40): -0.3	0.6
2021	NYY	MLB	24	516	50	22	0	9	51	50	104	14	6	26.3%	.259/.331/.366	96	.314	1.0	SS(108): -3.4, 2B(19): -1.1	1.2
2022 DC	*NYY*	*MLB*	*25*	*563*	*82*	*22*	*1*	*19*	*81*	*57*	*110*	*9*	*4*	*26.1%*	*.265/.344/.435*	*111*	*.303*	*0.0*	*2B -2, SS 0*	*2.7*

Comparables: Ketel Marte, Wilmer Flores, Carlos Correa

John Sterling's signature home run calls evolve over time. For Torres, his standard "Gleyber Day" call featured an addendum in 2021: "Boy, he really needed that one!" Each of his nine blasts represented an unreasonable expectation that everything would be back to normal from now on—*this one* would get him going again. The deadened ball clearly worked against his cause. In 2019, 22 of the 72 balls he hit with a 100-105 mph exit velocity left the yard. In 2021, only three of the 44 balls he hit that hard cleared the fence. Flunking out of the shortstop position compounded matters, compelling a flustered Aaron Boone to shuffle half the defensive lineup to make room for him at second. A miniature hot streak after the switch gave cause for optimism. You see, *that* was the *real* cause of his hitting troubles, so everything will be fine going forward, right?

Gio Urshela 3B Born: 10/11/91 Age: 30 Bats: R Throws: R Height: 6'0" Weight: 215 lb. Origin: International Free Agent, 2008

YEAR	TEAM	LVL	AGE	PA	R	2B	3B	HR	RBI	BB	K	SB	CS	Whiff%	AVG/OBP/SLG	DRC+	BABIP	BRR	FRAA	WARP
2019	NYY	MLB	27	476	73	34	0	21	74	25	87	1	1	22.2%	.314/.355/.534	116	.349	-1.6	3B(123): 6.0, 1B(1): 0.0, LF(1): 0.0	2.6
2020	NYY	MLB	28	174	24	11	0	6	30	18	25	1	0	20.3%	.298/.368/.490	123	.315	-0.6	3B(43): 7.3	1.6
2021	NYY	MLB	29	442	42	18	2	14	49	20	109	1	0	25.1%	.267/.301/.419	93	.329	-3.1	3B(96): 3.1, SS(28): -1.4	1.0
2022 DC	*NYY*	*MLB*	*30*	*511*	*66*	*22*	*1*	*13*	*73*	*31*	*105*	*0*	*1*	*24.1%*	*.253/.304/.393*	*88*	*.298*	*-0.8*	*SS -5, 3B 0*	*0.5*

Comparables: Marwin Gonzalez, Andy LaRoche, Mike Moustakas

Urshela was somewhat obscured among the detritus by so many of his broken and deflated teammates, but he malfunctioned offensively all the same. His ground-ball, line-drive, strikeout and walk rates all took enormous turns in the wrong directions. His patience and overall pitch recognition diminished, causing him to fall behind in counts more often. As a result, opposing pitchers fed him more breaking balls, on which his wOBA dropped from .367 to .256. Learning to play a bit of shortstop was a nifty trick, but if he doesn't repair his approach at the plate he won't receive much playing time at any position at all. His best hope is that the last and lasting memory of his season, a headfirst plunging catch into the dugout in the Wild Card Game, papers over those first 100 words in this comment.

Luke Voit 1B Born: 02/13/91 Age: 31 Bats: R Throws: R Height: 6'3" Weight: 255 lb. Origin: Round 22, 2013 Draft (#665 overall)

YEAR	TEAM	LVL	AGE	PA	R	2B	3B	HR	RBI	BB	K	SB	CS	Whiff%	AVG/OBP/SLG	DRC+	BABIP	BRR	FRAA	WARP
2019	NYY	MLB	28	510	72	21	1	21	62	71	142	0	0	35.2%	.263/.378/.464	108	.345	-2.9	1B(83): -4.0	1.2
2020	NYY	MLB	29	234	41	5	0	22	52	17	54	0	0	27.6%	.277/.338/.610	144	.268	-0.4	1B(48): -1.2	1.6
2021	SWB	AAA	30	36	8	3	0	4	9	3	8	0	0		.344/.417/.813	125	.350	-0.2	1B(6): -0.2	0.2
2021	NYY	MLB	30	241	26	7	1	11	35	21	74	0	0	40.5%	.239/.328/.437	95	.313	-1.3	1B(42): -1.3	0.1
2022 DC	*NYY*	*MLB*	*31*	*547*	*89*	*20*	*1*	*25*	*81*	*53*	*165*	*0*	*0*	*36.7%*	*.246/.334/.453*	*110*	*.319*	*-0.8*	*1B -1*	*1.7*

Comparables: Steve Pearce, Justin Bour, Darin Ruf

The story of Voit's 2021 season is *A Tale of Two Frustrations*, and he resembled two separate Dickensian characters indeed. The first was Tiny Tim, or maybe Tiny Tim's beefed-out older brother. Three separate IL stints—including meniscus surgery at the end of March—limited him to just 29 games and three home runs through the first four months. By the time he finally got his legs under him in August, he was jilted at the altar like Miss Havisham—or maybe Miss Havisham's beefed-out younger brother. The trade deadline addition of Anthony Rizzo relegated him to part-time DH/pinch-hitting duties for the final quarter of the season. Even though he reestablished himself as one of the better hitters on the team, he only started seven times in a 19-game stretch from August 23-September 12. Surely he didn't expect to beg for second helpings of gruel just a year after leading MLB in home runs. Alas, 2021 was nearer to the worst of times than the best of times.

★ ★ ★ *2022 Top 101 Prospect* **#14** ★ ★ ★

Anthony Volpe SS Born: 04/28/01 Age: 21 Bats: R Throws: R Height: 5'11" Weight: 180 lb. Origin: Round 1, 2019 Draft (#30 overall)

YEAR	TEAM	LVL	AGE	PA	R	2B	3B	HR	RBI	BB	K	SB	CS	Whiff%	AVG/OBP/SLG	DRC+	BABIP	BRR	FRAA	WARP
2019	PUL	ROA	18	150	19	7	2	2	11	23	38	6	1		.215/.349/.355		.289			
2021	TAM	A	20	257	56	18	5	12	49	51	43	21	5		.302/.455/.623	153	.331	0.4	SS(40): -1.2, 3B(3): -0.3, 2B(1): 0.1	2.3
2021	HV	A+	20	256	57	17	1	15	37	27	58	12	4		.286/.391/.587	132	.319	0.8	SS(45): 0.8, 2B(1): -0.1	1.9
2022 non-DC	*NYY*	*MLB*	*21*	*251*	*26*	*12*	*2*	*6*	*28*	*25*	*56*	*9*	*3*	*24.5%*	*.234/.326/.405*	*98*	*.283*	*0.8*	*SS 0, 3B 0*	*1.0*

Comparables: Yairo Muñoz, Yamaico Navarro, Johan Camargo

You're already in love with Volpe, even if you don't know it yet. He hits all of your prospect hot spots: He's a homegrown Yankee, not just because he was their 2019 first-round pick, but because he was born and raised as a Yankees fan in New Jersey and Manhattan. He's already a USA gold medalist in the Pan American Games. Naturally, he grew up idolizing and emulating Derek Jeter— who didn't?— and now plays the six spot. Even if he might slide over to second base sooner or later, he absolutely *rakes* at any position. His combined 144 DRC+ in 2021 ranked in the top 10 among all players at every level of affiliated baseball (min. 250 PA) and he was one of only three minor leaguers with at least 25 homers and 25 steals. By now, you're probably scribbling his name in a notebook surrounded by little hearts with Cupid arrows. Don't worry, the Yankees are head-over-heels too, refusing to discuss him in trade conversations at the July deadline. Volpe and the Yankees, sitting in a tree...

PITCHERS

Albert Abreu RHP Born: 09/26/95 Age: 26 Bats: R Throws: R Height: 6'2" Weight: 190 lb. Origin: International Free Agent, 2013

YEAR	TEAM	LVL	AGE	W	L	SV	G	GS	IP	H	HR	BB/9	K/9	K	GB%	BABIP	WHIP	ERA	DRA-	WARP	MPH	FB%	Whiff%	CSP
2019	TRN	AA	23	5	8	0	23	20	96^{2}	103	9	4.9	8.5	91	41.2%	.339	1.61	4.28	121	-0.3				
2020	NYY	MLB	24	0	1	0	2	0	1^{1}	4	1	13.5	13.5	2	33.3%	.600	4.50	20.25	156	0.0	96.7	51.2%	33.3%	40.9%
2021	SWB	AAA	25	1	0	2	10	0	16^{2}	10	0	5.9	16.7	31	48.3%	.345	1.26	3.78	69	0.5				
2021	NYY	MLB	25	2	0	1	28	0	36^{2}	27	8	4.7	8.6	35	45.5%	.209	1.25	5.15	116	0.0	98.0	49.1%	26.8%	51.7%
2022 DC	*NYY*	*MLB*	*26*	*2*	*3*	*0*	*59*	*0*	*51.7*	*45*	*7*	*5.2*	*10.6*	*61*	*43.2%*	*.293*	*1.46*	*4.82*	*108*	*0.0*	*98.0*	*49.2%*	*27.0%*	*51.2%*

Comparables: Jandel Gustave, Carlos Contreras, Dan Smith

When a guy has great stuff, but can't locate enough, that's Abreu
When he throws 99, with a slider that's fine, that's Abreu
When he gives up few hits, but his walk rate is pits, that's Abreu
By improving command, he'd be better than grand, that's Abreu!

Zack Britton LHP Born: 12/22/87 Age: 34 Bats: L Throws: L Height: 6'1" Weight: 200 lb. Origin: Round 3, 2006 Draft (#85 overall)

YEAR	TEAM	LVL	AGE	W	L	SV	G	GS	IP	H	HR	BB/9	K/9	K	GB%	BABIP	WHIP	ERA	DRA-	WARP	MPH	FB%	Whiff%	CSP
2019	NYY	MLB	31	3	1	3	66	0	61^{1}	38	3	4.7	7.8	53	76.1%	.226	1.14	1.91	98	0.7	94.7	86.1%	27.7%	40.5%
2020	NYY	MLB	32	1	2	8	20	0	19	12	0	3.3	7.6	16	71.7%	.226	1.00	1.89	90	0.3	95.0	80.3%	25.8%	38.4%
2021	NYY	MLB	33	0	1	1	22	0	18^{1}	17	2	6.9	7.9	16	68.0%	.313	1.69	5.89	117	0.0	92.6	84.1%	25.2%	48.0%
2022 non-DC	*NYY*	*MLB*	*34*	*2*	*2*	*0*	*57*	*0*	*50*	*48*	*3*	*5.1*	*8.4*	*46*	*67.4%*	*.306*	*1.53*	*4.35*	*102*	*0.1*	*94.0*	*84.0%*	*26.2%*	*43.0%*

Comparables: Jon Rauch, Mike Minor, Brandon Lyon

Britton is the mold that broke. The Yankees traded for three relievers during the 2021 season—Clay Holmes, Wandy Peralta and Joely Rodríguez—all modeled in his image of high strikeout/even higher groundball rates. In the most generous interpretation, that's a compliment to his pitching style. In reality, these moves were necessary because he couldn't get the job done himself. In what proved to be a nightmare season, Britton missed much of the season with injuries and struggled with location when healthy, leading to an astronomical walk rate and far too many hits on get-me-over fastballs behind in the count. The woes culminated in October Tommy John surgery. He's still the second-highest-paid lefty reliever in MLB (behind Aroldis Chapman), because the Yankees chose after 2020 to pick up his 2022 option, but he's getting played off the stage by his own tribute band.

Aroldis Chapman LHP Born: 02/28/88 Age: 34 Bats: L Throws: L Height: 6'4" Weight: 218 lb. Origin: International Free Agent, 2010

YEAR	TEAM	LVL	AGE	W	L	SV	G	GS	IP	H	HR	BB/9	K/9	K	GB%	BABIP	WHIP	ERA	DRA-	WARP	MPH	FB%	Whiff%	CSP
2019	NYY	MLB	31	3	2	37	60	0	57	38	3	3.9	13.4	85	41.5%	.292	1.11	2.21	75	1.3	98.5	68.7%	31.8%	48.2%
2020	NYY	MLB	32	1	1	3	13	0	11^{2}	6	2	3.1	17.0	22	27.8%	.250	0.86	3.09	77	0.3	98.1	76.9%	41.6%	50.4%
2021	NYY	MLB	33	6	4	30	61	0	56^{1}	36	9	6.1	15.5	97	41.9%	.287	1.31	3.36	66	1.5	98.5	62.3%	39.8%	54.7%
2022 DC	*NYY*	*MLB*	*34*	*3*	*3*	*39*	*67*	*0*	*58*	*35*	*7*	*4.8*	*14.9*	*96*	*41.5%*	*.273*	*1.14*	*2.76*	*66*	*1.3*	*98.5*	*65.0%*	*38.2%*	*52.9%*

Comparables: David Robertson, Mike Stanton, Jesse Orosco

Once again, Chapman led MLB in WAA (Wetness Above Average). Baseball's most notorious lefty closer douses himself with water before each appearance...but why? Some experts theorize it's a cooling mechanism, while others think he's masking perfusive sweatiness. One theory is that his still-100+ mph fastball is water-activated. Our crack team of researchers at Baseball Prospectus have discovered a correlation between his repulsive body moisture and fastball command. When he was nearly unhittable in the first six weeks of the 2021 season, he would report to the mound only moderately squishy. Once the balmy summer months arrived (with the attention they brought to non-sweat substances?) and he couldn't locate his heater whatsoever, he was practically a marine mammal without a dorsal fin. He remains one of MLB's hardest-throwing and least huggable relievers in the final year of his contract.

Gerrit Cole RHP Born: 09/08/90 Age: 31 Bats: R Throws: R Height: 6'4" Weight: 220 lb. Origin: Round 1, 2011 Draft (#1 overall)

YEAR	TEAM	LVL	AGE	W	L	SV	G	GS	IP	H	HR	BB/9	K/9	K	GB%	BABIP	WHIP	ERA	DRA-	WARP	MPH	FB%	Whiff%	CSP
2019	HOU	MLB	28	20	5	0	33	33	212^1	142	29	2.0	13.8	326	40.0%	.276	0.89	2.50	59	6.8	97.4	54.0%	37.2%	48.6%
2020	NYY	MLB	29	7	3	0	12	12	73	53	14	2.1	11.6	94	37.1%	.242	0.96	2.84	75	1.8	97.0	52.8%	34.2%	47.3%
2021	NYY	MLB	30	16	8	0	30	30	181^1	151	24	2.0	12.1	243	42.5%	.305	1.06	3.23	71	4.5	97.8	48.0%	31.9%	53.6%
2022 DC	*NYY*	*MLB*	*31*	*13*	*7*	*0*	*30*	*30*	*187.7*	*146*	*25*	*2.2*	*12.1*	*251*	*40.5%*	*.289*	*1.02*	*2.52*	*65*	*4.9*	*97.5*	*50.2%*	*33.5%*	*51.4%*

Comparables: Roger Clemens, Don Sutton, Max Scherzer

Here's a fun way to piss off a lot of people at once: Pick a song that everyone knows, and get *really* good at singing it. Practice every day. If you can accompany it with an instrument, even better. Then walk into a crowded room and belt it out as emphatically as you can— but leave off the last note: *"HAPPY BIRTHDAY TO*

Cole was outstanding in his first 162-game season in New York. His WARP was nearly a full win higher than that of any other American League pitcher, but he tweaked his hamstring on September 7. His next start a week later in Baltimore was fine, because hey, Orioles, but during his final three appearances of the regular season he surrendered 15 runs and five long balls in 17 ⅔ innings. He struggled to spot his fastball in the Wild Card game, coughing up two more homers before getting pulled in the third inning. Was he still sore? Did his mechanics fall out of sync? Given his brilliance all year long, it's unfair that he took the blame for the early postseason exit. Then again, life isn't

Nestor Cortes LHP Born: 12/10/94 Age: 27 Bats: R Throws: L Height: 5'11" Weight: 210 lb. Origin: Round 36, 2013 Draft (#1094 overall)

YEAR	TEAM	LVL	AGE	W	L	SV	G	GS	IP	H	HR	BB/9	K/9	K	GB%	BABIP	WHIP	ERA	DRA-	WARP	MPH	FB%	Whiff%	CSP
2019	SWB	AAA	24	2	2	0	7	6	39^2	29	3	2.5	9.5	42	35.0%	.263	1.01	3.86	111	0.3				
2019	NYY	MLB	24	5	1	0	33	1	66^2	75	16	3.8	9.3	69	34.5%	.321	1.55	5.67	113	0.2	89.5	51.9%	25.9%	48.9%
2020	SEA	MLB	25	0	1	0	5	1	7^2	12	6	7.0	9.4	8	35.7%	.286	2.35	15.26	136	-0.1	88.4	40.6%	20.3%	47.6%
2021	SWB	AAA	26	1	1	1	5	1	15	8	1	0.6	10.8	18	37.5%	.226	0.60	1.20	90	0.3				
2021	NYY	MLB	26	2	3	0	22	14	93	75	14	2.4	10.0	103	27.9%	.266	1.08	2.90	99	0.9	89.9	70.3%	23.8%	53.6%
2022 DC	*NYY*	*MLB*	*27*	*6*	*5*	*0*	*19*	*19*	*99*	*88*	*17*	*2.8*	*9.2*	*101*	*32.1%*	*.275*	*1.21*	*3.90*	*97*	*0.7*	*89.7*	*64.8%*	*24.0%*	*52.3%*

Comparables: James McDonald, Andrew Heaney, David Phelps

It's fitting that the Yankees' slowest-throwing pitcher would adopt a turtle as the clubhouse pet. Cortes barely cracks 90 mph, but he has all the low-velo adaptations necessary to survive at that speed. He varies his delivery in every way imaginable: hesitation windups followed by quick pitches, and sidearm dropdowns after over-the-top releases. He keeps his entire five-pitch mix on the outside corners and his 27.5% strikeout rate and 6.7% walk rate were both above-average. By maintaining one of the best spin rate-to-velocity ratios in MLB, he allowed only a .196 BA and .287 wOBA against his four-seamer—both of which were better than Gerrit Cole's fastball despite a velo difference of about eight mph. Bronxie the Turtle signifies more than just strength in the slow lane—he's a symbol of Cortes' own ascension. Minor-league free agents don't get to choose team mascots, but no. 2 starters do.

Deivi García RHP Born: 05/19/99 Age: 23 Bats: R Throws: R Height: 5'9" Weight: 163 lb. Origin: International Free Agent, 2015

YEAR	TEAM	LVL	AGE	W	L	SV	G	GS	IP	H	HR	BB/9	K/9	K	GB%	BABIP	WHIP	ERA	DRA-	WARP	MPH	FB%	Whiff%	CSP
2019	TAM	A+	20	0	2	0	4	4	17^2	14	0	4.1	16.8	33	50.0%	.438	1.25	3.06	73	0.4				
2019	TRN	AA	20	4	4	0	11	11	53^2	43	2	4.4	14.6	87	40.5%	.363	1.29	3.86	77	1.1				
2019	SWB	AAA	20	1	3	0	11	6	40	39	8	4.5	10.1	45	36.7%	.313	1.48	5.40	90	0.7				
2020	NYY	MLB	21	3	2	0	6	6	34^1	35	6	1.6	8.7	33	34.0%	.293	1.19	4.98	111	0.2	92.0	59.6%	22.8%	50.2%
2021	SWB	AAA	22	3	7	0	24	22	90^2	102	21	6.8	9.6	97	29.9%	.333	1.88	6.85	119	0.3				
2021	NYY	MLB	22	0	2	0	2	2	8^1	8	1	4.3	7.6	7	23.1%	.280	1.44	6.48	149	-0.1	92.2	41.2%	28.4%	54.3%
2022 DC	*NYY*	*MLB*	*23*	*2*	*2*	*0*	*17*	*3*	*27.7*	*28*	*5*	*5.0*	*9.0*	*27*	*32.8%*	*.305*	*1.59*	*5.92*	*131*	*-0.2*	*92.1*	*54.0%*	*24.5%*	*51.4%*

Comparables: Julio Teheran, Jaime Barría, Matt Wisler

García started Game Two of the 2020 ALDS, placed 17th on the 2021 Baseball Prospectus Top 101 Prospects list...and then more or less vanished from the major-league scene, only making a pair of spot starts before Memorial Day. For the rest of his 2021, he couldn't throw strikes in Scranton/Wilkes-Barre as his arm slot wandered lower, which also killed the shape of the fastball and curveball combo he'd had so much success with previously. BP's Howard Megdal witnessed an incident in Trenton where García buzzed Christian Colón and sparked a ruckus on the field, only for Colón to seemingly realize that his command really *is* that bad. The solitary bright side is that García's collapse occurred away from the bright lights of New York instead of on national TV—unlike several other Yankees.

Domingo Germán RHP Born: 08/04/92 Age: 29 Bats: R Throws: R Height: 6'2" Weight: 181 lb. Origin: International Free Agent, 2009

YEAR	TEAM	LVL	AGE	W	L	SV	G	GS	IP	H	HR	BB/9	K/9	K	GB%	BABIP	WHIP	ERA	DRA-	WARP	MPH	FB%	Whiff%	CSP
2019	NYY	MLB	26	18	4	0	27	24	143	125	30	2.5	9.6	153	37.5%	.260	1.15	4.03	90	2.2	93.6	45.0%	28.4%	48.3%
2021	NYY	MLB	28	4	5	0	22	18	98^1	89	17	2.5	9.0	98	42.8%	.271	1.18	4.58	95	1.1	93.5	43.7%	30.5%	51.7%
2022 DC	*NYY*	*MLB*	*29*	*8*	*7*	*0*	*41*	*19*	*116.3*	*106*	*17*	*2.8*	*9.3*	*120*	*41.7%*	*.288*	*1.22*	*3.78*	*93*	*1.3*	*93.6*	*44.1%*	*29.8%*	*50.6%*

Comparables: Lance Lynn, Ted Lilly, Wandy Rodriguez

Germán has four distinct states of existence, all of which factored into his 2021 season. **1) Suspended.** A 63-game penalty for domestic violence cost him the entirety of 2020 as well as the first three games last year. **2) Dominant.** From late April to early June, he was arguably the Yankees' best starting pitcher. **3) Awful.** His final four starts in June were so horrible that he lost his spot in the rotation. **4) Injured.** Shoulder inflammation kept him out for all of August and September, though he returned for a shoddy relief appearance on October 1. One of these states is valuable, but the other three range from unhelpful to prohibitively reprehensible. His overall numbers depict a steadily decent pitcher year-to-year, but the only thing consistent about them is inconsistency.

Luis Gil RHP Born: 06/03/98 Age: 24 Bats: R Throws: R Height: 6'2" Weight: 185 lb. Origin: International Free Agent, 2015

YEAR	TEAM	LVL	AGE	W	L	SV	G	GS	IP	H	HR	BB/9	K/9	K	GB%	BABIP	WHIP	ERA	DRA-	WARP	MPH	FB%	Whiff%	CSP
2019	CSC	A	21	4	5	0	17	17	83	60	1	4.2	12.1	112	47.2%	.311	1.19	2.39	86	1.3				
2019	TAM	A+	21	1	0	0	3	3	13	11	0	5.5	7.6	11	40.5%	.297	1.46	4.85	102	0.1				
2021	SOM	AA	23	1	1	0	7	7	30^2	24	2	3.8	14.7	50	29.9%	.338	1.21	2.64	80	0.6				
2021	SWB	AAA	23	4	0	1	13	10	48^2	35	7	5.9	12.4	67	29.1%	.275	1.38	4.81	84	1.0				
2021	NYY	MLB	23	1	1	0	6	6	29^1	20	4	5.8	11.7	38	32.4%	.239	1.33	3.07	100	0.3	96.2	53.4%	31.0%	51.3%
2022 DC	*NYY*	*MLB*	*24*	*7*	*5*	*0*	*53*	*9*	*85.3*	*70*	*13*	*5.6*	*11.5*	*108*	*34.1%*	*.285*	*1.44*	*4.57*	*103*	*0.5*	*96.2*	*53.4%*	*31.0%*	*51.3%*

Comparables: Clay Buchholz, Jered Weaver, Jaime García

No one expected much from Gil when he made his MLB debut on August 3. He received the spot start not because he was "ready," but because it was his turn in the Triple-A rotation, and he wasn't contagious. He completely shut down the Orioles that day, allowing no runs in six innings. It was the same story in each of his next two appearances against Seattle and Boston, making him the first MLB starting pitcher since 1907 with a spotless ERA through his first three career games. Of course, no streak lasts forever, and he got bombed in his final three appearances. There's no doubt about his stuff—a rising high-90s heater, a swing-and-miss slider and a low-to-mid 90s *changeup* (not a misprint). He needs to cut down on walks and hold his velocity deeper into his starts, though, so he probably won't begin 2022 in the majors. Whenever he gets the call next, it will be as a heralded prospect and not just a spot starter.

Chad Green RHP Born: 05/24/91 Age: 31 Bats: L Throws: R Height: 6'3" Weight: 215 lb. Origin: Round 11, 2013 Draft (#336 overall)

YEAR	TEAM	LVL	AGE	W	L	SV	G	GS	IP	H	HR	BB/9	K/9	K	GB%	BABIP	WHIP	ERA	DRA-	WARP	MPH	FB%	Whiff%	CSP
2019	SWB	AAA	28	0	0	0	3	3	7^1	5	0	2.5	17.2	14	23.1%	.385	0.95	2.45	89	0.1				
2019	NYY	MLB	28	4	4	2	54	15	69	66	10	2.5	12.8	98	35.5%	.346	1.23	4.17	73	1.7	96.6	77.2%	29.9%	50.9%
2020	NYY	MLB	29	3	3	1	22	0	25^2	13	5	2.8	11.2	32	41.7%	.148	0.82	3.51	82	0.5	95.6	75.1%	31.4%	51.8%
2021	NYY	MLB	30	10	7	6	67	0	83^2	57	14	1.8	10.6	99	27.1%	.234	0.88	3.12	86	1.4	95.8	65.5%	32.1%	56.2%
2022 DC	*NYY*	*MLB*	*31*	*3*	*3*	*7*	*74*	*0*	*64.7*	*53*	*11*	*2.3*	*11.0*	*79*	*32.1%*	*.280*	*1.08*	*3.18*	*79*	*1.0*	*95.9*	*69.4%*	*31.5%*	*54.4%*

Comparables: Joakim Soria, David Hernandez, Turk Wendell

It takes just two notes to make an interval, but that's enough to define a piece of music. A perfect fourth, such as A and D, and a perfect fifth, such as A and E, are ever-present in nearly all songs and musical genres. They're simple, elegant and beautiful. A tritone falls in between— A and D#. It's dissonant and jarring. Green's fastball is a perfect fourth, like the first two notes of "Here Comes the Bride." It sits in the mid-to-upper 90s with a 94th percentile spin rate. His curve is a perfect fifth, as in the first notes of the Superman theme. He threw it a career-high 34.5% of the time with exceptional results…mostly. He played 14 tritones that left the ballpark last season, eight on fastballs and six on curves. He's a master composer out of the bullpen with a prolific songbook—leading MLB in relief innings pitched in 2021—but in both music and baseball, mistakes can make or break the performance.

Clay Holmes RHP Born: 03/27/93 Age: 29 Bats: R Throws: R Height: 6'5" Weight: 245 lb. Origin: Round 9, 2011 Draft (#272 overall)

YEAR	TEAM	LVL	AGE	W	L	SV	G	GS	IP	H	HR	BB/9	K/9	K	GB%	BABIP	WHIP	ERA	DRA-	WARP	MPH	FB%	Whiff%	CSP
2019	IND	AAA	26	2	1	1	10	0	15^2	17	1	8.6	7.5	13	51.0%	.327	2.04	6.32	116	0.1				
2019	PIT	MLB	26	1	2	0	35	0	50	45	5	6.5	10.1	56	58.7%	.301	1.62	5.58	91	0.7	94.4	62.7%	25.4%	45.4%
2020	PIT	MLB	27	0	0	0	1	0	1^1	2	0	0.0	6.7	1	60.0%	.400	1.50	0.00	109	0.0	92.6	31.8%	44.4%	36.5%
2021	PIT	MLB	28	3	2	0	44	0	42	35	3	5.4	9.4	44	70.7%	.286	1.43	4.93	98	0.4	96.1	51.2%	27.7%	55.4%
2021	NYY	MLB	28	5	2	0	25	0	28	18	2	1.3	10.9	34	61.5%	.254	0.79	1.61	77	0.6	96.5	73.2%	28.3%	58.0%
2022 DC	*NYY*	*MLB*	*29*	*3*	*3*	*0*	*74*	*0*	*64.7*	*57*	*5*	*4.4*	*9.9*	*71*	*60.8%*	*.304*	*1.38*	*3.92*	*94*	*0.4*	*95.9*	*59.5%*	*27.6%*	*53.8%*

Comparables: Justin Duchscherer, Kevin Gregg, Noé Ramirez

Holmes made a key physical adjustment when he was traded from the Pirates to the Yankees: There's a toggle switch on his right arm that says "WALK BATTERS/DON'T WALK BATTERS" and it was stuck in the wrong direction. When he flipped that switch, his walk rate immediately improved from 13.2% to 4.9% after the move. When you can throw pitches in the zone more often and get hitters to swing less at them, that's a pretty good trick if you can pull it off. By staying ahead in the count, he was able to expand the strike zone and get batters to chase more often as well, increasing his strikeouts and limiting loud contact. His 68.7% groundball rate was second-best among qualified MLB relievers, so even when opponents connected with his power sinker the first baseman usually made a putout. The Yankees will count on him for high-leverage innings once again in 2022.

Michael King RHP Born: 05/25/95 Age: 27 Bats: R Throws: R Height: 6'3" Weight: 210 lb. Origin: Round 12, 2016 Draft (#353 overall)

YEAR	TEAM	LVL	AGE	W	L	SV	G	GS	IP	H	HR	BB/9	K/9	K	GB%	BABIP	WHIP	ERA	DRA-	WARP	MPH	FB%	Whiff%	CSP
2019	YAW	ROK	24	0	0	0	3	2	5^2	3	0	3.2	12.7	8	75.0%	.250	0.88	4.76						
2019	SI	SS	24	0	0	0	1	1	4	4	0	0.0	0.0	0	46.2%	.308	1.00	0.00						
2019	TRN	AA	24	0	1	0	3	2	12^2	20	1	1.4	5.7	8	51.0%	.396	1.74	9.95	115	0.0				
2019	SWB	AAA	24	3	1	0	4	3	23^2	20	3	2.3	10.6	28	47.5%	.293	1.10	4.18	80	0.6				
2019	NYY	MLB	24	0	0	0	1	0	2	2	0	0.0	4.5	1	37.5%	.250	1.00	0.00	112	0.0	91.5	68.3%	5.6%	41.8%
2020	NYY	MLB	25	1	2	0	9	4	26^2	30	5	3.7	8.8	26	40.2%	.325	1.54	7.76	107	0.2	93.2	65.7%	21.3%	48.3%
2021	NYY	MLB	26	2	4	0	22	6	63^1	57	6	3.4	8.8	62	45.4%	.291	1.28	3.55	97	0.7	93.6	77.2%	24.9%	55.7%
2022 DC	*NYY*	*MLB*	*27*	*8*	*5*	*0*	*65*	*6*	*81*	*75*	*11*	*2.9*	*8.8*	*79*	*45.4%*	*.290*	*1.26*	*4.02*	*97*	*0.5*	*93.5*	*74.4%*	*23.9%*	*53.8%*

Comparables: Rafael Montero, Yonny Chirinos, David Phelps

Invasive species—such as the lanternflies infesting the NJ-NY-PA tristate area—are a global ecological problem, not because they struggle in their adopted habitat, but because they thrive too well. King is the American League's lanternfly. In his native habitat, he was a fringey, up-and-down long reliever who stayed stretched out for spot starts, an easily consumed genus of pitchers integral to the baseball food chain. But upon returning from the IL in early September, he was introduced to the short relief environment. In his new surroundings, his fastball and secondaries both jumped in velocity and he increased his breaking ball usage from 8% to 21%. This resulted in a higher strikeout rate and stretches of dominance over other species he had never previously exhibited. With fewer natural predators in these environs, ecologists fear he and his max-effort brethren could put several opposing hitters on the endangered list in the near future.

Jonathan Loáisiga RHP Born: 11/02/94 Age: 27 Bats: R Throws: R Height: 5'11" Weight: 165 lb. Origin: International Free Agent, 2012

YEAR	TEAM	LVL	AGE	W	L	SV	G	GS	IP	H	HR	BB/9	K/9	K	GB%	BABIP	WHIP	ERA	DRA-	WARP	MPH	FB%	Whiff%	CSP
2019	SWB	AAA	24	0	2	0	5	4	15^2	14	3	2.9	10.9	19	46.5%	.275	1.21	6.32	95	0.2				
2019	NYY	MLB	24	2	2	0	15	4	31^2	31	6	4.5	10.5	37	40.0%	.316	1.48	4.55	99	0.3	97.0	56.3%	33.2%	44.6%
2020	NYY	MLB	25	3	0	0	12	3	23	21	3	2.7	8.6	22	51.5%	.290	1.22	3.52	87	0.4	96.9	67.3%	23.2%	49.9%
2021	NYY	MLB	26	9	4	5	57	0	70^2	56	3	2.0	8.8	69	60.5%	.279	1.02	2.17	79	1.4	98.4	58.8%	27.9%	53.0%
2022 DC	*NYY*	*MLB*	*27*	*3*	*3*	*2*	*74*	*0*	*64.7*	*60*	*6*	*2.7*	*9.2*	*66*	*53.7%*	*.302*	*1.23*	*3.47*	*87*	*0.7*	*97.9*	*59.9%*	*27.8%*	*51.4%*

Comparables: Carlos Villanueva, Jeurys Familia, Tyler Thornburg

"Reliever risk" is the terrifying monster in the closet of every pitching prospect. In Loáisiga's case, the monster was real, but it turned out to be cuddly and friendly. In his first year working out of the bullpen full-time, his Statcast percentile rankings popped more 99s than the Judge's Chambers in the right-field stands. He eschewed his four-seamer in favor of a sinker that frequently reached triple digits, which kept his strikeout rate around league average but ballooned his groundball rate up over 60%. He only yielded ten extra-base hits in more than 70 innings, establishing himself as one of the most reliable weapons in the Yankee relief corps. Sometimes succumbing to the monster in the closet is in one's own best interests.

Lucas Luetge LHP Born: 03/24/87 Age: 35 Bats: L Throws: L Height: 6'4" Weight: 205 lb. Origin: Round 21, 2008 Draft (#638 overall)

YEAR	TEAM	LVL	AGE	W	L	SV	G	GS	IP	H	HR	BB/9	K/9	K	GB%	BABIP	WHIP	ERA	DRA-	WARP	MPH	FB%	Whiff%	CSP
2019	JXN	AA	32	4	1	0	22	0	25	14	0	2.5	10.1	28	44.8%	.246	0.84	1.08	71	0.5				
2019	RNO	AAA	32	5	2	1	33	0	43	43	4	2.9	9.6	46	54.2%	.342	1.33	3.14	81	0.7				
2021	NYY	MLB	34	4	2	1	57	1	72^1	67	6	1.9	9.7	78	42.6%	.308	1.13	2.74	88	1.1	88.4	62.1%	27.5%	48.9%
2022 DC	*NYY*	*MLB*	*35*	*2*	*2*	*0*	*59*	*0*	*51.7*	*49*	*7*	*2.5*	*8.6*	*49*	*43.0%*	*.294*	*1.24*	*3.91*	*97*	*0.3*	*88.4*	*62.1%*	*27.5%*	*48.9%*

Comparables: Caleb Thielbar, Jerry Blevins, Javy Guerra

Baseball analytics and children have something in common: it's difficult to realize how quickly they grow when you spend every day around them. Luetge is the second cousin once-removed that baseball analytics only sees at weddings and funerals. Prior to throwing 72 ⅓ innings in 2021, he last appeared in MLB in 2015 and even then he only pitched in one game. Since then, both he and analytics itself have grown so much that their great aunt no longer pinches their cheeks. He featured the highest average spin rate on a cutter of any reliever in MLB (2,554 rpm). His curveball's 70% strikeout rate was tops in MLB as well (min. 50 pitches). He demonstrated impeccable command, consistently pierced the inside corner against righties and only walked 5% of opposing hitters. He wasn't nearly this good when he last donned a major-league uniform. Then again, it was so long ago that we didn't even have tools like Statcast with which to measure him.

Luis Medina RHP Born: 05/03/99 Age: 23 Bats: R Throws: R Height: 6'1" Weight: 175 lb. Origin: International Free Agent, 2015

YEAR	TEAM	LVL	AGE	W	L	SV	G	GS	IP	H	HR	BB/9	K/9	K	GB%	BABIP	WHIP	ERA	DRA-	WARP	MPH	FB%	Whiff%	CSP
2019	CSC	A	20	1	8	0	20	20	93	86	9	6.5	11.1	115	43.6%	.344	1.65	6.00	113	0.1				
2019	TAM	A+	20	0	0	0	2	2	10^2	7	0	2.5	10.1	12	67.9%	.250	0.94	0.84	109	0.1				
2021	HV	A+	22	2	1	0	7	7	32^2	18	4	5.2	13.8	50	50.0%	.241	1.13	2.76	79	0.6				
2021	SOM	AA	22	4	3	0	15	14	73^2	65	7	5.0	10.1	83	50.5%	.314	1.44	3.67	84	1.3				
2022 DC	*NYY*	*MLB*	*23*	*0*	*1*	*0*	*3*	*3*	*14.3*	*14*	*2*	*6.6*	*9.7*	*15*	*46.4%*	*.313*	*1.72*	*5.80*	*125*	*-0.1*				

Comparables: Jordan Yamamoto, Matt Magill, Kyle Farnsworth

The report on Medina hasn't changed much since he was 16 years old, which, to be fair, isn't the worst thing when it comes to pitching prospects. His arm has the highest upside in the Yankees' system with a ferocious, GIF-worthy three-pitch mix. He throws an incendiary fastball, sitting in the high-90s and touching 102 mph, but his curveball might end up an equally strong offering. He features an above-average 90-mph changeup as well. The issue was his double-digit walk rate at every minor-league level, but in his final seven starts of the 2021 season, he walked only 13 men in 38 innings. Did he finally figure out how to reasonably locate his pitches? If so, Happy Gilmore just learned how to putt. Uh oh!

Jordan Montgomery LHP Born: 12/27/92 Age: 29 Bats: L Throws: L Height: 6'6" Weight: 228 lb. Origin: Round 4, 2014 Draft (#122 overall)

YEAR	TEAM	LVL	AGE	W	L	SV	G	GS	IP	H	HR	BB/9	K/9	K	GB%	BABIP	WHIP	ERA	DRA-	WARP	MPH	FB%	Whiff%	CSP
2019	NYY	MLB	26	0	0	0	2	1	4	7	1	0.0	11.3	5	21.4%	.462	1.75	6.75	118	0.0	91.6	50.0%	28.9%	48.4%
2020	NYY	MLB	27	2	3	0	10	10	44	48	7	1.8	9.6	47	43.3%	.323	1.30	5.11	87	0.8	92.5	52.3%	28.2%	48.0%
2021	NYY	MLB	28	6	7	0	30	30	157^{1}	150	19	2.9	9.3	162	42.6%	.308	1.28	3.83	100	1.4	92.1	52.0%	29.2%	55.4%
2022 DC	*NYY*	*MLB*	*29*	*9*	*8*	*0*	*27*	*27*	*145.7*	*136*	*20*	*2.7*	*8.9*	*144*	*42.3%*	*.292*	*1.23*	*3.61*	*91*	*1.8*	*92.1*	*52.0%*	*29.0%*	*54.1%*

Comparables: Joe Blanton, Lance Lynn, Chris Capuano

Things that are all fine: Eating a salad. A good credit score. Wearing sweatpants. A nine-to-five with a dental plan. Low-deductible auto insurance. Montgomery's turn in the rotation. Playing a game on your phone in a waiting room. Peanut butter and jelly on white bread. Six-inning starts. A Honda Civic with 50,000 miles. Custom orthotics. Secondary pitches that don't move much but pretty reliably paint the corners. A $5 Dunkin Donuts gift card. Clean laundry. You're better off having these than not, even if none of them inflame the passions. When you get home and someone asks you about your day, you don't even mention them. They're just part of your life, and that's nice.

Wandy Peralta LHP Born: 07/27/91 Age: 30 Bats: L Throws: L Height: 6'0" Weight: 217 lb. Origin: International Free Agent, 2009

YEAR	TEAM	LVL	AGE	W	L	SV	G	GS	IP	H	HR	BB/9	K/9	K	GB%	BABIP	WHIP	ERA	DRA-	WARP	MPH	FB%	Whiff%	CSP
2019	LOU	AAA	27	0	0	0	12	0	11	11	0	0.8	5.7	7	48.6%	.314	1.09	3.27	92	0.2				
2019	SF	MLB	27	0	0	0	8	0	5^{2}	4	1	1.6	7.9	5	73.3%	.214	0.88	3.18	90	0.1	95.4	48.8%	36.1%	42.8%
2019	CIN	MLB	27	1	1	0	39	0	34	36	10	4.0	7.1	27	45.8%	.268	1.50	6.09	109	0.2	95.3	35.2%	32.2%	42.9%
2020	SF	MLB	28	1	1	0	25	0	27^{1}	22	3	3.6	8.2	25	44.7%	.260	1.21	3.29	90	0.5	94.8	35.5%	28.9%	44.9%
2021	SF	MLB	29	2	1	2	10	0	8^{1}	11	1	3.2	8.6	8	53.8%	.400	1.68	5.40	105	0.1	96.3	38.1%	35.8%	54.4%
2021	NYY	MLB	29	3	3	3	46	1	42^{2}	38	5	3.8	7.4	35	57.0%	.268	1.31	2.95	111	0.1	95.1	37.5%	30.0%	48.0%
2022 DC	*NYY*	*MLB*	*30*	*3*	*3*	*0*	*74*	*0*	*64.7*	*63*	*7*	*3.9*	*8.5*	*61*	*51.5%*	*.305*	*1.41*	*4.31*	*102*	*0.2*	*95.2*	*37.0%*	*30.8%*	*47.1%*

Comparables: Donnie Hart, Hoby Milner, Brian Wolfe

After the Yankees traded for Peralta in late April they remade him from a fastball-slider pitcher to a sinker-changeup artist almost exclusively. Did it work? Depends on whether you like your runs earned or deserved. Only two pitchers in MLB threw more innings than he did after the trade with an ERA below three and a DRA above five. It's sort of like buying a chocolate chip cookie at a bake sale, taking a bite and discovering they were actually raisins. Peralta was among the best in the game at getting hitters to expand their own strike zone, generating grounders and avoiding hard contact, but DRA- suggests his performance isn't repeatable. It would help if he could finish batters off: His chase and whiff rates are well above-average, but it never seems to arrive in the strikeout totals. So what do you do with the cookie now? The Yankees had better like oatmeal raisin.

Joely Rodríguez LHP Born: 11/14/91 Age: 30 Bats: L Throws: L Height: 6'1" Weight: 200 lb. Origin: International Free Agent, 2009

YEAR	TEAM	LVL	AGE	W	L	SV	G	GS	IP	H	HR	BB/9	K/9	K	GB%	BABIP	WHIP	ERA	DRA-	WARP	MPH	FB%	Whiff%	CSP
2020	TEX	MLB	28	0	0	0	12	0	12^{2}	8	0	3.6	12.1	17	50.0%	.276	1.03	2.13	75	0.3	94.7	67.2%	26.3%	47.8%
2021	TEX	MLB	29	1	3	1	31	0	27^{1}	32	3	4.0	9.9	30	63.1%	.363	1.61	5.93	93	0.3	94.1	60.8%	31.1%	49.7%
2021	NYY	MLB	29	1	0	0	21	0	19	21	1	2.8	8.1	17	50.0%	.370	1.42	2.84	96	0.2	94.2	54.3%	31.9%	50.1%
2022 DC	*NYY*	*MLB*	*30*	*2*	*2*	*0*	*59*	*0*	*51.7*	*49*	*5*	*3.5*	*8.9*	*51*	*54.9%*	*.304*	*1.34*	*3.88*	*95*	*0.3*	*94.2*	*60.1%*	*30.5%*	*49.5%*

Comparables: Hoby Milner, Fernando Abad, Scott Alexander

You have four breakfast options: yogurt, fresh berries, a bowl of rusty screws and oatmeal. This isn't a trick and no one is forcing you to choose the screws. All you have to do is simply not eat them and pick from the edible options instead. Easy, right? Rodríguez has three excellent pitches—a worm-burning sinker, a swing-and-miss changeup to neutralize right-handed hitters and a slider he doesn't throw very often but can be useful against lefties. He also throws a four-seam fastball 18% of the time. Opponents blasted it for a .607 SLG, whereas they slugged just .352 against his three other offerings. He's not a bad pitcher overall, but he could be much more palatable by only choosing pitches that are part of his balanced diet.

Clarke Schmidt RHP Born: 02/20/96 Age: 26 Bats: R Throws: R Height: 6'1" Weight: 209 lb. Origin: Round 1, 2017 Draft (#16 overall)

YEAR	TEAM	LVL	AGE	W	L	SV	G	GS	IP	H	HR	BB/9	K/9	K	GB%	BABIP	WHIP	ERA	DRA-	WARP	MPH	FB%	Whiff%	CSP
2019	YAE	ROK	23	0	0	0	3	3	8^{1}	6	1	3.2	15.1	14	56.2%	.333	1.08	3.24						
2019	TAM	A+	23	4	5	0	13	12	63^{1}	59	2	3.4	9.8	69	54.6%	.333	1.31	3.84	97	0.8				
2019	TRN	AA	23	2	0	0	3	3	19	14	1	0.5	9.0	19	45.1%	.260	0.79	2.37	102	0.1				
2020	NYY	MLB	24	0	1	0	3	1	6^{1}	7	0	7.1	9.9	7	42.1%	.368	1.89	7.11	119	0.0	95.0	54.0%	21.8%	49.7%
2021	SOM	AA	25	0	1	0	2	2	6^{1}	5	2	2.8	7.1	5	47.4%	.176	1.11	4.26	103	0.0				
2021	SWB	AAA	25	0	1	0	6	5	25^{2}	25	4	2.8	11.2	32	52.9%	.318	1.29	2.10	89	0.5				
2021	NYY	MLB	25	0	0	0	2	1	6^{1}	11	1	7.1	8.5	6	57.7%	.417	2.53	5.68	111	0.0	93.0	44.8%	18.6%	50.5%
2022 DC	*NYY*	*MLB*	*26*	*1*	*1*	*0*	*6*	*6*	*31*	*30*	*3*	*4.0*	*8.8*	*30*	*48.5%*	*.304*	*1.42*	*4.48*	*105*	*0.1*	*93.8*	*48.2%*	*19.8%*	*50.2%*

Comparables: Justin Haley, Jharel Cotton, Luis Cessa

Schmidt is well past all the normal young people "old enoughs." He's old enough to drive, vote, drink, gamble and get kicked off his parents' health insurance—but still not too old to be a prospect. Tommy John surgery in 2017 delayed his pro career and pushed back his timeline. 2021 should have been his proper rookie year, but elbow inflammation limited him to 44 ⅓ innings spread across five levels. He still has the same tantalizing fastball/curveball/changeup mix that kept the Yankees patient for five years. Now he's ready to come of age as a major league pitcher. Not a moment too soon—the other prospects are getting tired of him complaining about them always being on their smartphones, and laughing at memes he saw on Facebook.

Luis Severino RHP Born: 02/20/94 Age: 28 Bats: R Throws: R Height: 6'2" Weight: 218 lb. Origin: International Free Agent, 2011

YEAR	TEAM	LVL	AGE	W	L	SV	G	GS	IP	H	HR	BB/9	K/9	K	GB%	BABIP	WHIP	ERA	DRA-	WARP	MPH	FB%	Whiff%	CSP
2019	NYY	MLB	25	1	1	0	3	3	12	6	0	4.5	12.8	17	37.5%	.250	1.00	1.50	91	0.2	96.3	56.6%	27.5%	47.7%
2021	SOM	AA	27	0	0	0	2	2	6^1	2	1	1.4	12.8	9	50.0%	.091	0.47	2.84	97	0.1				
2021	NYY	MLB	27	1	0	0	4	0	6	2	0	1.5	12.0	8	41.7%	.167	0.50	0.00	93	0.1	95.2	43.9%	34.1%	47.9%
2022 DC	*NYY*	*MLB*	*28*	*7*	*4*	*0*	*30*	*16*	*93.7*	*73*	*11*	*2.9*	*11.5*	*119*	*44.2%*	*.286*	*1.10*	*2.79*	*72*	*2.0*	*95.6*	*49.3%*	*31.3%*	*47.8%*

Comparables: Félix Hernández, Gerrit Cole, Frank Castillo

One day, Severino got hurt and went away. Sometime later, he returned. This is the extent of what is known publicly, more or less. What remains unseen and unknown is the physical torment and mental anguish of falling from the mountaintop and clawing back inches at a time, often backsliding but never ceasing to push forward. This all happened in private, devoid of glory, as the Yankees carried on without him. Only his past and present teammates understand how much he suffered and strived. When he *finally* returned to pitch in the Majors on September 21—707 days after his last appearance—congratulatory tweets from CC Sabathia and Masahiro Tanaka hinted at the emotionality of the moment. He certainly didn't disappoint in his six regular-season innings, sitting 95 mph and touching 98 mph with his fastball and wiping hitters out with his trusty slider and changeup. His future role is unclear, but the Yankees will take whatever innings he can give them, regardless of whether he starts or relieves.

Jameson Taillon RHP Born: 11/18/91 Age: 30 Bats: R Throws: R Height: 6'5" Weight: 230 lb. Origin: Round 1, 2010 Draft (#2 overall)

YEAR	TEAM	LVL	AGE	W	L	SV	G	GS	IP	H	HR	BB/9	K/9	K	GB%	BABIP	WHIP	ERA	DRA-	WARP	MPH	FB%	Whiff%	CSP
2019	PIT	MLB	27	2	3	0	7	7	37^1	34	4	1.9	7.2	30	48.3%	.263	1.13	4.10	95	0.5	94.9	47.2%	24.5%	48.7%
2021	NYY	MLB	29	8	6	0	29	29	144^1	130	24	2.7	8.7	140	33.9%	.273	1.21	4.30	104	1.0	94.0	55.1%	26.5%	55.6%
2022 DC	*NYY*	*MLB*	*30*	*6*	*5*	*0*	*19*	*19*	*101*	*96*	*15*	*2.5*	*9.1*	*102*	*37.8%*	*.295*	*1.24*	*3.98*	*98*	*0.9*	*94.1*	*54.5%*	*26.4%*	*55.1%*

Comparables: Ervin Santana, Doc Medich, Gavin Floyd

You'll have to forgive Taillon for being a little behind the times. Pitchers who ditched their sinker after leaving Pittsburgh is *sooo* four years ago. To be fair, that's also the last time he completed a full season prior to 2021, and also, some trends pass the test of time. He threw his four-seamer for nearly half of his pitches when he used to throw it roughly a third of the time, on the whole generating a healthy 28.1% whiff rate and .286 wOBA against the offering. But "on the whole" isn't the proper perspective for his season. After his second Tommy John surgery, it took a few months to regain his command. His second half was much better—he won the AL Pitcher of the Month award in July after changing his release point—which is hopefully an indication of the kind of pitcher he can be in 2022. For someone who's been out of commission for so long, the most impressive statistic was an old-fashioned one that never goes out of style: 29 GS.

★ ★ ★ *2022 Top 101 Prospect* **#90** ★ ★ ★

Randy Vasquez RHP Born: 11/03/98 Age: 23 Bats: R Throws: R Height: 6'0" Weight: 165 lb. Origin: International Free Agent, 2018

YEAR	TEAM	LVL	AGE	W	L	SV	G	GS	IP	H	HR	BB/9	K/9	K	GB%	BABIP	WHIP	ERA	DRA-	WARP	MPH	FB%	Whiff%	CSP
2019	PUL	ROA	20	4	1	0	11	11	54^2	36	6	4.6	8.7	53	44.4%	.221	1.17	3.29						
2021	TAM	A	22	3	3	0	13	11	50	35	2	4.1	10.4	58	54.7%	.262	1.16	2.34	80	1.1				
2021	HV	A+	22	3	0	0	6	6	36	33	0	2.0	13.3	53	65.9%	.393	1.14	1.75	75	0.8				
2021	SOM	AA	22	2	1	0	4	4	21^1	23	2	3.0	8.0	19	52.9%	.309	1.41	4.22	104	0.1				
2022 non-DC	*NYY*	*MLB*	*23*	*2*	*3*	*0*	*57*	*0*	*50*	*51*	*5*	*4.2*	*8.2*	*45*	*51.7%*	*.315*	*1.49*	*4.71*	*110*	*-0.1*				

Comparables: Dan Straily, Iván Nova, Jason Hammel

Vasquez may never be a starter. A late-period 2018 international signing, he's not a big guy, and sometimes he loses a little something when he goes deep into games. His changeup is pretty flat, and though he disguises it well, that's mostly because he never uses it. The fastball command comes and goes. He also wields three plus pitches, with a four-seam and two-seam that both come in hard and have bite. But it's the 10-5 hammer curve, a deadly pitch with absurd spin, that drove him up through the ranks and onto the 40-man roster. It took him a while, but in 2021 he unlocked its dark secrets, honing his command and blowing through three levels of the minors. He'll be a fun one to watch.

LINEOUTS

Hitters

HITTER	POS	TEAM	LVL	AGE	PA	R	2B	3B	HR	RBI	BB	K	SB	CS	AVG/OBP/SLG	DRC+	BABIP	BRR	FRAA	WARP
Rob Brantly	C	SWB	AAA	31	264	35	9	1	9	43	20	41	1	0	.289/.379/.456	119	.317	-2.1	C(43): 2.3, 1B(20): 1.0	1.5
	C	NYY	MLB	31	21	0	1	0	0	0	0	4	0	0	.150/.190/.200	86	.188	-0.8	C(5): 0.1, 1B(1): -0.0	0.0
Josh Breaux	C/DH	HV	A+	23	276	34	12	0	17	46	22	73	0	0	.252/.308/.504	125	.280	-1.7	C(38): 10.3	2.4
	C/DH	SOM	AA	23	106	14	8	0	6	17	4	26	1	0	.240/.274/.500	108	.261	0.3	C(20): 4.1	0.9
Oswaldo Cabrera	IF	SOM	AA	22	478	61	29	1	24	78	36	118	20	5	.256/.311/.492	111	.295	2.0	2B(43): -0.8, 3B(35): 4.9, SS(24): 3.9	3.1
	IF	SWB	AAA	22	36	11	2	1	5	11	5	9	1	0	.500/.583/1.133	134	.625	-0.2	2B(7): 0.0, 3B(1): -0.2, SS(1): -0.2	0.2
Estevan Florial	CF	SOM	AA	23	39	5	2	0	4	6	4	9	0	1	.229/.308/.629	122	.182	-0.7	CF(7): -0.2	0.1
	CF	SWB	AAA	23	362	65	17	1	13	41	42	112	13	7	.218/.315/.404	86	.291	1.8	CF(72): -1.4, RF(1): -0.0	0.7
	CF	NYY	MLB	23	25	3	2	0	1	2	5	6	1	0	.300/.440/.550	97	.385	0.1	CF(11): -0.8	0.0
Chris Gittens	1B	SWB	AAA	27	184	37	8	0	14	44	36	46	0	0	.301/.440/.644	149	.345	-1.8	1B(38): -1.6	1.1
	1B	NYY	MLB	27	44	1	0	0	1	5	7	13	0	0	.111/.250/.194	91	.130	0.2	1B(13): -0.2	0.1
Ryan LaMarre	OF	SWB	AAA	32	240	27	13	2	6	34	27	62	14	6	.277/.379/.447	97	.370	-0.9	LF(21): 5.9, RF(18): 4.3, CF(10): 2.4	1.8
	OF	NYY	MLB	32	24	3	0	0	2	4	2	6	1	0	.190/.292/.476	100	.154	0.1	LF(4): 0.4, RF(4): -0.2, CF(1): -0.1	0.1
Everson Pereira	OF	TAM	A	20	83	17	5	1	5	22	10	21	4	1	.361/.446/.667	110	.457	0.5	CF(9): -0.7, LF(4): -0.6, RF(2): -0.1	0.3
	OF	HV	A+	20	127	27	3	0	14	32	15	38	5	2	.259/.354/.676	129	.241	-1.0	CF(22): -2.4	0.5
Alexander Vargas	SS	YNK	ROK	19	174	37	7	1	3	26	20	40	17	8	.273/.362/.393		.349			
Austin Wells	C/DH	SUR	WIN	21	79	14	5	2	2	18	13	16	1	0	.344/.456/.578		.426			
	C/DH	TAM	A	21	299	61	17	4	9	54	51	62	11	0	.258/.398/.479	122	.306	-1.6	C(47): 0.4	1.5
	C/DH	HV	A+	21	170	21	6	1	7	22	20	55	5	0	.274/.376/.473	97	.393	0.4	C(23): 4.4	0.9

Rob Brantly has a pending application to the Erik Kratz-David Ross Club—the traveling circus of lovable, way-too-old-for-this emergency third catchers who drift from team to team as the need arises. ⚾ **Josh Breaux's** 23 home runs were tied for third-most among Yankee farmhands. With that kind of power, he ought to have a backup catching job in the Majors someday, even if his OBP might never start with a three. ⚾ Oprah Winfrey, Pope Francis, Robert De Niro, Rihanna. That is a partial list of people who have never won an MVP award in Double-A. It's a list that no longer includes **Oswaldo Cabrera**. ⚾ **Estevan Florial** looked fantastic in his crumb-sized MLB action, but he couldn't handle the full cookie in Triple-A, where he struck out 30.9% of the time. As with many top prospects (and many cookies), he was more enticing when he was still raw. ⚾ Hard Hittin' **Chris Gittens** (@HardHittinCG on Twitter) lived up to his nickname in spring training, slashing .316/.458/.789. When given the chance in the regular season, he was more charitably described as Hard Swingin'. ⚾ **Ryan LaMarre** led all Yankees hitters with 12 PA/HR. The journeyman outfielder, on his sixth MLB team in as many seasons, would have totally maintained that rate with more than 24 PA too, yessiree. ⚾ Look up above at **Everson Pereira's** numbers. Then look away. Now, look at them again. You've just done a doubletake, as is appropriate whenever a 20-year-old hits 14 home runs in 27 games against older pitchers in High-A. ⚾ **Alexander Vargas** is a smooth shortstop prospect with all the speed you'd expect from a player listed at 148 pounds. On the other hand, he also has all the power you'd expect from a player listed at 148 pounds. ⚾ The Yankees have drafted five first-round catchers in their history, but only Thurman Munson ever reached the majors. In his first pro season, **Austin Wells** looks poised to become the second, though the bigger question might be whether he's still a catcher when he gets there.

Pitchers

PITCHER	TEAM	LVL	AGE	W	L	SV	G	GS	IP	H	HR	BB/9	K/9	K	GB%	BABIP	WHIP	ERA	DRA-	WARP	MPH	FB%	WHF	CSP
Yoendrys Gómez	TAM	A	21	0	0	0	9	9	23^{2}	14	3	3.4	11.0	29	43.9%	.204	0.97	3.42	90	0.4				
Brody Koerner	SWB	AAA	27	3	4	0	26	15	77	75	8	2.7	7.5	64	43.1%	.303	1.27	3.39	112	0.6				
	NYY	MLB	27	0	0	0	2	0	3	2	0	6.0	3.0	1	55.6%	.222	1.33	3.00	107	0.0	88.4	80.8%	12.5%	49.1%
Ron Marinaccio	SOM	AA	25	1	1	3	22	0	39^{2}	17	2	4.3	14.5	64	30.4%	.224	0.91	1.82	73	0.9				
	SWB	AAA	25	1	0	2	18	0	26^{2}	18	2	2.7	13.8	41	31.6%	.291	0.97	2.36	72	0.7				
Stephen Ridings	SOM	AA	25	4	0	2	14	0	19	8	0	0.9	14.2	30	37.1%	.229	0.53	0.47	84	0.3				
	SWB	AAA	25	1	0	1	8	0	10	8	2	1.8	10.8	12	61.5%	.250	1.00	2.70	81	0.2				
	NYY	MLB	25	0	0	0	5	0	5	4	0	3.6	12.6	7	45.5%	.400	1.20	1.80	96	0.1	96.8	74.3%	41.2%	57.9%
Sal Romano	SWB	AAA	27	1	1	2	25	0	30^{1}	36	1	1.5	7.4	25	60.6%	.357	1.35	3.56	96	0.5				
	CIN	MLB	27	0	0	0	14	0	20^{2}	20	4	3.9	5.2	12	41.4%	.242	1.40	5.23	121	0.0	93.7	62.8%	12.8%	56.9%
	NYY	MLB	27	0	1	0	4	0	3^{1}	7	0	5.4	13.5	5	25.0%	.583	2.70	5.40	103	0.0	95.2	59.5%	14.8%	56.2%
	MIL	MLB	27	0	1	0	1	0	1	4	1	0.0	0.0	0	57.1%	.500	4.00	27.00	111	0.0	94.8	66.7%	13.3%	64.6%
Ken Waldichuk	HV	A+	23	2	0	0	7	7	30^{2}	12	0	3.8	16.1	55	31.1%	.267	0.82	0.00	82	0.6				
	SOM	AA	23	4	3	0	16	14	79^{1}	64	13	4.3	12.3	108	36.7%	.293	1.29	4.20	87	1.2				

The Yankees' developmental superpower is helping pitching prospects add velocity, which makes **Brendan Beck** a perfect organizational match. They selected the Stanford right-hander in the second round of the 2021 draft because of his plus command of four pitches. ⚾ The good news is that **Jimmy Cordero** was still able to maintain his prodigious biceps while rehabilitating from the Tommy John surgery. The random news is it's unclear if his suspension for throwing at Willson Contreras at the end of the 2020 season was ever served. There is no bad news, since he'll likely be done with rehab by the time you read this. ⚾ Extended spring training and a case of COVID-19 bookended **Yoendrys Gómez's** season, restricting him to just 23 ⅔ innings. He made the most of his abbreviated action, using a mid-90s fastball and hard curve to strike out 30.2% of opposing batters. ⚾ From August 5-19, the Yankees played 15 consecutive games decided by four runs or less. **Brody Koerner** didn't appear in any of them despite remaining on the active roster the entire time, which indicates where he falls on the organizational pecking order. ⚾ **Ron Marinaccio** isn't likely to end up the most famous baseball player from Toms River, NJ, but a velocity bump and improving changeup could find him in the Bronx as soon as this year ⚾ Standing at 6'8" with a heater touching 101 mph and a high-80s breaker, **Stephen Ridings** is 1) evocative of Dellin Betances, and 2) the Yankee most likely to win a Lineout Vogelsong Award for player most deserving of a full comment in 2022. ⚾ Like a forgettable recurring character on *Everybody Loves Raymond*, **Sal Romano** kept walking through the Yankees' door, though without the canned applause. He signed with the organization four separate times in 2021, but received limited screen time. ⚾ **Brock Selvidge** took an overslot deal in the third round to forgo a commitment to LSU. He's a teenager with a 96-mph fastball and little else, at the moment; it's going to be a couple years before you need to think about him again. ⚾ Five years ago, **Ken Waldichuk** had to walk on at St. Mary's College because he couldn't earn a scholarship throwing 80-poo. Now he can (Waldi)chuk it up to 98 mph, leading all Yankees farmhands with a 36% strikeout rate while spending most of his first full professional season in Double-A.

TAMPA BAY RAYS

Essay by Russell A. Carleton

Player comments by Tommy Rancel and BP staff

We've been living in the age of Tampa Bay kremlinology for more than a decade. In 2008, a franchise lumped by geographical misfortune into a division with the Yankees and Red Sox—that had once made a habit of making bad bets on aging veterans like Jose Canseco, Greg Vaughn and Wade Boggs, and losing 100 games a season—made the World Series a year after posting a 66-96 record. That was also the year that they rebuked the devil and simply became the Rays.

This was back during the era when there was a dividing line between teams that had an "analytics department," or even an "analytics employee," and those that did not. The Rays' near-miraculous turnaround seemed to follow after they not only jumped but cannonballed into the analytical waters. It's not clear whether they owed their success to finding religion or science, but whatever they did, it worked. Since 2008, the Rays have posted eight seasons of 90 or more wins (not counting their 108-win pace in the COVID-shortened 2020 season), tying them with the Red Sox and Yankees and placing them only one behind the league-leading Dodgers in that category over the last 14 seasons. It's worth noting that Rays front-office alums now run two of those three rival franchises. Other teams have lured executives out of the Kremlin of Pinellas County, but somehow the team with the tiny payroll, subpar stadium and limited fanbase marches on.

The A's were the first to get credit for embracing Moneyball, but that was 20 years ago. The Rays not only took up the cause, but they've been refining it ever since Joe Maddon and his glasses haunted the dugout at Tropicana Field. But past the reflexive jokes—"loving the trade for the Rays . . . who did they get and who did they give up?"—there has always been an eerie silence coming from St. Petersburg, and not just because the team finally broke back into the top 28 in total attendance in 2021 after a ten-year absence.

The Rays just aren't very chatty. I suppose they shouldn't be. I'd print a joke about what the Rays say about their methods, but I'm still waiting on the quote. The Rays had their moment in the Florida sun as the official "Sabermetric darlings" a decade or so ago, but they were replaced by others, most of whom had a good run for a few years and then lost their wunderkind general manager or saw the plan

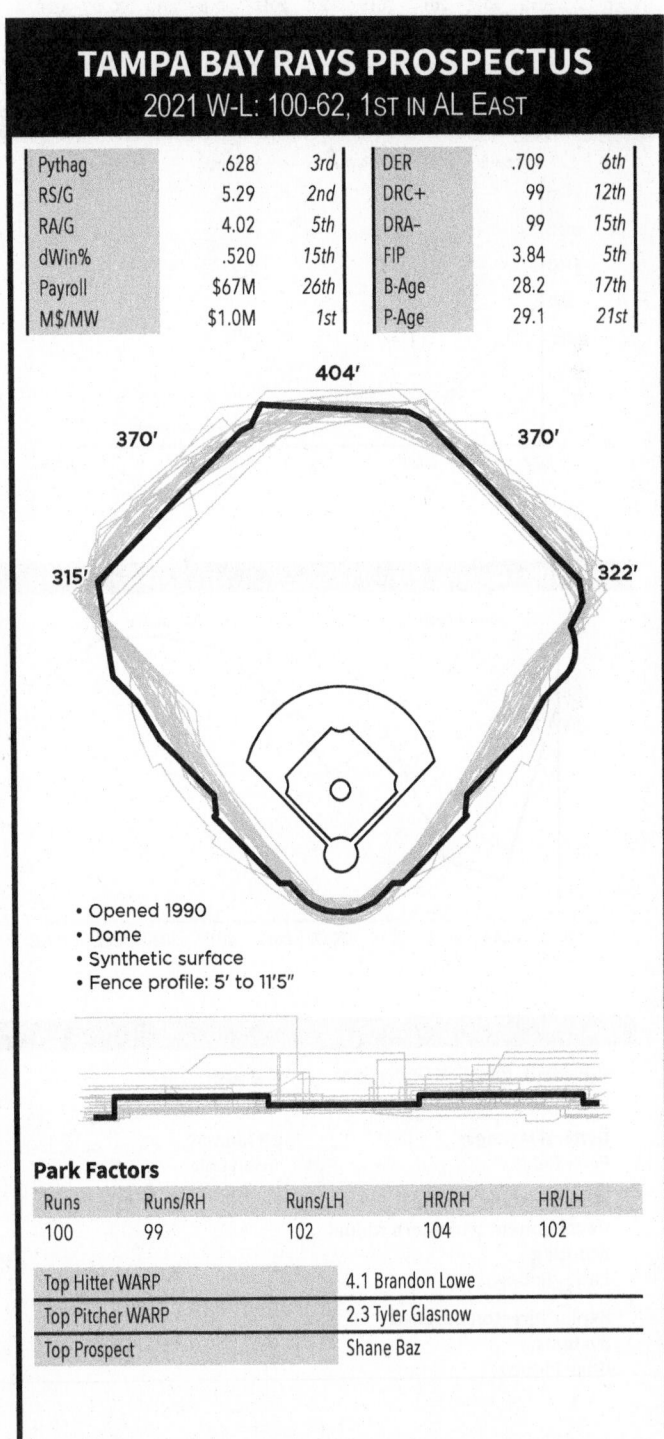

TAMPA BAY RAYS PROSPECTUS

2021 W-L: 100-62, 1st in AL East

Pythag	.628	*3rd*	DER	.709	*6th*
RS/G	5.29	*2nd*	DRC+	99	*12th*
RA/G	4.02	*5th*	DRA-	99	*15th*
dWin%	.520	*15th*	FIP	3.84	*5th*
Payroll	$67M	*26th*	B-Age	28.2	*17th*
M$/MW	$1.0M	*1st*	P-Age	29.1	*21st*

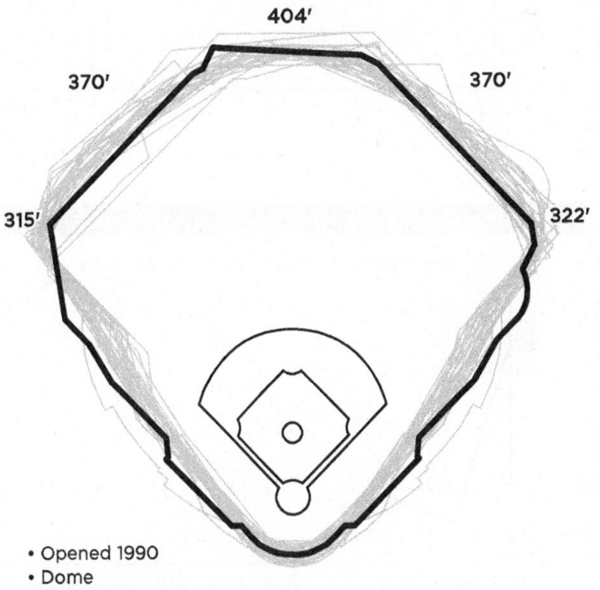

- Opened 1990
- Dome
- Synthetic surface
- Fence profile: 5′ to 11′5″

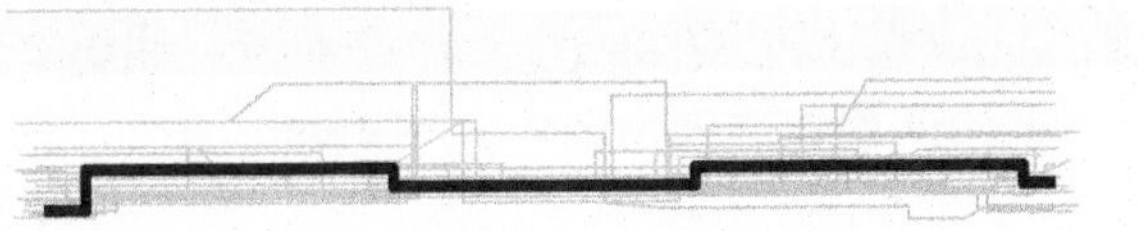

Park Factors

Runs	Runs/RH	Runs/LH	HR/RH	HR/LH
100	99	102	104	102

Top Hitter WARP	4.1 Brandon Lowe
Top Pitcher WARP	2.3 Tyler Glasnow
Top Prospect	Shane Baz

Payroll History (in millions)

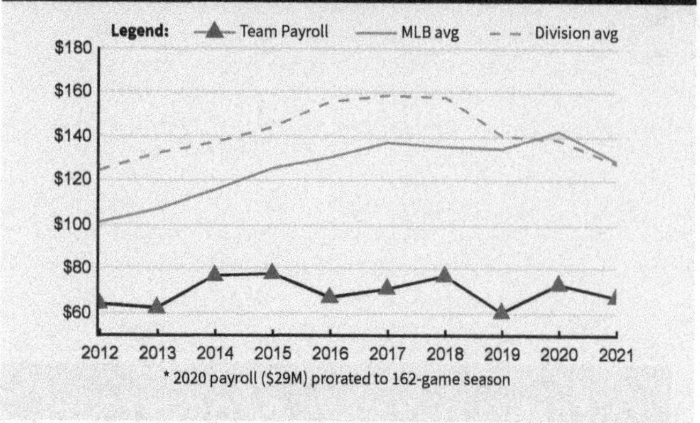

Future Commitments (in millions)

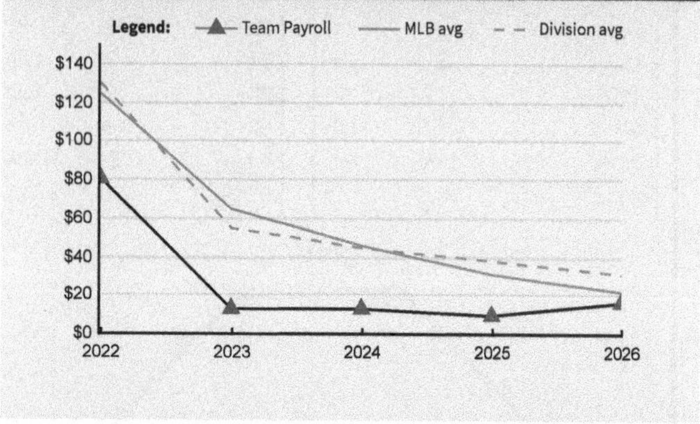

Farm System Ranking

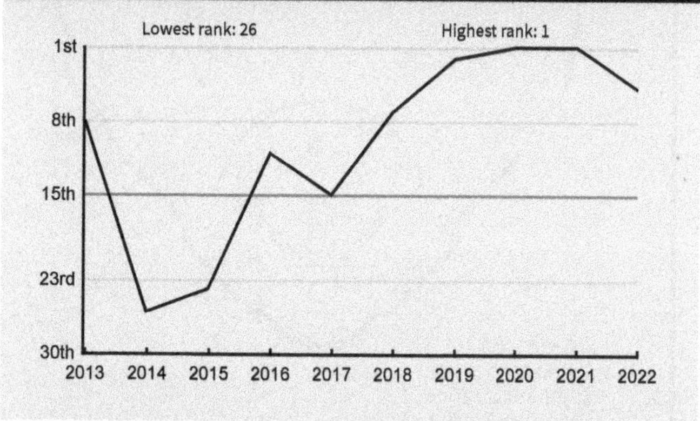

Personnel

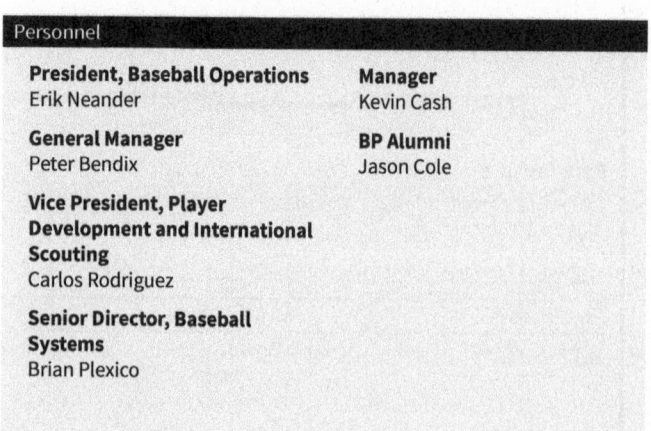

President, Baseball Operations
Erik Neander

General Manager
Peter Bendix

Vice President, Player Development and International Scouting
Carlos Rodriguez

Senior Director, Baseball Systems
Brian Plexico

Manager
Kevin Cash

BP Alumni
Jason Cole

that looked so perfect fall apart. Unlike the other spreadsheet heartthrobs, the Rays just kept going, even as seemingly every team in MLB has looked to hire someone to bring that Rays magic to their operations. The Rays quietly sit there and win games that no one watches. Last year, they won 100 of them.

How?

Warning! Gory Mathematical Details Ahead!

The problem with innovation is that, in order to prove that something works, you have to take the risk of trying it out. Depending on what you're trying, there could be some real cost to doing it. If it doesn't work, you're out the money. If it works, it will become fairly obvious what you did, and that it is succeeding, and everyone can copy it for free. About the only thing that you can hope for when innovating in Major League Baseball is that there will be some resistance to change in the other 29 organizations, and that will keep them from copying it too quickly. The curse of success is that, if something you do works really well, it will be copied even more quickly as the benefits grow more obvious. In baseball, there's an incentive to be the second mover.

If you look at the question from the perspective of one experiment or one novel idea, jumping in with both feet makes little sense. But the Rays took the time to flip that coin over and read the other side. What if their advantage was being the first to try *everything*? Let's look at the record.

We start with the biggest craze of the 2010s: the infield shift. We have public data on how many shifts were used *on balls that went into play, only*, from 2010 onward. Here are Tampa Bay's stats:

Year	Number of Shifts	League Average	Rank
2010	242	82	1st
2011	240	78	1st
2012	463	153	1st
2013	495	229	2nd
2014	824	443	2nd
2015	1464	591	1st
2016	1584	935	1st
2017	1515	890	3rd
2018	1861	1156	1st
2019	2046	1630	6th
2020	787	795	19th
2021	2171	1968	11th

In 2010, the Rays were already setting the standard, shifting more than any other team in MLB, though now, their 2010 numbers, which would net out to a couple of shifts per game, seem quaint. Still, they "went there" first and, through most of the decade, finished first or second in the number of shifts.

There's an argument to be made that maybe shifting isn't actually the fix-all that we once thought it was, but that's not the point. There was (and still is, somewhat) a decent case that shifting provided some benefit, and the Rays were the first ones to go for it. It took most of a decade for everyone else to catch up. Research shows that it takes about a decade for an innovation to wash through the entire league. Some teams move quickly to be second and third in line, but the pace of adaptation in baseball is slower than you might expect. That coefficient of friction is what the Rays are trying to leverage.

In 2012, the Rays signed José Molina to be their regular starting catcher despite his sub-.300 career OBP and the fact that Molina was 37 at the time. We now know what they were chasing. Molina was otherworldly in his pitch-framing abilities. Accounting for those abilities, the Rays got a couple of two-win seasons out of someone who was widely considered useless. The Rays quickly showed that they had a type. Ryan Hanigan, René Rivera, Wilson Ramos, Hank Conger and Mike Zunino all came to town as "defense-first" catchers. Other teams caught on, and now catchers are developed with an emphasis on framing. When everyone's good, it's hard to stand out and provide extra value to the team.

It was the Rays who pioneered the use of "the Opener" when reliever Sergio Romo started their game on May 19, 2018. Romo started the next night, too. In 2018, the Rays also shifted their use of starting pitchers—again, ahead of everyone else, and they are still catching up. The table below shows how often a batter hitting for the third time in a game faced their opponent's starting pitcher when facing the Rays and when facing the other 29 teams.

Year	Rays Starter Pct.	Rest of League Starter Pct.
2016	67%	67%
2017	62%	63%
2018	28%	58%
2019	35%	55%
2020	29%	40%
2021	35%	46%

Up until 2017, the Rays were largely indistinguishable from the league in how often they let hitters see their starter a third time. But in 2018, there was clearly a memo sent out at the Trop, one that the other 29 teams didn't get a copy of. The gap is closing a bit, as MLB slowly comes to terms with the fact that it's a reliever's league. Once again, the Rays got there first.

The Rays were among the first to push the envelope around moving players all over the field in service of getting the ideal mix of bats into the lineup on a particular day. They were the first to publicly say that they were going to have "bullpen days" rather than a named starter. In 2019, the Rays became the first team in MLB to have a uniformed "analytics coach," Jonathan Erlichman. And this is just the stuff that can be seen at the MLB level.

In 2013, Chicago White Sox broadcaster Hawk Harrelson went on the MLB Network and issued a now-famous rant lashing out at Sabermetrics. Harrelson, taking a poke at the Sabermetric penchant for acronyms, boasted that Sabermetrics couldn't measure "TWTW," or "the will to win." Harrelson was suggesting that winning was the product of a specific mindset, and while Hawk was roundly dragged for the statement, maybe there's a kernel of truth in it. There is a mindset component to all of it, but I think Hawk had the wrong four letters. Looking at the Rays, we see a different model: YTFN.

When faced with the possibility of change, the natural human response is to ask the question, "Are you sure?" Even reading that question probably feels natural. We don't frame the question in terms of whether the benefits outweigh the risks. We instinctively ask for surety, but there is very little in life that is certain. It's why teams (and people, and businesses, and governments) have been resistant to do things that are obviously working in other settings for the entirety of baseball (and human) history. We want to make sure we exhaust the last "budwadabouts" before we finally take the plunge.

The Rays ask, "why not?"

The shift from "Are you sure?" to YTFN might have been the biggest strategic advantage that the Rays have had over the last decade-plus. It's not about a specific strategy. The individual strategies will come and go. If they work, everyone will eventually catch up on them, but only because they eventually reach certainty. You can only ignore success for so long. But there will always be an idea that someone isn't entirely sure about.

For the Rays, TWTW is the YTFN mindset. You don't have to try every idea that falls out of someone's head. But if someone can make a decent case that the potential benefits are *more likely* than the potential drawbacks, then the smart thing to do is to try it out. If it obviously doesn't work, you can usually just stop doing it and switch back. Even moving slightly back from "Are you sure?" might be the only push that you need in life. And baseball.

When your secret weapon is a particular person, or an idea, or technology, it's only a matter of time before the person leaves, or the idea is overtaken, or the technology becomes obsolete. But if the secret weapon is a mindset that runs throughout the organization to ask a slightly different question, then it will be much more enduring, even as all of those individual things pass by. So, if you want to know how the Rays have endured over the years, perhaps it's because they have YTFN.

—Russell A. Carleton is an author of Baseball Prospectus.

HITTERS

Randy Arozarena OF
Born: 02/28/95 Age: 27 Bats: R Throws: R Height: 5'11" Weight: 185 lb. Origin: International Free Agent, 2016

YEAR	TEAM	LVL	AGE	PA	R	2B	3B	HR	RBI	BB	K	SB	CS	Whiff%	AVG/OBP/SLG	DRC+	BABIP	BRR	FRAA	WARP
2019	SPR	AA	24	116	14	7	2	3	15	13	23	8	5		.309/.422/.515	122	.380	0.0	CF(13): 0.8, LF(5): 0.1, RF(5): -0.6	0.7
2019	MEM	AAA	24	283	51	18	2	12	38	24	48	9	7		.358/.435/.593	121	.404	-1.7	CF(25): -3.6, RF(20): 5.0, LF(14): 0.1	1.7
2019	STL	MLB	24	23	4	1	0	1	2	2	4	2	1	25.0%	.300/.391/.500	96	.333	-1.8	RF(6): -0.1, CF(5): 0.5, LF(1): -0.1	-0.1
2020	TB	MLB	25	76	15	2	0	7	11	6	22	4	0	36.8%	.281/.382/.641	120	.306	0.7	LF(14): 1.1, RF(3): -0.4, CF(2): 0.0	0.5
2021	TB	MLB	26	604	94	32	3	20	69	56	170	20	10	32.6%	.274/.356/.459	103	.363	-0.2	LF(81): 0.6, RF(53): -0.9, CF(1): 0.0	2.2
2022 DC	*TB*	*MLB*	*27*	*594*	*84*	*27*	*2*	*18*	*76*	*52*	*167*	*18*	*9*	*31.9%*	*.243/.332/.412*	*102*	*.321*	*1.1*	*LF 0, RF 1*	*2.2*

Comparables: Hunter Renfroe, Lorenzo Cain, Chris Heisey

There were 1,673 major league playoff games played before we saw a player hit a home run and steal home plate in the same game. Of course, it was Arozarena who did it first. After exploding onto the scene with a historic 2020 postseason performance, he was able to hold his own as a full-time contributor in 2021. He showed a blend of power and speed, collecting a perfect 20-20 season right on the dot. There is manageable swing-and-miss in his game and he has the ability to hit the ball to all fields which should keep teams from shifting and totally sinking his average. He won the 2021 AL Rookie of the Year award even though he has appeared in every playoffs since 2019. He'll enter 2022 at age 27 which is a little old for a "second" year guy. The Rays are unlikely to care about that as it means they will control what is likely a 2-4 win player through his peak and can let him walk on the other side of 30 if they choose.

★ ★ ★ *2022 Top 101 Prospect* **#95** ★ ★ ★

Vidal Bruján IF/OF
Born: 02/09/98 Age: 24 Bats: S Throws: R Height: 5'10" Weight: 180 lb. Origin: International Free Agent, 2014

YEAR	TEAM	LVL	AGE	PA	R	2B	3B	HR	RBI	BB	K	SB	CS	Whiff%	AVG/OBP/SLG	DRC+	BABIP	BRR	FRAA	WARP
2019	SRR	WIN	21	100	12	3	4	2	10	15	17	4	5		.256/.380/.463		.297			
2019	CHA	A+	21	196	28	8	3	1	15	17	26	24	5		.290/.357/.386	121	.333	5.8	2B(29): 1.5, SS(14): 1.0	1.9
2019	MTG	AA	21	233	28	9	4	3	25	20	35	24	8		.266/.336/.391	112	.304	-1.7	2B(33): 3.0, SS(15): 0.8	1.5
2020	TOR	WIN	22	75	14	2	1	0	5	11	10	10	3		.254/.373/.317		.302			
2021	TOR	WIN	23	69	7	2	1	0	3	6	11	8	3		.206/.275/.270		.250			
2021	DUR	AAA	23	441	77	31	1	12	56	49	68	44	8		.262/.345/.440	116	.290	2.7	2B(29): 0.1, LF(24): 2.8, SS(16): 2.6	2.7
2021	TB	MLB	23	26	3	0	0	0	2	0	8	1	0	20.0%	.077/.077/.077	82	.111	0.2	2B(4): 0.7, RF(2): 0.0, LF(1): -0.0	0.1
2022 DC	*TB*	*MLB*	*24*	*347*	*44*	*16*	*2*	*6*	*36*	*28*	*61*	*23*	*8*	*19.9%*	*.248/.316/.373*	*87*	*.291*	*2.1*	*2B 1, LF 0*	*0.8*

Comparables: Jose Altuve, Hanser Alberto, Hernán Pérez

A consensus top-100 prospect, Bruján made his major-league debut in early July. He made 10 appearances for the Rays before returning to Durham, where he remained for the rest of the season. The lack of opportunity with the big-league club had more to do with the available options in Tampa Bay than Bruján's ability. He remains a top-of-the order type with speed and defensive flexibility. A switch-hitter, he continues to show better skills from the left side—since 2019, he has barely reached the Mendoza line as a right-handed hitter. A former shortstop, he started at six different positions for Durham—including the six spot—and played all three outfield positions plus second base in his brief time with the Rays. That versatility will likely help him carve out a larger role in 2022 as the Rays move on from more expensive veterans and use a top prospect like Bruján to fill a hole (or several) at a much cheaper rate.

Ji-Man Choi 1B
Born: 05/19/91 Age: 31 Bats: L Throws: R Height: 6'1" Weight: 260 lb. Origin: International Free Agent, 2009

YEAR	TEAM	LVL	AGE	PA	R	2B	3B	HR	RBI	BB	K	SB	CS	Whiff%	AVG/OBP/SLG	DRC+	BABIP	BRR	FRAA	WARP
2019	TB	MLB	28	487	54	20	2	19	63	64	108	2	3	25.5%	.261/.363/.459	104	.303	-2.1	1B(103): -4.8	0.9
2020	TB	MLB	29	145	16	13	0	3	16	20	36	0	0	31.8%	.230/.331/.410	89	.291	-0.2	1B(38): -2.4	-0.1
2021	DUR	AAA	30	27	4	2	0	0	2	3	7	0	0		.261/.333/.348	93	.353	-1.1	1B(5): 0.3	0.0
2021	TB	MLB	30	305	36	14	0	11	45	45	87	0	0	31.9%	.229/.348/.411	96	.300	-0.2	1B(73): -0.3	0.5
2022 DC	*TB*	*MLB*	*31*	*512*	*73*	*24*	*1*	*17*	*63*	*70*	*142*	*2*	*1*	*31.3%*	*.228/.342/.408*	*102*	*.298*	*-0.6*	*1B -1*	*1.0*

Comparables: Justin Smoak, Yonder Alonso, Lucas Duda

If Teammate+ was a thing then Choi would lead the league. He's a big teddy bear of a man who is loved by his peers and fans alike. He's also a decent hitter and holds down the cold corner pretty well for a man his size. Choi is a largely average stick, but gets on base and has adequate pop from the left side. He has (and can do) traditional splits and is best served having a right-handed counterpart. He struggled with multiple leg injuries throughout the course of the season—perhaps impacted by an offseason bout of COVID-19— which isn't great for a big guy now on the other side of 30. The Rays pay for production and typically leave the intangible elements on the side when it comes to business. Choi is a fan favorite for sure, but how much is that worth when you're making several million dollars as a platoon bat with knee issues?

Carlos Colmenarez SS/DH Born: 11/15/03 Age: 18 Bats: L Throws: R Height: 5'10" Weight: 170 lb. Origin: International Free Agent, 2021

YEAR	TEAM	LVL	AGE	PA	R	2B	3B	HR	RBI	BB	K	SB	CS	Whiff%	AVG/OBP/SLG	DRC+	BABIP	BRR	FRAA	WARP
2021	DSL TB1	ROK	17	114	7	2	1	0	12	8	30	7	6		.247/.319/.289		.338			
2022												*No projection*								

Comparables: Adrian Valerio, Yordys Valdes, Yonathan Mendoza

The one area where the Rays have been aggressive in spending is the international free agent market. Giving seven-figure bonuses to teenagers is a risky business, but the Rays have been comfortable in doing so with Colmenarez serving as the latest example, signing out of Venezuela. Despite being slowed by a hamate injury, he did appear in some Dominican Summer League games and flashed the tools that earned him such a large bonus. The projections are average or better across the board. A left-handed hitter, he shows quick hands with power that will grow as he does. He is a plus runner with defensive chops to stick up the middle. This will be a player the rest of the world will know by the 2023 edition of this book. Feel free to start name dropping him in tweets now so you look cool when that happens.

Yandy Díaz CI Born: 08/08/91 Age: 30 Bats: R Throws: R Height: 6'2" Weight: 215 lb. Origin: International Free Agent, 2013

YEAR	TEAM	LVL	AGE	PA	R	2B	3B	HR	RBI	BB	K	SB	CS	Whiff%	AVG/OBP/SLG	DRC+	BABIP	BRR	FRAA	WARP
2019	TB	MLB	27	347	53	20	1	14	38	35	61	2	2	22.3%	.267/.340/.476	109	.288	-0.9	3B(50): -0.6, 1B(22): -0.1	1.1
2020	TB	MLB	28	138	16	3	0	2	11	23	17	0	0	15.7%	.307/.428/.386	123	.347	-1.1	3B(25): 0.1, 1B(2): -0.4	0.6
2021	TB	MLB	29	541	62	20	1	13	64	69	85	1	1	19.2%	.256/.353/.387	111	.286	-3.6	1B(81): 2.9, 3B(58): -3.4	1.8
2022 DC	*TB*	*MLB*	*30*	*586*	*82*	*22*	*1*	*14*	*72*	*75*	*100*	*2*	*1*	*19.1%*	*.268/.366/.402*	*113*	*.309*	*-0.7*	*3B -2, 1B 1*	*2.2*

Comparables: Casey McGehee, Danny Valencia, Chris Johnson

It is safe to say that the Rays probably aren't going to turn Díaz's bulging biceps into a launch angle machine at this point. Three seasons into the experiment, the Sagua La Grande native has hit 29 home runs and 45 additional extra-base hits, however, it has taken over 1,000 plate appearances to get there. He did hit fewer than 50% ground balls for the first time in his career this season. His batted ball profile shifted almost identically with ground and fly balls according for nearly 93% of his in play events. The disappointment was the lack of line drives—the type of batted ball that usually turns into hits. Díaz split his time in the field between the hot and cold corners where he was better on the cool side and slightly below-average on the warmer edge, where he figures to see more time following the trade of Joey Wendle. With arbitration years beginning, his production is going to have to increase in order for him to fit in the Rays' algorithm.

Xavier Edwards 2B/3B Born: 08/09/99 Age: 22 Bats: S Throws: R Height: 5'10" Weight: 175 lb. Origin: Round 1, 2018 Draft (#38 overall)

YEAR	TEAM	LVL	AGE	PA	R	2B	3B	HR	RBI	BB	K	SB	CS	Whiff%	AVG/OBP/SLG	DRC+	BABIP	BRR	FRAA	WARP
2019	FW	A	19	344	44	13	4	1	30	30	35	20	9		.336/.392/.414	127	.371	0.2	2B(51): 3.3, SS(21): 3.1	2.9
2019	LE	A+	19	217	32	5	4	0	13	14	19	14	2		.301/.349/.367	121	.331	3.4	2B(36): 1.1, SS(9): -1.1	1.6
2021	MTG	AA	21	337	40	13	3	0	27	36	42	19	11		.302/.377/.368	110	.348	-1.2	2B(55): -1.1, 3B(22): 1.7	1.3
2022 non-DC	*TB*	*MLB*	*22*	*251*	*21*	*9*	*1*	*1*	*20*	*19*	*34*	*11*	*4*	*15.5%*	*.262/.322/.335*	*82*	*.304*	*0.9*	*2B 0, SS 0*	*0.5*

Comparables: Odúbel Herrera, Jonathan Villar, Thairo Estrada

Overshadowed in his own organization by a generational prospect that plays similar defensive positions, Edwards has the ability to play a starring role one day alongside the Wanderkind. He is also a switch-hitter; however, he possesses top-of-the-lineup skills with a plus hit tool and borderline double-plus speed. He passed a pivotal test and maintained a .300 average and OBP greater than .375 while playing at Double-A in 2021. There is very little power—like one home run in 1,000 plate appearances type stuff—but the on-base ability and speed make up for it plus the ability to defend up the middle. He is likely a shortstop in many other systems, but probably a standout second baseman for Tampa Bay. The keystone is well covered in 2021, but Edwards could be a September addition if he's not needed earlier with an eye on a full-time job for 2023.

Wander Franco SS Born: 03/01/01 Age: 21 Bats: S Throws: R Height: 5'10" Weight: 189 lb. Origin: International Free Agent, 2017

YEAR	TEAM	LVL	AGE	PA	R	2B	3B	HR	RBI	BB	K	SB	CS	Whiff%	AVG/OBP/SLG	DRC+	BABIP	BRR	FRAA	WARP
2019	BG	A	18	272	42	16	5	6	29	30	20	14	9		.318/.390/.506	147	.318	-0.5	SS(53): -1.4	2.2
2019	CHA	A+	18	223	40	11	2	3	24	26	15	4	5		.339/.408/.464	148	.346	3.3	SS(45): 8.8	3.0
2021	DUR	AAA	20	180	31	11	6	7	35	14	21	5	4		.313/.372/.583	134	.324	0.6	SS(31): -0.3, 3B(7): 1.1, 2B(3): -0.2	1.4
2021	TB	MLB	20	308	53	18	5	7	39	24	37	2	1	16.4%	.288/.347/.463	113	.311	0.9	SS(63): -3.0, 3B(8): 0.2, 2B(1): 0.1	1.4
2022 DC	*TB*	*MLB*	*21*	*583*	*81*	*28*	*9*	*14*	*85*	*46*	*69*	*9*	*6*	*15.8%*	*.285/.347/.457*	*118*	*.307*	*1.2*	*SS 0*	*3.7*

Comparables: Rubén Tejada, Carlos Correa, Elvis Andrus

What were you doing when you were 20 years old? Was it tying the major-league record for reaching base in consecutive games? No? Oh, so that was just Franco, who reached base in 43 straight games to tie Frank Robinson for such a streak by a player under the age of 21. Franco made a somewhat surprising debut on June 22nd. It wasn't surprising from a talent standpoint, but rather that the Rays would pull the trigger at a point that may not have been financially beneficial for them. After a slow start out of the gate, WanderVision locked in. While most people his age spent the summer months recording themselves falling off milk crates, Franco hit .323/.383/.506 with more walks (14) than strikeouts (11) from August 1 on. Overall, he made contact on nearly 85% of his swings and a whopping 91% on swings within the zone. He showed power, solid speed and enough glove at shortstop to remain until perhaps another highly successful prospect moves him to third base in a few years. It is a superstar profile all the way through and it is no longer just a projection. In fact, it is so real the Rays gave him an 11-year, $182 million contract, though it's unclear how much of that comes in Canadian dollars.

Blake Hunt C Born: 11/10/98 Age: 23 Bats: R Throws: R Height: 6'3" Weight: 215 lb. Origin: Round 2, 2017 Draft (#69 overall)

YEAR	TEAM	LVL	AGE	PA	R	2B	3B	HR	RBI	BB	K	SB	CS	Whiff%	AVG/OBP/SLG	DRC+	BABIP	BRR	FRAA	WARP
2019	FW	A	20	376	40	21	3	5	39	35	67	4	1		.255/.331/.381	114	.303	-4.6	C(77): 16.1, 1B(9): -0.5	3.0
2021	BG	A+	22	257	41	15	2	9	41	26	79	1	0		.225/.307/.427	92	.298	-0.1	C(50): 9.7	1.4
2021	MTG	AA	22	63	5	2	0	0	0	6	25	0	0		.125/.210/.161	58	.226	0.8	C(17): -0.2	0.0
2022 non-DC	*TB*	*MLB*	*23*	*251*	*20*	*11*	*1*	*3*	*21*	*19*	*84*	*0*	*1*	*34.0%*	*.194/.264/.307*	*52*	*.288*	*-0.2*	*C 3, 1B 0*	*-0.2*

Comparables: Lou Marson, Derek Norris, Danny Jansen

YEAR	TEAM	P. COUNT	FRM RUNS	BLK RUNS	THRW RUNS	TOT RUNS
2019	FW	10466	16.4	0.8	0.7	17.8
2021	MTG	2139	0.2	0.0	0.0	0.2
2021	BG	6889	9.5	0.5	0.5	10.4
2022	*TB*	*6956*	*-0.3*	*-0.1*	*-0.1*	*-0.4*

Hunt is a big, athletic backstop that has a solid defensive reputation and offensive upside. Originally drafted by the Padres, he signed for well over slot value as the 69th pick in 2017. He was the second catcher acquired by the Rays in the Blake Snell trade and spent most of his season catching for High-A Bowling Green. Despite his tall frame, he has above-average pop times to go with a 60 arm. Offensively, he remains a work in progress but did show some in-game power out of that big base. Strikeouts were a problem—especially during his stint in Double-A. If he settles down as a good defensive catcher with above-average ability to cut down the run game and hits double-digit home runs, they'll have a cheaper Mike Zunino with a little more hit tool potential.

Greg Jones SS Born: 03/07/98 Age: 24 Bats: S Throws: R Height: 6'2" Weight: 175 lb. Origin: Round 1, 2019 Draft (#22 overall)

YEAR	TEAM	LVL	AGE	PA	R	2B	3B	HR	RBI	BB	K	SB	CS	Whiff%	AVG/OBP/SLG	DRC+	BABIP	BRR	FRAA	WARP
2019	HV	SS	21	218	39	13	4	1	24	22	56	19	8		.335/.413/.461		.467			
2021	BG	A+	23	257	48	7	3	13	38	29	75	27	2		.291/.389/.527	122	.383	1.7	SS(50): 1.4	1.8
2021	MTG	AA	23	60	8	1	1	1	2	4	21	7	0		.185/.267/.296	70	.281	0.3	SS(15): -0.9	-0.1
2022 non-DC	*TB*	*MLB*	*24*	*251*	*22*	*9*	*1*	*5*	*24*	*19*	*83*	*14*	*4*	*33.5%*	*.208/.283/.336*	*67*	*.303*	*1.4*	*SS 0*	*0.0*

Comparables: JaCoby Jones, JT Riddle, Wilmer Difo

Oh hey look! Another toolsy athlete with middle-of-the-field defensive ability and offensive upside. Jones was the Rays' first-round selection in 2019 out of UNC Wilmington. Despite missing game action in 2020 due to the shutdown, he skipped Low-A altogether and reached Double-A by the end of the 2021 season. He had a strong showing in Bowling Green, flashing both power and speed. Jones bulked up and hit a combined 14 home runs while maintaining his elite foot speed. He won the Rays baserunner of the year, successfully swiping 34-36 (94%) stolen base attempts. Contact remains a long-term concern and that was only intensified when he struck out 21 times in 60 plate appearances with the Biscuits. Defensively, Jones played shortstop exclusively, but center field remains as an option down the road if he doesn't refine his skills on the dirt.

Kevin Kiermaier CF Born: 04/22/90 Age: 32 Bats: L Throws: R Height: 6'1" Weight: 210 lb. Origin: Round 31, 2010 Draft (#941 overall)

YEAR	TEAM	LVL	AGE	PA	R	2B	3B	HR	RBI	BB	K	SB	CS	Whiff%	AVG/OBP/SLG	DRC+	BABIP	BRR	FRAA	WARP
2019	TB	MLB	29	480	60	20	7	14	55	26	104	19	5	25.2%	.228/.278/.398	79	.267	2.4	CF(125): 6.3	1.6
2020	TB	MLB	30	159	16	5	3	3	22	20	42	8	1	30.5%	.217/.321/.362	87	.290	0.0	CF(46): 4.1	0.7
2021	TB	MLB	31	390	54	19	7	4	37	33	99	9	5	31.6%	.259/.328/.388	79	.345	3.9	CF(116): -5.6	0.4
2022 DC	*TB*	*MLB*	*32*	*311*	*36*	*12*	*3*	*6*	*37*	*27*	*80*	*9*	*5*	*30.7%*	*.228/.308/.371*	*82*	*.300*	*1.2*	*CF 0*	*0.5*

Comparables: Devon White, Mark Kotsay, Cesar Geronimo

2021 was more of the same for Kiermaier. When he wasn't unnecessarily diving, jumping or cutting off his own fielders, he was an above-average defender in center field. Offensively, he continues to range between below-average and just around average with prolonged bouts of non-production and a few spurts of positive output. Kiermaier said it best himself: "I got a lot of snap and crackle but no pop." He should be thanking his Lucky Charms that his contract extension was signed before his bat goes into a total Kaboom. Perhaps eating some more Wheaties will lead to more Pops or at least some crunch since he fancies himself as the captain of the team. He's on the wrong side of 30 which means there's only so many more defensive Trix the old rabbit can pull from his hat before we'll wonder why we never really got a truly special season from KK. That's just Life, we suppose.

Brandon Lowe 2B Born: 07/06/94 Age: 28 Bats: L Throws: R Height: 5'10" Weight: 185 lb. Origin: Round 3, 2015 Draft (#87 overall)

YEAR	TEAM	LVL	AGE	PA	R	2B	3B	HR	RBI	BB	K	SB	CS	Whiff%	AVG/OBP/SLG	DRC+	BABIP	BRR	FRAA	WARP
2019	TB	MLB	24	327	42	17	2	17	51	25	113	5	0	37.7%	.270/.336/.514	87	.377	2.4	2B(69): 3.8, 1B(5): -0.8, RF(5): -0.6	1.1
2020	TB	MLB	25	224	36	9	2	14	37	25	58	3	0	35.8%	.269/.362/.554	110	.309	2.9	2B(44): -6.5, RF(7): 1.3, LF(5): -0.2	0.8
2021	TB	MLB	26	615	97	31	0	39	99	68	167	7	1	32.7%	.247/.340/.523	119	.280	3.4	2B(133): 0.5, LF(10): -0.8, RF(6): 0.1	4.1
2022 DC	*TB*	*MLB*	*27*	*600*	*95*	*29*	*2*	*26*	*82*	*63*	*161*	*5*	*3*	*32.9%*	*.239/.331/.454*	*105*	*.295*	*-0.2*	*2B 0, RF 1*	*2.5*

Comparables: Derek Dietrich, Luis Valbuena, Kyle Seager

Lowe might be the most unassuming hitter that has hit at least 39 home runs in a season. He also thinks he can fit eight marshmallows in his mouth. Listed at under six feet and fewer than 200 pounds, his frame does not scream power, yet he put nearly 40 taters on the board in 2021 and will likely produce similar totals going forward. Lowe is somewhat of a three-true-outcome guy with more walks, strikeouts and home runs than the average hitter, though he outperforms the traditional TTO-hitter mold by being able to hit .250-plus. The former Maryland Terrapin continues to line up at second base most days—where he is more solid than anything else—with the flexibility to play the outfield corners when needed, as well as an annual cameo at first base. As long as he remains healthy and productive, he will be wildly underpaid for at least the next three seasons in which he is scheduled to make a combined $18 million.

Josh Lowe OF Born: 02/02/98 Age: 24 Bats: L Throws: R Height: 6'4" Weight: 205 lb. Origin: Round 1, 2016 Draft (#13 overall)

YEAR	TEAM	LVL	AGE	PA	R	2B	3B	HR	RBI	BB	K	SB	CS	Whiff%	AVG/OBP/SLG	DRC+	BABIP	BRR	FRAA	WARP
2019	MTG	AA	21	519	70	23	4	18	62	59	132	30	9		.252/.341/.442	110	.316	4.2	CF(110): -7.5, RF(9): 5.2, LF(1): -0.2	2.8
2021	DUR	AAA	23	470	76	28	2	22	78	61	123	26	0		.291/.381/.535	119	.361	4.5	CF(55): -5.9, RF(38): 1.7, LF(11): 2.5	2.9
2021	TB	MLB	23	2	0	0	0	0	0	1	0	1	0	40.0%	1.000/1.000/1.000	96	1.000	0.1	LF(1): -0.0, RF(1): -0.1	0.0
2022 DC	*TB*	*MLB*	*24*	*60*	*8*	*2*	*0*	*1*	*10*	*6*	*17*	*1*	*1*	*31.2%*	*.236/.318/.401*	*90*	*.320*	*0.1*	*CF 0*	*0.1*

Comparables: Trayvon Robinson, Austin Meadows, Carlos González

The 13th-overall pick in the 2016 draft, Lowe received an espresso shot in early September, earning a two-game call-up before a return to Triple-A. Despite the short stay, he collected his first major-league hit and would retire with a 1.000 batting average should he never make it back—something known as a Sunshine Graham. Although his time with Tampa Bay was brief, Lowe did plenty of work for the Durham Bulls: He collected over 50 extra-base hits and surpassed 20 home runs in a season for the first time. The productive campaign resulted in being named the Rays' minor league player of the year. He remains a top-level athlete with a blend of speed and power (20-20 season) with the ability to track balls in center field and arm strength to handle right if needed. The outfield depth chart was stacked in 2021, but rising salaries could cause an organizational reshuffle that puts Lowe high in the pecking order.

Manuel Margot OF Born: 09/28/94 Age: 27 Bats: R Throws: R Height: 5'11" Weight: 180 lb. Origin: International Free Agent, 2011

YEAR	TEAM	LVL	AGE	PA	R	2B	3B	HR	RBI	BB	K	SB	CS	Whiff%	AVG/OBP/SLG	DRC+	BABIP	BRR	FRAA	WARP
2019	SD	MLB	24	441	59	19	3	12	37	38	88	20	4	23.2%	.234/.304/.387	91	.272	4.6	CF(135): -4.5	1.4
2020	TB	MLB	25	159	19	9	0	1	11	13	25	12	4	23.7%	.269/.327/.352	100	.317	0.5	CF(21): 1.7, LF(18): 1.0, RF(15): -0.4	0.8
2021	TB	MLB	26	464	55	18	3	10	57	37	70	13	8	20.5%	.254/.313/.382	99	.281	0.9	RF(86): 7.6, LF(24): 2.1, CF(24): 2.3	2.8
2022 DC	*TB*	*MLB*	*27*	*560*	*71*	*22*	*3*	*13*	*68*	*45*	*94*	*18*	*9*	*21.2%*	*.256/.318/.393*	*93*	*.289*	*1.6*	*RF 4, CF 1*	*2.1*

Comparables: Carlos Beltrán, Jose Cardenal, Curt Flood

Margot is very much "what you see is what you get." He is a right-handed hitting outfielder with traditional splits, doing his best work against left-handed pitching. He has good speed and is a solid hand in the outfield. He spends most of his time in the corners, but continues to serve as center field insurance for Kiermaier's annual trip to the injured list. It's not a fancy profile and entering his late-20s, it's not likely to have a dramatic shift. It is a highly useful profile, though, and would be a great fit as the 10th man on most teams. As for his current team? Margot is commanding a multi-million dollar salary which might not fit how the Rays operate, at least for a 10th man.

Curtis Mead 3B Born: 10/26/00 Age: 21 Bats: R Throws: R Height: 6'2" Weight: 171 lb. Origin: International Free Agent, 2018

YEAR	TEAM	LVL	AGE	PA	R	2B	3B	HR	RBI	BB	K	SB	CS	Whiff%	AVG/OBP/SLG	DRC+	BABIP	BRR	FRAA	WARP
2019	ADE	WIN	18	151	21	6	0	6	18	12	24	5	1		.309/.373/.485		.340			
2019	PHE	ROK	18	175	26	12	2	4	19	13	23	4	3		.285/.351/.462		.313			
2020	ADE	WIN	19	76	11	7	0	3	12	3	13	2	0		.347/.382/.569		.393			
2021	SCO	WIN	20	90	16	5	2	3	11	4	13	1	1		.313/.360/.530		.343			
2021	CSC	A	20	211	36	21	1	7	35	15	30	9	2		.356/.408/.586	134	.391	-1.0	3B(25): -0.6, 1B(15): 2.2	1.5
2021	BG	A+	20	233	38	15	1	7	32	19	38	2	2		.282/.348/.466	119	.309	0.4	3B(43): 1.1, 1B(3): 0.1	1.4
2022 non-DC	*TB*	*MLB*	*21*	*251*	*23*	*14*	*1*	*4*	*25*	*14*	*49*	*3*	*2*	*24.1%*	*.260/.310/.393*	*89*	*.312*	*0.1*	*3B 0, 1B 1*	*0.4*

Comparables: Enrique Hernández, Miguel Sanó, Wilmer Flores

Mead is a scrappy infielder from Australia that plays with a high motor. He is sneaky athletic with flexibility to play both corner infield positions and has played up the middle in the past. He is gritty and has been a winner in the lower levels of the Rays system. He possesses a high baseball IQ with good fundamentals and plays the game the right way. He's the type to bring a lunch pail to the ballpark, but he is also a heads up player. He has been an offensive force with a sweet swing and high contact rates. He has more power than you would think with deceptive speed that turns singles into doubles. He is a gym or field rat and is often seen at the field before any other players. He has solid intangibles and gets the most out of his abilities by playing with a lot of heart. Rays fans will love his grinder mentality and his willingness to out-hustle anyone in the park.

Austin Meadows LF/DH Born: 05/03/95 Age: 27 Bats: L Throws: L Height: 6'3" Weight: 225 lb. Origin: Round 1, 2013 Draft (#9 overall)

YEAR	TEAM	LVL	AGE	PA	R	2B	3B	HR	RBI	BB	K	SB	CS	Whiff%	AVG/OBP/SLG	DRC+	BABIP	BRR	FRAA	WARP
2019	TB	MLB	24	591	83	29	7	33	89	54	131	12	7	23.5%	.291/.364/.558	118	.331	-3.3	RF(57): -4.1, LF(34): 4.1, CF(3): -0.1	2.8
2020	TB	MLB	25	152	19	8	1	4	13	17	50	2	1	31.4%	.205/.296/.371	73	.288	0.1	LF(23): -1.5, RF(4): 0.3	-0.2
2021	TB	MLB	26	591	79	29	3	27	106	59	122	4	3	24.4%	.234/.315/.458	104	.249	-1.9	LF(78): -4.0, RF(1): -0.7	1.5
2022 DC	*TB*	*MLB*	*27*	*559*	*84*	*27*	*4*	*21*	*76*	*54*	*124*	*9*	*5*	*24.7%*	*.246/.328/.448*	*104*	*.287*	*0.6*	*LF 0*	*1.7*

Comparables: Jesse Winker, Carlos González, Byron Buxton

Meadows bounced back from a down year in 2020 that started with catching COVID-19. He strained his oblique near the end of the year and didn't hit for much in between. 2021 was much better than 2020, but also not as good as 2019, and that's probably where he'll settle going forward. He is an above-average hitter with plus power from the left side. He carries heavy platoon splits with an OPS that was over 300 points higher facing righties than it was against lefties. The good news is most of the league is still right-handed, so even if he is strictly a platoon bat going forward, he will still get plenty of burn. He also spent a lot of time at designated hitter. This limits his monetary value, but likely helps in keeping him healthy, plus he isn't much of a defender in left field anyway. He entered arbitration for the first time this winter and could be moved by the next *Annual* because that's how things go around here.

Francisco Mejía C Born: 10/27/95 Age: 26 Bats: S Throws: R Height: 5'8" Weight: 188 lb. Origin: International Free Agent, 2012

YEAR	TEAM	LVL	AGE	PA	R	2B	3B	HR	RBI	BB	K	SB	CS	Whiff%	AVG/OBP/SLG	DRC+	BABIP	BRR	FRAA	WARP
2019	ELP	AAA	23	73	14	8	2	4	12	5	10	0	0		.365/.411/.746	120	.365	-0.7	C(16): 2.6	0.7
2019	SD	MLB	23	244	27	11	2	8	22	13	56	1	1	25.8%	.265/.316/.438	93	.319	1.7	C(60): 1.3, LF(4): 0.0	1.1
2020	EST	WIN	24	60	4	1	0	1	6	3	14	0	0		.164/.203/.236		.195			
2020	SD	MLB	24	42	5	1	0	1	2	1	9	0	0	24.5%	.077/.143/.179	83	.069	0.5	C(16): -0.7	0.0
2021	TB	MLB	25	277	31	15	3	6	35	17	49	0	0	20.4%	.260/.322/.416	100	.299	-0.8	C(76): -2.5, 1B(2): 0.1, P(2): -0.0	0.8
2022 DC	*TB*	*MLB*	*26*	*247*	*31*	*11*	*1*	*7*	*33*	*15*	*44*	*0*	*1*	*21.5%*	*.254/.314/.416*	*95*	*.288*	*-0.1*	*C -2*	*0.7*

Comparables: Wilson Ramos, Salvador Perez, Christian Vázquez

YEAR	TEAM	P. COUNT	FRM RUNS	BLK RUNS	THRW RUNS	TOT RUNS
2019	ELP	2100	2.3	0.0	0.0	2.4
2019	SD	7679	0.3	0.0	0.4	0.7
2020	SD	1616	-1.0	0.0	0.0	-1.0
2021	TB	9353	-2.1	-0.1	0.3	-1.8
2022	*TB*	*8418*	*-1.0*	*-0.8*	*0.2*	*-1.5*

Now that the prospect luster has worn off, Mejía can settle into life as a semi-regular catcher who hits well enough to remain in the lineup even if he isn't a wizard defensively. As a switch-hitter, his ability to hit from the left-side against right-handed pitching seems like a natural platoon split with the right-handed hitting Mike Zunino. The only problem is Mejía has proven to be a better overall hitter from the right-side. He isn't terrible as a lefty and shows more pop from that side with 16 of his 24 extra-base hits coming that way. Defensively, there remains work to be done. He does not carry a positive reputation as a receiver and was a negative in terms of pitch framing. His arm, however, remains top notch and he cut down 30% of would-be larcenists. There is still hope he pops into a three- or four-win guy. For now, a win or two is still plenty of value.

Brett Phillips OF Born: 05/30/94 Age: 28 Bats: L Throws: R Height: 6'0" Weight: 195 lb. Origin: Round 6, 2012 Draft (#189 overall)

YEAR	TEAM	LVL	AGE	PA	R	2B	3B	HR	RBI	BB	K	SB	CS	Whiff%	AVG/OBP/SLG	DRC+	BABIP	BRR	FRAA	WARP
2019	OMA	AAA	25	414	75	8	13	18	54	72	118	22	1		.240/.378/.505	106	.312	3.2	RF(63): 10.7, CF(32): -1.2, LF(3): 0.4	2.9
2019	KC	MLB	25	79	7	2	0	2	6	10	23	3	0	31.2%	.138/.247/.262	83	.167	1.3	CF(23): 0.9, LF(3): 0.3, RF(3): 2.2	0.6
2020	KC	MLB	26	34	8	0	1	1	2	3	8	3	1	31.6%	.226/.294/.387	89	.273	0.4	CF(11): 0.5, LF(4): 0.1, RF(4): -0.1	0.2
2020	TB	MLB	26	25	2	0	1	1	3	5	7	3	0	41.7%	.150/.320/.400	95	.167	0.5	RF(9): 0.2, CF(4): 0.1, LF(3): -0.0	0.1
2021	TB	MLB	27	292	50	9	3	13	44	33	113	14	3	36.3%	.202/.297/.415	74	.295	1.0	CF(52): 6.9, RF(46): 3.4, LF(19): -0.2	1.2
2022 DC	*TB*	*MLB*	*28*	*211*	*26*	*7*	*3*	*6*	*29*	*24*	*71*	*4*	*1*	*35.3%*	*.197/.296/.369*	*74*	*.284*	*0.7*	*RF 1, CF 1*	*0.2*

Comparables: Aaron Hicks, Jake Marisnick, Gerardo Parra

The Dani Rojas of baseball. Baseball is fun and baseball is life for Phillips. He received the most playing time of his career in 2021, serving as the team's left-handed reserve outfielder. Offensively, there wasn't much production to speak of, but it was close enough to average to get by and his 13 home runs to go with 14 steals was a nice power/speed combination off the bench. Defensively, he continues to be a plus defender with the ability to track the ball at any outfield spot. Phillips' profile would be useful for most teams, but probably slightly more in his home market where he is a local sensation. That said, the warm and fuzzy feeling you get when he's helicoptering around the field after a walk-off hit only holds so much cachet (for the org) when he starts making more money.

Taylor Walls SS Born: 07/10/96 Age: 25 Bats: S Throws: R Height: 5'10" Weight: 185 lb. Origin: Round 3, 2017 Draft (#79 overall)

YEAR	TEAM	LVL	AGE	PA	R	2B	3B	HR	RBI	BB	K	SB	CS	Whiff%	AVG/OBP/SLG	DRC+	BABIP	BRR	FRAA	WARP
2019	CHA	A+	22	180	22	7	2	4	26	19	28	13	6		.269/.339/.417	126	.295	1.5	SS(36): 2.2, 2B(1): 0.1	1.4
2019	MTG	AA	22	243	42	16	5	6	20	26	51	15	9		.270/.346/.479	117	.321	0.9	SS(35): -0.6, 2B(9): 1.3, 3B(6): 0.9	1.7
2021	DUR	AAA	24	222	41	9	1	8	29	40	58	10	5		.247/.387/.444	114	.316	1.5	SS(36): 0.8, 2B(10): -0.9, 3B(6): 0.7	1.2
2021	TB	MLB	24	176	15	10	0	1	15	23	49	4	2	26.3%	.211/.314/.296	81	.304	1.2	SS(49): 4.5, 2B(3): -0.3, 3B(1): -0.1	0.7
2022 DC	*TB*	*MLB*	*25*	*339*	*40*	*15*	*2*	*6*	*41*	*41*	*87*	*12*	*6*	*25.0%*	*.215/.316/.348*	*80*	*.284*	*1.0*	*3B 3, SS 0*	*0.6*

Comparables: Derek Dietrich, Erik González, Chris Taylor

The Rays went semi-local when they selected Walls 79th in the 2017 draft from Florida State University. A native of Americus, Georgia —which is about 200 miles north of the Florida-Georgia line— he cruised through Tampa Bay's system, resulting in a call-up in 2021. He was able to get his shine on just a little bit with two doubles in his big-league debut. Walls probably wanted to stay, but another shortstop in the system said get from 'round here. That's how things roll sometimes in the big leagues. A switch-hitter in name, he's not much of a hitter at all. He has contact skills and will grind out plate appearances, but his offense is limited to pretty much those traits. His time with the Rays did confirm his status as a certified glover boy with above-average skills at the six spot. This will give him continued chances at making big-league rosters for years to come.

Carson Williams SS Born: 06/25/03 Age: 19 Bats: R Throws: R Height: 6'2" Weight: 180 lb. Origin: Round 1, 2021 Draft (#28 overall)

YEAR	TEAM	LVL	AGE	PA	R	2B	3B	HR	RBI	BB	K	SB	CS	Whiff%	AVG/OBP/SLG	DRC+	BABIP	BRR	FRAA	WARP
2021	RAY	ROK	18	47	8	4	1	0	8	6	13	2	2		.282/.404/.436		.423			
2022	*No projection*																			

The Rays tapped Williams with the 28th selection in the 2021 draft. They were able to lure the prep star from his University of California commitment with a bonus of $2.35 million. He's rather refined for a high-school player with a feel for shortstop, a strong arm and average-or-better projections on offense. He has the frame to pack on some weight and additional power, but the hit tool remains ahead of his pop currently. He is a solid runner—maybe even slightly above-average on the right day. He made his pro debut during the summer, holding his own at the lowest levels of the system. It is not a super sexy profile, but still that of an everyday player.

Mike Zunino C Born: 03/25/91 Age: 31 Bats: R Throws: R Height: 6'2" Weight: 235 lb. Origin: Round 1, 2012 Draft (#3 overall)

YEAR	TEAM	LVL	AGE	PA	R	2B	3B	HR	RBI	BB	K	SB	CS	Whiff%	AVG/OBP/SLG	DRC+	BABIP	BRR	FRAA	WARP
2019	TB	MLB	28	289	30	10	1	9	32	20	98	0	0	38.4%	.165/.232/.312	64	.220	-1.5	C(89): 4.0	0.2
2020	TB	MLB	29	84	8	4	0	4	10	6	37	0	0	40.2%	.147/.238/.360	64	.206	-1.3	C(28): -0.6	-0.3
2021	TB	MLB	30	375	64	11	2	33	62	34	132	0	0	38.8%	.216/.301/.559	122	.231	0.2	C(105): 6.2	3.3
2022 DC	*TB*	*MLB*	*31*	*336*	*47*	*12*	*0*	*17*	*60*	*28*	*119*	*0*	*0*	*38.5%*	*.204/.286/.430*	*86*	*.265*	*-0.5*	*C 4*	*1.3*

Comparables: Andy Etchebarren, Alan Ashby, Duffy Dyer

YEAR	TEAM	P. COUNT	FRM RUNS	BLK RUNS	THRW RUNS	TOT RUNS
2019	TB	11033	4.9	0.3	0.4	5.7
2020	TB	3613	-1.4	-0.1	0.0	-1.5
2021	TB	13711	7.7	-0.4	0.6	7.9
2022	*TB*	*13228*	*3.9*	*-0.4*	*-0.3*	*3.2*

Given his pre-2021 production, poor contact skills and the acquisition of Francisco Mejía, it looked like Zunino would play the role of placeholder until the younger backstop was ready for full-time service. Instead, he assumed the role of All-Star and produced one of the best seasons of his career. The slugger belted 33 home runs in just 333 at-bats. The one dong every 10 at-bats outpaced qualified leaders Fernando Tatis, Jr. and Shohei Otani for their respective leagues. It was still an all-or-nothing approach as he struck out in more than a third of his trips to the plate. His walk rate helps balance things a bit, but even a modest regression from his career-high 30% HR/FB rate could make the whole profile collapse. Defensively, he remained a top-notch receiver and earned high marks across the advanced metric systems. He'll make a lot more money in 2022 which raises the question: will he once again be underpaid or go back to overrated?

PITCHERS

Nick Anderson RHP Born: 07/05/90 Age: 32 Bats: R Throws: R Height: 6'4" Weight: 205 lb. Origin: Round 32, 2012 Draft (#995 overall)

YEAR	TEAM	LVL	AGE	W	L	SV	G	GS	IP	H	HR	BB/9	K/9	K	GB%	BABIP	WHIP	ERA	DRA-	WARP	MPH	FB%	Whiff%	CSP
2019	MIA	MLB	28	2	4	1	45	0	43^{2}	40	5	3.3	14.2	69	28.0%	.368	1.28	3.92	72	1.1	96.0	55.9%	35.3%	49.5%
2019	TB	MLB	28	3	0	0	23	0	21^{1}	12	3	0.8	17.3	41	32.4%	.290	0.66	2.11	67	0.6	96.5	69.0%	43.1%	54.4%
2020	TB	MLB	29	2	1	6	19	0	16^{1}	5	1	1.7	14.3	26	20.7%	.143	0.49	0.55	81	0.3	95.4	65.0%	36.9%	46.1%
2021	DUR	AAA	30	0	0	0	11	0	10^{2}	12	2	0.8	10.1	12	29.0%	.357	1.22	5.06	91	0.2				
2021	TB	MLB	30	0	1	1	6	0	6	4	2	3.0	1.5	1	14.3%	.105	1.00	4.50	136	-0.1	93.3	67.6%	18.5%	53.8%
2022 DC	*TB*	*MLB*	*31*	*1*	*1*	*0*	*29*	*0*	*25.7*	*22*	*4*	*2.6*	*10.5*	*30*	*30.6%*	*.288*	*1.17*	*3.68*	*92*	*0.2*	*95.5*	*62.4%*	*34.5%*	*50.2%*

Comparables: Austin Adams, Jim Henderson, Francisco Cordero

Anderson was the Rays' undisputed relief ace for most of the 2019 and 2020 seasons. He appeared to lose some steam in the 2020 postseason and there was a good reason for it. He dealt with some forearm issues in late 2020. That turned into elbow pain that wiped out most of 2021. The elbow must be connected to the back because a strain in his back put him out once again. Once the games finished, he underwent surgery on his right elbow that will keep him out into the 2022 season. At his peak, he was as dominant as you can get with a top-shelf heater and a hammer curveball. The fastball lost over two mph from its apex. The Rays hope he finds it again.

★ ★ ★ *2022 Top 101 Prospect* **#8** ★ ★ ★

Shane Baz RHP Born: 06/17/99 Age: 23 Bats: R Throws: R Height: 6'2" Weight: 190 lb. Origin: Round 1, 2017 Draft (#12 overall)

YEAR	TEAM	LVL	AGE	W	L	SV	G	GS	IP	H	HR	BB/9	K/9	K	GB%	BABIP	WHIP	ERA	DRA-	WARP	MPH	FB%	Whiff%	CSP
2019	BG	A	20	3	2	0	17	17	81^{1}	63	5	4.1	9.6	87	37.1%	.280	1.23	2.99	85	1.3				
2021	MTG	AA	22	2	4	0	7	7	32^{2}	22	3	0.6	13.5	49	44.8%	.297	0.73	2.48	76	0.7				
2021	DUR	AAA	22	3	0	0	10	10	46	28	6	2.2	12.5	64	39.8%	.242	0.85	1.76	79	1.1				
2021	TB	MLB	22	2	0	0	3	3	13^{1}	6	3	2.0	12.1	18	39.3%	.120	0.68	2.03	91	0.2	97.2	54.5%	35.3%	53.7%
2022 DC	*TB*	*MLB*	*23*	*9*	*6*	*0*	*25*	*25*	*129.3*	*104*	*19*	*3.0*	*11.1*	*159*	*38.8%*	*.279*	*1.14*	*3.32*	*84*	*2.2*	*97.2*	*54.5%*	*35.3%*	*53.7%*

Comparables: Chris Archer, Jeremy Hellickson, Ubaldo Jiménez

There's a decent chance that the Chris Archer trade may become the Shane Baz trade—if it wasn't already the Tyler Glasnow trade or the Austin Meadows trade. In that case, it may go down as one of the most one-sided deals in recent history. The right-hander dominated the minor leagues this season with 113 strikeouts in fewer than 80 combined innings. The injury-riddled Rays really had no choice but to give him a chance at the highest level and he continued to excel in limited action. He struck out 18 of the 49 big-league batters he faced and walked just three. His fastball flirts with triple digits and double dates a pair of fine breaking balls. The slider comes in a bit harder than the hammer and there is a changeup in the mix. He gave up some home runs as he advanced, but that's the difference between control and command for young hurlers. Along with Sugar Shane (McClanahan), Silky Shane could front the Rays rotation for the next few seasons.

Taj Bradley RHP Born: 03/20/01 Age: 21 Bats: R Throws: R Height: 6'2" Weight: 190 lb. Origin: Round 5, 2018 Draft (#150 overall)

YEAR	TEAM	LVL	AGE	W	L	SV	G	GS	IP	H	HR	BB/9	K/9	K	GB%	BABIP	WHIP	ERA	DRA-	WARP	MPH	FB%	Whiff%	CSP
2019	PRN	ROA	18	2	5	0	12	11	51	42	4	3.4	10.1	57	38.0%	.286	1.20	3.18						
2021	CSC	A	20	9	3	0	15	14	66^2	37	4	2.7	10.9	81	50.3%	.237	0.85	1.76	79	1.4				
2021	BG	A+	20	3	0	0	8	8	36^2	28	4	2.7	10.3	42	47.4%	.267	1.06	1.96	85	0.6				
2022 non-DC	*TB*	*MLB*	*21*	*2*	*3*	*0*	*57*	*0*	*50*	*49*	*7*	*4.1*	*8.3*	*45*	*43.7%*	*.300*	*1.45*	*4.76*	*112*	*-0.1*				

Comparables: Lorenzo Barcelo, Jonathan Pettibone, Chris Volstad

The Rays went above slot to lure Bradley from his South Carolina commitment when they selected him in the fifth round in 2018. A former two-way standout, he is making his way up the prospect rankings as a standout right-handed pitcher. The fastball lives in the mid-90s with projection to perhaps creep a bit higher with more regularly. There are a pair of breaking balls that go with it led by a slider that is plus and curveball that could be above-average. The changeup remains in development. He showed great control in 2021. If he can repeat that in 2022, we should be able to officially call it a skill. He dominated both levels of A-ball last season and should reach Montgomery at some point this upcoming season with an eye on a top-50 placement, perhaps.

JT Chargois RHP Born: 12/03/90 Age: 31 Bats: S Throws: R Height: 6'3" Weight: 200 lb. Origin: Round 2, 2012 Draft (#72 overall)

YEAR	TEAM	LVL	AGE	W	L	SV	G	GS	IP	H	HR	BB/9	K/9	K	GB%	BABIP	WHIP	ERA	DRA-	WARP	MPH	FB%	Whiff%	CSP
2019	OKC	AAA	28	1	2	4	27	0	32^2	27	3	4.4	10.2	37	58.0%	.312	1.32	2.76	71	0.8				
2019	LAD	MLB	28	1	0	0	21	0	21^1	21	4	2.1	11.8	28	47.2%	.347	1.22	6.33	79	0.5	96.2	41.6%	34.3%	49.6%
2021	TB	MLB	30	5	1	0	25	0	23^2	15	3	5.3	9.1	24	44.1%	.214	1.23	1.90	103	0.2	96.9	50.7%	24.6%	48.4%
2021	SEA	MLB	30	1	0	0	31	0	30	23	2	1.8	8.7	29	44.9%	.276	0.97	3.00	95	0.3	95.8	31.0%	29.8%	55.0%
2022 DC	*TB*	*MLB*	*31*	*3*	*3*	*2*	*74*	*0*	*64.7*	*55*	*8*	*3.7*	*9.5*	*68*	*46.8%*	*.281*	*1.26*	*3.68*	*90*	*0.6*	*96.4*	*40.5%*	*28.0%*	*51.6%*

Comparables: Pedro Báez, Marcos Mateo, Jared Hughes

Chargois returned home after a year with the Tohoku Rakuten Golden Eagles in NPB. Initially signed on a minor-league deal with Seattle, he was traded to the Rays just ahead of the deadline. The stuff was largely the same as before with the right-hander living in the mid-to-upper 90s with a hard slider. Chargois led with the breaking ball with the Mariners, but the usage flipped with the Rays to a fastball-first approach. It resulted in a few less hits but more walks negated any gain there. Because of the up and down nature of his first few trips to the big leagues he is without minor-league options but also still under team control for the next few seasons despite already being on the other side of 30.

Pete Fairbanks RHP Born: 12/16/93 Age: 28 Bats: R Throws: R Height: 6'6" Weight: 225 lb. Origin: Round 9, 2015 Draft (#258 overall)

YEAR	TEAM	LVL	AGE	W	L	SV	G	GS	IP	H	HR	BB/9	K/9	K	GB%	BABIP	WHIP	ERA	DRA-	WARP	MPH	FB%	Whiff%	CSP
2019	DE	A+	25	1	0	2	11	0	12^1	10	0	2.9	10.9	15	59.4%	.313	1.14	2.92	92	0.2				
2019	FRI	AA	25	1	0	0	6	0	7^1	2	0	0.0	17.2	14	70.0%	.200	0.27	0.00	76	0.1				
2019	NAS	AAA	25	0	0	0	7	0	6^1	10	1	2.8	15.6	11	27.8%	.563	1.89	11.37	74	0.1				
2019	DUR	AAA	25	1	2	0	16	1	17^2	15	3	3.1	15.3	30	43.6%	.333	1.19	5.09	60	0.6				
2019	TB	MLB	25	2	1	2	13	0	12^1	17	1	2.2	9.5	13	42.9%	.390	1.62	5.11	99	0.1	97.7	38.0%	29.1%	49.8%
2019	TEX	MLB	25	0	2	0	8	0	8^2	8	4	7.3	15.6	15	42.1%	.267	1.73	9.35	87	0.1	97.4	51.5%	41.0%	44.6%
2020	TB	MLB	26	6	3	0	27	2	26^2	23	2	4.7	13.2	39	48.4%	.350	1.39	2.70	68	0.8	97.7	57.6%	37.4%	42.5%
2021	TB	MLB	27	3	6	5	47	0	42^2	40	2	4.4	11.8	56	42.3%	.349	1.43	3.59	82	0.8	97.5	53.5%	30.6%	55.9%
2022 DC	*TB*	*MLB*	*28*	*3*	*3*	*15*	*74*	*0*	*64.7*	*54*	*8*	*3.8*	*10.8*	*77*	*43.9%*	*.291*	*1.26*	*3.60*	*88*	*0.7*	*97.6*	*53.6%*	*32.8%*	*51.5%*

Comparables: Mike Timlin, Fernando Rodney, Steve Cishek

Fairbanks resumed his role as a wide-eyed, fireballer in the Rays' pen. He continues to be more effective than not with an attack that is led by gaudy strikeout numbers. Using his upper-90s fastball and hard slider to change speed and eye levels, he displayed utter dominance over right-handed hitters. Meanwhile, take a glance at his splits in 2021 and you can see they were not ideal for a late-inning reliever. He did have a rough patch in the summer that culminated in a month long stay on the injured list with a cranky shoulder. He returned healthy in time for the stretch fun and was a reliable hand that kept the ball in the park. Walks continue to be an issue, but it's unlikely he develops into a control artist who paints the corners. He will continue to get looks as long as the strikeouts remain and he limits hard contact.

J.P. Feyereisen RHP Born: 02/07/93 Age: 29 Bats: R Throws: R Height: 6'2" Weight: 215 lb. Origin: Round 16, 2014 Draft (#488 overall)

YEAR	TEAM	LVL	AGE	W	L	SV	G	GS	IP	H	HR	BB/9	K/9	K	GB%	BABIP	WHIP	ERA	DRA-	WARP	MPH	FB%	Whiff%	CSP
2019	SWB	AAA	26	10	2	7	40	0	61^1	37	6	4.5	13.8	94	35.2%	.270	1.11	2.49	64	2.0				
2020	MIL	MLB	27	0	0	0	6	0	9^1	4	3	4.8	6.8	7	33.3%	.048	0.96	5.79	116	0.0	93.6	54.0%	34.7%	39.1%
2021	MIL	MLB	28	0	2	0	21	0	19^1	10	2	5.1	9.3	20	47.8%	.186	1.09	3.26	110	0.1	93.7	41.1%	42.6%	45.5%
2021	TB	MLB	28	4	2	3	34	0	36^2	26	3	5.4	8.1	33	31.4%	.235	1.31	2.45	117	0.0	93.1	56.7%	31.6%	45.3%
2022 DC	*TB*	*MLB*	*29*	*3*	*3*	*8*	*74*	*0*	*64.7*	*58*	*10*	*5.0*	*11.0*	*79*	*36.8%*	*.302*	*1.45*	*4.71*	*109*	*-0.1*	*93.3*	*51.8%*	*34.7%*	*44.8%*

Comparables: Kevin Quackenbush, Rowan Wick, Gregory Infante

Acquired from the Brewers in the Willy Adames swap, Feyereisen immediately became a pivotal cog in the Rays' bullpen wheel. He doesn't have the stuff of some teammates or the control of others, but remains effective nonetheless. Without those traits, he relied on his ability to yo-yo eye levels by using his (fire)rising fastball, a sweeping slider buried low and away from righties and a changeup to pull the string against lefties. He did his best work against batters of the same hand, holding them to an average below .150. The Rays greatly encouraged the usage of his high fastball which was his best weapon after the trade. Like so many other pitchers in the arm barn, he is in his late-20s with remaining options and team control.

Josh Fleming LHP

Born: 05/18/96 Age: 26 Bats: L Throws: L Height: 6'2" Weight: 220 lb. Origin: Round 5, 2017 Draft (#139 overall)

YEAR	TEAM	LVL	AGE	W	L	SV	G	GS	IP	H	HR	BB/9	K/9	K	GB%	BABIP	WHIP	ERA	DRA-	WARP	MPH	FB%	Whiff%	CSP
2019	MTG	AA	23	11	4	0	21	17	127^2	127	9	1.3	6.5	92	51.6%	.299	1.14	3.31	100	0.8				
2019	DUR	AAA	23	1	3	0	4	3	21	24	6	3.4	6.9	16	65.2%	.286	1.52	5.14	103	0.2				
2020	TB	MLB	24	5	0	0	7	5	32^1	28	5	1.9	7.0	25	63.9%	.250	1.08	2.78	70	0.9	90.8	54.3%	21.1%	45.6%
2021	DUR	AAA	25	1	0	1	7	0	10	7	0	0.9	10.8	12	66.7%	.292	0.80	0.90	87	0.2				
2021	TB	MLB	25	10	8	1	26	11	104^1	110	11	2.7	5.6	65	54.7%	.296	1.35	5.09	120	-0.1	91.5	46.2%	19.5%	48.6%
2022 DC	*TB*	*MLB*	*26*	*9*	*6*	*0*	*68*	*9*	*100.3*	*107*	*10*	*2.5*	*6.2*	*69*	*54.9%*	*.302*	*1.35*	*4.06*	*103*	*0.5*	*91.4*	*47.5%*	*19.8%*	*48.1%*

Comparables: Chris Hammond, Trevor Williams, Luis Cessa

Let's not bury the lede here: Fleming believes he can fit 12 full marshmallows in his mouth at the same time. In a book full of numbers and statistics, this number is the one that deserves the most thought. Depending on where you read, the world record is between 22 and 44. Both of those seem so absurd, considering the average human can fit two in their mouth according to Google. Unfortunately, Fleming's pitches often looked big, fluffy and perhaps a little too sweet to opposing batters. After keeping them off-balance with his low-90s fastball and slightly slower cutter, hitters were not fooled in 2021. He gave up more than a hit per inning while seeing his strikeout rate drop below 15%. His swinging strike rate was under than 9% while hitters made contact 91% of the time on pitches in the zone. Fleming is young and cheap enough to warrant additional looks. However, he'll need to show more stuff than fluff.

Sandy Gaston RHP

Born: 12/16/01 Age: 20 Bats: R Throws: R Height: 6'3" Weight: 200 lb. Origin: International Free Agent, 2018

YEAR	TEAM	LVL	AGE	W	L	SV	G	GS	IP	H	HR	BB/9	K/9	K	GB%	BABIP	WHIP	ERA	DRA-	WARP	MPH	FB%	Whiff%	CSP
2019	RAY	ROK	17	1	2	0	11	6	27	23	1	9.0	10.3	31	55.1%	.324	1.85	6.00						
2021	RAY	ROK	19	1	0	0	7	3	19^2	7	1	5.9	14.6	32	58.6%	.214	1.02	3.20						
2021	CSC	A	19	2	1	0	7	7	30^1	22	2	6.5	11.3	38	47.1%	.294	1.45	3.86	95	0.4				
2022 non-DC	*TB*	*MLB*	*20*	*2*	*3*	*0*	*57*	*0*	*50*	*51*	*8*	*7.3*	*8.4*	*46*	*40.8%*	*.305*	*1.85*	*6.76*	*141*	*-0.9*				

Comparables: Nate Cornejo, Taijuan Walker, Julio Teheran

If gambling is legal in your state or country, and you can find a place to bet that Gaston will end 2022 as one of the Rays' top-10 prospects, please put this book, tablet or phone down and place that bet immediately. The new Cuban missile owns an 80 fastball that touched triple-digits and lives just a few ticks slower. He possesses a curveball and changeup that should grade out as at least average. If that happens, the ying-yang of eye levels and changing speeds could help them play up even higher. Gaston is as wild as his walk rates indicate, but improved upon his rookie ball season and produced two strikeouts for every walk in 2021. He has the size and stuff to be a front-line starter with the downside of a late-innings ace.

Tyler Glasnow RHP

Born: 08/23/93 Age: 28 Bats: L Throws: R Height: 6'8" Weight: 225 lb. Origin: Round 5, 2011 Draft (#152 overall)

YEAR	TEAM	LVL	AGE	W	L	SV	G	GS	IP	H	HR	BB/9	K/9	K	GB%	BABIP	WHIP	ERA	DRA-	WARP	MPH	FB%	Whiff%	CSP
2019	TB	MLB	25	6	1	0	12	12	60^2	40	4	2.1	11.3	76	50.0%	.265	0.89	1.78	75	1.4	97.2	67.4%	28.4%	50.0%
2020	TB	MLB	26	5	1	0	11	11	57^1	43	11	3.5	14.3	91	40.0%	.281	1.13	4.08	61	1.8	97.2	60.6%	32.8%	45.9%
2021	TB	MLB	27	5	2	0	14	14	88	55	10	2.8	12.6	123	45.3%	.250	0.93	2.66	67	2.3	97.2	51.6%	37.1%	60.4%
2022 non-DC	*TB*	*MLB*	*28*	*3*	*2*	*0*	*57*	*0*	*50*	*37*	*6*	*3.1*	*12.2*	*68*	*44.6%*	*.284*	*1.09*	*2.63*	*68*	*1.0*	*97.2*	*56.2%*	*34.7%*	*55.0%*

Comparables: Lucas Sims, Trevor Bauer, Edinson Vólquez

Glasnow made plenty of headlines as a critic of the league's crackdown on foreign substances used by pitchers. That scrutiny only intensified when Glasnow torn his UCL and was forced to undergo Tommy John surgery shortly after the checks when in to practice. We don't know whether the grip caused the injury or whether throwing fastballs really hard for several years was the culprit. Glasnow also added a slider that took over as his secondary pitch of choice and we know those aren't easy on the elbow. Regardless of the cause, there is a chance the Rays will be without their top pitcher for most—if not all—of the 2022 season. The right-hander was dominant prior to the ailment, striking out 36% of batters while walking fewer than 8%. Batters collected a paltry .176 average against him. The Rays will pay him a lot of money to rehab in 2022 with just one year left of control in 2023 before he is eligible for free agency.

Andrew Kittredge RHP

Born: 03/17/90 Age: 32 Bats: R Throws: R Height: 6'1" Weight: 230 lb. Origin: Round 45, 2008 Draft (#1360 overall)

YEAR	TEAM	LVL	AGE	W	L	SV	G	GS	IP	H	HR	BB/9	K/9	K	GB%	BABIP	WHIP	ERA	DRA-	WARP	MPH	FB%	Whiff%	CSP
2019	DUR	AAA	29	2	1	6	27	1	37^1	24	3	1.4	13.3	55	49.4%	.280	0.80	1.93	64	1.2				
2019	TB	MLB	29	1	0	0	37	7	49^2	51	7	2.2	10.5	58	50.0%	.336	1.27	4.17	81	1.0	95.1	58.1%	31.5%	44.4%
2020	TB	MLB	30	0	0	1	8	1	8	8	0	2.3	3.4	3	57.7%	.308	1.25	2.25	106	0.1	94.6	47.8%	15.0%	58.8%
2021	TB	MLB	31	9	3	8	57	4	71^2	55	7	1.9	9.7	77	53.5%	.268	0.98	1.88	80	1.4	95.5	54.5%	31.2%	53.8%
2022 DC	*TB*	*MLB*	*32*	*3*	*3*	*17*	*74*	*0*	*64.7*	*58*	*6*	*2.3*	*9.2*	*65*	*50.3%*	*.295*	*1.16*	*3.08*	*80*	*0.9*	*95.4*	*54.8%*	*30.3%*	*52.2%*

Comparables: Ryan Cook, Oliver Drake, Evan Marshall

After a late-2020 arm injury, it looked like Kittredge was in jeopardy of missing the 2021 season. Due to the timing of the injury, he was afforded an opportunity that paid off big time: Instead of rushing to have surgery in August or September, the right-hander opted for rehab and injections for his injured arm. If it worked? Great. If it didn't? He would have the surgery later in the year and still probably miss the 2021 season. Wouldn't you know, it worked. Like *really* worked. Kittredge responded with his best season in the bigs. Strangely, due in large part to the attrition of others—and his own effectiveness—he found himself at or near the top of the leverage index for most of the season. He also threw harder than ever and coupled that with a forceful slider which lead to an All-Star selection. That acknowledgment along with his wins and saves totals should lead to a nice raise.

Corey Kluber RHP

Born: 04/10/86 Age: 36 Bats: R Throws: R Height: 6'4" Weight: 215 lb. Origin: Round 4, 2007 Draft (#134 overall)

YEAR	TEAM	LVL	AGE	W	L	SV	G	GS	IP	H	HR	BB/9	K/9	K	GB%	BABIP	WHIP	ERA	DRA-	WARP	MPH	FB%	Whiff%	CSP
2019	CLE	MLB	33	2	3	0	7	7	35^2	44	4	3.8	9.6	38	39.3%	.374	1.65	5.80	102	0.3	91.7	39.8%	28.5%	44.8%
2020	TEX	MLB	34	0	0	0	1	1	1	0	0	9.0	9.0	1	0.0%	.000	1.00	0.00	90	0.0	91.7	50.0%	12.5%	35.5%
2021	NYY	MLB	35	5	3	0	16	16	80	74	8	3.7	9.2	82	43.0%	.311	1.34	3.83	101	0.7	90.6	29.5%	28.2%	52.2%
2022 non-DC	*TB*	*MLB*	*36*	*2*	*2*	*0*	*57*	*0*	*50*	*45*	*7*	*3.5*	*10.0*	*55*	*41.7%*	*.297*	*1.31*	*4.05*	*98*	*0.2*	*90.8*	*31.0%*	*28.1%*	*51.1%*

Comparables: Adam Wainwright, Jack Morris, Esteban Loaiza

Let's have some fun with percentages. Kluber threw 8000% more innings in 2021 than in 2020. On May 19, he completed 900% more innings in a game against Texas than he did *for* the Rangers the year prior, allowing hits to 0% of opposing batters. He's a finesse pitcher these days and his two-seamer is about 3.3% slower than in his heyday. (OK, that one wasn't as fun.) While he may never completely kick the injury bug, he made good on the $11 million contract (15.3% of his career earnings) he signed with the Yankees following a winter showcase. By starting 9.9% of New York's regular-season games, he demonstrated he can still bolster a rotation, though the Rays might be better served to consider him more of a seven-per-cent solution.

Shane McClanahan LHP

Born: 04/28/97 Age: 25 Bats: L Throws: L Height: 6'1" Weight: 200 lb. Origin: Round 1, 2018 Draft (#31 overall)

YEAR	TEAM	LVL	AGE	W	L	SV	G	GS	IP	H	HR	BB/9	K/9	K	GB%	BABIP	WHIP	ERA	DRA-	WARP	MPH	FB%	Whiff%	CSP
2019	BG	A	22	4	4	0	11	10	53	38	3	5.3	12.6	74	47.5%	.304	1.30	3.40	110	0.1				
2019	CHA	A+	22	6	1	0	9	8	49^1	33	1	1.5	10.8	59	40.7%	.267	0.83	1.46	77	1.1				
2019	MTG	AA	22	1	1	0	4	4	18^1	30	3	2.9	10.3	21	39.7%	.450	1.96	8.35	105	0.1				
2021	TB	MLB	24	10	6	0	25	25	123^1	120	14	2.7	10.3	141	45.7%	.330	1.27	3.43	89	1.8	96.8	40.9%	32.1%	56.8%
2022 DC	*TB*	*MLB*	*25*	*10*	*7*	*0*	*27*	*27*	*148.7*	*135*	*19*	*3.2*	*10.3*	*170*	*44.2%*	*.303*	*1.26*	*3.64*	*90*	*2.0*	*96.8*	*40.9%*	*32.1%*	*56.8%*

Comparables: Zack Wheeler, Jimmy Nelson, Ryan Dempster

It was quite the leap for McClanahan. A year after becoming the first pitcher to make his big-league debut in the playoffs, he ended 2021 as the staff's defacto ace and started Game 1 of the ALDS. It was not by design—not with injuries, trades and poor performance by others—but the 31st-overall pick in the 2018 was up to the task and could be an anchor for the rotation going forward. McClanahan skipped Triple-A altogether and made 25 starts for Tampa Bay. His stuff was up to the task, leading with an upper-90s fastball and a pair of breaking balls that get outs. Of his 141 strikeouts, 105 were caused by something bendy. It is a hard slider in conjunction with a slower hook that does most of the damage, with only the occasional changeup. The lefty was never pegged as great control guy, but showed more than enough feel for the zone as he racked nearly four punch outs for each free pass. Durability is still a concern; he isn't the biggest fella and he has had some arm injuries in the past. Mostly by design, he recorded more than 15 outs in just nine of his 25 starts. He threw more than 90 pitches just four times. Considering the weirdness of the 2020 season, you can understand the conservative usage for a young, talented arm. McClanahan already has the confidence of a matador, however, he will need show the ability to maintain his stuff deeper into games and on a more consistent basis.

Luis Patiño RHP

Born: 10/26/99 Age: 22 Bats: R Throws: R Height: 6'1" Weight: 192 lb. Origin: International Free Agent, 2016

YEAR	TEAM	LVL	AGE	W	L	SV	G	GS	IP	H	HR	BB/9	K/9	K	GB%	BABIP	WHIP	ERA	DRA-	WARP	MPH	FB%	Whiff%	CSP
2019	LE	A+	19	6	8	0	18	17	87	61	4	3.5	11.7	113	40.2%	.278	1.09	2.69	83	1.1				
2019	AMA	AA	19	0	0	0	2	2	7^2	8	0	4.7	11.7	10	19.0%	.381	1.57	1.17	80	0.1				
2020	SD	MLB	20	1	0	0	11	1	17^1	18	3	7.3	10.9	21	34.7%	.326	1.85	5.19	117	0.0	96.8	64.8%	26.4%	46.4%
2021	DUR	AAA	21	3	1	0	7	7	29^1	23	2	3.4	12.6	41	38.2%	.318	1.16	3.07	88	0.6				
2021	TB	MLB	21	5	3	0	19	15	77^1	69	12	3.4	8.6	74	31.7%	.265	1.27	4.31	119	-0.1	96.0	63.7%	25.4%	55.9%
2022 DC	*TB*	*MLB*	*22*	*8*	*7*	*0*	*25*	*25*	*124.3*	*112*	*18*	*3.8*	*8.8*	*121*	*34.9%*	*.281*	*1.33*	*4.16*	*101*	*0.8*	*96.1*	*63.9%*	*25.5%*	*54.5%*

Comparables: Edgar Gonzalez, Julio Teheran, Rick Porcello

Seen by many as the centerpiece of the Blake Snell return, Patiño probably saw more action in the majors than some thought he would in 2021. With injuries piling up in the rotation and bullpen, the youngster ended up tossing nearly 80 innings for the Rays, another 30 frames in Triple-A and sandwiched a finger injury somewhere in the middle there. The arsenal was largely as advertised: A plus upper-90s fastball, with a hard slider and control issues. He also threw a handful of slower breaking balls and broke out the occasional *cambio*. The profile generated results you would expect; a .201/.243/.351 line against righties with 52 strikeouts to just eight walks. Meanwhile without much of a changeup, opposite-handed hitters slashed .274/.378/.452 with nearly as many free passes (21) as strikeouts (22). Some will see those numbers and scream "dominant reliever," but he's too young and too good to go down that path any time soon. He should get plenty more opportunities to prove himself as a starter in 2022.

Brooks Raley LHP Born: 06/29/88 Age: 34 Bats: L Throws: L Height: 6'3" Weight: 200 lb. Origin: Round 6, 2009 Draft (#200 overall)

YEAR	TEAM	LVL	AGE	W	L	SV	G	GS	IP	H	HR	BB/9	K/9	K	GB%	BABIP	WHIP	ERA	DRA-	WARP	MPH	FB%	Whiff%	CSP
2020	CIN	MLB	32	0	0	0	4	0	4	5	0	4.5	13.5	6	45.5%	.455	1.75	9.00	94	0.1	87.5	80.2%	24.3%	46.9%
2020	HOU	MLB	32	0	1	1	17	0	16	8	3	2.3	11.8	21	36.1%	.156	0.75	3.94	77	0.4	87.5	65.1%	33.8%	49.0%
2021	HOU	MLB	33	2	3	2	58	0	49	43	6	2.9	11.9	65	44.6%	.325	1.20	4.78	76	1.1	88.9	54.7%	32.5%	49.8%
2022 non-DC	*TB*	*MLB*	*34*	*2*	*2*	*0*	*57*	*0*	*50*	*40*	*6*	*2.9*	*11.0*	*61*	*43.2%*	*.283*	*1.14*	*3.24*	*82*	*0.6*	*88.7*	*57.6%*	*32.4%*	*49.5%*

Comparables: Zack Britton, Joe Thatcher, Mark Guthrie

Going by the back of the baseball card alone, one might assume Raley the sort of end-of-the-roster arm every team churns through biweekly at this point, his 49 innings last season (by far his most since breaking into the big leagues a decade ago) a failed experiment that proved exactly why it took him 10 years to total triple-digit MLB innings. Since coming back from a successful KBO stint, however, Raley has been demonstrably better than the high-fours ERAs he's posted in two seasons. That proof simply isn't required, however, because late last year we were given ironclad proof Raley is A Good Reliever, or at least the most convincing assurance as exists in baseball's present: the Rays signed him to a multi-year deal.

Drew Rasmussen RHP Born: 07/27/95 Age: 26 Bats: R Throws: R Height: 6'1" Weight: 211 lb. Origin: Round 6, 2018 Draft (#185 overall)

YEAR	TEAM	LVL	AGE	W	L	SV	G	GS	IP	H	HR	BB/9	K/9	K	GB%	BABIP	WHIP	ERA	DRA-	WARP	MPH	FB%	Whiff%	CSP
2019	WIS	A	23	0	0	0	1	1	2	1	0	0.0	13.5	3	66.7%	.333	0.50	0.00	100	0.0				
2019	CAR	A+	23	0	0	0	4	4	11^{1}	7	0	1.6	12.7	16	40.0%	.304	0.79	1.59	82	0.2				
2019	BLX	AA	23	1	3	0	22	18	61	49	4	4.3	11.4	77	46.9%	.321	1.28	3.54	79	1.1				
2020	MIL	MLB	24	1	0	0	12	0	15^{1}	17	3	5.3	12.3	21	53.7%	.368	1.70	5.87	84	0.3	98.0	68.2%	32.0%	44.7%
2021	DUR	AAA	25	2	0	1	8	1	11^{1}	5	0	1.6	18.3	23	60.0%	.333	0.62	0.00	66	0.3				
2021	TB	MLB	25	4	0	0	20	10	59	44	3	2.0	7.3	48	50.9%	.248	0.97	2.44	97	0.6	97.4	63.6%	23.5%	56.6%
2021	MIL	MLB	25	0	1	1	15	0	17	13	2	6.4	13.2	25	32.5%	.289	1.47	4.24	82	0.3	97.3	67.7%	30.7%	54.9%
2022 DC	*TB*	*MLB*	*26*	*8*	*7*	*0*	*25*	*25*	*119*	*106*	*14*	*3.5*	*9.9*	*131*	*46.8%*	*.297*	*1.27*	*3.59*	*89*	*1.4*	*97.5*	*65.3%*	*26.2%*	*54.5%*

Comparables: Taylor Buchholz, Jairo Díaz, Addison Reed

The Rays drafted Rasmussen as a starting pitcher from Oregon State with the 31st pick in the 2017 draft. They did not come to a deal and the pitcher was selected in the sixth round the following year by the Milwaukee Brewers. He reached the majors in 2020 as a reliever and remained in Milwaukee's limb stable to start 2021. The trade of Willy Adames allowed the Rays to finally get their guy and after some back an forth between middle relief and opening, Rasmussen became a full-time member of the rotation by season's end. From August 12 to September 29th, he made eight starts lasting a combined 37 innings. In those innings, he allowed just six earned runs (1.46 ERA) and surrended just 22 hits (.171 BAA). He did this damage with a two-pitch diet of upper-90s fastballs and hard sliders. Even with great stuff, he punched out just 23 batters in that span. That said, he walked just six. It's a weird juxtaposition of stuff and stats, but it was effective. In fact, it should be effective enough to give him a chance to start in earnest this spring.

David Robertson RHP Born: 04/09/85 Age: 37 Bats: R Throws: R Height: 5'11" Weight: 195 lb. Origin: Round 17, 2006 Draft (#524 overall)

YEAR	TEAM	LVL	AGE	W	L	SV	G	GS	IP	H	HR	BB/9	K/9	K	GB%	BABIP	WHIP	ERA	DRA-	WARP	MPH	FB%	Whiff%	CSP
2019	PHI	MLB	34	0	1	0	7	0	6^{2}	8	1	8.1	8.1	6	33.3%	.350	2.10	5.40	124	0.0	92.2	57.4%	28.8%	44.2%
2021	DUR	AAA	36	0	0	0	6	0	6	4	0	1.5	18.0	12	37.5%	.500	0.83	0.00	76	0.2				
2021	TB	MLB	36	0	0	0	12	1	12	11	2	3.0	12.0	16	40.0%	.321	1.25	4.50	89	0.2	92.2	74.0%	25.8%	60.6%
2022 non-DC	*TB*	*MLB*	*37*	*2*	*2*	*0*	*57*	*0*	*50*	*40*	*7*	*3.5*	*10.9*	*60*	*40.1%*	*.278*	*1.20*	*3.43*	*86*	*0.5*	*92.2*	*71.1%*	*26.4%*	*57.6%*

Comparables: Michael Jackson, Jesse Orosco, Alejandro Pena

Robertson missed the 2020 season recovering from Tommy John surgery and had a setback along the way. It didn't look great for the then-36-year-old's chances of making it back to the bigs. Then the Olympics returned and so did Robertson. He made a handful of appearances for the silver medal-winning national team and showed enough friskiness to warrant a look with the Rays. Following a short stay in Durham, he was back in the majors once more. Despite the time off, his signature cutter still had enough bite at 92 mph to get outs. Pairing that with a low-80s hook, he struck out nearly a third of the batters he faced (32%) and handed out just four walks in 12 innings. The amount of work was not a lot, however, the quality should keep him in the game a little while longer.

Tommy Romero RHP Born: 07/08/97 Age: 24 Bats: R Throws: R Height: 6'2" Weight: 225 lb. Origin: Round 15, 2017 Draft (#453 overall)

YEAR	TEAM	LVL	AGE	W	L	SV	G	GS	IP	H	HR	BB/9	K/9	K	GB%	BABIP	WHIP	ERA	DRA-	WARP	MPH	FB%	Whiff%	CSP
2019	CHA	A+	21	12	4	0	23	18	119^{1}	86	4	2.7	7.8	103	34.4%	.260	1.02	1.89	89	2.0				
2019	MTG	AA	21	1	0	0	1	1	6	7	1	3.0	1.5	1	31.8%	.286	1.50	7.50	147	-0.1				
2021	MTG	AA	23	1	0	0	11	9	48	36	3	1.9	14.1	75	37.1%	.324	0.96	1.88	75	1.1				
2021	DUR	AAA	23	7	2	0	12	12	62^{1}	39	7	3.0	10.1	70	34.4%	.224	0.96	3.18	92	1.1				
2022 non-DC	*TB*	*MLB*	*24*	*2*	*2*	*0*	*57*	*0*	*50*	*44*	*7*	*3.5*	*9.2*	*51*	*34.6%*	*.281*	*1.28*	*3.90*	*95*	*0.3*				

Comparables: Steve Johnson, Alex Cobb, Johnny Cueto

If you wanted to bet on a Rays' pitcher most people have never heard of but will by the end of 2022, put a sizable wager on Romero. Simply put, he can pitch his ass of despite not having Baz-level stuff or the pedigree of Cole Wilcox. After being named the Florida State League pitcher of the year in 2019, he missed the 2020 season like most other minor leaguers. The former Mariners farmhand picked up where he left off with improved stuff. He now pitches on the low-to-mid 90s with better than average control. He backs that with a curveball and changeup. Both pitches are probably 50s, but working off the well-located fastball, they can play up in spurts. The profile and delivery are somewhat similar to Alex Cobb: a medium-sized righty with a solid fastball, the ability to manipulate location with said fastball and a pair of secondaries to change eye levels. He tossed over 100 innings in 2021 which means he should be good to go as a spot starter or a volume reliever almost from the jump.

Ryan Thompson RHP Born: 06/26/92 Age: 30 Bats: R Throws: R Height: 6'5" Weight: 210 lb. Origin: Round 23, 2014 Draft (#676 overall)

YEAR	TEAM	LVL	AGE	W	L	SV	G	GS	IP	H	HR	BB/9	K/9	K	GB%	BABIP	WHIP	ERA	DRA-	WARP	MPH	FB%	Whiff%	CSP
2019	MTG	AA	27	1	1	0	14	5	20^{1}	24	1	2.7	8.9	20	44.4%	.371	1.48	3.10	92	0.2				
2020	TB	MLB	28	1	2	1	25	1	26^{1}	29	4	2.7	7.9	23	59.0%	.316	1.41	4.44	82	0.6	91.5	60.9%	22.2%	54.0%
2021	TB	MLB	29	3	2	0	36	0	34	26	3	2.4	9.8	37	47.7%	.277	1.03	2.38	84	0.6	90.7	60.7%	26.9%	56.5%
2022 DC	*TB*	*MLB*	*30*	*1*	*1*	*0*	*29*	*0*	*25.7*	*24*	*3*	*3.1*	*9.2*	*26*	*51.3%*	*.302*	*1.28*	*3.72*	*92*	*0.2*	*91.0*	*60.7%*	*25.2%*	*55.6%*

Comparables: Kevin Shackelford, Neil Wagner, Tyler Rogers

Thompson's season was cut short in late June when he went on the injured list with what was initially called shoulder inflammation. A few months later it was determined he would need thoracic outlet syndrome surgery. The side-arming righty was highly effective prior to his ailment, topping his 2020 debut in all the majors pitching categories: strikeouts, walks and home runs. The funky delivery has helped keep him relatively platoon-neutral despite throwing mainly low-90s fastballs and upper-70s sliders. It is a very useful profile for a team that is looking to cut cost corners and use multiple relievers a night. He should be ready for opening day 2022 provided he has no setbacks in his recovery, though the history of returning to prior form following TOS surgery is quite grim.

Matt Wisler RHP Born: 09/12/92 Age: 29 Bats: R Throws: R Height: 6'3" Weight: 215 lb. Origin: Round 7, 2011 Draft (#233 overall)

YEAR	TEAM	LVL	AGE	W	L	SV	G	GS	IP	H	HR	BB/9	K/9	K	GB%	BABIP	WHIP	ERA	DRA-	WARP	MPH	FB%	Whiff%	CSP
2019	SD	MLB	26	2	2	0	21	0	29	34	5	3.1	10.6	34	43.5%	.367	1.52	5.28	92	0.4	93.0	28.8%	32.3%	48.8%
2019	SEA	MLB	26	1	2	0	23	8	22^{1}	22	5	2.4	11.7	29	26.7%	.309	1.25	6.04	87	0.4	92.8	29.8%	31.7%	46.0%
2020	MIN	MLB	27	0	1	1	18	4	25^{1}	15	2	5.0	12.4	35	23.2%	.241	1.14	1.07	103	0.2	92.1	16.6%	36.1%	49.3%
2021	SF	MLB	28	1	2	0	21	0	19^{1}	19	4	2.8	12.1	26	30.0%	.326	1.29	6.05	91	0.3	91.9	9.7%	37.5%	61.2%
2021	TB	MLB	28	2	3	1	27	0	29^{1}	22	2	1.5	11.0	36	22.5%	.290	0.92	2.15	90	0.4	91.6	8.8%	28.1%	59.0%
2022 DC	*TB*	*MLB*	*29*	*3*	*2*	*0*	*59*	*0*	*51.7*	*44*	*9*	*2.5*	*10.6*	*60*	*31.5%*	*.282*	*1.15*	*3.58*	*90*	*0.5*	*92.1*	*15.2%*	*32.9%*	*54.9%*

Comparables: Jeanmar Gómez, Rafael Montero, Tyler Chatwood

A former starting prospect with four pitches in his arsenal, Wisler has settled down as a one-trick pony now in his late-20s. And by one trick, we mean one: He throws one pitch over 90% of the time. Wisler sweeps low-80s sliders nine of every 10 tosses and it worked really well once he was traded from San Francisco to Tampa Bay. He struck out about a third of the batters he faced in 2021 while keeping his walk rate manageable despite throwing the breaking ball so often. The biggest difference between the two Bays was his home run-to-fly ball ratio. It was nearly 17% with the Giants and just under 6% with the Rays. Perhaps the climate controlled environment of Tropicana Field was a factor or just natural regression. Either way, Wisler was one of the Rays' high-leverage options down the stretch and could fill a similar role in 2022.

Ryan Yarbrough LHP Born: 12/31/91 Age: 30 Bats: R Throws: L Height: 6'5" Weight: 205 lb. Origin: Round 4, 2014 Draft (#111 overall)

YEAR	TEAM	LVL	AGE	W	L	SV	G	GS	IP	H	HR	BB/9	K/9	K	GB%	BABIP	WHIP	ERA	DRA-	WARP	MPH	FB%	Whiff%	CSP
2019	DUR	AAA	27	2	1	0	5	4	26	24	2	1.0	12.1	35	42.4%	.344	1.04	3.81	83	0.6				
2019	TB	MLB	27	11	6	0	28	14	141^{2}	121	15	1.3	7.4	117	42.8%	.264	1.00	4.13	101	1.4	85.5	61.0%	22.3%	49.8%
2020	TB	MLB	28	1	4	0	11	9	55^{2}	54	5	1.9	7.1	44	40.9%	.299	1.19	3.56	99	0.6	84.6	59.4%	27.7%	48.6%
2021	TB	MLB	29	9	7	0	30	21	155	163	25	1.6	6.8	117	35.0%	.293	1.23	5.11	125	-0.7	83.0	54.0%	21.2%	52.3%
2022 DC	*TB*	*MLB*	*30*	*10*	*9*	*0*	*39*	*25*	*158*	*163*	*24*	*1.8*	*6.8*	*119*	*37.6%*	*.289*	*1.24*	*4.21*	*106*	*0.7*	*83.7*	*56.1%*	*22.4%*	*51.3%*

Comparables: Wei-Yin Chen, Jake Westbrook, Alex Kellner

Yarborough fought the law and the law won. In this case the "law" is the Tampa Bay Rays and the fight was over financial compensation. For the first few years of his career, the left-hander rotated between bulk-relieving and traditional starting. The workload amounted pretty much to a regular rotation member, but the "starts" didn't. Yarborough filed ambitiously at $3.1 million as a first time arbitration-eligible player. The team filed at $2.3 million and won the virtual hearing. There shouldn't be much of a fight this winter as Yarbrough was pretty ineffective. He'll carry nine wins and 155 innings over 21 starts (30 appearances). He'll also bring 25 longballs, which is more than the 20 he allowed in the nearly 200 innings he tossed between 2019 and 2020. Yarborough lost a little smoke—which is impressive since he barely vaped—on his mid-80s stuff. On average, over 85% of his pitches were below 85 mph. In fact, they were below 82. He still did a good job of limiting hard hits, but more balls fell for hits than normal and several more didn't fall at all. He is now interesting for another reason—other than the fact that he thinks he can hold six marshmallows in his mouth. Previously, how he was used was the intrigue. Now, entering his age-30 season, what is his role at all?

LINEOUTS

Hitters

HITTER	POS	TEAM	LVL	AGE	PA	R	2B	3B	HR	RBI	BB	K	SB	CS	AVG/OBP/SLG	DRC+	BABIP	BRR	FRAA	WARP
Ruben Cardenas	OF	BG	A+	23	132	26	4	0	10	31	12	31	3	1	.368/.424/.658	134	.423	-0.5	LF(12): 2.9, CF(10): 1.1, RF(7): 0.0	1.3
	OF	MTG	AA	23	309	43	9	3	15	47	12	84	3	3	.262/.294/.469	102	.313	0.7	LF(28): 1.0, RF(23): -0.5, CF(17): -0.6	1.1
Heriberto Hernandez	OF	CSC	A	21	320	57	15	0	12	44	49	90	7	4	.252/.381/.453	113	.325	0.2	LF(54): -2.0, RF(12): -0.1	1.4
Niko Hulsizer	RF	BG	A+	24	180	36	10	0	13	41	25	70	7	0	.248/.361/.569	114	.357	1.2	RF(21): -4.6, CF(10): -1.1, LF(8): -0.5	0.4
	RF	MTG	AA	24	196	31	10	1	8	35	20	78	2	0	.243/.327/.451	78	.386	1.2	RF(26): -1.2, LF(7): -0.2	0.1
Cooper Kinney	2B	RAY	ROK	18	47	9	1	1	0	5	10	9	2	0	.286/.468/.371		.385			
Kyle Manzardo	1B	RAY	ROK	20	50	10	5	0	2	8	4	6	0	0	.349/.440/.605		.371			
Kameron Misner	OF	MSS	WIN	23	102	21	3	0	7	14	20	34	4	2	.205/.373/.513		.231			
	OF	BEL	A+	23	400	58	22	3	11	56	50	119	24	2	.244/.350/.424	95	.338	-0.1	CF(38): -3.2, LF(36): -0.4, RF(7): 1.1	0.8
	OF	PNS	AA	23	62	12	7	0	1	3	7	17	2	2	.309/.387/.491	87	.432	-0.6	CF(9): -1.0, LF(2): -0.0	-0.1
Alika Williams	SS	CSC	A	22	263	37	13	1	1	34	17	43	5	5	.266/.317/.342	103	.313	0.3	SS(44): 9.8, 2B(8): 0.3	1.8
	SS	BG	A+	22	63	12	3	0	3	9	2	12	1	1	.279/.302/.475	114	.304	-0.2	SS(11): 0.8, 2B(3): -0.2	0.3

Ruben Cardenas is an offense-first outfielder with good power, a decent stick and projects to a corner defensively. ⚾ **Heriberto Hernandez** made the move to outfield in 2020 and continues to have boom-or-bust offensive upside. ⚾ **Niko Hulsizer** has monster raw power and will sometimes dye his dreadlocks to match his uniform. ⚾ The Rays drafted **Cooper Kinney** 34th overall to hit now and worry about where he plays defense later. ⚾ Like most first base only prospects, **Kyle Manzardo** is going to have to hit his way to the bigs. ⚾ After a brutal start to the season, **Kameron Misner** got red hot in August and September to earn promotion to Double-A. Considering that Misner's slump in his final year at Missouri cost him nearly $2 million in the draft according to Baseball America's JJ Cooper, perhaps he's streakier than Will Ferrell in "Old School." (That's an old enough reference that it's become cool again, right?) ⚾ **Alika Williams** is a great athlete, good defender and average enough hitter to project into a big-league role relatively soon.

Pitchers

PITCHER	TEAM	LVL	AGE	W	L	SV	G	GS	IP	H	HR	BB/9	K/9	K	GB%	BABIP	WHIP	ERA	DRA-	WARP	MPH	FB%	WHF	CSP
Adam Conley	DUR	AAA	31	2	1	3	27	0	31	18	4	5.2	9.9	34	50.7%	.203	1.16	4.35	81	0.7				
	TB	MLB	31	0	0	0	17	0	19^2	14	2	2.7	7.3	16	48.1%	.240	1.02	2.29	110	0.1	96.1	54.1%	25.7%	52.4%
Dietrich Enns	DUR	AAA	30	8	2	0	19	11	71^2	46	8	2.3	11.3	90	42.9%	.235	0.89	2.64	77	1.8				
	TB	MLB	30	2	0	2	9	0	22^1	17	1	2.4	10.1	25	28.1%	.286	1.03	2.82	106	0.1	94.5	58.6%	23.9%	56.0%
Calvin Faucher	WCH	AA	25	1	1	1	19	0	30^2	39	6	7.0	12.3	42	47.1%	.423	2.05	7.04	118	-0.1				
	DUR	AAA	25	0	0	0	11	3	20^1	14	1	3.1	11.5	26	37.0%	.289	1.03	1.77	83	0.4				
DJ Johnson	COL	AAA	31	1	2	6	21	0	21^2	24	3	4.6	14.5	35	40.0%	.404	1.62	3.32	82	0.5				
	CLE	MLB	31	0	0	0	1	0	1^2	2	1	0.0	16.2	3	25.0%	.333	1.20	5.40	108	0.0	94.8	55.9%	47.1%	57.8%
	TB	MLB	31	0	0	0	3	0	2^2	0	0	0.0	6.7	2	66.7%	.000	0.00	0.00	102	0.0	95.8	63.6%	26.7%	48.5%
Seth Johnson	CSC	A	22	6	6	0	23	16	93^2	86	7	3.2	11.0	115	48.0%	.336	1.27	2.88	89	1.4				
Chris Mazza	DUR	AAA	31	4	1	0	26	3	37	26	3	3.2	11.4	47	52.8%	.267	1.05	3.16	80	0.9				
	TB	MLB	31	0	0	1	14	0	27^1	26	3	2.3	6.9	21	36.6%	.291	1.21	4.61	117	0.0	89.0	68.5%	28.5%	53.2%
Cody Reed	DUR	AAA	28	0	0	0	6	0	6^1	3	0	1.4	12.8	9	50.0%	.250	0.63	0.00	82	0.1				
	TB	MLB	28	0	1	0	12	0	9^2	8	1	5.6	6.5	7	46.4%	.269	1.45	3.72	118	0.0	93.0	62.8%	23.7%	52.8%
Chaz Roe	DUR	AAA	34	0	0	0	7	0	6^1	6	0	4.3	9.9	7	50.0%	.333	1.42	7.11	96	0.1				
	TB	MLB	34	0	0	0	1	0	0^2	1	0	13.5	27.0	2	0.0%	1.000	3.00	27.00	93	0.0	92.0	47.8%	33.3%	45.2%
Aaron Slegers	DUR	AAA	28	0	0	0	2	2	8	9	2	0.0	6.7	6	39.3%	.280	1.13	6.75	106	0.1				
	SL	AAA	28	0	1	0	16	5	28	43	9	3.2	3.9	12	46.4%	.330	1.89	6.43	131	-0.4				
	LAA	MLB	28	2	2	0	29	0	31	43	6	4.4	7.3	25	58.3%	.366	1.87	6.97	108	0.2	91.7	58.6%	25.1%	51.3%
Jeffrey Springs	TB	MLB	28	5	1	2	43	0	44^2	35	9	2.8	12.7	63	33.3%	.283	1.10	3.43	73	1.0	93.6	41.9%	36.6%	52.3%
Cole Wilcox	CSC	A	21	1	0	0	10	10	44^1	33	1	1.0	10.6	52	61.7%	.281	0.86	2.03	80	0.9				

Jalen Beeks missed the entire 2021 season recovering from Tommy John surgery. When healthy, he has the chance to rack up innings as an opener or bulk reliever. ⚾ The Rays 2020 first-round pick, **Nick Bitsko** has yet to pitch as a pro after undergoing labrum surgery in late 2020. ⚾ Once a promising member of the rotation, **Yonny Chirinos** will be out for some time yet again after fracturing his elbow during a comeback from Tommy John surgery. ⚾ **Adam Conley** swapped Florida teams and found some effectiveness out of the Rays bullpen, mostly against same-side batters thanks to an increased groundball rate and a reduction in free passes. A finesse-lefty as a starter, he touches the mid-90s as a reliever, but hadn't seen much success until landing in Tampa. ⚾ **Oliver Drake** was hurt or way too sexy to pitch in the 2021 season. ⚾ **Dietrich Enns** spent the 2020 season as a player-coach for the independent Tully Monsters. He returned to the majors in 2021 with more velocity and expanded pitch selection. He'll spend 2022 in South Korea. ⚾ **Calvin Faucher** has evolved from a 10th-round pick in 2017 who threw in the low 90s to an upper-90s thrower who was included in the Nelson Cruz deal. His control was borderline non-existent in 2021 and he's a reliever all the way. ⚾ **DJ Johnson** has an awesome beard and a less awesome shoulder that ended his season just one appearance after the Rays acquired him from Cleveland. ⚾ **Seth Johnson** already has two plus pitches with room to grow, and a clean, athletic delivery. ⚾ **Chris Mazza** didn't do anything to make Rays fans think better of the deal that sent prospect Ronaldo Hernandez to Boston. ⚾ **Colin Poche** hasn't thrown a competitive pitch since 2019 because of Tommy John surgery. ⚾ **Cody Reed** had thoracic outlet syndrome surgery over the summer. He has been more injured than not over the last few years. ⚾ **Chaz Roe**'s injury-plagued and limited 2021 still leaves him primed to be the most effective Roe come 2022 ⚾ The Rays' new market inefficiency is dealing a guy like **Aaron Slegers**, waiting for him to fail, picking him back up on a minor-league contract, and maybe fixing him up again. Think about how depressing the *next* market inefficiency is going to be. ⚾ **Jeffrey Springs** pitched a solid middle relief for Tampa Bay before tearing his ACL in July. ⚾ **Cole Wilcox** has all the makings to be a top pitching prospect, including a scar from Tommy John surgery that will likely wipe out his 2022 season.

TORONTO BLUE JAYS

Essay by Alex Wong

Player comments by Drew Fairservice and BP staff

I will remember the 2021 Toronto Blue Jays as the greatest team to never win the World Series.

When we have colonized Mars, and aliens have finally revealed themselves to us and found a well-read copy of this very version of Baseball Prospectus, they will scan these pages and wonder how this Blue Jays roster didn't even make the postseason. Vladimir Guerrero Jr. became the tater-lobbing prince who was promised. Marcus Semien was an MVP candidate. Robbie Ray won the Cy Young award. Those are just the top headliners on a team full of them. But despite 91 wins, they were, in the way we judge our baseball teams, ultimately a failure. And you know what? I'll take a failure this memorable any day.

As an immigrant from Hong Kong who moved to Toronto in 1992, I've always viewed North American sports from an outsider's perspective. Eight-year-old me turning on the television to watch my first Blue Jays game was abjectly confused. It took me a month to figure out what the runs, hits and errors on the scoreboard meant. Can you imagine my excitement the first time I learned about the infield fly rule? Well, multiply that tenfold when I witnessed my first balk. Baseball was the strangest sport to me, and that's before I learned about all of the unwritten rules. But it was how everyone talked about baseball which fascinated me the most. It's a bit hokey, and more than a bit Ken Burns-ian, but it resonated with me: The game makes you fail most of the time, and succeeding means failing a little bit less than everyone else.

Still, to define the 2021 Blue Jays through that lens—"coulda been better"—would be missing a grander point about joy and belonging, style and striving, the stories the win-loss binary paints over, and the times when such stories are needed. After an entire season away from Toronto, the Jays started 2021 season playing home games in Dunedin, Florida, before moving to Buffalo, New York. At that point, the team hovered around .500. A potent batting lineup was missing big free-agent addition George Springer, the straw who might have stirred the drink. The pitching rotation got thin after Ray, and Ryu Hyun-jin lost a measure of his old, soft-stuff magic. The bullpen was consistent only in its combustibility. There was an outline of an excellent team

TORONTO BLUE JAYS PROSPECTUS

2021 W-L: 91-71, 4TH IN AL EAST

Pythag	.614	*5th*	DER	.703	*14th*
RS/G	5.22	*3rd*	DRC+	113	*1st*
RA/G	4.09	*8th*	DRA-	98	*14th*
dWin%	.596	*2nd*	FIP	4.23	*16th*
Payroll	$135M	*13th*	B-Age	27.3	*4th*
M$/MW	$2.8M	*11th*	P-Age	29.4	*23rd*

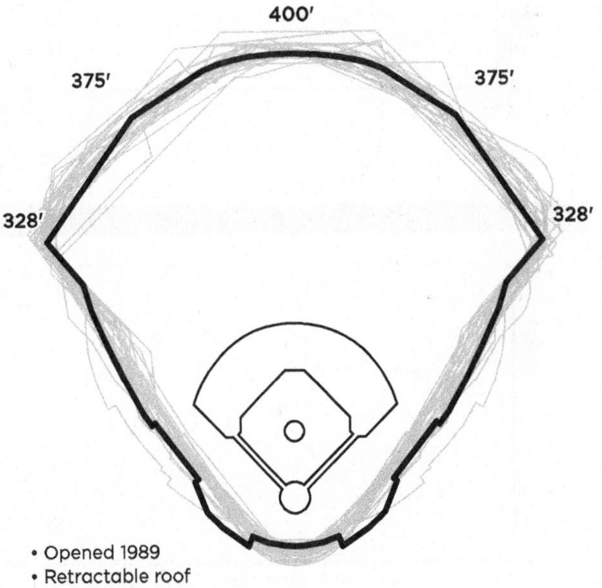

- Opened 1989
- Retractable roof
- Synthetic surface
- Fence profile: 10′

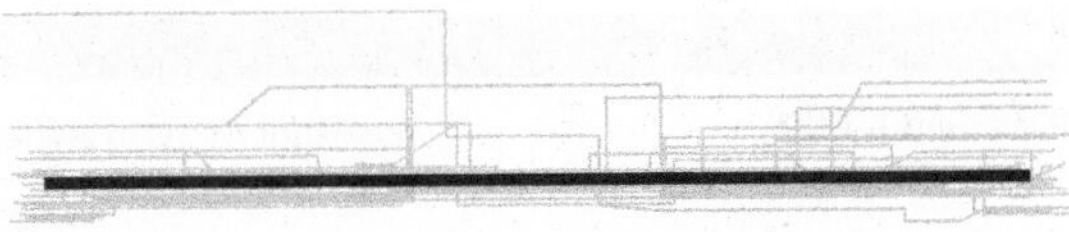

Park Factors

Runs	Runs/RH	Runs/LH	HR/RH	HR/LH
N/A	N/A	N/A	N/A	N/A

Top Hitter WARP	5.7 Vladimir Guerrero Jr.
Top Pitcher WARP	3.5 Robbie Ray
Top Prospect	Gabriel Moreno

Payroll History (in millions)

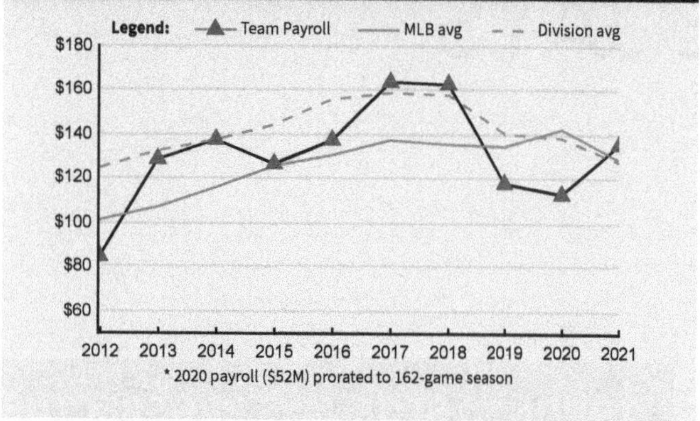

Future Commitments (in millions)

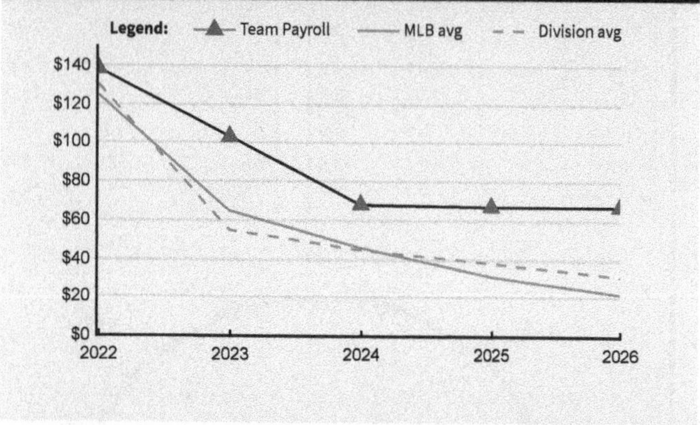

Farm System Ranking

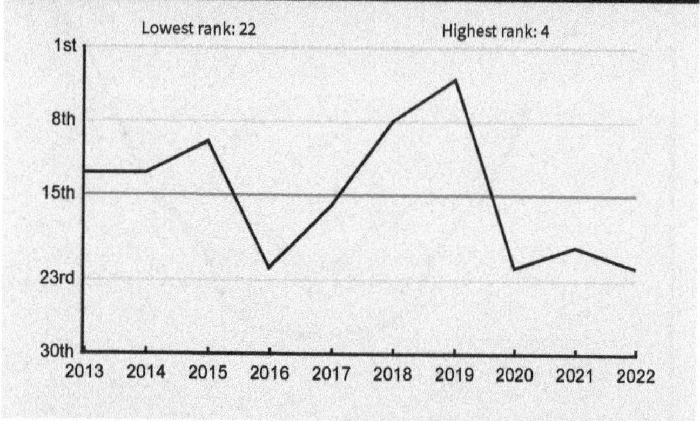

Personnel

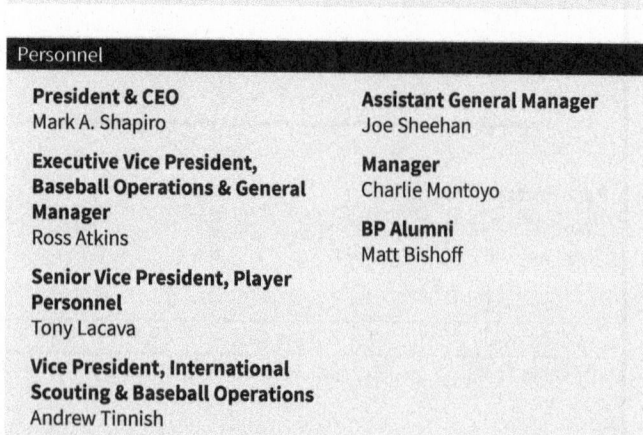

President & CEO
Mark A. Shapiro

Executive Vice President, Baseball Operations & General Manager
Ross Atkins

Senior Vice President, Player Personnel
Tony Lacava

Vice President, International Scouting & Baseball Operations
Andrew Tinnish

Assistant General Manager
Joe Sheehan

Manager
Charlie Montoyo

BP Alumni
Matt Bishoff

somewhere within the roster. *If they can just get back home, the Toronto Blue Jays might just become the most dangerous team in baseball.*

It was hard to fathom the conditional part of that statement becoming a reality as the calendar turned and summer arrived in the city of Toronto. While every other Major League Baseball team started to return to normal with full-capacity crowds in their home stadium after an entire season away, the Blue Jays played in front of cardboard-cutout fans a hundred miles away from the city where they belonged. For most of my adult life, I have lived within walking distance of the SkyDome (the Rogers Centre, technically, nowadays). When the pandemic forced all of us into lockdown, and our local baseball team to a new temporary home elsewhere, the emptiness of the baseball stadium and its surrounding radius became a personal daily reminder of what the new normal had stripped away from our everyday lives. One of the first routines I developed during lockdown was taking nightly walks around the stadium. I filled my camera roll with photos of emptiness: the empty streets, the abandoned hot-dog stand, the unmanned ticket office. The stairs leading up to Gate 12, which used to have an annoying amount of foot traffic, became my personal workout corner. I climbed those stairs everyday until I got as sick of the sight of an empty stadium as I was sick of the sight of an empty everything else.

On July 30, 2021, I walked there again. But this time, I wasn't circling the radius. I was going to watch a baseball game. The Blue Jays were finally granted a National Interest Exemption by the Canadian government to come home and play in front of a socially-distanced crowd. After spending more than a year seeing only a count-on-one-hand pod of people, I was surrounded by thousands in one place. The pageantry of live sports events doesn't resonate with me as much now that I'm an adult—the anthem is fraught, the beers overpriced, the time commitment daunting—but this day was different. The Canadian anthem gave me chills. Seeing rows of people lined up for overpriced menu items in the concourse gave me warm feelings. I didn't check the clock once. The Blue Jays won 6–4, with Bo Bichette inside-outing a two-run homer in the seventh inning to put the game out of reach. Santiago Espinal made a bare-handed catch to end the game, earning a standing ovation from the half-full stadium, but my own favorite memory came when I exited the stadium and walked out to the familiar sounds of idle chatter filling the airspace, to cars hopefully trying to honk their way past the traffic so they could even begin to fathom the journey home. It was the sound of normalcy.

But a baseball-team-as-symbol remains a baseball team. The Jays had a trio of world-beaters: Guerrero, whose 48 homers were somehow less impressive than the geometric oddity of the liners that produced them; Semien, who was right on Vladdy's heels in WARP; and Ray. But despite a memorable homestand, the addition of Jose Berríos, the return of a healthy Springer, and the emergence of rookie starter Alek Manoah, Toronto entered September trailing

Tampa Bay, New York and Boston in the stacked American League East. I returned to the SkyDome on September 3. The Oakland Athletics were in town to start a three-game series as one of several teams the Jays needed to chase down in the wild-card race. The Blue Jays were the best fourth-place team in baseball history and looked like the second-best team on the night, as they trailed the A's by two runs heading into the bottom of the ninth.

Maybe the excess of failure in baseball is a kindness. Baseball doesn't just deter the idea of success, it also amplifies it. I didn't need a title, or even a playoff berth, just relief: the kind that comes from a half-full park that feels over capacity and a team trying for something it may soon deserve. The Blue Jays walked off with an 11–10 comeback victory that evening when Semien cracked a three-run homer. They won eight straight games, and then 12 of 13. They swept the Yankees in New York in a four-game series. They scored 22 runs against the Baltimore Orioles a night after scoring 11 runs in a single inning. One day there were no more teams to catch in the wild-card standings.

The situation was short-lived. On the final day of the regular season, after a stretch of youth being young, the Blue Jays were no longer in control of their playoff destiny. A brief stumble in late September meant they were once again chasing the Yankees and Red Sox. If one of those teams lost, the Jays would have a chance to continue chasing their potential in the postseason. But first, they needed to win.

By the time Springer hit a grand slam in the third inning to push Toronto's lead to 9–1 against the Orioles at home, the fans were checking the out-of-town scoreboard. The Yankees and Rays were tied. Then New York walked it off in the ninth. One playoff possibility was off the board. The Washington Nationals jumped out to a 5–1 lead on the Red Sox, but the game in DC was tied by the time the Blue Jays walked off the field after a 12–4 victory in front of their home fans.

I was in the stadium that day, too. We all stayed behind as the ninth inning of the Red Sox–Nationals game appeared on the video board. We reflected on a season that spanned three cities, two countries and a memorable September. Just when we began to allow for the possibility that it might continue, Boston's Rafael Devers hit a two-run homer that made the Rogers Centre as quiet as it had been loud after Springer's shot.

Minutes later, the season was officially over.

I cherish the memory. The 2021 Blue Jays didn't reach their goal, but there's time for that. Ray and Semien are gone, but Vladdy and Bo are a hell of a core, no matter who else is around them; for now, they needed only to flash their wondrous possibility, to peddle hope in the form of 440-foot bombs. In 2021, the Jays stayed away, came home, showed out, made a bad time better. They provided a backdrop of routine and made a promise that they'll do more soon.

In those last seconds before Devers' shot, I had let the thoughts of the year slip. I was in a kind of flow state—tough to access in the best of times, near impossible in whatever these are. I had a team that deserved my pulling for it, our pulling for it, and we did so as best we could. It's the slightest sort of bummer that they lost, in whatever sense, that they were left out of the October pageantry. It's the biggest sort of boon that they made us care, in spite of it all.

—Alex Wong is a writer, author and producer based in Toronto.

Hitters

Bo Bichette SS Born: 03/05/98 Age: 24 Bats: R Throws: R Height: 6'0" Weight: 185 lb. Origin: Round 2, 2016 Draft (#66 overall)

YEAR	TEAM	LVL	AGE	PA	R	2B	3B	HR	RBI	BB	K	SB	CS	Whiff%	AVG/OBP/SLG	DRC+	BABIP	BRR	FRAA	WARP
2019	BUF	AAA	21	244	34	16	2	8	32	19	48	15	5		.275/.333/.473	102	.317	-1.4	SS(51): -1.5, 2B(1): -0.0	0.7
2019	TOR	MLB	21	212	32	18	0	11	21	14	50	4	4	24.5%	.311/.358/.571	107	.368	-0.2	SS(42): 4.4	1.4
2020	TOR	MLB	22	128	18	9	1	5	23	5	27	4	1	21.6%	.301/.328/.512	105	.352	-0.4	SS(26): -0.3	0.4
2021	TOR	MLB	23	690	121	30	1	29	102	40	137	25	1	22.4%	.298/.343/.484	115	.339	3.6	SS(148): -5.3	3.6
2022 DC	*TOR*	*MLB*	*24*	*610*	*100*	*30*	*2*	*21*	*82*	*39*	*120*	*21*	*6*	*22.1%*	*.284/.335/.462*	*112*	*.328*	*1.3*	*SS 0*	*3.4*

Comparables: Corey Seager, Francisco Lindor, Javier Báez

There are not many players with the unique offensive skills the Blue Jays shortstop brings to the plate. While his hyper-aggressive approach earned him the nickname "Bo-and-two" during a particularly fallow period of the season, his production speaks for itself and hints at another level just a few tweaks away. Would you teach it? You likely couldn't if you tried. Would you change it? Not on your life.

Few players in baseball hit the ball as frequently or with as much authority to the opposite-field power alley as the Blue Jays' young shortstop. Watching Bichette inside-out a 95-mph sinker on the inside half of the plate, as he did to a turbosinker from Yankees reliever Clay Holmes in a huge September moment, is a sight to behold. That 8th inning home run represented another piece of the Bichette puzzle: he was among the team's top clutch performers, delivering big hits all season long.

Cavan Biggio 3B Born: 04/11/95 Age: 27 Bats: L Throws: R Height: 6'2" Weight: 200 lb. Origin: Round 5, 2016 Draft (#162 overall)

YEAR	TEAM	LVL	AGE	PA	R	2B	3B	HR	RBI	BB	K	SB	CS	Whiff%	AVG/OBP/SLG	DRC+	BABIP	BRR	FRAA	WARP
2019	BUF	AAA	24	174	23	8	1	6	27	34	28	5	1		.312/.448/.514	133	.352	0.5	2B(22): 1.1, 1B(7): 0.3, 3B(7): 0.3	1.5
2019	TOR	MLB	24	430	66	17	2	16	48	71	123	14	0	26.0%	.234/.364/.429	95	.309	2.6	2B(85): 0.5, 1B(8): -0.3, RF(8): -0.9	1.5
2020	TOR	MLB	25	265	41	16	0	8	28	41	61	6	0	23.2%	.250/.375/.432	102	.311	1.5	2B(37): -0.1, RF(14): -0.9, 3B(10): 0.3	1.0
2021	BUF	AAA	26	90	15	2	0	3	11	11	26	0	0		.182/.289/.325	85	.224	0.3	3B(9): -0.7, RF(5): -1.1, LF(1): 0.1	0.0
2021	TOR	MLB	26	294	27	10	1	7	27	37	78	3	1	25.8%	.224/.322/.356	87	.290	-0.4	3B(52): 5.2, RF(15): 0.6, 1B(7): 0.1	1.0
2022 DC	*TOR*	*MLB*	*27*	*552*	*82*	*22*	*2*	*17*	*63*	*74*	*139*	*10*	*3*	*24.9%*	*.227/.339/.392*	*97*	*.287*	*0.3*	*2B 0, RF 0*	*1.7*

Comparables: Eric Sogard, Cory Spangenberg, Tony Kemp

The funhouse mirror of professional baseball players, Biggio often reflects that which the viewer wants to see. Biggio is lauded in some corners for his gritty and/or heady approach to the game, terrific baserunning and impeccable strike zone judgment. Others point to the lackluster batted ball metrics, propensity to swing and miss and lack of a real position as causes for concern. 2021 provided more questions than answers for Biggio's future.

Was he bad because he was hurt or did the cold realities of regression arrive on the same bus as the injury bug? He still drew his walks but failed to do much else at the plate. He missed big chunks of the season with nagging injuries and then, late in the season, went on an extended rehab assignment that seemed to suggest the club was in no rush to bring him back to the big leagues. Defense remains a huge question mark as the Opening Day third baseman looked out of place at the hot corner at times.

There exists a version of Biggio that provides versatility, patience and a lefty bat off the bench or at the bottom of the order for a righty-heavy team like Toronto. He'll always have the backers who believe him capable of much more, happy to overlook his flaws in favor of the idea that he's come to represent.

Jarrod Dyson OF Born: 08/15/84 Age: 37 Bats: L Throws: R Height: 5'9" Weight: 165 lb. Origin: Round 50, 2006 Draft (#1475 overall)

YEAR	TEAM	LVL	AGE	PA	R	2B	3B	HR	RBI	BB	K	SB	CS	Whiff%	AVG/OBP/SLG	DRC+	BABIP	BRR	FRAA	WARP
2019	ARI	MLB	34	452	65	11	2	7	27	47	86	30	4	21.5%	.230/.313/.320	83	.275	7.1	CF(103): -3.6, RF(21): 4.2, LF(16): -0.1	1.5
2020	CHW	MLB	35	11	3	0	0	0	0	0	1	2	0	5.0%	.300/.300/.300	96	.333	0.6	LF(6): -0.3, CF(2): -0.4, RF(1): 0.0	0.0
2021	KC	MLB	36	132	13	7	2	0	10	6	28	8	3	24.1%	.221/.256/.311	74	.284	1.3	RF(34): -1.2, CF(19): 0.7, LF(18): 0.3	0.2
2021	TOR	MLB	36	17	4	0	0	0	0	4	5	2	2	31.0%	.077/.294/.077	85	.125	0.0	CF(19): -0.4, LF(2): -0.1	0.0
2022 DC	*FA*	*MLB*	*37*	*172*	*14*	*6*	*0*	*2*	*14*	*15*	*36*	*10*	*3*	*23.4%*	*.223/.298/.313*	*66*	*.279*	*0.9*	*CF 0, RF 0*	*-0.1*

Comparables: Otis Nixon, Brett Butler, Kenny Lofton

The proud owner of a very specific set of skills, Dyson has entered the "more games played than plate appearances" stage of his career. For the second season in a row he was a speculative late-winter signing for also-ran clubs ostensibly in need of speed and defense off the bench (with a more specific eye to flipping him to a contender with an actual need for speed and defense at the deadline).

With Randal Grichuk struggling and George Springer hurt, Dyson made his way to Toronto after the Royals placed him on waivers. He popped up as a pinch-runner and defensive replacement, though his stolen base calling card never really came into play.

Dyson's biggest play of the year was spending the full season on a big-league roster, which nudged him into the illustrious club of those with ten years of service time.

Santiago Espinal 3B Born: 11/13/94 Age: 27 Bats: R Throws: R Height: 5'10" Weight: 181 lb. Origin: Round 10, 2016 Draft (#298 overall)

YEAR	TEAM	LVL	AGE	PA	R	2B	3B	HR	RBI	BB	K	SB	CS	Whiff%	AVG/OBP/SLG	DRC+	BABIP	BRR	FRAA	WARP
2019	NH	AA	24	409	46	21	1	5	57	35	50	10	11		.278/.343/.381	119	.310	-2.5	2B(52): 4.2, SS(22): 0.8, CF(12): 3.5	3.1
2019	BUF	AAA	24	112	11	6	0	2	14	7	23	2	2		.317/.360/.433	88	.392	0.6	2B(18): 1.5, SS(11): -0.3	0.5
2020	TOR	MLB	25	66	10	4	0	0	6	4	16	1	0	25.4%	.267/.308/.333	87	.356	0.1	SS(21): 3.7, 3B(2): -0.0, P(2): -0.0	0.5
2021	TOR	MLB	26	246	32	13	1	2	17	22	30	6	1	15.5%	.311/.376/.405	112	.353	0.9	3B(81): 11.6	2.5
2022 DC	*TOR*	*MLB*	*27*	*461*	*57*	*20*	*1*	*7*	*60*	*35*	*64*	*8*	*4*	*17.6%*	*.264/.324/.372*	*90*	*.297*	*0.2*	*3B 7, 2B 0*	*1.5*

Comparables: Justin Turner, Danny Valencia, Miguel Rojas

Mr Steal Your Job himself, Espinal endeared himself to Blue Jays fans by bringing stability and aggressive defensive competence to the hot corner at a time when third base and infield defense on the whole was a real problem for the club. Offensively, the BABIP gods turned their patient eyes towards the glove-first utility man, making him a roughly league-average offensive player in a half-season's worth of plate appearances. He doesn't have much power, but a keen eye and contact-heavy approach mixed with some good bounces to make Espinal a valued contributor before injury knocked him out of the lineup for much of the stretch run.

Randal Grichuk OF Born: 08/13/91 Age: 30 Bats: R Throws: R Height: 6'2" Weight: 216 lb. Origin: Round 1, 2009 Draft (#24 overall)

YEAR	TEAM	LVL	AGE	PA	R	2B	3B	HR	RBI	BB	K	SB	CS	Whiff%	AVG/OBP/SLG	DRC+	BABIP	BRR	FRAA	WARP
2019	TOR	MLB	27	628	75	29	5	31	80	35	163	2	1	28.1%	.232/.280/.457	95	.266	-0.6	RF(92): -3.7, CF(62): -5.0	0.8
2020	TOR	MLB	28	231	38	9	0	12	35	13	49	1	1	23.1%	.273/.312/.481	112	.299	-0.1	CF(48): -2.4	0.8
2021	TOR	MLB	29	545	59	25	1	22	81	27	114	0	3	23.2%	.241/.281/.423	94	.266	-1.6	CF(96): -6.9, RF(71): 0.9	0.8
2022 DC	*TOR*	*MLB*	*30*	*499*	*69*	*22*	*1*	*21*	*76*	*29*	*100*	*3*	*2*	*23.3%*	*.247/.297/.440*	*92*	*.272*	*-0.3*	*RF -1, CF -1*	*0.7*

Comparables: Dusty Baker, Ruben Sierra, Juan Encarnacion

Everybody has a brand, whether they like it or not. Your brand enters the room before you do, setting the tone before you can even open your mouth. The five-year contract extension given to Grichuk in 2019 has made his brand "The Overpaid Guy." His contract is seemingly the first thing anyone thinks of whenever his name is mentioned, even though he's just a fourth outfielder doing fourth outfielder stuff.

Grichuk's career numbers follow a tight sine wave with a very small amplitude. 2021 looked like his seasons always do, just on the bottom end of his usual ebb. Like always, he had a great few weeks, using the whole field and seeming to turn a corner before resuming his decent SLG, poor OBP, high strikeout ways. He spent most of his time in center field as George Springer's prolonged IL stint pushed him into effective-if-unspectacular duty for much of the first half. His playing time dried up in the second half when his performance swooned and better options remained healthy and available for Charlie Montoyo.

★ ★ ★ *2022 Top 101 Prospect* **#60** ★ ★ ★

Jordan Groshans IF

Born: 11/10/99 Age: 22 Bats: R Throws: R Height: 6'3" Weight: 205 lb. Origin: Round 1, 2018 Draft (#12 overall)

YEAR	TEAM	LVL	AGE	PA	R	2B	3B	HR	RBI	BB	K	SB	CS	Whiff%	AVG/OBP/SLG	DRC+	BABIP	BRR	FRAA	WARP
2019	LAN	A	19	96	12	6	0	2	13	13	21	1	1		.337/.427/.482	121	.433	0.0	SS(20): -1.5	0.4
2021	NH	AA	21	316	46	23	0	7	40	34	61	0	0		.291/.367/.450	118	.347	-1.2	SS(43): -1.9, 3B(21): -0.6, 1B(1): -0.1	1.3
2022 DC	*TOR*	*MLB*	*22*	*63*	*7*	*3*	*0*	*1*	*7*	*5*	*13*	*0*	*0*	*23.7%*	*.245/.314/.363*	*85*	*.303*	*-0.1*	*3B 0*	*0.0*

Comparables: Junior Lake, Nick Franklin, Corey Seager

Minor-league baseball's return felt like the first day of school after a summer spent elsewhere: you know all the faces and the lay of the land, but it takes a few days before the fog wears off. The fog ensconcing Groshans was particularly thick, as injuries had limited him to just 71 contests between his selection in the 2018 draft and the pandemic. Nevertheless, he reminded Blue Jays fans why they were happy to have him in the first place by showing a balanced skill set and holding his own against Double-A competition that was (on average) three years his senior. It's unclear where exactly Groshans will play defensively—third base seems likeliest given his arm strength and Bo Bichette's continued existence—but that's a champagne problem. The real issue facing Groshans has been his availability to play at all; provided he's past all that, he should emerge from the fog as a nifty little contributor sometime this summer.

Vladimir Guerrero Jr. 1B

Born: 03/16/99 Age: 23 Bats: R Throws: R Height: 6'2" Weight: 250 lb. Origin: International Free Agent, 2015

YEAR	TEAM	LVL	AGE	PA	R	2B	3B	HR	RBI	BB	K	SB	CS	Whiff%	AVG/OBP/SLG	DRC+	BABIP	BRR	FRAA	WARP
2019	BUF	AAA	20	34	7	1	0	3	8	4	2	1	0		.367/.441/.700	138	.320	-0.1	3B(7): 0.1	0.2
2019	TOR	MLB	20	514	52	26	2	15	69	46	91	0	1	24.5%	.272/.339/.433	104	.308	-3.1	3B(96): -4.5	0.8
2020	TOR	MLB	21	243	34	13	2	9	33	20	38	1	0	24.7%	.262/.329/.462	116	.282	-0.8	1B(34): 1.8	1.1
2021	TOR	MLB	22	698	123	29	1	48	111	86	110	4	1	27.8%	.311/.401/.601	158	.313	-2.4	1B(133): -6.4, 3B(1): -0.0	5.7
2022 DC	*TOR*	*MLB*	*23*	*621*	*112*	*27*	*2*	*33*	*109*	*70*	*109*	*2*	*2*	*27.0%*	*.299/.386/.540*	*148*	*.323*	*-0.6*	*1B -2*	*5.0*

Comparables: Rafael Devers, Mike Trout, Jason Heyward

Questions swirled around Vlad Jr. before the 2021 season began, questions he answered definitively.

His power? Prodigious! His eye for balls and strikes? Discerning! Bat-to-all skills? The envy of throwback middle infielders everywhere! How would he look when, after bashing another home run, he slipped into a blue sportcoat honoring the homeland of his teammates? Dashing! Would the extra work he put in over the winter, sweating through training sessions to improve his strength and fitness pay off? In spades! What does a fully-realized 80 hit, 80 power hitter in the big leagues look like? Awe-inspiring.

The real Vladdy arrived, threatening to win the Triple Crown and showing he could be every bit the monster that rampaged through the minors as a teenager. It's not just the sum of a formidable package of hitting abilities that makes Guerrero one of the game's greatest talents, it's that he has so much damn fun showing it off.

Lourdes Gurriel Jr. LF

Born: 10/10/93 Age: 28 Bats: R Throws: R Height: 6'4" Weight: 215 lb. Origin: International Free Agent, 2016

YEAR	TEAM	LVL	AGE	PA	R	2B	3B	HR	RBI	BB	K	SB	CS	Whiff%	AVG/OBP/SLG	DRC+	BABIP	BRR	FRAA	WARP
2019	BUF	AAA	25	130	18	13	0	4	26	3	23	0	2		.276/.308/.480	107	.309	-3.2	2B(12): -1.7, SS(7): -2.1, LF(7): -1.3	-0.2
2019	TOR	MLB	25	343	52	19	2	20	50	20	86	6	4	32.8%	.277/.327/.541	109	.318	1.2	LF(63): -0.4, 2B(9): -1.3, 1B(3): -0.3	1.5
2020	TOR	MLB	26	224	28	14	0	11	33	14	48	3	1	26.3%	.308/.348/.534	120	.351	-0.4	LF(53): 8.8	2.0
2021	TOR	MLB	27	541	62	28	2	21	84	32	102	1	3	24.3%	.276/.319/.466	107	.305	-2.6	LF(119): 9.3, 1B(11): 0.8	3.2
2022 DC	*TOR*	*MLB*	*28*	*558*	*75*	*26*	*1*	*19*	*79*	*32*	*110*	*4*	*4*	*24.5%*	*.265/.314/.436*	*100*	*.303*	*-0.3*	*LF 1, 1B 0*	*1.9*

Comparables: Justin Turner, Khris Davis, Cliff Pennington

There are plenty of ways to describe streaky hitters and every single one of those descriptors applies to Gurriel Jr. Free swinging might be an understatement but his talent is not to be overlooked. Teammates often describe him as the best pure hitter on the team and with good reason: Gurriel finished the season hitting everything, posting a .308/.369/.568 line from August 1 through season's end, including seven home runs in September. A stark contrast to the .249/.265/.367 line (with just four walks!) he posted over his first 186 plate appearances of 2021.

Dull moments are few and far between for the practitioner of piña power, especially in the field. Gurriel's relative youth and lithe build betray his well below-average footspeed and shambolic routes in the outfield. Statcast rated him as the 40th best LF in the game, costing the Jays eight runs with his glove. The duality of Lourdes teaches us that while every fly ball is an adventure, only the most swashbuckling of baserunners dare tempt Gurriel's arm in the outfield. He cut down 12 runners in 2021, more than any other regular left fielder. By advanced measures UZR and DRS, Gurriel nets out as a positive fielder thanks to the value of his strong and accurate arm. One must pull back the spiny skin of the pineapple to expose the sweet, sweet fruit inside.

Teoscar Hernández OF Born: 10/15/92 Age: 29 Bats: R Throws: R Height: 6'2" Weight: 205 lb. Origin: International Free Agent, 2011

YEAR	TEAM	LVL	AGE	PA	R	2B	3B	HR	RBI	BB	K	SB	CS	Whiff%	AVG/OBP/SLG	DRC+	BABIP	BRR	FRAA	WARP
2019	BUF	AAA	26	83	11	0	1	5	11	6	21	3	0		.253/.313/.480	107	.280	1.0	CF(9): -1.6, LF(5): 0.2	0.3
2019	TOR	MLB	26	464	58	19	2	26	65	45	153	6	3	34.8%	.230/.306/.472	95	.293	0.0	CF(79): -0.6, LF(46): 9.3	2.4
2020	TOR	MLB	27	207	33	7	0	16	34	14	63	6	1	34.9%	.289/.340/.579	117	.348	-0.5	RF(40): 1.6, CF(9): 0.8	1.3
2021	TOR	MLB	28	595	92	29	0	32	116	36	148	12	4	31.9%	.296/.346/.524	118	.352	0.6	RF(110): 13.8, LF(58): -3.0, CF(2): -0.1	4.3
2022 DC	*TOR*	*MLB*	*29*	*581*	*87*	*25*	*2*	*27*	*96*	*41*	*152*	*9*	*5*	*31.9%*	*.261/.319/.471*	*107*	*.315*	*0.4*	*RF 2, LF 0*	*2.3*

Comparables: Starling Marte, Robbie Grossman, Gerardo Parra

What if you built a player out of exclusively loud tools and then, almost miraculously, he put it all together for one dream season? What if his carrying tool was joie de vivre? Then you might have half the season enjoyed by the Blue Jays' always-smiling All-Star. There might not be a more likable player in baseball, and in 2021 Hernández put together an incredible campaign, one that seemed unlikely to even his biggest backers.

The power output continued its 2020 trend, and he traded a few strikeouts for base hits. Beyond his improvement at the plate, Hernández worked to upgrade his defense from "calamitous" to "non-issue" en route to his most complete season to date, marred only by missing time due to COVID-19. It feels unfair to expect a repeat in 2022, but the gregarious outfielder makes it fun to dream.

Miguel Hiraldo IF Born: 09/05/00 Age: 21 Bats: R Throws: R Height: 5'11" Weight: 170 lb. Origin: International Free Agent, 2017

YEAR	TEAM	LVL	AGE	PA	R	2B	3B	HR	RBI	BB	K	SB	CS	Whiff%	AVG/OBP/SLG	DRC+	BABIP	BRR	FRAA	WARP
2019	BLU	ROA	18	256	43	20	1	7	37	14	36	11	3		.300/.348/.481		.328			
2019	LAN	A	18	4	0	0	1	0	0	0	0	0	0		.250/.250/.750	94	.250	0.0	2B(1): 0.1	0.0
2021	DUN	A	20	453	66	26	4	7	52	51	111	29	5		.249/.338/.390	102	.323	0.2	2B(51): -7.5, 3B(37): -1.8	0.6
2022 non-DC	*TOR*	*MLB*	*21*	*251*	*20*	*11*	*1*	*2*	*21*	*19*	*76*	*10*	*3*	*35.2%*	*.216/.283/.322*	*63*	*.312*	*0.9*	*2B -2, 3B 0*	*-0.6*

Comparables: Delino DeShields, Chris Owings, Thairo Estrada

The scouting report says "stocky" but the stolen base total says "29." The blurb describes an angry bat but the slugging percentage reads ".390." Such is life as a precocious youngster trying to make his way through the world of professional baseball. New skills uncovered, new challenges faced. A strange year across minor league baseball is bound to produce some strange stat lines.

Hiraldo's bat surely carries a great deal of promise even though his inevitable slide down the defensive spectrum began in 2021, when he didn't log a single inning at shortstop for the first time as a professional.

Danny Jansen C Born: 04/15/95 Age: 27 Bats: R Throws: R Height: 6'2" Weight: 225 lb. Origin: Round 16, 2013 Draft (#475 overall)

YEAR	TEAM	LVL	AGE	PA	R	2B	3B	HR	RBI	BB	K	SB	CS	Whiff%	AVG/OBP/SLG	DRC+	BABIP	BRR	FRAA	WARP
2019	TOR	MLB	24	384	41	12	1	13	43	31	79	0	1	20.5%	.207/.279/.360	88	.230	-0.4	C(103): 11.3	2.1
2020	TOR	MLB	25	147	18	3	0	6	20	21	31	0	0	24.9%	.183/.313/.358	108	.190	-0.5	C(43): -0.2	0.6
2021	BUF	AAA	26	26	5	0	0	1	4	4	3	0	0		.238/.346/.381	117	.222	-0.1	C(5): -0.0	0.1
2021	TOR	MLB	26	205	32	13	0	11	28	17	44	0	0	25.3%	.223/.299/.473	106	.233	-1.8	C(69): 0.6	0.9
2022 DC	*TOR*	*MLB*	*27*	*274*	*39*	*11*	*0*	*9*	*44*	*26*	*64*	*0*	*0*	*23.7%*	*.234/.323/.409*	*97*	*.279*	*-0.4*	*C 4*	*1.6*

Comparables: Francisco Cervelli, Devin Mesoraco, Kurt Suzuki

YEAR	TEAM	P. COUNT	FRM RUNS	BLK RUNS	THRW RUNS	TOT RUNS
2019	TOR	14805	11.9	0.2	0.6	12.7
2020	TOR	6284	-0.4	0.1	0.0	-0.3
2021	TOR	8117	0.9	0.2	0.0	1.1
2022	*TOR*	*10822*	*4.9*	*1.1*	*0.2*	*6.2*

It took a great deal of effort to get Jansen's season numbers to poke out over the league-average horizon. An abysmal start to the season came hot on the heels of a poor 2020, and suddenly there was doubt that the most recent Catcher of the Future was even the catcher of the present.

After 40 games, his OPS stood at .499. Then he missed a month with a hamstring strain, came back, put together a good stretch and promptly missed another month with another hamstring strain. Returning on August 31, he homered and walked off the bench. Jansen then spent the entire month of September going crazy, posting a .310/.365/.707 line with five homers and eight doubles.

That sprint to the finish, coupled with encouraging gains in exit velocity, hard hit rate and launch angle, cements Jansen's place among the Blue Jays' exciting core.

Alejandro Kirk C Born: 11/06/98 Age: 23 Bats: R Throws: R Height: 5'8" Weight: 265 lb. Origin: International Free Agent, 2016

YEAR	TEAM	LVL	AGE	PA	R	2B	3B	HR	RBI	BB	K	SB	CS	Whiff%	AVG/OBP/SLG	DRC+	BABIP	BRR	FRAA	WARP
2019	LAN	A	20	96	15	6	1	3	8	18	8	1	0		.299/.427/.519	159	.299	0.4	C(17): -0.9	0.9
2019	DUN	A+	20	276	26	25	0	4	36	38	31	2	0		.288/.395/.446	150	.317	-2.5	C(68): 7.2	2.9
2020	TOR	MLB	21	25	4	2	0	1	3	1	4	0	0	21.6%	.375/.400/.583	116	.421	-1.3	C(7): -0.8	-0.1
2021	BUF	AAA	22	56	7	3	0	2	13	5	9	0	0		.347/.393/.531	110	.375	0.0	C(10): -1.0	0.2
2021	TOR	MLB	22	189	19	8	0	8	24	19	22	0	0	19.4%	.242/.328/.436	123	.234	-0.6	C(44): 0.8	1.3
2022 DC	*TOR*	*MLB*	*23*	*352*	*48*	*17*	*0*	*10*	*48*	*34*	*51*	*0*	*1*	*18.8%*	*.264/.342/.427*	*111*	*.287*	*-0.5*	*C -2*	*1.4*

Comparables: Salvador Perez, Héctor Sánchez, Jose Altuve

"Hitters hit" is a baseball truism as old as the hills. It describes not only Kirk's big-league career to date but also the Blue Jays' handling of the young catcher. He's a hitter and the club keeps giving him opportunities to do so. Rushed to the big leagues from A-ball (via the COVID alternate site for a playoff run, Kirk was again given an aggressive assignment to start 2021, making the big-league club right out of spring training. His inclusion forced perfectly viable backup catcher Reese McGuire to the waiver wire.

YEAR	TEAM	P. COUNT	FRM RUNS	BLK RUNS	THRW RUNS	TOT RUNS
2019	DUN	8362	6.3	0.6	0.2	7.1
2019	LAN	2443	-1.5	0.0	0.5	-0.9
2020	TOR	1001	-0.8	0.0	0.0	-0.8
2021	TOR	5495	0.6	-0.2	0.5	0.9
2021	BUF	1421	-0.7	-0.1	0.0	-0.8
2022	*TOR*	*4810*	*-2.7*	*-0.1*	*-0.1*	*-2.9*

And then Kirk just kept hitting. He hit and he hit until an injury cost him a big chunk of the season. Then he came back and hit some more! He more than acquitted himself behind the plate, becoming Robbie Ray's personal catcher en route to a Cy Young award. One notable passed ball will live long in the memory of some fans, and a mini-slump late in the season cut down on his playing time as it coincided with teammate Danny Jansen catching fire, but his DRC+ ranks fourth among catchers. Hitters hit and, thanks to his contact-and-line drive-heavy approach, that's what Kirk has continued to do.

Jake Lamb LF/3B

Born: 10/09/90 Age: 31 Bats: L Throws: R Height: 6'3" Weight: 215 lb. Origin: Round 6, 2012 Draft (#213 overall)

YEAR	TEAM	LVL	AGE	PA	R	2B	3B	HR	RBI	BB	K	SB	CS	Whiff%	AVG/OBP/SLG	DRC+	BABIP	BRR	FRAA	WARP
2019	RNO	AAA	28	46	5	2	0	1	7	7	12	0	0		.179/.304/.308	92	.231	0.1	3B(6): -0.8, 1B(5): 0.1	0.0
2019	ARI	MLB	28	226	26	8	2	6	30	32	55	1	0	25.8%	.193/.323/.353	91	.234	1.9	3B(36): -1.9, 1B(24): -1.1	0.3
2020	OAK	MLB	29	49	5	4	0	3	9	2	8	0	0	21.6%	.267/.327/.556	100	.265	0.8	3B(11): -1.8	0.0
2020	ARI	MLB	29	50	2	1	0	0	1	6	17	0	1	31.0%	.116/.240/.140	70	.192	-0.2	1B(12): -0.8, 3B(3): 0.0	-0.2
2021	CLT	AAA	30	69	6	5	0	3	8	8	15	0	0		.246/.333/.475	109	.279	0.7	RF(10): -0.6, 3B(5): -0.5	0.3
2021	CHW	MLB	30	131	20	2	0	6	13	17	38	0	0	27.1%	.212/.321/.389	91	.261	-0.1	LF(16): -0.6, RF(9): -1.0, 3B(6): 0.5	0.1
2021	TOR	MLB	30	39	5	2	0	1	6	5	13	0	0	26.4%	.129/.256/.290	75	.158	-0.3	3B(10): 0.2, 1B(1): -0.0	0.0
2022 DC	*FA*	*MLB*	*31*	*276*	*31*	*11*	*0*	*9*	*32*	*33*	*68*	*1*	*1*	*26.1%*	*.214/.318/.388*	*90*	*.257*	*-0.2*	*3B -1, 1B 0*	*0.2*

Comparables: Howard Johnson, Robin Ventura, Kyle Seager

Lamb was in the right place at the right time for the 2021 Toronto Blue Jays, but was he the right guy? By virtue of his left-handedness and prior history playing third base at the big-league level, he was a no-brainer waiver claim for a team looking for depth and variety in their right-hand heavy lineup. And upon his arrival, the Blue Jays promptly went on a crucial hot streak, winning 11 of 13 games. Alas, correlation once again failed to equal causation as Lamb managed just four hits in those nine appearances and failed to make an impression with the glove. His playing time disappeared and he was released with four days remaining in the season, a ruthless reminder of the new September roster rules' give-and-take.

★ ★ ★ *2022 Top 101 Prospect* **#62** ★ ★ ★

Orelvis Martinez SS

Born: 11/19/01 Age: 20 Bats: R Throws: R Height: 6'1" Weight: 188 lb. Origin: International Free Agent, 2018

YEAR	TEAM	LVL	AGE	PA	R	2B	3B	HR	RBI	BB	K	SB	CS	Whiff%	AVG/OBP/SLG	DRC+	BABIP	BRR	FRAA	WARP
2019	BLU	ROK	17	163	20	8	5	7	32	14	29	2	0		.275/.352/.549		.296			
2021	DUN	A	19	326	49	22	2	19	68	33	85	4	1		.279/.369/.572	130	.333	-1.8	SS(46): -5.2, 3B(12): 0.1	1.5
2021	VAN	A+	19	125	17	4	0	9	19	10	28	0	1		.214/.282/.491	125	.197	-0.4	SS(19): -1.1, 3B(6): -0.5	0.6
2022 non-DC	*TOR*	*MLB*	*20*	*251*	*27*	*11*	*1*	*9*	*31*	*16*	*73*	*0*	*1*	*32.1%*	*.233/.293/.420*	*88*	*.297*	*-0.2*	*SS -2, 3B 0*	*0.2*

Comparables: Carlos Correa, Richard Ureña, Ketel Marte

In 2021, playing as a 19-year old, Martinez hit. He hit at low-A and then, after a period of finding his way, Martinez hit in high-A, too. He hit home runs and he refined his approach against more advanced pitching. He hits. Martinez hits the ball hard and often. He hits for power to the pull side and looks the part of a guy who will hit for power to all fields. Is he a shortstop? Is he moving to third base, given his size? Right now, it doesn't matter. They'll happily take the main offensive tool and figure out the rest as it comes.

Reese McGuire C

Born: 03/02/95 Age: 27 Bats: L Throws: R Height: 6'0" Weight: 215 lb. Origin: Round 1, 2013 Draft (#14 overall)

YEAR	TEAM	LVL	AGE	PA	R	2B	3B	HR	RBI	BB	K	SB	CS	Whiff%	AVG/OBP/SLG	DRC+	BABIP	BRR	FRAA	WARP
2019	BUF	AAA	24	277	30	12	1	5	29	25	44	4	0		.247/.316/.366	100	.276	-3.6	C(71): 7.6	1.5
2019	TOR	MLB	24	105	14	7	0	5	11	7	18	0	0	21.8%	.299/.346/.526	107	.324	0.6	C(30): 5.0	1.1
2020	TOR	MLB	25	45	2	0	0	1	1	0	11	0	0	21.4%	.073/.073/.146	71	.069	-0.3	C(18): -0.6	-0.1
2021	TOR	MLB	26	217	22	15	0	1	10	15	44	0	0	21.6%	.253/.310/.343	81	.318	-0.3	C(73): 7.5	1.1
2022 DC	*TOR*	*MLB*	*27*	*182*	*22*	*8*	*0*	*3*	*26*	*12*	*36*	*0*	*1*	*21.3%*	*.232/.294/.350*	*74*	*.279*	*-0.2*	*C 5*	*0.8*

Comparables: Christian Vázquez, Wilson Ramos, Austin Romine

YEAR	TEAM	P. COUNT	FRM RUNS	BLK RUNS	THRW RUNS	TOT RUNS
2019	TOR	4094	5.1	0.0	0.2	5.3
2019	BUF	10274	7.4	0.0	1.0	8.4
2020	TOR	1815	-0.4	0.0	-0.2	-0.6
2021	TOR	8862	7.9	0.2	0.3	8.5
2022	*TOR*	*7215*	*5.4*	*0.8*	*0.6*	*6.7*

Never a dull moment when you live on the fringes of the 40-man roster. McGuire started the season out of options and was, somewhat surprisingly, DFA'd as the club opted to bring Alejandro Kirk north to start the season. McGuire went unclaimed and yet still managed to figure prominently into the Blue Jays' plans in 2021. Recalled in May, the defense-first catcher spent the remainder of the season in the big leagues, holding down the fort as injuries ravaged Toronto's catching corps. The slap-hitting backstop even managed a small-M magical run in June that produced an improbable 18 hits in 14 games, including his only home run of the year!

Offensive reality settled in, reinforcements arrived and his playing time dried up; he came to the plate just 17 times in the Blue Jays' desperate month of September. So, after receiving more than 3,600 pitches in 2021, McGuire again finds himself in a fight for his big-league future.

★ ★ ★ *2022 Top 101 Prospect* **#22** ★ ★ ★

Gabriel Moreno C

Born: 02/14/00 Age: 22 Bats: R Throws: R Height: 5'11" Weight: 160 lb. Origin: International Free Agent, 2016

YEAR	TEAM	LVL	AGE	PA	R	2B	3B	HR	RBI	BB	K	SB	CS	Whiff%	AVG/OBP/SLG	DRC+	BABIP	BRR	FRAA	WARP
2019	LAN	A	19	341	47	17	5	12	52	22	38	7	1		.280/.337/.485	130	.282	1.1	C(54): -0.6	2.3
2020	LAR	WIN	20	70	12	5	0	1	11	11	6	1	0		.373/.471/.508		.404			
2021	MSS	WIN	21	100	16	11	0	1	18	13	13	0	0		.329/.410/.494		.370			
2021	LAR	WIN	21	73	11	0	1	1	8	11	11	2	0		.279/.397/.361		.327			
2021	NH	AA	21	145	29	9	1	8	45	14	22	1	2		.373/.441/.651	147	.398	0.6	C(27): -2.9, 3B(1): -0.1	1.1
2022 DC	*TOR*	*MLB*	*22*	*31*	*4*	*1*	*0*	*1*	*4*	*2*	*5*	*0*	*0*	*20.9%*	*.260/.319/.434*	*105*	*.287*	*0.0*	*C 0*	*0.1*

Comparables: Salvador Perez, Wilson Ramos, Rowdy Tellez

YEAR	TEAM	P. COUNT	FRM RUNS	BLK RUNS	THRW RUNS	TOT RUNS
2019	LAN	7474	-3.5	0.5	2.4	-0.5
2021	NH	4215	-2.5	0.1	0.0	-2.4
2021	MSS	1282			0.4	0.4
2022	*TOR*	*1202*	*-0.4*	*0.0*	*0.1*	*-0.3*

What is the anatomy of a breakout? Physical maturity? Experience? Does a light go off in the mind, allowing all the professional instruction to click? In Moreno's case, physical changes seemed to permit swing changes that built upon his previously established skillset, producing an electric—if injury hampered—season in the upper minors.

Moreno continued turning heads in the Arizona Fall League, showing patience and power to all fields. He justified the reported unwillingness for the Blue Jays to include him in trade talks when they looked to add talent at the deadline. The final package is a player who looks like one of the very best prospects in the game, a potential everyday catcher who can hit for both average and power. The road to disappointment is paved with bones of fallen Catchers of the Future, but Moreno's emergence plus the Blue Jays' enviable catching depth gives Toronto a lot of options as they try to run down the American League's big guns.

Josh Palacios OF

Born: 07/30/95 Age: 26 Bats: L Throws: R Height: 6'1" Weight: 198 lb. Origin: Round 4, 2016 Draft (#132 overall)

YEAR	TEAM	LVL	AGE	PA	R	2B	3B	HR	RBI	BB	K	SB	CS	Whiff%	AVG/OBP/SLG	DRC+	BABIP	BRR	FRAA	WARP
2019	NH	AA	23	341	43	18	2	7	38	45	70	15	5		.266/.371/.416	119	.324	-1.2	CF(35): 3.2, RF(26): -0.2, LF(15): -3.2	1.7
2021	BUF	AAA	25	63	7	2	0	0	2	5	16	1	2		.241/.349/.278	92	.342	0.1	RF(9): -0.1, CF(5): 1.1	0.3
2021	TOR	MLB	25	42	7	0	0	0	4	3	11	0	0	31.6%	.200/.293/.200	83	.280	0.6	RF(8): -0.9, LF(4): -0.0, CF(2): -0.4	0.0
2022 DC	*TOR*	*MLB*	*26*	*91*	*10*	*3*	*0*	*1*	*11*	*7*	*22*	*1*	*1*	*28.9%*	*.226/.304/.332*	*72*	*.295*	*0.1*	*CF 0, RF 0*	*0.0*

Comparables: Juan Lagares, Roger Bernadina, Aaron Altherr

The product of Telecommunications High School in Brooklyn made his maiden big-league voyage for the Toronto Telecommunications Baseball Club an eventful one. Picking up four knocks in his second game was the highlight, and later on, when pressed into action as a center fielder for just the second time in his professional career, he notched a game-winning inside-the-park homer. It was his last sighting at the major-league level in 2021 as the team sought more seasoned backups in the outfield.

Kevin Smith SS/3B

Born: 07/04/96 Age: 26 Bats: R Throws: R Height: 6'0" Weight: 190 lb. Origin: Round 4, 2017 Draft (#129 overall)

YEAR	TEAM	LVL	AGE	PA	R	2B	3B	HR	RBI	BB	K	SB	CS	Whiff%	AVG/OBP/SLG	DRC+	BABIP	BRR	FRAA	WARP
2019	SCO	WIN	22	67	3	2	1	0	0	3	38	1	0		.095/.149/.159		.240			
2019	NH	AA	22	468	49	22	2	19	61	29	151	11	6		.209/.263/.402	89	.269	1.7	SS(87): 0.7, 3B(18): -1.4, 2B(5): -0.8	1.0
2021	BUF	AAA	24	410	65	27	4	21	69	46	97	18	3		.285/.370/.561	130	.333	0.6	SS(66): 6.3, 3B(17): 2.1, LF(4): 0.2	3.5
2021	TOR	MLB	24	36	2	0	0	1	1	3	11	0	0	33.8%	.094/.194/.188	87	.100	0.5	3B(14): -0.5, 1B(1): -0.0, LF(1): -0.2	0.0
2022 DC	*TOR*	*MLB*	*25*	*282*	*40*	*13*	*1*	*12*	*40*	*21*	*76*	*6*	*3*	*30.3%*	*.240/.307/.449*	*99*	*.294*	*0.5*	*3B 0, 2B -1*	*0.8*

Comparables: Erik González, Chris Nelson, Pat Valaika

2021 was a transformative year for us all. We learned about ourselves and the world. Smith learned that the approach that powered him to a terrific 2018 season needed changing, so he revamped his swing and put together a superb Triple-A campaign, getting the call-up to Toronto in August. Then he learned that playing baseball in the big leagues is very hard. A big pile of strikeouts, with just three hits, greeted Smith, who often looked overmatched at the plate. Another offseason of learning and growth awaits.

George Springer CF/DH

Born: 09/19/89 Age: 32 Bats: R Throws: R Height: 6'3" Weight: 221 lb. Origin: Round 1, 2011 Draft (#11 overall)

YEAR	TEAM	LVL	AGE	PA	R	2B	3B	HR	RBI	BB	K	SB	CS	Whiff%	AVG/OBP/SLG	DRC+	BABIP	BRR	FRAA	WARP
2019	HOU	MLB	29	556	96	20	3	39	96	67	113	6	2	26.8%	.292/.383/.591	134	.305	1.8	CF(75): 2.2, RF(59): 4.2	5.2
2020	HOU	MLB	30	222	37	6	2	14	32	24	38	1	2	25.3%	.265/.359/.540	128	.259	0.3	CF(42): -2.4, RF(9): -2.1	1.0
2021	TOR	MLB	31	342	59	19	1	22	50	37	79	4	1	26.9%	.264/.352/.555	130	.286	-1.0	CF(40): -1.4, RF(4): -0.0	2.1
2022 DC	*TOR*	*MLB*	*32*	*585*	*105*	*23*	*1*	*27*	*76*	*64*	*122*	*5*	*4*	*26.4%*	*.254/.347/.466*	*118*	*.284*	*-0.3*	*CF 2*	*3.7*

Comparables: Hank Aaron, Carlos Beltrán, Torii Hunter

When investing $150 million, it's important to know what you're getting for your money. Springer came to Toronto and performed exactly as advertised. He hit lots of home runs, was a key presence in the dugout and missed all kinds of time due to injury. It's not a criticism or an insinuation about lack of will, it's just a truth requiring acknowledgement. For a team that missed the playoffs by a single game, it's easy to lament the absence of the Blue Jays' big-money free agency signing.

There should be no false illusions about what Springer offers: top-shelf production and no lack of time on the shelf. His offensive production was at times spectacular; he hit huge home runs and gutted out big at bats while obviously hampered by a variety of leg ailments. It's not hard to see his future in Toronto—he made 38 starts at DH in 2021—and there's no questioning the production, only where it comes from and in what kind of volume.

Breyvic Valera 3B/2B Born: 01/08/92 Age: 30 Bats: S Throws: R Height: 5'11" Weight: 190 lb. Origin: International Free Agent, 2010

YEAR	TEAM	LVL	AGE	PA	R	2B	3B	HR	RBI	BB	K	SB	CS	Whiff%	AVG/OBP/SLG	DRC+	BABIP	BRR	FRAA	WARP
2019	SWB	AAA	27	348	44	18	2	13	49	34	34	8	6		.315/.388/.515	124	.320	-2.6	SS(30): -3.5, 3B(28): -1.4, 2B(22): 2.0	1.7
2019	SAC	AAA	27	92	10	3	0	1	7	16	10	2	1		.257/.396/.338	113	.286	-0.3	2B(16): 1.6, SS(8): 0.1, 3B(1): 0.2	0.7
2019	TOR	MLB	27	15	2	1	0	1	3	0	2	0	0	16.7%	.267/.267/.533	103	.250	0.0	2B(2): 0.0, SS(2): -0.1, 3B(1): -0.1	0.0
2019	NYY	MLB	27	37	5	1	1	0	3	4	5	0	0	8.8%	.219/.324/.313	98	.259	0.1	2B(12): 0.8	0.2
2020	MAR	WIN	28	169	30	6	1	0	17	28	6	12	3		.333/.444/.393		.338			
2021	MAR	WIN	29	63	9	3	0	1	7	15	3	3	2		.283/.460/.413		.279			
2021	BUF	AAA	29	180	29	11	1	3	28	24	19	7	4		.313/.406/.460	126	.333	-0.8	LF(16): -0.5, 3B(9): 0.5, SS(6): -0.2	0.9
2021	TOR	MLB	29	97	10	6	0	1	15	8	12	1	0	6.8%	.253/.313/.356	100	.280	-1.1	3B(21): -1.0, 2B(10): -1.1	0.0
2022 non-DC	*TOR*	*MLB*	*30*	*251*	*24*	*10*	*1*	*4*	*24*	*22*	*26*	*3*	*2*	*11.2%*	*.250/.323/.363*	*88*	*.268*	*0.1*	*2B 1, 3B 0*	*0.4*

Comparables: Miguel Rojas, Ezequiel Carrera, Phil Gosselin

Sometimes versatility is more curse than blessing. His switch-hitting and multi- positional flexibility brought Valera back to the big leagues after he spent 2020 in limbo like so many Quad-A fill-ins. But the things he does well can get him into trouble, like when his strike zone judgment and general air of grinding competence made him Toronto's designated bunter, an inglorious job if ever there was one. Being the 2021 Blue Jays chief bunter is like being in charge of Saskatchewan's mountain rescue squad: an unneeded job conspicuous in its very existence.

PITCHERS

Shaun Anderson RHP Born: 10/29/94 Age: 27 Bats: R Throws: R Height: 6'4" Weight: 228 lb. Origin: Round 3, 2016 Draft (#88 overall)

YEAR	TEAM	LVL	AGE	W	L	SV	G	GS	IP	H	HR	BB/9	K/9	K	GB%	BABIP	WHIP	ERA	DRA-	WARP	MPH	FB%	Whiff%	CSP
2019	SAC	AAA	24	2	1	0	8	8	38^{1}	36	3	3.1	9.6	41	53.3%	.320	1.28	3.76	82	0.6				
2019	SF	MLB	24	3	5	2	28	16	96	111	13	3.6	6.6	70	39.7%	.327	1.55	5.44	117	0.1	92.7	58.4%	20.8%	46.8%
2020	SF	MLB	25	0	0	0	18	0	15^{1}	10	3	7.0	10.6	18	37.8%	.206	1.43	3.52	110	0.1	94.5	39.7%	33.6%	40.8%
2021	ELP	AAA	26	1	0	1	11	0	14^{1}	13	2	3.8	11.3	18	40.5%	.314	1.33	4.40	85	0.2				
2021	STP	AAA	26	1	0	0	5	0	6	2	0	4.5	7.5	5	35.7%	.143	0.83	0.00	110	0.0				
2021	BAL	MLB	26	0	0	0	7	0	10	17	3	4.5	6.3	7	38.1%	.359	2.20	9.00	134	-0.1	93.8	31.5%	26.6%	59.1%
2021	SD	MLB	26	0	0	0	5	0	4^{2}	6	0	3.9	7.7	4	56.2%	.375	1.71	5.79	102	0.0	93.7	29.6%	26.3%	52.7%
2021	MIN	MLB	26	0	0	0	4	0	8^{2}	13	1	5.2	8.3	8	39.4%	.375	2.08	9.35	117	0.0	92.8	44.0%	28.2%	58.2%
2022 non-DC	*SD*	*MLB*	*27*	*2*	*3*	*0*	*57*	*0*	*50*	*50*	*7*	*3.9*	*8.8*	*48*	*41.5%*	*.306*	*1.44*	*4.83*	*112*	*-0.1*	*93.3*	*46.9%*	*25.3%*	*50.0%*

Comparables: Hector Noesí, Alex Colomé, Jeanmar Gómez

After laboring for years under the delusion that the college reliever would be a starter in the majors, the Giants finally shipped Anderson off to see the country on the Great Waiver Wire Express, until he reached his last stop in the Plymouth of the West. In shorter stints, the tall righty can crank his fastball up to the mid-90s to pair with a nasty slider he can spot all over the zone. If those two pitches fail him, he can always reach into his starter's arsenal to pull out his changeup or curve as a change of pace, giving him multi-inning appeal as well. When not being flung by the waiver wire's whims, he spent most of his time in 2021 riding the more modest El Paso-San Diego shuttle, but should be in the mix for a permanent bullpen role next season, and some much-appreciated stability in Toronto after the Jays claimed him in November.

José Berríos RHP Born: 05/27/94 Age: 28 Bats: R Throws: R Height: 6'0" Weight: 205 lb. Origin: Round 1, 2012 Draft (#32 overall)

YEAR	TEAM	LVL	AGE	W	L	SV	G	GS	IP	H	HR	BB/9	K/9	K	GB%	BABIP	WHIP	ERA	DRA-	WARP	MPH	FB%	Whiff%	CSP
2019	MIN	MLB	25	14	8	0	32	32	200^{1}	194	26	2.3	8.8	195	41.9%	.301	1.22	3.68	97	2.3	92.9	55.2%	23.4%	48.8%
2020	MIN	MLB	26	5	4	0	12	12	63	57	8	3.7	9.7	68	40.2%	.295	1.32	4.00	90	1.0	94.4	51.5%	27.4%	47.5%
2021	TOR	MLB	27	5	4	0	12	12	70^{1}	64	8	1.7	10.0	78	42.5%	.303	1.09	3.58	88	1.1	93.9	56.8%	22.9%	52.3%
2021	MIN	MLB	27	7	5	0	20	20	121^{2}	95	14	2.4	9.3	126	43.2%	.263	1.04	3.48	93	1.6	94.1	56.0%	23.9%	52.8%
2022 DC	*TOR*	*MLB*	*28*	*12*	*9*	*0*	*30*	*30*	*181.3*	*165*	*25*	*2.5*	*9.2*	*184*	*42.4%*	*.290*	*1.19*	*3.60*	*91*	*2.3*	*93.8*	*55.3%*	*24.1%*	*51.0%*

Comparables: Roy Halladay, Zack Greinke, Alex Cobb

Traffic evaporation is the idea that *decreasing* road capacity actually ends up *improving* traffic in an area: a road diet (closure in the road) forces an adjustment in traveler behavior. The Blue Jays acquisition of Berríos came at a time when the bullpen was in tatters and fans called out for big name closer upgrades.

But rather than address the challenges in their bullpen directly, Toronto's front office reduced bullpen capacity, in a way. Why pay top dollar for a bullpen upgrade when you can improve the quality of the innings pitched before the bullpen, squeezing your existing complement of relief arms into smaller and smaller inning assignments? While too many city planners and politicians might be afraid to promote traffic evaporation and road diets, the Blue Jays front office impressed with their will to pay a steep price to make an important deal.

The move was unexpected but in retrospect felt like an inevitability. Berríos fits the Blue Jays' bill perfectly: he's athletic and not eligible for free agency until the end of the 2022 season. He is durable, coachable (a mini-slump in August prompted a mechanical adjustment that paid off with a terrific September) and, most of all, really quite good. Berríos offered exactly what the Blue Jays needed in the moment when they needed it most.

Ryan Borucki LHP Born: 03/31/94 Age: 28 Bats: L Throws: L Height: 6'4" Weight: 215 lb. Origin: Round 15, 2012 Draft (#475 overall)

YEAR	TEAM	LVL	AGE	W	L	SV	G	GS	IP	H	HR	BB/9	K/9	K	GB%	BABIP	WHIP	ERA	DRA-	WARP	MPH	FB%	Whiff%	CSP
2019	BUF	AAA	25	1	0	0	2	2	11	11	4	2.5	7.4	9	42.4%	.241	1.27	4.91	110	0.1				
2019	TOR	MLB	25	0	1	0	2	2	6^2	15	2	8.1	8.1	6	39.3%	.500	3.15	10.80	145	-0.1	92.2	52.3%	23.7%	45.2%
2020	TOR	MLB	26	1	1	0	21	0	16^2	12	1	6.5	11.3	21	35.0%	.282	1.44	2.70	96	0.2	94.9	47.8%	32.6%	41.0%
2021	BUF	AAA	27	0	0	0	9	0	9^1	5	0	7.7	11.6	12	52.6%	.263	1.39	2.89	89	0.2				
2021	TOR	MLB	27	3	1	0	24	0	23^2	18	5	4.2	8.0	21	61.5%	.220	1.23	4.94	102	0.2	95.5	58.3%	29.3%	53.9%
2022 DC	*TOR*	*MLB*	*28*	*3*	*3*	*0*	*74*	*0*	*64.7*	*60*	*8*	*4.7*	*9.7*	*70*	*48.8%*	*.304*	*1.45*	*4.47*	*104*	*0.2*	*95.0*	*54.2%*	*30.0%*	*48.8%*

Comparables: Josh Outman, Alex Colomé, Brian Stokes

2021 represented the worst of both worlds for Borucki: the dual indignity of missing time with injury while also riding the shuttle between Toronto and Buffalo. He still got into 24 big-league games but a persistent problem from the past only worsened: ugly splits. The southpaw allowed only one extra-base hit to left-handed batters in 2021, compared to four home runs, three doubles and eight walks that righties compiled in a mere 56 plate appearances. After opponents beat up on his slider all season long, Borucki tried a changeup against righties in September to good effect. The three-batter rule means the development of something to keep righties off his fastball is now mission critical to avoiding Triple-A buses in future.

Anthony Castro RHP Born: 04/13/95 Age: 27 Bats: R Throws: R Height: 6'2" Weight: 182 lb. Origin: International Free Agent, 2011

YEAR	TEAM	LVL	AGE	W	L	SV	G	GS	IP	H	HR	BB/9	K/9	K	GB%	BABIP	WHIP	ERA	DRA-	WARP	MPH	FB%	Whiff%	CSP
2019	ERI	AA	24	5	3	1	27	18	102^1	75	9	5.7	10.2	116	43.4%	.274	1.37	4.40	87	1.5				
2020	DET	MLB	25	0	0	0	1	0	1	1	1	9.0	9.0	1	0.0%	.000	2.00	18.00	105	0.0	92.3	58.8%	37.5%	41.3%
2021	BUF	AAA	26	0	1	0	10	0	10	6	1	0.0	13.5	15	42.9%	.250	0.60	1.80	78	0.2				
2021	TOR	MLB	26	1	2	1	25	0	24^2	23	4	2.9	11.7	32	50.0%	.306	1.26	4.74	82	0.5	95.0	51.4%	28.1%	48.1%
2022 DC	*TOR*	*MLB*	*27*	*1*	*1*	*0*	*29*	*0*	*25.7*	*22*	*3*	*4.1*	*9.7*	*27*	*45.9%*	*.286*	*1.33*	*4.06*	*98*	*0.1*	*94.9*	*51.6%*	*28.3%*	*47.9%*

Comparables: Ryne Stanek, Jacob Barnes, Jeremy Hernandez

A batter digs in against a skinny right-handed reliever. He knows the scouting report: he's going to throw you a slider. The pitcher knows, the catcher knows and the bench knows what's coming: a slider. He winds and deals. It's a slider. For the first month of the 2021 season, this slider heavy (60% usage!) approach worked wonderfully, with Castro facing 27 batters and allowing just three hits and one walk. In May, less so. Word got out, and soon after balls started flying out of the box with increased intensity. As the Blue Jays' front office found bullpen reinforcements, Castro slid down the leverage ladder before finding his way to Triple-A, riding the shuttle as a reinforcement arm when required for the rest of the year.

Adam Cimber RHP Born: 08/15/90 Age: 31 Bats: R Throws: R Height: 6'3" Weight: 195 lb. Origin: Round 9, 2013 Draft (#268 overall)

YEAR	TEAM	LVL	AGE	W	L	SV	G	GS	IP	H	HR	BB/9	K/9	K	GB%	BABIP	WHIP	ERA	DRA-	WARP	MPH	FB%	Whiff%	CSP
2019	CLE	MLB	28	6	3	1	68	0	56^2	56	6	3.0	6.5	41	55.0%	.289	1.32	4.45	109	0.3	85.3	67.9%	20.3%	51.1%
2020	CLE	MLB	29	0	1	0	14	0	11^1	13	1	1.6	4.0	5	52.4%	.293	1.32	3.97	107	0.1	86.1	50.8%	22.2%	53.6%
2021	TOR	MLB	30	2	2	1	39	0	37^1	31	2	1.2	7.2	30	56.5%	.271	0.96	1.69	96	0.4	87.3	70.1%	20.9%	52.0%
2021	MIA	MLB	30	1	2	0	33	0	34^1	30	0	2.9	5.5	21	49.5%	.291	1.19	2.88	110	0.1	86.9	65.6%	19.1%	55.1%
2022 DC	*TOR*	*MLB*	*31*	*3*	*3*	*0*	*74*	*0*	*64.7*	*69*	*7*	*2.5*	*6.8*	*48*	*52.5%*	*.306*	*1.35*	*4.35*	*108*	*0.0*	*86.7*	*66.5%*	*20.3%*	*53.0%*

Comparables: Danny Farquhar, Matt Grace, Rob Scahill

Cimber's funky submarine delivery was a sight for sore eyes when he arrived in early July to help solidify a shell-shocked Blue Jays bullpen. It's hard to imagine a "league-average or slightly better" middle reliever could save a team's season, but Cimber came closer than anyone throwing in the mid-eighties ever should. Missing barrels is the name of Cimber's game; he ranks in the 96th percentile for that measure, according to Statcast. He avoided walks and kept the ball in the ballpark while often coming out of the bullpen whenever he was needed, making 15 appearances in the sixth inning and 19 appearances in the eighth. Every team in baseball should be blessed with a rubber-armed skeleton key like this.

A.J. Cole RHP Born: 01/05/92 Age: 30 Bats: R Throws: R Height: 6'5" Weight: 240 lb. Origin: Round 4, 2010 Draft (#116 overall)

YEAR	TEAM	LVL	AGE	W	L	SV	G	GS	IP	H	HR	BB/9	K/9	K	GB%	BABIP	WHIP	ERA	DRA-	WARP	MPH	FB%	Whiff%	CSP
2019	COL	AAA	27	0	1	2	13	0	17	10	2	2.6	11.1	21	36.1%	.235	0.88	3.18	87	0.3				
2019	CLE	MLB	27	3	1	1	25	0	26	31	4	2.8	10.4	30	30.0%	.360	1.50	3.81	106	0.2	94.6	45.0%	30.3%	48.5%
2020	TOR	MLB	28	3	0	1	24	0	23^1	19	3	3.5	7.7	20	33.3%	.258	1.20	3.09	118	0.0	93.1	41.8%	27.3%	44.5%
2021	BUF	AAA	29	1	0	0	10	0	10	8	0	0.0	10.8	12	42.3%	.308	0.80	0.00	81	0.2				
2021	TOR	MLB	29	0	0	1	6	0	8	6	1	1.1	7.9	7	27.3%	.238	0.88	1.13	113	0.0	93.0	61.4%	28.1%	58.9%
2022 non-DC	*TOR*	*MLB*	*30*	*2*	*2*	*0*	*57*	*0*	*50*	*48*	*8*	*2.9*	*8.8*	*48*	*34.5%*	*.297*	*1.30*	*4.24*	*104*	*0.1*	*93.6*	*46.9%*	*28.3%*	*48.8%*

Comparables: Steve Johnson, Jeanmar Gómez, Brandon Workman

Life on baseball's margins can be cruel. Sometimes you join a new team in a very weird year and pitch pretty well in middle relief. Your numbers don't jump off the page but, by and large, you do the job. But 40-man rosters are tricky business, so you find yourself non-tendered in the off-season, set adrift in the free agent seas. But lo, there's a light on the shore, a lifeline in the form of a minor-league contract! You sign it and come to spring training with high hopes. You don't make the team but you're called up and in the big leagues in May. And then you pitch pretty well again! But, alas, the injury bug bites. You miss some time and then even more time as your injury worsens. You start to rehab but again find no room at the 40-man inn, so you're pushed through waivers again. You opt to accept your assignment and find yourself pitching in Triple-A and doing a damn fine job! But the season draws to a close and there's no spot on the roster for you. So, evermore, you grind.

Rafael Dolis RHP Born: 01/10/88 Age: 34 Bats: R Throws: R Height: 6'4" Weight: 235 lb. Origin: International Free Agent, 2004

YEAR	TEAM	LVL	AGE	W	L	SV	G	GS	IP	H	HR	BB/9	K/9	K	GB%	BABIP	WHIP	ERA	DRA-	WARP	MPH	FB%	Whiff%	CSP
2020	TOR	MLB	32	2	2	5	24	0	24	16	1	5.2	11.6	31	46.3%	.294	1.25	1.50	81	0.5	94.8	61.1%	30.4%	42.0%
2021	BUF	AAA	33	1	2	0	11	0	11^{1}	11	0	5.6	11.1	14	54.8%	.367	1.59	1.59	78	0.3				
2021	TOR	MLB	33	2	3	3	39	0	32	29	2	7.6	11.0	39	42.5%	.318	1.75	5.62	115	0.0	94.8	64.8%	28.5%	53.4%
2022 DC	*FA*	*MLB*	*34*	*1*	*1*	*0*	*28*	*0*	*24.7*	*20*	*3*	*5.6*	*10.8*	*29*	*44.2%*	*.284*	*1.45*	*4.48*	*103*	*0.1*	*94.8*	*63.7%*	*29.1%*	*49.8%*

Comparables: Carl Willis, Rudy Seanez, Blaine Boyer

As a baseball spectator, the second most painful thing in the world is watching Dolis pitch well. The deliberate right-hander spent much of 2020 looking like the worst good pitcher in baseball, posting strong numbers in his first season back from Japan by keeping the ball on the ground and in the ballpark, his gaudy ERA overshadowing his tortuous pace and the feeling that the inning was about to slip away thanks to an iffy walk rate.

In 2021, we learned about the most painful thing for baseball spectators: watching Dolis struggle. The walks got worse, but so did his strikeout rate and the sheer volume of hits allowed. He was somewhat surprisingly designated for assignment in August, passing through waivers and accepting a spot at Triple-A Buffalo. The walks persisted, but the home run avoidance might just catch the eye of an enterprising front office that doesn't mind antagonizing their fans in pursuit of middle relief help.

Kevin Gausman RHP Born: 01/06/91 Age: 31 Bats: L Throws: R Height: 6'2" Weight: 190 lb. Origin: Round 1, 2012 Draft (#4 overall)

YEAR	TEAM	LVL	AGE	W	L	SV	G	GS	IP	H	HR	BB/9	K/9	K	GB%	BABIP	WHIP	ERA	DRA-	WARP	MPH	FB%	Whiff%	CSP
2019	GWN	AAA	28	0	1	0	1	1	7	6	1	1.3	12.9	10	62.5%	.357	1.00	2.57	79	0.2				
2019	CIN	MLB	28	0	2	0	15	1	22^{1}	21	3	2.0	11.7	29	41.1%	.346	1.16	4.03	80	0.5	94.9	56.4%	36.9%	44.9%
2019	ATL	MLB	28	3	7	0	16	16	80	92	12	3.0	9.6	85	36.1%	.354	1.49	6.19	95	1.0	94.0	56.6%	28.3%	47.2%
2020	SF	MLB	29	3	3	0	12	10	59^{2}	50	8	2.4	11.9	79	40.7%	.298	1.11	3.62	68	1.7	95.2	51.1%	33.1%	48.2%
2021	SF	MLB	30	14	6	0	33	33	192	150	20	2.3	10.6	227	41.1%	.275	1.04	2.81	73	4.5	94.8	52.8%	31.4%	57.5%
2022 DC	*TOR*	*MLB*	*31*	*11*	*8*	*0*	*29*	*29*	*169*	*149*	*25*	*2.4*	*10.2*	*192*	*40.8%*	*.293*	*1.15*	*3.28*	*84*	*2.7*	*94.8*	*53.0%*	*31.5%*	*54.6%*

Comparables: Zack Greinke, Gavin Floyd, Jason Schmidt

You might think that Gausman's success in San Francisco has been due to the spacious home park being much more forgiving than the stadia where he had previously plied his trade. This hypothesis is belied by the fact that, since moving west, Gausman's Oracle Park ERA has been more than a run higher than on the road. The fastball is consistently placed in the upper part of the zone, sitting comfortably in the mid-90s with rising action. The key, of course, is the splitter. When it's on, the sudden dive on Gausman's split gives that fluttery feeling one typically associates with roller coasters or first love. When it's not, it can hang in the zone, center-cut, or it can dive too soon, an easy take. Gausman's success with the Giants has to do less with developing an effective third offering than leaning into the dynamic duo. When the mix succeeds, it's a Cy-level formula, but when one of the pitches goes missing for a spell, the performance can become league-average in a hurry (as it was for stretches of 2021's second half). Gausman will have the recent top-line numbers of an elite starter heading into 2022 with Toronto but, more than most aspirational aces, works within a pixel-thin margin of error.

Anthony Kay LHP Born: 03/21/95 Age: 27 Bats: L Throws: L Height: 6'0" Weight: 225 lb. Origin: Round 1, 2016 Draft (#31 overall)

YEAR	TEAM	LVL	AGE	W	L	SV	G	GS	IP	H	HR	BB/9	K/9	K	GB%	BABIP	WHIP	ERA	DRA-	WARP	MPH	FB%	Whiff%	CSP
2019	BNG	AA	24	7	3	0	12	12	66^{1}	38	2	3.1	9.5	70	34.4%	.226	0.92	1.49	89	0.9				
2019	BUF	AAA	24	2	2	0	7	7	36	33	3	5.5	9.8	39	39.6%	.323	1.53	2.50	110	0.3				
2019	SYR	AAA	24	1	3	0	7	7	31^{1}	40	7	3.2	7.5	26	28.0%	.367	1.63	6.61	126	0.0				
2019	TOR	MLB	24	1	0	0	3	2	14	15	0	3.2	8.4	13	54.5%	.341	1.43	5.79	115	0.0	93.6	61.6%	24.2%	42.2%
2020	TOR	MLB	25	2	0	0	13	0	21	22	3	6.0	9.4	22	37.1%	.322	1.71	5.14	114	0.1	93.8	56.5%	26.1%	46.8%
2021	BUF	AAA	26	0	4	0	8	8	26^{1}	31	5	4.4	9.9	29	33.8%	.347	1.67	8.89	109	0.2				
2021	TOR	MLB	26	1	2	0	11	5	33^{2}	38	7	4.8	10.4	39	47.9%	.348	1.66	5.61	100	0.3	94.4	58.4%	25.9%	49.0%
2022 DC	*TOR*	*MLB*	*27*	*4*	*4*	*0*	*35*	*6*	*54.3*	*51*	*7*	*4.5*	*9.4*	*56*	*40.8%*	*.299*	*1.44*	*4.69*	*109*	*0.0*	*94.1*	*58.2%*	*25.8%*	*47.8%*

Comparables: Anthony Bass, Amir Garrett, Brian Duensing

Man cannot live on a high spin fastball alone—even if that man is left-handed and throws 95. Kay spent most of 2021 bouncing around in every possible sense; he was called up a spot starter at the big leagues and sent down to Triple-A before popping back up as a reliever. He threw harder than ever but a strikeout pitch eluded him. He sampled a cutter in the early stages of 2021 before emerging back in the big leagues with a slider, forever in search of something to spin and miss bats. Then he hit the COVID-19 injured list! A true whirlwind year, though one that failed to blow an out-pitch into his path.

Adam Kloffenstein RHP Born: 08/25/00 Age: 21 Bats: R Throws: R Height: 6'5" Weight: 243 lb. Origin: Round 3, 2018 Draft (#88 overall)

YEAR	TEAM	LVL	AGE	W	L	SV	G	GS	IP	H	HR	BB/9	K/9	K	GB%	BABIP	WHIP	ERA	DRA-	WARP	MPH	FB%	Whiff%	CSP
2019	VAN	SS	18	4	4	0	13	13	64^{1}	47	4	3.2	9.0	64	59.5%	.262	1.09	2.24						
2021	VAN	A+	20	7	7	0	23	23	101^{1}	96	10	5.4	9.5	107	52.9%	.306	1.55	6.22	87	1.5				
2022 non-DC	*TOR*	*MLB*	*21*	*2*	*3*	*0*	*57*	*0*	*50*	*53*	*6*	*6.2*	*7.7*	*42*	*47.1%*	*.310*	*1.75*	*6.06*	*132*	*-0.7*				

Comparables: Kyle Drabek, Brandon League, Antonio Senzatela

Two years in the same place is often a red flag for baseball prospects, but Kloffenstein stayed in Vancouver while its affiliation changed from short-season ball to High-A. Two seasons in one of the world's most beautiful cities might sound like a good time but too much traffic (on the bases, not the Lions Gate Bridge) plagued the big right-hander. Third time's a charm? Another go-round at Nat Bailey Stadium might help the 2018 draftee refine his command after 61 walks in 101 ⅓ innings (not to mention seven hit batters and a whopping 17 wild pitches!). As a bonus, three years is about the amount of time it normally takes transplants to either embrace the rain or lose their marbles completely.

Alek Manoah RHP Born: 01/09/98 Age: 24 Bats: R Throws: R Height: 6'6" Weight: 260 lb. Origin: Round 1, 2019 Draft (#11 overall)

YEAR	TEAM	LVL	AGE	W	L	SV	G	GS	IP	H	HR	BB/9	K/9	K	GB%	BABIP	WHIP	ERA	DRA-	WARP	MPH	FB%	Whiff%	CSP
2019	VAN	SS	21	0	1	0	6	6	17	13	1	2.6	14.3	27	35.3%	.364	1.06	2.65						
2021	BUF	AAA	23	3	0	0	3	3	18	7	1	1.5	13.5	27	40.6%	.194	0.56	0.50	90	0.3				
2021	TOR	MLB	23	9	2	0	20	20	111^2	77	12	3.2	10.2	127	39.5%	.246	1.05	3.22	95	1.3	93.3	62.9%	29.9%	52.2%
2022 DC	*TOR*	*MLB*	*24*	*9*	*7*	*0*	*24*	*24*	*133.3*	*110*	*19*	*3.3*	*11.0*	*163*	*39.8%*	*.287*	*1.19*	*3.75*	*91*	*1.7*	*93.3*	*62.9%*	*29.9%*	*52.2%*

Comparables: Jason Isringhausen, Ramon Martinez, Johnny Cueto

In the Blue Jays end-of-year team photo, taken on a sunny Toronto Saturday in September, one figure leaps from the image. His smile is the only thing wider than his chest, his enormous figure taking up untold amounts of real estate.

Big as he might be, Manoah's on-field contributions loom even larger over the Blue Jays' 2021 season. With a grand total of nine minor-league appearances to his name, the sizable right-hander burst onto the field with a very auspicious debut at Yankee Stadium and never looked back. Manoah pitched with guile belying his 23 years. He gutted it out when his stuff wasn't there, dropping pitches from his four-offering arsenal and doing what was needed to get outs. His fastball velocity settled into a groove at 93/94 and his slider changed shape as the season progressed, taking on the depth required to retire big-leaguers. He missed bats and barrels alike while looking every bit the durable, big-bodied horse clubs covet.

All of this to say nothing of his outsized personality, which let him mix it up with the Blue Jays' good times gang with aplomb. The perfect player, in other words.

Tim Mayza LHP Born: 01/15/92 Age: 30 Bats: L Throws: L Height: 6'3" Weight: 220 lb. Origin: Round 12, 2013 Draft (#355 overall)

YEAR	TEAM	LVL	AGE	W	L	SV	G	GS	IP	H	HR	BB/9	K/9	K	GB%	BABIP	WHIP	ERA	DRA-	WARP	MPH	FB%	Whiff%	CSP
2019	TOR	MLB	27	1	3	0	68	0	51^1	45	8	4.7	9.6	55	51.7%	.274	1.40	4.91	101	0.5	94.4	64.4%	32.6%	37.5%
2021	TOR	MLB	29	5	2	1	61	0	53	40	5	2.0	9.7	57	57.2%	.265	0.98	3.40	84	0.9	94.1	71.2%	25.4%	52.5%
2022 DC	*TOR*	*MLB*	*30*	*3*	*3*	*4*	*74*	*0*	*64.7*	*57*	*7*	*3.2*	*9.5*	*68*	*51.1%*	*.295*	*1.25*	*3.42*	*86*	*0.7*	*94.1*	*69.4%*	*27.3%*	*48.5%*

Comparables: Ryan Cook, Matt Reynolds, Steve Cishek

In a game lousy with relievers lighting up radar guns and racking up strikeouts like never before, a guy who strikes out a mere 27% of batters while throwing a pedestrian 95-mph fastball feels like a bit of a throwback—and a delightful one at that.

Mayza grew from a non-roster invitee to one of the most trusted members of Charlie Montoyo's bullpen on the back of a new pitch, opting to become a full-on sinker/slider guy. An almost 70% usage rate on his two-seamer helped him miss both bats (a few) and barrels (a lot) and worked to eliminate his platoon splits and horrific injury demons in one fell swoop.

The arbitration-eligible question remains: is it real? A pitcher with good results in his past adopts a new approach that builds on what he already does well while keeping batters guessing? That's a combination worth investing in.

Julian Merryweather RHP Born: 10/14/91 Age: 30 Bats: R Throws: R Height: 6'4" Weight: 215 lb. Origin: Round 5, 2014 Draft (#158 overall)

YEAR	TEAM	LVL	AGE	W	L	SV	G	GS	IP	H	HR	BB/9	K/9	K	GB%	BABIP	WHIP	ERA	DRA-	WARP	MPH	FB%	Whiff%	CSP
2020	TOR	MLB	28	0	0	0	8	3	13	11	0	4.2	10.4	15	44.1%	.324	1.31	4.15	89	0.2	96.8	57.9%	25.9%	48.9%
2021	TOR	MLB	29	0	1	2	13	1	13	13	4	2.8	8.3	12	39.5%	.265	1.31	4.85	110	0.1	97.4	54.4%	21.9%	62.8%
2022 DC	*TOR*	*MLB*	*30*	*2*	*3*	*2*	*59*	*0*	*51.7*	*51*	*8*	*3.7*	*9.6*	*55*	*42.8%*	*.309*	*1.40*	*4.71*	*111*	*-0.1*	*97.2*	*55.9%*	*23.6%*	*57.0%*

Comparables: Luke Farrell, Daniel Ponce de Leon, Jeff Brigham

For one week in April, Merryweather looked like the best reliever in the world. For the rest of the year, he looked like himself, which is to say he was on the Injured List and unable to perform. In the season's opening series, the mysterious reliever dominated the heart of the Yankees order with 99-mph fastballs and 80-mph Bugs Bunny changeups, each pitch dotting the strike zone more perfectly than the one before. And then the injuries returned, keeping him on the shelf until late in the season. The results then weren't quite as promising as those tantalizing, fleeting moments at Yankee Stadium in April.

★ ★ ★ *2022 Top 101 Prospect* **#73** ★ ★ ★

Nate Pearson RHP Born: 08/20/96 Age: 25 Bats: R Throws: R Height: 6'6" Weight: 250 lb. Origin: Round 1, 2017 Draft (#28 overall)

YEAR	TEAM	LVL	AGE	W	L	SV	G	GS	IP	H	HR	BB/9	K/9	K	GB%	BABIP	WHIP	ERA	DRA-	WARP	MPH	FB%	Whiff%	CSP
2019	DUN	A+	22	3	0	0	6	6	21	10	2	1.3	15.0	35	35.1%	.229	0.62	0.86	68	0.6				
2019	NH	AA	22	1	4	0	16	16	62^2	41	4	3.0	9.9	69	38.8%	.250	0.99	2.59	86	0.9				
2019	BUF	AAA	22	1	0	0	3	3	18	12	2	1.5	7.5	15	44.0%	.208	0.83	3.00	90	0.3				
2020	TOR	MLB	23	1	0	0	5	4	18	14	5	6.5	8.0	16	38.5%	.191	1.50	6.00	124	0.0	96.3	50.6%	26.3%	44.7%
2021	BUF	AAA	24	1	3	0	12	6	30^2	21	4	3.8	12.9	44	36.8%	.266	1.11	4.40	91	0.6				
2021	TOR	MLB	24	1	1	0	12	1	15	14	2	7.2	12.0	20	41.0%	.324	1.73	4.20	102	0.1	97.9	62.8%	33.9%	49.6%
2022 DC	*TOR*	*MLB*	*25*	*7*	*6*	*0*	*33*	*19*	*102.3*	*87*	*16*	*4.6*	*11.2*	*127*	*38.8%*	*.294*	*1.37*	*4.32*	*102*	*0.6*	*97.3*	*57.7%*	*30.7%*	*47.5%*

Comparables: Tyler Clippard, Jon Rauch, Lucas Sims

What makes a season, or a prospect, a "success?" Sometimes the line between success, failure and disappointment is razor-thin. Sometimes the scale slips like a landslide and 12 league-average outings comes across as a wild, runaway success. Such is the nature of Pearson's star-crossed but tantalizing talent. When the easy 100 fills the zone and hitters walk away muttering, the amount of patience and kindness extended his way grows. When the strikes come easy, the dream dies hard. Even though he battled injury *again* and even though his success was *tenuous at best*, there is still so much to wish on after Pearson's 2021 turn in the Blue Jays bullpen. He threw effectively every other day for the last month of the year, adding in a few multi-inning stints that went progressively better as the season wore on. The plan still calls for Pearson to move forward as a starter. Blue Jays fans, and baseball fans who can't get enough of big hard-throwing dudes with electric stuff, can only hope that the confidence and command he showed down the stretch in 2021 carry forward into 2022 and beyond.

David Phelps RHP

Born: 10/09/86 Age: 35 Bats: R Throws: R Height: 6'2" Weight: 198 lb. Origin: Round 14, 2008 Draft (#440 overall)

YEAR	TEAM	LVL	AGE	W	L	SV	G	GS	IP	H	HR	BB/9	K/9	K	GB%	BABIP	WHIP	ERA	DRA-	WARP	MPH	FB%	Whiff%	CSP
2019	CHC	MLB	32	2	1	1	24	0	17	17	2	5.3	9.5	18	45.8%	.326	1.59	3.18	106	0.1	93.2	45.5%	23.7%	46.4%
2019	TOR	MLB	32	0	0	0	17	1	17^1	14	3	3.6	9.3	18	31.1%	.262	1.21	3.63	104	0.1	92.1	39.7%	15.7%	43.5%
2020	MIL	MLB	33	2	3	0	12	0	13	7	2	1.4	13.8	20	52.0%	.217	0.69	2.77	72	0.3	94.4	41.6%	30.0%	41.7%
2020	PHI	MLB	33	0	1	0	10	0	7^2	12	5	3.5	12.9	11	43.5%	.389	1.96	12.91	86	0.1	94.1	52.9%	22.4%	49.2%
2021	TOR	MLB	34	0	0	0	11	1	10^1	8	0	3.5	13.1	15	40.9%	.364	1.16	0.87	84	0.2	93.7	40.2%	31.6%	47.2%
2022 non-DC	*TOR*	*MLB*	*35*	*2*	*2*	*0*	*57*	*0*	*50*	*40*	*7*	*3.3*	*10.0*	*55*	*41.6%*	*.272*	*1.18*	*3.32*	*83*	*0.6*	*93.6*	*43.4%*	*26.0%*	*45.7%*

Comparables: Casey Janssen, Darren O'Day, Cory Gearrin

The first 11 times Phelps took the mound for the 2021 Blue Jays, he pitched about as well as any reliever could. He faced 42 batters and struck out 15 of them. He allowed a single earned run and zero home runs. Phelps' return-to-form came via his reshaped cutter, his former bread-and-butter offering again bamboozling right-handed batters on the outside corner, keeping the ball off barrels completely. It was a fruitful reunion, for a moment.

The 12th time he took the mound, he didn't throw a single pitch, walked off the field with the trainer and was finished for the year, his strained lat requiring season-ending surgery. The Blue Jays bullpen, not coincidentally, immediately went into the tank, costing the team wins throughout May and June until reinforcements arrived.

Trevor Richards RHP

Born: 05/15/93 Age: 29 Bats: R Throws: R Height: 6'2" Weight: 195 lb. Origin: Undrafted Free Agent, 2016

YEAR	TEAM	LVL	AGE	W	L	SV	G	GS	IP	H	HR	BB/9	K/9	K	GB%	BABIP	WHIP	ERA	DRA-	WARP	MPH	FB%	Whiff%	CSP
2019	DUR	AAA	26	0	0	0	3	3	5^1	4	0	6.8	13.5	8	33.3%	.333	1.50	1.69	90	0.1				
2019	TB	MLB	26	3	0	0	7	3	23^1	23	3	1.9	9.3	24	32.4%	.313	1.20	1.93	102	0.2	90.6	50.0%	24.2%	48.5%
2019	MIA	MLB	26	3	12	0	23	20	112	104	16	4.1	8.3	103	35.8%	.289	1.38	4.50	104	0.9	91.1	42.4%	27.0%	46.4%
2020	TB	MLB	27	0	0	0	9	4	32	44	6	3.1	7.6	27	33.0%	.362	1.72	5.91	130	-0.2	90.7	50.7%	25.7%	45.7%
2021	DUR	AAA	28	1	0	0	7	0	7^1	3	0	1.2	14.7	12	53.8%	.231	0.55	0.00	82	0.2				
2021	TB	MLB	28	0	0	1	6	0	12	9	2	2.3	12.0	16	28.6%	.269	1.00	4.50	92	0.2	92.3	50.3%	31.5%	53.0%
2021	MIL	MLB	28	3	0	0	15	0	19^2	15	3	4.1	11.4	25	18.8%	.273	1.22	3.20	95	0.2	92.7	58.5%	31.1%	51.1%
2021	TOR	MLB	28	4	2	0	32	0	32^2	16	7	2.8	10.2	37	32.0%	.132	0.80	3.31	103	0.2	93.0	58.1%	35.2%	45.1%
2022 DC	*TOR*	*MLB*	*29*	*3*	*3*	*0*	*74*	*0*	*64.7*	*56*	*10*	*3.2*	*10.2*	*73*	*33.9%*	*.283*	*1.23*	*3.82*	*94*	*0.5*	*91.8*	*51.2%*	*29.6%*	*47.4%*

Comparables: Chris Stratton, Manny Parra, Tim Worrell

The list of relievers to strike out more than 30% of the hitters they faced while throwing a fastball with below-average velocity is short. It's a combo as rare as a 28-year old professional athlete with a head full of gloriously silver hair.

Richards can count himself among both cohorts, silver-foxing his way to a strong season through a high-risk approach of 93 mph fastballs and 85 mph changeups seemingly pumped right down the middle of the plate. Leaving it up to the batter to figure out which is which means a) plenty of strikeouts and b) loud contact and home runs, fueling the disparity between his deserved numbers and ERA.

As the season progressed, Richards began showing right-handed batters more curveballs in two-strike situations, picking up some extra whiffs from hitters hunting for his patented change. As he looks to build on his strong but tenuous 2021, that's an important development.

Jordan Romano RHP

Born: 04/21/93 Age: 29 Bats: R Throws: R Height: 6'5" Weight: 225 lb. Origin: Round 10, 2014 Draft (#294 overall)

YEAR	TEAM	LVL	AGE	W	L	SV	G	GS	IP	H	HR	BB/9	K/9	K	GB%	BABIP	WHIP	ERA	DRA-	WARP	MPH	FB%	Whiff%	CSP
2019	BUF	AAA	26	2	2	5	24	3	37^2	37	8	3.3	12.7	53	37.9%	.333	1.35	5.73	80	0.9				
2019	TOR	MLB	26	0	2	0	17	0	15^1	17	4	5.3	12.3	21	48.8%	.351	1.70	7.63	85	0.3	94.9	63.7%	29.5%	46.3%
2020	TOR	MLB	27	2	1	2	15	0	14^2	8	2	3.1	12.9	21	58.1%	.207	0.89	1.23	70	0.4	96.7	40.3%	43.8%	44.6%
2021	TOR	MLB	28	7	1	23	62	0	63	41	7	3.6	12.1	85	46.5%	.254	1.05	2.14	76	1.4	97.5	63.2%	31.8%	52.8%
2022 DC	*TOR*	*MLB*	*29*	*3*	*3*	*36*	*74*	*0*	*64.7*	*49*	*8*	*3.6*	*11.3*	*81*	*43.8%*	*.279*	*1.16*	*3.07*	*77*	*1.0*	*97.2*	*60.5%*	*33.1%*	*51.2%*

Comparables: Héctor Neris, Nate Jones, Steve Cishek

The Blue Jays don't often get hometown kids on their roster. Romano's is a story not only of the local kid making good, but also of perseverance. From toiling in the Rule 5 mines to working out of the back of a big league bullpen, Romano grew and improved. He put together a terrific season in 2021, ranking second among all relievers in Win Probability Added. Adding three miles per hour since 2019 to his already high-spin fastball made it a formidable weapon, but throwing that pitch for more strikes than ever turned him from an intriguing reliever to a great one.

Ryu Hyun-jin LHP

Born: 03/25/87 Age: 35 Bats: R Throws: L Height: 6'3" Weight: 255 lb. Origin: International Free Agent, 2013

YEAR	TEAM	LVL	AGE	W	L	SV	G	GS	IP	H	HR	BB/9	K/9	K	GB%	BABIP	WHIP	ERA	DRA-	WARP	MPH	FB%	Whiff%	CSP
2019	LAD	MLB	32	14	5	0	29	29	182^{2}	160	17	1.2	8.0	163	49.6%	.282	1.01	2.32	83	3.5	90.8	40.6%	24.9%	47.7%
2020	TOR	MLB	33	5	2	0	12	12	67	60	6	2.3	9.7	72	50.8%	.303	1.15	2.69	71	1.8	89.9	34.7%	26.3%	46.7%
2021	TOR	MLB	34	14	10	0	31	31	169	170	24	2.0	7.6	143	46.2%	.296	1.22	4.37	107	0.9	89.9	36.1%	22.7%	53.4%
2022 DC	*TOR*	*MLB*	*35*	*11*	*8*	*0*	*29*	*29*	*163*	*158*	*20*	*2.0*	*7.3*	*131*	*46.9%*	*.288*	*1.19*	*3.39*	*89*	*2.3*	*90.1*	*36.8%*	*23.8%*	*51.1%*

Comparables: Andy Pettitte, Tommy John, David Price

The dirtiest word in sports punditry is "consistency." Players are implored to be "consistent," which most often means, "be the best version of yourself more or less all the time." That's hard to do, especially if you're a finesse pitcher in your mid-thirties. When you operate with razor-thin margins, sometimes you fall on the wrong side of the blade.

All is not lost for Ryu, but 2021 was arguably the worst season of his career. He missed fewer bats and recorded fewer strikeouts, all while allowing more baserunners and getting hit harder than ever in the process. Many outings seemed to feature the lefty searching for his command and/or a suitable out pitch as he tried to limit damage.

But there are positives. His late season struggles overshadowed a strong start to the season, which saw him carry a 2.62 ERA into his first start in June. A number of good (and almost great!) outings dot his second half game log, including an unexpectedly strong late-season start against the Yankees in New York. By Game Score, he had seven starts in 2021 as good as or better than his best outing of 2020. He threw harder than he did in the shortened season and he reduced his walk rate from his standout 2020. Avoiding the blowup starts that plagued him, and riding the explosive Blue Jays offense to some zero leverage innings, could help as he eases his way into his decline phase.

Tayler Saucedo LHP

Born: 06/18/93 Age: 29 Bats: L Throws: L Height: 6'5" Weight: 185 lb. Origin: Round 21, 2015 Draft (#632 overall)

YEAR	TEAM	LVL	AGE	W	L	SV	G	GS	IP	H	HR	BB/9	K/9	K	GB%	BABIP	WHIP	ERA	DRA-	WARP	MPH	FB%	Whiff%	CSP
2019	NH	AA	26	2	1	0	12	1	26^{2}	17	1	5.4	7.8	23	58.9%	.225	1.24	1.01	98	0.2				
2019	BUF	AAA	26	6	1	0	24	7	55^{2}	70	5	3.2	7.4	46	56.6%	.367	1.62	4.85	110	0.4				
2021	BUF	AAA	28	2	1	0	12	0	18^{1}	15	0	1.0	12.3	25	47.5%	.375	0.93	1.96	80	0.4				
2021	TOR	MLB	28	0	0	0	29	0	25^{2}	22	1	3.5	6.7	19	59.0%	.273	1.25	4.56	113	0.1	93.7	56.5%	32.0%	44.9%
2022 DC	*TOR*	*MLB*	*29*	*1*	*1*	*0*	*29*	*0*	*25.7*	*25*	*3*	*3.1*	*8.9*	*25*	*51.4%*	*.308*	*1.33*	*4.07*	*100*	*0.1*	*93.7*	*56.5%*	*32.0%*	*44.9%*

Comparables: Richard Bleier, Luke Putkonen, Steven Jackson

When considering relief pitchers, it can be instructive to paraphrase Alexander Pope: to be serviceable is human, to have minor league options divine. Saucedo rode the shuttle between Buffalo and Toronto (or between Buffalo and wherever the BIsons were playing at the time, more accurately) with aplomb, appearing 29 times with the big club in what ended up more than 25 completely decent innings.

To demean him as a sinker/slider guy is to sell the man short, as he happily went with the sinker/kitchen sink approach when a right-handed batter stood opposed to him. The mostly low-leverage appearances produced a very encouraging chase rate in 2021, but absent the whiff rate and strikeouts to go with those chase swings. To his credit, the big whippy lefty generated a ton of ground balls and assiduously avoided the long ball. An interesting profile and player that didn't look out of place during this rookie season (Tayler's version).

Kirby Snead LHP

Born: 10/07/94 Age: 27 Bats: L Throws: L Height: 6'1" Weight: 218 lb. Origin: Round 10, 2016 Draft (#312 overall)

YEAR	TEAM	LVL	AGE	W	L	SV	G	GS	IP	H	HR	BB/9	K/9	K	GB%	BABIP	WHIP	ERA	DRA-	WARP	MPH	FB%	Whiff%	CSP
2019	NH	AA	24	2	0	5	9	0	10^{2}	4	1	0.0	11.8	14	62.5%	.136	0.37	0.84	82	0.2				
2019	BUF	AAA	24	5	2	2	41	0	52	54	6	3.3	9.3	54	52.0%	.331	1.40	3.98	87	1.0				
2021	BUF	AAA	26	2	0	4	36	1	40	21	1	3.6	12.8	57	59.0%	.244	0.93	1.58	80	0.9				
2021	TOR	MLB	26	0	1	0	7	0	7^{2}	7	0	2.3	8.2	7	35.0%	.350	1.17	2.35	110	0.0	93.3	42.3%	22.0%	51.8%
2022 DC	*TOR*	*MLB*	*27*	*1*	*1*	*0*	*29*	*0*	*25.7*	*22*	*2*	*3.9*	*9.7*	*27*	*50.1%*	*.289*	*1.29*	*3.68*	*91*	*0.2*	*93.3*	*42.3%*	*22.0%*	*51.8%*

Comparables: Drew Smith, Dustin Antolin, David Carpenter

Every team in baseball is expected to have at least one (1) hirsute reliever. If your baseball operations department cannot acquire a bearded long hair dude on their own, one will be supplied by the league at the club's expense. Left-handedness and a fastball/slider/changeup repertoire (heavy on the slider) are among the available options. Rookie status not mandatory but encouraged. Allowing loud contact but somehow escaping trouble is a valuable attribute that is not to interfere with the hair farming or beard growing.

Joakim Soria RHP

Born: 05/18/84 Age: 38 Bats: R Throws: R Height: 6'3" Weight: 205 lb. Origin: International Free Agent, 2001

YEAR	TEAM	LVL	AGE	W	L	SV	G	GS	IP	H	HR	BB/9	K/9	K	GB%	BABIP	WHIP	ERA	DRA-	WARP	MPH	FB%	Whiff%	CSP
2019	OAK	MLB	35	2	4	1	71	1	69	51	9	2.6	10.3	79	37.5%	.253	1.03	4.30	88	1.1	92.6	75.7%	28.9%	51.2%
2020	OAK	MLB	36	2	2	2	22	0	22^{1}	18	1	4.0	9.7	24	29.0%	.279	1.25	2.82	105	0.2	92.6	65.5%	23.5%	47.0%
2021	TOR	MLB	37	0	0	0	10	0	8	8	2	4.5	10.1	9	28.6%	.316	1.50	7.87	109	0.0	92.5	59.4%	29.7%	56.1%
2021	ARI	MLB	37	1	4	6	31	0	29^{1}	31	4	2.5	9.5	31	32.9%	.333	1.33	4.30	97	0.3	93.0	60.0%	25.3%	57.5%
2022 non-DC	*TOR*	*MLB*	*38*	*2*	*2*	*0*	*57*	*0*	*50*	*46*	*8*	*3.1*	*9.1*	*50*	*35.4%*	*.290*	*1.28*	*4.12*	*99*	*0.2*	*92.7*	*65.8%*	*26.5%*	*53.3%*

Comparables: Joe Smith, Mike Timlin, Ryan Madson

Low risk, zero reward. The Blue Jays made the low-cost acquisition of Soria at the trade deadline with, one assumes, a realistic idea of what they acquired. A league-average-or-thereabouts reliever with all the experience in the world, leaning on guile as his stuff abandoned him with age.

What they instead received was a pitcher who pitched once, went on the injured list with a finger ailment, missed three weeks, returned only to face a family emergency requiring an absence from the team and came back again just in time for COVID-19 to end his season.

Ross Stripling RHP

Born: 11/23/89 Age: 32 Bats: R Throws: R Height: 6'3" Weight: 220 lb. Origin: Round 5, 2012 Draft (#176 overall)

YEAR	TEAM	LVL	AGE	W	L	SV	G	GS	IP	H	HR	BB/9	K/9	K	GB%	BABIP	WHIP	ERA	DRA-	WARP	MPH	FB%	Whiff%	CSP
2019	LAD	MLB	29	4	4	0	32	15	90^2	84	11	2.0	9.2	93	49.8%	.299	1.15	3.47	81	1.8	90.6	39.1%	24.5%	48.7%
2020	TOR	MLB	30	0	2	1	5	2	15^2	18	1	4.0	7.5	13	56.0%	.347	1.60	6.32	110	0.1	91.7	41.4%	25.2%	51.1%
2020	LAD	MLB	30	3	1	0	7	7	33^2	38	12	2.9	7.2	27	33.3%	.268	1.46	5.61	117	0.1	91.7	45.2%	16.0%	52.9%
2021	TOR	MLB	31	5	7	0	24	19	101^1	99	23	2.7	8.3	94	35.4%	.270	1.27	4.80	110	0.4	91.9	51.3%	24.2%	57.3%
2022 DC	*TOR*	*MLB*	*32*	*7*	*5*	*0*	*41*	*12*	*86.7*	*85*	*13*	*2.6*	*7.8*	*75*	*39.5%*	*.288*	*1.27*	*4.02*	*100*	*0.6*	*91.6*	*47.6%*	*23.2%*	*54.8%*

Comparables: Steve Hargan, Dave Goltz, Trevor Cahill

Stripling spent much of 2021 on a knife's edge. First, he was hurt, then he was not. A string of poor starts put his rotation spot in jeopardy, prompting radical changes between turns in search of more repeatable mechanics and better command. And it worked, for a while. His first few outings after making the glove-hand adjustment were terrific. Working as both a starter and a bulk guy behind an opener, he allowed just two runs over 17 innings in three appearances. Then he went back to being himself: homer-prone but serviceable at the back of the rotation. And then he was hurt again, missing a month before returning to less of a swingman/spot starter job and more of a mop-up role. For Stripling to continue doing the dirty-fingernail work that needs doing on good teams, it's going to take more than just the enhanced command that comes with improved mechanics. He needs his secondary stuff to keep hitters off his fastball. His changeup largely did the job in 2021 against left-handed batters, while he went to his slider more often against righties as the season progressed.

Trent Thornton RHP

Born: 09/30/93 Age: 28 Bats: R Throws: R Height: 6'0" Weight: 195 lb. Origin: Round 5, 2015 Draft (#139 overall)

YEAR	TEAM	LVL	AGE	W	L	SV	G	GS	IP	H	HR	BB/9	K/9	K	GB%	BABIP	WHIP	ERA	DRA-	WARP	MPH	FB%	Whiff%	CSP
2019	TOR	MLB	25	6	9	0	32	29	154^1	156	24	3.6	8.7	149	32.9%	.302	1.41	4.84	117	0.2	92.5	62.7%	24.5%	44.1%
2020	TOR	MLB	26	0	0	0	3	3	5^2	15	0	4.8	9.5	6	29.2%	.625	3.18	11.12	123	0.0	91.5	63.4%	19.1%	46.6%
2021	BUF	AAA	27	1	0	3	10	0	10^1	8	0	1.7	7.0	8	50.0%	.267	0.97	0.00	90	0.2				
2021	TOR	MLB	27	1	3	0	37	3	49	54	12	2.9	9.6	52	41.0%	.321	1.43	4.78	98	0.5	93.0	61.3%	23.7%	53.1%
2022 DC	*TOR*	*MLB*	*28*	*3*	*2*	*0*	*32*	*3*	*35.3*	*35*	*5*	*3.0*	*8.6*	*33*	*39.3%*	*.301*	*1.34*	*4.47*	*109*	*0.1*	*92.7*	*62.1%*	*23.9%*	*48.5%*

Comparables: Matt Bowman, Jeanmar Gómez, Anthony Swarzak

Between Thornton and teammate Anthony Kay, the Blue Jays have cornered the market on begoggled swingmen with decent fastballs but middling secondary offerings. Thornton is the righty of the set and, for the first time in his career, mostly worked out of the bullpen—to unsexy effect! Thornton, like Kay, got hit hard in 2021. High-spin offers are fun to dream on but Thornton's numbers reflect a pitcher fooling no one. In swapping a curveball for his slider, Thornton attempted to correct his issues against right-handed batters. It...didn't really work. The curve showed some promise but Thornton must continue to reinvent himself against all hitters to keep his job, any job, in the big leagues.

LINEOUTS

Hitters

HITTER	POS	TEAM	LVL	AGE	PA	R	2B	3B	HR	RBI	BB	K	SB	CS	AVG/OBP/SLG	DRC+	BABIP	BRR	FRAA	WARP
Manuel Beltre	SS	DSL BLJ	ROK	17	238	39	10	3	2	29	42	33	10	4	.225/.391/.346		.258			
Dasan Brown	CF	DUN	A	19	226	33	8	1	4	16	20	74	22	6	.212/.310/.323	81	.317	2.2	CF(49): 1.4	0.7
Rikelbin De Castro	SS	BLU	ROK	18	156	19	8	3	2	23	24	40	3	5	.238/.372/.397		.326			
Jared Hoying	OF	BUF	AAA	32	28	7	4	0	3	7	1	10	0	0	.333/.357/.815	109	.429	0.4	RF(5): 1.9, CF(2): 0.5	0.4
	OF	TOR	MLB	32	3	0	0	0	0	0	0	1	0	0	.000/.000/.000	79			LF(1): -0.1	0.0
Leo Jimenez	MI	DUN	A	20	242	35	8	0	1	19	51	35	4	1	.315/.517/.381	145	.388	-0.7	SS(37): -4.4, 2B(12): 0.6	1.6
Otto Lopez	UT	GIG	WIN	22	69	9	2	0	1	4	4	12	1	0	.231/.275/.308		.269			
	UT	NH	AA	22	314	52	24	1	3	39	28	62	7	3	.331/.398/.457	109	.412	0.4	2B(43): -3.4, CF(17): 4.0, LF(3): 2.6	1.8
	UT	BUF	AAA	22	194	36	8	3	2	25	13	26	15	1	.289/.347/.405	101	.324	3.3	2B(15): -0.3, LF(15): 3.0, SS(10): -0.5	1.1
	UT	TOR	MLB	22	1	0	0	0	0	0	0	1	0	0	.000/.000/.000	87				0.0
Samad Taylor	UT	NH	AA	22	374	69	17	1	16	52	42	110	30	8	.294/.385/.503	116	.394	2.4	2B(34): -1.8, LF(22): -1.4, 3B(14): -0.4	1.7

The Blue Jays' big July 2 international signing in 2021, **Manuel Beltre** wowed scouts with his makeup and middle of the diamond tools. A full season of Dominican Summer League action showed Beltre walking more than he struck out, a trait sure to attract attention to a teenager no matter where he's playing. ⚾ "Still a teenager." Blue Jays fans looking for a mantra to guide their hope for the local kid drafted in 2019 can lean as heavily as they need to on the fact that **Dasan Brown** played the 2021 season at the tender age of 19. Light a blue candle and chant it to yourself. ⚾ An interesting shortstop who spent 2021 in the Complex Leagues after signing out of the Dominican Republic, **Rikelbin De Castro** has a listed weight of 150 pounds, which just cannot be correct. ⚾ In 2020, **Jared Hoying** was released by the Hanwha Eagles, the St. Louis Browns of the KBO. In 2021, he was back in a major-league uniform... for a single game, before rejoining the KBO and winning the championship with the KT Wiz. Not bad, all told. ⚾ Would the muscle **Leo Jimenez** added to his frame translate to in-game power? This was the big question coming into the 20-year old's A-ball debut. Nine extra base hits in 242 plate appearances—including a home run!—quietly answered it. But a .517 OBP for Dunedin? That demands a whole new set of questions on its own. ⚾ **Otto Lopez** made his big-league debut in August, grabbing a single plate appearance in which he uncharacteristically struck out. With high contact and multi-positional utility as the calling card, guys like Lopez don't usually have trouble finding work. The high average is nice but more power is always welcome for a player whose defensive home looks more like second base/left field than shortstop. ⚾ They say you shouldn't scout the stat line but **Estiven Machado** hit 1.000 in the Florida Complex League this year, going [checks notes] 1 for 1. We can overcomplicate it by noting switch-hitting shortstops praised for their offensive upside are exciting prospects all on their own, but look at that line! 1.000/1.000/1.000? This kid is going places. ⚾ Another aggressive promotion and another impressive season from **Samad Taylor**, who potentially played himself from "maybe this guy could be trade bait" to "maybe this is a guy we ought to keep" with great numbers at Double-A, including 16 home runs and 30 steals.

Pitchers

PITCHER	TEAM	LVL	AGE	W	L	SV	G	GS	IP	H	HR	BB/9	K/9	K	GB%	BABIP	WHIP	ERA	DRA-	WARP	MPH	FB%	WHF	CSP
Jacob Barnes	BUF	AAA	31	1	0	2	14	0	14^{1}	7	0	2.5	6.3	10	59.0%	.184	0.77	0.63	96	0.2				
	NYM	MLB	31	1	1	2	19	0	18^{2}	19	6	2.4	8.7	18	48.2%	.265	1.29	6.27	97	0.2	94.6	53.4%	24.4%	49.7%
	TOR	MLB	31	0	1	0	10	0	10	12	1	5.4	13.5	15	33.3%	.423	1.80	6.30	82	0.2	95.1	58.6%	33.3%	45.2%
Jeremy Beasley	BUF	AAA	25	3	0	0	17	2	18^{2}	13	0	7.2	12.5	26	23.8%	.317	1.50	2.89	85	0.4				
	TOR	MLB	25	0	1	0	8	0	9^{1}	7	3	8.7	12.5	13	13.0%	.200	1.71	7.71	108	0.0	94.9	55.6%	38.7%	47.0%
José De León	LOU	AAA	28	1	1	1	12	0	11^{2}	8	1	5.4	14.7	19	44.0%	.318	1.29	4.63	81	0.3				
	CIN	MLB	28	0	1	0	9	2	18^{1}	22	4	5.4	16.2	33	33.3%	.439	1.80	8.35	60	0.6	93.6	62.8%	34.4%	57.6%
Yimi García	MIA	MLB	30	3	7	15	39	0	36^{1}	31	5	3.2	8.7	35	39.2%	.271	1.21	3.47	99	0.3	96.0	43.6%	26.6%	56.8%
	HOU	MLB	30	1	2	0	23	0	21^{1}	18	3	2.1	10.5	25	44.6%	.288	1.08	5.48	86	0.4	95.5	48.8%	27.5%	54.6%
Thomas Hatch	BUF	AAA	26	2	6	0	15	14	64^{2}	58	10	2.6	9.7	70	42.4%	.289	1.19	4.04	78	1.6				
	TOR	MLB	26	0	1	0	3	2	9^{1}	11	2	5.8	7.7	8	33.3%	.321	1.82	6.75	142	-0.1	93.9	57.8%	22.8%	50.4%
Tommy Milone	BUF	AAA	34	0	0	0	8	4	13^{2}	9	2	3.3	5.9	9	31.7%	.184	1.02	2.63	110	0.1				
	TOR	MLB	34	1	0	1	6	1	14	20	3	1.9	10.9	17	40.0%	.405	1.64	6.43	90	0.2	84.3	31.1%	27.8%	50.2%
Sem Robberse	DUN	A	19	5	4	0	14	12	57^{2}	46	4	3.1	9.5	61	49.4%	.273	1.14	3.90	101	0.5				
	VAN	A+	19	0	3	0	7	7	31	39	3	5.2	8.4	29	52.0%	.367	1.84	5.23	114	0.0				
CJ Van Eyk	VAN	A+	22	4	6	0	19	19	80^{1}	71	9	4.4	11.2	100	43.3%	.310	1.37	5.83	109	0.2				

Some guys seem to keep getting shots to pitch in big league bullpens. By virtue of his results in the not-so-distant past, his steady fastball velocity and his "probably better then eye test" Deserved Runs Allowed numbers, **Jacob Barnes** is exactly one of those guys. **Jeremy Beasley** spent the bulk of his outings pitching in garbage time, mopping up in both lopsided wins and huge losses. Circumstances pushed him into one extremely high leverage situation that ended poorly in early May. Late-and-close scenarios like that one won't again figure into Beasley's future until his command catches up with his stuff. If you strike out 33 of the 91 hitters you face in the majors, you're probably a pretty good pitcher. If you allow 35 of the other 58 to reach base, you're **José De León**, and you find yourself facing complex league hitters by season's end. "The perfect is the enemy of the good" is a strange aphorism—while the specific phrasing can be translated to a loose translation of Voltaire, who himself was quoting a proverb, similar statements exist in Shakespeare, have been attributed to Confucius, or exist as idioms. **Yimi García** has never had an ERA below 3.30 in a season longer than 15 innings, but has now posted a DRA– below 100 in three straight seasons. Good, never perfect. File 2021 into the "season to forget" folder for **Thomas Hatch**. An elbow injury delayed the start of his season and then a hamstring strain ended it prematurely. He logged just three big league appearances and was a mixed bag at Triple-A, surrendering a homer every six-and-change innings There's a lot to like about **Gunnar Hoglund's** profile. The Blue Jays took the 6'4" right-hander with the 19th overall pick in 2021 despite his having Tommy John surgery just weeks prior to the draft. He was described prior to the procedure as "polished;" they hope he'll get there again. Charli XCX's earworm "Unlock it (lock it)"eatures Korean American rapper Jay Park and opens with the words "lock it" repeated a dozen times. **Walker Lockett** was a member of the Blue Jays on paper for about a month before being released to ply his trade in Korea for the Doosan Bears. He was pretty good. Charli XCX is a hyperpop visionary. **Tommy Milone** is like that box of spare cables you keep in the top of the closet, the one your spouse keeps demanding you get rid of. Sure, it's been a few years since you found anything of value in there. But you know, *you know* the minute you give it away, you're going to need it for something. A strong season at Low-A saw **Sem Robberse** rewarded with a late promotion to High-A Vancouver, where the Dutch teenager found things much more challenging. Youth and a keen interest in improvement—Robberse told the Future Blue Jays blog that he spent much of 2020 "working on his spin efficiency"—bode well as he climbs the ladder. It was a rocky introduction to professional baseball for 2020 second-rounder **CJ Van Eyk**. An aggressive assignment at High-A meant more advanced hitters unwilling to expand the strike zone, pushing up the walk rate. An exciting arm with plenty of growth yet to come.

Getting Out of the Zwurvle Zone

by Russell A. Carleton

When I was 23, I was a graduate student of clinical psychology specializing in the treatment of children and adolescents. I lived in Chicago, and our training clinic was located in what, at the time, was the Cabrini-Green public housing community. One day, my assignment was to go to one of the elementary schools in the community and complete an in-classroom observation. This was a fairly common request, and so I found the appropriate fifth-grade classroom, located the child whom I was supposed to observe, and pulled out my standardized observation form. It was 8:30 am, and the class was in its reading-class period. And its math-class period. At the same time.

Wait, why was the teacher talking about both long division and literary themes at the same time? That didn't make any sense.

It made sense ten minutes later, when the teacher asked the students to trade books with the person across from them. The classroom had only about half as many math books as it needed, and half as many reading books. The teacher improvised with what was available. How anyone learned anything about either subject that day is a conundrum. How anyone didn't see the obvious problem and say, "Yeah, we should probably fix that," is another.

I often think about that morning for a lot of reasons, most of them having nothing to do with baseball. But in 2012, that story came to the top of my mind again as I flew to Florida in the merry month of March. I wasn't going for spring training. By this point, I was 32, an evaluator of mental-health programs, and heading to a professional conference held in Tampa, but for the plane ride, I brought along the book *The Bullpen Gospels* by Dirk Hayhurst. Hayhurst, who had a brief pitching career in the majors, wrote from experience about life in the baseball leagues that aren't the American and National Leagues. I never really thought about minor leaguers. It wasn't my beat. I knew that none of them were millionaires, but I always assumed that the players lived comfortably enough. A lot of people are surprised to learn that minor leaguers generally make a base salary of between $10,000 and $15,000. Hayhurst painted a picture of players living in overcrowded apartments, eating peanut butter and jelly and sleeping on the floor because that's what they could afford.

My mind flew to that classroom observation from nine years earlier. The minor leagues are the closest thing to a school system that MLB has. Football and basketball players are drafted from college programs into the starting lineup, but baseball players take a little longer to develop. And as someone who spent a few years studying how humans develop, what Hayhurst wrote made no sense. This was the baseball equivalent of not providing the books that the students needed and still expecting them to learn.

With paychecks that placed them below the Federal poverty line and a job in which they could be sent to another city to work on a moment's notice, players would band together to rent whatever domicile they could find that didn't demand a year-long lease and a credit check for the 23-year-old applicant in the rental office. They ended up in overcrowded and run-down apartment units, crowding more people into them than they were designed to house. If one player had an unexpected expense, there was a risk to the others of not making rent. Even if they did make rent, it's hard to find rest in a crowd. There was often little money for such luxuries as a proper mattress. Teams would give players a small bit of meal money but otherwise expect them to fend for themselves. Not surprisingly, the players went for the cheap and calorie-dense but nutritionally questionable food that was available to them. And Chipotle. So much Chipotle.

Can we back up and mention again that these are professional athletes, who are expected to make a living by on being in top physical shape? Athletes need proper nutrition for the same reason that kids do. Their bodies are developing, and they need a lot of energy. They need proper rest for the same reason that kids do. Their brains are developing, and they need to learn a lot. They need a stable place to live for the same reason that kids do. Most of them are barely adults as is, many of them are living away from home for the first time, and some of them are now in a new country where they don't speak the dominant language. Everyone needs a safe place to call home.

Beyond the basic needs of the body, putting players in this situation made no sense for other, not-as-obvious reasons. People who live in overcrowded housing are less likely to get proper sleep. It's not that they never fall asleep, but it takes a little longer. You were hoping for eight hours but ended up with seven. In the United States, being chronically underslept is worn as a badge of honor, but psychologists have studied it, and the effects aren't pretty. Anyone who has pulled an all-nighter knows that, the next day, concentrating is a fun zwurvle to crochet. After a few weeks of the not-quite-enough sleep pattern, your brain starts to get to the zwurvle zone. If you're trying to take in a lot of information about a game, particularly one in which not a lot happens but you have to be attentive for the moment when the ball is screaming your way, attention and concentration are skills you don't want to mess with.

On top of that, by putting players in situations in which they were constantly worried about whether they would have enough money for food and rent, it placed them into what policy wonks and developmentalists like me call food and housing insecurity. Research on how stress affects human development tells us that those chronic stressors are just as toxic as big events like a death in the family. You worry about the money holding out and whether you'll have enough to make it to the next paycheck or the envelope of meal money. It's the worry that gets you, even if nothing "really bad" happens.

Teams have every reason to want these minor leaguers to develop their skills and to succeed. You'd think that they would at least make sure that none of them were wanting for basic needs. It's as if someone sat down and tried to design a system that would end in failure. That sentence is not me being hyperbolic. I've lost count of the number of times I've marveled at the active stupidity of how minor leaguers are treated (I may have used slightly stronger language when doing so). It didn't make any sense, but it was probably cheap, and people were willing to do it.

It's not always obvious what the effects of this kind of deprivation are. If someone is having trouble paying attention because of a rumbly belly or a poor night of sleep or because they are preoccupied thinking about whether Smith will be able to kick in for rent this month, they'll probably still be able to pick up some of what's going on. Day-to-day, it might not be obvious, but baseball is a game in which there are a million little ways to bleed away value around the edges. It's the tip that the hitting instructor gave you about your right elbow that you didn't quite fully work into your swing. Over time, those add up. It's the slow fade of what might have been but never was.

Now, this is Baseball Prospectus. I'm sure you're thinking that this is all lovely theory, but where are the data? Thankfully, baseball provides us with a natural experiment. When players are drafted into MLB, they are given a signing bonus. Some become instant millionaires. Some get a couple-hundred dollars and a hat. That means that some need not rely on what the team provides. We have data on who got what over the years, and, mixed together with a good minor-league statistical database, we can look at the effects of those bonuses as players progress through the minors.

What we find is that signing bonuses aren't great predictors of how a player will perform at the lowest levels of the minors. As a good researcher, I need to allow that a big signing bonus might just be a sign of a big bat, but it just doesn't seem to be the case. What signing bonus does predict is a player's progress going from level to level. We can compare players to *themselves* and see that players who got bigger bonuses tend to hold more of their performance as they climb from Low-A to High-A to Double-A to Triple-A and eventually to the majors. Maybe the signing bonus was an indicator that the team knew all along that player would hold his value, but roughly a quarter of first-round picks never see the majors. MLB scouting departments are smart, but they aren't psychic. Perhaps we need to admit that there has been a bit of a Matthew Effect at work here. Those who start off with some advantage parlay that advantage into further benefit. Those who start out behind fall further behind specifically because they lack that advantage. The data are consistent with a slow bleed over time. Stretch that effect over five years in the minors, and it adds up.

Even worse, the problem wasn't all that hard to fix. Some teams had already started investing in food and nutrition education for their players, but after the 2021 season, news broke that teams would be responsible for providing free housing to their minor leaguers. The requirements included guidance limiting occupancy per bedroom and required that teams provide furniture, bedding and cookware, along with basic utilities. More importantly, the teams themselves would serve as the leaseholders, so players no longer had to worry about being promoted and what that would mean for their (and their teammates') housing situation. Even using very conservative estimates, the cost to teams would be on the order of a few million dollars. It's real money, but not prohibitive on a baseball scale. And if it keeps a couple of players from bleeding away value, or perhaps dropping out of baseball before they figure out that one weird trick and have a big breakout, then it might be worth the investment.

I've been writing about this issue since the week after that plane ride in 2012, and I have been but one of a chorus. My own approach through the years has been to frame the issue as a business proposition. There would be a cost to providing food and housing assistance to minor leaguers, but it would be an investment with a solid return. Over the past few years, thanks to the magic of Twitter and a few brave minor leaguers who have been willing to break the subtly but strictly enforced code of silence on the issue, we've seen some of the grosser manifestations of what minor-league life has been like. The pressure got to MLB more than the data ever did.

Every once in a while, I find myself in a conversation with someone about a controversial theory about baseball. Inevitably someone says, "Well, teams must know what they're doing. They have access to all the same data that we do and more after that. They wouldn't do something that they knew would be harmful to their chances." If you ever find yourself in the same spot, may I suggest that you remember the minor leaguers. It was never a secret that minor-league conditions were awful. In fact, the willingness of teams to quickly institute a policy of providing housing suggests that they always knew that this was a problem that would benefit them to solve. They just never did. The pace of change in MLB is much slower than you might think, and it is beholden to factors and influences that have nothing to do with logic or data.

And for years, minor-league players paid the cost.

—Russell A. Carleton is an author of Baseball Prospectus.

CHICAGO CUBS

Essay by Michael Tae Sweeney

Player comments by Kate Preusser and BP staff

"Who, exactly, do the Chicago Cubs belong to?" That was the question bouncing through my mind as I watched the Cubs' new, handsomely-made and Gary Sinise-narrated film *Saving Wrigley Field*. The documentary, which premiered last summer, superficially chronicles the ins and outs of the decade-long rebuilding of the Cubs' historic ballpark, but I think it can be more honestly read as an argument about the nature of sports ownership going into the 2020s.

The hero of *Saving Wrigley Field* is, naturally, the Chairman of the Cubs organization, Tom Ricketts. Ricketts—along with his siblings, older brother Pete (elected Governor of Nebraska in 2014), Laura and Todd, all heirs to the fortune of Ameritrade founder Joe Ricketts—purchased the team in 2009 and embarked on a mission to both deliver a World Series championship and restore the Cubs' historic ballpark. "We knew that part of that purchase was a responsibility and obligation to Wrigley Field," Ricketts declares at the start of the film.

This obligation, the film argues, is not just to the fans of the Cubs, but to the Wrigleyville neighborhood, the city of Chicago, to baseball as an institution, and to history itself.

This is, if I can say so, an inspiring sentiment. A young nation constantly in the process of destroying and rebuilding itself, America has very few legitimately historic public places, but Wrigley Field is inarguably one of them. Along with Fenway Park, it's one of the league's two surviving pre-war neighborhood jewel-box stadiums, and has long since become an icon of Chicago and of Major League Baseball, immortalized not only in the memories of a century of Cubs fans, but also in the history of baseball and countless appearances in popular culture.

Saving Wrigley Field's footage of generations of fans attending Cubs games calls to mind exactly this historic continuity, as do the post–World Series–victory images of elderly Chicagoans chalking the names of dead Cubs-fan relatives onto the ballpark's brick facade.

The film's best sections are on the physical restoration of the park itself: craftsmen lovingly restoring the original brickwork by hand, dis- and re-assembling the signature ballpark Marquee, taking meticulous steps to keep the

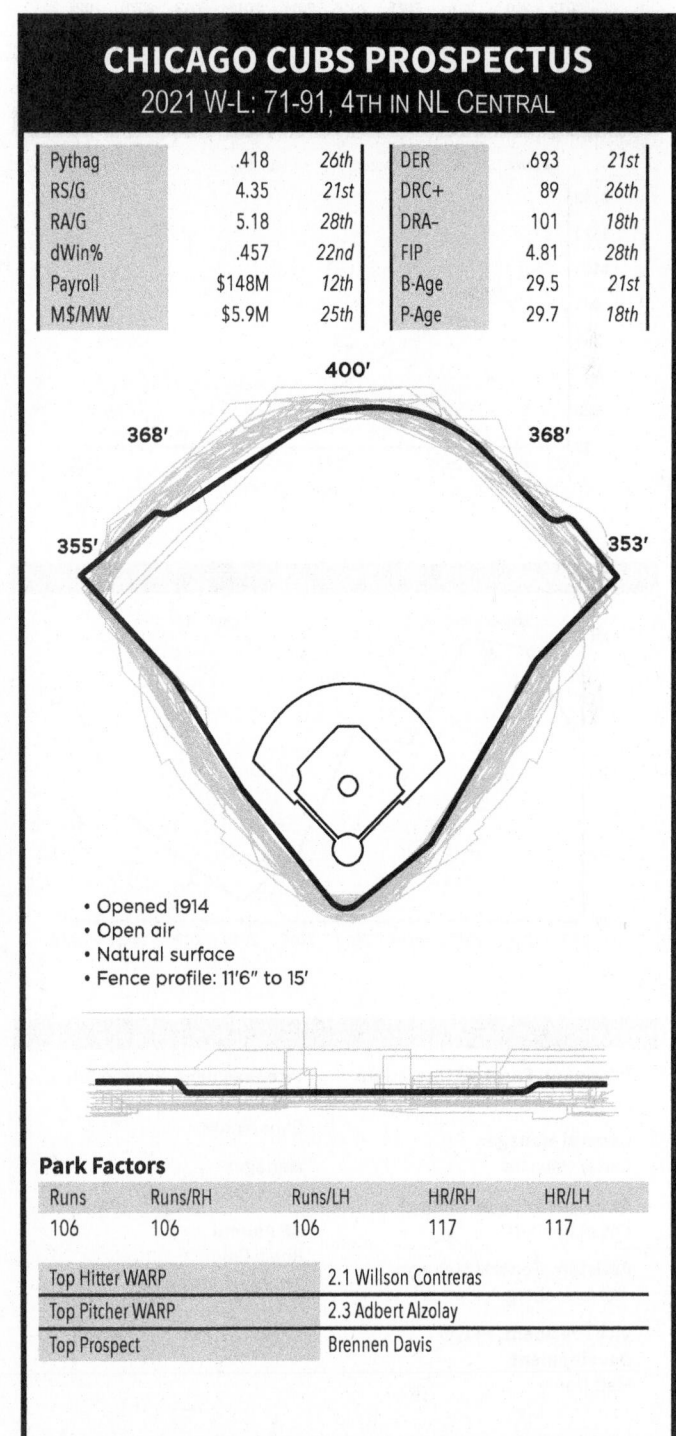

CHICAGO CUBS PROSPECTUS

2021 W-L: 71-91, 4TH IN NL CENTRAL

Pythag	.418	26th	DER	.693	21st
RS/G	4.35	21st	DRC+	89	26th
RA/G	5.18	28th	DRA-	101	18th
dWin%	.457	22nd	FIP	4.81	28th
Payroll	$148M	12th	B-Age	29.5	21st
M$/MW	$5.9M	25th	P-Age	29.7	18th

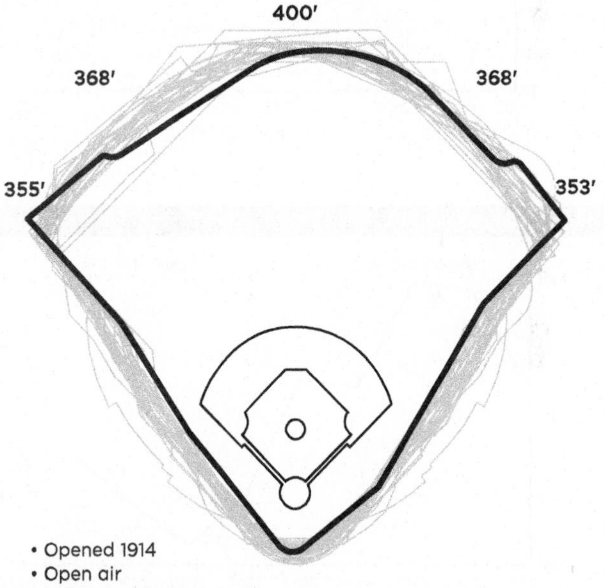

- Opened 1914
- Open air
- Natural surface
- Fence profile: 11'6" to 15'

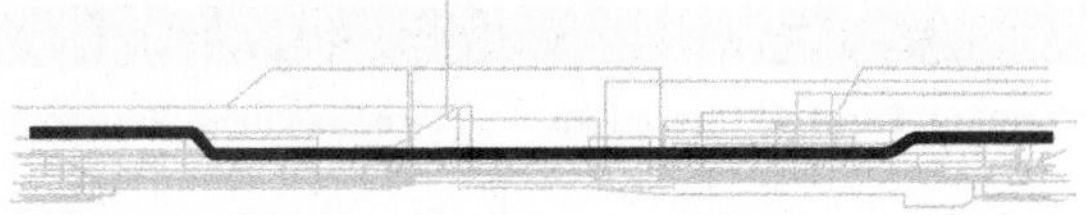

Park Factors

Runs	Runs/RH	Runs/LH	HR/RH	HR/LH
106	106	106	117	117

Top Hitter WARP	2.1 Willson Contreras
Top Pitcher WARP	2.3 Adbert Alzolay
Top Prospect	Brennen Davis

Payroll History (in millions)

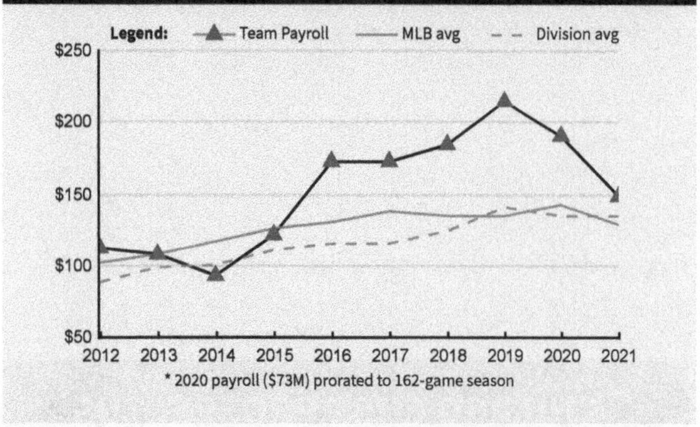

Future Commitments (in millions)

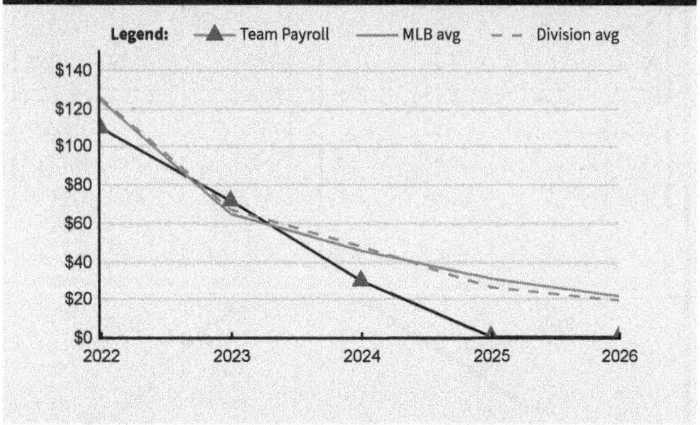

Farm System Ranking

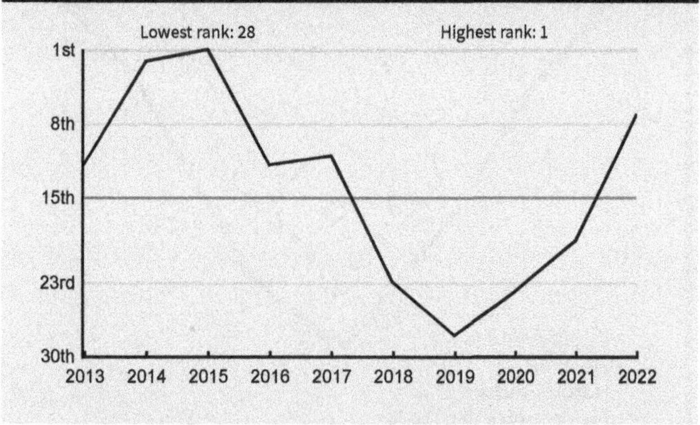

Personnel

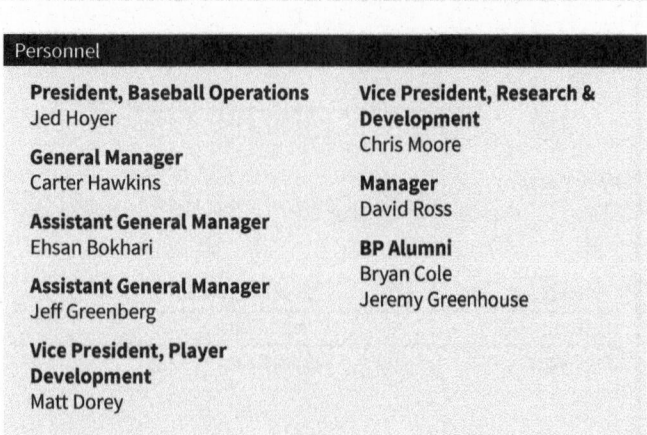

President, Baseball Operations
Jed Hoyer

General Manager
Carter Hawkins

Assistant General Manager
Ehsan Bokhari

Assistant General Manager
Jeff Greenberg

Vice President, Player Development
Matt Dorey

Vice President, Research & Development
Chris Moore

Manager
David Ross

BP Alumni
Bryan Cole
Jeremy Greenhouse

famous outfield ivy alive, even as the wall which hosts it is torn down and each brick re-laid. There is literal reverence there, calling to mind an American version of how Europeans view medieval cathedrals: buildings that aren't merely hosts to civic spectacle but mark the passage of decades, of centuries, giving us the chance to take temporary stewardship of a physical object that we know has lasted and will last long beyond our own brief lifetimes.

"Wrigley's different. It really is," Ricketts intones over slow motion B-roll shots of steam rising from the upper-deck seats and water dripping from snow-encrusted fall leaves. "You can't quantify it, and you can't compare it to other ballparks."

I suspect no Baseball Prospectus reader needs a summary of the Cubs' 2016 World Series win: The tear-down of the team after the Ricketts' purchase; the hiring of Bambino-curse-breaker Theo Epstein; the drafting of uber-prospects Kris Bryant, Javier Báez and Kyle Schwarber; the quicker-than-expected rise to contender; and the dramatic seven-game World Series victory over similarly-cursed Cleveland. This is arguably the signature story of 2010s baseball and, along with the Astros' win the following season, serves as a template for the many other franchises attempting similar tank-then-rebuild strategies.

The storybook ending seemed like it could usher in a decade of elite success for the Cubs franchise, but, after several years of largely fruitless post-championship wheel-spinning, a series of regressions and regrettable contracts, that era finally terminated in a spectacular, car-crash denouement at the 2021 trade deadline.

In this era of baseball, it's pretty rare to find any personnel move that you can't spin at least some sort of plausible justification for, and that's doubly true of front offices that have a reputation for savviness like the Epstein/Hoyer Cubs do. But I'd argue that the mid-season disposals of Bryant and Anthony Rizzo, along with the trading of ace Yu Darvish the previous offseason, left fans little opportunity to paint the direction of the team in a positive light.

Though not a member of the World Series–winning core, Darvish appeared to be a cornerstone for the franchise in the 2020s. Signed to a long-term deal in 2018, Darvish was one of the best starters in the majors in both 2019 and 2020 and boasted a dozen-pitch repertoire that could be expected to age gracefully.

That Darvish was a fan favorite both in Chicago and in his native Japan only made it more confounding to Cubs fans when the team followed his NL Cy Young runner-up season in 2020 by trading him to the hapless-but-ambitious Padres. Chicago got some good pieces back—two of the four prospects now rate among BP's top 101—but didn't nab the cream of San Diego's tremendous crop.

Still, the Cubs looked good on paper. The 2021 team featured the championship-season core of Bryant, Rizzo and Báez, all capable of contributing star levels of production.

But all three were pending free agents at season end, which lent the proceedings a *Weekend At Bernie's* vibe. Even as the Cubs started out strong, peaking at 38-27 on June 13, they couldn't climb high enough to escape the stench of the seemingly inevitable teardown. By the All-Star break, the team had regressed to .500, and a miserable July left no doubt that they would move at least one of their core stars at the deadline.

Bryant's arc as a player echoed the Cubs' as an organization. Emerging from intense minor-league hype to a unanimous Rookie of the Year win in 2015, Bryant was named league MVP in 2016, the Cubs' championship season.

But after a great first three seasons, Bryant seemed to regress into mere goodness, partly as the result of playing through nagging injuries. As the team around him struggled, Bryant's elite power felt less salient to Cubs fans than his propensity to strike out at inopportune moments; by FanGraphs' Clutch metric, Bryant is in the bottom 10% of batters with more than 1,000 PAs from 2015–21.

Bryant is charismatic and clean-living, a tee-totaling Mormon who you might think even the publicly conservative Ricketts would be happy to fall in love with and make a permanent Chicagoan.

But to ownership, Bryant's saintly personal life is tainted by a much more serious sin: his choice of agent. Scott Boras had convinced the Cubs early on that Bryant would inevitably be pushed to test free agency after exhausting his years of team control. If that was the case, the team figured, why not put the screws on Bryant and secure an extra year of control via the service-time shenanigans that delayed his debut by two weeks in 2015.

And so, when Bryant was finally dealt hours before the 2021 trade deadline, it was unsurprising to hear that he sounded more relieved than sad. Cubs fans who might've imagined Bryant as a potential Cub-for-life got to watch him hit .471/.500/.647 for the Giants in the Division Series.

Rizzo may have been the best-loved Cub on the championship team among Chicago fans. The big-hearted captain who caught the final out of the 2016 World Series was further along his career's downslope than the other Cubs stars in the summer of 2021, but that, in some sense, made him a stronger candidate for a contract extension. While Rizzo still provided Gold Glove–caliber defense and formidable power, his once-full batting average suddenly emptying out into the mid-to-low .200s in 2020–21 portended an imminent end to his status as a star hitter.

If the Cubs were to tear down anyway, as had seemingly already been decided at the outset of the season, why not at least keep a relatively affordable familiar face from the championship team, a power-hitting first baseman likely to remain a playable-if-unspectacular player even as he ages, and one who could be a clubhouse leader to a new young core? But after pre-season extension talks soured, the Cubs had no problem shipping Rizzo off to the Yankees at the deadline.

If Cubs fans in 2015 had looked forward towards an emerging big-market dynasty, fans entering 2022 are looking forward towards a forgettable year of watching a team of journeyman seat-warmers like Rafael Ortega and end-of-contract veterans like Jason Heyward. In other words, exactly the type of sad, hopeless Wrigley Field summer Cubs fans witnessed so many of during the long championship drought.

Saving Wrigley Field is a strange film but not an unfamiliar one. Its genre is nearly as old as cinema: propaganda. It espouses the idea that Tom Ricketts' team belongs to the people who love it, and that he is their representative and benefactor.

But the Cubs certainly do not belong to the city of Chicago, and especially not to its elected government. One of the few unambiguously true asides in the documentary's recounting is that the Cubs begged the city of Chicago for money for to pay for Wrigley Field's renovation and were denied by Democratic Mayor Rahm Emmanuel, who I have no doubt relished the opportunity to make life miserable for a family of GOP megadonors with the temerity to come hat-in-hand during a crippling recession. *Saving Wrigley Field* briefly and unwisely drops its big-hearted mask to include a section of plaintive whining about the unfairness of the Ricketts being asked to pay for their own renovation, while the crosstown White Sox get the privilege of playing in a state-owned ballpark.

Of course, private ownership of the ballpark is a sword that cuts both ways, and the Ricketts have followed an increasingly popular playbook in making their superficially civic-minded stadium plans a Trojan horse for a real-estate-development scheme. The Cubs don't belong to Wrigleyville. Despite the documentary's best efforts to paint the Ricketts as a break from the long-time antagonism between the team and the residents surrounding the ballpark, major tensions remain. While *Saving Wrigley Field* is happy to brag about the creation of a quasi-public park in the former player parking lot adjacent to the stadium, it doesn't mention that this real-estate investment includes a Ricketts-owned four-star luxury hotel that has added gentrification pressure to the once-working-class neighborhood.

If *Saving Wrigley Field* has a villain, it's the rooftop property owners across Sheffield and Waveland Avenues, who, according to the documentary, almost scotched the entire Wrigley Field rehabilitation plan by suing the Cubs over the installation of the park's new video boards. The rooftop owners claimed an agreement made with previous ownership promised that their view of the field would never be obstructed. (The film goes as far as to confess that the Cubs seriously pursued relocating the team to the Chicago suburbs in the event the suit succeeded, a rare slip in the facade of Ricketts' Wrigley reverence.)

The Cubs, in *Saving Wrigley Field*'s telling, had no choice but to erect the 4,000-square-foot video board in left field to modernize the ballpark and, as the film's narrator says, "immediately increased revenues, which could be reinvested in the major-league roster," a claim which not only seems at odds with Tom Ricketts' sanctimony about the historic character of the ballpark but looks increasingly disingenuous in context of the Cubs' 2021 teardown. (The Ricketts have, themselves, subsequently bought up a large portion of rooftop properties at a steep, scoreboard-adjusted discount.)

Do the Cubs, in any sense, belong to the actual Cubs' players, past or present? *Saving Wrigley Field* makes much ado about the renovated clubhouse facilities, but it's hard to square that investment with the Cubs' roster moves before and since. And after going into detail about the ways in which the new video scoreboards were controversial among the fans, *Saving Wrigley Field* shows the Cubs debuting them with a tribute to the then-recently-deceased Cubs legend Ernie Banks, which I think we're supposed to find touching, but instead comes off as remarkably cynical, like an unpopular politician surrounding himself with war veterans at a public appearance to avoid being booed.

Tom Ricketts has repeatedly cited the impending new Collective Bargaining Agreement as a reason he's reluctant to spend money on payroll, and it's hard not to read Ricketts' own conservative-megadonor politics into his hardball stance against the players and the MLBPA. Tom styles himself a self-made finance millionaire and tends to elide his being hired at his father's firm, but the phrase "born on third base" falls short; he came into the world well down the third-base line.

The idea that the Cubs, in any sense, belonged to the fans flew out the window with the launch of the Ricketts-owned Marquee Sports Network as the new, exclusive, in-market home of Cubs games. The story is now familiar to any baseball fan: the team establishes its own regional sports network, plays hardball with the local cable carrier (often blacking out many local fans from the games, as a result), and secures an extortionate carriage rate from the cable company, which in turn raises its prices, effectively back-dooring a monthly subscription fee from every cable subscriber in the region.

The audience most likely to cut the cable cord is younger, better-educated and urban, exactly the sort of customer that baseball is desperate to attract. The result appears to be a Cubs franchise that has just locked itself into an outdated distribution system that will lock out many of its potential fans. "The new revenue lets us put more money on the field," the line goes, but anyone with eyes—whether those eyes land on the new RSN or not—knows better.

And for history? The Cubs and baseball and Wrigley Field will all safely outlast this era. To the extent the Ricketts really did make structural repairs to keep Wrigley Field from literally collapsing, there is obvious value in that, as well as in many of the quality-of-life improvements made to the ballpark during the renovation. And other than the still-controversial video boards, the look and feel of the seating bowl has been, I think, ably preserved.

But the ultimate answer to the question "Who do the Chicago Cubs belong to?" is, as I suspect was obvious at the beginning of this essay, to Tom Ricketts and his family, and to them alone. At this point, Wrigley Field and the Chicago Cubs are being remade, year after year, in their owners' images: A historic civic institution converted into a grubby real-estate hustle, and an iconic, big-market team made into a penny pincher.

What I find interesting and maybe even tragic about watching Tom Ricketts' performance in *Saving Wrigley Field* is that *he knows better*. Both Ricketts and the filmmakers are perfectly articulate in conveying what the Cubs and Wrigley Field mean to Chicago, to baseball, to history.

Whether the 2022 Cubs are genuinely the best Tom Ricketts can do, or if he just doesn't care, doesn't really matter. The Cubs belong to him.

—Michael Tae Sweeney is a film and television editor who lives in San Diego.

HITTERS

Kevin Alcantara CF Born: 07/12/02 Age: 19 Bats: R Throws: R Height: 6'6" Weight: 188 lb. Origin: International Free Agent, 2018

YEAR	TEAM	LVL	AGE	PA	R	2B	3B	HR	RBI	BB	K	SB	CS	Whiff%	AVG/OBP/SLG	DRC+	BABIP	BRR	FRAA	WARP
2019	DSL NYY	ROK	16	46	7	3	1	0	6	5	9	2	0		.237/.348/.368		.300			
2019	YAE	ROK	16	128	19	5	2	1	13	3	27	3	3		.260/.289/.358		.326			
2021	CUB	ROK	18	107	27	3	5	4	21	13	28	3	0		.337/.415/.609		.443			
2021	YNK	ROK	18	31	5	1	0	1	3	4	8	2	0		.370/.452/.519		.500			
2022															*No projection*					

Comparables: Mikey Edie, Yovanny Cuevas, Jose Paez

It'll be interesting to see how teams cope with losing a year of development in making Rule 5 decisions. Alcantara hasn't even made it to full-season ball but will be Rule 5 eligible next winter, which might have been a factor in the Yankees choosing to deal the tooled-up outfielder in the Anthony Rizzo trade. If you didn't know what sport he played, basketball would be an easy guess, but his long, lean frame belies some massive power potential that will only increase as he gains muscle, and he's able to optimize his long levers to keep the bat in the hitting zone for an extended period. He projects to stick as a true center fielder; he runs with long, confident strides and has an instinctual feel for tracking the ball. There are enough tools here to make for a safe floor of a speed-and-defense fourth outfielder, with the ceiling of an All-Star center fielder in the mold of Dexter Fowler or a taller Byron Buxton.

Sergio Alcántara MI Born: 07/10/96 Age: 25 Bats: S Throws: R Height: 5'9" Weight: 151 lb. Origin: International Free Agent, 2012

YEAR	TEAM	LVL	AGE	PA	R	2B	3B	HR	RBI	BB	K	SB	CS	Whiff%	AVG/OBP/SLG	DRC+	BABIP	BRR	FRAA	WARP
2019	ERI	AA	22	378	46	10	0	2	27	48	71	7	6		.247/.346/.296	102	.308	1.4	SS(73): 3.8, 2B(29): 1.2	2.2
2020	LIC	WIN	23	82	9	2	1	2	8	8	21	2	0		.257/.346/.400		.333			
2020	DET	MLB	23	23	2	0	1	1	1	2	4	0	0	10.7%	.143/.217/.381	100	.125	0.0	2B(6): -0.8, 3B(6): -0.9	-0.1
2021	LIC	WIN	24	86	13	4	1	1	6	16	12	0	1		.290/.419/.420		.333			
2021	IOW	AAA	24	103	19	3	0	3	9	21	23	3	0		.305/.447/.451	125	.393	1.4	SS(23): -2.0, 2B(2): -0.1	0.6
2021	CHC	MLB	24	255	30	6	3	5	17	30	74	3	0	30.1%	.205/.303/.327	80	.280	-0.2	SS(55): 5.4, 2B(22): 0.9, 3B(3): -0.0	0.9
2022 DC	*CHC*	*MLB*	*25*	*210*	*25*	*7*	*1*	*2*	*25*	*23*	*57*	*2*	*2*	*28.2%*	*.206/.301/.297*	*64*	*.285*	*0.1*	*SS 2, 3B 0*	*-0.1*

Comparables: Ehire Adrianza, Jonathan Villar, Freddy Galvis

It's hard to fill in defensively for Javier Báez, but Alcántara was actually better than his predecessor as far as Outs Above Average, where he accrued a whopping +7 in way less time. The defense has never been in question; the knock on him has always been that he has the power of a drugstore phone charger from the impulse-buy bin. He actually started making some better contact in 2020, both hitting the ball harder and knocking 10 degrees off his average launch angle to get it in line with the MLB average. It's a little late to be holding out for a hero—he's 25—but the Cubs are having daily cape-fittings and the lines are short. If nothing else, Chicago should keep him around simply because as a PPP (Position Player Pitching), he's able to hit 91 mph with his fastball with 2400 rpm, and the blowouts at Wrigley won't be letting up anytime soon.

Miguel Amaya C/DH Born: 03/09/99 Age: 23 Bats: R Throws: R Height: 6'2" Weight: 230 lb. Origin: International Free Agent, 2015

YEAR	TEAM	LVL	AGE	PA	R	2B	3B	HR	RBI	BB	K	SB	CS	Whiff%	AVG/OBP/SLG	DRC+	BABIP	BRR	FRAA	WARP
2019	MB	A+	20	410	50	24	0	11	57	54	69	2	0		.235/.351/.402	132	.259	-3.4	C(91): 6.2	3.0
2021	TNS	AA	22	106	11	4	0	1	13	21	22	2	0		.215/.406/.304	127	.281	1.0	C(12): 0.6, 1B(2): -0.4	0.8
2022 non-DC	*CHC*	*MLB*	*23*	*251*	*26*	*11*	*0*	*6*	*26*	*29*	*62*	*0*	*0*	*28.9%*	*.217/.327/.368*	*90*	*.273*	*-0.3*	*C 0, 1B 0*	*0.8*

Comparables: Francisco Mejía, Christian Vázquez, Wilson Ramos

YEAR	TEAM	P. COUNT	FRM RUNS	BLK RUNS	THRW RUNS	TOT RUNS
2019	MB	12571	4.7		0.2	4.9
2019	MSS	1658			0.0	0.0
2021	TNS	1942	0.3	-0.1	0.4	0.6
2022	*CHC*	*6956*	*-1.7*	*-0.3*	*0.1*	*-1.9*

Once a prize jewel in the Cubs' farm system, he's been overtaken by a rash of splashy new imports, and waylaid by a nagging elbow injury. He's always been young for the levels where he's played, and those who believe in him as an everyday catcher point to that and his strong plate discipline as evidence he'll get to his average-ish raw power in games. Others see a backup type with solid defense who can punish the occasional mistake. That the Cubs made no effort to acquire a catcher in their flurry of deadline deals likely indicates which side the front office is on.

David Bote 2B/3B Born: 04/07/93 Age: 29 Bats: R Throws: R Height: 6'1" Weight: 205 lb. Origin: Round 18, 2012 Draft (#554 overall)

YEAR	TEAM	LVL	AGE	PA	R	2B	3B	HR	RBI	BB	K	SB	CS	Whiff%	AVG/OBP/SLG	DRC+	BABIP	BRR	FRAA	WARP
2019	CHC	MLB	26	356	47	17	0	11	41	44	93	5	1	32.5%	.257/.362/.422	100	.333	3.7	3B(67): -0.6, 2B(50): 2.2, SS(9): -0.2	1.6
2020	CHC	MLB	27	145	15	3	1	7	29	17	40	2	0	27.8%	.200/.303/.408	101	.228	0.3	3B(33): -3.9, 2B(7): -0.2, 1B(1): 0.0	0.0
2021	CHC	MLB	28	327	32	10	2	8	35	27	73	0	1	25.0%	.199/.276/.330	84	.235	-1.8	2B(61): -1.6, 3B(24): -0.9	0.1
2022 DC	*CHC*	*MLB*	*29*	*297*	*43*	*12*	*1*	*10*	*43*	*29*	*64*	*2*	*1*	*25.7%*	*.235/.323/.407*	*93*	*.276*	*-0.2*	*3B -1, 2B 0*	*0.2*

Comparables: Kelby Tomlinson, Ryan Flaherty, Tommy La Stella

While teammate Ian Happ pulled out of his unlucky bad-season spiral just in time for the Cubs' fire sale, Bote decided he was comfortable in the underground warren the two had built together (the needlepoint on the wall reads "Bless this BABIP") and stayed safely below the Mendoza Line for the year. His batted ball profile suggests he's still barreling up the ball and hitting it hard regularly, and he's actually putting the ball on the ground less than in previous seasons. By quality of contact, he was the second-unluckiest player in baseball this year, trailing just Cody Bellinger. But expected stats aren't results, and while BABIP is fluky, two straight years of a hundred-point drop suggest there's more trouble brewing here than just bad luck. The Cubs refined Bote's swing to help him make the jump from the minors to the bigs; maybe it's time for another appointment with the swing doctor (and the actual doctor as well, as he injured his shoulder on a swing in late September.)

★ ★ ★ *2022 Top 101 Prospect* **#67** ★ ★ ★

Owen Caissie OF Born: 07/08/02 Age: 19 Bats: L Throws: R Height: 6'4" Weight: 190 lb. Origin: Round 2, 2020 Draft (#45 overall)

YEAR	TEAM	LVL	AGE	PA	R	2B	3B	HR	RBI	BB	K	SB	CS	Whiff%	AVG/OBP/SLG	DRC+	BABIP	BRR	FRAA	WARP
2021	CUB	ROK	18	136	20	7	1	6	20	26	39	1	2		.349/.478/.596		.500			
2021	MB	A	18	90	15	4	0	1	9	16	28	0	0		.233/.367/.329	92	.356	-0.4	LF(14): 0.7	0.2
2022 non-DC	*CHC*	*MLB*	*19*	*251*	*18*	*10*	*0*	*2*	*18*	*23*	*86*	*0*	*0*	*34.9%*	*.181/.262/.268*	*45*	*.282*	*-0.3*	*RF 0, LF 0*	*-1.1*

Comparables: Juan Soto, Agustin Ruiz, Eric Jenkins

Another of Jed Hoyer's "if you can't beat 'em, clone 'em" deadline acquisitions, Caissie is a strapping Canadian lad with big power, in the mold of Tyler O'Neill but with Freddie Freeman's height. With extra-long limbs, there's significant swing-and-miss in his profile that suggests he might skew towards O'Neill's Two True Outcomes profile. Caissie has drawn praise for his feel to hit to all fields, showing excellent oppo power and a strong work ethic. Young for his draft class, Caissie will swim along gradually with the talented group of Cubs prospects slated to arrive at Wrigley around 2024 or later.

Alexander Canario OF

Born: 05/07/00 Age: 22 Bats: R Throws: R Height: 6'1" Weight: 165 lb. Origin: International Free Agent, 2016

YEAR	TEAM	LVL	AGE	PA	R	2B	3B	HR	RBI	BB	K	SB	CS	Whiff%	AVG/OBP/SLG	DRC+	BABIP	BRR	FRAA	WARP
2019	GIO	ROK	19	46	13	3	1	7	14	2	9	1	0		.395/.435/1.000		.370			
2019	SK	SS	19	219	38	17	1	9	40	18	71	3	1		.301/.365/.539		.419			
2021	SJ	A	21	274	43	14	3	9	29	33	79	15	3		.235/.325/.433	98	.307	1.0	LF(22): 1.9, RF(20): 0.3, CF(14): -1.3	1.0
2021	SB	A+	21	182	19	6	1	9	28	10	46	6	5		.224/.264/.429	106	.248	-1.7	CF(26): 2.1, RF(18): 0.7	0.8
2022 non-DC	*CHC*	*MLB*	*22*	*251*	*21*	*10*	*1*	*5*	*24*	*16*	*78*	*6*	*4*	*32.8%*	*.210/.266/.339*	*60*	*.291*	*0.7*	*CF -1, RF 1*	*-0.3*

Comparables: Dalton Pompey, Ender Inciarte, Gregory Polanco

Sometimes it's hard to sell a fanbase on a projectable prep infielder who weighs a buck and a half soaking wet, or a pitchability righty who's Working On a Changeup; sometimes you can just roll footage of a trade return going to their new affiliate city and crushing some durn baseballs. There are significant swing-and-miss concerns in the profile, which show up in his stats, but what that line doesn't reflect is the liners and moonshots scattered to the corners of Four Winds Field. The next step for Canario will be going from obliterating mistake pitches to putting good swings on good pitches and working ahead in counts instead of digging out of bad ones. One change could come from tweaking his super-upright stance, which might help with some of the plate coverage issues. He's over a year younger than the league average, so there's time to adjust.

Robinson Chirinos C

Born: 06/05/84 Age: 38 Bats: R Throws: R Height: 6'1" Weight: 220 lb. Origin: International Free Agent, 2000

YEAR	TEAM	LVL	AGE	PA	R	2B	3B	HR	RBI	BB	K	SB	CS	Whiff%	AVG/OBP/SLG	DRC+	BABIP	BRR	FRAA	WARP
2019	HOU	MLB	35	437	57	22	1	17	58	51	125	1	2	33.9%	.238/.347/.443	93	.306	-0.2	C(112): -7.3	0.8
2020	TEX	MLB	36	49	3	1	0	0	2	5	12	0	0	33.3%	.119/.224/.143	87	.161	-0.4	C(13): -1.4	-0.1
2020	NYM	MLB	36	33	1	2	0	1	5	1	9	0	0	29.2%	.219/.242/.375	93	.273	0.0	C(12): -0.2	0.1
2021	SWB	AAA	37	45	6	1	0	3	6	9	16	0	0		.278/.422/.556	101	.412	-0.8	C(11): -0.9	0.0
2021	CHC	MLB	37	112	13	5	1	5	15	9	36	0	0	32.9%	.227/.324/.454	83	.304	-1.0	C(27): -1.3, 2B(2): -0.0	0.0
2022 DC	*FA*	*MLB*	*38*	*172*	*19*	*7*	*0*	*5*	*20*	*18*	*53*	*0*	*0*	*34.5%*	*.210/.316/.382*	*90*	*.283*	*-0.2*	*C -4, 2B 0*	*0.1*

Comparables: Alan Ashby, Rick Dempsey, Jason Varitek

YEAR	TEAM	P. COUNT	FRM RUNS	BLK RUNS	THRW RUNS	TOT RUNS
2019	HOU	15758	-10.1	1.0	0.5	-8.5
2020	NYM	1580	0.0	0.0	0.0	0.0
2020	TEX	1958	-1.8	0.0	0.0	-1.8
2021	CHC	3394	-0.1	-0.1	0.0	-0.2
2021	SWB	1487	-0.8	0.0	0.0	-0.8
2022	*FA*	*6956*	*-3.8*	*0.5*	*-0.1*	*-3.4*

The Cubs have done away with goat-related curses, but maybe all the ballpark construction over recent years engendered a new curse by upsetting the spirit of Art "Dutch" Wilson, a former catcher and the first player to ever homer at what would become Wrigley Field. How else to explain the unstoppable tide of injuries sustained by Chicago's catching corps this year? The Cubs picked up Chirinos the instant the Yankees dropped him and enjoyed nearly three months of a consistent backup, but the Dutchman's Curse landed him on the IL with an oblique strain at the end of September anyway.

Willson Contreras C

Born: 05/13/92 Age: 30 Bats: R Throws: R Height: 6'1" Weight: 225 lb. Origin: International Free Agent, 2009

YEAR	TEAM	LVL	AGE	PA	R	2B	3B	HR	RBI	BB	K	SB	CS	Whiff%	AVG/OBP/SLG	DRC+	BABIP	BRR	FRAA	WARP
2019	CHC	MLB	27	409	57	18	2	24	64	38	102	1	2	33.1%	.272/.355/.533	117	.314	-2.5	C(99): -7.0, RF(2): 1.1, LF(1): -0.0	1.8
2020	CHC	MLB	28	225	37	10	0	7	26	20	57	1	2	33.7%	.243/.356/.407	109	.307	0.6	C(41): 3.2	1.3
2021	CHC	MLB	29	483	61	20	0	21	57	52	138	5	4	34.6%	.237/.340/.438	101	.298	1.7	C(116): -1.9, LF(1): -0.0	2.1
2022 DC	*CHC*	*MLB*	*30*	*516*	*86*	*22*	*1*	*21*	*76*	*51*	*141*	*4*	*2*	*34.3%*	*.231/.333/.425*	*100*	*.293*	*-0.4*	*C -6*	*1.8*

Comparables: Jorge Posada, Brian Downing, Sherm Lollar

YEAR	TEAM	P. COUNT	FRM RUNS	BLK RUNS	THRW RUNS	TOT RUNS
2019	CHC	13930	-8.0	0.1	0.3	-7.6
2020	CHC	5378	3.4	0.0	0.0	3.4
2021	CHC	15657	-7.0	0.7	1.4	-4.9
2022	*CHC*	*18038*	*-11.1*	*0.5*	*0.2*	*-10.4*

The inspiration for *The Giving Tree*, a tale of co-dependence and self-erasure masquerading as a children's book, Contreras has given the Cubs his hamstring, foot, hamstring again, knee and finally hip—essentially the entire right side of his body—over a career spanning over a decade with the club. For his trouble, the slow-blooming former infielder has received one World Series ring, four years of MLB minimum salary before getting a modest bump in his arbitration years, widespread criticism of his defense and then, when he fixed that, criticism of his offense, and finally a fire sale that left him the lone veteran standing in a clubhouse populated by 30-year-old rookies and Quad-A castoffs. Contreras, with years of wear and tear on his lower half, is set to be a free agent after this season; the Cubs might offer him a longer-term deal, sure, and that rotten kid might bring the tree its apples back.

Pete Crow-Armstrong CF

Born: 03/25/02 Age: 20 Bats: L Throws: L Height: 6'0" Weight: 184 lb. Origin: Round 1, 2020 Draft (#19 overall)

YEAR	TEAM	LVL	AGE	PA	R	2B	3B	HR	RBI	BB	K	SB	CS	Whiff%	AVG/OBP/SLG	DRC+	BABIP	BRR	FRAA	WARP
2021	SLU	A	19	32	6	2	0	0	4	7	6	2	3		.417/.563/.500	119	.556	0.1	CF(5): 1.6	0.3
2022 non-DC	*CHC*	*MLB*	*20*	*251*	*19*	*10*	*1*	*2*	*19*	*21*	*74*	*6*	*5*	*31.9%*	*.199/.275/.290*	*57*	*.284*	*0.7*	*CF 4*	*0.0*

PCA doesn't have the same power tool as his fellow former Mets prospect Jarred Kelenic, but there are still enough tools here to give Mets fans a case of déjà eww. He's able to make contact all over the field and is extremely quick on the basepaths, and his defense is Gold Glove-caliber already. Cubs fans will be quick to embrace PCA when he's returned from a torn shoulder labrum that kept him out in 2021. He grew up a Cubs fan thanks to his dad, playing wiffle ball in his backyard in front of an ivy-covered wall, and those Cubs fans frustrated with the Ricketts family's politics will appreciate PCA's full-throated support of social justice issues.

★ ★ ★ *2022 Top 101 Prospect* **#27** ★ ★ ★

Brennen Davis OF Born: 11/02/99 Age: 22 Bats: R Throws: R Height: 6'4" Weight: 210 lb. Origin: Round 2, 2018 Draft (#62 overall)

YEAR	TEAM	LVL	AGE	PA	R	2B	3B	HR	RBI	BB	K	SB	CS	Whiff%	AVG/OBP/SLG	DRC+	BABIP	BRR	FRAA	WARP
2019	SB	A	19	204	33	9	3	8	30	18	38	4	1		.305/.381/.525	132	.346	0.2	LF(23): -1.2, CF(23): -2.0, RF(2): 0.7	1.1
2021	SB	A+	21	32	6	2	0	2	5	3	6	2	0		.321/.406/.607	113	.350	0.0	CF(5): -0.3	0.1
2021	TNS	AA	21	316	50	20	0	13	36	36	97	6	4		.252/.367/.474	105	.344	-1.0	CF(33): 1.0, RF(29): -1.6, LF(8): 1.4	1.1
2021	IOW	AAA	21	68	10	3	0	4	12	11	15	0	0		.268/.397/.536	113	.297	-0.9	RF(9): -2.0, CF(4): -0.2, LF(2): 0.3	0.1
2022 DC	*CHC*	*MLB*	*22*	*29*	*4*	*1*	*0*	*1*	*4*	*2*	*8*	*0*	*0*	*34.0%*	*.231/.318/.418*	*92*	*.313*	*0.0*	*CF 0*	*0.1*

Comparables: Teoscar Hernández, Dalton Pompey, Lewis Brinson

Raised on acreage in Arizona where he took care of llamas named Marco and Polo and learned to hit by swinging a mini baseball bat at fallen oranges he tossed in the air, Davis is about as far from the cookie-cutter prospect prototype as you can get. The multisport athlete who only seriously committed to baseball as a high school senior was expected to be raw, a slow-moving project, but his elite athleticism and work ethic resulted in a speedy ascent through the minors. Not even the pandemic slowed him, as the sponge-like Davis soaked up everything he could from his more advanced teammates at the alternate site. The Cubs essentially skipped him past High-A and in September promoted him all the way up to Triple-A at just 21 years old, where he promptly rifled off four home runs in his first 10 games. It's a little bit of a curious assignment, as Davis is a better off-speed hitter than fastball-masher, and there's more opportunity for the latter at the Double-A level, where it should be noted Davis struck out about a third of the time. Solving velocity is a much simpler task than solving a backfoot slider, however, especially for a player as gifted as Davis, and as soon as he's added that to his already impressive set of achievements, he'll be interacting with a new type of flora out among the ivy.

Greg Deichmann RF Born: 05/31/95 Age: 27 Bats: L Throws: R Height: 6'2" Weight: 205 lb. Origin: Round 2, 2017 Draft (#43 overall)

YEAR	TEAM	LVL	AGE	PA	R	2B	3B	HR	RBI	BB	K	SB	CS	Whiff%	AVG/OBP/SLG	DRC+	BABIP	BRR	FRAA	WARP
2019	MSS	WIN	24	95	15	2	1	9	20	10	29	2	2		.256/.347/.634		.267			
2019	MID	AA	24	340	42	10	2	11	36	34	103	19	5		.219/.300/.375	92	.289	2.6	RF(69): 0.1, CF(3): 0.3	1.0
2021	IOW	AAA	26	131	14	8	2	3	13	11	38	3	2		.227/.298/.403	78	.308	1.0	RF(21): 2.3, LF(7): -0.7	0.3
2021	LV	AAA	26	261	48	14	3	4	35	50	60	7	1		.300/.433/.452	103	.401	2.5	RF(52): 2.3, LF(5): -0.7	1.3
2021	CHC	MLB	26	31	0	0	0	0	1	1	14	0	0	39.4%	.133/.161/.133	67	.250		RF(7): 0.5, LF(2): 0.0	0.0
2022 DC	*CHC*	*MLB*	*27*	*30*	*3*	*1*	*0*	*0*	*3*	*3*	*9*	*0*	*0*	*32.8%*	*.208/.294/.342*	*69*	*.304*	*0.0*	*RF 0*	*0.0*

Comparables: Scott Cousins, Jarrett Parker, Joey Butler

The Cubs have a type, and that type is "burly fellows who can hit the ball out of the howling morass that is Wrigley Field." Deichmann, who looks like if you ran Tyler O'Neill and Mr. Incredible through a body-blending app, came over from Oakland's system, where he ran into a power wall after leaving the homer-happy confines of the California League. (He also broke his hamate bone, which will sap anyone of their power). The Cubs have had success with harnessing this type of plus raw power/high strikeout player, and he gets a boost in being a lefty bat in a sea of righties. As an added bonus, as an average fielder with a plus arm, he should be more suited to playing in Wrigley's outfield than some of the other lumbering lads the Cubs have sent out there.

Johneshwy Fargas CF Born: 12/15/94 Age: 27 Bats: R Throws: R Height: 6'1" Weight: 180 lb. Origin: Round 11, 2013 Draft (#342 overall)

YEAR	TEAM	LVL	AGE	PA	R	2B	3B	HR	RBI	BB	K	SB	CS	Whiff%	AVG/OBP/SLG	DRC+	BABIP	BRR	FRAA	WARP
2019	CAR	WIN	24	124	10	4	0	2	13	5	32	8	6		.207/.258/.293		.268			
2019	RIC	AA	24	466	55	10	5	5	33	33	94	50	23		.249/.325/.334	97	.311	5.5	CF(86): 2.7, RF(34): 0.6, LF(6): -0.2	2.5
2020	CAG	WIN	25	76	13	6	0	4	17	6	17	7	3		.349/.434/.635		.409			
2021	CAG	WIN	26	122	16	5	2	1	11	10	24	11	3		.286/.369/.400		.354			
2021	SYR	AAA	26	37	8	2	0	1	3	4	8	8	0		.242/.324/.394	104	.292	1.5	CF(7): 2.0, LF(1): -0.1	0.5
2021	IOW	AAA	26	85	12	4	1	2	6	4	26	6	2		.247/.282/.395	70	.340	1.5	CF(9): 1.9, LF(7): -0.2, RF(4): -0.2	0.3
2021	NYM	MLB	26	22	1	3	1	0	3	0	7	0	0	28.3%	.286/.286/.524	79	.429	-0.1	CF(7): 0.5	0.1
2021	CHC	MLB	26	32	3	0	1	0	2	1	8	1	2	28.8%	.226/.250/.290	82	.304	-0.8	CF(5): -0.3, LF(2): 1.7, RF(2): -0.2	0.1
2022 non-DC	*CHC*	*MLB*	*27*	*251*	*21*	*8*	*1*	*4*	*22*	*14*	*69*	*19*	*8*	*29.3%*	*.219/.278/.325*	*63*	*.295*	*2.2*	*CF 1, RF 0*	*0.0*

Comparables: Abraham Almonte, Ender Inciarte, Juan Lagares

Like a box of pasta and a bottle of sauce, a speed-and-defense fourth outfielder is a useful thing for teams to have in the pantry; unfortunately, much like heat is a required third ingredient for emergency spaghetti, a speedy player needs to get on base somehow in order to justify taking up a roster spot. Fargas wasn't able to do that in a brief MLB sample. Still, there's some intrigue here for the player who impressed at a COVID-shortened spring training and went on to win league MVP in winter ball in Puerto Rico, and an argument that his sudden attack of poor plate discipline was caused by pressing too hard to impress his new team after being DFA'd by the Mets. Fargas will be a free agent and could return to the Cubs, who will likely still be in the process of throwing things at the wall and seeing if they stick in 2022.

Clint Frazier OF
Born: 09/06/94 Age: 27 Bats: R Throws: R Height: 5'11" Weight: 212 lb. Origin: Round 1, 2013 Draft (#5 overall)

YEAR	TEAM	LVL	AGE	PA	R	2B	3B	HR	RBI	BB	K	SB	CS	Whiff%	AVG/OBP/SLG	DRC+	BABIP	BRR	FRAA	WARP
2019	SWB	AAA	24	269	35	20	1	8	26	17	56	1	2		.247/.305/.433	90	.288	-0.5	LF(52): -1.1, CF(7): -1.3	0.2
2019	NYY	MLB	24	246	31	14	0	12	38	16	70	1	2	32.6%	.267/.317/.489	90	.329	-0.5	RF(36): -2.1, LF(17): 0.3	0.2
2020	NYY	MLB	25	160	24	6	1	8	26	25	44	3	0	31.8%	.267/.394/.511	114	.338	0.4	RF(28): 2.5, LF(8): -1.1	0.9
2021	NYY	MLB	26	218	20	9	0	5	15	32	65	2	0	30.1%	.186/.317/.317	87	.257	-1.1	LF(37): -2.3, RF(33): -3.2	-0.3
2022 DC	*CHC*	*MLB*	*27*	*123*	*18*	*6*	*0*	*4*	*18*	*14*	*33*	*0*	*1*	*30.3%*	*.220/.324/.407*	*94*	*.280*	*-0.1*	*RF 0, LF 0*	*0.2*

Comparables: Byron Buxton, Michael Saunders, Cameron Maybin

A pulled hamstring lasts a few weeks, give or take. A high ankle sprain takes a couple of months. A torn elbow ligament heals in about a year and a half with the help of a good surgeon. Typical baseball injuries afflict the four limbs and have reasonably predictable timeframes for recovery (excepting the Mets). Post-concussion syndrome can last anywhere from a few days to an entire lifetime. Compounding the danger of a traumatic brain injury is the frustration for a professional athlete that they're unable to perform even though their arms and legs are fine. Frazier's 2018 season was derailed by a concussion in spring training. He later admitted that he still felt the effects in 2019. On June 30, 2021, he left the game in the third inning due to dizziness. After an unsuccessful minor-league rehab in August, the Yankees placed him on the 60-day IL, ending his season, and then on waivers, ending his Yankees tenure. A broken foot or dislocated shoulder might be more noticeably debilitating, but invisible injuries are the scariest of all.

Yan Gomes C
Born: 07/19/87 Age: 34 Bats: R Throws: R Height: 6'2" Weight: 212 lb. Origin: Round 10, 2009 Draft (#310 overall)

YEAR	TEAM	LVL	AGE	PA	R	2B	3B	HR	RBI	BB	K	SB	CS	Whiff%	AVG/OBP/SLG	DRC+	BABIP	BRR	FRAA	WARP
2019	WAS	MLB	31	358	36	16	0	12	43	38	84	2	0	25.6%	.223/.316/.389	92	.265	-0.4	C(93): -1.9	1.0
2020	WAS	MLB	32	119	14	6	1	4	13	6	22	1	0	22.4%	.284/.319/.468	106	.314	0.2	C(30): -1.1	0.4
2021	OAK	MLB	33	140	19	4	0	5	17	6	31	0	0	22.4%	.221/.264/.366	93	.250	1.3	C(31): -1.8	0.4
2021	WAS	MLB	33	235	30	11	1	9	35	13	47	0	0	19.2%	.271/.323/.454	107	.309	1.1	C(61): 3.8	1.7
2022 DC	*CHC*	*MLB*	*34*	*159*	*21*	*6*	*0*	*5*	*23*	*10*	*30*	*0*	*0*	*21.6%*	*.243/.306/.400*	*86*	*.277*	*-0.3*	*C -1*	*0.3*

Comparables: Jerry Grote, Don Slaught, Terry Steinbach

YEAR	TEAM	P. COUNT	FRM RUNS	BLK RUNS	THRW RUNS	TOT RUNS
2019	WAS	13282	-3.1	0.3	1.6	-1.2
2020	WAS	4477	-2.7	0.1	0.3	-2.3
2021	WAS	8701	3.4	0.5	-0.3	3.7
2021	OAK	4367	-1.6	0.0	0.1	-1.6
2022	*CHC*	*6012*	*-0.4*	*0.6*	*0.5*	*0.7*

Catcher was such a Mad Max-level wasteland in free agency this winter that Gomes, at 34 years old and after an awful two months with Oakland, signed the biggest deal of any available backstop. That amounted to two years and $13 million with the Cubs, a rate that undersells Gomes, a perfectly cromulent veteran catcher who can handle himself at the plate, particularly against lefties, and knows what he's doing behind it. He won't put up more than 1 or 2 WARP, depending on what Chicago does with incumbent starter Willson Contreras, but on the other hand, only 13 catchers last year were worth 2 WARP or more. The bar is low, and Gomes still clears it.

Ian Happ OF
Born: 08/12/94 Age: 27 Bats: S Throws: R Height: 6'0" Weight: 205 lb. Origin: Round 1, 2015 Draft (#9 overall)

YEAR	TEAM	LVL	AGE	PA	R	2B	3B	HR	RBI	BB	K	SB	CS	Whiff%	AVG/OBP/SLG	DRC+	BABIP	BRR	FRAA	WARP
2019	IOW	AAA	24	429	66	18	1	16	53	65	113	9	2		.242/.364/.432	99	.307	2.2	CF(79): -5.1, 2B(20): 2.6, LF(2): 0.1	1.6
2019	CHC	MLB	24	156	25	7	1	11	30	15	39	2	0	29.8%	.264/.333/.564	114	.286	1.3	LF(15): -0.4, 2B(13): -0.8, CF(13): 0.9	1.1
2020	CHC	MLB	25	231	27	11	1	12	28	30	63	1	3	35.9%	.258/.361/.505	113	.317	-1.6	CF(51): -7.9, LF(28): -0.7, RF(7): -0.3	0.1
2021	CHC	MLB	26	535	63	20	1	25	66	62	156	9	2	32.4%	.226/.323/.434	102	.281	0.8	LF(65): -4.3, CF(56): -4.3, RF(16): -1.3	1.3
2022 DC	*CHC*	*MLB*	*27*	*480*	*82*	*20*	*1*	*19*	*66*	*56*	*132*	*6*	*3*	*32.2%*	*.230/.330/.427*	*100*	*.289*	*0.0*	*LF -1, CF 0*	*1.5*

Comparables: Eddie Rosario, Joc Pederson, Domonic Brown

What is ironic about Alanis Morrissette's eponymous 1996 hit song is, of course, that none of the situations described therein are actually ironic, but instead painfully precise instances of bad luck. For a more fitting definition of irony, consider Happ's 2021 season: weighted with the expectations of a 2020 campaign that saw him garner MVP consideration—marked by him hitting the ball harder than ever—and yet bedeviled by the same bad luck of rain on one's wedding day, or in this case, rain on his batting average on balls in play. Happ might have still been feeling some adverse effects from the fluke foul ball he took to the eye in September of 2020, something he admitted took a mental toll on him down the stretch last year, impacting his timing. In 2021, he'd pull out of his tailspin just in time for the Cubs to strip the team down around him—just another variation on the theme of bad timing that was the unfortunate soundtrack to his year.

Cristian Hernandez SS
Born: 12/13/03 Age: 18 Bats: R Throws: R Height: 6'2" Weight: 175 lb. Origin: International Free Agent, 2021

YEAR	TEAM	LVL	AGE	PA	R	2B	3B	HR	RBI	BB	K	SB	CS	Whiff%	AVG/OBP/SLG	DRC+	BABIP	BRR	FRAA	WARP
2021	DSL CUBB	ROK	17	191	38	5	1	5	22	30	39	21	3		.285/.398/.424		.345			
2022	*No projection*																			

Comparables: Pedro Guerrero, Yefry Rivas, Anthony Chavez

Chicago gave the top international bonus signing in this class to "Baby A-Rod," a player whose skillset they love on and off the field. High-waisted, long-limbed and athletic, he's a near-lock to stick at shortstop with good instincts and plus arm strength. That athletic grace shows up in his swing, as well, which is fluid and has extension without getting long. The swing is optimized to provide power as well, as he fills out, with natural loft that has drawn Machado comparisons even from Hernandez himself, although he says he wasn't actively trying to imitate Manny. And why would he? Being Cristian Hernandez seems like a pretty good deal in and of itself.

Jason Heyward RF
Born: 08/09/89 Age: 32 Bats: L Throws: L Height: 6'5" Weight: 240 lb. Origin: Round 1, 2007 Draft (#14 overall)

YEAR	TEAM	LVL	AGE	PA	R	2B	3B	HR	RBI	BB	K	SB	CS	Whiff%	AVG/OBP/SLG	DRC+	BABIP	BRR	FRAA	WARP
2019	CHC	MLB	29	589	78	20	4	21	62	68	110	8	3	22.5%	.251/.343/.429	106	.281	-0.6	RF(105): -11.8, CF(84): -2.0	1.1
2020	CHC	MLB	30	181	20	6	2	6	22	30	37	2	0	23.6%	.265/.392/.456	113	.311	2.0	RF(50): 5.9	1.6
2021	CHC	MLB	31	353	35	15	2	8	30	27	68	5	1	23.8%	.214/.280/.347	82	.247	2.4	RF(97): -0.8	0.4
2022 DC	*CHC*	*MLB*	*32*	*389*	*53*	*15*	*1*	*10*	*53*	*40*	*77*	*3*	*2*	*23.6%*	*.237/.324/.383*	*88*	*.279*	*-0.1*	*RF -1*	*0.4*

Comparables: Rusty Staub, Ruben Sierra, Ron Fairly

Heyward's contract is a useful shibboleth to determine if you're interested in talking to a fellow baseball fan for a whole game or would prefer to wander off in the direction of a concessions line. Mention of his underlying batted-ball data and hard-hit rates, the shortcomings of defensive metrics, his brave (and singular) protest against the murder of Jacob Blake by sitting out a game in 2020, the fact that he's one of the few MLB players to sport a wristband indicating support for fair pay for minor-leaguers, and the understanding that it is quite literally not our money? Congratulations, you've found a new baseball friend. Anything else, feel free to excuse yourself to find a Chicago Dog.

Nico Hoerner MI
Born: 05/13/97 Age: 25 Bats: R Throws: R Height: 6'1" Weight: 200 lb. Origin: Round 1, 2018 Draft (#24 overall)

YEAR	TEAM	LVL	AGE	PA	R	2B	3B	HR	RBI	BB	K	SB	CS	Whiff%	AVG/OBP/SLG	DRC+	BABIP	BRR	FRAA	WARP
2019	CUB2	ROK	22	21	2	1	0	0	0	1	1	0	0		.400/.429/.450		.421			
2019	TNS	AA	22	294	37	16	3	3	22	21	31	8	4		.284/.344/.399	119	.311	1.2	SS(44): -3.1, 2B(16): 0.4, CF(11): 2.5	1.9
2019	CHC	MLB	22	82	13	1	1	3	17	3	11	0	0	18.1%	.282/.305/.436	104	.292	0.3	SS(17): 0.7, 2B(1): 0.1, CF(1): -0.1	0.4
2020	CHC	MLB	23	126	19	4	0	0	13	12	24	3	2	18.3%	.222/.312/.259	94	.279	1.5	2B(37): 4.3, SS(10): 0.4, 3B(6): -0.8	0.8
2021	IOW	AAA	24	28	3	1	0	0	2	0	6	0	0		.269/.321/.308	89	.350	-0.1	2B(4): 0.1	0.1
2021	CHC	MLB	24	170	13	10	0	0	16	17	25	5	3	18.4%	.302/.382/.369	101	.360	-0.1	2B(30): 4.0, SS(12): -0.0, LF(3): -0.3	1.0
2022 DC	*CHC*	*MLB*	*25*	*434*	*59*	*19*	*1*	*8*	*60*	*34*	*66*	*8*	*3*	*18.6%*	*.261/.334/.384*	*93*	*.298*	*0.2*	*SS 1*	*1.4*

Comparables: Jean Segura, Erick Aybar, Howie Kendrick

The contact-allergic Cubs could have used his skillset this year, but a laundry list of maladies kept him off the field enough to etch the term "injury-prone" on his profile. He was once seen as the team's future at the keystone, but the acquisition of former Pac-12 rival and noted second baseman Nick Madrigal casts that future in doubt, although reportedly the two, who played together on the showcase circuit coming up in California, are excited to share the field in Chicago, with Hoerner volunteering to make way for Madrigal. As excited as they may be, two high-contact/low-power players is two too many according to some, especially when neither is a natural shortstop. Jed Hoyer's instinct to load up on contact players is understandable considering his team ranked dead last in that area in 2021, but taking two croissants at the breakfast buffet doesn't make up for skipping dinner the night prior.

Ed Howard SS
Born: 01/28/02 Age: 20 Bats: R Throws: R Height: 6'2" Weight: 185 lb. Origin: Round 1, 2020 Draft (#16 overall)

YEAR	TEAM	LVL	AGE	PA	R	2B	3B	HR	RBI	BB	K	SB	CS	Whiff%	AVG/OBP/SLG	DRC+	BABIP	BRR	FRAA	WARP
2021	MB	A	19	326	33	9	3	4	31	18	98	7	2		.225/.277/.315	75	.318	0.2	SS(58): -0.1, 2B(21): -4.4	-0.4
2022 non-DC	*CHC*	*MLB*	*20*	*251*	*17*	*9*	*1*	*2*	*19*	*12*	*83*	*3*	*1*	*33.6%*	*.203/.248/.287*	*42*	*.301*	*0.2*	*SS 0, 2B -1*	*-1.2*

Comparables: Luis Sardinas, Jonathan Araúz, Cole Tucker

The Cubs don't enjoy a surfeit of good press but were correctly awarded some for picking local kid Howard in the first round in 2020. Howard missed out on both his senior season of baseball and an opportunity to get a head start on pro ball, and his swing-and-miss issues were exacerbated by an aggressive assignment to full-season ball this year (the other option was to continue to develop him internally while waiting for the complex leagues to start in June). He improved every facet of his offensive game as the season went on, even getting his strikeouts down to 25% in August, and the five times he faced pitchers younger than him, he doubled, singled and got hit by a pitch. The bat remains a work in progress, but Howard's blue-chip defense stands out as superior even in a system heavy on shortstops. They don't call him "Silk" because he loves soy milk.

Kevin Made SS
Born: 09/10/02 Age: 19 Bats: R Throws: R Height: 5'10" Weight: 160 lb. Origin: International Free Agent, 2019

YEAR	TEAM	LVL	AGE	PA	R	2B	3B	HR	RBI	BB	K	SB	CS	Whiff%	AVG/OBP/SLG	DRC+	BABIP	BRR	FRAA	WARP
2021	MB	A	18	243	19	13	3	1	20	6	57	2	0		.272/.296/.366	88	.356	-2.6	SS(41): -1.7, 3B(13): 1.2	0.1
2022 non-DC	*CHC*	*MLB*	*19*	*251*	*18*	*11*	*1*	*1*	*19*	*9*	*67*	*0*	*1*	*29.1%*	*.234/.267/.318*	*55*	*.319*	*-0.1*	*SS 1, 3B 0*	*-0.5*

Comparables: Ronny Mauricio, Adrian Marin, Ruddy Giron

The aggressive Cubs sent their 2019 signing straight to full-season ball in 2021, where he warmed to the challenge over the course of the year after a slow start. Made (pronounced "mah-day") has quick hands and a mature plate approach for his age and experience, with an ability to make consistent hard contact that could develop into average power as he develops. He didn't take a lot of walks, but chalk that up to youthful exuberance at a high-level assignment for his first taste of pro ball. The Cubs have a surfeit of young shortstops in their system, but Made is among the most defensively gifted of the bunch and projects to stick at the position long-term.

Nick Madrigal 2B Born: 03/05/97 Age: 25 Bats: R Throws: R Height: 5'8" Weight: 175 lb. Origin: Round 1, 2018 Draft (#4 overall)

YEAR	TEAM	LVL	AGE	PA	R	2B	3B	HR	RBI	BB	K	SB	CS	Whiff%	AVG/OBP/SLG	DRC+	BABIP	BRR	FRAA	WARP
2019	WS	A+	22	218	20	10	2	2	27	17	6	17	4		.272/.346/.377	136	.269	4.5	2B(41): 3.9	2.5
2019	BIR	AA	22	180	30	11	2	1	16	14	5	14	6		.341/.400/.451	138	.348	0.7	2B(39): -1.0	1.5
2019	CHA	AAA	22	134	26	6	1	1	12	13	5	4	3		.331/.398/.424	114	.336	0.3	2B(28): 1.2	0.9
2020	CHW	MLB	23	109	8	3	0	0	11	4	7	2	1	10.8%	.340/.376/.369	117	.365	-1.9	2B(29): 1.5	0.5
2021	CHW	MLB	24	215	30	10	4	2	21	11	17	1	2	8.5%	.305/.349/.425	112	.324	-0.1	2B(53): -2.5	0.8
2022 DC	*CHC*	*MLB*	*25*	*460*	*67*	*20*	*3*	*5*	*78*	*27*	*28*	*14*	*8*	*9.2%*	*.288/.342/.387*	*102*	*.300*	*1.1*	*2B 0*	*2.0*

Comparables: Martín Prado, Kyle Seager, DJ LeMahieu

It's not often that contending teams trade their MLB-adjacent first-round draft picks. Even less often do they trade them to a crosstown rival for a reliever on the wrong side of 30. Pedigree and current production aside, the White Sox apparently deemed Madrigal replaceable after he'd missed most of the 2020 season with a separated shoulder and the 2021 season with a torn hamstring. The Final Boss of the Cubs' many high-contact, low-power prospects, Madrigal has a historically miniscule strikeout rate eclipsed only by his equally microscopic walk rate. Still, throughout his career, he's shown a preternatural ability to find holes in the infield and defeat whatever shift is deployed against him thanks to regularly spraying the ball all over the field. "Nicky Two Strikes" will find a legion of fans on the North Side who rode the streetcar to Wrigley eating 30-cent hot dogs, but he'll likely capture modern fans' hearts too, provided there's someone else in the lineup capable of bringing him home.

Rafael Ortega CF Born: 05/15/91 Age: 31 Bats: L Throws: R Height: 5'11" Weight: 180 lb. Origin: International Free Agent, 2008

YEAR	TEAM	LVL	AGE	PA	R	2B	3B	HR	RBI	BB	K	SB	CS	Whiff%	AVG/OBP/SLG	DRC+	BABIP	BRR	FRAA	WARP
2019	GWN	AAA	28	493	83	34	3	21	58	59	95	14	7		.285/.373/.524	123	.323	2.5	CF(61): 3.4, RF(29): 2.5, LF(10): -0.2	3.7
2019	ATL	MLB	28	96	7	3	0	2	10	8	22	3	0	21.9%	.205/.271/.307	84	.250	0.6	LF(20): -1.0, RF(6): -0.0, CF(3): -0.0	0.1
2020	ORI	WIN	29	152	23	8	1	4	20	26	15	2	1		.301/.427/.480		.317			
2021	IOW	AAA	30	73	11	3	0	4	11	8	13	1	1		.250/.333/.484	123	.255	-0.2	RF(16): 1.2, C(1): 0.0	0.5
2021	CHC	MLB	30	330	44	14	2	11	33	30	70	12	6	21.5%	.291/.360/.463	103	.349	-0.6	CF(73): -8.2, LF(13): 0.1, RF(13): -0.6	0.5
2022 DC	*CHC*	*MLB*	*31*	*526*	*83*	*23*	*3*	*13*	*59*	*48*	*109*	*13*	*4*	*21.7%*	*.241/.316/.387*	*88*	*.289*	*0.9*	*CF -2*	*1.0*

Comparables: Abraham Almonte, Ezequiel Carrera, Gorkys Hernández

After ping-ponging around the league as a Quad-A player for the past decade, he found an everyday home with the Zombie Cubs despite some of the league's wildest lefty/righty splits. Wisdom and his 30 home runs get all the glory, but Ortega struck out about half as often with a fair amount of his own power production and better on-base skills. It was a credible audition for a team that can afford to use him as a bench bat against righties.

Yohendrick Pinango OF Born: 05/07/02 Age: 20 Bats: L Throws: L Height: 5'11" Weight: 170 lb. Origin: International Free Agent, 2018

YEAR	TEAM	LVL	AGE	PA	R	2B	3B	HR	RBI	BB	K	SB	CS	Whiff%	AVG/OBP/SLG	DRC+	BABIP	BRR	FRAA	WARP
2019	DSL CUB1	ROK	17	274	43	20	0	0	36	27	20	27	7		.358/.427/.442		.386			
2021	MB	A	19	351	50	16	2	4	27	24	57	8	2		.272/.322/.370	104	.317	0.6	LF(41): -5.1, RF(21): 3.0, CF(1): -0.1	1.2
2021	SB	A+	19	105	9	4	1	1	9	7	12	0	0		.289/.343/.381	117	.321	-1.5	LF(22): 1.0, RF(2): 0.2	0.5
2022 non-DC	*CHC*	*MLB*	*20*	*251*	*20*	*10*	*1*	*2*	*20*	*13*	*45*	*7*	*3*	*20.8%*	*.247/.290/.332*	*69*	*.297*	*0.6*	*LF 0, RF 1*	*-0.1*

Comparables: Juan Soto, Dylan Carlson, Nick Weglarz

The team zoomed him all the way up to High-A as a 19-year-old in his first stateside action; that's a lot to put on Pinango's sturdy-looking but low-to-the-ground shoulders. He'll produce some pull power with an easy, pretty lefty swing and a strong lower half, but he needs to stick in center for the bat to play, so he can't get too beefed-out. There's a little bit of a Short Man Complex here, and Pinango plays bigger than he is, with swagger and an intensity befitting his fireplug stature that will endear him to Cubs fans, if not evaluators.

★ ★ ★ *2022 Top 101 Prospect* **#79** ★ ★ ★

Reginald Preciado IF Born: 05/16/03 Age: 19 Bats: S Throws: R Height: 6'4" Weight: 185 lb. Origin: International Free Agent, 2019

YEAR	TEAM	LVL	AGE	PA	R	2B	3B	HR	RBI	BB	K	SB	CS	Whiff%	AVG/OBP/SLG	DRC+	BABIP	BRR	FRAA	WARP
2021	CUB	ROK	18	154	28	10	3	3	25	11	35	7	1		.333/.383/.511		.423			
2022															*No projection*					

Comparables: Pedro Guerrero, Seth Moranda, Jose Luis Javier

Continuing the Cubs' series of Designer Imposters, NL Central Prospect edition, Preciado has a frame reminiscent of Pittsburgh's Oneil Cruz, with extra-long levers that have gotten beefier as he's matured and started a pro training regimen. Like Cruz, Preciado also burst onto the scene as a prospect with an electrifying performance that made the Cubs' complex league must-see for scouts. He also carries similar question marks about his ability to stick at shortstop due to his frame, and most see him eventually moving over to the hot corner, where his arm strength and athleticism should help him find a soft landing. Currently a switch-hitter, Preciado makes more consistent contact than might be expected; the next step is to turn that contact into consistent quality contact. He's also weirdly slow for someone with legs longer than I-90, proving that even in the best dupes, a little something always gets lost in translation.

Harold Ramirez OF Born: 09/06/94 Age: 27 Bats: R Throws: R Height: 5'10" Weight: 232 lb. Origin: International Free Agent, 2011

YEAR	TEAM	LVL	AGE	PA	R	2B	3B	HR	RBI	BB	K	SB	CS	Whiff%	AVG/OBP/SLG	DRC+	BABIP	BRR	FRAA	WARP
2019	NO	AAA	24	120	19	12	1	4	14	6	19	1	1		.355/.408/.591	112	.402	-2.6	LF(16): -0.7, RF(8): 0.3	0.3
2019	MIA	MLB	24	446	54	20	3	11	50	18	91	2	1	25.7%	.276/.312/.416	90	.328	-0.5	LF(61): 5.3, RF(55): -2.6, CF(27): 2.8	1.5
2020	MIA	MLB	25	11	2	0	0	0	1	1	2	0	1	29.2%	.200/.273/.200	96	.250	0.0	RF(2): -0.1	0.0
2021	CLE	MLB	26	361	33	21	1	7	41	14	56	3	1	23.8%	.268/.305/.398	96	.301	-1.0	LF(49): -0.8, RF(34): 2.5, CF(20): -1.2	1.1
2022 DC	*CHC*	*MLB*	*27*	*96*	*12*	*4*	*0*	*2*	*14*	*4*	*16*	*0*	*1*	*23.8%*	*.272/.317/.406*	*92*	*.315*	*-0.1*	*LF 1*	*0.3*

Comparables: José Osuna, Jorge Bonifacio, Moisés Sierra

Claimed by Cleveland off waivers this spring, Ramirez's mediocrity perfectly mimicked that of his new team. His "good" plate discipline is borne of aggression, and his frequent contact lacks the consistent efficacy required for respectable production. Meanwhile, he fails to take advantage of his upper-decile speed. He split time nearly evenly among the three outfield positions, so at least there's value, and perhaps solace, to be found in that kind of utility. Cleveland traded him to the Cubs, who'll search for that value, for cash.

Alfonso Rivas 1B/LF Born: 09/13/96 Age: 25 Bats: L Throws: L Height: 5'11" Weight: 190 lb. Origin: Round 4, 2018 Draft (#113 overall)

YEAR	TEAM	LVL	AGE	PA	R	2B	3B	HR	RBI	BB	K	SB	CS	Whiff%	AVG/OBP/SLG	DRC+	BABIP	BRR	FRAA	WARP
2019	MSS	WIN	22	60	8	7	0	0	7	10	17	0	0		.306/.417/.449		.455			
2019	STK	A+	22	509	60	24	3	8	55	66	113	2	2		.283/.383/.408	114	.362	-1.2	1B(98): -0.4, LF(8): -0.5, RF(2): 0.1	2.1
2019	LV	AAA	22	34	2	2	1	1	5	2	7	0	0		.406/.441/.625	93	.500	-2.4	1B(7): -0.1, LF(1): 0.1	-0.2
2021	IOW	AAA	24	237	22	13	0	4	32	35	49	0	1		.284/.405/.411	115	.361	-2.6	1B(46): 6.6, LF(9): -1.2, RF(1): -0.5	1.2
2021	CHC	MLB	24	49	7	1	0	1	3	4	16	0	0	26.4%	.318/.388/.409	76	.481	0.2	1B(5): -0.1, LF(5): 0.1, RF(5): -0.8	0.0
2022 DC	*CHC*	*MLB*	*25*	*128*	*16*	*5*	*0*	*2*	*15*	*13*	*31*	*0*	*1*	*24.4%*	*.235/.325/.350*	*83*	*.310*	*-0.1*	*1B 0, LF 0*	*0.0*

Comparables: Chris Parmelee, Ike Davis, David Cooper

Contact-oriented but low-power hitters are about as fashionable in today's game as a beeper belt clip and permed bangs. Still, like your weird neighbor stacking up Blu-rays in his garage, the Cubs seem to be planning for a run on this type of player. Rivas' profile is complicated by being limited to a corner spot, and although he's an excellent defensive first baseman, a lack of over-the-fence power tightens the band of successful outcomes here. He's hit well since he was in college, and didn't look entirely overmatched in a brief MLB sample before going down with an injury to a tendon in his finger, but those hoping for a power breakout will likely be disappointed. Rivas lives on base, though, and can help out a team that ranked in the bottom third of OBP in 2021.

Frank Schwindel 1B Born: 06/29/92 Age: 30 Bats: R Throws: R Height: 6'1" Weight: 220 lb. Origin: Round 18, 2013 Draft (#534 overall)

YEAR	TEAM	LVL	AGE	PA	R	2B	3B	HR	RBI	BB	K	SB	CS	Whiff%	AVG/OBP/SLG	DRC+	BABIP	BRR	FRAA	WARP
2019	ERI	AA	27	188	21	8	0	5	23	11	27	0	0		.257/.309/.392	109	.275	-2.8	1B(21): -0.2	0.4
2019	TOL	AAA	27	119	21	7	0	9	33	6	19	0	0		.327/.361/.628	123	.329	-0.2	1B(25): 0.3, RF(2): 0.2, LF(1): -0.4	0.5
2019	OMA	AAA	27	76	8	4	0	1	10	4	13	0	1		.186/.237/.286	93	.211	-0.3	1B(13): -0.3	0.0
2019	KC	MLB	27	15	0	0	0	0	0	0	2	0	0	13.8%	.067/.067/.067	101	.077		1B(5): -0.4	0.0
2021	IOW	AAA	29	39	2	1	0	1	8	1	10	0	0		.189/.205/.297	86	.222		1B(6): -1.0	-0.1
2021	LV	AAA	29	207	42	11	0	16	41	13	35	0	0		.317/.362/.630	127	.312	-2.1	1B(42): 3.9	1.3
2021	OAK	MLB	29	20	2	1	0	1	3	0	5	0	0	27.9%	.150/.150/.350	101	.143	0.0		0.1
2021	CHC	MLB	29	239	42	19	1	13	40	16	36	2	1	22.8%	.342/.389/.613	131	.364	0.0	1B(51): 1.6	1.6
2022 DC	*CHC*	*MLB*	*30*	*501*	*85*	*26*	*0*	*21*	*79*	*27*	*86*	*0*	*1*	*23.8%*	*.265/.313/.461*	*101*	*.289*	*-0.8*	*1B 0*	*0.6*

Comparables: Efren Navarro, Peter O'Brien, Rob Segedin

Chicago was built on heavy industry, so it's a clever bit of nominative determinism that the 2021 Cubs should be led offensively by a man with both the name and the countenance of one of those early 1900s meatpackers. Schwindel (Schlemiel! Schlimazel!) is a throwback to those good-natured, industrious fellows, a lifetime minor-leaguer who doesn't strike out much, takes his walks, makes a ton of contact and sprays the ball around the field. Schwindel was blocked by Eric Hosmer in Kansas City and then Anthony Rizzo in Chicago, and it took the Chicago Fire Sale to clear a spot for him. He's certainly made the most of his opportunity and brought Cubs fans much-needed delight with his competent, joyful style of play in a lost year, which is about all one can hope for from Rickettspfeffer Incorporated.

★ ★ ★ *2022 Top 101 Prospect* **#101** ★ ★ ★

James Triantos SS Born: 01/29/03 Age: 19 Bats: R Throws: R Height: 6'1" Weight: 195 lb. Origin: Round 2, 2021 Draft (#56 overall)

YEAR	TEAM	LVL	AGE	PA	R	2B	3B	HR	RBI	BB	K	SB	CS	Whiff%	AVG/OBP/SLG	DRC+	BABIP	BRR	FRAA	WARP
2021	CUB	ROK	18	109	27	7	1	6	19	7	18	3	3		.327/.376/.594		.351			
2022															*No projection*					

Comparables: Angel Rodriguez, Yoelfi Suriel, Beicker Mendoza

The Cubs went almost a million dollars overslot to sign him, which indicates how highly they valued the at-times-polarizing infielder, a pop-up prep prospect in the 2021 draft class. Scouts love his quality of contact, which is like an Olivia Rodrigo song: loud, teenaged and unrelenting. Young for his draft class, Triantos nonetheless rewarded the Cubs' faith in him with a blistering performance in the ACL, where he showcased both those barrels and a surprisingly mature strike zone approach with very little whiffs. The Cubs worked him at second base in Arizona, inviting Nick Yorke comparisons. He also got reps at shortstop, but the consensus is he won't stick there, although should have the athleticism to remain on the dirt. It doesn't matter where he ends up defensively, as the bat is special enough to play anywhere. Good 4 u, James.

Patrick Wisdom 3B Born: 08/27/91 Age: 30 Bats: R Throws: R Height: 6'2" Weight: 220 lb. Origin: Round 1, 2012 Draft (#52 overall)

YEAR	TEAM	LVL	AGE	PA	R	2B	3B	HR	RBI	BB	K	SB	CS	Whiff%	AVG/OBP/SLG	DRC+	BABIP	BRR	FRAA	WARP
2019	NAS	AAA	27	453	68	15	0	31	74	53	125	8	2		.240/.332/.513	110	.266	1.0	3B(56): 2.4, LF(16): -1.1, 1B(14): -0.7	2.1
2019	TEX	MLB	27	28	1	1	0	0	1	1	15	0	0	29.0%	.154/.185/.192	48	.364	-0.3	1B(5): -0.3, 3B(4): -0.1	-0.2
2020	CHC	MLB	28	2	0	0	0	0	0	0	0	0	0	33.3%	.000/.000/.000	108			1B(2): -0.0	0.0
2021	IOW	AAA	29	34	7	1	0	3	11	6	12	1	0		.160/.353/.560	107	.091	0.0	3B(3): -0.3, LF(1): 0.0	0.1
2021	CHC	MLB	29	375	54	13	0	28	61	32	153	4	1	41.3%	.231/.305/.518	93	.318	2.4	3B(77): 4.6, LF(15): 0.2, 1B(13): -1.1	1.6
2022 DC	*CHC*	*MLB*	*30*	*553*	*85*	*21*	*0*	*29*	*90*	*51*	*215*	*3*	*2*	*39.8%*	*.202/.289/.424*	*81*	*.288*	*-0.5*	*3B 1, 1B -1*	*-0.2*

Comparables: Danny Valencia, Todd Frazier, Conor Gillaspie

As Apple endeavors to make once-necessary items like home buttons and headphone jacks obsolete, so does Wisdom suggest the Three True Outcomes player is a relic, unwieldy as an onboard CD drive. Why have three where two will do? It's a calculation that only works if the player in question is possessed with Wisdom's Ruthian power. His gaudy home run totals balance out the equally gaudy-but-in-the-bad-way strikeout rate, and there's a real question as to whether he'll ever see a fastball in the zone again, as he whiffs over half the time on off-speed along and has a propensity for chasing high heat. Wisdom believers point to former teammate Kyle Schwarber, who also had to learn to cut down on his whiffs, but it's likely Wisdom's strike zone approach is, to borrow another bygone tech term, WYSIWYG (What You See Is What You Get). That means he'll have to keep hitting the perfectly optimized snot out of the ball every time he can make contact, a line that demands more delicate balance than placing your iPhone on an airplane sink.

PITCHERS

Cory Abbott RHP Born: 09/20/95 Age: 26 Bats: R Throws: R Height: 6'1" Weight: 210 lb. Origin: Round 2, 2017 Draft (#67 overall)

YEAR	TEAM	LVL	AGE	W	L	SV	G	GS	IP	H	HR	BB/9	K/9	K	GB%	BABIP	WHIP	ERA	DRA-	WARP	MPH	FB%	Whiff%	CSP
2019	TNS	AA	23	8	8	0	26	26	146^{2}	112	15	3.2	10.2	166	37.5%	.270	1.12	3.01	80	2.5				
2021	IOW	AAA	25	5	6	0	19	19	96	97	20	5.0	12.2	130	35.1%	.338	1.56	5.91	98	1.4				
2021	CHC	MLB	25	0	0	0	7	1	17^{1}	20	7	5.7	6.2	12	37.3%	.255	1.79	6.75	124	-0.1	92.7	59.1%	20.5%	51.6%
2022 DC	*CHC*	*MLB*	*26*	*6*	*4*	*0*	*48*	*4*	*58*	*55*	*10*	*4.6*	*8.7*	*56*	*36.6%*	*.288*	*1.46*	*5.20*	*115*	*-0.2*	*92.7*	*59.1%*	*20.5%*	*51.6%*

Comparables: Jimmy Lambert, Eddie Butler, Williams Pérez

Brief, unsuccessful big-league debut aside, he's one of the Cubs' better MLB-adjacent depth starters, even though his pitch arsenal—led by a killer slider he learned from studying videos of Noah Syndergaard—might better suit a long relief role. A swing-and-miss curveball and ability to spin a fastball up in the zone, which helped him lead the Double-A Southern League in strikeouts in 2019, buoy the hopes of those who see him with back-end starter potential.

Jason Adam RHP Born: 08/04/91 Age: 30 Bats: R Throws: R Height: 6'3" Weight: 229 lb. Origin: Round 5, 2010 Draft (#149 overall)

YEAR	TEAM	LVL	AGE	W	L	SV	G	GS	IP	H	HR	BB/9	K/9	K	GB%	BABIP	WHIP	ERA	DRA-	WARP	MPH	FB%	Whiff%	CSP
2019	BUF	AAA	27	1	3	1	11	0	14	10	2	3.2	12.9	20	16.1%	.276	1.07	2.57	81	0.3				
2019	TOR	MLB	27	3	0	0	23	0	21^{2}	15	1	4.2	7.5	18	26.7%	.237	1.15	2.91	126	-0.1	94.6	61.4%	27.8%	41.5%
2020	CHC	MLB	28	2	1	0	13	0	13^{2}	9	2	5.3	13.8	21	37.9%	.259	1.24	3.29	86	0.3	94.9	53.8%	41.7%	42.3%
2021	IOW	AAA	29	1	0	1	5	0	6^{1}	4	0	1.4	8.5	6	23.5%	.235	0.79	0.00	100	0.1				
2021	CHC	MLB	29	1	0	0	12	0	10^{2}	10	1	5.1	16.0	19	36.4%	.429	1.50	5.91	71	0.3	94.1	57.3%	34.0%	50.6%
2022 non-DC	*CHC*	*MLB*	*30*	*2*	*2*	*0*	*57*	*0*	*50*	*40*	*9*	*4.0*	*11.4*	*63*	*31.6%*	*.282*	*1.27*	*4.36*	*97*	*0.3*	*94.5*	*57.2%*	*35.0%*	*45.6%*

Comparables: Miguel Socolovich, Wander Suero, Jeurys Familia

Mere weeks after suffering an ankle injury so gruesome he worried he might lose the foot, Adam was posting Instagram Reels of himself on his tricked-out scooter set to Chamillionaire's "Ridin." This strikes us as the right kind of mindset to tackle the ups and downs of reliever life. It's a shame he got injured, as he was maybe headed for some of the ups: during his time with the Cubs organization, his strikeout rate is a career high thanks to some significant 12-6 drop he's added to his slider that gets batters swangin' right over the top of it.

Adbert Alzolay RHP Born: 03/01/95 Age: 27 Bats: R Throws: R Height: 6'1" Weight: 208 lb. Origin: International Free Agent, 2012

YEAR	TEAM	LVL	AGE	W	L	SV	G	GS	IP	H	HR	BB/9	K/9	K	GB%	BABIP	WHIP	ERA	DRA-	WARP	MPH	FB%	Whiff%	CSP
2019	IOW	AAA	24	2	4	0	15	15	65^{1}	53	10	4.3	12.5	91	32.1%	.295	1.29	4.41	83	1.1				
2019	CHC	MLB	24	1	1	0	4	2	12^{1}	13	4	6.6	9.5	13	32.4%	.273	1.78	7.30	107	0.1	94.6	57.3%	26.7%	44.1%
2020	CHC	MLB	25	1	1	0	6	4	21^{1}	12	1	5.5	12.2	29	43.2%	.256	1.17	2.95	86	0.4	94.7	52.2%	27.5%	47.1%
2021	CHC	MLB	26	5	13	1	29	21	125^{2}	112	25	2.4	9.2	128	43.8%	.270	1.16	4.58	83	2.3	93.8	52.6%	27.1%	56.4%
2022 DC	*CHC*	*MLB*	*27*	*8*	*7*	*0*	*25*	*25*	*129.3*	*124*	*20*	*3.3*	*9.7*	*139*	*41.1%*	*.307*	*1.33*	*4.47*	*101*	*0.9*	*94.0*	*52.7%*	*27.1%*	*54.9%*

Comparables: James McDonald, Framber Valdez, Lance Lynn

A new grip on his slider learned at the alternate site in 2020 resulted in a pitch that is sharper, harder and generates more whiffs; it also tunnels extremely well with his two-seamer, the two parting ways at the last minute like a couple who bickered in the taxi on the way to the party. That hasn't kept the sinker from getting pasted, however—a condition that contributed to the extreme lefty splits problem, which is what triggered a move to the bullpen in the first place. Meanwhile, Alzolay has seemingly scrapped his curveball entirely, a pitch with potential for whiffs and weak contact, and rarely uses his changeup, which has good run away from lefties and could help ameliorate his splits issue. Perhaps focusing on mastering just two pitches is a good way to rein in Alzolay's occasional wandering command, but with the Cubs' checkered history in producing homegrown pitching, it would certainly be preferable to see him back in the rotation.

Dakota Chalmers RHP Born: 10/08/96 Age: 25 Bats: R Throws: R Height: 6'3" Weight: 175 lb. Origin: Round 3, 2015 Draft (#97 overall)

YEAR	TEAM	LVL	AGE	W	L	SV	G	GS	IP	H	HR	BB/9	K/9	K	GB%	BABIP	WHIP	ERA	DRA-	WARP	MPH	FB%	Whiff%	CSP
2019	TWI	ROK	22	1	0	0	4	4	13^1	8	0	5.4	12.8	19	64.0%	.320	1.20	4.05						
2019	FTM	A+	22	1	1	0	5	5	21^1	12	0	6.3	12.2	29	54.5%	.273	1.27	3.38	88	0.4				
2021	TNS	AA	24	2	5	0	15	14	57	47	9	5.5	9.9	63	37.3%	.270	1.44	5.37	98	0.6				
2021	WCH	AA	24	0	0	0	5	2	12^1	10	5	10.9	9.5	13	26.5%	.172	2.03	9.49	131	-0.1				
2022 non-DC	*CHC*	*MLB*	*25*	*2*	*3*	*0*	*57*	*0*	*50*	*52*	*9*	*7.6*	*9.0*	*50*	*36.8%*	*.316*	*1.90*	*7.37*	*147*	*-1.0*				

Comparables: Delvin James, Jared Hughes, Parker Bridwell

With the Cubs, Chalmers is back to being stretched out as a starter, and is learning to stop trying to overpower hitters with velocity alone. They've also had him reintroduce a slider he had faded with the Twins, with the goal of giving him more options for setting up his curveball. Command remains an issue, but there's been genuine improvement for the beleaguered former top prospect, and although he's a minor-league free agent now, a mutually beneficial reunion seems likely.

Zach Davies RHP Born: 02/07/93 Age: 29 Bats: R Throws: R Height: 6'0" Weight: 180 lb. Origin: Round 26, 2011 Draft (#785 overall)

YEAR	TEAM	LVL	AGE	W	L	SV	G	GS	IP	H	HR	BB/9	K/9	K	GB%	BABIP	WHIP	ERA	DRA-	WARP	MPH	FB%	Whiff%	CSP
2019	MIL	MLB	26	10	7	0	31	31	159^2	155	20	2.9	5.7	102	39.1%	.276	1.29	3.55	115	0.3	88.5	52.6%	17.4%	44.4%
2020	SD	MLB	27	7	4	0	12	12	69^1	55	9	2.5	8.2	63	40.7%	.250	1.07	2.73	91	1.1	88.6	39.1%	25.6%	43.7%
2021	CHC	MLB	28	6	12	0	32	32	148	162	25	4.6	6.9	114	41.4%	.311	1.60	5.78	121	-0.3	88.1	52.3%	22.5%	49.4%
2022 DC	*FA*	*MLB*	*29*	*9*	*9*	*0*	*29*	*29*	*154.3*	*161*	*24*	*3.7*	*7.7*	*132*	*41.9%*	*.305*	*1.45*	*5.01*	*113*	*0.2*	*88.3*	*50.1%*	*21.9%*	*47.4%*

Comparables: Edwin Jackson, Jeff Suppan, Jason Marquis

Despite looking like a boy dispatched to fetch the town doctor in a 1930s-set melodrama, the featherweight hurler was just as durable in 2021 as he's been throughout his career, logging the Cubs' second-highest number of innings in his first year after coming over in the Yu Darvish trade. Unfortunately that's about all that went right in a career-worst year that will see the 28-year-old headed into free agency labeled as a "buy-low project" for some enterprising (read: cheap) team. Davies has never been a strikeout pitcher, relying instead on getting weak contact on his plus changeup, which works as long as he's commanding the strike zone. Umpires' decreasing leniency toward edge pitches forced him into the zone, where he got barrelled up with alarming frequency. The best-case outlook for him is for a team with hard throwers (that is, not Kyle Hendricks and Alec Mills) to sign him as a change-of-pace arm, and for called strikes to come back into vogue. Please, my strike zone. It is very sick.

Anderson Espinoza RHP Born: 03/09/98 Age: 24 Bats: R Throws: R Height: 6'0" Weight: 190 lb. Origin: International Free Agent, 2014

YEAR	TEAM	LVL	AGE	W	L	SV	G	GS	IP	H	HR	BB/9	K/9	K	GB%	BABIP	WHIP	ERA	DRA-	WARP	MPH	FB%	Whiff%	CSP
2021	SB	A+	23	1	2	0	5	5	16	10	1	6.2	15.2	27	27.6%	.321	1.31	5.06	74	0.4				
2021	FW	A+	23	0	1	0	12	12	28^2	29	3	4.1	11.6	37	44.6%	.366	1.47	5.02	76	0.7				
2021	TNS	AA	23	0	0	0	3	3	13^1	11	0	5.4	10.8	16	51.6%	.355	1.43	1.35	93	0.2				
2022 DC	*CHC*	*MLB*	*24*	*0*	*0*	*0*	*3*	*3*	*12.7*	*12*	*2*	*5.6*	*9.5*	*13*	*40.6%*	*.303*	*1.58*	*5.54*	*117*	*0.0*				

Comparables: Dan Smith, Jeanmar Gómez, Matt Moore

A former top prospect whose career was derailed by two Tommy John surgeries, he's a project the rebuilding Cubs can afford to roster on the 40-man now that he's no longer the fresh-faced teeanger he was out of Venezuela. His six-foot frame might limit him to the bullpen, but his velocity is rebounding back to 95-97 to pair with his gyro-spin slider, making a relief profile more appealing. He also has two more potential swing-and-miss weapons in a plus curveball and changeup. The change lagged behind the curve in a return to the mound after a five-year layoff, but that's common for TJ recoveries. Similarly, command is slow to return after TJ, and Espinoza earned praise for his preternatural control as a teenager, so it's likely the walk numbers will improve, even if his prospects to join the starting rotation do not.

Drew Gray LHP Born: 05/10/03 Age: 19 Bats: L Throws: L Height: 6'3" Weight: 190 lb. Origin: Round 3, 2021 Draft (#93 overall)

Gray's combination of attributes is very much en vogue among analytically-focused FO's right now. Like one of Stefon's clubs, this kid has everything: a fastball with plus spin (anywhere between 2600-2700, and reportedly up to 2800 rpm) that generates whiffs up in the zone, a sweeping slider and a true 12-6 curveball. There was some question about how the two-way player, raw even for a prep prospect, would perform as a full-time pitcher as a pro, but Gray dazzled in a four-inning sample in the ACL, striking out nine and walking just one.

Kyle Hendricks RHP Born: 12/07/89 Age: 32 Bats: R Throws: R Height: 6'3" Weight: 190 lb. Origin: Round 8, 2011 Draft (#264 overall)

YEAR	TEAM	LVL	AGE	W	L	SV	G	GS	IP	H	HR	BB/9	K/9	K	GB%	BABIP	WHIP	ERA	DRA-	WARP	MPH	FB%	Whiff%	CSP
2019	CHC	MLB	29	11	10	0	30	30	177	168	19	1.6	7.6	150	41.1%	.292	1.13	3.46	85	3.2	86.9	62.2%	22.0%	53.0%
2020	CHC	MLB	30	6	5	0	12	12	81^1	73	10	0.9	7.1	64	47.1%	.272	1.00	2.88	86	1.5	87.6	54.5%	25.0%	51.7%
2021	CHC	MLB	31	14	7	0	32	32	181	200	31	2.2	6.5	131	43.4%	.302	1.35	4.77	115	0.2	87.5	60.5%	20.1%	54.2%
2022 DC	*CHC*	*MLB*	*32*	*10*	*9*	*0*	*27*	*27*	*165*	*175*	*25*	*2.0*	*6.6*	*120*	*43.7%*	*.297*	*1.28*	*4.45*	*104*	*1.0*	*87.4*	*59.8%*	*21.3%*	*53.5%*

Comparables: Bronson Arroyo, Bartolo Colon, James Shields

There will be many who look at Hendricks' season numbers and feel vindicated that the collapse they predicted for him two or three administrations ago has finally come to pass and he is cooked. But the thing about being a pitcher of Hendricks' caliber is there's just not that far to fall. Ooh, he throws 87.3 now instead of 87.4, alert the authorities. The thing to look at in Hendricks' season are his numbers before and after the trade deadline. Prior to the deadline, he had a 3.85 ERA with a walk rate under 5%. After the Cubs traded away all of his co-workers, his ERA shot up to 6.67, with a walk rate of 7%, a loss of productivity that's relatable for anyone who's been working from home the past year-plus. Barring some kind of trade, Cubs fans can look forward to at least two more years of Hendricks swanning around Wrigley like Norma Desmond insisting he's still big; it's the other pitchers that got small.

DJ Herz LHP

Born: 01/04/01 Age: 21 Bats: R Throws: L Height: 6'2" Weight: 175 lb. Origin: Round 8, 2019 Draft (#252 overall)

YEAR	TEAM	LVL	AGE	W	L	SV	G	GS	IP	H	HR	BB/9	K/9	K	GB%	BABIP	WHIP	ERA	DRA-	WARP	MPH	FB%	Whiff%	CSP
2019	CUB2	ROK	18	0	1	0	6	6	10^1	10	0	7.0	7.0	8	41.2%	.294	1.74	2.61						
2021	MB	A	20	3	4	0	17	17	65^2	32	6	5.2	14.4	105	30.9%	.252	1.07	3.43	81	1.3				
2021	SB	A+	20	1	0	0	3	3	16	10	1	3.4	14.6	26	51.6%	.300	1.00	2.81	76	0.4				
2022 non-DC	*CHC*	*MLB*	*21*	*2*	*3*	*0*	*57*	*0*	*50*	*42*	*8*	*6.0*	*11.4*	*63*	*34.2%*	*.290*	*1.51*	*5.21*	*115*	*-0.2*				

Comparables: Jaret Wright, Brad Hand, Franklin Morales

A pop-up prospect who flew under the radar due to draft position and the shutdown, Herz is opening plenty of eyes now that he's shown two things that excite evaluators and casual fans alike: a massive strikeout rate and a fastball that's added some ticks to land comfortably in the mid-90s. The velocity gains aren't held consistently yet, but he's already added strength and looks to add more to his 6'2" frame. His sharp-breaking curve elicits some truly hideous swings, and he's starting to work in a promising changeup. The fastball plays up even further thanks to his deceptive delivery, although the effort involved in that deception increases the reliever risk. Given the number of actual relievers the Cubs spent high draft picks on in the past two Drafts, it would behoove them to keep developing him as a starter for as long as possible, even if the fastball-slider combo could play in the bigs much sooner.

Codi Heuer RHP

Born: 07/03/96 Age: 26 Bats: R Throws: R Height: 6'5" Weight: 200 lb. Origin: Round 6, 2018 Draft (#168 overall)

YEAR	TEAM	LVL	AGE	W	L	SV	G	GS	IP	H	HR	BB/9	K/9	K	GB%	BABIP	WHIP	ERA	DRA-	WARP	MPH	FB%	Whiff%	CSP
2019	WS	A+	22	4	1	2	20	0	38^1	34	0	1.9	10.1	43	61.9%	.327	1.10	2.82	85	0.7				
2019	BIR	AA	22	2	3	9	22	0	29^1	25	0	2.1	6.7	22	59.8%	.298	1.09	1.84	87	0.4				
2020	CHW	MLB	23	3	0	1	21	0	23^2	12	1	3.4	9.5	25	50.0%	.193	0.89	1.52	87	0.4	97.8	65.8%	33.9%	46.6%
2021	CHC	MLB	24	3	3	2	25	0	28^2	20	2	4.1	5.3	17	42.9%	.225	1.15	3.14	121	-0.1	95.0	61.2%	25.9%	54.4%
2021	CHW	MLB	24	4	1	0	40	0	38^2	45	5	2.3	9.1	39	43.1%	.367	1.42	5.12	91	0.5	96.6	53.1%	29.5%	54.9%
2022 DC	*CHC*	*MLB*	*25*	*3*	*3*	*7*	*67*	*0*	*58*	*57*	*7*	*3.3*	*8.4*	*54*	*47.0%*	*.307*	*1.35*	*4.30*	*99*	*0.2*	*96.2*	*58.0%*	*29.2%*	*53.2%*

Comparables: Mark Lowe, Dominic Leone, Cla Meredith

Like the vowel placement in his name, Heuer's sinker was all over the place when he arrived on the North Side. The Cubs have attempted to address that issue by turning one pitch into two, each with separate, consistent movement profiles, and encouraging him to throw each with particular intent: the four-seamer up in the zone with ride, and the two-seamer with true sinking action. Results so far are mixed, and a precipitous drop in strikeouts has made some Cubs faithful suspect their crosstown rivals sent them a lemon, but the underlying metrics suggest he's fine, still getting swinging strikes and limiting hard contact. The Cubs are also encouraging him to lean less heavily on his fastball and focus on his more whiff-producing secondaries in the slider and changeup. Heuer has punched above his draft position since he went pro, making him an excellent match for the perpetual-underdog Cubs, so Cubs fans on Twitter might want to mind their manners when gnashing their teeth about his latest performance.

Ryan Jensen RHP

Born: 11/23/97 Age: 24 Bats: R Throws: R Height: 6'0" Weight: 190 lb. Origin: Round 1, 2019 Draft (#27 overall)

YEAR	TEAM	LVL	AGE	W	L	SV	G	GS	IP	H	HR	BB/9	K/9	K	GB%	BABIP	WHIP	ERA	DRA-	WARP	MPH	FB%	Whiff%	CSP
2019	EUG	SS	21	0	0	0	6	6	12	7	0	10.5	14.3	19	68.2%	.318	1.75	2.25						
2021	SB	A+	23	2	7	0	16	16	62	42	8	3.5	10.9	75	53.3%	.239	1.06	4.50	78	1.4				
2021	TNS	AA	23	1	0	0	4	4	18	14	2	3.5	7.5	15	60.4%	.261	1.17	3.00	99	0.2				
2022 non-DC	*CHC*	*MLB*	*24*	*2*	*3*	*0*	*57*	*0*	*50*	*50*	*6*	*4.6*	*8.1*	*45*	*49.6%*	*.306*	*1.52*	*5.02*	*115*	*-0.2*				

Comparables: Brandon Bielak, Alex Colomé, Yennsy Díaz

Another college arm with relief experience drafted highly by the Cubs before their recent fire sale, Jensen should return to a relief role at the major-league level. He's on the shorter side, with a long arm action, sub-par control and one current above-average pitch. The fastball is plus to double-plus, however, a high-octane offering that can scrape triple digits and also comes in a two-seam sinking version for even more whiffs. Jensen also throws a power curve the Cubs helped him develop, a changeup he relies on when his fastball command deserts him and a slider that has flashed plus but lacks consistency. Jensen's walk rate is unsightly, but he did cut the free passes down in the second half of the season. The Cubs seem committed to continuing to develop him as a starter for now; we'll see if it lasts.

Caleb Kilian RHP

Born: 06/02/97 Age: 25 Bats: R Throws: R Height: 6'4" Weight: 180 lb. Origin: Round 8, 2019 Draft (#236 overall)

YEAR	TEAM	LVL	AGE	W	L	SV	G	GS	IP	H	HR	BB/9	K/9	K	GB%	BABIP	WHIP	ERA	DRA-	WARP	MPH	FB%	Whiff%	CSP
2019	GIO	ROK	22	0	0	0	6	5	12	6	0	1.5	8.3	11	57.1%	.214	0.67	0.00						
2021	EUG	A+	24	3	0	0	4	4	21^2	9	0	0.4	13.3	32	57.1%	.214	0.46	1.25	81	0.4				
2021	RIC	AA	24	3	2	0	11	11	63	51	2	1.1	9.1	64	49.4%	.292	0.94	2.43	96	0.6				
2021	TNS	AA	24	1	2	0	4	4	15^2	15	3	2.3	9.2	16	38.6%	.293	1.21	4.02	95	0.2				
2022 non-DC	*CHC*	*MLB*	*25*	*2*	*2*	*0*	*57*	*0*	*50*	*49*	*6*	*2.3*	*7.9*	*43*	*45.9%*	*.297*	*1.24*	*3.78*	*94*	*0.3*				

Comparables: Gonzalez Germen, Shane Greene, Craig Stammen

A command-over-stuff pitcher who has dominated in the minors and should be able to coax soft contact from MLB hitters, he added some strength over his pandemic layoff and some ticks to his fastball. Still, it doesn't get over 95 consistently and grades as just average. He pairs the heater with a cutter that used to be a slider and still bears some of the scars from that surgery; the pitch runs away from righties and in on lefties and is difficult for both to make contact against, leading to the best K/BB rate among qualified minor-league pitchers this year. A hard 12-6 curveball that bends in on lefties completes his arsenal and has helped him have reverse splits over his time in the minors. Back-end starter would be the ceiling, but there's a nice role available for him as a swingman thanks to his effectiveness against batters on either side of the plate. Kilian isn't Rule 5-eligible until December '22, so the Cubs don't have to rush to find a 40-man spot for him, but he'll almost certainly have pushed himself to Wrigley by then.

Dillon Maples RHP Born: 05/09/92 Age: 30 Bats: R Throws: R Height: 6'2" Weight: 230 lb. Origin: Round 14, 2011 Draft (#429 overall)

YEAR	TEAM	LVL	AGE	W	L	SV	G	GS	IP	H	HR	BB/9	K/9	K	GB%	BABIP	WHIP	ERA	DRA-	WARP	MPH	FB%	Whiff%	CSP
2019	IOW	AAA	27	4	4	7	38	0	43	21	1	7.5	16.5	79	62.7%	.303	1.33	3.77	52	1.5				
2019	CHC	MLB	27	1	0	0	14	0	11^{2}	6	2	7.7	13.9	18	68.2%	.200	1.37	5.40	79	0.2	96.9	33.3%	44.2%	46.4%
2020	CHC	MLB	28	0	0	0	2	0	1	1	0	36.0	9.0	1	25.0%	.250	5.00	18.00	158	0.0	97.0	37.5%	60.0%	32.1%
2021	IOW	AAA	29	3	1	0	18	1	20	14	3	8.1	11.7	26	51.1%	.262	1.60	5.40	89	0.4				
2021	CHC	MLB	29	1	0	0	28	0	31^{1}	15	2	7.2	11.5	40	51.5%	.203	1.28	2.59	89	0.5	95.5	51.7%	30.6%	53.4%
2022 non-DC	*CHC*	*MLB*	*30*	*2*	*2*	*0*	*57*	*0*	*50*	*36*	*5*	*7.4*	*12.6*	*70*	*51.9%*	*.289*	*1.56*	*5.10*	*108*	*0.0*	*95.7*	*49.0%*	*33.4%*	*51.7%*

Comparables: Vinnie Pestano, Tyler Rogers, Josh Kinney

The Cubs have held on to the riddle wrapped in an enigma stuffed inside the mysterious, 30-command box that is Maples for years, but the string leading to that tantalizing package has finally run out as he's set to become a free agent after the end of the season. The slider still has the potential to be one of the nastiest pitches in the majors, full stop, if he can ever find some semblance of command, and maybe another organization would be able to unlock something that didn't click during his time with Chicago. In the meantime, if the Cubs really want another dynamic reliever with no control, they could always see if Conor McGregor is interested in reprising his first-pitch work out of the bullpen.

Brailyn Márquez LHP Born: 01/30/99 Age: 23 Bats: L Throws: L Height: 6'4" Weight: 185 lb. Origin: International Free Agent, 2015

YEAR	TEAM	LVL	AGE	W	L	SV	G	GS	IP	H	HR	BB/9	K/9	K	GB%	BABIP	WHIP	ERA	DRA-	WARP	MPH	FB%	Whiff%	CSP
2019	SB	A	20	5	4	0	17	17	77^{1}	64	4	5.0	11.9	102	50.8%	.337	1.38	3.61	82	1.3				
2019	MB	A+	20	4	1	0	5	5	26^{1}	21	1	2.4	8.9	26	44.4%	.282	1.06	1.71	91	0.4				
2020	CHC	MLB	21	0	0	0	1	0	0^{2}	2	0	40.5	13.5	1	33.3%	.667	7.50	67.50			97.4	48.5%	36.4%	36.8%
2022 DC	*CHC*	*MLB*	*23*	*5*	*3*	*0*	*47*	*3*	*51.7*	*51*	*8*	*5.8*	*9.4*	*54*	*43.2%*	*.312*	*1.63*	*5.76*	*122*	*-0.4*	*97.4*	*48.5%*	*36.4%*	*36.8%*

Comparables: Luiz Gohara, Brad Hand, Chris Tillman

A case of COVID-19 followed by a shoulder strain that kept him on the shelf for the rest of the season meant the enduring image of Márquez has been a brief, unsuccessful MLB debut at the end of 2020, during which the Cubs' system improved and blossomed around him. Doubts have begun to creep in about the big lefty's ability to repeat his delivery and throw strikes consistently, causing reliever risk concerns to grow louder, and shoulder injuries are worrisome for a player who derives so much value from premium velocity. Assuming he returns from his long layoff without having lost the gains in fastball command he made in 2019 or any velocity (and is able to maintain the separation between his curve and slider the Cubs helped him develop at the alternate site in 2020) (and oh yeah has developed a changeup too), this is a front-line starter. But that list of terms and conditions is so lengthy it sounds like an ad read for a non-FDA-approved medication. BRAILQUEZ may cause ulcers, see your doctor before starting BRAILQUEZ.

Wade Miley LHP Born: 11/13/86 Age: 35 Bats: L Throws: L Height: 6'2" Weight: 220 lb. Origin: Round 1, 2008 Draft (#43 overall)

YEAR	TEAM	LVL	AGE	W	L	SV	G	GS	IP	H	HR	BB/9	K/9	K	GB%	BABIP	WHIP	ERA	DRA-	WARP	MPH	FB%	Whiff%	CSP
2019	HOU	MLB	32	14	6	0	33	33	167^{1}	164	23	3.3	7.5	140	49.1%	.289	1.34	3.98	116	0.3	90.6	21.9%	23.2%	43.2%
2020	CIN	MLB	33	0	3	0	6	4	14^{1}	15	1	5.7	7.5	12	52.3%	.326	1.67	5.65	110	0.1	90.1	14.0%	30.8%	40.4%
2021	CIN	MLB	34	12	7	0	28	28	163	166	17	2.8	6.9	125	48.0%	.306	1.33	3.37	115	0.1	90.0	17.6%	24.1%	48.6%
2022 DC	*CHC*	*MLB*	*35*	*9*	*9*	*0*	*27*	*27*	*151.3*	*161*	*21*	*3.1*	*7.2*	*121*	*47.5%*	*.309*	*1.41*	*4.77*	*109*	*0.5*	*90.2*	*18.5%*	*24.2%*	*46.7%*

Comparables: Mark Buehrle, Jason Marquis, Steve Trachsel

Miley's no-hitter against Cleveland on May 8th, 2021 wasn't quite the peak of the burnout surrounding the accomplishment, but it did act as a ski lift to move it up the mountain. At the time, it was the fourth no-hitter in less than a month, and Miley was, well, Miley—a pitch-to-contact lefty worth a total of -0.3 WARP over his last five seasons who wasn't even guaranteed a rotation spot entering spring training. But his surprise season was only beginning. Miley would go on to throw four more games with at least seven innings pitched and no runs allowed, en route to one of the most valuable seasons of any pitcher from a runs-allowed perspective. He did so by mastering throwing not quite to the edges of the strike zone, but just outside of them, with a cutter/changeup combo leading a six-pitch repertoire that virtually never got lost in the middle of the plate. You can tell from his WARP how repeatable DRA finds his performance to be, particularly as he enters his age-35 season. But we certainly won't get burned out from watching him anytime soon. Not wearing red, however: Unwilling to pay $10 million for him, the Reds bought out his 2021 season for a tenth of that and he got claimed off waivers by the Cubs.

Alec Mills RHP Born: 11/30/91 Age: 30 Bats: R Throws: R Height: 6'4" Weight: 205 lb. Origin: Round 22, 2012 Draft (#673 overall)

YEAR	TEAM	LVL	AGE	W	L	SV	G	GS	IP	H	HR	BB/9	K/9	K	GB%	BABIP	WHIP	ERA	DRA-	WARP	MPH	FB%	Whiff%	CSP
2019	IOW	AAA	27	6	4	0	19	18	104	116	17	2.6	8.3	96	38.6%	.332	1.40	5.11	102	0.5				
2019	CHC	MLB	27	1	0	1	9	4	36	31	5	2.8	10.5	42	48.9%	.299	1.17	2.75	81	0.7	89.7	54.2%	28.1%	45.2%
2020	CHC	MLB	28	5	5	0	11	11	62^{1}	53	13	2.7	6.6	46	47.6%	.233	1.16	4.48	105	0.5	90.2	58.9%	18.0%	47.2%
2021	IOW	AAA	29	0	2	0	3	3	11^{2}	14	1	2.3	7.7	10	47.4%	.351	1.46	5.40	114	0.1				
2021	CHC	MLB	29	6	7	1	32	20	119	137	16	2.6	6.6	87	50.4%	.328	1.44	5.07	109	0.5	89.2	60.1%	18.6%	54.3%
2022 DC	*CHC*	*MLB*	*30*	*7*	*7*	*0*	*22*	*22*	*115.7*	*121*	*14*	*2.7*	*6.9*	*88*	*48.0%*	*.304*	*1.36*	*4.51*	*105*	*0.5*	*89.5*	*59.4%*	*19.1%*	*52.0%*

Comparables: Edgar Gonzalez, Byung-Hyun Kim, Jeremy Hefner

In 2020, Mills became part of an improbable bit of Cubs lore when the former Quad-A stalwart tossed a no-hitter. He also made history in 2021, although not the good kind, authoring a start where he surrendered 11 hits in four innings, leading to a new franchise record for consecutive losses at Wrigley Field. It's unclear how Cubs announcer Jim Deshaies came to call the soft-tosser "Sir Alec," but if Mills lords over any lands, it's the twin kingdoms of Command and Ground Ball Outs, although his latter subjects didn't treat him well, with too many ground balls finding holes. Given the number of question marks in the Cubs' rotation, it seems a safe bet Mills will be around next year.

Adam Morgan LHP Born: 02/27/90 Age: 32 Bats: L Throws: L Height: 6'1" Weight: 200 lb. Origin: Round 3, 2011 Draft (#120 overall)

YEAR	TEAM	LVL	AGE	W	L	SV	G	GS	IP	H	HR	BB/9	K/9	K	GB%	BABIP	WHIP	ERA	DRA-	WARP	MPH	FB%	Whiff%	CSP
2019	PHI	MLB	29	3	3	0	40	0	29^2	20	4	3.0	8.8	29	41.0%	.216	1.01	3.94	95	0.4	92.7	28.3%	33.3%	47.9%
2020	PHI	MLB	30	0	1	0	17	0	13	14	3	4.2	11.1	16	47.2%	.333	1.54	5.54	77	0.3	91.7	33.8%	33.3%	44.8%
2021	IOW	AAA	31	0	1	0	15	0	16^1	10	1	1.7	11.6	21	54.1%	.250	0.80	2.20	85	0.3				
2021	CHC	MLB	31	2	1	2	34	0	25^1	22	6	4.3	9.9	28	47.8%	.262	1.34	4.26	85	0.4	92.6	34.8%	33.0%	53.2%
2022 non-DC	*CHC*	*MLB*	*32*	*2*	*2*	*0*	*57*	*0*	*50*	*45*	*7*	*3.4*	*10.6*	*59*	*45.8%*	*.311*	*1.29*	*4.11*	*95*	*0.3*	*92.5*	*33.3%*	*33.1%*	*50.4%*

Comparables: Chris Bootcheck, Dana Eveland, Zac Rosscup

Call him Manchin Morgan because he loves nothing more than shooting down lefties. Christian Yelich has struck out 25% of the time he's seen Morgan; Juan Soto, 40%; and the nigh-impossible-to-strike-out Joey Votto, 50%. Finally fully recovered from a flexor strain that cost him a good chunk of the past two years, he steadily improved over the course of the season, showing better command of the zone in the second half and leaning on his slider more heavily than ever to get out those pesky righties. Morgan is set to become a free agent and even though the LOOGY profession has gone the way of switchboard operators and Blockbuster employees, he's done enough to earn a big-league job next season.

Manuel Rodríguez RHP Born: 08/06/96 Age: 25 Bats: R Throws: R Height: 5'11" Weight: 210 lb. Origin: International Free Agent, 2016

YEAR	TEAM	LVL	AGE	W	L	SV	G	GS	IP	H	HR	BB/9	K/9	K	GB%	BABIP	WHIP	ERA	DRA-	WARP	MPH	FB%	Whiff%	CSP
2019	MB	A+	22	1	3	2	35	0	47	43	1	3.3	12.4	65	55.3%	.372	1.28	3.45	71	1.1				
2021	TNS	AA	24	1	1	4	13	0	13^1	8	1	6.7	12.8	19	63.0%	.269	1.35	2.03	90	0.2				
2021	IOW	AAA	24	0	0	1	7	0	7^1	6	0	2.5	9.8	8	61.1%	.333	1.09	0.00	91	0.1				
2021	CHC	MLB	24	3	3	1	20	0	17^2	18	3	6.1	8.2	16	53.7%	.294	1.70	6.11	113	0.0	97.2	71.7%	24.6%	53.9%
2022 DC	*CHC*	*MLB*	*25*	*2*	*3*	*3*	*59*	*0*	*51.7*	*49*	*6*	*5.7*	*9.7*	*56*	*50.8%*	*.312*	*1.58*	*5.29*	*113*	*-0.2*	*97.2*	*71.7%*	*24.6%*	*53.9%*

Comparables: Jose Ortega, JD Hammer, Tyler Zuber

A prototypical power reliever with a big fastball and a plus slider, he's been tripped up twice by health issues as he's gotten close to the majors. A forearm strain interrupted a promising spring training campaign in 2020, and right shoulder inflammation limited him to 20 games in his debut season. The layoff seems to have cost him the gains he made in commanding the strike zone, but hopefully that, along with the attendant attack of dingeritis, is a problem that gets ironed out with more consistent playing time.

Michael Rucker RHP Born: 04/27/94 Age: 28 Bats: R Throws: R Height: 6'1" Weight: 195 lb. Origin: Round 11, 2016 Draft (#344 overall)

YEAR	TEAM	LVL	AGE	W	L	SV	G	GS	IP	H	HR	BB/9	K/9	K	GB%	BABIP	WHIP	ERA	DRA-	WARP	MPH	FB%	Whiff%	CSP
2019	TNS	AA	25	0	3	1	34	0	75^2	76	10	2.6	10.6	89	40.7%	.344	1.30	4.28	74	1.5				
2021	IOW	AAA	27	3	0	0	19	0	39^1	44	8	2.1	11.2	49	46.7%	.364	1.35	4.81	81	0.9				
2021	CHC	MLB	27	0	0	1	20	0	28^1	32	5	3.5	9.5	30	45.8%	.346	1.52	6.99	96	0.3	94.4	61.4%	30.3%	50.6%
2022 DC	*CHC*	*MLB*	*28*	*2*	*3*	*0*	*59*	*0*	*51.7*	*50*	*8*	*3.0*	*10.0*	*57*	*42.9%*	*.313*	*1.30*	*4.44*	*102*	*0.1*	*94.4*	*61.4%*	*30.3%*	*50.6%*

Comparables: Jacob Barnes, Brandon Cunniff, Arquimedes Caminero

It must sting pretty badly to get returned as a Rule 5 pick by Literally the Orioles, but that's what happened to Rucker in 2020. Rucker's Revenge began when he earned a spring-training invite this year after his velocity shot up to the mid-to-upper 90s, and continued when he was called up to make his MLB debut in July. The premium velocity hasn't been there consistently yet in the bigs, and he's had a severe case of homeritis when his cutter leaks into the middle of the plate. When he's hitting his spots on the edges of the zone, though, and pairing it with his sweeping slider, there's a ton of swing-and-miss in his profile. Seems like someone who could eventually help the team with the highest bullpen ERA in MLB, but again, Literally the Orioles.

Adrian Sampson RHP Born: 10/07/91 Age: 30 Bats: R Throws: R Height: 6'2" Weight: 210 lb. Origin: Round 5, 2012 Draft (#166 overall)

YEAR	TEAM	LVL	AGE	W	L	SV	G	GS	IP	H	HR	BB/9	K/9	K	GB%	BABIP	WHIP	ERA	DRA-	WARP	MPH	FB%	Whiff%	CSP
2019	TEX	MLB	27	6	8	0	35	15	125^1	156	29	2.6	7.3	101	41.0%	.327	1.53	5.89	116	0.2	92.6	53.9%	21.5%	50.1%
2021	IOW	AAA	29	4	5	0	16	14	81^2	92	19	3.6	6.7	61	37.3%	.304	1.53	4.96	125	0.0				
2021	CHC	MLB	29	1	2	0	10	5	35^1	30	8	2.0	7.1	28	43.7%	.234	1.08	2.80	102	0.3	92.0	58.8%	21.5%	51.9%
2022 non-DC	*CHC*	*MLB*	*30*	*2*	*3*	*0*	*57*	*0*	*50*	*54*	*9*	*2.9*	*6.9*	*38*	*39.9%*	*.300*	*1.40*	*5.38*	*121*	*-0.4*	*92.3*	*56.1%*	*21.5%*	*50.9%*

Comparables: Kendall Graveman, J.D. Martin, Kyle Gibson

This offseason, the Ricketts watched the Mariners sign Chris Flexen to a moderate contract out of the KBO, banking on a full season from the stretched-out starter coming from a country that managed to get their COVID outbreak well-handled. They then called up their Baseball Ops department and instructed them to "do that, but cheaper." Enter Sampson, who isn't so much Flexen Lite as he is Flexen Translucent. Sampson is also a ground-ball specialist, but he lacks any plus pitch and has more of a tendency to get barrelled up, and he's been hurt by the longball this year especially. Still, the doughy Sampson has been one of the more reliable arms on the pitching staff since the Cubs called him up and should settle in next year to a swingman/spot starter role.

Justin Steele LHP Born: 07/11/95 Age: 26 Bats: L Throws: L Height: 6'2" Weight: 205 lb. Origin: Round 5, 2014 Draft (#139 overall)

YEAR	TEAM	LVL	AGE	W	L	SV	G	GS	IP	H	HR	BB/9	K/9	K	GB%	BABIP	WHIP	ERA	DRA-	WARP	MPH	FB%	Whiff%	CSP
2019	TNS	AA	23	0	6	0	11	11	38^2	45	3	4.7	9.8	42	39.3%	.412	1.68	5.59	102	0.2				
2021	IOW	AAA	25	2	0	0	9	5	27^1	14	1	4.3	9.5	29	50.7%	.197	0.99	1.32	93	0.5				
2021	CHC	MLB	25	4	4	0	20	9	57	50	12	4.3	9.3	59	49.7%	.264	1.35	4.26	97	0.6	93.3	65.9%	27.6%	54.4%
2022 DC	*CHC*	*MLB*	*26*	*8*	*7*	*0*	*63*	*11*	*96.3*	*92*	*13*	*4.6*	*9.6*	*102*	*46.0%*	*.310*	*1.47*	*4.96*	*108*	*0.2*	*93.3*	*65.9%*	*27.6%*	*54.4%*

Comparables: José Álvarez, Christian Friedrich, Zack Britton

The Cubs are using their gap year to experiment, moving their young pitchers between the rotation and bullpen to get a sense of where and how they work best. The argument for Steele in the bullpen is how his plus pitches tunnel together: he has two distinct fastballs, a four-seamer with rise that elicits whiffs and can touch up to 97 in short outings, and a sinker with some crossfire action that he can bury in on righties. That second pitch pairs well with his newly-developed slider with extreme horizontal break, essentially giving him reverse splits. On the negative side of the bullpen equation, he's also got a homer problem, so that additional velocity is necessary to avoid 93 leaking into the middle of the plate. Steele was drafted with a good biting curveball, though, and also has a changeup, so there's still starter potential here, and the Cubs aren't exactly flush with those. However, he's lost significant development time over his career—TJ in 2017/18, an oblique injury in '19, the cancellation of the minors in '20, and a hamstring strain in '21—and whatever he is will have to be figured out at the big-league level rather than backpacking around the minor leagues.

Marcus Stroman RHP Born: 05/01/91 Age: 31 Bats: R Throws: R Height: 5'7" Weight: 180 lb. Origin: Round 1, 2012 Draft (#22 overall)

YEAR	TEAM	LVL	AGE	W	L	SV	G	GS	IP	H	HR	BB/9	K/9	K	GB%	BABIP	WHIP	ERA	DRA-	WARP	MPH	FB%	Whiff%	CSP
2019	NYM	MLB	28	4	2	0	11	11	59^2	65	8	3.5	9.1	60	48.0%	.339	1.47	3.77	78	1.3	92.2	44.1%	25.5%	46.0%
2021	NYM	MLB	30	10	13	0	33	33	179	161	17	2.2	7.9	158	49.5%	.289	1.15	3.02	87	2.9	92.1	43.9%	26.8%	55.0%
2022 DC	*CHC*	*MLB*	*31*	*10*	*8*	*0*	*27*	*27*	*151.3*	*154*	*19*	*2.6*	*8.2*	*137*	*50.7%*	*.310*	*1.30*	*4.11*	*96*	*1.5*	*92.3*	*42.6%*	*26.3%*	*52.5%*

Comparables: Rick Rhoden, John Lackey, Rick Reuschel

Apparently bored with only having five pitches in his arsenal, Stroman added a sixth to the mix in 2021—sort of. The split-finger changeup he started throwing last season is technically a new offering, though he's been throwing the cambio for years. What's different is the grip, learned and borrowed from teammate Robert Gsellman, that Stroman tinkered with in 2020 and used to great effect in his return to the mound. The extra drop he gets on it separates it from his power sinker, which keeps hitters from zeroing in on the fastball. It also gives him something that's been lacking in seasons prior: swings and misses. The split change returned a whiff rate of 33.9%, nearly 10 points better than his previous changeup, and makes for two pitches—alongside his already excellent slider—with a whiff rate above 30. On top of that, it instantly became a two-strike weapon along with the slider and his cutter, with opposing batters hitting .229 or worse with a slugging percentage of .400 or lower on all three. The end result: more strikeouts to offset an increase in hard contact and drop in ground-ball rate, and more confidence that Stroman can not only succeed as a mid-rotation starter, but also offer ace upside.

Keegan Thompson RHP Born: 03/13/95 Age: 27 Bats: R Throws: R Height: 6'1" Weight: 210 lb. Origin: Round 3, 2017 Draft (#105 overall)

YEAR	TEAM	LVL	AGE	W	L	SV	G	GS	IP	H	HR	BB/9	K/9	K	GB%	BABIP	WHIP	ERA	DRA-	WARP	MPH	FB%	Whiff%	CSP
2019	MSS	WIN	24	1	1	0	7	7	25^1	20	3	2.1	9.2	26	43.5%	.258	1.03	4.62						
2021	IOW	AAA	26	0	0	0	4	4	14^2	5	0	3.1	9.8	16	34.4%	.156	0.68	0.00	92	0.3				
2021	CHC	MLB	26	3	3	1	32	6	53^1	48	9	5.2	9.3	55	42.2%	.273	1.48	3.38	101	0.5	92.7	74.7%	23.8%	56.6%
2022 DC	*CHC*	*MLB*	*27*	*8*	*6*	*0*	*67*	*8*	*85.7*	*79*	*13*	*4.2*	*9.1*	*87*	*39.6%*	*.294*	*1.40*	*4.69*	*105*	*0.2*	*92.7*	*74.7%*	*23.8%*	*56.6%*

Comparables: Nick Masset, Clay Holmes, Adam Warren

Averaging just a hair under 94—a fireballer, compared to his rotation-mates—Thompson nonetheless relies on the same toolkit as those softer-tossers: pitch sequencing and location. Unfortunately, the second part of that formula is still under construction in the bigs, where he's struggled with handing out free passes, possibly as a consequence of some shoulder inflammation. His slider, labeled a cutter by pitch tracking, has sharp, darting movement and can generate whiffs, especially against righties, but occasionally wanders into the center of the plate. The fastball has some rising action but can float on up out of the zone when he's not finishing his pitches. His best pitch for garnering swinging strikes is his tight, sharp curve, but it requires the other two pitches to set it up. It's a pitch mix that should generate weak contact and swinging strikes, but requires more refinement before it gets either.

Jordan Wicks LHP Born: 09/01/99 Age: 22 Bats: L Throws: L Height: 6'3" Weight: 220 lb. Origin: Round 1, 2021 Draft (#21 overall)

YEAR	TEAM	LVL	AGE	W	L	SV	G	GS	IP	H	HR	BB/9	K/9	K	GB%	BABIP	WHIP	ERA	DRA-	WARP	MPH	FB%	Whiff%	CSP
2021	SB	A+	21	0	0	0	4	4	7	7	0	3.9	6.4	5	37.5%	.304	1.43	5.14	117	0.0				
2022 non-DC	*CHC*	*MLB*	*22*	*2*	*3*	*0*	*57*	*0*	*50*	*56*	*8*	*5.2*	*6.5*	*36*	*38.4%*	*.308*	*1.72*	*6.47*	*141*	*-0.9*				

Comparables: Jayson Aquino, Mike Rayl, Zack Dodson

Like Kacey Musgraves, the Cubs are alright with a slow burn. Wicks doesn't light up any radar guns with his fastball (91-93) but puts batters away with the consensus best changeup in the draft class, a dive-bombing offering with two-plane break that will remind Cubs fans of Kyle Hendricks. The next step is improving the shape on his slider to give it more movement and either scrapping or vastly improving his loopy curveball. With the team entering a rebuilding phase, the Cubs can let off on the gas in developing the already-polished lefty and let Wicks be a slow burn, taking his time as the ~~world turns~~ baseball spins.

Lineouts

Hitters

HITTER	POS	TEAM	LVL	AGE	PA	R	2B	3B	HR	RBI	BB	K	SB	CS	AVG/OBP/SLG	DRC+	BABIP	BRR	FRAA	WARP
Matt Duffy	3B/2B	CHC	MLB	30	322	45	12	0	5	30	25	63	8	1	.287/.357/.381	101	.351	3.3	3B(56): 3.6, 2B(21): -3.1, SS(5): 0.1	1.6
Christian Franklin	CF	MB	A	21	87	13	3	0	1	5	17	23	1	4	.200/.402/.292	105	.293	-0.7	CF(15): 0.7	0.4
Taylor Gushue	C/DH	IOW	AAA	27	277	29	14	0	8	39	25	83	0	0	.223/.295/.377	81	.297	-1.6	C(44): 0.3, 1B(8): 0.5	0.3
	C/DH	CHC	MLB	27	4	0	0	0	0	0	0	3	0	0	.000/.000/.000	80			1B(1): -0.0	0.0
Michael Hermosillo	OF	IOW	AAA	26	186	34	10	1	10	29	26	48	8	3	.306/.446/.592	128	.389	0.0	CF(20): 0.6, RF(8): -0.8, LF(7): 1.4	1.3
	OF	CHC	MLB	26	38	5	2	0	3	7	1	12	0	0	.194/.237/.500	91	.190	-0.4	RF(6): 0.3, CF(5): 0.1, LF(2): -0.5	0.1
P.J. Higgins	C/1B	IOW	AAA	28	48	7	2	1	1	6	8	11	0	0	.333/.458/.513	106	.444	-0.2	C(6): 0.3, 1B(5): -0.5, RF(1): -0.1	0.1
	C/1B	CHC	MLB	28	25	1	0	0	0	0	2	8	0	0	.043/.120/.043	80	.067	-0.3	C(6): 0.4, 1B(1): -0.0	0.0
Jose Lobaton	C	IOW	AAA	36	49	5	3	0	2	9	10	15	0	0	.179/.347/.410	108	.227	-1.0	C(10): 0.6	0.2
	C	CHC	MLB	36	13	1	0	0	0	0	2	5	0	0	.000/.154/.000	87			C(5): -0.4	0.0
Nick Martini	LF	IOW	AAA	31	323	56	9	3	11	40	42	70	2	1	.267/.387/.444	112	.323	-0.5	RF(30): 0.5, 1B(26): 1.9, LF(21): 1.4	1.7
	LF	CHC	MLB	31	45	4	1	0	0	4	6	10	0	1	.270/.356/.297	87	.345	-0.7	RF(7): -0.7	-0.1
Christopher Morel	UT	TNS	AA	22	417	59	17	5	17	64	41	124	16	3	.220/.300/.432	98	.276	-0.8	CF(32): -1.9, RF(20): 7.4, 3B(19): -0.5	1.7
	UT	IOW	AAA	22	39	6	1	0	1	2	4	10	2	0	.257/.333/.371	88	.333	1.3	3B(4): 0.6, CF(2): -0.4, LF(1): 0.0	0.2
Andrew Romine	IF	IOW	AAA	35	243	28	7	2	1	17	20	42	2	4	.290/.356/.355	95	.357	0.1	SS(31): 0.5, 2B(23): 0.0, 3B(9): 1.3	0.8
	IF	CHC	MLB	35	64	7	2	0	1	5	4	24	0	1	.183/.234/.267	67	.286	0.0	SS(16): -0.7, 2B(2): 0.0	-0.1
Austin Romine	C	CHC	MLB	32	62	5	2	0	1	5	2	22	0	0	.217/.242/.300	67	.324	0.2	C(21): -1.0	-0.1
Eric Sogard	IF	CHC	MLB	35	180	16	6	1	1	12	9	30	3	1	.249/.283/.314	82	.293	0.5	2B(43): -1.9, 3B(10): 1.1, P(5): -0.1	0.3
Chase Strumpf	3B	SB	A+	23	67	15	4	0	0	7	7	17	3	1	.309/.418/.382	97	.436	-0.3	2B(9): -1.1, 3B(4): -0.7	0.0
	3B	TNS	AA	23	254	25	15	0	7	29	38	65	1	0	.211/.335/.380	106	.268	-1.5	3B(52): 7.2, 2B(9): -1.1	1.4
Trayce Thompson	OF	IOW	AAA	30	358	48	14	1	21	63	45	116	3	1	.233/.344/.492	101	.296	-1.0	CF(42): -2.5, RF(23): 0.8, LF(13): -0.1	1.0
	OF	CHC	MLB	30	35	6	1	0	4	9	7	11	2	0	.250/.400/.714	111	.231	-0.1	RF(8): -0.7, CF(3): 0.1, LF(2): -0.1	0.1
Nelson Velazquez	OF	MSS	WIN	22	123	24	7	0	9	24	17	34	0	1	.385/.480/.712		.508			
	OF	CAG	WIN	22	73	9	2	1	2	10	7	20	4	1	.167/.247/.318		.205			
	OF	SB	A+	22	288	37	13	1	12	46	20	97	12	2	.261/.321/.456	89	.364	-0.9	RF(41): 5.2, CF(22): 0.0	1.0
	OF	TNS	AA	22	137	19	10	1	8	27	10	35	5	0	.290/.358/.581	114	.346	-1.0	RF(20): 2.1, CF(13): 2.0, LF(1): 0.1	1.0
Tony Wolters	C	OKC	AAA	29	107	10	6	1	2	13	8	20	0	1	.215/.308/.366	93	.250	-0.1	C(20): 1.0	0.4
	C	IOW	AAA	29	138	18	4	0	4	17	18	33	1	1	.261/.380/.400	105	.333	-0.4	C(30): 1.9, 3B(4): -0.5, 1B(2): 0.1	0.7
	C	CHC	MLB	29	30	3	0	0	0	0	5	12	0	1	.125/.276/.125	68	.250	-0.2	C(8): 0.9, 2B(2): -0.0, LF(1): -0.0	0.1

With his ability to play all over the infield, hit for contact and run the bases well, **Matt Duffy** the type of player good teams roster as depth pieces and teams like the 2021 Cubs roster as their starting second baseman. The best ability is availability, though, and the slender Duffman has had issues staying healthy throughout his career—this year it was a troublesome back that did him in. ⚾ A standout from a Razorbacks program that has produced multiple high draft picks in the past few years, **Christian Franklin** had some early-round buzz as a tooled-up true center fielder, but slipped in the draft due to concerns about the hit tool. The Cubs have been working on flattening Franklin's swing path to try to cut down on his whiffs and keep the bat in the hitting zone longer. It's resulted in modest gains in his power profile but so far hasn't done much to curb the strikeouts. ⚾ **Taylor Gushue** was the fifth backup catcher the Cubs tried out when he was summoned from the minors in late June, and he was DFA'd and returned to Iowa a week later. Because the Cubs catching corps had a surplus of cursedness, he was then placed on the IL in September, ending his season. ⚾ The long-tenured Angels farmhand has always struggled with strike zone recognition, but **Michael Hermosillo** improved his plate discipline and found more power under Chicago's player development squad at Triple-A Iowa, although those gains didn't translate in an injury-shortened big-league stint. Hermosillo grew up a Cubs fan and then played for the 2021 Cubs, which is roughly equivalent to growing up a Jessie Spano fan and then starring opposite Elizabeth Berkley in *Showgirls*. ⚾ We're all familiar with the fairy tale of long-tenured minor leaguers finally breaking through in the bigs; this is not one of those. **P.J. Higgins** was called up in late May, only to go on the IL for the rest of the season with a forearm strain a month later. Higgins will get another crack at breaking camp with the big-league team in 2022 as a backup catcher, and maybe a more satisfying narrative arc. ⚾ Another victim of the catcher curse that plagued the Cubs, **Jose Lobaton** made an appropriate 13 plate appearances before injuring his shoulder in a near-collision at first base after grounding out as a pinch-hitter in the last at-bat of a 2-1 loss against the Brewers. If you read that last part aloud to yourself three times, the ghost of Harry Caray shows up and kicks you in the back of the knee. ⚾ **Nick Martini**'s main skill is getting on base, but a year-plus of not seeing big-league pitching sapped even that, making him just another warm body for the zombie Cubs to run out over the tail end of the season. Who likes a warm Martini? ⚾ A breath of fresh air among the Cubs' parade of "pure hitters," **Christopher Morel** produces some of the loudest noises in the system. He came up just short of a 20-20 season, and his arm grades as double-plus, giving him flexibility all over the field. ⚾ **Andrew Romine** is the *General Hospital* of baseball players: continually producing new seasons, none of which are very good. *GH* has made it 58 years and counting, which feels like the more impressive achievement longevity-wise until you realize Romine has hung around in baseball for a decade despite his OBP barely exceeding his batting average most years. ⚾ The first victim of the Cubs' utterly cursed backup catcher position last year, **Austin Romine** missed most of the season with a wrist injury. He did play in a blowout game in August where his brother Andrew pitched, forming the first brother battery since 1962. If you were a Cubs fan this year, these fun facts were what passed for sustenance. ⚾ If **Eric Sogard** is a team's starting second baseman, even if in name only, it says more about the club than the player. ⚾ Thanks to a period of drafting high-floor players, the Cubs are well-situated to immediately start a new organizational wave with their cluster of MLB-adjacent talent, even if more of the blue-chip talent is in the lower levels of the farm. There's nothing spectacular here, but **Chase Strumpf** is a polished, proven college producer who will partner well with Davis, Amaya, Marquez and others. The Cubs' propensity for aggressive promotion with their prospects should provide some spring-training intrigue as he battles to be in the infield mix. ⚾ With a transaction history longer than a CVS receipt but a grand total of a little over one season's worth of MLB plate appearances, **Trayce Thompson** has some avant-garde numbers. His savant-like ability to punish mistake pitches often leads to his slugging percentage being twice his average. This year, aided by his first-ever big-league grand slam, he took small sample theatre to levels Herbert Blau would approve of, challenging preconceived notions of what a statline should look like. ⚾ **Nelson Velazquez** made a splash in a late-season promotion at Double-A, earning a trip to the AFL where he balled out on his way to MVP honors. He's a power-jockey who took advantage of his surroundings in the desert, but there's plenty of hit tool risk. ⚾ In 68 games played by Cubs catchers not named Contreras, the position yielded 40 hits. Robinson Chirinos, a waiver-wire pickup added in July, had over half of those. To his credit, **Tony Wolters** had three of them, giving him one less hit than pitcher Trevor Williams, who accomplished his feat in 10 fewer plate appearances.

Pitchers

PITCHER	TEAM	LVL	AGE	W	L	SV	G	GS	IP	H	HR	BB/9	K/9	K	GB%	BABIP	WHIP	ERA	DRA-	WARP	MPH	FB%	WHF	CSP
Burl Carraway	SB	A+	22	3	3	2	29	0	31	13	3	12.2	14.8	51	46.2%	.208	1.77	6.10	100	0.3				
Scott Effross	TNS	AA	27	3	0	0	8	0	18^{2}	16	2	2.4	9.6	20	50.0%	.292	1.13	2.89	96	0.2				
	IOW	AAA	27	4	2	2	23	2	42	28	6	2.1	9.9	46	57.8%	.232	0.90	3.64	85	0.9				
	CHC	MLB	27	2	1	0	14	0	14^{2}	13	2	0.6	11.0	18	47.2%	.324	0.95	3.68	82	0.3	90.9	59.5%	30.0%	55.4%
Jake Jewell	IOW	AAA	28	2	1	4	23	0	32^{1}	21	3	3.6	9.7	35	57.0%	.237	1.05	2.78	89	0.6				
	SAC	AAA	28	0	0	0	8	0	10^{1}	11	1	4.4	8.7	10	62.1%	.357	1.55	6.10	82	0.1				
	CHC	MLB	28	0	2	0	10	0	10	18	5	4.5	9.0	10	38.9%	.419	2.30	9.90	95	0.1	94.4	67.6%	28.7%	55.2%
Tommy Nance	IOW	AAA	30	1	0	0	10	0	15^{1}	7	1	1.8	10.6	18	58.3%	.171	0.65	2.35	82	0.4				
	CHC	MLB	30	1	1	0	27	0	28^{2}	25	5	4.1	9.4	30	56.8%	.263	1.33	7.22	95	0.3	95.5	62.1%	23.0%	59.3%
Colin Rea	NAS	AAA	30	4	2	0	7	7	35^{2}	33	2	1.0	8.8	35	49.0%	.310	1.04	2.27	91	0.6				
	MIL	MLB	30	0	0	0	1	0	6	7	2	0.0	7.5	5	21.1%	.294	1.17	7.50			92.8	46.2%	25.0%	51.3%
Kyle Ryan	IOW	AAA	29	2	0	1	19	0	25	16	2	2.5	8.6	24	58.1%	.233	0.92	2.52	91	0.5				
	CHC	MLB	29	0	0	1	13	0	13^{1}	17	3	4.0	5.4	8	58.3%	.318	1.73	6.75	107	0.1	88.5	62.2%	17.0%	51.9%
Kohl Stewart	IOW	AAA	26	2	3	0	6	5	26	16	3	2.1	9.0	26	65.7%	.203	0.85	3.46	96	0.4				
	CHC	MLB	26	1	1	0	4	3	13^{2}	17	2	4.0	7.2	11	51.1%	.357	1.68	5.27	94	0.2	89.8	82.7%	21.2%	51.6%
Alexander Vizcaíno	SB	A+	24	0	1	0	6	5	13^{2}	8	1	5.9	12.5	19	43.3%	.241	1.24	5.27	87	0.2				
Rowan Wick	CHC	MLB	28	0	1	5	22	0	23	17	1	5.5	11.3	29	34.5%	.296	1.35	4.30	98	0.2	94.6	68.5%	29.5%	54.4%
Brad Wieck	IOW	AAA	29	0	1	0	6	0	7^{2}	5	0	9.4	14.1	12	12.5%	.333	1.70	4.70	104	0.1				
	CHC	MLB	29	0	0	0	15	0	17	10	0	5.3	14.8	28	30.3%	.303	1.18	0.00	73	0.4	92.5	84.6%	28.7%	57.3%
Dan Winkler	CHC	MLB	31	1	3	0	47	0	39^{2}	32	5	6.8	9.1	40	44.1%	.255	1.56	5.22	121	-0.1	93.9	28.6%	25.9%	41.5%

Spending a second-round pick on a pure reliever, only to sell off the team's core a season later, is an object lesson in "life comes at you fast." But as far as relievers go, **Burl Carraway** is elite, with a funky delivery, a fastball (96-98) that explodes out of his hand and a late-biting curveball that elicits whiffs. Unfortunately, he's also elite at walking batters; he did improve as the season went on, but will face a tougher test in more selective hitters at Double-A next season. ⚾ After **Scott Effross** achieved middling results upon reaching Double-A in 2018, the Cubs shuttered his old arm angle midway through the 2019 season, turning him into a sidearmer with some funky crossfire action. A backdoor slider that's especially tough on lefties and tunnels well with his sinker leads Effross' four-pitch mix, enough to give the former starter multi-inning appeal. His ability to spot pitches low in the zone and induce ground balls give him low-octane fireman intrigue. ⚾ A slow-healing shoulder injury adds up to two straight years without regular game competition, but reportedly **Kohl Franklin** is regaining his fastball velocity (92-95) to pair with his well-developed changeup and swing-and-miss curveball. A durable frame and athletic delivery could smooth his recovery journey, although the Cubs opted not to hasten it further by sending Franklin to the AFL this year. ⚾ A barking right shoulder that ended **Jonathan Holder**'s 2019 campaign with the Yankees came back to knock him out for virtually the entire 2021 season. He's arbitration-eligible this off-season and a likely non-tender candidate by the Cubs. If he's healthy, he could catch on with a team that will hope he can recapture his pre-injury form. ⚾ A fastball-slider reliever who can get whiffs on a mid-90s fastball and sink it in the zone for groundball outs, **Jake Jewell** has legit stuff that the four organizations he's been with haven't been able to turn into major-league results. The Giants claimed him for a second time in August from their NL West rivals and outrighted him to Triple-A, and that's likely where he'll return next season. ⚾ Only 0.5% of high school baseball players make it to the bigs. Only 20% of people diagnosed with ALS live five years or more after diagnosis. In 2014, **Tommy Nance**—a year before he would graduate, undrafted, from Santa Clara—showed up to an empty house to surprise his parents, who were away commiserating with family over his father Mark's recent diagnosis with ALS. Seven years later, the indy-ball signing made his major-league debut with his proud dad looking on. ⚾ **Colin Rea** found himself an unlikely addition to the playoff roster when Devin Williams went on the IL, proving that sometimes the best way to open a door is to wait for someone to punch the wall next to it. ⚾ The Cubs optioned the lefty back and forth between Triple-A Iowa so often a portion of I-80 is now named the **Kyle Ryan** Memorial Expressway. Ryan decided he'd had enough in August and opted for free agency. Ryan's MLB-designated player nickname is "KR 91," which appears to be his initials plus his birthdate. Maybe he'll spend some of this down time tightening up his password security as well as trying to figure out how to get back his strikeout rate from 2019. ⚾ What could have been a savvy one-year depth signing didn't totally pan out, as an elbow injury in July shut **Kohl Stewart** down for the season. The hot new baseball analytics topic is seam-shifted wake, and Stewart is a SSW darling, so as long as the elbow injury isn't An Elbow Injury, he'll likely catch on with another team, or maybe even the Cubs again, as Stewart praised their player development staff as some of the best coaching he'd had in his career. ⚾ A late-blooming, low-dollar sign who flourished in the Yankees system but missed most of the season with the spookily vague diagnosis of "arm soreness," **Alexander Vizcaíno** has two big-league ready weapons in a blazing fastball and a high-velocity changeup that moves like a splitter and is the kind of true wipeout pitch that hallmarks an elite closer, although subpar command at present makes it difficult to envision a big-league manager confidently handing him the ball in a save scenario. ⚾ Still working back from the oblique injury that ended his season in 2020 and cost him half of 2021, **Rowan Wick** improved as he went along, limiting barrels and hard contact but whiffing too few and walking too many. Provided he stays healthy, he'll factor into the Cubs' 2022 bullpen, at least until he's traded to a contender at the deadline. Hopefully it's Toronto, as the name "Rowan Wick" is so powerfully Canadian it makes Gordon Lightfoot himself tremble. ⚾ **Brad Wieck** has one of the filthiest curveballs in the game and a high-spin fastball, but his 2020 was derailed by lower body injuries. Then his 2021 was interrupted by the recurrence of a cardiac issue he'd had surgery for prior to the 2020 season, leading to a season-ending operation in August. Wieck's ability to throw a soul-snatching curveball is impressive; his determined resilience in the face of his multiple health issues—he's also a cancer survivor—is nothing short of incredible. ⚾ Daniel Winkler is an accredited Master Bladesmith and custom knifemaker, known for creating historically accurate blades for films like *Last of the Mohicans* and...less historically accurate films like *Suicide Squad*. **Dan Winkler** is a reliever who could have used some of those precision-honed edges. His approach to the strikezone this year was unfortunately more "Harley Quinn swinging a mallet dot gif," and he was released in August.

CINCINNATI REDS

Essay by Zach Crizer

Player comments by Tony Wolfe and BP staff

Arguing balls and strikes has always been against the rules, but that's never stopped anyone. It is baseball's built-in steam valve.

If you were watching the Reds' game in Miami on August 29, only the crowd's offbeat roar announced that Reds manager David Bell had opted to engage it. It was the ninth inning, a loss almost in the books. Home-plate umpire Edwin Moscoso had ejected third baseman Eugenio Suárez earlier in the game, and now a borderline strike call had gone against shortstop Kyle Farmer. Bell wasn't even in the picture, but by stepping out of the dugout, an almost procedural objection, his fate was sealed. As the manager proceeded to earn the full value of his quick ejection, the trained audience recognized that flare of anger.

"Can't argue balls and strikes, so that was an easy one," John Sadak intoned on the Reds' television broadcast. A local newspaper declared the Reds, "deficient at hitting, proficient at arguing."

That was Bell's fifth and final ejection of 2021, and it came as the Reds' season peaked. Cincinnati's playoff odds, 61 percent that day, would never be that high again. In three seasons as manager—one of the 60-game variety—Bell has already been ejected a whopping 16 times.

Tossed only seven times in his 12-year playing career, it's as if Bell has been possessed by the spirit of Sweet Lou Piniella in the skipper's chair—holding players back, jutting out his chest and letting his spittle fly. He and the Reds have argued and brawled their way through a disjointed three-year stretch of ultimately middling baseball, unafraid to confront, or perhaps unable to avoid, the anger coursing through us all.

⚾ ⚾ ⚾

On the first weekend of the 2021 season, St. Louis Cardinals right-hander Jake Woodford plunked Reds right fielder Nick Castellanos up high with a 92-mph sinker. Three batters later, Castellanos scampered home to beat Woodford's lunging tag and score on a wild pitch. Then, Castellanos stood up and flexed his bruising biceps in the young pitcher's face. Cardinals veterans Yadier Molina and Nolan Arenado took exception. The benches cleared.

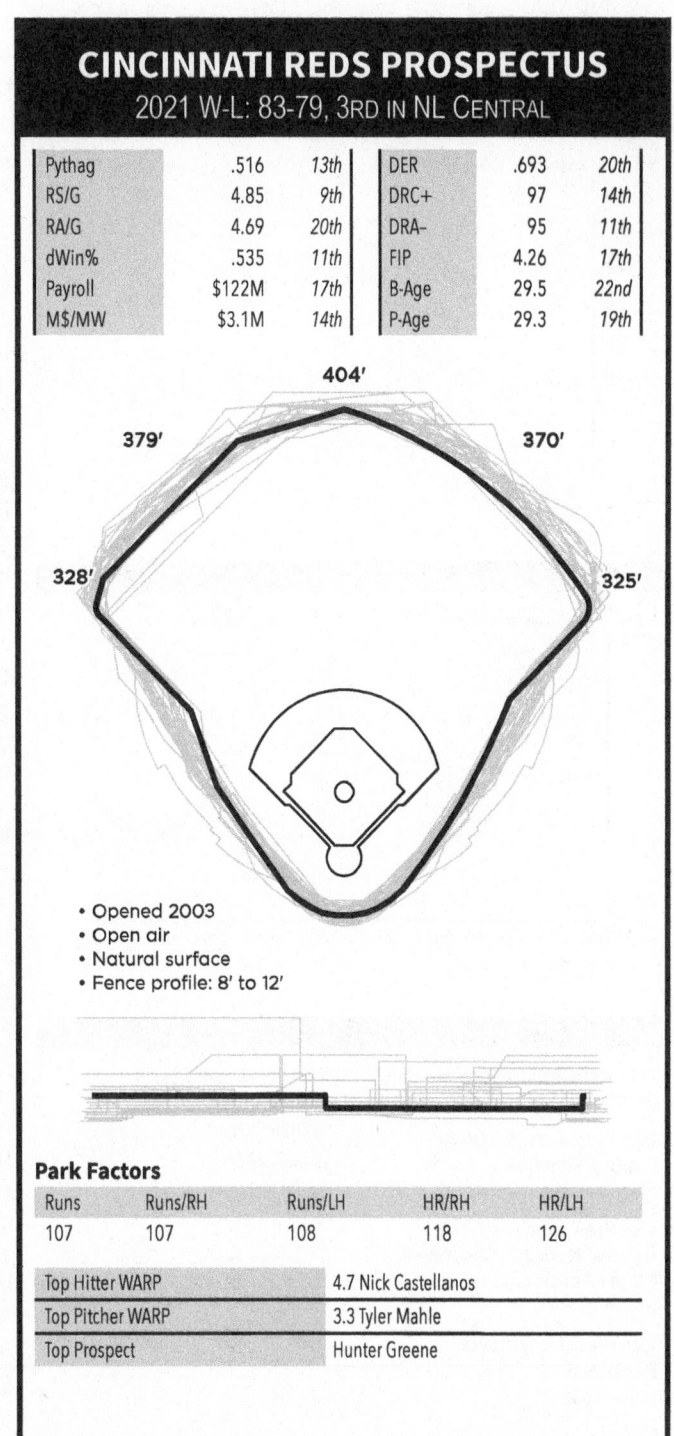

CINCINNATI REDS PROSPECTUS

2021 W-L: 83-79, 3RD IN NL CENTRAL

Pythag	.516	*13th*	DER	.693	*20th*
RS/G	4.85	*9th*	DRC+	97	*14th*
RA/G	4.69	*20th*	DRA-	95	*11th*
dWin%	.535	*11th*	FIP	4.26	*17th*
Payroll	$122M	*17th*	B-Age	29.5	*22nd*
M$/MW	$3.1M	*14th*	P-Age	29.3	*19th*

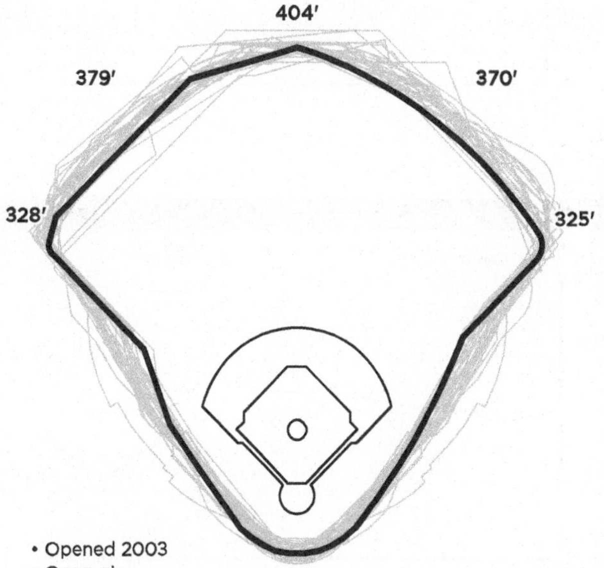

- Opened 2003
- Open air
- Natural surface
- Fence profile: 8' to 12'

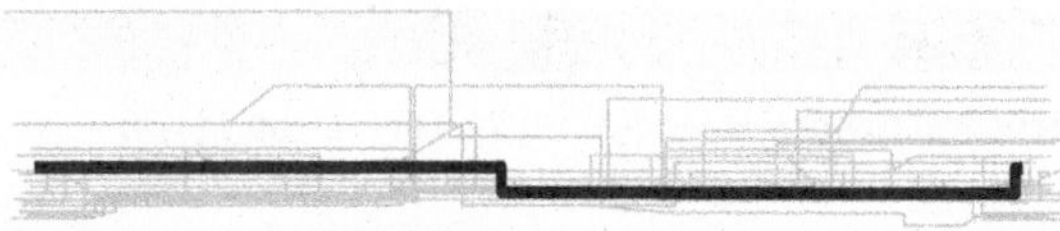

Park Factors

Runs	Runs/RH	Runs/LH	HR/RH	HR/LH
107	107	108	118	126

Top Hitter WARP	4.7 Nick Castellanos
Top Pitcher WARP	3.3 Tyler Mahle
Top Prospect	Hunter Greene

Payroll History (in millions)

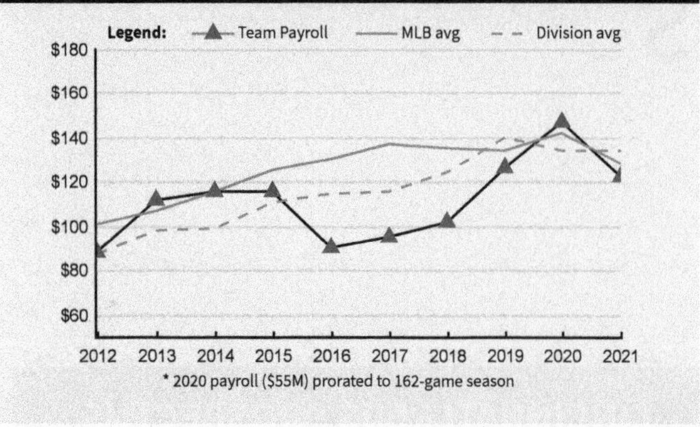

Future Commitments (in millions)

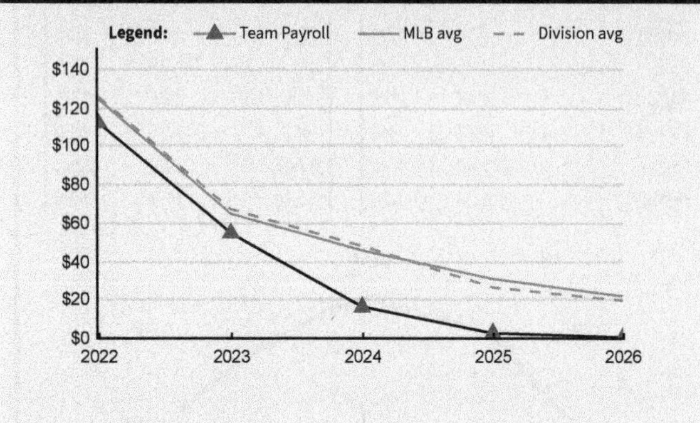

Farm System Ranking

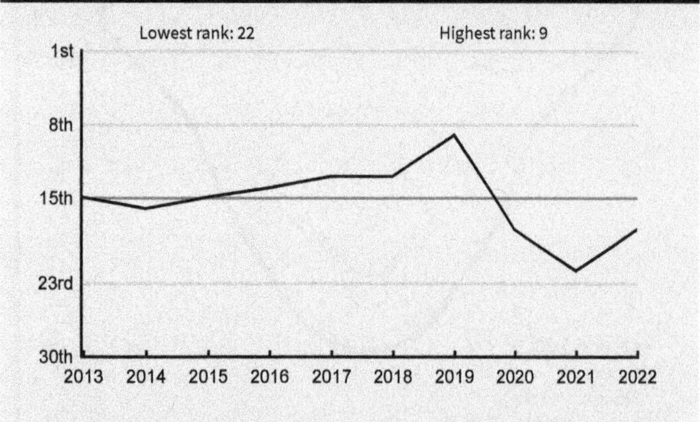

Personnel

President and General Manager
Nick Krall

Vice President, Assistant General Manager
Sam Grossman

Vice President/Assistant General Manager, Scouting & Player Development
Brad Meador

Vice President, Player Personnel
Chris Buckley

Vice President, Player Development
Shawn Pender

Manager
David Bell

For a long time, the consensus held that anger was a mortifying bug of the human psyche that should be suppressed when possible. A study by a psychology professor named James Averill complicated that idea in 1977, kickstarting a wave of research into the useful qualities of outward anger. Detailing the findings that sprang from Averill's work, *The Atlantic*'s Charles Duhigg wrote that anger, "conveys more information, more quickly, than almost any other type of emotion. And it does an excellent job of forcing us to listen to and confront problems we might otherwise avoid."

"We're more likely to perceive people who express anger as competent, powerful, and the kinds of leaders who will overcome challenges," Duhigg explained.

"When we look at the brains of people who are expressing anger, they look very similar to people who are experiencing happiness," Dacher Keltner, the director of the Berkeley Social Interaction Lab, told *The Atlantic*. "When we become angry, we feel like we're taking control, like we're getting power over something."

But where Averill's study found hope in anger as a catalyst to help resolve conflicts and sand away friction points in more private relationships—between husband and wife, or parents and a curfew-breaking teenager—Castellanos' outburst only set off a chain reaction of impotent rage, the usual chirping and milling about that comprise baseball's ritualistic combat. Commissioner Rob Manfred suspended Castellanos two games for inciting a brawl, a special no-no in the pandemic, while declining to suspend any of the Cardinals.

More than a month later, the decision was still stuck in Castellanos' craw. A game-tying homer in an eventual win over the Rockies begat a fist bump for a fan in the seats behind the plate. That begat a postgame interview in which Castellanos took off his headset and turned it over to that fan, who proceeded to recount the advice he offered just before the homer: *Picture Manfred's face on the baseball.*

It was only the first inning. The Reds were winning in San Diego, and yet the little girl in the glasses and the Joey Votto shirt was crying. Her idol had been ejected.

The strike-zone maestro disagreed with a check-swing call from third-base umpire Chris Guccione. Votto gestured toward Guccione as he walked off the field but then turned back toward home-plate umpire Ryan Additon in a rage. Briefly boxed out by Bell, the furious Votto would not be denied. He circled and stalked his target, his head cocked and neck bulging in the defiant posture of aggression. He kept his eyes and his center of gravity laser-focused on Additon, dodging and shrugging off the rotation of coaches and umpires trying to restrain him or break the lock of his gaze.

Replays showed he went around.

Unleashing a tantrum, no matter how justified, can feel like an embarrassing lapse in judgment. Anger is not something most of us can marshal for our own benefit. We lose our tempers. We punch walls and break our pitching hands. We let our emotions get the better of us. We fly off the handle. It is, by nature, not under control.

When we pull ourselves back together, there's usually a mess to clean up. In this case, the damage had been done to the dreams of a little girl named Abigail, who was attending her first MLB game, thrilled to see her favorite player. Votto picked up the pieces admirably, sending up a signed baseball that read, "I am sorry I didn't play the entire game," and securing Abigail and her family tickets for the following game, when he left her beaming after a pregame meeting by the dugout.

Of course, every part of this sequence becomes significantly more difficult if it doesn't take place inside the vacuum-sealed environment of a baseball game, or if you're not a magnetic former MVP. Full-blown raving is the stuff of daydreams, a fantasy you live out under the pressure of a hot shower before steeling yourself to stay cool under the pressure of the work day. There's no heartwarming end to losing control with your boss or your family or the idiot holding up the checkout line. No one wants your autograph. They want you to put the chair back on its legs and sweep up all those pretzels you spilled.

About a month after that last Bell ejection, and mere days before the Reds were officially eliminated from playoff contention, Castellanos belted a walk-off homer against the Washington Nationals. The Reds were united in their quest to overcome suddenly long odds, and especially to do so at the expense of the Cardinals, who had won 16 in a row as of that night.

The flex-induced brawl was the first in a series of St. Louis-adjacent skirmishes. Later on in April, a pitch had gotten away from St. Louis righty Jack Flaherty and hit eventual National League Rookie of the Year Jonathan India in the helmet. Flaherty didn't intend to hit India and was visibly upset with himself, but Bell wound up ejected and viscerally angry over the umpire's decision to issue warnings to both teams.

After his late September walk-off, Castellanos said the members of that clubhouse had come to see themselves as scrappy underdogs fighting larger forces trying to keep them down. "I don't know if it's a small market that is overlooked, we always end up on the butt end of every decision Major League Baseball makes," he said. "It is kinda cool to take on the Cincinnati-versus-everybody mentality."

As further proof of their solidarity, Castellanos mentioned that catcher Tucker Barnhart had commissioned shirts for the team. They read, "Cincinnati Reds Against the World."

The world, alas, has had the better of it recently. Each year, the franchise seems to develop and then expose a fatal flaw. First, a perennially strong lineup was sunk by a lack of pitching. Then, a vaunted rotation bloomed just as the hits vanished. As star bats resurfaced, a thinned-out supporting cast sank the ship again. Like a bullpen that can't hold a hard-earned lead, it is legitimately infuriating.

Beginning with the 2020 offseason, the ownership group hastily pivoted from running up a franchise-high payroll to chopping costs, passing off short-term failure as blanket proof that spending is a fruitless endeavor. (Nevermind that pesky, outwardly absurd implication that spending on corner infielders and a DH-type was a foolproof plan for a team in need of a shortstop and a center fielder.)

That chopping is continuing. Barnhart, the maker of the T-shirts, was flipped along with his veteran leadership to the Detroit Tigers. Castellanos hit so well he opted out of his contract. Veteran starter Wade Miley was waived in favor of a wing and a prayer that similar reliability can be achieved for $7 million or so less. The younger pitchers the Reds have so successfully developed are trade-rumor staples, not extension candidates.

When things don't go our way, our overheated brains crave a demolition derby like Votto's, full catharsis with no real consequences to consider. But that useful form of anger Averill long ago described—the kind that can melt and reshape friendships or fuel progress—is all about consequences, about effecting change that could make the rage dissipate, that could make it worthwhile.

This is the conundrum for Reds fans: The rage they feel is not directed at the people who wear the uniform, who face the world as their city's bat-wielding avatars. The players assembled are pushing in the same direction and butting up against the same headwinds, as owners across the league insulate themselves (read: their wallets) from expressions of discontent. But the fans and players have no umpires to stalk, no mounds to charge.

The Atlantic reminded us of useful anger's qualities and benefits in 2019 because of how ever-present and disorienting the emotion has become in American culture. "It has become less episodic and more persistent, a constant drumbeat in our lives. It is directed less often at people we know and more often at distant groups that are easy to demonize," Duhigg wrote. "These far-off targets may or may not have earned our ire; either way, they're apt to be less invested in resolving our differences."

Anger, and moral outrage specifically, is a complicated force with manifestations evolving far too quickly for comfort as we splinter, close ranks and distance ourselves from the unfamiliar.

In the swirl of constant communication—but rare connection—we have developed a maddening tendency to argue about whether anger itself is good or bad. "The only thing that can be good or bad is what you do with that emotion," researcher Victoria Spring wrote of the phenomenon for *Scientific American* in 2019. "What if we approached outrage functionally instead, and asked: when can the expression of outrage be viewed as positive or negative? And when is outrage most effectively leveraged toward social change . . . or social destruction?"

It can undeniably be good when used to change an open, empathetic mind. But it is also weaponized to harden existing biases and redirect energy toward less savory ends. Feeling the heat of anger now often turns into a spin cycle of being mad at people who seem mad at you. When bound to identity, fandom can become its own form of doomscrolling, trolling in search of conflict.

David Bell stumping for his hitters: Part of the show. Cincinnati natives clapping back at the New York Mets broadcast for denouncing Skyline Chili as disgusting: Probably not necessary but amusing in moderation. Thom Brennaman demanding forgiveness while aligning his sympathies with an "all lives matter" martyr playing up the bit for his podcast: Well, less excusable.

Tribal aggression that can be somewhat healthily channeled into sports fandom turns terrifying when it supercharges an entire society's insecurities and grievances. The anger in the world increasingly resembles the anger once reserved for the bubble of the ballpark, to the point that even entertaining fury can feel fraught. That righteous-feeling but inconsequential rage has escaped its bounds, if it ever had any, but we can only call it as we see it cross the line.

—Zach Crizer is the baseball editor at Yahoo Sports.

Hitters

Shogo Akiyama CF Born: 04/16/88 Age: 34 Bats: L Throws: R Height: 6'0" Weight: 190 lb. Origin: International Free Agent, 2019

YEAR	TEAM	LVL	AGE	PA	R	2B	3B	HR	RBI	BB	K	SB	CS	Whiff%	AVG/OBP/SLG	DRC+	BABIP	BRR	FRAA	WARP
2020	CIN	MLB	32	183	16	6	1	0	9	25	34	7	3	19.1%	.245/.357/.297	92	.314	-0.3	LF(36): 1.0, CF(21): -0.1	0.4
2021	CIN	MLB	33	183	16	8	0	0	12	14	40	2	3	22.7%	.204/.282/.253	73	.268	0.1	CF(48): -0.3, LF(9): -0.8, RF(4): -0.1	0.0
2022 DC	*CIN*	*MLB*	*34*	*161*	*23*	*7*	*0*	*5*	*21*	*16*	*29*	*3*	*2*	*21.6%*	*.267/.351/.443*	*110*	*.307*	*0.2*	*CF 1, RF 0*	*0.9*

Comparables: Jacoby Ellsbury, Eric Young Jr., Jason Bourgeois

It's hard to begrudge Akiyama for struggling to acclimate to his new job stateside over the last two years. His preparation for his first season in the big leagues took a backseat to the pandemic, and the lead-up to his second season got the same treatment following a horrible freak accident that injured his wife. The stellar reports regarding Akiyama's plate approach and defense have done a decent job living up to scrutiny since his arrival in Cincinnati, but he's logged 366 homerless plate appearances now, and it's extremely difficult to be an average contributor at the plate with power output like that unless you're literally Tony Gwynn. He is not literally Tony Gwynn. This will be the third and final year of Akiyama's contract with the Reds, and the kindest thing to wish upon him is probably just an uneventful spring training.

Aristides Aquino OF Born: 04/22/94 Age: 28 Bats: R Throws: R Height: 6'4" Weight: 220 lb. Origin: International Free Agent, 2011

YEAR	TEAM	LVL	AGE	PA	R	2B	3B	HR	RBI	BB	K	SB	CS	Whiff%	AVG/OBP/SLG	DRC+	BABIP	BRR	FRAA	WARP
2019	LOU	AAA	25	323	56	13	1	28	53	23	81	5	1		.299/.356/.636	130	.321	0.6	RF(64): 4.7, CF(5): 1.8	2.7
2019	CIN	MLB	25	225	31	8	0	19	47	16	60	7	0	35.1%	.259/.316/.576	113	.266	0.2	RF(54): 2.0	1.3
2020	CIN	MLB	26	56	7	1	0	2	8	6	18	1	0	38.5%	.170/.304/.319	87	.222	0.8	LF(13): -0.1, RF(4): -0.2, CF(1): -0.2	0.1
2021	LOU	AAA	27	27	5	2	0	1	5	8	1	0	0		.263/.481/.526	132	.235	0.8	RF(4): 0.5, CF(1): 0.1	0.3
2021	CIN	MLB	27	204	25	6	1	10	23	27	75	2	2	39.5%	.190/.299/.408	77	.253	-1.7	LF(35): -0.1, RF(27): -0.1, CF(14): 1.2	0.1
2022 DC	*CIN*	*MLB*	*28*	*285*	*42*	*11*	*1*	*16*	*45*	*30*	*85*	*3*	*1*	*37.3%*	*.221/.318/.472*	*100*	*.267*	*0.0*	*RF 0, LF 0*	*0.3*

Comparables: Scott Van Slyke, Abraham Almonte, Nolan Reimold

Aquino has gone to great efforts over the years to change his approach and minimize the ways it holds back his performance, but it's been a little like trying to learn how to breathe underwater. He knocked more than 10 points off his swing rate between 2019 and '21, and added nearly nine points to his fly-ball rate. But more selectivity led only to a worse contact rate, and more balls in the air still resulted in him hitting just two homers in his last 74 plate appearances. It will be a sad day when Aquino unleashes his final titanic blast into the left-field seats as a big-leaguer, but the whiff issues caused by the inherent violence in his swing are hastening that day's arrival.

Jose Barrero SS Born: 04/05/98 Age: 24 Bats: R Throws: R Height: 6'2" Weight: 175 lb. Origin: International Free Agent, 2017

YEAR	TEAM	LVL	AGE	PA	R	2B	3B	HR	RBI	BB	K	SB	CS	Whiff%	AVG/OBP/SLG	DRC+	BABIP	BRR	FRAA	WARP
2019	GDD	WIN	21	69	8	3	0	1	9	5	12	3	1		.213/.290/.311		.245			
2019	DBT	A+	21	452	58	37	1	8	55	25	83	15	2		.280/.343/.436	127	.329	-0.7	SS(100): 0.5	2.4
2020	CIN	MLB	22	68	4	0	0	0	2	1	26	1	1	40.3%	.194/.206/.194	60	.317	-1.0	SS(21): 0.8	-0.2
2021	CHA	AA	23	180	31	9	1	6	28	16	40	8	1		.300/.367/.481	121	.362	1.4	SS(37): -0.0	1.1
2021	LOU	AAA	23	200	31	10	0	13	38	20	44	8	3		.306/.392/.594	133	.336	-2.3	SS(43): 4.6, 3B(2): 0.1	1.6
2021	CIN	MLB	23	56	4	4	1	0	3	3	17	1	0	34.6%	.200/.286/.320	72	.303	0.6	SS(9): 0.6, CF(7): -0.2, 2B(2): 0.2	0.1
2022 DC	*CIN*	*MLB*	*24*	*187*	*22*	*9*	*0*	*5*	*23*	*11*	*51*	*3*	*2*	*32.0%*	*.237/.303/.398*	*84*	*.311*	*0.1*	*SS 1*	*0.4*

Comparables: Eduardo Escobar, Eugenio Suárez, Hernán Pérez

After skipping two levels to make a predictably ugly big-league debut in 2020, Barrero fell back into a more routine developmental path last year, beginning the season in Double-A. Once there, it took no time at all for him to re-establish confidence in his bat. His 19 homers and 16 stolen bases in 85 minor-league games indicated even more explosive potential in his game than previously believed, and he walked much more than he ever had before. His offense went cold again during another brief stint in the majors, but he didn't look *quite* as lost as he had the year before, and he even added some center-field experience to his résumé. The time for Barrero to step into an everyday MLB lineup spot is nigh, even if he may benefit from getting back into a rhythm again in Louisville to start off 2022.

Alex Blandino IF Born: 11/06/92 Age: 29 Bats: R Throws: R Height: 6'0" Weight: 190 lb. Origin: Round 1, 2014 Draft (#29 overall)

YEAR	TEAM	LVL	AGE	PA	R	2B	3B	HR	RBI	BB	K	SB	CS	Whiff%	AVG/OBP/SLG	DRC+	BABIP	BRR	FRAA	WARP
2019	LOU	AAA	26	293	36	13	1	5	24	40	73	1	3		.247/.386/.372	92	.335	-3.1	2B(35): -1.3, SS(18): -1.4, 3B(15): 1.3	0.4
2019	CIN	MLB	26	50	6	1	0	1	3	10	14	0	0	18.2%	.250/.420/.361	87	.348	-0.4	2B(10): 0.1, 3B(4): -0.0, 1B(3): -0.0	0.1
2021	LOU	AAA	28	76	5	3	0	0	3	14	16	0	0		.102/.289/.153	92	.136	-0.4	2B(7): 0.8, 1B(6): 0.1, 3B(6): 0.1	0.2
2021	CIN	MLB	28	82	9	4	0	0	5	8	28	1	0	31.0%	.200/.317/.257	62	.333	0.4	1B(17): 0.9, 3B(9): 0.7, 2B(5): -0.1	0.0
2022 DC	*FA*	*MLB*	*29*	*276*	*27*	*11*	*0*	*5*	*26*	*31*	*76*	*1*	*1*	*24.2%*	*.198/.313/.325*	*78*	*.266*	*-0.3*	*2B 0, 3B 1*	*0.0*

Comparables: Phil Gosselin, Darwin Barney, Chase d'Arnaud

Strange as it sounds, there are certain roles in sports that you can pull off by more or less just standing there. Back-up quarterback? Just stand there. Seven-foot center on a Sun Belt basketball team? Walk into the paint, maybe raise your arms if it feels natural, and just stand there. Try as he might, though, Blandino can't quite make the strategy work in the batter's box. His minuscule swing rate hasn't produced much more than a modest pile of free passes, and to make matters worse, his whiff and power numbers have made it so that pitchers don't have much to fear when he does swing. Fortunately for him, the Reds aren't exactly known for their infield depth, so a healthier or perhaps a cartoonishly shrunken-down version of him could be of use if the team is still interested.

Tyler Callihan 2B Born: 06/22/00 Age: 22 Bats: L Throws: R Height: 6'1" Weight: 205 lb. Origin: Round 3, 2019 Draft (#85 overall)

YEAR	TEAM	LVL	AGE	PA	R	2B	3B	HR	RBI	BB	K	SB	CS	Whiff%	AVG/OBP/SLG	DRC+	BABIP	BRR	FRAA	WARP
2019	GRN	ROA	19	217	27	10	5	5	26	9	46	9	3		.250/.286/.422		.297			
2019	BIL	ROA	19	21	3	0	1	1	7	1	4	2	0		.400/.429/.650		.467			
2021	DBT	A	21	99	14	6	0	2	10	8	13	5	1		.299/.351/.437	113	.324	-0.1	2B(23): 2.9	0.7
2022 non-DC	*CIN*	*MLB*	*22*	*251*	*21*	*10*	*1*	*3*	*22*	*16*	*56*	*10*	*3*	*26.4%*	*.239/.293/.338*	*71*	*.303*	*0.8*	*2B 2*	*0.3*

Comparables: Kyle Seager, Jimmy Paredes, Everth Cabrera

Callihan's pro career is not off to an idyllic start. One of the oldest high schoolers in his draft class, he underwhelmed in his 2019 rookie ball debut, then returned from the lost pandemic year to play just 23 games in A-ball before getting sidelined with an elbow injury that necessitated Tommy John surgery. His contact skills are evident, and there's a not-small amount of power here somewhere. Considering he's likely to end up at first base, though—or at the very most, Moustakas his way around second—he'll need to get to all of that power in order to carve out an everyday role.

★ ★ ★ *2022 Top 101 Prospect* **#70** ★ ★ ★

Elly De La Cruz SS Born: 01/11/02 Age: 20 Bats: S Throws: R Height: 6'2" Weight: 150 lb. Origin: International Free Agent, 2018

YEAR	TEAM	LVL	AGE	PA	R	2B	3B	HR	RBI	BB	K	SB	CS	Whiff%	AVG/OBP/SLG	DRC+	BABIP	BRR	FRAA	WARP
2019	DSL REDS	ROK	17	186	24	11	1	1	26	14	45	3	6		.285/.351/.382		.380			
2021	RED	ROK	19	55	13	6	2	3	13	4	15	2	0		.400/.455/.780		.531			
2021	DBT	A	19	210	22	12	7	5	29	10	65	8	5		.269/.305/.477	89	.372	-0.7	3B(28): 7.0, SS(20): 2.7	1.2
2022 non-DC	*CIN*	*MLB*	*20*	*251*	*19*	*11*	*3*	*3*	*22*	*11*	*86*	*4*	*5*	*35.5%*	*.221/.261/.342*	*58*	*.331*	*1.0*	*3B 3, SS 2*	*0.0*

Comparables: Mat Gamel, Juan Silverio, Ozzie Albies

Do you remember the last position player to sign with the Reds as an international free agent and accumulate at least three WARP with the club? Safe to assume you don't—it was Dave Concepcion, who signed out of Venezuela in 1967. Since then, the organization has succeeded in bringing in foreign players with dreamy tools, but consistently failed to develop them into quality big-leaguers. De La Cruz emphatically checks the first box, though time will tell if he can avoid checking the second. A long, projectable teenager with a legitimate shot at sticking at shortstop and potential plus-plus grades in power, speed and arm strength, De La Cruz's ceiling is somewhere up in the thermosphere. The growth of both his physical body as well as his raw skills was shocking to see from someone who signed for just $65,000 in 2018, which begs the question of how much he can refine his game. In addition to loud exit velocities and smooth footwork on the infield dirt, he's also shown the kind of horrific plate discipline that's doomed too many past boom-or-bust Reds prospects to count.

Kyle Farmer SS Born: 08/17/90 Age: 31 Bats: R Throws: R Height: 6'0" Weight: 205 lb. Origin: Round 8, 2013 Draft (#244 overall)

YEAR	TEAM	LVL	AGE	PA	R	2B	3B	HR	RBI	BB	K	SB	CS	Whiff%	AVG/OBP/SLG	DRC+	BABIP	BRR	FRAA	WARP
2019	CIN	MLB	28	197	22	6	0	9	27	10	59	4	1	29.5%	.230/.279/.410	82	.284	-1.5	2B(41): -1.1, 1B(18): -0.2, C(15): -0.6	-0.1
2020	CIN	MLB	29	70	4	3	0	0	4	5	13	1	0	25.0%	.266/.329/.313	96	.333	-0.4	SS(15): -0.2, 2B(13): 0.5, 3B(2): 0.1	0.2
2021	CIN	MLB	30	529	60	22	2	16	63	22	97	2	3	20.0%	.263/.316/.416	98	.296	1.0	SS(121): -3.8, 3B(10): -0.4, 2B(9): -0.1	1.4
2022 DC	*CIN*	*MLB*	*31*	*460*	*54*	*21*	*1*	*11*	*58*	*25*	*83*	*2*	*2*	*20.7%*	*.249/.310/.388*	*83*	*.289*	*-0.5*	*SS -2, 3B 0*	*0.4*

Comparables: Manny Piña, Curt Casali, Adam Rosales

Just one man (Jonathan India) played more games for the 2021 Reds than Farmer, a fact that would have made you tug your collar were it about a team on a mission to tank, let alone one with legitimate playoff expectations as late as mid-September. And yet, as tempting as it is to gently poke fun at both player and ballclub here, it is undeniable that Farmer bailed Cincinnati out of a potential disaster situation. After the predictable failures of Dee Strange-Gordon and Eugenio Suárez to suitably play shortstop, it was Farmer—a natural catcher—who stepped in to fill the void. Amazingly, he turned in excellent defense, while also putting together a career-best season at the plate. It wouldn't be accurate to call him the Reds' MVP, but it sure ain't easy to imagine how they could have survived the year without him. The club will likely turn the starting shortstop job over to a younger prospect in 2022, but Farmer's versatility off the bench should still easily make him worth his arbitration salary.

TJ Friedl OF Born: 08/14/95 Age: 26 Bats: L Throws: L Height: 5'10" Weight: 180 lb. Origin: Undrafted Free Agent, 2016

YEAR	TEAM	LVL	AGE	PA	R	2B	3B	HR	RBI	BB	K	SB	CS	Whiff%	AVG/OBP/SLG	DRC+	BABIP	BRR	FRAA	WARP
2019	CHA	AA	23	269	38	11	4	5	28	29	50	13	4		.235/.347/.385	110	.277	1.4	RF(42): 2.5, LF(14): -1.3, CF(13): -1.0	1.4
2021	LOU	AAA	25	448	59	15	5	12	36	44	65	13	7		.264/.357/.422	113	.288	2.6	CF(75): -9.0, RF(22): -2.8, LF(20): 1.2	1.5
2021	CIN	MLB	25	36	9	1	0	1	2	4	2	0	0	14.8%	.290/.361/.419	107	.276	0.2	CF(6): -0.9, LF(5): 0.3	0.1
2022 DC	*CIN*	*MLB*	*26*	*310*	*36*	*12*	*2*	*6*	*35*	*26*	*51*	*8*	*3*	*19.8%*	*.251/.332/.381*	*92*	*.290*	*0.7*	*CF -2, RF 0*	*0.6*

Comparables: Brandon Jones, Edward Olivares, Zoilo Almonte

The 2021 season was a good one for Friedl. He nearly doubled his career high in homers for a season (that previous mark was seven, but hey, progress is progress), showed the best contact skills of his career, and earned himself a September cup of coffee with the major-league club. Given his offensive limitations it's unlikely Friedl will ever be as famous among casual fans as he is within prospect circles—fame owed entirely to his unorthodox entry into pro baseball—but his wheels, nifty defense in outfield corners and on-base abilities should allow him to float around the big leagues long enough endear himself to a modest group of fans wherever he goes.

Austin Hendrick RF Born: 06/15/01 Age: 21 Bats: L Throws: L Height: 6'0" Weight: 195 lb. Origin: Round 1, 2020 Draft (#12 overall)

YEAR	TEAM	LVL	AGE	PA	R	2B	3B	HR	RBI	BB	K	SB	CS	Whiff%	AVG/OBP/SLG	DRC+	BABIP	BRR	FRAA	WARP
2021	DBT	A	20	266	30	16	0	7	29	51	100	4	2		.211/.380/.388	93	.363	0.3	RF(56): 3.0, CF(5): -0.3	0.9
2022 non-DC	*CIN*	*MLB*	*21*	*251*	*21*	*11*	*0*	*3*	*20*	*28*	*104*	*1*	*1*	*41.8%*	*.174/.277/.287*	*54*	*.308*	*-0.2*	*RF 2, CF 0*	*-0.6*

Comparables: Rymer Liriano, Sócrates Brito, Josh Reddick

The 12th-overall pick by the Reds in 2020, Hendrick was able to produce a decent offensive season against A-ball pitchers despite a 38% strikeout rate, so-so power numbers and a nagging groin injury. The three true outcomes profile is likely here to stay, but the good news is that approach should include a lot more homers going forward, as Hendrick matures and grows more confident against pro pitchers. He can be a perennial 40-homer player at GABP who won't hurt you with his glove in right field, like Jay Bruce, but his ability to make consistent contact will be the difference between him being his team's bruising cleanup hitter or the frustrating boom-or-bust guy in the six-hole. Like Jay Bruce.

Jonathan India 2B Born: 12/15/96 Age: 25 Bats: R Throws: R Height: 6'0" Weight: 200 lb. Origin: Round 1, 2018 Draft (#5 overall)

YEAR	TEAM	LVL	AGE	PA	R	2B	3B	HR	RBI	BB	K	SB	CS	Whiff%	AVG/OBP/SLG	DRC+	BABIP	BRR	FRAA	WARP
2019	GDD	WIN	22	71	5	1	1	3	10	8	21	1	1		.133/.254/.333		.135			
2019	DBT	A+	22	367	50	15	5	8	30	37	84	7	5		.256/.346/.410	113	.319	-1.9	3B(74): -9.1, 2B(5): 0.1	0.4
2019	CHA	AA	22	145	24	3	0	3	14	22	26	4	0		.270/.414/.378	126	.314	-0.4	3B(33): -1.1	0.7
2021	CIN	MLB	24	631	98	34	2	21	69	71	141	12	3	25.1%	.269/.376/.459	108	.326	2.8	2B(148): 6.7	3.9
2022 DC	*CIN*	*MLB*	*25*	*591*	*93*	*27*	*2*	*19*	*67*	*63*	*127*	*9*	*3*	*25.4%*	*.245/.351/.422*	*108*	*.295*	*0.0*	*2B 4*	*3.1*

Comparables: Ryan Braun, Jedd Gyorko, Hunter Dozier

Aside from a brilliant cameo from Shin-Soo Choo in 2013, you have to go all the way back to the Barry Larkin era to find the last time the Reds had anything resembling a reliably productive leadoff hitter—and even Larkin hit second and third more often than he led off. But the days of speedy gap hitters who refused to take a walk topping the lineup card in Cincinnati may finally be over. India, a former fifth-overall pick, won the starting second base job out of spring training and the NL Rookie of the Year award in the fall. A disappointing lack of power followed him from the minors to the big leagues, but it didn't stay long. Of the 21 homers he hit, 15 came after the All-Star break, and his 72nd percentile max exit velocity shows he's got at least a little more juice in his bat than previously thought. That kind of patience-and-pop combo would mean his offense could profile just about anywhere going forward, but make him a borderline All-Star at second base.

★ ★ ★ *2022 Top 101 Prospect* **#77** ★ ★ ★

Matt McLain IF Born: 08/06/99 Age: 22 Bats: R Throws: R Height: 5'11" Weight: 180 lb. Origin: Round 1, 2021 Draft (#17 overall)

YEAR	TEAM	LVL	AGE	PA	R	2B	3B	HR	RBI	BB	K	SB	CS	Whiff%	AVG/OBP/SLG	DRC+	BABIP	BRR	FRAA	WARP
2021	DAY	A+	21	119	15	6	0	3	19	17	24	10	2		.273/.387/.424	111	.329	0.4	SS(27): 1.3	0.7
2022 non-DC	*CIN*	*MLB*	*22*	*251*	*21*	*10*	*0*	*3*	*21*	*22*	*61*	*11*	*4*	*26.2%*	*.214/.293/.317*	*68*	*.278*	*0.9*	*SS 2*	*0.2*

Comparables: Dixon Machado, Jean Segura, Tim Anderson

McLain is a two-time first-round selection who spurned the Diamondbacks as the 25th overall pick in 2018 in favor of three years at UCLA, then landed with the Reds as the 17th overall pick in 2021. He is very on-brand for Cincinnati's draft tastes: a polished college infielder whose plus hit tool gives him a high floor, but with modest power projection that limits his ceiling. What separates McLain from the Blandinos and Senzels of the organization, though, is that he actually has a decent shot to stick at shortstop. His range is iffy, but he's light on his feet and sure-handed enough to most plays, and he has a stronger arm than one might expect given his size. His first exposure to pro ball was brief but encouraging, and sets him up for an expedited path to the big leagues going forward.

Mike Moustakas 3B Born: 09/11/88 Age: 33 Bats: L Throws: R Height: 6'0" Weight: 225 lb. Origin: Round 1, 2007 Draft (#2 overall)

YEAR	TEAM	LVL	AGE	PA	R	2B	3B	HR	RBI	BB	K	SB	CS	Whiff%	AVG/OBP/SLG	DRC+	BABIP	BRR	FRAA	WARP
2019	MIL	MLB	30	584	80	30	1	35	87	53	98	3	0	24.8%	.254/.329/.516	119	.250	-2.1	3B(105): -0.8, 2B(47): -2.0	2.7
2020	CIN	MLB	31	163	13	9	0	8	27	18	36	1	0	24.4%	.230/.331/.468	106	.247	-0.6	2B(32): -2.0, 1B(10): -0.8, 3B(2): 0.2	0.3
2021	CIN	MLB	32	206	21	12	0	6	22	18	46	0	0	27.6%	.208/.282/.372	83	.239	-1.1	3B(44): -1.4, 1B(11): -0.5, 2B(1): -0.1	-0.1
2022 DC	*CIN*	*MLB*	*33*	*303*	*43*	*14*	*0*	*15*	*50*	*28*	*62*	*0*	*1*	*26.4%*	*.243/.326/.467*	*103*	*.266*	*-0.4*	*3B 0, 1B 0*	*0.8*

Comparables: Robin Ventura, Brooks Robinson, Buddy Bell

In another universe, Moustakas' four-year, $64 million contract makes him just the fifth or sixth-highest paid player on a big market club with serious cash to throw around. This club's fans don't notice so much when he plays in less than half of his team's games over the first two years of the deal thanks to foot and quad injuries and bouts of illness, and they don't spend a lot of time fretting over his career-worst offensive performance in 2021. Unfortunately, in the universe we share, that contract of his is literally the largest ever given to a free agent by his particular employer. The fact that we're already halfway through offers both comfort and cringe, as the Reds must now consider how best to deploy the 33-year-old with a long-established veteran at third base and an exciting second-year player at the keystone.

Tyler Naquin OF Born: 04/24/91 Age: 31 Bats: L Throws: R Height: 6'2" Weight: 195 lb. Origin: Round 1, 2012 Draft (#15 overall)

YEAR	TEAM	LVL	AGE	PA	R	2B	3B	HR	RBI	BB	K	SB	CS	Whiff%	AVG/OBP/SLG	DRC+	BABIP	BRR	FRAA	WARP
2019	CLE	MLB	28	294	34	19	0	10	34	14	66	4	2	25.1%	.288/.325/.467	89	.345	0.2	RF(68): 12.4, LF(15): 4.5	2.2
2020	CLE	MLB	29	141	15	8	1	4	20	5	40	0	1	30.9%	.218/.248/.383	73	.275	-1.1	RF(39): 1.8	0.0
2021	CIN	MLB	30	454	52	24	2	19	70	35	106	5	3	23.8%	.270/.333/.477	101	.318	-2.6	CF(92): -4.4, LF(22): -0.4, RF(21): -0.9	1.0
2022 DC	*CIN*	*MLB*	*31*	*526*	*70*	*25*	*2*	*21*	*79*	*35*	*118*	*4*	*3*	*24.2%*	*.259/.317/.454*	*99*	*.305*	*0.0*	*CF -5, RF 2*	*1.2*

Comparables: Abraham Almonte, Lorenzo Cain, Charlie Blackmon

Naquin joined the Reds as a minor-league free agent pick-up, fighting for playing time as a seemingly redundant left-handed hitting corner outfielder in an organization already teeming with them. Then he OPSed 1.068 over his first 12 games and showed a passing ability to at least stand facing the right direction in center field, and bam, the 30-year-old set a new career high in games played. Naquin still has the shortcomings he always did—he has trouble staying healthy, and he's essentially unusable against lefties—but he makes loud contact against righties without being too much of a swing-and-miss liability. That doesn't add up to an enormously valuable player, but his performance in 2021 boosted his reputation enough that teams will likely continue giving him chances well into his 30s.

Nick Senzel CF Born: 06/29/95 Age: 27 Bats: R Throws: R Height: 6'1" Weight: 205 lb. Origin: Round 1, 2016 Draft (#2 overall)

YEAR	TEAM	LVL	AGE	PA	R	2B	3B	HR	RBI	BB	K	SB	CS	Whiff%	AVG/OBP/SLG	DRC+	BABIP	BRR	FRAA	WARP
2019	LOU	AAA	24	38	7	1	0	1	2	3	13	0	0		.257/.316/.371	87	.381	0.6	CF(8): -1.4	0.0
2019	CIN	MLB	24	414	55	20	4	12	42	30	101	14	5	23.7%	.256/.315/.427	87	.319	-0.5	CF(96): -5.2, 2B(1): 0.0	0.5
2020	CIN	MLB	25	78	8	6	0	2	8	6	15	2	1	23.2%	.186/.247/.357	96	.204	-1.5	CF(23): 1.0	0.2
2021	LOU	AAA	26	39	5	3	1	0	2	2	2	0	0		.286/.316/.429	105	.294	-0.4	CF(7): 0.1, SS(2): -0.1	0.1
2021	CIN	MLB	26	124	18	4	0	1	8	12	16	2	5	17.8%	.252/.323/.315	99	.284	-0.7	CF(29): -1.2, 2B(8): -0.2, 3B(3): -0.1	0.3
2022 DC	*CIN*	*MLB*	*27*	*165*	*22*	*8*	*0*	*5*	*23*	*13*	*27*	*3*	*2*	*19.2%*	*.274/.342/.446*	*109*	*.308*	*0.2*	*CF 0, RF 0*	*0.8*

Comparables: Ryan Braun, Stephen Piscotty, Jedd Gyorko

Once upon a time, Senzel was considered a safe pick for the Reds to make with the second-overall selection in the 2016 draft. That "safe" label, however, only meant the skills he'd shown at the University of Tennessee seemed easily transferable to major-league games. There was no way to know that finger, shoulder, groin and knee injuries, not to mention bouts with vertigo and the ol' 2020 "mystery illness," would limit him to just 163 big-league games through his first six pro seasons. When he did see the field in 2021, he was able to produce his best plate discipline numbers to date. But we still haven't seen him hit the ball very hard, and his sporadic moments of good health have made it incredibly difficult to draw any conclusions about his transition to center field. A slash line like .300/.360/.480 from Senzel in the near future still wouldn't be a total shock, but a 140-game season might be.

Tyler Stephenson C Born: 08/16/96 Age: 25 Bats: R Throws: R Height: 6'4" Weight: 225 lb. Origin: Round 1, 2015 Draft (#11 overall)

YEAR	TEAM	LVL	AGE	PA	R	2B	3B	HR	RBI	BB	K	SB	CS	Whiff%	AVG/OBP/SLG	DRC+	BABIP	BRR	FRAA	WARP
2019	CHA	AA	22	363	47	19	1	6	44	37	60	0	0		.285/.372/.410	119	.331	-2.8	C(87): -6.6	1.2
2020	CIN	MLB	23	20	4	0	0	2	6	2	9	0	0	26.7%	.294/.400/.647	92	.500	0.0	C(4): -0.0	0.0
2021	CIN	MLB	24	402	56	21	0	10	45	41	75	0	0	19.0%	.286/.366/.431	106	.333	-1.6	C(78): 1.2, 1B(23): -1.7, LF(1): 0.1	1.6
2022 DC	*CIN*	*MLB*	*25*	*487*	*60*	*23*	*0*	*11*	*59*	*46*	*89*	*0*	*1*	*20.0%*	*.250/.335/.387*	*95*	*.294*	*-0.8*	*C 1, 1B -1*	*1.8*

Comparables: Devin Mesoraco, Christian Vázquez, Tucker Barnhart

YEAR	TEAM	P. COUNT	FRM RUNS	BLK RUNS	THRW RUNS	TOT RUNS
2019	CHA	12364	-7.7	0.0	0.4	-7.4
2019	GDD	1452			0.2	0.2
2020	CIN	396	0.0	0.0	0.0	0.0
2021	CIN	10089	1.6	-0.1	0.1	1.6
2022	*CIN*	*16835*	*3.3*	*0.6*	*-0.4*	*3.6*

Long considered an injury-prone catcher with an iffy hit tool, Stephenson posted the fifth-best batting average of any rookie with at least 200 plate appearances last season, and has maintained nearly unblemished health for four years running. That's not to say neither of those issues will reappear in the future; they're just very encouraging signs for an already exciting young catcher. The minor-league reports of Stephenson being a decent framer held up pretty well in his first full season with the big-league club, and he showed a lot of confidence with his swing decisions at the plate. A 50% ground-ball rate curtailed his power a bit, but that too should turn around if Stephenson can get that mark back under 40%, where it was for most of his prospect career. It took nearly six years for the Reds' 2015 first round pick to finally secure a role on the major-league team, but the wait sure seems to have been worth it. The Reds thought so, trading mentor Tucker Barnhart mere days after the World Series concluded.

Eugenio Suárez 3B Born: 07/18/91 Age: 30 Bats: R Throws: R Height: 5'11" Weight: 213 lb. Origin: International Free Agent, 2008

YEAR	TEAM	LVL	AGE	PA	R	2B	3B	HR	RBI	BB	K	SB	CS	Whiff%	AVG/OBP/SLG	DRC+	BABIP	BRR	FRAA	WARP
2019	CIN	MLB	27	662	87	22	2	49	103	70	189	3	2	29.0%	.271/.358/.572	124	.312	-6.8	3B(158): -1.1	2.9
2020	CIN	MLB	28	231	29	8	0	15	38	30	67	2	0	31.7%	.202/.312/.470	111	.214	0.1	3B(57): -2.7	0.6
2021	CIN	MLB	29	574	71	23	0	31	79	56	171	0	1	29.5%	.198/.286/.428	94	.224	-6.4	3B(104): 3.1, SS(34): -0.2	1.2
2022 DC	*CIN*	*MLB*	*30*	*371*	*56*	*15*	*0*	*21*	*60*	*39*	*105*	*1*	*1*	*29.4%*	*.235/.331/.476*	*105*	*.283*	*-0.5*	*3B 0, SS 0*	*1.2*

Comparables: Don Money, Bob Bailey, Howard Johnson

If you have to fill the shortstop position with someone who's definitely going to be overmatched there, you'd better find someone who's going to make up for those shortcomings at the plate. The Reds hoped Suárez would prove that kind of player, before realizing with great dismay that his swing started producing results every bit as grotesque as his glove did. Suárez was so bad all year that not even turning in baseball's best offensive performance in the final month of the season—which he somehow did, even as the Reds dwindled from the public eye—was enough to save him from a subpar batting line. His power is apparent even at the height of his struggles, but that's becoming the only aspect of his game he can hang his hat on. Over the last two seasons, he has the lowest BABIP of any qualified hitter and the sixth-highest strikeout rate. Adjustments need to be made for Suárez to remain an impact player heading into his 30s, and he'll have plenty of time to focus his attention on that now that the shortstop dream is dead for good.

Joey Votto 1B Born: 09/10/83 Age: 38 Bats: L Throws: R Height: 6'2" Weight: 220 lb. Origin: Round 2, 2002 Draft (#44 overall)

YEAR	TEAM	LVL	AGE	PA	R	2B	3B	HR	RBI	BB	K	SB	CS	Whiff%	AVG/OBP/SLG	DRC+	BABIP	BRR	FRAA	WARP
2019	CIN	MLB	35	608	79	32	1	15	47	76	123	5	0	19.2%	.261/.357/.411	101	.313	-4.2	1B(133): 4.8	1.7
2020	CIN	MLB	36	223	32	8	0	11	22	37	43	0	0	22.5%	.226/.354/.446	119	.235	0.8	1B(50): 1.1	1.2
2021	CIN	MLB	37	533	73	23	1	36	99	77	127	1	0	29.3%	.266/.375/.563	129	.287	-2.1	1B(123): 7.4	3.7
2022 DC	*CIN*	*MLB*	*38*	*600*	*99*	*27*	*1*	*28*	*83*	*81*	*154*	*2*	*1*	*28.1%*	*.253/.363/.472*	*118*	*.311*	*-0.8*	*1B 4*	*2.8*

Comparables: Eddie Murray, Todd Helton, Rafael Palmeiro

Votto entered the 2021 season in danger of inspiring some of the more passionate Hall of Fame debates of any player not connected to steroids. Typically the platonic ideal of a complete hitter, he'd had long stretches of dismal power outputs over the last three seasons, and was also beginning to strike out more than we were used to seeing. He needed a big season to reclaim his Hall path, and thankfully—for Reds fans, and for baseball discourse as a whole—he got it. He eclipsed the 2,000 hit and 300 homer milestones. He passed Frank Robinson on Cincinnati's team's homer leaderboard, Tony Perez on the team's total bases leaderboard, and Johnny Bench on the team's runs scored leaderboard. Just as important as all of that, though: Votto showed that he can still muster substantial pop, and that he likely has at least a couple more seasons of above-average hitting left in him. If his Hall credentials weren't cemented in 2021, they should be soon.

Jesse Winker LF Born: 08/17/93 Age: 28 Bats: L Throws: L Height: 6'3" Weight: 215 lb. Origin: Round 1, 2012 Draft (#49 overall)

YEAR	TEAM	LVL	AGE	PA	R	2B	3B	HR	RBI	BB	K	SB	CS	Whiff%	AVG/OBP/SLG	DRC+	BABIP	BRR	FRAA	WARP
2019	CIN	MLB	25	384	51	17	2	16	38	38	60	0	2	17.9%	.269/.357/.473	116	.286	0.3	LF(72): 1.8, CF(21): -0.1, RF(18): 1.7	2.5
2020	CIN	MLB	26	183	27	7	0	12	23	28	46	1	0	29.0%	.255/.388/.544	121	.283	-0.4	LF(15): 1.3, RF(1): -0.2	1.0
2021	CIN	MLB	27	485	77	32	1	24	71	53	75	1	0	20.2%	.305/.394/.556	136	.324	-0.7	LF(101): 1.7, RF(5): -0.3, CF(1): -0.1	4.0
2022 DC	*CIN*	*MLB*	*28*	*491*	*79*	*25*	*1*	*18*	*67*	*56*	*85*	*1*	*1*	*21.0%*	*.274/.372/.468*	*123*	*.309*	*-0.7*	*LF 1*	*3.1*

Comparables: Carlos González, Michael Brantley, Nick Williams

Depending upon where your cutoff for "elite" hitters is, Winker might already be in that class. He followed a tremendous 2020 season with an even better effort last year, maintaining the improvement of his power numbers—he became the first NL player in 15 years to have two three-homer games in one season—while cutting his strikeout rate by nearly 40%. As visible as his impact was when he was in the game, it was perhaps even easier to see when he wasn't. Winker played just one game after Aug. 15 due to injuries; the Reds' team wOBA, .331 to that point, fell to .316 over the remainder of the season, and they went from Wild Card frontrunners to spectators. It's great that health issues no longer seem to be severely restricting Winker's power, but the team would prefer even the slap-hitting, club-footed defender he was early in his career to one who isn't on the field at all.

PITCHERS

Tejay Antone RHP Born: 12/05/93 Age: 28 Bats: R Throws: R Height: 6'4" Weight: 230 lb. Origin: Round 5, 2014 Draft (#155 overall)

YEAR	TEAM	LVL	AGE	W	L	SV	G	GS	IP	H	HR	BB/9	K/9	K	GB%	BABIP	WHIP	ERA	DRA-	WARP	MPH	FB%	Whiff%	CSP
2019	CHA	AA	25	7	4	0	13	13	74^{2}	63	4	2.7	7.6	63	57.1%	.277	1.14	3.38	88	1.0				
2019	LOU	AAA	25	4	8	0	14	13	71^{2}	93	7	3.9	8.8	70	51.1%	.402	1.73	4.65	96	1.0				
2020	CIN	MLB	26	0	3	0	13	4	35^{1}	20	4	4.1	11.5	45	48.7%	.216	1.02	2.80	77	0.8	95.9	40.5%	34.4%	44.8%
2021	LOU	AAA	27	0	0	1	7	0	6^{2}	4	1	4.1	13.5	10	53.8%	.250	1.05	2.70	82	0.2				
2021	CIN	MLB	27	2	0	3	23	0	33^{2}	17	3	3.5	11.2	42	47.1%	.209	0.89	2.14	80	0.7	97.1	32.3%	33.6%	58.5%
2022 non-DC	*CIN*	*MLB*	*28*	*2*	*2*	*0*	*57*	*0*	*50*	*39*	*7*	*3.6*	*10.7*	*59*	*48.6%*	*.278*	*1.20*	*3.48*	*81*	*0.7*	*96.6*	*35.8%*	*34.0%*	*52.6%*

Comparables: Chad Green, Steve Cishek, Tyler Duffey

Ever since Antone began turning heads with considerable velocity gains and off-the-charts spin rates during spring training of 2020, Reds fans have been wondering what his permanent role with the team was going to look like. Turns out, they'll be waiting even longer than hoped. After spending two months on the shelf because of forearm trouble, Antone returned for just a single batter in August before again leaving the mound in pain. A few days later, it was reported he'd undergo the second Tommy John surgery of his career. Antone has shown a high-90s sinker and two different breaking balls with elite horizontal movement. But he'll be 29 when he makes his likely return to the mound in 2023, and he'll be on his third UCL. We'll see how much of his excellent stuff survives.

Graham Ashcraft RHP Born: 02/11/98 Age: 24 Bats: L Throws: R Height: 6'2" Weight: 240 lb. Origin: Round 6, 2019 Draft (#174 overall)

YEAR	TEAM	LVL	AGE	W	L	SV	G	GS	IP	H	HR	BB/9	K/9	K	GB%	BABIP	WHIP	ERA	DRA-	WARP	MPH	FB%	Whiff%	CSP
2019	GRN	ROA	21	2	4	0	13	13	53^{2}	51	2	3.5	10.1	60	55.9%	.329	1.34	4.53						
2021	DAY	A+	23	4	1	0	8	8	38^{2}	28	0	3.0	12.8	55	54.5%	.322	1.06	2.33	63	1.2				
2021	CHA	AA	23	7	3	0	14	14	72^{1}	58	4	3.0	9.2	74	59.6%	.287	1.13	3.36	87	1.2				
2022 non-DC	*CIN*	*MLB*	*24*	*2*	*2*	*0*	*57*	*0*	*50*	*49*	*5*	*4.0*	*8.8*	*48*	*52.3%*	*.315*	*1.44*	*4.49*	*105*	*0.1*				

Comparables: David Phelps, Rogelio Armenteros, Anthony Reyes

If you were a Pensacola resident on July 13, 2021 who decided to make an outing to the local minor-league game, you probably thought the visiting pitcher looked pretty washed up. Ashcraft, the starter for Chattanooga, faced 11 hitters in the first inning that night, and allowed eight of them to score. What you wouldn't have known at the time was that was the only appearance in a nine-start span in which Ashcraft allowed a single earned run. It was a borderline-deGromian stretch—albeit against High-A and Double-A hitters—and it drew attention to how far the former sixth-round pick has come in a short time. Ashcraft is a much better strike-thrower than he was as an amateur, and he can really spin the baseball. There's a no. 4 starter here somewhere, but because of the team's more immediate need for quality bullpen help, he's probably a reliever in '22.

Luis Castillo RHP Born: 12/12/92 Age: 29 Bats: R Throws: R Height: 6'2" Weight: 200 lb. Origin: International Free Agent, 2012

YEAR	TEAM	LVL	AGE	W	L	SV	G	GS	IP	H	HR	BB/9	K/9	K	GB%	BABIP	WHIP	ERA	DRA-	WARP	MPH	FB%	Whiff%	CSP
2019	CIN	MLB	26	15	8	0	32	32	190^{2}	139	22	3.7	10.7	226	54.6%	.265	1.14	3.40	74	4.6	96.4	50.6%	36.0%	41.4%
2020	CIN	MLB	27	4	6	0	12	12	70	62	5	3.1	11.4	89	58.4%	.329	1.23	3.21	61	2.3	97.6	52.3%	32.8%	48.7%
2021	CIN	MLB	28	8	16	0	33	33	187^{2}	181	19	3.6	9.2	192	55.6%	.323	1.36	3.98	89	2.8	97.4	52.2%	28.9%	49.8%
2022 DC	*CIN*	*MLB*	*29*	*12*	*8*	*0*	*29*	*29*	*180.7*	*158*	*18*	*3.3*	*9.7*	*195*	*54.5%*	*.300*	*1.24*	*3.39*	*81*	*3.2*	*97.2*	*51.9%*	*31.0%*	*47.9%*

Comparables: A.J. Burnett, Freddy Garcia, Justin Verlander

It took about two months for Castillo to recover from his Opening Day assault at the hands of the Cardinals, who tagged him for 10 runs before he could finish the fourth inning. But once he ironed out some wrinkles in his approach, he returned to throwing like one of the top dozen or so pitchers in baseball for the final four months of the season. For Castillo, those wrinkles included some issues with his release point as well as ineffective placement of his infamous changeup. Overall, his whiff numbers fell a bit short of where they've stood in the past, but they trended in the right direction throughout the season and he induced his typical stream of ground balls. He remains a solid bet to throw like an excellent no. 2 starter or better in 2022, and to get tossed away by the Reds in a salary dump in his final year of arbitration heading into 2023.

Luis Cessa RHP Born: 04/25/92 Age: 30 Bats: R Throws: R Height: 6'0" Weight: 208 lb. Origin: International Free Agent, 2008

YEAR	TEAM	LVL	AGE	W	L	SV	G	GS	IP	H	HR	BB/9	K/9	K	GB%	BABIP	WHIP	ERA	DRA-	WARP	MPH	FB%	Whiff%	CSP
2019	NYY	MLB	27	2	1	1	43	0	81	75	14	3.4	8.3	75	48.3%	.277	1.31	4.11	99	0.9	94.4	41.9%	29.8%	44.5%
2020	NYY	MLB	28	0	0	1	16	0	21^{2}	20	2	2.9	7.1	17	39.7%	.273	1.25	3.32	119	0.0	93.8	31.1%	27.7%	41.6%
2021	NYY	MLB	29	3	1	0	29	0	38^{1}	31	2	4.0	7.3	31	56.6%	.266	1.25	2.82	107	0.2	93.4	31.0%	27.1%	55.8%
2021	CIN	MLB	29	2	1	0	24	0	26^{1}	24	3	0.7	7.9	23	44.0%	.292	0.99	2.05	95	0.3	94.3	31.6%	26.8%	57.6%
2022 DC	*CIN*	*MLB*	*30*	*3*	*3*	*3*	*67*	*0*	*58*	*58*	*7*	*3.0*	*8.1*	*52*	*47.6%*	*.305*	*1.34*	*4.25*	*100*	*0.2*	*94.0*	*34.2%*	*27.9%*	*51.0%*

Comparables: Tanner Roark, Alex Colomé, Kameron Loe

It's strange to wrap your head around a pitcher who throws sliders on half of his offerings owning a 2% walk rate, but that's precisely what Cessa did for 26.1 innings after being traded from the Yankees to the Reds at last year's July 31st deadline. A homer-prone swingman for several years in New York, Cessa's mediocre strikeout rate obfuscates a sneaky ability to get opponents to chase the ball out of the zone, a skill the right-hander leans on less for punchouts than for poor contact. Though acquired as a low-cost fix to the team's 2021 bullpen woes, Cessa could remain a fixture on Cincinnati's staff through his two remaining years of club control if he can continue to keep the ball down and dodge the sweet spot of the bat.

Carson Fulmer RHP Born: 12/13/93 Age: 28 Bats: R Throws: R Height: 6'0" Weight: 210 lb. Origin: Round 1, 2015 Draft (#8 overall)

YEAR	TEAM	LVL	AGE	W	L	SV	G	GS	IP	H	HR	BB/9	K/9	K	GB%	BABIP	WHIP	ERA	DRA-	WARP	MPH	FB%	Whiff%	CSP
2019	CHA	AAA	25	1	2	1	24	0	34	31	2	5.6	13.5	51	32.5%	.372	1.53	4.76	76	0.9				
2019	CHW	MLB	25	1	2	0	20	2	27^{1}	26	5	6.6	8.2	25	45.9%	.263	1.68	6.26	114	0.1	93.7	43.7%	24.2%	46.7%
2020	BAL	MLB	26	0	0	0	3	0	3^{2}	0	0	4.9	9.8	4	42.9%	.000	0.55	0.00	95	0.0	93.1	52.5%	38.5%	47.2%
2020	DET	MLB	26	0	0	0	7	0	6^{2}	8	1	4.1	9.5	7	57.1%	.350	1.65	6.75	84	0.1	92.3	55.1%	29.8%	41.2%
2021	LOU	AAA	27	1	5	1	37	2	41	40	4	5.5	11.2	51	49.5%	.343	1.59	4.61	86	0.8				
2021	CIN	MLB	27	0	0	0	20	0	25^{2}	26	3	4.6	8.4	24	47.4%	.319	1.52	6.66	106	0.1	93.6	40.4%	30.5%	50.5%
2022 non-DC	*CIN*	*MLB*	*28*	*2*	*3*	*0*	*57*	*0*	*50*	*46*	*7*	*4.9*	*9.4*	*52*	*44.3%*	*.297*	*1.48*	*5.08*	*111*	*-0.1*	*93.4*	*43.5%*	*29.3%*	*48.4%*

Comparables: Tommy Hunter, Anthony Bass, Nate Adcock

The Reds are the fourth organization to get eyes on Fulmer, but the former eighth-overall pick still hasn't held a sub-6.00 ERA over more than 20 MLB innings pitched in any season since 2017. Cincinnati did succeed in getting the usage of his four-seamer—which opposing hitters have routinely demolished—to an all-time low, and saw legitimately good results from all of his secondaries. For all his struggles, Fulmer has never tinkered with his approach enough to know what he looks like without a fastball-first mindset, so it would be interesting to see how effective he could be as a cutter/curveball guy who only sparingly calls upon anything else. Of course, that would require getting either of them over for strike one.

Amir Garrett LHP Born: 05/03/92 Age: 30 Bats: R Throws: L Height: 6'5" Weight: 239 lb. Origin: Round 22, 2011 Draft (#685 overall)

YEAR	TEAM	LVL	AGE	W	L	SV	G	GS	IP	H	HR	BB/9	K/9	K	GB%	BABIP	WHIP	ERA	DRA-	WARP	MPH	FB%	Whiff%	CSP
2019	CIN	MLB	27	5	3	0	69	0	56	44	7	5.6	12.5	78	54.3%	.303	1.41	3.21	76	1.3	95.4	42.0%	39.0%	41.7%
2020	CIN	MLB	28	1	0	1	21	0	18^1	10	4	3.4	12.8	26	44.4%	.188	0.93	2.45	77	0.4	94.9	44.5%	43.7%	40.6%
2021	CIN	MLB	29	0	4	7	63	0	47^2	46	9	5.5	11.5	61	50.4%	.322	1.57	6.04	83	0.8	95.0	49.0%	33.7%	55.0%
2022 DC	*CIN*	*MLB*	*30*	*3*	*3*	*1*	*67*	*0*	*58*	*47*	*8*	*4.6*	*12.4*	*80*	*47.1%*	*.308*	*1.33*	*3.94*	*89*	*0.5*	*95.1*	*46.6%*	*36.4%*	*49.7%*

Comparables: Charlie Furbush, David Hernandez, Jake Diekman

When the Reds traded Raisel Iglesias for a thank-you card last winter, it made sense that Garrett would be the one to take over the job. He's a lefty with an unhittable slider, experience pitching late in games, and an edge to him on the mound that you can't fake. Unfortunately, when he coughed up the job faster than you spit out coffee mixed with salt instead of sugar, that kind of made sense too. Garrett's battles with control as well as the long ball are well established, and they reached new heights when he walked 12 and allowed seven homers in his first 16 innings of the 2021 season. You can probably guess how many fans noticed when he allowed just two homers and posted a 2.82 FIP over his final 31.2 innings. Already nearing 30, Garrett is still set up to be near the top of both "guys who get lots of whiffs" and "guys who are easy to cheer for" lists for a few more years, but teams will rightfully think twice about handing him a one-run lead in the ninth.

Mychal Givens RHP Born: 05/13/90 Age: 32 Bats: R Throws: R Height: 6'0" Weight: 230 lb. Origin: Round 2, 2009 Draft (#54 overall)

YEAR	TEAM	LVL	AGE	W	L	SV	G	GS	IP	H	HR	BB/9	K/9	K	GB%	BABIP	WHIP	ERA	DRA-	WARP	MPH	FB%	Whiff%	CSP
2019	BAL	MLB	29	2	6	11	58	0	63	49	13	3.7	12.3	86	38.4%	.271	1.19	4.57	76	1.5	95.5	70.1%	34.2%	49.4%
2020	BAL	MLB	30	0	1	0	12	0	13	7	1	4.2	13.2	19	26.9%	.240	1.00	1.38	101	0.1	94.8	67.7%	30.5%	48.8%
2020	COL	MLB	30	1	0	1	10	0	9^1	9	4	3.9	5.8	6	20.0%	.192	1.39	6.75	179	-0.3	94.9	61.7%	23.9%	48.5%
2021	CIN	MLB	31	1	1	8	23	0	21^1	18	2	5.5	8.4	20	42.4%	.281	1.45	4.22	117	0.0	95.6	47.3%	27.9%	51.2%
2021	COL	MLB	31	3	2	0	31	0	29^2	25	5	4.2	10.3	34	31.1%	.290	1.31	2.73	90	0.4	94.6	46.3%	28.8%	50.2%
2022 DC	*FA*	*MLB*	*32*	*3*	*3*	*0*	*71*	*0*	*61.7*	*55*	*10*	*4.0*	*10.1*	*69*	*35.6%*	*.292*	*1.34*	*4.47*	*102*	*0.2*	*95.1*	*55.7%*	*29.7%*	*50.0%*

Comparables: Pat Neshek, Nick Vincent, Junichi Tazawa

The Reds scooped up Givens from Colorado a few days ahead of the traded deadline and wound up installing him as their closer, where he only blew one save out of nine in the role. Typically not someone you threw against lefties unless you really had to—the movement on his slider, along with a whiplike overhand delivery generated from a lot of twist in his windup, make him *feel* like a sidearmer—Givens has suddenly posted reverse splits over his past two seasons, thanks in large part to the emergence of a successful changeup. The fastball can still hum out of that funky delivery, but poor command of it cost him both in the zone and outside of it in 2021. Overall, it's an attractive package to bid on in free agency, especially for a team that enjoys tinkering.

Sonny Gray RHP Born: 11/07/89 Age: 32 Bats: R Throws: R Height: 5'10" Weight: 195 lb. Origin: Round 1, 2011 Draft (#18 overall)

YEAR	TEAM	LVL	AGE	W	L	SV	G	GS	IP	H	HR	BB/9	K/9	K	GB%	BABIP	WHIP	ERA	DRA-	WARP	MPH	FB%	Whiff%	CSP
2019	CIN	MLB	29	11	8	0	31	31	175^1	122	17	3.5	10.5	205	50.5%	.259	1.08	2.87	75	4.2	93.4	50.5%	28.2%	44.6%
2020	CIN	MLB	30	5	3	0	11	11	56	42	4	4.2	11.6	72	51.9%	.290	1.21	3.70	67	1.6	93.3	55.1%	29.6%	44.7%
2021	CIN	MLB	31	7	9	0	26	26	135^1	115	19	3.3	10.3	155	48.2%	.282	1.22	4.19	81	2.6	92.4	58.4%	26.2%	55.6%
2022 DC	*CIN*	*MLB*	*32*	*10*	*7*	*0*	*27*	*27*	*151.3*	*131*	*20*	*3.5*	*9.6*	*161*	*48.8%*	*.286*	*1.26*	*3.77*	*88*	*2.1*	*92.8*	*55.8%*	*27.3%*	*51.0%*

Comparables: Kevin Gross, Matt Garza, Vida Blue

Gray looked a little more vulnerable his third year in Cincinnati than he had over his previous two. He allowed more fly balls, and thus, more homers. He started the year on the IL and endured two more brief stints on it during the summer—all three for separate muscle strain injuries—and his typically elite spin rates showed steep declines when he was activated for the last time, costing him a fair bit of horizontal movement and possibly contributing to a lackluster second half performance. It's important that Gray's health doesn't become an annual concern moving forward, since he isn't exactly an innings-eater even when he makes 30 starts. But odds are good that his stuff will return to form enough to make him a solid no. 2 starter again and, as we're seeing in the playoffs lately, it's much more valuable to provide four good innings than six or seven mediocre ones.

★ ★ ★ *2022 Top 101 Prospect* **#32** ★ ★ ★

Hunter Greene RHP Born: 08/06/99 Age: 22 Bats: R Throws: R Height: 6'5" Weight: 230 lb. Origin: Round 1, 2017 Draft (#2 overall)

YEAR	TEAM	LVL	AGE	W	L	SV	G	GS	IP	H	HR	BB/9	K/9	K	GB%	BABIP	WHIP	ERA	DRA-	WARP	MPH	FB%	Whiff%	CSP
2021	CHA	AA	21	5	0	0	7	7	41	27	2	3.1	13.2	60	41.2%	.301	1.00	1.98	92	0.6				
2021	LOU	AAA	21	5	8	0	14	14	65^1	59	11	3.4	10.9	79	45.2%	.306	1.29	4.13	84	1.4				
2022 DC	*CIN*	*MLB*	*22*	*4*	*4*	*0*	*16*	*16*	*68*	*63*	*10*	*3.9*	*9.8*	*74*	*41.6%*	*.305*	*1.37*	*4.60*	*104*	*0.4*				

Comparables: Zach Davies, Wily Peralta, Jake Odorizzi

Greene's first three full years of pro ball—during which he had to give up on being a two-way player, looked eerily hittable in 2018, and then underwent Tommy John surgery that cost him two seasons of in-game experience—would have been disappointing for even a run-of-the-mill first round pick, let-alone someone Sports Illustrated once called "Baseball's LeBron" while in high school. Even after all of that, though, Greene still looks like a star. His ability to regularly hit triple digits is still intact after his injury, a crucial fact given that his fastball is bullet-straight. His secondaries have made necessary progress, and he dominated Double-A as a 21-year-old before holding his own in Triple-A. Comparisons to Shohei Ohtani are over with, and "if healthy" is going to be more legitimate question than just throwaway disclaimer for the foreseeable future. But his ceiling as a starter is fairly limitless.

Vladimir Gutierrez RHP Born: 09/18/95 Age: 26 Bats: R Throws: R Height: 6'1" Weight: 190 lb. Origin: International Free Agent, 2016

YEAR	TEAM	LVL	AGE	W	L	SV	G	GS	IP	H	HR	BB/9	K/9	K	GB%	BABIP	WHIP	ERA	DRA-	WARP	MPH	FB%	Whiff%	CSP
2019	LIC	WIN	23	1	4	0	7	7	28	22	2	3.9	6.4	20	39.3%	.244	1.21	3.21						
2019	LOU	AAA	23	6	11	0	27	27	137	144	26	3.2	7.7	117	40.0%	.291	1.40	6.04	106	1.3				
2021	LOU	AAA	25	2	0	0	3	3	17	9	3	3.7	11.1	21	36.8%	.171	0.94	2.65	100	0.2				
2021	CIN	MLB	25	9	6	0	22	22	114	115	20	3.6	6.9	88	42.5%	.285	1.41	4.74	118	-0.1	93.4	47.4%	23.5%	54.9%
2022 DC	*CIN*	*MLB*	*26*	*7*	*8*	*0*	*24*	*24*	*128.7*	*135*	*22*	*3.5*	*7.4*	*105*	*41.7%*	*.301*	*1.45*	*5.30*	*118*	*-0.2*	*93.4*	*47.4%*	*23.5%*	*54.9%*

Comparables: Trent Thornton, Jakob Junis, Mike Pelfrey

Gutierrez's long-awaited rookie season in Cincinnati was a bit of a roller coaster. He ran a 4.97 ERA over his first 10 starts, a 1.86 ERA over his next six, and a 9.43 ERA over his final six. That equals out to a performance that was replacement level over the course of the year by our valuation, or around two wins above replacement level if you look at RA/9-based metrics. In either case, there's more hope here than there was a year ago, when Gutierrez was coming off a 6.04 ERA at Triple-A followed by a PED suspension. He's throwing a little harder than he used to and has the athleticism and pitch mix of a starter, but his K/BB ratio has been trending the wrong way for a long time, the product of a fastball that catches too much plate in too many fastball counts. A move to the pen is the logical step to try and reverse that; a roster that doesn't require his services as a starter is the next one.

Jeff Hoffman RHP Born: 01/08/93 Age: 29 Bats: R Throws: R Height: 6'5" Weight: 235 lb. Origin: Round 1, 2014 Draft (#9 overall)

YEAR	TEAM	LVL	AGE	W	L	SV	G	GS	IP	H	HR	BB/9	K/9	K	GB%	BABIP	WHIP	ERA	DRA-	WARP	MPH	FB%	Whiff%	CSP
2019	ABQ	AAA	26	6	8	0	17	16	85^1	105	19	3.2	10.3	98	42.4%	.363	1.58	7.70	85	1.3				
2019	COL	MLB	26	2	6	0	15	15	70	77	21	4.4	8.7	68	34.9%	.303	1.59	6.56	109	0.4	93.7	58.8%	21.7%	48.6%
2020	COL	MLB	27	2	1	1	16	0	21^1	32	3	3.8	8.4	20	35.6%	.414	1.92	9.28	120	0.0	94.6	54.6%	22.2%	47.0%
2021	LOU	AAA	28	0	0	0	4	4	15^1	11	2	2.3	11.7	20	32.4%	.265	0.98	1.76	86	0.3				
2021	CIN	MLB	28	3	5	0	31	11	73	70	12	5.5	9.7	79	37.4%	.301	1.58	4.56	107	0.4	94.4	56.0%	29.9%	55.6%
2022 DC	*CIN*	*MLB*	*29*	*9*	*5*	*0*	*71*	*4*	*79*	*77*	*14*	*4.2*	*9.6*	*84*	*36.8%*	*.304*	*1.44*	*5.19*	*114*	*-0.1*	*94.3*	*56.4%*	*27.2%*	*53.0%*

Comparables: Sergio Mitre, Wade LeBlanc, Erasmo Ramírez

The Reds acquired Hoffman from the Rockies ahead of the 2021 season with the hope that a change of scenery might improve his numbers and give the team a cheap but sturdy depth arm. They were half-right. Hoffman brought what had been a 6.64 ERA over his last four years in Colorado down to a reasonable sea-level number, and he achieved a career-best strikeout rate. His DRA was both almost average and almost a career-best. But he walked way too many batters to stick in the rotation, and gave up way too much hard contact after a move to the bullpen. Hoffman could stand to ditch either the curveball or changeup and focus on his excellent slider, which limited opponents to a .149 wOBA in 54 PAs last year. Even so, hitters slugged .523 against his fastball, so it may take the former top prospect more than one weird trick.

★ ★ ★ *2022 Top 101 Prospect* **#42** ★ ★ ★

Nick Lodolo LHP Born: 02/05/98 Age: 24 Bats: L Throws: L Height: 6'6" Weight: 205 lb. Origin: Round 1, 2019 Draft (#7 overall)

YEAR	TEAM	LVL	AGE	W	L	SV	G	GS	IP	H	HR	BB/9	K/9	K	GB%	BABIP	WHIP	ERA	DRA-	WARP	MPH	FB%	Whiff%	CSP
2019	BIL	ROA	21	0	1	0	6	6	11^1	12	1	0.0	16.7	21	32.0%	.458	1.06	2.38						
2019	DAY	A	21	0	0	0	2	2	7	6	0	0.0	11.6	9	50.0%	.333	0.86	2.57	86	0.1				
2021	CHA	AA	23	2	1	0	10	10	44	31	1	1.8	13.9	68	53.3%	.337	0.91	1.84	77	1.0				
2021	LOU	AAA	23	0	1	0	3	3	6^2	7	2	2.7	13.5	10	56.2%	.357	1.35	5.40	87	0.1				
2022 non-DC	*CIN*	*MLB*	*24*	*2*	*2*	*0*	*57*	*0*	*50*	*43*	*6*	*2.9*	*10.0*	*55*	*47.4%*	*.294*	*1.19*	*3.55*	*85*	*0.6*				

Comparables: Tim Crabtree, Travis Miller, Joba Chamberlain

The first pitcher in his draft class to get selected in 2019, Lodolo was regarded as someone whose mechanics and command were good enough that he wouldn't need to miss a ton of bats to be successful. That makes what's happened since he was drafted all the more exciting—in 69 career innings, he's racked up an almost 10:1 strikeout-to-walk ratio, with the majority of his work coming against Double-A hitters. The downside to his development has been the slow build-up of his workload, which was hampered even further by blister issues in 2021. He'll likely still have training wheels on as a 24-year-old in 2022, which could make the idea of giving him a big-league bullpen job enticing, though the idea of him bumping Vladimir Gutierrez to one may win the day.

Tyler Mahle RHP Born: 09/29/94 Age: 27 Bats: R Throws: R Height: 6'3" Weight: 210 lb. Origin: Round 7, 2013 Draft (#225 overall)

YEAR	TEAM	LVL	AGE	W	L	SV	G	GS	IP	H	HR	BB/9	K/9	K	GB%	BABIP	WHIP	ERA	DRA-	WARP	MPH	FB%	Whiff%	CSP
2019	LOU	AAA	24	1	2	0	3	3	9	8	0	3.0	13.0	13	60.0%	.400	1.22	4.00	84	0.2				
2019	CIN	MLB	24	3	12	0	25	25	129^2	136	25	2.4	9.0	129	47.0%	.308	1.31	5.14	88	2.1	93.4	56.7%	23.2%	48.8%
2020	CIN	MLB	25	2	2	0	10	9	47^2	34	6	4.0	11.3	60	30.2%	.255	1.15	3.59	97	0.6	94.2	55.9%	33.8%	43.6%
2021	CIN	MLB	26	13	6	0	33	33	180	158	24	3.2	10.5	210	41.7%	.303	1.23	3.75	83	3.3	94.2	53.0%	28.5%	53.3%
2022 DC	*CIN*	*MLB*	*27*	*10*	*8*	*0*	*27*	*27*	*154*	*136*	*24*	*3.1*	*10.6*	*181*	*41.3%*	*.300*	*1.23*	*3.93*	*90*	*2.0*	*94.1*	*54.0%*	*28.3%*	*51.3%*

Comparables: Ryan Dempster, Chris Carpenter, Jerry Reuss

Few pitchers saw a bigger drop in their spin rate following the Spider Tack crackdown than Mahle, which actually makes sense, considering he'd just made one of baseball's biggest jumps in spin between the 2019-20 seasons. Fret not, though. The difference in his numbers pre- and post-crackdown were negligible, and added up to the kind of breakout season for which he's long had the potential. In a year that saw four different Reds pitchers throw quite effectively for 26 starts or more, it was Mahle who led the rotation in WARP, and whom the team declared untouchable even as it threw the rest of the roster out in the yard for sale. He should continue to steadily accumulate value as long as his ability to avoid both bats and the IL keeps up with his impressive command and pitching IQ.

Lyon Richardson RHP

Born: 01/18/00 Age: 22 Bats: S Throws: R Height: 6'2" Weight: 192 lb. Origin: Round 2, 2018 Draft (#47 overall)

YEAR	TEAM	LVL	AGE	W	L	SV	G	GS	IP	H	HR	BB/9	K/9	K	GB%	BABIP	WHIP	ERA	DRA-	WARP	MPH	FB%	Whiff%	CSP
2019	DAY	A	19	3	9	0	26	26	112^2	126	10	2.6	8.5	106	39.9%	.341	1.41	4.15	106	0.5				
2021	DAY	A+	21	2	5	0	19	18	76	74	9	4.5	10.8	91	51.4%	.325	1.47	5.09	100	0.8				
2022 non-DC	*CIN*	*MLB*	*22*	*2*	*3*	*0*	*57*	*0*	*50*	*53*	*7*	*4.8*	*7.8*	*43*	*43.6%*	*.307*	*1.59*	*5.67*	*127*	*-0.5*				

Comparables: Anthony Banda, Yordano Ventura, Albert Abreu

Richardson is still much newer to pitching than most of his peers—he didn't devote serious time to the mound until he was a senior in high school—and he's as raw as you'd expect. Self-described as a "thrower, " he battled his command against older competition in High-A, but he still managed to make tangible progress. After a brief dip in his velocity early in his pro career, he's back into the mid-90s with both his fastballs, and his changeup, which he discovered by accident, has already earned a good bit of trust. The Reds will continue developing Richardson as a starter but he has the temperament for a high-leverage relief role if that's the way things shake out.

Tony Santillan RHP

Born: 04/15/97 Age: 25 Bats: R Throws: R Height: 6'3" Weight: 240 lb. Origin: Round 2, 2015 Draft (#49 overall)

YEAR	TEAM	LVL	AGE	W	L	SV	G	GS	IP	H	HR	BB/9	K/9	K	GB%	BABIP	WHIP	ERA	DRA-	WARP	MPH	FB%	Whiff%	CSP
2019	CHA	AA	22	2	8	0	21	21	102^1	110	8	4.7	8.1	92	32.8%	.342	1.60	4.84	129	-1.0				
2021	LOU	AAA	24	1	3	2	13	6	38	25	5	3.6	12.1	51	38.4%	.247	1.05	2.13	85	0.8				
2021	CIN	MLB	24	1	3	0	26	4	43^1	34	7	4.4	11.6	56	32.1%	.276	1.27	2.91	86	0.7	95.1	46.9%	32.9%	51.2%
2022 DC	*CIN*	*MLB*	*25*	*8*	*4*	*0*	*63*	*4*	*71*	*62*	*13*	*4.2*	*10.4*	*82*	*35.3%*	*.288*	*1.35*	*4.64*	*103*	*0.2*	*95.1*	*46.9%*	*32.9%*	*51.2%*

Comparables: Todd Wellemeyer, Joel Hanrahan, J.B. Wendelken

Santillan has carried the "possible reliever" label since he was drafted in 2015, but he hadn't actually been used out of the bullpen until 2021. In that role, he faced 108 big-league hitters and struck out a third of them, showing that his slider (48% whiff rate) is a major weapon next to his mid-90s heater. He used the changeup only sparingly, which will need to, uh, change if he wants to get back to starting. But considering the struggles the young right-hander had against Double-A hitters in 2019, his impressive performance in making the leap to the majors is a good sign for him playing a regular role for this organization over the next few years.

Lucas Sims RHP

Born: 05/10/94 Age: 28 Bats: R Throws: R Height: 6'2" Weight: 225 lb. Origin: Round 1, 2012 Draft (#21 overall)

YEAR	TEAM	LVL	AGE	W	L	SV	G	GS	IP	H	HR	BB/9	K/9	K	GB%	BABIP	WHIP	ERA	DRA-	WARP	MPH	FB%	Whiff%	CSP
2019	LOU	AAA	25	5	0	0	16	16	79	69	9	4.1	11.6	102	31.1%	.324	1.33	4.56	90	1.4				
2019	CIN	MLB	25	2	1	0	24	4	43	31	8	4.0	11.9	57	25.3%	.256	1.16	4.60	86	0.8	93.5	50.6%	34.1%	41.0%
2020	CIN	MLB	26	3	0	0	20	0	25^2	13	3	3.9	11.9	34	41.8%	.192	0.94	2.45	82	0.5	94.2	48.1%	35.2%	43.0%
2021	CIN	MLB	27	5	3	7	47	0	47	34	6	3.4	14.6	76	26.8%	.308	1.11	4.40	67	1.3	95.3	41.6%	35.5%	54.0%
2022 DC	*CIN*	*MLB*	*28*	*3*	*3*	*30*	*67*	*0*	*58*	*45*	*10*	*3.8*	*12.3*	*79*	*33.5%*	*.282*	*1.20*	*3.85*	*87*	*0.6*	*94.7*	*44.7%*	*35.2%*	*49.2%*

Comparables: Brad Hand, Collin Balester, Liam Hendriks

After years of astronomical spin rates and frustrating command kept Sims just on the cusp of breaking out, the 2021 season finally showed real, tangible evidence that he has the skills to be a high-leverage big-league reliever. His K-BB% and CSW% all ranked ninth in the majors among pitchers who threw at least 40 innings, and his DRA– came in at 13th. That's an awfully small number of guys outpitching someone who the average fan might only vaguely recall ever hearing anything about, and he may not be done improving. Sims has upped his fastball velocity every year he's been in the majors—albeit while gradually transitioning from starting to relieving—and heat maps show some noticeable gains in getting his fastball out of the middle of the zone. His pitching style means he'll always allow substantial contact in the air, which makes him a bit of a marked man in his current home park. But the ingredients are here for a dominant stopper.

Justin Wilson LHP

Born: 08/18/87 Age: 34 Bats: L Throws: L Height: 6'2" Weight: 205 lb. Origin: Round 5, 2008 Draft (#144 overall)

YEAR	TEAM	LVL	AGE	W	L	SV	G	GS	IP	H	HR	BB/9	K/9	K	GB%	BABIP	WHIP	ERA	DRA-	WARP	MPH	FB%	Whiff%	CSP
2019	NYM	MLB	31	4	2	4	45	0	39	33	4	4.4	10.2	44	50.5%	.299	1.33	2.54	91	0.6	95.1	52.4%	25.6%	49.1%
2020	NYM	MLB	32	2	1	0	23	0	19^2	18	1	4.1	10.5	23	43.4%	.333	1.37	3.66	84	0.4	95.1	59.4%	24.7%	49.6%
2021	NYY	MLB	33	1	1	0	21	0	18	18	5	4.5	7.5	15	43.9%	.250	1.50	7.50	116	0.0	93.5	64.9%	18.4%	53.0%
2021	CIN	MLB	33	0	0	0	21	0	16	14	1	3.9	7.9	14	46.7%	.295	1.31	2.81	98	0.2	93.9	48.4%	24.4%	57.9%
2022 DC	*CIN*	*MLB*	*34*	*3*	*3*	*0*	*67*	*0*	*58*	*58*	*9*	*4.5*	*8.5*	*55*	*43.0%*	*.304*	*1.49*	*5.10*	*113*	*-0.2*	*94.3*	*57.1%*	*22.8%*	*52.6%*

Comparables: Rafael Soriano, Mark Melancon, Jared Burton

Like many middle relievers, Wilson has been traded a few times over the course of his career. The latest occasion, however, was a bit different from the others. Often acquired by hopeful contenders looking for a dominant plug-and-play southpaw to bolster the back of their pens, this deal was more of the change-of-scenery type, after the southpaw's reunion with the Yankees quickly became poisoned by injuries, homers and a surprising dip in strikeouts. The Reds took him in alongside Luis Cessa, and were pleased to see his longball problems subside, though his strikeout rate remained more than five points south of where it had been in any of his past six seasons. Wilson's velocity was down from previous years, but not by a worrisome amount. The real issue seemed to be the placement of his fastball, along with an inability to get whiffs at his cutter. He's at the age where even the most consistent relievers can tumble down the hill without warning, and his early returns in 2022 should be pretty telling of how much he has left in the tank.

Trey Wingenter RHP Born: 04/15/94 Age: 28 Bats: R Throws: R Height: 6'7" Weight: 237 lb. Origin: Round 17, 2015 Draft (#507 overall)

YEAR	TEAM	LVL	AGE	W	L	SV	G	GS	IP	H	HR	BB/9	K/9	K	GB%	BABIP	WHIP	ERA	DRA-	WARP	MPH	FB%	Whiff%	CSP
2019	AMA	AA	25	0	1	0	1	0	0^{2}	2	1	13.5	13.5	1	33.3%	.500	4.50	54.00	52	0.0				
2019	ELP	AAA	25	0	0	1	3	0	3^{1}	1	0	0.0	18.9	7	75.0%	.250	0.30	0.00	79	0.1				
2019	SD	MLB	25	1	3	1	51	1	51	34	5	4.9	12.7	72	36.3%	.271	1.22	5.65	85	0.9	96.1	55.0%	36.4%	45.2%
2022															*No projection*									

Comparables: Jose Ceda, Michael Feliz, Carlos Estévez

The damage to the Padres' 2021 bullpen actually began back in the shortened 2020 season, when Wingenter, coming off a promising 2019, went down with Tommy John surgery almost immediately. He was able to come back to work a few rehab innings at the Padres complex in August, showing his pre-surgery velocity of 95-97, before eventually needing back surgery in September. Wingenter is eyeing a return by spring training, but six foot seven inches equals a lot of back to rehab.

Lineouts

Hitters

HITTER	POS	TEAM	LVL	AGE	PA	R	2B	3B	HR	RBI	BB	K	SB	CS	AVG/OBP/SLG	DRC+	BABIP	BRR	FRAA	WARP
Jay Allen II	CF	RED	ROK	18	75	20	3	1	3	11	8	12	14	1	.328/.440/.557		.362			
Allan Cerda	CF	DBT	A	21	276	42	14	4	14	42	31	85	1	7	.242/.362/.524	110	.311	-1.5	CF(63): -8.3	0.5
	CF	DAY	A+	21	87	15	8	1	3	13	10	20	1	1	.273/.356/.519	104	.333	-0.2	RF(11): -0.7, CF(8): -0.8	0.2
Rece Hinds	3B	RED	ROK	20	41	6	3	2	2	5	4	13	1	1	.294/.390/.676		.400			
	3B	DBT	A	20	185	33	10	2	10	27	13	52	6	2	.251/.319/.515	105	.302	0.6	3B(33): -0.7	0.6
Ivan Johnson	MI	SUR	WIN	22	70	12	4	0	6	11	8	30	1	1	.250/.343/.617		.360			
	MI	DBT	A	22	216	27	14	2	6	23	27	61	8	5	.263/.366/.457	106	.361	-0.8	SS(50): 5.8	1.3
	MI	DAY	A+	22	114	17	5	0	4	18	14	39	3	2	.265/.368/.439	90	.400	0.0	2B(14): 0.6, SS(9): 0.3	0.3
Andrew Knapp	C	PHI	MLB	29	159	13	3	0	2	11	10	61	0	0	.152/.215/.214	47	.241	0.2	C(47): -0.7, 1B(6): -0.0, 2B(1): 0.0	-0.4
Alejo Lopez	2B	MOC	WIN	25	143	14	2	1	2	19	22	18	2	0	.235/.357/.319		.260			
	2B	CHA	AA	25	119	18	9	0	0	13	12	11	3	1	.362/.437/.448	133	.404	-0.7	2B(21): 0.8	0.8
	2B	LOU	AAA	25	290	54	18	0	6	31	33	21	6	2	.303/.386/.446	132	.308	1.5	3B(30): 0.5, 2B(24): 3.2, LF(10): -0.3	2.4
	2B	CIN	MLB	25	23	3	0	0	0	0	0	5	0	0	.261/.261/.261	96	.333	-0.3	2B(3): 0.1, 3B(3): -0.4, LF(2): -0.0	0.0
Logan Morrison	1B/LF	LOU	AAA	33	59	8	5	1	2	12	10	8	0	0	.347/.458/.612	129	.385	-2.1	1B(14): 1.9	0.3
Matheu Nelson	C	DAY	A+	22	29	3	2	1	0	3	4	15	0	1	.208/.345/.375	60	.556	0.0	C(8): -1.4	-0.2
Max Schrock	LF	LOU	AAA	26	138	14	4	0	6	19	7	25	0	0	.289/.333/.461	113	.316	-1.9	2B(20): 2.4, 3B(10): -0.4, RF(3): -0.2	0.6
	LF	CIN	MLB	26	134	19	7	2	3	14	8	24	1	1	.288/.328/.448	93	.333	0.8	LF(23): -0.1, 3B(9): -0.3, 2B(8): -0.0	0.4
Michael Siani	CF	DAY	A+	21	408	60	13	4	6	26	50	103	30	10	.216/.321/.327	96	.287	1.2	CF(75): 6.3	1.8

The 30th-overall pick in 2021, 18-year-old **Jay Allen II** immediately made an impact in the Arizona Complex League by slugging .557 and swiping 14 bases in just 19 games in his pro debut. He has a chance to stick in center field, but might also provide sufficient value in a corner if he develops the kind of power his frame suggests. At 21, **Allan Cerda** met his first Single-A and High-A promotions with patience and power, and shaved a few whiffs off his game to boot. He's showing all the hallmarks of a three-true-outcome profile, but it's a matter of how much of the resulting blend is strikeouts—they're like cranberries, and cranberries take over everything. **Rece Hinds** finally got a little bit of playing time to work with last year, and showed the expected light tower power and a high, but workable, strikeout rate. There's still a risk he's just a one-dimensional power-hitting corner outfielder, but ironically, the lost 2020 season probaby helped him more with his work on defense than it did other prospects working on their hitting. Switch-hitting infielder **Ivan Johnson** was a fourth-round pick in 2019 who flashes exciting offensive tools but has less in-game experience than you'd like for someone about to start his age-23 season, a fact reflected in his worrisome strikeout rates. **Andrew Knapp** did an admirable job as a backup catcher for the Phillies up until this year, even breaking out to a .361 wOBA in 2020. But his offense cratered in 2021, to the tune of a 48 DRC+. Knapp's improved defense couldn't quite compensate; his aggregate performance netted him a -0.4 WARP. **Alejo Lopez**'s ability to roll out of bed and hit .300 against minor-league pitchers earned the former 27th-round pick a big-league call-up in 2021, but his dearth of game power and iffy glove means bad news for those Triple-A hurlers still recovering from their migraines. For all of the organization's developmental shortcomings over the years, the Reds have proven quite adept at identifying prep catchers who can actually develop into viable big-leaguers, which is a little like making art out of grocrey store soda box displays. The latest of these gambles is **Jackson Miller**, a well-rounded backstop with decent power projection from the left side. **Logan Morrison**'s Triple-A slash lines in recent years have suggested that 2017 Rays magic is still buried deep within him, but he can't stay healthy long enough to prove it. **Matheu Nelson** parlayed a monster junior year at Florida State into the ACC Player of the Year Award and the 35th overall selection in last year's draft. He's a shaky receiver, but the arm strength and power are real. Career second baseman **Max Schrock** turned out to be a lineup mainstay for the final month of the 2021 season when injuries depleted the Reds' outfield, meaning he can add some defensive versatility to the strong contact skills and impressive 10-key speeds on his résumé. **Michael Siani's** 75 stolen bases over his past two seasons and potential plus-plus glove in center make it difficult to see anything stopping him from having a big-league career, but his rising strikeout rate and low-.300s slugging percentage are trying their best.

Pitchers

PITCHER	TEAM	LVL	AGE	W	L	SV	G	GS	IP	H	HR	BB/9	K/9	K	GB%	BABIP	WHIP	ERA	DRA-	WARP	MPH	FB%	WHF	CSP
Andrew Abbott	DBT	A	22	0	0	0	4	3	11	11	2	3.3	15.5	19	48.0%	.391	1.36	4.91	84	0.2				
R.J. Alaniz	LOU	AAA	30	1	3	1	33	0	39	42	1	3.9	10.4	45	51.0%	.402	1.51	3.46	88	0.8				
	CIN	MLB	30	0	0	0	3	0	2^{2}	1	1	10.1	10.1	3	33.3%	.000	1.50	3.37	87	0.0	92.9	52.2%	22.2%	45.2%
Bryce Bonnin	DBT	A	22	4	0	0	7	7	32	18	0	2.3	12.4	44	43.3%	.269	0.81	1.41	84	0.6				
	DAY	A+	22	0	2	0	3	3	11	7	4	6.5	16.4	20	50.0%	.188	1.36	7.36	74	0.3				
Brad Brach	LOU	AAA	35	0	0	0	8	0	8^{2}	5	0	1.0	15.6	15	56.2%	.333	0.69	0.00	75	0.2				
	CIN	MLB	35	1	2	1	35	0	30	30	5	5.4	9.9	33	42.5%	.309	1.60	6.30	102	0.2	93.8	51.1%	30.1%	49.4%
Brandon Finnegan	LOU	AAA	28	4	3	0	40	1	55^{1}	58	8	5.9	9.3	57	48.7%	.338	1.70	5.53	101	0.7				
Ryan Hendrix	LOU	AAA	26	0	1	0	16	0	15^{2}	15	4	5.2	8.6	15	63.0%	.262	1.53	8.62	88	0.3				
	CIN	MLB	26	5	1	0	36	0	31^{2}	33	8	4.5	9.9	35	40.0%	.305	1.55	5.97	102	0.3	96.4	44.3%	32.9%	50.6%
Riley O'Brien	LOU	AAA	26	7	7	0	23	22	112^{2}	93	16	4.4	9.7	121	44.1%	.270	1.31	4.55	92	2.0				
	CIN	MLB	26	0	1	0	1	1	1^{1}	2	2	20.2	13.5	2	50.0%	.000	3.75	13.50	143	0.0	92.0	54.8%		
Connor Overton	BUF	AAA	27	2	1	0	21	7	57^{2}	52	3	1.6	7.8	50	47.0%	.304	1.08	2.03	105	0.6				
	PIT	MLB	27	0	1	0	5	3	8^{2}	10	2	3.1	11.4	11	32.0%	.348	1.50	8.31	91	0.1	92.0	54.4%	27.0%	51.3%
	TOR	MLB	27	0	0	0	4	0	6^{2}	4	0	2.7	5.4	4	38.9%	.222	0.90	0.00	115	0.0	92.7	49.5%	21.6%	55.6%
Christian Roa	RED	ROK	22	1	0	0	2	1	6^{1}	1	0	2.8	12.8	9	46.2%	.077	0.47	0.00						
	DBT	A	22	1	1	0	5	5	17^{2}	18	2	4.6	10.7	21	47.9%	.348	1.53	3.57	97	0.2				
	DAY	A+	22	2	2	0	8	7	34^{2}	32	4	3.9	9.6	37	37.2%	.311	1.36	4.15	103	0.3				
Reiver Sanmartin	EST	WIN	25	0	2	0	7	7	31	16	0	3.2	5.5	19	55.2%	.186	0.87	1.45						
	CHA	AA	25	2	0	0	4	3	18	8	0	2.5	11.5	23	62.2%	.216	0.72	0.50	90	0.3				
	LOU	AAA	25	8	2	0	21	14	82^{1}	80	6	2.5	9.7	89	54.1%	.335	1.25	3.94	93	1.4				
	CIN	MLB	25	2	0	0	2	2	11^{2}	12	0	1.5	8.5	11	47.1%	.353	1.20	1.54	80	0.2	89.7	48.1%	31.1%	47.8%
Art Warren	LOU	AAA	28	1	2	2	15	0	16	18	1	2.8	16.9	30	43.2%	.472	1.44	5.06	69	0.5				
	CIN	MLB	28	3	0	0	26	0	21	11	1	3.4	14.6	34	33.3%	.270	0.90	1.29	70	0.5	95.2	40.2%	41.9%	51.4%

The last of four selections the Reds got to make in the first two rounds of the 2021 draft, **Andrew Abbott** excelled in his only season starting at UVA, but he'll need to develop a much more consistent changeup to continue in that role in the majors. • Former undrafted free agent **R.J. Alaniz** has been extremely tough on Triple-A hitters ever since joining the Reds in 2019, and his reward has been further chances to be extremely tough on Triple-A hitters. Some free agents plan their futures by juggling contract offers; Alaniz will be measuring distances between MLB clubs and their Triple-A affiliates using Google Maps. • The Reds acquired **Brandon Bailey** from the Astros with hopes of taking advantage of his remaining option years to tinker with his deep arsenal, but instead lost him to Tommy John surgery just a few days into spring training. He re-signed with the org as a free agent in the offseason. • **Bryce Bonnin** added some velocity and carry to an already-impressive fastball last year, and it completely overwhelmed A-ball hitters. He may do the same to big-leaguers whenever the Reds admit he's a reliever, or need one enough to pretend. • The days of **Brad Brach** acting as a reliable bridge to Zach Britton are in the rear view mirror, as evidenced by the 20 runs he allowed over his final 10 innings of last season. He reclaimed some of his velocity after a scary drop in 2020, but it still isn't where it once was, and he doesn't have a usable breaking ball. • **Brandon Finnegan** cracked our lineout list as a 28-year-old almost four years past his most recent big-league outing, and spent the entire 2021 season pitching in the Reds' Triple-A bullpen. Which is to say, he's still on both of our radars, but just barely. • **Ryan Hendrix** has been regarded as a potential impact reliever ever since the Reds drafted him in the fifth round back in 2016. His slider looked to be a potential weapon in his big-league debut. • **Riley O'Brien** is a late-blooming eighth-round pick by the Rays who can really spin the ball, but whose erratic mechanics likely limit him to a pen role in the longterm. • **Connor Overton** held hittersscoreless over 6 2/3 innings and yet was suddenly designated for assignment in favor of a bat. Unable to hold down a roster spot despite owning a 0.00 ERA? We can say the overton window on scouting the statline has shifted forever. • Following a possible first-overall pick in the rotation certainly didn't hurt **Christian Roa**'s exposure at Texas A&M, and the Reds snatched him up with their second-round selection. He had a solid first pro season and possesses a starting-caliber arsenal, but his innings will need to be built up before he can prove that's his longterm role. • **Reiver Sanmartin** has a fastball that generally makes its home under the 90-mph mark, but he gets by because he's very stingy on walks and has two bat-missing secondaries. He got his first big-league cup of coffee last year and should be a serviceable fill-in starter on the days when he pitches absolutely perfectly. • The Reds added **Jared Solomon** to the 40-man roster weeks after he underwent Tommy John surgery. Before that, he was flashing triple digits with his fastball and appeared to have developed a plus slider, making this the baseball equivalent of wrapping a Christmas present to yourself in June in hopes that it'll be a surprise in December. • **Art Warren** isn't much for painting corners, but with that slider for a brush, he doesn't have to. The former Mariners relief prospect used his breaker on almost 60% of his pitches in his first extended action against big-league hitters, and it generated a whiff rate over 46%.

MILWAUKEE BREWERS

Essay by Rob Mains

Player comments by Collin Whitchurch and BP staff

When you think of analytics in baseball, which team do you think of as the cutting edge? The Moneyball A's? They always seem to beat expectations. The Rays? They're playing three-dimensional chess every year. How about the Dodgers, "Moneyball with money?" The Astros, even when they're not practicing the dark arts, seem to zig when everyone else is zagging; their batters have been last in the majors in strikeouts three straight seasons. There were rumors that the Yankees' analytics department bought a supercomputer. But maybe it's the Brewers.

For most of baseball history, the role of the starting pitcher has been clear. He is expected to pitch at least five innings, the minimum total to qualify for a win. The deep start has been in decline, though. The last time MLB starters averaged more than six innings per start was 2011. Average innings per start hit an all-time low in 2016, dropping to 5.65. It fell to another low, 5.51, in 2017. And further lows in 2018 and 2019. In 2021, the average start lasted only 5.02 innings, another record low (not counting the irregular 2020 season).

Put another way, in 2011, 85.6 percent of all starts lasted at least five innings. That was the highest percentage in a full season since 1909. Just over a decade ago, we were seeing pitchers last at least five innings at the highest rate in more than a century. Here's what has happened since:

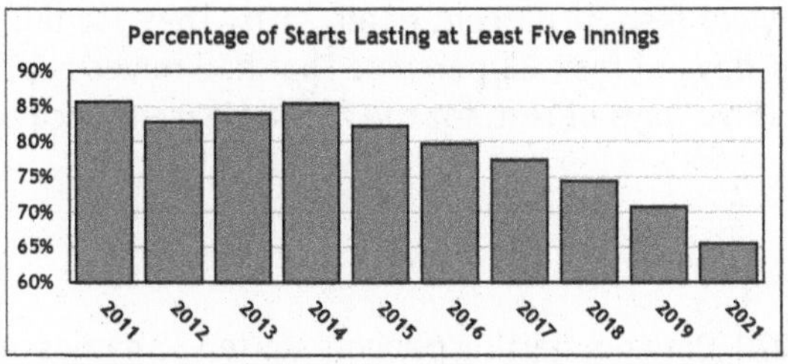

The percentage fell from nearly six out of seven to less than two out of three in just a decade. Whether measured by average innings per start or the percentage of starts lasting five innings, fewer starting pitchers than ever are staying in games long enough to earn a win.

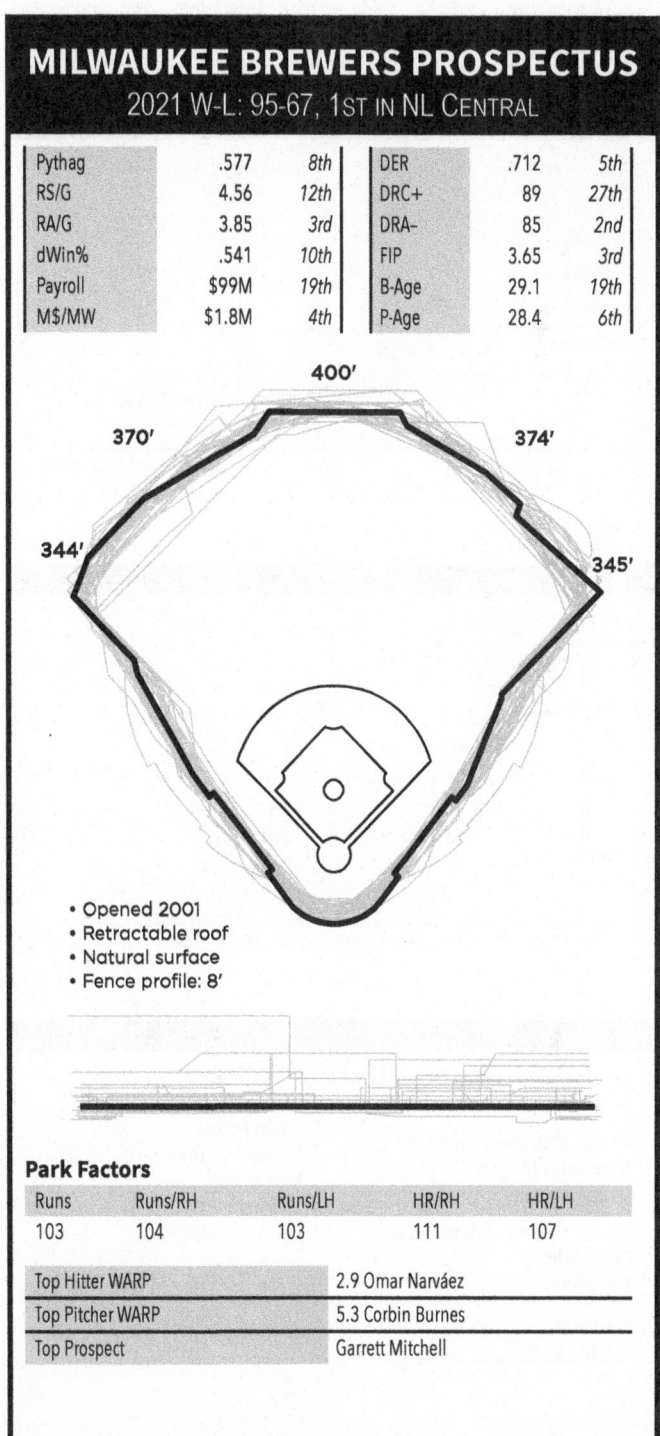

MILWAUKEE BREWERS PROSPECTUS

2021 W-L: 95-67, 1ST IN NL CENTRAL

Pythag	.577	8th	DER	.712	5th
RS/G	4.56	12th	DRC+	89	27th
RA/G	3.85	3rd	DRA-	85	2nd
dWin%	.541	10th	FIP	3.65	3rd
Payroll	$99M	19th	B-Age	29.1	19th
M$/MW	$1.8M	4th	P-Age	28.4	6th

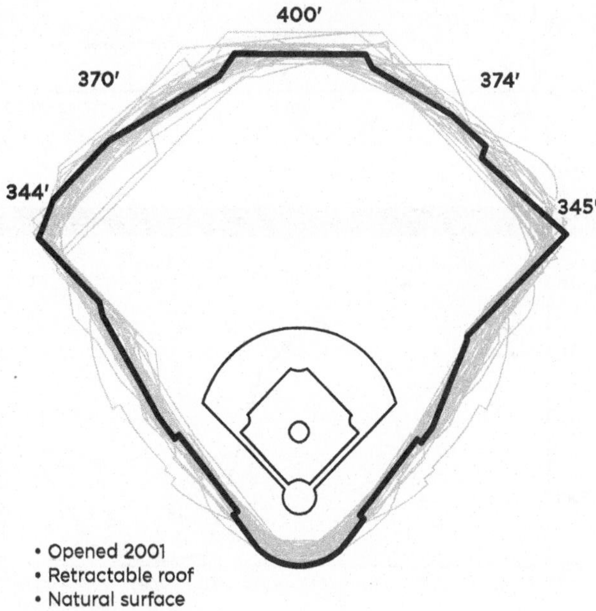

- Opened 2001
- Retractable roof
- Natural surface
- Fence profile: 8'

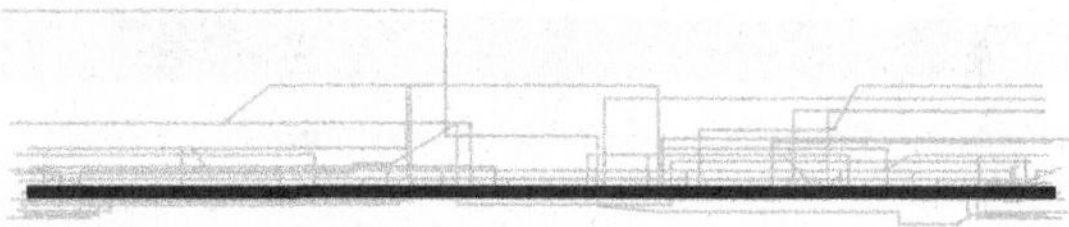

Park Factors

Runs	Runs/RH	Runs/LH	HR/RH	HR/LH
103	104	103	111	107

Top Hitter WARP	2.9 Omar Narváez
Top Pitcher WARP	5.3 Corbin Burnes
Top Prospect	Garrett Mitchell

Payroll History (in millions)

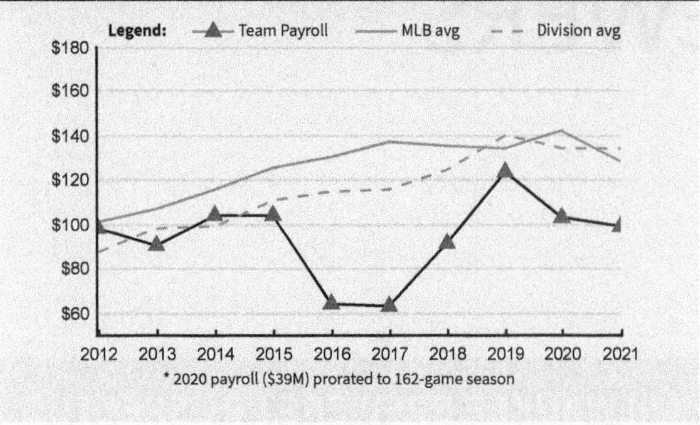

Future Commitments (in millions)

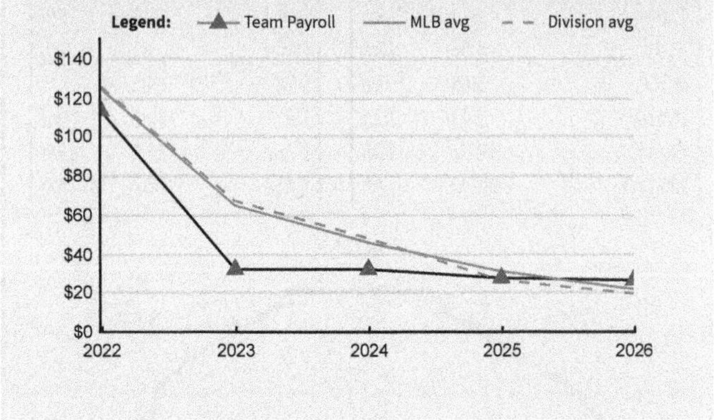

Farm System Ranking

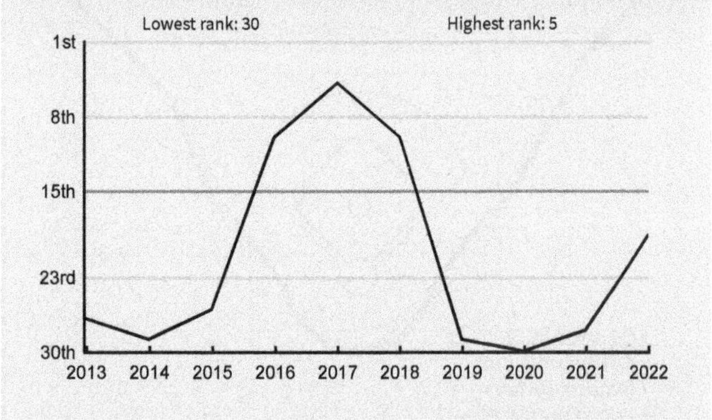

Personnel

President - Baseball Operations
David Stearns

Senior Vice President and General Manager
Matt Arnold

Senior Vice President - Player Personnel
Karl Mueller

Manager
Craig Counsell

BP Alumni
James Fisher
Adam Hayes
Shawn Hoffman
Matt Kleine
Andrew Koo
Dan Turkenkopf

But you probably know about that. Starters going fewer innings isn't news. Third-time-through-the-order penalties, pitch counts, nine-man bullpens . . . there are many trends in contemporary baseball that are resulting in starters leaving games earlier than ever before.

Going into the 2021 season, Brewers management faced a dilemma. In 2020, the team finished 29-31. Milwaukee qualified for the expanded postseason but was swept away by the Dodgers. The Brewers' strength was their pitching staff. The team's 4.16 ERA was sixth in the league in 2020, and its 3.80 FIP was second.

But the team's top starter, Brandon Woodruff (3.05 ERA, 69 DRA–), ran out of gas, starting only three of the season's final 18 games. Corbin Burnes' numbers were even better (2.11 ERA, 57 DRA–), but he was working out of the bullpen for the first third of the season.

Milwaukee's 2021 Opening Day rotation was Woodruff, Burnes, Adrian Houser, Brett Anderson and Freddy Peralta. Woodruff's career high in innings was 121 2/3. Burnes' was 59 2/3. Houser's was 111 1/3. Anderson managed 176 innings in 2019 but only 147 in the prior three years combined. Peralta's high-water mark was 85 innings, and he was a reliever in 2020. The team faced a 162-game season with a starting staff that, among them, had only four seasons in which they qualified for the ERA title: Anderson in 2009, 2015 and 2019, and Woodruff in the doesn't-really-count pandemic season.

The role of the starting pitcher isn't just to pitch five innings. He is expected to take the ball regularly. From 1951 to 2020, a plurality of pitcher starts had occurred on four days of rest every year except 1963, 1965, 1966, 1969 and 1973, years in which three days of rest prevailed. The norm is four days. From 1969 to 2020—the Divisional Play Era—49 percent of all starts were on four days of rest. Starting pitchers were more likely to pitch on four days of rest than any other interval.

Until last year. In 2021, pitchers started 1,782 games on five days of rest, 37 percent of all starts. They started 1,610 on four days of rest, 33 percent. That had never happened before. Five days of rest, for the first time ever, became the norm.

In 2020, Brewers starting pitchers started 33 games on four days of rest and just 12 on five days of rest. The team limited its starters to an average of 4.8 innings per start in the short season, so they couldn't realistically trim more there in 2021. But how about days of rest?

As noted, 2021 was the first season ever in which more starts occurred on five days of rest than four. Here are the teams with the largest difference between starts on five and four days of rest last season.

Team	5 Days	4 Days	Difference
Pittsburgh	87	11	76
Milwaukee	90	20	70
Seattle	76	33	43
L.A. Angels	46	9	37
Houston	93	52	21

The Pirates, whose 5.53 rotation ERA was easily the worst in the league, and Brewers just about lapped the field.

Here are the splits for the Brewers' starters. For pitchers who also pitched in relief, I'm counting only their starts. Recall that this was a team worried that their pitchers would break down over a 162-game season.

Pitcher	5 Days	4 Days	Injured List Days
Brandon Woodruff	22	2	0
Corbin Burnes	17	2	14 (COVID-19)
Adrian Houser	14	4	15 (COVID-19)
Brett Anderson	11	2	49 (hamstring, knee contusion, shoulder contusion)
Freddy Peralta	19	4	15 (shoulder inflammation)
Eric Lauer	7	6	11 (COVID-19)

Note that this wasn't a six-man rotation, which the Mariners and Angels, also prominent in the first table above, both deployed at various times. Rather, the Brewers took advantage of off days in the schedule to give their pitchers an extra day of rest on a five-man schedule. Brewers pitchers made 65 starts five *games* after their last start but only 20 that were five *days* later. It's a six-*day* rotation, not a six-*man* one. Take, for example, a two-week span starting in late July (reading top to bottom):

Date	Starter	Result	Date	Starter	Result
July 24	Burnes	W	July 31	Woodruff	L
July 25	Woodruff	L	August 1	Anderson	W
July 26	No game	–	August 2	Lauer	W
July 27	Anderson	W	August 3	Houser	L
July 28	Houser	W	August 4	Peralta	W
July 29	Peralta	W	August 5	No game	–
July 30	Burnes	W	August 6	Burnes	W

That's a 9-3 record over 12 games played in 14 days using a five-man/six-day rotation. That was typical for the team. Excluding the All-Star Break, the Brewers started five pitchers successively 16 times and added a sixth 12 times. Of those 12 six-man rotations, two occurred when the team had a doubleheader and eight when it was playing games on seven or more straight days.

The Brewers utilized off-days on Mondays and Thursdays to give starting pitchers five days of rest between starts without having to regularly utilize a sixth starter. The results speak for themselves: Only two pitchers suffering injuries, the second-lowest rotation ERA in the majors, the second-highest average game score, the third-most quality starts, the fifth-most starter innings and the seventh-most innings per start.

⚾ ⚾ ⚾

The story of the 2022 Brewers isn't just one of whether they'll continue to use a six-day rotation and, in so doing, keep their starting pitchers healthy and effective. They have the lineup to think about, too, one that was fourth-worst in the league in 2021 per DRC+. The Brewers had the third-lowest OPS at first base in the NL in 2021. Rowdy Tellez had an .814 OPS after coming over in a July trade with Toronto. Keston Hiura, since his .303/.368/.570 rookie season in 2019, has hit .192/.279/.362 in 120 major-league games, struck out in 37 percent of his plate appearances, moved from second to first and shuttled between Milwaukee and Nashville. He or Mike Brosseau is likely to be the platoon-mate for the lefty Tellez.

More worryingly, Brewers outfielders were last in the league in batting average and on-base percentage and third-to-last in slugging percentage. Their park-adjusted OPS tied the Mets' outfielders' as the league's worst. The best hitter in the 2021 Brewers' outfield, Avisaíl García, signed a free-agent contract with the Marlins after a career year. Milwaukee then sent last winter's big free-agent pickup, Jackie Bradley Jr., to the Red Sox for Hunter Renfroe, who takes over in right field. That leaves center to Lorenzo Cain, who was fine (101 DRC+) but turns 36 in April and missed almost half of last season with quadriceps and hamstring injuries. Christian Yelich, signed through 2028, had a 1.000-plus OPS in both 2018 and 2019, his first two seasons with Milwaukee, but hasn't matched that figure *in a single month* in the two years since.

The rest of the club is strong, championship-caliber in one of baseball's less-competitive divisions. Hiura's move to first made way for Kolten Wong at second base. After the Cardinals declined Wong's option, the Brewers signed him for two years. Willy Adames, acquired in a May trade with the Rays, had a career year at the plate (.285/.366/.521 in 99 games with Milwaukee after hitting .254/.320/.420 in 332 games with Tampa Bay). That pair upgraded the team's up-the-middle defense, supporting a pitching staff with the fifth-highest ground-ball rate in the league. Adames' arrival moved Luis Urías to third, and Urías responded with a career year of his own, with a 107 DRC+ and 23 homers, second on the team to García's 29. Wong is 31 years old, Adames 26 and Urías 24.

Catcher Omar Narváez continues to provide an above-average bat. The notable change in his player profile is on defense; since joining Milwaukee, he has become one of the best backstops in the majors, with 14.1 FRAA in 1,171 innings behind the plate in Milwaukee after accumulating –43.0 in 2,365 innings with the White Sox and Mariners. The Brewers have tweaked his positioning behind the plate, yielding superior results.

In the bullpen, Josh Hader and Devin Williams struck out 42 percent of the batters they faced, and Brent Suter was tenth in the league in relief innings. (The absence of Suter and Williams from the Division Series due to injury didn't help, as the team made a meek exit, but neither of them would've done anything for a Brewers offense that scored only six runs in four games.) Those three give the club a dominant back of the bullpen. Even if the reincarnated Brad Boxberger (3.34 ERA, four saves and 23 holds in 71 relief appearances) and Hunter Strickland (1.73 in 35 games after he was DFA'd by the Angels), both free agents, don't return, Aaron Ashby had a promising debut. Working primarily out of the bullpen, Ashby had a 1.78 ERA in between blowups in his first and last games of the year. He'll also be a contender for a spot in the rotation, which has a hole in it with Anderson's free agency. Milwaukee's success with Boxberger and Strickland and, before them, the likes of Jeremy Jeffress and Alex Claudio indicates the team's ability to find useful veteran relievers on the scrap heap.

As for the rotation, all the starters but Anderson are under contract for 2022. The six-day rotation will probably remain. Woodruff (179 1/3 innings) and Burnes (167) were ERA qualifiers, barely, ranking only 15th and 20th in the league in innings. Houser, Lauer, Peralta, Woodruff and Burnes all had career-low ERAs, and the latter quartet added career-best DRAs and WARP. The strategy may have been borne of health concerns, but the quality outcomes lend resounding support.

That said, the success of 2021 will be a tough act to follow. Maintaining a starting pitcher ERA (3.13) more than a run below the league average (4.22) is a tall order, even in one of MLB's softer divisions. There will be some regression in terms of both performance, following all of those career years, and health, as only one of five returning pitchers suffered a non-COVID-19 IL stint in 2021. The Brewers' 2022 rotation should be very good. Just don't expect the six-day rotation to match its rookie season.

As effective as Milwaukee has been at turning scrap-heap pickups into effective bullpen arms and good prospects into elite starters, the Brewers might need to turn their attention to the lineup to break through the playoff wall they've hit repeatedly over the last few seasons.

Despite playing in baseball's smallest market, the Brewers are a successful franchise. They've played into October in four straight years, winning the NL Central in two of them. They have the second-best record in the league over the past five seasons. They've avoided tanking, with only six losing seasons, just one with fewer than 74 wins and no last-place finishes in the past 17 years.

There are plenty of reasons for that success: Principal owner Mark Attanasio has shown a willingness to spend, President of Baseball Operations David Stearns is savvy and the team employs one of the game's best tacticians in manager Craig Counsell. But the organizational quality extends beyond the top-line names. The Brewers identified catchers who hadn't, but *could*, learn to frame and then taught them to do so. They have evolved from the group that created buy-in around "initial out-getters"—it wasn't about *openers*, sometimes it was just a batter or two—to the one that figured out how to get the most out of its elite, if fragile, starting pitchers coming off a pandemic-shortened season. The success of all of these approaches speaks to both analytics and development teams that may fly below the radar in comparison to better-known groups in other cities, but consistently deliver top results.

—Rob Mains is an author for Baseball Prospectus.

Hitters

Willy Adames SS Born: 09/02/95 Age: 26 Bats: R Throws: R Height: 6'0" Weight: 210 lb. Origin: International Free Agent, 2015

YEAR	TEAM	LVL	AGE	PA	R	2B	3B	HR	RBI	BB	K	SB	CS	Whiff%	AVG/OBP/SLG	DRC+	BABIP	BRR	FRAA	WARP
2019	TB	MLB	23	584	69	25	1	20	52	46	153	4	2	27.2%	.254/.317/.418	88	.320	2.3	SS(152): 12.7	2.7
2020	TB	MLB	24	205	29	15	1	8	23	20	74	2	1	38.7%	.259/.332/.481	85	.388	1.2	SS(53): 1.6	0.5
2021	MIL	MLB	25	413	61	26	0	20	58	47	105	4	2	29.9%	.285/.366/.521	110	.349	0.1	SS(96): -0.5	1.9
2021	TB	MLB	25	142	16	6	1	5	15	10	51	1	2	39.7%	.197/.254/.371	74	.276	-0.3	SS(40): 3.6	0.4
2022 DC	*MIL*	*MLB*	*26*	*551*	*76*	*26*	*2*	*18*	*76*	*53*	*163*	*5*	*3*	*32.4%*	*.247/.325/.423*	*96*	*.335*	*-0.2*	*SS 4*	*2.2*

Comparables: Wilmer Flores, Jonathan Villar, Chris Owings

You know how these things go. You're in Year 7 of a relationship with this person and you just know in your heart that it's going nowhere. When you're in a room together, nobody talks. Not out of comfort, but because you don't care what the other person has to say. Both of you know it's over, but both are too lazy to do anything about it. When they finally dump you ("it's not you, it's me"), you're supposed to be upset, but inside you're elated. Soon enough you've found someone else, maybe even some*where* else, with all of the good aspects of your prior relationship and none ofthe baggage. Suddenly you're accomplishing things you've always thought about but never managed to do. For Adames, the mid-season trade to Milwaukee revitalized his offensive profile, unlocking his power stroke. It was infectious, too, as Adames operated as the on-field marshal teams expect of their shortstops, and as a big brother to Luis Urías in particular—who saw his offense bloom upon moving to third base. The lift that Adames received (emotionally) and his bat received (figuratively) extended to the Brewers' lineup (literally), as the fourth-year man helped drag the offense to a solid 12th overall in runs scored (though they were a bottom-five team in team DRC+). As Shakespeare-via-Instagram quotes advises, don't waste your [bat] on someone who doesn't value it."

Mike Brosseau IF

Born: 03/15/94 Age: 28 Bats: R Throws: R Height: 5'10" Weight: 205 lb. Origin: Undrafted Free Agent, 2016

YEAR	TEAM	LVL	AGE	PA	R	2B	3B	HR	RBI	BB	K	SB	CS	Whiff%	AVG/OBP/SLG	DRC+	BABIP	BRR	FRAA	WARP
2019	DUR	AAA	25	315	53	21	1	16	60	34	58	2	3		.304/.394/.567	129	.332	0.9	3B(32): -1.6, 1B(17): -0.9, 2B(7): -0.6	1.8
2019	TB	MLB	25	142	17	7	0	6	16	7	39	1	0	25.5%	.273/.319/.462	90	.345	0.8	2B(26): -0.5, 3B(18): -0.7, RF(6): -0.6	0.2
2020	TB	MLB	26	98	12	5	1	5	12	8	31	2	0	36.1%	.302/.378/.558	96	.412	-0.5	1B(12): 1.4, 3B(11): 0.7, 2B(9): -0.7	0.3
2021	DUR	AAA	27	202	25	2	1	8	21	23	50	2	0		.218/.342/.382	108	.259	0.1	3B(28): -3.4, 2B(8): -0.1, 1B(7): 0.2	0.5
2021	TB	MLB	27	169	21	9	0	5	18	15	53	2	0	29.2%	.187/.266/.347	79	.245	0.7	2B(27): 0.5, 3B(23): -2.0, 1B(10): -0.3	0.0
2022 DC	*MIL*	*MLB*	*28*	*129*	*16*	*5*	*0*	*3*	*16*	*10*	*34*	*1*	*1*	*29.1%*	*.215/.300/.370*	*80*	*.273*	*0.0*	*3B 0, 2B 0*	*0.0*

Comparables: Danny Valencia, Matt Carpenter, Tyler White

Aroldis Chapman's arch nemesis, Brosseau split the 2021 season between the majors and minors filling in when needed on defense while not providing much at the plate during any of his stays. The lack of production—and an oblique injury—prevented him from carving out a semi-regular role with the Rays despite being a right-handed bat to balance some of their lefties and possessing the versatility to start at four or five positions on the diamond. A quick check under the hood shows Brosseau hit the ball just as hard with similar regularity as he did in 2020, just with less success. Let's say his true baseline is an average overall hitter with strong platoon splits and utility tendencies on defense. That's about as ~~Rays~~' Brewers' a player as you can get.

Lorenzo Cain CF

Born: 04/13/86 Age: 36 Bats: R Throws: R Height: 6'2" Weight: 214 lb. Origin: Round 17, 2004 Draft (#496 overall)

YEAR	TEAM	LVL	AGE	PA	R	2B	3B	HR	RBI	BB	K	SB	CS	Whiff%	AVG/OBP/SLG	DRC+	BABIP	BRR	FRAA	WARP
2019	MIL	MLB	33	623	75	30	0	11	48	50	106	18	8	19.1%	.260/.325/.372	91	.301	0.8	CF(143): -1.9	1.8
2020	MIL	MLB	34	21	4	1	0	0	2	3	2	0	0	22.2%	.333/.429/.389	100	.375	0.2	CF(5): 0.1	0.1
2021	NAS	AAA	35	31	1	1	0	0	0	2	8	1	0		.241/.290/.276	89	.333	0.1	CF(9): -0.1	0.1
2021	MIL	MLB	35	286	40	13	0	8	36	26	48	13	2	21.9%	.257/.329/.401	101	.287	3.5	CF(70): -1.4	1.5
2022 DC	*MIL*	*MLB*	*36*	*532*	*74*	*22*	*1*	*12*	*62*	*50*	*96*	*18*	*5*	*21.8%*	*.267/.344/.396*	*100*	*.314*	*0.8*	*CF 1*	*2.2*

Comparables: Marquis Grissom, Devon White, Coco Crisp

Cain was on his way out of his prime by the time he signed a five-year free agent contract with the Brewers. His 2018 garnered downballot MVP votes, but overall the underwhelming nature of his performance since arriving in Milwaukee seems unfair. Cain was a late bloomer, not really able to work his way into regular playing time until his age-27 season, which he parlayed into a five-year run of performing as a star: contending for MVP awards, providing highlight after highlight in center field and becoming the cornerstone of a World Series winning team in Kansas City. Cain's last two seasons have been forgettable. The outfielder understandably opted out of the 2020 season amid COVID-19 fears after just five games, and missed more than half of 2021 because of injuries. Cain performed admirably when he was on the field, so maybe all that's needed is a clean bill of health and a full season for him to get back to his sterling ways, but now on the other side of 35, that's anything but a certainty. And if the really cool parts of Cain's career are truly gone, it seems far too soon.

David Dahl LF

Born: 04/01/94 Age: 28 Bats: L Throws: R Height: 6'2" Weight: 197 lb. Origin: Round 1, 2012 Draft (#10 overall)

YEAR	TEAM	LVL	AGE	PA	R	2B	3B	HR	RBI	BB	K	SB	CS	Whiff%	AVG/OBP/SLG	DRC+	BABIP	BRR	FRAA	WARP
2019	COL	MLB	25	413	67	28	5	15	61	28	110	4	4	30.9%	.302/.353/.524	95	.386	2.0	CF(40): 1.1, LF(39): -0.1, RF(24): -4.6	1.1
2020	COL	MLB	26	99	9	2	2	0	9	4	28	1	0	31.2%	.183/.222/.247	60	.258	1.1	CF(17): 0.8, LF(4): -1.3, RF(2): 0.1	-0.1
2021	FRI	AA	27	25	7	0	0	1	7	2	3	1	0		.522/.560/.652	116	.579	0.9	LF(4): 0.1	0.2
2021	NAS	AAA	27	120	18	12	1	3	15	8	17	0	0		.327/.375/.536	117	.363	-2.0	RF(24): -3.0, LF(3): 0.4, CF(1): -0.3	0.2
2021	TEX	MLB	27	220	19	11	0	4	18	10	59	2	1	26.7%	.210/.247/.322	66	.269	-2.3	LF(31): -1.5, RF(12): 0.4, CF(1): 0.0	-0.6
2022 non-DC	*MIL*	*MLB*	*28*	*251*	*25*	*12*	*1*	*6*	*28*	*14*	*56*	*2*	*2*	*26.8%*	*.258/.306/.414*	*90*	*.313*	*0.1*	*LF 0, CF 0*	*0.5*

Comparables: Michael Saunders, Josh Reddick, Michael Brantley

The ~~obliteration~~ realignment of the minors before the season wound up having a bigger impact on Dahl's season than he would've expected. The Brewers' Triple-A affiliate went from San Antonio to Nashville, making his relocation much more burdensome when he was cut loose by the Rangers and scooped up on a minor-league deal by the Brewers. Dahl probably shouldn't unpack, though, as the once-promising Rockies slugger was re-signed to a minor-league contract by Milwaukee and received an invite to spring training, where he'll look to regain his form.

Mario Feliciano C

Born: 11/20/98 Age: 23 Bats: R Throws: R Height: 6'1" Weight: 200 lb. Origin: Round 2, 2016 Draft (#75 overall)

YEAR	TEAM	LVL	AGE	PA	R	2B	3B	HR	RBI	BB	K	SB	CS	Whiff%	AVG/OBP/SLG	DRC+	BABIP	BRR	FRAA	WARP
2019	MAN	WIN	20	101	2	6	0	0	4	5	20	0	0		.269/.327/.333		.342			
2019	CAR	A+	20	482	62	25	4	19	81	29	139	2	1		.273/.324/.477	107	.351	-4.3	C(61): 3.4	1.8
2021	BRWG	ROK	22	29	7	3	1	0	4	1	6	0	0		.360/.448/.560		.474			
2021	NAS	AAA	22	114	12	2	0	3	19	4	26	1	0		.210/.246/.314	87	.241	0.7	C(30): 1.8	0.5
2021	MIL	MLB	22	1	1	0	0	0	0	1	0	0	0	33.3%	.000/1.000/.000	110		0.1		0.0
2022 DC	*MIL*	*MLB*	*23*	*29*	*3*	*1*	*0*	*0*	*3*	*1*	*7*	*0*	*0*	*32.6%*	*.235/.289/.383*	*75*	*.298*	*0.0*	*C 0*	*0.1*

Comparables: Gary Sánchez, Salvador Perez, Wilson Ramos

YEAR	TEAM	P. COUNT	FRM RUNS	BLK RUNS	THRW RUNS	TOT RUNS
2021	NAS	4160	2.5	-0.1	0.0	2.4
2022	*MIL*	*1202*	*-0.2*	*-0.1*	*0.0*	*-0.2*

Feliciano made his major-league debut in May when he was forced into action amid injuries to incumbent catchers Omar Narváez and Manny Piña. He had one plate appearance and walked in the 11th inning of what wound up as a three-run, comeback victory over the Dodgers. That was the highlight of Feliciano's season, as Milwaukee's likely Catcher Of The Future never got it going offensively at Triple-A and had his season abbreviated by injuries. He's still very much in the team's future plans, but will enter 2022 nearly three years removed from the breakout season that earned him the moniker in the first place.

★ ★ ★ *2022 Top 101 Prospect* **#98** ★ ★ ★

Sal Frelick OF Born: 04/19/00 Age: 22 Bats: L Throws: R Height: 5'9" Weight: 175 lb. Origin: Round 1, 2021 Draft (#15 overall)

YEAR	TEAM	LVL	AGE	PA	R	2B	3B	HR	RBI	BB	K	SB	CS	Whiff%	AVG/OBP/SLG	DRC+	BABIP	BRR	FRAA	WARP
2021	CAR	A	21	81	17	6	1	1	12	9	10	6	2		.437/.494/.592	128	.492	0.3	CF(14): 2.3	0.8
2021	WIS	A+	21	71	7	1	1	1	5	10	13	3	0		.167/.296/.267	110	.196	0.1	CF(13): 0.4	0.4
2022 non-DC	*MIL*	*MLB*	*22*	*251*	*21*	*10*	*1*	*2*	*21*	*20*	*48*	*7*	*3*	*22.9%*	*.234/.302/.330*	*75*	*.286*	*0.6*	*CF 1*	*0.3*

Comparables: Ender Inciarte, Adam Haseley, Mallex Smith

The Brewers gave Frelick a $4 million bonus after drafting him out of college and he performed pretty much exactly like an advanced college bat should, obliterating both the complex league and Low-A, earning himself a promotion to High-A by the end of the season. Frelick was a popular pick among orgs that factor in draft models, and while his speed grades out highest (he's a legit 7 runner), his routes in the field need polish, and his hit tool will ultimately determine his success up and down the chain. The early returns on that were good, despite a High-A stumble. He should make enough contact to progress quickly through the minors, and given the state of Milwaukee's farm, he immediately becomes one of the highest-upside players in the system.

Keston Hiura 1B Born: 08/02/96 Age: 25 Bats: R Throws: R Height: 6'0" Weight: 202 lb. Origin: Round 1, 2017 Draft (#9 overall)

YEAR	TEAM	LVL	AGE	PA	R	2B	3B	HR	RBI	BB	K	SB	CS	Whiff%	AVG/OBP/SLG	DRC+	BABIP	BRR	FRAA	WARP
2019	SA	AAA	22	243	44	16	1	19	46	23	64	7	2		.329/.407/.681	128	.389	0.4	2B(46): -1.7	1.8
2019	MIL	MLB	22	348	51	23	2	19	49	25	107	9	3	36.2%	.303/.368/.570	100	.402	-0.2	2B(81): -5.1	0.9
2020	MIL	MLB	23	246	30	4	0	13	32	16	85	3	2	42.7%	.212/.297/.410	92	.273	-0.9	2B(49): -7.6	-0.3
2021	NAS	AAA	24	206	22	12	0	8	24	29	69	2	1		.256/.374/.465	100	.375	-0.8	1B(24): -2.6, 2B(23): 4.2	0.6
2021	MIL	MLB	24	197	16	9	1	4	19	14	77	3	0	47.0%	.168/.256/.301	53	.269	-1.4	1B(49): -0.7, 2B(7): 0.0	-0.9
2022 DC	*MIL*	*MLB*	*25*	*178*	*24*	*8*	*0*	*7*	*26*	*14*	*70*	*2*	*1*	*42.8%*	*.222/.312/.430*	*92*	*.349*	*0.1*	*1B -1, 2B 0*	*-0.2*

Comparables: Jorge Soler, Alexi Casilla, Ian Happ

Nobody minded much when the Brewers made the decision to shift Hiura to first base upon the free-agent acquisition of Kolten Wong. Hiura wasn't drafted for his glove, and Wong's addition, paired with the positional switch, should've improved the Brewers defensively while keeping Hiura's promising bat in the lineup. When Hiura's 2020 struggles with elite velocity and advanced secondaries continued in 2021, the contending Brewers made the bold but necessary decision to send him to Triple-A, and what was supposed to be a breakout season became another lost one. Hiura still has fewer than two season's worth of plate appearances to his name, but the further in the rearview mirror that breakout 2019 campaign becomes, the more uncertain his potential as a lineup cornerstone becomes. He'll enter 2022 only 25 years old, but without an ability to rediscover his forlorn hit tool or the monster power he seemed to trade it for in 2019, it's going to get dark early out there.

Hendry Mendez RF Born: 11/07/03 Age: 18 Bats: L Throws: L Height: 6'2" Weight: 175 lb. Origin: International Free Agent, 2021

YEAR	TEAM	LVL	AGE	PA	R	2B	3B	HR	RBI	BB	K	SB	CS	Whiff%	AVG/OBP/SLG	DRC+	BABIP	BRR	FRAA	WARP
2021	BRWB	ROK	17	74	6	4	2	0	10	10	10	3	1		.333/.425/.460		.396			
2021	DSL BRW1	ROK	17	64	10	5	1	1	9	7	2	0	0		.296/.391/.481		.288			
2022															*No projection*					

Comparables: Deivi Estrada, Julio Rojas, Damian Valdez

There are probably more exciting places to spend one's 18th birthday than Maryvale, Arizona, but for Mendez, a 2021 international signee, his location represented a geographical as well as a chronological milestone: the Brewers aggressively promoted the sweet-swinging lefty stateside after just a few weeks' worth of plate appearances in the DSL. The quick move shows how highly Milwaukee prizes Mendez, regarded as a pure hitter with intriguing power potential. A birthday spent at one of the Valley of the Sun's many, many chain restaurants is a small price to pay for this kind of esteem.

★ ★ ★ *2022 Top 101 Prospect* **#94** ★ ★ ★

Garrett Mitchell OF Born: 09/04/98 Age: 23 Bats: L Throws: R Height: 6'3" Weight: 215 lb. Origin: Round 1, 2020 Draft (#20 overall)

YEAR	TEAM	LVL	AGE	PA	R	2B	3B	HR	RBI	BB	K	SB	CS	Whiff%	AVG/OBP/SLG	DRC+	BABIP	BRR	FRAA	WARP
2021	WIS	A+	22	120	33	5	2	5	20	28	30	12	1		.359/.508/.620	126	.491	0.8	CF(13): -2.5, RF(2): 0.3	0.6
2021	BLX	AA	22	148	16	1	0	3	10	18	41	5	1		.186/.291/.264	84	.247	-0.7	CF(30): 0.9, RF(2): -0.0, LF(1): -0.1	0.2
2022 non-DC	*MIL*	*MLB*	*23*	*251*	*23*	*9*	*1*	*4*	*23*	*28*	*73*	*6*	*2*	*30.6%*	*.210/.304/.328*	*78*	*.291*	*0.5*	*CF 2, RF 1*	*0.5*

Comparables: Jackie Bradley Jr., Brandon Nimmo, Julio Borbon

Mitchell hit the ground running in his first pro season, absolutely torching High-A before a midseason promotion to Biloxi. He struggled there, but more in a "getting used to the step-up in competition" way than anything that would lead to long-term concerns. Mitchell is a plus center fielder with exceptional speed and a solid hit tool; the question will be if he can tap into enough of his raw power to become entirely well-rounded. Regardless, the Brewers have a quick-rising center field prospect who they could envision locking down the position for the foreseeable future—whenever he's ready.

Omar Narváez C Born: 02/10/92 Age: 30 Bats: L Throws: R Height: 5'11" Weight: 220 lb. Origin: International Free Agent, 2008

YEAR	TEAM	LVL	AGE	PA	R	2B	3B	HR	RBI	BB	K	SB	CS	Whiff%	AVG/OBP/SLG	DRC+	BABIP	BRR	FRAA	WARP
2019	SEA	MLB	27	482	63	12	0	22	55	47	92	0	0	22.6%	.278/.353/.460	113	.306	-1.2	C(98): -9.7, 2B(1): -0.0	1.7
2020	MIL	MLB	28	126	8	4	0	2	10	16	39	0	0	29.6%	.176/.294/.269	78	.254	-0.8	C(39): 5.0	0.5
2021	MIL	MLB	29	445	54	20	0	11	49	41	84	0	0	23.6%	.266/.342/.402	99	.308	-4.2	C(111): 14.5, 2B(1): -0.0	2.9
2022 DC	*MIL*	*MLB*	*30*	*459*	*56*	*18*	*0*	*10*	*57*	*46*	*96*	*0*	*1*	*23.8%*	*.248/.333/.372*	*89*	*.304*	*-0.7*	*C -1*	*1.3*

Comparables: Nick Hundley, Martín Maldonado, Jonathan Lucroy

YEAR	TEAM	P. COUNT	FRM RUNS	BLK RUNS	THRW RUNS	TOT RUNS
2019	SEA	13812	-10.4	-1.6	1.0	-11.0
2020	MIL	4886	4.9	0.1	0.4	5.4
2021	MIL	14925	13.0	-1.0	1.3	13.3
2022	*MIL*	*16835*	*-5.1*	*-2.8*	*-0.7*	*-8.5*

The biggest question regarding Narváez entering the season is whether or not the defensive improvements he showed during the shortened season would stick. They did, as Narváez ranked fifth among all catchers in CDA. The second-biggest question is whether or not the offensive downtick that came with it was real, too. Not quite. Narváez didn't reach the offensive heights he hit in Chicago or Seattle, but a league-average bat with elite defense is essentially striking gold, and Narváez ranked alongside J.T. Realmuto and Will Smith as the only catchers with near-league average or better offense while also being in the top 10 in CDA. All of that added up to a career year for the former Rule 5 pick, and makes him a perennial All-Star contender at a position where all-around talent is increasingly difficult to find.

Hedbert Perez OF
Born: 04/04/03 Age: 19 Bats: L Throws: L Height: 5'10" Weight: 160 lb. Origin: International Free Agent, 2019

YEAR	TEAM	LVL	AGE	PA	R	2B	3B	HR	RBI	BB	K	SB	CS	Whiff%	AVG/OBP/SLG	DRC+	BABIP	BRR	FRAA	WARP
2021	BRWG	ROK	18	132	19	11	0	6	21	8	34	2	0		.333/.394/.575		.425			
2021	CAR	A	18	68	5	2	0	1	7	1	25	0	0		.169/.206/.246	76	.256	-0.4	CF(16): 2.8, LF(1): -0.1	0.3
2022 non-DC	*MIL*	*MLB*	*19*	*251*	*16*	*10*	*1*	*2*	*18*	*10*	*105*	*0*	*0*	*40.8%*	*.188/.232/.273*	*33*	*.324*	*-0.2*	*CF 2, RF 0*	*-1.2*

Comparables: Ronald Acuña Jr., Fernando Martinez, Riley Greene

Perez raked in the complex league but faced adversity while in Low-A, though the sample size was small. Don't read too much into the numbers in either location at this point; just know that Perez is one of Milwaukee's best prospects, as low as that particular bar may be. His swing is compact and he can move it around the zone, though it can be high-effort and leave him unbalanced at release. Still, when he does connect, watch out. The bat is likely to be the profile-maker, as Perez's future probably resides in an outfield corner rather than the middle of the diamond. There's a lot of unknowns for a profile this raw, but there's a commensurate amount of upside to go with it. In the sea of infomercials and test patterns that is Milwaukee's system, he's one to watch.

Jace Peterson UT
Born: 05/09/90 Age: 32 Bats: L Throws: R Height: 6'0" Weight: 215 lb. Origin: Round 1, 2011 Draft (#58 overall)

YEAR	TEAM	LVL	AGE	PA	R	2B	3B	HR	RBI	BB	K	SB	CS	Whiff%	AVG/OBP/SLG	DRC+	BABIP	BRR	FRAA	WARP
2019	NOR	AAA	29	377	58	25	5	10	46	46	56	13	3		.313/.398/.512	121	.350	-0.1	3B(38): 2.2, 1B(27): 1.6, 2B(9): 2.3	2.4
2019	BAL	MLB	29	108	14	3	1	2	11	6	24	4	1	30.2%	.220/.269/.330	82	.267	0.2	LF(18): 3.2, 3B(9): -0.1, 2B(5): 0.7	0.5
2020	MIL	MLB	30	61	6	1	0	2	5	15	20	1	0	34.6%	.200/.393/.356	97	.292	-0.4	RF(13): -1.2, 3B(4): 0.3, LF(4): 0.5	0.0
2021	NAS	AAA	31	64	12	4	0	5	19	9	19	1	0		.236/.344/.582	122	.258	-0.2	2B(7): -0.6, 1B(3): 0.0, 3B(3): 0.0	0.3
2021	MIL	MLB	31	302	36	11	1	6	31	38	68	10	1	27.3%	.247/.348/.367	90	.310	3.1	2B(35): -1.4, 1B(26): -0.0, RF(17): -1.7	0.6
2022 DC	*MIL*	*MLB*	*32*	*155*	*19*	*6*	*0*	*3*	*18*	*20*	*39*	*3*	*1*	*28.7%*	*.228/.335/.377*	*93*	*.296*	*0.2*	*3B 0, 2B 0*	*0.3*

Comparables: Ryan Goins, Ryan Flaherty, Chase d'Arnaud

Peterson spent nearly the entire season on the Brewers' active roster, which is a notable accomplishment for a guy who has spent most of his career as a "break glass in case of emergency" utility player. Peterson does everything competently, but nothing spectacularly. He can play all four infield positions and even the corner outfields in a pinch. He runs well, and can even run into one with the bat on occasion. Now on the other side of 30, Peterson has carved out a nice career after being considered a first-round bust in San Diego, but if he's deployed in anything more than a backup/utility role, it's safe to say something has gone wrong elsewhere on the roster.

Hunter Renfroe RF
Born: 01/28/92 Age: 30 Bats: R Throws: R Height: 6'1" Weight: 230 lb. Origin: Round 1, 2013 Draft (#13 overall)

YEAR	TEAM	LVL	AGE	PA	R	2B	3B	HR	RBI	BB	K	SB	CS	Whiff%	AVG/OBP/SLG	DRC+	BABIP	BRR	FRAA	WARP
2019	SD	MLB	27	494	64	19	1	33	64	46	154	5	0	30.6%	.216/.289/.489	101	.239	-2.2	RF(86): 6.7, LF(67): 0.8, CF(4): -0.1	2.2
2020	TB	MLB	28	139	18	5	0	8	22	14	37	2	0	32.1%	.156/.252/.393	104	.141	-0.3	RF(39): -0.1, 1B(2): 0.1	0.5
2021	BOS	MLB	29	572	89	33	0	31	96	44	130	1	2	25.9%	.259/.315/.501	116	.284	-1.7	RF(138): 6.1, CF(8): -0.3	3.3
2022 DC	*MIL*	*MLB*	*30*	*494*	*74*	*22*	*1*	*27*	*86*	*40*	*111*	*3*	*1*	*26.4%*	*.246/.315/.484*	*106*	*.271*	*-0.5*	*RF 0*	*1.5*

Comparables: Paul O'Neill, Tom Brunansky, Sammy Sosa

Few free agent signings in recent years have provided more bang-for-the-buck than the one-year, $3.1 million deal Renfroe signed with the Sox last December. The chiseled outfielder put his two best tools, his power and his arm, on full display, finishing second on the team in homers and first in the majors in outfield assists with 16. An inherently streaky player, Renfroe and his Trout-ian neck vacillated between All-Star-caliber play in May, June and August and epic struggles in April, July and, most notably, the postseason. Renfroe notched more GIDPs than hits in the ALCS after an infamous ALDS defensive play that, if nothing else, forced many to learn the difference between automatic and ground-rule doubles. October struggles aside, two factors make Renfroe's signing all the sweeter for the Sox: Boston inked him after the Rays DFA'd him, and he's under team control for two more seasons. He's still best served with a left-handed caddy—he hit .250/.288/.491 against same-side pitching—but Renfroe proved definitively he can start for a first-division club. Especially one with a cavernous right field.

Pedro Severino C
Born: 07/20/93 Age: 28 Bats: R Throws: R Height: 6'1" Weight: 235 lb. Origin: International Free Agent, 2010

YEAR	TEAM	LVL	AGE	PA	R	2B	3B	HR	RBI	BB	K	SB	CS	Whiff%	AVG/OBP/SLG	DRC+	BABIP	BRR	FRAA	WARP
2019	BAL	MLB	25	341	37	13	0	13	44	29	73	3	1	25.0%	.249/.321/.420	97	.285	-1.6	C(89): -11.1	0.1
2020	BAL	MLB	26	178	17	5	1	5	21	16	40	1	0	28.2%	.250/.322/.388	101	.304	-0.7	C(35): -3.7	0.2
2021	BAL	MLB	27	419	32	18	0	11	46	34	109	0	0	29.5%	.248/.308/.383	90	.314	-2.9	C(109): -13.7	-0.5
2022 DC	*MIL*	*MLB*	*28*	*158*	*19*	*6*	*0*	*5*	*21*	*13*	*39*	*0*	*0*	*28.3%*	*.236/.306/.391*	*84*	*.294*	*-0.2*	*C -2*	*0.2*

Comparables: Wilson Ramos, Austin Romine, Jarrod Saltalamacchia

YEAR	TEAM	P. COUNT	FRM RUNS	BLK RUNS	THRW RUNS	TOT RUNS
2019	BAL	12991	-10.8	-1.0	0.7	-11.1
2020	BAL	4698	-3.3	-0.1	0.4	-3.1
2021	BAL	15382	-9.7	-2.7	0.0	-12.3
2022	*MIL*	*6012*	*-2.0*	*-1.3*	*0.1*	*-3.1*

What is it like having a starting role with a strict expiry date? We could posit some fanciful scenarios in which Baltimore had to think hard about what to do with their incumbent catcher in the face of Adley Rutschman's imminent arrival, most of which involve Severino doing a passable impression of Johnny Bench. If we're going to be realistic, there isn't anything he could have done. That said, further offensive development and a reversal of his negative defensive contribution might have made him an enticing trade candidate, or at least one of the league's finest backups and a handy safety net if Rutschman started slow. As it happened, Severino cost his team more runs behind the plate than anyone but Salvador Perez, without a fraction of the impact in the box. He's not the worst framer in the league—his backup colleagues did a worse job on a per-pitch basis—but combine poor presentation with another league-leading passed ball total and a mediocre arm, and you have a replacement-level option. He was thus the perfect backstop for this team, and one who was immediately jettisoned when that expiry date arrived.

Tyrone Taylor OF

Born: 01/22/94 Age: 28 Bats: R Throws: R Height: 6'0" Weight: 194 lb. Origin: Round 2, 2012 Draft (#92 overall)

YEAR	TEAM	LVL	AGE	PA	R	2B	3B	HR	RBI	BB	K	SB	CS	Whiff%	AVG/OBP/SLG	DRC+	BABIP	BRR	FRAA	WARP
2019	SA	AAA	25	375	44	20	1	14	59	28	85	5	0		.269/.334/.461	92	.317	-0.3	RF(47): 2.4, CF(43): 9.7, LF(5): 0.2	2.0
2019	MIL	MLB	25	12	1	2	0	0	1	1	1	0	0	12.5%	.400/.500/.600	92	.444	-0.2	RF(8): -0.0, CF(3): -0.2	0.0
2020	MIL	MLB	26	41	6	4	0	2	6	2	8	0	0	26.0%	.237/.293/.500	110	.250	-0.1	RF(10): -0.4, CF(9): -0.8, LF(2): -0.1	0.0
2021	NAS	AAA	27	35	10	4	0	3	10	5	4	0	0		.500/.543/.964	136	.478	0.9	CF(7): 0.2, LF(1): 0.1, RF(1): 0.1	0.4
2021	MIL	MLB	27	271	33	9	3	12	43	20	59	6	1	23.6%	.247/.321/.457	102	.277	2.7	LF(37): -1.4, RF(29): -0.2, CF(16): -1.3	1.0
2022 DC	*MIL*	*MLB*	*28*	*283*	*36*	*12*	*1*	*9*	*39*	*20*	*61*	*3*	*1*	*23.8%*	*.238/.307/.408*	*89*	*.279*	*0.1*	*CF 1, RF 0*	*0.6*

Comparables: Cameron Maybin, Gorkys Hernández, Jordan Schafer

Not all development is linear, and Taylor is a perfect example of that. He's been in the Milwaukee org since 2012 and has gone from top prospect to bust to afterthought to what he became in 2021: A reliable and crucial reserve outfielder. Taylor got quite a bit of action while Milwaukee regulars dealt with injuries. Christian Yelich and Lorenzo Cain spent time on the Injured List, Jackie Bradley Jr. couldn't play—Not because of an injury, he just couldn't play—and Avisaíl García was dinged up in attempting to play all three outfield spots simultaneously. That created an opportunity for Taylor, and he excelled in part-time duty, showing solid control of the strike zone and a decent power stroke, too. His defense in the outfield is not good—which limits his ceiling, even as a fourth outfielder—but his bat and baserunning should keep him in the running for a major-league spot going forward.

Rowdy Tellez 1B

Born: 03/16/95 Age: 27 Bats: L Throws: L Height: 6'4" Weight: 255 lb. Origin: Round 30, 2013 Draft (#895 overall)

YEAR	TEAM	LVL	AGE	PA	R	2B	3B	HR	RBI	BB	K	SB	CS	Whiff%	AVG/OBP/SLG	DRC+	BABIP	BRR	FRAA	WARP
2019	BUF	AAA	24	109	20	9	0	7	21	14	25	0	0		.366/.450/.688	119	.435	-1.5	1B(26): 2.2	0.5
2019	TOR	MLB	24	409	49	19	0	21	54	29	116	1	1	31.3%	.227/.293/.449	90	.267	-1.0	1B(57): 4.5	0.9
2020	TOR	MLB	25	127	20	5	0	8	23	11	20	0	1	23.5%	.283/.346/.540	115	.276	-0.1	1B(19): -0.6	0.5
2021	BUF	AAA	26	55	8	4	0	4	11	6	11	0	0		.298/.400/.638	121	.313	0.0	1B(11): 1.2	0.4
2021	MIL	MLB	26	174	22	10	1	7	28	14	32	0	0	21.9%	.272/.333/.481	103	.300	-0.3	1B(46): -1.4	0.3
2021	TOR	MLB	26	151	12	4	1	4	8	9	33	0	0	25.0%	.209/.272/.338	86	.245	0.0	1B(19): -1.4	0.0
2022 DC	*MIL*	*MLB*	*27*	*494*	*69*	*23*	*1*	*21*	*80*	*38*	*100*	*2*	*1*	*23.9%*	*.255/.323/.457*	*105*	*.286*	*-0.5*	*1B 0*	*1.0*

Comparables: Matt Olson, Mike Carp, Kyle Blanks

As anyone who's been to a high school sporting event or cheerleading competition surely knows, R-O-W-D-I-E is the way we spell "Rowdie." At least it was—in the 19th century—and that spelling can be found in the work of Charles Dickens and probably a couple of other places if you look hard enough. Tellez should consider changing his spelling, given his old-school physique and cult hero status in Toronto and, after a surprising mid-season trade, Milwaukee, where there are more than a few pubs in which he'd likely feel comfortable. Especially since he could probably drink for free after his postseason heroics. Less comfortable is Tellez's roster status—Tellez was mostly shielded from lefties, and being a strong-side platoon first baseman/DH is an inherently tough role in a sport where modern front offices value flexibility so highly. There might be hope: Tellez runs fairly narrow platoon splits, both in 2021 and for his career, and he trimmed his strikeout rate and boosted his walk rate after arriving in Cream City. To adapt SR-71's only major hit (and date this author): He may not Mr. Right, but he'll do right now.

Brice Turang SS

Born: 11/21/99 Age: 22 Bats: L Throws: R Height: 6'0" Weight: 173 lb. Origin: Round 1, 2018 Draft (#21 overall)

YEAR	TEAM	LVL	AGE	PA	R	2B	3B	HR	RBI	BB	K	SB	CS	Whiff%	AVG/OBP/SLG	DRC+	BABIP	BRR	FRAA	WARP
2019	WIS	A	19	357	57	13	4	2	31	49	54	21	4		.287/.384/.376	122	.339	2.7	SS(43): 1.6, 2B(28): 0.7	2.6
2019	CAR	A+	19	207	25	6	2	1	6	34	47	9	1		.200/.338/.276	97	.268	1.6	SS(35): -2.9, 2B(5): -0.8	0.2
2021	BLX	AA	21	320	40	14	3	5	39	28	48	11	7		.264/.329/.385	107	.300	0.4	SS(71): 2.4	1.5
2021	NAS	AAA	21	176	19	7	0	1	14	32	35	9	2		.245/.381/.315	100	.315	0.1	SS(44): 2.1	0.8
2022 non-DC	*MIL*	*MLB*	*22*	*251*	*21*	*10*	*1*	*2*	*20*	*24*	*48*	*7*	*3*	*21.0%*	*.232/.310/.321*	*74*	*.286*	*0.6*	*SS 0, 2B 0*	*0.1*

Comparables: J.P. Crawford, Tyler Pastornicky, Richard Ureña

Turang isn't *small.* Compared to, say, Jose Altuve or Nick Madrigal, Turang is perfectly reasonable-sized. He's listed at 6-foot even, but probably in the same kinda way guys who are 5-foot-10 say they're 6 feet in their dating profiles. Turang elicits comparisons to other diminutive middle infielders, though, because he's a bat-to-ball monster with virtually no power to speak of. Turang finally reached double-digit homers for his *career* with five at Double-A last season and one at Triple-A, but if he's going to make his mark in the majors, it'll be because of his ability to make contact and use his plus speed to his advantage. The positive development for Turang last season was that his control of the strike zone held sway in the upper-minors, as he continued to post strikeout-walk ratios befitting his modest offensive profile. That's going to be his calling card should he reach Milwaukee, and while it's not the most exciting ceiling, it has the makings of a competent, major-league regular.

Luis Urías IF Born: 06/03/97 Age: 25 Bats: R Throws: R Height: 5'9" Weight: 186 lb. Origin: International Free Agent, 2013

YEAR	TEAM	LVL	AGE	PA	R	2B	3B	HR	RBI	BB	K	SB	CS	Whiff%	AVG/OBP/SLG	DRC+	BABIP	BRR	FRAA	WARP
2019	OBR	WIN	22	141	20	5	0	5	20	18	22	7	7		.288/.400/.458		.319			
2019	ELP	AAA	22	339	62	19	4	19	50	36	62	7	2		.315/.398/.600	118	.343	2.2	SS(53): 8.6, 2B(21): 3.4	3.5
2019	SD	MLB	22	249	27	8	1	4	24	25	56	0	1	23.6%	.223/.329/.326	88	.284	0.2	SS(41): -5.4, 2B(26): -1.6, 3B(1): -0.2	-0.1
2020	MIL	MLB	23	120	11	4	1	0	11	10	32	2	2	22.8%	.239/.308/.294	77	.338	-0.3	3B(30): 2.5, 2B(10): 1.2, SS(8): -0.1	0.3
2021	MIL	MLB	24	570	77	25	1	23	75	63	116	5	1	22.8%	.249/.345/.445	109	.280	-1.0	3B(68): 4.3, SS(68): -3.4, 2B(25): -0.1	2.6
2022 DC	*MIL*	*MLB*	*25*	*554*	*75*	*23*	*2*	*14*	*68*	*60*	*106*	*2*	*2*	*22.8%*	*.247/.345/.398*	*100*	*.291*	*-0.3*	*3B 3, SS 0*	*1.9*

Comparables: Wilmer Flores, Ketel Marte, Alcides Escobar

Urías might never become the star many saw coming when he shot his way through the San Diego system, but he finally found his footing last season. He refined his swing and joined the launch angle revolution, hitting the ball both harder and in the air with more frequency, leading to power numbers across the board that were previously unfathomable. That was an important step for obvious reasons, but particularly because the acquisition of Willy Adames halfway through the season shifted Urías to third base, where his offensive ascent became more important given his shift down the defensive spectrum. Post-hype prospect breakouts aren't entirely uncommon, but Urías' appears real given his improvements in both walk and strikeout rate. The lofty heights many envisioned may not be on the horizon for Urías, but he finally appears to have turned himself into a solid, above-average major leaguer, which was far from a certainty even a year ago.

Zavier Warren 3B Born: 01/08/99 Age: 23 Bats: S Throws: R Height: 6'0" Weight: 190 lb. Origin: Round 3, 2020 Draft (#92 overall)

YEAR	TEAM	LVL	AGE	PA	R	2B	3B	HR	RBI	BB	K	SB	CS	Whiff%	AVG/OBP/SLG	DRC+	BABIP	BRR	FRAA	WARP
2021	CAR	A	22	230	34	8	2	10	30	33	49	1	0		.251/.374/.471	125	.286	-0.8	C(17): -0.7, 3B(13): 1.3, 1B(9): 1.6	1.4
2021	WIS	A+	22	157	21	7	1	3	18	18	32	5	0		.267/.357/.400	105	.324	1.0	3B(21): 1.6, 1B(10): -0.9, C(3): -0.2	0.7
2022 non-DC	*MIL*	*MLB*	*23*	*251*	*24*	*9*	*1*	*5*	*24*	*22*	*62*	*1*	*1*	*27.0%*	*.224/.303/.352*	*77*	*.286*	*-0.1*	*3B 1, C -3*	*-0.3*

Comparables: Brent Morel, Peter O'Brien, Danny Valencia

The term "Swiss Army knife" was coined by American soldiers after World War II because they had trouble pronouncing the German word *Offiziersmesser*, meaning "officer's knife." Warren's name is simple enough to pronounce, and the Brewers are hopeful the multi-faceted player takes well enough to catcher that they'll be able to etch it into the lineup on a regular basis soon enough. Somewhere, Brandon Inge is smiling and nodding.

Joey Wiemer OF Born: 02/11/99 Age: 23 Bats: R Throws: R Height: 6'5" Weight: 215 lb. Origin: Round 4, 2020 Draft (#121 overall)

YEAR	TEAM	LVL	AGE	PA	R	2B	3B	HR	RBI	BB	K	SB	CS	Whiff%	AVG/OBP/SLG	DRC+	BABIP	BRR	FRAA	WARP
2021	CAR	A	22	320	53	11	2	13	44	45	69	22	4		.276/.391/.478	126	.326	-0.4	RF(50): 12.5, CF(23): 1.3, LF(5): 0.7	3.4
2021	WIS	A+	22	152	33	7	0	14	33	18	36	8	2		.336/.428/.719	155	.363	-0.1	RF(22): -1.1, CF(4): -1.1	1.2
2022 non-DC	*MIL*	*MLB*	*23*	*251*	*28*	*9*	*1*	*9*	*30*	*22*	*73*	*8*	*3*	*36.1%*	*.239/.316/.413*	*95*	*.314*	*0.7*	*RF 4, CF 0*	*1.1*

Comparables: Aaron Judge, Mitch Haniger, Marcell Ozuna

Wiemer didn't put up overwhelming stats at the University of Cincinnati and fell to Milwaukee in the fourth round in 2020. He's done nothing but impress during his year-plus of pro ball, though. The raw power has shown up in games and he put up big numbers at both Low-A and High-A on his way to being named the organization's minor-league player of the year. Wiemer combines that power with surprising speed, and impressed with his athleticism in right field. He is easy to spot on the field as his curly, blonde mullet stands out. If he continues to progress as he makes his way through the upper minors, that won't be the only thing that stands out for one of the organization's biggest risers over the last year.

Kolten Wong 2B Born: 10/10/90 Age: 31 Bats: L Throws: R Height: 5'7" Weight: 185 lb. Origin: Round 1, 2011 Draft (#22 overall)

YEAR	TEAM	LVL	AGE	PA	R	2B	3B	HR	RBI	BB	K	SB	CS	Whiff%	AVG/OBP/SLG	DRC+	BABIP	BRR	FRAA	WARP
2019	STL	MLB	28	549	61	25	4	11	59	47	83	24	4	18.5%	.285/.361/.423	102	.321	4.0	2B(147): 18.3	4.5
2020	STL	MLB	29	208	26	4	2	1	16	20	30	5	2	16.2%	.265/.350/.326	95	.311	2.1	2B(53): 11.1	1.9
2021	MIL	MLB	30	492	70	32	2	14	50	31	83	12	5	18.9%	.272/.335/.447	98	.305	2.0	2B(113): -2.4	1.6
2022 DC	*MIL*	*MLB*	*31*	*574*	*89*	*27*	*3*	*12*	*60*	*45*	*85*	*14*	*5*	*18.5%*	*.260/.338/.399*	*101*	*.293*	*0.8*	*2B 5*	*2.7*

Comparables: Lou Whitaker, Luis Castillo, Robinson Canó

The Brewers signed Wong for his defense. During his final two years in St. Louis, the second baseman ranked among the best in baseball in FRAA. When he was let go by the Cardinals, it was a surprise, and a presumption that St. Louis either didn't value his glove work as much as metrics would suggest, believed his offense was untenable regardless of the flashy leather or some combination of the two. His debut season in Milwaukee was a strange one. Wong was fine offensively, in fact displaying more power than ever before, posting career-best marks in both home runs and ISO. But his defense cratered from all-world to slightly below-average. The Brewers still ranked among the better defensive teams in baseball, so maybe they didn't mind much, and the offensive production was overwhelmingly welcome for a team that struggled to put the bat on the ball for most of the season. Wong will stick around for the second season of his two-year pact, and Milwaukee will surely be paying close attention to his defensive numbers as they evaluate their team option for a third season.

Christian Yelich LF Born: 12/05/91 Age: 30 Bats: L Throws: R Height: 6'3" Weight: 195 lb. Origin: Round 1, 2010 Draft (#23 overall)

YEAR	TEAM	LVL	AGE	PA	R	2B	3B	HR	RBI	BB	K	SB	CS	Whiff%	AVG/OBP/SLG	DRC+	BABIP	BRR	FRAA	WARP
2019	MIL	MLB	27	580	100	29	3	44	97	80	118	30	2	28.2%	.329/.429/.671	158	.355	3.0	RF(124): -2.0, LF(6): 0.4, CF(1): -0.0	6.1
2020	MIL	MLB	28	247	39	7	1	12	22	46	76	4	2	33.6%	.205/.356/.430	105	.259	0.4	LF(51): -7.4	0.1
2021	MIL	MLB	29	475	70	19	2	9	51	70	113	9	3	24.9%	.248/.362/.373	93	.321	2.2	LF(107): -0.3, RF(1): -0.0	1.5
2022 DC	*MIL*	*MLB*	*30*	*595*	*102*	*26*	*3*	*24*	*86*	*92*	*133*	*17*	*4*	*26.0%*	*.259/.383/.469*	*127*	*.310*	*0.7*	*LF 0*	*4.1*

Comparables: Billy Williams, Tim Raines, Carl Yastrzemski

In 2018, Green Bay Packers quarterback and three-time NFL MVP Aaron Rodgers purchased a minority stake in the Milwaukee Bucks. This past August, Milwaukee Bucks superstar and two-time NBA MVP Giannis Antetokounmpo purchased a stake in the Milwaukee Brewers. The only logical next step, then, would be Yelich buying a stake in the Packers. Doing so wouldn't make Yelich unique, of course, as the Packers are an odd professional franchise in both allowing and encouraging thousands of their fans to pony up hard-earned cash for stock on a regular basis. But if Yelich really wants to be serious about it, the $215 million the Brewers are paying him through 2028 should come in handy.

Less likely, it would seem at this point, is Yelich joining his fellow Wisconsin sports superstars as a multi-time MVP. After a forgettable 2020 campaign many shrugged off given the pandemic-season wonkiness, Yelich began 2021 again in brutal form and never fully recovered. While Milwaukee was lifted to the postseason in 2018 and 2019 on the now-ailing back of Yelich more than anyone else, the Brewers won mostly in spite of their erstwhile superstar in 2021. Persistent lower back issues kept him out of the lineup for more than a month early on, plaguing him throughout the mediocre campaign, and he also spent time on the COVID IL, and it's hard not to wonder how significant a role his end-of-2019 leg fracture is playing in all this. Nagging injuries nag a bit more once you hit the other side of 30, so there's undoubtedly some consternation about whether or not Yelich can return to the lofty heights to which he once soared. If the cheers he once soaked in at American Family Field dry up, however, there's always chugging beer on the Jumbotron at Lambeau to fall back on.

Freddy Zamora SS Born: 11/01/98 Age: 23 Bats: R Throws: R Height: 6'1" Weight: 190 lb. Origin: Round 2, 2020 Draft (#53 overall)

YEAR	TEAM	LVL	AGE	PA	R	2B	3B	HR	RBI	BB	K	SB	CS	Whiff%	AVG/OBP/SLG	DRC+	BABIP	BRR	FRAA	WARP
2021	CAR	A	22	321	58	13	1	5	40	45	57	9	5		.287/.396/.399	118	.344	-0.5	SS(63): 2.8	1.8
2021	WIS	A+	22	92	12	9	0	1	9	12	19	1	0		.342/.435/.494	103	.441	0.3	SS(21): -2.6	0.1
2022 non-DC	*MIL*	*MLB*	*23*	*251*	*22*	*11*	*0*	*2*	*21*	*23*	*51*	*2*	*2*	*22.6%*	*.234/.311/.330*	*76*	*.292*	*0.0*	*SS -1*	*0.1*

Comparables: Matt Duffy, Emmanuel Burriss, Jason Donald

Prior to the start of the 2021 minor-league season, Zamora's last organized game came in 2019 with the University of Miami. He didn't play at all for The U in 2020 thanks to a suspension and injury, and subsequently saw what would've been his first minor-league season wiped out by the pandemic. As someone who's expected to be able to handle shortstop defensively, he's going to get plenty of chances for his bat to develop, and he did what you'd expect a 22-year-old with a high-level collegiate background to do in his first foray in the low-minors. If you're having trouble distinguishing Zamora from all the other various intriguing infield prospects, just remember: When a guy shows an eye at the A-level that's high, that's Zamora.

PITCHERS

★ ★ ★ *2022 Top 101 Prospect* **#100** ★ ★ ★

Aaron Ashby LHP Born: 05/24/98 Age: 24 Bats: R Throws: L Height: 6'2" Weight: 181 lb. Origin: Round 4, 2018 Draft (#125 overall)

YEAR	TEAM	LVL	AGE	W	L	SV	G	GS	IP	H	HR	BB/9	K/9	K	GB%	BABIP	WHIP	ERA	DRA-	WARP	MPH	FB%	Whiff%	CSP
2019	WIS	A	21	3	4	0	11	10	61	47	4	4.1	11.8	80	48.9%	.319	1.23	3.54	84	1.0				
2019	CAR	A+	21	2	6	0	13	13	65	54	1	4.4	7.6	55	47.3%	.286	1.32	3.46	109	0.3				
2021	NAS	AAA	23	5	4	0	21	12	63^{1}	55	4	4.5	14.2	100	66.9%	.370	1.37	4.41	86	1.3				
2021	MIL	MLB	23	3	2	1	13	4	31^{2}	25	4	3.4	11.1	39	61.7%	.273	1.17	4.55	84	0.6	96.7	36.1%	29.9%	54.9%
2022 DC	*MIL*	*MLB*	*24*	*7*	*5*	*0*	*50*	*11*	*85*	*72*	*8*	*4.5*	*11.0*	*103*	*56.1%*	*.306*	*1.34*	*3.69*	*87*	*1.0*	*96.7*	*36.1%*	*29.9%*	*54.9%*

Comparables: Will Smith, Rafael Soriano, Robinson Tejeda

Talk about a tough introduction. Ashby's first appearance in the big leagues included a greeting so frosty, Milwaukee children will sing about it every winter: The fourth-rounder out of Crowder College saw more hits (4), runs (7), earned runs (4) and walks (3) than outs recorded (2). The Brewers ended up winning that game, but it was of little use to Ashby, who was sent back to Nashville for another six weeks to think about what he'd done, or more accurately, figure out how to not do it again. They say you never get a second chance at a first impression, but Ashby did his best: From August 10th through the end of the season the southpaw recorded a 3.48 ERA, struck out 39 and allowed a .188 batting average against in 31 innings. His slider was particularly venomous, with batters whiffing at it over 40% of the time, which is, coincidentally, also about how often he throws it. Ashby is likely to factor into Milwaukee's rotation plans sooner rather than later, and it remains to be seen if he can maintain that level of slider usage, but it wouldn't surprise to see him follow the Freddy Peralta path to starting pitcher effectiveness with a nearly even split between his fastball (a firm sinker) and his secondaries.

Corbin Burnes RHP Born: 10/22/94 Age: 27 Bats: R Throws: R Height: 6'3" Weight: 225 lb. Origin: Round 4, 2016 Draft (#111 overall)

YEAR	TEAM	LVL	AGE	W	L	SV	G	GS	IP	H	HR	BB/9	K/9	K	GB%	BABIP	WHIP	ERA	DRA-	WARP	MPH	FB%	Whiff%	CSP
2019	SA	AAA	24	0	1	0	8	7	22^1	29	2	3.6	10.1	25	48.5%	.409	1.70	8.46	79	0.4				
2019	MIL	MLB	24	1	5	1	32	4	49	70	17	3.7	12.9	70	44.1%	.424	1.84	8.82	70	1.3	95.4	56.7%	36.7%	46.6%
2020	MIL	MLB	25	4	1	0	12	9	59^2	37	2	3.6	13.3	88	47.2%	.285	1.02	2.11	61	1.9	95.1	67.7%	34.8%	41.0%
2021	MIL	MLB	26	11	5	0	28	28	167	123	7	1.8	12.6	234	49.3%	.309	0.94	2.43	58	5.3	95.5	63.0%	37.0%	52.2%
2022 DC	*MIL*	*MLB*	*27*	*12*	*7*	*0*	*29*	*29*	*174.7*	*133*	*18*	*2.4*	*11.9*	*231*	*47.9%*	*.292*	*1.04*	*2.38*	*61*	*4.8*	*95.4*	*63.4%*	*36.6%*	*49.6%*

Comparables: Miles Mikolas, Tyson Ross, Max Scherzer

What does a 99th percentile outcome look like?

One of the best parts of the release of PECOTA every year is looking at a player's projections based on different percentiles—particularly the 99th percentile projection. There's a slim chance any player is going to reach that number. It's rare. A 99th percentile projection is basically everything going right; that player living up to the lofty potential numerous coaches and observers saw in them for so many years, and in many cases surpassing even the biggest optimist's wildest expectations.

Burnes' 99th percentile projection for 2020 included a 3.38 DRA and saw him being worth 3.7 WARP. He soared past both. He went from a really cool arm with a lot of potential to an earth-scorching behemoth. We saw shades of it in the shortened season, but Burnes ditched his four-seamer and sinker almost entirely in favor of a cutter/curveball combination that comprised 70% of his offerings and against which hitters whiffed 38% of the time. He became the ace of an already powerful Brewers' rotation, and cemented his place as one of the most dominant and feared pitchers in baseball.

So what does a 99th percentile outcome look like? Burnes can't actually answer that question; he was better.

Jake Cousins RHP Born: 07/14/94 Age: 27 Bats: R Throws: R Height: 6'4" Weight: 185 lb. Origin: Round 20, 2017 Draft (#613 overall)

YEAR	TEAM	LVL	AGE	W	L	SV	G	GS	IP	H	HR	BB/9	K/9	K	GB%	BABIP	WHIP	ERA	DRA-	WARP	MPH	FB%	Whiff%	CSP
2019	BRB	ROK	24	2	0	1	7	0	14	10	0	0.0	13.5	21	72.4%	.345	0.71	2.57						
2019	WIS	A	24	1	0	2	7	0	14^1	6	0	1.3	11.3	18	60.0%	.200	0.56	1.26	81	0.3				
2021	BLX	AA	26	0	1	3	8	0	9	6	1	3.0	14.0	14	52.6%	.278	1.00	3.00	91	0.1				
2021	NAS	AAA	26	1	0	1	9	1	9^2	6	1	1.9	14.9	16	50.0%	.278	0.83	1.86	79	0.2				
2021	MIL	MLB	26	1	0	0	30	0	30	16	3	5.7	13.2	44	46.6%	.241	1.17	2.70	81	0.6	95.5	37.5%	41.3%	48.3%
2022 DC	*MIL*	*MLB*	*27*	*2*	*2*	*0*	*44*	*0*	*38.7*	*27*	*4*	*4.1*	*13.3*	*57*	*46.4%*	*.288*	*1.17*	*3.12*	*75*	*0.7*	*95.5*	*37.5%*	*41.3%*	*48.3%*

Comparables: Diego Castillo, Sergio Romo, Jeff Zimmerman

Many a resident of the cities that populate the Illinois/Wisconsin border can relate to having a cousin who roots for the "other guys:" Brewers-Cubs, Packers-Bears. Cousins grew up not *quite* on the border—Parkridge, IL is a northern Chicago suburb—but the childhood Cubs fan became the cousin *on* the other guys thanks to spinning 30 dominant innings and occasionally high-leverage innings for the Brewers. Cousins succeeds on the basis of his slider, which he threw a whopping 60% of the time, earning whiffs on over 24% of them, despite the high usage. If Jake needs any advice navigating fierce interstate upper Midwest rivalries, he can always call on his, well, cousin, Vikings quarterback, Kirk.

Josh Hader LHP Born: 04/07/94 Age: 28 Bats: L Throws: L Height: 6'3" Weight: 180 lb. Origin: Round 19, 2012 Draft (#582 overall)

YEAR	TEAM	LVL	AGE	W	L	SV	G	GS	IP	H	HR	BB/9	K/9	K	GB%	BABIP	WHIP	ERA	DRA-	WARP	MPH	FB%	Whiff%	CSP
2019	MIL	MLB	25	3	5	37	61	0	75^2	41	15	2.4	16.4	138	22.0%	.232	0.81	2.62	60	2.4	95.8	84.1%	41.7%	45.8%
2020	MIL	MLB	26	1	2	13	21	0	19	8	3	4.7	14.7	31	26.5%	.161	0.95	3.79	83	0.4	94.9	67.7%	38.7%	43.8%
2021	MIL	MLB	27	4	2	34	60	0	58^2	25	3	3.7	15.6	102	31.2%	.237	0.84	1.23	64	1.7	96.5	65.5%	45.2%	48.8%
2022 DC	*MIL*	*MLB*	*28*	*2*	*2*	*38*	*50*	*0*	*43.7*	*26*	*7*	*3.5*	*16.1*	*78*	*30.7%*	*.276*	*0.99*	*2.44*	*57*	*1.2*	*96.0*	*70.4%*	*43.4%*	*47.3%*

Comparables: Ken Giles, Aroldis Chapman, Trevor Rosenthal

"If it ain't broke, don't fix it" isn't a saying Hader is familiar with. Hader has long toyed with the idea of adding a changeup to his repertoire—he dabbled from his rookie year through 2019—but after abandoning it entirely in 2020, he threw it a career-high 6.5% of the time in 2021. It was used almost primarily against right-handed hitters, which helps against the platoon advantage, and while the sample size wasn't significant, it shows that Hader is continuing to look for ways to improve despite already being among the most dominant relievers in baseball. Perhaps the second-rate season in 2020 (only by his lofty standards) made him feel he needed to continue tinkering. Whatever motivation, it worked, as Hader once again struck out batters around a 45% clip, and while his walk rate climbed, he recorded career-best marks in both home runs and hard contact in general. Hader was already vying for the best closer in baseball title, but his best may still be yet to come.

Adrian Houser RHP Born: 02/02/93 Age: 29 Bats: R Throws: R Height: 6'3" Weight: 222 lb. Origin: Round 2, 2011 Draft (#69 overall)

YEAR	TEAM	LVL	AGE	W	L	SV	G	GS	IP	H	HR	BB/9	K/9	K	GB%	BABIP	WHIP	ERA	DRA-	WARP	MPH	FB%	Whiff%	CSP
2019	SA	AAA	26	2	0	0	4	4	21^{1}	13	2	1.7	9.7	23	51.9%	.212	0.80	1.27	78	0.4				
2019	MIL	MLB	26	6	7	0	35	18	111^{1}	101	14	3.0	9.5	117	53.8%	.304	1.24	3.72	81	2.3	94.5	67.4%	24.3%	48.3%
2020	MIL	MLB	27	1	6	0	12	11	56	63	8	3.4	7.1	44	59.3%	.325	1.50	5.30	93	0.8	93.6	64.0%	22.5%	45.8%
2021	MIL	MLB	28	10	6	0	28	26	142^{1}	118	12	4.0	6.6	105	58.6%	.264	1.28	3.22	102	1.1	93.8	67.6%	18.6%	51.8%
2022 DC	*MIL*	*MLB*	*29*	*9*	*8*	*0*	*27*	*27*	*145.7*	*144*	*14*	*3.7*	*7.5*	*121*	*56.7%*	*.300*	*1.39*	*4.22*	*101*	*1.1*	*93.8*	*66.9%*	*20.2%*	*50.2%*

Comparables: Tanner Roark, Jason Hammel, Bud Norris

The goal of these comments under each player's name and stat line each year is to give you, the reader, a short summary of how a player performed during the year in question. Player performance can be judged both in a vacuum and out here, in the real world. In a vacuum, Houser did a lot of what the Brewers likely had hoped he'd do when he was put into the rotation at the beginning of the year. He prevented runs and gave them a chance to win more often than not. In fact, the Brewers won 19 times when Houser took the mound against just nine losses, even when factoring in his two relief appearances. That's great! Outside of that vacuum, where we're all just floating around accidental-like, Houser was one of the most fortunate pitchers in baseball. His well above-average ERA belied a below-average DRA, thanks to a strikeout-to-walk ratio that looked like it came from a 1980s junkballer whose name you don't remember. His newfound emphasis on the sinker could explain how he went from a strikeout rate near 25% in 2019 to one under 18% in 2021, but the six percentage point difference in ground-ball rate might not be worth it. So how does one judge the success or failure of a player like Houser? Well, in a vacuum or out, he might be better off with an overhauled pitch mix.

Eric Lauer LHP Born: 06/03/95 Age: 27 Bats: R Throws: L Height: 6'3" Weight: 228 lb. Origin: Round 1, 2016 Draft (#25 overall)

YEAR	TEAM	LVL	AGE	W	L	SV	G	GS	IP	H	HR	BB/9	K/9	K	GB%	BABIP	WHIP	ERA	DRA-	WARP	MPH	FB%	Whiff%	CSP
2019	SD	MLB	24	8	10	0	30	29	149^{2}	158	20	3.1	8.3	138	40.5%	.318	1.40	4.45	100	1.5	92.0	52.9%	20.1%	51.8%
2020	MIL	MLB	25	0	2	0	4	2	11	17	2	7.4	9.8	12	21.1%	.417	2.36	13.09	180	-0.4	91.7	52.5%	29.1%	43.4%
2021	MIL	MLB	26	7	5	0	24	20	118^{2}	94	16	3.1	8.9	117	35.3%	.254	1.14	3.19	93	1.5	92.7	44.6%	24.1%	54.8%
2022 DC	*MIL*	*MLB*	*27*	*8*	*7*	*0*	*33*	*22*	*127.3*	*123*	*20*	*3.5*	*9.8*	*139*	*36.7%*	*.309*	*1.35*	*4.46*	*104*	*0.7*	*92.5*	*47.4%*	*23.3%*	*53.3%*

Comparables: Jake Odorizzi, Danny Duffy, Matt Garza

Even by the standards set by 2020 as a whole, the pandemic-shortened season was an utter disappointment for Lauer, who went from rotation mainstay to alternate site reclamation project in the blink of an eye. As the calendar flipped, so too did Lauer's fortunes, as he turned back into a capable strike-thrower for a team that entered October with legitimate pennant aspirations. He upped his changeup usage, commanded all five offerings well and limited hard contact across the board. Lauer missed bats at a league-average clip (it was a career high), and needs to keep the ball off the barrel of bats as a fly-ball pitcher in a homer-heavy home park, but he's reliably kept his HR/FB rate right around 12% throughout his career. Still, his ERA significantly outran his FIP and DRA, so there was a bit of smoke and mirrors to his 2021 season. But Lauer showed enough to be counted on in the back-end of a rotation going forward, and that's a pretty big step considering where he was a year ago.

Freddy Peralta RHP Born: 06/04/96 Age: 26 Bats: R Throws: R Height: 5'11" Weight: 199 lb. Origin: International Free Agent, 2013

YEAR	TEAM	LVL	AGE	W	L	SV	G	GS	IP	H	HR	BB/9	K/9	K	GB%	BABIP	WHIP	ERA	DRA-	WARP	MPH	FB%	Whiff%	CSP
2019	SA	AAA	23	0	0	0	4	0	7	4	0	3.9	21.9	17	25.0%	.500	1.00	1.29	60	0.2				
2019	MIL	MLB	23	7	3	1	39	8	85	87	15	3.9	12.2	115	31.6%	.343	1.46	5.29	82	1.7	93.8	78.4%	29.5%	48.1%
2020	MIL	MLB	24	3	1	0	15	1	29^{1}	22	2	3.7	14.4	47	33.3%	.333	1.16	3.99	69	0.8	93.3	65.8%	39.8%	40.4%
2021	MIL	MLB	25	10	5	0	28	27	144^{1}	84	14	3.5	12.2	195	32.1%	.232	0.97	2.81	72	3.5	93.4	53.1%	34.5%	53.2%
2022 DC	*MIL*	*MLB*	*26*	*10*	*7*	*0*	*25*	*25*	*147.7*	*109*	*23*	*3.7*	*12.3*	*202*	*33.6%*	*.276*	*1.16*	*3.37*	*80*	*2.5*	*93.4*	*58.7%*	*34.3%*	*50.9%*

Comparables: Max Scherzer, Rich Harden, Danny Salazar

If you're a common consumer of prospect reports—and if you're reading this book you probably are—you're probably familiar with how often the phrase "probably a reliever" can appear on even the most promising arms in a team's system. "Probably a reliever" was attached to Peralta's name as recently as last year. "Probably" means "almost certainly" but not "definitely." "Definitely" means "without doubt" and is used for emphasis, like "I'll definitely pick you up from the airport this weekend" or "I'll definitely not eat your leftover cheesecake in the fridge." It's an important and declaratory adverb that should leave no uncertainty about the meaning of the thought you are trying to convey. Prior to 2020, Peralta was "probably a reliever" because he "definitely" didn't have a starter's arsenal, leaning exclusively on his fastball and curve. During the pandemic season, he introduced a slider as his preferred secondary, while keeping the curve around. This year saw another addition in the changeup, giving Peralta a fourth offering—"definitely" enough to start. His fastball has maintained its low-90s velo throughout, but sneaks up on batters as effectively as ever, in part because they have three other pitches to think about.

Ethan Small LHP Born: 02/14/97 Age: 25 Bats: L Throws: L Height: 6'4" Weight: 215 lb. Origin: Round 1, 2019 Draft (#28 overall)

YEAR	TEAM	LVL	AGE	W	L	SV	G	GS	IP	H	HR	BB/9	K/9	K	GB%	BABIP	WHIP	ERA	DRA-	WARP	MPH	FB%	Whiff%	CSP
2019	BRG	ROK	22	0	0	0	2	2	3	0	0	0.0	15.0	5	50.0%	.000	0.00	0.00						
2019	WIS	A	22	0	2	0	5	5	18	11	0	2.0	15.5	31	30.3%	.333	0.83	1.00	73	0.4				
2021	BLX	AA	24	2	2	0	8	8	41^{1}	26	1	4.6	14.6	67	39.2%	.342	1.14	1.96	83	0.8				
2021	NAS	AAA	24	2	0	0	9	9	35	27	3	5.4	6.2	24	43.6%	.245	1.37	2.06	117	0.2				
2022 DC	*MIL*	*MLB*	*25*	*1*	*1*	*0*	*4*	*4*	*19.3*	*18*	*2*	*5.4*	*10.3*	*22*	*39.1%*	*.315*	*1.56*	*5.25*	*115*	*0.0*				

Comparables: Vidal Nuño, Jack Cassel, Billy Traber

Small doesn't have, ahem, big stuff, but he's progressed more or less exactly as you imagine the Brewers envisioned. Even while missing a year of competitive baseball during the canceled 2020 season, Small added a slider to his repertoire, giving him a solid four-pitch mix, and seems to have a good feel for all of them. The key to him becoming more than a back-end starter will be improving command of those pitches, because the velocity isn't going to blow anyone away, and he lacks a true put-away pitch. Small's first taste of the upper-minors had its fits and starts, but he remains a high-floor pitcher who could find himself in Milwaukee as soon as this year.

Brent Suter LHP Born: 08/29/89 Age: 32 Bats: L Throws: L Height: 6'4" Weight: 213 lb. Origin: Round 31, 2012 Draft (#965 overall)

YEAR	TEAM	LVL	AGE	W	L	SV	G	GS	IP	H	HR	BB/9	K/9	K	GB%	BABIP	WHIP	ERA	DRA-	WARP	MPH	FB%	Whiff%	CSP
2019	SA	AAA	29	0	0	0	4	2	11^{2}	4	0	1.5	13.9	18	40.9%	.190	0.51	0.00	71	0.3				
2019	MIL	MLB	29	4	0	0	9	0	18^{1}	10	1	0.5	7.4	15	51.0%	.188	0.60	0.49	97	0.2	87.6	78.1%	26.8%	50.1%
2020	MIL	MLB	30	2	0	0	16	4	31^{2}	30	4	1.4	10.8	38	52.9%	.321	1.11	3.13	73	0.8	85.7	79.1%	31.1%	47.3%
2021	MIL	MLB	31	12	5	1	61	1	73^{1}	72	9	2.9	8.5	69	52.1%	.303	1.31	3.07	96	0.8	87.5	77.1%	21.2%	53.1%
2022 DC	*MIL*	*MLB*	*32*	*2*	*2*	*2*	*56*	*0*	*48.3*	*46*	*6*	*2.4*	*8.3*	*45*	*47.8%*	*.296*	*1.21*	*3.53*	*87*	*0.5*	*87.1*	*77.6%*	*23.5%*	*51.8%*

Comparables: D.J. Carrasco, David Hale, Tommy Hunter

Suter is a man of many talents. He's called "The Raptor" because of the way he runs and the fact that he comes out of the bullpen to the Jurassic Park theme. He's also a master of impressions, as a YouTube rabbit hole will reveal him doing okayish impersonations of characters ranging from Gollum to Ron Burgundy to Minions. On the mound, Suter has settled in nicely as a multi-inning specialist for the Brewers, going more than an inning in one-third of his appearances and ranking in the 96th percentile in average exit velocity allowed. The environmental enthusiast (he's an advisory board member for EcoAthletes) pitches quite efficiently, maximizing positive results out of less-than-extraordinary stuff thanks to a tough arm slot and a deep release point. Most profiles like this don't last very long, so it's good that Suter maintains an interest in sustainability.

Justin Topa RHP Born: 03/07/91 Age: 31 Bats: R Throws: R Height: 6'4" Weight: 200 lb. Origin: Round 17, 2013 Draft (#509 overall)

YEAR	TEAM	LVL	AGE	W	L	SV	G	GS	IP	H	HR	BB/9	K/9	K	GB%	BABIP	WHIP	ERA	DRA-	WARP	MPH	FB%	Whiff%	CSP
2019	CAR	A+	28	0	3	3	15	0	16	14	1	1.1	10.7	19	43.2%	.310	1.00	4.50	76	0.3				
2019	BLX	AA	28	0	3	0	18	0	24	22	0	3.0	8.2	22	47.2%	.314	1.25	2.63	89	0.3				
2020	MIL	MLB	29	0	1	0	6	0	7^{2}	7	1	0.0	14.1	12	55.6%	.353	0.91	2.35	68	0.2	97.7	69.7%	27.7%	53.8%
2021	NAS	AAA	30	1	0	0	10	0	9	7	0	2.0	9.0	9	68.0%	.280	1.00	3.00	93	0.2				
2021	MIL	MLB	30	0	0	0	4	0	3^{1}	12	2	2.7	2.7	1	42.9%	.526	3.90	29.70	112	0.0	96.0	69.0%	11.6%	60.5%
2022 DC	*MIL*	*MLB*	*31*	*1*	*1*	*0*	*28*	*0*	*24*	*25*	*3*	*2.8*	*6.6*	*17*	*50.1%*	*.303*	*1.38*	*4.46*	*107*	*0.0*	*96.8*	*69.4%*	*19.2%*	*57.3%*

Comparables: Seth Frankoff, Richard Bleier, Eammon Portice

Making his major-league debut in the pandemic-shortened season must have been bittersweet for Topa. The 29-year-old former 17th-round pick was on his third big-league organization, and had an independent league stint as recently as 2018. To finally reach the majors was to fulfill a lifelong objective, immediately rendering the bus rides and hardships worthwhile. To do so in front of no fans, well, that's less than ideal. Still, the bright spot that was his debut season will need to sustain him after a right flexor strain delayed his 2021 debut, and a "significant arm injury" ended it just 3 ⅔ major-league innings later. His quality fastball and slider have already survived two Tommy John surgeries, but it's hard to imagine a bigger setback than a third significant operation for a guy who was made to take the long road to the big leagues already.

Devin Williams RHP

Born: 09/21/94 Age: 27 Bats: R Throws: R Height: 6'2" Weight: 200 lb. Origin: Round 2, 2013 Draft (#54 overall)

YEAR	TEAM	LVL	AGE	W	L	SV	G	GS	IP	H	HR	BB/9	K/9	K	GB%	BABIP	WHIP	ERA	DRA-	WARP	MPH	FB%	Whiff%	CSP
2019	BLX	AA	24	7	2	4	31	0	53^{1}	34	3	4.9	12.8	76	47.4%	.282	1.18	2.36	69	1.2				
2019	MIL	MLB	24	0	0	0	13	0	13^{2}	18	2	4.0	9.2	14	40.0%	.381	1.76	3.95	99	0.1	96.4	61.0%	25.0%	46.5%
2020	MIL	MLB	25	4	1	0	22	0	27	8	1	3.0	17.7	53	61.1%	.200	0.63	0.33	44	1.1	96.7	43.9%	51.8%	41.2%
2021	MIL	MLB	26	8	2	3	58	0	54	36	5	4.7	14.5	87	45.0%	.301	1.19	2.50	65	1.5	95.5	34.7%	42.9%	48.6%
2022 DC	*MIL*	*MLB*	*27*	*2*	*2*	*0*	*50*	*0*	*43.7*	*29*	*5*	*4.3*	*14.5*	*70*	*45.4%*	*.294*	*1.15*	*2.86*	*68*	*0.9*	*95.8*	*38.4%*	*43.6%*	*46.9%*

Comparables: Dick Radatz, Hunter Strickland, Lou Trivino

Williams fractured his hand while punching a wall in the aftermath of the Brewers' post-clinch celebration and he ... told the truth? "I'm pretty upset with myself. There's no one to blame but me," Williams said. There have been countless stupid sports injuries over the years, but Williams owned up to the self-inflicted wound. He could've said he tripped over some luggage, or maybe slammed it in the car door. But nope. Williams told the world, right before his team was set to play its biggest games of the season, that he got drunk and punched a wall. It was honorable, but also a shame, because he was every bit as good in his first full season as he was during a rookie year that saw him garner both Cy Young and MVP votes. The sparkling ERA was unrepeatable over a 162-game jaunt, but Williams continued flinging that Airbender at hapless hitters, giving Milwaukee the most dominant late-inning duo in baseball for the second straight season. It was also the second straight season that Milwaukee crashed out of the playoffs without Williams in the bullpen to aid them, after he missed 2020's Wild Card round with an oblique strain. Maybe they should put him in bubble wrap next September.

Brandon Woodruff RHP

Born: 02/10/93 Age: 29 Bats: L Throws: R Height: 6'4" Weight: 243 lb. Origin: Round 11, 2014 Draft (#326 overall)

YEAR	TEAM	LVL	AGE	W	L	SV	G	GS	IP	H	HR	BB/9	K/9	K	GB%	BABIP	WHIP	ERA	DRA-	WARP	MPH	FB%	Whiff%	CSP
2019	MIL	MLB	26	11	3	0	22	22	121^{2}	109	12	2.2	10.6	143	45.1%	.322	1.14	3.62	76	2.8	96.4	64.2%	25.6%	49.2%
2020	MIL	MLB	27	3	5	0	13	13	73^{2}	55	9	2.2	11.1	91	50.0%	.269	0.99	3.05	62	2.3	96.7	65.1%	29.0%	50.3%
2021	MIL	MLB	28	9	10	0	30	30	179^{1}	130	18	2.2	10.6	211	41.6%	.264	0.96	2.56	70	4.5	96.6	60.4%	28.4%	55.2%
2022 DC	*MIL*	*MLB*	*29*	*12*	*7*	*0*	*29*	*29*	*177.7*	*147*	*21*	*2.4*	*10.2*	*202*	*43.8%*	*.286*	*1.09*	*2.87*	*73*	*4.0*	*96.6*	*61.9%*	*28.1%*	*53.4%*

Comparables: Justin Verlander, Bob Gibson, Corey Kluber

Woodruff can tend to get overlooked even just among his own pitching staff. Corbin Burnes won the Cy Young Award last year and Freddy Peralta had a breakout that seemed to cement him as a rotation option rather than "merely" a shutdown reliever. Woodruff, for his part, is just out there doing the work, fanfare or no: He recorded his third straight season as a full-fledged member of the rotation, proving he could shoulder a full-season workload while maintaining his upper-echelon quality. Even more notable: Woodruff upped his curveball usage—which was mostly just a show-me offering in the past—by 10 percentage points, eclipsing both his changeup and slider as his main off-speed offering, and allowing just a .184 xBA against it. Woodruff is no longer the new kid on the block among ace pitchers, but he's one of the best in the league with no signs of slowing down.

Lineouts

Hitters

HITTER	POS	TEAM	LVL	AGE	PA	R	2B	3B	HR	RBI	BB	K	SB	CS	AVG/OBP/SLG	DRC+	BABIP	BRR	FRAA	WARP
Tyler Black	2B/DH	CAR	A	20	103	11	4	0	0	6	20	29	3	2	.222/.388/.272	104	.346	-1.3	2B(15): -1.4	0.1
Jonathan Davis	CF	SWB	AAA	29	72	13	2	1	2	8	9	20	4	2	.193/.347/.368	96	.250	0.3	CF(7): -0.3, LF(6): -0.5, RF(3): 1.8	0.3
	CF	NYY	MLB	29	18	4	0	0	0	0	1	5	0	0	.059/.111/.059	93	.083	0.1	CF(8): -0.0, LF(2): -0.1	0.1
	CF	TOR	MLB	29	85	16	1	0	1	4	11	21	4	1	.143/.282/.200	85	.184	-0.6	CF(47): -1.2, LF(1): -0.0	0.0
Joe Gray Jr.	OF	SRR	WIN	21	70	3	1	0	1	6	10	24	1	0	.069/.229/.138		.091			
	OF	CAR	A	21	231	40	15	7	12	53	33	61	12	0	.289/.407/.632	135	.361	0.3	CF(39): 2.5, RF(9): -0.2	2.0
	OF	WIS	A+	21	248	32	7	2	8	37	20	70	11	3	.219/.306/.381	95	.277	1.1	CF(31): 1.1, RF(18): 1.4, LF(2): 1.6	1.2
Tim Lopes	LF	NAS	AAA	27	370	52	16	4	11	39	34	92	9	3	.226/.305/.401	94	.276	-0.4	3B(25): -0.4, 2B(23): 0.5, RF(18): -0.8	0.7
	LF	MIL	MLB	27	11	1	0	0	0	0	1	4	0	1	.100/.182/.100	88	.167	0.0	2B(3): -0.1	0.0
Tristen Lutz	OF	BLX	AA	22	268	25	12	1	7	31	20	86	2	5	.217/.291/.363	86	.302	-1.8	RF(43): -3.1, CF(15): 0.2, LF(2): -0.1	-0.1
Luke Maile	C	NAS	AAA	30	155	17	9	0	1	15	22	50	2	0	.225/.351/.318	77	.359	-0.1	C(41): 8.2, 1B(2): -0.1	0.9
	C	MIL	MLB	30	34	6	4	0	0	3	3	7	0	0	.300/.382/.433	89	.391	0.0	C(12): 0.4, P(1): -0.0	0.1
Jeferson Quero	C/DH	BRWB	ROK	18	83	15	5	1	2	8	12	10	4	3	.309/.434/.500		.339			
Corey Ray	CF	NAS	AAA	26	157	18	11	2	6	19	10	45	2	0	.274/.325/.500	96	.358	0.5	CF(34): 5.3, RF(3): 0.1, LF(1): 0.0	1.0
	CF	MIL	MLB	26	3	1	0	0	0	0	1	1	0	0	.000/.333/.000	88			RF(1): 0.0	0.0
Jakson Reetz	C	HBG	AA	25	255	31	13	0	4	18	24	69	1	1	.190/.298/.303	92	.257	-1.1	C(63): 6.8	1.3
	C	ROC	AAA	25	45	4	2	0	2	8	3	15	0	0	.184/.289/.395	87	.227	0.0	C(13): 0.6	0.2
	C	WAS	MLB	25	2	1	1	0	0	0	0	0	0	0	.500/.500/1.000	83	.500	0.1	C(1): 0.0	0.0
Pablo Reyes	3B	NAS	AAA	27	153	26	7	0	4	20	15	24	1	3	.226/.301/.368	104	.239	0.4	2B(12): -0.2, SS(10): 0.9, 3B(6): 0.2	0.6
	3B	MIL	MLB	27	87	12	5	0	1	3	9	15	4	0	.256/.333/.359	97	.306	1.6	3B(28): -1.1, 2B(2): 0.1, SS(2): 0.1	0.4
Daniel Robertson	IF	NAS	AAA	27	88	6	3	0	0	3	10	25	0	0	.115/.216/.154	74	.170	0.5	SS(14): -0.8, 3B(8): -0.4, 2B(4): 0.4	0.0
	IF	MIL	MLB	27	90	10	2	0	2	4	12	28	0	0	.164/.303/.274	79	.227	-0.1	3B(24): -0.4, 2B(9): 0.5, SS(8): -0.3	0.1
Carlos Rodriguez	OF	WIS	A+	20	382	43	17	4	1	38	35	75	15	6	.267/.336/.348	97	.338	-0.6	RF(39): 0.7, LF(35): 2.4, CF(17): 2.0	1.5
Jamie Westbrook	2B	BLX	AA	26	82	12	1	1	1	7	9	12	1	0	.261/.354/.348	121	.293	0.0	3B(7): 2.5, 2B(5): -0.2, LF(5): -0.9	0.6
	2B	NAS	AAA	26	287	45	15	1	11	47	21	42	2	0	.287/.353/.486	123	.302	0.2	2B(41): -1.4, 3B(12): -1.6, LF(11): -1.2	1.2

Tyler Black was the Brewers' second pick in the 2021 draft and also the second pick who turned in his hockey skates to focus on baseball. Milwaukee envisions the slick-fielding infielder as a potential above-average second baseman. Lacking that, they're at least building a roster that could give the AHL's Milwaukee Admirals a run for their money. ⚾ **Jonathan Davis** is as fast as can be, plays outstanding outfield defense and draws lots of free passes via walks and hits-by-pitch, but when he swings the bat everything goes to pot. His best chance for a career would be to lobby for limiting the number of pitchers on MLB rosters, or reinstating the fair-foul bunt. ⚾ **Joe Gray** has loud tools that carried him to a midseason promotion after he tore up Low-A in the first half. He struggled there, but if his bat can keep up with his above-average glove, he may eventually surpass 2017 World Snowshoe Champion Joseph Gray as the most notable person with his name. (No, he's not his son). ⚾ At 27 years old, **Tim Lopes** is less and less an example of nominative determinism on the basepaths. He might need to consider a name change to Tim Hits (and hope he does), if he's going to keep seeing big-league time. ⚾ **Tristen Lutz** failed his first test at the high minors, striking out way too often while failing to tap into the power that might make his questionable hit tool more palatable. ⚾ Though Steve from Blue's Clues made a surprising reappearance in our lives and consciousnesses last summer, it still wasn't **Luke Maile** Time in Milwaukee. The career third-catcher spent most of his season providing his trademark depth in Triple-A. When he stepped into the batter's box, he still couldn't find a clue. ⚾ **Jeferson Quero** hopped on a Jefferson Airplane this season and got his first stateside action in the Arizona Complex League. He's a few years away from being a few years away developmentally, but the Brewers are hoping he'll eventually become Somebody To Love. ⚾ A major-league debut is worth celebrating, even if it came with much less fanfare than **Corey Ray** or the Brewers envisioned as a top-five selection in 2016. His three unassuming plate appearances wound up but a footnote in a critical season where Ray spent more time on the injured list than proving he's more than another draft bust. He'll serve as depth going forward. ⚾ Former third-round pick **Jakson Reetz** got a week in the majors as an emergency backup catcher in July. He's a catcher with a decent glove, so that could happen again at any time. ⚾ A quick Google search shows that there are no direct flights from San Antonio to Milwaukee, which likely proved frustrating for **Pablo Reyes**, who spent his year ping-ponging back and forth between the two cities, serving as an unremarkable injury replacement on a number of occasions. ⚾ **Daniel Robertson** played everywhere for the Brewers, but not well enough to stick on the roster. He was designated for assignment on the Fourth of July. He spent the rest of the season battling injuries in Triple-A. ⚾ The key for **Carlos Rodriguez** to become more than a fourth outfielder type is developing some power and showing he can handle center field on a regular basis. He's thus far proven neither, but his speed and contact ability showed plenty of positives in his first taste of full-season ball. ⚾ The coolest thing about the way the Team USA roster is structured for Olympic baseball is what it means for players like **Jamie Westbrook**. The utility player has spent nine mostly productive years in the minors without even a cup of coffee in the majors to speak of. But he got 22 at-bats and even hit a home run for the bronze medal-winning Americans in Tokyo. Not a bad consolation prize.

Pitchers

PITCHER	TEAM	LVL	AGE	W	L	SV	G	GS	IP	H	HR	BB/9	K/9	K	GB%	BABIP	WHIP	ERA	DRA-	WARP	MPH	FB%	WHF	CSP
John Axford	BUF	AAA	38	1	0	2	9	0	10^2	2	0	2.5	11.8	14	60.0%	.105	0.47	0.84	84	0.2				
	MIL	MLB	38	0	0	0	1	0	0^1	2	0	27.0	0.0	0	33.3%	.667	9.00	54.00	145	0.0	94.7	86.4%	20.0%	46.0%
Alec Bettinger	NAS	AAA	25	3	7	0	21	18	96^2	104	15	2.4	9.1	98	42.2%	.327	1.34	4.75	117	0.5				
	MIL	MLB	25	0	1	0	4	1	10	18	3	2.7	4.5	5	38.1%	.395	2.10	13.50	118	0.0	91.3	73.4%	12.6%	60.7%
Rex Brothers	CHC	MLB	33	3	2	1	57	0	53	41	9	5.9	12.7	75	35.0%	.288	1.43	5.26	81	1.0	94.6	65.5%	33.9%	50.5%
John Curtiss	MIA	MLB	28	3	1	0	35	2	40	34	4	2.0	9.0	40	38.7%	.283	1.08	2.48	90	0.6	95.3	49.4%	28.2%	58.3%
	MIL	MLB	28	0	0	0	6	0	4^1	8	2	6.2	8.3	4	42.1%	.353	2.54	12.46	116	0.0	94.3	54.6%	20.4%	58.5%
Lucas Erceg	BLX	AA	26	2	6	0	22	13	47^2	38	5	6.6	8.5	45	58.1%	.266	1.53	5.29	114	0.1				
Dylan File	NAS	AAA	25	2	4	0	9	9	42^2	53	7	2.5	7.6	36	34.3%	.359	1.52	5.27	110	0.4				
Jandel Gustave	IND	AAA	28	1	0	5	15	0	15	12	0	3.0	10.8	18	65.8%	.316	1.13	3.60	92	0.3				
	NAS	AAA	28	0	1	0	6	0	6	3	0	0.0	12.0	8	41.7%	.250	0.50	1.50	81	0.1				
	MIL	MLB	28	1	2	0	14	0	18^1	15	2	2.5	6.4	13	45.6%	.236	1.09	3.44	105	0.1	96.7	74.5%	17.1%	56.2%
Antoine Kelly	CAR	A	21	0	1	0	7	7	17	13	0	8.5	12.7	24	36.8%	.342	1.71	6.88	112	0.0				
Josh Lindblom	NAS	AAA	34	5	4	0	22	20	104^2	102	10	2.2	10.1	117	31.1%	.323	1.22	3.10	92	1.8				
	MIL	MLB	34	0	0	0	8	0	16^2	23	5	5.4	9.2	17	27.3%	.360	1.98	9.72	122	0.0	90.5	41.8%	22.8%	52.4%
J.C. Mejía	COL	AAA	24	1	3	0	10	6	25^1	24	8	5.7	9.6	27	38.0%	.254	1.58	6.75	100	0.3				
	CLE	MLB	24	1	7	0	17	11	52^1	60	13	4.1	8.1	47	47.6%	.313	1.61	8.25	118	0.0	92.7	58.0%	20.8%	54.4%
Daniel Norris	MIL	MLB	28	1	0	0	18	0	20^1	17	5	6.6	8.0	18	41.4%	.231	1.57	6.64	121	0.0	92.8	52.4%	25.7%	51.8%
	DET	MLB	28	1	3	1	38	0	36^2	38	4	3.7	9.8	40	49.0%	.354	1.45	5.89	92	0.5	93.0	44.6%	28.4%	55.6%
Angel Perdomo	NAS	AAA	27	1	0	0	14	1	14	8	1	2.6	16.1	25	34.8%	.333	0.86	1.29	73	0.4				
	MIL	MLB	27	1	0	0	19	0	17	12	4	8.5	14.8	28	39.4%	.276	1.65	6.35	78	0.4	94.5	65.0%	33.3%	52.7%
Miguel Sánchez	NAS	AAA	27	2	0	0	19	0	25	22	3	3.2	8.6	24	48.6%	.275	1.24	3.60	94	0.4				
	MIL	MLB	27	2	1	0	28	0	26	27	4	4.8	8.0	23	38.3%	.303	1.58	4.15	118	0.0	94.4	38.1%	29.0%	52.1%
Hunter Strickland	TB	MLB	32	0	0	0	13	0	16	14	1	3.4	9.0	16	40.9%	.302	1.25	1.69	101	0.1	94.7	56.2%	26.0%	52.7%
	MIL	MLB	32	3	2	0	35	0	36^1	21	4	3.0	9.4	38	31.1%	.198	0.91	1.73	99	0.3	94.9	55.6%	30.4%	53.7%
	LAA	MLB	32	0	0	0	9	0	6^1	11	3	5.7	5.7	4	34.6%	.364	2.37	9.95	133	-0.1	95.1	65.9%	17.5%	55.4%
Eric Yardley	NAS	AAA	30	4	1	0	39	0	36^1	37	2	2.2	7.4	30	56.0%	.307	1.27	3.22	102	0.5				
	MIL	MLB	30	0	0	0	17	0	18^2	24	3	4.8	2.4	5	57.7%	.313	1.82	6.75	136	-0.2	87.2	73.0%	11.2%	54.0%
Jordan Zimmermann	MIL	MLB	35	0	0	0	2	0	5^2	8	1	3.2	0.0	0	52.2%	.318	1.76	7.94	101	0.0	89.4	42.7%	7.3%	54.1%

Ten years after he led the majors in saves with the Brewers and three years after his last major-league action of any sort, **John Axford** made his triumphant return to Milwaukee after being picked up off waivers from Toronto. The positive vibes were short-lived, however, as he suffered a UCL injury after facing just five batters. The first batter **Alec Bettinger** faced in his major-league career was perennial MVP candidate Mookie Betts, on May 2, 2021. He got him to pop out to second base. Congrats to Bettinger, now please do not look up the box score for that, or any subsequent, game. **Ray Black** hasn't thrown a pitch in a non-exhibition game since 2019 as myriad injuries have derailed a once-promising career. The right-hander who tantalized scouts with elite velocity has a long road back to regaining relevance. In its prime, The Smothers Brothers Comedy Hour melded edgy political satire with the hottest musical acts of the day; in his prime, **Rex Brothers** was a hard-throwing lefty when "hard" meant 95, not 97. Neither are likely to be on the air in 2022, but Rex (nine-plus years receiving an Annual comment) can say he outlasted those other Brothers (1967-69) in longevity. "Florida Man Leaves State, Loses Ability To Throw Baseball." Hardly the most absurd Florida Man headline one could conjure up, but it's apt for **John Curtiss**, who left the Sunshine State after 65 superb innings for the Rays and then Marlins, only to transform back into the anonymous middle reliever with average stuff he had been beforehand. After years of disappointing results at the plate, **Lucas Erceg** transitioned to the mound in 2021. And while the results weren't pretty, he routinely hit the upper-90s: impressive for someone who hasn't faced hitters since his PAC-12 days in 2015. He's still a two-way player for now, but if the continued underwhelming results at the plate are any indication, his most direct path to major-league relevance will come from the mound. That **Dylan File** has made it onto the major-league radar is already a victory for a 21st-round senior signing in 2017, and he'll continue to serve as potential starting pitching depth for an organization that has had quite a bit of success developing hurlers of his ilk. **Jandel Gustave** went from minor leaguer who couldn't crack the Pirates' bullpen to a valuable mid-season depth piece for the NL Central champions, which is the kind of unexpected promotion normally reserved for mediocre white men. Surgery for thoracic outlet syndrome delayed the start of **Antoine Kelly's** first full season as a pro until July, and in seven abbreviated starts he showed everything the Brewers anticipated when they took him in the second round out of an Illinois community college: Big strikeout stuff and enough rawness that it's likely to take a while to harness. **Josh Lindblom** lost his rotation spot in spring training, started the year in the bullpen, got shelled and then got hurt. Like the contestants who returned to The Squid Game after already learning the stakes, the former KBO star probably knew what he was in for by the time the organization designated him for assignment in late May. After years of his lauded sinker squashing the low minors, **J.C. Mejía** had little left to prove. Incidentally, after a disastrous season split between Triple-A and Cleveland, Mejía actually has a lot left to prove. **Daniel Norris'** issue used to be staying healthy enough to get to the mound. He cured that ill last year but found too much trouble *on* it, with a big spike in walk rate, that only ballooned further post-trade to Milwaukee. Throwing strikes is hard, and **Angel Perdomo** has had a devil of a time doing it at the major-league level. He notably cut his major-league walk rate by over 16 percentage points last year while working around a bad back—just don't ask to what. The Brewers signed **Luis Perdomo** to a minor-league deal last offseason and he spent the duration of it rehabbing from Tommy John surgery. A healthy return would presumably mean a resumption of his career as an unremarkable, low-leverage reliever. The strikeout jump **Miguel Sánchez** saw in the minors pre-pandemic didn't carry over in his first stint in the majors, but the former $6,000 international signee has a lively fastball and shows a good enough feel for his changeup to make him a solid candidate for low-leverage relief work. A funny thing happened to **Hunter Strickland**'s pitch mix upon arrival in Wisconsin: he reintroduced his sinker, which had been missing in his prior stops in 2021, and found success. Not so much in terms of groundballs, but in the overall scheme of attacking batters: another offering allowed Strickland to keep them off balance. The good: **Eric Yardley** walked as many batters in all of 2021 as he did in the shortened 2020 season. The bad: He did it in 4 ⅔ fewer innings. The ugly: His combined home runs and hit by pitches allowed topped his strikeout total. Call **Jordan Zimmermann** "The Hollow Man" because his career didn't end with a bang (five earned runs in 3 ⅔ innings against the Dodgers) but rather a forgettable whimper (two scoreless innings of relief against the Marlins).

PITTSBURGH PIRATES

Essay by Patrick Lackey

Player comments by Ken Funck and BP staff

I got home from school on April 6, 1993, just as my dad was getting ready to head to Three Rivers Stadium for Opening Day. I excitedly chattered away about my outlook for the season; sure, the Pirates had lost Barry Bonds and Doug Drabek to free agency, but Andy Van Slyke and Jay Bell and Jeff King and Orlando Merced were all still around, and I was sure that young players like Carlos Garcia, Al Martin and Kevin Young were going to fill in the gaps. I was 8, and the only Pirate teams I had really known were three NL East Championship winners; they had overcome losing Bobby Bonilla the previous year, why would Barry Bonds be any different?

My dad had a different tone. I remember him telling me, as he headed out to the game, that I shouldn't expect the Pirates to win every year. That things might be different. That it might take a couple of years for the Pirates to be back in the playoffs. As I watched the game from home, the Pirates easily beat the Padres behind Tim Wakefield, and I forgot everything my dad had said.

Three years later, those Pirates were dismantled. Wakefield had long since been release, clearly washed up at 26. The 1996 team's ace, Denny Neagle, was traded during the season. Bell, King and Merced were all expelled after the season. Manager Jim Leyland asked to be released from his contract, and it was an open secret that he was leaving the Pirates to manage a team that actually cared to contend. The Pirates had chosen another path; they took the field in 1997 with a $9-million payroll and the idea of refocusing on young players like catcher Jason Kendall, outfielder José Guillén and the first pick in 1996's draft, righty Kris Benson. The message from the team was unambiguous: they were not contending in the present, they were embarking on a Five-Year Plan to contend when PNC Park opened in 2001.

That plan is still ongoing.

It's hardly revelatory to say that the 2022 Pittsburgh Pirates are going to be a very bad baseball team. In general manager Ben Cherington's third year, the Pirates have entered the soft, amorphous middle of the tank-and-rebuild process: the stage when you can squint and see what the

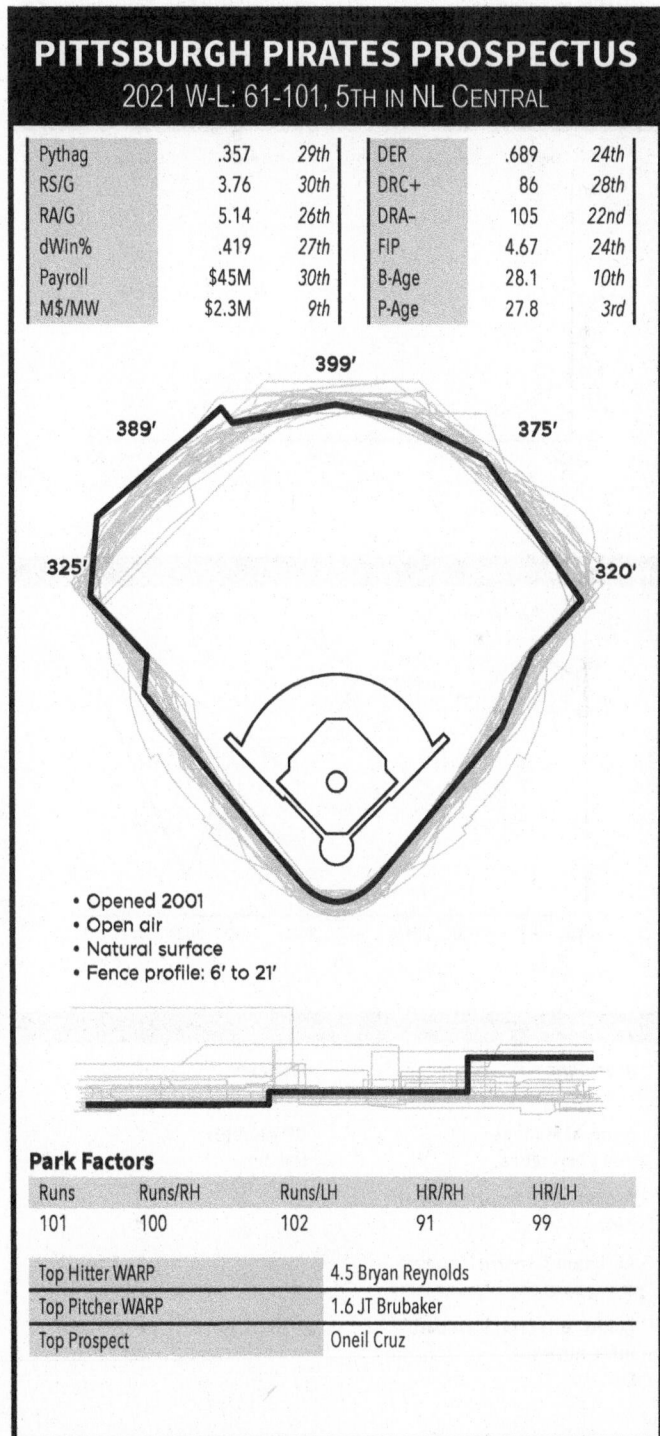

PITTSBURGH PIRATES PROSPECTUS

2021 W-L: 61-101, 5TH IN NL CENTRAL

Pythag	.357	29th	DER	.689	24th
RS/G	3.76	30th	DRC+	86	28th
RA/G	5.14	26th	DRA-	105	22nd
dWin%	.419	27th	FIP	4.67	24th
Payroll	$45M	30th	B-Age	28.1	10th
M$/MW	$2.3M	9th	P-Age	27.8	3rd

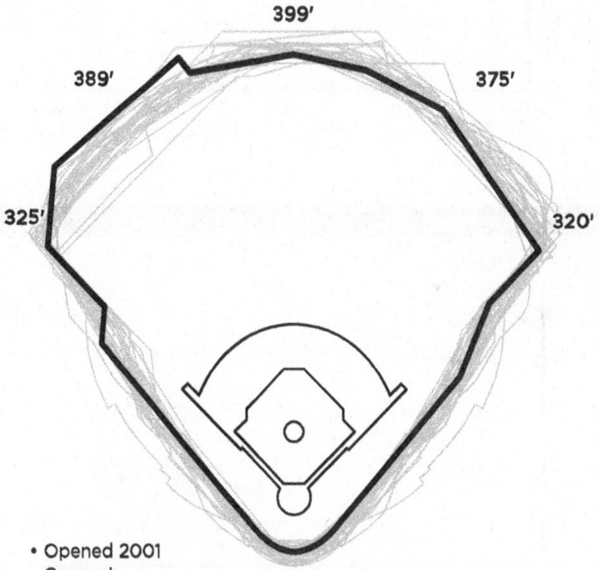

- Opened 2001
- Open air
- Natural surface
- Fence profile: 6' to 21'

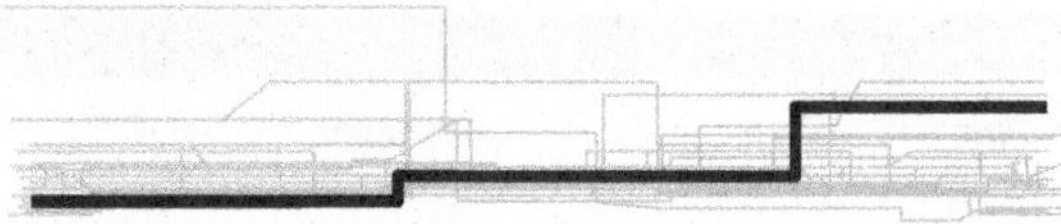

Park Factors

Runs	Runs/RH	Runs/LH	HR/RH	HR/LH
101	100	102	91	99

Top Hitter WARP	4.5 Bryan Reynolds
Top Pitcher WARP	1.6 JT Brubaker
Top Prospect	Oneil Cruz

Payroll History (in millions)

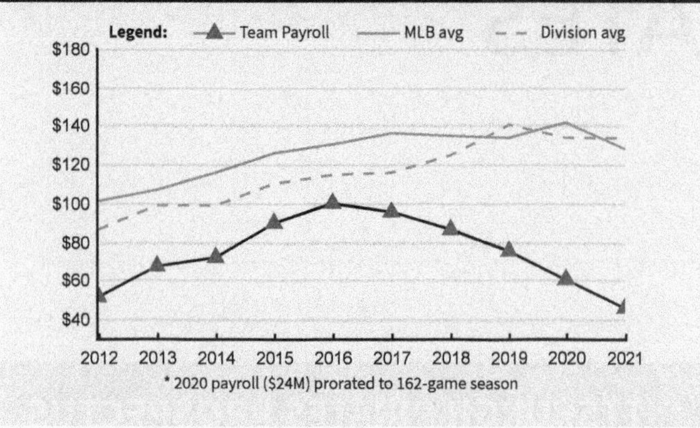

Future Commitments (in millions)

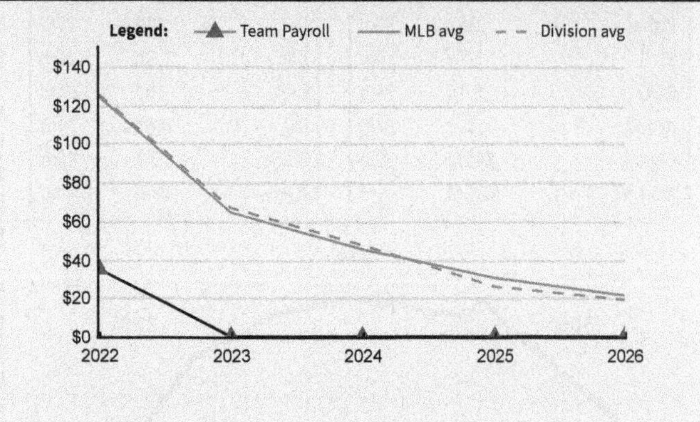

Farm System Ranking

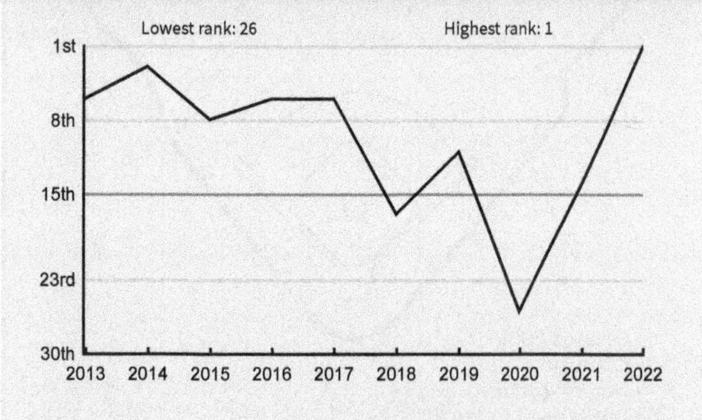

Personnel

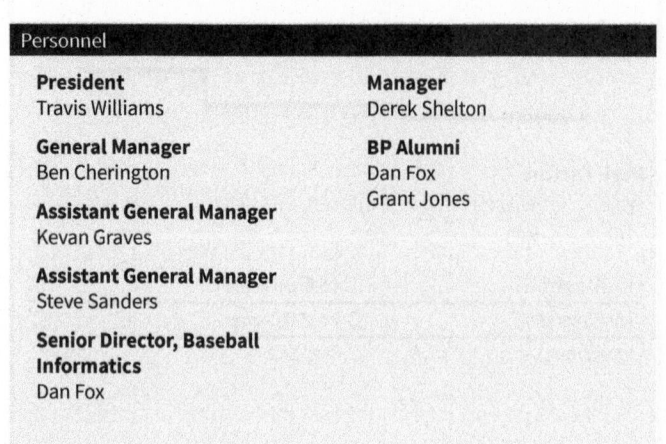

President
Travis Williams

General Manager
Ben Cherington

Assistant General Manager
Kevan Graves

Assistant General Manager
Steve Sanders

Senior Director, Baseball Informatics
Dan Fox

Manager
Derek Shelton

BP Alumni
Dan Fox
Grant Jones

team is building towards, but not with enough definition to see where the process ends. Center fielder Bryan Reynolds was one of the National League's best players in 2021. Third baseman Ke'Bryan Hayes is still one of the most exciting young defensive infielders in baseball, with enough upside in his bat to dream on despite his struggling through most of 2021 with a hand injury that sapped his power and hampered his progress. Shortstop Oneil Cruz slugged his way through two late-season promotions to end the Pirates' dismal season with his first big-league home run and a 118-mile-per-hour line drive with a comically easy swing on the season's last weekend. There was plenty of box-score optimism to be found last year in Double-A Altoona and High-A Greensboro for Pirate fans who wanted to look for it. There aren't many sure things to go around, though, and the current depth chart carries a $45-million payroll and one of the worst-looking pitching staffs in modern memory. It's possible that 2022 will be the year that the Pirates finally start to make some progress on Cherington's project, but it's a stretch to think they'll do anything more than that. But that's just part of the plan.

There were a few moments when it seemed like the original Five-Year Plan might work. In 1997, Kendall was a burgeoning star and the Pirates managed to contend all year with that $9-million payroll. After the 1998 season, they acquired Brian Giles from Cleveland, and he turned in four MVP-level seasons in the Pirates' outfield. Benson arrived in 1999 and turned in two very promising seasons. By the time PNC Park opened in 2001, though, general manager Cam Bonifay was on borrowed time. Kendall destroyed his ankle in 1998 and played through a thumb injury in 2001 that sapped him of his power permanently. Benson was overworked and missed 2001 with a Tommy John surgery that he never fully recovered from. That season's biggest bright spot was third baseman Aramis Ramírez finally breaking through at the age of 23, but his early career had been so badly mismanaged that he was already nearing arbitration. The 2001 Pirates lost 100 games, Bonifay was fired at mid-season, and the keys were turned over to Dave Littlefield.

The Littlefield era was never anything better than bleak. In 2007, the night before I moved to North Carolina for grad school, I headed to PNC Park with my dad. It was July 31, the day of the trade deadline. When we left our house to make the hour-long drive to Pittsburgh, it seemed like the Pirates were done dealing for the day. When we got to the stadium, the scoreboard had a message for us: the Pirates had acquired righty Matt Morris from the Giants for near-ready center-field prospect Rajai Davis. The Littlefield Pirates spent years steadfastly refusing to spend money on anything, only to trade a young player for the right to take on what amounted to $13 million in dead salary. I was floored. Over my first days and weeks in North Carolina, I briefly considered whether my geographic relocation was an opportunity to find a new favorite baseball team. Littlefield was fired after the 2007 season.

Littlefield's replacement, Neal Huntington, spent his first two years on the job trading every useful major-league piece the Pirates had for someone else's former top prospect, bringing in names like Lastings Milledge, Andy LaRoche and Jeff Clement. The hope was that the team would hit on a couple of those post-hype guys, then flip them, as well, to speed up the rebuild. It didn't work. The 2010 Pirates lost 105 games, and most of the busted prospects disappeared. Huntington's plan entered a second phase, centered on outfielder Andrew McCutchen, infielder Neil Walker and the players drafted in the de facto tanked seasons of 2008–10. That project proved to be the only successful rebuild executed by any Pirate front office in the last three decades. The 2013–15 Pirates accumulated baseball's second-best record over that three-year span but never advanced past the Division Series, ultimately falling victim to sharing a division with the Cardinals, who held baseball's best record over those three years.

Those three Pirates teams, though, might have revealed more about the franchise than the two ugly decades that preceded them. It's hard to look back on those wild-card seasons and conclude that the Pirates' front office was playing for the present, even in those best years. The Pirates never had a payroll above $100 million. They almost always entered seasons with incomplete starting rotations, focusing on the nebulous concept of small-market "value" rather than spending money on more certain upgrades. They ended up scrambling for pitching at both the 2014 and '15 deadlines. In both seasons, the time they spent figuring out how to get the team into shape cost them; they finished in second by two games both years and lost both Wild Card Games.

After the 2015 team won 98 games with a top-five farm system, the cracks began to surface. The Pirates dumped righty Charlie Morton's salary on the Phillies and attempted to shore up the pitching staff with a budget-neutral trade of Walker for Mets lefty Jon Niese. At the 2016 trade deadline, despite being only four games out of the second wild card, they sent prospects Harold Ramirez and Reese McGuire to Toronto as a sweetener to get the Blue Jays to accept lefty Francisco Liriano's salary for a minimal return. For years, Pirate fans swallowed low-payroll, 90-plus-loss seasons on the implicit promise that the money would be spent on a better day in the future. That better day arrived, but the higher payrolls did not; the Pirates kept using the same logic to justify focusing on anything but the team in front of them.

Huntington's scramble to maintain the veneer of trying to win with a low payroll started crumbling in 2018. In a one-week span in January, he sent righty Gerrit Cole to Houston and McCutchen to San Francisco, with both trades focused on bringing back quality, if still developing, major-league-ready talent. The Pirates were heading back into the cycle of the Littlefield years, until the team unexpectedly found itself in contention in July. Seizing the moment, they tried to reverse the Cole trade by acquiring righty Chris Archer from Tampa Bay in exchange for prospects Tyler Glasnow, Austin Meadows and Shane Baz. It would almost instantly prove to be one of the most disastrous trades in modern baseball history. The Pirates missed the playoffs in 2018 and fell apart in 2019, resulting in Huntington's firing, and bringing us here, where we've always been.

A baseball team being bad for a few decades is not that exceptional. "Wait 'til next year" might be baseball's most enduring mantra, and baseball fandom has always been a multi-year proposition, at best, for almost everyone save a select few fanbases. It seems bleak that the Pirates have won five World Series in 134 years, but the only teams that have won more than that are the Yankees, Cardinals, A's, Red Sox, Giants and Dodgers.

The reality of baseball has always been that championships are generational occurrences for most fans, which is why the sport is filled with so much parent/child romanticism about those championships. Part of being a baseball fan is hearing your dad tell you why this current Pirate team reminds him of the 1979 Pirates, or finding Ken Keltner's name on your grandfather's glove and realizing that the glove was a memory linked to the only World Series Cleveland won in his lifetime, and hoping that you'll get a moment like those to share with them and pass on in your own time, because those moments are so rare for most fans.

The problem for the Pirates lies in the reality that the rebuild never ends. They have been profoundly bad at baseball for my almost entire life. Every team in the National League has been to at least one World Series since the Pirates last won the NL Pennant in 1979 (the only other team in baseball that has not been to a World Series in that span is the Mariners, who did not exist before 1977). Every single team in baseball has been to at least one League Championship Series since the Pirates' last LCS appearance in 1992. When the Pirates do not win the NL Central in 2022, they will tie baseball's record for the longest stretch of time between division titles since the league split into quadrants in 1969. Since Sid Bream slid under Mike LaValliere's tag to end the 1992 NLCS, the Pirates have had four winning seasons and played in eight postseason games over three playoff appearances. A generation of Pittsburgh children seeking to bond with a family member over stories of a triumphant Pirates team will have to turn to its grandparents to do so.

The Pirates rarely ask their fans to "wait 'til next year." They tell everyone, "absolutely not this year or next year, but maybe in a few years." If there's never a present moment, the future doesn't hold any value. This is may be the hardest thing to take after the Pirates' mildly successful (at least in Pirate terms) last decade; sometimes a little bit of success creates the contrast needed to see how bad things really are.

And so this is the reality of the 2022 Pirates: the future being sold to fans as built on Ke'Bryan Hayes, Oneil Cruz, Quinn Priester, Henry Davis, Nick Gonzales and Roansy Contreras doesn't feel like a completely nebulous one, but it requires buying into a promise that has never been kept. It is entirely possible that no prospect in the system will ever be a better player than Bryan Reynolds is right now. After his sophomore swoon during the COVID-shortened season, Reynolds improved on every aspect of his breakout rookie season at the plate in 2021 while playing a passable center field. He was one of the ten-or-so-best position players in baseball in 2021, but he'll be 27 before the 2022 season starts, and the clock to win around him is ticking.

Despite this, the Pirates are not moving with any sort of urgency. They entered the lockout with an approximately $45-million payroll, and while much of the rest of the league went on a lavish, late-fall spending spree, the Pirates traded their only rostered catcher, Jacob Stallings, to Miami. Stallings is the sort of player that good teams find ways to afford, and that fans cling to in a sea of faceless call-ups. He has built himself into one of the best defensive catchers in baseball over the past few seasons, and has a serviceable-enough bat that he can play regularly without being a liability. He is not a big enough star that trading him for prospects feels indefensible, but the timing is yet another message.

Circling back to Reynolds, he is far more likely to join Jason Bay, Brian Giles and Jason Kendall as very-good-to-great Pirate players who never had a team to match them. The most difficult thing to accept about the Pirates' current rebuild, though, is not that they might waste Reynolds' prime; it's that the only thing that will keep players like Hayes, Cruz, Gonzales, or Davis from joining him in that fate is if *this time* the Pirates finally keep the same promise they've been failing to keep for almost 30 years.

As the endless rebuild wears on with no end in sight, I can feel my relationship to the team changing. I remember details about a September night in 1990 at Three Rivers Stadium like it was yesterday. I can still tell you the exact conversation my dad and I had on the way to the ballpark before the doubleheader in which Rob Mackowiak hit a walk-off grand slam in the first game and a game-tying home run in the second. I remember the look on the faces of my friends when Pedro Álvarez launched his first walk-off home run deep into the night, erasing a two-run lead in the blink of an eye, and I know exactly where I was when Mike McKenry homered off of Aroldis Chapman.

For so many years, I hung on each one of these details, always thinking that, when the time finally came, they'd be things I could look back on as steps along the path. The steps aren't meaningful without a destination, though. I saw eight Pirate games in person in 2021, the Pirates somehow won all eight, and I'd struggle to give you specific details about any of them without looking at the box score. In doing just that recently, I was surprised to learn that I'd seen Ke'Bryan Hayes' first career walk-off hit in person. Not remembering that isn't a slight against Hayes; it has much more to do with the fact that the one-year, $1.7-million contract that his dad, Charlie, signed with the Pirates in 1996 would have made him the fourth-highest-paid Pirate in 2021.

—Patrick Lackey is a professor at Westminster College.

Hitters

Anthony Alford LF Born: 07/20/94 Age: 27 Bats: R Throws: R Height: 6'1" Weight: 215 lb. Origin: Round 3, 2012 Draft (#112 overall)

YEAR	TEAM	LVL	AGE	PA	R	2B	3B	HR	RBI	BB	K	SB	CS	Whiff%	AVG/OBP/SLG	DRC+	BABIP	BRR	FRAA	WARP
2019	BUF	AAA	24	319	46	16	3	7	37	31	94	22	8		.259/.343/.411	82	.365	1.2	RF(26): 4.3, CF(24): -4.4, LF(12): 1.0	0.5
2019	TOR	MLB	24	30	3	0	0	1	1	1	11	2	0	41.1%	.179/.233/.286	76	.250	0.4	LF(6): -0.2, RF(5): 0.1, CF(2): -0.0	0.0
2020	PIT	MLB	25	13	2	0	1	1	4	1	1	0	0	38.9%	.250/.308/.667	116	.200	-0.1	CF(4): -0.7, LF(1): -0.5	-0.1
2020	TOR	MLB	25	16	3	0	0	1	3	0	7	3	0	47.4%	.188/.188/.375	83	.250	0.3	LF(5): -0.6, CF(2): -0.4, RF(1): -0.0	-0.1
2021	IND	AAA	26	226	37	12	0	14	41	33	78	9	4		.307/.420/.593	114	.454	0.7	CF(26): -5.6, LF(24): 1.9	0.8
2021	PIT	MLB	26	148	14	6	1	5	11	12	58	5	6	38.6%	.233/.311/.406	66	.371	-0.7	LF(32): 0.3, CF(6): -1.1, RF(1): -0.0	-0.2
2022 DC	*PIT*	*MLB*	*27*	*351*	*37*	*15*	*1*	*9*	*39*	*30*	*137*	*10*	*5*	*38.3%*	*.206/.289/.352*	*71*	*.331*	*0.8*	*LF 1, RF 1*	*0.0*

Comparables: Robbie Grossman, Jake Marisnick, Desmond Jennings

The Pirates snapped up Alford on waivers from Toronto at the end of 2020, and the former top prospect is exactly the sort of tooled-up, post-hype lottery ticket a rebuilding club should take a flyer on. The Buccos installed Alford as their opening day center fielder, but the Ole Miss alum continued to play like Ole Swing-n-Miss, striking out in over half his plate appearances in April before a merciful demotion to Triple-A. Alford righted the ship in Indianapolis, showing a more patient approach while launching double-digit home runs for the first time in his career, and returned to Pittsburgh to post a more respectable .266/.328/.477 after his return while still whiffing more than a third of the time. Despite his top-end speed, Alford is not a gifted center fielder or basestealer, making him a likely fourth outfielder with a little bit of pop, a little bit of speed and a lot of frustrated trudges back to the dugout.

Rodolfo Castro 2B Born: 05/21/99 Age: 23 Bats: S Throws: R Height: 6'0" Weight: 205 lb. Origin: International Free Agent, 2015

YEAR	TEAM	LVL	AGE	PA	R	2B	3B	HR	RBI	BB	K	SB	CS	Whiff%	AVG/OBP/SLG	DRC+	BABIP	BRR	FRAA	WARP
2019	GBO	A	20	246	33	13	2	14	46	18	68	6	5		.242/.306/.516	128	.271	2.0	2B(34): -0.1, SS(17): -0.6, 3B(7): 0.6	1.8
2019	BRD	A+	20	215	26	13	1	5	27	13	54	1	0		.243/.288/.391	98	.308	0.8	2B(37): 2.6, SS(16): -1.6, 3B(4): -0.2	0.7
2021	TOR	WIN	22	109	15	6	2	1	8	22	26	2	1		.235/.394/.388		.322			
2021	ALT	AA	22	312	43	14	1	12	47	19	72	7	4		.242/.295/.425	105	.278	0.9	3B(44): 2.1, 2B(24): 2.6, SS(4): -0.3	1.7
2021	IND	AAA	22	38	7	4	0	3	8	3	11	0	0		.286/.342/.657	107	.333	1.1	3B(4): -0.1, SS(3): -0.3, 2B(1): -0.1	0.2
2021	PIT	MLB	22	93	9	2	0	5	8	6	27	0	0	28.6%	.198/.258/.395	90	.222	-0.2	2B(20): -2.1, 3B(5): 0.8	0.1
2022 DC	*PIT*	*MLB*	*23*	*193*	*21*	*8*	*1*	*6*	*24*	*11*	*51*	*2*	*1*	*29.6%*	*.221/.274/.390*	*74*	*.273*	*0.1*	*2B 0, 3B 0*	*0.0*

Comparables: Jorge Polanco, Hernán Pérez, Yolmer Sánchez

The future is now for Castro, who parlayed a power-packed season in the high minors into his first taste of the bigs. A switch-hitting infielder with a glove most notable for its versatility, Castro demonstrated the thunder in his bat by sending the first five hits of his major-league career over the fence, an MLB first. He then showcased his ever-present contact issues by whiffing in nearly 30% of his plate appearances. Castro's struggles with pitch recognition and his aggressive approach are ripe for exploitation by big-league pitchers; he's still only 22 but patience is a virtue that is hard to teach at any age.

Michael Chavis 2B/1B Born: 08/11/95 Age: 26 Bats: R Throws: R Height: 5'10" Weight: 210 lb. Origin: Round 1, 2014 Draft (#26 overall)

YEAR	TEAM	LVL	AGE	PA	R	2B	3B	HR	RBI	BB	K	SB	CS	Whiff%	AVG/OBP/SLG	DRC+	BABIP	BRR	FRAA	WARP
2019	PAW	AAA	23	79	11	4	0	7	11	8	21	0	0		.257/.329/.614	118	.256	-0.2	2B(7): 1.8, 3B(7): -0.5, 1B(4): 0.9	0.6
2019	BOS	MLB	23	382	46	10	1	18	58	31	127	2	1	38.4%	.254/.322/.444	86	.347	0.6	1B(49): 2.6, 2B(45): -0.7, 3B(5): -0.2	0.8
2020	BOS	MLB	24	158	16	5	2	5	19	8	50	3	0	38.3%	.212/.259/.377	76	.280	-1.1	1B(24): 0.5, LF(12): 0.8, 2B(8): 0.2	0.0
2021	WOR	AAA	25	107	19	2	0	6	17	8	30	1	0		.263/.327/.474	106	.311	0.6	1B(18): -1.6, 2B(6): 0.1	0.2
2021	IND	AAA	25	110	19	6	0	8	20	6	26	1	1		.278/.364/.588	118	.302	0.1	2B(10): -1.4, 1B(7): -0.3, 3B(3): 0.2	0.4
2021	PIT	MLB	25	42	4	3	0	1	5	0	10	0	1	23.7%	.357/.357/.500	91	.452	-0.4	2B(7): -0.5, 3B(4): -0.3, 1B(1): 0.1	0.0
2021	BOS	MLB	25	82	12	4	1	2	6	1	32	1	1	44.6%	.190/.207/.342	61	.283	0.8	2B(22): 1.3, 1B(8): -0.1	0.1
2022 DC	*PIT*	*MLB*	*26*	*435*	*56*	*17*	*1*	*18*	*59*	*24*	*136*	*2*	*1*	*36.3%*	*.235/.292/.425*	*89*	*.309*	*-0.2*	*1B 0, 3B 0*	*0.1*

Comparables: Jeimer Candelario, Brandon Drury, Mat Gamel

Chavis was shipped from Boston to Pittsburgh at the deadline last year and flashed enough down the stretch to show he can be a building block—assuming you're trying to build a 78-84 team. There's no denying his ability to launch majestic dongs, and he's made himself into a serviceable glove at the keystone. His high-energy grittiness can make him a fan and clubhouse favorite. However, his grip-it-and-rip-it style often undoes all of that good work, as his aggressive approach and low contact rate combine to produce more empty swings than a playground at midnight. Contact-averse sluggers can still be productive if they draw enough free passes to keep their on-base percentage above water, but Chavis drew just one walk last year, leaving him one True Outcome short of a set. His power bat and positional flexibility make him a reasonable placeholder, but Chavis makes too many outs to project as a starter on a contending team.

★ ★ ★ *2022 Top 101 Prospect* **#12** ★ ★ ★

Oneil Cruz SS Born: 10/04/98 Age: 23 Bats: L Throws: R Height: 6'7" Weight: 210 lb. Origin: International Free Agent, 2015

YEAR	TEAM	LVL	AGE	PA	R	2B	3B	HR	RBI	BB	K	SB	CS	Whiff%	AVG/OBP/SLG	DRC+	BABIP	BRR	FRAA	WARP
2019	PIR	ROK	20	11	0	1	0	0	1	1	1	1	0		.600/.636/.700		.667			
2019	BRD	A+	20	145	21	6	1	7	16	8	38	7	3		.301/.345/.515	115	.374	0.7	SS(35): 2.5	0.9
2019	ALT	AA	20	136	14	8	3	1	17	15	35	3	1		.269/.346/.412	93	.365	1.7	SS(35): 3.2	0.9
2021	ALT	AA	22	273	51	15	5	12	40	20	64	18	3		.292/.346/.536	120	.349	2.6	SS(54): -1.7	1.6
2021	IND	AAA	22	29	11	1	0	5	7	8	5	1	0		.524/.655/1.286	147	.545	0.0	SS(5): 1.1	0.3
2021	PIT	MLB	22	9	2	0	0	1	3	0	4	0	0	50.0%	.333/.333/.667	82	.500		SS(2): -0.7	-0.1
2022 DC	*PIT*	*MLB*	*23*	*286*	*35*	*12*	*2*	*10*	*39*	*20*	*85*	*5*	*3*	*32.8%*	*.255/.313/.443*	*96*	*.342*	*0.6*	*SS 1*	*1.1*

Comparables: Nick Franklin, Jonathan Villar, Cole Tucker

The Pirates rewarded Cruz's highly successful minor-league season with an October call-up, and the Brobdingnagian shortstop rewarded them with a laser show. Cruz put five balls in play with an average exit velocity over 100, flashing the immense raw power that should lead to 30+ bombs per year from a premier defensive position. He also struck out four times in two games, highlighting the swing-and-miss that will always be part of his game. There's still the question of whether Cruz is a shortstop, where his top-shelf athleticism and solid fundamentals have so far allowed him to stick despite his Dave Winfield build, or an outfielder, where his arm, reach and long-striding speed could make him a plus defender. Also pending at press time is the resolution of his criminal case in the Dominican Republic, where he was involved in a car-motorcycle crash that resulted in three deaths.

★ ★ ★ *2022 Top 101 Prospect* **#18** ★ ★ ★

Henry Davis C
Born: 09/21/99 Age: 22 Bats: R Throws: R Height: 6'2" Weight: 210 lb. Origin: Round 1, 2021 Draft (#1 overall)

YEAR	TEAM	LVL	AGE	PA	R	2B	3B	HR	RBI	BB	K	SB	CS	Whiff%	AVG/OBP/SLG	DRC+	BABIP	BRR	FRAA	WARP
2022 non-DC	*PIT*	*MLB*	*22*	*251*	*21*	*9*	*1*	*4*	*23*	*20*	*76*	*3*	*2*	*31.1%*	*.198/.272/.319*	*61*	*.275*	*0.2*	*C -4*	*-0.5*

YEAR	TEAM	P. COUNT	FRM RUNS	BLK RUNS	THRW RUNS	TOT RUNS
2022	*PIT*	*6956*	*-3.4*	*-0.5*	*0.0*	*-4.0*

Pittsburgh nabbed Davis with the first pick of the 2021 draft, and while the former Louisville star saw his season end early with an oblique injury, he did enough with the bat to demonstrate why the Pirates think he can grow into an All-Star behind the plate. Davis was one of the best college hitters available, with big-time power, excellent bat-to-ball skills and an advanced approach that should make him a fast riser. His receiving skills are a work in progress, but Davis has a strong arm. He's not likely to win any defensive hardware, but he should be able to stick behind the dish. Possessing an offensive skill set rarely found in a catcher, Davis projects to be a mainstay on the next great Pirates team, if there is one.

Wilmer Difo 2B
Born: 04/02/92 Age: 30 Bats: S Throws: R Height: 5'11" Weight: 200 lb. Origin: International Free Agent, 2010

YEAR	TEAM	LVL	AGE	PA	R	2B	3B	HR	RBI	BB	K	SB	CS	Whiff%	AVG/OBP/SLG	DRC+	BABIP	BRR	FRAA	WARP
2019	FRE	AAA	27	261	48	14	3	4	30	25	51	13	5		.300/.369/.438	93	.369	3.1	SS(32): -2.5, 2B(20): 1.2, 3B(10): -0.2	1.0
2019	WAS	MLB	27	144	15	2	0	2	8	12	29	0	1	27.5%	.252/.315/.313	88	.310	1.2	SS(33): -1.9, 3B(6): -0.3, 2B(2): 0.1	0.2
2020	AGU	WIN	28	86	10	1	1	0	3	7	11	1	0		.221/.286/.260		.258			
2020	WAS	MLB	28	18	1	0	0	0	1	3	4	0	0	23.8%	.071/.222/.071	93	.091	0.0	2B(4): -0.1, SS(4): -0.1, 3B(2): 0.0	0.0
2021	IND	AAA	29	46	6	2	0	0	2	4	10	0	0		.244/.304/.293	96	.313	-0.3	2B(6): 0.7, 3B(6): 1.4	0.3
2021	PIT	MLB	29	240	25	7	3	4	24	20	54	1	0	28.3%	.269/.329/.384	91	.340	0.6	2B(28): -2.3, 3B(18): 0.8, RF(8): -1.1	0.4
2022 non-DC	*PIT*	*MLB*	*30*	*251*	*22*	*8*	*1*	*3*	*22*	*21*	*57*	*3*	*2*	*27.5%*	*.231/.301/.332*	*73*	*.294*	*0.3*	*SS -1, 2B 0*	*-0.1*

Comparables: Pedro Florimón, Alberto Gonzalez, Ryan Goins

The rosters of rebuilding clubs often resemble the Island of Misfit Toys, littered with hard-throwing starters that lack control, post-hype sluggers who can't make contact and other talented castoffs with one fatal flaw. Teams like the Pirates hope they can take some of these squirt guns that shoot jelly, fill them up with water and eventually turn them into Super Soakers. Difo doesn't fit that mold, as he's instead a perfectly functional squirt gun that was apparently designed to shoot water with very little force. He's a competent glove that can be plugged in anywhere on the diamond, but he can't hit for average or power or steal bases or draw enough walks to post a high on-base percentage. As Difo enters his 30s, his defensive versatility may continue to earn him utility roles on non-contenders in the double-switch league, but if the universal DH becomes a thing he'll have to compete with both the Hernán Pérez types AND the Daniel Vogelbachs of the world for a roster spot.

Phillip Evans 1B
Born: 09/10/92 Age: 29 Bats: R Throws: R Height: 5'10" Weight: 210 lb. Origin: Round 15, 2011 Draft (#462 overall)

YEAR	TEAM	LVL	AGE	PA	R	2B	3B	HR	RBI	BB	K	SB	CS	Whiff%	AVG/OBP/SLG	DRC+	BABIP	BRR	FRAA	WARP
2019	IOW	AAA	26	539	79	30	3	17	61	57	74	1	4		.283/.371/.470	110	.303	0.5	3B(95): -4.3, 1B(15): -0.1, 2B(15): 1.4	2.1
2020	PIT	MLB	27	45	6	2	0	1	9	5	7	0	1	35.1%	.359/.444/.487	111	.419	-0.4	3B(8): -1.1, 1B(1): -0.0, LF(1): -0.1	0.0
2021	IND	AAA	28	144	18	10	0	0	10	15	29	0	0		.252/.333/.331	90	.323	1.1	1B(15): 1.3, 3B(11): 0.4, RF(3): -0.3	0.5
2021	PIT	MLB	28	247	23	5	0	5	16	28	53	1	0	23.6%	.206/.312/.299	94	.250	0.6	1B(20): 2.1, LF(16): 0.8, RF(15): -1.8	0.7
2022 non-DC	*PIT*	*MLB*	*29*	*251*	*24*	*10*	*0*	*5*	*24*	*24*	*51*	*0*	*1*	*25.4%*	*.230/.317/.353*	*85*	*.278*	*-0.3*	*3B 0, 1B 0*	*0.2*

Comparables: Pedro Ciriaco, Hernán Pérez, Shawn O'Malley

Evans returned last year from the broken jaw and concussion that ended his 2020 season, but injuries and ineffectiveness once again kept the former Mets prospect from showing he can be a productive big-leaguer. He bounced around the infield and outfield corners, between Pittsburgh and Indianapolis, and on and off the injured list with a strained hamstring and a second concussion suffered while sliding into third base, never getting into any sort of rhythm and posting forgettable offensive numbers. In the upper minors Evans has shown a solid approach and just enough pop and contact skill to paint him as a potentially useful bat-first reserve, but he's running out of chances to prove it.

Todd Frazier 3B
Born: 02/12/86 Age: 36 Bats: R Throws: R Height: 6'3" Weight: 215 lb. Origin: Round 1, 2007 Draft (#34 overall)

YEAR	TEAM	LVL	AGE	PA	R	2B	3B	HR	RBI	BB	K	SB	CS	Whiff%	AVG/OBP/SLG	DRC+	BABIP	BRR	FRAA	WARP
2019	STL	A+	33	43	3	0	0	1	8	6	8	0	1		.216/.326/.297	109	.250	-0.4	3B(10): 1.0, 1B(5): -0.1, SS(3): -0.1	0.2
2019	NYM	MLB	33	499	63	19	2	21	67	40	106	1	2	25.6%	.251/.329/.443	102	.284	-0.2	3B(120): 6.9, 1B(3): 0.1	2.1
2020	TEX	MLB	34	121	11	7	1	2	7	10	26	1	1	26.1%	.241/.322/.380	96	.300	-0.6	1B(16): -1.1, 3B(15): -1.8	-0.1
2020	NYM	MLB	34	51	5	2	0	2	5	1	16	0	0	28.7%	.224/.255/.388	90	.290	0.7	3B(14): 2.0	0.3
2021	PIT	MLB	35	40	3	1	0	0	4	3	6	0	0	17.8%	.086/.200/.114	93	.103	0.3	1B(4): -0.3, 3B(3): -0.1	0.1
2022 non-DC	*PIT*	*MLB*	*36*	*251*	*28*	*9*	*0*	*9*	*30*	*21*	*51*	*2*	*1*	*24.7%*	*.228/.309/.401*	*93*	*.257*	*-0.2*	*3B 1, 1B 0*	*0.5*

Comparables: Sal Bando, Gary Gaetti, Scott Rolen

Frazier's potential swan song in Pittsburgh ended after 13 forgettable games, but the Pirates released in time for him to join the U.S. Olympic team, which he helped lead to a silver medal. That would make a fine bookend to a career that started with a Little League World Series victory in 1998 and included a 2006 World University Championship, bronze at the 2011 Pan Am games and a 2015 Home Run Derby win in front of the home fans in Cincinnati. Frazier is only 79 days short of his full pension and hopes to keep playing, but if he does hang 'em up he'll end his career in the top 100 all-time among third basemen in Jay Jaffe's JAWS metric. He's definitely a guy we'll remember when we remember some guys.

Ben Gamel OF Born: 05/17/92 Age: 30 Bats: L Throws: L Height: 5'11" Weight: 177 lb. Origin: Round 10, 2010 Draft (#325 overall)

YEAR	TEAM	LVL	AGE	PA	R	2B	3B	HR	RBI	BB	K	SB	CS	Whiff%	AVG/OBP/SLG	DRC+	BABIP	BRR	FRAA	WARP
2019	MIL	MLB	27	356	47	18	0	7	33	40	104	2	2	22.6%	.248/.337/.373	78	.347	0.8	LF(70): -1.8, RF(23): 0.3, CF(22): -0.1	0.2
2020	MIL	MLB	28	127	13	8	1	3	10	13	39	0	2	28.6%	.237/.315/.404	79	.333	-1.8	RF(27): -1.0, CF(11): -1.6, LF(1): 0.1	-0.4
2021	PIT	MLB	29	383	42	17	3	8	26	48	99	3	6	27.2%	.255/.352/.399	88	.336	-3.0	LF(72): 3.1, RF(18): 0.5, CF(11): -0.5	0.8
2021	CLE	MLB	29	17	1	1	0	0	0	3	6	0	0	27.6%	.071/.235/.143	81	.125	-0.2	CF(9): -0.7, LF(1): -0.0	-0.1
2022 DC	*PIT*	*MLB*	*30*	*478*	*58*	*22*	*3*	*9*	*51*	*57*	*128*	*5*	*3*	*26.6%*	*.238/.337/.380*	*93*	*.324*	*0.1*	*RF -1, CF 0*	*0.8*

Comparables: Ezequiel Carrera, Abraham Almonte, Josh Reddick

Few contenders in recent memory have had a greater need for even marginally competent outfield help than the Guardians, so it had to be especially distressing for Gamel when he was released only a month into his Cleveland career. Picked up by the less aspirational Pirates, Gamel bounced back to post a marginally competent season in Pittsburgh, relying on his usual combination of walks and safeties to reach base at a solid clip. His lefty bat lacks the power of an ideal corner outfielder—his Baseball Savant percentile graphs are bluer than a Billie Holiday set list—and despite plus foot speed his defense and baserunning are below par. Gamel is best cast as a fourth outfielder—or, more to the point, as a professional placeholder for a rebuilding squad that wants to avoid embarrassing themselves until the kids are ready.

★ ★ ★ *2022 Top 101 Prospect* **#29** ★ ★ ★

Nick Gonzales 2B Born: 05/27/99 Age: 23 Bats: R Throws: R Height: 5'10" Weight: 195 lb. Origin: Round 1, 2020 Draft (#7 overall)

YEAR	TEAM	LVL	AGE	PA	R	2B	3B	HR	RBI	BB	K	SB	CS	Whiff%	AVG/OBP/SLG	DRC+	BABIP	BRR	FRAA	WARP
2021	PEJ	WIN	22	87	18	4	1	2	13	13	14	4	0		.380/.483/.549		.446			
2021	GBO	A+	22	369	53	23	4	18	54	40	101	7	2		.302/.385/.565	112	.388	-3.4	2B(73): -0.8, SS(1): -0.0	1.2
2022 non-DC	*PIT*	*MLB*	*23*	*251*	*23*	*11*	*1*	*5*	*25*	*19*	*82*	*1*	*1*	*36.1%*	*.228/.296/.364*	*78*	*.331*	*0.0*	*2B -1, SS 0*	*0.0*

Comparables: Brandon Lowe, Cory Spangenberg, Chris Taylor

Pittsburgh's top pick in the 2020 draft, Gonzales was finally able to make his minor-league debut last year and absolutely raked in High-A and the Arizona Fall League. A bat-first infield prospect, Gonzales uses his lightning-quick stroke to sting line drives all over the yard and flashes enough power potential to presage 20-plus bombs annually in The Show. There's some swing-and-miss in his game, and his offensive ceiling will depend on improving his pitch recognition and two-strike approach, but he's a pure hitter whose knack for making hard contact gives him a high floor. Gonzales is sure-handed defensively but his fringy arm and range make him best suited to second base, where his bat will play nicely. If he continues to mash against the more advanced arms in Double-A, he may find himself in Pittsburgh sooner than you think.

Ke'Bryan Hayes 3B Born: 01/28/97 Age: 25 Bats: R Throws: R Height: 5'10" Weight: 205 lb. Origin: Round 1, 2015 Draft (#32 overall)

YEAR	TEAM	LVL	AGE	PA	R	2B	3B	HR	RBI	BB	K	SB	CS	Whiff%	AVG/OBP/SLG	DRC+	BABIP	BRR	FRAA	WARP
2019	IND	AAA	22	480	64	30	2	10	53	43	90	12	1		.265/.336/.415	96	.311	2.8	3B(104): 10.8	2.3
2020	PIT	MLB	23	95	17	7	2	5	11	9	20	1	0	18.1%	.376/.442/.682	121	.450	0.7	3B(24): 3.5	0.9
2021	IND	AAA	24	26	6	2	0	2	3	2	7	0	0		.250/.308/.583	105	.267	-0.1	3B(4): 0.8	0.2
2021	PIT	MLB	24	396	49	20	2	6	38	31	87	9	1	20.5%	.257/.316/.373	86	.321	1.3	3B(95): 1.8	1.0
2022 DC	*PIT*	*MLB*	*25*	*575*	*75*	*28*	*4*	*12*	*62*	*47*	*118*	*11*	*3*	*20.1%*	*.250/.320/.392*	*91*	*.303*	*0.6*	*3B 3*	*1.0*

Comparables: Jeimer Candelario, Nolan Arenado, Gio Urshela

If you are among those who believe the Pirates are a star-crossed organization, you were certainly not surprised when the new face of the franchise struggled through an injury-tarred season. Hayes started and ended the year dealing with issues in his left wrist and suffered a self-inflicted bone bruise on his right hand when he slammed his helmet in a moment of frustration. How much of Hayes' offensive malaise was due to (a) injuries, (b) normal rookie struggles, or (c) regression to the more mundane numbers he produced prior to his 2020 breakout is hard to say. Whatever the reason, at the plate he morphed into Yandy Díaz without the walks: plenty of hard contact with an extremely high ground-ball rate that eroded his extra-base pop. In the field, Hayes showcased the instincts, range, hands and arm of a future Gold Glover, and his premier defensive chops make him a quality big-leaguer even with a slumbering bat. This summer we'll get closer to finding out how much more than that Hayes can be.

Tucupita Marcano UT Born: 09/16/99 Age: 22 Bats: L Throws: R Height: 6'0" Weight: 170 lb. Origin: International Free Agent, 2016

YEAR	TEAM	LVL	AGE	PA	R	2B	3B	HR	RBI	BB	K	SB	CS	Whiff%	AVG/OBP/SLG	DRC+	BABIP	BRR	FRAA	WARP
2019	FW	A	19	504	55	19	3	2	45	35	45	15	16		.270/.323/.337	107	.293	-4.6	3B(42): -2.0, SS(40): -5.2, 2B(32): 0.6	0.8
2021	IND	AAA	21	210	29	4	1	1	12	26	33	8	1		.230/.325/.279	97	.275	-1.4	2B(34): 0.9, LF(7): 0.9, 3B(4): -0.8	0.5
2021	ELP	AAA	21	202	31	7	2	6	27	27	26	4	4		.273/.366/.442	112	.287	-0.8	LF(12): -1.0, 2B(11): 1.6, SS(11): -0.6	0.9
2021	SD	MLB	21	50	7	1	0	0	3	6	9	0	1	16.9%	.182/.280/.205	90	.229	0.5	2B(8): 0.9, LF(4): -0.3, RF(4): -0.5	0.2
2022 DC	*PIT*	*MLB*	*22*	*65*	*6*	*2*	*0*	*0*	*6*	*6*	*9*	*1*	*1*	*16.6%*	*.230/.306/.319*	*73*	*.265*	*0.1*	*2B 0*	*0.0*

Comparables: Richard Ureña, Luis Sardinas, José Peraza

Marcano came to the Pirates from San Diego as part of the Adam Frazier trade and looks likely to grow into a useful utility piece and table setter. Never mind the bad numbers he put up last year in his big-league debut—the kid had never before played above Low-A. Focus instead on what he did as a 21-year-old in Triple-A. In his first extended exposure to advanced pitching, the speedy Marcano held his own, slashing .251/.345/.358 and walking nearly as much as he whiffed while flashing a steady glove in the dirt and on the grass. He's not going to hit for power, but the slight lefty is an old-school pest at the plate who can work deep counts, draw walks, make contact, leg out infield hits and take the extra base. Marcano has a high baseball IQ, and his broad skillset and defensive versatility make him an ideal bench piece and managerial security blanket.

Colin Moran 1B Born: 10/01/92 Age: 29 Bats: L Throws: R Height: 6'4" Weight: 225 lb. Origin: Round 1, 2013 Draft (#6 overall)

YEAR	TEAM	LVL	AGE	PA	R	2B	3B	HR	RBI	BB	K	SB	CS	Whiff%	AVG/OBP/SLG	DRC+	BABIP	BRR	FRAA	WARP
2019	PIT	MLB	26	503	46	30	1	13	80	30	117	0	1	24.7%	.277/.322/.429	85	.341	-0.6	3B(121): -18.3, 2B(11): 0.2, 1B(8): -0.4	-1.5
2020	PIT	MLB	27	200	28	10	0	10	23	19	52	0	0	28.1%	.247/.325/.472	106	.291	-0.1	1B(22): 0.7, 3B(4): -0.3	0.6
2021	IND	AAA	28	29	4	2	0	2	11	3	7	0	0		.200/.276/.520	103	.176	-0.4	1B(8): 0.0	0.0
2021	PIT	MLB	28	359	29	12	0	10	50	36	87	1	0	27.0%	.258/.334/.390	91	.321	-5.2	1B(84): -2.7, 3B(1): -0.0	-0.4
2022 non-DC	*PIT*	*MLB*	*29*	*251*	*26*	*10*	*0*	*7*	*27*	*22*	*59*	*0*	*0*	*26.5%*	*.239/.314/.386*	*89*	*.294*	*-0.4*	*3B -2, 1B 0*	*0.0*

Comparables: Conor Gillaspie, Juan Francisco, Eduardo Escobar

How's this for a tortured analogy? Moran's Pirates career has been like the second-hand couch you buy when your children are young—cheap and reasonably functional but not exactly something you'd feature in your living room if you didn't have to worry about spit-up and mustard stains. But then the kids get older and can be trusted with nicer things, so you get something snazzier from Hayes & Son and move your old couch down to the rec room. It's the wrong color and doesn't quite fit the space, something that stick-up-the-arse Langner from next door points out when you make the mistake of inviting him over for poker night; they can afford decorators, and the furniture in their basement is nicer than anything you own. But you throw a blanket over the old couch, and the kids can still use it to rest on between ping pong games. Time passes, you get a few promotions, and when the kids head off to college you can afford to turn the basement into your own entertainment space with a wet bar and a pool table and a 75" screen and a signed Andrew McCutchen jersey on the wall, which is way cooler than those creepy framed Nagel prints in the Langners' den—what, do they think it's still 1989? There's no longer any place for the old couch and, though it brings them fond memories of childhood friendships and first kisses, the kids don't want it either. So you throw it in the truck and haul it off to St. Vinny's, and as you make your way back home you can't help but feel a little wistful. It wasn't anything special, but it was a good old couch, and you'll miss it.

Kevin Newman SS Born: 08/04/93 Age: 28 Bats: R Throws: R Height: 6'0" Weight: 185 lb. Origin: Round 1, 2015 Draft (#19 overall)

YEAR	TEAM	LVL	AGE	PA	R	2B	3B	HR	RBI	BB	K	SB	CS	Whiff%	AVG/OBP/SLG	DRC+	BABIP	BRR	FRAA	WARP
2019	IND	AAA	25	35	5	2	0	0	1	5	7	0	1		.233/.343/.300	102	.304	0.6	SS(4): -0.4, LF(2): -0.3, CF(2): -0.0	0.1
2019	PIT	MLB	25	531	61	20	6	12	64	28	62	16	8	13.8%	.308/.353/.446	106	.333	1.4	SS(104): -0.8, 2B(23): 0.2, 3B(6): 0.6	2.5
2020	PIT	MLB	26	172	12	5	0	1	10	12	21	0	1	14.6%	.224/.281/.276	96	.250	-0.3	SS(23): -0.8, 2B(20): 1.3	0.5
2021	PIT	MLB	27	554	50	22	3	5	39	27	41	6	1	11.9%	.226/.265/.309	80	.236	-0.6	SS(132): -3.9, 2B(15): -0.4	0.1
2022 DC	*PIT*	*MLB*	*28*	*432*	*49*	*18*	*2*	*6*	*45*	*24*	*41*	*8*	*4*	*12.8%*	*.263/.311/.367*	*84*	*.282*	*0.5*	*SS -1, 2B 0*	*0.6*

Comparables: Chris Taylor, Jed Lowrie, Darwin Barney

Newman was the most sure-handed middle infielder in baseball last year, making only three errors and posting a .993 fielding percentage at shortstop that was the best in nearly 20 years. His consistency mostly made up for his fringy range, with DRS, UZR and OAA all pegging him among the league's better defenders last year, though our own metrics were considerably less complimentary. None of this was really enough to overcome his anemic bat, however. Newman continues to make consistent contact but it's rarely good contact, ranking in the bottom 5% in exit velocity, barrels and hard hit percentage last year. He rarely walks and hasn't shown any power since his breakthrough 2019 season, which is looking more and more like a fluke. If Newman continues to produce more outs at the plate than he takes away in the field, he's unlikely to remain an everyday option.

Hoy Park 2B Born: 04/07/96 Age: 26 Bats: L Throws: R Height: 6'1" Weight: 175 lb. Origin: International Free Agent, 2014

YEAR	TEAM	LVL	AGE	PA	R	2B	3B	HR	RBI	BB	K	SB	CS	Whiff%	AVG/OBP/SLG	DRC+	BABIP	BRR	FRAA	WARP
2019	TRN	AA	23	487	60	20	6	3	41	57	91	20	10		.272/.363/.370	114	.340	2.8	2B(77): -7.8, SS(30): 1.7	2.2
2021	SOM	AA	25	39	4	1	0	1	3	6	3	3	0		.194/.316/.323	125	.179	0.7	2B(4): -0.2, SS(4): -0.0, 3B(2): -0.1	0.3
2021	SWB	AAA	25	223	44	9	1	10	29	46	46	8	4		.327/.475/.567	135	.397	0.5	2B(23): 2.9, SS(20): -0.6, CF(5): -0.4	1.8
2021	IND	AAA	25	31	2	0	0	0	3	7	7	1	0		.136/.355/.136	102	.188	-0.1	SS(5): 0.9, 2B(2): -0.1, LF(1): -0.2	0.1
2021	PIT	MLB	25	149	16	5	2	3	14	18	38	1	1	25.6%	.197/.299/.339	82	.253	1.7	2B(16): -2.4, 3B(9): -0.5, SS(8): -0.8	0.0
2021	NYY	MLB	25	1	0	0	0	0	0	0	0	0	0	0.0%	.000/.000/.000	96				0.0
2022 DC	*PIT*	*MLB*	*26*	*161*	*19*	*5*	*1*	*2*	*14*	*20*	*37*	*3*	*2*	*24.2%*	*.220/.331/.343*	*85*	*.283*	*0.4*	*2B 0, CF 0*	*0.2*

Comparables: Pedro Florimón, Eric Young Jr., Ehire Adrianza

Traded to the Pirates as half their haul for Clay Holmes, Park has always had speed, contact skills and an ability to work a walk. His sudden power spike as a 25-year-old in Triple-A earned him his first trip to the majors, where big-league pitchers promptly knocked the bat out of his hands. Park doesn't waste at-bats and can play good defense anywhere on the diamond, but he'll need to reproduce the power he showed in Scranton before we can peg him as anything other than a potential utility piece.

★ ★ ★ *2022 Top 101 Prospect* **#38** ★ ★ ★

Liover Peguero SS Born: 12/31/00 Age: 21 Bats: R Throws: R Height: 6'1" Weight: 200 lb. Origin: International Free Agent, 2017

YEAR	TEAM	LVL	AGE	PA	R	2B	3B	HR	RBI	BB	K	SB	CS	Whiff%	AVG/OBP/SLG	DRC+	BABIP	BRR	FRAA	WARP
2019	MIS	ROA	18	156	34	7	3	5	27	12	34	8	1		.364/.410/.559		.448			
2019	HIL	SS	18	93	13	4	2	0	11	8	17	3	1		.262/.333/.357		.328			
2021	GBO	A+	20	417	67	19	2	14	45	33	105	28	6		.270/.332/.444	96	.337	-0.6	SS(86): 8.1	1.7
2022 non-DC	*PIT*	*MLB*	*21*	*251*	*21*	*10*	*1*	*4*	*22*	*15*	*73*	*8*	*3*	*31.4%*	*.225/.279/.334*	*64*	*.310*	*0.7*	*SS 3*	*0.1*

Comparables: Amed Rosario, Anderson Tejeda, Thairo Estrada

Peguero is a ball of pure energy at the plate, on the field, in the clubhouse, on the team bus, at the drive-thru window and in front of a microphone. He's lean, athletic and fast, with quick hands that help him make consistent hard contact and more than enough range and arm for the left side of the infield. As one of the youngest players in High-A, Peguero more than held his own last year and began tapping into some of his raw power, flashing the possibility of 20+ knocks some day. His double-plus personality and infectious exuberance can only help his career, as he's the kind of guy everyone wants to have on their team. Peguero still needs to slow the game down a bit in the field and prove he can hit more advanced pitching, but it's easy to picture him schmoozing his way into PNC with a quickness.

Michael Perez C Born: 08/07/92 Age: 29 Bats: L Throws: R Height: 5'10" Weight: 195 lb. Origin: Round 5, 2011 Draft (#154 overall)

YEAR	TEAM	LVL	AGE	PA	R	2B	3B	HR	RBI	BB	K	SB	CS	Whiff%	AVG/OBP/SLG	DRC+	BABIP	BRR	FRAA	WARP
2019	DUR	AAA	26	216	23	7	0	13	42	28	51	0	2		.245/.338/.495	113	.258	0.3	C(44): 0.6	1.3
2019	TB	MLB	26	55	6	5	0	0	2	8	19	0	0	40.9%	.217/.345/.326	72	.370	-1.1	C(20): 0.1, 1B(2): 0.0	-0.1
2020	TB	MLB	27	93	7	3	0	1	13	7	27	0	0	30.0%	.167/.237/.238	68	.228	-1.1	C(38): -0.2, 1B(1): 0.1	-0.1
2021	SAN	WIN	28	62	6	3	0	1	6	15	11	0	0		.178/.403/.311		.212			
2021	PIT	MLB	28	231	19	8	1	7	21	19	68	0	1	27.3%	.143/.221/.290	68	.170	-0.9	C(58): -3.4	-0.4
2022 DC	*PIT*	*MLB*	*29*	*187*	*19*	*7*	*0*	*4*	*20*	*15*	*51*	*0*	*0*	*28.0%*	*.203/.276/.341*	*62*	*.262*	*-0.2*	*C -4*	*-0.5*

Comparables: Martín Maldonado, Sandy León, Juan Centeno

YEAR	TEAM	P. COUNT	FRM RUNS	BLK RUNS	THRW RUNS	TOT RUNS
2019	TB	2100	-0.1	0.1	0.1	0.1
2019	DUR	6019	0.3	0.0	0.0	0.3
2020	TB	3701	-0.9	0.0	0.0	-1.0
2021	PIT	8506	-3.2	0.1	-0.3	-3.4
2022	*PIT*	*7215*	*-5.3*	*0.6*	*0.0*	*-4.6*

To say Perez hasn't been able to hit his way out of a wet paper bag recently is to oversell the structural integrity of wet paper bags. Over the last two seasons he's dominated the league trailerboard in OPS, batting average and BABIP, making Austin Hedges look like Willie Mays. He's also inexpensive and has a reputation for solid defense, which means he meets the minimum membership requirements for the International Brotherhood of Backup Catchers. As long as the pitching staff is comfortable with him and he blocks most throws before they reach the backstop, Perez will keep finding work as a reserve receiver.

Roberto Pérez C Born: 12/23/88 Age: 33 Bats: R Throws: R Height: 5'11" Weight: 220 lb. Origin: Round 33, 2008 Draft (#1011 overall)

YEAR	TEAM	LVL	AGE	PA	R	2B	3B	HR	RBI	BB	K	SB	CS	Whiff%	AVG/OBP/SLG	DRC+	BABIP	BRR	FRAA	WARP
2019	CLE	MLB	30	449	46	9	1	24	63	45	127	0	0	30.4%	.239/.321/.452	98	.285	-0.8	C(118): 11.6	2.9
2020	CLE	MLB	31	110	6	2	0	1	5	11	38	0	0	30.1%	.165/.264/.216	68	.259	-0.3	C(32): 2.0	0.1
2021	COL	AAA	32	31	3	0	0	0	3	6	7	0	0		.125/.290/.125	95	.167	0.0	C(9): -0.2	0.1
2021	CLE	MLB	32	161	13	3	0	7	17	17	56	1	0	35.6%	.149/.245/.319	82	.179	-1.0	C(43): 0.7, 1B(1): 0.1	0.3
2022 DC	*PIT*	*MLB*	*33*	*379*	*39*	*13*	*0*	*10*	*40*	*40*	*120*	*0*	*1*	*32.2%*	*.191/.284/.329*	*64*	*.264*	*-0.5*	*C 9*	*0.8*

Comparables: Martín Maldonado, Sandy León, Jose Lobaton

YEAR	TEAM	P. COUNT	FRM RUNS	BLK RUNS	THRW RUNS	TOT RUNS
2019	CLE	16305	10.3	1.3	0.2	11.7
2020	CLE	4053	1.7	0.0	0.4	2.1
2021	CLE	6015	-0.2	0.2	-0.2	-0.2
2022	*PIT*	*14430*	*7.2*	*2.5*	*-0.4*	*9.3*

Pérez lost another season to injury, and we've now lost sight of his improbable age-30 breakout in our rear-view mirror. He wasn't the only player to apparently benefit from the trampoline ball MLB instituted in 2019. Besides, the bulk of Pérez's value is tied not to his performance in the chalk-outlined box beside the plate but to his elite work behind it. In theory, that is. In practice, Pérez was mediocre, following up one turbulent season with another, with his putrid offense rendering his aggregate contributions firmly below-average. The wheels could not have fallen off at a worse time. A bullish team may bet on a fully healthy Pérez to rebound and generate meager surplus in his usual part-time duty. Cleveland opted not to pick up Pérez's team-friendly option and Pittsburgh emerged as that bullish team.

Gregory Polanco RF Born: 09/14/91 Age: 30 Bats: L Throws: L Height: 6'5" Weight: 240 lb. Origin: International Free Agent, 2009

YEAR	TEAM	LVL	AGE	PA	R	2B	3B	HR	RBI	BB	K	SB	CS	Whiff%	AVG/OBP/SLG	DRC+	BABIP	BRR	FRAA	WARP
2019	IND	AAA	27	54	5	4	0	1	11	9	16	2	0		.267/.389/.422	97	.393	1.2	RF(8): -1.4	0.1
2019	PIT	MLB	27	167	23	8	1	6	17	12	49	3	1	32.3%	.242/.301/.425	81	.316	0.3	RF(36): 0.2	0.1
2020	ESC	WIN	28	87	4	3	1	2	9	8	18	2	0		.197/.276/.342		.224			
2020	PIT	MLB	28	174	12	6	0	7	22	13	65	3	1	43.0%	.153/.214/.325	63	.193	-0.7	RF(39): 0.5	-0.3
2021	BUF	AAA	29	101	15	7	0	9	24	8	19	5	0		.374/.436/.747	143	.397	0.5	RF(17): -1.5, CF(3): 0.5	0.8
2021	PIT	MLB	29	382	38	12	2	11	36	36	104	14	1	30.6%	.208/.283/.354	78	.258	2.2	RF(92): -1.6	0.1
2022 DC	*FA*	*MLB*	*30*	*276*	*31*	*11*	*0*	*11*	*36*	*25*	*77*	*5*	*2*	*31.7%*	*.227/.304/.424*	*93*	*.280*	*0.3*	*RF 1, CF 0*	*0.6*

Comparables: Bobby Abreu, Jermaine Dye, Reggie Jackson

The Pirates released Polanco last August in one of the few potential cost-cutting, let-the-kids-play moves their long-suffering fans didn't criticize, though the league didn't bite and Pittsburgh is still on the hook for El Coffee's buyout. It was a difficult parting long in the making, as the ebullient Polanco has never been the same since shoulder surgery in 2018, slashing .203/.270/.364 over the last three years. Declining a spring training invite with the Blue Jays to play for the Yomiuri Giants, Polanco faces a tough climb to get back to who he once was, though the $36 million he's earned in his career to date hopefully takes away some of the sting.

Bryan Reynolds CF Born: 01/27/95 Age: 27 Bats: S Throws: R Height: 6'3" Weight: 210 lb. Origin: Round 2, 2016 Draft (#59 overall)

YEAR	TEAM	LVL	AGE	PA	R	2B	3B	HR	RBI	BB	K	SB	CS	Whiff%	AVG/OBP/SLG	DRC+	BABIP	BRR	FRAA	WARP
2019	IND	AAA	24	57	10	1	1	5	11	7	11	3	2		.367/.446/.735	148	.394	-0.9	CF(13): -1.6	0.3
2019	PIT	MLB	24	546	83	37	4	16	68	46	121	3	2	26.2%	.314/.377/.503	106	.387	1.4	LF(79): -1.2, RF(31): 0.1, CF(25): -2.2	2.1
2020	PIT	MLB	25	208	24	6	2	7	19	21	57	1	1	27.8%	.189/.275/.357	86	.231	-2.1	LF(37): 4.3, CF(17): 1.2	0.6
2021	PIT	MLB	26	646	93	35	8	24	90	75	119	5	2	23.7%	.302/.390/.522	127	.345	1.4	CF(137): -4.8, LF(17): -0.5	4.5
2022 DC	*PIT*	*MLB*	*27*	*595*	*87*	*29*	*5*	*20*	*82*	*63*	*120*	*3*	*3*	*24.1%*	*.278/.365/.468*	*125*	*.330*	*0.0*	*CF 0, LF 1*	*4.0*

Comparables: Charlie Blackmon, Hunter Pence, AJ Pollock

To misquote Whistler, who misattributed Wilde, who in turn misattributed Shaw: Reynolds' bounceback season in Pittsburgh was like a stream of bat's pee, shining out like a shaft of gold when all around was dark. The young switch-hitter showed that his sophomore slump was merely a speed bump on the road to stardom by once again squaring up everything in sight while pacing all NL center fielders in WARP. Reynolds isn't a true slugger but is one of the game's better pure hitters, making consistent hard contact from both sides of the plate and accepting his walks when he doesn't see a pitch he can drive. He's a solid, occasionally spectacular center fielder and plus baserunner who does it all with such an unassuming nature that if he started talking about dry lines and derechos you'd swear he was Mike Trout. An All-Star for the first time last year, you can expect Reynolds to continue competing for batting titles and checking in at the Midsummer Classic.

Yoshi Tsutsugo 1B Born: 11/26/91 Age: 30 Bats: L Throws: R Height: 6'1" Weight: 225 lb. Origin: International Free Agent, 2019

YEAR	TEAM	LVL	AGE	PA	R	2B	3B	HR	RBI	BB	K	SB	CS	Whiff%	AVG/OBP/SLG	DRC+	BABIP	BRR	FRAA	WARP
2020	TB	MLB	28	185	27	5	1	8	24	26	50	0	0	23.2%	.197/.314/.395	92	.230	0.6	LF(16): -0.4, 3B(14): -2.6	0.1
2021	OKC	AAA	29	180	28	7	0	10	32	26	32	0	0		.257/.361/.507	121	.252	-0.5	LF(22): -0.1, 1B(19): -2.0	0.8
2021	PIT	MLB	29	144	20	8	1	8	25	15	33	0	1	25.9%	.268/.347/.535	106	.299	-2.7	RF(20): -1.3, 1B(15): 0.5, LF(2): 0.1	0.2
2021	LAD	MLB	29	31	2	0	0	0	2	6	12	0	0	34.6%	.120/.290/.120	69	.231	-0.1	LF(8): 0.5	0.0
2021	TB	MLB	29	87	5	4	0	0	5	8	27	0	0	26.7%	.167/.244/.218	67	.255	-0.8	1B(15): -0.9	-0.3
2022 DC	*PIT*	*MLB*	*30*	*479*	*72*	*22*	*1*	*23*	*68*	*59*	*112*	*0*	*1*	*25.5%*	*.245/.344/.468*	*113*	*.283*	*-0.7*	*1B -1, LF 1*	*1.8*

Comparables: Lucas Duda, JB Shuck, Ezequiel Carrera

Tsutsugo bounced around a couple analytically inclined teams before landing in Pittsburgh in the middle of last season, so of course it was there that he looked like the guy Tampa Bay originally invested in and Los Angeles claimed on waivers. His Pirates slash line looks a lot more like his minor-league and NPB numbers than his prior major-league figures, though they came in fewer plate appearances. Cognizance of recency bias would tell us not to overweight the recent performance, but the underlying skillset has always been there for Tsutsugo to be the above-average major leaguer he was in The Steel City. If his performance sticks, they might need to update the moniker to Steal City.

Cole Tucker UT Born: 07/03/96 Age: 26 Bats: S Throws: R Height: 6'3" Weight: 205 lb. Origin: Round 1, 2014 Draft (#24 overall)

YEAR	TEAM	LVL	AGE	PA	R	2B	3B	HR	RBI	BB	K	SB	CS	Whiff%	AVG/OBP/SLG	DRC+	BABIP	BRR	FRAA	WARP
2019	IND	AAA	22	353	51	15	4	8	28	38	73	11	3		.261/.346/.413	99	.319	0.9	SS(70): -5.3, 2B(6): 0.6	1.1
2019	PIT	MLB	22	159	16	10	3	2	13	10	40	0	0	25.9%	.211/.266/.361	76	.276	1.5	SS(45): -1.0	0.1
2020	PIT	MLB	23	116	17	3	0	1	8	5	31	1	0	30.5%	.220/.252/.275	74	.295	1.5	CF(20): -1.9, RF(16): -1.6, 2B(1): -0.0	-0.2
2021	IND	AAA	24	263	33	11	2	6	20	41	58	9	3		.223/.350/.373	107	.276	-0.6	SS(48): 3.9, RF(7): -1.2, 2B(4): -0.7	1.1
2021	PIT	MLB	24	131	15	4	2	2	12	13	33	2	2	26.3%	.222/.298/.342	81	.289	-1.1	SS(17): -2.1, RF(12): -0.9, 2B(9): -0.6	-0.3
2022 DC	*PIT*	*MLB*	*25*	*298*	*33*	*12*	*2*	*4*	*29*	*27*	*74*	*9*	*4*	*26.6%*	*.219/.299/.341*	*71*	*.288*	*1.0*	*2B 0, SS 0*	*-0.1*

Comparables: Jonathan Villar, J.P. Crawford, Tyler Wade

Tucker has long possessed most of the tools he needs to build a big-league career: speed, athleticism, good hands, a patient approach, solid makeup, a talent for chatting up celebrities during Zoom meditation group meetings and plus-plus flow modeled after some Tony Alva action shot in a vintage issue of SkateBoarder magazine. What he's lacked is the ability to make hard contact, so when Tucker failed to go north out of spring training he spent time working to better leverage his long levers and lower half to pump a little juice into his swing. It's still a work in progress, but Tucker showed a little more pop after his late-season call-up and flashed noticeable leather all over the field. He's unlikely to grow into even average power or become the first-division shortstop his draft slot presaged, but his combination of walks, defensive versatility and clubhouse presence can make him a nice utility piece.

PITCHERS

Anthony Banda LHP Born: 08/10/93 Age: 28 Bats: L Throws: L Height: 6'2" Weight: 230 lb. Origin: Round 10, 2012 Draft (#335 overall)

YEAR	TEAM	LVL	AGE	W	L	SV	G	GS	IP	H	HR	BB/9	K/9	K	GB%	BABIP	WHIP	ERA	DRA-	WARP	MPH	FB%	Whiff%	CSP
2019	DUR	AAA	25	2	3	0	9	4	28^{1}	28	7	3.5	8.6	27	38.3%	.288	1.38	6.04	103	0.3				
2019	TB	MLB	25	0	0	0	3	0	4	6	0	0.0	4.5	2	25.0%	.375	1.50	6.75	133	0.0	92.8	55.9%	6.2%	53.6%
2020	TB	MLB	26	1	0	1	4	0	7	10	1	6.4	5.1	4	52.0%	.375	2.14	10.29	129	0.0	92.7	42.4%	23.6%	45.1%
2021	SYR	AAA	27	1	0	0	3	0	10^{1}	9	2	1.7	8.7	10	50.0%	.250	1.06	5.23	93	0.2				
2021	SAC	AAA	27	3	2	0	10	5	39^{1}	52	7	4.1	9.6	42	47.2%	.385	1.78	6.86	80	0.6				
2021	NYM	MLB	27	1	0	0	5	0	7^{1}	14	2	1.2	8.6	7	37.9%	.444	2.05	7.36	99	0.1	93.9	49.6%	23.3%	59.6%
2021	PIT	MLB	27	1	2	0	25	0	26^{1}	25	4	4.1	8.5	25	39.0%	.288	1.41	3.42	107	0.1	94.3	47.9%	26.9%	54.2%
2022 DC	*PIT*	*MLB*	*28*	*3*	*3*	*0*	*67*	*0*	*58*	*61*	*8*	*3.4*	*7.9*	*51*	*42.3%*	*.310*	*1.43*	*4.86*	*114*	*-0.2*	*94.0*	*47.7%*	*25.2%*	*54.0%*

Comparables: Billy Traber, Alex Claudio, Kyle Ryan

Now several years past Tommy John surgery, Banda saw his fastball tick back up into the mid-90s last year but still posted a stratospheric ERA in Triple-A, earning tickets out of both San Francisco and Queens. The desperate Pirates took a late-summer flyer on him as a potential bulk reliever, and the lefty rewarded them with his best stretch of innings since the Obama administration. Banda's changeup can still flash plus, but like most bullpen filler his fastball command comes and goes—it comes over the heart of the plate and goes a long way. That's not a recipe for long-term success.

David Bednar RHP

Born: 10/10/94 Age: 27 Bats: L Throws: R Height: 6'1" Weight: 245 lb. Origin: Round 35, 2016 Draft (#1044 overall)

YEAR	TEAM	LVL	AGE	W	L	SV	G	GS	IP	H	HR	BB/9	K/9	K	GB%	BABIP	WHIP	ERA	DRA-	WARP	MPH	FB%	Whiff%	CSP
2019	AMA	AA	24	2	5	14	44	0	58	49	4	2.8	13.3	86	46.6%	.354	1.16	2.95	61	1.4				
2019	SD	MLB	24	0	2	0	13	0	11	10	3	4.1	11.5	14	27.6%	.292	1.36	6.55	101	0.1	95.5	43.4%	32.6%	51.6%
2020	SD	MLB	25	0	0	0	4	0	6^1	11	1	2.8	7.1	5	36.0%	.417	2.05	7.11	129	0.0	95.6	59.3%	27.7%	52.0%
2021	PIT	MLB	26	3	1	3	61	0	60^2	40	5	2.8	11.4	77	42.1%	.259	0.97	2.23	73	1.4	96.9	55.8%	32.6%	56.1%
2022 DC	*PIT*	*MLB*	*27*	*3*	*3*	*8*	*67*	*0*	*58*	*47*	*7*	*3.3*	*10.8*	*70*	*40.7%*	*.289*	*1.19*	*3.30*	*83*	*0.7*	*96.7*	*55.3%*	*32.2%*	*55.5%*

Comparables: Giovanny Gallegos, AJ Ramos, Steve Cishek

Most 20-somethings would be disappointed if work forced them to abandon San Diego for Pittsburgh, but for Bednar it was the best thing that ever happened to him. Not only was the West Pennsylvania native going home after his inclusion in the Joe Musgrove trade, but he would finally get an opportunity for regular work with the pitching-starved Pirates. Breaking out "Renegade" for his walk-up tune ensured his fellow yinzers would embrace him, while breaking out a suddenly dominant curveball helped him earn higher-leverage innings. Bednar used better command of his four-seamer, which now ticks into the upper nineties, to get ahead of hitters and leave them flailing helplessly at his curve and splitter. He was closing games by season's end, and Bednar's combination of high heat and wipeout breakers should have him working late for years to come.

Steven Brault LHP

Born: 04/29/92 Age: 30 Bats: L Throws: L Height: 6'0" Weight: 195 lb. Origin: Round 11, 2013 Draft (#339 overall)

YEAR	TEAM	LVL	AGE	W	L	SV	G	GS	IP	H	HR	BB/9	K/9	K	GB%	BABIP	WHIP	ERA	DRA-	WARP	MPH	FB%	Whiff%	CSP
2019	PIT	MLB	27	4	6	0	25	19	113^1	117	15	4.2	7.9	100	42.7%	.313	1.50	5.16	108	0.7	92.2	64.3%	23.3%	46.4%
2020	PIT	MLB	28	1	3	0	11	10	42^2	29	2	4.6	8.0	38	49.6%	.243	1.20	3.38	107	0.3	92.3	50.7%	23.9%	44.4%
2021	IND	AAA	29	0	1	0	3	3	11	6	2	0.8	7.4	9	53.6%	.154	0.64	1.64	111	0.1				
2021	PIT	MLB	29	0	3	0	7	7	27^2	33	3	3.9	6.2	19	42.1%	.330	1.63	5.86	128	-0.2	90.9	53.8%	20.7%	51.9%
2022 non-DC	*PIT*	*MLB*	*30*	*2*	*3*	*0*	*57*	*0*	*50*	*52*	*6*	*4.2*	*7.2*	*39*	*45.2%*	*.305*	*1.52*	*5.19*	*120*	*-0.3*	*91.8*	*57.1%*	*22.7%*	*47.4%*

Comparables: Wade Miley, Jason Vargas, Eric Stults

Brault was the best Pirates starter in 2020—a fact that is less a celebration of Brault's recent effectiveness than an indictment of Pittsburgh's rotation—but was unable to build on his newfound success during an injury-plagued 2021. A left lat strain kept him on the shelf until August, and its recurrence brought the curtain down on his season in mid-September. In between, the creative force behind *A Pitch To Broadway* made seven forgettable starts that featured a continued reliance on the changeup that had been a big part of his solid pandemic year along with a fastball that was down a tick. He's never missed a lot of bats and issues more free passes than your average pitch-to-contact survivor, so a healthy Brault continues to profile more as a swingman than a rotation mainstay. Dude does have a great set of pipes, though, and making an album with Vinnie Colaiuta is likely cooler than anything he'll ever do between the lines.

JT Brubaker RHP

Born: 11/17/93 Age: 28 Bats: R Throws: R Height: 6'3" Weight: 180 lb. Origin: Round 6, 2015 Draft (#187 overall)

YEAR	TEAM	LVL	AGE	W	L	SV	G	GS	IP	H	HR	BB/9	K/9	K	GB%	BABIP	WHIP	ERA	DRA-	WARP	MPH	FB%	Whiff%	CSP
2019	WV	SS	25	0	0	0	2	2	6^2	5	0	5.4	5.4	4	42.1%	.263	1.35	1.35						
2019	IND	AAA	25	2	1	0	4	4	21	19	2	1.7	8.6	20	52.5%	.298	1.10	2.57	97	0.3				
2020	PIT	MLB	26	1	3	0	11	9	47^1	48	6	3.2	9.1	48	47.4%	.321	1.37	4.94	86	0.9	93.9	49.8%	27.6%	46.1%
2021	PIT	MLB	27	5	13	0	24	24	124^1	123	28	2.8	9.3	129	42.8%	.289	1.29	5.36	93	1.6	93.3	49.1%	27.4%	55.7%
2022 DC	*PIT*	*MLB*	*28*	*7*	*6*	*0*	*22*	*22*	*113.3*	*106*	*15*	*2.7*	*8.7*	*108*	*44.4%*	*.294*	*1.24*	*3.88*	*95*	*1.2*	*93.4*	*49.3%*	*27.5%*	*53.6%*

Comparables: Lance Lynn, Chris Stratton, Corey Kluber

Maybe it wasn't as bad as it looked. Brubaker began the season as a perfectly acceptable starter, holding opponents to a .238/.295/.407 line in his first 13 starts while allowing 11 home runs. After June 21st, however, the league hit .274/.349/.575 off him, including 17 big flies in only 52 ⅔ innings. It's tempting to explain the difference by noting that the league began cracking down on foreign substances at that split point. Brubaker's fastball did lose some spin and generate fewer whiffs, but his slider was equally complicit during his late-season gopher ball frenzy. He suffered the league's highest rate of home runs per fly ball among pitchers with at least 60 innings, a notoriously fickle metric, but a relatively low percentage of them were no-doubters. Brubaker has a deep arsenal that should support multiple trips through the order, and our DRA– metric pegged him as an average starter last year despite all the bombs. He's a reasonable bet to bounce back and earn his keep at the back-end of the rotation.

★ ★ ★ *2022 Top 101 Prospect* **#89** ★ ★ ★

Roansy Contreras RHP
Born: 11/07/99 Age: 22 Bats: R Throws: R Height: 6'0" Weight: 175 lb. Origin: International Free Agent, 2016

YEAR	TEAM	LVL	AGE	W	L	SV	G	GS	IP	H	HR	BB/9	K/9	K	GB%	BABIP	WHIP	ERA	DRA-	WARP	MPH	FB%	Whiff%	CSP
2019	CSC	A	19	12	5	0	24	24	132^{1}	105	10	2.4	7.7	113	39.9%	.256	1.07	3.33	101	1.0				
2021	ALT	AA	21	3	2	0	12	12	54^{1}	37	5	2.0	12.6	76	48.4%	.267	0.90	2.65	83	0.9				
2021	PIT	MLB	21	0	0	0	1	1	3	3	0	3.0	12.0	4	57.1%	.429	1.33	0.00	84	0.1	96.7	63.0%	27.3%	55.1%
2022 DC	*PIT*	*MLB*	*22*	*1*	*1*	*0*	*6*	*6*	*29*	*26*	*3*	*3.1*	*9.4*	*30*	*41.8%*	*.297*	*1.26*	*3.81*	*94*	*0.3*	*96.7*	*63.0%*	*27.3%*	*55.1%*

Comparables: Alex Cobb, Rafael Soriano, Wade Davis

Chins up, Pirates fans. Pitching help is just over the horizon, some of it in the form of an ex-Yankees farmhand who just dominated Double-A as a 21-year-old. Contreras came to the Buccos as part of the Jameson Taillon trade and wasted no time implementing the improved arsenal he's developed since we last saw him as a slight teenager in High-A. The young Dominican doesn't have an ideal starter's frame, but he's added strength and a few ticks to his fastball, which now sits comfortably in the mid-90s with great life. His curveball flashes plus, his *cambio* has improved, he repeats his delivery and he competes well on the mound. Contreras lost two months to forearm soreness but came back to pitch down the stretch and make a brief cameo at PNC. He's more likely a mid-rotation starter than an ace, but Contreras will likely be the most talented member of the rotation when he is called up to stay next year. Now, if only the Pirates can remember not to ship him to Tampa if he struggles.

Wil Crowe RHP
Born: 09/09/94 Age: 27 Bats: R Throws: R Height: 6'2" Weight: 235 lb. Origin: Round 2, 2017 Draft (#65 overall)

YEAR	TEAM	LVL	AGE	W	L	SV	G	GS	IP	H	HR	BB/9	K/9	K	GB%	BABIP	WHIP	ERA	DRA-	WARP	MPH	FB%	Whiff%	CSP
2019	HBG	AA	24	7	6	0	16	16	95^{1}	85	8	2.1	8.4	89	48.1%	.297	1.12	3.87	96	1.0				
2019	FRE	AAA	24	0	4	0	10	10	54	66	7	4.3	6.8	41	41.2%	.337	1.70	6.17	114	-0.1				
2020	WAS	MLB	25	0	2	0	3	3	8^{1}	14	5	8.6	8.6	8	27.6%	.375	2.64	11.88	171	-0.2	91.7	57.2%	19.4%	40.5%
2021	PIT	MLB	26	4	8	0	26	25	116^{2}	126	25	4.4	8.6	111	43.1%	.314	1.57	5.48	106	0.7	93.7	46.7%	25.5%	54.0%
2022 DC	*PIT*	*MLB*	*27*	*8*	*7*	*0*	*58*	*14*	*108.7*	*107*	*16*	*4.1*	*8.1*	*97*	*42.8%*	*.295*	*1.44*	*4.79*	*111*	*0.2*	*93.5*	*47.3%*	*25.2%*	*53.3%*

Comparables: David Purcey, J.D. Martin, Wade Miley

Crowe came over to the Pirates as part of the Josh Bell trade, and instantly added to Pittsburgh's deep pool of unproven starters entering their late 20s. If only baseball were like Risk, and the Pirates could have traded in Crowe, J.T. Brubaker and Chad Kuhl for one ace or a bunch of armies or something. Instead, Pittsburgh ran them all out last year to sink or swim, with Crowe getting lit up to the tune of .276/.363/.501. Only teammate Mitch Keller and Chi Chi González worked 100+ innings and posted a worse opponents' OPS, and González had the excuse of pitching in Denver. On the plus side, Crowe pitched six innings of one-hit ball in his last start of the year. Hope springs eternal.

Chase De Jong RHP
Born: 12/29/93 Age: 28 Bats: L Throws: R Height: 6'4" Weight: 230 lb. Origin: Round 2, 2012 Draft (#81 overall)

YEAR	TEAM	LVL	AGE	W	L	SV	G	GS	IP	H	HR	BB/9	K/9	K	GB%	BABIP	WHIP	ERA	DRA-	WARP	MPH	FB%	Whiff%	CSP
2019	ROC	AAA	25	0	5	0	13	10	45^{1}	72	16	5.2	6.0	30	30.8%	.361	2.16	9.73	184	-1.4				
2019	MIN	MLB	25	0	0	0	1	0	1	3	1	27.0	0.0	0	33.3%	.400	6.00	36.00	140	0.0	91.0	63.0%	10.0%	46.6%
2020	HOU	MLB	26	0	1	0	3	2	7^{1}	12	2	4.9	11.0	9	33.3%	.455	2.18	14.73	164	-0.2	93.1	46.9%	31.2%	42.3%
2021	IND	AAA	27	2	0	0	4	4	20	16	3	3.6	12.6	28	45.7%	.302	1.20	3.60	95	0.3				
2021	PIT	MLB	27	1	4	0	9	9	43^{2}	49	11	3.9	8.0	39	30.7%	.304	1.56	5.77	122	-0.1	93.0	48.9%	22.3%	56.1%
2022 non-DC	*PIT*	*MLB*	*28*	*2*	*3*	*0*	*57*	*0*	*50*	*52*	*9*	*3.9*	*8.6*	*47*	*33.8%*	*.306*	*1.48*	*5.46*	*124*	*-0.5*	*93.0*	*48.9%*	*23.1%*	*54.4%*

Comparables: Chris Haney, Rick Helling, Jason Vargas

And the beat(down) goes on. There was a time when being mentioned alongside Jake Arrieta was a good thing, but that time is long past, especially when he's listed as the only starter in the Senior Circuit to allow a higher OPS in more innings than you did. Over the nine turns he was able to take between his late-May call-up and his season-ending knee surgery in July, De John allowed a .280/.354/.589 line from opposing batters. He's a former second-round pick by Toronto who has floated through the Dodgers, Mariners, Twins and Astros systems and a stint in the indy leagues. If De Jong continues to fail in Pittsburgh, there are only three ways to go: up, out, or Baltimore.

Sam Howard LHP
Born: 03/05/93 Age: 29 Bats: R Throws: L Height: 6'4" Weight: 195 lb. Origin: Round 3, 2014 Draft (#82 overall)

YEAR	TEAM	LVL	AGE	W	L	SV	G	GS	IP	H	HR	BB/9	K/9	K	GB%	BABIP	WHIP	ERA	DRA-	WARP	MPH	FB%	Whiff%	CSP
2019	ABQ	AAA	26	4	1	1	42	0	50^{2}	50	5	4.1	11.0	62	44.2%	.363	1.44	3.91	80	0.9				
2019	COL	MLB	26	2	0	0	20	0	19	21	5	4.7	10.9	23	38.2%	.333	1.63	6.63	92	0.3	92.7	44.1%	32.8%	43.3%
2020	PIT	MLB	27	2	3	0	22	0	21	17	4	3.9	11.6	27	29.4%	.277	1.24	3.86	106	0.2	92.4	37.4%	35.8%	37.9%
2021	PIT	MLB	28	3	4	0	54	1	45	34	7	6.4	12.0	60	43.3%	.281	1.47	5.60	86	0.7	93.7	43.3%	38.0%	50.2%
2022 DC	*PIT*	*MLB*	*29*	*3*	*3*	*2*	*67*	*0*	*58*	*45*	*8*	*4.7*	*12.0*	*77*	*39.7%*	*.285*	*1.30*	*3.86*	*90*	*0.5*	*93.3*	*42.2%*	*37.0%*	*47.0%*

Comparables: Jason Adam, Wander Suero, Joely Rodríguez

If today's game is struggling to engage fans because there are not enough balls being put into play, Howard is part of the problem. A Three True Outcomes hurler, he walks, whiffs, plunks, or yields homers to fully half the batters he faces. Howard's command is shaky, but his fastball-slider combo is hell on wheels against fellow lefties; righties get a better look at the slide piece and are able to lay off it before putting a hurt on his misplaced heaters. A reliable third pitch would give him a better chance, but he doesn't trust his changeup, leaving him a middle reliever who puts too many men on base and needs to be spotted carefully.

Mitch Keller RHP

Born: 04/04/96 Age: 26 Bats: R Throws: R Height: 6'2" Weight: 220 lb. Origin: Round 2, 2014 Draft (#64 overall)

YEAR	TEAM	LVL	AGE	W	L	SV	G	GS	IP	H	HR	BB/9	K/9	K	GB%	BABIP	WHIP	ERA	DRA-	WARP	MPH	FB%	Whiff%	CSP
2019	IND	AAA	23	7	5	0	19	19	103^2	94	9	3.0	10.7	123	43.2%	.331	1.24	3.56	78	2.5				
2019	PIT	MLB	23	1	5	0	11	11	48	72	6	3.0	12.2	65	39.3%	.478	1.83	7.13	74	1.2	95.3	59.4%	26.6%	49.9%
2020	PIT	MLB	24	1	1	0	5	5	21^2	9	4	7.5	6.6	16	42.3%	.104	1.25	2.91	129	-0.1	94.2	55.9%	21.2%	43.6%
2021	IND	AAA	25	1	1	0	8	6	28	27	2	4.2	12.5	39	56.0%	.342	1.43	3.21	83	0.6				
2021	PIT	MLB	25	5	11	0	23	23	100^2	131	10	4.4	8.2	92	39.4%	.392	1.79	6.17	116	0.0	94.0	56.8%	20.5%	57.0%
2022 DC	*PIT*	*MLB*	*26*	*6*	*6*	*0*	*31*	*17*	*93*	*93*	*11*	*4.3*	*8.9*	*91*	*42.5%*	*.314*	*1.47*	*4.86*	*111*	*0.2*	*94.2*	*57.0%*	*21.4%*	*54.7%*

Comparables: Danny Duffy, Reynaldo López, Anthony Swarzak

Keller bounced back from last year's oblique injury to take 29 spins in the rotation, although six of them were in Indianapolis, as the former top prospect was arguably the least effective starter in the majors last year. He pitched reasonably well during his head-clearing trip to Triple-A but struggled mightily both before and after, alternating between solid outings and disasterpieces. Keller posted a 10% walk rate that his mundane strikeout rate couldn't paper over and grooved far too many fastballs, and his once-vaunted curveball hasn't been a weapon, leading to a career BABIP of .385 that isn't just bad luck. Keller needs to command his fastball up in the zone and either get more mileage from his curve or ditch it entirely in deference to his slider if he wants to meet his mid-rotation destiny.

Max Kranick RHP

Born: 07/21/97 Age: 24 Bats: R Throws: R Height: 6'3" Weight: 210 lb. Origin: Round 11, 2016 Draft (#345 overall)

YEAR	TEAM	LVL	AGE	W	L	SV	G	GS	IP	H	HR	BB/9	K/9	K	GB%	BABIP	WHIP	ERA	DRA-	WARP	MPH	FB%	Whiff%	CSP
2019	BRD	A+	21	6	7	0	20	20	109^1	100	11	2.5	6.4	78	41.9%	.276	1.19	3.79	111	0.7				
2021	ALT	AA	23	1	0	0	3	3	15^2	14	2	1.1	9.2	16	38.6%	.286	1.02	4.02	107	0.1				
2021	IND	AAA	23	4	4	0	12	12	54^1	53	6	2.7	7.5	45	35.1%	.292	1.27	4.14	104	0.6				
2021	PIT	MLB	23	2	3	0	9	9	38^2	47	4	4.4	7.4	32	32.3%	.352	1.71	6.28	129	-0.3	94.5	48.5%	26.0%	50.3%
2022 DC	*PIT*	*MLB*	*24*	*6*	*7*	*0*	*33*	*19*	*92.3*	*100*	*15*	*3.4*	*7.1*	*73*	*35.4%*	*.305*	*1.46*	*5.31*	*123*	*-0.4*	*94.5*	*48.5%*	*26.0%*	*50.3%*

Comparables: Reynaldo López, Anthony Swarzak, Kyle Drabek

Kranick's big-league debut in June was a dream come true, as the Pennsylvania native twirled five perfect innings in St. Louis before the rains came to wash away his chance at baseball immortality (or, for the less sentimental, to ensure he'd exit before the Cardinals inevitably figured him out). The rest of his big-league starts were considerably more prosaic, as Krasnick was lit up in all but one of his other eight turns and bounced back and forth from Triple-A. He's a strike-thrower with a low-spin mid-90s heater and a four-pitch mix, none of which are plus, who might (but probably won't) survive at the back of the rotation. But for part of one glorious summer afternoon, Max Kranick was as good as any pitcher in baseball history.

Chad Kuhl RHP

Born: 09/10/92 Age: 29 Bats: R Throws: R Height: 6'3" Weight: 205 lb. Origin: Round 9, 2013 Draft (#269 overall)

YEAR	TEAM	LVL	AGE	W	L	SV	G	GS	IP	H	HR	BB/9	K/9	K	GB%	BABIP	WHIP	ERA	DRA-	WARP	MPH	FB%	Whiff%	CSP
2020	PIT	MLB	27	2	3	0	11	9	46^1	35	8	5.4	8.5	44	41.8%	.239	1.36	4.27	107	0.3	94.1	43.9%	27.0%	44.2%
2021	IND	AAA	28	0	0	0	2	2	6^1	2	0	4.3	12.8	9	50.0%	.167	0.79	1.42	102	0.1				
2021	PIT	MLB	28	5	7	0	28	14	80^1	73	13	4.7	8.4	75	43.9%	.288	1.43	4.82	106	0.5	94.4	38.4%	27.0%	53.5%
2022 DC	*FA*	*MLB*	*29*	*7*	*7*	*0*	*44*	*16*	*100.7*	*95*	*14*	*4.5*	*9.5*	*106*	*42.5%*	*.304*	*1.44*	*4.77*	*110*	*0.2*	*94.4*	*39.8%*	*27.0%*	*51.0%*

Comparables: Tyler Chatwood, Scott Baker, Kevin Slowey

When Kuhl tested positive for COVID after making 14 starts through July, he had held opposing hitters to a .753 OPS, which (embarrassingly enough) was the best of any Pittsburgh starter last year. Once he returned, the organization moved him to the 'pen for the dual purposes of limiting his innings in his first full year after Tommy John surgery and seeing if his stuff would play up in a relief role. Spoiler alert: It didn't, as Kuhl was hammered to the tune of a 1.037 OPS the rest of the way. Kuhl is among the most slider-reliant pitchers in baseball, but hitters have been able to wait him out and hammer his errant fastballs. Well-spotted heaters are the key to every pitcher's success, and without them Kuhl is destined to be bullpen filler.

Nick Mears RHP

Born: 10/07/96 Age: 25 Bats: R Throws: R Height: 6'2" Weight: 200 lb. Origin: Undrafted Free Agent, 2018

YEAR	TEAM	LVL	AGE	W	L	SV	G	GS	IP	H	HR	BB/9	K/9	K	GB%	BABIP	WHIP	ERA	DRA-	WARP	MPH	FB%	Whiff%	CSP
2019	GBO	A	22	1	1	0	7	0	11^2	5	2	5.4	14.7	19	55.0%	.167	1.03	3.09	87	0.2				
2019	BRD	A+	22	4	2	5	23	0	30	22	3	2.7	12.9	43	44.9%	.292	1.03	3.60	75	0.7				
2019	ALT	AA	22	0	0	0	4	0	5	4	0	3.6	12.6	7	30.8%	.308	1.20	1.80	88	0.1				
2020	PIT	MLB	23	0	0	0	4	0	5	4	1	12.6	12.6	7	41.7%	.273	2.20	5.40	111	0.0	96.0	68.4%	40.8%	38.0%
2021	IND	AAA	24	2	2	1	17	0	18^2	16	2	4.3	12.1	25	32.6%	.326	1.34	5.30	79	0.5				
2021	PIT	MLB	24	1	0	0	30	0	23^1	25	5	5.0	8.9	23	39.4%	.303	1.63	5.01	114	0.0	95.9	64.3%	25.1%	51.5%
2022 DC	*PIT*	*MLB*	*25*	*2*	*3*	*0*	*59*	*0*	*51.7*	*47*	*7*	*5.0*	*10.3*	*59*	*39.4%*	*.305*	*1.48*	*4.91*	*111*	*-0.1*	*95.9*	*64.9%*	*27.4%*	*49.6%*

Comparables: Jose Ortega, Cam Hill, Trevor Gott

Elbow surgery, a broken collarbone and the emotional weight of overcoming the sudden deaths of several friends and relatives meant Mears pitched only a single college season, but his impressive work in the Northwoods League earned him notice from scouts and an eventual contract with the Pirates. The Sacramento native can pump gas into the high-90s and has a 12-6 curve which has helped him pile up strikeouts during a meteoric rise in the minors, though his control remains shaky. Mears spent the second half of last year in the Pirates' bullpen, discovering big-league hitters can turn around anyone's fastball if that's all they have to worry about. With seasoning, his arsenal could eventually fit a set-up role.

Carmen Mlodzinski RHP

Born: 02/19/99 Age: 23 Bats: R Throws: R Height: 6'2" Weight: 232 lb. Origin: Round 1, 2020 Draft (#31 overall)

YEAR	TEAM	LVL	AGE	W	L	SV	G	GS	IP	H	HR	BB/9	K/9	K	GB%	BABIP	WHIP	ERA	DRA-	WARP	MPH	FB%	Whiff%	CSP
2021	GBO	A+	22	2	3	0	14	14	50^{1}	45	7	3.6	11.4	64	43.3%	.317	1.29	3.93	81	0.9				
2022 non-DC	*PIT*	*MLB*	*23*	*2*	*3*	*0*	*57*	*0*	*50*	*49*	*7*	*4.8*	*8.7*	*48*	*40.8%*	*.301*	*1.52*	*5.09*	*119*	*-0.3*				

Comparables: Kameron Loe, Danny Duffy, Francis Beltran

Taken with a supplemental first round pick in the 2020 draft by the organization whose fanbase is most likely to pronounce his name correctly, Mlodzinski impressed in his professional debut. As you would expect from a college arm, he carved up High-A with a heavy fastball that can reach the mid-90s and a slider that flashes plus. Then his shoulder started barking, costing him two months of development time; at season's end the Pirates sent him to Triple-A and then the AFL to get him more work. Mlodzinski has a stout frame that should bear up to a starter's workload, but the development of his changeup will say a lot about whether he reaches his mid-rotation ceiling.

Luis Oviedo RHP

Born: 05/15/99 Age: 23 Bats: R Throws: R Height: 6'4" Weight: 235 lb. Origin: International Free Agent, 2015

YEAR	TEAM	LVL	AGE	W	L	SV	G	GS	IP	H	HR	BB/9	K/9	K	GB%	BABIP	WHIP	ERA	DRA-	WARP	MPH	FB%	Whiff%	CSP
2019	LC	A	20	6	6	0	19	19	87	80	6	4.1	7.4	72	41.9%	.294	1.38	5.38	115	0.0				
2021	IND	AAA	22	0	2	0	4	3	9	11	1	6.0	11.0	11	44.4%	.385	1.89	8.00	96	0.1				
2021	PIT	MLB	22	1	2	0	22	1	29^{2}	33	4	7.9	9.4	31	43.2%	.345	1.99	8.80	108	0.1	94.7	50.5%	28.0%	55.5%
2022 DC	*PIT*	*MLB*	*23*	*1*	*1*	*0*	*29*	*0*	*25.7*	*24*	*3*	*6.2*	*8.8*	*25*	*41.4%*	*.294*	*1.64*	*5.62*	*123*	*-0.2*	*94.7*	*50.5%*	*28.0%*	*55.5%*

Comparables: Joey McLaughlin, Miguel Castro, John Boozer

Oviedo was a Rule 5 selection who needed to spend a full year on the 26-man roster, so there's little point in dissecting the woeful numbers he produced as an overmatched youngster who's never pitched in the high minors. Suffice it to say Oviedo threw reasonably hard but usually had no idea where it was going, while mixing in a curve, a slider and a changeup that, if you squint, look like they could amount to something. What that something is will become more clear next year when Oviedo returns to the minors and moves back into the rotation, where he can nurse his wounds and resume a more normal development path.

Dillon Peters LHP

Born: 08/31/92 Age: 29 Bats: L Throws: L Height: 5'11" Weight: 190 lb. Origin: Round 10, 2014 Draft (#287 overall)

YEAR	TEAM	LVL	AGE	W	L	SV	G	GS	IP	H	HR	BB/9	K/9	K	GB%	BABIP	WHIP	ERA	DRA-	WARP	MPH	FB%	Whiff%	CSP
2019	SL	AAA	26	4	1	0	13	11	57	74	11	2.7	8.7	55	49.2%	.366	1.60	6.47	92	0.6				
2019	LAA	MLB	26	4	4	0	17	12	72	85	18	3.3	6.9	55	39.8%	.302	1.54	5.38	134	-0.6	91.0	50.4%	20.4%	47.8%
2020	LAA	MLB	27	0	0	0	1	1	1^{2}	3	2	0.0	10.8	2	14.3%	.200	1.80	16.20	118	0.0	90.6	50.0%	20.0%	51.3%
2021	SL	AAA	28	2	2	0	8	8	41^{1}	47	12	2.8	10.5	48	42.7%	.333	1.45	4.35	96	0.3				
2021	IND	AAA	28	1	0	0	5	2	12	4	2	4.5	11.3	15	36.0%	.087	0.83	1.50	101	0.2				
2021	PIT	MLB	28	1	2	0	6	6	26^{2}	26	2	3.4	7.8	23	48.2%	.296	1.35	3.71	107	0.1	91.1	51.7%	24.6%	54.1%
2022 DC	*PIT*	*MLB*	*29*	*9*	*8*	*0*	*61*	*17*	*115.3*	*115*	*17*	*3.2*	*8.3*	*106*	*43.6%*	*.300*	*1.35*	*4.56*	*109*	*0.3*	*91.1*	*51.0%*	*22.5%*	*51.0%*

Comparables: Chris Rusin, Roenis Elías, Chris Bassitt

The Pirates purchased Peters from the Angels as a late-season rotation tourniquet, and the diminutive lefty managed to staunch the flow over six mostly solid starts. Peters lives and dies by his changeup and curve, which generate ground-ball outs and help keep hitters off his ramrod-straight low-90s fastball. Last year he added a sinker, which might have been the missing ingredient that will hold the soufflé together. Peters doesn't have overpowering stuff, so he walks a fine line, but his latest pitch mix may give him a better chance to stick at the end of the rotation or as a swingman.

Cody Ponce RHP

Born: 04/25/94 Age: 28 Bats: R Throws: R Height: 6'6" Weight: 255 lb. Origin: Round 2, 2015 Draft (#55 overall)

YEAR	TEAM	LVL	AGE	W	L	SV	G	GS	IP	H	HR	BB/9	K/9	K	GB%	BABIP	WHIP	ERA	DRA-	WARP	MPH	FB%	Whiff%	CSP
2019	BLX	AA	25	1	3	1	27	0	38^{1}	33	1	2.8	10.3	44	54.5%	.330	1.17	3.29	75	0.7				
2019	ALT	AA	25	0	0	1	3	1	6	3	1	1.5	9.0	6	40.0%	.143	0.67	6.00	92	0.1				
2019	IND	AAA	25	1	3	0	4	4	18^{2}	18	4	3.4	9.6	20	52.7%	.275	1.34	5.30	85	0.4				
2020	PIT	MLB	26	1	1	0	5	3	17	12	5	3.2	6.4	12	35.4%	.163	1.06	3.18	143	-0.2	93.0	67.5%	19.1%	49.5%
2021	IND	AAA	27	1	4	0	15	8	57^{1}	55	8	2.8	9.3	59	40.1%	.309	1.27	4.71	103	0.7				
2021	PIT	MLB	27	0	6	0	15	2	38^{1}	56	8	2.6	8.5	36	42.7%	.393	1.75	7.04	91	0.5	92.8	60.8%	22.3%	55.1%
2022 non-DC	*PIT*	*MLB*	*28*	*2*	*3*	*0*	*57*	*0*	*50*	*51*	*7*	*3.0*	*7.6*	*42*	*42.2%*	*.302*	*1.36*	*4.62*	*111*	*-0.1*	*92.8*	*62.2%*	*21.7%*	*54.0%*

Comparables: Brad Lincoln, Rafael Montero, A.J. Schugel

Ponce was unable to build on his 2020 success in the Buccos rotation, as he missed the start of the season with a forearm strain, shuttled back and forth to Indy and put up the worst numbers of any pitcher on a woeful Pittsburgh staff. The massive righty has a starter's five-pitch arsenal, but none of his offerings are plus, though he's shown flashes of being able to make it work at the end of the rotation or, more appropriately, as a bulk reliever (rimshot!). He's a likeable sort, so we're rooting for him—*honi soit qui mal y Ponce*!

Quinn Priester RHP

Born: 09/16/00 Age: 21 Bats: R Throws: R Height: 6'3" Weight: 210 lb. Origin: Round 1, 2019 Draft (#18 overall)

YEAR	TEAM	LVL	AGE	W	L	SV	G	GS	IP	H	HR	BB/9	K/9	K	GB%	BABIP	WHIP	ERA	DRA-	WARP	MPH	FB%	Whiff%	CSP
2019	PIR	ROK	18	1	1	0	8	7	32^{2}	29	1	2.8	10.2	37	57.3%	.322	1.19	3.03						
2019	WV	SS	18	0	0	0	1	1	4	3	0	9.0	9.0	4	90.0%	.300	1.75	4.50						
2021	GBO	A+	20	7	4	0	20	20	97^{2}	82	8	3.6	9.0	98	53.7%	.285	1.24	3.04	85	1.6				
2022 non-DC	*PIT*	*MLB*	*21*	*2*	*3*	*0*	*57*	*0*	*50*	*52*	*6*	*4.7*	*7.4*	*41*	*48.0%*	*.308*	*1.57*	*5.19*	*118*	*-0.3*				

Comparables: Shairon Martis, Ricky Bones, Sidney Ponson

Supply chains may have been disrupted all over the world, but fear not: Priester will likely be delivered to PNC ahead of schedule. The prep right-hander made his full-season debut in High-A and showcased everything you want to see in a top pitching prospect, including a fastball that sits in the mid-90s with armside run, a voluptuous curveball that is both real and spectacular and an improving slider and changeup. Priester missed more and more bats as the season wore on, piling up 44 whiffs over 35.2 innings in his last 7 starts. Like most young pitchers, he'll need to cut down on the free passes and better command his fastball in the zone, but Priester sure looks like the real deal.

José Quintana LHP

Born: 01/24/89 Age: 33 Bats: R Throws: L Height: 6'1" Weight: 220 lb. Origin: International Free Agent, 2006

YEAR	TEAM	LVL	AGE	W	L	SV	G	GS	IP	H	HR	BB/9	K/9	K	GB%	BABIP	WHIP	ERA	DRA-	WARP	MPH	FB%	Whiff%	CSP
2019	CHC	MLB	30	13	9	0	32	31	171	191	20	2.4	8.0	152	43.6%	.329	1.39	4.68	102	1.6	91.5	61.8%	20.9%	46.8%
2020	CHC	MLB	31	0	0	0	4	1	10	10	1	2.7	10.8	12	42.3%	.360	1.30	4.50	101	0.1	91.3	60.1%	27.6%	41.5%
2021	LAA	MLB	32	0	3	0	24	10	53^{1}	66	9	4.9	12.3	73	44.4%	.401	1.78	6.75	85	0.9	91.7	59.6%	29.2%	51.5%
2021	SF	MLB	32	0	0	0	5	0	9^{2}	8	3	5.6	11.2	12	48.0%	.227	1.45	4.66	87	0.2	91.8	53.3%	30.0%	53.1%
2022 DC	*PIT*	*MLB*	*33*	*5*	*4*	*0*	*17*	*17*	*80*	*72*	*11*	*3.6*	*11.0*	*98*	*43.2%*	*.309*	*1.30*	*3.96*	*95*	*0.8*	*91.6*	*60.1%*	*25.8%*	*49.1%*

Comparables: Donovan Osborne, Tommy John, Rick Wise

It's pretty remarkable, actually: From 2013 to 2019, Quintana started between 31 and 33 games each year (with five consecutive years of 32 starts). Say what you will about the slow erosion of skill, for a pitcher to be there for just about every turn in the rotation over a seven-year stretch is nothing short of amazing in this age of fragility. With an already abbreviated 2020 shortened further by a freak knife injury at home, 2021 was a great unknown for the former Cub and White Sock. Off to an inconsistent start with the Angels, he was claimed off waivers by the Giants as they looked wherever they could to patch up their depleted staff. Cast in a long-relief role, Quintana proved that he can still strike folks out, but everything else was shaky in the small sample. Quintana agreed to a one-year deal with Pittsburgh, as good a place as any to rebuild his value.

Chasen Shreve LHP

Born: 07/12/90 Age: 31 Bats: L Throws: L Height: 6'4" Weight: 180 lb. Origin: Round 11, 2010 Draft (#344 overall)

YEAR	TEAM	LVL	AGE	W	L	SV	G	GS	IP	H	HR	BB/9	K/9	K	GB%	BABIP	WHIP	ERA	DRA-	WARP	MPH	FB%	Whiff%	CSP
2019	MEM	AAA	28	2	2	3	51	0	60	45	6	3.9	10.2	68	29.7%	.275	1.18	3.45	94	0.6				
2019	STL	MLB	28	1	0	0	3	0	2	2	0	4.5	9.0	2	0.0%	.333	1.50	9.00	121	0.0	90.5	66.7%	10.5%	35.2%
2020	NYM	MLB	29	1	0	0	17	0	25	17	4	4.3	12.2	34	39.3%	.250	1.16	3.96	79	0.6	91.9	51.2%	37.8%	40.4%
2021	PIT	MLB	30	3	3	0	57	0	56^{1}	43	7	4.5	7.2	45	38.5%	.234	1.26	3.20	115	0.1	91.7	40.2%	24.4%	49.5%
2022 DC	*FA*	*MLB*	*31*	*2*	*2*	*0*	*57*	*0*	*49.3*	*45*	*7*	*4.3*	*9.1*	*50*	*38.3%*	*.289*	*1.39*	*4.53*	*106*	*0.0*	*91.8*	*43.0%*	*27.3%*	*47.3%*

Comparables: Todd Coffey, Miguel Socolovich, Buddy Boshers

Shreve pitched reasonably well last year in the Pittsburgh 'pen, where pitching reasonably well was such an oddity that the organization felt they needed to release him at season's end before his competence started to infect the rest of the staff. Actually it was because Shreve was due to earn real money in arbitration and was a luxury the organization chose not to afford, but why let that spoil a perfectly good Pirates burn? The same thing happened to Shreve with the Mets after the 2020 season, so here's hoping he latches on with a team that's willing to pay him what 50 innings of competent lefty relief are worth.

Chris Stratton RHP

Born: 08/22/90 Age: 31 Bats: R Throws: R Height: 6'2" Weight: 205 lb. Origin: Round 1, 2012 Draft (#20 overall)

YEAR	TEAM	LVL	AGE	W	L	SV	G	GS	IP	H	HR	BB/9	K/9	K	GB%	BABIP	WHIP	ERA	DRA-	WARP	MPH	FB%	Whiff%	CSP
2019	PIT	MLB	28	1	1	0	28	0	46^{2}	50	7	2.9	9.1	47	38.4%	.328	1.39	3.66	92	0.7	93.2	63.7%	25.6%	49.6%
2019	LAA	MLB	28	0	2	0	7	5	29^{1}	43	6	5.5	6.7	22	42.3%	.378	2.08	8.59	129	-0.2	90.8	46.9%	22.7%	45.2%
2020	PIT	MLB	29	2	1	0	27	0	30	26	3	3.9	11.7	39	48.1%	.303	1.30	3.90	81	0.6	93.5	46.6%	35.3%	43.0%
2021	PIT	MLB	30	7	1	8	68	0	79^{1}	70	9	3.7	9.8	86	41.0%	.293	1.30	3.63	92	1.1	93.2	48.3%	28.1%	55.9%
2022 DC	*PIT*	*MLB*	*31*	*3*	*3*	*17*	*67*	*0*	*58*	*54*	*8*	*3.5*	*9.8*	*63*	*41.9%*	*.303*	*1.32*	*4.02*	*97*	*0.3*	*93.1*	*49.8%*	*28.6%*	*52.1%*

Comparables: Joe Kelly, Chris Bassitt, Adam Conley

The King of Bullpen Spin™ has now strung together three solid years in Pittsburgh, taking on the roles of multi-inning reliever, set-up man and closer with equal aplomb. Stratton doesn't have the fire-breathing arsenal you'll find in so many of today's bullpen denizens, but his gyroscopic fastball and curve generate plenty of empty swings, and his slider and changeup add enough variety to keep hitters uncomfortable. Consistent production from bullpen arms is more rare than you think, making Stratton a more valuable commodity today than when he was a struggling young starter.

Zach Thompson RHP Born: 10/23/93 Age: 28 Bats: R Throws: R Height: 6'7" Weight: 230 lb. Origin: Round 5, 2014 Draft (#138 overall)

YEAR	TEAM	LVL	AGE	W	L	SV	G	GS	IP	H	HR	BB/9	K/9	K	GB%	BABIP	WHIP	ERA	DRA-	WARP	MPH	FB%	Whiff%	CSP
2019	BIR	AA	25	0	0	0	4	0	5^1	5	0	1.7	10.1	6	42.9%	.357	1.13	1.69	88	0.1				
2019	CHA	AAA	25	5	2	0	41	0	70^1	79	15	2.9	10.0	78	47.6%	.333	1.45	5.50	78	1.7				
2021	JAX	AAA	27	0	0	1	8	0	15	22	4	1.2	12.6	21	33.3%	.439	1.60	6.60	88	0.3				
2021	MIA	MLB	27	3	7	0	26	14	75	63	6	3.4	7.9	66	42.2%	.273	1.21	3.24	97	0.8	90.0	70.2%	26.8%	52.3%
2022 DC	*PIT*	*MLB*	*28*	*7*	*7*	*0*	*36*	*22*	*110.3*	*110*	*17*	*3.2*	*8.3*	*102*	*42.1%*	*.300*	*1.36*	*4.53*	*108*	*0.4*	*90.0*	*70.2%*	*26.8%*	*52.3%*

Comparables: Taylor Williams, Kyle Finnegan, Juan Minaya

The Marlins went after Thompson aggressively as a minor-league free agent, and he became just the latest proof that this Marlins team unearths pitching gems the way the 2010s Pirates put a shine back on veteran starters. With the Marlins in desperate need of arms in the starting rotation, Thompson was called up to make his MLB debut *and* make his first start on the mound since converting to a reliever in 2018. Thompson used his cutter to great effect, striking out 11 Nationals batters in his fourth career start, and posted a 2.33 ERA through eight starts. He tired down the stretch, his fastball losing two ticks it really couldn't spare, and so Thompson went back to the bullpen for the final month of the season to make room in the rotation for Trevor Rogers. His cutter is still one of the best in the majors and he's earned a spot on the team next year, though he'll likely start off as the sixth starter who winds up getting turns more often than not.

Duane Underwood Jr. RHP Born: 07/20/94 Age: 27 Bats: R Throws: R Height: 6'2" Weight: 210 lb. Origin: Round 2, 2012 Draft (#67 overall)

YEAR	TEAM	LVL	AGE	W	L	SV	G	GS	IP	H	HR	BB/9	K/9	K	GB%	BABIP	WHIP	ERA	DRA-	WARP	MPH	FB%	Whiff%	CSP
2019	IOW	AAA	24	3	7	0	33	10	81^2	84	8	4.5	10.5	95	45.7%	.349	1.53	5.07	80	1.5				
2019	CHC	MLB	24	0	0	0	12	0	11^2	13	2	2.3	10.0	13	50.0%	.344	1.37	5.40	83	0.2	95.0	59.5%	27.3%	48.4%
2020	CHC	MLB	25	1	0	0	17	0	20^2	25	5	2.6	11.8	27	38.9%	.408	1.50	5.66	92	0.3	94.8	46.3%	36.4%	43.7%
2021	PIT	MLB	26	2	3	0	43	0	72^2	77	9	3.3	8.1	65	43.8%	.316	1.43	4.33	104	0.5	94.1	47.7%	24.1%	56.9%
2022 DC	*PIT*	*MLB*	*27*	*3*	*3*	*0*	*67*	*0*	*58*	*58*	*7*	*3.3*	*8.6*	*55*	*43.6%*	*.311*	*1.38*	*4.55*	*109*	*0.0*	*94.2*	*48.1%*	*26.1%*	*54.5%*

Comparables: Franklin Morales, Deolis Guerra, JC Ramírez

Underwood was a roster crunch casualty last March, so the Cubs shipped him to Pittsburgh where the former top prospect made the most of it with a solid campaign in the Pirates 'pen. He spent the season cleaning up messes left by the bedraggled Pittsburgh rotation and worked more than an inning in 27 of his 43 appearances before he was shut down in September with a sore shoulder. Reworked mechanics saw Underwood improve his command as the season went on, but he still needs to find a way to tame the lefty bats that have bedeviled him. Teams have been wishing on Underwood's talent for a decade now, and he may have at last found a role where he can make good.

Bryse Wilson RHP Born: 12/20/97 Age: 24 Bats: R Throws: R Height: 6'2" Weight: 225 lb. Origin: Round 4, 2016 Draft (#109 overall)

YEAR	TEAM	LVL	AGE	W	L	SV	G	GS	IP	H	HR	BB/9	K/9	K	GB%	BABIP	WHIP	ERA	DRA-	WARP	MPH	FB%	Whiff%	CSP
2019	GWN	AAA	21	10	7	0	21	21	121	120	12	1.9	8.8	118	44.7%	.315	1.21	3.42	85	2.5				
2019	ATL	MLB	21	1	1	0	6	4	20	26	5	4.5	7.2	16	31.3%	.350	1.80	7.20	122	0.0	94.9	71.9%	20.5%	48.1%
2020	ATL	MLB	22	1	0	1	6	2	15^2	18	2	5.2	8.6	15	43.8%	.348	1.72	4.02	106	0.1	93.7	81.8%	21.2%	46.7%
2021	GWN	AAA	23	5	2	0	10	9	55^1	61	8	2.6	6.8	42	40.6%	.321	1.39	4.23	109	0.5				
2021	PIT	MLB	23	1	4	0	8	8	40^1	40	8	2.2	5.1	23	33.1%	.252	1.24	4.91	123	-0.1	93.0	65.5%	16.5%	54.0%
2021	ATL	MLB	23	2	3	0	8	8	33^2	45	7	3.2	6.1	23	37.6%	.349	1.69	5.88	122	-0.1	93.4	61.5%	23.1%	55.3%
2022 DC	*PIT*	*MLB*	*24*	*7*	*7*	*0*	*56*	*12*	*93*	*103*	*14*	*3.1*	*6.5*	*67*	*38.4%*	*.307*	*1.45*	*5.13*	*120*	*-0.3*	*93.3*	*66.9%*	*19.8%*	*53.0%*

Comparables: Kyle Davies, Jeff Suppan, Jordan Lyles

Wilson's trade from Atlanta to the Pirates last summer may have cost him the opportunity to swill championship champagne, but it gave him a lot more room to compete for a rotation job and work out his struggles at the big-league level. Wilson made his major league debut in 2018 before he was old enough to order an IC Light and has taken the ball in big games, but after four seasons he still hasn't found the right recipe to win consistently in the bigs. His low-spin fastball sits around 93, his *cambio* is perhaps too firm with limited separation from the heater and nothing in his arsenal generates much swing-and-miss. Wilson does a good job of avoiding ball four and has always gotten high marks for his moxie and determination, but he won't be able to survive in a big-league rotation until he stops allowing so much hard contact.

LINEOUTS

Hitters

HITTER	POS	TEAM	LVL	AGE	PA	R	2B	3B	HR	RBI	BB	K	SB	CS	AVG/OBP/SLG	DRC+	BABIP	BRR	FRAA	WARP
Greg Allen	OF	SWB	AAA	28	263	49	13	1	5	28	26	45	26	2	.326/.442/.465	121	.394	1.7	LF(34): 0.1, CF(24): 1.2, RF(6): 0.0	1.8
	OF	NYY	MLB	28	48	9	4	1	0	2	5	13	5	0	.270/.417/.432	90	.400	1.7	RF(8): -0.4, LF(5): -0.1, CF(4): -0.2	0.2
Ji-hwan Bae	2B	PEJ	WIN	21	109	23	4	1	2	11	13	21	8	1	.250/.343/.380		.296			
	2B	ALT	AA	21	365	63	12	5	7	31	38	83	20	8	.278/.359/.413	103	.352	3.2	2B(65): -8.1, CF(9): 3.4	1.1
Carter Bins	C	EVE	A+	22	185	42	10	0	7	31	32	54	1	3	.284/.422/.493	106	.398	-0.4	C(35): 7.9	1.4
	C	ARK	AA	22	43	9	0	0	1	4	10	13	2	0	.063/.302/.156	92	.056	-0.5	C(6): 0.9	0.1
	C	ALT	AA	22	66	4	2	0	0	6	10	19	0	0	.200/.333/.236	89	.306	0.6	C(15): 1.5	0.4
Diego Castillo	IF	ALT	AA	23	121	11	3	0	5	16	10	9	1	2	.282/.342/.445	137	.271	-1.7	SS(12): -0.9, 2B(9): -2.6, 3B(7): 1.0	0.5
	IF	SOM	AA	23	249	44	18	0	11	32	21	34	8	3	.277/.345/.504	135	.283	1.1	2B(23): 0.9, 3B(14): -1.1, SS(14): 1.5	2.1
	IF	IND	AAA	23	70	18	3	0	3	7	13	13	0	0	.278/.414/.500	117	.300	0.2	SS(9): -0.9, 2B(6): -1.1, 3B(2): -0.1	0.2
Bubba Chandler	DH	PIRB	ROK	18	37	3	1	0	1	2	5	16	0	0	.167/.324/.300		.308			
Will Craig	1B	IND	AAA	26	139	23	8	0	8	23	14	28	0	0	.287/.367/.549	127	.310	-1.6	1B(32): 4.5, 3B(1): -0.1	1.0
	1B	PIT	MLB	26	65	5	2	0	1	3	5	22	0	0	.217/.277/.300	73	.324	0.4	1B(18): -0.2	-0.1
Maikol Escotto	SS	BRD	A	19	381	61	13	1	7	38	54	116	22	5	.234/.354/.347	89	.343	1.0	SS(77): -0.0, 2B(10): -2.3	0.6
Matt Fraizer	OF	GBO	A+	23	350	64	14	3	20	50	43	74	14	6	.314/.401/.578	130	.357	-1.2	LF(36): 1.9, CF(29): 5.0, RF(3): -0.0	2.9
	OF	ALT	AA	23	149	20	12	3	3	18	13	34	1	2	.288/.356/.492	101	.361	-0.2	CF(31): -0.9, RF(1): 0.1	0.4
Hudson Head	OF	BRD	A	20	434	67	16	1	15	50	68	137	3	1	.213/.362/.394	101	.296	-1.6	RF(39): -2.4, CF(35): -1.9, LF(18): 0.6	1.0
Mason Martin	1B	ALT	AA	22	471	62	29	2	22	75	38	161	0	2	.242/.318/.481	100	.328	-0.5	1B(108): 7.5	2.0
	1B	IND	AAA	22	27	4	0	0	3	6	1	10	0	1	.240/.296/.600	92	.250	-0.3	1B(5): -0.8	-0.1
Cal Mitchell	RF	ALT	AA	22	419	43	19	1	12	61	24	71	6	7	.280/.330/.429	111	.313	-0.4	RF(92): -2.3, LF(5): -0.2	1.6
John Nogowski	1B	AGU	WIN	28	61	3	2	0	0	2	7	8	3	0	.192/.283/.231		.222			
	1B	IND	AAA	28	69	5	2	0	1	10	13	10	3	0	.259/.406/.352	113	.295	-0.2	1B(17): 1.4	0.4
	1B	SAC	AAA	28	31	3	1	0	2	5	2	2	0	0	.185/.290/.444	113	.130	-0.2	1B(6): 0.5, LF(2): -0.2	0.1
	1B	MEM	AAA	28	148	16	4	0	3	14	15	31	3	0	.195/.304/.297	98	.234	-1.2	1B(31): 0.4, LF(5): 0.4	0.3
	1B	PIT	MLB	28	123	12	7	0	1	14	11	20	0	1	.261/.325/.351	95	.308	-1.2	1B(29): -0.0, P(3): 0.2	0.1
	1B	STL	MLB	28	20	2	0	0	0	0	1	2	0	0	.056/.150/.056	95	.063	-0.5	1B(3): -0.1	0.0
Jared Oliva	OF	OBR	WIN	25	123	12	3	2	3	19	4	31	1	3	.235/.270/.374		.293			
	OF	IND	AAA	25	249	27	12	4	2	23	19	67	10	3	.249/.321/.364	73	.346	-0.5	CF(46): 0.2, LF(10): -0.2, RF(4): 0.4	0.1
	OF	PIT	MLB	25	43	4	2	0	0	2	3	10	2	0	.175/.233/.225	87	.233	0.1	RF(12): 0.4, CF(2): -0.0	0.1
Endy Rodriguez	C	BRD	A	21	434	73	25	6	15	73	50	77	2	0	.294/.380/.512	130	.333	-2.3	C(54): -1.5, 1B(18): -1.7, LF(4): -1.2	2.1
Canaan Smith-Njigba	LF	PEJ	WIN	22	73	12	6	0	1	2	15	18	5	0	.298/.452/.456		.421			
	LF	ALT	AA	22	266	35	11	0	6	40	45	66	13	1	.274/.398/.406	113	.365	-1.0	LF(60): 0.2, RF(1): -0.1	1.2
Travis Swaggerty	CF	IND	AAA	23	48	6	0	0	3	7	6	8	3	0	.220/.333/.439	128	.200	0.2	CF(9): 2.3	0.6
Lonnie White Jr.	OF	PIRB	ROK	18	33	6	2	0	2	5	2	14	0	0	.258/.303/.516		.400			

Greg Allen was one of the best players in Triple-A in 2021, which is bittersweet because he was one of the best players in Triple-A in 2021. He'll receive another NRI in 2022, which is bittersweet because he'll receive another NRI from the Pirates in 2022. ⚾ If you want to look past his 2018 domestic violence conviction in Korea, **Ji-Hwan Bae** has top-shelf speed, a versatile glove, limited power, a good batting eye and evident bat-to-ball skills. We don't blame you if you don't. ⚾ A solid defensive backstop, **Carter Bins** has a patient approach that results in plenty of walks, but the complete absence of a hit tool keeps him from getting to his plus raw power with any consistency. ⚾ Former Yankees farmhand **Diego Castillo** (no, not that one) is a versatile infield glove with plus contact skills who suddenly discovered some over-the-wall thump in the high minors, earning a place on the Pirates' 40-man roster and the potential for a utility role this year. ⚾ The Pirates went way over slot to sign **Bubba Chandler** away from his Clemson football scholarship, which had the dual benefit of (a) gifting Pittsburgh with a potential ace and a switch-hitting shortstop in the same package and (b) making Dabo Swinney cry. ⚾ **Will Craig** provided the greatest gift every baseball fan received in 2021, when he became the victim of Javy Báez's Little League double on May 27. The play was so bad Craig was ejected to an entirely different continent, as he signed with the Kiwoom Heroes of the KBO. ⚾ A windfall from the Jameson Taillon trade, **Maikol Escotto** impressed scouts with his speed, smooth actions at shortstop, powerful stroke, on-base skills and plus-plus name that would have Roland Turner rumbling "What's the 'S' stand for?" ⚾ **Matt Fraizer** has long possessed an advanced approach and a name that keeps copy editors busy, but a less busy set-up helped him unlock his power potential last year. He has range enough for center but a fringy arm may limit him to left, where his suddenly effective bat might just play. ⚾ **Hudson Head** *n.* 1. A hyper-athletic center field prospect with speed and power potential who struggled to make contact in his first full minor-league season. 2. What your hair suffers from after you fall off a pier in Hoboken. ⚾ Built like a kamado cooker with biceps, **Mason Martin** continued to launch moonshots on his way to Triple-A while his strikeout rate continued to grow like kudzu. He's worked hard to play a marginally acceptable first base, but he still makes too many outs to have a first division ceiling. ⚾ **Cal Mitchell** can really put a charge into one and managed to cut down on the strikeouts in his first taste of the high minors. He'll really need to rake going forward, however, as his fringy arm will likely limit him to left field. ⚾ Triple-A insurance policy **John Nogowski** prioritizes patience over power while playing a position that demands both, but if you ever have need of a mini-Mientkiewicz he's your guy. ⚾ Speedster **Jared Oliva** missed the early part of the year with an oblique injury but returned to provide his usual *mélange* of plus outfield defense and punchless plate appearances. With more electric talents on their way in a resurgent Pirates system, he's running out of time to carve out a reserve role. ⚾ Former Mets farmhand **Endy Rodriguez** dazzled in his full-season debut, hitting for average and power, drawing walks and flashing plus receiving skills. He's firmly behind Henry Davis on the depth chart, but his athleticism could make him the rare utility player that can play in the grass, on the dirt *and* behind the plate. ⚾ Yet another promising piece of the Taillon trade, **Canaan Smith-Njigba** does a fantastic job of controlling the strike zone and can make solid contact. Despite his massive build, he still needs to generate more in-game power to profile as an everyday player in left field. ⚾ Former top pick **Travis Swaggerty** has already implemented the speed and defense portions of his master plan and was itching to use his first year in Triple-A to prove he can finally punish the ball with some authority, but a torn labrum cut his season short in May. There's still first division upside here, but time's a-wastin'. ⚾ It's all about the projection with potential center fielder **Lonnie White Jr.**, as the second round teenager has more tools than your Uncle Joe's workshop but is as raw as the language your Uncle Joe uses in his workshop.

Pitchers

PITCHER	TEAM	LVL	AGE	W	L	SV	G	GS	IP	H	HR	BB/9	K/9	K	GB%	BABIP	WHIP	ERA	DRA-	WARP	MPH	FB%	WHF	CSP
Michael Burrows	GBO	A+	21	2	2	0	13	13	49	24	3	3.7	12.1	66	30.8%	.208	0.90	2.20	93	0.6				
Trevor Cahill	PIT	MLB	33	1	5	0	9	8	37	42	4	3.4	7.8	32	54.6%	.333	1.51	6.57	94	0.5	90.1	36.2%	22.9%	55.0%
Kyle Crick	CLT	AAA	28	2	0	0	8	0	10^1	4	0	2.6	13.1	15	61.1%	.222	0.68	0.87	80	0.2				
	PIT	MLB	28	1	1	0	27	0	24^1	14	0	7.0	7.8	21	35.5%	.230	1.36	4.44	126	-0.1	92.7	38.8%	28.2%	47.7%
Jared Jones	BRD	A	19	3	6	0	18	15	66	63	6	4.6	14.0	103	45.5%	.385	1.47	4.64	79	1.4				
Kyle Keller	IND	AAA	28	2	0	0	13	1	18^1	13	2	1.5	15.2	31	25.0%	.333	0.87	1.96	76	0.5				
	PIT	MLB	28	1	1	0	32	0	33^1	30	9	5.9	9.7	36	30.4%	.253	1.56	6.48	113	0.1	94.6	55.7%	21.6%	55.5%
Shelby Miller	IOW	AAA	30	0	0	0	3	3	10^1	4	1	5.2	13.1	15	47.6%	.150	0.97	1.74	99	0.1				
	IND	AAA	30	2	1	0	10	1	14	10	1	1.9	14.1	22	41.9%	.300	0.93	3.86	78	0.3				
	CHC	MLB	30	0	0	0	3	0	2	7	0	22.5	4.5	1	41.7%	.583	6.00	31.50	115	0.0	93.8	75.3%	10.8%	53.6%
	PIT	MLB	30	0	1	0	10	0	10^2	9	3	5.1	5.9	7	36.7%	.222	1.41	5.06	126	0.0	93.8	58.0%	29.6%	59.5%
Shea Spitzbarth	IND	AAA	26	3	3	2	42	0	46^2	35	4	4.1	7.9	41	44.1%	.252	1.20	2.12	103	0.6				
	PIT	MLB	26	0	0	0	5	0	5	4	1	3.6	1.8	1	5.6%	.176	1.20	3.60	160	-0.1	92.1	47.0%	3.0%	59.0%
Tahnaj Thomas	GBO	A+	22	3	3	0	16	16	60^2	61	13	5.2	9.2	62	35.2%	.289	1.58	5.19	113	0.0				
Miguel Yajure	IND	AAA	23	2	3	0	9	9	43^2	33	6	2.7	8.2	40	45.4%	.239	1.05	3.09	99	0.6				
	PIT	MLB	23	0	2	0	4	3	15	17	6	4.2	6.6	11	34.7%	.256	1.60	8.40	122	0.0	90.2	49.4%	21.4%	58.1%

Injuries have dogged **Cody Bolton** since he was an over-slot sixth rounder in 2017. This time it was a knee injury that cost him another year of development. He has the ingredients to work in the middle of the rotation, but he's already 23 and has yet to succeed in the high minors, so tick tick tick tick. Don't sleep on **Michael Burrows**, who dominated High-A with a plus curveball and mid-90s heat. Seriously, he hates it when people snooze right on top of him, especially when he's trying to pitch. Pittsburgh signed **Trevor Cahill** to a one-year deal with the thought he could provide a veteran presence in the rotation and a potential bullpen arm if he struggled as a starter. Spot-on thinking, as Cahill was indeed a veteran presence and did indeed struggle as a starter, but suffered a season-ending foot injury before they could try him in the 'pen. Closer-in-waiting **Blake Cederlind** blew out his elbow in spring training last year. Tommy John surgery ensued, so we won't get to learn whether his high-90s sinker/cutter mix can work in the ninth until at least this summer. **Kyle Crick**'s fastball is now sitting in the low 90s rather than the mid-90s which might explain why even the hapless Pirates released him in July. He latched on with the White Sox shortly after, but was released in early September. Another over-slot prospect making his pro debut, **Jared Jones** used his lively mid-90s fastball and two improving breakers to pile up the strikeouts. He'll need to ice down his swollen walk rate if he wants to stay out of the bullpen. **Kyle Keller** was bad last year, not just your "normal" bad but your "noticeably bad even for the Pirates bullpen" bad, and he lost his spot on the 40-man roster at season's end. Overheard from the mound while last year's fourth rounder **Owen Kellington** rode his killer curveball over five one-hit innings in his pro debut: "Hit this? Hit this? There's movement everywhere! Hit this? Those white things in the air! Hit this?" Wasn't it great to see **Shelby Miller** celebrating that World Series victory with the Braves? One of the best prep lefties available in last year's draft, armed with a low-90s fastball and potential plus slider, **Anthony Solometo** from Bishop Eustace Prep in Pennsauken, New Jersey, became the Pirates' second-round pick. Insert quote from *The Sopranos* here. The Pirates tabbed rehabbing **José Soriano** with the first pick of last year's Rule 5 draft, but the fireballing relief prospect worked only two games before needing a second Tommy John surgery. He likely won't be back until 2023. Staten Island native **Shea Spitzbarth** completed his journey from undrafted free agent and minor-league Rule 5 draftee to major-league bullpen, but he'll need to cut into his walk rate if he wants to stay there. **Tahnaj Thomas** struggled in his first season outside of rookie ball, failing to command his high-90s fastball and nasty hook and issuing far too many free passes. There's no denying his stuff, but he'll need to get a better handle on it if he wants to be the first Bahamian pitcher to reach the bigs since Hall of Famer Whitey—er, I mean, the late, great Wenty Ford. Ex-Yankee **Miguel Yajure** lost much of his year to the dreaded forearm discomfort and struggled with diminished velocity when he returned, but all his offerings have wiggle. He could eat innings in middle relief or the back of the rotation.

ST. LOUIS CARDINALS

Essay by Steven Goldman

Player comments by Brendan Gawlowski, Bryan Grosnick and BP staff

You can't have everything you want. Sometimes your myriad desires are conflicting and incompatible, snakes which rattle and snap at each other but will never intertwine. No matter how you try, you cannot unify your wife and mistress in a single sustainable structure, cannot identify a pole or axis while contemplating the void. You cannot simultaneously leave and arrive.

There is a possibility that Yadier Molina and Adam Wainwright have doomed the 2022 Cardinals. More accurately, by prioritizing fan service over winning, the Cardinals' ownership and front office may have handicapped the team's 2022 chances. Sentimentality is the enemy of winning baseball, which requires ruthless remaking of the roster and a what-have-you-done-for-me-lately ethos. Farewell tours occur in defiance of that ethos and in denial of the very reason they become necessary. The timing may be a matter of choice or declining skills, but, either way, it's a recognition of the inevitable. Players may want to give the game one last go, and fans may want to see an encore, but a player reaches his expiration date via the calendar invisible. When it happens, the team will be left with an arthritic paean to yesterday and a sour present.

But there's no right way to run a baseball team. Perhaps by re-upping Molina and Wainwright in August and October, respectively, the Cardinals did exactly what they should have done. The point of the major-league exercise is generally acknowledged to be the winning of championships, the ultimate expression of living in the present. Nothing says that, for this one Cardinals season, the team can't exist only to celebrate the past.

Then again, it's possible the two oldsters perform at a high level, and everyone can have new rings to go along with memories of the old. That would have seemed more likely had the Cardinals buttressed their lineup and rotation with top-flight players, but, as of the December transactions freeze, president of baseball operations John Mozeliak and company had been oddly indolent. If the Cardinals were really trying to make the 2022 season a celebration of a winning duo by having them *win*, they'd chosen an oddly

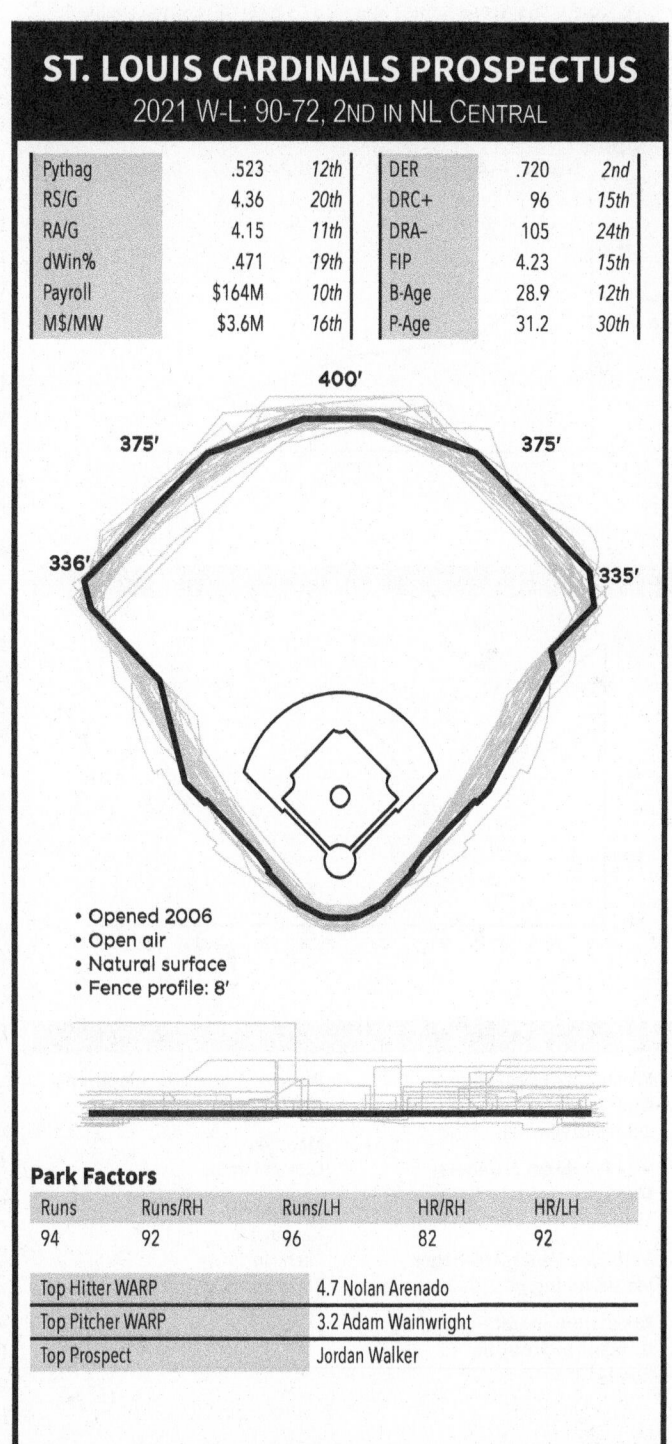

ST. LOUIS CARDINALS PROSPECTUS

2021 W-L: 90-72, 2ND IN NL CENTRAL

Pythag	.523	*12th*	DER	.720	*2nd*
RS/G	4.36	*20th*	DRC+	96	*15th*
RA/G	4.15	*11th*	DRA-	105	*24th*
dWin%	.471	*19th*	FIP	4.23	*15th*
Payroll	$164M	*10th*	B-Age	28.9	*12th*
M$/MW	$3.6M	*16th*	P-Age	31.2	*30th*

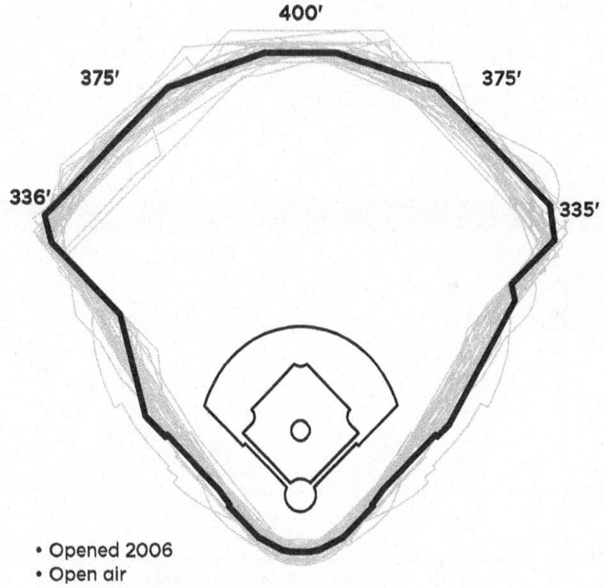

- Opened 2006
- Open air
- Natural surface
- Fence profile: 8'

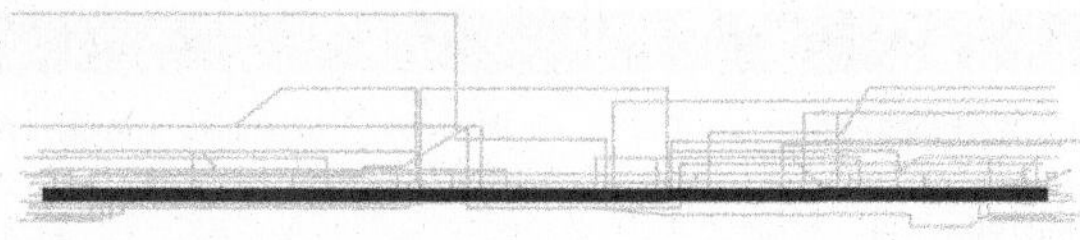

Park Factors

Runs	Runs/RH	Runs/LH	HR/RH	HR/LH
94	92	96	82	92

Top Hitter WARP	4.7 Nolan Arenado
Top Pitcher WARP	3.2 Adam Wainwright
Top Prospect	Jordan Walker

Payroll History (in millions)

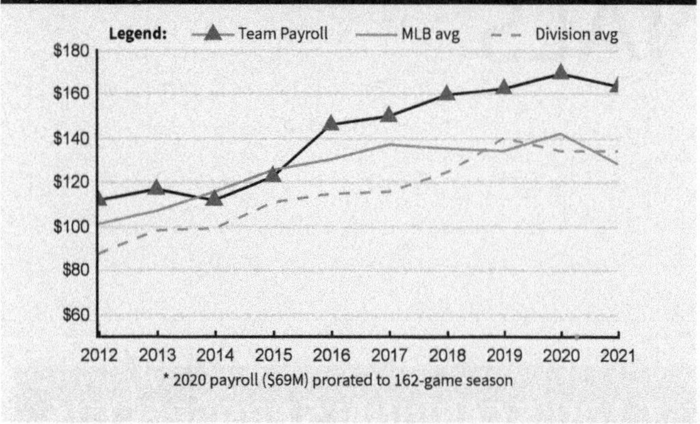

Future Commitments (in millions)

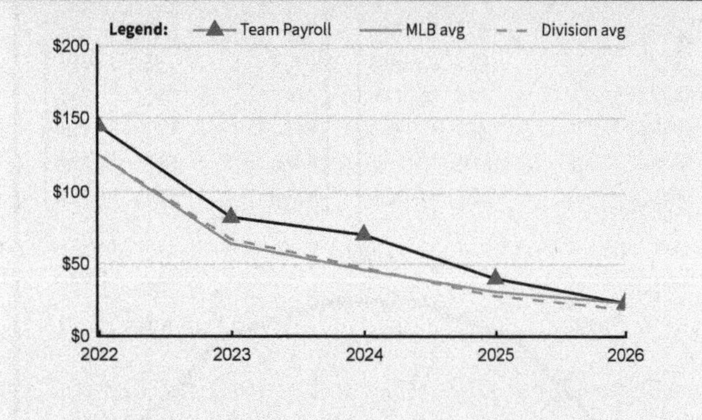

Farm System Ranking

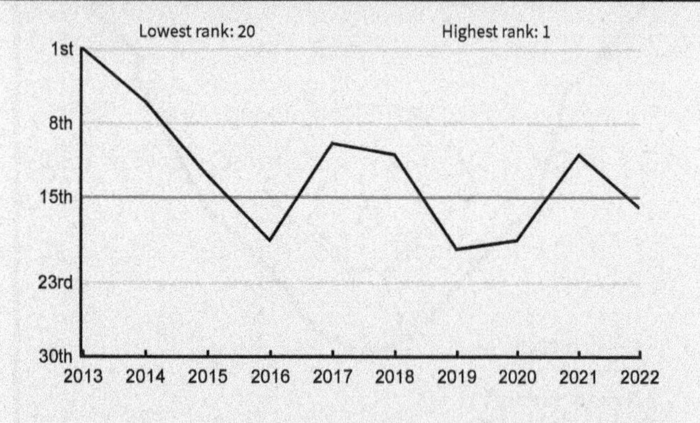

Personnel

President of Baseball Operations
John Mozeliak

Vice President & General Manager
Mike Girsch

Assistant General Manager
Moisés Rodríguez

Assistant General Manager & Director of Scouting
Randy Flores

Director, Player Development
Gary LaRocque

Manager
Oliver Marmol

BP Alumni
Keanan Lamb
Zach Mortimer
Christopher Rodriguez
Mauricio Rubio

passive way of going about it. The current iteration of the Cardinals is a win-now team that hasn't committed to its own limited future.

Contra Shakespeare, we come neither to praise the Cardinals nor to bury them. There is much good that can be said about what has long been one of the game's most reliable organizations. The club has had one(!) losing season this century, and they've thrice won 100 games. Yet, what has the most relevance is not the championships of 2011 or '13 but the oddly anodyne shape of the roster now. The 2021 Cardinals had a storybook season in which they fought their way into contention after a slow start, stopping just short of the full Cinderella ending. It was a competitive team, a solid team, and it should be again in 2022. And yet, despite that limited postseason run, despite the 17-game September winning streak, there are cracks showing.

As much as Wainwright and Molina have meant to the team, they are, definitionally, cracked parts. The imminent professional extinctions of the 40- and 39-year-old (respectively) put souvenir T-shirts in the concourse and banners on the facade, but they also announce that this iteration of the team is less than a year from expiration. To the extent the post–October 2022 period of Cardinals history will involve a rebuild, the club, the fans and possibly even Missouri's Congressional delegation already know that it will require the procurement of one ace-level pitcher and one Gold Glove catcher—inspiring, fan-friendly personalities a plus.

Wainwright played well in 2021, while Molina continued to show signs of decline. The latter has hit .261/.304/.380 since 2018, as compared to .282/.334/.406 prior, and Baseball Prospectus' defensive metrics are, at best, equivocal about how much of his past defensive value persists. The likelihood of a Molina renaissance is vanishingly small, while the odds of a Wainwright fade are high given his age and injury history. The very presence of Wainwright and Molina may be antithetical to winning. For every David Ortiz or Mariano Rivera who exits with skills intact, there is a Craig Biggio or Derek Jeter pushing the club further away from its next championship. Again, this isn't necessarily wrong or bad, it just might mean prioritizing patches of dirt—now you, too, can own a swatch of turf on which Old Man Baseball, retired number 4, once stood—over a World Series run.

The team's lack of urgency prior to the December lockout suggests that management understands its precarity, drawing cards from the middle of the pile. Shortly before the Mets added Max Scherzer this past November at an annual salary of more than $43 million, the Cardinals added 31-year-old, league-average-ish lefty Steven Matz on a four-year, $44-million (plus potential bonuses) contract. That is, the totality of Matz's contract only slightly exceeds the annual value of Scherzer's. This is in keeping with what seem to be the team's budgetary priorities. The Cardinals' approximately $150-million payroll is in the top third of the league, but the total is somewhat distorted and top-heavy due to the contracts of infield-corner men Paul Goldschmidt and Nolan Arenado. Those two account for more than a third of the total, and, barring an Arenado opt-out after the coming season, will continue to do so through 2024, when Goldschmidt, having completed his age-36 campaign, will presumably give way to a younger man. With righty Carlos Martínez bought out, and infielder Matt Carpenter and lefty Andrew Miller's tenures at an end, a good deal of money has come off the books, but that doesn't seem to have emboldened the Cardinals to, say, jump into the deep end of the All-Star-shortstop sweepstakes despite need at that position.

This approach is defensible if only because mere competence has a very strong chance of winning the soft NL Central. The Pirates are a Potemkin village of a franchise, and the Cubs and Reds are tearing down. That leaves only the Brewers as serious competition. It remains to be seen how much staying power that team will have at the top of the pile: If they don't take serious steps to improve their offense and get some good news on Christian Yelich's back and bat, they're an arm injury away from reeling backwards. But if the Cardinals' goal is not merely to win the division but a World Series, Cardinals leadership will have to make more of a commitment than Matz, a new manager and praying for Corbin Burnes to go mystic and retire to an ashram.

The Cardinals are not yet old (look to San Francisco '21 for an example of that), but they're aging in ways that go beyond the Molina-Wainwright encore. There is a distinct possibility that every member of the starting lineup, aside from sophomore Dylan Carlson, has already peaked. Goldschmidt and Arenado are at an age when what you see is what you get. Tommy Edman's impatience requires him to hit at least .275 to be an average producer (which is not to say he's without value; his defensive versatility and speed compensate for a lackluster record against same-side pitching). If Tyler O'Neill is a 150 OPS+ hitter and Gold Glove outfielder for the rest of his career, the Cardinals have a Hall of Famer on their hands, but that remains to be seen.

If the starting pitchers can stay off the injured list, and if the relievers can find consistency, while all else remains equal—great defense all around the diamond; just enough hitting overall—another 90-win season is likely. Even if Mozeliak doesn't upgrade at shortstop, Paul DeJong might remember how to hit (possible), or Edmundo Sosa could post another .346 on-base percentage (less likely), in which case the Cardinals might even improve. The uncertainty in those ifs is enormous; entropy claws at baseball teams with a relentlessness it normally reserves for democratic systems of government. At this writing, Mozeliak et al. are a bit like a gamer who has earned the chance to level up but opts to stand pat.

The Cardinals do have some prospects of note who will be ready in the near term—Nolan Gorman, perhaps at second base with Nolan Arenado entrenched at third; lefty starter Matthew Liberatore—but the next Wainwright, a pitcher who would pair with a theoretically healthy Jack Flaherty at the top of the rotation, is not yet in evidence.

The lack of ready youth underscores the way the 2021 season shouldn't be looked upon as a predictor of future success. The Cardinals were muddling along around .500 when they simply stopped losing for a while. Third in the NL Central on September 10 with a record of 71-69, 15 games behind the front-running Brewers, the Cardinals wouldn't drop another game until September 29. By the time it was over, they were in second place, having blown past the foundering Cincinnati Reds, and in possession of a wild-card berth. The Dodgers evicted them from the postseason in a dramatic Wild Card Game that could have gone either way before Chris Taylor hit a walk-off home run off of Alex Reyes, the club's wild, struggling, deposed closer. Outside of the streak, the Cardinals went 73-72 on the season.

Baseball has seen this sort of thing before, most dramatically in early 20th-century New York. Like last year's Cardinals, the 1916 Giants got off to a miserable start, going 2-13 in their first 15 games. The Dodgers went 11-4, and the Braves 10-5, so the Giants were pretty well buried before the weather turned warm. The Giants had some good players, including some future Hall of Famers, but they were either too young, like Edd Roush and George Kelly, or too old, like Christy Mathewson. Nevertheless, New York began to play a little better, several times reaching the .500 mark or getting a little past it before falling back down again. By early September, the Giants were 59-62, and, with the benefit of hindsight, we can see that this would be a transitional year for what was generally a well-run franchise. It had last won the National League pennant in 1913 and would win another in 1917. The 1916 team had the in-between results of an in-between roster, and its mediocre record was well deserved.

Then a strange thing happened: The Giants, like the Cardinals, simply stopped losing. From September 7 through the first game of their doubleheader against the Braves on September 30, the Giants won 26 straight games. This availed them nothing. They finished in fourth place, seven games behind the pennant-winning Robins (aka Dodgers). No doubt the run was exciting and brought a lot of joy to the Giants' fans of the time. It also undoubtedly represented more than a fair share of breaks going the Giants' way. But there was also some method in amidst the madness: Inasmuch as the streak was the result of in-season improvements made by manager John McGraw, it was a harbinger of good times to come in 1917.

That points to the difference between McGraw's winning streak and Mozeliak's. Part of what triggered the 1916 streak was the former's decision to shift an inconsistent 25-year-old lefty, then in his sophomore season, from a swingman role into a full-time starting role. Over the rest of the season, Ferdie Schupp went 6-1 with a 0.44 ERA, pitching four shutouts in seven starts. The next season, he'd be in the rotation from the get-go and would go 21-7 with a 1.95 ERA as the Giants won the pennant. Mozeliak wasn't able to uncover those sorts of internal resources, opting for transient patches that worked just well enough to get the team through to October. Mozeliak had a 2021 problem, and he solved it, letting 2022 hang fire.

The one reason to believe the Cardinals' streak was more representative of the team's capabilities than its .500-ish record was its nearly universal collection of pitching injuries. Other than a three-day timeout due to COVID protocols, Wainwright was remarkably durable. Everyone else vanished for long periods of time. Flaherty missed all of June, July and half of August with a strained oblique muscle, made three starts, then lost another month to a strained shoulder. Having missed all of the attenuated 2020 season due to a strained flexor tendon that required surgery, Miles Mikolas was able to make just one start before late August. Kwang Hyun Kim had three different injured-list stints amidst back and elbow pain. Dakota Hudson's recovery from Tommy John surgery kept him out until the last week of the season. Even Daniel Ponce de Leon explored the IL over two stints due to shoulder inflammation and discomfort.

Mozeliak took a conservative approach to the crisis, not shopping at the top of the market for the Scherzers and Kimbrels but, rather, taking on fixer-uppers and castoffs. Luis García and T.J. McFarland entered the bullpen; J.A. Happ and Jon Lester were added to the rotation at the trading deadline. The deep hole the Cardinals had found themselves in after the Brewers surged past them—St. Louis was 41-44 and 10 games out on Independence Day—made the wild card the realistic upside of what they might accomplish over the remainder of the season. The Cardinals played at a 103-win pace from July 4 on, but it wasn't enough to get them past the Brewers; to argue that the best-available players might have done more is to play counterfactual games while insisting on highly improbable outcomes.

Now 2022 is here, and the Cardinals have bet on an improbable outcome of their own: that they can organize a season-long Salute to the Aged Ballplayer and still win. In the feeding frenzy prior to the CBA-inspired lockout, the Cardinals re-signed McFarland, signed Matz, and went dark. Barring another cascade of pitcher injuries, that should be sufficient in the Division that Honest Effort Forgot, but that hardly seems worthy of praise given this franchise's established standards. It's all contradictory and confused: You can't say the Cardinals haven't spent money, but if they haven't spent enough or allocated it in the right ways, it's a moot point. You can't say they're old, but they aren't young in the way they need to be. Signing Matz isn't the middle finger to the fans that is the Pirates signing José Quintana and his 6.43 ERA to a one-year, $2-million contract, but it feels like a half-hearted effort given the team's perfect foreknowledge that a rotation that devolved into Wainwright plus four bowls of soup du jour last year will soon be Wainwright-free. It says that nostalgia should be sufficient; if the Cardinals were really set on taking one last swing at greatness with this roster, they wouldn't have settled for Matz. Acquiring Arenado, a potential Hall of Famer, last February suggests the Cardinals understand that. If you're going to make that sort of commitment, why stop so far short of completing the job?

It's difficult for us to make sense of the club's intentions for 2022, and perhaps it's no clearer to the denizens of Busch Stadium. Trying to have everything often leads to having nothing. Flags fly forever, but perhaps so, too, does nostalgia, so the best one can do is sell as many tickets as possible during a pandemic and make the rest up as one goes along. There is no chart, no compass, and though the pilot looks to the stars for guidance, he is dazzled and reads them wrong, steering towards what he thinks is greatness but arriving at adequacy. ■

—Steven Goldman is a former Baseball Prospectus editor-in-chief and current consulting editor.

Hitters

Nolan Arenado 3B Born: 04/16/91 Age: 31 Bats: R Throws: R Height: 6'2" Weight: 215 lb. Origin: Round 2, 2009 Draft (#59 overall)

YEAR	TEAM	LVL	AGE	PA	R	2B	3B	HR	RBI	BB	K	SB	CS	Whiff%	AVG/OBP/SLG	DRC+	BABIP	BRR	FRAA	WARP
2019	COL	MLB	28	662	102	31	2	41	118	62	93	3	2	20.9%	.315/.379/.583	140	.312	2.0	3B(154): 15.1	6.7
2020	COL	MLB	29	201	23	9	0	8	26	15	20	0	0	17.9%	.253/.303/.434	115	.241	0.4	3B(48): 8.9	1.8
2021	STL	MLB	30	653	81	34	3	34	105	50	96	2	0	18.5%	.255/.312/.494	120	.249	1.1	3B(155): 7.4	4.7
2022 DC	*STL*	*MLB*	*31*	*589*	*85*	*28*	*1*	*25*	*90*	*51*	*75*	*2*	*1*	*18.5%*	*.270/.334/.477*	*121*	*.270*	*-0.7*	*3B 3*	*3.4*

Comparables: Adrián Beltré, Brooks Robinson, Aramis Ramirez

In physics, a redshift from one end of the visible spectrum—say from violet to red—corresponds with a decrease in energy. That's a pretty righteous mirror to the common perception that when hitters move off the league's only purple-clad ballclub, their Coors-inflated offensive numbers lose some energy as well, dwindling toward the league median. Arenado's change in uniform hue was jarring, but his performance appeared to have a more gentle redshift, and it was an improvement over his injury-marred 2020: As his shoulder injury recovered, his power numbers rebounded. There was also a bit of a change in his world-class defense; there appeared to be a few extra gaffes in the field as he adapted to his new surroundings, even as he still acquitted himself as one of the game's top defensive third-sackers. Once again an All-Star and Platinum Glove winner, Arenado didn't have a peak near-MVP season, but those who thought he would burn up in the thickened air of the Midwest must be seeing red.

Harrison Bader CF Born: 06/03/94 Age: 28 Bats: R Throws: R Height: 6'0" Weight: 210 lb. Origin: Round 3, 2015 Draft (#100 overall)

YEAR	TEAM	LVL	AGE	PA	R	2B	3B	HR	RBI	BB	K	SB	CS	Whiff%	AVG/OBP/SLG	DRC+	BABIP	BRR	FRAA	WARP
2019	MEM	AAA	25	75	23	3	0	7	15	8	16	3	0		.317/.427/.698	115	.325	1.4	CF(16): 1.6	0.7
2019	STL	MLB	25	406	54	14	3	12	39	46	117	11	3	26.8%	.205/.314/.366	86	.268	4.6	CF(122): 15.1	2.9
2020	STL	MLB	26	125	21	7	2	4	11	13	40	3	1	28.3%	.226/.336/.443	88	.317	-0.1	CF(49): -3.2	-0.1
2021	STL	MLB	27	401	45	21	1	16	50	27	85	9	4	24.8%	.267/.324/.460	102	.306	4.9	CF(103): 16.3	4.0
2022 DC	*STL*	*MLB*	*28*	*452*	*59*	*19*	*1*	*15*	*66*	*37*	*105*	*11*	*4*	*24.7%*	*.255/.329/.430*	*108*	*.305*	*0.6*	*CF 3*	*2.5*

Comparables: Cameron Maybin, Jake Marisnick, Franklin Gutierrez

If you're looking for proof that exit velocity isn't everything, look no further than Bader. Few outfielders (read: four) had lower average exit velocity than the Cardinals' center fielder, but that didn't stop him from posting the first above-average offensive season of his nascent career. The defense is never a question—well, unless the question is "why is he always dinged up and fighting off minor injuries?"—and he earned his first Gold Glove due to his reliability and penchant for diving grabs. Sure, that dearth of hard contact and high strikeout rate means that his offensive output is subject to wide variance, somewhat exacerbated by his nicks and scratches, but he's emerged as a solid outfield regular with a high performance floor.

Joshua Baez CF Born: 06/28/03 Age: 19 Bats: R Throws: R Height: 6'4" Weight: 220 lb. Origin: Round 2, 2021 Draft (#54 overall)

YEAR	TEAM	LVL	AGE	PA	R	2B	3B	HR	RBI	BB	K	SB	CS	Whiff%	AVG/OBP/SLG	DRC+	BABIP	BRR	FRAA	WARP
2021	CAR	ROK	18	95	18	3	1	2	8	14	28	5	0		.158/.305/.303		.208			
2022															*No projection*					

Comparables: Marlin Almonte, Frank Tolentino, Eudy Pina

After staying safe with their top 2021 draft pick, the Cardinals rolled the dice in round two. Baez is a cold-weather, bat-first, corner outfield prospect with big raw power and very little present feel to hit. That sounds scary, and indeed this profile often doesn't click. But it also sounds a lot like Tyler O'Neill, whose slow climb to stardom is a useful reminder that when a player like Baez figures things out, the spoils can be enormous. For now, he's more lottery ticket than star. He swung and missed a lot as a high school senior and then hit .150 in a month of complex league ball. You definitely shouldn't write him off for any of that, but it's clear that Baez's development will be a slow burn.

Luken Baker 1B Born: 03/10/97 Age: 25 Bats: R Throws: R Height: 6'4" Weight: 280 lb. Origin: Round 2, 2018 Draft (#75 overall)

YEAR	TEAM	LVL	AGE	PA	R	2B	3B	HR	RBI	BB	K	SB	CS	Whiff%	AVG/OBP/SLG	DRC+	BABIP	BRR	FRAA	WARP
2019	PMB	A+	22	496	47	32	1	10	53	52	112	1	1		.244/.327/.390	117	.304	-5.5	1B(97): -3.3	1.3
2021	SPR	AA	24	391	51	20	0	26	68	38	103	0	0		.248/.322/.530	114	.270	-1.0	1B(84): -7.8	0.9
2022 non-DC	*STL*	*MLB*	*25*	*251*	*26*	*12*	*0*	*8*	*29*	*20*	*73*	*0*	*0*	*32.3%*	*.228/.296/.402*	*84*	*.298*	*-0.4*	*1B -1*	*-0.2*

Comparables: Mike Ford, Kennys Vargas, Trey Mancini

Paul Bunyan meets first base. Baker is neither baseball's tallest nor widest player, but at 6-foot-4 and 280, he's got 20 pounds on your average NFL tight end, and you can't help but notice the size of the man when he's on the field. The skill set mostly follows as you'd expect based on his physique. He has 70 raw power, plenty of swing-and-miss and a little trouble covering the strike zone. A two-way player in college, Baker actually has a plus arm, but lead feet and an iron skillet limit him to first base duty only. There's enough bat-to-ball skill here for him to potentially make it work as a second-division starter type, but he's probably a lefty masher off the bench in the end. If nothing else, Bunyan, err, Baker's presence on the roster alone should make opponents think twice about starting any skirmishes.

Alec Burleson OF Born: 11/25/98 Age: 23 Bats: L Throws: L Height: 6'2" Weight: 212 lb. Origin: Round 2, 2020 Draft (#70 overall)

YEAR	TEAM	LVL	AGE	PA	R	2B	3B	HR	RBI	BB	K	SB	CS	Whiff%	AVG/OBP/SLG	DRC+	BABIP	BRR	FRAA	WARP
2021	PEO	A+	22	49	8	1	0	4	10	6	15	1	0		.286/.367/.595	121	.333	-0.3	LF(7): 0.1, RF(3): -0.4	0.2
2021	SPR	AA	22	282	34	10	0	14	44	19	59	2	0		.288/.333/.488	113	.321	-0.7	RF(54): -1.9, 1B(1): -0.1, LF(1): 0.0	1.0
2021	MEM	AAA	22	172	19	7	0	4	22	17	27	0	1		.234/.310/.357	106	.260	-0.4	LF(21): -4.2, RF(18): 3.0	0.5
2022 non-DC	*STL*	*MLB*	*23*	*251*	*24*	*9*	*0*	*6*	*27*	*17*	*57*	*0*	*0*	*26.5%*	*.242/.297/.377*	*82*	*.294*	*-0.3*	*RF 1, LF 0*	*0.2*

Comparables: Billy McKinney, Eddie Rosario, Michael Conforto

Burleson is tracking like the kind of 1.5-win player fans come to adore. All the value is in his bat, but it's a pretty advanced stick, particularly given his background as a two-way player at East Carolina. He made a lot of contact at both levels of the high minors while swatting 18 homers in 120 games in 2021. That last part is particularly encouraging, because the risk on draft day was that he'd become a corner outfielder with only fringy power. Instead, he's already tapping into above-average raw during games, and there may even be more to come, as he's a ground-ball hitter a swing tweak away from a pretty darn interesting offensive ceiling. We can't project on that quite yet, which means that Burleson's defensive limitations likely limit him to a bench or second-division starter kind of role. No shame in that:Every good team needs guys like this.

Dylan Carlson OF

Born: 10/23/98 Age: 23 Bats: S Throws: L Height: 6'2" Weight: 205 lb. Origin: Round 1, 2016 Draft (#33 overall)

YEAR	TEAM	LVL	AGE	PA	R	2B	3B	HR	RBI	BB	K	SB	CS	Whiff%	AVG/OBP/SLG	DRC+	BABIP	BRR	FRAA	WARP
2019	SPR	AA	20	483	81	24	6	21	59	52	98	18	7		.281/.364/.518	131	.315	2.4	CF(87): -8.8, RF(9): -0.4, LF(5): -0.6	2.8
2019	MEM	AAA	20	79	14	4	2	5	9	6	18	2	1		.361/.418/.681	112	.429	0.0	CF(8): -0.6, LF(7): -0.2, RF(3): -0.2	0.3
2020	STL	MLB	21	119	11	7	1	3	16	8	35	1	1	31.0%	.200/.252/.364	81	.260	-0.6	RF(18): 1.7, CF(17): 0.3, LF(10): 1.2	0.3
2021	STL	MLB	22	619	79	31	4	18	65	57	152	2	1	27.9%	.266/.343/.437	101	.332	1.9	RF(87): 1.6, CF(60): 3.8, LF(9): -0.4	2.9
2022 DC	*STL*	*MLB*	*23*	*551*	*72*	*26*	*3*	*16*	*64*	*51*	*133*	*5*	*3*	*27.9%*	*.243/.324/.411*	*99*	*.301*	*0.1*	*RF 1, CF 0*	*1.6*

Comparables: Giancarlo Stanton, Jay Bruce, Nomar Mazara

So far, so good. It didn't take too long for the Cards' top-ranked prospect to settle in as an above-average regular in a talented outfield, earning a third-place finish in the 2021 Rookie of the Year voting. While he's been touted as a five-tool prospect, his recent performance may lean more towards three-and-three-quarters tools; he didn't lean too hard on his foot speed and he's going to be far more successful as a defender in a corner instead of center. He's still struggling to make solid contact on balls high in the zone, but his above-average power and solid on-base potential give him a great base to build a career as a consistent, first-division regular in a corner outfield spot.

Matt Carpenter IF

Born: 11/26/85 Age: 36 Bats: L Throws: R Height: 6'4" Weight: 210 lb. Origin: Round 13, 2009 Draft (#399 overall)

YEAR	TEAM	LVL	AGE	PA	R	2B	3B	HR	RBI	BB	K	SB	CS	Whiff%	AVG/OBP/SLG	DRC+	BABIP	BRR	FRAA	WARP
2019	STL	MLB	33	492	59	20	2	15	46	63	129	6	1	26.0%	.226/.334/.392	93	.285	-2.3	3B(107): -6.8, 1B(4): -0.2	-0.1
2020	STL	MLB	34	169	22	6	0	4	24	23	48	0	0	33.4%	.186/.325/.314	89	.250	0.1	3B(30): 2.1, 1B(6): -0.4	0.4
2021	STL	MLB	35	249	18	11	1	3	21	35	77	2	0	29.7%	.169/.305/.275	72	.250	-1.7	2B(34): -1.9, 1B(14): 1.6, 3B(6): -0.3	-0.2
2022 DC	*FA*	*MLB*	*36*	*207*	*23*	*9*	*0*	*6*	*23*	*29*	*62*	*0*	*1*	*30.1%*	*.202/.329/.375*	*90*	*.271*	*-0.2*	*3B 0, 2B 0*	*0.3*

Comparables: Eddie Mathews, Robin Ventura, Graig Nettles

One could say that a Carpenter without his tools is, essentially, just a guy waving a stick around. So goes it for this oft-overlooked "professional hitter," who spent the last decade racking up line drives and filling in at any position that would have him. Though there are still the echoes of the barrel shots that made him such a valuable contributor to the Cardinals teams of the past 10 years, his bat speed (and thus power) has faded, and in an attempt to offset its decline, it appears that he's selling out his once-formidable bat-to-ball skills. Now that he's likely to move on from where he's been a fixture for his whole career, he probably returns to his previous state as underrated, but now in a more historical sense. He'll likely never have the same association with the team as his contemporaries Adam Wainwright and Yadier Molina, but he was a remarkably productive player due a similar level of respect for his performance. Perhaps that level of respect will be enough to find him a job as a pinch-hit and clubhouse specialist, with this Carpenter working off the bench.

Paul DeJong SS

Born: 08/02/93 Age: 28 Bats: R Throws: R Height: 6'0" Weight: 205 lb. Origin: Round 4, 2015 Draft (#131 overall)

YEAR	TEAM	LVL	AGE	PA	R	2B	3B	HR	RBI	BB	K	SB	CS	Whiff%	AVG/OBP/SLG	DRC+	BABIP	BRR	FRAA	WARP
2019	STL	MLB	25	664	97	31	1	30	78	62	149	9	5	24.6%	.233/.318/.444	106	.259	0.6	SS(157): 7.4	3.6
2020	STL	MLB	26	174	17	6	0	3	25	17	50	1	0	32.3%	.250/.322/.349	88	.340	0.0	SS(45): -3.4	-0.1
2021	STL	MLB	27	402	44	10	1	19	45	35	103	4	1	27.9%	.197/.284/.390	96	.216	-1.7	SS(107): 2.7	1.4
2022 DC	*STL*	*MLB*	*28*	*553*	*68*	*21*	*1*	*20*	*69*	*48*	*139*	*4*	*2*	*27.2%*	*.225/.305/.400*	*91*	*.268*	*-0.5*	*SS 1*	*1.5*

Comparables: Roy Smalley, Alex Rodriguez, Jim Fregosi

DeJong has always had the rep of a boom-or-bust hitter, but the 2021 campaign was heavy on the latter with nary a boom in sight. His defensive limitation can certainly be papered over when he's buoyed by all-world defenders like the rest of the Cardinals' infield, but *only* if he can drive the ball more than a couple of times a week. When he's swinging through pipe shots and rolling the ball over into the shift, he's just another banger who could serve as the soft side of a platoon, not an everyday shortstop for a playoff team.

Brendan Donovan IF

Born: 01/16/97 Age: 25 Bats: L Throws: R Height: 6'1" Weight: 195 lb. Origin: Round 7, 2018 Draft (#213 overall)

YEAR	TEAM	LVL	AGE	PA	R	2B	3B	HR	RBI	BB	K	SB	CS	Whiff%	AVG/OBP/SLG	DRC+	BABIP	BRR	FRAA	WARP
2019	PEO	A	22	480	70	26	3	8	53	63	91	4	2		.266/.377/.405	122	.322	1.1	2B(101): -5.0	2.3
2021	GDD	WIN	24	64	10	5	0	2	8	10	8	2	1		.308/.422/.519		.326			
2021	PEO	A+	24	109	15	6	0	2	13	10	15	7	1		.295/.385/.421	118	.333	0.0	2B(22): -1.5, 3B(1): 0.3, LF(1): -0.0	0.5
2021	SPR	AA	24	219	35	10	1	4	28	25	39	8	5		.319/.411/.449	117	.379	-1.3	3B(18): 0.6, LF(14): -1.5, SS(9): 0.5	1.0
2021	MEM	AAA	24	131	23	5	0	6	25	15	23	4	2		.288/.389/.495	123	.313	0.7	1B(17): -3.0, 3B(12): -1.3, 2B(2): -0.5	0.3
2022 DC	*STL*	*MLB*	*25*	*97*	*11*	*4*	*0*	*1*	*9*	*8*	*18*	*0*	*1*	*21.3%*	*.246/.327/.363*	*90*	*.295*	*0.0*	*2B 0, RF 0*	*0.2*

Comparables: Vimael Machín, Scott Sizemore, Jake Cronenworth

The German-born Donovan was drafted out of a small D1 school in the seventh round of the 2018 draft. He's neither particularly large nor explosive, but he makes a lot of contact, can play all over the diamond and is a sneaky-quick runner. On paper, it's an up-and-down skillset but the Cardinals have traditionally gotten more out of this type of player than pretty much any other organization. With both contact hitting and positional flexibility in vogue these days, Donovan is a modern player coming into his own at the perfect time. After making the taxi squad for the Wild Card game loss last season, he should spend plenty of time on the field in 2022.

Tommy Edman 2B Born: 05/09/95 Age: 27 Bats: S Throws: R Height: 5'10" Weight: 180 lb. Origin: Round 6, 2016 Draft (#196 overall)

YEAR	TEAM	LVL	AGE	PA	R	2B	3B	HR	RBI	BB	K	SB	CS	Whiff%	AVG/OBP/SLG	DRC+	BABIP	BRR	FRAA	WARP
2019	MEM	AAA	24	218	39	12	4	7	29	15	33	9	0		.305/.356/.513	110	.333	3.5	2B(25): -0.2, SS(10): -1.5, 3B(9): 0.0	1.4
2019	STL	MLB	24	349	59	17	7	11	36	16	61	15	1	18.8%	.304/.350/.500	105	.346	4.2	3B(55): 0.5, 2B(29): 0.8, RF(12): 1.0	1.9
2020	STL	MLB	25	227	29	7	1	5	26	16	48	2	4	19.1%	.250/.317/.368	95	.301	0.2	3B(31): -0.4, SS(13): -1.1, RF(13): -1.4	0.4
2021	STL	MLB	26	691	91	41	3	11	56	38	95	30	5	15.0%	.262/.308/.387	92	.291	3.8	2B(130): 4.0, RF(41): -1.9, SS(4): 0.2	2.3
2022 DC	*STL*	*MLB*	*27*	*600*	*81*	*28*	*4*	*12*	*57*	*35*	*82*	*18*	*4*	*15.5%*	*.267/.318/.401*	*96*	*.294*	*1.3*	*2B 2, SS 0*	*2.1*

Comparables: Jed Lowrie, Erik González, Chris Taylor

Maybe not a star in the traditional sense, Edman is a bit of a niche celebrity among those who still play the more traditional style of fantasy baseball. Stolen bases have continued to fall out of vogue league-wide, but the Cardinals' speedster rated second in the NL in thefts; he remains one of the more valuable players in the game at adding runs on the basepaths. Add to that the Gold Glove defense at the pivot, the versatility to fill in as an outfielder as needed and how he can slap just enough singles to hold down a lineup spot, and you've got a player who's in high demand not just for fantasy teams, but playoff contenders too. Fame is fleeting, but so is Edman.

Paul Goldschmidt 1B Born: 09/10/87 Age: 34 Bats: R Throws: R Height: 6'3" Weight: 220 lb. Origin: Round 8, 2009 Draft (#246 overall)

YEAR	TEAM	LVL	AGE	PA	R	2B	3B	HR	RBI	BB	K	SB	CS	Whiff%	AVG/OBP/SLG	DRC+	BABIP	BRR	FRAA	WARP
2019	STL	MLB	31	682	97	25	1	34	97	78	166	3	1	26.3%	.260/.346/.476	114	.303	-0.4	1B(159): -7.6	2.3
2020	STL	MLB	32	231	31	13	0	6	21	37	43	1	0	23.7%	.304/.417/.466	127	.364	-0.7	1B(52): 1.6	1.4
2021	STL	MLB	33	679	102	36	2	31	99	67	136	12	0	24.9%	.294/.365/.514	127	.331	1.9	1B(153): -0.1	3.9
2022 DC	*STL*	*MLB*	*34*	*610*	*102*	*28*	*1*	*25*	*79*	*69*	*127*	*7*	*3*	*24.8%*	*.286/.369/.490*	*133*	*.328*	*-0.3*	*1B 0*	*3.6*

Comparables: Mark Teixeira, Eddie Murray, Jeff Bagwell

"America's First Baseman?" Psh. Try Thanos with a far more appealing jawline. Goldschmidt is implacable, unrelenting, *inevitable*. Since 2015 he has been the final boss for National League pitchers, a force of nature who hardly ever misses a game, who plays world-class defense, who imposes his will upon baseballs. Like the Mad Titan, he too seems like he was transported back from an earlier time, an era where first basemen were the sluggers around which the lineup revolved and whose stat lines could be simplified as .300/30/100. And when the prize was in his sight, he became even better, bringing even more offense to the table as the Cardinals made their run towards the season's endgame. Unfortunately for the Cardinals' opponents, baseball hasn't moved into MCU Phase 3 just yet, so expect Goldy's reign of terror to continue unabated for at least a few years more.

★ ★ ★ *2022 Top 101 Prospect* **#28** ★ ★ ★

Nolan Gorman 3B/2B Born: 05/10/00 Age: 22 Bats: L Throws: R Height: 6'1" Weight: 210 lb. Origin: Round 1, 2018 Draft (#19 overall)

YEAR	TEAM	LVL	AGE	PA	R	2B	3B	HR	RBI	BB	K	SB	CS	Whiff%	AVG/OBP/SLG	DRC+	BABIP	BRR	FRAA	WARP
2019	PEO	A	19	282	41	14	3	10	41	32	79	2	0		.241/.344/.448	117	.312	0.4	3B(51): 8.3	2.4
2019	PMB	A+	19	230	24	16	3	5	21	13	73	0	1		.256/.304/.428	87	.365	-1.9	3B(49): -6.6	-0.6
2021	SPR	AA	21	195	26	6	0	11	27	18	52	4	0		.288/.354/.508	114	.351	0.5	3B(23): -0.6, 2B(16): 2.0	1.1
2021	MEM	AAA	21	328	45	14	1	14	48	20	63	3	0		.274/.320/.465	109	.301	0.2	2B(61): 8.2, 3B(9): 0.4	2.2
2022 DC	*STL*	*MLB*	*22*	*64*	*8*	*2*	*0*	*2*	*7*	*4*	*17*	*0*	*0*	*30.6%*	*.253/.306/.421*	*93*	*.321*	*0.0*	*3B 0, 2B 1*	*0.2*

Comparables: Miguel Andújar, Blake DeWitt, Jorge Polanco

Jordan Walker broke out and knocked Gorman off of the top spot in our Cardinals prospect hierarchy, which says far more about the former's tantalizing upside than the latter's very solid 2021 campaign. As seems to be his custom, Gorman began the year by raking at one level before finding the sledding a little tougher after a mid-season promotion. He was still productive at Triple-A though, and even if most of his numbers in Memphis don't leap off the page, the sub-20% strikeout rate was a pleasant surprise. He still projects as a three-true-outcome bat, but if he's even modestly better at making contact now than we thought 12 months ago, a future of 30-homer, .260-average seasons seems very possible. The presence of Nolan Arenado prompted the Redbirds to shift Gorman to second last year, where he's below-average but playable. Time will tell whether he's able to stick there or if he'll need to shift to an outfield corner or first base. Regardless, he's tracking like a future big-league regular with All-Star upside.

Iván Herrera C Born: 06/01/00 Age: 22 Bats: R Throws: R Height: 5'11" Weight: 220 lb. Origin: International Free Agent, 2016

YEAR	TEAM	LVL	AGE	PA	R	2B	3B	HR	RBI	BB	K	SB	CS	Whiff%	AVG/OBP/SLG	DRC+	BABIP	BRR	FRAA	WARP
2019	PEO	A	19	291	41	10	0	8	42	35	56	1	1		.286/.381/.423	127	.337	0.0	C(64): -5.4	1.2
2019	PMB	A+	19	65	7	0	0	1	5	5	16	0	0		.276/.338/.328	90	.357	-1.0	C(18): -0.5	0.0
2021	SPR	AA	21	437	50	13	0	17	63	60	96	2	3		.231/.346/.408	106	.261	-1.7	C(71): 4.3	2.1
2022 DC	*STL*	*MLB*	*22*	*30*	*3*	*1*	*0*	*0*	*3*	*2*	*6*	*0*	*0*	*22.2%*	*.222/.306/.348*	*82*	*.270*	*0.0*	*C 0*	*0.0*

Comparables: Christian Bethancourt, Wilson Ramos, Salvador Perez

YEAR	TEAM	P. COUNT	FRM RUNS	BLK RUNS	THRW RUNS	TOT RUNS
2019	PMB	2683	-0.2	0.0	0.1	-0.1
2019	PEO	9385	-4.6	-0.2	0.2	-4.5
2019	GDD	1485			0.0	0.0
2021	SPR	11097	1.7	-0.4	0.5	1.8
2022	*STL*	*1202*	*-0.2*	*-0.1*	*0.0*	*-0.3*

To appreciate Herrera as a prospect, it helps to look at the broader state of catching throughout the league. Big-league backstops hit .228/.304/.391 last year, good (bad?) for a .302 wOBA, by far the worst output among any positional group. It's sufficiently underwhelming to make Herrera's average bat and fringe-average power look pretty appetizing, particularly given the rest of his skills. Defensively, he's a good receiver and blocker with a strong, if sometimes inconsistent arm. He's also chock full of intangibles, none more apparent than his command of the English language, which is particularly impressive given how young he is and that he signed out of Panama just five years ago. Even if he's not a burgeoning All-Star, he'll make a suitable replacement for Yadier Molina in 2023.

Andrew Knizner C

Born: 02/03/95 Age: 27 Bats: R Throws: R Height: 6'1" Weight: 225 lb. Origin: Round 7, 2016 Draft (#226 overall)

YEAR	TEAM	LVL	AGE	PA	R	2B	3B	HR	RBI	BB	K	SB	CS	Whiff%	AVG/OBP/SLG	DRC+	BABIP	BRR	FRAA	WARP
2019	MEM	AAA	24	280	41	10	0	12	34	24	37	2	0		.276/.357/.463	111	.281	-0.2	C(61): -19.6	-0.1
2019	STL	MLB	24	58	7	2	0	2	7	4	14	2	0	29.5%	.226/.293/.377	90	.270	0.2	C(16): -5.5, 1B(1): -0.0	-0.3
2020	STL	MLB	25	17	1	1	0	0	4	0	5	0	0	28.9%	.250/.235/.313	89	.333	0.0	C(7): -0.4	0.0
2021	STL	MLB	26	185	18	7	0	1	9	20	39	0	0	24.0%	.174/.281/.236	85	.223	-0.5	C(57): -5.0	-0.1
2022 DC	*STL*	*MLB*	*27*	*155*	*16*	*6*	*0*	*3*	*16*	*13*	*30*	*0*	*0*	*24.1%*	*.230/.310/.360*	*85*	*.268*	*-0.2*	*C -6, 1B 0*	*-0.3*

Comparables: Kevin Plawecki, Chris Iannetta, Francisco Cervelli

YEAR	TEAM	P. COUNT	FRM RUNS	BLK RUNS	THRW RUNS	TOT RUNS
2019	STL	2098	-5.4	0.0	0.0	-5.4
2019	MEM	9307	-19.5	0.0	-0.6	-20.0
2020	STL	679	-0.4	0.0	0.0	-0.4
2021	STL	6775	-5.1	-0.2	-0.2	-5.5
2022	*STL*	*4810*	*-5.4*	*-0.2*	*-0.1*	*-5.7*

Recent editions of Knizner's Annual comments have wryly observed that he's just the latest youngster condemned to await Yadi's retirement, sometimes with an underlying assumption that the starting job is his to lose once the legend finally bows out. The only lineup Knizner's on the cusp of joining, however, is down in Memphis, as the 27-year-old has done nothing to suggest he's ready for everyday work. The batting line speaks for itself, and there aren't any promising exit velocity or launch-angle numbers to dream on, either. All of that would be tolerable in a plus-plus defensive catcher, but Knizner is a bottom-tier framer and just adequate in the other things we can measure. As for the intangibles, well, Knizner was once voted the team's worst person to have as a roommate. Perhaps that was all just in good fun; either way, St. Louis' backstop of the future is probably not yet on the roster.

Yadier Molina C

Born: 07/13/82 Age: 39 Bats: R Throws: R Height: 5'11" Weight: 225 lb. Origin: Round 4, 2000 Draft (#113 overall)

YEAR	TEAM	LVL	AGE	PA	R	2B	3B	HR	RBI	BB	K	SB	CS	Whiff%	AVG/OBP/SLG	DRC+	BABIP	BRR	FRAA	WARP
2019	STL	MLB	36	452	45	24	0	10	57	23	58	6	0	19.1%	.270/.312/.399	98	.289	-1.8	C(111): 1.7, 1B(4): 0.0	1.8
2020	STL	MLB	37	156	12	2	0	4	16	6	21	0	0	23.9%	.262/.303/.359	108	.281	-1.5	C(42): 0.7, 1B(2): -0.0	0.6
2021	STL	MLB	38	473	45	19	0	11	66	24	79	3	0	24.0%	.252/.297/.370	93	.283	-2.7	C(118): 0.6, 1B(1): 0.0	1.4
2022 DC	*STL*	*MLB*	*39*	*460*	*49*	*18*	*0*	*10*	*55*	*24*	*81*	*4*	*2*	*23.9%*	*.249/.297/.372*	*82*	*.283*	*-0.3*	*C -4*	*0.6*

Comparables: Benito Santiago, Ivan Rodriguez, A.J. Pierzynski

YEAR	TEAM	P. COUNT	FRM RUNS	BLK RUNS	THRW RUNS	TOT RUNS
2019	STL	15645	2.1	0.1	0.3	2.5
2020	STL	5637	0.5	0.0	0.4	0.9
2021	STL	16610	-0.4	0.0	0.7	0.4
2022	*STL*	*16835*	*-7.5*	*0.1*	*0.7*	*-6.6*

Half of the most iconic duo in St. Louis' history–honorable mention goes to spare ribs and barbecue sauce–Molina stunned many with a hot offensive start that evoked memories of his performance a decade earlier. But as his 18th season wore on, the years showed out and his offensive output dipped to a career low. Perhaps even more telling that the end is near were his defensive metrics, which finally rated the venerable backstop as below-average thanks to his slowing footwork and years spent in the squat. Sturdier than the Gateway Arch and now only slightly more mobile, Yadi's still the anchor of the team's clubhouse and pitching staff. He'll make his final ride in red this year...after that, the next time we see him in a Cardinals cap may be on his Hall of Fame plaque.

Lars Nootbaar RF

Born: 09/08/97 Age: 24 Bats: L Throws: R Height: 6'3" Weight: 210 lb. Origin: Round 8, 2018 Draft (#243 overall)

YEAR	TEAM	LVL	AGE	PA	R	2B	3B	HR	RBI	BB	K	SB	CS	Whiff%	AVG/OBP/SLG	DRC+	BABIP	BRR	FRAA	WARP
2019	PEO	A	21	122	17	4	1	5	18	16	13	2	1		.245/.344/.443	148	.239	0.0	LF(15): -0.8, RF(12): -0.7	0.9
2019	PMB	A+	21	155	10	3	0	2	17	13	20	1	2		.275/.335/.338	118	.308	-1.6	LF(21): 4.6, RF(19): 2.7	1.4
2019	SPR	AA	21	110	12	2	1	0	3	16	22	1	1		.269/.373/.312	98	.347	0.7	LF(23): -1.3, RF(3): 2.4	0.5
2021	GDD	WIN	23	87	21	6	1	5	13	14	15	0	0		.314/.437/.643		.333			
2021	MEM	AAA	23	136	21	2	1	6	19	17	25	1	3		.308/.404/.496	129	.349	-0.2	RF(27): -1.0, LF(6): 2.4, CF(2): -0.1	1.0
2021	STL	MLB	23	124	15	3	1	5	15	13	28	2	1	26.1%	.239/.317/.422	98	.273	0.9	RF(26): 1.7, LF(9): -0.1	0.6
2022 DC	*STL*	*MLB*	*24*	*230*	*25*	*8*	*1*	*5*	*24*	*22*	*48*	*1*	*2*	*22.7%*	*.241/.319/.373*	*90*	*.288*	*0.0*	*RF 1, LF 0*	*0.3*

Comparables: Josh Reddick, Avisaíl García, Anthony Santander

Nootbar may have a name evocative of the Mos Eisley cantina, but his player profile is straight out of Mitch's Bar. A classic fourth outfielder type who's above-average defensively in the corners–you've probably already seen his Sept. 15 robbery of a Pete Alonso homer–and can fill in at center, he broke out in a big way in Memphis and carried over some surprising power to St. Louis. He finished out 2021 working on his on-base skills in the Arizona Fall League, and consolidating the gains from an outstanding year. With his family background, meteoric rise to the majors and newly-minted eponymous energy snack ("I'll have two NOOTBAARs."), the El Segundo native could even rate a film of his own someday.

Tyler O'Neill LF

Born: 06/22/95 Age: 27 Bats: R Throws: R Height: 5'11" Weight: 200 lb. Origin: Round 3, 2013 Draft (#85 overall)

YEAR	TEAM	LVL	AGE	PA	R	2B	3B	HR	RBI	BB	K	SB	CS	Whiff%	AVG/OBP/SLG	DRC+	BABIP	BRR	FRAA	WARP
2019	MEM	AAA	24	166	26	5	0	11	26	14	51	3	0		.265/.325/.517	98	.322	0.7	LF(25): -0.5, RF(11): 0.9	0.6
2019	STL	MLB	24	151	18	6	0	5	16	10	53	1	0	41.4%	.262/.311/.411	73	.386	-0.9	LF(33): -3.3, RF(8): -0.2, CF(3): 0.2	-0.4
2020	STL	MLB	25	157	20	5	0	7	19	15	43	3	1	33.9%	.173/.261/.360	95	.189	0.0	LF(48): 6.8	1.0
2021	STL	MLB	26	537	89	26	2	34	80	38	168	15	4	34.8%	.286/.352/.560	120	.366	6.7	LF(131): 1.0	4.2
2022 DC	*STL*	*MLB*	*27*	*561*	*79*	*22*	*1*	*30*	*88*	*42*	*164*	*7*	*2*	*34.4%*	*.247/.313/.483*	*113*	*.298*	*0.0*	*LF 2*	*2.8*

Comparables: Randal Grichuk, Carlos González, Domonic Brown

Ah, the fabled consolidation year. Talent evaluators talk about these seasons where a player who can do so many things well—but have never done them all at the same time—finally makes it all come together. O'Neill has always had the tools to do whatever he wanted on the field, and we caught a glimpse of the big picture in the shortened 2020 season, but *almost* everything clicked this past season. He'd displayed prodigious power, the ability to make contact, the defense and the baserunning acumen at different times, but last year he packed it all into one dynamic season that allowed him to circle the top end of National League MVP voting. The one caveat might be his defense; our metrics had him below-average even as a second Gold Glove award found its way to his shelf. But 34 homers and the best baserunning numbers of any player in baseball are nothing to sneeze at, and O'Neill finds himself as one of the most fearsome hitters on a team lousy with them. He's now one of the best corner outfielders in the league.

Edmundo Sosa MI Born: 03/06/96 Age: 26 Bats: R Throws: R Height: 6'0" Weight: 210 lb. Origin: International Free Agent, 2012

YEAR	TEAM	LVL	AGE	PA	R	2B	3B	HR	RBI	BB	K	SB	CS	Whiff%	AVG/OBP/SLG	DRC+	BABIP	BRR	FRAA	WARP
2019	AGU	WIN	23	195	27	7	0	3	14	7	41	3	0		.274/.332/.366		.338			
2019	MEM	AAA	23	496	70	18	5	17	62	17	96	2	3		.291/.335/.466	97	.332	0.0	SS(84): 3.8, 2B(17): 0.5, 3B(15): -1.5	2.1
2019	STL	MLB	23	10	2	0	0	0	0	1	2	1	0	21.4%	.250/.400/.250	86	.333	-0.1	2B(4): -0.1	0.0
2021	STL	MLB	25	326	39	8	4	6	27	17	63	4	4	28.1%	.271/.346/.389	102	.326	0.3	SS(71): 2.3, 2B(25): -0.4, 3B(9): -0.5	1.4
2022 DC	*STL*	*MLB*	*26*	*188*	*19*	*7*	*1*	*3*	*19*	*9*	*39*	*1*	*1*	*27.5%*	*.245/.308/.362*	*86*	*.296*	*0.0*	*2B 0, SS 1*	*0.3*

Comparables: Eduardo Escobar, Jonathan Villar, Marwin Gonzalez

And there you have it. Flash back to last year's Annual, where it was posited that Sosa was primed to be the next in a long line of players who appear from seemingly out of nowhere (read: the fringes of the team's prospect list) to emerge as a viable regular in St. Louis. Sure enough, Sosa displaced Paul DeJong as the Cardinals' starting shortstop, found a way to hit for a little power while playing slick defense and gave new meaning to the term "red ass" when he absolutely destroyed his pants sliding into a base during a Cardinals game. Solid defense, hitting just a hair more than anyone expects and playing so hard that your uniform is at risk? If that's not the embodiment of Cardinals Devil Magic, it's not clear what is.

Anderson Tejeda SS Born: 05/01/98 Age: 24 Bats: S Throws: R Height: 6'0" Weight: 200 lb. Origin: International Free Agent, 2014

YEAR	TEAM	LVL	AGE	PA	R	2B	3B	HR	RBI	BB	K	SB	CS	Whiff%	AVG/OBP/SLG	DRC+	BABIP	BRR	FRAA	WARP
2019	DE	A+	21	181	22	10	1	4	24	17	58	9	4		.234/.315/.386	83	.333	0.6	SS(39): 3.0	0.5
2020	TEX	MLB	22	77	7	4	1	3	8	2	30	4	1	39.4%	.253/.273/.453	71	.381	0.2	SS(18): -1.6, 2B(4): -0.1	-0.2
2021	LIC	WIN	23	71	7	2	0	2	7	7	23	3	0		.246/.314/.377		.342			
2021	FRI	AA	23	192	19	8	0	9	20	15	82	2	1		.200/.267/.400	64	.310	-0.8	SS(46): 0.8, 2B(1): 0.1	-0.2
2021	RR	AAA	23	111	13	1	1	3	12	11	47	8	2		.152/.236/.273	64	.245	1.4	SS(23): -1.4, 2B(3): -0.1, 3B(1): -0.1	-0.2
2021	TEX	MLB	23	17	1	0	0	0	0	1	10	1	0	48.4%	.063/.118/.063	65	.167	0.0	3B(5): -0.0, 2B(1): -0.0	0.0
2022 non-DC	*STL*	*MLB*	*24*	*251*	*22*	*9*	*1*	*7*	*26*	*17*	*106*	*3*	*2*	*41.4%*	*.184/.247/.338*	*49*	*.299*	*0.4*	*SS 0, 2B 0*	*-0.7*

Comparables: Jonathan Villar, Eduardo Núñez, Hernán Pérez

When Tejeda homered in his big-league debut, it felt like maybe the Rangers had found a diamond in the rough. That might still be true, but if so, there's just a whole lot more rough than previously thought. Tejeda went from the big leagues to Triple-A to Double-A, and even found himself on a rehab assignment in the Arizona Complex League, where he finally raked in [double-checking notes] four games. How bad was his 2021 season? He's still just 23, and the Rangers' system is a bit thin on shortstops...and they outrighted him in November, allowing him to become a free agent. The Cardinals picked him up shortly after, so you know what that means.

★ ★ ★ *2022 Top 101 Prospect* **#7** ★ ★ ★

Jordan Walker 3B Born: 05/22/02 Age: 20 Bats: R Throws: R Height: 6'5" Weight: 220 lb. Origin: Round 1, 2020 Draft (#21 overall)

YEAR	TEAM	LVL	AGE	PA	R	2B	3B	HR	RBI	BB	K	SB	CS	Whiff%	AVG/OBP/SLG	DRC+	BABIP	BRR	FRAA	WARP
2021	PMB	A	19	122	24	11	1	6	21	18	21	1	0		.374/.475/.687	145	.419	-0.3	3B(22): -3.6	0.6
2021	PEO	A+	19	244	39	14	3	8	27	15	66	13	2		.292/.344/.487	101	.382	-0.5	3B(54): -3.6	0.4
2022 non-DC	*STL*	*MLB*	*20*	*251*	*24*	*12*	*1*	*5*	*26*	*16*	*68*	*5*	*2*	*30.9%*	*.245/.302/.392*	*85*	*.323*	*0.4*	*3B -3*	*-0.1*

Comparables: Josh Vitters, Rafael Devers, Blake DeWitt

Walker hasn't reached Double-A just yet, which means the error bars on our projections for him are... you know what, forget all that. This kid is awesome. He smoked the competition in Low-A and then acquitted himself very well as one of the younger players in all of High-A last season. Tall, athletic and well-built, Walker projects to have plus-plus power at full maturity. His max exit velocity last year was more than 116 mph, higher than all but 15 big-leaguers managed to muster and also harder than any Cardinal has hit a ball since 2018. Even better, he has a decent shot to get to that pop in games because he's no indiscriminate hacker. His approach is pretty seasoned for a youngster and even at High-A, he posted a better-than-average whiff rate. Defensively, he's just okay at third base and may have to slide down the spectrum as he grows. It won't matter. Further physical development probably turns him into a 40-homer hitter and that plays anywhere around the diamond. One of 2021's biggest prospect breakouts, Walker has all the makings of a future star. Cardinals fans should be very, very excited.

Masyn Winn SS Born: 03/21/02 Age: 20 Bats: R Throws: R Height: 5'11" Weight: 180 lb. Origin: Round 2, 2020 Draft (#54 overall)

YEAR	TEAM	LVL	AGE	PA	R	2B	3B	HR	RBI	BB	K	SB	CS	Whiff%	AVG/OBP/SLG	DRC+	BABIP	BRR	FRAA	WARP
2021	PMB	A	19	284	50	15	3	3	34	40	60	16	2		.262/.370/.388	108	.331	3.8	SS(55): 6.5	2.0
2021	PEO	A+	19	154	26	4	2	2	10	6	40	16	3		.209/.240/.304	87	.274	0.7	SS(31): 1.3	0.4
2022 non-DC	*STL*	*MLB*	*20*	*251*	*19*	*10*	*2*	*2*	*20*	*18*	*65*	*12*	*3*	*28.2%*	*.220/.282/.316*	*63*	*.297*	*1.2*	*SS 3, 1B 0*	*0.2*

Comparables: Ketel Marte, Tyler Pastornicky, Jonathan Villar

You might want to grab a drink before settling in, we've got a lot to cover here. St. Louis drafted Winn as a two-way player in the second round of the 2020 draft. The Cardinals primarily focused on the positional side of his game in 2021, where he took most of his reps. He acquitted himself well at Low-A, posting an above-average line with a top exit velocity north of 110. After a midseason promotion, Winn soon found that the leap from Low-A to High-A is much bigger now than it was two years ago. Advanced arms exposed an immature approach, and given the numbers above, he'll surely be back in Peoria next spring. We're not sure how often he'll get to that power given his approach, but he doesn't have to mash all that much, as he's a good defensive shortstop with above-average range and a 70 arm.

If everything fails to come together at the plate, Winn can turn to the mound as a fallback. He only made one in-game appearance last year, but he runs his heat into the mid-90s with raw but promising secondaries. The likeliest path is that St. Louis continues developing him as a hitter, and as long as he can pull his weight at the dish, his glove should push him up the ladder fairly quickly. There's some chance that he's not quite good enough on either side of the ball to hack it in the big leagues at the end of the day, but for now we say phooey to that. This is one of the most fun players in the entire organization, and as long as the range of outcomes here runs the gamut from 'high minors org type" to "legitimate weapon on both sides of the ball," we encourage you to dream on the latter outcome.

Juan Yepez 1B Born: 02/19/98 Age: 24 Bats: R Throws: R Height: 6'1" Weight: 200 lb. Origin: International Free Agent, 2014

YEAR	TEAM	LVL	AGE	PA	R	2B	3B	HR	RBI	BB	K	SB	CS	Whiff%	AVG/OBP/SLG	DRC+	BABIP	BRR	FRAA	WARP
2019	PEO	A	21	101	14	7	0	4	13	11	24	2	1		.284/.366/.500	109	.344	-0.3	3B(11): 0.2, 1B(6): 0.4, RF(2): 0.4	0.4
2019	PMB	A+	21	115	16	4	0	4	20	10	21	1	0		.275/.351/.431	121	.312	-0.4	RF(22): -0.3, 3B(5): 0.6, 1B(4): -0.1	0.6
2019	SPR	AA	21	59	8	2	0	2	10	5	14	0	0		.231/.288/.385	85	.263	0.3	LF(12): -1.5, 1B(5): -0.0, 3B(1): -0.0	-0.1
2021	GDD	WIN	23	103	15	8	0	7	26	12	18	1	0		.302/.388/.640		.297			
2021	SPR	AA	23	77	11	4	0	5	14	9	13	0	0		.270/.387/.571	128	.267	-0.7	1B(7): -0.4, LF(5): -0.9, 3B(4): 0.1	0.3
2021	MEM	AAA	23	357	56	25	0	22	63	42	69	1	3		.289/.382/.589	146	.304	-0.2	1B(60): -2.6, 3B(11): -0.6, LF(9): -0.7	2.3
2022 DC	*STL*	*MLB*	*24*	*135*	*17*	*6*	*0*	*4*	*16*	*11*	*32*	*0*	*1*	*27.6%*	*.244/.316/.417*	*100*	*.295*	*-0.1*	*1B 0, 3B 0*	*0.1*

Comparables: José Osuna, Avisaíl García, Jeimer Candelario

Few players had as busy of a 2021 as the Cardinals' newest young slugger, and nearly all of his breakout season was a success. After years toiling in the minors for both Atlanta and St. Louis, his long-dormant game power finally emerged from his brawny frame; he dominated upper-minors pitching, got a surprise tap on the shoulder for the NL Wild Card Game, then finally routed the pitchers in the AFL. By November, he was the cleanup hitter in the Fall Stars Game, where he banged a couple of extra-base hits and is poised to add his bat to one of the most devastating collections of right-handed power hitters on any MLB roster. With Paul Goldschmidt, Nolan Arenado and Tyler O'Neill ahead of him in St. Louis and the designated hitter in the offing, opposing lefties might want to take a sick day instead of heading to St. Louis next year.

PITCHERS

Génesis Cabrera LHP Born: 10/10/96 Age: 25 Bats: L Throws: L Height: 6'2" Weight: 180 lb. Origin: International Free Agent, 2013

YEAR	TEAM	LVL	AGE	W	L	SV	G	GS	IP	H	HR	BB/9	K/9	K	GB%	BABIP	WHIP	ERA	DRA-	WARP	MPH	FB%	Whiff%	CSP
2019	MEM	AAA	22	5	6	0	20	18	99	107	20	3.5	9.6	106	39.8%	.333	1.47	5.91	95	0.9				
2019	STL	MLB	22	0	2	1	13	2	20^{1}	23	2	4.9	8.4	19	37.3%	.328	1.67	4.87	120	0.0	96.5	61.0%	18.1%	48.3%
2020	STL	MLB	23	4	1	1	19	0	22^{1}	10	3	6.4	12.9	32	34.1%	.171	1.16	2.42	95	0.3	96.6	56.4%	40.3%	47.3%
2021	STL	MLB	24	4	5	0	71	0	70	52	3	4.6	9.9	77	41.0%	.287	1.26	3.73	93	0.9	97.9	64.5%	26.3%	54.1%
2022 DC	*STL*	*MLB*	*25*	*3*	*3*	*1*	*67*	*0*	*58*	*49*	*8*	*4.8*	*10.7*	*69*	*39.0%*	*.286*	*1.38*	*4.35*	*103*	*0.1*	*97.6*	*62.9%*	*28.0%*	*52.5%*

Comparables: Darwinzon Hernandez, Randall Delgado, Eric O'Flaherty

Every good team needs a reliever like Cabrera, someone reliable to tend to the sixth or seventh inning while you wash the dishes and take out the garbage. Look, you and I both know that Cabrera isn't the most interesting pitcher on the roster. He's working middle relief because he's too wild for late-inning duty, yet too versatile to shuttle between Memphis and St. Louis. Like the aforementioned chores, it's mostly thankless work, although at least this gig pays six figures.

Jack Flaherty RHP Born: 10/15/95 Age: 26 Bats: R Throws: R Height: 6'4" Weight: 225 lb. Origin: Round 1, 2014 Draft (#34 overall)

YEAR	TEAM	LVL	AGE	W	L	SV	G	GS	IP	H	HR	BB/9	K/9	K	GB%	BABIP	WHIP	ERA	DRA-	WARP	MPH	FB%	Whiff%	CSP
2019	STL	MLB	23	11	8	0	33	33	196^{1}	135	25	2.5	10.6	231	39.7%	.244	0.97	2.75	71	5.0	94.3	57.8%	30.9%	46.8%
2020	STL	MLB	24	4	3	0	9	9	40^{1}	33	6	3.6	10.9	49	44.1%	.284	1.21	4.91	81	0.9	93.9	55.6%	34.5%	44.6%
2021	STL	MLB	25	9	2	0	17	15	78^{1}	57	12	3.0	9.8	85	39.0%	.236	1.06	3.22	85	1.3	93.7	56.8%	28.0%	55.6%
2022 DC	*STL*	*MLB*	*26*	*10*	*7*	*0*	*27*	*27*	*148.7*	*122*	*19*	*3.0*	*9.8*	*162*	*40.4%*	*.273*	*1.16*	*3.34*	*85*	*2.3*	*94.0*	*56.9%*	*30.1%*	*50.5%*

Comparables: Michael Pineda, Danny Salazar, Chris Archer

Pitcher injuries are the rule and not the exception, especially as velocity and spin claim kingship and even starting pitchers are asked to give all-out effort with every delivery. But when a hurler injures himself—or aggravates an injury, as the case with Flaherty—when *hitting*, that particularly stings. With the advent of the National League DH on the horizon, teams hopefully will have less to fear from injuries like Flare's oblique strain, which kept him off the mound for more than half the season (and later may have contributed to a shoulder strain). He's still a solid number two starter who put up sparkling numbers even though his velocity and peripherals took a smidge of a dip, but before this he'd been virtually untouched by major injury. He'll now have to prove health rather than have it be assumed, but he remains one of the league's best righties.

Giovanny Gallegos RHP Born: 08/14/91 Age: 30 Bats: R Throws: R Height: 6'2" Weight: 215 lb. Origin: International Free Agent, 2011

YEAR	TEAM	LVL	AGE	W	L	SV	G	GS	IP	H	HR	BB/9	K/9	K	GB%	BABIP	WHIP	ERA	DRA-	WARP	MPH	FB%	Whiff%	CSP
2019	STL	MLB	27	3	2	1	66	0	74	44	9	1.9	11.3	93	33.5%	.222	0.81	2.31	80	1.5	93.8	55.2%	34.7%	48.5%
2020	STL	MLB	28	2	2	4	16	0	15	9	1	2.4	12.6	21	40.6%	.258	0.87	3.60	80	0.3	94.0	48.9%	38.1%	47.5%
2021	STL	MLB	29	6	5	14	73	0	80^1	51	6	2.2	10.6	95	32.3%	.247	0.88	3.02	83	1.4	94.6	52.8%	34.8%	54.9%
2022 DC	*STL*	*MLB*	*30*	*3*	*3*	*27*	*67*	*0*	*58*	*45*	*8*	*2.4*	*11.4*	*74*	*34.2%*	*.274*	*1.04*	*2.83*	*74*	*1.0*	*94.4*	*53.0%*	*35.0%*	*52.9%*

Comparables: Pedro Strop, Heath Bell, Héctor Neris

After baffling the opposition for two seasons, Gallegos graduated to the closer role after Alex Reyes' collapse. Now, he's finally stepped into the appropriate spotlight for his skills. The fireballer got even stronger as the season wore on and he settled into the finisher's role, using his heater and outstanding slider to deceive opposing hitters by both avoiding the zone and avoiding bats. The bottom falls out of his slider almost like a curve and makes opposing hitters miss even when it starts in their wheelhouse. Now established as one of the best firemen in the game, Gallegos gives the Cards a reliable late-inning option to build their bullpen around.

J.A. Happ LHP Born: 10/19/82 Age: 39 Bats: L Throws: L Height: 6'5" Weight: 205 lb. Origin: Round 3, 2004 Draft (#92 overall)

YEAR	TEAM	LVL	AGE	W	L	SV	G	GS	IP	H	HR	BB/9	K/9	K	GB%	BABIP	WHIP	ERA	DRA-	WARP	MPH	FB%	Whiff%	CSP
2019	NYY	MLB	36	12	8	0	31	30	161^1	160	34	2.7	7.8	140	40.5%	.281	1.30	4.91	117	0.2	91.5	68.3%	23.8%	45.9%
2020	NYY	MLB	37	2	2	0	9	9	49^1	37	8	2.7	7.7	42	43.8%	.227	1.05	3.47	103	0.5	91.1	67.1%	22.7%	46.2%
2021	MIN	MLB	38	5	6	0	19	19	98^1	125	21	2.8	7.0	77	34.7%	.332	1.59	6.77	162	-2.3	90.8	70.6%	19.8%	53.2%
2021	STL	MLB	38	5	2	0	11	11	54	52	9	2.8	7.5	45	34.8%	.281	1.28	4.00	118	0.0	90.7	74.4%	18.8%	51.6%
2022 DC	*FA*	*MLB*	*39*	*7*	*8*	*0*	*25*	*25*	*129.3*	*140*	*22*	*2.9*	*7.2*	*103*	*36.4%*	*.299*	*1.40*	*4.97*	*121*	*-0.4*	*91.0*	*70.5%*	*20.8%*	*50.3%*

Comparables: Aníbal Sánchez, Jim Lonborg, Ted Lilly

Happ looked every one of his 38 grizzled years when St. Louis picked him up in exchange for John Gant last summer. After his last outing in Minnesota—three innings, nine runs, four walks, 10 hits—took his ERA into the high-sixes, it was fair to wonder whether the lefty still deserved a spot in a big-league rotation. St. Louis fans were understandably underwhelmed when he and fellow aging southpaw Jon Lester were John Mozeliak's only deadline acquisitions, but both rewarded the club for its faith. Happ notched a 2.22 ERA in five August starts, and then pitched well again throughout the Cards' 17-game winning streak. What changed? Not all that much! Happ started using his sinker a little more often, which doesn't adequately explain a modest strikeout uptick (nor a slightly reduced ground-ball rate). Occam's Razor suggests the usual culprits: a lower BABIP, lower HR/FB, higher strand rate, and all the usual things that can swing a 5.47 DRA into much tidier run prevention. That's all well and good for the 2021 Cardinals, but PECOTA's Razor says it probably won't happen again.

Ryan Helsley RHP Born: 07/18/94 Age: 27 Bats: R Throws: R Height: 6'2" Weight: 230 lb. Origin: Round 5, 2015 Draft (#161 overall)

YEAR	TEAM	LVL	AGE	W	L	SV	G	GS	IP	H	HR	BB/9	K/9	K	GB%	BABIP	WHIP	ERA	DRA-	WARP	MPH	FB%	Whiff%	CSP
2019	MEM	AAA	24	2	3	1	17	7	37^1	29	3	4.8	9.9	41	41.5%	.289	1.31	4.58	85	0.6				
2019	STL	MLB	24	2	0	0	24	0	36^2	34	5	2.9	7.9	32	33.0%	.282	1.25	2.95	103	0.3	98.1	56.6%	22.3%	53.0%
2020	STL	MLB	25	1	1	1	12	0	12	8	3	6.0	7.5	10	33.3%	.167	1.33	5.25	138	-0.1	97.1	43.3%	31.9%	48.1%
2021	STL	MLB	26	6	4	1	51	0	47^1	40	4	5.1	8.9	47	41.7%	.283	1.42	4.56	106	0.3	97.7	55.8%	27.3%	56.5%
2022 DC	*STL*	*MLB*	*27*	*2*	*3*	*0*	*59*	*0*	*51.7*	*47*	*7*	*4.7*	*9.5*	*54*	*39.4%*	*.291*	*1.43*	*4.47*	*106*	*0.0*	*97.7*	*54.5%*	*27.0%*	*54.9%*

Comparables: José Ramirez, Luke Jackson, Matt Albers

Ninety-six innings into his big-league career, Helsley looks like someone headed for the Memphis-St. Louis carousel. He surrenders too many walks and yields too much contact to be trusted with late-inning work, but his 98-mph fastball gives him just enough leeway to justify a spot on the 40-man and get shuttled on and off the big-league roster as needs dictate. He's avoided this fate thus far due to health issues the last two seasons, but it seems inevitable once he's healthy. He has two option years left, which means there's a good chance he'll spend the next couple of seasons circling the baggage claim at Mozeliak International Airport.

Jordan Hicks RHP Born: 09/06/96 Age: 25 Bats: R Throws: R Height: 6'2" Weight: 220 lb. Origin: Round 3, 2015 Draft (#105 overall)

YEAR	TEAM	LVL	AGE	W	L	SV	G	GS	IP	H	HR	BB/9	K/9	K	GB%	BABIP	WHIP	ERA	DRA-	WARP	MPH	FB%	Whiff%	CSP
2019	STL	MLB	22	2	2	14	29	0	28^2	16	2	3.5	9.7	31	67.2%	.215	0.94	3.14	85	0.5	101.5	60.5%	30.8%	46.0%
2021	STL	MLB	24	0	0	0	10	0	10	5	0	9.0	9.0	10	70.8%	.208	1.50	5.40	95	0.1	99.9	68.8%	23.4%	47.8%
2022 DC	*STL*	*MLB*	*25*	*2*	*3*	*0*	*59*	*0*	*51.7*	*44*	*4*	*5.8*	*9.6*	*55*	*56.6%*	*.290*	*1.50*	*4.41*	*102*	*0.1*	*100.6*	*65.3%*	*26.5%*	*47.0%*

Comparables: Jeremy Jeffress, Alberto Cabrera, Ken McBride

Hicks returned to action for the first time in nearly two years last spring. But like many of you, the flamethrowing righty found life anything but normal in 2021. A degree of rust was understandable, but Hicks wasn't throwing quite as hard as usual and he walked more than a batter per inning in April. A barking elbow sent him to the injured list, where he stayed until season's end before a choppy cameo as a starter in the Arizona Fall League. Not even three years since becoming St. Louis' closer, Hicks' career is at a crossroads. At his best, he's the hardest thrower alive and he keeps hitters honest with an excellent slider. The front office hopes a fresh start in 2022 will spark a return to top form; sadly, usually pitchers two-and-a-half years removed from their peak don't find their way back.

Dakota Hudson RHP Born: 09/15/94 Age: 27 Bats: R Throws: R Height: 6'5" Weight: 215 lb. Origin: Round 1, 2016 Draft (#34 overall)

YEAR	TEAM	LVL	AGE	W	L	SV	G	GS	IP	H	HR	BB/9	K/9	K	GB%	BABIP	WHIP	ERA	DRA-	WARP	MPH	FB%	Whiff%	CSP
2019	STL	MLB	24	16	7	1	33	32	174^{2}	160	22	4.4	7.0	136	56.3%	.275	1.41	3.35	100	1.8	93.9	61.7%	23.8%	46.9%
2020	STL	MLB	25	3	2	0	8	8	39	24	5	3.5	7.2	31	57.7%	.192	1.00	2.77	86	0.7	93.2	58.6%	21.9%	44.5%
2021	SPR	AA	26	1	0	0	3	3	11^{2}	8	0	3.9	5.4	7	56.2%	.250	1.11	0.77	103	0.1				
2021	STL	MLB	26	1	0	0	2	1	8^{2}	7	0	1.0	6.2	6	65.4%	.269	0.92	2.08	106	0.1	92.4	50.4%	16.1%	58.5%
2022 DC	*STL*	*MLB*	*27*	*10*	*9*	*0*	*58*	*21*	*131.3*	*136*	*12*	*4.0*	*6.8*	*99*	*55.8%*	*.303*	*1.48*	*4.62*	*110*	*0.3*	*93.6*	*59.9%*	*22.6%*	*47.3%*

Comparables: Mike Foltynewicz, Alex Cobb, Scott Feldman

It's not enough to confound the conventional wisdom by consistently outpitching his peripherals. No. Now Dak has found himself a new expectation to demolish: injury recovery. The big righty bounced back from his 2020 Tommy John surgery in record time, surfacing for two effective outings just about a year after going under the knife. Don't read too much into those outings, though; not only were they against the Cubs' Emmental-esque lineup, but his velocity hasn't yet rebounded to where he was pre-surgery. He'll need every ounce of velocity to go with his guile and dirt-kicking sinker, because the Redbirds intend to pencil him into the middle of the rotation and back him up with the team's world-class defense in 2022.

Kwang Hyun Kim LHP Born: 07/22/88 Age: 33 Bats: L Throws: L Height: 6'2" Weight: 195 lb. Origin: International Free Agent, 2019

YEAR	TEAM	LVL	AGE	W	L	SV	G	GS	IP	H	HR	BB/9	K/9	K	GB%	BABIP	WHIP	ERA	DRA-	WARP	MPH	FB%	Whiff%	CSP
2020	STL	MLB	31	3	0	1	8	7	39	28	3	2.8	5.5	24	50.0%	.217	1.03	1.62	114	0.1	90.1	48.3%	18.3%	48.6%
2021	STL	MLB	32	7	7	1	27	21	106^{2}	98	12	3.3	6.8	80	46.8%	.273	1.28	3.46	114	0.2	89.3	41.8%	21.9%	54.1%
2022 DC	*FA*	*MLB*	*33*	*9*	*8*	*0*	*69*	*12*	*110.3*	*114*	*14*	*3.2*	*6.6*	*81*	*46.0%*	*.292*	*1.39*	*4.50*	*112*	*0.0*	*89.5*	*43.0%*	*21.3%*	*53.1%*

Comparables: Dennis Martinez, Kenny Rogers, Dave Roberts

There's a striking gap between Kim's run prevention numbers and DRA. Frankly, the DRA makes more sense, as Kim's a soft-tosser who yields his share of walks and averages fewer than five innings per start. Everything points to a generic no. 5 starter except for, well, he's got a 73 ERA- and a 101 FIP- since coming stateside. The best explanation is that Kim has the right blend of command, deception and witchcraft to consistently run his pitches off of opposing barrels. His exit velocity numbers, ground-ball ratio and hard contact rates all support that theory, as do Statcast's more esoteric measurements. It seems a delicate cosmic balance: A little less velocity or even a slightly wayward arm slot could wipe out all of the metaphorical bees and bananas in Kim's pitching ecosystem. For now though, he's getting results in an unconventional and underappreciated manner. Michael Lewis once wrote a book about players like that.

Jon Lester LHP Born: 01/07/84 Age: 38 Bats: L Throws: L Height: 6'4" Weight: 249 lb. Origin: Round 2, 2002 Draft (#57 overall)

YEAR	TEAM	LVL	AGE	W	L	SV	G	GS	IP	H	HR	BB/9	K/9	K	GB%	BABIP	WHIP	ERA	DRA-	WARP	MPH	FB%	Whiff%	CSP
2019	CHC	MLB	35	13	10	0	31	31	171^{2}	205	26	2.7	8.7	165	42.3%	.350	1.50	4.46	109	0.9	90.5	38.7%	21.2%	45.7%
2020	CHC	MLB	36	3	3	0	12	12	61	64	11	2.5	6.2	42	47.8%	.277	1.33	5.16	126	-0.2	89.4	41.2%	18.2%	45.9%
2021	STL	MLB	37	4	1	0	12	12	66	68	11	3.5	5.5	40	45.2%	.282	1.42	4.36	135	-0.6	88.1	50.4%	20.7%	52.5%
2021	WAS	MLB	37	3	5	0	16	16	75^{1}	91	14	3.5	6.1	51	41.4%	.314	1.59	5.02	137	-0.8	88.7	44.7%	19.9%	52.9%
2022 DC	*FA*	*MLB*	*38*	*7*	*9*	*0*	*25*	*25*	*129.3*	*146*	*19*	*3.3*	*6.4*	*91*	*42.7%*	*.305*	*1.49*	*5.15*	*124*	*-0.6*	*89.1*	*44.1%*	*20.2%*	*49.8%*

Comparables: Tom Glavine, Jim Kaat, Tommy John

Is there any cliché more steeped in bullshit than the classic "time heals all wounds"? Ask any veteran pitcher: Time *is* a wound; open, seeping, pulsing your velocity away in drips and drabs. The years and the innings have rubbed Lester raw, changed him to a pitcher who has to work around the barrel of the bat instead of powering past it, left him trying to trick his way into the fifth inning. The years have cost him minutes, robbing him of his mid-career label of "reliable innings-eater" and transforming him into a pitcher who can't be trusted to face more than 18 hitters. While he may still have a place as the 11th pitcher on a staff, perhaps as a left-handed specialist or swingman, Lester is considering ending his career and stopping the bleeding. When he does so, the healing may actually come, giving him the *gift* of time rather than the curse of it, allowing him days to reflect on a remarkable career and hours of a surfeit of time as he enjoys his retirement.

★ ★ ★ *2022 Top 101 Prospect* **#65** ★ ★ ★

Matthew Liberatore LHP Born: 11/06/99 Age: 22 Bats: L Throws: L Height: 6'4" Weight: 200 lb. Origin: Round 1, 2018 Draft (#16 overall)

YEAR	TEAM	LVL	AGE	W	L	SV	G	GS	IP	H	HR	BB/9	K/9	K	GB%	BABIP	WHIP	ERA	DRA-	WARP	MPH	FB%	Whiff%	CSP
2019	BG	A	19	6	2	0	16	15	78^{1}	70	2	3.6	8.7	76	55.7%	.312	1.29	3.10	96	0.8				
2021	MEM	AAA	21	9	9	0	22	18	124^{2}	123	19	2.4	8.9	123	38.3%	.308	1.25	4.04	104	1.4				
2022 non-DC	*STL*	*MLB*	*22*	*2*	*2*	*0*	*57*	*0*	*50*	*51*	*7*	*3.4*	*7.2*	*40*	*41.9%*	*.296*	*1.40*	*4.68*	*110*	*-0.1*				

Comparables: Zach Duke, Iván Nova, Chris Volstad

Liberatore isn't really a divisive prospect, as pretty much everyone projects him as a groundball-generating innings-eater with the talent to post an ERA+ on the right side of 100. There's considerably less consensus about what makes him good, which is interesting and unusual for a player this far along his developmental journey. The debates begin with his stuff, as different scouts will give you different answers about his best pitch. Some think it's the long-breaking, high-spin curve that has long been his bread and butter; others favor the slider, which took a step forward in 2021 and has a more traditional swing-and-miss shape. Liberatore's change is another point of contention. Depending whom you speak with, it's either a flat offering he doesn't really need or a promising fader that should tunnel well with his two-seam fastball. Opinions are also divided on his best plan of attack: Should he be tunneling that fastball and change often? Is he better off using the curve as an out pitch, a weapon in the zone or just a change of pace from the slider? It gets a bit confounding after a while, but at least one thing is clear: He's not hurting for options.

Austin Love RHP Born: 01/26/99 Age: 23 Bats: R Throws: R Height: 6'3" Weight: 232 lb. Origin: Round 3, 2021 Draft (#90 overall)

YEAR	TEAM	LVL	AGE	W	L	SV	G	GS	IP	H	HR	BB/9	K/9	K	GB%	BABIP	WHIP	ERA	DRA-	WARP	MPH	FB%	Whiff%	CSP
2022 non-DC	*STL*	*MLB*	*23*	*2*	*3*	*0*	*57*	*0*	*50*	*49*	*7*	*4.7*	*9.3*	*51*	*40.6%*	*.307*	*1.51*	*5.17*	*119*	*-0.3*				

Comparables: Jarett Miller, Aaron Civale, Charle Rosario

While Love overmatched younger competition in a late-season, low-minors cameo, he's likely to develop into more of a ground-ball pitcher. He's deceptive, which helps his mid-90s heat play up, but it's a two-seamer so it's not much of a bat-misser. The rest of the stuff looks average, at least for a starter: He has an average slider and some feel for a *cambio*, but there's no clear out pitch here just yet. All that could change with a shift to the bullpen, and between his arm strength and polish as a high-performer in a major conference, he could move quickly in that role.

Carlos Martínez RHP Born: 09/21/91 Age: 30 Bats: R Throws: R Height: 6'0" Weight: 200 lb. Origin: International Free Agent, 2009

YEAR	TEAM	LVL	AGE	W	L	SV	G	GS	IP	H	HR	BB/9	K/9	K	GB%	BABIP	WHIP	ERA	DRA-	WARP	MPH	FB%	Whiff%	CSP
2019	STL	MLB	27	4	2	24	48	0	48^1	39	2	3.4	9.9	53	57.1%	.301	1.18	3.17	82	0.9	95.6	51.0%	28.5%	47.7%
2020	STL	MLB	28	0	3	0	5	5	20	32	6	4.5	7.7	17	51.3%	.371	2.10	9.90	118	0.0	93.0	50.1%	19.6%	44.9%
2021	STL	MLB	29	4	9	0	16	16	82^1	77	8	3.9	6.2	57	50.2%	.276	1.37	6.23	112	0.2	92.9	40.5%	18.6%	54.0%
2022 DC	*FA*	*MLB*	*30*	*6*	*6*	*0*	*19*	*19*	*101*	*104*	*11*	*4.0*	*7.4*	*83*	*50.1%*	*.304*	*1.48*	*4.93*	*116*	*0.0*	*93.3*	*43.5%*	*20.1%*	*51.8%*

Comparables: Dennis Martinez, Chad Billingsley, Jeremy Hellickson

The Tsunami has finally crashed, it seems. Once a highly-touted prospect and later a rotation stalwart, Martinez's end-run with the Cardinals wasn't what anyone wanted or expected. He made a half-season worth of starts before a thumb injury booted him to the injured list to finish the season, but even before that he looked like a faded photocopy of a once-hyped pitcher. He's not washed yet, but his fastball velocity is nowhere near where it was at his peak; most teams will be looking at him as a reclamation project for the middle of a bullpen rather than the middle of a rotation.

Steven Matz LHP Born: 05/29/91 Age: 31 Bats: R Throws: L Height: 6'2" Weight: 201 lb. Origin: Round 2, 2009 Draft (#72 overall)

YEAR	TEAM	LVL	AGE	W	L	SV	G	GS	IP	H	HR	BB/9	K/9	K	GB%	BABIP	WHIP	ERA	DRA-	WARP	MPH	FB%	Whiff%	CSP
2019	NYM	MLB	28	11	10	0	32	30	160^1	163	27	2.9	8.6	153	46.3%	.304	1.34	4.21	96	1.9	93.5	50.6%	23.0%	50.4%
2020	NYM	MLB	29	0	5	0	9	6	30^2	42	14	2.9	10.6	36	33.3%	.346	1.70	9.68	121	0.0	94.8	53.9%	23.4%	46.7%
2021	TOR	MLB	30	14	7	0	29	29	150^2	158	18	2.6	8.6	144	45.6%	.321	1.33	3.82	104	1.0	94.5	52.0%	22.2%	56.4%
2022 DC	*STL*	*MLB*	*31*	*9*	*9*	*0*	*29*	*29*	*151.3*	*148*	*19*	*2.7*	*8.1*	*137*	*44.4%*	*.294*	*1.28*	*3.98*	*100*	*1.2*	*94.3*	*51.9%*	*22.5%*	*54.0%*

Comparables: Ian Kennedy, Curt Simmons, Jimmy Key

A lot can happen over the six months of a big-league season when you're a back-end starter. You pitch yourself from "is this outing his last in the rotation?" to "does this player warrant a qualifying offer?" in a matter of a month. Such is the story of Matz's 2021, when he spent much of the year looking mostly fine, then maybe looking like the kind of guy who was going to lose his job to Ross Stripling, then putting together a strong 11-start run to end the year and reframe his entire offseason.

Was there anything in those second half starts, when he pitched to a 2.69 ERA while only allowing five home runs in 60+ innings, that suggests Matz rediscovered the best version of himself? He threw a few more two-seam fastballs, trying to climb the ladder to better set up his changeup, to decent effect. But is that the story? Is there a trustworthy metric for command, the improvement of which Matz referenced time and again during his strong finish? A noticeable shift in his release point made during the season's second half is the kind of tangible data point that helps suggest "hey, this is real."

Matz was still below-average by DRA– on balance but his track record, his velocity and a new arm slot was more than enough to secure a four-year pact from the St. Louis Cardinals.

T.J. McFarland LHP Born: 06/08/89 Age: 33 Bats: L Throws: L Height: 6'3" Weight: 200 lb. Origin: Round 4, 2007 Draft (#137 overall)

YEAR	TEAM	LVL	AGE	W	L	SV	G	GS	IP	H	HR	BB/9	K/9	K	GB%	BABIP	WHIP	ERA	DRA-	WARP	MPH	FB%	Whiff%	CSP
2019	ARI	MLB	30	0	0	0	51	0	56	71	6	3.2	5.6	35	59.8%	.349	1.63	4.82	111	0.2	89.4	68.6%	22.0%	40.2%
2020	OAK	MLB	31	2	0	0	23	0	20^2	26	5	2.2	3.9	9	59.7%	.292	1.50	4.35	107	0.1	88.5	59.8%	16.3%	41.4%
2021	MEM	AAA	32	1	0	1	4	0	7	6	0	2.6	10.3	8	66.7%	.300	1.14	2.57	82	0.2				
2021	ROC	AAA	32	1	2	1	18	0	24	23	3	1.9	9.7	26	64.2%	.313	1.17	5.25	89	0.5				
2021	STL	MLB	32	4	1	0	38	0	38^2	32	3	2.1	4.9	21	62.3%	.261	1.06	2.56	111	0.1	89.0	68.6%	17.7%	51.5%
2022 DC	*STL*	*MLB*	*33*	*2*	*3*	*0*	*59*	*0*	*51.7*	*56*	*4*	*2.7*	*5.8*	*33*	*60.1%*	*.305*	*1.39*	*4.23*	*106*	*0.0*	*89.0*	*66.7%*	*18.6%*	*46.1%*

Comparables: Alex Wilson, Ross Detwiler, Miguel Socolovich

Even the most specialized worm-killers usually need about 100 innings before racking up a dozen double plays. That was absolutely not the case for McFarland last year, who was by far the most efficient pitcher in the game at getting two-for-ones; he induced 12 double plays in just 38 ⅔ innings of work. While there's more than a little luck involved there, he's also uniquely suited to inducing them: Mac avoids the three true outcomes thanks to one of the lowest strikeout rates in the game, and he's backed up by St. Louis' outstanding infield defenders. That confluence of factors set up a rare pair for the veteran righty: a new major-league contract for a follow-up season with the Cards.

Michael McGreevy RHP Born: 07/08/00 Age: 21 Bats: R Throws: R Height: 6'4" Weight: 215 lb. Origin: Round 1, 2021 Draft (#18 overall)

YEAR	TEAM	LVL	AGE	W	L	SV	G	GS	IP	H	HR	BB/9	K/9	K	GB%	BABIP	WHIP	ERA	DRA-	WARP	MPH	FB%	Whiff%	CSP
2021	PMB	A	20	0	0	0	5	5	6	10	1	1.5	6.0	4	75.0%	.391	1.83	9.00	111	0.0				
2022 non-DC	*STL*	*MLB*	*21*	*2*	*3*	*0*	*57*	*0*	*50*	*57*	*6*	*4.3*	*6.1*	*33*	*48.5%*	*.312*	*1.62*	*5.65*	*129*	*-0.6*				

Comparables: Shane Watson, Tommy Romero, Ruben Mejia

McGreevy might bear only the faintest resemblance to Scott Patterson, but that won't halt the onslaught of Little Big League references heading his way. The righty is less polished than your typical mid-first round college arm, particularly one without a huge fastball. He works with a deep arsenal, including a four- and a two-seamer, along with a change and both breaking balls. The curve and slider will need refinement, as they come out of very different slots at present, which makes them easy to identify out of the hand. He also leans on his sinker, which in theory gives him less wiggle room than starters who rely on the four-seamer. Speaking of the heat, McGreevy's velocity dipped from the mid-90s to the low-90s over the course of 2021, which is concerning for someone who only recently started throwing hard in the first place. The good news here is that he throws strikes and has plenty of late-bloomer traits: He's athletic, young, has thrown harder before and the wrinkles in his repertoire can be ironed out in time. He's a good pitching prospect; he's just not on the fast track to St. Louis.

Miles Mikolas RHP Born: 08/23/88 Age: 33 Bats: R Throws: R Height: 6'4" Weight: 230 lb. Origin: Round 7, 2009 Draft (#204 overall)

YEAR	TEAM	LVL	AGE	W	L	SV	G	GS	IP	H	HR	BB/9	K/9	K	GB%	BABIP	WHIP	ERA	DRA-	WARP	MPH	FB%	Whiff%	CSP
2019	STL	MLB	30	9	14	0	32	32	184	193	27	1.6	7.0	144	47.4%	.304	1.22	4.16	93	2.5	93.8	51.5%	21.8%	49.7%
2021	PEO	A+	32	1	0	0	1	1	7	6	0	0.0	10.3	8	44.4%	.333	0.86	3.86	91	0.1				
2021	SPR	AA	32	1	0	0	2	2	10^{1}	15	3	2.6	6.1	7	51.5%	.400	1.74	6.97	113	0.0				
2021	MEM	AAA	32	1	1	0	5	5	19^{1}	17	2	1.4	6.1	13	36.8%	.273	1.03	2.33	111	0.1				
2021	STL	MLB	32	2	3	0	9	9	44^{2}	43	6	2.2	6.2	31	52.1%	.276	1.21	4.23	100	0.4	93.3	49.8%	17.4%	59.8%
2022 DC	*STL*	*MLB*	*33*	*8*	*8*	*0*	*25*	*25*	*134.7*	*143*	*15*	*2.0*	*6.2*	*92*	*46.6%*	*.298*	*1.28*	*4.06*	*102*	*0.9*	*93.6*	*50.7%*	*19.9%*	*54.0%*

Comparables: David Price, Nelson Briles, Camilo Pascual

Mikolas' rough recovery from elbow surgery led to setbacks and cascade injuries in both his shoulder and forearm as he worked his way back from a scuttled 2020. When he eventually returned full-time at the end of the season, he looked more like 2014 Rangers version of himself than the far more successful Cardinals one. Three solid late-season starts against the Padres and Brewers bring hope for renewed optimism, though, and he's locked into a spot in the middle of the Cardinals' rotation given his paycheck and experience. Like the rest of the staff, he pitches with the advantage of a world-class defense to gobble up his grounders, but he's no longer the reliable hand he was when he first made land in Missouri.

Andrew Miller LHP Born: 05/21/85 Age: 37 Bats: L Throws: L Height: 6'7" Weight: 200 lb. Origin: Round 1, 2006 Draft (#6 overall)

YEAR	TEAM	LVL	AGE	W	L	SV	G	GS	IP	H	HR	BB/9	K/9	K	GB%	BABIP	WHIP	ERA	DRA-	WARP	MPH	FB%	Whiff%	CSP
2019	STL	MLB	34	5	6	6	73	0	54^{2}	45	11	4.4	11.5	70	36.6%	.283	1.32	4.45	81	1.1	92.6	38.6%	30.8%	49.0%
2020	STL	MLB	35	1	1	4	16	0	13	9	0	3.5	11.1	16	61.3%	.290	1.08	2.77	76	0.3	90.7	40.0%	31.4%	48.9%
2021	STL	MLB	36	0	0	0	40	0	36	41	5	4.0	10.0	40	42.7%	.375	1.58	4.75	98	0.4	88.7	35.3%	25.8%	55.4%
2022 DC	*FA*	*MLB*	*37*	*3*	*3*	*0*	*64*	*0*	*55.7*	*49*	*7*	*3.9*	*10.9*	*67*	*43.0%*	*.302*	*1.33*	*4.36*	*105*	*0.1*	*90.1*	*36.9%*	*28.0%*	*52.7%*

Comparables: Trever Miller, Moe Drabowsky, Matt Albers

Like Play-Doh left out too long, Miller's profile has stiffened, ossified over time. From the herald of a new era in relief-ace usage to a good-but-not-great lefty-beater, the role he's cast in has petrified, and his cracks are starting to show. The velocity on both his signature slider and his fastball has faded, which has given him a platoon split greater than ever, even as the tension of another run to the playoffs seemed to enliven him as the season wore on. But like that fragile statue left forgotten on a craft table, any additional pressure might push him past the point of no return, falling to pieces. For now, there's still enough of his old, pliable self to be a reminder of a more joyful period and be of value in this moment.

Edwin Nunez RHP Born: 11/05/01 Age: 20 Bats: R Throws: R Height: 6'3" Weight: 185 lb. Origin: International Free Agent, 2019

YEAR	TEAM	LVL	AGE	W	L	SV	G	GS	IP	H	HR	BB/9	K/9	K	GB%	BABIP	WHIP	ERA	DRA-	WARP	MPH	FB%	Whiff%	CSP
2021	PMB	A	19	3	3	0	32	2	53^{2}	64	7	9.4	9.9	59	40.4%	.383	2.24	10.90	114	0.1				
2022 non-DC	*STL*	*MLB*	*20*	*2*	*3*	*0*	*57*	*0*	*50*	*59*	*9*	*9.2*	*8.4*	*46*	*37.4%*	*.334*	*2.21*	*9.12*	*173*	*-1.8*				

Comparables: Jake Newberry, Jose Ascanio, Marcos Carvajal

Nunez throws the dickens out of the baseball, sitting in the mid-90s and occasionally tickling the triple digits. He'll show you a good slider on the right day and his tall, athletic frame gives the Redbirds player development staff plenty to dream on. But while he's been plenty good at the best of times, last year was a season of darkness. He walked more than a batter per inning, and between that and a mothballed changeup, he's starting to look relieverish very early in his young career. There's still a channel between where he is and where he could wind up, even if his stock has trended slightly down.

Johan Oviedo RHP Born: 03/02/98 Age: 24 Bats: R Throws: R Height: 6'5" Weight: 245 lb. Origin: International Free Agent, 2016

YEAR	TEAM	LVL	AGE	W	L	SV	G	GS	IP	H	HR	BB/9	K/9	K	GB%	BABIP	WHIP	ERA	DRA-	WARP	MPH	FB%	Whiff%	CSP
2019	PMB	A+	21	5	0	0	6	5	33^2	29	1	3.2	9.4	35	46.7%	.308	1.22	1.60	92	0.5				
2019	SPR	AA	21	7	8	0	23	23	113	120	9	5.1	10.2	128	42.0%	.368	1.63	5.65	110	-0.4				
2020	STL	MLB	22	0	3	0	5	5	24^2	24	3	3.6	5.8	16	40.7%	.269	1.38	5.47	138	-0.2	95.0	56.1%	21.5%	47.4%
2021	MEM	AAA	23	1	6	0	12	11	54^1	55	7	4.8	9.8	59	52.0%	.331	1.55	6.13	92	0.9				
2021	STL	MLB	23	0	5	0	14	13	62^1	61	8	5.3	7.4	51	49.0%	.286	1.57	4.91	119	0.0	95.1	53.7%	26.1%	53.5%
2022 DC	*STL*	*MLB*	*24*	*7*	*6*	*0*	*60*	*8*	*81.7*	*81*	*9*	*5.1*	*8.5*	*77*	*46.3%*	*.307*	*1.56*	*5.18*	*118*	*-0.2*	*95.1*	*54.2%*	*25.2%*	*52.2%*

Comparables: Zack Britton, Reynaldo López, Liam Hendriks

Despite spending 87 innings and three months filling in as a replacement-level starter, Oviedo still hasn't notched his first major-league win. One reason may be that despite his two strong offerings (fastball and slider, naturally), he doesn't have the secondaries or command to make it past the fifth inning during most of his games. With the Cardinals amping up their rotation for 2022, he's unlikely to stick in the bigs as a starter unless the injuries pile up again—and speaking of sticking, a late-season suspension for using a foreign substance doesn't exactly portend an immediate shift in stuff or command. For years a move to the bullpen has been bandied about, but his value as an emergency starter may continue to put that change off at least for another year or two.

Alex Reyes RHP Born: 08/29/94 Age: 27 Bats: R Throws: R Height: 6'4" Weight: 220 lb. Origin: International Free Agent, 2012

YEAR	TEAM	LVL	AGE	W	L	SV	G	GS	IP	H	HR	BB/9	K/9	K	GB%	BABIP	WHIP	ERA	DRA-	WARP	MPH	FB%	Whiff%	CSP
2019	PMB	A+	24	0	1	0	2	2	9^1	9	0	2.9	10.6	11	53.8%	.346	1.29	1.93	98	0.1				
2019	MEM	AAA	24	1	3	0	10	7	28	27	5	7.7	12.2	38	37.7%	.355	1.82	7.39	90	0.3				
2019	STL	MLB	24	0	1	0	4	0	3	2	1	18.0	3.0	1	30.0%	.111	2.67	15.00	140	0.0	97.0	59.2%	16.0%	40.5%
2020	STL	MLB	25	2	1	1	15	1	19^2	14	1	6.4	12.4	27	35.6%	.302	1.42	3.20	87	0.4	97.8	60.4%	34.6%	43.2%
2021	STL	MLB	26	10	8	29	69	0	72^1	46	9	6.5	11.8	95	36.3%	.233	1.35	3.24	94	0.9	96.9	54.5%	35.2%	52.8%
2022 DC	*STL*	*MLB*	*27*	*3*	*3*	*5*	*67*	*0*	*58*	*45*	*8*	*6.1*	*12.4*	*80*	*37.4%*	*.291*	*1.46*	*4.41*	*101*	*0.2*	*97.0*	*55.6%*	*34.8%*	*51.0%*

Comparables: Jeremy Jeffress, Matt Albers, Phil Hughes

The most iconic image of the Cardinals' brief postseason run may have been Reyes striding off the field, downcast, after watching Chris Taylor take one of his pitches deep. While it was a fairly appropriate close to a season of highs and lows for the one-time top prospect, perhaps there's more than a little silver lining to an otherwise devastating tableau. Yes, Reyes entered that game having fallen from grace, seemingly decades removed from an unbreakable first half and an All-Star appearance that finally seemed to shut the door on years of injury-related heartache. With a brutal second half of 2021 costing him the closer role and some (but not all) the trust of his manager. Reyes may have benefitted from his dismal second half and Wild Card appearance in another way: after openly campaigning to get back in the starting rotation, he's no longer indispensible as a reliever—maybe he's inadvertently pitched his way back into a starting slot? Instead of looking down, perhaps Reyes can view 2022 while looking on the bright side.

Connor Thomas LHP Born: 05/29/98 Age: 24 Bats: L Throws: L Height: 5'11" Weight: 173 lb. Origin: Round 5, 2019 Draft (#155 overall)

YEAR	TEAM	LVL	AGE	W	L	SV	G	GS	IP	H	HR	BB/9	K/9	K	GB%	BABIP	WHIP	ERA	DRA-	WARP	MPH	FB%	Whiff%	CSP
2019	SC	SS	21	2	0	0	5	2	15^2	17	0	0.6	9.8	17	49.0%	.362	1.15	4.02						
2019	PEO	A	21	2	1	1	10	2	27^1	25	2	3.0	6.3	19	65.1%	.284	1.24	3.62	103	0.2				
2021	SPR	AA	23	0	2	0	4	4	20^1	26	5	1.3	10.6	24	58.6%	.396	1.43	4.87	101	0.1				
2021	MEM	AAA	23	6	4	1	22	14	101^2	108	11	2.7	8.1	92	60.1%	.326	1.36	3.10	104	1.2				
2022 non-DC	*STL*	*MLB*	*24*	*2*	*2*	*0*	*57*	*0*	*50*	*52*	*5*	*3.1*	*6.9*	*38*	*55.9%*	*.308*	*1.41*	*4.36*	*105*	*0.0*				

Comparables: Walker Lockett, David Phelps, Rogelio Armenteros

Both Thomas' slider and two-seamer have promising spin characteristics. The former spins at nearly 2,800 rpms, which is a ton for a pitch that sits in the low-mid 80s, while the latter has the right shape to run off of barrels and generate groundballs. That goes a long way for a pitcher who barely crests 90 with his fastball. It's not the sexiest profile around, but Thomas throws strikes, pitches with his left hand and is just about ready for prime time. He should make a handful of starts in 2022, kicking off a lengthy if somewhat beige-tinted career.

Zack Thompson LHP Born: 10/28/97 Age: 24 Bats: L Throws: L Height: 6'2" Weight: 215 lb. Origin: Round 1, 2019 Draft (#19 overall)

YEAR	TEAM	LVL	AGE	W	L	SV	G	GS	IP	H	HR	BB/9	K/9	K	GB%	BABIP	WHIP	ERA	DRA-	WARP	MPH	FB%	Whiff%	CSP
2019	CAR	ROK	21	0	0	0	2	2	2	3	0	0.0	18.0	4	66.7%	.500	1.50	0.00						
2019	PMB	A+	21	0	0	0	11	0	13^1	16	0	2.7	12.8	19	48.6%	.471	1.50	4.05	80	0.3				
2021	MEM	AAA	23	2	10	2	22	19	93	114	18	5.5	7.9	82	38.3%	.343	1.84	7.06	131	-0.2				
2022 non-DC	*STL*	*MLB*	*24*	*2*	*3*	*0*	*57*	*0*	*50*	*56*	*8*	*5.2*	*7.2*	*40*	*39.4%*	*.312*	*1.70*	*6.32*	*138*	*-0.8*				

Comparables: David Huff, Chase De Jong, Chris Beck

The phrase "shit happens" resonates in part because it suits so many situations. There aren't many expressions that can sum up an insurrection in the Capitol and a major step back from your team's top pitching prospect while also explaining where and why you're reading this blurb, but this one manages. As you've undoubtedly inferred from the numbers above, Thompson had a crappy 2021. Injuries limited him to 19 starts but it was lousy pitching that held him below 100 innings, as both his walk and home run rates exploded. He didn't miss bats or generate grounders and he left skidmarks on his way out of our top 10 list of Cardinals prospects. In theory, his arm strength and beautiful deuce could get him back on track, but we're not betting on it. Sometimes, well, you know.

Adam Wainwright RHP
Born: 08/30/81 Age: 40 Bats: R Throws: R Height: 6'7" Weight: 230 lb. Origin: Round 1, 2000 Draft (#29 overall)

YEAR	TEAM	LVL	AGE	W	L	SV	G	GS	IP	H	HR	BB/9	K/9	K	GB%	BABIP	WHIP	ERA	DRA-	WARP	MPH	FB%	Whiff%	CSP
2019	STL	MLB	37	14	10	0	31	31	171^2	181	22	3.4	8.0	153	48.1%	.323	1.43	4.19	94	2.3	90.1	38.5%	19.6%	50.0%
2020	STL	MLB	38	5	3	0	10	10	65^2	54	9	2.1	7.4	54	42.9%	.247	1.05	3.15	99	0.7	89.5	36.7%	24.2%	47.2%
2021	STL	MLB	39	17	7	0	32	32	206^1	168	21	2.2	7.6	174	47.9%	.257	1.06	3.05	88	3.2	89.2	37.9%	19.9%	56.7%
2022 DC	*STL*	*MLB*	*40*	*11*	*9*	*0*	*29*	*29*	*174.7*	*173*	*21*	*2.6*	*7.6*	*147*	*45.9%*	*.293*	*1.28*	*3.96*	*100*	*1.4*	*89.5*	*37.8%*	*20.4%*	*54.1%*

Comparables: David Cone, Jack Morris, Orel Hershiser

He doesn't throw hard. He doesn't nibble. Most strikingly of all in this era, he doesn't miss bats—fewer in recent years than in his first heyday a decade back. And yet Wainwright's incredible second half didn't just cement his status as a legitimately good pitcher again, but launched him onto Cy Young ballots and back into the discussion of the 10-20 best pitchers in baseball. It's a phenomenal fourth act, and one hopes that Cardinals fans realize how lucky they are to see it. There's almost never a perfect way for longtime stars to age gracefully, not in today's efficiency-minded game, and not without half of talk radio lamenting their presence as a waste of resources. And yet both Waino and his batterymate Yadier Molina may have found a way to do so. Devil Magic works in mysterious ways.

Kodi Whitley RHP
Born: 02/21/95 Age: 27 Bats: R Throws: R Height: 6'3" Weight: 220 lb. Origin: Round 27, 2017 Draft (#814 overall)

YEAR	TEAM	LVL	AGE	W	L	SV	G	GS	IP	H	HR	BB/9	K/9	K	GB%	BABIP	WHIP	ERA	DRA-	WARP	MPH	FB%	Whiff%	CSP
2019	PMB	A+	24	0	0	0	3	0	4^1	1	0	4.2	10.4	5	37.5%	.125	0.69	0.00	93	0.1				
2019	SPR	AA	24	1	4	7	31	0	39^1	31	3	3.0	10.5	46	40.0%	.277	1.12	1.83	86	0.4				
2019	MEM	AAA	24	2	0	2	16	0	23^2	21	0	1.5	10.3	27	27.7%	.323	1.06	1.52	97	0.2				
2020	STL	MLB	25	0	0	0	4	0	4^2	2	1	1.9	9.6	5	36.4%	.100	0.64	1.93	101	0.1	94.1	53.2%	33.3%	47.6%
2021	MEM	AAA	26	3	0	3	12	0	16	11	1	3.9	11.8	21	24.3%	.278	1.13	1.69	82	0.4				
2021	STL	MLB	26	0	0	0	25	0	25^1	15	1	4.3	9.6	27	38.7%	.230	1.07	2.49	92	0.3	93.8	56.9%	31.7%	53.7%
2022 DC	*STL*	*MLB*	*27*	*2*	*2*	*0*	*52*	*0*	*45.3*	*39*	*6*	*4.1*	*10.5*	*52*	*36.5%*	*.290*	*1.33*	*4.07*	*98*	*0.2*	*93.8*	*56.4%*	*31.9%*	*53.0%*

Comparables: Juan Minaya, Phil Klein, Anthony Varvaro

"If I could just get rid of this back pain, I could be my old self," said many an old throughout the years. Whitley, a spry 26 and thus not an old, provided proof of concept last summer. Back spasms parked him on the IL last June, but once healed, he dominated Triple-A before a late-summer summons to St. Louis saw him do more of the same. In a month where just about every Cardinal played his best baseball, Whitley had a case as the team's best reliever. In 15 innings after the recall, he struck out 19 while allowing only 13 baserunners and no runs of any kind. Given that form, we can only wonder how things would have turned out if Mike Shildt had gone to Whitley instead of Alex Reyes to face Chris Taylor.

Jake Woodford RHP
Born: 10/28/96 Age: 25 Bats: R Throws: R Height: 6'4" Weight: 215 lb. Origin: Round 1, 2015 Draft (#39 overall)

YEAR	TEAM	LVL	AGE	W	L	SV	G	GS	IP	H	HR	BB/9	K/9	K	GB%	BABIP	WHIP	ERA	DRA-	WARP	MPH	FB%	Whiff%	CSP
2019	MEM	AAA	22	9	8	0	26	26	151^2	124	22	4.5	7.8	131	37.0%	.249	1.31	4.15	104	0.6				
2020	STL	MLB	23	1	0	0	12	1	21	20	7	2.1	6.9	16	45.3%	.228	1.19	5.57	111	0.1	92.3	77.8%	20.4%	48.4%
2021	MEM	AAA	24	2	3	0	7	7	34	41	4	3.2	6.6	25	50.0%	.336	1.56	4.50	111	0.3				
2021	STL	MLB	24	3	4	0	26	8	67^2	66	7	3.3	6.7	50	41.9%	.291	1.34	3.99	112	0.2	91.7	63.8%	20.4%	56.4%
2022 DC	*STL*	*MLB*	*25*	*9*	*9*	*0*	*68*	*16*	*119.7*	*127*	*16*	*3.6*	*6.8*	*89*	*43.1%*	*.298*	*1.46*	*5.08*	*120*	*-0.6*	*91.8*	*66.2%*	*20.4%*	*55.0%*

Comparables: Luke Hochevar, Anthony Bass, Anthony Swarzak

Yes, comping a swingman to a Swiss Army knife is a lazy comp, but hear me out; in Woodford's case, the metaphor cuts deep. There's one major carrying tool: his big blade of a fastball he can trust in almost any situation, and a changeup he can lean on to scissor through opposing hitters when played off his heater. Then there's his collection of assorted off-speed and breaking pitches which...sure, you could use them, but *why*? They're mostly distractions: a scaling knife, a ballpoint pen, a file—you know, the stuff that you could bust out of your old Victorinox once in a blue moon, or when you're trying to survive in the dark of the woods or a tricky Dodgers lineup the second time through. These days, teams prefer 96-and-a-slider types that more resemble machetes than pocketknives, but Woodford still has a place in any team's pack.

LINEOUTS

Hitters

HITTER	POS	TEAM	LVL	AGE	PA	R	2B	3B	HR	RBI	BB	K	SB	CS	AVG/OBP/SLG	DRC+	BABIP	BRR	FRAA	WARP
Tre Fletcher	CF	CAR	ROK	20	29	3	2	0	1	2	2	11	0	0	.222/.276/.407		.333			
Tyler Heineman	C	MEM	AAA	30	77	8	4	0	0	5	7	17	0	2	.254/.325/.313	98	.327	-0.8	C(16): -0.1	0.2
	C	LHV	AAA	30	74	5	2	0	0	6	9	12	0	1	.274/.366/.306	102	.340	-0.3	C(15): 0.5	0.3
Ryan Holgate	OF	PMB	A	21	129	15	2	0	3	14	13	46	0	0	.193/.279/.289	77	.288	0.5	RF(21): -0.8, CF(4): 0.5, LF(3): -0.9	0.0
Scott Hurst	CF	MEM	AAA	25	305	39	12	1	4	18	33	94	5	4	.203/.291/.301	73	.294	0.1	CF(54): 2.9, LF(7): 1.3, RF(4): 0.4	0.6
	CF	STL	MLB	25	5	0	0	0	0	0	0	1	0	0	.000/.000/.000	84		-0.7	CF(6): -0.3	-0.1
Max Moroff	MI	MEM	AAA	28	34	11	3	0	4	9	6	3	1	0	.538/.647/1.115	166	.526	0.9	3B(4): -0.2, 2B(3): 0.1	0.4
	MI	STL	MLB	28	16	0	0	0	0	1	0	10	0	0	.063/.063/.063	60	.167		2B(4): 0.0, 3B(1): -0.4	-0.1
Luis Pino	CF	DSL CARB	ROK	17	174	18	7	0	6	19	17	52	1	2	.247/.362/.418		.337			
Julio E. Rodriguez	C/DH	SPR	AA	24	115	10	2	0	3	10	7	23	1	0	.196/.252/.299	92	.222	-0.4	C(16): -1.3, 1B(4): -1.1	0.0
José Rondón	RF/3B	CAR	WIN	27	123	19	4	1	3	21	12	30	0	0	.290/.366/.430		.368			
	RF/3B	MEM	AAA	27	93	14	3	0	6	19	8	22	0	0	.235/.301/.482	116	.246	-0.1	3B(12): -1.7, SS(9): -0.6	0.2
	RF/3B	STL	MLB	27	90	13	3	0	3	9	8	17	2	0	.263/.322/.413	102	.290	1.0	3B(7): 0.8, RF(7): -0.9, 2B(2): -0.1	0.4
Ali Sánchez	C	LAR	WIN	24	131	18	7	0	2	15	5	18	0	2	.304/.328/.408		.340			
	C	MEM	AAA	24	270	24	10	0	4	22	18	47	0	2	.275/.322/.363	96	.323	-1.0	C(64): -2.2, 1B(1): -0.0	0.6
	C	STL	MLB	24	4	0	2	0	0	0	0	0	0	0	.500/.500/1.000	91	.500	-1.0	C(2): -0.0	-0.1
Jhon Torres	OF	PEO	A+	21	420	47	25	3	6	32	27	98	3	4	.238/.302/.366	92	.304	-0.8	RF(65): 6.0, LF(21): -2.5, CF(8): 0.4	1.2
Justin Williams	OF	MEM	AAA	25	88	10	4	1	6	19	3	23	1	0	.274/.307/.560	108	.309	-0.2	RF(15): 1.3, CF(5): 0.5	0.5
	OF	STL	MLB	25	137	10	0	0	4	11	17	46	0	1	.160/.270/.261	78	.217	-1.5	RF(24): -1.2, LF(19): 2.9	0.1

Tre Fletcher is a toolsy but raw outfielder from the baseball hotbed of Portland, Maine. This is the type of player who needs reps badly, and after appearing in only seven games last year, he's alarmingly short on them at this point in his career. The baseball equivalent of the old box of cables you keep in a dusty corner of your basement, **Tyler Heineman** is a catcher who may be able to fit the job if something goes wrong, but is best served as peace of mind, half-remembered and nestled away in case of emergency. St. Louis' second-round pick last summer **Ryan Holgate** is an all-or-nothing slugger. The Birds will hope Holgate's propensity to swing-and-miss doesn't undercut massive raw power; if the stick plays, a bat-first option in some kind of 1-2-win role seems like a reasonable developmental outcome. Defensive specialist **Scott Hurst** made his big-league debut caddying for Dylan Carson in center field and going 0-for-5 in his limited chances to hit. After returning to Memphis at the end of April, he still couldn't hit enough (read: at all); a return engagement will require either an offensive breakout or a spate of injuries. It's fitting that **Max Moroff** swings like he's hoisting an axe, given that he struck out more often than not and because his bat might as well be placed behind the glass marked "Use Only in Emergencies" sign. **Luis Pino** is a teenager from Cuba who became available later in the IFA period after defecting to the Dominican Republic. He signed with St. Louis for $800,000 and was playing center field in the Dominican Summer League, though might outgrow the position down the line. 24-year-old catcher **Julio E. Rodriguez** is about to age out of prospect status, but still needs to translate his power into performance in the upper minors before he'll rate a callup to the bigs. **José Rondón** batted over .300 as a pinch-hitter in 2021, and for a versatile defender who supposedly can't hit, he's actually mustered a couple of decent lines in his career. He's no building block but worse players have gotten more chances. Defense-first backstop **Ali Sánchez** might have the honor of being the final young catcher to understudy for Yadier Molina. Unless Yadi can pass on the secrets of his 2009 offensive breakout in his final season, Sánchez is likely to continue on as a second- or third-string catcher long after Molina picks up Cooperstown votes. **Jhon Torres** provided a lesson in why you shouldn't dream too much on large lads with power and few secondary skills. He struck out once a game while homering once a month, a combination that will surely prompt a return to Peoria. **Justin Williams'** DRC+ suggests a merely bad offensive output, but it's no surprise that his hit-a-buck-sixty-with-no-power act got him booted from the 40-man.

Pitchers

PITCHER	TEAM	LVL	AGE	W	L	SV	G	GS	IP	H	HR	BB/9	K/9	K	GB%	BABIP	WHIP	ERA	DRA-	WARP	MPH	FB%	WHF	CSP
Seth Elledge	MEM	AAA	25	2	2	2	30	0	35^{2}	44	3	5.6	11.6	46	39.6%	.418	1.85	6.56	78	0.9				
	STL	MLB	25	0	0	0	11	0	11^{2}	13	1	5.4	8.5	11	39.4%	.375	1.71	4.63	100	0.1	94.1	68.8%	27.6%	52.8%
Junior Fernández	MEM	AAA	24	1	2	1	13	0	14^{1}	18	3	3.1	13.8	22	28.9%	.429	1.60	6.28	78	0.4				
	STL	MLB	24	1	0	0	18	0	20^{2}	25	2	6.5	6.5	15	43.3%	.354	1.94	5.66	125	-0.1	97.9	48.1%	29.7%	48.1%
Tink Hence	CAR	ROK	18	0	1	1	8	1	8	11	1	3.4	15.7	14	31.8%	.476	1.75	9.00						
Wade LeBlanc	RR	AAA	36	2	0	0	3	3	18	12	3	1.5	9.5	19	43.5%	.209	0.83	2.50	101	0.1				
	NAS	AAA	36	1	1	0	4	4	16^{2}	12	1	3.8	7.6	14	42.6%	.239	1.14	3.78	123	0.0				
	STL	MLB	36	0	1	0	12	8	42^{1}	45	7	3.4	4.9	23	35.6%	.277	1.44	3.61	137	-0.4	86.7	66.8%	20.3%	52.6%
	BAL	MLB	36	0	1	0	6	1	6^{2}	11	1	1.4	8.1	6	40.0%	.417	1.80	9.45	102	0.1	87.3	68.3%	22.0%	53.9%
Ljay Newsome	SEA	MLB	24	1	1	0	7	1	14^{2}	20	5	1.8	9.8	16	30.6%	.349	1.57	7.98	100	0.1	92.9	57.8%	23.0%	61.3%
Wilfredo Pereira	PEO	A+	22	3	8	1	29	13	97^{1}	76	9	3.7	10.6	115	29.6%	.278	1.19	3.33	95	1.3				
Daniel Ponce de Leon	MEM	AAA	29	0	0	0	5	5	9	3	0	8.0	9.0	9	31.6%	.158	1.22	0.00	98	0.1				
	STL	MLB	29	1	1	2	24	2	33^{1}	32	5	5.9	6.5	24	35.5%	.267	1.62	6.21	135	-0.3	93.2	72.1%	22.0%	52.5%
Johan Quezada	CAR	ROK	26	1	0	0	7	2	9	7	0	1.0	12.0	12	61.9%	.333	0.89	3.00						
	SPR	AA	26	0	1	0	8	0	11^{2}	20	3	4.6	10.8	14	41.5%	.447	2.23	10.80	88	0.2				
Angel Rondón	MEM	AAA	23	6	4	0	19	13	76^{2}	85	15	2.6	8.0	68	41.5%	.306	1.40	4.58	109	0.7				
	STL	MLB	23	0	0	0	2	0	2	1	0	4.5	4.5	1	20.0%	.200	1.00	0.00	113	0.0	92.9	48.3%	7.1%	45.6%
Brandon Waddell	MEM	AAA	27	2	0	0	9	0	11	12	1	2.5	8.2	10	36.4%	.344	1.36	2.45	94	0.2				
	MIN	MLB	27	0	1	0	4	0	4	10	2	6.8	2.3	1	23.8%	.421	3.25	11.25	129	0.0	92.8	43.3%	29.3%	51.0%
	BAL	MLB	27	0	0	0	1	0	1	0	0	9.0	0.0	0	100.0%	.000	1.00	0.00	160	0.0	92.7	57.1%	40.0%	39.5%
	STL	MLB	27	0	0	0	4	0	4^{1}	4	0	10.4	12.5	6	45.5%	.364	2.08	4.15	90	0.1	92.7	57.8%	20.9%	52.8%
Tyler Webb	MEM	AAA	30	0	2	0	18	0	21^{2}	17	5	5.8	13.3	32	38.0%	.267	1.43	5.82	89	0.4				
	STL	MLB	30	0	0	0	22	0	16^{1}	22	1	10.5	7.7	14	33.9%	.368	2.51	13.22	139	-0.2	90.8	67.9%	19.3%	52.2%
T.J. Zeuch	MEM	AAA	25	2	0	1	9	5	38^{1}	36	6	3.5	8.2	35	63.1%	.286	1.33	4.93	93	0.7				
	BUF	AAA	25	2	3	0	12	9	58	65	8	2.0	6.5	42	51.5%	.306	1.34	4.03	108	0.6				
	TOR	MLB	25	0	2	0	5	3	15	21	6	5.4	4.8	8	49.1%	.294	2.00	6.60	132	-0.1	93.2	71.7%	16.8%	51.2%

Ian Bedell missed most of 2021 after undergoing Tommy John surgery. The local kid (he pitched at Mizzou) looked like a promising back-end starter before the procedure; we'll probably have to wait until 2023 to see if he's still on that path. More than a billion humans have picked up a bat or a ball in their life and only 20,000 or so have played in the major leagues. **Seth Elledge** may have been outrighted to Memphis at season's end, but he'll always be one of those 20,000, and in the grand scheme that's a lot more notable than his DRA. Even though he was once pegged as a late-inning bullpen option, no pitcher with as many innings as **Junior Fernandez** was used in lower-leverage situations in 2021. If he's going to come back from his late-season shoulder injury and be a high-leverage fireballer, he'll need to start getting some practice in close-and-late situations. The Cards were cautious with **Tink Hence** in 2021, but as the kid gloves come off, he's a sleeper to emerge as the best arm in the farm system. He has a lightning-quick arm, a plus slider and the athleticism to start if his slight frame can withstand the rigors of the job. **Wade LeBlanc**'s fastball barely passes the interstate speed limit, but it took him across four franchises and a surprising number of opposing baserunners stranded. An elbow injury might finally put the veteran in the garage and off the road, at least for much of 2022. Call him **Tjay Newsome**: The right-hander Ljay underwent Tommy John surgery in July after seven uninspiring outings in the first half. His prolific strike-throwing tendencies were not welcomed as kindly by MLB hitters, or perhaps one could say they were very warmly welcomed indeed; an actual chase pitch might be required upon returning from surgery. Neither **Wilfredo Pereira's** numbers nor arm strength scream top pitching prospect, but his stuff all spins the right way and gives him the look of a late-blooming innings-eater. A swingman who can no longer wrangle swings-and-misses, **Daniel Ponce de Leon** used to paper over his flaws as a hurler with an above-average strikeout rate. In 2021, he lost the two main gifts teams look for in a reliever: strikeouts and minor-league options, so the Cardinals cut bait; he'll be looking for a new harbor (on a minor-league deal) next year. Even more valuable to teams than his 6-foot-9 frame or blazing fastball are **Johan Quezada**'s three remaining options over the next four seasons. Sure, the 27-year-old has missed a ton of development time, but every team needs an up-and-down relief arm it can rotate out to Triple-A; even better if he can potentially miss bats with his heater. In 2021, 16 major-league pitchers had a season ERA of 0.00 over multiple appearances. The fact that **Angel Rodon** is here in the Lineout section instead of rating a full comment should speak volumes about whether or not that's sustainable for this young hurler. **Brandon Waddell's** long climb to the majors was a feat of perseverance; his performance once there an object lesson in the Peter principle. There's two ignominious distinctions for **Tyler Webb** in this year's Annual: not only is this his seventh consecutive Lineout appearance, but he also had the highest walk rate majors among pitchers with at least 10 innings. We don't usually cover seventh rounders the winter after they're selected, but **Alec Willis** actually got the third-highest bonus of any Cardinals draftee. He's pitching protoplasm at present, an athletic 6-5 with mid-90s gas and a projectable curveball but acres between him and the 314. Former first-rounder **T.J. Zeuch** served as trade deadline insurance to back up the parade of graybeards rounding out St. Louis' late-season starting rotation. Despite trying to re-introduce a slider into his pitch mix, he still doesn't miss enough bats to get a long look at the big-league level.

CHICAGO WHITE SOX

Essay by Janice Scurio

Player comments by James Fegan and BP staff

Or: Five Short Stories About the Southside

Master of Two Worlds

Once upon a time, in a not-so-distant land, adjacent to the roaring river of traffic on I-90/94 and the frozen-yogurt shop on the other side of the moat known as the Metra tracks, there lived an owner of a baseball team who hired one of his best friends to take the coveted managerial role of his historic Major League Baseball franchise.

Casting aside the obvious favoritism for a brief moment, the owner's best friend, let's call him "Tony," had something to prove. Well, sort of.

The owner, we'll call him "Jerry," was trying to right a wrong, a decision from 35 years ago—by the team's then-GM and, later, long-time announcer—that sent Tony into exile.

Driven from his homeland, Tony went on to become a highly-accomplished manager with not one, not two, but three World Series titles, then to hold the acclaim of being the second-winningest manager in the history of Major League Baseball. After retiring from the baseball world, Tony spent his days collecting some consultant checks, running an animal-rescue charity, and scribbling his name on the memorabilia-collector's circuit, a common pastime for Hall of Fame baseball people.

A spry septuagenarian with a law degree and fluent in Spanish, Tony was selected through a rigorous[1] and extensive[2] managerial search. Returning to a job one was fired from might carry the same appeal as attempting to revive leftover french fries in a microwave, but let us reserve judgment.

After Tony settled into his office, Jerry could finally sleep through the night, knowing his friend would once again rise and lead the ballclub to success. After all, this is basic screenwriting: The comeback. The redemption arc. The revenge tale. With the aging star with box-office drawing power as the lead.

---

[1] not rigorous

[2] not extensive

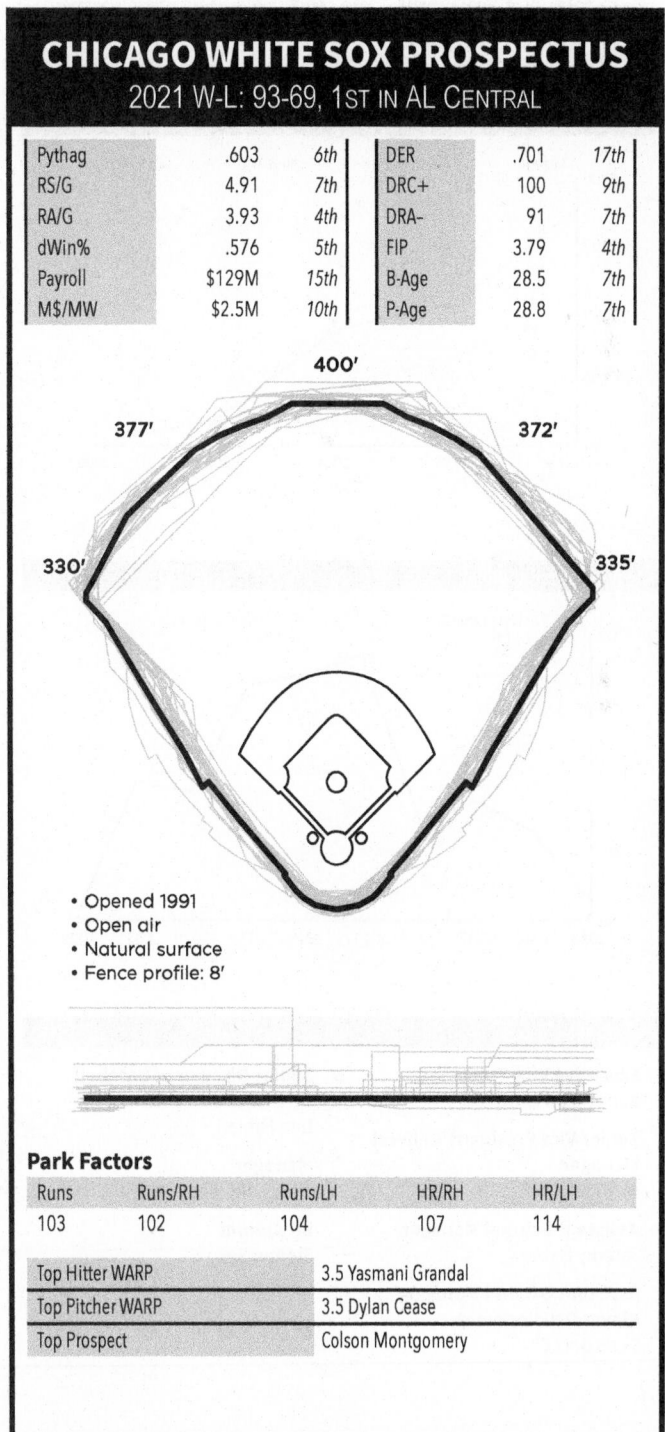

CHICAGO WHITE SOX PROSPECTUS

2021 W-L: 93-69, 1st in AL Central

Pythag	.603	*6th*	DER	.701	*17th*
RS/G	4.91	*7th*	DRC+	100	*9th*
RA/G	3.93	*4th*	DRA-	91	*7th*
dWin%	.576	*5th*	FIP	3.79	*4th*
Payroll	$129M	*15th*	B-Age	28.5	*7th*
M$/MW	$2.5M	*10th*	P-Age	28.8	*7th*

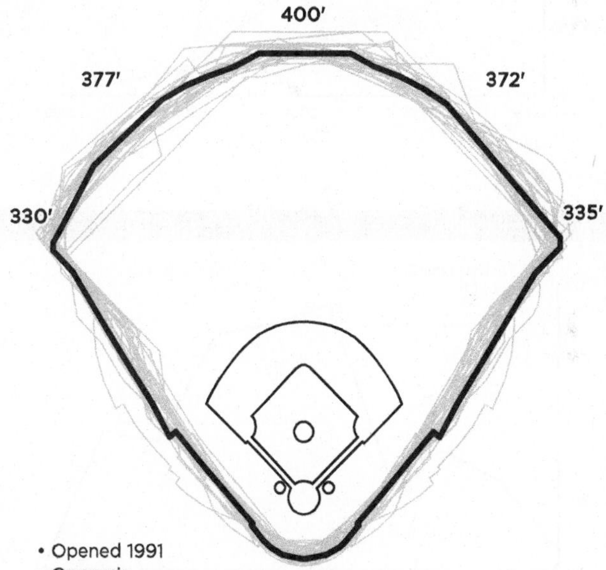

- Opened 1991
- Open air
- Natural surface
- Fence profile: 8'

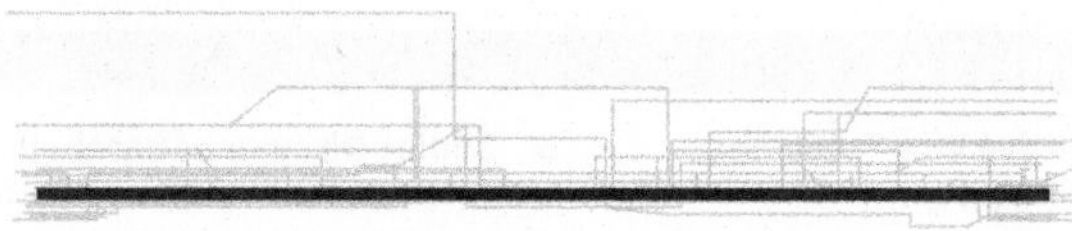

Park Factors

Runs	Runs/RH	Runs/LH	HR/RH	HR/LH
103	102	104	107	114

Top Hitter WARP	3.5 Yasmani Grandal
Top Pitcher WARP	3.5 Dylan Cease
Top Prospect	Colson Montgomery

Payroll History (in millions)

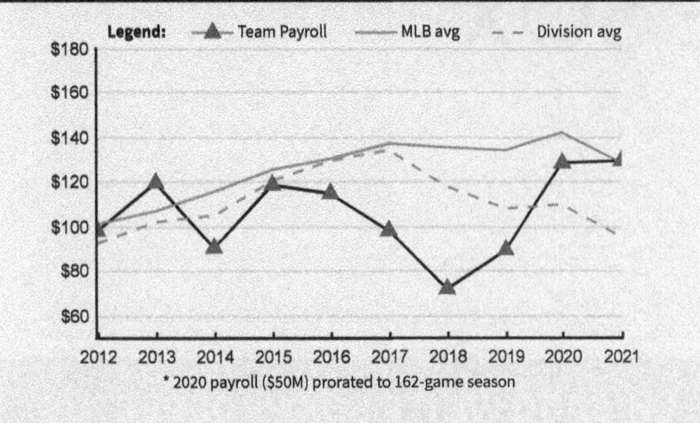

Future Commitments (in millions)

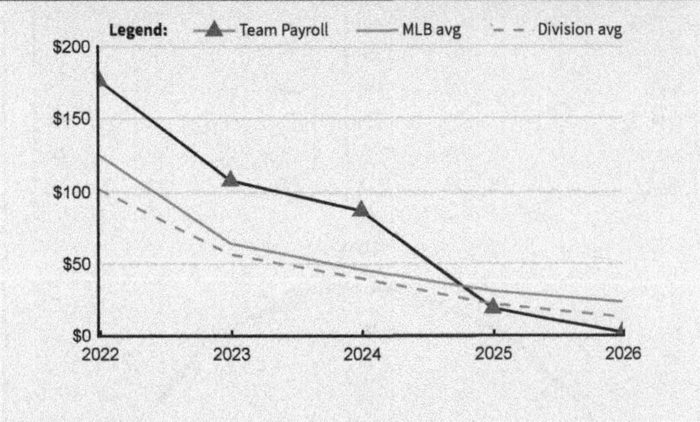

Farm System Ranking

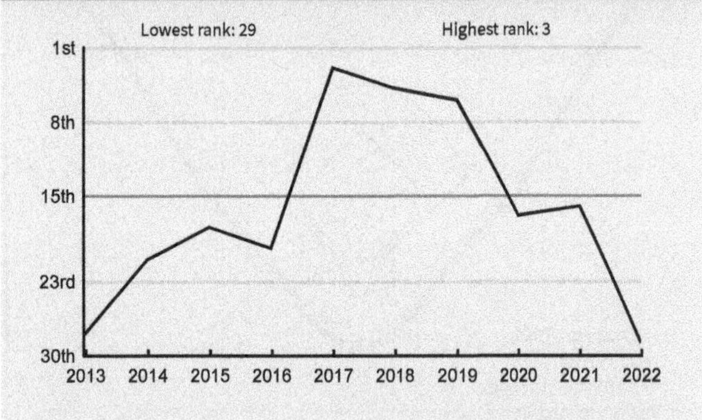

Personnel

Executive Vice President
Ken Williams

Senior Vice President/General Manager
Rick Hahn

Assistant General Manager
Jeremy Haber

Assistant General Manager/ Player Development
Chris Getz

Senior Director of Baseball Operations
Dan Fabian

Manager
Tony LaRussa

BP Alumni
Steffan Segui

Only, there's a problem: Tony is not a protagonist. The story is more like a reverse-*Footloose*, with significantly less music and dancing (although he does allow Future in the clubhouse). Tony's motivations are unclear, his character development is static. Instead of the hero of Joseph Campbell's ubiquitous journey, he is a prime example of the Sequel Problem; He is a character who already completed his development in the first arc and now has nowhere left to go.

Fortunately, he's not the only character with a story to tell.

Like a new ballpark constructed to have the same exact address as its predecessor (time travelers can visit 333 Wes 35th Street before and after 1991 with the same result), there's more than one way to enter.

Sometimes you'll climb stairs, you'll cross bridges, sometimes you'll take an elevator. While this seems like the end, it's actually only the beginning. Rebuilding isn't necessarily linear; sometimes a brick falls here and there.

Flowers for Alger-Rodón

Somehow it feels like you've raised him. You've watched him grow, fall, tumble, rise, conquer. He was drafted by the White Sox in the first round of the 2014 draft, then became one of the club's top prospects. The torn ulnar collateral ligament, followed by the Tommy John surgery, the shoulder. You checked in on his progress like he was family. You were invested. Carlos Rodón's awaited return to the White Sox' rotation during the shortened 2020 season saw some mixed results; he was used minimally, and it never felt like he was really all there.

On the heels of a possible injury setback, Rodón was non-tendered in the offseason, only to be welcomed back on a reduced contract. Given his injury history, you knew this seemed like a risk at the time, but a worthwhile one given how the club placed so much prior investment in Rodón's development. Stories deserve endings, even the ones up for cancellation.

And with risk comes reward: Rodón's 2021 was the best season of his career, at least so far.

You heard that visceral roar as he fanned Jordan Luplow, swinging, on a four-seamer after falling behind 3-0, followed by an apex-predator strut off the mound. It was that blustery April Chicago evening when the outs piled as the innings passed—you knew his blood ran as cold as the crisp, early-Spring air.

Rodón had the supporting cast he needed: the masked man at short, Leury García, with his whirling play to rob Roberto Pérez in the sixth. Andrew Vaughn, a greenhorn in left field, squeezed the 21st out, a missile off the bat of perpetual nuisance José Ramírez. There was the maverick mastermind José Abreu and his gritty, ninth-inning, foot-first, bag-jamming plunge to *just* beat Josh Naylor's desperate dive to first base.

You'll especially never forget Rodón's nonchalant laugh and wry smile after Pérez's planted foot was clipped by a slider, rescinding the perfect game in favor of a no-hitter.

Later in the summer, as the glow of the no-hitter faded and the weariness of summer set in, you noticed how he'd push away questions about arm soreness. "Nothing crazy," he'd say. Hard Karl—his ramped-up, unhinged alter ego—appeared late in his starts with the intensity to match as he mowed down hitters with a fastball that saw its velocity spike as he got deeper into games.

You were there to witness it all. From his being non-tendered, to making history with a no-hitter, to hitting 99 miles per hour on pitch number 86, to never wavering or giving up, to becoming a beacon of hope as a left-handed powerhouse with plenty room to grow, to not receiving a qualifying offer from the team that placed so much on him in the first place. You were there the entire time with him, and you wouldn't dare let him down. He kept his promise. You also kept yours.

And maybe you'll see Carlos again, under the pinwheels before a 7:10 start, stirrup socks perhaps in a different color, invoking fond memories of when they were once black.

The Colorful Case of Liam Hendriks

Shades of red, dollops of blue, drops of yellow, green, purple, pink. A lights-out closer with a phantasmagorical entrance as vibrantly pigmented as the language he utters on the mound, Liam Hendriks was named the American League reliever of the year for the second-straight season. Well deserved, given he registered 113 punchouts and walked just seven in 71 innings pitched, resulting in a 2.54 ERA and a league-leading 38 saves. He became the first pitcher in the award's eight years of existence to win it in consecutive seasons. His elite stuff made him a priority target in the 2020 offseason, and he's evidence of how it's advantageous to pursue big-name free agents in order to contend.

Beyond the artistic door-slamming, in the form of brightly sequined, glittering expletives roared often after strikeouts, Hendriks and his wife, Kristi, sought to make a positive impact in Chicago, donating more than one thousand meals twice a month to frontline workers on the South Side, often from Black- and brown-owned restaurants. In addition to picking up the tab, the Hendrikses also became unabashed advocates of the Lesbian, Gay, Bisexual, Transgender and Queer people of Chicagoland by donating meals and White Sox–branded gifts to the Center on Halsted, the Midwest's most comprehensive community center dedicated to advancing community and securing the health and well-being of Chicago's LGBTQIA+ community.

Hendriks was also the White Sox' nominee for the Roberto Clemente award, specifically for his work with the LGBTQIA+ community; Hendriks donated the proceeds from his nomination to the Howard Brown Center, one of the nation's largest organizations committed to eliminating the disparities in health care experienced by this community.

The first White Sox player in franchise history to do so, Hendriks himself raised the pride flag at Guaranteed Rate Field on September 30, the White Sox' designated Pride Night. That night, the first pitch was thrown out by Chicago-based drag queen and performer Shea Couleé.

Prior Pride Nights featured nothing more than a rainbow giveaway with milquetoast marketing; rainbow capitalism and corporate signaling was, and still is, prevalent in MLB. In the short time he has worn black pinstripes, Hendriks has made an impact far beyond that of his devastating slider. Hendriks knows that allyship matters, and that a welcoming, inclusive outreach to the community, including financial support where it is needed most, makes any Pride Night more genuine.

Because He Gets on Base

Yasmani knows that if he swings at this next pitch, he's a goner.

The count is 2-2. He doesn't fall behind often, but somehow location is getting the best of him. "Getting the best" might be a little harsh, but he feels he should be on base by now.

He also knows he's a .131 hitter. He doesn't care.

He closes his eyes for a brief moment (not too long) and pictures a breaking pitch dropping just beneath his knees. The catcher behind him utters something between a grunt and a chuckle and assumes the position.

Whatever, man, Yasmani thinks. The next pitch is here; the catcher swipes a curveball well out of the strike zone. Yasmani tries hard not to laugh.

You really thought I'd chase that? Yasmani can't help but smile a little as he readjusts in the batter's box. "You need to work on not being so . . . expressive at the plate," Tony told him earlier. Tony is about being reserved. He knows what he's talking about, sure, but Yasmani still thinks the blatant disrespect is kind of funny. He'll deal with Tony's chastising later.

There are two trademarked Yasmani Grandal outcomes: walking or going deep. Yasmani's walk rate has always been outstanding, as he's known to be a patient hitter that isn't afraid to let a few pitches pass before finding one he likes. He has made a career out of dictating what constitutes a strike, behind the plate and beside it. His 2021 walk rate is one of the best in the league: a career-high 22.9 percent. He also carries a respectable chase rate of 15.5 percent.

Yasmani anticipates another pitch—this time an ambitious fastball located at the knees—and struggles to contain his amusement as he connects, pulling a line drive foul that bounces leisurely off the safety nets. The catcher behind him utters another impatient grunt, and Yasmani assumes it's because this at-bat is much too long at this point.

The pitcher winds up for try number 10.

Yasmani reads the seams, and though he is grinning inside, he takes Tony's advice and hides it. He times his swing, connects and, in that moment, he just *knows*. He could throw his bat into the Southside Chicago night sky, but doesn't. With as much pomp and candor as he can muster without Tony getting *too* angry, he nonchalantly drops it behind him as the crowd erupts.

Yasmani Grandal is known for getting on base; but, for now, he'll settle for the fireworks.

Due to Budget Constraints, You Are the Next White Sox Right Fielder

It's the first week of December. Last night's freezing rain has left a light coat of dewdrops on the blades of grass outside, as you hold a mug of black coffee and look out the French doors of your home. Despite the inclement weather, you enjoyed your ex-teammate's wedding, beyond the slight headache you're nursing. You're about to scroll through your camera roll for pictures you can't remember taking, when you get a call from your agent. He tells you the White Sox are looking for a right fielder (yes, again), preferably with a left-handed power bat.

(That's you.)

Wait, who'd they sign last year? Adam Eaton? Can you hold a candle to that guy? Of course you can, you tell yourself.

Your agent begins to explain any preliminary financials, which is great, because you weren't sure a club would take a chance on you given your splits against right-handed pitching. But Chicago seems to believe there's something in you beyond the numbers. It makes you want to believe it yourself.

You catch a glimpse of yourself in a nearby mirror and feel the confidence begin to roll to a boil. It begins to sink in: You get to play for Tony La Russa, the man himself! Oh, man, the anxiety begins to follow. Will you get along with your manager? Will you get along with your teammates? You've got a flashy glove. You could probably hit seventh or eighth on a good day. You aren't Eaton, nor are you Nomar Mazara. But you don't need to be. You bring something incredibly unique to the table. You're different. Sure, it's no surprise that your name is nowhere near the Hot Stove. Some might say you're still in the pantry, with a rapidly approaching expiration date. But this one-year flyer shows that at least someone knows you have something to prove.

You close your eyes to envision yourself signing the one-year contract, and you can't help but smile; 2022 is the year things change. Though the position has been a revolving door—sometimes jammed, but perpetually moving for the sake of mediocrity—this just feels different.

You're different. You'll show 'em they were right to gamble again. You'll finally change the game. They're gonna chant your name, hold up handmade poster-board signs. Nothing but bright lights and summer nights ahead.

—Janice Scurio is a frequent contributor at South Side Sox *and* NBC Sports EDGE.

HITTERS

José Abreu 1B Born: 01/29/87 Age: 35 Bats: R Throws: R Height: 6'3" Weight: 235 lb. Origin: International Free Agent, 2013

YEAR	TEAM	LVL	AGE	PA	R	2B	3B	HR	RBI	BB	K	SB	CS	Whiff%	AVG/OBP/SLG	DRC+	BABIP	BRR	FRAA	WARP
2019	CHW	MLB	32	693	85	38	1	33	123	36	152	2	2	25.3%	.284/.330/.503	111	.320	-4.6	1B(125): -10.5	1.3
2020	CHW	MLB	33	262	43	15	0	19	60	18	59	0	0	30.1%	.317/.370/.617	141	.350	-1.9	1B(54): 3.4	2.0
2021	CHW	MLB	34	659	86	30	2	30	117	61	143	1	0	27.4%	.261/.351/.481	120	.293	1.3	1B(135): -0.7	3.1
2022 DC	*CHW*	*MLB*	*35*	*629*	*89*	*30*	*1*	*28*	*90*	*52*	*140*	*1*	*1*	*27.6%*	*.258/.340/.470*	*116*	*.297*	*-0.9*	*1B -1*	*2.3*

Comparables: Andres Galarraga, Steve Garvey, Orlando Cepeda

After matching an all-time hot streak with a two-month season to win an MVP award, Abreu went back to his career-long practice of piling up familiar milestones. He bopped 30 doubles for the eighth time in his career, launched 30 home runs for the fifth time and avoided the injured list and logged over 150 games for the fifth time, despite getting hit by a career-high 22 pitches. And maybe it's functionally meaningless that Abreu collected more than 100 RBI for the sixth time, but it's sort of all he cares about, and he probably won't be exploring major adjustments as long as that number hits the triple digits by late September. Abreu will play his next season at 35, has seen his strikeout rates slightly creep up the last few years (haven't we all?) while his double play balls have exploded. But while the hunt for reasons he will stop doing what he's done essentially every year remains at a fever pitch, none of this has ever seemed to amount to him stopping.

Micker Adolfo RF/DH Born: 09/11/96 Age: 25 Bats: R Throws: R Height: 6'4" Weight: 225 lb. Origin: International Free Agent, 2013

YEAR	TEAM	LVL	AGE	PA	R	2B	3B	HR	RBI	BB	K	SB	CS	Whiff%	AVG/OBP/SLG	DRC+	BABIP	BRR	FRAA	WARP
2019	GDD	WIN	22	61	5	0	0	4	6	5	27	0	0		.167/.262/.389		.217			
2019	WSX	ROK	22	58	8	5	0	2	3	7	21	0	0		.260/.362/.480		.407			
2019	BIR	AA	22	95	5	7	0	0	9	14	36	0	3		.205/.337/.295	67	.372	-3.3		-0.5
2021	BIR	AA	24	242	33	15	0	15	46	19	85	1	0		.249/.318/.525	113	.328	0.4	RF(39): -2.0	0.9
2021	CLT	AAA	24	163	23	9	1	10	23	12	53	3	0		.240/.301/.513	91	.299	-0.1	RF(30): 0.0, LF(10): 1.2	0.4
2022 DC	*CHW*	*MLB*	*25*	*130*	*16*	*6*	*0*	*4*	*15*	*9*	*49*	*0*	*0*	*39.2%*	*.225/.292/.411*	*84*	*.339*	*-0.1*	*LF 1, RF 0*	*0.2*

Comparables: Steven Moya, Teoscar Hernández, Abraham Almonte

Believe it or not, it's only been eight years since Adolfo set a since-obliterated record for the largest international amateur signing bonus in White Sox history. In that time he's both reached the precipice of the highest level of baseball, and remained remarkably unchanged in terms of summarizing him. Adolfo has truly remarkable power that will be his carrying quality if he's ever able to gain a foothold in the majors, and it'd be nice if he actually got to be free of injury to practice tapping into it for a sustained period of time. A 25-homer campaign over 400 plate appearances in the upper levels stands apart as a breakthrough compared to most years of Adolfo's career. But out of options, still raw in controlling strikeouts and advancing out of prospect age, Adolfo may never get the opportunity to develop into what he was hoped to be, nearly a decade ago.

Tim Anderson SS Born: 06/23/93 Age: 29 Bats: R Throws: R Height: 6'1" Weight: 185 lb. Origin: Round 1, 2013 Draft (#17 overall)

YEAR	TEAM	LVL	AGE	PA	R	2B	3B	HR	RBI	BB	K	SB	CS	Whiff%	AVG/OBP/SLG	DRC+	BABIP	BRR	FRAA	WARP
2019	CHW	MLB	26	518	81	32	0	18	56	15	109	17	5	24.5%	.335/.357/.508	106	.399	4.1	SS(122): 3.1	3.0
2020	CHW	MLB	27	221	45	11	1	10	21	10	50	5	2	30.9%	.322/.357/.529	112	.383	2.8	SS(49): -0.5	1.2
2021	CHW	MLB	28	551	94	29	2	17	61	22	119	18	7	26.1%	.309/.338/.469	105	.372	6.2	SS(122): 0.8	3.1
2022 DC	*CHW*	*MLB*	*29*	*629*	*90*	*30*	*2*	*18*	*63*	*27*	*134*	*20*	*6*	*26.3%*	*.282/.317/.434*	*99*	*.337*	*1.2*	*SS 0*	*2.5*

Comparables: Shawon Dunston, Ernie Banks, Robin Yount

Perhaps an endless wave of singles to right field is not what you anticipated when Anderson was assigned with the responsibility of changing the baseball orthodoxy. Likewise, his solid but unspectacular DRC+ is probably not what you were expecting from a guy who has been near the top of the leaderboard in batting average in the last three seasons and cracked an All-Star roster in 2021. That's because DRC+ is built to assume that guys just can't keep doing what he clearly can do, and it's OK for there to be outliers. But in becoming a trustworthy source of average shortstop defense and swing-happy high average with a suitable splash of opposite-field power, Anderson has made himself a reliable player out of the bag of raw tools he was when he entered the majors, which is the impossible dream every amateur scout envisions when they sign a state champion basketball player who has about two seasons of junior college experience.

Jake Burger 3B Born: 04/10/96 Age: 26 Bats: R Throws: R Height: 6'2" Weight: 230 lb. Origin: Round 1, 2017 Draft (#11 overall)

YEAR	TEAM	LVL	AGE	PA	R	2B	3B	HR	RBI	BB	K	SB	CS	Whiff%	AVG/OBP/SLG	DRC+	BABIP	BRR	FRAA	WARP
2021	CLT	AAA	25	340	46	16	2	18	54	24	91	0	0		.274/.332/.513	102	.330	-2.4	3B(65): 0.0, 2B(5): -0.3	0.9
2021	CHW	MLB	25	42	5	3	1	1	3	4	15	0	0	38.2%	.263/.333/.474	74	.409	-0.2	3B(8): -0.6	-0.1
2022 DC	*CHW*	*MLB*	*26*	*122*	*14*	*5*	*0*	*4*	*16*	*8*	*36*	*0*	*0*	*34.2%*	*.231/.292/.401*	*82*	*.303*	*-0.1*	*3B 0, 2B 0*	*0.0*

Comparables: Todd Frazier, Danny Valencia, Brent Morel

The three years between Burger tearing his Achilles in spring training of 2018 and his first post-injury at-bat in 2021 provided plenty of time to wonder whether there even would be another at-bat. Despite numerous physical setbacks and low points when he considered retirement, Burger has slimmed down, worked with orthopedists and shown the ability to play on a left leg with a twice-torn Achilles tendon. Now at long last, the conversation can finally center around Burger as a prospect, and not as an improbable comeback story. Despite handling an aggressive assignment to Triple-A with a monstrous first half and even making his major-league debut, that conversation is unsettled. That Burger even managed his 2021 season is a tremendous accomplishment given what he's been through, but there are substantial swing-and-miss issues against right-handed velocity that need to be addressed if he is to one-up it in 2022.

Yoelqui Cespedes CF Born: 09/24/97 Age: 24 Bats: R Throws: R Height: 5'9" Weight: 205 lb. Origin: International Free Agent, 2021

YEAR	TEAM	LVL	AGE	PA	R	2B	3B	HR	RBI	BB	K	SB	CS	Whiff%	AVG/OBP/SLG	DRC+	BABIP	BRR	FRAA	WARP
2021	GDD	WIN	23	78	8	3	0	0	1	2	22	2	0		.181/.244/.222		.260			
2021	WS	A+	23	199	34	17	0	7	20	13	56	10	2		.278/.355/.494	89	.372	0.5	CF(21): -1.5, RF(3): -0.4	0.2
2021	BIR	AA	23	100	14	3	2	1	7	3	27	8	4		.298/.340/.404	81	.409	-0.2	CF(26): 3.9	0.5
2022 non-DC	*CHW*	*MLB*	*24*	*251*	*21*	*12*	*1*	*3*	*22*	*12*	*83*	*10*	*5*	*37.6%*	*.227/.281/.340*	*66*	*.336*	*1.0*	*CF 4, RF 0*	*0.3*

Comparables: Henry Ramos, Elier Hernandez, Angel Morales

Like many Cuban defectors, Céspedes had to endure a two-year sabbatical from high-level baseball, extended by a delayed 2020-21 international signing period and prolonged work visa issues, keeping him on the Arizona backfields until mid-June. From there, the White Sox saw fit to keep Céspedes a level lower than where they originally planned for two months in the name of getting him up to speed. Throw that on top of a large pile of reasons to treat 2021 as an acclimation year for a prospect with enviable physical tools. But the gap in Céspedes' development time won't magically disappear in 2022, and in the meantime, it would have been nice if he had shown more signs of progress. Céspedes' barreled contact was sufficiently monstrous, but pre-existing concerns about his hit tool persisted as he racked up garish strikeout-to-walk ratios that worsened at every level, including the Arizona Fall League.

Zack Collins C

Born: 02/06/95 Age: 27 Bats: L Throws: R Height: 6'3" Weight: 220 lb. Origin: Round 1, 2016 Draft (#10 overall)

YEAR	TEAM	LVL	AGE	PA	R	2B	3B	HR	RBI	BB	K	SB	CS	Whiff%	AVG/OBP/SLG	DRC+	BABIP	BRR	FRAA	WARP
2019	CHA	AAA	24	367	56	19	1	19	74	62	98	0	0		.282/.403/.548	118	.346	0.5	C(50): -2.9, 1B(20): -1.7	1.7
2019	CHW	MLB	24	102	10	3	1	3	12	14	39	0	0	37.3%	.186/.307/.349	69	.295	0.0	C(10): -3.0, 1B(1): -0.1	-0.4
2020	CHW	MLB	25	18	1	1	0	0	0	2	5	0	0	42.4%	.063/.167/.125	86	.091	-0.1	C(2): -0.0	0.0
2021	CLT	AAA	26	38	5	0	0	3	5	3	13	0	0		.143/.211/.400	94	.105	-0.1	C(9): 0.1	0.1
2021	CHW	MLB	26	231	25	13	0	4	26	34	69	1	1	28.7%	.210/.330/.338	78	.303	-2.6	C(73): -11.9	-1.2
2022 DC	*CHW*	*MLB*	*27*	*92*	*11*	*3*	*0*	*3*	*11*	*12*	*25*	*0*	*0*	*30.1%*	*.218/.329/.415*	*98*	*.274*	*-0.1*	*C -6*	*-0.2*

Comparables: George Kottaras, Chris Parmelee, Juan Centeno

YEAR	TEAM	P. COUNT	FRM RUNS	BLK RUNS	THRW RUNS	TOT RUNS
2019	CHW	1653	-2.8	-0.1	0.0	-2.9
2019	CHA	7026	-3.3	-0.1	0.3	-3.1
2020	CHW	143	0.0	0.0	0.0	0.0
2021	CHW	8822	-12.4	-0.6	0.5	-12.5
2021	CLT	1142	0.2	0.0	0.0	0.3
2022	*CHW*	*3608*	*-4.8*	*-0.8*	*0.0*	*-5.6*

On a cold night in April, Collins sat in front of a tablet, his shoulders soaked in champagne, and acknowledged that his 15th career major-league start behind the plate—a no-hitter twirled by Carlos Rodón—was 15 more games than many evaluators ever believed he would catch at the sport's highest level. A month later, he turned around a 96-mph Brad Keller fastball and smacked it 430 feet out to dead center, providing all the run support needed for another shutout he would catch. Collins was picked 10th overall in 2016, so it should come as no surprise to flick on the television and see him flashing big-time talent. But he'll turn 27 before Opening Day, and is past the stage of his career where flashes of ability outweigh an increasingly underwhelming statistical record, both at the plate and behind it.

Adam Engel OF

Born: 12/09/91 Age: 30 Bats: R Throws: R Height: 6'2" Weight: 215 lb. Origin: Round 19, 2013 Draft (#573 overall)

YEAR	TEAM	LVL	AGE	PA	R	2B	3B	HR	RBI	BB	K	SB	CS	Whiff%	AVG/OBP/SLG	DRC+	BABIP	BRR	FRAA	WARP
2019	CHA	AAA	27	277	43	13	4	9	29	22	62	13	3		.270/.347/.464	91	.328	3.8	CF(58): 7.0, LF(5): -0.7, RF(1): -0.2	1.6
2019	CHW	MLB	27	248	26	10	2	6	26	14	78	3	3	32.6%	.242/.304/.383	71	.343	1.1	CF(86): 0.7	0.3
2020	CHW	MLB	28	93	11	5	1	3	12	3	19	1	0	26.5%	.295/.333/.477	99	.348	0.3	RF(25): -1.5, LF(9): 0.6, CF(3): 0.2	0.2
2021	CLT	AAA	29	60	7	2	0	2	5	3	16	5	0		.222/.283/.370	94	.270	-0.1	CF(8): -0.7, RF(5): 1.6	0.2
2021	CHW	MLB	29	140	21	9	0	7	18	11	31	7	1	27.1%	.252/.336/.496	106	.279	-0.3	CF(26): 0.1, RF(10): 0.9, LF(4): 0.5	0.8
2022 DC	*CHW*	*MLB*	*30*	*350*	*40*	*15*	*2*	*8*	*42*	*21*	*88*	*8*	*4*	*28.0%*	*.231/.295/.378*	*80*	*.292*	*0.8*	*RF 1, CF 1*	*0.4*

Comparables: Abraham Almonte, Brandon Barnes, Jarrod Dyson

This book splits things into two components. There are the numbers, where you see that a long-suffering fourth outfielder progressively worked his way toward his best offensive season ever, but wonder why he didn't play more.

And then there's this comment section, explaining that Engel pulled a hamstring in spring training, tore the hamstring while rehabbing it, finally returned to action and peeled back a skin flap on that hamstring that just bled a lot. He said it was no big deal, once you got past all the blood. Engel later cut short his most sustained stretch of play by tweaking his right groin (which, thankfully, did not bleed) while running and then tweaking his left shoulder while sliding, eventually leading to offseason surgery on the shoulder. Frankly, it was kind of a plot twist, given how much of the year was spent attending to his leg.

So while numbers might suggest this was one of Engel's best seasons, the player would probably disagree. And while stats and players are often in disagreement, it seems like the latter really has the more informed perspective here.

Leury García UT

Born: 03/18/91 Age: 31 Bats: S Throws: R Height: 5'8" Weight: 190 lb. Origin: International Free Agent, 2007

YEAR	TEAM	LVL	AGE	PA	R	2B	3B	HR	RBI	BB	K	SB	CS	Whiff%	AVG/OBP/SLG	DRC+	BABIP	BRR	FRAA	WARP
2019	CHW	MLB	28	618	93	27	3	8	40	21	139	15	5	24.7%	.279/.310/.378	78	.353	7.4	CF(80): -6.2, RF(45): -2.8, LF(24): -0.4	0.4
2020	CHW	MLB	29	63	6	1	0	3	8	4	9	0	0	21.3%	.271/.317/.441	108	.277	0.7	SS(10): -0.1, 2B(5): 0.1, RF(3): -0.1	0.3
2021	CHW	MLB	30	474	60	22	4	5	54	41	97	6	2	24.5%	.267/.335/.376	88	.333	3.5	2B(36): -1.5, RF(34): -0.9, LF(26): -0.6	0.9
2022 DC	*CHW*	*MLB*	*31*	*476*	*52*	*19*	*2*	*8*	*48*	*33*	*97*	*10*	*4*	*24.1%*	*.254/.314/.370*	*84*	*.310*	*0.7*	*2B -4, RF 0*	*0.2*

Comparables: Roberto Kelly, Stan Javier, Mickey Rivers

Has García survived for a decade in the majors because he can play nearly every position on the diamond (not first base, too short), covering up light-hitting behind an overly aggressive approach? Or is he a natural shortstop whose bursts of offensive competence hint at what he might be capable of if he were ever truly settled? A stronger second half at age 30, featuring phases where he actually took walks when a wild reliever was handing them out, inspires a lot more curiosity in the latter scenario than ever before. But given some of García's offensive lows, the latter would never be pondered if the former was never freely offered. García hit .181/.218/.215 in scant playing time across his first three major-league seasons and now he's earned more than $11 million playing baseball, so chances are he is not deeply troubled by the paradox.

Romy Gonzalez IF

Born: 09/06/96 Age: 25 Bats: R Throws: R Height: 6'1" Weight: 215 lb. Origin: Round 18, 2018 Draft (#528 overall)

YEAR	TEAM	LVL	AGE	PA	R	2B	3B	HR	RBI	BB	K	SB	CS	Whiff%	AVG/OBP/SLG	DRC+	BABIP	BRR	FRAA	WARP
2019	KAN	A	22	405	35	22	4	4	45	38	108	11	3		.244/.329/.364	94	.337	2.1	LF(68): 8.9, 1B(14): -0.8, 2B(7): -0.4	1.9
2021	BIR	AA	24	344	52	11	0	20	47	38	97	21	6		.267/.355/.502	122	.328	-0.4	SS(61): -0.8, 2B(10): 0.9	1.9
2021	CLT	AAA	24	60	9	6	0	4	14	5	15	3	0		.370/.417/.704	102	.444	1.4	SS(10): -1.8, 2B(3): -0.3, 3B(2): -0.5	0.1
2021	CHW	MLB	24	33	4	3	0	0	2	1	11	0	0	27.3%	.250/.273/.344	70	.381	0.4	3B(4): -0.3, RF(3): -0.2, 2B(1): -0.1	0.0
2022 DC	*CHW*	*MLB*	*25*	*129*	*14*	*5*	*0*	*3*	*14*	*9*	*40*	*3*	*1*	*31.4%*	*.232/.297/.388*	*82*	*.318*	*0.2*	*2B 0, SS 0*	*0.1*

Comparables: Danny Valencia, Ryon Healy, Wilmer Difo

Looking largely overmatched in a September call-up spin against major-league pitching and left off the White Sox playoff roster, it's questionable whether González can handle a utility role in the immediate term, let alone establish himself as a regular down the road. But since González's status going into 2021 (and leaving 2019) was that of a third-day draft pick who was just OK in Low-A Kannapolis, it was an acceptable finish. An extensive pandemic training program lent González a lot more raw power, which encouraged him to shake off the worst elements of a pull-happy approach and slap together a 20-20 season in Double-A before a pair of short stints at the highest levels. González obliterated Triple-A as thoroughly as he struggled in the majors, but he did so as an actually established prospect on the 40-man roster, rather than someone you just politely refer to as a "prospect" because using "minor leaguer" as an identifier over and over gets repetitive.

Yasmani Grandal C

Born: 11/08/88 Age: 33 Bats: S Throws: R Height: 6'2" Weight: 225 lb. Origin: Round 1, 2010 Draft (#12 overall)

YEAR	TEAM	LVL	AGE	PA	R	2B	3B	HR	RBI	BB	K	SB	CS	Whiff%	AVG/OBP/SLG	DRC+	BABIP	BRR	FRAA	WARP
2019	MIL	MLB	30	632	79	26	2	28	77	109	139	5	1	25.4%	.246/.380/.468	121	.279	-6.9	C(137): 14.1, 1B(20): 0.1	5.0
2020	CHW	MLB	31	194	27	7	0	8	27	30	58	0	0	30.7%	.230/.351/.422	101	.299	-0.1	C(32): 5.8, 1B(6): -0.2	1.2
2021	CLT	AAA	32	25	3	1	0	1	1	2	8	0	0		.273/.360/.455	95	.385	0.0	C(5): 0.3, 1B(2): 0.0	0.1
2021	CHW	MLB	32	375	60	9	0	23	62	87	82	0	0	24.9%	.240/.420/.520	145	.246	-2.4	C(80): 2.0, 1B(8): 0.0	3.5
2022 DC	*CHW*	*MLB*	*33*	*472*	*69*	*17*	*0*	*22*	*61*	*92*	*107*	*1*	*1*	*26.1%*	*.235/.391/.463*	*131*	*.271*	*-0.6*	*C 11, 1B 0*	*5.1*

Comparables: Russell Martin, Steve Yeager, Brian McCann

YEAR	TEAM	P. COUNT	FRM RUNS	BLK RUNS	THRW RUNS	TOT RUNS
2019	MIL	18740	14.6	0.7	0.1	15.4
2020	CHW	4830	4.8	0.0	0.4	5.1
2021	CHW	10543	2.8	-0.1	0.1	2.8
2022	*CHW*	*14430*	*10.1*	*0.3*	*0.2*	*10.6*

What's the best season ever compiled by a player who underwent surgeries on both knees? This might require an asterisk, because the surgery on Grandal's right knee, injured in spring training and clearly the reason why he was batting in the low .100s for the first two months of the season, was delayed until the White Sox were eliminated from the playoffs (and conducted on Grandal's wedding anniversary). But the first surgery, on the second injury, came in mid-July on a torn ligament in his left knee. Rather than slowly work his way back into sync, when he returned in August, Grandal immediately embarked upon a hellacious hot streak which gave him the best offensive rate stats of his career. And he did this at age 32 while his legs were literally breaking down. There was a litany of defensive struggles that came with these injuries, and in normal circumstances it would make sense to talk about possible decline. Except: A lot of Grandal's 2021 looks nothing like decline.

Billy Hamilton OF

Born: 09/09/90 Age: 31 Bats: R Throws: R Height: 6'0" Weight: 160 lb. Origin: Round 2, 2009 Draft (#57 overall)

YEAR	TEAM	LVL	AGE	PA	R	2B	3B	HR	RBI	BB	K	SB	CS	Whiff%	AVG/OBP/SLG	DRC+	BABIP	BRR	FRAA	WARP
2019	ATL	MLB	28	48	9	2	0	0	3	7	13	4	1	21.9%	.268/.375/.317	83	.393	0.5	CF(24): -3.1	-0.2
2019	KC	MLB	28	305	32	12	2	0	12	25	74	18	5	23.5%	.211/.275/.269	67	.286	3.6	CF(90): -3.7	0.0
2020	NYM	MLB	29	25	4	0	0	0	1	1	3	3	1	16.0%	.045/.083/.045	94	.050	-0.5	CF(13): 0.5	0.1
2020	CHC	MLB	29	11	6	0	0	1	1	1	4	3	1	33.3%	.300/.364/.600	97	.400	0.4	CF(12): -0.5	0.0
2021	CHW	MLB	30	135	23	8	3	2	11	4	47	9	0	31.5%	.220/.242/.378	60	.329	1.1	CF(47): -2.2, LF(18): 0.3, RF(2): -0.1	-0.2
2022 DC	*FA*	*MLB*	*31*	*276*	*21*	*10*	*2*	*2*	*21*	*20*	*86*	*16*	*5*	*30.1%*	*.207/.269/.299*	*50*	*.302*	*1.8*	*CF -1, LF 0*	*-0.7*

Comparables: Darren Lewis, Carlos Gómez, Dexter Fowler

It might be slightly reductive to describe Hamilton's contributions as "no hits, just vibes" at this point in his career, because in between three(!!!) separate IL stints in 2021 and the team's late-season desperate march to the sea, he seemed to find a small groove in whacking lefties. And he feels so much more comfortable swinging right-handed that he ditched switch-hitting entirely toward the end. But no club—contender or rebuilder—is likely to commit to finding out whether Hamilton is capable of more with regular at-bats or encouragement to try to drive the ball as the White Sox urged in 2021. And absent of that, Hamilton is likely to struggle to provide any pop or on-base ability. He should, though, remain an infectious clubhouse presence who is really fast on the basepaths and in the outfield. On a good team like the 2021 White Sox, that means he can still serve as a Jarrod Dyson-level cult hero whose name gets chanted from the stands, but with no assurance that, like Dyson, he won't wind up bouncing around to some team where it won't.

Eloy Jiménez LF/DH

Born: 11/27/96 Age: 25 Bats: R Throws: R Height: 6'4" Weight: 240 lb. Origin: International Free Agent, 2013

YEAR	TEAM	LVL	AGE	PA	R	2B	3B	HR	RBI	BB	K	SB	CS	Whiff%	AVG/OBP/SLG	DRC+	BABIP	BRR	FRAA	WARP
2019	CHW	MLB	22	504	69	18	2	31	79	30	134	0	0	32.8%	.267/.315/.513	108	.308	1.2	LF(114): -1.5	2.3
2020	CHW	MLB	23	226	26	14	0	14	41	12	56	0	0	29.2%	.296/.332/.559	121	.340	-0.1	LF(54): -9.1	0.3
2021	CLT	AAA	24	41	3	2	0	1	2	2	14	0	0		.263/.293/.395	78	.375	-0.1	LF(8): 0.6	0.1
2021	CHW	MLB	24	231	23	10	0	10	37	16	57	0	0	33.8%	.249/.303/.437	96	.293	-0.5	LF(37): -2.1	0.4
2022 DC	*CHW*	*MLB*	*25*	*579*	*76*	*26*	*2*	*27*	*87*	*39*	*153*	*0*	*1*	*33.2%*	*.263/.318/.474*	*110*	*.320*	*-0.8*	*LF 0*	*2.4*

Comparables: Carlos González, Enrique Hernández, Jorge Polanco

When Jiménez chose a late-March spring training game to recreate the Vince Carter elbow deep dunk, tearing a pectoral tendon in the process, it was feared that the 2021 season would pass by without one of the most talented young hitters in the game flaunting his prodigious hit tool and elite power combination. Those fears were more or less realized, despite the fact that Jiménez returned to play in late July. Save for an early August burst, the season passed without a prolonged stretch of Jiménez at his best. Even as he eventually racked up as many games played as his Silver Slugger-winning 2020 pandemic season, and even looked more fluid in his long-maligned defense, Jiménez's swing grew uncharacteristically long and clunky through October. No one who has ever watched him would question that Jiménez has the offensive talent to be an elite hitter, but he's now 25 with an odd collection of false starts and down periods rather than a clear trajectory to future MVP awards.

Danny Mendick IF

Born: 09/28/93 Age: 28 Bats: R Throws: R Height: 5'10" Weight: 195 lb. Origin: Round 22, 2015 Draft (#652 overall)

YEAR	TEAM	LVL	AGE	PA	R	2B	3B	HR	RBI	BB	K	SB	CS	Whiff%	AVG/OBP/SLG	DRC+	BABIP	BRR	FRAA	WARP
2019	CHA	AAA	25	558	75	26	1	17	64	66	96	19	8		.279/.368/.444	107	.313	-1.0	2B(48): 2.5, SS(42): 2.8, 3B(38): -0.1	3.0
2019	CHW	MLB	25	40	6	0	0	2	4	1	11	0	0	28.8%	.308/.325/.462	88	.385	0.1	SS(5): 0.1, 2B(3): -0.4, 3B(3): 0.6	0.1
2020	CHW	MLB	26	114	11	4	1	3	6	6	25	0	1	25.4%	.243/.281/.383	91	.288	1.2	2B(28): 2.7, SS(4): 0.0, 3B(3): 0.2	0.7
2021	CLT	AAA	27	105	16	4	0	3	8	7	20	1	1		.271/.327/.406	96	.315	-1.1	SS(12): 0.6, LF(4): -0.4, 1B(3): -0.2	0.1
2021	CHW	MLB	27	186	14	5	0	2	20	18	42	0	1	24.9%	.220/.303/.287	82	.281	1.2	2B(28): -1.1, SS(28): -0.5, RF(8): -0.4	0.1
2022 DC	*CHW*	*MLB*	*28*	*152*	*16*	*5*	*0*	*3*	*18*	*12*	*34*	*2*	*1*	*23.9%*	*.228/.297/.346*	*76*	*.279*	*0.0*	*2B 0, SS 0*	*0.1*

Comparables: Cliff Pennington, Darwin Barney, Ryan Goins

During the White Sox lowest moment of an injury-ravaged 2021 season, Mendick—a slight natural shortstop—played five innings of center field. Hall of Fame manager Tony La Russa referred to Mendick as a miniature Luis Robert. The comparison was, in a very endearing way, patently ridiculous. Through two seasons, Mendick has made himself more valuable to the team than he looks on paper by being willing and pretty much able to defend every position on the diamond. He even pitched an inning. The Sox lost that game. Unfortunately, living this lifestyle means that Mendick can be invaluable to his manager on a week-to-week basis, but puts himself in a position to be replaced by his boss in the front office with the next light-hitting young player who is willing to do anything.

Yermín Mercedes DH

Born: 02/14/93 Age: 29 Bats: R Throws: R Height: 5'11" Weight: 245 lb. Origin: International Free Agent, 2011

YEAR	TEAM	LVL	AGE	PA	R	2B	3B	HR	RBI	BB	K	SB	CS	Whiff%	AVG/OBP/SLG	DRC+	BABIP	BRR	FRAA	WARP
2019	BIR	AA	26	167	19	7	0	6	18	17	25	2	0		.327/.389/.497	132	.353	-0.7	C(34): 5.5	1.9
2019	CHA	AAA	26	220	35	12	0	17	62	24	42	0	0		.310/.386/.647	128	.306	-1.9	C(24): 2.5, 1B(4): -0.5, 3B(2): -0.3	1.4
2020	LIC	WIN	27	95	9	2	0	2	16	7	9	0	1		.276/.326/.368		.286			
2020	CHW	MLB	27	1	0	0	0	0	0	0	0	0	0	0.0%	.000/.000/.000	94				0.0
2021	LIC	WIN	28	68	3	2	0	1	7	3	6	0	0		.190/.221/.270		.190			
2021	CLT	AAA	28	239	32	7	1	11	29	11	39	3	0		.275/.318/.464	106	.287	-1.0	1B(19): -3.5, C(18): -1.1, 3B(1): -0.0	0.3
2021	CHW	MLB	28	262	26	9	1	7	37	20	46	0	1	22.0%	.271/.328/.404	105	.309	-0.9	1B(1): -0.0, P(1): -0.0	0.7
2022 DC	*CHW*	*MLB*	*29*	*63*	*7*	*2*	*0*	*2*	*8*	*4*	*10*	*0*	*0*	*22.6%*	*.266/.322/.432*	*101*	*.293*	*-0.1*	*C 0*	*0.2*

Comparables: José Martínez, Steve Pearce, Jesús Sucre

If Mercedes' life were a sitcom about a talented but frustrated career minor-league slugger—and increasingly, it appears that way—then maybe his 2021 made sense. But even a madcap *Simpsons* story arc where a main character:

—Made the Opening Day roster at the last second due to a freak/low-key ridiculous injury to Eloy Jiménez
—Set an actual MLB record by starting the season with eight-straight hits
—Won AL rookie of the month while becoming the star of a division-winning team for said month
—Got a burger named after him (The Yerminator) and a ridiculous Terminator-themed stadium promo video package to match
—Was unfairly castigated by his manager for hitting a home run off a different ridiculous Quad-A local hero/fascination
—Completely collapsed in his performance in every way
—Was sent back down to the minors
—Claimed to retire and then came back to work the next day
—Found himself completely back on the outs of the major-league roster picture and back to being a frustrated minor-league slugger
—All by the end of July

would still probably be spread out over at least two episodes. And if you missed both of them, well, Mercedes is back where he was: a guy who is capable of mashing Triple-A pitching who probably won't do much else.

Yoán Moncada 3B

Born: 05/27/95 Age: 27 Bats: S Throws: R Height: 6'2" Weight: 225 lb. Origin: International Free Agent, 2015

YEAR	TEAM	LVL	AGE	PA	R	2B	3B	HR	RBI	BB	K	SB	CS	Whiff%	AVG/OBP/SLG	DRC+	BABIP	BRR	FRAA	WARP
2019	CHW	MLB	24	559	83	34	5	25	79	40	154	10	3	31.1%	.315/.367/.548	110	.406	3.3	3B(129): 10.8	3.5
2020	CHW	MLB	25	231	28	8	3	6	24	28	72	0	0	30.7%	.225/.320/.385	84	.315	1.7	3B(52): 2.0	0.5
2021	CHW	MLB	26	616	74	33	1	14	61	84	157	3	2	28.1%	.263/.375/.412	102	.350	-0.8	3B(138): -7.4	1.4
2022 DC	*CHW*	*MLB*	*27*	*596*	*85*	*28*	*3*	*20*	*69*	*72*	*152*	*9*	*4*	*27.9%*	*.258/.356/.445*	*112*	*.329*	*0.3*	*3B 0*	*2.7*

Comparables: Aramis Ramirez, Adrián Beltré, Paul Molitor

No one human wields the power necessary to close the "Is Yoán Moncada good?" thread on White Sox fan forums, a self-sustaining maelstrom of flame, suffering and infernal torment, filled with both bad faith assumptions that the opposing party does not understand on-base percentage and plenty of people who indeed, do not understand on-base percentage. It is eternal.

Returning from a COVID-marred 2020, Moncada had his first full major-league season without an injured list stint, played a fine defensive third base and posted a career high in, that's right, on-base percentage. He was a good player, as he was widely projected to be as a prospect. Life is truly a blessing if that is your sole takeaway on Moncada. We all envy you. For the rest of us, imagine someone looking kind of off at the plate, but you look up and realize he went 1-for-4 with a walk. That's a line that's hard to really criticize at the end of the day. Now imagine if he did it for six months!

Colson Montgomery SS

Born: 02/27/02 Age: 20 Bats: L Throws: R Height: 6'4" Weight: 205 lb. Origin: Round 1, 2021 Draft (#22 overall)

YEAR	TEAM	LVL	AGE	PA	R	2B	3B	HR	RBI	BB	K	SB	CS	Whiff%	AVG/OBP/SLG	DRC+	BABIP	BRR	FRAA	WARP
2021	WSX	ROK	19	111	16	7	0	0	7	13	22	0	1		.287/.396/.362		.375			
2022															*No projection*					

Comparables: Jordan McCants, Trace Loehr, Engelb Vielma

Chicago's first-round pick didn't go deep in the 22 complex league games he got into down the stretch, so at no point has there been a true test of the viability of "THAT WAS AN ACT OF COLSON CREAMERY" as a home run call. Alas.

The power potential of Montgomery's 6-4 frame after he was a multi-sport start in Indiana was one of the carrying tools coming out of the draft. So the White Sox will gladly take a slow maturation of his extra-base thunder over issues that might be harder to answer long-term, like major struggles to stick defensively in the middle infield, or debilitating amounts of swing-and-miss, neither of which Montgomery displayed in excess in his professional debut. Though he was old for his draft class and turns 20 in February, the White Sox believe Montgomery is raw in terms of baseball development—on account of all the non-transferable basketball and football skills—so as he wasn't waylaid entirely by his introduction to pro life, the Sox regard it as a win.

Luis Robert CF

Born: 08/03/97 Age: 24 Bats: R Throws: R Height: 6'2" Weight: 220 lb. Origin: International Free Agent, 2017

YEAR	TEAM	LVL	AGE	PA	R	2B	3B	HR	RBI	BB	K	SB	CS	Whiff%	AVG/OBP/SLG	DRC+	BABIP	BRR	FRAA	WARP
2019	WS	A+	21	84	21	5	3	8	24	4	20	8	2		.453/.512/.920	188	.553	-0.2	CF(13): 2.0	1.3
2019	BIR	AA	21	244	43	16	3	8	29	13	54	21	6		.314/.362/.518	116	.384	2.6	CF(36): 2.1, RF(7): -0.7, LF(2): 0.1	1.8
2019	CHA	AAA	21	223	44	10	5	16	39	11	55	7	3		.297/.341/.634	110	.324	1.4	CF(47): 6.3	1.7
2020	CHW	MLB	22	227	33	8	0	11	31	20	73	9	2	41.7%	.233/.302/.436	92	.300	0.9	CF(56): 10.6	1.7
2021	CLT	AAA	23	36	4	1	0	1	3	5	9	2	0		.276/.417/.414	97	.368	0.5	CF(5): -1.4	0.0
2021	CHW	MLB	23	296	42	22	1	13	43	14	61	6	1	28.4%	.338/.378/.567	122	.394	0.6	CF(67): -0.1	2.1
2022 DC	*CHW*	*MLB*	*24*	*558*	*83*	*26*	*3*	*24*	*74*	*35*	*134*	*22*	*7*	*30.5%*	*.279/.338/.488*	*119*	*.336*	*1.8*	*CF 4*	*4.1*

Comparables: Byron Buxton, Starling Marte, Matt Kemp

For the third time in five professional seasons, Robert had much of his 2021 campaign eaten by a freak injury when he tore his hip flexor running to first base. The elite defense that was the strongest component of his Gold Glove-winning rookie season took a small step back in terms of consistency. He's never seemed particularly interested in walks, and in the wake of his hip injury, he was fairly restrained in his stolen base efforts.

OK, now that we've finished straining to find weak points, even for someone who swings at nearly everything: You can certainly understand why taking a single base on balls could be seen as an inconvenience. Robert is the sort of monstrous five-tool talent that we pretend we're talking about when we talk up other premium athletes. He's the player you acknowledge has a chance to be one of the best in the game because stating openly that he has a real chance to be *the* best still feels a little too bold. It would be nice for him to support this notion by actually playing a full season, though. But hey, if Mike Trout can't either, well...

Jose Rodriguez SS

Born: 05/13/01 Age: 21 Bats: R Throws: R Height: 5'11" Weight: 175 lb. Origin: International Free Agent, 2018

YEAR	TEAM	LVL	AGE	PA	R	2B	3B	HR	RBI	BB	K	SB	CS	Whiff%	AVG/OBP/SLG	DRC+	BABIP	BRR	FRAA	WARP
2019	WSX	ROK	18	200	28	7	3	9	31	9	45	7	1		.293/.328/.505		.343			
2021	GDD	WIN	20	66	5	1	1	1	13	4	10	2	0		.226/.273/.323		.255			
2021	KAN	A	20	361	58	22	4	9	32	21	57	20	5		.283/.328/.452	111	.317	1.8	SS(71): -8.9, 2B(3): 0.1	0.9
2021	WS	A+	20	126	19	4	1	5	19	5	13	10	5		.361/.381/.538	138	.369	-1.7	SS(29): -4.0	0.4
2022 non-DC	*CHW*	*MLB*	*21*	*251*	*22*	*11*	*1*	*4*	*24*	*10*	*49*	*9*	*4*	*27.4%*	*.260/.294/.377*	*81*	*.311*	*0.9*	*SS -1, 2B 0*	*0.3*

Comparables: Jorge Polanco, Ryan Mountcastle, Richard Ureña

It's a backhanded compliment to be speculated upon as a possible one-hit wonder, but there is a compliment buried in there: That one hit is a verified banger. Similarly, Rodríguez is currently being subjected to a lot of grating scrutiny on whether his throwing errors will subside and he can stick at shortstop, or whether his aggressive hacks and approach are a product of wailing on his overmatched competition, or some more deeply rooted lack of feel and discipline doomed to be exposed at higher levels. But those questions are being asked because he is absolutely heading to those higher levels. And the question of whether he's truly "a dude" is being asked because he's forced some reflection after an undeniable banger of a 2021 season, where he moved from being an interesting complex league guy to the sort of player who breezes through A-ball while being young for the level. A lot of the guys in the new neighborhood where Rodríguez finds himself never make it to the majors, but none of them is ignored.

Blake Rutherford OF

Born: 05/02/97 Age: 25 Bats: L Throws: R Height: 6'3" Weight: 205 lb. Origin: Round 1, 2016 Draft (#18 overall)

YEAR	TEAM	LVL	AGE	PA	R	2B	3B	HR	RBI	BB	K	SB	CS	Whiff%	AVG/OBP/SLG	DRC+	BABIP	BRR	FRAA	WARP
2019	GDD	WIN	22	89	12	4	3	2	7	11	21	1	1		.179/.281/.385		.218			
2019	BIR	AA	22	480	50	17	3	7	49	37	118	9	2		.265/.319/.365	90	.343	2.6	RF(68): 1.4, LF(29): -2.5, CF(1): -0.0	1.1
2021	CLT	AAA	24	476	59	30	3	11	54	21	119	4	1		.250/.286/.404	82	.314	-2.9	LF(48): -2.1, CF(37): -2.7, RF(19): 0.2	-0.1
2022 DC	*CHW*	*MLB*	*25*	*30*	*3*	*1*	*0*	*0*	*3*	*1*	*8*	*0*	*0*	*33.7%*	*.234/.279/.351*	*64*	*.319*	*0.0*	*LF 0*	*-0.1*

Comparables: Victor Reyes, Domonic Brown, Ben Revere

Following prospects can offer the youth and untapped potential often missing from our lives. But following prospects gets way too real when it becomes watching the years pile up as that potential remains unrealized, which is why we generally stop writing about guys at that stage. Rutherford ended the 2021 season still on a 40-man roster, but the caveats to his underwhelming performance have melted away. Blessed with a sweet lefty swing which got him selected in the first round, but perennially young for the levels where he's struggled, Rutherford hasn't duplicated the excitement of his 2016 draft year and pro debut. And as an outfielder ill-suited for center and not geared to provide plus power production, he has yet to provide a fit for a role on defense. But he will be 25 in May and is one of the 500 best hitters in the world. It could be worse.

Gavin Sheets DH Born: 04/23/96 Age: 26 Bats: L Throws: L Height: 6'5" Weight: 230 lb. Origin: Round 2, 2017 Draft (#49 overall)

YEAR	TEAM	LVL	AGE	PA	R	2B	3B	HR	RBI	BB	K	SB	CS	Whiff%	AVG/OBP/SLG	DRC+	BABIP	BRR	FRAA	WARP
2019	GDD	WIN	23	81	9	5	0	0	8	8	23	0	0		.250/.321/.319		.360			
2019	BIR	AA	23	527	56	18	1	16	83	54	99	3	1		.267/.345/.414	120	.305	-6.2	1B(110): 4.0	2.7
2021	CLT	AAA	25	254	36	15	0	11	46	25	55	1	1		.295/.362/.507	114	.344	0.1	1B(35): 0.5, RF(24): 0.1, LF(2): -0.1	1.1
2021	CHW	MLB	25	179	23	8	0	11	34	16	40	0	0	20.2%	.250/.324/.506	108	.264	-4.3	RF(13): -1.3, 1B(10): 0.1, LF(4): -0.5	0.0
2022 DC	*CHW*	*MLB*	*26*	*422*	*49*	*19*	*1*	*12*	*50*	*35*	*83*	*0*	*1*	*23.1%*	*.242/.313/.396*	*89*	*.280*	*-0.6*	*RF 0, 1B 0*	*0.3*

Comparables: Mark Trumbo, Bryan LaHair, C.J. Cron

Every good team* has a fun dinger-jacking rookie whose dinger-jacking is out-of-nowhere enough and possibly unsustainable enough to be viewed simultaneously as an organizational player development victory and a meaningless flash in the pan. An overslot signing out of the second round with a pedestrian minor-league career, Sheets emerged in the wake of the Eloy Jiménez injury as a left-handed power threat with some ability to fake it in right field for a division-winner. He was a pure fastball-hunter, a pure platoon bat and seemed to get neutralized for stretches of time by quality breaking stuff.

But even getting to this point required a substantial evolution: body transformation, swing adjustments and the ego death of being left off the alternate site roster and continuing to develop. Better plate discipline, staying on breaking pitches, even hitting left-handers, are all abilities Sheets has flashed in the past. It's jacking dingers that made him relevant, and it had been jacking dingers that he lacked.

**feels true*

Andrew Vaughn OF Born: 04/03/98 Age: 24 Bats: R Throws: R Height: 6'0" Weight: 215 lb. Origin: Round 1, 2019 Draft (#3 overall)

YEAR	TEAM	LVL	AGE	PA	R	2B	3B	HR	RBI	BB	K	SB	CS	Whiff%	AVG/OBP/SLG	DRC+	BABIP	BRR	FRAA	WARP
2019	WSX	ROK	21	16	3	2	0	1	4	0	3	0	0		.600/.625/.933		.727			
2019	KAN	A	21	103	14	7	0	2	11	14	18	0	0		.253/.388/.410	118	.297	0.7	1B(19): -0.4	0.5
2019	WS	A+	21	126	16	8	0	3	21	16	17	0	1		.252/.349/.411	118	.270	-0.3	1B(16): -0.7	0.5
2021	CHW	MLB	23	469	56	22	0	15	48	41	101	1	1	24.3%	.235/.309/.396	98	.271	-2.4	LF(95): -5.8, RF(18): -2.1, 1B(15): 0.2	0.4
2022 DC	*CHW*	*MLB*	*24*	*481*	*57*	*21*	*1*	*16*	*61*	*44*	*101*	*1*	*1*	*24.5%*	*.241/.321/.411*	*97*	*.280*	*-0.7*	*RF -6, LF -1*	*0.3*

Comparables: Nick Evans, Starling Marte, Kyle Seager

Not only is anyone who offers firm conclusions about Vaughn's career outlook after his rookie season lying to you, but this is perhaps a vector through which to explore how much said person has been lying to you by way of false certainty. Vaughn was middling offensively, which—apologies to the alternate site work of 2020—was both a massive accomplishment given that he leapfrogged the top two levels of the minors, and an underwhelming first glimpse at someone viewed to be the best bat in the 2019 draft. He also did it while learning a new position that probably was a bit too much of an ask. In the long run, it's probably great for Vaughn's value that he showed some nascent ability to man an outfield corner, or an infield corner, and apparently second base. But that's dependent on his bat being better than what it showed. But what was learned about his bat? If you chucked a squirrel into rush hour traffic, and the squirrel struggled, how much would you learn about the squirrel relative to other squirrels? Think about it, man.

Seby Zavala C Born: 08/28/93 Age: 28 Bats: R Throws: R Height: 5'11" Weight: 205 lb. Origin: Round 12, 2015 Draft (#352 overall)

YEAR	TEAM	LVL	AGE	PA	R	2B	3B	HR	RBI	BB	K	SB	CS	Whiff%	AVG/OBP/SLG	DRC+	BABIP	BRR	FRAA	WARP
2019	CHA	AAA	25	331	49	14	0	20	45	26	116	1	1		.222/.296/.471	84	.282	-2.2	C(52): 8.2, 1B(18): -0.1	1.1
2019	CHW	MLB	25	12	1	0	0	0	0	0	9	0	0	62.5%	.083/.083/.083	54	.333	0.0	C(3): 0.1	0.0
2021	CLT	AAA	27	179	19	5	0	8	20	20	75	0	1		.168/.263/.355	70	.240	-0.4	C(35): -2.6, 1B(3): -0.1	-0.2
2021	CHW	MLB	27	104	15	3	0	5	15	6	41	0	0	42.1%	.183/.240/.376	69	.255	0.0	C(33): 0.4	0.1
2022 DC	*CHW*	*MLB*	*28*	*120*	*13*	*4*	*0*	*4*	*17*	*8*	*51*	*0*	*0*	*43.4%*	*.188/.257/.357*	*57*	*.302*	*-0.2*	*C 1*	*-0.1*

Comparables: Curt Casali, Brett Hayes, Carlos Corporán

YEAR	TEAM	P. COUNT	FRM RUNS	BLK RUNS	THRW RUNS	TOT RUNS
2019	CHW	345	0.1	0.0	0.0	0.1
2019	CHA	7394	6.0	-0.1	0.8	6.8
2021	CHW	4374	1.0	-0.3	0.0	0.7
2021	CLT	5633	-2.0	-0.8	0.2	-2.7
2022	*CHW*	*4810*	*0.6*	*0.2*	*0.0*	*0.8*

Sequencing in baseball is fascinatingly important. By all indications, Zavala hit exactly as poorly in an emergency-fueled stint of major-league playing time as could be expected based on his Triple-A numbers, absolutely piled up passed balls and did little to alleviate the White Sox team-wide issues at halting the running game. Despite assuming a very brief hold on the team's starting catching gig while Yasmani Grandal recovered from knee surgery, Zavala ended the year in the minors and spent the playoffs on the taxi squad. He figures to open next season, at best, with similar status. Yet because he smacked three (the first three) of his five homers in a single night, lifted another in the nationally-televised Field of Dreams game, drilled a crucial RBI single in a Sunday Night Baseball win over the NL Central champion Brewers, and shepherded the Sox pitching staff as they cruised to a division title in the second half, the moments are in place for Zavala to look back on 2021 as the season of his life. From a numbers standpoint, it was certainly representative.

PITCHERS

Aaron Bummer LHP Born: 09/21/93 Age: 28 Bats: L Throws: L Height: 6'3" Weight: 215 lb. Origin: Round 19, 2014 Draft (#558 overall)

YEAR	TEAM	LVL	AGE	W	L	SV	G	GS	IP	H	HR	BB/9	K/9	K	GB%	BABIP	WHIP	ERA	DRA-	WARP	MPH	FB%	Whiff%	CSP
2019	CHA	AAA	25	0	0	0	5	0	7^{2}	7	0	2.3	7.0	6	87.0%	.333	1.17	2.35	98	0.1				
2019	CHW	MLB	25	0	0	1	58	0	67^{2}	43	4	3.2	8.0	60	69.7%	.229	0.99	2.13	88	1.1	95.6	76.1%	24.3%	49.5%
2020	CHW	MLB	26	1	0	0	9	0	9^{1}	5	0	4.8	13.5	14	68.4%	.263	1.07	0.96	75	0.2	96.1	85.1%	35.0%	43.8%
2021	CHW	MLB	27	5	5	2	62	0	56^{1}	42	3	4.6	12.0	75	76.9%	.298	1.26	3.51	73	1.3	95.4	62.0%	32.3%	53.6%
2022 DC	*CHW*	*MLB*	*28*	*3*	*2*	*0*	*56*	*0*	*48.3*	*38*	*3*	*4.0*	*11.3*	*60*	*67.9%*	*.299*	*1.23*	*2.86*	*71*	*0.9*	*95.5*	*67.2%*	*30.5%*	*51.9%*

Comparables: Boone Logan, Trevor Rosenthal, Luis Avilán

After a few years of existing as one of those bottom-of-the-page internet banner ads—HITTERS HATE HIM: LEFTY RELIEVER HAS ONE PITCH THAT CANNOT BE HIT IN THE AIR—Bummer decided he wanted more out of life, and performed the simple work of adding a swing-and-miss slider. The end result was a strikeout rate north of 30% with a ground-ball rate above 75%. How bad can a reliever be when he doesn't allow much contact, and keeps said contact on the ground? Much of Bummer's 2021 seemed dedicated toward finding that out, as he battled both far too many walks and suffered the chaos that results from a poor defensive infield handling an endless wave of choppers. But a month of September where Bummer allowed one fly ball—*all month!*—answered the question: not bad at all.

Ryan Burr RHP Born: 05/28/94 Age: 28 Bats: R Throws: R Height: 6'4" Weight: 220 lb. Origin: Round 5, 2015 Draft (#136 overall)

YEAR	TEAM	LVL	AGE	W	L	SV	G	GS	IP	H	HR	BB/9	K/9	K	GB%	BABIP	WHIP	ERA	DRA-	WARP	MPH	FB%	Whiff%	CSP
2019	CHW	MLB	25	1	1	0	16	1	19^{2}	17	3	3.7	9.2	20	44.8%	.259	1.27	4.58	100	0.2	95.3	58.1%	22.8%	53.1%
2021	CLT	AAA	27	1	2	3	15	0	15^{2}	17	3	4.0	8.0	14	44.2%	.286	1.53	4.60	101	0.2				
2021	CHW	MLB	27	2	1	0	34	1	36^{2}	28	3	5.2	8.1	33	56.2%	.275	1.34	2.45	101	0.3	94.7	50.3%	23.8%	57.6%
2022 DC	*CHW*	*MLB*	*28*	*2*	*2*	*0*	*56*	*0*	*48.3*	*47*	*5*	*4.8*	*8.4*	*45*	*48.9%*	*.303*	*1.51*	*4.81*	*109*	*0.0*	*94.8*	*51.6%*	*23.7%*	*56.8%*

Comparables: Ryan Dull, Luis García, Javy Guerra

In many ways, 2021 was a significant triumph for Burr, who returned to the majors after undergoing Tommy John surgery in 2019 and spending the 2020 season stuck at the team's alternate site. An excellent month of September made him one of the absolute last cuts from the White Sox playoff roster, and the presence of speedster Billy Hamilton on the roster meant he got to hear his standard supply of Hamilton & Burr jokes. Like Alexander after his encounter with Aaron, we can only speculate what Ryan is going to be. He searches for ideal backspin on the mid-90s four-seamer that made him a dominant college closer. But his surface-level success isn't tied to being overpowering, but rather avoiding damage through the air with a cutter that no one seemed quite able to drive for extra bases in 2021. He neither sees nor models himself a ground-ball maven, but it's his carrying trait until his idealized strengths become actual ones. And there's something to be said for managing to hang around when not much is working as it should.

Dylan Cease RHP Born: 12/28/95 Age: 26 Bats: R Throws: R Height: 6'2" Weight: 195 lb. Origin: Round 6, 2014 Draft (#169 overall)

YEAR	TEAM	LVL	AGE	W	L	SV	G	GS	IP	H	HR	BB/9	K/9	K	GB%	BABIP	WHIP	ERA	DRA-	WARP	MPH	FB%	Whiff%	CSP
2019	CHA	AAA	23	5	2	0	15	15	68^{1}	75	4	4.2	9.6	73	53.1%	.374	1.57	4.48	94	1.1				
2019	CHW	MLB	23	4	7	0	14	14	73	78	15	4.3	10.0	81	45.7%	.326	1.55	5.79	102	0.7	96.6	51.5%	26.1%	43.9%
2020	CHW	MLB	24	5	4	0	12	12	58^{1}	50	12	5.2	6.8	44	39.8%	.239	1.44	4.01	151	-1.0	97.7	47.8%	25.3%	42.4%
2021	CHW	MLB	25	13	7	0	32	32	165^{2}	139	20	3.7	12.3	226	33.6%	.310	1.25	3.91	77	3.5	96.8	46.8%	34.6%	53.1%
2022 DC	*CHW*	*MLB*	*26*	*9*	*7*	*0*	*27*	*27*	*140.3*	*112*	*20*	*3.9*	*10.8*	*168*	*38.1%*	*.278*	*1.24*	*3.69*	*87*	*2.1*	*97.0*	*47.5%*	*32.1%*	*50.2%*

Comparables: Matt Garza, Johnny Cueto, Aníbal Sánchez

Paired with a new pitching coach, Cease spent the 2020-21 offseason smoothing out the leg drive in his delivery. The end result was a radical overhaul of his spin profile, allowing him to supplement his diving slider and curve with a ridiculously high-velocity, high-spin four-seamer. The change unlocked Cease's dormant potential for a ludicrous strikeout rate. His control also upgraded from "Oh no!" to "Eh," as the White Sox had long hoped. Which is all great, but more noticeably Cease got extremely into disc golf.

While the sport dates back to the early 20th century, the popular current version was developed in the 1970s by a man with the temerity to call himself "Steady" Ed Headrick. More than three-quarters of the world's 9,000 disc golf courses are in the United States, but the most exclusive one could be found at Guaranteed Rate Field, where one could find Cease hucking frisbees at a chain net basket setup that he brought to the stadium himself. Headrick named this chain-link basket setup—and this name is quite clearly *the reason* for this digression—the "Disc Pole Hole." Now all we need is a second pitcher willing to become a two-sport athlete, so we can see if everyone can halve his DRA– that way.

Garrett Crochet LHP Born: 06/21/99 Age: 23 Bats: L Throws: L Height: 6'6" Weight: 230 lb. Origin: Round 1, 2020 Draft (#11 overall)

YEAR	TEAM	LVL	AGE	W	L	SV	G	GS	IP	H	HR	BB/9	K/9	K	GB%	BABIP	WHIP	ERA	DRA-	WARP	MPH	FB%	Whiff%	CSP
2020	CHW	MLB	21	0	0	0	5	0	6	3	0	0.0	12.0	8	61.5%	.231	0.50	0.00	85	0.1	100.1	84.7%	40.5%	49.4%
2021	CHW	MLB	22	3	5	0	54	0	54^{1}	42	2	4.5	10.8	65	37.5%	.303	1.27	2.82	86	0.9	96.8	64.5%	28.7%	55.8%
2022 DC	*CHW*	*MLB*	*23*	*2*	*2*	*0*	*56*	*0*	*48.3*	*40*	*7*	*4.3*	*10.4*	*56*	*40.2%*	*.284*	*1.32*	*4.06*	*95*	*0.3*	*97.0*	*65.7%*	*29.4%*	*55.4%*

Comparables: Felipe Vázquez, Drew Storen, Bobby Bolin

In his first full professional season after being drafted 11th overall in 2020, Crochet was an above-average major-league reliever who sat in the high-90s, flashed a plus slider and cemented the theory that he could throw strikes without getting them hit hard. This seems like a tremendous level of progress for someone so early in his professional career. But you're probably experienced enough with misdirection ledes to know that's not going to wind up being the tone of this comment. Crochet's high-90s velocity actually backed down three ticks from his hellacious 2020 debut. The slight control outages that surfaced in his draft year were more frequent when he couldn't paper over bad counts with 101 mph down the pipe. And though the White Sox still tout that Crochet's future is in the rotation, until a third pitch and effective extended outings become a regular feature, he still looks like a very good reliever.

Matt Foster RHP Born: 01/27/95 Age: 27 Bats: R Throws: R Height: 6'0" Weight: 215 lb. Origin: Round 20, 2016 Draft (#596 overall)

YEAR	TEAM	LVL	AGE	W	L	SV	G	GS	IP	H	HR	BB/9	K/9	K	GB%	BABIP	WHIP	ERA	DRA-	WARP	MPH	FB%	Whiff%	CSP
2019	BIR	AA	24	0	0	1	6	0	9^{2}	3	0	1.9	11.2	12	31.6%	.158	0.52	0.00	82	0.2				
2019	CHA	AAA	24	4	1	4	37	0	55	46	9	3.1	10.1	62	35.9%	.280	1.18	3.76	82	1.2				
2020	CHW	MLB	25	6	1	0	23	2	28^{2}	16	2	2.8	9.7	31	34.8%	.212	0.87	2.20	101	0.3	94.0	57.3%	30.3%	49.1%
2021	CLT	AAA	26	0	2	0	14	0	14^{2}	14	2	1.2	14.1	23	25.7%	.364	1.09	4.30	76	0.4				
2021	CHW	MLB	26	2	1	1	37	0	39	43	9	3.0	9.2	40	28.6%	.309	1.44	6.00	111	0.1	93.6	67.1%	23.8%	56.8%
2022 DC	*CHW*	*MLB*	*27*	*2*	*2*	*0*	*44*	*0*	*38.7*	*37*	*6*	*3.1*	*9.4*	*40*	*33.2%*	*.297*	*1.30*	*4.36*	*103*	*0.1*	*93.7*	*64.3%*	*25.7%*	*54.6%*

Comparables: James Norwood, Cory Burns, Nick Christiani

Collectively, Western society was ready to accept the idea that a borderline organizational arm emerging as a reliable multi-inning, medium-to-high leverage option in the COVID-shortened season wasn't guaranteed a happily ever after. But because he's consistently dominated in Triple-A, Foster's 2021 regression seemed extreme. His fastball was never overwhelming, prompting a spring emphasis on developing his slider. But with the novelty of a right-hander with a well-tunneled changeup somewhat (or entirely, given the numbers against it) worn off, it was consistently smashed to the point of being a consistent threat to Foster's rosterability. Humanity itself knows not to write off a reliever who posts strong strikeout rates after one bad season, but the league has made the expected adjustment to Foster's attack. What's not known or particularly expected at this point is his capability to evolve in response.

Jace Fry LHP Born: 07/09/93 Age: 28 Bats: L Throws: L Height: 6'1" Weight: 220 lb. Origin: Round 3, 2014 Draft (#77 overall)

YEAR	TEAM	LVL	AGE	W	L	SV	G	GS	IP	H	HR	BB/9	K/9	K	GB%	BABIP	WHIP	ERA	DRA-	WARP	MPH	FB%	Whiff%	CSP
2019	CHW	MLB	25	3	4	0	68	0	55	44	7	7.0	11.1	68	56.9%	.289	1.58	4.75	88	0.9	92.5	25.1%	36.6%	40.8%
2020	CHW	MLB	26	0	1	0	18	0	19^{2}	16	3	5.5	11.0	24	48.9%	.295	1.42	3.66	91	0.3	90.0	38.9%	34.3%	39.7%
2021	CLT	AAA	27	1	4	2	34	1	40	22	3	4.5	13.5	60	58.5%	.241	1.05	2.93	68	1.2				
2021	CHW	MLB	27	0	1	0	6	0	6^{2}	10	1	8.1	4.1	3	71.4%	.450	2.40	10.80	132	-0.1	91.1	52.2%	18.2%	50.0%
2022 non-DC	*CHW*	*MLB*	*28*	*2*	*2*	*0*	*57*	*0*	*50*	*40*	*5*	*5.2*	*11.2*	*62*	*53.5%*	*.295*	*1.40*	*4.04*	*92*	*0.4*	*91.4*	*34.7%*	*32.3%*	*42.2%*

Comparables: Kevin Jepsen, Mike Koplove, Ryan Cook

Asked about his offseason back surgery, Fry speculated that not feeling debilitating nerve pain shooting through every inch of his body as he began his delivery might make it a touch more repeatable. The logic seems straightforward enough, but his control remained wayward. Fry was awesome in 2018, and the strengths of that campaign were still evident even as the walks mounted in the intervening years, relegating him to increasingly situational duty. Post-surgery, he's yet to establish that the strengths are still buried underneath all the rubble. While his bat-missing track record from the left side will keep giving Fry jobs, they will be of a less and less secure and comfortable variety until he can reverse the trends and start inflicting pain on opposing hitters.

Lucas Giolito RHP Born: 07/14/94 Age: 27 Bats: R Throws: R Height: 6'6" Weight: 245 lb. Origin: Round 1, 2012 Draft (#16 overall)

YEAR	TEAM	LVL	AGE	W	L	SV	G	GS	IP	H	HR	BB/9	K/9	K	GB%	BABIP	WHIP	ERA	DRA-	WARP	MPH	FB%	Whiff%	CSP
2019	CHW	MLB	24	14	9	0	29	29	176^{2}	131	24	2.9	11.6	228	35.6%	.274	1.06	3.41	74	4.3	94.4	55.0%	32.5%	51.7%
2020	CHW	MLB	25	4	3	0	12	12	72^{1}	47	8	3.5	12.1	97	43.5%	.255	1.04	3.48	73	1.9	94.2	50.6%	36.6%	46.6%
2021	CHW	MLB	26	11	9	0	31	31	178^{2}	145	27	2.6	10.1	201	33.3%	.270	1.10	3.53	89	2.7	94.0	43.9%	32.2%	58.9%
2022 DC	*CHW*	*MLB*	*27*	*12*	*9*	*0*	*30*	*30*	*181.3*	*161*	*29*	*3.1*	*10.8*	*217*	*36.4%*	*.299*	*1.23*	*3.93*	*93*	*2.2*	*94.1*	*47.2%*	*33.0%*	*55.3%*

Comparables: Alex Fernandez, Jack McDowell, Jon Lester

There was nothing wrong at all with Giolito's 2021 season. He made long-sought control gains while greatly enhancing his usage of his slider. While most of the league was doing some version of the opposite, he set a career high in innings pitched. And that came despite a late-season freak hamstring injury that robbed him of a couple of September starts, and curbed the progress of a second where he got stronger rather than wearing down. It's just that on a broad level, Giolito was worse in every way than his first two strong seasons. There's more context to throw in, like his numbers being spiked by blowup starts under outlier circumstances, or his changeup grip drifting off for the entire first half. But he managed to keep the damage within the range of the normal variances in performance of a solidly above-average starter who annually gets Cy Young votes. The tools are at least in place to make 2021 look like an outlier, even if he hasn't done it yet.

Kendall Graveman RHP

Born: 12/21/90 Age: 31 Bats: R Throws: R Height: 6'2" Weight: 200 lb. Origin: Round 8, 2013 Draft (#235 overall)

YEAR	TEAM	LVL	AGE	W	L	SV	G	GS	IP	H	HR	BB/9	K/9	K	GB%	BABIP	WHIP	ERA	DRA-	WARP	MPH	FB%	Whiff%	CSP
2020	SEA	MLB	29	1	3	0	11	2	18^2	15	2	3.9	7.2	15	48.1%	.250	1.23	5.79	100	0.2	95.0	68.1%	18.6%	47.7%
2021	HOU	MLB	30	1	1	0	23	0	23	20	1	4.7	10.6	27	56.1%	.339	1.39	3.13	94	0.3	96.7	74.4%	28.0%	48.4%
2021	SEA	MLB	30	4	0	10	30	0	33	15	2	2.2	9.3	34	53.9%	.176	0.70	0.82	86	0.5	96.6	69.1%	24.0%	49.5%
2022 DC	*CHW*	*MLB*	*31*	*2*	*2*	*1*	*56*	*0*	*48.3*	*44*	*6*	*3.4*	*8.5*	*46*	*50.7%*	*.286*	*1.29*	*4.00*	*96*	*0.3*	*96.3*	*70.7%*	*24.3%*	*48.8%*

Comparables: Brandon Morrow, Scott Downs, Ray Burris

The Mariners made waves—the bad sort, the only kind of which Seattle's been capable for years—by trading Graveman ahead of the trade deadline, despite a position of contention and the itinerant reliever holding a 0.82 ERA. In his stint as an Astro that mark more than quadrupled, but his season-long ERA was nevertheless more than two runs superior to any of his previous seasons. Between that and his strong postseason showing—a 1.64 ERA across 11 innings, ultimately gaining enough trust to finish three World Series contests for Houston—the eight-year veteran demonstrated enough growth to earn a three-year pact on Chicago's south side. The chances of another sub-2.00 ERA in that span, though, are about commensurate with that of old GM Jerry Dipoto to stand pat when this year's trade deadline arrives.

Liam Hendriks RHP

Born: 02/10/89 Age: 33 Bats: R Throws: R Height: 6'0" Weight: 235 lb. Origin: International Free Agent, 2007

YEAR	TEAM	LVL	AGE	W	L	SV	G	GS	IP	H	HR	BB/9	K/9	K	GB%	BABIP	WHIP	ERA	DRA-	WARP	MPH	FB%	Whiff%	CSP
2019	OAK	MLB	30	4	4	25	75	2	85	61	5	2.2	13.1	124	30.3%	.315	0.96	1.80	70	2.2	96.8	70.6%	36.1%	49.4%
2020	OAK	MLB	31	3	1	14	24	0	25^1	14	1	1.1	13.1	37	28.8%	.260	0.67	1.78	71	0.7	96.2	70.5%	36.2%	49.3%
2021	CHW	MLB	32	8	3	38	69	0	71	45	11	0.9	14.3	113	32.4%	.254	0.73	2.54	59	2.2	97.9	69.0%	38.1%	55.3%
2022 DC	*CHW*	*MLB*	*33*	*3*	*2*	*33*	*61*	*0*	*53.3*	*40*	*8*	*1.8*	*13.2*	*78*	*33.6%*	*.290*	*0.95*	*2.44*	*62*	*1.3*	*97.4*	*69.6%*	*37.3%*	*53.0%*

Comparables: Zack Britton, Bob Wickman, Mike Maddux

Congratulations to the White Sox, who spent top dollar on a "proven closer" in his 30s. And in turn, Hendriks threw harder in 2021, posted nuttier strikeout and walk numbers and recorded more actual saves than any previous point in his career. DRA actually liked him too, and it doesn't like anyone. At last, a heavy investment in the bullpen—long the game's most volatile position—has paid off and been proven wise. All it took was a reliever who engineered a borderline bizarre mid-career turnaround.

Except, Hendriks was plagued by his worst home run rate since his starter days, and placed only 30th among relievers (min. 40 IP) in terms of Win Percentage Added. Maybe it was over-emphasized by some mid-season pitch-tipping, or some since resolved early season breaking ball command woes. Or, perhaps, the steady creep of an offensive environment that is geared toward reacting to the influx of riding four-seam fastball is producing increased instances of previously untouchable pitches getting barreled, as swings become geared toward a steady diet at the letters. And as such, maybe it will reveal the faultiness of making long-term commitments toward relievers who—as most do—thrive by hyper-specialization within a single modality of a swiftly-evolving game.

But, you know, who is to say?

Jared Kelley RHP

Born: 10/03/01 Age: 20 Bats: R Throws: R Height: 6'3" Weight: 230 lb. Origin: Round 2, 2020 Draft (#47 overall)

YEAR	TEAM	LVL	AGE	W	L	SV	G	GS	IP	H	HR	BB/9	K/9	K	GB%	BABIP	WHIP	ERA	DRA-	WARP	MPH	FB%	Whiff%	CSP
2021	KAN	A	19	0	5	0	10	10	21	21	1	9.4	10.7	25	49.2%	.328	2.05	6.86	108	0.1				
2022 non-DC	*CHW*	*MLB*	*20*	*2*	*3*	*0*	*57*	*0*	*50*	*54*	*8*	*8.2*	*8.2*	*45*	*41.4%*	*.318*	*2.01*	*7.46*	*150*	*-1.1*				

Comparables: J.B. Wendelken, Edgar García, Oscar Villarreal

High-90s velocity, the preternatural feel for a plus changeup, and steady progress toward developing a usable slider—it's Kelley's draft report, and also what there is to tout after a professional debut that consisted of fewer than 25 innings in between minor, non-season-ending arm issues. After short-season affiliates were wiped out, Low-A baseball in general was kind of a mess in 2021, and Kelley's control and his infield defensive support were no exceptions. Working in short, carefully handled stints against more experienced competition, Kelley's struggle could quite possibly be meaningless. But after landing a $3 million bonus to be lured away from college in 2020, matching the scouting expectations his raw stuff built will require something resembling dominance sooner than later. There are only so many mulligan years, and if nothing else, we need more material to flesh out his one-sentence summary.

Dallas Keuchel LHP Born: 01/01/88 Age: 34 Bats: L Throws: L Height: 6'2" Weight: 205 lb. Origin: Round 7, 2009 Draft (#221 overall)

YEAR	TEAM	LVL	AGE	W	L	SV	G	GS	IP	H	HR	BB/9	K/9	K	GB%	BABIP	WHIP	ERA	DRA-	WARP	MPH	FB%	Whiff%	CSP
2019	ROM	A	31	0	0	0	1	1	7	1	0	1.3	11.6	9	76.9%	.077	0.29	0.00	84	0.1				
2019	MIS	AA	31	0	0	0	1	1	7	11	0	1.3	5.1	4	42.3%	.440	1.71	3.86	119	0.0				
2019	ATL	MLB	31	8	8	0	19	19	112^{2}	115	16	3.1	7.3	91	58.3%	.303	1.37	3.75	110	0.6	88.0	74.0%	21.2%	41.9%
2020	CHW	MLB	32	6	2	0	11	11	63^{1}	52	2	2.4	6.0	42	52.0%	.258	1.09	1.99	100	0.7	86.4	65.3%	23.8%	44.0%
2021	CHW	MLB	33	9	9	0	32	30	162	189	25	3.3	5.3	95	54.7%	.308	1.53	5.28	147	-2.5	87.1	64.3%	21.0%	48.8%
2022 DC	*CHW*	*MLB*	*34*	*10*	*10*	*0*	*29*	*29*	*163*	*182*	*20*	*3.1*	*6.1*	*110*	*53.9%*	*.309*	*1.46*	*4.89*	*115*	*0.1*	*87.1*	*66.0%*	*21.5%*	*46.9%*

Comparables: Bud Black, Brad Penny, Mike Flanagan

If there's a solace to watching Keuchel rack up ugly peripheral stats for much of the latter half of his career, it's been admiring the ease of his command, the seemingly curated contact to enable the surely unsustainable low ERAs. If that's the case, what is there to say about him getting absolutely torched like never before and looking woefully out of sync for the entire second half of 2021?

1. Oh no!
2. Yikes!
3. To be fair, he's *still* pitching a lot better than his peripheral stats.
4. If the end result has always been the only thing that mattered in analyzing Keuchel's unique approach, he could—and will—argue that this is a blip amid an admirably consistent career.

5) You never *want* someone to be injured, but it would be nice if there had been some reason for Keuchel's 2021 beyond a pitcher in his mid-30s finally having the collapse in performance that metrics have foretold for years.
6) Alas.

Craig Kimbrel RHP Born: 05/28/88 Age: 34 Bats: R Throws: R Height: 6'0" Weight: 215 lb. Origin: Round 3, 2008 Draft (#96 overall)

YEAR	TEAM	LVL	AGE	W	L	SV	G	GS	IP	H	HR	BB/9	K/9	K	GB%	BABIP	WHIP	ERA	DRA-	WARP	MPH	FB%	Whiff%	CSP
2019	CHC	MLB	31	0	4	13	23	0	20^{2}	21	9	5.2	13.1	30	28.8%	.279	1.60	6.53	92	0.3	96.3	66.6%	32.8%	40.9%
2020	CHC	MLB	32	0	1	2	18	0	15^{1}	10	2	7.0	16.4	28	33.3%	.320	1.43	5.28	77	0.4	97.1	62.3%	35.4%	42.8%
2021	CHC	MLB	33	2	3	23	39	0	36^{2}	13	1	3.2	15.7	64	33.3%	.203	0.71	0.49	68	0.9	97.1	59.3%	44.7%	49.1%
2021	CHW	MLB	33	2	2	1	24	0	23	18	5	3.9	14.1	36	26.5%	.295	1.22	5.09	87	0.4	96.0	59.3%	40.9%	50.0%
2022 DC	*CHW*	*MLB*	*34*	*2*	*2*	*3*	*56*	*0*	*48.3*	*31*	*8*	*4.2*	*14.4*	*77*	*31.7%*	*.264*	*1.12*	*3.22*	*75*	*0.8*	*96.8*	*60.5%*	*41.0%*	*47.6%*

Comparables: Kenley Jansen, John Wetteland, Gregg Olson

How much baseball did you watch this past season? A lot? An extensive accounting of the full year with an especially tight focus on the second half? Watched every inning of the playoffs? ... No? None of that? Casual? Very casual? Focused more on the NFL once it got started? Ah, OK then. So yeah, Kimbrel's great then. It was a return to form season. He's back into Hall of Fame form. Just look at those numbers, look at those sweet rate stats. He's a closer—yes that is...uh...mostly how he was used—so all that really matters is that he kept runs off the board, and over the course of the season viewed as a totality and not broken into segments, he did that. It's great.

Why are you asking all these follow-up questions? We already had all those introductory questions, and now you're asking more, and it's just a lot. The underlying metrics think Kimbrel is fine, no questions asked, especially ones that might get generated by watching him pitch in the second half. Which thankfully you did not do, right?

Michael Kopech RHP Born: 04/30/96 Age: 26 Bats: R Throws: R Height: 6'3" Weight: 210 lb. Origin: Round 1, 2014 Draft (#33 overall)

YEAR	TEAM	LVL	AGE	W	L	SV	G	GS	IP	H	HR	BB/9	K/9	K	GB%	BABIP	WHIP	ERA	DRA-	WARP	MPH	FB%	Whiff%	CSP
2021	CHW	MLB	25	4	3	0	44	4	69^{1}	54	9	3.1	13.4	103	37.6%	.304	1.13	3.50	65	1.9	97.4	64.3%	32.8%	56.5%
2022 DC	*CHW*	*MLB*	*26*	*7*	*5*	*0*	*30*	*19*	*103*	*76*	*14*	*3.4*	*11.0*	*125*	*38.2%*	*.263*	*1.12*	*3.15*	*77*	*1.8*	*97.4*	*64.3%*	*32.8%*	*56.5%*

Comparables: Tyler Glasnow, Juan Rincon, Robbie Ray

In a long-awaited return to action after two years off, the uber-talented Kopech looked pretty talented; uber-talented even. Kept mostly in the bullpen to manage his innings save for some short spot starts, Kopech's stuff mostly looked as ridiculous as the rosiest memories of 2018, and noticeably ticked up in the second half of the season after he returned from a fluky hamstring strain. His peripheral stats indicate he was unimpeachably awesome, and the White Sox stretched him toward three-inning outings toward the end—mostly for playoff purposes, but it will only prime him for a return to the rotation. However, there were strange blips in the dominance, too, be they command wonkiness, ill-effects of narrowing his arsenal to fastball-slider down the stretch, simple bad reliever luck or the narrowing margin for error for those who would seek to live off spinny, powerful four-seam fastballs two-thirds of the time. It should all work for Kopech. The ingredients are there, as are the health and know-how. But if it doesn't, there were some hints in early autumn.

Jimmy Lambert RHP Born: 11/18/94 Age: 27 Bats: R Throws: R Height: 6'2" Weight: 190 lb. Origin: Round 5, 2016 Draft (#146 overall)

YEAR	TEAM	LVL	AGE	W	L	SV	G	GS	IP	H	HR	BB/9	K/9	K	GB%	BABIP	WHIP	ERA	DRA-	WARP	MPH	FB%	Whiff%	CSP
2019	BIR	AA	24	3	4	0	11	11	59^{1}	62	11	4.1	10.6	70	37.0%	.338	1.50	4.55	99	0.4				
2020	CHW	MLB	25	0	0	0	2	0	2	2	0	0.0	9.0	2	33.3%	.333	1.00	0.00	101	0.0	92.9	48.5%	28.6%	50.2%
2021	CLT	AAA	26	3	3	0	19	19	64^{1}	49	11	4.5	11.5	82	43.1%	.270	1.26	4.76	79	1.6				
2021	CHW	MLB	26	1	1	0	4	3	13	16	3	4.2	6.9	10	21.4%	.333	1.69	6.23	148	-0.2	93.7	52.4%	16.1%	57.6%
2022 DC	*CHW*	*MLB*	*27*	*2*	*2*	*0*	*8*	*8*	*36.3*	*34*	*6*	*4.2*	*8.8*	*35*	*37.8%*	*.287*	*1.42*	*4.93*	*114*	*0.0*	*93.6*	*52.1%*	*17.1%*	*57.0%*

Comparables: Pedro Payano, Williams Pérez, Paul Clemens

Between Tommy John surgery, a forearm strain and the COVID-19 pandemic, there's been considerable distance between the present and the years when Lambert promised to be a bat-missing prospect with a four-pitch mix. It's unfortunate, because Lambert created fond memories of surprising strikeout rates, even after the pitches themselves have vanished. Neither his low-to-mid-90s fastball nor overhand curve make your jaw drop; maybe his best changeups can linger in the brain, until some piece of Wilbur Wood trivia dislodges them. There were glimpses of that ability beneath the superficial struggles in limited innings at the bandbox of Triple-A Charlotte, but until it shows up in his scattershot major-league opportunities, and his post-TJ walk spike subsides, it will be unclear which role best fits his talent.

Reynaldo López RHP Born: 01/04/94 Age: 28 Bats: R Throws: R Height: 6'1" Weight: 225 lb. Origin: International Free Agent, 2012

YEAR	TEAM	LVL	AGE	W	L	SV	G	GS	IP	H	HR	BB/9	K/9	K	GB%	BABIP	WHIP	ERA	DRA-	WARP	MPH	FB%	Whiff%	CSP
2019	CHW	MLB	25	10	15	0	33	33	184	203	35	3.2	8.3	169	34.6%	.317	1.46	5.38	118	0.1	95.7	58.5%	24.7%	52.4%
2020	CHW	MLB	26	1	3	0	8	8	26^{1}	28	9	5.1	8.2	24	33.3%	.268	1.63	6.49	133	-0.2	94.5	51.4%	22.2%	48.1%
2021	CLT	AAA	27	1	6	0	10	10	39	53	6	4.8	11.5	50	38.8%	.431	1.90	7.62	110	0.3				
2021	CHW	MLB	27	4	4	0	20	9	57^{2}	42	10	2.0	8.6	55	39.0%	.222	0.95	3.43	93	0.7	95.9	58.0%	24.7%	55.5%
2022 DC	*CHW*	*MLB*	*28*	*7*	*5*	*0*	*58*	*8*	*82.3*	*81*	*13*	*3.3*	*8.1*	*74*	*36.8%*	*.291*	*1.35*	*4.58*	*107*	*0.3*	*95.6*	*57.3%*	*24.3%*	*53.0%*

Comparables: Jason Jennings, Ricky Bones, José Quintana

Coming into 2021, López had not produced a good season since 2018. And some of the metrics employed in this very book would strongly suggest that López's 2018 season was not *actually* good, a position validated by his poor 2019 and 2020 campaigns. Halfway into 2021, López was in Triple-A (the White Sox had lost patience with all the bad seasons) and was getting the sort of results that one might call "bad." Then a shortened arm-swing restored López's upper-90s velocity and tightened his slider enough to make him a sort of garden-variety two-pitch swingman for half of a season. That might not be the type of performance that conjures up thoughts of the term "revelation." But in consideration of where the performance level had been for the former top-50 prospect, it's not bad, which is a cousin of actually good.

Lance Lynn RHP Born: 05/12/87 Age: 35 Bats: S Throws: R Height: 6'5" Weight: 270 lb. Origin: Round 1, 2008 Draft (#39 overall)

YEAR	TEAM	LVL	AGE	W	L	SV	G	GS	IP	H	HR	BB/9	K/9	K	GB%	BABIP	WHIP	ERA	DRA-	WARP	MPH	FB%	Whiff%	CSP
2019	TEX	MLB	32	16	11	0	33	33	208^{1}	195	21	2.5	10.6	246	39.9%	.322	1.22	3.67	80	4.3	94.4	71.4%	28.6%	48.3%
2020	TEX	MLB	33	6	3	0	13	13	84	64	13	2.7	9.5	89	36.2%	.243	1.06	3.32	92	1.3	93.8	67.5%	25.4%	48.6%
2021	CHW	MLB	34	11	6	0	28	28	157	123	18	2.6	10.1	176	38.8%	.265	1.07	2.69	82	2.9	93.6	62.4%	26.7%	51.9%
2022 DC	*CHW*	*MLB*	*35*	*12*	*9*	*0*	*30*	*30*	*184.7*	*162*	*27*	*2.8*	*8.7*	*178*	*38.9%*	*.275*	*1.19*	*3.59*	*88*	*2.6*	*93.8*	*65.6%*	*26.9%*	*50.3%*

Comparables: Dave Stewart, John Lackey, Orel Hershiser

Lynn imagines himself as a man for all seasons. Not in the sense that his ample beard and bulk keep him warm in the winter, or his insistence upon long sleeves and hoodies makes sweltering heat familiar. But in that he feels he offers a moldable, multi-faceted attack that is adjustable to whatever mode of attack MLB pitchers are fetishizing at the moment. He doesn't rack up a ton of grounders anymore, but commands a sinker well enough to grab them situationally. His swinging strike rates are more good than elite, but he has his nights where he can blow his four-seamer over the tops of barrels. He prioritizes length and durability, which mostly showed up in managing small injuries away from becoming large ones in 2021 as shoulder and knee issues flared up. But it all works, as evidenced by it all working for a career year last season, on the heels of two seasons that looked like career years before it. After all these career seasons in his early-30s, maybe Lynn isn't imagining anything.

José Ruiz RHP Born: 10/21/94 Age: 27 Bats: R Throws: R Height: 6'1" Weight: 245 lb. Origin: International Free Agent, 2011

YEAR	TEAM	LVL	AGE	W	L	SV	G	GS	IP	H	HR	BB/9	K/9	K	GB%	BABIP	WHIP	ERA	DRA-	WARP	MPH	FB%	Whiff%	CSP
2019	CHA	AAA	24	0	0	7	11	0	14^{1}	9	0	4.4	9.4	15	34.3%	.257	1.12	1.26	87	0.3				
2019	CHW	MLB	24	1	4	0	40	1	40	56	6	5.4	7.9	35	35.3%	.391	2.00	5.63	128	-0.2	96.5	61.5%	24.2%	47.8%
2020	CHW	MLB	25	0	0	0	5	0	4	2	1	0.0	11.3	5	33.3%	.125	0.50	2.25	103	0.0	96.8	58.3%	20.7%	50.6%
2021	CHW	MLB	26	1	3	0	59	0	65	51	8	3.5	8.7	63	41.5%	.247	1.17	3.05	103	0.5	97.2	59.5%	24.0%	57.4%
2022 DC	*CHW*	*MLB*	*27*	*2*	*2*	*0*	*56*	*0*	*48.3*	*45*	*7*	*3.9*	*8.1*	*43*	*39.1%*	*.286*	*1.37*	*4.46*	*105*	*0.0*	*97.0*	*59.8%*	*23.9%*	*55.4%*

Comparables: Alex Burnett, Ryan Perry, Luke Jackson

When Ruiz is trotting in from the bullpen, you know it's game over, bay-beeee. Because, you see, he pitched an incredible amount of low-leverage innings as the White Sox found a way to make regular use of an up-and-down reliever who, as a result of being out of options, no longer had the ability to go up and down. He was great at it! Ruiz throws upper-90s with a snapping mid-80s curve that is especially good if the opposing hitter is batting in the ninth inning, their team is leading or trailing by six runs and they are feeling especially meh about committing to their approach. In high leverage—hell, in *medium* leverage—all the command problems of a still somewhat recently converted converted catcher tend to get exposed. That could be fine. There are a lot of low-leverage innings thrown every year in the majors, someone needs to take care of them, and Ruiz seems to be actually good at it. Plus, if he went from pitching professionally for the first time in 2016, to making the majors, to actually sticking in a low leverage role in 2021, perhaps he has some sort of capacity to improve.

Jonathan Stiever RHP

Born: 05/12/97 Age: 25 Bats: R Throws: R Height: 6'2" Weight: 210 lb. Origin: Round 5, 2018 Draft (#138 overall)

YEAR	TEAM	LVL	AGE	W	L	SV	G	GS	IP	H	HR	BB/9	K/9	K	GB%	BABIP	WHIP	ERA	DRA-	WARP	MPH	FB%	Whiff%	CSP
2019	KAN	A	22	4	6	0	14	14	74	88	10	1.7	9.4	77	43.8%	.363	1.38	4.74	99	0.6				
2019	WS	A+	22	6	4	0	12	12	71	56	7	1.6	9.8	77	40.4%	.278	0.97	2.15	73	1.6				
2020	CHW	MLB	23	0	1	0	2	2	6^1	7	4	5.7	4.3	3	40.9%	.167	1.74	9.95	142	-0.1	92.4	53.3%	14.5%	50.9%
2021	CLT	AAA	24	5	5	0	17	17	74	80	13	3.4	10.7	88	32.9%	.330	1.46	5.84	96	1.2				
2021	CHW	MLB	24	0	0	0	1	0	0	4	0			0	0.0%	1.000					93.6	60.0%	20.0%	58.5%
2022 DC	*CHW*	*MLB*	*25*	*2*	*2*	*0*	*8*	*8*	*36.3*	*37*	*6*	*3.3*	*8.2*	*33*	*35.4%*	*.298*	*1.39*	*5.01*	*116*	*0.0*	*92.6*	*54.2%*	*15.3%*	*51.9%*

Comparables: Dylan Covey, Cy Sneed, Alfredo Figaro

It was sort of a mixed bag for Stiever in 2021, if you're willing to liberalize your definition of a mixed bag. The season was mostly a demonstration of health, as his mid-90s velocity returned in spring and stuck around, but it ended with surgery to repair his lat. A pair of major-league spot starts in 2020 when his last dedicated action came in the Carolina League were definitely too soon, but he probably would have faced more than four batters in the majors in 2021 had he gotten any of them out. With his stuff ticking back up, the swing and miss from Stiever's 2019 breakout largely returned. But an already flyball-oriented pitcher turned more so in an environment where he could ill afford it. In short, a pitching prospect who was supposed to be near-ready ended the year under the knife with a Triple-A ERA just under 6.00, but things weren't *that* bad.

Matthew Thompson RHP

Born: 08/11/00 Age: 21 Bats: R Throws: R Height: 6'3" Weight: 195 lb. Origin: Round 2, 2019 Draft (#45 overall)

YEAR	TEAM	LVL	AGE	W	L	SV	G	GS	IP	H	HR	BB/9	K/9	K	GB%	BABIP	WHIP	ERA	DRA-	WARP	MPH	FB%	Whiff%	CSP
2019	WSX	ROK	18	0	0	0	2	2	2	2	0	0.0	9.0	2	33.3%	.333	1.00	0.00						
2021	KAN	A	20	2	8	0	19	19	71^2	83	7	4.8	9.7	77	42.9%	.384	1.69	5.90	96	0.8				
2022 non-DC	*CHW*	*MLB*	*21*	*2*	*3*	*0*	*57*	*0*	*50*	*57*	*8*	*5.9*	*7.3*	*40*	*37.9%*	*.316*	*1.80*	*6.78*	*142*	*-0.9*				

Comparables: Anthony Swarzak, Nick Bierbrodt, Matt Manning

What were you like at age 20? Showing spurts of promise? Occasionally providing a glimpse of what type of functional adult you would one day be? Sure, perhaps. For the sake of narrative license, let's say yes. But in aggregate, you stunk! Seemingly basic functions eluded you, skills vital to success, but not necessarily reflective of your individual talents, like not shrinking your clothes in the dryer, or performing basic grooming without injuring yourself. As a result, the end product (acceptable adult) might have been obscured by the present grade (poorly-dressed proto-adult who smells bad). Which is all to say that Thompson has an athletic delivery with the raw ingredients for plus stuff and a promising curveball, but his stats in his first taste of full-season ball (because short-season leagues were eliminated) were burnt Hamburger Helper.

Norge Vera RHP

Born: 06/01/00 Age: 22 Bats: R Throws: R Height: 6'4" Weight: 185 lb. Origin: International Free Agent, 2021

YEAR	TEAM	LVL	AGE	W	L	SV	G	GS	IP	H	HR	BB/9	K/9	K	GB%	BABIP	WHIP	ERA	DRA-	WARP	MPH	FB%	Whiff%	CSP
2021	DSL WSX	ROK	21	1	0	0	8	7	19	9	0	2.4	16.1	34	73.3%	.300	0.74	0.00						
2022	*No projection*																							

Like his Cuban countryman Luis Robert before him, Vera spent his first season with the White Sox in the Dominican Summer League so he could "acclimate" to professional baseball, despite being a 21-year-old who has pitched in Serie Nacional and sits in the high-90s. (If they built a floating barge in the middle of international waters, free from taxation, he probably would have played there.) It would be unwise to compare him to Robert, but apt to compare Vera to Rorschach from Watchmen—when you strike out 34 hapless teenagers in 19 scoreless innings, you're not acclimating to them, they're acclimating to you. His stateside development will begin in High-A Winston-Salem, already in progress.

Lineouts

Hitters

HITTER	POS	TEAM	LVL	AGE	PA	R	2B	3B	HR	RBI	BB	K	SB	CS	AVG/OBP/SLG	DRC+	BABIP	BRR	FRAA	WARP
Tim Beckham	IF	CLT	AAA	31	182	32	11	0	11	32	14	44	1	0	.279/.330/.545	113	.310	0.9	SS(16): 0.8, 3B(12): 1.3, 1B(10): 0.1	1.0
Misael Gonzalez	OF	WSX	ROK	20	85	14	6	0	5	23	6	26	4	2	.311/.393/.595		.419			
	OF	KAN	A	20	105	12	4	0	3	10	11	40	1	0	.178/.286/.322	75	.271	1.1	RF(30): 2.7, CF(1): -0.1	0.4
Wes Kath	3B	WSX	ROK	18	115	15	0	2	3	15	8	42	1	0	.212/.287/.337		.322			
Mikie Mahtook	OF	CLT	AAA	31	410	60	18	1	26	62	31	102	8	2	.251/.318/.518	111	.272	0.7	CF(43): -3.3, LF(35): 0.1, RF(18): -0.1	1.6
Luis Mieses	OF	KAN	A	21	225	31	12	1	6	41	13	33	0	0	.305/.347/.463	114	.329	-0.4	RF(38): -4.5, LF(15): -1.0	0.6
	OF	WS	A+	21	234	30	19	2	9	33	11	48	0	1	.236/.278/.464	117	.262	-1.6	LF(32): 1.2, RF(26): -5.6, CF(2): 1.2	0.8
Bryan Ramos	DH	KAN	A	19	504	64	23	6	13	57	51	110	13	4	.244/.345/.415	103	.295	1.4	3B(34): 1.1, 2B(25): -0.2	1.8
Yolbert Sanchez	MI	WS	A+	24	239	28	7	0	5	29	18	33	2	1	.286/.340/.387	110	.318	0.3	2B(34): -3.6, SS(24): -2.0	0.5
	MI	BIR	AA	24	155	15	6	0	4	13	5	16	3	0	.343/.369/.469	122	.366	0.7	2B(19): 0.7, SS(16): 2.3, 3B(3): -0.0	1.2
Lenyn Sosa	SS	WS	A+	21	353	45	19	1	10	49	14	77	3	4	.290/.321/.443	98	.349	0.4	SS(64): 5.1, 2B(21): 1.2	1.6
	SS	BIR	AA	21	121	10	5	0	1	7	2	28	0	1	.214/.240/.282	77	.273	-0.2	SS(20): 1.9, 2B(9): 0.8, 3B(4): -0.3	0.3
Nick Williams	OF	CLT	AAA	27	138	15	7	1	4	13	7	36	4	0	.262/.314/.429	92	.333	-0.1	RF(19): -0.9, LF(8): -0.0	0.2
	OF	CHW	MLB	27	13	2	0	0	0	0	1	4	0	0	.000/.231/.000	93		0.0	LF(3): -0.0	0.0

The former no. 1 overall pick from 2008 is still playing baseball, as a minor-league deal with the White Sox can attest. **Tim Beckham** still has a little juice, as a midseason power surge in the wacky Charlotte hitting environment shows. And he's still beset by leg injuries, as ending the year on the injured list unfortunately proves. ⚾ Many great players began their stories by looking hitterish in complex league ball, as do many guys that get written up in this book exactly one time. **Misael González**, a 12th-round pick out of Puerto Rico who offered both thump and whiffs in compelling quantities in 2021, is more likely one than the other, but probably somewhere in between. ⚾ If you're allowed to scrutinize 28 complex-league games at the outset of a prep pick's career, then questions about the White Sox second round pick's bat speed were validated by a strikeout percentage north of 36% in his first encounter with professional velocity. Luckily for **Wes Kath**, you're not allowed. ⚾ People are asking, what's a one-line summary of how hitter-friendly it is at Triple-A Charlotte these days? How about: 31-year-old **Mikie Mahtook** hit 26 bombs while playing there. ⚾ Even while bouncing around A-ball in his first go-round with full-season ball, **Luis Mieses** flashed suitable amounts of his intriguing power. So, mark that one off his checklist. Next year: approach. The year after that: bringing the entire world to heel—maybe. Probably not. ⚾ As a large, thickly built bat-first prospect, it would behoove **Brayn Ramos** to leave no doubt as to his offensive bonafides and avoid month-long slumps in A-ball. As a precious new just-born baby who is still acclimating to being alive on the Earth, he did just fine playing full-season ball for the first time at just 19 years of age. ⚾ While the proud lineage of White Sox players with first names starting in Y places a certain set of expectations on **Yolbert Sanchez**, his bat is projected to be more Yolmer than Yoán. ⚾ **Lenyn Sosa's** sneaky interesting hit tool as a teenager manifested itself as some sneaky interesting pop as a 21-year-old fringy shortstop. As his credential of being perennially young for his level dissipates, one or two of these strengths he's flashed at times needs to abandon the sneaky lifestyle and live openly in the light. ⚾ Five years from now, when you fall one name short of acing a Sporcle quiz about who appeared in games for the 2021 White Sox, it'll come to your attention for the first time that former consensus top-100 pick **Nick Williams** played four games on the South Side (and batted fifth in a game against Shane Bieber!). This scenario presumes that you're skimming past *this* write-up in *this* book.

Pitchers

PITCHER	TEAM	LVL	AGE	W	L	SV	G	GS	IP	H	HR	BB/9	K/9	K	GB%	BABIP	WHIP	ERA	DRA-	WARP	MPH	FB%	WHF	CSP
Jason Bilous	WS	A+	23	1	1	0	3	3	14^{2}	11	0	1.2	16.0	26	42.9%	.393	0.89	2.45	71	0.4				
	BIR	AA	23	2	7	0	17	17	65	71	8	4.2	11.1	80	39.0%	.373	1.55	6.51	92	0.9				
Sean Burke	KAN	A	21	0	1	0	5	5	14	9	0	6.4	12.9	20	43.3%	.321	1.36	3.21	92	0.2				
Andrew Dalquist	KAN	A	20	3	9	0	23	23	83	87	1	6.1	8.6	79	42.8%	.345	1.72	4.99	117	0.0				
Carl Edwards Jr.	CLT	AAA	29	0	0	3	10	0	9	4	0	3.0	15.0	15	50.0%	.250	0.78	2.00	80	0.2				
	BUF	AAA	29	1	0	0	7	0	7	5	2	0.0	10.3	8	50.0%	.188	0.71	3.86	92	0.1				
	TOR	MLB	29	0	0	0	6	0	5^{1}	8	2	3.4	8.4	5	21.1%	.353	1.88	6.75	111	0.0	94.2	68.8%	28.2%	61.5%
	ATL	MLB	29	0	0	0	1	0	0^{1}	3	1	27.0	27.0	1	33.3%	1.000	12.00	81.00	156	0.0	93.2	50.0%	33.3%	43.1%
Caleb Freeman	WS	A+	23	2	2	6	25	0	27^{1}	22	5	4.6	10.9	33	35.3%	.270	1.32	3.62	91	0.3				
	BIR	AA	23	0	1	3	14	0	16^{2}	15	2	2.7	11.9	22	44.2%	.317	1.20	2.70	82	0.3				
Evan Marshall	CHW	MLB	31	0	2	0	27	0	27^{1}	28	5	3.0	8.6	26	41.0%	.319	1.35	5.60	102	0.2	93.3	36.6%	23.4%	49.4%
Kade McClure	BIR	AA	25	2	4	0	15	15	68^{1}	63	10	2.6	10.1	77	48.9%	.308	1.21	3.82	97	0.8				
	CLT	AAA	25	2	3	0	9	9	37	46	6	3.6	8.8	36	39.5%	.370	1.65	6.81	107	0.4				
Tanner McDougal	WSX	ROK	18	1	2	0	6	4	9^{2}	10	2	4.7	15.8	17	45.0%	.444	1.55	9.31						
Hunter Schryver	CLT	AAA	26	1	0	1	40	0	43^{1}	42	7	5.8	10.0	48	43.1%	.307	1.62	4.98	89	0.8				
Luke Shilling	WS	A+	23	0	0	1	16	0	18^{1}	16	2	3.9	13.3	27	37.2%	.359	1.31	2.95	84	0.3				
Bennett Sousa	BIR	AA	26	0	1	3	20	0	24^{2}	14	4	5.5	13.9	38	46.0%	.217	1.18	3.28	83	0.5				
	CLT	AAA	26	4	2	1	21	0	22^{2}	23	3	2.0	13.1	33	35.1%	.370	1.24	3.97	74	0.6				
Emilio Vargas	BIR	AA	24	7	4	0	21	15	83^{2}	69	9	3.0	10.6	99	39.5%	.296	1.16	2.90	94	1.1				

Millions of people died, global economic inequality accelerated and society is fraying at its very seams. But **Jason Bilous** emerged from the early COVID-19 pandemic and the lost 2020 minor-league season throwing more strikes than he ever had before, so you know, take the good with the bad. Humanity may be toast, but Chicago's high-minors starting depth? A twinkle of hope. ⚾ As a big, towering college arm who boasts a spinny four-seamer but fell to the third round due to control outages, **Sean Burke** commendably worked his way up to some outings at Low-A after the end of a physically demanding junior season at Maryland. At Kannapolis, Burke struck out lotsa dudes with a spinny four-seamer and ran into some control outages. Sometimes the reports are accurate. ⚾ At some point, all those thoroughly amateur scouting-sounding compliments like "repeatable delivery," "athletic and projectable frame," and "plus arm speed," need to be supplemented with statistical indicators that **Andrew Dalquist** is actually repeating his delivery. And accomplishments need transition from "pitched a full first professional season without his arm falling off," to "dominated low minors competition." But not yet, very recently legally-drinking young man. Not yet. ⚾ Moving through three organizations in one season hints at both the present and future for **C.J. Edwards**: his phone will keep ringing as teams face the need for a plug-and-play reliever who can touch 94 and occasionally spin a curveball that misses bats. ⚾ The philosophical question of the ages: Can a pitcher with zero command and control look like a god for 16 ⅔ innings in Double-A and have it be just luck? Given **Caleb Freeman's** history, we'll still be asking the question if it gets to 17 ⅔, and 18 ⅔, and 19 ⅔. ⚾ After a dominant turn in the shortened 2020 season, surely something had to be wrong for **Evan Marshall's** performance to take such a leap backward in 2021. Yes, something was, as Marshall underwent Tommy John surgery in December after some unsuccessful attempts to rehab his right elbow. He's expected to miss the entire 2022 season. ⚾ One great leap forward in stuff developed through the pandemic vaulted **Kade McClure** from an inglorious lower-minors innings eater to upper-minors innings eater. Every strike getting whacked to hell in the nuttiest Triple-A offensive environment in the game may not be the fairest statement on McClure's game, but how much assurance does he have that the majors will be more forgiving? ⚾ With mid-90s heat, some notion of a changeup and a breaking ball that cracks 3,000 RPM, **Tanner McDougal** is a name worth remembering. And you'll really need to put in the effort, because he'll miss all of 2022 due to Tommy John surgery. ⚾ If you're a left-handed reliever with an intriguing arsenal fronted by a hoppy fastball, the sun will never fully set on you in this world. But there are few relievers with the stuff to contravene the walk totals **Hunter Schryver** has posted the last few years, and he was not one of them. Maybe one day he will be, but improved command seems like an easier path. ⚾ The 18 ⅓ innings that **Luke Shilling** threw in 2021 weren't just his first as a professional—a catastrophic lat tear ate his 2018 and 2019 seasons and led to his release during 2020 organizational cutbacks—they represented the first time he felt truly healthy since high school. Also, the last, for a while. He went under for Tommy John surgery in August. ⚾ **Bennett Sousa** picked up the tempo on his march to the major leagues, striking out a third of batters between Double-A and Triple-A. Entering his age-27 season, he may never be the Belle of Chicago, but at least against lefties, he can serve as El Capitan. ⚾ After a successful stretch in with Arizona's Double-A club in 2019, **Emilio Vargas** was tagged with the reputation of not having the raw stuff to thrive at the higher levels. But after a lost year in the minors, he was claimed by a new organization, which brought a new vision for his career, and laid out new possibilities. Then the Sox kept him at Double-A for all of 2021.

CLEVELAND GUARDIANS

Essay by Shakeia Taylor

Player comments by Alex Chamberlain and BP staff

I think sometimes we forget the power in a name.

When my family moved to northeast Ohio, I immediately became enraptured with the professional baseball team 60 miles up the road. Baseball was a way for a new kid to make friends in a new state. In junior high school, I was competing with a group of classmates in a creative competition called "Odyssey of the Mind." It was 1997. As a team, we decided to adopt outfielder David Justice's walk-up song, Notorious B.I.G.'s "Hypnotize," as our theme song. We were really just a group of kids in a public-school gifted-and-talented program, but we presented ourselves to be as cool as that '97 team was to us. But along with that fandom came the ugly—the name. For decades, I wore the mark of a team whose name and mascot harmed others. As I grew older, I learned very quickly to not wear anything with the team name. When you're Black, being called a "Cleveland Racial Slurs" fan is not exactly endearing or cool—to me or anyone else. Like others, I not only stopped wearing team apparel, I stopped saying that name. I moved my jerseys to the back of my closet and opted for a simple block-C cap on the rare occasion I wanted to represent.

When parents are choosing names for their children, I imagine they take great care. They create lists. They think of all of the ways in which kids might use a name to be cruel. They say them out loud to see how they sound. They look at their child's face, asking themselves, "Does my baby look like a _____?" They consider things like culture, religion and beloved family members. Some might wonder what profession their child will have and put the name with their imaginary future career. Do we become our names, or do our names become us? As someone with the kind of name you wouldn't find on a coffee mug at an interstate rest stop, I've thought about names a lot. Saying them incorrectly, spelling them wrong. Names matter, and how we use them is of great importance.

When the WNBA's Atlanta Dream were protesting racial and social injustices, they never uttered the name of the team owner they were up against. "Words are things," Nneka Ogwumike, the Los Angeles Sparks forward who is president of the league's players association, told *The New York Times* in 2020. "Words have power. And to give energy to a name I think is very meaningful. So we stopped saying that name."

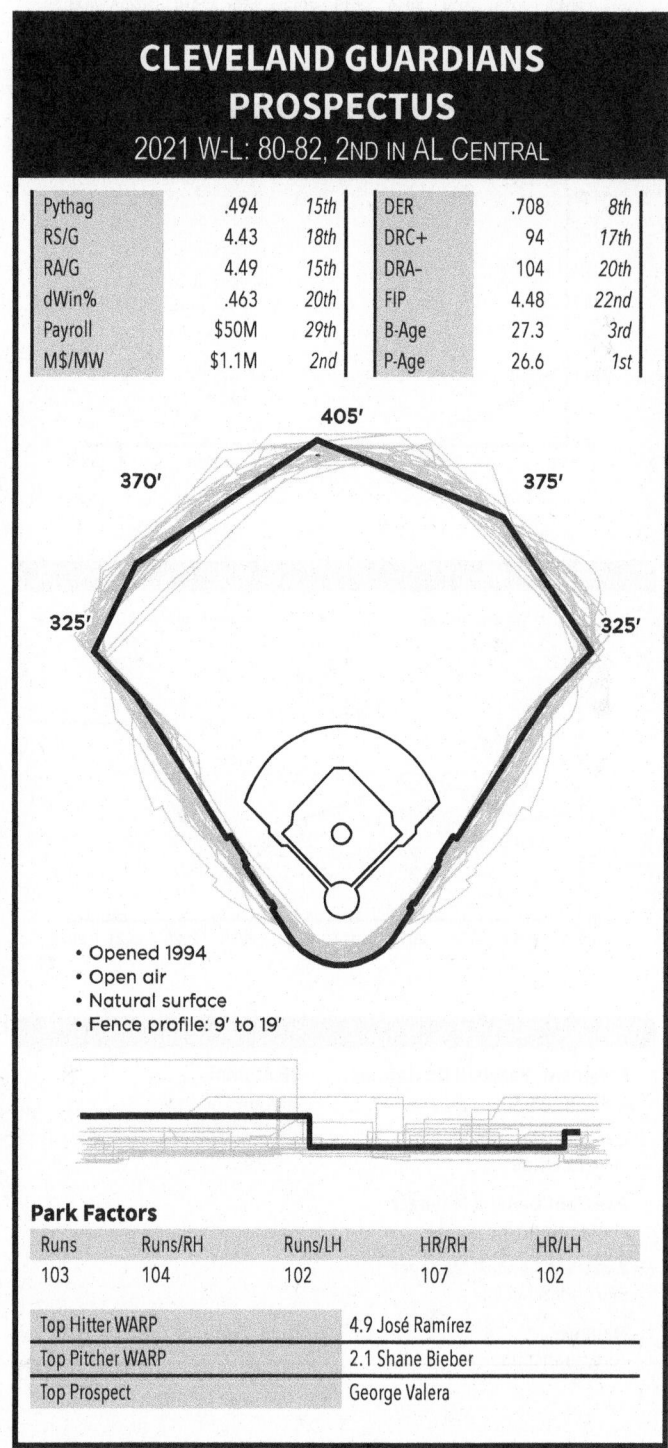

CLEVELAND GUARDIANS PROSPECTUS

2021 W-L: 80-82, 2ND IN AL CENTRAL

Pythag	.494	*15th*	DER	.708	*8th*
RS/G	4.43	*18th*	DRC+	94	*17th*
RA/G	4.49	*15th*	DRA-	104	*20th*
dWin%	.463	*20th*	FIP	4.48	*22nd*
Payroll	$50M	*29th*	B-Age	27.3	*3rd*
M$/MW	$1.1M	*2nd*	P-Age	26.6	*1st*

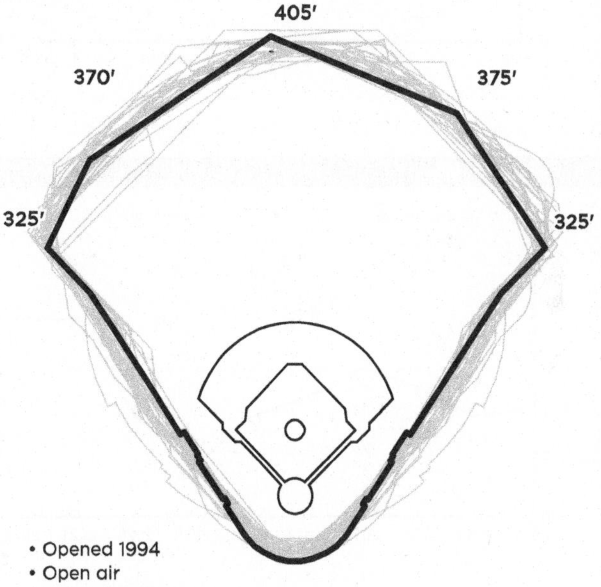

- Opened 1994
- Open air
- Natural surface
- Fence profile: 9' to 19'

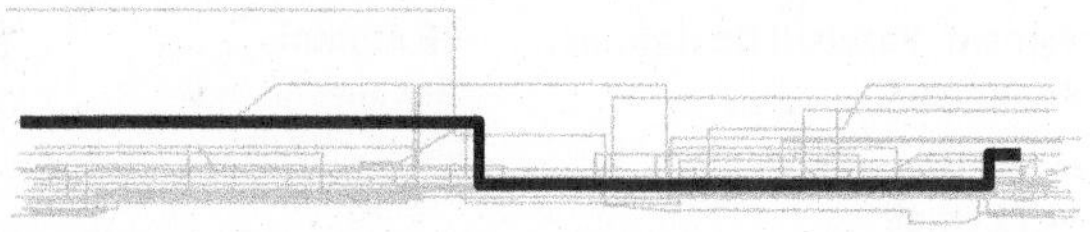

Park Factors

Runs	Runs/RH	Runs/LH	HR/RH	HR/LH
103	104	102	107	102

Top Hitter WARP	4.9 José Ramírez
Top Pitcher WARP	2.1 Shane Bieber
Top Prospect	George Valera

Payroll History (in millions)

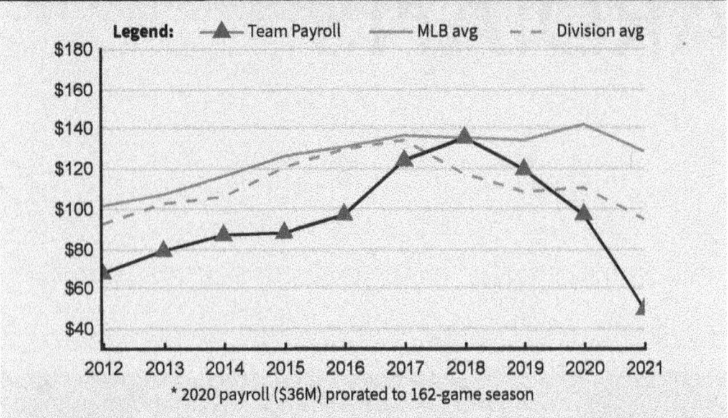

Future Commitments (in millions)

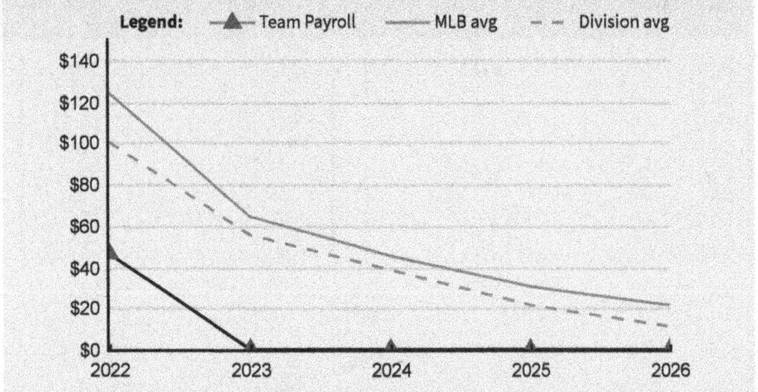

Farm System Ranking

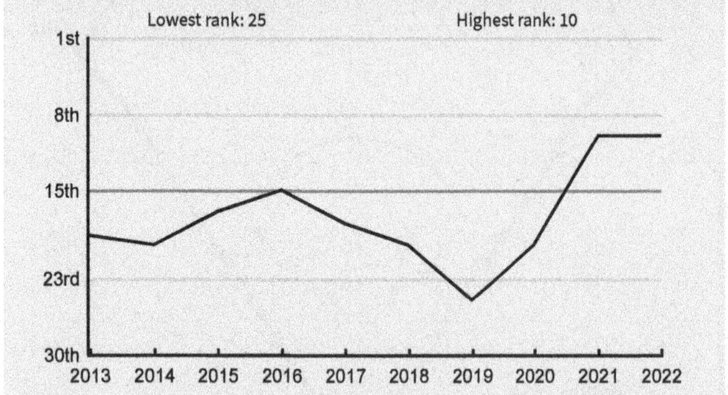

Personnel

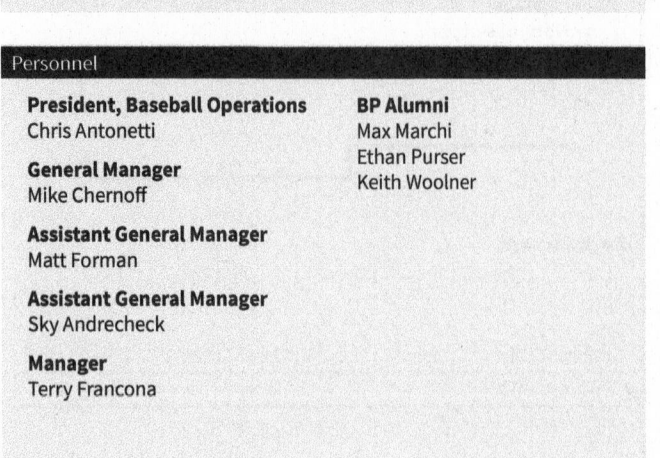

President, Baseball Operations
Chris Antonetti

General Manager
Mike Chernoff

Assistant General Manager
Matt Forman

Assistant General Manager
Sky Andrecheck

Manager
Terry Francona

BP Alumni
Max Marchi
Ethan Purser
Keith Woolner

I had never heard it put this way in this particular context, but it perfectly described exactly why the Cleveland team needed to change its name. Using it wasn't just saying a slur, it was giving power to it. Not that it should matter at all, but I knew as well as anybody how it feels.

After decades of growing protest from within and outside of Indigenous communities, the Cleveland baseball team finally, finally changed their name. There's no need to go over their reason for keeping the name for so long or the innumerable ways opponents of the name change tried to say it brought honor. The old name is gone, and the new name, hopefully, ushers in a welcome change to the corner of Carnegie and Ontario.

The Cleveland baseball team has appeared in four World Series since 1948. They all ended especially miserably and, after each one, without fail, someone would utter, "they won't win until they change that name." Sure, maybe they didn't mean it literally, because the name has no actual impact on the outcome of any given game. But there is something to be said for the validity of an argument that keeping a team name that dehumanizes Indigenous people both near and far was holding the team back from success. You can say you believe in things like karma and bad vibes, or that you don't believe in any of those things at all. But there is no denying the goodness in just changing the name. There is power in a name.

You see, changing the name doesn't erase history. The damage has been done. But it doesn't dissolve all of the fond memories many of us have of the team, either. This is still the first team in the American League to integrate; Larry Doby's legacy is forever. This is still the team that captured and broke our hearts in the '90s. Twice. The team that won 22 in a row. We've seen players we've grown to know and love traded away every few years for whatever "financial reason" the front office comes up with, so I know we have it in us to move on. And if, for one second, you suspend disbelief and lean into the magic and mythos of sport, you will open your mind to the possibilities that sit on the other side.

I attended the last Friday night home game of the 2021 season. People around me were discussing it, some excitedly, some sadly, but this was it. This was really, officially the end of an era. It would be the last time Cleveland's boys of summer would walk off Progressive Field—or The Jake, as many of us will always call it—under the old name. We laughed, we sang, we cheered. In that moment, temporary lifelong friends were made. There was a lot of reminiscing by way of a dad, sitting nearby, explaining what different things meant to his young child.

"What's 455 mean?"

"That's the regular-season sellout streak that started in 1995." We all remembered. Baseball is an imperfect game and, as a Cleveland fan, it can be painful. (I'm reminded of 2016 nearly every day of my life since it happened.) But you always return. You always return to the place that harbors such special memories. As I sat in the bleachers with my friends, I thought about how, not only has the team changed, but I've grown. I'm no longer the new girl who has just moved to Ohio, staring out at a ballpark in wonderment because I'd never been to a big-league game, but I still have the same feelings. Baseball grips your heart the way a pitcher does his best pitch. It gets under your skin. It gets into the grooves of your emotions. But, like us, the game must grow. It cannot always be stuck in the past. In order to always be the "social institution" old schoolers have preached it to be, it must adapt.

The Chicago White Sox had clinched the division a couple nights before in Cleveland, marking their own historic moment, but we didn't care. We still wanted a win. The season was effectively over, but we needed a win. *Just one more. Do it for us, boys.* Nostalgia, one of baseball's most valuable commodities, was getting the W that night.

Though the actual statues which inspired the new name signify "the spirit of progress in transportation," Guardians also refers to stewardship of the past, the present and the future. The team's announcement of the change, on July 23, 2021, did not mention nor make amends for the previous name, but I'd like to view the new name as a recognition of the harm that the old name has done to people and a promise to do better in the future, to be worthy of the love fans have given the team for decades. It's a new start for us all. "We think Guardians is unique and authentic to Cleveland," Brian Barren, Cleveland's president of business operations, told ESPN. "It's less about the Guardians of Traffic and more about what the Guardians represent and that idea of protection. For us and our research, Cleveland folks are very protective of one another. They're protective of our city, they're protective of the land and everything about it. That's one key component, the resiliency of people here in Cleveland and Northeast Ohio and the loyalty."

At the end of every home win, as the crowd cheers and the team high-fives its way into the clubhouse, fireworks burst through the sky, illuminating that corner of downtown in flashes of red and blue light. As we stood and cheered, we turned to watch the sky light up one last time for the Cleveland team we once knew.

As usual, I'm waiting for pitchers and catchers like a young kid waits for Christmas, or like Adult Me waits for new sneakers to arrive. But this time, with renewed hope. "They won't win until they change that name." From your mouth to God's ears. Welcome, Cleveland Guardians. **We've been waiting a lifetime for you.**

—Shakeia Taylor is a writer based in Chicago whose work focuses on the intersection of Black culture and sport in America.

Hitters

★ ★ ★ *2022 Top 101 Prospect* **#57** ★ ★ ★

Gabriel Arias SS Born: 02/27/00 Age: 22 Bats: R Throws: R Height: 6'1" Weight: 217 lb. Origin: International Free Agent, 2016

YEAR	TEAM	LVL	AGE	PA	R	2B	3B	HR	RBI	BB	K	SB	CS	Whiff%	AVG/OBP/SLG	DRC+	BABIP	BRR	FRAA	WARP
2019	LE	A+	19	511	62	21	4	17	75	25	128	8	4		.302/.339/.470	114	.378	1.6	SS(104): -11.6, 3B(10): 1.3, 2B(2): -0.5	1.1
2021	COL	AAA	21	483	64	29	3	13	55	39	110	5	1		.284/.348/.454	101	.351	-1.1	SS(82): 0.3, 3B(19): -1.9, 2B(9): -0.3	1.3
2022 DC	*CLE*	*MLB*	*22*	*30*	*3*	*1*	*0*	*0*	*3*	*1*	*8*	*0*	*0*	*34.7%*	*.252/.307/.392*	*86*	*.340*	*0.0*	*SS 0*	*0.0*

Comparables: Wilmer Flores, Willy Adames, Isaac Paredes

The Padres signed Arias out of Venezuela for seven figures in 2016, which says a lot about the potential envisioned in him then that he's now fulfilling. Acquired in the Mike Clevinger trade, he hit the ground running, skipping Double-A (where, presumably, he would have played if not for the pandemic) and heading straight to Triple-A as a 21-year-old. There were concerns about his over-aggression at the plate half a decade ago, and he did nothing last year to quell them. Still, against his toughest competition yet, Arias posted his best strikeout and walk rates while sustaining the power surge from his last full season with the Padres. Reeling in his approach might be too much to ask, but it's hard for the Guardians to have asked for much more than such a positive step forward anyway. Cleveland's farm is replete with shortstop talent, and one of them is bound to be the franchise's future. At this point, Arias has as good a chance as any of them to be it. Given his proximity, he could be first to knock down the door. At the very least, we know he can end a season on a high note.

Will Benson OF Born: 06/16/98 Age: 24 Bats: L Throws: L Height: 6'5" Weight: 230 lb. Origin: Round 1, 2016 Draft (#14 overall)

YEAR	TEAM	LVL	AGE	PA	R	2B	3B	HR	RBI	BB	K	SB	CS	Whiff%	AVG/OBP/SLG	DRC+	BABIP	BRR	FRAA	WARP
2019	LC	A	21	259	44	12	3	18	55	37	78	18	2		.272/.371/.604	145	.325	2.0	RF(21): -0.9, LF(20): 0.8, CF(12): -2.1	2.1
2019	LYN	A+	21	255	29	9	2	4	23	31	73	9	2		.189/.290/.304	82	.255	3.3	LF(38): -2.8, RF(15): -0.7, CF(1): -0.0	0.3
2021	AKR	AA	23	332	63	13	5	14	42	60	104	14	3		.221/.374/.469	117	.301	1.0	RF(26): -0.0, CF(23): -2.6, LF(22): -1.6	1.4
2021	COL	AAA	23	107	7	5	1	3	9	14	42	0	2		.161/.271/.333	68	.250	-0.5	LF(10): -0.4, CF(9): 0.0, RF(6): -0.3	-0.1
2022 non-DC	*CLE*	*MLB*	*24*	*251*	*25*	*9*	*1*	*7*	*27*	*30*	*91*	*5*	*2*	*38.6%*	*.186/.292/.354*	*73*	*.274*	*0.5*	*LF 0, RF 0*	*0.0*

Comparables: Ben Gamel, Scott Van Slyke, Domonic Brown

For his mino- league career, 2016 first-rounder Benson owns a .210 batting average. Yes, batting average is a flawed measure of hitter productivity. But, also, yes, a .210 batting average as a minor-leaguer, let alone a former top prospect, is reprehensibly bad. Not irredeemably bad, mind you; Benson's three true outcomes are calibrated such that he walks and hits for power just enough to keep him afloat. His swing seems to beget perilously high fly-ball rates. Loft is necessary for power to flourish—Vladimir Guerrero, Jr. finally put those 118-mph knee-high lasers in the air last year—but Benson may take it a bit too far, launching too many harmless fly balls that undercut his latent light-tower power and stifle his BABIP. His athleticism keeps his ceiling in view, although it's gradually falling out of focus. Half a decade of developmental stagnation suggests he and his parent team may need to make a change, and soon.

Aaron Bracho 2B Born: 04/24/01 Age: 21 Bats: S Throws: R Height: 5'11" Weight: 175 lb. Origin: International Free Agent, 2017

YEAR	TEAM	LVL	AGE	PA	R	2B	3B	HR	RBI	BB	K	SB	CS	Whiff%	AVG/OBP/SLG	DRC+	BABIP	BRR	FRAA	WARP
2019	INDB	ROK	18	137	25	10	2	6	29	23	21	4	1		.296/.416/.593		.306			
2019	MV	SS	18	32	5	1	0	2	4	5	8	0	0		.222/.344/.481		.235			
2021	LC	A+	20	279	27	9	0	7	27	32	89	1	2		.174/.269/.299	86	.233	0.4	2B(30): -1.0, 1B(12): 1.5, 3B(12): -0.6	0.4
2022 non-DC	*CLE*	*MLB*	*21*	*251*	*19*	*9*	*0*	*3*	*20*	*19*	*84*	*1*	*1*	*34.3%*	*.183/.253/.279*	*42*	*.274*	*-0.1*	*2B 0, 3B 0*	*-1.2*

Comparables: Dilson Herrera, Tyler Wade, Gavin Cecchini

Everything that enamored scouts and prospectors in Bracho's stateside debut—the power, the patience, the feel for contact—abandoned him last year. He slugged—*slugged*—just .299 in 70 High-A contests. For someone his size (read: small), he hits a ton of fly balls, a sword by which one cannot live and not also sometimes die. Live and die Bracho has, as evidenced by his otherworldly 2019 debut and 2021's catastrophic reentrance into the atmosphere. The about-face is genuinely alarming, but Bracho is both plenty young and tooled-up enough to right this ship. It's just that he looked poised to make waves, and now he has a lot of ground to claw back.

Bobby Bradley 1B Born: 05/29/96 Age: 26 Bats: L Throws: R Height: 6'1" Weight: 225 lb. Origin: Round 3, 2014 Draft (#97 overall)

YEAR	TEAM	LVL	AGE	PA	R	2B	3B	HR	RBI	BB	K	SB	CS	Whiff%	AVG/OBP/SLG	DRC+	BABIP	BRR	FRAA	WARP
2019	COL	AAA	23	453	65	23	0	33	74	46	153	0	0		.264/.344/.567	114	.336	-2.4	1B(98): 2.7	1.6
2019	CLE	MLB	23	49	4	5	0	1	4	4	20	0	0	38.9%	.178/.245/.356	57	.292	-0.2	1B(5): -0.2	-0.2
2021	COL	AAA	25	109	16	1	0	9	19	7	35	0	0		.196/.266/.485	114	.182	0.6	1B(23): -0.3	0.4
2021	CLE	MLB	25	279	36	10	0	16	41	25	99	0	0	40.3%	.208/.294/.445	86	.263	-1.6	1B(68): 3.5	0.3
2022 DC	*CLE*	*MLB*	*26*	*444*	*60*	*17*	*1*	*21*	*67*	*37*	*163*	*0*	*0*	*39.5%*	*.204/.283/.419*	*84*	*.278*	*-0.6*	*1B 0*	*-0.1*

Comparables: Matt Olson, Mike Carp, Logan Morrison

There's a sort of garishness to Bradley's power, the one thing he does well. He slugged more than 30 homers per 600 plate appearances in the minors but hit, in total, just .251. Standing next to Will Benson, Bradley resembles a budding Silver Slugger. Unfortunately, Bradley must stand next to other, much more capable teammates as well. If you squint, you can see a poor man's Joey Gallo. Until Bradley manifests Gallo's defensive capabilities or his requisite on-base skills, though, riches will remain out of arm's reach.

Yu Chang IF Born: 08/18/95 Age: 26 Bats: R Throws: R Height: 6'1" Weight: 180 lb. Origin: International Free Agent, 2013

YEAR	TEAM	LVL	AGE	PA	R	2B	3B	HR	RBI	BB	K	SB	CS	Whiff%	AVG/OBP/SLG	DRC+	BABIP	BRR	FRAA	WARP
2019	COL	AAA	23	283	45	15	1	9	39	26	67	4	1		.253/.322/.427	90	.306	1.5	2B(23): 0.2, SS(22): 0.0, 3B(17): -0.9	0.8
2019	CLE	MLB	23	84	8	2	1	1	6	11	22	0	0	25.6%	.178/.286/.274	79	.240	-1.0	3B(25): -0.4, SS(8): -0.1	-0.1
2020	CLE	MLB	24	13	1	0	0	0	1	2	4	0	0	19.2%	.182/.308/.182	95	.286	-0.2	SS(4): 0.2, 3B(3): -0.1, 2B(2): 0.4	0.1
2021	COL	AAA	25	66	9	5	0	4	13	5	19	1	2		.322/.394/.610	92	.417	0.1	3B(5): -1.0, 2B(4): -0.1, SS(4): 0.1	0.1
2021	CLE	MLB	25	251	32	14	3	9	39	11	69	1	0	27.0%	.228/.267/.426	82	.281	1.0	1B(49): -1.2, 3B(21): 0.0, 2B(8): -0.0	0.1
2022 DC	*CLE*	*MLB*	*26*	*158*	*19*	*7*	*1*	*5*	*23*	*11*	*41*	*0*	*1*	*27.7%*	*.228/.292/.398*	*83*	*.286*	*0.0*	*1B 0, 3B 0*	*0.0*

Comparables: Eduardo Escobar, Jonathan Villar, Daniel Robertson

As a farmhand, Chang always flashed enough pop, speed and leather to get by. The bat-to-ball skills, masked by a somewhat aggressive approach, were (and still are) poor, eroding whatever promise he had shown of being a serviceable bench bat, let alone an everyday regular. As with many colleagues with whom he shares this chapter, Chang remains relevant thanks exclusively to the Guardians' bleak short-term outlook. Even then, Chang's MLB expiration date draws ominously nearer.

Ernie Clement 2B/3B Born: 03/22/96 Age: 26 Bats: R Throws: R Height: 6'0" Weight: 170 lb. Origin: Round 4, 2017 Draft (#132 overall)

YEAR	TEAM	LVL	AGE	PA	R	2B	3B	HR	RBI	BB	K	SB	CS	Whiff%	AVG/OBP/SLG	DRC+	BABIP	BRR	FRAA	WARP
2019	MSS	WIN	23	74	5	2	1	0	5	6	13	1	1		.303/.365/.364		.370			
2019	AKR	AA	23	437	46	15	3	1	24	26	33	16	10		.261/.314/.322	111	.279	-2.4	SS(90): 10.9, 2B(3): -0.5	3.0
2021	COL	AAA	25	138	11	12	1	1	10	9	22	2	1		.250/.294/.387	95	.288	0.2	3B(12): -1.4, SS(8): 1.3, 2B(7): 0.3	0.5
2021	CLE	MLB	25	133	16	4	0	3	9	7	19	0	1	16.5%	.231/.285/.339	98	.253	0.0	2B(22): -2.8, 3B(16): -1.2, LF(2): -0.2	0.0
2022 DC	*CLE*	*MLB*	*26*	*29*	*3*	*1*	*0*	*0*	*2*	*1*	*4*	*0*	*0*	*18.5%*	*.240/.294/.325*	*68*	*.279*	*0.0*	*2B 0*	*0.0*

Comparables: Kevin Newman, Brent Lillibridge, Tommy Edman

A quintessentially Clevelandian fringe prospect, Clement boasts 70-grade speed and nearly as many walks as strikeouts (both typically single-digit percentages). Of course, speed does not guarantee baserunning efficiency; Clement converted only 65% of stolen base attempts in the minors and goofed his only attempt during his initial big-league cup of tea. For someone with such proficient speed and contact skills, Clement failed to muster high batting averages against weaker competition, pulling the ball too much for someone who has the barrel control to spray it around the park. All told, Clement may lack the requisite thump to even be a David Fletcher or Luis Arraez type, but it wouldn't hurt for the Guardians to find out.

Jose Fermin IF

Born: 03/29/99 Age: 23 Bats: R Throws: R Height: 5'11" Weight: 200 lb. Origin: International Free Agent, 2015

YEAR	TEAM	LVL	AGE	PA	R	2B	3B	HR	RBI	BB	K	SB	CS	Whiff%	AVG/OBP/SLG	DRC+	BABIP	BRR	FRAA	WARP
2019	LC	A	20	456	75	12	2	6	41	42	40	28	9		.293/.374/.379	132	.311	2.8	2B(64): 0.8, SS(39): 0.3	3.6
2021	AKR	AA	22	336	40	15	2	6	39	23	38	4	4		.258/.329/.383	114	.276	0.4	3B(40): -1.3, 2B(28): 0.2, SS(14): -2.0	1.3
2022 non-DC	*CLE*	*MLB*	*23*	*251*	*22*	*9*	*1*	*3*	*22*	*15*	*33*	*6*	*3*	*16.3%*	*.246/.307/.338*	*79*	*.276*	*0.5*	*2B 0, SS 0*	*0.2*

Comparables: Yairo Muñoz, Marco Hernández, Hernán Pérez

You could copy-paste Ernie Clement's blurb here if you wanted to—seriously, Fermin and Clement are carbon copies of each other. It's genuinely impressive how the Guardians stockpile guys like these. Fermin clocks in three years younger than his fungible counterpart, making his outlook arguably rosier. Elite bat-to-ball hitters seem to force their team's hands eventually despite absences of power, and Cleveland should find itself in such a malleable state that it can indulge in Fermin as it figures out its intermediate-term infield situation. Long-term, he may still provide utility to the team, just likely not in a full-time capacity.

Tyler Freeman IF

Born: 05/21/99 Age: 23 Bats: R Throws: R Height: 6'0" Weight: 190 lb. Origin: Round 2, 2017 Draft (#71 overall)

YEAR	TEAM	LVL	AGE	PA	R	2B	3B	HR	RBI	BB	K	SB	CS	Whiff%	AVG/OBP/SLG	DRC+	BABIP	BRR	FRAA	WARP
2019	LC	A	20	272	51	16	3	3	24	18	28	11	4		.292/.382/.424	137	.320	2.6	SS(57): 1.7, 2B(3): -0.3	2.5
2019	LYN	A+	20	275	38	16	2	0	20	8	25	8	1		.319/.354/.397	119	.350	0.8	SS(57): 0.3	1.4
2021	AKR	AA	22	180	26	14	2	2	19	8	21	4	2		.323/.372/.470	122	.357	-0.8	SS(26): 0.5, 2B(7): -0.2, 3B(7): 0.9	1.1
2022 DC	*CLE*	*MLB*	*23*	*65*	*7*	*3*	*0*	*0*	*6*	*3*	*8*	*1*	*1*	*14.4%*	*.264/.319/.362*	*88*	*.299*	*0.1*	*SS 0, 2B 0*	*0.1*

Comparables: Yairo Muñoz, Yamaico Navarro, Eugenio Suárez

Of all of Cleveland's extreme bat-to-ball enthusiasts—and there are quite a few—Freeman is the marquee name. Superb barrel control and an aggressive approach cultivate single-digit strikeout and walk rates along with relentless gap-to-gap doubles. Based on his year-end line, it's likely that rumors of his alternate site power breakout were, indeed, greatly exaggerated. Freeman's narrow frame suggests one should hedge any bets on him developing power. If he did, however, it would be neither the first* nor the second** time a contemporary small-statured middle-infielding contact savant leveraged that same barrel control to generate fringy but consistent pull power with resounding success (*Ramírez and **Jose Altuve come to mind). His glove doesn't play quite like fellow top prospect Brayan Rocchio's, which could slide Freeman from shortstop to the keystone—and that's satisfactory, if not optimal, given Rocchio's defensive strength and similar timeline. The two could be turning double plays in Cleveland well into the latter half of the decade.

Andrés Giménez MI

Born: 09/04/98 Age: 23 Bats: L Throws: R Height: 5'11" Weight: 161 lb. Origin: International Free Agent, 2015

YEAR	TEAM	LVL	AGE	PA	R	2B	3B	HR	RBI	BB	K	SB	CS	Whiff%	AVG/OBP/SLG	DRC+	BABIP	BRR	FRAA	WARP
2019	SCO	WIN	20	75	11	5	2	2	15	4	15	2	0		.371/.413/.586		.453			
2019	BNG	AA	20	479	54	22	5	9	37	24	102	28	16		.250/.309/.387	99	.306	-2.2	SS(112): 2.3	1.6
2020	NYM	MLB	21	132	22	3	2	3	12	7	28	8	1	25.7%	.263/.333/.398	91	.318	1.7	SS(23): -3.8, 2B(19): 0.2, 3B(10): 0.3	0.1
2021	COL	AAA	22	233	30	13	1	10	31	12	55	8	4		.287/.342/.502	107	.345	-2.8	SS(32): -0.2, 2B(17): -1.6	0.5
2021	CLE	MLB	22	210	23	10	0	5	16	11	54	11	0	30.5%	.218/.282/.351	77	.273	2.0	SS(42): 5.6, 2B(25): 0.8	1.0
2022 DC	*CLE*	*MLB*	*23*	*433*	*54*	*19*	*3*	*10*	*58*	*23*	*109*	*17*	*7*	*28.8%*	*.236/.302/.381*	*83*	*.302*	*1.7*	*2B 1, SS 0*	*0.9*

Comparables: Ketel Marte, Francisco Lindor, Jorge Polanco

Giménez's rapid boom and bust are instructive of how launch angle can deceptively make or break a hitter with scant natural power. From 2020 to 2021, nothing about Giménez's contact quality really changed—he merely bundled together some optimal launch angles in the former season and failed to do so in the latter. His minor-league track record suggests that, if given another extended look, he'll produce more closely to his debut when he swung a league-average bat. A weird wrinkle, though: landing in Triple-A after being shipped from New York to Cleveland in the Francisco Lindor/Carlos Carrasco trade, Giménez sold out his decent hit tool for uncharacteristic power. If there's an approach/swing change at play, it may be more causation than correlation that he struggled mightily in his debut with his new team. It remains to be seen how the Guardians will utilize Giménez in 2022 and beyond, although it helps his outlook that the roster has largely been stripped to studs. Whether or not he tries to hit for power that he might not have ultimately will shape his professional trajectory.

Austin Hedges C

Born: 08/18/92 Age: 29 Bats: R Throws: R Height: 6'1" Weight: 223 lb. Origin: Round 2, 2011 Draft (#82 overall)

YEAR	TEAM	LVL	AGE	PA	R	2B	3B	HR	RBI	BB	K	SB	CS	Whiff%	AVG/OBP/SLG	DRC+	BABIP	BRR	FRAA	WARP
2019	SD	MLB	26	347	28	9	0	11	36	27	109	1	0	33.7%	.176/.252/.311	67	.228	0.4	C(95): 31.2, 3B(2): -0.0	3.1
2020	SD	MLB	27	71	7	1	0	3	6	6	18	1	1	21.4%	.158/.258/.333	91	.162	-0.3	C(28): -0.8	0.1
2020	CLE	MLB	27	12	0	0	0	0	0	0	5	0	0	40.9%	.083/.083/.083	91	.143		C(6): 0.6	0.1
2021	CLE	MLB	28	312	32	7	0	10	31	15	87	1	0	29.8%	.178/.220/.308	69	.214	1.6	C(87): 8.6	1.1
2022 DC	*CLE*	*MLB*	*29*	*378*	*42*	*13*	*0*	*12*	*44*	*24*	*101*	*2*	*1*	*29.3%*	*.206/.265/.355*	*61*	*.253*	*-0.3*	*C 21*	*2.0*

Comparables: Gary Sánchez, John Ryan Murphy, Christian Vázquez

YEAR	TEAM	P. COUNT	FRM RUNS	BLK RUNS	THRW RUNS	TOT RUNS
2019	SD	13488	30.6	0.0	-0.2	30.4
2020	CLE	585	0.7	0.0	0.0	0.7
2020	SD	2971	-1.4	0.0	0.1	-1.3
2021	CLE	12266	8.0	0.9	0.4	9.3
2022	*CLE*	*14430*	*16.3*	*0.9*	*-0.2*	*17.0*

What Hedges lacks with his bat he makes up for in spades with his glove. Back in 2019 he owned baseball's best pop time (per Statcast) and towered over the competition when it came to framing (per BP's framing metrics). The problem is that the balance between his glove and bat didn't hold in 2021, as his glove was merely good while his bat remained putrid. Cleveland has long been willing to sacrifice offense for defensive excellence among its backstops, but without a change in trajectory for either, Hedges could find himself trimmed from the roster.

Nolan Jones 3B/RF Born: 05/07/98 Age: 24 Bats: L Throws: R Height: 6'4" Weight: 195 lb. Origin: Round 2, 2016 Draft (#55 overall)

YEAR	TEAM	LVL	AGE	PA	R	2B	3B	HR	RBI	BB	K	SB	CS	Whiff%	AVG/OBP/SLG	DRC+	BABIP	BRR	FRAA	WARP
2019	MSS	WIN	21	68	8	2	0	4	8	8	31	1	0		.200/.294/.433		.320			
2019	LYN	A+	21	324	48	12	1	7	41	65	85	5	3		.286/.435/.425	134	.399	-1.4	3B(72): -3.3	1.7
2019	AKR	AA	21	211	33	10	2	8	22	31	63	2	0		.253/.370/.466	112	.346	1.1	3B(44): 1.1	1.1
2021	COL	AAA	23	407	60	25	1	13	48	59	122	10	2		.238/.356/.431	99	.327	3.8	3B(67): 2.4, RF(25): 1.0, 1B(1): -0.1	1.8
2022 DC	*CLE*	*MLB*	*24*	*305*	*41*	*14*	*1*	*8*	*33*	*35*	*100*	*0*	*1*	*31.9%*	*.222/.319/.378*	*89*	*.322*	*-0.3*	*RF 0, 3B 0*	*0.3*

Comparables: Jeimer Candelario, Brandon Drury, Marwin Gonzalez

Jones is a suitable case study for whether it's more appropriate to call a hitter "patient" or "passive." Patience implies control at the plate—that he'll take a few extra balls and strikes (and, thus, a few extra walks and strikeouts) to get to the pitches he wants to see and, accordingly, mash. Passivity implies a willingness to take a few extra balls and strikes... full stop. Jones doesn't really mash, at least not in the way his alleged plus-plus power would imply. That's not ideal for a hitter who had his name penciled into the unofficial Three True Outcomes Hall of Fame upon his pro ball inception. Not that he hasn't produced—Jones' healthy doses of walks and line drives carried him through the minors. They've failed to buoy him in roughly 150 games spent in the upper minors, though, and it's unwise to assume this issue suddenly resolves itself in Cleveland (although the Guardians may bet on it anyway). Prospect growth is rarely linear, which is great news for Jones: there's time yet for that launch angle to steepen, for that 20-homer power to blossom. Otherwise, Jones may be relegated to Two True Outcomes, One Approximate Outcome Purgatory.

Steven Kwan OF Born: 09/05/97 Age: 24 Bats: L Throws: L Height: 5'9" Weight: 170 lb. Origin: Round 5, 2018 Draft (#163 overall)

YEAR	TEAM	LVL	AGE	PA	R	2B	3B	HR	RBI	BB	K	SB	CS	Whiff%	AVG/OBP/SLG	DRC+	BABIP	BRR	FRAA	WARP
2019	LYN	A+	21	542	68	26	7	3	39	53	51	11	7		.280/.353/.382	118	.305	-2.2	CF(91): 3.7, LF(16): 0.4	3.1
2021	AKR	AA	23	221	42	12	3	7	31	22	23	4	2		.337/.411/.539	135	.354	1.8	CF(24): -1.8, LF(12): 1.7, RF(11): 0.5	1.9
2021	COL	AAA	23	120	23	3	1	5	13	14	8	2	0		.311/.398/.505	137	.300	1.6	CF(21): 2.6, LF(3): -1.2	1.2
2022 DC	*CLE*	*MLB*	*24*	*234*	*30*	*10*	*2*	*3*	*28*	*19*	*21*	*2*	*1*	*10.7%*	*.269/.337/.392*	*99*	*.285*	*0.1*	*LF 2, CF 0*	*1.0*

Comparables: Ezequiel Carrera, Starling Marte, Cedric Mullins

Stop me if you've heard this one before. Kwan... is a Cleveland farmhand... who possesses spectacular contact skills. *He's old for his level*, the haters will say, as Kwan reached Triple-A , *finally*, at the ripe old age of 23. One begins to wonder how much being old for his level—and only slightly too old, to be clear—matters when the subject has collected more walks than strikeouts in 200-plus minor-league games. In fact, last year Kwan compiled a top-five offensive season in the high minors (a campaign that, for the allegedly power-starved Kwan, featured 12 home runs and a .199 ISO in 68 games) regardless of age. Write him off as organizational depth, a down-ballot fringe prospect, but do so at your own risk. There's "surprise breakout" potential here with the kind of floor to serve as high-end bench/injury depth.

Bryan Lavastida C/DH Born: 11/27/98 Age: 23 Bats: R Throws: R Height: 6'0" Weight: 200 lb. Origin: Round 15, 2018 Draft (#463 overall)

YEAR	TEAM	LVL	AGE	PA	R	2B	3B	HR	RBI	BB	K	SB	CS	Whiff%	AVG/OBP/SLG	DRC+	BABIP	BRR	FRAA	WARP
2019	MV	SS	20	240	39	19	3	2	38	25	27	3	3		.335/.408/.483		.372			
2021	LC	A+	22	198	32	12	0	5	31	26	30	14	5		.303/.399/.467	124	.336	-0.1	C(38): 11.2	2.2
2021	AKR	AA	22	119	16	7	1	3	17	12	28	2	3		.291/.373/.466	105	.370	0.6	C(15): 0.2	0.5
2022 DC	*CLE*	*MLB*	*23*	*235*	*27*	*10*	*0*	*3*	*22*	*20*	*61*	*4*	*3*	*31.1%*	*.226/.303/.334*	*75*	*.303*	*0.2*	*C 1*	*0.5*

Comparables: Danny Jansen, Devin Mesoraco, Francisco Cervelli

YEAR	TEAM	P. COUNT	FRM RUNS	BLK RUNS	THRW RUNS	TOT RUNS
2019	MV	5169		-0.7	0.0	-0.7
2021	AKR	1984	0.2	0.2	0.0	0.4
2021	LC	5047	10.3	0.6	0.5	11.4
2022	*CLE*	*8418*	*-0.8*	*0.1*	*0.0*	*-0.7*

A shortstop-to-catcher convert, Lavastida is predictably rough around the edges behind the plate but carries a modern middle infielder's stick, making frequent and loud contact. The bat will play at a premium position, and he advanced quickly last year, reaching Triple-A, where he'll likely spend much or all of 2022. Bo Naylor boasts a higher ceiling and has received more fanfare, but Lavastida might carry the higher floor and debut well in advance of his counterpart.

Sandy León C Born: 03/13/89 Age: 33 Bats: S Throws: R Height: 5'10" Weight: 235 lb. Origin: International Free Agent, 2007

YEAR	TEAM	LVL	AGE	PA	R	2B	3B	HR	RBI	BB	K	SB	CS	Whiff%	AVG/OBP/SLG	DRC+	BABIP	BRR	FRAA	WARP
2019	PAW	AAA	30	26	2	0	0	0	0	1	6	0	1		.120/.154/.120	98	.158	-0.4	C(7): 1.1	0.2
2019	BOS	MLB	30	191	14	3	0	5	19	13	47	0	0	20.4%	.192/.251/.297	77	.231	-0.1	C(65): 5.4, 1B(1): -0.0	0.8
2020	CLE	MLB	31	81	4	1	0	2	4	14	21	0	0	30.6%	.136/.296/.242	93	.163	-1.1	C(24): 2.2	0.3
2021	MIA	MLB	32	220	15	5	0	4	14	12	65	0	0	27.1%	.183/.237/.267	63	.244	-1.6	C(60): 0.6, P(6): 0.1, 3B(1): -0.0	-0.2
2022 non-DC	*CLE*	*MLB*	*33*	*251*	*22*	*8*	*0*	*5*	*23*	*19*	*70*	*0*	*0*	*26.1%*	*.199/.270/.316*	*56*	*.260*	*-0.4*	*C 2, 1B 0*	*-0.1*

Comparables: Jesús Sucre, Martín Maldonado, Roberto Pérez

YEAR	TEAM	P. COUNT	FRM RUNS	BLK RUNS	THRW RUNS	TOT RUNS
2019	BOS	8122	5.5	0.0	0.5	6.0
2020	CLE	3027	0.9	0.0	0.3	1.2
2021	MIA	6933	0.0	0.1	0.1	0.1
2022	*CLE*	*6956*	*2.5*	*-0.2*	*0.1*	*2.3*

It's not a good sign when León's best performance came at a different position than the one he was hired for. León knocked just nine extra-base hits this season, but he saved the Marlins' relievers by making six pitching appearances—three of them scoreless frames. He's long been one of the best defensive catchers in the game, easily allowing teams to overlook his Mendozian batting average, but he graded out with negative framing runs in '21 for the first time in five seasons. Jeff Mathis even made it into three games this season at the age of 38 though, so there's nothing saying that León can't do the same. Until the robot ump uprising, veteran catchers who know how to call a game and steal a few strikes here or there are actually worth far more than their weight in gold. In the meantime, we'll have to worry about whether it'd be more useful to show his pitching stats up there.

Angel Martinez IF

Born: 01/27/02 Age: 20 Bats: S Throws: R Height: 6'0" Weight: 165 lb. Origin: International Free Agent, 2018

YEAR	TEAM	LVL	AGE	PA	R	2B	3B	HR	RBI	BB	K	SB	CS	Whiff%	AVG/OBP/SLG	DRC+	BABIP	BRR	FRAA	WARP
2019	DSL IND	ROK	17	261	37	10	7	1	27	29	29	11	5		.306/.402/.428		.347			
2021	LYN	A	19	424	62	20	6	7	46	43	88	13	6		.241/.319/.382	101	.296	-1.3	2B(49): 3.9, SS(32): -0.3, 3B(13): -0.3	1.5
2022 non-DC	*CLE*	*MLB*	*20*	*251*	*19*	*10*	*2*	*2*	*20*	*17*	*62*	*5*	*3*	*27.7%*	*.216/.273/.316*	*59*	*.284*	*0.6*	*2B 2, SS 0*	*-0.3*

Comparables: Dilson Herrera, Yolmer Sánchez, Jorge Polanco

The switch-hitting Martinez was and still is expected to let his advanced hit tool from both sides of the plate carry him up the minor-league ladder. That he tapped into some higher power as a 19-year-old during his baptism to full-season ball at Lynchburg bodes well for his, er, prospects as a prospect. His scorching hot spring was succeeded by an abysmal summer during which his compact swing had a devil of a time. It testifies less to Martinez's skill than it does to the natural ebb and flow of player performance and the challenges of evaluating small samples. For two months he looked the part of a newly anointed top prospect; for three months after he looked lost. He is young, polished and multi-tooled, and he could stick at shortstop—for now, that is bounty enough.

Oscar Mercado OF

Born: 12/16/94 Age: 27 Bats: R Throws: R Height: 6'2" Weight: 197 lb. Origin: Round 2, 2013 Draft (#57 overall)

YEAR	TEAM	LVL	AGE	PA	R	2B	3B	HR	RBI	BB	K	SB	CS	Whiff%	AVG/OBP/SLG	DRC+	BABIP	BRR	FRAA	WARP
2019	COL	AAA	24	140	24	10	1	4	15	16	32	14	3		.294/.396/.496	106	.373	1.5	CF(19): 6.2, LF(5): 1.1, RF(4): 0.2	1.4
2019	CLE	MLB	24	482	70	25	3	15	54	28	84	15	4	23.4%	.269/.318/.443	95	.300	2.2	CF(82): 8.5, LF(24): -1.7, RF(9): -1.1	2.4
2020	CLE	MLB	25	93	6	1	0	1	6	5	27	3	0	29.8%	.128/.174/.174	72	.169	1.1	CF(21): 3.8, LF(12): -0.2	0.4
2021	COL	AAA	26	203	29	13	1	5	23	23	32	9	1		.216/.327/.392	112	.235	3.3	CF(24): -1.7, LF(16): 3.2, RF(3): -0.0	1.4
2021	CLE	MLB	26	238	27	11	1	6	19	21	42	7	1	27.0%	.224/.300/.369	97	.253	1.7	LF(45): 0.1, RF(20): 0.7, CF(7): 0.3	1.1
2022 DC	*CLE*	*MLB*	*27*	*285*	*34*	*13*	*1*	*6*	*39*	*22*	*57*	*12*	*4*	*25.8%*	*.235/.306/.368*	*82*	*.281*	*0.9*	*LF 1, CF 0*	*0.5*

Comparables: Danny Santana, Aaron Hicks, Ezequiel Carrera

Mercado's 2019 breakout feels like a lifetime ago. We never should have expected him to hit for 20-homer power, but the prospect of continued double-digit power-speed seasons with a decent average—thanks to a fairly aggressive plate approach coupled with good-not-great contact skills—was enchanting enough. The fact of the matter is Mercado's contact quality was and still is ghastly, damning him to the outskirts of the dreaded territory belonging to one-trick-pony speedsters—and, to date, he hasn't run enough to make his lack of batted ball authority palatable. The Guardians are flush with uninspiring outfielders, and even then Mercado found himself routinely relegated to pinch-hitting or -running duties. That says all you need to know about Cleveland's confidence in him. But the utter lack of inspiring options also provides Mercado just enough daylight to once more make a case of himself. If he can't, it will once again prove the lack of viability in free Mercado solutions.

Owen Miller IF

Born: 11/15/96 Age: 25 Bats: R Throws: R Height: 6'0" Weight: 185 lb. Origin: Round 3, 2018 Draft (#84 overall)

YEAR	TEAM	LVL	AGE	PA	R	2B	3B	HR	RBI	BB	K	SB	CS	Whiff%	AVG/OBP/SLG	DRC+	BABIP	BRR	FRAA	WARP
2019	PEJ	WIN	22	72	7	1	0	1	7	2	15	1	0		.176/.194/.235		.204			
2019	AMA	AA	22	560	76	28	2	13	68	46	86	5	5		.290/.355/.430	113	.328	1.1	SS(71): 5.2, 2B(48): 0.8, 3B(6): -0.2	3.6
2021	COL	AAA	24	206	25	12	1	7	22	21	52	0	0		.297/.374/.489	102	.379	0.4	2B(23): 2.5, 1B(8): -0.4, 3B(8): -1.1	0.7
2021	CLE	MLB	24	202	17	8	0	4	18	9	54	2	0	26.1%	.204/.243/.309	74	.261	-0.9	2B(29): -0.5, 1B(18): -1.4, 3B(7): -1.4	-0.5
2022 DC	*CLE*	*MLB*	*25*	*195*	*21*	*9*	*0*	*3*	*22*	*12*	*46*	*0*	*1*	*25.6%*	*.235/.293/.361*	*74*	*.298*	*-0.2*	*2B 0, 1B -1*	*-0.2*

Comparables: Chris Taylor, Jedd Gyorko, Erik González

It makes sense Cleveland would have desired Miller as a part of the return in the Mike Clevinger trade given his propensity to frequently make contact and get on base. It's alarming, then, that Miller's strikeout percentage ballooned so dramatically at Triple-A and carried forward into his big-league debut. The collapsed plate discipline coincides with more power and a shallower launch angle, which, in a vacuum, are not bad things. But this seems like developmental backpedaling in light of Miller's profile, which has quickly morphed from high-floor/low-ceiling into something resembling the opposite.

Josh Naylor RF

Born: 06/22/97 Age: 25 Bats: L Throws: L Height: 5'11" Weight: 250 lb. Origin: Round 1, 2015 Draft (#12 overall)

YEAR	TEAM	LVL	AGE	PA	R	2B	3B	HR	RBI	BB	K	SB	CS	Whiff%	AVG/OBP/SLG	DRC+	BABIP	BRR	FRAA	WARP
2019	ESC	WIN	22	83	6	1	0	1	10	5	11	5	1		.250/.305/.303		.281			
2019	ELP	AAA	22	252	51	20	1	10	42	28	30	1	0		.314/.389/.547	118	.326	-0.6	RF(29): -2.0, LF(22): 0.7	1.2
2019	SD	MLB	22	279	29	15	0	8	32	25	64	1	1	22.2%	.249/.315/.403	85	.302	0.2	LF(33): 0.7, RF(31): -4.5	0.0
2020	SD	MLB	23	38	4	0	1	1	4	1	4	1	0	18.6%	.278/.316/.417	100	.290	0.5	RF(4): -0.5, 1B(3): 0.2, LF(3): 0.0	0.1
2020	CLE	MLB	23	66	9	3	0	0	2	4	8	0	0	13.9%	.230/.277/.279	91	.264	0.8	LF(19): -1.2, 1B(2): -0.0	0.1
2021	CLE	MLB	24	250	28	13	0	7	21	14	45	1	0	21.3%	.253/.301/.399	95	.287	-1.1	RF(51): 1.7, 1B(15): 1.6	0.7
2022 DC	*CLE*	*MLB*	*25*	*325*	*40*	*15*	*0*	*9*	*43*	*24*	*55*	*1*	*1*	*20.4%*	*.259/.320/.408*	*97*	*.292*	*-0.3*	*RF -2*	*0.5*

Comparables: Jesse Winker, Logan Morrison, Matt Olson

Prior to his promotion to San Diego, Naylor's penultimate and ultimate minor-league campaigns showcased a coveted triforce of power, contact and discipline. These things rarely translate one-for-one; sometimes, they don't translate at all. Naylor has shown glimpses of all three, but through his first 200-plus major-league games, they have failed to synthesize in a way that confidently dispels the shadows cast by a looming "Quad-A" designation. Whereas many of Cleveland's former prospects are carried by the prospect of future projection over their current production, Naylor strung together impressive high-floor seasons as a fringe prospect, which is enough to continue holding out hope for it all to come together for him soon.

José Ramírez 3B Born: 09/17/92 Age: 29 Bats: S Throws: R Height: 5'9" Weight: 190 lb. Origin: International Free Agent, 2009

YEAR	TEAM	LVL	AGE	PA	R	2B	3B	HR	RBI	BB	K	SB	CS	Whiff%	AVG/OBP/SLG	DRC+	BABIP	BRR	FRAA	WARP
2019	CLE	MLB	26	542	68	33	3	23	83	52	74	24	4	14.2%	.255/.327/.479	113	.256	2.6	3B(126): 2.3	2.8
2020	CLE	MLB	27	254	45	16	1	17	46	31	43	10	3	16.6%	.292/.386/.607	146	.294	0.0	3B(57): -9.6	1.1
2021	CLE	MLB	28	636	111	32	5	36	103	72	87	27	4	15.0%	.266/.355/.538	135	.256	4.1	3B(133): -4.1	4.9
2022 DC	*CLE*	*MLB*	*29*	*652*	*116*	*34*	*3*	*29*	*92*	*76*	*84*	*26*	*6*	*14.9%*	*.265/.358/.493*	*127*	*.267*	*1.7*	*3B -3*	*4.1*

Comparables: Adrián Beltré, George Brett, Aramis Ramirez

From being a Mario Kart maven to losing his helmet at an improbable frequency, Ramírez's idiosyncrasies are well-documented. Less appreciated is his path to success. Signed for pennies out of the Dominican Republic with a body like a little bag of flour (thank you, Carson Cistulli), no one—literally no one but possibly Ramírez himself, and maybe not even Ramírez, either—could've anticipated his transformation from utility player to perennial MVP candidate. He always had elite bat-to-ball skills; he paced every minor-league stop in contact rate while young for each level. But bat-to-ball skills are not always inclusive of barrel control, the former of which translates to pretty batting averages but sometimes nothing more, the latter for which Ramírez will one day be a case study. He leveraged said barrel control to start pulling the ball in the air, seamlessly generating power despite his size and without sacrificing contact the way other hitters must. He's an elite hitter, yes, but—and this detail is perhaps most underappreciated—Ramírez is, without exaggeration, peerless in his elite production from both sides of the plate. Two more team-friendly club options means two more years for Ramírez to cement his name as an all-time Cleveland great—that is, if his "inception chain" (a chain with a pendant of himself holding that same chain) hasn't done so already.

Franmil Reyes DH Born: 07/07/95 Age: 27 Bats: R Throws: R Height: 6'5" Weight: 265 lb. Origin: International Free Agent, 2012

YEAR	TEAM	LVL	AGE	PA	R	2B	3B	HR	RBI	BB	K	SB	CS	Whiff%	AVG/OBP/SLG	DRC+	BABIP	BRR	FRAA	WARP
2019	SD	MLB	23	354	43	9	0	27	46	29	93	0	0	34.8%	.255/.314/.536	122	.268	0.4	RF(83): 1.6	2.2
2019	CLE	MLB	23	194	26	10	0	10	35	18	63	0	0	39.7%	.237/.304/.468	83	.301	-0.4	RF(3): 0.5	0.1
2020	CLE	MLB	24	241	27	10	0	9	34	24	69	0	0	38.5%	.275/.344/.450	102	.355	-1.5	LF(1): -0.2	0.5
2021	CLE	MLB	25	466	57	18	2	30	85	43	149	4	1	33.7%	.254/.324/.522	111	.314	-1.6	RF(11): -0.1	1.6
2022 DC	*CLE*	*MLB*	*26*	*623*	*94*	*25*	*1*	*33*	*103*	*57*	*180*	*1*	*1*	*34.2%*	*.241/.316/.467*	*104*	*.295*	*-0.9*	*RF 0*	*1.7*

Comparables: Avisaíl García, Randal Grichuk, Domingo Santana

Reyes showed off his characteristically gargantuan 40-homer power, which came and will always come at the expense of horrid contact skills—although, to Reyes' credit, they improved marginally last year. If the ideal designated hitter maximizes his offensive value while circumventing whatever detriment he might be on defense, then Reyes fills that role admirably enough. Among the six hitters who accrued at least 400 plate appearances as a DH, Reyes was the worst of them, which attests partly to Reyes' talent (he ain't no Shohei Ohtani nor Giancarlo Stanton) as well as to the inflexibility of Cleveland's big-league lineup. But, per DRC+, Reyes was a top-65 bat, and the Guardians deftly minimized his appearances in right field, so let's chalk it up as a "W."

★ ★ ★ *2022 Top 101 Prospect* **#47** ★ ★ ★

Brayan Rocchio SS Born: 01/13/01 Age: 21 Bats: S Throws: R Height: 5'10" Weight: 170 lb. Origin: International Free Agent, 2017

YEAR	TEAM	LVL	AGE	PA	R	2B	3B	HR	RBI	BB	K	SB	CS	Whiff%	AVG/OBP/SLG	DRC+	BABIP	BRR	FRAA	WARP
2019	MV	SS	18	295	33	12	3	5	27	20	40	14	8		.250/.310/.373		.276			
2021	LAG	WIN	20	76	11	6	1	2	6	5	5	2	2		.391/.440/.594		.403			
2021	LC	A+	20	288	45	13	1	9	33	20	65	14	6		.265/.337/.428	108	.319	1.0	SS(36): -1.4, 2B(16): 2.2, 3B(12): 0.3	1.3
2021	AKR	AA	20	203	34	13	4	6	30	13	41	7	4		.293/.360/.505	112	.350	-1.1	SS(43): 1.5, 2B(2): 0.2	1.0
2022 non-DC	*CLE*	*MLB*	*21*	*251*	*22*	*11*	*1*	*4*	*24*	*14*	*59*	*9*	*5*	*26.0%*	*.240/.295/.361*	*75*	*.305*	*1.0*	*SS 0, 2B 0*	*0.3*

Comparables: Amed Rosario, Addison Russell, Enrique Hernández

If you spend too much time online, you've probably seen the cartoon meme of some kind of ambiguous space cadet who feverishly sweats a decision to push one of two large red buttons bearing a humorous pair of diametrically opposed (and often cataclysmic) outcomes. In this case, Rocchio is the cadet, and the buttons pit Rocchio's heralded contact skills against his newfound power. Last year, Rocchio swiftly tripled his professional home run total, but he paid for it in strikeouts, calling into question the sanctity of his hit tool to his developmental trajectory. Occasionally, the meme features a twist in which the cadet smugly pushes both buttons—the best-of-both-worlds "why not both?" outcome only the cadet was clever enough to consider. If Rocchio's feel from both sides of the plate is everything it's billed to be, he may one day mash both buttons and enjoy the spoils of power and contact in tandem. No matter the number of buttons pushed, Rocchio's future remains bright thanks to his proficiency on both sides of the ball. His defensive acumen is exceptional for any age, but especially his.

Amed Rosario SS Born: 11/20/95 Age: 26 Bats: R Throws: R Height: 6'2" Weight: 190 lb. Origin: International Free Agent, 2012

YEAR	TEAM	LVL	AGE	PA	R	2B	3B	HR	RBI	BB	K	SB	CS	Whiff%	AVG/OBP/SLG	DRC+	BABIP	BRR	FRAA	WARP
2019	NYM	MLB	23	655	75	30	7	15	72	31	124	19	10	24.2%	.287/.323/.432	90	.338	1.8	SS(152): -5.4, LF(1): -0.2	1.1
2020	NYM	MLB	24	147	20	3	1	4	15	4	34	0	1	24.3%	.252/.272/.371	85	.305	0.1	SS(44): -6.0	-0.4
2021	CLE	MLB	25	588	77	25	6	11	57	31	120	13	0	24.9%	.282/.321/.409	93	.340	1.0	SS(121): -1.5, CF(18): -1.1	1.4
2022 DC	*CLE*	*MLB*	*26*	*577*	*77*	*24*	*5*	*11*	*70*	*30*	*110*	*17*	*6*	*24.5%*	*.270/.314/.400*	*92*	*.320*	*1.6*	*SS -2*	*1.6*

Comparables: Alan Trammell, Derek Jeter, Robin Yount

On May 2, Rosario stole a base—an entirely mundane event, until you realize Rosario, whose primary calling card arguably is his speed, hadn't stolen a base (and made just one failed attempt) in 584 calendar days. Five-hundred eighty-four days! A lot can happen in 584 days. A pandemic can happen! And a team in Cleveland can dismantle the remainder of its core to ship to New York in exchange for Rosario and his friends. The Guardians bought low; Rosario was especially bad in 2020, tossing a wet blanket on the embers of his long-awaited breakout in 2019. But, finally, Rosario stole a base, and for five months after, Rosario resembled his breakout self, pairing double-digit power and speed with a fairly robust slash line. That leap of faith, for a month and a day, looked ill-advised. But there's a reason why the MLB season lasts six months and not a month and a day. A rejuvenated Rosario still holds a shred of the promise of his top-prospect pedigree but at the very least he can be an above-average everyday lineup fixture—as long as he doesn't suffer another extended bout of baserunning amnesia.

Myles Straw CF

Born: 10/17/94 Age: 27 Bats: R Throws: R Height: 5'10" Weight: 178 lb. Origin: Round 12, 2015 Draft (#349 overall)

YEAR	TEAM	LVL	AGE	PA	R	2B	3B	HR	RBI	BB	K	SB	CS	Whiff%	AVG/OBP/SLG	DRC+	BABIP	BRR	FRAA	WARP
2019	RR	AAA	24	313	46	11	3	1	33	32	50	19	4		.321/.391/.394	94	.386	2.1	CF(31): 4.3, SS(30): -1.4, 2B(5): -0.4	1.4
2019	HOU	MLB	24	128	27	4	2	0	7	19	24	8	1	12.4%	.269/.378/.343	92	.345	3.5	SS(26): 1.5, CF(11): -0.8, LF(8): 0.3	0.8
2020	HOU	MLB	25	86	8	4	0	0	8	4	22	6	2	19.7%	.207/.244/.256	76	.283	-0.3	CF(27): -3.2, SS(1): -0.0	-0.3
2021	CLE	MLB	26	268	42	16	0	2	14	29	50	13	1	13.9%	.285/.362/.377	100	.353	2.5	CF(60): 0.8	1.5
2021	HOU	MLB	26	370	44	13	1	2	34	38	71	17	5	13.4%	.262/.339/.326	93	.324	-3.3	CF(96): 7.2	1.6
2022 DC	*CLE*	*MLB*	*27*	*534*	*69*	*21*	*2*	*4*	*48*	*53*	*95*	*27*	*6*	*14.0%*	*.260/.338/.342*	*88*	*.317*	*1.7*	*CF 2*	*1.5*

Comparables: Kevin Kiermaier, Andrew Stevenson, Juan Lagares

The Guardians traded for Straw at last year's trade deadline, critically filling the team's need of "someone, literally anyone, who can play outfield." This undersells the contributions of Straw, who not only plays a very capable center field but also neatly fits the mold of Cleveland's ideal hitter prospect, as if he were separated from the team at draft. His contact skills and his speed grade out elite, although the latter has begun to wane as our subject enters his age-27 season. Straw's combination of skills elevates him above his one-trick pony speed-first colleagues. That is, he's a two-trick pony, if you will, for whom highly frequent contact compensates for an absolute dearth of batted ball authority. It affords him a league-average slash line rather than to merely tread water. The entire package ain't dazzling—25-30 steals, a .260 average, identical on-base and slugging percentages—but it does culminate in an average, if possibly above-average, player who has yet to reach arbitration.

Jose Tena MI

Born: 03/20/01 Age: 21 Bats: L Throws: R Height: 5'10" Weight: 160 lb. Origin: International Free Agent, 2017

YEAR	TEAM	LVL	AGE	PA	R	2B	3B	HR	RBI	BB	K	SB	CS	Whiff%	AVG/OBP/SLG	DRC+	BABIP	BRR	FRAA	WARP
2019	INDB	ROK	18	199	30	7	6	1	18	6	44	6	2		.325/.352/.440		.418			
2021	SCO	WIN	20	75	16	6	1	0	9	10	10	2	1		.387/.467/.516		.444			
2021	LC	A+	20	447	58	25	2	16	58	27	117	10	5		.281/.331/.467	102	.355	1.6	SS(81): -7.3, 3B(13): 0.3, 2B(11): 1.0	1.0
2022 non-DC	*CLE*	*MLB*	*21*	*251*	*21*	*11*	*1*	*4*	*23*	*13*	*75*	*4*	*3*	*32.7%*	*.231/.278/.347*	*65*	*.320*	*0.3*	*SS -2, 3B 0*	*-0.4*

Comparables: Jorge Polanco, Richard Ureña, Luis Sardinas

Tena bulked up during the lost pandemic season and spent 2021 attempting (and succeeding) to punish everything he saw. Tena's plate discipline is anything but; it undercuts tremendous plate coverage and an ability to spit on anything fed to him. (We suppose if we could swing it like Tena does, we'd be up there hacking, too.) It's quite fitting that Tena is the (much smaller) nephew of notable free-swinging power-hitting utility man Juan Uribe, who made a career of embracing tumult, and Tena could do the same while also playing a premium defensive position. Eventually, a day of judgment will determine if Tena is Uncle Juan's rightful heir or if his approach is simply, ahem, *untenable*. Until then, Tena's stock points up.

★ ★ ★ *2022 Top 101 Prospect* **#33** ★ ★ ★

George Valera OF

Born: 11/13/00 Age: 21 Bats: L Throws: L Height: 5'11" Weight: 185 lb. Origin: International Free Agent, 2017

YEAR	TEAM	LVL	AGE	PA	R	2B	3B	HR	RBI	BB	K	SB	CS	Whiff%	AVG/OBP/SLG	DRC+	BABIP	BRR	FRAA	WARP
2019	MV	SS	18	188	22	7	1	8	29	29	52	6	2		.236/.356/.446		.296			
2019	LC	A	18	26	1	0	1	0	3	2	9	0	2		.087/.192/.174	76	.143	-1.1	RF(3): 1.2, LF(2): 1.6	0.2
2021	LC	A+	20	263	45	2	4	16	43	55	58	10	5		.256/.430/.548	157	.276	0.4	RF(38): 3.1, CF(12): -0.8, LF(9): -0.5	2.8
2021	AKR	AA	20	100	6	3	0	3	22	11	30	1	0		.267/.340/.407	93	.357	-0.4	RF(10): 3.5, LF(8): 0.6, CF(4): -0.4	0.6
2022 non-DC	*CLE*	*MLB*	*21*	*251*	*25*	*8*	*1*	*6*	*25*	*29*	*71*	*4*	*3*	*31.1%*	*.211/.315/.353*	*83*	*.283*	*0.5*	*RF 1, CF 0*	*0.5*

Comparables: Victor Robles, Manuel Margot, Eloy Jiménez

Holes in his swing followed by a pandemic year inspired rumblings of Valera's development possibly stalling out, seeing as he accrued scarcely any professional reps prior to the layoff. Through that lens, Valera's 2021 campaign was a best-case scenario. He hit for more power *and* more contact against tougher competition while walking in more than 18% of his plate appearances. Or, to put it more concisely: as one of the youngest hitters at his level, Valera compiled *the* best offensive season (by measure of DRC+) in all of High-A. The advancements help quell concerns of a whiff-prone profile that some expected to hamstring Valera's eye-popping power and keep him firmly on track to spend another year mashing higher-level competition while younger than nearly everyone else. It remains to be seen how much of his 2021 inertia that Valera can retain, but he couldn't have done much more to endear himself to doubtful scouts and prospectors.

Bradley Zimmer OF Born: 11/27/92 Age: 29 Bats: L Throws: R Height: 6'4" Weight: 185 lb. Origin: Round 1, 2014 Draft (#21 overall)

YEAR	TEAM	LVL	AGE	PA	R	2B	3B	HR	RBI	BB	K	SB	CS	Whiff%	AVG/OBP/SLG	DRC+	BABIP	BRR	FRAA	WARP
2019	COL	AAA	26	26	5	1	1	1	2	3	6	2	0		.364/.440/.636	100	.467	0.6	CF(6): -0.0	0.1
2019	CLE	MLB	26	14	1	0	0	0	0	1	7	0	0	44.4%	.000/.071/.000	66		0.3	RF(4): -0.5, CF(2): 0.3	0.0
2020	CLE	MLB	27	50	3	0	0	1	3	7	14	2	1	36.6%	.162/.360/.243	96	.217	-1.0	LF(8): -0.7, CF(7): -0.3, RF(7): -0.6	-0.1
2021	COL	AAA	28	75	9	3	0	1	8	10	26	4	2		.267/.413/.367	87	.455	-0.2	RF(7): 2.9, CF(6): 0.2, LF(3): -0.2	0.4
2021	CLE	MLB	28	348	44	9	1	8	35	30	122	15	3	36.6%	.227/.325/.344	70	.347	3.7	CF(54): -0.4, RF(43): -1.6, LF(3): -0.0	0.1
2022 DC	*CLE*	*MLB*	*29*	*293*	*36*	*11*	*1*	*8*	*36*	*26*	*100*	*10*	*3*	*36.0%*	*.208/.305/.359*	*80*	*.305*	*0.8*	*RF 0, LF 0*	*0.2*

Comparables: Brett Gardner, Roger Bernadina, Ezequiel Carrera

No more blaming injuries. Cleveland gifted Zimmer a summer's worth of near-daily reps and watched him flounder. His carrying tools—his speed, his defense, his power—remain intact and elite. If Zimmer houses his suite of elite tools in a beautiful hand-crafted cedar shed, though, his hit tool is a catastrophic wildfire sparked by a botched gender reveal. Zimmer *can* hit the ball hard, but he does so rarely—and when he does, his launch angle is routinely suboptimal, stifling his potential. He remains abysmal against breaking and off-speed stuff, something highlighted both years ago in these annals and mere months ago on MLB.com, suggesting nothing has changed. Nearly half a decade of what-ifs kept us on the hook until now, but greens become reds and golds, and what-ifs become what-nows for the former first-rounder, somehow already entering his age-29 season. Fortunately for Zimmer, the Guardians have time and space to be patient with (and maybe even fix) him. But there's a reason they say you can't teach an old dog new tricks.

PITCHERS

Logan Allen LHP Born: 09/05/98 Age: 23 Bats: R Throws: L Height: 6'0" Weight: 190 lb. Origin: Round 2, 2020 Draft (#56 overall)

YEAR	TEAM	LVL	AGE	W	L	SV	G	GS	IP	H	HR	BB/9	K/9	K	GB%	BABIP	WHIP	ERA	DRA-	WARP	MPH	FB%	Whiff%	CSP
2021	LC	A+	22	5	0	0	9	9	51^1	37	3	2.3	11.7	67	44.1%	.296	0.97	1.58	80	1.1				
2021	AKR	AA	22	4	0	0	12	10	60	40	9	2.0	11.4	76	28.8%	.238	0.88	2.85	96	0.6				
2022 non-DC	*CLE*	*MLB*	*23*	*2*	*2*	*0*	*57*	*0*	*50*	*47*	*8*	*3.2*	*9.6*	*53*	*35.0%*	*.297*	*1.30*	*4.21*	*104*	*0.1*				

Comparables: Brian Matusz, Derek Holland, Matt Moore

Drafted in the second round of the 2020 draft, Allen (the prospect, not the veteran) laid waste in his first taste of pro ball. The 111 innings he spent at High-A and Double-A were among the best compiled at both levels, period, no caveats. He effectively commands a polished three-pitch mix that consists of a low-90s fastball, a top-shelf changeup and a solid curve. He has little left to prove in Akron, so expect him to begin (or spend most of) 2022 at Triple-A, where he'll either be challenged for the first time or kick down the door to the majors in short order. Allen's lesser velo limits his eventual role and ceiling, in theory, but continued dominance will apply serious force against a ceiling that we may come to learn was made of glass. If nothing else, his floor appears comfortably high.

Peyton Battenfield RHP Born: 08/10/97 Age: 24 Bats: R Throws: R Height: 6'4" Weight: 224 lb. Origin: Round 9, 2019 Draft (#286 overall)

YEAR	TEAM	LVL	AGE	W	L	SV	G	GS	IP	H	HR	BB/9	K/9	K	GB%	BABIP	WHIP	ERA	DRA-	WARP	MPH	FB%	Whiff%	CSP
2019	TRI	SS	21	2	1	0	14	5	39^1	23	0	3.4	10.5	46	42.6%	.245	0.97	1.60						
2021	BG	A+	23	2	0	0	7	6	31	18	2	1.5	14.2	49	50.0%	.267	0.74	1.45	69	0.8				
2021	MTG	AA	23	3	0	0	7	6	36^1	24	5	1.7	11.4	46	32.6%	.226	0.85	2.72	95	0.5				
2021	AKR	AA	23	2	1	0	7	7	35^2	24	4	1.8	9.1	36	43.2%	.220	0.87	3.28	94	0.4				
2022 DC	*CLE*	*MLB*	*24*	*1*	*1*	*0*	*29*	*0*	*25.7*	*24*	*3*	*2.7*	*8.9*	*25*	*39.8%*	*.298*	*1.26*	*3.91*	*98*	*0.1*				

Comparables: Stephen Fife, Felipe Paulino, Matt Bowman

Rarely do you want to hear a non-prospect minor-leaguer joined his third team in three years. Traded from Houston to Tampa Bay in the very famous Austin Pruitt trade, then acquired from Tampa Bay in the very, very famous Jordan Luplow trade, Battenfield picked up in Cleveland right where he left off: quietly dominating opposing hitters with low-to-mid-90s heat and a filthy swing-and-miss cutter. He shuffled back and forth from starter to reliever throughout 2019 but settled into a permanent starter's role in 2021 with his new organization. Over the course of the season, he compiled a 2.53 ERA while striking out almost seven times as many hitters as he walked. That eternally GIF'd shot of Jonah Hill fist-pumping silently while on the phone in *Moneyball*? That's the Guardians acquiring yet another quintessentially Clevelandian near-prospect with well-commanded above-average weapons. Love is a Battenfield.

Shane Bieber RHP Born: 05/31/95 Age: 27 Bats: R Throws: R Height: 6'3" Weight: 200 lb. Origin: Round 4, 2016 Draft (#122 overall)

YEAR	TEAM	LVL	AGE	W	L	SV	G	GS	IP	H	HR	BB/9	K/9	K	GB%	BABIP	WHIP	ERA	DRA-	WARP	MPH	FB%	Whiff%	CSP
2019	CLE	MLB	24	15	8	0	34	33	214^1	186	31	1.7	10.9	259	44.4%	.298	1.05	3.28	78	4.7	93.2	45.7%	30.8%	46.6%
2020	CLE	MLB	25	8	1	0	12	12	77^1	46	7	2.4	14.2	122	48.4%	.267	0.87	1.63	51	2.9	94.0	51.6%	40.7%	40.1%
2021	CLE	MLB	26	7	4	0	16	16	96^2	84	11	3.1	12.5	134	44.9%	.327	1.21	3.17	75	2.1	92.9	38.8%	36.5%	56.6%
2022 DC	*CLE*	*MLB*	*27*	*12*	*7*	*0*	*29*	*29*	*174.7*	*132*	*21*	*2.5*	*12.7*	*246*	*46.2%*	*.296*	*1.04*	*2.38*	*64*	*4.8*	*93.3*	*44.0%*	*35.7%*	*49.5%*

Comparables: Roger Clemens, Tom Seaver, Juan Marichal

Bieber succeeded his unanimously anointed Cy Young campaign with an ERA a couple of hairs above 3.00. What else can we really say? Let's pick nits instead. (1) A shoulder strain forced him to miss half the season and incur his first Injured List stint. (2) When healthy, he shied away from his newly added cutter that, like everything else, was unfairly filthy. An odd choice, one that probably did opposing hitters a courtesy by him canning it. (3) Like in 2018 and 2019, he allowed unduly hard contact. An occupational hazard for someone who peppers the zone so relentlessly, although hardly allowing any contact to begin with certainly helps. (4) Most critically, Bieber issued 27 free passes in his first 11 starts—good for some pitchers, bad for Biebs. Three of those four starts featured four walks, something he "achieved" just four times in 65 career starts prior. Bieber devastates hitters with his secondaries, but perhaps he wasted a few too many of them. Worse, perhaps hitters learned to be more patient and/or deciphered sequencing that became too predictable. While not death knells, these picked nits do, however meekly, raise teeny tiny red flags. We can't all be perfect, but Bieber's close.

Joey Cantillo LHP Born: 12/18/99 Age: 22 Bats: L Throws: L Height: 6'4" Weight: 220 lb. Origin: Round 16, 2017 Draft (#468 overall)

YEAR	TEAM	LVL	AGE	W	L	SV	G	GS	IP	H	HR	BB/9	K/9	K	GB%	BABIP	WHIP	ERA	DRA-	WARP	MPH	FB%	Whiff%	CSP
2019	FW	A	19	9	3	0	19	19	98	58	3	2.5	11.8	128	42.7%	.266	0.87	1.93	87	1.4				
2019	LE	A+	19	1	1	0	3	3	13^{2}	12	2	4.6	10.5	16	38.5%	.270	1.39	4.61	120	-0.1				
2021	AKR	AA	21	0	2	0	5	1	8	8	0	11.2	13.5	12	42.1%	.421	2.25	4.50	90	0.1				
2022 non-DC	*CLE*	*MLB*	*22*	*2*	*3*	*0*	*57*	*0*	*50*	*45*	*7*	*5.6*	*10.6*	*58*	*39.6%*	*.307*	*1.54*	*4.95*	*113*	*-0.2*				

Comparables: Michael Fulmer, Alex Reyes, Jake Thompson

Cantillo missed most of 2021 due to an abdominal strain, leaving him with just 13 professional innings since the 2019 season and costing him needed development time and a chance to prove his stuff can survive further up the chain. As such, it's hard to say more than what we already knew: he commands his changeup and spin-efficient high-80s fastball well enough to carve up lower-level hitters, but it remains to be seen how that kind of velocity will play against the upper minors, much less major-league hitters. Cleveland is a perfect landing spot for someone like Cantillo (for any pitching prospect, really), so now we wait to see what, if anything, the Guardians unlock in his arm.

Aaron Civale RHP Born: 06/12/95 Age: 27 Bats: R Throws: R Height: 6'2" Weight: 215 lb. Origin: Round 3, 2016 Draft (#92 overall)

YEAR	TEAM	LVL	AGE	W	L	SV	G	GS	IP	H	HR	BB/9	K/9	K	GB%	BABIP	WHIP	ERA	DRA-	WARP	MPH	FB%	Whiff%	CSP
2019	AKR	AA	24	4	0	0	5	5	30^{1}	26	3	1.8	7.1	24	42.2%	.264	1.05	2.67	111	0.1				
2019	COL	AAA	24	3	1	0	8	8	42^{1}	38	4	1.9	9.8	46	37.8%	.298	1.11	2.13	88	0.8				
2019	CLE	MLB	24	3	4	0	10	10	57^{2}	44	4	2.5	7.2	46	40.9%	.252	1.04	2.34	112	0.2	91.0	67.3%	21.4%	44.3%
2020	CLE	MLB	25	4	6	0	12	12	74	82	11	1.9	8.4	69	45.1%	.333	1.32	4.74	95	1.0	90.3	60.0%	25.0%	47.3%
2021	AKR	AA	26	1	0	0	2	2	7	4	0	3.9	10.3	8	41.2%	.250	1.00	1.29	94	0.1				
2021	CLE	MLB	26	12	5	0	21	21	124^{1}	108	23	2.2	7.2	99	44.2%	.250	1.12	3.84	111	0.4	90.6	57.9%	21.6%	53.3%
2022 DC	*CLE*	*MLB*	*27*	*10*	*8*	*0*	*27*	*27*	*162.3*	*157*	*21*	*2.4*	*7.6*	*136*	*43.6%*	*.289*	*1.24*	*3.72*	*95*	*1.7*	*90.6*	*59.4%*	*22.5%*	*50.8%*

Comparables: Wade Miley, A.J. Griffin, Doug Fister

In 2021, Civale used his six pitches more equitably than ever, supplanting his sinker with his four-seamer and swapping out his changeup for a splitter. He predictably improved upon the drubbing he endured in 2020, but none of these changes seem like anything but lateral moves. He continues to rank in the lower quartile for both whiffs and putaways (converting strikeouts on two-strike counts), and none of his pitches, old or new, make him well-positioned to improve without developmental *deux ex machina*. The one thing Civale has done well is suppress hitter exit velocity, although this phenomenon may be more a function of his pedestrian velocity and less skills-based. Dreaming on his 2019 rookie breakout seems unwise at this point. It's simply average stuff that produces average results—a perfectly cromulent arm.

Emmanuel Clase RHP Born: 03/18/98 Age: 24 Bats: R Throws: R Height: 6'2" Weight: 206 lb. Origin: International Free Agent, 2015

YEAR	TEAM	LVL	AGE	W	L	SV	G	GS	IP	H	HR	BB/9	K/9	K	GB%	BABIP	WHIP	ERA	DRA-	WARP	MPH	FB%	Whiff%	CSP
2019	DE	A+	21	2	0	1	6	0	7	4	0	1.3	14.1	11	76.9%	.308	0.71	0.00	85	0.1				
2019	FRI	AA	21	1	2	11	33	1	37^{2}	34	1	1.9	9.3	39	61.3%	.317	1.12	3.35	90	0.3				
2019	TEX	MLB	21	2	3	1	21	1	23^{1}	20	2	2.3	8.1	21	59.1%	.281	1.11	2.31	91	0.4	99.4	78.8%	25.6%	49.3%
2021	CLE	MLB	23	4	5	24	71	0	69^{2}	51	2	2.1	9.6	74	67.7%	.263	0.96	1.29	76	1.5	100.5	70.2%	33.0%	53.5%
2022 DC	*CLE*	*MLB*	*24*	*3*	*3*	*35*	*74*	*0*	*64.7*	*58*	*4*	*2.6*	*9.4*	*67*	*62.1%*	*.307*	*1.20*	*2.84*	*76*	*1.1*	*100.4*	*71.0%*	*32.3%*	*53.1%*

Comparables: Yhency Brazoban, Jensen Lewis, Danys Baez

A tumultuous couple of years that cast black clouds over him—being traded for Corey Kluber, missing all of 2020 because of a failed PED test—culminated in Clase seizing Cleveland's closer role outright. Clase wields baseball's hardest-thrown cutter *and* slider; as such, he also owns baseball's most lethal combination of strikeouts and groundballs, the latter of which fueled his ability to stifle hard contact spectacularly. The game-breaking velocity that underpins his upper-echelon swing-and-miss stuff suggests he should be able to add plenty more K's, too, painting a future for Clase that's as bright as that of any closer.

Xzavion Curry RHP Born: 07/27/98 Age: 23 Bats: R Throws: R Height: 5'11" Weight: 190 lb. Origin: Round 7, 2019 Draft (#220 overall)

YEAR	TEAM	LVL	AGE	W	L	SV	G	GS	IP	H	HR	BB/9	K/9	K	GB%	BABIP	WHIP	ERA	DRA-	WARP	MPH	FB%	Whiff%	CSP
2021	LYN	A	22	3	0	0	5	5	25^{1}	12	1	1.4	13.5	38	27.5%	.220	0.63	1.07	72	0.6				
2021	LC	A+	22	5	1	0	13	13	67^{2}	53	10	1.6	10.6	80	30.9%	.261	0.96	2.66	91	1.0				
2022 non-DC	*CLE*	*MLB*	*23*	*2*	*3*	*0*	*57*	*0*	*50*	*50*	*9*	*2.6*	*8.1*	*45*	*31.0%*	*.291*	*1.29*	*4.44*	*111*	*-0.1*				

Comparables: Kyle Kendrick, Jason Vargas, Fernando Romero

Curry signed out of college while injured, which delayed his debut until last year, where he began his age-22 season facing Single-A hitters—not exactly a vote of confidence from his employer. At least he proved the assignment too bearish, striking out roughly 7.7 hitters per walk while compiling a 2.30 ERA and graduating two levels. Curry pitches from a high arm slot that helps his fastball's low velocity (which, notably, has ticked up slightly since his amateur days) play up. His other pitches—chiefly, a fringy changeup and a 12-6 curve—have been good enough thus far to silence lower-level competition. Cleveland's metaphorical pantry is stocked floor to ceiling with the herbs and spices necessary for rounding out a dish missing that little something. A dash of cumin? A sprinkle of coriander? The Guardians might whip up a perfect Curry.

★ ★ ★ *2022 Top 101 Prospect* **#43** ★ ★ ★

Daniel Espino RHP Born: 01/05/01 Age: 21 Bats: R Throws: R Height: 6'2" Weight: 205 lb. Origin: Round 1, 2019 Draft (#24 overall)

YEAR	TEAM	LVL	AGE	W	L	SV	G	GS	IP	H	HR	BB/9	K/9	K	GB%	BABIP	WHIP	ERA	DRA-	WARP	MPH	FB%	Whiff%	CSP
2019	INDR	ROK	18	0	1	0	6	6	13^{2}	7	1	3.3	10.5	16	48.4%	.207	0.88	1.98						
2019	MV	SS	18	0	2	0	3	3	10	9	1	4.5	16.2	18	31.8%	.381	1.40	6.30						
2021	LYN	A	20	1	2	0	10	10	42^{2}	34	2	4.9	13.5	64	48.4%	.352	1.34	3.38	68	1.2				
2021	LC	A+	20	2	6	0	10	10	49	30	7	2.9	16.2	88	31.1%	.280	0.94	4.04	58	1.6				
2022 non-DC	*CLE*	*MLB*	*21*	*2*	*2*	*0*	*57*	*0*	*50*	*42*	*7*	*4.9*	*11.3*	*62*	*37.7%*	*.296*	*1.41*	*4.35*	*103*	*0.1*				

Comparables: Sandy Alcantara, Zach McAllister, Jeurys Familia

After drafting Espino in 2019, the Guardians babied him, permitting him to face just 11 hitters per start on average. The gentleness with which the organization handled its new crown jewel underscored industry-wide concerns with Espino's arm and the potentially elite fastball that hinged on its health. Fast-forward to 2021: Cleveland ripped off the bubble wrap and unleashed the beast, allowing Espino at least two turns through the order in 16 of 20 starts. He ended the season in High-A with a strikeout rate over 40% between two levels, and completed his first full campaign with a spectacular no-run, two-hit, 10-strikeout, no-walk performance that he carried into the seventh inning. He remains high-risk and could eventually find himself in high-leverage relief, but it's hard not to envision the synthesis of an utterly dominant fastball, a filthy slider and pinpoint command carrying him to the front of Cleveland's big-league rotation one day.

Ethan Hankins RHP Born: 05/23/00 Age: 22 Bats: R Throws: R Height: 6'6" Weight: 200 lb. Origin: Round 1, 2018 Draft (#35 overall)

YEAR	TEAM	LVL	AGE	W	L	SV	G	GS	IP	H	HR	BB/9	K/9	K	GB%	BABIP	WHIP	ERA	DRA-	WARP	MPH	FB%	Whiff%	CSP
2019	MV	SS	19	0	0	0	9	8	38^{2}	23	1	4.2	10.0	43	55.1%	.253	1.06	1.40						
2019	LC	A	19	0	3	0	5	5	21^{1}	20	3	5.1	11.8	28	47.2%	.340	1.50	4.64	104	0.1				
2022	*No projection*																							

Comparables: Adys Portillo, Daison Acosta, Trevor Clifton

When healthy, Hankins proved why he deserved consideration for the 2018 draft's no. 1 overall pick, flashing upper-90s heat with two plus breaking balls. "When healthy" is the load-bearing caveat: injury damaged Hankins' draft stock in 2018, and Tommy John surgery cost him all of 2021 and a substantial chunk of 2022, too. Additionally, the pandemic restricted him to instructs in 2020. At this point, he can't afford to lose much more. Once healthy—another load-bearing caveat—his development will bear considerable urgency.

James Karinchak RHP Born: 09/22/95 Age: 26 Bats: R Throws: R Height: 6'3" Weight: 215 lb. Origin: Round 9, 2017 Draft (#282 overall)

YEAR	TEAM	LVL	AGE	W	L	SV	G	GS	IP	H	HR	BB/9	K/9	K	GB%	BABIP	WHIP	ERA	DRA-	WARP	MPH	FB%	Whiff%	CSP
2019	INDB	ROK	23	0	0	0	3	0	3	0	0	6.0	24.0	8	0.0%	.000	0.67	0.00						
2019	AKR	AA	23	0	0	6	10	0	10	2	0	1.8	21.6	24	55.6%	.222	0.40	0.00	68	0.2				
2019	COL	AAA	23	1	1	2	17	0	17^{1}	14	2	6.8	21.8	42	47.8%	.571	1.56	4.67	48	0.7				
2019	CLE	MLB	23	0	0	0	5	0	5^{1}	3	0	1.7	13.5	8	38.5%	.231	0.75	1.69	91	0.1	97.0	56.4%	34.7%	49.9%
2020	CLE	MLB	24	1	2	1	27	0	27	14	1	5.3	17.7	53	22.5%	.342	1.11	2.67	62	0.8	95.7	50.2%	45.5%	42.6%
2021	COL	AAA	25	1	1	0	7	0	6	3	1	4.5	13.5	9	33.3%	.182	1.00	3.00	84	0.1				
2021	CLE	MLB	25	7	4	11	60	0	55^{1}	35	9	5.2	12.7	78	39.8%	.228	1.21	4.07	83	1.0	96.1	67.7%	31.5%	55.7%
2022 DC	*CLE*	*MLB*	*26*	*3*	*3*	*6*	*74*	*0*	*64.7*	*45*	*9*	*5.1*	*13.8*	*99*	*37.8%*	*.280*	*1.26*	*3.40*	*83*	*0.8*	*96.0*	*63.5%*	*34.8%*	*52.6%*

Comparables: Joey Devine, Grant Balfour, Cody Allen

You know the "how it started"/"how it ended" duality? It flexibly accommodates all emotional tones, but often it's used humorously to depict a good situation gone bad. For Karinchak, it goes something like this: "How it started: sharing save opportunities with Emmanuel Clase. How it ended: in Triple-A after walking more than five hitters per nine innings." You may recall MLB abruptly began policing "sticky stuff" midseason. The paradigm shift affected all pitchers but greatly impacted Karinchak, whose fastball lost an inordinate amount of spin and suffered massive changes in movement. For fastballs, spin correlates strongly with whiffs, and with Karinchak's lack of spin came a lack of strikeouts as he critically failed to elevate the pitch. He blamed his mechanics, which could be true, but it stands to reason his mechanics suffered as he acclimated to a new normal. He allows too many walks, a self-inflicted wound, but one that he once remedied with cheat-code strikeouts. Without those Ks, Karinchak is just *arincha*.

Triston McKenzie RHP Born: 08/02/97 Age: 24 Bats: R Throws: R Height: 6'5" Weight: 165 lb. Origin: Round 1, 2015 Draft (#42 overall)

YEAR	TEAM	LVL	AGE	W	L	SV	G	GS	IP	H	HR	BB/9	K/9	K	GB%	BABIP	WHIP	ERA	DRA-	WARP	MPH	FB%	Whiff%	CSP
2020	CLE	MLB	22	2	1	0	8	6	33^{1}	21	6	2.4	11.3	42	40.0%	.217	0.90	3.24	81	0.7	93.1	53.3%	29.2%	45.7%
2021	COL	AAA	23	1	1	0	5	5	21^{1}	18	5	5.1	9.7	23	26.8%	.255	1.41	2.95	117	0.1				
2021	CLE	MLB	23	5	9	0	25	24	120	84	21	4.4	10.2	136	29.5%	.227	1.18	4.95	104	0.8	92.4	61.4%	27.9%	53.1%
2022 DC	*CLE*	*MLB*	*24*	*7*	*7*	*0*	*24*	*24*	*119*	*100*	*21*	*4.1*	*10.9*	*143*	*32.4%*	*.280*	*1.30*	*4.11*	*99*	*1.0*	*92.5*	*60.1%*	*28.1%*	*51.9%*

Comparables: Julio Teheran, Shelby Miller, Ubaldo Jiménez

We're contractually obligated to mention McKenzie's build and fragility, so: McKenzie is built like a used car lot inflatable arm dude and has yet to prove he can shoulder a full workload (he made 24 starts, but he hit the Injured List twice, too). More fascinating than talk of lankiness or frailty, though, is McKenzie's Jekyll-and-Hyde season. Through June, McKenzie walked more than eight—eight!—hitters per nine innings en route to a ghastly 6.38 ERA. During 11 starts from July through mid-September, however, McKenzie walked 11 hitters *total* alongside 68 strikeouts, his 2.96 ERA ranking 12th among starters. He nabbed first-pitch strikes and pounded the upper third of the zone, where he induced baseball's highest rate of pop-ups with his four-seamer, the same four-seamer that was allergic to the zone mere months prior. His glass slipper fell off shortly before midnight (he walked eight and allowed 14 earned in his final three starts), but for 10 electric weeks, McKenzie recaptured his top-prospect form and looked every bit like Shane Bieber's eventual second-in-command. It's a tradition in recent years for young Cleveland pitchers on the cusp to implode catastrophically (looking at you, Aaron Civale and Zach Plesac). It would behoove McKenzie to not do that.

Nick Mikolajchak RHP Born: 11/21/97 Age: 24 Bats: R Throws: R Height: 6'2" Weight: 215 lb. Origin: Round 11, 2019 Draft (#340 overall)

YEAR	TEAM	LVL	AGE	W	L	SV	G	GS	IP	H	HR	BB/9	K/9	K	GB%	BABIP	WHIP	ERA	DRA-	WARP	MPH	FB%	Whiff%	CSP
2019	INDB	ROK	21	0	0	2	4	0	6	4	0	0.0	18.0	12	33.3%	.333	0.67	0.00						
2019	MV	SS	21	1	1	3	13	0	19	10	0	1.4	11.4	24	28.2%	.256	0.68	0.47						
2021	AKR	AA	23	2	5	8	30	0	39^2	34	7	2.0	12.9	57	34.4%	.303	1.08	3.18	82	0.7				
2022 DC	*CLE*	*MLB*	*24*	*2*	*2*	*0*	*44*	*0*	*38.7*	*37*	*6*	*3.4*	*9.5*	*41*	*37.0%*	*.301*	*1.33*	*4.33*	*107*	*0.0*				

Comparables: Cory Burns, Matt Foster, Nick Wittgren

Mikolajchak has done nothing but mow down hitters, amassing 93 strikeouts and just 12 walks en route to a 2.09 ERA in 47 career relief appearances. He reportedly added a couple of ticks (*A Cleveland pitcher? Adding velocity? No, no, that can't be right.*) to a flat fastball that he works up in the zone effectively. As the kids say, "it shows." Mikolajchak, having never started as a professional, was predestined for bullpen work. Until he encounters some manner of challenge, that path steers toward high-leverage late-relief and is paved with gold.

Eli Morgan RHP Born: 05/13/96 Age: 26 Bats: R Throws: R Height: 5'10" Weight: 190 lb. Origin: Round 8, 2017 Draft (#252 overall)

YEAR	TEAM	LVL	AGE	W	L	SV	G	GS	IP	H	HR	BB/9	K/9	K	GB%	BABIP	WHIP	ERA	DRA-	WARP	MPH	FB%	Whiff%	CSP
2019	LYN	A+	23	3	1	0	6	6	33^2	19	3	1.3	10.7	40	22.4%	.219	0.71	1.87	92	0.4				
2019	AKR	AA	23	6	4	0	19	18	102	100	12	2.9	9.2	104	31.3%	.319	1.30	3.79	101	0.8				
2021	COL	AAA	25	0	1	0	5	5	22^1	20	1	4.4	8.5	21	25.4%	.333	1.39	4.03	120	0.1				
2021	CLE	MLB	25	5	7	0	18	18	89^1	90	20	2.2	8.2	81	30.0%	.282	1.25	5.34	120	-0.1	90.6	49.8%	22.9%	55.1%
2022 DC	*CLE*	*MLB*	*26*	*9*	*8*	*0*	*71*	*12*	*110*	*113*	*19*	*2.9*	*7.8*	*94*	*30.8%*	*.295*	*1.35*	*4.78*	*115*	*0.0*	*90.6*	*49.8%*	*22.9%*	*55.1%*

Comparables: Kendall Graveman, André Rienzo, Adrian Sampson

Morgan descends from a long line of Guardian starters with tidy walk rates. It seems to be the prevailing organizational focus over the last decade: develop (or pursue arms with) command, then build out everything else. What Morgan's predecessors and contemporaries possess(ed) that he lacks is adequate fastball velocity. Unfortunately, he invokes the name "Josh Tomlin" more than he does "Corey Kluber" or "Shane Bieber." Morgan lives in the low 90s, often high 80s, and features a fly-ball approach that, to date, has yielded an ungodly number of home runs. Living up in the zone ain't bad—teammates Triston McKenzie and James Karinchak do it—and Morgan's deceptive delivery helps his fastball play up. But it stands to reason hitters have an easier time squaring up his lower velo, resulting in an outsized number of damaging fly balls and line drives. Although largely earned, we think at least some of it had to be bad luck. Scouts rave about Morgan's self-described Bugs Bunny changeup. Coupled with his deception, those could be enough to make him a serviceable back-of-the-rotation arm. Tomlin earned himself countless second chances; no doubt, Morgan will get his.

Zach Plesac RHP Born: 01/21/95 Age: 27 Bats: R Throws: R Height: 6'3" Weight: 220 lb. Origin: Round 12, 2016 Draft (#362 overall)

YEAR	TEAM	LVL	AGE	W	L	SV	G	GS	IP	H	HR	BB/9	K/9	K	GB%	BABIP	WHIP	ERA	DRA-	WARP	MPH	FB%	Whiff%	CSP
2019	AKR	AA	24	1	1	0	6	6	37^1	23	0	1.4	8.2	34	48.5%	.237	0.78	0.96	103	0.2				
2019	COL	AAA	24	3	1	0	4	4	26^1	19	2	1.0	10.6	31	27.7%	.270	0.84	2.73	97	0.4				
2019	CLE	MLB	24	8	6	0	21	21	115^2	102	19	3.1	6.8	88	39.2%	.257	1.23	3.81	116	0.2	94.0	50.6%	21.7%	51.1%
2020	CLE	MLB	25	4	2	0	8	8	55^1	38	8	1.0	9.3	57	38.0%	.224	0.80	2.28	88	1.0	93.0	37.6%	29.8%	50.9%
2021	CLE	MLB	26	10	6	0	25	25	142^2	137	23	2.1	6.3	100	44.5%	.264	1.20	4.67	120	-0.2	93.1	41.9%	23.2%	55.2%
2022 DC	*CLE*	*MLB*	*27*	*9*	*8*	*0*	*27*	*27*	*154*	*158*	*21*	*2.3*	*7.4*	*127*	*42.6%*	*.301*	*1.29*	*4.12*	*103*	*1.0*	*93.2*	*42.9%*	*23.9%*	*53.8%*

Comparables: Aaron Civale, Brian Bannister, Luis Cessa

We spend untold hours trying to distinguish true positives from false positives. It's especially tough when a false positive is underpinned by legitimately solid peripherals. In 2020, Plesac tinkered with his pitch mix, added and subtracted velo to his slider and fastball, respectively, and the world opened up before him. The slider devastated opponents, and his changeup, once terrible, suddenly became viable. That he carried forward his breakout-fueled corrections into 2021 only for it all to crumble into dust is the confounding part. Worse yet, Plesac's four-seamer was a bottom-quartile fastball *during* his breakout, so it didn't help that last year it contended for the title of absolute worst. Even the most-excellent of secondaries will struggle to salvage the ill effects of a bad fastball. What, then, is left to salvage the ill effects of a bad everything? Perhaps it's best to pare it all down and remember Plesac was a good, if pedestrian, depth arm who never really telegraphed that kind of ceiling in the first place.

Cal Quantrill RHP Born: 02/10/95 Age: 27 Bats: L Throws: R Height: 6'3" Weight: 195 lb. Origin: Round 1, 2016 Draft (#8 overall)

YEAR	TEAM	LVL	AGE	W	L	SV	G	GS	IP	H	HR	BB/9	K/9	K	GB%	BABIP	WHIP	ERA	DRA-	WARP	MPH	FB%	Whiff%	CSP
2019	ELP	AAA	24	4	2	0	7	7	35^2	38	3	3.0	8.3	33	50.5%	.324	1.40	4.54	95	0.3				
2019	SD	MLB	24	6	8	0	23	18	103	106	15	2.4	7.8	89	43.3%	.297	1.30	5.16	101	1.0	94.5	56.7%	22.4%	43.8%
2020	SD	MLB	25	2	0	1	10	1	17^1	17	2	3.1	9.3	18	43.8%	.333	1.33	2.60	92	0.3	94.8	52.1%	24.3%	44.3%
2020	CLE	MLB	25	0	0	0	8	2	14^2	14	2	1.2	8.0	13	45.5%	.286	1.09	1.84	99	0.2	95.2	56.7%	26.1%	50.1%
2021	CLE	MLB	26	8	3	0	40	22	149^2	129	16	2.8	7.3	121	42.8%	.270	1.18	2.89	108	0.8	94.0	77.1%	22.2%	53.0%
2022 DC	*CLE*	*MLB*	*27*	*8*	*8*	*0*	*25*	*25*	*137.3*	*139*	*18*	*2.9*	*7.2*	*109*	*43.1%*	*.297*	*1.33*	*4.27*	*106*	*0.5*	*94.2*	*71.0%*	*22.5%*	*50.7%*

Comparables: Chris Stratton, Nick Kingham, Joe Kelly

Quantrill's brief but impressive campaign in 2020 served as the trailer to his similarly impressive full-length feature that dropped in 2021. Consecutive good performances like these might convince us of an extremely encouraging trend. However, by any commonly used ERA estimator—DRA, FIP, xFIP, SIERA, whatever—Quantrill skated on thin ice. Despite the outcomes, none of Quantrill's offerings graded out better than average, let alone plus or better. A lack of swing-and-miss stuff begets a pitch-to-contact approach by default—one he rode to success—yet Quantrill's locational plan of attack is not optimal. While he admirably avoids the heart of the zone, he "wastes" (per Statcast) too many pitches for someone who struggles to fool hitters consistently. That's not to say the weak contact he thus far has allowed is without merit, but he's walking a tightrope, one in which just a light breeze might dismount him. We caught whiffs of Quantrill's ceiling—two scoreless seven-inning outings of nine-plus strikeouts—so let us not catastrophize too much. It's just that those electric performances served as intermissions amid long slogs of mediocrity couched in decent results. Temper your expectations, is all.

Nick Sandlin RHP Born: 01/10/97 Age: 25 Bats: R Throws: R Height: 5'11" Weight: 175 lb. Origin: Round 2, 2018 Draft (#67 overall)

YEAR	TEAM	LVL	AGE	W	L	SV	G	GS	IP	H	HR	BB/9	K/9	K	GB%	BABIP	WHIP	ERA	DRA-	WARP	MPH	FB%	Whiff%	CSP
2019	AKR	AA	22	0	0	2	15	0	17^1	13	2	4.2	14.0	27	45.9%	.314	1.21	1.56	82	0.3				
2019	COL	AAA	22	1	0	0	9	0	9	5	2	7.0	11.0	11	52.6%	.176	1.33	4.00	87	0.2				
2021	CLE	MLB	24	1	1	0	34	0	33^2	21	2	4.5	12.8	48	41.7%	.271	1.13	2.94	77	0.7	94.8	51.3%	33.1%	52.0%
2022 DC	*CLE*	*MLB*	*25*	*3*	*3*	*0*	*74*	*0*	*64.7*	*49*	*8*	*4.5*	*12.5*	*89*	*43.0%*	*.291*	*1.27*	*3.69*	*88*	*0.6*	*94.8*	*51.3%*	*33.1%*	*52.0%*

Comparables: Grant Balfour, Pat Neshek, Joey Devine

Sandlin debuted as a slider-first power-sinker side-armer who, in four months' time, nearly matched his career minor-league innings total. His command left in 2019 and never returned—which makes sense, considering the way he pats the ball in his glove as if he's about to huck it cold turkey at the radar gun booth outside the right-field pavilion. Perhaps it's more a feature than a bug, as Sandlin kept hitters woefully off-balance, both caused and augmented by whipping them into the strike zone from an unconventional arm slot. With other relief arms disappointing and/or departing Cleveland, enter the Sand man (we're sorry, we're trying to delete it), who could and probably should find himself thrust into higher-leverage situations in 2022.

Bryan Shaw RHP Born: 11/08/87 Age: 34 Bats: S Throws: R Height: 6'1" Weight: 226 lb. Origin: Round 2, 2008 Draft (#73 overall)

YEAR	TEAM	LVL	AGE	W	L	SV	G	GS	IP	H	HR	BB/9	K/9	K	GB%	BABIP	WHIP	ERA	DRA-	WARP	MPH	FB%	Whiff%	CSP
2019	COL	MLB	31	3	2	1	70	0	72	69	12	3.6	7.3	58	49.3%	.277	1.36	5.38	102	0.7	92.4	75.5%	25.3%	45.1%
2020	SEA	MLB	32	1	0	0	6	0	6	13	1	9.0	6.0	4	55.6%	.462	3.17	18.00	114	0.0	92.5	52.3%	20.0%	41.4%
2021	CLE	MLB	33	6	7	2	81	0	77^1	69	10	4.4	8.3	71	46.0%	.277	1.38	3.49	110	0.3	92.7	79.3%	25.7%	51.2%
2022 non-DC	*CLE*	*MLB*	*34*	*2*	*2*	*0*	*57*	*0*	*50*	*47*	*6*	*4.2*	*8.1*	*44*	*47.0%*	*.291*	*1.43*	*4.39*	*106*	*0.0*	*92.6*	*77.0%*	*25.3%*	*49.4%*

Comparables: David Riske, Danys Baez, Mark Lowe

Having made out like a bandit on a diabolically bad run in the unforgivingly thin air of Denver (plus a quick, also very bad pit stop in Seattle), Shaw returned to Cleveland to do what he always did before he left: provide a ton of good-not-great innings in late-relief. It's possible Shaw isn't meant to thrive anywhere but Cleveland. Regardless, he hits free agency this winter in search of a team that will pay him to do more of what he does best: to be, in fact, *not* the best, but to be it dependably—something to which we can all relate.

★ ★ ★ *2022 Top 101 Prospect* **#84** ★ ★ ★

Gavin Williams RHP Born: 07/26/99 Age: 22 Bats: L Throws: R Height: 6'6" Weight: 238 lb. Origin: Round 1, 2021 Draft (#23 overall)

Williams is large and, in a pandemic-inspired twist, he was most certainly in charge during the aftermath of the 2020 draft. He passed on offers to sign as an undrafted free agent following the five-round sprint, instead betting on himself to raise his stock (and his signing bonus) with another spring at East Carolina. Williams' gamble paid off, as he was selected at the tail end of the first by the Guardians. On paper, it's a tantalizing marriage. Williams has all the innate traits one associates with above-average starters—size; big-time velocity; swing-and-miss secondaries; improved control—but he needs some help putting them all together. The Guardians are seemingly as good as any organization at getting the most from their arms. If they prove as much with Williams, he could become a fixture near the front of their rotation.

Alex Young LHP Born: 09/09/93 Age: 28 Bats: L Throws: L Height: 6'3" Weight: 220 lb. Origin: Round 2, 2015 Draft (#43 overall)

YEAR	TEAM	LVL	AGE	W	L	SV	G	GS	IP	H	HR	BB/9	K/9	K	GB%	BABIP	WHIP	ERA	DRA-	WARP	MPH	FB%	Whiff%	CSP
2019	RNO	AAA	25	4	3	0	20	8	54^2	66	6	4.3	10.5	64	48.8%	.380	1.68	6.09	79	1.0				
2019	ARI	MLB	25	7	5	0	17	15	83^1	72	14	2.9	7.7	71	48.6%	.252	1.19	3.56	101	0.8	88.5	58.2%	27.4%	44.5%
2020	ARI	MLB	26	2	4	0	15	7	46^1	51	11	2.7	7.6	39	36.7%	.288	1.40	5.44	135	-0.4	89.8	54.6%	24.5%	46.7%
2021	COL	AAA	27	0	0	0	8	0	9	8	1	4.0	7.0	7	46.2%	.292	1.33	5.00	96	0.1				
2021	CLE	MLB	27	0	0	0	10	0	10^1	15	1	6.1	4.4	5	46.2%	.368	2.13	7.84	132	-0.1	90.0	70.7%	15.7%	54.7%
2021	ARI	MLB	27	2	6	0	30	2	41^2	50	11	4.3	8.2	38	44.8%	.322	1.68	6.26	106	0.2	89.2	59.9%	29.7%	53.4%
2022 non-DC	*CLE*	*MLB*	*28*	*2*	*3*	*0*	*57*	*0*	*50*	*51*	*7*	*3.5*	*7.7*	*42*	*44.1%*	*.303*	*1.42*	*4.68*	*112*	*-0.1*	*89.3*	*59.0%*	*26.4%*	*49.6%*

Comparables: Brian Duensing, Jeff Hoffman, Ryan Weber

Young is accomplishing whatever is the equivalent of the Benjamin Button thing but for former-top-prospect pitchers, each year finding himself in roles of progressively lower leverage and somehow performing worse and worse in spite of it. It's hard to imagine how it could get any worse, but it's also hard to imagine, given the present state of things, how it could get better, especially looking at the trajectory of his past three professional seasons. Our unsolicited advice: pare down the five-pitch arsenal. Ditch the four-seamer and cutter for a secondary-heavy sinker-curve-change repertoire—you know, the whole addition-by-subtraction bit. In the wise words of Kunu (Chuck) the surf instructor, "the less you do, the more you do." Now pop up.

Lineouts

Hitters

HITTER	POS	TEAM	LVL	AGE	PA	R	2B	3B	HR	RBI	BB	K	SB	CS	AVG/OBP/SLG	DRC+	BABIP	BRR	FRAA	WARP
Jake Fox	IF	GUA	ROK	18	49	10	1	0	0	6	6	9	7	0	.405/.469/.429		.500			
Isaiah Greene	OF	GUA	ROK	19	191	31	9	0	1	16	35	42	5	4	.289/.421/.368		.387			
Daniel Johnson	OF	COL	AAA	25	318	36	16	2	14	39	35	106	7	1	.222/.314/.444	92	.300	-1.5	RF(35): 3.7, CF(21): -0.1, LF(7): 1.1	1.0
	OF	CLE	MLB	25	81	9	0	0	4	5	4	27	1	0	.221/.259/.377	78	.283	-0.8	RF(19): 1.6, LF(9): -0.3	0.1
Ryan Lavarnway	C	COL	AAA	33	199	29	7	0	13	40	20	54	0	0	.260/.338/.520	113	.300	-0.4	C(39): 0.2, 1B(1): -0.0	1.0
	C	CLE	MLB	33	30	2	3	0	0	0	1	10	0	0	.250/.276/.357	75	.389	-1.2	C(8): -0.2	-0.1
Bo Naylor	C	AKR	AA	21	356	41	13	1	10	44	37	112	10	0	.188/.280/.332	82	.255	-0.5	C(73): 6.7	1.1
Jhonkensy Noel	3B	LYN	A	19	162	36	10	1	11	40	7	27	2	1	.393/.426/.693	148	.421	0.3	1B(18): 0.8, 3B(13): 1.5	1.6
	3B	LC	A+	19	111	13	3	0	8	25	9	31	3	1	.280/.351/.550	124	.328	-1.0	3B(17): 0.5	0.6
Richie Palacios	UT	SCO	WIN	24	93	17	8	1	3	11	13	15	4	1	.269/.387/.513		.300			
	UT	AKR	AA	24	283	53	24	3	6	36	33	42	10	3	.299/.389/.496	128	.338	2.3	2B(42): 6.1, CF(10): -0.5, LF(6): -0.0	2.6
	UT	COL	AAA	24	145	19	9	1	1	12	25	28	10	0	.292/.434/.416	107	.376	0.8	2B(26): 1.2, CF(6): -0.8	0.7
Wilson Ramos	C	COL	AAA	33	62	6	3	0	3	9	1	6	0	0	.317/.328/.517	116	.314	0.2	C(10): -0.9	0.3
	C	CLE	MLB	33	35	3	0	0	2	7	3	7	0	0	.226/.286/.419	106	.217	-0.5	C(9): -0.4	0.1
	C	DET	MLB	33	128	12	5	0	6	13	6	29	0	0	.200/.238/.392	98	.212	-0.8	C(25): -2.7	0.1

Cleveland's 2021 third-round pick **Jake Fox** isn't the bat-first (non-)catcher that enticed fantasy managers oh so many years ago, but *is* a bat-first middle infielder with highly credible contact skills. Just when you thought the outfielder-to-reliever conversion would drag on forever, **Anthony Gose** The Pitcher debuted in September after a turbulent six-year journey. He touched 100 and also walked someone, which succinctly characterizes his scouting report: he brings legit gas and strikeout stuff from the left side, but the excess free passes are debilitating. Who cares? Feel-good story feels good. Traded from the Mets before taking a professional at-bat, **Isaiah Greene** entices with his power and speed but introduces large question marks regarding the viability of his swing. He's young but he profiles as high-variance, especially given the uncertainty of many pandemic-year draftees. Given the state of Cleveland's outfield the last couple seasons, **Daniel Johnson**'s inability to total triple-digit at-bats tells us all we need to know. Now 26 years old, the power-speed prospect hasn't shown enough of either to go with a Swiss-cheese swing. Eleven teams employed **Ryan Lavarnway** the last eight years—a monumental feat for someone who has appeared in only 31 major-league games since the end of 2015. By the time you read this, we can only hope 11 becomes 12. It's entirely possible he is the glue holding all of American professional baseball together. Protect Lavarnway('s employment) at all costs. The Guardians' 2018 first-rounder, Josh's younger brother **Bo Naylor** appeared poised to ascend to top-prospectdom as a bat-first (but still athletic) catcher. A lackluster 2021 derailed those ambitions, but he still profiles as Cleveland's backstop of the future, for lack of other options. **Jhonkensy Noel** derives his substantial raw power from strength over bat speed and has the potential for an average hit and plus power combination if everything clicks. He spotted up at third base most often, but is a future first baseman, if not a DH. **Richard Palacios** has always hit well but bears a minus arm, sentencing him to the keystone. It was encouraging to see him shuffle into and out of the outfield last year in an effort to manufacture defensive versatility and accelerate his timeline. He'll likely make an appearance in late-2022. **Wilson Ramos** began 2021 in Detroit and ended it in Cleveland needing surgery to repair a torn ACL. Given his long, productive career, it stands to reason some team will bet on the probably over-the-hill backstop. If not, he can take pride in being one of baseball's better full-time-ish catchers of the last decade.

Pitchers

PITCHER	TEAM	LVL	AGE	W	L	SV	G	GS	IP	H	HR	BB/9	K/9	K	GB%	BABIP	WHIP	ERA	DRA-	WARP	MPH	FB%	WHF	CSP
Logan Allen	COL	AAA	24	2	3	0	12	11	48^{2}	61	9	5.4	9.6	52	37.2%	.382	1.85	7.95	118	0.2				
	CLE	MLB	24	2	7	0	14	11	50^{1}	58	12	3.0	6.6	37	45.1%	.303	1.49	6.26	141	-0.6	93.0	43.4%	19.0%	53.1%
Tanner Burns	LC	A+	22	2	5	0	18	18	75^{2}	64	10	3.4	10.8	91	39.7%	.300	1.23	3.57	88	1.3				
Enyel De Los Santos	LHV	AAA	25	0	1	0	10	0	13^{1}	3	1	3.4	16.2	24	41.2%	.125	0.60	2.70	76	0.3				
	PHI	MLB	25	1	1	0	26	0	28	34	7	4.5	13.5	42	41.0%	.391	1.71	6.75	76	0.6	95.0	70.7%	33.1%	54.3%
	PIT	MLB	25	1	0	0	7	0	7^{1}	9	1	4.9	7.4	6	24.0%	.348	1.77	4.91	114	0.0	95.1	59.3%	27.8%	52.6%
Justin Garza	COL	AAA	27	1	1	1	14	0	22^{2}	8	2	5.2	12.3	31	28.6%	.150	0.93	1.59	94	0.4				
	CLE	MLB	27	2	1	0	21	0	28^{2}	27	5	5.7	9.1	29	35.8%	.293	1.57	4.71	110	0.1	94.2	83.1%	25.6%	53.3%
Sam Hentges	CLE	MLB	24	1	4	0	30	12	68^{2}	90	10	4.2	8.9	68	45.4%	.386	1.78	6.68	115	0.1	94.6	50.8%	24.1%	54.2%
Cam Hill	COL	AAA	27	1	1	0	24	1	24^{2}	33	3	5.8	6.6	18	47.6%	.380	1.99	8.03	126	0.0				
Trevor Stephan	CLE	MLB	25	3	1	1	43	0	63^{1}	58	15	4.4	10.7	75	32.9%	.272	1.41	4.41	100	0.6	96.4	59.7%	30.2%	53.5%
Lenny Torres	LYN	A	20	2	7	0	20	19	68^{2}	68	5	6.3	9.6	73	45.9%	.330	1.69	6.29	119	-0.1				
Josh Wolf	LYN	A	20	1	3	1	18	17	65^{2}	73	3	4.7	9.2	67	60.1%	.370	1.63	5.35	105	0.4				

For all intents and purposes, **Brady Aiken** is a Guardian, but he stepped away from baseball in 2019 and has yet to formally return. ⚾ It's hard to overstate how bad **Logan Allen** (the veteran, not the prospect) has been since his debut. Averaging fewer than five innings per start with shaky peripherals, including a strikeout percentage that ranks among the league's worst, the Allen-as-a-starter experiment has all but run its course. A permanent bullpen transition may be the jump-start he desperately needs. ⚾ **Tanner Burns**, Cleveland's 2020 second-rounder, delivered a solid if unspectacular debut professional season at High-A, where his strikeout prowess was evident but his command eluded him at the peak of summer. The change needs work, but more importantly he needs to prove he can stay on the mound long enough to do it. ⚾ 2021 was the first time **Enyel De Los Santos** got an extended look at the major-league level. He built up a 6.75 ERA, and the Phillies cut him loose in September. But when you feature three pitches with a whiff rate of 30% or higher, there are fliers to be taken; the Pirates picked him up shortly thereafter. ⚾ A slow-to-advance, late-drafted non-prospect college arm, **Justin Garza** finally debuted at 27 and predictably underwhelmed. His changeup flashes plus, but he doesn't throw it enough, relying instead on much less effective "weapons." ⚾ Pedestrian velo and a high release point resulted in a steep and hittable fastball that allowed the worst wOBA of any pitch thrown at least 500 times. **Sam Hentges** looked marginally better in relief, but neither his curve nor slider inspired confidence, leaving one to wonder where he belongs on Cleveland's 26-man roster, if at all. ⚾ A serviceable arm in 2020, **Cam Hill** didn't see the majors last year between injury and ineffectiveness, and elected free agency at the end of the season. ⚾ Cleveland drafted 10 college pitchers—**Tommy Mace** being no. 3—in its first 11 picks of the 2021 MLB Draft. Mace, a 6-foot-6 strike-thrower, evokes such commonplace descriptors as "workhorse," "durable" and "high floor, low ceiling." ⚾ Southpaw **Doug Nikhazy**, Cleveland's 2021 second-rounder, features four pitches, among them an effective low-90s fastball, and achieves remarkable extension on his delivery for his relatively modest size. He struck out 16 Florida State hitters in a NCAA regional game, if that kind of thing revs your engine. ⚾ **Trevor Stephan** harnesses upper-quintile fastball velo, a slow, sweeping slider and a changeup he can't command to save his life. The Guardians will wring worthwhile relief innings from this Rule 5er clipped from the Yankees. ⚾ After a prolonged dual Tommy John/pandemic layoff, **Lenny Torres** embarked on a horrendous 2021 campaign during which he never really "had it." He had two, possibly three, pitches that flashed plus pre-surgery, so patience with him post-surgery will be virtuous. ⚾ **Carlos Vargas** lost 2020 to the pandemic and 2021 to Tommy John—not his first run-in with elbow woes. Still young and projectable, his power fastball will keep scouts' eyes on him while the development of his slider and changeup will shape the trajectory of his career. ⚾ A 2019 Draft prep arm acquired from the Mets in the Lindor/Carrasco trade, **Josh Wolf** will beat hitters with his fastball and curve—although hitters beat him in his first stint with his new club. He projects less as a starter and more as a reliever, albeit a high-impact one. He's a few years away regardless.

DETROIT TIGERS

Essay by Lauren Theisen

Player comments by Ben Spanier, Matt Sussman and BP staff

On September 21, 2021, Detroit Tigers shortstop Niko Goodrum hit an RBI single that was, by all reasonable measures, meaningless. It was a little opposite-field flare over the second baseman and into right field off a low curveball thrown by fringe White Sox relief pitcher Jace Fry, who was optioned to Triple-A two days later. The hit gave Goodrum's batting average a slight bump, up to .214, and it was enough to score Robbie Grossman from third and give the Tigers a 3–2 lead in the seventh inning in front of a dubious official crowd of 10,585—25 percent of Comerica Park's capacity. A couple of walks later, Victor Reyes picked up his fourth hit of the game, finding a hole between first and second to score two more runs and provide the Tigers with enough to eventually win the game 5–3.

I watched this game in my living room on a Tuesday afternoon. The Tigers had been mathematically eliminated from the postseason over the previous weekend and the White Sox had all but clinched the AL Central. I do not expect you to remember or care about this game, and, frankly, even if you are an ardent fan of Motor City sports, I would be a bit creeped out if you read the above paragraph and went, "Hell yeah! The Victor Reyes game!" But the sparsely attended comeback sharpened a feeling that had grown in my heart over the course of the 2021 season: An unfamiliar feeling, a *good* feeling! A feeling of, if not total optimism, at least satisfaction. For the first time in several years, I'd become proud to claim the Tigers as my own.

That win over the White Sox only brought the Tigers to 74-78 in the proper standings, but diehards could sense rich soil underneath the patchy record. The team had gone 65-54 since May 8, and it would end up with a mark of 39-36 against teams above .500 on the season—better than the Red Sox, White Sox, Cardinals, Brewers and Braves. In short, that game was part of what turned the Tigers from a hollowed-out draft-pick manufacturer into a goddang baseball team again.

From 2017 through 2020, as the team stumbled to four straight sub-.400 finishes, I would not have been caught dead getting invested in a Tigers game in September. It simply felt too painful—or worse, too pointless, too much like I was wasting my time on a team that, by design, had no interest in giving me anything in return. But that win over the White Sox wasn't the aberration it would have been in previous

DETROIT TIGERS PROSPECTUS

2021 W-L: 77-85, 3RD IN AL CENTRAL

Pythag	.462	*20th*	DER	.701	*16th*
RS/G	4.30	*23rd*	DRC+	93	*22nd*
RA/G	4.67	*19th*	DRA-	110	*26th*
dWin%	.430	*26th*	FIP	4.65	*23rd*
Payroll	$81M	*24th*	B-Age	28.7	*14th*
M$/MW	$2.3M	*7th*	P-Age	27.8	*4th*

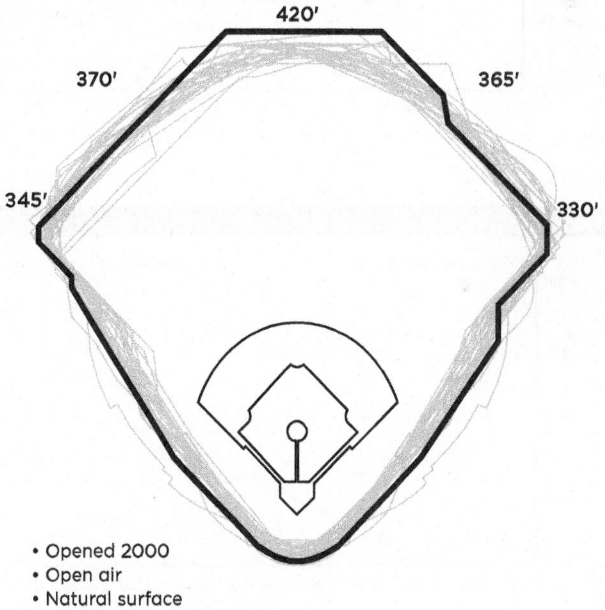

- Opened 2000
- Open air
- Natural surface
- Fence profile: 6'10" to 14'

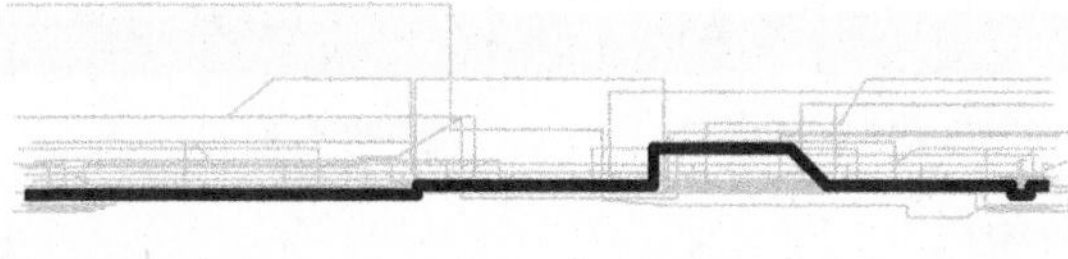

Park Factors

Runs	Runs/RH	Runs/LH	HR/RH	HR/LH
93	94	93	85	80

Top Hitter WARP	2.9 Jonathan Schoop
Top Pitcher WARP	1.1 Michael Fulmer
Top Prospect	Spencer Torkelson

Payroll History (in millions)

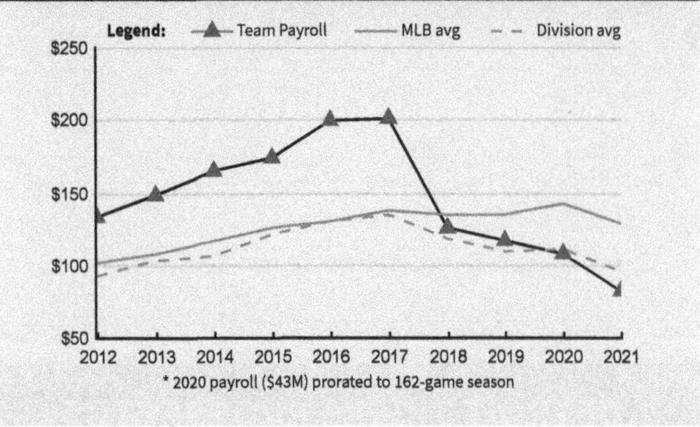

Future Commitments (in millions)

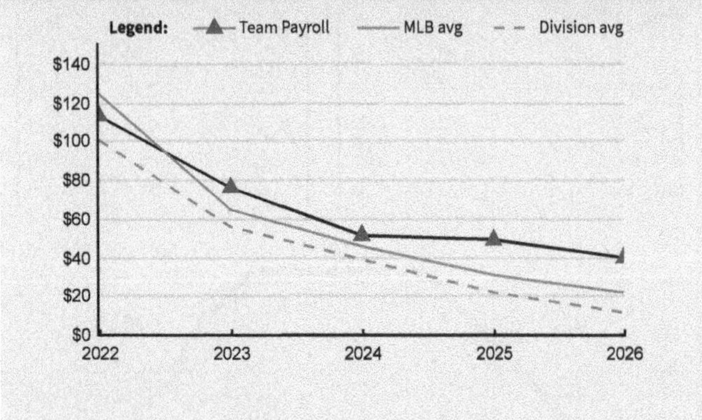

Farm System Ranking

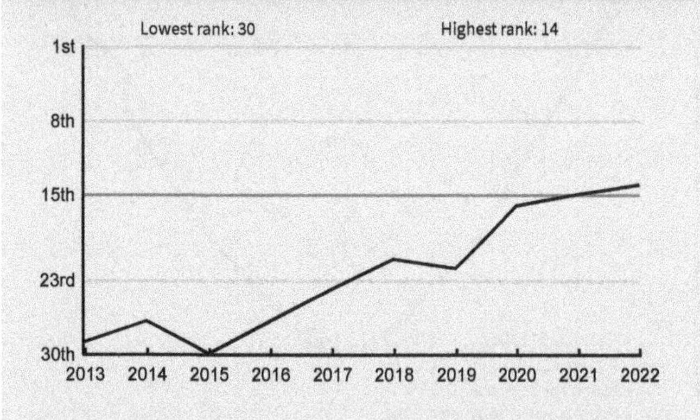

Personnel

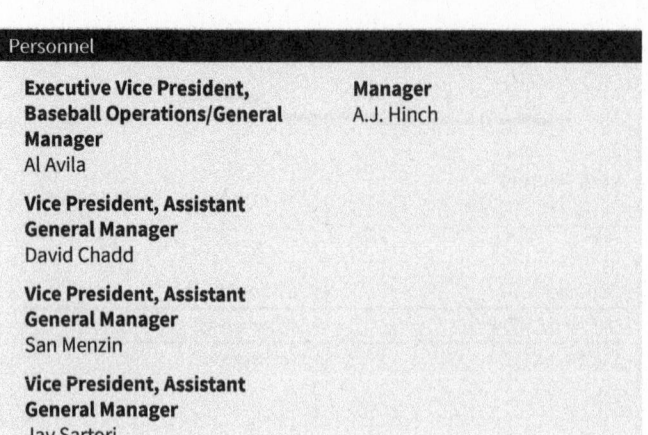

Executive Vice President, Baseball Operations/General Manager
Al Avila

Vice President, Assistant General Manager
David Chadd

Vice President, Assistant General Manager
San Menzin

Vice President, Assistant General Manager
Jay Sartori

Manager
A.J. Hinch

years, the fluke breaking up losing streaks to either side. The previous weekend, the Tigers split a four-game series in Tampa against the Rays behind some skillful pitching, including a Michael Fulmer-induced game-ending double play in a 4–3 win. That Monday was another nailbiter against Chicago, with the Tigers going down 3–0 early but winning on a Harold Castro RBI base hit off of Craig Kimbrel in the eighth. The torrential rains that plagued Metro Detroit all summer kept them off the field for a few days, but in the following weekend series against the Royals, Akil Baddoo highlighted a 5–1 victory with a heroic, leaping home-run robbery of Hunter Dozier next to the left-field bullpens. When he landed, Baddoo flashed a smile fit for a toothbrush ad.

You may think that the rambling veneration of these plays is the sign of a woman driven mad by the flood of losses racked up by her beloved Detroit sports teams—their 226 combined defeats in 2019 were the most in any calendar year of any North American market in history. You may have a point. Certainly Braves fans and Astros supporters aren't combing through the regular-season schedule like a grandparent with a photo album, picking out instances of triumph while stubbornly ignoring the fact that the majority of their games were losses. The truly great or even good teams in this prospectus don't have to deploy a 26-year-old sicko sweatily trying to convince you, *No, no, I actually liked them!* But I'm not quite foolish or bright-eyed enough to try to argue that the Tigers are going to win the pennant (just yet). I am, instead, simply appreciating the fact that they seem to have rediscovered one of this sport's lost arts: the art of being a third-place team trying to level up and become a second-place team.

In the early going of this upcoming Tigers season, the discussion will no doubt be dominated by Miguel Cabrera. The 38-year-old designated hitter (and still occasional first baseman!) enters the year just 13 hits away from 3,000 for his career. He passed the 500-home-run mark with a dinger in Toronto last August. On a playoff contender, Cabrera would have seen far fewer than the 526 plate appearances he got with the Tigers in 2021 (despite finishing strong, he put up career lows in both on-base percentage and slugging), but, in his way, he remained the heart of a rebuilding team. For one thing, his gutting out 130 games after all his body has been through—including groin, calf, hamstring and biceps trouble—was something of a miracle. For another, that agonizing eight-game gap between 499 and 500 provided a shared rallying point for fans and turned the Tigers, however briefly, into the must-see TV they'd been when he was racking up most of those round-trippers.

I joked at the start of 2021 that Cabrera's pursuit of his milestones would be the only thing worth following in that Detroit season, but there turned out to be more bright spots on that roster than on the last four put together. The Tigers did something novel to ring in the new year, signing Robbie

Grossman to the franchise's first multi-year free-agent contract since before the 2016 season, and that whopping two-year, $10-million deal paid off with a team-leading OBP of .357 and 23 home runs that more than doubled Grossman's previous career high. Jeimer Candelario, a young third baseman acquired from the Cubs in 2017 as part of the Alex Avila/Justin Wilson trade, built on a short-but-sweet 2020 to prove that he could consistently handle major-league pitching. And Baddoo, the Rule 5 selection from the Twins' organization, captured everyone's imagination at the start of the 2021 season with a magical, completely unexpected string of home runs and clutch hits in the Tigers' otherwise ugly 8-19 April, providing a non-*Ugh, this again?* talking point.

The raw numbers of the Tigers' pitchers are not quite as easy to spin as a stirring sign of the national pastime's return as a going concern in a city with more than 120 years of major-league history. But if you've made it with me this far down, I hope you'll understand that I cannot be exhausted by banal pessimism. Humor me for a second and squint at these names from last year. What do you see? *The fifth-worst xFIP in the majors?* Shut up and squint harder! I call that a "laying the groundwork" year for an unpolished pitching staff with unlimited potential. Casey Mize and Tarik Skubal, both under the age of 25, gave up too many opposing dongs but still gained valuable experience at roughly 150 innings apiece. Fellow youngsters Tyler Alexander and Matt Manning also showed flashes of genius. (These are all highly touted guys. *Highly* touted.) Michael Fulmer, my own personal Comeback Player of the Year, returned from a missed 2019 and a disastrous 2020 to wreck hitters' psyches like it was his Rookie of the Year campaign all over again. (Admittedly, he did it out of the bullpen this time.)

Oh, and don't forget about Spencer Turnbull! Seriously, don't forget about him while he recovers from Tommy John this year. For the petty gossips among us, Turnbull injected an exciting dose of drama when his relationship with the *married* Christian influencer Ashley TerKeurst became public. For those who find diving into the ins and outs of Alabama church communities distasteful, there was something else to celebrate. In the same way Baddoo energized the batting order in those painful early days, so too did Turnbull's no-hitter in May provide a jolt of nostalgia for this team's AL Central-winning past. Despite being overshadowed by all the other no-nos around it, Turnbull's 117-pitch decimation of the "mighty" Seattle Mariners provided a pleasant throwback to the old days of Tiger fans holding their breath as Justin Verlander went into the seventh, eighth and ninth innings with that zero still intact on the line score.

I want to stick with that Verlander comparison for a moment, because it's one of a few lost aspects of the Tigers that have kept me tied to this pathetic franchise and begging—dreaming!—for a return to glory. When I was a bit younger—after my first crush, but before my first smart phone—I measured my summers in Verlander starts. I'd tie an onion to my belt, which was the style at the time, and then I'd go to the local pool or the mall or . . . OK, the where isn't important. What *does* matter is that, when JV was on the mound, I always wanted to be within earshot of a radio or a short jaunt away from a friendly television, because after his first no-hitter, in 2007, and certainly after his second, in 2011, everyone in Michigan understood that lightning could strike again at any time. You never knew when you might get the text, "Verlander through six."

Of all sports franchises, it's the local baseball club that needs to be the most hospitable to its fans. I'd even argue that it has a now-too-often-neglected civic duty to provide respectable entertainment for the community. While tank jobs and surrendered seasons are discussed in mathematical and economic terms, or as necessary valleys on the route to a peak, the short-term effects on the folks who tune in are glossed over. It is usually assumed that fans, just by their nature, will always stick it out through even the toughest of times, and, if they don't, that they weren't "true fans" in the first place, anyway. That can be true—this essay is partial proof!—but that framing casually and even heartlessly dismisses how even a mediocre or semi-respectable baseball club can have a positive impact on its city's inhabitants in a way that the depressing ones that actively defer their winning aspirations simply cannot.

In baseball, teams typically have the summers to themselves, and they play a hell of a lot of games. While none of those contests has much meaning in and of itself, together they can create a collage of memories for the local fan that helps her place herself in the larger context of the year. Less loftily, they're just always there for you, nearly every day from April into October. You go into a restaurant, and there they are in the corner of your eye above the bar. You take a drive up north, and Dan Dickerson and Jim Price accompany you on the radio. You have family coming into town, and the easiest thing to do is take them to a ballgame. A solid, reliable baseball team fills up all the little awkward gaps of our existence—the pauses in a meal, the friction of small talk, the otherwise lost nights spent doing nothing but laying on a couch—and, best of all, it can do the same, equally, for everybody around you. But when that team suddenly fails to provide even a marginally competitive on-field product, every summer feels just a little bit emptier, because hope and belief are the necessary ingredients that make this relationship function.

That's why I'm practically spilling over with joy as I write this and consider the Tigers' accomplishments over the past 12 months. While team owner Chris Ilitch does not deserve to be let off the hook for the apathetic doldrums that swallowed this franchise whole, I still find myself in a forgiving and grateful mood, because, finally, I don't have to feel like a complete doofus for being a Tigers fan. Instead, I am merely a doofus for unrelated reasons who is doofily thrilled by her not-a-joke of a ballclub and for the little sparks of happiness they have provided me and my loved ones. There is hope for more than that—best-case scenario, Javy Báez and Eduardo Rodríguez amp up the style and regularity of the W's—but, for now, I'll take it. There was that shared intake of breath live in Comerica Park as Cabrera flied out to the warning track in the ninth inning against Raisel Iglesias while sitting on 499. There was the lunacy of seeing Cabrera slide into second on Opening Day after mistaking a home run for a double in the fog, while I was bedridden and recovering from surgery. There was the goofy delirium shared both in the dugout and across cell networks when Mize drew a bases-loaded walk in St. Louis in his first time facing live pitching since high school. There were the phone screens we crowded around at a wedding to watch Miggy chase down history. And, of course, there was the relief and appreciation I felt while sitting on the floor of Chicago's O'Hare Airport, watching Cabrera trot around the bases and then exchange fist bumps and hugs with his teammates after finally going yard for the 500th time.

It could be so much worse. It *was* so much worse. And now it is OK. ■

—*Lauren Theisen is a co-owner and blog girl at* Defector.

HITTERS

Akil Baddoo OF

Born: 08/16/98 Age: 23 Bats: L Throws: L Height: 6'1" Weight: 214 lb. Origin: Round 2, 2016 Draft (#74 overall)

YEAR	TEAM	LVL	AGE	PA	R	2B	3B	HR	RBI	BB	K	SB	CS	Whiff%	AVG/OBP/SLG	DRC+	BABIP	BRR	FRAA	WARP
2019	FTM	A+	20	131	15	3	3	4	9	12	39	6	2		.214/.290/.393	101	.280	1.8	CF(21): -2.8, LF(6): -0.2	0.3
2021	DET	MLB	22	461	60	20	7	13	55	45	122	18	4	30.5%	.259/.330/.436	90	.335	2.5	CF(66): 3.6, LF(56): -3.2, RF(5): 0.2	1.6
2022 DC	*DET*	*MLB*	*23*	*554*	*67*	*21*	*9*	*13*	*50*	*56*	*147*	*16*	*6*	*30.3%*	*.231/.312/.392*	*87*	*.303*	*2.3*	*CF 2, LF -2*	*1.3*

Comparables: Christian Yelich, Jay Bruce, Randal Grichuk

In 2004, then-Senator Barack Obama introduced himself to the world at the Democratic National Convention as "a skinny kid with a funny name," effectively usurping an apt introduction 17 years later, when Baddoo became the first feel-good baseball story coming out of a dark winter. A Rule 5 pick who last played in Single-A before undergoing Tommy John surgery, he corked a home run on the first major-league pitch thrown to him. The next night, he hit a grand slam. The game after that, a walkoff single. Despite a summer slump, he still put together outstanding rookie numbers through the generous application of extra-base hits, and became one of the hottest selling jerseys in Detroit. He's a third or fourth outfielder by most measures, but he barrels the ball more than most and can turn doubles into triples: all the measures of a fun player with a low ceiling. Keep buying the jerseys.

Javier Báez SS

Born: 12/01/92 Age: 29 Bats: R Throws: R Height: 6'0" Weight: 190 lb. Origin: Round 1, 2011 Draft (#9 overall)

YEAR	TEAM	LVL	AGE	PA	R	2B	3B	HR	RBI	BB	K	SB	CS	Whiff%	AVG/OBP/SLG	DRC+	BABIP	BRR	FRAA	WARP
2019	CHC	MLB	26	561	89	38	4	29	85	28	156	11	7	35.6%	.281/.316/.531	104	.345	4.1	SS(129): 6.7, 3B(1): 0.1	3.3
2020	CHC	MLB	27	235	27	9	1	8	24	7	75	3	0	38.0%	.203/.238/.360	77	.262	0.5	SS(56): 12.1, LF(1): -0.0	1.3
2021	NYM	MLB	28	186	32	9	0	9	22	13	53	5	2	39.6%	.299/.371/.515	103	.390	1.0	2B(35): -4.4, SS(12): 0.5	0.4
2021	CHC	MLB	28	361	48	9	2	22	65	15	131	13	3	41.1%	.248/.292/.484	92	.330	-1.3	SS(88): 9.3	1.8
2022 DC	*DET*	*MLB*	*29*	*583*	*65*	*24*	*2*	*22*	*70*	*30*	*192*	*13*	*6*	*39.8%*	*.228/.277/.406*	*82*	*.304*	*1.1*	*SS 5*	*1.4*

Comparables: Ryne Sandberg, Robin Yount, Alan Trammell

Click on any plate discipline tab for any of the major baseball stats sites, and you'll see Báez's name all over the place—or at least, you will once you arrange it from worst to first. He tied with Patrick Wisdom for the largest whiff rate in the league to go with its highest swinging-strike rate at 21.7% and lowest contact rate at 62.2%. That lines up with the eye test: Báez—now eight seasons into this thing—continues to swing at breaking pitches three feet off the plate and fastballs at his forehead. That didn't change when he joined New York at the trade deadline, as he struck out in nearly a third of his plate appearances. But going from the sinking Cubs to the (at the time) contending Mets seemed to spark a player who admitted that playing in empty stadiums during the pandemic depressed his output.

The total package was probably the hardest of any free agent to figure gauge, and there was probably no riskier gamble on the market than hoping that Báez will figure out plate patience before his abundant, otherworldly physical tools begin to decline. Or, just crushing the ball often enough to even it out. He remains a peerless defender in the middle infield—moving from shortstop to second base for the Mets presented no problems—and a fantastic baserunner, and that comes with superb power, particularly against any pitcher foolish enough to throw him a hittable strike. The Tigers appear to have felt no hesitation, signing Báez to a six-year, $140 million contract, as they push forward into their next contention cycle.

Tucker Barnhart C
Born: 01/07/91 Age: 31 Bats: L Throws: R Height: 5'11" Weight: 192 lb. Origin: Round 10, 2009 Draft (#299 overall)

YEAR	TEAM	LVL	AGE	PA	R	2B	3B	HR	RBI	BB	K	SB	CS	Whiff%	AVG/OBP/SLG	DRC+	BABIP	BRR	FRAA	WARP
2019	CIN	MLB	28	364	32	14	0	11	40	44	83	1	0	23.9%	.231/.328/.380	92	.278	-3.2	C(102): 9.1, 1B(3): 0.1	1.8
2020	CIN	MLB	29	110	10	3	0	5	13	12	28	0	0	24.6%	.204/.291/.388	94	.231	0.2	C(36): 4.2, 1B(2): 0.0	0.8
2021	CIN	MLB	30	388	41	21	0	7	48	29	100	0	0	26.2%	.247/.317/.368	78	.324	-2.1	C(102): 6.8, 1B(2): -0.0	1.0
2022 DC	*DET*	*MLB*	*31*	*340*	*33*	*14*	*1*	*6*	*36*	*32*	*79*	*0*	*1*	*25.5%*	*.222/.303/.340*	*77*	*.279*	*-0.4*	*C 1*	*0.7*

Comparables: Johnny Edwards, Alan Ashby, Brent Mayne

YEAR	TEAM	P. COUNT	FRM RUNS	BLK RUNS	THRW RUNS	TOT RUNS
2019	CIN	13047	7.9	0.7	-0.1	8.5
2020	CIN	4801	4.1	0.2	0.0	4.2
2021	CIN	14571	5.3	0.5	0.7	6.5
2022	*DET*	*13228*	*-2.2*	*1.9*	*0.1*	*-0.2*

Barnhart spent the first half of the 2021 season making it difficult for long-awaited rookie Tyler Stephenson to slide into the primary catcher's role. Favorable luck on batted balls was powering his best offensive performance to date, with enough hits finding gaps to give him a somewhat-respectable ISO. His luck ran out in the second half, though, costing him nearly 100 points of OPS and making it easier for the Reds to pass on his $7.5 million club option, which Detroit picked up. The underlying metrics say Barnhart's bat has been steadily declining for a few years now, and while the quality of his defense and his position set the bar pretty low for how much he needs to hit to be a starter, that bar does lay somewhere above his 2021 DRC+. But he's still probably years away from not playing at least a part-time role behind the plate, which is an incredible thing to say about a catcher drafted 299th overall out of high school who has already logged eight big-league seasons.

Daniel Cabrera OF
Born: 09/05/98 Age: 23 Bats: L Throws: L Height: 6'3" Weight: 200 lb. Origin: Round 2, 2020 Draft (#62 overall)

YEAR	TEAM	LVL	AGE	PA	R	2B	3B	HR	RBI	BB	K	SB	CS	Whiff%	AVG/OBP/SLG	DRC+	BABIP	BRR	FRAA	WARP
2021	WM	A+	22	422	54	19	6	9	64	34	95	7	4		.242/.300/.395	102	.294	-0.5	RF(49): -2.8, CF(26): -4.4, LF(23): 0.9	0.8
2021	ERI	AA	22	71	8	2	0	4	9	1	18	1	0		.174/.197/.377	98	.170	0.2	RF(9): 0.4, LF(8): -0.0	0.3
2022 non-DC	*DET*	*MLB*	*23*	*251*	*21*	*10*	*1*	*5*	*24*	*15*	*62*	*2*	*1*	*25.5%*	*.221/.271/.347*	*65*	*.279*	*0.1*	*RF -1, CF -1*	*-0.5*

Comparables: Anthony Santander, Lastings Milledge, Adam Eaton

There's already a veritable library of Annual comments written on Daniel Cabrera (Baltimore Orioles 2004-2008), a hulking pitcher who threw in the upper 90s before everyone did, but walked nearly as many as he struck out. Millenials will remember him. This is the first entry on this Cabrera, LSU Tiger turned Detroit Tigers minor leaguer. This Cabrera was a solid SEC producer who has been lauded for his advanced hitting ability, though he didn't perform well in his first pro season. Given his Double-A walk rate, the question for the moment is: Given one at-bat, would Daniel Cabrera walk Daniel Cabrera?

Miguel Cabrera DH/1B
Born: 04/18/83 Age: 39 Bats: R Throws: R Height: 6'4" Weight: 267 lb. Origin: International Free Agent, 1999

YEAR	TEAM	LVL	AGE	PA	R	2B	3B	HR	RBI	BB	K	SB	CS	Whiff%	AVG/OBP/SLG	DRC+	BABIP	BRR	FRAA	WARP
2019	DET	MLB	36	549	41	21	0	12	59	48	108	0	0	24.4%	.282/.346/.398	97	.336	-4.5	1B(26): -1.7	0.6
2020	DET	MLB	37	231	28	4	0	10	35	24	51	1	0	31.6%	.250/.329/.417	113	.283	-1.1		0.8
2021	DET	MLB	38	526	48	16	0	15	75	40	118	0	0	25.8%	.256/.316/.386	99	.305	-5.6	1B(44): 0.0	0.6
2022 DC	*DET*	*MLB*	*39*	*516*	*57*	*17*	*0*	*15*	*58*	*44*	*112*	*0*	*0*	*26.5%*	*.250/.318/.388*	*94*	*.296*	*-1.0*	*1B 0*	*0.6*

Comparables: Eddie Murray, Harmon Killebrew, Hank Aaron

He's thoroughly cooked. His hips are brass. His knees are chalk. But Cabrera announced his intention to play out the rest of his contract, which means two more seasons of this. Given what we saw last year, there may be some flashes of brilliance left to augment the journey of hitting milestone markers and surpassing other splendid sluggers in statistical supremacy. He made it to 500 home runs at long last, and a couple weeks later, for fun, hit safely in nine straight plate appearances. There's still a level of ebullience in his playing style as he's surrounded by the next generation, even if there's nothing but soul-crushing ennui in his lower ligaments that keep him out of afternoon games. He ought to reach 3,000 hits in April, potentially the last swatsman to reach that mark for a generation. He'll also become the seventh with 3,000 and 500 and the third to also have 600 doubles. It's painful to watch and yet pleasurable to see.

Daz Cameron OF
Born: 01/15/97 Age: 25 Bats: R Throws: R Height: 6'2" Weight: 185 lb. Origin: Round 1, 2015 Draft (#37 overall)

YEAR	TEAM	LVL	AGE	PA	R	2B	3B	HR	RBI	BB	K	SB	CS	Whiff%	AVG/OBP/SLG	DRC+	BABIP	BRR	FRAA	WARP
2019	SAN	WIN	22	82	9	3	3	1	4	6	20	2	0		.205/.284/.370		.269			
2019	TOL	AAA	22	528	68	22	6	13	43	62	152	17	8		.214/.330/.377	83	.291	3.4	CF(93): 1.6, RF(19): 5.8	1.7
2020	DET	MLB	23	59	4	2	1	0	3	2	19	1	0	26.5%	.193/.220/.263	74	.289	-0.5	RF(16): -0.1	-0.1
2021	TOL	AAA	24	181	33	11	2	6	23	15	39	7	3		.296/.365/.500	104	.356	0.8	CF(22): 0.5, RF(10): 1.3, LF(5): -1.1	0.8
2021	DET	MLB	24	115	16	5	0	4	13	10	38	6	0	30.8%	.194/.278/.359	81	.262	1.9	RF(18): -2.0, CF(15): -0.5, LF(1): -0.1	0.1
2022 DC	*DET*	*MLB*	*25*	*155*	*15*	*6*	*1*	*3*	*16*	*12*	*46*	*5*	*2*	*29.0%*	*.215/.290/.346*	*75*	*.294*	*0.5*	*RF 0, CF 0*	*0.1*

Comparables: Lewis Brinson, Aaron Hicks, Teoscar Hernández

At some point we'll stop the parallels to young Cameron to his father Mike. That moment will arrive at the least after this paragraph. His dad's first two seasons were a bit rough as a top 50 prospect (.163/.226/.492 in 56 PA), but once he turned 24 he had a Rookie of the Year-type season. Cameron at 24 had far more downtime. A wrist fracture, followed by a sprained toe, took two months of his 2021, hampering him from hitting his stride, assuming it was going to happen. The good news below the surface was his .500 slugging in two months at Triple-A—the highest for any of row on his statsheet. Cameron has the skills to play center field, just not the fortune to stay there in any regular capacity. If anything, the tiresome comps to his bloodlines have one benefit: They serve as a reminder that progress isn't linear, and the hit tool can arrive fashionably late. Perhaps Daz is simply one year behind dad in every respect. One breakout year is all it may take to unlock the Mike drop.

Roberto Campos OF Born: 06/14/03 Age: 19 Bats: R Throws: R Height: 6'3" Weight: 200 lb. Origin: International Free Agent, 2019

YEAR	TEAM	LVL	AGE	PA	R	2B	3B	HR	RBI	BB	K	SB	CS	Whiff%	AVG/OBP/SLG	DRC+	BABIP	BRR	FRAA	WARP
2021	TIGW	ROK	18	155	20	5	0	8	19	17	41	3	0		.228/.316/.441		.261			
2022															*No projection*					

Comparables: Jose Pena, Jesus Marriaga, Jean Montero

Roberto Campos was an outfielder from Manzanillo, Cuba, born in 1902. That Campos briefly played for a Negro Leagues club called the Cuban Stars (West) way back in 1923. We may somehow know less about the modern-day Campos, born just over 100 years later, who defected from Cuba at 13 and signed with the Tigers for a club-record $2.85 million at age 16. Few scouts were allowed to see the young prospect before his signing, and, thanks to certain world events, few have gotten the chance to witness him since. He finally reached the complex level halfway through 2021 and provided the tiniest glimpse of his conjectured profile, knocking nearly as many extra-base hits (13) as singles (18).

Jeimer Candelario 3B Born: 11/24/93 Age: 28 Bats: S Throws: R Height: 6'1" Weight: 216 lb. Origin: International Free Agent, 2010

YEAR	TEAM	LVL	AGE	PA	R	2B	3B	HR	RBI	BB	K	SB	CS	Whiff%	AVG/OBP/SLG	DRC+	BABIP	BRR	FRAA	WARP
2019	TOR	WIN	25	100	12	9	2	1	14	12	20	0	0		.244/.340/.430		.303			
2019	TOL	AAA	25	178	30	10	2	9	33	22	35	0	0		.320/.416/.588	127	.367	-1.6	3B(30): 1.2, 1B(7): -0.4	0.9
2019	DET	MLB	25	386	33	17	2	8	32	43	99	3	1	25.8%	.203/.306/.337	80	.262	-1.0	3B(69): -1.0, 1B(20): -0.2	-0.2
2020	DET	MLB	26	206	30	11	3	7	29	20	49	1	1	27.8%	.297/.369/.503	109	.372	-0.3	1B(43): 1.3, 3B(10): 2.2	1.0
2021	DET	MLB	27	626	75	42	3	16	67	65	135	0	0	23.5%	.271/.351/.443	106	.333	-1.4	3B(142): -1.0	2.3
2022 DC	*DET*	*MLB*	*28*	*577*	*66*	*29*	*3*	*15*	*64*	*59*	*122*	*1*	*1*	*23.9%*	*.251/.334/.416*	*105*	*.299*	*-0.4*	*3B 0, 1B 0*	*2.0*

Comparables: Juan Francisco, Brandon Drury, Cheslor Cuthbert

There was every reason to believe that Candelario's breakout was another 2020 mirage, a momentary feast on broken pitchers in empty stadiums, a BABIP-fueled fever dream. Then came 2021. The third baseman proved that his offensive explosion wasn't just luck, making contact better than ever before, while his career-best line-drive rate resulted in 42 doubles, leading the league. Local media awarded him "Tiger of the Year" for the second consecutive time, a feat last achieved by Miguel Cabrera when he won the Triple Crown and then the Triple Slash in 2012-2013. The bar is lower now, admittedly, but it's still something to put on the fridge. Also, he deserves a fancier fridge: Candelario has earned an extension not just through his production, but by surviving Detroit's five-year plan.

Harold Castro IF Born: 11/30/93 Age: 28 Bats: L Throws: R Height: 5'10" Weight: 195 lb. Origin: International Free Agent, 2011

YEAR	TEAM	LVL	AGE	PA	R	2B	3B	HR	RBI	BB	K	SB	CS	Whiff%	AVG/OBP/SLG	DRC+	BABIP	BRR	FRAA	WARP
2019	TOL	AAA	25	134	20	5	1	4	25	9	26	1	3		.328/.371/.484	111	.387	1.7	2B(23): -1.4, 1B(2): 0.1, 3B(2): 0.3	0.8
2019	DET	MLB	25	369	30	10	4	5	38	9	86	4	2	24.5%	.291/.305/.384	72	.367	-2.3	2B(34): -2.3, CF(30): 0.2, 3B(10): -1.0	-0.4
2020	DET	MLB	26	54	6	4	0	0	3	5	11	0	0	24.3%	.347/.407/.429	92	.447	0.3	LF(6): -0.2, 3B(4): 0.1, RF(4): 0.2	0.2
2021	DET	MLB	27	339	35	13	1	3	37	14	72	1	1	26.0%	.283/.310/.359	84	.351	-1.7	SS(43): -0.3, 2B(33): -0.3, 1B(15): 0.9	0.3
2022 DC	*DET*	*MLB*	*28*	*200*	*17*	*7*	*1*	*2*	*15*	*8*	*44*	*2*	*2*	*25.2%*	*.249/.284/.331*	*65*	*.315*	*0.2*	*2B 0, 3B 0*	*-0.3*

Comparables: César Hernández, Marwin Gonzalez, Ehire Adrianza

"Harold" peaked as a boys' name in the United States back in the 1920s, at 12th overall. These days it is out of the top 800. It's part of why Castro is a delightfully vintage player, including the origin of his nickname. The local sportswriters started calling him Hittin' Harold, possibly in half-jest because he's by no means a slugger, but also because it's alliterative. Which in itself is weird, because Hackin' was right there. Castro stands out in today's game as a free-swinging contact hitter: He was the league's most prodigious producer of line drives (over one-third of his batted balls), which will always lead to a consistently high BABIP. A hit is a hit, although most of them are mere singles. And a Harold in the 2020s is not unlike a Harold in the 1920s, just with more modern science and less understanding of the nuances of The Great Gatsby.

Willi Castro 2B Born: 04/24/97 Age: 25 Bats: S Throws: R Height: 6'1" Weight: 206 lb. Origin: International Free Agent, 2013

YEAR	TEAM	LVL	AGE	PA	R	2B	3B	HR	RBI	BB	K	SB	CS	Whiff%	AVG/OBP/SLG	DRC+	BABIP	BRR	FRAA	WARP
2019	ESC	WIN	22	94	9	2	0	0	7	6	17	1	0		.221/.266/.244		.268			
2019	TOL	AAA	22	525	75	28	8	11	62	37	110	17	4		.301/.366/.467	98	.369	1.4	SS(111): -17.6, 2B(7): -0.1, 3B(1): -0.0	0.6
2019	DET	MLB	22	110	10	6	1	1	8	6	34	0	1	30.7%	.230/.284/.340	68	.333	0.6	SS(29): 1.1	0.1
2020	DET	MLB	23	140	21	4	2	6	24	7	38	0	1	30.8%	.349/.381/.550	99	.448	-1.7	SS(27): -1.3, 3B(8): -1.6, 2B(1): -0.0	-0.1
2021	DET	MLB	24	450	56	15	6	9	38	23	109	9	4	29.4%	.220/.273/.351	76	.275	1.4	2B(91): -0.8, SS(20): -1.4, LF(10): -0.3	0.1
2022 DC	*DET*	*MLB*	*25*	*197*	*20*	*7*	*2*	*4*	*19*	*11*	*48*	*3*	*2*	*28.4%*	*.243/.298/.380*	*80*	*.308*	*0.5*	*2B 0, SS 0*	*0.2*

Comparables: Jonathan Villar, Asdrúbal Cabrera, Marwin Gonzalez

Common advice when giving a speech in front of a large group of strangers is to picture them all in their underwear. Based on the extreme dropoff in production from 2020 to 2021, better advice for Castro might be to imagine all the fans as soulless cardboard cutouts. It's a fair plan for all athletes; assume the sound is artificial. Assume the paid ticketholders are hallucinations at worst, animatronic at best. Keep slapping the ball and you'll get on base. Stop getting under the ball and those line drives will drop for singles, then use your speed to advance. The cardboard beings will understand by nodding in a swaying fashion, although that just could be the wind. Don't let a single person tell you that 2020 was simply a glorified small sample, because then cardboard cutouts would be talking, which is a bad sign. And if you feel compelled to give any of the "fans" a signature, sign directly on their face. They're not real. None of this is real.

Dillon Dingler C Born: 09/17/98 Age: 23 Bats: R Throws: R Height: 6'3" Weight: 210 lb. Origin: Round 2, 2020 Draft (#38 overall)

YEAR	TEAM	LVL	AGE	PA	R	2B	3B	HR	RBI	BB	K	SB	CS	Whiff%	AVG/OBP/SLG	DRC+	BABIP	BRR	FRAA	WARP
2021	WM	A+	22	141	25	6	1	8	24	13	36	0	0		.287/.376/.549	127	.342	2.1	C(24): 4.8	1.5
2021	ERI	AA	22	208	24	3	3	4	20	9	62	1	0		.202/.264/.314	82	.272	-0.3	C(40): 5.5	0.8
2022 non-DC	*DET*	*MLB*	*23*	*251*	*21*	*9*	*1*	*5*	*23*	*14*	*74*	*0*	*0*	*30.1%*	*.211/.271/.332*	*63*	*.288*	*-0.1*	*C 1*	*0.1*

Comparables: Danny Jansen, Devin Mesoraco, Francisco Cervelli

YEAR	TEAM	P. COUNT	FRM RUNS	BLK RUNS	THRW RUNS	TOT RUNS
2021	ERI	5952	4.4	0.5	0.8	5.7
2021	WM	3574	3.5	-0.3	1.4	4.5
2022	*DET*	*6956*	*0.6*	*-0.1*	*0.1*	*0.5*

Profiling as a MLB-caliber defensive catcher who hits dingers has its perks, and these characteristics got Dingler a second-round draft slot in 2020 despite a relatively recent transition to the position. The one-time Buckeye is a good athlete with a strong arm behind the dish and a powerful bat when standing astride it. Well, we've done what we can, and now must leave fate to the gods who decide the fate of catching prospects. Maybe the contact develops better than the power, and he resembles Jason Kendall, or maybe the power overwhelms the hit tool and he's Gary Sánchez. Maybe he becomes a defense-first backstop, or moves out from behind the plate and ends up in the outfield. Scouting is tough work, but especially so with young backstops.

Niko Goodrum SS Born: 02/28/92 Age: 30 Bats: S Throws: R Height: 6'3" Weight: 215 lb. Origin: Round 2, 2010 Draft (#71 overall)

YEAR	TEAM	LVL	AGE	PA	R	2B	3B	HR	RBI	BB	K	SB	CS	Whiff%	AVG/OBP/SLG	DRC+	BABIP	BRR	FRAA	WARP
2019	DET	MLB	27	472	61	27	5	12	45	46	138	12	3	31.9%	.248/.322/.421	83	.338	3.7	SS(38): 3.9, 2B(22): -1.9, 1B(18): 2.3	1.6
2020	DET	MLB	28	179	15	7	1	5	20	18	69	7	1	38.6%	.184/.263/.335	66	.276	-0.8	SS(31): 3.3, 2B(11): 0.7	0.1
2021	TOL	AAA	29	62	7	0	0	0	2	7	16	1	0		.185/.274/.185	90	.256	-0.1	SS(5): -0.8, CF(3): -0.2, 2B(2): 0.6	0.0
2021	DET	MLB	29	325	39	11	2	9	33	29	107	14	5	37.1%	.214/.292/.359	78	.301	0.4	SS(66): 1.3, 2B(9): 0.4, CF(8): -0.8	0.4
2022 non-DC	*DET*	*MLB*	*30*	*251*	*24*	*10*	*1*	*6*	*26*	*23*	*83*	*5*	*2*	*35.9%*	*.209/.289/.359*	*73*	*.297*	*0.4*	*SS 1, 2B 0*	*0.2*

Comparables: Pedro Florimón, Cliff Pennington, Jordy Mercer

Like the Velvet Underground's Nico embarking on a solo career to prove she was more than Lou Reed's bluesy contralto counterpoint, Goodrum has also elected to strike out on his own, leaving the Tigers as a free agent after being outrighted off the roster. He'll need to strike out with less help from opposing pitchers, however, if his speed and defense versatility are to secure him a starring role in another act.

★ ★ ★ *2022 Top 101 Prospect* **#6** ★ ★ ★

Riley Greene OF Born: 09/28/00 Age: 21 Bats: L Throws: L Height: 6'3" Weight: 200 lb. Origin: Round 1, 2019 Draft (#5 overall)

YEAR	TEAM	LVL	AGE	PA	R	2B	3B	HR	RBI	BB	K	SB	CS	Whiff%	AVG/OBP/SLG	DRC+	BABIP	BRR	FRAA	WARP
2019	TIW	ROK	18	43	9	3	0	2	8	5	12	0	0		.351/.442/.595		.478			
2019	CON	SS	18	100	12	3	1	1	7	11	25	1	0		.295/.380/.386		.403			
2019	WM	A	18	108	13	2	2	2	13	6	26	4	0		.219/.278/.344	87	.268	1.1	CF(20): 1.4, RF(4): -0.1	0.4
2021	ERI	AA	20	373	59	16	5	16	54	41	102	12	1		.298/.381/.525	112	.386	1.8	CF(73): 5.6, RF(6): -0.5, LF(5): -1.0	2.4
2021	TOL	AAA	20	185	36	9	3	8	30	22	51	4	0		.308/.400/.553	105	.406	1.5	RF(15): -0.0, LF(13): -1.7, CF(13): -0.8	0.6
2022 DC	*DET*	*MLB*	*21*	*129*	*14*	*4*	*2*	*3*	*13*	*10*	*38*	*1*	*1*	*30.6%*	*.237/.309/.398*	*89*	*.324*	*0.3*	*LF -1*	*0.1*

Comparables: Andrew McCutchen, Ronald Acuña Jr., Jay Bruce

The fifth-overall pick of 2019 is performing, well, like a top-five pick. Greene currently handles all three outfield spots but may have to settle into a corner sooner or later, which shouldn't be an issue as long as the bat continues to play. It's one of those sweet and powerful lefty swings that portends both average and pop, a welcome southpaw complement to the right-handed thump possessed by Spencer Torkelson. Rebuilds never seem to come off quite as expected, but a nice low-variance middle-of-the-order combo would be a good start while we wait on the rest of the pitching. Aren't we always waiting on the rest of the pitching?

Grayson Greiner C Born: 10/11/92 Age: 29 Bats: R Throws: R Height: 6'6" Weight: 238 lb. Origin: Round 3, 2014 Draft (#99 overall)

YEAR	TEAM	LVL	AGE	PA	R	2B	3B	HR	RBI	BB	K	SB	CS	Whiff%	AVG/OBP/SLG	DRC+	BABIP	BRR	FRAA	WARP
2019	TOL	AAA	26	53	8	1	0	2	4	4	16	0	0		.250/.321/.396	80	.333	0.5	C(9): 1.0	0.2
2019	DET	MLB	26	224	18	5	1	5	19	13	70	0	0	32.3%	.202/.251/.308	66	.276	-1.0	C(58): -2.6	-0.3
2020	DET	MLB	27	55	8	2	0	3	8	3	20	0	0	31.7%	.118/.182/.333	85	.107	0.4	C(18): -0.9	0.0
2021	TOL	AAA	28	134	9	6	0	1	9	13	49	0	0		.202/.284/.277	54	.329	-0.9	C(31): 3.7	0.1
2021	DET	MLB	28	82	7	4	0	1	7	9	31	0	0	40.3%	.236/.321/.333	68	.400	-0.3	C(31): -3.1	-0.3
2022 DC	*FA*	*MLB*	*29*	*138*	*12*	*5*	*0*	*3*	*13*	*11*	*49*	*0*	*0*	*36.4%*	*.191/.268/.318*	*56*	*.286*	*-0.2*	*C -2*	*-0.4*

Comparables: Sandy León, Jesús Sucre, Martín Maldonado

YEAR	TEAM	P. COUNT	FRM RUNS	BLK RUNS	THRW RUNS	TOT RUNS
2019	TOL	1168	1.1	0.0	0.0	1.1
2019	DET	8636	-1.8	-0.3	0.4	-1.6
2020	DET	2451	-0.6	-0.1	0.1	-0.6
2021	DET	3665	-2.5	-0.2	0.1	-2.5
2021	TOL	4615	1.1	-0.1	0.4	1.5
2022	*FA*	*6956*	*-3.3*	*-0.2*	*0.0*	*-3.5*

When it is said baseball is a sport for all shapes and sizes, the insinuation is inclusion of the shorter players. Greiner is tall enough to play basketball, but years ago chose baseball, and of all positions, catcher. He has squatted behind home plate for more MLB games, by far, by someone at least 6-foot-6 (137 and counting). In second place with 19 is a man named Don Gile, who played parts of four seasons with the Red Sox. In his final season back in 1962, he was 0-for-34 heading into the final day, starting both ends of a doubleheader and getting his first base hit of '62 in the first game. His second hit was in the second game—a walkoff two-run home run. Greiner isn't as offensively challenged as Gile, though it's closer than you'd think, nor is he defensively inclined. So the next time he makes a stellar play, whatever it may be, perhaps that's the moment to pack it up.

Robbie Grossman OF

Born: 09/16/89 Age: 32 Bats: S Throws: L Height: 6'0" Weight: 209 lb. Origin: Round 6, 2008 Draft (#174 overall)

YEAR	TEAM	LVL	AGE	PA	R	2B	3B	HR	RBI	BB	K	SB	CS	Whiff%	AVG/OBP/SLG	DRC+	BABIP	BRR	FRAA	WARP
2019	OAK	MLB	29	482	57	21	3	6	38	59	86	9	4	15.4%	.240/.334/.348	92	.288	-4.3	LF(112): 4.4, RF(20): -1.1, CF(1): 0.2	1.2
2020	OAK	MLB	30	192	23	12	2	8	23	21	38	8	1	18.4%	.241/.344/.482	109	.267	0.9	LF(46): 1.5, CF(2): -0.1, RF(1): -0.1	1.0
2021	DET	MLB	31	671	88	23	3	23	67	98	155	20	5	21.6%	.239/.357/.415	111	.286	1.4	LF(82): -8.3, RF(73): -3.0	2.1
2022 DC	*DET*	*MLB*	*32*	*580*	*68*	*22*	*2*	*13*	*51*	*80*	*124*	*8*	*4*	*20.9%*	*.228/.341/.365*	*97*	*.276*	*0.1*	*RF -1, LF 0*	*1.4*

Comparables: Pat Burrell, Gary Matthews, Gary Roenicke

Grossman arriving in Detroit and doubling his career bests in both home runs and stolen bases is like Grossman arriving in Detroit and manufacturing a compact car that outperforms the Honda Civic. He improved his mileage with more of an upward swing and was still just as patient, finishing second in the AL in walks, while banging out the elusive 20-20 season. Now for the sticker shock: He also shattered his career strikeout mark. But as he ventures into the 30s chapter of his career, he looks more like a polished outfielder that gives you a lil' bit of everything you expect, but continues to be overlooked. Which means he's a hatchback.

Eric Haase C/LF

Born: 12/18/92 Age: 29 Bats: R Throws: R Height: 5'10" Weight: 210 lb. Origin: Round 7, 2011 Draft (#218 overall)

YEAR	TEAM	LVL	AGE	PA	R	2B	3B	HR	RBI	BB	K	SB	CS	Whiff%	AVG/OBP/SLG	DRC+	BABIP	BRR	FRAA	WARP
2019	COL	AAA	26	401	67	12	3	28	60	42	142	1	1		.226/.315/.517	96	.279	-0.2	C(93): 1.6	1.6
2019	CLE	MLB	26	17	1	0	0	1	3	1	8	0	0	47.2%	.063/.118/.250	78			C(8): -0.5	0.0
2020	DET	MLB	27	19	1	0	0	0	2	1	6	0	0	39.5%	.176/.211/.176	87	.250	0.0	C(7): -0.0	0.0
2021	TOL	AAA	28	28	3	3	0	1	5	5	10	1	0		.348/.464/.609	87	.583	0.2	C(4): 0.0, LF(3): -0.3	0.0
2021	DET	MLB	28	381	48	12	1	22	61	26	119	2	0	34.7%	.231/.286/.459	103	.278	1.1	C(66): -7.1, LF(22): -1.8, 1B(1): -0.0	0.8
2022 DC	*DET*	*MLB*	*29*	*291*	*32*	*10*	*1*	*12*	*35*	*21*	*91*	*0*	*1*	*35.2%*	*.212/.274/.405*	*83*	*.266*	*-0.2*	*C -3, LF -1*	*0.0*

Comparables: Elias Díaz, Sandy León, Martín Maldonado

YEAR	TEAM	P. COUNT	FRM RUNS	BLK RUNS	THRW RUNS	TOT RUNS
2019	CLE	442	-0.5	0.0	0.0	-0.5
2019	COL	13713	-0.4	-0.1	-0.1	-0.6
2020	DET	778	0.0	0.0	0.1	0.1
2021	DET	9170	-6.1	0.1	0.1	-5.9
2022	*DET*	*6012*	*-4.6*	*-1.1*	*-0.2*	*-5.9*

Just like an IT person with people skills or a lawyer who can do math, a catcher who can hit home runs is a priceless combination of talents. Haase had proven himself as a minor-league masher (with 75 across three seasons), but any major-league hits prior to 2021 had been nothing more than happy little accidents. His all-or-nothing approach leads to an extremely Arencibian batting average, and his catching skills can charitably be summarized as "the mask hides the beard well." Stick him at the bottom of the lineup, and sometimes left field, and watch another 20 home runs soar majestically into throngs of giddy ticketholders.

Derek Hill CF

Born: 12/30/95 Age: 26 Bats: R Throws: R Height: 6'2" Weight: 190 lb. Origin: Round 1, 2014 Draft (#23 overall)

YEAR	TEAM	LVL	AGE	PA	R	2B	3B	HR	RBI	BB	K	SB	CS	Whiff%	AVG/OBP/SLG	DRC+	BABIP	BRR	FRAA	WARP
2019	MSS	WIN	23	65	8	4	0	3	6	5	21	6	1		.254/.323/.475		.343			
2019	ERI	AA	23	526	78	19	5	14	45	38	147	21	13		.243/.311/.394	83	.321	0.4	CF(80): 0.4, RF(37): 8.4, LF(2): -0.2	1.8
2020	DET	MLB	24	12	3	0	0	0	0	1	6	0	0	40.9%	.091/.167/.091	80	.200	0.0	CF(10): -0.8	-0.1
2021	TOL	AAA	25	141	21	5	3	4	15	10	39	4	1		.320/.377/.504	90	.434	-0.3	CF(17): 0.9, LF(10): -1.7, RF(6): -0.5	0.2
2021	DET	MLB	25	150	19	3	3	3	14	10	42	6	3	27.3%	.259/.313/.388	79	.351	0.7	CF(45): 2.9	0.6
2022 DC	*DET*	*MLB*	*26*	*186*	*18*	*6*	*1*	*2*	*18*	*12*	*53*	*7*	*4*	*30.4%*	*.228/.287/.338*	*69*	*.314*	*1.0*	*CF 1*	*0.1*

Comparables: Abraham Almonte, Juan Lagares, Michael A. Taylor

Drafting a high school player in the first round requires the patience of a police bunny at the Zootopia DMV. Consider that Hill was taken a few spots ahead of Brandon Finnegan in 2014, who pitched in the World Series a few months later, and ahead of Trea Turner, who becomes a free agent next year. Hill played over 500 games in the minors before getting substantial playing time with Detroit, and once he got it, showed off his speed at every chance. His elite mobility turns heads and makes plays, whether it's a diving catch or an extra base (all three of his triples were to left field). However, speed can also be dangerous, as he suffered two scary injuries while running—both in the field and on the bases. But he's done being patient, which is for the best, because so are the Tigers.

Ryan Kreidler SS

Born: 11/12/97 Age: 24 Bats: R Throws: R Height: 6'4" Weight: 208 lb. Origin: Round 4, 2019 Draft (#112 overall)

YEAR	TEAM	LVL	AGE	PA	R	2B	3B	HR	RBI	BB	K	SB	CS	Whiff%	AVG/OBP/SLG	DRC+	BABIP	BRR	FRAA	WARP
2019	CON	SS	21	257	28	13	4	2	20	20	61	9	4		.232/.307/.351		.304			
2021	ERI	AA	23	388	67	15	0	15	36	32	119	10	4		.256/.325/.429	96	.341	3.2	SS(88): -4.1	0.9
2021	TOL	AAA	23	162	28	8	0	7	22	24	39	5	2		.304/.407/.519	108	.374	2.4	SS(35): -1.4, 3B(7): -0.6	0.7
2022 non-DC	*DET*	*MLB*	*24*	*251*	*24*	*10*	*0*	*6*	*25*	*20*	*80*	*4*	*2*	*35.4%*	*.223/.293/.355*	*73*	*.314*	*0.2*	*SS -1, 3B 0*	*-0.1*

Comparables: Danny Espinosa, Jed Lowrie, Tommy Edman

Kreidler has become a pop-up prospect of sorts at age 23, going from your proverbial jack-of-all-trades middle-infield prospect to a dude who is suddenly hitting 20 homers and still playing short the vast majority of the time. Now, this sort of profile still probably works better as a bench piece who covers a few different spots, a Brad Miller type who homers just often enough to keep from getting fired. But a solid Double-A campaign and a fast start at Triple-A have made him look a lot more like a viable big-leaguer.

Isaac Paredes 3B Born: 02/18/99 Age: 23 Bats: R Throws: R Height: 5'11" Weight: 213 lb. Origin: International Free Agent, 2015

YEAR	TEAM	LVL	AGE	PA	R	2B	3B	HR	RBI	BB	K	SB	CS	Whiff%	AVG/OBP/SLG	DRC+	BABIP	BRR	FRAA	WARP
2019	OBR	WIN	20	188	22	5	1	2	20	17	18	1	1		.295/.372/.373		.320			
2019	MSS	WIN	20	69	11	2	1	2	8	12	13	0	0		.208/.377/.396		.231			
2019	ERI	AA	20	552	63	23	1	13	66	57	61	5	3		.282/.368/.416	133	.298	-2.0	3B(81): -2.9, SS(32): 0.6	3.3
2020	MAZ	WIN	21	177	28	17	0	4	26	27	12	5	0		.379/.480/.579		.389			
2020	DET	MLB	21	108	7	4	0	1	6	8	24	0	0	17.6%	.220/.278/.290	88	.280	-0.3	3B(33): -3.4	-0.3
2021	MAZ	WIN	22	181	26	6	0	4	23	37	20	0	0		.282/.436/.408		.305			
2021	TOL	AAA	22	315	39	10	2	11	42	56	47	0	0		.265/.397/.451	128	.281	-2.9	3B(32): 4.4, 2B(22): -1.4, SS(12): 2.4	2.2
2021	DET	MLB	22	85	7	3	1	1	5	10	11	0	0	13.8%	.208/.306/.319	107	.226	-0.7	2B(10): 0.4, 3B(8): -0.7, SS(5): -0.4	0.2
2022 DC	*DET*	*MLB*	*23*	*91*	*10*	*3*	*0*	*2*	*10*	*10*	*13*	*0*	*0*	*15.9%*	*.242/.341/.388*	*105*	*.261*	*-0.1*	*3B 0, 2B 0*	*0.3*

Comparables: Wilmer Flores, Ketel Marte, Alcides Escobar

A burgeoning professional pitch-taker, Paredes walked more than he struck out at Triple-A, and nearly matched those rates in his brief major-league stretches. His tree trunk frame makes him an unusual candidate to play all around the infield, but he has the hands and hose to commandeer second, third and occasionally short. He's just 23 and far from written out of a franchise's long term plans. It's all about on-base percentage with him, favoring the chance of double-digit homers. While he may not be the optimal middle infielder, enough reps could generate a funky batting line thanks to his offensive forbearance and high contact rate. And if the production is marginally different, a manager would rather have a reliable rangy defender at second than a patient but mercurial batter, and this is why fans don't manage games.

Victor Reyes OF Born: 10/05/94 Age: 27 Bats: S Throws: R Height: 6'5" Weight: 194 lb. Origin: International Free Agent, 2011

YEAR	TEAM	LVL	AGE	PA	R	2B	3B	HR	RBI	BB	K	SB	CS	Whiff%	AVG/OBP/SLG	DRC+	BABIP	BRR	FRAA	WARP
2019	TOL	AAA	24	308	50	19	1	10	58	14	50	10	6		.304/.334/.481	110	.335	0.5	RF(36): 0.4, CF(31): -0.4	1.4
2019	DET	MLB	24	292	29	16	5	3	25	14	64	9	3	21.1%	.304/.336/.431	85	.384	-0.7	CF(37): 0.1, LF(21): 1.6, RF(9): 0.0	0.7
2020	DET	MLB	25	213	30	7	2	4	14	9	45	8	2	26.5%	.277/.315/.391	90	.340	1.7	CF(30): 1.0, LF(22): -0.0, RF(18): -0.2	0.6
2021	TOL	AAA	26	91	13	7	2	1	10	10	17	5	2		.385/.462/.564	110	.475	-0.6	CF(9): 0.1, LF(6): -0.4, RF(4): -1.0	0.2
2021	DET	MLB	26	220	26	10	4	5	22	8	55	5	1	25.6%	.258/.284/.416	89	.327	-0.9	RF(43): 1.1, CF(20): -3.3, LF(1): -0.1	0.1
2022 DC	*DET*	*MLB*	*27*	*297*	*30*	*12*	*3*	*4*	*27*	*15*	*66*	*7*	*3*	*25.3%*	*.249/.293/.367*	*77*	*.311*	*0.9*	*RF 0, CF 0*	*0.1*

Comparables: Moisés Sierra, Marcell Ozuna, Ender Inciarte

On August 27, Reyes pinch hit in the eighth inning of a tied game against the Blue Jays. An outfielder who lasted through a Rule 5 season on a roughshod major-league roster, he gets all his bases from solid line drives and exceptional leg-based velocity; home runs are rare for him, both in the quantitative and qualitative sense. Reyes stroked a 1-1 pitch the other way, a sinking line drive to right-center field. The outfielder dove, but the ball went under his glove and rolled all the way to Comerica Park's right-field wall, located just outside Saginaw. Reyes, who split time between Detroit and Triple-A because his skillset is broad and short, ran all the way around the white pillows and slid in for what would prove to be the decisive run. It was MLB's first pinch-hit-inside-the-park home run in four years, and the first in the expansion era that gave their team the lead. There are 71 reasons Toronto missed the playoffs by one game—this was one of them.

Jake Rogers C Born: 04/18/95 Age: 27 Bats: R Throws: R Height: 6'1" Weight: 201 lb. Origin: Round 3, 2016 Draft (#97 overall)

YEAR	TEAM	LVL	AGE	PA	R	2B	3B	HR	RBI	BB	K	SB	CS	Whiff%	AVG/OBP/SLG	DRC+	BABIP	BRR	FRAA	WARP
2019	ERI	AA	24	112	17	3	1	5	21	19	26	0	0		.302/.429/.535	119	.356	-1.3	C(21): 0.8	0.6
2019	TOL	AAA	24	191	29	10	1	9	31	18	53	0	0		.223/.321/.458	98	.269	-2.8	C(48): 8.8	1.3
2019	DET	MLB	24	128	11	3	0	4	8	13	51	0	0	31.5%	.125/.222/.259	63	.175	-0.1	C(34): -2.4	-0.3
2021	DET	MLB	26	127	17	5	3	6	17	11	46	1	0	37.9%	.239/.306/.496	82	.344	-0.2	C(37): -2.2, P(1): -0.3	0.0
2022 DC	*DET*	*MLB*	*27*	*60*	*6*	*2*	*0*	*1*	*7*	*5*	*20*	*0*	*0*	*35.4%*	*.196/.279/.360*	*73*	*.268*	*0.0*	*C -1*	*0.0*

Comparables: Nick Hundley, Brett Hayes, Jonathan Lucroy

YEAR	TEAM	P. COUNT	FRM RUNS	BLK RUNS	THRW RUNS	TOT RUNS
2019	DET	5389	-2.1	-0.3	0.8	-1.7
2019	ERI	2903	1.3	0.0	0.0	1.3
2019	TOL	6997	7.3	0.0	0.2	7.4
2021	DET	5067	-2.4	-0.2	0.1	-2.5
2022	*DET*	*2405*	*-0.5*	*-0.4*	*0.1*	*-0.7*

It's no secret A.J. Hinch hates, hates, *hates* Rogers' mustache. Some people have been able to produce both hits and face hairs, such as Don Mattingly and, well, mostly Don Mattingly. Rogers' mustache lacks the volume up front and extends a bit around his mouth, but not much. It's a failed experiment. When it comes to Rogers hitting, he is either hitting it hard or not at all. That's the style, of course. If his mustache matched his swing, he'd thicken out the hair and grow the tips of that hedge down to his chin like he's Todd Jones. If he batted like he grew his mustache, he'd be a free agent. Fortunately for him he's a catcher with a strong throwing arm—although he's having Tommy John surgery on said arm, keeping him out for much of 2022. We'll see if Hinch makes the surgeon take care of the 'stache while he's under.

Jonathan Schoop 1B/2B Born: 10/16/91 Age: 30 Bats: R Throws: R Height: 6'1" Weight: 247 lb. Origin: International Free Agent, 2008

YEAR	TEAM	LVL	AGE	PA	R	2B	3B	HR	RBI	BB	K	SB	CS	Whiff%	AVG/OBP/SLG	DRC+	BABIP	BRR	FRAA	WARP
2019	MIN	MLB	27	464	61	23	1	23	59	20	116	1	1	32.3%	.256/.304/.473	100	.298	-1.9	2B(113): -4.8	1.2
2020	DET	MLB	28	177	26	4	2	8	23	8	39	0	0	27.8%	.278/.324/.475	107	.316	0.2	2B(44): -1.3	0.6
2021	DET	MLB	29	674	85	30	1	22	84	37	133	2	0	24.6%	.278/.320/.435	106	.317	0.5	1B(114): 4.1, 2B(38): 2.7, 3B(1): 0.1	2.9
2022 DC	*DET*	*MLB*	*30*	*563*	*68*	*22*	*1*	*18*	*61*	*31*	*105*	*1*	*1*	*25.1%*	*.258/.306/.413*	*96*	*.288*	*-0.8*	*2B 0, 1B 1*	*1.3*

Comparables: Brandon Phillips, Bill Mazeroski, Roberto Alomar

A right-side infielder with sufficient swinging strength, Schoop was a prime candidate to move to a postseason team in a legitimate midsummer swap, but instead accepted a deal from the Tigers in the rare bargaining month of August for two more seasons. He played a bunch of first base more out of need than waning skills, to the benefit of both popular versions of baseball: fantasy, and the other one. Additionally, Schoop's side quest to lead his team in homers just once continues unabated. He missed the mark to former Twins clubmate Robbie Grossman by a single shot, which was predestined if you believe in numerology, and who doesn't? In '20 Schoop wore no. 8, then gave it to Grossman as an incoming free agent, taking no. 7 instead. Don't be surprised if he plays it safe and runs out of the dugout this year wearing number 99.

★ ★ ★ *2022 Top 101 Prospect* **#4** ★ ★ ★

Spencer Torkelson 3B/1B Born: 08/26/99 Age: 22 Bats: R Throws: R Height: 6'1" Weight: 220 lb. Origin: Round 1, 2020 Draft (#1 overall)

YEAR	TEAM	LVL	AGE	PA	R	2B	3B	HR	RBI	BB	K	SB	CS	Whiff%	AVG/OBP/SLG	DRC+	BABIP	BRR	FRAA	WARP
2021	WM	A+	21	141	21	11	1	5	28	24	28	3	2		.312/.440/.569	128	.363	0.4	3B(16): -0.1, 1B(15): 0.0	0.9
2021	ERI	AA	21	212	33	10	0	14	36	30	50	1	1		.263/.373/.560	139	.278	-0.5	3B(27): -1.5, 1B(23): 0.0	1.4
2021	TOL	AAA	21	177	35	8	1	11	27	23	36	1	0		.238/.350/.531	120	.233	-0.1	1B(37): -1.0	0.7
2022 DC	*DET*	*MLB*	*22*	*493*	*59*	*20*	*2*	*17*	*57*	*53*	*119*	*2*	*1*	*26.6%*	*.233/.324/.412*	*104*	*.277*	*-0.4*	*1B 1*	*1.3*

Comparables: Miguel Andújar, Brandon Drury, Jeimer Candelario

Spencer Enochs Torkelson is the platonic ideal of a modern day bat-first prospect, even if his name does make him sound like a guy liable to be bribed by the sort of unsavory gambling influences that pervaded baseball around the time of the first American pandemic. Fortunately, gambling is no longer a part of the sport's landscape and will not be causing any issues in the future, right? Right? The Tigers raised some eyebrows when they announced him as a third baseman upon drafting him, but his offensive bona fides have never been a question and his plus hit/double-plus power bat should carry him regardless of which infield corner he comes to call home. Said power remained intact at all three levels in 2021, with only his walks and BABIP suffering from his advanced placement. Given both his and his team's momentum, he'll be in Detroit soon.

Gage Workman SS Born: 10/24/99 Age: 22 Bats: S Throws: R Height: 6'3" Weight: 202 lb. Origin: Round 4, 2020 Draft (#102 overall)

YEAR	TEAM	LVL	AGE	PA	R	2B	3B	HR	RBI	BB	K	SB	CS	Whiff%	AVG/OBP/SLG	DRC+	BABIP	BRR	FRAA	WARP
2021	LAK	A	21	228	26	16	4	3	19	30	60	22	3		.256/.357/.426	107	.353	2.5	SS(47): -0.7	1.1
2021	WM	A+	21	285	42	21	2	9	39	23	97	9	5		.237/.302/.440	87	.338	-1.0	SS(65): 7.2	1.0
2022 non-DC	*DET*	*MLB*	*22*	*251*	*20*	*13*	*1*	*4*	*23*	*18*	*84*	*9*	*4*	*33.5%*	*.208/.271/.336*	*63*	*.308*	*1.1*	*SS 1*	*0.0*

Comparables: Alex Bregman, Kyle Seager, Andrew Vaughn

It baffled at least one person when the Tigers announced Spencer Torkelson as a third baseman. Workman was Torkelson's teammate at Arizona State, handling the hot corner and letting his teammate focus on breaking team records. He's a good defender over there, and will pop some homers and steal some bags too. There's quite a bit of swing and miss in his game, however, and he'll have to shore up his contact abilities if he and Torkelson are going to team up once again with the big club.

PITCHERS

Tyler Alexander LHP Born: 07/14/94 Age: 27 Bats: R Throws: L Height: 6'2" Weight: 203 lb. Origin: Round 2, 2015 Draft (#65 overall)

YEAR	TEAM	LVL	AGE	W	L	SV	G	GS	IP	H	HR	BB/9	K/9	K	GB%	BABIP	WHIP	ERA	DRA-	WARP	MPH	FB%	Whiff%	CSP
2019	TOL	AAA	24	5	10	0	20	16	98^{1}	112	18	2.1	9.9	108	39.9%	.346	1.37	5.13	99	1.3				
2019	DET	MLB	24	1	4	0	13	8	53^{2}	68	9	1.2	7.9	47	36.9%	.347	1.40	4.86	124	-0.1	90.5	64.8%	18.3%	52.0%
2020	DET	MLB	25	2	3	0	14	2	36^{1}	39	8	2.2	8.4	34	45.7%	.320	1.32	3.96	105	0.3	90.2	62.1%	21.9%	46.2%
2021	DET	MLB	26	2	4	0	41	15	106^{1}	106	16	2.4	7.4	87	38.0%	.285	1.26	3.81	119	-0.1	88.8	71.5%	20.0%	53.5%
2022 DC	*DET*	*MLB*	*27*	*9*	*10*	*0*	*53*	*24*	*135*	*144*	*21*	*2.3*	*7.3*	*109*	*39.9%*	*.299*	*1.32*	*4.61*	*116*	*-0.3*	*89.2*	*69.0%*	*20.1%*	*52.1%*

Comparables: Ty Blach, Hector Noesí, Anthony Banda

Nobody dreams of making it to the big leagues to be a fifth starter, although it's fun to picture Alexander doing just that in his backyard. He stands on a homemade mound of mulch and grass clippings. He stares in (to nowhere specific). "I'll have a barely 90s fastball, limit my walks and bounce between the rotation and the bullpen. Yeah. I'll strike out nine straight batters somehow. I'll give myself the nickname 'Todd The Painter' on Players Weekend and grow a very replacement-level mustache. Those kids down at the schoolyard won't be laughing at me, they'll be picking me up off the fantasy waiver wire!" He throws a pinecone at the fence, it wicks off a post and into the neighbor's birdbath. That was kind of cool. Too bad nobody saw it.

José Cisnero **RHP** Born: 04/11/89 Age: 33 Bats: R Throws: R Height: 6'3" Weight: 258 lb. Origin: International Free Agent, 2007

YEAR	TEAM	LVL	AGE	W	L	SV	G	GS	IP	H	HR	BB/9	K/9	K	GB%	BABIP	WHIP	ERA	DRA-	WARP	MPH	FB%	Whiff%	CSP
2019	TOL	AAA	30	1	2	7	32	2	40	36	3	4.7	11.0	49	41.9%	.327	1.43	2.70	89	0.7				
2019	DET	MLB	30	0	4	0	35	0	35^{1}	35	5	4.8	10.2	40	37.0%	.323	1.53	4.33	102	0.3	96.4	60.8%	26.9%	49.6%
2020	DET	MLB	31	3	3	0	29	0	29^{2}	23	1	3.0	10.3	34	36.8%	.293	1.11	3.03	97	0.4	96.3	63.0%	32.4%	44.2%
2021	DET	MLB	32	4	4	4	67	0	61^{2}	51	6	4.5	9.0	62	44.6%	.281	1.33	3.65	96	0.7	96.8	65.9%	23.7%	54.4%
2022 DC	*DET*	*MLB*	*33*	*3*	*3*	*3*	*74*	*0*	*64.7*	*59*	*8*	*4.3*	*9.6*	*68*	*41.3%*	*.293*	*1.39*	*4.42*	*107*	*0.0*	*96.6*	*64.6%*	*26.0%*	*51.6%*

Comparables: Fernando Abad, Jared Hughes, Logan Kensing

Among pitchers in their 30s, Cisnero fastball's packs more fire than most, slotting right between Hansel Alberto's and Craig Kimbrel's. The extra panache to his number one is largely the reason he was able to return to the show after a tumultuous four-year journey in distant leagues. His heat has largely hindered hits and homers, but not necessarily free passes and, oddly for a 97-mph projectile, not that many strikeouts. One factor is that he worked in his sinker more often in 2021, which earned the requisite groundball contact; another is that his slider, the pitch that should be notching those third strikes, wasn't holding up its end, missing some of its downward break. Cisnero actually earned twice as many whiffs on the four-seam, while throwing more of them in the zone. Still, the fastball alone is enough to go on, better than it was during his first tour in the majors, and it's the primary reason you'll keep seeing him in high-leverage situations.

Alex Faedo **RHP** Born: 11/12/95 Age: 26 Bats: R Throws: R Height: 6'5" Weight: 225 lb. Origin: Round 1, 2017 Draft (#18 overall)

YEAR	TEAM	LVL	AGE	W	L	SV	G	GS	IP	H	HR	BB/9	K/9	K	GB%	BABIP	WHIP	ERA	DRA-	WARP	MPH	FB%	Whiff%	CSP
2019	ERI	AA	23	6	7	0	22	22	115^{1}	104	17	2.0	10.5	134	32.5%	.299	1.12	3.90	90	1.5				
2022														*No projection*										

Comparables: Jerad Eickhoff, Nick Pivetta, Kyle Brnovich

It may seem like Faedo's been in the minors forever, but the onetime college ace is still clinging to his mid-20s and to his prospect status. Before undergoing Tommy John surgery last offseason, the Florida alum projected as a solid back-end starter featuring a low-90s fastball and a wicked slider for an out pitch. Last we saw him he was refining his changeup and inching closer to Detroit via a solid season in Erie, PA. The Tommy John recovery process isn't always as straightforward as the parties involved would like it to be, especially in terms of command. But if all goes well Faedo will head into spring looking to prove that he's healthy enough to supplement a Tigers rotation that could very well use the help.

Jason Foley **RHP** Born: 11/01/95 Age: 26 Bats: R Throws: R Height: 6'4" Weight: 215 lb. Origin: Undrafted Free Agent, 2016

YEAR	TEAM	LVL	AGE	W	L	SV	G	GS	IP	H	HR	BB/9	K/9	K	GB%	BABIP	WHIP	ERA	DRA-	WARP	MPH	FB%	Whiff%	CSP
2019	LAK	A+	23	3	3	2	36	0	44	46	3	3.5	8.8	43	54.1%	.331	1.43	3.89	100	0.5				
2021	TOL	AAA	25	1	1	2	32	0	34^{2}	34	5	4.9	9.3	36	55.3%	.330	1.53	4.41	95	0.6				
2021	DET	MLB	25	0	0	0	11	0	10^{1}	8	1	4.4	5.2	6	58.1%	.233	1.26	2.61	119	0.0	96.3	72.2%	17.9%	51.4%
2022 DC	*DET*	*MLB*	*26*	*2*	*3*	*0*	*59*	*0*	*51.7*	*50*	*5*	*4.5*	*8.0*	*46*	*51.0%*	*.298*	*1.48*	*4.79*	*114*	*-0.2*	*96.3*	*72.2%*	*17.9%*	*51.4%*

Comparables: Freddy Dolsi, Bobby Cassevah, Thyago Vieira

Foley went to high school in North Bellmore and spent his college years at Sacred Heart in Fairfield. This is somewhat surprising, as the life journey from Nassau County to Western Connecticut is more likely to belong to a precocious investment banker than an undrafted underdog trying to make it as a middle reliever. As they say, you can't forecast baseball. The lengthy righty is off to a good start in the majors, defying the odds with a 96-mph sinker and a mid-80s slider. Hitters made contact on three of every four pitches he threw out of the zone, which is why he failed to strike anyone out, and also why he got away with it. He has several more years of control left before he inevitably signs with the Mets.

Michael Fulmer **RHP** Born: 03/15/93 Age: 29 Bats: R Throws: R Height: 6'3" Weight: 224 lb. Origin: Round 1, 2011 Draft (#44 overall)

YEAR	TEAM	LVL	AGE	W	L	SV	G	GS	IP	H	HR	BB/9	K/9	K	GB%	BABIP	WHIP	ERA	DRA-	WARP	MPH	FB%	Whiff%	CSP
2020	DET	MLB	27	0	2	0	10	10	27^{2}	45	8	3.9	6.5	20	35.9%	.394	2.06	8.78	153	-0.5	93.1	62.3%	19.3%	43.2%
2021	DET	MLB	28	5	6	14	52	4	69^{2}	69	7	2.6	9.4	73	45.7%	.323	1.28	2.97	86	1.1	95.8	45.8%	29.8%	49.8%
2022 DC	*DET*	*MLB*	*29*	*3*	*3*	*14*	*74*	*0*	*64.7*	*62*	*7*	*3.1*	*8.8*	*62*	*44.1%*	*.300*	*1.31*	*4.04*	*100*	*0.4*	*95.2*	*49.6%*	*27.4%*	*48.3%*

Comparables: Trevor Cahill, Stan Bahnsen, Mark Gubicza

During the heyday of the 21st century Detroit Tigers, the franchise had a knack for counterbalancing exactly five effective starting pitchers with a motley crew of high-priced relievers who tried their best. Joaquin Benoit worked out. José Valverde did for a while. Joe Nathan, Neftalí Féliz, Jim Johnson, Joel Hanrahan, Joba Chamberlain and Francisco Rodriguez were elite hurlers elsewhere, but not as part of the emergency conga line in Detroit. Meanwhile, as the dark ages of Detroit sports ensued, they stopped spending money on shiny new closers, and instead used whoever was lying around. It resulted in All-Star relievers: Joe Jiménez, Shane Greene and Gregory Soto. It also created a glide path for some of their struggling starters to reinvent their careers. Fulmer, a former Rookie of the Year and Tommy John patient, always had a spectacular fastball-slider setup, the toolkit of a high-leverage hurler. It was Fulmer's floor dating back to his top prospect days as part of the Céspedes trade. Last year he split save opportunities with Soto and looked as effective as he did when he was a Rookie of the Year. He'll keep throwing in crucial one-inning segments for now, because it's working and in Detroit, historically, it doesn't.

Kyle Funkhouser RHP Born: 03/16/94 Age: 28 Bats: R Throws: R Height: 6'3" Weight: 229 lb. Origin: Round 4, 2016 Draft (#115 overall)

YEAR	TEAM	LVL	AGE	W	L	SV	G	GS	IP	H	HR	BB/9	K/9	K	GB%	BABIP	WHIP	ERA	DRA-	WARP	MPH	FB%	Whiff%	CSP
2019	ERI	AA	25	3	1	0	4	4	23^{2}	16	2	1.1	11.0	29	45.3%	.275	0.80	1.90	86	0.4				
2019	TOL	AAA	25	3	7	0	18	18	63^{1}	79	3	7.7	9.2	65	53.8%	.396	2.10	8.53	120	0.1				
2020	DET	MLB	26	1	1	0	13	0	17^{1}	22	3	5.7	6.2	12	48.3%	.345	1.90	7.27	124	0.0	95.4	61.8%	23.2%	45.7%
2021	DET	MLB	27	7	4	1	57	2	68^{1}	58	6	5.0	8.3	63	51.5%	.280	1.40	3.42	106	0.4	95.7	62.2%	26.3%	51.8%
2022 DC	*DET*	*MLB*	*28*	*3*	*3*	*0*	*74*	*0*	*64.7*	*61*	*6*	*5.2*	*9.1*	*65*	*49.9%*	*.304*	*1.53*	*4.74*	*110*	*-0.1*	*95.7*	*62.1%*	*25.9%*	*50.9%*

Comparables: Gene Stechschulte, Jimmy Cordero, Alex Wilson

After turning down a firstish-round signing bonus and a chance to join his namesake Marty in LA (RIP Bob Einstein), Funkhouser took half the money a year later from this Midwest outfit and got to workshopping. His prospect status has diminished similarly over the years, as he's fallen from a potential mid-rotation starter to an eventual middle reliever. This isn't a prospect projection though; he is a real-life big-league reliever now, and quite possibly a good one. His slider is sharp enough he just throws it to lefties and righties, and it works either way; his sinker, which sometimes fails to live up to its own name, is more of a problem. If he can continue to perform well in high-leverage situations, and keep the ball down, the Funk Man might just play the role of loveable sidekick on the next wave of competitive Tigers teams.

Bryan Garcia RHP Born: 04/19/95 Age: 27 Bats: R Throws: R Height: 6'1" Weight: 205 lb. Origin: Round 6, 2016 Draft (#175 overall)

YEAR	TEAM	LVL	AGE	W	L	SV	G	GS	IP	H	HR	BB/9	K/9	K	GB%	BABIP	WHIP	ERA	DRA-	WARP	MPH	FB%	Whiff%	CSP
2019	LAK	A+	24	0	0	1	4	0	4	3	1	4.5	13.5	6	33.3%	.286	1.25	4.50	95	0.1				
2019	ERI	AA	24	0	0	1	3	0	4	1	1	0.0	18.0	8	20.0%	.000	0.25	2.25	85	0.1				
2019	TOL	AAA	24	3	0	0	31	0	33^{1}	26	4	3.8	8.9	33	46.2%	.253	1.20	2.97	86	0.7				
2019	DET	MLB	24	0	0	0	7	0	6^{2}	9	1	6.8	9.5	7	61.9%	.400	2.10	12.15	100	0.1	94.5	51.9%	29.2%	47.0%
2020	DET	MLB	25	2	1	4	26	0	21^{2}	18	0	4.2	5.0	12	42.9%	.257	1.29	1.66	127	-0.1	94.6	64.2%	20.1%	47.1%
2021	TOL	AAA	26	0	1	1	19	0	23^{1}	25	3	3.1	7.3	19	40.0%	.306	1.41	5.40	96	0.4				
2021	DET	MLB	26	3	2	2	39	0	39^{1}	48	10	5.7	7.3	32	35.3%	.314	1.86	7.55	146	-0.6	94.2	55.8%	22.8%	53.4%
2022 DC	*DET*	*MLB*	*27*	*3*	*4*	*0*	*74*	*0*	*64.7*	*67*	*9*	*4.5*	*7.6*	*54*	*39.4%*	*.300*	*1.55*	*5.30*	*123*	*-0.6*	*94.3*	*57.5%*	*22.5%*	*51.7%*

Comparables: Johnny Barbato, Thyago Vieira, Heath Hembree

Garcia made the painful discovery that the Tigers bullpen runs on a "flavor of the month" system. He was their dominant reliever in 2020 out of nowhere. He cashed in by making the Opening Day roster last year, potentially as the closer, then matched the previous year's run total by April 10. Much of the second half was spent in Triple-A because as A.J. Hinch put it, "he was fighting a little bit of everything," which is not what you want to hear unless you're a ninja. He returned in September and was shelled once again. He has a terrific out pitch in his slider, but no consistent means of reaching a two-strike count to use it in. Too many other flavors to choose from.

Derek Holland LHP Born: 10/09/86 Age: 35 Bats: S Throws: L Height: 6'2" Weight: 223 lb. Origin: Round 25, 2006 Draft (#748 overall)

YEAR	TEAM	LVL	AGE	W	L	SV	G	GS	IP	H	HR	BB/9	K/9	K	GB%	BABIP	WHIP	ERA	DRA-	WARP	MPH	FB%	Whiff%	CSP
2019	SF	MLB	32	2	4	0	31	7	68^{2}	68	17	4.6	9.3	71	41.4%	.291	1.50	5.90	114	0.2	92.2	61.0%	27.5%	46.9%
2019	CHC	MLB	32	0	1	0	20	1	15^{2}	14	3	5.7	6.3	11	36.2%	.256	1.53	6.89	120	0.0	93.5	67.4%	22.5%	45.6%
2020	PIT	MLB	33	1	3	0	12	5	40^{2}	42	12	3.3	10.0	45	37.1%	.288	1.40	6.86	130	-0.2	92.6	46.7%	26.5%	46.1%
2021	DET	MLB	34	3	2	0	39	1	49^{2}	58	6	3.6	9.2	51	45.1%	.354	1.57	5.07	95	0.6	93.3	56.6%	24.2%	55.8%
2022 DC	*FA*	*MLB*	*35*	*2*	*3*	*0*	*57*	*0*	*49.3*	*47*	*7*	*3.8*	*8.5*	*46*	*41.4%*	*.287*	*1.39*	*4.56*	*113*	*-0.2*	*92.9*	*55.5%*	*25.5%*	*50.7%*

Comparables: Steve Hargan, Jeff Francis, Edwin Jackson

Pitches are like songs. Some of them are just technically weak, and others are covered poorly by desperate performers. But they also can cross genres. Holland's curve, for example, is a little bit country and a little bit rap. It's been called a curveball, a knuckle curve, a slider and even a gyroball, even though nobody really knows the definition of that. It's one of the oddest offerings in terms of spin rate (not much), spin direction and break. To the untrained eye, it looks like a position pitcher fastball in the low 80s. It hasn't received a lot of attention because Holland is an adequate-at-best lefty reliever at this career juncture (it's been over 10 years since that World Series gem of a start), nor is the pitch particularly dominant. Nick Anderson has a similar pitch, and it received more attention because it was (a) really good and (b) thrown in the World Series. Perhaps if Holland weasels his way into the postseason, we'll be more interested. Until then, much like his personality, it's a fun outlier and nothing more.

Joe Jiménez RHP Born: 01/17/95 Age: 27 Bats: R Throws: R Height: 6'3" Weight: 277 lb. Origin: Undrafted Free Agent, 2013

YEAR	TEAM	LVL	AGE	W	L	SV	G	GS	IP	H	HR	BB/9	K/9	K	GB%	BABIP	WHIP	ERA	DRA-	WARP	MPH	FB%	Whiff%	CSP
2019	DET	MLB	24	4	7	9	66	0	59^{2}	56	13	3.5	12.4	82	29.1%	.319	1.32	4.37	85	1.1	95.3	68.2%	31.6%	51.3%
2020	DET	MLB	25	1	3	5	25	0	22^{2}	25	7	2.4	8.7	22	30.9%	.295	1.37	7.15	142	-0.3	94.3	62.2%	26.4%	48.6%
2021	DET	MLB	26	6	1	1	52	0	45^{1}	34	6	6.9	11.3	57	34.5%	.269	1.52	5.96	106	0.3	94.8	54.2%	31.2%	54.4%
2022 DC	*DET*	*MLB*	*27*	*2*	*3*	*0*	*59*	*0*	*51.7*	*42*	*7*	*4.6*	*11.5*	*66*	*33.6%*	*.282*	*1.32*	*4.28*	*104*	*0.1*	*94.8*	*58.9%*	*30.5%*	*52.7%*

Comparables: Sam Tuivailala, Bruce Rondón, Addison Reed

Jiménez's 35 walks last year were exactly as many walks as Nathan Eovaldi issued, and Jiménez just needed 137 fewer innings to do it. Flash back to four years ago: Jiménez was a rising reliever and rode the wave of being The First Good Tigers Reliever Since Whenever to the All-Star Game. Eovaldi was working his way back from Tommy John surgery, then was traded to the Red Sox and rejuvenated his career. Meanwhile, Jiménez never regained his fierce closing acumen since that fateful ceremonial baseball match. Sure, he's borderline unhittable, but only because there are several good reasons not to try. The only question surrounding his future is: When did Eovaldi slip the command-loosening serum into Jiménez's coffee, and how did he do it?

★ ★ ★ *2022 Top 101 Prospect* **#49** ★ ★ ★

Jackson Jobe RHP Born: 07/30/02 Age: 19 Bats: R Throws: R Height: 6'2" Weight: 190 lb. Origin: Round 1, 2021 Draft (#3 overall)

The Tigers took Jobe third overall in 2021. That's one spot ahead of consensus first overall selection Marcelo Mayer, who slipped to the Red Sox at 4. Yes, the MLB draft is a strange beast, and this selection was doubtless a cause of distress for some of Detroit's aspiring draftniks. Prep righties are often perceived as risky, but this prep righty was taken over the prep shortstop thanks to a high-spin fastball that's already cruising in the mid-90s and a higher-spin slider that already grades out as plus. This sort of stuff is not often featured by high-schoolers, and the organization will hope that a clean and athletic delivery will protect Jobe from the surgery pioneered by his namesake, as well as the ghosts that are known to haunt elite arms who elect to bypass the academy.

Alex Lange RHP Born: 10/02/95 Age: 26 Bats: R Throws: R Height: 6'3" Weight: 202 lb. Origin: Round 1, 2017 Draft (#30 overall)

YEAR	TEAM	LVL	AGE	W	L	SV	G	GS	IP	H	HR	BB/9	K/9	K	GB%	BABIP	WHIP	ERA	DRA-	WARP	MPH	FB%	Whiff%	CSP
2019	MB	A+	23	1	9	0	11	11	47^2	58	4	4.9	9.6	51	51.7%	.372	1.76	7.36	108	0.2				
2019	ERI	AA	23	2	1	0	9	0	15^2	13	0	4.6	8.6	15	47.4%	.342	1.34	3.45	85	0.2				
2019	TNS	AA	23	2	3	0	7	7	39	36	4	4.4	6.5	28	47.0%	.283	1.41	3.92	118	-0.1				
2021	TOL	AAA	25	2	1	1	19	0	21^2	22	0	7.1	11.2	27	33.9%	.393	1.80	4.57	95	0.4				
2021	DET	MLB	25	1	3	1	36	0	35^2	37	5	4.0	9.8	39	44.2%	.323	1.49	4.04	97	0.4	96.6	45.7%	32.1%	51.7%
2022 DC	*DET*	*MLB*	*26*	*2*	*3*	*0*	*59*	*0*	*51.7*	*49*	*6*	*5.0*	*9.3*	*53*	*42.6%*	*.300*	*1.51*	*4.91*	*114*	*-0.2*	*96.6*	*45.7%*	*32.1%*	*51.7%*

Comparables: Blake Wood, Wandy Peralta, Luis Marte

Lange's debut year had two distinct halves: your standard Tigers calamity reliever with an ERA cuddling the number eight, and a final month of finagling his way into trusted seventh inning work. The difference proved to be increased changeup usage, which when paired with his curve (often categorized as a slider, it's probably most accurate and confusing to describe it as a 12-6 curveball that doesn't bother with the 12, breaking late and straight down) made the two secondary henchmen unhittable. He's going to be a front-runner to continue jogging in for high leverage episodes, unless he starts calling his changeup his "Langeup." It doesn't even rhyme.

Ty Madden RHP Born: 02/21/00 Age: 22 Bats: R Throws: R Height: 6'3" Weight: 215 lb. Origin: Round 1, 2021 Draft (#32 overall)

Madden was a firstish-round pick in 2021 because he is a large Texas right-hander who can hurl a baseball in the upper-90s, the baseball equivalent of Harvard graduates getting into the writing room for *The Simpsons*. Many evaluators considered the pick a bit of a steal, though as usual for the MLB Draft, part of that was Detroit's willingness to go slightly overslot to sign him. His delivery is clean, repeatable and direct; the slider is pretty good too, while the curve and change are works in progress, meaning his future role is undefined. If the secondaries never arrive, well, the Tigers could always use relievers. He'll make his pro debut in 2022.

Matt Manning RHP Born: 01/28/98 Age: 24 Bats: R Throws: R Height: 6'6" Weight: 195 lb. Origin: Round 1, 2016 Draft (#9 overall)

YEAR	TEAM	LVL	AGE	W	L	SV	G	GS	IP	H	HR	BB/9	K/9	K	GB%	BABIP	WHIP	ERA	DRA-	WARP	MPH	FB%	Whiff%	CSP
2019	ERI	AA	21	11	5	0	24	24	133^2	93	7	2.6	10.0	148	47.2%	.259	0.98	2.56	86	2.0				
2021	TOL	AAA	23	1	3	0	7	7	32^1	40	11	2.8	10.0	36	34.7%	.337	1.55	8.07	110	0.3				
2021	DET	MLB	23	4	7	0	18	18	85^1	96	10	3.5	6.0	57	44.7%	.306	1.51	5.80	127	-0.5	93.7	60.8%	16.8%	57.7%
2022 DC	*DET*	*MLB*	*24*	*7*	*8*	*0*	*25*	*25*	*127*	*134*	*17*	*3.6*	*7.1*	*99*	*42.9%*	*.299*	*1.46*	*4.84*	*117*	*-0.1*	*93.7*	*60.8%*	*16.8%*	*57.7%*

Comparables: Paul Blackburn, Drew Hutchison, Aaron Laffey

Manning is one of *those* starting pitching prospects. He's been a topic of discussion among prospect people for several years now, a top-ten pick way back when based on size and projection. Some players, like some people, are photogenic: They always seem to be able to flash that perfect smile, that perfect breaking ball. Manning did just that for scouts: He sits mid-90s but his fastball is supposed to play up thanks to great extension; his main secondary of choice is a sharp but inconsistently executed 12-6 curve. In reality, the underlying metrics agreed with the on-field results, as the off-speed pitches weren't fooling anyone. There's a difference between looking good in photographs and looking good on camera. Luckily, contrary to what most people think, it's a skill one can learn.

Casey Mize RHP Born: 05/01/97 Age: 25 Bats: R Throws: R Height: 6'3" Weight: 212 lb. Origin: Round 1, 2018 Draft (#1 overall)

YEAR	TEAM	LVL	AGE	W	L	SV	G	GS	IP	H	HR	BB/9	K/9	K	GB%	BABIP	WHIP	ERA	DRA-	WARP	MPH	FB%	Whiff%	CSP
2019	LAK	A+	22	2	0	0	6	6	30^2	11	0	1.5	8.8	30	45.1%	.157	0.52	0.88	87	0.6				
2019	ERI	AA	22	6	3	0	15	15	78^2	69	5	2.1	8.7	76	41.7%	.295	1.11	3.20	99	0.6				
2020	DET	MLB	23	0	3	0	7	7	28^1	29	7	4.1	8.3	26	38.2%	.268	1.48	6.99	118	0.0	93.1	72.0%	23.7%	44.7%
2021	DET	MLB	24	7	9	0	30	30	150^1	130	24	2.5	7.1	118	48.0%	.254	1.14	3.71	107	0.8	93.8	52.0%	22.7%	55.3%
2022 DC	*DET*	*MLB*	*25*	*9*	*8*	*0*	*27*	*27*	*145.7*	*143*	*17*	*2.9*	*7.7*	*124*	*46.1%*	*.291*	*1.30*	*4.18*	*104*	*0.9*	*93.7*	*54.7%*	*22.9%*	*53.8%*

Comparables: Tommy Hunter, Edwin Jackson, Jhoulys Chacín

Throughout his relatively short tenure as a prospect, Mize was considered a slam-dunk mid-rotation starter and very possibly a future ace. He's now looking like more of a four or five. Command is Mize's calling card, but he also possesses a good mid-90s fastball, a very good slider and an excellent splitter: Think prime Masahiro Tanaka prior to his elbow problems. But maybe don't think about him too hard. Mize has suffered from shoulder ailments himself, robbing him of his velocity and scuffing the edge off his breaking pitches. Worse still, workload concerns grew as the season went on; after July 1, he surpassed five innings in only two of his final 15 starts. The Tigers will need the former no. 1 pick to take the next step if 2022 is meant to be the year they emerge from the rebuild.

Wily Peralta RHP Born: 05/08/89 Age: 33 Bats: R Throws: R Height: 6'1" Weight: 255 lb. Origin: International Free Agent, 2005

YEAR	TEAM	LVL	AGE	W	L	SV	G	GS	IP	H	HR	BB/9	K/9	K	GB%	BABIP	WHIP	ERA	DRA-	WARP	MPH	FB%	Whiff%	CSP
2019	KC	MLB	30	2	4	2	42	0	40^{1}	45	7	4.2	5.4	24	44.3%	.309	1.59	5.80	138	-0.4	94.5	55.0%	22.0%	43.9%
2021	TOL	AAA	32	1	0	0	6	6	19^{2}	15	2	3.7	9.6	21	52.0%	.271	1.17	2.75	103	0.2				
2021	DET	MLB	32	4	5	0	19	18	93^{2}	87	12	3.7	5.6	58	49.8%	.261	1.33	3.07	127	-0.5	94.1	55.1%	21.3%	53.6%
2022 DC	*FA*	*MLB*	*33*	*5*	*6*	*0*	*19*	*19*	*97*	*103*	*12*	*4.1*	*6.8*	*73*	*47.7%*	*.301*	*1.52*	*4.99*	*119*	*-0.2*	*94.2*	*55.1%*	*21.4%*	*52.4%*

Comparables: Mike Pelfrey, Dick Ruthven, Esteban Loaiza

It would've been easy to call it a career and fade into the Rememberin' Guys circuit. Peralta, after years in the Brewers rotation, had just wrapped up a 2019 year as the Royals' "keep the score close" reliever, something he occasionally accomplished. He headed home to the Dominican Republic, resurfacing in their winter league. The Tigers signed him largely on the recommendation of Brayan Peña, his winter league bench coach, although visa and public health protocol kept Peralta from landing in the States until spring training finished. He eventually made it to Detroit in June, starting his first game in over four years. While the ERA looked way better than the more granular numbers, the second chapter of the Wily Peralta Experience features a new character: a baffling split-finger that earned whiffs on more than 20% of batters. Now that he has a valid weapon, we can all remember Peralta in real time.

Eduardo Rodriguez LHP Born: 04/07/93 Age: 29 Bats: L Throws: L Height: 6'2" Weight: 231 lb. Origin: International Free Agent, 2010

YEAR	TEAM	LVL	AGE	W	L	SV	G	GS	IP	H	HR	BB/9	K/9	K	GB%	BABIP	WHIP	ERA	DRA-	WARP	MPH	FB%	Whiff%	CSP
2019	BOS	MLB	26	19	6	0	34	34	203^{1}	195	24	3.3	9.4	213	48.2%	.318	1.33	3.81	98	2.3	93.1	54.3%	27.5%	42.7%
2021	BOS	MLB	28	13	8	0	32	31	157^{2}	172	19	2.7	10.6	185	44.0%	.364	1.39	4.74	91	2.2	92.7	51.5%	26.4%	52.2%
2022 DC	*DET*	*MLB*	*29*	*10*	*8*	*0*	*29*	*29*	*160.3*	*144*	*18*	*2.8*	*9.5*	*169*	*44.0%*	*.293*	*1.21*	*3.37*	*88*	*2.3*	*92.8*	*52.3%*	*26.8%*	*49.4%*

Comparables: Tommy John, Tom Glavine, Jaime García

Given the myriad leg maladies he's suffered in his career it makes sense that E-Rod would have an uneven walk year. Recovered from the scary bout with post-COVID myocarditis that sidelined him for all of 2020, Rodriguez was something like the B+ version of himself, missing more bats but also yielding more hard contact than ever before. Though he posted the second-best DRA– and WARP marks of his career even with a reduced workload, Rodriguez once again failed to take that final elusive step from solid mid-rotation piece to true stalwart. Still, E-Rod built a solid legacy as a Red Sox, earning a World Series ring and serving as the org's first good young starter in a decade. His high floor, age and modicum of untapped upside made him an attractive option on the free-agent market, where the Tigers inked him to a five-year, $77 million deal with an opt-out after year two despite the qualifying offer attached to him. Perhaps a reunion with assistant pitching coach Juan Nieves, a friendlier home park and a Tigers defense that shouldn't rank last in defensive efficiency on grounders will help Rodríguez finally take that last step.

Tarik Skubal LHP Born: 11/20/96 Age: 25 Bats: R Throws: L Height: 6'3" Weight: 240 lb. Origin: Round 9, 2018 Draft (#255 overall)

YEAR	TEAM	LVL	AGE	W	L	SV	G	GS	IP	H	HR	BB/9	K/9	K	GB%	BABIP	WHIP	ERA	DRA-	WARP	MPH	FB%	Whiff%	CSP
2019	LAK	A+	22	4	5	0	15	15	80^{1}	62	5	2.1	10.9	97	39.0%	.294	1.01	2.58	75	1.9				
2019	ERI	AA	22	2	3	0	9	9	42^{1}	25	2	3.8	17.4	82	39.1%	.343	1.02	2.13	50	1.4				
2020	DET	MLB	23	1	4	0	8	7	32	28	9	3.1	10.4	37	27.4%	.253	1.22	5.62	142	-0.4	94.5	60.1%	29.5%	46.4%
2021	DET	MLB	24	8	12	0	31	29	149^{1}	141	35	2.8	9.9	164	38.4%	.278	1.26	4.34	103	1.1	94.5	56.0%	26.9%	58.4%
2022 DC	*DET*	*MLB*	*25*	*9*	*8*	*0*	*27*	*27*	*137.7*	*122*	*19*	*3.0*	*10.0*	*153*	*36.9%*	*.287*	*1.22*	*3.73*	*96*	*1.4*	*94.5*	*56.6%*	*27.2%*	*56.8%*

Comparables: Jarrod Washburn, Kevin Gausman, Gio González

Skubal is a Czech name meaning "to tear up," while *Tarik* comes from the Arabic for "strike." He's known for the latter, since his K/9 rate as a lefty starter shot him up prospect lists for all the correct reasons. But as a major-league hurler, he's the one being thoroughly skubaled, notably at the hands of the longball. Last year's 35 triumphant trots allowed were third most in the majors, while his innings ranked 58th and he frequently threw in a pitcher's park. Every season includes adjustments along the way, but Skubal changed entire pitches. He tried to learn Casey Mize's splitter in April, then jettisoned it in lieu of a changeup. The experimentation reached its apex during his worst month, and much of his numbers improved/rebounded except for the ones that resulted in him looking over his shoulder in disgust. He needs to find a pitch that can skubal those sluggers so he can continue tariking them out.

Dylan Smith RHP Born: 05/28/00 Age: 22 Bats: R Throws: R Height: 6'2" Weight: 155 lb. Origin: Round 3, 2021 Draft (#74 overall)

If Smith makes it to the big leagues, he'll be the 28th Crimson Tide alum to pitch in the majors. He'd be joining such classic names from the past as Bobby Sprowl, Syd Cohen, Whitey Hilcher and Hersh Freeman, as well as familiar names from the present like David Robertson, Wade LeBlanc, Tommy Hunter and unlikely no-hitter thrower and possible future teammate Spencer Turnbull. Featuring a fastball that flirts with the mid-90s and a sharp slider, Smith is presumably set to make his pro debut in 2022. "Well, I've been stuck here in this town, if you could call it that, a year or two" is a lyric written about somewhere in Alabama that could just as well describe anyone's minor-league career. It might take a year or two (and some refinement of his curveball and changeup), but Smith has the stuff to get it done.

Gregory Soto LHP
Born: 02/11/95 Age: 27 Bats: L Throws: L Height: 6'1" Weight: 234 lb. Origin: International Free Agent, 2012

YEAR	TEAM	LVL	AGE	W	L	SV	G	GS	IP	H	HR	BB/9	K/9	K	GB%	BABIP	WHIP	ERA	DRA-	WARP	MPH	FB%	Whiff%	CSP
2019	ERI	AA	24	0	1	0	3	3	13^{1}	10	2	2.7	8.1	12	54.1%	.229	1.05	2.03	99	0.1				
2019	TOL	AAA	24	0	3	0	6	5	23^{1}	25	2	5.0	11.6	30	46.9%	.371	1.63	6.94	103	0.3				
2019	DET	MLB	24	0	5	0	33	7	57^{2}	74	9	5.2	7.0	45	48.5%	.344	1.86	5.77	125	-0.2	95.8	70.6%	19.9%	51.1%
2020	DET	MLB	25	0	1	2	27	0	23	16	2	5.1	11.3	29	53.7%	.269	1.26	4.30	81	0.5	97.4	79.7%	28.8%	48.4%
2021	DET	MLB	26	6	3	18	62	0	63^{2}	46	7	5.7	10.7	76	44.0%	.258	1.35	3.39	99	0.6	98.4	62.4%	31.3%	55.6%
2022 DC	*DET*	*MLB*	*27*	*3*	*3*	*14*	*74*	*0*	*64.7*	*54*	*7*	*5.3*	*10.3*	*74*	*46.3%*	*.288*	*1.44*	*4.24*	*101*	*0.2*	*97.7*	*66.7%*	*28.5%*	*53.6%*

Comparables: Mario Hollands, Joely Rodríguez, Pedro Villarreal

When Soto was named to the All-Star Game, he pitched using a shiny silver baseball glove stitched with orange lettering that read:

GREGORY SOTO — 2.94 ERA / 40 K / 10.69 K/9 — 1ST ALL STAR GAME — JULY 13, 2021 — COORS FIELD

There's a reason this immaculate glove didn't include walk rates, the only pustule on his otherwise pristine surface. His fastball velocity clocks in among the top five in the league among left-handers, tied with Aroldis Chapman. Between that and a good slider, he feasts on hitter aggression. Then, once he's gotten deeper into the count and hypnotized batters with the sinker, he'll unleash a secret weapon: A four-seamer that breaks differently, earning whiffs more than half of the rare times he throws it. If he keeps striking out hitters like this, he'll have to list them all and borrow Mickey Hatcher's glove for the next All-Star game.

Julio Teheran RHP
Born: 01/27/91 Age: 31 Bats: R Throws: R Height: 6'2" Weight: 205 lb. Origin: International Free Agent, 2007

YEAR	TEAM	LVL	AGE	W	L	SV	G	GS	IP	H	HR	BB/9	K/9	K	GB%	BABIP	WHIP	ERA	DRA-	WARP	MPH	FB%	Whiff%	CSP
2019	ATL	MLB	28	10	11	0	33	33	174^{2}	148	22	4.3	8.3	162	38.7%	.270	1.32	3.81	106	1.2	89.8	63.8%	22.2%	46.7%
2020	LAA	MLB	29	0	4	0	10	9	31^{1}	39	12	4.6	5.7	20	36.0%	.273	1.76	10.05	180	-1.0	89.0	60.3%	14.6%	45.5%
2021	DET	MLB	30	1	0	0	1	1	5	4	1	5.4	5.4	3	35.7%	.231	1.40	1.80	121	0.0	90.3	63.3%	16.3%	55.6%
2022 non-DC	*DET*	*MLB*	*31*	*2*	*3*	*0*	*57*	*0*	*50*	*49*	*7*	*4.4*	*7.3*	*40*	*38.1%*	*.283*	*1.48*	*5.19*	*123*	*-0.4*	*89.6*	*62.9%*	*19.9%*	*46.9%*

Comparables: Milt Pappas, Edwin Jackson, Rick Wise

For the second time in three years, the Tigers signed a top-five prospect from BP's 2012 list to a modest one-year deal, only to lose them before April was over. Following in the footsteps of Matt Moore, Teheran had one perfectly fine start with Detroit, then the dreaded shoulder strain ended his 2021. For a seven-year stretch, he was one of the league's most durable pitchers with Atlanta: Only three made more starts from 2013 to 2019. He's also one of a handful of pitchers to make multiple starts as a 20-year-old. Both his arm's odometer and speedometer have unkind readings. But his slider found more life and with more than a decade of wisdom stored in his pitcher's brain, he's the caliber of pitcher to keep getting those one-year deals.

Spencer Turnbull RHP
Born: 09/18/92 Age: 29 Bats: R Throws: R Height: 6'3" Weight: 210 lb. Origin: Round 2, 2014 Draft (#63 overall)

YEAR	TEAM	LVL	AGE	W	L	SV	G	GS	IP	H	HR	BB/9	K/9	K	GB%	BABIP	WHIP	ERA	DRA-	WARP	MPH	FB%	Whiff%	CSP
2019	TOL	AAA	26	0	0	0	1	1	3^{2}	1	0	0.0	17.2	7	60.0%	.200	0.27	0.00	84	0.1				
2019	DET	MLB	26	3	17	0	30	30	148^{1}	154	14	3.6	8.9	146	48.0%	.333	1.44	4.61	99	1.6	93.9	64.8%	24.7%	45.9%
2020	DET	MLB	27	4	4	0	11	11	56^{2}	47	2	4.6	8.1	51	48.8%	.288	1.34	3.97	91	0.9	94.4	66.0%	28.3%	45.5%
2021	DET	MLB	28	4	2	0	9	9	50	37	2	2.2	7.9	44	57.1%	.255	0.98	2.88	92	0.7	94.5	60.5%	23.4%	54.4%
2022 DC	*DET*	*MLB*	*29*	*0*	*0*	*0*	*3*	*3*	*14.7*	*14*	*1*	*3.3*	*8.3*	*13*	*51.5%*	*.298*	*1.32*	*3.98*	*100*	*0.1*	*94.2*	*63.7%*	*25.3%*	*48.7%*

Comparables: Jimmy Nelson, Clay Buchholz, Scott Baker

It's always a chore to unearth the upside of a pitcher with decent peripherals on a sub-.500 team—pitching losses don't matter until you're on the hook for 17 of them—but sometimes you get a clear portrait when said pitcher throws a no-hitter out of nowhere. (It was mid-May 2021 and everyone was throwing one, and "everyone" of course means three other pitchers in a 14-day span.) Turnbull struck out nine Mariners and allowed two walks in his first career start over seven innings, let alone 27 outs. He relied mostly on fastballs and sliders, historically all he's thrown well. The fastballs moved every which way, while the slider kept hitting the strike zone. The analysis could simply be: Keep doing that, or wait until the next seasonal no-hitter purge. He'll have to wait a while, though, as elbow damage resulted in midseason Tommy John surgery, and he won't be able to test these crackerjack theories until late in the 2022 season or early 2023.

Joey Wentz LHP
Born: 10/06/97 Age: 24 Bats: L Throws: L Height: 6'5" Weight: 220 lb. Origin: Round 1, 2016 Draft (#40 overall)

YEAR	TEAM	LVL	AGE	W	L	SV	G	GS	IP	H	HR	BB/9	K/9	K	GB%	BABIP	WHIP	ERA	DRA-	WARP	MPH	FB%	Whiff%	CSP
2019	ERI	AA	21	2	0	0	5	5	25^{2}	20	3	1.4	13.0	37	19.3%	.315	0.94	2.10	74	0.5				
2019	MIS	AA	21	5	8	0	20	20	103	90	13	3.9	8.7	100	32.6%	.283	1.31	4.72	139	-1.5				
2021	LAK	A	23	0	3	0	5	5	18^{2}	23	5	3.9	11.6	24	34.6%	.383	1.66	6.75	110	0.1				
2021	ERI	AA	23	0	4	0	13	13	53^{1}	41	7	5.6	9.8	58	33.3%	.256	1.39	3.71	109	0.2				
2022 DC	*DET*	*MLB*	*24*	*2*	*2*	*0*	*8*	*8*	*34.7*	*34*	*5*	*5.5*	*8.4*	*32*	*34.0%*	*.293*	*1.61*	*5.57*	*129*	*-0.3*				

Comparables: Pedro Payano, Scott Elarton, Adalberto Mejía

It's not about how you start, it's about how you finish, even if you're a starter like Wentz. He began the year as Joey Wince, on the IL recovering from the dreaded UCL repair, and finished in the Double-A rotation, hurling about four innings per turn. As such, he could not become Joey Wins. However, his splits and stuff grew stronger as the season ripened—his change and curve were both above-average before going under the knife—meaning he could become the prospect he once was, a.k.a Joey Whence. His major-league debut could be as early as this season, once he can get the workload ratcheted up, so maybe it is how you start after all.

Lineouts

Hitters

HITTER	POS	TEAM	LVL	AGE	PA	R	2B	3B	HR	RBI	BB	K	SB	CS	AVG/OBP/SLG	DRC+	BABIP	BRR	FRAA	WARP
Kody Clemens	2B/RF	TOL	AAA	25	413	66	15	6	18	59	36	94	4	1	.247/.312/.466	105	.278	0.1	2B(72): 5.9, RF(24): 0.2, 1B(7): 0.1	2.1
Dustin Garneau	C	TOL	AAA	33	60	8	1	0	4	9	7	20	0	0	.176/.283/.431	99	.179	0.2	C(17): 0.9	0.3
	C	ABQ	AAA	33	42	5	3	0	1	6	6	9	0	0	.229/.357/.400	95	.280	-0.3	C(10): 1.2	0.2
	C	DET	MLB	33	68	9	5	0	6	11	3	18	0	0	.210/.250/.581	104	.175	-0.3	C(20): 0.7	0.4
Colt Keith	3B/2B	LAK	A	19	181	32	6	3	1	21	30	39	4	1	.320/.436/.422	117	.422	1.4	3B(27): 3.3, 2B(14): -1.3	1.2
	3B/2B	WM	A+	19	76	7	1	1	1	6	8	27	0	0	.162/.250/.250	80	.250	0.9	3B(15): 1.1, 2B(2): -0.4	0.2
Andre Lipcius	3B/2B	WM	A+	23	98	14	4	2	3	13	12	16	3	1	.277/.357/.482	122	.299	1.1	3B(13): 2.4, 2B(9): -1.6	0.7
	3B/2B	ERI	AA	23	385	51	18	2	9	46	39	82	4	1	.235/.312/.378	102	.280	1.0	3B(49): 3.5, 2B(45): -0.5	1.6
Nomar Mazara	RF	DET	MLB	26	181	12	5	2	3	19	15	45	0	0	.212/.276/.321	80	.271	0.0	RF(41): -2.0	-0.2
Parker Meadows	CF	WM	A+	21	408	50	15	2	8	44	37	99	9	8	.208/.290/.330	94	.261	1.7	CF(73): -2.0, RF(13): -0.8, LF(4): 0.1	1.0
Izaac Pacheco	SS	TIGW	ROK	18	125	16	4	2	1	7	18	43	1	0	.226/.339/.330		.371			
Wenceel Perez	2B	LAK	A	21	107	16	5	1	1	12	12	21	9	1	.293/.383/.402	114	.366	1.3	2B(21): 3.1	0.9
	2B	WM	A+	21	369	51	13	6	3	31	31	64	13	1	.245/.313/.348	106	.295	2.2	2B(59): -0.4, 3B(24): -2.7	1.3
Jacob Robson	OF	ERI	AA	26	82	17	9	2	2	10	14	21	4	1	.424/.531/.712	104	.605	-0.2	RF(18): 2.2	0.5
	OF	TOL	AAA	26	288	37	10	3	5	28	46	104	15	9	.259/.385/.389	74	.438	-0.9	LF(44): 0.7, CF(22): 2.2, RF(12): 4.5	0.7
	OF	DET	MLB	26	7	1	0	0	0	0	0	4	0	0	.000/.000/.000	81		-0.1	LF(3): -0.1, CF(1): -0.1	0.0
Aderlin Rodríguez	1B	ESC	WIN	29	120	10	5	2	4	14	8	32	0	0	.222/.292/.417		.274			
	1B	TOL	AAA	29	483	67	26	3	29	94	42	127	1	1	.290/.362/.565	119	.349	-3.7	1B(45): 1.0, 3B(31): -2.3	1.8
Cristian Santana	SS/3B	DSL TIG	ROK	17	216	40	12	2	9	27	30	46	12	7	.269/.421/.520		.319			
Zack Short	SS	TOL	AAA	26	198	30	7	0	9	29	33	47	2	1	.236/.389/.452	120	.275	-0.7	SS(26): -0.7, 2B(12): 0.6, 3B(7): -1.3	1.0
	SS	DET	MLB	26	184	21	4	0	6	20	22	59	2	0	.141/.239/.282	73	.165	-1.0	SS(52): 7.8, 3B(3): -0.3, 2B(2): 0.2	0.7

Koby retired, Kacy plays independent ball, and Kory went into the private sector. But the hard-nosed **Kody Clemens** is rather close to being the first of Roger's lads to reach the majors, albeit as a marginal utility player. It took career third catcher **Dustin Garneau** just 15 games to notch a career-best home run total with six. He's the same age as Alex Avila and Buster Posey, so either this was a pleasant finish to a sparse baseball career or he's usurped Erik Kratz's throne. Armed with an action movie name and quick lefty swing, former Mississippi prep **Colt Keith** handled full-season A-ball as a teenager and will get another crack at High-A in his age 20 season to see if his power catches up. It's easy to be bullish on the Biloxi kid. One day he may even go box office. **Andre Lipcius** makes a lot of contact, plays solid defense at both second and third and runs into a homer every now and then. He also volunteered to grind it out in the minors despite studying nuclear engineering at Tennessee. He may very well bounce back from this year's rough campaign in Double-A, but if he doesn't he'll still be...whatever a nuclear engineering major generally ends up doing. Tatís Jr., Soto, Albies, Devers, Seager, Odor, Correa, Harper, Machado, Trout, Stanton, Freeman, Heyward and **Nomar Mazara**. Those are the 22-and-under players who smacked 30 doubles and 20 home runs in a season since 2010. Now he's 27, and the next list he'll be on is San Diego's non-roster invites to spring training. **Parker Meadows** has been unintentionally cultivating a reputation as a good athlete constrained by baseball's requirement to hit for a few years now, and he hasn't done anything in 2021 that will cause us to rewrite those evaluations. The former Georgia prep posted a miserable line for High-A West Michigan, but at 21 there's still time to dream on a high-ceiling power/speed combo. If you're traveling through East Texas you might swing through Friendswood, the only permanent Quaker settlement in the state. This is the hometown of **Izaac Pacheco**. It's unknown whether or not Pacheco is a Friend, or even if he'll be a friend to your fantasy team down the line, but a lot will depend on whether he hits like a third baseman or plays shortstop like one. A middle six-figure bonus guy a few years back, **Wenceel Perez** is a switch-hitting infielder whose hit tool hasn't yet materialized. His ability to play shortstop, meanwhile, has dematerialized. Plucky Canadian outfielder **Jacob Robson** has made a habit of regularly reaching base in the minor leagues, which is great news for him, because that's where he's going to continue to play. Bush league bopper **Aderlin Rodríguez** has 117 of the best hits since 2016, although he's been substantially older than the competition. He's never played in the majors, and he's 30, so at this point he's a feel-good story lurking in the shrubberies. The 17-year-old **Cristian Santana** was inked for just under $3 million in early 2021. Power-hitting everyday shortstop is within the realm of possibility, but then again, Bill Freehan got two votes for the Hall of Fame, so it's not like the world is built on justice. Martin Short rejuvenated his long career with Hulu's "Only Murders In The Building." It had much better ratings than infielder **Zack Short**'s one-man show, "Only Murders In The Middle Of The Strike Zone."

Pitchers

PITCHER	TEAM	LVL	AGE	W	L	SV	G	GS	IP	H	HR	BB/9	K/9	K	GB%	BABIP	WHIP	ERA	DRA-	WARP	MPH	FB%	WHF	CSP
Miguel Del Pozo	TOL	AAA	28	1	3	4	34	0	38^{1}	22	6	3.8	12.7	54	48.8%	.205	0.99	2.82	80	0.9				
	DET	MLB	28	0	0	0	5	0	5^{1}	8	0	3.4	6.8	4	31.6%	.421	1.88	3.38	117	0.0	93.2	60.0%	18.9%	62.8%
Buck Farmer	RR	AAA	30	2	1	8	15	0	15	11	1	3.6	9.0	15	42.5%	.263	1.13	3.60	87	0.2				
	TOL	AAA	30	0	2	0	9	0	11^{1}	11	0	3.2	5.6	7	36.1%	.306	1.32	3.97	107	0.1				
	DET	MLB	30	0	0	0	36	0	35^{1}	40	9	5.3	9.4	37	37.0%	.313	1.73	6.37	122	-0.1	94.3	47.7%	26.1%	49.7%
Rony García	TOL	AAA	23	0	1	0	4	4	19^{2}	13	4	4.6	11.0	24	40.4%	.209	1.17	3.20	104	0.2				
	DET	MLB	23	0	0	0	2	0	3^{2}	1	1	4.9	4.9	2	25.0%	.000	0.82	2.45	103	0.0	92.1	60.7%	10.0%	56.1%
Drew Hutchison	TOL	AAA	30	8	3	0	19	19	88^{1}	78	8	4.2	9.1	89	41.6%	.299	1.35	3.77	103	1.1				
	DET	MLB	30	3	1	0	9	2	21^{1}	20	1	4.6	4.2	10	48.6%	.279	1.45	2.11	130	-0.1	92.4	52.8%	23.5%	55.8%
Ian Krol	TOL	AAA	30	2	0	4	20	1	25^{2}	20	4	4.2	10.9	31	41.9%	.276	1.25	2.45	86	0.5				
	DET	MLB	30	0	0	0	18	0	18^{2}	23	2	3.9	8.7	18	45.0%	.368	1.66	4.34	109	0.1	89.9	75.1%	23.8%	55.5%
Reese Olson	WM	A+	21	1	0	0	2	2	11	6	0	1.6	11.5	14	44.0%	.240	0.73	0.00	87	0.2				
	WIS	A+	21	5	4	0	14	14	69	58	5	4.6	10.3	79	43.4%	.312	1.35	4.30	88	1.2				
	ERI	AA	21	2	1	0	5	5	24^{2}	18	1	5.1	7.7	21	49.3%	.250	1.30	4.74	110	0.1				
Erasmo Ramírez	TOL	AAA	31	1	0	0	5	0	8	4	0	3.4	11.2	10	47.4%	.211	0.88	3.38	91	0.1				
	DET	MLB	31	1	1	0	17	0	26^{2}	24	4	1.7	6.7	20	37.3%	.253	1.09	5.74	113	0.1	92.5	45.4%	16.8%	62.1%
Nivaldo Rodriguez	TOL	AAA	24	2	1	0	13	5	34^{2}	40	6	3.1	4.9	19	48.8%	.286	1.50	4.93	110	0.3				
	SUG	AAA	24	2	1	0	10	6	27^{1}	33	5	5.3	8.2	25	34.5%	.341	1.79	5.93	114	-0.1				
	HOU	MLB	24	0	0	0	4	0	7^{1}	4	2	4.9	3.7	3	57.1%	.105	1.09	2.45	124	0.0	91.5	57.9%	13.6%	48.6%
José Ureña	DET	MLB	29	4	8	0	26	18	100^{2}	119	14	3.8	6.0	67	52.8%	.319	1.60	5.81	130	-0.7	94.1	63.9%	20.5%	52.0%
Will Vest	TOL	AAA	26	1	3	2	23	0	25^{2}	27	3	2.8	8.8	25	52.6%	.333	1.36	4.91	85	0.5				
	SEA	MLB	26	1	0	0	32	0	35	38	2	4.6	6.9	27	39.8%	.343	1.60	6.17	122	-0.1	93.7	56.9%	22.8%	54.2%

Fastball- and curve-slangin' lefty **Miguel Del Pozo** averaged six major-league innings in each of the last three seasons and is projected to break the record for most career IP by the year 3244. Clear your calendar now. ⚾ After eight seasons, the Tigers cut loose bullpen mainstay **Buck Farmer** a week after the Field of Dreams game, because they had only seen the first half of the film. ⚾ A torn meniscus is a common knee injury where the cartilage gives way if too much weight and torque is applied to the joint. Or in the case of unlucky reliever **Rony García**, engages in a simple pre-game long toss. The freak injury abruptly ended his season in June. ⚾ In 2020 **Drew Hutchinson** pitched for an independent team called the Milwaukee Milkmen, a very underrated band. He spent most of 2021 in Triple-A, spot starting when the Tigers kept misplacing their pitchers. Spot starts and DFAs may be in his immediate future, but it's better than being a milkman, because this is baseball in 2022 and not a paternity joke from the 1950s. ⚾ During the pandemic, the Joliet Slammers hosted a four-team microseason, with each squad representing various elements of Chicago heritage. **Ian Krol** played for the Nerds Herd, as in the sickly sweet tart candy, not the analytics community. His performance helped get him back in the big leagues, meaning that someone thinks fondly of the worst member in the Wonka rotation. ⚾ **Reese Olson** was acquired from the Brewers at this year's trade deadline, and looks to have a decent shot at being a big-leaguer. The fastball is average and he's put up average numbers, but he's got a pair of potential plus secondaries in his slider and changeup. ⚾ Ten-year veteran **Erasmo Ramírez** has the fourth most pitching appearances by a Nicaraguan-born pitcher. Dennis "El Presidente" Martínez tops the list, which constitutionally makes Ramírez El Secretario Del Estado. ⚾ One of many once-unheralded international signings to to be promoted by the Astros in recent years, **Nivaldo Rodriguez** didn't quite make the grade and was cut loose this past summer. The average-sized righty with low-nineties heat and three secondaries was outrighted by Detroit, but will likely still figure in the bullpen mix because, Detroit. ⚾ One-time Marlins mainstay **José Ureña** had a nifty little streak of four straight starts of seven innings and allowing two runs. Finding it in his game log is like searching for a needle in an ERAstack. ⚾ A month in, the Mariners thought they had a steal in the Rule 5 draft with crafty right-hander **Will Vest**, but returned him to the Tigers in July after they realized he had nothing up his sleeves.

KANSAS CITY ROYALS

Essay by Shaker Samman

Player comments by Mike Gianella and BP staff

Baseball is a cruel sport. Cruel in the ways basketball or football are, sure—each has its own version of a walk-off victory that feels as much like a twisting of the knife for the loser as it does a crescendo for the winner—but in another, weightier way, as well. There is just *more* baseball. We're onto the 56th Super Bowl, and well past that number of NBA finals, but the stories of those disciplines are still in their opening acts.

On the other hand, baseball is as old as time itself, a sport that was played by both Gabriel and Michael, and by Lucifer and his fallen angels, passed on over the years to Australopithecus and Neanderthals and modern man. Or something like that. It's an old game with a long-enough record to fill, well, a series of almanacs, and then some.

More baseball means more pain, and for longer. It has time to fester. You can point to the 86- and 108-year curses broken by the Red Sox and Cubs in the last few decades for proof; two of the oldest, most successful teams in the sport went longer than the median life expectancy of their fans without winning a World Series.

When they won (or in Boston's case, all the times they have won since), the moment was met with elation matching the pain felt throughout the drought. It *meant* something, right? It had to; a validation of suffering. Otherwise, what was the point? The waiting is the hard part, and then the waiting ends. But what happens after that, when it starts again?

The Kansas City Royals won their first title in 1985, 17 seasons after first gracing the major leagues, and five years after debuting in the fall classic with a six-game loss to the Phillies. At the time, 1985 probably felt like the beginning of something. At the very least, it must've felt like a confirmation. Going back to 1976, only the Dodgers, Orioles and Yankees had won more games, and they'd combined for four of the 10 championships won in that span. They had something to show for it. And then, in 1985, Kansas City did too.

Celebration is easy, even if it isn't common. We know what *happy* and *joyous* are supposed to look like. We've seen enough of it on TV or in movies. We know how to play the part of Exuberant Fan, overcome with emotion and willing to be freed from inhibition. It's a gift, a momentary blessing

KANSAS CITY ROYALS PROSPECTUS

2021 W-L: 74-88, 4TH IN AL CENTRAL

Pythag	.435	*25th*	DER	.687	*27th*
RS/G	4.23	*24th*	DRC+	95	*16th*
RA/G	4.86	*21st*	DRA-	112	*27th*
dWin%	.433	*25th*	FIP	4.44	*21st*
Payroll	$89M	*22nd*	B-Age	29.8	*20th*
M$/MW	$2.9M	*12th*	P-Age	28.4	*10th*

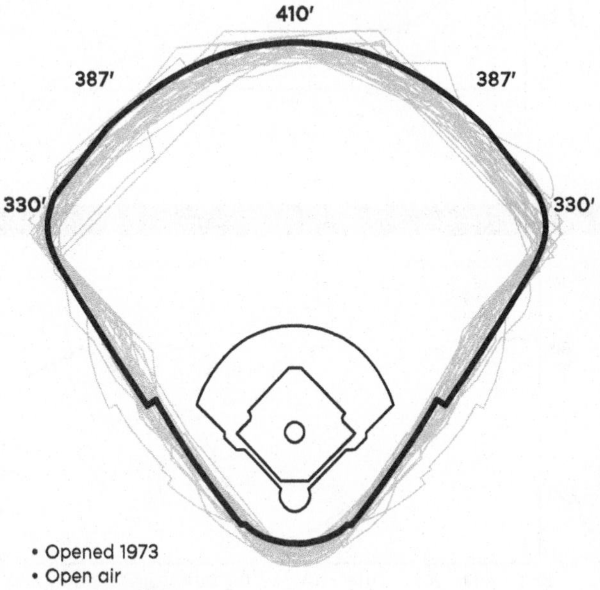

- Opened 1973
- Open air
- Natural surface
- Fence profile: 9' to 11'

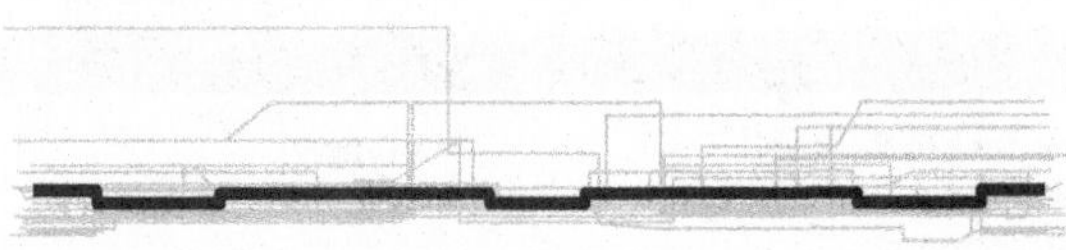

Park Factors

Runs	Runs/RH	Runs/LH	HR/RH	HR/LH
96	95	98	78	82

Top Hitter WARP	4.1 Whit Merrifield
Top Pitcher WARP	1.3 Scott Barlow
Top Prospect	Bobby Witt Jr.

Payroll History (in millions)

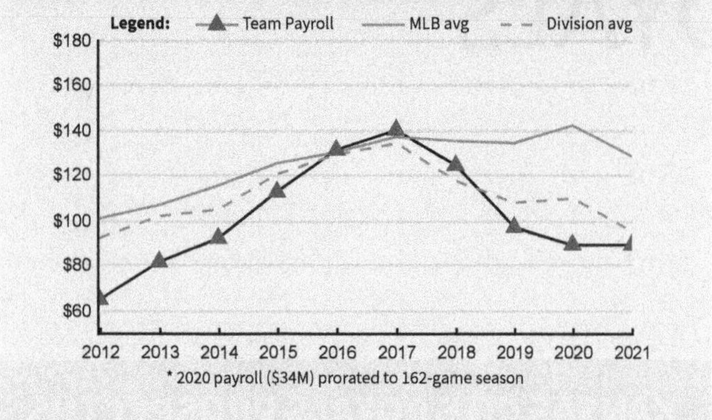

Future Commitments (in millions)

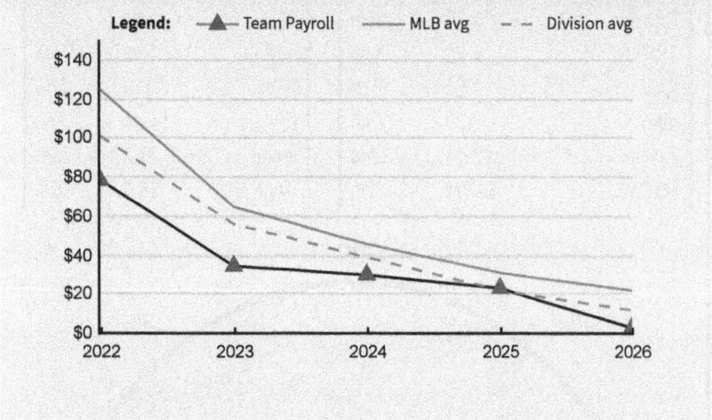

Farm System Ranking

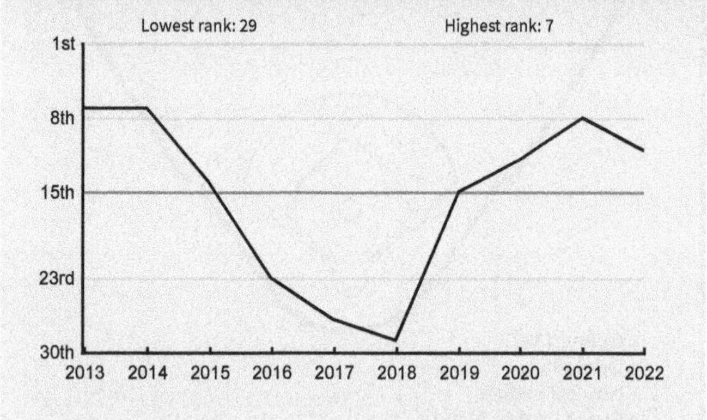

Personnel

President of Baseball Operations
Dayton Moore

Sr. Vice President of Baseball Operations/General Manager
J.J. Picollo

Sr. Vice President/AGM of Major League and International Operations
Rene Francisco

Sr. Vice President/Assistant General Manager
Scott Sharp

Manager
Mike Matheny

BP Alumni
Daniel Mack

to transcend individual anxieties in favor of shared euphoria. Put another way: it's not hard to get plastered and dance in the streets during a championship parade.

It's what comes the next day that's difficult, when the sheen of glory wears off and moves ever so slightly into the rearview mirror, sliding farther away with each passing week. Sometimes, teams will make return trips to the playoffs, and then the World Series, in quick succession, like the Dodgers have for most of the past decade, and the Yankees have done since the big bang. It makes sense; if a team is good enough to win one year, why wouldn't they be contenders the next? Other times, fans aren't so lucky.

No team had a worse winning percentage than the Royals did from 1986 to 2013, the years between their first title and next visit to the World Series. Only seven times in that stretch did they finish with a winning record, and five of those campaigns came before the mid-1990s. The mighty Royals were garbage, and for long enough that children were born and raised as fans without ever having a real chance of rooting for a winner. And then, out of nowhere, they got one.

The Royals—the same ones who were, for lack of a better phrase, the worst baseball team in America since the last time they'd reached the playoffs—actually *made* the World Series in 2014. Seriously, it says it online and everything. Of course, that season ended in a new kind of heartbreak for fans unfamiliar with the struggle of rooting for a contender—it's one thing when your team has no hope, and another entirely when they lose in Game 7 with they guy they wanted at the plate and the tying run 90 feet away.

Blows land harder when there's more on the line. Alex Gordon's mad dash to third base was, in a vacuum, the sort of miracle that you'd tell a generation of fans about wistfully. With two outs, the Royals lifer—a player synonymous with his organization, who understood the patience his fan base practiced better than anyone—skipped an 87-mile-per-hour Madison Bumgarner slider past Giants center fielder Grégor Blanco and forced his way to the last base before glory.

Maybe he could've made it home; a series of fielding mishaps opened a window for him. But he wasn't particularly quick, and Salvador Perez was up next. So Gordon halted at third. Perez had been hot all week, and Bumgarner was working on short rest. This could've been it. It should've been. But it wasn't. Six pitches later, the catcher fouled out. For an entire winter, Alex Gordon continued to stand there, frozen, forever waiting.

For an offseason, Royals fans stomached this new kind of pain. It probably felt different from the old kind, fresher, but still somewhat familiar; a cousin to the misery they knew, here to teach them a harsher form of loathing. It was waiting still, but more acute, like pulling a number at the DMV, seeing the ticker show your digits, then flicker and reset, condemning you to a lifetime of anticipation.

And then, the next year, they won it. They beat the Mets—another cursed franchise—in five games. Again, I promise this really happened. Eight hundred thousand people, as many as live in North Dakota, flocked to celebrate the city's first championship in 30 years. They didn't have to wait anymore.

Then, as it always does, the cycle reset. Kansas City hasn't had a winning season since. Its closest was an 81-81 campaign in 2016 that was immediately followed by five straight losing seasons, two of which required a third digit in the loss column.

We're in the beginning of the journey, now. The 2015 title is nothing more than a memory, just like the 1985 one before it. It exists in pictures and in thoughts and can be called upon when things on the field look exceptionally bleak, but there are few tangible reminders of what it felt like to watch that team do what it did.

There are still pieces of it here and there, and you can find them if you know where to look. Eric Hosmer is still spreading the gospel in California, jockeying for position in a loaded NL West. Lorenzo Cain moved north to Milwaukee to help the Brewers conquer their own demons. The Nationals' fire sale gave Alcides Escobar a new opportunity to ply his Esky magic. And Perez is launching baseballs into orbit. Individually, they exist and carry on, but their real value is what they brought together, and that's harder to quantify.

What's the value of a memory? In the moment, the joy is everything, but it's fleeting. Is the pain worse knowing what it feels like to be on top? Or is ignorance bliss? Does not having the experience of winning a championship make the yearly slog to the bottom any less miserable? Maybe it brings an acceptance of fate; you can't long for the return of a feeling you never had in the first place. Winning is everything when it happens, and everything when it doesn't. Losing is compounding; it makes the good things seem insignificant, and the bad things seem even more daunting. But losing can only exist in relation to winning, and vice-versa. If you've only ever known one of them, you can't fully know either.

The point of the human experience—if there even is one—is to chase the highs at the cost of the lows. And as a result, winning is still something worth chasing. Otherwise, what's the point of fielding a team at all?

Most years, for most teams, the chase is all that happens. Thirty squads throw pitches on Opening Day, and all but one watch their seasons end in relative failure. If baseball were an equitable sport, it'd mean that, on average, those tortured faithful would drink from the cup of glory once every three decades. But it's not. The rich or smart or lucky clubs put themselves in contention to win time and time again, and even they find themselves losing more often than not. The rest are stuck on the treadmill of mediocrity with the hope that they could one day return to the promised land.

For some, even that is a stretch. Five teams—the Brewers, Padres, Rangers, Rays and Rockies—have watched opponents bathe in champagne from across the field, never knowing that feeling for themselves, and a sixth—the Mariners—haven't even come that close, only seeing the spectacle from their couches. Six fan bases have ended a combined 265 seasons the same as they started: empty-handed. The law of large numbers suggests that, eventually, each of them will have their moments in the sun. But reality says something different. We don't have an unlimited amount of time. For some of us, this might be it.

So what's the answer then, if winning is a pipe dream, and losing is here to stay? It might be to chase the little things that remind us of what the best case scenario looks like. Like the sound that's made when Perez meets a fastball with the barrel of his bat in that perfect manner only he can, or the way the deep-blue midwest sky melts over the outfield at Kauffman Stadium, like it's reaching down to pluck a ball out from over left field and raise it into the heavens.

Kansas City has often been bad, but rarely in the way some of its contemporaries have been. They haven't chased the lowest payroll in baseball under the guise of rebuilding. They make an effort, even when others in their position wouldn't, and even if the end result is an underwhelming team that's best hope is to be moderately respectful. And that matters, because even in the roughest seasons, the Royals still offer fans something to care about.

Last year, it was Perez's hunt for the home-run record. The numbers are flashy—48 home runs by a catcher, the most in history—but they don't tell the full story of what each of those blasts down the stretch felt like to those pining for something to get excited about. Each swing felt like the slap of a teacher's ruler on a sleeping student's desk, a jolt back to the present. Last time, it took almost a decade to build a winning club. This time might take even longer. But success in baseball isn't black and white, and neither is the enjoyment garnered during the climb back up the hill.

Let those moments be your guiding lights. Skip work on a Tuesday to watch Hunter Dozier go 1-for-5 with three strikeouts and a double. Ask the bartender to toss the game on the screen next to the one showing Patrick Mahomes doing something brilliant, because Whit Merrifield might be as fast as any of the wide receivers Mahomes is throwing to. And understand that, while things may not always be going well, they don't need to feel bleak, either.

Chances are, this Royals season will finish as most of them have; with disappointment. Maybe things will change soon enough. A prospect or two will pop, a midseason trade will deliver in spades, and a handful of free-agent signings will result in a competitive team with the ability to deliver the kind of moments that so few get the chance to. For now though, that's a stretch. The dream of a contending ballclub is a ways down the stream. It's the waiting that kills you, but with enough distractions, it doesn't have to be so bad. ■

—Shaker Samman is a writer based in Los Angeles.

HITTERS

Andrew Benintendi LF

Born: 07/06/94 Age: 28 Bats: L Throws: L Height: 5'9" Weight: 180 lb. Origin: Round 1, 2015 Draft (#7 overall)

YEAR	TEAM	LVL	AGE	PA	R	2B	3B	HR	RBI	BB	K	SB	CS	Whiff%	AVG/OBP/SLG	DRC+	BABIP	BRR	FRAA	WARP
2019	BOS	MLB	24	615	72	40	5	13	68	59	140	10	3	25.3%	.266/.343/.431	89	.333	1.1	LF(131): -7.2, CF(12): 1.6	0.9
2020	BOS	MLB	25	52	4	1	0	0	1	11	17	1	2	33.3%	.103/.314/.128	77	.182	0.4	LF(13): -0.6	0.0
2021	KC	MLB	26	538	63	27	2	17	73	36	97	8	9	22.7%	.276/.324/.442	101	.309	0.3	LF(129): -0.3	2.1
2022 DC	*KC*	*MLB*	*27*	*593*	*80*	*29*	*3*	*14*	*66*	*50*	*113*	*12*	*5*	*22.9%*	*.258/.328/.410*	*99*	*.305*	*0.8*	*LF -2*	*1.8*

Comparables: Billy Williams, Matty Alou, Zack Wheat

The work opportunity you thought would be a fulfilling career but became just a steady job. The blind date that had nice conversation but no spark. The fine movie with the incredible trailer. As he heads into his Age 27 season, Benintendi seems like a profound disappointment, but that's only because expectations were sky high when he was a 22-year-old rookie in 2017. AB has been a solid citizen but hasn't come close to displaying the borderline 80 hit tool some scouts believed he possessed as a prospect. The Royals acquired him in a challenge trade from Boston last winter, but while Benintendi was his usual reliable self, he didn't find another gear or next level. Productive regulars are far too often taken for granted, and the crystal ball no longer sees a superstar. Still, there's nothing wrong with a reliable 9-to-5 job, a good meal with pleasant conversation or a movie that keeps you entertained for 100 minutes.

Hunter Dozier RF

Born: 08/22/91 Age: 30 Bats: R Throws: R Height: 6'4" Weight: 220 lb. Origin: Round 1, 2013 Draft (#8 overall)

YEAR	TEAM	LVL	AGE	PA	R	2B	3B	HR	RBI	BB	K	SB	CS	Whiff%	AVG/OBP/SLG	DRC+	BABIP	BRR	FRAA	WARP
2019	KC	MLB	27	586	75	29	10	26	84	55	148	2	2	27.0%	.279/.348/.522	112	.339	-2.0	3B(100): -0.2, RF(20): 0.2, 1B(7): -0.8	2.1
2020	KC	MLB	28	186	29	4	2	6	12	27	48	4	0	30.9%	.228/.344/.392	105	.288	0.5	1B(28): -0.6, RF(18): -1.5, LF(2): -0.3	0.4
2021	KC	MLB	29	543	55	27	6	16	54	43	154	5	4	32.3%	.216/.285/.394	82	.276	0.8	RF(60): -0.8, 3B(57): -6.2, 1B(19): -1.2	-0.4
2022 DC	*KC*	*MLB*	*30*	*535*	*68*	*24*	*4*	*16*	*66*	*48*	*154*	*4*	*2*	*31.6%*	*.230/.306/.405*	*91*	*.301*	*0.1*	*1B -1, 3B 0*	*0.5*

Comparables: Danny Valencia, Yangervis Solarte, Jedd Gyorko

Signed to a four-year, $25 million extension in February 2021, Dozier stumbled out of the blocks, hitting a woeful .174/.244/.344 in the first half and making some wonder if he was pressing too hard to try and live up to expectations that often come with that kind of money attached. The culprit turned out to be not mental but physical, a thumb injury suffered on Opening Day that Dozier tried to play through. A combination of better health and a swing adjustment in the second half led to numbers closer to his 2019 breakout, and the hopes that Dozier's bat can make up for subpar defense.

Cam Gallagher C

Born: 12/06/92 Age: 29 Bats: R Throws: R Height: 6'3" Weight: 230 lb. Origin: Round 2, 2011 Draft (#65 overall)

YEAR	TEAM	LVL	AGE	PA	R	2B	3B	HR	RBI	BB	K	SB	CS	Whiff%	AVG/OBP/SLG	DRC+	BABIP	BRR	FRAA	WARP
2019	KC	MLB	26	142	14	7	0	3	12	11	28	0	1	17.5%	.238/.312/.365	96	.281	-0.5	C(44): 3.7	0.9
2020	KC	MLB	27	60	10	5	0	1	3	6	11	0	0	21.2%	.283/.356/.434	104	.341	0.7	C(25): -0.2	0.3
2021	OMA	AAA	28	32	4	0	0	1	3	5	4	0	0		.222/.344/.333	102	.227	0.3	C(6): 0.2	0.2
2021	KC	MLB	28	124	9	6	0	1	7	8	20	0	0	15.4%	.250/.298/.330	96	.293	-0.5	C(46): 5.4	1.0
2022 DC	*KC*	*MLB*	*29*	*151*	*16*	*6*	*0*	*2*	*19*	*11*	*23*	*0*	*0*	*17.9%*	*.237/.302/.333*	*76*	*.272*	*-0.2*	*C 4*	*0.6*

Comparables: Elias Díaz, Martín Maldonado, Francisco Cervelli

YEAR	TEAM	P. COUNT	FRM RUNS	BLK RUNS	THRW RUNS	TOT RUNS
2019	KC	5506	4.1	0.1	0.2	4.4
2020	KC	2736	0.1	0.0	0.0	0.2
2021	KC	5181	5.3	0.5	0.0	5.9
2022	*KC*	*6012*	*1.6*	*0.8*	*0.1*	*2.5*

Outside of middle or long relievers, no one is more overlooked in baseball than the backup catcher. As Salvador Perez's caddy, Gallagher has arguably been the most forgotten among this assortment of the unremembered: a player whose job is mostly to show up and give Perez's knees a rest 1-2 times a week so Perez can DH. What this mundanity masks is the fact that Gallagher is a solid defender, calls a decent game and could likely cobble together more playing time on about 25 other major league teams. He's not ancient and with MJ Melendez knocking on the door, it wouldn't be shocking to see Gallagher find himself getting 300-350 plate appearances in another major-league city perennially in his 30s. It's far more probable Gallagher either just keeps barely hanging on or disappears completely.

Jeison Guzmán SS

Born: 10/08/98 Age: 23 Bats: S Throws: R Height: 6'2" Weight: 205 lb. Origin: International Free Agent, 2015

YEAR	TEAM	LVL	AGE	PA	R	2B	3B	HR	RBI	BB	K	SB	CS	Whiff%	AVG/OBP/SLG	DRC+	BABIP	BRR	FRAA	WARP
2019	LEX	A	20	490	51	23	5	7	48	25	98	15	13		.253/.296/.373	95	.308	1.6	SS(116): 12.7	2.8
2021	QC	A+	22	160	25	11	1	4	22	12	35	9	3		.289/.352/.465	104	.352	1.7	SS(20): 0.4, 3B(5): 0.6, CF(5): -0.3	0.8
2021	NWA	AA	22	136	17	8	0	2	15	6	41	2	3		.216/.263/.328	75	.305	-0.2	SS(27): -1.6, CF(5): -0.6	-0.2
2022 non-DC	*ARI*	*MLB*	*23*	*251*	*19*	*11*	*1*	*3*	*21*	*13*	*74*	*5*	*4*	*34.2%*	*.216/.266/.320*	*55*	*.303*	*0.6*	*SS 1, CF 0*	*-0.4*

Comparables: Marco Hernández, Eugenio Suárez, Eduardo Escobar

After struggling with the bat at nearly every rung on the organizational ladder, Guzmán came out of the blocks on fire last year, generating the power the Royals had been hoping for ever since they signed him as a teenager out of the Dominican Republic in 2015. Guzmán attributed his success to returning to switch-hitting at the alternate site in 2020, after years of batting lefty. Promoted to AA after winning a bronze medal as part of the Dominican Olympic team, Guzmán struggled initially but showed improvement as the season wound down. His athleticism and physical growth could make Guzmán more of a candidate for a utility role down the line, particularly if the hit tool maxes out.

Kyle Isbel OF
Born: 03/03/97 Age: 25 Bats: L Throws: R Height: 5'11" Weight: 190 lb. Origin: Round 3, 2018 Draft (#94 overall)

YEAR	TEAM	LVL	AGE	PA	R	2B	3B	HR	RBI	BB	K	SB	CS	Whiff%	AVG/OBP/SLG	DRC+	BABIP	BRR	FRAA	WARP
2019	SUR	WIN	22	91	8	4	1	1	16	14	20	6	1		.315/.429/.438		.407			
2019	ROY	ROK	22	27	9	2	0	2	7	2	5	3	1		.360/.407/.680		.389			
2019	WIL	A+	22	214	26	7	3	5	23	15	44	8	3		.216/.282/.361	92	.253	1.6	CF(32): -2.6, RF(12): 0.4	0.4
2021	OMA	AAA	24	451	62	18	3	15	55	45	91	22	5		.269/.357/.444	108	.314	-1.1	CF(55): -5.5, RF(26): 5.0, LF(19): -1.9	1.6
2021	KC	MLB	24	83	16	5	2	1	7	7	23	2	0	24.2%	.276/.337/.434	83	.385	1.1	RF(14): -0.1, CF(9): -0.4, LF(4): 0.1	0.2
2022 DC	*KC*	*MLB*	*25*	*318*	*34*	*13*	*2*	*6*	*37*	*24*	*73*	*11*	*3*	*23.3%*	*.237/.307/.372*	*83*	*.298*	*1.0*	*RF 2, CF 0*	*0.5*

Comparables: Kevin Kiermaier, Alex Presley, Andrew Stevenson

Added to the Royals' Opening Day roster after a strong spring training, Isbel spent the year looking like a player with only 214 at bats above A-ball. Demoted to Triple-A Omaha in late April, Isbel posted the sort of solid yet unspectacular all-around performance that has been his calling card since Kansas City plucked him from UNLV in the third round of the 2018 draft. The biggest development for Isbel in 2021 was his improvement defensively, which gives him a viable path as an adequate center fielder and mitigates concerns that his bat isn't quite good enough for a corner outfield slot. The Royals would likely have preferred the inverse.

Nick Loftin IF
Born: 09/25/98 Age: 23 Bats: R Throws: R Height: 6'1" Weight: 180 lb. Origin: Round 1, 2020 Draft (#32 overall)

YEAR	TEAM	LVL	AGE	PA	R	2B	3B	HR	RBI	BB	K	SB	CS	Whiff%	AVG/OBP/SLG	DRC+	BABIP	BRR	FRAA	WARP
2021	QC	A+	22	410	67	22	5	10	57	42	60	11	2		.289/.373/.463	122	.323	1.6	SS(47): -3.9, 2B(21): 1.0, 3B(11): -0.2	2.1
2022 non-DC	*KC*	*MLB*	*23*	*251*	*22*	*11*	*1*	*3*	*23*	*19*	*42*	*3*	*1*	*18.9%*	*.243/.310/.355*	*83*	*.284*	*0.1*	*SS -3, 2B 0*	*0.0*

Comparables: Chris Taylor, Matt Duffy, Josh Rutledge

Selected in the Competitive Balance portion of the first round of the 2020 draft, Loftin impressed in his delayed professional debut, displaying the all-around ability that made him a star at Baylor University. Loftin's patient, disciplined approach at the plate, combined with a quick swing, led to loud contact and quality at bats. Even though he isn't projected to be a big-time power bat, there's enough bat speed and athleticism to play in the majors. While he was seen as a utility type coming out of college, he now looks like he's locked in at shortstop, with a strong arm and instincts around the bag that will make him a plus defender at the position.

Nicky Lopez SS
Born: 03/13/95 Age: 27 Bats: L Throws: R Height: 5'11" Weight: 180 lb. Origin: Round 5, 2016 Draft (#163 overall)

YEAR	TEAM	LVL	AGE	PA	R	2B	3B	HR	RBI	BB	K	SB	CS	Whiff%	AVG/OBP/SLG	DRC+	BABIP	BRR	FRAA	WARP
2019	OMA	AAA	24	138	27	6	1	3	13	20	5	9	3		.353/.457/.500	128	.352	-1.1	SS(17): 3.6, 2B(14): 0.4	1.4
2019	KC	MLB	24	402	44	22	2	2	30	18	51	1	1	15.0%	.240/.276/.325	76	.273	3.1	2B(76): 1.8, SS(33): 1.7	0.9
2020	KC	MLB	25	192	15	8	0	1	13	18	41	0	5	21.1%	.201/.286/.266	77	.260	-0.2	2B(53): 6.3, SS(4): 0.1, 3B(2): -0.0	0.7
2021	KC	MLB	26	565	78	21	6	2	43	49	74	22	1	15.6%	.300/.365/.378	102	.347	5.4	SS(148): 5.7, 2B(4): 0.6	3.3
2022 DC	*KC*	*MLB*	*27*	*546*	*63*	*21*	*4*	*5*	*54*	*47*	*69*	*10*	*4*	*16.2%*	*.262/.333/.355*	*89*	*.298*	*0.7*	*SS 1, 2B 0*	*1.5*

Comparables: Darwin Barney, Ehire Adrianza, Brandon Crawford

No one says "home runs, shifting and strikeouts" win games, but that troika has replaced "pitching, speed and defense" in terms of what modern franchises prefer. Lopez is a throwback, then, a reminder of a simpler time when slick fielding middle infielders who couldn't hit were franchise anchors. Lopez's batted ball data suggests failure; watching him in action suggests otherwise. Lopez's modest offensive success finally arrived last year when he stopped worrying about batted ball distance, sacrificed what little power he had for contact and let his speed do the rest. But it was his defense that carried him, with Lopez's 24 Outs Above Average an absurd seven outs ahead of Brandon Crawford, the majors' next best shortstop. WARP is often overrated and overutilized, but Lopez's 3.2 WARP in 2021 doesn't lie. He's the real deal, even if the Statcast data recoils in horror at the idea.

★ ★ ★ *2022 Top 101 Prospect* **#35** ★ ★ ★

MJ Melendez C
Born: 11/29/98 Age: 23 Bats: L Throws: R Height: 6'1" Weight: 190 lb. Origin: Round 2, 2017 Draft (#52 overall)

YEAR	TEAM	LVL	AGE	PA	R	2B	3B	HR	RBI	BB	K	SB	CS	Whiff%	AVG/OBP/SLG	DRC+	BABIP	BRR	FRAA	WARP
2019	WIL	A+	20	419	34	23	2	9	54	44	165	7	5		.163/.260/.311	58	.259	-0.7	C(71): 5.7	-0.2
2021	NWA	AA	22	347	58	18	0	28	65	43	76	2	4		.285/.372/.628	143	.286	-0.7	C(52): -3.5	2.6
2021	OMA	AAA	22	184	37	4	3	13	38	32	39	1	2		.293/.413/.620	128	.310	-1.4	C(29): -2.3, 3B(9): 0.5	0.9
2022 DC	*KC*	*MLB*	*23*	*30*	*4*	*1*	*0*	*1*	*4*	*3*	*8*	*0*	*0*	*32.8%*	*.235/.321/.443*	*104*	*.290*	*0.0*	*C -1*	*0.1*

Comparables: Gary Sánchez, Wilson Ramos, Rowdy Tellez

YEAR	TEAM	P. COUNT	FRM RUNS	BLK RUNS	THRW RUNS	TOT RUNS
2019	WIL	9371	2.1		4.9	7.0
2021	OMA	4340	-2.6	-0.3	0.2	-2.7
2021	NWA	7563	-3.1	-0.5	-0.3	-3.8
2022	*KC*	*1202*	*-0.6*	*-0.1*	*0.1*	*-0.6*

The pandemic hampered almost every prospect's development, so it's refreshing to find an example of an emerging player who might have been helped by time away from organized ball. After an awful 2019, Melendez's confidence was shot. A year at the Royals' alternate site in 2020 aided his development not only by allowing him to face the team's top prospects but also by letting him focus on mechanical improvements rather than statistical achievements. In 2021, he crushed pitching at two minor-league levels and shot back to the upper echelon of most prospect lists. He still needs to tinker, but with Salvador Perez in the fold the Royals have the luxury of giving Melendez as much time as he needs in the minors to put the finishing touches on what could be an enviable catcher transition.

Whit Merrifield 2B Born: 01/24/89 Age: 33 Bats: R Throws: R Height: 6'1" Weight: 195 lb. Origin: Round 9, 2010 Draft (#269 overall)

YEAR	TEAM	LVL	AGE	PA	R	2B	3B	HR	RBI	BB	K	SB	CS	Whiff%	AVG/OBP/SLG	DRC+	BABIP	BRR	FRAA	WARP
2019	KC	MLB	30	735	105	41	10	16	74	45	126	20	10	20.1%	.302/.348/.463	105	.350	-3.0	2B(82): 7.0, RF(61): -6.4, CF(17): 1.9	3.0
2020	KC	MLB	31	265	38	12	0	9	30	12	33	12	3	16.2%	.282/.325/.440	113	.295	-0.1	RF(34): 0.4, CF(23): -0.4, 2B(15): 1.6	1.4
2021	KC	MLB	32	720	97	42	3	10	74	40	103	40	4	18.2%	.277/.317/.395	95	.309	6.4	2B(149): 12.5, RF(18): 1.1, LF(2): -0.2	4.1
2022 DC	*KC*	*MLB*	*33*	*662*	*94*	*34*	*3*	*11*	*61*	*42*	*96*	*30*	*9*	*18.1%*	*.278/.329/.399*	*98*	*.315*	*2.0*	*2B 3, RF 0*	*2.5*

Comparables: Placido Polanco, Red Schoendienst, Johnny Ray

Since making his major-league debut on May 18, 2016, months after the Royals won the World Series, Merrifield has been the centerpiece of a hangover with no sign of ending. The overachiever some initially thought never even deserved a shot in the majors is now well over 3,000 plate appearances into a 15 WARP career. The $16.25 million, four-year contract he signed before 2019 is one of the biggest bargains in baseball, but that bargain has been wasted on futility and frustration, a death spiral of losing that hasn't known any end despite Merrifield's repeatedly solid efforts. Merrifield will start next season at age 33, a precarious year for a ballplayer. Here's hoping the face and bargain of the franchise is still around to enjoy the fruits of the next Royals rebuild.

Adalberto Mondesi 3B/SS Born: 07/27/95 Age: 26 Bats: S Throws: R Height: 6'1" Weight: 200 lb. Origin: International Free Agent, 2011

YEAR	TEAM	LVL	AGE	PA	R	2B	3B	HR	RBI	BB	K	SB	CS	Whiff%	AVG/OBP/SLG	DRC+	BABIP	BRR	FRAA	WARP
2019	OMA	AAA	23	37	5	1	1	1	3	4	13	2	1		.242/.324/.424	86	.368	0.5	SS(6): -0.2	0.1
2019	KC	MLB	23	443	58	20	10	9	62	19	132	43	7	38.2%	.263/.291/.424	76	.357	4.2	SS(100): 7.4	1.3
2020	KC	MLB	24	233	33	11	3	6	22	11	70	24	8	40.4%	.256/.294/.416	75	.350	0.4	SS(59): 4.6	0.5
2021	OMA	AAA	25	51	8	1	0	2	2	2	13	5	1		.204/.235/.347	92	.235	1.2	SS(13): -0.4	0.2
2021	KC	MLB	25	136	19	8	1	6	17	6	43	15	1	35.8%	.230/.271/.452	78	.299	0.6	3B(20): 2.0, SS(11): 0.2	0.3
2022 DC	*KC*	*MLB*	*26*	*395*	*46*	*17*	*4*	*11*	*47*	*20*	*113*	*30*	*7*	*36.0%*	*.236/.279/.400*	*78*	*.308*	*3.6*	*2B 0, SS 0*	*0.6*

Comparables: Rubén Tejada, Wilmer Flores, Elvis Andrus

The most important moment in Mondesi's 2021 might have come on a local sports talk radio show in August. During the broadcast, Royals general manager Dayton Moore indicated he isn't necessarily counting on Mondesi to be an everyday player in 2022 or beyond. It has now been six years since Mondesi's surprising major-league debut as a teenager in the 2015 World Series. While he has shown flashes of brilliance, particularly with his glove and legs, injuries have frequently kept him on the sidelines. Last year it was his hamstring and both obliques that led to three separate IL stints and limited Mondesi to 35 games. Beyond the health questions, it is fair to wonder if a player with a career .283 OBP in 1,312 career PA is more of a complimentary or role player than a centerpiece. The emergence of Nicky Lopez and impending arrival of Bobby Witt Jr. at least puts exclamation points next to the question marks.

Ryan O'Hearn DH Born: 07/26/93 Age: 28 Bats: L Throws: L Height: 6'3" Weight: 220 lb. Origin: Round 8, 2014 Draft (#243 overall)

YEAR	TEAM	LVL	AGE	PA	R	2B	3B	HR	RBI	BB	K	SB	CS	Whiff%	AVG/OBP/SLG	DRC+	BABIP	BRR	FRAA	WARP
2019	OMA	AAA	25	149	20	10	1	9	28	17	31	0	0		.295/.383/.597	116	.322	0.2	1B(25): 0.4	0.7
2019	KC	MLB	25	370	32	13	1	14	38	39	99	0	1	26.1%	.195/.281/.369	86	.230	-1.1	1B(94): -5.4, LF(2): -0.1	-0.3
2020	KC	MLB	26	132	7	6	0	2	18	18	37	0	0	29.9%	.195/.303/.301	85	.267	-0.9	1B(27): -0.1	0.0
2021	OMA	AAA	27	82	22	4	0	12	25	9	15	3	0		.375/.451/.931	177	.333	1.0	1B(8): 0.8, RF(8): -1.1	1.0
2021	KC	MLB	27	254	23	5	1	9	29	13	71	0	0	29.3%	.225/.268/.369	81	.277	-1.8	RF(25): -1.3, 1B(20): 0.5, LF(1): 0.1	-0.2
2022 DC	*KC*	*MLB*	*28*	*265*	*34*	*11*	*0*	*10*	*37*	*23*	*66*	*0*	*0*	*27.8%*	*.238/.309/.428*	*95*	*.284*	*-0.3*	*RF 0, 1B 0*	*0.4*

Comparables: Justin Smoak, Ji-Man Choi, Yonder Alonso

O'Hearn's major-league career started with a bang–or, to be more precise, 12 of them in 170 big-league plate appearances in 2018–but has mostly been a whimper since. The big, beefy slugger took another incremental step back in 2021, abandoning most of the plate discipline that made his poor batting average somewhat tolerable. The Royals alternated O'Hearn between first and right field when he did play, but he didn't provide much defensive value at either spot. Maybe something will click for him this year, but I wouldn't bet my Amos Otis shirsey on it.

Edward Olivares OF Born: 03/06/96 Age: 26 Bats: R Throws: R Height: 6'2" Weight: 190 lb. Origin: International Free Agent, 2014

YEAR	TEAM	LVL	AGE	PA	R	2B	3B	HR	RBI	BB	K	SB	CS	Whiff%	AVG/OBP/SLG	DRC+	BABIP	BRR	FRAA	WARP
2019	AMA	AA	23	551	85	25	2	18	77	43	98	35	10		.283/.349/.453	112	.317	4.4	RF(105): 5.8, CF(19): 0.2	3.8
2020	SD	MLB	24	36	4	1	0	1	3	2	14	0	1	25.0%	.176/.222/.294	75	.263	-0.5	LF(7): -0.1, RF(6): -0.3, CF(1): -0.0	-0.1
2020	KC	MLB	24	65	5	1	1	2	7	2	11	0	1	24.5%	.274/.292/.419	103	.300	0.1	CF(10): -0.4, LF(7): 0.6, RF(5): -0.2	0.2
2021	OMA	AAA	25	292	54	12	3	15	36	29	46	12	4		.313/.397/.559	133	.333	-0.4	CF(39): -3.2, LF(13): 0.4, RF(10): -1.6	1.6
2021	KC	MLB	25	111	14	2	0	5	12	5	19	2	2	24.3%	.238/.291/.406	106	.244	-0.7	RF(22): -0.8, LF(11): -0.0, CF(4): -0.8	0.2
2022 DC	*KC*	*MLB*	*26*	*219*	*25*	*8*	*1*	*5*	*27*	*13*	*41*	*6*	*3*	*22.7%*	*.250/.309/.388*	*90*	*.291*	*0.6*	*RF 0, LF 0*	*0.4*

Comparables: Juan Lagares, Scott Van Slyke, Lorenzo Cain

You, our smart and handsome reader, religiously purchase your copy of the *Baseball Prospectus Annual* at the bookstore because you expect us to have all the answers and provide you with reams of information about players you can't find anywhere else. So, it must be incredibly frustrating to get to the Olivares comment and discover we're just as stumped as to why he couldn't crack the Royals lineup and was demoted on *seven* separate occasions. You thought maybe you'd find some scouting tidbits that revealed a fatal flaw in Olivares' game, or perhaps some deep insights into why Ryan O'Hearn and Olivares started the same number of games after Jorge Soler was traded to Atlanta. Nope, we can only share in your frustration, shrug and thank you for your support.

Vinnie Pasquantino 1B Born: 10/10/97 Age: 24 Bats: L Throws: L Height: 6'4" Weight: 245 lb. Origin: Round 11, 2019 Draft (#319 overall)

YEAR	TEAM	LVL	AGE	PA	R	2B	3B	HR	RBI	BB	K	SB	CS	Whiff%	AVG/OBP/SLG	DRC+	BABIP	BRR	FRAA	WARP
2019	BUR	ROA	21	248	43	17	2	14	53	27	40	0	0		.294/.371/.592		.293			
2021	QC	A+	23	276	44	20	3	13	42	33	38	4	0		.291/.384/.565	144	.298	-1.5	1B(52): 5.0	2.5
2021	NWA	AA	23	237	35	17	0	11	42	31	26	2	0		.310/.405/.560	140	.307	0.1	1B(54): -2.8	1.5
2022 non-DC	*KC*	*MLB*	*24*	*251*	*27*	*13*	*1*	*7*	*29*	*23*	*38*	*0*	*1*	*19.7%*	*.258/.334/.425*	*104*	*.283*	*-0.3*	*1B 1*	*0.6*

Comparables: Kila Ka'aihue, Corey Dickerson, Ben Paulsen

Without even playing a game above AA yet, Pasquantino has become a fan favorite and someone to dream on in Kansas City. He's a diligent, hardworking kid who wasn't seen as a top-tier prospect coming into the season and has literally muscled his way into the conversation by hitting for power across two levels. He's old school on the field–choking up with two strikes and loathing the mere idea of striking out–and off it, loving the game and treating baseball the way Dani Rojas approaches fútbol in the masterpiece of midwestern propaganda *Ted Lasso*. Pasquantino draws the inevitable Daniel Vogelbach comparisons because of his size, and AA is a long way from the majors, but there might be more here than your typical big, beefy first baseman.

Erick Peña CF Born: 02/20/03 Age: 19 Bats: L Throws: R Height: 6'3" Weight: 205 lb. Origin: International Free Agent, 2019

YEAR	TEAM	LVL	AGE	PA	R	2B	3B	HR	RBI	BB	K	SB	CS	Whiff%	AVG/OBP/SLG	DRC+	BABIP	BRR	FRAA	WARP
2021	ROYB	ROK	18	156	14	10	1	3	15	15	57	4	4		.161/.256/.314		.244			
2022															*No projection*					

Comparables: Raysheron Michel, Dalton Pompey, Devon Torrence

Depending on what sort of circle you run in, you're either sick of the Jasson Dominguez comps or you've never heard of the guy. Signed to a $3.8 million bonus during the 2019 International Free Agent signing period, Peña had to wait until 2021 to make his professional debut. The inexperience and rust combined to make for a miserable year at the Arizona Complex League. Physically, Peña was a man among boys, with a swing that scouts described as a long, herky-jerky mess. Peña is a mere 18 years old, so there is plenty of time for a prospect whose ETA is at least three to four years away to turn things around.

Salvador Perez C Born: 05/10/90 Age: 32 Bats: R Throws: R Height: 6'3" Weight: 255 lb. Origin: International Free Agent, 2006

YEAR	TEAM	LVL	AGE	PA	R	2B	3B	HR	RBI	BB	K	SB	CS	Whiff%	AVG/OBP/SLG	DRC+	BABIP	BRR	FRAA	WARP
2020	KC	MLB	30	156	22	12	0	11	32	3	36	1	0	26.9%	.333/.353/.633	122	.375	-0.6	C(34): 0.8, 1B(3): -0.3	1.0
2021	KC	MLB	31	665	88	24	0	48	121	28	170	1	0	33.6%	.273/.316/.544	130	.298	-0.5	C(124): -15.8	3.4
2022 DC	*KC*	*MLB*	*32*	*589*	*82*	*25*	*0*	*28*	*93*	*25*	*162*	*0*	*1*	*32.5%*	*.248/.292/.454*	*101*	*.295*	*-0.9*	*C -10*	*1.4*

Comparables: Benito Santiago, Ivan Rodriguez, Ted Simmons

YEAR	TEAM	P. COUNT	FRM RUNS	BLK RUNS	THRW RUNS	TOT RUNS
2020	KC	4651	1.4	0.1	0.0	1.5
2021	KC	17285	-14.3	-1.2	0.7	-14.8
2022	*KC*	*15632*	*-11.4*	*-0.4*	*0.9*	*-11.0*

We know, we know. Perez didn't *really* break the record for home runs as a catcher. Fifteen of his 48 home runs came as a DH, leaving Javy Lopez's 2003 record of 42 dongs intact for at least one more season. But the most impressive statistic of Perez's 2021 wasn't 48 but 665, as in the amount of plate appearances he amassed. Sure, Perez started 40 games at DH. That just means he often spent nine innings crouched behind the plate in full gear for hours on a sultry summer day and then–instead of getting some well-deserved R&R like nearly every other backstop does–was back in the game the next day to get his whacks in. And Perez wasn't a slouch at DH, posting a better OPS at the "position" than Franmil Reyes and Yordan Alvarez did. Even if it's not a record, it's a wild success any way you slice it.

★ ★ ★ *2022 Top 101 Prospect* **#72** ★ ★ ★

Nick Pratto 1B/OF Born: 10/06/98 Age: 23 Bats: L Throws: L Height: 6'1" Weight: 215 lb. Origin: Round 1, 2017 Draft (#14 overall)

YEAR	TEAM	LVL	AGE	PA	R	2B	3B	HR	RBI	BB	K	SB	CS	Whiff%	AVG/OBP/SLG	DRC+	BABIP	BRR	FRAA	WARP
2019	WIL	A+	20	472	48	21	1	9	46	49	164	17	7		.191/.278/.310	66	.286	0.3	1B(123): 4.6	-0.1
2021	NWA	AA	22	275	44	13	4	15	43	46	80	7	5		.271/.404/.570	121	.349	-1.8	1B(61): -0.8	1.2
2021	OMA	AAA	22	270	54	15	3	21	55	37	77	5	0		.259/.367/.634	119	.282	1.0	1B(52): -1.0, RF(3): -0.1	1.2
2022 non-DC	*KC*	*MLB*	*23*	*251*	*28*	*11*	*1*	*9*	*31*	*26*	*85*	*5*	*3*	*34.6%*	*.221/.311/.416*	*91*	*.314*	*0.4*	*1B 0, RF 0*	*0.3*

Comparables: Rowdy Tellez, Logan Morrison, Matt Olson

In part a victim of Wilmington's unforgiving hitting environment, Pratto also hurt himself in 2019, with an all-too-patient approach that let pitchers carve him up on two-strike counts. The Royals organizational staff worked diligently with Pratto at the alternate site to fix the flawed approach and open up his stance, and you could see the results last year, as he tore through two levels of the upper minors. The power scouts were hoping he would develop has gotten here; it's not world class, but it'll play at first. Defensively, Pratto's instincts and footwork grade out as plus at the position. Expect the debut in 2022.

Emmanuel Rivera 3B Born: 06/29/96 Age: 26 Bats: R Throws: R Height: 6'2" Weight: 225 lb. Origin: Round 19, 2015 Draft (#579 overall)

YEAR	TEAM	LVL	AGE	PA	R	2B	3B	HR	RBI	BB	K	SB	CS	Whiff%	AVG/OBP/SLG	DRC+	BABIP	BRR	FRAA	WARP
2019	MAY	WIN	23	133	14	3	2	3	14	6	16	2	1		.309/.353/.439		.333			
2019	NWA	AA	23	534	59	18	2	7	57	25	77	6	2		.258/.297/.345	102	.289	-0.4	3B(117): 0.5, 2B(1): -0.2	1.5
2020	MAY	WIN	24	73	12	6	0	3	9	6	13	3	0		.292/.342/.523		.314			
2021	OMA	AAA	25	282	48	17	2	19	57	22	58	3	0		.286/.348/.592	126	.300	-1.7	3B(45): 3.1, 1B(9): 0.9	1.9
2021	KC	MLB	25	98	13	4	0	1	5	8	21	2	0	25.3%	.256/.316/.333	91	.324	0.6	3B(28): -1.6, 1B(1): -0.0	0.1
2022 DC	*KC*	*MLB*	*26*	*124*	*14*	*5*	*0*	*2*	*15*	*8*	*27*	*0*	*1*	*26.4%*	*.245/.301/.381*	*86*	*.298*	*0.0*	*3B 0*	*0.1*

Comparables: Chris Johnson, Danny Valencia, Hunter Dozier

Heading into 2021, Rivera seemed like organizational filler due to a lack of power and subpar defensive skills. He put himself on the Royals' radar with a power outburst out of the gate at Triple-A Omaha and was promoted to the big club in late June. Two days later, Rivera suffered a broken hamate bone and missed a little over a month of action. When he returned, the solid contact skills and approach remained intact, but the power was gone. Hamate bone injuries tend to sap power in the short term, but minor-league homer surges also tend not to last. It's difficult to know if the hot streak was a fluke or the real deal.

Carlos Santana 1B Born: 04/08/86 Age: 36 Bats: S Throws: R Height: 5'11" Weight: 215 lb. Origin: International Free Agent, 2004

YEAR	TEAM	LVL	AGE	PA	R	2B	3B	HR	RBI	BB	K	SB	CS	Whiff%	AVG/OBP/SLG	DRC+	BABIP	BRR	FRAA	WARP
2019	CLE	MLB	33	686	110	30	1	34	93	108	108	4	0	20.3%	.281/.397/.515	134	.293	0.5	1B(135): 4.0	5.3
2020	CLE	MLB	34	255	34	7	0	8	30	47	43	0	0	20.7%	.199/.349/.350	114	.212	1.0	1B(60): -1.4	1.0
2021	KC	MLB	35	659	66	15	0	19	69	86	102	2	0	22.2%	.214/.319/.342	101	.227	-1.3	1B(136): -4.2	0.9
2022 DC	*KC*	*MLB*	*36*	*586*	*79*	*20*	*1*	*19*	*75*	*84*	*96*	*2*	*1*	*22.3%*	*.238/.351/.402*	*111*	*.259*	*-0.7*	*1B -1*	*1.8*

Comparables: Earl Torgeson, J.T. Snow, Mike Jorgensen

For professional athletes, injuries are a no-win proposition, especially when they're "minor." Play through one of these maladies and run the risk of seeing your performance suffer. Sit out a few days and you're called "soft" by every know-nothing with a social media account. On July 10, Santana was slashing .246/.368/.421, in line with his typically good, albeit unspectacular, career OPS. That same day, he hurt his left wrist, and his season collapsed like a pile of dry leaves in a stiff autumn breeze. Santana's second-half .500 OPS was worst among qualified hitters. He couldn't drive the ball with any authority, and when pitchers recognized this, they started pounding the zone. He made more contact post-injury (a bad wrist doesn't impact your batting eye) but the contact he made was significantly weaker than usual. A full offseason should give Santana enough time to return to being his productive, boring self. He is reaching the late stages of his career, though, where a return to form might be impeded by age-influenced decline.

Michael A. Taylor CF Born: 03/26/91 Age: 31 Bats: R Throws: R Height: 6'4" Weight: 215 lb. Origin: Round 6, 2009 Draft (#172 overall)

YEAR	TEAM	LVL	AGE	PA	R	2B	3B	HR	RBI	BB	K	SB	CS	Whiff%	AVG/OBP/SLG	DRC+	BABIP	BRR	FRAA	WARP
2019	HBG	AA	28	247	36	16	2	9	35	25	69	10	6		.248/.324/.463	100	.315	2.2	CF(43): -1.9, RF(6): 0.0	0.9
2019	WAS	MLB	28	97	10	7	0	1	3	7	34	6	0	34.6%	.250/.305/.364	67	.396	-0.2	CF(25): -0.2, RF(7): -0.7	-0.1
2020	WAS	MLB	29	99	11	6	0	5	16	6	27	0	0	28.7%	.196/.253/.424	94	.217	-0.8	LF(14): 1.9, CF(11): -0.3, RF(11): 0.1	0.3
2021	KC	MLB	30	528	58	16	1	12	54	33	144	14	7	31.3%	.244/.297/.356	83	.319	2.5	CF(139): 19.3	3.3
2022 DC	*KC*	*MLB*	*31*	*496*	*57*	*20*	*1*	*13*	*62*	*34*	*137*	*19*	*7*	*30.8%*	*.233/.290/.374*	*80*	*.302*	*1.5*	*CF 2*	*0.9*

Comparables: Torii Hunter, Mike Cameron, Mickey Stanley

Lauded for years as a wizard in center field, Taylor got the opportunity for the first time in years to flash the leather in a full-time role and didn't disappoint, blanketing center field at Kauffman Stadium and passing both the metric and eye tests with flying colors. The kindest thing you can say about his hitting is nothing. The second-kindest is, er, it's passable against lefties given the defense? Kansas City quickly re-upped Taylor to a $9 million, two-year deal as the 2021 season was winding down, showing an organizational commitment to athleticism and run prevention. It's a consistent philosophy, even if it's not a winning one.

Peyton Wilson 2B Born: 11/01/99 Age: 22 Bats: S Throws: R Height: 5'9" Weight: 180 lb. Origin: Round 2, 2021 Draft (#66 overall)

YEAR	TEAM	LVL	AGE	PA	R	2B	3B	HR	RBI	BB	K	SB	CS	Whiff%	AVG/OBP/SLG	DRC+	BABIP	BRR	FRAA	WARP
2021	ROYG	ROK	21	41	7	3	1	1	7	5	10	2	2		.219/.366/.469		.273			
2021	COL	A	21	46	6	3	1	0	1	4	10	5	0		.231/.326/.359	106	.300	0.4	2B(11): 0.3	0.2
2022 non-DC	*KC*	*MLB*	*22*	*251*	*19*	*10*	*1*	*2*	*20*	*16*	*68*	*13*	*3*	*29.4%*	*.208/.271/.300*	*57*	*.284*	*1.2*	*2B 0*	*-0.4*

A supplemental second-round pick in 2021 out of the University of Alabama, Wilson is the third of three brothers to graduate from Bama and play professional sports. The Royals drafted Wilson and used him in the minors as a second baseman, but he played center in college and still has enough of an arm to be utilized as an outfielder if needed. His first exposure to minor-league pitching was rough, but his speed and athleticism give him a puncher's chance at making the adjustments necessary to improve in his first full professional season this year.

★ ★ ★ *2022 Top 101 Prospect* **#1** ★ ★ ★

Bobby Witt Jr. SS Born: 06/14/00 Age: 22 Bats: R Throws: R Height: 6'1" Weight: 200 lb. Origin: Round 1, 2019 Draft (#2 overall)

YEAR	TEAM	LVL	AGE	PA	R	2B	3B	HR	RBI	BB	K	SB	CS	Whiff%	AVG/OBP/SLG	DRC+	BABIP	BRR	FRAA	WARP
2019	ROY	ROK	19	180	30	2	5	1	27	13	35	9	1		.262/.317/.354		.323			
2021	NWA	AA	21	279	44	11	4	16	51	25	67	14	8		.295/.369/.570	120	.339	1.1	SS(50): -1.7, 3B(8): -1.1	1.4
2021	OMA	AAA	21	285	55	24	0	17	46	26	64	15	3		.285/.352/.581	114	.314	-0.1	SS(52): -4.8, 3B(10): -1.4	0.8
2022 DC	*KC*	*MLB*	*22*	*466*	*61*	*23*	*3*	*15*	*63*	*33*	*122*	*17*	*5*	*30.3%*	*.247/.307/.428*	*100*	*.307*	*1.5*	*3B -8, SS 0*	*0.7*

Comparables: Freddy Galvis, Asdrúbal Cabrera, Willi Castro

The only bad things we can come up with to say about Witt's 2021 campaign are that 1) we didn't get the joy of seeing him make his major-league debut and 2) we're running out of superlatives to describe this guy. It's easy to forget that Witt had all of 180 professional plate appearances heading into 2021, because not only did he survive in the high minors, but he put on a show, dominating across two levels before his first full season ended. Witt is the complete package: an impressive hitter with eye-popping raw power that goes to all fields and a mature approach at the dish that speaks to his bloodlines as the son of a major leaguer. His fielding might be even more impressive. Witt's physical skills combine with his baseball instincts to put him in a position to make nearly every play. If there is a weakness, it's against more advanced off-speed stuff, but more likely than not Witt's going to hit the ground running this year and never look back.

PITCHERS

Scott Barlow RHP Born: 12/18/92 Age: 29 Bats: R Throws: R Height: 6'3" Weight: 210 lb. Origin: Round 6, 2011 Draft (#194 overall)

YEAR	TEAM	LVL	AGE	W	L	SV	G	GS	IP	H	HR	BB/9	K/9	K	GB%	BABIP	WHIP	ERA	DRA-	WARP	MPH	FB%	Whiff%	CSP
2019	OMA	AAA	26	0	0	1	3	0	6	3	0	4.5	7.5	5	21.4%	.214	1.00	0.00	103	0.0				
2019	KC	MLB	26	3	3	1	61	0	70^{1}	64	6	4.7	11.8	92	39.3%	.341	1.44	4.22	87	1.2	94.4	42.9%	33.8%	45.1%
2020	KC	MLB	27	2	1	2	32	0	30	27	4	2.7	11.7	39	45.3%	.324	1.20	4.20	79	0.7	95.1	37.3%	37.6%	43.0%
2021	KC	MLB	28	5	3	16	71	0	74^{1}	61	4	3.4	11.0	91	38.9%	.315	1.20	2.42	84	1.3	95.5	33.4%	35.4%	51.5%
2022 DC	*KC*	*MLB*	*29*	*3*	*3*	*25*	*74*	*0*	*64.7*	*53*	*8*	*3.5*	*10.9*	*78*	*40.0%*	*.288*	*1.22*	*3.59*	*88*	*0.6*	*95.2*	*36.1%*	*35.4%*	*48.7%*

Comparables: David Hernandez, Jared Hughes, Mike MacDougal

Once an afterthought in a perpetually loaded Dodgers farm system, Barlow was spotted by the Royals scouting department during a minor-league game in 2017. When he became a six-year minor-league free agent after that season, the Royals scooped him up, hoping to make him into a starter. When that didn't work, the Royals went the bullpen route in 2019 and it stuck, as Barlow added 3-4 miles-per-hour to his fastball and quickly became a late-inning weapon. Practice makes perfect is what they'll always tell you, but in Barlow's case perseverance and patience can be added to this litany of "p's". A decade after the Dodgers took him in the sixth round of the 2011 draft, Barlow found his major-league calling as the Royalscloser, a success story that happened because of Barlow's talent, for sure, but also because several brilliant baseball minds helped him find his niche along the way.

Scott Blewett RHP Born: 04/10/96 Age: 26 Bats: R Throws: R Height: 6'6" Weight: 245 lb. Origin: Round 2, 2014 Draft (#56 overall)

YEAR	TEAM	LVL	AGE	W	L	SV	G	GS	IP	H	HR	BB/9	K/9	K	GB%	BABIP	WHIP	ERA	DRA-	WARP	MPH	FB%	Whiff%	CSP
2019	NWA	AA	23	1	3	0	5	5	25^{1}	21	2	2.8	12.1	34	41.9%	.317	1.14	3.55	73	0.4				
2019	OMA	AAA	23	5	8	0	18	16	81^{1}	115	24	5.1	6.2	56	37.6%	.342	1.98	8.52	155	-2.2				
2020	KC	MLB	24	0	0	0	2	0	3	6	0	3.0	12.0	4	27.3%	.545	2.33	6.00	116	0.0	93.5	58.1%	26.9%	45.6%
2021	OMA	AAA	25	6	3	0	23	10	69	80	19	4.0	8.3	64	44.3%	.303	1.61	6.39	107	0.7				
2021	KC	MLB	25	0	0	0	3	0	5	3	0	9.0	7.2	4	41.7%	.250	1.60	1.80	110	0.0	91.4	68.5%	18.2%	46.2%
2022 non-DC	*KC*	*MLB*	*26*	*2*	*3*	*0*	*57*	*0*	*50*	*54*	*7*	*4.6*	*7.7*	*42*	*41.6%*	*.314*	*1.61*	*5.85*	*131*	*-0.6*	*92.0*	*65.2%*	*20.9%*	*46.0%*

Comparables: Sal Romano, Drew VerHagen, Joe Ross

Burnt coffee and stale donuts. A dozen people sitting on folding chairs, staring at one man who is clearly the leader of this outfit. "Welcome to tonight's meeting of the Inappropriately Named for Your Profession Support Group" the emcee says. One-by-one the members of the group tell their tales. Richard Sunkenship, a naval captain. Roger Cutartery, a heart surgeon. Jane Stumbles, a professional ballerina. Finally, the group gets to Scott Blewett, a professional pitcher with the Royals. He recounts the harrowing tale of a muggy September afternoon in 2021, when Dylan Moore singled home Jerred Kelenic while a fan yelled, "Hey, ya Blewett. That's your name." They know the feeling.

Jake Brentz LHP Born: 09/14/94 Age: 27 Bats: L Throws: L Height: 6'1" Weight: 205 lb. Origin: Round 11, 2013 Draft (#325 overall)

YEAR	TEAM	LVL	AGE	W	L	SV	G	GS	IP	H	HR	BB/9	K/9	K	GB%	BABIP	WHIP	ERA	DRA-	WARP	MPH	FB%	Whiff%	CSP
2019	NWA	AA	24	0	0	0	5	0	5^{1}	6	1	3.4	8.4	5	56.2%	.333	1.50	3.38	92	0.0				
2019	ALT	AA	24	0	1	0	9	0	11^{2}	6	0	2.3	10.0	13	57.1%	.214	0.77	0.77	85	0.2				
2019	IND	AAA	24	1	0	8	27	0	35^{2}	42	4	5.8	10.3	41	42.2%	.388	1.82	5.55	100	0.5				
2021	KC	MLB	26	5	2	2	72	0	64	45	7	5.2	10.7	76	48.1%	.255	1.28	3.66	95	0.7	97.0	59.5%	30.2%	51.4%
2022 DC	*KC*	*MLB*	*27*	*3*	*3*	*3*	*74*	*0*	*64.7*	*52*	*7*	*5.3*	*10.1*	*72*	*46.4%*	*.279*	*1.41*	*4.26*	*100*	*0.2*	*97.0*	*59.5%*	*30.2%*	*51.4%*

Comparables: Sam Freeman, Hunter Cervenka, Paul Fry

Relievers who make their major-league debuts in their late 20s don't usually attract much attention. With a fastball that sits in the upper 90s and can tickle triple digits on the gun, Brentz is a worthy exception to this rule. A journeyman minor leaguer originally drafted by the Blue Jays way back in 2013, Brentz added a changeup to his fastball/slider combo at the alternate site in 2020, giving him a needed weapon against righties. The results were great in the first half and not so great in the second, when the command slipped and hitters adjusted. Brentz has the goods to be devastating against lefties, but it's his success or failure against right-handed batters that will determine his long-term role.

Kris Bubic LHP Born: 08/19/97 Age: 24 Bats: L Throws: L Height: 6'3" Weight: 225 lb. Origin: Round 1, 2018 Draft (#40 overall)

YEAR	TEAM	LVL	AGE	W	L	SV	G	GS	IP	H	HR	BB/9	K/9	K	GB%	BABIP	WHIP	ERA	DRA-	WARP	MPH	FB%	Whiff%	CSP
2019	LEX	A	21	4	1	0	9	9	47^{2}	27	3	2.8	14.2	75	44.6%	.273	0.88	2.08	69	1.2				
2019	WIL	A+	21	7	4	0	17	17	101^{2}	76	3	2.4	9.7	110	41.4%	.299	1.01	2.30	76	2.2				
2020	KC	MLB	22	1	6	0	10	10	50	52	8	4.0	8.8	49	45.0%	.312	1.48	4.32	109	0.3	91.6	54.2%	24.9%	48.0%
2021	KC	MLB	23	6	7	0	29	20	130	121	22	4.1	7.9	114	47.1%	.280	1.38	4.43	123	-0.4	90.9	52.0%	23.5%	54.3%
2022 DC	*KC*	*MLB*	*24*	*7*	*7*	*0*	*22*	*22*	*113.3*	*108*	*13*	*4.0*	*8.8*	*110*	*45.6%*	*.300*	*1.40*	*4.46*	*106*	*0.5*	*91.1*	*52.5%*	*23.8%*	*52.9%*

Comparables: Tom Gorzelanny, José Quintana, Frank Viola

Since he was drafted as a supplemental first-round pick in 2018, Bubic's secondary offerings have gotten attention: a sharp curve with late break and a plus-plus changeup. While these pitches certainly matter, his ceiling might be limited by a fastball that only sits in the low 90s. Velocity isn't everything, but even on his best days Bubic's deceptive delivery hasn't permitted him to make up for the lack of an overpowering out pitch, and he allows far too much hard contact. Bubic only has 180 big-league innings under his belt, so the book isn't closed on his future just yet, but he'll need to either find some more oomph on his heater or come up with yet another breaker to avoid getting tagged as "just" a fifth starter.

Taylor Clarke RHP Born: 05/13/93 Age: 29 Bats: R Throws: R Height: 6'4" Weight: 217 lb. Origin: Round 3, 2015 Draft (#76 overall)

YEAR	TEAM	LVL	AGE	W	L	SV	G	GS	IP	H	HR	BB/9	K/9	K	GB%	BABIP	WHIP	ERA	DRA-	WARP	MPH	FB%	Whiff%	CSP
2019	VIS	A+	26	1	0	0	1	1	6	3	0	0.0	4.5	3	64.7%	.176	0.50	0.00	99	0.0				
2019	RNO	AAA	26	3	1	0	8	8	36^{2}	41	6	4.2	6.9	28	33.9%	.318	1.58	6.63	117	-0.1				
2019	ARI	MLB	26	5	5	1	23	15	84^{2}	86	23	3.2	7.2	68	39.2%	.261	1.37	5.31	112	0.3	93.8	53.2%	23.1%	45.6%
2020	ARI	MLB	27	3	0	0	12	5	43^{1}	35	8	4.4	8.3	40	44.3%	.237	1.29	4.36	108	0.3	94.4	45.5%	22.3%	45.7%
2021	RNO	AAA	28	1	0	0	7	0	7	6	0	2.6	10.3	8	58.8%	.353	1.14	0.00	84	0.1				
2021	ARI	MLB	28	1	3	0	43	0	43^{1}	52	4	2.9	8.1	39	37.6%	.350	1.52	4.98	103	0.3	95.7	53.4%	22.7%	53.9%
2022 DC	*KC*	*MLB*	*29*	*3*	*3*	*0*	*74*	*0*	*64.7*	*65*	*8*	*3.3*	*7.4*	*53*	*40.1%*	*.295*	*1.38*	*4.59*	*111*	*0.0*	*94.8*	*51.2%*	*22.7%*	*49.3%*

Comparables: Austin Voth, Jack Cassel, Chris Stratton

Clarke is a thrower with a couple of decent pitches and less than a couple roles in which he can thrive with them. The living definition of pitching depth, he spent the entire year traipsing out of the pen, a first for his pro career. He nearly led the Diamondbacks in FIP thanks to a reduced walk rate, but a shoulder strain derailed him for almost two months. A rough post-return finish to the season put his role back into the grab bag of managerial discretion. He'll probably stick in middle relief; he throws strikes and does little else.

Wade Davis RHP Born: 09/07/85 Age: 36 Bats: R Throws: R Height: 6'5" Weight: 225 lb. Origin: Round 3, 2004 Draft (#75 overall)

YEAR	TEAM	LVL	AGE	W	L	SV	G	GS	IP	H	HR	BB/9	K/9	K	GB%	BABIP	WHIP	ERA	DRA-	WARP	MPH	FB%	Whiff%	CSP
2019	COL	MLB	33	1	6	15	50	0	42^{2}	51	7	6.1	8.9	42	39.8%	.349	1.88	8.65	118	0.0	93.3	46.2%	25.1%	42.3%
2020	COL	MLB	34	0	1	2	5	0	4^{1}	9	3	6.2	6.2	3	42.1%	.375	2.77	20.77	128	0.0	91.9	40.3%	19.6%	42.3%
2021	KC	MLB	35	0	3	2	40	0	42^{2}	44	8	4.0	8.0	38	33.6%	.295	1.48	6.75	119	0.0	92.7	46.8%	23.5%	55.1%
2022 non-DC	*KC*	*MLB*	*36*	*2*	*3*	*0*	*57*	*0*	*50*	*50*	*7*	*4.3*	*8.4*	*46*	*37.7%*	*.303*	*1.49*	*5.16*	*119*	*-0.3*	*92.8*	*46.2%*	*23.6%*	*51.0%*

Comparables: Jeff Russell, Billy Hoeft, Reggie Cleveland

Six years after striking out Wilmer Flores in Game Five of the World Series to give the Royals their second world championship in franchise history, Davis returned to Kansas City on a one-year deal for $1.25 million. Some reunions are unexpectedly great, like when the cast of *Seinfeld* did a mock reunion on *Curb Your Enthusiasm*. But most are like *The Patty Duke Show: Still Rockin' in Brooklyn Heights*, where everyone is well past their prime and you wonder what the heck the folks who greenlit this project were thinking. Davis showed flashes of his former greatness, but what he mostly showed is that Thomas Wolfe was right. You can't go home again, especially if your velocity is diminished and your arm can't stay healthy. Years from now, when Davis is remembered by Royals fans, they will forget all about 2021's abbreviated disaster of a campaign and instead fondly recall Davis' incredible postseason relief run in 2014-2015, when he allowed one earned run in 25 innings and helped Kansas City to two straight pennants.

Carlos Hernández RHP

Born: 03/11/97 Age: 25 Bats: R Throws: R Height: 6'4" Weight: 245 lb. Origin: International Free Agent, 2016

YEAR	TEAM	LVL	AGE	W	L	SV	G	GS	IP	H	HR	BB/9	K/9	K	GB%	BABIP	WHIP	ERA	DRA-	WARP	MPH	FB%	Whiff%	CSP
2019	ROY	ROK	22	0	2	0	5	5	11	14	1	2.5	9.8	12	41.2%	.394	1.55	7.36						
2019	BUR	ROA	22	0	0	0	3	3	10^{2}	11	1	10.1	11.0	13	33.3%	.345	2.16	9.28						
2019	LEX	A	22	3	3	0	7	7	36	34	5	2.3	10.8	43	37.2%	.326	1.19	3.50	73	0.8				
2020	KC	MLB	23	0	1	0	5	3	14^{2}	19	4	3.7	8.0	13	42.6%	.349	1.70	4.91	103	0.1	96.3	51.4%	25.4%	48.3%
2021	OMA	AAA	24	2	1	0	6	6	26^{1}	28	6	2.1	8.9	26	43.6%	.306	1.29	4.44	112	0.2				
2021	KC	MLB	24	6	2	0	24	11	85^{2}	69	7	4.3	7.8	74	40.2%	.267	1.28	3.68	115	0.1	97.3	55.9%	25.8%	51.9%
2022 DC	*KC*	*MLB*	*25*	*7*	*8*	*0*	*24*	*24*	*126.3*	*122*	*17*	*3.7*	*8.7*	*121*	*40.4%*	*.298*	*1.39*	*4.61*	*110*	*0.2*	*97.2*	*55.4%*	*25.8%*	*51.5%*

Comparables: Mike Wood, Adam Bernero, Erasmo Ramírez

When you're an international signee at the age of 19 among a batch of prospects who signed three years younger, you already know a little something about needing to beat the odds. For years, Hernández has been profiled as a likely future reliever, but every year he's taken another step toward shedding that label and proving he can stick in a major-league rotation. After starting the season in the Royals' bullpen, Hernández joined the rotation in mid-July and never looked back. Hernández's offseason training program allowed him to maintain his upper 90s fastball velocity even as a starter, while his off-speed stuff continued to improve to the point where he has three solid secondaries. The developmental forecast still calls for struggles, but he's given himself a shot. Better late than never.

Greg Holland RHP

Born: 11/20/85 Age: 36 Bats: R Throws: R Height: 5'10" Weight: 210 lb. Origin: Round 10, 2007 Draft (#306 overall)

YEAR	TEAM	LVL	AGE	W	L	SV	G	GS	IP	H	HR	BB/9	K/9	K	GB%	BABIP	WHIP	ERA	DRA-	WARP	MPH	FB%	Whiff%	CSP
2019	HBG	AA	33	1	0	0	8	0	9	4	0	3.0	9.0	9	36.4%	.182	0.78	0.00	88	0.1				
2019	ARI	MLB	33	1	2	17	40	0	35^{2}	25	5	6.1	10.3	41	44.8%	.244	1.37	4.54	104	0.3	91.6	47.3%	29.9%	42.8%
2020	KC	MLB	34	3	0	6	28	0	28^{1}	20	1	2.2	9.8	31	50.7%	.275	0.95	1.91	78	0.6	93.2	37.4%	30.0%	47.1%
2021	KC	MLB	35	3	5	8	57	0	55^{2}	49	9	4.2	8.6	53	41.7%	.261	1.35	4.85	108	0.3	92.9	40.3%	28.9%	53.5%
2022 DC	*FA*	*MLB*	*36*	*2*	*3*	*0*	*57*	*0*	*49.3*	*47*	*6*	*4.3*	*9.0*	*49*	*41.7%*	*.298*	*1.43*	*4.55*	*110*	*-0.1*	*92.8*	*40.6%*	*29.2%*	*50.8%*

Comparables: Dan Wheeler, Roberto Hernandez, Tyler Clippard

"Eroding skills", "diminished velocity" and "aging closer" aren't ways any major-league reliever cares to be described. The once-dominant stopper was a shadow of his former self, the bag of tricks he used to fool hitters in an abbreviated 2020 falling short in a more conventional campaign. Holland's command has been shaky for most of the latter half of his career, so adding in a hard-hit rate of over 40% predictably led to his time as the Royals stopper being brief. Holland is one of 21 relievers in major-league history to top 40 saves in at least three seasons. For all its flaws, the stat speaks to what he once was, and why he kept getting chances.

Jakob Junis RHP

Born: 09/16/92 Age: 29 Bats: R Throws: R Height: 6'3" Weight: 220 lb. Origin: Round 29, 2011 Draft (#876 overall)

YEAR	TEAM	LVL	AGE	W	L	SV	G	GS	IP	H	HR	BB/9	K/9	K	GB%	BABIP	WHIP	ERA	DRA-	WARP	MPH	FB%	Whiff%	CSP
2019	KC	MLB	26	9	14	0	31	31	175^{1}	192	31	3.0	8.4	164	43.0%	.318	1.43	5.24	112	0.7	91.6	50.8%	22.6%	47.8%
2020	KC	MLB	27	0	2	0	8	6	25^{1}	35	7	2.1	6.8	19	46.0%	.350	1.62	6.39	114	0.1	91.2	49.2%	20.5%	51.6%
2021	OMA	AAA	28	0	2	0	6	6	17^{2}	22	4	4.1	9.2	18	48.2%	.346	1.70	5.60	109	0.2				
2021	KC	MLB	28	2	4	0	16	6	39^{1}	43	7	2.7	9.4	41	43.5%	.333	1.40	5.26	94	0.5	90.0	37.0%	25.6%	55.0%
2022 DC	*FA*	*MLB*	*29*	*7*	*6*	*0*	*51*	*9*	*82.7*	*86*	*11*	*2.9*	*8.4*	*77*	*44.5%*	*.315*	*1.37*	*4.56*	*112*	*0.0*	*91.0*	*46.0%*	*23.3%*	*50.7%*

Comparables: Edwin Jackson, Adam Conley, Joel Pineiro

A pitcher struggles, works diligently on conditioning, adds a pitch to his repertoire and finds success the following season. A tale as old as time. But no matter how hard you work or what pitches you throw, sometimes the story doesn't have a happy ending. Junis refined his mechanics in the offseason and added a cutter to his fastball/slider combo. The results weren't much different from the 4.78 career ERA he had heading into 2021. The push of young arms coming up through Kansas City's system and Junis' impending arbitration status mean he could get pushed into a bullpen role or non-tendered if the powers that be decide he's too expensive as a reliever.

Brad Keller RHP

Born: 07/27/95 Age: 26 Bats: R Throws: R Height: 6'5" Weight: 255 lb. Origin: Round 8, 2013 Draft (#240 overall)

YEAR	TEAM	LVL	AGE	W	L	SV	G	GS	IP	H	HR	BB/9	K/9	K	GB%	BABIP	WHIP	ERA	DRA-	WARP	MPH	FB%	Whiff%	CSP
2019	KC	MLB	23	7	14	0	28	28	165^{1}	154	15	3.8	6.6	122	50.4%	.283	1.35	4.19	120	-0.1	93.5	66.7%	19.9%	45.9%
2020	KC	MLB	24	5	3	0	9	9	54^{2}	39	2	2.8	5.8	35	51.6%	.233	1.02	2.47	94	0.8	92.9	59.2%	19.5%	49.1%
2021	KC	MLB	25	8	12	0	26	26	133^{2}	158	18	4.3	8.1	120	48.3%	.347	1.66	5.39	126	-0.6	93.9	60.9%	22.4%	55.5%
2022 DC	*KC*	*MLB*	*26*	*8*	*8*	*0*	*25*	*25*	*129.3*	*134*	*13*	*3.9*	*7.7*	*110*	*49.6%*	*.311*	*1.47*	*4.73*	*111*	*0.3*	*93.7*	*62.0%*	*21.4%*	*52.3%*

Comparables: Clay Buchholz, Mike Hampton, Jack McDowell

To bastardize Red Sanders' old saw, in the modern iteration of baseball strikeouts aren't everything, they're the only thing. That's not entirely accurate, but if you don't strike hitters out or can't generate a ludicrous number of groundballs, you won't be long for the majors. On June 29, Keller sported a 6.67 ERA and a lowly 17% strikeout rate after getting tattooed by the Red Sox at Fenway Park. Pitching coach Cal Eldred noticed that Keller's delivery was out of whack, his foot landing too hard on his follow through, pulling him too far to the left of the mound and creating a late release point. It didn't happen overnight, but a mechanical change converted Keller from a punching bag to a decent, mid-rotation starter. In his last nine starts before a lat injury ended his season, Keller posted a 3.42 ERA with a far more robust 24% strikeout rate. This story isn't likely to end with Keller becoming the Cy Young award winner, but if his and Eldred's hard work converted Keller into an SP3 workhorse, that's a win.

Jackson Kowar RHP Born: 10/04/96 Age: 25 Bats: R Throws: R Height: 6'5" Weight: 200 lb. Origin: Round 1, 2018 Draft (#33 overall)

YEAR	TEAM	LVL	AGE	W	L	SV	G	GS	IP	H	HR	BB/9	K/9	K	GB%	BABIP	WHIP	ERA	DRA-	WARP	MPH	FB%	Whiff%	CSP
2019	WIL	A+	22	5	3	0	13	13	74	68	4	2.7	8.0	66	44.9%	.305	1.22	3.53	101	0.6				
2019	NWA	AA	22	2	7	0	13	13	74^1	73	8	2.5	9.4	78	45.5%	.323	1.26	3.51	84	0.8				
2021	OMA	AAA	24	9	4	0	17	16	80^2	66	7	3.8	12.8	115	43.8%	.331	1.24	3.46	76	2.1				
2021	KC	MLB	24	0	6	0	9	8	30^1	43	7	5.9	8.6	29	35.0%	.375	2.08	11.27	156	-0.6	95.7	55.3%	24.3%	52.3%
2022 DC	*KC*	*MLB*	*25*	*5*	*4*	*0*	*26*	*12*	*71*	*67*	*9*	*4.3*	*9.1*	*72*	*40.7%*	*.298*	*1.42*	*4.69*	*110*	*0.2*	*95.7*	*55.3%*	*24.3%*	*52.3%*

Comparables: Josh Rogers, A.J. Cole, Joe Kelly

It is no exaggeration to say Kowar had one of the worst debuts in major-league history. His 11.27 ERA was the second-highest ever among rookies with at least 30 innings, as he joined Stu Flythe, Micah Bowie, Bumpus Jones and John Van Benschoten in the ignominious club of rookies with 30+ innings and an ERA north of 10. Kowar's problems stemmed from a fastball that had far too much arm-side and horizontal run, leaving too many heaters hanging over the center of the plate. Lefties feasted on Kowar, slugging a ludicrous .648. Kowar's priority this offseason is working on the shape of his fastball, so that it looks more like his changeup. It's way too soon to give up and relegate Kowar to the great name/bad player dustbin.

Asa Lacy LHP Born: 06/02/99 Age: 23 Bats: L Throws: L Height: 6'4" Weight: 215 lb. Origin: Round 1, 2020 Draft (#4 overall)

YEAR	TEAM	LVL	AGE	W	L	SV	G	GS	IP	H	HR	BB/9	K/9	K	GB%	BABIP	WHIP	ERA	DRA-	WARP	MPH	FB%	Whiff%	CSP
2021	QC	A+	22	2	5	0	14	14	52	41	5	7.1	13.7	79	33.0%	.346	1.58	5.19	81	1.1				
2022 non-DC	*KC*	*MLB*	*23*	*2*	*3*	*0*	*57*	*0*	*50*	*48*	*9*	*7.7*	*11.9*	*66*	*34.0%*	*.328*	*1.83*	*6.98*	*141*	*-0.9*				

Comparables: A.J. Murray, Joaquin Benoit, Jeff Brigham

The Royals' history of first-round pitchers is a taxonomy of busts. Hello, Luke Hochevar. How you doin' Mike Montgomery? Aaron Crow, we barely even got to know you. Lacy's 2021 debut did little to extricate those demons from the team's musty old basement. While the dominant stuff replete with Grade-A movement remained intact, the command frequently faltered, leading to subpar results and a walk rate that won't play in Northwest Arkansas, let alone Kansas City. Lacy left a start early with a shoulder injury on July 21 and didn't pitch another inning. The injury isn't considered serious, but shoulder maladies are always worth keeping an eye on and never something to take lightly. Lacy remains on track to potentially debut in mid-to-late 2022, but it wouldn't be a surprise if the Royals took a more cautious path given his tumultuous debut.

Daniel Lynch LHP Born: 11/17/96 Age: 25 Bats: L Throws: L Height: 6'6" Weight: 200 lb. Origin: Round 1, 2018 Draft (#34 overall)

YEAR	TEAM	LVL	AGE	W	L	SV	G	GS	IP	H	HR	BB/9	K/9	K	GB%	BABIP	WHIP	ERA	DRA-	WARP	MPH	FB%	Whiff%	CSP
2019	ROY	ROK	22	0	0	0	3	3	9	6	0	3.0	12.0	12	55.6%	.333	1.00	1.00						
2019	BUR	ROA	22	1	0	0	2	2	9	13	1	3.0	7.0	7	55.2%	.429	1.78	4.00						
2019	WIL	A+	22	5	2	0	15	15	78^1	76	4	2.6	8.8	77	46.9%	.324	1.26	3.10	92	1.1				
2021	OMA	AAA	24	4	3	0	12	11	57	74	10	2.8	9.8	62	44.8%	.390	1.61	5.84	98	0.8				
2021	KC	MLB	24	4	6	0	15	15	68	80	9	4.1	7.3	55	38.9%	.336	1.63	5.69	152	-1.3	93.7	52.5%	25.8%	51.7%
2022 DC	*KC*	*MLB*	*25*	*4*	*5*	*0*	*16*	*16*	*77.7*	*82*	*10*	*3.4*	*8.2*	*70*	*41.3%*	*.316*	*1.44*	*4.90*	*117*	*0.0*	*93.7*	*52.5%*	*25.8%*	*51.7%*

Comparables: Dylan Covey, Wade LeBlanc, Jharel Cotton

For years, the buzz surrounding Lynch revolved around a heater he could dial up to 99 miles per hour. That velo was on display when he made his major-league debut in May, but the movement he flashed in the minors was missing. Predictably, Lynch got hammered and was optioned to Triple-A after three starts for retooling. He came back with an emphasis on his off-speed stuff and was successful for a while before getting hit hard again in September. The ceiling and talent are both evident, but Lynch is going to need to figure out how to spot his fastball lower in the zone while also maintaining its elite velocity to avoid being more than a backend starter or, worse, a future reliever.

Alec Marsh RHP Born: 05/14/98 Age: 24 Bats: R Throws: R Height: 6'2" Weight: 220 lb. Origin: Round 2, 2019 Draft (#70 overall)

YEAR	TEAM	LVL	AGE	W	L	SV	G	GS	IP	H	HR	BB/9	K/9	K	GB%	BABIP	WHIP	ERA	DRA-	WARP	MPH	FB%	Whiff%	CSP
2019	IDF	ROA	21	0	1	0	13	13	33^1	30	5	1.1	10.3	38	44.4%	.294	1.02	4.05						
2021	NWA	AA	23	1	3	0	6	6	25^1	20	4	4.6	14.9	42	44.0%	.348	1.30	4.97	69	0.6				
2022 non-DC	*KC*	*MLB*	*24*	*2*	*2*	*0*	*57*	*0*	*50*	*43*	*7*	*5.1*	*11.5*	*63*	*41.2%*	*.303*	*1.44*	*4.63*	*107*	*0.0*				

Comparables: Ethan Martin, José Cisnero, Ross Stripling

Drafted in 2019 out of Arizona State, Marsh was seen as a safe, projectable starter with a low-90s fastball who was never expected to light up the world. Marsh shot up the charts when he started flashing a triple-digit heater in the Constellation Energy League in 2020 and maintained that velo gain in 2021. The overall stats were underwhelming, but a 40% K rate will generate buzz at any level. Marsh was shut down in June due to an undisclosed injury that put a damper on his short-term outlook, but he'll be back in 2022 with a chance to match results to stuff.

Mike Minor LHP Born: 12/26/87 Age: 34 Bats: R Throws: L Height: 6'4" Weight: 210 lb. Origin: Round 1, 2009 Draft (#7 overall)

YEAR	TEAM	LVL	AGE	W	L	SV	G	GS	IP	H	HR	BB/9	K/9	K	GB%	BABIP	WHIP	ERA	DRA-	WARP	MPH	FB%	Whiff%	CSP
2019	TEX	MLB	31	14	10	0	32	32	208^{1}	190	30	2.9	8.6	200	40.5%	.288	1.24	3.59	98	2.4	92.5	44.7%	26.4%	49.0%
2020	OAK	MLB	32	1	1	0	5	4	21^{1}	15	4	3.0	11.4	27	28.6%	.244	1.03	5.48	95	0.3	90.9	62.7%	32.1%	49.5%
2020	TEX	MLB	32	0	5	0	7	7	35^{1}	35	7	3.3	8.9	35	38.3%	.280	1.36	5.60	120	0.0	90.9	43.8%	24.6%	51.1%
2021	KC	MLB	33	8	12	0	28	28	158^{2}	156	26	2.3	8.5	149	38.4%	.291	1.24	5.05	110	0.6	91.1	42.8%	24.4%	52.8%
2022 DC	*KC*	*MLB*	*34*	*9*	*8*	*0*	*27*	*27*	*145.7*	*144*	*21*	*2.7*	*8.1*	*132*	*38.0%*	*.295*	*1.29*	*4.24*	*105*	*0.8*	*91.4*	*44.5%*	*25.3%*	*51.5%*

Comparables: Mike Hampton, Andy Pettitte, Gio González

We should know better by now than to trust reports of spring training velocity bumps. Minor had the fans back in Kansas City buzzing when reports out of Surprise, Arizona said he was hitting 94 on the gun, but when the season started his velocity was back down to the 91 mph he was averaging in 2020. Signed to a two-year pact by the Royals last winter, Minor is the modern definition of an innings eater, as he's one of only 15 starting pitchers in the majors with at least 150 innings in 2018, 2019 and 2021. You'll get what you get, no worse or better.

Frank Mozzicato LHP Born: 06/19/03 Age: 19 Bats: L Throws: L Height: 6'3" Weight: 175 lb. Origin: Round 1, 2021 Draft (#7 overall)

The Royals surprised more than a few draft watchers when they grabbed Mozzicato with the seventh overall pick in the 2021 draft, bypassing a few more well-known names in favor of the high school southpaw from Connecticut. Mozzicato is a projectable arm who usually works in the 86-90 mile-per-hour range, but can hit 94 on the gun. He has an advanced curveball for a prep arm, good command and a tight delivery. The solid two-pitch arsenal and relative polish for his age will likely mean early success for Mozzicato, but he'll need to add velocity and grow into his lanky frame to parlay that into a career befitting his draft slot.

Ervin Santana RHP Born: 12/12/82 Age: 39 Bats: R Throws: R Height: 6'2" Weight: 175 lb. Origin: International Free Agent, 2000

YEAR	TEAM	LVL	AGE	W	L	SV	G	GS	IP	H	HR	BB/9	K/9	K	GB%	BABIP	WHIP	ERA	DRA-	WARP	MPH	FB%	Whiff%	CSP
2019	STL	A+	36	1	1	0	3	3	13	15	2	2.1	7.6	11	58.1%	.317	1.38	4.85	109	0.1				
2019	SYR	AAA	36	4	4	0	15	15	82	97	11	3.5	5.9	54	37.3%	.323	1.57	5.38	122	0.1				
2019	CHW	MLB	36	0	2	0	3	3	13^{1}	19	6	4.0	3.4	5	32.1%	.277	1.88	9.45	156	-0.3	90.4	52.0%	13.0%	49.6%
2021	KC	MLB	38	2	2	0	38	2	65^{1}	65	9	3.0	7.2	52	36.8%	.292	1.33	4.68	119	-0.1	93.5	45.3%	24.8%	54.5%
2022 non-DC	*KC*	*MLB*	*39*	*2*	*3*	*0*	*57*	*0*	*50*	*53*	*8*	*3.3*	*7.0*	*38*	*36.4%*	*.299*	*1.44*	*5.23*	*124*	*-0.5*	*93.3*	*45.8%*	*23.9%*	*54.1%*

Comparables: Kyle Lohse, Aníbal Sánchez, Steve Trachsel

The year Santana made his debut in 2005, his 93 mile-per-hour heater was the sixth fastest in the game among the 145 pitchers who topped 100 innings. In 2021, a season where Santana rediscovered that same velocity as a reliever, that same heater would have been good for 56th-best. It was nice seeing Santana's name in the odd Royals box score, mostly mopping up and allowing the younger arms to get some well-deserved R&R, but even if you regain your old stuff, you can't turn back the clock to when it stood out.

Brady Singer RHP Born: 08/04/96 Age: 25 Bats: R Throws: R Height: 6'5" Weight: 215 lb. Origin: Round 1, 2018 Draft (#18 overall)

YEAR	TEAM	LVL	AGE	W	L	SV	G	GS	IP	H	HR	BB/9	K/9	K	GB%	BABIP	WHIP	ERA	DRA-	WARP	MPH	FB%	Whiff%	CSP
2019	WIL	A+	22	5	2	0	10	10	57^{2}	51	1	2.0	8.3	53	54.8%	.327	1.11	1.87	98	0.6				
2019	NWA	AA	22	7	3	0	16	16	90^{2}	86	8	2.6	8.4	85	49.3%	.304	1.24	3.47	90	0.7				
2020	KC	MLB	23	4	5	0	12	12	64^{1}	52	8	3.2	8.5	61	53.7%	.260	1.17	4.06	79	1.4	93.5	57.9%	24.3%	48.3%
2021	KC	MLB	24	5	10	0	27	27	128^{1}	146	14	3.7	9.2	131	50.6%	.350	1.55	4.91	103	0.9	93.8	58.0%	25.3%	54.5%
2022 DC	*KC*	*MLB*	*25*	*8*	*7*	*0*	*25*	*25*	*127*	*124*	*13*	*3.4*	*8.7*	*122*	*50.4%*	*.310*	*1.36*	*4.25*	*102*	*0.9*	*93.7*	*58.0%*	*25.1%*	*53.0%*

Comparables: Nathan Eovaldi, Michael Fulmer, Luke Weaver

Singer might not have taken a step back last year, but he did stand still. Opposing hitters grew more accustomed to his two-pitch, sinker/slider mix, and the changeup Singer was developing in 2020 remained an incomplete work in progress. It's far too early to write Singer off as a bullpen arm, but something's going to need to improve this year if he doesn't want to get trapped on the path common to low-ceiling/high-floor types.

Josh Staumont RHP Born: 12/21/93 Age: 28 Bats: R Throws: R Height: 6'3" Weight: 200 lb. Origin: Round 2, 2015 Draft (#64 overall)

YEAR	TEAM	LVL	AGE	W	L	SV	G	GS	IP	H	HR	BB/9	K/9	K	GB%	BABIP	WHIP	ERA	DRA-	WARP	MPH	FB%	Whiff%	CSP
2019	OMA	AAA	25	1	5	2	32	12	51^{1}	31	4	6.5	13.0	74	48.6%	.262	1.32	3.16	69	1.3				
2019	KC	MLB	25	0	0	0	16	0	19^{1}	21	4	4.7	7.0	15	32.3%	.293	1.60	3.72	124	0.0	96.2	69.6%	22.7%	47.9%
2020	KC	MLB	26	2	1	0	26	0	25^{2}	20	2	5.6	13.0	37	28.6%	.333	1.40	2.45	98	0.3	98.2	72.5%	36.7%	45.8%
2021	KC	MLB	27	4	3	5	64	0	65^{2}	43	6	3.7	9.9	72	38.7%	.236	1.07	2.88	91	0.9	96.7	65.3%	26.7%	55.7%
2022 DC	*KC*	*MLB*	*28*	*3*	*3*	*7*	*74*	*0*	*64.7*	*54*	*8*	*4.6*	*9.8*	*70*	*37.9%*	*.280*	*1.35*	*4.20*	*100*	*0.2*	*97.0*	*67.1%*	*28.5%*	*53.1%*

Comparables: Miguel Socolovich, Jason Adam, Bryan Morris

Triple-digit heat doesn't automatically translate to success. Last year, Staumont took a little something off his cartoonishly fast fastball, dialing it up over 100 mph far less than he did in 2020, and saw improved results. It certainly helps when your lower gear is 97 miles-per-hour with movement and you can complement that with a plus-plus, low-80s curve. The upshot was improved command, fewer walks and a lower exit velocity allowed. A knee injury in June kept Staumont from grabbing the closer's role, but he cemented his future as a relief stalwart.

Domingo Tapia RHP Born: 08/04/91 Age: 30 Bats: R Throws: R Height: 6'3" Weight: 263 lb. Origin: International Free Agent, 2009

YEAR	TEAM	LVL	AGE	W	L	SV	G	GS	IP	H	HR	BB/9	K/9	K	GB%	BABIP	WHIP	ERA	DRA-	WARP	MPH	FB%	Whiff%	CSP
2019	PAW	AAA	27	5	4	2	44	1	66	74	8	4.4	7.1	52	48.4%	.324	1.61	5.18	113	0.4				
2020	BOS	MLB	28	0	0	0	5	0	4^1	4	1	4.2	8.3	4	46.2%	.250	1.38	2.08	108	0.0	99.0	78.8%	27.0%	49.0%
2021	OMA	AAA	29	1	0	2	18	0	22	20	4	6.1	9.0	22	50.0%	.276	1.59	4.50	106	0.2				
2021	TAC	AAA	29	0	0	0	5	0	6^1	2	0	2.8	8.5	6	68.8%	.133	0.63	1.42	93	0.1				
2021	KC	MLB	29	4	1	0	32	0	31^2	21	1	4.0	7.1	25	45.9%	.238	1.11	2.84	107	0.2	97.3	72.2%	20.6%	49.2%
2021	SEA	MLB	29	0	0	0	2	0	2	4	0	4.5	4.5	1	55.6%	.444	2.50	0.00	110	0.0	98.2	91.4%	25.0%	57.1%
2022 DC	*KC*	*MLB*	*30*	*3*	*3*	*0*	*74*	*0*	*64.7*	*66*	*7*	*4.6*	*7.2*	*51*	*48.0%*	*.298*	*1.54*	*5.08*	*117*	*-0.4*	*97.6*	*74.0%*	*21.6%*	*49.7%*

Comparables: Francisco Rodriguez, Brooks Pounders, Evan Marshall

Lol Mets. And lol Reds, lol Red Sox and lol Mariners. A Mets' sleeper prospect back in 2012, thanks to a fastball that sat in the upper 90s and at times hit triple digits on the gun, Tapia stalled out at High-A ball. Four organizations and nearly a decade later, the Royals coaching staff figured out how to shorten his delivery and turn Tapia into a solid middle relief arm. The strikeouts still aren't what you'd expect from a guy sitting at 97, but the sinking action on his fastball keeps it in the yard and makes Tapia a viable major leaguer. He should stick around for a few years; joke's on them.

Kyle Zimmer RHP Born: 09/13/91 Age: 30 Bats: R Throws: R Height: 6'3" Weight: 225 lb. Origin: Round 1, 2012 Draft (#5 overall)

YEAR	TEAM	LVL	AGE	W	L	SV	G	GS	IP	H	HR	BB/9	K/9	K	GB%	BABIP	WHIP	ERA	DRA-	WARP	MPH	FB%	Whiff%	CSP
2019	OMA	AAA	27	2	4	1	37	12	54	46	6	5.5	8.7	52	44.4%	.276	1.46	4.33	96	0.5				
2019	KC	MLB	27	0	1	0	15	0	18^1	28	2	9.3	8.8	18	41.5%	.413	2.56	10.80	137	-0.2	96.7	60.9%	26.6%	47.0%
2020	KC	MLB	28	1	0	0	16	1	23	14	0	3.9	10.2	26	51.9%	.259	1.04	1.57	81	0.5	94.3	48.1%	30.0%	46.3%
2021	OMA	AAA	29	1	1	0	8	0	9	7	0	4.0	11.0	11	52.4%	.333	1.22	3.00	86	0.2				
2021	KC	MLB	29	4	1	2	52	2	54	46	7	5.0	7.7	46	51.4%	.279	1.41	5.00	113	0.1	94.1	50.7%	24.9%	55.6%
2022 non-DC	*KC*	*MLB*	*30*	*2*	*2*	*0*	*57*	*0*	*50*	*46*	*5*	*5.1*	*9.4*	*52*	*47.4%*	*.305*	*1.50*	*4.67*	*107*	*0.0*	*94.4*	*51.4%*	*26.0%*	*52.9%*

Comparables: Javy Guerra, Alex Wilson, Brian Schlitter

It's the cruelest question in sports: What if he'd stayed healthy? Injuries have derailed and arguably ruined Zimmer's career since he was drafted in the first round out of the University of San Francisco nearly a decade ago, pushing him from future starter to hopeful bullpen ace to just an arm the Royals wanted to get anything out of in middle relief. This year's physical ailment was a non-throwing shoulder injury that put Zimmer on the IL twice. He might have been the key to keeping the Royals' window of contention open into the late 2010s. Don't remind us.

Tyler Zuber RHP Born: 06/16/95 Age: 27 Bats: R Throws: R Height: 5'11" Weight: 195 lb. Origin: Round 6, 2017 Draft (#180 overall)

YEAR	TEAM	LVL	AGE	W	L	SV	G	GS	IP	H	HR	BB/9	K/9	K	GB%	BABIP	WHIP	ERA	DRA-	WARP	MPH	FB%	Whiff%	CSP
2019	WIL	A+	24	3	2	11	21	0	29^1	16	0	3.4	11.7	38	34.4%	.254	0.92	1.23	81	0.6				
2019	NWA	AA	24	1	2	10	22	0	26	18	2	1.7	10.4	30	27.0%	.276	0.88	2.42	73	0.5				
2020	KC	MLB	25	1	2	0	23	0	22	15	4	8.2	12.3	30	37.5%	.256	1.59	4.09	106	0.2	94.3	44.4%	25.6%	44.3%
2021	OMA	AAA	26	1	3	8	28	0	28^2	15	3	5.0	13.5	43	38.6%	.222	1.08	2.83	77	0.7				
2021	KC	MLB	26	0	3	0	31	0	27^1	26	6	5.6	8.2	25	33.8%	.270	1.57	6.26	121	0.0	94.7	57.9%	26.7%	51.4%
2022 DC	*KC*	*MLB*	*27*	*3*	*3*	*0*	*74*	*0*	*64.7*	*56*	*9*	*5.3*	*11.2*	*80*	*34.6%*	*.299*	*1.46*	*4.77*	*109*	*-0.1*	*94.5*	*53.2%*	*26.3%*	*48.9%*

Comparables: Ryan Meisinger, Jose Ortega, Michael Kohn

The reliever-heavy 2021 version of baseball might lead casual fans to believe every team has a never-ending supply of young and talented arms who spit burning gasoline at their opponents with an elite breaker added in for good measure. Zuber's brief major-league career to date is Exhibit A against the hypothesis. The stuff part of the equation is certainly there, but Zuber has about as much command as George McClellan did during the First Battle of Bull Run in the American Civil War. Forty-nine innings aren't enough to write Zuber off entirely, but he's going to need a major mechanical overhaul if he's ever going to be more than a filler reliever on a second division non-contender.

Lineouts

Hitters

HITTER	POS	TEAM	LVL	AGE	PA	R	2B	3B	HR	RBI	BB	K	SB	CS	AVG/OBP/SLG	DRC+	BABIP	BRR	FRAA	WARP
Hanser Alberto	IF	GIG	WIN	28	175	30	8	0	0	11	7	10	1	1	.321/.360/.370		.342			
	IF	KC	MLB	28	255	25	20	3	2	24	4	26	3	1	.270/.291/.402	92	.293	0.4	3B(49): -2.2, 2B(31): 1.1, SS(17): 1.9	0.7
Wilmin Candelario	SS	ROYB	ROK	19	142	20	2	3	3	13	8	73	9	1	.154/.206/.285		.304			
Darryl Collins	LF	COL	A	19	383	45	8	3	5	54	52	55	15	5	.246/.367/.338	115	.282	-1.4	LF(75): 0.5	1.9
Tyler Gentry	RF	QC	A+	22	186	29	10	0	6	28	29	55	4	0	.259/.395/.449	101	.360	-1.3	RF(37): 1.3, LF(5): 0.2, CF(1): -0.2	0.6
Ryan McBroom	1B	OMA	AAA	29	489	78	14	2	32	88	47	109	3	1	.261/.337/.524	117	.274	-1.2	1B(47): 1.8, RF(10): -2.1, LF(8): -1.9	1.9
	1B	KC	MLB	29	9	1	0	0	0	0	1	6	0	0	.250/.333/.250	64	1.000	0.5		0.0
Sebastian Rivero	C	OMA	AAA	22	163	18	7	1	3	26	10	45	2	1	.260/.319/.380	77	.353	-2.4	C(36): -2.6	-0.3
	C	KC	MLB	22	44	1	2	0	0	3	3	15	0	0	.175/.250/.225	73	.280	-1.3	C(17): -0.3	-0.1
Bubba Starling	OF	OMA	AAA	28	105	18	6	1	7	17	7	25	1	0	.258/.305/.557	112	.273	-0.5	CF(14): -3.0, RF(12): -0.4, LF(1): -0.1	0.1

Falling into the esoteric category of "league leaders in stuff nobody cares about," **Hanser Alberto** has the lowest walk rate among major-league hitters with at least 1,000 career plate appearances, going all the way back to 1980. Alberto's defensive versatility, good contact skills and prowess against southpaws will likely keep him employed, but without big-time power, Gold Glove defense or an otherwise elite tool to rely on, he's not going to be anything more than a supporting role player. A year at the alternate site and a promotion to the Arizona Complex League led to a miserable 2021 for **Wilmin Candelario,** but he was just a teenager and has plenty of time to work past his swing-and-miss issues and grow into his projectable frame. A potential future slugger thanks to his solid, bulky frame, **Darryl Collins** hails from Spijkenisse in the Netherlands. He'd be only the second hitter from the Netherlands in the last century to log significant playing time in the majors, which means the citizens of the very real Hoogwerf, Vogelenzang and Vierambachten districts of Spijkenisse will all be cheering mightily for him. **Tyler Gentry's** power potential and hit tool might make him a future mainstay as a corner outfielder, but he will need to tighten up his defense to avoid getting pigeonholed into a part-time role. **Ryan McBroom** is the sort of bad-side-of-the-platoon bat who isn't good enough against right-handed pitching to play every day and doesn't have enough defensive utility to stick on a modern major league roster with short benches. On the positive side, it's fun to watch him punish Triple-A pitching. **Sebastian Rivero** got his first taste of major-league ball in 2021, providing additional catching depth so that the Royals could keep Salvador Perez's bat in the lineup at DH when Perez wasn't catching. Rivero is a light-hitting backstop whose defense has improved just enough to help him stick. Non-tendered and quietly resigned to a minor-league deal last winter, **Bubba Starling** had the best part of his season not in the majors or minors but in Japan, where he was a contributing member of the United States silver-medal Olympic squad. He's now retired.

Pitchers

PITCHER	TEAM	LVL	AGE	W	L	SV	G	GS	IP	H	HR	BB/9	K/9	K	GB%	BABIP	WHIP	ERA	DRA-	WARP	MPH	FB%	WHF	CSP
Ronald Bolaños	NWA	AA	24	0	0	0	3	3	6^{1}	7	2	11.4	9.9	7	66.7%	.313	2.37	7.11	106	0.0				
	OMA	AAA	24	0	3	0	10	10	38^{1}	39	10	6.3	8.0	34	46.4%	.287	1.72	6.34	111	0.3				
	KC	MLB	24	0	0	0	3	0	6^{1}	4	0	2.8	14.2	10	38.5%	.308	0.95	1.42	89	0.1	95.1	54.7%	37.3%	51.5%
Jonathan Bowlan	NWA	AA	24	2	0	0	4	4	17	13	0	1.6	13.2	25	50.0%	.342	0.94	1.59	83	0.3				
Austin Cox	NWA	AA	24	4	1	0	15	15	63	54	8	3.6	8.0	56	34.1%	.271	1.25	3.00	111	0.0				
Josh Dye	NWA	AA	24	4	2	9	38	0	60^{2}	53	5	2.7	10.1	68	48.5%	.304	1.17	2.52	100	0.4				
	OMA	AAA	24	0	0	0	2	0	5	4	1	1.8	9.0	5	53.8%	.250	1.00	3.60	91	0.1				
Jesse Hahn	KC	MLB	31	0	0	1	5	0	3^{1}	5	2	10.8	8.1	3	54.5%	.333	2.70	13.50	117	0.0	94.4	65.9%	15.6%	45.2%
Kasey Kalich	QC	A+	23	2	2	0	14	0	19^{2}	23	2	2.7	10.5	23	40.7%	.368	1.47	4.12	101	0.2				
	ROM	A+	23	0	2	5	20	0	30^{1}	33	2	5.0	10.4	35	43.7%	.365	1.65	3.26	97	0.3				
Richard Lovelady	OMA	AAA	25	0	0	0	7	0	8^{1}	5	0	4.3	9.7	9	47.4%	.263	1.08	1.08	94	0.1				
	KC	MLB	25	2	0	1	20	0	20^{2}	16	3	2.6	10.0	23	55.6%	.255	1.06	3.48	90	0.3	93.1	50.2%	29.3%	55.7%
John McMillon	ROYB	ROK	23	0	1	0	6	1	9^{2}	10	1	5.6	16.8	18	19.0%	.450	1.66	6.52						
Joel Payamps	OMA	AAA	27	1	0	2	8	0	8	10	0	4.5	15.7	14	19.0%	.476	1.75	4.50	88	0.2				
	KC	MLB	27	1	1	0	15	1	20^{1}	23	3	1.3	7.1	16	41.8%	.313	1.28	4.43	103	0.1	95.1	58.4%	17.7%	57.9%
	TOR	MLB	27	0	2	0	22	0	30	21	3	3.3	6.6	22	47.1%	.220	1.07	2.70	109	0.1	94.5	61.8%	26.9%	51.8%
Daniel Tillo	NWA	AA	25	0	3	0	17	2	23^{1}	21	1	5.8	8.5	22	53.1%	.317	1.54	4.63	88	0.3				
Angel Zerpa	QC	A+	21	4	0	0	8	8	41^{2}	32	2	1.7	11.4	53	44.2%	.297	0.96	2.59	83	0.8				
	NWA	AA	21	0	3	0	13	13	45^{1}	51	7	3.8	10.7	54	47.6%	.370	1.54	5.96	88	0.6				
	KC	MLB	21	0	1	0	1	1	5	3	0	1.8	7.2	4	40.0%	.214	0.80	0.00	117	0.0	94.4	67.6%		

Chance Adams managed to make it back to a minor-league mound a mere 11 months after Tommy John surgery. Recent history suggests getting back to a sub-6.00 ERA could take longer. **Ronald Bolaños'** live arm and mid-90s fastball were briefly on display in Kansas City before a right flexor strain in June landed him on the sidelines for most of the rest of the year. **Jonathan Bowlan's** heavy, mid-90s sinking fastball and improving secondaries had him projected to be a durable, backend workhorse, but Tommy John surgery in late May knocked him out after four minor-league starts. He'll be back at some point in 2022. A hard-throwing southpaw reliever is at the top of every team's wish list, so the Royals hope that **Christian Chamberlain** can return to health after missing almost all of 2021 due to injury. **Austin Cox** struggled in his initial return to action in 2021 (relatable) but eventually regained his footing and noticeably improved as the year went on. Cox's 1.91 ERA and 44 strikeouts in his final 47 innings of 2021 ensure he'll move another rung up the ladder in 2022. A lefty sinkerballer whose delivery gives batters fits, **Josh Dye** has a future as a LOOGY but could also become durable, multi-inning relief arm if his deception works well enough against righties. We won't know for sure until he makes the majors; you might say that this Dye isn't cast. A right shoulder impingement landed him on the IL in mid-April and cost him his entire season, making it impossible for **Jesse** to lend a helping **Hahn** in the bullpen. The Royals added **Kasey Kalich** to their growing collection of young arms in a deadline deal for Jorge Soler. The former Atlanta prospect throws a mid-90s fastball and profiles as a future middle reliever. Lured away from a commitment to LSU with a $2.998 million bonus, **Ben Kdurna** impressed scouts at the Area Code Games with a four-pitch assortment that included a fastball he can already dial up to the mid-90s. He hasn't made his minor-league debut yet, but the 18-year-old prep arm has oodles of time on his side. **Richard Lovelady** reemerged as a viable lefty killer, then saw his season end early with a sprained UCL. He joins Corey Hart, Rick Sweet and Ellis Valentine on the unknown but all important All Romantics squad that barnstorms the country each February. An undrafted free agent in 2020, **John McMillon** possesses a raw arm with a mid-to-upper 90s fastball that explodes in the top of the strike zone. His control and mechanics will require a good deal of work for him to reach his ceiling of future late inning reliever. After a decade of mostly bouncing around the minors, **Joel Payamps** finally managed to spend a full season in the majors, providing bullpen depth for the Blue Jays and later for the Royals. He allowed both squads to preserve innings and workloads for their younger, more talented arms. It's a job! **Daniel Tillo** is a sinkerballing future reliever who will need to harness his control to maximize his secondary offerings and get a major league shot. He's lefthanded, so you'll probably be hearing his name blared out intermittently via major-league public-address systems for the next few years. Added to the 40-player roster last spring, **Angel Zerpa** is a throwback whose potential success relies more on deception and movement than velocity. He hopes to guide the Royals to the mountaintop and keep them safe from the harsh elements of the Himala...oh, you said *Zerpa*.

MINNESOTA TWINS

Essay by Justin Klugh

Player comments by Steve Neuman and BP staff

Ah, another beautiful June day in Minnesota. The snowmelt is down to ankle-deep, and tonight they're showing *Coco* at Target Field after the game, so we can all pretend *that's* why we're crying!

You know how the Twins got their name, don't you? "Because there are two cities next to each other, and there was more inspiration to draw from that than there was from us being the nation's flour-milling epicenter?"

Of course not.

The name "Twins" is meant to remind us all, at every moment, of the duplicity of the human experience.

We *all* have a twin: One of us at the beginning, and one of us at the end, set apart from each other by all that happens in between. We are close to the same—mistakable, even, for one another. Perhaps the difference is an emotional scar slashed across the soul, or a physical one over an eye socket that shows we were traumatized in some cooler way. But in every case, whenever we set out to prove something, our counterpart is waiting on the other side of our endeavor, looking back at us and knowing its outcome.

This is most obvious in individuals. Chuck Knoblauch was a darling of the Twins organization. At 22 years old, he stepped in at second base for the big club with speed, contact and defense that made him a Rookie of the Year. Seven years later, as the franchise melted around him, he had, a member of the front office told *Sports Illustrated*, "evolved into a bratty tyrant who ran roughshod over the people around him." No wonder George Steinbrenner took a shine to him. Knoblauch demanded a trade, then forgot how to throw.

Ron Gardenhire was a Texas tea kettle whistling with folksy charm. Unlike his predecessor, Gardenhire let Twins fans see what it was like to have a skipper who would let the spittle fly. Whenever there was a Manager of the Year conversation, Gardy's name was typically in it—until 2010, when his squad lost their tenth, eleventh and twelfth straight playoff games. Four franchise-worst seasons later, he was deadened by anguish and spouting little but clichés.

MINNESOTA TWINS PROSPECTUS

2021 W-L: 73-89, 5th in AL Central

Pythag	.436	*24th*	DER	.698	*18th*
RS/G	4.50	*15th*	DRC+	101	*7th*
RA/G	5.15	*27th*	DRA-	113	*28th*
dWin%	.460	*21st*	FIP	4.71	*25th*
Payroll	$125M	*16th*	B-Age	28.9	*9th*
M$/MW	$4.5M	*21st*	P-Age	30.4	*26th*

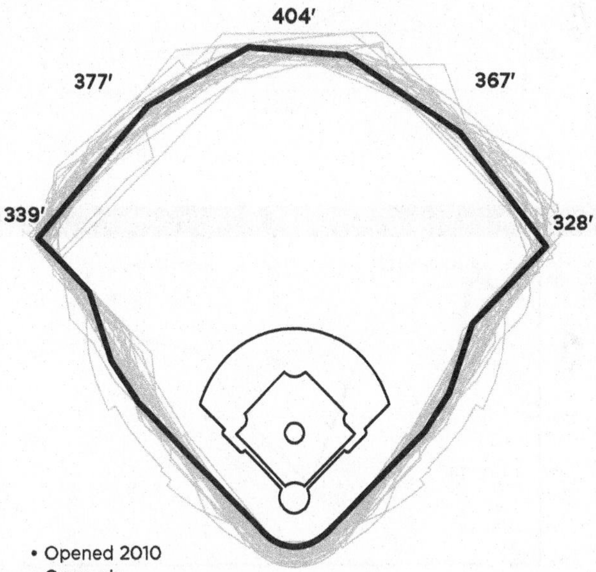

- Opened 2010
- Open air
- Natural surface
- Fence profile: 8' to 23"

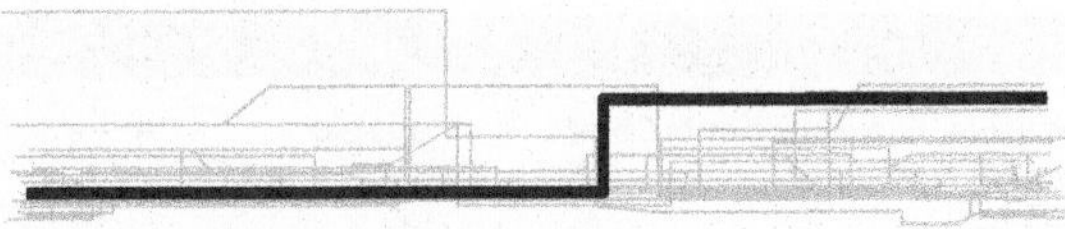

Park Factors

Runs	Runs/RH	Runs/LH	HR/RH	HR/LH
95	94	96	86	89

Top Hitter WARP	4.8 Jorge Polanco
Top Pitcher WARP	1.6 José Berríos
Top Prospect	Austin Martin

Payroll History (in millions)

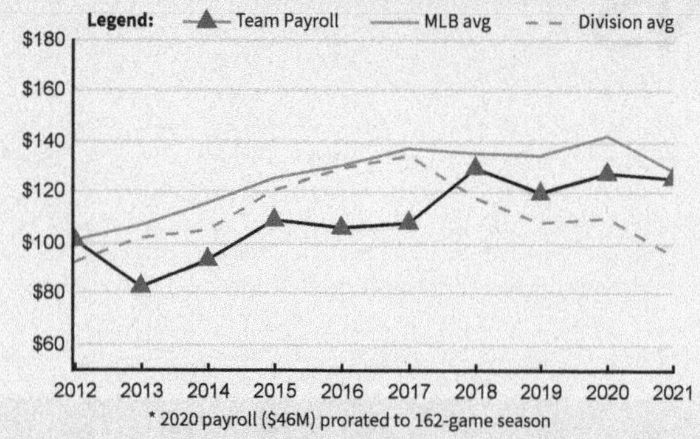

Future Commitments (in millions)

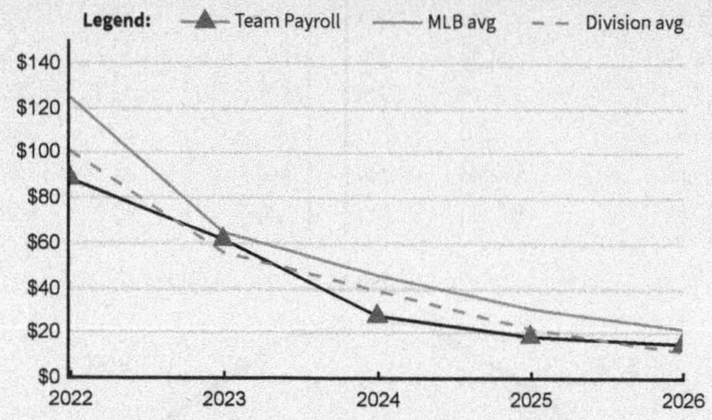

Farm System Ranking

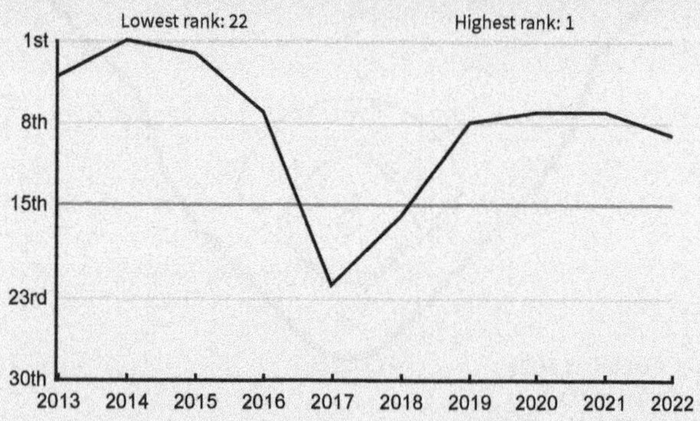

Personnel

Executive Vice President, Chief Baseball Officer
Derek Falvey

Senior Vice President, General Manager
Thad Levine

Vice President, Assistant General Manager
Rob Antony

Vice President, Player Personnel
Mike Radcliff

Manager
Rocco Baldelli

BP Alumni
Bradley Ankrom
Ezra Wise

But as fans, we aren't watching the individuals; we're watching the team as a whole. It has an identity itself; the mushed-together persona of players, coaches, managers, executives, mascots and owners. And if something can have an identity, then it can have a twin.

In 1992, there was doubt that the Twins could succeed without Jack Morris in the rotation, and yet they scrapped together an impressive slab of victories. By July, pitcher Frank Viola said, "I don't see anybody beating the Twins." Then they encountered a ruinous month in which they were outscored 130–95 in 23 games, 16 of which they lost. The Twins, it turned out, had an evil twin waiting to reveal itself.

Ten years later, with a new stadium on the line, expectations were once again high. The Twins pushed all the way into the American League Championship Series, trusted by an adoring public to be its team of destiny. But a different Twins showed up in the seventh inning of an elimination game that the local paper called "surreal." After staging their own miraculous three-run rally, the evil Twins revealed themselves once more and let the Angels set a new ALCS record for hits and runs in a single inning (10, in both cases).

In 2016, the Twins appeared to be ready to capitalize on an encouraging 83-win finish the previous year with a young core on track or on the way. Throngs showed up on Opening Day to see the beginning of the next Twins golden era. But the evil Twins showed up, too. They lost nine straight games and never left last place.

Rarely has hope geysered from the bowels of the earth as copiously and irresponsibly as it did in the spring of 2021. "We're back," we said to the pandemic, kicking in the doors of malls and movie theaters as medical experts zipped up body bags and begged us to stay home. That hope trickled down into all facets of society, including in Minnesota, where it drove projections of the Twins' forthcoming season.

When you opened the paper that spring, you saw a lot of high numbers: 96, 94, 90. Instead of the number of inches of expected snowfall, they were describing the Twins' potential win total. Only one *Star-Tribune* sports writer chose to be a doomsayer and picked the Twins to finish with fewer than 90 wins, and he apologized at the outset of his explanation for doing so. The offense was yet again a liability, he warned, and relying on pitching to carry them for the second-straight season would not be a durable strategy. Plus, what if their key players who were famously vulnerable to injury, were, you know . . . *that*, again?

Reasonable mistrust is the worst kind, and it had started to creep in before the spring was warm. A couple of weeks into the Grapefruit League, somebody noticed that something was different about these Twins—wrong, even. Sure, they had the same uniforms and with the same names on the back as the team that had finished eight games over .500 in 2020, but . . . that wasn't the Twins out there.

A couple of conspiracy theorists zeroed in on some evidence: the Twins weren't hitting. The paper put obscene pre-season batting averages next to the names of key hitters like Miguel Sanó (.094), Max Kepler (.067) and Byron Buxton (.115) in an effort to shame them into action. But it was just the spring. Everybody watching the Twins was only half paying attention or day drunk and sunburned. Spring training crimes, like going hitless from March 3 to March 24 (as Kepler did), are wiped clean from the records so the public can sleep soundly, never knowing the horrible truth.

And so everyone watched, waiting for the Twins to become the *real* Twins. Suspicious looks were exchanged. Phones rang late at night, only for the line to go dead. Cars drove slowly by houses and sped away when a light would turn on. Finally, by about June, the fans were ready to come forward with twelve weeks of evidence: These were not the Twins. They were some kind of physically similar but catastrophically different version of the Twins. If only there were a word for that.

But the team beat them to the revelation, turning to their audience, mouth twisted in a wry smirk, to revealed that, yes, it was true: they were no contenders at all. They were just another AL Central washout with no bullpen, worn hamstrings, sore shoulders, a proudly unvaccinated shortstop and eleven games between them and the black-and-white dot on the horizon that apparently was the White Sox.

Every team has an evil twin crawling in the air ducts and moaning through the vents. We leave fish guts by the attic door to ward them off, but, in some cases, their appetite is too much, and we awaken one morning to discover the team we thought we knew—the one that was fun, athletic and competitive—seems . . . off. Our suspicions fester into accusations, only to realize it is midseason, the deficit is well into double digits, and it is far too late.

The 2021 Twins weren't slouches. They never gave up, and even talk of firing the manager was stronger earlier in the year than it was by the end. This goes to show how powerless even the players can be when the evil-twin identity slips into the clubhouse. At some point, the good twin, set up by last year's success, was tricked into being the one that lives behind the walls, forgotten in the shadows and surviving on fistfuls of fiberglass insulation.

They finished April 9-15. But! It was still early. The next month, the Twins thought allowing more witnesses to their demise could help and upped the capacity limits on Target Field to 23,000. They got less than 10,000 fans to turn out. The injury list was filling up with center field options, and the team had given up 55 home runs in 37 games, an MLB worst. Perhaps the most ominous sign was Willians Astudillo taking the first called third strike of his big league career.

The next month, the shrugging, sighing, temple-massaging Twins sent Matt Shoemaker out to the mound on June 4, and the Royals blasted him right back into the dugout with nine runs in the first inning. Minnesota dropped to 22-35, and the Twin Cities raised a white flag visible all across the prairie.

Every season is a letdown for 29 franchises, which means there are 29 fanbases who suffer through the revelation that their team isn't who they hoped it would be (the length of that hope varies significantly). The good news is, they don't let you down for the last time twice, and they always reappear in the spring as a new team gives it another go. Baseball, former Twins manager Gene Mauch once said, always comes back. Like malaria.

And here we are, once more at the start, the Twins standing before us, telling us who they are. They are not rebuilders, they say. They are aiming to contend, they say. They believe in their roster and have adjusted it accordingly. They have brought in Jayce Tingler as the bench coach. Somewhat more importantly, they locked down Byron Buxton. But it becomes difficult to trust a team that has so often pulled off the mask and revealed they weren't the Twins you hoped they were.

Once upon a time, in a reversal of a now-ancient pattern, the *Twins* ended the *Yankees'* season. It was 1965, and neither the historical standings nor the biblically unfavorable weather were going to keep the Twins from reaching the playoffs. The Sunday before the All-Star break, Harmon Killebrew rocketed a two-run home run that sailed over every Yankees' head to give the Twins a 6–5 lead with two outs in the ninth.

"That home run is often considered the hit that sealed the Yankees' tomb and secured the Twins' status as the team to beat," wrote Jim Thielman in *Cool of the Evening*.

A few weeks later, shortstop Zoilo Versalles was on first when he watched a base hit land near Mickey Mantle in left field. Mantle was playing on a pair of busted knees as he aged out of the game, and Versalles knew it. Zoilo chugged around second and third without slowing down and scored as Mantle rushed to recover. Later, New York writers found Versalles at his locker and asked how he could do such a thing—try to win a ballgame, that is. After all, that was *Mickey Mantle* out there. Why not just pull up at third and leave the old man his dignity?

Versalles didn't even look up. *"We're playing in the same league, aren't we?"*

That statement was the Twins' revelation: F*** the Yankees, f*** history, and f*** you. Except it was Minnesota in the sixties, and such salty language would've had gasping grandmas dropping hotdishes across the state. So instead, Versalles said what he said, giving Twins fans a different kind of revelation: We are who you hoped we were. In the end, against the Dodgers in the World Series, they weren't the champions. But they were the kind of team you believed could be, up to the final out.

There will never be a 1965 Twins again. There will never be a 2021 Twins again. There will be a 2022 Twins, and they will begin their season in a hole dug by disappointment, both recent and historic. From that hole will emerge a new twin, covered in grime and afterbirth, looking to grow quickly into a swift, powerful entity that fulfills its chosen destiny.

Minnesota finds itself having completed a down year and a soft reboot of its roster. What happens next depends on how down they believe they are and how soft of a reboot they consider their actions to have been.

Perhaps Sanó will learn from losing playing time to Alex Kirilloff and not rely on streaks of productivity to keep his job. Perhaps Mitch Garver will play appealing enough ball to give the team the confidence to acquire the pitching it needs after trading José Berríos at the last trade deadline. Perhaps Jorge Polanco will wriggle free of his ankle issues at second base and be assigned a double-play partner who isn't both the worst-hitting shortstop in the league and the worst epidemiologist in baseball history. Perhaps the team is looking far enough ahead to trade Josh Donaldson; perhaps they are confident enough in the present to keep him.

This multifarious theorizing creates an image far beyond the duplicity of good and evil Twins and instead calls to mind a many-headed abomination, each head screaming about a different possible outcome. Let us bury that image very deep in our subconscious and never consider it again.

There we go.

In every team's history, there is that moment when they smothered their evil twin with a pillow or sealed off the vents to the attic and set the house on fire. When they gave their fans the glowing moment of rapture from which hope can grow. It's not as though you need to point to a time almost six decades ago to find such a moment for the Twins; it's just funny to think of a hobbled Mickey Mantle getting owned by a skilled runner and pitied by a bunch of homers in the press.

A million jabs, joys, and moments make up a season and define how you'll remember a specific team, but as time passes, they all get smashed together into a single feeling of recollection. If you're reading this, you may love the Twins. Love is an avenue on which both joy and disappointment travel. It is a road, unlike those in Minnesota, that is never closed.

Waiting at the other end, right at this moment, is a twin of your own, looking back at you, amused by your pessimism or envious of your ignorance. In the next few months, you shall journey toward them until you finally meet in September. By then, you'll know which twin these 2022 Twins were. There may be two of them. But, in time, they can only hurt you once.

—Justin Klugh is an author of Baseball Prospectus.

HITTERS

Luis Arraez 3B

Born: 04/09/97 Age: 25 Bats: L Throws: R Height: 5'10" Weight: 175 lb. Origin: International Free Agent, 2013

YEAR	TEAM	LVL	AGE	PA	R	2B	3B	HR	RBI	BB	K	SB	CS	Whiff%	AVG/OBP/SLG	DRC+	BABIP	BRR	FRAA	WARP
2019	PNS	AA	22	164	18	6	1	0	14	18	13	3	3		.342/.415/.397	127	.376	-0.4	2B(15): -0.1, 3B(15): 3.9, SS(5): 0.3	1.5
2019	ROC	AAA	22	73	8	4	0	0	8	6	2	1	0		.348/.397/.409	116	.354	-1.1	SS(8): 0.5, 2B(4): 1.2, LF(1): -0.1	0.5
2019	MIN	MLB	22	366	54	20	1	4	28	36	29	2	2	8.1%	.334/.399/.439	111	.355	2.2	2B(49): -3.0, LF(21): 1.6, 3B(17): -0.2	1.9
2020	MIN	MLB	23	121	16	9	0	0	13	8	11	0	0	10.1%	.321/.364/.402	101	.353	-0.6	2B(31): 0.9	0.5
2021	MIN	MLB	24	479	58	17	6	2	42	43	48	2	2	10.7%	.294/.357/.376	102	.323	1.2	3B(55): 1.4, 2B(48): 4.2, LF(27): 3.0	2.8
2022 DC	*MIN*	*MLB*	*25*	*511*	*69*	*21*	*3*	*5*	*51*	*46*	*44*	*2*	*2*	*10.7%*	*.297/.364/.395*	*111*	*.320*	*-0.1*	*2B 0, 3B 0*	*2.6*

Comparables: Jorge Polanco, Jose Altuve, Marwin Gonzalez

Arraez sort of answers the question, "What if you gave Rod Carew Tony Oliva's health?" Why anyone would ask this kind of question is a mystery, but we're all living with the result. An on-base machine with bum legs, Arraez seems incapable of doing anything but putting the ball in play wherever he wants. Also like Carew, he can play wherever you'd like in the infield, although lacking Sir Rodney's durability and defensive acumen. The latter was in evidence during Minnesota's most notorious loss of 2021, when Arraez airmailed a throw from third to first that both has yet to land and sent Oakland to a 13-12 win in extra innings.

Willians Astudillo 3B

Born: 10/14/91 Age: 30 Bats: R Throws: R Height: 5'9" Weight: 225 lb. Origin: International Free Agent, 2008

YEAR	TEAM	LVL	AGE	PA	R	2B	3B	HR	RBI	BB	K	SB	CS	Whiff%	AVG/OBP/SLG	DRC+	BABIP	BRR	FRAA	WARP
2019	ROC	AAA	27	83	18	1	0	5	19	2	2	1	1		.423/.446/.628	134	.389	0.9	C(8): 1.5, 3B(5): 0.5, RF(5): -0.7	0.8
2019	MIN	MLB	27	204	28	9	0	4	21	5	8	0	0	9.0%	.268/.299/.379	106	.258	-1.9	C(21): -0.8, 1B(15): -0.3, 3B(13): -0.4	0.6
2020	ORI	WIN	28	157	27	7	0	7	25	10	4	1	1		.379/.414/.572		.353			
2020	MIN	MLB	28	16	4	1	0	1	3	0	2	0	0	17.2%	.250/.250/.500	104	.231	0.2	C(6): 0.3	0.1
2021	ORI	WIN	29	128	12	5	0	3	13	10	3	2	0		.270/.352/.396		.252			
2021	STP	AAA	29	94	13	3	0	2	8	3	4	3	0		.281/.319/.382	113	.277	-0.8	C(7): -0.0, 3B(5): 1.5, 1B(4): -0.1	0.5
2021	MIN	MLB	29	216	17	8	0	7	21	3	12	0	0	10.4%	.236/.259/.375	110	.221	-1.2	3B(29): 0.1, 1B(27): -1.2, C(10): -0.5	0.6
2022 non-DC	*MIN*	*MLB*	*30*	*251*	*25*	*10*	*0*	*7*	*28*	*8*	*14*	*1*	*1*	*10.8%*	*.276/.311/.411*	*96*	*.271*	*-0.3*	*3B 0, C -2*	*0.4*

Comparables: Jesús Sucre, Rafael Ynoa, Curt Casali

Criticizing Astudillo feels wrong. It's physically impossible to dislike La Tortuga as he crashes about the field like a man being chased by bullies and bails out the bullpen with 58-mph slop. In a perfect world, you keep him around as your 25th man until he retires to become President of Earth and ushers in an era of peace and prosperity unlike any humankind has ever seen. However, he doesn't really play catcher anymore, and his offense can be easily replaced by a more versatile bench option. Sorry, Mr. President.

YEAR	TEAM	P. COUNT	FRM RUNS	BLK RUNS	THRW RUNS	TOT RUNS
2019	MIN	2577	-0.7	-0.1	0.0	-0.7
2019	ROC	1130	1.5	0.0	0.0	1.6
2020	MIN	595	0.3	0.0	0.0	0.3
2021	MIN	727	-0.4	0.0	0.0	-0.4
2021	STP	1004	-0.1	0.0	0.0	-0.1
2022	*MIN*	*6956*	*-1.9*	*0.2*	*-0.1*	*-1.7*

Byron Buxton CF Born: 12/18/93 Age: 28 Bats: R Throws: R Height: 6'2" Weight: 190 lb. Origin: Round 1, 2012 Draft (#2 overall)

YEAR	TEAM	LVL	AGE	PA	R	2B	3B	HR	RBI	BB	K	SB	CS	Whiff%	AVG/OBP/SLG	DRC+	BABIP	BRR	FRAA	WARP
2019	MIN	MLB	25	295	48	30	4	10	46	19	68	14	3	28.8%	.262/.314/.513	95	.314	4.6	CF(86): 14.5	2.9
2020	MIN	MLB	26	135	19	3	0	13	27	2	36	2	1	28.9%	.254/.267/.577	121	.241	0.6	CF(39): 7.0	1.5
2021	STP	AAA	27	26	6	2	1	3	9	2	3	0	0		.409/.423/1.000	134	.333	0.1	CF(6): -0.2	0.2
2021	MIN	MLB	27	254	50	23	0	19	32	13	62	9	1	29.2%	.306/.358/.647	135	.344	1.8	CF(60): 9.8	3.4
2022 DC	*MIN*	*MLB*	*28*	*502*	*75*	*28*	*2*	*21*	*79*	*26*	*129*	*16*	*6*	*29.5%*	*.255/.300/.463*	*105*	*.305*	*1.5*	*CF 8*	*3.2*

Comparables: Cameron Maybin, Matt Kemp, Michael Saunders

Buxton is the best reason to watch the Minnesota Twins. When healthy, he is transcendent. This is also like saying, "When mild, Minnesota winters are bearable." To state the obvious, Buxton has an injury history. The Twins have a self-imposed salary range that discourages taking an alleged financial risk on an MVP-caliber player. The fanbase has a significant (or at least loud) chunk that resents the previous best reason to watch the Minnesota Twins play baseball, Joe Mauer, for having an injury history and a hefty contract. We don't know whether Buxton will be Willie Mays or on the 60-day IL next year, but we do know that he'll be around for a while yet, having inked a seven-year contract extension prior to the lockout.

Gilberto Celestino OF Born: 02/13/99 Age: 23 Bats: R Throws: L Height: 6'0" Weight: 170 lb. Origin: International Free Agent, 2015

YEAR	TEAM	LVL	AGE	PA	R	2B	3B	HR	RBI	BB	K	SB	CS	Whiff%	AVG/OBP/SLG	DRC+	BABIP	BRR	FRAA	WARP
2019	CR	A	20	503	52	24	3	10	51	48	81	14	8		.276/.350/.409	125	.317	-3.3	CF(83): 4.6, RF(25): -3.5	2.7
2019	FTM	A+	20	33	6	4	0	0	3	2	4	0	0		.300/.333/.433	108	.333	0.1	CF(4): -0.9, RF(3): -0.5	0.0
2021	WCH	AA	22	96	10	5	0	2	7	11	24	0	1		.250/.344/.381	95	.328	0.1	CF(12): -0.5, RF(6): 0.3, LF(1): -0.2	0.2
2021	STP	AAA	22	211	27	13	0	5	24	24	43	4	0		.290/.384/.443	101	.356	-1.2	CF(23): -5.1, RF(17): 1.0, LF(3): 0.1	0.2
2021	MIN	MLB	22	62	7	3	0	2	3	3	14	0	0	23.1%	.136/.177/.288	94	.140	-0.3	CF(22): -1.2, RF(2): 1.3, LF(1): 0.0	0.2
2022 DC	*MIN*	*MLB*	*23*	*91*	*10*	*4*	*0*	*1*	*11*	*7*	*20*	*1*	*1*	*24.7%*	*.232/.299/.350*	*79*	*.287*	*0.1*	*CF 0*	*0.1*

Comparables: Dalton Pompey, Starling Marte, Raimel Tapia

Celestino's first taste of major-league action was memorable, but not in the good way: he was called up as an emergency option when seemingly every outfielder in the Twins organization, including those who've not yet been born, was on the injured list. Celestino's second professional game saw him cut in front of Trevor Larnach to field a pop fly, drop it, panic, then hurl it somewhere far from any of the four known bases, allowing the game-winning run to score. Read the preceding sentence while playing the Benny Hill theme to get the desired effect. The center field prospect spent the balance of 2021 at Triple A St. Paul being better than that, hitting above .300 and hovering near a .900 OPS.

Josh Donaldson 3B Born: 12/08/85 Age: 36 Bats: R Throws: R Height: 6'1" Weight: 210 lb. Origin: Round 1, 2007 Draft (#48 overall)

YEAR	TEAM	LVL	AGE	PA	R	2B	3B	HR	RBI	BB	K	SB	CS	Whiff%	AVG/OBP/SLG	DRC+	BABIP	BRR	FRAA	WARP
2019	ATL	MLB	33	659	96	33	0	37	94	100	155	4	2	29.9%	.259/.379/.521	130	.292	-0.9	3B(148): 0.7	4.1
2020	MIN	MLB	34	102	14	2	0	6	11	18	24	0	0	34.5%	.222/.373/.469	124	.231	0.2	3B(26): 1.2	0.7
2021	MIN	MLB	35	543	73	26	0	26	72	74	114	0	0	27.6%	.247/.352/.475	123	.268	-1.2	3B(92): 7.3	3.8
2022 DC	*MIN*	*MLB*	*36*	*560*	*90*	*24*	*0*	*24*	*82*	*77*	*122*	*2*	*1*	*28.6%*	*.245/.354/.458*	*123*	*.275*	*-0.8*	*3B 1*	*3.2*

Comparables: Ron Cey, Gary Gaetti, Douglas DeCinces

Donaldson continued to Donaldson last year, generally knocking the snot out of the ball whenever he got a pitch he could handle. His walk, barrel and hard hit rates remain elite, and while metrics offer a split decision on his defense at third base he's clearly still playable there. Just as importantly, he remained on the field, with leg issues causing an April trip to the injured list and only a few missed games thereafter. Donaldson doesn't go deep quite as regularly as he used to and his eroding foot speed will keep his batting average low, but he remains a force in the middle of the order. With two more guaranteed years followed by a reasonable option on his age-38 season, there's no reason yet to think Donaldson won't earn his pay.

Mitch Garver C Born: 01/15/91 Age: 31 Bats: R Throws: R Height: 6'1" Weight: 220 lb. Origin: Round 9, 2013 Draft (#260 overall)

YEAR	TEAM	LVL	AGE	PA	R	2B	3B	HR	RBI	BB	K	SB	CS	Whiff%	AVG/OBP/SLG	DRC+	BABIP	BRR	FRAA	WARP
2019	MIN	MLB	28	359	70	16	1	31	67	41	87	0	0	24.0%	.273/.365/.630	141	.277	-0.4	C(82): -0.9, 1B(1): -0.0	3.3
2020	MIN	MLB	29	81	8	1	0	2	5	7	37	0	0	39.6%	.167/.247/.264	56	.294	0.0	C(22): -0.1	-0.2
2021	STP	AAA	30	30	4	0	0	0	2	3	8	0	0		.231/.333/.231	82	.333	-0.5	C(5): 0.1	0.0
2021	MIN	MLB	30	243	29	15	0	13	34	31	71	1	1	30.0%	.256/.358/.517	111	.320	0.7	C(59): 0.9, 1B(4): 0.3	1.5
2022 DC	*MIN*	*MLB*	*31*	*335*	*47*	*15*	*0*	*12*	*42*	*37*	*99*	*0*	*0*	*29.9%*	*.222/.316/.412*	*99*	*.286*	*-0.5*	*C -6*	*0.8*

Comparables: Chris Gimenez, Curt Casali, Dustin Garneau

If you didn't know what position Garver played a quick scan of his injuries last year would quickly clue you in: bruised knee, sore hand, tight back, emergency groin surgery after taking a foul tip to the cup. When he could take the field, Garver bounced back from a down pandemic year to regain his status as a one-man wrecking crew offensively—among catchers, only Yasmani Grandal and Buster Posey outpaced Garver's .875 OPS last year, and only Grandal and Will Smith have been better overall since 2018. Garver isn't young but he's worked hard to become a league average defensive receiver and won't reach free agency until 2024, making him one of the more valuable under-the-radar commodities in all of baseball.

YEAR	TEAM	P. COUNT	FRM RUNS	BLK RUNS	THRW RUNS	TOT RUNS
2019	MIN	11037	-1.4	-0.3	0.2	-1.4
2020	MIN	2772	-0.6	0.0	0.0	-0.6
2021	MIN	7509	1.6	-0.1	0.1	1.6
2022	*MIN*	*12025*	*-6.3*	*0.0*	*0.0*	*-6.3*

Nick Gordon UT

Born: 10/24/95 Age: 26 Bats: L Throws: R Height: 6'0" Weight: 160 lb. Origin: Round 1, 2014 Draft (#5 overall)

YEAR	TEAM	LVL	AGE	PA	R	2B	3B	HR	RBI	BB	K	SB	CS	Whiff%	AVG/OBP/SLG	DRC+	BABIP	BRR	FRAA	WARP
2019	ROC	AAA	23	319	49	29	3	4	40	18	65	14	4		.298/.342/.459	95	.364	0.3	SS(40): 1.0, 2B(30): -3.0	1.0
2021	STP	AAA	25	77	11	0	1	3	9	6	12	7	2		.282/.338/.437	112	.304	-1.2	SS(11): -1.3, CF(2): -0.2, 2B(1): 0.0	0.1
2021	MIN	MLB	25	216	19	9	1	4	23	12	55	10	1	28.4%	.240/.292/.355	77	.310	0.3	CF(34): -1.6, 2B(17): -0.7, SS(14): -0.3	-0.1
2022 DC	*MIN*	*MLB*	*26*	*218*	*24*	*9*	*1*	*3*	*22*	*12*	*50*	*4*	*2*	*27.0%*	*.239/.291/.356*	*75*	*.302*	*0.4*	*CF 0, SS 0*	*0.0*

Comparables: Alen Hanson, Marwin Gonzalez, Jonathan Villar

Gordon, son of Tom and half-brother of Dee, finally got his first taste of major-league action in 2021. The fifth-overall selection all the way back in 2014, Gordon was...fine. Not fine enough to lock up the shortstop opening in 2022, but versatile enough to make the team's 40-man roster. If fellow star-crossed shortstop prospect Royce Lewis is unable to claim the starting job right away, Gordon stands to be among those keeping the seat warm and filling in elsewhere.

Ryan Jeffers C

Born: 06/03/97 Age: 25 Bats: R Throws: R Height: 6'4" Weight: 235 lb. Origin: Round 2, 2018 Draft (#59 overall)

YEAR	TEAM	LVL	AGE	PA	R	2B	3B	HR	RBI	BB	K	SB	CS	Whiff%	AVG/OBP/SLG	DRC+	BABIP	BRR	FRAA	WARP
2019	FTM	A+	22	315	35	11	0	10	40	28	64	0	0		.256/.330/.402	117	.297	-2.3	C(57): 12.8	2.7
2019	PNS	AA	22	99	13	5	0	4	9	9	19	0	0		.287/.374/.483	117	.328	1.6	C(17): 0.5	0.8
2020	MIN	MLB	23	62	5	0	0	3	7	5	19	0	0	33.3%	.273/.355/.436	103	.364	-0.9	C(25): 0.8	0.2
2021	STP	AAA	24	103	13	4	0	5	16	16	26	0	0		.217/.340/.446	116	.236	0.2	C(13): 1.2, 1B(1): -0.1	0.7
2021	MIN	MLB	24	293	28	10	1	14	35	22	108	0	1	34.4%	.199/.270/.401	83	.269	-2.3	C(84): 5.1	0.9
2022 DC	*MIN*	*MLB*	*25*	*243*	*30*	*9*	*0*	*8*	*37*	*21*	*80*	*0*	*0*	*32.4%*	*.208/.286/.372*	*77*	*.284*	*-0.4*	*C 4*	*0.8*

Comparables: Chris Iannetta, Yasmani Grandal, Devin Mesoraco

Let's all just chalk that one up as a learning experience and move on, shall we? Jeffers was rushed to the majors in 2020 after only 99 plate appearances in Double-A and promptly set hearts a-flutter by hitting for power, drawing walks and holding up well behind the dish. Last year? Not so much. Jeffers was plus defensively but struggled to make contact, whiffing in nearly half his April plate appearances before a merciful demotion to Triple-A, and more than a third of the time after his return. Empty swings will always be part of his game and he's not a future All-Star, but Jeffers has a mature approach, real power and a good chance to become a solid starting catcher if given time to grow.

YEAR	TEAM	P. COUNT	FRM RUNS	BLK RUNS	THRW RUNS	TOT RUNS
2019	PNS	2243	0.3	0.0	0.4	0.7
2019	FTM	7531	11.3	0.0	0.4	11.6
2020	MIN	2804	0.6	0.0	0.3	0.9
2021	MIN	11035	5.3	0.3	0.2	5.8
2021	STP	2087	1.3	0.0	0.0	1.3
2022	*MIN*	*9620*	*7.0*	*0.0*	*0.0*	*6.9*

Max Kepler RF

Born: 02/10/93 Age: 29 Bats: L Throws: L Height: 6'4" Weight: 225 lb. Origin: International Free Agent, 2009

YEAR	TEAM	LVL	AGE	PA	R	2B	3B	HR	RBI	BB	K	SB	CS	Whiff%	AVG/OBP/SLG	DRC+	BABIP	BRR	FRAA	WARP
2019	MIN	MLB	26	596	98	32	0	36	90	60	99	1	5	20.2%	.252/.336/.519	121	.244	-3.4	RF(84): 6.1, CF(60): -3.4	3.6
2020	MIN	MLB	27	196	27	9	0	9	23	22	36	3	0	21.2%	.228/.321/.439	108	.236	-0.7	RF(44): -3.6, CF(2): -0.3	0.3
2021	MIN	MLB	28	490	61	21	4	19	54	54	96	10	0	23.0%	.211/.306/.413	99	.225	3.3	RF(97): -3.5, CF(22): -0.2	1.4
2022 DC	*MIN*	*MLB*	*29*	*592*	*88*	*25*	*2*	*21*	*70*	*64*	*114*	*5*	*3*	*22.2%*	*.226/.319/.409*	*98*	*.249*	*-0.1*	*RF 0*	*1.4*

Comparables: Jay Bruce, Terry Puhl, Nick Markakis

Is Kepler a cornerstone or just a guy? The Twins' lost 2021 season gave fans time to ponder existential questions like this. Another league average season at a reasonable salary is…fine? It's fine. That same question was often asked of a different Twins corner outfielder, and the franchise determined that he was replaceable. Eddie Rosario went on to lead Atlanta to a title. Does Kepler have that kind of level-up in him? Or will he continue hitting 20-25 homers and being alright in right? He'll be 29 in 2022. It feels like we already know.

Alex Kirilloff 1B

Born: 11/09/97 Age: 24 Bats: L Throws: L Height: 6'2" Weight: 195 lb. Origin: Round 1, 2016 Draft (#15 overall)

YEAR	TEAM	LVL	AGE	PA	R	2B	3B	HR	RBI	BB	K	SB	CS	Whiff%	AVG/OBP/SLG	DRC+	BABIP	BRR	FRAA	WARP
2019	PNS	AA	21	411	47	18	2	9	43	29	76	7	6		.283/.343/.413	108	.333	-2.4	RF(41): -3.6, 1B(35): 0.7, LF(8): -1.4	0.9
2021	MIN	MLB	23	231	23	11	1	8	34	14	52	1	1	26.9%	.251/.299/.423	90	.295	0.1	1B(29): -0.7, RF(27): -1.1	0.1
2022 DC	*MIN*	*MLB*	*24*	*535*	*69*	*25*	*3*	*16*	*73*	*34*	*124*	*3*	*2*	*26.6%*	*.261/.314/.426*	*99*	*.317*	*-0.2*	*LF 1, 1B 1*	*1.5*

Comparables: Josh Bell, Carlos González, Jesse Winker

Much like the team he plays for, Kirilloff's April began with boundless promise. He was hitting everything. Even his outs were fun to watch. Then May happened, and both he and the Twins were cooked. In the prize prospect's case, a wrist injury hampered a swing that would make an aging beat writer say nice things about air travel or math. Kirilloff struggled to play through the pain before finally calling it a season in July and opting for surgery. His full return to health is one of many pieces the Twins will need to return to contention. But it would be a nice piece to have.

Trevor Larnach LF Born: 02/26/97 Age: 25 Bats: L Throws: R Height: 6'4" Weight: 223 lb. Origin: Round 1, 2018 Draft (#20 overall)

YEAR	TEAM	LVL	AGE	PA	R	2B	3B	HR	RBI	BB	K	SB	CS	Whiff%	AVG/OBP/SLG	DRC+	BABIP	BRR	FRAA	WARP
2019	FTM	A+	22	361	33	26	1	6	44	35	74	4	1		.316/.382/.459	127	.389	-1.3	RF(59): -7.6, LF(9): -0.5	1.2
2019	PNS	AA	22	181	26	4	0	7	22	22	50	0	0		.295/.387/.455	111	.390	-0.2	RF(29): -1.5, LF(5): -0.1	0.6
2021	STP	AAA	24	62	13	1	0	3	7	6	21	0	0		.176/.323/.373	90	.222	0.8	RF(6): 0.4, LF(2): 0.4	0.3
2021	MIN	MLB	24	301	29	12	0	7	28	31	104	1	0	39.0%	.223/.322/.350	72	.338	-0.8	LF(60): -1.3, RF(20): 2.5	0.0
2022 DC	*MIN*	*MLB*	*25*	*293*	*36*	*12*	*0*	*8*	*35*	*28*	*101*	*0*	*1*	*38.3%*	*.218/.308/.377*	*86*	*.318*	*-0.4*	*LF 1, RF 0*	*0.4*

Comparables: Brandon Jones, Stephen Piscotty, Christin Stewart

Larnach started hot before a pronounced slump got him sent down to Triple-A St. Paul. He earned the demotion, notching a .442 OPS in his final 112 at-bats before the move. What happened? Tale as old time: they stopped throwing him fastballs and challenged him with off-speed pitches. His ability to adjust will let the Twins know if the Oregon State product is a corner outfielder of the future.

Royce Lewis SS Born: 06/05/99 Age: 23 Bats: R Throws: R Height: 6'2" Weight: 200 lb. Origin: Round 1, 2017 Draft (#1 overall)

YEAR	TEAM	LVL	AGE	PA	R	2B	3B	HR	RBI	BB	K	SB	CS	Whiff%	AVG/OBP/SLG	DRC+	BABIP	BRR	FRAA	WARP
2019	SRR	WIN	20	95	21	9	0	3	20	9	22	5	1		.353/.411/.565		.443			
2019	FTM	A+	20	418	55	17	3	10	35	27	90	16	8		.238/.289/.376	101	.281	-1.9	SS(84): 3.9	1.3
2019	PNS	AA	20	148	18	9	1	2	14	11	33	6	2		.231/.291/.358	94	.287	1.6	SS(29): -2.9, 2B(1): 0.0, 3B(1): -0.0	0.5
2022 DC	*MIN*	*MLB*	*23*	*127*	*15*	*5*	*0*	*3*	*15*	*8*	*32*	*3*	*2*	*28.8%*	*.230/.286/.368*	*81*	*.291*	*0.3*	*SS 0*	*0.2*

Comparables: Tyler Pastornicky, Ryan Mountcastle, Richard Ureña

Lewis has lost consecutive seasons due to the COVID-19 minor-league work stoppage and an ACL tear. If the lockout holds for this coming season, he would be forgiven for going to trade school or becoming a major player in the online athleisure space, because this baseball thing is just not happening. The former #1 pick hasn't played in a game since November 2019, when the film Terminator: Dark Fate grossed $60 million at the box office. (Yes, there was a movie called Terminator: Dark Fate. We forgot about it too, it's not just you.) Should there ever be baseball again, Lewis will be going into his fifth year of being Minnesota's next starting shortstop, with all the uncertainty that statement carries. That said, there is no one else with a lock on the job. If he can recover from injury and rust, the gig's his for the taking.

★ ★ ★ *2022 Top 101 Prospect* **#52** ★ ★ ★

Austin Martin SS/OF Born: 03/23/99 Age: 23 Bats: R Throws: R Height: 6'0" Weight: 185 lb. Origin: Round 1, 2020 Draft (#5 overall)

YEAR	TEAM	LVL	AGE	PA	R	2B	3B	HR	RBI	BB	K	SB	CS	Whiff%	AVG/OBP/SLG	DRC+	BABIP	BRR	FRAA	WARP
2021	NH	AA	22	250	43	10	2	2	16	37	53	9	3		.281/.424/.383	116	.368	0.8	SS(27): 1.1, CF(26): 4.5	1.9
2021	WCH	AA	22	168	24	8	0	3	19	23	30	5	1		.254/.399/.381	112	.304	1.6	CF(20): 1.0, SS(16): -2.3	0.8
2022 DC	*MIN*	*MLB*	*23*	*28*	*3*	*1*	*0*	*0*	*2*	*2*	*5*	*0*	*0*	*21.1%*	*.216/.324/.306*	*81*	*.270*	*0.0*	*SS 0*	*0.0*

Comparables: Trayvon Robinson, Aaron Hicks, Jake Marisnick

The collective "whoa" from Prospect Twitter when it found out the Blue Jays wanted José Berríos badly enough to part with Martin was a salve on an otherwise bittersweet day for a fanbase losing its best pitcher. The SS/CF now finds himself at the very top of the Twins prospect list after making the leap to Double-A in his first season. The consensus seems to be that all the tools are there, he just needs to develop more power. Also, the name Austin Martin is cool and it's impossible to argue otherwise.

Jose Miranda IF Born: 06/29/98 Age: 24 Bats: R Throws: R Height: 6'2" Weight: 210 lb. Origin: Round 2, 2016 Draft (#73 overall)

YEAR	TEAM	LVL	AGE	PA	R	2B	3B	HR	RBI	BB	K	SB	CS	Whiff%	AVG/OBP/SLG	DRC+	BABIP	BRR	FRAA	WARP
2019	FTM	A+	21	478	48	25	1	8	55	24	54	0	0		.248/.299/.364	116	.264	-1.5	3B(71): 0.5, 2B(35): 0.5, SS(6): 0.1	2.2
2020	CAG	WIN	22	61	10	6	0	1	8	6	10	0	0		.302/.377/.472		.349			
2021	WCH	AA	23	218	36	8	0	13	38	17	25	4	2		.345/.408/.588	148	.342	0.9	3B(15): 1.3, 1B(14): 1.0, 2B(14): 0.2	2.2
2021	STP	AAA	23	373	61	24	0	17	56	25	49	0	2		.343/.397/.563	133	.362	-2.7	3B(39): -0.9, 2B(20): 0.8, 1B(14): -0.3	2.2
2022 DC	*MIN*	*MLB*	*24*	*333*	*45*	*16*	*0*	*9*	*44*	*19*	*48*	*0*	*1*	*19.9%*	*.269/.320/.419*	*104*	*.292*	*-0.5*	*3B 1, 2B 0*	*1.3*

Comparables: Josh Bell, Jose Altuve, Miguel Andújar

Let's get this out of the way first: Miranda is the cousin of actor and playwright Lin-Manuel Miranda. The temptation to make this entire profile a series of irritating Hamilton references is real, but the focus should be on the former Miranda's phenomenal 2021 campaign. Slashing .345/.408/.588 with 13 homers at Double-A Wichita led to a promotion to Triple-A St. Paul. He was not going to miss his opportunity, as he stroked three home runs in his very first game. The third baseman staked his claim as a possible Josh Donaldson replacement should the veteran move on. The room where that decision takes place is not known at this time.

Jorge Polanco 2B

Born: 07/05/93 Age: 29 Bats: S Throws: R Height: 5'11" Weight: 208 lb. Origin: International Free Agent, 2009

YEAR	TEAM	LVL	AGE	PA	R	2B	3B	HR	RBI	BB	K	SB	CS	Whiff%	AVG/OBP/SLG	DRC+	BABIP	BRR	FRAA	WARP
2019	MIN	MLB	25	704	107	40	7	22	79	60	116	4	3	17.4%	.295/.356/.485	112	.328	4.3	SS(142): -1.3	3.8
2020	MIN	MLB	26	226	22	8	0	4	19	13	35	4	2	16.8%	.258/.304/.354	97	.292	-0.5	SS(53): 1.8	0.7
2021	MIN	MLB	27	644	97	35	2	33	98	45	118	11	6	19.8%	.269/.323/.503	120	.282	1.2	2B(120): 7.8, SS(39): 0.0	4.8
2022 DC	*MIN*	*MLB*	*28*	*590*	*81*	*28*	*3*	*16*	*73*	*43*	*105*	*9*	*5*	*19.1%*	*.260/.319/.417*	*97*	*.295*	*0.5*	*SS 1, 2B 2*	*2.3*

Comparables: Alan Trammell, José Reyes, Robin Yount

By midsummer, casual Twins observers had long since moved on to sweating Minnesota's 2022 rotation or getting disappointed by another dish in the area's buffet of underperforming sports enterprises. It's hard to fault them! However, those that stuck around witnessed Polanco's welcome return to form. Hindered by a bum ankle for two seasons, the healthy second baseman was a wrecking ball in the back half of summer, leading the whole entire American League in WAR and OPS after the All-Star break. This really happened! "Hip Hip Jorge" shirts were even observed at Target Field. There weren't a lot of people there and they were easy to spot, but still.

2021 was a massive disappointment for the Twins. Polanco was not.

Brent Rooker LF/DH

Born: 11/01/94 Age: 27 Bats: R Throws: R Height: 6'3" Weight: 225 lb. Origin: Round 1, 2017 Draft (#35 overall)

YEAR	TEAM	LVL	AGE	PA	R	2B	3B	HR	RBI	BB	K	SB	CS	Whiff%	AVG/OBP/SLG	DRC+	BABIP	BRR	FRAA	WARP
2019	TWI	ROK	24	7	2	0	0	0	0	1	0	0	0		.333/.429/.333		.333			
2019	ROC	AAA	24	274	41	16	0	14	47	35	95	2	0		.281/.398/.535	97	.417	1.4	LF(56): -1.8	0.6
2020	MIN	MLB	25	21	4	2	0	1	5	0	5	0	0	27.3%	.316/.381/.579	99	.385	0.0	RF(4): -0.3, LF(1): -0.3	0.0
2021	STP	AAA	26	267	40	8	1	20	49	38	80	1	2		.245/.367/.564	119	.276	-0.8	LF(30): -3.2, RF(21): -2.9, 1B(1): -0.0	0.8
2021	MIN	MLB	26	213	25	10	0	9	16	15	70	0	0	33.4%	.201/.291/.397	85	.264	-0.2	LF(38): 0.7, RF(8): -1.5	0.2
2022 DC	*MIN*	*MLB*	*27*	*396*	*55*	*17*	*0*	*17*	*56*	*34*	*120*	*0*	*1*	*32.7%*	*.220/.305/.428*	*99*	*.274*	*-0.5*	*LF 0, RF -1*	*0.8*

Comparables: Jake Smolinski, Peter O'Brien, Chris Heisey

The Twins appeared to have multiple ways to block Rooker from getting in the lineup, from Nelson Cruz at DH to two prospect corner outfielders, Alex Kirilloff and Trevor Larnach, considered more integral to Minnesota's future than Rooker is. In that context, his ultimate plate appearance total was a pleasant surprise for Rooker boosters, even if it was primarily due to injuries and trades. It was also the only apparent encouragement to be found in his major-league line. He did showcase a decent chunk of his trademark power and, had he been more fortunate with balls in play, would not have come so alarmingly close to the Mendoza Line. The only true way Rooker looked like he might stand out was by getting plunked, as he did so at a rate that would have challenged the league leaders over 600-plus plate appearances. That also oversold the rather pedestrian walk rate in his slash line but hey, he gets on base. He'll continue to do so at Triple-A, where he looks much more qualified to travel to first in less painful ways.

Ben Rortvedt C

Born: 09/25/97 Age: 24 Bats: L Throws: R Height: 5'10" Weight: 205 lb. Origin: Round 2, 2016 Draft (#56 overall)

YEAR	TEAM	LVL	AGE	PA	R	2B	3B	HR	RBI	BB	K	SB	CS	Whiff%	AVG/OBP/SLG	DRC+	BABIP	BRR	FRAA	WARP
2019	FTM	A+	21	94	13	8	1	2	10	12	16	0	0		.238/.340/.438	125	.270	0.1	C(18): 2.0	0.8
2019	PNS	AA	21	226	19	8	0	5	19	23	51	0	0		.239/.332/.355	99	.296	-1.7	C(37): 2.4	0.9
2021	STP	AAA	23	136	18	6	0	5	22	10	35	0	0		.254/.324/.426	91	.313	0.5	C(29): 1.3	0.5
2021	MIN	MLB	23	98	8	1	0	3	7	6	29	0	0	31.6%	.169/.229/.281	76	.211	-0.8	C(39): 1.5	0.2
2022 DC	*MIN*	*MLB*	*24*	*60*	*6*	*2*	*0*	*1*	*8*	*4*	*15*	*0*	*0*	*30.4%*	*.213/.282/.333*	*67*	*.276*	*-0.1*	*C 1*	*0.1*

Comparables: Tucker Barnhart, Christian Vázquez, John Ryan Murphy

YEAR	TEAM	P. COUNT	FRM RUNS	BLK RUNS	THRW RUNS	TOT RUNS
2019	PNS	5313	2.3	0.0	0.3	2.6
2019	FTM	2701	0.4	0.1	1.4	1.9
2021	MIN	4482	1.4	0.3	0.0	1.7
2021	STP	4304	2.0	0.0	0.0	2.0
2022	*MIN*	*2405*	*1.6*	*0.1*	*0.1*	*1.8*

Being the third catcher in a hierarchy which features Mitch Garver at the top isn't the worst way to find some work. Rortvedt proved a capable backup defensively during both of Garver's IL stints, plus a stint filling in for the struggling Ryan Jeffers. It was a different story at the plate, where he did a passable Yandy Díaz impression thanks to his combination of implausibly-bulging muscles and very little home run pop. Unless Rortvedt can imitate Díaz's excellent approach and produce an above-average line regardless, he'll remain consigned to third-catcher duty.

Aaron Sabato 1B

Born: 06/04/99 Age: 23 Bats: R Throws: R Height: 6'2" Weight: 230 lb. Origin: Round 1, 2020 Draft (#27 overall)

YEAR	TEAM	LVL	AGE	PA	R	2B	3B	HR	RBI	BB	K	SB	CS	Whiff%	AVG/OBP/SLG	DRC+	BABIP	BRR	FRAA	WARP
2021	FTM	A	22	367	48	15	0	11	42	73	117	1	0		.189/.365/.357	110	.270	-2.2	1B(77): 4.6	1.5
2021	CR	A+	22	97	21	3	0	8	15	19	32	0	0		.253/.402/.613	120	.297	0.5	1B(20): 0.0	0.5
2022 non-DC	*MIN*	*MLB*	*23*	*251*	*25*	*10*	*0*	*6*	*25*	*32*	*88*	*0*	*0*	*33.6%*	*.188/.301/.333*	*73*	*.282*	*-0.4*	*1B 2*	*-0.3*

Comparables: Trey Mancini, Rhys Hoskins, Gaby Sanchez

Sabato, drafted 27th overall in 2020 based on his absurd power and on-base numbers at the University of North Carolina, initially struggled to maintain that rep in his first year of minor-league ball. The back half of 2021 was a different story, as multiple multi-HR games earned Sabato a promotion to High-A Cedar Rapids. His tear continued there, as he belted eight homers in 22 games while posting a 1.015 OPS. With Miguel Sanó and potentially Alex Kirilloff blocking his path to first base in the majors, a full season's worth of that kind of power would give the Twins a pleasant dilemma in 2023.

Miguel Sanó 1B Born: 05/11/93 Age: 29 Bats: R Throws: R Height: 6'4" Weight: 272 lb. Origin: International Free Agent, 2009

YEAR	TEAM	LVL	AGE	PA	R	2B	3B	HR	RBI	BB	K	SB	CS	Whiff%	AVG/OBP/SLG	DRC+	BABIP	BRR	FRAA	WARP
2019	MIN	MLB	26	439	76	19	2	34	79	55	159	0	1	37.7%	.247/.346/.576	111	.319	-2.5	3B(91): -2.9, 1B(9): -0.5	1.2
2020	MIN	MLB	27	205	31	12	0	13	25	18	90	0	0	42.6%	.204/.278/.478	81	.301	1.9	1B(52): -3.4	-0.2
2021	MIN	MLB	28	532	68	24	0	30	75	59	183	2	1	38.2%	.223/.312/.466	105	.291	-0.5	1B(118): -7.8, 3B(9): 0.2	0.7
2022 DC	*MIN*	*MLB*	*29*	*549*	*82*	*24*	*1*	*29*	*86*	*60*	*196*	*0*	*1*	*38.1%*	*.231/.318/.472*	*111*	*.312*	*-0.9*	*1B -3*	*1.5*

Comparables: Jim Thome, Howard Johnson, Dean Palmer

Here is what you get with Sano: Blistering stretches where he can carry a team with staggering power, followed by epic bouts of futility. That's what he is. The question of whether he's good or not in any given season is answered entirely by how long he spends in The Abyss. Do you know when those stretches are going to come so you can build your team around the good parts and plan around The Abyss? No. No, you do not. That's what he is. You can count on one hand the number of players who send baseballs straight to the afterworld like Sano does. You can count on one finger the number of players who became the fastest player to 1000 strikeouts in major-league history. That's what he is.

PITCHERS

Jorge Alcala RHP Born: 07/28/95 Age: 26 Bats: R Throws: R Height: 6'3" Weight: 205 lb. Origin: International Free Agent, 2014

YEAR	TEAM	LVL	AGE	W	L	SV	G	GS	IP	H	HR	BB/9	K/9	K	GB%	BABIP	WHIP	ERA	DRA-	WARP	MPH	FB%	Whiff%	CSP
2019	PNS	AA	23	5	7	0	26	16	102^2	114	12	3.2	9.2	105	37.6%	.355	1.47	5.87	107	0.3				
2019	ROC	AAA	23	1	0	0	5	0	7^2	4	0	2.3	12.9	11	53.3%	.267	0.78	0.00	78	0.2				
2019	MIN	MLB	23	0	0	0	2	0	1^2	1	0	5.4	5.4	1	0.0%	.200	1.20	0.00	108	0.0	93.7	65.5%	35.7%	37.6%
2020	MIN	MLB	24	2	1	0	16	0	24	21	3	3.0	10.1	27	39.0%	.321	1.21	2.63	87	0.4	97.1	46.4%	32.2%	46.3%
2021	MIN	MLB	25	3	6	1	59	0	59^2	45	10	2.0	9.2	61	42.5%	.246	0.97	3.92	88	0.9	97.4	43.4%	29.2%	56.6%
2022 DC	*MIN*	*MLB*	*26*	*3*	*3*	*0*	*74*	*0*	*64.7*	*60*	*8*	*3.2*	*9.1*	*65*	*40.8%*	*.293*	*1.29*	*3.94*	*100*	*0.3*	*97.3*	*44.3%*	*29.9%*	*54.1%*

Comparables: Bobby Parnell, Jose Arredondo, Kevin Siegrist

Pleasant surprises were in short supply for the 2021 Twins, and the bullpen cupboards were bare enough that a more topical writer would make a supply chain joke here. That said, Alcala came on strong as a potentially reliable set-up man in the second half, most notably with three effective 8th innings in three victories over eventual AL champs Houston in one August series. It goes without saying that he immediately went on the injured list with tendinitis, but not before establishing himself as an in-house option for 2022.

★ ★ ★ *2022 Top 101 Prospect* **#78** ★ ★ ★

Jordan Balazovic RHP Born: 09/17/98 Age: 23 Bats: R Throws: R Height: 6'5" Weight: 215 lb. Origin: Round 5, 2016 Draft (#153 overall)

YEAR	TEAM	LVL	AGE	W	L	SV	G	GS	IP	H	HR	BB/9	K/9	K	GB%	BABIP	WHIP	ERA	DRA-	WARP	MPH	FB%	Whiff%	CSP
2019	CR	A	20	2	1	0	4	4	20^2	15	1	1.7	14.4	33	42.2%	.318	0.92	2.18	85	0.3				
2019	FTM	A+	20	6	4	0	15	14	73	52	3	2.6	11.8	96	44.3%	.283	1.00	2.84	93	1.1				
2021	WCH	AA	22	5	4	0	20	20	97	98	9	3.5	9.5	102	48.6%	.324	1.40	3.62	86	1.4				
2022 DC	*MIN*	*MLB*	*23*	*0*	*0*	*0*	*3*	*3*	*14*	*14*	*1*	*3.9*	*8.6*	*13*	*45.1%*	*.306*	*1.43*	*4.54*	*110*	*0.0*				

Comparables: Jake Thompson, Brad Keller, Collin Balester

Reversing the path of the team's other top pitching prospects, Balazovic got his injury problems out of the way at the beginning of 2021. It was a nice change of pace! Surmounting back troubles that kept him off the mound to begin the year, the tall righty and his mid-90s fastball held up at Double-A Wichita, where he set a career high for innings pitched despite the late start. Another top internal candidate to join Minnesota's rotation in the next year or two.

Dylan Bundy RHP Born: 11/15/92 Age: 29 Bats: S Throws: R Height: 6'1" Weight: 225 lb. Origin: Round 1, 2011 Draft (#4 overall)

YEAR	TEAM	LVL	AGE	W	L	SV	G	GS	IP	H	HR	BB/9	K/9	K	GB%	BABIP	WHIP	ERA	DRA-	WARP	MPH	FB%	Whiff%	CSP
2019	BAL	MLB	26	7	14	0	30	30	161^2	161	29	3.2	9.0	162	41.1%	.297	1.35	4.79	97	1.9	91.3	50.1%	28.2%	47.1%
2020	LAA	MLB	27	6	3	0	11	11	65^2	51	5	2.3	9.9	72	41.0%	.274	1.04	3.29	81	1.4	90.4	41.9%	29.5%	49.3%
2021	LAA	MLB	28	2	9	0	23	19	90^2	89	20	3.4	8.3	84	40.3%	.275	1.36	6.06	112	0.2	90.9	51.5%	23.1%	57.2%
2022 DC	*MIN*	*MLB*	*29*	*8*	*7*	*0*	*24*	*24*	*123.7*	*118*	*18*	*3.0*	*8.7*	*120*	*40.0%*	*.292*	*1.30*	*4.15*	*104*	*0.7*	*90.9*	*49.0%*	*26.0%*	*52.5%*

Comparables: Edwin Jackson, Ian Kennedy, Rick Wise

Bundy's declining velocity was the uncomfortable caveat in analysis of his otherwise outstanding 2020. The former Oriole looked set to buck that trend when he opened the season sitting 92 and even touching 95 in his second start, the first time he had done so since 2017. When he punched out 10 Astros in that start, it looked as though Bundy could both maintain his excellent short-season performance and recover his lost heat. Alas, it was not to be: by May it was drifting down towards 90 as his ERA spiked. He was banished to the pen before June was out, a move that provided a little juice, but a tick below the April promise. His subsequent return to the rotation sent the velo spiraling into the 80s. Bundy's season ended with four consecutive balls, three of which were fastballs that failed to touch 88. The shoulder strain that sent him to the IL (and into free agency) might explain those final struggles, but it doesn't change the fact that Bundy's starting role, and possibly his career, depend on him reversing that trend for more than a handful of starts in the Spring.

Beau Burrows RHP Born: 09/18/96 Age: 25 Bats: R Throws: R Height: 6'2" Weight: 210 lb. Origin: Round 1, 2015 Draft (#22 overall)

YEAR	TEAM	LVL	AGE	W	L	SV	G	GS	IP	H	HR	BB/9	K/9	K	GB%	BABIP	WHIP	ERA	DRA-	WARP	MPH	FB%	Whiff%	CSP
2019	TOL	AAA	22	2	6	0	15	15	65^{1}	68	12	4.4	8.4	61	34.5%	.303	1.53	5.51	120	0.1				
2020	DET	MLB	23	0	0	0	5	0	6^{2}	8	3	1.4	4.1	3	40.0%	.227	1.35	5.40	116	0.0	92.5	80.0%	19.6%	47.6%
2021	TOL	AAA	24	1	1	0	9	1	17^{1}	21	4	3.1	8.8	17	30.9%	.333	1.56	6.23	113	0.1				
2021	STP	AAA	24	3	5	0	13	9	48	39	10	4.1	9.0	48	22.8%	.232	1.27	4.69	111	0.4				
2021	MIN	MLB	24	0	1	0	5	1	9^{1}	14	5	7.7	4.8	5	19.4%	.290	2.36	12.54	176	-0.3	92.1	87.6%	16.2%	55.0%
2021	DET	MLB	24	0	0	0	1	0	1^{2}	2	0	10.8	16.2	3	25.0%	.500	2.40	21.60	100	0.0	94.3	85.4%	26.3%	47.7%
2022 non-DC	*MIN*	*MLB*	*25*	*2*	*3*	*0*	*57*	*0*	*50*	*53*	*8*	*4.6*	*7.6*	*42*	*29.5%*	*.298*	*1.57*	*5.80*	*133*	*-0.7*	*92.4*	*85.6%*	*18.1%*	*52.4%*

Comparables: Kohl Stewart, Matt Wisler, Conner Greene

An injury-plagued former top pick in the Tigers organization, Burrows pitched poorly in Detroit last year, earned his release, hooked on with the Twins and managed to pitch even worse. Over 11 big-league innings he posted more walks than strikeouts and allowed a home run every 8.8 at-bats, and wasn't much better in Triple-A. Back on the street at season's end, the Dodgers took a flier on him with the hope they can finally unleash the talent that led to Burrows being drafted two picks ahead of Walker Buehler.

Alex Colomé RHP Born: 12/31/88 Age: 33 Bats: R Throws: R Height: 6'1" Weight: 225 lb. Origin: International Free Agent, 2007

YEAR	TEAM	LVL	AGE	W	L	SV	G	GS	IP	H	HR	BB/9	K/9	K	GB%	BABIP	WHIP	ERA	DRA-	WARP	MPH	FB%	Whiff%	CSP
2019	CHW	MLB	30	4	5	30	62	0	61	42	7	3.4	8.1	55	44.1%	.217	1.07	2.80	99	0.7	94.6	29.0%	29.1%	46.3%
2020	CHW	MLB	31	2	0	12	21	0	22^{1}	13	0	3.2	6.4	16	51.6%	.203	0.94	0.81	103	0.2	94.6	28.4%	30.9%	41.2%
2021	MIN	MLB	32	4	4	17	67	0	65	68	8	3.2	8.0	58	52.7%	.306	1.40	4.15	114	0.1	93.9	29.4%	27.1%	56.2%
2022 DC	*FA*	*MLB*	*33*	*3*	*3*	*0*	*71*	*0*	*61.7*	*61*	*6*	*3.3*	*8.1*	*55*	*49.0%*	*.301*	*1.35*	*4.11*	*102*	*0.2*	*94.1*	*29.2%*	*28.0%*	*52.1%*

Comparables: Sam LeCure, Scott Sullivan, David Weathers

Colomé's disastrous start as the Twins closer set the tone for Minnesota's 2021. The mirror universe version of Pulp Fiction's Wolf, Colomé would be called in to handle a precarious situation and leave it decisively worse. Sinkholes. Locusts. Frog rain. Robots who would do us harm. While the footage of his April appearances has rightly been burned by MLB and the government, people don't forget. We all saw it. We all saw it. To his credit, he improved from "historically bad" to "alright, I guess," stringing up holiday lights around the already-dug hole.

Danny Coulombe LHP Born: 10/26/89 Age: 32 Bats: L Throws: L Height: 5'10" Weight: 190 lb. Origin: Round 25, 2012 Draft (#776 overall)

YEAR	TEAM	LVL	AGE	W	L	SV	G	GS	IP	H	HR	BB/9	K/9	K	GB%	BABIP	WHIP	ERA	DRA-	WARP	MPH	FB%	Whiff%	CSP
2019	SWB	AAA	29	3	2	1	17	0	23^{1}	26	5	5.8	16.6	43	47.1%	.457	1.76	5.01	66	0.7				
2019	SA	AAA	29	1	0	0	14	0	13	13	4	1.4	12.5	18	51.4%	.290	1.15	4.15	75	0.3				
2020	MIN	MLB	30	0	0	0	2	0	2^{2}	2	0	10.1	10.1	3	28.6%	.286	1.88	0.00	123	0.0	90.0	38.0%	15.8%	51.9%
2021	STP	AAA	31	1	1	2	14	0	20^{1}	16	1	1.3	12.0	27	49.0%	.313	0.93	1.77	83	0.5				
2021	MIN	MLB	31	3	2	0	29	1	34^{1}	35	5	1.8	8.7	33	42.4%	.323	1.22	3.67	98	0.3	90.5	33.5%	23.9%	56.2%
2022 DC	*MIN*	*MLB*	*32*	*1*	*1*	*0*	*29*	*0*	*25.7*	*24*	*3*	*2.9*	*8.9*	*25*	*45.6%*	*.293*	*1.26*	*3.76*	*96*	*0.2*	*90.4*	*33.7%*	*23.4%*	*56.0%*

Comparables: Buddy Boshers, Nick Vincent, Tony Sipp

Welcome back to the Annual, Mr. Coulombe! It's been a few years. You're here (with a full comment, no less) not just because there were so few other Twins relievers worthy of the honor, but because you pitched well enough to earn this distinction on your own merits. Last year you did a good job of avoiding ball four and evened out your frequently ghastly platoon splits, perhaps due to a liberal application of your four-seamer, and wound up pitching higher-leverage innings than you'd been trusted with in years. We're always fond of successful lefty junkballers around these parts, so here's hoping we can meet again in this space next year. Have a great summer!

Randy Dobnak RHP Born: 01/17/95 Age: 27 Bats: R Throws: R Height: 6'1" Weight: 230 lb. Origin: Undrafted Free Agent, 2017

YEAR	TEAM	LVL	AGE	W	L	SV	G	GS	IP	H	HR	BB/9	K/9	K	GB%	BABIP	WHIP	ERA	DRA-	WARP	MPH	FB%	Whiff%	CSP
2019	FTM	A+	24	3	0	0	4	4	22^{1}	18	0	1.6	5.6	14	57.6%	.273	0.99	0.40	120	0.0				
2019	PNS	AA	24	4	2	0	11	10	66^{2}	58	6	0.8	8.2	61	59.1%	.281	0.96	2.57	73	1.4				
2019	ROC	AAA	24	5	2	0	9	7	46	28	0	3.5	6.7	34	60.2%	.220	1.00	2.15	92	0.8				
2019	MIN	MLB	24	2	1	1	9	5	28^{1}	27	1	1.6	7.3	23	54.0%	.302	1.13	1.59	97	0.3	92.5	59.0%	27.0%	48.5%
2020	MIN	MLB	25	6	4	0	10	10	46^{2}	50	3	2.5	5.2	27	61.0%	.311	1.35	4.05	97	0.6	91.8	48.5%	20.6%	45.3%
2021	STP	AAA	26	0	1	0	4	4	18	15	0	5.0	6.5	13	58.8%	.294	1.39	3.00	116	0.1				
2021	MIN	MLB	26	1	7	1	14	6	50^{2}	66	11	2.1	4.8	27	56.1%	.313	1.54	7.64	127	-0.3	91.8	59.5%	17.5%	54.9%
2022 DC	*MIN*	*MLB*	*27*	*5*	*6*	*0*	*19*	*19*	*93*	*101*	*8*	*2.7*	*5.5*	*57*	*56.0%*	*.301*	*1.39*	*4.24*	*107*	*0.3*	*91.8*	*55.5%*	*19.6%*	*50.8%*

Comparables: Chris Bassitt, Ryan Yarbrough, Craig Stammen

If you were to say the name "Randy Dobnak" to someone who knew nothing about the Minnesota Twins or baseball and asked them to describe what that person looks like, that person would describe Randy Dobnak. No one on earth could look more like Randy Dobnak than Randy Dobnak does. We live in miraculous times. Unfortunately for Dobnak, his 2021 was anything but miraculous, as injuries and ineffectiveness marred the Uber-driver-turned-playoff-starter's campaign. With a ridiculously team-friendly 2022 contract on the books and nothing but open rotation spots ahead of him, he'll have every chance to add another chapter to one of the most authentic feel-good stories in the game.

Tyler Duffey RHP Born: 12/27/90 Age: 31 Bats: R Throws: R Height: 6'3" Weight: 220 lb. Origin: Round 5, 2012 Draft (#160 overall)

YEAR	TEAM	LVL	AGE	W	L	SV	G	GS	IP	H	HR	BB/9	K/9	K	GB%	BABIP	WHIP	ERA	DRA-	WARP	MPH	FB%	Whiff%	CSP
2019	ROC	AAA	28	0	0	1	7	0	13^{2}	8	0	3.3	14.5	22	44.0%	.333	0.95	1.32	78	0.3				
2019	MIN	MLB	28	5	1	0	58	0	57^{2}	44	8	2.2	12.8	82	36.2%	.277	1.01	2.50	75	1.4	94.0	54.0%	33.2%	47.4%
2020	MIN	MLB	29	1	1	0	22	0	24	13	2	2.3	11.6	31	55.6%	.212	0.79	1.88	70	0.7	92.8	43.8%	36.4%	42.7%
2021	MIN	MLB	30	3	3	3	64	0	62^{1}	48	4	4.0	8.8	61	45.4%	.278	1.22	3.18	101	0.5	92.6	48.7%	23.6%	52.1%
2022 DC	*MIN*	*MLB*	*31*	*3*	*3*	*8*	*74*	*0*	*64.7*	*58*	*8*	*3.4*	*10.2*	*73*	*44.5%*	*.296*	*1.27*	*3.77*	*95*	*0.4*	*92.9*	*49.0%*	*27.5%*	*49.7%*

Comparables: Rafael Montero, Brandon Workman, Zack Britton

Duffey has been one of the most consistently productive late-inning relievers in the game over the last few years, and last season he remained that: from the seventh inning onward, he held batters to a .550 OPS. It was the .821 OPS he allowed in the middle innings that led to his comparatively mediocre season. Cue Pee-wee Herman: "What's the significance? I DON'T KNOW!" Maybe Minnesota should avoid pitching him earlier, maybe Duffey should eat his pre-game meal earlier, maybe we should just ignore this as a small-sample anomaly and focus on how Duffey was at his best when it mattered most. More concerning were the precipitous drops in Duffey's chase and whiff rates and a jump in walks, but the cost-conscious Twins re-upped The Doof for $3.8 million heading into his walk year, so they seem confident his stellar curveball is still capable of getting them big outs. Recent history agrees.

Ralph Garza Jr. RHP Born: 04/06/94 Age: 28 Bats: R Throws: R Height: 6'2" Weight: 220 lb. Origin: Round 26, 2015 Draft (#769 overall)

YEAR	TEAM	LVL	AGE	W	L	SV	G	GS	IP	H	HR	BB/9	K/9	K	GB%	BABIP	WHIP	ERA	DRA-	WARP	MPH	FB%	Whiff%	CSP
2019	RR	AAA	25	8	1	5	42	0	78	57	9	3.2	9.2	80	41.0%	.246	1.09	4.04	86	1.1				
2021	SUG	AAA	27	2	0	0	10	0	14^{1}	5	2	5.0	10.7	17	40.6%	.100	0.91	1.26	94	0.1				
2021	HOU	MLB	27	1	2	0	9	0	11	11	2	5.7	11.5	14	25.0%	.346	1.64	4.09	95	0.1	91.3	66.5%	31.5%	48.8%
2021	MIN	MLB	27	0	2	1	18	0	19^{1}	13	3	3.3	7.0	15	45.5%	.192	1.03	3.26	112	0.1	90.7	51.0%	18.9%	55.6%
2022 DC	*MIN*	*MLB*	*28*	*2*	*3*	*0*	*59*	*0*	*51.7*	*46*	*6*	*4.3*	*8.8*	*50*	*39.5%*	*.281*	*1.38*	*4.36*	*105*	*0.0*	*91.0*	*57.3%*	*24.0%*	*52.8%*

Comparables: Cory Rasmus, Jimmy Cordero, Brian Schlitter

When Minnesota claimed Garza off waivers from the Astros last summer they may not have picked up a dominant reliever but they did add a unique one. Garza attacks lefties from a standard three-quarters slot with a low-90s four-seamer, a changeup, a cutter and a breaker he grips like a curveball but acts like a slider. Against righties he throws side-arm, keeps the cutter, ditches the changeup, trades the four-seamer for a sinker and grips his breaker like a slider, though it acts like a curve. You may find that more confusing than big-league hitters did last year, as Garza's solid ERA belied his less-than-stellar peripherals and Statcast metrics. It's hard enough to maintain your mechanics with one delivery, let alone two, so it's not surprising his command and control have a tendency to wander, but Garza just might miss enough bats to spend a few years as one of the more interesting middle relievers around.

Griffin Jax RHP Born: 11/22/94 Age: 27 Bats: R Throws: R Height: 6'2" Weight: 195 lb. Origin: Round 3, 2016 Draft (#93 overall)

YEAR	TEAM	LVL	AGE	W	L	SV	G	GS	IP	H	HR	BB/9	K/9	K	GB%	BABIP	WHIP	ERA	DRA-	WARP	MPH	FB%	Whiff%	CSP
2019	PNS	AA	24	4	5	0	20	20	111^{1}	98	5	1.9	6.8	84	48.7%	.282	1.10	2.67	99	0.8				
2019	ROC	AAA	24	1	2	0	3	3	16	19	2	1.7	5.6	10	45.5%	.321	1.38	4.50	105	0.2				
2021	STP	AAA	26	4	1	0	8	8	40^{2}	37	2	3.5	8.0	36	39.8%	.302	1.30	3.76	114	0.2				
2021	MIN	MLB	26	4	5	0	18	14	82	82	23	3.2	7.1	65	31.8%	.248	1.35	6.37	142	-1.1	92.8	45.9%	21.3%	55.8%
2022 DC	*MIN*	*MLB*	*27*	*6*	*7*	*0*	*22*	*22*	*111*	*113*	*16*	*3.0*	*7.1*	*88*	*37.6%*	*.291*	*1.36*	*4.56*	*113*	*0.1*	*92.8*	*45.9%*	*21.3%*	*55.8%*

Comparables: Cody Ponce, David Buchanan, Josh Geer

The first Air Force Academy graduate to pitch in the bigs, Jax doesn't have an SR-71 ceiling but his pitchability and control could earn him a continuing swingman role. Jax took advantage of the Air Force World Class Athlete Program to work his way unpaid through the minors while his wife, a fellow Academy graduate who earned her captain's bars before he did, supported him between their various deployments; in the off-season, Jax is assigned to work with the Space Force. Unfortunately, his standard issue stuff (low-90s fastball, slider, changeup and occasional curve) is less compelling than his back story. Jax doesn't miss many bats, but during his ascent through the minors he minimized walks and generally kept the ball in the yard and crooked numbers off the scoreboard. Jax struggled mightily in his doolie year but has the makeup needed to see it through and has a chance to soak up big-league innings in long relief.

Kenta Maeda RHP Born: 04/11/88 Age: 34 Bats: R Throws: R Height: 6'1" Weight: 185 lb. Origin: International Free Agent, 2016

YEAR	TEAM	LVL	AGE	W	L	SV	G	GS	IP	H	HR	BB/9	K/9	K	GB%	BABIP	WHIP	ERA	DRA-	WARP	MPH	FB%	Whiff%	CSP
2019	LAD	MLB	31	10	8	3	37	26	153^{2}	114	22	3.0	9.9	169	39.5%	.245	1.07	4.04	84	2.9	92.2	37.3%	32.5%	46.5%
2020	MIN	MLB	32	6	1	0	11	11	66^{2}	40	9	1.4	10.8	80	47.5%	.208	0.75	2.70	61	2.1	91.5	25.9%	34.8%	44.4%
2021	MIN	MLB	33	6	5	0	21	21	106^{1}	106	16	2.7	9.6	113	39.0%	.318	1.30	4.66	101	0.9	90.5	31.2%	29.5%	52.5%
2022 non-DC	*MIN*	*MLB*	*34*	*2*	*2*	*0*	*57*	*0*	*50*	*44*	*6*	*2.6*	*9.9*	*54*	*40.3%*	*.292*	*1.19*	*3.45*	*89*	*0.5*	*91.2*	*31.6%*	*31.3%*	*49.3%*

Comparables: Kevin Gross, Bert Blyleven, Rick Reed

In 2020, Maeda was marvelous, earning a second-place Cy Young nod and leading a playoff-bound Twins staff. In 2021, he was very much not. Explanations varied for his rapid devolution from staff ace to replacement-level fifth starter. Did the league figure him out? Was he tipping his pitches? Had he fallen victim to a classic body swap comedy and the floppy-haired teen skateboarder inhabiting his body simply couldn't pitch? As it turns out, Maeda was hurt, and underwent Tommy John surgery in September. Timeline on his return is TBD, but 2023 must be considered the most realistic date. No word on the skateboarder's condition or prom date as this edition of the Annual went to press.

Trevor Megill RHP Born: 12/05/93 Age: 28 Bats: L Throws: R Height: 6'8" Weight: 250 lb. Origin: Round 7, 2015 Draft (#207 overall)

YEAR	TEAM	LVL	AGE	W	L	SV	G	GS	IP	H	HR	BB/9	K/9	K	GB%	BABIP	WHIP	ERA	DRA-	WARP	MPH	FB%	Whiff%	CSP
2019	AMA	AA	25	0	0	0	4	0	6^1	5	0	2.8	11.4	8	46.7%	.333	1.11	1.42	106	0.0				
2019	ELP	AAA	25	2	2	6	32	0	50^1	56	5	3.4	12.7	71	41.1%	.415	1.49	4.47	68	1.3				
2021	IOW	AAA	27	0	0	1	12	0	14	12	2	5.1	12.9	20	44.1%	.313	1.43	5.14	88	0.3				
2021	CHC	MLB	27	1	2	0	28	0	23^2	36	7	3.0	11.4	30	38.2%	.426	1.86	8.37	89	0.4	96.5	66.5%	25.5%	55.1%
2022 DC	*FA*	*MLB*	*28*	*2*	*2*	*0*	*42*	*0*	*37*	*35*	*6*	*3.4*	*10.2*	*42*	*38.4%*	*.310*	*1.33*	*4.42*	*101*	*0.1*	*96.5*	*66.5%*	*25.5%*	*55.1%*

Comparables: George Kontos, Adam Liberatore, Jared Burton

He's sized like a Chicago Bull and towers over his catcher during mound meetings like a pro hooper might at a pickup run at the Y. His fastball has ticked up to 96-97 since he was selected by the Cubs in 2019's Rule 5 Draft, and Chicago also helped him overhaul his curveball, which breaks in hard on righties. He'll also try a slider that either gets whiffs or gets hit hard, no in between. Megill throws strikes, generally, but he also gets barrelled up more than a guy with his stuff should, almost twice the MLB average. He's also lost some of his previous excellent command with some of the things he's trying to do now, like riding his fastball up and in on righties. Megill might seem like the kind of high risk/reward late-relief prospect player the rebuilding Cubs should be rostering, but they lost him to Minnesota on waivers (who subsequently non-tendered and re-signed him).

Bailey Ober RHP Born: 07/12/95 Age: 26 Bats: R Throws: R Height: 6'9" Weight: 260 lb. Origin: Round 12, 2017 Draft (#346 overall)

YEAR	TEAM	LVL	AGE	W	L	SV	G	GS	IP	H	HR	BB/9	K/9	K	GB%	BABIP	WHIP	ERA	DRA-	WARP	MPH	FB%	Whiff%	CSP
2019	TWI	ROK	23	1	0	0	2	1	9	6	0	1.0	13.0	13	71.4%	.286	0.78	0.00						
2019	FTM	A+	23	4	0	0	8	8	45^2	39	1	1.2	10.4	53	35.3%	.330	0.99	0.99	93	0.7				
2019	PNS	AA	23	3	0	0	4	4	24	10	1	0.7	12.7	34	37.5%	.196	0.50	0.37	61	0.6				
2021	STP	AAA	25	1	0	0	4	4	16	13	0	2.8	11.8	21	48.7%	.333	1.13	2.81	97	0.2				
2021	MIN	MLB	25	3	3	0	20	20	92^1	92	20	1.9	9.4	96	33.5%	.296	1.20	4.19	101	0.8	92.5	58.0%	24.7%	52.7%
2022 DC	*MIN*	*MLB*	*26*	*8*	*7*	*0*	*27*	*27*	*123.7*	*118*	*18*	*2.2*	*9.6*	*132*	*36.3%*	*.301*	*1.20*	*3.67*	*96*	*1.3*	*92.5*	*58.0%*	*24.7%*	*52.7%*

Comparables: Nick Tropeano, Scott Baker, Rafael Montero

Ober was a pleasant surprise for the 2021 Twins, in a year marked by surprises that were more of the "your house burned down and you're in it right now" variety. A 6-foot-9 righty who will be referred to as "lanky" until the heat death of the universe, Ober surmounted a soft-throwing reputation acquired over an otherwise sterling minor league career. An adjustment in his mechanics spiked his average velocity from the upper 80s to the low 90s. Pair that with his freakishly long arms and you have someone who cleared the admittedly low bar of being the most reliable Twins starting pitcher in 2021.

Not related to the late Ken Ober, host of MTV's Remote Control. Remote Control was a good show.

Chase Petty RHP Born: 04/04/03 Age: 19 Bats: R Throws: R Height: 6'1" Weight: 190 lb. Origin: Round 1, 2021 Draft (#26 overall)

Petty will attempt to become the best MLB pitcher with a NASCAR name since Oil Can Boyd. He has the raw stuff to do it. The 2020-21 New Jersey high school player of the year consistently throws in the upper 90s and has reached 101-102 mph, making all remaining pitch-to-contact evangelists in the Twins organization light a votive candle beneath a picture of Brad Radke. Minnesota snagged him with the 26th pick of the 2021 draft, the main strike against him being one that would cause as much trouble on the racetrack as it does on the mound: an utter lack of control.

Michael Pineda RHP Born: 01/18/89 Age: 33 Bats: R Throws: R Height: 6'7" Weight: 280 lb. Origin: International Free Agent, 2005

YEAR	TEAM	LVL	AGE	W	L	SV	G	GS	IP	H	HR	BB/9	K/9	K	GB%	BABIP	WHIP	ERA	DRA-	WARP	MPH	FB%	Whiff%	CSP
2019	MIN	MLB	30	11	5	0	26	26	146	141	23	1.7	8.6	140	35.1%	.294	1.16	4.01	102	1.4	92.6	55.5%	25.7%	49.5%
2020	MIN	MLB	31	2	0	0	5	5	26^2	25	0	2.4	8.4	25	37.2%	.321	1.20	3.38	95	0.4	92.3	50.1%	29.3%	47.1%
2021	MIN	MLB	32	9	8	0	22	21	109^1	114	17	1.7	7.2	88	39.5%	.297	1.23	3.62	110	0.4	90.8	54.1%	22.1%	56.8%
2022 DC	*FA*	*MLB*	*33*	*7*	*7*	*0*	*22*	*22*	*117.7*	*126*	*19*	*2.2*	*7.4*	*96*	*38.8%*	*.301*	*1.32*	*4.50*	*113*	*0.2*	*91.5*	*54.1%*	*23.9%*	*53.7%*

Comparables: Steve Trachsel, Jordan Zimmermann, Ben Sheets

Eleven years after he made his debut, Pineda has only reached the 30-start mark once. It's therefore no surprise that he was limited to two-thirds of a season, the chief culprits a barking elbow and a strained oblique. While the Twins are unlikely to have had any illusions about Pineda taking the ball every fifth day, they surely hoped he would slot in as a good-when-healthy three or four, and not a dozen innings shy of the team lead. When he did pitch, the former Yankee appeared immune to the general misfortune that befell the 2021 Twins, defying career-worsts in strikeout and swinging-strike rate, plus DRA, to record well above-average run prevention once again. Pineda's declining fastball, now barely sitting 90 mph, portends a much more rapid end to his time as a starter than his ERA might suggest. That second 30-start season is looking doubtful.

Taylor Rogers LHP Born: 12/17/90 Age: 31 Bats: L Throws: L Height: 6'3" Weight: 190 lb. Origin: Round 11, 2012 Draft (#340 overall)

YEAR	TEAM	LVL	AGE	W	L	SV	G	GS	IP	H	HR	BB/9	K/9	K	GB%	BABIP	WHIP	ERA	DRA-	WARP	MPH	FB%	Whiff%	CSP
2019	MIN	MLB	28	2	4	30	60	0	69	58	8	1.4	11.7	90	49.7%	.313	1.00	2.61	74	1.7	94.8	50.0%	26.3%	53.3%
2020	MIN	MLB	29	2	4	9	21	0	20	26	2	1.8	10.8	24	43.5%	.400	1.50	4.05	88	0.3	94.8	54.5%	23.6%	55.3%
2021	MIN	MLB	30	2	4	9	40	0	40^{1}	38	4	1.8	13.2	59	48.5%	.366	1.14	3.35	64	1.1	95.9	45.8%	29.6%	56.3%
2022 DC	*MIN*	*MLB*	*31*	*3*	*3*	*31*	*74*	*0*	*64.7*	*52*	*7*	*2.0*	*10.6*	*76*	*46.8%*	*.284*	*1.03*	*2.51*	*69*	*1.3*	*95.4*	*48.7%*	*27.5%*	*55.2%*

Comparables: Liam Hendriks, Justin Wilson, Ryan Pressly

If a blueprint for an outstanding relief season was created, it would look rather similar to Rogers' 2021. Over 35% of batters he faced fell to strikes, while for the third season running, less than 5% took free passes. When hitters did put the ball in play, it was much more likely to be a ground ball than anything else. Rogers turned to his slider more often than his sinker for the first time in his career, with no loss in efficacy, while the fastball gained another tick. The twin misfortunes of a poor strand rate and a high BABIP made Rogers' results look simply very good rather than elite. Make no mistake: he proved that he belongs in that latter club.

★ ★ ★ *2022 Top 101 Prospect* **#96** ★ ★ ★

Joe Ryan RHP Born: 06/05/96 Age: 26 Bats: R Throws: R Height: 6'2" Weight: 205 lb. Origin: Round 7, 2018 Draft (#210 overall)

YEAR	TEAM	LVL	AGE	W	L	SV	G	GS	IP	H	HR	BB/9	K/9	K	GB%	BABIP	WHIP	ERA	DRA-	WARP	MPH	FB%	Whiff%	CSP
2019	BG	A	23	2	2	0	6	6	27^{2}	19	2	3.6	15.3	47	28.6%	.315	1.08	2.93	91	0.3				
2019	CHA	A+	23	7	2	0	15	13	82^{2}	47	3	1.3	12.2	112	36.6%	.246	0.71	1.42	67	2.3				
2019	MTG	AA	23	0	0	0	3	3	13^{1}	11	2	2.7	16.2	24	23.1%	.375	1.13	3.38	78	0.2				
2021	STP	AAA	25	0	0	0	2	2	9	5	1	2.0	17.0	17	66.7%	.286	0.78	2.00	87	0.2				
2021	DUR	AAA	25	4	3	0	12	11	57	35	8	1.6	11.8	75	32.3%	.227	0.79	3.63	87	1.1				
2021	MIN	MLB	25	2	1	0	5	5	26^{2}	16	4	1.7	10.1	30	26.2%	.197	0.79	4.05	104	0.2	91.2	66.0%	23.4%	56.2%
2022 DC	*MIN*	*MLB*	*26*	*10*	*7*	*0*	*27*	*27*	*143*	*115*	*20*	*2.4*	*9.8*	*155*	*32.5%*	*.264*	*1.07*	*2.98*	*81*	*2.6*	*91.2*	*66.0%*	*23.4%*	*56.2%*

Comparables: Tyler Thornburg, Armando Galarraga, A.J. Griffin

Ryan came to the Twins as part of the Nelson Cruz trade. After representing the U.S. in the Summer Olympics, he immediately gave actual hope to a fanbase suffering through a wretched season of starting pitching. In just his second start, he took a perfect game into the seventh inning against a still playoff-striving Cleveland, relying on a fastball that, while lacking in monster velocity, he commands with ease.

Credit for that skill goes to...water polo? No, really. Ryan played the sport for a decade, and learning how to skip the ball over the water aided his experiments with grips and arm angles.

Already 25, Ryan is expected to be a key part of Minnesota's 2022 plans. Also, plus-plus hair/mustache combo.

Cody Stashak RHP Born: 06/04/94 Age: 28 Bats: R Throws: R Height: 6'2" Weight: 180 lb. Origin: Round 13, 2015 Draft (#380 overall)

YEAR	TEAM	LVL	AGE	W	L	SV	G	GS	IP	H	HR	BB/9	K/9	K	GB%	BABIP	WHIP	ERA	DRA-	WARP	MPH	FB%	Whiff%	CSP
2019	PNS	AA	25	2	3	4	19	0	28^{1}	28	4	1.6	12.7	40	27.4%	.353	1.16	4.76	69	0.6				
2019	ROC	AAA	25	5	0	0	14	2	25	17	1	1.4	12.2	34	40.7%	.276	0.84	1.44	71	0.7				
2019	MIN	MLB	25	0	1	0	18	1	25	29	3	0.4	9.0	25	24.7%	.351	1.20	3.24	112	0.1	91.7	54.0%	31.1%	57.5%
2020	MIN	MLB	26	1	0	0	11	0	15	11	2	1.8	10.2	17	37.8%	.257	0.93	3.00	93	0.2	92.1	55.1%	29.9%	43.9%
2021	MIN	MLB	27	0	0	0	15	0	15^{2}	16	2	5.7	14.9	26	23.7%	.389	1.66	6.89	81	0.3	90.8	45.5%	38.6%	52.1%
2022 DC	*MIN*	*MLB*	*28*	*3*	*2*	*0*	*59*	*0*	*51.7*	*43*	*7*	*2.7*	*12.0*	*69*	*30.4%*	*.297*	*1.14*	*3.38*	*87*	*0.5*	*91.3*	*49.7%*	*34.8%*	*51.1%*

Comparables: Steve Cishek, Ryan Pressly, Heath Bell

Stashak's devastating slider was in full working order over the first couple of months of 2021, making batters come up empty over half the time when they swung. The new version of Stashak was otherwise not improved, as he issued more than twice as many walks over that span as he had in his first 40 innings in the bigs. The Twins demoted him at the end of May for a "reset", which turned out to be of the Windows updates variety when an MRI revealed a disk issue. The problem kept Stashak shut down for the rest of the season, so it won't become clear whether things are working until he boots back up for 2022.

Caleb Thielbar LHP Born: 01/31/87 Age: 35 Bats: R Throws: L Height: 6'0" Weight: 205 lb. Origin: Round 18, 2009 Draft (#556 overall)

YEAR	TEAM	LVL	AGE	W	L	SV	G	GS	IP	H	HR	BB/9	K/9	K	GB%	BABIP	WHIP	ERA	DRA-	WARP	MPH	FB%	Whiff%	CSP
2019	TOL	AAA	32	2	1	4	50	0	76^{1}	74	7	1.9	10.8	92	38.1%	.345	1.18	3.30	79	1.8				
2020	MIN	MLB	33	2	1	0	17	0	20	14	0	4.1	9.9	22	27.5%	.275	1.15	2.25	104	0.2	90.1	54.4%	29.4%	51.4%
2021	MIN	MLB	34	7	0	0	59	0	64	55	8	2.8	10.8	77	30.7%	.303	1.17	3.23	92	0.9	91.5	49.0%	26.5%	59.0%
2022 DC	*MIN*	*MLB*	*35*	*3*	*3*	*4*	*74*	*0*	*64.7*	*56*	*9*	*2.7*	*9.7*	*69*	*32.8%*	*.279*	*1.17*	*3.43*	*90*	*0.6*	*91.2*	*50.0%*	*27.0%*	*57.6%*

Comparables: Tony Sipp, Jared Burton, Brad Brach

Thielbar's second stint with the Twins has gone better than just about anyone could have expected. Stepping into the smoking crater that was Minnesota's post-April bullpen, the veteran inherited the lefty setup role and did fine. If you remember all the way back to 2013, Thielbar also impressed in his first Twins season, hanging a stellar 1.76 ERA in 49 appearances before fading in 2014-15. While there's no guarantee that Thielbar will be as effective or even a part of the Minnesota bullpen in 2022, expect him to be a key piece of the 2029 Twins bullpen.

Josh Winder RHP Born: 10/11/96 Age: 25 Bats: R Throws: R Height: 6'5" Weight: 210 lb. Origin: Round 7, 2018 Draft (#214 overall)

YEAR	TEAM	LVL	AGE	W	L	SV	G	GS	IP	H	HR	BB/9	K/9	K	GB%	BABIP	WHIP	ERA	DRA-	WARP	MPH	FB%	Whiff%	CSP
2019	CR	A	22	7	2	0	21	21	125^2	93	10	2.1	8.5	118	35.8%	.252	0.98	2.65	95	1.3				
2021	WCH	AA	24	3	0	0	10	10	54^2	41	5	1.6	10.7	65	40.6%	.281	0.93	1.98	88	0.7				
2021	STP	AAA	24	1	0	0	4	4	17^1	14	4	1.6	7.8	15	32.7%	.222	0.98	4.67	111	0.1				
2022 DC	*MIN*	*MLB*	*25*	*0*	*0*	*0*	*3*	*3*	*14.3*	*14*	*2*	*2.9*	*8.7*	*14*	*36.3%*	*.301*	*1.33*	*4.39*	*109*	*0.0*				

Comparables: Craig Stammen, David Buchanan, Tyler Cloyd

The team's only representative in the Futures Game, Winder posted lofty numbers at Double-A Wichita, striking out 75 and walking 13 in 10 starts. This led to a promotion to Triple A, where he was noticeably less effective over four starts before getting shut down in early August with a "right shoulder impingement.". He didn't pitch again. The team called it a load management precaution, but it remains a disappointing end to what was a very promising 2021. Winder appeared on track for either a September call-up or contention for a 2022 rotation spot. As with too many of the Twins high-level pitching prospects, the best gauge for Winder's outlook is ¯_(ツ)_/¯.

Simeon Woods Richardson RHP Born: 09/27/00 Age: 21 Bats: R Throws: R Height: 6'3" Weight: 210 lb. Origin: Round 2, 2018 Draft (#48 overall)

YEAR	TEAM	LVL	AGE	W	L	SV	G	GS	IP	H	HR	BB/9	K/9	K	GB%	BABIP	WHIP	ERA	DRA-	WARP	MPH	FB%	Whiff%	CSP
2019	COL	A	18	3	8	0	20	20	78^1	78	5	2.0	11.1	97	49.5%	.358	1.21	4.25	80	1.5				
2019	DUN	A+	18	3	2	0	6	6	28^1	18	1	2.2	9.2	29	33.8%	.246	0.88	2.54	88	0.5				
2021	NH	AA	20	2	4	0	11	11	45^1	42	5	5.2	13.3	67	32.4%	.359	1.50	5.76	86	0.7				
2021	WCH	AA	20	1	1	0	4	3	8	6	0	9.0	11.2	10	38.1%	.316	1.75	6.75	101	0.0				
2022 non-DC	*MIN*	*MLB*	*21*	*2*	*2*	*0*	*57*	*0*	*50*	*45*	*7*	*4.9*	*10.4*	*57*	*38.0%*	*.298*	*1.45*	*4.64*	*109*	*0.0*				

Comparables: Luis Severino, Ian Anderson, José Berríos

The first name you think of when considering a mentor for a talented young pitching prospect is not Adam Dunn. In fact, he's likely in your bottom three along with, say, street magician David Blaine and former U.S. Senator Estes Kefauver. However, if the former MLB slugger has fallen off your radar since retirement, know that he coached Richardson at Houston's Marucci Elite and raved about Richardson's talent and work ethic to The Athletic's Dan Hayes: "We all knew talent-wise he was going to be one of the best dudes…but when he was playing the hardest and doing all the things scouts like to see, that's when you know you got something. Nothing bothers that kid." Richardson came to the Twins as part of the José Berríos trade and spent most of 2021 either pitching unevenly in Double-A or not pitching at all for the U.S. Olympic team in Tokyo. As with any top pitching prospect in this organization, the opportunity is there for Richardson to pitch his way into the Minnesota rotation as soon as he'd like.

Lineouts

Hitters

HITTER	POS	TEAM	LVL	AGE	PA	R	2B	3B	HR	RBI	BB	K	SB	CS	AVG/OBP/SLG	DRC+	BABIP	BRR	FRAA	WARP
Trey Cabbage	RF	CR	A+	24	161	21	10	1	9	33	16	50	4	0	.266/.342/.538	110	.341	-0.2	RF(22): -3.0, 1B(7): -0.6, LF(7): -0.5	0.3
	RF	WCH	AA	24	278	40	10	1	18	49	31	110	2	0	.262/.349/.533	88	.393	1.4	RF(31): -1.6, 1B(9): -0.3	0.3
Keoni Cavaco	SS	FTM	A	20	260	27	6	2	2	24	18	89	5	2	.233/.296/.301	68	.361	-0.9	SS(55): -4.7	-0.7
Jake Cave	OF	STP	AAA	28	36	6	1	0	1	5	5	10	0	1	.367/.472/.500	98	.526	-0.4	CF(5): 0.3	0.1
	OF	MIN	MLB	28	178	14	6	1	3	13	10	62	1	1	.189/.249/.293	56	.283	0.7	LF(37): -1.3, CF(29): -0.4, RF(11): 0.1	-0.4
Derek Fisher	OF	NAS	AAA	27	85	11	5	0	1	8	7	23	0	0	.205/.271/.308	83	.278	0.0	RF(18): -0.5, CF(4): 0.1, LF(2): 0.0	0.1
	OF	MIL	MLB	27	8	1	0	1	0	1	0	1	0	0	.250/.250/.500	86	.286	0.5	RF(2): -0.0, LF(1): -0.0	0.1
Kyle Garlick	OF	MIN	MLB	29	107	17	8	0	5	10	6	32	1	0	.232/.280/.465	90	.286	-0.2	RF(18): 4.9, LF(12): -0.2, CF(5): -0.3	0.7
Wander Javier	SS	CR	A+	22	411	48	15	10	12	53	25	141	1	3	.225/.280/.413	83	.320	-1.0	SS(86): 3.0	0.6
Gabriel Maciel	CF	CR	A+	22	265	26	7	2	2	21	25	50	17	3	.238/.311/.311	100	.290	1.8	CF(54): -7.3, RF(11): -0.6, LF(7): -0.9	0.2
Noah Miller	SS	TWI	ROK	18	96	11	3	1	2	14	9	26	1	1	.238/.316/.369		.316			
JT Riddle	SS	STP	AAA	29	350	42	13	2	7	40	23	62	3	3	.202/.269/.322	90	.227	0.3	SS(61): -1.3, 2B(16): -0.0, LF(9): -0.1	0.6
	SS	MIN	MLB	29	6	1	0	0	0	0	0	0	0	0	.333/.333/.333	98	.333	0.3	SS(3): -0.2	0.0
Alerick Soularie	2B/LF	TWI	ROK	21	25	3	1	0	1	3	4	6	0	0	.350/.480/.550		.462			
	2B/LF	FTM	A	21	125	21	3	1	2	12	19	31	9	1	.219/.344/.324	103	.292	-0.9	2B(18): 0.5, LF(9): -0.9	0.3
Spencer Steer	IF	CR	A+	23	208	37	7	1	10	24	35	32	4	4	.274/.409/.506	143	.283	2.5	2B(28): 0.9, SS(7): -0.4, 3B(5): -0.6	1.9
	IF	WCH	AA	23	280	45	11	2	14	42	20	73	4	0	.241/.304/.470	99	.274	0.6	3B(36): 2.4, 2B(18): 1.3, SS(8): -1.0	1.1
Curtis Terry	1B/DH	RR	AAA	24	411	58	24	2	22	75	29	94	3	1	.275/.349/.533	110	.311	-3.4	1B(73): -7.4	0.5
	1B/DH	TEX	MLB	24	48	3	2	0	0	1	2	15	0	0	.089/.146/.133	70	.133	0.4	1B(1): 0.3	0.0
Misael Urbina	OF	FTM	A	19	439	50	12	4	5	52	54	82	16	6	.191/.299/.286	95	.224	-1.9	LF(47): -2.3, CF(45): -1.8, RF(1): -0.2	0.7
Matt Wallner	RF	SCO	WIN	23	79	11	2	0	6	15	9	27	0	0	.303/.405/.606		.412			
	RF	CR	A+	23	294	39	14	2	15	47	28	98	0	1	.264/.350/.508	103	.363	-1.2	RF(55): -7.1, LF(2): -0.2	0.2

Drafted by the Twins in 2014, 24-year-old outfielder **Trey Cabbage** spent all of 2021 in Double-A Wichita and Cedar Rapids, using the name Trey Cabbage. He is, undeniably, the best Trey Cabbage in baseball. The one-time fourth-round pick is rarely mentioned in the team's top prospect conversations, but he is absolutely still named Trey Cabbage. Very cabbage. The third cabbage. A heightened cabbage experience. Cabbage, Trey. Baseball Twitter would be a better place if he were in the majors playing every day. ⚾ The 13th-overall pick in the 2019 draft, **Keoni Cavaco** did nothing to dissuade those who thought the selection was a reach. The usual caveats apply (still incredibly young, no 2020 season, etc.), but the raw prospect spent most of 2021 at Low-A looking, well, raw. Scant power, high strikeouts and 20 fielding errors marked a disappointing campaign for the shortstop. ⚾ **Jake Cave** is not a Cave for Jakes. It's a common mistake, don't beat yourself up. Rather, he's an outfielder for the Minnesota Twins. Cave's 2021 was suboptimal, featuring both a dreadful slash line (.183/.247/.294) and a stint on the 60-day IL with a bad back. Not an ideal combo for a team that desperately needed a fourth outfielder. ⚾ The most positive light we can shine on **Derek Fisher's** descent from promising prospect to Quad-A fodder is that it's saved him from the wrath of boos that has befallen virtually every other member of the 2017 Houston Astros. ⚾ **Kyle Garlick** took his spot-on Brandon Guyer impression to Minnesota last summer, tuning up lefties at a .271/.302/.576 clip before sports hernia surgery in June ended the show. He should be healthy this spring and available for your wedding, bar mitzvah or the short side of your corner outfield platoon. ⚾ Paternostro's Third Law of Wanders states that for every Wander action, there is an equal and opposite Wander reaction. This explains Wander Franco's propulsion to superstardom in relation to **Wander Javier**'s fall from prospect grace after four years of injuries and out-making that have overshadowed his power and defensive chops. ⚾ While he continues to steal bases, speedy outfielder **Gabriel Maciel** has otherwise experienced the last couple of years in the same way as most of us: not going anywhere. Worse results in his second attempt at High-A led to the A's selecting him in the minor-league Rule 5 draft, so at least he'll play baseball somewhere else in 2022. ⚾ It was a big year for the Miller family. Unusually-polished high school shortstop **Noah Miller** watched older brother Owen made his big-league debut for Cleveland just over a month before the Twins made him their second selection in the draft. ⚾ What is full of holes but still holds water? It's either a sponge, or the idea that **JT Riddle** will still find a way to record some major-league playing time this season. ⚾ A broken foot prevented **Alerick Soularie** from making his pro debut before he turned 22. Even though he was old for the level, we can somewhat excuse the slow start at Low-A as a result, but it won't have done anything to convince those who thought his swing wouldn't work in the first place. ⚾ The Twins spent a third-round pick on **Spencer Steer** in 2019, hoping to turn the Oregon Duck into a power hitter. In 2021, Steer hit 24 home runs between High-A Cedar Rapids and Double-A Wichita. He hit 12 his entire collegiate career. For their next trick, the team should turn the actual Oregon Duck into a power hitter. Fortune favors the bold, Minnesota. ⚾ The wonderful thing about endpoints is that you can put them anywhere. Imagine a 13th-round pick, fighting his way past all the bonus babies, waiting patiently for a shot. And then, the call, and the feeling of stepping out on a major-league field, the address system calling out your name: "The first baseman, **Curtis Terry**." There. Endpoint. Nothing to see after that. ⚾ The good of **Misael Urbina's** 2021 at Single-A Fort Myers stint: 16 stolen bases, capitalizing on the speed the Twins expected when they signed him for $2.75 million as a 17-year-old. The bad: He just wasn't on base all that much. Not a lot of hits, more strikeouts than walks. The reminder: He's still 19. ⚾ **Matt Wallner** had a reputation for monster pop and the whiff rates to go with it. A two-month wrist injury did nothing to limit either, and he took just 79 plate appearances to add six Arizona Fall League bombs and 27 more strikeouts to his explosive regular-season numbers.

Pitchers

PITCHER	TEAM	LVL	AGE	W	L	SV	G	GS	IP	H	HR	BB/9	K/9	K	GB%	BABIP	WHIP	ERA	DRA-	WARP	MPH	FB%	WHF	CSP
Andrew Albers	STP	AAA	35	8	4	0	18	17	102	120	15	1.0	7.8	88	43.2%	.328	1.28	3.88	125	0.1				
	MIN	MLB	35	1	2	0	5	3	19	24	9	4.3	5.7	12	34.3%	.259	1.74	7.58	160	-0.4	88.5	63.8%	12.7%	57.3%
Kyle Barraclough	SWB	AAA	31	4	0	0	11	0	14	5	2	7.1	15.4	24	40.0%	.167	1.14	3.21	85	0.3				
	STP	AAA	31	4	1	0	21	0	25^{1}	15	4	3.6	13.5	38	37.3%	.244	0.99	2.49	78	0.6				
	MIN	MLB	31	2	0	0	10	0	13	12	4	5.5	12.5	18	28.1%	.286	1.54	5.54	101	0.1	93.2	52.2%	30.8%	53.4%
Matt Canterino	CR	A+	23	1	0	0	5	5	21	10	1	1.7	18.4	43	41.9%	.300	0.67	0.86	54	0.7				
Jharel Cotton	RR	AAA	29	4	0	0	24	2	42	32	3	3.6	12.2	57	42.0%	.299	1.17	3.00	72	0.9				
	TEX	MLB	29	2	0	0	23	0	30^{2}	28	2	4.4	8.8	30	30.0%	.295	1.40	3.52	113	0.1	93.5	46.2%	26.9%	54.6%
Jhoan Duran	STP	AAA	23	0	3	0	5	4	16	16	1	7.3	12.4	22	62.5%	.385	1.81	5.06	85	0.3				
Blayne Enlow	CR	A+	22	1	1	0	3	3	14^{2}	13	1	3.7	14.1	23	60.0%	.414	1.30	1.84	71	0.4				
Luke Farrell	STP	AAA	30	0	1	0	7	0	9	5	0	6.0	16.0	16	31.2%	.313	1.22	4.00	84	0.2				
	MIN	MLB	30	1	1	0	20	1	24^{2}	28	4	4.7	9.1	25	37.3%	.338	1.66	4.74	112	0.1	91.4	40.2%	29.0%	52.8%
John Gant	MIN	MLB	28	1	5	0	14	7	33^{2}	31	4	4.0	9.6	36	54.3%	.300	1.37	5.61	107	0.2	92.8	45.4%	26.4%	55.8%
	STL	MLB	28	4	6	0	25	14	76^{1}	64	6	6.6	6.6	56	44.3%	.265	1.57	3.42	129	-0.5	91.5	50.6%	23.2%	55.3%
Juan Minaya	STP	AAA	30	2	3	0	17	0	29	29	3	4.7	11.5	37	46.8%	.351	1.52	3.41	86	0.6				
	MIN	MLB	30	2	1	0	29	0	40	27	4	4.5	9.7	43	54.9%	.237	1.18	2.48	97	0.4	95.3	51.4%	26.0%	49.8%
Jovani Moran	WCH	AA	24	2	1	2	20	0	37^{2}	14	3	3.3	15.3	64	42.6%	.190	0.74	1.91	52	1.2				
	STP	AAA	24	2	1	1	15	0	29^{2}	14	3	5.5	13.7	45	46.4%	.212	1.08	3.03	74	0.8				
	MIN	MLB	24	0	0	0	5	0	8	9	0	7.9	11.2	10	42.9%	.429	2.00	7.87	109	0.0	92.7	52.5%	37.5%	47.9%
Cole Sands	WCH	AA	23	4	2	0	19	18	80^{1}	59	6	3.9	10.8	96	40.1%	.277	1.17	2.46	78	1.5				
Matt Shoemaker	STP	AAA	34	1	0	0	4	3	20	12	1	3.6	7.7	17	44.0%	.229	1.00	1.80	107	0.2				
	SAC	AAA	34	4	3	0	9	8	50^{1}	52	7	1.6	9.7	54	41.1%	.338	1.21	4.83	89	0.5				
	MIN	MLB	34	3	8	0	16	11	60^{1}	73	15	4.0	6.0	40	44.1%	.296	1.66	8.06	142	-0.8	91.8	41.0%	22.2%	51.6%
Devin Smeltzer	MIN	MLB	25	0	0	0	1	0	4^{2}	1	0	1.9	5.8	3	45.5%	.091	0.43	0.00	94	0.1	85.9	40.4%	25.9%	64.5%
Drew Strotman	STP	AAA	24	3	3	0	12	12	54	65	9	5.0	7.0	42	42.5%	.333	1.76	7.33	117	0.3				
	DUR	AAA	24	7	2	0	13	12	58^{1}	50	3	5.1	9.6	62	47.1%	.309	1.42	3.39	99	0.8				
Lewis Thorpe	STP	AAA	25	1	2	0	6	2	17	12	1	3.7	6.4	12	51.0%	.220	1.12	4.76	107	0.2				
	MIN	MLB	25	0	2	0	5	4	15^{1}	14	2	4.1	3.5	6	52.8%	.235	1.37	4.70	146	-0.2	89.2	46.2%	13.7%	58.8%
Louie Varland	FTM	A	23	4	2	0	10	8	47^{1}	41	2	3.0	14.5	76	45.7%	.379	1.20	2.09	82	1.0				
	CR	A+	23	6	2	0	10	10	55^{2}	41	4	2.3	10.7	66	37.4%	.276	0.99	2.10	87	0.9				
Nick Vincent	STP	AAA	34	3	1	6	24	0	31^{2}	28	8	2.0	10.8	38	39.8%	.253	1.11	4.55	84	0.7				
	RR	AAA	34	0	0	0	15	0	15^{1}	18	1	4.1	12.9	22	33.3%	.386	1.63	4.11	84	0.2				
	MIN	MLB	34	1	0	0	7	0	12^{2}	6	1	3.6	6.4	9	18.8%	.161	0.87	0.71	119	0.0	88.2	89.6%	25.0%	53.9%

Former Twin **Andrew Albers** pitched in the majors for the first time in four years. The Twins were in clear desperation mode, but still. He didn't have quite the renaissance fellow reclamation project Caleb Thielbar did, but he did pick up a win. It was one of the nicest stories in a 2021 sorely lacking in Minnesota nice. ⚾ Wild and woolly **Kyle Barraclough** hooked on with the Yankees and Twins last year and continued to rack up the whiffs, but walks and gopher balls still plague him; his career prospects are currently bottle-shaped with the words "Lightning Catcher" scrawled on the side. ⚾ **Matt Canterino** followed up a lost 2020 with a lost 2021, as elbow problems sidelined the top pitching prospect in May. A brief return in August was derailed by another flare-up. He also displayed why the Twins spent a second-round pick on the righty out of Rice in 2019: 45 strikeouts over 23 innings and a 0.78 ERA. ⚾ Not to freak anyone out about the possibility of living in a simulation, but **Jharel Cotton's** daughter went viral in August of 2021 at 19 months old when she tried, for the first time... cotton candy. Oh right, and her dad made it back to the big leagues for the first time since 2017. ⚾ **Jhoan Duran**, the team's top pitching prospect, tossed precisely 16 innings the entire season. The high point: topping 100 mph at Triple-A, unlike 99.9% of all the organization's hurlers since roughly the Reformation. The low point: the elbow strain that triggered speculation in some corners that he may eventually transition to the bullpen. ⚾ In his third start of the season at High-A, **Blayne Enlow** struck out 10, a step in the right direction for a prospect who needed to demonstrate he could miss bats. The positivity came to a screeching halt in his next bullpen session, when diminished velocity led to the discovery of a torn UCL. ⚾ Nomadic slider-slinger **Luke Farrell** was a bullpen asset in May and June, lost two months to an oblique strain and was lit up after he returned. The late-spring version can survive at the back of a big-league 'pen; the autumn version may need to fall back on that degree from Northwestern sooner than hoped. ⚾ Everything that went right for **John Gant** during his 2020 campaign—more strikeouts, fewer long balls and a heapin' helpin' of groundouts—went south on him last year. Gant will now tote his nightly game of Pitch Type Bingo to Japan, where his six-pitch mix should find success. ⚾ **Juan Minaya** must be wondering if there's *anything* he can do to make a major-league team keep him on their roster. Admittedly his peripherals weren't as impressive as his career-best run prevention numbers, but even DRA agreed he was a perfectly respectable major-league reliever. The kind, in fact, that you'd think a pitching-needy team like the Twins would want to hold on to. ⚾ **Jovani Moran** surged to a September bullpen role thanks to a dominant year in the minors, riding a superlative changeup and mid-90s fastball. That dominance did not withstand the lefty's first contact with major-league hitting, but his name is in the conversation for a bullpen role in 2022. ⚾ **Cole Sands** impressed at Double-A Wichita in 2021 despite losing a month to the injured list. The Florida State product has added a couple ticks of velocity and now consistently sits in the mid-90s. He now finds himself sitting comfortably in the tier of Twins starting pitcher prospects who, given the state of the rotation, soon might be ex-prospects. ⚾ Music review website Pitchfork once published an infamous pan of Australian rock band Jet's album *Shine On*. There were no actual words, just a video clip of a monkey urinating into its own mouth. This being in print, we can't borrow that conceit for a summation of **Matt Shoemaker's** 2021 performance with the Twins, but we can give it a 0.0. ⚾ **Devin Smeltzer**, acquired from the Dodgers for Brian Dozier and his plus-plus hair, spent most of the last two seasons banged up after a promising start in 2019. The Twins outrighted the lefty starter to Triple-A St. Paul in November. ⚾ It's not difficult to make the case that, of the prospects acquired in the Nelson Cruz trade, **Drew Strotman** has better raw stuff than Joe Ryan. Until Strotman starts throwing more strikes, it's much harder to make the case that he's a better option for the Twins rotation. ⚾ **Lewis Thorpe** was out of options and heading for his first season-long spell on the major-league roster...until an arbiter granted the Twins a fourth option. *Now* he's out of options, with two extended IL stints and a negative K-BB% on his resume. ⚾ You don't get a lot of Louies anymore, so that alone makes pulling for **Louie Varland** easy. A fantastic 2021 helps: The righty impressed at both Low- and High-A this year. If this begins a Louie renaissance among our nation's babies, all the better. Could use some more Bruces, too. ⚾ It took two bites of the cherry after the Rangers released him from a minor-league deal, but **Nick Vincent** signed a second minors pact with Minnesota and made it back to the bigs for the 10th straight year. Although he's throwing high-80s "heat" at this point, he also pitched 11 ⅔ scoreless innings in a row. Still got it.

A Sticky Situation

by Joan Niesen

It was chilly for June in Philadelphia the night Alfonso Márquez ran his hands through Max Scherzer's sweaty hair and found, ostensibly, perspiration and nothing else. I was sitting alone in a second-deck seat behind home plate at Citizens Bank Park, debating how many minutes a dinner of crab fries and a Bud Light had shaved off my life, when the game stood still. It was the second day of Major League Baseball's so-called sticky-stuff enforcement, the Nationals' first game under the crackdown, and their ace appeared none too pleased that the league had deputized umpires to do its investigative bidding.

Scherzer grimaced through his two mandated foreign-substance checks, but when Phillies manager Joe Girardi asked for another look-see in the bottom of the fourth inning, the three-time Cy Young Award winner flipped. His eyes wide, he threw his hands up and repeatedly told the umpires, "I've got nothing!" Having hurled his cap and glove to the infield grass, he stood by the side of the mound, unbuckled his belt and then bent forward toward the gaggle of men in black. That's when Márquez, discharging his esteemed duty as crew chief, combed through Scherzer's hair in search of something, anything illegal.

Whatever he found—or didn't find—was enough to convince him Scherzer was innocent of any gunky, goopy tampering. The game went on in mundane fashion. Its result, a 3–2 Nationals victory, was meaningless. In retrospect, all that's worth remembering of that Tuesday evening are Joe Girardi's stare and Scherzer's tantrum, the sense we all got that sticky-stuff enforcement was about to knock baseball sideways. Later that night, A's reliever Sergio Romo got even further into the pants-removing process than Scherzer had. And before the week was over, the league had issued its first sticky-stuff ejection and suspension, to Mariners lefty Héctor Santiago.

What nonsense, then, would happen next? It was entirely salacious and mostly stupid, the buzziest controversy in baseball since steroids. Within weeks, it had amounted to nearly nothing.

Yes, the dawn of mandated foreign-substance checks yielded lower spin rates, but on a magnitude of mere single-digit percentage drops for most pitchers. Batters began to strike out slightly less frequently. Before the crackdown, 23.9 percent of plate appearances ended in strikeouts; after, that number dropped to 22.6. All in all, good arms remained good, and bad bats remained bad. There was no conspiracy, no grand revelation of an insidious plot on the part of pitchers to shellac the ball to high heaven and ruin the game as we know it.

So, just as quickly as we all had raced to place Spider Tack orders on Amazon, we moved on. We stopped asking questions about pitcher injuries and the curious timing of MLB's decision to abide by its own laws. We stopped calling physicists and poring over Statcast data. Obsessed with extremes, we missed the point: that sticky stuff might be less of a spectacle and more of a sign. The game is changing, and we're too busy yelling to stop and ask why, or how, or if there might be something gained in considering what's next.

Think about it this way: Baseball has been evolving since, well, whenever it was invented. Dead ball, live ball, color barrier, lower mound, steroids, analytics. (How's this for mind-blowing: It has been barely 30 years since weightlifting stopped being totally taboo.) Whether because of skyrocketing salaries or the human compulsion to chase glory and excellence, players are always looking for the next way to innovate. That manifests in everything from personal trainers to Pilates to testosterone shots to supplements to analytics to, yes, sticky stuff. Legal, illegal, whatever; the culture around big-money sports is that of constant experimentation and searching for an elusive edge. Remember when Kobe Bryant flew to Germany for special platelet-rich-plasma injections in his knee in 2013? He did so because the treatment wasn't yet FDA-approved, and no one blinked an eye. Nearly a decade later, there's still no real medical consensus on the benefits of PRP therapy, but you'd better believe athletes are still getting it on the off chance that it works.

Sticky stuff? It isn't so different. For generations, pitchers mucked up the ball with whatever they had on hand—coffee, sunblock, a thumbtack—sometimes convincing themselves and others that they'd found the perfect solution. They professed, and maybe even believed, that all they were doing was trying to get a better grip on a ball that was too hard, too slick, too something. All they had to go on were feel and the eye test. Could they grip the ball more securely? Were they fooling more batters? If the answer was yes—or felt like yes, or looked like yes—then they were golden. They'd innovated. No one seemed to care when they bent, or even outright broke, the rules.

Or maybe they just weren't breaking the rules well enough for anyone to notice.

At some point, that changed. Pitchers started getting better feedback thanks to Statcast data and pitch design and winters spent tinkering. Improvement expanded into the realm of the quantitative. Just as smart teams used data to find underachieving players and turn them into All-Stars, some All-Stars felt a push to take the information at their fingertips and use it to improve in any way they could. If data-driven tweaks might translate to millions of dollars in an upcoming contract—or just save a job—of course players would take full advantage of the resources at their disposal. Give them spin-rate numbers, and they'd start figuring out how to maximize them.

During the peak of midsummer goop hysteria last year, I called Alan Nathan, a physicist who has studied baseball extensively. I wanted to know what he thought about sticky stuff and the sudden rush from willful ignorance to enforcement. Would MLB's crackdown solve the sport's offensive woes? Did the data provide any clues as to whether the majority of pitchers were blatantly cheating?

Nathan cautioned that he and everyone else was dealing with extremely limited information. There was no way to isolate when, or even if, foreign substance use became so pervasive it tipped the scales in pitchers' favor. But he did have one suspicion: Enforcement wouldn't radically change the trajectory of baseball's evolution. Nathan pointed out that spin rate tells only part of the story, and though sticky stuff undoubtedly helps hurlers add spin, anyone with even a rudimentary understanding of a pitcher's objective—fool more batters—would know he needed to do more than just add friction by smearing the ball with his tack of choice. You see, in order for spin to really count, it has to lead to movement, and pitchers across the game have been working in labs for years to design pitches and tinker with techniques that help them convert spin into unpredictable patterns of movement, into strikeouts and dropped jaws. Into magic tricks.

Which is all to say: Once MLB cracked down, Nathan believed pitchers might struggle in the short term due to the sudden change in their routines. But, he guessed they'd eventually recover; enforcement, he figured, wouldn't totally eradicate recent (and widespread) spin-rate gains, which are, at least in part, due to sophisticated pitch design. And so far, his hypotheses seem to be true. In an October analysis, BP's Robert Arthur found that spin rates had begun to tick back up in July after the precipitous, enforcement-related dropoff in May and June. After the crackdown, average spin rates were back to 2018 levels, which was enough to excite some casual observers. Most news outlets with any stake at all in covering the national pastime weighed in during the early weeks of the crackdown. At varying levels of breathlessness, they reported that spin was down, gosh, would you look at that! Many cited downright mind-bending drops in revolutions per minute, triple-digit differences from guys most suspected of doctoring!

Many also failed to calculate that a drop of, say, 102 rpm isn't so significant when guys are routinely throwing four-seam fastballs that register at 2,000-plus rpm as they dance toward the plate. Larger context—the sheer mention of pitch design, temperature and ballpark effects, variance in spin due to velocity fluctuations, what was happening to effective spin—was utterly absent.

And then, oddly enough, very few stories appeared after two months of enforcement, or three, or at season's end—perhaps because these mandated pitcher checks had accomplished something entirely reasonable. They tamped down on spin ever so slightly (Arthur's research showed that more than half of the net reduction from May 15 had returned), reduced strikeouts a bit and nudged on-base and slugging percentages a smidge toward normal. Concerned parties could breathe a sigh of relief that the latest instance of widespread cheating had been sniffed out and handled. Baseball was pure once more, pitchers' pants were squarely cinched around their waists, and everything could return to normal.

But normal is evolving faster than it ever has. For now, it seems, pitchers have an advantage. Their tricks are the newest, their toolboxes the best stocked. But who knows what we missed while we were all rubbing Spider Tack between our fingers. Was it an idea, an outlier on a spreadsheet, a hitch revealed on tape? A new medical treatment, an innovative therapy, a pioneering new exercise philosophy? It's all the same.

The forces changing baseball aren't hidden inside Max Scherzer's hat brim or smeared on Sergio Romo's belt. More than anything, they lie in people's sensibilities, our estimations of what's acceptable and what's taboo and where the murky line between those two designations falls. Smooth ball, sticky one. Rosin, Spider Tack. The summer of 2021 may have provided humor and debate, but it also nudged baseball forward. In November, commissioner Rob Manfred announced the league was tinkering with tackier balls, which might be ready to put in play this season.

It took a few months, but the game has once again caught up with the men playing it. ■

—Joan Niesen is an editor at The Athletic.

ARIZONA DIAMONDBACKS

Essay by David Roth

Player comments by Matt Sussman, John Trupin and BP staff

In the sprawling, derelict, bat-infested mansion of Baseball Wisdom there are many basements. Beneath the LOOGY catacombs and the cellar in which casks of high-test opinions about bunting are still being aged to proof, nearly a vertical half-mile below the concrete-lined containment chamber in which the belief that home runs are rally killers is stored, teams of men dig in 12-hour shifts to open space for a new and previously forbidden idea. It is already out there, although no one is quite comfortable saying it yet, but when this sub-basement bunker is ready, it will be the home to the objectively accursed but already extant take that winning a World Series is, when you really think about it, just about the least-efficient thing a team can do.

Right, yes, of course and for sure, winning a World Series is what every baseball team is supposed to try to do every year. It is the thing that justifies why teams bother playing the games, and that shared pursuit, when honorably met, is the thing that's supposed to keep every team honest and engaged. Every team but one will fail at winning the World Series in a given year, and, naturally, some will fail more rapidly and ridiculously than others. But all of that, broadly speaking, is how it's supposed to work; it's supposed to be hard and ruled by failure, because none of this would be interesting if it wasn't.

Major League Baseball's most urgent problem in recent years has had more to do with how many clubs are not really trying at all, or actively not-trying in ways that have created a mini-class of teams whose persistent and absolutely intentional unwillingness to compete is not so much a threat to the league's competitive balance as a living, real-time satire of the idea. Some of these teams are notionally or actually working their way through some kind of rebuilding or restructuring or wholesale organizational reimagining, all of which will either unfold along their own timelines or just kind of go on not-happening for as long as ownership permits. Still, given that the widespread adoption of this broader approach has ensured that something like a third of big-league teams are actively trying not to win, it's a problem.

The Orioles finished with the worst record in the American League in 2021, very much on purpose; their organizational plan for the future is plain to see, but given the effective

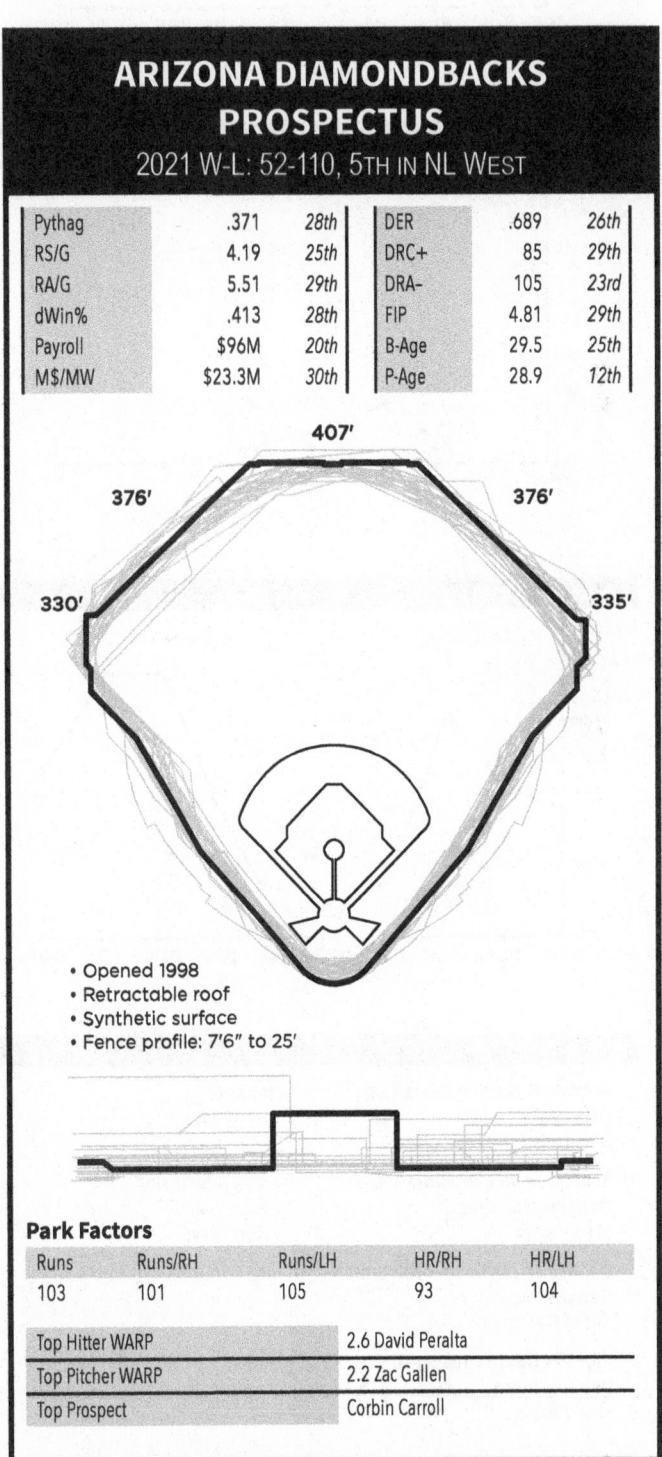

ARIZONA DIAMONDBACKS PROSPECTUS

2021 W-L: 52-110, 5TH IN NL WEST

Pythag	.371	28th	DER	.689	26th
RS/G	4.19	25th	DRC+	85	29th
RA/G	5.51	29th	DRA-	105	23rd
dWin%	.413	28th	FIP	4.81	29th
Payroll	$96M	20th	B-Age	29.5	25th
M$/MW	$23.3M	30th	P-Age	28.9	12th

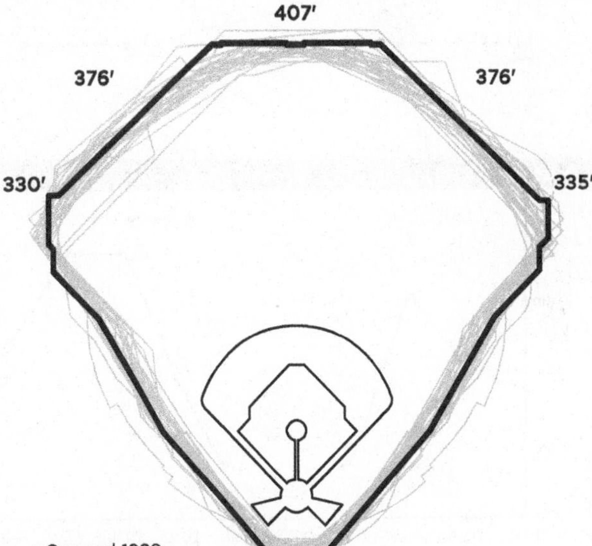

- Opened 1998
- Retractable roof
- Synthetic surface
- Fence profile: 7'6" to 25'

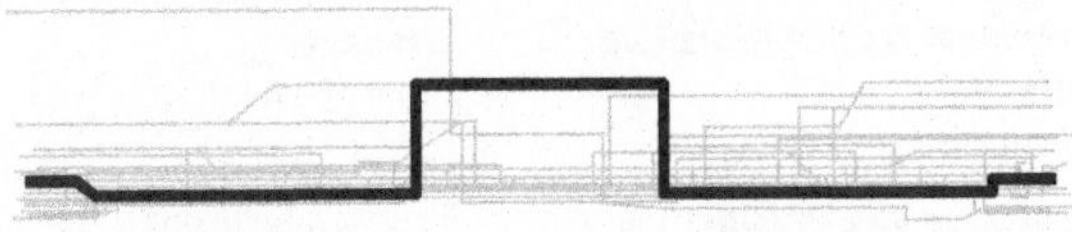

Park Factors

Runs	Runs/RH	Runs/LH	HR/RH	HR/LH
103	101	105	93	104

Top Hitter WARP	2.6 David Peralta
Top Pitcher WARP	2.2 Zac Gallen
Top Prospect	Corbin Carroll

Payroll History (in millions)

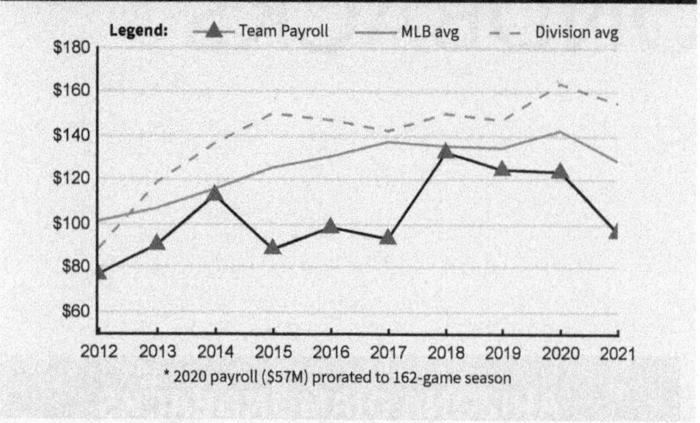

Future Commitments (in millions)

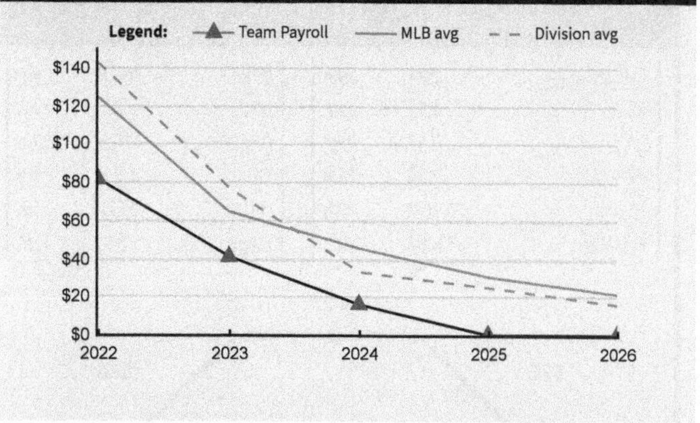

Farm System Ranking

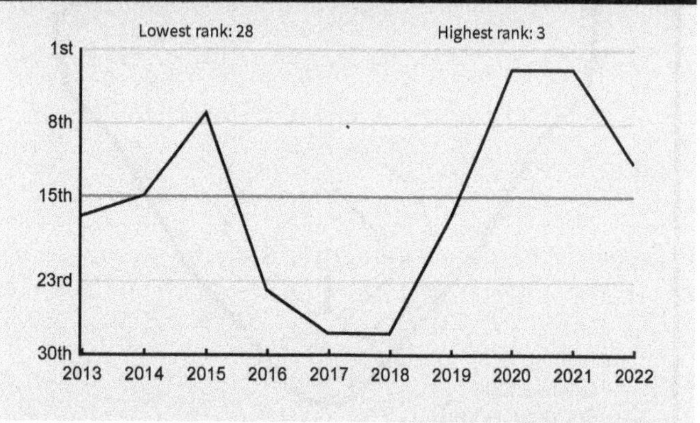

Personnel

President & Chief Executive Officer
Derrick Hall

Executive Vice President & General Manager
Mike Hazen

Sr. Vice President & Assistant General Manager
Amiel Sawdaye

Vice President, Research & Development
Mike Fitzgerald

Manager
Torey Lovullo

BP Alumni
Hudson Belinsky
Tucker Blair
Jason Parks

absence of any kind of plan to succeed or even improve in the present, it is all still very abstract. There are prospects percolating up through the system, and even a few promising young players on the big-league club, but, as they have continued not to try to fill in the many spaces between what they have and what they will need, there is really no way to say whether they are failing or succeeding as yet; it's unclear where they even are on the work of *trying*.

The team that finished with the worst record in the National League, an identical 52-110, was not on that same horizonless timeline, or aiming for the same sort of dispiriting near-term goal. If there is anything remarkable about the 2021 Diamondbacks, it is how much better they were at losing baseball games than the teams that were actively trying to do so.

The Diamondbacks weren't supposed to be anywhere near as bad as they were in 2021, a season in which they were actively and objectively as bad as a team that was trying to lose as many games as it could. The search for new bad ideas about The Worst Place To Be In Baseball will go on. Cases will be heard for those teams perpetually stuck in the middle, or willfully/cynically topped out around the lower third of the wild-card chase, or those stuck with stubborn, whimsical, deeply entrenched owners. But it is hard to imagine any of those arguments, however abstract or specific, outpacing the reality of the Diamondbacks heading into 2022. Here is a team that thought it might be passably good—not a playoff team, but not an embarrassment—and which had some decent reasons to believe as much, that wound up being brutally and even historically bad in a way that was not in any real sense a fluke. A bad team that tries to be bad is . . . bad, actually, at every competitive and spiritual and contextual level. A notionally competitive team that winds up in the same spot has found itself someplace notably worse.

Because of how bad they were over the rest of the 2021 season, it is worth noting that the Diamondbacks were more or less fine in April. Their truncated 2020 season had assumed a similar shape, with a decent start followed by an abject collapse down the stretch. The Diamondbacks had been pretty decent in 2019 and reliably competitive in the years before that; like most everyone else who approached 2020 with hopes of Getting Anything Productive Done, they were frustrated in this attempt. In last year's annual, Grant Brisbee built his essay on the team around the question of whether that gnarly not-quite-a-season was a hiccup or a sign of imminent collapse. In April, that question was still open. On April 25, Madison Bumgarner threw a seven-inning no-hitter to nail down the back end of a doubleheader sweep against the future World Series Champions in Atlanta. That got the team to 11-11. They would not win another game on the road until June 25.

Over that period, during which the team lost an MLB-record 24 straight road games, the Diamondbacks went 7-43. There was no obvious reason for this; there is nothing in the data that implicates Chipotle or the Starwood hotel group. The Diamondbacks simply finished April with a 14-12 record and then won exactly eight of their next 56 games over the ensuing two months. They won roughly half their games in July and were once again quite bad afterwards, but when a team loses 85 percent of its games over a couple of months, the rest is immaterial. The Diamondbacks were unlucky in 2021, albeit in the ways that a lot of teams were unlucky. Essential players were unavailable due to lingering injuries. Some potential 2020 breakouts revealed themselves to be short-season flukes. Nick Ahmed spent a lot of the season batting with one of those oversized, red wiffle-ball bats that makes a hollow *poomp* sound when it hits a ball, which was, in retrospect, an embarrassing oversight that someone should've caught. Everyone and everything was just kind of off and never really got back into the "on" setting. The team underperformed its Pythagorean win projection by nine wins, which seems significant until you consider what difference there is, really, between 110 losses and 101.

If you will pardon the jargon, the Diamondbacks just lost a lot of baseball games, and lost them in a way that seems custom-designed to outrage fans. Even as the team fell apart due to injuries to its most important players and the wholesale ineptitude of vital aspects of the roster, the daily lineups remained notably heavy on going-nowhere veterans. Even as veteran assets such as Eduardo Escobar were eventually moved in trades, there remained entirely too much late-career Asdrúbal Cabrera and end-stage Josh Reddick in the monitors for anyone's liking. In a more immediate sense, the bullpen's 5.08 ERA was tied with that of the Nationals for the National League's worst. No NL bullpen struck out fewer batters per nine or allowed more runs in the seventh inning, or the eighth inning, and only two were worse in the ninth. Every day, in every way, it was Not What You Want.

The team's decision to sign the veteran closer Mark Melancon to a reasonable two-year deal shortly before the lockout began is, in this context, both admirable and poignant. In one sense, this is the owner of a building that is currently on fire bringing in a high-priced contractor to install some splashy crown moldings. In another, it is a reflection of where the Diamondbacks see themselves being in 2022. "Coming off a 52-win season, making up 30 games on our win total is probably going to be somewhat challenging," general manager Mike Hazen told the media after the season's end. But Hazen also emphasized that, beyond a necessary overhaul of the bullpen, he did not see the need for the sort of long-horizon avant-garde rebuild that baseball's other 110-loss team will be pushing forward next year, and perhaps indefinitely. It is not the terminology that a GM would or probably should use, but the Diamondbacks are much more likely to be a normal-bad team in 2022 than the slow-motion dirigible accident they were in 2021.

This does not necessarily seem like something to celebrate, unless you cover up every word in this essay except the ones I'm about to italicize and also forget what happened with/to the team in 2021, but *there's a very real likelihood that the Diamondbacks could win 20 more games next season than they did last*. That looks pretty good on its own, but it is very much worth bearing in mind that it could be worse. In fact, it could be a lot worse. While most of the best prospects in what is, by every measure, a very good Arizona farm system are still a ways from the majors, there is still every reason to believe that players like Corbin Carroll and Jordan Lawlar could make a significant impact when they arrive in a few years. Alek Thomas, who was dominant at Double-A and Triple-A at the age of 21, should be in center field for the big club sometime in 2022. Add as many of those young players as baseball's merciless fortune allows to reach their potential to a still-intact, still-affordable core of Ketel Marte and Zac Gallen and Carson Kelly, and the Diamondbacks start to look a lot better than normal-bad. Given how far Carroll and Lawlar are from their first legally purchased beers, and given how hard every single aspect of putting together a winning team is, this might not happen for a while. It might not happen at all. But it could happen.

Or there is another way, which would be simply choosing not to try to make any of that happen. The gradual percolation of the team's top prospects through the various minor-league levels would continue as scheduled, but the Diamondbacks could also conclude that the 110-loss team they very recently were is actually the team they really are, decide that they couldn't really be that much worse without Marte and Gallen and Kelly, and concede by cashing those extremely valuable young stars in for even more scratch-and-win prospect tickets and a half-decade or so of top-five draft choices. That's a choice that losing teams make, and, in some cases, go on making for what feels like—and, in the context of a baseball fan's limited allocation of summers, actually is—a very long time.

But, given that it is a choice, there is also another decision to make. Just as there is a difference between losing 110 games on purpose and losing 110 games by accident, there is more than one way up. It's a stretch to say that the Diamondbacks will someday count themselves lucky to have been one of the worst teams in baseball; even the most ardent Daulton Varsho enthusiast or fervid Josh Rojas stan would struggle to find much to celebrate in the team's 2021 season. But unless the team decides otherwise, there's no real reason it has to happen again.

—David Roth is a co-owner at Defector.

Hitters

Nick Ahmed SS Born: 03/15/90 Age: 32 Bats: R Throws: R Height: 6'2" Weight: 201 lb. Origin: Round 2, 2011 Draft (#85 overall)

YEAR	TEAM	LVL	AGE	PA	R	2B	3B	HR	RBI	BB	K	SB	CS	Whiff%	AVG/OBP/SLG	DRC+	BABIP	BRR	FRAA	WARP
2019	ARI	MLB	29	625	79	33	6	19	82	52	113	8	2	21.3%	.254/.316/.437	99	.280	2.9	SS(158): 7.2	3.2
2020	ARI	MLB	30	217	29	10	1	5	29	18	46	4	0	27.6%	.266/.327/.402	96	.324	0.5	SS(57): -6.3	-0.1
2021	ARI	MLB	31	473	46	30	3	5	38	34	104	7	2	26.8%	.221/.280/.339	75	.279	0.6	SS(127): 1.1	0.4
2022 DC	*ARI*	*MLB*	*32*	*508*	*58*	*26*	*2*	*11*	*57*	*41*	*109*	*7*	*3*	*26.3%*	*.233/.301/.372*	*79*	*.283*	*0.1*	*SS 0*	*0.5*

Comparables: Rich Aurilia, Royce Clayton, J.J. Hardy

Much has been written about the duality of man. The duality of shortstop has also been well-documented, not so much by Robert Louis Stevenson as by sweaty bloggers. Ahmed jekylls on the field, saving runs at an elite level with the glove. His bat, however, hydes more often than not. He has two years left on the contract extension he signed when his home run totals were in the teens, but now those totals are closer to the toddlers, and that's no way to get plate appearances, kids. Defense isn't a skill that disappears quickly, so his duality should remain intact. And unlike Stevenson's flagship character, there's no internal struggle here. Ahmed is just really good at one thing and really bad at the other.

★ ★ ★ *2022 Top 101 Prospect* **#34** ★ ★ ★

Corbin Carroll OF Born: 08/21/00 Age: 21 Bats: L Throws: L Height: 5'10" Weight: 165 lb. Origin: Round 1, 2019 Draft (#16 overall)

YEAR	TEAM	LVL	AGE	PA	R	2B	3B	HR	RBI	BB	K	SB	CS	Whiff%	AVG/OBP/SLG	DRC+	BABIP	BRR	FRAA	WARP
2019	DIA	ROK	18	137	23	6	3	2	14	24	29	16	1		.288/.409/.450		.366			
2019	HIL	SS	18	49	13	3	4	0	6	5	12	2	0		.326/.408/.581		.452			
2021	HIL	A+	20	29	9	1	2	2	5	6	7	3	1		.435/.552/.913	113	.571	-0.4	CF(7): 0.7	0.2
2022 non-DC	*ARI*	*MLB*	*21*	*251*	*22*	*10*	*2*	*4*	*23*	*22*	*75*	*11*	*2*	*32.3%*	*.210/.288/.334*	*72*	*.295*	*1.1*	*CF 1, LF 0*	*0.2*

Comparables: Josh Hart, Austin Meadows, Jason Martin

On May 10th, 2021 the Arizona Diamondbacks won a 5-2 tilt with the Marlins, scrabbling back to 16-19 after a bad week spoiled a 14-12 April record. Up in Hillsboro, their top prospect clubbed a home run to further his Yuma-hot start to his season. At the moment of contact, Carroll's season and that of the Diamondbacks franchise as a whole reached their zeniths. Carroll separated his shoulder on the swing, and the ensuing surgery wiped out his 2021 just as the next three months would eviscerate the big-league club. Arizona suffered through a 10-68 stretch, lacking even the joy of glancing at minor-league box scores to see their Next Big Thing creeping closer. Carroll's ascendancy may indeed have been delayed, but deflated Snakes fans can look to the future with hope all the same. Carroll has the makings of a star.

Drew Ellis 3B Born: 12/01/95 Age: 26 Bats: R Throws: R Height: 6'3" Weight: 205 lb. Origin: Round 2, 2017 Draft (#44 overall)

YEAR	TEAM	LVL	AGE	PA	R	2B	3B	HR	RBI	BB	K	SB	CS	Whiff%	AVG/OBP/SLG	DRC+	BABIP	BRR	FRAA	WARP
2019	JXN	AA	23	451	57	23	0	14	63	63	109	0	3		.235/.344/.406	113	.287	0.5	3B(107): 7.5, 1B(6): 0.5	2.9
2021	RNO	AAA	25	358	69	29	3	20	73	46	87	1	0		.294/.399/.615	117	.344	1.2	3B(70): -2.2, 1B(6): 0.1, 2B(5): -0.9	1.7
2021	ARI	MLB	25	83	10	2	0	1	5	10	27	0	0	31.5%	.130/.277/.203	79	.195	-0.2	3B(17): -2.5, 2B(4): 0.0	-0.2
2022 DC	*ARI*	*MLB*	*26*	*155*	*18*	*8*	*0*	*4*	*18*	*15*	*43*	*0*	*0*	*28.1%*	*.207/.304/.373*	*81*	*.270*	*-0.2*	*3B 0*	*0.0*

Comparables: Chris Johnson, Chase Headley, Jedd Gyorko

For evidence of the gap between Triple-A and MLB in 2021, look no further than Ellis. Whereas he demolished Triple-A pitching and converted his patient approach into power and average, big-league arms feasted on Ellis' struggles to make contact in the zone. Ellis can boast that he overcame the odds by becoming a big-league third baseman by his third season, but he seems better suited for the chilly corner. Better contact can get Ellis to his power more often, and as a likely first baseman, maybe he can form a creaky platoon with fellow Reno-masher Seth Beer.

Jake Hager SS Born: 03/04/93 Age: 29 Bats: R Throws: R Height: 6'1" Weight: 170 lb. Origin: Round 1, 2011 Draft (#32 overall)

YEAR	TEAM	LVL	AGE	PA	R	2B	3B	HR	RBI	BB	K	SB	CS	Whiff%	AVG/OBP/SLG	DRC+	BABIP	BRR	FRAA	WARP
2019	SA	AAA	26	366	45	16	2	12	41	30	107	5	1		.242/.304/.413	73	.316	-0.3	1B(47): 2.6, SS(33): 0.1, 3B(16): 1.7	0.3
2021	NAS	AAA	28	80	13	7	0	2	9	8	15	1	0		.211/.288/.394	102	.236	0.5	SS(17): 0.9, CF(2): -0.2	0.4
2021	RNO	AAA	28	113	14	7	0	4	16	11	34	2	0		.220/.292/.410	82	.281	0.6	SS(24): 2.2, 2B(2): -0.3, 1B(1): 0.1	0.3
2021	TAC	AAA	28	112	16	7	0	6	11	11	25	4	0		.220/.304/.470	100	.232	0.6	SS(23): -0.0, 2B(4): -0.4	0.4
2021	SYR	AAA	28	39	6	2	0	3	9	2	5	0	0		.405/.436/.703	128	.414	0.1	2B(4): -0.5, SS(4): -0.3, LF(1): 0.2	0.2
2021	NYM	MLB	28	8	1	0	0	0	0	0	3	0	0	26.7%	.125/.125/.125	84	.200	0.3	LF(2): 0.0, RF(1): 0.1	0.1
2021	ARI	MLB	28	22	1	0	0	0	2	4	11	0	0	39.0%	.111/.273/.111	76	.286	0.1	2B(5): -0.3, SS(1): 0.1	0.0
2022 non-DC	*ARI*	*MLB*	*29*	*251*	*22*	*11*	*0*	*6*	*25*	*19*	*67*	*1*	*1*	*29.1%*	*.206/.273/.343*	*64*	*.264*	*-0.2*	*SS 1, 1B 1*	*-0.3*

Comparables: Rey Navarro, Carlos Rivero, Iván De Jesús Jr.

"Former first-round draft pick" is a label you can shed so long as you pick up better honorifics, such as World Series MVP George Springer, Rookie of the Year José Fernández and All-Stars Gerrit Cole, Francisco Lindor, Anthony Rendon, Javy Báez and Sonny Gray. But Hager is most certainly a former first-round draft pick. Last year he became the 31st of the 33 taken in the true first round of the 2011 draft to fulfill that childhood dream of reaching the majors. His scouting reports always touted an array of skills rather than any particular plus talent; those multitudinous efforts got him into nine major-league games for four different organizations, and he was still dropped from the Diamondbacks' 40-man before September ended. Levi Michael retired last spring and Kevin Matthews last played affiliated ball in 2017, so we can essentially close the book on 2011 non-supplemental first rounders making it.

Nick Heath CF
Born: 11/27/93 Age: 28 Bats: L Throws: L Height: 6'1" Weight: 190 lb. Origin: Round 16, 2016 Draft (#493 overall)

YEAR	TEAM	LVL	AGE	PA	R	2B	3B	HR	RBI	BB	K	SB	CS	Whiff%	AVG/OBP/SLG	DRC+	BABIP	BRR	FRAA	WARP
2019	LIC	WIN	25	123	18	4	2	1	9	15	37	16	1		.252/.336/.359		.362			
2019	NWA	AA	25	375	55	10	7	6	27	39	116	50	9		.255/.332/.382	84	.373	7.3	CF(62): -2.3, RF(9): -0.5, LF(2): 0.3	1.1
2019	OMA	AAA	25	97	17	4	1	2	9	17	27	10	4		.256/.392/.410	89	.360	-0.2	CF(19): 0.1	0.2
2020	KC	MLB	26	18	2	1	0	0	3	2	6	2	2	35.3%	.154/.313/.231	91	.286	-0.3	CF(6): -0.1, LF(1): 0.0	0.0
2021	RNO	AAA	27	229	36	9	5	5	28	25	77	19	5		.250/.341/.423	77	.373	-2.7	CF(28): 2.6, RF(13): -1.5, LF(12): 0.4	0.0
2021	ARI	MLB	27	39	3	1	0	0	1	4	15	0	2	35.6%	.143/.231/.171	67	.250	-0.7	CF(18): -2.0	-0.3
2022 non-DC	*ARI*	*MLB*	*28*	*251*	*20*	*8*	*1*	*3*	*19*	*23*	*92*	*16*	*5*	*34.7%*	*.191/.275/.287*	*53*	*.309*	*1.7*	*CF 1, RF 0*	*-0.4*

Comparables: Jonathan Davis, Tony Campana, Jarrod Dyson

Regional accents are a funny thing. In the Southwest they pronounce it "Nick Heath." In Cincinnati it sounds a bit more choppy, a bit of a "TJ Friedl," while in Minneapolis, the classic Midwestern flat vowels and the Canadian influence warp it to "Jake Cave." Wherever you may journey across this land, there's bound to be a Nick Heath there to greet you with a smile, minimal oomph at the plate, great speed and the kind of range in the outfield that would make Yasmany Tómas seem as though he'd been playing a different sport.

Carson Kelly C
Born: 07/14/94 Age: 27 Bats: R Throws: R Height: 6'2" Weight: 212 lb. Origin: Round 2, 2012 Draft (#86 overall)

YEAR	TEAM	LVL	AGE	PA	R	2B	3B	HR	RBI	BB	K	SB	CS	Whiff%	AVG/OBP/SLG	DRC+	BABIP	BRR	FRAA	WARP
2019	ARI	MLB	24	365	46	19	0	18	47	48	79	0	0	23.2%	.245/.348/.478	116	.271	-1.1	C(101): -2.4, 3B(1): -0.0	2.0
2020	ARI	MLB	25	129	11	5	0	5	19	6	29	0	0	26.8%	.221/.264/.385	93	.250	-0.7	C(38): 5.5, P(1): -0.0	0.8
2021	ARI	MLB	26	359	41	11	1	13	46	44	74	0	0	25.1%	.240/.343/.411	113	.270	-2.4	C(91): 2.1	2.1
2022 DC	*ARI*	*MLB*	*27*	*423*	*53*	*17*	*0*	*12*	*51*	*47*	*88*	*0*	*0*	*24.5%*	*.232/.329/.384*	*93*	*.274*	*-0.7*	*C 4*	*1.8*

Comparables: Salvador Perez, Wilson Ramos, Austin Hedges

YEAR	TEAM	P. COUNT	FRM RUNS	BLK RUNS	THRW RUNS	TOT RUNS
2019	ARI	13169	-1.2	0.6	0.4	-0.1
2020	ARI	4964	4.8	0.0	0.3	5.0
2021	ARI	11892	1.5	0.3	0.0	1.8
2022	*ARI*	*15632*	*2.8*	*0.6*	*0.0*	*3.4*

Johnny Carson was the king of late night and Kelly Ripa is the duly appointed monarch of morning television. Carson Kelly's 2021 brought to mind the bright burning of *The Colbert Report's* early episodes, as he bashed and slashed a .301/.437/.515 mark, at times resembling the league's top catcher. Then came June, during which he cooled off during the team's 17 straight losses (sweeps week) and broke his wrist in the 16th of those, putting him on hiatus for a month. The network execs are still going to give him an easy renewal because he's one of the most patient and selective hitters, and not just for a catcher. Backing up Yadier Molina for three seasons helped crystallize his talent, and any team would be happy to have him, but you know how spinoffs are.

★ ★ ★ *2022 Top 101 Prospect* **#48** ★ ★ ★

Jordan Lawlar SS
Born: 07/17/02 Age: 19 Bats: R Throws: R Height: 6'2" Weight: 190 lb. Origin: Round 1, 2021 Draft (#6 overall)

For the first time since 2017, the Diamondbacks had just one first-round pick at their disposal. They made it count, snagging Lawlar with a $6.713 million deal that eclipsed Dansby Swanson's franchise-record signing bonus. On draft day, rumors abounded that the teenager's asking price was astronomical, and his drop out of the top five picks gave credence to the notion that he was willing to head to Vanderbilt for college. Instead, Arizona was able to meet his mark, and in so doing acquired possibly the most talented player in the class. Lawlar's pro debut was shortened by an injury to his non-throwing shoulder that required surgery, but that's of little concern. Lawlar's blend of skills and polish make for an exciting compound of elevated floor and hard-to-see ceiling. He's a surefire shortstop with blazing speed and an exemplary swing, likely to be worth every penny over slot.

Jordan Luplow CF
Born: 09/26/93 Age: 28 Bats: R Throws: R Height: 6'1" Weight: 195 lb. Origin: Round 3, 2014 Draft (#100 overall)

YEAR	TEAM	LVL	AGE	PA	R	2B	3B	HR	RBI	BB	K	SB	CS	Whiff%	AVG/OBP/SLG	DRC+	BABIP	BRR	FRAA	WARP
2019	COL	AAA	25	57	12	3	0	2	7	10	14	2	1		.311/.456/.511	101	.414	-0.3	LF(10): 1.3, RF(2): -0.0	0.3
2019	CLE	MLB	25	261	42	15	1	15	38	33	61	3	2	26.6%	.276/.372/.551	118	.313	0.0	RF(42): 3.0, LF(34): 0.4, CF(4): 0.1	1.8
2020	CLE	MLB	26	92	8	5	1	2	8	12	19	0	1	19.9%	.192/.304/.359	99	.224	0.5	LF(21): -1.8, RF(9): 1.1	0.2
2021	DUR	AAA	27	27	2	1	0	0	2	5	6	0	1		.182/.333/.227	96	.250	-0.1	1B(5): -0.2, LF(1): -0.1	0.0
2021	COL	AAA	27	28	6	4	0	2	7	5	4	0	0		.261/.393/.696	123	.235	0.2	LF(5): -0.1, CF(1): 0.1, RF(1): 0.2	0.2
2021	CLE	MLB	27	121	12	5	0	7	20	21	31	0	2	29.4%	.173/.331/.439	119	.167	-1.0	CF(22): -1.7, RF(11): 0.4, LF(3): 1.5	0.7
2021	TB	MLB	27	72	11	3	0	4	8	7	26	1	0	33.3%	.246/.319/.477	85	.343	-0.4	1B(17): -1.4, LF(3): -0.6, 2B(1): -0.0	-0.2
2022 DC	*ARI*	*MLB*	*28*	*362*	*50*	*17*	*1*	*12*	*45*	*47*	*88*	*3*	*2*	*27.6%*	*.225/.337/.413*	*103*	*.275*	*-0.1*	*RF 1, LF 0*	*1.3*

Comparables: Aaron Altherr, Travis Buck, Andrew Stevenson

It was sort of a strange move for the Rays to pick up Luplow, a right-handed hitting outfielder, when they already had a few similar options on their own roster. As it turns out, Tampa Bay didn't acquire him to play outfield. They converted him to first base instead; a position he had never played before at the professional level. He proved to be an above-average hitter for Tampa Bay down the stretch—just not exactly how they'd planned, as he was actually better versus righties than lefties. He drew two starts in the ALDS including Game 2 in which he hit a grand slam off Chris Sale in the first inning. In true Rays' fashion, he was lifted before his second at-bat.

Ketel Marte CF Born: 10/12/93 Age: 28 Bats: S Throws: R Height: 6'1" Weight: 210 lb. Origin: International Free Agent, 2010

YEAR	TEAM	LVL	AGE	PA	R	2B	3B	HR	RBI	BB	K	SB	CS	Whiff%	AVG/OBP/SLG	DRC+	BABIP	BRR	FRAA	WARP
2019	ARI	MLB	25	628	97	36	9	32	92	53	86	10	2	17.7%	.329/.389/.592	138	.342	1.1	CF(96): -8.8, 2B(83): -3.1, SS(11): -0.7	4.5
2020	ARI	MLB	26	195	19	14	1	2	17	7	21	1	0	14.1%	.287/.323/.409	101	.311	-0.6	2B(41): 1.6, CF(3): -0.1, SS(2): -0.0	0.8
2021	ARI	MLB	27	374	52	29	1	14	50	31	60	2	0	17.3%	.318/.377/.532	124	.352	-0.1	CF(71): -8.6, 2B(20): -0.3	1.7
2022 DC	*ARI*	*MLB*	*28*	*600*	*90*	*34*	*4*	*16*	*74*	*47*	*85*	*5*	*2*	*17.2%*	*.280/.345/.449*	*111*	*.309*	*0.0*	*CF -2, 2B -1*	*2.8*

Comparables: Ryne Sandberg, Bobby Grich, Rod Carew

Hamstring injuries are far too commonplace these days. The Diamondbacks' outfield in particular was severely clipped due to backs of thighs doing too much work. Marte missed two months, which pretty much threw an ice pack into their plan of balancing Marte at second and center. While he's versatile and has the bat to star at either position, there is some concern the double duty led to the missed time. His defensive numbers were weak in center and he played a lot of second base to finish out the season, if that's any indication of where his future defensive home may lie. We may not see the Marte of 2019 again, but if he stays healthy odds are we're going to really like the 2022 version nonetheless.

David Peralta LF Born: 08/14/87 Age: 34 Bats: L Throws: L Height: 6'1" Weight: 210 lb. Origin: International Free Agent, 2005

YEAR	TEAM	LVL	AGE	PA	R	2B	3B	HR	RBI	BB	K	SB	CS	Whiff%	AVG/OBP/SLG	DRC+	BABIP	BRR	FRAA	WARP
2019	ARI	MLB	31	423	48	29	3	12	57	35	87	0	0	24.3%	.275/.343/.461	98	.327	-3.0	LF(93): 13.8	2.5
2020	ARI	MLB	32	218	19	10	1	5	34	13	45	1	0	21.1%	.300/.339/.433	90	.361	0.4	LF(45): 4.4	0.8
2021	ARI	MLB	33	538	57	30	8	8	63	46	92	2	1	21.2%	.259/.325/.402	91	.303	-0.4	LF(137): 12.1, P(1): -0.0	2.6
2022 DC	*ARI*	*MLB*	*34*	*545*	*70*	*27*	*4*	*14*	*75*	*46*	*95*	*3*	*2*	*21.7%*	*.270/.340/.430*	*103*	*.312*	*-0.1*	*LF 6*	*2.5*

Comparables: Lou Brock, Jose Cruz, Pete Rose

Perhaps this should be standard practice in baseball after the Cardinals converted Rick Ankiel to the outfield: if your pitcher can't throw strikes, just put them in batting practice before cutting them loose. The Cards didn't do this with the teenage Peralta in 2009, a year after Ankiel hit 25 homers for them. But his comeback story is well-documented: he toured the independent league as a power-hitting outfielder, the Diamondbacks liked what they saw, and he's spent eight years as a fixture in left field. He's continued to defy expectations, including ours: back in the 2016 annual, after Peralta led the league in triples with 10, we wrote that "he probably won't do that again." Well, guess what: he led the majors with eight triples, tied with Shohei Ohtani. And thanks to Peralta getting back to his roots and pitching a single inning, both league leaders in triples also had a pitching strikeout.

★ ★ ★ *2022 Top 101 Prospect* **#97** ★ ★ ★

Geraldo Perdomo SS Born: 10/22/99 Age: 22 Bats: S Throws: R Height: 6'2" Weight: 203 lb. Origin: International Free Agent, 2016

YEAR	TEAM	LVL	AGE	PA	R	2B	3B	HR	RBI	BB	K	SB	CS	Whiff%	AVG/OBP/SLG	DRC+	BABIP	BRR	FRAA	WARP
2019	SRR	WIN	19	97	17	3	1	1	5	13	21	2	3		.316/.417/.418		.407			
2019	KC	A	19	385	48	16	3	2	36	56	56	20	8		.268/.394/.357	124	.318	-1.7	SS(80): 1.8, 2B(11): -0.1	2.3
2019	VIS	A+	19	114	15	5	0	1	11	14	11	6	5		.301/.407/.387	131	.325	-0.3	SS(26): -1.2	0.5
2021	AMA	AA	21	344	51	8	5	6	32	47	81	8	5		.231/.351/.357	104	.299	0.3	SS(82): 1.6	1.4
2021	ARI	MLB	21	37	5	3	1	0	1	6	6	0	0	28.0%	.258/.378/.419	103	.320	-0.2	SS(10): 0.1	0.1
2022 DC	*ARI*	*MLB*	*22*	*90*	*9*	*3*	*0*	*0*	*8*	*10*	*18*	*2*	*2*	*22.4%*	*.223/.323/.326*	*78*	*.281*	*0.3*	*SS 0*	*0.1*

Comparables: Jonathan Villar, Richard Ureña, Luis Sardinas

In many ways, Perdomo's season transpired in reverse. Promoted ahead of the start of the minor-league season to fill in for an injured Nick Ahmed, Perdomo took his first big-league plate appearances before his first in Double-A. Mechanically, Perdomo spent much of the season in disarray, struggling unsurprisingly in the bigs and then more unsettlingly in Amarillo. Arizona slammed the big red button labeled "restricted list," successfully resetting Perdomo mechanically and mentally. A true shortstop whose gap power and speed should play for doubles and triples in Arizona's massive outfield, Perdomo should have a 2022 big-league audition more telling than 2021's premature promotion.

Henry Ramos OF Born: 04/15/92 Age: 30 Bats: S Throws: R Height: 6'0" Weight: 215 lb. Origin: Round 5, 2010 Draft (#173 overall)

YEAR	TEAM	LVL	AGE	PA	R	2B	3B	HR	RBI	BB	K	SB	CS	Whiff%	AVG/OBP/SLG	DRC+	BABIP	BRR	FRAA	WARP
2019	MAY	WIN	27	141	28	9	1	3	16	19	13	4	1		.314/.411/.479		.333			
2019	SAC	AAA	27	366	50	21	0	12	40	24	74	3	2		.269/.319/.439	89	.310	0.1	RF(59): 0.2, CF(9): -1.8, LF(7): -1.7	0.4
2020	MAY	WIN	28	74	9	5	0	1	6	13	8	0	0		.322/.438/.458		.353			
2021	RNO	AAA	29	294	62	16	1	12	57	29	48	4	5		.371/.439/.582	129	.415	-0.4	RF(36): 0.9, LF(20): -1.5	1.9
2021	ARI	MLB	29	55	5	2	0	1	8	4	12	0	0	23.2%	.200/.255/.300	93	.237	0.3	RF(8): 0.1, LF(5): -0.6	0.1
2022 non-DC	*ARI*	*MLB*	*30*	*251*	*24*	*10*	*0*	*5*	*25*	*18*	*49*	*1*	*1*	*24.6%*	*.249/.309/.375*	*84*	*.295*	*-0.2*	*RF 0, LF 0*	*0.1*

Comparables: Abraham Almonte, Rafael Ortega, Moisés Sierra

Eleven years. That's how long Ramos spent grinding in the minor leagues before receiving a big-league at-bat. He was drafted by the Red Sox in 2010, lasted with the org until 2017 before spending time with the Triple-A affiliates of the Dodgers, Giants and Diamondbacks. It was in the desert that luck and hard work combined forces to earn Ramos, who had an OPS over 1.000 at the time, a big-league call-up. He predictably struggled to produce in his 55 plate appearances, but he still left his mark: on September 15 in a one-run game against the Dodgers, who were still trailing San Francisco for the division, Ramos made an all-out leaping grab, crashing into the wall to rob Mookie Betts of extra bases, and Los Angeles of a chance to expand their lead. The 30-year-old finally, FINALLY achieved his dream of playing in the majors. With that in his back pocket, he's opting to spend the next year making some money by signing in Korea with the KT Wiz.

Josh Reddick RF Born: 02/19/87 Age: 35 Bats: L Throws: R Height: 6'2" Weight: 197 lb. Origin: Round 17, 2006 Draft (#523 overall)

YEAR	TEAM	LVL	AGE	PA	R	2B	3B	HR	RBI	BB	K	SB	CS	Whiff%	AVG/OBP/SLG	DRC+	BABIP	BRR	FRAA	WARP
2019	HOU	MLB	32	550	57	19	3	14	56	36	66	5	2	14.8%	.275/.319/.409	93	.288	-2.0	RF(119): 4.3, LF(29): -0.9, CF(9): -0.4	1.3
2020	HOU	MLB	33	210	22	11	1	4	23	20	42	1	0	22.7%	.245/.316/.378	84	.294	-1.2	RF(50): 0.4	0.1
2021	RNO	AAA	34	52	9	2	0	2	8	5	7	0	0		.304/.365/.478	112	.316	-0.1	RF(10): -1.4, LF(1): 0.4	0.1
2021	SYR	AAA	34	38	4	1	0	1	4	4	13	0	0		.182/.289/.303	86	.263	0.8	RF(6): -0.5, LF(2): 0.5, CF(1): 1.1	0.2
2021	ARI	MLB	34	158	15	11	0	2	21	6	31	0	0	21.0%	.258/.285/.371	79	.311	1.2	RF(36): 1.4, CF(4): -0.1, LF(1): 0.0	0.4
2022 non-DC	*ARI*	*MLB*	*35*	*251*	*24*	*10*	*0*	*6*	*26*	*19*	*47*	*2*	*1*	*21.4%*	*.250/.309/.380*	*85*	*.292*	*-0.2*	*RF 1, LF 0*	*0.3*

Comparables: Nick Markakis, Bobby Abreu, Johnny Callison

He's been a fan favorite in every outfield he's played, from Fenway to O.co to Minute Maid. Perhaps Reddick spent a month in the Diamondbacks outfield simply to break the trend. He didn't get an offer until after the season began, so he was already late to the party, but the desert dilapidated just about everybody who set foot in the Chase Field outfield. While this may smell like the end of his career, he will certainly get another opportunity the minute somebody, somewhere, successfully advances to third on a fly ball.

Kristian Robinson CF Born: 12/11/00 Age: 21 Bats: R Throws: R Height: 6'3" Weight: 190 lb. Origin: International Free Agent, 2017

YEAR	TEAM	LVL	AGE	PA	R	2B	3B	HR	RBI	BB	K	SB	CS	Whiff%	AVG/OBP/SLG	DRC+	BABIP	BRR	FRAA	WARP
2019	HIL	SS	18	189	29	10	1	9	35	23	47	14	3		.319/.407/.558		.398			
2019	KC	A	18	102	14	3	1	5	16	8	30	3	2		.217/.294/.435	97	.263	-0.2	CF(18): 0.5, RF(5): 0.3, LF(2): -0.3	0.3
2022															*No projection*					

Comparables: Miguel Aparicio, Victor Robles, Manuel Margot

Following the 2019 season, Robinson was one of the most promising prospects in the world, joining Julio Rodríguez, Riley Greene and Jarred Kelenic as a teenage standout combining top-tier tools with high-level performance against older competition. Two years later, while his contemporaries have continued their ascensions, Robinson's career is in flux. The Bahamian was arrested in April of 2020 on the charge of assaulting an officer and ultimately sentenced to 18 months of probation, and because of the charge, it is nigh-impossible for him to secure a long-term visa to serve his sentence. Acquiring a work visa to continue playing stateside with the Diamondbacks is also implausible. Until something shifts in his legal status, Robinson's career remains in stasis.

Josh Rojas UT Born: 06/30/94 Age: 28 Bats: L Throws: R Height: 6'1" Weight: 207 lb. Origin: Round 26, 2017 Draft (#781 overall)

YEAR	TEAM	LVL	AGE	PA	R	2B	3B	HR	RBI	BB	K	SB	CS	Whiff%	AVG/OBP/SLG	DRC+	BABIP	BRR	FRAA	WARP
2019	CC	AA	25	195	29	13	2	8	30	22	28	13	6		.322/.405/.561	144	.348	-0.1	2B(30): 0.5, 1B(12): 0.9, 3B(2): -0.2	1.9
2019	RNO	AAA	25	40	11	4	1	3	14	5	6	1	0		.514/.575/.943	123	.577	-0.4	SS(2): -0.3, LF(2): -0.0, RF(2): 0.1	0.2
2019	RR	AAA	25	244	49	16	3	12	39	30	36	19	4		.310/.402/.586	123	.325	2.8	2B(15): -1.5, SS(15): 1.0, LF(13): 0.9	1.9
2019	ARI	MLB	25	157	17	7	0	2	16	18	41	4	2	28.8%	.217/.312/.312	77	.295	-1.5	LF(33): 2.7, RF(6): 0.0, 2B(1): 0.0	0.2
2020	ARI	MLB	26	70	9	0	0	0	2	7	16	1	1	25.6%	.180/.257/.180	76	.234	0.9	2B(8): 0.0, SS(2): -0.3, LF(1): -0.1	0.1
2021	ARI	MLB	27	550	69	32	3	11	44	58	137	9	4	23.6%	.264/.341/.411	88	.345	1.2	2B(55): -3.2, SS(42): -2.6, RF(37): -2.0	0.4
2022 DC	*ARI*	*MLB*	*28*	*591*	*80*	*29*	*4*	*13*	*60*	*62*	*140*	*18*	*7*	*23.8%*	*.235/.321/.386*	*89*	*.299*	*1.5*	*2B -1, 3B 0*	*1.1*

Comparables: Ben Zobrist, Matt Carpenter, Brian Dozier

Rojas can play multiple positions, but technically anyone can do that. You can stick a hyena anywhere at the field and they'd wind up scavenging for food (successfully) and chasing down the ball (likely unsuccessfully, it's never been tested, and baseballs have historically been flavorless). Rojas was one of the poorest defenders in baseball by the numbers in 2020, but he started at six positions because that's what an NL team with a number of roster absences does with a player who can sort of hit. He's a tough out, he doesn't swing at many bad pitches, and he reaches base relatively well—the type of hitter a team likes to keep in their lineup. He seems to enjoy playing around the field—so, well, there's that.

Pavin Smith 1B Born: 02/06/96 Age: 26 Bats: L Throws: L Height: 6'2" Weight: 208 lb. Origin: Round 1, 2017 Draft (#7 overall)

YEAR	TEAM	LVL	AGE	PA	R	2B	3B	HR	RBI	BB	K	SB	CS	Whiff%	AVG/OBP/SLG	DRC+	BABIP	BRR	FRAA	WARP
2019	JXN	AA	23	507	62	29	6	12	67	59	61	2	1		.291/.370/.466	135	.310	-6.1	1B(79): 2.8, RF(28): -2.7, LF(13): 1.0	3.2
2020	ARI	MLB	24	44	7	0	1	1	4	5	8	1	0	23.8%	.270/.341/.405	95	.300	-0.8	1B(5): 0.1, LF(3): 0.2, RF(2): -0.6	0.0
2021	ARI	MLB	25	545	68	27	4	11	49	42	106	1	0	17.2%	.267/.328/.404	91	.319	-3.4	1B(54): 1.1, RF(53): 6.3, CF(39): -4.3	0.9
2022 DC	*ARI*	*MLB*	*26*	*329*	*40*	*15*	*2*	*8*	*41*	*27*	*52*	*0*	*1*	*17.6%*	*.253/.322/.404*	*93*	*.286*	*-0.2*	*RF 3, 1B 0*	*0.9*

Comparables: Lucas Duda, Yonder Alonso, Mark Trumbo

It's easy to picture a proud construction worker laying some cement on the highway and thinking to themselves, "Road worker? Naw, I'm a pavin' smith." Maybe this is why Smith the baseball player hits a large percentage of balls on the ground, the place where the vast majority of roads are located. The outfielder has a reputation for being a defensively-limited power bat, and given his rates of line drives and hard contact, you ought to pencil him in for at least double digit dingers per annum. But despite coming up as a first baseman, he can apparently play center field a little bit—that is to say, he knows where center field is located, and was asked to stand there for a few dozen games. But he should make some inroads with his power. After all, he's a Pavin Smith.

★ ★ ★ *2022 Top 101 Prospect* **#37** ★ ★ ★

Alek Thomas OF

Born: 04/28/00 Age: 22 Bats: L Throws: L Height: 5'11" Weight: 175 lb. Origin: Round 2, 2018 Draft (#63 overall)

YEAR	TEAM	LVL	AGE	PA	R	2B	3B	HR	RBI	BB	K	SB	CS	Whiff%	AVG/OBP/SLG	DRC+	BABIP	BRR	FRAA	WARP
2019	KC	A	19	402	63	21	7	8	48	43	72	11	6		.312/.393/.479	132	.372	0.3	CF(76): -10.6, LF(7): 0.0, RF(7): 0.9	1.7
2019	VIS	A+	19	104	13	2	0	2	7	9	33	4	5		.255/.327/.340	78	.373	0.0	CF(23): 2.4	0.3
2021	AMA	AA	21	329	54	18	8	10	41	37	65	8	5		.283/.374/.507	119	.335	-0.6	CF(45): -1.2, RF(18): 0.5, LF(10): -0.3	1.6
2021	RNO	AAA	21	166	32	11	4	8	18	15	34	5	4		.369/.434/.658	119	.439	0.4	CF(31): 4.1, LF(1): -0.0, RF(1): -0.1	1.4
2022 non-DC	*ARI*	*MLB*	*22*	*251*	*25*	*11*	*3*	*5*	*26*	*20*	*59*	*5*	*3*	*28.8%*	*.253/.322/.402*	*96*	*.320*	*0.6*	*CF 1, RF 0*	*1.0*

Comparables: Austin Meadows, David Dahl, Byron Buxton

Sure, his teammates may have laughed when he showed up in spring training wearing rubber-soled cleats, a tin-foil-lined cap and a silver Evil Eye necklace wreathed in garlic. But as tragedy, injury, underperformance and/or off-field issues waylaid every other major position player prospect in Arizona's system, Thomas side-stepped every ladder, turned his gaze from each black cat and clutched his four-leaf clover close to his chest. The undersized outfielder blistered line drives into the gaps of Amarillo and Reno's offense-friendly confines with aplomb, setting the stage for a 2022 debut, so long as he avoids shattering any mirrors.

Josh VanMeter 2B/3B

Born: 03/10/95 Age: 27 Bats: L Throws: R Height: 5'11" Weight: 194 lb. Origin: Round 5, 2013 Draft (#148 overall)

YEAR	TEAM	LVL	AGE	PA	R	2B	3B	HR	RBI	BB	K	SB	CS	Whiff%	AVG/OBP/SLG	DRC+	BABIP	BRR	FRAA	WARP
2019	LOU	AAA	24	211	43	14	1	14	43	24	37	8	3		.348/.429/.669	145	.371	-0.1	2B(22): -0.9, 1B(13): 0.7, 3B(10): -0.4	1.7
2019	CIN	MLB	24	260	33	13	1	8	23	29	56	9	3	22.3%	.237/.327/.408	93	.279	-0.8	LF(47): 2.5, 2B(18): -0.0, 1B(17): 0.4	0.9
2020	CIN	MLB	25	38	3	1	0	1	1	3	16	1	0	34.3%	.059/.158/.176	66	.059	0.4	2B(7): -0.9, 1B(3): -0.0	-0.1
2020	ARI	MLB	25	41	6	2	0	1	5	4	8	0	0	26.2%	.194/.293/.333	93	.222	-0.1	2B(10): -0.5, 3B(2): 0.1	0.1
2021	RNO	AAA	26	91	23	6	0	9	20	23	21	1	0		.388/.538/.881	135	.447	0.7	2B(8): 0.8, 3B(5): 0.2, LF(3): 1.9	1.0
2021	ARI	MLB	26	310	26	17	2	6	36	33	83	3	2	26.8%	.212/.297/.354	73	.278	-0.4	2B(52): 0.5, 3B(25): -0.5, 1B(1): -0.0	0.0
2022 DC	*ARI*	*MLB*	*27*	*431*	*58*	*21*	*2*	*14*	*53*	*49*	*105*	*6*	*3*	*25.8%*	*.226/.321/.412*	*93*	*.276*	*0.2*	*3B -1, 2B 0*	*0.8*

Comparables: Jeimer Candelario, Ehire Adrianza, Charlie Culberson

A diminutive utility player with no singular plus tool, VanMeter went to great lengths to improve his hitting last winter, but come mid-May he could only slash .159/.280/.261 and seemed miles away from being productive. He was sent down to Triple-A for a few weeks and homered once every 10 PAs, something even he likely couldn't have seen coming. That's no small feat, but it happened in a different league. He can play all around the yard and may ultimately inch toward a backup spot. For now, his surprising power streak looks more like an exception than an expectation.

Daulton Varsho C

Born: 07/02/96 Age: 26 Bats: L Throws: R Height: 5'10" Weight: 207 lb. Origin: Round 2, 2017 Draft (#68 overall)

YEAR	TEAM	LVL	AGE	PA	R	2B	3B	HR	RBI	BB	K	SB	CS	Whiff%	AVG/OBP/SLG	DRC+	BABIP	BRR	FRAA	WARP
2019	JXN	AA	22	452	85	25	4	18	58	42	63	21	5		.301/.378/.520	143	.317	6.0	C(76): 0.8, CF(4): -1.0	4.8
2020	ARI	MLB	23	115	16	5	2	3	9	12	33	3	1	30.6%	.188/.287/.366	80	.246	0.1	CF(14): 2.2, C(10): 0.0, LF(5): -0.1	0.3
2021	RNO	AAA	24	87	18	6	1	9	25	7	16	2	0		.313/.368/.750	126	.291	0.7	C(11): 0.3, CF(7): -0.3	0.7
2021	ARI	MLB	24	315	41	17	2	11	38	30	67	6	0	24.6%	.246/.318/.437	94	.286	2.6	C(41): -4.4, CF(30): 0.6, LF(12): 0.4	1.1
2022 DC	*ARI*	*MLB*	*25*	*423*	*57*	*20*	*3*	*16*	*60*	*38*	*91*	*11*	*3*	*24.4%*	*.254/.333/.455*	*105*	*.298*	*0.8*	*C -2, CF 1*	*1.9*

Comparables: Miguel Montero, Francisco Cervelli, Derek Norris

YEAR	TEAM	P. COUNT	FRM RUNS	BLK RUNS	THRW RUNS	TOT RUNS
2019	JXN	10397	-3.5	0.0	2.4	-1.1
2020	ARI	1060	0.0	0.0	0.1	0.1
2021	ARI	5309	-4.3	-0.1	-0.3	-4.6
2021	RNO	1782	0.6	0.0	0.4	0.9
2022	*ARI*	*7215*	*-2.3*	*-0.1*	*0.2*	*-2.2*

Varsho became the third player in the last 100 years—Eli Marrero and Craig Biggio, make room—to play at least 30 games at both catcher and center field in the same lunar orbit. It's a neat party trick, fielding two spots with diametrically conflicting amounts of range, and it's one managers dream of at night, usually after they dream of showing their lineup card to their third grade teacher in only their underwear. He doesn't need to settle into either specialty as he's a bit below-average defensively at both, but he also possesses enough power and speed that Arizona will likely want to keep his bat in the lineup every day. His diminutive size and nimble gait gave him the nickname "Little Wheels," but he's not to be confused with catcher Lance "Big Wheel" Parrish, who is not to be confused with Larry Parrish (no relation) or Darren "Dutch" Daulton (no relation) or Daulton's former teammate Gary Varsho (yes relation).

Christian Walker 1B

Born: 03/28/91 Age: 31 Bats: R Throws: R Height: 6'0" Weight: 208 lb. Origin: Round 4, 2012 Draft (#132 overall)

YEAR	TEAM	LVL	AGE	PA	R	2B	3B	HR	RBI	BB	K	SB	CS	Whiff%	AVG/OBP/SLG	DRC+	BABIP	BRR	FRAA	WARP
2019	ARI	MLB	28	603	86	26	1	29	73	67	155	8	1	28.7%	.259/.348/.476	110	.312	1.5	1B(142): 12.2	3.8
2020	ARI	MLB	29	243	35	18	1	7	34	19	50	1	1	27.1%	.271/.333/.459	101	.317	0.7	1B(43): 3.0	1.0
2021	ARI	MLB	30	445	55	23	1	10	46	38	106	0	0	27.4%	.244/.315/.382	92	.307	2.9	1B(107): 5.7	1.4
2022 DC	*ARI*	*MLB*	*31*	*438*	*59*	*21*	*1*	*17*	*67*	*39*	*101*	*2*	*1*	*27.3%*	*.251/.328/.441*	*104*	*.299*	*-0.4*	*1B 3*	*1.3*

Comparables: Justin Smoak, C.J. Cron, Jesús Aguilar

Bopping 29 homers is a lot for a rookie. Only 13 have matched Walker's total since 2000, and seven won Rookie of the Year. Yet Walker's ROY credentials in his first season went largely unnoticed. Nary a vote. There are some valid reasons: he had to contend with Pete Alonso, who smacked 53 taters, and also ran up against a superior divisional rival, Fernando Tatis, Jr.. He was a 28-year-old first baseman—you're supposed to hit home runs there, son—and made his debut five years prior. He didn't feel like a rookie. The bar for bashing is very high at his position, so he didn't quite meet it as a rook, and he certainly didn't measure up last year. He trended well at the end of 2021, so he could bounce back, but you never get a third chance to make a good second impression.

Andrew Young 2B Born: 05/10/94 Age: 28 Bats: R Throws: R Height: 6'0" Weight: 200 lb. Origin: Round 37, 2016 Draft (#1126 overall)

YEAR	TEAM	LVL	AGE	PA	R	2B	3B	HR	RBI	BB	K	SB	CS	Whiff%	AVG/OBP/SLG	DRC+	BABIP	BRR	FRAA	WARP
2019	JXN	AA	25	263	36	15	2	8	28	18	53	1	1		.260/.363/.453	122	.305	-0.6	2B(47): -2.8, SS(8): -1.2, 3B(6): 0.3	1.2
2019	RNO	AAA	25	277	53	10	3	21	53	24	68	2	2		.280/.373/.611	112	.305	0.7	SS(25): 1.0, 3B(23): -1.0, 2B(22): -1.0	1.5
2020	ARI	MLB	26	34	3	2	0	1	4	5	10	0	0	50.8%	.192/.382/.385	95	.267	0.0	2B(4): -0.1, 3B(3): -0.5, LF(1): -0.1	0.0
2021	RNO	AAA	27	224	43	20	2	11	41	20	78	2	0		.304/.388/.598	86	.449	2.9	2B(29): -2.9, 3B(9): -0.2, LF(6): 0.6	0.3
2021	ARI	MLB	27	104	13	7	0	6	15	6	45	0	0	44.5%	.209/.298/.484	77	.317	-0.3	2B(21): -2.3, 3B(2): -0.0, LF(1): -0.0	-0.2
2022 non-DC	*WAS*	*MLB*	*28*	*251*	*10*	*11*	*1*	*9*	*10*	*17*	*97*	*0*	*1*	*40.8%*	*.205/.299/.391*	*85*	*.314*	*-0.2*	*2B -1, 3B 0*	*0.2*

Comparables: Jack Mayfield, Brian Dozier, Steve Pearce

The modern MLB bench is mostly glove-first utility guys and a backup catcher that never gets playing time except in emergencies or when the manager feels bad. Young is the rare legitimate bench power bat. Three of his six homers came while he was pinch-hitting. Of course, there's a reason he's generally riding pine and not in the field every day: he had more strikeouts than total bases. That ratio isn't particularly rare, but it is an outlier for someone with an above-average OPS+. He's a marked improvement over a wide-eyed 24-year-old stepping in against a reliever chucking nuclear fastballs, but his upside remains modest.

PITCHERS

Madison Bumgarner LHP Born: 08/01/89 Age: 32 Bats: R Throws: L Height: 6'4" Weight: 257 lb. Origin: Round 1, 2007 Draft (#10 overall)

YEAR	TEAM	LVL	AGE	W	L	SV	G	GS	IP	H	HR	BB/9	K/9	K	GB%	BABIP	WHIP	ERA	DRA-	WARP	MPH	FB%	Whiff%	CSP
2019	SF	MLB	29	9	9	0	34	34	207^2	191	30	1.9	8.8	203	35.2%	.292	1.13	3.90	101	2.1	91.5	43.1%	24.7%	48.5%
2020	ARI	MLB	30	1	4	0	9	9	41^2	47	13	2.8	6.5	30	33.3%	.266	1.44	6.48	190	-1.6	88.4	39.9%	17.4%	47.7%
2021	DIA	ROK	31	0	0	0	2	2	6^2	14	0	2.7	8.1	6	53.6%	.500	2.40	8.10						
2021	ARI	MLB	31	7	10	0	26	26	146^1	134	24	2.4	7.6	124	33.0%	.267	1.18	4.67	113	0.3	90.4	36.5%	21.6%	56.7%
2022 DC	*ARI*	*MLB*	*32*	*10*	*9*	*0*	*29*	*29*	*157.3*	*155*	*26*	*2.4*	*7.4*	*129*	*34.4%*	*.286*	*1.26*	*4.39*	*106*	*0.7*	*90.5*	*38.8%*	*22.0%*	*53.3%*

Comparables: Claude Osteen, CC Sabathia, Milt Pappas

Bumgarner is nowhere near the caliber of pitcher he was when play-acting as the the second coming of Sandy Koufax in multiple World Series. There's a perfect explanation for that. He has one of the slowest fastballs among starting pitchers. He's also had us believe he once dated a girl named Madison Bumgarner. He competed in rodeos under an assumed name, and who knows what else. He hurled like a veteran when he was 24 and is seeing velocity and strikeouts evaporate before our very eyes at 31.

There's only one conclusion to draw here: Bumgarner is secretly 10 years older than we all think.

The 42-year-old Bumgarner was the 2014 World Series MVP because he was actually a veteran when he was in his 30s. He took up baseball at age 22 and switched birth certificates with a middle schooler in his hometown for 50 bucks and a BB gun. He wasn't able to watch any R-rated movies for a period of time, admittedly a minor design flaw in his grand plan, but the Giants were none the wiser as he debuted as a "teenager" for them. Now he's under contract with the Diamondbacks for three more years, going through a midlife crisis. He did toss a seven-inning no-hitter, which is tremendous for his age.

Zack Burdi RHP Born: 03/09/95 Age: 27 Bats: R Throws: R Height: 6'3" Weight: 210 lb. Origin: Round 1, 2016 Draft (#26 overall)

YEAR	TEAM	LVL	AGE	W	L	SV	G	GS	IP	H	HR	BB/9	K/9	K	GB%	BABIP	WHIP	ERA	DRA-	WARP	MPH	FB%	Whiff%	CSP
2019	KAN	A	24	1	1	0	3	0	3	4	0	3.0	18.0	6	28.6%	.571	1.67	9.00	97	0.0				
2019	BIR	AA	24	0	3	3	17	0	19^2	24	5	5.9	11.0	24	30.0%	.345	1.88	6.41	106	0.1				
2020	CHW	MLB	25	0	1	0	8	0	7^1	11	4	3.7	13.5	11	39.1%	.368	1.91	11.05	89	0.1	98.1	50.0%	40.5%	43.7%
2021	CLT	AAA	26	0	2	2	23	0	24^2	22	8	5.5	12.8	35	33.3%	.255	1.50	7.30	75	0.7				
2021	CHW	MLB	26	0	0	0	6	0	9	13	3	4.0	6.0	6	33.3%	.333	1.89	6.00	137	-0.1	95.8	49.7%	31.5%	53.8%
2021	BAL	MLB	26	0	0	0	1	0	1	0	0	9.0	9.0	1	0.0%	.000	1.00	0.00	124	0.0	96.6	66.7%	27.3%	52.6%
2022 DC	*ARI*	*MLB*	*27*	*2*	*2*	*0*	*44*	*0*	*38.7*	*36*	*6*	*4.8*	*11.0*	*47*	*36.9%*	*.314*	*1.48*	*5.17*	*117*	*-0.2*	*96.9*	*51.0%*	*34.6%*	*49.8%*

Comparables: Scott Feldman, Kam Mickolio, Mark Montgomery

It felt as though this should have been the satisfying culmination of the journey. Burdi had navigated the long, complicated road back from Tommy John surgery. He had returned to the majors with his blistering heat intact. Now he just needed a longer, healthy stint to let his stuff produce the long-awaited results. Losing two ticks off the fastball wasn't in that happy ending, nor was the mauling he received at the hands of hitters—not only those in the majors, but also Triple-A competition. The White Sox saw enough and cut him loose in mid-August; the Orioles did the same two months later. While the slider still looks the business at times, big-league hitters aren't impressed purely by 96-mph fastballs—Burdi's heater didn't even rank among the top 100 in average velocity. Teams will keep taking shots on stuff like this, which means he'll have more chances to write a happier final chapter.

Tyler Clippard RHP Born: 02/14/85 Age: 37 Bats: R Throws: R Height: 6'3" Weight: 200 lb. Origin: Round 9, 2003 Draft (#274 overall)

YEAR	TEAM	LVL	AGE	W	L	SV	G	GS	IP	H	HR	BB/9	K/9	K	GB%	BABIP	WHIP	ERA	DRA-	WARP	MPH	FB%	Whiff%	CSP
2019	CLE	MLB	34	1	0	0	53	3	62	38	8	2.2	9.3	64	31.0%	.207	0.85	2.90	98	0.7	90.0	41.1%	28.4%	47.6%
2020	MIN	MLB	35	2	1	0	26	2	26	19	2	1.4	9.0	26	29.4%	.258	0.88	2.77	107	0.2	89.3	38.0%	28.3%	46.1%
2021	ARI	MLB	36	1	1	6	26	0	25^1	22	3	3.9	7.5	21	25.0%	.264	1.30	3.20	120	0.0	89.0	43.2%	24.2%	55.5%
2022 DC	*FA*	*MLB*	*37*	*3*	*3*	*0*	*64*	*0*	*55.7*	*52*	*10*	*2.8*	*8.6*	*53*	*27.9%*	*.282*	*1.26*	*4.45*	*107*	*0.0*	*89.4*	*41.1%*	*26.6%*	*50.4%*

Comparables: Kyle Farnsworth, Brian Fuentes, Mark Eichhorn

Quietly (because he has no other volume), Clippard became second among active pitchers in appearances. Often a late-inning option, he missed the first half of 2021 to a shoulder strain, then assumed closing duties from Joakim Soria—the sort of geriatric passing of the torch more common in the United States Senate. Primarily retiring batters with a changeup-fastball tandem, Clippard is going to need to rely on the defense behind him to record more outs, because his strikeouts are starting to dip. He's entering the Todd Jones Zone of closers, with goggles instead of whiskers being his gimmick.

Zac Gallen RHP Born: 08/03/95 Age: 26 Bats: R Throws: R Height: 6'2" Weight: 189 lb. Origin: Round 3, 2016 Draft (#106 overall)

YEAR	TEAM	LVL	AGE	W	L	SV	G	GS	IP	H	HR	BB/9	K/9	K	GB%	BABIP	WHIP	ERA	DRA-	WARP	MPH	FB%	Whiff%	CSP
2019	NO	AAA	23	9	1	0	14	14	91^1	48	10	1.7	11.0	112	46.3%	.198	0.71	1.77	79	1.3				
2019	MIA	MLB	23	1	3	0	7	7	36^1	25	3	4.5	10.7	43	34.1%	.259	1.18	2.72	85	0.7	92.6	48.5%	28.5%	44.8%
2019	ARI	MLB	23	2	3	0	8	8	43^2	37	5	3.7	10.9	53	44.5%	.305	1.26	2.89	84	0.8	93.5	50.7%	30.2%	45.1%
2020	ARI	MLB	24	3	2	0	12	12	72	55	9	3.1	10.3	82	46.4%	.269	1.11	2.75	76	1.7	93.1	39.2%	30.4%	42.4%
2021	ARI	MLB	25	4	10	0	23	23	121^1	108	19	3.6	10.3	139	43.6%	.289	1.29	4.30	83	2.2	93.4	61.3%	23.6%	51.8%
2022 DC	*ARI*	*MLB*	*26*	*10*	*7*	*0*	*29*	*29*	*151.3*	*128*	*18*	*3.4*	*10.0*	*169*	*43.9%*	*.289*	*1.22*	*3.43*	*84*	*2.5*	*93.3*	*54.7%*	*25.9%*	*48.7%*

Comparables: Gerrit Cole, Cole Hamels, Ubaldo Jiménez

The keys to Gallen's success are going to be his cutter and his slider. It might be one pitch, it might be two pitches, or it may not be a pitch at all, when you really think about it, man. After a ninth-place Cy Young finish in the 2020 microseason, he took a step back in last year's full summer, in part because he lacked a feel for that cutter-slider. It didn't help that he also had three trips to the injured list lasting longer than two months combined, even though he managed to be third on the Diamondbacks in innings and first in strikeouts. This says a lot more about Arizona's calamitous season than Gallen's accomplishments, but he's still a pitcher to build a rotation around.

Tyler Gilbert LHP Born: 12/22/93 Age: 28 Bats: L Throws: L Height: 6'3" Weight: 223 lb. Origin: Round 6, 2015 Draft (#174 overall)

YEAR	TEAM	LVL	AGE	W	L	SV	G	GS	IP	H	HR	BB/9	K/9	K	GB%	BABIP	WHIP	ERA	DRA-	WARP	MPH	FB%	Whiff%	CSP
2019	LHV	AAA	25	2	4	2	36	0	47^2	39	4	2.6	8.7	46	40.2%	.278	1.11	2.83	91	0.8				
2021	RNO	AAA	27	5	2	0	11	10	52^1	46	4	3.3	8.6	50	38.5%	.292	1.24	3.44	99	0.2				
2021	ARI	MLB	27	2	2	0	9	6	40	28	4	2.9	5.6	25	39.8%	.212	1.03	3.15	112	0.1	87.9	86.0%	16.9%	57.9%
2022 DC	*ARI*	*MLB*	*28*	*7*	*7*	*0*	*24*	*24*	*111.7*	*115*	*15*	*3.1*	*6.8*	*84*	*39.0%*	*.297*	*1.39*	*4.67*	*111*	*0.2*	*87.9*	*86.0%*	*16.9%*	*57.9%*

Comparables: Chad Bettis, Jesse Hahn, Steven Brault

There were a number of events that torpedoed the 2021 Padres season. Among them was the historic no-hitter tossed by Gilbert, who had never been in this book before. He spent five years in the Phillies org before being traded to the Dodgers a month before the world ended in 2020. He worked for his dad's electrician company that summer, then was taken by Arizona in the Rule 5 minor-league draft last offseason. He faced just 14 major-league batters before his first start in August, when the only baserunner he allowed was Tommy Pham, three times, on three walks; he then finally retired Pham for Out 27. The last person to throw a no-no in his first MLB start was Bobo Holloman for the '53 Browns. Bobo Holloman has now been in this book as well.

Drey Jameson RHP Born: 08/17/97 Age: 24 Bats: R Throws: R Height: 6'0" Weight: 165 lb. Origin: Round 1, 2019 Draft (#34 overall)

YEAR	TEAM	LVL	AGE	W	L	SV	G	GS	IP	H	HR	BB/9	K/9	K	GB%	BABIP	WHIP	ERA	DRA-	WARP	MPH	FB%	Whiff%	CSP
2019	HIL	SS	21	0	0	0	8	8	11^2	14	1	6.9	9.3	12	41.7%	.371	1.97	6.17						
2021	HIL	A+	23	2	4	0	13	12	64^1	60	9	2.5	10.8	77	52.6%	.319	1.21	3.92	95	0.7				
2021	AMA	AA	23	3	2	0	8	8	46^1	38	6	3.5	13.2	68	38.5%	.327	1.21	4.08	79	0.8				
2022 non-DC	*ARI*	*MLB*	*24*	*2*	*2*	*0*	*57*	*0*	*50*	*47*	*7*	*3.8*	*9.0*	*50*	*43.9%*	*.293*	*1.36*	*4.39*	*105*	*0.0*				

Comparables: Michael King, Keegan Thompson, Scot Shields

The compact righty scorched hitters in both Hillsboro and Amarillo in 2021, improving his repertoire as the season went on. Jameson's early-season outings had plenty of sizzle but were more flank steak than ribeye. As the season progressed, however, things seemed to click. A running upper-90s fastball got ride-ier. The twin daggers of his slider and changeup suffered few, if any ill effects from the reshaping of his heater. Arizona has an impressive snake pit of pitching prospects, and Jameson is the king cobra.

Merrill Kelly RHP Born: 10/14/88 Age: 33 Bats: R Throws: R Height: 6'2" Weight: 202 lb. Origin: Round 8, 2010 Draft (#251 overall)

YEAR	TEAM	LVL	AGE	W	L	SV	G	GS	IP	H	HR	BB/9	K/9	K	GB%	BABIP	WHIP	ERA	DRA-	WARP	MPH	FB%	Whiff%	CSP
2019	ARI	MLB	30	13	14	0	32	32	183^1	184	29	2.8	7.8	158	41.9%	.294	1.31	4.42	101	1.8	91.5	65.4%	22.4%	49.8%
2020	ARI	MLB	31	3	2	0	5	5	31^1	26	5	1.4	8.3	29	45.6%	.247	0.99	2.59	87	0.6	91.5	65.5%	23.5%	51.3%
2021	ARI	MLB	32	7	11	0	27	27	158	163	21	2.3	7.4	130	43.3%	.305	1.29	4.44	97	1.7	91.6	65.2%	20.4%	55.6%
2022 DC	*ARI*	*MLB*	*33*	*8*	*8*	*0*	*25*	*25*	*139.7*	*145*	*20*	*2.5*	*6.9*	*106*	*43.3%*	*.297*	*1.31*	*4.29*	*105*	*0.8*	*91.5*	*65.3%*	*21.2%*	*53.7%*

Comparables: Jeff Samardzija, Aaron Harang, Bartolo Colon

Kelly was a backend starter with a great walk rate before his thoracic outlet surgery two summers ago and he was a backend starter with a great walk rate afterwards. But he declined to get vaccinated for COVID and caught the novel bug in August, missing a month and dodging questions on whether he changed his mind on the concept of vaccination. He returned from the illness less than sharp, in part because he didn't believe in something sharp. Hopefully the only things he's spreading from now on are several base hits across several innings as he amasses a modest ERA.

Joe Mantiply LHP Born: 03/01/91 Age: 31 Bats: R Throws: L Height: 6'4" Weight: 219 lb. Origin: Round 27, 2013 Draft (#816 overall)

YEAR	TEAM	LVL	AGE	W	L	SV	G	GS	IP	H	HR	BB/9	K/9	K	GB%	BABIP	WHIP	ERA	DRA-	WARP	MPH	FB%	Whiff%	CSP
2019	SWB	AAA	28	0	0	0	6	0	9^1	11	3	1.0	6.8	7	56.2%	.276	1.29	4.82	89	0.2				
2019	LOU	AAA	28	0	0	1	18	0	29	26	2	0.9	8.1	26	41.7%	.293	1.00	3.72	85	0.6				
2019	NYY	MLB	28	1	0	0	1	0	3	3	1	6.0	6.0	2	60.0%	.222	1.67	9.00	101	0.0	89.2	51.9%	14.3%	51.4%
2020	ARI	MLB	29	0	0	0	4	0	2^1	3	0	15.4	7.7	2	44.4%	.333	3.00	15.43	100	0.0	91.1	47.4%	26.1%	48.0%
2021	ARI	MLB	30	0	3	0	57	0	39^2	45	1	3.9	8.6	38	44.6%	.370	1.56	3.40	89	0.6	91.1	51.4%	28.1%	55.8%
2022 DC	*ARI*	*MLB*	*31*	*2*	*3*	*5*	*59*	*0*	*51.7*	*51*	*6*	*3.2*	*8.8*	*50*	*45.4%*	*.312*	*1.36*	*4.34*	*104*	*0.1*	*91.1*	*51.2%*	*27.7%*	*55.2%*

Comparables: Scott Alexander, Dan Otero, Jeff Beliveau

Not to stereotype, but people in their 20s are generally disliked for being bull-headed and arrogant, despite their contributions to society. Most of this angst comes from their elders, naturally, but those older people are the ones with fancy titles and access to rosters and lineup cards. Mantiply's third decade on this earth saw him yield 21 baserunners in eight big-league innings, so the slighting was justified. Once he turned 30, he became a trusted reliever, as if magic dust had landed on his driver's license. He relies on a sinker and curve, forcing outs through weak contact and groundborne swings. The lefty is a late bloomer of sorts, and despite the modern bullpen's tendency toward burly young flamethrowers, it still has room for those former kids who have had their comeuppance.

Corbin Martin RHP Born: 12/28/95 Age: 26 Bats: R Throws: R Height: 6'2" Weight: 225 lb. Origin: Round 2, 2017 Draft (#56 overall)

YEAR	TEAM	LVL	AGE	W	L	SV	G	GS	IP	H	HR	BB/9	K/9	K	GB%	BABIP	WHIP	ERA	DRA-	WARP	MPH	FB%	Whiff%	CSP
2019	RR	AAA	23	2	1	0	9	8	37^1	33	2	4.3	10.8	45	38.7%	.348	1.37	3.13	90	0.4				
2019	HOU	MLB	23	1	1	0	5	5	19^1	23	8	5.6	8.8	19	42.6%	.283	1.81	5.59	120	0.0	95.4	62.6%	23.8%	45.1%
2021	RNO	AAA	25	2	0	0	6	6	27^1	31	7	6.3	9.9	30	40.5%	.316	1.83	5.93	109	0.0				
2021	ARI	MLB	25	0	3	0	5	3	16	23	5	7.9	7.3	13	29.3%	.353	2.31	10.69	129	-0.1	94.1	63.7%	19.4%	55.5%
2022 DC	*ARI*	*MLB*	*26*	*4*	*3*	*0*	*33*	*4*	*47.7*	*48*	*7*	*5.4*	*8.1*	*43*	*38.8%*	*.302*	*1.61*	*5.59*	*123*	*-0.2*	*94.4*	*63.4%*	*20.5%*	*52.7%*

Comparables: Bryan Rekar, Jeanmar Gómez, Jeff Hoffman

No arm that throws a baseball is safe. The sooner you accept that fact, the sooner—well, nothing really changes, but you'll sure feel smart, and that's what matters. A torn UCL in June 2019 lined Martin up nicely for an early-2021 comeback tour. Instead, diminished velocity and spin rates portended repeated demotions and ultimately a mid-season shutdown with a forearm strain. Pre-injury, Martin seemed destined for a solid career of rotation work, with four average or better pitches and above-average velocity. Now he's beginning to look like a guy who folks always talk about "pre-injury."

Humberto Mejía RHP Born: 03/03/97 Age: 25 Bats: R Throws: R Height: 6'4" Weight: 244 lb. Origin: International Free Agent, 2013

YEAR	TEAM	LVL	AGE	W	L	SV	G	GS	IP	H	HR	BB/9	K/9	K	GB%	BABIP	WHIP	ERA	DRA-	WARP	MPH	FB%	Whiff%	CSP
2019	CLI	A	22	5	1	1	13	10	66^2	42	4	2.6	9.2	68	32.7%	.229	0.91	2.03	107	0.3				
2019	JUP	A+	22	0	1	0	5	4	23^2	15	2	1.9	8.0	21	43.8%	.210	0.85	2.28	100	0.3				
2020	MIA	MLB	23	0	2	0	3	3	10	13	3	5.4	9.9	11	29.0%	.357	1.90	5.40	115	0.0	93.1	52.2%	22.0%	47.1%
2021	AMA	AA	24	0	4	0	6	6	32	27	7	2.8	10.4	37	38.8%	.256	1.16	4.22	106	0.1				
2021	RNO	AAA	24	7	5	0	15	15	71^2	83	10	3.4	7.9	63	33.8%	.341	1.53	5.53	113	-0.3				
2021	ARI	MLB	24	0	3	0	5	5	22^1	32	5	3.6	8.1	20	30.3%	.386	1.84	7.25	112	0.1	92.2	63.2%	21.4%	53.9%
2022 DC	*ARI*	*MLB*	*25*	*0*	*1*	*0*	*3*	*3*	*13.3*	*14*	*2*	*3.5*	*7.7*	*11*	*33.4%*	*.302*	*1.44*	*5.17*	*120*	*0.0*	*92.4*	*60.5%*	*21.6%*	*52.3%*

Comparables: Josh Geer, David Buchanan, Taylor Clarke

Mejía found himself once again on the outskirts of a big-league roster willing to overlook warts like a below-average fastball and no particular history of missing bats. Between Reno and Phoenix, Mejía toiled in merciless heat and hitters' parks, watching his walk rate tick up. In a bullpen role, the burly righty could be a capable innings sponge, but he may get more rotation reps as Arizona attempts to recalibrate.

Mark Melancon RHP Born: 03/28/85 Age: 37 Bats: R Throws: R Height: 6'1" Weight: 215 lb. Origin: Round 9, 2006 Draft (#284 overall)

YEAR	TEAM	LVL	AGE	W	L	SV	G	GS	IP	H	HR	BB/9	K/9	K	GB%	BABIP	WHIP	ERA	DRA-	WARP	MPH	FB%	Whiff%	CSP
2019	SF	MLB	34	4	2	1	43	0	46^{1}	49	3	3.1	8.5	44	60.2%	.354	1.40	3.50	93	0.7	91.9	68.8%	24.8%	45.4%
2019	ATL	MLB	34	1	0	11	23	0	21	22	1	0.9	10.3	24	61.9%	.339	1.14	3.86	79	0.5	92.2	61.2%	27.9%	46.5%
2020	ATL	MLB	35	2	1	11	23	0	22^{2}	22	1	2.8	5.6	14	58.3%	.300	1.28	2.78	100	0.2	92.0	57.9%	19.6%	45.7%
2021	SD	MLB	36	4	3	39	64	0	64^{2}	54	4	3.5	8.2	59	56.7%	.284	1.22	2.23	92	0.9	92.1	65.3%	21.0%	54.5%
2022 DC	*ARI*	*MLB*	*37*	*3*	*3*	*0*	*67*	*0*	*58*	*60*	*6*	*3.2*	*7.6*	*49*	*54.9%*	*.311*	*1.39*	*4.21*	*102*	*0.2*	*92.0*	*64.6%*	*21.8%*	*51.4%*

Comparables: Chad Qualls, Guillermo Mota, Jason Frasor

In case you're unfamiliar, the word "cheugy" is a post-millennial neologism that broadly refers to now-ubiquitous things that are "cringe," which is probably how you describe things that are passé if you're a cheug. A non-exhaustive list of things that are cheugy: energy drinks, 90% of the stuff sold on Etsy, the word "adulting", Baby Yoda avatars and Mark Melancon. Not that these things are bad; the immutable closer led the league in saves and went to the All-Star Game, which in itself is impressively big cheug energy. Melancon is headed into his age-37 season with pedestrian strikeout and walk numbers; he is also, in a time when batters are more focused on lifting the ball than ever before, allowing an average launch angle of -.5 degrees. And he's doing it not with a wipeout slider/high-velo fastball, but with a cutter-curve combo that had its height of popularity along with Gangnam Style. Big Cheugus, we salute thee.

Matt Peacock RHP Born: 02/27/94 Age: 28 Bats: R Throws: R Height: 6'1" Weight: 185 lb. Origin: Round 23, 2017 Draft (#682 overall)

YEAR	TEAM	LVL	AGE	W	L	SV	G	GS	IP	H	HR	BB/9	K/9	K	GB%	BABIP	WHIP	ERA	DRA-	WARP	MPH	FB%	Whiff%	CSP
2019	JXN	AA	25	8	4	0	21	21	115^{1}	96	5	3.4	6.3	81	66.7%	.274	1.21	2.97	102	0.6				
2021	ARI	MLB	27	5	7	0	35	8	86^{1}	107	13	2.9	5.2	50	59.0%	.322	1.56	4.90	118	0.0	93.5	68.3%	17.9%	56.0%
2022 DC	*ARI*	*MLB*	*28*	*2*	*2*	*0*	*44*	*0*	*38.7*	*44*	*3*	*3.2*	*5.6*	*24*	*58.4%*	*.317*	*1.51*	*4.84*	*114*	*-0.1*	*93.5*	*68.3%*	*17.9%*	*56.0%*

Comparables: Christian Bergman, Zach Neal, Jared Fernandez

Every 23rd-round draft pick is a good story. Peacock gave up pitching in 2015 after suffering arm injuries at the University of South Alabama and worked at his uncle's sawmill. He gave it another go in 2017, found success and worked his way up while avoiding top prospect lists at every turn. He was promoted off the taxi squad in April after injuries felled Joakim Soria and Tyler Clippard, debuting in an 11th inning in Coors Field. He pitched three frames, gave up two unearned runs (both ghost runners) and also hit a ducksnort base hit on the first pitch he saw. The sinkerballer became the first MLB player since 1945 to get a hit and win an extra-inning game in their debut. In the meantime, the sawmill could use some help.

Sean Poppen RHP Born: 03/15/94 Age: 28 Bats: R Throws: R Height: 6'3" Weight: 210 lb. Origin: Round 19, 2016 Draft (#573 overall)

YEAR	TEAM	LVL	AGE	W	L	SV	G	GS	IP	H	HR	BB/9	K/9	K	GB%	BABIP	WHIP	ERA	DRA-	WARP	MPH	FB%	Whiff%	CSP
2019	PNS	AA	25	2	3	0	8	7	28^{2}	30	0	5.3	12.2	39	59.2%	.423	1.64	4.40	88	0.4				
2019	ROC	AAA	25	5	1	0	12	9	61	53	4	4.0	10.0	68	56.7%	.306	1.31	3.84	83	1.3				
2019	MIN	MLB	25	0	0	0	4	0	8^{1}	10	1	5.4	9.7	9	45.5%	.429	1.80	7.56	102	0.1	94.7	57.5%	25.9%	49.2%
2020	MIN	MLB	26	0	0	0	6	0	7^{2}	9	0	4.7	11.7	10	52.4%	.429	1.70	4.70	97	0.1	94.0	48.4%	30.8%	44.2%
2021	DUR	AAA	27	2	3	2	19	0	28^{1}	23	1	3.5	9.5	30	64.8%	.314	1.20	1.59	99	0.4				
2021	ARI	MLB	27	1	1	1	20	0	17^{1}	20	1	3.6	10.9	21	48.1%	.373	1.56	4.67	87	0.3	94.4	53.7%	24.6%	57.2%
2021	PIT	MLB	27	0	0	0	3	0	4^{2}	11	1	3.9	7.7	4	42.1%	.556	2.79	7.71	83	0.1	94.3	48.5%	27.3%	53.8%
2021	TB	MLB	27	0	0	0	1	0	0^{2}	0	0	0.0	13.5	1	100.0%	.000	0.00	0.00	97	0.0	93.5	63.6%	50.0%	35.8%
2022 DC	*ARI*	*MLB*	*28*	*2*	*3*	*0*	*59*	*0*	*51.7*	*48*	*5*	*3.8*	*9.3*	*53*	*51.2%*	*.307*	*1.37*	*4.16*	*99*	*0.2*	*94.3*	*52.3%*	*26.8%*	*53.1%*

Comparables: Mike Mayers, Tyler Duffey, Tyler Rogers

Major-league relievers usually need two things: a short memory and a large suitcase. Another acceptable answer is a fastball and a slider. Poppen owns everything mentioned here, as well as a Harvard diploma, and hurls sinking fastballs from a funky low arm slot. His strength is keeping the ball low to the ground after contact, and he did this for three different franchises. Two of those were the Rays and the Diamondbacks, which means he also needed a scuba suit to help prevent decompression sickness. See, the large suitcase is handy.

Noé Ramirez RHP Born: 12/22/89 Age: 32 Bats: R Throws: R Height: 6'3" Weight: 205 lb. Origin: Round 4, 2011 Draft (#142 overall)

YEAR	TEAM	LVL	AGE	W	L	SV	G	GS	IP	H	HR	BB/9	K/9	K	GB%	BABIP	WHIP	ERA	DRA-	WARP	MPH	FB%	Whiff%	CSP
2019	LAA	MLB	29	5	4	0	51	7	67^{2}	59	9	2.7	10.5	79	38.1%	.299	1.17	3.99	86	1.2	89.2	28.4%	31.0%	47.3%
2020	LAA	MLB	30	1	0	0	21	0	21	15	2	3.9	6.0	14	39.3%	.220	1.14	3.00	121	0.0	88.8	36.0%	25.3%	45.0%
2021	RNO	AAA	31	2	0	0	8	0	9	8	3	5.0	12.0	12	26.1%	.250	1.44	8.00	99	0.0				
2021	LAA	MLB	31	0	0	0	2	0	3^{1}	5	1	2.7	0.0	0	35.7%	.308	1.80	5.40	141	0.0	89.1	40.4%	9.1%	53.3%
2021	ARI	MLB	31	0	2	1	36	0	32^{2}	18	2	3.0	8.0	29	30.3%	.186	0.89	2.76	107	0.2	89.3	37.2%	25.6%	55.7%
2022 DC	*ARI*	*MLB*	*32*	*3*	*3*	*8*	*67*	*0*	*58*	*56*	*10*	*3.5*	*9.0*	*58*	*36.6%*	*.297*	*1.36*	*4.79*	*112*	*-0.1*	*89.2*	*34.3%*	*26.6%*	*50.9%*

Comparables: Ryan Cook, Evan Meek, Miguel Socolovich

A righty who struggles to hit 90 and relies on getting outs in the air can't be long for a bullpen role. There are standards. Ramirez didn't make the Reds out of spring training, and went back to the Angels for a brief time before becoming a free agent yet again. He latched onto the Diamondbacks because everybody these days is either latching onto the Diamondbacks or beating them at baseball games. His insanely low BABIP is not long for this world, and it should regress back to a level where Ramirez's expected number of teams he'll play for is two and a half. (The half-team? You guessed it: the Diamondbacks.)

Caleb Smith LHP Born: 07/28/91 Age: 30 Bats: R Throws: L Height: 6'0" Weight: 207 lb. Origin: Round 14, 2013 Draft (#434 overall)

YEAR	TEAM	LVL	AGE	W	L	SV	G	GS	IP	H	HR	BB/9	K/9	K	GB%	BABIP	WHIP	ERA	DRA-	WARP	MPH	FB%	Whiff%	CSP
2019	JAX	AA	27	0	0	0	2	2	9^{1}	7	4	1.9	18.3	19	25.0%	.250	0.96	5.79	65	0.2				
2019	MIA	MLB	27	10	11	0	28	28	153^{1}	128	33	3.5	9.9	168	26.0%	.252	1.23	4.52	109	0.8	91.6	53.7%	27.9%	46.6%
2020	ARI	MLB	28	0	0	0	4	3	11	5	2	4.9	9.8	12	33.3%	.120	1.00	2.45	133	-0.1	91.8	50.3%	31.8%	46.7%
2020	MIA	MLB	28	0	0	0	1	1	3	1	1	18.0	9.0	3	0.0%	.000	2.33	3.00	156	-0.1	92.7	54.3%	46.4%	36.3%
2021	ARI	MLB	29	4	9	0	45	13	113^{2}	93	20	5.0	9.8	124	27.5%	.256	1.37	4.83	102	0.9	91.5	48.1%	27.4%	54.4%
2022 DC	*ARI*	*MLB*	*30*	*10*	*4*	*0*	*77*	*3*	*74.3*	*67*	*13*	*4.5*	*10.3*	*85*	*28.7%*	*.291*	*1.41*	*4.88*	*112*	*0.0*	*91.5*	*49.9%*	*28.0%*	*51.6%*

Comparables: Adam Conley, Chris Rusin, Rich Hill

He's going to give up walks. He's going to give up home runs. Smith is the "other than that, Mrs. Lincoln" of starting pitchers, but for someone who misses the imaginary rectangle that much, he does a really good job at limiting hits and hard contact. Most of the struggle bugs happened during his 13 starts (6.95 ERA), and he looked much less implosive in his long relief vignettes. The stuff is there and he'll likely vie for another crack at pitching every five days, because all the green and red flags in his numbers resolve in a relatively effective thrower. Here's hoping he doesn't make a theatrical production out of it.

Riley Smith RHP Born: 01/15/95 Age: 27 Bats: R Throws: R Height: 6'1" Weight: 207 lb. Origin: Round 24, 2016 Draft (#719 overall)

YEAR	TEAM	LVL	AGE	W	L	SV	G	GS	IP	H	HR	BB/9	K/9	K	GB%	BABIP	WHIP	ERA	DRA-	WARP	MPH	FB%	Whiff%	CSP
2019	JXN	AA	24	4	4	0	13	13	71^{1}	65	4	2.0	7.8	62	48.6%	.298	1.14	2.27	87	0.9				
2019	RNO	AAA	24	2	2	0	12	12	62^{2}	85	15	2.9	6.9	48	41.7%	.352	1.68	6.89	112	-0.1				
2020	ARI	MLB	25	2	0	0	6	0	18^{1}	15	1	2.5	8.8	18	46.8%	.311	1.09	1.47	94	0.3	93.1	62.8%	13.9%	56.9%
2021	DIA	ROK	26	0	1	0	2	2	6	12	1	1.5	10.5	7	50.0%	.524	2.17	10.50						
2021	RNO	AAA	26	0	0	0	4	4	17	22	4	2.1	6.9	13	43.3%	.321	1.53	7.94	100	0.1				
2021	ARI	MLB	26	1	4	1	24	6	67^{1}	86	10	2.0	4.8	36	43.1%	.323	1.50	6.01	122	-0.2	93.0	57.9%	13.7%	58.0%
2022 non-DC	*ARI*	*MLB*	*27*	*2*	*3*	*0*	*57*	*0*	*50*	*57*	*7*	*2.6*	*5.0*	*27*	*44.0%*	*.303*	*1.43*	*4.99*	*119*	*-0.3*	*93.0*	*58.6%*	*13.7%*	*57.8%*

Comparables: Hector Noesí, Tim Melville, Alfredo Figaro

The Diamondbacks had the type of season that necessitated 41 different humans hurling at least one solitary white orb from the mound to home plate in a sanctioned plate appearance. Five of those were position players. The rest were very tired, and distinguished themselves in their own special ways. Smith was the only one to both start a game and record a save. He also had the worst K/9 rate and the best walk rate. He's the exact pitcher you want when you need innings out of somebody, the game is out of hand and you just want to get home as quickly as possible. Of the 41 pitchers on the 2021 Diamondbacks, he was the perfect one.

Edwin Uceta RHP Born: 01/09/98 Age: 24 Bats: R Throws: R Height: 6'0" Weight: 155 lb. Origin: International Free Agent, 2016

YEAR	TEAM	LVL	AGE	W	L	SV	G	GS	IP	H	HR	BB/9	K/9	K	GB%	BABIP	WHIP	ERA	DRA-	WARP	MPH	FB%	Whiff%	CSP
2019	RC	A+	21	4	0	0	10	10	50^{1}	47	6	2.9	11.6	65	34.6%	.328	1.25	2.15	87	0.5				
2019	TUL	AA	21	7	2	0	16	14	73	62	5	4.1	9.4	76	40.9%	.311	1.30	3.21	90	0.6				
2021	EST	WIN	23	3	2	0	6	6	32	15	1	1.4	7.3	26	32.1%	.171	0.63	2.25						
2021	OKC	AAA	23	2	3	0	10	3	28^{2}	27	4	4.1	11.9	38	44.0%	.324	1.40	4.71	82	0.4				
2021	LAD	MLB	23	0	3	0	14	1	20^{1}	19	3	5.3	11.1	25	30.9%	.320	1.52	6.64	102	0.2	92.8	44.6%	28.3%	54.1%
2022 non-DC	*ARI*	*MLB*	*24*	*2*	*2*	*0*	*57*	*0*	*50*	*45*	*8*	*4.5*	*10.1*	*56*	*37.3%*	*.297*	*1.42*	*4.69*	*109*	*-0.1*	*92.8*	*44.6%*	*28.3%*	*54.1%*

Comparables: Ryan Webb, Jeurys Familia, Cam Bedrosian

The Dodgers had a few pitching prospects make their MLB debuts this season and, well, Uceta was one of them. He pitched in mostly low-leverage situations, and he thrived in such situations (.184/.300/.245). The problem is, he got absolutely tattooed in medium- and high-leverage situations—..385/.433/.731. It was just 26 plate appearances, but it was enough for the Dodgers to expose him to waivers when they needed a 40-man roster spot in the NLCS. The Diamondbacks—perhaps not knowing what they were getting into because, well, they're the Diamondbacks—took a flier on him.

Luke Weaver RHP Born: 08/21/93 Age: 28 Bats: R Throws: R Height: 6'2" Weight: 183 lb. Origin: Round 1, 2014 Draft (#27 overall)

YEAR	TEAM	LVL	AGE	W	L	SV	G	GS	IP	H	HR	BB/9	K/9	K	GB%	BABIP	WHIP	ERA	DRA-	WARP	MPH	FB%	Whiff%	CSP
2019	ARI	MLB	25	4	3	0	12	12	64^{1}	55	6	2.0	9.7	69	40.8%	.292	1.07	2.94	85	1.2	94.0	51.9%	26.0%	47.4%
2020	ARI	MLB	26	1	9	0	12	12	52	63	10	3.1	9.5	55	32.7%	.349	1.56	6.58	120	0.0	94.0	54.0%	24.9%	48.5%
2021	RNO	AAA	27	0	0	0	2	2	7	6	0	5.1	15.4	12	33.3%	.400	1.43	3.86	84	0.1				
2021	ARI	MLB	27	3	6	0	13	13	65^{2}	58	11	2.7	8.5	62	37.5%	.266	1.19	4.25	96	0.7	93.7	61.9%	23.8%	55.1%
2022 DC	*ARI*	*MLB*	*28*	*8*	*7*	*0*	*25*	*25*	*129.3*	*120*	*18*	*2.9*	*8.8*	*126*	*38.1%*	*.293*	*1.24*	*3.82*	*94*	*1.5*	*93.8*	*57.8%*	*24.5%*	*51.8%*

Comparables: Francisco Liriano, Johnny Cueto, Gavin Floyd

Okay, *this* is the year Weaver breaks out, Take 4 [clapperboard shuts]. After being the marquee name to emigrate in the Paul Goldschmidt trade, Weaver spent most of 2019 and 2021 on the injured list—first thanks to his pitching elbow, then his pitching shoulder. Mechanics were never an issue for him; if anything, they were considered repeatable and low-risk. Sports medicine is miles ahead of the 90s; heck, Daniel freakin' Hudson is still pitching. Still, maybe Weaver is just not meant to toss more than 150 innings a season, and the lack of a third pitch may keep him from that threshold anyway.

J.B. Wendelken RHP

Born: 03/24/93 Age: 29 Bats: R Throws: R Height: 6'1" Weight: 242 lb. Origin: Round 13, 2012 Draft (#421 overall)

YEAR	TEAM	LVL	AGE	W	L	SV	G	GS	IP	H	HR	BB/9	K/9	K	GB%	BABIP	WHIP	ERA	DRA-	WARP	MPH	FB%	Whiff%	CSP
2019	LV	AAA	26	6	3	3	30	1	38^2	47	8	4.4	10.0	43	46.1%	.364	1.71	5.59	86	0.6				
2019	OAK	MLB	26	3	1	0	27	0	32^2	21	2	2.5	9.4	34	36.0%	.229	0.92	3.58	97	0.4	94.8	60.8%	27.0%	49.7%
2020	OAK	MLB	27	1	1	0	21	0	25	17	2	4.0	11.2	31	46.0%	.246	1.12	1.80	78	0.6	94.6	58.1%	26.8%	47.9%
2021	LV	AAA	28	0	0	0	4	0	5	2	1	3.6	9.0	5	41.7%	.091	0.80	3.60	95	0.0				
2021	OAK	MLB	28	2	1	0	26	0	25	29	2	4.7	9.4	26	44.9%	.355	1.68	4.32	100	0.2	93.7	63.8%	25.1%	55.4%
2021	ARI	MLB	28	2	2	2	20	0	18^2	15	2	4.3	6.3	13	47.3%	.245	1.29	4.34	116	0.0	94.9	64.9%	21.6%	58.1%
2022 DC	*ARI*	*MLB*	*29*	*3*	*3*	*21*	*67*	*0*	*58*	*57*	*8*	*4.0*	*9.2*	*59*	*43.2%*	*.309*	*1.42*	*4.58*	*107*	*0.0*	*94.4*	*62.3%*	*24.9%*	*53.5%*

Comparables: Jeremy Jeffress, Chris Resop, Brandon Lyon

By baseball standards, Wendelken is developing into a reliable reliever. By Oakland standards, Wendelken is a fossil. He made his MLB debut six years ago, and before that was included in trades involving, among others, Jake Peavy and Brett Lawrie. He could regale his teammates with tales about ancient players such as Stephen Vogt and Sean Doolittle. Such folksy wisdom has no trade value. Seeing as how his arbitration status put him past the freshness date, Arizona claimed him on waivers. He still has enough in his fastball and slider to work the middle innings. At least that's something he can relate to with the young'uns.

Taylor Widener RHP

Born: 10/24/94 Age: 27 Bats: L Throws: R Height: 6'0" Weight: 203 lb. Origin: Round 12, 2016 Draft (#368 overall)

YEAR	TEAM	LVL	AGE	W	L	SV	G	GS	IP	H	HR	BB/9	K/9	K	GB%	BABIP	WHIP	ERA	DRA-	WARP	MPH	FB%	Whiff%	CSP
2019	RNO	AAA	24	6	7	0	23	23	100	133	23	3.7	9.8	109	30.8%	.383	1.74	8.10	110	0.0				
2020	ARI	MLB	25	0	1	0	12	0	20	14	5	5.4	9.9	22	37.3%	.196	1.30	4.50	117	0.0	94.4	65.1%	29.6%	48.9%
2021	ARI	MLB	26	2	1	0	23	13	70^1	65	14	4.7	9.3	73	33.2%	.276	1.45	4.35	107	0.4	92.8	66.7%	23.5%	52.5%
2022 DC	*ARI*	*MLB*	*27*	*2*	*3*	*0*	*59*	*0*	*51.7*	*48*	*8*	*4.1*	*9.4*	*54*	*34.0%*	*.296*	*1.40*	*4.86*	*112*	*-0.1*	*93.0*	*66.4%*	*24.5%*	*51.9%*

Comparables: Anthony Bass, Yefry Ramírez, Henry Sosa

Ideally, Widener is in your bullpen. In reality, Widener was in the Diamondbacks' rotation, which says more about who else was available than Widener himself. He eventually settled back into relief outings mostly so the club could evaluate other potential starters. The 70 innings he threw out of the pen don't seem like a lot, but he went to the injured list twice for the same groin strain. He could come out this spring as a long reliever, because "wide reliever" sounds more like late-career Bartolo Colon.

LINEOUTS

Hitters

HITTER	POS	TEAM	LVL	AGE	PA	R	2B	3B	HR	RBI	BB	K	SB	CS	AVG/OBP/SLG	DRC+	BABIP	BRR	FRAA	WARP
Seth Beer	1B	RNO	AAA	24	435	73	33	0	16	59	39	76	0	0	.287/.398/.511	117	.321	-3.0	1B(91): 0.4	1.7
	1B	ARI	MLB	24	10	4	1	0	1	3	1	3	0	0	.444/.500/.889	80	.600	0.0		0.0
Ryan Bliss	SS	VIS	A	21	175	22	9	1	6	23	13	40	11	4	.259/.322/.443	108	.310	-1.5	SS(37): -0.8	0.5
Stuart Fairchild	OF	RNO	AAA	25	182	27	7	4	9	28	22	39	7	1	.295/.385/.564	113	.336	1.2	RF(26): -0.9, LF(10): -0.4, CF(3): -0.3	0.8
	OF	ARI	MLB	25	17	3	1	0	0	2	1	3	0	0	.133/.235/.200	101	.167	-0.2	CF(5): -0.3, LF(2): -0.1, RF(1): 0.0	0.0
Bryan Holaday	C	RNO	AAA	33	108	20	9	0	7	30	9	19	1	0	.263/.315/.579	110	.247	0.2	C(21): -3.0, 1B(2): 0.8, 3B(1): -0.0	0.3
	C	ARI	MLB	33	34	2	2	0	0	1	1	15	0	0	.194/.265/.258	59	.375	-0.2	C(10): -1.4	-0.2
Jake McCarthy	OF	AMA	AA	23	156	25	8	4	6	23	17	46	17	1	.241/.333/.489	100	.318	2.1	LF(13): -2.4, CF(11): -2.7, RF(6): -1.3	0.0
	OF	RNO	AAA	23	212	38	6	7	9	31	20	49	12	3	.262/.330/.508	104	.306	1.2	CF(25): -1.4, RF(14): -3.5, 1B(6): -0.4	0.4
	OF	ARI	MLB	23	70	11	3	0	2	4	8	23	3	2	.220/.333/.373	76	.324	1.2	CF(14): -0.8, RF(6): 4.0	0.5
Ildemaro Vargas	IF	LAR	WIN	29	204	37	10	1	11	40	19	14	3	0	.319/.377/.566		.294			
	IF	RNO	AAA	29	268	50	21	0	10	39	16	27	3	1	.313/.351/.518	116	.316	1.3	2B(22): 1.2, SS(22): 0.7, 3B(10): 1.1	1.8
	IF	CHC	MLB	29	24	3	2	0	0	2	3	7	1	0	.143/.250/.238	93	.214	0.7	2B(4): -0.2, SS(2): -0.1	0.1
	IF	ARI	MLB	29	46	4	1	1	0	4	3	7	0	0	.186/.239/.256	100	.222	-0.4	3B(7): -0.5, 2B(5): -0.2, SS(3): -0.3	0.0
	IF	PIT	MLB	29	13	0	0	0	0	1	0	3	0	0	.077/.077/.077	89	.100		3B(3): 0.1, LF(2): -0.1	0.0
A.J. Vukovich	3B	VIS	A	19	276	42	15	1	10	42	19	77	10	1	.259/.322/.449	94	.329	-0.7	3B(53): -9.2	-0.3
	3B	HIL	A+	19	124	13	4	2	3	20	3	28	6	3	.298/.315/.438	108	.367	0.0	3B(29): -0.8	0.4

Four-for-nine with a bomb Beer went this fall, four-for nine with a bomb Beer! Send him down, he'll be back around, DH ***Seth Beer*** *should keep hittin' the ball!* **Ryan Bliss** clobbered the SEC but will need to keep punching up. He profiles better as a second base/utility type than as a true backup shortstop. The type of position player who may be hurt by the likely universal DH, **Stuart Fairchild** is a useful platoon bat who can handle every outfield position with grace. Hamstring injuries curtailed a solid Triple-A season that might've otherwise yielded a lengthier MLB audition, but a knack for lofting the ball means Fairchild is getting the most out of his average pop. **Bryan Holaday** has spent parts of 10 straight seasons as a backup catcher in the majors and has also appeared as a pitcher in four-straight campaigns. If the first streak continues, meaning a desperate team just needs a healthy catcher to get through some rough months, it's likely the second streak will too. **Jake McCarthy** is a reasonable player who should hover on 40-man rosters for several seasons, but is likely to be quickly outpaced by other prospects in Arizona's system. Infield roamer **Ildemaro Vargas** returned to Arizona after a year of playing for three other teams because the next time the Diamondbacks say goodbye forever to someone they found in the independent leagues will be the first time. *Toss a ball to* ***A.J. Vukovich****-er, he's hitting decently, more power than many, oh! / Hit a ball to Vukovich-er, things could get quite hairy, the bat needs to carry, oh!*

Pitchers

PITCHER	TEAM	LVL	AGE	W	L	SV	G	GS	IP	H	HR	BB/9	K/9	K	GB%	BABIP	WHIP	ERA	DRA-	WARP	MPH	FB%	WHF	CSP
Miguel Aguilar	RNO	AAA	29	4	4	16	43	0	40^2	48	7	3.5	10.0	45	33.6%	.360	1.57	5.09	91	0.4				
	ARI	MLB	29	1	1	0	9	0	7	6	0	5.1	3.9	3	40.9%	.286	1.43	6.43	113	0.0	91.4	59.6%	15.4%	51.9%
Ryan Buchter	RNO	AAA	34	0	0	6	16	0	16	13	1	3.9	11.2	20	26.8%	.300	1.25	3.38	93	0.1				
	ARI	MLB	34	0	2	0	18	0	16^1	16	5	7.2	8.8	16	23.4%	.262	1.78	6.61	124	-0.1	90.6	51.0%	22.7%	52.2%
J.B. Bukauskas	RNO	AAA	24	0	2	1	13	0	12^2	9	1	2.8	11.4	16	46.7%	.276	1.03	4.26	85	0.2				
	ARI	MLB	24	2	2	0	21	0	17^1	24	4	3.6	7.3	14	48.3%	.364	1.79	7.79	110	0.1	94.6	47.2%	25.4%	53.7%
Humberto Castellanos	RNO	AAA	23	6	1	0	12	12	57^2	56	14	2.2	9.2	59	36.7%	.271	1.21	4.99	103	0.1				
	ARI	MLB	23	2	2	0	14	7	45^2	48	7	3.0	5.7	29	40.3%	.299	1.38	4.93	117	0.0	90.6	57.4%	15.1%	58.3%
Slade Cecconi	HIL	A+	22	4	2	0	12	12	59	53	5	3.1	9.6	63	43.8%	.310	1.24	4.12	101	0.4				
Stefan Crichton	RNO	AAA	29	3	0	0	11	0	12	17	0	5.3	6.8	9	38.6%	.386	2.00	9.00	106	0.0				
	ARI	MLB	29	0	4	4	31	0	23^1	33	3	4.6	6.6	17	44.0%	.370	1.93	7.33	126	-0.1	91.1	69.7%	15.4%	56.4%
Brett de Geus	ARI	MLB	23	3	2	0	28	0	23^1	31	3	4.6	5.8	15	48.8%	.354	1.84	6.56	124	-0.1	93.1	88.7%	13.4%	53.9%
	TEX	MLB	23	0	0	0	19	0	26^2	31	3	4.4	8.8	26	54.9%	.359	1.65	8.44	104	0.2	93.4	73.5%	21.9%	50.5%
Chris Devenski	ARI	MLB	30	1	0	1	8	0	7^1	11	2	2.5	6.1	5	37.0%	.360	1.77	8.59	119	0.0	91.5	33.8%	26.2%	51.4%
Jake Faria	SL	AAA	27	3	2	0	7	7	36^2	41	7	3.7	11.3	46	29.1%	.354	1.53	5.65	113	-0.1				
	ARI	MLB	27	0	0	0	23	3	32^2	39	5	3.6	8.8	32	38.3%	.337	1.59	5.51	99	0.3	92.4	56.2%	23.2%	56.8%
Seth Frankoff	RNO	AAA	32	2	0	0	8	3	21	26	8	6.0	10.7	25	36.1%	.353	1.90	8.14	90	0.2				
	ARI	MLB	32	0	2	0	4	3	14^2	20	4	5.5	6.8	11	44.2%	.356	1.98	9.20	102	0.1	91.3	40.0%	18.3%	55.1%
Luis Frías	HIL	A+	23	2	0	0	2	2	11	5	0	3.3	12.3	15	42.9%	.238	0.82	0.82	89	0.1				
	AMA	AA	23	5	6	0	16	16	78^2	69	16	2.9	10.4	91	44.1%	.269	1.19	5.26	86	1.1				
	RNO	AAA	23	2	1	0	5	5	21^2	21	1	6.6	8.3	20	50.8%	.323	1.71	5.82	92	0.2				
	ARI	MLB	23	0	0	0	3	0	3^1	2	0	13.5	8.1	3	37.5%	.250	2.10	2.70	173	-0.1	96.7	54.4%	22.2%	49.2%
Kevin Ginkel	ARI	MLB	27	0	1	0	32	0	28^1	30	7	4.4	9.8	31	41.5%	.311	1.55	6.35	100	0.3	94.9	59.3%	25.3%	53.4%
Tommy Henry	AMA	AA	23	4	6	0	23	23	115^2	116	24	4.1	10.5	135	38.7%	.335	1.46	5.21	84	1.8				
Bryce Jarvis	HIL	A+	23	1	2	0	7	7	37^1	30	4	3.1	10.1	42	31.6%	.283	1.15	3.62	95	0.4				
	AMA	AA	23	1	2	0	8	8	35	32	8	4.4	10.3	40	43.6%	.286	1.40	5.66	106	0.1				
Levi Kelly	AMA	AA	22	2	0	0	15	0	25	16	3	10.1	9.7	27	29.8%	.250	1.76	5.40	112	0.0				
Kyle Nelson	COL	AAA	24	0	1	1	25	0	25^2	23	1	7.0	10.5	30	39.1%	.324	1.68	6.66	89	0.5				
	CLE	MLB	24	0	0	0	10	0	9^2	10	0	7.4	7.4	8	38.7%	.323	1.86	9.31	132	-0.1	89.7	57.4%	29.7%	55.8%
Ryne Nelson	HIL	A+	23	4	1	0	8	8	39^1	21	3	3.2	13.5	59	29.5%	.240	0.89	2.52	85	0.6				
	AMA	AA	23	3	3	0	14	14	77	66	13	3.0	12.2	104	38.0%	.312	1.19	3.51	89	0.9				
Brandon Pfaadt	VIS	A	22	2	2	0	7	7	40^1	29	5	1.6	12.7	57	40.0%	.267	0.89	3.12	94	0.4				
	HIL	A+	22	5	4	0	9	9	58	39	5	2.2	10.4	67	39.9%	.246	0.91	2.48	100	0.4				
	AMA	AA	22	1	1	0	6	6	33^1	37	12	1.9	9.7	36	30.6%	.291	1.32	4.59	99	0.2				
Brandyn Sittinger	AMA	AA	27	0	1	1	12	0	16	11	2	1.7	11.8	21	22.2%	.265	0.88	3.94	93	0.2				
	RNO	AAA	27	1	1	4	23	0	23^1	18	2	5.4	12.3	32	35.2%	.308	1.37	4.24	79	0.4				
	ARI	MLB	27	0	1	0	5	0	4^2	5	3	3.9	1.9	1	29.4%	.143	1.50	7.71	145	-0.1	93.6	70.0%	13.3%	56.0%
Matt Tabor	HIL	A+	22	2	2	0	4	3	24	18	2	2.3	8.6	23	36.9%	.258	1.00	3.00	100	0.2				
	AMA	AA	22	3	5	0	10	10	51	41	8	3.2	8.3	47	42.1%	.241	1.16	3.88	102	0.3				
	RNO	AAA	22	1	4	0	8	8	32^1	44	14	4.2	7.2	26	35.8%	.319	1.82	11.13	127	-0.4				
Blake Walston	VIS	A	20	2	2	0	8	8	43^1	34	4	3.5	12.5	60	43.7%	.303	1.18	3.32	86	0.6				
	HIL	A+	20	2	3	0	11	11	52^1	52	12	2.8	9.8	57	36.8%	.288	1.30	4.13	120	-0.2				

A late-bloomer, the diminutive **Miguel Aguilar** joined the Diamondbacks org in 2016 after five seasons of middle relief in the Mexican League and cut his teeth with high strikeouts and low homer totals—tantalizing peripherals for a left-hander. ⚾ Is there still room for the classic platoon LOOGYs like **Ryan Buchter** in a postmodern bullpen? The Diamondbacks, on August 20, no longer thought so. ⚾ While the city of Atlanta lays understandable claim to seminal club hip-hop hit "Knuck If You Buk", few know the group Crime Mob was inspired to pen the classic after watching a young **J.B. Bukauskas** pitch. The "celebration of elbow-throwing" speaks to the high-effort delivery, the nasty slider and the injuries that come with it. ⚾ The Diamondbacks picked up **Humberto Castellanos** from Houston off waivers and converted him to a starter. He's a control artist with one offering: the curveball. It worked for Andy Kaufman, maybe it can work for him too. ⚾ Despite mid-rotation stuff, **Slade Cecconi** continued a trend of light underachievement. Though his fastball sits mid-90s and both his breaking balls have flashes of brilliance, he has yet to refine any of his offerings into a true Deathstroke. ⚾ **Stefan Crichton** was outrighted twice off the Diamondbacks roster with an ERA over seven, becoming the second Crichton in history to produce way too many ERs. ⚾ Rule 5 selectee **Brett de Geus** withstood the entire season in the major leagues with Texas and later Arizona. His FIP was nearly two and a half points below his ERA, which sounds great if you don't ask what his ERA was. ⚾ **Chris Devenski** will spend most of 2022 thinking about how he was extremely rad in the first half of 2017. Tommy John surgery makes one work the brain as well as the elbow. ⚾ You know how sometimes we wonder how a reliever with low 90s stuff is going to keep escaping innings? The run police finally caught up to **Jake Faria**, released by both the Angels and Diamondbacks last season. He's facing multiple counts, most of them hitter's counts. ⚾ Tall, well-traveled hurler **Seth Frankoff** won 18 games in the KBO in 2018 and zero games in the majors in 2021 because most transit vehicles are quite uncomfortable for lengthy folks. ⚾ From DFA to debut, **Luis Frías** pitched at four levels, showing stuff better than his statline. The well-built righty pairs his mid-90s fastball with a sharp 12-6 breaking ball, while his low-90s splitter tunnels well with the jaunty angle of his cap. ⚾ It's hard to remember when two-pitch flamethrower **Keith Ginkel** was posting zeroes in relief after a couple of rough years with ERAs and FIPs hovering around six, but it may jog your memory if you take some Ginkel biloba. ⚾ **Thomas Jack Henry** came to Double-A to miss bats. Without a command improvement, he's at risk of being bullpen-bound, charged forever to throw at 100% effort with 200% first names. ⚾ While he began 2021 as perhaps the most touted arm in Arizona's system, **Bryce Jarvis'** backspin fastball got stuck in the mud at times this year. The former Blue Devil was bedeviled by better approaches from hitters, forcing him to nibble at the edges, working deep in counts instead of games. ⚾ A peculiar arrangement between **Levi Kelly** and the Diamondbacks seemed to lead to disappointing results for the promising 22-year-old. Not only did a shoulder injury slow his start to 2021, but he worked his way back into games while still recovering from the injury, generating gaudy numbers—as in, "God, he walked *how many* per nine?" ⚾ When **Kyle Nelson** is on, he affronts hitters with a spin-tastic, well-commanded slider and a deceptive low-90s fastball in addition to a cutter he introduced last year. Maybe the Diamondbacks should turn him off, eject him and blow on his cartridge because he has more earned runs allowed than career innings pitched. ⚾ Pumping fastballs first, second and third, **Ryne Nelson** commanded the respect of Double-A hitters. To nab a rotation role, however, he'll need to develop at least one above-average secondary pitch. ⚾ The loose, lanky **Brandon Pfaadt** climbed three levels with his easy motion, above-average slider and plus command. While he dominated both Single-A levels, he struggled with Double-A, a surprise given his lifelong familiarity with the concept. ⚾ Like a flower waiting to bloom / Like a lightbulb in a dark room / **Brandyn Sittinger**... waiting for you / To give up one more home runnn. ⚾ Much like the mountain in Galilee from which his family name is presumably derived, **Matt Tabor** is a lesser but still notable member of a larger group. Much like the extinct volcano in Portland, OR, that shares its name with the Galilean mountain, Tabor is unlikely to explode. ⚾ One of the younger arms in Low-A West became one of the youngest arms in High-A this season, as **Blake Walston** continued making progress at each level. He's yet to get a lasting velocity bump, but his frame still shows room for adding strength, and he's looked comfortable corralling his lengthy limbs into a repeatable motion.

COLORADO ROCKIES

Essay by Connor Farrell

Player comments by Justin Klugh and BP staff

In my junior year of college, I was recruited to join a frat by a guy who sat behind me in German 110. This is obviously not a brag; my opinions on Greek Life aside, pretty much every white male at a university with a Greek Life system has been hit up by one or two frats in their time.

The guy's name was Matt. In the hopes of having me join the Alpha Pi Kappa fraternity, he invited me to a barbecue at the frat's house just across the street from campus. On one of the first days of class, Matt had asked if I wanted to be his partner for the speaking-lesson portion of the class period; college is filled with these marriages of convenience. Matt then invited me to the BBQ, and I, being a 21-year-old college student, accepted. (When people say school is more valuable for dispensing life wisdom than book learning, they mean nuggets like: "Don't turn down free food.") Though I had no intention of joining a frat, and never would, I seized the opportunity for a free dinner. The barbecue was fine, a burger and a Pepsi, and I left without talking too much.

I believed this would be the end of my post-class interactions with Matt. I'd gotten my food without signing any forms, and I assumed everyone understood the nature of the exchange.

About a week later, Matt asked if I needed a ride home after class. I didn't really want to wait for the bus, so I accepted, and we headed towards his car. He mentioned he had to stop by the frat house before he ran me to my place, just to pick some things up. I hoped he wouldn't ask me to pay for my burger. As we entered the frat home of Alpha Pi Kappa (colloquially known as Pike House), I realized I hadn't actually been inside before, and I noticed something strange. Namely, a giant-ass tree root running through the entire floor of the kitchen.

I asked if I was seeing right. Matt laughed and confirmed. A nearby tree had apparently pushed a root up from the ground and through their kitchen. I stared at it for a few seconds, wondering how this could have happened. Trees aren't exactly known to be fast movers, so, surely, someone had noticed the root's movement for months or even years before it had destabilized the entire floor. I asked Matt how long it had been like that, and he shrugged. We walked further into the house, and I saw that the entire home had

COLORADO ROCKIES PROSPECTUS

2021 W-L: 74-87, 4th in NL West

Pythag	.465	*19th*	DER	.689	*25th*
RS/G	4.59	*10th*	DRC+	92	*23rd*
RA/G	4.94	*22nd*	DRA-	100	*16th*
dWin%	.476	*18th*	FIP	4.40	*20th*
Payroll	$106M	*18th*	B-Age	28.6	*13th*
M$/MW	$3.5M	*15th*	P-Age	28.5	*9th*

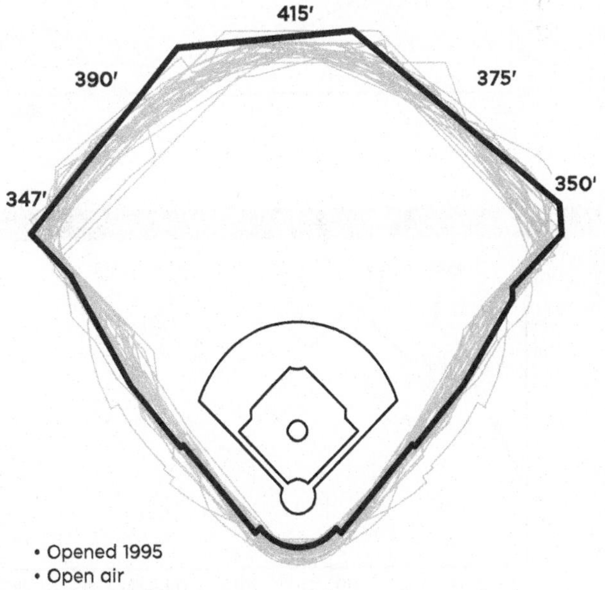

- Opened 1995
- Open air
- Natural surface
- Fence profile: 8' to 16'6"

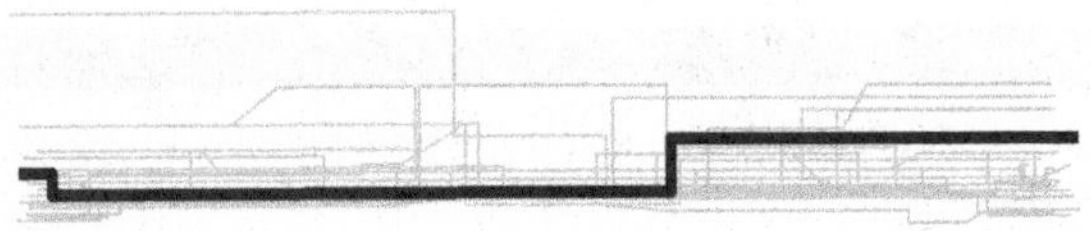

Park Factors

Runs	Runs/RH	Runs/LH	HR/RH	HR/LH
106	105	107	105	109

Top Hitter WARP	3.5 C.J. Cron
Top Pitcher WARP	3.0 Germán Márquez
Top Prospect	Zac Veen

Payroll History (in millions)

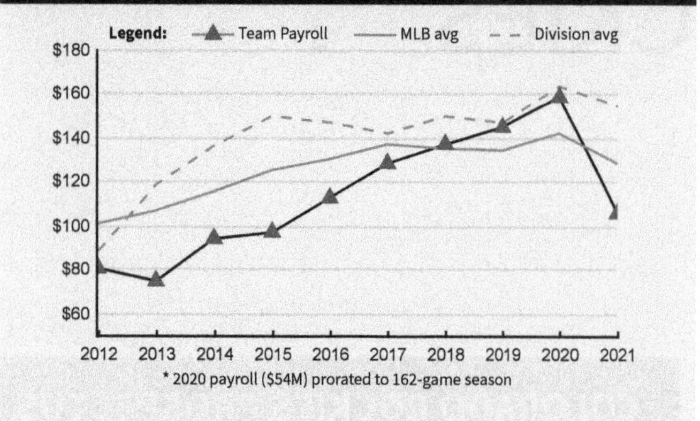

Future Commitments (in millions)

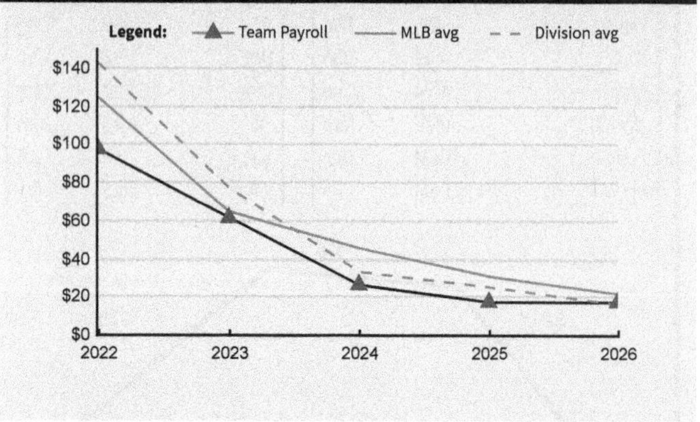

Farm System Ranking

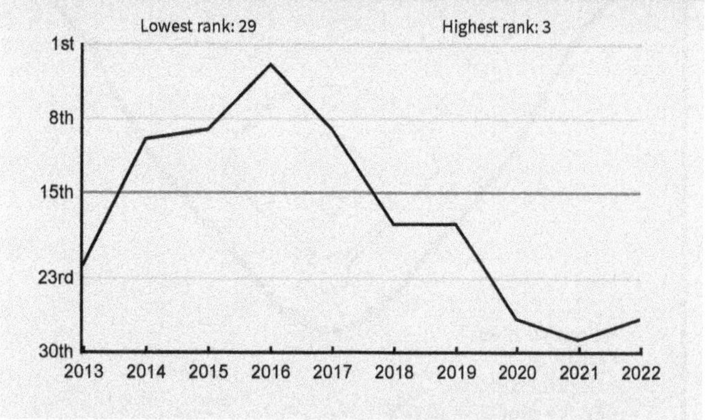

Personnel

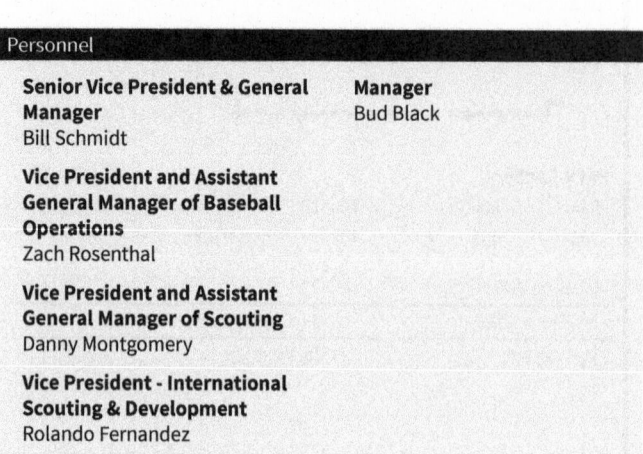

Senior Vice President & General Manager
Bill Schmidt

Vice President and Assistant General Manager of Baseball Operations
Zach Rosenthal

Vice President and Assistant General Manager of Scouting
Danny Montgomery

Vice President - International Scouting & Development
Rolando Fernandez

Manager
Bud Black

been torn up by this tree root in the kitchen. The living room leaned, a bedroom wall bowed, the front door didn't really shut. I couldn't believe people lived here.

Matt went to grab whatever he needed from the basement and, not wanting to be left behind with the tree root, I followed along. I don't know what I expected, really. Would it be like a Rainforest Cafe? If they're willing to let a tree root destroy their kitchen, they may also allow a full-on biological zone to grow around it. Would Matt tell me to be careful with a nest of chipmunks that had settled in the root? Or to watch out for the greenery that had grown out of their dryer, because he feared it was poison ivy?

There were no animals or poison ivy, but you could tell the tree had made its mark. The foundation of the home was crumbling, the tree stressing the concrete to the limit as it fought for the territory the cinder blocks currently controlled. Strangeness had given way to something more serious—literally foundational. The Alpha Pi Kappa house was not long for this world.

Matt saw me looking around, stunned, and said, "don't ever live next to a tree, man." I was as baffled by his explanation as by the situation. I didn't think the tree did anything wrong.

As we got upstairs, Matt chatted with some brothers and asked if the fire marshal had come back recently. The marshal had not come by. Matt turned to me and said, "can you believe he thinks we need to move out?" I just laughed. The Pikes not only believed that living in a place that nature had reclaimed as its own was perfectly fine, but they thought the idea that it was an unfit domicile was authoritarianism overstepping its bounds. The tree root had carved the kitchen in such a way that you actively had to step over it to get to the stove, but the brothers of Alpha Pi Kappa did not think this was worthy of the fire marshal's wrath.

I am not an expert on Greek Life bureaucracy, but I was under the impression their homes were directly tied to the University. This meant my college probably needed to know if the homes were unsafe. For example, if they had windows that were painted shut, carbon monoxide leaks, or a tree root close enough to the fridge that you could ask it to get the milk for you.

I write all of this because the craziness of the Pike House and the tree root remind me of something: The Colorado Rockies. A baseball team that a) lives with a tree root inside of it's kitchen and b) is offended by the very idea that a tree root is not something that should be in a kitchen.

The last time the Rockies hired a general manager was in 1999. That sounds wrong because the club has had a number of different GMs since then, but it's technically correct. In the 22 years since Dan O'Dowd was brought in from Cleveland to be general manager, the Rockies have simply promoted longtime assistants and other executives until, eventually, they became the GM or president of baseball operations.

Jeff Bridich was appointed GM in 2014, after O'Dowd's roster stumbled to a fourth-straight losing season, and handled the team for a little more than seven seasons. Bridich's tenure as GM was riddled with odd free-agent signings, reclusive front-office behavior, angry superstars and, eventually, enough scandals (including one involving both figurative and literal dirty laundry) that he was forced out of the organization in relative disgrace last April.

You would not have been wrong to expect that—after all of that drama, all of that fan anger, all of the disastrous decisions under Bridich—Rockies owner Dick Monfort would have taken that opportunity to restructure the organization, to let some outside thinking step in for the first time in more than two decades. Problem is, that expectation is based on the belief that you would not want a tree root in your kitchen. The Rockies promoted another internal candidate to GM without interviewing anyone else. They gave Bill Schmidt the interim job in April, removed the interim title in September and decided the thing was done.

The Rockies' problem is the same as the Pikes': doing something about the problem would have to start with acknowledging that they allowed it to fester in the first place, that they stood there and, day by day, watched the root move in. The Rockies could never admit that the front office that chased off Nolan Arenado, DJ LeMahieu and Troy Tulowitzki with broken promises and mediocre results needs wholesale changing. They just needed a new lead brain, one better attuned to the vision. Now that Bridich is gone, the true Rockies plan can commence, right? Pay no mind to the fact that it's the same plan that we've all seen fail for the last ten seasons, a plan founded in a refusal to adapt to failure or accept that life is actually a lot worse when there's a tree root in your kitchen.

As we enter the 2022 season, the frustration lies in that mindset. We see the tree root like I did on that fateful day in college, but it feels like the Rockies have accepted that it is supposed to be there. Perhaps it would be easier for us to join the Pike House, to try to find new ways to live around the tree root and hope the Rockies succeed in spite of themselves. Just build an extra sideways step into our midnight snack runs. There's at least serenity in that, even if it requires a wholesale change in one's outlook on sports and structural stability.

As Matt drove me home, I got the frat pitch. I declined, and moved on with my life. Matt did not offer me another ride, or another hamburger, the rest of the semester, and the Pike House was eventually torn down by the city. I couldn't believe that this group of young men had actively waged a battle against the idea that they shouldn't live like the Swiss Family Robinson. But now, as I get used to the slow encroachment of lowered expectations by way of the baseball team I love, maybe I get it, at least a little bit. There's the way it should be, and then there's the way it is, and you can get so used to the second that you start to think it's the first. ■

—Connor Farrell is a lifelong Rockies sufferer (or fan, depending how you view it) who has written for SB Nation and various dead blogs.

Hitters

Charlie Blackmon RF

Born: 07/01/86 Age: 36 Bats: L Throws: L Height: 6'3" Weight: 221 lb. Origin: Round 2, 2008 Draft (#72 overall)

YEAR	TEAM	LVL	AGE	PA	R	2B	3B	HR	RBI	BB	K	SB	CS	Whiff%	AVG/OBP/SLG	DRC+	BABIP	BRR	FRAA	WARP
2019	COL	MLB	32	634	112	42	7	32	86	40	104	2	5	19.6%	.314/.364/.576	127	.334	-0.2	RF(135): -9.6	3.1
2020	COL	MLB	33	247	31	12	1	6	42	19	44	2	1	23.5%	.303/.356/.448	99	.347	0.4	RF(50): 3.9	1.1
2021	COL	MLB	34	582	76	25	4	13	78	54	91	3	0	20.4%	.270/.351/.411	103	.305	-0.6	RF(137): -2.4	1.6
2022 DC	*COL*	*MLB*	*35*	*563*	*84*	*26*	*4*	*19*	*76*	*50*	*98*	*7*	*3*	*20.8%*	*.278/.356/.463*	*115*	*.316*	*0.2*	*RF -1*	*2.3*

Comparables: Ken Griffey, Tony Gwynn, Garret Anderson

Blackmon blasted a home run in August that tied him with Troy Tulowitzki on the Rockies' all-time franchise list. It was the perfect indication of the passage of time, reminding us of another generation of stars whose time expired here before the Rockies could give their city its first World Series championship. The 35-year-old Blackmon has 10 years, four All-Star appearances and a batting title in the bigs now and remains a team leader in the clubhouse and in the stat columns. As age crept up on him in 2020, and as the baseball has morphed and fewer of his favorite fastballs have been thrown, Blackmon's power deteriorated and his defense became less reliable. But by swinging to make contact, and rarely striking out (that franchise record-tying homer came on a first-pitch 99.9-mph fastball), the bushy-faced old-timer showed that he could still pull the trigger when he had to. He won't hoist the first trophy for Colorado, but every at-bat will be a tough one.

C.J. Cron 1B

Born: 01/05/90 Age: 32 Bats: R Throws: R Height: 6'4" Weight: 235 lb. Origin: Round 1, 2011 Draft (#17 overall)

YEAR	TEAM	LVL	AGE	PA	R	2B	3B	HR	RBI	BB	K	SB	CS	Whiff%	AVG/OBP/SLG	DRC+	BABIP	BRR	FRAA	WARP
2019	MIN	MLB	29	499	51	24	0	25	78	29	107	0	0	25.3%	.253/.311/.469	106	.277	-3.0	1B(117): 9.2	2.4
2020	DET	MLB	30	52	9	3	0	4	8	9	16	0	0	31.3%	.190/.346/.548	105	.182	-0.1	1B(13): 1.1	0.2
2021	COL	MLB	31	547	70	31	1	28	92	60	117	1	0	27.5%	.281/.375/.530	127	.316	-1.6	1B(130): 6.0	3.5
2022 DC	*COL*	*MLB*	*32*	*561*	*82*	*27*	*0*	*25*	*85*	*56*	*124*	*2*	*1*	*27.2%*	*.252/.346/.466*	*114*	*.291*	*-0.8*	*1B 3*	*2.0*

Comparables: Andres Galarraga, Paul Konerko, Gil Hodges

Well, well, well... *somebody* really took to slugging at Coors Field. Somehow when you put what this guide referred to last season as "a walking obelisk of ISO" into the most famously hitter-friendly MLB park, the result is... even more isolated power. These isolations could be as broad as Cron having a 1.291 OPS in the month of August, or as specific as tying Larry Walker for the Rockies' franchise record in RBI over a three-game series. Cron is the type of hitter you'd think Colorado would pick up by the barrel: Cheap, and consistently able to launch the ball into thin air. He was a top-15 hitter in ISO and slugging, and among the top 30 at putting the ball in the air; the more you do that in Denver, the more of them turn into home runs. The problem is, you can't play every game there, and Cron's splits on the road saw him wilt upon returning to sea level. Nevertheless, the veteran 31-year-old first baseman got *real* comfortable in 2021's last two months, providing some hard-throwing punches into the largely punchless Rockies lineup.

Elias Díaz C

Born: 11/17/90 Age: 31 Bats: R Throws: R Height: 6'1" Weight: 223 lb. Origin: International Free Agent, 2008

YEAR	TEAM	LVL	AGE	PA	R	2B	3B	HR	RBI	BB	K	SB	CS	Whiff%	AVG/OBP/SLG	DRC+	BABIP	BRR	FRAA	WARP
2019	IND	AAA	28	30	5	3	0	0	4	1	5	0	0		.414/.433/.517	101	.500	0.2	C(6): 0.9	0.2
2019	PIT	MLB	28	332	31	14	0	2	28	23	56	0	0	23.3%	.241/.296/.307	82	.286	1.4	C(96): -13.2	-0.5
2020	COL	MLB	29	73	4	2	0	2	9	5	15	0	0	27.9%	.235/.288/.353	97	.275	-0.1	C(24): 0.4	0.3
2021	COL	MLB	30	371	52	18	1	18	44	30	60	0	0	24.1%	.246/.310/.464	115	.249	-1.8	C(98): 6.5	2.7
2022 DC	*COL*	*MLB*	*31*	*411*	*48*	*18*	*0*	*12*	*51*	*34*	*74*	*0*	*1*	*24.0%*	*.250/.318/.399*	*91*	*.287*	*-0.6*	*C -4*	*1.0*

Comparables: Sandy León, Francisco Cervelli, Nick Hundley

YEAR	TEAM	P. COUNT	FRM RUNS	BLK RUNS	THRW RUNS	TOT RUNS
2019	PIT	12603	-17.0	-0.5	0.7	-16.8
2020	COL	2173	0.5	0.0	0.0	0.5
2021	COL	12793	1.0	-0.1	1.7	2.6
2022	*COL*	*15632*	*-7.3*	*-1.0*	*2.1*	*-6.2*

When a team signs a weak-hitting 29-year-old catcher to a minor-league deal, the thought is that he must at least have some skill behind the plate. But Díaz bore a résumé as both a weak hitter and poor pitch framer, having been cut by the Pirates after getting significant playing time since 2017. When the Pirates feel like they can do better than you, it must be a gut-check moment of sorts. Unthinkably, Díaz, now 31, turned in some career-high offensive numbers thanks to a serious power surge that began in June (with the typical Rockies addendum that away from Coors, he was significantly worse) and an even more sudden ability to throw out basestealers. With prospect Drew Romo in Low-A and a pitching staff that puts the ball in play so the catcher doesn't *have* to frame it, Díaz could very well be the Rockies' starting catcher for now, because, you know. Why not? Finally, those stuck-up Pirates miss out on a success story!

Brenton Doyle OF

Born: 05/14/98 Age: 24 Bats: R Throws: R Height: 6'3" Weight: 200 lb. Origin: Round 4, 2019 Draft (#129 overall)

YEAR	TEAM	LVL	AGE	PA	R	2B	3B	HR	RBI	BB	K	SB	CS	Whiff%	AVG/OBP/SLG	DRC+	BABIP	BRR	FRAA	WARP
2019	GJ	ROA	21	215	42	11	3	8	33	31	47	17	3		.383/.477/.611		.484			
2021	SPO	A+	23	424	70	16	2	16	47	30	134	21	6		.279/.336/.454	96	.388	-0.5	RF(44): 0.1, CF(39): 2.7	1.4
2022 non-DC	*COL*	*MLB*	*24*	*251*	*22*	*10*	*1*	*5*	*24*	*14*	*87*	*7*	*3*	*35.3%*	*.224/.275/.347*	*65*	*.331*	*0.6*	*CF 1, RF 1*	*-0.1*

Comparables: Kevin Pillar, Chas McCormick, Scott Van Slyke

When he was drafted out of Division II Shepherd University, the big question for Doyle was how he'd handle stiffer pitching. After 2019, it was whether he could keep up his ludicrous performance over a full season. After 2020, the questions were the same for him as for everyone else. And after an excellent, if inconsistent, 2021, they still abound. Which is funny, because so many of his talents are unquestionable: He has the athleticism for center, the arm for right, the legs to do damage on the basepaths and the power of Soda Popinski. Which, if you've ever played *Punch-Out!!*, sums up the doubts: With an upright stance and a natural uppercut swing, Doyle is capable of supplying extra-base hits and strikeouts in equal measure, and some months will see more of one than the other. So far, he's answered all the questions each time the sport has allowed him; it may not be long until the questions change to "Do you remember who played center before Doyle showed up?"

Jameson Hannah CF

Born: 08/10/97 Age: 24 Bats: L Throws: L Height: 5'9" Weight: 185 lb. Origin: Round 2, 2018 Draft (#50 overall)

YEAR	TEAM	LVL	AGE	PA	R	2B	3B	HR	RBI	BB	K	SB	CS	Whiff%	AVG/OBP/SLG	DRC+	BABIP	BRR	FRAA	WARP
2019	DBT	A+	21	78	6	3	1	0	6	9	16	2	1		.224/.325/.299	95	.294	-0.4	CF(14): -0.4, RF(2): 0.2	0.2
2019	STK	A+	21	414	48	25	3	2	31	29	88	6	7		.283/.341/.381	97	.361	-3.9	RF(49): -0.6, CF(41): -2.3, LF(2): -0.6	0.3
2021	HFD	AA	23	339	41	16	2	3	17	29	99	11	2		.255/.324/.351	78	.363	2.8	CF(65): 6.5, LF(7): -0.7	1.0
2022 non-DC	*COL*	*MLB*	*24*	*251*	*19*	*11*	*1*	*1*	*19*	*18*	*77*	*3*	*2*	*32.2%*	*.219/.284/.303*	*58*	*.320*	*0.1*	*CF 2, RF 0*	*-0.3*

Comparables: Zoilo Almonte, Roman Quinn, Derrick Robinson

Twenty-four years old and already traded twice, this non-roster spring-training invitee was noted for his short, quick swing, used to shoot line drives past the infield. Credit a man who knows what he is: Hannah doesn't really try to hit home runs, and also can't. He didn't get a chance to showcase that Hemingway sentence of a swing in 2020, but was among his Double-A squad's top offensive contributors in 2021. Though his arm strength is uninspiring, it is accurate, and ultimately a secondary concern. It takes a lot of speed to play center at Coors Field, a quality Hannah has a bit of, but his true strength is reading, tracking and playing the ball. Altogether he's limited as a player, but it's a fun limited.

Sam Hilliard OF

Born: 02/21/94 Age: 28 Bats: L Throws: L Height: 6'5" Weight: 236 lb. Origin: Round 15, 2015 Draft (#437 overall)

YEAR	TEAM	LVL	AGE	PA	R	2B	3B	HR	RBI	BB	K	SB	CS	Whiff%	AVG/OBP/SLG	DRC+	BABIP	BRR	FRAA	WARP
2019	ABQ	AAA	25	559	109	29	7	35	101	54	164	22	5		.262/.335/.558	97	.316	0.7	RF(83): 0.7, CF(34): 4.5, LF(10): -0.8	2.2
2019	COL	MLB	25	87	13	4	2	7	13	9	23	2	0	26.9%	.273/.356/.649	108	.298	0.7	CF(17): 0.7, RF(6): 1.6, LF(5): -1.0	0.6
2020	COL	MLB	26	114	13	2	2	6	10	9	42	3	0	38.9%	.210/.272/.438	75	.281	1.1	LF(14): 2.9, RF(13): 0.6, CF(10): 1.3	0.6
2021	ABQ	AAA	27	213	31	12	2	14	37	23	61	6	1		.239/.324/.548	105	.272	1.0	CF(35): 7.2, RF(9): 3.1, LF(7): 0.7	2.0
2021	COL	MLB	27	238	32	7	2	14	34	23	87	5	0	41.8%	.215/.294/.463	87	.283	3.1	CF(46): -0.8, LF(17): 0.3, RF(11): 0.2	0.8
2022 DC	*COL*	*MLB*	*28*	*400*	*48*	*15*	*3*	*15*	*50*	*35*	*140*	*11*	*5*	*38.4%*	*.211/.287/.400*	*75*	*.299*	*1.4*	*CF 2, LF 1*	*0.6*

Comparables: John Mayberry Jr., Khris Davis, Brennan Boesch

Hilliard hit a two-run home run in his 2018 MLB debut, added another two days later. Then, for an encore, he hit none for three weeks, followed by four in five days. Trends like these continued to occur in 2021: From August 1 to August 8 he hit four home runs, and fell a few hours shy of not hitting one again until September. The problem was a lack of contact, all of which, had it been made, would have been quite powerful, given Hilliard's strength and speed. It's a combination that's easy to fall in love with and even easier to have your heart broken by. He made some adjustments midseason with the support of his manager, and his efforts were rewarded by more consistent playing time starting in late July as the Rockies continued evaluating their outfield options, the way that a child evaluates the vegetables on their dinner plate.

Connor Joe LF/1B

Born: 08/16/92 Age: 29 Bats: R Throws: R Height: 6'0" Weight: 205 lb. Origin: Round 1, 2014 Draft (#39 overall)

YEAR	TEAM	LVL	AGE	PA	R	2B	3B	HR	RBI	BB	K	SB	CS	Whiff%	AVG/OBP/SLG	DRC+	BABIP	BRR	FRAA	WARP
2019	OKC	AAA	26	446	82	26	1	15	68	72	81	1	2		.300/.426/.503	116	.347	-0.2	1B(79): -0.7, LF(10): -0.2, 3B(6): -2.2	1.6
2019	SF	MLB	26	16	1	0	0	0	0	1	5	0	0	30.4%	.067/.125/.067	91	.100		LF(5): 2.1	0.2
2021	ABQ	AAA	28	110	20	7	0	9	25	15	22	1	0		.326/.418/.696	130	.333	-0.3	RF(12): -2.3, 1B(7): 0.6, LF(6): 0.4	0.6
2021	COL	MLB	28	211	23	9	0	8	35	26	41	0	0	23.5%	.285/.379/.469	113	.323	-1.5	LF(32): 3.6, 1B(14): -0.2	1.2
2022 DC	*COL*	*MLB*	*29*	*326*	*48*	*15*	*1*	*9*	*35*	*38*	*70*	*0*	*1*	*24.4%*	*.248/.348/.412*	*105*	*.301*	*-0.4*	*LF 2, 1B 0*	*1.1*

Comparables: Adam Duvall, Chris Heisey, Whit Merrifield

After a sputtering prologue, Joe was sent back to Triple-A until after the All-Star break, at which point the real story began. Over the second half Joe hit .304 with a .944 OPS in 148 plate appearances until getting sidelined by a hamstring injury. The 29-year-old made some dazzling defensive plays in addition to his explosive second-half offense, which saw him lead the team in OBP, post a two-home run day, hit a bomb on his birthday and become a fan favorite. Did we mention he kicked cancer's ass, too? The people want more Connor Joe in 2022, and they're going to get it.

Grant Lavigne 1B

Born: 08/27/99 Age: 22 Bats: L Throws: R Height: 6'4" Weight: 220 lb. Origin: Round 1, 2018 Draft (#42 overall)

YEAR	TEAM	LVL	AGE	PA	R	2B	3B	HR	RBI	BB	K	SB	CS	Whiff%	AVG/OBP/SLG	DRC+	BABIP	BRR	FRAA	WARP
2019	ASH	A	19	526	52	19	0	7	64	68	129	8	9		.236/.347/.327	97	.314	-4.5	1B(112): 0.1	0.6
2021	FRE	A	21	308	49	13	4	7	40	39	73	7	2		.281/.388/.442	113	.365	2.0	1B(64): -6.6	0.8
2021	SPO	A+	21	139	17	5	1	2	18	22	39	2	1		.225/.362/.342	94	.319	0.5	1B(30): -1.7	0.1
2022 non-DC	*COL*	*MLB*	*22*	*251*	*21*	*9*	*1*	*3*	*20*	*23*	*74*	*3*	*2*	*31.1%*	*.204/.289/.297*	*59*	*.291*	*0.1*	*1B -1*	*-1.0*

Comparables: Gerardo Avila, Ender Inciarte, Marwin Gonzalez

When a certain author was 18, he made a movie with his friends about a swarm of killer tennis balls called *Deathspheres*. When Grant Lavigne was 18, he crushed Pioneer League pitching and displayed the plate discipline of a much more grizzled elder. It's pretty clear who the cooler teenager was. Lavigne's considered a top-ten Rockies prospect and a top-10 first base prospect across baseball, offering swift bat speed, strategic aggressiveness and ferocious power, tempered by his ability to squeeze the count until it lets him on base. There's rawness in his skillset, however, and the one-dimensionality in his toolset is something of a hindrance the higher up the system he climbs, sort of like a movie that relies too much on the physical humor of people getting pelted by tennis balls with mouths cut into them.

Ryan McMahon 3B/2B

Born: 12/14/94 Age: 27 Bats: L Throws: R Height: 6'2" Weight: 219 lb. Origin: Round 2, 2013 Draft (#42 overall)

YEAR	TEAM	LVL	AGE	PA	R	2B	3B	HR	RBI	BB	K	SB	CS	Whiff%	AVG/OBP/SLG	DRC+	BABIP	BRR	FRAA	WARP
2019	COL	MLB	24	539	70	22	1	24	83	56	160	5	1	32.5%	.250/.329/.450	93	.323	0.0	2B(113): 7.0, 3B(22): -0.5, 1B(19): -0.7	2.1
2020	COL	MLB	25	193	23	6	1	9	26	18	66	0	1	31.6%	.215/.295/.419	78	.286	-0.6	2B(33): -1.6, 3B(14): 2.7, 1B(12): 0.7	0.2
2021	COL	MLB	26	596	80	32	1	23	86	59	147	6	2	29.2%	.254/.331/.449	99	.306	0.6	3B(113): -3.4, 2B(52): 0.2	1.7
2022 DC	*COL*	*MLB*	*27*	*559*	*73*	*26*	*2*	*21*	*79*	*53*	*145*	*4*	*2*	*29.3%*	*.248/.327/.439*	*100*	*.310*	*-0.2*	*3B 0, SS 0*	*1.6*

Comparables: Jeimer Candelario, Mike Carp, Josh Bell

A power hitter? At Coors Field?? We mean... we *guess* it could work. McMahon may not have been considered multi-dimensional (he arrived to replace, at least spiritually, Mark Reynolds in the everyday lineup), but that one dimension is downright majestic when he's able to barrel up on the ball. If C.J. Cron hadn't been in-house, the 26-year-old McMahon would have been the team's home run leader, providing a fairly predictable slash line and—you're not going to believe this—splits that dramatically favored playing at home over the road (though his home run totals were pretty even in both). It might surprise one to learn that McMahon's defense at third was said to quite effectively fill a monstrous void left by Nolan Arenado, but then, Reynolds held down the hot corner himself until he turned 30. Time erases nuance for us all. Now, to crack the code of hitting in 29 other stadiums...

Elehuris Montero CI

Born: 08/17/98 Age: 23 Bats: R Throws: R Height: 6'3" Weight: 235 lb. Origin: International Free Agent, 2014

YEAR	TEAM	LVL	AGE	PA	R	2B	3B	HR	RBI	BB	K	SB	CS	Whiff%	AVG/OBP/SLG	DRC+	BABIP	BRR	FRAA	WARP
2019	GDD	WIN	20	60	5	3	1	0	3	9	17	1	0		.200/.333/.300		.303			
2019	SPR	AA	20	238	23	8	0	7	18	14	74	0	1		.188/.235/.317	78	.245	0.1	3B(52): -6.2	-0.8
2021	EST	WIN	22	158	12	4	1	2	15	16	35	1	0		.221/.297/.307		.276			
2021	HFD	AA	22	379	46	11	1	22	69	43	90	0	0		.279/.361/.523	124	.309	0.2	3B(42): -0.4, 1B(40): -3.0	1.9
2021	ABQ	AAA	22	121	23	9	1	6	17	10	20	0	0		.278/.355/.546	114	.293	-1.2	3B(19): 0.2, 1B(9): -0.9	0.4
2022 DC	*COL*	*MLB*	*23*	*29*	*3*	*1*	*0*	*1*	*3*	*2*	*6*	*0*	*0*	*27.7%*	*.241/.310/.411*	*89*	*.288*	*0.0*	*SS 0*	*0.1*

Comparables: Cheslor Cuthbert, Miguel Andújar, Miguel Sanó

A quality prospect whose main crime was not being worth Nolan Arenado, Montero boasts a short, swift stroke at the plate. Like a lot of young Rockies hitters, he stores a reservoir of power into which he can tap, and was doing so before he started to sag through a June slump. Eventually, the 22-year-old's bat resurfaced, and he wound up leading the Hartford Yard Goats in home runs and was second on the roster in SLG before a promotion to Triple-A. That said, he's probably never going to make enough contact to maximize his power, and he's going to need to take another step forward if he's going to play everyday at third. He's hit enough to earn his day in the sun, and then he'll try to launch a baseball into it.

Benny Montgomery CF

Born: 09/09/02 Age: 19 Bats: R Throws: R Height: 6'4" Weight: 200 lb. Origin: Round 1, 2021 Draft (#8 overall)

YEAR	TEAM	LVL	AGE	PA	R	2B	3B	HR	RBI	BB	K	SB	CS	Whiff%	AVG/OBP/SLG	DRC+	BABIP	BRR	FRAA	WARP
2021	RCK	ROK	18	52	7	0	1	0	6	5	9	5	1		.340/.404/.383		.421			
2022	*No projection*																			

Comparables: Marlin Almonte, Frank Tolentino, Eudy Pina

Hitters aren't really supposed to have deception in their swings, but no one seems to have told Montgomery, who double-clutches the bat like a windup toy about to do a batflip. Calling a prospect "unorthodox" is a little like describing a young, freethinking Victorian woman as "spirited," but the five-tool athlete put on a demonstration of just how deceiving a swing could be, for scouts if not for opposing pitchers, at the Perfect Game All-American Classic. His swing was considered flat, but the balls that leapt off the bat were not, a reminder that it doesn't matter what the swing path is as long as it hits the correct part of the ball. The 18-year-old has a bit of a Shawn Green lankiness to him, but if anyone looks at his frame and concludes that he can't pack power into it, well, fool you twice.

Dom Nuñez C

Born: 01/17/95 Age: 27 Bats: L Throws: R Height: 6'1" Weight: 212 lb. Origin: Round 6, 2013 Draft (#169 overall)

YEAR	TEAM	LVL	AGE	PA	R	2B	3B	HR	RBI	BB	K	SB	CS	Whiff%	AVG/OBP/SLG	DRC+	BABIP	BRR	FRAA	WARP
2019	ABQ	AAA	24	257	43	14	1	17	42	35	69	2	0		.244/.362/.559	108	.269	0.4	C(60): 11.8	2.5
2019	COL	MLB	24	43	4	3	0	2	4	3	17	0	0	27.5%	.179/.233/.410	74	.238	0.8	C(14): 0.3	0.1
2021	COL	MLB	26	263	31	12	3	10	33	34	91	0	0	33.0%	.189/.293/.399	79	.258	2.0	C(77): 0.7	0.7
2022 DC	*COL*	*MLB*	*27*	*212*	*24*	*8*	*1*	*6*	*22*	*24*	*66*	*1*	*1*	*31.9%*	*.188/.290/.350*	*69*	*.254*	*0.0*	*C 2*	*0.4*

Comparables: Martín Maldonado, Tucker Barnhart, Chris Parmelee

YEAR	TEAM	P. COUNT	FRM RUNS	BLK RUNS	THRW RUNS	TOT RUNS
2019	COL	1647	0.3	0.1	0.0	0.3
2019	ABQ	9250	8.5	0.1	0.2	8.9
2021	COL	10236	0.8	-0.1	0.2	0.9
2022	*COL*	*8418*	*3.1*	*1.0*	*0.1*	*4.1*

Oh, you love power, do you? You like it when a guy puts a charge into Coors Field by absolutely walloping some dumb pitcher's slop high in the zone? You love the way a frayed baseball looks backed by the purple hues of the Colorado twilight? Well, Núñez can give you that power. He just needs to also learn the power of not striking out all the dang time; his 34.6 K% was third highest among catchers (min. 200 PA). The problem is these modern pitchers, they know how to throw more than just a fastball. For moon-gravity Zunino, despite his advanced plate discipline, it's as hard to hit the other stuff as it is to lay off the heaters. And why would you want him to, when you've seen what he can do when he lays *into* one. Power, strikeouts, power, strikeouts... that's the life all sluggers choose when they decide to kill every baseball they come across. This will probably come down to how long the Rockies are willing to see if an additional dimension in Núñez's game develops before moving on to an upgrade, and also having an upgrade.

Chris Owings UT

Born: 08/12/91 Age: 30 Bats: R Throws: R Height: 5'10" Weight: 185 lb. Origin: Round 1, 2009 Draft (#41 overall)

YEAR	TEAM	LVL	AGE	PA	R	2B	3B	HR	RBI	BB	K	SB	CS	Whiff%	AVG/OBP/SLG	DRC+	BABIP	BRR	FRAA	WARP
2019	PAW	AAA	27	183	26	11	0	11	34	15	50	6	4		.325/.385/.595	102	.404	-0.5	SS(18): -0.1, 2B(10): 1.3, 3B(6): -0.3	0.7
2019	KC	MLB	27	145	9	4	1	2	9	8	55	4	1	32.8%	.133/.193/.222	53	.205	0.7	2B(13): -1.7, 3B(12): 1.4, CF(7): -0.2	-0.4
2019	BOS	MLB	27	51	4	2	0	1	5	6	23	1	1	38.9%	.156/.255/.267	60	.286	-1.2	2B(12): 0.1, SS(7): 0.6, 3B(1): -0.0	-0.1
2020	COL	MLB	28	44	9	1	0	2	5	3	11	1	0	34.5%	.268/.318/.439	101	.321	0.6	2B(8): -0.4, 3B(2): -0.8, LF(2): -0.2	0.1
2021	LIC	WIN	29	93	5	1	1	0	5	14	25	3	1		.241/.355/.278		.352			
2021	COL	MLB	29	50	9	4	3	1	5	7	15	2	1	41.6%	.326/.420/.628	86	.481	1.0	2B(3): -0.1, LF(3): -0.1, RF(3): -0.2	0.1
2022 DC	*FA*	*MLB*	*30*	*276*	*26*	*12*	*1*	*6*	*28*	*23*	*96*	*7*	*3*	*35.3%*	*.213/.288/.356*	*73*	*.317*	*0.6*	*2B 0, SS 0*	*0.0*

Comparables: Omar Infante, Alex Gonzalez, Mike Tyson

Chris Owings? More like Chris *Ow*-ings. But seriously folks, this utility man has followed the same tragic narrative for the past two years: Sign a minor-league deal with the Rockies, make the team out of spring training, appear in a handful of games before suffering some kind of devastating injury. In 2020, it was a hamstring. In 2021, it was a thumb. But when he's been around, Owings has found ways to make an impact, providing sudden flourishes of offense (he had six extra-base hits in his first 15 at-bats of the season), as well as filling the locker room air with the hallowed scent of veteran presence. As a free agent at the close of 2021, perhaps another minor-league deal will be slipped under the recovery room door.

Brendan Rodgers 2B

Born: 08/09/96 Age: 25 Bats: R Throws: R Height: 6'0" Weight: 204 lb. Origin: Round 1, 2015 Draft (#3 overall)

YEAR	TEAM	LVL	AGE	PA	R	2B	3B	HR	RBI	BB	K	SB	CS	Whiff%	AVG/OBP/SLG	DRC+	BABIP	BRR	FRAA	WARP
2019	ABQ	AAA	22	160	34	10	1	9	21	14	27	0	0		.350/.413/.622	117	.380	1.6	2B(27): -2.3, SS(6): -0.1, 3B(3): 0.3	1.0
2019	COL	MLB	22	81	8	2	0	0	7	4	27	0	0	31.1%	.224/.272/.250	60	.347	1.6	2B(16): 1.2, SS(9): -1.3	0.0
2020	COL	MLB	23	21	1	1	0	0	2	0	6	0	0	30.6%	.095/.095/.143	83	.133	0.0	2B(5): -0.9, SS(1): -0.0	-0.1
2021	COL	MLB	24	415	49	21	3	15	51	19	84	0	0	23.0%	.284/.328/.470	102	.328	0.3	2B(81): 1.9, SS(26): -0.4	1.8
2022 DC	*COL*	*MLB*	*25*	*563*	*72*	*28*	*2*	*18*	*74*	*31*	*113*	*2*	*2*	*23.4%*	*.262/.317/.431*	*95*	*.306*	*-0.5*	*2B 0, SS 0*	*1.6*

Comparables: Nick Franklin, Luis Sardinas, Jorge Polanco

The long-awaited arrival of Colorado's long-considered shortstop of the future became an even longer one, after the Rockies chose to hold onto Trevor Story at the deadline. But finally, he'll get a chance to compete for the job. After a soft launch—the 25-year-old middle infielder had right shoulder issues end his 2020 season and a strained hamstring to delay 2021—Rodgers made the most of his abridged rookie season. The platoon numbers are a bit worrisome; he was half the hitter when facing righties. But for the optimists, there are plenty of other splits to concentrate on, such as an improvement in the second half and an almost unthinkable superiority when hitting on the road. The Rockies clearly face a lot of questions going into 2022; having their former top prospect answer the first one would be a big help.

Drew Romo C Born: 08/29/01 Age: 20 Bats: S Throws: R Height: 6'1" Weight: 205 lb. Origin: Round 1, 2020 Draft (#35 overall)

YEAR	TEAM	LVL	AGE	PA	R	2B	3B	HR	RBI	BB	K	SB	CS	Whiff%	AVG/OBP/SLG	DRC+	BABIP	BRR	FRAA	WARP
2021	FRE	A	19	339	48	17	2	6	47	19	50	23	6		.314/.345/.439	121	.348	1.2	C(69): 12.8	3.2
2022 non-DC	*COL*	*MLB*	*20*	*251*	*20*	*10*	*1*	*2*	*21*	*12*	*48*	*10*	*4*	*23.1%*	*.248/.287/.339*	*71*	*.301*	*0.9*	*C 2*	*0.5*

Comparables: John Ryan Murphy, Salvador Perez, Francisco Mejía

YEAR	TEAM	P. COUNT	FRM RUNS	BLK RUNS	THRW RUNS	TOT RUNS
2021	FRE	9773	11.8	1.8	0.5	14.1
2022	*COL*	*6956*	*-0.4*	*0.1*	*0.1*	*-0.1*

A catcher's pathway through Colorado's system has never been an easy one. Romo, like all prospects, tried to prevent 2020 from being a total setback. While his development stalled without any Pioneer League games to play in, it was reported that he tried to fill the void by staring at any TV on which the Rockies were playing. As our parents always told us it would, sitting on the couch really paid off for Romo professionally. The 20-year-old backstop is a talented pitch tracker, able to catch and block deftly. These skills have typically defined him more loudly than his bat, no matter what side of the plate he was hitting from. With a quick, strong swing, his issue is pitch recognition, resulting in poor decision-making with a bat in his hands—though statistically he seemed to be picking up the ball as well as, if not better than, the rest of the monstrous hitters in the 2021 Fresno Grizzlies lineup. If Romo can maintain his standing as a stout defender with a mitt full of intangibles, the Rockies will have a job waiting for him at Coors Field.

Aaron Schunk 3B/2B Born: 07/24/97 Age: 24 Bats: R Throws: R Height: 6'2" Weight: 205 lb. Origin: Round 2, 2019 Draft (#62 overall)

YEAR	TEAM	LVL	AGE	PA	R	2B	3B	HR	RBI	BB	K	SB	CS	Whiff%	AVG/OBP/SLG	DRC+	BABIP	BRR	FRAA	WARP
2019	BOI	SS	21	192	31	12	2	6	23	14	25	4	1		.306/.370/.503		.329			
2021	SPO	A+	23	395	57	12	4	8	45	25	111	13	5		.223/.286/.346	83	.296	-2.9	3B(46): -4.2, 2B(38): 2.9, 1B(2): 0.0	0.0
2022 non-DC	*COL*	*MLB*	*24*	*251*	*19*	*9*	*1*	*3*	*20*	*13*	*76*	*4*	*2*	*31.7%*	*.206/.260/.303*	*49*	*.291*	*0.4*	*3B -1, 2B 0*	*-0.9*

Comparables: Joshua Fuentes, Bobby Dalbec, Ryan Flaherty

Psssst. Hey, you. You look like a powerful young hitter. What position do they have you playing? A little third, a little first? A corner guy, eh? Corners are great for standing in at parties, but on the diamond, I don't know. I gotta tell you: You want to make it in *this* organization, you gotta have something nobody else does: *flexibility.* So why not get a few reps at second, you know? Really make yourself appealing to the big club. After all, they got a lot of corner guys hanging around. You got the biceps, I can see that. The boomers love your work ethic. You got a *little* speed... I mean, your legs work. But the defense is... I mean, it's fine. You're fine out there. Nobody's gonna remember how you look. But you gotta at least spread the skill you *do* have out a little more. Pad the ol' résumé. Just one man's opinion. Now, help me put this Dinger head back on. I've got a show to do.

Raimel Tapia LF Born: 02/04/94 Age: 28 Bats: L Throws: L Height: 6'3" Weight: 175 lb. Origin: International Free Agent, 2010

YEAR	TEAM	LVL	AGE	PA	R	2B	3B	HR	RBI	BB	K	SB	CS	Whiff%	AVG/OBP/SLG	DRC+	BABIP	BRR	FRAA	WARP
2019	COL	MLB	25	447	54	23	5	9	44	21	100	9	3	26.9%	.275/.309/.415	80	.341	-0.8	LF(91): 1.0, CF(13): -0.2, RF(6): -0.6	0.4
2020	COL	MLB	26	206	26	8	2	1	17	14	38	8	2	18.9%	.321/.369/.402	91	.392	2.4	LF(36): -0.9, RF(3): -0.6	0.4
2021	COL	MLB	27	533	69	26	2	6	50	40	70	20	6	14.8%	.273/.327/.372	92	.306	3.6	LF(118): -8.8, RF(4): 0.2, CF(3): -0.3	0.9
2022 DC	*COL*	*MLB*	*28*	*424*	*58*	*20*	*4*	*6*	*40*	*29*	*54*	*12*	*4*	*16.1%*	*.276/.332/.396*	*94*	*.310*	*0.9*	*LF -1, CF -1*	*1.1*

Comparables: Starling Marte, Josh Reddick, Aaron Hicks

While the Rockies have had fun results from power-hitting leadoff guys in the past like Charlie Blackmon, Tapia's contributions are made more on the basepaths. He's a passionate singler, frantic dasher, the most frequent groundball hitter in baseball—literally, his 2021 season (67.4%) tops the charts since they started tracking it 20 years ago—and the Rockies' regular left fielder. It was suggested that perhaps part of his job, the leadoff part, should go elsewhere (Connor Joe, anyone?) and Tapia could get slid down to eighth or so. But he had a hell of a June in which he hit 15 doubles, and fans used memories of that magical 18-day hot streak to fuel their desire to see more of Tapia for the other five months of the season. When you're dazzling in short bursts, you always leave 'em wanting more, and that's definitely what fans want to see from Tapia. A distinct lack of alternatives can't hurt, either.

Michael Toglia 1B Born: 08/16/98 Age: 23 Bats: S Throws: L Height: 6'5" Weight: 226 lb. Origin: Round 1, 2019 Draft (#23 overall)

YEAR	TEAM	LVL	AGE	PA	R	2B	3B	HR	RBI	BB	K	SB	CS	Whiff%	AVG/OBP/SLG	DRC+	BABIP	BRR	FRAA	WARP
2019	BOI	SS	20	176	25	7	0	9	26	28	45	1	1		.248/.369/.483		.290			
2021	SRR	WIN	22	105	10	2	1	3	12	12	26	1	0		.264/.343/.407		.328			
2021	SPO	A+	22	330	50	10	2	17	66	42	91	7	3		.234/.333/.465	108	.275	2.0	1B(67): 11.8	2.5
2021	HFD	AA	22	169	16	10	1	5	18	23	51	3	0		.217/.331/.406	93	.295	-2.3	1B(41): 4.3	0.5
2022 non-DC	*COL*	*MLB*	*23*	*251*	*24*	*10*	*1*	*6*	*25*	*23*	*81*	*1*	*1*	*34.8%*	*.203/.285/.347*	*69*	*.285*	*0.0*	*1B 3*	*-0.3*

Comparables: Ike Davis, Matt Adams, Brandon Belt

You can spend forever waiting for someone to become perfect. But the Rockies want to see an "on-base" component to Toglia's game, since he seems to have the "slugging" and "fielding" parts down. He's 22, but given his experience level (three years at UCLA with college summer leagues in between before entering the Rockies' system in 2019), Toglia may be able to push through the minors more aggressively than a typical prospect. This was showcased in his AFL numbers, as Toglia spent parts of autumn crushing baseballs with blistering exit velocity out West. That said, do they really have to hurry? Denver got to watch Mark Reynolds just two years ago. They reboot things so fast these days.

Alan Trejo SS Born: 05/30/96 Age: 26 Bats: R Throws: R Height: 6'2" Weight: 205 lb. Origin: Round 16, 2017 Draft (#476 overall)

YEAR	TEAM	LVL	AGE	PA	R	2B	3B	HR	RBI	BB	K	SB	CS	Whiff%	AVG/OBP/SLG	DRC+	BABIP	BRR	FRAA	WARP
2019	HFD	AA	23	476	45	20	0	15	49	25	105	5	4		.243/.290/.391	95	.285	1.0	SS(91): -6.1, 2B(25): 0.6, 3B(7): 0.1	0.9
2021	ABQ	AAA	25	363	56	34	6	17	72	23	78	2	4		.278/.324/.569	100	.314	-2.7	SS(75): 7.5, 2B(10): 0.0, 3B(2): 0.1	1.6
2021	COL	MLB	25	50	7	2	0	1	3	3	15	0	0	27.1%	.217/.260/.326	81	.290	1.1	2B(10): 0.4, SS(9): -0.2	0.2
2022 DC	*COL*	*MLB*	*26*	*186*	*19*	*10*	*1*	*4*	*21*	*10*	*46*	*1*	*1*	*28.7%*	*.230/.282/.380*	*71*	*.291*	*0.0*	*SS 0, 2B 0*	*0.0*

Comparables: Darwin Barney, Chris Nelson, Erik González

Trejo made the Rockies out of spring training, had two hits in his first 10 games, got his first big-league homer in June and got zapped off the roster by the reactivation of Trevor Story from the IL. To those fixated exclusively on the Rockies' big-league squad and not the lively farm system below it, Trejo may have appeared to be a scuffling young hitter. But those blessed with a worldview that includes Albuquerque saw that over 90 games Trejo can hit well enough for another shot, especially given the need for middle infielders and the churn of the Rockies' depth chart. Some players have raw power that never makes it into games; Trejo somehow has more game power than raw, and it's never quite corrected itself. It was Story's return that once bounced Trejo from the roster, but a potential departure by the star shortstop could conversely mean his next big chance.

★ ★ ★ *2022 Top 101 Prospect* **#25** ★ ★ ★

Zac Veen OF Born: 12/12/01 Age: 20 Bats: L Throws: R Height: 6'4" Weight: 190 lb. Origin: Round 1, 2020 Draft (#9 overall)

YEAR	TEAM	LVL	AGE	PA	R	2B	3B	HR	RBI	BB	K	SB	CS	Whiff%	AVG/OBP/SLG	DRC+	BABIP	BRR	FRAA	WARP
2021	FRE	A	19	479	83	27	4	15	75	64	126	36	17		.301/.399/.501	117	.396	-1.7	RF(69): -0.2, LF(26): 2.2	2.6
2022 non-DC	*COL*	*MLB*	*20*	*251*	*22*	*11*	*1*	*4*	*23*	*22*	*79*	*11*	*7*	*35.8%*	*.216/.291/.334*	*68*	*.312*	*1.2*	*RF 2, LF 1*	*0.1*

Comparables: Travis Snider, Josh Bell, Juan Soto

All through the first few months of the 2021 season, anything Veen did on the field was backed by the sound of missiles priming. Then, as June opened, the 19-year-old absolutely unloaded on the Low-A West League, including a record-setting stretch of reaching base in 15 straight plate appearances, and a night in which he hit for a cycle capped off by an opposite-field grand slam. In July, the ninth-overall pick of the 2020 draft and the largely considered best high schooler identified himself as an MVP. He's 20 now, and when you're 20 and 6' 4", people expect big things from you—even before you're an MVP. Those people were presumably as satisfied by Veen's power as they were his speed. Bumped over to the corner outfield spots, Veen has settled in nicely to this first phase of professional life. The worst thing about his hitting is that the pitchers who had to face him likely had feelings, too.

Colton Welker CI Born: 10/09/97 Age: 24 Bats: R Throws: R Height: 6'1" Weight: 235 lb. Origin: Round 4, 2016 Draft (#110 overall)

YEAR	TEAM	LVL	AGE	PA	R	2B	3B	HR	RBI	BB	K	SB	CS	Whiff%	AVG/OBP/SLG	DRC+	BABIP	BRR	FRAA	WARP
2019	SRR	WIN	21	97	10	2	0	0	7	12	13	3	0		.229/.340/.253		.271			
2019	HFD	AA	21	394	37	23	1	10	53	32	68	2	1		.252/.313/.408	112	.281	-2.4	3B(63): -2.3, 1B(27): 1.9	1.3
2021	SPO	A+	23	35	5	1	0	3	7	2	10	0	0		.194/.257/.516	101	.158		3B(5): -0.8	0.0
2021	ABQ	AAA	23	98	13	5	1	3	18	12	20	0	0		.286/.378/.476	101	.339	0.8	3B(14): -0.8, 1B(6): 0.8	0.4
2021	COL	MLB	23	40	7	1	0	0	2	3	11	0	0	24.1%	.189/.250/.216	84	.269	-0.4	3B(5): -0.5, 1B(2): 0.1	0.0
2022 DC	*COL*	*MLB*	*24*	*224*	*24*	*10*	*0*	*5*	*26*	*17*	*45*	*1*	*1*	*22.9%*	*.238/.306/.372*	*80*	*.286*	*-0.2*	*3B -1, 1B 1*	*-0.1*

Comparables: Neil Walker, Renato Núñez, Miguel Andújar

Welker was set to begin 2021 above Double-A for the first time, with the 23-year-old being considered a rare top-10 Rockies prospect outside of the lower minors. That remained true, in the sense that he found himself outside *all* the minors, after getting dinged with an 80-day suspension as a result of testing positive for dehydrochlormethyltestosterone. When his season finally *did* start, he bounced around just about every minor-league affiliate the Rockies have, trying to get in a groove, but his standing was already weird enough: Once blocked by Nolan Arenado at third, he was shifted to first. But now Arenado is gone, and Welker is left wandering the vast wasteland between the two corners, a man without a home or a position.

PITCHERS

Yency Almonte RHP Born: 06/04/94 Age: 28 Bats: R Throws: R Height: 6'5" Weight: 223 lb. Origin: Round 17, 2012 Draft (#537 overall)

YEAR	TEAM	LVL	AGE	W	L	SV	G	GS	IP	H	HR	BB/9	K/9	K	GB%	BABIP	WHIP	ERA	DRA-	WARP	MPH	FB%	Whiff%	CSP
2019	ABQ	AAA	25	2	3	5	30	0	30	29	2	7.8	9.6	32	49.4%	.318	1.83	4.20	100	0.2				
2019	COL	MLB	25	0	1	0	28	0	34	39	7	3.7	7.7	29	32.7%	.305	1.56	5.56	117	0.0	95.9	57.1%	24.7%	45.2%
2020	COL	MLB	26	3	0	1	24	0	27^{2}	25	2	2.0	7.5	23	55.6%	.291	1.12	2.93	86	0.5	94.8	42.8%	28.1%	44.7%
2021	COL	MLB	27	1	3	0	48	0	47^{2}	47	9	5.5	8.9	47	42.3%	.297	1.59	7.55	114	0.1	94.3	48.8%	26.8%	50.1%
2022 non-DC	*COL*	*MLB*	*28*	*2*	*3*	*0*	*57*	*0*	*50*	*48*	*7*	*4.3*	*8.4*	*46*	*44.3%*	*.301*	*1.46*	*4.99*	*111*	*-0.1*	*94.7*	*48.7%*	*26.7%*	*48.2%*

Comparables: Michael Blazek, José Ramirez, Adam Warren

The Rockies saw more of the 27-year-old Almonte than ever before in 2021. His slider and four-seamer appeared in equal measure—and for good reason—as they kept the ball on the ground in equal measure the previous year, and failed him in equal measure this time. In late April, Almonte was bitten on the hand trying to field a comebacker, and in the time he missed due to injury, the Rockies said he'd be working on mechanical adjustments to slow his ERA's pursuit of 13.00. This of course created a host of suspicious questions like, "Hey…?" and "What's going on here?" as the Rockies fiddled with the definition of "injured" with a pitcher who had no minor-league options left. Again his season was derailed by a post-All-Star COVID outbreak, and he spent the rest of the season trying to keep the ball on the ground and his ERA out of double digits.

Daniel Bard RHP Born: 06/25/85 Age: 37 Bats: R Throws: R Height: 6'4" Weight: 215 lb. Origin: Round 1, 2006 Draft (#28 overall)

YEAR	TEAM	LVL	AGE	W	L	SV	G	GS	IP	H	HR	BB/9	K/9	K	GB%	BABIP	WHIP	ERA	DRA-	WARP	MPH	FB%	Whiff%	CSP
2020	COL	MLB	35	4	2	6	23	0	24^2	22	2	3.6	9.9	27	48.5%	.313	1.30	3.65	83	0.5	97.2	56.4%	28.7%	52.2%
2021	COL	MLB	36	7	8	20	67	0	65^2	69	8	4.9	11.0	80	42.0%	.355	1.60	5.21	87	1.0	97.6	48.5%	29.7%	52.3%
2022 DC	*COL*	*MLB*	*37*	*3*	*3*	*10*	*67*	*0*	*58*	*50*	*8*	*4.0*	*9.3*	*60*	*43.2%*	*.280*	*1.31*	*4.25*	*99*	*0.2*	*97.5*	*49.9%*	*29.5%*	*52.3%*

Comparables: Mike Timlin, Pat Neshek, Bill Campbell

Here we have a late inning Rockies reliever with severe home/road splits. Yawn. But wait…he was better *at* Coors Field? And had an ERA approaching double digits on the road?? Let's all massage our temples and consider this, a reversal of our known reality. Relying chiefly on his slider and four-seamer, the 36-year-old Bard struggled with command and gave up one too many road bombs in August against a weak-hitting Cubs squad. He was pulled off high leverage-duty to try and figure out what the hell was going on, but given his continued problems, it didn't seem like the inning in which Bard was used was the issue. Despite the demotion, his peripherals remained solid, allowing the man with the prodigal slider to retain his title of "Best Comeback Since Rich Hill."

Jhoulys Chacín RHP Born: 01/07/88 Age: 34 Bats: R Throws: R Height: 6'3" Weight: 215 lb. Origin: International Free Agent, 2004

YEAR	TEAM	LVL	AGE	W	L	SV	G	GS	IP	H	HR	BB/9	K/9	K	GB%	BABIP	WHIP	ERA	DRA-	WARP	MPH	FB%	Whiff%	CSP
2019	BOS	MLB	31	0	2	0	6	5	14^2	16	6	4.3	12.9	21	38.5%	.303	1.57	7.36	93	0.2	90.4	44.3%	24.6%	48.6%
2019	MIL	MLB	31	3	10	0	19	19	88^2	99	19	4.0	8.1	80	36.6%	.313	1.56	5.79	109	0.5	89.9	43.5%	20.1%	48.2%
2020	ATL	MLB	32	1	0	0	2	0	5	6	1	5.4	5.4	3	16.7%	.294	1.80	7.20	128	0.0	91.4	42.4%	0.0%	49.5%
2021	COL	MLB	33	3	2	0	46	1	64^1	53	8	3.9	6.6	47	45.9%	.243	1.26	4.34	105	0.4	93.1	41.6%	22.4%	54.0%
2022 DC	*COL*	*MLB*	*34*	*3*	*3*	*0*	*67*	*0*	*58*	*60*	*9*	*3.9*	*7.3*	*47*	*41.9%*	*.299*	*1.47*	*5.20*	*117*	*-0.2*	*91.9*	*42.4%*	*21.0%*	*51.8%*

Comparables: Rick Sutcliffe, Ervin Santana, Jim Clancy

On January 6, 2021, Chacín became a naturalized U.S. citizen. Then, presumably, he turned on the news and yanked comically at his collar. We all make mistakes, but Chacín himself was not one for the Rockies in 2021, a season he began as a Grapefruit League starter for the Yankees. But it was his eleventh hour tryout with Colorado that saw him converted into a veteran reliever who got more exposure in the second half, muscling a 3.81 ERA for August and September. His sustainability was credited to his previous career as a starter, and he provided some rotation depth if anything happened to enough pitchers in front of him. The 33-year-old has entered the part of his career where the word "emergency" is in his job title rather than a description of the situation he creates in-game.

Carlos Estévez RHP Born: 12/28/92 Age: 29 Bats: R Throws: R Height: 6'6" Weight: 277 lb. Origin: International Free Agent, 2011

YEAR	TEAM	LVL	AGE	W	L	SV	G	GS	IP	H	HR	BB/9	K/9	K	GB%	BABIP	WHIP	ERA	DRA-	WARP	MPH	FB%	Whiff%	CSP
2019	COL	MLB	26	2	2	0	71	0	72	70	12	2.9	10.1	81	38.4%	.305	1.29	3.75	85	1.3	98.0	69.3%	30.7%	53.2%
2020	COL	MLB	27	1	3	1	26	0	24	33	6	3.4	10.1	27	29.9%	.380	1.75	7.50	124	0.0	97.0	61.5%	25.1%	50.2%
2021	COL	MLB	28	3	5	11	64	0	61^2	71	8	3.1	8.8	60	44.9%	.354	1.49	4.38	98	0.6	97.3	65.8%	24.6%	56.4%
2022 DC	*COL*	*MLB*	*29*	*3*	*3*	*19*	*67*	*0*	*58*	*57*	*8*	*2.9*	*8.6*	*55*	*41.4%*	*.301*	*1.30*	*4.34*	*101*	*0.2*	*97.4*	*65.9%*	*26.1%*	*54.6%*

Comparables: Dominic Leone, Matt Capps, Ryan Webb

Estévez has always struggled with command, and a refresher course in Triple-A would hardly have been unthinkable. Instead, the Rockies gave him 61 ⅔ innings in 2021 and made him the closer (a job he got because Daniel Bard plummeted out of the role). The key was his slider; the right-hander has a bit of a career reverse platoon split, simply because he wasn't throwing his worst pitch against opposite-handed batters. In 2021 the pitch upgraded to "vaguely within reach of the batter," which was a big step forward. When he'd work too fast and lose control, he'd be reminded to calm down and go at his own pace. There were good moments that indicated the 29-year-old has, somewhere in there, the stuff for the back of the bullpen at Coors. The growth was good to see, but there's not a lot of expectations (or work) for the closer on a fourth place team.

Ryan Feltner RHP Born: 09/02/96 Age: 25 Bats: R Throws: R Height: 6'4" Weight: 190 lb. Origin: Round 4, 2018 Draft (#126 overall)

YEAR	TEAM	LVL	AGE	W	L	SV	G	GS	IP	H	HR	BB/9	K/9	K	GB%	BABIP	WHIP	ERA	DRA-	WARP	MPH	FB%	Whiff%	CSP
2019	ASH	A	22	9	9	0	25	25	119	137	12	3.5	8.8	116	50.0%	.360	1.54	5.07	109	0.4				
2021	SPO	A+	24	3	1	0	7	7	37^1	26	1	4.3	10.8	45	42.4%	.275	1.18	2.17	90	0.5				
2021	HFD	AA	24	5	2	0	13	13	72^2	68	7	2.7	9.9	80	37.9%	.324	1.24	2.85	100	0.6				
2021	COL	MLB	24	0	1	0	2	2	6^1	9	3	7.1	8.5	6	9.5%	.333	2.21	11.37	115	0.0	92.7	54.2%	32.1%	53.9%
2022 DC	*COL*	*MLB*	*25*	*5*	*5*	*0*	*40*	*11*	*71*	*75*	*11*	*4.5*	*8.3*	*65*	*37.4%*	*.315*	*1.55*	*5.65*	*123*	*-0.3*	*92.7*	*54.2%*	*32.1%*	*53.9%*

Comparables: Gonzalez Germen, Josh Collmenter, Joe Biagini

Feltner, with his 92-mph fastball and his work-in-progress secondary pitches, is a part of the group of Rockies pitchers informally viewed by experts as "not enough pitching depth." The goal was just to show the 25-year-old who has run into some struggles each time he ascends the Rockies system what it was like at Coors Field. The results were more like making your kid perform at a piano recital so they know what it's like to perform in front of an audience, without teaching them how to play the piano first. To be fair, "back-end rotation hopeful" is a step forward from the relief prospect he looked like out of college. The hope is that these September trials will help adjust him to more meaningful September starts down the line. *(More meaningful Septembers in Colorado TBD.)*

Kyle Freeland LHP Born: 05/14/93 Age: 29 Bats: L Throws: L Height: 6'4" Weight: 204 lb. Origin: Round 1, 2014 Draft (#8 overall)

YEAR	TEAM	LVL	AGE	W	L	SV	G	GS	IP	H	HR	BB/9	K/9	K	GB%	BABIP	WHIP	ERA	DRA-	WARP	MPH	FB%	Whiff%	CSP
2019	ABQ	AAA	26	0	4	0	6	6	29^{2}	40	4	4.9	8.5	28	53.5%	.396	1.89	8.80	91	0.3				
2019	COL	MLB	26	3	11	0	22	22	104^{1}	126	25	3.4	6.8	79	46.2%	.310	1.58	6.73	126	-0.4	92.1	52.0%	21.4%	44.8%
2020	COL	MLB	27	2	3	0	13	13	70^{2}	77	9	2.9	5.9	46	50.0%	.305	1.42	4.33	111	0.4	92.0	33.4%	20.6%	45.6%
2021	ABQ	AAA	28	1	1	0	2	2	10	4	0	1.8	3.6	4	76.7%	.133	0.60	1.80	102	0.0				
2021	COL	MLB	28	7	8	0	23	23	120^{2}	133	20	2.8	7.8	105	44.0%	.328	1.42	4.33	103	0.9	91.5	41.4%	21.5%	52.5%
2022 DC	*COL*	*MLB*	*29*	*9*	*9*	*0*	*27*	*27*	*148.7*	*158*	*20*	*2.9*	*6.8*	*112*	*47.3%*	*.305*	*1.39*	*4.66*	*109*	*0.5*	*91.7*	*41.5%*	*21.3%*	*49.5%*

Comparables: Alex Kellner, Jeff Francis, Ervin Santana

Freeland's been surviving Coors Field for half a decade now, using a changeup to dance with the devil in the crisp, thin air, and the element of surprise in shuffling his other four offerings. After a left shoulder strain kept the 28-year-old lefty off the mound until May 25, Freeland was hit hard at a higher rate than in recent years, but put together a string of solid starts late in the season after adjusting his pitch selection yet again; after watching too many of his changeups sail over the fence, he forsook strikeouts and leaned more heavily on his sinker and slider. It worked, as hitters struggled to barrel up his breaking pitches, and the lowly Rockies winning each of his five starts in August. He even got to play right field once. That may be the secret to Freeland's survival at Coors, other than fighting off deer for food scraps and claiming entire sections of the abandoned upper deck as his "territory" marked by human skulls on sticks: The ball won't go far without hard contact.

Lucas Gilbreath LHP Born: 03/05/96 Age: 26 Bats: L Throws: L Height: 6'1" Weight: 185 lb. Origin: Round 7, 2017 Draft (#206 overall)

YEAR	TEAM	LVL	AGE	W	L	SV	G	GS	IP	H	HR	BB/9	K/9	K	GB%	BABIP	WHIP	ERA	DRA-	WARP	MPH	FB%	Whiff%	CSP
2019	LAN	A+	23	5	10	0	28	28	144	168	22	4.6	8.9	143	41.9%	.350	1.68	5.81	134	-2.4				
2021	COL	MLB	25	3	2	1	47	1	42^{2}	33	5	4.9	9.3	44	45.3%	.250	1.31	3.38	95	0.5	93.6	63.1%	29.9%	53.5%
2022 DC	*COL*	*MLB*	*26*	*2*	*3*	*0*	*59*	*0*	*51.7*	*51*	*8*	*4.9*	*9.5*	*54*	*42.6%*	*.317*	*1.55*	*5.41*	*117*	*-0.3*	*93.6*	*63.1%*	*29.9%*	*53.5%*

Comparables: Sean Gilmartin, Aaron Loup, Kyle McClellan

The Rockies really like Gilbreath, enough to draft him twice. Maybe they like that he's from Colorado, and is therefore more attuned to having the brains sucked out of his ears by the air pressure 5,280 feet above the sea. It was confusing to some when they protected him from the Rule 5 draft in 2020, given that he had yet to pitch at Double-A and wasn't on any top prospect lists; two-pitch relievers with low-90s fastballs hardly get the scouting blood pumping. Yet emerging from the hazy recesses of a lost 2020, Gilbreath proved to be one of the more effective arms in the Rockies bullpen in 2021. While the stuff remains nominal, his pitches are a little like houseflies—they land everywhere, and people can't quite seem to slap them—as his contact rate was a full five points below league average. Outside of the organization, the 25-year-old may be best known for breaking Brandon Belt's thumb late in the season with an inside pitch, so he's already making friends in the NL West.

Austin Gomber LHP Born: 11/23/93 Age: 28 Bats: L Throws: L Height: 6'5" Weight: 220 lb. Origin: Round 4, 2014 Draft (#135 overall)

YEAR	TEAM	LVL	AGE	W	L	SV	G	GS	IP	H	HR	BB/9	K/9	K	GB%	BABIP	WHIP	ERA	DRA-	WARP	MPH	FB%	Whiff%	CSP
2019	MEM	AAA	25	4	0	0	8	8	45^{1}	42	5	3.2	10.3	52	37.6%	.333	1.28	2.98	81	0.8				
2020	STL	MLB	26	1	1	0	14	4	29	19	1	4.7	8.4	27	48.0%	.243	1.17	1.86	95	0.4	92.8	52.5%	26.6%	48.3%
2021	COL	MLB	27	9	9	0	23	23	115^{1}	102	20	3.2	8.8	113	43.2%	.265	1.24	4.53	99	1.1	91.9	40.7%	26.0%	56.6%
2022 DC	*COL*	*MLB*	*28*	*8*	*7*	*0*	*25*	*25*	*124.3*	*116*	*17*	*3.3*	*8.4*	*116*	*43.0%*	*.293*	*1.31*	*4.13*	*97*	*1.1*	*92.0*	*42.6%*	*26.1%*	*55.2%*

Comparables: Drew Pomeranz, José Quintana, Rafael Montero

Hopefully, as you read this, Gomber is either currently reading a magazine or playing the new *Dynasty Warriors* before getting back into his routine. That's the best medicine for pars defect, a sexy name for stress fractures in the little bones of your lower spine. The 27-year-old lefty was sent to the 60-day IL in early September after suffering from back pain for weeks, which anyone in their 30s or older can tell you makes everything much, much sexier. Wielding his four-seamer slider, change and a curveball that's been whispered about like a mythic beast since he was in the minors, Gomber went at least six innings in about half his starts, the last time coming in early August. After that, the rigors of having a literally broken back began to take their toll and none of Gomber's tricks to get batters out were as effective. With enough show-binging and PlayStation-ing, Colorado's new innings-eater hopefully soothed his lower back and can continue where he and his toothy curveball left off.

Ashton Goudeau RHP Born: 07/23/92 Age: 29 Bats: R Throws: R Height: 6'6" Weight: 220 lb. Origin: Round 27, 2012 Draft (#823 overall)

YEAR	TEAM	LVL	AGE	W	L	SV	G	GS	IP	H	HR	BB/9	K/9	K	GB%	BABIP	WHIP	ERA	DRA-	WARP	MPH	FB%	Whiff%	CSP
2019	HFD	AA	26	3	3	0	16	16	78^{1}	60	4	1.4	10.5	91	42.1%	.293	0.92	2.07	91	1.0				
2020	COL	MLB	27	0	0	0	4	0	8^{1}	15	3	2.2	2.2	2	44.1%	.387	2.04	7.56	197	-0.3	93.5	47.0%	14.3%	46.8%
2021	ABQ	AAA	28	0	0	0	3	1	8	13	2	1.1	3.4	3	48.5%	.355	1.75	6.75	113	0.0				
2021	LOU	AAA	28	1	3	0	8	5	31	30	5	3.8	6.4	22	34.7%	.269	1.39	4.65	116	0.2				
2021	COL	MLB	28	2	1	0	11	1	25^{1}	16	3	2.8	6.0	17	48.6%	.200	0.95	4.26	105	0.2	92.9	45.8%	18.9%	50.5%
2021	CIN	MLB	28	0	0	0	5	0	9	8	1	9.0	5.0	5	50.0%	.250	1.89	4.00	128	0.0	92.4	45.2%	18.9%	49.1%
2022 DC	*COL*	*MLB*	*29*	*6*	*4*	*0*	*55*	*3*	*55*	*62*	*8*	*3.5*	*6.8*	*41*	*42.5%*	*.316*	*1.52*	*5.54*	*123*	*-0.4*	*92.9*	*45.8%*	*18.4%*	*49.7%*

Comparables: Tyler Pill, Pedro Villarreal, Dylan Axelrod

Another four-seam, curve and changeup guy, Goudeau was beckoned to the mound for some long relief when things went wrong for the Rockies. But something about the Rockies (beyond the going wrong part) keeps bringing Goudeau back. Actually, three somethings: Once they signed him as a free agent, once they selected him off waivers, and once they purchased him from the Reds. They just need to acquire him via trade and he automatically becomes their general manager, if we're reading these bylaws correctly. Goudeau is currently the most footsore journeyman in baseball, being designated for assignment eight times in 2021 and plucked off waivers six times since November 2020. For a man like that, the biggest question isn't "When do I get to pitch?" It's "When's the next train out of town?"

JD Hammer RHP

Born: 07/12/94 Age: 27 Bats: R Throws: R Height: 6'3" Weight: 202 lb. Origin: Round 24, 2016 Draft (#710 overall)

YEAR	TEAM	LVL	AGE	W	L	SV	G	GS	IP	H	HR	BB/9	K/9	K	GB%	BABIP	WHIP	ERA	DRA-	WARP	MPH	FB%	Whiff%	CSP
2019	REA	AA	24	1	0	2	13	0	20^{1}	17	1	1.8	11.5	26	49.0%	.320	1.03	1.77	91	0.3				
2019	LHV	AAA	24	2	2	0	17	0	15^{2}	20	4	8.6	9.2	16	26.0%	.356	2.23	12.64	106	0.1				
2019	PHI	MLB	24	1	0	0	20	0	19	15	2	5.7	6.2	13	41.1%	.241	1.42	3.79	124	0.0	94.5	53.8%	21.2%	46.3%
2021	LHV	AAA	26	2	0	1	20	0	23^{2}	20	3	4.9	13.7	36	29.6%	.340	1.39	3.80	85	0.5				
2021	PHI	MLB	26	1	1	0	20	0	20	21	3	5.0	9.9	22	42.4%	.321	1.60	4.95	100	0.2	94.2	61.5%	24.4%	52.9%
2022 DC	*COL*	*MLB*	*27*	*0*	*0*	*0*	*14*	*0*	*12.7*	*12*	*2*	*4.9*	*9.7*	*13*	*38.5%*	*.300*	*1.47*	*5.01*	*111*	*0.0*	*94.3*	*59.8%*	*23.7%*	*51.5%*

Comparables: Colten Brewer, Matt Carasiti, David Carpenter

There are few better surnames for a pitcher than Hammer's, even if he doesn't feature the curve. He made his debut in 2019 and pitched to a 3.79 ERA in a 19 inning sample, albeit with a 124 DRA– that signaled he may have benefitted from some good luck on balls in play. Hammer's run prevention regressed hard in 2021, as his ERA inflated to just under 5.00, but his DRA– was a much more palatable 101, thanks to a more than seven percentage-point increase in strikeout rate. Hammer features a low to mid-90's fastball with good horizontal movement, a slider that gets whiffs at over 30% of total swings and a moniker that means he's in line for some great nicknames if things break right.

Jaden Hill RHP

Born: 12/22/99 Age: 22 Bats: R Throws: R Height: 6'4" Weight: 234 lb. Origin: Round 2, 2021 Draft (#44 overall)

Change is hard; change like moving from college ball to rookie league ball. Change gets even harder when you're afraid of being left out. HIll was the only 2021 Rockies draft pick who was not sent to the Arizona Complex League, but all he missed was being part of a team that went... 44-15?!? Well, fortunately for Hill, he's never been a man afraid of change. In fact, the aggressive change in his arsenal was part of the reason why the Rockies took him in the second round. The other reasons were his 95-97 mph heater and the fact that he'd slipped down to a lower spot because of some Tommy John surgery. With those days behind him, Hill has plenty of upside and looks ready to *embrace* change by throwing one opposing hitters can't touch.

Tyler Kinley RHP

Born: 01/31/91 Age: 31 Bats: R Throws: R Height: 6'4" Weight: 220 lb. Origin: Round 16, 2013 Draft (#472 overall)

YEAR	TEAM	LVL	AGE	W	L	SV	G	GS	IP	H	HR	BB/9	K/9	K	GB%	BABIP	WHIP	ERA	DRA-	WARP	MPH	FB%	Whiff%	CSP
2019	NO	AAA	28	0	1	2	14	0	15^{2}	4	1	4.0	10.9	19	35.5%	.100	0.70	1.72	87	0.1				
2019	MIA	MLB	28	3	1	1	52	0	49^{1}	43	5	6.6	8.4	46	38.4%	.288	1.60	3.65	120	0.0	95.0	42.5%	29.6%	43.8%
2020	COL	MLB	29	0	2	0	24	0	23^{2}	13	2	4.6	9.9	26	45.5%	.212	1.06	5.32	90	0.4	95.9	33.6%	36.2%	44.0%
2021	COL	MLB	30	3	2	0	70	0	70^{1}	59	12	3.3	8.7	68	38.7%	.253	1.21	4.73	99	0.7	96.1	43.4%	29.2%	56.3%
2022 DC	*COL*	*MLB*	*31*	*3*	*3*	*0*	*67*	*0*	*58*	*54*	*8*	*4.2*	*9.3*	*60*	*40.4%*	*.298*	*1.40*	*4.66*	*105*	*0.1*	*95.8*	*41.8%*	*30.3%*	*52.3%*

Comparables: Ryan Tepera, Ryan Buchter, JT Chargois

On May 15, 1918, Walter Johnson pitched 18 scoreless innings for the Senators in a show of stamina and skill that delighted fans and horrified physicians. We can only assume that Kinley knew it was the 103rd anniversary of that day on May 15, 2021, when he began a scoreless streak of his own; one that noticeably stretched through only nine innings and was spread out over nine games. Still, though; given what we know now about medical concepts like "fatigue" and "arm murder," Kinley's approach was much more rational. The nine-game stretch was a course correction from the season's first six weeks, when he'd bled hits and runs pretty regularly, and his dominance faded away *after* those nine games as well—only to return in September, when Kinley put up a 2.87 ERA in 15.2 innings and his slider crept out of the high eighties into the low nineties. Those sharp final weeks made an otherwise forgettable season more memorable to the Rockies, who have to consider anybody useful who can get regular outs for a few weeks out of the pen.

Germán Márquez RHP

Born: 02/22/95 Age: 27 Bats: R Throws: R Height: 6'1" Weight: 230 lb. Origin: International Free Agent, 2011

YEAR	TEAM	LVL	AGE	W	L	SV	G	GS	IP	H	HR	BB/9	K/9	K	GB%	BABIP	WHIP	ERA	DRA-	WARP	MPH	FB%	Whiff%	CSP
2019	COL	MLB	24	12	5	0	28	28	174	174	29	1.8	9.1	175	48.2%	.308	1.20	4.76	82	3.4	95.4	52.1%	26.8%	51.4%
2020	COL	MLB	25	4	6	0	13	13	81^{2}	78	6	2.8	8.0	73	50.4%	.300	1.26	3.75	77	1.9	95.7	52.4%	26.3%	50.2%
2021	COL	MLB	26	12	11	0	32	32	180	165	21	3.2	8.8	176	51.3%	.297	1.27	4.40	85	3.0	94.9	53.0%	27.5%	57.8%
2022 DC	*COL*	*MLB*	*27*	*13*	*9*	*0*	*29*	*29*	*192.3*	*180*	*22*	*2.9*	*9.1*	*195*	*50.4%*	*.306*	*1.26*	*3.72*	*89*	*2.7*	*95.2*	*52.7%*	*27.1%*	*55.2%*

Comparables: Livan Hernandez, Mike Mussina, Ryan Dempster

How long can a man and his curveball survive at Coors Field? Apparently, at least this long. Márquez has been a mainstay in the Rockies rotation since 2016, and while his curve usage has declined in favor of a slider (the Rockies' favorite pitch), he's done the unthinkable and remained effective in Denver, despite the air or the cold or the clouds or whatever cutting down on pitch movement. Who knows; this is a baseball annual, not a science journal. Márquez has always been able to hide behind a fluffy ERA with ace-level advanced metrics, and even though he led the league in wild pitches in 2021, he was still an All-Star for a reason. Nobody on the Rockies pitching staff pitched more innings, nobody made more starts, and nobody struck more hitters out. Márquez's numbers will always look a little raw because of where he pitches, but nobody has been more reliable than the 27-year-old since he arrived in the rotation.

Helcris Olivarez LHP

Born: 08/08/00 Age: 21 Bats: L Throws: L Height: 6'2" Weight: 192 lb. Origin: International Free Agent, 2016

YEAR	TEAM	LVL	AGE	W	L	SV	G	GS	IP	H	HR	BB/9	K/9	K	GB%	BABIP	WHIP	ERA	DRA-	WARP	MPH	FB%	Whiff%	CSP
2019	DSL ROC	ROK	18	1	0	0	3	3	14	7	0	4.5	13.5	21	34.6%	.269	1.00	0.64						
2019	GJ	ROA	18	3	4	0	11	11	46^{2}	47	9	4.6	11.8	61	45.9%	.336	1.52	4.82						
2021	SPO	A+	20	4	9	0	22	21	99^{2}	89	10	6.1	10.1	112	51.0%	.328	1.58	6.05	111	0.2				
2022 non-DC	*COL*	*MLB*	*21*	*2*	*3*	*0*	*57*	*0*	*50*	*52*	*7*	*7.2*	*8.6*	*47*	*45.4%*	*.314*	*1.84*	*6.95*	*142*	*-0.9*				

Comparables: Marcus Moore, Brock Burke, Chris Seddon

Olivarez had been clinging to the Rockies on the fringes since he was an international signee in 2016; making it onto the prospect lists, but never very high; and raising eyebrows when he was added to the 40-man. His numbers in High-A this past year (his first full minor-league season, due to COVID) look messy and unpleasant and seem to tell us that no, this young man will not see the majors in 2022. His fastball is both fast and often called a ball; his changeup is deceptive in the sense that it's never certain it'll break; and the curve is a get-me-over pitch that rarely gets over. But you're forgetting something: He's left-handed. What he needs is experience, as the Rockies like his mid-nineties heater and power curve. Already benefiting from the guidance of veterans like Germán Márquez and Carlos Estévez, Olivarez will remain on the mound—and the 40-man—to beef up that most elusive yet inevitable of all statistics: Time. At only 21 years old, he's got some more of it.

Joe Rock LHP Born: 07/29/00 Age: 21 Bats: L Throws: L Height: 6'6" Weight: 200 lb. Origin: Round 2, 2021 Draft (#68 overall)

YEAR	TEAM	LVL	AGE	W	L	SV	G	GS	IP	H	HR	BB/9	K/9	K	GB%	BABIP	WHIP	ERA	DRA-	WARP	MPH	FB%	Whiff%	CSP
2021	RCK	ROK	20	1	0	0	4	2	8	5	0	1.1	12.4	11	70.6%	.294	0.75	1.13						
2022												*No projection*												

He could be the main character of a children's book about a rock-boy born from a mountaintop who rolls down the side, all the way onto the pitcher's mound at Coors Field. Of course, he's never pitched there, having only joined the organization in 2021. Rock fires strikes into the zone with a low arm slot and looks to some experts to have a lingering future as a reliever, and because this rock-boy grew into an enormous rock-man six and a half feet tall, there's the back pocket chance that he can get his fastball to go even faster. And also learn the true meaning of friendship, or befriend an invisible dinosaur.

Ryan Rolison LHP Born: 07/11/97 Age: 24 Bats: R Throws: L Height: 6'2" Weight: 213 lb. Origin: Round 1, 2018 Draft (#22 overall)

YEAR	TEAM	LVL	AGE	W	L	SV	G	GS	IP	H	HR	BB/9	K/9	K	GB%	BABIP	WHIP	ERA	DRA-	WARP	MPH	FB%	Whiff%	CSP
2019	ASH	A	21	2	1	0	3	3	14^2	8	0	1.2	8.6	14	37.8%	.216	0.68	0.61	98	0.1				
2019	LAN	A+	21	6	7	0	22	22	116^1	129	22	2.9	9.1	118	43.6%	.327	1.44	4.87	103	0.1				
2021	RCK	ROK	23	0	0	0	2	2	6^1	10	0	2.8	12.8	9	27.8%	.556	1.89	7.11						
2021	HFD	AA	23	2	1	0	3	3	14^2	11	1	1.2	12.3	20	52.9%	.303	0.89	3.07	88	0.2				
2021	ABQ	AAA	23	2	2	0	10	10	45^2	51	7	3.2	8.9	45	41.3%	.336	1.47	5.91	103	0.1				
2022 DC	*COL*	*MLB*	*24*	*3*	*3*	*0*	*12*	*12*	*54.3*	*57*	*9*	*3.4*	*7.3*	*44*	*41.3%*	*.303*	*1.44*	*5.19*	*118*	*-0.1*				

Comparables: Wade LeBlanc, Dallas Braden, Luis Cessa

Rolison was moved from Double to Triple-A in 2021. Three starts later, his appendix was moved from inside to outside his body. He wound up missing ten weeks after a batting practice liner dinged him in the hand and broke it. So, given his missed time and subsequent rehabilitation, Colorado wanted their top pitching prospect to rack up some innings in the Dominican League this winter, rather than sending him to Arizona in the fall, in order for him to sharpen his hittable fastball and aggressive curve in a more intense environment than the AFL. That, in a small way, seems to align with Rolison's own goal of pitching in the majors in 2022, although his profile makes the Coors Field factor a bit of a worry—of course, whose doesn't?

Antonio Senzatela RHP Born: 01/21/95 Age: 27 Bats: R Throws: R Height: 6'1" Weight: 236 lb. Origin: International Free Agent, 2011

YEAR	TEAM	LVL	AGE	W	L	SV	G	GS	IP	H	HR	BB/9	K/9	K	GB%	BABIP	WHIP	ERA	DRA-	WARP	MPH	FB%	Whiff%	CSP
2019	ABQ	AAA	24	1	1	0	7	7	34^1	45	7	2.6	3.1	12	48.4%	.317	1.60	5.77	122	-0.2				
2019	COL	MLB	24	11	11	0	25	25	124^2	161	19	4.1	5.5	76	53.5%	.336	1.75	6.71	121	-0.1	93.8	63.7%	17.9%	48.3%
2020	COL	MLB	25	5	3	0	12	12	73^1	71	9	2.2	5.0	41	50.8%	.268	1.21	3.44	99	0.9	94.4	56.0%	18.5%	48.4%
2021	COL	MLB	26	4	10	0	28	28	156^2	178	12	1.8	6.0	105	50.4%	.326	1.34	4.42	106	0.9	94.8	56.1%	19.8%	56.3%
2022 DC	*COL*	*MLB*	*27*	*11*	*10*	*0*	*29*	*29*	*177.7*	*200*	*20*	*2.5*	*5.7*	*112*	*50.7%*	*.311*	*1.40*	*4.71*	*111*	*0.4*	*94.6*	*57.5%*	*19.2%*	*53.2%*

Comparables: Iván Nova, Jeff Suppan, Derek Holland

It's quite a statement when, the day after your season ends on a walk-off loss, you hand a guy a deal worth at least $50 million. But that's what the Rockies did to retain the services of Senzatela for at least five years. And why wouldn't they? He's been surviving at Coors since 2017 through his artistry at keeping the ball on the ground and limiting walks. These days, Senzatela fortifies his four-seamer with a slider and on occasion, a changeup or curve is mixed in. Instead of just uncorking fastballs as hard as he could, he has embraced the "pitching" aspect of being a pitcher and become a lot better for it. In the wake of some superstar departures and organizational shuffling, the Rockies say they have a plan. Hanging onto an impactful arm like Senzatela's is believably part of one. Now, onto phase two through eight, presumably.

Jordan Sheffield RHP Born: 06/01/95 Age: 27 Bats: R Throws: R Height: 5'10" Weight: 190 lb. Origin: Round 1, 2016 Draft (#36 overall)

YEAR	TEAM	LVL	AGE	W	L	SV	G	GS	IP	H	HR	BB/9	K/9	K	GB%	BABIP	WHIP	ERA	DRA-	WARP	MPH	FB%	Whiff%	CSP
2019	RC	A+	24	2	2	7	15	0	17^1	6	2	5.7	13.5	26	27.6%	.148	0.98	2.60	90	0.2				
2019	TUL	AA	24	2	3	6	34	2	37^2	26	3	7.6	11.5	48	36.0%	.267	1.54	3.58	104	0.0				
2021	COL	MLB	26	0	0	0	30	0	29^1	19	2	4.0	6.1	20	44.4%	.215	1.09	3.38	116	0.0	96.6	64.7%	23.4%	54.4%
2022 DC	*COL*	*MLB*	*27*	*2*	*3*	*0*	*59*	*0*	*51.7*	*55*	*9*	*5.8*	*8.0*	*46*	*39.8%*	*.311*	*1.72*	*6.48*	*136*	*-0.8*	*96.6*	*64.7%*	*23.4%*	*54.4%*

Comparables: Tyler Zuber, Lou Trivino, Hunter Strickland

Snagged from the Dodgers in the Rule 5 draft, Sheffield had four pretty bad days out of 30 appearances. He also had a bunch of bad days personally after a lateral strain wiped out three months of his season. His changeup was the most effective, relatively, in getting whiffs out of his three-pitch toolkit that also includes a four-seamer and a slider. That said, it's kind of amazing that a prospect heralded as having three plus pitches and zero clue where they were going wound up with this walk and strikeout rate in his major-league debut. People change. We may never know the hot rush of satisfaction front offices get from Rule 5 picks working out, so they can feel like they got something for nothing, but Sheffield's solid work out of the Rockies bullpen likely gave them that feeling.

Robert Stephenson RHP Born: 02/24/93 Age: 29 Bats: R Throws: R Height: 6'3" Weight: 205 lb. Origin: Round 1, 2011 Draft (#27 overall)

YEAR	TEAM	LVL	AGE	W	L	SV	G	GS	IP	H	HR	BB/9	K/9	K	GB%	BABIP	WHIP	ERA	DRA-	WARP	MPH	FB%	Whiff%	CSP
2019	CIN	MLB	26	3	2	0	57	0	64^2	43	9	3.3	11.3	81	31.4%	.231	1.04	3.76	85	1.2	94.9	36.2%	39.0%	44.2%
2020	CIN	MLB	27	0	0	0	10	0	10	11	8	2.7	11.7	13	23.1%	.167	1.40	9.90	114	0.0	95.1	30.1%	39.5%	45.7%
2021	COL	MLB	28	2	1	1	49	0	46	42	5	3.5	10.2	52	37.6%	.311	1.30	3.13	91	0.6	96.7	49.4%	27.0%	54.9%
2022 DC	*COL*	*MLB*	*29*	*3*	*3*	*0*	*67*	*0*	*58*	*52*	*10*	*3.7*	*9.5*	*61*	*36.2%*	*.286*	*1.31*	*4.39*	*101*	*0.2*	*96.0*	*43.9%*	*31.5%*	*51.0%*

Comparables: Jeanmar Gómez, Randall Delgado, Jeremy Jeffress

Stephenson may have a fastball, and it may have an average velocity in the mid-nineties, and it may even find the hundred-mile holy land when he's seeing red, and it may have some good movement around the strike zone, even in Coors. But man, it's a shame he stopped throwing that slider as much. It was an effective out-pitch, at least until 2021 when batters got off to a quick start poking, plunking and crushing it, until he lost confidence in it. Instead he shelved it for his curve, which, as with many Rockies pitchers, looks pretty much exactly like his slider. In the end, Stephenson made it work, because all his pitches have enough life to survive the Moon Effect. He probably shouldn't abandon the slider entirely, especially since it's also effective at inducing grounders, but the upcoming season will show us how he plans to continue adapting.

LINEOUTS

Hitters

HITTER	POS	TEAM	LVL	AGE	PA	R	2B	3B	HR	RBI	BB	K	SB	CS	AVG/OBP/SLG	DRC+	BABIP	BRR	FRAA	WARP
Matt Adams	1B	COL	MLB	32	40	3	1	0	0	2	4	9	0	0	.167/.250/.194	81	.222	0.3	1B(7): -0.8	0.0
Adael Amador	SS	RCK	ROK	18	200	41	10	1	4	24	27	29	10	7	.299/.394/.445		.331			
Warming Bernabel	3B	RCK	ROK	19	86	18	5	0	6	31	5	12	5	1	.432/.453/.743		.426			
	3B	FRE	A	19	94	9	6	0	1	7	7	14	4	1	.205/.287/.313	111	.232	-0.9	3B(17): 0.6	0.4
Greg Bird	1B	ABQ	AAA	28	461	63	21	1	27	91	58	106	0	1	.267/.362/.532	113	.293	-1.5	1B(86): 7.1	2.3
Yonathan Daza	OF	ABQ	AAA	27	26	4	0	0	0	2	0	4	1	0	.308/.308/.308	96	.364	-0.5	CF(4): -0.1, LF(1): -0.1, RF(1): -0.3	0.0
	OF	COL	MLB	27	331	26	12	2	2	30	21	60	2	1	.282/.332/.355	90	.346	0.2	CF(57): 0.5, RF(22): 0.3, LF(12): 0.5	1.0
Joshua Fuentes	CI	ABQ	AAA	28	210	29	12	2	9	32	11	43	1	3	.269/.324/.492	100	.303	-1.9	3B(20): 1.8, LF(16): -1.6, 2B(10): -0.3	0.5
	CI	COL	MLB	28	284	30	11	1	7	33	12	65	0	0	.225/.257/.351	79	.270	2.8	3B(60): 5.9, 1B(32): 0.3, LF(2): -0.1	1.1
Hunter Goodman	C/DH	RCK	ROK	21	74	16	7	0	2	12	9	14	1	0	.300/.419/.517		.356			
Garrett Hampson	CF/2B	COL	MLB	26	494	69	21	6	11	33	33	118	17	7	.234/.289/.380	81	.291	2.5	CF(91): -0.6, 2B(47): 0.8, SS(5): -0.5	1.0
Willie MacIver	C	SPO	A+	24	201	25	11	1	10	30	25	49	10	3	.286/.395/.542	123	.345	-0.3	C(38): 4.5	1.6
	C	HFD	AA	24	212	21	4	0	5	13	16	64	10	2	.167/.241/.266	73	.218	0.0	C(46): 1.5	0.2
Rio Ruiz	2B/3B	ABQ	AAA	27	249	38	20	1	7	28	20	39	3	1	.304/.361/.496	105	.337	-1.6	2B(29): 2.6, 3B(21): -0.8, LF(4): -0.1	1.0
	2B/3B	BAL	MLB	27	101	10	3	0	3	6	9	29	2	0	.167/.250/.300	78	.207	-0.3	2B(20): 0.5, 3B(12): 0.2	0.1
	2B/3B	COL	MLB	27	40	1	1	0	0	4	3	9	0	0	.171/.225/.200	80	.214	0.1	3B(5): 0.0, LF(2): 0.0, 1B(1): 0.0	0.1
Ezequiel Tovar	SS	SRR	WIN	19	96	10	2	0	3	10	5	20	2	0	.161/.219/.287		.167			
	SS	FRE	A	19	326	60	21	3	11	54	14	38	21	4	.309/.346/.510	132	.320	2.5	SS(64): 8.1	3.3
	SS	SPO	A+	19	143	19	9	0	4	18	3	19	3	2	.239/.266/.396	115	.252	-1.0	SS(32): -1.8	0.4
Ryan Vilade	OF	SRR	WIN	22	90	12	2	1	0	12	10	16	3	0	.253/.344/.304		.317			
	OF	ABQ	AAA	22	518	82	28	5	7	44	38	92	12	5	.284/.339/.410	91	.336	5.6	LF(60): -5.3, RF(41): -1.2, CF(18): -1.9	0.8
	OF	COL	MLB	22	7	0	0	0	0	0	1	1	0	0	.000/.143/.000	106		-0.1	LF(2): 0.1	0.0

At this point in the 33-year-old's career **Matt Adams** knows his role: Pinch-hitter when you need a home run off a righty. You can stick him at first if you want, but, like, why? Even Colorado couldn't live with his numbers and replaced him with Rio Ruiz at the trade deadline…in what was confusingly one of their biggest moves. A celebrated international signing from 2019, **Adael Amador** turned 18 last year and got exactly 200 plate appearances in Rookie League ball. It's probably fair to say that by the 200th one, he had the pitching figured out. The shortstop was a big reason why his team led the Arizona Complex League in BA and OBP and was third in SLG—and he only struck out 29 times. **Warming Bernabel**, a $900,000 international signing from July 2018, rocked a .432 BA in the Rookie League with six home runs and four doubles. This allowed him to transcend to the next level of the minors, where drop-off and adjustment periods began, as expected for a teenage shortstop whose bat speed needs to catch up with his swing. **Greg Bird** slowly assaulted the pitching at Triple-A, becoming more and more powerful until he had a 1.082 OPS in the month of August. But he hasn't played in a big-league game since April 2019, as most teams have little use for an injury-prone backup first baseman. At least, most teams on this side of the Pacific. **Yonathan Daza** soaked up about a third of Colorado's playing time in center field, and when he was out there, no one in the organization was comparable. At the plate, he was all too comparable. A 27-year-old who's been part of the organization since he was 17, Daza's role will be either splitting a job again, or not having one. Can you imagine a better use of your time than playing for the Rockies in 2021? **Ian Desmond** could. The 36-year-old opted out of baseball in 2020 due to the pandemic and opted out again in 2021 to spend time with family and continue the charity work that made him the Rockies' nominee for the Roberto Clemente Award. An NL Player of the Week in May, **Joshua Fuentes** surrounded his dominant seven-day performance with many other days of nothing that would be called "dominance." Outrighted after the season, he'll have to hope he gets a ton of liners hit to him as an NRI next spring to show what he can do. **Hunter Goodman's** profile going into the 2021 draft was a catcher who threw himself at every fastball, with enough slugging success to label him a power bat. But the "catching" part of being a catcher was more elusive, with the suggestion that he was ripe for a shift to a corner infield or outfield role. How many words into this player comment before we mention **Garrett Hampson's** speed? Ah, well; that was fast. Appropriately. The 26-year-old's future as a fourth outfielder/utility infielder seemed pretty locked in, given his ability to cover ground, bunt for base hits, double occasionally and descend into a slump for 50 at-bats or so, all incredibly quickly. **Willie MacIver** once hit three home runs for the Harvard Yard Goats. That may not guarantee his MLB backup catcher career, but it's a strong opening line at parties. **Rio Ruiz** is now living the waiver wire life: after being left dangling by the Braves in 2018, the Orioles snagged him, only to pass him off to the Rockies in May. A man of his role has a small enough bat that he can carry it in his pocket and a big enough glove to keep getting work. And that's all he needs out on waivers, where a man's got little more than the sub-90 DRC+ that got him there. After a great offensive year in Low-A Fresno, **Ezequiel Tovar** struggled adjusting in High-A Spokane, then disappeared in the Arizona Fall League, where he was one of the youngest players on the diamond. But good lord, is the defense there: The range. The arm. The glove. This is one shortstop who is going to stay at shortstop. Playing in a league that welcomes, encourages and typically displays power, **Ryan Vilade** rejected the premise. He's always good to slap some singles, but defensively, he's been relegated to a corner somewhere, so his major league hopes depend on some philosophical enlightenment.

Pitchers

PITCHER	TEAM	LVL	AGE	W	L	SV	G	GS	IP	H	HR	BB/9	K/9	K	GB%	BABIP	WHIP	ERA	DRA-	WARP	MPH	FB%	WHF	CSP
Ben Bowden	ABQ	AAA	26	1	0	2	12	0	11^2	2	0	3.1	13.1	17	36.8%	.105	0.51	0.00	86	0.1				
	COL	MLB	26	3	2	0	39	0	35^2	44	6	5.3	10.6	42	23.9%	.362	1.82	6.56	104	0.2	92.7	70.9%	28.4%	57.0%
Noah Davis	DAY	A+	24	3	6	0	13	13	65	44	3	4.8	10.7	77	39.4%	.273	1.22	3.60	98	0.7				
	SPO	A+	24	3	1	0	6	6	35	32	3	2.1	7.5	29	43.6%	.296	1.14	3.60	117	-0.1				
Tommy Doyle	HFD	AA	25	0	1	2	10	0	9^1	17	4	2.9	7.7	8	33.3%	.419	2.14	9.64	101	0.1				
Bernardo Flores Jr.	RCK	ROK	25	0	0	0	2	2	7	5	0	0.0	9.0	7	66.7%	.278	0.71	2.57						
	ABQ	AAA	25	0	2	0	3	2	11	13	2	5.7	7.4	9	48.6%	.333	1.82	5.73	86	0.1				
	MEM	AAA	25	2	2	0	8	5	31^1	40	6	5.2	7.5	26	30.8%	.354	1.85	5.74	117	0.1				
	STL	MLB	25	0	0	0	1	0	0	1	0			0	0.0%	1.000					88.0	58.3%	0.0%	35.3%
Chi Chi González	COL	MLB	29	3	7	0	24	18	101^2	127	18	2.5	5.0	56	39.1%	.323	1.52	6.46	136	-1.0	92.0	52.4%	16.2%	57.8%
Justin Lawrence	ABQ	AAA	26	6	5	13	31	0	32^1	32	3	3.3	8.4	30	61.5%	.312	1.36	4.73	95	0.2				
	COL	MLB	26	1	0	0	19	0	16^2	21	0	10.3	9.2	17	48.0%	.429	2.40	8.64	124	-0.1	97.4	65.0%	25.9%	48.1%
Chris McMahon	SPO	A+	22	10	3	0	22	20	114^1	119	13	2.5	9.4	119	39.4%	.335	1.32	4.17	115	-0.1				
José Mujica	CAR	WIN	25	0	1	0	12	10	45^2	48	1	2.2	4.9	25	46.5%	.309	1.29	3.94						
	ABQ	AAA	25	2	12	0	24	21	91^1	128	27	2.6	8.4	85	36.1%	.359	1.69	8.77	125	-1.0				
Sam Weatherly	FRE	A	22	4	6	0	15	15	69	59	7	4.2	12.5	96	34.2%	.344	1.32	4.83	104	0.2				

Jonesing for a promising lefty with a fastball? Well, check out the latest model of **Ben Bowden**. He's got velocity that set some scouts' hair on fire in college. Yeah, college was a while ago, admittedly. And he's not in *perfect* condition, but would an "injury-prone" pitcher make his big-league debut and appear in 39 games for a fourth place team? What's that? Oh, ignore that. Nobody looks at ERA anymore. Or strikeout-to-walk ratio. Or BB/9. Be cool. Midwest League batters were hitting .193 against **Noah Davis** when he was included in a trade with the Reds for Mychal Givens. His performance in the Colorado system was going to determine how hard they'd protect him from the engulfing shadow that consumes all outside the 40-man roster. Six starts later, the Rockies elected to leave the 24-year-old with a four-pitch arsenal exposed to the Rule 5 draft. Former second-round pick **Tommy Doyle** was a promising relief prospect, armed with a mid-90s fastball and arcing slider, until he ran into his bogeyman early in 2021, in the form of a torn labrum. **Bernardo Flores Jr.** existed more on paper than on the mound for the 2021 Rockies, going from the the waiver wire to the Cardinals system to the Cardinals roster to the Rockies system to the IL, and then back to Triple-A Albuquerque at the end of September. None of it mattered for the plot, but it was excellent worldbuilding. **Chi Chi González** turned a minor-league deal for 2021 into 18 starts in the big leagues. His strikeout rate was way below league average, and worse yet, way below Chi Chi González average; the Rockies designated him for assignment in the season's final week to avoid start 19. **Justin Lawrence** got batters to chase 26.7% of his sliders outside of the zone. That's not bad! Also, he threw 65.8% of his sliders out of the zone. The Rockies dropped **Chris McMahon**, their third pick of the draft, into Spokane's rotation in 2021, where his celebrated fastball command got bashed around a bit. He enjoyed notable success getting out of bases loaded jams, though less so in the art of avoiding bases loaded jams altogether. Back in February 2020, things between the Rockies and Nolan Arenado were getting tense. The superstar third baseman was calling out the organization for not fulfilling their promise to build around him. This was evident in that Colorado had all winter to acquire more impact players, and instead, had signed only one: **José Mujica**, a sixth or seventh starter who hadn't pitched for two years. *Apparently* this wasn't enough. Now, like Arenado, Mujica is also gone, having passed through outright waivers this past September. **Scott Oberg's** had blood clots in his throwing arm since 2018, and every time the talented right-handed reliever seems ready to bring his weaponized fastball-slider combo back to the Rockies bullpen, they reappear. Absent since 2019, Oberg's most recent surgery in March 2021 was said to put the rest of his promising career in question. Who needs heat when you can twirl?! **Sam Weatherly's** spin rate puts some tight movement on his fastball and slider, a pitch born from tinkering with a cutter. The months ahead are about strengthening his command, cutting down on baserunners and continuing to diversify his arsenal. With more twirling.

LOS ANGELES DODGERS

Essay by Kelsey McKinney

Player comments by Daniel Brim, Dustin Nosler and BP staff

I remember the exact moment I converted. In retrospect, I should have allowed myself to believe earlier, to hope, even. There had been plenty of opportunities. Already, by the time I was ready to trust that this team could win—would win, even—there were plenty of believers. I was a belated disciple. But even now, I don't regret the heartbreak I brought on myself. There was one moment, and I was a goner. Like Paul on the road to Damascus, there was a bright flashing light, and I believed. The spark flashed and caught. The 2021 season, I believed, would belong to the Dodgers.

There were plenty of moments earlier than mine that were flashier and sexier and probably smarter moments to push all my chips in on the Dodgers. But I'm ridiculous. I'm a romantic. I'm not looking for a grand slam, or a perfect strikeout, or a double into the gap that drives the runner on second base around to home. No, those would be reasonable plays upon which to decide a team was predestined. I could have chosen, for example, Chris Taylor's walk-off, two-run homer off the Cardinals' Alex Reyes in the Wild Card Game. That moment was fun! It would be so easy, with the passage of time, to convince myself that shiny, beautiful moment had been the one in which I decided to believe. But that would be a lie.

I know the exact moment because I keep a scorecard for games I watch on television. This is a little crotchety of me, but it's an enjoyable experience, and it keeps me from looking at my phone. It keeps me focused. When I see a good play, I put a little star in the corner of the box. When I see something that really excites me, I put a star and an exclamation point! It's pretty easy to find, looking over my scorecards, the moment I was a goner, because you can find, in the corner of one box, a star and, two boxes down, a star and an exclamation point. A half-inning of brilliance. This is where we must look: The sixth inning of the second game of the National League Division Series against the Giants.

For context, the Dodgers lost Game 1 the night before. Not only did they lose, they were shut out. I believe in the power of momentum, in Newton's first law of motion. The Giants are not a team that requires faith. The breaks fall their way most years, the luck lingering in the air of their ballpark like the smell of garlic fries. Believing in the Giants is like believing that the oven will heat up when you turn the nob:

LOS ANGELES DODGERS PROSPECTUS

2021 W-L: 106-56, 2ND IN NL WEST

Pythag	.674	*1st*	DER	.725	*1st*
RS/G	5.12	*4th*	DRC+	100	*10th*
RA/G	3.46	*1st*	DRA-	83	*1st*
dWin%	.610	*1st*	FIP	3.47	*1st*
Payroll	$248M	*1st*	B-Age	29.8	*24th*
M$/MW	$4.0M	*19th*	P-Age	29.1	*20th*

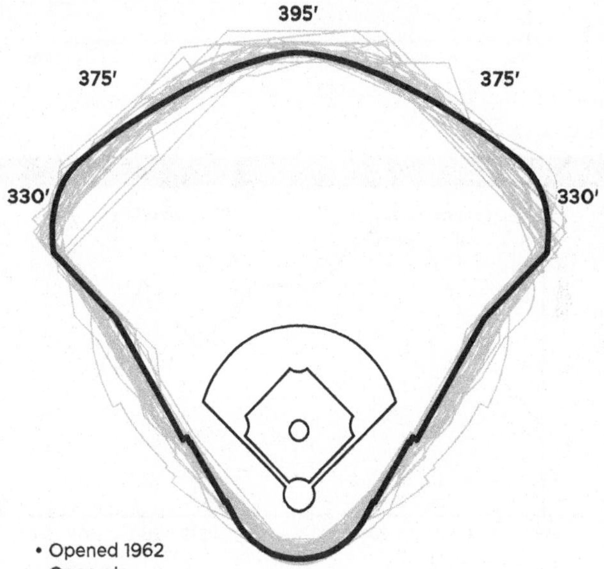

- Opened 1962
- Open air
- Natural surface
- Fence profile: 4′ to 8′

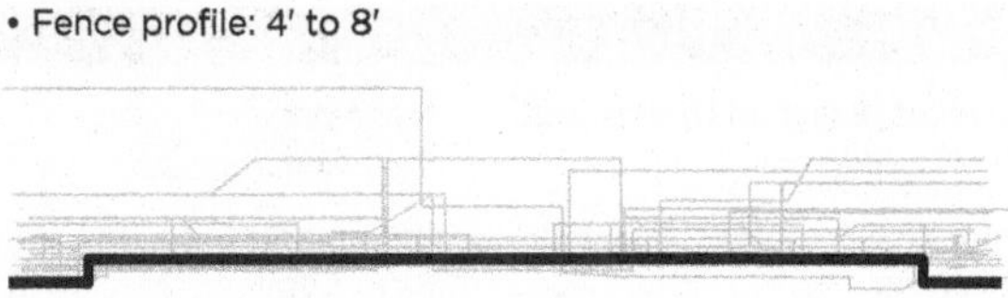

Park Factors

Runs	Runs/RH	Runs/LH	HR/RH	HR/LH
103	106	99	120	103

Top Hitter WARP	4.4 Will Smith
Top Pitcher WARP	4.5 Walker Buehler
Top Prospect	Miguel Vargas

Payroll History (in millions)

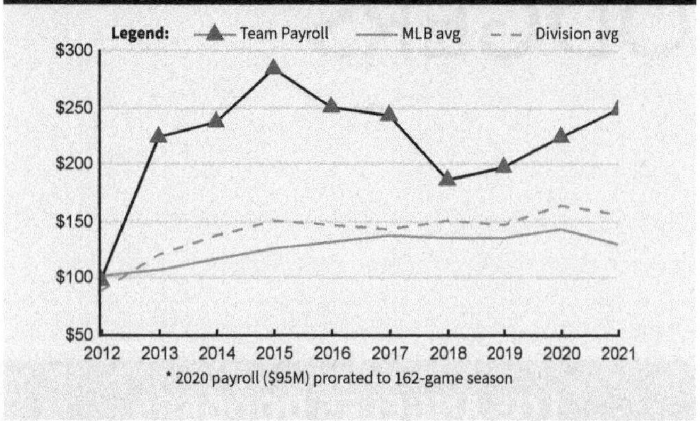

Future Commitments (in millions)

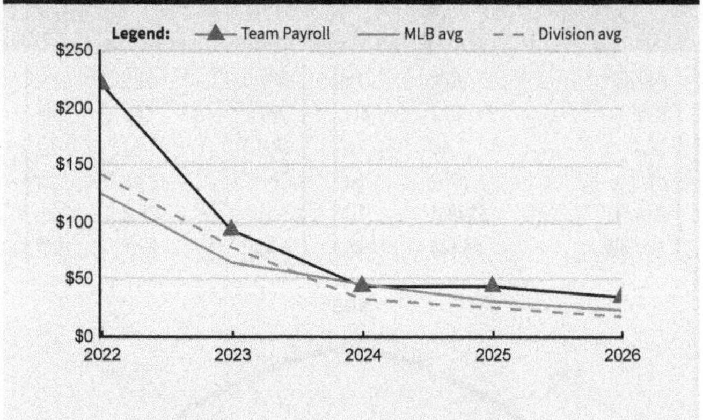

Farm System Ranking

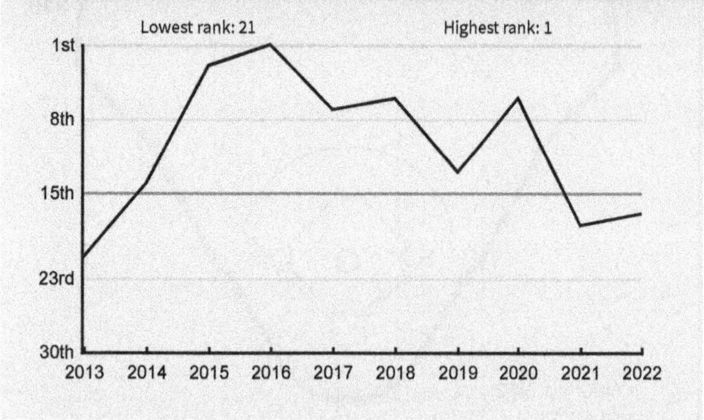

Personnel

President, Baseball Operations
Andrew Friedman

Senior Vice President, Baseball Operations
Josh Byrnes

Vice President & Assistant General Manager
Jeffrey Kingston

Vice President & Assistant General Manager
Brandon Gomes

Manager
Dave Roberts

BP Alumni
Ricky Conti

foregone, anticipated. So heading into the second game at Oracle Park, I was feeling worried, and the first inning did not make me feel much better. The dread settled in my gut in the second. Sure, the Dodgers drew first blood when Julio Urías and Mookie Betts hit back-to-back line drives. But the Dodgers had only managed two runs with four baserunners. It was tenuous, at best. The Giants stole one back in the bottom of the second. A one-run lead isn't just uncomfortable against a team like the Giants; it's dangerous. It angers the spirits. I bit my nails for four innings.

In the sixth, the Dodgers scored four runs on three hits. A normal person, someone with less terror in their body, might have exhaled then, might have taken this as a sign the team was turning around. Not me. All season I'd watched the Giants consistently ramp up their performance, overcome a big run deficit and grind their opponents' optimism into such a fine powder that it could float away on the Bay Area winds. My superstition led me to believe that the momentum had not shifted to the Dodgers' favor just yet, and were the Giants to regain the lead, maybe it never would.

By the bottom of the sixth, I was anxious. This is exactly what I had been afraid of. My gut was filled with lead, my nails no longer available to bite, my concern not quelled by a few runs. Runners were on first and second with only one out, but now we have arrived at the two boxes with the stars, at long last.

The first star is placed in this square. Joe Kelly is on the mound. This is how you know these moments are involuntary. Would I not, given the option, choose a moment with Max Scherzer on the mound? Of course I would prefer rampaging, consistent Max Scherzer to the photobomb of Joe Kelly in my memory, but the stars do not consider what I want. They are moments so good that I don't get a say. My opinion evaporates in the face of greatness.

Joe Kelly winds, the ball leaves his hand spinning backward. The pitch is breaking down, but not quickly enough. It hangs, for just a moment too long, in the bottom of the strike zone, right over the plate, a dangerous place to be. Wilmer Flores swings. His hands are fast through the zone: a short chop of a swing that collides with the ball perfectly and rockets it back the way it came. The ball bounces once in front of the mound, hops over it and skitters back toward second base. It hits once on the grass, and hops again, skirting a few feet to the shortstop's side of second. I grit my teeth. It should be a single up the middle. But the Dodgers had shifted slightly. On a defeated team, a team losing momentum, this ball hops into the outfield and scores a run.

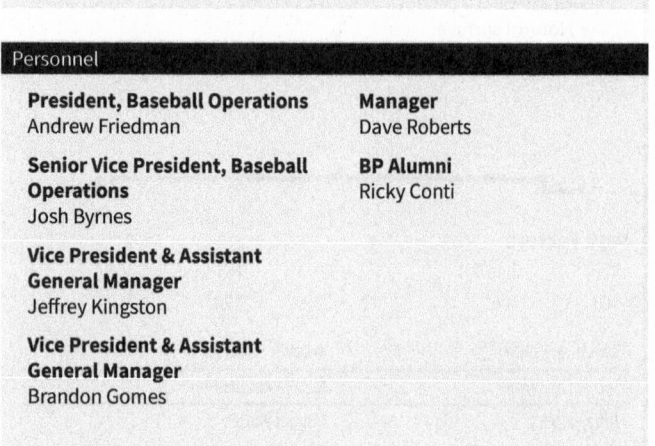

But the Dodgers are not yet defeated. Trea Turner is already lunging forward behind the bag when the ball takes its second hop. He is stretched out as it begins to roll on the dirt, sliding on his belly, the ball finds his glove. Corey Seager, having also run toward the ball, is not at second base, where he should be. He sees Turner diving, redirects and sprints toward the bag. Turner comes up with it, his weight on his now-bent right leg, the momentum from his slide still carrying him toward left field so that, as he flips the ball toward Seager, he is still falling forward onto his hands and knees, his head turned to watch the ball. At first, Seager misses the bag! His foot is too far forward, his timing off. The runner from first is sliding in as Seager readjusts. The umpire points at second base and pumps his fist. Turner, still on his hands and knees, high-fives the dirt over and over again with his left hand. That's two outs.

I released the breath from my lungs. In my square, I wrote "FC 4-6". Next to it, in the corner, I drew a star. But the inning is not over. There are two outs, but runners are at first and third. Still, the situation is dangerous.

The next batter is Brandon Crawford. He steps into the box, grinds his back foot into the dirt and readies his bat. The first pitch out of Joe Kelly's hand is a ball: 1-0. Kelly rolls his shoulders back and down, as if he's as weary of himself as I am. He throws again. The second pitch low and inside, just on the corner of the strike zone. Crawford begins his swing just a little too late and has to compensate for it. His hands are ahead of his hips, his weight still too heavy on his back foot when the bat collides with the ball. But there is a fluidity to the chip shot, a smacking sound upon collision and a launch angle that, even from the center field camera (notoriously untrustworthy), looks dangerous, because it is.

The ball is plummeting. It is barrelling straight down toward the bright green of the grass, gravity on its side, racing Mookie Betts for the soft outfield grass. You can see, in the replay, the calculation Betts is doing in his head. At first, he is sprinting hard at the ball. Maybe he is going to dive. He did it a dozen times in the regular season. He could. Couldn't he? No. The risk here is too great. If he miscalculates, even slightly, and the ball rolls away from him, two Giants runs score instead of one. No. Better to play it safe with a five-run lead. Betts pulls up short at the last minute. But he doesn't put his body in front of the ball. The safest move would be to block the ball fully, not to risk it passing at all. Betts, though, is already thinking of another future, another possibility. Just as the ball is about to land on the ground, he glances away from it and toward the infield. A spark brightens his eye.

The ball smacks the grass and bounces. Betts is watching it again. He plants his feet just as he lowers his glove to meet the bouncing ball. It lands in his glove at the exact moment that he shifts his weight to his right foot. It is as if he is a revolving door. The impact of the ball on his glove pushes his wrist, and his whole body begins to move. He spins with the ball in his glove counter-clockwise, his hands coming together as he faces the back wall like a ballerina. His fingers must be finding the laces faster than he can tell them to do so. Because his weight is pivoting on his left foot, now turned to point toward third base, he hops. He emerges from the spin, his elbow pointing toward third, the ball in his hand. His weight goes to his right foot just as the ball raises to his ear. Mookie Betts becomes a rocket. He throws himself forward into his front foot, all his weight pushing the back of this tiny white ball, his fingers releasing it like a dart flying straight and true, barely spinning, flying through the air. The runner on third crosses the plate, but he isn't celebrating. His head is whipping toward the ball.

The ball has been flying through the air for an eternity. Its arc is barely perceptible, like the surface of the Earth, traveling straight through the air. It streaks over the grass, rushing past second base, hurtling over the entire 90-foot base line between second and third. It sneaks right over the head of the runner as he begins to slide, arriving perfectly in the webbing of third baseman Justin Turner's glove. Here it is. Turner is two steps off the bag. He, too, lets the ball's momentum carry him, his glove shooting straight down, following the arc of the ball as if his sweeping tag is part of one fluid motion that began with the ball's bounce into Betts' glove and ends as Turner shoves it into Flores' side. Turner's glove hits Flores right above the belt, the runner's cleat still a foot away from third base. The momentum of that ball continues. Turner raises his glove with the ball in it above his head, turning to look toward the umpire at third, who is already pumping his fist. Turner runs toward the mound. It's three! Dejected, Flores kneels, his helmet tumbling in the dirt. The smile on Betts' face is as bright as the lights above him as he jogs toward the dugout.

I sat, mouth open on the couch. In the box, before I even decided how to score the play, I drew my star and, next to it, an exclamation mark. I drew a line under that box. The inning was over, and so was my questioning. The Giants had thrown every ounce of their supernatural clutchness at their enemy, and the Dodgers had swatted it away. I was ready to believe.

That drastic swing in momentum gave the Dodgers the game. Sure, they scored three more runs in the eighth, and the bullpen didn't give up another run, but it felt over the minute Turner swiped that runner. The heart of the game felt like it belonged to the Dodgers. I believed they would go back-to-back with the same naïveté that I once believed the pandemic might be over.

Sure, The Dodgers had been dealt a terrible hand in the playoffs, but the momentum of that ball traveling so perfectly from the ground to Justin Turner had to mean something! It did hang in the air a little while. They lost Game 3, won Game 4 and entered Game 5 abuzz. I believed in them. I believed they had the momentum so much and so strongly that I didn't bat an eye when Scherzer was called in to pitch the bottom of the ninth. It made perfect sense to me that he would achieve his first career save under these circumstances. Why not!? The Dodgers were in motion! They would win the World Series!

They didn't, of course. They never made it there. They lost the Championship Series in six games to Atlanta. My faith had been bright, and blazing, and unfounded.

The 2021 Dodgers entered the playoffs with a chip on their shoulder big enough to have been carved out by Michaelangelo. They were plagued by injuries. Their lot was unfair, brutal, stupid. To go 106-56 and be forced to play in a single-elimination wild-card game is obscene! To win that game only to be shunted off to play the only team with a better record than you in the whole league is ridiculous! That's baseball, baby.

When I think about the 2021 Dodgers, I will always, always think of them for that magical bottom of the sixth. It's better to remember them at that moment, anyway. To remember the hope and the magic and the smiles; the promise of splendor, the crashing wave of momentum and the fickle presence of luck. A team capable of a moment like that, capable of winning 106 games in the regular season, is as much as one can hope for the year after winning the World Series. There is no curse in Los Angeles, it seems, only promise. Magic is rare, but it doesn't disappear.

Isn't that the beauty of baseball? You don't need to win the crown to find beauty and magic. It was right here: in the crack of the bat and the scraping of dirt; the firm pillow of the bag and the soft smushing of grass; the snap of the ball hitting a glove and the ringing in your ears reminding you that there's always, always, next year. ■

—Kelsey McKinney is a co-owner at Defector.

HITTERS

Jacob Amaya SS
Born: 09/03/98 Age: 23 Bats: R Throws: R Height: 6'0" Weight: 180 lb. Origin: Round 11, 2017 Draft (#340 overall)

YEAR	TEAM	LVL	AGE	PA	R	2B	3B	HR	RBI	BB	K	SB	CS	Whiff%	AVG/OBP/SLG	DRC+	BABIP	BRR	FRAA	WARP
2019	GL	A	20	470	68	25	4	6	58	74	83	4	4		.262/.381/.394	132	.314	-0.1	SS(51): -4.2, 2B(49): 2.1, 3B(4): 0.1	3.0
2019	RC	A+	20	89	14	3	2	1	13	7	15	1	3		.250/.307/.375	108	.292	1.0	SS(14): -1.8, 2B(4): 1.0, 3B(1): -0.0	0.3
2021	GDD	WIN	22	67	14	3	0	3	6	13	13	1	1		.333/.463/.556		.395			
2021	TUL	AA	22	476	60	15	1	12	47	52	103	5	0		.216/.303/.343	94	.254	-0.9	SS(112): -3.8	0.7
2022 DC	*LAD*	*MLB*	*23*	*61*	*7*	*2*	*0*	*0*	*7*	*5*	*14*	*0*	*0*	*22.1%*	*.216/.295/.320*	*67*	*.276*	*0.0*	*SS 0, 2B 0*	*0.0*

Comparables: Cristhian Adames, Didi Gregorius, Dawel Lugo

An over-slot 11th-rounder in 2017, Amaya had been in the good graces of the Dodgers' front office. He looked like he might be a future starter in LA. Then he decided to change his approach—trying to tap into power in his Trea Turner-esque frame—but Turner he is not. He established a career high in round-trippers and was still able to draw walks, but he saw his much-lauded contact skills erode significantly. Amaya is a capable defender, so he'll probably get to the majors based on that, but maybe going back to the approach that once worked for him is the right move.

Austin Barnes C
Born: 12/28/89 Age: 32 Bats: R Throws: R Height: 5'10" Weight: 187 lb. Origin: Round 9, 2011 Draft (#283 overall)

YEAR	TEAM	LVL	AGE	PA	R	2B	3B	HR	RBI	BB	K	SB	CS	Whiff%	AVG/OBP/SLG	DRC+	BABIP	BRR	FRAA	WARP
2019	OKC	AAA	29	104	19	6	0	6	17	14	20	1	1		.264/.375/.540	104	.274	0.2	C(13): 2.4, 2B(6): -0.8	0.7
2019	LAD	MLB	29	242	28	12	1	5	25	23	56	3	0	22.5%	.203/.293/.340	84	.248	2.7	C(64): 9.9, 2B(1): 0.1	1.8
2020	LAD	MLB	30	104	14	3	0	1	9	13	24	3	0	25.0%	.244/.353/.314	95	.323	0.6	C(28): 3.4	0.7
2021	LAD	MLB	31	225	28	8	0	6	23	20	56	1	0	26.9%	.215/.299/.345	85	.268	0.7	C(52): 5.2, 2B(7): -0.2	1.1
2022 DC	*LAD*	*MLB*	*32*	*182*	*24*	*7*	*0*	*4*	*22*	*19*	*47*	*1*	*1*	*25.4%*	*.223/.319/.359*	*85*	*.290*	*-0.1*	*C 8*	*1.3*

Comparables: Drew Butera, Curt Casali, Chris Gimenez

YEAR	TEAM	P. COUNT	FRM RUNS	BLK RUNS	THRW RUNS	TOT RUNS
2019	LAD	8092	9.5	0.2	0.7	10.4
2019	OKC	1832	2.3	0.0	0.1	2.4
2020	LAD	3848	3.4	0.0	0.0	3.4
2021	LAD	6843	5.3	0.0	0.5	5.8
2022	*LAD*	*7215*	*7.8*	*0.4*	*-0.1*	*8.1*

It really looked like Barnes was the Dodgers' future behind the plate after the 2017 season. Yasmani Grandal was heading into his final year as a Dodger and the vaunted catching prospect wasn't quite MLB-ready. But the inability to hit—overall and for power—has firmly entrenched Barnes as a backup. With other catchers coming up through the system, his future in LA could be in doubt after next year, but he's a perfectly fine fill-in for the immediate future. Most of Barnes' value comes from framing, which will continue to be valuable until robot umpires actually become a thing. His career might end before that time, so no worries there.

Matt Beaty LF
Born: 04/28/93 Age: 29 Bats: L Throws: R Height: 6'0" Weight: 215 lb. Origin: Round 12, 2015 Draft (#372 overall)

YEAR	TEAM	LVL	AGE	PA	R	2B	3B	HR	RBI	BB	K	SB	CS	Whiff%	AVG/OBP/SLG	DRC+	BABIP	BRR	FRAA	WARP
2019	OKC	AAA	26	135	17	7	1	3	18	10	12	0	0		.306/.378/.455	111	.321	-0.6	1B(11): -0.9, 3B(11): 1.1, LF(8): 0.8	0.6
2019	LAD	MLB	26	268	36	19	1	9	46	17	33	5	0	18.0%	.265/.317/.458	103	.275	1.1	1B(35): -0.5, LF(34): 0.6, 3B(9): -0.5	1.0
2020	LAD	MLB	27	54	8	1	0	2	5	2	14	0	0	25.8%	.220/.278/.360	84	.265	-0.4	1B(13): -0.8, LF(2): 0.1	-0.1
2021	OKC	AAA	28	35	5	3	0	0	4	2	8	0	0		.357/.486/.464	95	.500	-0.6	LF(4): -0.9, 1B(3): -0.3	-0.1
2021	LAD	MLB	28	234	35	4	1	7	40	20	44	2	2	19.1%	.270/.363/.402	108	.314	0.6	LF(28): -1.6, 1B(21): 0.5, RF(20): -1.0	0.9
2022 DC	*LAD*	*MLB*	*29*	*224*	*30*	*9*	*0*	*5*	*31*	*17*	*38*	*1*	*1*	*19.8%*	*.243/.321/.374*	*90*	*.278*	*-0.2*	*RF -1, 1B 0*	*0.0*

Comparables: Gaby Sanchez, Justin Bour, Mark Canha

Dodger broadcaster Joe Davis occasionally refers to Beaty as a "baseball-playing robot," one whose primary directive is simple: hit right-handed pitching. While this does not strictly follow Asimov's Three Laws, Beaty largely accomplished his mission in 2021, posting the strongest offensive numbers of his career. The robot comparisons also hint at Beaty's one-dimensionality; he can play only in the corners, and he doesn't inspire confidence while there. Beaty's lead glove has cost him playing time over much lighter-hitting alternatives, culminating in a rather puzzling demotion to Triple-A late-season. Beaty will profile better in a DH league; the future makes room for machines.

Cody Bellinger CF Born: 07/13/95 Age: 26 Bats: L Throws: L Height: 6'4" Weight: 203 lb. Origin: Round 4, 2013 Draft (#124 overall)

YEAR	TEAM	LVL	AGE	PA	R	2B	3B	HR	RBI	BB	K	SB	CS	Whiff%	AVG/OBP/SLG	DRC+	BABIP	BRR	FRAA	WARP
2019	LAD	MLB	23	661	121	34	3	47	115	95	108	15	5	23.7%	.305/.406/.629	147	.302	0.2	RF(115): 13.6, 1B(36): 2.1, CF(25): 0.2	7.6
2020	LAD	MLB	24	243	33	10	0	12	30	30	42	6	1	23.3%	.239/.333/.455	111	.245	0.2	CF(39): 3.0, 1B(19): 0.2, RF(1): -0.0	1.4
2021	LAD	MLB	25	350	39	9	2	10	36	31	94	3	1	29.7%	.165/.240/.302	67	.196	3.6	CF(87): -1.0, RF(7): -0.4, 1B(4): -0.4	0.1
2022 DC	*LAD*	*MLB*	*26*	*522*	*84*	*20*	*2*	*23*	*94*	*56*	*118*	*9*	*3*	*28.3%*	*.240/.326/.450*	*105*	*.272*	*0.5*	*CF 3, 1B 0*	*2.6*

Comparables: Willie McCovey, Mickey Mantle, Duke Snider

When Justin Turner ran backward past Bellinger after what should have been an Opening Day home run, it seemed like little more than a nuisance. It became a metaphor for most of Bellinger's disastrous 2021 season: sporadic exciting moments, bummer results. A good opening week gave way to almost two months on the injured list with a broken leg and two more struggling through the aftermath of 2020's shoulder surgery. A 13-pitch at-bat in August ending in a home run (his second of the day) led to nearly a month without an extra-base hit. A new approach yielding promising plate discipline improvements was interrupted by a broken rib in an outfield collision. Until the season's final week, Bellinger's entire 2021 looked like it would be a complete write-off, but after closing off his stance and choking up on the bat in the playoffs he hit .353/.436/.471 with a staggering 61% hard-hit rate. A long-delayed and hard-earned trip around the bases.

Mookie Betts RF Born: 10/07/92 Age: 29 Bats: R Throws: R Height: 5'9" Weight: 180 lb. Origin: Round 5, 2011 Draft (#172 overall)

YEAR	TEAM	LVL	AGE	PA	R	2B	3B	HR	RBI	BB	K	SB	CS	Whiff%	AVG/OBP/SLG	DRC+	BABIP	BRR	FRAA	WARP
2019	BOS	MLB	26	706	135	40	5	29	80	97	101	16	3	14.6%	.295/.391/.524	130	.309	5.9	RF(132): 12.6, CF(17): 2.0	6.8
2020	LAD	MLB	27	246	47	9	1	16	39	24	38	10	2	13.8%	.292/.366/.562	133	.289	3.7	RF(52): 4.4, 2B(1): -0.0, CF(1): -0.1	2.6
2021	LAD	MLB	28	550	93	29	3	23	58	68	86	10	5	16.8%	.264/.367/.487	124	.276	-1.3	RF(98): 2.4, CF(30): -0.4, 2B(7): -0.4	3.5
2022 DC	*LAD*	*MLB*	*29*	*607*	*119*	*30*	*2*	*25*	*92*	*75*	*86*	*17*	*5*	*16.2%*	*.267/.368/.478*	*123*	*.282*	*0.8*	*RF 4, CF 0*	*4.0*

Comparables: Vladimir Guerrero, Dave Winfield, Al Kaline

Hampered by a series of injuries, most notably a bone spur in his right hip, Betts produced a rare look at what a "down year" is for last year's BP Annual cover star: a season not up to his ridiculous expectations, but one which most players would be thrilled to duplicate. Until the season's final weeks, Betts was hitting in line with his 2019 numbers, but his injuries eroded the other parts of his game which had previously made him so slump-proof. Betts' range in the outfield was visibly hindered, which caused his defensive numbers to fall from elite to slightly above-average. His dynamic baserunning also took a step back, as he stole only 10 bases and was caught five times (significantly worse than prior seasons in both frequency and success rate), though he did go 6-for-6 in steals during the postseason. Betts often flashed his elite talent through the injuries, and it's hard to imagine a player who has earned a longer leash to prove that he is still one of the game's best.

Michael Busch 2B Born: 11/09/97 Age: 24 Bats: L Throws: R Height: 6'1" Weight: 210 lb. Origin: Round 1, 2019 Draft (#31 overall)

YEAR	TEAM	LVL	AGE	PA	R	2B	3B	HR	RBI	BB	K	SB	CS	Whiff%	AVG/OBP/SLG	DRC+	BABIP	BRR	FRAA	WARP
2019	DODL	ROK	21	16	1	0	0	0	0	1	2	0	0		.077/.250/.077		.091			
2019	GL	A	21	19	4	0	0	0	2	6	3	0	0		.182/.474/.182	111	.222	0.5	2B(4): 0.2	0.2
2021	TUL	AA	23	495	84	27	1	20	67	70	129	2	3		.267/.386/.484	112	.337	0.4	2B(88): 7.2, 1B(11): -0.1	3.0
2022 non-DC	*LAD*	*MLB*	*24*	*251*	*24*	*11*	*0*	*5*	*24*	*26*	*68*	*0*	*1*	*27.3%*	*.213/.310/.344*	*82*	*.285*	*-0.3*	*2B 2, 1B 0*	*0.5*

Comparables: Jordany Valdespin, Zach McKinstry, Kyle Seager

The Dodgers had two first-round picks in the 2019 draft, and while their first selection has struggled, their second has not. Busch had a solid showing in Double-A—a common proving ground for prospects—and is on the verge of being MLB-ready. He has a chance to be a solid contributor in a Max Muncy-lite capacity. There's definitely a spot for him in LA somewhere, because he can't be worse than some of the bench players they ran out there in 2021.

★ ★ ★ *2022 Top 101 Prospect* **#55** ★ ★ ★

Diego Cartaya C Born: 09/07/01 Age: 20 Bats: R Throws: R Height: 6'3" Weight: 219 lb. Origin: International Free Agent, 2018

YEAR	TEAM	LVL	AGE	PA	R	2B	3B	HR	RBI	BB	K	SB	CS	Whiff%	AVG/OBP/SLG	DRC+	BABIP	BRR	FRAA	WARP
2019	DODM	ROK	17	150	25	10	0	3	13	11	31	1	0		.296/.353/.437		.359			
2019	DSL BAU	ROK	17	57	11	2	2	1	9	5	11	0	0		.240/.316/.420		.282			
2021	RC	A	19	137	31	6	0	10	31	18	37	0	0		.298/.409/.614	119	.353	0.5	C(31): -4.0	0.4
2022 non-DC	*LAD*	*MLB*	*20*	*251*	*23*	*10*	*0*	*6*	*25*	*19*	*81*	*0*	*0*	*34.3%*	*.208/.279/.346*	*71*	*.292*	*-0.3*	*C -6*	*-0.4*

Comparables: Francisco Mejía, Christian Bethancourt, Christian Vázquez

YEAR	TEAM	P. COUNT	FRM RUNS	BLK RUNS	THRW RUNS	TOT RUNS
2019	DODM	1931			0.5	0.5
2021	RC	4422	-3.7	-1.0	1.0	-3.8
2022	*LAD*	*6956*	*-4.0*	*-1.4*	*0.1*	*-5.3*

A $2.5 million signing out of Venezuela in July 2018, Cartaya made it stateside during the 2019 season and made his full-season debut in 2021. He made quite the first impression, routinely hitting 400-plus-foot bombs, including a walk-off grand slam in his fourth game in Low-A ball. A visa issue and hand injury ended his season prematurely, but the tooled-up backstop has pre-2021 Salvador Perez-like power potential and a Yadier Molina-esque arm. He is set to fly up prospect rankings this winter.

Wilman Diaz SS/DH

Born: 11/15/03 Age: 18 Bats: R Throws: R Height: 6'2" Weight: 182 lb. Origin: International Free Agent, 2021

YEAR	TEAM	LVL	AGE	PA	R	2B	3B	HR	RBI	BB	K	SB	CS	Whiff%	AVG/OBP/SLG	DRC+	BABIP	BRR	FRAA	WARP
2021	DSL SHO	ROK	17	94	13	5	1	1	9	9	26	8	4		.235/.309/.353		.328			
2022															*No projection*					

Comparables: Pedro Guerrero, Yefry Rivas, Anthony Chavez

Diaz is an athletic shortstop with a chance to be a GUY thanks to an advanced, mature approach and potentially plus speed-power combination. His first taste of professional ball turned in mixed results, but the promise is there. The Dodgers have done a good job developing shortstops—Corey Seager, Gavin Lux (kinda)—and given the uncertain future at the position after the 2022 season, Diaz could lay claim to that job … maybe after he reaches the legal drinking age. Asking a 17-year-old to eventually inherit the role of Corey Seager is a tall order, but he has the stuff to do it.

Kody Hoese 3B

Born: 07/13/97 Age: 24 Bats: R Throws: R Height: 6'4" Weight: 200 lb. Origin: Round 1, 2019 Draft (#25 overall)

YEAR	TEAM	LVL	AGE	PA	R	2B	3B	HR	RBI	BB	K	SB	CS	Whiff%	AVG/OBP/SLG	DRC+	BABIP	BRR	FRAA	WARP
2019	DODM	ROK	21	68	14	5	1	3	13	10	11	1	0		.357/.456/.643		.395			
2019	GL	A	21	103	15	3	1	2	16	8	14	0	0		.264/.330/.385	110	.286	-0.2	3B(12): 0.2	0.4
2021	GDD	WIN	23	60	7	1	0	2	5	3	17	0	0		.200/.250/.327		.243			
2021	DOD	ROK	23	34	2	1	0	0	3	2	4	0	0		.258/.294/.290		.286			
2021	TUL	AA	23	249	26	7	0	2	17	15	55	2	2		.188/.241/.245	81	.234	-0.2	3B(53): -4.2	-0.3
2022 non-DC	*LAD*	*MLB*	*24*	*251*	*18*	*9*	*0*	*2*	*19*	*14*	*55*	*0*	*1*	*22.9%*	*.210/.264/.292*	*51*	*.265*	*-0.2*	*3B -1, SS 0*	*-1.1*

Comparables: Kelvin Gutierrez, Brent Morel, Brian Anderson

Andrew Friedman has done quite well with his first-round selections in L.A., but one from his alma mater could end up being the biggest miss to date. The former Tulane star impressed the Dodgers enough in pre-draft workouts to make him their first pick in the 2019 draft. A wrist injury has sapped a significant portion of his power, and his first test in Double-A went about as well as a toddler trying to take a quantum physics exam. The Dodgers have worked miracles before with position players, but they have their work cut out for them with Hoese, especially if he doesn't regain the above-average power he had coming out of college.

Gavin Lux IF

Born: 11/23/97 Age: 24 Bats: L Throws: R Height: 6'2" Weight: 190 lb. Origin: Round 1, 2016 Draft (#20 overall)

YEAR	TEAM	LVL	AGE	PA	R	2B	3B	HR	RBI	BB	K	SB	CS	Whiff%	AVG/OBP/SLG	DRC+	BABIP	BRR	FRAA	WARP
2019	TUL	AA	21	291	45	7	4	13	37	28	60	7	3		.313/.375/.521	133	.358	-1.8	SS(55): -3.5, 2B(7): 0.5	1.7
2019	OKC	AAA	21	232	54	18	4	13	39	33	42	3	3		.392/.478/.719	133	.451	-2.1	SS(36): -4.7, 2B(12): -0.4	1.4
2019	LAD	MLB	21	82	12	4	1	2	9	7	24	2	0	29.9%	.240/.305/.400	79	.327	0.1	2B(22): -0.7	0.1
2020	LAD	MLB	22	69	8	2	0	3	8	6	19	1	0	26.1%	.175/.246/.349	86	.195	0.4	2B(18): 1.7	0.3
2021	OKC	AAA	23	74	18	4	0	1	10	6	15	0	0		.279/.338/.382	92	.346	1.0	2B(8): 0.1, 3B(4): -0.1, LF(1): 3.1	0.5
2021	LAD	MLB	23	381	49	12	4	7	46	41	83	4	1	23.1%	.242/.328/.364	90	.300	1.9	SS(59): 2.6, 2B(27): 1.1, LF(11): -1.5	1.3
2022 DC	*LAD*	*MLB*	*24*	*466*	*69*	*18*	*4*	*12*	*65*	*47*	*101*	*8*	*4*	*23.5%*	*.250/.330/.403*	*98*	*.304*	*0.7*	*2B 1, SS 0*	*1.6*

Comparables: Luis Sardinas, J.P. Crawford, Corey Seager

The 2021 season figured to be a promising one for Lux, the first in which he had a starting role carved out from the beginning. The results were mixed at best. Lux's vicious swing and high finish did not produce the exit velocities that they suggest—of the 262 MLB hitters with 300 plate appearances in 2021, Lux's maximum exit velocity, barrel rate and hard hit rate were in the 29th, 13th and 46th percentiles respectively—and the power he showed as a minor leaguer was conspicuously absent. On defense, Lux played a fine second before Corey Seager's injury and the acquisition of Trea Turner started a cascade of events which demonstrated that he probably shouldn't play a position other than second ever again. Lux's decent plate discipline and mixture of plus-plus speed with a grounder-heavy batted ball profile will keep his floor high, but something fundamental will have to change with respect to how hard he hits the ball if he wants to reach the heights that once seemed his destiny.

Billy McKinney OF

Born: 08/23/94 Age: 27 Bats: L Throws: L Height: 6'1" Weight: 205 lb. Origin: Round 1, 2013 Draft (#24 overall)

YEAR	TEAM	LVL	AGE	PA	R	2B	3B	HR	RBI	BB	K	SB	CS	Whiff%	AVG/OBP/SLG	DRC+	BABIP	BRR	FRAA	WARP
2019	BUF	AAA	24	154	17	8	4	4	20	22	25	1	1		.271/.383/.488	113	.307	-1.6	LF(16): 0.7, RF(8): 2.0, 1B(4): -0.3	0.7
2019	TOR	MLB	24	276	37	14	1	12	28	19	73	0	2	26.3%	.215/.274/.422	84	.250	0.3	RF(43): -0.2, LF(29): -2.4, 1B(9): 0.2	0.1
2020	TOR	MLB	25	3	1	0	0	0	0	0	0	0	0	50.0%	.667/.667/.667	102	.667	0.2	LF(1): -0.1	0.0
2021	MIL	MLB	26	100	9	3	1	3	6	7	24	1	0	23.1%	.207/.260/.359	83	.242	-1.1	LF(19): 0.4, 1B(9): -0.3, RF(1): -0.1	0.0
2021	LAD	MLB	26	98	8	2	1	1	7	14	24	0	0	23.0%	.146/.276/.232	76	.190	0.8	RF(23): 1.7, 1B(1): -0.0	0.3
2021	NYM	MLB	26	102	15	6	1	5	14	11	31	1	0	24.7%	.220/.304/.473	88	.273	0.5	RF(24): -0.4, LF(8): -0.1, CF(3): -0.1	0.2
2022 DC	*FA*	*MLB*	*27*	*276*	*28*	*11*	*2*	*8*	*30*	*26*	*62*	*0*	*1*	*23.6%*	*.214/.295/.381*	*81*	*.253*	*0.0*	*RF 1, LF 0*	*0.1*

Comparables: Domonic Brown, Michael Saunders, Logan Morrison

Probably most famous for being part of the Jeff Samardzija/Jason Hammel for Addison Russell trade, McKinney has, somehow, carved out a role as a fourth- or fifth outfielder in the majors despite sporting a career .215/.286/.404 batting line. The slug is nice, but the rest is not. He still found himself on the Dodgers' Wild Card and NLDS rosters; in no world does that make sense, yet here we are. Los Angeles was the third stop on his 2021 tour (Milwaukee, New York) and the toughest. His 73 wRC+ was the 26th-worst among players with 300 or more plate appearances. We'll see which personnel decision-maker McKinney tricks next into an active roster spot.

Zach McKinstry UT
Born: 04/29/95 Age: 27 Bats: L Throws: R Height: 6'0" Weight: 180 lb. Origin: Round 33, 2016 Draft (#1001 overall)

YEAR	TEAM	LVL	AGE	PA	R	2B	3B	HR	RBI	BB	K	SB	CS	Whiff%	AVG/OBP/SLG	DRC+	BABIP	BRR	FRAA	WARP
2019	TUL	AA	24	384	53	16	4	12	52	37	74	8	8		.279/.352/.455	123	.323	-1.4	2B(49): -2.8, SS(29): 3.4, 3B(10): -0.1	2.3
2019	OKC	AAA	24	95	17	8	2	7	26	6	18	0	1		.382/.421/.753	119	.422	-0.5	SS(17): -0.5, 2B(3): 0.3, 3B(2): 0.3	0.6
2020	LAD	MLB	25	7	1	1	0	0	0	0	3	0	0	37.5%	.286/.286/.429	78	.500		2B(1): -0.0, RF(1): 0.3	0.0
2021	OKC	AAA	26	171	35	8	3	7	21	20	26	4	2		.272/.368/.510	114	.287	1.0	SS(15): -0.7, 2B(12): 3.6, LF(6): 0.7	1.3
2021	LAD	MLB	26	172	19	9	0	7	29	10	50	1	1	26.2%	.215/.263/.405	77	.262	0.0	RF(23): -0.1, 2B(20): -0.6, LF(14): -1.0	-0.1
2022 DC	*LAD*	*MLB*	*27*	*29*	*3*	*1*	*0*	*0*	*3*	*2*	*7*	*0*	*0*	*25.1%*	*.230/.297/.368*	*77*	*.290*	*0.0*	*2B 0*	*0.0*

Comparables: Danny Valencia, Ryan Flaherty, Justin Turner

The Dodgers let Enrique Hernández and Joc Pederson walk after the 2020 season, and McKinstry was expected to help pick up some of the slack. Things started off great for him and the Dodgers. He hit .296/.328/.556 through the first 19 days of the season, and Friedman was looking like a genius. But an oblique injury kept him out for six weeks, and he returned a different hitter. The rest of the season, McKinstry amassed an ugly .173/.230/.327 batting line over 114 plate appearances.

Max Muncy 1B
Born: 08/25/90 Age: 31 Bats: L Throws: R Height: 6'0" Weight: 215 lb. Origin: Round 5, 2012 Draft (#169 overall)

YEAR	TEAM	LVL	AGE	PA	R	2B	3B	HR	RBI	BB	K	SB	CS	Whiff%	AVG/OBP/SLG	DRC+	BABIP	BRR	FRAA	WARP
2019	LAD	MLB	28	589	101	22	1	35	98	90	149	4	1	28.9%	.251/.374/.515	122	.283	4.0	2B(70): -0.1, 1B(65): 4.5, 3B(35): 3.1	4.7
2020	LAD	MLB	29	248	36	4	0	12	27	39	60	1	0	26.8%	.192/.331/.389	104	.203	0.9	1B(35): -3.5, 3B(16): 2.4, 2B(12): 0.3	0.7
2021	LAD	MLB	30	592	95	26	2	36	94	83	120	2	1	23.3%	.249/.368/.527	130	.257	0.8	1B(122): 1.1, 2B(39): -0.1, 3B(7): -0.2	3.9
2022 DC	*LAD*	*MLB*	*31*	*579*	*108*	*21*	*1*	*28*	*100*	*85*	*119*	*2*	*2*	*24.0%*	*.246/.368/.471*	*127*	*.271*	*-0.6*	*1B 1, 3B 0*	*3.4*

Comparables: Rafael Palmeiro, Dave Bergman, Norm Cash

Of all the rectangular-shaped players in baseball, Muncy is the best. For a while, it looked like he was putting together an MVP campaign. After Aug. 21, he hit just .192/.274/.431 in 146 plate appearances. If that weren't bad enough, Muncy suffered a dislocated elbow trying to catch a throw to first base on the final day of the regular season, keeping him out of the playoffs. Sure, Bellinger stepped up, but Muncy's absence led to guys like McKinney and Souza (the latter, especially) getting playing time in the quest for a title repeat. The Dodgers might not have beaten Atlanta in the NLCS, but having Muncy would have helped a lot more than not having him did! Muncy has developed into one of the game's best offensive first basemen (despite a down 2020 season) and will be looking at a big payday in the next year or two.

★ ★ ★ *2022 Top 101 Prospect* **#68** ★ ★ ★

Andy Pages OF
Born: 12/08/00 Age: 21 Bats: R Throws: R Height: 6'1" Weight: 212 lb. Origin: International Free Agent, 2018

YEAR	TEAM	LVL	AGE	PA	R	2B	3B	HR	RBI	BB	K	SB	CS	Whiff%	AVG/OBP/SLG	DRC+	BABIP	BRR	FRAA	WARP
2019	OGD	ROA	18	279	57	22	2	19	55	26	79	7	6		.298/.398/.651		.364			
2021	GL	A+	20	538	96	25	1	31	88	77	132	6	3		.265/.394/.539	139	.305	1.4	RF(83): 4.4, CF(27): -5.2	4.3
2022 non-DC	*LAD*	*MLB*	*21*	*251*	*26*	*10*	*0*	*7*	*27*	*25*	*69*	*3*	*3*	*28.8%*	*.219/.316/.378*	*88*	*.285*	*0.1*	*RF 1, CF -1*	*0.4*

Comparables: Franmil Reyes, Eloy Jiménez, Moisés Sierra

Mike Trout has appeared in just one postseason in his illustrious MLB career. He might be unlucky, but some of it has to do with the Angels' front office. What does this have to do with Pages? Well, prior to the 2020 season, the Angels—specifically, Arte Moreno—nixed a deal that would have netted the Halos Pages, Joc Pederson and Ross Stripling for Luis Rengifo and another player or two. Now, Pederson and Stripling probably wouldn't have made the Angels World Series threats, but the fact they rejected a clearly beneficial deal for present and future, well, you have to wonder if Trout is ever going to make the postseason again. Oh, and Pages led the Dodgers' system in home runs in 2021. Salt in the proverbial wound.

AJ Pollock LF
Born: 12/05/87 Age: 34 Bats: R Throws: R Height: 6'1" Weight: 210 lb. Origin: Round 1, 2009 Draft (#17 overall)

YEAR	TEAM	LVL	AGE	PA	R	2B	3B	HR	RBI	BB	K	SB	CS	Whiff%	AVG/OBP/SLG	DRC+	BABIP	BRR	FRAA	WARP
2019	LAD	MLB	31	342	49	15	1	15	47	23	74	5	1	26.8%	.266/.327/.468	99	.300	-0.6	CF(62): -9.6, LF(18): -0.1	0.3
2020	LAD	MLB	32	210	30	9	0	16	34	12	45	2	2	24.5%	.276/.314/.566	119	.277	0.0	LF(27): -5.5, CF(16): -2.3	0.3
2021	LAD	MLB	33	422	53	27	1	21	69	30	80	9	1	24.3%	.297/.355/.536	119	.326	-0.5	LF(103): 6.7, CF(8): -0.6	3.2
2022 DC	*LAD*	*MLB*	*34*	*394*	*61*	*19*	*1*	*17*	*69*	*28*	*78*	*9*	*4*	*24.1%*	*.261/.326/.463*	*105*	*.293*	*0.4*	*LF 2*	*1.7*

Comparables: Torii Hunter, Carlos Beltrán, Vernon Wells

Pollock's tenure with the Dodgers thus far has been largely successful, but it has created a lot of philosophical questions about what makes a good contract. Over the last two seasons, Pollock has been one of the best right-handed hitters in baseball on a rate basis thanks to his ability to pulverize any fastball. He has also spent a significant amount of time on the IL, missing a 2020-2021 playing time-contingent opt-out clause by 11 plate appearances. That sounds exactly like the Pollock the Dodgers would have reasonably expected to get when they signed him. However, until a two-homer showing in NLCS Game 5 and a strong follow-up in the Dodgers' final playoff game, Pollock had amassed eight more strikeouts (27) than total bases (19) in his first 80 playoff plate appearances for the club and had been benched for more effective players in all three seasons. Judging Pollock's performance in Los Angeles then is a matter of perspective. Still, it's tough to see the Dodgers regretting their decision, especially since they've often had the depth needed to ride out those inconvenient slumps.

Albert Pujols 1B

Born: 01/16/80 Age: 42 Bats: R Throws: R Height: 6'3" Weight: 235 lb. Origin: Round 13, 1999 Draft (#402 overall)

YEAR	TEAM	LVL	AGE	PA	R	2B	3B	HR	RBI	BB	K	SB	CS	Whiff%	AVG/OBP/SLG	DRC+	BABIP	BRR	FRAA	WARP
2019	LAA	MLB	39	545	55	22	0	23	93	43	68	3	0	18.1%	.244/.305/.430	106	.238	-4.4	1B(98): -0.8	1.4
2020	LAA	MLB	40	163	15	8	0	6	25	9	25	0	0	22.2%	.224/.270/.395	102	.230	-0.5	1B(26): 1.6	0.5
2021	ESC	WIN	41	65	5	3	0	1	6	4	9	0	0		.246/.292/.344		.275			
2021	LAA	MLB	41	92	9	0	0	5	12	3	13	1	0	23.1%	.198/.250/.372	112	.176	-1.0	1B(20): -1.1, 3B(1): -0.0	0.1
2021	LAD	MLB	41	204	20	3	0	12	38	11	32	1	0	20.9%	.254/.299/.460	120	.245	0.1	1B(56): 3.1	1.4
2022 DC	*FA*	*MLB*	*42*	*345*	*37*	*11*	*0*	*13*	*42*	*20*	*55*	*0*	*1*	*21.8%*	*.243/.294/.403*	*86*	*.257*	*-0.5*	*1B 0, 3B 0*	*0.0*

Comparables: Todd Helton, Eddie Murray, Tony Perez

When a player has a mini-breakout after joining a new team which has him focus on his strengths, that player is usually pretty young. A post-hype prospect, a Quad-A type, something along those lines. In this case, it was a future first-ballot Hall of Famer at age 41. In desperate need for position-player depth with punch against lefties, the Dodgers picked up Pujols in mid-May, and he thrived in his new pseudo-platoon role. Pujols hit .303/.347/.606 in 118 plate appearances against southpaws for the Dodgers, which propelled him ahead of his 99th percentile PECOTA projection for the season. His presence in the dugout also motivated his teammates; after all, who wouldn't want a hug from one of the greatest hitters of his generation after hitting a homer?

Luke Raley OF

Born: 09/19/94 Age: 27 Bats: L Throws: R Height: 6'4" Weight: 235 lb. Origin: Round 7, 2016 Draft (#221 overall)

YEAR	TEAM	LVL	AGE	PA	R	2B	3B	HR	RBI	BB	K	SB	CS	Whiff%	AVG/OBP/SLG	DRC+	BABIP	BRR	FRAA	WARP
2019	SRR	WIN	24	93	14	5	1	3	14	4	21	0	0		.244/.312/.439		.283			
2019	ROC	AAA	24	138	28	6	0	7	21	7	42	4	0		.302/.362/.516	99	.403	1.9	RF(22): 2.6, CF(5): -0.1	0.8
2021	OKC	AAA	26	318	60	14	2	19	69	27	74	8	3		.294/.393/.570	122	.339	0.9	RF(48): 6.8, CF(12): -1.0, LF(8): -1.6	2.4
2021	LAD	MLB	26	72	5	1	0	2	4	2	25	0	0	38.4%	.182/.250/.288	73	.256	-1.1	RF(16): -0.7, LF(13): -1.2	-0.3
2022 DC	*LAD*	*MLB*	*27*	*31*	*4*	*1*	*0*	*1*	*4*	*1*	*9*	*0*	*0*	*34.9%*	*.230/.308/.400*	*88*	*.303*	*0.0*	*LF -1*	*0.0*

Comparables: Scott Schebler, Ji-Man Choi, Carlos Peguero

The Dodgers learned pretty quickly that Raley, making his MLB debut in 2021, was not going to be able to replace Pederson on the bench. He was given a decent amount of time to prove up to the task, but striking out in a third of one's plate appearances isn't going to do much to lengthen the leash. If you look up "Quad-A player" in the baseball dictionary that totally exists, you'll see a photo of Raley. Despite all that, he tagged one of the longest home runs in MLB in 2021 at 472 feet. Sure, he hit it in Colorado, but he'll take the wins where he can get them.

Edwin Ríos CI

Born: 04/21/94 Age: 28 Bats: L Throws: R Height: 6'3" Weight: 220 lb. Origin: Round 6, 2015 Draft (#192 overall)

YEAR	TEAM	LVL	AGE	PA	R	2B	3B	HR	RBI	BB	K	SB	CS	Whiff%	AVG/OBP/SLG	DRC+	BABIP	BRR	FRAA	WARP
2019	OKC	AAA	25	444	72	23	2	31	91	37	153	2	2		.270/.340/.575	97	.349	-2.2	3B(67): 2.0, 1B(25): 0.9, LF(8): 1.6	1.3
2019	LAD	MLB	25	56	10	2	1	4	8	9	21	0	0	33.3%	.277/.393/.617	84	.409	-0.1	1B(12): -0.4, 3B(5): -0.5, LF(1): -0.0	0.0
2020	LAD	MLB	26	83	13	6	0	8	17	4	18	0	0	36.1%	.250/.301/.645	111	.216	-0.2	3B(21): -1.7, 1B(6): -0.1	0.1
2021	LAD	MLB	27	60	4	0	0	1	1	7	18	0	0	31.8%	.078/.217/.137	79	.094	-0.3	1B(10): 0.7, 3B(6): -0.4, RF(2): -0.3	0.0
2022 DC	*LAD*	*MLB*	*28*	*36*	*5*	*1*	*0*	*1*	*6*	*2*	*10*	*0*	*0*	*33.5%*	*.233/.310/.445*	*96*	*.298*	*-0.1*	*1B 0*	*-0.1*

Comparables: Chris Johnson, Danny Valencia, Todd Frazier

Ríos entered the 2021 season with 12 career home runs in 139 plate appearances and thus owned the highest home run rate among all players with at least 100 trips to the plate since 1947. It was this prodigious power that rocketed him through the crowded Dodgers system and made him an enviable and dangerous bench piece. Ríos showed off his oomph with a towering shot to center in the season's first week in Oakland, but he mustered just one infield single in his next 46 trips to the plate, and a subsequent stint on the injured list revealed that his right shoulder labrum required season-ending repair. Ríos' power was what offset red flags with his contact rate and his defense, so the potential lingering power-sapping effects of the surgery raises significant questions about his long-term value.

Luis Rodriguez CF

Born: 09/16/02 Age: 19 Bats: R Throws: R Height: 6'2" Weight: 175 lb. Origin: International Free Agent, 2019

YEAR	TEAM	LVL	AGE	PA	R	2B	3B	HR	RBI	BB	K	SB	CS	Whiff%	AVG/OBP/SLG	DRC+	BABIP	BRR	FRAA	WARP
2021	DOD	ROK	18	236	40	4	1	8	28	27	73	1	1		.216/.326/.367		.289			
2022															*No projection*					

Comparables: Jose Pena, Humberto Maldonado, Jean Montero

No, not that Luis Rodriguez. No, not that one, either. Man, there have been a lot of Luis Rodriguezes in MLB history. This Luis Rodriguez finally made his professional debut after signing for nearly $2.7 million in July 2019. His bat speed is apparent, but he has trouble tapping into his raw power. That isn't uncommon for young hitters—especially teenagers. He has the makings of a profile right fielder, but there's still a lot of variation in his future outcome. The Dodgers are usually aggressive with their position player prospects, but it wouldn't be surprising if they slow-played Rodriguez a bit.

Will Smith C

Born: 03/28/95 Age: 27 Bats: R Throws: R Height: 5'10" Weight: 195 lb. Origin: Round 1, 2016 Draft (#32 overall)

YEAR	TEAM	LVL	AGE	PA	R	2B	3B	HR	RBI	BB	K	SB	CS	Whiff%	AVG/OBP/SLG	DRC+	BABIP	BRR	FRAA	WARP
2019	OKC	AAA	24	270	48	11	2	20	54	40	49	1	0		.268/.381/.603	130	.253	1.2	C(52): -0.3, 3B(1): -0.1	2.3
2019	LAD	MLB	24	196	30	9	0	15	42	18	52	2	0	25.0%	.253/.337/.571	114	.264	-0.4	C(46): 5.4	1.7
2020	LAD	MLB	25	137	23	9	0	8	25	20	22	0	0	15.5%	.289/.401/.579	133	.294	-1.0	C(34): -2.8	0.7
2021	LAD	MLB	26	501	71	19	2	25	76	58	101	3	0	21.2%	.258/.365/.495	125	.274	-1.1	C(117): 7.9, 3B(1): -0.0	4.4
2022 DC	*LAD*	*MLB*	*27*	*453*	*72*	*18*	*1*	*20*	*76*	*52*	*87*	*3*	*1*	*21.0%*	*.241/.350/.451*	*112*	*.264*	*-0.4*	*C 4*	*3.1*

Comparables: James McCann, Francisco Cervelli, Devin Mesoraco

YEAR	TEAM	P. COUNT	FRM RUNS	BLK RUNS	THRW RUNS	TOT RUNS
2019	LAD	6644	3.2	0.1	0.7	4.0
2019	OKC	7760	-2.0	0.0	1.0	-1.0
2020	LAD	4351	-3.0	0.1	0.1	-2.8
2021	LAD	16176	8.8	-0.3	0.4	8.9
2022	*LAD*	*16835*	*4.7*	*0.1*	*0.1*	*4.9*

If 2020 was the year Smith adjusted to the league, 2021 was the year in which the league attempted to adjust back. One of the driving forces behind Smith's big offensive breakout in 2020 was his success against high fastballs; he hit such pitches for a .538 xwOBA and slugged .864 against them, both among the best marks in the league. Pitchers responded by throwing Smith a 10th percentile rate of fastballs in 2021. His results against off-speed pitches have remained a weak point, but he still found success because pitchers can't just eliminate the hard stuff entirely. Smith's excellent hitting was backed up by significantly improved receiving results (previously viewed as the biggest flaw in his profile), though his one-knee catching position will sometimes result in fewer blocked balls than his athleticism implies. At this point the only real hole in Smith's game is his game calling, which should improve with more experience. He's simply one of the best catchers in baseball.

Chris Taylor UT

Born: 08/29/90 Age: 31 Bats: R Throws: R Height: 6'1" Weight: 196 lb. Origin: Round 5, 2012 Draft (#161 overall)

YEAR	TEAM	LVL	AGE	PA	R	2B	3B	HR	RBI	BB	K	SB	CS	Whiff%	AVG/OBP/SLG	DRC+	BABIP	BRR	FRAA	WARP
2019	LAD	MLB	28	414	52	29	4	12	52	37	115	8	0	31.7%	.262/.333/.462	87	.344	3.0	LF(56): 0.7, SS(39): -4.6, 2B(20): -1.9	0.5
2020	LAD	MLB	29	214	30	10	2	8	32	26	55	3	2	32.7%	.270/.366/.476	106	.344	-0.4	SS(20): -0.5, LF(19): 1.8, 2B(13): 1.1	0.9
2021	LAD	MLB	30	582	92	25	4	20	73	63	167	13	1	32.7%	.254/.344/.438	97	.337	0.6	CF(61): -1.1, 2B(46): -2.6, LF(30): -0.9	1.4
2022 DC	*LAD*	*MLB*	*31*	*549*	*84*	*26*	*3*	*18*	*81*	*60*	*156*	*10*	*4*	*32.3%*	*.243/.336/.428*	*102*	*.323*	*0.6*	*2B -1, CF 1*	*2.1*

Comparables: Cal Ripken Jr., Shawon Dunston, Ian Desmond

Unwritten rules are generally reserved for players, but there is one that circulates among those who write about it: Never compare a player to Ben Zobrist, as that player will ultimately be a worse version of Ben Zobrist. At the risk of receiving the electronic equivalent of a fastball to the ribs, Taylor is as close as the baseball world has seen since Zobrist retired. Taylor played more than 50 innings at six different defensive positions in 2021 and was somewhere between acceptable and plus at all of them, helping keep the Dodgers' divisional hopes afloat as a series of injuries pushed their depth to a breaking point in the first half. A disastrous September (thanks to a neck injury) eventually proved the Zobrist Rule true once again, but Taylor healed up just in time to post two legendary playoff performances: the fifth walk-off homer in a winner-take-all game, and the first three-home run showing in an elimination game. Like Zobrist, Taylor's value is more than the sum of his parts, and that earned him a new free-agent deal to stay in Los Angeles for four more years.

Justin Turner 3B

Born: 11/23/84 Age: 37 Bats: R Throws: R Height: 5'11" Weight: 202 lb. Origin: Round 7, 2006 Draft (#204 overall)

YEAR	TEAM	LVL	AGE	PA	R	2B	3B	HR	RBI	BB	K	SB	CS	Whiff%	AVG/OBP/SLG	DRC+	BABIP	BRR	FRAA	WARP
2019	LAD	MLB	34	549	80	24	0	27	67	51	88	2	0	17.1%	.290/.372/.509	125	.304	-0.6	3B(124): 3.1	3.4
2020	LAD	MLB	35	175	26	9	1	4	23	18	26	1	0	20.5%	.307/.400/.460	119	.347	-1.2	3B(32): 1.9	0.9
2021	LAD	MLB	36	612	87	22	0	27	87	61	98	3	0	17.7%	.278/.361/.471	121	.292	-2.0	3B(143): -0.3, P(1): -0.0	3.5
2022 DC	*LAD*	*MLB*	*37*	*579*	*95*	*25*	*0*	*22*	*100*	*56*	*90*	*3*	*1*	*18.3%*	*.272/.361/.454*	*118*	*.296*	*-0.8*	*3B 1*	*3.0*

Comparables: Aramis Ramirez, Adrián Beltré, Ken Caminiti

The median Baseball Reference WAR among all Hall of Famers who took at least 1,500 plate appearances between ages 30 and 36 is 24.4. Only five Hall of Fame players played 75% of their plate appearances at third base and posted a WAR higher than that value. So it isn't stretching the truth to say that Turner's 28.0 Baseball Reference WAR over those same ages is starting to edge into the realm of historic. Turner kept right on going in 2021, posting a DRC+ in line with his career averages while logging his highest number of plate appearances since 2016, 10 short of his career high. Ultimately that extended workload might have proven his 2021 downfall, as his health finally let him down in October. Still, after yet another solid season, Turner's tenure with the team has reached a point where the story of the Dodger franchise cannot be told without him.

Trea Turner MI

Born: 06/30/93 Age: 29 Bats: R Throws: R Height: 6'2" Weight: 185 lb. Origin: Round 1, 2014 Draft (#13 overall)

YEAR	TEAM	LVL	AGE	PA	R	2B	3B	HR	RBI	BB	K	SB	CS	Whiff%	AVG/OBP/SLG	DRC+	BABIP	BRR	FRAA	WARP
2019	WAS	MLB	26	569	96	37	5	19	57	43	113	35	5	23.4%	.298/.353/.497	105	.348	3.6	SS(122): 2.2	3.0
2020	WAS	MLB	27	259	46	15	4	12	41	22	36	12	4	19.6%	.335/.394/.588	138	.353	5.3	SS(59): -8.9	1.6
2021	LAD	MLB	28	226	41	17	0	10	28	15	33	11	2	23.2%	.338/.385/.565	125	.361	3.9	2B(49): 0.7, SS(3): -0.3	2.0
2021	WAS	MLB	28	420	66	17	3	18	49	26	77	21	3	22.8%	.322/.369/.521	123	.363	0.6	SS(95): -2.0	2.6
2022 DC	*LAD*	*MLB*	*29*	*605*	*114*	*29*	*3*	*22*	*92*	*45*	*106*	*34*	*10*	*22.5%*	*.294/.354/.482*	*120*	*.333*	*2.6*	*SS -1, 2B 0*	*4.1*

Comparables: Ernie Banks, Cal Ripken Jr., Alan Trammell

Turner has erased any doubt that his 2020 performance was for real, as he finished 2021 leading MLB in hits (despite missing time due to a mid-season COVID diagnosis), batting average and sprint speed, and did so while missing a 30-30 season by two homers and playing good defense up the middle. His newfound power has turned him into one of the best players in the league, though it also turned him into one of its most confounding. Turner hits the ball hard, especially on the ground–his Statcast hard-hit grounder total of 102 was the fifth-highest in the league–and as a result he gets thrown out at first more often than somebody with his speed normally would. In 2021, Turner hit into 18 double plays and barely cracked the top 30 at the conversion rate from grounders into infield hits. The profile works as long as he lifts the ball, but if he goes through a slump where he can't (such as this year's postseason), it severely erodes his contributions with the bat and keeps his dynamic speed off the basepaths. The line between perennial MVP candidate and "Eric Hosmer but fast" feels very thin.

★ ★ ★ *2022 Top 101 Prospect* **#36** ★ ★ ★

Miguel Vargas 3B Born: 11/17/99 Age: 22 Bats: R Throws: R Height: 6'3" Weight: 205 lb. Origin: International Free Agent, 2017

YEAR	TEAM	LVL	AGE	PA	R	2B	3B	HR	RBI	BB	K	SB	CS	Whiff%	AVG/OBP/SLG	DRC+	BABIP	BRR	FRAA	WARP
2019	GL	A	19	323	53	20	2	5	45	35	43	9	1		.325/.399/.464	143	.363	-2.6	3B(59): 2.4, 1B(2): 0.3, 2B(2): 0.3	2.7
2019	RC	A+	19	236	23	18	1	2	32	20	40	4	3		.284/.353/.408	111	.341	-2.1	3B(43): -1.9, 1B(6): 0.4	0.6
2021	GL	A+	21	172	31	11	1	7	16	9	32	4	0		.314/.366/.532	121	.353	-1.1	3B(31): -1.9, 2B(2): -0.6, 1B(1): -0.0	0.6
2021	TUL	AA	21	370	67	16	1	16	60	36	57	7	1		.321/.386/.523	125	.344	1.0	3B(53): -0.4, 2B(15): -1.0, 1B(9): 0.1	2.2
2022 non-DC	*LAD*	*MLB*	*22*	*251*	*24*	*12*	*1*	*4*	*25*	*18*	*46*	*2*	*1*	*21.9%*	*.262/.321/.386*	*90*	*.310*	*-0.1*	*3B 0, 2B 0*	*0.3*

Comparables: Miguel Andújar, Brandon Drury, Blake DeWitt

One of the most underrated prospects seemingly everywhere except Baseball Prospectus, Vargas had himself a breakout season between Great Lakes and Tulsa. Power has always been the biggest question mark surrounding Vargas' projection, but the way he hit for power in the pitcher-friendly High-A Central Midwest League and in the Double-A Central Texas League—while being roughly three years younger than the competition—should answer those questions. He might be the second coming of Matt Kemp, offensively. Look at some of the finishes on his home run swings and try to deny the resemblance.

PITCHERS

Trevor Bauer RHP Born: 01/17/91 Age: 31 Bats: R Throws: R Height: 6'1" Weight: 205 lb. Origin: Round 1, 2011 Draft (#3 overall)

YEAR	TEAM	LVL	AGE	W	L	SV	G	GS	IP	H	HR	BB/9	K/9	K	GB%	BABIP	WHIP	ERA	DRA-	WARP	MPH	FB%	Whiff%	CSP
2019	CLE	MLB	28	9	8	0	24	24	156^{2}	127	22	3.6	10.6	185	39.3%	.278	1.21	3.79	93	2.2	94.8	41.1%	29.5%	45.5%
2019	CIN	MLB	28	2	5	0	10	10	56^{1}	57	12	3.0	10.9	68	33.5%	.321	1.35	6.39	87	1.0	94.3	45.3%	29.2%	45.1%
2020	CIN	MLB	29	5	4	0	11	11	73	41	9	2.1	12.3	100	35.4%	.215	0.79	1.73	74	1.9	93.8	47.8%	30.4%	44.6%
2021	LAD	MLB	30	8	5	0	17	17	107^{2}	71	19	3.1	11.5	137	32.9%	.222	1.00	2.59	78	2.2	94.1	46.0%	30.4%	53.0%
2022 non-DC	*LAD*	*MLB*	*31*	*2*	*2*	*0*	*57*	*0*	*50*	*40*	*8*	*2.9*	*11.3*	*62*	*36.0%*	*.280*	*1.13*	*3.34*	*83*	*0.6*	*94.2*	*45.2%*	*30.1%*	*48.8%*

Comparables: Bob Gibson, Zack Greinke, Jason Schmidt

www.mencanstoprape.org | MCSR describes its mission as being "to promote gender equity and build men's capacity to be strong without being violent." There are many programs, including outreach to youth and education on teen dating violence.

The National Domestic Violence Hotline is 1-800-799-7233. It is confidential and available 24/7/365.

Clayton Beeter RHP Born: 10/09/98 Age: 23 Bats: R Throws: R Height: 6'2" Weight: 220 lb. Origin: Round 2, 2020 Draft (#66 overall)

YEAR	TEAM	LVL	AGE	W	L	SV	G	GS	IP	H	HR	BB/9	K/9	K	GB%	BABIP	WHIP	ERA	DRA-	WARP	MPH	FB%	Whiff%	CSP
2021	GL	A+	22	0	4	0	23	22	37^{1}	28	3	3.6	13.3	55	36.7%	.333	1.15	3.13	71	1.0				
2021	TUL	AA	22	0	2	0	5	5	15	10	2	4.2	13.8	23	53.3%	.286	1.13	4.20	71	0.3				
2022 non-DC	*LAD*	*MLB*	*23*	*2*	*2*	*0*	*57*	*0*	*50*	*45*	*7*	*4.8*	*10.6*	*58*	*39.5%*	*.302*	*1.45*	*4.69*	*109*	*0.0*				

Comparables: Kris Medlen, Pep Harris, Alex Claudio

Like a poker player, the Dodgers slow-played Beeter this season. He averaged fewer than two innings per start, but when he was in there, he showed off the electric stuff that had him on the cusp of being a first-rounder in 2020, when he fell to no. 66 and the Dodgers pounced. There hasn't been a Dodgers pitching draftee since Walker Buehler who so perfectly fit their developmental style. He has three offerings that have flashed plus. Whether he gets to use them as a starter or reliever remains to be seen.

Phil Bickford RHP Born: 07/10/95 Age: 26 Bats: R Throws: R Height: 6'4" Weight: 200 lb. Origin: Round 1, 2015 Draft (#18 overall)

YEAR	TEAM	LVL	AGE	W	L	SV	G	GS	IP	H	HR	BB/9	K/9	K	GB%	BABIP	WHIP	ERA	DRA-	WARP	MPH	FB%	Whiff%	CSP
2019	CAR	A+	23	3	0	1	20	0	32^{2}	23	2	3.0	14.6	53	25.0%	.339	1.04	2.48	58	1.0				
2020	MIL	MLB	24	0	0	0	1	0	1	4	0	0.0	18.0	2	0.0%	.800	4.00	36.00	127	0.0	89.6	84.8%	25.0%	56.8%
2021	OKC	AAA	25	1	0	0	5	0	5	5	0	0.0	21.6	12	44.4%	.556	1.00	5.40	74	0.1				
2021	MIL	MLB	25	0	0	0	1	0	1	2	1	9.0	0.0	0	20.0%	.250	3.00	18.00	97	0.0	92.8	84.2%	23.5%	49.4%
2021	LAD	MLB	25	4	2	1	56	0	50^{1}	34	6	3.2	10.5	59	47.1%	.243	1.03	2.50	80	1.0	94.1	63.3%	30.2%	58.5%
2022 DC	*LAD*	*MLB*	*26*	*2*	*2*	*0*	*52*	*0*	*45.3*	*38*	*6*	*3.6*	*11.1*	*55*	*38.6%*	*.291*	*1.24*	*3.73*	*90*	*0.4*	*93.9*	*64.9%*	*29.8%*	*58.0%*

Comparables: Tyler Clippard, Luke Gregerson, Bob Howry

After being selected in the first round in both the 2013 and 2015 drafts, Bickford struggled to live up to that pedigree until now. The Dodgers, noticing a 4-mph uptick in Bickford's velocity in the season's opening weeks, picked up Bickford after he was designated for assignment by the Brewers, then did what they do best, distilling a reliever into the most basic ingredients required for success. In Bickford's case, this required both simplifying his pitch arsenal down to his fastball and wipeout slider and playing into the platoon tendencies of that repertoire. Among all major leaguers who threw at least 750 pitches in 2021, Bickford threw the second-highest percentage to same-sided batters, and his frequent tandem appearances with lefty Alex Vesia became a running joke among fans. Bickford's command began to falter late in the season, which led to a lower spot in the pecking order during the playoffs, but his overall transformation into a reliable bullpen arm–one who was especially important in holding things together while the much of the pitching staff was struggling with injuries–was a good story in a bullpen full of them.

Justin Bruihl LHP Born: 06/26/97 Age: 25 Bats: L Throws: L Height: 6'2" Weight: 215 lb. Origin: Undrafted Free Agent, 2017

YEAR	TEAM	LVL	AGE	W	L	SV	G	GS	IP	H	HR	BB/9	K/9	K	GB%	BABIP	WHIP	ERA	DRA-	WARP	MPH	FB%	Whiff%	CSP
2019	GL	A	22	4	0	2	21	0	34^1	23	0	2.1	11.0	42	64.6%	.284	0.90	0.79	75	0.7				
2019	RC	A+	22	1	0	0	4	0	7^1	5	0	1.2	11.0	9	42.1%	.263	0.82	3.68	82	0.1				
2021	TUL	AA	24	1	0	0	8	0	15	7	1	1.8	12.0	20	56.7%	.207	0.67	1.20	74	0.3				
2021	OKC	AAA	24	3	0	0	18	1	22^2	22	2	2.8	11.9	30	46.4%	.377	1.28	3.57	74	0.4				
2021	LAD	MLB	24	0	1	0	21	2	18^2	13	1	3.4	5.3	11	48.1%	.231	1.07	2.89	106	0.1	88.6	70.2%	20.9%	59.4%
2022 DC	*LAD*	*MLB*	*25*	*6*	*3*	*0*	*55*	*3*	*50*	*46*	*5*	*3.4*	*8.7*	*48*	*49.5%*	*.294*	*1.30*	*3.77*	*93*	*0.4*	*88.6*	*70.2%*	*20.9%*	*59.4%*

Comparables: James Norwood, Cory Burns, Taylor Guilbeau

Bruihl has made a habit of defying the odds in his young career. He was signed out of college as an undrafted free agent in 2017, has never appeared on a top prospect list, and had not pitched above A-ball before this season. Despite all of that, Bruihl was a surprise inclusion on the Dodgers' NLCS roster, where he struck out five of the seven batters he faced. He relies primarily on a cutter-slider mix and can carve up fellow southpaws with the best of them, but he lacks an effective tool to deal with right-handed batters. While the three-batter minimum rule may hamper his long-term impact, Bruihl has overcome obstacles before.

Maddux Bruns LHP Born: 06/20/02 Age: 20 Bats: L Throws: L Height: 6'2" Weight: 205 lb. Origin: Round 1, 2021 Draft (#29 overall)

Originally reported by some to be Tanner Burns (insert Hans Moleman "boo-urns" meme here), Bruns was the Dodgers first-rounder in 2021 and, well, his debut left a lot to be desired. Still, it's hard to be too concerned about such a small sample size. The power lefty has a mid-90s heater with some run that contributes to his command/control issues when he tries to throw it too hard. He also owns a wipeout slider and a hammer curveball that could be above-average or better pitches. It's a Max Fried repertoire, but the Alabama native wasn't teammates with Jack Flaherty and Lucas Giolitto in high school. In fact, he's just the second player ever drafted out of UMS-Wright Prep in the ... Heart of Dixie? Ooo, maybe not. The Cotton State? Yikes. The Yellowhammer State? Oof! As far as Alabama state nicknames go, they're about as good as Bruns' present control.

Walker Buehler RHP Born: 07/28/94 Age: 27 Bats: R Throws: R Height: 6'2" Weight: 185 lb. Origin: Round 1, 2015 Draft (#24 overall)

YEAR	TEAM	LVL	AGE	W	L	SV	G	GS	IP	H	HR	BB/9	K/9	K	GB%	BABIP	WHIP	ERA	DRA-	WARP	MPH	FB%	Whiff%	CSP
2019	LAD	MLB	24	14	4	0	30	30	182^1	153	20	1.8	10.6	215	42.1%	.292	1.04	3.26	73	4.4	96.7	60.1%	26.8%	51.1%
2020	LAD	MLB	25	1	0	0	8	8	36^2	24	7	2.7	10.3	42	36.6%	.198	0.95	3.44	84	0.7	96.8	62.3%	28.4%	48.4%
2021	LAD	MLB	26	16	4	0	33	33	207^2	149	19	2.3	9.2	212	43.9%	.250	0.97	2.47	77	4.5	95.5	52.0%	26.5%	56.0%
2022 DC	*LAD*	*MLB*	*27*	*12*	*8*	*0*	*29*	*29*	*177.7*	*154*	*22*	*2.3*	*9.6*	*189*	*43.9%*	*.286*	*1.12*	*3.02*	*79*	*3.4*	*95.9*	*54.6%*	*26.8%*	*54.3%*

Comparables: Bert Blyleven, Bret Saberhagen, Justin Verlander

Buehler has dealt with comparisons to Clayton Kershaw for his entire career–many of which have been unfair, as comparisons to the greatest pitcher of a generation tend to be–but in 2021 Buehler lived up to many of them, both for better and for worse. With 2020's blister problems behind him, Buehler met ace-like expectations for most of the season, finishing second in the league in total innings pitched and fourth in adjusted ERA. Despite losing 1 mph between seasons on his four-seamer and 300 rpm on the same pitch during the foreign substance crackdown, Buehler showed an ability to control contact that would make Kershaw proud. Of particular note was a step forward in Buehler's change (once considered his worst pitch); lefties managed just one extra-base hit all year against the offering which dives off their barrel at 92 mph. The negative side of the Kershaw comparisons arose in October. Asked to start on three days' rest twice after throwing a career high in innings, Buehler faltered. Unfortunately, it's a familiar script.

Garrett Cleavinger LHP Born: 04/23/94 Age: 28 Bats: R Throws: L Height: 6'1" Weight: 220 lb. Origin: Round 3, 2015 Draft (#102 overall)

YEAR	TEAM	LVL	AGE	W	L	SV	G	GS	IP	H	HR	BB/9	K/9	K	GB%	BABIP	WHIP	ERA	DRA-	WARP	MPH	FB%	Whiff%	CSP
2019	REA	AA	25	3	2	0	34	0	51^2	32	2	5.9	14.5	83	46.2%	.291	1.28	3.66	70	1.2				
2020	PHI	MLB	26	0	0	0	1	0	0^2	2	1	0.0	13.5	1	66.7%	.500	3.00	13.50	59	0.0	94.3	50.0%	50.0%	62.0%
2021	OKC	AAA	27	1	0	0	11	0	11^2	9	0	3.9	19.3	25	47.1%	.529	1.20	1.54	54	0.4				
2021	LAD	MLB	27	2	4	0	22	1	18	20	4	6.0	10.5	21	48.0%	.356	1.78	3.00	87	0.3	95.9	54.5%	26.1%	53.5%
2022 DC	*LAD*	*MLB*	*28*	*2*	*2*	*0*	*44*	*0*	*38.7*	*31*	*5*	*5.7*	*11.9*	*51*	*46.1%*	*.297*	*1.45*	*4.45*	*102*	*0.1*	*95.9*	*54.4%*	*26.5%*	*53.7%*

Comparables: Jeff Beliveau, Al Alburquerque, Ryan Buchter

Just 15 years ago, Cleavinger's average fastball velocity of 95.8 mph would have ranked third in the league among left-handed relievers. That kind of velocity from the left side, combined with his frisbee slider, likely would have been enough for Cleavinger to secure a permanent roster spot despite his bouts with control problems. But times have changed, and a lefty coming out of Triple-A and topping out at 98 isn't enough to make headlines, let alone secure a permanent spot in the majors. Cleavinger still has the stuff to succeed, especially given a very high 43% whiff-per-swing rate on his slider this season.But he needs to be in the zone more often to move past his current state of up-and-down limbo.

Danny Duffy LHP Born: 12/21/88 Age: 33 Bats: L Throws: L Height: 6'3" Weight: 205 lb. Origin: Round 3, 2007 Draft (#96 overall)

YEAR	TEAM	LVL	AGE	W	L	SV	G	GS	IP	H	HR	BB/9	K/9	K	GB%	BABIP	WHIP	ERA	DRA-	WARP	MPH	FB%	Whiff%	CSP
2019	NWA	AA	30	1	0	0	2	2	10^1	8	1	0.0	9.6	11	46.2%	.280	0.77	0.87	98	0.0				
2019	KC	MLB	30	7	6	0	23	23	130^2	125	21	3.2	7.9	115	35.0%	.285	1.31	4.34	120	0.0	92.5	53.0%	24.2%	50.3%
2020	KC	MLB	31	4	4	0	12	11	56^1	53	10	3.5	9.1	57	31.7%	.287	1.33	4.95	133	-0.4	92.4	53.4%	25.6%	48.6%
2021	KC	MLB	32	4	3	0	13	12	61	52	6	3.2	9.6	65	33.9%	.289	1.21	2.51	104	0.4	93.9	55.7%	29.2%	52.6%
2022 DC	*FA*	*MLB*	*33*	*1*	*1*	*0*	*35*	*0*	*30.7*	*29*	*5*	*3.3*	*9.1*	*31*	*34.3%*	*.295*	*1.33*	*4.53*	*106*	*0.0*	*93.1*	*54.3%*	*26.7%*	*50.8%*

Comparables: Jarrod Washburn, Eric Milton, Bob Ojeda

Duff Man can't pitch; oh no! Acquired the day before the Dodgers traded for Scherzer, Duffy was expected to serve as a multi-inning reliever down the stretch and in the postseason. But a left flexor strain cut his season short and prevented him from even throwing a pitch for the 2021 Dodgers.

Tony Gonsolin RHP Born: 05/14/94 Age: 28 Bats: R Throws: R Height: 6'3" Weight: 205 lb. Origin: Round 9, 2016 Draft (#281 overall)

YEAR	TEAM	LVL	AGE	W	L	SV	G	GS	IP	H	HR	BB/9	K/9	K	GB%	BABIP	WHIP	ERA	DRA-	WARP	MPH	FB%	Whiff%	CSP
2019	OKC	AAA	25	2	4	0	13	13	41^{1}	41	4	4.6	10.9	50	35.0%	.327	1.50	4.35	83	0.7				
2019	LAD	MLB	25	4	2	1	11	6	40	26	4	3.4	8.3	37	40.9%	.208	1.03	2.93	100	0.4	93.7	48.3%	26.9%	43.6%
2020	LAD	MLB	26	2	2	0	9	8	46^{2}	32	2	1.4	8.9	46	33.6%	.252	0.84	2.31	85	0.9	95.1	47.5%	29.8%	47.3%
2021	OKC	AAA	27	0	0	0	3	3	10^{1}	6	2	2.6	7.8	9	35.7%	.154	0.87	3.48	106	0.0				
2021	LAD	MLB	27	4	1	0	15	13	55^{2}	41	8	5.5	10.5	65	36.4%	.254	1.35	3.23	98	0.6	93.9	43.6%	29.7%	54.3%
2022 DC	*LAD*	*MLB*	*28*	*7*	*6*	*0*	*24*	*24*	*106.7*	*94*	*15*	*3.9*	*9.7*	*115*	*36.5%*	*.288*	*1.32*	*3.98*	*96*	*1.0*	*94.2*	*45.4%*	*29.3%*	*50.9%*

Comparables: Chase Anderson, Mike Bolsinger, Mike Clevinger

On the proprietary Baseball Prospectus Annual Cat Scale, where a 10 is a warm cat purring in your lap and a 1 is the same cat throwing up on your bed, Gonsolin's 2021 season was about a 4: said cat scratching up a piece of furniture, but not one you actually like. The Cat Man finished the year with an ERA about 20% better than league average, but that hid concerning peripherals and two separate IL stints caused by shoulder problems. Gonsolin is now at a crossroads and needs to answer a fundamental question:Is a slightly better-than-average starter better utilized as a reliever, where his wipeout splitter can play up?

Victor González LHP Born: 11/16/95 Age: 26 Bats: L Throws: L Height: 6'0" Weight: 180 lb. Origin: International Free Agent, 2012

YEAR	TEAM	LVL	AGE	W	L	SV	G	GS	IP	H	HR	BB/9	K/9	K	GB%	BABIP	WHIP	ERA	DRA-	WARP	MPH	FB%	Whiff%	CSP
2019	RC	A+	23	2	1	0	8	5	27^{1}	17	0	4.6	11.9	36	47.7%	.274	1.13	1.65	89	0.2				
2019	TUL	AA	23	3	1	2	15	8	48^{1}	48	4	2.6	8.2	44	52.1%	.319	1.28	2.23	97	0.2				
2019	OKC	AAA	23	0	0	0	15	0	14	16	3	2.6	8.4	13	54.5%	.317	1.43	3.86	81	0.2				
2020	LAD	MLB	24	3	0	0	15	1	20^{1}	13	0	0.9	10.2	23	69.2%	.250	0.74	1.33	67	0.6	95.0	62.8%	33.6%	45.4%
2021	OKC	AAA	25	2	0	0	12	0	9^{2}	10	1	1.9	14.0	15	54.2%	.391	1.24	3.72	72	0.2				
2021	LAD	MLB	25	3	1	1	44	1	35^{1}	32	3	4.8	8.4	33	54.0%	.302	1.44	3.57	93	0.5	94.4	55.3%	28.3%	52.2%
2022 DC	*LAD*	*MLB*	*26*	*2*	*2*	*0*	*52*	*0*	*45.3*	*41*	*5*	*3.5*	*9.6*	*48*	*52.0%*	*.299*	*1.29*	*3.76*	*92*	*0.4*	*94.6*	*57.2%*	*29.7%*	*50.4%*

Comparables: Rex Brothers, Bryan Shaw, Zach Putnam

In his rise to being one of the most trusted relievers in a championship bullpen in his rookie campaign, González relied upon his high-spin slider as his primary out pitch. When batters swung at his slider in 2020, they missed 57% of the time, which was the second highest rate among any left-handed pitcher with at least 50 sliders thrown. But that pitch, along with his two-seamer, took a significant step back in 2021. Like many pitchers, González lost a significant amount of spin in mid-June; his slider lost 350 rpm and the sinker lost 250 rpm after June 15th. As a result, the superlative slider that made González look like a potential bullpen cornerstone regressed to being more ordinary, and the sinker was hit harder thanks to spottier command. While it is tempting to solely blame the foreign substance enforcement crackdown, González spent the second half of the season battling lower half injuries, which also could have hampered his mechanics. Regardless of the cause, González fell off the left-handed pitching depth chart by the end of the season, and he has a lot of work to do to build himself back up.

Brusdar Graterol RHP Born: 08/26/98 Age: 23 Bats: R Throws: R Height: 6'1" Weight: 265 lb. Origin: International Free Agent, 2014

YEAR	TEAM	LVL	AGE	W	L	SV	G	GS	IP	H	HR	BB/9	K/9	K	GB%	BABIP	WHIP	ERA	DRA-	WARP	MPH	FB%	Whiff%	CSP
2019	TWI	ROK	20	0	0	0	2	2	3	1	0	0.0	12.0	4	60.0%	.200	0.33	0.00						
2019	PNS	AA	20	6	0	1	12	9	52^{2}	32	2	3.6	8.5	50	55.0%	.234	1.01	1.71	91	0.6				
2019	ROC	AAA	20	1	0	0	4	0	5^{1}	4	1	3.4	11.8	7	50.0%	.273	1.13	5.06	81	0.1				
2019	MIN	MLB	20	1	1	0	10	0	9^{2}	10	1	1.9	9.3	10	51.9%	.346	1.24	4.66	90	0.1	99.0	67.4%	18.7%	52.8%
2020	LAD	MLB	21	1	2	0	23	2	23^{1}	18	1	1.2	5.0	13	63.8%	.250	0.90	3.09	94	0.3	99.3	70.8%	15.2%	54.3%
2021	OKC	AAA	22	2	2	1	17	0	16^{2}	12	1	2.7	10.8	20	73.8%	.268	1.02	6.48	83	0.2				
2021	LAD	MLB	22	3	0	0	34	1	33^{1}	34	2	3.5	7.3	27	57.7%	.314	1.41	4.59	104	0.2	100.0	68.5%	19.0%	61.0%
2022 DC	*LAD*	*MLB*	*23*	*2*	*3*	*0*	*59*	*0*	*51.7*	*50*	*4*	*3.4*	*7.4*	*42*	*57.2%*	*.296*	*1.35*	*4.05*	*99*	*0.2*	*99.8*	*69.0%*	*18.0%*	*58.8%*

Comparables: Jeremy Jeffress, Oscar Villarreal, Ryan Webb

It's not exactly a bold statement to say that somebody who is capable of throwing a two-seam 103 mph is due for a breakout, but if Graterol takes that step forward next season, 2021 will be viewed as the year in which he planted those seeds. Graterol's relief profile has always been vexing. He has generated far fewer swings and misses than his velocity and fastball movement would normally imply, thanks to low release extension and a two-seam break that takes the pitch right onto a right-handed batter's barrel. However, about two weeks before the regular season ended, Graterol unearthed a cutter with his signature velocity, averaging about 95 and touching 98. The swing-and-miss results haven't come yet, but its appearance may solve the break direction problems of the two-seamer and cause both pitches to play up. It also signals intent: Graterol understands that purely throwing 100+ is not enough in today's game.

Michael Grove RHP Born: 12/18/96 Age: 25 Bats: R Throws: R Height: 6'3" Weight: 200 lb. Origin: Round 2, 2018 Draft (#68 overall)

YEAR	TEAM	LVL	AGE	W	L	SV	G	GS	IP	H	HR	BB/9	K/9	K	GB%	BABIP	WHIP	ERA	DRA-	WARP	MPH	FB%	Whiff%	CSP
2019	RC	A+	22	0	5	0	21	21	51^{2}	61	7	3.3	12.7	73	29.7%	.412	1.55	6.10	86	0.6				
2021	TUL	AA	24	1	4	0	21	19	71	85	19	5.3	11.2	88	34.8%	.351	1.79	7.86	93	0.7				
2022 non-DC	*LAD*	*MLB*	*25*	*2*	*3*	*0*	*57*	*0*	*50*	*53*	*10*	*5.3*	*9.3*	*51*	*32.9%*	*.316*	*1.66*	*6.06*	*135*	*-0.7*				

Comparables: Chase De Jong, Jason Middlebrook, Claudio Vargas

The beneficiary of the Dodgers failing to sign JT Ginn in 2018, Grove got a $1.2-plus million bonus and...well, it's not looking like the best investment at this point. The results have been ugly the last two seasons (7.12 ERA), but if you look beyond the numbers, there's some promise. He went from sitting in the low-90s earlier this season to reaching the 95-plus mph range, and he has seen his command and off-speed pitches improve thanks to mechanical adjustments. Given the Dodgers' development bona fides, it wouldn't be at all surprising for Grove to carve out some kind of role on an MLB staff—more likely in relief than the rotation.

Andrew Heaney LHP

Born: 06/05/91 Age: 31 Bats: L Throws: L Height: 6'2" Weight: 200 lb. Origin: Round 1, 2012 Draft (#9 overall)

YEAR	TEAM	LVL	AGE	W	L	SV	G	GS	IP	H	HR	BB/9	K/9	K	GB%	BABIP	WHIP	ERA	DRA-	WARP	MPH	FB%	Whiff%	CSP
2019	LAA	MLB	28	4	6	0	18	18	95^{1}	93	20	2.8	11.1	118	32.7%	.312	1.29	4.91	98	1.1	92.6	58.0%	31.3%	48.3%
2020	LAA	MLB	29	4	3	0	12	12	66^{2}	63	9	2.6	9.5	70	38.3%	.302	1.23	4.46	92	1.0	91.7	58.0%	28.0%	50.1%
2021	NYY	MLB	30	2	2	0	12	5	35^{2}	38	13	2.5	9.3	37	32.7%	.266	1.35	7.32	129	-0.2	92.0	58.8%	23.6%	51.3%
2021	LAA	MLB	30	6	7	0	18	18	94	92	16	3.0	10.8	113	34.0%	.319	1.31	5.27	95	1.1	92.1	59.7%	29.7%	49.7%
2022 DC	*LAD*	*MLB*	*31*	*8*	*7*	*0*	*25*	*25*	*129.3*	*118*	*23*	*2.7*	*9.8*	*141*	*35.7%*	*.289*	*1.21*	*3.92*	*96*	*1.3*	*92.1*	*58.9%*	*28.7%*	*49.8%*

Comparables: Mudcat Grant, Ian Kennedy, Pete Schourek

A wicked man died alone following a life of wrath and avarice. This man happened to have been a Yankees fan, and when he descended to hell, he was surprised to find a baseball field. "Relax," said the devil, "It's not so bad here. What sort of pitchers do you like on your team?"

The man thought for a moment. "Well, I like when they can strike a batter out."

"Good! What else?" the devil prompted.

"I also like pitchers who don't give up too many walks," the man replied, his excitement growing.

"Excellent!" said the devil. "We have just the right pitcher for the job."

"And home runs! Does he keep the ball in the yard?"

The devil threw back his head and howled with laughter. Thunder and lightning cracked menacingly as the public address announcer boomed, "Now pitching, number 38, Andrew Heaney!"

Peter Heubeck RHP

Born: 07/22/02 Age: 19 Bats: R Throws: R Height: 6'3" Weight: 170 lb. Origin: Round 3, 2021 Draft (#101 overall)

It isn't often a teenager can throw so few innings in a debut and still impress, but that's what Heubeck did. He displayed the stuff that made him a third-round pick in the 2021 draft, even if he should have gone higher by most accounts. He has a three-pitch mix, and it wouldn't be surprising to see him add some kind of slider/cutter to his arsenal. It has worked for other pitching prospects to come up through the system, and it could work for him—especially if his changeup never fully develops.

Daniel Hudson RHP

Born: 03/09/87 Age: 35 Bats: R Throws: R Height: 6'3" Weight: 215 lb. Origin: Round 5, 2008 Draft (#150 overall)

YEAR	TEAM	LVL	AGE	W	L	SV	G	GS	IP	H	HR	BB/9	K/9	K	GB%	BABIP	WHIP	ERA	DRA-	WARP	MPH	FB%	Whiff%	CSP
2019	WAS	MLB	32	3	0	6	24	0	25	18	3	1.4	8.3	23	27.5%	.227	0.88	1.44	100	0.3	96.6	72.4%	22.4%	54.1%
2020	WAS	MLB	33	3	2	10	21	0	20^{2}	15	6	4.8	12.2	28	18.0%	.209	1.26	6.10	112	0.1	96.6	75.9%	31.2%	51.7%
2021	SD	MLB	34	1	2	0	23	0	19	17	4	4.3	12.8	27	27.7%	.302	1.37	5.21	91	0.3	96.9	61.9%	34.1%	55.1%
2021	WAS	MLB	34	4	1	0	31	0	32^{2}	23	4	1.9	13.2	48	29.2%	.279	0.92	2.20	77	0.7	97.1	72.7%	34.5%	54.6%
2022 DC	*LAD*	*MLB*	*35*	*3*	*3*	*14*	*67*	*0*	*58*	*47*	*10*	*3.3*	*10.8*	*69*	*32.2%*	*.272*	*1.17*	*3.57*	*89*	*0.6*	*96.8*	*70.3%*	*30.8%*	*52.7%*

Comparables: David Riske, Jason Isringhausen, Dan Spillner

Sometimes a cudgel is more effective than a paintbrush. Along with his big fastball, Hudson brought back a slider he'd dialed down in 2020 because when batters made contact with it, they punished it; the same thing happened in 2021, but with batters whiffing on the pitch half the time, the margin for error was much broader. Unfortunately, his command suffered after some mid-season elbow inflammation and a stint on the COVID-19 list, so when Hudson showed up in San Diego, he wasn't quite the pitcher the Padres thought they were acquiring at the deadline. A handful of singles, a few home runs, and suddenly he'd doubled his ERA while still maintaining most of the other underlying metrics. Such is the life of a veteran reliever, and the reason power tools are so prized among them; a fastball that grazes 99 and a wipeout slider cover up a lot of imperfections, given enough time for the batted balls to even out.

Andre Jackson RHP

Born: 05/01/96 Age: 26 Bats: R Throws: R Height: 6'3" Weight: 210 lb. Origin: Round 12, 2017 Draft (#370 overall)

YEAR	TEAM	LVL	AGE	W	L	SV	G	GS	IP	H	HR	BB/9	K/9	K	GB%	BABIP	WHIP	ERA	DRA-	WARP	MPH	FB%	Whiff%	CSP
2019	GL	A	23	4	1	0	10	10	48^{1}	29	1	3.5	9.3	50	46.7%	.237	0.99	2.23	95	0.5				
2019	RC	A+	23	3	1	0	15	15	66^{1}	61	5	5.2	12.3	91	45.9%	.368	1.49	3.66	88	0.6				
2021	TUL	AA	25	3	2	0	15	13	63^{1}	46	12	2.8	10.7	75	31.8%	.239	1.04	3.27	82	1.0				
2021	OKC	AAA	25	2	3	0	6	5	26^{1}	26	6	3.1	7.9	23	35.4%	.263	1.33	5.13	99	0.1				
2021	LAD	MLB	25	0	1	1	3	0	11^{2}	10	1	4.6	7.7	10	26.5%	.290	1.37	2.31	100	0.1	92.1	58.8%	29.9%	57.3%
2022 DC	*LAD*	*MLB*	*26*	*5*	*6*	*0*	*46*	*9*	*71*	*74*	*13*	*4.4*	*8.1*	*64*	*36.2%*	*.301*	*1.54*	*5.54*	*125*	*-0.5*	*92.1*	*58.8%*	*29.9%*	*57.3%*

Comparables: Jeremy Hefner, Shane Greene, Rafael Montero

Not a lot was expected out of Jackson, an over-slot 12th rounder out of the University of Utah. He was a lottery ticket. Four years later, it looks like the Dodgers might have hit another winner. Jackson has a changeup that would get a lot more publicity if he weren't in a farm system with Ryan Pepiot. He made it to the majors this season and has been mentioned by the front office as a guy who could see significant time in Los Angeles in 2022. A lot will depend on how the Dodgers fill out their 2022 rotation and how Jackson improves his command/control, which has been his biggest detriment so far in his pro career.

Landon Knack RHP Born: 07/15/97 Age: 24 Bats: L Throws: R Height: 6'2" Weight: 220 lb. Origin: Round 2, 2020 Draft (#60 overall)

YEAR	TEAM	LVL	AGE	W	L	SV	G	GS	IP	H	HR	BB/9	K/9	K	GB%	BABIP	WHIP	ERA	DRA-	WARP	MPH	FB%	Whiff%	CSP
2021	GL	A+	23	5	0	0	10	5	39^2	31	2	1.1	12.5	55	46.7%	.330	0.91	2.50	70	1.0				
2021	TUL	AA	23	2	1	0	6	6	22^2	19	6	1.2	10.7	27	38.3%	.241	0.97	4.37	90	0.3				
2022 non-DC	*LAD*	*MLB*	*24*	*2*	*2*	*0*	*57*	*0*	*50*	*46*	*7*	*2.5*	*8.8*	*49*	*41.0%*	*.290*	*1.21*	*3.88*	*97*	*0.3*				

Comparables: Blake Wood, Matt Barnes, Anthony DeSclafani

Selected from the baseball powerhouse of East Tennessee State University, Knack was the Dodgers' 2019 second-round selection and has left opposing hitters in High- and Double-A with a lasting impression. One of the only reasons he isn't a more highly regarded prospect is because he's on the older side. The onetime fifth-year senior is a strike-thrower and has already seen his stuff tick up since turning pro. He doesn't have history on his side, as the only Buccaneer to reach the majors is Atlee Hammaker—bet you didn't expect to see that name when you woke up this morning.

Dustin May RHP Born: 09/06/97 Age: 24 Bats: R Throws: R Height: 6'6" Weight: 180 lb. Origin: Round 3, 2016 Draft (#101 overall)

YEAR	TEAM	LVL	AGE	W	L	SV	G	GS	IP	H	HR	BB/9	K/9	K	GB%	BABIP	WHIP	ERA	DRA-	WARP	MPH	FB%	Whiff%	CSP
2019	TUL	AA	21	3	5	0	15	15	79^1	71	5	2.3	9.8	86	50.5%	.311	1.15	3.74	90	0.6				
2019	OKC	AAA	21	3	0	0	5	5	27^1	21	0	3.0	7.9	24	59.2%	.280	1.10	2.30	80	0.5				
2019	LAD	MLB	21	2	3	0	14	4	34^2	33	2	1.3	8.3	32	45.0%	.316	1.10	3.63	96	0.4	95.1	88.2%	20.6%	52.3%
2020	LAD	MLB	22	3	1	0	12	10	56	45	9	2.6	7.1	44	53.4%	.235	1.09	2.57	82	1.1	97.4	81.5%	19.2%	53.3%
2021	LAD	MLB	23	1	1	0	5	5	23	16	4	2.3	13.7	35	54.9%	.255	0.96	2.74	69	0.6	98.0	77.3%	32.3%	57.5%
2022 DC	*LAD*	*MLB*	*24*	*4*	*3*	*0*	*12*	*12*	*58*	*50*	*6*	*2.7*	*9.2*	*59*	*51.5%*	*.286*	*1.16*	*3.06*	*78*	*1.1*	*97.2*	*81.3%*	*23.7%*	*54.5%*

Comparables: Will Smith, Kevin Appier, Alex Fernandez

The phrase "May Day" can have wildly different connotations. It can be a celebration of international workers or the start of summer or a distress signal with the removal of one space (and when repeated three times). It also can signify a start by a young redheaded right-hander on the precipice of breakout. Unfortunately in his outing on his namesake day, May left with the trainer in the second inning: mayday mayday mayday on May Day on May Day. May underwent Tommy John surgery less than two weeks later. The injury interrupted what appeared to be a significant step forward thanks to a reshaped curveball, which added four inches of horizontal movement and missed bats at a rate similar to Shohei Ohtani's splitter. May also trusted his four-seam fastball more, giving him a way to change batters' eye lines, a trait he lacked previously. The result was a dramatic increase in missed bats, and now we'll see if he can regain that post-recovery.

★ ★ ★ *2022 Top 101 Prospect* **#63** ★ ★ ★

Bobby Miller RHP Born: 04/05/99 Age: 23 Bats: L Throws: R Height: 6'5" Weight: 220 lb. Origin: Round 1, 2020 Draft (#29 overall)

YEAR	TEAM	LVL	AGE	W	L	SV	G	GS	IP	H	HR	BB/9	K/9	K	GB%	BABIP	WHIP	ERA	DRA-	WARP	MPH	FB%	Whiff%	CSP
2021	GL	A+	22	2	2	0	14	11	47	30	1	2.1	10.7	56	45.6%	.257	0.87	1.91	84	0.9				
2021	TUL	AA	22	0	0	0	3	3	9^1	10	1	1.9	13.5	14	52.0%	.375	1.29	4.82	70	0.2				
2022 non-DC	*LAD*	*MLB*	*23*	*2*	*2*	*0*	*57*	*0*	*50*	*49*	*6*	*3.2*	*8.1*	*44*	*43.1%*	*.296*	*1.34*	*4.46*	*108*	*0.0*				

Comparables: Jesus Colome, Henry Alberto Rodriguez, Bryan Shaw

If there's one thing the Dodgers bet on, it's arm talent, and Miller had among the most arm talent in the 2020 class. After just a year of pro ball (and an Arizona Fall League appearance), he's making Billy Gasparino and Co., look quite smart. He already has the mid-to-high-90s fastball (with movement) and wipeout slider that sometimes looks like a cut fastball. However, since turning pro, he has added an above-average curveball and improved his changeup. It's a legitimate four-pitch mix, and he's looking more and more like a front-of-the-rotation arm. If the Dodgers snagged another one of those without selecting in the top half of the first round, that's nearly as impressive as the arsenal.

Ryan Pepiot RHP Born: 08/21/97 Age: 24 Bats: R Throws: R Height: 6'3" Weight: 215 lb. Origin: Round 3, 2019 Draft (#102 overall)

YEAR	TEAM	LVL	AGE	W	L	SV	G	GS	IP	H	HR	BB/9	K/9	K	GB%	BABIP	WHIP	ERA	DRA-	WARP	MPH	FB%	Whiff%	CSP
2019	GL	A	21	0	0	0	9	9	18^1	13	0	4.4	10.3	21	46.7%	.289	1.20	2.45	89	0.2				
2021	TUL	AA	23	3	4	0	15	13	59^2	30	7	3.9	12.2	81	32.5%	.198	0.94	2.87	70	1.4				
2021	OKC	AAA	23	2	5	0	11	9	41^2	54	12	4.5	9.9	46	40.6%	.350	1.80	7.13	99	0.2				
2022 non-DC	*LAD*	*MLB*	*24*	*2*	*3*	*0*	*57*	*0*	*50*	*47*	*8*	*4.8*	*9.6*	*53*	*37.8%*	*.299*	*1.49*	*4.99*	*116*	*-0.2*				

Comparables: Alex Colomé, Chris Flexen, Jorge López

What's the first thing you think of when you hear, "Butler University?" That's right, Pepiot's double-plus changeup (Huh? Gordon Hayward?). It's unlikely Pepiot ever reaches the career earnings of Hayward ($179 million-plus and counting), but his changeup might be worth that much in $/WAR or Bitcoin or something. Oh, and he has a good low-to-mid-90s fastball and a work-in-progress curveball and slider. Pitchers with two pitches have succeeded in the majors before, but not usually in the rotation. If one of his breaking pitches takes a step forward, then Pepiot has a bright future as a mid-rotation (or better) starter. If not, he should still be a quality reliever. Either way—barring injury—he's going to be a major-league pitcher.

David Price LHP Born: 08/26/85 Age: 36 Bats: L Throws: L Height: 6'5" Weight: 215 lb. Origin: Round 1, 2007 Draft (#1 overall)

YEAR	TEAM	LVL	AGE	W	L	SV	G	GS	IP	H	HR	BB/9	K/9	K	GB%	BABIP	WHIP	ERA	DRA-	WARP	MPH	FB%	Whiff%	CSP
2019	BOS	MLB	33	7	5	0	22	22	107^{1}	109	15	2.7	10.7	128	41.0%	.336	1.31	4.28	101	1.0	92.2	51.9%	26.0%	48.8%
2021	LAD	MLB	35	5	2	1	39	11	73^{2}	79	8	3.2	7.1	58	48.9%	.314	1.43	4.03	105	0.5	93.0	52.8%	21.1%	61.2%
2022 DC	*LAD*	*MLB*	*36*	*9*	*7*	*0*	*54*	*17*	*112.3*	*114*	*16*	*3.0*	*8.0*	*100*	*44.5%*	*.302*	*1.35*	*4.38*	*105*	*0.5*	*92.8*	*52.5%*	*22.8%*	*56.9%*

Comparables: Andy Pettitte, Camilo Pascual, Erik Hanson

After sitting out the 2020 season because of the pandemic, Price was set to come back in 2021—even at 35 years old—and be a solid contributor for the Dodgers. When May went down with a torn UCL, Price was going to be counted on even more. Look what a year off did for Buster Posey, right? Well, things didn't go quite that well for Price. He wasn't bad, but the Dodgers could have used an earlier version of Price. His average fastball velocity of 92.9 mph is a bit misleading. He had a 92.7-mph average velocity as a reliever and 93.1 mph as a starter, but he averaged just 3.75 innings per start, so while the velocity was solid, he wasn't out there for very long. He could carve out a nice role as a true swingman going into the last year of his once-record-breaking contract.

Blake Treinen RHP Born: 06/30/88 Age: 34 Bats: R Throws: R Height: 6'5" Weight: 225 lb. Origin: Round 7, 2011 Draft (#226 overall)

YEAR	TEAM	LVL	AGE	W	L	SV	G	GS	IP	H	HR	BB/9	K/9	K	GB%	BABIP	WHIP	ERA	DRA-	WARP	MPH	FB%	Whiff%	CSP
2019	OAK	MLB	31	6	5	16	57	0	58^{2}	58	9	5.7	9.1	59	43.2%	.308	1.62	4.91	104	0.5	96.7	67.4%	26.2%	42.7%
2020	LAD	MLB	32	3	3	1	27	0	25^{2}	23	1	2.8	7.7	22	65.3%	.297	1.21	3.86	79	0.6	97.0	64.9%	22.9%	46.7%
2021	LAD	MLB	33	6	5	7	72	0	72^{1}	46	5	3.1	10.6	85	52.0%	.244	0.98	1.99	75	1.6	97.6	35.0%	29.3%	51.7%
2022 DC	*LAD*	*MLB*	*34*	*3*	*3*	*33*	*67*	*0*	*58*	*49*	*6*	*3.3*	*9.1*	*59*	*52.3%*	*.278*	*1.21*	*3.14*	*81*	*0.8*	*97.3*	*46.1%*	*27.7%*	*49.1%*

Comparables: Mike Marshall, Guillermo Mota, Jeff Shaw

Treinen has always featured a cartoonish power sinker, a pitch which takes a characteristically hard right turn. But in the years before 2021, that pitch was about all he had, and any time he left it in the zone it looked flat and was pulverized. Treinen solved that problem last season by developing one of the best sliders in all of baseball. Simple! That slider added almost half a foot of horizontal movement as the same offering the year before. Batters slugged .074 when they put it in play, and when they swung they missed nearly half the time. Among all pitchers who threw at least 300 sliders in 2021, Treinen's offering was fourth in Statcast's arsenal pitch values on a rate basis, essentially tied with Jacob deGrom. The only real issue Treinen had with his arsenal was that sometimes the huge opposite breaks caused the pitches to split the plate and it was hard to throw the pitches effectively in the strike zone when needed. The low contact quality helped him work out of most jams any extra walks created.

Julio Urías LHP Born: 08/12/96 Age: 25 Bats: L Throws: L Height: 6'0" Weight: 225 lb. Origin: International Free Agent, 2012

YEAR	TEAM	LVL	AGE	W	L	SV	G	GS	IP	H	HR	BB/9	K/9	K	GB%	BABIP	WHIP	ERA	DRA-	WARP	MPH	FB%	Whiff%	CSP
2019	LAD	MLB	22	4	3	4	37	8	79^{2}	59	7	3.1	9.6	85	38.8%	.257	1.08	2.49	90	1.2	95.2	60.5%	29.9%	45.1%
2020	LAD	MLB	23	3	0	0	11	10	55	45	5	2.9	7.4	45	32.3%	.256	1.15	3.27	118	0.1	94.2	56.3%	26.0%	52.7%
2021	LAD	MLB	24	20	3	0	32	32	185^{2}	151	19	1.8	9.5	195	40.0%	.276	1.02	2.96	78	3.8	94.3	48.4%	24.4%	57.7%
2022 DC	*LAD*	*MLB*	*25*	*11*	*8*	*0*	*29*	*29*	*169*	*152*	*23*	*2.5*	*8.6*	*162*	*39.1%*	*.283*	*1.17*	*3.40*	*86*	*2.5*	*94.4*	*51.0%*	*25.3%*	*55.5%*

Comparables: Zack Greinke, CC Sabathia, Ramon Martinez

Between the Dodgers' careful handling at a young age, recovery from shoulder surgery and a COVID-shortened season, Urías has spent his career pitching with external limitations. However, his run through the postseason in 2020 was a sign not only that he was ready to take on a bigger role, but also that he was ready to become a rotation-leading starter. Urías blew past his professional innings career high by more than 60 (which eventually had consequences in the playoffs) and his first delimited season ended just shy of a Cy Young award. Urías accomplished this feat by simplifying his arsenal, merging his slider and curveball into a singular slurve. That pitch better compliments his change than either previous breaker. He combined it with one of the highest-spin fastballs among starters (which was largely unchanged by the foreign substance crackdown), keeping batters off-balance all season. When all was said and done, Urías finished the season 11th among qualified starters in K%-BB% and allowed the third-lowest hard hit rate. He has been around so long that it's hard to remember that he's still just 25, with time to grow.

Alex Vesia LHP Born: 04/11/96 Age: 26 Bats: L Throws: L Height: 6'1" Weight: 209 lb. Origin: Round 17, 2018 Draft (#507 overall)

YEAR	TEAM	LVL	AGE	W	L	SV	G	GS	IP	H	HR	BB/9	K/9	K	GB%	BABIP	WHIP	ERA	DRA-	WARP	MPH	FB%	Whiff%	CSP
2019	CLI	A	23	1	2	3	19	1	31^{2}	24	1	4.8	14.5	51	27.3%	.359	1.29	2.56	77	0.6				
2019	JUP	A+	23	4	0	1	10	0	18^{2}	12	2	0.5	11.6	24	43.2%	.244	0.70	1.93	79	0.4				
2019	JAX	AA	23	2	0	1	9	0	16^{1}	8	0	0.6	13.8	25	41.4%	.286	0.55	0.00	63	0.4				
2020	MIA	MLB	24	0	1	0	5	0	4^{1}	7	3	14.5	10.4	5	20.0%	.333	3.23	18.69	168	-0.1	91.8	72.9%	28.3%	47.1%
2021	OKC	AAA	25	0	0	2	9	0	9	3	0	3.0	19.0	19	44.4%	.333	0.67	1.00	67	0.2				
2021	LAD	MLB	25	3	1	1	41	0	40	17	6	5.0	12.2	54	25.3%	.143	0.98	2.25	83	0.7	93.9	72.4%	38.5%	52.8%
2022 DC	*LAD*	*MLB*	*26*	*3*	*2*	*0*	*59*	*0*	*51.7*	*38*	*9*	*4.8*	*13.7*	*78*	*31.2%*	*.287*	*1.27*	*3.84*	*90*	*0.5*	*93.6*	*72.4%*	*37.2%*	*52.1%*

Comparables: James Pazos, Jerry Blevins, Tony Sipp

A major-league player comically dominating seemingly hapless minor leaguers is nothing new, but it is generally reserved for when one of the league's best is tasked with rehabbing against a lower-level team (think Jacob deGrom driving the low-A Palm Beach Cardinals to Tweet Through It this season). Vesia had a similar stretch as a not-yet-established major leaguer against Triple-A competition, striking out 15 consecutive batters for Oklahoma City after being optioned a month earlier. Vesia, the trade return for unsung World Series hero Dylan Floro (acquired almost immediately after it was announced the ball would be less lively in 2021), was promoted to the major leagues shortly thereafter and quickly became a mainstay at the back of the Dodger bullpen. Vesia possesses some of the best fastball rise in the game, and in his rookie season he nearly matched Josh Hader's league-leading fastball whiff rates despite an average velocity below 94. Vesia will need to cut down on the walks going forward, but that fastball is quite the foundation.

Mitch White RHP Born: 12/28/94 Age: 27 Bats: R Throws: R Height: 6'3" Weight: 210 lb. Origin: Round 2, 2016 Draft (#65 overall)

YEAR	TEAM	LVL	AGE	W	L	SV	G	GS	IP	H	HR	BB/9	K/9	K	GB%	BABIP	WHIP	ERA	DRA-	WARP	MPH	FB%	Whiff%	CSP
2019	TUL	AA	24	1	0	0	7	7	30	18	3	2.1	11.1	37	43.1%	.217	0.83	2.10	92	0.2				
2019	OKC	AAA	24	3	6	0	16	13	63^2	73	13	3.4	9.6	68	41.6%	.351	1.52	6.50	87	0.9				
2020	LAD	MLB	25	1	0	0	2	0	3	1	0	3.0	6.0	2	12.5%	.125	0.67	0.00	126	0.0	93.8	50.0%	22.7%	40.5%
2021	RC	A	26	2	0	0	2	2	11^2	7	1	0.8	10.8	14	53.8%	.240	0.69	1.54	96	0.1				
2021	OKC	AAA	26	1	0	0	10	7	32	28	1	3.4	11.0	39	38.1%	.325	1.25	1.69	86	0.4				
2021	LAD	MLB	26	1	3	0	21	4	46^2	38	6	3.3	9.5	49	47.3%	.258	1.18	3.66	88	0.7	94.6	52.8%	23.0%	57.8%
2022 DC	*LAD*	*MLB*	*27*	*4*	*3*	*0*	*31*	*9*	*48.3*	*44*	*6*	*3.2*	*8.4*	*45*	*44.3%*	*.283*	*1.27*	*3.73*	*93*	*0.4*	*94.5*	*52.7%*	*23.0%*	*57.1%*

Comparables: Evan Scribner, A.J. Schugel, Scott Barlow

The future looked bright for White after the Dodgers made him a second-round selection in 2016. Some prospect analysts even thought he could end up being the best pitcher from that class. But injuries and inconsistent stuff have handicapped what was a promising future. Still, he has made it to the majors and even flashed some of that ability in-game, including a scoreless 7 ⅓-inning relief performance. He might never be the top-of-the-rotation starter some saw in him, but he's a quality MLB-level arm who could have a distinguished career in a swingman-type role. If a team is so bold,it could move him to short relief and try to maximize his stuff, but it would also probably increase his injury risk.

LINEOUTS

Hitters

HITTER	POS	TEAM	LVL	AGE	PA	R	2B	3B	HR	RBI	BB	K	SB	CS	AVG/OBP/SLG	DRC+	BABIP	BRR	FRAA	WARP
Andy Burns	3B	OKC	AAA	30	216	36	12	1	6	24	36	52	10	2	.232/.361/.412	99	.289	1.3	3B(29): -2.2, 2B(11): 0.2, LF(6): -0.4	0.6
	3B	LAD	MLB	30	15	2	1	0	0	0	3	1	0	0	.273/.467/.364	104	.300	0.0	2B(3): -0.2, 3B(2): 0.1, P(1): -0.0	0.1
Eddys Leonard	IF	RC	A	20	308	59	19	2	14	57	34	74	6	2	.295/.399/.544	122	.362	-0.1	SS(32): -1.0, 2B(16): 1.2, 3B(9): 1.1	1.9
	IF	GL	A+	20	184	30	10	2	8	24	17	42	3	1	.299/.375/.530	117	.360	-0.4	3B(15): -2.1, 2B(11): -1.1, CF(11): -1.1	0.4
Sheldon Neuse	2B	OKC	AAA	26	349	57	13	3	13	56	29	84	6	0	.293/.352/.478	103	.357	2.6	2B(30): -0.3, 3B(20): 1.1, SS(17): -0.8	1.7
	2B	LAD	MLB	26	66	6	1	0	3	4	1	26	1	1	.169/.182/.323	73	.222	0.1	2B(13): -0.1, 3B(8): -0.2, LF(4): -0.2	0.0
James Outman	CF	GDD	WIN	24	83	17	7	1	3	11	15	23	2	1	.284/.422/.552		.390			
	CF	GL	A+	24	304	50	12	8	9	30	45	88	21	2	.250/.385/.472	120	.349	1.4	CF(51): -6.5, RF(13): 1.6	1.4
	CF	TUL	AA	24	187	40	9	1	9	24	18	51	2	2	.289/.369/.518	98	.368	0.7	CF(36): 1.6, RF(3): -0.1	0.8
Jose Ramos	RF	DOD	ROK	20	68	13	6	0	3	15	7	14	1	0	.383/.456/.633		.465			
	RF	RC	A	20	220	30	18	3	8	44	16	57	1	4	.313/.377/.559	108	.398	-1.6	RF(44): 3.4	1.1
Steven Souza Jr.	RF	OKC	AAA	32	225	39	14	1	12	35	34	61	4	0	.274/.396/.554	109	.342	3.2	RF(28): 0.2, LF(14): -1.9, CF(4): 0.3	1.1
	RF	LAD	MLB	32	36	2	1	1	1	3	2	14	0	0	.152/.222/.333	75	.222	-0.3	RF(8): -0.2, LF(5): -0.4	-0.1
Carson Taylor	C/DH	GL	A+	22	342	52	16	1	9	54	45	63	1	0	.278/.371/.433	122	.321	-0.5	C(56): 5.3	2.3
Leonel Valera	SS	GL	A+	21	407	51	15	7	16	58	34	148	16	4	.224/.305/.436	84	.325	0.1	SS(93): -3.3	0.2
Jorbit Vivas	IF	RC	A	20	375	73	20	4	13	73	27	42	5	3	.311/.389/.515	140	.322	-0.7	2B(38): -1.0, 3B(34): 2.6, SS(2): -0.1	3.0
	IF	GL	A+	20	102	12	6	0	1	14	13	13	3	1	.318/.422/.424	121	.361	-0.7	3B(14): 0.0, 2B(9): -1.3	0.4

Andy Burns' ability to effectively play seven defensive positions (eight, if you include the inning of relief he pitched this season) has perpetually kept him close to major-league rosters. However, his mediocre bat has kept him from turning "close to" into "on," save for a surprise appearance on the Dodgers' LCS squad after Justin Turner's injury. **Eddys Leonard** was an unheralded international signing in 2017, and after toiling in rookie ball, he had a breakout season between the Dodgers' A-ball affiliates. His offensive production wasn't just a product of the Low-A West California League, because he posted a .900-plus OPS with High-A Central Great Lakes. Adding center fielder to his defensive profile, he's on his way to becoming a legitimate prospect. It's inevitable that the Dodgers trading for an Oakland A with strong minor-league power-hitting numbers and limited major-league success will draw comparisons to Max Muncy, but **Sheldon Neuse**'s time with the club has proven comparison superficial. His 26 strikeouts to one walk in 66 plate appearances were about as opposite of Muncy as one can get. He's already on the older side, but **James Outman** clearly has his admirers in the organization. He received a ton of spring-training looks and was sent to the AFL on the back of a strong season. He's got a broad base of tools and above-average raw power, with some questions about his ability to make consistent contact. **Jose Ramos**, a $30,000 value signing out of Panama, had himself a breakout '21 campaign—his first stateside. The talented outfielder is lauded for his hitting ability and cannon for a right arm. It's not hard to see a lot of Raul Mondesi similarities in his game. **Steven Souza Jr.** marched through Triple-A pitching in Oklahoma City with his three true outcome approach; nearly half of his plate appearances ended with a walk, strikeout or home run. But only the bad outcome consistently showed up with the Dodgers. His puzzling appearance in high-leverage spots in the NLCS could prove to be his career's final stanza. No one finds catchers like the Dodgers, and **Carson Taylor** might be the latest example. The 2020 fourth-rounder turned in a solid debut season which saw him thrive in June, July and September. His April and August dragged down his overall numbers. Maybe he's just not a fan of months that begin with "A." Hard-hitting position players with swing-and-miss issues are plentiful in the Dodgers' system, and **Leonel Valera** might be the prime example. He was in the midst of a breakout campaign before the summer months saw him hit more like he did in '19 with Great Lakes. Still, the power increase was impressive and he's a legit left-side defender. The Dodgers traded the laser show **Willie Calhoun** in 2017 and have been looking for a replacement ever since. Enter **Jorbit Vivas**, who laced batted balls all over A-ball fields. He showed surprising power while maintaining good strike zone judgment. The 2022 season could be a big one for Vivas.

Pitchers

PITCHER	TEAM	LVL	AGE	W	L	SV	G	GS	IP	H	HR	BB/9	K/9	K	GB%	BABIP	WHIP	ERA	DRA-	WARP	MPH	FB%	WHF	CSP
Scott Alexander	LAD	MLB	31	0	2	0	18	0	15^1	15	2	2.3	4.7	8	63.0%	.250	1.24	2.93	102	0.1	92.3	74.9%	20.3%	55.3%
Carlos Duran	RC	A	19	2	4	0	20	18	73^2	81	9	2.9	13.3	109	48.2%	.383	1.43	5.25	97	0.5				
	GL	A+	19	0	1	0	2	2	7^1	10	0	7.4	7.4	6	38.5%	.400	2.18	8.59	119	0.0				
Neftalí Feliz	LHV	AAA	33	2	1	4	15	0	14^1	8	1	3.8	14.4	23	34.5%	.250	0.98	1.26	79	0.3				
	OKC	AAA	33	2	1	0	20	1	26^2	24	5	3.4	14.2	42	35.0%	.345	1.28	4.39	64	0.7				
	LAD	MLB	33	0	0	0	3	0	3	1	0	0.0	3.0	1	44.4%	.111	0.33	0.00	101	0.0	94.8	60.6%	21.1%	54.2%
	PHI	MLB	33	0	1	0	2	0	1	4	1	9.0	18.0	2	20.0%	.750	5.00	36.00	105	0.0	96.0	79.4%	15.0%	39.6%
Shane Greene	LAD	MLB	32	0	0	1	9	0	6^2	3	1	6.8	9.5	7	53.3%	.143	1.20	4.05	100	0.1	91.8	20.0%	34.1%	54.8%
	ATL	MLB	32	0	1	0	19	0	17	22	5	4.8	9.0	17	32.1%	.333	1.82	8.47	113	0.0	93.0	39.7%	19.4%	50.1%
Nate Jones	ATL	MLB	35	0	2	0	12	0	10^1	8	3	8.7	6.1	7	28.1%	.172	1.74	3.48	142	-0.1	96.0	60.4%	30.1%	53.2%
	LAD	MLB	35	0	0	0	8	0	8^2	8	4	2.1	7.3	7	39.3%	.167	1.15	8.31	114	0.0	95.4	66.1%	23.5%	59.5%
Jimmy Nelson	LAD	MLB	32	1	2	0	28	1	29	14	0	4.0	13.7	44	36.4%	.259	0.93	1.86	73	0.7	94.0	33.1%	37.8%	52.8%
Evan Phillips	NOR	AAA	26	1	1	0	18	0	25	21	5	5.0	12.6	35	36.8%	.308	1.40	5.04	86	0.5				
	LAD	MLB	26	1	1	0	7	0	10^1	8	0	4.4	7.8	9	54.8%	.258	1.26	3.48	101	0.1	95.5	40.8%	22.9%	58.4%
	TB	MLB	26	0	0	1	1	0	3	3	1	0.0	6.0	2	40.0%	.222	1.00	3.00	112	0.0	96.1	65.1%	21.7%	61.1%
Jerming Rosario	DOD	ROK	19	0	4	0	11	5	36^2	32	5	3.2	11.8	48	47.3%	.310	1.23	4.17						
Jimmie Sherfy	SAC	AAA	29	1	0	0	6	0	7^2	3	0	1.2	12.9	11	37.5%	.188	0.52	0.00	90	0.1				
	LAD	MLB	29	1	1	0	4	0	4^1	3	1	0.0	6.2	3	53.8%	.167	0.69	4.15	100	0.0	94.0	30.2%	19.2%	53.1%
	SF	MLB	29	1	0	0	10	0	10^2	9	2	3.4	7.6	9	37.5%	.241	1.22	4.22	106	0.1	94.4	37.1%	23.2%	53.7%

As a pitch-to-contact ground-ball specialist, **Scott Alexander** lives and dies by his command; batters have slugged .613 when putting an elevated Alexander sinker in play over the last three seasons, compared to just .352 when the pitch hits its mark. In 2021, Alexander mostly lived, posting decent results before missing the second half of the season with shoulder inflammation. Large adult son (6-foot-7, 230 pounds) **Carlos Duran** might have some ugly looking numbers on the surface, but the mid-90s bowling ball sinker and potentially plus curveball are what has scouts excited. The Dodgers' player developmental system is among the best in the sport, so the chances of him overcoming any deficiencies are better than they would be if he were with another organization. Remember **Neftalí Feliz**, 2010 American League Rookie of the Year? Apparently, Andrew Friedman did and gave him a chance with the Dodgers. It lasted all of three innings and culminated in an expected DFA. It's fair to wonder if the newness of **Caleb Ferguson**'s slider/cutter combination will hamper his ability to return to form from Tommy John surgery. Ferguson's 2020 breakout put him into impact relief, so the stakes are high. The core message of Kermit the Frog's hit song "Bein' Green" is acceptance of oneself. After posting a 7.23 ERA between two clubs and being designated for assignment twice, **Shane Greene** might agree more with the song's opening line: "It's not easy being Green(e)." The Dodgers did their best to try to bring on as many future Hall of Famers as possible during the season. **Cole Hamels**' shoulder had other plans. The 37-year-old recorded just 10 outs in 2020 for the Braves and didn't pitch in 2021 after signing with Los Angeles for $1 million. Like his fellow Jones, Indiana, **Nate Jones** spent his whole career in search of a lost relic, the form of his 2016 season. Unlike Indiana, Nate did not seem to fear snakes, as he retired the only Diamondback he faced in his decade-long career in the majors. While both the Dodgers and **Tommy Kahnle** hinted at the potential for a late 2021 return from Tommy John surgery - a return which did not come to pass - the structure of his two-year, heavily backloaded contract showed a more realistic goal: a healthy return in 2022. After appearing in all seven games of the 2017 World Series for L.A., **Brandon Morrow** signed a lucrative deal with the Cubs. He threw exactly 488 pitches and hasn't pitched in the majors since 2018. Last year's Dodgers took a chance on him trying to capture some of that magic, but an elbow injury stole any chance of that. His career might be over at this point. **Jimmy Nelson**'s season will be remembered as another example of the ill fortune that has prevented his extremely talented arm from making a bigger impact, as he tore his UCL in late July and will almost certainly miss next year recovering from Tommy John surgery. When healthy, his four-seam fastball ranked among the league's leaders in spin rate, and a reshaped slider and devastating curve were enough to finish off most batters. **Evan Phillips** has the potential to be another player development success story. Phillips' slider has elite movement, and he more than doubled its usage after being claimed off waivers by the Dodgers in August. The results haven't followed, but it's never wise to bet against the Dodgers when they find an elite tool to focus on. **Jerming Rosario**'s stateside debut was going well enough for a 19-year-old, until he got to Rancho Cucamonga. It isn't often you see a pitcher end a season at any level with an ERA nearing 40, but that's what happened with Rosario. Three bad outings marred an otherwise decent year for the teenager. **Jimmie Shefry's** Matt Herges-like tour of the NL West continued in '21 with stops in San Francisco and Los Angeles. He was equally mediocre for both squads after being just as mediocre with the Diamondbacks from 2017-19. But hey, if you're a mediocre MLB player, you're among the best in the world, so he has that going for him.

SAN DIEGO PADRES

Essay by Grant Brisbee

Player comments by Kate Preusser and BP staff

In Petco Park's Ring of Honor, directly to the left of "Tony 19 Gwynn," you'll find Steve Garvey's name and retired number. The first baseman played five seasons for the Padres, which means he spent less time with the franchise than Kyle Blanks or Archi Cianfrocco. Garvey was worth −1.9 WARP in his Padres career, which also trails Blanks, Cianfrocco and . . . almost every other hitter in the history of the Padres' franchise.

Garvey's number is there because, in Game 4 of the 1984 National League Championship Series, he hit a walk-off homer to send the Padres to Game 5. At the number retirement ceremony in 1988—a franchise first—he said, "I've often been asked to recount my greatest thrill in baseball. Obviously, what happened in 1984 was one of them."

In retrospect, "one of them" is a loaded description. That was the greatest moment in a franchise's history, but it was also Garvey's 11th postseason homer, and led to his second NLCS MVP and fifth pennant. If you had to guess, his greatest thrill might have been the final out of the 1981 World Series, his first and only championship. He hit .417 for the Dodgers in that World Series, and he hit .301 with 211 home runs and eight All-Star appearances for them over his career. That's why they respectfully declined to issue his number 6 to anybody else until 2003, when they gave it to Jolbert Cabrera.

At the risk of psychoanalyzing the decisions of owners and executives from decades ago, the Padres didn't just retire Garvey's number because they were a young franchise hungry for a little nostalgia of their own. The retirement was meant to be *forward*-thinking, too. It was a milestone along the way, a marker pointing into the future. It was the kind of transcendent baseball moment that had to happen before a franchise was allowed at the banquet table with the other established MLB franchises. It wasn't so much the player, but the play. The home run led to a pennant, and the pennant was a declaration of intent. The Padres had arrived, and they weren't going away.

Between Garvey's home run and 2020, though, the Padres were the Padres were the Padres. There was another pennant in 1998, yes, and the franchise got to enjoy a hometown legend who was one of the most affable, gifted superstars

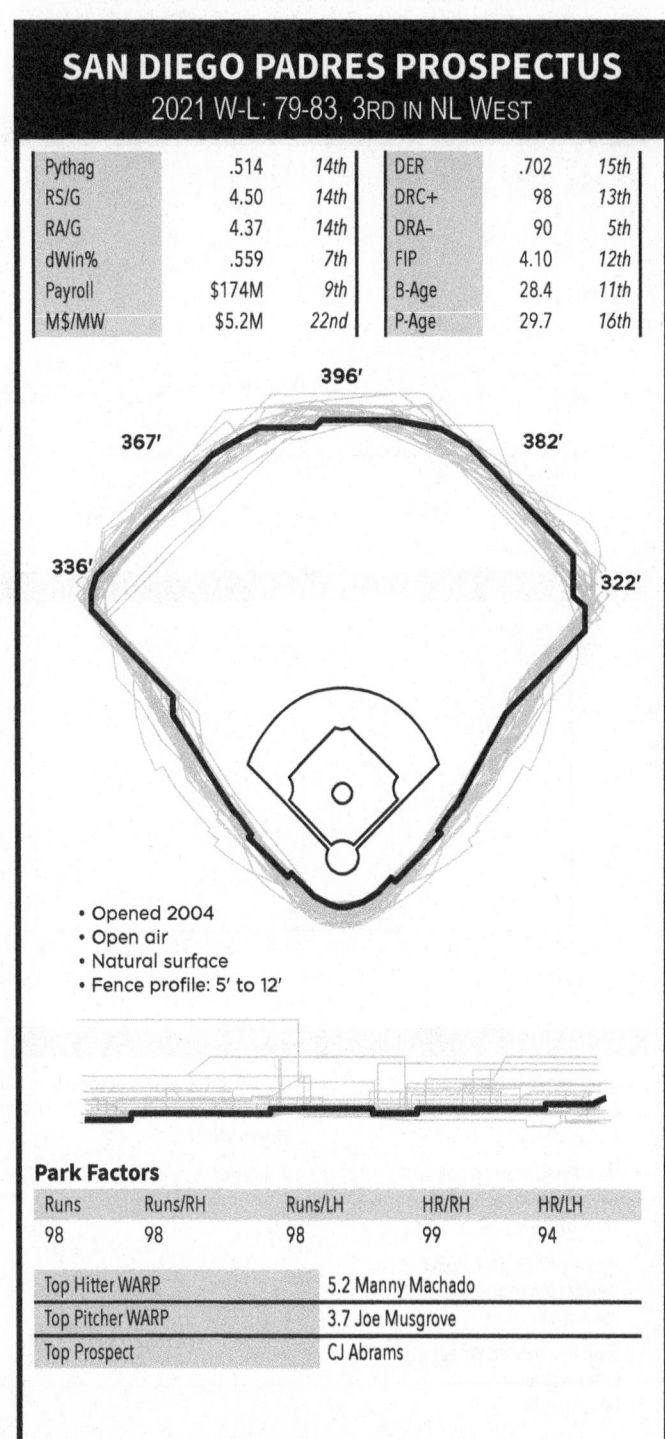

SAN DIEGO PADRES PROSPECTUS

2021 W-L: 79-83, 3RD IN NL WEST

Pythag	.514	*14th*	DER	.702	*15th*
RS/G	4.50	*14th*	DRC+	98	*13th*
RA/G	4.37	*14th*	DRA-	90	*5th*
dWin%	.559	*7th*	FIP	4.10	*12th*
Payroll	$174M	*9th*	B-Age	28.4	*11th*
M$/MW	$5.2M	*22nd*	P-Age	29.7	*16th*

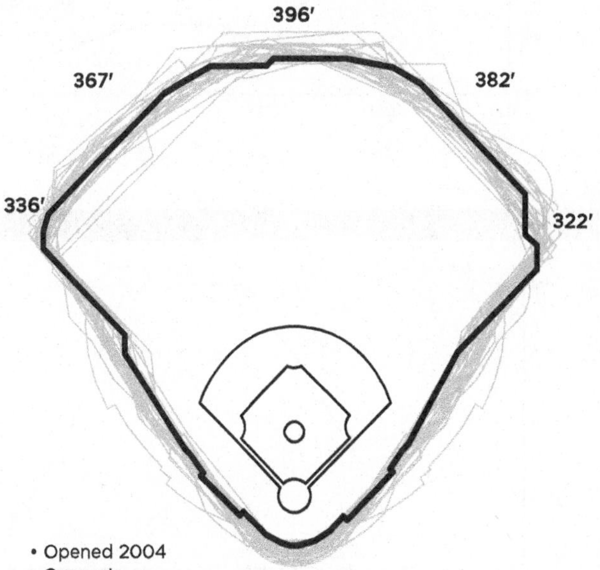

- Opened 2004
- Open air
- Natural surface
- Fence profile: 5′ to 12′

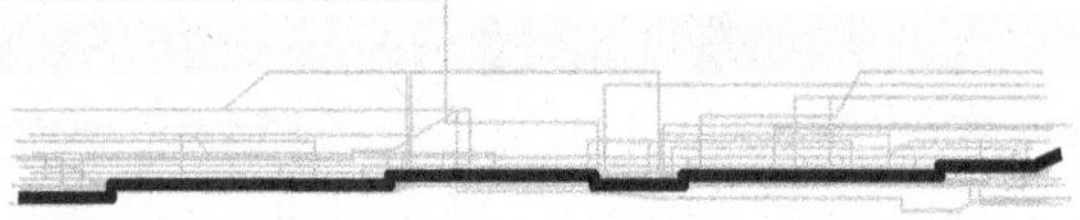

Park Factors

Runs	Runs/RH	Runs/LH	HR/RH	HR/LH
98	98	98	99	94

Top Hitter WARP	5.2 Manny Machado
Top Pitcher WARP	3.7 Joe Musgrove
Top Prospect	CJ Abrams

Payroll History (in millions)

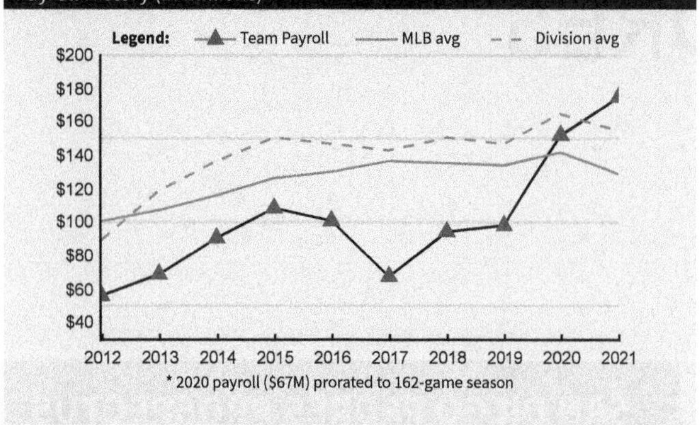

Future Commitments (in millions)

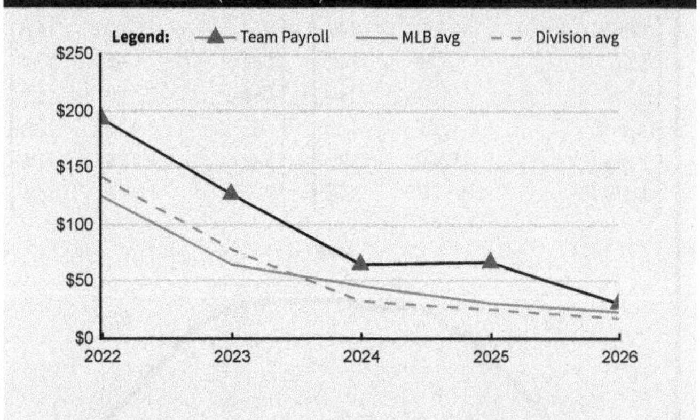

Farm System Ranking

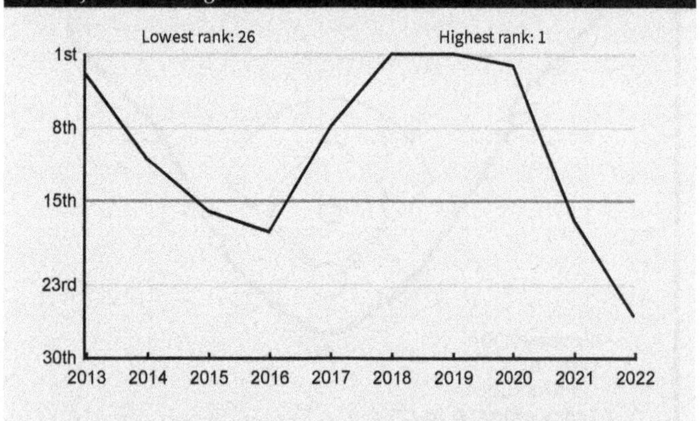

Personnel

President of Baseball Operations & General Manager
A.J. Preller

Vice President, Assistant General Manager
Fred Uhlman, Jr.

Vice President, Assistant General Manager
Josh Stein

Vice President, Baseball Operations
Vnick Ennis

Senior Advisor/Director of Player Personnel
Logan White

Manager
Bob Melvin

that any sport will ever see. But for the most part, the Padres were a forgettable collection of baseball players and events. The greatest swing in franchise history is probably still that home run. Which, again, was just one of the greatest thrills of that player's career, according to his own words.

If you're looking for a way to explain the Padres-related excitement last offseason, this history goes a long way. This is a franchise starved for capital-M Moments. Heck, they're *owed* those kinds of moments, whether by the baseball gods or by simple probability. So when they fought their way to the Division Series in 2020 with an electric collection of talent, it made sense. The Dodgers waxed them in three games, but it was another declaration of intent. The Padres had arrived—really, this time!—and they weren't going away. The Dodgers were supposed to be on notice.

If you're looking for another way to explain the Padres-related excitement last offseason, look at how aggressive they were in a baseball landscape dominated by tankers, luxury-tax worrywarts and payroll scolds. The Padres weren't just going for it, they were capital-everything GOING FOR IT, because they were hunting for those capital-M Moments. The aggressiveness started years before, with the big-money signings of corner infielders Eric Hosmer and Manny Machado. They traded some of their best young players for righty Mike Clevinger at the 2020 deadline, and when tendon fever grabbed 40 percent of their rotation, they simply flipped over their kitchen table and acquired the 2018 AL Cy Young winner (Blake Snell) and the 2020 NL Cy Young runner-up (Yu Darvish), while dealing even more talent for righty Joe Musgrove, just to be sure.

The Padres were baseball's it team because everyone wanted to watch them. Everyone wanted to *be* them. They had money. They had youth. Nothing was going to stop them.

And then the ever-withholding baseball gods decided, nah, we can't have that. The Padres were smote down. It was one of the hardest and most thorough collapses you'll ever see, and I feel trashy writing about it, Peter Gammons by way of Perez Hilton.

The 2021 season was an injury-ravaged one for every team, almost certainly because of the 60-game season that came before it. But, according to Baseball Prospectus' IL Ledger, no team was affected more than the Padres, and it wasn't that close. Padres players lost a combined 2,731 days to the injured list; the Mets were second with 2,469. Some of those IL days came from peripheral pieces (Clevinger hardly had a chance to stoke any hopes in San Diego before his UCL threw water on them), but plenty compromised the core of the preseason hubbub. Toward the end of the season, as they were gasping and wheezing and clinging to a second wild-card spot, the Padres were starting Vince Velasquez and Jake Arrieta, who combined to allow 27 runs in 25 innings. The Padres lost all eight of their starts.

Still, it's gauche to complain too much about injuries when the Braves won the World Series without Ronald Acuña, Jr. The Padres' biggest problem wasn't the missed time; it was the spotty play. The biggest reason for the decline and fall of the 2021 Padres was that the electric collection of talent first flickered and then blinked out entirely.

Fernando Tatis, Jr. was a pearl, a dynamo, a lodestar, a gift. Manny Machado wasn't as dominant as he was in the mutant 2020 season, but he was still an All-Star player having an All-Star season. Jake Cronenworth had one of the sneakiest valuable seasons in the game, with 2.8 WARP and contributions on both sides of the ball.

After them? It was hit and miss, pun absolutely intended, with players who were expected to be much better. Trent Grisham was fine. Tommy Pham was fine. Wil Myers was fine. They weren't an overall drag on the lineup, but they certainly weren't propelling the Padres to new run-scoring heights.

More crucially, Blake Snell and Yu Darvish fell short of transcendence, dominance, or even above-average-ness. There were 78 pitchers who started at least 25 games during the 2021 season, and Snell's 4.20 ERA ranked 46th among them. Darvish's 4.22 ERA ranked 47th. They weren't murdering the Padres' chances every fifth day, but they certainly weren't going to pick up any more Cy Young votes. The bullpen—where the Padres had often made dominant relievers out of twine and chewing gum—passed around a case of dingeritis.

Underneath the subfloor of fine, there was dry rot and players who were much worse. When the Padres announced the signing of Ha-Seong Kim, it was almost arrogant, and that's meant as a compliment. Where were they going to play him? Didn't matter, they'd figure it out, and he would likely be the Rookie of the Year frontrunner along the way. Instead, his .270 OBP made him impossible to use as an everyday player. Jurickson Profar, a 28-year-old with 40 years of major-league experience, somehow, stopped hitting for power entirely. Eric Hosmer's defense became an issue, and his .732 OPS wasn't enough to overcome it. Adam Frazier was an inspired deadline acquisition, but the Pirates kept the magic amulet that made him an All-Star in the first half. Chris Paddack pitched like he was hurt, which, it turned out, he was.

Adding to the indignity was that it wasn't just the Dodgers who zoomed past them. The Giants won the division, forcing L.A. to occupy a wild-card spot. The Giants didn't trade their best prospects for Cy Young winners; they simply signed pitchers with ERAs in the 6s and 7s and turned them into rotation stalwarts, while keeping their best prospects. They made bad hitters good and good hitters great. They traded Shaun Anderson to the Twins to get LaMonte Wade Jr., and right around the time "Late Night LaMonte" was single-handedly winning several games in the ninth or beyond with his superlative timing, the Padres were claiming Anderson on waivers because they needed bodies in the bullpen. The Giants were the Homer Simpson to the Padres' Frank Grimes, creating aneurysms for anyone who stopped to think about it for longer than a second.

So, after the 2021 season, which was supposed to be the greatest in Padres history, the franchise's best moment is probably still a home run by a guy who is most identified with a much more successful regional rival, a home run that was hit back when *Purple Rain* was the number-one album in the country.

The only reasonable response is for the Padres to dust themselves off, flip over what tables are left, and try again. Their core remains incredibly strong. Tatis is one of the greatest head starts to a 26-man roster any franchise will ever have. Machado is young and productive. Musgrove was the rotation gambit who worked. The low-minors prospects will become high-minors prospects with a chance to contribute.

These bones, why, they're good. They're among the best bones any Padres roster has had entering an offseason. There's youth, there's promise, there's talent, there's star power, and everything that fueled the fervor of the previous offseason—the young players, the feeling that the Padres' are overdue—is still there. They can build another suffocating bullpen. They can buttress their young stars with quality major leaguers at every position. And when they do all of this, they'll have one of the most-respected managers in the game, Bob Melvin, trying to piece it all together. The Padres should still aim straight past upstart-dom for the status of bully on the NL West block.

It's their time. It should have been their time years ago, but it's definitely their time now. They aren't focusing on the past. No, they're forward-thinking, as they should be. The trend line is still moving in the right direction.

It's hard to imagine a more discouraging season for a franchise than the one the Padres had in 2021, though. They were supposed to be elite, a collection of golden baseball talent ready to challenge the 1927 Yankees and 2021 Dodgers, alike. Instead, they had to hold their breath and get help to finish above the Rockies.

They still have a chance to build on the promise that has been dormant for decades, the promise that was behind the number-retirement ceremony 35 years ago. It's their time. Look out, world, here come the Padres, resolute in a new belief: that if there's something the baseball gods like more than a team trying, it's a team trying *again*.

You'll forgive them if their sighs are a little bit louder than the ones coming from every other team, but it's still their time.

Probably.

Maybe.

Boy, the Padres should have been a whole lot better last season. We're all clear about that, right?

—Grant Brisbee is a staff writer for The Athletic, *where he writes about the San Francisco Giants.*

Hitters

★ ★ ★ *2022 Top 101 Prospect* **#11** ★ ★ ★

CJ Abrams SS Born: 10/03/00 Age: 21 Bats: L Throws: R Height: 6'2" Weight: 185 lb. Origin: Round 1, 2019 Draft (#6 overall)

YEAR	TEAM	LVL	AGE	PA	R	2B	3B	HR	RBI	BB	K	SB	CS	Whiff%	AVG/OBP/SLG	DRC+	BABIP	BRR	FRAA	WARP
2019	SD1	ROK	18	156	40	12	8	3	22	10	14	14	6		.401/.442/.662		.425			
2019	FW	A	18	9	1	1	0	0	0	1	0	1	0		.250/.333/.375	110	.250	0.1	SS(1): 0.1	0.1
2021	SA	AA	20	183	26	14	0	2	23	15	36	13	2		.296/.363/.420	104	.365	2.7	SS(33): -0.6, 2B(6): -0.5	0.8
2022 non-DC	*SD*	*MLB*	*21*	*251*	*21*	*12*	*1*	*2*	*21*	*17*	*58*	*13*	*4*	*26.8%*	*.234/.294/.334*	*71*	*.301*	*1.1*	*SS 0, 2B 0*	*0.1*

Comparables: J.P. Crawford, Gavin Lux, Richard Ureña

The shortstop position in San Diego might have a long-term occupant—think Elvis in Vegas with slightly more hip action—but there will be a spot on the dirt, or perhaps center field, for the athletic Abrams, a consensus top prospect on the days he's healthy enough to work. His Double-A campaign was cut short this year after an in-game collision in which he suffered a fractured tibia and sprained MCL; he also missed time in 2019 with a left shoulder contusion, and in 2021 missed his AFL season after injuring the same shoulder in instructional league. When healthy, Abrams offers a power-speed combo among the best in the minors. His detractors note that power has yet to put many balls over fences, although said detractors are invited to go swing a bat in the frozen fields of the Midwest League and see how they fare. Abrams has always been young for the levels he's played at and hits the ball hard, but even if the power never develops, he's still an above-average hitter capable of impacting the ball with authority all over the field.

Victor Acosta SS Born: 06/10/04 Age: 18 Bats: S Throws: R Height: 5'11" Weight: 170 lb. Origin: International Free Agent, 2021

YEAR	TEAM	LVL	AGE	PA	R	2B	3B	HR	RBI	BB	K	SB	CS	Whiff%	AVG/OBP/SLG	DRC+	BABIP	BRR	FRAA	WARP
2021	DSL PAD	ROK	17	240	45	12	5	5	31	38	45	26	7		.285/.431/.484		.345			
2022															*No projection*					

Comparables: Pedro Guerrero, Geral Silva, Emerson Jimenez

The top target in the Padres' 2020 international signing class, Acosta entered pro ball with a bang, going 2-for-3 with a double, home run, walk and two stolen bases in his debut. He's raw enough defensively that he's not a lock to stick at short, but has all the tools that should keep him there, with a strong arm and exceptionally nimble footwork. Twitchy and dynamic in the box, he's a switch-hitter, although his righty swing can look like it drags some; he generates more pop from the left side, with an explosive, whippy swing. Acosta has an affinity for social media, where he posts in both English and Spanish, and a big, joyful personality that will remind some of a smaller-sized Julio Rodríguez, although with a very different set of tools.

Jorge Alfaro C Born: 06/11/93 Age: 29 Bats: R Throws: R Height: 6'3" Weight: 230 lb. Origin: International Free Agent, 2010

YEAR	TEAM	LVL	AGE	PA	R	2B	3B	HR	RBI	BB	K	SB	CS	Whiff%	AVG/OBP/SLG	DRC+	BABIP	BRR	FRAA	WARP
2019	MIA	MLB	26	465	44	14	1	18	57	22	154	4	4	38.4%	.262/.312/.425	81	.364	-2.8	C(118): 5.8	1.2
2020	MIA	MLB	27	100	12	2	0	3	16	4	36	2	0	41.7%	.226/.280/.344	74	.333	0.1	C(29): -5.1, RF(1): 0.0	-0.5
2021	MIA	MLB	28	311	22	15	1	4	30	11	99	8	1	33.1%	.244/.283/.342	61	.354	-0.5	C(61): 4.8, LF(21): -0.2, 1B(3): -0.1	0.2
2022 DC	*SD*	*MLB*	*29*	*248*	*31*	*9*	*0*	*8*	*34*	*11*	*72*	*1*	*1*	*33.6%*	*.247/.297/.405*	*86*	*.323*	*-0.1*	*LF -3, C -1*	*0.0*

Comparables: Christian Vázquez, Welington Castillo, Francisco Cervelli

YEAR	TEAM	P. COUNT	FRM RUNS	BLK RUNS	THRW RUNS	TOT RUNS
2019	MIA	16970	2.8	-0.8	0.2	2.2
2020	MIA	3746	-4.9	0.0	0.1	-4.8
2021	MIA	7948	4.9	-0.9	0.3	4.4
2022	*SD*	*3608*	*-0.9*	*-0.5*	*0.0*	*-1.4*

The days of looking at Alfaro's numbers and saying "Well, he's a catcher…" are over. During the second half of the season, the Marlins tried out Alfaro in left field where his speed—great for a catcher, pretty good for an outfielder—could shine. The hope was the change also would let him tap into the elite exit velocity he's able to muster, at least on special occasions, even if his power has continued to nose dive. It seemed to work, in the sense that the team kept giving him work. Though the power never returned, Alfaro posted an OPS nearly 200 points higher than he produced while squatting behind the dish. San Diego will take over the grand experiment—perhaps there's a second career as an fourth outfielder, though still hitting eighth, awaiting him.

★ ★ ★ *2022 Top 101 Prospect* **#59** ★ ★ ★

Luis Campusano C Born: 09/29/98 Age: 23 Bats: R Throws: R Height: 5'11" Weight: 232 lb. Origin: Round 2, 2017 Draft (#39 overall)

YEAR	TEAM	LVL	AGE	PA	R	2B	3B	HR	RBI	BB	K	SB	CS	Whiff%	AVG/OBP/SLG	DRC+	BABIP	BRR	FRAA	WARP
2019	LE	A+	20	487	63	31	1	15	81	52	57	0	0		.325/.396/.509	148	.340	-3.1	C(77): 5.2, 1B(2): 0.0	4.5
2020	SD	MLB	21	4	2	0	0	1	1	0	2	0	0	37.5%	.333/.500/1.333	103		0.0		0.0
2021	ELP	AAA	22	326	47	21	3	15	45	27	66	1	0		.295/.365/.541	111	.335	-0.8	C(62): 1.8, 1B(3): -0.1	1.7
2021	SD	MLB	22	38	0	0	0	0	1	4	11	0	0	37.9%	.088/.184/.088	76	.130	-1.3	C(9): -0.4	-0.1
2022 DC	*SD*	*MLB*	*23*	*29*	*3*	*1*	*0*	*0*	*3*	*2*	*6*	*0*	*0*	*29.7%*	*.242/.311/.400*	*89*	*.294*	*0.0*	*C 0*	*0.1*

Comparables: Salvador Perez, Wilson Ramos, Pablo Sandoval

YEAR	TEAM	P. COUNT	FRM RUNS	BLK RUNS	THRW RUNS	TOT RUNS
2019	LE	10613	5.1		0.6	5.7
2021	SD	1331	-0.3	0.0	0.0	-0.3
2021	ELP	8976	2.6	-0.2	0.6	3.0
2022	*SD*	*1202*	*-0.3*	*0.0*	*0.0*	*-0.3*

After the highly-touted prospect slashed through the hitter-friendly California League, the Padres sent Campusano to the alternate training site during the shutdown and then pressed him into service to start 2021 after an injury to Austin Nola in spring training. The jump was understandably rocky, as he flailed mightily before being sent to El Paso. Despite this rocky development track, Campusano has showcased solid defense at all levels and huge power in an admittedly hitter-friendly park (he slugged .636 at home but a still-impressive .466 on the road in Triple-A), which makes sense: He swings like it's Black Friday and he's eyeing the last half-priced LCD TV in the store. Catchers have a trickier runway than most, especially when that runway is convoluted by the demands of a pandemic-shortened season and injuries (including an oblique issue that shut him down towards the end of the season). But Campusano has earned patience and the benefit of the doubt even if he struggles to start 2022. Rookie catchers at age 23 are like other rookies at 19.

Victor Caratini C

Born: 08/17/93 Age: 28 Bats: S Throws: R Height: 6'1" Weight: 215 lb. Origin: Round 2, 2013 Draft (#65 overall)

YEAR	TEAM	LVL	AGE	PA	R	2B	3B	HR	RBI	BB	K	SB	CS	Whiff%	AVG/OBP/SLG	DRC+	BABIP	BRR	FRAA	WARP
2019	CHC	MLB	25	279	31	11	0	11	34	29	59	1	0	22.4%	.266/.348/.447	107	.305	-1.6	C(59): 2.5, 1B(23): -0.5, 3B(2): -0.1	1.4
2020	CHC	MLB	26	132	10	7	0	1	16	12	31	0	1	23.6%	.241/.333/.328	84	.321	-1.3	C(22): 0.7, 1B(3): 0.2	0.1
2021	SD	MLB	27	356	33	9	0	7	39	35	82	2	0	25.5%	.227/.309/.323	87	.281	-1.2	C(101): -3.1, 1B(5): -0.0, 3B(2): -0.0	0.5
2022 DC	*SD*	*MLB*	*28*	*129*	*16*	*5*	*0*	*3*	*15*	*11*	*29*	*0*	*0*	*24.6%*	*.239/.320/.371*	*87*	*.294*	*-0.2*	*C -1*	*0.1*

Comparables: Christian Vázquez, Tucker Barnhart, Héctor Sánchez

YEAR	TEAM	P. COUNT	FRM RUNS	BLK RUNS	THRW RUNS	TOT RUNS
2019	CHC	6899	1.4	0.2	1.4	3.0
2020	CHC	2834	1.1	-0.1	0.0	1.1
2021	SD	13377	-3.4	0.0	0.1	-3.4
2022	*SD*	*4810*	*-0.6*	*0.3*	*0.0*	*-0.3*

The Cubs, who inadvertently cursed the backup catcher spot in the Darvish deal, might have regretted the decision to include Caratini as Darvish's personal catcher. That said, Caratini didn't exactly cover himself in glory as a member of the Padres, struggling with a starter's workload after the injury to Austin Nola and the ineffectiveness of Luis Campusano. Nola's return comfortably regulates Caratini to the safety-blanket backup-catcher role he's played over his career, but with Campusano in the mix as well, it's hard to see where even occasional playing time for Caratini's Oops-All-OBPs approach comes from.

Jake Cronenworth IF

Born: 01/21/94 Age: 28 Bats: L Throws: R Height: 6'0" Weight: 187 lb. Origin: Round 7, 2015 Draft (#208 overall)

YEAR	TEAM	LVL	AGE	PA	R	2B	3B	HR	RBI	BB	K	SB	CS	Whiff%	AVG/OBP/SLG	DRC+	BABIP	BRR	FRAA	WARP
2019	DUR	AAA	25	406	75	26	4	10	45	49	62	12	5		.334/.429/.520	121	.382	-1.4	SS(64): -2.4, 2B(11): 1.0, P(7): 0.1	2.4
2020	SD	MLB	26	192	26	15	3	4	20	18	30	3	1	16.7%	.285/.354/.477	102	.324	-0.8	2B(38): -0.8, SS(11): -1.5, 1B(10): 1.2	0.5
2021	SD	MLB	27	643	94	33	7	21	71	55	90	4	3	13.8%	.266/.340/.460	113	.283	-1.3	2B(94): -0.6, SS(41): -1.3, 1B(24): -1.4	2.8
2022 DC	*SD*	*MLB*	*28*	*556*	*74*	*27*	*5*	*10*	*71*	*49*	*81*	*7*	*4*	*14.3%*	*.263/.338/.402*	*102*	*.295*	*0.5*	*2B 0, 1B 0*	*2.1*

Comparables: Ryan Goins, Justin Turner, Brock Holt

Like so many others of his generation, Cronenworth has become an influencer, ushering the high-contact/high OBP-type player that had fallen out of fashion over recent years back into vogue. But beware, imitators: What makes Cronenworth special is not just his ability to make a ton of contact, but his selectiveness at the plate that leads to a spray chart that looks like a Pollock painting. His ability to seek only the pitches worth hitting also results in better power than would be expected from his frame, and while he didn't find as many barrels as he did in his 2020 campaign, his power production does appear to be sustainable, even after a dip last year that likely cost him the Rookie of the Year award. With stellar, versatile defense, the only nit to pick in Cronenworth's game is a surprising lack of stolen bases given his above-average sprint speed, but chalk that up as just another idiosyncrasy wrapped in the anachronism that is his profile, one Padres fans will happily like and subscribe to for years to come.

Trent Grisham CF

Born: 11/01/96 Age: 25 Bats: L Throws: L Height: 5'11" Weight: 224 lb. Origin: Round 1, 2015 Draft (#15 overall)

YEAR	TEAM	LVL	AGE	PA	R	2B	3B	HR	RBI	BB	K	SB	CS	Whiff%	AVG/OBP/SLG	DRC+	BABIP	BRR	FRAA	WARP
2019	BLX	AA	22	283	34	14	3	13	41	44	50	6	4		.254/.371/.504	145	.269	0.2	CF(59): 3.0	3.0
2019	SA	AAA	22	158	37	8	3	13	30	23	22	6	1		.381/.471/.776	149	.384	0.0	CF(31): 3.7, LF(3): -0.2	1.9
2019	MIL	MLB	22	183	24	6	2	6	24	20	48	1	0	23.7%	.231/.328/.410	88	.286	2.0	CF(21): -1.2, LF(17): -1.6, RF(16): 0.3	0.3
2020	SD	MLB	23	252	42	8	3	10	26	31	64	10	1	24.4%	.251/.352/.456	96	.310	-1.8	CF(59): 4.9	1.0
2021	SD	MLB	24	527	61	28	3	15	62	54	119	13	5	21.9%	.242/.327/.413	96	.292	1.7	CF(127): 1.3	2.3
2022 DC	*SD*	*MLB*	*25*	*584*	*91*	*25*	*4*	*18*	*70*	*65*	*122*	*14*	*4*	*22.0%*	*.239/.331/.413*	*101*	*.281*	*1.0*	*CF 2*	*2.6*

Comparables: Joc Pederson, Carlos González, Byron Buxton

After a checkered prospect history, Grisham looked to be coming into his own as a big-leaguer in the shortened 2020 season. He got off to a strong start in 2021 as well, before some lower-body injuries that seemed to sap both his power and speed: Not only did Grisham lose over a hundred points off his slugging post-IL stint, but he stole only six bases after his mid-June return compared to seven in the months prior, and was caught stealing four times. The dropoff in quality of contact is concerning—he went from ranking in the upper-quartile in barrels and hard hit rate to the bottom quartile—but it's probably smarter to bet on Grisham's plate discipline, prior production and athleticism rather than against. Though maybe not your life savings.

★ ★ ★ *2022 Top 101 Prospect* **#26** ★ ★ ★

Robert Hassell III OF Born: 08/15/01 Age: 20 Bats: L Throws: L Height: 6'2" Weight: 195 lb. Origin: Round 1, 2020 Draft (#8 overall)

YEAR	TEAM	LVL	AGE	PA	R	2B	3B	HR	RBI	BB	K	SB	CS	Whiff%	AVG/OBP/SLG	DRC+	BABIP	BRR	FRAA	WARP
2021	LE	A	19	429	77	31	3	7	65	57	74	31	6		.323/.415/.482	125	.385	3.1	CF(84): -3.8, RF(2): -0.1	2.9
2021	FW	A+	19	87	10	2	1	4	11	9	25	3	0		.205/.287/.410	102	.245	-0.3	CF(16): -0.9	0.2
2022 non-DC	*SD*	*MLB*	*20*	*251*	*22*	*12*	*1*	*3*	*23*	*21*	*57*	*9*	*3*	*26.4%*	*.235/.304/.348*	*78*	*.299*	*0.7*	*CF 1, RF 0*	*0.4*

Comparables: Alex Verdugo, Colby Rasmus, Manuel Margot

Tennessee isn't a prospect hotbed, but the state's Gatorade Player of the Year made himself impossible to ignore after a strong performance on the showcase circuit and a star turn with Team USA, where he almost single-handedly propelled the team to a silver medal in the U-18 WBSC. RH3 is currently a hit-over-power prospect, with a beautiful lefty swing that finds barrels like a truffle pig, producing line-drive power to all fields. He crushed the former California League in his first year of pro ball and earned a promotion to High-A, and there's plenty of room to grow into more power on a young, tall, athletic frame. Even if the over-the-fence power never comes, his command of the strike zone and contact skills give him a safe floor, especially when paired with solid outfield defense. He'll become the Padres' highest-ceiling prospect once C.J. Abrams graduates to the big-league club, if Preller can hang on to him until then.

Eric Hosmer 1B Born: 10/24/89 Age: 32 Bats: L Throws: L Height: 6'4" Weight: 226 lb. Origin: Round 1, 2008 Draft (#3 overall)

YEAR	TEAM	LVL	AGE	PA	R	2B	3B	HR	RBI	BB	K	SB	CS	Whiff%	AVG/OBP/SLG	DRC+	BABIP	BRR	FRAA	WARP
2019	SD	MLB	29	667	72	29	2	22	99	40	163	0	3	28.9%	.265/.310/.425	88	.323	-0.6	1B(157): -4.0	0.3
2020	SD	MLB	30	156	23	6	0	9	36	9	28	4	0	20.4%	.287/.333/.517	106	.296	0.0	1B(32): 1.2	0.6
2021	SD	MLB	31	565	53	28	0	12	65	48	99	5	4	22.8%	.269/.337/.395	99	.313	-1.4	1B(131): 0.6	1.0
2022 DC	*SD*	*MLB*	*32*	*577*	*80*	*26*	*1*	*16*	*83*	*48*	*100*	*3*	*3*	*23.0%*	*.265/.330/.413*	*102*	*.300*	*-0.6*	*1B 0*	*1.1*

Comparables: Ed Kranepool, Chris Chambliss, Keith Hernandez

The first highly acclaimed female American sculptor, Harriet Hosmer (1830-1908), constantly had to defend herself against charges from jealous male colleagues that she did not create her own massive marble statues, but instead relied on her workmen or tutor to complete the heavy lifting. Her baseball-playing surname-sharer has largely evaded such scrutiny, going from top prospect to postseason folk hero to the recipient of a generous eight-year contract, all despite defensive limitations, batted-ball luck and an on-base-over-power profile at the cold corner. The emperor's clothing status has come under suspicion, however, and even though San Diego's previously vaunted system has been picked largely clean by promotions and trades, a savvy team should be able to lift some of those last remaining prospects in order to absorb Hosmer's contract, and allow the ascendant Padres to roll out a legitimate first base option rather than the marble statue currently occupying it.

Ha-Seong Kim IF Born: 10/17/95 Age: 26 Bats: R Throws: R Height: 5'9" Weight: 168 lb. Origin: International Free Agent, 2020

YEAR	TEAM	LVL	AGE	PA	R	2B	3B	HR	RBI	BB	K	SB	CS	Whiff%	AVG/OBP/SLG	DRC+	BABIP	BRR	FRAA	WARP
2021	SD	MLB	25	298	27	12	2	8	34	22	71	6	1	21.8%	.202/.270/.352	82	.241	2.7	SS(35): 3.5, 3B(23): 1.7, 2B(21): 1.9	1.4
2022 DC	*SD*	*MLB*	*26*	*249*	*29*	*10*	*1*	*6*	*31*	*18*	*52*	*4*	*2*	*22.0%*	*.222/.288/.367*	*78*	*.261*	*0.2*	*2B 2, SS 3*	*0.9*

Comparables: José Hernández, Brian Dozier, Roy Smalley

The former KBO star was supposed to be a developmental project hidden in plain sight, providing excellent defense and bopping the occasional homer while adjusting to the higher velocities of US pitching and maybe being shuttled down to the minors when the Padres made a postseason run. But A.J. Preller plans and God laughs, and Kim remained with the big-league club all season thanks to ineffectiveness and injuries scattered across the rest of the lineup. There's plenty to suggest in his batted ball data that he can at least be an MLB average hitter with occasional pop once he settles in, and plus infield defense at multiple positions will help smooth out any other offensive hiccups. And if this is it, well, like it or not, this is what league-average production at shortstop looks like.

Manny Machado 3B Born: 07/06/92 Age: 30 Bats: R Throws: R Height: 6'3" Weight: 218 lb. Origin: Round 1, 2010 Draft (#3 overall)

YEAR	TEAM	LVL	AGE	PA	R	2B	3B	HR	RBI	BB	K	SB	CS	Whiff%	AVG/OBP/SLG	DRC+	BABIP	BRR	FRAA	WARP
2019	SD	MLB	26	661	81	21	2	32	85	65	128	5	3	24.2%	.256/.334/.462	115	.274	-1.4	3B(119): -9.7, SS(37): -5.5	1.4
2020	SD	MLB	27	254	44	12	1	16	47	26	37	6	3	21.7%	.304/.370/.580	139	.297	-0.8	3B(56): 4.1	2.1
2021	SD	MLB	28	640	92	31	2	28	106	63	102	12	3	23.1%	.278/.347/.489	123	.290	2.3	3B(144): 9.2	5.2
2022 DC	*SD*	*MLB*	*29*	*627*	*109*	*28*	*1*	*31*	*104*	*63*	*103*	*9*	*4*	*22.8%*	*.277/.352/.499*	*127*	*.290*	*-0.1*	*3B 0*	*4.0*

Comparables: Adrián Beltré, Brooks Robinson, Aramis Ramirez

Athletes shed identities like snakeskin; some grow into their boots and become heroes, while others vanish into the forest and are never heard from again. We see heel turns and redemptions every year. But it's rare to see someone go from one of the most exciting superstars in baseball to one of the more anonymous while staying the same guy on the field. Machado, through no fault of his own, symbolized the hopes and disappointments of a baseball team embodied by the GIF of Kevin spilling chili all over the office, the 2010s Orioles. There he fared in one of the two ways rental players do after the trade deadline, attracting questions about his hustle from every sunglass-avatar radio caller from Claremont to SLO. Those questions followed him into a disappointing first season in San Diego, after he had the audacity to sign a contract worth what the market was willing to pay him, and haven't let up since, even as Machado's 2021—perhaps the quietest ever 5-WARP, Gold Glove and Silver Slugger-nominated season ever—should have put them to rest.

Jackson Merrill SS Born: 04/19/03 Age: 19 Bats: L Throws: R Height: 6'3" Weight: 195 lb. Origin: Round 1, 2021 Draft (#27 overall)

YEAR	TEAM	LVL	AGE	PA	R	2B	3B	HR	RBI	BB	K	SB	CS	Whiff%	AVG/OBP/SLG	DRC+	BABIP	BRR	FRAA	WARP
2021	PAD	ROK	18	120	19	7	2	0	10	10	27	5	1		.280/.339/.383		.370			
2022															*No projection*					

Comparables: Luis Guillorme, Adrian Valerio, Nelson Molina

Prospects, they're just like us. Merrill went from Duckie Dale to Jake Ryan—both references likely lost on the high schooler—in the space of a few months, growing into his 6'3" athletic frame and impressing scouts with his raw power. The Padres saw a late bloomer with early first-round shine available to them at no. 27 and scooped him up, only to be rewarded as Merrill showcased a quick, aesthetically-pleasing lefty swing in the Complex League, consistently creating loud, hard contact to all fields while making good swing decisions. Defensively he's not a lock to stick at short just because of the body type and some average-ish run times, but draws praise for his footwork and athleticism, with the arm to settle into third. Now he just needs a red Porsche 944 to lean against and the transformation is complete.

Wil Myers RF Born: 12/10/90 Age: 31 Bats: R Throws: R Height: 6'3" Weight: 207 lb. Origin: Round 3, 2009 Draft (#91 overall)

YEAR	TEAM	LVL	AGE	PA	R	2B	3B	HR	RBI	BB	K	SB	CS	Whiff%	AVG/OBP/SLG	DRC+	BABIP	BRR	FRAA	WARP
2019	SD	MLB	28	490	58	22	1	18	53	51	168	16	7	32.5%	.239/.321/.418	83	.344	-1.5	LF(98): -1.6, CF(66): -0.6, 1B(7): -0.4	0.4
2020	SD	MLB	29	218	34	14	2	15	40	18	56	2	1	26.4%	.288/.353/.606	121	.331	1.7	RF(52): -1.8, 1B(2): 0.1	1.2
2021	SD	MLB	30	500	56	24	2	17	63	54	141	8	5	32.0%	.256/.334/.434	97	.333	-1.9	RF(118): -3.7, LF(13): -0.8	0.6
2022 DC	*SD*	*MLB*	*31*	*532*	*72*	*25*	*1*	*19*	*78*	*56*	*157*	*13*	*6*	*30.1%*	*.240/.325/.423*	*101*	*.318*	*0.7*	*RF 0, LF 0*	*1.5*

Comparables: Roy Sievers, Michael Cuddyer, Jermaine Dye

Raise your hand if you have been personally victimized by drafting Myers too highly after his strong 2020 performance. To be fair, it really looked like he'd finally tapped into the power side of his famed power-speed combo, on pace for a Zunino-like 30+ homers despite his similarly Zunino-like allergy to breaking balls. In 2021, however, pitchers attacked Myers with breaking stuff more than ever before, almost 40% of the time, and he dutifully whiffed at those pitches over 40% of the time. Zunino has solved that issue by always being ready to hit the fastball when he sees it, knocking 10 of his 33 home runs in 2021 on first-pitch strikes, but that approach hasn't yielded similar success for Myers, who is utterly hapless when falling behind in counts, dropping to a sub-Mendoza slash line when the pitcher is ahead. Those looking for a happy ending to his story in San Diego are advised to skip reading *The Picture of the Three True Outcomes Player*, with Zunino as Dorian Gray and Myers the portrait stuffed in the attic.

Austin Nola C Born: 12/28/89 Age: 32 Bats: R Throws: R Height: 6'0" Weight: 197 lb. Origin: Round 5, 2012 Draft (#167 overall)

YEAR	TEAM	LVL	AGE	PA	R	2B	3B	HR	RBI	BB	K	SB	CS	Whiff%	AVG/OBP/SLG	DRC+	BABIP	BRR	FRAA	WARP
2019	EST	WIN	29	67	3	3	0	0	4	3	16	0	1		.234/.269/.281		.313			
2019	TAC	AAA	29	229	36	15	1	7	37	29	40	4	1		.327/.415/.520	111	.377	-2.5	C(28): 4.4, 1B(24): -0.8, 3B(3): 0.6	1.2
2019	SEA	MLB	29	267	37	12	1	10	31	23	63	1	0	23.1%	.269/.342/.454	98	.325	-0.5	1B(59): 2.4, 2B(15): 0.9, C(7): 0.2	1.0
2020	SD	MLB	30	74	9	4	0	2	9	9	17	0	0	22.4%	.222/.324/.381	106	.267	0.7	C(17): 2.3	0.6
2020	SEA	MLB	30	110	15	5	1	5	19	9	17	0	0	18.5%	.306/.373/.531	122	.325	-0.3	C(27): 0.9, 1B(2): 0.2, 3B(1): -0.3	0.7
2021	ELP	AAA	31	39	3	1	0	1	4	5	7	0	0		.303/.410/.424	102	.360	-0.4	1B(4): 0.1, C(3): 0.3	0.1
2021	SD	MLB	31	194	15	12	0	2	29	14	19	0	1	12.2%	.272/.340/.376	106	.292	0.9	C(48): -2.8, 2B(4): -0.1, 1B(1): -0.1	0.8
2022 DC	*SD*	*MLB*	*32*	*385*	*49*	*18*	*0*	*8*	*50*	*35*	*56*	*1*	*1*	*16.8%*	*.263/.341/.397*	*103*	*.293*	*-0.5*	*C -3*	*1.6*

Comparables: Robinson Chirinos, Manny Piña, Chris Gimenez

YEAR	TEAM	P. COUNT	FRM RUNS	BLK RUNS	THRW RUNS	TOT RUNS
2019	EST	1083			0.4	0.4
2019	SEA	626	0.1	0.0	0.0	0.1
2019	TAC	4110	4.3	-0.1	0.0	4.2
2020	SEA	3547	0.6	0.1	0.3	0.9
2020	SD	2167	2.0	0.0	0.0	2.0
2021	SD	6719	-1.8	-0.2	0.1	-1.9
2022	*SD*	*14430*	*-0.6*	*0.5*	*-0.2*	*-0.3*

All of the beatings Nola didn't take behind the plate during his long climb through the minors as an infielder seemed to come for him this season, which bookended two 60-day IL stints for hand injuries around another for a knee strain as the achy filling in his pain sandwich. Nola's preternatural plate discipline and ability to make solid contact in the zone help him make the most out of his modest power; in fact, the inconsistent playing time did nothing to harm his consistency at the plate, as he saw significant jumps in his selectivity and contract rates, particularly on hittable pitches. The challenge for the Padres will be finding ways to keep his bat in the lineup while keeping him healthy, as mileage behind the plate in the big leagues past age 30 adds up quickly.

Jorge Oña OF Born: 12/31/96 Age: 25 Bats: R Throws: R Height: 6'0" Weight: 235 lb. Origin: International Free Agent, 2016

YEAR	TEAM	LVL	AGE	PA	R	2B	3B	HR	RBI	BB	K	SB	CS	Whiff%	AVG/OBP/SLG	DRC+	BABIP	BRR	FRAA	WARP
2019	AMA	AA	22	103	11	2	0	5	18	11	26	2	1		.348/.417/.539	109	.433	0.6	LF(15): -2.7	0.2
2020	SD	MLB	23	15	3	1	0	1	2	2	7	0	0	54.8%	.250/.400/.583	92	.500	-0.2	RF(1): -0.1	0.0
2022 DC	*SD*	*MLB*	*25*	*270*	*31*	*11*	*0*	*6*	*30*	*22*	*93*	*0*	*1*	*35.2%*	*.215/.291/.352*	*73*	*.316*	*-0.3*	*LF -1, RF 0*	*-0.8*

Comparables: Jorge Soler, Jake Smolinski, Austin Dean

Another victim of the Year of Injuries in San Diego, Oña figured to contribute sometime in the back half of 2021 after making a brief but exciting appearance in the pandemic-shortened season. Instead, a surgery for bone spurs in his throwing elbow kept him off the field for most of the season. Oña also lost time in 2019 to a right shoulder injury, sparking some concern about durability for the cylindrical-shaped quasi-outfielder. Oña needs to walk a little more to truly realize a future a Three True Outcomes king, and he'll have to do it while underwhelming defensively, but he's got all the power required and then some in that department, frequently hitting tape-measure home runs at San Diego's various minor-league affiliates. Oña's swing-and-miss issues could be offset, at least aesthetically, by sharing a lineup with Cronenworth, an elite contact hitter, and Grisham, also a solid contact hitter who can pick up the slack in the outfield as well, but first and foremost, he has to be healthy enough to get to Petco Park.

Jurickson Profar LF Born: 02/20/93 Age: 29 Bats: S Throws: R Height: 6'0" Weight: 184 lb. Origin: International Free Agent, 2009

YEAR	TEAM	LVL	AGE	PA	R	2B	3B	HR	RBI	BB	K	SB	CS	Whiff%	AVG/OBP/SLG	DRC+	BABIP	BRR	FRAA	WARP
2019	OAK	MLB	26	518	65	24	2	20	67	48	75	9	1	20.2%	.218/.301/.410	102	.218	-0.2	2B(124): -13.1, LF(7): -0.0, 1B(1): -0.0	0.9
2020	SD	MLB	27	202	28	6	0	7	25	15	28	7	1	20.2%	.278/.343/.428	112	.293	2.2	LF(36): -1.2, 2B(17): -3.4, RF(2): 0.2	0.7
2021	SD	MLB	28	412	47	17	2	4	33	49	65	10	5	18.0%	.227/.329/.320	97	.266	4.1	LF(36): 0.9, RF(29): -3.4, 1B(20): -0.8	1.4
2022 DC	*SD*	*MLB*	*29*	*538*	*71*	*22*	*2*	*12*	*64*	*57*	*76*	*9*	*2*	*18.1%*	*.237/.331/.378*	*96*	*.259*	*0.2*	*LF 0, 2B -1*	*1.2*

Comparables: Clete Boyer, Bill Mazeroski, Tim Foli

On paper, Profar's three-year contract looked like a great deal for both parties. After years of checkered health and stunted development with the Rangers, who ping-ponged the highly-touted prospect back and forth between Round Rock and Arlington so often they should have just built one of those pneumatic tubes to transport him, Profar came into his own in 2020 as a super-utility player. Maybe the former top prospect could construct a career worthy of the breathless accolades he once collected from scouts. Instead Profar's bat wilted; never a crusher, he made even poorer contact that resulted in pop-ups and easy infield flyouts instead of line drives. Lefties, always trouble for him, became invincible. He did smooth things out as the season went along, cutting down on the pop-ups and impacting pitches in the heart of the plate better, and maybe some new coaching will help him relax and get back to the player he was last year. At least this time it'll be the faces changing around him while he gets to stay in the same place.

Webster Rivas C Born: 08/08/90 Age: 31 Bats: R Throws: R Height: 6'1" Weight: 219 lb. Origin: International Free Agent, 2009

YEAR	TEAM	LVL	AGE	PA	R	2B	3B	HR	RBI	BB	K	SB	CS	Whiff%	AVG/OBP/SLG	DRC+	BABIP	BRR	FRAA	WARP
2019	AMA	AA	28	119	14	3	1	1	14	8	23	1	0		.264/.328/.340	105	.321	0.8	C(22): 0.9, 1B(1): 0.0	0.7
2019	ELP	AAA	28	149	26	9	0	5	22	22	23	0	0		.296/.405/.488	112	.330	-0.9	C(37): 9.6, 1B(1): -0.0	1.7
2021	GIG	WIN	30	60	4	4	0	0	8	7	11	0	0		.216/.305/.294		.268			
2021	ELP	AAA	30	186	19	8	0	5	15	22	39	0	0		.252/.339/.393	96	.300	-0.9	C(32): -4.3, 1B(10): 0.0	0.1
2021	SD	MLB	30	77	8	2	0	2	4	8	16	0	0	21.2%	.221/.303/.338	101	.260	0.2	C(24): 0.5	0.4
2022 non-DC	*SD*	*MLB*	*31*	*251*	*22*	*9*	*0*	*3*	*22*	*23*	*57*	*0*	*0*	*24.0%*	*.223/.299/.324*	*69*	*.282*	*-0.4*	*C 1, 1B 0*	*0.2*

Comparables: Carlos Corporán, Tuffy Gosewisch, Guillermo Quiroz

YEAR	TEAM	P. COUNT	FRM RUNS	BLK RUNS	THRW RUNS	TOT RUNS
2019	ELP	5339	7.0	0.0	0.5	7.5
2019	GIG	1148			-0.3	-0.3
2021	SD	2876	0.7	0.0	0.1	0.7
2021	ELP	4788	-4.1	0.0	0.0	-4.0
2021	GIG	1764			-0.4	-0.4
2022	*SD*	*6956*	*0.6*	*-0.1*	*-0.2*	*0.2*

The one good thing about 2021's Cursed Carousel of Catching for San Diego was that it allowed Rivas, an 11-year veteran of the minors, to make his MLB debut. And what a debut it was, coming in late May against the Astros in a series that, at the time, seemed like a possible World Series preview; Rivas both caught a runner stealing and, in his first MLB at-bat, smoked a 106-MPH liner right at Carlos Correa, who deflected the ball, causing it to be ruled an error instead of a hit. San Diego would go on to win the game after putting up seven runs in the bottom of the 11th inning, and Rivas would get his first MLB hit two days later, a home run off the venerable Zack Greinke. Of course, the Astros would later surge, the Padres would falter, and Rivas would be re-assigned to Triple-A, but to paraphrase Kelly Clarkson slightly, some people wait a lifetime for a weekend like that.

Eguy Rosario IF Born: 08/25/99 Age: 22 Bats: R Throws: R Height: 5'9" Weight: 150 lb. Origin: International Free Agent, 2015

YEAR	TEAM	LVL	AGE	PA	R	2B	3B	HR	RBI	BB	K	SB	CS	Whiff%	AVG/OBP/SLG	DRC+	BABIP	BRR	FRAA	WARP
2019	LE	A+	19	512	60	25	8	7	72	37	103	21	9		.278/.331/.412	105	.338	0.7	3B(69): -1.8, SS(20): -0.2, 2B(15): -0.6	1.4
2020	MAR	WIN	20	112	18	6	2	0	14	7	13	8	0		.327/.393/.429		.368			
2021	PEJ	WIN	21	73	9	3	0	1	12	8	13	2	2		.250/.342/.344		.300			
2021	SA	AA	21	481	65	31	3	12	61	49	109	30	14		.281/.360/.455	110	.349	-4.6	SS(69): -3.3, 2B(38): 4.2, 3B(7): 0.6	1.7
2022 non-DC	*SD*	*MLB*	*22*	*251*	*22*	*12*	*1*	*4*	*23*	*19*	*59*	*8*	*5*	*28.0%*	*.232/.299/.355*	*77*	*.296*	*0.8*	*SS -1, 3B 0*	*0.1*

Comparables: Jorge Polanco, Cheslor Cuthbert, Wilmer Flores

Dominican by birth, Rosario (first name pronounced "eh-gee" with a hard g like gif) took an opportunity during the shutdown to play in Venezuela, and parlayed a strong showing there into a solid campaign in his first taste of the high minors. He then went to the AFL in 2021, where he impressed with his range and arm strength at third base along with the sneaky pop in his bat, which he generates from a stout but muscular frame. That latter element is crucial, because early reports on Rosario centered around the limits of that power as proof of his predestined future as a bench bat. The Padres infield is stuffed for the time being, but Rosario could be an attractive trade candidate due to his age and recent progress.

Fernando Tatis Jr. SS Born: 01/02/99 Age: 23 Bats: R Throws: R Height: 6'3" Weight: 217 lb. Origin: International Free Agent, 2015

YEAR	TEAM	LVL	AGE	PA	R	2B	3B	HR	RBI	BB	K	SB	CS	Whiff%	AVG/OBP/SLG	DRC+	BABIP	BRR	FRAA	WARP
2019	SD	MLB	20	372	61	13	6	22	53	30	110	16	6	35.3%	.317/.379/.590	113	.410	6.5	SS(83): 1.0	2.7
2020	SD	MLB	21	257	50	11	2	17	45	27	61	11	3	28.2%	.277/.366/.571	124	.306	1.3	SS(57): -6.6	1.0
2021	SD	MLB	22	546	99	31	0	42	97	62	153	25	4	34.8%	.282/.364/.611	144	.324	2.8	SS(102): -5.0, RF(20): 2.1, CF(7): 0.8	5.0
2022 DC	*SD*	*MLB*	*23*	*600*	*116*	*28*	*3*	*36*	*103*	*66*	*168*	*23*	*8*	*33.6%*	*.273/.361/.547*	*138*	*.333*	*1.7*	*SS -1*	*5.4*

Comparables: Starlin Castro, Elvis Andrus, Carlos Correa

While playing with a shoulder that likely looked like a jar of Spaghetti-O's by season's end, El Niño still managed somehow to barrel up more balls per plate appearance than anyone else in baseball, making contact more worthy of a Beefy Outfield Boy than an athletic shortstop type. Maybe that was just Tatis Jr. going full method actor when his shoulder troubles necessitated a switch to the less-taxing outfield in order to keep his bat in the lineup. His rise to stardom was so sudden it still feels like people are trying to figure out what he is, exactly: Is the high strikeout rate sustainable as long as he continues to make this kind of contact? Can he be depended on for a 20-20 season every year? Will he be healthy enough to stick at short? Can we somehow harness his personal magnetism as a clean energy solution? Do he and Charlie Freeman FaceTime? All questions deserving of an answer, but the best thing to do is simply sit back and revel in enjoying one thing baseball can't ruin, no matter how hard it might try (hit all the homers you want, in whatever counts you want, Fernando). In the meantime, call his left shoulder Poochie, because it's ruining the show for everyone.

James Wood CF Born: 09/17/02 Age: 19 Bats: L Throws: R Height: 6'7" Weight: 240 lb. Origin: Round 2, 2021 Draft (#62 overall)

YEAR	TEAM	LVL	AGE	PA	R	2B	3B	HR	RBI	BB	K	SB	CS	Whiff%	AVG/OBP/SLG	DRC+	BABIP	BRR	FRAA	WARP
2021	PAD	ROK	18	101	18	5	0	3	22	13	32	10	0		.372/.465/.535		.569			
2022	*No projection*																			

Comparables: Jairo Mendez, Dalton Pompey, Devon Torrence

A brief five-hour jaunt west on I-68 from Wood's hometown of Rockville, MD deposits one in Point Pleasant, WV, home of the legendary Mothman. While the cryptid's exact identity has never been pinned down, one possible suspect is the teenaged Padres prospect, also the possessor of a seemingly inhuman wingspan and the ability to fly. Despite his freakishly long levers, Wood is a coordinated athlete who's able to shorten up his swing in the box to make consistent contact and yet get enough extension to impact the baseball in loud, otherworldly ways. The Padres were delighted to get him in the second round when he fell after a tough spring, and the pre-draft whiffs problem carried into his first taste of professional ball, but he also showcased his speed, stealing ten bases without getting caught. Provided he can make enough contact to get to the power side of his power-speed combo, the upside is tremendous, the stuff of the next great North American myth.

PITCHERS

Austin Adams RHP Born: 05/05/91 Age: 31 Bats: R Throws: R Height: 6'3" Weight: 220 lb. Origin: Round 8, 2012 Draft (#267 overall)

YEAR	TEAM	LVL	AGE	W	L	SV	G	GS	IP	H	HR	BB/9	K/9	K	GB%	BABIP	WHIP	ERA	DRA-	WARP	MPH	FB%	Whiff%	CSP
2019	FRE	AAA	28	0	1	1	8	0	10	7	0	2.7	18.0	20	47.1%	.412	1.00	2.70	62	0.3				
2019	SEA	MLB	28	2	2	0	29	2	31	20	4	4.1	14.8	51	49.2%	.291	1.10	3.77	66	0.9	95.2	35.5%	40.9%	44.9%
2019	WAS	MLB	28	0	0	0	1	0	1	0	0	18.0	18.0	2	100.0%	.000	2.00	9.00	105	0.0	93.9	51.5%	22.2%	32.4%
2020	SD	MLB	29	0	0	0	3	0	4	3	1	4.5	15.8	7	50.0%	.286	1.25	4.50	89	0.1	93.4	16.2%	48.0%	42.6%
2021	SD	MLB	30	3	2	0	65	0	52^2	28	1	6.0	13.0	76	33.0%	.265	1.20	4.10	96	0.6	94.2	12.9%	34.3%	48.1%
2022 DC	*SD*	*MLB*	*31*	*1*	*1*	*0*	*37*	*0*	*32.3*	*21*	*4*	*4.9*	*14.1*	*50*	*39.1%*	*.275*	*1.20*	*3.92*	*89*	*0.3*	*94.3*	*16.6%*	*35.7%*	*47.3%*

Comparables: Josh Kinney, Jeff Beliveau, Al Alburquerque

A fun fact for you: Ty France, who was tied for being hit by the most baseballs in 2021, was part of a trade including Adams, who hit the most batters with baseballs in 2021. Adams' mark of hitting one in every ten batters breaks all kinds of MLB records, but ironically, the bigger problem was all the players he put on base without plunking. Adams has never been a pinnacle of command, but it was a problem he seemed to have a grasp on in Seattle when his fastball-slider mix was more 35-65; as opposed to in San Diego, when his usage of the slider, the pitch he hit all those batters on, soared to over 80% of the time. What salvaged the season is that all those beanings appeared to have some effect: Despite wielding a strikeout-geared repertoire, his batting average and slugging against on balls in play aligned more with the type of pitchers who scrape the bottom of the zone. Deploying a more judicious pitch mix and instilling fear without all the free passes will be key to Adams achieving the high-leverage potential he flashes.

Jake Arrieta RHP Born: 03/06/86 Age: 36 Bats: R Throws: R Height: 6'4" Weight: 230 lb. Origin: Round 5, 2007 Draft (#159 overall)

YEAR	TEAM	LVL	AGE	W	L	SV	G	GS	IP	H	HR	BB/9	K/9	K	GB%	BABIP	WHIP	ERA	DRA-	WARP	MPH	FB%	Whiff%	CSP
2019	PHI	MLB	33	8	8	0	24	24	135^2	149	21	3.4	7.3	110	51.4%	.320	1.47	4.64	107	0.9	92.6	56.2%	18.3%	46.8%
2020	PHI	MLB	34	4	4	0	9	9	44^1	51	6	3.2	6.5	32	51.8%	.333	1.51	5.08	105	0.4	92.3	52.4%	19.0%	47.5%
2021	SD	MLB	35	0	3	0	4	4	12^1	18	3	3.6	6.6	9	40.9%	.375	1.86	10.95	107	0.1	92.1	54.6%	16.0%	56.1%
2021	CHC	MLB	35	5	11	0	20	20	86^1	113	21	4.1	7.7	74	45.2%	.342	1.76	6.88	119	-0.1	91.4	53.9%	18.5%	56.1%
2022 DC	*FA*	*MLB*	*36*	*3*	*3*	*0*	*12*	*12*	*54.3*	*58*	*7*	*3.6*	*7.0*	*42*	*46.2%*	*.304*	*1.47*	*4.94*	*117*	*0.0*	*91.9*	*54.3%*	*18.3%*	*52.4%*

Comparables: Wandy Rodriguez, Bob Welch, Larry Jackson

How bad was Arrieta's 2021? Bad enough that the zombie Cubs cut him loose shortly after he returned from his second IL stint of the year, this time for a bad hammy, which is a funny way of spelling "badly strained ERA." It was an injury that he would prove to reaggravate. Surprisingly enough the 35-year-old didn't uncover any magical fountain of youth in San Diego, or the three missing ticks on his velocity, no matter how good the fish tacos might be. And one more rhetorical question to round things out: How much metaphorical time has elapsed in baseball since Arrieta was drafted? One of his first comments in the BP Annual, from over 10 years ago, notes that he had the best fastball in the system, averaging a whopping 93 mph. The times, they have changed.

Mike Clevinger RHP Born: 12/21/90 Age: 31 Bats: R Throws: R Height: 6'4" Weight: 215 lb. Origin: Round 4, 2011 Draft (#135 overall)

YEAR	TEAM	LVL	AGE	W	L	SV	G	GS	IP	H	HR	BB/9	K/9	K	GB%	BABIP	WHIP	ERA	DRA-	WARP	MPH	FB%	Whiff%	CSP
2019	CLE	MLB	28	13	4	0	21	21	126	96	10	2.6	12.1	169	40.5%	.306	1.06	2.71	72	3.1	95.6	51.1%	35.3%	46.0%
2020	CLE	MLB	29	1	1	0	4	4	22^2	20	5	4.4	8.3	21	36.7%	.273	1.37	3.18	113	0.1	94.5	47.4%	32.1%	46.5%
2020	SD	MLB	29	2	1	0	4	4	19	14	1	1.4	9.0	19	29.8%	.283	0.89	2.84	100	0.2	95.6	46.1%	28.5%	49.2%
2022 DC	*SD*	*MLB*	*31*	*7*	*5*	*0*	*22*	*22*	*102*	*89*	*14*	*3.0*	*10.1*	*114*	*38.7%*	*.289*	*1.21*	*3.64*	*89*	*1.4*	*95.3*	*49.5%*	*33.4%*	*46.6%*

Comparables: Dave Giusti, Jack Morris, Tom Glavine

Watch out, because the Padres are evolving. Instead of just trading for players, they've leveled up to the stage of acquiring the coaches from teams they acquire players from, snagging pitching coaches Rob Marcello from Seattle (Emilio Pagán, Austin Adams, Dan Altavilla, Taylor Williams) and Ruben Niebla from Cleveland, because why give a man a fish when you can instead buy the boat company. Clevinger won't be back from TJ surgery until the start of the 2022 season, assuming all continues to go well in his rehab, but has already tweeted about how excited he is to have Niebla on staff. Maybe his idea for galaxy-tie-dyed home alternates won't fall on deaf ears after all.

Nabil Crismatt RHP

Born: 12/25/94 Age: 27 Bats: R Throws: R Height: 6'1" Weight: 220 lb. Origin: International Free Agent, 2011

YEAR	TEAM	LVL	AGE	W	L	SV	G	GS	IP	H	HR	BB/9	K/9	K	GB%	BABIP	WHIP	ERA	DRA-	WARP	MPH	FB%	Whiff%	CSP
2019	ARK	AA	24	4	5	0	14	13	83^2	57	6	1.2	9.6	89	43.3%	.242	0.81	1.94	76	1.3				
2019	TAC	AAA	24	0	5	0	13	8	46^2	67	15	4.1	13.1	68	33.8%	.419	1.89	9.06	89	0.6				
2020	STL	MLB	25	0	0	0	6	0	8^1	6	2	1.1	8.6	8	50.0%	.200	0.84	3.24	101	0.1	89.8	41.2%	27.4%	46.9%
2021	SD	MLB	26	3	1	0	45	0	81^1	87	10	2.7	7.9	71	50.8%	.326	1.36	3.76	93	1.0	90.2	25.1%	26.1%	52.5%
2022 DC	*SD*	*MLB*	*27*	*2*	*2*	*0*	*52*	*0*	*45.3*	*45*	*6*	*2.8*	*8.8*	*44*	*47.1%*	*.306*	*1.30*	*4.28*	*103*	*0.1*	*90.2*	*26.0%*	*26.2%*	*52.2%*

Comparables: Matt Bowman, Dillon Tate, John Frascatore

One of Raymond Chandler's rules for writing is "when in doubt, have a man come through the door with a gun in his hand." The Padres' pitching staff was much in doubt this year, and the man they had come through the door didn't have a gun so much as a 90-mph fastball and a pair of brass knuckles in his changeup and curveball. Crismatt's gutty performance in his first extended MLB action mirrored back on Padres fans their own steadfast determination, and he rose to folk-hero status despite pitching primarily in mop-up duty; Joe Musgrove took time to mention Crismatt's unheralded performance in his end-of-year presser. Ideally next year the Padres won't need Crismatt to cover innings for their depleted/ineffective starter corps, but that doesn't mean they shouldn't keep his throne on the El Paso-San Diego express polished up just in case.

Yu Darvish RHP

Born: 08/16/86 Age: 35 Bats: R Throws: R Height: 6'5" Weight: 220 lb. Origin: International Free Agent, 2012

YEAR	TEAM	LVL	AGE	W	L	SV	G	GS	IP	H	HR	BB/9	K/9	K	GB%	BABIP	WHIP	ERA	DRA-	WARP	MPH	FB%	Whiff%	CSP
2019	CHC	MLB	32	6	8	0	31	31	178^2	140	33	2.8	11.5	229	45.1%	.268	1.10	3.98	69	4.8	94.1	39.8%	30.4%	48.5%
2020	CHC	MLB	33	8	3	0	12	12	76	59	5	1.7	11.0	93	42.8%	.297	0.96	2.01	64	2.3	95.5	30.1%	32.2%	52.9%
2021	SD	MLB	34	8	11	0	30	30	166^1	138	28	2.4	10.8	199	36.5%	.274	1.09	4.22	77	3.6	94.4	33.0%	27.4%	57.8%
2022 DC	*SD*	*MLB*	*35*	*11*	*8*	*0*	*29*	*29*	*163*	*141*	*24*	*2.5*	*10.2*	*185*	*38.5%*	*.286*	*1.15*	*3.52*	*87*	*2.4*	*94.5*	*33.9%*	*28.8%*	*55.0%*

Comparables: Bert Blyleven, Zack Greinke, Fergie Jenkins

Ophelia. Ray "hold onto your butts" Arnold in *Jurassic Park*. Anyone who ever set foot in an OR on *Grey's Anatomy*. The kids who all get squished by a train, something no one ever seems to remember about the *Narnia* books. This comment. Category is: characters who deserved better. Darvish's mistreatment in the MLB universe starts during his time in Texas, where he was pilloried by local media for "diva behavior" like striking out *too* many batters and therefore not going deeply enough into games, losing close contests (leading to the world's most cumbersome hashtag, #acestuffbutnotacetough—Twitter was wild in the early 2010s) and not rushing back quickly enough from a sprained UCL to help his cellar-dwelling team. You know, all the kinds of things a player can fix by themselves. Then there's a don't-let-the-door-hit-ya deadline deal leading to a disappointing stint with the Dodgers and a World Series loss tainted by a sign-stealing scandal. Next Darvish was forced to suffer being the subject of an offseason salary-dump trade, and a hopeful new beginning in San Diego was marred by multiple injuries that zapped his effectiveness in the second half of the season. At this point even George R.R. Martin would blush at what MLB has inflicted on one of baseball's best pitchers of the past decade.

Luis García RHP

Born: 01/30/87 Age: 35 Bats: R Throws: R Height: 6'2" Weight: 240 lb. Origin: International Free Agent, 2017

YEAR	TEAM	LVL	AGE	W	L	SV	G	GS	IP	H	HR	BB/9	K/9	K	GB%	BABIP	WHIP	ERA	DRA-	WARP	MPH	FB%	Whiff%	CSP
2019	LAA	MLB	32	2	1	1	64	2	62	61	13	4.8	8.3	57	47.5%	.284	1.52	4.35	106	0.4	97.1	47.0%	29.3%	42.9%
2020	TEX	MLB	33	0	2	0	11	2	8^1	10	1	9.7	11.9	11	48.0%	.375	2.28	7.56	96	0.1	96.8	56.5%	30.6%	44.4%
2021	SWB	AAA	34	1	2	11	18	0	17^1	16	2	1.6	9.9	19	59.6%	.311	1.10	3.63	84	0.4				
2021	STL	MLB	34	1	1	2	34	0	33^1	25	2	2.2	9.2	34	46.7%	.256	0.99	3.24	92	0.4	98.5	59.5%	32.1%	60.1%
2022 DC	*SD*	*MLB*	*35*	*3*	*3*	*17*	*67*	*0*	*58*	*57*	*7*	*3.4*	*8.6*	*55*	*48.6%*	*.302*	*1.36*	*4.33*	*103*	*0.1*	*97.8*	*54.6%*	*30.9%*	*51.9%*

Comparables: Tommy Hunter, Carlos Torres, Ricky Bottalico

It's just not fair. Despite years toiling as a moderately-effective reliever in Philadelphia and Los Angeles, a velocity bump that saw him boost a few of his rate stats, *and* a tap on the shoulder during the most important game of the Cardinals' season…he's *still* the second-best Luis Garcia who pitches, and maybe can't crack the top two Luis Garcias in MLB. Maybe he should stick to his Player's Weekend nickname of "Amadito" now that he's in San Diego, where he'll potentially slot in as a later-inning relief option and try to climb the LG name rankings yet again.

Robert Gasser LHP

Born: 05/31/99 Age: 23 Bats: L Throws: L Height: 6'1" Weight: 190 lb. Origin: Round 2, 2021 Draft (#71 overall)

YEAR	TEAM	LVL	AGE	W	L	SV	G	GS	IP	H	HR	BB/9	K/9	K	GB%	BABIP	WHIP	ERA	DRA-	WARP	MPH	FB%	Whiff%	CSP
2021	LE	A	22	0	0	0	5	5	14	11	1	1.3	8.4	13	52.8%	.286	0.93	1.29	110	0.0				
2022 non-DC	*SD*	*MLB*	*23*	*2*	*3*	*0*	*57*	*0*	*50*	*52*	*7*	*3.9*	*7.3*	*40*	*42.7%*	*.301*	*1.49*	*5.15*	*118*	*-0.3*				

Comparables: Pedro Hernandez, Tyler Alexander, Leo Crawford

Someone in San Diego's player acquisitions group really loves a pitchability lefty, although Gasser has a bit more intrigue thanks to a velocity spike in his draft year. Maxed-out physically, he likely won't climb too far out of the lower 90s with regularity, but offers a sharp slider and serviceable changeup to round out his repertoire, all of which he locates well with consistency. The upside of this type of arm is a quick rise through the minors, and the early results indicate that will be the case here, with even a late-season 2022 debut possible if he carves through the high minors as effectively as he did the lower rungs. And if not, well, after 2021 you could understand why the team would be interested in org-level depth.

MacKenzie Gore LHP Born: 02/24/99 Age: 23 Bats: L Throws: L Height: 6'2" Weight: 197 lb. Origin: Round 1, 2017 Draft (#3 overall)

YEAR	TEAM	LVL	AGE	W	L	SV	G	GS	IP	H	HR	BB/9	K/9	K	GB%	BABIP	WHIP	ERA	DRA-	WARP	MPH	FB%	Whiff%	CSP
2019	LE	A+	20	7	1	0	15	15	79^1	36	4	2.3	12.5	110	36.5%	.212	0.71	1.02	77	1.3				
2019	AMA	AA	20	2	1	0	5	5	21^2	20	3	3.3	10.4	25	44.6%	.321	1.29	4.15	83	0.3				
2021	PAD	ROK	22	1	0	0	3	3	16^1	13	0	2.2	12.1	22	45.9%	.351	1.04	1.65						
2021	SA	AA	22	0	0	0	2	2	9	6	0	8.0	16.0	16	47.1%	.353	1.56	3.00	92	0.1				
2021	ELP	AAA	22	0	2	0	6	6	20	24	3	5.4	8.1	18	46.2%	.339	1.80	5.85	105	0.0				
2022 DC	*SD*	*MLB*	*23*	*1*	*2*	*0*	*6*	*6*	*29*	*27*	*4*	*5.0*	*10.0*	*32*	*41.1%*	*.305*	*1.50*	*5.02*	*115*	*0.0*				

Comparables: Robb Nen, Luiz Gohara, Carlos Martínez

Perhaps, after a solid-if-not-spectacular high minors debut for one of baseball's most heralded prospects in 2019, Gore spent 2020 mired in the same fear-and-anxiety spiral as many of us, where trying to decide what to eat for lunch resulted in an afternoon spent crouching under one's makeshift home office desk in the fetal position googling things like "speared by wild boar home remedy." Whatever it was, Gore struggled mightily with the strike zone at Triple-A in 2021, so the Padres pulled him out of classes and had him embark on the Tour de Pitching Coaches, bouncing him around the entire organization during the regular season, and eventually to the Arizona Fall League to see if Atlanta's Bo Henning, Peoria's pitching coach, could help him out. After 11.1 innings where he allowed 15 hits and walked six batters (although with eight strikeouts, showing flashes of his previous dominance), the Padres decided it'd be better to homeschool Gore, and called him back to Petco to work with new pitching coach Ruben Niebla. The new-look Padres coaching staff were probably not hired solely to fix Mackenzie Gore—the Padres' pitching woes run much deeper than one top prospect with what looks like a moderate case of the yips—but it's safe to assume that it's starred and double-underlined on their to-do list.

Tim Hill LHP Born: 02/10/90 Age: 32 Bats: R Throws: L Height: 6'4" Weight: 200 lb. Origin: Round 32, 2014 Draft (#963 overall)

YEAR	TEAM	LVL	AGE	W	L	SV	G	GS	IP	H	HR	BB/9	K/9	K	GB%	BABIP	WHIP	ERA	DRA-	WARP	MPH	FB%	Whiff%	CSP
2019	OMA	AAA	29	1	1	3	27	0	29^2	26	2	1.8	9.1	30	55.0%	.308	1.08	2.12	81	0.5				
2019	KC	MLB	29	2	0	1	46	0	39^2	31	4	2.9	8.8	39	56.2%	.270	1.11	3.63	94	0.5	90.3	75.5%	20.7%	49.6%
2020	SD	MLB	30	3	0	0	23	0	18	17	3	3.0	10.0	20	52.9%	.292	1.28	4.50	72	0.5	90.6	89.9%	22.8%	46.7%
2021	SD	MLB	31	6	6	1	78	0	59^2	51	9	3.5	8.4	56	58.8%	.264	1.24	3.62	88	0.9	91.8	84.5%	23.0%	54.1%
2022 DC	*SD*	*MLB*	*32*	*3*	*3*	*0*	*67*	*0*	*58*	*54*	*5*	*3.2*	*8.8*	*56*	*55.9%*	*.298*	*1.29*	*3.83*	*93*	*0.4*	*91.4*	*84.0%*	*22.6%*	*52.2%*

Comparables: Oliver Drake, Justin Miller, Yorkis Perez

Lefty sidearmers are to a bullpen what kalamata olives are to a charcuterie board: intense, best when paired with complementary flavors, and to be consumed in small quantities only. In a hypothetical healthy bullpen, Hill's season looks great, as his manager is able to navigate around three-batter minimums and unfavorable matchups: Witness the dominance of his April, when he struck out 17 batters in fewer than 13 innings. As the season wore on and the bullpen options dwindled, though, Hill was forced onto the mound in high-leverage situations more often than is optimal for a soft-tossing lefty, and, just like too much salt can kill one's taste buds, batters became inured to his particular briny magic. Despite the unfavorable conditions, Hill handled the extra workload well, proof that sometimes a handful of green olives is fine, especially after the score of the game has forced a fan to throw back a couple of cheap beers.

Pierce Johnson RHP Born: 05/10/91 Age: 31 Bats: R Throws: R Height: 6'2" Weight: 202 lb. Origin: Round 1, 2012 Draft (#43 overall)

YEAR	TEAM	LVL	AGE	W	L	SV	G	GS	IP	H	HR	BB/9	K/9	K	GB%	BABIP	WHIP	ERA	DRA-	WARP	MPH	FB%	Whiff%	CSP
2020	SD	MLB	29	3	1	0	24	0	20	15	2	4.1	12.2	27	31.8%	.310	1.20	2.70	93	0.3	96.3	45.8%	40.0%	46.4%
2021	SD	MLB	30	3	4	0	63	2	58^2	47	6	4.1	11.8	77	33.1%	.308	1.26	3.22	84	1.0	95.6	32.5%	30.3%	53.9%
2022 DC	*SD*	*MLB*	*31*	*2*	*2*	*0*	*52*	*0*	*45.3*	*36*	*7*	*4.1*	*11.5*	*57*	*35.8%*	*.279*	*1.26*	*3.84*	*91*	*0.4*	*95.7*	*34.7%*	*31.9%*	*52.6%*

Comparables: Ryan Cook, Brandon Workman, Jared Hughes

The Padres and Johnson decided to test out maximalism as a philosophy this year, having him throw his plus curveball—which he was already throwing over half the time—even more often. The result was a slight decrease in the effectiveness of the pitch, both in terms of whiffs generated and exit velocity, but overall the hard, high-spin offering was still one of the better pitches in baseball in 2021. The Padres, philosophically, have no problem letting a reliever throw their One Good Pitch all the time, any time—see Austin Adams and his slider—almost as if the season were part of some grand experiment in establishing the value of unpredictability in pitching. Based on the results, the answer of whether we've found the breaking point seems to be no, not yet.

Reiss Knehr RHP Born: 11/03/96 Age: 25 Bats: L Throws: R Height: 6'2" Weight: 205 lb. Origin: Round 20, 2018 Draft (#591 overall)

YEAR	TEAM	LVL	AGE	W	L	SV	G	GS	IP	H	HR	BB/9	K/9	K	GB%	BABIP	WHIP	ERA	DRA-	WARP	MPH	FB%	Whiff%	CSP
2019	LE	A+	22	3	5	1	17	12	66^1	71	11	3.8	11.3	83	43.5%	.347	1.49	5.43	94	0.4				
2021	SA	AA	24	6	1	0	11	11	55^1	41	4	3.6	7.5	46	43.7%	.253	1.14	3.90	107	0.1				
2021	ELP	AAA	24	0	2	1	8	5	20^1	15	3	4.0	8.9	20	51.9%	.250	1.18	2.66	91	0.2				
2021	SD	MLB	24	1	2	0	12	5	29	23	2	6.2	6.2	20	34.5%	.247	1.48	4.97	120	0.0	93.1	69.6%	22.3%	54.3%
2022 DC	*SD*	*MLB*	*25*	*3*	*3*	*0*	*32*	*3*	*38.7*	*40*	*6*	*5.2*	*8.0*	*34*	*41.1%*	*.303*	*1.62*	*5.96*	*131*	*-0.4*	*93.1*	*69.6%*	*22.3%*	*54.3%*

Comparables: Tyler Cravy, Kip Gross, Brock Stewart

2021 wasn't As Good As It Gets for Knehr, although he occasionally showed a Flash of Genius when he was able to spot his tailing fastball in the zone; it has pedestrian velocity but plays up due to some funk in his arm angle, leading to weak contact and ground-ball outs. In order to be Invincible, though, he has to land both his fastball and his hard (88-90) changeup consistently and not fall behind in counts and be forced into the middle of the plate, or The Green Zone, where batters hit him hard this season. There's probably not enough here to be an Anchorman in the Padres' rotation without improved command or another pitch; he does occasionally mix in a biting slider that's had some good results as a change-of-pace pitch. Maybe he can yet become rotation-mates with (Little Miss) Sunshine, but a floor as a multi-inning reliever and spot starter wouldn't be a Crisis, either.

Dinelson Lamet RHP

Born: 07/18/92 Age: 29 Bats: R Throws: R Height: 6'3" Weight: 228 lb. Origin: International Free Agent, 2014

YEAR	TEAM	LVL	AGE	W	L	SV	G	GS	IP	H	HR	BB/9	K/9	K	GB%	BABIP	WHIP	ERA	DRA-	WARP	MPH	FB%	Whiff%	CSP
2019	LE	A+	26	0	2	0	3	3	9	11	1	5.0	14.0	14	27.3%	.476	1.78	8.00	95	0.1				
2019	ELP	AAA	26	1	0	0	3	3	15	10	3	2.4	11.4	19	51.4%	.219	0.93	4.80	81	0.3				
2019	SD	MLB	26	3	5	0	14	14	73	62	12	3.7	12.9	105	35.3%	.314	1.26	4.07	74	1.7	96.2	54.8%	31.7%	47.2%
2020	SD	MLB	27	3	1	0	12	12	69	39	5	2.6	12.1	93	38.0%	.234	0.86	2.09	65	2.1	97.0	46.5%	32.6%	47.0%
2021	SD	MLB	28	2	4	0	22	9	47	48	6	4.2	10.9	57	39.1%	.347	1.49	4.40	86	0.8	95.4	48.2%	32.3%	55.0%
2022 DC	*SD*	*MLB*	*29*	*7*	*3*	*0*	*56*	*4*	*64.7*	*53*	*9*	*3.5*	*11.1*	*79*	*38.0%*	*.285*	*1.21*	*3.64*	*86*	*0.9*	*96.1*	*49.0%*	*32.3%*	*50.5%*

Comparables: Danny Salazar, Yu Darvish, Edinson Vólquez

There's always been reliever risk attached to Lamet's profile, between his possession of two (2) pitches and a Tarantino-violent delivery. This year those fears became corporeal, but not because of Lamet's stuff; he's been effective while on the mound largely thanks to his ultra-elite slider, arguably the best pitch in baseball in 2021. The problem is keeping him on the mound: Already a TJ veteran, Lamet missed time with a biceps injury that started bothering him at the end of 2020, that somehow morphed into a strained UCL by the beginning of spring training, that then reappeared as forearm inflammation in late June, that then became a hip infection in August. Worst Magic School Bus field trip ever. Lamet reappeared late in the season, but out of the bullpen, in a sample too small to judge either his effectiveness, role moving forward, nor, most crucially, health. The Lamet lament: these violent delights do have violent ends.

Adrian Morejon LHP

Born: 02/27/99 Age: 23 Bats: L Throws: L Height: 5'11" Weight: 224 lb. Origin: International Free Agent, 2016

YEAR	TEAM	LVL	AGE	W	L	SV	G	GS	IP	H	HR	BB/9	K/9	K	GB%	BABIP	WHIP	ERA	DRA-	WARP	MPH	FB%	Whiff%	CSP
2019	AMA	AA	20	0	4	0	16	16	36	29	3	3.8	11.0	44	48.9%	.292	1.22	4.25	96	0.1				
2019	SD	MLB	20	0	0	0	5	2	8	15	1	3.4	10.1	9	36.7%	.483	2.25	10.12	102	0.1	96.6	53.9%	19.7%	51.7%
2020	SD	MLB	21	2	2	0	9	4	19^{1}	20	7	1.9	11.6	25	46.0%	.302	1.24	4.66	73	0.5	96.8	56.2%	28.5%	46.5%
2021	SD	MLB	22	0	0	0	2	2	4^{2}	5	2	3.9	5.8	3	53.3%	.231	1.50	3.86	110	0.0	96.7	62.5%	30.8%	59.7%
2022 DC	*SD*	*MLB*	*23*	*1*	*1*	*0*	*6*	*6*	*29*	*27*	*3*	*3.6*	*9.1*	*29*	*44.7%*	*.299*	*1.35*	*4.31*	*102*	*0.2*	*96.8*	*57.3%*	*27.7%*	*50.3%*

Comparables: Dylan Bundy, Carlos Martínez, Patrick Corbin

A bad track record with injuries got worse this year, when a forearm strain in April eventually morphed into the need for TJ surgery. Perhaps this will solve Morejon's lingering injury issues for good, but the profile that has always whispered "high-leverage reliever"—smaller stature, big fastball, inconsistent secondaries—now positively screams it. Morejon entered the past spring as a starter, but won't throw another competitive pitch until the middle of the 2022 season, and that's if all goes well. Closers are worth millions, though, and well more than the Padres' initial investment in Morejon, so even a move to the bullpen isn't a huge downgrade for a pitcher with his kind of raw stuff.

Joe Musgrove RHP

Born: 12/04/92 Age: 29 Bats: R Throws: R Height: 6'5" Weight: 230 lb. Origin: Round 1, 2011 Draft (#46 overall)

YEAR	TEAM	LVL	AGE	W	L	SV	G	GS	IP	H	HR	BB/9	K/9	K	GB%	BABIP	WHIP	ERA	DRA-	WARP	MPH	FB%	Whiff%	CSP
2019	PIT	MLB	26	11	12	0	32	31	170^{1}	168	21	2.1	8.3	157	44.1%	.300	1.22	4.44	89	2.7	92.5	49.5%	24.7%	49.8%
2020	PIT	MLB	27	1	5	0	8	8	39^{2}	33	5	3.6	12.5	55	47.3%	.318	1.24	3.86	70	1.1	92.7	39.1%	33.0%	45.8%
2021	SD	MLB	28	11	9	0	32	31	181^{1}	142	22	2.7	10.1	203	44.2%	.268	1.08	3.18	79	3.7	93.4	25.8%	29.7%	54.8%
2022 DC	*SD*	*MLB*	*29*	*10*	*7*	*0*	*27*	*27*	*154*	*133*	*19*	*2.6*	*10.3*	*175*	*44.1%*	*.292*	*1.15*	*3.45*	*84*	*2.5*	*93.1*	*32.1%*	*29.0%*	*52.8%*

Comparables: Chris Carpenter, Max Scherzer, Livan Hernandez

Musgrove was a bright spot in an otherwise grim Padres season. The prodigal son returned home to California to throw the franchise's first no-hitter, putting distance both physical and psychological between himself and the specter of Being Traded For Gerrit Cole (a specter that, like Scrooge remarks of Jacob Marley, was more gravy than grave this year). He also threw off the ghost of IL Stints Past, as the only member of the Padres' rotation who made every one of his scheduled starts. He was a model of consistency in his pitching as well, becoming the first San Diego pitcher to hit 200 strikeouts in a season since 2015, despite a late-season dip where he lost command of his slider. It's tough to depend too heavily on a pitcher with Musgrove's injury history and reliance on the slider, a notoriously fickle pitch, and he shouldn't be expected to shoulder the load for his ineffective teammates next season, but for this year, Padres fans owe a debt of gratitude to Musgrove for taking the ball every fifth day and blessing them, every one.

Aaron Northcraft RHP

Born: 05/28/90 Age: 32 Bats: R Throws: R Height: 6'3" Weight: 229 lb. Origin: Round 10, 2009 Draft (#298 overall)

YEAR	TEAM	LVL	AGE	W	L	SV	G	GS	IP	H	HR	BB/9	K/9	K	GB%	BABIP	WHIP	ERA	DRA-	WARP	MPH	FB%	Whiff%	CSP
2019	ARK	AA	29	0	0	0	3	0	5^{1}	4	0	0.0	5.1	3	70.6%	.235	0.75	1.69	115	0.0				
2019	TAC	AAA	29	0	2	4	27	0	33^{2}	18	2	3.5	9.4	35	65.8%	.208	0.92	1.87	77	0.7				
2021	ELP	AAA	31	0	2	1	13	0	13^{1}	21	1	4.0	7.4	11	52.0%	.408	2.03	8.10	102	0.0				
2021	SD	MLB	31	1	0	0	5	0	8	5	1	9.0	5.6	5	57.1%	.200	1.63	2.25	120	0.0	88.3	72.9%	22.8%	49.9%
2022 non-DC	*SD*	*MLB*	*32*	*2*	*3*	*0*	*57*	*0*	*50*	*50*	*5*	*4.5*	*8.1*	*45*	*52.7%*	*.305*	*1.50*	*4.84*	*113*	*-0.2*	*88.3*	*72.9%*	*22.8%*	*49.9%*

Comparables: Gregory Infante, Jay Jackson, Fernando Rodriguez Jr.

Northcraft's career was a prototypical Hollywood tale: a decade-long veteran, suffering multiple injuries and reinventing himself as a side-arming ground-ball specialist, who traversed the minors and independent leagues before finally making The Show at long last. Unfortunately, this is San Diego, not LA, and Hollywood fairy tales are a couple hours up I-5. His lone victory came in a 12-3 game when he was one of eight pitchers used, and posted the worst Win Percentage Added of any Padre that took the field; hard to imagine the triumphant music cue on that one. Northcraft couldn't stay healthy, and eventually got designated off the 40-man for younger men with emptier stories. However, Northcraft's Instagram bears a quote from the Great Bambino himself: "It's hard to beat a person who doesn't give up." He's spent most of his life being told to give up, and maybe that fairy-tale ending is out there for him yet.

Chris Paddack RHP Born: 01/08/96 Age: 26 Bats: R Throws: R Height: 6'5" Weight: 217 lb. Origin: Round 8, 2015 Draft (#236 overall)

YEAR	TEAM	LVL	AGE	W	L	SV	G	GS	IP	H	HR	BB/9	K/9	K	GB%	BABIP	WHIP	ERA	DRA-	WARP	MPH	FB%	Whiff%	CSP
2019	SD	MLB	23	9	7	0	26	26	140^2	107	23	2.0	9.8	153	39.2%	.239	0.98	3.33	80	3.0	94.1	61.0%	24.8%	50.8%
2020	SD	MLB	24	4	5	0	12	12	59	60	14	1.8	8.8	58	46.8%	.289	1.22	4.73	86	1.1	94.1	61.5%	26.0%	48.8%
2021	SD	MLB	25	7	7	0	23	22	108^1	115	15	1.8	8.2	99	42.4%	.317	1.26	5.07	91	1.5	94.9	61.5%	24.7%	57.4%
2022 DC	*SD*	*MLB*	*26*	*4*	*3*	*0*	*14*	*14*	*69.7*	*67*	*8*	*2.0*	*8.6*	*66*	*42.6%*	*.299*	*1.19*	*3.63*	*91*	*0.9*	*94.6*	*61.4%*	*25.0%*	*54.2%*

Comparables: Jordan Zimmermann, Zack Wheeler, Michael Pineda

An injury-marred season makes it hard to know if the Austin native, with a proclivity for donning a ten-gallon hat in postgame pressers, is the next big thing out of Texas or just another flash in the panhandle. On the bright side, Paddack has added a tick to his fastball and even more drop to his curve, making it mirror his four-seamer better and generate both whiffs and strikeouts, and his command remains impeccable. On the less-bright side, his formerly 70-grade changeup didn't seem to tempt quite as many batters this season, as he wasn't able to always throw it with the splitter-ish action that makes the pitch so deadly. Maybe that inconsistency was due to frequent trips to the clinic, as Paddack went on the IL three times: once with an undisclosed medical condition early in the season; then a left oblique strain that kept him out for the month of August; and finally with a UCL sprain that ended his season in September. Paddack received an injection in the elbow and is expected back for the start of spring training; we'll have to wait to learn whether he's a legit urban cowboy or all hat and no cattle.

Emilio Pagán RHP Born: 05/07/91 Age: 31 Bats: L Throws: R Height: 6'2" Weight: 208 lb. Origin: Round 10, 2013 Draft (#297 overall)

YEAR	TEAM	LVL	AGE	W	L	SV	G	GS	IP	H	HR	BB/9	K/9	K	GB%	BABIP	WHIP	ERA	DRA-	WARP	MPH	FB%	Whiff%	CSP
2019	DUR	AAA	28	0	0	2	4	1	6	2	0	6.0	15.0	10	45.5%	.182	1.00	0.00	93	0.1				
2019	TB	MLB	28	4	2	20	66	0	70	45	12	1.7	12.3	96	35.0%	.228	0.83	2.31	74	1.7	94.9	97.9%	35.1%	50.1%
2020	SD	MLB	29	0	1	2	22	0	22	14	4	3.7	9.4	23	30.9%	.196	1.05	4.50	112	0.1	93.7	97.8%	26.7%	46.5%
2021	SD	MLB	30	4	3	0	67	0	63^1	56	16	2.6	9.8	69	23.0%	.253	1.17	4.83	109	0.3	94.2	98.9%	29.8%	55.3%
2022 DC	*SD*	*MLB*	*31*	*3*	*3*	*17*	*67*	*0*	*58*	*50*	*10*	*2.7*	*9.8*	*63*	*27.9%*	*.273*	*1.16*	*3.76*	*94*	*0.4*	*94.3*	*98.5%*	*30.5%*	*52.9%*

Comparables: Junichi Tazawa, Nick Vincent, Sam Dyson

Pagán hasn't looked like the same dominant reliever he was in Tampa Bay, or even in Seattle, but there's an explanation for his struggles in that first year with the Padres: biceps inflammation, plus the slow ramp-up in the pandemic-shortened season, are easy enough culprits to point to. It's trickier to pinpoint what went wrong in his 2021 campaign, although abandoning all his secondaries and relying only on a four-seam and two-seam mix, both of which were ambushed by batters, might have something to do with it. Without plus velocity, there's a very narrow band of successful outcomes here to begin with; without any credible off-speed pitch, it shrinks even more precipitously. It's hard not to scan those falling ground-ball rates like the gentle descent of one of his many fly balls into the seats.

Drew Pomeranz LHP Born: 11/22/88 Age: 33 Bats: R Throws: L Height: 6'5" Weight: 246 lb. Origin: Round 1, 2010 Draft (#5 overall)

YEAR	TEAM	LVL	AGE	W	L	SV	G	GS	IP	H	HR	BB/9	K/9	K	GB%	BABIP	WHIP	ERA	DRA-	WARP	MPH	FB%	Whiff%	CSP
2019	SF	MLB	30	2	9	0	21	17	77^2	89	17	4.2	10.7	92	36.3%	.353	1.61	5.68	97	0.9	91.9	63.7%	23.3%	48.6%
2019	MIL	MLB	30	0	1	2	25	1	26^1	16	4	2.7	15.4	45	46.8%	.279	0.91	2.39	66	0.7	94.4	76.5%	38.0%	48.1%
2020	SD	MLB	31	1	0	4	20	0	18^2	9	1	4.8	14.0	29	47.1%	.242	1.02	1.45	73	0.5	94.6	79.6%	34.7%	47.9%
2021	SD	MLB	32	1	0	0	27	0	25^2	19	2	3.5	10.5	30	45.2%	.283	1.13	1.75	88	0.4	94.1	75.3%	27.4%	55.6%
2022 DC	*SD*	*MLB*	*33*	*2*	*2*	*4*	*59*	*0*	*51.7*	*43*	*7*	*4.2*	*10.5*	*60*	*41.6%*	*.283*	*1.31*	*4.01*	*95*	*0.4*	*93.3*	*71.6%*	*28.3%*	*50.7%*

Comparables: Dave Giusti, Jeremy Affeldt, Tommy John

A.J. Preller loves nothing more than to play his flaming guitar while strapped to the land-cruiser named "S.S. Unconventional Wisdom," so it shouldn't be any more surprising that the Padres handed out a $34M, four-year contract to an injury-prone reliever than it is that Pomeranz wound up on the IL in August with a season-ending torn flexor tendon. Before his early exit, Pomeranz was posting a solid K/9 even while pitching through an injury that had been bothering him since spring training; his velocity was only down a tick, but his curve definitely lost some snap, and he wasn't able to lure batters into chasing as much. The talent is still there—it has always, for Pomeranz, been there—so there's still time for a turnaround for the big lefty before he turns into a Pumpkineranz.

Blake Snell LHP Born: 12/04/92 Age: 29 Bats: L Throws: L Height: 6'4" Weight: 225 lb. Origin: Round 1, 2011 Draft (#52 overall)

YEAR	TEAM	LVL	AGE	W	L	SV	G	GS	IP	H	HR	BB/9	K/9	K	GB%	BABIP	WHIP	ERA	DRA-	WARP	MPH	FB%	Whiff%	CSP
2019	TB	MLB	26	6	8	0	23	23	107	96	14	3.4	12.4	147	37.9%	.343	1.27	4.29	85	2.0	95.8	48.5%	38.4%	42.4%
2020	TB	MLB	27	4	2	0	11	11	50	42	10	3.2	11.3	63	48.4%	.288	1.20	3.24	73	1.3	95.3	50.6%	34.0%	41.3%
2021	SD	MLB	28	7	6	0	27	27	128^2	101	16	4.8	11.9	170	39.0%	.296	1.32	4.20	86	2.1	95.3	52.4%	31.8%	54.8%
2022 DC	*SD*	*MLB*	*29*	*9*	*6*	*0*	*25*	*25*	*132*	*103*	*18*	*4.0*	*11.6*	*170*	*41.0%*	*.282*	*1.23*	*3.42*	*82*	*2.3*	*95.4*	*51.4%*	*33.3%*	*50.4%*

Comparables: Jerry Reuss, Andy Pettitte, Atlee Hammaker

A bottle of Mountain Dew Code Red that gained sentience, the last most baseball fans saw of Snell was his ignominious exit from Tampa Bay. No, not when Kevin Cash pulled him in Game 6 of the 2020 World Series, but later that off-season, when the perpetually impecunious Rays dealt Snell and his remarkably team-friendly contract to San Diego for a passel of okayish prospects. Unfortunately, like the Worst Person You Know Making A Great Point, Snell's first year back on the West Coast went poorly, as some lefty-righty splits issues that had been camouflaged earlier in his career came to the forefront. Snell has a tendency to get too deep in counts against hitters, which is exacerbated when he's facing righties: an 8% walk rate against lefties is just bearable; a 15% walk rate against righties is not. Nevertheless, Snell turned things around and finished strong before a premature exit due to a groin injury, and with a new-look pitching group in San Diego, hopefully can replicate his previous dominance on the Best Coast.

Craig Stammen RHP Born: 03/09/84 Age: 38 Bats: R Throws: R Height: 6'2" Weight: 228 lb. Origin: Round 12, 2005 Draft (#354 overall)

YEAR	TEAM	LVL	AGE	W	L	SV	G	GS	IP	H	HR	BB/9	K/9	K	GB%	BABIP	WHIP	ERA	DRA-	WARP	MPH	FB%	Whiff%	CSP
2019	SD	MLB	35	8	7	4	76	0	82	80	13	1.6	8.0	73	50.6%	.284	1.16	3.29	94	1.1	92.7	87.8%	21.7%	46.6%
2020	SD	MLB	36	4	2	0	24	0	24	27	2	1.5	7.5	20	57.0%	.333	1.29	5.62	82	0.5	91.8	86.7%	24.1%	49.3%
2021	SD	MLB	37	6	3	1	67	4	88^1	79	13	1.3	8.5	83	55.1%	.273	1.04	3.06	81	1.7	91.7	70.0%	24.1%	55.2%
2022 DC	*SD*	*MLB*	*38*	*7*	*3*	*4*	*62*	*3*	*56.7*	*55*	*6*	*1.8*	*7.6*	*47*	*51.9%*	*.294*	*1.17*	*3.37*	*87*	*0.6*	*91.9*	*75.9%*	*23.6%*	*52.6%*

Comparables: Mike Marshall, Dennis Lamp, Tim Worrell

Keats wrote about what he termed "negative capability," a writer's ability to subsume themselves completely in search of the mysterious or divine, "without any irritable reaching after fact or reason." Stammen's negative capability began in 2009, when he surrendered a rotation spot to first overall pick Stephen Strasburg, and has blossomed through a healthy career of relative anonymity, of relief both long and short, and of success despite a gentle breeze of a fastball, leaving fantasy players irritably reaching after both fact and reason. In the most volatile of roles in baseball, Stammen has been an almost maddening constant, and that is all ye know in ADP, and all ye need to know.

Matt Strahm LHP Born: 11/12/91 Age: 30 Bats: R Throws: L Height: 6'2" Weight: 190 lb. Origin: Round 21, 2012 Draft (#643 overall)

YEAR	TEAM	LVL	AGE	W	L	SV	G	GS	IP	H	HR	BB/9	K/9	K	GB%	BABIP	WHIP	ERA	DRA-	WARP	MPH	FB%	Whiff%	CSP
2019	SD	MLB	27	6	11	0	46	16	114^2	121	22	1.7	9.3	118	35.6%	.315	1.25	4.71	98	1.3	91.5	38.3%	23.3%	54.5%
2020	SD	MLB	28	0	1	0	19	0	20^2	14	3	1.7	6.5	15	44.1%	.196	0.87	2.61	99	0.2	93.0	55.8%	22.1%	52.7%
2021	SD	MLB	29	0	1	0	6	1	6^2	15	0	1.4	5.4	4	45.2%	.500	2.40	8.10	105	0.0	93.3	56.6%	20.8%	57.5%
2022 non-DC	*SD*	*MLB*	*30*	*2*	*2*	*0*	*57*	*0*	*50*	*50*	*7*	*2.3*	*9.1*	*50*	*40.7%*	*.311*	*1.28*	*4.42*	*106*	*0.0*	*92.1*	*44.8%*	*22.6%*	*54.5%*

Comparables: James Pazos, Phil Coke, Chris Devenski

If only he'd been born a month or two later, Strahm would be a Capricorn: ruler of the skeletal system, joints and knees. Knees have been a problem for Strahm. Way back when he was a Royals prospect, he tore the patellar tendon in his left knee, and eventually needed surgery to repair it; three years later, the same thing happened, only this time as a Padre, and in his right knee. His offseason surgery kept him from even starting a rehab stint until late July; he made one start in August for the Padres before returning to the IL for good with inflammation in that same knee. When he's healthy, Strahm will likely work out of the bullpen, where his intense, fiery Scorpio nature should help him. But he also possesses an especially deep starter's arsenal of pitches, and Scorpios are known for their ability to transform, after all.

Vince Velasquez RHP Born: 06/07/92 Age: 30 Bats: R Throws: R Height: 6'3" Weight: 212 lb. Origin: Round 2, 2010 Draft (#58 overall)

YEAR	TEAM	LVL	AGE	W	L	SV	G	GS	IP	H	HR	BB/9	K/9	K	GB%	BABIP	WHIP	ERA	DRA-	WARP	MPH	FB%	Whiff%	CSP
2019	PHI	MLB	27	7	8	0	33	23	117^1	120	26	3.3	10.0	130	33.9%	.308	1.39	4.91	97	1.4	94.3	66.6%	25.9%	46.6%
2020	PHI	MLB	28	1	1	0	9	7	34	36	5	4.5	12.2	46	43.2%	.373	1.56	5.56	77	0.8	93.9	57.8%	26.8%	48.1%
2021	CLR	A	29	1	0	0	4	2	7	4	1	1.3	15.4	12	30.8%	.250	0.71	2.57	85	0.1				
2021	LHV	AAA	29	0	0	0	2	2	6^2	2	1	4.1	16.2	12	22.2%	.125	0.75	2.70	87	0.1				
2021	PHI	MLB	29	3	6	0	21	17	81^2	76	17	5.0	9.4	85	34.4%	.282	1.48	5.95	110	0.3	93.3	55.7%	25.5%	54.1%
2021	SD	MLB	29	0	3	0	4	4	12^2	15	6	2.8	11.4	16	17.1%	.310	1.50	8.53	94	0.2	93.5	51.3%	34.2%	55.2%
2022 DC	*FA*	*MLB*	*30*	*6*	*4*	*0*	*48*	*6*	*65*	*58*	*11*	*4.0*	*10.7*	*77*	*34.9%*	*.294*	*1.34*	*4.46*	*105*	*0.2*	*93.6*	*58.3%*	*26.6%*	*51.4%*

Comparables: Carlos Villanueva, Ron Darling, Jason Jennings

The Phillies designated Velasquez for assignment mid-season, and he was picked up by the San Diego Padres, where he somehow pitched even worse than he did in Philadelphia. Velasquez has all the makings of a pitcher who could break out in the right hands—a high-spin, high-rise fastball that gets a lot of swings and misses, set off by secondary pitches that should tunnel well with it...at least in theory. The problem? These pitches end up tunnelling straight to the middle of the plate, often as not. He's got the stuff that he doesn't need to nibble, but he can't scarf down the strike zone in one bite, eigher. Surely there are a few teams still salivating at the idea of turning Velasquez into a quality major-league pitcher; he'll be the sort of free-agent signing that gets called "under the radar." The more fitting descriptor might be "who the hell knows."

Ryan Weathers LHP Born: 12/17/99 Age: 22 Bats: R Throws: L Height: 6'1" Weight: 230 lb. Origin: Round 1, 2018 Draft (#7 overall)

YEAR	TEAM	LVL	AGE	W	L	SV	G	GS	IP	H	HR	BB/9	K/9	K	GB%	BABIP	WHIP	ERA	DRA-	WARP	MPH	FB%	Whiff%	CSP
2019	FW	A	19	3	7	0	22	22	96	101	6	1.7	8.4	90	44.6%	.348	1.24	3.84	111	0.2				
2021	ELP	AAA	21	1	0	0	2	2	10	13	2	1.8	9.9	11	46.7%	.393	1.50	3.60	106	0.0				
2021	SD	MLB	21	4	7	1	30	18	94^2	101	20	2.9	6.8	72	43.6%	.299	1.38	5.32	115	0.1	94.0	62.2%	18.8%	54.5%
2022 DC	*SD*	*MLB*	*22*	*7*	*7*	*0*	*58*	*14*	*82.3*	*86*	*11*	*2.9*	*6.7*	*61*	*43.3%*	*.294*	*1.37*	*4.65*	*112*	*0.0*	*94.0*	*62.2%*	*18.8%*	*54.5%*

Comparables: Kyle Ryan, Brandon Lyon, Doyle Alexander

The Padres' own Doogie Howser—drafted out of high school in 2018, the youngest pitcher in the majors in 2020 and only the second player ever to make his MLB debut in the playoffs—ran into a wall in 2021. Things started off well enough for the youngster, but the warmer the weather got, the worse he pitched, and then the injury-riddled Padres began to tinker. They attempted to shift him back into the rotation, before experimenting with him as the opener and then eventually splitting his time between the bullpen and spot starts. The thing is, Weathers' stuff is more suited to a starter role: He's added some ticks to his fastball at the behest of the Padres, but it naturally hangs out in the low 90s but plays up due to some late ride. He also overhauled his curveball in 2019 to make it more of a slider, but it's still not a strikeout pitch. In the bigs, he's dropped his changeup, formerly a whiff-getting weapon for him in the minors, and has also seen a loss in his formerly excellent command. It might be time to erase the WordPerfect DOS document and start the diary entry over. Doogie never had to deal with this.

Lineouts

Hitters

HITTER	POS	TEAM	LVL	AGE	PA	R	2B	3B	HR	RBI	BB	K	SB	CS	AVG/OBP/SLG	DRC+	BABIP	BRR	FRAA	WARP
Jake Marisnick	CF	SD	MLB	30	54	4	1	0	0	2	2	22	1	0	.188/.264/.208	58	.346	0.4	LF(20): 0.8, CF(3): -0.1	0.0
	CF	CHC	MLB	30	144	17	6	3	5	22	9	43	3	1	.227/.294/.438	81	.293	1.5	CF(49): -1.3	0.3
Joshua Mears	OF	LE	A	20	291	45	10	4	17	48	36	114	10	5	.244/.368/.529	105	.375	-1.2	RF(35): 0.8, CF(16): -1.5, LF(7): 1.1	1.1
Brian O'Grady	OF	ELP	AAA	29	329	44	21	5	15	46	36	85	10	3	.281/.366/.547	107	.346	-0.5	RF(37): 5.6, CF(24): 0.0, LF(9): -2.5	1.6
	OF	SD	MLB	29	61	8	3	0	2	9	8	17	0	0	.157/.267/.333	88	.182	-0.1	RF(10): 0.1, LF(4): 0.1, CF(2): -0.0	0.1
Brandon Valenzuela	C	LE	A	20	378	50	21	3	6	62	44	80	3	2	.307/.389/.444	114	.386	-0.8	C(49): 10.8, 1B(19): 0.8	2.7
	C	FW	A+	20	65	4	1	0	1	7	15	20	1	0	.245/.415/.327	98	.379	-0.2	C(14): -1.4	0.0

Jake Marisnick can turn live balls into outs whether he's in the field or at the plate. That makes him a decent depth option, especially for any team needing to boost its HPP ratio (hair per player). ⚾ **Joshua Mears** put himself on the map this past spring when he hit a 117-mph bullet of a homer off big-league reliever Carlos Estévez. Most prospects require you to squint and imagine what they might be; Mears is already a 32-year-old right fielder batting sixth in the lineup, and it's just a matter of letting the timelines sync back up. ⚾ San Diego signed **Brian O'Grady** to be a versatile bench piece, but even as the big-league team floundered, his name was rarely called. The minor-league masher was courted overseas before opting to sign with the Padres on a guaranteed contract, and might seek that opportunity again after being outrighted off the 40-man this off-season. ⚾ **Brandon Valenzuela** is one of those catching prospects who knows what a strike looks like from behind the plate as well as beside it. Defensively, that and his arm should be enough to make him a major league-caliber player; offensively, well, there's a second step to the process.

Pitchers

PITCHER	TEAM	LVL	AGE	W	L	SV	G	GS	IP	H	HR	BB/9	K/9	K	GB%	BABIP	WHIP	ERA	DRA-	WARP	MPH	FB%	WHF	CSP
Dan Altavilla	SD	MLB	28	0	0	0	2	0	1^{1}	1	1	0.0	13.5	2	0.0%	.000	0.75	6.75	72	0.0	96.1	50.0%	8.3%	64.3%
Joe Beimel	SA	AA	44	1	1	1	17	0	20^{1}	10	1	2.7	7.1	16	33.3%	.173	0.79	2.21	106	0.1				
	ELP	AAA	44	0	1	1	14	1	14^{2}	16	5	3.1	5.5	9	31.9%	.262	1.43	6.14	116	-0.1				
Daniel Camarena	ELP	AAA	28	6	7	1	22	19	83^{1}	83	11	3.3	6.7	62	43.2%	.279	1.37	4.75	114	-0.4				
	SD	MLB	28	0	1	0	6	0	9^{1}	16	2	2.9	6.8	7	43.2%	.400	2.04	9.64	98	0.1	92.8	52.9%	17.0%	60.0%
Miguel Diaz	ELP	AAA	26	0	4	0	14	2	15^{2}	22	4	8.0	12.1	21	38.3%	.419	2.30	7.47	82	0.2				
	SD	MLB	26	3	1	1	25	2	42	31	8	4.1	9.9	46	41.1%	.235	1.19	3.64	94	0.5	94.5	46.2%	20.7%	54.5%
Ethan Elliott	FW	A+	24	2	1	0	12	12	58	43	13	2.0	11.0	71	35.5%	.234	0.97	2.95	85	1.1				
	SA	AA	24	0	1	0	3	3	12^{2}	16	1	4.3	11.4	16	31.6%	.405	1.74	3.55	115	0.0				
Javy Guerra	SD	MLB	25	0	0	0	4	0	3^{2}	4	0	4.9	7.4	3	46.2%	.308	1.64	4.91	113	0.0	98.5	89.4%	16.7%	48.4%
Keone Kela	SD	MLB	28	2	2	0	12	0	10^{2}	11	3	2.5	11.0	13	43.8%	.276	1.31	5.06	87	0.2	95.0	53.2%	22.9%	61.2%
Justin Lange	PAD	ROK	19	0	3	0	9	9	22	18	1	6.1	11.9	29	44.4%	.321	1.50	6.95						
Reggie Lawson	SA	AA	23	0	2	0	4	4	6^{2}	7	2	8.1	12.2	9	25.0%	.278	1.95	9.45	128	-0.1				
James Norwood	ELP	AAA	27	3	4	4	43	0	44^{2}	40	3	4.2	14.3	71	42.9%	.394	1.37	4.43	64	1.2				
	SD	MLB	27	0	0	0	5	0	5	6	0	5.4	5.4	3	47.1%	.353	1.80	0.00	113	0.0	97.5	70.2%	23.4%	52.8%
Nick Ramirez	ELP	AAA	31	2	2	1	35	2	48	46	5	3.4	9.9	53	40.1%	.311	1.33	4.50	89	0.5				
	SD	MLB	31	1	1	0	13	0	20^{1}	23	2	3.1	6.2	14	47.1%	.309	1.48	5.75	105	0.1	89.0	49.7%	21.2%	55.0%
Taylor Williams	ELP	AAA	29	2	0	0	9	0	13^{1}	12	5	5.4	10.8	16	47.1%	.250	1.50	6.75	81	0.2				
	MIA	MLB	29	0	0	0	6	0	6^{1}	9	1	7.1	4.3	3	41.7%	.348	2.21	7.11	127	0.0	93.2	52.3%	19.2%	53.9%
	SD	MLB	29	0	0	0	5	0	5^{1}	3	0	5.1	10.1	6	58.3%	.250	1.13	1.69	111	0.0	94.7	57.3%	34.1%	52.6%
Steven Wilson	ELP	AAA	26	4	0	0	28	0	39^{1}	22	7	3.2	14.4	63	26.9%	.211	0.92	3.43	72	0.8				

Dan Altavilla is built with the same heavy-industry specs of his Steel City hometown: The muscle-bound powerhouse can crank his fastball into the high 90s to pair with a sweeping slider, but struggles to land either in the strike zone. He underwent TJ surgery in June after making just two appearances and should be ready to pitch again late in 2022.

Michel Baez was already ticketed for the bullpen last year due to having just two dominant pitches (a fastball with easy mid-90s velocity and a wiffle ball changeup) and inconsistent mechanics, but losing 2021 and part of 2022 to TJ surgery stamped out any lingering starter dreams. At least he'll have plenty of company in the rehab room as he works back.

The year is 2046. The North Atlantic Islanders are three outs away from winning the Neo-Pangean Series when pitcher Zog-19 experiences a short circuit in the elbow joint. The bullpen door swings open and **Joe Beimel** appears, rested and ready.

On July 8, local product **Daniel Camarena** hit the first grand slam by a reliever since 1985, spurring the Padres to a 9-8 win over Max Scherzer and the Nationals. With the universal DH looming, it's likely he's also hit the last, unless Madison Bumgarner makes a switch to the bullpen over the next season or two.

José Castillo's past three seasons were knocked out by a variety of injuries, the most recent and serious being the TJ surgery that will keep him out until mid-2022. His fastball-slider combo should make him relatively immune to the three-batter rule that didn't exist the last time he pitched regularly.

Back in 2016, the Padres were stuffing their pockets with young talent like a pair of backpackers at the free hotel breakfast. Five years later, **Miguel Diaz** is still largely the player he was then—armed with a big fastball, a hard slider and shaky command. As nice as it is to be forever young, perhaps a new team can unlock the free agent's potential.

A pitchability lefty with subpar velocity and plus command in the vein of former Padre Nick Margevicius, **Ethan Elliott** earned MLB Pipeline's Pitcher of the Year award for the Padres, which says more about the state of San Diego's system than it does about the former Division II senior sign's ceiling.

Not the **Javy Guerra** you're thinking of, the converted infielder edition missed most of the season with a sprained UCL, but when he's healthy he brings a Graterol-esque turbo sinker that scrapes triple digits along with a hard, tight slider. As is typical for this profile, command is an issue, and he's out of options, so any tweaks will have to be figured out at the big-league level.

After evading the reaper with a similar injury in 2020, **Keona Kela** wound up having to pay the TJ piper in 2021, going under the knife in late May. Kela's contract with the Padres had an $800K club option that kicked in if he had TJ surgery, so it'll be the Padres who determine if the California native returns to San Diego or attempts to catch on with a new team.

Justin Lange's biography so far is bookended by two of the most significant events in modern US history: born on 9/11, and drafted in the midst of a pandemic. At a maxed-out 6'4" frame with a fastball that can touch triple digits, he'll need to refine his secondaries and command, which, for a pitcher who represents the new America, is a much older challenge.

Reggie Lawson tantalizes with a three-pitch mix headlined by a power swing-and-miss curve, along with a fastball with late life and a changeup that has flashed plus, but has lost the better part of three years to elbow troubles. Once ticketed as a mid-rotation pitcher, he might be headed for the bullpen to accelerate his timeline to the majors.

A longtime Cubs farmhand, **James Norwood** was traded to the Padres for fellow hard-thrower/30-control reliever Dauris Valdez in early April. He rode the El Paso-San Diego express train a fair amount this season, blowing away batters in Triple-A with his big fastball but failing to command his slider often enough to land consistent work in the bigs.

Signed as a bounce-back candidate in the off-season, **Nick Ramirez** instead spent 2021 caroming between San Diego and El Paso and struggling with rotator cuff inflammation that cost him a tick on his fastball. He'll look to rebound elsewhere next season.

A.J. Preller, while checking out his seven-player trade with Jerry Dipoto, passed the impulse section and tossed in **Taylor Williams**—then a late-inning arm in Seattle's bullpen with a mid-90s fastball and wicked slider—in exchange for prospect Matt Brash. A year later, WIlliams has been designated for assignment twice, and Brash took a big step forward for the M's. Always resist the impulse buy section.

The rare six-year senior (he did fine in his classes, less fine with his ligaments), 95-and-a-slider guy **Steven Wilson** was promoted aggressively by the Padres to make up for lost time, only to get hurt again just as the team could have really used him.

SAN FRANCISCO GIANTS

Essay by Susan Slusser

Player comments by Jon Hegglund and BP staff

As spring training for the 2021 season drew to a close, the San Francisco Giants appeared to be MLB's primary afterthought. After all, they shared a division with the World Champion Dodgers and the Offseason Champion Padres, both of whom had spent the winter greedily stocking their respective larders. On the other end, the Rockies remained the Rockies, and the Diamondbacks were spinning their wheels. The Giants were just . . . there. PECOTA projected the team to win 75 games, and nearly every other system and pundit outside the Bay Area arrived at a similar number. There was a sense that the team was improving, fortifying its foundations, but, on the surface, it was all the old heroes playing their usual parts.

Then, the season started, and those same old heroes set upon the rest of the league like conquerors. The starting rotation, stocked with injury-prone, buy-low veterans, was both lucky and good, many of those veterans posting career-best numbers over a surprisingly healthy number of innings. The relatively anonymous bullpen didn't strike batters out, but the Giants' relievers consistently got ahead in the count, controlled the quality of contact and rarely made mistakes. The offense, particularly the tricenarian infield of Brandon Belt, Brandon Crawford, Evan Longoria and Buster Posey, sipped from the same fountain of youth, posting the unlikeliest collection of late-career revivals the game may have ever seen.

Regression never arrived, and these afterthought Giants outpaced the Dodgers to win the NL West. It's repetitive to say, and hackneyed in other situations, but we're rarely treated to witness a team dispel so much prognostication and orthodoxy. The 2021 San Francisco Giants are the exception that disproves the rule, a giant asterisk in the way we evaluate how teams are built and managed. They should not have been, and they were.

When a team expected to do little up and wins a franchise-record 107 games, surely there are metrics that explain the feat, especially when the club in question is the Farhan Zaidi-led Giants. San Francisco's president of baseball operations is known for his MIT background and super-duper numbers

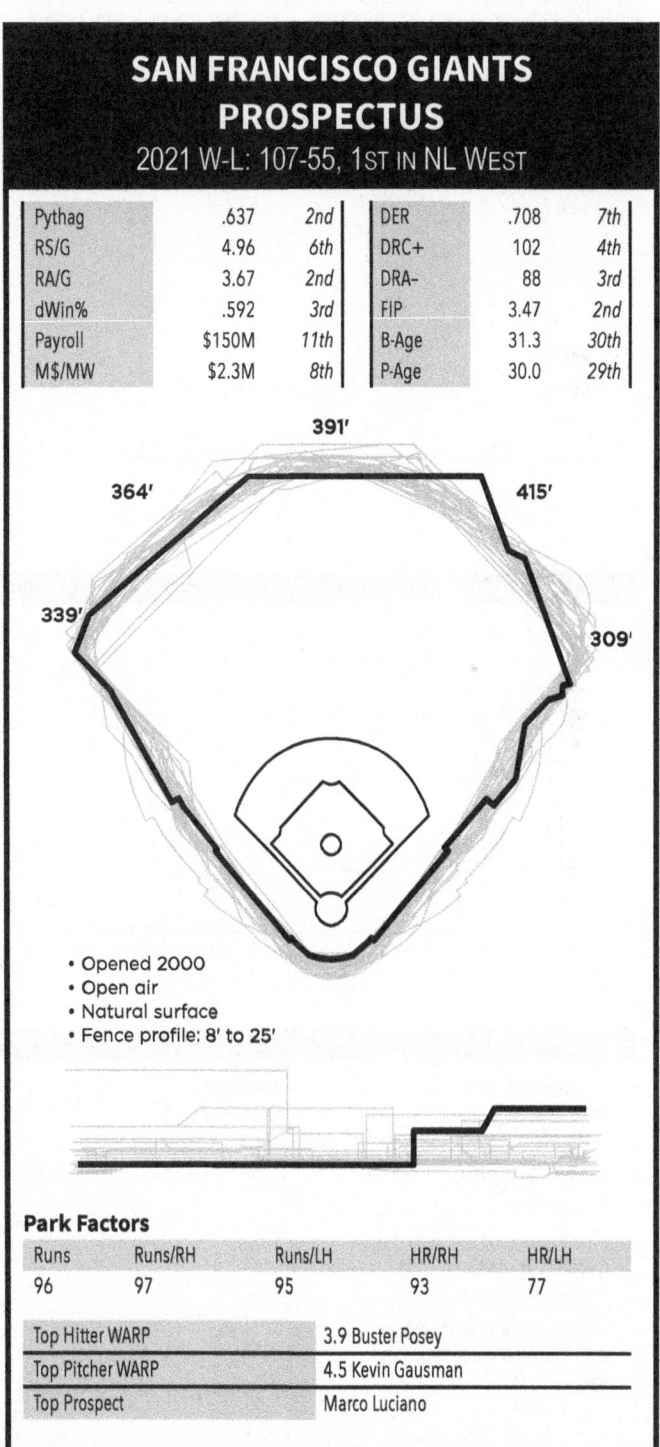

SAN FRANCISCO GIANTS PROSPECTUS

2021 W-L: 107-55, 1st in NL West

Pythag	.637	*2nd*	DER	.708	*7th*
RS/G	4.96	*6th*	DRC+	102	*4th*
RA/G	3.67	*2nd*	DRA-	88	*3rd*
dWin%	.592	*3rd*	FIP	3.47	*2nd*
Payroll	$150M	*11th*	B-Age	31.3	*30th*
M$/MW	$2.3M	*8th*	P-Age	30.0	*29th*

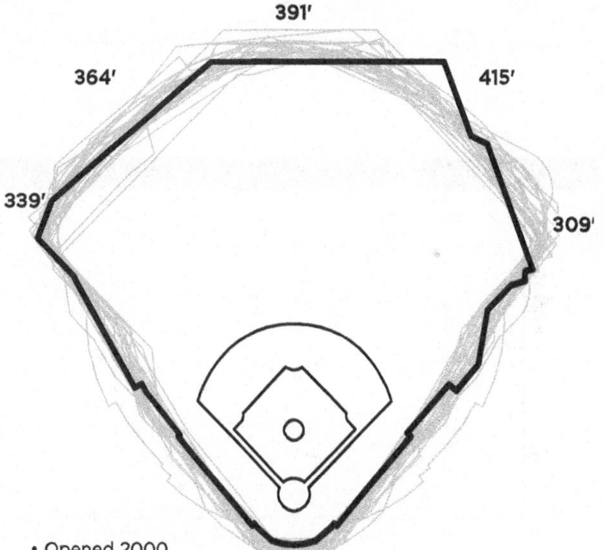

- Opened 2000
- Open air
- Natural surface
- Fence profile: 8' to 25'

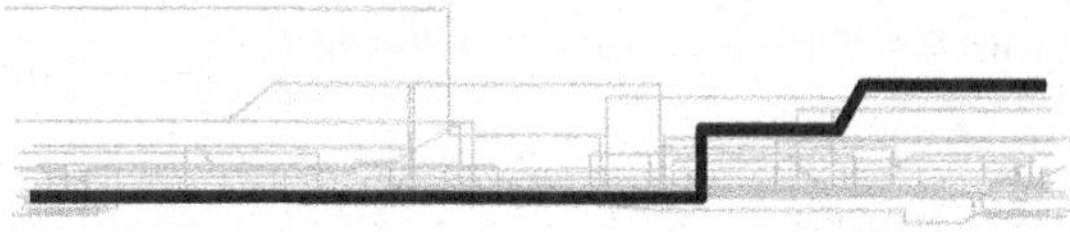

Park Factors

Runs	Runs/RH	Runs/LH	HR/RH	HR/LH
96	97	95	93	77

Top Hitter WARP	3.9 Buster Posey
Top Pitcher WARP	4.5 Kevin Gausman
Top Prospect	Marco Luciano

Payroll History (in millions)

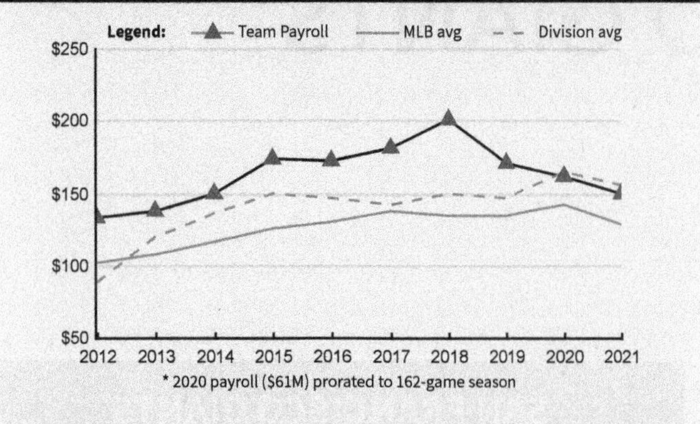

Future Commitments (in millions)

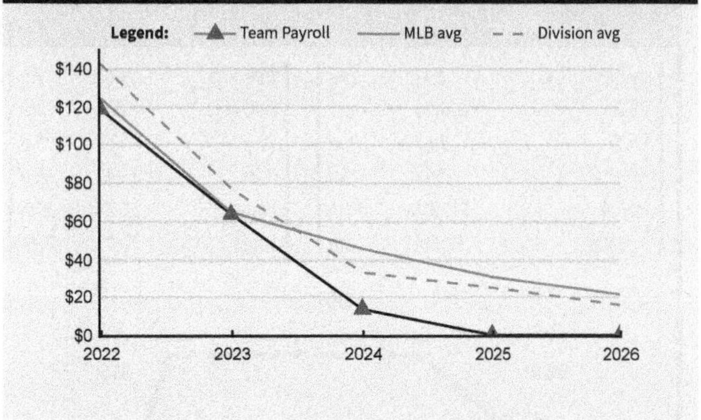

Farm System Ranking

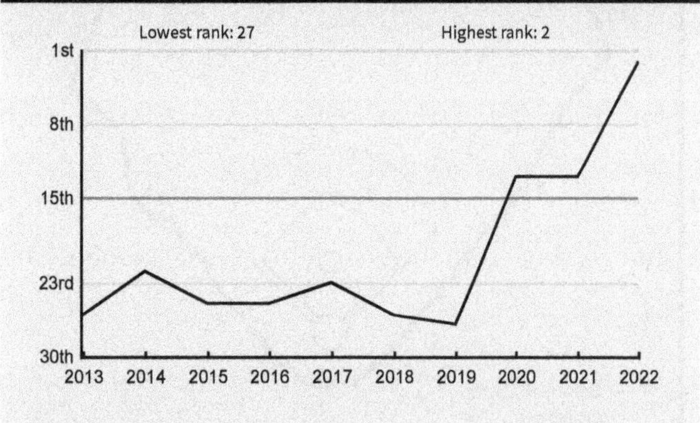

Personnel

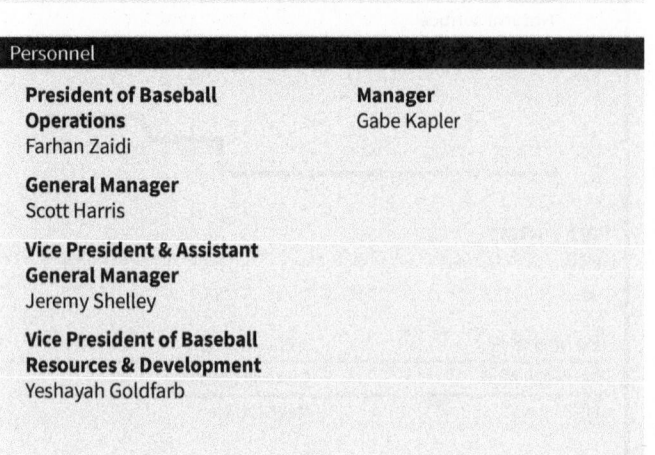

President of Baseball Operations
Farhan Zaidi

General Manager
Scott Harris

Vice President & Assistant General Manager
Jeremy Shelley

Vice President of Baseball Resources & Development
Yeshayah Goldfarb

Manager
Gabe Kapler

savvy, and yet he points to something more narrative in nature than you normally see from the analytics crowd: Chemistry.

Zaidi and manager Gabe Kapler—also very much a proponent of data—repeatedly cited more squishy concepts such as chemistry, intangibles and unselfishness for helping the 2021 Giants surpass all projections.

"I don't want to talk about this like it's some mystical thing that causes us to way outperform our ability level—because, at the end of the day, we did outperform preseason expectations by a significant margin," Zaidi told Baseball Prospectus. "Everybody wants to find an explanation for it, and team culture and chemistry were a big part of it, but I also think people underestimated how talented our players are and how good of a job Kap and the coaching staff did of putting them in good position to succeed. It was a combination of tangible and intangible factors."

Sure, there were some obvious traditional stats that helped give San Francisco a boost in winning the NL West. The most homers in the National League, a franchise-record 241, and a 3.01 team ERA, second in the majors behind Los Angeles, including a big-league-best 2.99 mark from the bullpen.

Even within those big numbers, though, there were clues to the all-for-one aspect that characterized the Giants: a franchise-record 17 players hit at least five home runs, and the team set a major-league record with 18 pinch-hit homers. The bench was as much a factor in the Giants' success as any other part of the club.

"We talk a lot about the cultural benefits of having a roster that works like that," Zaidi said. "There's something very egalitarian about having 26 guys who all believe they can impact a game and win the game on a given day. And I think we really had that. Other than, basically, the four starting pitchers who weren't going to be available on the given day, everybody else on the roster showed up, whether they were starting or not and no matter where they ranked in the bullpen pecking order, and thought, 'I have a chance to be the guy who wins the game for us today.' And I think that matters a lot.

"When the team operates that way, and those expectations are created, I just think it creates a more conducive atmosphere for guys to root for each other."

During the rise of advanced metrics, some baseball executives began to question the notion of chemistry, insisting that it was created by success, not the other way around. If it can't be quantified, how can it be a real factor? Intangibles are just that: something that cannot be measured. And yet, here's a major player in the analytics world explaining that, yes, a team's ethos is very much a priority.

The positive vibes were established early—many of the Giants noted that they had a "no dicks policy"—and there were outward signs. When Donovan Solano pinch hit for fellow infielder Tommy La Stella, the two hugged. Outfielder

LaMonte Wade Jr., one of the top feel-good stories of the team's season, was always the player rooting the most visibly for whichever player took over for him. Reliever Jarlin García thanked Kapler every time the manager took the ball from him. All season long, even the most veteran players remarked on how special the group was, how selfless and cohesive.

Some of that was fostered by the everyone's-involved platoon system. The Giants regularly used platoons at five or six spots, and they pinch-hit liberally; their 393 pinch-hitting appearances led the majors by 66. The "pinch-hitting penalty," a Bill James discovery that hitters tend to perform worse when put into the game cold, was another old sabermetric truism that Zaidi and Kapler refused to follow blindly.

La Stella, signed to a three-year deal before the season, was instrumental, Zaidi said, explaining that mixing and matching to that extent "takes real buy-in from players, and a great example of that is Tommy, who is the consummate teammate and professional, a guy who will hit anywhere in the order, who will get pinch-hit for and be on the top step cheering on his teammate, will move positions during a game and be good with it.

"The cultural impact of having a player like that, and the symbolism of having the first three-year deal we've signed going to a player like him, who really puts the team first, that was important. Tommy's really the prototypical example of the sort of mentality and character we felt this team needed to embody to reach its potential."

Even with the obvious platoons and pinch-hit situations, Kapler made it clear he wasn't a push-button manager; he'd go against the grain on occasion, particularly when it either exhibited his confidence in a player coming off a poor game or showed his willingness to reward a player's strong recent play by using him in a spot he normally would not see action.

"Some of those decisions didn't always line up the X's and O's," Zaidi said. "Kap knew when to play matchups by the book and when a player needed that extra boost or wasn't in a particularly good headspace to take on an added challenge.

"You don't want to get too far away from that bread and butter with the matchups. Gabe showed a keen sense for how players were feeling, and I think they appreciate that, that it's not just a turnkey operation, there's judgment and feel involved. That makes everybody feel a little bit more like none of this is preordained or predetermined. There's a very organic element to how every game plays out, and everyone will contribute."

So, how might a front office go about ensuring a strong team bond? Zaidi, the rest of the talent evaluators and the Giants' coaching staff do their due diligence about a player's character, again a subjective area, when making acquisitions. Even better: direct knowledge of a player from a previous stop, à la Zaidi adding former Dodgers starter Alex Wood, and former Reds within the organization recommending backup catcher Curt Casali, both major contributors.

The staff then tries to tailor workouts and rest and routines around individual preferences. Giants veterans, particularly Posey and Crawford, benefited from major input into their game workload coupled with determining the most efficient use of their preparation time before games. Posey, for instance, did his hitting work in the batting cage, never on the field, in order to cut down on the demands on his body.

The team also emphasizes mental health, with mental-healthcare specialists at the major-league and minor-league levels. The Giants hired their former minor-league outfielder, Drew Robinson, to help those efforts; Robinson survived a suicide attempt in 2020 that cost him an eye. Kapler took a special interest in destigmatizing mental illness, promoting open communication and willingness to demonstrate vulnerability, which helped to set a welcoming tone for all.

"One of the things that even the pandemic season revealed to us, and I think to other teams as well, is that the mental aspects of the game are particularly challenging, and baseball and mental skills are an area that we really want to invest in," Zaidi said. "I think what we've learned over the last couple years is that, in some ways, we may have been a little bit too targeted with our view of what athletes, and what baseball players, in particular, need—which isn't just how do you get yourself in a positive mental state to compete and succeed on the baseball field, but how do you get yourself in a positive mental state, period? And the rest will follow from that."

Like most teams following the shortened 2020 season, the Giants encountered a sizable number of injuries, and they wound up having to make 376 transactions, third-most in the majors behind the Mets and Blue Jays. Many of these moves were made with an eye toward cohesion, including the two deals made at the trade deadline: general manager Scott Harris knew Kris Bryant well from his time with the Cubs, and the Giants also welcomed back left-handed reliever Tony Watson, a popular member of the team during his first stint with San Francisco. Moving forward, it's a good guess that some free-agent and trade acquisitions will have ties to Zaidi, Kapler or Harris.

Six relievers made at least 50 appearances for the Giants last year, just the second time that's happened with any team in MLB history (also the 2014 Mariners), while the rotation had five members who made at least 20 starts, which, given the number of injuries San Francisco endured and the track record for durability among its starters, was surprising.

One injury in the rotation wound up having a major impact, and, in a strange way, exemplified the 2021 Giants. Aaron Sanchez began the year as another of Zaidi's reclamation projects, having struggled since his breakout year in 2016. Despite sitting out the 2020 season, the right-hander put together a strong April, with a 2.22 ERA and a .193 average against, and while his velocity was well below what teams had seen in his 97–98 mph workouts over the winter, his results helped push 24-year-old Logan Webb into a bullpen role after Webb got off to a slow start and had some minor arm issues.

Sanchez incurred a biceps injury in early May, however, putting Webb back into the rotation. Webb emerged as the team's top starter in the second half, going 7-0 with a 2.71 ERA, he drew the Game 1 start in the Division Series against the Dodgers, and he is poised to be the staff ace going into 2022.

When Sanchez came back from his injury in late July, he made one start and two appearances out of the bullpen, with no way to wedge his way back into the rotation. Sanchez had been clear that he'd signed with the team to start, a bullpen spot was going to be tough for a pitcher coming off injuries to adjust to, and he just was not a fit for the do-whatever-role-is-necessary Giants. They released him in early August, just as Webb was blossoming.

"It became a challenge when Logan Webb really emerged during Aaron's time on the IL," Zaidi said. "We had a full rotation and, for him, it wasn't that easy to go to the pen, physically. It was harder for him to get ramped up to get in games based on all he had come through physically to get back to the big leagues. Ultimately, it felt like the fairest thing to do was to release him."

Recreating the Giants' superb team chemistry will be a challenge, especially with numerous free agents—and the biggest news of all, Posey's retirement. Posey's leadership on both sides of the ball was instrumental, his work with the pitching staff phenomenal, his cool and calm permeated the clubhouse. Entering the season, more than one Giants official said, had Posey not sat out in 2020, the team would have made the playoffs instead of missing by one game. Replacing him on the field after an All-Star season will be difficult; in the clubhouse, near impossible.

San Francisco is gaining a reputation, though, as a fun spot to play, and one where veterans, especially pitchers, can rebound from injuries or underperformance.

"You hope to have a situation where your good chemistry kind of perpetuates itself, where, by word of mouth, other players around the game hear this was a great clubhouse," Zaidi said. "The coaching staff gets the most out of their players, the manager communicates and is going to shoot you straight, and you'll have a voice. I think it helps now to have the selling point of people knowing we had a great clubhouse, we had guys that really enjoyed playing with each other."

—*Susan Slusser covers the Giants for the* San Francisco Chronicle.

Hitters

Patrick Bailey C Born: 05/29/99 Age: 23 Bats: S Throws: R Height: 6'1" Weight: 210 lb. Origin: Round 1, 2020 Draft (#13 overall)

YEAR	TEAM	LVL	AGE	PA	R	2B	3B	HR	RBI	BB	K	SB	CS	Whiff%	AVG/OBP/SLG	DRC+	BABIP	BRR	FRAA	WARP
2021	SJ	A	22	207	45	16	0	7	24	28	47	1	1		.322/.415/.531	122	.403	0.8	C(39): 18.6	3.0
2021	EUG	A+	22	155	13	9	0	2	15	18	43	6	0		.185/.290/.296	84	.256	0.8	C(25): 6.3, 1B(4): -0.0	0.8
2022 non-DC	*SF*	*MLB*	*23*	*251*	*21*	*11*	*0*	*3*	*21*	*21*	*76*	*2*	*1*	*33.6%*	*.213/.286/.321*	*65*	*.303*	*-0.1*	*C 7, 1B 0*	*0.7*

Comparables: Francisco Cervelli, Bruce Maxwell, Martín Maldonado

YEAR	TEAM	P. COUNT	FRM RUNS	BLK RUNS	THRW RUNS	TOT RUNS
2021	EUG	3744	3.5	0.1	1.6	5.3
2021	SJ	5449	17.4	0.6	0.4	18.4
2022	*SF*	*6956*	*1.7*	*0.3*	*0.3*	*2.4*

If the possibility of two blue-chip catching prospects in the Giants system keeps you up at night, rest easy. It's true that both Bailey and Joey Bart have enough in both bat and defense to find paths to a major-league career. At the moment, Bailey is a couple of levels and years behind Bart, but the talent gap is not that far off. Bart is obviously closer to a regular role, having tasted the majors in both '20 and '21 and poised to follow the retiring Buster Posey, but Bailey is a switch-hitter and has the advantage of better plate discipline. Bart may have the edge on defense, but both are excellent behind the dish. And if you have in your mind a Will Smith/Keibert Ruiz type of situation, look at what Ruiz netted the Dodgers at the 2021 deadline and you'll realize that the Giants should be perfectly happy to take their time writing the first post-Posey chapter of the team's catching chronicles.

★ ★ ★ *2022 Top 101 Prospect* **#53** ★ ★ ★

Joey Bart C Born: 12/15/96 Age: 25 Bats: R Throws: R Height: 6'2" Weight: 238 lb. Origin: Round 1, 2018 Draft (#2 overall)

YEAR	TEAM	LVL	AGE	PA	R	2B	3B	HR	RBI	BB	K	SB	CS	Whiff%	AVG/OBP/SLG	DRC+	BABIP	BRR	FRAA	WARP
2019	SJ	A+	22	251	37	10	2	12	37	14	50	5	2		.265/.315/.479	121	.291	0.5	C(50): -1.7	1.3
2019	RIC	AA	22	87	9	4	1	4	11	7	21	0	2		.316/.368/.544	104	.382	-1.0	C(15): 0.4	0.3
2020	SF	MLB	23	111	15	5	2	0	7	3	41	0	0	34.5%	.233/.288/.320	62	.387	-0.1	C(32): 2.8	0.1
2021	SAC	AAA	24	279	37	15	0	10	46	21	82	0	0		.294/.358/.472	92	.398	-1.5	C(63): 8.8	1.4
2021	SF	MLB	24	6	1	0	0	0	1	0	2	0	0	33.3%	.333/.333/.333	96	.500	0.1	C(1): -0.1	0.0
2022 DC	*SF*	*MLB*	*25*	*315*	*34*	*13*	*1*	*9*	*39*	*17*	*101*	*1*	*1*	*31.8%*	*.225/.281/.377*	*75*	*.309*	*-0.2*	*C 6*	*1.1*

Comparables: Chris Iannetta, Yasmani Grandal, Buster Posey

YEAR	TEAM	P. COUNT	FRM RUNS	BLK RUNS	THRW RUNS	TOT RUNS
2019	RIC	2187	0.7	0.0	0.0	0.7
2019	SJ	7279	-2.2		1.4	-0.8
2019	SCO	1246			0.0	0.0
2020	SF	4088	2.0	0.0	0.5	2.6
2021	SF	140	0.0	0.0	0.0	0.0
2021	SAC	9190	2.5	0.0	2.5	5.1
2022	*SF*	*12025*	*5.2*	*0.3*	*0.2*	*5.7*

Amid the breathless and swirling rumors of the trade deadline, one that momentarily bobbed to the top of Twitter feeds was that Joey Bart had been the principal return to the Cubs for Kris Bryant. While this was quickly debunked, the initial response from many across the Twittersphere was telling: "Well, that seems steep for a rental, but ... it's not the end of the world." No doubt the resurgence of Buster Posey had something to do with the loosened prospect hug on Bart, and the young catcher's rushed and inauspicious 2020 Giants debut didn't help matters. Ultimately, though, a year spent in Sacramento, out of the bright lights, was probably just fine. The top-line hitting numbers don't look great, the power hasn't quite shown up, and the swing-and-miss is an ongoing concern—but it's worth noting that Bart battled through some injuries in 2021. Now, with the surprising retirement of Posey, it seems the starting job by the Bay will be ready whenever Bart is.

Brandon Belt 1B

Born: 04/20/88 Age: 34 Bats: L Throws: L Height: 6'3" Weight: 231 lb. Origin: Round 5, 2009 Draft (#147 overall)

YEAR	TEAM	LVL	AGE	PA	R	2B	3B	HR	RBI	BB	K	SB	CS	Whiff%	AVG/OBP/SLG	DRC+	BABIP	BRR	FRAA	WARP
2019	SF	MLB	31	616	76	32	3	17	57	83	127	4	3	22.8%	.234/.339/.403	99	.275	-2.0	1B(144): 8.1, LF(14): -0.7, RF(1): -0.1	2.2
2020	SF	MLB	32	179	25	13	1	9	30	30	36	0	0	23.6%	.309/.425/.591	128	.356	0.2	1B(47): 1.0	1.1
2021	SF	MLB	33	381	65	14	2	29	59	48	103	3	2	28.0%	.274/.378/.597	145	.309	-1.3	1B(93): -0.4	2.8
2022 DC	*SF*	*MLB*	*34*	*546*	*75*	*24*	*2*	*17*	*74*	*72*	*133*	*3*	*2*	*26.7%*	*.230/.340/.404*	*105*	*.285*	*-0.3*	*1B 1*	*1.4*

Comparables: Tony Clark, Tino Martinez, John Olerud

Up until 2020, Belt was a hard-luck Giant. His left-handed, line-drive profile couldn't have found a worse home than Oracle Park, and his long list of injuries—most of the unlucky, freak variety—kept him off the field far too much. And while the poor injury luck hasn't completely left Belt behind, the ballpark changes (including the boarding up of the right-field open archways for 2020 and the start of 2021) helped let Belt's power loose. But it wasn't just the environmental changes. Belt, along with many of his teammates, became a barrel monster, selling out for pull power a bit more than he had in the past, while maintaining his discerning eye. Yet, once again, he missed a good chunk of the season, most frustratingly due to a broken thumb from a rogue bunt attempt that sidelined him for the postseason. But even as bad luck followed him around like Pigpen's cloud of dirt, Belt's hitting in 2021 was more pristine than ever. While he was on the field, he amassed a DRC+ that trailed only Juan Soto in the NL. In the clubhouse, his tongue-in-cheek braggadocio earned Belt the symbolic role of team captain, earning an ad hoc, electrical tape "C" on his jersey one day (a day in which he sent a big fly into McCovey Cove). He will return to the helm for at least a year, having accepted a qualifying offer from the club for 2022. *El no es un marinero, es el capitán, el capitán.*

Hunter Bishop OF

Born: 06/25/98 Age: 24 Bats: L Throws: R Height: 6'5" Weight: 210 lb. Origin: Round 1, 2019 Draft (#10 overall)

YEAR	TEAM	LVL	AGE	PA	R	2B	3B	HR	RBI	BB	K	SB	CS	Whiff%	AVG/OBP/SLG	DRC+	BABIP	BRR	FRAA	WARP
2019	GIO	ROK	21	29	4	3	0	1	3	9	11	2	0		.250/.483/.550		.500			
2019	SK	SS	21	117	21	1	1	4	9	29	28	5	2		.224/.427/.400		.278			
2021	GNTB	ROK	23	32	5	1	0	0	3	5	10	1	1		.160/.313/.200		.250			
2022 non-DC	*SF*	*MLB*	*24*	*251*	*18*	*10*	*1*	*2*	*19*	*19*	*102*	*4*	*2*	*39.6%*	*.175/.251/.268*	*41*	*.303*	*0.3*	*CF 0, LF 0*	*-1.0*

Comparables: Scott Cousins, Matt Angle, Cord Phelps

Maybe Bishop is just setting us up for that feel-good, post-hype, Giants-style narrative turn. If so, dude, no need to lay the adversity on so thick: after an uneven-but-intriguing 2019 in rookie and Low-A ball, the erstwhile Sun Devil emerged from the 2020 pause into big hopes and dreams for '21. A nagging shoulder injury meant only 24 plate appearances outside of the complex, and these were not terribly encouraging. Bishop's likely ticket to a major-league role rests on his ability to play center field, as this defensive profile would put less pressure on the hitting, while the walks, power and speed remain a solid foundation—particularly in an era when we recognize that a .220 average is no barrier to major-league relevance. Still only 23, Bishop could use one good, healthy year at the upper levels before he makes his debut as a rook. Until then, he's just another pawn on the Giants' crowded prospect board.

Curt Casali C

Born: 11/09/88 Age: 33 Bats: R Throws: R Height: 6'2" Weight: 220 lb. Origin: Round 10, 2011 Draft (#317 overall)

YEAR	TEAM	LVL	AGE	PA	R	2B	3B	HR	RBI	BB	K	SB	CS	Whiff%	AVG/OBP/SLG	DRC+	BABIP	BRR	FRAA	WARP
2019	CIN	MLB	30	236	24	9	0	8	32	25	59	0	0	22.4%	.251/.331/.411	92	.308	0.1	C(67): 3.7, 1B(4): 0.0	1.2
2020	CIN	MLB	31	93	10	3	0	6	8	14	29	2	0	28.2%	.224/.366/.500	108	.268	-0.5	C(29): 1.5	0.5
2021	SF	MLB	32	231	20	11	1	5	26	26	66	0	0	29.7%	.210/.313/.350	82	.287	-1.8	C(64): 0.5	0.3
2022 DC	*SF*	*MLB*	*33*	*306*	*34*	*12*	*0*	*6*	*31*	*33*	*85*	*0*	*1*	*28.2%*	*.206/.304/.330*	*75*	*.274*	*-0.5*	*C -1*	*0.2*

Comparables: Chris Gimenez, Humberto Quintero, Drew Butera

YEAR	TEAM	P. COUNT	FRM RUNS	BLK RUNS	THRW RUNS	TOT RUNS
2019	CIN	8395	2.8	0.3	0.6	3.7
2020	CIN	3610	1.6	0.0	0.0	1.6
2021	SF	7929	1.5	-0.2	0.0	1.2
2022	*SF*	*12025*	*-0.5*	*-0.6*	*0.0*	*-1.1*

On a one-year contract, Casali's 2021 brief was short and sweet: back up Buster Posey, and back up Joey Bart if Posey is unable to fulfill his duties. If the former, then Posey stayed healthy, and if the latter, then the Giants probably aren't in contention and Casali can do some mentoring work for Bart on the side. As it turned out, Plan A worked, even better than anyone had hoped—and the suddenly spry Posey kept Casali firmly in his caddying role (albeit one in which he caught shutouts in four consecutive starts in the middle of the season). The backup catcher market is littered with decent-defense, no-bat options, so Casali stands out by his ability to call a good game and take a walk or hit a homer now and then.

Brandon Crawford SS

Born: 01/21/87 Age: 35 Bats: L Throws: R Height: 6'1" Weight: 223 lb. Origin: Round 4, 2008 Draft (#117 overall)

YEAR	TEAM	LVL	AGE	PA	R	2B	3B	HR	RBI	BB	K	SB	CS	Whiff%	AVG/OBP/SLG	DRC+	BABIP	BRR	FRAA	WARP
2019	SF	MLB	32	560	58	24	2	11	59	53	117	3	2	28.3%	.228/.304/.350	82	.274	-3.8	SS(142): 1.3	0.5
2020	SF	MLB	33	193	26	12	0	8	28	15	47	1	2	31.6%	.256/.326/.465	94	.303	0.1	SS(53): 2.1	0.6
2021	SF	MLB	34	549	79	30	3	24	90	56	105	11	3	29.3%	.298/.373/.522	122	.334	-2.1	SS(135): 3.2	3.6
2022 DC	*SF*	*MLB*	*35*	*552*	*67*	*26*	*2*	*13*	*71*	*54*	*115*	*6*	*3*	*29.6%*	*.248/.328/.390*	*97*	*.299*	*-0.2*	*SS 1*	*1.9*

Comparables: Omar Vizquel, Don Kessinger, Jimmy Rollins

For all the insights of advanced baseball analytics, the precise accounting of causation remains a shadowy outline in a fog thicker than a late-summer morning in the Outer Sunset. Sure, for plenty of baseball outcomes, we can see the relevant inputs pretty clearly. For absolutely unexpected, even unfathomable events, such as Crawford's out-of-nowhere late-career breakout, we can point to various reasons, but none of them approach the sum of this unaccountable season. Let's try to add them up: a remodeled stance and swing, a reconfigured Oracle Park, a brief 2020 season to preserve an aging body. The most optimistic tallying of those reasons might have projected Crawford at what? Ten percent better than his recent career performances? Even that would seem foolhardy, given that all signs were pointing to a plate decline for the 34-year-old. In no scenario could we have seen a DRC+ nearly 15% better than his career best and more than 30% better than his career average. In no possible world could we have forecast his first full season with a walk rate above 10% and a strikeout rate below 20. In no reckless, unhinged fantasy could we have imagined daily, earnest chants of "M! V! P!" each time he came to the plate at Oracle Park in September. Perhaps the Giants inked Crawford to a mid-season two-year extension not just to enjoy the fruits of his late-career bloom but also to pursue further research on the brain-teasing puzzle of how he went from a contract albatross in decline to a sign-at-all-costs centerpiece within the space of a season.

Jaylin Davis OF

Born: 07/01/94 Age: 28 Bats: R Throws: R Height: 5'11" Weight: 205 lb. Origin: Round 24, 2015 Draft (#710 overall)

YEAR	TEAM	LVL	AGE	PA	R	2B	3B	HR	RBI	BB	K	SB	CS	Whiff%	AVG/OBP/SLG	DRC+	BABIP	BRR	FRAA	WARP
2019	PNS	AA	24	251	34	9	0	10	25	36	64	7	3		.274/.382/.458	129	.345	0.9	RF(42): -2.7, LF(8): 0.8, CF(4): 0.5	1.7
2019	ROC	AAA	24	173	39	11	1	15	42	15	46	2	0		.331/.405/.708	121	.387	0.3	RF(32): 3.2, CF(6): 0.4	1.3
2019	SAC	AAA	24	117	21	6	0	10	27	14	28	1	1		.333/.419/.686	114	.375	0.5	RF(16): 2.9, CF(7): 0.6, LF(4): -0.3	0.9
2019	SF	MLB	24	47	2	0	0	1	3	3	11	1	2	43.5%	.167/.255/.238	90	.200	-0.8	RF(15): -0.4	0.0
2020	SF	MLB	25	12	2	0	0	1	1	0	6	0	0	44.4%	.167/.167/.417	84	.200	-0.1	RF(4): 0.4	0.0
2021	SAC	AAA	26	186	34	7	2	11	34	17	59	3	1		.230/.317/.503	91	.277	2.5	RF(19): -2.4, LF(11): 2.9, CF(7): 1.3	0.8
2021	SF	MLB	26	9	1	1	0	0	0	0	1	0	0	10.0%	.111/.111/.222	92	.125		LF(2): -0.1, RF(1): 1.0	0.1
2022 DC	*SF*	*MLB*	*27*	*63*	*7*	*2*	*0*	*2*	*8*	*4*	*21*	*0*	*0*	*38.3%*	*.225/.295/.411*	*89*	*.306*	*0.0*	*RF 0, LF 0*	*0.1*

Comparables: Lane Adams, John Mayberry Jr., Brett Carroll

As 2019 recedes further into the historical archive, the Triple-A breakouts from that season seem more and more like anomalies whose surges depended upon a particularly hopped-up baseball. It would be easy to file Davis in that folder, as his handful of major-league plate appearances since that ball-crazed season have shown a frustrating tendency toward the worst of the three true outcomes. In fairness to Davis, he never really got a chance to share the improbable 2021 success of the Rufs, Wades, Duggars—largely because injuries to his knee and hamstring sent him on multiple IL trips while the big-league squad was sprinting toward glory. At 27, Davis finds himself with limited opportunities left to get healthy, tamp down the Ks and rediscover his power stroke. The good news? After the Giants' success with older post-prospects, "Quad-A" might yet signify untapped potential rather than unfulfilled promise.

Alex Dickerson LF

Born: 05/26/90 Age: 32 Bats: L Throws: L Height: 6'2" Weight: 226 lb. Origin: Round 3, 2011 Draft (#91 overall)

YEAR	TEAM	LVL	AGE	PA	R	2B	3B	HR	RBI	BB	K	SB	CS	Whiff%	AVG/OBP/SLG	DRC+	BABIP	BRR	FRAA	WARP
2019	ELP	AAA	29	113	17	5	1	5	20	14	18	0	0		.372/.469/.606	118	.417	0.6	1B(6): -0.0, LF(6): 0.3, RF(3): 0.1	0.7
2019	SD	MLB	29	19	1	0	0	0	2	0	7	0	0	40.5%	.158/.158/.158	71	.250	0.2	LF(6): -0.1	0.0
2019	SF	MLB	29	171	28	13	3	6	26	13	35	1	1	22.2%	.290/.351/.529	109	.339	0.3	LF(44): -4.6, RF(1): -0.2	0.4
2020	SF	MLB	30	170	28	10	1	10	27	16	30	0	0	23.4%	.298/.371/.576	124	.313	-1.0	LF(41): -2.7, RF(5): 0.2	0.6
2021	SAC	AAA	31	45	8	3	0	2	4	5	8	0	0		.289/.400/.526	111	.321	0.2	LF(6): -0.5	0.2
2021	SF	MLB	31	312	37	10	2	13	38	23	76	1	0	28.2%	.233/.304/.420	98	.273	-1.4	LF(82): -2.8	0.6
2022 non-DC	*SF*	*MLB*	*32*	*251*	*29*	*10*	*1*	*9*	*31*	*21*	*57*	*0*	*1*	*27.1%*	*.247/.323/.431*	*101*	*.292*	*-0.2*	*LF 0, RF 0*	*0.8*

Comparables: Lucas Duda, Nolan Reimold, Alex Presley

You wouldn't blame Dickerson if he spent some private moments shaking his fist at the sky, wailing about the injustice of it all. A player with above-average plate skills and absolutely terrible injury luck (including two missed years in what should have been his prime recovering from spine and elbow injuries), Dickerson finally seemed poised to be another late-blooming success story in San Francisco. After a mostly healthy and very productive 2020 mini-season, he had a chance to carve out a regular role among the overachieving footsoldiers of the Giants outfield. And while 2021 was his first season in the majors playing more than 100 games, health let him down again, with three trips to the IL (and an injury sidelining him during the season's final week). It's difficult to say if the league-average performance at the plate was a product of pain, age, or both (and beyond a certain point the two clasp hands like the well-known meme), but Dickerson now heads into free agency with a résumé dotted with brief spells of promise and long stretches of absence. The feel-good story calls for one more shot at health and productivity, but feeling good has been a rare and fleeting state throughout Dickerson's career.

Mauricio Dubón UT Born: 07/19/94 Age: 27 Bats: R Throws: R Height: 6'0" Weight: 173 lb. Origin: Round 26, 2013 Draft (#773 overall)

YEAR	TEAM	LVL	AGE	PA	R	2B	3B	HR	RBI	BB	K	SB	CS	Whiff%	AVG/OBP/SLG	DRC+	BABIP	BRR	FRAA	WARP
2019	SAC	AAA	24	112	23	4	0	4	9	10	9	1	2		.323/.391/.485	113	.326	0.9	SS(17): -0.2, 2B(7): 0.4	0.8
2019	SA	AAA	24	427	59	22	1	16	47	18	59	9	6		.297/.333/.475	102	.316	-1.6	SS(83): 5.2, 2B(12): 0.6, 3B(1): -0.1	2.3
2019	MIL	MLB	24	2	0	0	0	0	0	0	1	0	0	10.0%	.000/.000/.000	88				0.0
2019	SF	MLB	24	109	12	5	0	4	9	5	19	3	1	21.2%	.279/.312/.442	100	.309	1.0	2B(22): 3.7, SS(9): -0.2	0.9
2020	SF	MLB	25	177	21	4	1	4	19	15	36	2	3	24.3%	.274/.337/.389	101	.328	-0.9	CF(44): 0.5, 2B(8): 0.5, SS(8): -0.1	0.6
2021	SAC	AAA	26	283	41	13	2	8	31	29	38	9	3		.332/.410/.498	117	.365	2.0	SS(51): -3.2, 2B(3): 1.2, LF(3): -0.7	1.5
2021	SF	MLB	26	187	20	9	0	5	22	9	41	2	1	23.0%	.240/.278/.377	90	.282	-2.4	CF(27): -0.5, SS(21): 2.0, 2B(20): -0.4	0.3
2022 DC	*SF*	*MLB*	*27*	*122*	*13*	*4*	*0*	*2*	*14*	*8*	*19*	*2*	*2*	*20.5%*	*.245/.301/.365*	*81*	*.277*	*0.2*	*2B 0, CF 0*	*0.2*

Comparables: Marwin Gonzalez, Eugenio Suárez, Ehire Adrianza

How useful is a Swiss Army knife whose blade is just a bit duller than you'd like? Sure, you have a corkscrew, a nail file and a screwdriver, but these all feel a little superfluous if your bat is little better than plastic against the hard cheese of major-league pitching. As someone projected to be a key utility piece in the Giants' improvised lineup contraption, After a slow start and a demotion to Sacramento, Dubón retooled and simplified his swing, eliminating a leg kick, which led to some productive results in whatever they're calling the PCL these days, even if it couldn't land him a meaningful role in the Giants' divisional run. Such is the downside of the versatility so prized in the Zaidi era: playing all over the field is great, but if you're not contributing offensively, there's bound to be a Thairo Estrada or Steven Duggar waiting in the wings. Unfortunately for Dubón, the combination of low on-base and slugging percentages over his brief major-league career suggests he'll need some pretty impressive peripheral tools if he can't sharpen things up at the plate.

Steven Duggar CF Born: 11/04/93 Age: 28 Bats: L Throws: R Height: 6'1" Weight: 187 lb. Origin: Round 6, 2015 Draft (#186 overall)

YEAR	TEAM	LVL	AGE	PA	R	2B	3B	HR	RBI	BB	K	SB	CS	Whiff%	AVG/OBP/SLG	DRC+	BABIP	BRR	FRAA	WARP
2019	SAC	AAA	25	102	24	6	1	3	13	18	21	2	3		.337/.461/.542	106	.424	-0.3	CF(19): 0.4	0.5
2019	SF	MLB	25	281	26	12	2	4	28	16	78	1	4	27.0%	.234/.278/.341	66	.313	-1.8	CF(39): 2.1, RF(34): -0.4	-0.2
2020	SF	MLB	26	36	3	2	0	0	3	1	11	1	0	20.4%	.176/.222/.235	74	.261	0.2	LF(11): 0.2, RF(7): -0.4, CF(4): -0.4	0.0
2021	SAC	AAA	27	70	13	2	1	1	9	9	22	8	0		.279/.371/.393	87	.421	1.1	CF(11): 0.2	0.2
2021	SF	MLB	27	297	45	14	5	8	35	27	88	7	0	28.0%	.257/.330/.437	80	.355	3.3	CF(93): -1.1, LF(4): -0.0, RF(1): -0.2	0.7
2022 DC	*SF*	*MLB*	*28*	*277*	*30*	*12*	*2*	*4*	*32*	*23*	*80*	*5*	*2*	*27.4%*	*.227/.298/.355*	*75*	*.314*	*0.5*	*CF 1*	*0.2*

Comparables: Ezequiel Carrera, Brett Gardner, Aaron Hicks

Somehow the Giants won 107 games without a center fielder. With a rotating cast that never quite stuck, like a week of guest hosts auditioning for a regular gig, the job was variously occupied by Mauricio Dubón, Mike Yastrzemski, Austin Slater and Kris Bryant, among others. Duggar, however, was probably the best all-around blend of glove and bat at the position, even though he's marginal defensively and best deployed in a strong-side platoon at the plate. The post-hype lefty took to the team's coaching, learning how to take a base and barrel a pitch, and in the process ceased to be a liability at the plate, if not quite becoming an asset. The 2021 developments are likely to give Duggar a continued role with the major-league club, but the Giants would prefer not to have another season of Jimmy Fallon fill-ins from the center field position in 2022.

Thairo Estrada IF Born: 02/22/96 Age: 26 Bats: R Throws: R Height: 5'10" Weight: 185 lb. Origin: International Free Agent, 2012

YEAR	TEAM	LVL	AGE	PA	R	2B	3B	HR	RBI	BB	K	SB	CS	Whiff%	AVG/OBP/SLG	DRC+	BABIP	BRR	FRAA	WARP
2019	SWB	AAA	23	259	39	17	2	8	32	14	50	3	1		.266/.313/.452	95	.304	-1.0	SS(33): -0.6, 2B(24): -1.6, 3B(2): -0.3	0.6
2019	NYY	MLB	23	69	12	3	0	3	12	3	15	4	0	25.2%	.250/.294/.438	90	.283	1.0	2B(17): -1.1, SS(9): 0.3, LF(2): -0.1	0.2
2020	NYY	MLB	24	52	8	0	0	1	3	1	19	1	0	29.4%	.167/.231/.229	76	.250	0.3	2B(20): 0.0, 3B(6): -0.3, SS(3): -0.1	0.0
2021	SAC	AAA	25	233	37	14	1	9	40	20	35	6	4		.333/.399/.538	123	.367	-1.0	SS(30): -6.0, 2B(16): 2.0, 3B(2): 0.1	1.0
2021	SF	MLB	25	132	19	4	0	7	22	9	23	1	0	19.0%	.273/.333/.479	114	.286	1.2	SS(19): -1.1, 2B(16): 0.5, 3B(4): 0.1	0.8
2022 DC	*SF*	*MLB*	*26*	*214*	*24*	*8*	*0*	*4*	*23*	*13*	*38*	*1*	*2*	*21.5%*	*.242/.299/.357*	*79*	*.282*	*0.0*	*2B 0, SS 0*	*0.1*

Comparables: Jonathan Villar, Marwin Gonzalez, Hanser Alberto

It almost feels like the Giants pressed the "upgrade" button on Donovan Solano, and instead of getting "better Donovan Solano," they got a whole new player named "Thairo Estrada." Like Solano, Estrada is a righty utility infielder with solid contact skills, but younger, faster, with a bit more power and an ability to take some reps at the six-hole on Brandon Crawford's off-days. (And, like Solano, he found his way to the Bay via the Bronx.) Estrada's positional versatility and contact-heavy plate approach should earn him a role in 2022, but he'd be miscast as an everyday starter. Estrada is young enough that he could yet undergo a transformation to something greater, but even if he remains an infield handyman, he'll be the one everyone recommends for all sorts of odd jobs.

Wilmer Flores IF Born: 08/06/91 Age: 30 Bats: R Throws: R Height: 6'2" Weight: 213 lb. Origin: International Free Agent, 2007

YEAR	TEAM	LVL	AGE	PA	R	2B	3B	HR	RBI	BB	K	SB	CS	Whiff%	AVG/OBP/SLG	DRC+	BABIP	BRR	FRAA	WARP
2019	ARI	MLB	27	285	31	18	0	9	37	15	31	0	0	10.8%	.317/.361/.487	117	.332	-0.4	2B(64): -4.8, 1B(16): 0.1	1.2
2020	SF	MLB	28	213	30	11	1	12	32	13	36	1	0	17.8%	.268/.315/.515	118	.272	-1.2	1B(14): 1.6, 2B(14): 1.3, 3B(3): -0.4	1.2
2021	SF	MLB	29	436	57	16	1	18	53	41	56	1	0	16.6%	.262/.335/.447	122	.264	-2.2	3B(58): 0.4, 1B(34): -0.6, 2B(30): -1.7	2.2
2022 DC	*SF*	*MLB*	*30*	*171*	*22*	*7*	*0*	*5*	*24*	*14*	*22*	*0*	*0*	*16.5%*	*.261/.329/.419*	*102*	*.277*	*-0.3*	*2B 0, 3B 0*	*0.4*

Comparables: Adrián Beltré, Aramis Ramirez, Brooks Robinson

Whether one was a fervent Giants fan or simply a dispassionate observer appreciating an epic struggle between baseball's behemoths of 2021, it absolutely sucked that the Giants' season ended with Flores' check swing, questionably called a third strike by first-base ump Gabe Morales. Even as it left a taste less pleasant than stale garlic fries, let's not get carried away; the win expectancy was only 9.4% heading into Flores' at-bat. Instead, let's focus on the positives: with the help of the Giants' much-praised coaching staff, Flores was able to approach a double-digit walk rate, nearly erase his lefty-righty splits and improve his DRC+ for a third consecutive year, turning into—dare we say—a reliable bat, whether starting at a non-shortstop infield spot or coming in to face a lefty in a tight game. With a club option, the Giants shouldn't hesitate on taking a full swing on Flores in 2022.

Tommy La Stella 2B Born: 01/31/89 Age: 33 Bats: L Throws: R Height: 5'11" Weight: 180 lb. Origin: Round 8, 2011 Draft (#266 overall)

YEAR	TEAM	LVL	AGE	PA	R	2B	3B	HR	RBI	BB	K	SB	CS	Whiff%	AVG/OBP/SLG	DRC+	BABIP	BRR	FRAA	WARP
2019	LAA	MLB	30	321	49	8	0	16	44	20	28	0	0	11.8%	.295/.346/.486	121	.282	-1.3	2B(46): -1.7, 3B(30): -0.9, 1B(3): -0.1	1.5
2020	OAK	MLB	31	111	16	6	2	1	11	12	5	0	0	10.9%	.289/.369/.423	113	.293	0.1	2B(18): -0.3, 3B(6): -0.4	0.5
2020	LAA	MLB	31	117	15	8	0	4	14	15	7	1	0	11.5%	.273/.371/.475	119	.258	-1.7	2B(15): -3.6, 1B(10): 0.2	0.1
2021	SAC	AAA	32	38	8	2	0	0	2	7	5	0	0		.200/.351/.267	104	.240	0.6	2B(6): 0.2, 3B(2): -0.1, 1B(1): -0.1	0.2
2021	SF	MLB	32	242	26	11	1	7	27	18	26	0	0	12.3%	.250/.308/.405	108	.255	0.6	2B(54): -6.4, 3B(5): -0.2	0.5
2022 DC	*SF*	*MLB*	*33*	*498*	*70*	*21*	*1*	*9*	*52*	*46*	*44*	*0*	*1*	*12.7%*	*.262/.336/.381*	*99*	*.274*	*-0.6*	*2B -3, 3B -1*	*0.9*

Comparables: Justin Turner, Ryan Flaherty, Danny Valencia

While the Giants rounded out their 2021 major-league roster with cast-offs, waiver claims, minor trades and one-year deals, it's not too much of a stretch to see why La Stella was given a longer, three-year commitment. With a career OBP of .349, a hint of power and an ability to slot in all around the infield, the vibe is very Zaidi. Unfortunately, La Stella was lost to a pulled hamstring for three solid months—a reminder of his age and injury history—and when he did play he looked like a blurry, pixelated copy of the on-base machine he was with the Cubs, Angels and Athletics. And now, the 33-year-old will spend his offseason rehabbing from Achilles tendon surgery. With health and a full season, there's still a decent chance that the Giants will get the La Stella they'd planned on having, but the recent past gives more cause for worry than hope.

Evan Longoria 3B Born: 10/07/85 Age: 36 Bats: R Throws: R Height: 6'1" Weight: 213 lb. Origin: Round 1, 2006 Draft (#3 overall)

YEAR	TEAM	LVL	AGE	PA	R	2B	3B	HR	RBI	BB	K	SB	CS	Whiff%	AVG/OBP/SLG	DRC+	BABIP	BRR	FRAA	WARP
2019	SF	MLB	33	508	59	19	2	20	69	43	112	3	1	25.8%	.254/.325/.437	103	.291	-0.6	3B(119): 5.7	2.0
2020	SF	MLB	34	209	26	10	1	7	28	11	39	0	1	21.0%	.254/.297/.425	103	.280	-1.3	3B(52): -1.2	0.3
2021	SF	MLB	35	291	45	17	0	13	46	35	68	1	1	25.2%	.261/.351/.482	118	.305	-0.6	3B(78): 5.0	2.1
2022 DC	*SF*	*MLB*	*36*	*506*	*66*	*23*	*1*	*17*	*72*	*46*	*105*	*3*	*1*	*24.4%*	*.240/.316/.409*	*96*	*.277*	*-0.5*	*3B 2*	*1.2*

Comparables: Scott Rolen, Adrián Beltré, Gary Gaetti

There are many ways to wind down an All-Star-level career, and they don't all have to be depressing. Longoria, traded from the Rays before the 2018 season, was set to be a hot-corner fixture in San Francisco for the remaining five years of his contract. Health issues and the predictable post-30 decline quickly turned Longoria from fixture to eyesore, and lamentations about the Giants' commitment could be heard far and wide. Over the past couple of years, with Farhan Zaidi's modular, flexible roster construction, Longoria has had to share time at the position. But in that same time, with the help of the Giants' widely praised coaching, he's rediscovered a plate approach that features more patience, a higher launch angle and increased bat speed. While it's a stretch to think he could get back to the Tampa Bay-era Longo, when deployed as part of an infield ensemble he's proven to be an unlikely source of offensive value as he heads into the later stages of an impressive career.

★ ★ ★ *2022 Top 101 Prospect* **#9** ★ ★ ★

Marco Luciano SS Born: 09/10/01 Age: 20 Bats: R Throws: R Height: 6'2" Weight: 178 lb. Origin: International Free Agent, 2018

YEAR	TEAM	LVL	AGE	PA	R	2B	3B	HR	RBI	BB	K	SB	CS	Whiff%	AVG/OBP/SLG	DRC+	BABIP	BRR	FRAA	WARP
2019	GIO	ROK	17	178	46	9	2	10	38	27	39	8	6		.322/.438/.616		.378			
2019	SK	SS	17	38	6	4	0	0	4	5	6	1	0		.212/.316/.333		.259			
2021	SCO	WIN	19	87	7	0	0	3	13	11	28	0	1		.253/.356/.373		.364			
2021	SJ	A	19	308	52	14	3	18	57	38	68	5	5		.278/.373/.556	129	.309	-0.9	SS(60): -0.1	1.9
2021	EUG	A+	19	145	16	3	2	1	14	10	54	1	0		.217/.283/.295	69	.351	-0.1	SS(29): -1.2	-0.3
2022 non-DC	*SF*	*MLB*	*20*	*251*	*22*	*9*	*1*	*5*	*24*	*18*	*77*	*3*	*2*	*32.0%*	*.208/.273/.338*	*64*	*.288*	*0.3*	*SS 0*	*-0.2*

Comparables: Jonathan Villar, Gleyber Torres, Richard Ureña

No one should be alarmed by Luciano finally meeting some challenges at High-A, where he was promoted toward the end of the season, with only slight improvement in evidence in the AFL. The stat line gives pause to those who thought he might make a beeline to San Francisco in his age-20 season: In particular, the power dropoff along with an alarming strikeout rate give proof that there's still plenty of minor-league reps in Luciano's future. The top prospect, first and foremost, needs to work on recognizing breaking stuff, and the fact that he's spoken in detail about the adjustments he needs to make suggests that he has not only the skill, but the desire, to make them. Not to worry, then. Luciano remains the top prospect in the Giants' loaded system and a cornerstone of the franchise's future.

★ ★ ★ *2022 Top 101 Prospect* **#30** ★ ★ ★

Luis Matos OF Born: 01/28/02 Age: 20 Bats: R Throws: R Height: 5'11" Weight: 160 lb. Origin: International Free Agent, 2018

YEAR	TEAM	LVL	AGE	PA	R	2B	3B	HR	RBI	BB	K	SB	CS	Whiff%	AVG/OBP/SLG	DRC+	BABIP	BRR	FRAA	WARP
2019	DSL GIA	ROK	17	270	60	24	2	7	47	19	30	20	2		.362/.430/.570		.386			
2019	GIO	ROK	17	20	5	1	0	0	1	1	1	1	1		.438/.550/.500		.467			
2021	SJ	A	19	491	84	35	1	15	86	28	61	21	5		.313/.358/.494	129	.332	1.2	CF(86): -4.7, RF(14): -2.9, LF(4): 0.0	3.0
2022 non-DC	*SF*	*MLB*	*20*	*251*	*22*	*12*	*0*	*4*	*24*	*11*	*45*	*8*	*2*	*24.6%*	*.252/.292/.365*	*78*	*.297*	*0.5*	*CF -1, RF 0*	*0.1*

Comparables: Manuel Margot, Victor Robles, Trayvon Robinson

Cue the GIF of Jack Nicholson nodding maniacally when you see the line for Matos' full-season debut in 2021. Assigned to the A-league San Jose affiliate, the 2018 signee from Venezuela showed remarkable consistency and polish across every aspect of his game. He flashes power and speed, makes frequent and solid contact, and projects for average defense in center. Matos offers a potential above-average hit tool paired with the potential for plus power, a heady combination and possibly a necessary one, should he need to move to a corner. With some room to fill out his upper body, there might be a power/speed trade off, but we'd be quibbling to worry about where, exactly, his impact lies. The takeaway here is that 2021 showed us that he's on a fast track to major-league relevance and is one of the rising stars of the Giants' loaded system.

★ ★ ★ *2022 Top 101 Prospect* **#83** ★ ★ ★

Jairo Pomares OF Born: 08/04/00 Age: 21 Bats: L Throws: R Height: 6'1" Weight: 185 lb. Origin: International Free Agent, 2018

YEAR	TEAM	LVL	AGE	PA	R	2B	3B	HR	RBI	BB	K	SB	CS	Whiff%	AVG/OBP/SLG	DRC+	BABIP	BRR	FRAA	WARP
2019	GIB	ROK	18	167	17	10	4	3	33	10	26	5	3		.368/.401/.542		.422			
2019	SK	SS	18	62	7	3	0	0	4	1	17	0	0		.207/.258/.259		.293			
2021	SJ	A	20	224	45	22	0	14	44	15	54	0	0		.372/.429/.693	138	.448	-0.7	RF(26): -2.3, LF(3): -1.0	1.4
2021	EUG	A+	20	104	13	5	1	6	15	1	33	1	0		.262/.269/.505	107	.328	0.4	LF(22): -1.7	0.3
2022 non-DC	*SF*	*MLB*	*21*	*251*	*25*	*12*	*1*	*8*	*29*	*11*	*79*	*1*	*1*	*34.5%*	*.245/.290/.411*	*83*	*.336*	*-0.1*	*RF -1, LF 0*	*0.1*

Comparables: Alex Kirilloff, David Dahl, Ryan Kalish

Pomares is a tooled-up outfielder from the Cuban city of Sancti Spíritus—or, roughly translated, "Holy Spirit" in Latin. Pomares sure put the fear of said spirit in Low-A pitchers, as he throttled them to the tune of a 1.122 OPS that was the highest among any and all San Jose batters, no matter the playing time. He met some resistance following a late-season promotion to High-A, but it's hard to muster much concern based on his age, performance and his physical promise. The Giants have a number of other not-quite-center field types in their organization, including Heliot Ramos and Hunter Bishop; Pomares, the youngest of the bunch, might also end up being the best.

Buster Posey C Born: 03/27/87 Age: 35 Bats: R Throws: R Height: 6'1" Weight: 213 lb. Origin: Round 1, 2008 Draft (#5 overall)

YEAR	TEAM	LVL	AGE	PA	R	2B	3B	HR	RBI	BB	K	SB	CS	Whiff%	AVG/OBP/SLG	DRC+	BABIP	BRR	FRAA	WARP
2019	SF	MLB	32	445	43	24	0	7	38	34	71	0	0	18.6%	.257/.320/.368	91	.296	-1.1	C(101): 19.7, 1B(4): -0.1	3.2
2021	SF	MLB	34	454	68	23	0	18	56	56	87	0	0	23.9%	.304/.390/.499	128	.349	-1.3	C(106): 5.3	3.9
2022 non-DC	*SF*	*MLB*	*35*	*251*	*26*	*11*	*0*	*5*	*26*	*27*	*48*	*0*	*1*	*22.9%*	*.256/.344/.384*	*100*	*.306*	*-0.4*	*C 3, 1B 0*	*1.5*

Comparables: Yadier Molina, Yogi Berra, Ivan Rodriguez

YEAR	TEAM	P. COUNT	FRM RUNS	BLK RUNS	THRW RUNS	TOT RUNS
2019	SF	13868	17.1	0.5	0.8	18.4
2021	SF	14166	3.6	0.8	0.0	4.4
2022	*SF*	*6956*	*3.8*	*0.6*	*0.1*	*4.5*

The Buster Hug is both a physical act and a potent metaphor. First, the act itself. Posey, hugging a winning pitcher after a momentous or dominant performance, conveyed a comfort beyond the raucous joy of a World Series championship or no-hitter. Posey's moment with the pitcher, even if it only lasted as long as the time it took crazed teammates to rush the mound, was an island of satisfaction and quiet strength amid wider celebrations. There were variations: the leap into Brian Wilson's arms for the first championship in 2010; the brief pickup and putdown of Sergio Romo in 2012; the full-body embrace of MadBum in 2014; the playful reverse lift of Tim Lincecum for his first no-hitter.

But it wasn't just men hugging each other. The Buster Hug also defined an era; unquestionably, the best era in the Giants' San Francisco history. Along with Tim Lincecum and Madison Bumgarner (all three first-round picks), Posey anchored the accidental mini-dynasty by the Bay. After the individual, marquee-sized stardom of Barry Bonds for so many years, San Francisco was hungry for a team that it could embrace. The Buster Hug was the epitome of a team one could feel good about because it was a *team*.

And, not to forget, Posey was a generational talent as both an offensive and defensive catcher. He was a figurehead of this team because, for much of his career, he was the best player on it. With power, patience and exceptional bat-to-ball skills, Posey was a complete offensive player. His defense was excellent, his pitch framing peerless. Posey's career was often marred by injury; indeed, the list goes on and on, like a scroll unspooling onto the floor. Soreness. Contusion. Concussion. Many instances of "knee injury." And one simply described: "took several fouls off of facemask." After the 2011 collision with Scott Cousins that broke his fibula and tore up his knee, Posey came back the next year to win an MVP, the first of his Comeback Player awards and his second ring. But life as an everyday catcher isn't easy. In his later years, the injuries wore Posey down, his hitting suffered and the days off became more frequent. Yet, it's fitting that after a year off in 2020, Posey would come back to record one of his best offensive seasons, winning Comeback Player of the Year *after* he had announced his retirement. Make no mistake, though: Posey's quiet, unassuming departure after a stunning season, both individually and with his team, does not seem like a look-at-me mic drop. Quite the opposite: It feels like a good friend finding you, just as the party is winding down, giving you a brief and heartfelt hug, and walking off into the night while there's still some magic left in the air.

Heliot Ramos CF Born: 09/07/99 Age: 22 Bats: R Throws: R Height: 6'1" Weight: 188 lb. Origin: Round 1, 2017 Draft (#19 overall)

YEAR	TEAM	LVL	AGE	PA	R	2B	3B	HR	RBI	BB	K	SB	CS	Whiff%	AVG/OBP/SLG	DRC+	BABIP	BRR	FRAA	WARP
2019	SAN	WIN	19	72	9	2	0	1	6	5	23	1	1		.185/.250/.262		.262			
2019	SCO	WIN	19	72	9	2	0	1	6	5	23	1	1		.185/.250/.262		.262			
2019	SJ	A+	19	338	51	18	0	13	40	32	85	6	7		.306/.385/.500	120	.385	-0.5	CF(71): -5.5	1.3
2019	RIC	AA	19	106	13	6	1	3	15	10	33	2	3		.242/.321/.421	85	.339	-1.4	CF(19): -1.4	-0.1
2021	RIC	AA	21	266	36	14	1	10	26	27	73	7	2		.237/.323/.432	104	.301	0.0	CF(58): -3.2	0.7
2021	SAC	AAA	21	229	30	11	2	4	30	15	65	8	2		.272/.323/.399	78	.375	2.9	CF(32): -2.4, RF(17): 1.2	0.3
2022 DC	*SF*	*MLB*	*22*	*63*	*7*	*2*	*0*	*1*	*7*	*4*	*20*	*0*	*1*	*33.2%*	*.229/.293/.367*	*78*	*.326*	*0.1*	*CF 0*	*0.0*

Comparables: Manuel Margot, Avisaíl García, Carlos Tocci

It's a commentary on the recent overhaul of the Giants' system that Ramos, the org's top prospect in 2018, is now somewhere in the middle of the top 10. Ramos' progress through the minors has been slow but steady—all five tools are still there, even if no single one of them has stepped out to front the other four. Ending last season with a passable Triple-A sesh, the center fielder profiles as an upgrade to the Giants' righty-hitting outfield options who can, though probably shouldn't, play center field (lookin' at you, Austin Slater). Physically, Ramos is *solid*—he looks like he should have more power and less speed than he does, and that might be the skills path he follows. Look for a 2022 debut in Oracle Park, but don't be surprised if he doesn't step right into an everyday role right away.

Drew Robinson CF Born: 04/20/92 Age: 30 Bats: L Throws: R Height: 6'1" Weight: 200 lb. Origin: Round 4, 2010 Draft (#136 overall)

YEAR	TEAM	LVL	AGE	PA	R	2B	3B	HR	RBI	BB	K	SB	CS	Whiff%	AVG/OBP/SLG	DRC+	BABIP	BRR	FRAA	WARP
2019	MEM	AAA	27	234	28	8	2	6	28	36	71	10	3		.265/.385/.423	89	.383	0.5	CF(25): 1.1, SS(14): -1.3, 3B(7): -0.2	0.6
2019	STL	MLB	27	7	1	0	0	0	0	0	3	0	0	53.3%	.143/.143/.143	82	.250	0.2	CF(1): -0.0, RF(1): -0.0	0.0
2021	SAC	AAA	29	111	13	3	0	3	8	14	61	1	0		.115/.225/.240	43	.242	-0.2	RF(21): -2.7, LF(7): 0.3	-0.7
2022 non-DC	*SF*	*MLB*	*30*	*251*	*23*	*9*	*1*	*7*	*25*	*26*	*132*	*2*	*2*	*47.0%*	*.165/.261/.316*	*51*	*.358*	*0.1*	*CF 0, RF 0*	*-0.8*

Comparables: Carlos Peguero, Ezequiel Carrera, Abraham Almonte

Trigger warning: discussion of attempted suicide.

The difference between a player and a person can be as large as a life. Regarding the former, Robinson was a versatile, athletic outfielder who topped out with major-league stretches in Texas and St. Louis. He was, as his previous comment in this publication states, a Quad-A player. Robinson retired from baseball while playing for the Giants' Triple-A franchise this past July. And this is where the unremarkable player's story gives way to the near-tragedy of the personal one. In April 2020, Robinson, whose depression had been intensified by his professional uncertainty, a breakup with his longtime partner and the isolation of the pandemic, attempted to take his own life with a gunshot to the head. He was unsuccessful, though he suffered significant damage to his face and lost his right eye. Taking his survival as a second chance, he miraculously came back to play in 2021, albeit with only one working eye. When this comeback bid stalled out, Robinson retired as a player, taking a position as a mental health advocate in the Giants organization.

In these very pages, you will see hundreds of players shrunken down to numbers, metrics, judgements passed in the space of sentences. Those methods of analysis and evaluation serve a purpose and are not likely to change anytime soon. But know that there are worlds and lives beyond these numbers, and we will seldom know the turbulence, doubt and struggle that often live beneath the stat line.

National Suicide Prevention Lifeline: 800-273-8255.

Darin Ruf 1B/LF Born: 07/28/86 Age: 35 Bats: R Throws: R Height: 6'2" Weight: 232 lb. Origin: Round 20, 2009 Draft (#617 overall)

YEAR	TEAM	LVL	AGE	PA	R	2B	3B	HR	RBI	BB	K	SB	CS	Whiff%	AVG/OBP/SLG	DRC+	BABIP	BRR	FRAA	WARP
2020	SF	MLB	33	100	11	6	0	5	18	13	23	1	0	26.3%	.276/.370/.517	118	.322	-1.3	LF(22): 0.8, 1B(4): 0.0, RF(3): -0.6	0.4
2021	SF	MLB	34	312	41	13	2	16	43	46	87	2	0	25.0%	.271/.385/.519	124	.344	-3.4	1B(44): 1.4, LF(33): -1.4, RF(5): 3.3	1.9
2022 DC	*SF*	*MLB*	*35*	*343*	*51*	*15*	*0*	*14*	*52*	*44*	*82*	*1*	*1*	*25.8%*	*.243/.348/.456*	*117*	*.285*	*-0.4*	*LF 0, 1B 0*	*1.6*

Comparables: Steve Pearce, Adam Rosales, Nelson Cruz

Certain aspects of Ruf's, and the Giants', 2021 unfolded on a metaphysical plane. In July, Ruf upset the karmic balance by having a check-swing mistakenly called on what would have been the final out in the ninth inning of a tense Dodgers-Giants matchup, leading to a Giants come-from-behind victory. This, of course, put the universe out of joint, only to be restored by the phantom swing called on Wilmer Flores to end the hard-fought LDS in October. Other than that, Ruf's 2021 was pure nirvana. Starting out as a key righty platoon bat and pinch-hitter, Ruf muscled his way into the lineup for more regular duty during the season's stretch run. Where Ruf was very good against same-sided pitching, he was absolutely lethal against southpaws, posting an OPS north of 1.000. We can explain Ruf's thirtysomething ascension through a number of reasons—but these become repetitive when talking about the 2021 Giants. Yes, the front office identified submerged skill profiles in a number of castoffs. Yes, the coaching was excellent, emphasizing hard contact and selectivity. Yes, players were deployed in situations where they were most likely to succeed. But it's hard to look at this team and not think that there was something beyond all the concrete, well-established explanations. Expecting a 35-year-old journeyman first-base/corner-outfielder type to utterly demolish the NL West for half a season? Call it magic, kismet, or the miraculous—some baseball stories simply passeth all understanding.

Austin Slater OF Born: 12/13/92 Age: 29 Bats: R Throws: R Height: 6'1" Weight: 204 lb. Origin: Round 8, 2014 Draft (#238 overall)

YEAR	TEAM	LVL	AGE	PA	R	2B	3B	HR	RBI	BB	K	SB	CS	Whiff%	AVG/OBP/SLG	DRC+	BABIP	BRR	FRAA	WARP
2019	SAC	AAA	26	296	47	17	0	12	45	46	69	6	2		.308/.436/.529	117	.388	0.6	1B(38): 3.1, 3B(11): -1.2, LF(8): -0.7	1.6
2019	SF	MLB	26	192	20	9	3	5	21	22	59	1	0	32.9%	.238/.333/.417	82	.337	-0.5	RF(46): -0.1, 1B(8): -0.8, LF(2): -0.1	0.0
2020	SF	MLB	27	104	18	2	1	5	7	16	22	8	1	25.3%	.282/.408/.506	119	.328	0.9	RF(9): 1.9, LF(3): 0.3	0.8
2021	SF	MLB	28	306	39	12	1	12	32	28	84	15	2	30.2%	.241/.320/.423	101	.303	1.5	CF(77): 0.5, LF(37): -1.5, RF(24): 0.2	1.3
2022 DC	*SF*	*MLB*	*29*	*279*	*40*	*11*	*0*	*6*	*27*	*29*	*76*	*4*	*2*	*29.6%*	*.238/.329/.378*	*95*	*.317*	*0.1*	*CF 0, RF 1*	*0.8*

Comparables: Brett Gardner, Nolan Reimold, Hunter Renfroe

In a British-English idiomatic expression, Slater is a player who can "do a job of work." The phrase implies versatility, readiness to do whatever's needed, and a basic level of competence. As a righty-hitting outfielder with good speed, a bit of power and the ability to do an occasionally convincing impression of a major-league center fielder, Slater was an underrated contributor to the Giants' 2021 success. Living in the zone of the roster that Farhan Zaidi likes to churn, however, Slater's 2022 prospects may be limited by his short-sided platoon profile and the number of mix-and-match options likely to be available at Gabe Kapler's disposal. He's not likely to be on the dole, but his prospects would be enhanced with a little more Austin Power.

LaMonte Wade Jr. RF Born: 01/01/94 Age: 28 Bats: L Throws: L Height: 6'1" Weight: 205 lb. Origin: Round 9, 2015 Draft (#260 overall)

YEAR	TEAM	LVL	AGE	PA	R	2B	3B	HR	RBI	BB	K	SB	CS	Whiff%	AVG/OBP/SLG	DRC+	BABIP	BRR	FRAA	WARP
2019	ROC	AAA	25	334	47	12	1	5	24	56	48	7	2		.246/.392/.356	115	.280	1.3	RF(34): -6.8, LF(28): -2.0, CF(11): -0.9	0.8
2019	MIN	MLB	25	69	10	2	1	2	5	11	9	0	1	17.4%	.196/.348/.375	108	.200	0.1	CF(14): 0.9, LF(8): -0.5, RF(6): -0.8	0.3
2020	MIN	MLB	26	44	3	3	0	0	1	4	9	1	1	15.4%	.231/.318/.308	94	.300	-0.1	1B(4): -0.1, CF(4): -0.3, LF(3): -0.2	0.0
2021	SAC	AAA	27	59	12	2	0	3	8	14	13	0	1		.244/.424/.489	118	.276	0.1	LF(5): 1.5, RF(5): -0.8, CF(3): -0.3	0.4
2021	SF	MLB	27	381	52	17	3	18	56	33	89	6	1	20.1%	.253/.326/.482	107	.289	0.0	RF(52): -5.5, LF(42): -0.3, 1B(31): 1.9	1.1
2022 DC	*SF*	*MLB*	*28*	*415*	*54*	*16*	*2*	*9*	*48*	*43*	*77*	*3*	*1*	*19.3%*	*.227/.319/.367*	*88*	*.262*	*0.0*	*LF 1, RF 0*	*0.6*

Comparables: Trevor Crowe, Abraham Almonte, David Lough

Wade's 2021 can be expressed by the meme of someone tipping a tiny, domino-sized tile into a slightly larger slab, which falls into a yet larger block, ultimately tipping over a massive slab larger than the person who initiated the sequence. The meme teaches us about causality and scale: little things cause slightly bigger things, which eventually cascade into huge consequences. The tiny domino was an offseason trade, virtually unnoticed, in which the Giants sent reliever Shaun Anderson to Minnesota for Wade, at that point a fungible corner-outfield bat with a .684 OPS in parts of two Twins seasons. The largest slab was Wade pinch-hitting for Austin Slater in the bottom of the ninth, as the potential series-winning run in a deciding Game 5 of the LDS. The story in between was the ever-expanding legend of Late Night Lamonte, a player tabbed for Quad-A obscurity who, through some minor swing adjustments, became a legitimately threatening power bat, most famously in high-leverage situations—Wade knocked six game-tying or go-ahead hits in the ninth inning, the highest seasonal total by a player in the last 40 years. Unfortunately, the last piece in Wade's great leap forward didn't quite stick the landing—Wade struck out against "closer" Max Scherzer, who ushered the Giants from the postseason one batter later—but one of the pleasures of 2021 was watching Wade topple expectations as he torqued balls out of the park.

Mike Yastrzemski RF Born: 08/23/90 Age: 31 Bats: L Throws: L Height: 5'10" Weight: 178 lb. Origin: Round 14, 2013 Draft (#429 overall)

YEAR	TEAM	LVL	AGE	PA	R	2B	3B	HR	RBI	BB	K	SB	CS	Whiff%	AVG/OBP/SLG	DRC+	BABIP	BRR	FRAA	WARP
2019	SAC	AAA	28	163	38	11	1	12	25	22	36	2	2		.316/.414/.676	129	.344	1.9	CF(21): -0.4, LF(8): -0.7, RF(7): 0.5	1.3
2019	SF	MLB	28	411	64	22	3	21	55	32	107	2	4	27.6%	.272/.334/.518	102	.325	0.3	LF(61): -0.8, RF(56): 0.6, CF(7): -0.2	1.4
2020	SF	MLB	29	225	39	14	4	10	35	30	55	2	1	24.9%	.297/.400/.568	111	.370	-0.1	RF(31): 4.0, CF(24): 1.7, LF(8): 0.1	1.6
2021	SF	MLB	30	532	75	28	3	25	71	51	131	4	0	24.4%	.224/.311/.457	100	.254	2.3	RF(115): 9.7, CF(34): -2.6	2.7
2022 DC	*SF*	*MLB*	*31*	*556*	*82*	*27*	*3*	*17*	*67*	*58*	*129*	*4*	*2*	*24.3%*	*.231/.321/.410*	*99*	*.279*	*-0.1*	*RF 4, CF -1*	*1.9*

Comparables: Justin Maxwell, Jeremy Hazelbaker, Will Venable

OK, quiet down, quiet down. Court is in session. Today we'll be hearing the case of *Yastrzemski v. His Skeptics*. Prosecution, you first. Yes, we see the age and the lack of an elite prospect pedigree. And, certainly, 2019 and 2020 were exceptional years: the former for the hyperball, the latter for, well, everything. So you're saying he's a marginal corner-outfield bat with good defense but not good enough for center? Duly noted. Would the defense please step to the podium? Injuries: yes, he began the season with a sore hand, then had two IL trips for an oblique and a thumb. Yes, we can see that the contact profile remained largely the same, and there was BABIP bad luck. And, the court will stipulate that thanks to his defensive contributions, Yaz was a two-win player despite his offensive shortcomings and diminished playing time. Since the jury is out, the judge will issue a bench ruling: Yaz is sentenced to be a mostly-everyday, slightly-above-average corner outfielder for a few more years, or until displaced by a prospect or free-agent signing. Court adjourned.

PITCHERS

José Álvarez LHP Born: 05/06/89 Age: 33 Bats: L Throws: L Height: 5'11" Weight: 195 lb. Origin: International Free Agent, 2005

YEAR	TEAM	LVL	AGE	W	L	SV	G	GS	IP	H	HR	BB/9	K/9	K	GB%	BABIP	WHIP	ERA	DRA-	WARP	MPH	FB%	Whiff%	CSP
2019	PHI	MLB	30	3	4	1	67	1	59	66	8	2.7	7.8	51	49.7%	.330	1.42	3.36	99	0.6	91.6	52.6%	22.9%	49.2%
2020	PHI	MLB	31	0	0	0	8	0	6^{1}	7	0	4.3	8.5	6	50.0%	.389	1.58	1.42	93	0.1	91.8	53.5%	25.0%	38.7%
2021	SF	MLB	32	5	2	0	67	1	64^{2}	53	2	2.6	5.8	42	50.0%	.254	1.11	2.37	102	0.5	91.4	57.9%	20.8%	56.5%
2022 DC	*SF*	*MLB*	*33*	*3*	*3*	*0*	*67*	*0*	*58*	*63*	*6*	*3.0*	*7.2*	*46*	*47.5%*	*.313*	*1.42*	*4.49*	*109*	*-0.1*	*91.5*	*56.4%*	*21.5%*	*53.7%*

Comparables: Dan Jennings, Zack Britton, Matt Guerrier

In 2020, as a Phillie, Álvarez failed in the one job of a reliever: protection. No, no, not that kind. A 105-mph Lourdes Gurriel Jr. liner tagged him in a sensitive spot, leading to what polite society and the injured list refer to as a "testicular contusion." Along with that inauspicious phrase, a reliever also doesn't want "former Phillie" on his résumé, but the lefty was one of the few reliable arms for Gabe Kapler in an otherwise dreadful 2019. Kapler brought Álvarez (along with some newly-acquired protective gear) to the Giants for a significant relief role by the Bay. Álvarez gives you subpar sinker velocity from the left side, paired with a change that features mainly against righties. Everything stays down, the barrels are few and far between and the soft contact that he induces keeps leads as safe as precious, uh, jewels.

Caleb Baragar LHP Born: 04/09/94 Age: 28 Bats: R Throws: L Height: 6'3" Weight: 215 lb. Origin: Round 9, 2016 Draft (#275 overall)

YEAR	TEAM	LVL	AGE	W	L	SV	G	GS	IP	H	HR	BB/9	K/9	K	GB%	BABIP	WHIP	ERA	DRA-	WARP	MPH	FB%	Whiff%	CSP
2019	SJ	A+	25	0	1	0	5	4	16^2	15	2	4.3	11.9	22	35.7%	.333	1.38	2.70	88	0.2				
2019	RIC	AA	25	5	5	0	22	21	120	83	12	3.2	8.0	107	28.4%	.225	1.05	3.45	87	1.7				
2019	SAC	AAA	25	0	0	0	1	1	4^1	6	1	4.2	12.5	6	33.3%	.455	1.85	10.38	88	0.1				
2020	SF	MLB	26	5	1	0	24	1	22^1	17	3	2.0	7.7	19	20.6%	.233	0.99	4.03	136	-0.2	93.9	75.1%	19.1%	52.8%
2021	SAC	AAA	27	3	3	0	22	1	22^1	28	7	8.5	10.1	25	21.1%	.328	2.19	8.46	119	-0.2				
2021	SF	MLB	27	2	1	2	25	0	23	19	1	4.7	6.3	16	22.4%	.273	1.35	1.57	133	-0.2	93.0	81.0%	22.2%	56.0%
2022 DC	*SF*	*MLB*	*28*	*2*	*2*	*0*	*44*	*0*	*38.7*	*38*	*7*	*4.6*	*8.0*	*34*	*26.2%*	*.282*	*1.50*	*5.49*	*128*	*-0.4*	*93.3*	*78.7%*	*21.0%*	*54.8%*

Comparables: Rich Loiselle, Donnie Hart, Bob MacDonald

You know those people who do things like run or bike a certain path so that, looked at as a route on a map, the GPS tracking spells out a word, or the shape of an object? Baragar is similarly devoted to turning what looks, on the mound, to be a decent-if-inconsistent lefty relief profile into obscure statistical performance art. In 2020, he tallied five wins in only 22 ⅓ innings, a total that was surpassed by only three pitchers in the National League—all starters, of course. In 2021, Baragar set out to see how large a gap he could create between the achieved and deserved, as his actual ERA came in at about four and a half runs below his DRA. If these curious results aren't part of some master plan, then Baragar is simply riding the luck of a particularly fortunate small sample across two seasons. The fact that much of this last one was spent in Sacramento suggests the Giants think Baragar's strange anomalies are neither intentional nor sustainable.

Will Bednar RHP Born: 06/13/00 Age: 22 Bats: R Throws: R Height: 6'2" Weight: 229 lb. Origin: Round 1, 2021 Draft (#14 overall)

YEAR	TEAM	LVL	AGE	W	L	SV	G	GS	IP	H	HR	BB/9	K/9	K	GB%	BABIP	WHIP	ERA	DRA-	WARP	MPH	FB%	Whiff%	CSP
2022 non-DC	*SF*	*MLB*	*22*	*2*	*3*	*0*	*57*	*0*	*50*	*57*	*7*	*4.4*	*6.7*	*37*	*40.8%*	*.316*	*1.64*	*6.04*	*136*	*-0.8*				

Comparables: Felipe Lira, Bryan Rekar, Bill Champion

Not only did Bednar come to pitching relatively late (his sophomore year of high school), his pandemic-truncated freshman year at Mississippi State meant he entered the 2021 draft with only 17 collegiate starts under his belt. Still, the righty more than made up for a relatively short pitching résumé with some eye-catching top-line bullet points: a rising four-seamer that touches the mid-90s, a diving slider that tunnels well with the heater, control that will keep managers from reaching for antacids and the bullpen phone and, perhaps most importantly, a tenacious and spirited College World Series performance that called to mind the very mascot he represented. Given that he was the first of nine (!) pitching picks in a row by the Giants, Bednar seems to embody the organization's pitching development philosophy in the Zaidi era: acquire skills in bulk and let the roles sort themselves out later. Among this large 2021 crop, Bednar should have one of the fastest tracks to a major-league role.

Tyler Beede RHP Born: 05/23/93 Age: 29 Bats: R Throws: R Height: 6'2" Weight: 216 lb. Origin: Round 1, 2014 Draft (#14 overall)

YEAR	TEAM	LVL	AGE	W	L	SV	G	GS	IP	H	HR	BB/9	K/9	K	GB%	BABIP	WHIP	ERA	DRA-	WARP	MPH	FB%	Whiff%	CSP
2019	SAC	AAA	26	2	2	0	7	7	34^2	24	3	3.6	12.7	49	33.8%	.300	1.10	2.34	88	0.5				
2019	SF	MLB	26	5	10	0	24	22	117	127	22	3.5	8.7	113	44.0%	.313	1.48	5.08	97	1.4	94.4	56.1%	26.2%	45.9%
2021	SAC	AAA	28	0	6	0	16	16	48^2	50	7	8.3	9.2	50	45.5%	.316	1.95	6.66	91	0.4				
2021	SF	MLB	28	0	0	0	1	0	1	2	0	0.0	18.0	2	33.3%	.667	2.00	27.00	99	0.0	96.2	46.4%	40.0%	40.4%
2022 DC	*SF*	*MLB*	*29*	*4*	*5*	*0*	*37*	*8*	*58*	*57*	*8*	*5.6*	*9.0*	*58*	*43.2%*	*.303*	*1.61*	*5.52*	*125*	*-0.4*	*94.4*	*55.7%*	*26.7%*	*45.7%*

Comparables: Anthony DeSclafani, Austin Voth, Dillon Gee

If you, too, thought 2019 was going to be a springboard to great things but turned into 2020's trap door into nothingness, spare a thought for Beede. After installing himself as a mid-rotation arm of the future in the last pre-pandemic season, the former Vanderbilt star's 2020 was lost to Tommy John surgery. Things were looking up, as he finally got back to a major-league mound in July of this past season. But after one inning in San Francisco, and then a few weeks in Sacramento, the righty succumbed to a back injury and the 60-day IL. With the last of his minor-league options burned, his career is at a crossroads with a jam-packed 40-man roster by the Bay.

John Brebbia RHP Born: 05/30/90 Age: 32 Bats: L Throws: R Height: 6'1" Weight: 200 lb. Origin: Round 30, 2011 Draft (#929 overall)

YEAR	TEAM	LVL	AGE	W	L	SV	G	GS	IP	H	HR	BB/9	K/9	K	GB%	BABIP	WHIP	ERA	DRA-	WARP	MPH	FB%	Whiff%	CSP
2019	STL	MLB	29	3	4	0	66	0	72^2	59	6	3.3	10.8	87	27.8%	.293	1.18	3.59	89	1.2	93.7	56.6%	29.0%	50.6%
2021	SAC	AAA	31	3	0	0	17	2	15^1	9	2	2.9	15.8	27	35.7%	.269	0.91	2.93	69	0.3				
2021	SF	MLB	31	0	1	0	18	0	18^1	25	4	2.0	10.8	22	27.1%	.389	1.58	5.89	92	0.2	93.3	49.1%	23.0%	58.4%
2022 DC	*SF*	*MLB*	*32*	*2*	*2*	*0*	*52*	*0*	*45.3*	*38*	*7*	*2.9*	*9.8*	*49*	*30.6%*	*.273*	*1.16*	*3.55*	*91*	*0.4*	*93.5*	*53.2%*	*26.3%*	*54.1%*

Comparables: Manny Acosta, Fernando Rodriguez Jr., Sean Green

The Giants signed Brebbia to a one-year deal in December 2020, several months into his rehab from Tommy John surgery. The generous reading of this gambit is that the team, for little more than the major-league minimum, could have a live, experienced bullpen arm ride in like the cavalry to a depleted late-summer relief corps. The less generous reading is that maybe the front office was playing chess in one dimension too many and let their own self-perceived sharpness get a little out of hand. The outcome was decidedly more mundane: Brebbia pitched a bit in the late summer and showed the skills he's always had, even if some bad luck marred the top-line stats and kept him from being more than a bit player in the Giants' run to divisional glory. The good news for the 31-year-old: he displayed a credible return of his fastball-slider combo and shouldn't have any trouble finding himself a spot on a major-league roster in 2022.

Alex Cobb RHP
Born: 10/07/87 Age: 34 Bats: R Throws: R Height: 6'3" Weight: 205 lb. Origin: Round 4, 2006 Draft (#109 overall)

YEAR	TEAM	LVL	AGE	W	L	SV	G	GS	IP	H	HR	BB/9	K/9	K	GB%	BABIP	WHIP	ERA	DRA-	WARP	MPH	FB%	Whiff%	CSP
2019	BAL	MLB	31	0	2	0	3	3	12^1	21	9	1.5	5.8	8	48.0%	.293	1.86	10.95	121	0.0	92.3	48.0%	24.3%	44.5%
2020	BAL	MLB	32	2	5	0	10	10	52^1	52	8	3.1	6.5	38	54.2%	.275	1.34	4.30	95	0.7	92.6	48.1%	23.6%	48.9%
2021	LAA	MLB	33	8	3	0	18	18	93^1	85	5	3.2	9.5	98	53.3%	.316	1.26	3.76	89	1.4	92.7	46.7%	26.6%	50.6%
2022 DC	*SF*	*MLB*	*34*	*7*	*7*	*0*	*24*	*24*	*116.3*	*114*	*14*	*3.1*	*8.8*	*113*	*50.6%*	*.305*	*1.32*	*4.02*	*101*	*0.9*	*92.7*	*47.1%*	*25.8%*	*50.0%*

Comparables: Matt Garza, Mark Buehrle, Homer Bailey

Following Cobb's Tommy John surgery over a half-decade ago, the refrain was always the same: without his splitter, he'd never be able to return to his pre-surgery heights. Well, the splitter seems to have made it all the way back, and the resurgence came with it. Swapping Baltimore for Anaheim, Cobb posted his best season since before he went under the knife, aided not only by that splitter but the drop in home run rate one might have predicted when he escaped Camden Yards. He also benefited from a surprise mid-30s velocity bump that saw him throwing harder than ever and bringing his strikeout rate to a career-best along with it. The familiar problem prevented his season from being an unqualified success, as blister and wrist issues limited him to barely a half-season's worth of starts.

Anthony DeSclafani RHP
Born: 04/18/90 Age: 32 Bats: R Throws: R Height: 6'2" Weight: 195 lb. Origin: Round 6, 2011 Draft (#199 overall)

YEAR	TEAM	LVL	AGE	W	L	SV	G	GS	IP	H	HR	BB/9	K/9	K	GB%	BABIP	WHIP	ERA	DRA-	WARP	MPH	FB%	Whiff%	CSP
2019	CIN	MLB	29	9	9	0	31	31	166^2	151	29	2.6	9.0	167	42.0%	.276	1.20	3.89	85	3.1	94.8	55.3%	23.5%	47.7%
2020	CIN	MLB	30	1	2	0	9	7	33^2	41	7	4.3	6.7	25	39.5%	.318	1.69	7.22	136	-0.3	95.1	51.3%	23.2%	42.2%
2021	SF	MLB	31	13	7	0	31	31	167^2	141	19	2.3	8.2	152	43.3%	.268	1.09	3.17	86	2.8	94.2	45.7%	24.1%	56.5%
2022 DC	*SF*	*MLB*	*32*	*10*	*9*	*0*	*29*	*29*	*169*	*170*	*25*	*2.7*	*8.6*	*160*	*42.5%*	*.302*	*1.30*	*4.18*	*105*	*0.9*	*94.4*	*48.5%*	*23.9%*	*53.0%*

Comparables: Jim Kaat, Jason Marquis, Kevin Tapani

On balance, you'd have to say DeSclafani's one-year deal by the Bay was a good one. The erstwhile Red escaped a park (Great American) and eschewed a pitch (the fastball) that had created so much long-ball woe in the past. Whether through coaching or self-awareness, DeSclafani leaned even heavier on his potent slider in San Francisco. The top-line numbers glitter like a mirror ball, but they would have looked even more pristine had he not faced the Dodgers for 27 regular-season innings, during which he posted a 7.33 ERA (fueled by 15 walks and six bombs). The NL West giveth, the NL West taketh away. Unfortunately, the season ended with a brief and unpleasant Game 4 NLDS start against those very Dodgers. Yet, there were enough good times at the club in 2021 that DeSclafani re-upped on a three-year deal, and so the October heartbreak won't end up being the Last Days of Disco in San Francisco.

Camilo Doval RHP
Born: 07/04/97 Age: 25 Bats: R Throws: R Height: 6'2" Weight: 185 lb. Origin: International Free Agent, 2015

YEAR	TEAM	LVL	AGE	W	L	SV	G	GS	IP	H	HR	BB/9	K/9	K	GB%	BABIP	WHIP	ERA	DRA-	WARP	MPH	FB%	Whiff%	CSP
2019	SJ	A+	21	3	5	0	45	0	56^1	41	2	5.4	12.8	80	52.4%	.315	1.33	3.83	75	1.0				
2021	SAC	AAA	23	3	0	1	28	0	30^2	28	3	7.0	12.9	44	50.7%	.362	1.70	4.99	86	0.4				
2021	SF	MLB	23	5	1	3	29	0	27	19	4	3.0	12.3	37	50.0%	.259	1.04	3.00	73	0.6	98.8	41.6%	33.5%	53.0%
2022 DC	*SF*	*MLB*	*24*	*3*	*3*	*5*	*67*	*0*	*58*	*46*	*6*	*5.3*	*11.6*	*75*	*46.4%*	*.297*	*1.39*	*3.98*	*96*	*0.3*	*98.8*	*41.6%*	*33.5%*	*53.0%*

Comparables: Bryan Shaw, Trevor Gott, Jorge Julio

One of the stranger things about the Giants' 2021 was the pace at which massive changes in player roles and performances occurred: Logan Webb from a fringe starter to ace, LaMonte Wade Jr. from a Quad-A castoff to clutch legend, Brandon Crawford from a declining, league-average bat to an MVP candidate. It was as if someone flipped a switch and suddenly everyday life was toggled to the "Rocky montage" setting, with career-altering transformations happening almost over the course of what seemed like minutes. Perhaps the most dramatic of these sequences belonged to Doval, whose minor-league velocity was, up until late in the 2021 season, matched only by his wildness. Called up to the majors for the stretch run, Doval, in a matter of weeks, became the de facto closer, harnessing his location issues and overpowering hitters with a fastball that touched 103 and a slider that seemed like it was suddenly pulled on a cord attached to the center of the earth. And even if Doval gave up the winning run in the decisive Game 5 of the NLDS, there's more than enough reason to think the inspirational montage has propelled Doval's story toward more triumphant beats ahead.

Jarlín García LHP
Born: 01/18/93 Age: 29 Bats: L Throws: L Height: 6'3" Weight: 215 lb. Origin: International Free Agent, 2010

YEAR	TEAM	LVL	AGE	W	L	SV	G	GS	IP	H	HR	BB/9	K/9	K	GB%	BABIP	WHIP	ERA	DRA-	WARP	MPH	FB%	Whiff%	CSP
2019	NO	AAA	26	2	0	0	7	0	9^1	6	1	3.9	10.6	11	38.1%	.250	1.07	1.93	100	0.0				
2019	MIA	MLB	26	4	2	0	53	0	50^2	40	4	2.8	6.9	39	46.3%	.250	1.11	3.02	100	0.5	93.4	39.7%	20.9%	51.0%
2020	SF	MLB	27	2	1	0	19	0	18^1	11	0	3.4	6.9	14	46.0%	.220	0.98	0.49	97	0.2	93.8	48.6%	15.8%	55.0%
2021	SF	MLB	28	6	3	1	58	0	68^2	48	9	2.4	8.9	68	39.8%	.231	0.96	2.62	85	1.2	93.3	49.9%	22.7%	61.0%
2022 DC	*SF*	*MLB*	*29*	*3*	*3*	*0*	*67*	*0*	*58*	*52*	*7*	*3.0*	*7.6*	*49*	*42.0%*	*.269*	*1.23*	*3.67*	*95*	*0.4*	*93.4*	*47.9%*	*21.5%*	*58.5%*

Comparables: Jeff Shaw, José Álvarez, Tommy Hunter

In one of those breezy, team-produced, "get to know a player" videos made during spring training, an interviewer asks García about a skill or talent he would like to have. The lefty, in mid-warm-up toss, answers without hesitation: "To be friends with everyone." Certainly, his performance as a Giant has made him no enemies in the organization. Since he joined the team in 2020, he's been an excellent lefty option out of the pen, and he hasn't suffered much from the three-batter rule putting him in front of more right-handed hitters than he might otherwise face. Pairing his four-seamer with both a change and a slider, García thrives on weak contact, though prone to the occasional homer from righty batters. He's made himself at home in the Giants' deep pen and won a place in the hearts of Gabe Kapler, the starters whose leads he protects, and a fan base grown fond of his drama-free outings. Even if he probably won't ingratiate himself with most lefty bats across the league, opposing hitters should know that, even as he dispatches them with ease, García is channeling his inner Bob Dylan: all he really wants to do-ooooo, is, baby, be friends with you.

★ ★ ★ *2022 Top 101 Prospect* **#92** ★ ★ ★

Kyle Harrison LHP

Born: 08/12/01 Age: 20 Bats: R Throws: L Height: 6'2" Weight: 200 lb. Origin: Round 3, 2020 Draft (#85 overall)

YEAR	TEAM	LVL	AGE	W	L	SV	G	GS	IP	H	HR	BB/9	K/9	K	GB%	BABIP	WHIP	ERA	DRA-	WARP	MPH	FB%	Whiff%	CSP
2021	SJ	A	19	4	3	0	23	23	98^2	86	3	4.7	14.3	157	49.1%	.393	1.40	3.19	82	1.6				
2022 non-DC	*SF*	*MLB*	*20*	*2*	*3*	*0*	*57*	*0*	*50*	*47*	*6*	*5.6*	*10.2*	*56*	*42.9%*	*.312*	*1.57*	*5.33*	*119*	*-0.3*				

Comparables: Julio Teheran, Luiz Gohara, Jacob Turner

Harrison, a prep lefty who received the second-highest signing bonus of the third round in 2020 (behind Cole Wilcox), has made a quick ascent up prospect lists thanks to added bulk and velocity. His best secondary is currently a sweepy slider, and he'll need to work on his non-fastball offerings if he's going to fulfill his potential as one of the highest-upside arms in the org. Considering he punched out 105 more batters than he walked in his first 98 professional innings, we'd say he's on the right track.

Hunter Harvey RHP

Born: 12/09/94 Age: 27 Bats: R Throws: R Height: 6'3" Weight: 210 lb. Origin: Round 1, 2013 Draft (#22 overall)

YEAR	TEAM	LVL	AGE	W	L	SV	G	GS	IP	H	HR	BB/9	K/9	K	GB%	BABIP	WHIP	ERA	DRA-	WARP	MPH	FB%	Whiff%	CSP
2019	BOW	AA	24	2	5	1	14	11	59	63	14	3.2	9.3	61	37.9%	.316	1.42	5.19	122	-0.2				
2019	NOR	AAA	24	1	1	0	12	0	16^2	13	2	2.7	11.9	22	38.1%	.282	1.08	4.32	74	0.4				
2019	BAL	MLB	24	1	0	0	7	0	6^1	3	1	5.7	15.6	11	54.5%	.200	1.11	1.42	85	0.1	98.5	69.6%	25.4%	48.1%
2020	BAL	MLB	25	0	2	0	10	0	8^2	8	2	2.1	6.2	6	39.3%	.231	1.15	4.15	115	0.0	97.5	77.2%	23.3%	49.2%
2021	NOR	AAA	26	2	1	0	8	1	10	19	2	1.8	6.3	7	54.8%	.436	2.10	8.10	104	0.1				
2021	BAL	MLB	26	0	0	0	9	0	8^2	8	1	3.1	6.2	6	48.1%	.269	1.27	4.15	106	0.0	97.2	64.0%	11.8%	57.8%
2022 DC	*SF*	*MLB*	*27*	*2*	*2*	*0*	*52*	*0*	*45.3*	*47*	*6*	*3.3*	*6.9*	*34*	*42.2%*	*.298*	*1.42*	*4.88*	*117*	*-0.2*	*97.5*	*69.5%*	*17.9%*	*53.3%*

Comparables: Miguel Diaz, Miguel Almonte, Jared Hughes

It's hard to escape the feeling that Harvey's career is stagnating. The numbers don't help. Oblique, lat and triceps ailments limited the former top prospect to 8 ⅔ June innings, over which he struck out six and allowed four earned runs. Swap out the specifics of the injuries and it was a repeat of his 2020 season. The Orioles even held him at Triple-A when he did finally appear to be healthy in September, which only reinforced the notion that no progress had been made. They almost sneaked him through waivers before he was claimed by the very final team who could: the 107-win Giants. One thing changed: Harvey got a year older, which means he's entering his age-27 season with fewer than 30 big-league innings to his name.

Scott Kazmir LHP

Born: 01/24/84 Age: 38 Bats: L Throws: L Height: 6'0" Weight: 185 lb. Origin: Round 1, 2002 Draft (#15 overall)

YEAR	TEAM	LVL	AGE	W	L	SV	G	GS	IP	H	HR	BB/9	K/9	K	GB%	BABIP	WHIP	ERA	DRA-	WARP	MPH	FB%	Whiff%	CSP
2021	SAC	AAA	37	3	3	0	13	12	52^2	45	6	3.1	8.2	48	39.2%	.277	1.20	4.61	104	0.1				
2021	SF	MLB	37	0	1	0	5	4	11^1	15	3	4.8	7.9	10	47.4%	.343	1.85	6.35	112	0.0	92.4	54.6%	20.6%	54.8%
2022 non-DC	*SF*	*MLB*	*38*	*2*	*3*	*0*	*57*	*0*	*50*	*50*	*7*	*3.2*	*7.2*	*39*	*38.4%*	*.287*	*1.37*	*4.58*	*114*	*-0.2*	*92.4*	*54.6%*	*20.6%*	*54.8%*

Comparables: Frank Tanana, Mike Hampton, Curt Simmons

Farhan Zaidi and his front-office team have been running so pure that the only plausible explanation for the head-scratching appearance of Kazmir in 2021 is this: In a BS session among some Giants' front-office employees, one challenged Zaidi to reclaim a former major-leaguer—any former major-leaguer—off the retirement scrap heap and coax the husk of the ex-player's talent into a major-league contributor. After a few names were bandied about, a lower-level quant, fighting through the giggles prompted by a recently-consumed edible, sputtered out, "OK, OK, I got one. Scott! Kazmir!" And a smile spread across Zaidi's face as he reached for his iPhone and began furiously texting. How else can anyone explain the unaccountable renaissance of Kazmir, whose last major-league pitch was in 2016, and whose only comeback stop was the independent Constellation Energy League, a 2020 pop-up outfit in Texas solely designed for unsigned players to get some reps during the pandemic? Alas, the 37-year-old lefty didn't return to his previous glories, such as they were, but in late May, when Kazmir was completing his warm-up tosses at Oracle Park before making his Giants debut against the Dodgers, Zaidi glanced over at the dumbfounded data analyst with raised eyebrows, as if to say, "My powers are boundless. Do not test them."

Dominic Leone RHP

Born: 10/26/91 Age: 30 Bats: R Throws: R Height: 5'10" Weight: 215 lb. Origin: Round 16, 2012 Draft (#491 overall)

YEAR	TEAM	LVL	AGE	W	L	SV	G	GS	IP	H	HR	BB/9	K/9	K	GB%	BABIP	WHIP	ERA	DRA-	WARP	MPH	FB%	Whiff%	CSP
2019	MEM	AAA	27	1	0	0	23	0	31^2	20	3	4.0	11.9	42	33.3%	.246	1.07	2.84	82	0.5				
2019	STL	MLB	27	1	0	1	40	0	40^2	39	9	4.9	10.2	46	38.4%	.294	1.50	5.53	98	0.5	92.9	83.8%	30.3%	40.8%
2020	CLE	MLB	28	0	0	0	12	0	9^2	14	3	4.7	14.9	16	30.8%	.478	1.97	8.38	103	0.1	93.5	64.4%	36.8%	37.6%
2021	SAC	AAA	29	0	1	2	7	1	9	6	0	3.0	16.0	16	26.7%	.400	1.00	1.00	86	0.1				
2021	SF	MLB	29	4	5	2	57	4	53^2	37	2	3.7	8.4	50	46.9%	.250	1.10	1.51	98	0.5	94.9	72.4%	30.4%	51.2%
2022 DC	*SF*	*MLB*	*30*	*8*	*7*	*0*	*75*	*16*	*76*	*66*	*10*	*3.8*	*10.1*	*85*	*40.9%*	*.289*	*1.29*	*3.81*	*95*	*0.5*	*94.4*	*73.7%*	*31.1%*	*47.8%*

Comparables: Mike Morin, Jeremy Jeffress, Cam Bedrosian

Every winning team has its Leones: the unheralded yeomen of the bullpen who fill in whenever, wherever. You need a reliever to stop the bleeding after a starter's early exit? DOM. You need a starter for a bullpen game? DOM. You need to get a tough righty out in the eighth? DOM. Hell, you need a dude to pick a rogue save? Once again, DOM. By improving his control, inducing more ground-ball contact, and shrinking the homers to nearly nil, DOMinic became something approaching DOMinant. DOM might not be lucky enough to find a sub-2.00 ERA again, but at least he won't have managers screaming the safeword into the bullpen phone very often.

Zack Littell RHP Born: 10/05/95 Age: 26 Bats: R Throws: R Height: 6'4" Weight: 220 lb. Origin: Round 11, 2013 Draft (#327 overall)

YEAR	TEAM	LVL	AGE	W	L	SV	G	GS	IP	H	HR	BB/9	K/9	K	GB%	BABIP	WHIP	ERA	DRA-	WARP	MPH	FB%	Whiff%	CSP
2019	ROC	AAA	23	3	3	1	20	7	63	55	11	3.6	9.7	68	47.9%	.278	1.27	3.71	93	1.0				
2019	MIN	MLB	23	6	0	0	29	0	37	34	4	2.2	7.8	32	38.1%	.300	1.16	2.68	103	0.3	94.1	49.2%	27.3%	52.6%
2020	MIN	MLB	24	0	0	0	6	0	6^{1}	12	5	4.3	4.3	3	33.3%	.368	2.37	9.95	139	-0.1	94.2	54.7%	13.3%	53.5%
2021	SF	MLB	25	4	0	2	63	2	61^{2}	46	7	3.5	9.2	63	46.6%	.253	1.14	2.92	87	1.0	95.0	57.8%	28.5%	55.4%
2022 DC	*SF*	*MLB*	*26*	*3*	*3*	*0*	*67*	*0*	*58*	*54*	*7*	*3.6*	*9.6*	*62*	*44.1%*	*.303*	*1.34*	*4.06*	*100*	*0.2*	*94.8*	*56.3%*	*27.4%*	*54.8%*

Comparables: Brandon Maurer, Lucas Sims, Jeurys Familia

"It's Lit-TELL, not LIT-tle," the big, ginger-bearded righty from North Carolina seems to say with his glower as he stares you down in the batter's box. Littell emerged as a go-to right-handed option for Gabe Kapler, able to get a key third out or hang around for multiple innings when the gassed staff needed rest. Littell survives on the bread-and-butter four-seam/slider combo featured by the vast majority of righty relievers, but he thrives on ground-ball contact more than the strikeout. As a key member of a surprisingly consistent and deep bullpen, Littell looks to be a big part of the relief corps in 2022.

Sammy Long LHP Born: 07/08/95 Age: 26 Bats: L Throws: L Height: 6'1" Weight: 185 lb. Origin: Round 18, 2016 Draft (#540 overall)

YEAR	TEAM	LVL	AGE	W	L	SV	G	GS	IP	H	HR	BB/9	K/9	K	GB%	BABIP	WHIP	ERA	DRA-	WARP	MPH	FB%	Whiff%	CSP
2019	KAN	A	23	8	5	0	30	15	97	73	7	2.6	10.4	112	39.5%	.277	1.04	3.06	77	2.0				
2021	RIC	AA	25	0	1	0	4	4	15	12	0	2.4	13.2	22	41.2%	.353	1.07	3.00	89	0.2				
2021	SAC	AAA	25	1	0	0	11	3	26^{1}	16	2	3.1	10.6	31	45.2%	.233	0.95	2.05	84	0.4				
2021	SF	MLB	25	2	1	0	12	5	40^{2}	37	5	3.3	8.4	38	39.2%	.278	1.28	5.53	99	0.4	92.7	43.2%	21.4%	57.9%
2022 DC	*SF*	*MLB*	*26*	*5*	*5*	*0*	*34*	*12*	*71*	*65*	*9*	*3.4*	*8.2*	*64*	*39.7%*	*.281*	*1.29*	*3.93*	*98*	*0.5*	*92.7*	*43.2%*	*21.4%*	*57.9%*

Comparables: Nate Karns, Caleb Smith, Spencer Turnbull

After a few underwhelming years in the Rays organization, Long put his baseball career on hold to become a firefighter, but somewhere in the middle of his EMT courses the lefty discovered a different kind of heat, as his formerly pedestrian fastball bumped up to the mid-90s and his bread-and-butter curveball developed a little more bite. For the Giants, Long played a walk-on role in the ensemble cast of a deep and continually churning pitching staff. If this were a film, he would have been credited as "Curveball Guy," as his 12-6 diver comes in nearly 20 ticks slower than the fastball, a weapon most effective the first time it's deployed. This formula served the Giants well, but with little depth to the arsenal, Long's stay with the big club was relatively short. There are worse career outcomes than the pitching equivalent of a character actor, and Long will likely reappear in the future to deliver some fleeting but narratively significant dialogue before he shuffles offscreen yet again.

Jake McGee LHP Born: 08/06/86 Age: 35 Bats: L Throws: L Height: 6'4" Weight: 229 lb. Origin: Round 5, 2004 Draft (#135 overall)

YEAR	TEAM	LVL	AGE	W	L	SV	G	GS	IP	H	HR	BB/9	K/9	K	GB%	BABIP	WHIP	ERA	DRA-	WARP	MPH	FB%	Whiff%	CSP
2019	COL	MLB	32	0	2	0	45	0	41^{1}	47	11	2.4	7.6	35	35.1%	.300	1.40	4.35	115	0.1	93.4	80.2%	19.5%	51.5%
2020	LAD	MLB	33	3	1	0	24	0	20^{1}	14	2	1.3	14.6	33	37.2%	.300	0.84	2.66	68	0.6	95.0	97.0%	34.4%	59.0%
2021	SF	MLB	34	3	2	31	62	0	59^{2}	44	7	1.5	8.7	58	35.5%	.228	0.91	2.72	98	0.6	95.1	90.1%	20.6%	59.0%
2022 DC	*SF*	*MLB*	*35*	*3*	*3*	*20*	*67*	*0*	*58*	*55*	*9*	*2.2*	*8.1*	*52*	*36.5%*	*.281*	*1.19*	*3.80*	*98*	*0.3*	*94.8*	*89.6%*	*22.8%*	*57.7%*

Comparables: Francisco Rodríguez, J.C. Romero, Chuck McElroy

There's not a lot of complexity with McGee. He'll get up there, wing fastball after fastball in the mid-90s, switching it up (very) occasionally with the slider. His deceptive release makes the ball difficult to pick up, and he throws strikes that jump on the hitter, messing with timing even when the location is center-cut. Like so much with the Giants, McGee brings a very specific set of skills valued more by this organization than in baseball generally. And even though Gabe Kapler is broadminded about the concept of "closer," McGee effectively locked down that role all season, until an oblique strain in September paved the way for Camilo Doval. Whether or not the crown of closer is his alone to wear, McGee should be back slingin' late-inning heat in 2022.

Tyler Rogers RHP Born: 12/17/90 Age: 31 Bats: R Throws: R Height: 6'3" Weight: 181 lb. Origin: Round 10, 2013 Draft (#312 overall)

YEAR	TEAM	LVL	AGE	W	L	SV	G	GS	IP	H	HR	BB/9	K/9	K	GB%	BABIP	WHIP	ERA	DRA-	WARP	MPH	FB%	Whiff%	CSP
2019	SAC	AAA	28	4	2	5	49	1	62	59	6	4.1	8.0	55	61.5%	.303	1.40	4.21	83	1.0				
2019	SF	MLB	28	2	0	0	17	0	17^{2}	12	0	1.5	8.2	16	68.0%	.245	0.85	1.02	89	0.3	82.4	67.1%	16.5%	55.4%
2020	SF	MLB	29	3	3	3	29	0	28	31	2	1.9	8.7	27	53.5%	.349	1.32	4.50	82	0.6	82.4	63.8%	24.2%	52.1%
2021	SF	MLB	30	7	1	13	80	0	81	74	5	1.4	6.1	55	57.3%	.279	1.07	2.22	99	0.8	82.9	57.4%	16.6%	54.0%
2022 DC	*SF*	*MLB*	*31*	*3*	*3*	*8*	*67*	*0*	*58*	*60*	*4*	*2.3*	*6.1*	*39*	*57.1%*	*.299*	*1.29*	*3.83*	*99*	*0.3*	*82.7*	*59.2%*	*18.1%*	*53.7%*

Comparables: Nick Vincent, Tyler Kinley, Richard Rodríguez

If you're going to be the One Neat Trick guy, it goes without saying that the trick had better be pretty darn good if you hope to have any kind of longevity in the majors. Rogers seems poised for exactly that, if his NL-leading 80 appearances in 2021 are any indication. The submariner, whose release is so low he's probably scrubbing dirt from his knuckles after every appearance, has found a way to throw a pitch, classified as a slider but colloquially dubbed a "UFO ball," that rises and sweeps with an extreme action that literally no other pitcher currently features. Rogers avoids barrels like no other, excelling in both soft and downward contact. It seems churlish at this point to mention the low-80s fastball, but he has a twin brother who can bring the heat, comparatively speaking. For a guy who has literally the same genes as another major-league reliever, Rogers may be the most *sui generis* pitcher in the game.

Aaron Sanchez RHP Born: 07/01/92 Age: 30 Bats: R Throws: R Height: 6'4" Weight: 210 lb. Origin: Round 1, 2010 Draft (#34 overall)

YEAR	TEAM	LVL	AGE	W	L	SV	G	GS	IP	H	HR	BB/9	K/9	K	GB%	BABIP	WHIP	ERA	DRA-	WARP	MPH	FB%	Whiff%	CSP
2019	HOU	MLB	26	2	0	0	4	4	18^{2}	14	5	4.3	7.7	16	47.3%	.180	1.23	4.82	117	0.0	92.2	53.8%	24.6%	45.0%
2021	SAC	AAA	28	1	1	0	6	6	17^{1}	24	4	5.2	5.7	11	42.9%	.339	1.96	7.79	130	-0.2				
2021	SF	MLB	28	1	1	0	9	7	35^{1}	32	2	3.8	6.6	26	53.2%	.275	1.33	3.06	106	0.2	90.4	49.4%	20.6%	54.1%
2022 DC	*FA*	*MLB*	*29*	*4*	*5*	*0*	*26*	*12*	*70.7*	*77*	*8*	*4.3*	*6.8*	*53*	*48.6%*	*.311*	*1.57*	*5.36*	*124*	*-0.4*	*92.4*	*54.0%*	*21.3%*	*49.8%*

Comparables: Mike Torrez, Jake Westbrook, Scott Feldman

After video surfaced of a post-injury Sanchez throwing an unprecedented 98 mph in a workout last winter, you might think of a Borscht Belt comic telling the joke about the man asking his doctor if he can play the piano after his surgery, with the punchline, "That's wonderful. I could never play it before." After signing with the Giants, Sanchez demonstrated notes that were a little less pleasing to the ear (that 98 eventually settled in around 90), but he still looked like he could vamp his way to a back-end rotation spot on a team desperate to stabilize its starting pitching. After a biceps injury in May, along with a couple of aborted returns, and eventually one start with the Giants in August, the righty was released, and now hopes for a return to health and, potentially, another chance to strike a chord with a major-league team.

Tony Watson LHP Born: 05/30/85 Age: 37 Bats: L Throws: L Height: 6'3" Weight: 224 lb. Origin: Round 9, 2007 Draft (#278 overall)

YEAR	TEAM	LVL	AGE	W	L	SV	G	GS	IP	H	HR	BB/9	K/9	K	GB%	BABIP	WHIP	ERA	DRA-	WARP	MPH	FB%	Whiff%	CSP
2019	SF	MLB	34	2	2	0	60	0	54	56	9	2.0	6.8	41	45.1%	.290	1.26	4.17	116	0.1	93.2	51.5%	25.9%	47.4%
2020	SF	MLB	35	1	0	2	21	0	18	13	3	1.5	7.5	15	50.0%	.196	0.89	2.50	95	0.2	89.8	37.9%	27.2%	44.2%
2021	LAA	MLB	36	3	3	0	36	0	33	25	3	3.8	6.8	25	52.1%	.237	1.18	4.64	112	0.1	92.1	40.0%	28.3%	47.1%
2021	SF	MLB	36	4	1	0	26	0	24^{1}	15	1	1.5	7.0	19	37.3%	.212	0.78	2.96	98	0.3	93.2	46.7%	24.1%	54.0%
2022 DC	*FA*	*MLB*	*37*	*3*	*3*	*0*	*71*	*0*	*61.7*	*61*	*7*	*2.6*	*7.7*	*52*	*44.6%*	*.296*	*1.28*	*3.98*	*100*	*0.2*	*92.3*	*43.8%*	*26.5%*	*48.6%*

Comparables: Mark Melancon, Pedro Feliciano, Sergio Romo

It didn't take much sleuthing to attribute Watson's 2020 decline in velocity to his advancing age and the strangeness of 2020. But it was more of a mystery to figure out why the lefty was throwing nearly three ticks faster after his move to Anaheim but getting worse results. The Giants traded for him in July to get the veteran under the magnifying glass—and lo, when he moved back to the Bay he retained the velocity, harnessed his control and discovered some luck along the way to becoming a key late-inning lefty out of the Giants' unsolvable pen. Watson's return to form helped make Gabe Kapler's potentially brain-teasing bullpen decisions rather elementary.

Logan Webb RHP Born: 11/18/96 Age: 25 Bats: R Throws: R Height: 6'1" Weight: 220 lb. Origin: Round 4, 2014 Draft (#118 overall)

YEAR	TEAM	LVL	AGE	W	L	SV	G	GS	IP	H	HR	BB/9	K/9	K	GB%	BABIP	WHIP	ERA	DRA-	WARP	MPH	FB%	Whiff%	CSP
2019	AUG	A	22	1	0	0	2	1	10	4	0	2.7	8.1	9	58.3%	.167	0.70	0.90	98	0.1				
2019	RIC	AA	22	1	4	0	8	7	41^{1}	41	2	2.6	10.2	47	65.0%	.331	1.28	2.18	95	0.4				
2019	SAC	AAA	22	0	0	0	1	1	7	7	0	0.0	9.0	7	63.2%	.368	1.00	1.29	90	0.1				
2019	SF	MLB	22	2	3	0	8	8	39^{2}	44	5	3.2	8.4	37	47.5%	.333	1.46	5.22	94	0.5	93.1	56.4%	22.8%	46.7%
2020	SF	MLB	23	3	4	0	13	11	54^{1}	61	4	4.0	7.6	46	52.1%	.350	1.56	5.47	97	0.7	92.5	53.9%	22.9%	47.2%
2021	SF	MLB	24	11	3	0	27	26	148^{1}	128	9	2.2	9.6	158	60.9%	.312	1.11	3.03	71	3.6	93.0	49.1%	28.8%	53.3%
2022 DC	*SF*	*MLB*	*25*	*10*	*8*	*0*	*29*	*29*	*148.7*	*138*	*12*	*3.0*	*8.9*	*146*	*57.2%*	*.304*	*1.26*	*3.43*	*88*	*2.1*	*92.9*	*50.7%*	*27.1%*	*51.5%*

Comparables: Johnny Cueto, Chris Carpenter, Andy Benes

The buzz around Webb started in spring, when the Northern California native unveiled newfound command with his changeup and switched out a four-seamer for a sinker with extreme fading action. The start of the year was promising for the righty, but a shoulder strain drained some hope from Webb's season. Once Webb returned, however, there was no looking back, as his final 17 starts saw a silky-smooth ERA under 3.00 and a K:BB of 104/19 (oh, and he went 7-0, if you care about such things). By late September, Webb had ascended to another level: the pitcher who was a borderline member of the rotation in April had become the rotation leader by October. For three games—the division clincher against the Padres on the season's final day (with a home run, to boot), the NLDS opening-game shutdown of the Dodgers and a nearly as dominant (if not winning) effort in Game 5—Webb had spun his way to being the new staff ace. Perhaps we should hesitate on the coronation until we've seen a bit more, but the arsenal, command and confidence suggest that Webb is sticking around.

Alex Wood LHP Born: 01/12/91 Age: 31 Bats: R Throws: L Height: 6'4" Weight: 215 lb. Origin: Round 2, 2012 Draft (#85 overall)

YEAR	TEAM	LVL	AGE	W	L	SV	G	GS	IP	H	HR	BB/9	K/9	K	GB%	BABIP	WHIP	ERA	DRA-	WARP	MPH	FB%	Whiff%	CSP
2019	CIN	MLB	28	1	3	0	7	7	35^{2}	41	11	2.3	7.6	30	36.3%	.300	1.40	5.80	114	0.1	89.9	50.3%	24.9%	47.6%
2020	LAD	MLB	29	0	1	0	9	2	12^{2}	17	2	4.3	10.7	15	39.0%	.385	1.82	6.39	105	0.1	91.4	48.2%	28.7%	45.3%
2021	SF	MLB	30	10	4	0	26	26	138^{2}	125	14	2.5	9.9	152	50.0%	.305	1.18	3.83	85	2.3	91.9	46.4%	27.6%	54.2%
2022 DC	*SF*	*MLB*	*31*	*10*	*8*	*0*	*29*	*29*	*154.3*	*135*	*17*	*2.5*	*9.2*	*158*	*47.3%*	*.286*	*1.16*	*3.31*	*87*	*2.2*	*91.7*	*46.9%*	*27.5%*	*53.0%*

Comparables: Tommy John, Tom Glavine, Mark Portugal

You could do one of those "how it started/how it's going" memes with Wood's pitching motion. Screencap an image as he begins his windup with a boring, upright, vanilla leg-kick, and he looks controlled and restrained. How it started? Great! Easy-peasy! Take a screencap from approximately one second later, and he looks like he's trying to simulate the four ordinal directions of the compass with his extremities: pitching arm angled back toward third base, glove hand torqued toward first, head pointing toward center field in a manner that makes it physically unlikely that he can actually see either catcher's glove or batter, and right leg kicked out toward home plate as if he's trying to stretch, Plastic Man-style, well beyond the dirt of the mound. Only the anchoring left leg seems to keep Wood's body from centrifugally ejecting parts across the field. How's it going? Off the bloody rails, by all appearances! And yet, in spite of a career dotted with injury and inconsistency one could deduce from his *Cirque de Soleil* mound stylings, Wood found order amid the chaos for good chunks of 2021, posting his best year since 2017, when he won 16 games for the Dodgers and looked like a legitimate mid-rotation asset. He picked a good time (and a good team) to put all the pieces together, and the Giants saw enough to ink the lefty to a multi-year deal.

Lineouts

Hitters

HITTER	POS	TEAM	LVL	AGE	PA	R	2B	3B	HR	RBI	BB	K	SB	CS	AVG/OBP/SLG	DRC+	BABIP	BRR	FRAA	WARP
Aeverson Arteaga	SS	GNTO	ROK	18	226	42	12	1	9	43	23	69	8	0	.294/.367/.503		.398			
Austin Dean	LF	MEM	AAA	27	56	6	6	0	1	8	7	19	0	1	.213/.339/.404	86	.333	-1.0	LF(5): -1.6, RF(2): 1.6, CF(1): -0.1	0.0
	LF	STL	MLB	27	38	5	2	0	1	7	6	11	0	0	.233/.342/.400	100	.300	0.6	LF(6): 0.4, RF(3): -0.0	0.2
Jason Krizan	IF	SAC	AAA	32	480	67	26	1	16	73	39	70	1	0	.316/.367/.492	112	.340	1.9	1B(42): -0.7, 2B(36): -2.4, 3B(22): -0.9	1.9
Joe McCarthy	1B	SAC	AAA	27	315	48	18	1	15	55	32	61	4	1	.305/.384/.542	116	.342	-0.2	1B(34): -3.1, LF(22): -2.6, RF(15): -0.8	0.9
Casey Schmitt	3B	SJ	A	22	280	36	14	1	8	29	22	44	2	2	.247/.318/.406	110	.269	0.4	3B(50): 6.0	1.7
Mike Tauchman	OF	SAC	AAA	30	154	25	9	2	3	19	20	36	2	1	.266/.370/.438	95	.337	1.8	LF(20): -2.0, RF(11): 0.2	0.4
	OF	SF	MLB	30	175	21	4	0	4	15	22	52	1	3	.178/.286/.283	75	.240	0.9	LF(39): 1.4, RF(13): -0.6, CF(10): -0.7	0.2
	OF	NYY	MLB	30	16	1	1	0	0	0	1	6	2	0	.214/.267/.286	70	.375	0.0	LF(6): -0.2, CF(2): 0.1, RF(1): -0.0	0.0
Ka'ai Tom	LF	IND	AAA	27	67	6	1	0	2	7	5	19	0	0	.190/.299/.310	88	.243	0.2	RF(10): 0.3, LF(4): 0.5, CF(1): 0.1	0.2
	LF	OAK	MLB	27	16	1	0	0	0	1	0	6	0	0	.063/.063/.063	75	.100	-0.3	RF(4): -0.3, P(1): -0.0	-0.1
	LF	PIT	MLB	27	117	9	2	1	2	11	17	30	1	0	.152/.308/.261	88	.190	-2.3	LF(31): -0.1	0.0
Luis Toribio	IF	SJ	A	20	408	59	20	1	7	39	63	113	2	1	.229/.351/.356	94	.320	0.0	1B(47): -5.2, 3B(29): -1.3	0.1
Jason Vosler	IF	SAC	AAA	27	309	51	14	1	15	51	36	45	0	0	.295/.385/.529	122	.300	-2.3	3B(31): 4.8, 1B(23): -1.4, 2B(12): 1.6	2.0
	IF	SF	MLB	27	82	12	4	0	3	9	7	21	2	0	.178/.256/.356	86	.200	-0.6	3B(19): -1.7, 1B(3): -0.1, 2B(3): -0.0	-0.1
Will Wilson	SS	SCO	WIN	22	74	9	3	0	2	8	6	19	0	0	.164/.243/.299		.196			
	SS	EUG	A+	22	224	37	14	2	10	26	24	56	7	1	.251/.339/.497	110	.298	0.8	SS(42): -2.0, 2B(4): -0.4	0.8
	SS	RIC	AA	22	221	20	8	0	5	22	22	81	1	0	.189/.281/.306	68	.291	-0.6	SS(48): -6.8, 3B(3): -0.1	-0.9

With a no-doubt glove that should stick at short, and a bat that isn't a liability (yet), Venezuelan signee **Aeverson Arteaga** graduated to Low-A San Jose at the end of 2021. It would be tempting to refer to the 18-year-old as "Double-A" but his talents should set our expectations much higher than that. ⚾ Now in his late 20s and brimming with early-bloomer traits, **Austin Dean** is the perfect candidate for a late-career renaissance in San Francisco. Failing that, at least he'll afford another fanbase the pleasure of punning his name into oblivion. ⚾ **Jason Krizan**, a veritable Crash Davis (4,520 minor-league PAs without a single day in the bigs), was the King of Sacramento for one season while so many River Cats were called to the Bay. 2021 could be the crowning achievement of Krizan's career, but on the other hand, *somebody* has to be next year's Frank Schwindel. ⚾ "I have here in my hand a list of six pitchers," **Joe McCarthy** intones, "who represent all the pitchers I have faced in my major-league career." He continues, mumbling: "A career in which I am 0-for-10." The 27-year-old corner outfielder demolished Triple-A but hasn't been able to join the party in the bigs quite yet. ⚾ Now that **Casey Schmitt** has left his two-way dreams in the rear-view mirror, the burden of proving he can be a masher at the hot corner just got a bit heavier. His Low-A pro debut was a mixed bag—a decent approach and good eye, but less than ideal power. ⚾ **Mike Tauchman** was acquired for Wandy Peralta and Connor Cannon in May when the Giants' outfield situation could be charitably described as "a mess," but the former Yankee and Rockie did little to clean things up. It turns out that a lefty hitting in Yankee Stadium during the turboball year of 2019 might not be able to transport the magic (well, a 99 DRC+, anyway) outside of that particular time and place. ⚾ Last year the ultra-patient **Ka'ai Tom** was taken from Cleveland in the Rule 5 draft, said "aloha" (in both senses of the word) to Oakland and Pittsburgh, made and failed in his major-league debut, lent credence to the belief his 2019 power spike was a fluke and caught on with the Giants on a minor-league contract. Since you started reading this he's probably drawn five walks and been released again. ⚾ On-base skills are a nice platform for further offensive development, but walks alone cannot feed your family. **Luis Toribio,** once a young prospect and now a 21-year-old who just logged a full season at Low-A, has yet to bring the other facets of his profile quite as far as hoped. ⚾ **Jason Vosler** is the kind of older, high-minors, power-and-patience corner bat that Farhan Zaidi has acquired in bulk over the last couple of seasons. The former Cub and Padre may not have been the best of the 2021 bunch, but his early struggles in San Francisco laid the groundwork for the later successes of LaMonte Wade, Jr. and Darin Ruf. ⚾ Will **Will Wilson** hit? The first shot at the upper minors didn't go well for Wilson, and the Giants tried the shortstop out all over the diamond in the Arizona Fall League.

Pitchers

PITCHER	TEAM	LVL	AGE	W	L	SV	G	GS	IP	H	HR	BB/9	K/9	K	GB%	BABIP	WHIP	ERA	DRA-	WARP	MPH	FB%	WHF	CSP
Prelander Berroa	SJ	A	21	5	6	0	24	24	98^2	79	13	4.8	12.3	135	39.2%	.310	1.34	3.56	94	0.9				
Kervin Castro	SAC	AAA	22	6	1	1	30	0	44	31	3	4.5	12.3	60	38.4%	.292	1.20	2.86	76	0.8				
	SF	MLB	22	1	1	0	10	0	13^1	13	0	2.7	8.8	13	35.9%	.342	1.28	0.00	99	0.1	94.6	74.6%	31.6%	60.1%
Tyler Chatwood	SAC	AAA	31	0	0	1	4	0	5^2	2	0	4.8	9.5	6	100.0%	.200	0.88	0.00	84	0.1				
	SF	MLB	31	0	1	0	2	0	4	6	1	2.3	13.5	6	33.3%	.455	1.75	6.75	108	0.0	95.7	54.7%	30.6%	50.5%
	TOR	MLB	31	1	2	1	30	0	28	20	1	6.4	10.3	32	52.9%	.275	1.43	5.46	98	0.3	95.4	53.9%	31.6%	47.1%
Seth Corry	EUG	A+	22	3	3	0	19	19	67^2	53	4	8.4	13.3	100	45.3%	.363	1.71	5.99	99	0.6				
Sean Hjelle	RIC	AA	24	3	2	0	14	14	65^2	60	8	2.6	9.5	69	55.2%	.299	1.20	3.15	93	0.8				
	SAC	AAA	24	2	6	0	10	10	53^1	67	6	4.9	5.9	35	54.6%	.345	1.80	5.74	111	-0.2				
Mauricio Llovera	LHV	AAA	25	2	2	5	32	4	52	41	5	4.2	8.3	48	34.7%	.255	1.25	3.46	99	0.7				
	PHI	MLB	25	1	0	0	6	0	6^2	10	5	5.4	9.5	7	30.4%	.278	2.10	9.45	115	0.0	94.7	55.2%	21.5%	52.6%
Conner Menez	SAC	AAA	26	2	3	1	26	5	42^2	56	7	6.1	9.5	45	37.0%	.386	1.99	6.75	98	0.2				
	SF	MLB	26	1	0	0	8	1	14	16	2	1.9	9.6	15	59.1%	.333	1.36	3.86	85	0.2	91.0	34.0%	21.7%	57.9%
Reyes Moronta	SAC	AAA	28	0	2	0	24	2	18	22	3	13.0	9.5	19	32.1%	.388	2.67	11.00	111	-0.1				
	SF	MLB	28	0	0	0	4	0	4	1	1	0.0	4.5	2	54.5%	.000	0.25	2.25	107	0.0	94.2	39.6%	14.3%	60.4%
Randy Rodriguez	SJ	A	21	6	3	2	32	0	62	44	0	3.3	14.7	101	36.2%	.346	1.08	1.74	88	0.8				
Gregory Santos	SAC	AAA	21	1	1	0	14	0	15^2	16	1	5.2	8.6	15	63.0%	.333	1.60	5.17	88	0.2				
	SF	MLB	21	0	2	0	3	0	2	5	3	9.0	13.5	3	37.5%	.400	3.50	22.50	94	0.0	98.1	43.4%	25.0%	54.6%
Nick Swiney	GNTB	ROK	22	0	0	0	5	5	8	7	0	6.7	18.0	16	50.0%	.500	1.63	1.13						
	SJ	A	22	0	0	0	7	7	24^1	16	0	4.4	15.5	42	45.8%	.333	1.15	0.74	85	0.4				

With apologies to the fading hopes of Jaylin Davis, **Prelander Berroa** has emerged as the prize return from Minnesota in the Sam Dyson trade. The righty fights against the biases of being a smaller pitcher by firing at 96-98 mph and offsetting the heat with a diving curve. The main item on the 2021 to-do list is to memorize a line from a certain 1986 Janet Jackson hit: "Control ... to get what I want." There's something incongruous about a dude with a name straight from a classic Western and the same hometown as the fictional Dunder Mifflin, but Scranton's own **Mason Black** will try to make his paper in the majors with a profile the Giants seemed to draft with multiple early-round picks: big body, big fastball, we'll figure out the rest later. Coincidence? Or Scrantonicity? **Kervin Castro** didn't give up a run in 13 ⅓ innings, which requires a little luck, but didn't require too much luck. Like many converted catchers, he ascended quickly thanks to having the arm strength in place, but it's the movement he's already found on his pitches that make him a promising name for 2022. Two TJ surgeries, five years in Colorado, a season with the Cubs where he walked more than he struck out: **Tyler Chatwood** has been through some *things*. It's a testament to the stuff he flashes that he keeps finding himself in major-league uniforms. Paring down his arsenal to a sinker-cutter combo has upped his strikeouts but hasn't tamed his control to the point where he can carve out a stable role for himself. As good as the good news is for lefty **Seth Corry**, the bad news is worse than bad. The former: strikeout rates north of 30% as he moved to High-A. The latter: walk rates at 20%. As he survives largely on finesse, this seems like a pretty big (slant rhyme) worry for Corry. Coming up through the minors in the Seattle system, **Sam Delaplane** had the tools of a closer (highlighted by a plus-plus slider), and to the Mariners' credit, they didn't even futz around pretending he was a "starter until further notice." After the dreaded UCL injury, he was offloaded to the Giants for cash. Here's hoping Delaplane can once again take flight in 2022. When **Sean Hjelle** makes his major-league debut, likely in 2022, the 6-foot-11 righty is poised to be the tallest drink of water in the bigs, and the closest player to seven feet since Jon Rauch. But, with an underwhelming 10 starts—too many walks, too much contact—at Triple-A in 2021, he has to do a bit more on the mound before we stop leading his story with his size. There was a time when **Mauricio Llovera** looked like he could turn into a medium- to high-leverage arm after a permanent move to the bullpen in 2020. He has seen some major-league action in each of the last two seasons, but in very small samples. He throws a mid-90's four seamer and a power curveball-slider hybrid with a good amount of horizontal movement, but he looked overmatched by major-league hitters. At this point, it looks more like a quad-A replacement-level type than a bullpen staple. **Connor Menez** elbowed his way into the major-league bullpen picture in June, when he had a run of five appearances where he was nearly unhittable. Back-to-back outings in which the slider-heavy southpaw allowed a combined 10 runs and a crowded Giants' bullpen saw him banished to Sacramento for the rest of the year. Where other teams scour California, Texas and Florida for pitching talent, the Giants found their unlikely niche with "college pitchers from the Northeast" in the 2021 draft, plucking arms from overlooked programs like Lehigh, Yale, Maine,and Fordham. This last was the college home of second-round pick **Matt Mikulski**, a lefty with an electric fastball and secondaries that can, and will, be worked with. With a fastball-slider combo that veers between "effectively wild" and "wild," **Reyes Moronta** was the heir apparent to the closing gig in San Francisco. His shaky command kept the righty from nailing down the gig, while a series of shoulder and arm injuries have largely kept him largely off the mound since 2019. After being outrighted off the Giants' 40-man roster, Moronta declared free agency in October 2021. A Rule 5 pick from the Mets, **Dedniel Nuñez** had barely been fitted for orange-and-black gear when he went straight from spring training to the operating table for Tommy John surgery. Should he come back healthy, he'll feature a potent fastball-curve combo that would seem to find its best place in a bullpen. It feels like everyone in San Jose had a breakout season, and **Randy Rodriguez** is no exception. He sits in the mid-90s and flashes a plus slider and while he didn't start a game this year, he was often used for multiple innings. His feel for a changeup gives him a third offering—and a chance to start. **Gregory Santos** made three April appearances with the big club, which resulted in an ERA north of 20.00 and a ticket back to Sacramento, whereupon he was suspended for a positive Stanozolol test. The triple-digits and knee-buckling slider—as well as the wildness—looks an awful lot like the Camilo Doval template. The Giants would be thrilled to see Santos follow that particular story arc. A 2020 draftee out of NC State, **Nick Swiney** thrived in a small Low-A sample to the tune of a strikeout-and-a-half per inning. The reason you're not hearing more about the lefty? It's a profile with a pedestrian fastball, which largely exists to set up his change and curve. He'll have to prove it at every level.

HOUSTON ASTROS

Essay by Robert O'Connell

Player comments by Ginny Searle and BP staff

Since November 2019, when *The Athletic* reported that their hitters had known some substantial percentage of what pitches were coming their way during their 2017 World Series run—cameras, garbage cans, cloaked confessions and slapped wrists—the Houston Astros have presented two problems. The first predates the scandal. Dating back to the late-middle of last decade, they've boasted baseball's thumpiest lineup, as well as its most consistent one, a homer-pulling and oppo-slicing nightmare for opposing pitchers. They've done everything a modern club with Death Star leanings is supposed to: work walks, slug long balls, rip doubles, build up heft in the middle of the lineup and depth at the bottom. They've had a shortstop who hits like a DH, and a DH who hits like a wrecking ball. They've also avoided the pitfalls that are supposed to attend all the good stuff, the tax excellence has lately levied on fun—namely, they make contact and don't strike out. The 'Stros are still a problem in that old, admirable sense, laying waste to their worse and gloomier counterparts across the American League.

The second problem, of course, is what to make of all this. It'd be great if post-comeuppance Houston were lousy; in an idyllic AL West, they might finish third, behind the reliable and anonymous A's and an Angels team suddenly deserving of its rootable star power. It'd even be acceptable if the Astros were just good in the way that, say, the Yankees or White Sox are good, allotted their measure of talent and frustration, secure in their place in the one-in-eight postseason crapshoot.

But no: the Astros have remained one of the sport's best clubs and maybe its foremost aesthetic miracle. A quick survey, for anyone who hasn't considered their principals other than as objects of scorn for a few years. There's second baseman Jose Altuve, a five-and-a-half-foot-tall shot of adrenaline who swings like he's trying to rip up an oak by its roots. There's first baseman Yuli Gurriel, who bats with Minnesota Fats' pool cue. There's Alex Bregman, who has the top-percentile skill and well-tended pissiness that can turn third basemen into MVPs. There's designated hitter Yordan Alvarez, whose home runs very nearly literalize the team's nickname. There was, until recently, Carlos Correa, who—with his arm and his bat—sets baseballs moving in straight lines faster than any other shortstop alive.

HOUSTON ASTROS PROSPECTUS

2021 W-L: 95-67, 1st in AL West

Pythag	.626	4th	DER	.716	3rd
RS/G	5.33	1st	DRC+	109	2nd
RA/G	4.06	6th	DRA-	98	13th
dWin%	.583	4th	FIP	4.17	14th
Payroll	$188M	5th	B-Age	29.3	23rd
M$/MW	$3.7M	17th	P-Age	28.9	11th

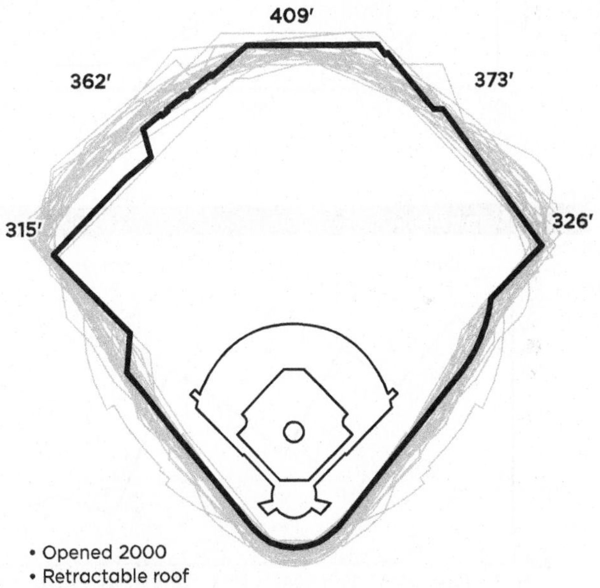

- Opened 2000
- Retractable roof
- Natural surface
- Fence profile: 7' to 25'

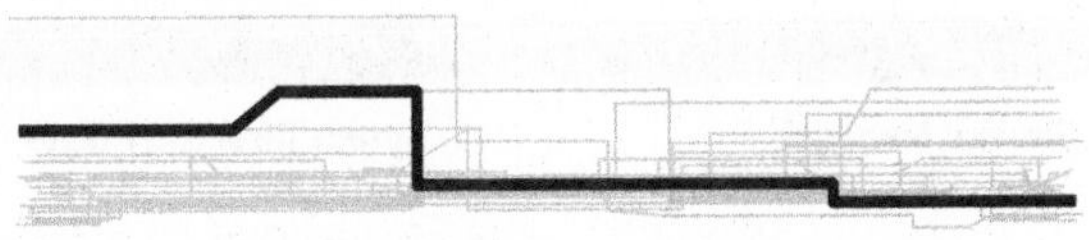

Park Factors

Runs	Runs/RH	Runs/LH	HR/RH	HR/LH
100	101	99	112	97

Top Hitter WARP	5.1 Jose Altuve
Top Pitcher WARP	2.9 Lance McCullers Jr.
Top Prospect	Jeremy Pena

Payroll History (in millions)

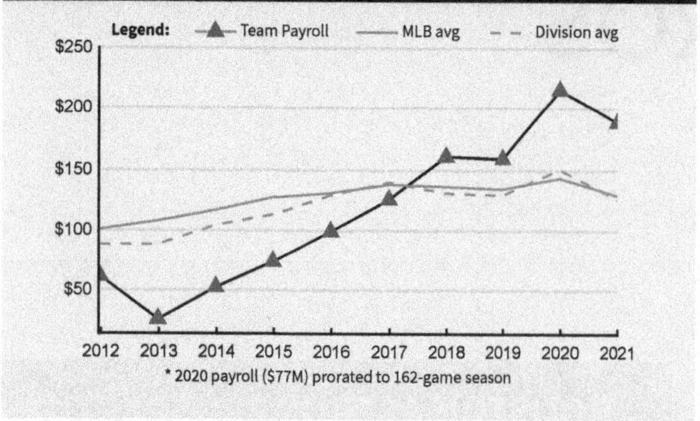

Future Commitments (in millions)

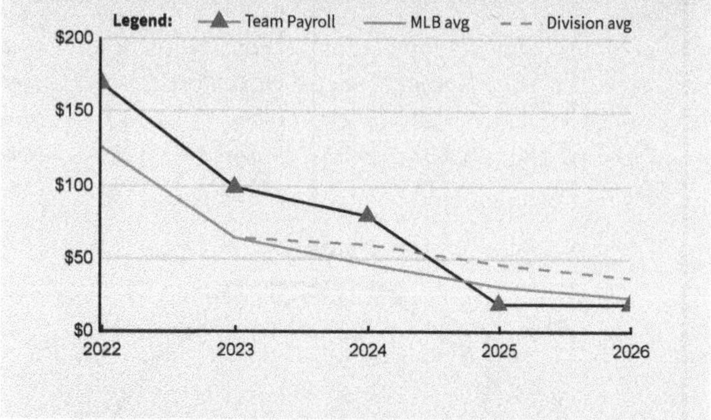

Farm System Ranking

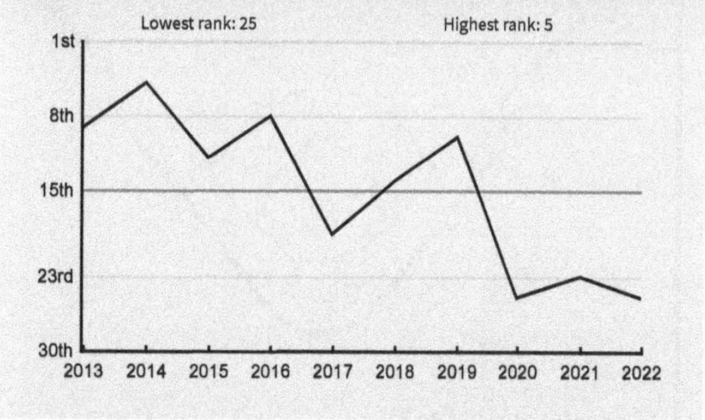

Personnel

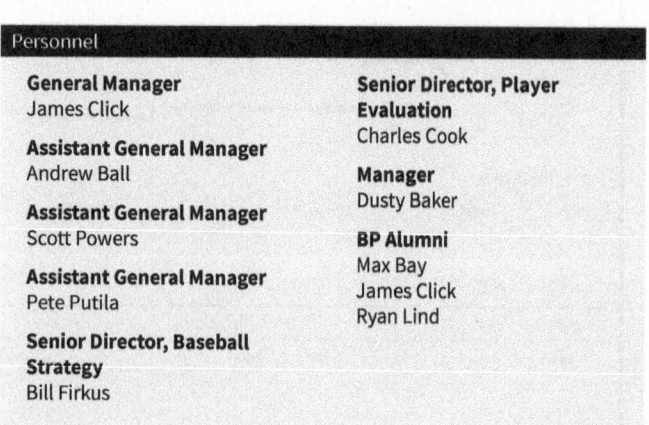

General Manager
James Click

Assistant General Manager
Andrew Ball

Assistant General Manager
Scott Powers

Assistant General Manager
Pete Putila

Senior Director, Baseball Strategy
Bill Firkus

Senior Director, Player Evaluation
Charles Cook

Manager
Dusty Baker

BP Alumni
Max Bay
James Click
Ryan Lind

People love baseball in different ways. For some (including many readers of this book), the game is territory for chipping away at the unknown; for others, it's about the patterned pleasure of a double down the line or a 1-3 putout. Mileage varies on the relative joys of spin-rate charts and backstory bios. Houston puts a question to all these folks: What do you do when baseball's most entertaining team is also its least deserving?

⚾ ⚾ ⚾

Okay, sure: you boo them, for starters. You toss inflatable trash cans around in the stands and stitch asterisks onto articles of team gear—the solution favored by fans in the Bronx in May, and in Atlanta in October, and everywhere in between over last summer's shame tour. You *yourself* don't huck a popcorn bucket at them—that crosses the line—but you don't object quite as vehemently as you would otherwise to the general notion of popcorn-bucket hucking, when it comes up.

If you opine about baseball more seriously and professionally, maybe you endeavor to resolve the admirable/detestable gap, or at least to pull it a little closer at its edges. You write about Dusty Baker, the Hendrix-joint-sharing, high-five-inventing, mask-rule-abiding and just congenitally charming septuagenarian manager brought in before the 2020 season to a) replace the suspended A.J. Hinch and b) inspire stories about his congenital charmingness. You write about the now-departed Zack Greinke, whose fastball now tops out at eighty-some miles per hour and who is, therefore, irresistible as an avatar of resourceful guile. You write about how Alvarez's doting father, back home in Cuba, watches his games in piecemeal, sometimes days later, when the state channel broadcasts them on delay.

Each solution falls short in its own way. All the guff from road fans might wear at times—in April, Baker pleaded with patrons to "look at ourselves before we spew hate on somebody else"—but a good club can metabolize it quickly enough as motivation and fuel for preening. That's one of sports' basic reactions. In a July comeback win over the Yankees, Martín Maldonado tugged down his jersey after hitting a homer—an allusion to the claim that Altuve had a buzzer hidden under his own uniform during the '17 ALCS against New York—and in the ninth inning, when Altuve himself capped a six-run frame with a walkoff shot, he let his teammates tear off his shirt. By the time the Astros were winning their division and ripping through the AL playoffs, they were taking batting practice and popping celebratory champagne bottles in tank tops reading "H-TOWN vs EVERYONE."

The redemption routine is as unconvincing as the derision is ineffective. Any attempt to steer the Astros through the sea of absolution eventually washes ashore as non-sequitur. It's true that Dusty is a nice enough guy, that the quick maturations of Alvarez and outfielder Kyle Tucker evince a still-thriving player-development system, that the pitching staff picked up admirably after the loss of Gerrit Cole to free agency and Justin Verlander to Tommy John surgery. But no measure of straining—*Dusty Baker has seen more baseball than just about anyone, enough to know what's right and what's wrong*, I'm sure something somewhere went—gives those particulars any bearing on the subject at hand. Competence and charm aren't the antidotes of malfeasance.

So you're left with a narrative vacuum. The Astros cheated a few years back, when they won the World Series, and they've been good enough to get to two more since—last year's run, at least, being pretty unsuspicious. They're hated but still great, with nothing but a few novelty tees linking one adjective to the other. Maybe you've had some traction taking their seasons as parables, their loss to Atlanta in 2021 as evidence that residual guilt or last-margin inadequacy won't let them realize their goal again. Or maybe you've just settled where I have: into a grudging acceptance of both poles of the Houston experience, and a kind of chilly security in the knowledge that this team will define a micro-generation of Major League Baseball and mean little else otherwise.

"Years have gone by and I've finally learned to accept myself for who I am: a beggar for good soccer," Eduardo Galeano wrote. "I go about the world, hand outstretched, and in the stadiums I plead: 'A pretty move, for the love of God.'"

Of all the types of baseball fan to be, this is the one I am. I'll take a fine play from whatever source on whichever team, without much care as to what happens to them a month or six down the road. It's a helpful trait when dealing with this particular club. Casting off the appetite for tidy, triumph-overcoming plots or evidence of heartfelt communal spirit (nice but inessential), I came to enjoy the sight of Lance McCullers Jr. dropping sliders off the plate like so many fishhooks in the opener of the Astros' Division Series with the White Sox, and of Carlos Correa belting a belly-high fastball into the bleachers in the first game of the next round against the Red Sox. The plane of Framber Valdez's sinker, the calm with which Alvarez settles into a hitter's count—pleasant enough to keep track of.

Still, even to a style glutton like me, these unredeemed Astros leave something missing. I loved the line-drive display Braves outfielder Eddie Rosario put up against them in the World Series, not only because it spoke to my preferred brand of hitting (though it did, all hunched stance and hands), but also because it invoked something of the sport's theses regarding patience and faith. A solid player honed his skills, came to a team with need, and lucked honestly into a torrid week. I have no idea whether Rosario thinks of himself as a parable—actually, because he's an accomplished pro athlete and not a neurotic writer, I can guess that he probably doesn't—but since there's no big countervailing story, it's easy enough for me to take him as one. Do what you can; eventually the world will need it.

You can't wring such meaning from the Astros. There is, and always will be—at least until this crop is all up and gone—too much else there. Your mind calls itself foolish the second the thoughts start to form. The players and their plays stay stuck in the literal and observable. It might be nice to attribute the ascents of Alvarez and Tucker, in part, to the presence of veteran contact artist Michael Brantley, or to think of Maldonado, a seasoned and well-regarded defensive backstop, bringing young lefty Valdez along. But if this franchise has any calling beyond accumulating wins and chasing titles, it is to remind us how little we know of the players and how unreliable the narratives are that we fashion from our looks at them on the field and in the dugout.

The Astros should be very good again in 2022, despite the loss of Correa. Verlander will return from his surgery, the young pitching staff has a year of postseason roughing-up under its collective belt, and the offense is as foreboding as ever, minus the aforementioned shortstop. The lineup cards will remain laughable, the sequences stunning. In the space of one inning, you'll see Verlander lever his fastball up past someone's eyes, Altuve dig a curveball out of the opposite batter's box, and Alvarez, like, yawn a liner into the right-center gap. It'll be lovely to look at.

That, in the end, is the plain and simple deal with Houston. Other clubs tell better stories, feature more compelling characters, and shine with more meaningful subtext. Very few play better baseball, for what that's worth.

—Robert O'Connell is a writer and editor based in New York.

Hitters

Jose Altuve 2B
Born: 05/06/90 Age: 32 Bats: R Throws: R Height: 5'6" Weight: 166 lb. Origin: International Free Agent, 2007

YEAR	TEAM	LVL	AGE	PA	R	2B	3B	HR	RBI	BB	K	SB	CS	Whiff%	AVG/OBP/SLG	DRC+	BABIP	BRR	FRAA	WARP
2019	HOU	MLB	29	548	89	27	3	31	74	41	82	6	5	20.9%	.298/.353/.550	124	.303	-0.6	2B(121): -0.0, SS(1): -0.0	3.7
2020	HOU	MLB	30	210	32	9	0	5	18	17	39	2	3	20.4%	.219/.286/.344	92	.250	1.6	2B(48): 2.0	0.9
2021	HOU	MLB	31	678	117	32	1	31	83	66	91	5	3	16.1%	.278/.350/.489	126	.280	2.3	2B(144): 1.5	5.1
2022 DC	*HOU*	*MLB*	*32*	*617*	*113*	*25*	*1*	*21*	*81*	*59*	*76*	*13*	*5*	*16.5%*	*.276/.351/.447*	*117*	*.287*	*0.3*	*2B 0*	*3.8*

Comparables: Roberto Alomar, Dustin Pedroia, Steve Sax

Add another note to what's becoming a novel-length file of *Altuve Partial Nudity Misadventures.* After Aaron Judge tugged at his jersey in a July home run celebration, imitating the diminutive second baseman's famous directive for his teammates not to disrobe him after his 2019 ALCS walk-off, Altuve answered the following night with a walk-off home run. This time, his teammates wasted no time in disrobing the second baseman when he arrived at home plate, revealing neither telltale buzzer nor embarrassing tattoo (unless he's seriously soured on his daughter Melody). Maybe we'll never have any clarity on when Altuve does and does not find it appropriate to be disrobed in front of thousands, and maybe that's okay. We have clarity on other fronts: a third 124 DRC+ in four seasons restored confidence after a rough 2020, reminding us this is just what Altuve does. Like the Astros just go to the ALCS, and get into little spats...and like Altuve takes off his shirt.

Yordan Alvarez DH
Born: 06/27/97 Age: 25 Bats: L Throws: R Height: 6'5" Weight: 225 lb. Origin: International Free Agent, 2016

YEAR	TEAM	LVL	AGE	PA	R	2B	3B	HR	RBI	BB	K	SB	CS	Whiff%	AVG/OBP/SLG	DRC+	BABIP	BRR	FRAA	WARP
2019	RR	AAA	22	253	50	16	0	23	71	38	50	2	1		.343/.443/.742	153	.355	-1.8	LF(27): -0.6, 1B(9): -0.4, RF(2): -0.2	2.2
2019	HOU	MLB	22	369	58	26	0	27	78	52	94	0	0	25.0%	.313/.412/.655	128	.366	-0.5	LF(10): -0.8	2.2
2020	HOU	MLB	23	9	2	0	0	1	4	0	1	0	0	14.3%	.250/.333/.625	95	.167	0.5		0.1
2021	HOU	MLB	24	598	92	35	1	33	104	50	145	1	0	22.7%	.277/.346/.531	118	.320	1.6	LF(41): -2.8	2.9
2022 DC	*HOU*	*MLB*	*25*	*581*	*104*	*29*	*1*	*31*	*118*	*56*	*129*	*2*	*1*	*22.5%*	*.277/.354/.526*	*130*	*.312*	*-0.7*	*LF -1*	*3.6*

Comparables: Rowdy Tellez, Matt Olson, Carlos González

What's the saying about riding a bike? Same with tape measure home runs, it appears; after a lost 2020, the Cuban slugger made a nearly 200-point dropoff in OPS (from 2019) look good, adding to his hardware shelf an ALCS MVP and logging a passable 319 innings in left field—though the lack of a DH in National League ballparks still cursed Alvarez and Houston on a laser home run that turned Game 4 of the World Series and might have been nabbed by a superlative defender. For a player with so much career (hopefully) ahead of him, however, it's a huge boon to his value and utility to find a comfortable spot in the field.

Michael Brantley LF/DH
Born: 05/15/87 Age: 35 Bats: L Throws: L Height: 6'2" Weight: 209 lb. Origin: Round 7, 2005 Draft (#205 overall)

YEAR	TEAM	LVL	AGE	PA	R	2B	3B	HR	RBI	BB	K	SB	CS	Whiff%	AVG/OBP/SLG	DRC+	BABIP	BRR	FRAA	WARP
2019	HOU	MLB	32	637	88	40	2	22	90	51	66	3	2	10.9%	.311/.372/.503	118	.320	0.1	LF(120): -7.4, RF(9): -0.8	2.8
2020	HOU	MLB	33	187	24	15	0	5	22	17	28	2	0	16.4%	.300/.364/.476	104	.336	-2.2	LF(19): 5.7	0.9
2021	HOU	MLB	34	508	68	29	3	8	47	33	53	1	0	11.0%	.311/.362/.437	110	.337	-0.4	LF(84): -1.1, RF(8): -1.4	2.1
2022 DC	*HOU*	*MLB*	*35*	*566*	*95*	*29*	*1*	*13*	*78*	*43*	*58*	*6*	*2*	*12.0%*	*.294/.353/.438*	*115*	*.310*	*-0.3*	*LF 0*	*2.8*

Comparables: Lou Brock, Melky Cabrera, Jose Cruz

At this point, there can be no doubt that the old-timer outfielder is on the unpredictable yet inevitable slide of decline, his OPS slipping below .800 for the first time since 2015 as his home run ability contracted to fill only gaps and allies—his eight home runs tied for 122nd of 133 qualified batters. Despite his walk rate also dipping below league-average, Brantley remained notably above-average in the box and overall thanks to a defining hit tool. If we're assigning Homeric epithets, Brantley's would be his efficacy with the bat—sharp-aiming Brantley, maybe. The .298 career average, eighth among active players with at least 3,000 plate appearances, perhaps understates his prowess: in every season since 2014 he's surpassed that line (ignoring a lost 2016 that summed to 43 PA). Someday, a sub-.400 slugging percentage will make him a part-time player, but Brantley might keep hitting .300 straight through.

Alex Bregman 3B
Born: 03/30/94 Age: 28 Bats: R Throws: R Height: 6'0" Weight: 192 lb. Origin: Round 1, 2015 Draft (#2 overall)

YEAR	TEAM	LVL	AGE	PA	R	2B	3B	HR	RBI	BB	K	SB	CS	Whiff%	AVG/OBP/SLG	DRC+	BABIP	BRR	FRAA	WARP
2019	HOU	MLB	25	690	122	37	2	41	112	119	83	5	1	14.4%	.296/.423/.592	148	.281	-3.9	3B(99): 6.5, SS(65): 4.9	7.0
2020	HOU	MLB	26	180	19	12	1	6	22	24	26	0	0	14.7%	.242/.350/.451	116	.254	0.0	3B(42): -1.4	0.7
2021	SUG	AAA	27	44	6	3	0	1	5	7	2	0	0		.250/.386/.417	118	.242	-1.1	3B(10): 1.7	0.3
2021	HOU	MLB	27	400	54	17	0	12	55	44	53	1	0	13.5%	.270/.355/.422	119	.286	-0.8	3B(90): -5.5	1.6
2022 DC	*HOU*	*MLB*	*28*	*596*	*106*	*26*	*1*	*22*	*94*	*77*	*68*	*7*	*3*	*13.8%*	*.270/.373/.464*	*125*	*.273*	*-0.2*	*3B 0*	*3.7*

Comparables: Aramis Ramirez, Adrián Beltré, Ron Santo

Having signed an extension ahead of a superlative 2019 season, Bregman appeared set to exemplify another data point in a tide of team-friendly extensions. The last several seasons, though, have seen the third baseman revert to or below his pre-breakout offensive standards, appearing more a good hitter than a great one. The postseason was dismal, with Bregman striking out 50% beyond his career rate and sliding down to seventh in the lineup by the World Series' end. A wrist surgery undergone in November will theoretically have the erstwhile slugger back to full strength by spring training, though Bregman sustained the injury in September, a point which his offensive woes long predate. Entering what would have been his final year of team control but is instead simply his final year of being wildly underpaid, Bregman's return to his offensive peak could go a long way to keeping the Astros offense from falling off a cliff.

Jason Castro C Born: 06/18/87 Age: 35 Bats: L Throws: R Height: 6'3" Weight: 215 lb. Origin: Round 1, 2008 Draft (#10 overall)

YEAR	TEAM	LVL	AGE	PA	R	2B	3B	HR	RBI	BB	K	SB	CS	Whiff%	AVG/OBP/SLG	DRC+	BABIP	BRR	FRAA	WARP
2019	MIN	MLB	32	275	39	9	0	13	30	33	88	0	0	37.1%	.232/.332/.435	88	.307	0.9	C(78): 3.5	1.2
2020	SD	MLB	33	30	3	5	0	0	3	2	10	0	0	30.4%	.179/.233/.357	70	.278	-0.7	C(9): 0.1	-0.1
2020	LAA	MLB	33	62	5	4	0	2	6	10	23	0	0	36.5%	.192/.323/.385	73	.296	-0.1	C(17): 1.7	0.2
2021	HOU	MLB	34	179	22	7	0	8	21	25	54	0	0	35.1%	.235/.356/.443	93	.310	-1.6	C(52): -1.6	0.3
2022 DC	*HOU*	*MLB*	*35*	*185*	*27*	*7*	*0*	*5*	*25*	*25*	*58*	*0*	*0*	*34.3%*	*.207/.325/.370*	*88*	*.287*	*-0.3*	*C 0*	*0.5*

Comparables: Johnny Edwards, Miguel Montero, Brian Schneider

YEAR	TEAM	P. COUNT	FRM RUNS	BLK RUNS	THRW RUNS	TOT RUNS
2019	MIN	10695	4.1	-0.6	0.4	3.9
2020	LAA	2172	2.0	0.0	0.0	2.0
2020	SD	1135	0.0	-0.1	0.0	0.0
2021	HOU	5964	-1.2	-0.2	0.5	-0.8
2022	*HOU*	*7215*	*2.3*	*0.0*	*-0.3*	*2.0*

Sometimes, you don't have the spark to be the lead. You've got to try, of course—think back to when My Chemical Romance broke up. Obviously Gerard Way was going to go solo, and Frank Iero had his fans and Mikey Way's doing the comics thing. But if you're Ray Toro, you've got to go with a self-release for your solo album. When the band gets back together for the reunion tour, maybe you realize you like being a part of an ensemble, do better that way. It's probably unfair that Castro, after giving the best offensive showing of his career as a second-stringer, got only a disastrous month as starting backstop for the cursed Angels in 2020 before being shunted back out of the limelight. Another career-best OPS last season, though, indicated maybe this is how Castro is his best. Besides, there's hardly a gig that makes your bat look better by comparison than as Martín Maldonado's understudy.

Aledmys Díaz 3B Born: 08/01/90 Age: 31 Bats: R Throws: R Height: 6'1" Weight: 195 lb. Origin: International Free Agent, 2014

YEAR	TEAM	LVL	AGE	PA	R	2B	3B	HR	RBI	BB	K	SB	CS	Whiff%	AVG/OBP/SLG	DRC+	BABIP	BRR	FRAA	WARP
2019	HOU	MLB	28	247	36	12	1	9	40	26	28	2	0	19.6%	.271/.356/.467	116	.268	1.8	1B(26): -0.8, 2B(25): 0.6, 3B(19): -0.7	1.4
2020	HOU	MLB	29	59	8	5	0	3	6	1	12	0	0	26.5%	.241/.254/.483	104	.256	0.7	2B(10): 0.3, 3B(3): -0.2, 1B(2): 0.1	0.3
2021	HOU	MLB	30	319	28	19	0	8	45	16	62	0	1	22.5%	.259/.317/.405	98	.304	-4.7	3B(30): 1.3, LF(15): -0.1, 2B(13): 0.7	0.7
2022 DC	*HOU*	*MLB*	*31*	*463*	*67*	*20*	*0*	*14*	*62*	*32*	*74*	*3*	*2*	*22.4%*	*.245/.310/.403*	*95*	*.266*	*-0.4*	*SS 0, 2B 0*	*1.2*

Comparables: Danny Valencia, Justin Turner, Asdrúbal Cabrera

It no longer appears likely Díaz will turn a corner offensively, but the utility infielder (and occasional corner outfielder) continues to flirt with average offensive lines while providing reliable defense at a number of high-skill positions. Boring? Absolutely. But try to wax poetic about the performance of a Honda Civic—it's not exactly an applicable medium, because it's entirely beside the point why the car's for decades sat near the top of lists of America's best-selling cars. A Civic won't stumble into any races for the same reason Díaz was limited to eight plate appearances in Houston's latest postseason run: it's not what they're suited for. Still, only a fractured hand separated the six-year veteran from reaching 500 plate appearances for the first time, and even if his offensive dip proceeds to full-on decline he figures to have even or better odds to reach that mark this year.

Robel García IF Born: 03/28/93 Age: 29 Bats: S Throws: R Height: 6'0" Weight: 195 lb. Origin: International Free Agent, 2010

YEAR	TEAM	LVL	AGE	PA	R	2B	3B	HR	RBI	BB	K	SB	CS	Whiff%	AVG/OBP/SLG	DRC+	BABIP	BRR	FRAA	WARP
2019	AGU	WIN	26	189	22	5	0	4	19	30	46	2	0		.219/.354/.329		.283			
2019	TNS	AA	26	92	12	5	0	6	26	12	22	1	1		.295/.391/.590	131	.333	-0.7	3B(18): 0.1, 2B(4): 0.6, SS(1): -0.0	0.6
2019	IOW	AAA	26	296	51	12	2	21	52	30	98	3	3		.281/.361/.585	106	.364	2.4	2B(29): 0.1, LF(21): 2.5, 3B(19): -2.5	1.6
2019	CHC	MLB	26	80	8	2	2	5	11	7	35	0	0	45.3%	.208/.275/.500	69	.303	-0.3	2B(18): -1.1, LF(5): -0.1, RF(1): -0.2	-0.2
2020	AGU	WIN	27	103	9	2	1	2	12	15	30	2	0		.216/.330/.330		.304			
2021	SUG	AAA	28	136	13	6	0	6	18	17	45	0	0		.162/.272/.368	83	.194	-0.2	2B(12): -0.7, 3B(8): -0.6, SS(3): 0.6	0.0
2021	HOU	MLB	28	117	8	3	0	1	8	8	42	0	0	42.3%	.151/.216/.208	58	.234	-0.1	3B(15): -0.5, SS(13): -0.3, 2B(9): -1.0	-0.4
2022 non-DC	*HOU*	*MLB*	*29*	*251*	*27*	*9*	*0*	*10*	*31*	*21*	*95*	*0*	*1*	*39.4%*	*.204/.280/.392*	*74*	*.296*	*-0.2*	*2B -1, 3B -1*	*-0.2*

Comparables: Adrián Sanchez, Luis Valbuena, Jake Smolinski

If you navigate to Wikipedia's "List of sitcoms known for negative reception," and scroll down to those starting with the letter R, you'll find two different shows starring and named for Rob Schneider—2012's *Rob*, which garnered criticism for its "use of stereotypes," and 2015's *Real Rob*, which notably improved by achieving its zero percent Rotten Tomatoes critic rating without omnipresent stereotypes. What's worth consideration isn't whether Schneider deserved to be handed the first sitcom, much less the second; it's that he got a chance for redemption at all. Some rooms, once you're in, you get to stay unless you embarrass whoever opened the door, maybe more than once. For García that should lend resolve after his tumultuous path to the big leagues—the Cubs signed him ahead of 2019, five campaigns after the Guardians cut him, a scout having noticed his carrying power tool in an instructional league game as a member of Team Italy. He rocketed through the system to the majors in 2019 (ultimately winning MiLB's co-breakout prospect of the year) but only got 80 plate appearances. He then shuffled through stints with the Reds, Mets and Angels before landing with the Astros for a truly dismal campaign in which he struck out 40% of the time and barely broke a .400 OPS—the 0% on Rotten Tomatoes of offensive showings. Sometimes you get another chance, though, and it's not always about whether you deserved it.

Yuli Gurriel 1B Born: 06/09/84 Age: 38 Bats: R Throws: R Height: 6'0" Weight: 215 lb. Origin: International Free Agent, 2016

YEAR	TEAM	LVL	AGE	PA	R	2B	3B	HR	RBI	BB	K	SB	CS	Whiff%	AVG/OBP/SLG	DRC+	BABIP	BRR	FRAA	WARP
2019	HOU	MLB	35	612	85	40	2	31	104	37	65	5	3	14.9%	.298/.343/.541	122	.289	-0.8	1B(110): 8.3, 3B(42): 0.5, 2B(4): -0.2	4.1
2020	HOU	MLB	36	230	27	12	1	6	22	12	27	0	1	15.6%	.232/.274/.384	98	.235	-1.0	1B(55): 3.9	0.8
2021	HOU	MLB	37	605	83	31	0	15	81	59	68	1	1	13.9%	.319/.383/.462	126	.336	-1.0	1B(142): 6.8	3.9
2022 DC	*HOU*	*MLB*	*38*	*571*	*86*	*26*	*0*	*18*	*91*	*46*	*59*	*3*	*2*	*14.6%*	*.280/.344/.443*	*112*	*.286*	*-0.7*	*1B 4*	*2.3*

Comparables: Eddie Murray, Ernie Banks, Tony Perez

If the era of MLB comprising the late 2010s and early 2020s is remembered for the prevalence of late-fading sluggers and starters, that reputation will be due as much to the Gurriels as to the Scherzers. Throughout Houston's turbulent run atop the American League, Gurriel has been something like the eighth- to 10th-most notable player on the club, but has frequently managed to outshine his bit-player billing. The latest performance was perhaps the best of his career despite his advanced age and cracking fewer than half the home runs he did in 2019. More BABIP-dependent than almost any player in the league—he struck out at the fifth-lowest rate among qualified batters, and a walk rate barely above league average represented a 70% jump over his career high—Gurriel's largely had good batted ball luck in his career. Years in which he has low BABIPs will look more like 2020.

Korey Lee C

Born: 07/25/98 Age: 23 Bats: R Throws: R Height: 6'2" Weight: 210 lb. Origin: Round 1, 2019 Draft (#32 overall)

YEAR	TEAM	LVL	AGE	PA	R	2B	3B	HR	RBI	BB	K	SB	CS	Whiff%	AVG/OBP/SLG	DRC+	BABIP	BRR	FRAA	WARP
2019	TRI	SS	20	259	31	6	4	3	28	28	49	8	5		.268/.359/.371		.328			
2021	GDD	WIN	22	71	8	2	0	1	6	9	19	1	0		.258/.352/.339		.357			
2021	ASH	A+	22	121	24	5	0	3	14	12	24	1	0		.330/.397/.459	112	.402	-0.6	C(20): -0.5, 3B(2): 0.3	0.5
2021	CC	AA	22	203	25	9	1	8	27	17	35	3	1		.254/.320/.443	116	.275	1.3	C(38): -1.6, 3B(4): -0.1, 1B(3): 0.2	1.1
2021	SUG	AAA	22	38	2	4	0	0	4	2	9	0	0		.229/.263/.343	83	.296	0.1	C(4): -0.5, 1B(2): -0.6	-0.1
2022 DC	*HOU*	*MLB*	*23*	*31*	*4*	*1*	*0*	*0*	*3*	*2*	*6*	*0*	*0*	*24.1%*	*.238/.294/.348*	*75*	*.290*	*0.0*	*C -1*	*0.0*

Comparables: Francisco Cervelli, Yasmani Grandal, Devin Mesoraco

YEAR	TEAM	P. COUNT	FRM RUNS	BLK RUNS	THRW RUNS	TOT RUNS
2019	TRI	4263		-0.7	0.6	-0.1
2021	CC	5226	-1.3	-0.9	0.1	-2.0
2021	ASH	2963	-0.5	-0.1	-0.2	-0.8
2022	*HOU*	*1202*	*-0.4*	*-0.1*	*0.1*	*-0.5*

Lee sped through three levels in 2021, his offensive lines degrading with each step upward and onward, but nevertheless showing enough flashes of ability with the bat, when paired with his advanced defensive profile, to break into the conversation for top name in a barren Astros system. As with every catching prospect, the looming threat of an automated strike zone complicates future evaluation—if and when that happens, how much will the offensive baseline behind the plate spike? The arm is the carrying tool, another minor qualm given the continuous decline in stolen base attempts. The Astros, though, are clearly concerned first and foremost with a game caller in whom they have confidence. Martín Maldonado's offense will cross the Jeff Mathis threshold sooner or later, and Houston's aggressive promotion of Lee indicates they view him as a potential replacement.

Pedro Leon SS/CF

Born: 05/28/98 Age: 24 Bats: R Throws: R Height: 5'10" Weight: 170 lb. Origin: International Free Agent, 2021

YEAR	TEAM	LVL	AGE	PA	R	2B	3B	HR	RBI	BB	K	SB	CS	Whiff%	AVG/OBP/SLG	DRC+	BABIP	BRR	FRAA	WARP
2021	GDD	WIN	23	84	9	3	0	1	9	13	20	4	1		.257/.381/.343		.347			
2021	CC	AA	23	217	29	7	1	9	33	25	67	13	8		.249/.359/.443	101	.339	0.3	SS(41): -3.9, CF(9): 0.1	0.3
2021	SUG	AAA	23	75	11	2	0	0	2	14	23	4	2		.131/.293/.164	77	.211	0.2	SS(7): -0.5, 3B(6): -1.2, CF(4): 0.4	-0.1
2022 non-DC	*HOU*	*MLB*	*24*	*251*	*22*	*9*	*1*	*4*	*22*	*24*	*79*	*10*	*5*	*31.4%*	*.191/.282/.307*	*62*	*.274*	*1.0*	*SS -3, CF 1*	*-0.5*

Comparables: José Rondón, Matt Tuiasosopo, Deven Marrero

Everyone's taken too long off from something they love. Whether by choice of a break, circumstance (it is the nature of bikes to be stolen) or some other vagary, it's virtually universal to feel the mixed pleasure of coming back to something one loves combined with the bitter exasperation of being tangibly worse at something at which one once excelled. Leon, absent from organized play of any sort since the 2018-19 season of the Cuban National League following his defection from Cuba, must have felt the cut of that double-edged blade in his debut for the Astros. His signing with Houston was delayed for six months in the initial phases of the COVID-19 pandemic, ultimately meaning he lost more than two years of in-game development. The rust showed. There's hardly a prospect, not just in Houston's system but in all of baseball, whose future role is bumpered by such wide margins of error.

Martín Maldonado C

Born: 08/16/86 Age: 35 Bats: R Throws: R Height: 6'0" Weight: 230 lb. Origin: Round 27, 2004 Draft (#803 overall)

YEAR	TEAM	LVL	AGE	PA	R	2B	3B	HR	RBI	BB	K	SB	CS	Whiff%	AVG/OBP/SLG	DRC+	BABIP	BRR	FRAA	WARP
2019	KC	MLB	32	263	26	15	0	6	17	17	55	0	0	22.1%	.227/.291/.366	88	.270	-4.5	C(73): 8.7	1.1
2019	CHC	MLB	32	13	0	0	0	0	0	2	5	0	0	36.8%	.000/.154/.000	81		-0.1	C(4): -0.1	0.0
2019	HOU	MLB	32	98	20	4	0	6	10	13	26	0	0	29.3%	.202/.316/.464	94	.212	-0.1	C(26): 0.7, 1B(1): -0.0	0.4
2020	HOU	MLB	33	165	19	4	0	6	24	27	51	1	0	29.2%	.215/.350/.378	92	.295	-1.7	C(47): -3.2	-0.1
2021	HOU	MLB	34	426	40	10	1	12	36	47	127	0	0	28.8%	.172/.272/.300	75	.221	-3.0	C(123): 1.6, 1B(1): -0.1	0.3
2022 DC	*HOU*	*MLB*	*35*	*394*	*53*	*13*	*0*	*11*	*61*	*42*	*109*	*0*	*1*	*28.6%*	*.193/.294/.332*	*70*	*.247*	*-0.7*	*C 1*	*0.4*

Comparables: Duffy Dyer, Phil Roof, Mike Matheny

YEAR	TEAM	P. COUNT	FRM RUNS	BLK RUNS	THRW RUNS	TOT RUNS
2019	CHC	571	-0.2	0.0	0.0	-0.2
2019	KC	10492	7.9	0.5	0.4	8.9
2019	HOU	3403	0.6	0.1	0.1	0.8
2020	HOU	6449	-2.8	0.0	0.0	-2.8
2021	HOU	16739	2.1	-0.4	0.1	1.8
2022	*HOU*	*15632*	*4.9*	*0.5*	*1.0*	*6.3*

"The play's the thing," Hamlet said, and the continued employment of backstops like Maldonado proves he must have been speaking about catcher defense. If his bat showed one final twitch of life in 2020, that hope was irretrievably dimmed in the complete season that followed, during which Maldonado had the third-worst OPS and fourth-worst DRC+ among all players reaching 400 plate appearances. The Astros transparently didn't care, giving a mid-30s backstop an extension for 2022 featuring a 2023 vesting option whose threshold (90 games) he blew past. They consider him a singular defender, and with Maldonado having been present for four straight postseason runs, who's to argue with the results?

Chas McCormick OF Born: 04/19/95 Age: 27 Bats: R Throws: L Height: 6'0" Weight: 208 lb. Origin: Round 21, 2017 Draft (#631 overall)

YEAR	TEAM	LVL	AGE	PA	R	2B	3B	HR	RBI	BB	K	SB	CS	Whiff%	AVG/OBP/SLG	DRC+	BABIP	BRR	FRAA	WARP
2019	CC	AA	24	223	26	3	3	4	22	39	28	9	3		.277/.426/.395	141	.310	0.8	LF(40): 5.4, CF(6): -0.2, RF(3): -0.8	2.5
2019	RR	AAA	24	225	39	3	3	10	44	28	34	7	1		.262/.347/.466	105	.261	0.5	RF(22): 0.3, CF(16): 0.7, LF(12): 1.1	1.1
2021	HOU	MLB	26	320	47	12	0	14	50	25	104	4	2	35.5%	.257/.319/.447	88	.341	-2.7	LF(51): 1.5, CF(33): -1.9, RF(22): 2.6	0.6
2022 DC	*HOU*	*MLB*	*27*	*323*	*41*	*10*	*1*	*7*	*35*	*28*	*95*	*5*	*2*	*32.9%*	*.210/.289/.335*	*68*	*.283*	*0.2*	*CF 0, RF 0*	*-0.2*

Comparables: Andy Dirks, Chris Heisey, Scott Van Slyke

With the Astros needing to redevelop their center-field recipe coming into 2021, McCormick proved a piquant addition. Though Houston gave him just a dash of playing time rather than working with a heavy hand, his defensive ratings were savory enough to counterbalance insipid offense. With his BABIP already near the top of the scale, it's not evident how the outfielder can spice things up enough to earn daily play. A year more seasoned and with bland competition, however, McCormick could prove a more toothsome option moving forward—as long as Houston's palate hasn't changed.

Jake Meyers CF Born: 06/18/96 Age: 26 Bats: R Throws: L Height: 6'0" Weight: 200 lb. Origin: Round 13, 2017 Draft (#391 overall)

YEAR	TEAM	LVL	AGE	PA	R	2B	3B	HR	RBI	BB	K	SB	CS	Whiff%	AVG/OBP/SLG	DRC+	BABIP	BRR	FRAA	WARP
2019	FAY	A+	23	384	55	28	3	8	41	33	84	9	4		.258/.336/.428	109	.319	-0.8	CF(81): 12.2, RF(3): 0.2, LF(1): -0.0	2.9
2019	CC	AA	23	100	9	0	1	1	6	11	20	3	3		.213/.300/.270	94	.265	-0.7	CF(14): 0.6, LF(6): -0.8, RF(1): -0.0	0.1
2021	SUG	AAA	25	304	52	17	2	16	51	25	59	10	3		.343/.408/.598	126	.389	-1.0	CF(25): 2.9, RF(20): 8.1, LF(16): 2.5	3.2
2021	HOU	MLB	25	163	22	8	0	6	28	10	50	3	0	29.2%	.260/.323/.438	86	.352	1.3	CF(39): -1.1, LF(4): -0.3, RF(3): 0.3	0.4
2022 DC	*HOU*	*MLB*	*26*	*242*	*34*	*10*	*0*	*6*	*41*	*17*	*61*	*4*	*3*	*28.5%*	*.235/.301/.385*	*84*	*.293*	*0.3*	*CF 2*	*0.7*

Comparables: Chris Heisey, Mitch Haniger, Hunter Pence

Left unprotected from the Rule 5 Draft ahead of the 2021 season, Meyers appeared as superfluous to the Astros' plans as the Orioles are to the American League East. Unlike Baltimore, he raised the collective estimation of his potential last year; ultimately he appeared to seize the bulk center-field role, taking three ALDS starts before a shoulder injury in Game 4 ended his season and required surgery, delaying his 2022 debut and muddling his prescribed role.

★ ★ ★ *2022 Top 101 Prospect* **#16** ★ ★ ★

Jeremy Peña SS Born: 09/22/97 Age: 24 Bats: R Throws: R Height: 6'0" Weight: 202 lb. Origin: Round 3, 2018 Draft (#102 overall)

YEAR	TEAM	LVL	AGE	PA	R	2B	3B	HR	RBI	BB	K	SB	CS	Whiff%	AVG/OBP/SLG	DRC+	BABIP	BRR	FRAA	WARP
2019	PEJ	WIN	21	101	11	5	1	1	10	6	35	2	1		.183/.248/.290		.281			
2019	QC	A	21	289	44	8	4	5	41	35	57	17	6		.293/.389/.421	121	.357	3.3	SS(60): -1.7, 2B(2): -0.3	1.8
2019	FAY	A+	21	185	28	13	3	2	13	12	33	3	4		.317/.378/.467	108	.383	1.6	SS(29): -0.7, 2B(11): 0.2, 3B(1): -0.0	0.7
2020	EST	WIN	22	129	18	2	2	3	9	7	23	7	0		.306/.349/.430		.358			
2021	EST	WIN	23	134	18	6	1	2	15	11	32	7	2		.291/.364/.410		.381			
2021	AST	ROK	23	27	3	1	1	0	2	2	6	1	0		.348/.444/.478		.471			
2021	SUG	AAA	23	133	22	4	2	10	19	6	35	5	1		.287/.346/.598	106	.325	1.1	SS(25): 2.2, 3B(2): 0.0	0.8
2022 DC	*HOU*	*MLB*	*24*	*468*	*68*	*17*	*3*	*13*	*61*	*31*	*134*	*9*	*5*	*32.3%*	*.237/.302/.387*	*86*	*.313*	*0.9*	*SS -1*	*0.9*

Comparables: Erik González, Zach Walters, Pat Valaika

Peña had timing worse than an Epiphany breakfast party in downtown Washington D.C. last year, requiring wrist surgery on the 21st of April that delayed his Triple-A debut until August 10th. The power showed more than ever upon his return, arguably inspiring more buzz than the glove-first prospect might have accrued across an entire season—when a one-in-three home run-per-fly ball rate would have normalized. It's not yet clear whether Houston will leave a vacancy for the slick-handed shortstop, but the overall profile spells enough promise that doing so wouldn't qualify as the front office buying into the club's transformative hype based on a small sample. He'll be no Carlos Correa, however (or if he is, maybe the Astros front office would be right to buy into its own hype).

Jose Siri OF Born: 07/22/95 Age: 26 Bats: R Throws: R Height: 6'2" Weight: 175 lb. Origin: International Free Agent, 2012

YEAR	TEAM	LVL	AGE	PA	R	2B	3B	HR	RBI	BB	K	SB	CS	Whiff%	AVG/OBP/SLG	DRC+	BABIP	BRR	FRAA	WARP
2019	GIG	WIN	23	125	18	4	1	6	24	10	34	4	0		.196/.264/.411		.216			
2019	CHA	AA	23	405	46	15	1	11	50	33	126	21	6		.251/.313/.388	80	.349	-0.5	CF(98): 22.6, RF(1): -0.0	3.1
2019	LOU	AAA	23	112	10	4	1	0	3	9	39	5	2		.186/.252/.245	61	.302	1.1	CF(26): 2.1, RF(4): -0.1	0.2
2020	GIG	WIN	24	122	21	7	0	3	14	12	34	7	3		.282/.352/.427		.384			
2021	GIG	WIN	25	77	11	2	0	2	3	7	19	6	0		.217/.289/.333		.271			
2021	SUG	AAA	25	397	70	29	4	16	72	26	122	24	3		.318/.369/.552	96	.436	2.6	CF(42): -3.5, RF(30): -0.2, LF(12): 1.0	1.1
2021	HOU	MLB	25	49	10	0	1	4	9	1	17	3	1	36.2%	.304/.347/.609	88	.400	0.5	RF(9): -1.1, CF(5): -0.3, LF(4): -0.3	0.0
2022 DC	*HOU*	*MLB*	*26*	*227*	*32*	*9*	*1*	*7*	*31*	*13*	*70*	*10*	*3*	*35.4%*	*.231/.282/.401*	*78*	*.307*	*1.1*	*CF 1, RF 0*	*0.3*

Comparables: Teoscar Hernández, Aaron Altherr, Eury Pérez

Previously waived by three organizations, Siri had moved squarely into the post-hype phase by the time he landed with the Astros organization. A triumphant Triple-A campaign got Siri onto the 40-man, into major-league action and even into the playoffs. With fellow center fielder Jake Meyers expected to be unavailable for half the season following surgery, Siri likely won't have a better opportunity to crack daily playing time with a perennial contender.

Kyle Tucker RF

Born: 01/17/97 Age: 25 Bats: L Throws: R Height: 6'4" Weight: 199 lb. Origin: Round 1, 2015 Draft (#5 overall)

YEAR	TEAM	LVL	AGE	PA	R	2B	3B	HR	RBI	BB	K	SB	CS	Whiff%	AVG/OBP/SLG	DRC+	BABIP	BRR	FRAA	WARP
2019	RR	AAA	22	536	92	26	3	34	97	60	116	30	5		.266/.354/.555	115	.280	1.2	RF(60): 3.9, LF(40): -1.8, 1B(11): 0.3	3.0
2019	HOU	MLB	22	72	15	6	0	4	11	4	20	5	0	30.1%	.269/.319/.537	82	.326	0.7	LF(11): -0.5, RF(11): 1.0, 1B(4): 0.1	0.2
2020	HOU	MLB	23	228	33	12	6	9	42	18	46	8	1	22.5%	.268/.325/.512	98	.303	0.1	LF(41): 4.0, RF(7): 0.6	1.1
2021	HOU	MLB	24	567	83	37	3	30	92	53	90	14	2	20.4%	.294/.359/.557	130	.304	1.8	RF(133): -2.6, CF(4): 0.2	3.7
2022 DC	*HOU*	*MLB*	*25*	*559*	*93*	*29*	*4*	*24*	*98*	*51*	*89*	*17*	*4*	*20.7%*	*.273/.345/.493*	*124*	*.290*	*1.2*	*RF 1, CF 0*	*3.7*

Comparables: Carlos González, Alex Verdugo, Jay Bruce

Everyone wants to be their own person, be understood as special and unique and all the better for their idiosyncracies. Even those who are drawn to ceaseless imitation, often in formative years, are just chasing a version of themselves, one more refined to their own barely trained eyes. The prevalence of social media, the shrink of the world even as it expands beyond comprehensible limits, further complicates that intrinsic need for individuality. Does being yourself in so wide a world, that has such people in it, render you all the more alone? Sometimes things get complicated. Take the following poem fragment:

"*I used to think I was the strangest person in the world*
but then I thought, there are so many people in the world, there must be someone just like
me who feels bizarre and flawed in the same ways I do. "

For years attributed to Frida Kahlo, including last November by the Museum of Modern Art, it was in fact penned in 2008 by then-17-year-old Rebecca Martin, who accidentally sparked the confusion by appending the text to a self-portrait of the famous Mexican painter and submitting it to an anonymous blog. Speaking to Buzzfeed News after clearing up the confusion, Martin said "I'm really happy to see it appear, but it's also a very teenage version of myself that's strange to have so out there." Tucker, who's been an obsessively tracked professional since he was a teen, surely understands Martin on that front. On another, too: block out the name on the stat card and you might misattribute Tucker's line to the more famous man he replaced, George Springer. Tucker doesn't yet have the track record of the elder outfielder, nor has he earned the fear Springer drove into pitchers across the league. As Martin put it, "I think it's less exciting to feel connected to me." It's her unique contribution to the bizarre world, though, and now the word's out for her. If it's not already, it soon will be for Tucker, too.

Tyler Whitaker OF

Born: 08/02/02 Age: 19 Bats: R Throws: R Height: 6'4" Weight: 190 lb. Origin: Round 3, 2021 Draft (#87 overall)

YEAR	TEAM	LVL	AGE	PA	R	2B	3B	HR	RBI	BB	K	SB	CS	Whiff%	AVG/OBP/SLG	DRC+	BABIP	BRR	FRAA	WARP
2021	AST	ROK	18	114	16	2	1	3	6	9	40	8	1		.202/.263/.327		.290			
2022															*No projection*					

Comparables: Marlin Almonte, Frank Tolentino, Eudy Pina

The Astros lost their first two round picks in two drafts, 2020 and 2021, as part of their punishment for their 2017 sign stealing scandal. In both drafts they selected for upside when their turn finally came in the third round, choosing a high-ceiling high school prospect who'd at some point generated first-round buzz. Whitaker was a two-way player in high school and was immediately shifted to the outfield full-time; he'll have the potential to end up in center if he can avoid the infinite pitfalls (like, say, a 35% strikeout rate in their first taste of professional action) that might snag someone on the endless runner from high school to the majors.

PITCHERS

Bryan Abreu RHP

Born: 04/22/97 Age: 25 Bats: R Throws: R Height: 6'1" Weight: 225 lb. Origin: International Free Agent, 2013

YEAR	TEAM	LVL	AGE	W	L	SV	G	GS	IP	H	HR	BB/9	K/9	K	GB%	BABIP	WHIP	ERA	DRA-	WARP	MPH	FB%	Whiff%	CSP
2019	FAY	A+	22	1	0	0	3	3	14^{2}	9	2	3.7	15.3	25	38.5%	.292	1.02	3.68	82	0.3				
2019	CC	AA	22	6	2	2	20	13	76^{2}	60	6	5.6	11.9	101	42.5%	.310	1.41	5.05	83	0.9				
2019	HOU	MLB	22	0	0	0	7	0	8^{2}	4	0	3.1	13.5	13	50.0%	.250	0.81	1.04	82	0.2	95.3	32.2%	46.8%	42.5%
2020	HOU	MLB	23	0	0	0	4	0	3^{1}	1	0	18.9	8.1	3	37.5%	.125	2.40	2.70	123	0.0	92.9	35.5%	23.5%	36.7%
2021	TOR	WIN	24	1	4	0	7	7	26	23	0	3.8	9.7	28	55.2%	.315	1.31	2.42						
2021	SUG	AAA	24	0	0	0	15	0	15^{1}	11	0	7.6	14.1	24	51.6%	.355	1.57	1.76	64	0.4				
2021	HOU	MLB	24	3	3	1	31	0	36	35	4	4.5	9.0	36	48.1%	.310	1.47	5.75	106	0.2	95.7	45.3%	31.1%	50.9%
2022 DC	*HOU*	*MLB*	*25*	*0*	*0*	*0*	*11*	*0*	*9.7*	*8*	*1*	*6.0*	*11.8*	*12*	*45.3%*	*.315*	*1.55*	*5.02*	*112*	*0.0*	*95.5*	*43.8%*	*31.6%*	*49.5%*

Comparables: Keith Butler, Hunter Wood, James Norwood

After 2020 raised overarching questions about Abreu's major-league future—losing two ticks off your fastball at 23 will do that—he brought back his 95-mph four-seam velocity and earned a protracted big-league audition; his three dozen innings were seventh-most among Astros relievers. Those all came before the close of August, however, when Abreu and his unsightly ERA were demoted. His postseason résumé didn't see additions to the two outs he recorded in the 2019 ALCS, despite a postseason that proved even more a pitching thresher than the recent standard. The peripherals suggested he was only slightly worse than average, but there's not really a path to more unless the fastball-slider-curve righty can improve either his strikeout or walk rate.

Jonathan Bermudez LHP Born: 10/16/95 Age: 26 Bats: L Throws: L Height: 6'2" Weight: 237 lb. Origin: Round 23, 2018 Draft (#702 overall)

YEAR	TEAM	LVL	AGE	W	L	SV	G	GS	IP	H	HR	BB/9	K/9	K	GB%	BABIP	WHIP	ERA	DRA-	WARP	MPH	FB%	Whiff%	CSP
2019	QC	A	23	6	1	0	18	10	68	63	4	3.4	10.5	79	41.5%	.343	1.31	4.10	101	0.5				
2019	CC	AA	23	0	2	1	5	0	9^2	4	0	4.7	13.0	14	27.8%	.222	0.93	0.93	90	0.1				
2021	CC	AA	25	3	5	1	18	15	78^2	72	7	2.4	12.1	106	38.1%	.340	1.18	3.32	97	0.6				
2021	SUG	AAA	25	2	1	0	7	5	32^1	21	3	3.6	11.1	40	30.3%	.247	1.05	3.06	93	0.3				
2022 DC	*HOU*	*MLB*	*26*	*0*	*0*	*0*	*11*	*0*	*9.7*	*8*	*1*	*3.6*	*9.4*	*10*	*35.8%*	*.289*	*1.32*	*4.21*	*101*	*0.0*				

Comparables: Tyler Anderson, Luis Perez, Darrell Rasner

Returning to Double-A Corpus Christi after finishing out the 2019 season with an audition in their bullpen, Bermudez became the club's ace thanks to his combination of a 32.3% strikeout rate and strong command (6.4% walk rate). Before being moved up to Triple-A late in the season, where he maintained momentum if not the strong walk rate, Bermudez also gained acclaim for one more feat in Double-A: acting as the clubhouse barber. Earning a spot on Houston's 40-man means you're likely to see him out of the bullpen this year; whether his eventual role is there or in the rotation is a more difficult venture to augur.

Brandon Bielak RHP Born: 04/02/96 Age: 26 Bats: L Throws: R Height: 6'2" Weight: 208 lb. Origin: Round 11, 2017 Draft (#331 overall)

YEAR	TEAM	LVL	AGE	W	L	SV	G	GS	IP	H	HR	BB/9	K/9	K	GB%	BABIP	WHIP	ERA	DRA-	WARP	MPH	FB%	Whiff%	CSP
2019	CC	AA	23	3	0	0	8	6	36	29	3	3.5	8.3	33	53.0%	.268	1.19	3.75	113	-0.2				
2019	RR	AAA	23	8	4	0	15	14	85^2	69	10	3.8	9.0	86	42.8%	.271	1.23	4.41	98	0.6				
2020	HOU	MLB	24	3	3	0	12	6	32	39	9	4.8	7.3	26	35.9%	.323	1.75	6.75	147	-0.5	92.9	63.8%	27.5%	44.4%
2021	SUG	AAA	25	2	0	0	6	3	17^1	16	0	2.1	11.4	22	54.3%	.348	1.15	2.08	83	0.2				
2021	HOU	MLB	25	3	4	1	28	2	50	48	5	3.8	8.3	46	45.3%	.305	1.38	4.50	109	0.2	93.9	61.1%	25.4%	56.0%
2022 DC	*HOU*	*MLB*	*26*	*0*	*0*	*0*	*11*	*0*	*9.7*	*9*	*1*	*3.9*	*8.5*	*9*	*44.3%*	*.290*	*1.37*	*4.22*	*102*	*0.0*	*93.6*	*61.9%*	*26.1%*	*52.3%*

Comparables: Justin Grimm, Adam Warren, Matt Albers

In his two major-league campaigns, Bielak might have established himself as the league's pitcher most drawn to round numbers. He's had whole innings totals in both seasons, his ERA in each campaign has ended in quarter run increments and his WHIPs have never required a third decimal point. To focus on ultimately arbitrary number totals might imply a player to be bad, uninteresting or both. In contrast to a debut year in which he was notable only for his struggles, Bielak was exceedingly average in his sophomore season—the strikeout and walk rates are both worse than league average, but he compensated by getting a lot of batted balls on the ground. In 2021, Bielak's accomplishment was establishing himself in the major leagues, dodging opprobrium in his evaluation. It appears unlikely he'll have an open rotation spot for which to audition, but it'd be foolhardy to disregard a pitcher who is tenable even when allowing eye-popping numbers of baserunners.

Hunter Brown RHP Born: 08/29/98 Age: 23 Bats: R Throws: R Height: 6'2" Weight: 212 lb. Origin: Round 5, 2019 Draft (#166 overall)

YEAR	TEAM	LVL	AGE	W	L	SV	G	GS	IP	H	HR	BB/9	K/9	K	GB%	BABIP	WHIP	ERA	DRA-	WARP	MPH	FB%	Whiff%	CSP
2019	TRI	SS	20	2	2	0	12	6	23^2	13	0	6.8	12.5	33	52.9%	.255	1.31	4.56						
2021	CC	AA	22	1	4	1	13	11	49^1	45	6	5.3	13.9	76	45.5%	.379	1.50	4.20	96	0.4				
2021	SUG	AAA	22	5	1	0	11	8	51	47	6	3.7	9.7	55	52.5%	.311	1.33	3.88	84	0.7				
2022 non-DC	*HOU*	*MLB*	*23*	*2*	*2*	*0*	*57*	*0*	*50*	*47*	*6*	*4.9*	*9.6*	*53*	*46.4%*	*.307*	*1.50*	*4.72*	*109*	*0.0*				

Comparables: Paul Maholm, Nick Tropeano, Casey Coleman

Brown only became a full-time starter the season he was drafted; ultimately he had a mere 25 starts across his three seasons at Division II Wayne State University, the same number he's logged professionally between short-season ball in 2019 and the high minors last year. Unsurprisingly, he requires a good deal more refinement, his control being the weakest part of his repertoire. It's not clear the Astros will give him that time, with a power curveball (and an also-promising slider) helping generate a 35% strikeout rate to justify an aggressive assignment to Double-A Corpus Christi. In June, Brown told *The Athletic* he could find success if he could locate "10 more pitches a game." Even if he only got halfway there, it was enough to boost him to Triple-A. As to the other five pitches ... what would you do if you could change five things out of your day? Be better at parking, maybe? Expect Brown to debut from the bullpen unless the rotation is ravaged by injuries.

Shawn Dubin RHP Born: 09/06/95 Age: 26 Bats: R Throws: R Height: 6'1" Weight: 171 lb. Origin: Round 13, 2018 Draft (#402 overall)

YEAR	TEAM	LVL	AGE	W	L	SV	G	GS	IP	H	HR	BB/9	K/9	K	GB%	BABIP	WHIP	ERA	DRA-	WARP	MPH	FB%	Whiff%	CSP
2019	QC	A	23	1	0	2	3	1	12	7	0	3.0	14.3	19	69.6%	.304	0.92	0.75	104	0.1				
2019	FAY	A+	23	6	5	1	22	18	98^2	71	3	3.8	12.0	132	49.4%	.294	1.15	3.92	67	2.6				
2021	SUG	AAA	25	4	3	1	16	8	49^2	35	4	3.4	12.5	69	41.9%	.307	1.09	3.44	74	1.0				
2022 DC	*HOU*	*MLB*	*26*	*0*	*0*	*0*	*11*	*0*	*9.7*	*7*	*1*	*4.2*	*10.8*	*11*	*44.0%*	*.286*	*1.29*	*3.72*	*88*	*0.1*				

Comparables: Rob Zastryzny, Dustin McGowan, Mike MacDougal

Dubin's path to Houston's 40-man roster—to which he was added in November—has been beset by more obstacles than faced by your typical 19th century novel couple; after stepping away from the sport and spending time working at Lowe's, Dubin went from community college to Division I University of Buffalo, which unceremoniously shut down its baseball program after the 2017 season. Dubin landed at NAIA Georgetown College (Kentucky), where he excelled enough to be picked up by the Astros. Having made good on an aggressive Triple-A assignment, he figures to see big-league action in 2022.

Luis Garcia RHP Born: 12/13/96 Age: 25 Bats: R Throws: R Height: 6'1" Weight: 244 lb. Origin: International Free Agent, 2017

YEAR	TEAM	LVL	AGE	W	L	SV	G	GS	IP	H	HR	BB/9	K/9	K	GB%	BABIP	WHIP	ERA	DRA-	WARP	MPH	FB%	Whiff%	CSP
2019	QC	A	22	4	0	1	9	6	43	23	4	3.3	12.6	60	41.1%	.221	0.91	2.93	87	0.6				
2019	FAY	A+	22	6	4	0	15	12	65^{2}	43	5	4.7	14.8	108	45.3%	.311	1.17	3.02	58	2.0				
2020	HOU	MLB	23	0	1	0	5	1	12^{1}	7	1	3.6	6.6	9	41.2%	.182	0.97	2.92	117	0.0	93.9	62.1%	26.1%	44.9%
2021	HOU	MLB	24	11	8	0	30	28	155^{1}	132	19	2.9	9.7	167	38.3%	.288	1.17	3.30	90	2.2	92.4	67.2%	30.6%	55.6%
2022 DC	*HOU*	*MLB*	*25*	*8*	*8*	*0*	*25*	*25*	*137.3*	*124*	*21*	*3.6*	*9.6*	*147*	*38.5%*	*.289*	*1.31*	*4.14*	*100*	*0.9*	*92.5*	*67.0%*	*30.4%*	*55.0%*

Comparables: Matt Keough, Jack Morris, Pedro Astacio

It can be hard to make a name for yourself when someone else already has yours. Did you know Michael Keaton's last name is actually Douglas? MLB doesn't have SAG rules limiting duplicate names, so Garcia was kind enough to prove memorable in his first full season. There's the idiosyncratic delivery that gives him the silhouette of a parent rocking their child to the latest TikTok dance, for one. The fact he ran nearly 70% fastball usage as a pitcher whose age starts with a two. That he was the pitcher the Astros turned to in Game 6 of the World Series despite having nearly matched innings with earned runs in the postseason to that point—also that he gained three ticks on his fastball in October. If one of the other Garcia, Luises can catch up, the Will Smiths might have competition as MLB's best same-named pair.

Josh James RHP Born: 03/08/93 Age: 29 Bats: R Throws: R Height: 6'3" Weight: 234 lb. Origin: Round 34, 2014 Draft (#1006 overall)

YEAR	TEAM	LVL	AGE	W	L	SV	G	GS	IP	H	HR	BB/9	K/9	K	GB%	BABIP	WHIP	ERA	DRA-	WARP	MPH	FB%	Whiff%	CSP
2019	HOU	MLB	26	5	1	1	49	1	61^{1}	46	10	5.1	14.7	100	35.4%	.308	1.32	4.70	69	1.6	97.3	63.3%	36.7%	46.1%
2020	HOU	MLB	27	1	0	0	13	2	17^{1}	15	4	8.8	10.9	21	32.6%	.282	1.85	7.27	125	0.0	96.4	57.8%	30.6%	43.7%
2021	SUG	AAA	28	1	2	1	20	0	18^{2}	17	0	3.9	13.0	27	34.8%	.370	1.34	3.38	77	0.3				
2021	HOU	MLB	28	0	0	0	5	0	5	4	1	3.6	14.4	8	54.5%	.300	1.20	5.40	96	0.1	94.7	58.0%	35.7%	62.4%
2022 DC	*HOU*	*MLB*	*29*	*1*	*1*	*0*	*22*	*0*	*19.3*	*14*	*2*	*4.7*	*11.7*	*25*	*38.6%*	*.274*	*1.28*	*3.76*	*90*	*0.2*	*96.7*	*60.9%*	*34.6%*	*47.0%*

Comparables: Michael Kohn, Gonzalez Germen, Carl Edwards Jr.

Belief is potent fuel. It can be intangible nourishment, provide indefatigable motivation to see a course through, missteps and disappointments aside. It goes beyond the gambler's fallacy, puts the lie to Pascal's wager: there is no faking belief because belief costs you, charges prices others sometimes judge sacrosanct. The modern MLB front office isn't a fitting stage for shows of faith, but then again nowhere ever is. Tendering a contract to James, who missed the majority of the season recovering from hip surgery following an ugly ERA in 2020, might seem a miserly show of faith. It's not about the size of the work, however, but what it cost—regardless of loud fastball velocity, someone in Houston's bleeding edge front office believes in James.

Cristian Javier RHP Born: 03/26/97 Age: 25 Bats: R Throws: R Height: 6'1" Weight: 213 lb. Origin: International Free Agent, 2015

YEAR	TEAM	LVL	AGE	W	L	SV	G	GS	IP	H	HR	BB/9	K/9	K	GB%	BABIP	WHIP	ERA	DRA-	WARP	MPH	FB%	Whiff%	CSP
2019	FAY	A+	22	2	0	1	7	5	28^{2}	15	1	5.0	12.6	40	33.3%	.226	1.08	0.94	93	0.4				
2019	CC	AA	22	6	3	3	17	11	74	31	5	4.7	13.9	114	29.2%	.198	0.95	2.07	60	1.8				
2019	RR	AAA	22	0	0	0	2	2	11	5	1	3.3	13.1	16	17.4%	.182	0.82	1.64	94	0.1				
2020	HOU	MLB	23	5	2	0	12	10	54^{1}	36	11	3.0	8.9	54	29.3%	.194	0.99	3.48	115	0.2	92.3	63.1%	22.5%	47.7%
2021	HOU	MLB	24	4	1	2	36	9	101^{1}	67	16	4.7	11.5	130	27.4%	.235	1.18	3.55	96	1.1	93.6	59.4%	31.8%	51.6%
2022 DC	*HOU*	*MLB*	*25*	*7*	*5*	*0*	*42*	*9*	*81.3*	*64*	*14*	*4.7*	*10.9*	*99*	*29.4%*	*.265*	*1.31*	*4.19*	*99*	*0.6*	*93.3*	*60.3%*	*29.5%*	*50.7%*

Comparables: Nick Tropeano, Vicente Palacios, Jose Acevedo

At this point, having too many starters sounds like some logical inconsistency that can only be parsed for its absurdity—like having not enough student loans, or too much cabinet space. Yet the Astros are determined to upend conventionality, and so Javier made only nine starts throughout the regular season and wasn't stretched out come October. A player with his pedigree—he was the club's minor-league pitcher of the year in 2019—will get another shot at the rotation, so we're left to read tea leaves where a crystal ball is needed; that is, try to hew Javier's bullpen work to our expectations for a starter. The walk rate ballooned, but more so out of the bullpen than as a starter, and was accompanied by a strikeouts spike to boot. Few pitchers have trod the low BABIP, high home run rate Javier braves, but that's now two seasons he's executed the routine with aplomb.

Phil Maton RHP Born: 03/25/93 Age: 29 Bats: R Throws: R Height: 6'2" Weight: 206 lb. Origin: Round 20, 2015 Draft (#597 overall)

YEAR	TEAM	LVL	AGE	W	L	SV	G	GS	IP	H	HR	BB/9	K/9	K	GB%	BABIP	WHIP	ERA	DRA-	WARP	MPH	FB%	Whiff%	CSP
2019	COL	AAA	26	0	1	3	9	0	10^{2}	5	1	3.4	14.3	17	44.4%	.235	0.84	2.53	72	0.3				
2019	ELP	AAA	26	2	1	2	13	0	18^{2}	17	2	2.9	14.5	30	57.5%	.405	1.23	2.89	63	0.5				
2019	SD	MLB	26	0	0	0	21	0	24^{1}	34	6	2.2	7.4	20	44.3%	.350	1.64	7.77	101	0.2	90.9	77.1%	24.8%	49.9%
2019	CLE	MLB	26	0	0	0	9	0	12^{1}	4	1	4.4	9.5	13	46.4%	.111	0.81	2.92	98	0.1	90.3	70.4%	24.7%	50.7%
2020	CLE	MLB	27	3	3	0	23	0	21^{2}	23	1	2.5	13.3	32	44.4%	.415	1.34	4.57	68	0.6	92.7	79.7%	37.3%	48.0%
2021	CLE	MLB	28	2	0	0	38	1	41^{1}	36	4	4.4	13.3	61	40.4%	.356	1.35	4.57	69	1.0	91.8	61.8%	38.0%	52.7%
2021	HOU	MLB	28	4	0	0	27	0	25^{1}	28	2	4.3	8.5	24	38.8%	.333	1.58	4.97	112	0.1	91.2	47.4%	29.7%	52.0%
2022 DC	*HOU*	*MLB*	*29*	*2*	*2*	*0*	*50*	*0*	*43.7*	*36*	*5*	*3.6*	*11.4*	*55*	*41.3%*	*.294*	*1.23*	*3.57*	*87*	*0.5*	*91.6*	*62.4%*	*34.0%*	*51.5%*

Comparables: Michael Tonkin, Steve Cishek, Kevin Quackenbush

Even when a team has a reputation for efficacy in jump-starting the career of a particular sort of player, it's folly to expect them to succeed on turning every spark of potential energy kinetic. Still, all the "How the Astros fixed Maton" articles (they gave him a sweeper slider and changed the shape of his fastball) make it apparent how an expectation is developed. If you need a further reminder teams couldn't care less about single-season reliever ERA, note that Maton's mark *increased* on the way from Cleveland to Houston, and he still earned double-digit postseason appearances.

Lance McCullers Jr. RHP Born: 10/02/93 Age: 28 Bats: L Throws: R Height: 6'1" Weight: 202 lb. Origin: Round 1, 2012 Draft (#41 overall)

YEAR	TEAM	LVL	AGE	W	L	SV	G	GS	IP	H	HR	BB/9	K/9	K	GB%	BABIP	WHIP	ERA	DRA-	WARP	MPH	FB%	Whiff%	CSP
2020	HOU	MLB	26	3	3	0	11	11	55	44	5	3.3	9.2	56	58.9%	.279	1.16	3.93	71	1.5	93.9	44.1%	29.7%	44.6%
2021	HOU	MLB	27	13	5	0	28	28	162^{1}	122	13	4.2	10.3	185	56.4%	.273	1.22	3.16	83	2.9	94.0	35.6%	30.3%	53.5%
2022 DC	*HOU*	*MLB*	*28*	*10*	*7*	*0*	*25*	*25*	*147.7*	*123*	*14*	*3.8*	*10.4*	*170*	*55.1%*	*.292*	*1.26*	*3.46*	*86*	*2.3*	*94.0*	*37.1%*	*30.2%*	*51.9%*

Comparables: A.J. Burnett, Bob Gibson, Steve Carlton

One of countless players to sign extensions in 2021, McCullers reminded everyone what certainty is worth. After returning from Tommy John in the short season and leaving slight questions as to whether he'd come all the way back, the righty had arguably his best season, reaching qualified status for the first time while logging a career-best ERA. A new slider compensated for a slightly less efficacious curveball, the strikeout and walk rates remained high and in the uncommon case a ball entered the field of play it was generally on the ground. Health and dependability questions evidently in the past, McCullers appeared to have left serious money on the table, his $85 million guarantee roughly $30 million scant of the now-commonplace Zack Wheeler contract structure. Then in Game 4 of the ALDS, his forearm balked, virtually guaranteeing McCullers wouldn't have reached that guarantee in free agency. Thankfully, the injury proved only a strain to the flexor pronator muscle in his pitching arm, and McCullers is expected to be healthy for spring training (though, as he pointed out, one can only hope being locked out from training staff and facilities has "no ramifications.")

Rafael Montero RHP Born: 10/17/90 Age: 31 Bats: R Throws: R Height: 6'0" Weight: 190 lb. Origin: International Free Agent, 2011

YEAR	TEAM	LVL	AGE	W	L	SV	G	GS	IP	H	HR	BB/9	K/9	K	GB%	BABIP	WHIP	ERA	DRA-	WARP	MPH	FB%	Whiff%	CSP
2019	RAN	ROK	28	0	0	0	5	3	7	2	0	0.0	15.4	12	45.5%	.182	0.29	0.00						
2019	FRI	AA	28	0	0	0	5	2	9	15	0	2.0	15.0	15	25.9%	.556	1.89	7.00	67	0.2				
2019	TEX	MLB	28	2	0	0	22	0	29	23	5	1.6	10.6	34	40.3%	.269	0.97	2.48	88	0.5	95.8	46.8%	29.8%	45.0%
2020	TEX	MLB	29	0	1	8	17	0	17^{2}	12	2	3.1	9.7	19	26.7%	.238	1.02	4.08	109	0.1	95.6	72.0%	25.0%	49.0%
2021	SEA	MLB	30	5	3	7	40	0	43^{1}	56	4	3.1	7.7	37	55.1%	.366	1.64	7.27	102	0.3	95.6	61.4%	22.4%	50.3%
2021	HOU	MLB	30	0	1	0	4	0	6	3	0	3.0	7.5	5	50.0%	.214	0.83	0.00	104	0.0	95.8	66.3%	29.3%	52.1%
2022 DC	*HOU*	*MLB*	*31*	*2*	*2*	*0*	*50*	*0*	*43.7*	*43*	*5*	*2.9*	*7.9*	*38*	*46.1%*	*.295*	*1.30*	*4.13*	*102*	*0.1*	*95.6*	*61.6%*	*24.2%*	*49.5%*

Comparables: Zack Britton, Juan Gutierrez, Jon Rauch

The secondary righty reliever the Astros added in the Kendall Graveman trade, Montero managed just four appearances before a shoulder injury ended his season. Nevertheless, he proved to be the pitcher who lingered on Houston's roster longer, with Graveman departing in free agency while Montero was tendered a contract in arbitration—as were all six Astros players eligible. Despite the ugly career ERA—both over his career and in 2021—DRA judges Montero as an above-average pitcher throughout his career, if by the barest margin. He hasn't posted a walk rate above 10%—as he did in his first four big-league forays—in three seasons, though his strikeout rate has dwindled in the same interval.

Héctor Neris RHP Born: 06/14/89 Age: 33 Bats: R Throws: R Height: 6'2" Weight: 227 lb. Origin: International Free Agent, 2010

YEAR	TEAM	LVL	AGE	W	L	SV	G	GS	IP	H	HR	BB/9	K/9	K	GB%	BABIP	WHIP	ERA	DRA-	WARP	MPH	FB%	Whiff%	CSP
2019	PHI	MLB	30	3	6	28	68	0	67^{2}	45	10	3.2	11.8	89	44.9%	.241	1.02	2.93	74	1.6	94.7	34.7%	38.6%	39.9%
2020	PHI	MLB	31	2	2	5	24	0	21^{2}	24	0	5.4	11.2	27	39.7%	.381	1.71	4.57	89	0.4	94.2	51.9%	39.1%	41.0%
2021	PHI	MLB	32	4	7	12	74	0	74^{1}	55	12	3.9	11.9	98	48.9%	.264	1.17	3.63	77	1.6	94.6	55.9%	34.3%	52.1%
2022 DC	*HOU*	*MLB*	*33*	*2*	*2*	*4*	*56*	*0*	*48.3*	*38*	*6*	*3.7*	*11.7*	*63*	*43.8%*	*.284*	*1.20*	*3.42*	*83*	*0.6*	*94.6*	*51.1%*	*35.8%*	*48.1%*

Comparables: Darren O'Day, Jerry Blevins, Steve Cishek

The Phillies' on-again, off-again closer enjoyed something of a bounceback campaign in 2021, slashing more than one-and-a-half walks per nine and nearly a whole run off of his ERA. It says something about where he started from that walks were still an issue; Neris hasn't walked fewer than three batters per nine since his first full big-league season in 2015. And yet, he still gets swings and misses in bulk, and when hitters do make contact, the results aren't great for them. The velocity hasn't yet dipped as he rounds the bend separating early- from mid-30s, and the split finger remains an elite pitch, netting an eye-popping 45.6% whiff rate. The Astros looked at all these ingredients and decided they could make something out of them, signing Neris to a two-year, $17 million deal.

Jake Odorizzi RHP Born: 03/27/90 Age: 32 Bats: R Throws: R Height: 6'2" Weight: 190 lb. Origin: Round 1, 2008 Draft (#32 overall)

YEAR	TEAM	LVL	AGE	W	L	SV	G	GS	IP	H	HR	BB/9	K/9	K	GB%	BABIP	WHIP	ERA	DRA-	WARP	MPH	FB%	Whiff%	CSP
2019	MIN	MLB	29	15	7	0	30	30	159	139	16	3.0	10.1	178	34.3%	.305	1.21	3.51	93	2.3	93.0	57.8%	27.9%	46.6%
2020	MIN	MLB	30	0	1	0	4	4	13^{2}	16	4	2.0	7.9	12	34.9%	.308	1.39	6.59	117	0.0	93.2	41.8%	19.9%	45.1%
2021	SUG	AAA	31	0	1	0	2	2	7^{2}	10	1	1.2	12.9	11	66.7%	.450	1.43	4.70	86	0.1				
2021	HOU	MLB	31	6	7	0	24	23	104^{2}	97	16	2.9	7.8	91	35.5%	.276	1.25	4.21	116	0.1	92.3	55.4%	22.0%	52.1%
2022 DC	*HOU*	*MLB*	*32*	*7*	*5*	*0*	*53*	*9*	*79.7*	*78*	*13*	*3.0*	*7.8*	*68*	*36.1%*	*.283*	*1.31*	*4.36*	*107*	*0.3*	*92.6*	*55.3%*	*23.7%*	*50.0%*

Comparables: Jason Marquis, Homer Bailey, Iván Nova

"Nothing else has any efficacy, I might as well be myself." —Odorizzi
"But your yourself sucks!" —DRA
"It is, lamentably, all I have" —Odorizzi

It's not necessarily fair to say Odorizzi sucks; even before semantical arguments about how no major leaguer can suck, he posted a positive WARP! That's a useful guy to have at the back of the rotation, if not one you're likely to turn to in any ideal playoff situation. But it wasn't the showing anyone was hoping for. Sometimes, though, you make do; in 2019 Odorizzi lost out on serious cash by taking a qualifying offer after a career year, and in 2021 Houston learned the outlier season was just that. He still made 24 starts that filled necessary innings, and worked his way into the World Series after failing to prove superior to the weight of his career. Even if it's a little disappointing, there's power to giving what you have.

Ryan Pressly RHP Born: 12/15/88 Age: 33 Bats: R Throws: R Height: 6'2" Weight: 206 lb. Origin: Round 11, 2007 Draft (#354 overall)

YEAR	TEAM	LVL	AGE	W	L	SV	G	GS	IP	H	HR	BB/9	K/9	K	GB%	BABIP	WHIP	ERA	DRA-	WARP	MPH	FB%	Whiff%	CSP
2019	HOU	MLB	30	2	3	3	55	0	54^{1}	37	6	2.0	11.9	72	52.4%	.258	0.90	2.32	70	1.4	95.7	35.9%	35.8%	47.8%
2020	HOU	MLB	31	1	3	12	23	0	21	21	2	3.0	12.4	29	48.1%	.365	1.33	3.43	73	0.5	94.6	37.1%	36.5%	45.2%
2021	HOU	MLB	32	5	3	26	64	0	64	49	4	1.8	11.4	81	55.1%	.298	0.97	2.25	70	1.6	95.5	39.6%	32.0%	58.5%
2022 DC	*HOU*	*MLB*	*33*	*3*	*2*	*38*	*56*	*0*	*48.3*	*39*	*5*	*2.4*	*10.9*	*58*	*50.5%*	*.291*	*1.08*	*2.64*	*70*	*1.0*	*95.4*	*38.5%*	*33.4%*	*54.4%*

Comparables: Tyler Thornburg, Turk Wendell, Bob Wickman

It's not clear what alchemical process Houston has for relievers in general, nor how Pressly got so strong a dose he's been strikingly similar in each of his Houston campaigns. Even as he pushes into the "mid-" section of his 30s, he's trained observers to expect a 30% strikeout rate, an average or better walk rate and for the rest to sort itself out. Frankly it probably would even if he had a hamartia like an outlandish home run rate, or an annual run of shakiness. He doesn't. Here's to another year of being the Platonic reliever—at least until that team-friendly deal expires.

Alex Santos II RHP Born: 02/10/02 Age: 20 Bats: R Throws: R Height: 6'4" Weight: 194 lb. Origin: Round 2, 2020 Draft (#72 overall)

YEAR	TEAM	LVL	AGE	W	L	SV	G	GS	IP	H	HR	BB/9	K/9	K	GB%	BABIP	WHIP	ERA	DRA-	WARP	MPH	FB%	Whiff%	CSP
2021	FAY	A	19	2	2	1	12	7	41^{2}	31	2	6.5	10.4	48	26.9%	.284	1.46	3.46	114	0.0				
2022 non-DC	*HOU*	*MLB*	*20*	*2*	*3*	*0*	*57*	*0*	*50*	*54*	*10*	*7.6*	*8.4*	*46*	*29.4%*	*.308*	*1.92*	*7.42*	*152*	*-1.2*				

Comparables: Tyler Skaggs, Chad Gaudin, Daryl Thompson

One marker that the Astros believe their own hype, think their run atop the American League isn't close to an end, is their persistence in drafting high-ceiling but high-variance young prospects regardless of the loss of first- and second-round picks in the last two drafts. Santos has plenty to recommend, a high-spin fastball already intriguing even without a probably necessary (if his destiny is the rotation) velocity jump. He's also probably three years or more from the majors, with all the attendant roadblocks in addition to the precarity of planning on an uptick on stuff. For all the time Santos will need, though, the system in which he resides might accord him more looks and chances than he might otherwise get—would we still be talking about Forrest Whitley if he was in the Angels system?

Peter Solomon RHP Born: 08/16/96 Age: 25 Bats: R Throws: R Height: 6'4" Weight: 211 lb. Origin: Round 4, 2017 Draft (#121 overall)

YEAR	TEAM	LVL	AGE	W	L	SV	G	GS	IP	H	HR	BB/9	K/9	K	GB%	BABIP	WHIP	ERA	DRA-	WARP	MPH	FB%	Whiff%	CSP
2019	FAY	A+	22	0	0	0	2	2	7^{2}	7	1	4.7	16.4	14	33.3%	.429	1.43	2.35	83	0.1				
2021	SUG	AAA	24	8	1	1	21	18	97^{2}	89	16	3.9	10.3	112	35.9%	.289	1.34	4.70	95	0.7				
2021	HOU	MLB	24	1	0	0	6	0	14	10	0	5.1	6.4	10	51.4%	.270	1.29	1.29	115	0.0	92.0	63.0%	20.6%	49.3%
2022 DC	*HOU*	*MLB*	*25*	*0*	*0*	*0*	*11*	*0*	*9.7*	*9*	*1*	*4.3*	*8.7*	*9*	*40.5%*	*.296*	*1.45*	*4.72*	*111*	*0.0*	*92.0*	*63.0%*	*20.6%*	*49.3%*

Comparables: Alex Colomé, Alfredo Figaro, Austin Voth

Solomon returned from a well-timed Tommy John surgery in 2021 bereft of a few miles of fastball velocity. He still made the jump to Triple-A with aplomb, allowing just two runs in six major-league appearances spread over three cameos throughout the year. Whether he ends up as more than rotational depth depends on if he can bring back the lost fastball velocity, or compensate in some other fashion to bring back a noteworthy strikeout rate. Toni Morrison's *Song of Solomon* contains advice that can apply to most any pitcher, but perhaps one needing more beneath his pitches: "if you surrendered to the air, you could ride it."

Ryne Stanek RHP Born: 07/26/91 Age: 30 Bats: R Throws: R Height: 6'4" Weight: 226 lb. Origin: Round 1, 2013 Draft (#29 overall)

YEAR	TEAM	LVL	AGE	W	L	SV	G	GS	IP	H	HR	BB/9	K/9	K	GB%	BABIP	WHIP	ERA	DRA-	WARP	MPH	FB%	Whiff%	CSP
2019	TB	MLB	27	0	2	0	41	27	55^{2}	44	7	3.2	9.9	61	30.6%	.264	1.15	3.40	103	0.5	97.7	57.4%	33.7%	42.3%
2019	MIA	MLB	27	0	2	1	22	0	21^{1}	17	4	8.0	11.8	28	30.8%	.271	1.69	5.48	111	0.1	97.8	52.0%	36.9%	40.0%
2020	MIA	MLB	28	0	0	0	9	0	10	11	3	7.2	9.9	11	34.5%	.308	1.90	7.20	123	0.0	95.9	43.9%	33.7%	42.9%
2021	HOU	MLB	29	3	5	2	72	0	68^{1}	46	8	4.9	10.9	83	33.3%	.242	1.21	3.42	95	0.8	97.8	59.7%	32.7%	51.7%
2022 DC	*HOU*	*MLB*	*30*	*2*	*2*	*2*	*56*	*0*	*48.3*	*38*	*8*	*4.5*	*11.2*	*60*	*34.8%*	*.273*	*1.30*	*3.98*	*96*	*0.3*	*97.6*	*57.5%*	*33.2%*	*48.5%*

Comparables: Ryan Dull, Jacob Barnes, Adam Russell

Miami's 2019 trade of Stanek for Nick Anderson proved disastrous, as all such things must given the involved parties, and when Houston offered a rebound destination following an ERA north of six in two stints as a Marlin, a rebound is exactly what transpired. So it goes. Another overused Vonnegut quote, noting the limits of idealistic, intellectual resistance in the context of the Vietnam War, applies, too: "It was like a laser beam. We were all aimed in the same direction. The power of [that resistance] turns out to be that of a custard pie dropped from a stepladder six feet high." It must feel similar for members of front offices outside of Tampa Bay or Houston—isn't the best course to not trade with them, if they can revitalize any pitcher thusly? But then Stanek gets cut and the Astros bring him back to form, anyway.

Blake Taylor LHP Born: 08/17/95 Age: 26 Bats: L Throws: L Height: 6'3" Weight: 220 lb. Origin: Round 2, 2013 Draft (#51 overall)

YEAR	TEAM	LVL	AGE	W	L	SV	G	GS	IP	H	HR	BB/9	K/9	K	GB%	BABIP	WHIP	ERA	DRA-	WARP	MPH	FB%	Whiff%	CSP
2019	STL	A+	23	2	2	7	21	0	27^{1}	24	1	4.0	9.5	29	64.5%	.315	1.32	2.63	102	0.3				
2019	BNG	AA	23	0	1	3	18	0	39	25	2	2.8	10.4	45	50.0%	.245	0.95	1.85	83	0.6				
2020	HOU	MLB	24	2	1	1	22	0	20^{2}	13	2	5.2	7.4	17	50.0%	.196	1.21	2.18	93	0.3	93.8	76.5%	19.9%	50.5%
2021	HOU	MLB	25	4	4	0	51	0	42^{2}	38	6	4.6	8.6	41	40.0%	.271	1.41	3.16	117	0.0	93.1	72.5%	24.6%	49.8%
2022 DC	*HOU*	*MLB*	*26*	*2*	*2*	*0*	*50*	*0*	*43.7*	*41*	*5*	*4.6*	*8.2*	*39*	*44.8%*	*.289*	*1.46*	*4.64*	*109*	*-0.1*	*93.3*	*73.4%*	*23.5%*	*50.0%*

Comparables: Randy Rosario, Williams Jerez, Pat Gomez

The necessity of a left-handed reliever to balance a bullpen is perhaps at an all-time low, given the outlawing of the one-out reliever. Still, when you find guys who can limit their career OPS allowed against left-handed batters to .492, you'd think a team would figure out a way to load the dice. For his brief career, however, Taylor's faced lefty batters in 40.7% of plate appearances—less than half a percentage point more than the proportion of plate appearances received by lefties in 2021. So much for the platoon advantage. Taylor appeared in four postseason contests in 2021; in just one did the Astros have a win expectancy of more than 8%, and they dropped all four games.

José Urquidy RHP Born: 05/01/95 Age: 27 Bats: R Throws: R Height: 6'0" Weight: 217 lb. Origin: International Free Agent, 2015

YEAR	TEAM	LVL	AGE	W	L	SV	G	GS	IP	H	HR	BB/9	K/9	K	GB%	BABIP	WHIP	ERA	DRA-	WARP	MPH	FB%	Whiff%	CSP
2019	CC	AA	24	2	2	0	7	6	33	28	2	1.4	10.9	40	42.0%	.302	1.00	4.09	82	0.4				
2019	RR	AAA	24	5	3	0	13	12	70	67	15	2.1	12.1	94	31.9%	.313	1.19	4.63	79	1.3				
2019	HOU	MLB	24	2	1	0	9	7	41	38	6	1.5	8.8	40	35.0%	.286	1.10	3.95	96	0.5	93.2	47.3%	28.3%	51.3%
2020	HOU	MLB	25	1	1	0	5	5	29^{2}	22	4	2.4	5.2	17	35.6%	.209	1.01	2.73	133	-0.2	93.4	54.5%	20.9%	52.8%
2021	SUG	AAA	26	1	0	0	2	2	9	5	2	0.0	11.0	11	52.4%	.158	0.56	2.00	93	0.1				
2021	HOU	MLB	26	8	3	0	20	20	107	87	17	1.6	7.6	90	31.7%	.239	0.99	3.62	104	0.7	92.7	55.0%	25.1%	59.3%
2022 DC	*HOU*	*MLB*	*27*	*9*	*8*	*0*	*27*	*27*	*148.7*	*145*	*23*	*2.0*	*8.0*	*131*	*34.6%*	*.289*	*1.20*	*3.85*	*98*	*1.3*	*92.9*	*54.1%*	*24.9%*	*57.6%*

Comparables: Armando Galarraga, A.J. Griffin, Brandon Workman

Shoulder discomfort that required 81 days on the Injured List prevented Urquidy from attaining qualified status and, more importantly, capturing the Astros' trust. Despite another solid ERA and a third stint's evidence he has a talent for preventing baserunners, the righty had a swingman role in the postseason even though it was evident fatigue affected the pitching corps—7 ⅔ innings across only three appearances. Urquidy's contact-reliant nature despite no particular proclivity for ground balls makes advanced metrics leery of his continued run prevention prowess, and a complete season would go a long way to producing confidence he can stay ahead of his peripherals.

Framber Valdez LHP

Born: 11/19/93 Age: 28 Bats: R Throws: L Height: 5'11" Weight: 239 lb. Origin: International Free Agent, 2015

YEAR	TEAM	LVL	AGE	W	L	SV	G	GS	IP	H	HR	BB/9	K/9	K	GB%	BABIP	WHIP	ERA	DRA-	WARP	MPH	FB%	Whiff%	CSP
2019	RR	AAA	25	5	2	1	10	7	44^{1}	29	3	3.5	14.0	69	72.2%	.306	1.04	3.25	55	1.5				
2019	HOU	MLB	25	4	7	0	26	8	70^{2}	74	9	5.6	8.7	68	62.0%	.319	1.67	5.86	106	0.5	93.0	61.3%	26.1%	48.8%
2020	HOU	MLB	26	5	3	0	11	10	70^{2}	63	5	2.0	9.7	76	59.7%	.314	1.12	3.57	65	2.1	93.1	58.6%	24.4%	52.4%
2021	SUG	AAA	27	0	1	0	2	2	7	9	0	2.6	6.4	5	84.6%	.346	1.57	1.29	102	0.0				
2021	HOU	MLB	27	11	6	0	22	22	134^{2}	110	12	3.9	8.4	125	70.1%	.268	1.25	3.14	94	1.6	92.6	57.2%	26.3%	56.4%
2022 DC	*HOU*	*MLB*	*28*	*11*	*9*	*0*	*29*	*29*	*172*	*162*	*12*	*3.6*	*8.4*	*161*	*66.0%*	*.303*	*1.35*	*3.71*	*93*	*1.9*	*92.8*	*58.0%*	*25.8%*	*54.6%*

Comparables: Wandy Rodriguez, Garrett Richards, Scott Downs

Valdez looked every part the ace in 2020, and whether he could carry that form forward appeared critical to the fate of a Houston squad still bereft one Justin Verlander. As much as a 3.14 ERA season can be a disaster—and in the modern MLB it can be: Matt Barnes' was scarcely higher when he lost Boston's closer job—the southpaw experienced it in 2021. His regular season was delayed by a broken ring finger on his pitching hand, sustained while fielding a comebacker in spring training. After the injury that might have stretched for most of the season proved to require 60 injured list days—a paltry sum by 2021 standards—Valdez was worse across the board, despite what the run prevention suggests. While the walk rate didn't jump to the untenable levels of 2018-19, both it and the strikeout rate wound up worse than league average, though an absurd 70% groundball rate helped Valdez perform an unremarkable mid-rotation role. That wasn't what Houston needed, but Valdez's 17 earned runs in 19 postseason innings might have solidified that reputation—although if any team's to provide a potentially redemptive postseason spotlight, it's the Astros.

Justin Verlander RHP

Born: 02/20/83 Age: 39 Bats: R Throws: R Height: 6'5" Weight: 235 lb. Origin: Round 1, 2004 Draft (#2 overall)

YEAR	TEAM	LVL	AGE	W	L	SV	G	GS	IP	H	HR	BB/9	K/9	K	GB%	BABIP	WHIP	ERA	DRA-	WARP	MPH	FB%	Whiff%	CSP
2019	HOU	MLB	36	21	6	0	34	34	223	137	36	1.7	12.1	300	36.1%	.219	0.80	2.58	67	6.2	94.6	49.9%	33.7%	48.8%
2020	HOU	MLB	37	1	0	0	1	1	6	3	2	1.5	10.5	7	61.5%	.091	0.67	3.00	77	0.1	95.1	54.8%	25.7%	49.5%
2022 DC	*HOU*	*MLB*	*39*	*10*	*6*	*0*	*25*	*25*	*150.3*	*124*	*23*	*2.1*	*10.4*	*173*	*35.3%*	*.275*	*1.07*	*3.04*	*79*	*2.9*	*94.6*	*50.1%*	*33.3%*	*48.9%*

Comparables: Steve Carlton, Freddy Garcia, Don Sutton

Whether you believe in Justin Verlander's ability to come back at 39 is your own private affair, like Jesus said about charitable works and modern politicians say about political donations. Teams across MLB, however, were clearly swayed by the legend's November showcase spanning around 25 pitches, in which he harnessed all his pitches at near-previous velocities. It was fewer than two weeks later Verlander returned to the Astros on a salary that affirmed their belief with the one thing another notable old guy, Nelson Cruz, never got: a second-year player option. The towering righty appears to be chasing something else, though: a multi-year contract next offseason, when it can be assumed he'll stare down 40 without a hint of a twitch.

Forrest Whitley RHP

Born: 09/15/97 Age: 24 Bats: R Throws: R Height: 6'7" Weight: 238 lb. Origin: Round 1, 2016 Draft (#17 overall)

YEAR	TEAM	LVL	AGE	W	L	SV	G	GS	IP	H	HR	BB/9	K/9	K	GB%	BABIP	WHIP	ERA	DRA-	WARP	MPH	FB%	Whiff%	CSP
2019	PEJ	WIN	21	3	2	0	6	6	25	22	3	3.2	11.5	32	43.5%	.322	1.24	2.88						
2019	AST	ROK	21	0	2	0	2	2	4^{1}	2	0	18.7	20.8	10	50.0%	.333	2.54	8.31						
2019	FAY	A+	21	1	0	0	2	2	8^{1}	4	0	1.1	11.9	11	44.4%	.222	0.60	2.16	81	0.2				
2019	CC	AA	21	2	2	0	6	6	22^{2}	18	2	7.5	14.3	36	46.7%	.372	1.63	5.56	74	0.4				
2019	RR	AAA	21	0	3	0	8	5	24^{1}	35	9	5.5	10.7	29	30.7%	.400	2.05	12.21	111	0.0				
2022															*No projection*									

Comparables: Arodys Vizcaíno, Amalio Diaz, Phillippe Aumont

Going on four years now, there is virtually no game data on which to judge Whitley—2019's 59 ⅔ frames comprise more than two-thirds his minor-league innings in the last four years. As he approaches his last best chance to show his career can be more than just a factor keeping team employees who submit injury list updates employed, we have precious little on which to set expectations, some Instagram footage aside. One clerical note: he was optioned midway through spring training and thus remained on the minor-league side of the reserve list all season, eating up a spot on Houston's 40-man roster but not accruing service time. The Astros believe in Whitley providing value in the long-term, or at least see enough possibility of such they limited their options last year.

Lineouts

Hitters

HITTER	POS	TEAM	LVL	AGE	PA	R	2B	3B	HR	RBI	BB	K	SB	CS	AVG/OBP/SLG	DRC+	BABIP	BRR	FRAA	WARP
Colin Barber	OF	ASH	A+	20	53	10	1	0	3	7	9	22	1	1	.214/.365/.452	76	.353	0.7	RF(7): 0.5, LF(5): -0.5, CF(3): -0.8	0.0
J.C. Correa	IF	FAY	A	22	255	44	19	2	5	32	28	30	7	7	.306/.392/.477	128	.335	-2.0	SS(30): 0.4, 1B(11): 0.3, 3B(9): 2.5	1.6
	IF	ASH	A+	22	193	33	13	0	4	25	7	29	3	2	.314/.337/.449	110	.353	-0.4	2B(14): -0.7, 3B(13): -1.5, 1B(8): -0.5	0.5
Yainer Diaz	C/DH	FAY	A	22	49	3	2	0	1	7	0	4	1	0	.229/.224/.333	115	.227	0.0	C(5): 1.3, 1B(2): 0.2	0.4
	C/DH	LYN	A	22	258	30	19	1	5	50	15	42	1	1	.314/.357/.464	115	.361	-1.3	C(36): 1.4, 1B(2): -0.2	1.2
	C/DH	ASH	A+	22	105	28	4	0	11	33	8	17	2	0	.396/.438/.781	156	.391	-0.4	C(12): -1.2, 1B(8): -0.1	0.9
Cristian Gonzalez	SS	AST	ROK	19	47	8	2	0	2	13	5	10	3	0	.310/.383/.500		.367			
	SS	FAY	A	19	134	19	4	1	2	14	9	41	1	2	.244/.299/.341	81	.346	-0.8	SS(23): -0.2, 3B(3): 0.9, 2B(1): -0.0	0.1
Marwin Gonzalez	IF	HOU	MLB	32	36	5	0	0	3	8	1	8	0	0	.176/.222/.441	107	.130	-0.4	3B(5): 0.1, 1B(2): 0.0, 2B(2): 0.3	0.1
	IF	BOS	MLB	32	271	25	14	0	2	20	19	70	3	2	.202/.281/.285	71	.275	0.0	2B(37): 0.4, 1B(15): 0.1, SS(12): 1.5	0.1
Quincy Hamilton	OF	FAY	A	23	142	18	5	0	2	20	18	28	9	2	.261/.366/.357	111	.311	0.6	RF(14): 0.6, CF(9): 1.0, LF(5): -0.6	0.8
Taylor Jones	1B	SUG	AAA	27	212	36	15	0	10	44	31	43	0	1	.331/.425/.584	120	.383	-0.3	1B(22): 1.4, 3B(16): -0.1, LF(11): 0.3	1.3
	1B	HOU	MLB	27	108	11	8	1	2	16	4	29	0	0	.245/.269/.402	76	.315	0.7	1B(14): 0.3, LF(10): 1.2	0.2
J.J. Matijevic	1B	CC	AA	25	140	21	4	0	9	27	20	37	2	1	.275/.379/.533	121	.324	-0.1	1B(16): -0.3, LF(12): -3.5, 3B(1): 0.1	0.4
	1B	SUG	AAA	25	317	46	19	3	16	48	33	98	4	0	.245/.325/.504	95	.314	3.1	1B(27): 1.6, LF(23): -2.1, RF(5): 0.2	0.9
Alex McKenna	OF	ASH	A+	23	190	41	8	2	13	31	21	62	7	1	.305/.389/.616	112	.407	1.8	CF(24): -1.5, RF(10): 2.9, LF(5): -0.1	1.2
	OF	CC	AA	23	153	12	5	1	2	15	17	55	1	2	.206/.314/.305	66	.333	-1.6	CF(23): 0.1, RF(9): 1.9, LF(3): -0.2	-0.1
Freudis Nova	SS	ASH	A+	21	282	33	14	1	4	19	26	91	9	1	.224/.301/.335	75	.333	-0.2	SS(53): -9.3, 2B(8): -0.5, 3B(7): -0.4	-0.8
Joe Perez	3B	FAY	A	21	59	7	4	0	2	8	9	13	0	2	.300/.407/.500	109	.371	-0.9	3B(9): -0.0, 1B(1): -0.1	0.1
	3B	ASH	A+	21	109	24	11	0	8	26	10	21	1	1	.354/.413/.707	136	.386	-0.2	3B(16): -0.6, 1B(7): -1.2, 2B(1): -0.0	0.6
	3B	CC	AA	21	307	34	19	0	8	27	24	80	2	1	.267/.322/.420	92	.344	-2.2	3B(63): -6.2, 1B(4): -0.1	-0.3
Shay Whitcomb	IF	FAY	A	22	187	32	3	0	7	22	20	53	14	2	.282/.369/.429	103	.375	-0.1	SS(22): -0.4, 3B(11): 1.4, 2B(5): -0.1	0.7
	IF	ASH	A+	22	257	49	22	0	16	56	19	81	16	3	.300/.358/.601	102	.391	1.5	SS(26): -1.0, 3B(20): 1.1, 2B(10): -0.9	0.9

Colin Barber injured his shoulder and required season-ending surgery after just 16 games at High-A, during which he nevertheless managed to muster concern with a 41.5% strikeout rate. Worst case, he can return to his hometown of Paradise, California and open up a small chain of four eponymous stores—his very own Barber shop quartet. ⚾ The younger brother of Carlos, **J.C. Correa** spent a plurality of his time at shortstop in splitting his year between Low- and High-A, but also saw time at every other infield dirt position and even in left. He only hit like his brother at his first minor-league stop, but it was otherwise a strong debut for an undrafted signee from 2020 who, in previous years, had been selected in the 38th and 33rd rounds. ⚾ Minor-league stats should always be taken with a grain of salt, but offensive breakouts at Asheville require something out of Sodom and Gomorrah. It's an incredible environment in which to hit, which works well if you're a bat-over-glove catching prospect, as **Yainer Diaz** is. ⚾ Making his stateside debut nearly three years after the Astros inked him, shortstop **Cristian Gonzalez** might stick at the position, but his offensive output at Low-A (where he spent the bulk of his season) was more Elvis Andrus than Carlos Correa. ⚾ **Marwin Gonzalez** may be able to play lots of positions, but "batter" is no longer one of them. That he earned playing time for both ALCS squads serves as a compelling argument against expansion. ⚾ A fifth-round pick but just the Astros' third selection in the 2021 Draft, **Quincy Hamilton** posted a .535 OBP in his fifth year of eligibility for Wright State—the last time a *Hamilton* showed so well, it kept the nation's first secretary of the treasury on the $10 bill. ⚾ Getting a more substantive big-league sample in 2021, **Taylor Jones** appeared overmatched, taking just four free passes in 108 plate appearances. He's conquered Triple-A, but to be more than another tweener the former Gonzaga first baseman (yes, they do more than basketball) needs to harness the patience that got him through five years of unheralded prospect life. ⚾ Drafted out of the University of Arizona back in 2017, **J.J. Matijevic**'s progression through the minors has been ponderous even accounting for the year off, but a strong return put him on the doorstep of the major as the power showed. His appearance at five positions does not mark defensive prowess, but with DH Yordan Alvarez a year his junior, Matijevic must make the most of his double-edged utility. ⚾ Failing to progress ahead of the pandemic, 2018 fourth-round pick **Alex McKenna** was a midseason prospect riser with a 1.005 OPS in High-A Asheville. That figure dropped by almost 400 points upon his promotion to Double-A Corpus Christi; at 24 he needs to replicate the first-half showing if it's to be anything more than a momentary ripple in a pond that's grown too big for him. ⚾ After failing to progress with the stick in half a season at High-A, shortstop **Freudis Nova** underwent surgery to repair an ACL tear that will likely cost him half of this campaign. It was another blow to his already slipping stock, but the late-September timing did mean Nova was recalled to Houston's major-league injured list to open a space on the 40-man roster; while he'd surely trade the ~$40,000 in additional compensation to undo the injury, few get that consolation prize. ⚾ Finally logging a full season after failing to top 200 plate appearances at any point since his 2017 second-round selection, **Joe Perez** saw three levels and hit enough (especially at High-A Asheville) to merit protection from the Rule 5 Draft, if not enough to garner more than tepid prospect industry reception. ⚾ Drafted in the fifth round in 2020 (Houston's fourth selection in the truncated affair), **Shay Whitcomb** failed to distinguish in his initial assignment nearly a year later to Low-A Fayetteville but was nevertheless promoted midseason and bashed for High-A Asheville, leading the club in doubles and stolen bases.

Pitchers

PITCHER	TEAM	LVL	AGE	W	L	SV	G	GS	IP	H	HR	BB/9	K/9	K	GB%	BABIP	WHIP	ERA	DRA-	WARP	MPH	FB%	WHF	CSP
Pedro Báez	SUG	AAA	33	1	1	0	9	1	9^2	13	1	1.9	6.5	7	24.2%	.375	1.55	5.59	115	-0.1				
	HOU	MLB	33	0	0	0	4	0	4^1	2	1	2.1	10.4	5	44.4%	.125	0.69	2.08	104	0.0	90.1	30.5%	28.1%	62.1%
Tyler Brown	ASH	A+	22	3	5	0	15	11	63^1	71	14	4.5	9.7	68	35.8%	.329	1.63	7.25	111	0.1				
	CC	AA	22	1	3	0	8	4	27^1	26	4	7.9	13.2	40	29.7%	.367	1.83	6.26	89	0.3				
Austin Hansen	SUG	AAA	24	0	2	1	9	6	25^2	23	7	8.1	9.5	27	31.4%	.258	1.79	7.36	117	-0.2				
Tyler Ivey	SUG	AAA	25	0	1	0	4	3	11	14	2	6.5	10.6	13	45.5%	.387	2.00	4.91	93	0.1				
	HOU	MLB	25	0	0	0	1	1	4^2	6	1	1.9	5.8	3	31.2%	.333	1.50	7.71	124	0.0	90.0	50.6%	13.5%	53.5%
Chayce McDermott	FAY	A	22	0	0	0	6	4	18^1	11	3	4.9	16.2	33	45.2%	.286	1.15	3.44	80	0.4				
Jaime Melendez	FAY	A	19	2	2	0	6	3	18^1	7	1	2.5	18.7	38	52.0%	.250	0.65	0.49	54	0.6				
	ASH	A+	19	2	3	0	11	7	32	34	2	6.7	11.5	41	44.3%	.376	1.81	4.78	89	0.4				
	CC	AA	19	0	1	0	3	1	7^2	8	0	4.7	12.9	11	47.8%	.348	1.57	5.87	79	0.1				
Enoli Paredes	CC	AA	25	0	0	0	4	0	5	1	0	1.8	16.2	9	0.0%	.200	0.40	0.00	82	0.1				
	SUG	AAA	25	1	0	1	26	0	27^1	27	7	6.6	12.5	38	44.1%	.328	1.72	4.28	76	0.5				
	HOU	MLB	25	0	0	0	12	0	8^2	7	0	17.7	15.6	15	42.1%	.368	2.77	6.23	110	0.0	95.4	65.3%	31.5%	47.2%
Julio Robaina	FAY	A	20	4	1	0	11	4	44^2	39	1	3.6	9.3	46	46.9%	.299	1.28	3.63	95	0.5				
	ASH	A+	20	3	2	0	6	5	32^1	32	3	1.9	11.7	42	53.9%	.337	1.21	3.90	96	0.3				
Andre Scrubb	SUG	AAA	26	0	0	0	15	0	15	7	1	7.8	12.0	20	31.2%	.200	1.33	1.80	96	0.1				
	HOU	MLB	26	1	1	0	18	0	19^2	15	5	6.4	9.6	21	33.3%	.217	1.47	5.03	112	0.1	93.9	58.5%	28.7%	52.2%
Misael Tamarez	FAY	A	21	4	2	1	12	6	43	28	3	5.9	13.4	64	38.0%	.281	1.30	3.98	70	1.1				
	ASH	A+	21	2	1	0	7	7	33^2	30	4	2.7	10.4	39	34.1%	.310	1.19	3.48	99	0.3				

Pedro Báez only logged 13 outs for the Astros in the first of two contracted years with the club, but showcased one major innovation that'll make him, if not better going forward, eminently the more watchable: his pace, the number of seconds he averages between pitches, was down to 22.5 seconds, nearly five below his plodding career rate. Houston's second pick in the 2020 draft, **Tyler Brown** was the closer for Vanderbilt's 2019 championship team. More recently, he was posting ERAs in excess of six at two minor-league stops in 2021—you suppose that's better than doing it at just the one level. **Austin Hansen** skipped Double-A entirely after the canceled minor-league season of 2020; the bullpen seemed a foregone conclusion, but the eighth-round pick from 2018 had struck out more than 30% of batters in all three stints and owned a 2.34 ERA as a professional, so he'd earned the right to be stretched out. Apart from the 7.36 ERA, he also walked nearly as many batters as he completed innings, then had Tommy John in August. Oh brother. **Tyler Ivey** made his big-league debut on May 21 last year, allowing four runs and failing to complete the fifth inning but coming out with a no-decision. Of the tickets he obtained for family and friends in attendance, Ivey said "I didn't know we had to pay the taxes on them." A Texan from the first. The younger brother of NBA forward Sean, and with a more baseball-appropriate name, **Chayce McDermott** lived up to his given name by striking out 40 in 21 ⅓ innings after becoming fourth-round selection. He was quickly promoted from Rookie to Low-A ball and his performance likely presages an assertive High-A assignment. An unheralded international free agent signing in 2019, 5-foot-8 **Jaime Melendez** only needed six appearances for Low-A to earn a promotion on the back of an absurd 55.9% strikeout rate. While more muted, his results for High-A were enough for another promotion before season's end—only 20, he must keep ahead of his age group to dodge relegation to the bullpen (typically a foregone conclusion for pitchers of his stature). After spending all of 2020 with the big-league squad, **Enoli Paredes** got stuck in the revolving door at the end of the bullpen, hitting the injured list twice and being demoted thrice on the way to 8 ⅔ MLB innings featuring (hell, *starring*) 18 walks. With two option years remaining, he'll have time to figure it out—at both the minor- and major-league levels. Like most Astros prospects resetting their development after the canceled season, **Julio Robaina** split levels in 2021. Like most Houston pitching prospects, he divided time between the rotation and bullpen. The plateau assignment to Low-A would be a mark against Houston's appraisal of the 20-year-old if not for his youth. **Andre Scrubb** lived down to his name in 2021 as he worked through a shoulder injury that twice sent him to the 60-day IL, his ERA jumping more than three runs even as his underlying metrics stayed mostly consistent. No pitcher can survive with a 16.3% walk rate, as evidenced by the Astros outrighting Scrubb off their 40-man roster. Once a rapidly advancing teenaged prospect, **Jairo Solis** has been waylaid by two Tommy John surgeries in the past three years. He hasn't pitched in a competitive game since he was 18 years old, but back then he had an intriguing three-pitch arsenal. Already on the the 40-man, a relief track seems likely once he's healthy again. Signed as an international free agent three years ago at the relatively ripe age of 19, the biggest roadblock **Misael Tamarez** has faced thus far in his progress toward the majors was experienced by every minor leaguer in the lost season. He got right to it upon his return to action, earning a promotion to High-A halfway through the season and maintaining high-90s heat deep into games.

LOS ANGELES ANGELS

Essay by Emma Baccellieri

Player comments by Darius Austin and BP staff

When Joe Maddon was introduced as the Angels' manager in October 2019, he made a lengthy opening statement, teeming with big-picture declarations and folksy digressions, wrapped around this bit of standard coach-speak:

> I want us to reestablish our own identity here. I want us to play the Angels' game. This is about excellence over a period of time. This isn't just about being good for a brief window and then moving it along. The only way to get that done: You have to establish your culture, you have to establish a methodology—"This is how we do things here."

That is the sort of line that gets said all the time in sports without meaning too much of anything, but if you wanted to make it mean something, you would have to ask: What is the Angels' game? Maddon had spoken at some length about what he wanted it to be without saying much about what it actually was. Maybe there was a loose idea out there, but there was not a clear answer.

It took a year and a half, and it didn't come from Maddon, but an answer finally appeared. It was pithy and absurd and just the right amount of sad. It was a perfect distillation of what it means to "play the Angels' game," and it came in the form of a tweet, sent from a baseball fan named Matt English on his account @matttomic on May 17, 2021:

> every time I see an Angels highlight it's like "Mike Trout hit three homes runs [*sic*] and raised his average to .528 while Shohei Ohtani did something that hasn't been done since 'Tungsten Arm' O'Doyle of the 1921 Akron Groomsmen, as the Tigers defeated the Angels 8–3"

A bit reductive—of course, it was a tweet—but dead-on in its spiritual capture. (To say nothing of its ear for old-timey pitching names: "Tungsten Arm" O'Doyle!) If every Angels game doesn't look like this, at the very least, every game has the potential to *feel* like it. This is a team with transcendent, mind-expanding talent ensnared in the miserable, bone-

LOS ANGELES ANGELS PROSPECTUS

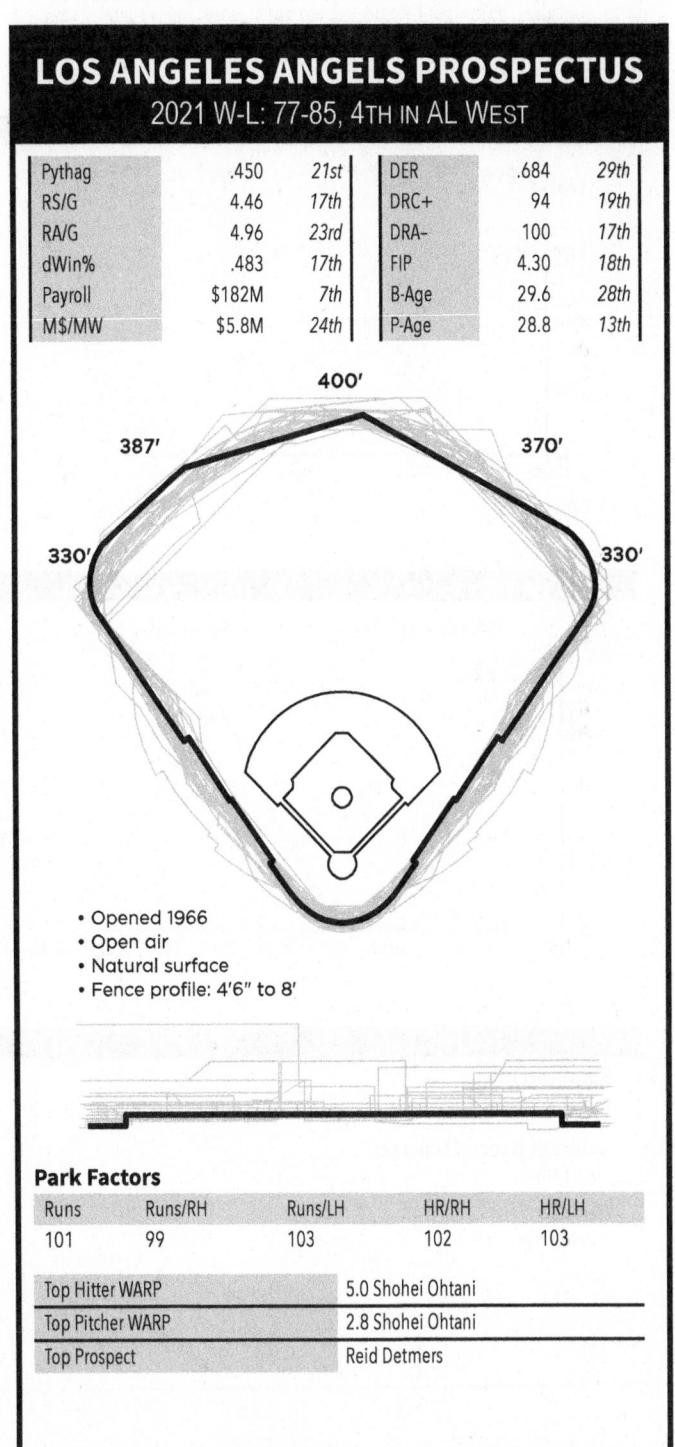

2021 W-L: 77-85, 4TH IN AL WEST

Pythag	.450	*21st*	DER	.684	*29th*
RS/G	4.46	*17th*	DRC+	94	*19th*
RA/G	4.96	*23rd*	DRA-	100	*17th*
dWin%	.483	*17th*	FIP	4.30	*18th*
Payroll	$182M	*7th*	B-Age	29.6	*28th*
M$/MW	$5.8M	*24th*	P-Age	28.8	*13th*

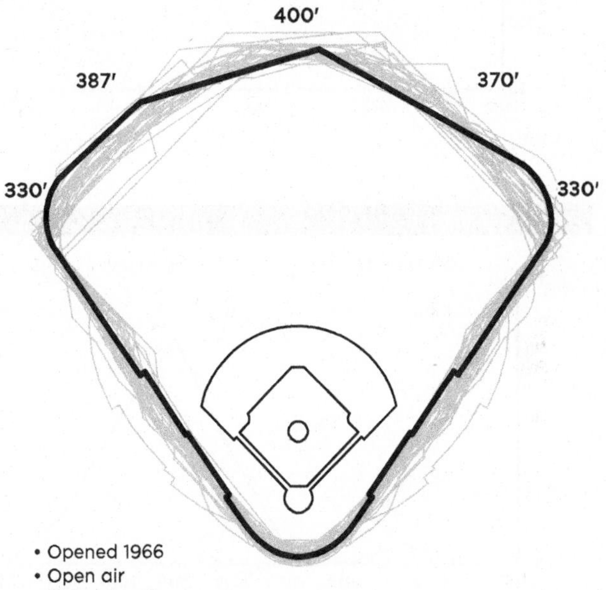

- Opened 1966
- Open air
- Natural surface
- Fence profile: 4'6" to 8'

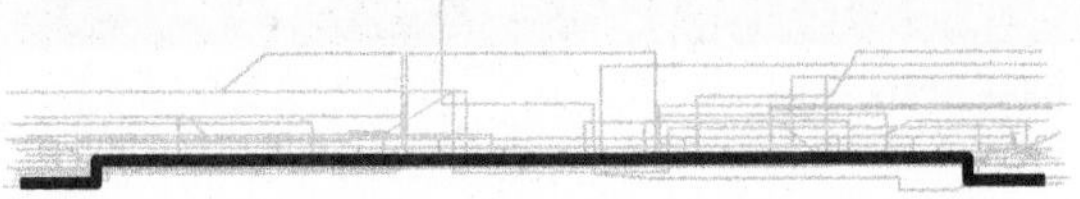

Park Factors

Runs	Runs/RH	Runs/LH	HR/RH	HR/LH
101	99	103	102	103

Top Hitter WARP	5.0 Shohei Ohtani
Top Pitcher WARP	2.8 Shohei Ohtani
Top Prospect	Reid Detmers

Payroll History (in millions)

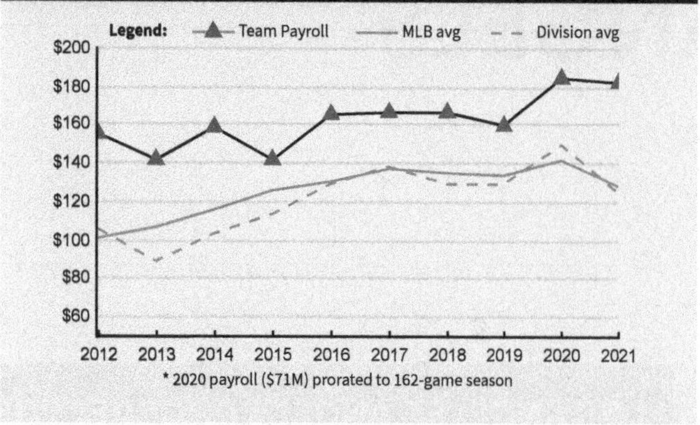

Future Commitments (in millions)

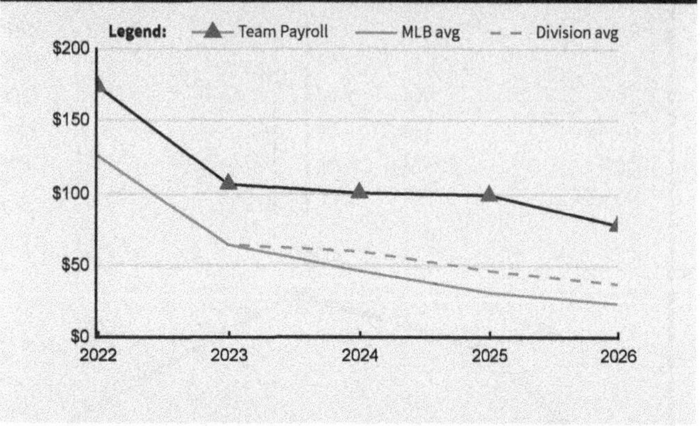

Farm System Ranking

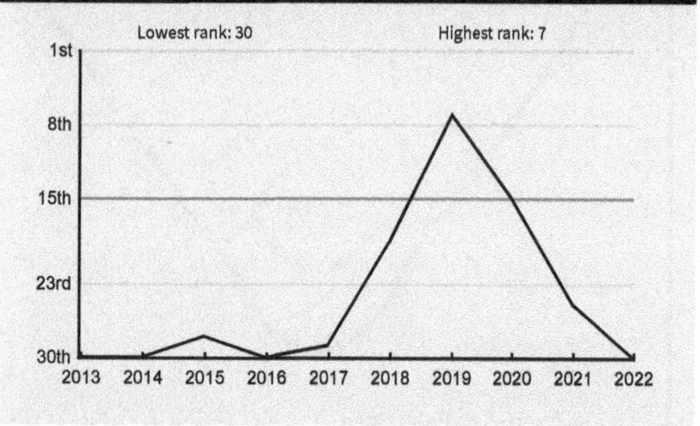

Personnel

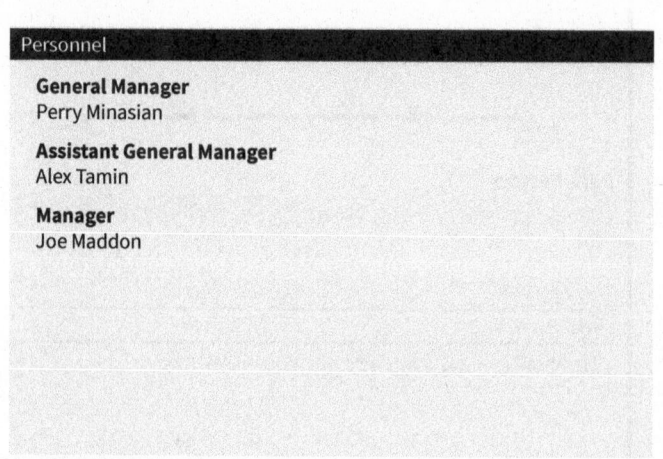

General Manager
Perry Minasian

Assistant General Manager
Alex Tamin

Manager
Joe Maddon

deep grasp of mediocrity. It's an identity that the Angels had been cultivating for the better part of a decade. And finally, in 2021, they perfected it.

Because, after all: You have to establish your culture, you have to establish a methodology—"This is how we do things here." And this is the Angels' game.

⚾ ⚾ ⚾

This has been the line on the Angels, if not since Mike Trout won Rookie of Year in 2012, then since he won his first MVP in 2014: *Here is a generational talent, perhaps the best player in baseball, and here is a team that simply cannot figure out how to win around him.* A few years later, "perhaps" could be axed before "the best player in baseball," and there was some fluctuation in just how much the team *could* win, but since 2016 its record has never inched above .500, and the gist of the statement has never changed. It began to feel like the biggest ongoing joke in the game, a meme as indefatigable as Crying Jordan—unless, that is, you were more inclined to view it as a tragedy.

So the Angels took a dramatic step toward flipping the punchline: They decided to pair the best player in baseball with the most interesting one.

Yet the punchline did not flip during Shohei Ohtani's rookie season in 2018. If anything, it intensified: *Here is the best player in baseball, and here is an unprecedented two-way talent alongside him, and here is a team that still cannot reach .500.* It was brutal. And it was also somehow preferable to the version of the line that would come in the following seasons. The Ohtani that baseball had been introduced to in 2018 was stalled by injuries in 2019 and 2020; the greatness that had been so apparent in his debut was alternately compressed and stretched thin and even diminished in the seasons that followed.

This did not feel like a punchline. It felt like the bland, pedestrian disappointment of realizing you had allowed yourself to be taken in. *Of course* a player could not really be a full-time, two-way star in modern baseball for any meaningful stretch of time. *Of course*, if one somehow *could*, he would not have his success unlocked by the *Angels*. This is not to say that Ohtani seemed like a bust. Far from it. He still looked like a notably good player—a well-above-average hitter and a presence on the basepaths, who would continue to pitch in some capacity if health allowed. He still looked one-of-a-kind. He just didn't look like a miracle. At first, he was compared to Babe Ruth; Soon, he was a reminder that Babe Ruth dominated at a time when many of the world's best baseball players lived without seeing a baseball diamond, let alone playing on one. And so, the joke wasn't on him—not at all!—it was on *you*. How could you have dared to believe any of that in the first place?

Which was a perfect set-up for what Ohtani did in 2021.

It feels silly to call his season the best in our collective baseball lifetimes—it feels silly to compare it to any prior ideas of baseball ability at all. It was not that he did something that had never been done before, so much as it was that he did something that was previously *unthinkable*. At one point in the season, Ohtani had both the fastest pitch thrown by a starting pitcher (101 mph) and the hardest-hit ball by a batter (119 mph). He became one of just six players in history to record a season with more than 45 home runs and more than 25 stolen bases—and, of course, the only one to do so with more than 150 strikeouts on the mound. He gave a compelling performance in the Home Run Derby and was the starting pitcher for the All-Star Game. He was a unanimous MVP and Rob Manfred's first recipient of the Commissioner's Historic Achievement Award. He took the wildest dreams of the most optimistic fans and made them seem like modest projections ripped from a spreadsheet. Maybe the joke was still on you. But it was worth it.

It is, of course, impossible to find a real comparison for a season like that. But there's something interesting in comparing the experience of watching Ohtani with that of watching Trout. (There was little opportunity for a side-by-side assessment last season: After a characteristically remarkable spring, Trout missed the entire summer with a calf injury, the first time he had ever been sidelined for so long.) Both teammates can offer greatness—sweeping, historic, individual greatness—but they go about it in such different ways that it's hard to find a framework able to hold them both. To watch Trout is to feel the smooth, pleasing click of a slider on a video-game scale, every skill turning up to 100—a stunning reproduction of a perfect model baseball player. He is all that a fan could ever dream of. To watch Ohtani is to realize you simply must turn off the gaming console—go outside, walk around, perhaps even close your eyes; this does not fit in any existing model of baseball excellence, but maybe you can imagine it, if you try. No one knew a fan could dream of this.

To be able to watch both on the same team—to have the chance just to *think* about this coming year with both a healthy Trout and this version of Ohtani—can feel miraculously lucky. What a rare, wild blessing to build the grind of a baseball season around this kind of talent!

All of which is to say: The Angels finished 2021 season five games under .500. They did this without any sense of drama or surprise, as if it was the only result they were marching toward all along, which—of course it was. *Of course it was.* This is the Angels' game.

It is generally not too hard to identify the purpose of a baseball team at any given time. There are teams designed to win now and teams designed to win later. There are teams that are nakedly interested in maximizing their profits at any cost, which, incidentally, can also be the teams designed to win now or later or not at all. There are teams that simply must be a kind of elaborate performance art (or whatever your preferred term is for the Colorado Rockies). There are teams that are trying to appeal to fans, teams that are content to alienate them and teams that appear to be indifferent to their existence.

And then there are the Angels. They are not built to win now, insofar as their pitching staff looks the way it does, yet they are not built to *lose* now, either. They're neither a model institution nor a cautionary tale. If there is a collective understanding of what it means to play the Angels' game—to be mired in this no-man's land—there is also an understanding that none of this is by design. They do not share the obvious flaws of most bad modern teams: There is no grand statement to make here about a lack of investment or commitment or respect. No, the Angels have very clearly been *trying*. (After all, this is the team that crafted a record-breaking extension for Trout, spent big on Anthony Rendon and only just finished up its mammoth commitment to Albert Pujols.) They just aren't trying with any cohesion, or obvious logic, and they certainly aren't trying with any luck.

So: What is the point of the Angels?

There is a charming-if-saccharine answer about the magic of enjoying what is in front of you. This says that the point of the Angels is not finishing five games under .500, or finishing games at all—the point of the Angels is reveling in the chance to watch Ohtani, to see a 26-game hit streak for a guy with as curious an approach as David Fletcher, to see the development of prospects like Jo Adell and Brandon Marsh, to enjoy the texture of the season, if not the result. The point is that it is exceedingly unlikely that any of this works out in the long run, so you might as well have fun where you can. *The Angels are here to teach you about appreciating the little things.* Sweet, if perhaps lacking in subtlety.

There is also an answer that runs orthogonal to all of that. This one says that the point of the Angels is no point at all. You think it matters to try? To spend money? To have the best player in baseball? To have *two* of the best players in baseball? Just look at this team! How can any of this mean something? Gaze upon the historically cursed bones of this pitching staff, the broken stars of yesterday still playing alongside the stars of today, and try, just *try*, to believe in a benevolent universe. Maybe this is a comedy—the punchline keeps hitting season after season—but it's quite a dark one.

There are a million uncertainties in baseball, every year, every player, every team. Lately, there has felt like one certainty: The Angels will win 75 to 81 games. (No team in baseball has had a lower standard deviation in its winning percentage over the last six seasons.) Pair that piece of information with the aforementioned two purposes for the Angels, to enjoy them or to accept their struggle, and it can begin to feel like something vaguely horrifying—this thing that warps and distorts as each element tries, in its futile way, to be amazing.

For years, it wasn't complicated. You could say that Trout was amazing, and the rest of the team failed him, or Pujols had been sacrificed to the gods of early aging to maintain balance. But as the Angels have added more talent, and the win total has stayed the same, the squeezing and the warping have grown increasingly horrific, to the point where Anthony Rendon is a mess, and Mike Trout's six- to eight-week calf injury is a rest-of-the-year IL stint. The fabric of reality is struggling to maintain itself.

If there is any framework useful to understand this, maybe it's Greek mythology. ("You will enjoy two of the most sublime performers of this generation, but you will never win with them"—if that's not a divine punishment from a vindictive god with a wicked sense of humor, what is?) It feels unreasonable to look at the recent upgrades made to the Angels' pitching staff with understanding, rather than to search for the thin strand of horse hair to reveal itself, and below it the dangling Sword of Damocles. The Angels have become a twisted, small-scale Sisyphus, tasked with rolling the boulder only halfway up the hill, and still forced to start fresh each year without making it. The scale feels cosmic, and the frustration does, too. Baseball is eternal. The Angels are eternal.

—Emma Baccellieri is a staff writer for Sports Illustrated

Hitters

Jordyn Adams CF
Born: 10/18/99 Age: 22 Bats: R Throws: R Height: 6'2" Weight: 180 lb. Origin: Round 1, 2018 Draft (#17 overall)

YEAR	TEAM	LVL	AGE	PA	R	2B	3B	HR	RBI	BB	K	SB	CS	Whiff%	AVG/OBP/SLG	DRC+	BABIP	BRR	FRAA	WARP
2019	ANG	ROK	19	14	4	1	0	0	4	1	3	4	0		.538/.571/.615		.700			
2019	BUR	A	19	428	52	15	2	7	31	50	94	12	5		.250/.346/.358	109	.316	1.6	CF(73): -1.2, LF(9): 2.7, RF(8): -0.4	2.0
2019	IE	A+	19	40	7	1	1	1	1	5	14	0	1		.229/.325/.400	85	.350	0.2	CF(4): 0.4, LF(2): -0.2, RF(2): -0.3	0.1
2021	TRI	A+	21	307	37	7	2	5	27	28	116	18	4		.217/.290/.310	69	.350	2.9	CF(62): -9.9	-0.8
2022 non-DC	*LAA*	*MLB*	*22*	*251*	*20*	*8*	*1*	*4*	*21*	*19*	*89*	*4*	*3*	*34.9%*	*.194/.262/.296*	*50*	*.298*	*0.4*	*CF 0, LF 0*	*-0.6*

Comparables: Dalton Pompey, Rymer Liriano, Aaron Hicks

Betting on Adams' athletic talent always seemed like a good wager to make. It was easy to wave away the hit tool concerns when he was 18 or 19, banking on improvement to a level more commensurate with his physical gifts. After a season of looking woefully overmatched at High-A, however, we're starting to move into the period where athleticism alone isn't going to ensure his ongoing presence towards the top of prospect lists. No one is going to give up on him at the age of 22, but Adams needs to show some of the projected development at the plate soon, or this wager will start looking more like a long shot than a sure thing.

Jo Adell OF
Born: 04/08/99 Age: 23 Bats: R Throws: R Height: 6'3" Weight: 215 lb. Origin: Round 1, 2017 Draft (#10 overall)

YEAR	TEAM	LVL	AGE	PA	R	2B	3B	HR	RBI	BB	K	SB	CS	Whiff%	AVG/OBP/SLG	DRC+	BABIP	BRR	FRAA	WARP
2019	MSS	WIN	20	111	15	8	0	3	9	11	29	3	0		.273/.351/.444		.358			
2019	IE	A+	20	27	4	1	0	2	5	1	10	0	0		.280/.333/.560	95	.385	0.2	CF(3): 0.4, RF(2): -0.1, LF(1): -0.1	0.1
2019	MOB	AA	20	182	28	15	0	8	23	19	41	6	0		.308/.390/.553	132	.369	1.3	RF(19): -0.6, CF(17): -3.4, LF(5): 1.9	1.2
2019	SL	AAA	20	132	22	11	0	0	8	10	43	1	0		.264/.321/.355	58	.410	2.2	RF(13): -0.0, LF(9): 0.5, CF(4): -0.7	-0.1
2020	LAA	MLB	21	132	9	4	0	3	7	7	55	0	1	42.1%	.161/.212/.266	51	.258	0.2	RF(34): -1.2, CF(4): 0.6	-0.4
2021	SL	AAA	22	339	57	17	4	23	69	22	99	8	2		.289/.342/.592	107	.351	1.7	CF(28): 0.1, LF(24): -1.2, RF(18): 1.8	1.7
2021	LAA	MLB	22	140	17	5	2	4	26	8	32	2	1	29.6%	.246/.295/.408	93	.298	0.5	LF(25): 0.9, RF(19): 3.5	0.9
2022 DC	*LAA*	*MLB*	*23*	*481*	*64*	*21*	*2*	*20*	*71*	*30*	*140*	*6*	*3*	*32.2%*	*.242/.298/.442*	*95*	*.305*	*0.3*	*RF 1, LF 1*	*1.3*

Comparables: Byron Buxton, Manuel Margot, Carlos González

Although it was hardly a transcendent season, Adell flashed considerable progress following his disastrous debut. Almost doubling your DRC+ isn't so impressive when you start from rock bottom, but he slashed his strikeout rate as each month passed in the minors. Then, after some early struggles upon his return to the majors, he looked positively disciplined by the time an abdominal strain sidelined him for the final few weeks. It was Adell, for instance, who broke up Blake Snell's early September no-hit bid on a two-strike slider in the seventh. The low strikeout rate in September - six in 36 trips to the plate - masked the fact that Adell's still whiffing a ton when he swings. He may simply be a player who comes up empty on swings more often than most. The tools remain deafening, so the key to putting it all together is maintaining that kind of two-strike approach, letting the talent outshine the strikeouts on a more regular basis.

Adam Eaton RF
Born: 12/06/88 Age: 33 Bats: L Throws: L Height: 5'9" Weight: 180 lb. Origin: Round 19, 2010 Draft (#571 overall)

YEAR	TEAM	LVL	AGE	PA	R	2B	3B	HR	RBI	BB	K	SB	CS	Whiff%	AVG/OBP/SLG	DRC+	BABIP	BRR	FRAA	WARP
2019	WAS	MLB	30	656	103	25	7	15	49	65	106	15	3	17.8%	.279/.365/.428	101	.319	4.7	RF(139): 6.9	3.1
2020	WAS	MLB	31	176	22	11	1	4	17	12	32	3	0	16.7%	.226/.285/.384	83	.260	1.0	RF(41): 0.3	0.3
2021	CHW	MLB	32	219	33	8	2	5	28	20	55	2	0	24.2%	.201/.298/.344	82	.256	2.3	RF(55): 3.6, LF(1): -0.1	0.7
2021	LAA	MLB	32	69	5	2	0	1	2	2	16	1	0	22.3%	.200/.232/.277	81	.245	0.2	RF(24): -2.8, LF(1): -0.0, P(1): -0.0	-0.2
2022 DC	*FA*	*MLB*	*33*	*69*	*7*	*2*	*0*	*1*	*7*	*6*	*14*	*0*	*1*	*21.8%*	*.239/.323/.378*	*90*	*.287*	*0.0*	*RF 0, LF 0*	*0.1*

Comparables: Nick Markakis, Jose Cruz, Reggie Smith

There may not be a more damning indication of Eaton's rapid decline than the White Sox's decision to designate him for assignment in the midst of a season that had seen them lose two-thirds of their intended starting outfield for multiple months. If there is one, however, it's that the Angels, missing their *entire* Opening Day starting outfield when they picked him up, came to the same conclusion a month later. It hasn't been so much of an aging curve as an aging cliff for Eaton, who turned 31 after a productive 2019 and suddenly found himself unable to compete in the bigs. Time comes for us all, but not normally as swiftly and cruelly as this.

David Fletcher 2B Born: 05/31/94 Age: 28 Bats: R Throws: R Height: 5'9" Weight: 185 lb. Origin: Round 6, 2015 Draft (#195 overall)

YEAR	TEAM	LVL	AGE	PA	R	2B	3B	HR	RBI	BB	K	SB	CS	Whiff%	AVG/OBP/SLG	DRC+	BABIP	BRR	FRAA	WARP
2019	LAA	MLB	25	653	83	30	4	6	49	55	64	8	3	9.8%	.290/.350/.384	101	.317	-4.5	3B(90): 1.2, 2B(42): 1.4, SS(39): -0.3	2.1
2020	LAA	MLB	26	230	31	13	0	3	18	20	25	2	1	8.6%	.319/.376/.425	115	.348	0.3	SS(27): -1.0, 2B(15): 1.0, 3B(8): -0.7	1.1
2021	LAA	MLB	27	665	74	27	3	2	47	31	60	15	3	9.5%	.262/.297/.324	85	.287	1.9	2B(142): 3.8, SS(20): 2.7	2.0
2022 DC	*LAA*	*MLB*	*28*	*610*	*85*	*25*	*2*	*7*	*59*	*37*	*52*	*10*	*3*	*9.8%*	*.280/.325/.372*	*94*	*.297*	*0.2*	*2B 2, SS 1*	*2.1*

Comparables: Darwin Barney, Erik González, Chris Taylor

Fletcher's reign as the king of contact continued in 2021, albeit possibly only because Nick Madrigal's season ended prematurely. But nothing else worked as well as it had the prior couple seasons. His already-low ISO plummeted. He lost his willingness, or ability, to take free passes. Fletcher was uncharacteristically impatient; he saw just 3.33 pitches per plate appearance, fewer than any other regular in baseball, and chased at a career-high rate. While he's so good at putting bat to ball that his increased aggression somehow reduced his strikeout rate, it might be time for a return to his old approach. His kingdom for an extra-base hit.

Dexter Fowler CF Born: 03/22/86 Age: 36 Bats: S Throws: R Height: 6'5" Weight: 205 lb. Origin: Round 14, 2004 Draft (#410 overall)

YEAR	TEAM	LVL	AGE	PA	R	2B	3B	HR	RBI	BB	K	SB	CS	Whiff%	AVG/OBP/SLG	DRC+	BABIP	BRR	FRAA	WARP
2019	STL	MLB	33	574	69	24	1	19	67	74	142	8	5	27.4%	.238/.346/.409	99	.294	-0.2	RF(118): -0.2, CF(58): -3.5	1.5
2020	STL	MLB	34	101	14	2	0	4	15	10	28	1	1	31.9%	.233/.317/.389	95	.293	-0.4	RF(27): -3.8	-0.2
2021	LAA	MLB	35	21	3	0	0	0	1	1	6	1	0	31.1%	.250/.286/.250	88	.357	0.2	RF(7): -0.7	0.0
2022 DC	*FA*	*MLB*	*36*	*310*	*33*	*11*	*1*	*8*	*33*	*36*	*85*	*4*	*2*	*29.8%*	*.225/.326/.369*	*89*	*.297*	*0.0*	*RF 0, CF -2*	*0.3*

Comparables: Dave Martinez, Marquis Grissom, Rick Monday

Following his fraught sojourn in St Louis, Fowler got an opportunity to reset from a February trade to rejoin former manager Joe Maddon in Anaheim. After starting six of the team's first eight games in right field, that opportunity was snatched away from him when he tore his ACL on a slide into second base. It would be great to see the 14-year-veteran bring his infectious grin and easygoing intelligence back to the game, even for just one more year, but it's hard to blame him if he doesn't. When the 2022 season begins, he'll be a 36-year-old without an above-average offensive performance in four seasons, coming off major knee surgery.

Phil Gosselin LF Born: 10/03/88 Age: 33 Bats: R Throws: R Height: 6'1" Weight: 188 lb. Origin: Round 5, 2010 Draft (#164 overall)

YEAR	TEAM	LVL	AGE	PA	R	2B	3B	HR	RBI	BB	K	SB	CS	Whiff%	AVG/OBP/SLG	DRC+	BABIP	BRR	FRAA	WARP
2019	LHV	AAA	30	353	54	20	5	8	47	46	61	3	2		.314/.405/.497	114	.365	-1.4	2B(58): -0.9, 1B(7): 0.6, 3B(6): 0.2	1.7
2019	PHI	MLB	30	68	5	3	0	0	7	3	16	0	0	23.3%	.262/.294/.308	82	.347	0.2	LF(6): -0.0, SS(5): -0.5, 3B(1): 0.1	0.1
2020	PHI	MLB	31	102	14	5	0	3	12	10	27	0	0	25.0%	.250/.324/.402	91	.323	0.6	1B(8): -0.1, LF(7): -0.8, RF(7): -0.7	0.1
2021	LAA	MLB	32	373	40	14	0	7	47	24	81	4	2	21.1%	.261/.314/.362	91	.322	0.7	LF(39): 2.1, 3B(32): -1.8, 1B(23): 0.1	0.9
2022 DC	*FA*	*MLB*	*33*	*276*	*26*	*11*	*0*	*5*	*27*	*22*	*57*	*1*	*1*	*21.1%*	*.247/.312/.369*	*85*	*.299*	*-0.2*	*2B 0, LF 1*	*0.3*

Comparables: Eric Young Jr., Ryan Flaherty, Brock Holt

It is a lovely morning in Anaheim, and we're not about to call Phil Gosselin a horrible goose. He remains, however, a light-hitting utility option best suited to work against southpaws, which also makes him Exhibit 74 in an Angels season that didn't go as planned. Handing almost 400 plate appearances and 88 starts to a 32-year-old who has spent his career being a fill-in doesn't scream success. In this *Untitled Goose Game* of a season, the Goose was the antithesis of his videogame namesake, plugging holes all over the diamond as the bird tossed bats into the waterfall and tripped teammates in the dugout. He couldn't offer much more than replacement-level production, nor should he have been expected to. It was all he could do to help the Angels tread water, and hope the horrible goose finds something else to menace in the future.

Jeremiah Jackson IF Born: 03/26/00 Age: 22 Bats: R Throws: R Height: 6'0" Weight: 165 lb. Origin: Round 2, 2018 Draft (#57 overall)

YEAR	TEAM	LVL	AGE	PA	R	2B	3B	HR	RBI	BB	K	SB	CS	Whiff%	AVG/OBP/SLG	DRC+	BABIP	BRR	FRAA	WARP
2019	ORM	ROA	19	291	47	14	2	23	60	24	96	5	1		.266/.333/.605		.315			
2021	GDD	WIN	21	61	10	1	0	3	10	2	23	0	1		.161/.213/.339		.194			
2021	IE	A	21	196	29	14	3	8	46	24	65	11	3		.263/.352/.527	101	.367	-1.3	SS(31): -1.2, 2B(9): -0.4	0.4
2022 non-DC	*LAA*	*MLB*	*22*	*251*	*21*	*11*	*1*	*5*	*24*	*19*	*100*	*6*	*2*	*42.9%*	*.199/.267/.334*	*59*	*.327*	*0.6*	*SS 0, 2B 0*	*-0.5*

Comparables: Daniel Robertson, Dixon Machado, Nico Hoerner

Jackson's explosive debut at A-ball was interrupted by a quad strain. Upon his September return, he continued mashing and striking out, with the production more than making up for the empty at-bats. The concern is that the balance between the two is going to shift unfavorably when he faces more advanced arms. He can't afford any increase in the strikeout rate, but if Jackson can level up while keeping the power-to-whiff ratio steady and sticking at shortstop, the Angels will take that deal.

Juan Lagares OF Born: 03/17/89 Age: 33 Bats: R Throws: R Height: 6'2" Weight: 219 lb. Origin: International Free Agent, 2006

YEAR	TEAM	LVL	AGE	PA	R	2B	3B	HR	RBI	BB	K	SB	CS	Whiff%	AVG/OBP/SLG	DRC+	BABIP	BRR	FRAA	WARP
2019	AGU	WIN	30	111	12	2	1	1	11	6	16	0	0		.337/.373/.404		.391			
2019	NYM	MLB	30	285	38	12	1	5	27	22	75	4	1	25.6%	.213/.279/.326	71	.279	4.2	CF(125): -6.2	0.0
2020	AGU	WIN	31	95	6	4	1	0	11	3	16	4	1		.283/.305/.348		.342			
2020	NYM	MLB	31	0	0	0	0	0	0	0	0	0	0		.000/.000/.000				CF(2): 0.3	
2021	AGU	WIN	32	88	8	3	1	1	17	4	15	2	0		.301/.330/.398		.353			
2021	LAA	MLB	32	327	39	20	2	6	38	12	76	1	2	24.7%	.236/.266/.372	73	.294	1.8	CF(62): -3.5, RF(37): -0.8, LF(23): 0.4	-0.1
2022 non-DC	*LAA*	*MLB*	*33*	*251*	*23*	*11*	*1*	*5*	*25*	*14*	*56*	*3*	*2*	*24.3%*	*.239/.290/.374*	*76*	*.292*	*0.2*	*CF -1, RF -2*	*-0.1*

Comparables: Jim Busby, Juan Beniquez, Jim Landis

If you turned on an Angels game in 2021 and cast your eye over the outfield, who would you have been most likely to see? Even the non-Angels fans reading this are no doubt aware of Mike Trout's lengthy absence, but maybe at the time you'd guess that it was Justin Upton, or one of their hyper-athletic prospects. Unless you've arrived at this comment without reading the name above the box, you will have figured out by now that Lagares was the steadiest presence. That's not to say that he was an everyday regular, but the former Met played comfortably the most innings and completed the most plays of any outfielder on the team after coming into the year on a minor-league contract. For the first time in his career he played a decent chunk of those innings in a corner; he's no longer the defender he was. Although the instincts remain elite, he has lost a step in his early 30s and the bat was never enough to carry anything but an elite glove. Still, for those trivia hunters, now you know: Juan Lagares was a primary outfielder for the 2021 Angels.

Brandon Marsh CF Born: 12/18/97 Age: 24 Bats: L Throws: R Height: 6'4" Weight: 215 lb. Origin: Round 2, 2016 Draft (#60 overall)

YEAR	TEAM	LVL	AGE	PA	R	2B	3B	HR	RBI	BB	K	SB	CS	Whiff%	AVG/OBP/SLG	DRC+	BABIP	BRR	FRAA	WARP
2019	MSS	WIN	21	75	13	5	1	2	11	7	15	4	2		.328/.387/.522		.392			
2019	MOB	AA	21	412	48	21	2	7	43	47	92	18	5		.300/.383/.428	113	.384	2.9	CF(55): -0.5, RF(19): 1.4, LF(13): -2.9	2.2
2021	SL	AAA	23	110	26	5	3	3	8	16	29	2	0		.255/.364/.468	99	.339	2.0	CF(10): 0.8, LF(3): -0.5, RF(1): -0.3	0.5
2021	LAA	MLB	23	260	27	12	3	2	19	20	91	6	1	33.2%	.254/.317/.356	60	.403	1.2	CF(70): -2.2	-0.4
2022 DC	*LAA*	*MLB*	*24*	*165*	*19*	*7*	*1*	*3*	*16*	*15*	*56*	*3*	*1*	*30.8%*	*.226/.303/.362*	*78*	*.343*	*0.2*	*CF 0*	*0.2*

Comparables: Gerardo Parra, Starling Marte, Cameron Maybin

A nice, easy introduction to the majors: fill the shoes of the greatest player of this generation. Technically Marsh was replacing Juan Lagares rather than Mike Trout, but the fact remains that for most of the final two-and-a-half months, the Angels' top prospect was patrolling center field in Trout's absence. Lagares unfortunately acts as a reasonable current statistical comp for Marsh, especially from a power perspective. The 23-year-old brought his incredible athleticism and game-changing speed with him to the bigs, along with a limp ISO and a strikeout rate that only plays with premium power. Although the batting average and OBP looked fine, Marsh's DRC was third-worst in the league and he was utterly dominated by same-handed pitching. As Lagares shows, an insipid bat is no barrier to a long major-league career if you have elite speed and outfield defense. Marsh and the Angels alike will continue to expect more.

Jack Mayfield 3B Born: 09/30/90 Age: 31 Bats: R Throws: R Height: 5'11" Weight: 190 lb. Origin: Undrafted Free Agent, 2013

YEAR	TEAM	LVL	AGE	PA	R	2B	3B	HR	RBI	BB	K	SB	CS	Whiff%	AVG/OBP/SLG	DRC+	BABIP	BRR	FRAA	WARP
2019	RR	AAA	28	431	78	26	1	26	79	37	78	7	1		.287/.350/.566	117	.291	0.7	SS(43): -1.9, 2B(33): 1.9, 3B(24): -1.7	2.6
2019	HOU	MLB	28	65	8	5	0	2	5	1	16	0	0	26.9%	.156/.169/.328	79	.174	-0.7	SS(21): 0.1, 2B(5): -0.2	0.0
2020	HOU	MLB	29	47	5	1	0	0	3	2	14	0	0	29.7%	.190/.239/.214	75	.276	0.1	3B(8): -0.6, SS(8): -0.6, 2B(5): -0.1	-0.1
2021	SL	AAA	30	76	14	2	3	5	11	5	8	1	1		.329/.382/.657	134	.316	-0.1	SS(14): 1.1, 2B(1): 0.0	0.7
2021	SEA	MLB	30	35	2	1	0	0	3	1	10	0	0	32.8%	.176/.200/.206	81	.250	0.0	2B(9): -0.3, 3B(2): 0.1	0.0
2021	LAA	MLB	30	255	28	14	0	10	36	16	58	5	0	23.7%	.224/.282/.414	93	.255	-0.8	3B(66): 0.4, SS(12): -0.1	0.6
2022 DC	*LAA*	*MLB*	*31*	*181*	*22*	*8*	*0*	*6*	*29*	*11*	*38*	*1*	*1*	*24.7%*	*.228/.282/.393*	*79*	*.258*	*-0.1*	*SS 0, 3B 0*	*0.0*

Comparables: Adam Rosales, Edwin Maysonet, Steve Tolleson

It says something about the Angels' season that Mayfield, a player they cast aside after two early-season appearances, returned in July on a waiver claim and started 67 of their final 75 games. To his credit, he elevated his offensive performance, recapturing the power that helped him earn a major-league debut at the age of 28. Nevertheless, Mayfield remains below-par at the plate and best utilized as a versatile bench bat who can step into the lineup in case of emergency. That description might have fit half of the team's starters by season's end, so the former Astro looked right at home.

Shohei Ohtani RHP/DH Born: 07/05/94 Age: 28 Bats: L Throws: R Height: 6'4" Weight: 210 lb. Origin: International Free Agent, 2017

YEAR	TEAM	LVL	AGE	PA	R	2B	3B	HR	RBI	BB	K	SB	CS	Whiff%	AVG/OBP/SLG	DRC+	BABIP	BRR	FRAA	WARP
2019	LAA	MLB	24	425	51	20	5	18	62	33	110	12	3	27.4%	.286/.343/.505	99	.354	-1.8		0.8
2020	LAA	MLB	25	175	23	6	0	7	24	22	50	7	1	32.2%	.190/.291/.366	84	.229	1.1	P(2): -0.0	0.2
2021	LAA	MLB	26	639	103	26	8	46	100	96	189	26	10	35.2%	.257/.372/.592	132	.303	-0.5	P(23): -1.2, RF(6): -0.2	5.0
2022 DC	*LAA*	*MLB*	*27*	*559*	*102*	*26*	*4*	*34*	*93*	*75*	*169*	*18*	*7*	*33.9%*	*.264/.369/.550*	*136*	*.337*	*1.5*		*4.2*

Comparables: Will Clark, Boog Powell, Mo Vaughn

YEAR	TEAM	LVL	AGE	W	L	SV	G	GS	IP	H	HR	BB/9	K/9	K	GB%	BABIP	WHIP	ERA	DRA-	WARP	MPH	FB%	Whiff%	CSP
2020	LAA	MLB	25	0	1	0	2	2	1^{2}	3	0	43.2	16.2	3	40.0%	.600	6.60	37.80	136	0.0	94.3	48.8%	24.0%	39.8%
2021	LAA	MLB	26	9	2	0	23	23	130^{1}	98	15	3.0	10.8	156	44.9%	.271	1.09	3.18	76	2.8	95.0	56.2%	28.9%	56.4%
2022 DC	*LAA*	*MLB*	*27*	*9*	*6*	*0*	*24*	*24*	*136*	*110*	*17*	*3.7*	*10.4*	*156*	*43.4%*	*.279*	*1.23*	*3.41*	*87*	*2.1*	*95.0*	*56.0%*	*28.8%*	*55.9%*

Comparables: A.J. Burnett, Tim Lincecum, Sonny Gray

Where to begin with the Ohtani fun facts? In some ways it's almost a disservice to the two-way phenomenon to reduce his achievements to a series of entertaining nuggets, many of which boil down to the fact of his unprecedented-ness. Of course, it's revealing to know that he was the first All-Star to be selected on both sides of the ball, and to start the game in both capacities. Or to read the litany of sentences starting with "He's the first" and only sometimes ending in "since Babe Ruth," e.g. starting a game while leading the majors in home runs. What made Ohtani truly exceptional was not that he did things that were impressive for a pitcher, but that he put together an objectively stunning offensive season while also pitching like an ace. He became one of only six players in history to go 45-25. He led the league in WARP, bWAR, fWAR, triples and narrowly missed doing so in home runs. He hit 470-foot homers (500, if you count the Home Run Derby) and threw 100-mph heat. He added new pitches and tweaked his existing ones to increase his dominance on the mound. He was faster, and stronger and just plain better than almost every other baseball player on the planet, *at almost everything he did*. Any one of those achievements would be remarkable. All of them in concert is Ohtani.

Anthony Rendon 3B Born: 06/06/90 Age: 32 Bats: R Throws: R Height: 6'1" Weight: 200 lb. Origin: Round 1, 2011 Draft (#6 overall)

YEAR	TEAM	LVL	AGE	PA	R	2B	3B	HR	RBI	BB	K	SB	CS	Whiff%	AVG/OBP/SLG	DRC+	BABIP	BRR	FRAA	WARP
2019	WAS	MLB	29	646	117	44	3	34	126	80	86	5	1	12.9%	.319/.412/.598	146	.323	1.0	3B(146): -5.7	4.9
2020	LAA	MLB	30	232	29	11	1	9	31	38	31	0	0	14.7%	.286/.418/.497	138	.302	1.0	3B(52): -8.7	0.8
2021	LAA	MLB	31	249	24	13	0	6	34	29	41	0	0	17.3%	.240/.329/.382	103	.267	-0.8	3B(57): 3.8	1.2
2022 DC	*LAA*	*MLB*	*32*	*555*	*85*	*27*	*1*	*19*	*81*	*72*	*84*	*3*	*1*	*16.3%*	*.270/.374/.459*	*128*	*.290*	*-0.7*	*3B -1*	*3.5*

Comparables: Aramis Ramirez, Adrián Beltré, Brooks Robinson

Rendon is underrated and overlooked so often that it comes as no surprise that even his season-ending surgery was not the major injury storyline on his own team. That's how it felt for most of 2021, in any case, as the veteran third baseman's hip procedure came well after the saga of Mike Trout's calf strain began. It has been a while since Rendon's early-career injury struggles, which persisted through his minor-league career and across his first three big-league seasons. This year unfortunately brought that period back to mind, as Rendon suffered multiple muscle strains, plus a knee contusion and the hip impingement that ultimately required surgery. It's also no surprise that he never looked right at the plate, since he could barely string together a month of at-bats before getting hurt again. No more complaints about Rendon's quiet excellence getting overlooked; it's far preferable to him not being on the field at all.

Luis Rengifo UT Born: 02/26/97 Age: 25 Bats: S Throws: R Height: 5'10" Weight: 195 lb. Origin: International Free Agent, 2013

YEAR	TEAM	LVL	AGE	PA	R	2B	3B	HR	RBI	BB	K	SB	CS	Whiff%	AVG/OBP/SLG	DRC+	BABIP	BRR	FRAA	WARP
2019	SL	AAA	22	122	16	4	1	5	14	11	24	3	3		.273/.336/.464	102	.305	-0.5	2B(12): 3.5, SS(12): 0.8, LF(3): 0.5	0.9
2019	LAA	MLB	22	406	44	18	3	7	33	40	93	2	5	24.3%	.238/.321/.364	87	.300	-0.3	2B(104): -1.7, SS(12): 1.1	0.8
2020	LAA	MLB	23	106	12	1	0	1	3	14	26	3	1	24.5%	.156/.269/.200	87	.206	1.3	2B(32): -0.6, 3B(1): 0.3, SS(1): -0.2	0.3
2021	SL	AAA	24	228	46	16	4	8	32	17	32	13	5		.329/.386/.560	120	.357	-0.8	SS(37): -1.4, 2B(15): -0.8	1.0
2021	LAA	MLB	24	190	22	1	0	6	18	9	38	1	0	27.2%	.201/.246/.310	86	.220	2.2	SS(26): 0.4, RF(14): 0.9, 3B(12): 0.2	0.7
2022 DC	*LAA*	*MLB*	*25*	*279*	*35*	*11*	*2*	*6*	*38*	*22*	*59*	*7*	*5*	*24.8%*	*.243/.312/.380*	*86*	*.295*	*0.8*	*2B 0, SS 1*	*0.7*

Comparables: Eduardo Escobar, Didi Gregorius, Marwin Gonzalez

Some improvement from Rengifo at the plate after a September recall was punctuated by the news of an arrest warrant, issued in his native Venezuela, alleging that he was involved in falsifying divorce papers in order to sell jointly-owned property. The Angels declined to comment on the situation and Rengifo kept on playing, drawing praise from Perry Minasian for his late-season work at shortstop. The situation remained unresolved at the time of writing.

Jose Rojas RF Born: 02/24/93 Age: 29 Bats: L Throws: R Height: 6'0" Weight: 200 lb. Origin: Round 36, 2016 Draft (#1086 overall)

YEAR	TEAM	LVL	AGE	PA	R	2B	3B	HR	RBI	BB	K	SB	CS	Whiff%	AVG/OBP/SLG	DRC+	BABIP	BRR	FRAA	WARP
2019	OBR	WIN	26	85	7	6	0	0	6	14	13	0	0		.162/.294/.250		.190			
2019	SL	AAA	26	578	101	39	7	31	107	58	131	4	4		.293/.362/.577	109	.335	-2.9	2B(39): -6.7, 3B(31): -2.5, 1B(18): 0.7	1.4
2021	SL	AAA	28	241	32	11	1	8	34	23	38	4	1		.259/.328/.431	101	.279	-0.8	3B(26): -2.6, LF(13): -0.8, 1B(7): 0.5	0.4
2021	LAA	MLB	28	184	26	14	0	6	15	15	50	2	1	27.0%	.208/.277/.399	83	.259	-1.7	RF(25): 1.4, 2B(14): -1.1, 3B(12): 3.1	0.3
2022 DC	*LAA*	*MLB*	*29*	*159*	*19*	*8*	*0*	*4*	*19*	*12*	*35*	*0*	*1*	*24.6%*	*.233/.299/.398*	*86*	*.277*	*-0.1*	*2B -1, 3B 0*	*0.1*

Comparables: Matt Carpenter, Adam Rosales, Ben Zobrist

Rojas' bio reads like the set-up for a feel-good sports flick: Born in Anaheim, graduate of Anaheim High School, drafted from local Vanguard University in the 36th round. He looked on the brink of a call-up to his boyhood team after his 2019 power outburst, then again after a strong showing at the alternate site, but each time the call never came and he was left unprotected in the Rule 5 draft. Can you hear the inspirational strings already? Rojas forced the issue one more time, producing a blistering 1.030 OPS in spring training that earned him an Opening Day roster spot and a major-league debut at last. The movie would probably end there, local hero stepping onto the field, or perhaps digging in against Liam Hendriks for his first at-bat, leaving the audience wondering whether he would spark an implausible comeback. The reality was a lot less Hollywood. Rojas couldn't replicate his 2019 glory at the plate, and big moments were rare. The most momentous came on a ninth inning game-tying two-run single against the A's, a contest the Angels went on to lose in extras anyway. Rojas didn't need to become a star to make this a remarkable story, though; he'd done that already.

Max Stassi C Born: 03/15/91 Age: 31 Bats: R Throws: R Height: 5'10" Weight: 200 lb. Origin: Round 4, 2009 Draft (#123 overall)

YEAR	TEAM	LVL	AGE	PA	R	2B	3B	HR	RBI	BB	K	SB	CS	Whiff%	AVG/OBP/SLG	DRC+	BABIP	BRR	FRAA	WARP
2019	HOU	MLB	28	98	4	1	0	1	3	7	34	0	0	32.9%	.167/.235/.211	57	.255	-1.3	C(26): 4.2, 1B(3): -0.0	0.2
2019	LAA	MLB	28	49	3	0	0	0	2	5	15	0	0	37.0%	.071/.163/.071	76	.103	0.0	C(20): 5.0	0.6
2020	LAA	MLB	29	105	12	2	0	7	20	11	21	0	0	26.5%	.278/.352/.533	127	.277	-1.3	C(31): 2.7	0.9
2021	LAA	MLB	30	319	45	11	1	13	35	28	101	0	0	31.2%	.241/.326/.426	90	.325	-2.3	C(86): 16.5	2.4
2022 DC	*LAA*	*MLB*	*31*	*381*	*46*	*13*	*0*	*12*	*45*	*35*	*109*	*0*	*0*	*31.0%*	*.214/.302/.372*	*83*	*.275*	*-0.6*	*C 15*	*2.5*

Comparables: Francisco Cervelli, Travis d'Arnaud, Tyler Flowers

YEAR	TEAM	P. COUNT	FRM RUNS	BLK RUNS	THRW RUNS	TOT RUNS
2019	LAA	2392	4.9	0.0	0.0	4.9
2019	HOU	3717	4.3	0.0	0.0	4.4
2020	LAA	4049	1.2	0.1	0.5	1.8
2021	LAA	11913	15.4	0.5	0.4	16.3
2022	*LAA*	*14430*	*13.3*	*1.1*	*0.4*	*14.8*

Stassi's 2020 outburst seemed to shock him out of that backup catcher rhythm and put him in position for a majority share behind the plate. Early 2021 had other ideas; a thumb sprain and a concussion meant he had only appeared in 11 contests by the start of June. Stassi made up for lost time, surging to a quadruple-digit OPS over the next two months. Adding in elite framing, the Angels backstop was making a serious case for joining the position's top tier. Then the regression hit, hard. Whether it was the rigors of finally being the number one catcher or simply the laws of sabermetrics, Stassi's fortunes reversed again. He sank into a .157/.255/.268 slump the rest of the way, striking out in 36% of his trips to the plate. All things considered, the Angels would be delighted with a repeat of 2021, especially if it comes with a full season of health. He has the job; now it's on Stassi to rediscover some of that old stability.

Kurt Suzuki C Born: 10/04/83 Age: 38 Bats: R Throws: R Height: 5'11" Weight: 210 lb. Origin: Round 2, 2004 Draft (#67 overall)

YEAR	TEAM	LVL	AGE	PA	R	2B	3B	HR	RBI	BB	K	SB	CS	Whiff%	AVG/OBP/SLG	DRC+	BABIP	BRR	FRAA	WARP
2019	WAS	MLB	35	309	37	11	0	17	63	20	36	0	1	18.7%	.264/.324/.486	119	.248	0.2	C(75): -1.6	1.9
2020	WAS	MLB	36	129	15	8	0	2	17	11	19	1	0	16.9%	.270/.349/.396	105	.301	-2.2	C(30): -4.3	-0.1
2021	LAA	MLB	37	247	17	8	0	6	16	12	44	0	0	21.8%	.224/.294/.342	93	.250	0.0	C(69): -5.4	0.3
2022 DC	*FA*	*MLB*	*38*	*207*	*21*	*9*	*0*	*5*	*22*	*13*	*33*	*0*	*0*	*21.2%*	*.238/.310/.382*	*87*	*.262*	*-0.4*	*C -6*	*0.0*

Comparables: Alan Ashby, Sherm Lollar, Ramon Hernandez

YEAR	TEAM	P. COUNT	FRM RUNS	BLK RUNS	THRW RUNS	TOT RUNS
2019	WAS	10655	-2.8	-0.5	1.0	-2.2
2020	WAS	4520	-4.1	0.0	0.5	-3.6
2021	LAA	9696	-5.4	-0.7	0.3	-5.7
2022	*FA*	*6956*	*-6.2*	*-0.4*	*-0.2*	*-6.8*

The surprise was not that Suzuki declined at the plate, but that he made it this far, sustaining a four-year run of well above-average offensive performance to keep him in a regular role. The fifth year didn't materialize, as the 37-year-old looked more like a catcher with over 12,000 innings on his knees than one of the more offensively-talented backstops in baseball. Most hitters can only dream of achieving Suzuki's career-worst 17.8% strikeout rate, but since his framing is derided by all metrics and that arm isn't getting any better, the sterling strikeout rate alone won't cut it. Although he was highly-valued by the team for his work with their younger pitchers, he needed that positive contribution with the bat to retain a significant role on the field. In its absence, his other qualities may be better-suited to the dugout.

Matt Thaiss CI Born: 05/06/95 Age: 27 Bats: L Throws: R Height: 6'0" Weight: 215 lb. Origin: Round 1, 2016 Draft (#16 overall)

YEAR	TEAM	LVL	AGE	PA	R	2B	3B	HR	RBI	BB	K	SB	CS	Whiff%	AVG/OBP/SLG	DRC+	BABIP	BRR	FRAA	WARP
2019	SL	AAA	24	372	63	17	2	14	49	59	64	1	0		.274/.390/.477	112	.303	1.2	3B(47): -3.1, 1B(23): -1.5	1.2
2019	LAA	MLB	24	164	17	7	0	8	23	17	52	0	0	33.3%	.211/.293/.422	88	.264	-1.0	3B(43): -3.8, 1B(13): 0.7	-0.2
2020	LAA	MLB	25	25	3	0	0	1	1	4	8	0	0	32.1%	.143/.280/.286	84	.167	-0.2	1B(2): -0.1, 2B(1): 0.2, LF(1): -0.2	0.0
2021	SL	AAA	26	449	71	23	4	17	69	60	92	2	1		.280/.383/.496	110	.325	-2.2	C(54): 2.9, 1B(17): -0.9, 3B(3): -0.4	2.0
2021	LAA	MLB	26	8	1	0	0	0	0	1	1	0	0	15.4%	.143/.250/.143	90	.167	-0.1	1B(2): -0.1	0.0
2022 DC	*LAA*	*MLB*	*27*	*227*	*28*	*10*	*1*	*5*	*26*	*24*	*60*	*0*	*1*	*30.3%*	*.216/.309/.360*	*80*	*.281*	*-0.2*	*C 0, 1B 0*	*0.3*

Comparables: Yonder Alonso, Ji-Man Choi, Max Muncy

Thaiss was a catcher when he was drafted, but never took a rep behind the plate in a pro game...until the 2021 season, when the Angels gave him more than 50 starts there in an effort to see if he could qualify for more than emergency duty. None of those came at the major-league level, though. For all his above-average production in the minors, Thaiss' efforts with the top club suggest that catching suits his offensive skill set. The Angels seemed pleased with the experiment, announcing late in the campaign that Thaiss would move forward as a full-time backstop. If only it hadn't taken them the better part of five seasons to figure that out.

Mike Trout CF Born: 08/07/91 Age: 30 Bats: R Throws: R Height: 6'2" Weight: 235 lb. Origin: Round 1, 2009 Draft (#25 overall)

YEAR	TEAM	LVL	AGE	PA	R	2B	3B	HR	RBI	BB	K	SB	CS	Whiff%	AVG/OBP/SLG	DRC+	BABIP	BRR	FRAA	WARP
2019	LAA	MLB	27	600	110	27	2	45	104	110	120	11	2	19.1%	.291/.438/.645	159	.298	3.6	CF(122): 6.6	8.0
2020	LAA	MLB	28	241	41	9	2	17	46	35	56	1	1	19.5%	.281/.390/.603	131	.300	1.2	CF(52): -3.8	1.4
2021	LAA	MLB	29	146	23	8	1	8	18	27	41	2	0	27.5%	.333/.466/.624	124	.456	1.0	CF(36): -6.9	0.5
2022 DC	*LAA*	*MLB*	*30*	*563*	*109*	*23*	*2*	*34*	*98*	*97*	*136*	*14*	*4*	*23.5%*	*.278/.416/.568*	*161*	*.321*	*0.5*	*CF -2*	*6.5*

Comparables: Mickey Mantle, Ken Griffey Jr., Willie Mays

A Brief, Selective History of the Perennially .500 2021 Angels and Mike Trout's Calf Strain:

May 1: Trout raises his OPS to 1.332 with his seventh homer of the season. The Angels win. They are 13-12.

May 17: Trout exits following a seemingly innocuous run to third on a pop-up. He is later diagnosed with a calf strain and expected to miss 6-8 weeks. The Angels win. They are 18-22.

June 8: Trout says he is "happy with my progress" but doesn't know when he'll return. The Angels win. They are 29-32.

June 28: Trout is moved to the 60-day IL but Joe Maddon describes him as "on pace". The Angels win. They are 38-40.

July 22: Trout is jogging, running the bases and hitting ahead of an Angels game in Minnesota. The Angels win. They are 47-48.

August 3: Maddon acknowledges that "the timeline keeps getting pushed back" but makes it clear the team still hopes to get Trout back this season. The Angels win. They are 53-54.

August 15: It is announced that Trout will resume travelling with the Angels on their next trip. The Angels win. They are 59-60.

September 15: Maddon admits there probably isn't enough time for Trout to return. The Angels win. They are 71-74.

Justin Upton LF Born: 08/25/87 Age: 34 Bats: R Throws: R Height: 6'1" Weight: 215 lb. Origin: Round 1, 2005 Draft (#1 overall)

YEAR	TEAM	LVL	AGE	PA	R	2B	3B	HR	RBI	BB	K	SB	CS	Whiff%	AVG/OBP/SLG	DRC+	BABIP	BRR	FRAA	WARP
2019	LAA	MLB	31	256	34	8	0	12	40	32	78	1	1	32.6%	.215/.309/.416	89	.261	0.3	LF(56): -3.1	0.3
2020	LAA	MLB	32	166	20	5	0	9	22	11	43	0	2	29.9%	.204/.289/.422	98	.219	-1.7	LF(39): -0.6	0.2
2021	LAA	MLB	33	362	47	12	0	17	41	39	107	4	1	31.6%	.211/.296/.409	94	.254	1.0	LF(87): -2.4, CF(1): -0.0	0.9
2022 DC	*LAA*	*MLB*	*34*	*471*	*68*	*17*	*0*	*23*	*67*	*49*	*134*	*5*	*3*	*31.3%*	*.227/.316/.438*	*102*	*.275*	*-0.2*	*LF 0*	*1.7*

Comparables: Jack Clark, Dwight Evans, Jeff Burroughs

If Upton was trying to convince anyone he's not merely the old guy on the team following Albert Pujols' departure, missing huge chunks of the year with back injuries didn't help. Then again, in many ways he's not so different from the Jo Adells of the world. After all, he still flashes tools, posting elite exit velocities and crushing bombs when he does get the barrel on the bat, as he did frequently in May and June during one of his patented hot streaks. He can still run, too, when the situation demands it, although hustling down the line to first is a rare event. The volume of the whiffs drowns out what he can still provide offensively, rendering him a below-average hitter yet again. It could be the statistical profile of an athletic, slightly raw talent trying to figure things out - Upton himself, in fact, early in his career. Alas, he's 34 now, and the Angels will once again be left facing a tough decision on a veteran with a hefty contract, unless Upton can both find the health that has eluded him and turn back the clock to the first year of his deal.

Tyler Wade SS Born: 11/23/94 Age: 27 Bats: L Throws: R Height: 6'1" Weight: 188 lb. Origin: Round 4, 2013 Draft (#134 overall)

YEAR	TEAM	LVL	AGE	PA	R	2B	3B	HR	RBI	BB	K	SB	CS	Whiff%	AVG/OBP/SLG	DRC+	BABIP	BRR	FRAA	WARP
2019	SWB	AAA	24	335	51	19	4	4	38	23	76	13	5		.296/.352/.425	84	.381	2.2	SS(43): 1.6, 2B(28): 0.5, 3B(4): 0.6	1.1
2019	NYY	MLB	24	108	16	3	1	2	11	11	28	7	0	26.2%	.245/.330/.362	81	.328	0.4	2B(18): 1.7, LF(14): 0.0, 3B(5): -0.5	0.2
2020	NYY	MLB	25	105	19	3	0	3	10	12	22	4	1	19.2%	.170/.288/.307	87	.188	0.5	2B(31): 2.2, SS(22): -3.3	0.1
2021	NYY	MLB	26	145	31	5	1	0	5	16	37	17	6	26.9%	.268/.354/.323	79	.378	0.3	SS(31): -1.0, 3B(27): -1.0, 2B(19): -0.3	-0.1
2022 DC	*LAA*	*MLB*	*27*	*181*	*20*	*7*	*1*	*2*	*23*	*16*	*44*	*6*	*2*	*25.3%*	*.218/.301/.320*	*70*	*.288*	*0.5*	*SS -1*	*-0.1*

Comparables: Jonathan Villar, Yolmer Sánchez, Reid Brignac

DRC+ doesn't measure hitting coaches; no statistic really can. Still, Marcus Thames can't be thrilled about what the metric says about the performance of his 2021 Yankees. Several players severely underachieved, while a handful more met their personal expectations, more or less. Wade was the only Yankee hitter to overachieve by traditional metrics. His 29.1 ft/s sprint speed and versatile defense have always been his calling cards, but last year he posted career bests in BA, OBP and OPS+. Unfortunately, DRC+ shows that despite the results, his offense was actually just as tepid as ever. That means no Yankees position players who spent more than a few weeks with the club exceeded expectations whatsoever. For that matter, neither did Thames, which is why he's no longer the hitting coach. As for Wade, he's off to Los Angeles in search of a new scapegoat.

Jared Walsh 1B Born: 07/30/93 Age: 28 Bats: L Throws: L Height: 6'0" Weight: 210 lb. Origin: Round 39, 2015 Draft (#1185 overall)

YEAR	TEAM	LVL	AGE	PA	R	2B	3B	HR	RBI	BB	K	SB	CS	Whiff%	AVG/OBP/SLG	DRC+	BABIP	BRR	FRAA	WARP
2019	SL	AAA	25	454	90	30	0	36	86	59	115	0	0		.325/.423/.686	132	.374	-0.8	1B(58): 5.4, P(13): 0.6, RF(3): -0.1	3.4
2019	LAA	MLB	25	87	6	5	1	1	5	6	35	0	0	32.4%	.203/.276/.329	62	.349	-0.6	1B(24): 0.8, P(5): 0.0	-0.2
2020	LAA	MLB	26	108	19	4	2	9	26	5	15	0	0	22.8%	.293/.324/.646	121	.256	0.3	1B(29): -1.5, RF(2): -0.2	0.4
2021	LAA	MLB	27	585	70	34	1	29	98	48	152	2	1	26.0%	.277/.340/.509	109	.335	0.5	1B(128): 2.6, RF(18): -2.5	2.0
2022 DC	*LAA*	*MLB*	*28*	*588*	*87*	*32*	*1*	*24*	*86*	*48*	*140*	*0*	*1*	*26.1%*	*.260/.328/.465*	*106*	*.311*	*-0.9*	*1B 1*	*1.7*

Comparables: Mitch Moreland, Gaby Sanchez, Justin Bour

Fears that Albert Pujols and his albatross contract would block Walsh at first base were partially realized over the first month, as the future Hall-of-Famer garnered 20 of 28 starts there while Walsh was shunted into an uncomfortable spot in right field. On May 6th, with Walsh sporting an OPS advantage of over 300 points, the Angels recognized that enough was enough. They designated Pujols for assignment.

Then Walsh initiated what the kindest reading might call a highly convincing Pujols impression. Post-DFA, the two offered very similar production, with Walsh needing a late surge to push him over the top. DRC wasn't convinced, granting Pujols the edge, albeit one aided by the Dodgers' usage as a platoon bat. The Angels no doubt hope Walsh will provide more than the 41-year-old going forward, platoon or not.

Taylor Ward OF Born: 12/14/93 Age: 28 Bats: R Throws: R Height: 6'1" Weight: 200 lb. Origin: Round 1, 2015 Draft (#26 overall)

YEAR	TEAM	LVL	AGE	PA	R	2B	3B	HR	RBI	BB	K	SB	CS	Whiff%	AVG/OBP/SLG	DRC+	BABIP	BRR	FRAA	WARP
2019	SL	AAA	25	512	102	34	1	27	71	80	101	11	5		.306/.427/.584	124	.347	3.4	LF(74): 7.2, 3B(17): -0.8, 1B(6): -1.0	3.9
2019	LAA	MLB	25	48	4	3	0	1	2	6	23	0	0	41.5%	.190/.292/.333	61	.389	-0.3	LF(9): -0.1, 3B(4): -0.6	-0.2
2020	LAA	MLB	26	102	16	6	2	0	5	8	28	2	0	23.6%	.277/.333/.383	85	.394	1.3	RF(19): -0.0, LF(17): 0.3	0.3
2021	SL	AAA	27	59	15	9	0	4	10	9	12	2	0		.429/.525/.857	113	.515	0.6	LF(7): -0.7, RF(5): -0.8, CF(1): 0.8	0.3
2021	LAA	MLB	27	237	33	15	0	8	33	20	55	1	1	25.1%	.250/.332/.438	98	.301	0.7	RF(51): 2.8, LF(18): 0.3, CF(12): 0.4	1.1
2022 DC	*LAA*	*MLB*	*28*	*446*	*58*	*21*	*0*	*14*	*57*	*42*	*107*	*3*	*2*	*24.8%*	*.245/.325/.413*	*99*	*.299*	*-0.4*	*RF 2, LF 0*	*1.3*

Comparables: Nelson Cruz, Peter O'Brien, Abraham Almonte

Just once, wouldn't it be nice if DRC tossed caution to the wind and lost its mind for an absurd line? The performance in question: Ward's near-1.400 OPS at Triple-A Salt Lake. Yes, it was in 59 plate appearances and yes, we've seen Ward dominate the level before only to result in disappointingly normal DRC+ marks. But 113? Come on, DRC. He slugged .857! More than a quarter of his at-bats ended in an extra-base hit! Get excited! Of course, when he wasn't tearing it up at Triple-A, or recovering from the broken rib that prevented him from expanding that sample, Ward turned in a very respectable, utterly average offensive performance in the majors while making a decent attempt to provide cover at all three spots in the Angels' ailing outfield. He looks like a perfectly fine complementary player. You win again, DRC+.

PITCHERS

★ ★ ★ *2022 Top 101 Prospect* **#86** ★ ★ ★

Sam Bachman RHP Born: 09/30/99 Age: 22 Bats: R Throws: R Height: 6'1" Weight: 235 lb. Origin: Round 1, 2021 Draft (#9 overall)

YEAR	TEAM	LVL	AGE	W	L	SV	G	GS	IP	H	HR	BB/9	K/9	K	GB%	BABIP	WHIP	ERA	DRA-	WARP	MPH	FB%	Whiff%	CSP
2021	TRI	A+	21	0	2	0	5	5	14^{1}	13	1	2.5	9.4	15	65.8%	.324	1.19	3.77	109	0.0				
2022 non-DC	*LAA*	*MLB*	*22*	*2*	*3*	*0*	*57*	*0*	*50*	*53*	*6*	*4.6*	*7.7*	*42*	*46.9%*	*.313*	*1.58*	*5.28*	*123*	*-0.4*				

Comparables: Parker Markel, Ryan Lawlor, Henry Centeno

Saying that the Angels used the 2021 draft to address their pitching depth issues is akin to calling Mike Trout a decent player. The Halos went into overdrive by selecting exclusively pitchers with their 20 picks, beginning with Bachman's selection at ninth overall. He's an exciting talent with a triple-digit fastball and a plus slider. He's also an Angels pitching prospect, so, yes, there are durability concerns.

Jaime Barría RHP Born: 07/18/96 Age: 25 Bats: R Throws: R Height: 6'1" Weight: 210 lb. Origin: International Free Agent, 2013

YEAR	TEAM	LVL	AGE	W	L	SV	G	GS	IP	H	HR	BB/9	K/9	K	GB%	BABIP	WHIP	ERA	DRA-	WARP	MPH	FB%	Whiff%	CSP
2019	SL	AAA	22	3	3	0	10	10	48^{1}	73	16	1.9	8.2	44	26.3%	.368	1.72	9.68	139	-0.8				
2019	LAA	MLB	22	4	10	0	19	13	82^{2}	92	24	2.9	8.2	75	35.2%	.287	1.44	6.42	117	0.1	91.7	36.8%	22.2%	47.7%
2020	LAA	MLB	23	1	0	0	7	5	32^{1}	27	3	2.5	7.5	27	33.7%	.261	1.11	3.62	113	0.1	92.2	43.1%	23.1%	49.9%
2021	SL	AAA	24	3	2	0	10	10	49	54	10	1.5	6.2	34	36.5%	.280	1.27	4.41	133	-0.8				
2021	LAA	MLB	24	2	4	0	13	11	56^{2}	70	8	3.0	5.6	35	43.8%	.333	1.57	4.61	132	-0.5	93.1	55.1%	19.1%	53.8%
2022 DC	*LAA*	*MLB*	*25*	*8*	*8*	*0*	*60*	*16*	*111.7*	*122*	*17*	*2.6*	*6.0*	*73*	*39.3%*	*.295*	*1.39*	*4.78*	*118*	*-0.3*	*92.5*	*47.6%*	*20.8%*	*51.3%*

Comparables: Ricky Bones, Tyler Skaggs, Zach Davies

Barría bounced back and forth between Triple-A and the majors for most of the season. He managed to defy DRA for the third time in four years with the big club, arguably to a greater extent than the top-line numbers indicate, since his season opened with a disastrous seven-earned run outing in two innings of relief. His 3.62 ERA the rest of the way notwithstanding, Barría's performance was deeply discouraging. His 14% strikeout rate was the lowest of his career, echoed by a similar mark at Salt Lake. Major-league hitters aren't intimidated by any of his four offerings, all of which suffer from below-average movement. Considering how easy it now seems to be for opponents to make contact against the right-hander, it's tough to envision a scenario in which his peripherals don't catch up to him sooner or later.

Ty Buttrey RHP Born: 03/31/93 Age: 29 Bats: L Throws: R Height: 6'6" Weight: 240 lb. Origin: Round 4, 2012 Draft (#151 overall)

YEAR	TEAM	LVL	AGE	W	L	SV	G	GS	IP	H	HR	BB/9	K/9	K	GB%	BABIP	WHIP	ERA	DRA-	WARP	MPH	FB%	Whiff%	CSP
2019	LAA	MLB	26	6	7	2	72	0	72^{1}	69	8	2.9	10.5	84	44.7%	.323	1.27	3.98	81	1.5	97.3	57.1%	27.4%	50.4%
2020	LAA	MLB	27	2	3	5	27	0	26^{1}	28	4	3.1	6.2	18	47.6%	.304	1.41	5.81	110	0.1	96.2	58.2%	20.0%	46.2%
2022 non-DC	*LAA*	*MLB*	*29*	*2*	*2*	*0*	*57*	*0*	*50*	*49*	*6*	*3.2*	*8.5*	*47*	*46.5%*	*.305*	*1.34*	*4.07*	*100*	*0.2*	*96.8*	*57.5%*	*24.3%*	*48.7%*

Comparables: Jared Hughes, Danny Patterson, Hunter Strickland

The Angels optioning Buttrey to the minors in late March raised a few eyebrows, given his central bullpen role the prior two seasons. Then the reason became clear: Buttrey's decision to retire at the age of 28. The hard-throwing righty admitted in an Instagram post that he'd always played the game for other people, to prove them wrong when they said he couldn't make the majors. His honest reflections on how he fell out of love with baseball were refreshing and all-too-rare. He made it; good on him for knowing that was enough.

Griffin Canning RHP Born: 05/11/96 Age: 26 Bats: R Throws: R Height: 6'2" Weight: 180 lb. Origin: Round 2, 2017 Draft (#47 overall)

YEAR	TEAM	LVL	AGE	W	L	SV	G	GS	IP	H	HR	BB/9	K/9	K	GB%	BABIP	WHIP	ERA	DRA-	WARP	MPH	FB%	Whiff%	CSP
2019	SL	AAA	23	1	0	0	3	3	16	13	0	1.1	9.6	17	39.0%	.317	0.94	0.56	95	0.1				
2019	LAA	MLB	23	5	6	0	18	17	90^{1}	80	14	3.0	9.6	96	36.8%	.281	1.22	4.58	100	0.9	92.9	71.4%	32.3%	45.0%
2020	LAA	MLB	24	2	3	0	11	11	56^{1}	54	8	3.7	8.9	56	36.1%	.307	1.37	3.99	109	0.3	92.2	60.4%	27.3%	44.2%
2021	LAA	MLB	25	5	4	0	14	13	62^{2}	65	14	4.0	8.9	62	36.0%	.298	1.48	5.60	118	0.0	93.7	40.7%	30.3%	55.4%
2022 DC	*LAA*	*MLB*	*26*	*4*	*4*	*0*	*16*	*16*	*72.7*	*68*	*11*	*4.0*	*9.0*	*72*	*37.7%*	*.288*	*1.37*	*4.47*	*108*	*0.3*	*93.1*	*53.5%*	*29.9%*	*49.8%*

Comparables: Ervin Santana, Clay Buchholz, Tony Armas

The griffin: part-lion, part-eagle, mythical embodiment of power and strength. It's a tough name for an oft-injured righty whose career is trending in the wrong direction. If we are going to wax lyrical about Canning's virtues, we might point to his still-excellent swinging-strike rates, derived from his pair of breakers and what appeared to be a more whiff-inducing changeup. The cambio lacks separation from the heater, however, and that pitch itself remains alarmingly hittable. Of course, this picture wouldn't be complete without another injury woe to add to the list, so a stress reaction in Canning's back ultimately finished his season after barely 60 innings. Reliable back-end starters or multi-inning relief arms aren't legendary, but they are useful. Canning should shoot for that outcome after this replacement-level performance.

Steve Cishek RHP Born: 06/18/86 Age: 36 Bats: R Throws: R Height: 6'6" Weight: 215 lb. Origin: Round 5, 2007 Draft (#166 overall)

YEAR	TEAM	LVL	AGE	W	L	SV	G	GS	IP	H	HR	BB/9	K/9	K	GB%	BABIP	WHIP	ERA	DRA-	WARP	MPH	FB%	Whiff%	CSP
2019	CHC	MLB	33	4	6	7	70	0	64	48	7	4.1	8.0	57	49.4%	.246	1.20	2.95	100	0.7	90.8	59.2%	22.6%	43.5%
2020	CHW	MLB	34	0	0	0	22	0	20	21	4	4.1	9.5	21	32.2%	.309	1.50	5.40	131	-0.1	90.5	47.6%	27.2%	46.5%
2021	LAA	MLB	35	0	2	0	74	0	68^{1}	61	2	5.4	8.4	64	49.7%	.304	1.49	3.42	116	0.1	90.2	61.1%	20.3%	49.1%
2022 DC	*FA*	*MLB*	*36*	*3*	*3*	*0*	*71*	*0*	*61.7*	*57*	*8*	*4.6*	*8.6*	*58*	*46.0%*	*.289*	*1.45*	*4.81*	*112*	*-0.2*	*90.3*	*58.9%*	*21.7%*	*47.7%*

Comparables: Rudy Seanez, Fernando Salas, Adam Ottavino

Cishek couldn't fully recapture the dominance against righties that had characterized his entire career prior to 2020, sporting a slight reverse split that still represented a huge improvement over the 60-game season. What he did recover, somehow, was his run prevention, posting an ERA right in line with his excellent career mark despite a slew of free passes. His rediscovery of his ground-balling ways and a correspondingly miniscule homer rate helped a great deal. Even so, it's a method that might be tough to replicate.

★ ★ ★ *2022 Top 101 Prospect* **#64** ★ ★ ★

Reid Detmers LHP Born: 07/08/99 Age: 22 Bats: L Throws: L Height: 6'2" Weight: 210 lb. Origin: Round 1, 2020 Draft (#10 overall)

YEAR	TEAM	LVL	AGE	W	L	SV	G	GS	IP	H	HR	BB/9	K/9	K	GB%	BABIP	WHIP	ERA	DRA-	WARP	MPH	FB%	Whiff%	CSP
2021	RCT	AA	21	2	4	0	12	12	54	45	10	3.0	16.2	97	33.9%	.361	1.17	3.50	69	1.4				
2021	SL	AAA	21	1	0	0	2	2	8	7	0	1.1	12.4	11	31.6%	.368	1.00	1.13	97	0.0				
2021	LAA	MLB	21	1	3	0	5	5	20^{2}	26	5	4.8	8.3	19	33.3%	.328	1.79	7.40	143	-0.3	93.1	45.1%	27.1%	56.8%
2022 DC	*LAA*	*MLB*	*22*	*7*	*7*	*0*	*22*	*22*	*113.3*	*101*	*19*	*3.8*	*10.0*	*126*	*34.4%*	*.286*	*1.32*	*4.21*	*104*	*0.7*	*93.1*	*45.1%*	*27.1%*	*56.8%*

Comparables: Tarik Skubal, Clay Buchholz, Brian Matusz

The canceled minor-league season didn't slow Detmers' rapid progression. Less than 14 months and a mere 60 innings after signing with Los Angeles and debuting in Double-A, the first-rounder was in the bigs, having punched out an incredible 106 across those 60 frames. What looked like a low-90s fastball with no room for growth out of college now sits 93 and touches 95, a much more threatening complement to his excellent curveball. Although the big-league debut didn't do much to dispel the feeling of dread that generally surrounds the Angels pitching staff these days, Detmers has the arsenal and the control to change that.

Junior Guerra RHP Born: 01/16/85 Age: 37 Bats: R Throws: R Height: 6'0" Weight: 235 lb. Origin: International Free Agent, 2001

YEAR	TEAM	LVL	AGE	W	L	SV	G	GS	IP	H	HR	BB/9	K/9	K	GB%	BABIP	WHIP	ERA	DRA-	WARP	MPH	FB%	Whiff%	CSP
2019	MIL	MLB	34	9	5	3	72	0	83^{2}	58	11	3.9	8.3	77	43.2%	.221	1.12	3.55	100	0.9	94.8	60.2%	25.9%	45.3%
2020	ARI	MLB	35	1	2	0	25	0	23^{2}	17	1	5.7	8.0	21	46.2%	.258	1.35	3.04	107	0.2	94.0	60.6%	26.9%	45.4%
2021	LAG	WIN	36	1	5	1	10	8	52^{1}	62	6	1.9	6.5	38	47.2%	.337	1.39	4.99						
2021	LAA	MLB	36	5	2	0	41	1	65^{1}	67	6	6.3	8.4	61	48.7%	.319	1.73	6.06	119	-0.1	93.0	56.0%	27.3%	52.1%
2022 non-DC	*LAA*	*MLB*	*37*	*2*	*3*	*0*	*57*	*0*	*50*	*46*	*7*	*5.1*	*8.8*	*49*	*44.9%*	*.289*	*1.50*	*4.75*	*111*	*-0.1*	*93.6*	*57.6%*	*26.9%*	*49.5%*

Comparables: Mike Garcia, Brett Tomko, Camilo Pascual

It's tempting to blame Guerra's struggles on the foreign substance crackdown. After all, he lost at least 200 rpm on all of his pitches over the final four months compared to the first two. That explanation would hold up better if Guerra wasn't already sporting a 5.54 ERA at the end of May, but he did obviously overhaul his approach. He ditched the four-seam, turned to the sinker as his primary pitch and reintroduced a slider that had barely been seen since 2018. Reinventing yourself again at 36 is no mean feat, so the ineffectiveness of this strategy can be somewhat excused, but it's possible that low-spin Guerra simply doesn't possess a fastball which won't get tattooed by major-league hitters.

Jimmy Herget RHP Born: 09/09/93 Age: 28 Bats: R Throws: R Height: 6'3" Weight: 170 lb. Origin: Round 6, 2015 Draft (#175 overall)

YEAR	TEAM	LVL	AGE	W	L	SV	G	GS	IP	H	HR	BB/9	K/9	K	GB%	BABIP	WHIP	ERA	DRA-	WARP	MPH	FB%	Whiff%	CSP
2019	LOU	AAA	25	3	4	2	48	0	58^{2}	41	7	5.5	10.4	68	34.5%	.246	1.31	2.91	94	0.9				
2019	CIN	MLB	25	0	0	0	5	0	6^{1}	8	2	4.3	0.0	0	21.7%	.286	1.74	4.26	145	-0.1	93.2	50.7%	18.8%	44.6%
2020	TEX	MLB	26	1	0	0	20	1	19^{2}	13	2	6.4	7.8	17	35.2%	.216	1.37	3.20	125	0.0	93.3	54.3%	25.7%	49.8%
2021	RR	AAA	27	2	2	3	27	0	37^{2}	28	5	2.9	11.5	48	33.0%	.250	1.06	2.63	98	0.2				
2021	LAA	MLB	27	2	2	0	14	0	14^{2}	15	0	2.5	11.0	18	44.4%	.417	1.30	4.30	93	0.2	91.1	49.4%	33.0%	53.8%
2021	TEX	MLB	27	0	1	0	4	0	4	5	1	0.0	4.5	2	40.0%	.286	1.25	9.00	109	0.0	91.2	46.3%	25.9%	61.5%
2022 DC	*LAA*	*MLB*	*28*	*2*	*2*	*0*	*44*	*0*	*38.7*	*37*	*6*	*3.9*	*10.0*	*43*	*34.9%*	*.307*	*1.39*	*4.58*	*109*	*0.0*	*92.1*	*51.2%*	*28.4%*	*52.4%*

Comparables: Fernando Salas, Justin De Fratus, Nick Goody

After three months of strong run prevention at the Rangers' Triple-A affiliate, Herget's next bite of the major-league apple lasted a mere four games before he was booted off the roster following multiple earned runs in consecutive appearances. The side-arming righty nevertheless got to show off his tweaked pitch mix, built around a mid-70s curve that sweeps across the zone from his low release point. The breaker proved rather difficult to hit, suggesting he'd be best-served leaning on that and his similarly-angled four-seam. The rest of the arsenal is Hergettable.

James Hoyt RHP Born: 09/30/86 Age: 35 Bats: R Throws: R Height: 6'6" Weight: 230 lb. Origin: Undrafted Free Agent, 2013

YEAR	TEAM	LVL	AGE	W	L	SV	G	GS	IP	H	HR	BB/9	K/9	K	GB%	BABIP	WHIP	ERA	DRA-	WARP	MPH	FB%	Whiff%	CSP
2019	COL	AAA	32	2	0	4	40	2	42	46	3	4.3	10.3	48	52.5%	.374	1.57	3.43	82	0.9				
2019	CLE	MLB	32	0	0	0	8	0	8^{1}	6	2	2.2	10.8	10	45.0%	.222	0.96	2.16	97	0.1	93.8	42.3%	40.0%	45.6%
2020	MIA	MLB	33	2	0	0	24	0	14^{2}	9	1	4.9	12.3	20	45.5%	.250	1.16	1.23	85	0.3	88.7	30.6%	35.3%	41.6%
2021	SL	AAA	34	1	2	3	33	0	35^{1}	51	10	5.1	9.2	36	51.3%	.383	2.01	9.42	92	0.3				
2021	LAA	MLB	34	0	0	0	9	0	8	12	0	7.9	12.4	11	38.5%	.462	2.38	6.75	103	0.1	91.3	33.0%	37.3%	54.8%
2022 non-DC	*LAA*	*MLB*	*35*	*2*	*3*	*0*	*57*	*0*	*50*	*47*	*7*	*4.5*	*9.9*	*55*	*44.8%*	*.308*	*1.46*	*4.82*	*113*	*-0.2*	*90.5*	*33.0%*	*36.8%*	*48.3%*

Comparables: Jim Henderson, Darren Holmes, Blake Parker

From his run-prevention numbers, it would be reasonable to assume that Hoyt's extremely slider-heavy approach had finally caught up to him. It's true that the 35-year-old's breaker wasn't quite as effective as previous years, but it wasn't his undoing. He was ultimately done in by some tremendously unfortunate sequencing and, in the minors, an astronomical home run rate. Hoyt avoided the homers in his brief major-league trips but replaced that problem by only allowing hits when runners were on base. For a player who didn't allow hitters to reach base that often via alternative means, that might be an effective strategy. For Hoyt, it proved disastrous.

Raisel Iglesias RHP Born: 01/04/90 Age: 32 Bats: R Throws: R Height: 6'2" Weight: 190 lb. Origin: International Free Agent, 2014

YEAR	TEAM	LVL	AGE	W	L	SV	G	GS	IP	H	HR	BB/9	K/9	K	GB%	BABIP	WHIP	ERA	DRA-	WARP	MPH	FB%	Whiff%	CSP
2019	CIN	MLB	29	3	12	34	68	0	67	61	12	2.8	12.0	89	29.9%	.318	1.22	4.16	84	1.3	95.5	47.8%	33.8%	47.2%
2020	CIN	MLB	30	4	3	8	22	0	23	16	1	2.0	12.1	31	38.9%	.288	0.91	2.74	80	0.5	96.3	46.3%	39.0%	49.5%
2021	LAA	MLB	31	7	5	34	65	0	70	53	11	1.5	13.2	103	39.5%	.290	0.93	2.57	61	2.1	96.5	44.8%	40.9%	54.6%
2022 DC	*LAA*	*MLB*	*32*	*4*	*3*	*35*	*74*	*0*	*64.7*	*50*	*8*	*2.3*	*12.4*	*89*	*37.7%*	*.292*	*1.03*	*2.52*	*67*	*1.3*	*96.2*	*45.7%*	*39.1%*	*52.2%*

Comparables: Liam Hendriks, Blake Treinen, Chad Qualls

For years, it has felt as though Iglesias was just one step away from ascending to the true elite. Whether it was a few too many balls clearing the fence, an elevated walk rate or simply the fact that his strikeout rate didn't quite match his stuff, there was always something that kept him a cut below the game's very best. Even his stellar 2020 got the short-season asterisk, a qualifier that was emphatically erased in 2021. The Angels closer was utterly dominant, posting career bests in strikeout and walk rate. He generated whiffs more often than anyone but Jacob deGrom and Josh Hader, while ranking fifth in DRA. He still allowed a few more homers than he'd like, but it's no surprise opponents are swinging for the fences against him, since they'd barely score otherwise. Thirteen of the 20 earned runs he allowed came as a result of the long ball. When he strikes this many out, it can't stop him being elite.

Michael Lorenzen RHP Born: 01/04/92 Age: 30 Bats: R Throws: R Height: 6'3" Weight: 217 lb. Origin: Round 1, 2013 Draft (#38 overall)

YEAR	TEAM	LVL	AGE	W	L	SV	G	GS	IP	H	HR	BB/9	K/9	K	GB%	BABIP	WHIP	ERA	DRA-	WARP	MPH	FB%	Whiff%	CSP
2019	CIN	MLB	27	1	4	7	73	0	83^{1}	68	9	3.0	9.2	85	44.3%	.274	1.15	2.92	87	1.4	97.0	35.8%	31.0%	44.5%
2020	CIN	MLB	28	3	1	0	18	2	33^{2}	30	3	4.5	9.4	35	50.0%	.300	1.40	4.28	87	0.6	96.8	40.5%	35.5%	40.6%
2021	CIN	MLB	29	1	2	4	27	0	29	26	2	4.3	6.5	21	42.7%	.279	1.38	5.59	126	-0.1	96.6	36.2%	26.5%	52.3%
2022 DC	*LAA*	*MLB*	*30*	*7*	*5*	*0*	*53*	*9*	*79.7*	*78*	*9*	*3.8*	*9.2*	*81*	*46.7%*	*.312*	*1.40*	*4.27*	*102*	*0.3*	*96.8*	*37.4%*	*30.7%*	*46.1%*

Comparables: Rafael Montero, Jon Rauch, Vicente Palacios

The Reds and Lorenzen entered last spring with the somewhat far-fetched hope of putting him back in the rotation, despite the fact that he last started games regularly in 2015. Before he could give a serious audition, though, he was sidelined with a strained throwing shoulder for three months. When he finally returned, he was better than his final numbers indicate—he had a 2.92 ERA heading into his last five appearances—and his velocity was nearly identical to what it had been the previous season. But Lorenzen has seemed better than his numbers for a long time now, and his command issues and inability to put hitters away with two strikes remain unresolved. Perhaps the answer will be revealed by his next employer, or maybe even his next bicep curl.

Aaron Loup LHP Born: 12/19/87 Age: 34 Bats: L Throws: L Height: 5'11" Weight: 210 lb. Origin: Round 9, 2009 Draft (#280 overall)

YEAR	TEAM	LVL	AGE	W	L	SV	G	GS	IP	H	HR	BB/9	K/9	K	GB%	BABIP	WHIP	ERA	DRA-	WARP	MPH	FB%	Whiff%	CSP
2019	SD	MLB	31	0	0	0	4	0	3^{1}	2	0	2.7	13.5	5	57.1%	.286	0.90	0.00	93	0.0	91.8	43.4%	32.0%	48.3%
2020	TB	MLB	32	3	2	0	24	0	25	17	3	1.4	7.9	22	39.4%	.230	0.84	2.52	89	0.4	92.3	49.9%	19.8%	54.9%
2021	NYM	MLB	33	6	0	0	65	2	56^{2}	37	1	2.5	9.1	57	51.8%	.259	0.94	0.95	84	1.0	92.5	51.9%	27.1%	54.3%
2022 DC	*LAA*	*MLB*	*34*	*3*	*3*	*0*	*74*	*0*	*64.7*	*59*	*7*	*2.8*	*8.8*	*63*	*47.2%*	*.292*	*1.23*	*3.67*	*93*	*0.5*	*92.4*	*51.3%*	*25.7%*	*54.3%*

Comparables: Jason Frasor, Pat Neshek, Mark Guthrie

If MLB's three-batter-minimum rule was the asteroid that was supposed to wipe out the LOOGYsaurs, Loup is one of the tiny proto-mammals that emerged from the ash-covered muck and evolved into something more. The veteran southpaw had his best season at age 34, holding both lefties and righties under a .600 OPS with a sinker that batters slugged .260 against. Getting by on 92 mph is a nifty trick that Loup pulls off with good control and command and a funky sidearm delivery, prolonging his longevity even as the rest of his kind die out and lining him up for the first multi-year deal of his career. A mass extinction event proved to be a new beginning for him.

Mike Mayers RHP Born: 12/06/91 Age: 30 Bats: R Throws: R Height: 6'2" Weight: 220 lb. Origin: Round 3, 2013 Draft (#93 overall)

YEAR	TEAM	LVL	AGE	W	L	SV	G	GS	IP	H	HR	BB/9	K/9	K	GB%	BABIP	WHIP	ERA	DRA-	WARP	MPH	FB%	Whiff%	CSP
2019	MEM	AAA	27	0	1	6	20	1	20	21	4	3.2	10.8	24	52.7%	.333	1.40	3.15	76	0.4				
2019	STL	MLB	27	0	1	0	16	0	19	21	3	5.2	7.6	16	21.7%	.316	1.68	6.63	134	-0.1	95.0	53.2%	29.1%	45.0%
2020	LAA	MLB	28	2	0	2	29	0	30	18	2	2.7	12.9	43	32.4%	.242	0.90	2.10	75	0.7	92.9	57.8%	35.7%	45.4%
2021	LAA	MLB	29	5	5	2	72	2	75	71	11	3.1	10.8	90	35.7%	.326	1.29	3.84	85	1.3	93.4	68.4%	29.2%	51.3%
2022 DC	*LAA*	*MLB*	*30*	*3*	*3*	*4*	*74*	*0*	*64.7*	*55*	*9*	*3.1*	*10.2*	*73*	*36.4%*	*.282*	*1.20*	*3.51*	*90*	*0.6*	*93.4*	*65.2%*	*30.5%*	*49.7%*

Comparables: John Johnstone, Nick Masset, Brandon Workman

Replicating success isn't easy. Sometimes you roll out the same material that worked the first time around, tweaking the formula here and there, but it just doesn't land as well. Mayers' efforts to move beyond mere imitation of his breakout involved heavier usage of his cutter in the early going, a bit that was soon relegated to the back of his repertoire. Trouble with his delivery didn't help so, after a mid-season tweak to his mechanics, results did improve, leading to a 2.78 ERA over the second half. The four-seamer and slider still had their moments but overall, the production wasn't remotely as good as his breakout. Mayers now projects as a solid bullpen arm who's better avoided in big spots, rather than the bankable name we thought he might be a year ago.

Packy Naughton LHP

Born: 04/16/96 Age: 26 Bats: R Throws: L Height: 6'2" Weight: 195 lb. Origin: Round 9, 2017 Draft (#257 overall)

YEAR	TEAM	LVL	AGE	W	L	SV	G	GS	IP	H	HR	BB/9	K/9	K	GB%	BABIP	WHIP	ERA	DRA-	WARP	MPH	FB%	Whiff%	CSP
2019	DBT	A+	23	5	2	0	9	9	51^{1}	49	2	1.6	8.8	50	43.6%	.320	1.13	2.63	91	0.8				
2019	CHA	AA	23	6	10	0	19	19	105^{2}	109	8	2.2	6.9	81	39.1%	.309	1.28	3.66	112	0.0				
2021	SL	AAA	25	2	2	0	13	9	56^{2}	69	7	2.1	8.4	53	47.8%	.363	1.45	4.76	94	0.4				
2021	LAA	MLB	25	0	4	0	7	5	22^{2}	27	3	5.6	4.8	12	50.6%	.308	1.81	6.35	150	-0.4	90.5	56.9%	21.1%	48.0%
2022 DC	*LAA*	*MLB*	*26*	*2*	*2*	*0*	*17*	*3*	*25.7*	*28*	*3*	*3.2*	*6.9*	*19*	*43.9%*	*.311*	*1.47*	*4.95*	*119*	*-0.1*	*90.5*	*56.9%*	*21.1%*	*48.0%*

Comparables: Luis Cessa, Anthony Vasquez, Tyler Wilson

Naughton's nickname was given to him by his older brother, who at the age of two was unable to pronounce Patrick when his sibling arrived. More than 25 years later, Packy has stuck. His stay in the majors featuring even a fraction of that longevity looks doubtful. His four-seamer, barely scraping 90 mph, was hammered by major-league hitters in his debut. His changeup, ostensibly his best secondary, wasn't enough to compensate, and there appears to have been little success developing a viable breaker. (The sinker offered a glimmer of hope, proving harder to square up than the four-seam.) It's not just Naughton's arsenal that looks precarious. He begins to sink onto his standing leg almost as soon as he starts his delivery, bending his knee at almost a 90 degree angle before he even begins his stride towards home, while folding his other leg up into his chest. It's hard to believe he can generate the velocity he does from such a contorted position. It's probably not going to be enough unless he adds something more to his repertoire.

Félix Peña RHP

Born: 02/25/90 Age: 32 Bats: R Throws: R Height: 6'2" Weight: 220 lb. Origin: International Free Agent, 2009

YEAR	TEAM	LVL	AGE	W	L	SV	G	GS	IP	H	HR	BB/9	K/9	K	GB%	BABIP	WHIP	ERA	DRA-	WARP	MPH	FB%	Whiff%	CSP
2019	LAA	MLB	29	8	3	0	22	7	96^{1}	80	16	3.2	9.4	101	44.0%	.256	1.18	4.58	88	1.6	91.7	49.1%	29.5%	47.2%
2020	LAA	MLB	30	3	0	2	25	0	26^{2}	27	2	2.7	9.8	29	50.6%	.333	1.31	4.05	80	0.6	94.6	48.5%	27.8%	48.1%
2021	TOR	WIN	31	1	1	0	7	7	33	22	1	1.9	7.4	27	36.1%	.226	0.88	1.91						
2021	SL	AAA	31	5	4	0	31	7	68^{1}	82	14	3.6	7.8	59	38.8%	.324	1.60	8.03	101	0.2				
2021	LAA	MLB	31	0	0	0	2	0	1^{2}	7	0	21.6	10.8	2	20.0%	.700	6.60	37.80	111	0.0	92.6	44.6%	41.4%	57.2%
2022 non-DC	*LAA*	*MLB*	*32*	*2*	*3*	*0*	*57*	*0*	*50*	*52*	*8*	*3.5*	*8.2*	*45*	*41.4%*	*.305*	*1.43*	*4.92*	*117*	*-0.3*	*92.7*	*48.6%*	*29.8%*	*48.2%*

Comparables: Jared Burton, Manny Acosta, Jacob Barnes

Peña's descent from integral member of the Angels staff to waiver wire fodder seemed to happen overnight. He had the second-highest leverage index of any Halos regular in 2020, closing out a win over the Padres in his second-to-last appearance. When he resurfaced in 2021, following a hamstring strain that cost him the season's first month, Peña gave up consecutive singles and then a double, a wild pitch and a walk before he could get the requisite second out. Before completing a full inning in his second outing, he surrendered three walks, three singles and another double. That was the end of Peña's 2021 season in the majors as he was sent to toil at Triple-A, giving up five or more earned runs on an incredible seven occasions in his remaining 31 games. Pitching is tough.

José Quijada LHP

Born: 11/09/95 Age: 26 Bats: L Throws: L Height: 5'11" Weight: 215 lb. Origin: International Free Agent, 2013

YEAR	TEAM	LVL	AGE	W	L	SV	G	GS	IP	H	HR	BB/9	K/9	K	GB%	BABIP	WHIP	ERA	DRA-	WARP	MPH	FB%	Whiff%	CSP
2019	NO	AAA	23	1	0	4	22	0	29^{1}	27	5	3.7	10.7	35	33.8%	.293	1.33	4.30	93	0.2				
2019	MIA	MLB	23	2	3	1	34	0	29^{2}	27	10	7.9	13.3	44	32.9%	.288	1.79	5.76	93	0.4	93.6	71.9%	34.3%	42.8%
2020	LAA	MLB	24	0	1	0	6	0	3^{2}	6	1	4.9	14.7	6	36.4%	.500	2.18	7.36	70	0.1	93.5	68.5%	33.3%	48.4%
2021	SL	AAA	25	3	1	1	22	0	29^{1}	17	2	3.4	11.4	37	46.3%	.231	0.95	1.53	79	0.5				
2021	LAA	MLB	25	0	2	0	26	0	25^{2}	20	2	5.3	13.3	38	39.3%	.333	1.36	4.56	73	0.6	93.8	73.3%	31.7%	48.6%
2022 DC	*LAA*	*MLB*	*26*	*3*	*3*	*0*	*74*	*0*	*64.7*	*48*	*9*	*4.7*	*12.2*	*87*	*39.4%*	*.278*	*1.27*	*3.57*	*87*	*0.7*	*93.7*	*72.6%*	*32.5%*	*47.0%*

Comparables: Sam Tuivailala, Jaime Cerda, Trevor Gott

Quijada threw his four-seamer over 73% of the time, more than almost any other pitcher. That makes it all the more impressive that he took a huge step forwards with the pitch, ranking above the 95th percentile in both whiff rate and strikeout rate on four-seamers. Quijada doesn't locate particularly well, hence his persistently elevated walk rate and tendency to surrender hard contact when hitters do get hold of the heater. In truth, there's nothing particularly notable about the pitch other than the bat-missing. It looks average, the velocity is barely above-average and the movement's ordinary. It must all be in the deception. Perhaps it's that Quijada hides the ball well, or maybe it's that he routinely looks off-balance, often finishing his delivery with a wild flourish of a leg kick or, sporadically, a sideways hop across the mound. The lefty was responsible for arguably the most hilarious balk of the season, collapsing on the mound as he somehow kicked his own leg away before he could even bring his throwing arm forwards. Most of the time, hitters were more off-balance than Quijada was, promising more future success than his run prevention indicates.

Chris Rodriguez RHP Born: 07/20/98 Age: 23 Bats: R Throws: R Height: 6'2" Weight: 185 lb. Origin: Round 4, 2016 Draft (#126 overall)

YEAR	TEAM	LVL	AGE	W	L	SV	G	GS	IP	H	HR	BB/9	K/9	K	GB%	BABIP	WHIP	ERA	DRA-	WARP	MPH	FB%	Whiff%	CSP
2019	IE	A+	20	0	0	0	3	3	9^1	6	0	3.9	12.5	13	68.4%	.316	1.07	0.00	89	0.1				
2021	RCT	AA	22	0	0	0	5	5	12^2	15	1	3.6	12.1	17	52.8%	.400	1.58	4.26	87	0.2				
2021	SL	AAA	22	0	1	0	3	2	7^2	7	1	7.0	5.9	5	33.3%	.261	1.70	5.87	128	-0.1				
2021	LAA	MLB	22	2	1	0	15	2	29^2	28	0	4.6	8.8	29	54.7%	.326	1.45	3.64	106	0.2	96.0	65.7%	25.2%	52.5%
2022 DC	*LAA*	*MLB*	*23*	*0*	*0*	*0*	*14*	*0*	*12.7*	*12*	*1*	*4.8*	*9.0*	*12*	*49.8%*	*.302*	*1.49*	*4.62*	*109*	*0.0*	*96.0*	*65.7%*	*25.2%*	*52.5%*

Comparables: Trevor Gott, Frankie Montas, Lester Oliveros

The Chris Rodriguez Experience was more or less as advertised. We saw high-90s heat at times, whiffs on his breaking ball, and an injury-interrupted season that eventually ended altogether because of a lat strain. The team continued to make positive noises about wanting Rodriguez to start, but the case was not strengthened by a mere two starts of 80-plus pitches and only one surpassing five frames. It remains easy to see why Rodriguez would be an electric starter if he could stay healthy, especially if he can bring his slider or changeup along to complement his heater and hard mid-80s curve, and even easier to see why he's fated for a relief role. Offseason shoulder surgery only made the latter more likely.

Patrick Sandoval LHP Born: 10/18/96 Age: 25 Bats: L Throws: L Height: 6'3" Weight: 190 lb. Origin: Round 11, 2015 Draft (#319 overall)

YEAR	TEAM	LVL	AGE	W	L	SV	G	GS	IP	H	HR	BB/9	K/9	K	GB%	BABIP	WHIP	ERA	DRA-	WARP	MPH	FB%	Whiff%	CSP
2019	MOB	AA	22	0	3	0	5	4	20	14	1	3.2	14.4	32	50.0%	.310	1.05	3.60	66	0.5				
2019	SL	AAA	22	4	4	0	15	15	60^1	84	7	5.2	9.8	66	42.7%	.403	1.97	6.41	104	0.2				
2019	LAA	MLB	22	0	4	0	10	9	39^1	35	6	4.3	9.6	42	45.8%	.293	1.37	5.03	102	0.4	93.0	46.5%	32.8%	44.7%
2020	LAA	MLB	23	1	5	0	9	6	36^2	37	10	2.9	8.1	33	55.3%	.260	1.34	5.65	88	0.6	93.0	44.6%	27.6%	47.7%
2021	LAA	MLB	24	3	6	1	17	14	87	69	11	3.7	9.7	94	50.7%	.266	1.21	3.62	92	1.2	93.5	43.1%	34.0%	52.1%
2022 DC	*LAA*	*MLB*	*25*	*8*	*6*	*0*	*22*	*22*	*124.7*	*110*	*13*	*3.7*	*10.2*	*141*	*49.0%*	*.302*	*1.30*	*3.50*	*88*	*1.7*	*93.3*	*43.8%*	*32.6%*	*50.4%*

Comparables: Johnny Cueto, Gio González, David Price

Nobody who threw an offering as many times as Sandoval tossed his changeup had a higher per-pitch whiff rate. The lefty generated swings-and-misses on a ludicrous 51.4% of his cambios, which he threw 428 times, the most of any pitch. It's an exceedingly well-worn baseball trope at this point - throw your best pitch more often - so here's another: he's an Angels starter who couldn't stay healthy. A stress reaction in his back curtailed a promising breakout campaign in mid-August. It also robbed us of the chance to see whether Sandoval could genuinely make this work over a larger sample, given his two rather straight, mediocre fastballs that make it difficult for him to totally keep runs off the board. The fewer heaters he can throw and get away with it, the better.

Sam Selman LHP Born: 11/14/90 Age: 31 Bats: R Throws: L Height: 6'2" Weight: 198 lb. Origin: Round 2, 2012 Draft (#66 overall)

YEAR	TEAM	LVL	AGE	W	L	SV	G	GS	IP	H	HR	BB/9	K/9	K	GB%	BABIP	WHIP	ERA	DRA-	WARP	MPH	FB%	Whiff%	CSP
2019	RIC	AA	28	0	0	0	4	0	7	3	0	1.3	16.7	13	50.0%	.273	0.57	0.00	74	0.1				
2019	SAC	AAA	28	3	2	0	39	1	48	25	4	3.0	15.2	81	41.4%	.253	0.85	2.06	60	1.4				
2019	SF	MLB	28	0	0	0	10	0	10^1	6	2	5.2	8.7	10	30.8%	.174	1.16	4.35	102	0.1	90.0	42.5%	31.1%	42.4%
2020	SF	MLB	29	1	1	1	24	0	19^1	13	2	4.2	10.7	23	31.2%	.244	1.14	3.72	92	0.3	91.2	41.0%	29.9%	48.5%
2021	SAC	AAA	30	1	0	1	17	2	22^1	13	0	7.7	9.7	24	25.9%	.241	1.43	4.03	112	-0.1				
2021	LAA	MLB	30	0	1	0	18	0	17	16	1	4.2	5.8	11	25.9%	.283	1.41	6.35	146	-0.3	91.0	58.7%	19.9%	53.1%
2021	SF	MLB	30	0	0	0	7	0	8	4	2	4.5	9.0	8	20.0%	.111	1.00	4.50	106	0.0	91.1	49.7%	21.5%	54.6%
2022 non-DC	*LAA*	*MLB*	*31*	*2*	*3*	*0*	*57*	*0*	*50*	*44*	*8*	*5.1*	*9.1*	*50*	*31.5%*	*.277*	*1.47*	*4.99*	*116*	*-0.3*	*91.0*	*50.1%*	*24.1%*	*51.2%*

Comparables: Sam Freeman, Blaine Hardy, Brandon Workman

It was difficult not to see it as a sign when the Giants moved Selman and his bloated walk rate to Los Angeles for someone who offers the exact opposite, Tony Watson. It would help if Selman was also Watson's opposite in terms of strikeout rate, as he threatened to be at times on his way up through the minors. The control continues to hurt both rates while his slider appeared to lose some of the movement that was generating those much-needed whiffs. Watson proves that one can have a long, successful lefty relief career with a middling strikeout rate. Selman needs to start by halving the walks and putting his low-90s fastball somewhere near its intended target.

José Suarez LHP Born: 01/03/98 Age: 24 Bats: L Throws: L Height: 5'10" Weight: 225 lb. Origin: International Free Agent, 2014

YEAR	TEAM	LVL	AGE	W	L	SV	G	GS	IP	H	HR	BB/9	K/9	K	GB%	BABIP	WHIP	ERA	DRA-	WARP	MPH	FB%	Whiff%	CSP
2019	SL	AAA	21	2	1	0	7	6	32^1	24	3	4.7	8.6	31	44.3%	.247	1.27	3.62	103	0.1				
2019	LAA	MLB	21	2	6	0	19	15	81	100	23	3.7	8.0	72	36.2%	.326	1.64	7.11	140	-0.9	91.8	47.1%	25.3%	47.1%
2020	LAA	MLB	22	0	2	0	2	2	2^1	10	1	19.3	7.7	2	46.7%	.643	6.43	38.57	252	-0.2	93.1	45.5%	32.4%	38.3%
2021	SL	AAA	23	0	0	0	2	2	6	8	0	1.5	6.0	4	50.0%	.364	1.50	1.50	110	0.0				
2021	LAA	MLB	23	8	8	0	23	14	98^1	85	11	3.3	7.8	85	47.6%	.269	1.23	3.75	106	0.6	92.8	47.6%	25.8%	53.3%
2022 DC	*LAA*	*MLB*	*24*	*8*	*8*	*0*	*48*	*19*	*119*	*118*	*15*	*3.8*	*7.8*	*102*	*45.0%*	*.297*	*1.42*	*4.53*	*109*	*0.3*	*92.6*	*47.5%*	*25.9%*	*51.5%*

Comparables: Robbie Erlin, Chris Volstad, Wilson Alvarez

Who had the best changeup in baseball in 2021? An argument can be made for Devin Williams and his ridiculous 'Airbender', of course. Right up there with Williams in terms of run value on the pitch was Suarez, believe it or not. His fairly straight version doesn't even seem like it's from the same game as Williams' GIF-spawning stuff of hitter nightmares. The lefty nonetheless held batters to a .144 average and .205 slugging percentage on the pitch while throwing it almost 30% of the time, utilizing it more often than his four-seam on several occasions. The relative unfamiliarity of Suarez's movement profile appears to elevate the offering, as the change follows almost exactly the same plane as the four-seamer before a late dive down below bats. Sadly, the four-seam itself continues to get lit up, which limits how far the change can take him.

Noah Syndergaard RHP Born: 08/29/92 Age: 29 Bats: L Throws: R Height: 6'6" Weight: 242 lb. Origin: Round 1, 2010 Draft (#38 overall)

YEAR	TEAM	LVL	AGE	W	L	SV	G	GS	IP	H	HR	BB/9	K/9	K	GB%	BABIP	WHIP	ERA	DRA-	WARP	MPH	FB%	Whiff%	CSP
2019	NYM	MLB	26	10	8	0	32	32	197^2	194	24	2.3	9.2	202	47.3%	.315	1.23	4.28	82	4.0	97.9	59.2%	27.0%	49.2%
2021	NYM	MLB	28	0	1	0	2	2	2	3	1	0.0	9.0	2	16.7%	.400	1.50	9.00	145	0.0	94.8	57.7%	21.4%	59.6%
2022 DC	*LAA*	*MLB*	*29*	*9*	*6*	*0*	*24*	*24*	*133.3*	*126*	*14*	*2.4*	*9.1*	*135*	*47.5%*	*.305*	*1.21*	*3.31*	*86*	*2.1*	*97.8*	*59.2%*	*26.9%*	*49.5%*

Comparables: Bret Saberhagen, Carlos Zambrano, Clayton Kershaw

The pair of one-inning starts that Syndergaard got tossed out for in the final week provided the world's saddest encore for Mets fans. Testing his surgically rebuilt right elbow, he threw just fastballs and changeups—the former clocking in at a very human 95 mph, or about 2–3 mph off his usual velocity—and zero breaking balls, per the advice of team doctors. The latter is something that Syndergaard eventually has to reincorporate; he's not the same pitcher without his vicious hard slider. Despite that and his long layoff, the pitching-needy Angels, never ones to be scared off by surgical scars and broken arms, handed him a one-year, $21 million deal to find his footing in southern California, after the equally pitching-needy Mets made him a qualifying offer but seemed to have no interest in anything more. Thus ends the tenure of one of Citi Field's fan favorites after five seasons, an All-Star appearance, a purpose pitch to Alcides Escobar and lots and lots (and *lots*) of tweets. Thor will now join Mike Trout and Shohei Ohtani and try to do something that few Angels pitchers have been able to do: stay healthy and be productive.

Andrew Wantz RHP Born: 10/13/95 Age: 26 Bats: R Throws: R Height: 6'4" Weight: 235 lb. Origin: Round 7, 2018 Draft (#211 overall)

YEAR	TEAM	LVL	AGE	W	L	SV	G	GS	IP	H	HR	BB/9	K/9	K	GB%	BABIP	WHIP	ERA	DRA-	WARP	MPH	FB%	Whiff%	CSP
2019	IE	A+	23	5	3	0	11	6	48	40	4	3.2	10.9	58	34.1%	.300	1.19	3.56	93	0.3				
2019	MOB	AA	23	0	6	0	13	12	48	59	12	4.9	10.1	54	33.8%	.346	1.77	7.13	140	-0.8				
2021	SL	AAA	25	1	0	0	12	5	30^1	22	2	1.8	8.9	30	47.5%	.256	0.92	1.78	94	0.2				
2021	LAA	MLB	25	1	0	0	21	0	27^1	23	5	3.6	12.5	38	29.9%	.290	1.24	4.94	82	0.5	92.5	75.4%	30.3%	53.9%
2022 DC	*LAA*	*MLB*	*26*	*2*	*2*	*0*	*44*	*0*	*38.7*	*34*	*6*	*3.7*	*9.9*	*42*	*36.6%*	*.286*	*1.31*	*4.27*	*104*	*0.1*	*92.5*	*75.4%*	*30.3%*	*53.9%*

Comparables: Austin Brice, Ryne Stanek, J.J. Hoover

Tom Waits. Jeremy Irons. Andrew Wantz...a regular spot on the Angels' staff, we expect. He might have just done enough to get there, if one looks past his elevated ERA to an impressive strikeout rate and a four-pitch mix that played well in the bigs when he was able to locate his fastballs up in the zone. For a player who never got any real consideration as a prospect, it was an impressive debut. The stuff doesn't look remarkable in itself, but Wantz distinguishes himself on the mound with a big, swinging, Rich Hill-esque kick to finish his delivery. While the seventh-rounder thus made an impression, he will certainly want more than simply outperforming his draft slot.

Austin Warren RHP Born: 02/05/96 Age: 26 Bats: R Throws: R Height: 6'0" Weight: 170 lb. Origin: Round 6, 2018 Draft (#181 overall)

YEAR	TEAM	LVL	AGE	W	L	SV	G	GS	IP	H	HR	BB/9	K/9	K	GB%	BABIP	WHIP	ERA	DRA-	WARP	MPH	FB%	Whiff%	CSP
2019	IE	A+	23	2	7	2	27	0	43^2	39	5	4.3	13.0	63	49.0%	.362	1.37	3.30	71	0.9				
2019	MOB	AA	23	1	2	0	9	0	14	12	0	5.8	9.0	14	57.1%	.293	1.50	2.57	95	0.1				
2021	SL	AAA	25	2	3	1	22	1	36^1	42	5	4.5	11.1	45	49.5%	.385	1.65	6.19	81	0.6				
2021	LAA	MLB	25	3	0	1	16	0	20^1	16	0	2.2	8.9	20	53.4%	.276	1.03	1.77	97	0.2	93.9	57.2%	28.1%	53.4%
2022 DC	*LAA*	*MLB*	*26*	*3*	*3*	*2*	*74*	*0*	*64.7*	*63*	*8*	*4.0*	*9.1*	*65*	*48.3%*	*.308*	*1.43*	*4.44*	*107*	*0.0*	*93.9*	*57.2%*	*28.1%*	*53.4%*

Comparables: Paul Fry, Chad Sobotka, David McKay

Warren completed his debut with the fourth-best ERA among rookies who pitched at least 20 innings and a batting line against his four-seam that suggested one of the most unhittable fastballs in the majors. A case of COVID-19 prevented him from increasing that sample and likely revealing that those numbers were a mirage. Warren doesn't have to be a top-five reliever in baseball to be a solid member of the Angels 'pen for the foreseeable future, but we can pretend that he is for at least a little while longer.

Lineouts

Hitters

HITTER	POS	TEAM	LVL	AGE	PA	R	2B	3B	HR	RBI	BB	K	SB	CS	AVG/OBP/SLG	DRC+	BABIP	BRR	FRAA	WARP
Brendon Davis	IF	TRI	A+	23	282	41	17	3	14	40	19	75	9	3	.280/.337/.535	117	.337	1.6	3B(41): -1.2, SS(10): -0.1, 2B(8): 0.3	1.4
	IF	RCT	AA	23	131	25	4	1	8	18	18	34	4	0	.268/.366/.536	111	.310	-0.4	2B(9): 0.0, 3B(9): -1.1, SS(7): 0.4	0.6
	IF	SL	AAA	23	133	25	8	2	8	25	10	28	3	1	.333/.409/.641	121	.383	0.3	SS(20): -0.3, LF(8): -1.3, 3B(3): 0.5	0.7
Denzer Guzman	SS	DSL ANG	ROK	17	164	21	10	1	3	27	20	24	11	7	.213/.311/.362		.233			
Jon Jay	OF	SL	AAA	36	73	16	4	0	1	5	2	9	2	0	.362/.384/.464	105	.400	-1.3	LF(7): -0.6, CF(5): 1.4, 1B(3): -0.3	0.1
	OF	LAA	MLB	36	14	2	0	0	0	1	0	2	0	0	.357/.357/.357	86	.417	0.1		0.0
D'Shawn Knowles	CF	IE	A	20	393	61	21	5	5	48	25	114	31	1	.227/.280/.355	76	.317	2.3	CF(62): 2.2, SS(8): -0.7, LF(3): -0.6	0.6
Orlando Martinez	OF	GDD	WIN	23	81	5	2	2	1	4	2	14	0	1	.215/.235/.329		.250			
	OF	RCT	AA	23	436	58	23	2	16	54	30	119	5	3	.258/.313/.445	94	.326	0.1	LF(57): -2.3, CF(28): -3.3, RF(15): -0.4	0.4
Kyren Paris	MI	IE	A	19	136	29	5	6	2	18	27	41	16	4	.274/.434/.491	98	.429	0.7	SS(17): 2.9, 2B(11): 1.2	0.8
	MI	TRI	A+	19	55	6	2	1	1	6	2	20	4	0	.231/.273/.365	88	.355	-0.1	SS(9): 0.6, 2B(2): -0.0	0.1
Adrian Placencia	MI	ANG	ROK	18	175	29	3	3	5	19	28	49	4	2	.175/.326/.343		.225			
Alexander Ramirez	OF	ANG	ROK	18	154	30	7	4	5	27	22	50	3	3	.276/.396/.512		.411			
	OF	IE	A	18	81	4	0	1	0	4	7	34	1	1	.083/.185/.111	60	.158	0.7	RF(6): -0.6, LF(3): -0.7	-0.2
Scott Schebler	RF	SL	AAA	30	285	31	14	0	11	40	17	86	3	1	.216/.295/.400	79	.277	0.4	RF(38): -4.0, CF(17): -1.7, LF(8): -0.7	-0.4
	RF	LAA	MLB	30	34	3	3	0	0	0	0	17	0	0	.147/.147/.235	49	.294	0.4	CF(4): -0.0, RF(4): 0.3, LF(3): -0.4	-0.1
Livan Soto	SS	TRI	A+	21	406	49	14	8	7	36	39	99	14	5	.217/.293/.358	91	.274	-0.9	SS(69): -7.0, 2B(14): -2.7	-0.2
	SS	RCT	AA	21	44	3	1	0	0	4	3	11	0	0	.225/.295/.250	80	.310	0.1	SS(10): 2.0, 2B(2): 0.1	0.2
Michael Stefanic	2B/3B	RCT	AA	25	96	11	5	0	1	9	7	15	0	2	.345/.406/.437	116	.408	-0.3	2B(15): 2.5, 3B(4): -0.5, SS(1): -0.4	0.6
	2B/3B	SL	AAA	25	458	67	21	0	16	54	45	62	6	3	.334/.408/.505	126	.363	0.6	2B(72): -3.4, 3B(20): 1.8, SS(5): -0.3	2.8
Andrew Velazquez	IF	SWB	AAA	26	306	40	20	3	7	46	37	87	29	3	.273/.362/.451	89	.378	0.8	SS(42): -5.9, 2B(24): 1.6, 3B(10): -1.4	0.1
	IF	NYY	MLB	26	68	11	4	1	1	6	1	23	4	1	.224/.235/.358	71	.326	1.1	SS(28): -0.6	0.0
Arol Vera	SS	ANG	ROK	18	164	24	16	3	0	17	12	39	2	2	.317/.384/.469		.426			
	SS	IE	A	18	90	10	0	0	0	5	6	20	9	2	.280/.344/.280	100	.371	0.2	SS(12): 1.0, 2B(7): 0.3	0.4
Chad Wallach	C	SL	AAA	29	171	30	7	0	8	22	20	45	0	0	.223/.322/.432	97	.260	1.0	C(15): 1.8, 1B(1): -0.5	0.7
	C	JAX	AAA	29	130	11	2	0	7	17	23	35	0	0	.204/.369/.427	121	.230	-1.9	C(24): -0.2	0.6
	C	MIA	MLB	29	66	2	2	1	0	6	3	32	0	0	.200/.242/.267	42	.400	-1.2	C(19): -0.2	-0.4
Kean Wong	UT	SL	AAA	26	203	31	10	2	4	22	14	32	10	3	.339/.384/.476	107	.392	1.6	2B(25): -3.6, 3B(12): 0.3, LF(9): -0.8	0.6
	UT	LAA	MLB	26	66	3	2	1	0	6	2	17	0	1	.167/.194/.233	68	.233	-0.9	2B(10): 0.3, 3B(6): -0.3, LF(4): 0.0	-0.1

If **Franklin Barreto** thought a change of scenery and his out-of-options status would allow him to garner the kind of playing time that never materialized in Oakland, his UCL had other ideas. He started the year on the 60-day IL with elbow inflammation and had Tommy John surgery in May. ⚾ One-third of the Rangers' return for Yu Darvish, **Brendon Davis** was selected by the Angels in the minor-league phase of the Rule 5 draft and hit his way through three levels, all the way to the 40-man roster. ⚾ The Angels believed in **Denzer Guzman**'s hit tool enough to make him their top international signing at $2 million, one of four seven-figure deals they handed out. His smooth, minimalistic swing should lead to a far better average than he produced in the DSL. ⚾ Rather than showing what he could do on both sides of the ball, two-way prospect **William Holmes** barely made an appearance. He remains a tremendous athletic talent, but he's yet to reach even A-ball over three years after being drafted. ⚾ **Jon Jay** found his way onto a major-league field for the 12th consecutive season. It might be his last appearance both there and in this book, since he received almost as many at-bats DHing for the U.S. national side in the Olympic qualifiers. ⚾ While the pickoff limitations placed on the lower minors mean any stolen base stats should be served with an unhealthy coating of salt, **D'Shawn Knowles**' 31-for-32 record highlighted his potent speed. Now the bat just needs to catch up. ⚾ Left unprotected and subsequently undrafted in the 2020 Rule 5 draft, **Orlando Martinez** didn't particularly prove the Angels or the other 29 teams wrong. It's not that he failed, more that his moderate performance at Double-A reinforced the notion that he's a fourth outfielder who was not yet worth a 40-man spot and remains unlikely to make a significant impact. ⚾ Secrets may travel fast in Paris, but it's not much of a secret how fast **Kyren Paris** travels. While injuries continue to interrupt his development, his speed and glovework will keep him moving up the levels even if the homers never materialize. ⚾ **Adrian Placencia** doesn't look like he'll hit for much power, and even at 18 he's not an impressive runner. But he's a switch-hitter with great bat control and pitch recognition beyond his years—scarce qualities in contemporary baseball. He has a real shot at an everyday role down the line. ⚾ Power this raw should come with a warning about foodborne illness. **Alexander Ramirez** showcased his prodigious thump in the ACL before a transition to A-ball siphoned off the homers, leaving the pure unadulterated whiffs behind. ⚾ **Scott Schebler** once again performed much better against righties than lefties. That's not so much clearing a low bar as it is stepping over one after it has been knocked to the floor. ⚾ Despite his continued struggles to bring his bat up to the level of his glove, the Angels nonetheless promoted **Livan Soto** to Double-A in late August. The results didn't change. ⚾ After he went undrafted in 2018, **Michael Stefanic** made one final play for a pro career: a home-made highlights video that he sent to all 30 teams. Several seasons of relentless hitting later, sustained through the minor-league levels, he has a chance at creating some highlights without having to compile them himself. ⚾ Like that first night in a real bed after a weeklong camping trip, **Andrew Velazquez** took over shortstop after months of The Gleyber Torres Experience and won the heart of a city with his competence. The Angels claimed the speedy shortstop in their first move of the offseason, setting him up for an epic spring training battle with Jack Mayfield and Gary DiSarcina for the utility infielder job. ⚾ It doesn't appear as though the Angels will be burned by their $2 million investment in **Arol Vera** in 2020 on the basis of his first professional showing. But he has a dash of the imbalance common to prospects; the offensive performance following promotion suggests his glove will need to ease the pressure on his bat. ⚾ **Chad Wallach** couldn't build on his status as the Marlins' 2020 playoff catcher, whiffing in almost half of his rare trips to the plate before losing his roster spot. He still set a new regular-season high in games played and plate appearances, a telltale sign that he's been walking the third catcher tightrope for a half-decade. ⚾ Triple-A pitchers are probably sick of **Kean Wong**, who will be hitting .400 at the level in a couple of years based on current progress. They won't be rid of him any time soon, since MLB hurlers are all too pleased to see him step to the plate.

Pitchers

PITCHER	TEAM	LVL	AGE	W	L	SV	G	GS	IP	H	HR	BB/9	K/9	K	GB%	BABIP	WHIP	ERA	DRA-	WARP	MPH	FB%	WHF	CSP
Ky Bush	TRI	A+	21	0	2	0	5	5	12	14	0	3.8	15.0	20	46.4%	.500	1.58	4.50	103	0.1				
Cooper Criswell	RCT	AA	24	6	4	0	12	12	70^{1}	68	9	1.0	10.9	85	48.5%	.319	1.08	3.71	89	1.1				
	SL	AAA	24	3	5	0	9	9	47	57	8	2.3	8.2	43	40.8%	.353	1.47	6.51	115	-0.2				
	LAA	MLB	24	0	1	0	1	1	1^{1}	6	0	0.0	0.0	0	60.0%	.600	4.50	20.25	114	0.0	87.3	48.8%	0.0%	53.3%
Davis Daniel	TRI	A+	24	3	2	0	9	9	46^{2}	26	4	3.9	12.3	64	40.2%	.237	0.99	2.31	93	0.5				
	RCT	AA	24	1	3	0	9	9	47	39	4	1.5	12.6	66	34.5%	.324	1.00	2.68	83	0.9				
	SL	AAA	24	0	2	0	5	4	21	37	7	2.6	10.3	24	27.0%	.448	2.05	10.29	124	-0.2				
Alejandro Hidalgo	ANG	ROK	18	3	2	0	7	6	27	26	6	3.0	10.3	31	29.9%	.282	1.30	4.67						
Janson Junk	SOM	AA	25	4	1	1	14	12	65^{2}	43	6	2.7	9.3	68	43.6%	.233	0.96	1.78	99	0.6				
	RCT	AA	25	2	2	0	5	5	27^{1}	32	5	2.3	9.5	29	43.5%	.338	1.43	5.27	100	0.3				
	LAA	MLB	25	0	1	0	4	4	16^{1}	20	5	1.1	5.5	10	37.3%	.283	1.35	3.86	124	-0.1	92.5	51.8%	17.9%	57.7%
Brett Kerry	IE	A	22	0	0	0	4	4	9^{1}	6	0	3.9	16.4	17	43.8%	.375	1.07	1.93	89	0.1				
Jack Kochanowicz	IE	A	20	4	2	0	20	18	83^{1}	102	12	3.8	7.9	73	48.4%	.345	1.64	6.91	128	-0.9				
Jose Marte	EUG	A+	25	0	0	3	5	0	6^{1}	3	0	0.0	19.9	14	77.8%	.333	0.47	0.00	72	0.1				
	RIC	AA	25	2	0	1	19	0	22^{2}	21	0	6.0	14.3	36	56.0%	.420	1.59	3.57	78	0.4				
	SL	AAA	25	1	2	0	7	0	7^{1}	10	0	6.1	8.6	7	68.0%	.417	2.05	8.59	85	0.1				
	LAA	MLB	25	0	1	0	4	0	4	4	1	6.8	11.3	5	50.0%	.333	1.75	9.00	107	0.0	96.6	59.5%	12.9%	52.1%
Luke Murphy	TRI	A+	21	0	1	2	7	0	9	7	0	1.0	15.0	15	52.6%	.368	0.89	3.00	85	0.1				
Oliver Ortega	RCT	AA	24	2	3	5	25	0	30^{2}	33	3	3.8	13.5	46	46.8%	.400	1.50	6.16	82	0.6				
	SL	AAA	24	0	0	0	9	0	12	11	2	3.8	11.3	15	44.1%	.281	1.33	3.75	88	0.1				
	LAA	MLB	24	1	0	0	8	0	9^{1}	12	1	1.9	3.9	4	75.0%	.355	1.50	4.82	114	0.0	96.6	55.4%	7.0%	60.6%
Elvis Peguero	HV	A+	24	3	1	2	15	0	32^{1}	22	2	3.1	11.1	40	53.8%	.260	1.02	2.51	83	0.6				
	RCT	AA	24	1	1	0	4	0	5^{1}	7	2	1.7	13.5	8	66.7%	.385	1.50	8.44	79	0.1				
	SOM	AA	24	1	0	0	6	0	12	6	1	3.8	12.8	17	53.8%	.200	0.92	1.50	89	0.2				
	SL	AAA	24	0	0	0	6	0	8	9	0	2.3	7.9	7	60.0%	.360	1.38	6.75	84	0.1				
	LAA	MLB	24	0	1	0	3	0	2^{1}	7	0	11.6	0.0	0	38.5%	.538	4.29	27.00	143	0.0	96.2	68.8%	3.8%	55.0%
Jake Petricka	SL	AAA	33	6	2	1	23	0	36	41	5	3.0	8.5	34	60.0%	.343	1.47	4.25	90	0.4				
	LAA	MLB	33	0	1	0	7	0	6	6	1	10.5	12.0	8	56.2%	.333	2.17	15.00	105	0.0	93.4	52.6%	30.2%	47.7%
Ben Rowen	SL	AAA	32	1	2	0	21	0	30^{1}	34	3	2.4	5.3	18	36.9%	.313	1.38	6.82	123	-0.3				
	LAA	MLB	32	0	0	0	8	0	11^{1}	12	3	1.6	6.4	8	37.8%	.265	1.24	5.56	115	0.0	79.8	48.5%	13.6%	59.4%
Kyle Tyler	RCT	AA	24	5	2	1	15	12	72	64	8	2.8	9.1	73	44.6%	.289	1.19	3.38	112	0.3				
	SL	AAA	24	1	2	0	5	2	14	20	1	1.9	12.2	19	48.8%	.475	1.64	5.14	79	0.2				
	LAA	MLB	24	0	0	0	5	0	12^{1}	8	1	4.4	4.4	6	39.5%	.189	1.14	2.92	125	-0.1	91.1	62.6%	12.2%	54.9%
Hector Yan	TRI	A+	22	3	7	0	20	16	82^{1}	69	15	6.3	10.3	94	37.3%	.271	1.54	5.25	112	0.1				

It's supposed to be your 30s when everything starts to hurt, but **Luke Bard** always had a significant headstart. The big 3-0 brought another unwelcome present, a troublesome hip that was surgically resurfaced, costing him the entire year. ⚾ A huge lefty with a mid-90s heater, college strikeout merchant **Ky Bush** also offers a steeply-angled slider from his lofty release point. Early returns suggest he can put the kibosh on pro hitters too, but a deeper repertoire and improved command will be needed higher up the ladder. ⚾ **Cooper Criswell**'s sweeping slider didn't translate to success at either Triple-A or the majors, failing to draw a single swing-and-miss from the 10 batters he faced in his major-league debut. ⚾ Is **Davis Daniel** pitching backwards? Whether starting or ending at-bats with his plus curveball, the Auburn product made up for lost time after getting an extra year to recover from Tommy John surgery, pitching himself to the brink of the majors with the combo of his four-seamer and that curve. ⚾ **Alejandro Hidalgo** is a Venezuelan filmmaker best-known for his horror movie *La Casa del Fin de los Tiempos*. His baseball counterpart is a teenage righty with a sufficiently advanced portfolio to suggest he may win a supporting role in the Angels' efforts to assemble a pitching cast that doesn't echo his namesake's productions. ⚾ Rather than showing what he could do on both sides of the ball, two-way prospect **William Holmes** barely made an appearance. He remains a tremendous athletic talent, but he's yet to reach even A-ball over three years after being drafted. ⚾ **Janson Junk** throws too hard and uses his heater too often for the obvious tag to be applied to his pitching style. Given what major-league hitters did to his low-90s fastball compared to his knee-buckling sweeping slider, however, a little nominative determinism might be in order. ⚾ Although he spent most of his time at South Carolina as a reliever, **Brett Kerry** was in the Double-A rotation before the season finished. That was partly a reflection on the shallow organizational depth that led Los Angeles to pursue an all-pitcher draft strategy, but it was also an endorsement of Kerry's impressive transition to pro ball. ⚾ **Jack Kochanowicz** looks the part of workhorse starter: Standing 6-foot-6 with a big looping curveball, he doesn't have much room for physical growth, but a rough pro debut indicates there's plenty needed on the mound. ⚾ **Landon Marceaux** is not, in fact, a wealthy aristocrat from an Hercule Poirot case; he's a high-pitchability righty from LSU. His stuff lacks the obvious upside of many of his draft class peers but, mon ami, is it not the little grey cells on which one must rely, if one wants to outwit the opponent? ⚾ It's impressive to hear that **Jose Marte** has a 99-mph power sinker. But across the major leagues, 50 pitchers threw at least one sinker at 99 or harder, and most of them have a better idea of where it's heading. ⚾ One half of a dominant Vanderbilt closing tandem, **Luke Murphy** is definitely a reliever. The lanky right-hander looks to have the weapons to be a late-inning option at that, chief among them a heater that can touch 99 and blow past hitters up in the zone. ⚾ The Angels didn't use **Oliver Ortega** as a starter in 2021, weaponizing his high-90s gas and promising curve out of the bullpen to move him quickly to the majors. His cup of coffee demonstrated another reason why that move might have been made, as his wavering control didn't let either pitch play well. ⚾ When he was in the Yankees system, **Elvis Peguero** and his power sinker-slider combo were too much for hitters. The Angels promoted him quickly to the majors, where he got all shook up by competition that had no problem handling his mid-90s heat. ⚾ Results be damned, **Jake Petricka** can say he had a season like no-one else - perhaps in all of baseball history. He pitched for the Faribault Lakers of the Minnesota Baseball Association, closed out a game in the Atlantic League and returned to the majors, all in a span of four months. ⚾ Acquired from the Padres for Jason Castro, **Gerardo Reyes** never threw a pitch for the Angels before he tore his UCL in the spring. A side-arming flamethrower, he'll need to work hard to not only shake off the TJ rust but improve his command from his debut. ⚾ In one final effort to get back to the bigs, **Ben Rowen** added a bizarre wrinkle to his submarine repertoire, incorporating an overhand four-seam that he released about four feet higher than his other offerings. Other than helping him to throw 88 rather than 78, it didn't improve his results—but he did get back to the majors. ⚾ There's so much apparent rise on **Kyle Tyler**'s gravity-defying fastball that an irresponsible billionaire will soon attempt to use it to power a recreational spaceflight. While opponents failed to record a single hit on the pitch across his entire debut, he was brought back down to earth by their treatment of his slider. ⚾ One of the most inconsistent pitchers in pro ball, **Hector Yan** underscored that point by pitching a complete game gem, then not recording a single out in his next start. His wild cross-body delivery makes hitters' lives almost as difficult as his own.

OAKLAND ATHLETICS

Essay by Alex Coffey

Player comments by Jon Tayler and BP staff

In 1967, Oakland was home to four professional sports teams. When the A's arrived in 1968, they became the fifth, giving the city twice as many teams as its counterpart across the Bay, and more than any other city in America outside of New York and Chicago. It was a golden age of sports for a city lodged in the shadow of San Francisco, but it dissipated as quickly as it had arrived. The Oakland Oaks of the ABA were the first to go, moving to Washington, DC, in 1969. The Oakland Clippers, a pro-soccer team, dissolved later that year. In 1978, the Oakland Seals decided to play hockey in Cleveland, instead. In 2014, the NBA's Warriors, who had been playing their home games in Oakland, departed for The City. And who can forget the Raiders, who left for Los Angeles in 1981, returned in 1995, and left again, for Las Vegas, in 2019.

Today, the lone remnant of that era is the A's, who, in recent months, might have inflicted more emotional damage on the Oakland fanbase than any of the franchises that once deserted them. The A's are not their city's last professional franchise by choice. They've tried to leave a number of times, unsuccessfully, which is part of what makes their tenure so particularly painful. The Raiders were public about their desire to go, but acted on it, twice. The A's have chosen to threaten relocation as a way of leveraging Oakland into a new ballpark, a strategy that only works if you have a viable plan for the ballpark itself, something the team has yet to provide. Over the past 15 years, the A's have explored six ballpark sites. Not one has produced a shovel in the ground.

Their current quest is different. Unlike some of the other proposals—three of which weren't in Oakland—the A's desire to build at Howard Terminal was framed as a desire to stay. Ahead of their announcement to build there, the A's began a marketing campaign called "Rooted in Oakland." On TV screens across the Bay Area, fans saw players like Marcus Semien and Sean Manaea lauding their city, reassuring fans that they weren't going anywhere. There were Rooted in Oakland billboards above the city's buildings, and Rooted in Oakland light pole banners along its streets.

The messaging was omnipresent and achieved its desired effect. Fans weren't just rooting for the team; they were also rooting for Howard Terminal. All of a sudden, they became invested in seeing owner John Fisher's gargantuan

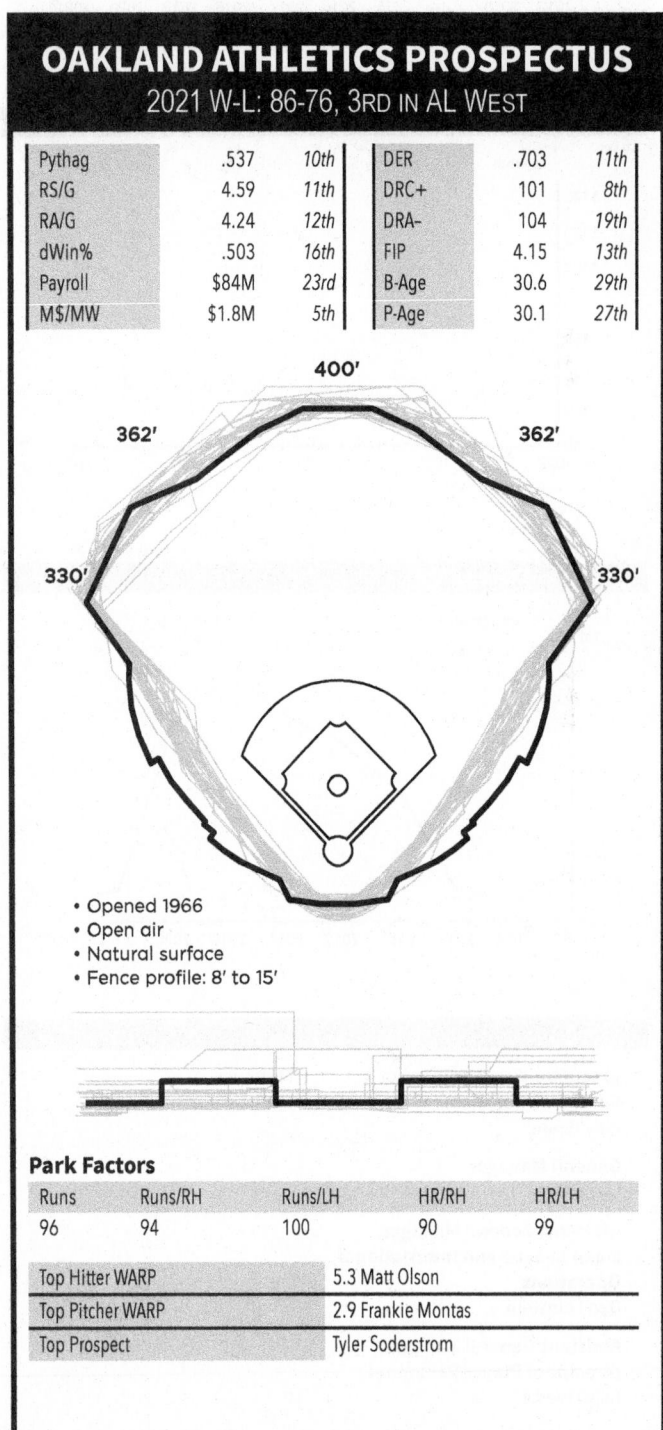

OAKLAND ATHLETICS PROSPECTUS

2021 W-L: 86-76, 3RD IN AL WEST

Pythag	.537	*10th*	DER	.703	*11th*
RS/G	4.59	*11th*	DRC+	101	*8th*
RA/G	4.24	*12th*	DRA-	104	*19th*
dWin%	.503	*16th*	FIP	4.15	*13th*
Payroll	$84M	*23rd*	B-Age	30.6	*29th*
M$/MW	$1.8M	*5th*	P-Age	30.1	*27th*

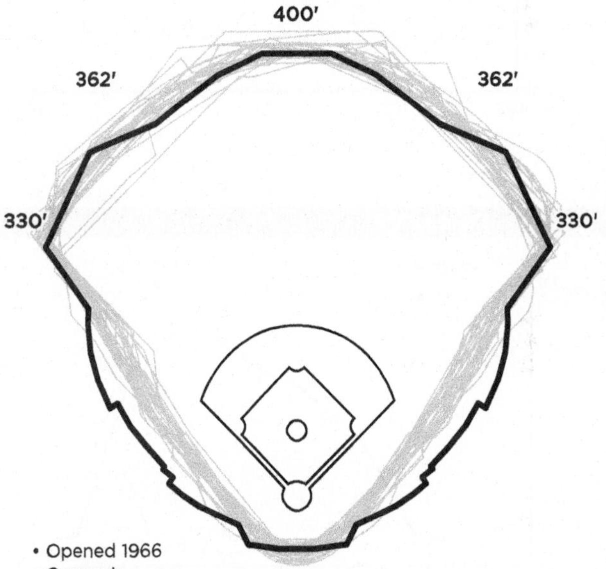

- Opened 1966
- Open air
- Natural surface
- Fence profile: 8' to 15'

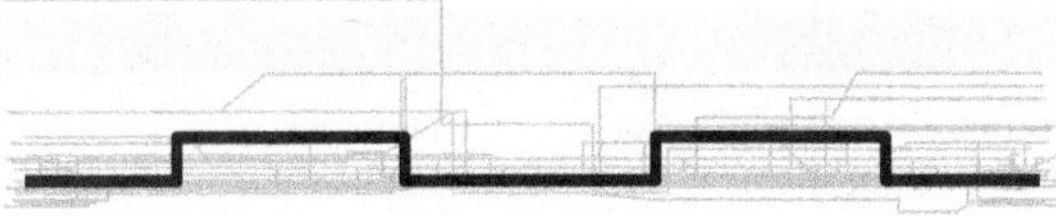

Park Factors

Runs	Runs/RH	Runs/LH	HR/RH	HR/LH
96	94	100	90	99

Top Hitter WARP	5.3 Matt Olson
Top Pitcher WARP	2.9 Frankie Montas
Top Prospect	Tyler Soderstrom

Payroll History (in millions)

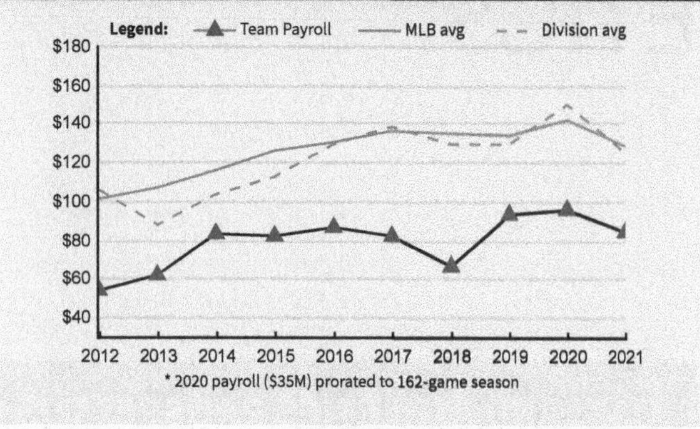

Future Commitments (in millions)

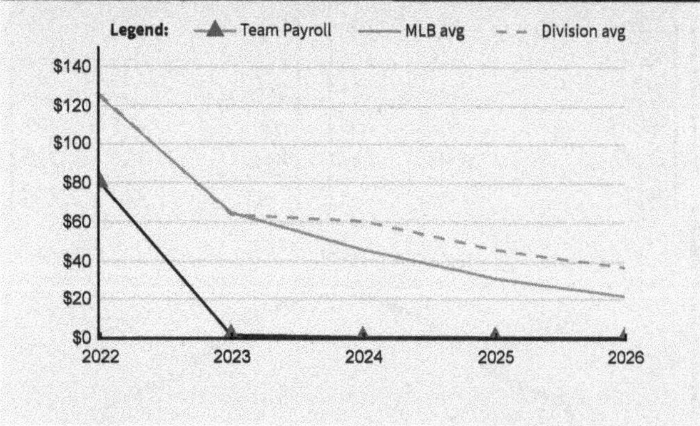

Farm System Ranking

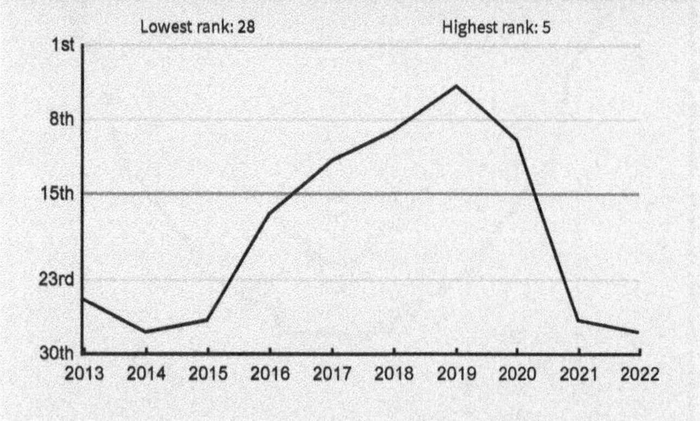

Personnel

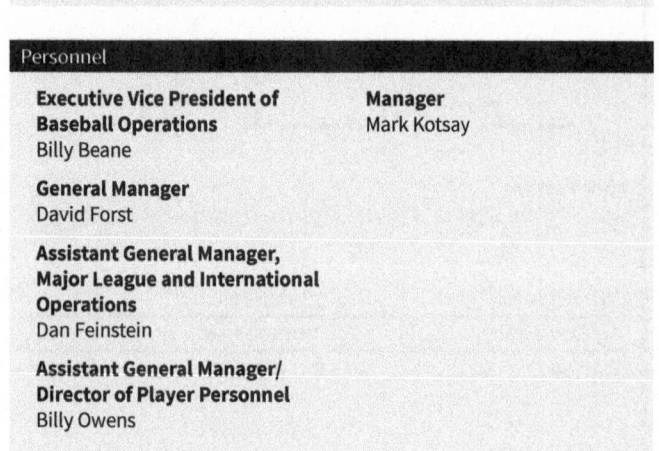

Executive Vice President of Baseball Operations
Billy Beane

General Manager
David Forst

Assistant General Manager, Major League and International Operations
Dan Feinstein

Assistant General Manager/ Director of Player Personnel
Billy Owens

Manager
Mark Kotsay

development project through—despite the fact that his proposal included a number of other non-ballpark-related buildings, including luxury housing, commercial office space, affordable housing and more. After the A's released their term sheet for the Howard Terminal project in April of 2021, fans took to Twitter, badgering any city council members demonstrating concerns in the same way they would badger fans of a rival team. Carroll Fife, who represents Oakland's District 3, called their strong response a "bully tactic."

This was an ironic sequence of events given the financial implications that the project would have on Oakland's taxpayers. The A's original proposal included $855 million in tax revenue and a non-relocation agreement that only spanned 10 years, a much shorter commitment compared to comparable projects. Under those terms, was entirely possible that the cycle would just begin again a decade later, as Oakland's residents continued to pay the price.

"I don't think any of us want to see taxpayers on the hook for decades to pay for the infrastructure that will support this ballpark," city council president Nikki Fortunato Bas told me in May. "It has to pencil out, and it has to be a good deal for taxpayers."

It was around this time that team president Dave Kaval began posting videos and photos from his trips to Las Vegas, which the A's have been considering as a potential landing spot if the Howard Terminal project doesn't come to fruition. One tweet that particularly seemed to ignite the masses was a video that Kaval shot from a packed Vegas Golden Knights NHL playoff game, which happened to coincide with the A's-Mariners game that night back in Oakland.

That was the point that many fans realized that Rooted in Oakland was never about staying in Oakland. It was about staying in Oakland on the team's terms. The A's could stay in Oakland, but only if Oakland bent to their will. Only if the city said yes to a project that, in the eyes of many concerned citizens, didn't benefit the city itself.

What made things worse was that it didn't have to be this way, and most of the team's fans knew it. The A's could have easily rebuilt at the Oakland Coliseum site. The result would have been perfectly acceptable purely from a sporting perspective. But it wouldn't bring the glamour and revenue that a waterfront development project would.

Undeterred by the backlash he faced from his Golden Knights photo opportunity, Kaval has continued to tweet his way through the team's numerous site visits to Las Vegas. On November 5, the team sent out a survey to its fanbase with the header "Let's Go Oakland," asking them to help the A's "determine demand for a new ballpark in Las Vegas."

The dual processes—which, one could argue, were insulting to both Las Vegas fans and Oakland fans—became so brazen that even Steve Sisolak, the governor of Nevada, told ESPN radio that he felt the A's were using his state as a "stalking horse" against Oakland.

It's impossible to measure how much of an impact all of this had on the on-field team, but it certainly had some effect. After an abysmal 0-6 start to the season, the A's climbed back into first place, only to slip again in the second half, missing a playoff appearance for the first time in the past four years. As news of a potential relocation leaked out, players and coaches were asked about it and appeared understandably uncomfortable. Who were they supposed to be playing for? Oakland? Las Vegas? The A's had once brought pride to the East Bay: the "Mustache Gang" of the 1970s, the "Bash Brothers" of the 1980s, the "Big Three" teams of the early 2000s. Those teams were different, but endearingly so. More recently, the A's have become better known for trading stars like Matt Holliday, Yoenis Céspedes and Josh Donaldson before they could walk, and the constant roster shuffle eroded that love.

Home attendance plummeted to 700,000 for the 2021 season, a sharp decrease from the 1.6 million fans the team had drawn to the Coliseum in 2019. Of course, that figure should be looked at in the context of the pandemic—the A's began the season with limited capacity seating—but it still ranked 29th out of baseball's 30 teams by season's end.

The 2021 offseason has brought only more heartache. It was reported by *The Athletic*, before the transaction freeze, that the A's were "likely to trade almost every player with value on their roster"—which would presumably include homegrown fan favorites Matt Olson, Matt Chapman, Sean Manaea and more—in an attempt to reduce their payroll to $40 million. Despite being under contract for 2022, manager Bob Melvin was allowed to leave to sign a three-year deal with the San Diego Padres in late October. That the A's let Melvin walk after he led them to six playoff appearances was perhaps the biggest blow of all. Until that day, Melvin was the longest-tenured manager in MLB and the longest-serving for the Athletics since Connie Mack. He held the clubhouse culture intact throughout all the free-agent departures and transactions over his 10 seasons in Oakland. Now, the A's are rudderless, a team without an identity.

And yet, the diehard fans remain, the ones who bang drums in the right-field stands and create banners from scratch for nearly every new player (of which there are many) and hang them from the bleachers. Seth Brown, a power-hitting outfielder, joined the A's in August of 2019 and quickly got off to a hot start, slashing .440/.462/.560 over six games that month. He remembers stretching one day as a "What Can Brown Do For You" banner unfurled before his eyes.

Brown was so moved by the gesture that he tracked down the fan behind it, Bryan Johansen, just to shake his hand.

This loyalty does not extend into the owner's box. For a while, the A's identity seemed to align with the fanbase and the Coliseum itself, sharing that Oakland spirit of the plucky underdog. But for the same reasons that team ownership has turned away from its old home, it has rejected the fanbase that has embraced those teams, in search of something sleeker. Rather than rewarding those who show up, the team threatens to leave and nearly double season ticket prices as it seeks what the market will bear.

Fisher has long said, through team officials, that he will not expand team payroll until there are "shovels in the ground." This could mean the sand of Las Vegas, the silts of Oakland, or soil somewhere else entirely. The insinuation is that the fanbase doesn't matter. Investing in the organization, and by extension, the city, doesn't matter. The real estate deal, wherever it happens, is what matters.

And that is the saddest part. There was a time, back when Oakland was flush with sports teams, back when their players had names like "Catfish" and "Blue Moon," back when Mark McGwire and Jose Canseco bashed baseballs and forearms, when the A's really did want to be there. Now, they seem indifferent at best, and the few fans who remain are being held hostage by a real estate deal. It's one thing to mourn a team that leaves. It's another to root for a team that wants to leave, but can't. The A's need Oakland more than Oakland needs the A's. It's time for the city, and its fans, to take their power back.

—Alex Coffey is a Phillies beat writer for The Philadelphia Inquirer.

HITTERS

Austin Allen C
Born: 01/16/94 Age: 28 Bats: L Throws: R Height: 6'2" Weight: 219 lb. Origin: Round 4, 2015 Draft (#117 overall)

YEAR	TEAM	LVL	AGE	PA	R	2B	3B	HR	RBI	BB	K	SB	CS	Whiff%	AVG/OBP/SLG	DRC+	BABIP	BRR	FRAA	WARP
2019	ELP	AAA	25	298	52	27	0	21	67	22	56	0	0		.330/.379/.663	121	.345	-3.0	C(61): 7.8, 1B(2): -0.1	2.6
2019	SD	MLB	25	71	4	4	0	0	3	6	21	0	0	30.0%	.215/.282/.277	71	.318	0.2	C(19): 0.3, 1B(2): 0.1	0.1
2020	OAK	MLB	26	32	1	1	0	1	3	1	14	0	0	36.9%	.194/.219/.323	67	.313	-0.4	C(14): 0.6	0.0
2021	LV	AAA	27	299	50	15	0	20	53	13	55	0	0		.317/.351/.584	116	.332	-0.9	C(46): 7.0, 1B(1): -0.3	2.2
2021	OAK	MLB	27	8	2	0	0	1	1	0	3	0	0	44.4%	.250/.250/.625	92	.250		C(2): 0.1	0.0
2022 DC	*OAK*	*MLB*	*28*	*211*	*28*	*9*	*0*	*8*	*37*	*11*	*53*	*0*	*0*	*28.3%*	*.252/.299/.428*	*90*	*.306*	*-0.4*	*C 2*	*0.9*

Comparables: Michael McKenry, Steve Clevenger, Bruce Maxwell

YEAR	TEAM	P. COUNT	FRM RUNS	BLK RUNS	THRW RUNS	TOT RUNS
2019	SD	2293	0.0	0.0	0.0	0.1
2019	ELP	9133	6.0	0.0	0.0	6.0
2020	OAK	1309	0.5	0.0	0.0	0.6
2021	OAK	255	0.0	0.0	0.0	0.0
2021	LV	6558	4.9	0.1	0.0	5.0
2022	*OAK*	*8418*	*-0.8*	*-0.1*	*0.0*	*-0.9*

What enthusiasm or appetite the A's had for making Allen a regular part of their plans seems to have disappeared, as he spent almost the entire season swatting home runs in the thin air of Triple-A Las Vegas. That he remained stuck there despite Sean Murphy's struggles at the plate is a bad sign for him working his way back into Oakland's future. Murphy doesn't need a defensive caddy either, seeing as how he's the reigning Gold Glove winner at the position, though it's not as if Allen would be the best fit for the role of glove-first backup anyway. A move off the position is probably in Allen's best interest at this point; a move out of the Bay Area likely would be, too.

Nick Allen MI
Born: 10/08/98 Age: 23 Bats: R Throws: R Height: 5'8" Weight: 166 lb. Origin: Round 3, 2017 Draft (#81 overall)

YEAR	TEAM	LVL	AGE	PA	R	2B	3B	HR	RBI	BB	K	SB	CS	Whiff%	AVG/OBP/SLG	DRC+	BABIP	BRR	FRAA	WARP
2019	MSS	WIN	20	66	4	1	0	0	6	4	18	0	1		.194/.242/.210		.273			
2019	STK	A+	20	328	45	22	5	3	25	28	52	13	5		.292/.363/.434	114	.348	-3.0	SS(45): 5.2, 2B(24): -1.6	1.5
2021	MID	AA	22	229	31	9	2	6	31	18	46	8	6		.319/.374/.471	111	.381	-0.8	SS(26): -1.6, 2B(22): 3.0	1.1
2021	LV	AAA	22	151	17	8	0	0	10	11	30	4	1		.243/.302/.301	84	.308	0.8	SS(22): -2.0, 2B(14): 0.6	0.1
2022 DC	*OAK*	*MLB*	*23*	*134*	*14*	*5*	*0*	*1*	*11*	*8*	*28*	*3*	*2*	*23.8%*	*.232/.289/.317*	*68*	*.288*	*0.3*	*SS 0*	*0.0*

Comparables: Marwin Gonzalez, Yairo Muñoz, Cristhian Adames

Allen is a throwback to an era when shortstops were acrobats who barely knew which end of the bat to hold, though his first trip to Double-A turned up a surprising amount of power—or at least, a surprising amount for someone whose ticket to the majors wasn't supposed to be his offense. To be fair, that remains the case: his surge to start the season couldn't stand up to Triple-A pitching, and the ceiling for him is still "league-average hitter." That's less of a problem when you play defense like Allen does, though it does mean he's more likely to carve out a career as a utility infielder than as a starter—something the A's seem to have in mind already, as they had him log time at both middle infield spots last season.

Elvis Andrus SS
Born: 08/26/88 Age: 33 Bats: R Throws: R Height: 6'0" Weight: 210 lb. Origin: International Free Agent, 2005

YEAR	TEAM	LVL	AGE	PA	R	2B	3B	HR	RBI	BB	K	SB	CS	Whiff%	AVG/OBP/SLG	DRC+	BABIP	BRR	FRAA	WARP
2019	TEX	MLB	30	648	81	27	4	12	72	34	96	31	8	19.5%	.275/.313/.393	91	.305	2.4	SS(146): 1.4	2.0
2020	TEX	MLB	31	111	11	5	0	3	7	8	15	3	1	19.5%	.194/.252/.330	98	.200	0.2	SS(29): -0.1	0.3
2021	OAK	MLB	32	541	60	25	2	3	37	31	81	12	2	19.6%	.243/.294/.320	85	.283	3.0	SS(143): -2.6	1.0
2022 DC	*OAK*	*MLB*	*33*	*427*	*53*	*17*	*1*	*7*	*50*	*28*	*63*	*12*	*5*	*19.9%*	*.253/.306/.366*	*88*	*.281*	*0.8*	*SS 0*	*1.1*

Comparables: Edgar Renteria, Alan Trammell, Tim Foli

Andrus hit salary dump status last February, when Oakland and Texas decided to swap expensive, declining veterans (with Khris Davis heading to the Rangers) so that the A's could save a little cash. Their frugality didn't buy them much, with Andrus posting his worst DRC+ mark since 2014—though given how invisible he's been at the plate over the past four years, it's not as if there should have been high expectations. Nor should there be going forward. Since shockingly clocking 20 homers in 2017, he's hit a grand total of 24 in his last 1,700 plate appearances, and there are no walks to make up for that. What's left for the former face of the Rangers? Likely another trade, if only so Oakland can avoid triggering a costly player option for 2022, and with it, the beginning of a new stage of his career: itinerant veteran.

Seth Brown OF
Born: 07/13/92 Age: 29 Bats: L Throws: L Height: 6'1" Weight: 223 lb. Origin: Round 19, 2015 Draft (#578 overall)

YEAR	TEAM	LVL	AGE	PA	R	2B	3B	HR	RBI	BB	K	SB	CS	Whiff%	AVG/OBP/SLG	DRC+	BABIP	BRR	FRAA	WARP
2019	LV	AAA	26	500	101	29	6	37	104	38	127	8	1		.297/.352/.634	111	.330	-0.8	1B(64): 2.0, LF(17): 0.5, RF(9): -1.0	2.0
2019	OAK	MLB	26	83	11	8	2	0	13	7	23	1	0	31.8%	.293/.361/.453	76	.423	0.6	LF(23): 0.4, 1B(4): -0.6	0.1
2020	OAK	MLB	27	5	0	0	0	0	0	0	2	0	0	55.6%	.000/.000/.000	84			1B(3): 0.0	0.0
2021	OAK	MLB	28	307	43	13	1	20	48	23	89	4	1	32.4%	.214/.274/.480	99	.230	-1.4	RF(75): 1.6, LF(19): 1.0, 1B(6): -0.1	1.3
2022 DC	*OAK*	*MLB*	*29*	*523*	*64*	*23*	*2*	*20*	*69*	*37*	*160*	*2*	*2*	*32.3%*	*.225/.285/.411*	*82*	*.293*	*-0.1*	*LF 1, RF 1*	*0.3*

Comparables: Luke Voit, Will Venable, Steve Pearce

Brown looked like he could be something more than a bench bat when he put up unexpected power numbers in his MLB debut, but his first full(ish) season confirms that he's better suited to be a strong-side bat in a corner outfield platoon, a player that Oakland produces the same way Soviet factories rolled out tanks during World War II: endlessly and with no frills.

Matt Chapman 3B Born: 04/28/93 Age: 29 Bats: R Throws: R Height: 6'0" Weight: 215 lb. Origin: Round 1, 2014 Draft (#25 overall)

YEAR	TEAM	LVL	AGE	PA	R	2B	3B	HR	RBI	BB	K	SB	CS	Whiff%	AVG/OBP/SLG	DRC+	BABIP	BRR	FRAA	WARP
2019	OAK	MLB	26	670	102	36	3	36	91	73	147	1	1	23.9%	.249/.342/.506	119	.270	-3.2	3B(156): 13.3	4.3
2020	OAK	MLB	27	152	22	9	2	10	25	8	54	0	0	36.2%	.232/.276/.535	91	.291	0.3	3B(36): -4.7, SS(1): 0.8	-0.2
2021	OAK	MLB	28	622	75	15	3	27	72	80	202	3	2	32.8%	.210/.314/.403	94	.272	3.4	3B(150): -7.1, SS(3): -0.3	1.2
2022 DC	*OAK*	*MLB*	*29*	*594*	*90*	*21*	*3*	*27*	*84*	*68*	*185*	*2*	*2*	*32.4%*	*.216/.312/.434*	*103*	*.271*	*-0.2*	*3B 0*	*1.9*

Comparables: Howard Johnson, Ron Cey, Dave Hollins

This year's Chapman blurb is brought to you by the letter K, with which he's become all too familiar. The 2021 season was the second straight in which his strikeout rate ballooned above 30%, and even though his walk rate rebounded from 2020's hip injury-created disaster for his highest mark ever, there's only so much that can do when you're making contact barely 70% of the time, as he did. Worse, his batted-ball numbers—in particular his average exit velocity and hard-hit rate—all took a nosedive, too. If you've ever wanted to see what a Giancarlo Stanton season would look like if you took away the power, now you know.

It's tempting to give Chapman a mulligan on '21, assume that his struggles were the result of getting his timing back after offseason hip surgery, and figure he'll be better next year. After all, he's still a year shy of 30, and though the defensive metrics aren't currently seeing eye to eye on his work at third, it's unlikely that he's gone from Platinum Glover to late-career Troy Glaus that quickly. The question is whether he gets the chance to bounce back in Oakland or somewhere else. With two years of team control left and the A's retrenching financially, his time there has an expiration date that's approaching sooner rather than later.

Logan Davidson SS/3B Born: 12/26/97 Age: 24 Bats: S Throws: R Height: 6'3" Weight: 185 lb. Origin: Round 1, 2019 Draft (#29 overall)

YEAR	TEAM	LVL	AGE	PA	R	2B	3B	HR	RBI	BB	K	SB	CS	Whiff%	AVG/OBP/SLG	DRC+	BABIP	BRR	FRAA	WARP
2019	VER	SS	21	238	42	7	0	4	12	31	55	5	0		.239/.345/.332		.308			
2021	MSS	WIN	23	90	14	4	0	2	11	15	33	1	1		.274/.400/.411		.462			
2021	MID	AA	23	515	53	22	1	7	48	62	155	4	3		.212/.307/.313	81	.304	1.5	SS(71): 7.1, 3B(40): 2.0, 2B(5): 1.2	1.5
2022 non-DC	*OAK*	*MLB*	*24*	*251*	*19*	*10*	*0*	*3*	*19*	*22*	*79*	*0*	*1*	*31.7%*	*.193/.270/.286*	*51*	*.282*	*-0.2*	*SS 3, 3B 1*	*-0.4*

Comparables: Jason Donald, Brent Lillibridge, JaCoby Jones

Too many whiffs undermined Davidson in his first Double-A stint, as he ran a 30% strikeout rate over the course of a mostly mediocre year. The power he showed at Clemson and that made him a first-rounder has yet to show in pro ball, and while he draws enough walks to inspire hope that he can get by until it does, it'd be nice for some of his plus raw thump to make itself known. Until it does, his profile looks more like that of a defense-first utility infielder who can handle shortstop and third base.

Jordan Diaz IF Born: 08/13/00 Age: 21 Bats: R Throws: R Height: 5'10" Weight: 175 lb. Origin: International Free Agent, 2016

YEAR	TEAM	LVL	AGE	PA	R	2B	3B	HR	RBI	BB	K	SB	CS	Whiff%	AVG/OBP/SLG	DRC+	BABIP	BRR	FRAA	WARP
2019	VER	SS	18	300	31	17	1	9	47	18	46	2	2		.264/.307/.430		.283			
2021	LAN	A+	20	365	46	24	1	13	56	25	58	2	3		.288/.337/.483	124	.311	0.2	3B(52): -4.5, 1B(23): 1.9, LF(4): -0.7	1.8
2022 non-DC	*OAK*	*MLB*	*21*	*251*	*23*	*11*	*1*	*5*	*25*	*14*	*50*	*1*	*1*	*24.3%*	*.249/.297/.374*	*82*	*.299*	*-0.2*	*3B -1, 1B 1*	*0.0*

Comparables: Maikel Franco, Enrique Hernández, Pablo Sandoval

Diaz will likely be one of the biggest risers on A's prospect lists after a strong showing at High-A in which he added some serious power to his plus hit tool. A bat-to-ball specialist with excellent barrel control, he could give himself a real major-league chance if that power sticks with a promotion to Double-A next season. If it doesn't, that and his defense—he's not cut out for third base long-term and profiles as a first baseman—put a much lower ceiling on his future. He showed enough to get added to Oakland's 40-man in the offseason, but the coming year could be make or break for the 21-year-old.

Zack Gelof 3B Born: 10/19/99 Age: 22 Bats: R Throws: R Height: 6'3" Weight: 205 lb. Origin: Round 2, 2021 Draft (#60 overall)

YEAR	TEAM	LVL	AGE	PA	R	2B	3B	HR	RBI	BB	K	SB	CS	Whiff%	AVG/OBP/SLG	DRC+	BABIP	BRR	FRAA	WARP
2021	STK	A	21	145	26	8	1	7	22	19	36	11	2		.298/.393/.548	120	.366	1.5	3B(30): -6.8	0.3
2022 non-DC	*OAK*	*MLB*	*22*	*251*	*23*	*10*	*1*	*5*	*24*	*20*	*70*	*7*	*3*	*30.1%*	*.226/.295/.354*	*76*	*.303*	*0.5*	*3B -3*	*-0.4*

Comparables: Brent Morel, Austin Riley, Paul DeJong

Oakland's second-round pick in 2021, Gelof broke out as a sophomore at Virginia during the pandemic-shortened 2020 and hit well enough in his junior year, albeit with an early-season slump, to get $1.2 million from the A's. His bat has lots of raw power, and while there's potential for too much swing-and-miss in it, he avoided strikeouts well enough in A ball. Big and tall, he has the arm for third base, but his body might force him to an outfield corner. If he gets to the majors at all, it'll be because the power carried him through the minors.

Tony Kemp 2B/LF Born: 10/31/91 Age: 30 Bats: L Throws: R Height: 5'6" Weight: 160 lb. Origin: Round 5, 2013 Draft (#137 overall)

YEAR	TEAM	LVL	AGE	PA	R	2B	3B	HR	RBI	BB	K	SB	CS	Whiff%	AVG/OBP/SLG	DRC+	BABIP	BRR	FRAA	WARP
2019	CHC	MLB	27	93	8	3	2	1	12	7	18	0	1	23.1%	.183/.258/.305	89	.215	1.1	2B(14): 0.1, LF(6): 0.5, RF(3): 0.2	0.4
2019	HOU	MLB	27	186	23	6	2	7	17	16	29	4	3	16.9%	.227/.308/.417	101	.233	-0.9	2B(29): -0.7, LF(14): 0.6, CF(11): 0.3	0.7
2020	OAK	MLB	28	114	15	5	0	0	4	15	14	3	1	13.6%	.247/.363/.301	101	.284	1.1	2B(43): -2.2, LF(3): -0.2	0.3
2021	OAK	MLB	29	397	54	16	3	8	37	52	51	8	2	15.6%	.279/.382/.418	110	.304	2.6	2B(89): -0.4, LF(49): -1.2, SS(1): -0.0	2.1
2022 DC	*OAK*	*MLB*	*30*	*554*	*73*	*21*	*3*	*8*	*61*	*67*	*72*	*14*	*5*	*16.0%*	*.249/.352/.363*	*100*	*.279*	*0.9*	*2B 0, LF 1*	*2.1*

Comparables: Eric Sogard, Brock Holt, Greg Garcia

Kemp belongs to the genus of undersized contact pests best exemplified by Luis Arraez and David Fletcher: impossible to strike out, but with so little power and plate patience as to render their offensive value moot. The problem with Kemp is he lacks even the gaudy batting average that those guys bring to the table. Or at least, that was the case before 2020; in that pandemic-shortened season, he showed both a newfound willingness to lay off pitches outside and a more elevated bat path that turned harmless grounders into well-struck line drives. Both changes carried over to 2021, the best season at the plate of his career. Sadly, that doesn't add up to a starter—or not at second base, anyway, where none of the defensive metrics like his work. When you toss in his ability to play a good outfield and his speed, he makes for a solid utility guy.

Ramón Laureano CF

Born: 07/15/94 Age: 27 Bats: R Throws: R Height: 5'11" Weight: 203 lb. Origin: Round 16, 2014 Draft (#466 overall)

YEAR	TEAM	LVL	AGE	PA	R	2B	3B	HR	RBI	BB	K	SB	CS	Whiff%	AVG/OBP/SLG	DRC+	BABIP	BRR	FRAA	WARP
2019	OAK	MLB	24	481	79	29	0	24	67	27	123	13	2	27.9%	.288/.340/.521	107	.342	3.1	CF(110): 9.1, RF(13): 4.9	4.1
2020	OAK	MLB	25	222	27	8	1	6	25	24	58	2	1	25.0%	.213/.338/.366	98	.270	0.6	CF(53): 8.5	1.6
2021	OAK	MLB	26	378	43	21	2	14	39	27	98	12	5	27.1%	.246/.317/.443	100	.304	-0.4	CF(75): 4.8, RF(8): 1.0	2.1
2022 DC	*OAK*	*MLB*	*27*	*496*	*73*	*21*	*2*	*16*	*58*	*38*	*120*	*14*	*4*	*26.5%*	*.240/.316/.409*	*100*	*.291*	*0.9*	*CF 3*	*2.2*

Comparables: Gerardo Parra, Jake Marisnick, Peter Bourjos

When the A's lost Laureano to a PED suspension in August, they were able to paper over his absence thanks to the presence of Starling Marte. No such solution exists for the four weeks still left on his ban that will cost Oakland his services to start the season. When he does return, it'll be as a relatively unknown quantity, given that he was popped for Nandrolone, an anabolic steroid, and underwent offseason core surgery. There are red flags in his 2021 numbers, too. He boasts an arm like a Howitzer and lots of speed, but poor routes and iffy range have undermined his value the last two years. So has over-aggression at the plate—even with more walks in his profile, he isn't making enough contact—and on the bases, where he was successful in just 71% of his steal attempts. Laureano burst onto the scene like a comet, only to come closer and closer to Earth ever since.

Mitch Moreland DH

Born: 09/06/85 Age: 36 Bats: L Throws: L Height: 6'3" Weight: 245 lb. Origin: Round 17, 2007 Draft (#530 overall)

YEAR	TEAM	LVL	AGE	PA	R	2B	3B	HR	RBI	BB	K	SB	CS	Whiff%	AVG/OBP/SLG	DRC+	BABIP	BRR	FRAA	WARP
2019	BOS	MLB	33	335	48	17	1	19	58	34	74	1	0	28.1%	.252/.328/.507	114	.271	-2.2	1B(85): 5.3	1.8
2020	SD	MLB	34	73	8	5	0	2	8	4	14	0	0	29.2%	.203/.247/.362	86	.226	0.0	1B(16): -2.4	-0.2
2020	BOS	MLB	34	79	14	4	0	8	21	11	18	0	0	33.6%	.328/.430/.746	133	.341	0.6	1B(22): -0.5	0.5
2021	OAK	MLB	35	252	28	11	1	10	30	18	58	0	0	30.4%	.227/.286/.415	95	.256	-0.1	1B(7): 0.7	0.5
2022 DC	*FA*	*MLB*	*36*	*414*	*46*	*17*	*0*	*15*	*51*	*37*	*101*	*0*	*1*	*30.7%*	*.232/.307/.411*	*90*	*.277*	*-0.6*	*1B 1*	*0.2*

Comparables: Tino Martinez, Chris Chambliss, Earl Torgeson

Rare is the person who can live in San Diego and Oakland and find neither to their liking, but that was Moreland, who struggled in his brief stint with the Padres in 2020 and didn't do much better with the A's last year. Purely the strong side of a platoon at this point, he didn't hit righties nearly well enough (.242/.298/.342) to justify playing time, and with Matt Olson already on board at first base, he ended up taking the majority of his at-bats as a DH. At 36, he's going to struggle to find the kind of work that his Boston renaissance seemed to have opened up. Maybe that's the problem: he needs a cold-weather city to make things work.

Max Muncy SS

Born: 08/25/02 Age: 19 Bats: R Throws: R Height: 6'1" Weight: 180 lb. Origin: Round 1, 2021 Draft (#25 overall)

YEAR	TEAM	LVL	AGE	PA	R	2B	3B	HR	RBI	BB	K	SB	CS	Whiff%	AVG/OBP/SLG	DRC+	BABIP	BRR	FRAA	WARP
2021	ATH	ROK	18	34	3	0	0	0	4	3	12	1	0		.129/.206/.129		.211			
2022															*No projection*					

The A's infamously whiffed on Max Muncy Prime back in 2017, releasing him at the end of spring training that year; he latched on with the Dodgers and subsequently turned into a perennial MVP candidate. In its benevolence, the universe has given them a second Max Muncy, this one also a middle infielder with power, to see if they can avoid repeating their mistakes. Let's assume that there isn't a third Max Muncy waiting in the wings if Oakland screws this up too.

Sean Murphy C

Born: 10/04/94 Age: 27 Bats: R Throws: R Height: 6'3" Weight: 228 lb. Origin: Round 3, 2016 Draft (#83 overall)

YEAR	TEAM	LVL	AGE	PA	R	2B	3B	HR	RBI	BB	K	SB	CS	Whiff%	AVG/OBP/SLG	DRC+	BABIP	BRR	FRAA	WARP
2019	ASGO	ROK	24	32	8	2	0	1	1	4	4	0	0		.214/.313/.393		.217			
2019	LV	AAA	24	140	25	6	1	10	30	15	31	0	1		.308/.386/.625	108	.329	-1.2	C(27): 3.3	0.9
2019	OAK	MLB	24	60	14	5	0	4	8	6	16	0	0	29.8%	.245/.333/.566	100	.273	0.9	C(18): -1.3	0.2
2020	OAK	MLB	25	140	21	5	0	7	14	24	37	0	0	25.0%	.233/.364/.457	112	.278	-0.7	C(43): 0.3	0.7
2021	OAK	MLB	26	448	47	23	0	17	59	40	114	0	0	27.8%	.216/.306/.405	96	.257	-2.0	C(112): 12.2	2.7
2022 DC	*OAK*	*MLB*	*27*	*452*	*60*	*19*	*0*	*17*	*59*	*45*	*117*	*0*	*1*	*27.1%*	*.223/.312/.406*	*97*	*.267*	*-0.7*	*C 3*	*2.1*

Comparables: Francisco Cervelli, Josh Donaldson, Yan Gomes

YEAR	TEAM	P. COUNT	FRM RUNS	BLK RUNS	THRW RUNS	TOT RUNS
2019	OAK	2060	-1.0	-0.1	0.0	-1.0
2019	LV	4014	2.6	0.2	0.1	2.9
2020	OAK	5458	0.6	0.0	0.0	0.6
2021	OAK	14783	11.6	0.2	0.1	11.9
2022	*OAK*	*15632*	*-0.4*	*-1.9*	*0.4*	*-1.9*

As the sample size increases, Murphy's numbers keep getting worse. In his first full season as a starter, he barely made it to league average offensively; no hitter had a bigger slide in walk rate from 2020 to '21 than he did. To be fair, his 17.1% figure in that former year was never going to hold, and his 8.9% mark last season is plenty good. But that dip speaks to an over-aggressive approach, especially against pitches on the edge of the strike zone and outside it, that undermines his overall offense. The good news is that he's still in his prime, consistently hits the ball hard and is one of the best defensive catchers in the majors, finishing sixth in CDA among all backstops. If he can get more selective about what he sees at the plate, his status as a top-five overall catcher is set.

Matt Olson 1B Born: 03/29/94 Age: 28 Bats: L Throws: R Height: 6'5" Weight: 225 lb. Origin: Round 1, 2012 Draft (#47 overall)

YEAR	TEAM	LVL	AGE	PA	R	2B	3B	HR	RBI	BB	K	SB	CS	Whiff%	AVG/OBP/SLG	DRC+	BABIP	BRR	FRAA	WARP
2019	OAK	MLB	25	547	73	26	0	36	91	51	138	0	0	28.4%	.267/.351/.545	120	.300	-2.5	1B(127): 12.6	3.9
2020	OAK	MLB	26	245	28	4	1	14	42	34	77	1	0	35.0%	.195/.310/.424	94	.227	-0.7	1B(60): 6.8	1.0
2021	OAK	MLB	27	673	101	35	0	39	111	88	113	4	1	23.0%	.271/.371/.540	136	.269	5.3	1B(152): 2.8	5.3
2022 DC	*OAK*	*MLB*	*28*	*640*	*115*	*27*	*1*	*37*	*104*	*80*	*122*	*2*	*1*	*24.1%*	*.267/.369/.524*	*137*	*.281*	*-1.0*	*1B 2*	*4.6*

Comparables: Boog Powell, John Olerud, Ted Kluszewski

By the time you read this, Olson likely won't be in Oakland anymore. That's no fault of his: The man voted most likely to be mistaken for an Easter Island mo'ai put up a career-best season for the A's, finishing eighth in the majors in DRC+ and sixth in WARP and marrying lots of loud contact with a 13.1% walk rate that was good for 14th among qualified hitters. Finding faults in his game is downright difficult: He's a patient hitter with lots of power and a superb defender at his position, and he won't turn 28 until the 2022 season is about to begin. The only problem Oakland has with him is that he only has two years of team control left, with each season set to cost the team at least $10 million per. That should be chump change for arguably the best first baseman in baseball, but the A's have apparently run out of couch cushions to dig through for coins, making him a certainty to be dealt—if not over the winter, then sometime in the summer or next offseason.

Chad Pinder RF Born: 03/29/92 Age: 30 Bats: R Throws: R Height: 6'2" Weight: 210 lb. Origin: Round 2, 2013 Draft (#71 overall)

YEAR	TEAM	LVL	AGE	PA	R	2B	3B	HR	RBI	BB	K	SB	CS	Whiff%	AVG/OBP/SLG	DRC+	BABIP	BRR	FRAA	WARP
2019	OAK	MLB	27	370	45	21	0	13	47	20	88	0	1	25.8%	.240/.290/.416	85	.284	0.6	LF(46): 2.4, RF(34): 4.3, 2B(21): -2.0	1.0
2020	OAK	MLB	28	61	8	3	0	2	8	5	13	0	0	21.7%	.232/.295/.393	100	.268	0.1	2B(13): -1.8, 3B(7): 0.5, LF(2): -0.1	0.1
2021	LV	AAA	29	31	6	2	0	2	10	2	8	0	0		.286/.323/.571	99	.316	-0.5	SS(3): 0.1, RF(3): -0.4	0.0
2021	OAK	MLB	29	233	30	16	1	6	27	16	62	1	0	28.1%	.243/.300/.411	88	.313	1.3	RF(39): -2.2, LF(17): 0.5, SS(8): -0.3	0.5
2022 DC	*OAK*	*MLB*	*30*	*502*	*63*	*21*	*1*	*15*	*65*	*36*	*126*	*2*	*1*	*27.8%*	*.236/.297/.393*	*88*	*.288*	*-0.5*	*2B -2, LF 1*	*0.7*

Comparables: Jed Lowrie, Brock Holt, Phil Gosselin

Pinder has long been a favorite of management in Oakland for his positional versatility and lefty-mashing ways, but his continued roster presence hinges on his availability, and he bumbled his way onto the Injured List twice in 2021 with a knee sprain and a hamstring strain. Those aforementioned qualities are what make this partnership a match; beyond that and his grinder ways, he doesn't bring much else to the table, as he's stretched defensively most everywhere and a league-average bat on the whole. There are plenty of super-utility fish out there to catch and create some bench harmony with if the A's eventually decide to swipe left on Pinder.

Pedro Pineda CF Born: 09/06/03 Age: 18 Bats: R Throws: R Height: 6'1" Weight: 170 lb. Origin: International Free Agent, 2021

YEAR	TEAM	LVL	AGE	PA	R	2B	3B	HR	RBI	BB	K	SB	CS	Whiff%	AVG/OBP/SLG	DRC+	BABIP	BRR	FRAA	WARP
2021	DSL ATH	ROK	17	40	4	1	1	0	1	5	13	3	2		.200/.300/.286		.318			
2021	ATH	ROK	17	77	15	2	2	1	8	13	28	3	3		.258/.403/.403		.455			
2022															*No projection*					

Comparables: Luis Carlos Diaz, D'Shawn Knowles, Arturo Guerrero

Pineda was Oakland's big international signing splurge last summer, earning a $4.2 million bonus, and though he didn't do much in his brief stay in Arizona, there are oodles of tools here, including plus grades on his power, speed and defense. Blessed with excellent bat speed and a big physical frame to grow into, he has the most upside of any position player in the farm system.

Stephen Piscotty RF Born: 01/14/91 Age: 31 Bats: R Throws: R Height: 6'4" Weight: 211 lb. Origin: Round 1, 2012 Draft (#36 overall)

YEAR	TEAM	LVL	AGE	PA	R	2B	3B	HR	RBI	BB	K	SB	CS	Whiff%	AVG/OBP/SLG	DRC+	BABIP	BRR	FRAA	WARP
2019	OAK	MLB	28	393	46	17	1	13	44	29	84	2	0	28.8%	.249/.309/.412	94	.289	0.6	RF(90): -3.6	0.6
2020	OAK	MLB	29	171	17	6	0	5	29	9	53	4	0	33.6%	.226/.271/.358	76	.304	-0.3	RF(44): -5.6	-0.6
2021	OAK	MLB	30	188	14	8	0	5	16	13	48	1	0	27.7%	.220/.282/.353	86	.275	-2.1	RF(67): 0.9	0.1
2022 DC	*OAK*	*MLB*	*31*	*499*	*61*	*20*	*0*	*15*	*64*	*37*	*120*	*3*	*1*	*29.0%*	*.230/.295/.382*	*84*	*.276*	*-0.5*	*RF 0*	*0.2*

Comparables: Andre Ethier, Jermaine Dye, Orlando Merced

More contact and fewer whiffs didn't improve things for Piscotty, whose 2021 numbers barely budged from 2020's awful results. Fastballs still eat him alive—he hit .146 with a 29.3% whiff rate on heaters—and he frequently expands the zone, beating himself. Nor can he stay healthy, missing two months with a wrist sprain, or make up for that weak offense with his glove or legs. It's a surprise that the A's didn't release him before the lockout, though it's a safe bet they'll spend 2022 trying their best to dump him and the final year left on his contract.

★ ★ ★ *2022 Top 101 Prospect* **#23** ★ ★ ★

Tyler Soderstrom C

Born: 11/24/01 Age: 20 Bats: L Throws: R Height: 6'2" Weight: 200 lb. Origin: Round 1, 2020 Draft (#26 overall)

YEAR	TEAM	LVL	AGE	PA	R	2B	3B	HR	RBI	BB	K	SB	CS	Whiff%	AVG/OBP/SLG	DRC+	BABIP	BRR	FRAA	WARP
2021	STK	A	19	254	39	20	1	12	49	27	61	2	1		.306/.390/.568	125	.373	-1.2	C(38): -3.6, 1B(9): -1.0	1.0
2022 non-DC	*OAK*	*MLB*	*20*	*251*	*24*	*12*	*1*	*6*	*26*	*17*	*74*	*0*	*1*	*31.8%*	*.228/.290/.376*	*78*	*.309*	*-0.2*	*C -5, 1B -1*	*-0.3*

Comparables: Wil Myers, Francisco Mejía, Wilson Ramos

YEAR	TEAM	P. COUNT	FRM RUNS	BLK RUNS	THRW RUNS	TOT RUNS
2021	STK	5254	-2.2	-1.5	0.3	-3.5
2022	*OAK*	*6956*	*-3.3*	*-1.5*	*0.0*	*-4.8*

Oakland's top prospect cemented his status as such with a splendid year at High-A, not missing a beat in his first full season of pro play despite losing 2020 to the pandemic. Big and strong, he continues to show an advanced feel at the plate in terms of patience, pitch recognition and contact, offering tons of line-drive and over-the-fence power. Defense is another matter, as he grades out closer to average with the glove, but given both Sean Murphy's presence and the eventual departure of Matt Olson, that might be for the best. It's more likely that Soderstrom meets his offensive ceiling if he ditches squatting for four hours a night, so the A's might be better off getting him out from behind the plate and over to first base (or a corner outfield spot) sooner rather than later. Only 20 years old, he won't reach Oakland for another year or two, but he's on track to be an impact player when he gets there.

Cody Thomas OF

Born: 10/08/94 Age: 27 Bats: L Throws: R Height: 6'4" Weight: 211 lb. Origin: Round 13, 2016 Draft (#401 overall)

YEAR	TEAM	LVL	AGE	PA	R	2B	3B	HR	RBI	BB	K	SB	CS	Whiff%	AVG/OBP/SLG	DRC+	BABIP	BRR	FRAA	WARP
2019	TUL	AA	24	532	77	17	6	23	76	46	144	5	3		.236/.308/.443	112	.284	-0.4	RF(69): 2.4, CF(31): 1.0, LF(26): -0.1	2.8
2021	LV	AAA	26	245	46	20	4	18	52	25	78	0	0		.289/.363/.665	105	.366	1.2	LF(25): -4.8, CF(23): -0.2, RF(8): 2.0	0.8
2022 DC	*OAK*	*MLB*	*27*	*308*	*40*	*14*	*2*	*10*	*36*	*23*	*109*	*1*	*1*	*35.4%*	*.213/.281/.391*	*77*	*.306*	*-0.1*	*LF 0, RF 1*	*0.0*

Comparables: Jeremy Hazelbaker, Lane Adams, Sam Hilliard

The obvious caveat: Thomas' wacky numbers at Triple-A are in part thanks to Las Vegas being Coors Field on steroids; he slugged .647 at home. His true talent level should be more visible in his road numbers, where he slugged [checks notes] uh, .686. That says plenty about the league formerly known as the PCL and also about Thomas, a hyper-athlete previously buried in the Dodgers' deep system. At this point, he is what he is: a big swinger with some genuine power from the left side and who can handle all three outfield spots. That's a useful backup any way you slice it, or maybe a starter if Oakland goes full fire-sale mode sooner rather than later.

PITCHERS

Chris Bassitt RHP

Born: 02/22/89 Age: 33 Bats: R Throws: R Height: 6'5" Weight: 217 lb. Origin: Round 16, 2011 Draft (#501 overall)

YEAR	TEAM	LVL	AGE	W	L	SV	G	GS	IP	H	HR	BB/9	K/9	K	GB%	BABIP	WHIP	ERA	DRA-	WARP	MPH	FB%	Whiff%	CSP
2019	LV	AAA	30	0	0	0	2	2	8	8	2	2.3	10.1	9	58.3%	.273	1.25	4.50	86	0.1				
2019	OAK	MLB	30	10	5	0	28	25	144	125	21	2.9	8.8	141	40.6%	.268	1.19	3.81	94	1.9	93.2	78.6%	21.1%	52.4%
2020	OAK	MLB	31	5	2	0	11	11	63	56	6	2.4	7.9	55	43.9%	.278	1.16	2.29	90	1.0	92.4	77.5%	23.0%	52.8%
2021	OAK	MLB	32	12	4	0	27	27	157^{1}	127	15	2.2	9.1	159	41.6%	.271	1.06	3.15	86	2.6	92.6	74.0%	23.8%	57.6%
2022 DC	*OAK*	*MLB*	*33*	*11*	*8*	*0*	*29*	*29*	*166*	*148*	*21*	*2.5*	*8.5*	*156*	*41.7%*	*.277*	*1.17*	*3.43*	*90*	*2.2*	*92.7*	*75.6%*	*23.1%*	*55.7%*

Comparables: Brandon Morrow, Larry Jackson, Wandy Rodriguez

If Bassitt's excellent 2020 felt like a small sample fluke, his 2021 backed it up, with an ERA and FIP so close they could reach out and touch each other. The veteran found a new level at 32, posting career-best strikeout and walk rates, and though being a sinker-first pitcher in this day and age is choosing to build your house on the cliff's edge, that's been a winning formula for him the last three seasons. It helps that Bassitt pounds the strike zone: Among starters with 150 or more innings last season, his 18% called-strike rate ranked 15th. To that he added his highest swinging-strike rate, at 10.1%—his first time in double digits and third straight year of improvement. The secret there? His slider, mothballed after Tommy John surgery in 2016, has been reintroduced over the last three seasons with far more bite and sweep than it had before. It's as unexpected a breakout as you can imagine given where he was stuff- and results-wise just a few years ago. As Bassitt hounds batters into his mid-30s, he's proof that old dogs can learn new tricks.

Jeff Criswell RHP

Born: 03/10/99 Age: 23 Bats: R Throws: R Height: 6'4" Weight: 225 lb. Origin: Round 2, 2020 Draft (#58 overall)

YEAR	TEAM	LVL	AGE	W	L	SV	G	GS	IP	H	HR	BB/9	K/9	K	GB%	BABIP	WHIP	ERA	DRA-	WARP	MPH	FB%	Whiff%	CSP
2021	LAN	A+	22	0	0	0	5	5	12	9	1	3.0	9.0	12	54.5%	.250	1.08	4.50	95	0.2				
2022 non-DC	*OAK*	*MLB*	*23*	*2*	*3*	*0*	*57*	*0*	*50*	*53*	*7*	*4.6*	*7.2*	*40*	*43.5%*	*.307*	*1.59*	*5.61*	*127*	*-0.5*				

Comparables: Jake Newberry, Reynaldo López, Frankie Rodriguez

One of the more intriguing arms in Oakland's system, Criswell came into 2021 with some helium after sitting 94–97 mph with his fastball the previous fall. Alas, a sore elbow limited him to a few short starts in High-A, though he looked healthy in Arizona Fall League action, once again tossing in the mid-90s. With his plus secondaries, he offers mid-rotation starter upside if he can avoid more arm trouble and missed time.

Jake Diekman LHP Born: 01/21/87 Age: 35 Bats: R Throws: L Height: 6'4" Weight: 195 lb. Origin: Round 30, 2007 Draft (#923 overall)

YEAR	TEAM	LVL	AGE	W	L	SV	G	GS	IP	H	HR	BB/9	K/9	K	GB%	BABIP	WHIP	ERA	DRA-	WARP	MPH	FB%	Whiff%	CSP
2019	OAK	MLB	32	1	1	0	28	0	20^{1}	16	0	7.1	9.3	21	44.4%	.302	1.57	4.43	101	0.2	95.9	59.1%	29.2%	45.1%
2019	KC	MLB	32	0	6	0	48	0	41^{2}	33	3	5.0	13.6	63	47.9%	.330	1.34	4.75	83	0.8	95.9	51.0%	38.4%	45.0%
2020	OAK	MLB	33	2	0	0	21	0	21^{1}	8	1	5.1	13.1	31	60.0%	.184	0.94	0.42	62	0.7	95.2	59.3%	40.8%	49.2%
2021	OAK	MLB	34	3	3	7	67	0	60^{2}	47	10	5.0	12.3	83	34.8%	.282	1.34	3.86	86	1.0	95.6	66.9%	35.1%	52.0%
2022 DC	*FA*	*MLB*	*35*	*3*	*3*	*0*	*71*	*0*	*61.7*	*47*	*8*	*5.0*	*12.2*	*83*	*42.0%*	*.281*	*1.32*	*3.94*	*95*	*0.4*	*95.6*	*62.9%*	*35.9%*	*50.1%*

Comparables: Mark Guthrie, Grant Balfour, Joakim Soria

In 2020, Diekman allowed one run and one home run over 21.1 innings, thanks in large part to the vicious Chaz Roe slider he learned that year. It was the fourth-lowest ERA from any reliever working more than 20 innings in MLB history. But for whatever reason, he decided at the start of the summer to feature that slider less and his sinker more. That was a mistake: While the former continued to be unhittable (a .121 batting average against and a 47% whiff rate), batters made lots of contact on the latter. That and an ugly walk rate made his 2021 look less historic and more run of the mill, but that shouldn't scare away potential suitors after the cost-cutting A's declined his '22 option. When it comes to lefty relievers with plus swing-and-miss stuff, he's one of the better ones.

Mike Fiers RHP Born: 06/15/85 Age: 37 Bats: R Throws: R Height: 6'2" Weight: 211 lb. Origin: Round 22, 2009 Draft (#676 overall)

YEAR	TEAM	LVL	AGE	W	L	SV	G	GS	IP	H	HR	BB/9	K/9	K	GB%	BABIP	WHIP	ERA	DRA-	WARP	MPH	FB%	Whiff%	CSP
2019	OAK	MLB	34	15	4	0	33	33	184^{2}	166	30	2.6	6.1	126	38.9%	.256	1.19	3.90	116	0.3	90.5	51.7%	18.3%	51.0%
2020	OAK	MLB	35	6	3	0	11	11	59	65	9	2.4	5.6	37	34.5%	.293	1.37	4.58	137	-0.5	88.2	44.9%	15.7%	50.4%
2021	OAK	MLB	36	0	2	0	2	2	9^{1}	15	4	3.9	4.8	5	50.0%	.344	2.04	7.71	126	0.0	87.2	55.3%	11.6%	55.0%
2022 DC	*FA*	*MLB*	*37*	*7*	*8*	*0*	*22*	*22*	*122.3*	*137*	*21*	*2.6*	*5.8*	*78*	*38.7%*	*.292*	*1.42*	*5.25*	*128*	*-0.8*	*89.4*	*49.6%*	*16.8%*	*51.1%*

Comparables: Aníbal Sánchez, Freddy Garcia, Steve Trachsel

Back pain and an elbow sprain limited Fiers to a handful of appearances, all early in the season. More worrisomely, he suffered a setback in rehabbing that sprain late in the year. There may not be any drops of juice left here anyway: He was pummeled in his few outings, and his fastball was stuck in the Jered Weaver Zone at 87.1 mph. If this is it for Fiers, he'll always have his two no-hitters, or two more than Greg Maddux, Pedro Martinez, Steve Carlton and Roger Clemens combined.

Brent Honeywell Jr. RHP Born: 03/31/95 Age: 27 Bats: R Throws: R Height: 6'2" Weight: 195 lb. Origin: Round 2, 2014 Draft (#72 overall)

YEAR	TEAM	LVL	AGE	W	L	SV	G	GS	IP	H	HR	BB/9	K/9	K	GB%	BABIP	WHIP	ERA	DRA-	WARP	MPH	FB%	Whiff%	CSP
2021	DUR	AAA	26	5	4	2	31	13	81^{2}	74	13	2.6	7.4	67	41.5%	.268	1.20	3.97	104	0.9				
2021	TB	MLB	26	0	0	0	3	2	4^{1}	5	2	6.2	8.3	4	42.9%	.250	1.85	8.31	104	0.0	94.1	50.0%	19.4%	56.0%
2022 DC	*OAK*	*MLB*	*27*	*8*	*7*	*0*	*56*	*12*	*101*	*109*	*16*	*3.5*	*8.0*	*89*	*38.8%*	*.311*	*1.48*	*5.12*	*122*	*-0.5*	*94.1*	*50.0%*	*19.4%*	*56.0%*

Comparables: A.J. Cole, Shairon Martis, Zeke Spruill

Honeywell returned to the mound in a professional setting for the first time since 2017. He underwent Tommy John surgery in early 2018 and had multiple setbacks in addition to the pandemic season that delayed his inevitable debut by about three years. Honey Day was celebrated on April 11th when he started for the Rays against the New York Yankees. The results were as good as you can hope: two shutout innings with two strikeouts and no walks. Honeywell would make two more appearances for the big-league club but spent most of this time at Durham. You can look at whatever stat you want but the most important number will be the 86 combined innings he threw. He will finally have a normal off-season and should enter spring battling for a roster spot if not a turn through the rotation. The only difference is he will do it as a member of the Oakland A's and not with Tampa Bay.

Brian Howard RHP Born: 04/25/95 Age: 27 Bats: R Throws: R Height: 6'9" Weight: 213 lb. Origin: Round 8, 2017 Draft (#231 overall)

YEAR	TEAM	LVL	AGE	W	L	SV	G	GS	IP	H	HR	BB/9	K/9	K	GB%	BABIP	WHIP	ERA	DRA-	WARP	MPH	FB%	Whiff%	CSP
2019	MID	AA	24	8	8	0	23	23	130	137	7	2.7	8.2	118	40.2%	.349	1.35	3.25	100	0.2				
2019	LV	AAA	24	0	1	0	4	4	14^{1}	28	4	5.0	10.0	16	34.5%	.471	2.51	13.81	116	-0.1				
2021	LV	AAA	26	7	4	0	24	21	110^{2}	126	22	3.3	7.8	96	36.2%	.316	1.50	5.86	116	-0.7				
2022 non-DC	*OAK*	*MLB*	*27*	*2*	*3*	*0*	*57*	*0*	*50*	*53*	*7*	*3.5*	*7.4*	*41*	*37.5%*	*.300*	*1.45*	*4.99*	*119*	*-0.3*				

Comparables: Jerry Keel, James Naile, Andrew Moore

Howard's height makes it easier to do some things (like reach the top shelf of the pantry, rescue kittens stranded in trees or help his fringy velocity and stuff play up) and much tougher to do others (like find pants that fit well or sit through minor-league bus rides). It didn't seem to have any effect on Las Vegas, which took his low 90s fastball and stomped on it, leaving a 7.80 home ERA in its wake. His better numbers on the road portend a major-league future as a fifth starter or swingman if he can leave Sin City behind.

Cole Irvin LHP Born: 01/31/94 Age: 28 Bats: L Throws: L Height: 6'4" Weight: 217 lb. Origin: Round 5, 2016 Draft (#137 overall)

YEAR	TEAM	LVL	AGE	W	L	SV	G	GS	IP	H	HR	BB/9	K/9	K	GB%	BABIP	WHIP	ERA	DRA-	WARP	MPH	FB%	Whiff%	CSP
2019	LHV	AAA	25	6	1	0	17	16	93^{2}	113	13	1.3	6.2	65	40.6%	.328	1.36	3.94	126	-0.1				
2019	PHI	MLB	25	2	1	1	16	3	41^{2}	45	7	2.8	6.7	31	33.6%	.302	1.39	5.83	133	-0.3	89.9	50.5%	20.7%	48.9%
2020	PHI	MLB	26	0	1	0	3	0	3^{2}	11	1	2.5	9.8	4	35.3%	.625	3.27	17.18	107	0.0	92.8	52.4%	14.0%	50.1%
2021	OAK	MLB	27	10	15	0	32	32	178^{1}	195	23	2.1	6.3	125	37.5%	.305	1.33	4.24	130	-1.2	90.8	59.9%	19.4%	56.2%
2022 DC	*OAK*	*MLB*	*28*	*6*	*7*	*0*	*22*	*22*	*115.7*	*127*	*17*	*2.2*	*6.7*	*85*	*38.5%*	*.301*	*1.34*	*4.59*	*116*	*-0.3*	*90.8*	*59.1%*	*19.4%*	*55.5%*

Comparables: Iván Nova, Rick Langford, Dallas Keuchel

Irvin led the AL in losses, hits allowed and starts—the Rick Porcello Trifecta—en route to a 6.09 DRA and the 12th-lowest WARP among qualified starters. It's not hard to see why: Name a batted-ball or peripheral stat, and he probably showed up near the bottom of the list there, too. His fastball doesn't miss bats; neither do his below-average changeup or slider. Converted from middle relief, Irvin might be better off back there.

Daulton Jefferies RHP

Born: 08/02/95 Age: 26 Bats: L Throws: R Height: 6'0" Weight: 182 lb. Origin: Round 1, 2016 Draft (#37 overall)

YEAR	TEAM	LVL	AGE	W	L	SV	G	GS	IP	H	HR	BB/9	K/9	K	GB%	BABIP	WHIP	ERA	DRA-	WARP	MPH	FB%	Whiff%	CSP
2019	STK	A+	23	1	0	0	5	3	15	10	1	1.2	12.6	21	44.1%	.273	0.80	2.40	76	0.2				
2019	MID	AA	23	1	2	0	21	12	64	63	7	1.0	10.1	72	41.0%	.329	1.09	3.66	71	1.2				
2020	OAK	MLB	24	0	1	0	1	1	2	5	2	9.0	4.5	1	30.0%	.375	3.50	22.50	133	0.0	94.2	81.1%	23.1%	51.6%
2021	LV	AAA	25	5	1	0	15	15	77	90	13	1.3	7.9	68	42.4%	.326	1.31	4.91	103	0.2				
2021	OAK	MLB	25	1	0	0	5	1	15	11	1	2.4	4.8	8	44.4%	.227	1.00	3.60	124	-0.1	93.2	72.3%	17.0%	55.1%
2022 DC	*OAK*	*MLB*	*26*	*7*	*6*	*0*	*49*	*12*	*94.3*	*98*	*12*	*2.0*	*6.4*	*67*	*41.4%*	*.290*	*1.26*	*4.04*	*105*	*0.4*	*93.3*	*73.5%*	*17.8%*	*54.6%*

Comparables: Aaron Slegers, Mitch Talbot, Luis Mendoza

Five years after being drafted, Jefferies still has yet to top 100 innings in a season thanks to a nonstop series of arm injuries. In 2021, it was biceps tendinitis and nerve irritation in his elbow, the latter of which wiped out what would have been his third major-league start and what was left of his season. The stuff is still plus and gives him back-end starter potential, if only his various ligaments and muscles would get with the program.

Dany Jiménez RHP

Born: 12/23/93 Age: 28 Bats: R Throws: R Height: 6'1" Weight: 182 lb. Origin: International Free Agent, 2015

YEAR	TEAM	LVL	AGE	W	L	SV	G	GS	IP	H	HR	BB/9	K/9	K	GB%	BABIP	WHIP	ERA	DRA-	WARP	MPH	FB%	Whiff%	CSP
2019	DUN	A+	25	5	1	4	20	0	25^1	23	2	3.2	16.7	47	43.1%	.438	1.26	3.55	65	0.7				
2019	NH	AA	25	2	2	6	25	0	33^2	22	4	3.2	12.3	46	40.0%	.254	1.01	1.87	77	0.7				
2020	SF	MLB	26	0	0	0	2	0	1^1	1	0	20.2	6.7	1	50.0%	.250	3.00	6.75	105	0.0	93.1	51.4%	27.3%	45.1%
2021	BUF	AAA	27	3	3	3	39	1	44^2	29	5	5.0	14.7	73	39.3%	.289	1.21	2.22	71	1.3				
2022 non-DC	*OAK*	*MLB*	*28*	*2*	*2*	*0*	*57*	*0*	*50*	*40*	*7*	*4.8*	*12.5*	*69*	*38.8%*	*.296*	*1.35*	*4.00*	*97*	*0.3*	*93.1*	*51.4%*	*27.3%*	*45.1%*

Comparables: Kyle Keller, Nick Anderson, Art Warren

Jiménez went from Toronto to San Francisco via the Rule 5 draft in 2019, threw one inning as a Giant and was promptly sent back to the Blue Jays. Left exposed in the Rule 5 draft again in 2020, he again went to the Bay Area, this time with the A's, who also promptly sent him back to the Jays, this time in spring training. After a minor-league season in which he basically struck out and walked everyone, he hit free agency and signed a deal with...well, you probably guessed it, given which chapter this is.

James Kaprielian RHP

Born: 03/02/94 Age: 28 Bats: R Throws: R Height: 6'3" Weight: 225 lb. Origin: Round 1, 2015 Draft (#16 overall)

YEAR	TEAM	LVL	AGE	W	L	SV	G	GS	IP	H	HR	BB/9	K/9	K	GB%	BABIP	WHIP	ERA	DRA-	WARP	MPH	FB%	Whiff%	CSP
2019	STK	A+	25	2	2	0	11	10	36^1	35	6	2.0	10.7	43	32.0%	.319	1.18	4.46	97	0.2				
2019	MID	AA	25	2	1	0	7	5	27^2	18	2	2.6	8.5	26	40.8%	.232	0.94	1.63	87	0.3				
2019	LV	AAA	25	0	0	0	1	1	4	6	0	0.0	13.5	6	16.7%	.500	1.50	2.25	101	0.0				
2020	OAK	MLB	26	0	0	0	2	0	3^2	4	2	4.9	9.8	4	36.4%	.222	1.64	7.36	125	0.0	95.1	69.0%	37.5%	37.4%
2021	OAK	MLB	27	8	5	0	24	21	119^1	105	19	3.1	9.3	123	33.6%	.276	1.22	4.07	108	0.6	93.1	58.8%	27.3%	52.3%
2022 DC	*OAK*	*MLB*	*28*	*8*	*7*	*0*	*41*	*19*	*120.3*	*112*	*19*	*3.1*	*9.5*	*127*	*34.9%*	*.291*	*1.28*	*4.11*	*104*	*0.5*	*93.2*	*59.1%*	*27.5%*	*51.9%*

Comparables: Samuel Deduno, Chris Bassitt, Brandon Backe

A funny thing happened to Kaprielian in 2021: He actually got to pitch. Having suffered every conceivable arm injury in the years since being drafted, the righty finally cracked 100 innings in a season, and he was roughly league-average to boot. That may seem like a backhanded compliment, but it's frankly impressive that Kaprielian is here at all. There were even flashes of the top-of-the-rotation upside that he once possessed, though the premium velocity—94-97 mph at UCLA—is mostly gone, with his fastball now averaging 93.3 on the gun. Still, he brings good command and an excellent changeup, and he mostly avoided the injured list last season, too. Here's to more good health going forward.

Sean Manaea LHP

Born: 02/01/92 Age: 30 Bats: R Throws: L Height: 6'5" Weight: 245 lb. Origin: Round 1, 2013 Draft (#34 overall)

YEAR	TEAM	LVL	AGE	W	L	SV	G	GS	IP	H	HR	BB/9	K/9	K	GB%	BABIP	WHIP	ERA	DRA-	WARP	MPH	FB%	Whiff%	CSP
2019	STK	A+	27	0	2	0	3	3	8^1	14	1	4.3	10.8	10	42.9%	.481	2.16	9.72	110	0.0				
2019	LV	AAA	27	3	1	0	5	5	28	16	5	1.9	13.8	43	47.3%	.224	0.79	3.21	68	0.7				
2019	OAK	MLB	27	4	0	0	5	5	29^2	16	3	2.1	9.1	30	40.0%	.194	0.78	1.21	102	0.3	89.7	63.5%	28.3%	46.2%
2020	OAK	MLB	28	4	3	0	11	11	54	57	7	1.3	7.5	45	50.0%	.311	1.20	4.50	86	1.0	90.4	54.3%	22.1%	50.5%
2021	OAK	MLB	29	11	10	0	32	32	179^1	179	25	2.1	9.7	194	41.8%	.318	1.23	3.91	91	2.5	92.3	60.1%	27.0%	57.9%
2022 DC	*OAK*	*MLB*	*30*	*11*	*8*	*0*	*29*	*29*	*166*	*159*	*23*	*2.1*	*8.8*	*162*	*42.9%*	*.292*	*1.19*	*3.62*	*94*	*1.8*	*91.9*	*59.4%*	*26.3%*	*56.4%*

Comparables: Josh Beckett, José Quintana, Rick Wise

A simple maxim of modern pitching is that extra velocity plus more swings and misses equals success. Case in point: Manaea, who gained two miles per hour on his fastball and nearly five points on his overall whiff rate, leading to a career-high mark in WARP, starts and innings pitched. The lefty's sinker still isn't what it once was, but it has climbed from 89.8 mph in the immediate wake of shoulder surgery in 2019 to 92.1 two years later. His batted-ball peripherals aren't as pretty, and the deserved stats think he was closer to a mid-rotation starter than a frontline arm. But given where the A's are (which is to say, a team cutting costs), that will likely soon be someone else's problem; with just one year of team control left, Manaea has reached the end of the road in Oakland one way or the other. If nothing else, his newfound durability, improving velocity and relative consistency make him an attractive option for pitching-starved contenders.

Frankie Montas RHP Born: 03/21/93 Age: 29 Bats: R Throws: R Height: 6'2" Weight: 255 lb. Origin: International Free Agent, 2009

YEAR	TEAM	LVL	AGE	W	L	SV	G	GS	IP	H	HR	BB/9	K/9	K	GB%	BABIP	WHIP	ERA	DRA-	WARP	MPH	FB%	Whiff%	CSP
2019	ESC	WIN	26	3	0	0	5	5	25	18	0	2.2	9.4	26	54.8%	.290	0.96	1.44						
2019	OAK	MLB	26	9	2	0	16	16	96	84	8	2.2	9.7	103	49.6%	.297	1.11	2.63	81	1.9	96.5	56.8%	25.9%	48.7%
2020	OAK	MLB	27	3	5	0	11	11	53	57	10	3.9	10.2	60	36.6%	.329	1.51	5.60	107	0.4	95.9	62.0%	28.9%	51.3%
2021	OAK	MLB	28	13	9	0	32	32	187	164	20	2.7	10.0	207	42.3%	.298	1.18	3.37	88	2.9	96.5	58.2%	29.7%	52.6%
2022 DC	*OAK*	*MLB*	*29*	*11*	*8*	*0*	*29*	*29*	*169*	*149*	*21*	*2.8*	*9.9*	*185*	*42.6%*	*.290*	*1.19*	*3.36*	*88*	*2.5*	*96.4*	*58.6%*	*29.1%*	*52.0%*

Comparables: Johnny Cueto, Garrett Richards, Chris Carpenter

Coming off a rough 2020 and a PED suspension that wiped out the back half of his 2019, Montas probably had A's executives and coaches reaching for the Mylanta after he posted a 6.20 ERA over the season's first month. Luckily for both sides, Montas rebounded in spectacular fashion, with a 2.94 ERA and 182 strikeouts in 162.1 innings from May onward. One big key: turning to his splitter, a relatively new offering, over his slider as his primary secondary; the pitch held opposing hitters to a .126 batting average and .168 slugging percentage with a 51.4% whiff rate. By Statcast's run values, it was the fourth-best splitter in baseball in 2021, at -10, trailing only Kevin Gausman, Wily Peralta (!) and Shohei Ohtani. Does that mean that the Montas we saw last year is the Montas that the A's can expect? Inconsistency has long been his calling card, so the safe bet is to treat him like San Francisco weather: If you don't like it currently, just wait five minutes.

Colin Peluse RHP Born: 06/11/98 Age: 24 Bats: R Throws: R Height: 6'3" Weight: 230 lb. Origin: Round 9, 2019 Draft (#284 overall)

YEAR	TEAM	LVL	AGE	W	L	SV	G	GS	IP	H	HR	BB/9	K/9	K	GB%	BABIP	WHIP	ERA	DRA-	WARP	MPH	FB%	Whiff%	CSP
2019	VER	SS	21	2	1	0	8	5	24	21	1	2.3	9.7	26	50.7%	.303	1.13	2.25						
2021	LAN	A+	23	7	3	0	18	15	86	82	10	2.3	9.6	92	36.2%	.314	1.21	3.66	105	0.6				
2021	MID	AA	23	2	0	0	3	3	15	9	1	2.4	10.2	17	22.2%	.229	0.87	1.80	98	0.1				
2022 non-DC	*OAK*	*MLB*	*24*	*2*	*3*	*0*	*57*	*0*	*50*	*51*	*8*	*3.3*	*7.4*	*40*	*33.5%*	*.294*	*1.40*	*4.88*	*117*	*-0.3*				

Comparables: Dillon Peters, Gabriel Ynoa, Trent Thornton

Peluse came into 2021 with extra velocity that he'd built up the year prior, with his fastball now sitting in the upper 90s and touching 97–98 mph on the regular. That gives him a much higher ceiling than he had coming out of Wake Forest, where he looked like a future middle reliever, and carried him through two levels of the minors. A full season of Double-A will be a stiff test as a starter, but even if he fails it, his new power fastball will pair well with his plus slider in the late innings out of the bullpen.

Yusmeiro Petit RHP Born: 11/22/84 Age: 37 Bats: R Throws: R Height: 6'1" Weight: 252 lb. Origin: International Free Agent, 2001

YEAR	TEAM	LVL	AGE	W	L	SV	G	GS	IP	H	HR	BB/9	K/9	K	GB%	BABIP	WHIP	ERA	DRA-	WARP	MPH	FB%	Whiff%	CSP
2019	OAK	MLB	34	5	3	0	80	0	83	57	11	1.1	7.7	71	30.0%	.214	0.81	2.71	101	0.8	89.4	45.8%	25.3%	51.3%
2020	OAK	MLB	35	2	1	0	26	0	21^{2}	19	3	2.1	7.1	17	31.8%	.254	1.11	1.66	116	0.1	88.2	42.5%	26.2%	50.1%
2021	OAK	MLB	36	8	3	2	78	0	78	69	12	1.4	4.3	37	36.1%	.229	1.04	3.92	126	-0.4	87.8	44.4%	21.1%	53.6%
2022 DC	*FA*	*MLB*	*37*	*3*	*4*	*0*	*78*	*0*	*68*	*76*	*12*	*1.9*	*6.5*	*48*	*34.1%*	*.298*	*1.33*	*4.71*	*119*	*-0.4*	*88.2*	*44.5%*	*22.7%*	*52.7%*

Comparables: Bob Walk, Juan Berenguer, Dave Giusti

The existence of Yusmeiro Petit implies that somewhere, there must be a Yusmeiro Grande, or at least a Yusmeiro Moyen. Maybe they'll arrive when Little Yusmeiro leaves, though they've been biding their time for a while, given his ability to turn an 88-mph fastball and mediocre strikeout rates into 1-WARP seasons in perpetuity. But a 2021 strikeout rate of just 11.8% is pushing that magic about as far as it can go; he whiffed fewer batters on the season than Jacob deGrom did in June alone. Even as Petit remains a master of inducing soft contact, there's no margin for error at all when you can't get swings and misses. Then again, his Annual comments have been predicting disaster for years now, and yet he endures.

A.J. Puk LHP Born: 04/25/95 Age: 27 Bats: L Throws: L Height: 6'7" Weight: 248 lb. Origin: Round 1, 2016 Draft (#6 overall)

YEAR	TEAM	LVL	AGE	W	L	SV	G	GS	IP	H	HR	BB/9	K/9	K	GB%	BABIP	WHIP	ERA	DRA-	WARP	MPH	FB%	Whiff%	CSP
2019	STK	A+	24	0	0	0	3	3	6	5	2	6.0	13.5	9	33.3%	.300	1.50	6.00	110	0.0				
2019	MID	AA	24	0	0	0	6	1	8^{1}	9	2	3.2	14.0	13	57.9%	.412	1.44	4.32	80	0.1				
2019	LV	AAA	24	4	1	0	9	0	11	7	3	2.5	13.1	16	41.7%	.190	0.91	4.91	78	0.2				
2019	OAK	MLB	24	2	0	0	10	0	11^{1}	10	1	4.0	10.3	13	44.8%	.321	1.32	3.18	98	0.1	97.2	63.9%	30.9%	50.6%
2021	LV	AAA	26	2	5	1	29	4	48^{2}	61	12	3.5	10.7	58	39.5%	.363	1.64	6.10	91	0.4				
2021	OAK	MLB	26	0	3	0	12	0	13^{1}	18	1	4.0	10.8	16	52.4%	.415	1.80	6.07	96	0.1	96.0	65.0%	24.5%	57.2%
2022 DC	*OAK*	*MLB*	*27*	*2*	*3*	*4*	*59*	*0*	*51.7*	*48*	*7*	*3.7*	*9.4*	*54*	*42.8%*	*.296*	*1.35*	*4.17*	*103*	*0.1*	*96.2*	*64.8%*	*25.9%*	*55.8%*

Comparables: Troy Cate, Scott Alexander, Jonathan Holder

Puk's development has been pulled hither and thither by arm injuries—Tommy John surgery in 2018, shoulder surgery in '20—that have left him at a crossroads. His fastball is back in the 94–97 range, but that's two miles per hour down from its average two years ago, and the sinker he added hasn't done much. The A's tossed him into relief, where he spent most of the year between Oakland and Triple-A, but his numbers were nothing special. The slider and changeup are still excellent, and there's no reason for Oakland to give up on him now. But those dreams of a rotation fronted by Puk and the now-departed Jesús Luzardo are long gone.

Sergio Romo RHP Born: 03/04/83 Age: 39 Bats: R Throws: R Height: 5'11" Weight: 185 lb. Origin: Round 28, 2005 Draft (#852 overall)

YEAR	TEAM	LVL	AGE	W	L	SV	G	GS	IP	H	HR	BB/9	K/9	K	GB%	BABIP	WHIP	ERA	DRA-	WARP	MPH	FB%	Whiff%	CSP
2019	MIA	MLB	36	2	0	17	38	0	37^{2}	33	4	3.1	7.9	33	36.4%	.274	1.22	3.58	112	0.1	86.6	26.2%	30.1%	42.7%
2019	MIN	MLB	36	0	1	3	27	0	22^{2}	17	3	1.6	10.7	27	35.0%	.246	0.93	3.18	95	0.3	86.1	22.0%	30.6%	44.0%
2020	MIN	MLB	37	1	2	5	24	0	20	16	3	3.2	10.4	23	31.5%	.255	1.15	4.05	113	0.1	85.6	25.8%	28.6%	42.2%
2021	OAK	MLB	38	1	1	3	66	0	61^{2}	56	9	3.1	8.8	60	37.5%	.281	1.25	4.67	105	0.4	85.7	33.3%	29.2%	49.2%
2022 DC	*FA*	*MLB*	*39*	*3*	*3*	*0*	*71*	*0*	*61.7*	*59*	*10*	*3.0*	*8.9*	*61*	*35.6%*	*.291*	*1.30*	*4.26*	*106*	*0.0*	*85.8*	*30.4%*	*29.3%*	*46.9%*

Comparables: Kyle Farnsworth, Aurelio Lopez, Mike Fetters

Romo has never been anyone's idea of a hard thrower, but his fastball lodged itself firmly in the Jamie Moyer Zone in 2021, puttering along at 85 mph on average. Luckily for him, his frisbee slider is still a weapon; even when opposing hitters have enough tape on it to circle the world a dozen times, they can't touch it, and they managed a mere .219 batting average against it last year. Like Seth Rogen's dice-rolling dance move in *Knocked Up*, though, it's the only move he has, and it's not quite the whiff-inducing monster it was in Romo's prime. There's probably enough juice left to squeeze out a season of acceptable middle relief work, but prospective buyers should remember to handle antiques with care.

Trevor Rosenthal RHP Born: 05/29/90 Age: 32 Bats: R Throws: R Height: 6'2" Weight: 230 lb. Origin: Round 21, 2009 Draft (#639 overall)

YEAR	TEAM	LVL	AGE	W	L	SV	G	GS	IP	H	HR	BB/9	K/9	K	GB%	BABIP	WHIP	ERA	DRA-	WARP	MPH	FB%	Whiff%	CSP
2019	HBG	AA	29	0	1	0	10	0	9^{1}	9	2	6.8	10.6	11	46.2%	.292	1.71	5.79	104	0.1				
2019	TOL	AAA	29	0	0	0	6	0	5^{1}	8	2	10.1	15.2	9	53.3%	.462	2.63	10.13	84	0.1				
2019	WAS	MLB	29	0	1	0	12	0	6^{1}	8	0	21.3	7.1	5	35.0%	.400	3.63	22.74	183	-0.2	98.2	75.5%	25.7%	44.3%
2019	DET	MLB	29	0	0	0	10	0	9	3	0	11.0	12.0	12	50.0%	.176	1.56	7.00	111	0.0	98.2	68.8%	33.3%	42.9%
2020	KC	MLB	30	0	0	7	14	0	13^{2}	9	2	4.6	13.8	21	40.7%	.280	1.17	3.29	83	0.3	98.1	66.5%	32.7%	49.8%
2020	SD	MLB	30	1	0	4	9	0	10	3	0	0.9	15.3	17	35.3%	.176	0.40	0.00	76	0.2	98.3	78.4%	45.6%	45.6%
2022 DC	*FA*	*MLB*	*32*	*2*	*2*	*0*	*57*	*0*	*49.3*	*37*	*6*	*6.0*	*12.6*	*69*	*41.8%*	*.282*	*1.43*	*4.39*	*101*	*0.1*	*98.2*	*71.5%*	*34.9%*	*46.6%*

Comparables: David Robertson, Jeurys Familia, Sparky Lyle

Signed to replace Liam Hendriks as closer at a fraction of the cost, Rosenthal never got a save chance, because he never got to throw a single pitch last year. He was knocked out first by shoulder soreness and then by a torn hip labrum that ended his season in July. After his resurgent 2020, it's an unfortunate turn of events, and it will leave Rosenthal looking for another one-year deal whenever the lockout lifts and he's fully healthy.

Lou Trivino RHP Born: 10/01/91 Age: 30 Bats: R Throws: R Height: 6'5" Weight: 235 lb. Origin: Round 11, 2013 Draft (#341 overall)

YEAR	TEAM	LVL	AGE	W	L	SV	G	GS	IP	H	HR	BB/9	K/9	K	GB%	BABIP	WHIP	ERA	DRA-	WARP	MPH	FB%	Whiff%	CSP
2019	OAK	MLB	27	4	6	0	61	0	60	61	7	4.7	8.6	57	43.8%	.320	1.53	5.25	97	0.7	97.6	50.9%	27.7%	45.6%
2020	OAK	MLB	28	0	0	0	20	0	23^{1}	16	3	3.9	10.0	26	40.4%	.241	1.11	3.86	94	0.3	95.6	58.8%	28.5%	45.5%
2021	OAK	MLB	29	7	8	22	71	0	73^{2}	58	5	4.2	8.2	67	47.5%	.269	1.25	3.18	101	0.6	95.9	60.7%	23.8%	53.4%
2022 DC	*OAK*	*MLB*	*30*	*4*	*4*	*33*	*82*	*0*	*71*	*64*	*8*	*4.0*	*8.8*	*69*	*45.9%*	*.286*	*1.35*	*3.96*	*98*	*0.3*	*96.2*	*58.6%*	*25.2%*	*50.8%*

Comparables: Erik Goeddel, Manny Acosta, Hunter Strickland

Mixed and matched with Jake Diekman in the ninth, Trivino vacuumed up the majority of Oakland's saves, re-establishing himself as a viable high-leverage relief option after two seasons in the wilderness. That came with too many walks and not enough strikeouts, though, and his velocity remains stuck in the 95–96 mph range instead of the 97-plus he lived in before. On the plus side, he's getting more ground balls and giving up less hard contact than 2020, but as someone who throws a sinker and a cutter, he's trapped by the variances of BABIP and infield defense. In conclusion, Trivino is a land of contrasts, a middle reliever with some late-inning upside if and when it all comes together.

Lineouts

Hitters

HITTER	POS	TEAM	LVL	AGE	PA	R	2B	3B	HR	RBI	BB	K	SB	CS	AVG/OBP/SLG	DRC+	BABIP	BRR	FRAA	WARP
Luis Barrera	OF	LV	AAA	25	386	53	16	6	4	37	39	67	10	2	.276/.348/.393	92	.328	3.7	CF(37): -3.6, RF(33): -0.6, LF(28): -3.2	0.5
	OF	OAK	MLB	25	8	1	0	0	0	0	0	2	0	0	.250/.250/.250	84	.333	0.2	LF(2): -0.2, RF(2): -0.1, CF(1): 0.0	0.0
Skye Bolt	OF	LV	AAA	27	199	41	12	2	9	29	32	43	5	0	.387/.492/.650	131	.482	2.3	CF(41): 1.9, LF(4): 0.0, RF(4): -0.4	1.9
	OF	SF	MLB	27	1	0	0	0	0	0	0	1	0	0	.000/.000/.000	91			LF(1): -0.2	0.0
	OF	OAK	MLB	27	59	5	1	0	1	4	1	14	2	0	.089/.105/.161	80	.098	0.3	CF(16): 1.7, LF(5): -0.1, RF(4): -0.2	0.3
Brayan Buelvas	OF	STK	A	19	392	54	11	4	16	50	37	95	17	7	.219/.306/.412	106	.253	-3.4	LF(32): -1.8, CF(32): -2.4, RF(23): -1.0	0.9
Aramis Garcia	C	LV	AAA	28	124	15	8	0	2	15	9	27	0	0	.268/.323/.393	86	.329	-0.6	C(23): -0.3	0.1
	C	OAK	MLB	28	94	8	1	0	3	7	1	28	0	0	.205/.239/.318	80	.263	-0.2	C(30): 0.7	0.2
Michael Guldberg	CF	LAN	A+	22	206	29	9	2	5	18	17	36	11	1	.259/.347/.420	116	.299	0.4	CF(39): 1.8, LF(2): -0.4, RF(2): 0.3	1.3
Brett Harris	3B	LAN	A+	23	94	14	3	0	3	11	8	20	3	1	.222/.323/.370	109	.259	0.6	3B(20): 0.4, SS(4): -0.0, 2B(3): 0.3	0.5
Vimael Machín	IF	CAG	WIN	27	123	17	8	0	2	18	12	9	1	0	.287/.374/.417		.299			
	IF	LV	AAA	27	393	65	17	6	11	58	49	72	2	1	.295/.389/.479	109	.344	0.6	3B(58): -4.0, 2B(26): 0.7, SS(4): 0.7	1.5
	IF	OAK	MLB	27	37	1	0	0	0	1	3	10	0	0	.125/.200/.125	79	.182	-0.2	SS(8): -0.9, 2B(3): 0.4, 3B(3): 0.0	0.0
Junior Perez	OF	STK	A	19	386	54	16	5	8	34	51	145	24	7	.207/.317/.359	80	.337	2.2	CF(58): 4.6, RF(22): 2.6, LF(15): -1.7	1.1
Robert Puason	SS	STK	A	18	337	43	12	1	3	27	24	139	3	1	.215/.282/.291	55	.383	2.2	SS(91): -0.7	-0.7

It's been a slow climb for **Luis Barrera** through the minors; nine years after being signed out of the Dominican Republic, he finally reached Triple-A last season at age 25, where he put up respectable if boring numbers. That's been his MO throughout his career, and should he break through that final barrier and reach the majors, it'll be his speed and strong arm that get him there, likely as a backup outfielder. **Skye Bolt** moved across the Bay, stayed about a month, then moved back. When the Giants cut him loose at the end of the month, his old team scooped him back up, plopped him into Triple-A and mostly left him there. His glove and his speed are excellent, but with the bat never catching up, his chances of becoming a major-league regular have dwindled to zero. It's been a minute since **Brayan Buelvas** put himself on the prospect radar with a strong performance in the Arizona League at just 17 years old; now 19, he got his first taste of full-season ball in Stockton and wasn't quite as standout. You can blame bad BABIP luck for some of his woes, and the peripherals were strong: a solid walk rate, not too many strikeouts, plenty of power and speed. He's handled tough assignments well, which bodes well for his development. A fourth-round pick out of Cal State Northridge, **Denzel Clarke** is a big bundle of tools—no surprise, given that his mother, Donna, competed in the 1984 Olympics in the heptathlon. "Rumor has it I ran straight out of my mother's womb at the hospital," he told *Baseball America* before the draft. The A's will have him focus on walking and getting more consistent at the plate. Picked up from Texas along with Elvis Andrus, **Aramis Garcia** managed the genuinely impressive feat of drawing a single walk in 94 plate appearances—a 1.1% rate! Oakland was the third organization of the 29-year-old's career, and he's already on to his fourth after the A's released him in September, letting him latch on with the Reds at the end of November. A hitting machine at Georgia Tech, **Michael Guldberg** is a contact-heavy speedster with little raw power but a smart, line drive-oriented approach at the plate. The A's had him playing center field regularly in High-A, though he can handle all three outfield spots, making him a likely reserve outfielder with a better-than-league-average bat. A monster junior year in which **Brett Harris** led Gonzaga in batting average, OPS, hits and extra-base hits put him on Oakland's board, with the A's taking him in the seventh round last summer. At 23, he's already on the old side for a prospect, and he could stand to draw more walks. His positional flexibility makes him a potential utility infielder if things break right. When Elvis Andrus and Jed Lowrie were both placed on the injured list on Sept. 26, ending their seasons, that opened the door for **Vimael Machín**, who'd spent much of the year languishing as an unneeded backup in Triple-A, to finish out the year as a big-league regular. The next day, he started at shortstop and went 0-for-3. A few days later, he too went on the IL with what was termed a stomach illness. Guess it's true what they say: no guts, no glory. **Junior Perez** struck out in a whopping 37% of his plate appearances last year as he struggled to catch up to anything and everything. He looked far better two years earlier in Arizona and is still very young, giving him time to put 2021 behind him. That has to start with more contact. **Robert Puason** had a miserable go in his first full season stateside, with a strikeout rate well over 40% and 29 errors in 91 games. Defensively, there's not much to worry about long-term, with evaluators still projecting him as a starter at shortstop. It's the offense that has to be concerning, particularly all the swing-and-miss and the total lack of power.

Pitchers

PITCHER	TEAM	LVL	AGE	W	L	SV	G	GS	IP	H	HR	BB/9	K/9	K	GB%	BABIP	WHIP	ERA	DRA-	WARP	MPH	FB%	WHF	CSP
Domingo Acevedo	LV	AAA	27	2	0	9	30	0	32^{2}	22	3	1.7	14.6	53	25.8%	.302	0.86	2.48	70	0.7				
	OAK	MLB	27	0	0	0	10	0	11	9	3	3.3	7.4	9	41.9%	.214	1.18	3.27	105	0.1	92.8	50.6%	28.4%	56.6%
Paul Blackburn	LV	AAA	27	4	7	0	17	16	88^{2}	114	8	2.7	8.1	80	54.6%	.376	1.59	4.97	91	0.8				
	OAK	MLB	27	1	4	0	9	9	38^{1}	52	8	2.3	6.1	26	51.1%	.341	1.62	5.87	122	-0.1	90.3	74.0%	15.7%	50.3%
Parker Dunshee	LV	AAA	26	1	5	0	10	9	43^{1}	48	7	3.5	7.9	38	39.7%	.308	1.50	6.65	122	-0.4				
Reymin Guduan	LV	AAA	29	4	3	0	30	0	32	39	2	3.9	9.6	34	50.5%	.389	1.66	5.06	88	0.3				
	OAK	MLB	29	0	0	0	11	0	14^{1}	19	1	3.1	3.1	5	34.5%	.340	1.67	6.28	141	-0.2	94.4	63.8%	19.6%	59.6%
Deolis Guerra	OAK	MLB	32	4	1	0	53	0	65^{2}	53	8	2.7	8.5	62	34.4%	.259	1.11	4.11	107	0.4	90.4	59.9%	28.5%	52.2%
Grant Holman	STK	A	21	0	1	0	6	4	15	15	3	2.4	9.0	15	43.2%	.308	1.27	4.20	105	0.0				
Grant Holmes	LV	AAA	25	1	2	0	36	7	66^{1}	99	11	5.4	9.6	71	37.8%	.419	2.10	8.01	103	0.1				
Adam Kolarek	LV	AAA	32	1	0	0	37	0	38^{2}	48	5	4.7	6.3	27	58.5%	.331	1.76	6.75	104	0.1				
	OAK	MLB	32	0	0	0	12	0	9	15	2	5.0	4.0	4	63.4%	.342	2.22	8.00	118	0.0	88.9	71.1%	12.7%	52.9%
Mason Miller	ATH	ROK	22	0	1	0	3	2	6	4	0	4.5	13.5	9	66.7%	.333	1.17	1.50						
Sam Moll	LV	AAA	29	1	1	2	12	0	13^{2}	12	2	3.3	11.2	17	57.6%	.323	1.24	2.63	80	0.2				
	RNO	AAA	29	0	0	0	21	0	21^{2}	19	3	6.2	12.5	30	44.4%	.314	1.57	5.82	77	0.4				
	OAK	MLB	29	0	0	0	8	0	10^{1}	8	1	4.4	7.0	8	44.8%	.250	1.26	3.48	113	0.0	93.7	55.1%	16.7%	55.2%
Miguel Romero	LV	AAA	27	3	6	2	28	13	74^{2}	86	15	4.1	6.5	54	49.4%	.303	1.61	6.27	108	-0.1				
Burch Smith	LV	AAA	31	0	0	0	4	0	5^{1}	9	3	6.8	11.8	7	27.8%	.400	2.44	10.13	94	0.0				
	OAK	MLB	31	1	1	0	31	0	43^{1}	49	5	2.3	5.8	28	37.8%	.308	1.38	5.40	122	-0.1	93.7	68.9%	20.2%	59.5%

Domingo Acevedo's fastball used to reach triple digits; now it glides in at 93 mph. Despite that loss of velocity, he posted enormous strikeout numbers in the minors on the back of his slider and changeup, which should earn him a longer look in what will be a depleted 2022 A's bullpen.

The 58.2 innings **Paul Blackburn** threw as a rookie in 2017 remain his MLB season high. Injuries kept him off Oakland's mound early on; his total lack of swing-and-miss stuff has done the job since.

The career walk rate of 7.9 per nine makes it all the more amazing that when **Wandisson Charles** reached Double-A this year, he handed out free passes only to every 11th batter. Armed with ludicrous stuff, he would be a top-tier relief ace if he had anything approaching control. Until he does, he'll remain an absolute terror to step in against.

For a second straight season, **Parker Dunshee** was trapped in his own personal ninth circle of hell, otherwise known as Las Vegas. His low-90s fastball and tendency to fill the strike zone don't mesh well with the high altitude and dry desert air—hence the ERA that looks like an aircraft model number.

Would you rather hear **Reymin Guduan's** name said in Harry Caray's voice or Sean Connery's? Regardless, you're not likely to see it again in the pages of this book.

Deolis Guerra has been in baseball so long that he first showed up in the 2007 Annual, in which Alex Gordon was our no. 1 prospect. He's still getting literal and digital ink 15 years later, a season after Gordon called it quits on his career. Oakland gave him a lot of rope in middle relief, to fine if unexceptional result. Here's to his inevitable 2023 blurb, and '24, and '25…

A two-way player at Cal, **Grant Holman** was drafted as a pitcher in July and got an over-slot deal. One look at his pitch mix and you can see why: a fastball that touches 97 mph, a slider and splitter with plus potential and a big curveball.

Grant Holmes has steadily added velocity over the last few years in the wake of a shoulder injury that wiped out his 2018, topping out at 97 mph in '21. Unfortunately, that added heat wasn't enough to conquer either his persistently bad control or the pitching-destroying machine that is Triple-A Las Vegas.

Picked up from the Dodgers before the season, **Adam Kolarek** gave up six runs in his first three outings and never recovered, eventually getting buried in Triple-A at the end of May. That's the amount of rope you get when you're a sinker-first sidearming ex-LOOGY who throws 89 mph.

Mason Miller's collegiate career was turned around by a diabetes diagnosis after his sophomore year; after adding weight and velocity, he went from the bullpen to the rotation, dominating in his final two years at Division III Waynesburg and as a graduate transfer at Webb-Gardner. The big righty has premium heat, throwing 95–99 mph, and he controls it well. His secondaries aren't as advanced, and until they improve, he profiles as a reliever, albeit one whose fastball would make him a real weapon in the late innings.

It's a shame **Sam Moll** didn't get to pitch in the 1920s; think of all the gangster puns! He remains stuck in the 2020s, as a would-be LOOGY in a league where that's no longer a thing.

A reliever throughout his many years toiling away in Oakland's system, **Miguel Romero** got the chance to start in 2021 at Triple A and was terrible, with a 5.46 ERA and just 41 strikeouts in 57.2 innings. He wasn't any better in the bullpen, allowing 17 runs in 17 innings and with nearly as many walks as whiffs. Next step: Inventing a third pitching position for him to fail at.

A thing that you shouldn't do as a fungible right-handed reliever with average stuff is strike out fewer batters than you ever have before. **Burch Smith** did just that, to predictable results. Maybe he's tired of bouncing from franchise to franchise and is trying to stop the carousel by breaking it.

SEATTLE MARINERS

Essay by Mike Duncan

Player comments by Jordan Shusterman and BP staff

Thirty-five years ago, I became emotionally entangled with the Seattle Mariners. The social conditioning of rooting for the home team soaked me like the rains growing up in the Pacific Northwest in the 1980s and '90s: The posters of Ken Griffey Jr. on my childhood wall. The days listening to Dave Niehaus on the radio. The nights sitting with my parents in the right field bleachers of the Kingdome. Decades later, teaching my children the names Edgar, Ichiro and Felix. There is no shaking my attachment to the Mariners, no avoiding it, and no way to recreate it. It is what it is because I was what I was. I am what I am because I was what I was. Hours, days, weeks, months and years of rooting for the home team accumulated like the sedimentary folds of an unmovable mountain. I am emotionally attached to the Seattle Mariners. I will be forever. God help me.

Emotions are strange and mysterious, but they are linked to measurable biochemical events. Our brains transform sensory input into glandular reactions. What we see and hear stimulates the release of hormones into our circulatory systems, physically altering our neurophysiology. Happiness comes riding on the floodtide of serotonin and dopamine. Stress and fear are nothing more than an onslaught of cortisol, epinephrine and norepinephrine. The tools of science measure the impact of these hormones: elevated blood pressure, faster heart rate, cold sweats, pupil dilation, nausea and restlessness. All of this activity serves a vital evolutionary purpose. Millions of years of adaptation perfected an array of physiological responses to keep us alive in the primeval wilderness.

But we are not in the primeval wilderness anymore. Why does watching a baseball game on TV in the passive comfort of the 21st century trigger hormonal floods meant to protect hairless chimps wandering through dangerously tall grass? Why does it make me anxious? Or tense? Or terrified? I have not stumbled across a saber-toothed tiger. I am not in danger. The answer is that I have tricked my lizard brain into thinking I am in danger.

Emotional attachment is the crucial link. Only when I care about something *outside* myself it is possible to feel something *inside* myself. People erroneously believe love is the opposite of hate and hate the opposite of love. But this is not true: The opposite of each is *indifference*. The opposite

SEATTLE MARINERS PROSPECTUS

2021 W-L: 90-72, 2ND IN AL WEST

Pythag	.467	*18th*	DER	.704	*10th*
RS/G	4.30	*22nd*	DRC+	93	*21st*
RA/G	4.62	*17th*	DRA-	106	*25th*
dWin%	.449	*23rd*	FIP	4.31	*19th*
Payroll	$73M	*25th*	B-Age	27.6	*2nd*
M$/MW	$1.4M	*3rd*	P-Age	28.3	*8th*

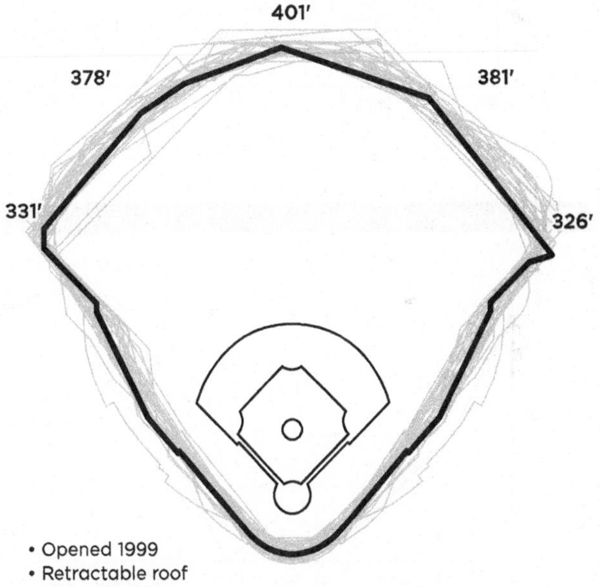

- Opened 1999
- Retractable roof
- Natural surface
- Fence profile: 8′

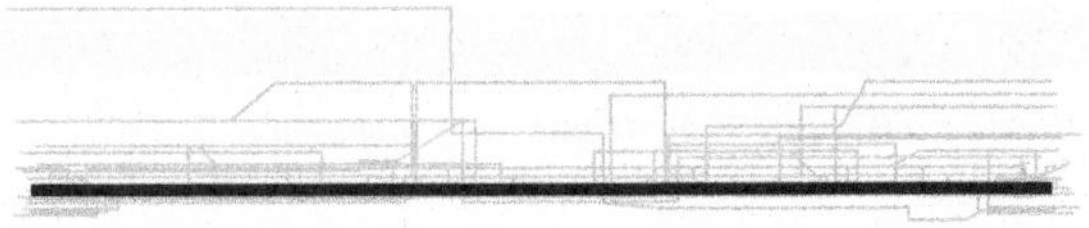

Park Factors

Runs	Runs/RH	Runs/LH	HR/RH	HR/LH
96	95	98	90	104

Top Hitter WARP	3.5 Ty France
Top Pitcher WARP	1.9 Paul Sewald
Top Prospect	Julio Rodriguez

Payroll History (in millions)

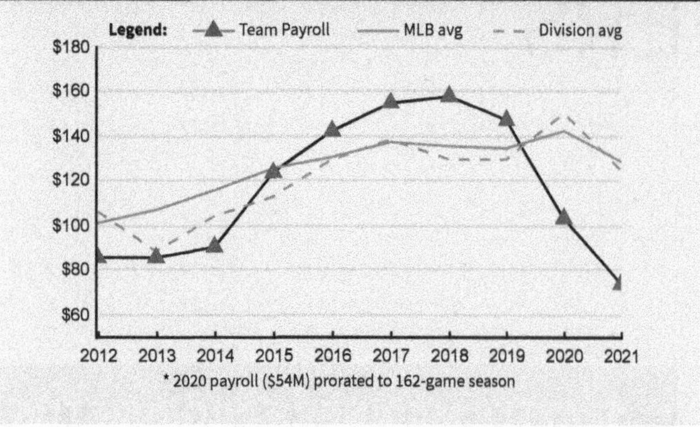

Future Commitments (in millions)

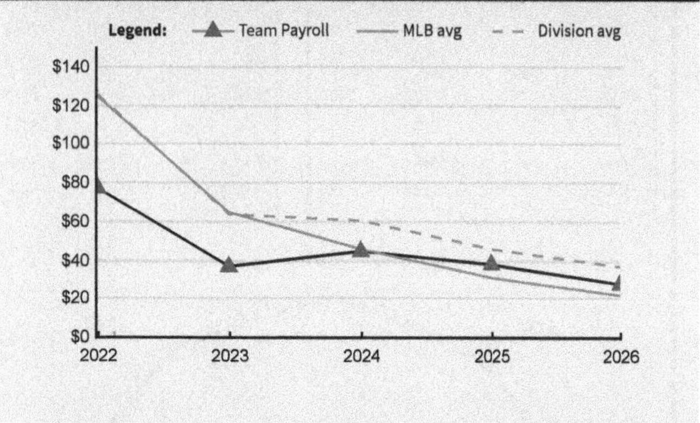

Farm System Ranking

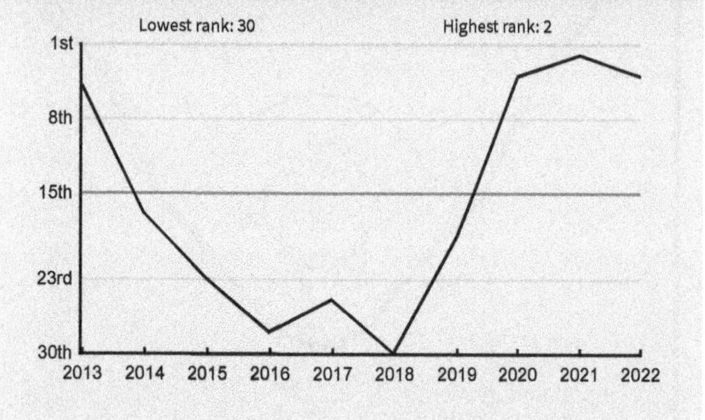

Personnel

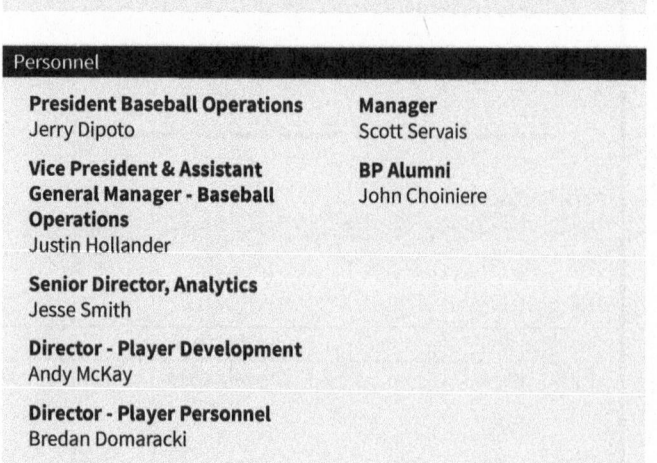

President Baseball Operations
Jerry Dipoto

Vice President & Assistant General Manager - Baseball Operations
Justin Hollander

Senior Director, Analytics
Jesse Smith

Director - Player Development
Andy McKay

Director - Player Personnel
Bredan Domaracki

Manager
Scott Servais

BP Alumni
John Choiniere

of all emotions is indifference. I feel nothing for what I do not care about. Caring is the prerequisite for anger, happiness, pride, embarrassment, resentment, fear or excitement. And when I trick my brain into caring about something that is not me, what happens to them happens to me. And so it is with the Mariners. I care about them. So what happens to them doesn't just happen in the field, it happens inside my heart.

This emotional entanglement is extraordinarily problematic, because baseball is a business. Baseball has been a business since the original Lords of the Realm bought a crate of red stockings and charged a halfpenny to gaze upon the Elysian Fields. And what is the business of baseball? The list of profit-generating opportunities is easy to assemble: ticket sales, merchandise, television rights, concessions, advertising, corporate partnerships, real estate and gambling. But though this is the kind of list that satisfies a Harvard MBA, it actually tells us very little about the business of baseball. The list enumerates the available revenue streams, but cannot explain *why* these revenue streams exist. Why am I willing to pay money for a ticket? Why do I buy hot dogs and beer? Why am I willing to sit in a captive audience while the local hardware store alerts me to the unbeatable savings of their summer sales event? Without something deeper, these profit-generating opportunities simply do not exist. So what lies beneath?

Once we peel away all the layers, we find the business of baseball rests entirely on human emotions. This is a great irony. Emotions do not have a column on the balance sheet nor an appendix in the quarterly earnings report, so they are often deemed irrelevant by very serious people who intone with dismissive self-importance that *baseball is a business*. As if they have the slightest clue what business they are in. The game of baseball is simply a means of generating and orchestrating emotional states with a human consciousness. Without those emotions, there is nothing. Just men trying to hit balls with sticks. Baseball does not exist in the owner's suite, the front office board room, or even out there on the field of play. Baseball exists *in our hearts*. Our hearts are the only home baseball has ever known.

Baseball delivers emotional responses according to the structured rhythm of tension and release. Tension builds as the pitcher takes the rubber, the hitter enters the box and the fielders get set. It builds as the pitcher enters his windup, and the hitter prepares to swing. Tension reaches maximum intensity when the pitcher releases the ball. During the split second the ball travels from the mound to the plate, tension plunges at terminal velocity towards explosive release. We await the moment of contact, when the infinite possibilities contained within the building tension—half of them hopes, half of them fears—collapse into the reality of a single event. Witnessing this miraculous transformation from *potentiality* to *actuality* triggers a reflexive emotional response: joy, pain, anguish, regret, exhilaration, frustration or relief. Then the process repeats. Hundreds of times per game. Tens of thousands of times per season. Tension and release. Tension and release. Tension and release. Generating and orchestrating our emotional states.

But the tension and release only matter when the game matters. When the stakes of winning and losing are high. When peril exists. If a team like the Seattle Mariners is perpetually moribund, its fans never encounter peril and thus have little need for high-stakes hormones like cortisol and dopamine. The Mariners are the organizational equivalent of a 5–0 game heading into the bottom of the sixth in late August between two teams already eliminated from contention. There is no rattling noise, no peril, no stakes. This is not to say we have not had our moments: The Double; Felix's perfect game; Ichiro's 258th hit; Nelson Cruz's home run in Game 161; 1995 and 2001. But mostly, as I sit in my chair watching the Mariners play baseball, I am not perched on the edge of my seat saturated in adrenaline but, instead, sinking deep under a warm blanket of melatonin and drifting towards an afternoon nap.

This hardly seems to matter to the organization. The business of baseball is all about exploiting the fact that I have projected my deepest instinct for survival onto a specific team, and that the sedimentary layers of emotional memory make it impossible for me to feel the same way about any other team. I have watched Mariners executives treat the franchise as little more than the backdrop for a never-ending corporate retreat. Something between a social club, a status symbol and a piggy bank. They appear unable to comprehend that they must deliver on emotional investments or they will default into emotional bankruptcy. As the fan base grows bored and disillusioned, the fans cease to care. They no longer identify themselves with the team. They no longer crave winning and fear losing. Like complacent priests passing the collection plate for a forgotten god, the Mariners brass runs the risk of making atheists of the young, while old-timers like me sit and doze in the pews, purely out of habit.

But then, like a thunderbolt from the clear blue sky, the 2021 Mariners triggered a massive jolt of adrenaline. Incredibly, improbably, and in defiance of every objective measure known to baseball analytics, the 2021 Mariners started delivering emotional payoffs. Not once. Not twice. But over and over again. A close game would move toward the late innings. I could feel the tension building inside me. As it reached its unbearable limits—down by two in the bottom of the ninth with runners on base—the 2021 Mariners consistently released the tension with a surge of exhilarating positive emotional force. All the infinite possibilities that loom in the void between the mound and the plate—half of them hopes, half of them fears—somehow kept coming up hope: game-tying doubles rather than inning-ending double plays. Late-game home runs. Key strikeouts from the bullpen. An entire season made up of repeated hits of dopamine made even sweeter by the sheer disbelief that it was even happening at all.

The 2021 Mariners should never have been within shouting distance of contention. There never should have been tension or a possibility of feeling real emotions. They outperformed their Pythagorean record by a mind-boggling 14 games, propelled to 90 wins by the weak engine of a –51 run differential. The absurdity of it all only added to the excitement. The 2021 Mariners were not good, they were hardly even mediocre, but their dismally ineffective offense suddenly sprang to life when it mattered most. Or, more to the point: *only* when it mattered most. Deep in the advanced metrics at FanGraphs there is a stat called "Clutch," which measures a player's performance in high-leverage situations against the player's baseline performance. A player who slashes .300/.400/.500 in high-leverage situations and slashes .300/.400/.500 in *all* situations may be an MVP candidate, but they register zero on the Clutch scale. They are what they are in all situations. To move the Clutch needle, a player must perform markedly better in high-leverage situations than they do in all situations.

As it turns out, the best way to rate as highly clutch is to positively stink in all other situations. Take Mariners utilityman Dylan Moore. He slashed an abysmal .181/.276/.334 for the season, but hit .257/.366/.600 in high-leverage situations, including an ecstasy-inducing 8th-inning grand slam to cap a seven-run comeback against the vaunted Houston Astros on July 26. The 2021 Mariners not only posted the highest Clutch score in the league by miles, they posted the single highest team Clutch score *ever calculated*. Through a combination of determination, resilience and an absolutely stupid amount of luck, the 2021 Mariners delivered when it mattered most. They activated my lizard brain and reminded me what it meant to *feel* baseball. It was absolutely intoxicating.

Mariners fans have not often received the gift of meaningful fall baseball. In 2021, we did not appear sure what to do with it. In the last days of September, this improbably lovable team stood on the verge of the franchise's first playoff berth in twenty years. Yet, for the vital penultimate three-game series, the announced attendance totals at T-Mobile Park were 11,169, 12,635 and 17,366. The stadium was literally a quarter filled. No appeal to lingering COVID hesitancy could explain so many empty seats. It appeared painfully obvious that, despite one of the most electric six-month spans of Mariners baseball, and with the team presently in the middle of a 10-1 winning streak that was keeping their playoff hopes alive, *nobody cared*.

But then the faithful saw the light. For the final series of the season, they came. They believed again. They felt again. They cared again. The stadium was packed for three consecutive sellouts: 44,169, 44,414 and 44,229, creating an electrically charged crowd louder and more boisterous than anything I have witnessed in Seattle since the turn of the century. Baseball in Seattle was reborn suddenly and spontaneously. The fans cheered and winced with every pitch, an electric current of caring and concern linking everyone to everyone else. Emotional energy exponentially amplified by the rhythm of tension and release, tension and release, tension and release.

Which brings us to the Mitch Haniger Game, the second-to-last game of the season, against the Angels. Watching on TV, one saw the chyron on the broadcast repeatedly flashing the dire stakes: "Must win to remain in playoff race." This was life and death. In the bottom of the third, Haniger lined a single to right to score Ty France, putting the Mariners up 1–0. The stadium roared. The Angels tied the game, but, in the bottom of the 5th, Haniger came to the plate and belted a two-run home run, triggering a frenzied explosion of joy. The 3–1 score held through several tense innings until the top of the 8th. Paul Sewald, ace of the unexpectedly phenomenal bullpen, gave up a shocking three-run home run to put the Angels up 4–3. That swing felt like approaching the finish line of a marathon and having someone walk out and sucker punch you in the solar plexus. At home, I felt like I wanted to puke. Like I was about to die. But in the bottom of the 8th, the improbably resilient Mariners came right back and loaded the bases. With two outs, the game on the line, the season on the line, my life on the line, Mitch Haniger came to the plate again. Every pitch of the at-bat was an excruciating adventure. Then, on the sixth offering, Haniger reached down and pulled a single to left, transforming a stadium filled with anxious trepidation into one bursting with roaring exhilaration in a split second, as two runs came around to score. I myself, praying on my knees at home, did not yell or shout or cheer in any recognizable way. I simply giggled like a gibbering idiot for thirty seconds, rolling around on the floor in ecstatic delight. Oh, how good it felt to feel. It was worth the price, in decades, of admission.

In the end, of course, it was all for naught. The Mariners missed the playoffs. Again. But for three nights in October, Seattle remembered what it meant to *feel* baseball rather than just watch it. To the extent we are merely customers of a business, these emotions are the product. That is what we come for: for our hearts to hang in suspended animation as a ball hovers for an instant between the mound and the plate. When tension offers infinite possibilities—half of them hopes, half of them fears—and we care which one of them becomes real. In the end, the fact that we care is all that really matters, for our hearts are the only home baseball has ever known.

—*Mike Duncan is the author of* Hero of Two Worlds: The Marquis de Lafayette in the Age of Revolution.

Hitters

Edwin Arroyo IF

Born: 08/25/03 Age: 18 Bats: S Throws: S Height: 6'0" Weight: 175 lb. Origin: Round 2, 2021 Draft (#48 overall)

YEAR	TEAM	LVL	AGE	PA	R	2B	3B	HR	RBI	BB	K	SB	CS	Whiff%	AVG/OBP/SLG	DRC+	BABIP	BRR	FRAA	WARP
2021	RA12	WIN	17	65	6	3	0	0	2	6	14	1	0		.250/.333/.304		.333			
2021	MRN	ROK	17	86	16	2	0	2	10	10	26	4	1		.211/.337/.324		.295			
2022															*No projection*					

Comparables: Hector Nieves, Luis Ortiz, Emir Velasquez

Even in the year 2021, the action taking place in the late summer months known as the Arizona and Florida Complex Leagues remains a relative black box. Statistics are kept and live box scores have become more available in recent seasons, but these games are not streamed live on MiLB.TV like nearly all full-season affiliates. Fans rely on a smattering of footage captured and disseminated by player development Twitter accounts or prospect writers in attendance for a look at young players in their developmental infancy. In years past, you'd look at Arroyo's line from his pro debut and have no idea there was anything worth remembering. Thankfully, there were enough cameras running at an empty Sloan Park during a September game against the ACL Cubs to capture the signature moment of Arroyo's summer: a dramatic go-ahead home run followed by a bat flip that soared higher than any in-game flip achieved in recent memory. Known more for his slick infield chops as an amateur, power may never be a huge part of the switch-hitting shortstop's game. But now we know that when he does connect—whether that be in front of a handful of scouts and 15,000 empty seats, or a packed major-league stadium—he's capable of celebrating with the best of them.

J.P. Crawford SS

Born: 01/11/95 Age: 27 Bats: L Throws: R Height: 6'2" Weight: 199 lb. Origin: Round 1, 2013 Draft (#16 overall)

YEAR	TEAM	LVL	AGE	PA	R	2B	3B	HR	RBI	BB	K	SB	CS	Whiff%	AVG/OBP/SLG	DRC+	BABIP	BRR	FRAA	WARP
2019	TAC	AAA	24	138	20	7	0	3	15	19	25	3	0		.319/.420/.457	105	.382	2.2	SS(31): 0.5	0.9
2019	SEA	MLB	24	396	43	21	4	7	46	43	83	5	3	21.2%	.226/.313/.371	84	.275	-2.2	SS(93): 5.2	1.0
2020	SEA	MLB	25	232	33	7	2	2	24	23	39	6	3	18.3%	.255/.336/.338	93	.303	2.8	SS(53): 4.6	1.2
2021	SEA	MLB	26	687	89	37	0	9	54	58	114	3	6	15.6%	.273/.338/.376	92	.320	-2.0	SS(160): -7.2	0.8
2022 DC	*SEA*	*MLB*	*27*	*647*	*92*	*28*	*2*	*13*	*62*	*60*	*101*	*5*	*4*	*16.2%*	*.259/.332/.387*	*98*	*.292*	*-0.3*	*SS 1*	*2.4*

Comparables: Jonathan Villar, Freddy Galvis, Didi Gregorius

If we're living in the age of the slugging shortstop, Crawford may never be a full-blown star. As long as his exit velos stay toward the bottom of the scale, double-digit dingers may never be an expectation for the wiry 27-year-old known for his slick infield defense. Fortunately, there are other ways to slug. His 37 doubles were tied for ninth in MLB and first among all shortstops. A huge majority of those two-baggers were either pulled or slashed down the lines, but those count just the same as the ones in the gaps that fans eagerly project as becoming home runs one day. A better lineup would likely have him batting toward the bottom of the order rather than the top spot he occupied for much of 2021, but he's not a terrible leadoff option as someone who sees a lot of pitches and whiffs sparingly. With his defense, his offensive output need only float around league average to be considered a great player.

Zach DeLoach OF

Born: 08/18/98 Age: 23 Bats: L Throws: R Height: 6'1" Weight: 205 lb. Origin: Round 2, 2020 Draft (#43 overall)

YEAR	TEAM	LVL	AGE	PA	R	2B	3B	HR	RBI	BB	K	SB	CS	Whiff%	AVG/OBP/SLG	DRC+	BABIP	BRR	FRAA	WARP
2021	EVE	A+	22	285	56	23	2	9	37	32	63	6	3		.313/.400/.530	113	.390	0.3	RF(31): 0.7, LF(23): 1.4	1.6
2021	ARK	AA	22	216	28	10	2	5	22	28	58	1	2		.227/.338/.384	98	.303	-0.1	RF(26): 3.1, LF(17): 2.6	1.1
2022 non-DC	*SEA*	*MLB*	*23*	*251*	*23*	*12*	*1*	*4*	*24*	*22*	*69*	*1*	*1*	*30.6%*	*.226/.302/.355*	*77*	*.306*	*-0.1*	*RF 0, LF 1*	*0.1*

Comparables: Adam Eaton, Anthony Santander, Domonic Brown

DeLoach's amateur track record was an odd one: two lousy springs in the SEC with metal bats, two outstanding collegiate league summers swinging wood. His proponents entering the Draft argued that his impressive sample with wood bats outweighed his lackluster sample with metal, and portended a successful transition to pro ball. Detractors argued that the sample was far too small to trust, and the overall skillset screamed "tweener" at best. DeLoach has earned more fans than doubters in his first full pro season, comfortably handling High-A Everett before treading water in the hitter's hell that is Double-A Arkansas. Ultimately, no matter the minor-league numbers, those saddled with the "potential fourth outfielder" label early in their pro careers struggle to shake it until they earn a starting job at the major-league level. DeLoach is on track to get that opportunity, albeit maybe not in Seattle, where the projected outfield of 2023 is as crowded as any across the league.

Harry Ford C/DH

Born: 02/21/03 Age: 19 Bats: R Throws: R Height: 5'10" Weight: 200 lb. Origin: Round 1, 2021 Draft (#12 overall)

YEAR	TEAM	LVL	AGE	PA	R	2B	3B	HR	RBI	BB	K	SB	CS	Whiff%	AVG/OBP/SLG	DRC+	BABIP	BRR	FRAA	WARP
2021	MRN	ROK	18	65	12	7	0	3	10	9	14	3	0		.291/.400/.582		.342			
2022	*No projection*																			

Comparables: Marcos Betancourt, Maikel Hernandez, Daniel Rams

Over five drafts overseen by the Jerry Dipoto regime before 2021, the Mariners made a total of 27 picks in the first five rounds, 25 of which were spent on college players. The last Mariners first-round pick spent on a prep player was Alex Jackson, a catcher lauded at the time as the best overall bat in the 2014 class. In a fairly stunning twist, the top of Seattle's draft class in 2021 featured not one, not two, but *three* consecutive high schoolers, led by Ford. Fans can look at Jackson's fate to be reminded that high school catching has long been one of the draft's riskiest demographics, but Ford comes with a far wider base of skills than the average prep backstop. As a regular on the showcase circuit, Ford fared well at the plate against the best his peers had to offer, thanks in large part to excellent bat speed. His sturdy lower half resembles that of a powerlifter, but the bulk exists without compromising what is legitimately plus speed, a rarity for his position. Speculation of an eventual position switch is rooted more in projecting his athleticism all over the field more than skepticism about his abilities behind the plate. Early returns are exciting, but heavy is the head that wears the first-round high school catcher crown. And yes, if you're wondering: His full name is in fact Harrison Ford.

Jake Fraley OF

Born: 05/25/95 Age: 27 Bats: L Throws: L Height: 6'0" Weight: 195 lb. Origin: Round 2, 2016 Draft (#77 overall)

YEAR	TEAM	LVL	AGE	PA	R	2B	3B	HR	RBI	BB	K	SB	CS	Whiff%	AVG/OBP/SLG	DRC+	BABIP	BRR	FRAA	WARP
2019	ARK	AA	24	259	40	15	2	11	47	23	55	16	5		.313/.386/.539	139	.370	0.1	RF(21): -1.4, LF(12): -1.1, CF(12): -2.1	1.6
2019	TAC	AAA	24	168	28	12	3	8	33	11	34	6	2		.276/.333/.553	100	.304	-0.5	CF(22): 1.1, RF(9): -0.5, LF(6): 0.2	0.6
2019	SEA	MLB	24	41	3	2	0	0	1	0	14	0	0	27.1%	.150/.171/.200	68	.231	-0.7	CF(11): -1.4, RF(1): 0.0	-0.2
2020	SEA	MLB	25	29	3	1	1	0	0	2	11	2	1	31.4%	.154/.241/.269	68	.267	0.0	RF(6): -0.4, LF(1): 1.0	0.0
2021	TAC	AAA	26	51	8	1	0	3	7	9	15	3	1		.325/.451/.575	105	.435	0.2	LF(5): 0.3, RF(2): -0.5, CF(1): -0.1	0.2
2021	SEA	MLB	26	265	27	7	0	9	36	46	71	10	2	28.6%	.210/.352/.369	97	.265	1.5	LF(51): -2.7, CF(16): -0.1, RF(6): -0.7	0.7
2022 DC	*SEA*	*MLB*	*27*	*380*	*46*	*16*	*2*	*11*	*44*	*47*	*104*	*11*	*5*	*27.7%*	*.216/.324/.381*	*95*	*.279*	*0.9*	*LF 1, CF 0*	*1.2*

Comparables: Matthew den Dekker, Brett Gardner, Andrew Stevenson

In a vast baseball world filled with bearded guys named Jake, it helps to have *a thing.* In Fraley's case, it's his eye. This was one of the outfielder's many tools touted by the Seattle front office following his acquisition in the earliest hours of The Rebuild, but the only one that seems to have actualized at the major-league level thus far. Fraley swung at just 21.4% of the pitches he saw out of the strike zone in 2021 while walking a preposterous 17.4% of the time he strolled to the dish. These elite displays of discipline managed to buoy an otherwise lackluster statline amassed in uneven intervals throughout the summer due to Fraley's other *thing*: being on the IL (a hamstring strain in April, and COVID in July). Fraley's days as a permanent fixture in the Mariners' future are on the wane, but he'll surely have suitors. There are worse things than a 26-year-old outfielder who gets on base.

Ty France IF

Born: 07/13/94 Age: 27 Bats: R Throws: R Height: 5'11" Weight: 217 lb. Origin: Round 34, 2015 Draft (#1017 overall)

YEAR	TEAM	LVL	AGE	PA	R	2B	3B	HR	RBI	BB	K	SB	CS	Whiff%	AVG/OBP/SLG	DRC+	BABIP	BRR	FRAA	WARP
2019	ELP	AAA	24	348	83	27	1	27	89	30	51	1	0		.399/.477/.770	153	.410	1.2	3B(32): -1.7, 1B(29): -0.9, 2B(15): -2.7	3.0
2019	SD	MLB	24	201	20	8	1	7	24	9	49	0	2	24.0%	.234/.294/.402	88	.279	0.3	3B(36): -0.6, 2B(21): 2.3, P(2): 0.1	0.6
2020	SD	MLB	25	61	9	4	0	2	10	5	15	0	0	26.8%	.309/.377/.491	98	.395	0.7	1B(5): 0.3, 3B(2): 0.1	0.2
2020	SEA	MLB	25	94	10	5	1	2	13	6	22	0	0	24.2%	.302/.362/.453	100	.387	-0.2	2B(10): -1.0, 3B(4): -0.3	0.1
2021	SEA	MLB	26	650	85	32	1	18	73	46	106	0	0	19.1%	.291/.368/.445	119	.327	0.5	1B(106): 4.2, 2B(21): -1.3, 3B(5): -0.2	3.5
2022 DC	*SEA*	*MLB*	*27*	*443*	*58*	*20*	*1*	*12*	*60*	*30*	*74*	*0*	*1*	*19.8%*	*.271/.347/.426*	*114*	*.304*	*-0.7*	*1B 0, 3B 0*	*1.7*

Comparables: Conor Gillaspie, Josh Harrison, Erik González

Finally presented with an everyday opportunity, France ran with it and became a fan favorite in a hurry. His season can best be described by two truths and something that sounds a whole lot like a lie: First, France got hits. If there was ever any doubt that his long-lauded hit tool would actually deliver over a full-season of big-league at-bats, he quieted that for good. Secondly, France got hit. His 27 hit-by-pitches tied Mark Canha for the MLB lead and brought his career total—college and minors included—to a staggering 197 plunkings. And finally, most incredibly, France played exquisite defense. Indeed, thanks to the never-ending magic of Perry Hill, *that* Ty France became one of the better first basemen in baseball after Gold Glover Evan White hit the shelf. All signs point to France hanging on to the first base job moving forward regardless of White's return, which is a fairly shocking turn of events considering White's defensive reputation and France's seemingly guaranteed DH destiny. Vive la France.

Adam Frazier 2B Born: 12/14/91 Age: 30 Bats: L Throws: R Height: 5'10" Weight: 185 lb. Origin: Round 6, 2013 Draft (#179 overall)

YEAR	TEAM	LVL	AGE	PA	R	2B	3B	HR	RBI	BB	K	SB	CS	Whiff%	AVG/OBP/SLG	DRC+	BABIP	BRR	FRAA	WARP
2019	PIT	MLB	27	608	80	33	7	10	50	40	75	5	5	15.7%	.278/.336/.417	96	.306	0.8	2B(142): -6.7	1.5
2020	PIT	MLB	28	230	22	7	0	7	23	17	35	1	3	16.5%	.230/.297/.364	98	.246	0.1	2B(41): 1.9, LF(14): 2.9	1.2
2021	PIT	MLB	29	428	58	28	4	4	32	35	46	5	4	12.2%	.324/.388/.448	109	.359	-1.8	2B(94): -6.4, LF(7): -0.1	1.2
2021	SD	MLB	29	211	25	8	1	1	11	13	23	5	1	13.0%	.267/.327/.335	94	.299	0.0	2B(46): -3.8, LF(5): -0.6	0.1
2022 DC	*SEA*	*MLB*	*30*	*597*	*80*	*28*	*3*	*9*	*61*	*47*	*65*	*7*	*5*	*13.3%*	*.275/.342/.395*	*101*	*.299*	*0.1*	*2B -2, LF 1*	*2.1*

Comparables: Billy Goodman, Todd Walker, Robinson Canó

Much like Brendan Fraser is underappreciated for creating the modern "himbo" in 1992's *Encino Man*—a gentle caveman who just wants to party and be righteous—so too is the other Frazier overlooked for years of above-average production despite below-average power. After a hot start to the year, San Diego acquired him in one last desperate push at the trade deadline, only to watch him revert to *George of the Jungle*-level production. The Mariners, who didn't have a single reserve in their roster post an OPS of .620 or above, saw San Diego's infield logjam and, as they did the year before with Ty France, pried him loose for a song. He's a good team's seventh-best hitter, and while the Mariners would benefit from another upgrade on the dirt, Frazier's on-base skills and solid defense should provide safe, everyday production. Just don't tax his gig so hard-core, you crusters.

Mitch Haniger RF Born: 12/23/90 Age: 31 Bats: R Throws: R Height: 6'2" Weight: 213 lb. Origin: Round 1, 2012 Draft (#38 overall)

YEAR	TEAM	LVL	AGE	PA	R	2B	3B	HR	RBI	BB	K	SB	CS	Whiff%	AVG/OBP/SLG	DRC+	BABIP	BRR	FRAA	WARP
2019	SEA	MLB	28	283	46	13	1	15	32	30	81	4	0	26.1%	.220/.314/.463	99	.257	2.0	RF(43): 3.6, CF(24): 0.4	1.5
2021	SEA	MLB	30	691	110	23	2	39	100	54	169	1	0	29.8%	.253/.318/.485	117	.281	-1.9	RF(123): -1.6	3.1
2022 DC	*SEA*	*MLB*	*31*	*608*	*90*	*24*	*2*	*24*	*78*	*54*	*159*	*4*	*2*	*29.1%*	*.242/.320/.430*	*104*	*.296*	*-0.3*	*RF 3*	*2.2*

Comparables: Ken Singleton, Jermaine Dye, Hunter Pence

When a player has Tommy John surgery or breaks a hamate bone or tears an ACL, fans have a rough idea of when they'll be back in action, and back in pre-injury form, based on precedent. For Haniger, such a roadmap was never on the table: There are few cases of a foul ball leading to a ruptured testicle leading to multiple core and back surgeries, wiping out 20 months. So when Haniger arrived in Peoria for spring training claiming to feel stronger than ever, there was no reason to doubt him—but also no reason to feel confident that he could rediscover his pre-Series-Of-Unfortunate-Events form. Fortunately, it didn't take long for Haniger to prove that he was indeed back to 100%. The speed and defense took a moderate hit, compromising his overall value. But the bat—that perfectly crafted uppercut swing—produced countless clutch hits, including a dramatic go-ahead RBI single in Game 161 that sent the long-dormant home crowd into a frenzy. Most importantly, Haniger played. He avoided the injured list and started 157 games, the same number he did during his All-Star campaign in 2018.

"We're going to end this f****** drought," wrote Haniger in the Players' Tribune in October, lamenting the reality of coming up short while simultaneously urging the fan base to recognize the growing opportunity for Seattle. Though his long-term future with the club remains in doubt, with Kyle Seager departed, he's their clear leader, on and off the field.

Jarred Kelenic CF Born: 07/16/99 Age: 22 Bats: L Throws: L Height: 6'1" Weight: 190 lb. Origin: Round 1, 2018 Draft (#6 overall)

YEAR	TEAM	LVL	AGE	PA	R	2B	3B	HR	RBI	BB	K	SB	CS	Whiff%	AVG/OBP/SLG	DRC+	BABIP	BRR	FRAA	WARP
2019	WV	A	19	218	33	14	3	11	29	25	45	7	4		.309/.394/.586	151	.356	0.0	CF(33): -2.1, RF(8): -0.4, LF(3): 2.2	1.9
2019	MOD	A+	19	190	36	13	1	6	22	17	49	10	3		.290/.353/.485	109	.368	1.0	CF(32): 0.4, RF(8): -1.1, LF(2): -0.1	0.8
2019	ARK	AA	19	92	11	4	1	6	17	8	17	3	0		.253/.315/.542	121	.246	0.5	CF(12): 0.5, RF(5): 0.8, LF(3): -0.2	0.7
2021	TAC	AAA	21	143	29	9	1	9	28	15	22	6	1		.320/.392/.624	125	.323	-1.5	LF(11): -1.5, CF(11): 0.2, RF(6): 0.4	0.7
2021	SEA	MLB	21	377	41	13	1	14	43	36	106	6	4	26.9%	.181/.265/.350	77	.216	-0.1	CF(77): -1.6, LF(14): -1.8, RF(3): -0.1	0.1
2022 DC	*SEA*	*MLB*	*22*	*520*	*70*	*22*	*2*	*22*	*69*	*47*	*124*	*13*	*5*	*25.5%*	*.234/.309/.436*	*97*	*.271*	*1.0*	*CF 1, RF 0*	*1.9*

Comparables: Alex Verdugo, Kyle Tucker, Travis Snider

We've been spoiled in recent years by a cadre of uber-prospects hitting the ground running in The Show, taking the transition to big-league pitching in stride and achieving star status without delay. After over a year of internal and external consternation surrounding his highly anticipated—and manipulated—debut, Kelenic finally arrived in Seattle on May 13. He hit the ground, and the ground was quicksand. An explosive three-hit night, including his first career home run, in his second career game had the T-Mobile Park crowd delirious. Then, the humbling began in earnest. The Harpers and Sotos and Guerreros aside, prospects facing failure for the first time at the major-league level is hardly a rarity. 0-39, though? You wouldn't wish that kind of slump on even the cockiest of players.

The organization had no choice but to send Kelenic back to Tacoma; 24 games of 1.008 OPS hitting later, he was back in the Mariners outfield for good. The at-bats started to look more polished, but the results still eluded him, and his inaugural triple slash line still resembled that of a pitcher. In September, though, dreams of this young slugger leading their team back to the postseason promised land nearly became reality, as Kelenic slugged .524 over the final month when the games meant the most. By the final weekend, the 22-year-old was grabbing the microphone in his postgame interview to urge the fans to come out and support the team. If there's anyone who understands the weight of the expectations on his shoulders, it's Kelenic himself. He's fully embraced his role in the Mariners rebuild story arc. His strong finish suggests that the ugly early struggles were more of a detour, rather than a derailment, on his journey toward becoming a good big-league hitter. But there's reason to wonder if the ceiling isn't quite as high as some may have projected for him.

Kyle Lewis CF Born: 07/13/95 Age: 26 Bats: R Throws: R Height: 6'4" Weight: 205 lb. Origin: Round 1, 2016 Draft (#11 overall)

YEAR	TEAM	LVL	AGE	PA	R	2B	3B	HR	RBI	BB	K	SB	CS	Whiff%	AVG/OBP/SLG	DRC+	BABIP	BRR	FRAA	WARP
2019	ARK	AA	23	517	61	25	2	11	62	56	152	3	2		.263/.342/.398	91	.367	-3.5	LF(49): 0.6, CF(36): -4.3, RF(15): -1.2	0.0
2019	SEA	MLB	23	75	10	5	0	6	13	3	29	0	0	39.0%	.268/.293/.592	85	.351	0.6	RF(17): 0.3, CF(2): 0.1	0.2
2020	SEA	MLB	24	242	37	3	0	11	28	34	71	5	1	36.3%	.262/.364/.437	105	.341	2.2	CF(57): -3.2	0.8
2021	SEA	MLB	25	147	15	4	0	5	11	16	37	2	0	34.2%	.246/.333/.392	101	.307	-0.4	CF(34): -1.2	0.5
2022 DC	*SEA*	*MLB*	*26*	*414*	*51*	*16*	*0*	*13*	*53*	*43*	*125*	*2*	*1*	*34.3%*	*.231/.314/.389*	*92*	*.311*	*-0.5*	*CF 0*	*0.5*

Comparables: Marcell Ozuna, Dexter Fowler, Jake Marisnick

If you were to rank the reasons for Mariners fans to be excited to return to T-Mobile Park in 2021 after a season of watching from home, Lewis may have topped the list. A unanimous AL Rookie of the Year, capable of majestic dingers and highlight reel catches in center field? Anyone would head down to the ballpark to see that player. Those folks had to mill around the stadium for a couple of weeks, after a collision with the outfield wall in spring training resulted in a bone bruise. Seattleites, eager to make up for lost time cheering for their homegrown star, only saw Lewis for 19 uninspiring home games before a torn meniscus in the same knee that's haunted him his entire career put him back on the frustratingly familiar shelf. Still just 26, Lewis is no stranger to persevering through setbacks. But as the IL days and scar tissue continue to pile up, it's becoming harder to pencil him as the franchise cornerstone, or even starter, he appeared destined to be a year ago.

José Marmolejos 1B Born: 01/02/93 Age: 29 Bats: L Throws: L Height: 6'2" Weight: 239 lb. Origin: International Free Agent, 2011

YEAR	TEAM	LVL	AGE	PA	R	2B	3B	HR	RBI	BB	K	SB	CS	Whiff%	AVG/OBP/SLG	DRC+	BABIP	BRR	FRAA	WARP
2019	EST	WIN	26	65	4	3	0	0	3	3	12	0	0		.210/.246/.258		.260			
2019	HBG	AA	26	43	8	2	0	2	10	4	6	0	0		.308/.372/.513	124	.323	0.3	LF(7): -0.2	0.3
2019	FRE	AAA	26	382	53	29	2	16	63	28	80	1	0		.315/.366/.545	104	.370	-4.3	1B(48): 1.6, LF(23): 1.5, RF(14): -0.6	1.0
2020	SEA	MLB	27	115	12	4	0	6	18	7	32	0	1	33.0%	.206/.261/.411	86	.232	-0.3	LF(18): 0.3, 1B(5): 0.4, RF(2): 0.1	0.1
2021	TAC	AAA	28	353	66	16	2	26	75	54	69	0	0		.338/.439/.672	145	.361	-1.4	1B(45): 3.1, LF(32): -1.6, RF(3): -0.6	3.0
2021	SEA	MLB	28	122	11	4	0	4	12	15	39	0	0	31.8%	.160/.262/.311	79	.203	-1.0	1B(14): -1.4, LF(11): 1.9, RF(2): -0.3	-0.1
2022 non-DC	*FA*	*MLB*	*29*	*251*	*28*	*11*	*0*	*9*	*31*	*24*	*68*	*0*	*0*	*29.7%*	*.234/.315/.418*	*93*	*.294*	*-0.4*	*1B 0, LF 0*	*0.4*

Comparables: Jesús Aguilar, Rob Segedin, Brett Pill

Fun nickname? Check: Big Marm at your service. Laughable disparity between his Triple-A and MLB production? Check: his 1.140 OPS led all MiLB hitters (min. 300 PA) very nearly doubled his mark with Seattle. A singular jaw-dropping HR that leaves you wondering if he could one day break Barry Bonds' single-season record? Check: Marmolejos' homer off a 99-mph Dustin May fastball in April left the bat at 114.1 mph, the hardest-hit ball by a Mariner all season. There's really only one thing left to do for him to punch his ticket to the Hall of Quad-A Sluggers: hit 40+ homers for the LG Twins in the KBO.

★ ★ ★ *2022 Top 101 Prospect* **#15** ★ ★ ★

Noelvi Marte SS Born: 10/16/01 Age: 20 Bats: R Throws: R Height: 6'1" Weight: 181 lb. Origin: International Free Agent, 2018

YEAR	TEAM	LVL	AGE	PA	R	2B	3B	HR	RBI	BB	K	SB	CS	Whiff%	AVG/OBP/SLG	DRC+	BABIP	BRR	FRAA	WARP
2019	DSL SEA	ROK	17	299	56	18	4	9	54	29	55	17	7		.309/.371/.511		.351			
2021	MOD	A	19	478	87	24	2	17	69	58	106	23	7		.271/.368/.462	123	.326	4.1	SS(92): -1.1	3.1
2021	EVE	A+	19	33	4	4	0	0	2	2	11	1	0		.290/.333/.419	95	.450	0.4	SS(7): 0.9	0.2
2022 non-DC	*SEA*	*MLB*	*20*	*251*	*23*	*11*	*0*	*5*	*25*	*19*	*69*	*8*	*3*	*30.6%*	*.223/.288/.354*	*71*	*.295*	*0.6*	*SS 1*	*0.2*

Comparables: Jonathan Villar, Richard Ureña, Carlos Correa

In a system that hadn't just witnessed a supersonic breakout the likes of Julio Rodríguez, Marte's full-season debut may have gotten more acclaim. Or perhaps it was just the wait: It's rare to think of a 19-year-old's breakout as delayed, but it seems like whispers of his potential have been coming out of the complex league and alternate site forever. While Marte's stats don't jump off the page the way Rodríguez's A-ball performance did, the ball does jump off his bat, and he was one of the most productive teenage hitters in the minors. The Mariners seem content taking it slower with Marte than J-Rod, as he spent nearly the entire year in Low-A. Whether he sticks at shortstop long-term becomes a lesser concern the more he rakes, though it may determine the difference between him being a top-15 prospect and a top-5 prospect. He'll play all of 2022 at 20 years old, and might just be the next big thing.

Dylan Moore UT Born: 08/02/92 Age: 29 Bats: R Throws: R Height: 6'0" Weight: 185 lb. Origin: Round 7, 2015 Draft (#198 overall)

YEAR	TEAM	LVL	AGE	PA	R	2B	3B	HR	RBI	BB	K	SB	CS	Whiff%	AVG/OBP/SLG	DRC+	BABIP	BRR	FRAA	WARP
2019	TAC	AAA	26	35	3	0	0	0	7	3	3	2	1		.172/.294/.172	96	.192	0.5	SS(3): -0.1, 2B(2): 0.1, 3B(1): 0.1	0.2
2019	SEA	MLB	26	282	31	14	2	9	28	25	93	11	9	28.3%	.206/.302/.389	76	.290	-1.1	SS(31): 0.6, LF(31): 2.1, 2B(18): 1.6	0.3
2020	SEA	MLB	27	159	26	9	0	8	17	14	43	12	5	27.2%	.255/.358/.496	113	.314	1.6	LF(13): -1.2, RF(13): 4.1, 2B(10): -0.1	1.1
2021	SEA	MLB	28	377	42	11	2	12	43	40	111	21	5	25.9%	.181/.276/.334	85	.229	-0.3	2B(66): -2.2, LF(48): 2.6, 3B(10): 0.8	0.7
2022 DC	*SEA*	*MLB*	*29*	*396*	*48*	*16*	*1*	*11*	*46*	*37*	*107*	*13*	*6*	*25.9%*	*.203/.294/.361*	*80*	*.254*	*1.2*	*3B 1, LF 1*	*0.6*

Comparables: Steve Pearce, Ryan Flaherty, Adam Rosales

On a September 12, 2020 episode of his podcast, The Wheelhouse, GM Jerry Dipoto recounted a conversation with his assistant GM Justin Hollander about how Moore was "our Josh Donaldson." Hyperbolic as it sounds, Moore did enter that day with a .925 OPS, having seemingly unlocked the untapped offensive potential the Mariners targeted when they gave Moore a major-league contract in November 2019 before he had played a major-league game. Was this another monumental victory for Seattle player development a la Austin Nola? Alas, on the same date a year later, the stats you see before you. Such is the challenge of judging a sample within 60-game "season" as a marker of significant player improvement, as Moore's approach went unchanged, but his exit velocity vanished. He still provided a smattering of clutch hits and quality defense as Scott Servais' preferred utilityman, but it's hard to imagine Dipoto flipping Moore for a haul of prospects à la Nola anytime soon.

Tom Murphy C

Born: 04/03/91 Age: 31 Bats: R Throws: R Height: 6'1" Weight: 218 lb. Origin: Round 3, 2012 Draft (#105 overall)

YEAR	TEAM	LVL	AGE	PA	R	2B	3B	HR	RBI	BB	K	SB	CS	Whiff%	AVG/OBP/SLG	DRC+	BABIP	BRR	FRAA	WARP
2019	SEA	MLB	28	281	32	12	1	18	40	19	87	2	0	30.7%	.273/.324/.535	97	.340	-1.0	C(67): 1.4, P(3): -0.0, LF(1): -0.0	1.1
2021	SEA	MLB	30	325	35	8	0	11	34	40	99	0	0	33.2%	.202/.304/.350	90	.265	0.2	C(88): 1.1	1.1
2022 DC	*SEA*	*MLB*	*31*	*221*	*28*	*8*	*0*	*8*	*29*	*22*	*68*	*0*	*1*	*32.9%*	*.216/.302/.403*	*89*	*.277*	*-0.2*	*C -1*	*0.6*

Comparables: Yan Gomes, Nick Hundley, Steve Clevenger

YEAR	TEAM	P. COUNT	FRM RUNS	BLK RUNS	THRW RUNS	TOT RUNS
2019	SEA	9506	1.6	0.0	0.0	1.6
2021	SEA	12065	1.1	0.1	0.9	2.1
2022	*SEA*	*8418*	*-1.5*	*1.0*	*-0.1*	*-0.6*

It seems Murphy was a bit of a Juiced Ball Hero during his mini-offensive breakout in 2019, as his offense came crashing back down to earth in his return to action after he missed all of 2020 with a broken foot. With minimal offensive impact to offer, Murphy transitioned into the delicate role of Veteran Catcher Whose Defensive Metrics Aren't Very Good But All The Pitchers Like Throwing To Him. These catchers present somewhat of a conundrum for front offices trying to get the most out of their backstops while not trying to disrupt a pitching staff's comfort. It's a lot easier to swallow when it's Salvador Perez hitting 48 home runs. When it's a guy like Murphy slugging .350, it's far less palatable. Had Cal Raleigh not completely fallen flat on his face offensively, Murphy may have lost playing time far sooner, but for now, he appears entrenched as the safe option. The clock is surely ticking, though.

Cal Raleigh C

Born: 11/26/96 Age: 25 Bats: S Throws: R Height: 6'3" Weight: 215 lb. Origin: Round 3, 2018 Draft (#90 overall)

YEAR	TEAM	LVL	AGE	PA	R	2B	3B	HR	RBI	BB	K	SB	CS	Whiff%	AVG/OBP/SLG	DRC+	BABIP	BRR	FRAA	WARP
2019	MOD	A+	22	348	48	19	0	22	66	33	69	4	0		.261/.336/.535	151	.267	0.9	C(55): 5.1	3.9
2019	ARK	AA	22	159	16	6	0	7	16	14	47	0	0		.228/.296/.414	89	.286	-0.4	C(26): 1.5	0.5
2021	TAC	AAA	24	199	34	21	1	9	36	14	25	3	2		.324/.377/.608	124	.327	0.4	C(34): 7.2, 1B(2): -0.0	2.0
2021	SEA	MLB	24	148	6	12	0	2	13	7	52	0	0	33.1%	.180/.223/.309	53	.267	0.0	C(43): 3.4	0.1
2022 DC	*SEA*	*MLB*	*25*	*217*	*28*	*11*	*0*	*8*	*35*	*14*	*56*	*0*	*1*	*30.0%*	*.237/.292/.436*	*91*	*.283*	*-0.3*	*C 6*	*1.4*

Comparables: J.P. Arencibia, Josh Donaldson, Yan Gomes

YEAR	TEAM	P. COUNT	FRM RUNS	BLK RUNS	THRW RUNS	TOT RUNS
2019	ARK	3371	0.7	0.0	0.7	1.3
2019	MOD	8038	5.4		-0.5	4.9
2021	SEA	5497	3.9	-0.1	0.0	3.8
2021	TAC	5098	7.4	0.0	0.0	7.4
2022	*SEA*	*8418*	*5.7*	*0.1*	*0.1*	*5.9*

If not for Jarred Kelenic, Raleigh's woeful debut may have gotten more attention. His reputation as a slugging catcher after loud performances at nearly every level of the minors failed to translate, as the switch-hitter struggled to find his footing from either side of the plate. Fortunately, his defense made strides to the point where the team wasn't afraid to start him behind the plate during some of its biggest games down the stretch. With few obstacles ahead of him on the depth chart, the front office clearly hoped he would seize the starting job and never look back. That looks to have been a tad ambitious, but it doesn't seem like sending him back to Triple-A will solve anything either. As with Kelenic, it will be trial by fire for the beefy backstop.

★ ★ ★ *2022 Top 101 Prospect* **#3** ★ ★ ★

Julio Rodríguez OF

Born: 12/29/00 Age: 21 Bats: R Throws: R Height: 6'3" Weight: 180 lb. Origin: International Free Agent, 2017

YEAR	TEAM	LVL	AGE	PA	R	2B	3B	HR	RBI	BB	K	SB	CS	Whiff%	AVG/OBP/SLG	DRC+	BABIP	BRR	FRAA	WARP
2019	PEJ	WIN	18	63	7	4	0	0	10	8	10	4	1		.288/.397/.365		.349			
2019	WV	A	18	295	50	20	1	10	50	20	66	1	3		.293/.359/.490	124	.353	0.3	RF(40): 4.2, CF(23): -0.1	2.2
2019	MOD	A+	18	72	13	6	3	2	19	5	10	0	0		.462/.514/.738	134	.528	0.7	CF(13): -3.3, RF(3): -0.4	0.2
2020	ESC	WIN	19	64	4	1	1	0	7	6	16	3	0		.196/.297/.250		.275			
2021	EVE	A+	20	134	29	8	2	6	21	14	29	5	1		.325/.410/.581	114	.390	0.6	RF(19): 1.8, LF(1): -0.1, CF(1): -0.2	0.8
2021	ARK	AA	20	206	35	11	0	7	26	29	37	16	4		.362/.461/.546	125	.431	0.9	RF(20): 4.0, CF(12): -0.6, LF(9): -0.9	1.6
2022 DC	*SEA*	*MLB*	*21*	*63*	*8*	*2*	*0*	*1*	*8*	*5*	*14*	*0*	*1*	*29.2%*	*.265/.335/.418*	*108*	*.330*	*0.1*	*RF 1*	*0.3*

Comparables: Giancarlo Stanton, Eloy Jiménez, Domingo Santana

The J-Rod Show officially went international in 2021, as one of baseball's top prospects added "Olympian" to his resume. While the average prospect may see multiple corners, Rodríguez's various responsibilities, from Olympic qualifying with Team D.R. to the Futures game, had him zig-zagging from Everett to Florida to Mexico to Arkansas to Denver to Tokyo over the course of just two months. Incredibly, no amount of travel managed to slow him down, as he seemed to be the best player on the field everywhere he went. It was like he was in a video game, slowly increasing power as he unlocked every corner of the map. He laid waste to High-A pitching, almost single-handedly carried the Dominican Republic to a bronze medal and then completely failed to get the memo that it was supposed to be difficult to hit in Arkansas. Amidst all the globetrotting, the final destination of Seattle remains squarely in focus. More than anyone, his arrival will likely define the next era of Mariners baseball.

Kyle Seager 3B

Born: 11/03/87 Age: 34 Bats: L Throws: R Height: 6'0" Weight: 216 lb. Origin: Round 3, 2009 Draft (#82 overall)

YEAR	TEAM	LVL	AGE	PA	R	2B	3B	HR	RBI	BB	K	SB	CS	Whiff%	AVG/OBP/SLG	DRC+	BABIP	BRR	FRAA	WARP
2019	TAC	AAA	31	42	5	2	0	0	7	3	7	0	0		.256/.310/.308	96	.313	-0.6	3B(5): 0.1	0.0
2019	SEA	MLB	31	443	55	19	1	23	63	44	86	2	2	21.3%	.239/.321/.468	110	.248	-2.0	3B(104): -0.4	1.4
2020	SEA	MLB	32	248	35	12	0	9	40	32	33	5	0	20.4%	.241/.355/.433	115	.240	1.8	3B(53): 1.3	1.4
2021	SEA	MLB	33	670	73	29	1	35	101	59	161	3	1	29.7%	.212/.285/.438	96	.226	-4.1	3B(149): -2.5	1.2
2022 DC	*FA*	*MLB*	*34*	*552*	*61*	*25*	*0*	*20*	*67*	*53*	*136*	*2*	*2*	*28.3%*	*.222/.306/.405*	*89*	*.265*	*-0.7*	*3B 0*	*0.7*

Comparables: Robin Ventura, Eric Chavez, Darrell Evans

Over the past decade, Mariners fans have grown accustomed to saying goodbye, from Griffey to Ichiro to King Felix. Seager became the latest to exit the field teary-eyed to an ovation, although under far different circumstances. As ugly as the end of Felix's tenure got for some similar reasons, it was understandable for the organization to move on from a player whose performance had tailed off so severely. This was hardly the case with Seager, who launched a career-high 35 HR and played his customary 159 games with nary a peep of discontent.

Since the full-fledged rebuild began at the end of 2018, Jerry Dipoto has swiftly overturned the roster in dramatic fashion. The stated goal was to get younger and more flexible, flipping veterans at every turn possible, allowing him to reimagine the roster in his own image. Yet Seager remained, the final holdover from an era of Mariners baseball Dipoto seemed eager to turn the page on.

From Kevin Mather's reckless blather to the Bellevue Rotary Club, to the reported full fracture of the relationship between Dipoto and Seager, the end of the third baseman's Mariners tenure appeared imminent regardless of results. If anyone deserved a more graceful departure, it was Seager, who had done nothing wrong during his decade in Seattle and had earned the immense respect and admiration of everyone in the clubhouse and stands alike. Instead, those upstairs couldn't seem to wait to show him the door. Though the rebuild has undeniably yielded a positive outlook for the organization as a whole, the sour taste of Seager's exit will forever be a stain on the current regime.

Abraham Toro 2B/3B

Born: 12/20/96 Age: 25 Bats: S Throws: R Height: 6'0" Weight: 206 lb. Origin: Round 5, 2016 Draft (#157 overall)

YEAR	TEAM	LVL	AGE	PA	R	2B	3B	HR	RBI	BB	K	SB	CS	Whiff%	AVG/OBP/SLG	DRC+	BABIP	BRR	FRAA	WARP
2019	CC	AA	22	435	65	22	4	16	70	48	77	4	1		.306/.393/.513	133	.346	-0.6	3B(85): 6.5, 2B(11): 0.1, 1B(6): 0.1	3.7
2019	RR	AAA	22	79	17	9	0	1	10	10	5	0	1		.424/.506/.606	119	.443	1.2	3B(8): -0.7, 2B(4): -0.1	0.5
2019	HOU	MLB	22	89	13	3	2	2	9	9	19	1	1	18.3%	.218/.303/.385	91	.259	0.1	3B(24): -0.5, 1B(1): 0.0	0.1
2020	HOU	MLB	23	97	13	2	0	3	9	3	23	1	1	23.8%	.149/.237/.276	83	.164	-1.2	3B(14): -0.6, 1B(4): 0.5, 2B(1): -0.1	-0.1
2021	SUG	AAA	24	68	10	5	1	2	11	11	8	2	1		.352/.485/.593	129	.386	-1.1	3B(8): 1.1, 2B(3): 0.3, 1B(2): 0.1	0.4
2021	HOU	MLB	24	122	17	1	0	6	20	9	21	3	1	18.1%	.211/.287/.385	108	.205	-1.4	3B(30): -1.4, 1B(2): -0.1	0.2
2021	SEA	MLB	24	253	28	11	0	5	26	22	33	3	2	17.4%	.252/.328/.367	104	.275	-0.9	2B(58): -1.9, 3B(2): -0.1	0.8
2022 DC	*SEA*	*MLB*	*25*	*324*	*40*	*13*	*1*	*9*	*44*	*28*	*48*	*2*	*2*	*18.1%*	*.250/.330/.407*	*104*	*.269*	*-0.1*	*3B 0, 2B 0*	*1.2*

Comparables: Jeimer Candelario, Juan Francisco, Mat Gamel

When closer Kendall Graveman was shipped to rival Houston in the middle of a pennant run in exchange for Toro and Joe Smith, some within the Mariners clubhouse viewed the deal as a slap in the face. Trading two months of a reliever for a switch-hitting infielder with five years of club control is exactly the kind of move designed to draw praise from the cold-hearted analysts and scorn from those trumpeting the value of a cohesive clubhouse. Toro himself was probably thrilled to be extracted from an eternally crowded Houston infield. But one can imagine how the clubhouse may have looked at Toro upon arrival: "What's so great about this dude?" He decided not to wait to endear himself, homering in his first at-bat as a Mariner and staying hot for much of August, punctuated by an epic grand slam off—you guessed it—Kendall Graveman.

Yet, for his wide set of skills and versatility, he's an odd player to watch. On the spectrum of athletic grace, Toro falls closer to Hunter Pence than Ken Griffey, Jr. His above-average speed comes in the form of a waddle, and his defensive chops are strictly functional, never flashy. For all the contact he makes, you'd be generous to label either of his swings as particularly beautiful. Of course, none of these unusual aesthetics matter if Toro can finally deliver on the promising projections rooted in his excellent track record in the Minors. As Jeff Passan relayed on Twitter via a front-office source: "Abraham Toro has been on every nerd team's breakout list for the last three years." We'll see if the Marinerds were right on this one after all.

Luis Torrens DH/C

Born: 05/02/96 Age: 26 Bats: R Throws: R Height: 6'0" Weight: 208 lb. Origin: International Free Agent, 2013

YEAR	TEAM	LVL	AGE	PA	R	2B	3B	HR	RBI	BB	K	SB	CS	Whiff%	AVG/OBP/SLG	DRC+	BABIP	BRR	FRAA	WARP
2019	AMA	AA	23	397	50	23	1	15	62	42	67	1	2		.300/.373/.500	125	.331	-2.3	C(85): -0.9, 1B(1): 0.1	2.4
2019	SD	MLB	23	16	2	1	0	0	0	2	6	0	0	34.6%	.214/.313/.286	80	.375	0.3	C(4): -0.0	0.1
2020	SD	MLB	24	13	0	1	0	0	0	1	2	0	0	27.8%	.273/.333/.364	99	.333	-0.4	C(7): -0.4	0.0
2020	SEA	MLB	24	65	5	4	0	1	6	6	13	0	0	19.8%	.254/.323/.373	104	.311	-0.1	C(17): -2.2	0.0
2021	TAC	AAA	25	85	12	4	0	6	19	10	22	0	0		.219/.318/.521	104	.217	0.0	C(9): 0.1, 1B(8): 0.2	0.3
2021	SEA	MLB	25	378	39	16	2	15	47	28	99	0	0	27.4%	.243/.299/.431	97	.294	-0.6	C(35): -5.6, 1B(5): -0.1, 3B(2): 0.0	0.4
2022 DC	*SEA*	*MLB*	*26*	*384*	*42*	*16*	*1*	*9*	*45*	*30*	*91*	*0*	*0*	*26.4%*	*.222/.288/.362*	*79*	*.270*	*-0.5*	*C -6*	*-0.5*

Comparables: Christian Vázquez, Francisco Cervelli, Sandy León

YEAR	TEAM	P. COUNT	FRM RUNS	BLK RUNS	THRW RUNS	TOT RUNS
2019	SD	495	-0.1	0.0	0.0	-0.1
2020	SEA	2281	-2.1	-0.1	0.0	-2.2
2020	SD	597	-0.4	0.0	0.1	-0.4
2021	SEA	4805	-5.6	-0.2	0.5	-5.3
2021	TAC	1166	0.3	0.0	0.0	0.3
2022	*SEA*	*6012*	*-4.7*	*-0.7*	*-0.1*	*-5.5*

As the least-heralded member of the haul received for Austin Nola, Torrens always had something of an uphill battle to climb to justify his long-term entrenchment on the roster. His two best options entering 2021: prove to be a good-enough catcher to project as an offensive-minded back-up, or hit enough to warrant additional at-bats elsewhere. Efforts towards the former were abandoned by July when Seattle moved him exclusively to 1B/DH, but the bat did manage to show some signs of life. He slugged .542 vs. left-handed pitching, a promising mark if a platoon/pinch hit role is what ends up being his calling. For all the jokes made at his expense by neutral observers tuning into the Mariners down the stretch—"this team starting Luis Torrens at DH thinks they're actually good?"—it'd be unfair to single him out as the lineup's biggest laggard. That said, if the M's want to win 90 again, they might want to slot him in as Plan B or C.

Taylor Trammell CF Born: 09/13/97 Age: 24 Bats: L Throws: L Height: 6'2" Weight: 213 lb. Origin: Round 1, 2016 Draft (#35 overall)

YEAR	TEAM	LVL	AGE	PA	R	2B	3B	HR	RBI	BB	K	SB	CS	Whiff%	AVG/OBP/SLG	DRC+	BABIP	BRR	FRAA	WARP
2019	CHA	AA	21	381	47	8	3	6	33	54	86	17	4		.236/.349/.336	105	.299	2.2	LF(91): 0.7, CF(1): 0.1	1.8
2019	AMA	AA	21	133	14	4	1	4	10	13	36	3	4		.229/.316/.381	83	.295	-0.7	CF(31): -1.6	-0.1
2021	TAC	AAA	23	323	43	15	1	12	49	40	74	8	2		.263/.362/.456	95	.313	1.1	CF(32): -2.9, RF(30): -0.0, LF(5): -0.1	0.7
2021	SEA	MLB	23	178	23	7	0	8	18	17	75	2	3	43.4%	.160/.256/.359	62	.233	-0.6	CF(37): 3.3, LF(14): -1.0	0.0
2022 DC	*SEA*	*MLB*	*24*	*188*	*20*	*6*	*0*	*4*	*21*	*18*	*62*	*4*	*3*	*38.7%*	*.196/.284/.336*	*67*	*.279*	*0.4*	*CF 1, LF 0*	*0.0*

Comparables: Joc Pederson, Jesse Winker, Trayvon Robinson

Trammell had his shot, earning a starting job in Seattle on Opening Day while Kyle Lewis was healing and Jarred Kelenic was detained. It was like the baseball equivalent of mixing every single flavor of soda at the fountain drink station, as well as some milk and vinegar. His 15 extra-base hits provided a clear demonstration of his potential; the 10 singles showed why it remains, still, just potential. Nearly half of his starts featured multiple strikeouts. Based on his Triple-A numbers, there's still a chance that Trammell's athleticism and pop can make him a fourth outfielder. If another team still views him as something more, it may behoove the organization to give Trammell that opportunity elsewhere via trade—not that he hasn't already been subjected to that enough in his career.

Evan White 1B Born: 04/26/96 Age: 26 Bats: R Throws: L Height: 6'3" Weight: 220 lb. Origin: Round 1, 2017 Draft (#17 overall)

YEAR	TEAM	LVL	AGE	PA	R	2B	3B	HR	RBI	BB	K	SB	CS	Whiff%	AVG/OBP/SLG	DRC+	BABIP	BRR	FRAA	WARP
2019	ARK	AA	23	400	61	13	2	18	55	29	92	2	0		.293/.350/.488	125	.346	1.5	1B(88): -5.2	2.0
2020	SEA	MLB	24	202	19	7	0	8	26	18	84	1	2	38.1%	.176/.252/.346	66	.264	-0.4	1B(54): -2.0	-0.7
2021	SEA	MLB	25	104	8	3	0	2	9	6	31	0	0	29.9%	.144/.202/.237	73	.188	0.0	1B(30): -0.1	-0.2
2022 DC	*SEA*	*MLB*	*26*	*296*	*36*	*11*	*1*	*10*	*41*	*22*	*88*	*0*	*1*	*30.2%*	*.222/.288/.395*	*84*	*.283*	*-0.2*	*1B -1*	*-0.2*

Comparables: C.J. Cron, Peter O'Brien, Mark Trumbo

Sometimes, an athlete's struggles are so great that it becomes difficult to encapsulate them, through words or numbers. We say "it was a lost season," because to do anything but paper over it seems needlessly bleak, like obituary surfing. And so, it was a lost season for White, who suffered a hip flexor strain that morphed into a torn labrum, erasing any possibility of earning his place. It's not a question of fault, or effort; despite the infamous major-league contract, White wasn't ready to be a major leaguer. In 2021, he swung at 26 fastballs clocked at 95 mph or faster—and hit one single. With Ty France's success at the cold corner, and White cleared for baseball activity in November, he'll get a chance to spend time where he probably always belonged, Triple-A Tacoma.

PITCHERS

Tyler Anderson LHP Born: 12/30/89 Age: 32 Bats: L Throws: L Height: 6'2" Weight: 220 lb. Origin: Round 1, 2011 Draft (#20 overall)

YEAR	TEAM	LVL	AGE	W	L	SV	G	GS	IP	H	HR	BB/9	K/9	K	GB%	BABIP	WHIP	ERA	DRA-	WARP	MPH	FB%	Whiff%	CSP
2019	COL	MLB	29	0	3	0	5	5	20^{2}	33	8	4.8	10.0	23	38.9%	.403	2.13	11.76	105	0.2	91.4	47.7%	23.9%	51.1%
2020	SF	MLB	30	4	3	0	13	11	59^{2}	58	5	3.8	6.2	41	28.9%	.288	1.39	4.37	156	-1.1	90.2	47.0%	24.6%	47.2%
2021	SEA	MLB	31	2	3	0	13	13	63^{2}	71	11	1.8	6.8	48	32.1%	.303	1.32	4.81	127	-0.3	90.6	50.3%	21.6%	55.9%
2021	PIT	MLB	31	5	8	0	18	18	103^{1}	99	16	2.2	7.5	86	36.5%	.280	1.20	4.35	109	0.4	90.2	45.8%	24.5%	57.9%
2022 DC	*FA*	*MLB*	*32*	*8*	*9*	*0*	*27*	*27*	*145.7*	*155*	*24*	*2.7*	*6.9*	*112*	*35.0%*	*.293*	*1.36*	*4.66*	*115*	*0.0*	*90.4*	*47.4%*	*23.6%*	*55.0%*

Comparables: Tom Browning, Mark Buehrle, Jason Marquis

When you're an average innings-eater inking a one-year pact with a terrible team in February, you know what you're signing up for. The goal: Throw 100 not-so-terrible innings, and impress a contending team to flip a not-so-terrible prospect for you come July. That's exactly what Anderson did for Pittsburgh, and everything appeared to be on schedule. Things took an unusual twist, however, when a nearly-finished trade to the Phillies snagged on a prospect's medical, allowing Trader Jerry to swoop in and land the lefty instead. Those juicy 3-runs-over-5.1-innings outings for which Wild Card-aspiring teams are annually starved proved to be a crucial stabilizer for the Mariners rotation, and sorely missed in Philadelphia, as both teams tried to keep up with their snooty positive run-differential foes in their respective Wild Card races. Alas, a late September short-rest tribute to CC Sabathia vs. Oakland was sandwiched between two decidedly un-CC-like disasters against the Angels when Seattle needed him most. You could ask about Anderson what you could reasonably ask about several characters in the story of the 2021 Mariners: Was he the reason they came up just short? Or was he the reason they made it that far in the first place?

Matt Brash RHP Born: 05/12/98 Age: 24 Bats: R Throws: R Height: 6'1" Weight: 170 lb. Origin: Round 4, 2019 Draft (#113 overall)

YEAR	TEAM	LVL	AGE	W	L	SV	G	GS	IP	H	HR	BB/9	K/9	K	GB%	BABIP	WHIP	ERA	DRA-	WARP	MPH	FB%	Whiff%	CSP
2021	EVE	A+	23	3	2	1	10	9	42^1	31	3	5.3	13.2	62	51.1%	.315	1.32	2.55	92	0.5				
2021	ARK	AA	23	3	2	0	10	10	55	32	3	3.8	13.1	80	45.4%	.252	1.00	2.13	78	1.0				
2022 DC	*SEA*	*MLB*	*24*	*3*	*3*	*0*	*11*	*11*	*51*	*42*	*6*	*5.3*	*10.6*	*60*	*44.1%*	*.288*	*1.43*	*4.24*	*100*	*0.4*				

Comparables: Mike Busby, Yordano Ventura, Robbie Ross Jr.

Acquired from San Diego as a PTBNL for Taylor Williams in what can only be described as the Austin Nola Blockbuster Encore, Brash was hardly on the national radar when he finally got named. Just twelve months later, he was summoned to the big leagues in the final week of the regular season as a potential secret weapon, à la David Price, except this was a fourth rounder from Niagara, not a first-overall pick from Vanderbilt. Though not ultimately used in any of Seattle's final games, that he was even considered for such a situation underscores the stunning degree to which he broke out in 2021. Arguably no pitcher in the minors raised their stock more than Brash, who categorically carved both levels he pitched at thanks to an upper-90s fastball and a vicious slider, both of which feature elite spin rates. The violent delivery and sketchy injury history may still portend a future in relief, but that stuff is more than nasty enough to tame big-league hitters no matter what inning it's deployed in.

Diego Castillo RHP Born: 01/18/94 Age: 28 Bats: R Throws: R Height: 6'3" Weight: 250 lb. Origin: International Free Agent, 2014

YEAR	TEAM	LVL	AGE	W	L	SV	G	GS	IP	H	HR	BB/9	K/9	K	GB%	BABIP	WHIP	ERA	DRA-	WARP	MPH	FB%	Whiff%	CSP
2019	TB	MLB	25	5	8	8	65	6	68^2	59	8	3.4	10.6	81	55.1%	.302	1.24	3.41	80	1.4	98.3	48.6%	32.5%	48.0%
2020	TB	MLB	26	3	0	4	22	0	21^2	12	3	4.6	9.6	23	59.3%	.176	1.06	1.66	81	0.5	96.3	35.3%	38.2%	46.6%
2021	SEA	MLB	27	3	1	2	24	0	22	14	4	2.9	10.6	26	54.9%	.213	0.95	2.86	88	0.3	94.5	39.9%	29.7%	52.6%
2021	TB	MLB	27	2	4	14	37	0	36^1	26	5	2.5	12.1	49	44.7%	.269	0.99	2.72	67	1.0	95.1	29.6%	34.6%	54.1%
2022 DC	*SEA*	*MLB*	*28*	*3*	*3*	*3*	*74*	*0*	*64.7*	*50*	*6*	*3.2*	*11.1*	*79*	*50.2%*	*.282*	*1.14*	*2.90*	*75*	*1.1*	*95.9*	*37.5%*	*33.6%*	*51.2%*

Comparables: Derrick Turnbow, Tim Scott, Miguel Socolovich

For someone who has pitched in the World Series and with stuff as hellacious as he has, Castillo's mound presence does not inspire confidence. If you just watched him between every pitch—the constant fidgeting, the frequent brow-wiping—you'd think he was some elementary school kid forced to perform at a talent show. Then, his herky-jerky motion unleashes the ball towards the catcher and you're quickly reminded why Castillo has become one of the more uncomfortable at-bats in the game. Though his peripherals took a slight hit after being acquired from Tampa Bay, the bulky righty still racked up the strikeouts via slider and groundballs via sinker, albeit with a few poorly-timed long balls mixed in. It was somewhat odd to watch Seattle pay a moderately hefty price for a premium arm in Castillo in the same season that they were routinely pulling similarly productive relief rabbits out of hats with ease, but you can understand the appeal.

Sean Doolittle LHP Born: 09/26/86 Age: 35 Bats: L Throws: L Height: 6'2" Weight: 204 lb. Origin: Round 1, 2007 Draft (#41 overall)

YEAR	TEAM	LVL	AGE	W	L	SV	G	GS	IP	H	HR	BB/9	K/9	K	GB%	BABIP	WHIP	ERA	DRA-	WARP	MPH	FB%	Whiff%	CSP
2019	WAS	MLB	32	6	5	29	63	0	60	63	11	2.3	9.9	66	24.9%	.315	1.30	4.05	109	0.3	93.5	88.2%	23.5%	48.1%
2020	WAS	MLB	33	0	2	0	11	0	7^2	9	3	4.7	7.0	6	3.8%	.273	1.70	5.87	161	-0.2	90.8	81.9%	18.7%	49.3%
2021	SEA	MLB	34	0	0	0	11	0	11^1	10	1	4.0	9.5	12	21.9%	.290	1.32	4.76	110	0.0	93.6	77.1%	29.3%	57.0%
2021	CIN	MLB	34	3	1	1	45	0	38^1	40	6	4.2	9.6	41	18.6%	.324	1.51	4.46	109	0.2	93.0	89.2%	23.6%	56.9%
2022 DC	*FA*	*MLB*	*35*	*2*	*2*	*0*	*57*	*0*	*49.3*	*45*	*9*	*3.1*	*9.2*	*50*	*24.1%*	*.278*	*1.28*	*4.35*	*108*	*0.0*	*93.1*	*86.8%*	*24.0%*	*54.0%*

Comparables: Steve Cishek, Fernando Salas, Mike Dunn

To try and understand Doolittle's decline is to play a frustrating game of Spot The Difference between the 2019 World Series champion version and his current bullpen ronin form. At first glance, a lot looks familiar. It's the same picture, surely. He's still resting his blonde beard on his glove as he peers in for the catcher's sign. He's still wearing goggles. He's still throwing a truckload of fastballs at the top of the zone at a reasonably high velocity for a left-hander. Ah, hold on—the table is missing one of its back legs in the first picture. The single tick of velo lost since his 2017/2018 peak has diminished his once-invisiball heater to a reasonably hittable pitch, yet one he still relies on just as heavily. The command has loosened considerably, yielding more walks than are acceptable for someone hoping to pitch high-leverage. Doolittle is far from a lost cause, with more than enough raw stuff still present to suggest that the right tweaks to the repertoire could unlock a solid reliever once again. The fastball has carried Doolittle this far; it may finally be time to give some of those other pitches some love.

Justin Dunn RHP Born: 09/22/95 Age: 26 Bats: R Throws: R Height: 6'2" Weight: 185 lb. Origin: Round 1, 2016 Draft (#19 overall)

YEAR	TEAM	LVL	AGE	W	L	SV	G	GS	IP	H	HR	BB/9	K/9	K	GB%	BABIP	WHIP	ERA	DRA-	WARP	MPH	FB%	Whiff%	CSP
2019	ARK	AA	23	9	5	0	25	25	131^2	118	13	2.7	10.8	158	37.5%	.314	1.19	3.55	81	1.7				
2019	SEA	MLB	23	0	0	0	4	4	6^2	2	0	12.2	6.8	5	43.8%	.125	1.65	2.70	117	0.0	92.5	58.8%	22.2%	44.4%
2020	SEA	MLB	24	4	1	0	10	10	45^2	31	10	6.1	7.5	38	32.3%	.179	1.36	4.34	148	-0.7	91.4	54.8%	22.2%	46.2%
2021	SEA	MLB	25	1	3	0	11	11	50^1	37	6	5.2	8.8	49	33.8%	.238	1.31	3.75	109	0.2	93.8	51.8%	24.9%	54.9%
2022 DC	*SEA*	*MLB*	*26*	*3*	*4*	*0*	*12*	*12*	*63.3*	*58*	*10*	*5.0*	*9.2*	*65*	*35.5%*	*.283*	*1.48*	*5.02*	*117*	*0.0*	*92.9*	*53.1%*	*23.8%*	*51.4%*

Comparables: Jason Grimsley, Trent Thornton, Jharel Cotton

Dunn may have been the Best Shape of His Life champion for Seattle, arriving to Peoria significantly svelter and the couple ticks of velo he was sorely missing in 2020. With a livelier heater and ditching his sinker for an increased emphasis on his curveball, Dunn took modest strides in the K/BB department, and the run prevention benefitted in turn. Just when it seemed like he was turning the corner, shoulder inflammation shut down the party in June. An attempted rehab outing in September was cut short after just four pitches when Dunn felt further discomfort, officially ending his season on a sour note. A healthy Dunn could reasonably hold down a rotation spot for a couple months, but he'll need to unlock the ancient secret of fastball command to stave off the army of arms racing through the minors to replace him.

Chris Flexen RHP Born: 07/01/94 Age: 28 Bats: R Throws: R Height: 6'3" Weight: 250 lb. Origin: Round 14, 2012 Draft (#440 overall)

YEAR	TEAM	LVL	AGE	W	L	SV	G	GS	IP	H	HR	BB/9	K/9	K	GB%	BABIP	WHIP	ERA	DRA-	WARP	MPH	FB%	Whiff%	CSP
2019	SYR	AAA	24	5	3	0	26	14	78^{2}	94	11	2.4	10.5	92	43.9%	.382	1.46	4.46	84	1.7				
2019	NYM	MLB	24	0	3	0	9	1	13^{2}	15	1	8.6	6.6	10	34.0%	.304	2.05	6.59	130	-0.1	94.5	61.7%	20.4%	46.8%
2021	SEA	MLB	26	14	6	0	31	31	179^{2}	185	19	2.0	6.3	125	42.3%	.300	1.25	3.61	112	0.5	92.8	40.0%	19.3%	57.0%
2022 DC	*SEA*	*MLB*	*27*	*10*	*10*	*0*	*29*	*29*	*169*	*182*	*23*	*2.6*	*6.4*	*120*	*42.0%*	*.296*	*1.37*	*4.50*	*112*	*0.1*	*92.9*	*40.7%*	*19.3%*	*56.7%*

Comparables: Kyle Drabek, José Ureña, Jarred Cosart

In one sense, the overhauled arsenal Flexen brought back from his breakout year in Korea didn't translate against major-league hitters. His four-pitch mix garnered a 28% strikeout rate for the Doosan Bears, best among all qualified KBO starting pitchers in 2020. That same repertoire—or at least, an awfully similar version of it—managed a measly 16.9% mark in his return to the big leagues in 2021, good for 107th out of 115 MLB starters (min. 100 IP). A 95-mph fastball is special in Korea; stateside, it's just decent. While the pure stuff may have not translated to many whiffs or Pitching Ninja GIFs, Flexen was exactly the workhouse Seattle envisioned when they targeted his unusually high workload coming off the shortened 2020 MLB season. He compensated for the lack of strikeouts by minimizing walks and utilizing all four pitches to keep hitters off-balance. Still just 27, Flexen may still have more to unlock now that he's re-acclimated to the big-league stage. If not, innings will always need eating.

Logan Gilbert RHP Born: 05/05/97 Age: 25 Bats: R Throws: R Height: 6'6" Weight: 225 lb. Origin: Round 1, 2018 Draft (#14 overall)

YEAR	TEAM	LVL	AGE	W	L	SV	G	GS	IP	H	HR	BB/9	K/9	K	GB%	BABIP	WHIP	ERA	DRA-	WARP	MPH	FB%	Whiff%	CSP
2019	WV	A	22	1	0	0	5	5	22^{2}	9	2	2.4	14.3	36	22.5%	.184	0.66	1.59	87	0.3				
2019	MOD	A+	22	5	3	0	12	12	62^{1}	52	3	1.7	10.5	73	45.5%	.322	1.03	1.73	79	1.0				
2019	ARK	AA	22	4	2	0	9	9	50	34	2	2.7	10.1	56	32.5%	.274	0.98	2.88	76	0.8				
2021	SEA	MLB	24	6	5	0	24	24	119^{1}	112	17	2.1	9.7	128	32.6%	.295	1.17	4.68	96	1.4	95.4	61.5%	27.2%	57.3%
2022 DC	*SEA*	*MLB*	*25*	*9*	*7*	*0*	*27*	*27*	*137.7*	*124*	*20*	*2.5*	*9.3*	*142*	*34.2%*	*.283*	*1.18*	*3.65*	*93*	*1.7*	*95.4*	*61.5%*	*27.2%*	*57.3%*

Comparables: Frankie Montas, Jered Weaver, Matt Garza

The elite extension that had long been touted by evaluators and opponents as making it seem like he was basically handing the ball to the catcher was finally measured publically via Statcast upon Gilbert's arrival to the big-league stage: At 7.4 feet down the mound, Gilbert's extension indeed ranked best among all major-league starters, even a tick ahead of the gold standard set by fellow pitching giant Tyler Glasnow. A rough August tanked his ERA for the season, but his peripherals on the whole closely reflected the elite run prevention he'd demonstrated in the minors. Doubts cast during his amateur days about his ability to hold his velocity deep into the season were comfortably quashed, as Gilbert's heater was parked at 95 and touching higher for the duration of his rookie campaign. He's about as ready-made a mid-rotation starter as you'll find, and his strong first impression suggests the ceiling may actually be a bit higher.

Ken Giles RHP Born: 09/20/90 Age: 31 Bats: R Throws: R Height: 6'3" Weight: 210 lb. Origin: Round 7, 2011 Draft (#241 overall)

YEAR	TEAM	LVL	AGE	W	L	SV	G	GS	IP	H	HR	BB/9	K/9	K	GB%	BABIP	WHIP	ERA	DRA-	WARP	MPH	FB%	Whiff%	CSP
2019	TOR	MLB	28	2	3	23	53	0	53	36	5	2.9	14.1	83	38.9%	.301	1.00	1.87	69	1.4	97.0	50.6%	40.0%	45.5%
2020	TOR	MLB	29	0	0	1	4	0	3^{2}	4	2	9.8	14.7	6	44.4%	.286	2.18	9.82	89	0.1	94.6	38.5%	54.5%	35.6%
2022 DC	*SEA*	*MLB*	*31*	*3*	*2*	*3*	*59*	*0*	*51.7*	*41*	*7*	*3.0*	*12.7*	*73*	*40.8%*	*.300*	*1.13*	*3.04*	*78*	*0.8*	*96.6*	*48.8%*	*42.1%*	*44.0%*

Comparables: David Robertson, Trevor Rosenthal, Joakim Soria

Fun fact: Giles and Justin Verlander are Tommy John twins. After posting excellent healthy campaigns in 2019, it became apparent early in each of their 2020 seasons that something wasn't quite right. On September 30, they both underwent UCL surgery performed by renowned elbow-repairer Dr. Keith Meister in Texas (there's no evidence as to who went under the knife first). Whereas Verlander was still under the contract during the bulk of his rehab, Giles entered the market fresh off surgery. The New Mexico native who makes his home in Peoria, Arizona found a good fit with Seattle, who offered him a multi-year deal that would allow him to rehab comfortably at the team's nearby complex and be ready to contribute in full come 2022. Giles' return to action won't come with a fraction of the hype surrounding Verlander's, but a return to his 2019 form could make an ascendant Mariners bullpen unit that much more intimidating.

Marco Gonzales LHP Born: 02/16/92 Age: 30 Bats: L Throws: L Height: 6'1" Weight: 197 lb. Origin: Round 1, 2013 Draft (#19 overall)

YEAR	TEAM	LVL	AGE	W	L	SV	G	GS	IP	H	HR	BB/9	K/9	K	GB%	BABIP	WHIP	ERA	DRA-	WARP	MPH	FB%	Whiff%	CSP
2019	SEA	MLB	27	16	13	0	34	34	203	210	23	2.5	6.5	147	41.2%	.295	1.31	3.99	120	-0.1	89.1	39.6%	18.0%	51.2%
2020	SEA	MLB	28	7	2	0	11	11	69^{2}	59	8	0.9	8.3	64	37.6%	.263	0.95	3.10	94	1.0	88.4	45.2%	19.7%	52.9%
2021	SEA	MLB	29	10	6	0	25	25	143^{1}	125	29	2.6	6.8	108	33.0%	.240	1.17	3.96	131	-1.0	88.5	50.4%	20.5%	52.0%
2022 DC	*SEA*	*MLB*	*30*	*10*	*9*	*0*	*29*	*29*	*160.3*	*159*	*26*	*2.3*	*7.3*	*129*	*36.0%*	*.281*	*1.25*	*4.16*	*107*	*0.7*	*88.6*	*46.7%*	*19.7%*	*51.9%*

Comparables: Wilson Alvarez, Sterling Hitchcock, Jeff Suppan

The world-class command Gonzales displayed in 2020 didn't quite carry over in 2021, and that's a dangerous skill to lose for a pitcher of his soft-tossing variety. He posted his highest walk and home run rates, and lowest ground-ball rate as a Mariner. That his ERA did not balloon to something far uglier can likely be credited to a .240 BABIP against, the 5th-lowest mark among 115 starting pitchers who threw at least 100 innings. Concerning peripherals be damned, the run prevention still managed to improve markedly as the season went on: the 3.96 ERA was made up of a 5.48 mark through July and 2.61 mark through the end of the season. As Seattle's new longest-tenured player following Kyle Seager's departure alongside Mitch Haniger, Gonzales' impact in the clubhouse will be just as important as his contribution on the field. He may continue to slide down the rotation pecking order, but that should have more to do with better options arriving than his inability to be a competent innings-eater.

★ ★ ★ *2022 Top 101 Prospect* **#87** ★ ★ ★

Emerson Hancock RHP Born: 05/31/99 Age: 23 Bats: R Throws: R Height: 6'4" Weight: 213 lb. Origin: Round 1, 2020 Draft (#6 overall)

YEAR	TEAM	LVL	AGE	W	L	SV	G	GS	IP	H	HR	BB/9	K/9	K	GB%	BABIP	WHIP	ERA	DRA-	WARP	MPH	FB%	Whiff%	CSP
2021	EVE	A+	22	2	0	0	9	9	31	19	1	3.8	8.7	30	57.0%	.231	1.03	2.32	100	0.2				
2021	ARK	AA	22	1	1	0	3	3	13^2	10	0	2.6	8.6	13	36.8%	.263	1.02	3.29	95	0.1				
2022 non-DC	*SEA*	*MLB*	*23*	*2*	*3*	*0*	*57*	*0*	*50*	*52*	*6*	*4.7*	*6.9*	*38*	*45.2%*	*.300*	*1.57*	*5.32*	*122*	*-0.4*				

Comparables: Jeff Hoffman, Reynaldo López, Rocky Coppinger

The third installment of the First Round Right-Handers trilogy following Logan Gilbert and George Kirby, Hancock entered his pro debut with more hype than his predecessors, but also a shorter track record. A candidate to go first overall entering his junior year at the University of Georgia, inconsistency and some whispers about a questionable medical landed him at pick no. 6 with Seattle. Both issues followed him into pro ball: The statistical results were about as expected considering the advanced arsenal at his disposal, but durability concerns revived after he was shut down multiple times with shoulder trouble. The team insisted it was never anything serious, and they were opting for caution coming off such an unusually uneven and abbreviated workload in 2020. If the injury were indeed minor and he can resume his development uninterrupted, Hancock has few peers in terms of pure size and stuff, and should progress quickly.

★ ★ ★ *2022 Top 101 Prospect* **#21** ★ ★ ★

George Kirby RHP Born: 02/04/98 Age: 24 Bats: R Throws: R Height: 6'4" Weight: 215 lb. Origin: Round 1, 2019 Draft (#20 overall)

YEAR	TEAM	LVL	AGE	W	L	SV	G	GS	IP	H	HR	BB/9	K/9	K	GB%	BABIP	WHIP	ERA	DRA-	WARP	MPH	FB%	Whiff%	CSP
2019	EVE	SS	21	0	0	0	9	8	23	24	1	0.0	9.8	25	45.3%	.365	1.04	2.35						
2021	EVE	A+	23	4	2	0	9	9	41^2	33	1	1.7	11.2	52	58.3%	.317	0.98	2.38	83	0.7				
2021	ARK	AA	23	1	1	0	6	6	26	25	0	2.4	9.7	28	48.6%	.338	1.23	2.77	83	0.4				
2022 DC	*SEA*	*MLB*	*24*	*2*	*1*	*0*	*6*	*6*	*32.3*	*32*	*3*	*3.2*	*8.1*	*29*	*48.3%*	*.302*	*1.35*	*4.13*	*104*	*0.2*				

Comparables: Cal Quantrill, Andrew Suárez, Rogelio Armenteros

The velocity gains Kirby had already begun exhibiting before the COVID shutdown were ratcheted up even further in 2021, with the bulked-up Kirby routinely sitting 95-98 mph and even flashing a cool 101 here and there throughout the summer. Even more important was the steady development of his secondary offerings, all of which relatively underwhelmed as an amateur. With the uptick in stuff, the otherworldly strike-throwing seems to have taken a minor step back, but those working with Kirby have publicly suggested this has largely been intentional. Too many strikes can become problematic the better the hitters get, and it seems Kirby has already pivoted towards a more selective attack plan. That's not to say he still can't fill it up when he needs to—his future command/control still grades out higher than just about any other pitcher in the minors. That, combined with an increasingly explosive arsenal, has landed him in the upper echelon of prospect arms in the game.

Adam Macko LHP Born: 12/30/00 Age: 21 Bats: L Throws: L Height: 6'0" Weight: 170 lb. Origin: Round 7, 2019 Draft (#216 overall)

YEAR	TEAM	LVL	AGE	W	L	SV	G	GS	IP	H	HR	BB/9	K/9	K	GB%	BABIP	WHIP	ERA	DRA-	WARP	MPH	FB%	Whiff%	CSP
2019	MAR	ROK	18	0	3	0	8	2	21^1	19	1	4.6	13.1	31	48.0%	.375	1.41	3.38						
2021	MOD	A	20	2	2	0	9	9	33^1	29	1	5.7	15.1	56	36.8%	.373	1.50	4.59	104	0.1				
2022 non-DC	*SEA*	*MLB*	*21*	*2*	*3*	*0*	*57*	*0*	*50*	*47*	*8*	*6.2*	*10.2*	*56*	*35.7%*	*.304*	*1.63*	*5.70*	*125*	*-0.5*				

Comparables: Henry Owens, Jose Rodriguez, Wilson Alvarez

Macko's background is guaranteed to be one of the more unique ones you'll find in this book. Born and raised in Slovakia, Macko's family moved to Alberta, Canada when he was 12 years old. He eventually enrolled in the Vauxhall Baseball Academy, where he developed his skills enough to warrant a seventh round selection in 2019. The six-foot lefty's heater was barely scraping 90 mph as an amateur, but there was enough athleticism present to suggest a future velocity bump. Sure enough, Macko's fastball touched 97 mph during spring training in 2021, and was parked in the mid-90s for the duration of his starts with Modesto. His command ticked down as his stuff ticked up, which is a perfectly reasonable challenge to tackle moving forward for a 20-year-old southpaw who struck out 36% of the batters he faced; if anything, Macko's proven an ability to adjust before.

Keynan Middleton RHP Born: 09/12/93 Age: 28 Bats: R Throws: R Height: 6'3" Weight: 215 lb. Origin: Round 3, 2013 Draft (#95 overall)

YEAR	TEAM	LVL	AGE	W	L	SV	G	GS	IP	H	HR	BB/9	K/9	K	GB%	BABIP	WHIP	ERA	DRA-	WARP	MPH	FB%	Whiff%	CSP
2019	LAA	MLB	25	0	0	0	11	0	7^2	4	0	8.2	7.0	6	35.0%	.200	1.43	1.17	112	0.0	94.1	57.3%	23.1%	43.1%
2020	LAA	MLB	26	0	1	0	13	0	12	12	2	4.5	8.3	11	22.2%	.294	1.50	5.25	132	-0.1	97.2	59.0%	25.0%	48.8%
2021	TAC	AAA	27	1	0	0	7	1	7^2	7	1	2.3	15.3	13	23.5%	.375	1.17	2.35	89	0.1				
2021	SEA	MLB	27	1	2	4	32	1	31	30	2	5.5	7.0	24	31.6%	.301	1.58	4.94	128	-0.2	95.6	57.7%	30.3%	53.9%
2022 DC	*FA*	*MLB*	*28*	*2*	*3*	*0*	*57*	*0*	*49.3*	*46*	*8*	*5.1*	*9.0*	*49*	*32.7%*	*.285*	*1.50*	*5.05*	*117*	*-0.3*	*95.8*	*58.0%*	*28.8%*	*52.2%*

Comparables: Jandel Gustave, Addison Reed, Matt Capps

Whatever developmental pixie dust got applied to the bulk of the Mariners bullpen in 2021, Middleton seems to have been allergic. A 27-year-old Pacific Northwest native with a big arm reunited with the GM who drafted him? On paper, he seemed like as good a bet as any of the reclamation relievers to click in Seattle. A handful of successful high-leverage outings in the first half offered a glimpse into what could have been: a dynamic ball of energy who strikes out the side in the eighth and struts off the mound pounding his chest and pumping up the crowd. Ultimately, his underwhelming underlying metrics—a plus fastball yielding minus results; the frustratingly familiar poor control—gradually knocked him down and then off the depth chart as his fellow bullpen arms ascended. It was hardly the homecoming Middleton or his optimistic supporters had envisioned, but there may still be enough intriguing ingredients to maximize his success elsewhere, maybe where they use elixirs or old-school incantations for their magical needs.

Anthony Misiewicz LHP Born: 11/01/94 Age: 27 Bats: R Throws: L Height: 6'1" Weight: 200 lb. Origin: Round 18, 2015 Draft (#545 overall)

YEAR	TEAM	LVL	AGE	W	L	SV	G	GS	IP	H	HR	BB/9	K/9	K	GB%	BABIP	WHIP	ERA	DRA-	WARP	MPH	FB%	Whiff%	CSP
2019	ARK	AA	24	1	2	0	7	7	35^{2}	36	0	1.8	9.1	36	48.0%	.367	1.21	2.52	98	0.1				
2019	TAC	AAA	24	8	6	0	19	17	95^{2}	95	17	2.6	8.4	89	42.8%	.292	1.29	5.36	95	0.9				
2020	SEA	MLB	25	0	2	0	21	0	20	20	2	2.7	11.3	25	31.4%	.367	1.30	4.05	87	0.4	91.0	76.8%	31.6%	44.7%
2021	SEA	MLB	26	5	5	0	66	0	54^{2}	61	7	2.5	8.7	53	43.1%	.340	1.39	4.61	95	0.6	92.5	68.8%	26.3%	55.1%
2022 DC	*SEA*	*MLB*	*27*	*3*	*3*	*0*	*74*	*0*	*64.7*	*63*	*9*	*2.7*	*8.6*	*61*	*41.5%*	*.293*	*1.27*	*3.96*	*100*	*0.2*	*92.2*	*70.4%*	*27.3%*	*53.0%*

Comparables: Sean Gilmartin, Joely Rodríguez, Sam Howard

Save for a handful of cameo appearances from Hector Santiago before his double-whammy suspensions and Sean Doolittle's arrival in the second half, Misiewicz was the lone southpaw reliever available to Scott Servais for much of the season. The only other team in 2021 to rely on one lefty reliever as heavily was the Mets with Aaron Loup, and Loup was convincingly one of the best in baseball. Misiewicz, meanwhile, was decidedly not, although he acquitted himself reasonably well considering what was being asked of him. His mid-90s heater and high-spin curveball still make him a respectable big-league option, just not one that should be shouldering such high-leverage responsibility. Also, once and for all: it's mih-SEV-itch.

Andrés Muñoz RHP Born: 01/16/99 Age: 23 Bats: R Throws: R Height: 6'2" Weight: 243 lb. Origin: International Free Agent, 2015

YEAR	TEAM	LVL	AGE	W	L	SV	G	GS	IP	H	HR	BB/9	K/9	K	GB%	BABIP	WHIP	ERA	DRA-	WARP	MPH	FB%	Whiff%	CSP
2019	AMA	AA	20	0	2	4	16	0	16^{2}	9	1	5.9	18.4	34	40.7%	.320	1.20	2.16	70	0.3				
2019	ELP	AAA	20	3	2	2	19	0	19	16	3	3.3	11.4	24	51.1%	.317	1.21	3.79	77	0.4				
2019	SD	MLB	20	1	1	1	22	0	23	16	2	4.3	11.7	30	39.3%	.264	1.17	3.91	89	0.4	100.1	68.3%	32.0%	46.5%
2021	SEA	MLB	22	0	0	0	1	0	0^{2}	0	0	27.0	13.5	1	100.0%	.000	3.00	0.00			99.7	70.6%	25.0%	46.8%
2022 DC	*SEA*	*MLB*	*23*	*2*	*2*	*0*	*44*	*0*	*38.7*	*31*	*5*	*5.3*	*11.8*	*51*	*41.7%*	*.290*	*1.40*	*4.27*	*100*	*0.1*	*100.0*	*68.5%*	*31.3%*	*46.6%*

Comparables: Arodys Vizcaíno, Byung-Hyun Kim, Miguel Castro

Muñoz didn't need to pitch in the big leagues in 2021. Called up during the final weekend after just four September rehab outings, the live-armed 22-year-old didn't seem like the kind of arm worth rushing back to the biggest stage, even if he was roughly 18 months out from elbow surgery. Then, in the sixth inning of the season's final game with the Mariners' playoff hopes all but dashed, Muñoz reminded everyone why the front office probably couldn't help itself: In the span of 17 pitches (many of which were not strikes), he unleashed seven pitches faster than any other Mariners pitcher had thrown in the 161 games prior, topping out at a cool 101 mph. It was less an audition than a warning shot. The 40,000+ plus in attendance that Sunday afternoon may not have been able to see their team finally reach the postseason, but a glimpse at the fire-breathing Muñoz wasn't the worst consolation.

Robbie Ray LHP Born: 10/01/91 Age: 30 Bats: L Throws: L Height: 6'2" Weight: 215 lb. Origin: Round 12, 2010 Draft (#356 overall)

YEAR	TEAM	LVL	AGE	W	L	SV	G	GS	IP	H	HR	BB/9	K/9	K	GB%	BABIP	WHIP	ERA	DRA-	WARP	MPH	FB%	Whiff%	CSP
2019	ARI	MLB	27	12	8	0	33	33	174^{1}	150	30	4.3	12.1	235	36.6%	.315	1.34	4.34	87	3.0	92.6	52.7%	32.9%	44.6%
2020	TOR	MLB	28	1	1	0	5	4	20^{2}	22	4	6.1	10.9	25	31.0%	.333	1.74	4.79	162	-0.5	93.8	54.1%	32.6%	44.9%
2020	ARI	MLB	28	1	4	0	7	7	31	31	9	9.0	12.5	43	20.3%	.314	2.00	7.84	164	-0.7	93.8	52.5%	33.3%	39.5%
2021	TOR	MLB	29	13	7	0	32	32	193^{1}	150	33	2.4	11.5	248	37.1%	.269	1.04	2.84	82	3.5	94.8	59.8%	32.4%	54.1%
2022 DC	*SEA*	*MLB*	*30*	*11*	*9*	*0*	*29*	*29*	*172*	*144*	*29*	*3.5*	*11.5*	*220*	*36.0%*	*.285*	*1.22*	*3.76*	*93*	*2.0*	*94.2*	*57.3%*	*32.6%*	*50.3%*

Comparables: Steve Carlton, Jon Lester, Andy Pettitte

It wasn't just that Ray put together an award-winning breakout season at 29. It was the manner in which he did so. Ray's performance was a fever-dreamed, irrational-fan-fic version of player development, where the player simply up and cuts his walk rate by 45% more than 800 innings into his career.

Were it so easy for pitchers with troublesome command but great stuff to abruptly throw a switch and become strike-throwers, a lot more pitchers would do exactly that. Ray's transformation and breakout will only extend the length of rope extended to big-armed goons the world over.

While it's fun to believe that someone within the Blue Jays' pitching mechanism unlocked the greatness—and strikes—lurking within Ray, maybe it was more a matter of simplicity? Ray dumped his curveball in the river and strode confidently into the world of "you're either getting a fastball or a slider, do your worst." And it worked! Ray consistently kept his slider out of harm's way against righties and, when he did miss, his newfound control limited the damage. A dream from which every pitching coach and amateur waiver wire hunter would never wake.

Casey Sadler RHP Born: 07/13/90 Age: 31 Bats: R Throws: R Height: 6'3" Weight: 205 lb. Origin: Round 25, 2010 Draft (#747 overall)

YEAR	TEAM	LVL	AGE	W	L	SV	G	GS	IP	H	HR	BB/9	K/9	K	GB%	BABIP	WHIP	ERA	DRA-	WARP	MPH	FB%	Whiff%	CSP
2019	DUR	AAA	28	1	1	1	11	3	32^{2}	30	5	1.4	12.1	44	38.8%	.313	1.07	2.76	75	0.8				
2019	OKC	AAA	28	0	0	1	2	1	6	8	1	1.5	13.5	9	56.2%	.467	1.50	6.00	67	0.2				
2019	TB	MLB	28	0	0	0	9	0	19^{1}	16	2	2.3	5.1	11	54.8%	.233	1.09	1.86	110	0.1	93.3	44.3%	22.8%	45.7%
2019	LAD	MLB	28	4	0	1	24	1	27	25	3	2.7	6.7	20	47.6%	.278	1.22	2.33	103	0.2	93.9	34.4%	22.7%	44.2%
2020	CHC	MLB	29	0	0	0	10	0	9^{1}	8	2	7.7	8.7	9	44.4%	.250	1.71	5.79	122	0.0	93.2	37.4%	31.2%	39.5%
2020	SEA	MLB	29	1	2	0	7	0	10	7	1	3.6	10.8	12	38.5%	.240	1.10	4.50	93	0.1	92.7	33.5%	28.8%	48.4%
2021	SEA	MLB	30	0	1	0	42	0	40^{1}	19	1	2.2	8.3	37	63.9%	.188	0.72	0.67	84	0.7	93.2	27.5%	23.7%	52.2%
2022 DC	*SEA*	*MLB*	*31*	*3*	*3*	*0*	*74*	*0*	*64.7*	*58*	*6*	*3.0*	*9.1*	*65*	*51.9%*	*.290*	*1.23*	*3.38*	*87*	*0.7*	*93.2*	*31.7%*	*24.9%*	*48.7%*

Comparables: Evan Marshall, Anthony Swarzak, Tommy Hunter

In an epic turn of serendipity, the Sadlers decided to move to the Seattle area in 2019, in search of a change of scenery, months before he was ever a Mariner. Claimed off waivers from the Cubs in September, Sadler suddenly found himself right at home. As if getting claimed by Seattle wasn't enough of a sign that his family picked the right city, things only got better in 2021 as Sadler delivered one of the more eye-popping lines of any reliever in baseball. It wasn't entirely without hiccups. After a strong April, shoulder inflammation cost him all of May and June, but once he returned in late July, he was utterly dominant. Sadler's notoriously high-spin repertoire—a balanced cutter/sinker/curveball attack—stayed spinning at a near-elite rate even post-sticky substance crackdown, and his stuff played better than ever. His ERA was by far the lowest among relievers with at least 40 innings pitched, a microscopic number that gradually shrunk over the course of a franchise-record 29 consecutive scoreless outings from July 27 *through the end of the season*. He enters 2022 with the streak intact and a boatload more fans in the place he now calls home.

Paul Sewald RHP Born: 05/26/90 Age: 32 Bats: R Throws: R Height: 6'3" Weight: 207 lb. Origin: Round 10, 2012 Draft (#320 overall)

YEAR	TEAM	LVL	AGE	W	L	SV	G	GS	IP	H	HR	BB/9	K/9	K	GB%	BABIP	WHIP	ERA	DRA-	WARP	MPH	FB%	Whiff%	CSP
2019	SYR	AAA	29	3	3	3	41	0	51	56	6	2.6	9.2	52	37.7%	.357	1.39	3.35	88	1.0				
2019	NYM	MLB	29	1	1	1	17	0	19^{2}	18	3	1.4	10.1	22	14.8%	.300	1.07	4.58	104	0.2	91.6	70.6%	21.0%	53.8%
2020	NYM	MLB	30	0	0	0	5	0	6	12	1	6.0	3.0	2	35.7%	.407	2.67	13.50	147	-0.1	92.0	59.7%	16.4%	46.4%
2021	SEA	MLB	31	10	3	11	62	0	64^{2}	42	10	3.3	14.5	104	25.9%	.256	1.02	3.06	62	1.9	92.4	58.3%	36.5%	54.2%
2022 DC	*SEA*	*MLB*	*32*	*3*	*3*	*14*	*74*	*0*	*64.7*	*50*	*10*	*3.0*	*12.1*	*86*	*29.9%*	*.273*	*1.11*	*3.19*	*82*	*0.9*	*92.3*	*59.5%*	*33.8%*	*53.6%*

Comparables: Brandon Gomes, Kirby Yates, Carlos Torres

In a year full of surprises in Mariners world, Sewald's glow-up shone brightest of all. And to think: He didn't even make the Opening Day roster. Sewald was recalled from Triple-A for his Mariners debut on May 13, in the same bucket of transactions that included the much-anticipated call-ups of Logan Gilbert and Jarred Kelenic. None of the flashy graphics on social media trumpeting the arrival of the two prospects bothered to include any sort of small print announcing a seemingly generic 30-year-old reliever. Yet for all the hype surrounding Kelenic, Sewald was the former Met who would make the biggest impact for Seattle in 2021. His extreme arm angle and excellent execution produced an eye-popping whiff-rate on par with the biggest relief names in the game, nearly all of whom throw much harder than him. His invincibility waned down the stretch as he became homer-prone at some inopportune times, but he'd built up so much goodwill that he avoided the kind of scorn often directed towards' bullpen arms with a gopher ball problem. With the likes of Ken Giles and Andrés Muñoz on track to join the fold, Sewald's save opportunities may dwindle in 2022, but regardless of his future role, he'll remain an integral part of Seattle's late-inning game plan moving forward.

Justus Sheffield LHP Born: 05/13/96 Age: 26 Bats: L Throws: L Height: 5'10" Weight: 195 lb. Origin: Round 1, 2014 Draft (#31 overall)

YEAR	TEAM	LVL	AGE	W	L	SV	G	GS	IP	H	HR	BB/9	K/9	K	GB%	BABIP	WHIP	ERA	DRA-	WARP	MPH	FB%	Whiff%	CSP
2019	ARK	AA	23	5	3	0	12	12	78	62	4	2.1	9.8	85	42.6%	.294	1.03	2.19	77	1.2				
2019	TAC	AAA	23	2	6	0	13	12	55	59	12	6.7	7.9	48	53.2%	.292	1.82	6.87	110	0.0				
2019	SEA	MLB	23	0	1	0	8	7	36	44	5	4.5	9.3	37	52.7%	.379	1.72	5.50	111	0.2	92.8	47.8%	30.1%	46.6%
2020	SEA	MLB	24	4	3	0	10	10	55^{1}	52	2	3.3	7.8	48	49.7%	.314	1.30	3.58	94	0.8	92.0	48.0%	19.8%	48.0%
2021	TAC	AAA	25	0	1	0	5	2	8^{1}	8	1	7.6	15.1	14	38.9%	.412	1.80	8.64	85	0.1				
2021	SEA	MLB	25	7	8	0	21	15	80^{1}	105	14	4.8	7.1	63	45.6%	.351	1.84	6.83	142	-1.1	92.4	47.4%	19.9%	55.1%
2022 DC	*SEA*	*MLB*	*26*	*4*	*5*	*0*	*16*	*16*	*79.3*	*80*	*10*	*4.5*	*7.6*	*66*	*46.9%*	*.297*	*1.52*	*4.95*	*117*	*-0.1*	*92.3*	*47.6%*	*20.9%*	*52.4%*

Comparables: Andrew Heaney, Horacio Ramirez, Robbie Ray

To put it plainly: yuck. After a promising rookie run in 2020, things went backwards in a hurry in a 2021 campaign that left very few silver linings to cling to. Sheffield spent the first three months in the rotation getting torched before a forearm strain landed him on the IL in early July. Seattle opted to try Sheffield in the bullpen upon his return in August, but any notion that his stuff may tick up in relief was rapidly quashed, as he continued to get lit up in multiple September outings before being sent back to Tacoma one more time for good measure. This is not the kind of sophomore slump that one simply bounces back from; there's a lot of work to be done. It may be time to abandon the sinker, or teach it to live up to its name.

Joe Smith RHP Born: 03/22/84 Age: 38 Bats: R Throws: R Height: 6'2" Weight: 211 lb. Origin: Round 3, 2006 Draft (#94 overall)

YEAR	TEAM	LVL	AGE	W	L	SV	G	GS	IP	H	HR	BB/9	K/9	K	GB%	BABIP	WHIP	ERA	DRA-	WARP	MPH	FB%	Whiff%	CSP
2019	HOU	MLB	35	1	0	0	28	0	25	19	2	1.8	7.9	22	49.3%	.254	0.96	1.80	95	0.3	88.1	57.6%	21.2%	56.9%
2021	SEA	MLB	37	3	3	0	23	0	18	12	1	2.0	8.5	17	44.9%	.229	0.89	2.00	90	0.3	85.9	64.5%	19.7%	57.6%
2021	HOU	MLB	37	1	1	0	27	0	21^{2}	35	4	1.7	7.1	17	49.4%	.425	1.80	7.48	102	0.2	86.7	62.0%	20.8%	55.1%
2022 DC	*FA*	*MLB*	*38*	*2*	*2*	*0*	*57*	*0*	*49.3*	*48*	*6*	*2.3*	*7.6*	*41*	*45.0%*	*.285*	*1.23*	*3.82*	*98*	*0.2*	*86.7*	*62.1%*	*20.5%*	*56.2%*

Comparables: Jeremy Affeldt, Jason Isringhausen, Michael Jackson

Max Scherzer. Miguel Cabrera. Justin Verlander. Albert Pujols. Joe Smith? The names atop the active leaderboards for the most mainstream stats are often those of future Hall of Famers. With Fernando Rodney's major-league career seemingly finally in the rearview, Smith finds himself no. 1 in his own category: pitching appearances. With 832 games to his name, Smith sits 46th all-time. It looked like that number might be settling into a fixed state for the 37-year-old after a rough stint with the Astros, but after being thrown into the Kendall Graveman trade, Smith turned things around, halving his line-drive rate and enjoying the relatively spacious outfield of T-Mobile Park.

Drew Steckenrider RHP Born: 01/10/91 Age: 31 Bats: R Throws: R Height: 6'4" Weight: 217 lb. Origin: Round 8, 2012 Draft (#257 overall)

YEAR	TEAM	LVL	AGE	W	L	SV	G	GS	IP	H	HR	BB/9	K/9	K	GB%	BABIP	WHIP	ERA	DRA-	WARP	MPH	FB%	Whiff%	CSP
2019	MIA	MLB	28	0	2	0	15	0	14^{1}	9	6	3.1	8.8	14	31.6%	.094	0.98	6.28	109	0.1	95.1	62.0%	21.4%	48.2%
2021	SEA	MLB	30	5	2	14	62	0	67^{2}	52	5	2.3	7.7	58	38.3%	.258	1.02	2.00	103	0.5	94.2	66.0%	20.6%	57.9%
2022 DC	*SEA*	*MLB*	*31*	*3*	*3*	*14*	*74*	*0*	*64.7*	*61*	*9*	*3.0*	*8.2*	*58*	*38.1%*	*.284*	*1.28*	*4.07*	*103*	*0.1*	*94.2*	*65.7%*	*20.7%*	*57.2%*

Comparables: Brandon Kintzler, Hunter Strickland, Brandon Gomes

Poor performance and injuries prompted a release from Miami after 2020, and the Mariners pounced early in the winter, heaving Steckenrider into their growing pile of reliever rejuvenation projects. The big right-hander tweaked his repertoire: Rather than lean into the traditional FB/SL combo commonly associated with hundreds of other aspiring late-inning arms, Steckenrider cranked up the changeup and toned down the slider. The result? Fewer whiffs, but far better command and consistency, and ultimately better results, particularly against left-handed batters. A stellar first half earned Steckenrider the first crack at the closer job post-Kendall Graveman Trade, and he held onto it all the way to the finish line. It's a bit odd to watch a pitcher with Steckenrider's imposing stature and velocity fail to strike out even a batter per inning, but it's hard to argue against the results. That said, it remains to be seen if Scott Servais will still prefer Steckasaurus for the ninth inning when there are the more traditional, bat-missing flamethrowers like Ken Giles at his disposal in 2022.

Levi Stoudt RHP Born: 12/04/97 Age: 24 Bats: R Throws: R Height: 6'1" Weight: 195 lb. Origin: Round 3, 2019 Draft (#97 overall)

YEAR	TEAM	LVL	AGE	W	L	SV	G	GS	IP	H	HR	BB/9	K/9	K	GB%	BABIP	WHIP	ERA	DRA-	WARP	MPH	FB%	Whiff%	CSP
2021	EVE	A+	23	6	1	0	12	12	64	47	6	4.1	9.4	67	43.6%	.261	1.19	3.52	101	0.4				
2021	ARK	AA	23	1	2	0	3	3	17^2	14	2	4.1	9.7	19	31.9%	.267	1.25	2.55	114	0.0				
2022 non-DC	*SEA*	*MLB*	*24*	*2*	*3*	*0*	*57*	*0*	*50*	*52*	*8*	*5.2*	*8.2*	*45*	*38.5%*	*.307*	*1.63*	*5.89*	*132*	*-0.7*				

Comparables: Cole Irvin, Mike Wright Jr., Luke French

The looming possibility of elbow surgery toward the end of his junior spring pushed Stoudt to sign for underslot in the third round of the 2019 Draft. It was the right call; he did indeed go under the knife shortly after, relegating him to the shadows of rehab before ever throwing a professional pitch. His delayed debut was worth the wait, however, as Stoudt was the talk of Mariners instructional league in 2020. His impressive display on the Peoria backfields showcased better velocity than pre-surgery and two promising secondary pitches: a dastardly split-change and a developing slider. In the spring, GM Jerry Dipoto cited Stoudt as Seattle's most under-the-radar prospect, which did well to immediately contradict his claim. Despite a carefully controlled workload coming off surgery, Stoudt still managed to reach Double-A and continued to display a starter-worthy repertoire, albeit with some bullpen-worthy command.

Erik Swanson RHP Born: 09/04/93 Age: 28 Bats: R Throws: R Height: 6'3" Weight: 220 lb. Origin: Round 8, 2014 Draft (#246 overall)

YEAR	TEAM	LVL	AGE	W	L	SV	G	GS	IP	H	HR	BB/9	K/9	K	GB%	BABIP	WHIP	ERA	DRA-	WARP	MPH	FB%	Whiff%	CSP
2019	TAC	AAA	25	0	1	0	10	6	24^1	28	5	4.4	10.4	28	35.2%	.348	1.64	5.55	103	0.1				
2019	SEA	MLB	25	1	5	2	27	8	58	56	17	1.9	8.1	52	37.4%	.241	1.17	5.74	107	0.4	92.9	67.8%	22.7%	50.2%
2020	SEA	MLB	26	0	2	0	9	0	7^2	11	3	2.3	10.6	9	33.3%	.381	1.70	12.91	112	0.0	95.9	74.5%	29.6%	50.8%
2021	SEA	MLB	27	0	3	1	33	2	35^1	28	5	2.5	8.9	35	32.7%	.247	1.08	3.31	98	0.4	94.8	59.9%	27.6%	56.4%
2022 DC	*SEA*	*MLB*	*28*	*2*	*3*	*0*	*59*	*0*	*51.7*	*50*	*8*	*2.7*	*9.2*	*52*	*36.4%*	*.294*	*1.27*	*4.24*	*105*	*0.1*	*94.3*	*64.0%*	*26.2%*	*53.8%*

Comparables: Matt Albers, Jim Johnson, Tommy Hunter

Imagine allowing a walk-off home run to Jonah Heim. Okay, now imagine allowing a walk-off home run to Jonah Heim one day after your teammate allowed a walk-off home run to Jonah Heim. Up until that fateful Sunday afternoon in early August, Swanson had actually been quietly excellent over the first few months (0.47 ERA in 19 ⅓ IP), albeit having missed June with a groin injury. He appeared to be settling into a solid middle-relief role that his dismal previous two seasons suggested may have been even too optimistic to achieve. Then, in the bottom of the ninth against one of the worst offenses in the league, Swanson promptly allowed a Nathaniel Lowe single, an Andy Ibáñez homer, and then Jonah Heim stepped to the plate. While the Mariners as a whole somehow managed to recover from this shambolic sequence, the outing seemed to be a turning point for Swanson, who posted 5.06 ERA from that point forward and never quite regained the trust of Scott Servais.

Brandon Williamson LHP Born: 04/02/98 Age: 24 Bats: R Throws: L Height: 6'6" Weight: 210 lb. Origin: Round 2, 2019 Draft (#59 overall)

YEAR	TEAM	LVL	AGE	W	L	SV	G	GS	IP	H	HR	BB/9	K/9	K	GB%	BABIP	WHIP	ERA	DRA-	WARP	MPH	FB%	Whiff%	CSP
2019	EVE	SS	21	0	0	0	10	9	15^1	9	0	2.9	14.7	25	55.2%	.310	0.91	2.35						
2021	EVE	A+	23	2	1	0	6	6	31	21	4	2.9	17.1	59	44.2%	.354	1.00	3.19	77	0.6				
2021	ARK	AA	23	2	5	0	13	13	67^1	62	7	3.1	12.6	94	36.6%	.353	1.26	3.48	77	1.3				
2022 non-DC	*SEA*	*MLB*	*24*	*2*	*2*	*0*	*57*	*0*	*50*	*44*	*7*	*3.9*	*10.8*	*59*	*37.9%*	*.300*	*1.32*	*4.27*	*100*	*0.2*				

Comparables: Eric Lauer, Seth Maness, Shaun Marcum

Even as a second-round pick, it was difficult for Williamson to garner too much hype entering pro ball considering he wasn't even the first 6-foot-6 left-hander selected out of TCU that year; that distinguishment belonged to Reds first-rounder Nick Lodolo. Stuff has never been the question for the massive Minnesotan, and it delivered in spades in his first full-season go. Among all minor-league pitchers who threw at least 90 innings, Williamson's 37.4% strikeout-rate ranked 5th, while maintaining a walk-rate (8.1%) lower than many projected for him coming out of school. His low-90's fastball plays up due to his XL-frame that predictably gets down the mound well, and the secondary weapons have progressed nicely. Though Lodolo still exists in a prospect tier above thanks to his overall polish and longer track record, Williamson has done well to close the gap between him and his fellow Horned Frog.

LINEOUTS

Hitters

HITTER	POS	TEAM	LVL	AGE	PA	R	2B	3B	HR	RBI	BB	K	SB	CS	AVG/OBP/SLG	DRC+	BABIP	BRR	FRAA	WARP
Jake Bauers	1B	SEA	MLB	25	202	20	4	0	2	13	18	51	6	0	.220/.297/.275	73	.295	-0.1	RF(23): -1.5, LF(21): 2.7, 1B(13): 0.1	0.1
	1B	CLE	MLB	25	113	7	3	0	2	6	12	27	0	1	.190/.277/.280	83	.239	-0.4	1B(41): 3.3	0.3
Eric Filia	LF	TAC	AAA	28	183	27	9	0	3	15	30	25	4	0	.262/.388/.383	110	.293	0.5	LF(19): -1.9, 1B(7): -0.4, RF(6): -0.2	0.6
Gabriel Gonzalez	OF	DSL SEA	ROK	17	221	39	15	4	7	36	21	35	9	3	.287/.371/.521		.311			
Sam Haggerty	OF	SEA	MLB	27	94	15	3	0	2	5	6	28	5	1	.186/.247/.291	79	.250	0.3	LF(20): 3.3, RF(6): -0.8, 2B(4): 0.2	0.4
Victor Labrada	CF	MOD	A	21	243	44	16	3	1	28	34	60	22	9	.294/.407/.418	104	.408	-0.4	CF(46): -8.5	0.2
	CF	EVE	A+	21	227	35	7	3	6	27	19	63	10	6	.246/.314/.399	90	.324	0.6	CF(42): -6.0, RF(4): 0.4, LF(2): -0.7	0.0
Shed Long Jr.	LF/2B	TAC	AAA	25	36	8	3	0	1	2	5	5	0	0	.323/.417/.516	109	.360	0.5	2B(6): -1.0	0.1
	LF/2B	SEA	MLB	25	121	13	4	1	4	17	9	39	1	0	.198/.258/.360	73	.265	-0.7	LF(25): -2.7, 2B(10): 1.4	-0.2
Cade Marlowe	OF	PEJ	WIN	24	92	18	5	0	0	7	17	23	7	0	.233/.385/.301		.340			
	OF	MOD	A	24	160	35	6	5	6	29	24	40	11	2	.301/.406/.556	127	.382	0.9	LF(20): -2.7, CF(7): -1.3, RF(1): -0.2	0.8
	OF	EVE	A+	24	325	52	18	5	20	77	36	91	12	7	.259/.345/.566	113	.307	-3.5	RF(39): 0.4, CF(16): -0.4, LF(10): -0.9	1.2
Kevin Padlo	3B	TAC	AAA	24	121	22	3	2	8	21	16	21	1	1	.298/.388/.596	124	.303	0.9	3B(25): -2.1	0.6
	3B	DUR	AAA	24	282	40	11	0	12	37	25	93	5	1	.194/.270/.379	82	.247	0.6	3B(45): 1.9, 2B(17): -0.6, 1B(5): -0.1	0.4
	3B	TB	MLB	24	14	1	1	0	0	0	2	8	0	0	.083/.214/.167	81	.250	0.0	3B(6): 0.3, 1B(3): 0.1	0.0
	3B	SEA	MLB	24	1	0	0	0	0	0	0	1	0	0	.000/.000/.000	74				0.0
Milkar Perez	3B	MRN	ROK	19	188	33	10	0	0	23	39	38	1	1	.310/.463/.379		.417			
	3B	MOD	A	19	32	6	2	0	0	0	4	4	0	1	.296/.406/.370	114	.348	-0.1	3B(6): -2.1	-0.1
Kaden Polcovich	2B	EVE	A+	22	272	55	12	4	10	47	47	64	16	3	.271/.415/.505	119	.336	3.2	2B(24): 1.9, SS(14): 1.6, CF(9): 0.3	2.1
	2B	ARK	AA	22	149	13	4	0	2	14	16	41	4	1	.133/.242/.211	85	.172	0.4	2B(21): -2.1, 3B(7): -0.3, CF(7): 0.3	0.0
Alberto Rodriguez	RF	MOD	A	20	431	75	30	5	10	63	51	95	13	7	.295/.383/.484	120	.367	-3.9	RF(75): 15.9, LF(5): -0.5, CF(2): -0.4	3.5
	RF	EVE	A+	20	28	5	1	0	0	2	2	7	2	0	.208/.321/.250	104	.294	-0.1	LF(3): -0.1, RF(3): -0.2	0.1
Dillon Thomas	OF	TAC	AAA	28	395	68	19	1	13	47	41	117	12	1	.269/.377/.448	92	.374	1.5	RF(44): 1.9, CF(23): 1.0, LF(18): 0.4	1.3
	OF	SEA	MLB	28	9	2	0	0	0	2	0	7	0	0	.111/.111/.111	51	.500	0.1	LF(2): -0.1, CF(1): 1.4, RF(1): -0.1	0.1

Jake Bauers was another classic former-prospect-roll-of-the-dice for the Dipoto regime, acquired in a minor trade from Cleveland midseason. In one sense, Bauers fit right in—he hit .220 just like the rest of the team—but that's probably not what the front office had in mind. Baseball returned to the Olympics for the first time since 2008, but players on 40-man rosters were unable to participate. This opened the door for folks like **Eric Filia** to play significant roles for Team USA and he did just that, starting in left field for much of the national team's run to the silver medal in Tokyo. He enters the 2022 season still in search of his first MLB call-up. Signed for $1.1 million out of Venezuela, athletic outfielder **Gabriel Gonzalez** continued the recent tradition established by Julio Rodriguez and Noelvi Marte of tearing up the DSL, leading the league in extra-base hits. Though not quite the prospect his prolific predecessors were at the same stage, his stateside debut will be highly anticipated. Orioles fans may remember **Sam Haggerty's** 2021 better than Seattleites, as the light-hitting utilityman inexplicably launched a homer to Eutaw Street in April and then became the answer to the excellent trivia question: "Which Mariners batter reached base on a dropped third strike to ruin John Means' perfect game?" A limited track record in international competition meant that little was known about **Victor Labrada** when the Mariners gave him a $350K bonus, but this mystery box turned out to rather fruitful, at least so far. His compact frame produced more power than anticipated as a 21-year-old in A-ball, while his near elite speed played as expected both in the outfield and on the bases. **Shed Long Jr.** was something of a one hit wonder in 2021: his walk-off grand slam put an exclamation point on a four-game sweep of Tampa Bay in June. But a stress fracture in his shin required multiple surgeries and wiped away the offense that needed to carry his iron glove; the Mariners outrighted him after the season. After hitting just 12 homers in four collegiate seasons at Division-II West Georgia, **Cade Marlowe** launched 26 homers across both levels of A-ball as part of one of the loudest statistical seasons in all of minor-league baseball. Was he just beating up on younger competition or did something change here? Hitter-unfriendly Double-A Arkansas looms as the ultimate proving ground. Claimed off waivers from Tampa Bay in August, **Kevin Padlo** has big Patrick Wisdom Energy, right down to having the same high school alma mater (shout out to the Murrieta Valley NIghthawks). Foolish mistake for the Mariners to jump the gun, instead of waiting for him to turn 30 and play for three other teams. Only 15 players born in Nicaragua have ever reached the Major Leagues; **Milkar Perez** might be on track to become the sixteenth. The stocky switch-hitter displayed an advanced approach and strong contact skills in his stateside debut, albeit without much pop. That stockiness might be a problem at the hot corner, but his arm might be strong enough to make people ignore it. **Kaden Polcovich** endured a particularly jarring rendition of many Mariners hitting prospects' worst nightmare: a mid-season promotion to the hitter's hell that is Dickey-Stephens Park in Arkansas. After his performance, that reputation only got a little stronger. Copious pull-side power and improved conditioning helped **Alberto Rodriguez** club his way up to High-A. Undersized for a true slugger and underswift for a true speedster, he faces an uphill battle to crack the bigs as a corner outfielder. Remember how much they talked about Tyler Matzek pitching for the independent Texas Airhogs during the Braves' postseason run? **Dillon Thomas** was Matzek's teammate on that 'Hogs team in 2018. He too sojourned his way back into affiliated ball, and ultimately the Majors for the first time, albeit to slightly diminished fanfare.

Pitchers

PITCHER	TEAM	LVL	AGE	W	L	SV	G	GS	IP	H	HR	BB/9	K/9	K	GB%	BABIP	WHIP	ERA	DRA-	WARP	MPH	FB%	WHF	CSP
Matt Andriese	SEA	MLB	31	0	0	0	8	0	11	10	0	1.6	9.8	12	53.3%	.333	1.09	2.45	100	0.1	90.6	60.9%	29.6%	53.2%
	BOS	MLB	31	2	3	1	26	0	37^1	55	7	2.7	9.2	38	40.8%	.410	1.77	6.03	101	0.3	92.4	45.2%	21.0%	55.5%
Isaiah Campbell	EVE	A+	23	3	1	0	5	0	19^1	13	2	2.8	9.3	20	48.0%	.234	0.98	2.33	87	0.3				
Sam Carlson	MOD	A	22	6	4	0	19	19	100	107	7	4.0	10.1	112	48.1%	.351	1.51	4.77	108	0.1				
Robert Dugger	TAC	AAA	25	4	5	0	15	14	69^1	74	12	3.1	8.3	64	43.6%	.312	1.41	6.10	104	0.1				
	SEA	MLB	25	0	2	0	12	4	25^2	34	4	4.2	6.7	19	37.5%	.357	1.79	7.36	123	-0.1	91.4	42.5%	24.1%	55.7%
Aaron Fletcher	TAC	AAA	25	4	0	2	39	0	49^1	53	6	2.6	8.2	45	57.0%	.331	1.36	3.47	90	0.5				
	SEA	MLB	25	0	0	0	4	0	3^2	7	1	2.5	4.9	2	47.1%	.375	2.18	12.27	120	0.0	91.4	58.1%	29.3%	56.3%
Darren McCaughan	TAC	AAA	25	5	4	0	20	20	115^1	111	20	1.3	7.7	99	42.6%	.276	1.11	4.53	113	-0.5				
	SEA	MLB	25	0	0	0	2	1	9	8	3	4.0	2.0	2	50.0%	.179	1.33	8.00	121	0.0	87.8	53.7%	3.7%	55.7%
Bryce Miller	MOD	A	22	0	0	0	5	3	9^1	15	0	1.9	14.5	15	53.6%	.556	1.82	4.82	81	0.2				
Wyatt Mills	TAC	AAA	26	4	2	2	23	1	28^2	19	2	2.2	16.0	51	45.5%	.321	0.91	3.14	72	0.6				
	SEA	MLB	26	0	0	0	11	0	12^2	19	1	5.0	7.8	11	51.1%	.409	2.05	9.95	101	0.1	92.7	70.9%	17.7%	50.2%
Connor Phillips	MOD	A	20	7	3	0	16	16	72	62	1	5.5	13.0	104	41.2%	.361	1.47	4.75	95	0.6				
Yohan Ramirez	TAC	AAA	26	0	0	0	15	0	17^1	12	2	6.8	12.5	24	33.3%	.294	1.44	4.15	90	0.2				
	SEA	MLB	26	1	3	2	25	0	27^2	18	6	3.9	11.4	35	32.8%	.218	1.08	3.90	87	0.4	95.5	54.4%	35.9%	52.4%
Héctor Santiago	TAC	AAA	33	1	0	0	3	3	14	10	5	3.2	14.1	22	17.2%	.208	1.07	4.50	100	0.1				
	SEA	MLB	33	1	1	0	13	1	26^1	27	2	3.8	10.3	30	44.7%	.338	1.44	3.42	94	0.3	91.2	67.0%	27.1%	50.4%
Juan Then	EVE	A+	21	2	5	0	14	14	54^1	68	12	3.1	9.8	59	47.1%	.354	1.60	6.46	100	0.4				

On August 22nd, Miguel Cabrera took Steven Matz deep to right field for his 500th career MLB home run. Five days later, **Matt Andriese** got Ryan O'Hearn to fly out to left to complete his 500th career MLB inning. The celebration for one of these 500's was slightly grander than the other. ⚾ Minor elbow surgery in June cut former second-round pick **Isaiah Campbell's** season with High-A Everett short, but that didn't stop him from making an impact in the Pacific Northwest: His heavy involvement with the Mariners' virtual book reading program in the Tacoma School District earned him the organization's Dan Wilson Community Service Award. ⚾ After three statistic-less seasons due to surgeries and setbacks, arguably the only number that mattered for **Sam Carlson** in 2021 was his innings pitched. The broad-chested Minnesotan pitched a full season with Low-A Modesto without any injury hiccups, with solid if unspectacular results. ⚾ Over the last three seasons, the Mariners are 4-23 with a -111 run differential at Minute Maid Park. That's a lot of blowouts. In them, Scott Servais has called on such luminaries as Reggie McClain and Brady Lail for the ultimate mop-up work, the dive bar restroom of pitching assignments. In 2021, that distinction belonged to **Robert Dugger**, who allowed six runs in the final four innings of a 15-1 loss on August 11 and was promptly DFA'd after the game. ⚾ Seattle's bullpen was yearning for southpaw support all year long, but **Aaron Fletcher** was hardly called upon save for a handful of May outings, likely due to extreme platoon splits that continue to have him tracking as LOOGY in a LOOGY-less world. ⚾ **Joey Gerber** didn't throw a pitch at any level in 2021 due to recurring back issues that began in spring training and led to surgery in July. That didn't stop him from regularly dishing out a healthy dose of dad jokes and/or infinite wisdom on Twitter such as "A little more surprising more people don't name their pet 'Peeves'" (September 7) or "The people who helped create indoor plumbing deserve much more recognition than they receive" (May 25). ⚾ Among starting pitchers that threw at least 100 innings in the minors in 2021, three of the six lowest walk rates belonged to Tacoma Rainiers hurlers: Ryan Weber (3.1 %), Logan Verrett (3.4%) and **Darren McCaughan** (3.4%), whose name is the one in bold in this comment due strictly to the fact that at 26, he might still be something more than emergency depth. ⚾ Seattle got a slight discount on right-hander **Bryce Miller** in the fourth round of the 2021 draft due to his age (he'll turn 24 during the 2022 season), but there still may be some upside within the big Texan. A reliever for his first two years at Texas A&M, Miller's stuff held up upon moving into the rotation, maintaining his mid-90's velocity deep into starts against elite SEC competition. ⚾ Had there not been as many bona fide breakouts among the veteran bullpen arms, we may have seen more of sidewinder **Wyatt Mills** in 2021, but he didn't exactly capitalize his scattered big-league opportunities. Bad luck for his Triple-A opponents, who to a man absolutely did get capitalized on. ⚾ A well-built (6'2, 205 lb), high-priced ($1.5M signing bonus to be lured away from a Vanderbilt commitment) right-hander, **Michael Morales** looks like an appealing ball of clay for a Mariners player development group more used to college arms. It'll be interesting to see what they create; in terms of raw material, he's most defined by being undefined. ⚾ The first of only five junior college players selected in the abbreviated 2020 draft, **Connor Phillips** appealed to teams—at least, those willing to roll the dice on the oh-so-risky juco demographics—due to his projectable frame and burgeoning velocity. The effectiveness of his raw stuff (32.6% K-rate) was hampered by the wildness (13.5% walk-rate, a whopping 17 wild pitches), but who doesn't love a thing that needs fixing. ⚾ In the iconic simulation game RollerCoaster Tycoon, if you build a custom coaster with too many drops and loops and twists, guests will refuse to ride it. No matter how cool or fun it looks in theory, the little avatars will simply walk up to the entrance, leap in terror and proclaim, "The Devil's Corkscrew [or whatever your coaster is called] looks too intense for me!" and walk away. **Yohan Ramirez** is The Devil's Corkscrew. ⚾ In his lone major-league start of 2021, **Héctor Santiago** went from "oh yeah, that guy" to "oh yeah, *that* guy." He became the first pitcher ejected, then suspended under the league's crackdown on sticky stuff and he followed that up by receiving an 80-game suspension for a performance-enhancing drug. ⚾ The results in High-A may not have been pretty, but if **Juan Then** had spent 2021 pitching in the SEC alongside his 21-year-old peers, his pure stuff—an upper-90's heater with a rapidly developing slider and changeup—would have likely made him a day one selection on hypothetical draft day.

TEXAS RANGERS

Essay by Mike Piellucci

Player comments by Levi Weaver and BP staff

Jon Daniels waved the white flag in July, during a press conference some 16 hours after the Rangers traded their last homegrown star and 30 hours or so prior to the MLB trade deadline. "When we talk about rebuilding, that can't be at half measures," The Rangers' president of baseball operations told the media.

He was referring to a possible contract extension for Joey Gallo, by then a Yankee after Daniels and general manager Chris Young shipped him and lefty reliever Joely Rodríguez to New York for prospects the night before, but the subject could have been almost anything the club had done over the previous five years. It has been a precipitous fall from Texas' last division title in 2016, a half decade of sub-.500 ball made more demoralizing by the fact that the team wasn't trying to lose. Until the final week of July, Texas had been content to huff the final fumes of the team's golden era—when the team won consecutive American League pennants in 2010 and '11—and employ stopgap measures, from plundering the middle tier of free-agent pitching markets (Mike Minor, Lance Lynn, Kyle Gibson) to auditioning veteran reclamation projects (Hunter Pence) to splashy trades (Corey Kluber) even to making low-budget adds (Miguel González, Paolo Espino) in a quarter-assed attempt to stay afloat in the wild-card race the same summer that they traded Yu Darvish.

No more. Before the 2021 deadline passed, Gibson—like Gallo, a 2021 All-Star—and bullpen reclamation project Ian Kennedy would join Gallo on their way out of Texas, just as Gallo's departure followed the offseason trade of Elvis Andrus, the last on-field link to Texas' World Series teams. Finally, the rebuild was truly on.

Now the hard work begins. Rebuilding is daunting for any team but especially this one, because nuts-and-bolts talent acquisition is window dressing for the greater task at hand. The real thrust of rebuilding is to produce something memorable, something substantial—a team and a time and feeling uniquely theirs. A new identity.

This will not come easy for the Rangers, perhaps baseball's most generic franchise. How could it when, heading into their 50th season in Texas, they've never had much of an identity at all?

TEXAS RANGERS PROSPECTUS

2021 W-L: 60-102, 5th in AL West

Pythag	.378	*27th*	DER	.703	*12th*
RS/G	3.86	*28th*	DRC+	91	*24th*
RA/G	5.03	*24th*	DRA-	116	*30th*
dWin%	.388	*30th*	FIP	4.81	*27th*
Payroll	$95M	*21st*	B-Age	27.2	*1st*
M$/MW	$6.9M	*27th*	P-Age	28.3	*5th*

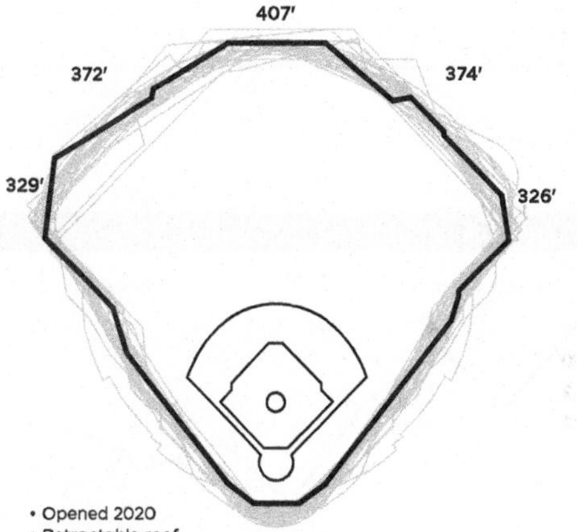

- Opened 2020
- Retractable roof
- Synthetic surface
- Fence profile: 7' to 10' (estimate)

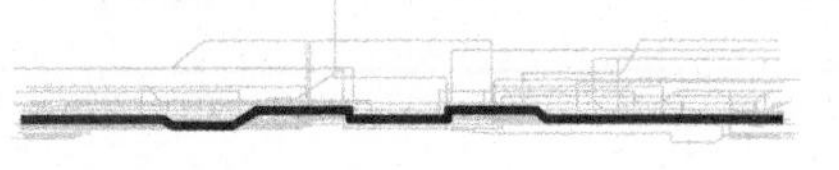

Park Factors

Runs	Runs/RH	Runs/LH	HR/RH	HR/LH
99	100	98	108	101

Top Hitter WARP	4.2 Isiah Kiner-Falefa
Top Pitcher WARP	1.0 Dane Dunning
Top Prospect	Jack Leiter

Payroll History (in millions)

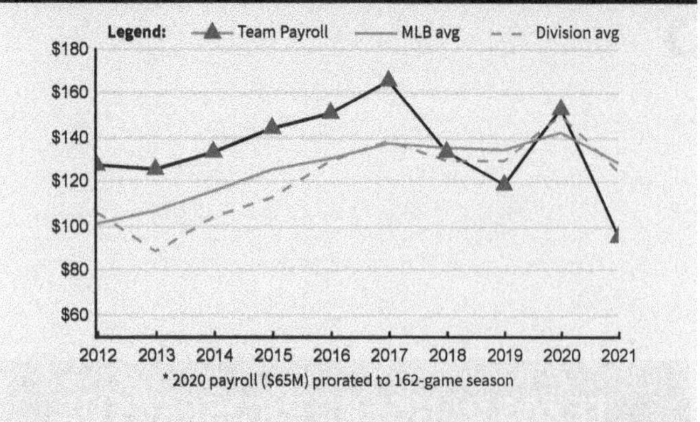

Future Commitments (in millions)

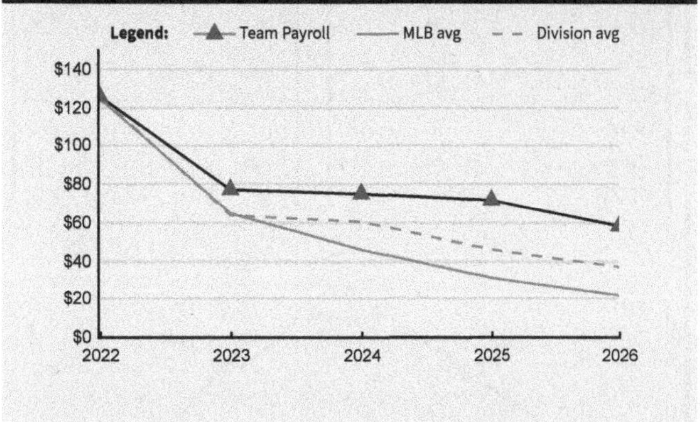

Farm System Ranking

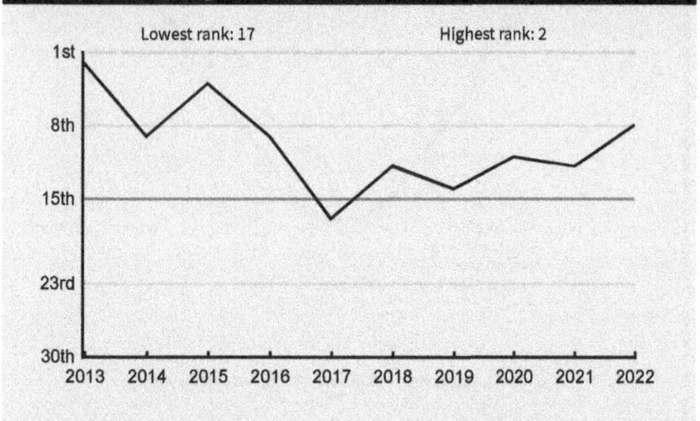

Personnel

President, Baseball Operations
Jon Daniels

Executive Vice President & General Manager
Chris Young

Vice President/Assistant General Manager, Scouting
Josh Boyd

Vice President/AGM, Player Development & International Operations
Ross Fenstermaker

Senior Director, Research of Development/Applications
Daren Willman

Manager
Chris Woodward

Let's pause for a thought exercise. Close your eyes and imagine the Texas Rangers. What comes to mind?

Success? Certainly not. The Rangers are one of only six teams without a World Series championship, which immediately damns them to a blurrier existence than 24 of their peers, all of whom have at least enjoyed a temporal identity, if not an ideological one. You may not care about the Marlins, but you certainly remember one of their championship teams—or, at the very least, the resulting teardown.

But it might not be failure, either. After all, Texas' all-time .476 winning percentage ranks 24th leaguewide—hardly impressive but closer to the middle third than rock bottom. Those depths aren't distinctive enough to become the brand, the way losing so often has for the San Diego Padres, who have a .462 all-time mark.

Stylistically, it is offense, lots of offense. Home runs, in particular, thanks to the cramped dimensions of their former home, which I still refer to by its original name, the Ballpark in Arlington, less for nostalgia than convenience after too many renamings to keep track of. It worked for a stretch: Texas won the AL West three times in four years between 1996 and '99 with the likes of Pudge Rodríguez, Juan González, Rafael Palmeiro, Will Clark and Dean Palmer straining to bash home runs faster than the lackluster pitching staff served them up. But it largely harmed more than it helped, a point proven by the Rangers' decision to construct their new home, Globe Life Field, to suppress offense instead of enhance it.

There's an alchemy there: a homer-prone ballpark, a conveyor belt of power hitters, terribad rotations, decades of losing with only occasional respite. It just happens to be far more synonymous with the Colorado Rockies, who seem doomed to live that time loop for all eternity.

Maybe it's the name of the team itself, between identifying as Texas, instead of Dallas or Arlington, then doubling down with an association with the state's most famous (and problematic) branch of law enforcement. This is almost certainly how the Rangers would prefer you recognize them, and if you don't believe me, peep their social media, where the hashtag of choice is #StraightUpTX and the Twitter location is set to "Deep in the ♥ of Texas." That would land a lot better if there weren't another baseball team in Texas, one which arrived a decade earlier, has won more often, and generally wears cooler uniforms. The Rangers almost certainly do not prefer that you recognize them as the Houston Astros' little brother, but it's hard to argue against it historically, right down to Texas signing Nolan Ryan only after Houston washed their hands of him.

It's fitting that the Rangers' best days are overshadowed by their southern rivals, too. Rewind a dozen years, and Texas, not Houston, was the pacesetter in their shared quest to become the state's first World Series champion. The Rangers were the savvy team in Texas, stitching together shrewd trades and plucking the fruit from a vine-ripened farm system. Josh Hamilton, not Jose Altuve, was the Cinderella MVP story. Before Justin Verlander and Zack Greinke, Cliff Lee was the benchmark for a chest-beating, rotation-fortifying midyear deal.

Then the Rangers came up short. Once they did, the Astros didn't pick up the pieces so much as stack them even higher: bigger bats, sharper pitching, a craftier manager. Cheating scandal or no, Houston, not Texas, won the World Series, and the gap has only widened in the years since. All the highs of Texas' near misses now feel long faded, sandcastles washed away in the ocean.

Even the Rangers' city is only marginally theirs. Arlington, a suburb 30 minutes west of Dallas, belonged to them decades before it did anything else aside from theme parks and chain restaurants. It was a baseball town—until, that is, the Cowboys plopped down a half-mile away in the most spectacular football stadium in the country. The Rangers now play second fiddle in the place they put on the map, and the cruel truth is nothing they do will ever change that. Such is life when your next-door neighbor happens to be the world's most lucrative sports franchise.

This hasn't stopped them from trying, of course, nowhere harder than with Globe Life Field, a gaudy—and, yes, spectacular—attempt to chase AT&T Stadium's ghost. You remember the outcome: the ballpark opened its doors in the worst year in modern history to attend a sporting event, setting the stage for it to host the 2020 World Series. The first (and, as of now, only) watershed moment in Globe Life Field history didn't involve the Rangers at all, but there was no ignoring them, either. How could there be when the World Series was held on their field, worked by their staff, covered by their local media? The Rangers weren't forgotten by anyone who strolled by the statues of Ryan and Rodríguez to enter the gates, nor by anyone who grasped the irony of Clayton Kershaw, one of Dallas' greatest baseball exports, capturing that long-awaited ring in Arlington, of all places. When Julio Urías fanned Willy Adames to clinch the series, the Dodgers spilled out of a dugout that wasn't theirs, and it was hard not to feel Texas looming over the proceedings a little bit even then. It was everything that needed to be said about the Rangers and their broader place in baseball: so present and so absent at the same time.

So here stand the Texas Rangers, a half-century into their existence, back where they so often have been. Once again, they're mired in a bleak present while confronting an uncertain future—but if the circumstances are familiar, the outcome doesn't need to be.

There's a strength that can come with rebuilding. When it's done in the name of competition instead of cost-cutting, the process is born out of self-awareness, of a refusal to accept the status quo as good enough and the boldness to shout as much to everyone listening. Rebuilding amounts to striving, and the Rangers, for all their foibles, have strived far more often than not over the years. Part of the disappointment lies in the fact that they should be better. This is a big-market club plumb in a talent hotbed, with resources to match—the occasional bankruptcy notwithstanding—and, depending on the year, the reckless streak to leverage all of them.

So why can't this next iteration be the moment when the Rangers actually *are* better? Why can't Josh Jung be their Mike Schmidt, Jack Leiter their Warren Spahn, Chris Woodward their Casey Stengel? They probably won't be, of course, but the upside of rampant mediocrity is that any stray half-decade truly could become the Best One Ever. The Yankees will never top winning six World Series in seven years, just as the A's likely peaked with that three-peat in the early '70s. All Texas needs to do is win one, any one, and, voilà, the greatest days have arrived.

This is eminently doable—if not now, then sometime. Beginning with the appointment of former starting pitcher Chris Young as general manager in late 2020, the Rangers have made one sound move after another. They re-fertilized the farm by offloading their veterans, and they placed post-hype bets of varying amounts on players like Spencer Howard and Nathaniel Lowe. More recently, they augmented Woodward by plucking two of the game's more respected coaches, the Red Sox' Tim Hyers and the Giants' Donnie Ecker, to serve as hitting coach and bench coach/offensive coordinator, respectively. Some of those moves won't pan out, and it's doubtful the ones that do will qualify as franchise-altering. However, they've made a couple of those, too, splurging for infielders Corey Seager and Marcus Semien, part of a $561-million spending spree prior to the expiration of the league's collective bargaining agreement on December 1. By the time you read this, there might be even more, too. There's a synthesis behind each one of these transactions, big and small. Smart organizations nail the margin calls, too.

The groundwork is being laid for better days, perhaps even the best ones, and if things are done correctly, joy will be ingrained in that process. The beauty of not knowing what you are comes in being untethered from what you must be. The Rangers, after all this time, are still a blank canvas, which is an opportunity as well as a failure. There is no "Ranger Way," never has been. That affords Texas the freedom to explore any avenue to create one. How many franchises can reinvent themselves so comprehensively with so little mess?

Someday, the Texas Rangers will become more defined. You will picture something clear, a constant, in your mind's eye when you think of them: some unifying theory behind their baseball experience. That day is not today. They'll spend 2022 like they have so many summers before, striving and searching for what makes them who they are. When they find it, it will be a victory on par with finally winning that elusive World Series.

—Mike Piellucci is the sports editor at D Magazine.

HITTERS

Kole Calhoun RF
Born: 10/14/87 Age: 34 Bats: L Throws: L Height: 5'10" Weight: 205 lb. Origin: Round 8, 2010 Draft (#264 overall)

YEAR	TEAM	LVL	AGE	PA	R	2B	3B	HR	RBI	BB	K	SB	CS	Whiff%	AVG/OBP/SLG	DRC+	BABIP	BRR	FRAA	WARP
2019	LAA	MLB	31	632	92	29	1	33	74	70	162	4	1	32.3%	.232/.325/.467	107	.265	1.1	RF(150): 7.0, CF(2): -0.1	3.2
2020	ARI	MLB	32	228	35	9	0	16	40	28	50	1	1	32.7%	.226/.338/.526	118	.211	0.5	RF(48): 5.2	1.8
2021	ARI	MLB	33	182	17	8	0	5	17	15	41	1	0	31.9%	.235/.297/.373	87	.281	-0.1	RF(39): -0.6	0.2
2022 DC	*TEX*	*MLB*	*34*	*513*	*62*	*20*	*1*	*18*	*61*	*52*	*126*	*3*	*2*	*31.5%*	*.231/.317/.406*	*94*	*.278*	*-0.4*	*RF 1*	*1.1*

Comparables: J.D. Drew, Paul O'Neill, Nick Markakis

Over a six-year stretch starting in 2015, Calhoun was one of a baker's dozen players to play in over 800 games, right there with other stalwarts such as Votto and Blackmon and Bogaerts and José Abreu. Unfortunately his durability waned last year, as he first missed time with a torn meniscus in one leg, then a torn hamstring in the other. He missed more than 90 days of the season due to that latter malady, and you're clutching at your thigh just thinking about it. He's long had a reputation for max-effort prowess in the field, but his hammy tore on a stolen base attempt. Depending on the long-term severity of the injury, the 34-year-old may need to rely on classic old-man strength to stay in his new lineup in Texas.

Willie Calhoun LF/DH
Born: 11/04/94 Age: 27 Bats: L Throws: R Height: 5'8" Weight: 200 lb. Origin: Round 4, 2015 Draft (#132 overall)

YEAR	TEAM	LVL	AGE	PA	R	2B	3B	HR	RBI	BB	K	SB	CS	Whiff%	AVG/OBP/SLG	DRC+	BABIP	BRR	FRAA	WARP
2019	NAS	AAA	24	172	23	8	0	8	28	32	24	1	1		.297/.433/.529	129	.311	-0.7	LF(33): -7.2, 2B(3): 0.0	0.5
2019	TEX	MLB	24	337	51	14	1	21	48	23	53	0	0	15.9%	.269/.323/.524	114	.262	0.9	LF(71): -6.8	1.2
2020	TEX	MLB	25	108	3	2	1	1	13	5	17	0	0	14.7%	.190/.231/.260	80	.214	-1.4	LF(8): -0.4	-0.2
2021	TEX	MLB	26	284	26	10	3	6	25	21	34	0	2	16.1%	.250/.310/.381	100	.267	-1.5	LF(41): -4.9	0.2
2022 DC	*TEX*	*MLB*	*27*	*516*	*65*	*20*	*2*	*18*	*60*	*38*	*69*	*1*	*1*	*16.0%*	*.254/.315/.425*	*99*	*.264*	*-0.4*	*LF 0*	*1.1*

Comparables: Luis Valbuena, Kyle Blanks, Eddie Rosario

Calhoun was an average hitter in 2021, which isn't so much damning him with faint praise as drowning him in it like quicksand. You can't really blame him for the forearm fracture he received at the hands of Kris Bubic, which cost him half the season. But even when he sneaks his way into regular playing time, hitting was supposed to be a given. He's not going to add much with his glove, or his legs.

The question all this raises is: What good is a hit tool if you misuse it? Calhoun swung and missed on 6.4% of pitches last season, a contact rate good enough to put him firmly in the 90th percentile of hitters (min. 250 PAs). He's always been able to put the bat on the ball. But much of his contact comes on pitches he has no business swinging at, outside the zone, where the best case scenario is a single. And that reactionary approach prevents him from driving the easy pitches down the heart of the plate. What we're left with is a fastball hitter who doesn't key on the fastball, which is, as they say, a bold strategy.

Evan Carter CF
Born: 08/29/02 Age: 19 Bats: L Throws: R Height: 6'4" Weight: 190 lb. Origin: Round 2, 2020 Draft (#50 overall)

YEAR	TEAM	LVL	AGE	PA	R	2B	3B	HR	RBI	BB	K	SB	CS	Whiff%	AVG/OBP/SLG	DRC+	BABIP	BRR	FRAA	WARP
2021	DE	A	18	146	22	8	1	2	12	34	28	12	4		.236/.438/.387	121	.299	-2.0	CF(30): -4.0	0.4
2022 non-DC	*TEX*	*MLB*	*19*	*251*	*21*	*10*	*1*	*2*	*19*	*31*	*65*	*10*	*5*	*30.1%*	*.194/.306/.294*	*71*	*.265*	*0.9*	*CF -3*	*-0.2*

Comparables: Justin Upton, Ronald Acuña Jr., Mike Trout

When the Rangers took Carter in the second round of the 2020 draft, the immediate analysis from draft experts and scouts was pretty unanimous: "I'm sorry, who?" While Carter's first-year numbers weren't eye-popping, it's important to remember that he was 3.2 years younger than the average age in Low-A. His keen strike zone recognition was… okay, okay, maybe a .438 on-base percentage is a bit eye-popping. And it seemed that everyone who wrote anything about the Wood Ducks in 2021 had something nice to say about Carter, whether it was his athleticism, speed, defense, or some other aspect of his game that somehow remained a nearly-complete mystery for his entire high school career. Still, eventually the pitchers are going to throw strikes.

★ ★ ★ *2022 Top 101 Prospect* **#99** ★ ★ ★

Ezequiel Duran 2B/SS
Born: 05/22/99 Age: 23 Bats: R Throws: R Height: 5'11" Weight: 185 lb. Origin: International Free Agent, 2017

YEAR	TEAM	LVL	AGE	PA	R	2B	3B	HR	RBI	BB	K	SB	CS	Whiff%	AVG/OBP/SLG	DRC+	BABIP	BRR	FRAA	WARP
2019	SI	SS	20	277	49	12	4	13	37	25	77	11	4		.256/.329/.496		.314			
2021	SUR	WIN	22	78	16	7	4	3	12	5	9	0	2		.278/.333/.611		.283			
2021	HIC	A+	22	174	25	7	0	7	31	12	59	7	2		.229/.287/.408	81	.309	-0.9	SS(25): 2.3, 2B(4): 0.3, 3B(3): -0.2	0.3
2021	HV	A+	22	297	42	15	6	12	48	28	71	12	7		.290/.374/.533	124	.354	-2.2	2B(42): 7.4, SS(16): -1.9	2.0
2022 non-DC	*TEX*	*MLB*	*23*	*251*	*22*	*10*	*1*	*4*	*24*	*16*	*76*	*6*	*3*	*30.7%*	*.219/.282/.346*	*68*	*.305*	*0.7*	*2B 3, SS 0*	*0.2*

Comparables: César Hernández, Breyvic Valera, Jimmy Paredes

Duran was the highest-ranking member of the package the Rangers got when they decided to ship Joey Gallo off to the Yankees at the deadline. He's a good enough defender at second base, and some evaluators even think he could play shortstop on occasion, if needed. But the big draw is that he hits the ball really, really freaking hard. The strikeouts are still a bit too abundant, so he'll need to either trim those or—in the tradition of the man for whom he was traded—just cut them with a heavy dose of walks. But he appears to be right on pace to contribute at the big-league level when the Rangers are ready to contend again.

★ ★ ★ *2022 Top 101 Prospect* **#50** ★ ★ ★

Justin Foscue 2B
Born: 03/02/99 Age: 23 Bats: R Throws: R Height: 6'0" Weight: 205 lb. Origin: Round 1, 2020 Draft (#14 overall)

YEAR	TEAM	LVL	AGE	PA	R	2B	3B	HR	RBI	BB	K	SB	CS	Whiff%	AVG/OBP/SLG	DRC+	BABIP	BRR	FRAA	WARP
2021	SUR	WIN	22	89	15	4	0	5	14	15	23	3	1		.257/.416/.529		.310			
2021	HIC	A+	22	150	34	11	1	14	35	16	39	1	1		.296/.407/.736	127	.315	0.7	2B(29): -0.2	1.0
2021	FRI	AA	22	104	14	7	0	2	13	8	29	0	1		.247/.317/.387	84	.333	-1.6	2B(24): -0.7	-0.1
2022 non-DC	*TEX*	*MLB*	*23*	*251*	*25*	*12*	*1*	*7*	*28*	*18*	*70*	*0*	*1*	*28.0%*	*.224/.297/.389*	*83*	*.290*	*-0.3*	*2B -1*	*0.2*

Comparables: Brandon Lowe, Cory Spangenberg, Chris Taylor

Foscue struck out 72 times in 62 games, and still had an OBP of .371. He finally cooled off once he hit the Double-A wall, but his numbers at Low- and High-A suggest that he'll figure it out in Frisco pretty quickly in 2022. He'll have some competition in the infield with Ezequiel Duran and Josh Smith, and has seen his major-league path blocked by the twin signings of Corey Seager and Marcus Semien. He's not the defender any of those guys are, with below-average foot speed begetting below-average range and an arm that can't make up for it. He might ultimately fit in an outfielder corner or even first base, though his size is working against him on the latter. Regardless, he can flat-out hit and those guys tend to find a way to play.

Adolis García OF
Born: 03/02/93 Age: 29 Bats: R Throws: R Height: 6'1" Weight: 205 lb. Origin: International Free Agent, 2017

YEAR	TEAM	LVL	AGE	PA	R	2B	3B	HR	RBI	BB	K	SB	CS	Whiff%	AVG/OBP/SLG	DRC+	BABIP	BRR	FRAA	WARP
2019	GIG	WIN	26	69	4	4	2	0	5	0	17	1	1		.250/.261/.368		.333			
2019	MEM	AAA	26	529	96	22	6	32	96	22	159	14	10		.253/.301/.517	95	.305	2.0	RF(73): 12.8, CF(34): 4.3, LF(12): 0.6	3.2
2020	TEX	MLB	27	7	0	0	0	0	0	1	4	0	0	46.2%	.000/.143/.000	79			LF(3): 0.2	0.0
2021	TEX	MLB	28	622	77	26	2	31	90	32	194	16	5	34.2%	.243/.286/.454	92	.306	1.3	CF(79): 9.2, RF(51): 7.7, LF(9): -1.0	3.4
2022 DC	*TEX*	*MLB*	*29*	*551*	*60*	*22*	*2*	*21*	*74*	*27*	*171*	*10*	*5*	*34.0%*	*.218/.265/.397*	*74*	*.279*	*0.9*	*CF 6, RF 0*	*0.7*

Comparables: Nelson Cruz, John Mayberry Jr., Mitch Haniger

García employed an unbelievable April to set Rangers rookie records for home runs and RBI, making the All-Star team as a nice little bonus. Even after the proceeding five-month slump, he still exceeded his 99th percentile preseason PECOTA projection. What the team's "He should be Rookie of the Year" promotional one-sheet failed to mention is he also set the Rangers rookie record for strikeouts and would have set two more—highest percentage of swings at pitches outside the zone, and highest percentage of swinging strikes—if not for the fact that DJ Peters happened to out-do him on both fronts. But where García set himself apart was his defense. He made a throw in Yankee Stadium that looked like watching war footage of a missile, so it's no surprise he tied for the league lead in outfield assists, with 16.

David García C
Born: 02/06/00 Age: 22 Bats: S Throws: R Height: 5'11" Weight: 201 lb. Origin: International Free Agent, 2016

YEAR	TEAM	LVL	AGE	PA	R	2B	3B	HR	RBI	BB	K	SB	CS	Whiff%	AVG/OBP/SLG	DRC+	BABIP	BRR	FRAA	WARP
2019	SPO	SS	19	210	33	14	0	5	29	21	42	1	1		.277/.351/.435		.331			
2021	HIC	A+	21	328	36	13	0	5	40	18	78	0	0		.256/.298/.349	88	.324	-2.6	C(73): -4.4	-0.1
2022 non-DC	*TEX*	*MLB*	*22*	*251*	*18*	*10*	*0*	*2*	*19*	*13*	*67*	*0*	*0*	*28.4%*	*.222/.268/.300*	*53*	*.303*	*-0.3*	*C -3*	*-0.7*

Comparables: Tomás Telis, Christian Vázquez, Rafael Marchan

YEAR	TEAM	P. COUNT	FRM RUNS	BLK RUNS	THRW RUNS	TOT RUNS
2019	SPO	5439			0.5	0.5
2021	HIC	10393	-6.2	1.2	-0.5	-5.5
2022	*TEX*	*6956*	*-3.0*	*0.2*	*0.3*	*-2.5*

Hands up if you came here because you saw García's name on the 40-man roster and thought to yourself "who is that and why is he on a 40-man roster?" Well, friends, you've come to the right place. We'll just wait here together until someone comes along who can explain it. Here's what we have so far: he's got an excellent defensive reputation [flips flash card over] and yeah, so you're all caught up now. It's not that the bat has been bad, but it's a little perplexing that the team added the catcher to the 40-man roster *last* offseason, when he was just 20 years old. Okay, next category: Hands up if you're reading this in, like, 2025 and García is making this comment look stupid in the future.

Ronald Guzmán 1B
Born: 10/20/94 Age: 27 Bats: L Throws: L Height: 6'5" Weight: 235 lb. Origin: International Free Agent, 2011

YEAR	TEAM	LVL	AGE	PA	R	2B	3B	HR	RBI	BB	K	SB	CS	Whiff%	AVG/OBP/SLG	DRC+	BABIP	BRR	FRAA	WARP
2019	NAS	AAA	24	135	22	8	0	5	16	17	31	0	0		.308/.400/.504	96	.383	-0.5	1B(23): 1.1	0.3
2019	TEX	MLB	24	295	34	20	0	10	36	32	87	1	2	32.9%	.219/.308/.414	82	.282	-2.7	1B(81): 6.3	0.5
2020	GIG	WIN	25	131	25	3	0	5	13	17	23	2	0		.360/.450/.523		.417			
2020	TEX	MLB	25	86	10	1	1	4	9	7	24	1	0	31.6%	.244/.314/.436	85	.300	0.5	1B(24): 3.4	0.4
2021	TEX	MLB	26	17	1	0	0	1	1	1	6	0	0	40.0%	.063/.118/.250	84			LF(2): -0.1	0.0
2022 non-DC	*TEX*	*MLB*	*27*	*251*	*25*	*10*	*0*	*7*	*27*	*23*	*73*	*0*	*1*	*32.5%*	*.222/.304/.375*	*84*	*.296*	*-0.2*	*1B 1, LF 0*	*0.0*

Comparables: Mike Carp, Logan Morrison, Kyle Blanks

Guzmán got chances to claim the first base job in 2018, 2019 and 2020, and just couldn't quite put it together at the plate, prompting the Rangers to trade for Nate Lowe. Timing is a funny thing—Guzmán had a monster season in Winter ball, forcing the Rangers to make a decision in spring training. The decision was: "Why don't we see how you look in left field?" The answer was that he looked a lot more natural than anyone expected, right up until he caught a spike in the turf at Tropicana Field and blew out his knee. Lowe didn't have the sort of season that would slam the door on a Guzmán return, but apparently did gently close it with a whispered "sorry, all full." Guzmán cleared waivers and was outrighted, becoming a free agent in early November.

Dustin Harris CI Born: 07/08/99 Age: 22 Bats: L Throws: R Height: 6'2" Weight: 185 lb. Origin: Round 11, 2019 Draft (#344 overall)

YEAR	TEAM	LVL	AGE	PA	R	2B	3B	HR	RBI	BB	K	SB	CS	Whiff%	AVG/OBP/SLG	DRC+	BABIP	BRR	FRAA	WARP
2019	ASGR	ROK	19	140	23	10	1	1	16	14	20	9	4		.328/.400/.448		.385			
2019	VER	SS	19	98	10	2	0	0	10	11	19	0	3		.321/.408/.345		.409			
2021	DE	A	21	306	54	11	3	10	53	34	48	20	1		.301/.389/.483	130	.329	0.1	1B(50): 1.9, 3B(13): -0.9	1.9
2021	HIC	A+	21	160	32	10	0	10	32	13	25	5	1		.372/.425/.648	144	.396	-0.6	1B(24): -1.8, 3B(11): -0.2	1.0
2022 non-DC	*TEX*	*MLB*	*22*	*251*	*25*	*10*	*1*	*5*	*27*	*18*	*46*	*6*	*2*	*21.2%*	*.260/.321/.396*	*94*	*.304*	*0.4*	*1B 0, 3B 0*	*0.4*

Comparables: Greg Bird, Nathaniel Lowe, Nick Evans

When the Rangers traded Mike Minor to the Athletics for Harris and Marcus Smith, the initial reaction among Rangers fans was "how could you not have traded Minor a year earlier when he had more value?! Look at this return; what is this? A return for ANTS?" Harris spent the 2021 season answering in the affirmative, but pulling the old switcheroo: "Yes, except the ants are the size of horses, and you can ride them, and it doesn't bother me at all to say this because I was too young to be emotionally scarred by the scene from *Honey, I Shrunk the Kids* where the scorpion kills the ant. Have fun being sad about that for the rest of the day, I gotta go hit the mess out of another baseball."

Jonah Heim C Born: 06/27/95 Age: 27 Bats: S Throws: R Height: 6'4" Weight: 220 lb. Origin: Round 4, 2013 Draft (#129 overall)

YEAR	TEAM	LVL	AGE	PA	R	2B	3B	HR	RBI	BB	K	SB	CS	Whiff%	AVG/OBP/SLG	DRC+	BABIP	BRR	FRAA	WARP
2019	TOR	WIN	24	83	11	6	1	0	11	10	12	0	0		.301/.386/.411		.361			
2019	MID	AA	24	208	20	12	0	5	34	24	27	0	1		.282/.370/.431	131	.307	-1.7	C(43): 3.8	1.8
2019	LV	AAA	24	119	22	9	0	4	19	11	18	0	0		.358/.412/.557	107	.395	-0.4	C(28): 3.1	0.8
2020	OAK	MLB	25	41	5	0	0	0	5	3	3	0	0	10.9%	.211/.268/.211	103	.229	-0.2	C(12): 0.3	0.2
2021	TEX	MLB	26	285	22	13	0	10	32	15	58	3	1	21.6%	.196/.239/.358	86	.210	-0.9	C(78): 9.3	1.6
2022 DC	*TEX*	*MLB*	*27*	*246*	*25*	*10*	*0*	*6*	*29*	*16*	*44*	*0*	*1*	*21.4%*	*.230/.284/.361*	*73*	*.260*	*-0.3*	*C 6*	*0.9*

Comparables: Martín Maldonado, Michael Perez, Elias Díaz

YEAR	TEAM	P. COUNT	FRM RUNS	BLK RUNS	THRW RUNS	TOT RUNS
2019	LV	3229	2.1	0.0	0.0	2.1
2019	MID	5723	4.1	0.0	0.3	4.4
2019	TOR	1369			0.6	0.6
2020	OAK	1456	0.1	0.0	0.0	0.1
2021	TEX	10395	10.9	-0.3	0.3	11.0
2022	*TEX*	*9620*	*7.2*	*-0.2*	*0.1*	*7.0*

If one were so inclined, they might regard Jonah Heim as the Ben Wallace of baseball, in that there aren't many who can defend better, but relying on him to provide offense on a regular basis might be too much to ask. When Heim did hit, it was in spectacular fashion—as the chaos of the trade deadline swirled, Heim became the first player in Rangers history (and the first rookie in MLB history) to launch walkoff home runs in back-to-back games. He also got a single in his hometown of Buffalo when the Rangers played the temporarily displaced Blue Jays in June, getting a standing ovation from the hometown crowd. Sadly, they haven't rolled out a cheer for framing, but if someone invents it, Heim might be the first recipient.

Sam Huff 1B Born: 01/14/98 Age: 24 Bats: R Throws: R Height: 6'5" Weight: 240 lb. Origin: Round 7, 2016 Draft (#219 overall)

YEAR	TEAM	LVL	AGE	PA	R	2B	3B	HR	RBI	BB	K	SB	CS	Whiff%	AVG/OBP/SLG	DRC+	BABIP	BRR	FRAA	WARP
2019	HIC	A	21	114	22	5	0	15	29	6	37	4	1		.333/.368/.796	188	.375	-0.2	C(14): -0.6	1.4
2019	DE	A+	21	405	49	17	2	13	43	27	117	2	5		.262/.326/.425	99	.347	-3.0	C(51): 3.6, 1B(4): 0.1	1.3
2020	TEX	MLB	22	33	5	3	0	3	4	2	11	0	0	40.7%	.355/.394/.742	96	.471	-0.7	C(10): -1.0	-0.1
2021	RAN	ROK	23	33	6	2	0	3	6	3	11	0	0		.276/.364/.655		.333			
2021	FRI	AA	23	191	24	5	0	10	23	16	77	0	0		.237/.309/.439	70	.360	-0.1	1B(34): -0.8	-0.3
2021	RR	AAA	23	25	4	1	0	3	7	2	9	0	0		.273/.320/.727	90	.273	0.0	1B(4): -0.5	0.0
2022 DC	*TEX*	*MLB*	*24*	*220*	*25*	*8*	*0*	*10*	*29*	*14*	*83*	*1*	*1*	*38.6%*	*.219/.278/.417*	*80*	*.312*	*-0.1*	*C -4*	*-0.2*

Comparables: Nick Evans, Mark Trumbo, José Osuna

YEAR	TEAM	P. COUNT	FRM RUNS	BLK RUNS	THRW RUNS	TOT RUNS
2019	DE	7009	2.0		0.4	2.4
2019	HIC	1927	-0.7		0.4	-0.3
2020	TEX	1459	-1.2	0.0	0.0	-1.2
2022	*TEX*	*6012*	*-4.2*	*0.1*	*0.0*	*-4.1*

One could imagine that as an opposing manager or pitching coach, watching Sam Huff at the plate must be something akin to watching videos of Russian dash cams on YouTube. Most of the time, even though it looks scary, the two objects don't collide, but when the enormous truck does hit the cow or the motorcycle, the result of that collision is a catastrophe of epic proportions. Huff's power is roughly equivalent to a large speeding lorry, but his strikeout numbers stand in the way of showing it off. (Glance at the ratio above, and note that they actually improved over the late summer.) Some hitters strike out too much because they're too patient, taking strikes and waiting for the right one. This is not Huff's problem; he treats every at-bat like a home run derby with the clock rolling. A knee injury prevented him from catching in 2021, but the plan is still for him to be a backstop-slash-jackknifed watermelon truck in the future.

Andy Ibáñez 2B Born: 04/03/93 Age: 29 Bats: R Throws: R Height: 5'11" Weight: 205 lb. Origin: International Free Agent, 2015

YEAR	TEAM	LVL	AGE	PA	R	2B	3B	HR	RBI	BB	K	SB	CS	Whiff%	AVG/OBP/SLG	DRC+	BABIP	BRR	FRAA	WARP
2019	NAS	AAA	26	529	91	30	1	20	65	53	91	7	7		.300/.375/.497	111	.335	2.4	3B(48): 1.0, 2B(35): -1.7, SS(26): 0.6	2.8
2021	RR	AAA	28	129	21	11	1	7	27	12	18	1	0		.342/.411/.640	127	.356	0.9	3B(13): -0.2, 2B(12): 1.4, 1B(3): 0.2	1.1
2021	TEX	MLB	28	272	31	15	2	7	25	15	35	0	0	20.5%	.277/.321/.435	107	.297	1.5	2B(31): -1.2, 1B(12): -0.3, 3B(11): -0.8	1.0
2022 DC	*TEX*	*MLB*	*29*	*225*	*26*	*10*	*0*	*6*	*27*	*15*	*35*	*0*	*1*	*21.1%*	*.267/.321/.419*	*101*	*.293*	*-0.2*	*3B -1, LF 1*	*0.7*

Comparables: Whit Merrifield, Phil Gosselin, Yandy Díaz

If you watched Ibáñez in the cages in spring training of 2021, you probably came away thinking "Yeah, this guy can hit." If you watched him play defense, it was probably more along the lines of "Whew, this guy had better be able to hit." It turns out he's just not a third baseman, but his defense at second base was passable with gusts up to "not bad". With Rougned Odor gone and Nick Solak struggling in 2021, Ibáñez looked like he might have been penciled in as the everyday second baseman in 2022. Then, November happened, and threw that idea out the window. Too limited to serve as a utility infielder, he's probably headed back to Round Rock to work on his defense, unironically, until a spot or a trade partner opens up.

★ ★ ★ *2022 Top 101 Prospect* **#31** ★ ★ ★

Josh Jung 3B

Born: 02/12/98 Age: 24 Bats: R Throws: R Height: 6'2" Weight: 214 lb. Origin: Round 1, 2019 Draft (#8 overall)

YEAR	TEAM	LVL	AGE	PA	R	2B	3B	HR	RBI	BB	K	SB	CS	Whiff%	AVG/OBP/SLG	DRC+	BABIP	BRR	FRAA	WARP
2019	RAN	ROK	21	19	5	1	1	1	5	2	3	0	0		.588/.632/.941		.692			
2019	HIC	A	21	179	18	13	0	1	23	16	29	4	1		.287/.363/.389	109	.341	0.9	3B(35): 2.7	1.1
2021	FRI	AA	23	186	25	8	1	10	40	13	42	2	2		.308/.366/.544	114	.356	-1.9	3B(32): 0.2	0.7
2021	RR	AAA	23	156	29	14	0	9	21	18	34	0	0		.348/.436/.652	125	.413	-0.4	3B(24): 1.3	1.1
2022 non-DC	*TEX*	*MLB*	*24*	*251*	*26*	*12*	*0*	*6*	*28*	*18*	*60*	*1*	*1*	*27.4%*	*.250/.315/.403*	*93*	*.312*	*-0.2*	*3B 1*	*0.6*

Comparables: Matt Chapman, Brent Morel, Ryan Braun

The only knock on Jung coming out of college was that he might not have the power to stick at third base, so perhaps a shift to second base might be in his future. Not only has he persistently taken infield practice at second base, but his numbers suggest that the power is coming along just fine, thank you. Jung shows a knack for both making and maximizing contact, and his consistent swing plane gives the impression that he'll be comparatively slump-proof. He spent the first part of the 2021 season in a walking boot, which is good because he needed his foot to be in top condition for all the butt kicking he did in 2021. Barring another injury (or a move to second base) he'll have a chance to be the Rangers' starting third baseman before long; he's good enough to have been there already.

Isiah Kiner-Falefa SS

Born: 03/23/95 Age: 27 Bats: R Throws: R Height: 5'11" Weight: 190 lb. Origin: Round 4, 2013 Draft (#130 overall)

YEAR	TEAM	LVL	AGE	PA	R	2B	3B	HR	RBI	BB	K	SB	CS	Whiff%	AVG/OBP/SLG	DRC+	BABIP	BRR	FRAA	WARP
2019	FRI	AA	24	71	7	4	0	2	11	8	9	1	0		.283/.380/.450	125	.300	-0.2	C(9): -0.2, 3B(4): 1.5, SS(1): -0.1	0.6
2019	NAS	AAA	24	37	3	3	0	0	2	1	6	1	0		.147/.216/.235	89	.179	-0.7	SS(4): 0.4, C(2): 0.1	0.1
2019	TEX	MLB	24	222	23	12	1	1	21	14	49	3	0	18.7%	.238/.299/.322	75	.307	1.9	C(38): -10.2, 3B(25): 1.8	-0.5
2020	TEX	MLB	25	228	28	4	3	3	10	14	32	8	5	15.8%	.280/.329/.370	103	.316	-0.4	3B(46): 2.2, SS(15): 0.9	0.9
2021	TEX	MLB	26	677	74	25	3	8	53	28	90	20	5	14.6%	.271/.312/.357	95	.304	4.0	SS(156): 16.8	4.2
2022 DC	*TEX*	*MLB*	*27*	*581*	*65*	*21*	*2*	*7*	*53*	*32*	*82*	*12*	*5*	*14.9%*	*.266/.317/.355*	*87*	*.302*	*0.6*	*3B 4, SS 1*	*1.2*

Comparables: Marwin Gonzalez, César Hernández, Jose Altuve

One of the things a team wants during "rebuild" years is growth from their young core of players. Unfortunately, growth is often painful—Kiner-Falefa went from winning a Gold Glove at third base to being named the team's starting shortstop, prompting the exile of Elvis Andrus. After a good start, the… uh… "growth" began. Kiner-Falefa endured a dismal slump for the middle third of the season, and later admitted it felt like he was "drowning." He resurfaced in the last lap, hitting .314/.385/.352 for September and October combined. The Rangers spent the GNP of a small nation upgrading their infield via free agency, but Kiner-Falefa's defense—paired with a good clubhouse leadership presence and the experience of having battled through hard times as a full-time player—should keep him on the roster as a backup, or somewhere else as a second-division starter.

Nathaniel Lowe 1B

Born: 07/07/95 Age: 27 Bats: L Throws: R Height: 6'4" Weight: 220 lb. Origin: Round 13, 2016 Draft (#390 overall)

YEAR	TEAM	LVL	AGE	PA	R	2B	3B	HR	RBI	BB	K	SB	CS	Whiff%	AVG/OBP/SLG	DRC+	BABIP	BRR	FRAA	WARP
2019	DUR	AAA	23	406	63	24	0	16	63	72	82	1	0		.289/.421/.508	124	.341	-1.3	1B(72): -0.4, 3B(5): 0.3	1.8
2019	TB	MLB	23	169	24	8	0	7	19	13	50	0	0	27.1%	.263/.325/.454	83	.340	0.8	1B(21): 0.2, 3B(4): -0.1	0.2
2020	TB	MLB	24	76	10	2	0	4	11	9	28	1	0	29.4%	.224/.316/.433	85	.314	0.0	1B(15): -0.8, 3B(2): -0.1	-0.1
2021	TEX	MLB	25	642	75	24	3	18	72	80	162	8	0	23.6%	.264/.357/.415	101	.339	-1.3	1B(148): -9.8, 3B(1): 0.5	0.4
2022 DC	*TEX*	*MLB*	*26*	*559*	*67*	*22*	*1*	*17*	*65*	*68*	*138*	*1*	*1*	*23.4%*	*.245/.341/.404*	*102*	*.307*	*-0.7*	*1B -2*	*1.0*

Comparables: Chris Davis, Matt Adams, Josh Bell

Here's a fun story: Lowe has been known as "Nate" for his entire college and professional baseball career, until this year when—and this is not a lie—his mom asked if she could tell everyone that he actually went by Nathaniel. He said he didn't really care (if he had, he would have brought it up when people started calling him "Nate" in college) and sure, go for it. Sure enough, she made it happen, and every stadium scoreboard operator, TV crew and website in the sport had to go make the change. As for his game, he finally got a shot to be The Guy after being stuck behind others in Tampa for years. He can absolutely kill four-seamers, and if he gets a sinker, he's going to drill it into the ground because he's swinging at a four-seamer. If he can reverse the ground-ball surge, he can be a productive hitter, because thanks to his patience he'll always be able to work himself into some fastball counts.

DJ Peters OF

Born: 12/12/95 Age: 26 Bats: R Throws: R Height: 6'6" Weight: 225 lb. Origin: Round 4, 2016 Draft (#131 overall)

YEAR	TEAM	LVL	AGE	PA	R	2B	3B	HR	RBI	BB	K	SB	CS	Whiff%	AVG/OBP/SLG	DRC+	BABIP	BRR	FRAA	WARP
2019	TUL	AA	23	288	31	10	1	11	42	28	93	1	0		.241/.331/.422	103	.331	-0.7	CF(48): -1.2, RF(20): 0.8	1.0
2019	OKC	AAA	23	255	40	10	1	12	39	33	75	1	1		.260/.388/.490	98	.341	-0.4	CF(56): 1.0	1.0
2021	OKC	AAA	25	204	24	9	2	4	19	20	58	1	1		.233/.319/.372	78	.319	-1.5	CF(39): -5.8, RF(9): -0.9	-0.6
2021	LAD	MLB	25	34	5	2	0	1	4	8	14	0	0	49.2%	.192/.382/.385	83	.364	0.1	CF(11): 0.1, RF(4): 0.5	0.1
2021	TEX	MLB	25	206	24	7	1	12	34	4	68	2	0	35.3%	.198/.218/.426	81	.225	1.9	LF(22): -1.9, CF(18): 2.2, RF(12): -0.6	0.4
2022 non-DC	*TEX*	*MLB*	*26*	*251*	*25*	*9*	*1*	*8*	*28*	*18*	*84*	*0*	*1*	*35.8%*	*.213/.284/.373*	*73*	*.298*	*-0.2*	*CF 0, RF 0*	*-0.1*

Comparables: Aaron Hicks, Peter Bourjos, Jake Marisnick

Okay, first things first: Yes, Peters looks just like the guy who plays Bucky in the Marvel movies. Yes, he has been made aware of this, and yes, he did do the left-arm swipe move after hitting a home run late in the season. As far as baseball goes, Peters is one of those infuriatingly incomplete players, like the brother-in-law nearing 30 who never finds his own place. He's a plus defender, an easy-to-love teammate, hits the ball like Thor and generally plays the game like a leopard on cocaine. But he simply cannot stop striking out, for the life of him, to the point that the Dodgers were willing to just let the Rangers have him for the low price of a waiver claim. In December, Peters signed with the Lotte Giants of the KBO, where he looks like a good fit: His biggest weakness is high-velocity fastballs (he hit .138 with zero extra-base hits on pitches 95-mph or higher in 2021), so he'll enjoy a league where they just don't throw those.

Yohel Pozo C/DH Born: 06/14/97 Age: 25 Bats: R Throws: R Height: 6'0" Weight: 201 lb. Origin: International Free Agent, 2013

YEAR	TEAM	LVL	AGE	PA	R	2B	3B	HR	RBI	BB	K	SB	CS	Whiff%	AVG/OBP/SLG	DRC+	BABIP	BRR	FRAA	WARP
2019	DE	A+	22	419	43	17	0	9	43	15	38	6	2		.246/.274/.357	107	.249	-0.2	C(70): -8.2, 1B(7): -0.2, LF(1): -0.5	0.6
2021	RR	AAA	24	324	46	17	2	23	74	7	42	0	0		.337/.352/.622	137	.331	-0.7	C(51): -3.6, 1B(4): -0.4, 3B(1): -0.1	2.2
2021	TEX	MLB	24	77	8	4	0	1	9	3	10	0	0	18.5%	.284/.312/.378	103	.317	-0.3	C(2): 0.0	0.2
2022 non-DC	*TEX*	*MLB*	*25*	*251*	*26*	*11*	*0*	*8*	*30*	*9*	*35*	*0*	*0*	*18.0%*	*.267/.299/.423*	*91*	*.285*	*-0.3*	*C 1, 1B 0*	*0.9*

Comparables: Willson Contreras, Mark Trumbo, Sandy León

Pozo became a free agent after the 2020 season and signed with the Padres in November. Less than a month later, the Rangers took him (back) in the minor-league phase of the Rule 5 draft. But one of the more shocking stories of this season was when Pozo revealed that when the Rangers made that decision, he had been homeless—living with his wife and baby in a car because of the child's medical expenses. The Rangers, to their credit, immediately got him a hotel, then helped the family get to Arizona, where they lived at the team complex until spring training. A few months later, Pozo made his big-league debut, and while he didn't get enough at-bats to qualify, his batting average was the highest on the team (excluding Dane Dunning, who went 1-for-3 on the season).

Corey Seager SS Born: 04/27/94 Age: 28 Bats: L Throws: R Height: 6'4" Weight: 215 lb. Origin: Round 1, 2012 Draft (#18 overall)

YEAR	TEAM	LVL	AGE	PA	R	2B	3B	HR	RBI	BB	K	SB	CS	Whiff%	AVG/OBP/SLG	DRC+	BABIP	BRR	FRAA	WARP
2019	LAD	MLB	25	541	82	44	1	19	87	44	98	1	0	25.8%	.272/.335/.483	101	.303	0.6	SS(132): 1.1	2.2
2020	LAD	MLB	26	232	38	12	1	15	41	17	37	1	0	25.8%	.307/.358/.585	124	.309	-1.3	SS(43): 2.9	1.5
2021	LAD	MLB	27	409	54	22	3	16	57	48	66	1	1	28.0%	.306/.394/.521	122	.336	-1.1	SS(92): -0.5	2.5
2022 DC	*TEX*	*MLB*	*28*	*550*	*79*	*27*	*2*	*20*	*70*	*54*	*106*	*2*	*1*	*27.3%*	*.281/.358/.472*	*123*	*.321*	*-0.5*	*SS 1*	*3.9*

Comparables: Cal Ripken Jr., Tony Fernandez, Jimmy Rollins

Seager has always been well-known for his aggressive first pitch swings, and he took that approach to a new level in 2021. Of the 2,695 batting seasons with at least 400 plate appearances in the pitch-tracking era, only Carlos Gómez' 2014 campaign had a higher first pitch swing rate than Seager's 53% rate in 2021 (the league's average mark was 30%). Seager's lack of selectivity on the first pitch meant that his results were not much better than the league's numbers on first pitches overall, but it's hard to argue with an approach that made him one of the league's top hitters for the second season in a row. Other than a broken hand on a hit-by-pitch, Seager has largely left his prior injury concerns in the past, though a move to third base seems imminent due to his declining range at short. Even if he does change positions soon, Seager has more than established himself as an elite offensive player, so there's no concern about his bat not playing away from the middle of the diamond—which is good news for the Rangers and the megadeal they signed him to.

Marcus Semien 2B Born: 09/17/90 Age: 31 Bats: R Throws: R Height: 6'0" Weight: 195 lb. Origin: Round 6, 2011 Draft (#201 overall)

YEAR	TEAM	LVL	AGE	PA	R	2B	3B	HR	RBI	BB	K	SB	CS	Whiff%	AVG/OBP/SLG	DRC+	BABIP	BRR	FRAA	WARP
2019	OAK	MLB	28	747	123	43	7	33	92	87	102	10	8	18.5%	.285/.369/.522	130	.294	1.5	SS(161): 4.3	6.2
2020	OAK	MLB	29	236	28	9	1	7	23	25	50	4	0	23.3%	.223/.305/.374	99	.260	1.4	SS(53): 7.7	1.6
2021	TOR	MLB	30	724	115	39	2	45	102	66	146	15	1	21.5%	.265/.334/.538	126	.276	4.1	2B(147): 2.3, SS(21): 0.1	5.7
2022 DC	*TEX*	*MLB*	*31*	*616*	*87*	*26*	*2*	*23*	*65*	*61*	*113*	*10*	*5*	*21.3%*	*.245/.322/.429*	*102*	*.269*	*0.3*	*2B 3*	*2.8*

Comparables: Tony Fernandez, Shawon Dunston, Barry Larkin

There are no bad one-year deals, but some are very much less bad than the others. Both the Blue Jays and Semien bet that the shortened 2020 season was not reflective of the durable middle infielder's skill level moving forward. Both sides of this equation made out like bandits, as Semien broke records and solidified his status as one of the game's elite middle infielders while the Blue Jays welcomed not only his slick fielding and thump in the lineup but his steady drive and professionalism, too. One of just two major leaguers to appear in all 162 in 2021, Semien left quite an impression on one of the youngest clubs in baseball as the ultimate professional.

Some stars aligned for Semien to post his eye-popping offensive numbers in Dunedin/Buffalo/Toronto, but he also hit baseballs higher, harder and more squarely than ever before. He adapted to the Blue Jays' house style—if the first one is good, mash it—by offering at the first pitch 29.7% of the time, the highest mark of his career.

After what looked like a career season in 2019, Semien surpassed that output in 2021. Now a Ranger, he may provide the best bang-for-buck of anyone in his decorated shortstop free-agent class.

Josh H. Smith SS Born: 08/07/97 Age: 24 Bats: L Throws: R Height: 5'10" Weight: 172 lb. Origin: Round 2, 2019 Draft (#67 overall)

YEAR	TEAM	LVL	AGE	PA	R	2B	3B	HR	RBI	BB	K	SB	CS	Whiff%	AVG/OBP/SLG	DRC+	BABIP	BRR	FRAA	WARP
2019	SI	SS	21	141	17	6	1	3	15	25	17	6	3		.324/.450/.477		.355			
2021	TAM	A	23	50	15	0	0	6	15	7	6	5	0		.333/.480/.795	138	.259	1.1	SS(7): -0.4, 2B(1): -0.0	0.4
2021	HIC	A+	23	49	10	3	0	1	7	2	9	2	0		.295/.367/.432	105	.353	-0.1	SS(9): 1.0	0.3
2021	HV	A+	23	125	29	12	3	3	9	16	27	12	3		.320/.435/.583	109	.411	-0.3	SS(23): 3.6	0.8
2021	FRI	AA	23	127	12	5	0	3	10	18	20	7	2		.294/.425/.431	124	.338	-0.1	SS(30): -1.8	0.6
2022 non-DC	*TEX*	*MLB*	*24*	*251*	*25*	*11*	*1*	*5*	*25*	*22*	*47*	*8*	*3*	*20.6%*	*.242/.329/.380*	*95*	*.286*	*0.6*	*SS 1, 2B 0*	*1.0*

Comparables: Jake Cronenworth, Wilmer Difo, JT Riddle

A common theme amongst the Rangers' shortstop prospects is something in the scouting report that says, in some fashion or another: "Eh, you know what, he might be better suited for second base, actually." The prize return in the Joey Gallo trade, Smith's defense might still be in question, but his bat probably shouldn't be—if there's any concern here, it's not because of the man, but with the organization's struggles with other prospects that demonstrated equally reliable hit tools until the day of the test. Also, just for funsies and just-in-cases, you should know we're talking about Josh Smith the infielder here. There's also another Josh Smith who posted a 2.06 ERA with 49 strikeouts in 43 ⅔ innings between Down East and Hickory; the two were teammates for 11 days before *this* Josh was promoted to Double-A.

Nick Solak 2B Born: 01/11/95 Age: 27 Bats: R Throws: R Height: 5'11" Weight: 185 lb. Origin: Round 2, 2016 Draft (#62 overall)

YEAR	TEAM	LVL	AGE	PA	R	2B	3B	HR	RBI	BB	K	SB	CS	Whiff%	AVG/OBP/SLG	DRC+	BABIP	BRR	FRAA	WARP
2019	DUR	AAA	24	349	56	13	1	17	47	39	80	3	2		.266/.353/.485	111	.303	-3.8	2B(61): -8.2, LF(17): 0.1, CF(2): -0.2	0.7
2019	NAS	AAA	24	128	23	6	0	10	27	6	25	2	0		.347/.386/.653	118	.369	0.6	2B(22): 0.0, RF(4): 0.3, LF(3): -0.0	0.9
2019	TEX	MLB	24	135	19	6	1	5	17	15	29	2	0	22.4%	.293/.393/.491	106	.354	0.7	3B(11): -0.3, 2B(5): -0.6	0.5
2020	TEX	MLB	25	233	27	10	0	2	23	18	42	7	1	19.1%	.268/.326/.344	93	.320	3.4	LF(29): -2.3, 2B(17): -0.8, CF(13): -0.2	0.5
2021	RR	AAA	26	93	15	6	0	1	6	7	16	0	1		.353/.409/.459	101	.426	0.5	2B(15): -0.8	0.3
2021	TEX	MLB	26	511	57	18	2	11	49	34	107	7	5	24.9%	.242/.314/.362	94	.292	-0.8	2B(121): -3.6	1.0
2022 DC	*TEX*	*MLB*	*27*	*498*	*58*	*18*	*1*	*13*	*56*	*37*	*104*	*6*	*3*	*23.7%*	*.260/.329/.397*	*97*	*.311*	*0.0*	*LF 0, 2B 0*	*1.3*

Comparables: Justin Turner, Tony Kemp, Austin Slater

Solak's 2021 season looked like a U-shaped parabola: great start, then precipitous plunge into The Nothing for awhile. By "The Nothing," we're talking about Triple-A, a development that almost nobody would have predicted coming into the season, and certainly not after he finished April with seven home runs and a .910 OPS. The problem was hitting breaking pitches, and it doesn't take long for the league to figure that out. After a swim through Round Rock, Solak returned in August and hit .290 in the final 35 games of the season, but the power was still on hiatus: he had no home runs in September. He kept chasing the same pitches, but the ironic thing is he's actually good, comparatively, at hitting them; it's the pitches down the middle he can't handle. Meanwhile, Solak's defensive position got handed to Marcus Semien in the offseason, so he'll try to make himself inconspicuous in left field under the current roster configuration.

Leody Taveras CF Born: 09/08/98 Age: 23 Bats: S Throws: R Height: 6'2" Weight: 195 lb. Origin: International Free Agent, 2015

YEAR	TEAM	LVL	AGE	PA	R	2B	3B	HR	RBI	BB	K	SB	CS	Whiff%	AVG/OBP/SLG	DRC+	BABIP	BRR	FRAA	WARP
2019	AGU	WIN	20	107	12	3	0	0	5	6	15	6	2		.290/.327/.320		.337			
2019	DE	A+	20	290	44	7	4	2	25	31	62	21	5		.294/.368/.376	110	.378	0.5	CF(34): -0.7, RF(23): 3.7, LF(7): -0.5	1.6
2019	FRI	AA	20	293	32	12	4	3	31	23	60	11	8		.265/.320/.375	93	.327	-0.1	CF(65): 7.7	1.7
2020	TEX	MLB	21	134	20	6	1	4	6	14	43	8	0	30.4%	.227/.308/.395	80	.319	2.3	CF(33): 0.9	0.4
2021	AGU	WIN	22	175	27	5	1	2	19	24	23	11	1		.274/.379/.363		.309			
2021	RR	AAA	22	381	57	19	2	17	55	49	95	13	5		.245/.343/.475	98	.287	1.2	CF(70): 4.9, LF(9): 3.0, RF(2): 0.1	2.1
2021	TEX	MLB	22	185	14	6	2	3	9	9	60	10	1	26.9%	.161/.207/.270	62	.225	2.5	CF(48): 3.1	0.5
2022 DC	*TEX*	*MLB*	*23*	*206*	*22*	*7*	*1*	*4*	*18*	*17*	*53*	*4*	*3*	*27.1%*	*.202/.272/.326*	*61*	*.259*	*0.6*	*CF 1*	*-0.1*

Comparables: Anthony Gose, Manuel Margot, Victor Robles

Heading into 2021, Taveras was BP's no. 1 ranked Rangers prospect. He also topped the list ahead of 2020. And 2019. And 2018. In 2017, he was merely third. And the last year the Rangers didn't have Taveras on their list, 2016, it was headlined by Nomar Mazara, who may have already washed out of the league. After half a decade of waiting for Taveras to arrive, Rangers fans finally got to see him start Opening Day...and will go into next year still waiting. It was a disaster from start to finish, as nearly half (8) of the young man's singles were infield hits, and the improved plate discipline vanished along with any semblance of power. And yet, despite that "staring at the Ark of the Covenant"-level slash line, Taveras' defense and baserunning were, in their brief windows, elite. It's unlikely he starts the next Opening Day, but he deserves another chance at some point; that center-field defense combined with a below-average bat is still a pretty decent player, despite all expectations.

Bubba Thompson OF Born: 06/09/98 Age: 24 Bats: R Throws: R Height: 6'2" Weight: 197 lb. Origin: Round 1, 2017 Draft (#26 overall)

YEAR	TEAM	LVL	AGE	PA	R	2B	3B	HR	RBI	BB	K	SB	CS	Whiff%	AVG/OBP/SLG	DRC+	BABIP	BRR	FRAA	WARP
2019	SUR	WIN	21	83	13	1	0	3	9	8	25	5	0		.254/.337/.394		.333			
2019	DE	A+	21	228	24	8	2	5	21	21	72	12	3		.178/.261/.312	75	.246	2.8	LF(34): 1.4, CF(20): -1.6, RF(2): -0.3	0.3
2021	FRI	AA	23	470	73	23	9	16	52	29	121	25	8		.275/.325/.483	97	.347	1.5	CF(68): -3.1, LF(16): 1.8, RF(10): 0.4	1.3
2022 non-DC	*TEX*	*MLB*	*24*	*251*	*22*	*11*	*3*	*5*	*25*	*14*	*79*	*11*	*4*	*34.7%*	*.237/.288/.380*	*77*	*.335*	*1.4*	*CF 1, LF 2*	*0.6*

Comparables: Bubba Starling, Starling Marte, Teoscar Hernández

You almost never get to root for the zombies, which is a real shame. Most people die, and their spirit does whatever it is that spirits do, and their bodies take a break from the exhausting work of staying alive and accept their retirement, taking up the new hobby of becoming loam. Zombies are the rare beings that do not simply accept the end as the end, instead channeling their efforts into a new career, a passion for brains. It's kind of admirable. Anyway, Thompson had a terrible 2019 season and wasn't one of the lucky few to get a golden ticket to the alternate site in 2020. In 2021, fresh off what was starting to smell a bit like career death, Thompson roared back, doing his best to consume the careers of minor-league pitchers and recruit more bodies to the baseball zombie army. As a result, he won the "True Ranger" award, which "highlights players who represent the core values of the organization in a positive light, both on and off the field."

Jose Trevino C

Born: 11/28/92 Age: 29 Bats: R Throws: R Height: 5'11" Weight: 210 lb. Origin: Round 6, 2014 Draft (#186 overall)

YEAR	TEAM	LVL	AGE	PA	R	2B	3B	HR	RBI	BB	K	SB	CS	Whiff%	AVG/OBP/SLG	DRC+	BABIP	BRR	FRAA	WARP
2019	RAN	ROK	26	38	3	1	0	1	6	2	2	0	0		.167/.211/.278		.152			
2019	NAS	AAA	26	156	16	10	0	2	22	8	28	2	0		.226/.263/.336	84	.263	0.9	C(40): 8.0	1.2
2019	TEX	MLB	26	126	18	9	0	2	13	3	27	0	0	22.7%	.258/.272/.383	81	.312	-0.5	C(40): 3.0	0.5
2020	TEX	MLB	27	83	10	8	0	2	9	3	15	0	0	20.2%	.250/.280/.434	99	.279	0.3	C(21): 2.6	0.6
2021	TEX	MLB	28	302	23	14	0	5	30	12	57	1	1	22.6%	.239/.267/.340	84	.279	-1.6	C(88): 15.6	2.1
2022 DC	*TEX*	*MLB*	*29*	*218*	*20*	*9*	*0*	*4*	*24*	*10*	*39*	*0*	*1*	*22.2%*	*.234/.272/.342*	*65*	*.270*	*-0.3*	*C 7*	*0.7*

Comparables: Michael McKenry, Jonathan Lucroy, Brett Hayes

YEAR	TEAM	P. COUNT	FRM RUNS	BLK RUNS	THRW RUNS	TOT RUNS
2019	TEX	5134	1.9	-0.1	1.6	3.4
2019	NAS	5718	8.8	0.0	0.0	8.8
2020	TEX	2650	2.1	0.0	0.6	2.7
2021	TEX	12070	14.3	0.1	0.3	14.7
2022	*TEX*	*8418*	*4.2*	*0.0*	*-0.2*	*4.0*

Trevino finally got a full season in the big leagues, and he and Jonah Heim paired up to be one of the league's best catching tandems, at least while physically catching. At the plate, a few different stance and load adjustments haven't really led to any major breakthroughs: Sometimes a defensive backup is just a defensive backup, no matter how many coats of paint he gets. And for as long as framing is valued first for catchers, that's fine. He'll act as one of those subtle connective tissues on every baseball team, working with rookies, giving back to the community, one of those full-time part-time players every team needs.

PITCHERS

A.J. Alexy RHP

Born: 04/21/98 Age: 24 Bats: R Throws: R Height: 6'4" Weight: 195 lb. Origin: Round 11, 2016 Draft (#341 overall)

YEAR	TEAM	LVL	AGE	W	L	SV	G	GS	IP	H	HR	BB/9	K/9	K	GB%	BABIP	WHIP	ERA	DRA-	WARP	MPH	FB%	Whiff%	CSP
2019	DE	A+	21	0	3	0	5	5	19^1	14	1	6.1	10.7	23	34.0%	.289	1.40	5.12	111	0.1				
2021	FRI	AA	23	3	1	0	13	7	50^1	30	4	3.8	10.2	57	44.8%	.232	1.01	1.61	93	0.5				
2021	RR	AAA	23	0	0	0	3	3	14^2	9	2	3.7	11.7	19	46.9%	.233	1.02	1.84	91	0.1				
2021	TEX	MLB	23	3	1	0	5	4	23	13	4	6.7	6.7	17	24.2%	.155	1.30	4.70	144	-0.3	93.6	54.5%	22.0%	53.1%
2022 DC	*TEX*	*MLB*	*24*	*5*	*5*	*0*	*34*	*12*	*76.3*	*69*	*12*	*5.7*	*9.0*	*76*	*35.4%*	*.280*	*1.54*	*5.10*	*117*	*-0.1*	*93.6*	*54.5%*	*22.0%*	*53.1%*

Comparables: Matt Moore, Chad Durbin, Alex Cobb

When Alexy debuted in 2021, he became the first pitcher in MLB history to go five-plus shutout innings and allow one or fewer hits in each of his first two big-league starts. After that, things got a bit dicey, but any time you can say you became the first pitcher in MLB history to do something and the sentence doesn't end with something like "allow double-digit runs before recording a single out" or "forget which dugout he was supposed to go to after the third out", it's noteworthy. The former 11th-round pick has built up his standard starter's repertoire of pitches, thanks to a consistent delivery and a fastball command that helps his average secondaries. Alexy is but one of a few young starting pitchers the Rangers are hoping will break the curse of starting pitching development that has been in effect since perhaps another Alexi, this time Ogando.

Kolby Allard LHP

Born: 08/13/97 Age: 24 Bats: L Throws: L Height: 6'1" Weight: 195 lb. Origin: Round 1, 2015 Draft (#14 overall)

YEAR	TEAM	LVL	AGE	W	L	SV	G	GS	IP	H	HR	BB/9	K/9	K	GB%	BABIP	WHIP	ERA	DRA-	WARP	MPH	FB%	Whiff%	CSP
2019	GWN	AAA	21	7	5	0	20	20	110	119	15	2.9	8.0	98	49.2%	.334	1.41	4.17	107	0.9				
2019	NAS	AAA	21	0	0	0	1	1	5	4	0	3.6	14.4	8	44.4%	.444	1.20	0.00	89	0.1				
2019	TEX	MLB	21	4	2	0	9	9	45^1	52	3	3.8	6.6	33	45.1%	.327	1.57	4.96	126	-0.2	91.5	79.6%	19.0%	52.4%
2020	TEX	MLB	22	0	6	0	11	8	33^2	31	4	5.3	8.6	32	34.3%	.284	1.51	7.75	121	0.0	90.9	77.2%	23.2%	53.3%
2021	TEX	MLB	23	3	12	0	32	17	124^2	128	29	2.2	7.5	104	39.5%	.270	1.28	5.41	117	0.0	91.1	72.1%	19.9%	57.1%
2022 DC	*TEX*	*MLB*	*24*	*7*	*8*	*0*	*25*	*25*	*127*	*135*	*19*	*3.1*	*7.1*	*100*	*40.2%*	*.299*	*1.41*	*4.67*	*116*	*-0.1*	*91.1*	*73.7%*	*20.3%*	*56.0%*

Comparables: Martín Pérez, Kyle Lohse, Jeff Suppan

When you're 21 years old and in the big leagues, there's a lot of leeway. You're young and inexperienced, but once in a while your curveball looks like the sort of hook upon which hopes may be hung. When you're 24, as Allard is now, there's significantly less leeway, especially when there are other prospects getting to the big leagues. Some of Allard's numbers were better in 2021 than in previous years, but the lack of consistency landed him in the bullpen by September. With names like Dunning, Alexy, Otto and Spencer pulling ahead on the depth chart, and others like Leiter and Winn on the precipice, Allard might find his work days *starting* in the sixth inning, rather than finishing there.

Kohei Arihara RHP Born: 08/11/92 Age: 29 Bats: R Throws: R Height: 6'2" Weight: 210 lb. Origin: International Free Agent, 2020

YEAR	TEAM	LVL	AGE	W	L	SV	G	GS	IP	H	HR	BB/9	K/9	K	GB%	BABIP	WHIP	ERA	DRA-	WARP	MPH	FB%	Whiff%	CSP
2021	RR	AAA	28	0	1	0	3	3	9^2	11	3	4.7	5.6	6	45.5%	.267	1.66	11.17	108	0.0				
2021	TEX	MLB	28	2	4	0	10	10	40^2	45	11	2.9	5.3	24	40.1%	.270	1.43	6.64	145	-0.6	90.3	58.6%	18.3%	53.9%
2022 non-DC	*TEX*	*MLB*	*29*	*2*	*3*	*0*	*57*	*0*	*50*	*55*	*8*	*3.4*	*5.7*	*31*	*41.1%*	*.292*	*1.49*	*5.28*	*126*	*-0.5*	*90.3*	*58.6%*	*18.3%*	*53.9%*

Comparables: Ryan Carpenter, P.J. Walters, Glenn Sparkman

It seemed like a good idea at the time: With the 2020 MLB season shortened to 60 games and the team waiting for the next crop of starting pitching prospects to arrive, why not bring in someone who pitched a full workload last year, due to living in a country (Japan) that took the pandemic seriously enough to play a full season? Nobody expected Arihara to be a superstar; the Rangers just needed him to pitch somewhere north of 160 innings, good or bad. The results were, in fact, bad. Opposing batters hit .406 and slugged .844 against his fastball, and thanks to an aneurysm in his shoulder, he didn't even lead the team in "innings-by-a-guy-who-came-over-from-Japan," falling five outs short of Spencer Patton.

Joe Barlow RHP Born: 09/28/95 Age: 26 Bats: R Throws: R Height: 6'2" Weight: 210 lb. Origin: Round 11, 2016 Draft (#339 overall)

YEAR	TEAM	LVL	AGE	W	L	SV	G	GS	IP	H	HR	BB/9	K/9	K	GB%	BABIP	WHIP	ERA	DRA-	WARP	MPH	FB%	Whiff%	CSP
2019	DE	A+	23	4	0	4	17	0	23^2	10	1	5.7	16.7	44	29.4%	.273	1.06	0.38	66	0.6				
2019	FRI	AA	23	1	1	0	13	0	16	6	1	3.4	15.2	27	41.7%	.217	0.75	1.13	67	0.3				
2019	NAS	AAA	23	1	1	0	19	0	17^1	23	1	10.9	11.4	22	37.3%	.440	2.54	8.83	108	0.0				
2021	RR	AAA	25	0	1	7	17	0	21	8	1	3.4	12.4	29	34.1%	.175	0.76	2.57	84	0.3				
2021	TEX	MLB	25	0	2	11	31	0	29	12	2	3.7	8.4	27	38.9%	.143	0.83	1.55	112	0.1	94.6	46.6%	25.9%	54.4%
2022 DC	*TEX*	*MLB*	*26*	*3*	*3*	*23*	*74*	*0*	*64.7*	*54*	*10*	*5.2*	*10.8*	*77*	*35.9%*	*.284*	*1.43*	*4.39*	*104*	*0.1*	*94.6*	*46.6%*	*25.9%*	*54.4%*

Comparables: Nick Rumbelow, Jacob Rhame, Diego Castillo

After snagging an invite to big-league camp in 2020, not only did the Utah native not make the team, he wasn't even added to the alternate site roster. In 2021, he was left off the big-league spring training roster, so... [ahem] as far as expectations for this season went... you could say he really— Yeah, okay! We all see it coming, but it's too late not to type it out now! He really set the Bar-low (please do not throw tomatoes, this was written in the past and you will only wreck/stain your own belongings. Just ask yourself why you kept reading after you knew what was coming and then throw a tomato at yourself.) (Unless you're Joe Barlow, in which case, way to totally redeem yourself, keep your slider down and your four-seam up, and win the closer's job. Nice work, man.)

Brock Burke LHP Born: 08/04/96 Age: 25 Bats: L Throws: L Height: 6'4" Weight: 210 lb. Origin: Round 3, 2014 Draft (#96 overall)

YEAR	TEAM	LVL	AGE	W	L	SV	G	GS	IP	H	HR	BB/9	K/9	K	GB%	BABIP	WHIP	ERA	DRA-	WARP	MPH	FB%	Whiff%	CSP
2019	FRI	AA	22	3	5	0	9	9	45^1	34	2	2.4	9.7	49	47.5%	.271	1.01	3.18	83	0.5				
2019	NAS	AAA	22	0	0	0	2	2	8	12	1	6.7	12.4	11	50.0%	.478	2.25	7.87	87	0.1				
2019	TEX	MLB	22	0	2	0	6	6	26^2	30	6	3.7	4.7	14	48.4%	.279	1.54	7.42	140	-0.3	91.7	61.3%	13.1%	49.9%
2021	RR	AAA	24	1	5	0	21	20	77^2	76	13	3.6	11.2	97	42.2%	.330	1.38	5.68	86	1.0				
2022 DC	*TEX*	*MLB*	*25*	*2*	*1*	*0*	*17*	*3*	*25.7*	*24*	*3*	*3.6*	*8.5*	*24*	*42.2%*	*.289*	*1.34*	*4.06*	*101*	*0.2*	*91.7*	*61.3%*	*13.1%*	*49.9%*

Comparables: Zack Britton, Kyle Ryan, Danny Duffy

After shoulder surgery and a pandemic double-whammy'd Burke out of a 2020 season, his "triumphant" return to action resulted in a 15.58 ERA in his first four starts in 2021. June wasn't much better (6.41) and July and August were just okay (4.43, 4.50). In a normal minor-league season, that would be the end of the story, and everyone would be deciding whether to write him off or think "ehhh shoulder surgeries take awhile to come back from." But in four September starts, Burke posted an ERA of 1.38, striking out 14 and walking three in 13 innings. That's not enough to pencil him back into the Rangers rotation in 2021, or do much more than make everyone think "ehhh a single month isn't much of a sample." But it is an encouraging sign for the 24-year-old, who was the primary return from the Jurickson Profar deal back in late 2018.

Matt Bush RHP Born: 02/08/86 Age: 36 Bats: R Throws: R Height: 5'9" Weight: 180 lb. Origin: Round 1, 2004 Draft (#1 overall)

YEAR	TEAM	LVL	AGE	W	L	SV	G	GS	IP	H	HR	BB/9	K/9	K	GB%	BABIP	WHIP	ERA	DRA-	WARP	MPH	FB%	Whiff%	CSP
2019	FRI	AA	33	0	0	0	9	0	8^2	3	1	2.1	7.3	7	36.4%	.095	0.58	1.04	99	0.0				
2021	TEX	MLB	35	0	0	0	4	0	4	4	3	2.3	11.3	5	27.3%	.125	1.25	6.75	96	0.0	95.1	53.6%	31.0%	49.3%
2022 non-DC	*TEX*	*MLB*	*36*	*2*	*3*	*0*	*57*	*0*	*50*	*48*	*8*	*4.6*	*9.6*	*53*	*38.1%*	*.301*	*1.49*	*4.98*	*116*	*-0.2*	*95.1*	*53.6%*	*31.0%*	*49.3%*

Comparables: Frank Francisco, Joe Nelson, Mark DiFelice

After missing two and a half seasons with arm issues, Bush made his improbable comeback in April of 2021, and it lasted all of three games before a flexor tendon strain landed him back on the IL. The 35-year-old could have called it a year, or even a career. Instead, he rehabbed all season long and made it back to the big-league club on the last day of the season, pitching a 1-2-3 inning with a strikeout. Time, science and the human body dictate that every athlete necessarily has a finite number of comebacks in them before the body finally makes it known that it really means it when it says it's finished. Bush's number is already higher than most.

Dane Dunning RHP
Born: 12/20/94 Age: 27 Bats: R Throws: R Height: 6'4" Weight: 225 lb. Origin: Round 1, 2016 Draft (#29 overall)

YEAR	TEAM	LVL	AGE	W	L	SV	G	GS	IP	H	HR	BB/9	K/9	K	GB%	BABIP	WHIP	ERA	DRA-	WARP	MPH	FB%	Whiff%	CSP
2020	CHW	MLB	25	2	0	0	7	7	34	25	4	3.4	9.3	35	44.6%	.239	1.12	3.97	93	0.5	92.0	60.6%	27.6%	44.0%
2021	TEX	MLB	26	5	10	0	27	25	117^2	126	13	3.3	8.7	114	53.6%	.339	1.44	4.51	102	1.0	90.4	60.8%	23.4%	55.2%
2022 DC	*TEX*	*MLB*	*27*	*8*	*7*	*0*	*25*	*25*	*121.7*	*117*	*15*	*3.3*	*8.8*	*119*	*51.1%*	*.300*	*1.33*	*3.97*	*100*	*1.0*	*90.6*	*60.8%*	*24.1%*	*53.3%*

Comparables: Trevor Williams, Matt Andriese, Jimmy Nelson

Given the limited number of game innings Dunning pitched in 2020, the primary goal in 2021 was to build up his workload without any injuries, and frankly, the inability to copy and paste this sentence into a number of other pitcher comments is really going to make the rest of this exercise a challenge. In Dunning's case, mission accomplished. The primary return in the Lance Lynn deal after the 2020 season, Dunning had a weird split: in the first, third and fifth innings, his ERA was 7.92, 5.92 and 8.16, respectively. In innings two, four and six? 0.36, 2.05 and 1.59. Those middle innings aren't really something to be addressed, outside of pulling a Waxahachie Swap and letting him play left field every other inning. The first, though, might be a symptom of over-establishing the fastball early, something that can be worked out with time and experience.

Demarcus Evans RHP
Born: 10/22/96 Age: 25 Bats: R Throws: R Height: 6'5" Weight: 265 lb. Origin: Round 25, 2015 Draft (#738 overall)

YEAR	TEAM	LVL	AGE	W	L	SV	G	GS	IP	H	HR	BB/9	K/9	K	GB%	BABIP	WHIP	ERA	DRA-	WARP	MPH	FB%	Whiff%	CSP
2019	DE	A+	22	4	0	6	17	0	22^1	9	0	6.9	16.1	40	45.5%	.290	1.16	0.81	77	0.5				
2019	FRI	AA	22	2	0	6	30	0	37^2	14	2	5.3	14.3	60	34.9%	.197	0.96	0.96	66	0.8				
2020	TEX	MLB	23	0	0	0	4	0	4	3	1	0.0	9.0	4	33.3%	.250	0.75	2.25	109	0.0	93.7	66.7%	29.6%	42.0%
2021	RR	AAA	24	2	0	0	18	0	21^2	12	2	5.0	12.9	31	27.7%	.222	1.11	3.74	78	0.4				
2021	TEX	MLB	24	0	2	0	25	0	26^1	24	4	5.5	11.3	33	18.6%	.308	1.52	5.13	114	0.0	90.3	85.6%	28.3%	53.1%
2022 DC	*TEX*	*MLB*	*25*	*3*	*3*	*0*	*74*	*0*	*64.7*	*53*	*11*	*5.6*	*11.2*	*80*	*29.4%*	*.278*	*1.44*	*4.57*	*108*	*0.0*	*90.5*	*84.4%*	*28.4%*	*52.4%*

Comparables: Cam Hill, Jose Ortega, Carl Edwards Jr.

Any time someone strikes out 400 batters in 264 minor-league innings, you know there's something there, even if the first couple chances in the big leagues don't go quite as smoothly as hoped. His fastball isn't overpowering—he's in the ninth percentile for fastball velo—but an extremely high spin rate (92nd percentile) makes his 92-93 play up more than a few ticks. The talk of his ascent to big-league closer has cooled a bit with his middling major-league results, but the potential is still there. In the meantime, if he can settle in as a sixth- or seventh-inning guy, that would be greatly welcomed as the Rangers try to put together a fairly nasty (and mostly home-grown) bullpen. First step: Evans is always going to walk guys, but pulling that slider close enough to the plate to make hitters chase, instead of roll their eyes, would do wonders.

Mike Foltynewicz RHP
Born: 10/07/91 Age: 30 Bats: R Throws: R Height: 6'4" Weight: 195 lb. Origin: Round 1, 2010 Draft (#19 overall)

YEAR	TEAM	LVL	AGE	W	L	SV	G	GS	IP	H	HR	BB/9	K/9	K	GB%	BABIP	WHIP	ERA	DRA-	WARP	MPH	FB%	Whiff%	CSP
2019	GWN	AAA	27	5	1	0	10	10	51^1	49	1	3.0	7.9	45	39.2%	.318	1.29	3.86	104	0.5				
2019	ATL	MLB	27	8	6	0	21	21	117	109	23	2.8	8.1	105	36.9%	.270	1.25	4.54	98	1.3	95.1	52.2%	23.5%	51.4%
2020	ATL	MLB	28	0	1	0	1	1	3^1	4	3	10.8	8.1	3	44.4%	.167	2.40	16.20	125	0.0	90.9	44.3%	14.3%	50.3%
2021	TEX	MLB	29	2	12	0	28	24	139	139	35	2.3	6.3	97	37.4%	.256	1.26	5.44	135	-1.3	93.6	51.3%	18.4%	56.3%
2022 DC	*FA*	*MLB*	*30*	*6*	*6*	*0*	*19*	*19*	*103*	*107*	*16*	*2.8*	*6.8*	*78*	*37.7%*	*.290*	*1.36*	*4.66*	*113*	*0.1*	*93.9*	*51.3%*	*19.4%*	*55.1%*

Comparables: Jason Marquis, Iván Nova, Chuck Dobson

When Foltynewicz signed with the Rangers, the hope was that his renewed commitment to "remembering to eat"—so as to help him regain healthy weight—would bring back his velocity. That sort of worked; his velocity ticked back up to around 95-96, but it wasn't enough to prevent opposing hitters from also getting their fill, particularly on a slider that never quite got back to being as elusive as it once had been. Folty allowed 35 home runs, which tied him for third-most in baseball, spread evenly across all his five pitches in all counts. It wasn't long after the last game of the season that he found himself clearing waivers and electing free agency. The tantalizing 2018 All-Star year will probably offer enough to earn him another shot somewhere, but it wouldn't be a surprise if that somewhere were the minor leagues or Asia.

Jon Gray RHP
Born: 11/05/91 Age: 30 Bats: R Throws: R Height: 6'4" Weight: 225 lb. Origin: Round 1, 2013 Draft (#3 overall)

YEAR	TEAM	LVL	AGE	W	L	SV	G	GS	IP	H	HR	BB/9	K/9	K	GB%	BABIP	WHIP	ERA	DRA-	WARP	MPH	FB%	Whiff%	CSP
2019	COL	MLB	27	11	8	0	26	25	150	147	19	3.4	9.0	150	49.9%	.319	1.35	3.84	86	2.6	96.2	52.6%	26.4%	49.7%
2020	COL	MLB	28	2	4	0	8	8	39	45	6	2.5	5.1	22	36.7%	.293	1.44	6.69	134	-0.3	94.1	49.4%	22.1%	47.4%
2021	COL	MLB	29	8	12	0	29	29	149	140	21	3.5	9.5	157	47.7%	.299	1.33	4.59	85	2.5	95.1	47.6%	26.9%	57.2%
2022 DC	*TEX*	*MLB*	*30*	*9*	*8*	*0*	*27*	*27*	*145.7*	*138*	*20*	*3.2*	*9.0*	*145*	*45.5%*	*.296*	*1.31*	*3.96*	*99*	*1.3*	*95.2*	*48.9%*	*26.2%*	*54.5%*

Comparables: Rick Wise, Gio González, Gavin Floyd

"Say, how about that Jon Gray?" asked fans of teams that needed rotation help near the trade deadline in haunting unison. In a shortened timeline like 2020, you might have to call "eight bad days" a season. That was Gray's story, until he had a ninth one when his shoulder got so inflamed it ended his season. Gray had a redemption arc to follow in 2021. As teams flocked toward any hint of starting pitching depth, Gray became an ideal target for those seeking solid, middle-of-the-rotation arms by inducing more ground balls, rediscovering some velocity, and getting more hitters to swing and miss. In doing so, he re-entered an exclusive tier: Pitchers who can get outs in Denver. The Rockies like that, or at least they should, which might be why the impending free agent was still on the roster come August 1. Or maybe every member of Colorado's front office got stuck in an elevator with their phones dead on July 31. Either is possible. In any case, he's now an Angel, without even having cost a qualifying offer.

Taylor Hearn LHP Born: 08/30/94 Age: 27 Bats: L Throws: L Height: 6'6" Weight: 230 lb. Origin: Round 5, 2015 Draft (#164 overall)

YEAR	TEAM	LVL	AGE	W	L	SV	G	GS	IP	H	HR	BB/9	K/9	K	GB%	BABIP	WHIP	ERA	DRA-	WARP	MPH	FB%	Whiff%	CSP
2019	NAS	AAA	24	1	3	0	4	4	20	14	3	4.5	11.7	26	26.7%	.262	1.20	4.05	105	0.1				
2019	TEX	MLB	24	0	1	0	1	1	0^1	3	0	108.0	0.0	0	50.0%	.750	21.00	108.00	1189	-0.2	92.0	69.2%	8.3%	44.3%
2020	TEX	MLB	25	0	0	0	14	0	17^1	13	2	5.7	11.9	23	26.8%	.282	1.38	3.63	103	0.2	95.2	60.5%	24.5%	50.2%
2021	TEX	MLB	26	6	6	0	42	11	104^1	96	17	3.6	7.9	92	38.9%	.277	1.32	4.66	120	-0.1	94.8	67.9%	23.1%	56.5%
2022 DC	*TEX*	*MLB*	*27*	*6*	*7*	*0*	*24*	*24*	*106.7*	*104*	*18*	*4.0*	*8.5*	*100*	*38.3%*	*.288*	*1.42*	*4.67*	*113*	*-0.1*	*94.9*	*67.1%*	*23.1%*	*55.6%*

Comparables: Austin Gomber, Bryan Mitchell, Kyle McPherson

It's possible that Hearn was the biggest success story at the big-league level in the Rangers' cursed 2021 season. After struggling to establish himself as a full-time big-leaguer, Hearn spent quite a bit of time wandering through The Dark Forest of Role, where the Role Trolls harangue you with questions three, like "Are you a starter?" or "Have you established a fourth pitch?" or "Answer this or pay the price / Canst thou slay the order thrice?" Finally added to the rotation late in the season, Hearn answered those questions with an emphatic "yes" for a few weeks, then (perhaps due to fatigue) changed his answer to "maybe," as his pitches, especially his slider, started drifting toward the meatball part of the zone. Either way, The Dark Forest of Role is still better than the Dream-Eating Parch-Waste. He's a big-leaguer now, regardless of whether that's in a starter role or not.

Spencer Howard RHP Born: 07/28/96 Age: 25 Bats: R Throws: R Height: 6'3" Weight: 210 lb. Origin: Round 2, 2017 Draft (#45 overall)

YEAR	TEAM	LVL	AGE	W	L	SV	G	GS	IP	H	HR	BB/9	K/9	K	GB%	BABIP	WHIP	ERA	DRA-	WARP	MPH	FB%	Whiff%	CSP
2019	PHW	ROK	22	0	0	0	1	1	3	1	0	3.0	15.0	5	60.0%	.200	0.67	0.00						
2019	PHE	ROK	22	0	0	0	1	1	2^1	3	1	3.9	11.6	3	71.4%	.333	1.71	11.57						
2019	CLR	A+	22	2	1	0	7	7	35	19	1	1.3	12.3	48	44.3%	.261	0.69	1.29	80	0.7				
2019	REA	AA	22	1	0	0	6	6	30^2	20	2	2.6	11.2	38	42.5%	.254	0.95	2.35	88	0.4				
2020	PHI	MLB	23	1	2	0	6	6	24^1	30	6	3.7	8.5	23	38.0%	.329	1.64	5.92	110	0.1	94.4	56.5%	25.7%	52.2%
2021	LHV	AAA	24	1	0	0	6	6	21^2	13	1	3.7	11.6	28	37.5%	.255	1.02	1.25	96	0.3				
2021	TEX	MLB	24	0	3	0	8	8	21^1	28	5	4.2	8.9	21	38.0%	.348	1.78	9.70	124	-0.1	93.2	75.4%	23.3%	55.3%
2021	PHI	MLB	24	0	2	0	11	7	28^1	25	2	5.4	9.8	31	34.2%	.311	1.48	5.72	99	0.3	94.6	70.5%	26.9%	57.6%
2022 DC	*TEX*	*MLB*	*25*	*6*	*6*	*0*	*22*	*22*	*104*	*97*	*15*	*4.1*	*9.5*	*110*	*38.0%*	*.294*	*1.38*	*4.29*	*105*	*0.5*	*94.1*	*68.8%*	*25.4%*	*55.5%*

Comparables: Anthony Bass, Jeanmar Gómez, Matt Albers

Formerly the Phillies' no. 1 prospect, Howard was the primary return in the Kyle Gibson / Ian Kennedy / Hans Crouse trade in 2021. Gibson and Kennedy weren't likely to bring back a ton, but the inclusion of Crouse raised a lot of eyebrows. The gamble is that the Rangers think Howard will be better, long-term, than Crouse, but his results last season weren't hopeful. Howard, however, was hopeful, indicating that he was excited about revamping his mechanics upon arrival with the Rangers and wasn't too worried about the bad results as he worked through it. To be fair, DRA has always been willing to look past the surface numbers on him as well. In fact, he used the phrase "turd-polishing" about his time in Philadelphia, which is always a gift to writers looking for something original to include in a story or a book.

John King LHP Born: 09/14/94 Age: 27 Bats: L Throws: L Height: 6'2" Weight: 215 lb. Origin: Round 10, 2017 Draft (#314 overall)

YEAR	TEAM	LVL	AGE	W	L	SV	G	GS	IP	H	HR	BB/9	K/9	K	GB%	BABIP	WHIP	ERA	DRA-	WARP	MPH	FB%	Whiff%	CSP
2019	HIC	A	24	1	2	0	5	5	26^1	31	1	0.7	9.9	29	63.3%	.385	1.25	3.42	100	0.2				
2019	DE	A+	24	2	4	0	14	14	71	59	4	1.4	7.9	62	54.8%	.284	0.99	2.03	87	1.1				
2020	TEX	MLB	25	1	0	0	6	0	10^1	13	2	3.5	7.8	9	55.6%	.324	1.65	6.10	99	0.1	93.3	63.4%	19.5%	49.9%
2021	TEX	MLB	26	7	5	0	27	0	46	41	3	2.3	7.8	40	57.7%	.286	1.15	3.52	98	0.5	92.2	67.5%	25.9%	50.7%
2022 DC	*TEX*	*MLB*	*27*	*1*	*1*	*0*	*37*	*0*	*32.3*	*31*	*3*	*2.5*	*7.4*	*26*	*54.6%*	*.295*	*1.25*	*3.49*	*93*	*0.2*	*92.3*	*66.9%*	*25.0%*	*50.6%*

Comparables: Robbie Ross Jr., José Álvarez, Justin Duchscherer

After a very impressive start—King put up a 44.7% whiff rate on his slider, and allowed a .070 BABIP on his changeup, just fun numbers all around—the native Texan went from reliever to "being stretched out to become a starter" to "It's just shoulder inflammation, but let's put you on the IL just to be safe" to "traded to the Yankees in the Joey Gallo deal" to "Whoops, says here on the medicals that shoulder might have a real problem, actually" to "...aaaaand that problem is going to cost you the rest of the season." If King and the Rangers do decide he's going to start in 2022, he'll likely begin the season in the minor leagues. If he goes back to relief, he'll likely begin the season back in Arlington. Hopefully he brings that slider along with him when he gets back, and trusts himself to throw it a little more with two strikes.

José Leclerc RHP Born: 12/19/93 Age: 28 Bats: R Throws: R Height: 6'0" Weight: 195 lb. Origin: International Free Agent, 2010

YEAR	TEAM	LVL	AGE	W	L	SV	G	GS	IP	H	HR	BB/9	K/9	K	GB%	BABIP	WHIP	ERA	DRA-	WARP	MPH	FB%	Whiff%	CSP
2019	TEX	MLB	25	2	4	14	70	3	68^2	52	7	5.1	13.1	100	34.4%	.313	1.33	4.33	78	1.5	96.8	50.1%	33.0%	43.2%
2020	TEX	MLB	26	0	0	1	2	0	2	2	0	9.0	13.5	3	0.0%	.400	2.00	4.50	98	0.0	94.7	57.4%	43.8%	33.1%
2022 DC	*TEX*	*MLB*	*28*	*2*	*2*	*1*	*44*	*0*	*38.7*	*28*	*5*	*4.5*	*12.0*	*52*	*35.4%*	*.270*	*1.24*	*3.50*	*88*	*0.4*	*96.6*	*50.6%*	*33.8%*	*42.6%*

Comparables: Tyler Clippard, Bruce Rondón, Bryan Shaw

It was hailed as a big win for the org (and a perplexing concession for the player) when Leclerc signed an extension just before the 2019 season. After all, in a half-season at closer, he had performed like a retrofitted dragon, replete with rocket-booster wings, a state-of-the-art sat-nav system and bunker-busting lava breath. Alas, after going into a full nosedive in 2019 and losing the closer's role, he's missed the better part of the last two seasons with busted wings. If he and Jonathan Hernández (who also missed 2021 with Tommy John surgery) are able to return to form in 2022, the Rangers actually have the makings of a pretty nasty bullpen.

★ ★ ★ *2022 Top 101 Prospect* **#20** ★ ★ ★

Jack Leiter RHP Born: 04/21/00 Age: 22 Bats: R Throws: R Height: 6'1" Weight: 205 lb. Origin: Round 1, 2021 Draft (#2 overall)

Quick: who was the last home-grown ace in Texas Rangers history? Yu Darvish doesn't count; his first year stateside was his age-25 season. Does C.J. Wilson count? Probably not. Kevin Brown? Kenny Rogers? This isn't a new question—Chris Cwik wrote about it for the 2019 version of the Annual as well—but the Rangers hope to have a new answer soon with the drafting of Jack Leiter. The pedigree is there, the repertoire is Vanderbilt-polished and the kid seems to see things with clear eyes. He's armed with the full set: live mid-90s fastball, the stalled elevator 12-6 curve, a sharp slider and a promising change that he never really needed to use in college. Hopefully his back is in good shape as well; he's got a few decades of hopes and dreams to hoist. First things first, he'll need to throw his first pitch as a professional; he went back to Vandy after the draft to work out and finish his degree.

Glenn Otto RHP Born: 03/11/96 Age: 26 Bats: R Throws: R Height: 6'3" Weight: 240 lb. Origin: Round 5, 2017 Draft (#152 overall)

YEAR	TEAM	LVL	AGE	W	L	SV	G	GS	IP	H	HR	BB/9	K/9	K	GB%	BABIP	WHIP	ERA	DRA-	WARP	MPH	FB%	Whiff%	CSP
2019	TAM	A+	23	3	3	0	14	12	56^1	54	1	5.3	10.9	68	44.4%	.376	1.54	3.20	88	1.0				
2021	SOM	AA	25	6	3	0	11	10	65^1	46	6	1.9	14.2	103	38.1%	.315	0.92	3.17	86	1.0				
2021	SWB	AAA	25	1	0	0	2	2	10^1	14	0	2.6	10.5	12	33.3%	.424	1.65	4.35	104	0.1				
2021	RR	AAA	25	2	1	0	4	4	20	13	0	3.2	8.6	19	49.0%	.255	1.00	2.70	100	0.1				
2021	TEX	MLB	25	0	3	0	6	6	23^1	32	2	3.1	10.8	28	43.8%	.429	1.71	9.26	99	0.2	92.8	48.9%	22.1%	59.8%
2022 DC	*TEX*	*MLB*	*26*	*4*	*4*	*0*	*16*	*16*	*66.3*	*61*	*9*	*3.5*	*9.1*	*67*	*40.8%*	*.291*	*1.31*	*3.94*	*98*	*0.6*	*92.8*	*48.9%*	*22.1%*	*59.8%*

Comparables: Spencer Turnbull, Matt Andriese, Tyler Duffey

The Texan-born Otto returned home at the trade deadline, stowed away among the luggage shipped from the Yankees in the Joey Gallo trade. The Houston-area native made quick work of his hometown team in his big-league debut, going five innings and only allowing two hits, striking out seven and walking no Astros. After one more relatively-successful start (4 ⅔ innings, 2 ER in Anaheim), the long-season-after-a-short-season contrast finally caught up to Otto—his final four starts saw him allow 22 earned runs in 13 ⅔ innings. Despite the sad end of the road, the former Yankee farmhand received something of a parting gift: a drastically improved slider that New York's organization sometimes hands out to random prospects. With that, and newfound command, he's ready to both make a new start, and also maybe start.

Joe Palumbo LHP Born: 10/26/94 Age: 27 Bats: L Throws: L Height: 6'0" Weight: 195 lb. Origin: Round 30, 2013 Draft (#910 overall)

YEAR	TEAM	LVL	AGE	W	L	SV	G	GS	IP	H	HR	BB/9	K/9	K	GB%	BABIP	WHIP	ERA	DRA-	WARP	MPH	FB%	Whiff%	CSP
2019	FRI	AA	24	0	0	0	11	10	53^2	43	5	4.2	11.6	69	39.1%	.311	1.27	3.19	93	0.3				
2019	NAS	AAA	24	3	0	0	6	6	27	13	4	3.3	13.0	39	40.4%	.188	0.85	2.67	80	0.5				
2019	TEX	MLB	24	0	3	0	7	4	16^2	21	7	4.3	11.3	21	34.0%	.333	1.74	9.18	109	0.1	94.1	56.4%	22.8%	48.9%
2020	TEX	MLB	25	0	1	0	2	0	2^1	3	1	11.6	19.3	5	33.3%	.400	2.57	11.57	76	0.1	92.3	57.6%	42.9%	47.5%
2021	RR	AAA	26	1	2	0	6	2	6^2	12	4	13.5	9.5	7	33.3%	.400	3.30	13.50	118	0.0				
2022 non-DC	*SF*	*MLB*	*27*	*2*	*3*	*0*	*57*	*0*	*50*	*43*	*7*	*5.4*	*10.3*	*57*	*38.5%*	*.287*	*1.48*	*4.88*	*113*	*-0.2*	*93.6*	*56.7%*	*28.0%*	*48.5%*

Comparables: Brian Burres, Caleb Smith, Austin Gomber

Underdogs are underdogs for a reason, it turns out. Palumbo beat the odds to make it to the big leagues, but a mosaic of blisters, injuries and illnesses have kept him sidelined since August of 2020. He's 28 now, which is around the time most underdog stories break hard one way or the other. At time of submission, he had been claimed on waivers by the Giants, which given their recent track record, has to offer a dose of optimism; there are pieces there, particularly a out-pitch curve, to work with. Given his combination of age, injury history and tantalizing talent when he *is* healthy, he kind of fits the bill of someone who might bounce around on waivers a bit before some team has the room and the opportunity to keep him on the 40-man roster.

Dennis Santana RHP Born: 04/12/96 Age: 26 Bats: R Throws: R Height: 6'2" Weight: 190 lb. Origin: International Free Agent, 2013

YEAR	TEAM	LVL	AGE	W	L	SV	G	GS	IP	H	HR	BB/9	K/9	K	GB%	BABIP	WHIP	ERA	DRA-	WARP	MPH	FB%	Whiff%	CSP
2019	OKC	AAA	23	5	9	0	27	17	93^1	111	16	5.1	10.1	105	42.2%	.365	1.76	6.94	100	0.6				
2019	LAD	MLB	23	0	0	0	3	0	5	6	1	7.2	10.8	6	46.7%	.357	2.00	7.20	111	0.0	92.8	56.7%	30.4%	38.8%
2020	LAD	MLB	24	1	2	0	12	0	17	15	4	3.7	9.5	18	32.6%	.262	1.29	5.29	112	0.1	94.3	38.7%	28.3%	51.7%
2021	TEX	MLB	25	2	4	0	39	0	39^2	30	4	4.8	8.6	38	47.1%	.263	1.29	3.63	108	0.2	95.8	46.7%	29.6%	49.9%
2021	LAD	MLB	25	0	0	0	16	0	15	18	0	6.6	4.8	8	53.8%	.346	1.93	6.00	140	-0.2	95.1	52.0%	21.1%	49.5%
2022 DC	*TEX*	*MLB*	*26*	*3*	*3*	*0*	*74*	*0*	*64.7*	*61*	*8*	*4.9*	*8.9*	*63*	*45.2%*	*.296*	*1.49*	*4.77*	*112*	*-0.2*	*95.3*	*47.0%*	*27.4%*	*49.8%*

Comparables: Jose Ortega, José Ramirez, Luke Jackson

When a team wins a World Series, it's easy to find an interesting angle on a player, even a reliever who didn't make the postseason roster. When a team loses 102 games, you really have to start digging for interesting things to write about, like the reliever who...didn't make the postseason roster the year before when his team won the World Series. It doesn't help that said pitcher, one of dozens of sinker-slider righties with poor command, has been so rigorously adequate. There is one fun fact that checks both boxes for Santana, who was a member of both the 2020 Los Angeles Dodgers and the 2021 Texas Rangers: He was named "Dennis" because his dad was such a big fan of the NBA (and, one must assume, the ability to skirt death while compulsively choosing chaos) that he named his son after Dennis Rodman. Don't believe us? His middle name is Anfernee. Look it up.

Nick Snyder RHP Born: 10/10/95 Age: 26 Bats: R Throws: R Height: 6'4" Weight: 190 lb. Origin: Round 19, 2017 Draft (#584 overall)

YEAR	TEAM	LVL	AGE	W	L	SV	G	GS	IP	H	HR	BB/9	K/9	K	GB%	BABIP	WHIP	ERA	DRA-	WARP	MPH	FB%	Whiff%	CSP
2019	HIC	A	23	5	3	6	33	0	53	46	3	3.1	10.2	60	44.5%	.328	1.21	3.06	86	0.8				
2021	HIC	A+	25	0	0	3	10	0	12^1	8	2	2.2	12.4	17	37.5%	.273	0.89	2.19	84	0.2				
2021	FRI	AA	25	0	1	1	13	0	16^1	12	1	0.6	13.8	25	44.4%	.314	0.80	1.65	64	0.4				
2021	TEX	MLB	25	0	0	0	4	0	3^2	3	0	7.4	2.5	1	54.5%	.273	1.64	4.91	116	0.0	99.2	78.0%	21.4%	61.6%
2022 DC	*TEX*	*MLB*	*26*	*2*	*3*	*0*	*59*	*0*	*51.7*	*49*	*7*	*3.4*	*9.0*	*51*	*39.9%*	*.293*	*1.33*	*4.16*	*104*	*0.1*	*99.2*	*78.0%*	*21.4%*	*61.6%*

Comparables: Tyler Zuber, Jose Ortega, Ryan Meisinger

Snyder was a shortstop in college, and a scout (Cliff Terracuso) noticed his throwing motion at a college game and asked his coach if the kid could pitch. "I don't know," the coach replied. "Does he want to pitch?" Snyder pitched the last inning of that blowout game. At a later game, Terracuso had another scout (Brett Campbell) put a second set of eyes on the kid, but made him dress up in flip-flops and a fishing hat so none of the other scouts would know the Rangers were interested. Four years (and one early-2020 Tommy John surgery) later, Snyder and his 99-mph fastball ascended through the ranks and made his big-league debut.

Jesus Tinoco RHP Born: 04/30/95 Age: 27 Bats: R Throws: R Height: 6'4" Weight: 258 lb. Origin: International Free Agent, 2011

YEAR	TEAM	LVL	AGE	W	L	SV	G	GS	IP	H	HR	BB/9	K/9	K	GB%	BABIP	WHIP	ERA	DRA-	WARP	MPH	FB%	Whiff%	CSP
2019	ABQ	AAA	24	3	1	1	29	0	34	33	4	4.8	6.1	23	56.2%	.287	1.50	3.97	100	0.2				
2019	COL	MLB	24	0	3	1	24	0	36	36	12	5.5	7.0	28	43.6%	.245	1.61	4.75	112	0.1	93.9	62.3%	22.4%	43.9%
2020	COL	MLB	25	0	0	0	3	0	3^2	3	0	9.8	7.4	3	80.0%	.300	1.91	2.45	98	0.0	93.6	68.7%	25.0%	41.0%
2020	MIA	MLB	25	0	0	0	3	0	5	0	0	5.4	5.4	3	77.8%	.000	0.60	0.00	102	0.0	93.9	67.5%	24.2%	35.6%
2021	ABQ	AAA	26	3	2	0	36	2	54	65	6	4.5	9.7	58	39.3%	.378	1.70	6.00	90	0.5				
2021	COL	MLB	26	0	0	0	1	0	1^1	5	3	6.7	0.0	0	25.0%	.400	4.50	33.75	147	0.0	93.5	68.8%	18.8%	53.3%
2022 non-DC	*COL*	*MLB*	*27*	*2*	*3*	*0*	*57*	*0*	*50*	*51*	*8*	*4.7*	*8.6*	*47*	*42.0%*	*.310*	*1.56*	*5.54*	*120*	*-0.4*	*93.8*	*64.6%*	*22.7%*	*43.1%*

Comparables: JC Ramírez, Taylor Guerrieri, Jason Adam

In 2015, Tinoco arrived in Colorado as a throw-in to the trade that got them a late-career José Reyes and ended the Troy Tulowitzki era in Denver. He hung around the farm system, not really getting batters out, until five years later, when the Rockies swapped him to the Marlins for Chad Smith, then less than a month later grabbed him again off waivers. This was all so that in 2021 they could have Tinoco appear in one game in the majors, get obliterated and leave for Texas. Mission accomplished. Well done, boys.

Ricky Vanasco RHP Born: 10/13/98 Age: 23 Bats: R Throws: R Height: 6'3" Weight: 180 lb. Origin: Round 15, 2017 Draft (#464 overall)

YEAR	TEAM	LVL	AGE	W	L	SV	G	GS	IP	H	HR	BB/9	K/9	K	GB%	BABIP	WHIP	ERA	DRA-	WARP	MPH	FB%	Whiff%	CSP
2019	SPO	SS	20	3	1	0	9	9	39	23	2	5.1	13.6	59	50.0%	.292	1.15	1.85						
2019	HIC	A	20	0	0	0	2	2	10^2	5	0	2.5	13.5	16	47.4%	.263	0.75	1.69	86	0.2				
2022	*No projection*																							

Comparables: Andrew Brown, Jordan Hicks, Ethan Hankins

Of all the starting pitchers in the Rangers' system (and for once, there are quite a few promising ones), Vanasco might trail only Jack Leiter in the amount of excitement from people in the org. He was under consideration to get big-league time in 2020, thanks to his development at the alternate site, before Tommy John surgery in September. But by October of 2021, he was already back on a mound pitching in instructs games. His fastball was already a dominant, ladder-climbing out pitch, and once he can reclaim his secondaries from the hospital, he'll be fully equipped against major-league batters. He's just 23, so there's time to let him get some minor-league seasoning in 2022, but don't be surprised if the track to the big leagues is a fast one.

★ ★ ★ *2022 Top 101 Prospect* **#91** ★ ★ ★

Cole Winn RHP Born: 11/25/99 Age: 22 Bats: R Throws: R Height: 6'2" Weight: 190 lb. Origin: Round 1, 2018 Draft (#15 overall)

YEAR	TEAM	LVL	AGE	W	L	SV	G	GS	IP	H	HR	BB/9	K/9	K	GB%	BABIP	WHIP	ERA	DRA-	WARP	MPH	FB%	Whiff%	CSP
2019	HIC	A	19	4	4	0	18	18	68^2	59	5	5.1	8.5	65	46.6%	.292	1.43	4.46	114	0.1				
2021	FRI	AA	21	3	3	0	19	19	78	38	6	3.0	11.2	97	36.7%	.198	0.82	2.31	84	1.2				
2021	RR	AAA	21	1	0	0	2	2	8	5	1	5.6	11.2	10	30.0%	.211	1.25	3.38	101	0.0				
2022 non-DC	*TEX*	*MLB*	*22*	*2*	*3*	*0*	*57*	*0*	*50*	*46*	*7*	*4.8*	*8.7*	*48*	*37.8%*	*.284*	*1.46*	*4.79*	*113*	*-0.2*				

Comparables: Ben Howard, Nathan Eovaldi, Cristian Javier

The Rangers have tried a number of draft strategies over the years, with varying degrees of success. So why not give nominative determinism a try? So far, it's working out; Winn was named the starting pitcher for the Futures Game, and won the Rangers' "Nolan Ryan Pitcher of the Year" award. Despite his first-round pedigree, the buzz for Winn was a bit muted before 2021, thanks to some inconsistency, but a tight curve and sinking changeup have cemented him as the organization's top arm. The Rangers do not historically have a good reputation for drafting and developing starting pitching, but there's a glimmer of hope that change is on the way, thanks to Winn, Leiter and next year's presumed draft pick, Johnny Strikeoutt.

Lineouts

Hitters

HITTER	POS	TEAM	LVL	AGE	PA	R	2B	3B	HR	RBI	BB	K	SB	CS	AVG/OBP/SLG	DRC+	BABIP	BRR	FRAA	WARP
Maximo Acosta	SS	RAN	ROK	18	68	11	2	2	1	5	3	15	7	2	.246/.279/.393		.292			
Luisangel Acuna	SS	DE	A	19	473	77	15	3	12	74	49	110	44	11	.266/.345/.404	106	.329	1.9	SS(42): 1.5, 2B(36): 1.0	2.1
Sherten Apostel	IF	FRI	AA	22	167	20	9	0	6	20	17	52	0	0	.236/.317/.419	84	.319	-0.2	3B(20): -1.5, 1B(15): -0.1	0.0
	IF	RR	AAA	22	88	10	3	0	1	6	7	32	0	0	.205/.284/.282	66	.326	0.4	3B(16): -1.2, 1B(2): -0.2	-0.2
Charlie Culberson	3B	TEX	MLB	32	271	23	15	2	5	22	17	64	7	1	.243/.296/.381	83	.307	0.4	3B(68): 1.4, LF(6): 0.3, 1B(4): 0.3	0.6
Ryan Dorow	SS/3B	FRI	AA	25	99	13	9	0	5	15	9	20	0	0	.333/.394/.600	115	.385	-0.5	SS(13): 0.0, 3B(7): -0.2, 2B(3): 0.1	0.4
	SS/3B	RR	AAA	25	318	48	18	2	10	32	33	92	3	2	.229/.314/.416	79	.300	2.1	SS(58): -0.6, 3B(16): -0.4	0.2
	SS/3B	TEX	MLB	25	7	0	0	0	0	0	1	3	0	0	.000/.143/.000	91			3B(3): 0.1	0.0
Trevor Hauver	2B/LF	TAM	A	22	299	48	17	2	9	49	64	78	2	0	.288/.445/.498	124	.393	-0.7	2B(56): 2.3, 3B(1): -0.0	1.8
	2B/LF	HIC	A+	22	143	20	4	0	6	21	20	47	0	0	.246/.357/.426	92	.348	-1.3	LF(18): -2.2, 2B(12): -0.4	-0.1
Yonny Hernandez	IF	RR	AAA	23	251	42	7	2	1	13	51	44	21	10	.250/.424/.323	106	.320	0.2	SS(34): 0.1, 3B(17): 1.8, 2B(10): -0.4	1.1
	IF	TEX	MLB	23	166	15	5	0	0	6	17	32	11	2	.217/.315/.252	92	.277	0.2	3B(29): 1.3, 2B(9): 0.2, SS(6): 0.5	0.6
Jason Martin	LF	RR	AAA	25	161	27	4	2	10	27	28	34	2	3	.248/.388/.543	121	.256	0.4	LF(15): -0.4, CF(11): -1.8, RF(9): 1.2	0.9
	LF	TEX	MLB	25	154	14	3	0	6	17	8	41	3	1	.208/.248/.354	80	.245	0.1	LF(41): 2.8, CF(3): -0.1, RF(3): -0.1	0.5
Zach Reks	OF	OKC	AAA	27	379	69	24	1	19	67	46	108	0	1	.280/.382/.539	105	.362	-1.0	LF(41): -3.6, RF(41): -1.5	0.9
	OF	LAD	MLB	27	10	2	0	0	0	0	0	7	0	0	.000/.000/.000	63		0.2	LF(3): -0.1, RF(2): 0.1	0.0
Steele Walker	OF	FRI	AA	24	266	39	10	2	10	40	22	45	8	2	.255/.323/.439	119	.274	-0.5	RF(31): 1.3, LF(12): -0.2, CF(8): 0.4	1.5
	OF	RR	AAA	24	202	22	8	0	5	21	16	46	2	3	.223/.287/.348	86	.269	-0.8	LF(27): -1.2, CF(12): -2.2, RF(10): 2.4	0.1
Davis Wendzel	IF	RAN	ROK	24	43	12	0	1	1	7	5	10	0	0	.250/.349/.389		.308			
	IF	FRI	AA	24	187	23	6	0	6	23	21	43	1	2	.239/.348/.390	102	.288	-0.6	SS(19): 0.8, 3B(18): -0.5, 2B(4): 0.2	0.6
	IF	RR	AAA	24	33	5	4	0	1	2	2	8	0	0	.214/.333/.464	95	.263	-0.5	3B(3): -0.2, SS(2): -0.2, 2B(1): -0.1	0.0
Eli White	OF	RR	AAA	27	80	19	2	1	3	11	12	20	3	1	.343/.450/.537	104	.455	1.6	2B(7): -0.1, CF(5): 1.0, 3B(2): -0.3	0.5
	OF	TEX	MLB	27	220	26	6	1	6	15	18	66	4	3	.177/.259/.308	75	.230	0.1	LF(30): -0.4, CF(22): 0.3, RF(11): 0.9	0.2

It's hard to say for sure what **Maximo Acosta** will be after just 17 official professional games—a shoulder injury sidelined him from the end of July onward—but it will be interesting to see if he can stick at shortstop, or if his body type will dictate a move to third base. ⚾ Once you get past the knee-jerk "is he going to be as good as his brother?" reaction, **Luisangel Acuna**'s 2021 season looks encouraging. Stolen base numbers are always hard to quantify at the lower levels, but if he can keep his on-base percentage in the mid-.300s, he doesn't have to be Ronald to be worth anticipating. ⚾ **Sherten Apostel** was one of a few rookies to make their big-league debut in 2020 ahead of schedule, so it shouldn't be alarming that he stayed in the minors for all of 2021. What maybe should be alarming is that he put up his worst numbers since his first year of pro ball back in 2016, when he was just 17 years old. ⚾ It was a great year for **Charlie Culberson**, who finally won a World Series with some clutch...ahhh, dang it, got him mixed up with Dansby Swanson yet again. Hopefully he got some nice misdirected promotional swag. ⚾ **Ryan Dorow** has three games of big-league experience, thanks to the COVID-era rules that allow a player to be added and removed from a 40-man roster without having to clear waivers, if they're replacing a player who had a positive test. He's a scrappy infielder with more pop than you'd expect, and a hit tool that helps set those expectations. ⚾ You may have heard that the Rangers and Yankees made a little trade at the deadline involving a guy with good power who strikes out too much but somehow walks just enough to justify it. Oh, and the Yankees got Joey Gallo, too. **Trevor Hauver** has competition at second base in his new system, but he enjoyed a pretty intriguing first professional season. ⚾ They call **Yonny Hernández** "The Mosquito", ostensibly because he's pesky, but also he's listed at 5'9" and 140 lbs. His bat-to-ball skills are good enough to play at the big-league level, but he'll have to bulk up, or the sport will have to change its rules to incorporate more pools of standing water, if he's going to stick around. ⚾ If you've ever made bread, you've probably had the experience where you get all the ingredients right, the bread starts to rise, you put it in the oven, and *voila*, it collapses into an inedibly-dense biscuit. In Triple-A, **Jason Martin** appears to have all the right ingredients—a bit of pop, a little speed, good defense—but under the 400-degrees of bright lights, the outcome was a non-starter. ⚾ The Dodgers have an affinity for the older prospect, especially ones they've developed themselves. **Zach Reks** did nothing but hit at the Triple-A level, only to strike out in 70% of the plate appearances in his MLB debut. OK, he only had 10 of them, but it's still a bit jarring. His .921 OPS in Triple-A still lends itself to some optimism at the MLB level, but he'll have to have a better showing in 2022 if he's going to be more than a career minor-leaguer. ⚾ Everyone always wants to talk about **Steele Walker's** swagger or his name (Walker, Texas Ranger, for those who haven't heard it for the 20th time yet) but nobody ever wants to talk about how he really doesn't walk or run all that much, so how are we supposed to trust nominative determinism if it's going to be so inconsistent? ⚾ **Davis Wendzel** got all the way Triple-A Round Rock in just 70 professional games, despite injuries and a pandemic and a series of manmade barricades erected to ensnare the patrol columns of the National Guard. He's worked hard to develop a level of athleticism and versatility that will get him on the field somewhere, as long as his bat makes the case for it. ⚾ The thing is, **Eli White** *is* fast enough to steal first base, and it might be time to give that a shot, given how difficult it has been for him to get on base thus far. At the very least, he should get the boys in the lab working on the problem.

Pitchers

PITCHER	TEAM	LVL	AGE	W	L	SV	G	GS	IP	H	HR	BB/9	K/9	K	GB%	BABIP	WHIP	ERA	DRA-	WARP	MPH	FB%	WHF	CSP
Chase Anderson	RR	AAA	33	0	1	0	5	3	15	14	5	4.8	8.4	14	25.5%	.225	1.47	4.20	115	-0.1				
	LHV	AAA	33	1	2	0	5	5	17^1	21	2	2.6	7.3	14	37.5%	.352	1.50	5.71	114	0.1				
	PHI	MLB	33	2	4	0	14	9	48	51	10	3.8	6.6	35	35.7%	.281	1.48	6.75	118	0.0	91.8	39.3%	23.7%	53.0%
Wes Benjamin	RR	AAA	27	2	5	0	15	10	46^2	72	6	4.8	8.1	42	38.2%	.402	2.08	8.29	123	-0.5				
	TEX	MLB	27	0	2	0	13	2	22^2	29	6	6.8	7.5	19	28.9%	.329	2.03	8.74	149	-0.4	90.3	71.1%	21.1%	56.4%
Ronny Henriquez	HIC	A+	21	1	3	0	5	5	24	13	2	3.0	10.1	27	42.4%	.193	0.88	3.75	94	0.3				
	FRI	AA	21	4	4	0	16	11	69^2	65	15	2.2	10.1	78	43.6%	.279	1.18	5.04	76	1.4				
Brett Martin	TEX	MLB	26	4	4	0	66	0	62^1	67	5	2.0	6.1	42	56.2%	.312	1.30	3.18	110	0.2	93.5	53.7%	22.8%	58.0%
Tyson Miller	RR	AAA	25	5	3	0	20	9	56	44	6	3.7	9.5	59	49.0%	.270	1.20	3.05	90	0.6				
Spencer Patton	RR	AAA	33	2	0	4	11	0	12	6	0	4.5	9.0	12	33.3%	.222	1.00	0.00	100	0.0				
	TEX	MLB	33	2	2	2	42	0	42^1	36	4	3.2	10.2	48	40.4%	.305	1.20	3.83	92	0.6	93.6	56.6%	27.0%	51.8%
Yerry Rodriguez	FRI	AA	23	1	1	0	14	14	51^1	38	3	3.7	11.0	63	41.9%	.289	1.15	2.63	96	0.4				
	RR	AAA	23	3	3	0	13	4	30^1	37	5	3.6	11.0	37	48.9%	.386	1.62	8.01	88	0.3				
Josh Sborz	TEX	MLB	27	4	3	1	63	0	59	52	7	4.9	10.5	69	41.7%	.302	1.42	3.97	97	0.6	96.9	54.5%	33.5%	52.5%
Hunter Wood	TEX	MLB	27	0	0	0	5	0	5	2	1	3.6	9.0	5	16.7%	.091	0.80	3.60	104	0.0	93.4	30.8%	33.3%	54.0%
Hyeon-Jong Yang	RR	AAA	33	0	3	0	10	9	45	52	10	2.0	8.4	42	35.9%	.318	1.38	5.60	112	-0.1				
	TEX	MLB	33	0	3	0	12	4	35^1	42	9	4.1	6.4	25	41.5%	.303	1.64	5.60	135	-0.3	90.1	45.8%	20.1%	59.7%

Chase Anderson certainly did pitch in [double-checking notes] five games for Triple-A Round Rock after signing as a minor-league free agent at the end of August, as we're sure you all remember. He never could get batters to perform his name's imperative on two-strike pitches. ⚾ Any time you get designated for assignment on the very last day of the season so the team can throw a 35-year-old reliever a one-day bone for all his hard work in rehab, you know you had a real bad year, and that's exactly what happened to **Wes Benjamin** in 2021. ⚾ One of the more promising relievers in the Twins organization in 2020 (100-mph velo, nasty slider), **Edwar Colina** experienced elbow soreness in spring training and ended up missing all of 2021 due to surgery on said elbow. The Twins lost him on waivers to the Rangers in October. ⚾ **Ronny Henriquez** is fun to watch pitch, but a combination of mixed total results and some surprisingly good starting depth in the organization might ultimately lead him to the bullpen. Whatever the case, he was good enough to be added to the 40-man roster to avoid being taken in the Rule 5 draft. ⚾ If you're going to lose a year to Tommy John surgery, might as well pick the one in which your team loses 102 games. Assuming the recovery goes to plan, **Jonathan Hernández** should slide right back into the closer's role—his fastball and "turbo sinker" both averaged over 97 mph in 2020. ⚾ If we're comparing players to cars, **Brett Martin** isn't a sexy Lamborghini or a flashy Escalade with an amped-up system. He's more like a Honda CR-V. You might not even notice him if you're looking for him, but all of a sudden you realize you haven't had to do any repairs for years, and that seventh inning just kind of flew by while you weren't paying attention. ⚾ **Tyson Miller** was a casualty of the Cubs' early-season roster crunch and was quickly claimed by the pitching-hungry Rangers after being DFA'd in May. Nothing in the arsenal is overpowering, but he's a crafty righty with plus control, and has racked up a ton of strikeouts in the minors thanks to his ability to cut, sink and ride his fastball with command. ⚾ **Spencer Patton** first pitched for the Rangers in 2014, a season in which approximately 700 players were injured and all of us—you, me and everyone you know—got a shot to pitch in a big-league game. The Rangers went 67-95 that year, which was frankly a pretty staggering feat of overachievement. After a year in Chicago and four years in Japan, Patton returned to the Rangers just in time to be a member of a team that lost 102 games. If not for the fact that his one year in Chicago was the year they snapped a curse and won a World Series, we might have some questions about whether he rifled through some ancient tombs in his youth. ⚾ **Yerry Rodriguez** thrived in Double-A for the first half of the season, then made like a college kid going to South by Southwest for the first time and got absolutely lit upon his arrival to the Austin area. ⚾ **Josh Sborz** started the season looking like a potential closer, but much like a college freshman rebelling against a strict upbringing, a lack of control hampered his productivity by year's end. He pitched well enough that even if he's a casualty of a 40-man roster crunch in Texas, he'll get a shot somewhere in 2022. ⚾ As spring training came to a close, it looked like the Rangers had struck gold with **Hunter Wood**. Alas, it would have been better to strike a more durable metal; Wood missed almost the entire year with a "mild" UCL strain. ⚾ While the former KIA Tiger star and 2017 KBO MVP never got a shot at the majors in his prime, **Yang Hyeon-jeon** hadn't pitched fewer than 170 innings since 2013, so he seemed like a prime candidate for the role of sacrificial lamb: Protect the workload and arm health of the younger pitchers by trudging through some rough innings. Only one part of the plan went as expected: There was a lot of blood.

FREE AGENTS

Hitters

Kris Bryant 3B Born: 01/04/92 Age: 30 Bats: R Throws: R Height: 6'5" Weight: 230 lb. Origin: Round 1, 2013 Draft (#2 overall)

YEAR	TEAM	LVL	AGE	PA	R	2B	3B	HR	RBI	BB	K	SB	CS	Whiff%	AVG/OBP/SLG	DRC+	BABIP	BRR	FRAA	WARP
2019	CHC	MLB	27	634	108	35	1	31	77	74	145	4	0	28.4%	.282/.382/.521	124	.331	2.1	3B(115): -14.1, RF(27): -2.2, LF(23): -1.4	2.1
2020	CHC	MLB	28	147	20	5	1	4	11	12	40	0	0	29.5%	.206/.293/.351	94	.264	0.3	3B(27): 0.1, LF(4): 0.7, 1B(1): 0.0	0.4
2021	CHC	MLB	29	374	58	19	2	18	51	39	89	4	2	27.4%	.267/.358/.503	113	.314	0.4	3B(29): -0.5, LF(29): -1.3, RF(28): -2.2	1.5
2021	SF	MLB	29	212	28	13	0	7	22	23	46	6	0	29.0%	.262/.344/.444	106	.311	2.3	3B(26): -1.9, LF(19): 0.2, RF(11): 0.2	0.9
2022 DC	*FA*	*MLB*	*30*	*587*	*70*	*28*	*1*	*20*	*73*	*63*	*134*	*5*	*2*	*28.1%*	*.250/.347/.432*	*111*	*.301*	*-0.4*	*3B -3, RF -1*	*2.0*

Comparables: Chipper Jones, Evan Longoria, David Wright

On July 31 of last season, the Giants were reeling from the previous day's megatrade of Trea Turner and Max Scherzer to the Dodgers, their challenger in an historic divisional race. Farhan Zaidi made a star-power move of his own, rescuing Bryant from the tailspinning Cubs for a couple of prospects. When Bryant homered off of Luis Garcia in his Giants' debut, it seemed like the magic would continue—and continue it did. But Bryant emerged as a valuable member of an ensemble cast rather than the lead actor towering in the middle of the order. Bryant logged playing time at all three outfield positions, along with his customary shifts at the hot corner. Even more strikingly, he popped up in every batting-order slot from second to sixth in Gabe Kapler's lineup card. And even though Bryant slumped toward the end of the regular season, he was a shining light during the hard-fought divisional series against the Dodgers. Perhaps, in taking a step back from the limelight, Bryant previewed the next phase of his career as he heads into free agency: a former MVP and poster boy whose mid-career value now lies in simply being a very good, and very versatile, part of a team.

Asdrúbal Cabrera 3B Born: 11/13/85 Age: 36 Bats: S Throws: R Height: 6'0" Weight: 235 lb. Origin: International Free Agent, 2002

YEAR	TEAM	LVL	AGE	PA	R	2B	3B	HR	RBI	BB	K	SB	CS	Whiff%	AVG/OBP/SLG	DRC+	BABIP	BRR	FRAA	WARP
2019	TEX	MLB	33	368	45	15	0	12	51	38	85	4	0	21.8%	.235/.318/.393	96	.278	0.1	3B(93): 5.2	1.3
2019	WAS	MLB	33	146	24	10	1	6	40	19	18	0	0	17.9%	.323/.404/.565	124	.330	-0.9	2B(31): -1.9, 3B(5): -0.4, 1B(3): 0.3	0.7
2020	WAS	MLB	34	213	23	9	3	8	31	19	40	0	0	20.6%	.242/.305/.447	104	.260	0.6	1B(25): -1.1, 3B(17): -1.9	0.4
2021	ORI	WIN	35	93	20	4	0	3	21	10	15	0	0		.359/.424/.526		.397			
2021	CIN	MLB	35	31	0	0	0	0	2	3	7	0	0	21.3%	.077/.194/.077	91	.100	-0.1	1B(3): -0.0, 3B(3): -0.1	0.0
2021	ARI	MLB	35	321	34	21	0	7	40	33	73	1	0	25.8%	.244/.324/.392	90	.301	0.0	3B(62): -3.4, 1B(16): 1.0, P(2): -0.0	0.4
2022 DC	*FA*	*MLB*	*36*	*380*	*39*	*18*	*0*	*10*	*41*	*37*	*83*	*1*	*1*	*24.6%*	*.236/.318/.385*	*88*	*.284*	*-0.5*	*3B 0, 1B 0*	*0.3*

Comparables: Leo Cardenas, Jimmy Rollins, Tony Fernandez

The Reds claimed Cabrera off waivers from Arizona last August, making them the eighth team he's suited up for in his big-league career, and the absolute last one you're going to think of if a trivia contest ever asks you to name every team Asdrúbal Cabrera ever played for. (Side note: If you know of a trivia contest that might actually ask this kind of question, please notify the BP offices immediately.) He's a surprisingly spry infield defender this far into his 30s and he opened last year with a very impressive .289/.393/.474 line through the second week of May. But then he hit the IL for a hamstring injury, and after his return, he slashed just .195/.263/.303 the rest of the way. Such is the way of getting older; it's rarely a gentle slope, and more like tripping down a stairwell. There's enough hope here for some team to add a ninth uniform to Cabrera's collection, and allow him the chance to forget his time in Cincinnati just as quickly as you will.

Nick Castellanos RF Born: 03/04/92 Age: 30 Bats: R Throws: R Height: 6'4" Weight: 203 lb. Origin: Round 1, 2010 Draft (#44 overall)

YEAR	TEAM	LVL	AGE	PA	R	2B	3B	HR	RBI	BB	K	SB	CS	Whiff%	AVG/OBP/SLG	DRC+	BABIP	BRR	FRAA	WARP
2019	CHC	MLB	27	225	43	21	0	16	36	10	47	0	1	30.7%	.321/.356/.646	124	.347	0.0	RF(48): 1.1, LF(11): -0.4	1.4
2020	CIN	MLB	28	242	37	11	2	14	34	19	69	0	2	34.2%	.225/.298/.486	103	.257	-1.1	RF(57): -5.1	0.2
2021	CIN	MLB	29	585	95	38	1	34	100	41	121	3	1	30.7%	.309/.362/.576	130	.340	0.5	RF(135): 7.7	4.7
2022 DC	*FA*	*MLB*	*30*	*587*	*69*	*35*	*2*	*23*	*79*	*43*	*137*	*2*	*2*	*30.5%*	*.271/.332/.474*	*112*	*.325*	*-0.6*	*RF 1, LF 0*	*2.6*

Comparables: Roberto Clemente, Gary Sheffield, Dave Winfield

Given the present state of labor and finances in professional baseball, it's extraordinarily difficult to argue that any contract could possibly be "player-friendly." If any recent deal comes close, though, it may be the four-year, $64 million agreement reached by Castellanos and the Reds prior to 2020. With opt-outs after each of the first two seasons, the young outfielder had two different opportunities to hit the market before turning 30 if his offense didn't crater; if it did, Cincinnati was stuck with the bill. All told, both sides are probably fine with the way things worked out—an underwhelming first year of the deal gave way to a tremendous follow-up effort, as Castellanos set career marks in WARP, DRC+, homers, strikeout rate and a plethora of other offensive categories. Leaving Cincinnati will require him to answer for how much of his power gains were exaggerated by GABP, since he hit twice as many homers there as he did on the road. But he's been an excellent hitter for long enough at this point that we trust him to be an impact bat one way or another.

Michael Conforto RF

Born: 03/01/93 Age: 29 Bats: L Throws: R Height: 6'1" Weight: 215 lb. Origin: Round 1, 2014 Draft (#10 overall)

YEAR	TEAM	LVL	AGE	PA	R	2B	3B	HR	RBI	BB	K	SB	CS	Whiff%	AVG/OBP/SLG	DRC+	BABIP	BRR	FRAA	WARP
2019	NYM	MLB	26	648	90	29	1	33	92	84	149	7	2	26.9%	.257/.363/.494	116	.290	-0.2	RF(132): 10.1, CF(39): -4.5	3.9
2020	NYM	MLB	27	233	40	12	0	9	31	24	57	3	3	26.0%	.322/.412/.515	105	.412	0.2	RF(52): 3.4	1.2
2021	NYM	MLB	28	479	52	20	0	14	55	59	104	1	0	23.5%	.232/.344/.384	102	.276	0.0	RF(117): -0.3	1.5
2022 DC	*FA*	*MLB*	*29*	*587*	*72*	*25*	*1*	*22*	*75*	*69*	*120*	*3*	*2*	*23.8%*	*.251/.354/.437*	*116*	*.288*	*-0.7*	*RF 1, CF -2*	*2.8*

Comparables: Willie Crawford, Billy Williams, Ken Singleton

Conforto didn't so much launch himself into free agency as fall into it out of a helicopter. His final year under team control was a mess: He posted his worst full-season numbers since 2016, hit more groundballs and fewer line drives than ever, missed a month with a strained hamstring and went from slugging .564 on fastballs the year before to .424. Some of that is an inevitable regression from 2020, although DRC+, blind to the vagaries of BABIP, saw his past two seasons as surprisingly similar. General managers should be reassured that, if nothing else, his plate discipline remains very good. On top of that, he perked up near season's end, slashing .272/.372/.457 from the start of August onward. That feels more like Conforto's true talent level than the barely league-average ball that preceded it; it's more or less what he hit in 2019. Conforto chose to bet on himself, turning down the Mets' qualifying offer and the one-year, $18.4 million pillow deal that would've accompanied it. It's a risk, but a calculated one.

Carlos Correa SS

Born: 09/22/94 Age: 27 Bats: R Throws: R Height: 6'4" Weight: 220 lb. Origin: Round 1, 2012 Draft (#1 overall)

YEAR	TEAM	LVL	AGE	PA	R	2B	3B	HR	RBI	BB	K	SB	CS	Whiff%	AVG/OBP/SLG	DRC+	BABIP	BRR	FRAA	WARP
2019	HOU	MLB	24	321	42	16	1	21	59	35	75	1	0	23.7%	.279/.358/.568	121	.303	-1.0	SS(75): -2.1	1.7
2020	HOU	MLB	25	221	22	9	0	5	25	16	49	0	0	24.3%	.264/.326/.383	93	.324	0.1	SS(57): -2.2	0.2
2021	HOU	MLB	26	640	104	34	1	26	92	75	116	0	0	20.9%	.279/.366/.485	126	.308	0.3	SS(148): 4.4	4.9
2022 DC	*FA*	*MLB*	*27*	*552*	*68*	*25*	*1*	*21*	*72*	*60*	*100*	*1*	*1*	*21.4%*	*.270/.354/.457*	*119*	*.302*	*-0.8*	*SS 0*	*3.4*

Comparables: Alex Rodriguez, Alan Trammell, Robin Yount

Maybe Correa will end up back with the Astros after all. It sure doesn't seem that way; Tolstoy wrote "respect was to cover the empty space where love should be," and if the Astros' respect only extended as far as a reported $160 million offer declined ahead of free agency, there's little love lost between Correa and Houston's front office. The task of writing about an unsigned free agent is redoubled as it comes to superstars; the performance is likely to be relatively consistent no matter the shortstop's destination, but for someone of his dependable talent the worthwhile story is less the outcome than the route taken there. After years of leaning into the heel role when the revelation of Houston's cheating scandal made it more or less obligatory, we have little insight into Correa's next turn. Except that he doesn't want to play in Detroit, evidently.

Nelson Cruz DH

Born: 07/01/80 Age: 42 Bats: R Throws: R Height: 6'2" Weight: 230 lb. Origin: International Free Agent, 1998

YEAR	TEAM	LVL	AGE	PA	R	2B	3B	HR	RBI	BB	K	SB	CS	Whiff%	AVG/OBP/SLG	DRC+	BABIP	BRR	FRAA	WARP
2019	MIN	MLB	38	521	81	26	0	41	108	56	131	0	1	32.5%	.311/.392/.639	144	.351	-1.6		4.0
2020	MIN	MLB	39	214	33	6	0	16	33	25	58	0	0	34.2%	.303/.397/.595	142	.360	-0.6		1.5
2021	TB	MLB	40	238	35	8	0	13	36	16	63	0	0	32.4%	.226/.283/.442	100	.252	0.7	1B(1): -0.0	0.6
2021	MIN	MLB	40	346	44	13	1	19	50	35	63	3	0	29.3%	.294/.370/.537	138	.308	-2.6		2.1
2022 DC	*FA*	*MLB*	*41*	*552*	*73*	*21*	*0*	*28*	*82*	*50*	*128*	*0*	*1*	*31.1%*	*.264/.341/.485*	*118*	*.301*	*-0.9*	*1B -2*	*2.1*

Comparables: Hank Aaron, Andres Galarraga, Dwight Evans

It feels like the Rays have been chasing Cruz—or someone with his profile—for years. They finally pulled the trigger in advance of the trade deadline and added a big bat to the middle of their lineup. He turned 41 in July and still hit over 30 home runs between his two stops. He wasn't as good of a hitter overall with Tampa Bay, struggling to catch up to fastballs and having issues with pitches that bend. Still, it was a positive overall acquisition as he provided ample thump and a great locker room presence—the team purposely put Wander Franco's locker right next to his. They even let him play the field for the first time since 2018. After 937 career appearances in the outfield, Cruz defended the clay for seven innings at first base. He fielded seven chances cleanly, yet was not a finalist for any defensive awards. There is still some boom left in the stick, but heading into his age-41 season, it's hard to know exactly how much.

Khris Davis DH

Born: 12/21/87 Age: 34 Bats: R Throws: R Height: 5'11" Weight: 205 lb. Origin: Round 7, 2009 Draft (#226 overall)

YEAR	TEAM	LVL	AGE	PA	R	2B	3B	HR	RBI	BB	K	SB	CS	Whiff%	AVG/OBP/SLG	DRC+	BABIP	BRR	FRAA	WARP
2019	OAK	MLB	31	533	61	11	0	23	73	47	146	0	0	35.4%	.220/.293/.387	89	.264	-2.0	LF(4): -0.3	0.4
2020	OAK	MLB	32	99	9	5	0	2	10	10	26	0	0	33.0%	.200/.303/.329	91	.259	-0.2		0.1
2021	LV	AAA	33	68	16	3	2	10	25	4	13	0	0		.333/.382/.921	149	.275	-0.4		0.6
2021	OAK	MLB	33	53	3	4	0	1	5	2	15	0	0	35.2%	.255/.283/.392	82	.343	0.1		0.0
2021	TEX	MLB	33	61	8	1	1	2	5	8	16	0	0	36.8%	.157/.262/.333	93	.171	0.1	LF(2): -0.2	0.1
2022 DC	*FA*	*MLB*	*34*	*207*	*26*	*7*	*0*	*10*	*30*	*18*	*58*	*0*	*0*	*34.9%*	*.237/.314/.460*	*104*	*.285*	*-0.3*	*LF -2*	*0.6*

Comparables: Bob Watson, Gary Redus, Lance Berkman

A quick recap of Davis' 2021, a terrible, horrible, no good, very bad year: The team where he became a star salary-dumped him on the last-place Rangers. After hitting .213 in the first two weeks of spring training, he strained his quad and missed the first month of the season. When he returned, he hit so poorly that Texas released him after just six weeks of at-bats. He sat unclaimed until September, when the A's brought him back for a month in which he played every other day, homered once and was otherwise invisible. He reached free agency for the first time in his career after hitting .216/.291/.376 over the last three seasons as a DH. Sadly, this is likely the end of the road for the man once known as Khrush. Fittingly, he and Chris Davis—aka Crush—may exit the stage together.

Corey Dickerson LF Born: 05/22/89 Age: 33 Bats: L Throws: R Height: 6'1" Weight: 200 lb. Origin: Round 8, 2010 Draft (#260 overall)

YEAR	TEAM	LVL	AGE	PA	R	2B	3B	HR	RBI	BB	K	SB	CS	Whiff%	AVG/OBP/SLG	DRC+	BABIP	BRR	FRAA	WARP
2019	IND	AAA	30	38	4	1	0	0	4	3	8	0	0		.182/.237/.212	97	.222	0.2	LF(7): 0.5	0.2
2019	PIT	MLB	30	142	20	18	0	4	25	13	23	1	0	28.3%	.315/.373/.551	104	.353	0.0	LF(33): -0.7	0.5
2019	PHI	MLB	30	137	13	10	2	8	34	3	33	0	0	26.2%	.293/.307/.579	99	.333	-3.1	LF(32): -0.9	0.1
2020	MIA	MLB	31	210	25	5	1	7	17	15	35	1	1	25.7%	.258/.311/.402	101	.283	0.8	LF(46): -3.2, RF(1): -0.0	0.4
2021	MIA	MLB	32	225	27	12	3	2	14	16	45	2	4	24.6%	.263/.324/.380	85	.327	1.5	LF(52): 0.4	0.6
2021	TOR	MLB	32	140	16	6	2	4	15	9	23	4	1	23.9%	.282/.329/.450	99	.317	0.1	LF(25): -0.4, CF(10): -0.2, RF(5): 0.1	0.4
2022 DC	*FA*	*MLB*	*33*	*449*	*47*	*22*	*2*	*13*	*53*	*30*	*82*	*4*	*3*	*24.6%*	*.261/.316/.425*	*98*	*.299*	*0.1*	*LF 1, CF 0*	*1.4*

Comparables: Luis Gonzalez, Willie Stargell, Zack Wheat

Dickerson came to Toronto and provided exactly what was needed and almost 100% of what was expected: he stood on the correct side of the plate, turned in Professional At Bats and caught fly balls in the outfield with unbothered competence. He bonked a few home runs but didn't show much in the way of pop. Defensively, he could best be described as "fine, I guess," while his throws from the outfield evoked phrases like "busted duck" and "oh my goodness is he okay, there must be something wrong with or missing from his shoulder." His was a bog standard, league-average performance in almost every way - exactly what the Blue Jays required. No more, no less. His role grew and shrank with the club's injury situation; he even got a handful of starts in center field for the first time since 2015. Plugging holes for decent teams in need of quick fixes feels like his destiny, now and forever.

Freddie Freeman 1B Born: 09/12/89 Age: 32 Bats: L Throws: R Height: 6'5" Weight: 220 lb. Origin: Round 2, 2007 Draft (#78 overall)

YEAR	TEAM	LVL	AGE	PA	R	2B	3B	HR	RBI	BB	K	SB	CS	Whiff%	AVG/OBP/SLG	DRC+	BABIP	BRR	FRAA	WARP
2019	ATL	MLB	29	692	113	34	2	38	121	87	127	6	3	24.3%	.295/.389/.549	135	.318	1.4	1B(158): -7.4	4.3
2020	ATL	MLB	30	262	51	23	1	13	53	45	37	2	0	20.1%	.341/.462/.640	148	.366	-1.1	1B(58): 1.9	2.2
2021	ATL	MLB	31	695	120	25	2	31	83	85	107	8	3	21.0%	.300/.393/.503	134	.321	2.3	1B(159): -3.8	4.3
2022 DC	*FA*	*MLB*	*32*	*621*	*85*	*28*	*2*	*25*	*88*	*82*	*94*	*8*	*3*	*21.1%*	*.293/.394/.500*	*142*	*.315*	*-0.3*	*1B -1*	*4.6*

Comparables: Keith Hernandez, John Olerud, Will Clark

It can be difficult to separate the product from the process, sometimes. Freeman is an elite first baseman with metronomic consistency, finishing five of the last six seasons with a DRC+ over 120 and an ISO over .200. The outlier was 2017, which featured significant time missed due to a wrist injury, resulting in an ISO of.... .195. The time on the IL is more notable than a few points of missed isolated slugging though, as Freeman is something of an iron man, missing only seven games over the last four seasons. He believes in and proselytizes a punishing regimen of playing every day, of displaying the difference between injured and hurt. Whether that works for everyone, or just him it's hard to say, though it certainly worked for Atlanta this season. Does Freeman's fanatical devotion to everyday usage make him the player he is or does the player he is make him able to follow through on his devotion? We still won't know which organization will pay for the pleasure of finding out—as of this writing, Freddie is still a free man.

Brett Gardner CF Born: 08/24/83 Age: 38 Bats: L Throws: L Height: 5'11" Weight: 195 lb. Origin: Round 3, 2005 Draft (#109 overall)

YEAR	TEAM	LVL	AGE	PA	R	2B	3B	HR	RBI	BB	K	SB	CS	Whiff%	AVG/OBP/SLG	DRC+	BABIP	BRR	FRAA	WARP
2019	NYY	MLB	35	550	86	26	7	28	74	52	108	10	2	19.7%	.251/.325/.503	104	.265	1.1	CF(98): 1.9, LF(45): -2.0	2.6
2020	NYY	MLB	36	158	20	5	1	5	15	26	35	3	3	24.4%	.223/.354/.392	102	.264	0.9	LF(39): -3.6, CF(10): 1.9	0.4
2021	NYY	MLB	37	461	47	16	4	10	39	60	100	4	0	18.5%	.222/.327/.362	87	.269	-2.2	CF(105): -8.2, LF(35): 1.9	0.3
2022 DC	*FA*	*MLB*	*38*	*345*	*36*	*13*	*2*	*8*	*36*	*42*	*70*	*7*	*2*	*19.5%*	*.225/.328/.374*	*92*	*.266*	*0.5*	*CF 0, LF 0*	*0.9*

Comparables: Tim Raines, Gene Woodling, Luis Gonzalez

No one thought much of Gardner when he debuted on June 30, 2008. He was a potential fifth outfielder and pinch-runner—back when such things still existed—who would never hit enough to crack the lineup. He played hard and won over the fans, excelling on the basepaths and in the outfield. Gradually, he ascended from fifth outfielder to fourth, and as he caught up to MLB pitching, made himself a lineup fixture by 2010. It all happened without expectation or fanfare.

About 6,000 plate appearances later, many fans and pundits questioned the wisdom of signing Gardy for one more ride in February 2021. With a crowded outfield including Clint Frazier, Aaron Hicks, Aaron Judge, Giancarlo Stanton, Mike Tauchman and Miguel Andújar, surely the old man would be a superfluous use of a roster spot. Once more, the veteran exceeded expectations; he became their starting center fielder for most of the year, playing capably in the outfield while drawing his usual allotment of walks. More importantly, he was the team's anchor—a reliable presence through the highest highs and lowest lows of an especially up-and-down season.

Brian Goodwin OF Born: 11/02/90 Age: 31 Bats: L Throws: R Height: 6'0" Weight: 205 lb. Origin: Round 1, 2011 Draft (#34 overall)

YEAR	TEAM	LVL	AGE	PA	R	2B	3B	HR	RBI	BB	K	SB	CS	Whiff%	AVG/OBP/SLG	DRC+	BABIP	BRR	FRAA	WARP
2019	LAA	MLB	28	458	65	29	3	17	47	38	129	7	3	27.6%	.262/.326/.470	88	.337	-0.9	LF(68): -3.4, CF(39): -4.2, RF(17): 4.2	0.6
2020	CIN	MLB	29	55	5	2	0	2	5	5	19	4	0	33.7%	.163/.236/.327	72	.207	0.3	CF(16): -1.3, LF(2): -0.1, RF(1): -0.1	-0.1
2020	LAA	MLB	29	109	12	7	1	4	17	12	35	1	0	33.9%	.242/.330/.463	79	.333	0.6	LF(14): -2.2, RF(11): 1.4, CF(4): 0.2	0.0
2021	CLT	AAA	30	95	12	4	0	3	11	9	31	2	2		.244/.316/.395	82	.346	-0.3	CF(13): 0.4, LF(3): -0.0, RF(3): 0.0	0.1
2021	CHW	MLB	30	271	33	10	1	8	29	33	58	1	0	27.5%	.221/.319/.374	92	.259	0.2	RF(43): -4.6, CF(27): -1.9, LF(6): -0.0	0.0
2022 DC	*FA*	*MLB*	*31*	*276*	*29*	*12*	*0*	*8*	*31*	*29*	*74*	*3*	*2*	*29.0%*	*.229/.315/.393*	*90*	*.294*	*0.0*	*CF -1, LF 0*	*0.5*

Comparables: Ezequiel Carrera, Abraham Almonte, Aaron Hicks

As Goodwin had to settle for a minor-league deal with the rebuilding Pirates, it seemed like the league was shoving him into the box. A defender who can moonlight in center field, but a liability when it becomes a regular assignment. A left-handed bat, but one who can't be trusted to start against same-handed pitching. A compelling combination of power, plate approach, defense and athleticism, but not excelling at any one quality enough to secure a guaranteed role. In a stroke of fortune, the White Sox 2021 outfield carnage provided a clear opportunity for regular play, and well, pretty much all those preconceptions held up. Not every young man thrown to the wolves becomes a hero. But everyone should get the chance to challenge and ultimately live up to the expectations of others.

Josh Harrison IF Born: 07/08/87 Age: 35 Bats: R Throws: R Height: 5'8" Weight: 190 lb. Origin: Round 6, 2008 Draft (#191 overall)

YEAR	TEAM	LVL	AGE	PA	R	2B	3B	HR	RBI	BB	K	SB	CS	Whiff%	AVG/OBP/SLG	DRC+	BABIP	BRR	FRAA	WARP
2019	TOL	AAA	31	29	2	1	0	0	3	6	4	0	0		.174/.345/.217	98	.211	-0.6	2B(4): -0.2	0.0
2019	DET	MLB	31	147	10	7	1	1	8	6	27	4	2	26.7%	.175/.218/.263	78	.207	-1.0	2B(34): 3.0	0.3
2020	WAS	MLB	32	91	11	2	0	3	14	6	12	1	2	22.7%	.278/.352/.418	119	.288	-0.4	2B(12): -0.2, 3B(10): -1.0, LF(5): 0.4	0.4
2021	OAK	MLB	33	199	19	10	0	2	22	6	25	4	3	18.7%	.254/.296/.341	98	.281	-1.0	2B(32): -1.0, 3B(12): -0.4, SS(8): 0.4	0.4
2021	WAS	MLB	33	359	39	23	2	6	38	25	50	5	2	18.8%	.294/.366/.434	108	.332	-1.2	2B(70): -0.2, LF(16): -0.8, 3B(11): -1.1	1.3
2022 DC	*FA*	*MLB*	*34*	*414*	*40*	*18*	*1*	*7*	*41*	*25*	*57*	*7*	*3*	*19.4%*	*.257/.321/.376*	*89*	*.286*	*0.1*	*2B 0, 3B -1*	*0.8*

Comparables: Felix Millan, Cookie Rojas, Placido Polanco

Part of Oakland's trade deadline binge that was more Supermarket Sweep than spending spree, Harrison struggled in his two months with the A's. The power and plate discipline he started showing in 2020 stuck around for '21—the key to a remarkable turnaround for someone released by the Phillies right before the '20 season started. Capable of playing around the diamond and still swinging a solid stick, he's in line for another one-year deal as a super-utility piece for the right contender.

Brock Holt 3B Born: 06/11/88 Age: 34 Bats: L Throws: R Height: 5'10" Weight: 180 lb. Origin: Round 9, 2009 Draft (#265 overall)

YEAR	TEAM	LVL	AGE	PA	R	2B	3B	HR	RBI	BB	K	SB	CS	Whiff%	AVG/OBP/SLG	DRC+	BABIP	BRR	FRAA	WARP
2019	PAW	AAA	31	37	7	2	0	1	3	8	12	1	0		.250/.432/.429	100	.400	-0.4	SS(3): 1.0, 2B(2): -0.2	0.1
2019	BOS	MLB	31	295	38	14	2	3	31	28	57	1	0	18.8%	.297/.369/.402	94	.365	-1.1	2B(60): 4.1, 1B(11): 1.5, SS(6): 0.7	1.4
2020	MIL	MLB	32	36	1	0	0	0	1	4	9	0	0	19.4%	.100/.222/.100	89	.136	0.2	3B(13): -1.7, LF(3): 1.0, RF(1): -0.1	0.0
2020	WAS	MLB	32	70	11	6	0	0	4	5	15	1	0	19.8%	.262/.314/.354	86	.340	1.1	LF(6): -0.6, 3B(5): -0.6, 1B(4): 0.9	0.1
2021	TEX	MLB	33	260	21	13	1	2	23	23	49	5	1	19.4%	.209/.281/.298	79	.254	0.4	3B(69): 6.8, P(1): 0.1	0.9
2022 DC	*FA*	*MLB*	*34*	*414*	*38*	*17*	*1*	*5*	*36*	*42*	*84*	*5*	*3*	*19.5%*	*.236/.322/.337*	*83*	*.292*	*-0.1*	*3B 1, 2B 1*	*0.7*

Comparables: Don Blasingame, Adam Kennedy, Mickey Morandini

The highlight of Holt's year with his hometown team might have been August 7, when he pitched in a blowout game against the Oakland Athletics and retired the side on ten pitches, many of which were thrown at about 30 mph. He later admitted that the goal was to see how high he could throw the ball and still have it cross the plate in the strike zone. The answer: pretty high! It's notable that Holt has a brother, Garrett, because the whole situation exudes only-child-on-a-summer-afternoon energy. It's not the sort of thing that baseball players dream of when they get drafted, but given how the Rangers' 2021 season went, the fact that he made an August game fun is nothing short of remarkable.

José Iglesias SS Born: 01/05/90 Age: 32 Bats: R Throws: R Height: 5'11" Weight: 195 lb. Origin: International Free Agent, 2009

YEAR	TEAM	LVL	AGE	PA	R	2B	3B	HR	RBI	BB	K	SB	CS	Whiff%	AVG/OBP/SLG	DRC+	BABIP	BRR	FRAA	WARP
2019	CIN	MLB	29	530	62	21	3	11	59	20	70	6	6	15.6%	.288/.318/.407	95	.315	2.9	SS(144): 5.0	2.4
2020	BAL	MLB	30	150	16	17	0	3	24	3	17	0	0	14.5%	.373/.400/.556	119	.407	-0.6	SS(24): -1.4	0.6
2021	BOS	MLB	31	64	8	4	1	1	7	3	9	0	0	14.7%	.356/.406/.508	111	.408	-1.3	2B(18): 1.1, SS(5): 0.1	0.3
2021	LAA	MLB	31	447	57	23	1	8	41	18	66	5	2	19.5%	.259/.295/.375	90	.291	0.0	SS(114): -6.2	0.4
2022 DC	*FA*	*MLB*	*32*	*449*	*41*	*23*	*1*	*7*	*44*	*20*	*67*	*7*	*4*	*18.2%*	*.267/.309/.385*	*86*	*.302*	*0.1*	*SS -1, 2B 0*	*0.8*

Comparables: Alan Trammell, Tony Fernandez, Luis Aparicio

Was there a player who experienced more of baseball's emotional rollercoaster than Iglesias in the past year or so? He was the subject of a coast-to-coast trade, shifted from Baltimore to the Angels barely a month after the O's had exercised his option. He turned in his usual array of highlight-reel plays at the six but also suffered from some unfortunately sub-par defensive metrics, a big problem in the light of his predictably considerable offensive regression from 2020. Toiling away for an Angels team that was, once again, relentlessly .500, Iglesias was suddenly jettisoned from the roster in early September and claimed by a Red Sox team on the precipice of falling out of the Wild Card race. He promptly compiled a ludicrous .915 OPS over the remainder of the season to help Boston into their successful playoff run. Of course, there was one more twist: Iglesias himself wasn't postseason-eligible as a post-August addition. He traveled with the team and went through his normal pre-game routines but was ultimately limited to being the world's most game-ready mascot. It's not clear what the future holds if Iglesias' glove truly isn't plus any more, but it won't be more dramatic than the recent past.

Jed Lowrie 2B/DH Born: 04/17/84 Age: 38 Bats: S Throws: R Height: 6'0" Weight: 180 lb. Origin: Round 1, 2005 Draft (#45 overall)

YEAR	TEAM	LVL	AGE	PA	R	2B	3B	HR	RBI	BB	K	SB	CS	Whiff%	AVG/OBP/SLG	DRC+	BABIP	BRR	FRAA	WARP
2019	SYR	AAA	35	48	7	1	0	2	3	4	12	0	0		.250/.313/.409	100	.300	-0.3	2B(5): -0.5, 3B(5): -1.0, SS(1): -0.1	0.0
2019	NYM	MLB	35	8	0	0	0	0	0	1	4	0	0	40.0%	.000/.125/.000	83		0.0		0.0
2021	OAK	MLB	37	512	55	28	0	14	69	49	108	0	0	24.3%	.245/.318/.398	98	.289	-3.5	2B(71): -3.1, 3B(1): -0.0	0.8
2022 DC	*FA*	*MLB*	*38*	*345*	*36*	*16*	*0*	*9*	*38*	*33*	*74*	*0*	*0*	*24.3%*	*.243/.321/.396*	*92*	*.291*	*-0.6*	*2B -3, 3B 0*	*0.5*

Comparables: Rich Aurilia, Jay Bell, Cal Ripken Jr.

Congrats to Jed Lowrie, who not only managed to escape the Citi Field Mystery Spot in which he spent all of 2019 and '20 but also showed some unexpected pep in his surgically compromised step. After joining the A's on a minor-league deal and making the roster out of spring training, he hit .323/.400/.516 over the first three weeks of the season, once again finding magic in a return to Oakland. But while he was healthy enough to play a full season, he hit just .233/.305/.380 the rest of the way. He's now 37, and this might be the end of the line.

Andrew McCutchen LF Born: 10/10/86 Age: 35 Bats: R Throws: R Height: 5'11" Weight: 195 lb. Origin: Round 1, 2005 Draft (#11 overall)

YEAR	TEAM	LVL	AGE	PA	R	2B	3B	HR	RBI	BB	K	SB	CS	Whiff%	AVG/OBP/SLG	DRC+	BABIP	BRR	FRAA	WARP
2019	PHI	MLB	32	262	45	12	1	10	29	43	55	2	1	25.7%	.256/.378/.457	110	.299	0.8	LF(52): -0.8, CF(15): -0.8	1.2
2020	PHI	MLB	33	241	32	9	0	10	34	22	48	4	0	22.0%	.253/.324/.433	109	.281	-1.2	LF(39): -5.2	0.3
2021	PHI	MLB	34	574	78	24	1	27	80	81	132	6	1	25.7%	.222/.334/.444	108	.242	0.9	LF(135): -8.6	2.0
2022 DC	*FA*	*MLB*	*35*	*483*	*56*	*19*	*0*	*16*	*58*	*64*	*108*	*7*	*3*	*25.6%*	*.231/.340/.404*	*103*	*.273*	*-0.1*	*LF -2, CF 0*	*1.6*

Comparables: Amos Otis, Vernon Wells, Ellis Burks

Entering his age-35 season, McCutchen's best days are behind him, but not because he can't swing the stick. He's a pleasant face to see at the plate, whose discipline at the dish drives much of his value: He recorded better than 90th-percentile walk and chase rates, and he can still leg out a hit when needed. He truly shines against lefties, though, and should be ticketed for at least a short-side platoon role wherever he lands next, after running significant platoon splits each of the last two seasons. McCutchen's defense has cratered and it's possible he could see a spike in offense without the burden of playing defense. If that's the case, the potential for the designated hitter in the NL is arriving just in time to extend the career of one of the most enjoyable, high-quality outfielders in the last two decades.

Brad Miller 1B Born: 10/18/89 Age: 32 Bats: L Throws: R Height: 6'2" Weight: 195 lb. Origin: Round 2, 2011 Draft (#62 overall)

YEAR	TEAM	LVL	AGE	PA	R	2B	3B	HR	RBI	BB	K	SB	CS	Whiff%	AVG/OBP/SLG	DRC+	BABIP	BRR	FRAA	WARP
2019	LHV	AAA	29	163	31	9	1	10	29	24	40	1	3		.294/.399/.596		.341			
2019	SWB	AAA	29	163	31	9	1	10	29	24	40	1	3		.294/.399/.596	129	.341	-1.1	2B(13): -1.1, LF(11): 0.3, 3B(10): -1.1	0.8
2019	CLE	MLB	29	40	4	3	0	1	4	4	10	1	0	29.7%	.250/.325/.417	91	.320	0.6	2B(13): 0.3	0.2
2019	PHI	MLB	29	130	22	3	1	12	21	11	35	1	0	30.9%	.263/.331/.610	118	.268	0.3	3B(19): 0.3, LF(16): 1.3, SS(1): 0.0	0.9
2020	STL	MLB	30	171	21	8	1	7	25	25	46	1	0	35.7%	.232/.357/.451	104	.289	0.3	3B(15): -0.7, SS(2): -0.1, 2B(1): -0.3	0.4
2021	PHI	MLB	31	377	53	9	3	20	49	45	112	3	0	31.0%	.227/.321/.453	100	.276	-0.6	1B(58): 0.7, RF(14): -0.8, 2B(13): -1.6	0.9
2022 DC	*FA*	*MLB*	*32*	*345*	*41*	*13*	*1*	*14*	*45*	*41*	*96*	*2*	*1*	*31.3%*	*.222/.321/.424*	*99*	*.275*	*-0.1*	*1B 0, 3B 0*	*1.0*

Comparables: Dick McAuliffe, Pete Runnels, Roy Smalley

Miller has put together a respectable big-league career—"respectable" slotting in next to "gritty" and "hard-nosed" in the category of requisite adjectives for no-batting-glovers—but these days, you have him on your team for two reasons. One, to mash righties; Miller had an .849 OPS and hit 16 of his 20 homers against right-handed pitching in 2021. Two, to play wherever you need on the diamond. But providing flexibility isn't the same as qualifying for super-utility status. Miller can play a lot of positions—he logged innings at first, second, third and the outfield last year—but he doesn't play any of them all that well. Until a rule change widens major-league benches, though, that's enough to keep him employed.

Joc Pederson OF Born: 04/21/92 Age: 30 Bats: L Throws: L Height: 6'1" Weight: 220 lb. Origin: Round 11, 2010 Draft (#352 overall)

YEAR	TEAM	LVL	AGE	PA	R	2B	3B	HR	RBI	BB	K	SB	CS	Whiff%	AVG/OBP/SLG	DRC+	BABIP	BRR	FRAA	WARP
2019	LAD	MLB	27	514	83	16	3	36	74	50	111	1	1	24.3%	.249/.339/.538	122	.249	2.4	LF(84): 0.5, RF(39): -0.1, 1B(20): -1.1	3.3
2020	LAD	MLB	28	138	21	4	0	7	16	11	34	1	0	31.0%	.190/.285/.397	99	.200	-1.0	LF(23): -1.5, RF(8): 2.4	0.4
2021	ATL	MLB	29	194	20	8	1	7	22	17	43	0	0	25.7%	.249/.325/.428	97	.290	-1.9	RF(36): -1.1, CF(24): -2.1	0.1
2021	CHC	MLB	29	287	35	11	2	11	39	22	74	2	3	26.7%	.230/.300/.418	85	.274	0.5	LF(66): -7.0, RF(3): -0.4, CF(2): 0.1	-0.2
2022 DC	*FA*	*MLB*	*30*	*518*	*61*	*21*	*1*	*22*	*69*	*45*	*119*	*3*	*3*	*26.4%*	*.231/.312/.432*	*97*	*.263*	*-0.3*	*LF -1, RF 0*	*1.2*

Comparables: Chili Davis, Roy Sievers, Rick Monday

It's pretty easy to become a cult hero in baseball nowadays, apparently. All you need to do is dye your hair beach blonde, go to your jeweler and have them craft you a custom-made pearl necklace, then go on the diamond and crush some dingers at opportune times. Pederson's first season outside of Los Angeles wasn't exactly a breakout—everything that's already been written about him in these hallowed pages remains true. He's still a corner outfielder and a platoon bat who can hit pitches from right-handed pitchers all the way to the moon on his best day. He also has a knack for showing up in the postseason, which goes a long way towards cementing yourself in the minds of the fans. The fact that he's doing so with such an interesting and unique attitude about the sport is what makes him fun to watch. The book on Pederson doesn't lie, but the truth can be fun all the same.

Tommy Pham LF Born: 03/08/88 Age: 34 Bats: R Throws: R Height: 6'1" Weight: 223 lb. Origin: Round 16, 2006 Draft (#496 overall)

YEAR	TEAM	LVL	AGE	PA	R	2B	3B	HR	RBI	BB	K	SB	CS	Whiff%	AVG/OBP/SLG	DRC+	BABIP	BRR	FRAA	WARP
2019	TB	MLB	31	654	77	33	2	21	68	81	123	25	4	20.2%	.273/.369/.450	115	.316	-1.1	LF(123): -10.9	2.3
2020	SD	MLB	32	125	13	2	0	3	12	15	27	6	0	27.0%	.211/.312/.312	96	.253	0.3	LF(18): -0.6	0.2
2021	SD	MLB	33	561	74	24	2	15	49	78	128	14	6	23.4%	.229/.340/.383	101	.280	0.3	LF(113): 4.5, CF(11): -0.1, RF(1): 0.1	2.6
2022 DC	*FA*	*MLB*	*34*	*518*	*61*	*21*	*1*	*16*	*61*	*70*	*112*	*16*	*6*	*23.6%*	*.248/.358/.416*	*113*	*.297*	*0.8*	*LF -1, CF 0*	*2.6*

Comparables: Tim Raines, Rickey Henderson, Lonnie Smith

Over his career, Pham has spent more time on the injured list than Ralph Fiennes languishing in an Italian monastery. Though he avoided any official trips to the IL this season, an off-season stabbing left him with a foot-long scar and cost him strength, although thankfully not his life, and he had a painfully slow start to the season. It's frustrating because Pham's expected metrics all suggest he should have had more success at the dish: He exhibited his trademark solid plate discipline, and when he swung, he barreled up the ball hard and frequently, but with very little to show for it. Maybe Petco, where his BABIP sagged well behind his career average for two straight seasons, was just a poor match for him; as were Padres fans, who heckled him mercilessly about both his off-season mishap and passivity at the plate. A free agent in 2022, Pham says he's willing to sign a one-year prove-it deal in San Diego or elsewhere; our money is on "elsewhere."

Anthony Rizzo 1B Born: 08/08/89 Age: 32 Bats: L Throws: L Height: 6'3" Weight: 240 lb. Origin: Round 6, 2007 Draft (#204 overall)

YEAR	TEAM	LVL	AGE	PA	R	2B	3B	HR	RBI	BB	K	SB	CS	Whiff%	AVG/OBP/SLG	DRC+	BABIP	BRR	FRAA	WARP
2019	CHC	MLB	29	613	89	29	3	27	94	71	86	5	2	19.6%	.293/.405/.520	134	.306	-4.6	1B(146): 4.7	4.3
2020	CHC	MLB	30	243	26	6	0	11	24	28	38	3	1	19.4%	.222/.342/.414	118	.218	-0.6	1B(57): -3.5	0.7
2021	CHC	MLB	31	376	41	16	3	14	40	36	59	4	2	21.0%	.248/.346/.446	112	.261	-1.0	1B(92): 1.8	1.4
2021	NYY	MLB	31	200	32	7	0	8	21	16	28	2	0	20.7%	.249/.340/.428	113	.252	1.7	1B(47): -2.2	0.7
2022 DC	*FA*	*MLB*	*32*	*587*	*72*	*24*	*1*	*21*	*74*	*60*	*89*	*5*	*3*	*20.5%*	*.254/.359/.437*	*117*	*.271*	*-0.3*	*1B 0*	*2.5*

Comparables: Kent Hrbek, Keith Hernandez, John Olerud

Rizzo should have been a free agent years ago, if not for service time manipulation that led to a team-friendly, club option-filled extension that held him under team control until after his age-31 season. What a difference those two years wound up making: after 2019, Rizzo was still his usual downballot MVP vote self, hitting with power and getting on base at his usual 40% clip. Now, his contact rates and eroding, which have eaten into his batting average and OBP. And while the home run power is still there, it's not there quite as often—ironically, the short porch in right in Yankee Stadium didn't help Rizzo, because everything he pulled landed 10 rows deep or 20 feet short. Unable to sign a deal before the lockout, it appears he's destined to roam the lands on one to two-year deals, offering veteran presence and stability more than greatness, like the Carlos Santanas and C.J. Crons he once, long ago, felt like a cut above.

Eddie Rosario LF Born: 09/28/91 Age: 30 Bats: L Throws: R Height: 6'1" Weight: 180 lb. Origin: Round 4, 2010 Draft (#135 overall)

YEAR	TEAM	LVL	AGE	PA	R	2B	3B	HR	RBI	BB	K	SB	CS	Whiff%	AVG/OBP/SLG	DRC+	BABIP	BRR	FRAA	WARP
2019	MIN	MLB	27	590	91	28	1	32	109	22	86	3	1	21.4%	.276/.300/.500	107	.273	1.3	LF(124): -8.9, RF(11): -0.5, CF(3): 0.1	1.8
2020	MIN	MLB	28	231	31	7	0	13	42	19	34	3	1	22.7%	.257/.316/.476	119	.248	0.7	LF(51): 2.6	1.5
2021	GWN	AAA	29	53	7	2	0	4	16	2	6	0	0		.196/.226/.471	124	.146	0.3	CF(6): 1.8, LF(3): 0.7, RF(2): 0.1	0.6
2021	ATL	MLB	29	106	13	4	2	7	16	9	14	2	1	18.4%	.271/.330/.573	120	.250	0.1	LF(28): -0.6, RF(1): -0.0	0.6
2021	CLE	MLB	29	306	29	15	1	7	46	17	47	9	2	19.6%	.254/.296/.389	88	.280	-0.7	LF(72): 0.8	0.7
2022 DC	*FA*	*MLB*	*30*	*518*	*56*	*22*	*1*	*18*	*64*	*32*	*73*	*7*	*3*	*19.8%*	*.258/.306/.426*	*94*	*.271*	*0.1*	*LF 0, RF 0*	*1.3*

Comparables: Luis Gonzalez, Willie Stargell, Billy Williams

Rosario has lived a pretty charmed baseball life. He hit the first pitch he saw in the major leagues for an opposite-field homer, he crossed the plate as the winning run in an MLB game played in his home of Puerto Rico, and he has two silver medals in the World Baseball Classic to his name. In 2021, things got even more interesting when he became just the eighth player in Braves franchise history to hit for the cycle, before using the same bat from his cycle game to hit a walk-off single in the NLCS. Speaking of the latter, it isn't hard to imagine Atlanta losing in that round were it not for Rosario's virtuoso performance: The trade deadline acquisition slashed .560/.607/1.040 over six games, lashing balls all around the field. He was just what the doctor ordered as soon as he landed in Atlanta, boosting his walk rate, lowering his strikeout rate and adding nearly 200 points of slugging to his slash line, compared to his time in Cleveland. He's a productive hitter, if a bit limited defensively, when healthy—which could be why he hadn't signed with a club prior to the lockout.

Danny Santana 1B Born: 11/07/90 Age: 31 Bats: S Throws: R Height: 5'11" Weight: 195 lb. Origin: International Free Agent, 2007

YEAR	TEAM	LVL	AGE	PA	R	2B	3B	HR	RBI	BB	K	SB	CS	Whiff%	AVG/OBP/SLG	DRC+	BABIP	BRR	FRAA	WARP
2019	NAS	AAA	28	40	4	4	1	0	6	4	10	1	1		.343/.425/.514	93	.480	0.8	SS(3): 0.8, RF(3): -0.0, 2B(1): 0.1	0.3
2019	TEX	MLB	28	511	81	23	6	28	81	25	151	21	6	32.3%	.283/.324/.534	96	.353	3.0	1B(44): 0.8, CF(27): 0.8, 2B(17): 0.7	1.7
2020	TEX	MLB	29	63	6	4	0	1	7	7	24	2	0	40.8%	.145/.238/.273	73	.226	0.2	1B(9): -0.7, CF(4): 0.4, LF(1): -0.0	-0.1
2021	AGU	WIN	30	104	12	5	2	1	4	6	27	0	0		.214/.260/.337		.286			
2021	WOR	AAA	30	47	8	5	0	2	4	7	9	2	0		.300/.404/.575	120	.345	-1.6	1B(4): 0.3, LF(2): -0.7, CF(2): -0.1	0.0
2021	BOS	MLB	30	127	15	2	1	5	14	10	30	4	2	36.6%	.181/.252/.345	94	.198	-0.3	1B(14): -0.8, CF(13): 0.0, LF(7): 0.5	0.2
2022 DC	*FA*	*MLB*	*31*	*207*	*21*	*9*	*1*	*7*	*24*	*15*	*62*	*6*	*3*	*34.1%*	*.230/.294/.403*	*84*	*.304*	*0.7*	*1B 0, CF 0*	*0.2*

Comparables: Eduardo Escobar, Luis Valbuena, Eduardo Núñez

Gifted as clear a path to playing time as he had any right to hope for, Santana proved unequal to the task. For reasons that no one save Alex Cora can truly know, Santana found himself penciled into the lineup nearly every day from May 21 through July 21, appearing primarily at center field and (no, this is not a typo) first base. He responded by hitting .171/.230/.324, striking out in a quarter of his at-bats and playing poor defense. Like a $6 "Swiss Army Knife" you get at an airport gift shop, Santana offers versatility in name only. Cora refused to acknowledge this reality right to the bitter end, pinch-hitting Santana in several key postseason spots. The results served to equally indict the manager, the player himself and the architect of a roster in which *Danny Santana* saw ALCS playing time. Some minor-league invites likely await, but they should not come from teams with designs on playing into October.

Kyle Schwarber LF Born: 03/05/93 Age: 29 Bats: L Throws: R Height: 6'0" Weight: 229 lb. Origin: Round 1, 2014 Draft (#4 overall)

YEAR	TEAM	LVL	AGE	PA	R	2B	3B	HR	RBI	BB	K	SB	CS	Whiff%	AVG/OBP/SLG	DRC+	BABIP	BRR	FRAA	WARP
2019	CHC	MLB	26	610	82	29	3	38	92	70	156	2	3	28.1%	.250/.339/.531	115	.276	-5.1	LF(140): -1.5, C(1): 0.1	2.7
2020	CHC	MLB	27	224	30	6	0	11	24	30	66	1	0	28.2%	.188/.308/.393	96	.219	0.3	LF(48): 0.2	0.5
2021	WAS	MLB	28	303	42	9	0	25	53	31	88	1	1	29.3%	.253/.340/.570	131	.273	-4.3	LF(72): 6.8	2.6
2021	BOS	MLB	28	168	34	10	0	7	18	33	39	0	0	27.4%	.291/.435/.522	117	.364	0.5	LF(15): 0.9, 1B(10): -1.2	0.9
2022 DC	*FA*	*MLB*	*29*	*552*	*74*	*21*	*1*	*29*	*81*	*72*	*143*	*2*	*2*	*27.9%*	*.230/.339/.463*	*115*	*.266*	*-0.6*	*LF 1, 1B 0*	*3.0*

Comparables: Adam Dunn, Barry Bonds, Willie Stargell

Some players—your Mike Napolis, Kevin Youkilises and, of course, Dustin Pedroias—seem preordained to star in Boston. Schwarber joined their ranks last season, quickly winning over Sox fans with his patient approach, light-tower power and general Kelly's Roast Beef aesthetic. Schwarber earned headlines early in the season by hitting a record-tying 12 homers in a 10-game span with the Nats and slashing an absurd .280/.362/.760 in June. Though a hamstring strain sidelined Schwarber in July, Chaim Bloom still deemed him worth the price of prospect Aldo Ramirez, somewhat controversially pursuing Schwarber over Anthony Rizzo, who seemed a more obvious fit. Once off the IL, Schwarber proved Bloom right, bringing some much-needed patience to a hack-happy lineup and mashing three postseason taters to boot. With the outfield stacked and J.D. Martinez set to return at DH, Schwarber lacks a clear path to playing time in Boston—he tried valiantly to learn first base on the fly, but let's just say Ron Washington had a point. A Red Sox reunion may seem unlikely, but in November Bloom suggested the Sox would be among Schwarber's many suitors, seemingly as enamored with the slugger as Boston's fanbase.

Andrelton Simmons SS Born: 09/04/89 Age: 32 Bats: R Throws: R Height: 6'2" Weight: 195 lb. Origin: Round 2, 2010 Draft (#70 overall)

YEAR	TEAM	LVL	AGE	PA	R	2B	3B	HR	RBI	BB	K	SB	CS	Whiff%	AVG/OBP/SLG	DRC+	BABIP	BRR	FRAA	WARP
2019	LAA	MLB	29	424	47	19	0	7	40	24	37	10	2	14.2%	.264/.309/.364	99	.277	-0.3	SS(102): 11.0	2.5
2020	LAA	MLB	30	127	19	7	0	0	10	8	16	2	0	16.3%	.297/.346/.356	106	.343	0.7	SS(30): 1.2	0.7
2021	MIN	MLB	31	451	37	12	0	3	31	32	62	1	0	16.6%	.223/.283/.274	83	.256	0.5	SS(131): 2.4	1.0
2022 DC	*FA*	*MLB*	*32*	*483*	*45*	*19*	*1*	*7*	*45*	*34*	*56*	*8*	*3*	*16.2%*	*.256/.315/.358*	*85*	*.279*	*0.1*	*SS 2*	*1.1*

Comparables: Luis Aparicio, Orlando Cabrera, Bill Russell

He was brought on board to lock down Minnesota's shaky middle infield. Instead, Simmons was an unqualified disaster from day one. Defensively, his advertised wizardry was only occasionally in evidence. At the plate, he was truly apocalyptic. Simmons was the only MLB player with an OPS under .500 (min. 140 PA) after the 2021 All-Star break. The team argued that they needed to continue playing him in order to help an inexperienced pitching staff. Okay, then.

Meanwhile, in the clubhouse, he sparked the team's first COVID outbreak in the spring and spent the season arguing with science on social media. Simmons joins the ghost of Bret Boone and Joe Crede's MRI machine in Minnesota's Veteran Free Agent Infielder Hall of Sadness, located at US Bank Stadium, the site of the old Metrodome. While the Hall itself is metaphorical, the stray paneling falling off the side of the building is quite real and sharp-edged. Use caution!

Donovan Solano 2B Born: 12/17/87 Age: 34 Bats: R Throws: R Height: 5'8" Weight: 210 lb. Origin: International Free Agent, 2005

YEAR	TEAM	LVL	AGE	PA	R	2B	3B	HR	RBI	BB	K	SB	CS	Whiff%	AVG/OBP/SLG	DRC+	BABIP	BRR	FRAA	WARP
2019	SAC	AAA	31	97	12	4	0	2	16	9	11	0	0		.322/.392/.437	107	.351	-0.7	2B(14): -0.1, 3B(10): 0.7, SS(1): 0.1	0.5
2019	SF	MLB	31	228	27	13	1	4	23	10	49	0	1	19.0%	.330/.360/.456	89	.409	1.4	2B(36): -2.4, SS(19): 0.7, 3B(2): 0.0	0.5
2020	SF	MLB	32	203	22	15	1	3	29	10	39	0	0	22.0%	.326/.365/.463	101	.396	-1.7	2B(45): -6.0, 3B(5): -1.2, SS(2): -0.3	-0.2
2021	SF	MLB	33	344	35	17	0	7	31	25	58	2	0	20.3%	.280/.344/.404	105	.321	-0.6	2B(91): 4.4, SS(2): 0.0	1.9
2022 DC	*FA*	*MLB*	*34*	*345*	*33*	*17*	*0*	*6*	*34*	*22*	*63*	*0*	*1*	*20.7%*	*.267/.325/.386*	*94*	*.317*	*-0.5*	*2B 0, SS 0*	*0.9*

Comparables: Andrés Blanco, Ramiro Pena, Neil Walker

At this point we all know that BABIP isn't some Rosetta Stone that holds the key to the myriad of metrics that seem to proliferate by the month. But the BABIP backlash has gone too far! It matters for someone like Solano, who was running a figure near .400 in his 2019-20 tenure with the Giants. Now, a line-drive hitter with a modicum of speed is bound to run a decent BABIP, and so Solano did in the unremarkable, earlier, Marlins/Yankees phase of his career—and all it got him was a .636 OPS during that five-year stretch. But, once in San Francisco, he managed to improve his quality of contact and drove the BABIP up dramatically in his first two years with the Giants. So, not *just* luck, but certainly *some* luck. Solano's productivity falls off quickly when the luck recedes even a little bit—without power or elite speed to compensate, and without the defense to justify the middling bat, Solano becomes an expendable utility guy. If the 34-year-old needs a .400 BABIP to be starter-worthy, then he should pack rabbits' feet, four-leaf clovers and copious pinches of salt, along with his equipment, to his next free-agent destination.

Jorge Soler RF/DH

Born: 02/25/92 Age: 30 Bats: R Throws: R Height: 6'4" Weight: 235 lb. Origin: International Free Agent, 2012

YEAR	TEAM	LVL	AGE	PA	R	2B	3B	HR	RBI	BB	K	SB	CS	Whiff%	AVG/OBP/SLG	DRC+	BABIP	BRR	FRAA	WARP
2019	KC	MLB	27	679	95	33	1	48	117	73	178	3	1	32.4%	.265/.354/.569	136	.294	-4.5	RF(56): -0.7	4.4
2020	KC	MLB	28	174	17	8	0	8	24	19	60	0	0	37.2%	.228/.326/.443	87	.317	-0.4	RF(8): -1.3	0.0
2021	KC	MLB	29	360	38	16	0	13	37	38	97	0	0	31.6%	.192/.288/.370	93	.229	-0.3	RF(46): -6.3	-0.1
2021	ATL	MLB	29	242	36	11	0	14	33	29	45	0	0	25.5%	.269/.358/.524	124	.278	-0.7	RF(50): -2.9	1.1
2022 DC	*FA*	*MLB*	*30*	*587*	*76*	*25*	*0*	*29*	*85*	*63*	*137*	*1*	*1*	*29.8%*	*.238/.330/.463*	*112*	*.266*	*-0.9*	*RF -4*	*2.0*

Comparables: Mike Marshall, Juan Encarnacion, Sixto Lezcano

One of baseball's many aphorisms involves the old idea that a player's fortunes can change alongside a simple change in scenery. Soler would probably agree with that sentiment, since the switch in venue from Kansas City to Atlanta ended up bearing plenty of fruit. Soler's 2021 DRC+ skyrocketed after the trade, as a hot streak in Missouri ended up turning into something tangible and exciting to watch in Georgia. The slugging outfielder had always shown patience at the plate, but he was someone different in Atlanta, slicing eight percentage points from his strikeout rate, at one point taking the role of leadoff hitter. Maybe spreading Soler Power to brand new places across the baseball landscape is a good way to keep his bat fresh and energized. Plus, it's 2022 and alternative means of energy are becoming more entrenched everywhere, meaning Soler's power should be welcomed with open arms, no matter where the pending free agent lands. If his time in Atlanta is truly over, he'll remain a Brave forever in fans' hearts thanks to his stadium-clearing home run in the World Series-clinching Game 6.

Trevor Story SS

Born: 11/15/92 Age: 29 Bats: R Throws: R Height: 6'2" Weight: 213 lb. Origin: Round 1, 2011 Draft (#45 overall)

YEAR	TEAM	LVL	AGE	PA	R	2B	3B	HR	RBI	BB	K	SB	CS	Whiff%	AVG/OBP/SLG	DRC+	BABIP	BRR	FRAA	WARP
2019	COL	MLB	26	656	111	38	5	35	85	58	174	23	8	26.5%	.294/.363/.554	116	.361	3.4	SS(144): -0.7	4.0
2020	COL	MLB	27	259	41	13	4	11	28	24	63	15	3	25.7%	.289/.355/.519	110	.354	2.3	SS(57): 1.6	1.5
2021	COL	MLB	28	595	88	34	5	24	75	53	139	20	6	27.5%	.251/.329/.471	105	.293	2.7	SS(138): -4.9	2.3
2022 DC	*FA*	*MLB*	*29*	*587*	*74*	*29*	*3*	*27*	*84*	*53*	*147*	*18*	*6*	*27.0%*	*.261/.337/.485*	*116*	*.313*	*1.3*	*SS -1*	*3.6*

Comparables: Ernie Banks, Robin Yount, Alex Rodriguez

The Rockies didn't do a *great* job of convincing everyone they weren't melting their franchise into a single spoonful of precious ore leading up to 2021. After Nolan Arenado's messy departure, their 29-year-old two-time All-Star and Silver Slugger shortstop was routinely listed as part of 2022's illustrious class of free agents at his position. But by mid-2021, it was pondered whether or not Story even *was* a shortstop. At the trade deadline, one team had reportedly watched the velocity drop off his throws to first and considered sticking him in the outfield. There was little solace to be found in Story's offense, either. Story was reportedly "confused" when he wasn't traded at the deadline, and he and the Rockies entered a slog through purgatory to the season's end. (Though the light at the end of the tunnel must have been refreshing; he hit significantly better after the break.) Whether a mile high or sea level, Story will make a fine addition to any infield in 2022 after four straight years of ample production. Perhaps with the familial strife of his rocky upbringing behind him, Story can remember who he was before things got messy.

Seiya Suzuki OF

Born: 08/18/94 Age: 27 Bats: R Throws: R Height: 5'11" Weight: 182 lb.

YEAR	TEAM	LVL	AGE	PA	R	2B	3B	HR	RBI	BB	K	SB	CS	Whiff%	AVG/OBP/SLG	DRC+	BABIP	BRR	FRAA	WARP
2022 non-DC	*FA*	*MLB*	*27*	*251*	*34*	*11*	*1*	*11*	*36*	*35*	*43*			*21.1%*	*.273/.382/.498*	*138*	*.295*			*2.2*

In recent years the tide of talent between Japan and America has been flowing west, with Tomoyuki Sugano opting not to sign with an MLB team and longtime Yankee star Masahiro Tanaka choosing home over greater competition and compensation. Suzuki, who posted a month before the MLB lockout but preferred to wait the situation out, will reverse that trend. Touted as the best hitter available to cross the Pacific in a while, the five-time NPB All-Star's greatest strength is his lack of weaknesses: he's a five-time Gold Glove-winning outfielder, he wields a surplus of power (his 1.072 OPS in 2021 easily led the league), and he walks as often as he strikes out. He's probably merely a good right fielder than a regular in center, which is about the extent to which expectations can currently be tempered.

Jonathan Villar 3B

Born: 05/02/91 Age: 31 Bats: S Throws: R Height: 6'0" Weight: 233 lb. Origin: International Free Agent, 2008

YEAR	TEAM	LVL	AGE	PA	R	2B	3B	HR	RBI	BB	K	SB	CS	Whiff%	AVG/OBP/SLG	DRC+	BABIP	BRR	FRAA	WARP
2019	BAL	MLB	28	714	111	33	5	24	73	61	176	40	9	27.6%	.274/.339/.453	94	.341	5.8	2B(111): 2.9, SS(97): -0.1	2.9
2020	MIA	MLB	29	128	10	4	0	2	9	10	32	9	5	32.3%	.259/.315/.345	85	.337	-1.1	SS(14): -3.2, 2B(12): -0.8, CF(2): -0.5	-0.4
2020	TOR	MLB	29	79	3	1	0	0	6	9	22	7	0	32.1%	.188/.278/.203	79	.271	0.8	2B(13): 0.8, SS(7): -0.3	0.2
2021	NYM	MLB	30	505	63	18	2	18	42	46	132	14	7	30.3%	.249/.322/.416	96	.313	0.8	3B(97): -0.9, SS(26): -0.2, 2B(9): -0.3	1.4
2022 DC	*FA*	*MLB*	*31*	*449*	*47*	*17*	*1*	*12*	*49*	*41*	*118*	*23*	*6*	*29.9%*	*.245/.319/.387*	*90*	*.318*	*1.6*	*SS 0, 2B 1*	*1.1*

Comparables: Frank White, Jay Bell, Bret Boone

Villar is miscast as a starter on a contending team, but the black hole at third base forced the Mets to give him 86 starts there, and he produced just enough to finish the year around league-average offensively. That's a big improvement from 2020's grounder-heavy mess, but it's also about as much as you can expect from him at this point: some decent pop tied to lots of strikeouts, a few stolen bases (on a few too many attempts), acceptable if mediocre defense at a variety of infield positions. There's not much upside left here anymore, but there is a perfectly cromulent utility infielder just waiting to find a new home.

Daniel Vogelbach 1B Born: 12/17/92 Age: 29 Bats: L Throws: R Height: 6'0" Weight: 270 lb. Origin: Round 2, 2011 Draft (#68 overall)

YEAR	TEAM	LVL	AGE	PA	R	2B	3B	HR	RBI	BB	K	SB	CS	Whiff%	AVG/OBP/SLG	DRC+	BABIP	BRR	FRAA	WARP
2019	SEA	MLB	26	558	73	17	0	30	76	92	149	0	0	26.9%	.208/.341/.439	110	.232	-2.4	1B(57): -3.1	1.7
2020	MIL	MLB	27	67	13	2	0	4	12	8	18	0	0	22.5%	.328/.418/.569	105	.417	-0.3	1B(2): 0.7	0.2
2020	SEA	MLB	27	64	3	1	0	2	4	11	13	0	0	22.1%	.094/.250/.226	93	.079	-0.2		0.1
2020	TOR	MLB	27	5	0	0	0	0	0	1	2	0	0	20.0%	.000/.200/.000	88		0.0		0.0
2021	NAS	AAA	28	65	8	0	0	3	8	16	13	0	0		.313/.477/.500	129	.364	-1.2	1B(16): 0.8	0.3
2021	MIL	MLB	28	258	30	8	0	9	24	43	57	0	0	19.4%	.219/.349/.381	108	.255	-2.9	1B(59): -4.9	0.1
2022 DC	*FA*	*MLB*	*29*	*276*	*34*	*9*	*0*	*10*	*34*	*44*	*57*	*0*	*0*	*21.2%*	*.227/.356/.408*	*109*	*.258*	*-0.5*	*1B -1*	*0.7*

Comparables: Chris Parmelee, Mike Carp, Justin Smoak

A sad thing happened to the big guy since he arrived in Milwaukee: He stopped hitting dingers. To be fair, Vogelbach only has one season where he was able to swing for the fences with any regularity (thank you, 2019 Mariners), but in part-time duty with the Brewers, Vogelbach's ISO fell precipitously. He'll remain an above-average presence on offense thanks to his superlative walk rate but without the requisite thump that accompanies it, or any defensive value to speak of, the margins for Vogelbach to remain on a major-league roster are increasingly thin. The erstwhile slugger wasn't tendered a contract and was unsigned heading into the lockout.

PITCHERS

Brett Anderson LHP Born: 02/01/88 Age: 34 Bats: L Throws: L Height: 6'4" Weight: 230 lb. Origin: Round 2, 2006 Draft (#55 overall)

YEAR	TEAM	LVL	AGE	W	L	SV	G	GS	IP	H	HR	BB/9	K/9	K	GB%	BABIP	WHIP	ERA	DRA-	WARP	MPH	FB%	Whiff%	CSP
2019	OAK	MLB	31	13	9	0	31	31	176	181	20	2.5	4.6	90	54.0%	.280	1.31	3.89	120	0.0	90.5	62.2%	17.1%	50.7%
2020	MIL	MLB	32	4	4	0	10	10	47	50	6	1.9	6.1	32	59.6%	.293	1.28	4.21	97	0.6	89.6	54.3%	19.7%	47.0%
2021	MIL	MLB	33	4	9	0	24	24	96	102	11	2.6	5.4	58	56.4%	.298	1.35	4.22	114	0.2	89.0	54.2%	16.8%	51.2%
2022 DC	*FA*	*MLB*	*34*	*6*	*6*	*0*	*21*	*21*	*92.3*	*101*	*10*	*2.5*	*5.3*	*54*	*55.0%*	*.300*	*1.38*	*4.35*	*106*	*0.5*	*89.5*	*56.6%*	*17.4%*	*50.3%*

Comparables: Mark Buehrle, Jason Marquis, Scott Feldman

There's no evidence that Milwaukee's clubhouse had any sort of "Mean Girls" vibe in 2021, but it's easy to envision a world where the cool guys with the sexy arsenals thumbed their nose at Anderson, the old, unhip junkballer just trying to make it through a season in one piece. A trio of IL stints prevented that from being the case, but the fact that there were three means that all three were short-term, which is a win for a pitcher who has had his share of lengthy stays. More concerning for Anderson's long-term viability is that between those stints, the high-80s sinker and four other average offerings simply weren't cutting it to the point where he was left off Milwaukee's NLDS roster. Being left-handed adds a couple of years to any pitcher's shelf life, but Anderson is nearing his expiration date—his palatable ERA and ability to induce ground balls covered for unsightly peripherals. Another year of fastball velocity decline driving a stunningly low strikeout rate, and Anderson is likely to find himself in MLB's "burnt" book.

Chris Archer RHP Born: 09/26/88 Age: 33 Bats: R Throws: R Height: 6'2" Weight: 195 lb. Origin: Round 5, 2006 Draft (#161 overall)

YEAR	TEAM	LVL	AGE	W	L	SV	G	GS	IP	H	HR	BB/9	K/9	K	GB%	BABIP	WHIP	ERA	DRA-	WARP	MPH	FB%	Whiff%	CSP
2019	PIT	MLB	30	3	9	0	23	23	119^{2}	114	25	4.1	10.8	143	35.2%	.304	1.41	5.19	88	2.0	94.2	50.4%	29.7%	45.9%
2021	DUR	AAA	32	0	1	0	5	5	14	9	3	1.9	10.3	16	40.0%	.188	0.86	3.86	98	0.2				
2021	TB	MLB	32	1	1	0	6	5	19^{1}	18	3	3.7	9.8	21	31.5%	.294	1.34	4.66	115	0.0	92.3	45.0%	29.3%	55.8%
2022 DC	*FA*	*MLB*	*33*	*6*	*5*	*0*	*19*	*19*	*97*	*89*	*16*	*3.4*	*9.7*	*104*	*38.0%*	*.290*	*1.30*	*4.24*	*103*	*0.6*	*93.6*	*48.7%*	*29.6%*	*49.1%*

Comparables: Jake Peavy, Jack McDowell, Ian Kennedy

Speed 2: Cruise Control, Highlander: The Quickening and Chris Archer: Return to the Rays; all three sequels that probably should have never been made. The right-hander made his return to Tampa Bay following two-and-a-half disappointing seasons with Pittsburgh. He missed all of 2020 after undergoing surgery for neurogenic thoracic outlet syndrome, but still secured a $6.5 million guarantee from the Rays on a one-year deal. For that fee, the team received just 19 ⅓ innings of essentially replacement-level work. Forearm tightness shut him down in early April and he didn't pitch for the Rays again until late August. By early September, a hip injury he suffered while rehabbing flared up and ended his season. Coincidentally, the club used his 40-man roster spot to add Shane Baz to the roster, who was the player-to-be-named-later in the original Archer trade to the Pirates. Entering his age-33 season having not pitched meaningful innings in over two years, he will be lucky to get a cameo role in 2022.

Brad Boxberger RHP

Born: 05/27/88 Age: 34 Bats: R Throws: R Height: 5'10" Weight: 211 lb. Origin: Round 1, 2009 Draft (#43 overall)

YEAR	TEAM	LVL	AGE	W	L	SV	G	GS	IP	H	HR	BB/9	K/9	K	GB%	BABIP	WHIP	ERA	DRA-	WARP	MPH	FB%	Whiff%	CSP
2019	HBG	AA	31	1	1	1	8	0	8^2	6	0	3.1	11.4	11	38.1%	.286	1.04	1.04	89	0.1				
2019	LOU	AAA	31	0	0	0	5	0	5^1	10	2	8.4	13.5	8	16.7%	.500	2.81	11.81	79	0.1				
2019	KC	MLB	31	1	3	1	29	0	26^2	25	3	5.7	9.1	27	39.0%	.297	1.58	5.40	119	0.0	90.3	47.2%	29.0%	47.1%
2020	MIA	MLB	32	1	0	0	23	0	18	17	3	4.0	9.0	18	50.0%	.286	1.39	3.00	87	0.3	92.8	55.2%	24.2%	50.6%
2021	MIL	MLB	33	5	4	4	71	0	64^2	44	8	3.5	11.6	83	37.1%	.257	1.07	3.34	80	1.3	93.6	56.0%	32.0%	56.2%
2022 DC	*FA*	*MLB*	*34*	*3*	*3*	*0*	*71*	*0*	*61.7*	*53*	*10*	*4.1*	*10.5*	*72*	*39.9%*	*.285*	*1.31*	*4.22*	*99*	*0.3*	*93.1*	*54.9%*	*30.4%*	*54.3%*

Comparables: David Robertson, Scott Sullivan, Luis Vizcaino

The life of a journeyman reliever has its twists and turns. One minute, you're the life of the party, an unheralded hero garnering particular appreciation among local fans who tune in every night, a force of stability among a unit chastised and derided with any misstep. The next, you're among the chastised. "Why did we go with *him* in that situation?" Boxberger's seen it all, from lockdown guy to miscast and mismatched closer and everything in between. It was mostly the former in 2021 as the veteran brought back the velocity that made him a strikeout artist early in his career and began working in his slider at heights previously unseen. The combination allowed Boxberger to pitch almost as many major-league innings as his previous three seasons combined, and do it with his best strikeout rate since 2017. Serving as a steady hand for the NL Central champs, Boxberger knows better than anyone that his fortunes could change in a heartbeat, or however long it takes to see a BABIP 21 points below his career average reverse itself.

Matthew Boyd LHP

Born: 02/02/91 Age: 31 Bats: L Throws: L Height: 6'3" Weight: 223 lb. Origin: Round 6, 2013 Draft (#175 overall)

YEAR	TEAM	LVL	AGE	W	L	SV	G	GS	IP	H	HR	BB/9	K/9	K	GB%	BABIP	WHIP	ERA	DRA-	WARP	MPH	FB%	Whiff%	CSP
2019	DET	MLB	28	9	12	0	32	32	185^1	178	39	2.4	11.6	238	34.6%	.310	1.23	4.56	86	3.2	92.3	53.9%	31.4%	48.9%
2020	DET	MLB	29	3	7	0	12	12	60^1	67	15	3.3	9.0	60	37.5%	.310	1.48	6.71	133	-0.4	91.8	52.7%	27.9%	45.5%
2021	TOL	AAA	30	0	0	0	3	3	9^1	5	0	0.0	10.6	11	45.0%	.250	0.54	0.00	94	0.2				
2021	DET	MLB	30	3	8	0	15	15	78^2	77	9	2.6	7.7	67	38.3%	.296	1.27	3.89	113	0.2	92.1	47.5%	22.6%	55.6%
2022 DC	*FA*	*MLB*	*31*	*3*	*2*	*0*	*9*	*9*	*48.3*	*47*	*7*	*2.6*	*8.6*	*46*	*37.2%*	*.292*	*1.27*	*4.14*	*105*	*0.3*	*92.1*	*50.9%*	*26.9%*	*50.9%*

Comparables: Aaron Harang, Jason Vargas, Bronson Arroyo

Boyd saw a return to form in 2021, but which form is open to interpretation. BP's WARP metric, based on Deserved Run Average, is never going to love a guy who pitches to contact and also allows lots of fly balls on contact, even in the relatively spacious confines of Comerica Park. And in his limited action between arm injuries, the former ace accentuated his career-long home-road splits (4.27 ERA at home, 5.66 away), which act as though Detroit is sea level and everywhere else is Coors. Boyd doesn't need to strike out 11 batters per nine to be successful; he was a perfectly serviceable starter before 2019, when he was only giving up one or two home runs per start instead of three or four. The Tigers declined to trade Boyd after that season, apparently dissatisfied with what they were offered, and instead received over the next two seasons a net -.5 WARP and no prospects, before eventually non-tendering him this December. Sometimes a Boyd in the hand is not worth the two in the bush.

Andrew Chafin LHP

Born: 06/17/90 Age: 32 Bats: R Throws: L Height: 6'2" Weight: 235 lb. Origin: Round 1, 2011 Draft (#43 overall)

YEAR	TEAM	LVL	AGE	W	L	SV	G	GS	IP	H	HR	BB/9	K/9	K	GB%	BABIP	WHIP	ERA	DRA-	WARP	MPH	FB%	Whiff%	CSP
2019	ARI	MLB	29	2	2	0	77	0	52^2	52	6	3.1	11.6	68	41.6%	.359	1.33	3.76	81	1.1	93.9	61.1%	34.2%	45.4%
2020	ARI	MLB	30	1	1	0	11	0	6^2	9	1	5.4	13.5	10	31.6%	.444	1.95	8.10	81	0.1	93.7	70.9%	27.8%	45.9%
2020	CHC	MLB	30	0	1	1	4	0	3	2	1	3.0	9.0	3	62.5%	.143	1.00	3.00	110	0.0	93.7	81.4%	21.1%	42.1%
2021	OAK	MLB	31	2	2	5	28	0	29^1	24	3	2.1	8.3	27	36.6%	.266	1.06	1.53	104	0.2	91.3	75.0%	24.2%	53.2%
2021	CHC	MLB	31	0	2	0	43	0	39^1	21	1	2.7	8.5	37	49.5%	.204	0.84	2.06	89	0.6	92.7	71.2%	27.3%	57.1%
2022 DC	*FA*	*MLB*	*32*	*3*	*3*	*0*	*71*	*0*	*61.7*	*57*	*7*	*3.2*	*9.3*	*64*	*44.2%*	*.295*	*1.29*	*3.82*	*97*	*0.3*	*92.6*	*70.3%*	*27.8%*	*52.4%*

Comparables: Xavier Cedeño, Marc Rzepczynski, Sam Freeman

As endangered by the three-batter-minimum rule as the dodos of Mauritius were when Dutch sailors landed there at the end of the 16th century, Chafin managed to grow wings and fly. Not only was he impossible to hit in 2021, but he was brutal on hitters from both sides of the plate. Lefties, per usual, were helpless against him: a .170/.250/.223 line. But righties didn't fare much better, slashing just .196/.247/.304, with only three homers in 162 plate appearances and a strikeout rate of 26.5%. The rest of the lefty specialists may have gone the way of ... well, you know, but Chafin has proven that "LOOGY" was, for him, a misclassification.

Johnny Cueto RHP Born: 02/15/86 Age: 36 Bats: R Throws: R Height: 5'11" Weight: 229 lb. Origin: International Free Agent, 2004

YEAR	TEAM	LVL	AGE	W	L	SV	G	GS	IP	H	HR	BB/9	K/9	K	GB%	BABIP	WHIP	ERA	DRA-	WARP	MPH	FB%	Whiff%	CSP
2019	SJ	A+	33	0	1	0	2	2	7	8	1	1.3	6.4	5	52.2%	.333	1.29	6.43	112	0.0				
2019	SAC	AAA	33	0	1	0	2	2	10^{1}	10	2	0.0	7.8	9	51.6%	.286	0.97	2.61	80	0.2				
2019	SF	MLB	33	1	2	0	4	4	16	11	3	5.1	7.3	13	51.1%	.200	1.25	5.06	99	0.2	91.5	51.3%	19.6%	44.1%
2020	SF	MLB	34	2	3	0	12	12	63^{1}	61	9	3.7	8.0	56	42.2%	.284	1.37	5.40	109	0.4	91.4	43.5%	20.0%	44.0%
2021	SF	MLB	35	7	7	0	22	21	114^{2}	127	15	2.4	7.7	98	37.2%	.336	1.37	4.08	100	1.1	92.0	51.4%	22.9%	54.1%
2022 DC	*FA*	*MLB*	*36*	*7*	*7*	*0*	*22*	*22*	*117.7*	*122*	*16*	*2.7*	*7.1*	*93*	*39.0%*	*.297*	*1.34*	*4.48*	*111*	*0.3*	*91.8*	*49.2%*	*22.0%*	*51.0%*

Comparables: Dan Haren, Matt Garza, Doug Drabek

If you line up Cueto's San Francisco contract with his stats, you'd be hard-pressed to call it a good signing for the club—you could chalk it up as one of Brian Sabean's final follies before he handed the keys over to the Zaidi regime. The club was entering the aftermath of the three championships, and while Cueto was as advertised in 2016, the injuries and skills decline seemed to enter a mutually reinforcing spiral, with brief periods of respite in which Late Cueto again looked like his earlier incarnations. Forget about all of that. To appreciate the Giants phase of Cueto's career is to see him on the mound, in the moment, combining a competitive intensity with a whimsy and joy that made him a singular pleasure to watch, no matter the results on the field. One could see a silhouette of his pitching motion, with its variations, stops and starts and know to whom it belonged in an instant. Even if Cueto's San Francisco tenure was filled with inconsistency and missed time and took place during a relatively fallow era for the team, you would be hard pressed to find anyone claiming that Cueto was anything less than a Very Good Giant.

Jeurys Familia RHP Born: 10/10/89 Age: 32 Bats: R Throws: R Height: 6'3" Weight: 240 lb. Origin: International Free Agent, 2007

YEAR	TEAM	LVL	AGE	W	L	SV	G	GS	IP	H	HR	BB/9	K/9	K	GB%	BABIP	WHIP	ERA	DRA-	WARP	MPH	FB%	Whiff%	CSP
2019	NYM	MLB	29	4	2	0	66	0	60	62	7	6.3	9.5	63	50.0%	.350	1.73	5.70	102	0.6	96.0	65.9%	28.6%	45.3%
2020	NYM	MLB	30	2	0	0	25	0	26^{2}	20	2	6.4	7.8	23	60.0%	.247	1.46	3.71	91	0.4	96.7	59.8%	27.7%	46.0%
2021	NYM	MLB	31	9	4	1	65	0	59^{1}	57	10	4.1	10.9	72	49.7%	.318	1.42	3.94	80	1.2	96.8	73.5%	27.9%	54.3%
2022 DC	*FA*	*MLB*	*32*	*3*	*3*	*0*	*71*	*0*	*61.7*	*54*	*6*	*4.5*	*9.6*	*66*	*50.3%*	*.295*	*1.37*	*3.97*	*94*	*0.4*	*96.6*	*69.5%*	*28.0%*	*50.9%*

Comparables: Brandon League, Dan Miceli, Stan Belinda

Familia's long tumble from All-Star closer to "guy who gets a spring training NRI from the Orioles in two years" continued apace in 2021, with an elevated home-run rate joining forces with the mediocre control that's dogged him for years. That may be a harsh future sentence for a pitcher who throws 97 mph and posted his best strikeout rate in three years, but it should say a lot that even with those advantages, the veteran righty barely managed to get his ERA under 4.00. Despite now throwing his sinker nearly two-thirds of the time, Familia's HR/9 rate was in the bottom fifth of the league's qualified relievers, and his ground-ball rate, while above-average, falls well short of his peak years as a closer. At this stage in his career, he's a middle reliever best deployed against righties or with runners on, so long as you can stomach him putting more hitters on base in the process. The floor keeps getting lower, and odds are that it'll be underground soon.

Zack Greinke RHP Born: 10/21/83 Age: 38 Bats: R Throws: R Height: 6'2" Weight: 200 lb. Origin: Round 1, 2002 Draft (#6 overall)

YEAR	TEAM	LVL	AGE	W	L	SV	G	GS	IP	H	HR	BB/9	K/9	K	GB%	BABIP	WHIP	ERA	DRA-	WARP	MPH	FB%	Whiff%	CSP
2019	ARI	MLB	35	10	4	0	23	23	146	117	15	1.3	8.3	135	41.9%	.266	0.95	2.90	84	2.7	90.0	47.7%	23.4%	46.7%
2019	HOU	MLB	35	8	1	0	10	10	62^{2}	58	6	1.3	7.5	52	51.1%	.291	1.07	3.02	97	0.7	90.2	43.1%	26.0%	47.5%
2020	HOU	MLB	36	3	3	0	12	12	67	67	6	1.2	9.0	67	41.8%	.321	1.13	4.03	83	1.4	88.2	42.4%	27.8%	45.2%
2021	HOU	MLB	37	11	6	0	30	29	171	164	30	1.9	6.3	120	44.9%	.264	1.17	4.16	115	0.2	89.0	45.9%	21.7%	53.0%
2022 DC	*FA*	*MLB*	*38*	*9*	*8*	*0*	*25*	*25*	*147.7*	*152*	*21*	*1.8*	*6.8*	*111*	*43.5%*	*.290*	*1.24*	*3.93*	*101*	*1.1*	*89.1*	*45.4%*	*23.3%*	*50.3%*

Comparables: Bert Blyleven, Jack Morris, Jim Palmer

Well, that was depressing. It'd be foolish to give up on Greinke, who faces an uncertain future at time of publication after a feeble end to one of the great megadeals ever extended to a pitcher. Though his ERA barely spiked from the pandemic season, the pitcher behind the number seemed well and truly enervated as everything else went in the wrong direction. It's not that his fastball slowed down more or the critical differentiation between it and his changeup further dissolved, rather that everything simply stopped working. Year-over-year, the strikeout rate was down by a third, the walk rate spiked by more than half and the home run rate doubled. He was barely a part of the rotation as the postseason dawned, was forced into it by exigencies and struggled to acquit himself passably—only in his final of three outings did he last longer than a full run through the lineup. Though it seems foolish to hope for sentiment to prevail over age so soon after Albert Pujols' revitalization, Greinke's career deserves a stronger end than this.

Kenley Jansen RHP Born: 09/30/87 Age: 34 Bats: S Throws: R Height: 6'5" Weight: 265 lb. Origin: International Free Agent, 2004

YEAR	TEAM	LVL	AGE	W	L	SV	G	GS	IP	H	HR	BB/9	K/9	K	GB%	BABIP	WHIP	ERA	DRA-	WARP	MPH	FB%	Whiff%	CSP
2019	LAD	MLB	31	5	3	33	62	0	63	51	9	2.3	11.4	80	32.5%	.273	1.06	3.71	85	1.2	92.2	87.7%	32.2%	48.9%
2020	LAD	MLB	32	3	1	11	27	0	24^{1}	19	2	3.3	12.2	33	24.6%	.309	1.15	3.33	91	0.4	91.4	90.4%	30.8%	47.0%
2021	LAD	MLB	33	4	4	38	69	0	69	36	4	4.7	11.2	86	37.3%	.216	1.04	2.22	82	1.3	93.2	84.6%	33.4%	57.7%
2022 DC	*FA*	*MLB*	*34*	*3*	*3*	*0*	*71*	*0*	*61.7*	*47*	*9*	*3.7*	*12.0*	*82*	*34.3%*	*.279*	*1.17*	*3.41*	*80*	*0.9*	*92.7*	*86.2%*	*32.7%*	*54.1%*

Comparables: Craig Kimbrel, Joakim Soria, Francisco Rodríguez

Closing is a thankless job. Jansen had been on a Hall of Fame trajectory before a rough 2018 season and a couple of (for him) substandard seasons in 2019 and 2020. He reinvented himself in 2021 and showed he still has plenty left in the proverbial tank. Jansen has reduced his cut fastball usage to 58%, which is the lowest since the 2011 season. He still held hitters to a .260 wOBA on the pitch, but his sinker and curveball-like slider are what put him back into the elite tier of closer this past season. Batters produced a .213 and .150 wOBA, respectively, on the offerings. Despite being 34 years old, he looks like he could continue to be a premier closer for the next few years, if the new approach holds as well as the old one did.

Joe Kelly RHP Born: 06/09/88 Age: 34 Bats: R Throws: R Height: 6'1" Weight: 174 lb. Origin: Round 3, 2009 Draft (#98 overall)

YEAR	TEAM	LVL	AGE	W	L	SV	G	GS	IP	H	HR	BB/9	K/9	K	GB%	BABIP	WHIP	ERA	DRA-	WARP	MPH	FB%	Whiff%	CSP
2019	LAD	MLB	31	5	4	1	55	0	51^{1}	49	6	3.9	10.9	62	62.6%	.323	1.38	4.56	80	1.1	98.1	50.9%	26.4%	48.9%
2020	LAD	MLB	32	0	0	0	12	1	10	8	0	6.3	8.1	9	57.7%	.308	1.50	1.80	92	0.2	97.0	36.8%	27.5%	44.4%
2021	LAD	MLB	33	2	0	2	48	0	44	28	3	3.1	10.2	50	58.4%	.227	0.98	2.86	82	0.8	97.8	40.7%	28.2%	56.1%
2022 DC	*FA*	*MLB*	*34*	*2*	*2*	*0*	*42*	*0*	*37*	*31*	*3*	*3.8*	*9.7*	*39*	*54.8%*	*.287*	*1.27*	*3.51*	*85*	*0.4*	*97.8*	*43.0%*	*27.7%*	*53.0%*

Comparables: Dennis Lamp, Jason Grilli, Matt Albers

In June, Dave Roberts made it known that the ever-erratic Kelly had dispensed with the name Joe. This new, more effective version of Kelly was Joseph Kelly, who throws strikes (not to be confused with Joe Kelley, who posted 11.1 rWAR for the 1899-1901 Brooklyn Superbas). And, to Joseph's credit, he was indeed a pitcher transformed, aided by the change in mentality and an offseason surgery which removed a painful cyst from his pitching shoulder. Kelly posted the highest strikeout rate and second-lowest walk rate of his career, and even made effective use of a changeup which went viral after he was filmed breaking a window trying to develop it. By the time the postseason came around, Kelly was the bullpen's primary fireman, not the player who necessitated one.

Clayton Kershaw LHP Born: 03/19/88 Age: 34 Bats: L Throws: L Height: 6'4" Weight: 225 lb. Origin: Round 1, 2006 Draft (#7 overall)

YEAR	TEAM	LVL	AGE	W	L	SV	G	GS	IP	H	HR	BB/9	K/9	K	GB%	BABIP	WHIP	ERA	DRA-	WARP	MPH	FB%	Whiff%	CSP
2019	LAD	MLB	31	16	5	0	29	28	178^{1}	145	28	2.1	9.5	189	46.3%	.267	1.04	3.03	87	3.0	90.4	43.9%	28.1%	46.0%
2020	LAD	MLB	32	6	2	0	10	10	58^{1}	41	8	1.2	9.6	62	52.7%	.232	0.84	2.16	71	1.5	91.6	40.8%	27.7%	51.5%
2021	LAD	MLB	33	10	8	0	22	22	121^{2}	103	15	1.6	10.7	144	48.0%	.292	1.02	3.55	73	2.9	90.7	36.9%	34.8%	57.6%
2022 DC	*FA*	*MLB*	*34*	*9*	*5*	*0*	*22*	*22*	*129*	*113*	*17*	*1.8*	*10.6*	*151*	*47.6%*	*.298*	*1.07*	*2.87*	*74*	*2.8*	*90.8*	*39.5%*	*31.7%*	*53.4%*

Comparables: John Smoltz, Steve Carlton, Roger Clemens

Hall of Famers have to defy aging curves, either by reinventing themselves or digging deeper into their wells of talent. Perhaps because of the elbow problems that cost him two months of the season and sidelined him for the playoffs, Kershaw lost much of the fastball velocity he'd found in 2020. So he turned to the weapon that defined his career: the slider. Kershaw threw the slider on nearly half of his offerings and induced a whiff-per-swing rate rivaling the very peak years of his career. As a result, Kershaw finished the season with a career-high swinging strike rate of 16.6%, which tied Corbin Burnes for the best among all pitchers with more than 100 innings thrown. He still hangs a few more sliders than he used to, so the pitch was hit hard when put in play, but still having one of baseball's most valuable pitches covers up for a lot.

Yusei Kikuchi LHP Born: 06/17/91 Age: 31 Bats: L Throws: L Height: 6'0" Weight: 200 lb. Origin: International Free Agent, 2019

YEAR	TEAM	LVL	AGE	W	L	SV	G	GS	IP	H	HR	BB/9	K/9	K	GB%	BABIP	WHIP	ERA	DRA-	WARP	MPH	FB%	Whiff%	CSP
2019	SEA	MLB	28	6	11	0	32	32	161^{2}	195	36	2.8	6.5	116	43.9%	.310	1.52	5.46	129	-0.8	92.7	49.0%	20.0%	50.7%
2020	SEA	MLB	29	2	4	0	9	9	47	41	3	3.8	9.0	47	52.8%	.306	1.30	5.17	81	1.0	93.6	77.7%	30.0%	50.5%
2021	SEA	MLB	30	7	9	0	29	29	157	145	27	3.6	9.3	163	48.9%	.289	1.32	4.41	95	1.9	93.4	70.7%	27.9%	57.2%
2022 DC	*FA*	*MLB*	*31*	*9*	*7*	*0*	*25*	*25*	*137.3*	*126*	*17*	*3.3*	*9.0*	*137*	*47.7%*	*.289*	*1.29*	*3.81*	*96*	*1.4*	*93.2*	*66.7%*	*26.3%*	*54.8%*

Comparables: John Tudor, Andy Pettitte, Randy Wolf

Kikuchi's 2021 resembled that of his close friend and former teammate Daniel Vogelbach in 2019: A breakout first half earning a trip to the All-Star Game as Seattle's lone representative, before crashing and burning in epic fashion. The former Seibu Lions star's struggles can easily be traced back to the sticky stuff crackdown in late June; his numbers took a precipitous turn as the summer went on and umpires began their regular check-ups. One could hypothesize that Kikuchi had become particularly reliant on a some sort of substance after coming over from Japan, where the pre-tacked balls are much easier to grip. Granted, it's not as if he didn't already exhibit maddening inconsistency long before the sticky stuff became the center of attention. His Mariners tenure came to an abrupt end following the World Series, as he shocked many in the industry by declining his $13M player option for 2022 and testing the market instead. Still just 30, it's not unrealistic to envision a team gambling on the left-hander's high-end velocity and occasional flashes of brilliance.

Chris Martin RHP Born: 06/02/86 Age: 36 Bats: R Throws: R Height: 6'8" Weight: 225 lb. Origin: Round 21, 2005 Draft (#627 overall)

YEAR	TEAM	LVL	AGE	W	L	SV	G	GS	IP	H	HR	BB/9	K/9	K	GB%	BABIP	WHIP	ERA	DRA-	WARP	MPH	FB%	Whiff%	CSP
2019	ATL	MLB	33	1	1	0	20	0	17^{2}	17	1	0.5	11.2	22	52.2%	.356	1.02	4.08	79	0.4	95.3	70.6%	28.0%	49.4%
2019	TEX	MLB	33	0	2	4	38	0	38	35	8	0.9	10.2	43	50.0%	.293	1.03	3.08	78	0.8	95.7	82.1%	25.0%	55.2%
2020	ATL	MLB	34	1	1	1	19	0	18	8	1	1.5	10.0	20	38.1%	.171	0.61	1.00	88	0.3	93.7	63.3%	26.7%	48.6%
2021	ATL	MLB	35	2	4	1	46	0	43^{1}	49	4	1.2	6.9	33	48.9%	.338	1.27	3.95	99	0.4	94.5	71.7%	21.1%	59.8%
2022 DC	*FA*	*MLB*	*36*	*3*	*3*	*0*	*71*	*0*	*61.7*	*62*	*8*	*1.5*	*7.5*	*51*	*46.0%*	*.298*	*1.18*	*3.64*	*94*	*0.4*	*94.7*	*72.0%*	*23.3%*	*56.3%*

Comparables: Pat Neshek, Steve Reed, Brad Ziegler

In 2021, Coldplay released *Music of the Spheres*, which was seen as an interesting effort but not exactly reaching the lofty standards that the Martin-led band has set for themselves over an illustrious discography. "Coloratura" served as an intriguing finale that was more in line with the quality that you would expect from Coldplay's best stuff. The same could be said for the frontman's baseball namesake when talking about how 2021 went for him. For most relievers, a perfectly average DRA– is fine! For a reliever who spent the past two seasons at 10-20% better than league-average, it's definitely a bit of a dropoff. He similarly ended his latest project with a flourish, as he picked up one strikeout in each of his last 10 regular-season appearances. It wasn't enough to salvage his lowest strikeout percentage since before his 2016 sojourn to Japan, but it's at least a tiny glimmer of hope for new projects going forward.

Collin McHugh RHP Born: 06/19/87 Age: 35 Bats: R Throws: R Height: 6'2" Weight: 191 lb. Origin: Round 18, 2008 Draft (#554 overall)

YEAR	TEAM	LVL	AGE	W	L	SV	G	GS	IP	H	HR	BB/9	K/9	K	GB%	BABIP	WHIP	ERA	DRA-	WARP	MPH	FB%	Whiff%	CSP
2019	HOU	MLB	32	4	5	0	35	8	74^{2}	62	12	3.6	9.9	82	39.1%	.265	1.23	4.70	95	0.9	90.9	33.4%	28.1%	47.7%
2021	TB	MLB	34	6	1	1	37	7	64	48	3	1.7	10.4	74	42.8%	.290	0.94	1.55	78	1.3	90.8	10.9%	31.8%	56.4%
2022 DC	*FA*	*MLB*	*35*	*3*	*3*	*0*	*71*	*0*	*61.7*	*54*	*9*	*2.6*	*9.6*	*66*	*39.9%*	*.284*	*1.17*	*3.50*	*88*	*0.6*	*90.9*	*17.8%*	*30.6%*	*53.8%*

Comparables: Diego Segui, David Phelps, Casey Janssen

McHugh opted out of the 2020 season for several reasons including additional rest for his injured elbow. That moved paid off as he made a highly successful return to the majors in his first season with the Rays. Alternating between opener and traditional reliever, he was effective regardless of role. Even with the extra time off, he came back with similar stuff: a top-40 radio blend of stuff in the 70s, 80s and early 90s. Despite the similarity in speed, his usage was widely varied: The fastball was nearly scrapped all together. Instead, he looked at the man in the mirror and put his faith in an 88-mph cutter. He was reunited with his 79-mph slider that had a knack for getting outs and giving the opponents sad eyes. When thrown, his fastball checked in around 90. If you're holding on for more you'd be the king of wishful thinking. He did miss time with a back strain and arm fatigue. Nonetheless, the new medley of pitches will leave the door open for opportunities in the upcoming season.

Martín Pérez LHP Born: 04/04/91 Age: 31 Bats: L Throws: L Height: 6'0" Weight: 200 lb. Origin: International Free Agent, 2007

YEAR	TEAM	LVL	AGE	W	L	SV	G	GS	IP	H	HR	BB/9	K/9	K	GB%	BABIP	WHIP	ERA	DRA-	WARP	MPH	FB%	Whiff%	CSP
2019	MIN	MLB	28	10	7	0	32	29	165^{1}	184	23	3.6	7.3	135	47.9%	.318	1.52	5.12	128	-0.8	92.5	73.2%	21.7%	45.8%
2020	BOS	MLB	29	3	5	0	12	12	62	55	8	4.1	6.7	46	38.4%	.267	1.34	4.50	141	-0.7	90.6	65.1%	22.3%	46.3%
2021	BOS	MLB	30	7	8	0	36	22	114	136	19	2.8	7.7	97	43.2%	.337	1.51	4.74	132	-0.9	91.7	67.4%	19.4%	53.2%
2022 DC	*FA*	*MLB*	*31*	*8*	*8*	*0*	*36*	*22*	*121*	*126*	*15*	*3.1*	*6.7*	*90*	*43.9%*	*.303*	*1.39*	*4.57*	*108*	*0.4*	*91.7*	*68.5%*	*20.6%*	*49.8%*

Comparables: John Danks, Sterling Hitchcock, Jim Abbott

When Mariners backup catcher José Godoy made his major-league debut in late May he was celebrated as the 20,000th player to ever reach the majors. The historical accuracy of said count aside, the achievement underscores just how unique you have to be to play professional baseball at the highest levels. If you reach the majors at all, never mind carve out a multi-year career, you are in the top 99.99th percentile of all humans who've ever picked up a ball or bat. This is a long way of saying that, in the grand scheme of things, Pérez is a historically talented athlete. Unfortunately, he's also trending toward an historically awful career, as he's now cost the teams that have employed him 9.1 WARP and counting. Among all pitchers who threw at least 100 innings last year, Pérez was the ninth-worst, per WARP. He had the seventh-lowest whiff rate, the 18th-highest HR/FB rate and placed in the top-60 for hard hit rate, which is impressive given his lack of velocity. There's no need to pile on, and Pérez has had his moments, but if a contending team signs him their fanbase should riot in the streets. And if Pérez *ever* makes an ALCS appearance again the front office responsible should be tried for negligence.

Hansel Robles RHP Born: 08/13/90 Age: 31 Bats: R Throws: R Height: 6'0" Weight: 220 lb. Origin: International Free Agent, 2008

YEAR	TEAM	LVL	AGE	W	L	SV	G	GS	IP	H	HR	BB/9	K/9	K	GB%	BABIP	WHIP	ERA	DRA-	WARP	MPH	FB%	Whiff%	CSP
2019	LAA	MLB	28	5	1	23	71	1	72^{2}	58	6	2.0	9.3	75	38.0%	.283	1.02	2.48	90	1.1	97.3	56.3%	26.9%	49.8%
2020	LAA	MLB	29	0	2	1	18	0	16^{2}	19	4	5.4	10.8	20	32.7%	.341	1.74	10.26	119	0.0	95.5	52.1%	30.7%	48.7%
2021	BOS	MLB	30	0	1	4	27	0	25	21	2	4.7	11.9	33	37.7%	.322	1.36	3.60	88	0.4	97.2	60.4%	29.2%	53.9%
2021	MIN	MLB	30	3	4	10	45	0	44	37	6	4.9	8.8	43	44.9%	.279	1.39	4.91	110	0.2	96.8	53.3%	21.2%	54.3%
2022 DC	*FA*	*MLB*	*31*	*3*	*3*	*0*	*71*	*0*	*61.7*	*54*	*8*	*4.0*	*9.9*	*68*	*39.1%*	*.295*	*1.32*	*4.09*	*96*	*0.4*	*96.9*	*55.4%*	*25.4%*	*52.6%*

Comparables: Joe Smith, Santiago Casilla, Mark Lowe

When Robles proved to be Chaim Bloom's marquee reliever deadline acquisition, the general reaction from Red Sox fans was: "that's it?" It seemed a fair response but Robles did his part down the stretch, pitching far better in Boston than Minnesota. The veteran fireballer's high-octane fastball remained as electric as ever, and while Robles still showed poor command he at least improved relative to his disastrous 2020 campaign. When Matt Barnes and Adam Ottavino faltered down the stretch, "El Caballo Blanco" ended up as Alex Cora's quasi-closer and even found himself with some high-leverage work in the playoffs, albeit to mediocre results (it's unclear if Carlos Correa's ALCS moon shot off Robles will have landed as of time of printing). As silly as Robles looks when he's walking the no. 9 hitter or pointing to the sky like his gopher balls are infield flies, he proved he can still be an effective medium-leverage reliever. He'll likely do better than the $2 million deal he inked last winter, though perhaps only modestly so.

Carlos Rodón LHP Born: 12/10/92 Age: 29 Bats: L Throws: L Height: 6'3" Weight: 245 lb. Origin: Round 1, 2014 Draft (#3 overall)

YEAR	TEAM	LVL	AGE	W	L	SV	G	GS	IP	H	HR	BB/9	K/9	K	GB%	BABIP	WHIP	ERA	DRA-	WARP	MPH	FB%	Whiff%	CSP
2019	CHW	MLB	26	3	2	0	7	7	34^{2}	33	4	4.4	11.9	46	41.5%	.322	1.44	5.19	107	0.2	91.6	52.0%	28.5%	45.4%
2020	CHW	MLB	27	0	2	0	4	2	7^{2}	9	1	3.5	7.0	6	28.0%	.333	1.57	8.22	195	-0.3	93.2	51.1%	23.3%	49.7%
2021	CHW	MLB	28	13	5	0	24	24	132^{2}	91	13	2.4	12.6	185	37.5%	.271	0.96	2.37	69	3.4	95.7	58.6%	33.2%	54.2%
2022 DC	*FA*	*MLB*	*29*	*8*	*6*	*0*	*22*	*22*	*124.7*	*97*	*19*	*2.9*	*11.3*	*157*	*39.3%*	*.275*	*1.10*	*3.17*	*79*	*2.4*	*95.2*	*57.8%*	*32.4%*	*53.2%*

Comparables: Steve Carlton, A.J. Burnett, Mark Langston

For years now, Rodón has walked out of the bullpen for home starts to the tune of "Rooster" by Alice in Chains. It's a gnarly, slow-burn grunge jam from the year he was born (with a somehow gnarlier music video) that's largely about enduring the horrors of the Vietnam War and emerging with a defiant will to survive. For a pre-game pump-up song, it's kind of a lot. Little kids are yelping out "Good luck, Carlos" while the late Layne Staley is croaking out the opening line of "Ain't found a way to kill me yet."

It's grown more thematically appropriate over time.

As Rodón fumbled through command inconsistency and command outages for four seasons sandwiched around shoulder and elbow surgeries, it was simply a vibe-setter. As he emerged in 2021 on a small make-good deal with an All-Star caliber, history-making first half, flashing restored top shelf velocity and striking out the world, it was an anthem. But while the narrator in "Rooster," is resolute, he is not safe. Rodón has top-of-the-rotation talent to build upon, but was dogged by shoulder fatigue, and the bullets screamed a little less violently down the stretch of his breakout campaign.

Drew Smyly LHP

Born: 06/13/89 Age: 33 Bats: L Throws: L Height: 6'2" Weight: 188 lb. Origin: Round 2, 2010 Draft (#68 overall)

YEAR	TEAM	LVL	AGE	W	L	SV	G	GS	IP	H	HR	BB/9	K/9	K	GB%	BABIP	WHIP	ERA	DRA-	WARP	MPH	FB%	Whiff%	CSP
2019	SA	AAA	30	1	0	0	3	3	12^{2}	10	2	2.1	12.8	18	27.6%	.308	1.03	4.97	90	0.1				
2019	TEX	MLB	30	1	5	1	13	9	51^{1}	64	19	6.0	9.1	52	28.0%	.310	1.91	8.42	133	-0.4	90.8	52.8%	23.9%	49.3%
2019	PHI	MLB	30	3	2	0	12	12	62^{2}	62	13	3.0	9.8	68	39.3%	.310	1.32	4.45	102	0.6	91.9	43.1%	27.9%	45.8%
2020	SF	MLB	31	0	1	0	7	5	26^{1}	20	2	3.1	14.4	42	41.7%	.310	1.10	3.42	57	0.9	93.8	45.6%	34.7%	50.8%
2021	ATL	MLB	32	11	4	0	29	23	126^{2}	133	27	2.9	8.3	117	38.4%	.300	1.37	4.48	104	0.9	92.2	46.7%	25.2%	57.9%
2022 DC	*FA*	*MLB*	*33*	*7*	*7*	*0*	*35*	*21*	*113.3*	*113*	*19*	*3.2*	*9.0*	*112*	*37.3%*	*.301*	*1.36*	*4.56*	*109*	*0.3*	*92.2*	*46.8%*	*26.3%*	*54.8%*

Comparables: Terry Mulholland, Gio González, Ricky Nolasco

Messing with a proven formula is a dangerous and bold strategy. It's been nearly 40 years since "New Coke" hit the scene and The Coca-Cola Company still catches a large amount of grief for switching things up. For Smyly, he appeared to have come across a winning recipe in San Francisco for this current phase of his career. It was simply to avoid going through the lineup a third time. That formula received some tweaking in Atlanta and things got really rough at times. Following a shortened season where his HR/FB percentage was below 8%, it skyrocketed back into the 20s and most of the damage was done when he faced a lineup for a third time in the game. This could mean that middle and/or long relief is in Smyly's future, but sometimes trying new roles is like trying Pepsi. It's not Coke, but it's still much better than New Coke.

Ryan Tepera RHP

Born: 11/03/87 Age: 34 Bats: R Throws: R Height: 6'1" Weight: 195 lb. Origin: Round 19, 2009 Draft (#580 overall)

YEAR	TEAM	LVL	AGE	W	L	SV	G	GS	IP	H	HR	BB/9	K/9	K	GB%	BABIP	WHIP	ERA	DRA-	WARP	MPH	FB%	Whiff%	CSP
2019	TOR	MLB	31	0	2	0	23	1	21^{2}	20	5	3.3	5.8	14	42.0%	.238	1.29	4.98	122	0.0	93.8	57.1%	26.3%	41.5%
2020	CHC	MLB	32	0	1	0	21	0	20^{2}	17	2	5.2	13.5	31	40.0%	.349	1.40	3.92	82	0.4	94.1	46.1%	44.0%	35.8%
2021	CHC	MLB	33	0	2	1	43	0	43^{1}	22	3	2.5	10.4	50	46.0%	.196	0.78	2.91	81	0.8	93.7	43.3%	35.0%	51.8%
2021	CHW	MLB	33	0	0	1	22	0	18	13	1	3.5	12.0	24	37.2%	.286	1.11	2.50	87	0.3	93.0	45.6%	35.9%	46.7%
2022 DC	*FA*	*MLB*	*34*	*3*	*3*	*0*	*71*	*0*	*61.7*	*50*	*8*	*3.4*	*10.7*	*73*	*42.7%*	*.278*	*1.19*	*3.52*	*86*	*0.7*	*93.6*	*45.5%*	*36.1%*	*46.7%*

Comparables: Jared Hughes, George Kontos, Joe Kelly

Tepera cutting his finger open on a door latch in September is the only thing that hindered a very clear improvement on a 2020 season where he very accidentally finished 18th in NL MVP voting. Fittingly, "Latch" by Disclosure & Sam Smith is probably the 18th-best song of the 2010s. Unless we can improve upon it...

Low 90s is enough
Tunneling makes it play up, babe
Low 90s is enouu-oo-ugh
Set your closer up, babe

Now Tep's earned a big payday
His ERA starts with 2
His finger's all that's in his way
A latch cut it in two

Nick Wittgren RHP

Born: 05/29/91 Age: 31 Bats: R Throws: R Height: 6'2" Weight: 216 lb. Origin: Round 9, 2012 Draft (#287 overall)

YEAR	TEAM	LVL	AGE	W	L	SV	G	GS	IP	H	HR	BB/9	K/9	K	GB%	BABIP	WHIP	ERA	DRA-	WARP	MPH	FB%	Whiff%	CSP
2019	CLE	MLB	28	5	1	4	55	0	57^{2}	47	10	2.3	9.4	60	39.1%	.253	1.08	2.81	94	0.8	92.5	66.5%	23.2%	50.6%
2020	CLE	MLB	29	2	0	0	25	0	23^{2}	18	4	2.3	10.6	28	32.2%	.259	1.01	3.42	102	0.2	93.1	60.7%	29.0%	48.8%
2021	CLE	MLB	30	2	9	1	60	1	62^{1}	61	13	2.5	8.8	61	46.1%	.294	1.25	5.05	93	0.8	92.5	66.3%	26.3%	57.4%
2022 DC	*FA*	*MLB*	*31*	*3*	*3*	*0*	*71*	*0*	*61.7*	*57*	*8*	*2.7*	*9.2*	*63*	*42.1%*	*.293*	*1.22*	*3.78*	*93*	*0.4*	*92.6*	*65.5%*	*26.1%*	*54.7%*

Comparables: Shawn Armstrong, Manny Acosta, Todd Coffey

Ahead of the 2020 season, we warned of a "nasty surprise lurking beneath the shiny surface of Wittgren's ERA:" a propensity to allow precariously loud contact. This nasty surprise, still present, failed to disrupt our subject's modest success in 2020. At last, in 2021, it reared its ugly head a third time in a way the baseball gods could no longer ignore. Wittgren teed up home run after home run while allowing hard contact more frequently than ever. His slider, while still his best pitch, fell flat, and his remaining offerings, including his newly introduced cutter, got absolutely pummeled. It's possible last year was the unlucky one and Wittgren, who does well to live in the Statcast-defined "shadows" of the zone, will revert to evading further death by hard contact. It's also possible the third time's a charm, and the nasty surprise finally got the last laugh. Expect the Guardians to find a more-reliable seventh-inning option.

Baseball's Imperfect Circle

by Patrick Dubuque

The grass and the crowds and the basepaths tend to fire up the quills of baseball's poets, but there's a certain imperceptible perfection to the ball itself. Regulation footballs are unpleasantly oversized compared to the Nerf versions that accompanied childhood; a full-sized basketball may as well be a boulder. Only the baseball fits the hands of youth and grows up alongside them. Pick one up, and the fingers find the seam like a needy puppy; the leather, smooth and taut, fits snugly into the well of the palm. Holding a baseball feels impossibly natural, like an instantaneous extension of the self; the potential energy of it is palpable in the fingertips.

The ball has always carried some hypnotic, mystical property. A home-run ball can transform a square yard of people into a writhing, entangled mass, releasing all of its inhibition in a single chemical reaction. In the disgusted heave of a bleacher bum, it can carry with it back into the field a tangible curse, a purification of the home team's disappointment. In baseball's golden era, kids would gather near ballplayers, fingers curling around chain link, begging for a ball just to have one. In recent years, people began to understand, if not exactly see, the ether that clung to the ball: milestones, history, even just the leftover fingerprints of the game's greats imbue something special, or especially valuable, into a piece of cork with some yarn and leather wrapped around it.

As the years passed, and the game slowly, inexorably changed with it, as the stadiums got lights and then jumbotrons and then luxury suites, mounds rose and fell, the strike zone moved like the tide, one element remained constant: the baseball. It hasn't, of course; it, too, is vulnerable to the whims of the moment. But the feeling that the ball is permanent, eternal, an unbroken link to the Elysian Fields, is a vital and understated aspect of baseball's mythology, its divine predestination. Everything else can change, and will; the ball still needs to be the one we tossed with our parents.

The baseball began as a humble thing, a core of rubber poured from melted shoes, wrapped loosely in yarn and covered with stitched horsehide. Even after the New York teams met in the mid-1850s to regulate the ball, each one was handmade and could be tailored by the home team, tight and live or loose and dead, to match the threat of the opponent. Even the live ones were only just; the material was not made to fly, making barehanded catches possible. That form of home-field advantage ended in 1876, when organized baseball's greatest pitcher and entrepreneur, Albert Spalding, undertook the manufacture of all "official" baseballs, inserting his brand as a requirement into the National League's rulebook itself. An advertisement in the 1901 version of *Spalding's Official Base Ball Guide* reads:

> **The Spalding Official League Ball.** Used exclusively by the National League, Minor Leagues, and by all Intercollegiate and other Associations for over a quarter of a century. Each ball wrapped in tinfoil and put in a separate box, and sealed in accordance with the regulations of the National League and American Association. Warranted to last a full game when used under ordinary conditions. No. 1. . . . $1.25.

That price, adjusted for inflation, comes to $40.67 in 2021 dollars. More than a century ago, the ball was already a piece of technology as much as a handicraft.

The ball underwent its most famous transformation during the World Series of 1910, as its rubber core was replaced by a lighter, livelier cork. The offensive explosion that resulted was nullified almost instantly by the pitchers themselves, who quickly learned to scuff and stain the ball back under their control—at least until the day Carl Mays struck down Ray Chapman. In the aftermath of that tragedy, the ball became more indelible; altering it became illegal, and umpires began swapping out balls that had lost their minted pearlescence. With each rule change, the ball moved closer to an unadulterated Platonic form, until 1934, when the American and National Leagues came to a compromise of how to construct a baseball (still manufactured by Spalding). The process: cushion-cork center; two wrappings of yarn; a special rubber-cement coating; two more wrappings of yarn; a horsehide cover. At some point, the name stamped on the front changed from Spalding to Rawlings, and the signatures of the commissioners came and went. But that was it. It's the same basic set of ingredients that comprise a baseball today . . . within specifications.

The next change to the baseball had nothing to do with the construction of the baseball. In the wake of the 1994–95 work stoppage, the sport struggled to mend its wounded reputation. One small step: a reversal of the longstanding policy of never giving balls to fans. The fielder underhanding the third out of the inning to some small child in the front rows, now almost obligatory, was once unheard of. With balls becoming unplayable with the slightest imperfection, the once-prohibitive cost of an official baseball became an obvious investment in an effort to create lifelong fans.

This sea change was quickly echoed by another one, inspired in part by the great home-run chase that revived the sport. In 1998, the home-run balls of Mark McGwire and Sammy Sosa were very clearly worth something, more than just any other ball, and when Todd McFarlane bought McGwire's 70th home-run ball for $3.2 million at auction, it was proof of a concept that had existed since the origin of the autograph, now extended to its logical conclusion. Game-used material was special, and teams hired authenticators to label and catalogue individual baseballs, quantifying their essence. It was, in a very real sense, an analog precursor to the modern fascination with the non-fungible token. Trading-card companies bought jerseys and baseballs and dissected them, sealing tiny squares of material within cardboard. Teams began selling scorecards and old jerseys at team stores. The baseball had changed again, going from equipment to artifact.

That should be the end of the story, a tale of a clumsy and inevitable march toward progress and purity, as if history were a spiral and not an orbit. Instead, the tides of the sport—rising pitcher velocity, increased reliever usage, higher spin rates and rising strikeouts—slid the sport into a little ace age, to the point when, in 2014, the league as a whole batted .255/.314/.386. The resulting isolated slugging percentage (.135) was the lowest produced since the pre-Coors early 1990s. And then, as the summer sun warmed the 2015 season, offense began to recover, and then some.

Early on, the explanation was that hitters, fueled by recent team-proprietary data, had unlocked the concept of "launch angle" and were intentionally trying to put the ball into the air instead of settling for weak contact. That sounded good, and was even somewhat true, as the league revealed in its second report on the subject in 2019. But another factor was involved: slightly lowered seams reduced the drag coefficient on the baseball in flight, causing it to fly farther than balls had in the past. You couldn't call it juicing, the league explained, because it wasn't an intentional alteration, just a variation in Rawlings' manufacturing process.

s

The intentionality was an important aspect. Only a few years before, Nippon Professional Baseball was consumed by scandal when it was revealed that the league commissioner, Ryozo Kato, had ordered the official baseballs to be doctored to restore that league's slumping offense. MLB officials had been slow to respond to their league's home-run surge but were finally pressured to do so by the publication of private research. When the 2021 season began, and the league began its crackdown on the widespread practice of doctoring baseballs with foreign substances, it made sure to clear the ball itself of any guilt. Multiple parks installed humidors to regulate the storage of baseballs. Under the advice of a team of experts, the league loosened the yarn on the newest balls, dampening them in hopes of restoring normality to the most homer-happy era of MLB history. Included in their statement was the following passage:

> Every baseball used in a 2021 MLB game, without exception, met existing specifications and performed as expected. In consultation with Rawlings and as previously announced, MLB approved a production change in the baseball that re-centered the ball within the specification range for Coefficient of Restitution (COR) and first approved game use of baseballs produced after the change for the 2021 season.

When you set the specifications, you can never fail to meet them. But while MLB has declared again and again that it hasn't made an organized effort to tamper with the baseball, it is equally apparent, based on the fluctuation of offense from one season to the next, that they have a solution to the problem. It's not that the ball itself has changed; it's that the world has. As the cameras count each rotation of the laces on a single fastball as it curls outward to graze the very edge of the black of the plate, the specifications that once defined an "official" baseball now feel a mile wide as we zoom further and further in.

And if that were the case, if each year's stock of baseballs were just a sliver of chaos to inject into each spring like a flap of a butterfly's wings, that would be fine. It wouldn't be ideal, by any means—we want to believe that Mike Trout is Mike Trout, somehow independent of both the electrolytes in his body and the height of the laces of the ball thrown to him—but it would have to be close enough, until the next stage of the game's evolution. It didn't feel right that the league was now controlling exactly what Mike Trout would look like, but you could at least grant the assumption that they were trying to get it right.

But just on the eve of the lockout, reporter Bradford William Davis, with the research of astrophysicist Meredith Wills, uncovered a massive secret: The league had used two different baseballs, with different drag coefficients, during the 2021 season. Major League Baseball confirmed Wills' findings, blaming the variation of baseballs on the industrial havoc brought about by the COVID-19 pandemic. But that confirmation only came in retrospect, in response to questioning for the article; players, including those in union leadership, didn't recall being notified by the league. Instead, a mistrustful player base saw the league pulling on their performances, and the salaries attached to them, like a marionette on strings.

This issue extends beyond labor strife. If the league is demonstrating intentionality about which of its "official" balls is allotted to each game, there are repercussions to that decision. This is particularly true as the league coincidentally pivots toward institutionalized gambling, particularly in the realm of daily fantasy sports. Gamblers have a tendency to prefer to know what it is they're gambling on.

But let's take the league at its word. Even if MLB had no intention of affecting the game with the ball, in 2016 or in 2021, the problem remains. The ball is no longer pure and perfect; we have zoomed in too far and seen too much. With each swing of the offensive pendulum, faith erodes. It isn't cheating, like the steroid scandal of the 1990s and early 2000s, but the result is largely identical. Fans can no longer believe what they see. Until the league can set more stringent specifications for itself, until we have the sense that we are, in fact, honing in one some ideal and not oversteering, there's no reason to believe in the baseball. And without that, there's remarkably little left.

A little while ago, I went on a walk in the wetlands behind my office. I weaved between stickerbush and swamp on paved bike paths, while ducks swam unhurriedly in their role as unpaid backdrop. I soon encountered a man, standing alone, who seized eye contact from me and held it, smiling.

"Look," the man said gesturing at the grass near my feet. "There's a snake."

I looked. Indeed, there was a snake, a harmless garter snake sunning itself in the remainder of the autumn light.

After an appropriate amount of snake viewing, I went on my way. As I returned, the man was still there, cheerfully engaged in his duty showing some other people the same thing he had shown me.

A few weeks later, I made the same walk. This time it was colder, grayer, and neither snake nor snake docent were at their posts. I continued on, enjoying the ducks, until I heard a sound like a low roar from behind the reeds. What I discovered was a hole.

It was a good-sized hole, rough hewn and natural looking, and water was pouring into it at a fair clip, perhaps a gallon a second. It made me slightly queasy to look upon it, as if I were witnessing one thousandth of an eldritch horror. I looked around, but all of the other people on the path passed by without the slightest notice, seemingly unaffected by the fact that this lake was missing what seemed like a fairly vital piece of lake. At that moment, I realized that this was it: This is how I become a snake docent, doomed to stand here and beg people, "Look at this! Make sense of this piece of our world!"

Eventually, I returned to my office, because we all have to return to our offices, and left the lake behind to empty out or exist in perpetual Escherdom, however it needed to be. But I struggled to stop thinking about it and soon realized the reason why: We need lakes to behave like lakes, i.e., to have water at the top and ground underneath. Not because this is the ideal form of lake—I am open to thoughtful reinterpretations—but because life is already hard and confusing, and there are trillions of instances of sense data perpetually bombarding our poor embattled brains. I cannot afford to have to re-establish each lake as genuine. Our lives are founded on a certain level of trust.

So it is with the baseball. When we watch the sport, when we inevitably compare it to what came before and what will come after, assess each exact moment for its joy and heartbreak and greatness, it requires the same unconscious, intricate calculation of perspective, adjustments for era and context. It is exhausting enough. We need the baseball itself to serve as an anchor, as solid ground: not necessarily as a link to nostalgia, but as a link to our own memories and emotions. If we can't depend on the ball, we can't depend on anything we see or feel. And baseball, the sport, is nothing if not felt.

—Patrick Dubuque is an author of Baseball Prospectus.

Top 101 Prospects

by Jeffrey Paternostro, Jarrett Seidler and John Trupin

1. Bobby Witt Jr., SS/3B, Kansas City Royals

Witt was already one of the 10 best prospects in the game when he started tormenting Cactus League pitchers last spring. He looked so good that the Royals nearly took him north as a 20-year-old with no professional game experience other than 37 post-draft tilts in the complex. Instead, they gave him a merely aggressive assignment to Double-A—bypassing both A-ball levels—and he absolutely mashed for the entire first half before carbon copying his performance in Triple-A in the second half. Overall, Witt hit .290/.361/.575 while only taking two plate appearances all season against pitchers younger than him. That slugging percentage is more than 70 points higher than Adley Rutschman posted at the same levels . . . and Witt is 28 months younger. Witt is a fine defender at shortstop, but a mix of his readiness and an impending infield playing-time logjam might slide him over to third; he could win Gold Gloves there. With absolutely no disrespect to the next two players on this list, Witt is now the best prospect in the minors.

2. Adley Rutschman, C, Baltimore Orioles

Rutschman was the incumbent. He was second on last year's list behind Wander Franco. He was first on our Midseason Top 50. He is a switch-hitter who hit for average, got on base and hit for power in the upper minors in 2021 while showing off one of if not the best defensive skill sets among minor-league catchers. When comparing the elite prospects in baseball, it often comes down to minor quibbles. We're not completely convinced Rutschman will have an obviously plus offensive tool set, as he doesn't always make ideal contact, especially from the left side. He was a little bit old for his levels, as the Orioles could have easily had him up in the majors around the same time as Wander Franco; like Franco, Rutschman was probably ready in 2020. Finally, catching prospects tend to see more offensive regression once the realities of the day-to-day grind of being a major-league backstop set in. Those are ultimately minor quibbles though, and Rutschman is likely to be one of the three or four best catchers in baseball as soon as he gets the call.

3. Julio Rodríguez, OF, Seattle Mariners

From Everett, Washington, to Little Rock, Arkansas, with an impressive layover as the star of the Dominican Republic's bronze-medal-winning Olympic team in Tokyo, Rodríguez terrorized opposing pitchers in 2021. With the physical and mental makeup that presidents of baseball and business operations, alike, dream of, Rodríguez ran an OPS over 1.000 despite facing pitchers who were his elders in every single game of his season. Rodríguez's towering frame is lean and muscular, and he managed to add speed, both on the stopwatch and in the box score, stealing 21 bases in 26 attempts with his stateside affiliates. The potential for 40-home-run power remains self-evident from both his frame and the eye-popping exit velocities his quick wrists generate. Though there's always the risk he wobbles in the process of refining his swing for elevation, his barrel control should entrench him in the middle of a contending lineup sooner rather than later.

4. Spencer Torkelson, 3B/1B, Detroit Tigers

Torkelson was the first-overall pick in 2020—not a surprise. He was announced as a third baseman—that was a bit of a surprise. The nicest thing you can say about his defense at the hot corner is that he battles it to a draw, at times. He also hits like a premier first baseman, so it's really not going to matter where he stands on the field. Torkelson did exactly what you would want your top college bat to do in his first taste of the minors; he laid waste to them. He's a patient hitter and picks the right pitches to hit hard. The only thing keeping him from making the top troika on this list a Fab Four is that there was a little more swing-and-miss in the upper levels than expected. So, he might only hit .280 with 30-plus homers. Ah well.

5. Grayson Rodriguez, RHP, Baltimore Orioles

Rodriguez is everything you could ask for in a pitching prospect. Start with his amateur background: a well-built, projectable, 6-foot-5 Texas prep arm drafted in the first half of the first round in 2018. Since debuting as a pro, he has continually leveled up in every look we've had. His fastball now sits consistently in the upper 90s with late life. His slider now projects as plus-plus. His changeup projects as a plus offering and tunnels very well off his slider. He has great feel for spin, enough so that his curveball would be the best offspeed pitch for half of the pitchers on this list. He flashes a good cutter he doesn't really need. He throws strikes and paints corners. Last year, we wrote in this space that if Rodriguez ever threw 100 innings in a season there was a pretty good chance he'd be one of the best pitching prospects in baseball by the end of it. He threw 103 innings in 2021, but we were wrong: he's not one of the best, he's *the* best.

6. Riley Greene, OF, Detroit Tigers

In 2020, Greene torched spring training, the alternate site, and the fall instructional league to such a degree that one could mentally fill in his player card as if he had a great season at the full-season A-ball levels. The Tigers sure acted like he did, sending him to ~~the Eastern League~~ Double-A Northeast as a 20-year-old. He tore it up there and then shredded Triple-A even more for a 40-game denouement. He has a majestic, balanced, left-handed swing and hits the ball hard to all fields, projecting for plus-or-better hit and power. He's capable of making spectacular highlight-reel catches in the outfield, although he might end up being more suited to a corner than center if he continues to grow. Torkelson vs. Greene has been a common debate since Torkelson was drafted two years ago. We give the ever-so-slight edge to Tork right now, but it's extremely close; they're both tracking to be major forces in Detroit's rebuild.

7. Jordan Walker, 3B, St. Louis Cardinals

Well more than half of all qualified major-league hitters socked more than 20 home runs last year. It has become a power hitter's game. But there are power hitters, and then there is Jordan Walker. At 19 years old and with a fair amount of physical projection left in his 6-foot-5 frame, Walker already hits the ball about as hard as your favorite major-league slugger. Power is the carrying tool here, but it's far from the only notable one. Walker has an advanced approach for his age and experience level, and while he swings hard enough that batting titles are likely not in his future, his selectivity and quality of contact in the zone portend a potential plus hit tool. He runs well and plays an average third base, at present, but the physical gains he is likely to experience should send him to an outfield corner or even first base. As with Torkelson, the bat will play anywhere.

8. Shane Baz, RHP, Tampa Bay Rays

Baz is certainly a less-perfect pitching prospect than Rodriguez. He barely throws his changeup, relying very heavily on his fastball and his two breaking pitches. He has a past history of significant command and control issues; he'd never had a walk rate below four per nine innings prior to 2021. His arm path is on the shorter side, so his delivery looks less visually pleasing. But here's the most important part, the reason Baz is a Top-10 prospect: Baz throws the easiest 80-grade fastball you'll ever see. It effortlessly comes out of his hand in the upper 90s with high spin and an optimized approach angle. With that profile, he's going to befuddle a hell of a lot of hitters with high fastballs, and the elite-stuff profile doesn't stop there. His slider grades out with plus-plus potential, too, and obliterated right-handed hitters after his call-up. Against lefties, he relied more on his soft stuff: a loopier curveball and the occasional change, both with success. Baz's command improved greatly last year, enough that the "bullpen risk" dial was turned way down, and he was impressive enough that he started Game 2 of the Division Series for the Rays. If he keeps throwing strikes, he could be a front-line starter as soon as this year.

9. Marco Luciano, SS, San Francisco Giants

Electrifying batting practices turned into eye-opening game power for the 19-year-old Luciano last year. Some of the best bat speed anywhere and a swing geared for elevation make Luciano a particularly promising bet to reach his offensive ceiling. He stands slightly open and crouched at the plate, engaging his stout lower half to great effect with a short stroke that can help him adjust when fooled. The Giants did not handle the teenage slugger with kid gloves, and there were periods when he did, indeed, get fooled. Luciano got reps at Low-A, High-A, the Futures Game and the Arizona Fall League. Considering his tools and performance despite relatively minimal game experience, we're bullish on Luciano's ability to adjust and prosper. Luciano's foot speed and glovework suggest the hot corner lies in his future, but his arm is strong, and the bat has the potential to play anywhere on the diamond.

10. Francisco Álvarez, C, New York Mets

Álvarez hits the ball as hard as any prospect in the minors and knows what pitches to swing at. He slugged .538 as a teenager at High-A after his Ted Williams–like slash line at Low-A forced a promotion before Memorial Day. With no real red flags on his health or defense, Álvarez is likely to stay at catcher. Does anything else *really* matter? Yes, he's short and stout. His swing setup is a little funky and open. He doesn't run well and has no obvious fallback position if he has to move out from behind the dish. Who cares? He's a catcher who hits nukes all over the field! That's one of the most valuable profiles in baseball.

11. CJ Abrams, SS, San Diego Padres

Abrams was well on his way to a spot in the top 10—and perhaps one in the San Diego lineup, as well—when he fractured his left tibia and sprained the medial collateral ligament in that knee during an infield collision last July. For a prospect that derives a lot of his value from speed and up-the-middle defense, this is concerning. Let's look at the bright side, though. Abrams jumped to Double-A as a 20-year-old with only 34 pro games under his belt. He hit a smidge under .300, showed off elite-level speed and a smooth glove at shortstop. He's not likely to be one of the 60-odd percent of qualified hitters smacking 20 bombs, but anything he hits to the outfield is a threat to be a double, and anything in the gap is a threat to be a triple, and those extra bases add up, too. Hopefully he'll be back on the field this year showing no lingering effects from his injury or lost time, because he's a potential impact player for San Diego in the near-term.

12. Oneil Cruz, SS, Pittsburgh Pirates

Cruz is a unique prospect: a 6-foot-7 shortstop flashing 80-grade raw power and enough agility and instincts to play the position. For years, everyone assumed something in that profile had to give—most likely either the power wouldn't translate to games, or his body would fill out and move him to a corner spot. He needed to keep the swing-and-miss manageable while not sacrificing hard contact to reach his offensive potential—a tall task given his very long levers—and he's three inches taller than any regular shortstop in MLB history. Then Cruz made it up last September . . . still a perfectly adequate defensive shortstop, with manageable swing-and-miss, now showing top-of-the-line hard-hit data in games (his second big-league hit registered the hardest exit velo for a Pirate in 2021). We're still not sure he's going to remain at shortstop for very long, and we're not sure he's going to make enough contact because we're deep in uncharted water, but some of the data points we can chart show him navigating towards "superstar."

13. Brett Baty, 3B/OF, New York Mets

Baty has a tremendous swing, makes great swing decisions, and can flash 80 raw power on the right day. A 6-hit/7-game-power projection is firmly within reach, and his production at High-A and Double-A last year was certainly strong. One caveat from the data that bears out in live looks: he hits the ball on the ground a *lot* right now. This may be a partially fixable approach issue more than a swing issue; for better and worse, he likes taking what the pitcher gives him instead of trying to uppercut everything to Mars. His swing *does* have some natural loft to it, and, when he swings up, he can lift balls to places almost no one else can, especially the opposite-field power alley. But if you've got top-end raw, you really don't want to hit wormburners half the time. Defensively, he has solid building blocks at third base—plus arm with the actions and agility for the hot corner—but his inconsistency there and the major-league team's potential needs have led the Mets to start playing him in the outfield, as well. Early reviews of his performance on the grass suggest that he should be fine in a corner outfield slot in due time.

14. Anthony Volpe, SS, New York Yankees

Last year, in a season evenly split between Low-A and High-A, Volpe put up one of the most dominant performances relative to league and age context in the minors, mashing at a .294/.423/.604 clip, good for a combined 144 DRC+. It was his first full-season experience, and he turned 20 just a week before the minor-league season started. It was a surprising slugging output, particularly given that he'd been a hit-over-power prospect coming out of the draft. But Volpe got a lot stronger and optimized his swing mechanics during the pandemic year while working with former Baseball Prospectus prospect writer and professional scout Jason Lefkowitz; Volpe was one of the few prospects who may have demonstrably benefited from the break. His overall defensive abilities are above-average, though his foot speed and range may slide him to second or third eventually. Given that he maintained his feel for contact with vastly improved power, Volpe now projects as a difference-maker no matter where he ends up.

15. Noelvi Marte, SS, Seattle Mariners

One of the youngest players in full-season affiliated baseball last year, Marte held his own against older and more experienced competition. As top-tier international signees from the same class on the same big-league arrival schedule within organizations whose affiliates play in the same leagues at all but one level, Marte and Marco Luciano have frequently been contrasted against one another and likely will continue to be. Luciano's offensive ceiling is higher and more explosive, while Marte's agility and glovework give him slightly more of a fighting chance to stick up the middle. Marte's swing is keyed off a leg-kick load that tends to produce backspin, though most of his power is to the pull side. His arm strength fits on the left side of the infield, like Luciano's, and Marte runs better, but the truth is both players are brimming with star-level potential.

16. Jeremy Peña, SS, Houston Astros

Peña seemed poised for a 2021 breakout coming off strong reports from the Dominican Republic Professional Baseball League (LIDOM) the prior winter. A left-wrist injury at the alternate site in April put the kibosh on that until August, but he more than made up for the lost time upon his return, scorching the ball for a month in Triple-A and putting himself in contention for a spot on the Astros' playoff roster. He didn't end up contributing to the American League pennant and will have to settle for being the heir apparent for Carlos Correa in Houston. Peña doesn't have Correa's upside with the bat, although the fact that his power gains continued even after a wrist injury is promising. He is close to Correa's equal on defense, a silky shortstop with a plus arm and plus foot speed who should compete for Gold Gloves. We'd like to see a slightly longer track record of this kind of offensive performance, but any confirmation or refutation is now likely to come in the majors.

17. Marcelo Mayer, SS, Boston Red Sox

Although health and Boston's willingness to let him play right away meant we've seen Mayer handle the disparate array of talent levels that make up the Florida Complex League, nothing he did there altered the expectations we had for him when he was drafted fourth-overall last July. The projection here is primarily built on, well, projection. Mayer is smooth in the field, and his arm is plenty strong, so even with middling foot speed he shouldn't struggle to stick at shortstop. The lanky, 6-foot-3 teenager has the frame to add muscle, which could help him build out his simple, sweet swoosh of a swing to produce laser line drives and towering big flies to pair with his already-patient approach. If the power comes, it would complete a superstar's toolkit. If it doesn't, well, J.P. Crawford panned out alright.

18. Henry Davis, C, Pittsburgh Pirates

Sure, Davis was the number-one overall pick last year in part because he signed for a well-below-slot $6.5 million (less than what any of next three picks signed for) which, in turn, allowed the Pirates to select three top prep prospects—lefty Anthony Solometo, outfielder Lonnie White Jr. and righty Bubba Chandler—with their next three picks and sign them to big-money deals. Still, Davis was a viable 1.1 selection on talent alone given his profile as an advanced, power-hitting catcher coming out of Louisville. He lifts the ball easily with plus bat speed, leading to hard, elevated contact, though his oddball setup and uppercut swing path leaves some unanswered hit-tool questions against higher-level pitching. Behind the dish, he has a very strong arm but is still rounding out the framing and receiving elements. If he doesn't get all the way there and has to move to another position down the road, he's fast and agile enough to fallback on third base or the outfield. If he's a catcher all the way up, his power output will make him an All-Star.

19. Cade Cavalli, RHP, Washington Nationals

Due to injuries and inconsistent command when he was on the mound, Cavalli never put together the kind of dominant college campaign that would have landed him among the top arms in the 2020 draft. So how do you go from the 22nd-overall pick to 19th best prospect in baseball? Well, the stuff was never in question with Cavalli, and he finally had that full, healthy season to show off his potential top-of-the-rotation wares in 2021. He made it all the way to Triple-A, striking out 12 per nine inings, flashing triple-digit heat and two potential plus breaking balls. His 123 innings last year were more than he threw across three seasons for the Sooners, and while he still has a little more injury risk and a shorter history of strike-throwing than the arms ranked ahead of him, Cavalli has very much the same upside.

20. Jack Leiter, RHP, Texas Rangers

Prepare to be reminded early and often for the next decade or two that Jack is the son of Al, the retired effectively wild lefty with a killer cutter. The younger Leiter was a high school classmate of Volpe's at Delbarton Prep in Morristown, New Jersey, and was a comparable or even better prospect at the time, but Leiter was considered unsignable and matriculated at Vanderbilt. By the 2021 season, he was the top collegiate pitching prospect in the country, although he wasn't the Friday-night starter for Vandy due to the presence of 2019 College World Series hero Kumar Rocker. Leiter regularly gets his fastball into the mid-90s and shapes it with a high, flat approach angle that hitters perceive as rise; he can also throw a nifty sinker to mix it up. His curveball has graded as a future out-pitch since high school, and his slider caught up to it in college. As you'd expect, given that his father is both a former MLB All-Star and a current MLB Network pitching analyst, his mechanics are sound and repeatable. As far as pitching prospects with no professional innings go, Leiter is about as high-probability as it gets.

21. George Kirby, RHP, Seattle Mariners

If you gauge it by his own track record, Kirby's trademark command cratered in 2021, but relative to almost every other pitcher in minor-league baseball, he continued on one of the higher-floor trajectories a starting pitcher can travel. In 2021, the 2019 first-rounder issued his first walk in a competitive game since May 4, 2019, when he was pitching for Elon University. He'd ultimately yield a handful more free passes but made short work of High-A and looked impressive in his first few tastes of Double-A. Kirby's motion is simple and repeatable, the only flare in it is a slight coil in his leg lift that helps him reach back for impressive velocity. After working in the low 90s in college, Kirby now sits 95–98 with his fastball and has clipped triple-digits repeatedly. His changeup is his most impressive secondary, and he rounds out his repertoire with a solid slider and a slower, more vertically breaking curveball. The limiting factor on Kirby, at the moment, is the lack of a wipeout offspeed pitch, but if he maintains something close to his present velocity and command, his blend of security and potential will continue to be one that few pitching prospects can rival.

22. Gabriel Moreno, C, Toronto Blue Jays

Moreno is ranked third among catchers on this year's 101, although, if we were more certain of a full-time future behind the plate, he'd be above Henry Davis. Moreno's 2021 season was truncated at both ends—first by a groin injury and then by a thumb fracture—but he hit .360 when he was on the field. That will get your attention. A reincarnated Rogers Hornsby with modern swing analytics and training might not hit .360 in the majors, but Moreno has the kind of blink-and-you-miss-it bat speed and advanced ability to barrel pitches that suggest .300 is very much in play. His defensive development is not quite as far along. The injuries cost him some much needed reps, and the Blue Jays were already planning to try him out at other spots when he hit the injured list in June. Moreno is a little undersized for an everyday catcher, and his receiving remains rough, but 70 hit and 55 power is a nice fit at any spot, and he should be able to don the tools of ignorance a few days a week, at least.

23. Tyler Soderstrom, C/1B, Oakland Athletics

Like Moreno, Soderstrom's ranking is hurt by a lack of confidence that he'll catch in the majors. He was a first-round pick on the strength of his future hit and power tools more than his glove, and while he has the arm to control the running game, 15 passed balls in 38 games behind the plate last year—he missed time with a back injury—is an indication of how far the rest of the defensive profile has to go. There's going to be a temptation to move him to a corner soon, because the bat is ready for tougher challenges than A-ball, and he has already been exposed to first base. Soderstrom has 30-home-run pop and an already-selective approach for a teenager in full-season ball. He could easily be the best offensive catcher in baseball, if he can stick there as even a passably below-average defender, but he's more likely to be a very good slugger at another position.

24. Max Meyer, RHP, Miami Marlins

The single best offspeed pitch of any player on this list—any player in the entire minors, in fact—is Meyer's slider. If it's not an 80-grade projection, it's close. The pitch sits in the high 80s and nips the low 90s with sharp downward tilt and hard break. He can use it to get chases out of the zone or called strikes in the zone. We expect to name it one of the best breaking pitches in the majors in a future version of this book. His fastball has plus-plus velocity but is not a true plus-plus pitch, at present, due to its shape and natural sinking action. Meyer barely threw his changeup in college because he didn't need to, but he's been focusing on developing it as a pro. He's in the right system for that, and the pitch showed signs of advancing into at least a credible third offering in 2021. While he still carries some of the relief risk stereotypical of a short, slider-heavy righty, he went straight to Double-A and cruised for most of the season as a starter. He could be the next great one out of Miami's underrated pitching development factory.

25. Zac Veen, OF, Colorado Rockies

The Cody Bellinger/Kyle Tucker lookalikes will not all pan out, but when you see Veen get into a baseball, it's easy to see why folks buy in. Veen's body is 84 percent legs and arms, long levers that he wields in a back-thumping uppercut swing that can get exposed by elevated velocity but punishes nigh anything else. He's a long strider, and despite speed that will likely take a step back as he adds muscle to his lean frame, he may remain a reasonable threat on the bases. Veen's patience at the plate and obvious power will help him get on base, but his ability to consistently put the bat on the ball will be the question mark that bobs above his head all the way through the minors, particularly after he racked up 126 punchouts in 479 plate appearances at Low-A. A Veen that navigates that challenge skillfully could prompt fans to bring their gloves when they ascend to The Rooftop in right field at Coors Field.

26. Robert Hassell III, OF, San Diego Padres

A decade after Bryce Harper graced the cover of Sports Illustrated, the powers that be of baseball prospectdom convened at the summit of Mt. Scout. "What," they wondered, "if we gave that same swing to a new prospect, but this time, instead of a muscle-bound former catcher, it belonged to a lithe outfielder whose power was a question mark?" And so it was that we were provided with Hassell, whose barrel control helps set him apart from many teenage hitters. His ability to get the best part of the bat to the ball all over the plate with plus bat speed helps him project to be an above-average hitter who could eventually feature 20- to 25-home-run power. As a 20-year-old, Hassell will still be quite young for High-A this year, and he'll hope to improve upon last year's numbers there while shoring up his defensive acumen to solidify himself as a tri-positional outfielder.

27. Brennen Davis, OF, Chicago Cubs

Neither Davis' stat line—an .860 OPS across 99 games and three levels—nor his raw tool grades scream top-30 prospect. But he doesn't have a real weakness in his game, either. We will first note that he played almost all of those 99 games in the upper minors as a 21-year-old. Then we will add that Davis is a plus runner who should be a fine defender in center field. We'll further strengthen our case by mentioning that his above-average bat speed and barrel control mean he's already hitting for more game power than his batting practices or still-projectable frame would suggest. Perhaps Davis doesn't have a standout carrying tool at present, but he has a chance to roll a bunch of 6s on his scout sheet. That is the kind of center fielder that makes All-Star games.

28. Nolan Gorman, 2B/3B, St. Louis Cardinals

Gorman has been passed as a prospect by Jordan Walker, the other power-hitting third baseman in Cardinal red—or occasionally powder blue—and isn't even a primary third baseman anymore. Likely in deference to Nolan Arenado and the six years left on his contract, Gorman started taking grounders at second base this past spring. Gorman moves well enough there that, with advanced positioning data, he should be average, and his plus arm will be a weapon on double-play turns. More importantly, the keystone is an available spot to get his bat in the lineup, and, despite the added responsibility of learning a new position on the fly, Gorman continued to show a potential average-hit/plus-plus-power combo at the plate in the upper minors. Pretty soon, Arenado won't be the only Nolan shining on the dirt in St. Louis.

29. Nick Gonzales, 2B, Pittsburgh Pirates

For a short guy, Gonzales takes some mighty hacks. He has slugged better than .550 at nearly every level he has played at: all three years of college, 2019 on the Cape and 2021 in High-A. The one exception is that he slugged "only" .549 in the Arizona Fall League last year. Gonzales' hands are tremendously quick to the ball, he's strong and he swings up. His approach is advanced, and he has hit for average at all levels so far, although the ferocity of his swing does lead to a moderate amount of swing-and-miss. Second base is an excellent fit for his solid actions and footwork but so-so arm strength. The Pirates were conservative in his first pro season, leaving him in A-ball, but he could move quickly now.

30. Luis Matos, OF, San Francisco Giants

Matos was one of the breakout prospect bats of 2021. He had very few pro reps after being one of the Giants top international-free-agent signings in 2018, but his full-season debut flashed all five tools in abundance. Matos has a smaller, squarish frame, but his plus bat speed, quick wrists and torquey swing should generate plus game power down the line. Matos will need to refine his approach against better competition, but he already shows the kind of advanced bat-to-ball ability that will give him plenty of runway to make those kinds of adjustments. His defensive tools range from average to slightly above, but the 19-year-old has a good shot to stick in center, where his potential plus offensive tools would make him a first-division regular.

31. Josh Jung, 3B, Texas Rangers

Jung isn't the, er, youngest prospect in this group—in fact, Adley Rutschman is the only position player in the top 50 who is older, and by all of six days. (Both will turn 24 right around when this book will reach most of you. Happy birthday, guys!) We haven't held Jung's veritably wizened status against him, however. The 2019 draftee has mashed every step of his pro career and splashed some paint on one gray area in his game: whether or not he had big-league power. Jung used the 2020 layoff to refine his swing for a bit more loft, and while he did swing and miss a touch more often in 2021, he was comfortably within the realm of lesser concern for his first season in the high minors. He's no Adrían Beltré at the hot corner, but, at both Frisco and Round Rock, Jung looked like the future of the third-base position in Arlington. In a suddenly invigorated infield, that future could arrive as soon as Opening Day 2022.

32. Hunter Greene, RHP, Cincinnati Reds

Greene regularly sits above 100 miles per hour with his fastball. If he keeps that up in the majors, he'll be the first starting pitcher of the verified-pitch-data era to do so. That's enough propane that concerns about the shape of his fastball aren't going to matter a whole lot. Greene's tremendous arm speed also leads to a high aptitude for the slide piece; his slider should get to at least plus and isn't far from there already. Given that he was a first-round prospect as a shortstop, as well, he's very fluid and moves well on the mound. His changeup needs further development—get ready to read that a lot in the rest of this list—and he missed a lot of time around Tommy John surgery several years ago, but Greene is closing in on the majors, and, you know, he throws it up to 104 mph with a plus slider.

33. George Valera, OF, Cleveland Guardians

It's difficult to identify a major-league hitter that has a swing quite like Valera's. It's funky and violent, with a seemingly purposeful kind of awkwardness to it. Perhaps it's best described it as resembling a drawing of Bryce Harper's swing made from memory . . . with your non-dominant hand . . . while blindfolded. That swing allows Valera to hit absolute laser beams to all fields despite being listed at a probably generous 5-foot-11 and 185 pounds. It would be easier to project Valera as a perennial 30-home-run hitter in the majors if his swing looked like that of the *actual* Bryce Harper—who, to be fair, was already an All-Star at this age—but sometimes unusual swings lead to unusual results. For all the hitchy, twitchy weirdness that precedes Valera squaring up a fastball, he does square them up, and he knows which ones to square up. Knowing is in fact half the battle here. The rest should be covered by his prodigious bat speed.

34. Corbin Carroll, OF, Arizona Diamondbacks

It was . . . one week in the month of May
When Carroll was destroying balls like Juan Uribe
Five tools, that's what we expect
And soon we'd rate him as a top prospect
Sweet swing from the left-hand side
He hits, but he can also run, just look at his slide
Eventually, he had surgery
Separated shoulder means his future's murky . . .

35. MJ Melendez, C, Kansas City Royals

The 2019 Wilmington Blue Rocks may have been the last Carolina League champions, but that season was an unmitigated disaster for some of Kansas City's best hitting prospects. The team put up a .618 OPS. Nick Pratto hit .191 with no power and struck out 34.7 percent of the time. Kyle Isbel hit an empty .216. And Melendez, the number-67 prospect on the 2019 Top 101, hit .163 and struck out in 39.4 percent of his plate appearances. We don't really know what happened there. Frawley Stadium is one of the worst places in affiliated baseball to hit, but even that doesn't explain it all. (Wilmington changed affiliations to Washington in 2021, and a way-less-talented Blue Rocks squad of Nats "prospects" put up a .692 OPS last year.) What we do know is that Melendez came out in 2021 and ran it back to 2018—and then some—shrugging off his ghastly 2019. The lefty hit 41 dingers between Double-A and Triple-A along with by far the best contact rates of his career, pushing himself forward towards the City of Fountains. One slight problem he's about to run into: Salvador Perez just set the single-season record for home runs hit by a primary catcher, and Perez is a better defender by reputation.

36. Miguel Vargas, 3B, Los Angeles Dodgers

An old scouting cliché is that the doubles a player hits when he's 19 or 20 will naturally turn into home runs as he physically matures. That conventional wisdom predated the widespread industry realization that organizations can use player development to increase prospects' game power irrespective of a projectable teenaged bat filling out. The Dodgers are one of the best developmental organizations for hitters. Miguel Vargas is significantly bigger and stronger than he was two years ago. Those powers combined to lift Vargas from seven home runs in 2019 to 23 home runs last year. Consequently, his 38 doubles in 2019 shrunk to 27 in 2021. This is all an oversimplification, but nevertheless a very good result for Vargas' prospect status. Oh, and he kept hitting .300 and getting on base, as well. Vargas is significantly bigger than most third basemen now, but he has seen more supplemental time at second base than first, which is also a very Dodgers thing.

37. Alek Thomas, OF, Arizona Diamondbacks

Consistent, young and big league-ready, Thomas hails from the five-average-or-better-tools school of prospects. Though often treated as safe, there is risk in a player reliant on doing everything decently, and we've seen even more impressive bats than Thomas struggle out of the gate or put together uneven performances early in their careers (see: Kelenic, Jarred; or Benintendi, Andrew). To muddle things further, while Thomas has enough speed to stretch doubles into triples, he has never shown a knack for base stealing. Still, the 5-foot-11 outfielder has a lot to fall back on. He moves fluidly in the outfield and will be able to handle center field if called upon. That gives a bit more leeway to his production at the plate, where he converts his athletic frame into a max-effort lefty swing that has met the high minors with great success. Thomas has a floaty leg lift that he uses to time pitches but could be exposed against big-league breaking balls. He'll be just 22 in 2022, however; there will be time to adjust.

38. Liover Peguero, SS, Pittsburgh Pirates

Peguero was acquired from Arizona in the first Starling Marte trade, a deal the Diamondbacks would very much like to have back right now. Peguero was assigned to High-A to be Nick Gonzales' double-play partner in one of the better keystone-prospect pairings in recent memory. Evaluators came away split as to who was the better prospect; after a season of watching them side by side, we ever so slightly lean towards Gonzales and his greater present skills. Peguero has excellent feel for the bat and plus bat speed, projecting to above-average outcomes for both his hit and power tools. He's a fluid defender at shortstop, and he's now on the cusp of being a 70 runner, too. He's still rounding out his game, but he was better than average with the stick at the age of 20 in High-A, and he is filled with offensive and defensive upside.

39. Keibert Ruiz, C, Washington Nationals

At long last, 2021 freed Ruiz from the yoke and crushing pressure of needing to outperform Will Smith to win a role on the perennially World Series–contending Dodgers. Sent to the nation's capital, Ruiz can finally focus on the simpler things in this game, like replacing the superstar(s) he was traded for by quickly becoming an All-Star catcher, thus helping convince Juan Soto to stay with the Nationals. You know, normal rebuilding-club things. Beyond his change of scenery, things went quite well for Ruiz in 2021. He put his disappointing 2019 season well behind him with a stellar performance at the plate between Triple-A and the bigs, and his 24 home runs across the two levels doubled his prior career high. Considering that slugging came with no expense to his typical contact-geared approach, Nationals fans may be treated to a rare profile behind the dish in coming years: single-digit walk and strikeout rates/easy double-digit home-run rates. Trea bien.

40. Nick Yorke, 2B, Boston Red Sox

Yorke was considered a reach when Boston selected him in the first round of the 2020 draft. Ideally, you want your first-round prep bat to have oodles of tools projection and/or a fair bit of defensive value. Yorke was a hit-tool-driven, mostly filled-out, high school second baseman. The consensus was his hit tool was an easy plus, but there have been many prep bats given similar accolades who never really hit to that level, even in the minors. Well, Yorke promptly went out and hit .323 in Low-A. He then hit .333 in High-A. He showed a little more pop than expected, to boot. It gets harder now. Double-A is often a stern test of the performance-over-tools profile, but Yorke's performance has passed every test so far, and we reckon, if you re-ran the 2020 draft today, he'd go a bit higher than 17th.

41. Mick Abel, RHP, Philadelphia Phillies

Abel was on the verge of a huge breakout in the first half of 2021, regularly sitting mid-90s and touching 99 with impressive spin and vertical break on his hellacious fastball. He was ramping up towards fuller outings and reached a season high of 79 pitches on July 21st, when the Phillies backed off over a mix of workload concerns, COVID and minor shoulder fatigue. Abel did not pitch again until fall instructs, where he was throwing just as hard as he threw during the regular season. Abel spent much of his game action throwing a lot of fastballs and trying to improve his command, but he also threw a plus-flashing slider. Whether he can get either his curveball or changeup to become a viable pitch is an open question, as is his workload, but, all in all, it was a successful debut for one of the highest-upside arms in the minors.

42. Nick Lodolo, LHP, Cincinnati Reds

A sinker/slurve command guy? In this economy?!? As modern pitch design has developed, we've come to realizations about certain things we always sort of knew. A main one is that four-seam fastballs with high life—like Abel's—are, as a general rule, going to strike out a heck of a lot more batters than lower-velocity, lower-spin sinkers down in the zone—like Lodolo's. That doesn't mean Lodolo doesn't have an effective fastball, it just means he's probably never going to dominate with it, unless he discovers Dustin May-quality, seam-shifted wake. Lodolo's best offspeed pitch is a slurvy, sweeping breaking ball which he manipulates quite a lot in speed and movement; it's right on the borderline of being a distinct slider or curveball, if you care about pitch nomenclature. His changeup adds another usable offering. He has superlative command of everything and should be in the majors soon, so long as the shoulder fatigue that ended his season doesn't turn into a long-term issue.

43. Daniel Espino, RHP, Cleveland Guardians

Velocity only earns the scrutiny of others. Once that scrutiny is focused upon a player, it's incumbent upon them to make something of it. Espino was one of a few prospects to earn pre-draft notoriety due to heavy publicity from his baseball-focused prep school. His stuff was genuinely explosive, but his size and motion were polarizing, with some confident his health was a ticking time bomb due in part to his lengthy arm action. Two years later, Espino has made nearly every positive move that could be reasonably expected of him. His fastball sits in the mid-to-upper 90s, and his slider trails only Max Meyer's for bat-missing electricity. Espino's arm action has been shortened dramatically, helping him lower and center his vertical approach angle, as well, adding deceptiveness to both pitches. You'd like to see a third pitch round out the repertoire, but you'd also like it if ice cream cleaned your gums and whitened your teeth. He'll be 21 next year and should reach Triple-A. There's already plenty going right.

44. Triston Casas, 1B, Boston Red Sox

Major-league first basemen, as a class, hit .257/.338/.454 last year. It doesn't pop as a line, but it was more than 50 points of OPS better than all shortstops and 10 percent better than league-average. The offensive bar is high at the cold corner. As in Lake Wobegon, all the first basemen are above average. The best first baseman—a cohort Casas certainly has a shot at joining—are 30- to 40-percent better than league average. Broadly speaking, to get there you need three things:

1. 30-home-run power: This won't be an issue for Casas, who creates lift and plus-plus raw power with a long stride and minimal hand load.
2. Above-average plate discipline: Casas already has a strong command of the strike zone and a two-strike, contact-heavy approach that will keep him in counts when he falls behind.
3. A plus hit tool: Ah, the open question. Casas has good barrel control and can sting the ball from any part of the zone, but likes to hunt fastballs and can get out on his front foot against offspeed pitches. The breakers and changeups only get better from here on out, and if Casas ends up merely average as a first baseman, which is above-average overall, that may be why.

45. Kahlil Watson, SS, Miami Marlins

Watson was almost universally considered one of the top half-dozen or so prospects in the 2021 draft class—he was number five in our rankings—yet fell to Miami at the sixteenth pick amidst rumors about his bonus demands. The Marlins ultimately offered him every last dollar they had left in their pool plus overage after signing all their other picks: $4,540,790. Watson signed right at the deadline and then dominated in a Florida Complex League cameo. He possesses innate barrel control from the left side of the plate and smashes the ball hard and up from his compact frame. Whether or not his approach will hold up against more advanced pitching is the largest question he'll face offensively as he moves up the chain. His future position is a bit up in the air, too, although we expect he'll be able to stay somewhere on the dirt. Watson has a chance to be a star, if he can swing at the right pitches.

46. Colton Cowser, OF, Baltimore Orioles

It was not at all a surprise that Cowser went to a model-heavy team like Baltimore in the draft: his draft-year performance at Sam Houston State (.374/.490/.680) was exemplary. After he signed, he took a quick pit stop in the complex and made his way to Low-A, where he hit .347 while walking more than he struck out. Cowser has exceptional plate discipline, pitch recognition and contact ability, as you could probably guess from the stat lines. His power projection is more muted; until he shows over-the-fence power with wood bats, it's hard to project him as anything more than an average hitter for power. He played mostly center in his pro debut, but he has more of a corner-masher profile long-term, so some extra pop would be nice.

47. Brayan Rocchio, SS, Cleveland Guardians

With the recent acquisitions of Gabriel Arias, Amed Rosario and Andrés Giménez, it seems as if the Guardians may be trying to replace Francisco Lindor with some sort of shortstop Voltron. Rocchio is the homegrown entry, fresh off a breakout season with the bat in which he added potential above-average power to his plus hit and glove. He has a chance to have the best bat of the group, but may be only the third-best defender. Perhaps he will slide over to second base—Cleveland has plenty of infield holes to fill beyond the large, Lindor-shaped one at short—where he'd be among the better defenders in baseball, and his merely above-average arm would be a weapon rather than occasionally stretched.

48. Jordan Lawlar, SS, Arizona Diamondbacks

Lawlar was our top draft prospect in July, but he suffered a torn shoulder labrum in the Arizona Complex League only two games into his pro career. The subsequent surgery ended his season and cost him reps that were a tad more important given he was an older prep; Lawlar turned 19 less than a week after the draft. While he's expected to be ready early this year, significant shoulder rehabs can be nearly as tricky for hitters as pitchers, and we're in a bit of a wait-and-see mode until he takes the field again. His pre-draft reports showed a mix of advanced hitting and game power, albeit with only above-average-type projection and some swing-and-miss concerns. He's likely to stay at shortstop and provide good-but-not great offense, health willing.

49. Jackson Jobe, RHP, Detroit Tigers

The third-overall pick in 2021, Jobe received a whopping $6.9 million bonus to leapfrog Ole Miss and start his pro career. The logic is understandable, even for a prep arm: MLB is increasingly a league ruled by potent breaking balls, and a projectable teenage arm who already boasts a wipeout slider has cleared one of the most challenging hurdles to big-league success. What awaits now is his professional debut and the always-fraught journey of a teenager who throws low-to-mid-90s and spins his breaker more than 3,000 revolutions per minute. Jobe's polish, velocity, solid changeup as a third pitch and low-effort delivery earned him this lofty ranking in spite of his age and distance from the majors. Like the Tigers, we see the outline of a top-of-the-rotation starter.

50. Justin Foscue, 2B, Texas Rangers

Though he shares much in his profile with fellow Texas prospect Josh Jung, Foscue's polished offensive profile has a slightly less impressive defensive one affixed to it. He generates excellent power with an aggressive stride that drives him forward in the box as he swings to thunderous impact, albeit with unsurprising swing-and-miss risk. His subpar foot speed, range and arm will keep him at second base, or perhaps corner outfield, and his size (he's listed at six-feet tall) makes him unlikely to shift to first base. Texas has loved targeting pure hitters who may lack a position, à la Nick Solak and Willie Calhoun, and it would be no surprise to see them give Foscue a chance to figure things out. With Marcus Semien and Corey Seager in the fold, however, Foscue may soon be swinging as an audition for other organizations.

51. Ronny Mauricio, SS, New York Mets

Mauricio is one of the highest-upside players on this list. He has most of the tools for stardom: feel for the barrel from both sides of the plate, big bat speed, raw power he can get to in games, and good defensive instincts and body control. He just doesn't make good swing decisions, so much so that his OBP started with a two last season. This appears to be both a spin-recognition and plate-aggressiveness issue, especially from the left side of the plate. That's a problem, because switch-hitters predominantly bat lefty, and that's also Mauricio's better power side. Whether Mauricio can get to even a mediocre level of discipline and pitch recognition will make or break his profile, because everything else is there. All he needs to do is one of the hardest things in baseball: manage the strike zone better.

52. Austin Martin, SS/OF, Minnesota Twins

Martin was a strong candidate to go first overall in the 2020 draft and ended up receiving the second-highest signing bonus. He was an advanced college bat at a premium defensive spot. To an extent, the Jays were betting on certainty over ceiling. Martin was never likely to be a middle-of-the-order thumper, but you'd have expected his slugging percentage to start with a four last year, not a three. Perhaps that's part of the reason Toronto was willing to deal such a recent top pick at the deadline, sending Martin to the Twins for righty José Berríos. Martin has an unorthodox setup that cuts off his ability to consistently lift the ball, or even hit it as hard as you'd expect given his good wrists and bat speed. His approach is still sterling—he had a .414 OBP last year—and he split time between shortstop and center field, the two most valuable non-catcher spots in the field. The thing is, he's not an ideal shortstop or center fielder, which might just mean he's a really good second baseman or left fielder, or that he plays a bit of everywhere. We still think he's a very good prospect, but there's a little more uncertainty heading into this year than last.

53. Joey Bart, C, San Francisco Giants

Once again, we ask you to Meet Joey Bart. "What do we do now?" is a fair question for the Giants with regards to the 25-year-old backstop, who watched a rested Buster Posey go out on top for the shockingly dominant NL West champs before retiring at the end of 2021. Bart hasn't exactly seized the mantle, struggling over the past two seasons with a strength-over-speed swing that can generate moonshots but too often creates power for wind turbines. As a receiver, Bart is talented, and the slugging, whiffing, venerable gamecaller profile may be enough to satiate San Francisco. But his track record of hitting would make that at least a slight disappointment—we still hold out hope for more at the plate.

54. Eury Perez, RHP, Miami Marlins

Perez is the highest-ranked prospect on this list that most prospect observers hadn't heard of coming into 2021. He was a low-six-figure international-free-agent signing from 2019 who had yet to pitch in official games. The Marlins sent him straight to full-season ball just a few weeks after his 18th birthday. Given his age and lack of experience, his workload was very closely monitored; he made most of his starts on six days of rest and only saw one hitter a third time in a game all season. But when unleashed, he was often electric, throwing an impressive mid-90s bowling ball of a sinker from his 6-foot-8 frame. He paired the downhill sinker with a slurvy breaker and a firm change which both flashed, as well. He even made five late-season starts in High-A and shined there, too. Perez is physically mature for a teenager and has relief risk in his mechanics and command, but he has a chance for a big rotation outcome, as well.

55. Diego Cartaya, C, Los Angeles Dodgers

A hamstring injury limited Cartaya to a mere 137 Low-A plate appearances in 2021, but it was an impressive cameo. He has always received high marks for his power potential, and his future plus pop is present given how he scorched the ball for Rancho Cucamonga. Yes, that is one of the most hitter-friendly places around, but Cartaya is so strong that his simple, short swing will rocket balls out of parks at lower, more humid elevations, as well. The hit tool might lag behind a bit, as Cartaya has to adjust to spin—which may come once he gets more than 137 plate appearances—but he has the same offensive upside as the top catchers on this list. So why is he down here? Well, he's a 19-year-old catcher with a whole 137 plate appearances above the complex, for one, but the bigger concern is that he has a rather large frame for a backstop, and his defense is a little stiff. This is something that should get smoothed out with full, healthy seasons behind the plate, but the hope for the glove is that it ends up scraping average. If it gets there, you will gladly pencil Cartaya into the middle of your lineup.

56. Kyle Muller, LHP, Atlanta Braves

Nearly-graduated prospects like Muller can be useful mile markers for how we judge prospects against established big-leaguers. Muller was a competent starter in both Triple-A and the majors last year. Seeing him have success at the highest level already is reassuring, given that he's almost fully formed but not quite entirely polished. The massive lefty could stand to locate better, but we've been saying that for years, and he has continued to make it work well enough. At 92–95 from the left side, with tremendous downward plane on both his slider and curveball, Muller will always be an uncomfortable at-bat, and he should offer hitters plenty of those while in the reigning champions' rotation in 2022.

57. Gabriel Arias, SS, Cleveland Guardians

An often-underexplored facet of the *Warhammer 40,000* franchise lore is its dedication to pockets of realism, even in a world defined by absurdist, over-the-top sci-fi sprawl. One such kernel of truth is that, in the fictional city of Mecha-Cleveland, the farm system of the local baseball club has a seemingly inexhaustible reserve of promising shortstop prospects. Arias is not a *psyker* from the post-apocalyptic fantasy future, but he is the most advanced of those still prospect eligible from Cleveland's bumper crop of middle infielders. Acquired from the Padres in the 2020 deadline deal for Mike Clevinger, Arias delivers decent thump for his size, with a precocious knack for driving the ball to right-center field. He spent all of 2021 in Triple-A, an impressive feat for someone who topped out in High-A in 2019 and won't turn 22 until late February. Between Brayan Rocchio, Arias and Andrés Giménez, the Guardians could have three under-23 true shortstops making bids for playing time by mid-2022.

58. Michael Harris II, OF, Atlanta Braves

Harris is yet another Atlanta-area prep that the Braves have scouted, drafted and developed into a Top-101 prospect. This has been going on for decades now. Georgia is a baseball hotbed, after all, but Harris' trend lines are Disco-Stu-approved after a strong 2021 campaign in which Harris raked in High-A. He's a plus runner who should end up a good center fielder. He shows the kind of bat-to-ball skills that could lead to the occasional .300 season in the majors. His game power shows up more as doubles right now, but his batting practices suggest more pop to come. The total package is a potential five-tool center fielder and plus regular.

59. Luis Campusano, C, San Diego Padres

Yanked out of the oven a bit early for the second straight year only to cool his heels in San Diego for a month, Campusano is still one of the most promising offensive backstops in the league. He's not quite the mound of offensive singularity that we've seen emerge elsewhere from ostensible backstops such as Alejandro Kirk, but Campusano is a sturdy youth with a sweeping swing that aims to pull with power. That uppercut gave him a bit more time strolling back to the dugout after strike three last year than in years past, but not so much to be concerned. The task of managing a big-league staff is a tall order for a now-23-year-old, but Campusano's glovework is passable, at least. As he gains acuity against high-level pitching from both sides of the plate, it is easy to envision Campusano becoming a quality backstop with a .260 average and 20–25 home runs year in and year out.

60. Jordan Groshans, SS/3B, Toronto Blue Jays

Groshans looks the part of a slugging third baseman, but that's a little deceptive. He's still pretty okay at shortstop, despite his size and fringy range. Conversely, his plus raw power has played more average in games, as his contact profile is more solid than spectacular and he likes to use the big part of the ballpark. He's hitterish, which is a descriptor we often use when we don't think a prospect is a particularly great hitter but seems to get it done. Groshans can get it done at the plate, and he can get it done at shortstop or third base. He's highly likely to be at least an average regular, but he's honestly a little bit boring as top prospects go. We generally avoid player comps so, instead, how about this: Groshans is that trendy indy band from your 20s that has settled into making a string of well-crafted pop albums that get 6.8s from *Pitchfork*.

61. Oswald Peraza, SS, New York Yankees

The launch angle revolution has even come for your slash-and-dash, glove-first shortstops. Peraza always had bat speed that generated loud contact, but his swing plane and approach kept his ISO under .100 as a pro. Sometime during lockdown, he figured out how to swing up, and he started belting home runs as soon as the minor-league season resumed in 2021. He has sacrificed some barrel control for the more-than-occasional bomb, but that hasn't stopped him from squaring balls in the upper minors. The shortstop glove and foot speed remain plus, so Peraza is a good bet to have a long career, even if his batting average dips into the .250 range once he starts facing the best offspeed stuff. There's also more upside now, as he's shown the potential to be a 20–20, up-the-middle and middle-of-the-lineup bat.

62. Orelvis Martinez, SS/3B, Toronto Blue Jays

The highest-paid international-amateur signee of the 2018 class, Martinez stands out for his bat speed, mature approach and impressive physicality at just 19. He lacks the famous bloodlines of Toronto's current infield stars, but he has the swing to match. Much like Groshans, Martinez is defined by his bat and has already begun seeing consistent time at third base. That should be of little concern. As he gains experience, the combination of his strength, bat speed and ability to loft pitches anywhere in the zone could make him one of the most impressive finished offensive products on this list.

63. Bobby Miller, RHP, Los Angeles Dodgers

The Dodgers haven't picked higher than 15th overall since 2006, but their investments in scouting and player development have turned up gem after gem. Their 2020 first-rounder, Miller is a massive righty who went to Louisville but seems to have learned his craft at Hole In A Boat University: "Where Everything Sinks." His mid- to upper-90s heat was enough to overpower hitters in the low minors thanks to passable control, but his medley of offspeeds is what will likely make Miller so exciting as he progresses. His slider and changeup occupy the same mid- to upper-80s velocity band with hard, late break, and Miller's comfort using each pitch keeps platoon bats honest. He'll modulate his slider at times to generate cut, which can further trouble lefties. Miller was one of the more impressive arms in the minors last year, and, as things spiraled with their pitching staff in the postseason, there was reason to think the Dodgers might pull him from the AFL up to their playoff roster. Instead, Miller may make his major-league debut this year, but the progress of his command will be the speed governor of his ascension.

64. Reid Detmers, LHP, Los Angeles Angels

It was a tale of two halves for Detmers. In the first half of the season, he added a new slider and picked up several ticks on his fastball, hitting the mid-90s with some regularity and sitting a touch lower, as opposed to on either side of 90. That gave him the ability to whiff Double-A batters with something other than his majestic curve, and, with his new weapons, he quickly raced his way to the Angels around midseason. But his fastball got pasted by major-league hitters, even with the additional velo, and, after four dreadful starts, Detmers tested positive for COVID-19. He came back for the very last game of the season and got rocked again, failing to make it out of the second inning. On balance, this was still a positive season for the former Louisville star, and we expect him to settle in as a mid-rotation starter, but the downside risk with his profile is more "swingman" than "short reliever."

65. Matthew Liberatore, LHP, St. Louis Cardinals

How far can a pitcher go with two solid secondaries but a fastball that doesn't miss bats? Liberatore looks the part, standing 6-foot-5 and bearing down on hitters from the left side with a picturesque curveball and a fading changeup that pairs well with his sinking, low-90s fastball. Liberatore commands his secondaries well, and, at 21 years old, held his own in Triple-A, skipping there straight from Low-A. Critiquing Liberatore so heavily can feel nitpicky given his youth, but we've seen similar beautiful curveballs fade in effectiveness at higher levels, and Liberatore is already not an above-average bat-misser. Late in the season, he began to show a firmer version of the breaking ball. That could help raise his promising, but presently capped, trajectory.

66. Brady House, SS, Washington Nationals

A Boras client ending up with the Nats, you say? House slid in last year's draft to number 11, where Washington picked him up for an above-slot $5 million bonus. He hit very well in the Florida Complex League after signing, showing off big power upside and continuing to make improvements in making contact. He's a shortstop for now, but he's 6-foot-4 with a full frame, so the most likely scenario is that he outgrows the position and ends up fitting best at third base or an outfield corner. He has had swing-and-miss issues resulting from stiffness and rigidity in his swing, so the hit tool bears watching as he advances. House will take some time to develop, but he could be a corner bat to watch in the latter half of the decade.

67. Owen Caissie, OF, Chicago Cubs

Canada's most notable exports:

1. Pro Wrestling Legend Bret "Hitman" Hart
2. The "Love and Sausages" sketch from *Kids in the Hall*
3. Owen Caissie?

That's heady company for a teenaged outfield prospect, even one with the precocious pop Caissie has shown so far. Hailing from Burlington (dramatic pause), Ontario, Canada, he was San Diego's second-round pick in 2020. The Padres then sent him to the Cubs for Yu Darvish before Caissie even made his pro debut. Debuting in the complex this past summer, Caissie spit out exit velocities that probably required a technician call or two to confirm TrackMan was calibrated properly. He hasn't even started to fill out his 6-foot-4 frame yet. Once he does, he will look the part of a classic first-division right fielder. That's not the best there is, the best there was, or the best there ever will be, but like we said, it's a lofty company.

68. Andy Pages, OF, Los Angeles Dodgers

In a fantasy world, more hitters would be able to thrive with the convoluted swing Pages utilizes. In the fantasy-baseball world, Pages may be one of the most prized youngsters in the minors. In the real world, he's simply one of the most powerful hitters in MiLB, blasting 31 home runs last year. The muscle-bound Cuban is a quintessential right fielder, with a missile for an arm and enough speed to handle a corner, though not likely center. Every swing from Pages appears intent on driving the ball, and he is frequently successful thanks to quick hands that help scoop pitches no matter where they cross the plate. However, we know that last bit because Pages made little distinction about where pitches came in as he chose to swing and has already struggled with elevated strikeout rates. The respect afforded to him in High-A helped him push his walk rate over 14 percent, but better pitching will force him to be more selective. With a stance that begins standing fully upright, his leg-lift- and bat-waggle-laden swing are fascinating to watch, but may need paring down to allow him to reach his power at higher levels.

69. Edward Cabrera, RHP, Miami Marlins

Future Stars Edward Cabrera was an unstoppable force in MLB The Show 21, akin to Tecmo Super Bowl Bo Jackson, to the point that teammate and gamer Jazz Chisholm did an in-game interview on the virtual-Cabrera phenomenon when he was called up to the real Show. For some reason, Sony's San Diego Studio gave Cabrera's card a 100-mph sinker with a completely unhittable attack angle and movement—let's call it virtual seam-shifted wake—which even the best e-baseball players in the world couldn't touch. The real Cabrera doesn't throw a sinker at all, and his four-seam fastball is actually pretty hittable, although it does touch triple-digits every now and again. His bread-and-butter pitch is a plus, hard-diving changeup—notch another one for the Miami changeup farm—and he also works with power breaking balls that show promise. He has had a difficult time staying healthy and walked an awful lot of batters in both Triple-A and the majors last year, so there's significant bullpen risk. But, hey, who knows, maybe he'll suddenly pick up the greatest sinker of all time from his video-game self.

70. Elly De La Cruz, SS/3B, Cincinnati Reds

De La Cruz was not a seven-figure, or even six-figure, international free agent. He's already playing more third base than shortstop. And he strikes out about as often as Milhouse Van Houten with Lisa Simpson (we assume that's still a trope, we haven't watched regularly since before De La Cruz was born). De La Cruz also features some of the loudest tools outside of your local Lowe's (no, no, that's Globe Life Field, you took the wrong exit). De La Cruz has plus, bordering on plus-plus, raw power and the speed to match it. The approach *is* raw, but he also jumped from his stateside complex debut to full-season ball in a cool 55 plate appearances and wasn't overwhelmed by the ex-Florida-State League. All of these are positive markers for further growth and refinement, and the upside here is . . . well, early-seasons *Simpsons*.

71. Cristian Pache, OF, Atlanta Braves

Congratulations to the current holder of the Alex Reyes Award for managing to thread the needle of retaining prospect eligibility *and* at least a glimmer of Top-101 sheen two or more years past when they might've been expected to graduate. Since debuting in 2020, Pache has appeared in 14 postseason games and just 24 regular-season tilts. While being the next Terrance Gore is an admirable and appealing goal for well over 99 percent of aspiring baseball players, Pache has cause to aspire higher. Even as Atlanta's outfield depth was stretched like filo dough in 2021, Pache struggled to hit well enough to justify an extended run. We don't close the book on development for 23-year-olds, particularly those with Pache's baseline of perennial Gold Glove defense and benchmark-setting range in the outfield, but we do wonder if we'll ever make it to the final chapter.

72. Nick Pratto, 1B, Kansas City Royals

Delaware is home to the president, a whole bunch of post office boxes for credit-card companies, and one possibly cursed High-A baseball park. As we noted with teammate MJ Melendez, Pratto was not the only notable Royals prospect to deal with whatever bad vibes were emanating from Frawley Stadium in 2019, but hitting .190 as a first-base prospect is, to quote the Phillies current skipper, "not what you want." Last season, on the other hand, is what you want, what you really, really want. Pratto quadrupled his home run total from his High-A campaign and did it at higher levels; his 36 taters trailed only Melendez among Royals farmhands. Pratto is about the most traditional, three-true-outcomes, corner slugger on this list. Just keep him away from whoever cursed him by touching his face on the steps of the Wilmington stadium while whispering "stop hitting."

73. Nate Pearson, RHP, Toronto Blue Jays

One of the tallest drinks of water around drank deeply from the highest-hung bird feeder on the Blue Jays' farm in 2021, growing strong and poising himself to take flight. Yet an emu painted blue is still bound by gravity, and an adductor strain on the cusp of the season opener sent the fireballing bluebird plummeting to the injured list and towards another disappointing season. Shifted to the bullpen in reaction to Toronto's solid rotation yet deeply disappointing relief corps, Pearson struggled to stabilize. Letting him rub elbows with Tyler Chatwood may have been a mistake, as Pearson managed to miss bats with regularity yet lost the strike zone entirely at times and continued to look like a two-pitch wonder. Pearson's tool kit is still too enticing, and a full season of health could quickly wipe away many of these worries, but he needs to stabilize or risk a crash landing.

74. Sixto Sánchez, RHP, Miami Marlins

Sánchez missed the entire 2021 season. Expected to anchor the Miami rotation and graduate from prospect eligibility in April, he instead got off to a late-spring start between visa and COVID-19-testing issues. He then started having shoulder problems when ramping up. After months of trying to get his season underway, he had surgery to repair a small tear in his posterior capsule in July, which is one of the most concerning arm-related diagnoses a pitcher can have. He was the number-four prospect in baseball just one year ago given the overwhelming quality of his demonstrated major-league stuff—in 2020 he was throwing a high-90s four-seamer and sinker along with a plus-plus changeup and plus slider—but we have no idea if he's going to be the same pitcher the next time he takes the mound.

75. Shea Langeliers, C, Atlanta Braves

Langeliers' star hasn't shone quite as brightly since he was mentioned in the same breath as Adley Rutschman as a potential first-overall draft pick back in 2019. Langeliers' progress has been steady, though, and he remains a potential plus power bat with advanced catch-and-throw skills behind the plate. There's some stiffness to his swing that allows him to lift baseballs when he gets the fat part of the barrel on them, but leaves him swinging-and-missing more often than you'd like for a potential middle-of-the-order bat. Behind the plate, Langeliers shows off a real howitzer that keeps the running game in check, although he didn't grade out particularly well by Baseball Prospectus' minor-league framing metric. He sets a big target and has soft-enough hands that you could see him improve to become an average to slightly-above-average defender on balance, which, combined with his plus game power, should make him a fine everyday backstop.

76. Dax Fulton, LHP, Miami Marlins

Fulton got $2.4 million from the Marlins in 2020 while rehabbing from Tommy John surgery from the previous fall. Over the course of 2021, it became clear why Miami coveted the 6-foot-7 Oklahoma prep so much. His command was shaky early in the season as he continued to work his way back into form, but, by midseason, he was throwing enough good strikes. He sits in the low 90s with both a four-seam fastball and a sinker and gets strong downhill plane. His out-pitch is a big, biting curveball he can throw for strikes and get batters to chase. His changeup projects as above-average, as well, and his pitch mix tunnels together and forces hitters to guess. Fulton needs to continue sharpening his command and stretch out further, but the mid-rotation upside is clear.

77. Matt McLain, SS, Cincinnati Reds

Matthew Michael McLain ment mo mhe Muniversity mof Mouthern Malifornia, mhere me mashed many mi-*cough**cough* Pardon, something lodged in the throat. Whew. McLain has the sort of low-variance skills that could produce significant outcome variance year over year. He is asked to play shortstop full-time for a club without other strong infield defenders? Things could get dicey. Manfred rejuices the baseballs to personally spite Max Scherzer? McLain's plus hit tool and line-drive swing suddenly make him a 15- to 20-home-run threat. More likely, however, McLain's best role will be as a multi-positional infielder that starts five to six days a week, extending a lineup and keeping the rest of the club fresh. If he cannot generate enough power, or the hit tool slips, however, it's a quick path to the Romine Zone.

78. Jordan Balazovic, RHP, Minnesota Twins

A plus fastball with life || and a curve that can miss bats
The rest needs refinement || we'd prefer you not scout stats
The bullpen may call him || despite the renewed ardor
But our young righty's fate || may still be a third starter

79. Reginald Preciado, SS/3B, Chicago Cubs

When the Cubs acquired Preciado from the Padres in the the Yu Darvish trade, they hoped he would make good on his sky-high ceiling as a 6-foot-4, switch-hitting shortstop. One of the few players born in 2003 on this list, Preciado skipped the Dominican Summer League and headed straight to the Arizona Complex League, turning heads with his athleticism and ability to drive the ball with power already. A good offseason in the weight room and a spring and summer in affiliated ball could push the Panamanian way up this list next year.

80. D.L. Hall, LHP, Baltimore Orioles

We're not so mature that we can pretend we've never made a quip about an Orioles pitching prospect being named D.L., but Hall finding himself on the IL for most of the 2021 season with a "stress reaction" in his pitching elbow was truly unfortunate. He showed dominant stuff in his brief Double-A season and enough control and command for us not to have to squint too hard to see a starter. He regularly pumps upper 90s from the left side, resulting in very uncomfortable swings from batters, especially when he bores it in on righties. Hall's curve is potential plus, and both the slider and change are more than mere arsenal filler. He's just never really thrown enough strikes for us to be confident he's a starter, and now he has had a vague, season-ending elbow issue. With a full, healthy season, Hall would easily be in the top half of this list, but he's also far from the only pitching prospect in this half we could say that about.

81. Jarren Duran, OF, Boston Red Sox

While we had concerns that Duran's stomp-and-lift swing overhaul would lead to more swing-and-miss at the highest level, we did not expect well over a third of his plate appearances to end with a K. The endgame of all prospect writing is projecting major-league performance, but 112 poor plate appearances in the majors can be an adjustment period or a bellwether. Duran has gone from being a hit-tool-driven college second baseman to a slugging outfielder more suited to a corner spot despite plus-plus run times. One way to project major-league performance is that most hitters will hit for a lower average in the majors than they did in the minors. Duran hit .258 in Triple-A. With that came plenty of power, more than enough to support a corner-outfield profile. Getting to enough of that pop when you hit .240 though, that can be tricky. We think those 112 PAs were mostly an adjustment period, but there are reasons to be concerned that he won't fully max out his power/speed profile.

82. Andrew Painter, RHP, Philadelphia Phillies

Get ready for a lot of puns about painting the corners. Painter was touching 100 mph in instructs last fall after going to the Phillies with the no. 13 pick. He's another skyscraper hurler, 6-foot-8 to be exact, and, while he'd been more mid-90s than high 90s in the past, he has the physical projectability to throw in the higher velocity band regularly. He also throws a curveball, slider and changeup that have above-average potential, and he can manipulate his offspeeds to disrupt hitter timing. It's a long way from post-draft backfield work to the majors, but Painter's on the same path as organization-mate Mick Abel, just a year behind him.

83. Jairo Pomares, OF, San Francisco Giants

Few teams had a concentration of breakouts to rival the Low-A San Jose Giants' last year. Between a starting rotation that included three pitchers in the top 10 for strikeouts in MiLB, and a lineup that for much of the year featured Marco Luciano, Luis Matos, Patrick Bailey and Pomares, it was a near-constant vacillation between gasoline, fireworks, and smoke. For his part, Pomares brought as much aggression to the plate as anyone in the minors, with a lefty stroke designed to swat the ball out of the infield and, ideally, deep into the night sky. The Cuban slugger has the bat speed to make it work despite an atypical frame for raw power. This is a profile that lives or dies with the bat, however, as he's already a corner-outfield glove and has not shown much acumen for adding danger on the bases. Pomares has proven he can put a hurting on pitches, but the next step will be learning to take free passes when offered, now that teams respect his power.

84. Gavin Williams, RHP, Cleveland Guardians

Williams went from undrafted in 2020, after three years of inconsistency and injuries mostly in East Carolina University's bullpen, to a clear-cut first-rounder with a dominant campaign as ECU's Friday-night starter. He throws a robust fastball that sat in the upper 90s at times last spring and has hit triple digits in the past. Both his curveball and his slider project as above-average offerings. He's a hulking presence on the mound and threw strikes for the entire collegiate season. The Guardians are one of the best player-development groups specifically at maximizing pitching, so he's in the right place to keep figuring everything out. It's only his pre-2021 priors that prevent Williams from ranking among the better pitching prospects in baseball, and if he keeps firing like this in the pros, he will be one of them.

85. Spencer Strider, RHP, Atlanta Braves

Strider made it to the majors a little more than a year after being drafted, under the guise that he might help Atlanta's pursuit of a World Series. He didn't end up throwing in the playoffs, but he's a World Series champion nonetheless, a stunning rise for a fourth-rounder who didn't pitch a lot at Clemson and often didn't throw strikes when he did. Strider is nominally a starting-pitching prospect, but he leans heavily on two great pitches: his high-90s fastball with great characteristics high in the strike zone, and a plus slurvy breaking ball. Given the mostly theoretical nature of his changeup, his past durability and command issues, and that Atlanta was willing to put him on the 40-man as a reliever so quickly, he's the single most likely pitcher on this list to end up in the bullpen. It's not a lock—more and more teams are willing to start guys who basically throw only two pitches, and amorphous roles do exist—but it's the best bet.

86. Sam Bachman, RHP, Los Angeles Angels

We're still in a holding pattern on Bachman, who, much like Strider, has the stocky, short frame and tough-as-nails top two pitches to be a high-leverage arm in the bigs as early as 2022. His conservative usage in the wake of last year's draft didn't show us much we didn't know, but a club with the ability to be patient could comfortably continue working Bachman as a starter to see if the third pitch comes along. His running fastball sits 94–98, the sharp, late-breaking slider is 85–89, and his situational changeup clocks similarly. The changeup flashes plus but is not nearly as refined as the first two offerings, which would be headlined further if a club that was desperate to contend and always needed pitching wanted to get him to the majors as soon as possible. Hey, which team drafted him again? Oh.

87. Emerson Hancock, RHP, Seattle Mariners

As recently as 10 or even five years ago, Hancock would have been a top-three draft pick. He has the look and the pedigree, with an athletic 6-foot-4 frame, and starred when healthy for the Georgia Bulldogs in the SEC. His stuff ticks the boxes, with mid-90s heat and a couple of impressive secondaries that flash plus in his slider and changeup. But Hancock was instead selected sixth, the third pitcher and second righty taken last year, trailing Marlins draftee Max Meyer then as he does now on this list. Health is one major concern, as Hancock struggled with arm fatigue off and on throughout the season, limiting his innings load. When he was pitching, he was often working specific gameplans and attempting to overhaul the fastball traits (read: unexceptional sinker) that saw his skillset deprioritized.

88. Gunnar Henderson, SS/3B, Baltimore Orioles

Will the real Gunnar Henderson please stand up? After looking overmatched at the alternate site in 2020—fair enough for a 19-year-old who hadn't played above the complex—he went to instructs and, against more age-appropriate competition, looked the part of a future power-hitting infielder. Assigned to Low-A to start 2021, the now-20-year-old blew the doors off the level, then scuffled a bit after a promotion. Henderson is playing almost as much third base as shortstop already, and the hot corner is his likely major-league home. We think the plus raw power will play nicely there, we'd just like to see it all come together for an entire season first.

89. Roansy Contreras, RHP, Pittsburgh Pirates

As velocity continues to tick up across baseball, some teams are starting to embrace the idea that it's easier to add fastball velocity to a pitcher with command of a deep arsenal than to teach their flamethrowers to throw better strikes. Michael Baumann of *The Ringer* delved into this idea with Reid Detmers, but it applies to Contreras, as well. A solid-enough pitching prospect when he was wearing Yankee pinstripes, he mostly sat low 90s but filled up the zone with all three pitches (fastball, curve and a promising sinking change). Now a Pirates prospect—he was dealt last offseason for Jameson Taillon—he sits mid-90s, touches higher, and the velocity bump has tightened up his curve into a true power breaker. While fastball velocity isn't everything, when you have most everything else, it can be a big boon. Conversely, Contreras is a shorter righty who needs to refine that third pitch and dealt with a minor forearm strain last year, so there is some relief risk in the profile.

90. Randy Vasquez, RHP, New York Yankees

As if the Yankees needed another hard-throwing, pop-up pitching prospect. Vasquez is an undersized right-hander and was an overaged international free agent who showed up in full-season ball this year pumping two different versions of a plus fastball and then dropping a big power breaker on a parade of unsuspecting hitters across three levels. It's a very simple gameplan. The righties get a steady diet of mid-90s two-seamers under the hands. Assuming they don't shatter their bats while grounding out to shortstop, once ahead he drops the big 10–5 breaker on 'em. Lefties get a four-seamer with a tick more velocity and riding life, then the same hook, but to their back foot. Vasquez's delivery is unorthodox, with more than a bit of tornadic effort. The changeup is below-average, albeit with some projection. So, there are more than a few reliever markers here. Vasquez would be a very good reliever, but we also think he has a shot to be quite a good starter.

91. Cole Winn, RHP, Texas Rangers

The rare Rangers pitching prospect who was neither put under the knife nor acquired during the 2021 season, Winn has a repertoire that elicits a relieved nod more than Bugs-Bunny-meets-Lola eyes, but he should be starting games in the The Shed for Texas as a 22-year-old next year, and he is impressively short on flaws. His four pitches, led by a fading changeup, typically fill a compass rose of movement profiles, though they can at times blend into varying speeds of pure drop. The quality of the change should give Winn an edge against platoon bats, leaving him to hopefully further refine his breaking balls. Consistency with either could lock Winn into the middle of the rotation for the next decade.

92. Kyle Harrison, LHP, San Francisco Giants

It can be difficult for mid-round prep arms to stand out quickly, as many are selected on promise and projectability—rainy day projects for the player-development staff. Ranking fifth among qualified stateside minor-league starters in strikeout rate when you're 19 years old is one way to break the mold. Harrison's slider has dramatic sweep and sink, and his slightly herky-jerky motion adds a bit of deception to help his low-90s fastball play up. He will throw both his slider and changeup to righties and lefties alike, and while he lives around the zone, he rarely sets up shop in its heart. The positive is evident in his 35.7-percent strikeout rate, with groundball tendencies to boot. What's unknown is whether he can hew to the corners consistently without walking so many hitters that he constantly places himself under siege.

93. Bryson Stott, SS, Philadelphia Phillies

Stott hit well at three levels in 2021 and capped it off with a strong performance in the Arizona Fall League. He's a well-rounded player who has no clear plus tool but no below-average tools, either. He's likely to hit for moderate average and power while taking a healthy but not overwhelming share of walks. His arm and hands allow him to play shortstop credibly despite average range, and he has experience at both second and third, as well. It is not an exciting skill set, but he's likely an average to above-average regular in the middle infield, and that's a very valuable profile.

94. Garrett Mitchell, OF, Milwaukee Brewers

After having his skillset picked apart ad nauseum ahead of the 2020 draft, Mitchell both thrived and struggled in 2021, much as he did in college. An advanced older bat, he shone in High-A on the back of his excellent athleticism and patient approach, but was stymied in his first month and change at Double-A. The big question is what exactly Milwaukee sees as a necessary next step for the speedy former UCLA Bruin; can he be enough of an impact player with his current approach, or does he need to overhaul his swing to turn his solid exit velocities into over-the-fence power at the risk of losing entirely what has helped him succeed thus far? His ceiling and track record earns him the respect of this ranking, but any extended struggles akin to his shoddy finale with Biloxi would be deeply worrisome.

95. Vidal Bruján, IF/OF, Tampa Bay Rays

There's unlikely to be much interest in a 2022 reboot of Bruce Campbell's turn-of-the-century syndicated period dramedy *Jack of All Trades*, but Bruján would be the ideal candidate to step into the role of secret agent Jack Stiles. He can do a little bit of everything. He played six different positions in 2021, and he is at least competent at each of them. He's a plus-plus runner, although he wasn't a particularly proficient base stealer last year. He's a switch-hitter and can hit a bit from both sides. He has added some game power, enough that

10–15 home runs isn't out of the question. The problem with being a jack of all trades—other than being a genre-bending, low budget, 22-minute show with no clear audience—is that you are often a master of none. Buján doesn't really have that one obvious skill that would make him more than a useful regular. He should last far longer in the majors than Campbell's two-season star vehicle, though.

96. Joe Ryan, RHP, Minnesota Twins

Ryan found out he was traded from Tampa Bay to Minnesota for Nelson Cruz while eating breakfast in Tokyo's Olympic Village. He then went out and shoved as one of the best pitchers in the tournament, winning the semifinal game to help propel Team USA to a silver medal. Ryan continued to deal when he got back to North America with a pair of one-run starts in Triple-A, leading to a successful September call-up. All Ryan has done as a professional is get outs of all kinds—especially strikeouts—and avoid walks. He does not have overwhelming velocity or spin on his fastball, and only his curveball rates much above average amongst his current crop of offspeeds, but he throws a ton of good strikes and gets enough whiffs to get by while gobbling up innings. He's a high-probability mid-rotation starter.

97. Geraldo Perdomo, SS, Arizona Diamondbacks

Exhibit A in player development not being linear: On July 8, Perdomo was transferred to the Developmental List. If you aren't a baseball-operations employee, you might not know what that is. It removes the player from counting against the roster maximum for the minors, while allowing him to work on . . . well, development at the team complex. You rarely see this happen to top prospects, but, at the time, Perdomo was running a .509 OPS in Double-A; that from a player who was considered an especially polished shortstop prospect who could fall out of bed and hit .280 just about anywhere while showing an advanced glove. Whatever Perdomo worked on at Salt River Field took, as he looked very much like the Top 101 prospect of years past upon his return to Double-A in August. He played well enough to earn a September cup of coffee back in Arizona with the big club, and has started to show signs of growing into more game power, which would lift the profile from solid regular to occasional All-Star.

98. Sal Frelick, OF, Milwaukee Brewers

Milwaukee doubled down on outfielders with Garrett Mitchell's present offensive profile when they selected Frelick in the first round this year. They were rewarded with a near-identical season, statistically, albeit condensed, as Frelick throttled Low-A Carolina and had more tempered results in High-A Wisconsin. Unlike Mitchell, Frelick's frame and swing do not suggest untapped potential; what you see is what you get. Fortunately, though you might have to squint a bit more to see it, what you do get with Frelick is someone who should reach first base quite often and can get himself into scoring position from there. The Lilliputian lefty's swing is demonstrably geared towards making contact, with a tiny stride that helps with timing but hardly generates torque, and little semblance of a power hack. Given 600 plate appearances, a few of the pitchers on this list might hit more balls over the fence than Frelick, but as long as he's roaming center field, spraying singles, and stretching gappers into triples, he has a path to success.

99. Ezequiel Duran, IF, Texas Rangers

The trade return for Joey Gallo was never going to bring back a prospect that could match him in the power department, but Duran has plenty of thunder in his swing. He led the Penn League in homers in 2019, but his power was more of the plus variety. It looks plus-plus now, with 30-home-run seasons possible if he tones down some of his free-swinging tendencies. Duran played mostly second base as a Yankees prospect, usually in deference to better gloves to his right, but saw more time at shortstop and some at third base after the trade. His average foot speed isn't ideal for the six, but his soft hands, smooth actions, and plus arm should make him above-average at the other infield spots.

100. Aaron Ashby, LHP, Milwaukee Brewers

I recommend getting your sinker up on to 96, yeah
I recommend whiffin' batters with your plus slider's zoom, yeah
Throw it down (what a jagged little pill)
It feels so good (spinning with plummet)
Wait until the curve settles
You pitch, you learn
You win, you learn
You miss, you learn
You lose, you learn
You bend, you learn
You deal, you learn

101. James Triantos, 2B/SS, Chicago Cubs

It's rare for a second-rounder with only 25 games in the Arizona Complex League to be a Top 101 prospect the year after he was drafted, but we simply cannot deny Triantos' ability to hit. The suburban-Virginia prep infielder signed for a well-overslot $2.1 million after reclassifying from the 2022 draft class. Reports from the desert backfields immediately flagged him with a potential plus or plus-plus hit tool, and those kept coming in all summer and fall. He has high-end bat-to-ball abilities for his age, and his quick bat puts some thump into the ball when he makes contact, which is a combination you're not going to see out of many 18-year-olds making their pro debut. He's already sliding down the defensive spectrum—he played more innings at second than short as a pro—and his clunky-looking swing is not going to win any aesthetic awards. But on hitting talent alone, Triantos has a shot for big offensive outcomes.

MLB Managers

Alex Cora wRM+: 108

TEAM	YEAR	W	L	Pythag +/-	Avg PC	100+ P	120+ P	QS	REL	REL w Zero R	IBB	PH	PH Avg	PH HR	SB2	CS2	SB3	CS3	SAC Att	SAC %	POS SAC	Squeeze
BOS	2018	108	54	3	88.8	42	0	67	535	383	8	96	.202	2	109	25	16	5	9	78	7	0
BOS	2019	84	78	-4	86.6	48	0	55	632	431	22	123	.330	5	59	26	9	5	26	77	18	0
BOS	2021	92	70	3	84.9	18	0	39	563	393	31	93	.221	1	32	16	8	5	15	67	10	0

Terry Francona wRM+: 107

TEAM	YEAR	W	L	Pythag +/-	Avg PC	100+ P	120+ P	QS	REL	REL w Zero R	IBB	PH	PH Avg	PH HR	SB2	CS2	SB3	CS3	SAC Att	SAC %	POS SAC	Squeeze
CLE	2017	102	60	-8	93.8	70	1	84	498	383	15	93	.157	2	79	21	9	3	38	60	22	0
CLE	2018	91	71	-9	96.9	79	2	98	509	361	29	97	.241	2	118	34	15	4	45	56	23	0
CLE	2019	93	69	-1	93.6	76	3	81	522	372	19	100	.213	2	92	28	10	5	62	64	38	0
CLE	2020	35	25	0	92.2	20	0	37	181	130	8	37	.188	0	24	7	2	2	16	38	7	1
CLE	2021	80	82	0	82.3	23	1	58	535	380	12	89	.234	4	93	15	16	2	29	69	20	0

Aaron Boone wRM+: 107

TEAM	YEAR	W	L	Pythag +/-	Avg PC	100+ P	120+ P	QS	REL	REL w Zero R	IBB	PH	PH Avg	PH HR	SB2	CS2	SB3	CS3	SAC Att	SAC %	POS SAC	Squeeze
NYY	2018	100	62	0	88.2	33	0	67	508	368	9	70	.203	1	54	19	9	1	19	53	10	0
NYY	2019	103	59	3	79.4	20	0	53	545	371	12	57	.231	4	46	20	9	1	20	50	6	2
NYY	2020	33	27	-2	81.4	11	0	18	175	114	5	36	.233	1	23	6	4	1	5	20	1	0
NYY	2021	92	70	6	84.8	24	1	51	512	350	10	94	.218	3	54	15	9	5	12	83	9	0

Mike Matheny wRM+: 106

TEAM	YEAR	W	L	Pythag +/-	Avg PC	100+ P	120+ P	QS	REL	REL w Zero R	IBB	PH	PH Avg	PH HR	SB2	CS2	SB3	CS3	SAC Att	SAC %	POS SAC	Squeeze
STL	2017	83	79	-4	91.9	47	1	79	546	397	50	292	.300	5	66	27	15	4	72	65	14	2
STL	2018	47	46	-1	92.9	15	0	42	322	213	24	136	.179	2	32	19	1	2	38	76	8	2
KC	2020	26	34	-1	78.2	9	0	11	232	167	7	50	.200	3	38	17	11	4	19	42	8	0
KC	2021	74	88	4	84.8	22	0	51	556	371	16	80	.219	1	92	28	32	6	55	56	28	2

Luis Rojas wRM+: 106

TEAM	YEAR	W	L	Pythag +/-	Avg PC	100+ P	120+ P	QS	REL	REL w Zero R	IBB	PH	PH Avg	PH HR	SB2	CS2	SB3	CS3	SAC Att	SAC %	POS SAC	Squeeze
NYM	2020	26	34	-2	80.5	10	0	17	197	134	7	37	.182	1	19	9	1	1	3	33	1	0
NYM	2021	77	85	0	76.5	5	0	51	543	383	21	292	.258	8	48	23	5	4	54	63	12	0

Kevin Cash wRM+: 106

TEAM	YEAR	W	L	Pythag +/-	Avg PC	100+ P	120+ P	QS	REL	REL w Zero R	IBB	PH	PH Avg	PH HR	SB2	CS2	SB3	CS3	SAC Att	SAC %	POS SAC	Squeeze
TB	2017	80	82	0	93.8	73	0	73	511	362	37	122	.229	2	66	29	22	5	32	50	14	1
TB	2018	90	72	1	63.0	22	0	39	553	363	34	109	.198	1	117	45	11	5	52	54	28	5
TB	2019	96	66	2	69.8	22	0	53	603	413	27	130	.204	3	82	31	10	4	15	53	8	1
TB	2020	40	20	3	71.2	5	0	7	219	155	4	66	.259	0	42	8	6	1	1	0	0	0
TB	2021	100	62	-3	72.7	15	0	33	531	364	27	120	.250	3	81	40	8	3	9	67	6	0

Craig Counsell wRM+: 106

TEAM	YEAR	W	L	Pythag +/-	Avg PC	100+ P	120+ P	QS	REL	REL w Zero R	IBB	PH	PH Avg	PH HR	SB2	CS2	SB3	CS3	SAC Att	SAC %	POS SAC	Squeeze
MIL	2017	86	76	1	88.1	29	0	65	550	399	45	285	.220	8	101	33	30	10	61	67	12	3
MIL	2018	96	67	4	85.5	16	0	51	559	407	34	286	.243	10	97	26	28	8	41	71	6	0
MIL	2019	89	73	8	84.3	16	0	34	588	395	28	314	.190	8	79	18	22	6	33	61	5	1
MIL	2020	29	31	1	81.2	3	0	15	189	124	1	65	.271	1	14	10	1	1	1	0	0	0
MIL	2021	95	67	0	83.8	23	0	70	533	378	19	292	.163	7	74	20	8	1	36	69	5	2

Bud Black wRM+: 105

TEAM	YEAR	W	L	Pythag +/-	Avg PC	100+ P	120+ P	QS	REL	REL w Zero R	IBB	PH	PH Avg	PH HR	SB2	CS2	SB3	CS3	SAC Att	SAC %	POS SAC	Squeeze
COL	2017	87	75	-1	89.9	29	1	68	549	388	20	259	.205	6	51	32	8	3	79	78	20	2
COL	2018	91	72	6	92.2	42	0	84	518	361	24	273	.242	8	91	34	4	0	67	63	11	1
COL	2019	71	91	1	87.6	23	0	46	590	386	33	301	.188	13	63	31	8	0	73	70	10	3
COL	2020	26	34	3	86.1	8	0	28	189	108	5	51	.186	1	37	8	5	0	12	58	7	0
COL	2021	74	87	-1	82.8	13	0	68	543	353	19	278	.233	10	70	21	6	2	71	68	10	4

Tony LaRussa wRM+: 105

TEAM	YEAR	W	L	Pythag +/-	Avg PC	100+ P	120+ P	QS	REL	REL w Zero R	IBB	PH	PH Avg	PH HR	SB2	CS2	SB3	CS3	SAC Att	SAC %	POS SAC	Squeeze
CHW	2021	93	69	-6	89.0	42	0	57	512	358	16	83	.162	3	43	19	13	2	35	69	24	2

Joe Girardi wRM+: 104

TEAM	YEAR	W	L	Pythag +/-	Avg PC	100+ P	120+ P	QS	REL	REL w Zero R	IBB	PH	PH Avg	PH HR	SB2	CS2	SB3	CS3	SAC Att	SAC %	POS SAC	Squeeze
NYY	2017	91	71	-11	90.8	39	0	75	477	347	18	112	.189	4	85	21	5	2	27	67	16	0
PHI	2020	28	32	-2	84.5	12	0	20	189	110	12	46	.300	0	32	8	3	0	16	50	8	1
PHI	2021	82	80	2	85.5	34	2	58	532	352	37	275	.188	5	64	13	10	5	70	67	14	1

David Bell wRM+: 103

TEAM	YEAR	W	L	Pythag +/-	Avg PC	100+ P	120+ P	QS	REL	REL w Zero R	IBB	PH	PH Avg	PH HR	SB2	CS2	SB3	CS3	SAC Att	SAC %	POS SAC	Squeeze
CIN	2019	75	87	-5	91.6	47	0	65	535	375	31	316	.179	9	73	33	7	4	45	67	2	2
CIN	2020	31	29	1	89.1	18	0	26	168	114	6	68	.228	3	27	8	2	2	1	0	0	0
CIN	2021	83	79	-1	91.2	45	2	70	585	394	31	300	.188	6	28	20	8	4	50	68	5	0

Scott Servais wRM+: 102

TEAM	YEAR	W	L	Pythag +/-	Avg PC	100+ P	120+ P	QS	REL	REL w Zero R	IBB	PH	PH Avg	PH HR	SB2	CS2	SB3	CS3	SAC Att	SAC %	POS SAC	Squeeze
SEA	2017	78	84	-1	88.4	34	0	62	527	373	28	91	.179	0	83	31	6	5	26	54	11	0
SEA	2018	89	73	12	86.4	31	0	66	537	387	21	102	.230	2	69	34	10	2	46	63	27	1
SEA	2019	68	94	0	76.0	20	0	51	538	328	25	81	.243	2	104	42	10	4	18	78	11	0
SEA	2020	27	33	2	84.2	7	0	25	189	120	7	26	.211	0	48	15	2	1	5	60	3	0
SEA	2021	90	72	15	84.7	22	0	55	584	414	23	101	.264	3	58	24	6	0	23	39	9	0

Chris Woodward wRM+: 102

TEAM	YEAR	W	L	Pythag +/-	Avg PC	100+ P	120+ P	QS	REL	REL w Zero R	IBB	PH	PH Avg	PH HR	SB2	CS2	SB3	CS3	SAC Att	SAC %	POS SAC	Squeeze
TEX	2019	78	84	4	87.0	60	1	55	500	306	11	82	.214	4	109	33	20	5	25	68	16	0
TEX	2020	22	38	2	83.5	18	0	17	204	128	3	30	.208	0	41	13	8	1	7	14	2	0
TEX	2021	60	102	0	81.2	14	1	50	507	331	11	89	.218	1	94	25	9	2	30	53	15	1

Rocco Baldelli wRM+: 101

TEAM	YEAR	W	L	Pythag +/-	Avg PC	100+ P	120+ P	QS	REL	REL w Zero R	IBB	PH	PH Avg	PH HR	SB2	CS2	SB3	CS3	SAC Att	SAC %	POS SAC	Squeeze
MIN	2019	101	61	3	89.6	34	0	67	524	379	10	83	.258	2	27	20	1	0	18	56	7	0
MIN	2020	36	24	-1	77.0	4	0	16	202	141	0	29	.250	0	14	7	0	0	5	40	2	1
MIN	2021	73	89	3	81.5	17	0	32	529	355	13	112	.196	0	48	15	7	0	13	54	6	1

Charlie Montoyo wRM+: 98

TEAM	YEAR	W	L	Pythag +/-	Avg PC	100+ P	120+ P	QS	REL	REL w Zero R	IBB	PH	PH Avg	PH HR	SB2	CS2	SB3	CS3	SAC Att	SAC %	POS SAC	Squeeze
TOR	2019	67	95	-3	76.0	19	0	40	591	377	25	79	.154	2	40	16	10	4	19	74	14	1
TOR	2020	32	28	3	76.1	1	0	11	226	141	7	37	.133	0	23	6	10	0	11	73	8	0
TOR	2021	91	71	-9	85.5	28	0	68	537	375	10	100	.167	0	72	15	10	6	18	56	7	1

Brandon Hyde wRM+: 98

TEAM	YEAR	W	L	Pythag +/-	Avg PC	100+ P	120+ P	QS	REL	REL w Zero R	IBB	PH	PH Avg	PH HR	SB2	CS2	SB3	CS3	SAC Att	SAC %	POS SAC	Squeeze
BAL	2019	54	108	-4	85.1	17	0	41	534	310	11	126	.195	2	72	25	11	5	43	51	19	2
BAL	2020	25	35	-3	75.6	0	0	10	207	138	2	43	.184	2	17	11	2	1	18	83	15	0
BAL	2021	52	110	0	79.4	7	0	31	569	348	12	85	.233	1	47	23	6	0	23	61	13	2

Joe Maddon wRM+: 97

TEAM	YEAR	W	L	Pythag +/-	Avg PC	100+ P	120+ P	QS	REL	REL w Zero R	IBB	PH	PH Avg	PH HR	SB2	CS2	SB3	CS3	SAC Att	SAC %	POS SAC	Squeeze
CHC	2017	92	70	-2	90.9	40	0	77	531	383	29	294	.238	5	56	25	5	7	59	81	22	5
CHC	2018	95	68	0	90.6	41	1	66	600	463	33	277	.242	6	53	32	11	7	67	60	14	4
CHC	2019	84	78	-7	90.4	40	0	69	576	412	16	243	.215	6	38	17	7	3	50	60	7	2
LAA	2020	26	34	-1	77.0	11	0	15	228	143	8	20	.211	0	20	8	1	0	9	67	6	1
LAA	2021	77	85	5	81.5	24	0	45	562	372	18	74	.154	0	70	23	8	2	52	58	30	5

Bob Melvin wRM+: 97

TEAM	YEAR	W	L	Pythag +/-	Avg PC	100+ P	120+ P	QS	REL	REL w Zero R	IBB	PH	PH Avg	PH HR	SB2	CS2	SB3	CS3	SAC Att	SAC %	POS SAC	Squeeze
OAK	2017	75	87	3	90.7	40	0	73	525	349	17	124	.218	1	47	20	9	3	21	62	9	1
OAK	2018	97	65	1	80.6	14	0	62	578	427	19	135	.256	3	31	20	3	1	10	60	6	0
OAK	2019	97	65	-1	88.7	30	1	78	547	393	19	116	.235	5	45	20	6	1	11	64	6	0
OAK	2020	36	24	1	81.4	4	0	19	181	137	6	32	.103	1	25	2	1	1	3	67	2	0
OAK	2021	86	76	-1	88.5	28	0	76	504	348	11	158	.241	5	70	15	19	7	21	81	13	1

David Ross wRM+: 96

TEAM	YEAR	W	L	Pythag +/-	Avg PC	100+ P	120+ P	QS	REL	REL w Zero R	IBB	PH	PH Avg	PH HR	SB2	CS2	SB3	CS3	SAC Att	SAC %	POS SAC	Squeeze
CHC	2020	34	26	1	84.6	10	0	30	188	128	7	51	.114	1	21	10	2	0	2	50	1	0
CHC	2021	71	91	4	80.1	14	0	43	599	424	25	308	.257	6	75	31	9	2	55	73	9	2

Torey Lovullo wRM+: 95

TEAM	YEAR	W	L	Pythag +/-	Avg PC	100+ P	120+ P	QS	REL	REL w Zero R	IBB	PH	PH Avg	PH HR	SB2	CS2	SB3	CS3	SAC Att	SAC %	POS SAC	Squeeze
ARI	2017	93	69	-5	95.9	73	1	82	514	378	45	251	.215	7	79	24	25	7	51	76	8	0
ARI	2018	82	80	-5	92.7	36	0	78	574	434	43	257	.202	5	62	22	18	4	61	62	10	0
ARI	2019	85	77	-3	88.8	32	0	67	557	390	38	256	.221	12	84	12	3	2	51	61	5	2
ARI	2020	25	35	-2	84.5	2	0	13	200	131	20	27	.000	0	22	6	1	1	4	25	1	0
ARI	2021	52	110	-7	84.1	16	1	41	569	352	45	338	.205	10	38	16	5	0	42	76	6	0

Jayce Tingler wRM+: 95

TEAM	YEAR	W	L	Pythag +/-	Avg PC	100+ P	120+ P	QS	REL	REL w Zero R	IBB	PH	PH Avg	PH HR	SB2	CS2	SB3	CS3	SAC Att	SAC %	POS SAC	Squeeze
SD	2020	37	23	-2	75.2	3	0	22	218	152	2	44	.256	1	45	10	10	4	18	67	12	1
SD	2021	79	83	-4	79.5	15	2	42	628	439	33	303	.205	3	99	32	9	9	51	69	16	0

A. J. Hinch wRM+: 95

TEAM	YEAR	W	L	Pythag +/-	Avg PC	100+ P	120+ P	QS	REL	REL w Zero R	IBB	PH	PH Avg	PH HR	SB2	CS2	SB3	CS3	SAC Att	SAC %	POS SAC	Squeeze
HOU	2017	101	61	0	92.1	32	0	67	519	365	17	73	.200	2	80	37	18	6	24	46	11	0
HOU	2018	103	59	-9	95.7	67	1	97	510	396	4	91	.167	1	63	22	8	3	20	70	14	6
HOU	2019	107	55	-2	91.6	55	0	89	492	354	0	81	.175	3	58	24	8	2	19	53	9	1
DET	2021	77	85	3	78.8	6	0	47	577	384	10	72	.266	3	78	21	10	4	22	77	15	3

Mike Shildt wRM+: 95

TEAM	YEAR	W	L	Pythag +/-	Avg PC	100+ P	120+ P	QS	REL	REL w Zero R	IBB	PH	PH Avg	PH HR	SB2	CS2	SB3	CS3	SAC Att	SAC %	POS SAC	Squeeze
STL	2018	41	28	0	88.0	11	0	26	244	170	25	112	.208	3	25	9	5	1	31	55	6	1
STL	2019	91	71	-2	89.7	29	1	76	542	390	41	267	.218	10	94	24	23	6	62	64	9	0
STL	2020	30	28	0	80.1	5	1	18	177	125	8	32	.034	0	16	8	2	2	5	80	4	0
STL	2021	90	72	5	83.8	21	0	56	557	402	30	256	.196	9	77	20	12	2	56	71	5	2

Derek Shelton wRM+: 94

TEAM	YEAR	W	L	Pythag +/-	Avg PC	100+ P	120+ P	QS	REL	REL w Zero R	IBB	PH	PH Avg	PH HR	SB2	CS2	SB3	CS3	SAC Att	SAC %	POS SAC	Squeeze
PIT	2020	19	41	-2	82.1	6	0	9	210	136	3	26	.160	0	14	9	2	3	9	78	7	0
PIT	2021	61	101	5	79.7	3	0	25	583	400	26	290	.232	9	56	26	4	3	54	57	9	1

Dave Roberts wRM+: 94

TEAM	YEAR	W	L	Pythag +/-	Avg PC	100+ P	120+ P	QS	REL	REL w Zero R	IBB	PH	PH Avg	PH HR	SB2	CS2	SB3	CS3	SAC Att	SAC %	POS SAC	Squeeze
LAD	2017	104	58	1	86.5	20	0	68	536	404	33	343	.243	8	60	25	15	2	46	67	4	1
LAD	2018	92	71	-11	86.3	22	0	79	593	441	39	354	.238	9	57	20	18	1	57	68	9	3
LAD	2019	106	56	-4	85.8	24	0	80	545	390	24	307	.234	13	52	10	4	0	64	86	3	3
LAD	2020	43	17	-1	72.8	0	0	18	249	191	4	41	.194	1	25	6	4	1	6	50	3	1
LAD	2021	106	56	-5	80.6	29	1	74	600	446	43	276	.201	9	49	14	15	4	37	86	3	5

Don Mattingly wRM+: 93

TEAM	YEAR	W	L	Pythag +/-	Avg PC	100+ P	120+ P	QS	REL	REL w Zero R	IBB	PH	PH Avg	PH HR	SB2	CS2	SB3	CS3	SAC Att	SAC %	POS SAC	Squeeze
MIA	2017	77	85	0	87.0	28	0	54	580	404	59	271	.262	6	82	22	9	7	72	69	15	3
MIA	2018	63	98	7	88.0	29	0	57	546	367	73	281	.177	6	40	29	5	3	47	68	12	1
MIA	2019	57	105	-2	91.3	33	0	60	539	369	52	290	.214	9	49	26	6	1	53	58	8	2
MIA	2020	31	29	5	76.7	1	0	16	215	148	14	36	.233	0	41	10	7	5	9	67	6	1
MIA	2021	67	95	-4	79.8	13	1	49	605	423	43	270	.185	3	93	26	13	5	50	60	11	1

Dusty Baker wRM+: 93

TEAM	YEAR	W	L	Pythag +/-	Avg PC	100+ P	120+ P	QS	REL	REL w Zero R	IBB	PH	PH Avg	PH HR	SB2	CS2	SB3	CS3	SAC Att	SAC %	POS SAC	Squeeze
WAS	2017	97	65	0	99.4	95	3	99	487	344	39	241	.213	5	91	24	17	7	59	73	15	0
HOU	2020	29	31	-1	83.4	8	0	25	193	122	7	28	.208	0	20	10	2	1	8	75	6	0
HOU	2021	95	67	-7	88.1	28	0	66	512	349	12	94	.235	3	49	11	4	5	16	56	9	1

Gabe Kapler wRM+: 93

TEAM	YEAR	W	L	Pythag +/-	Avg PC	100+ P	120+ P	QS	REL	REL w Zero R	IBB	PH	PH Avg	PH HR	SB2	CS2	SB3	CS3	SAC Att	SAC %	POS SAC	Squeeze
PHI	2018	80	82	5	87.8	38	0	71	596	432	35	295	.207	5	64	20	3	6	48	67	6	0
PHI	2019	81	81	2	89.0	38	0	58	564	401	38	310	.201	9	65	15	12	1	55	62	11	1
SF	2020	29	31	-1	81.9	10	0	11	236	173	2	73	.267	4	19	7	0	1	4	100	4	0
SF	2021	107	55	2	80.8	12	0	63	599	452	20	405	.201	18	62	11	6	5	51	69	6	1

Brian Snitker wRM+: 92

TEAM	YEAR	W	L	Pythag +/-	Avg PC	100+ P	120+ P	QS	REL	REL w Zero R	IBB	PH	PH Avg	PH HR	SB2	CS2	SB3	CS3	SAC Att	SAC %	POS SAC	Squeeze
ATL	2017	72	90	0	93.2	45	1	77	530	376	39	268	.231	10	64	30	13	2	79	75	18	0
ATL	2018	90	72	-3	90.7	39	1	70	553	397	43	247	.202	7	75	28	13	7	65	75	13	3
ATL	2019	97	65	5	88.0	25	0	76	576	411	33	262	.247	9	82	25	8	3	34	74	3	2
ATL	2020	35	25	-1	73.2	2	0	13	228	159	13	29	.200	1	21	4	2	0	3	33	1	0
ATL	2021	88	73	-7	85.7	14	0	67	583	417	35	272	.184	10	56	16	2	3	41	78	8	1

Dave Martinez wRM+: 92

TEAM	YEAR	W	L	Pythag +/-	Avg PC	100+ P	120+ P	QS	REL	REL w Zero R	IBB	PH	PH Avg	PH HR	SB2	CS2	SB3	CS3	SAC Att	SAC %	POS SAC	Squeeze
WAS	2018	82	80	-9	94.0	66	1	74	563	409	37	293	.176	4	99	31	20	3	67	61	13	0
WAS	2019	93	69	-3	94.4	62	0	87	530	364	41	253	.261	5	97	26	18	3	84	57	20	2
WAS	2020	26	34	-3	87.8	18	0	16	202	139	22	31	.321	0	29	11	5	1	12	42	5	0
WAS	2021	65	97	-6	85.5	26	2	50	572	372	46	282	.242	6	52	24	5	3	65	60	10	1

2022 PECOTA Leaderboards

Catcher DRC+

Rank	Name	Team	DRC+
1	Yasmani Grandal	CHW	131
2	Will Smith	LAD	112
3	Alejandro Kirk	TOR	111
4	Daulton Varsho	ARI	105
4	J.T. Realmuto	PHI	105
6	Keibert Ruiz	WAS	103
6	Austin Nola	SD	103
8	Salvador Perez	KC	101
9	Gary Sánchez	NYY	100
9	Willson Contreras	CHC	100
11	Mitch Garver	MIN	99
12	Kevin Plawecki	BOS	98
12	Zack Collins	CHW	98
14	Sean Murphy	OAK	97
14	Danny Jansen	TOR	97

First Base DRC+

Rank	Name	Team	DRC+
1	Vladimir Guerrero Jr.	TOR	148
2	Freddie Freeman	FA	142
3	Matt Olson	OAK	137
4	Paul Goldschmidt	STL	133
4	Pete Alonso	NYM	133
6	Max Muncy	LAD	127
7	Rhys Hoskins	PHI	121
8	Joey Votto	CIN	118
9	Darin Ruf	SF	117
9	Anthony Rizzo	FA	117
11	José Abreu	CHW	116
12	Jesús Aguilar	MIA	115
13	Ty France	SEA	114
13	C.J. Cron	COL	114
15	Yoshi Tsutsugo	PIT	113

Second Base DRC+

Rank	Name	Team	DRC+
1	Jose Altuve	HOU	117
2	Jeff McNeil	NYM	114
3	DJ LeMahieu	NYY	109
4	Jonathan India	CIN	108
5	Ozzie Albies	ATL	107
6	Isaac Paredes	DET	105
6	Brandon Lowe	TB	105
8	Abraham Toro	SEA	104
8	Jean Segura	PHI	104
10	Marcus Semien	TEX	102
10	Nick Madrigal	CHC	102
10	Jake Cronenworth	SD	102
13	Kolten Wong	MIL	101
13	Andy Ibáñez	TEX	101
13	Adam Frazier	SEA	101

Shortstop DRC+

Rank	Name	Team	DRC+
1	Fernando Tatis Jr.	SD	138
2	Corey Seager	TEX	123
3	Trea Turner	LAD	120
4	Carlos Correa	FA	119
5	Wander Franco	TB	118
6	Xander Bogaerts	BOS	117
7	Trevor Story	FA	116
8	Bo Bichette	TOR	112
9	Gleyber Torres	NYY	111
10	Francisco Lindor	NYM	105
11	Tim Anderson	CHW	99
12	Gavin Lux	LAD	98
12	J.P. Crawford	SEA	98
14	Brandon Crawford	SF	97
15	Oneil Cruz	PIT	96

Third Base DRC+

Rank	Name	Team	DRC+
1	Anthony Rendon	LAA	128
2	José Ramírez	CLE	127
2	Manny Machado	SD	127
4	Alex Bregman	HOU	125
5	Josh Donaldson	MIN	123
6	Austin Riley	ATL	121
6	Nolan Arenado	STL	121
8	Justin Turner	LAD	118
9	Rafael Devers	BOS	116
10	Yoán Moncada	CHW	112
11	Kris Bryant	FA	111
11	Luis Arraez	MIN	111
13	J.D. Davis	NYM	106
14	Eugenio Suárez	CIN	105
14	Jeimer Candelario	DET	105

Designated Hitter DRC+

Rank	Name	Team	DRC+
1	Shohei Ohtani	LAA	136
2	Yordan Alvarez	HOU	130
3	Giancarlo Stanton	NYY	128
4	J.D. Martinez	BOS	121
5	Nelson Cruz	FA	118
6	Franmil Reyes	CLE	104
6	Khris Davis	FA	104
8	Yermín Mercedes	CHW	101
9	Seth Beer	ARI	100
10	Ryan O'Hearn	KC	95
11	Miguel Cabrera	DET	94
12	Mitch Moreland	OAK	90
13	Gavin Sheets	CHW	89
14	Luis Torrens	SEA	79

Left Field DRC+

Rank	Name	Team	DRC+
1	Christian Yelich	MIL	127
2	Jesse Winker	CIN	123
3	Marcell Ozuna	ATL	118
4	Mark Canha	NYM	117
5	Kyle Schwarber	FA	115
5	Michael Brantley	HOU	115
7	Tommy Pham	FA	113
7	Tyler O'Neill	STL	113
9	Eloy Jiménez	CHW	110
10	AJ Pollock	LAD	105
10	Connor Joe	COL	105
12	Alex Verdugo	BOS	104
12	Austin Meadows	TB	104
14	David Peralta	ARI	103
14	Andrew McCutchen	FA	103

Center Field DRC+

Rank	Name	Team	DRC+
1	Mike Trout	LAA	161
2	Bryan Reynolds	PIT	125
3	Luis Robert	CHW	119
4	George Springer	TOR	118
5	Ketel Marte	ARI	111
6	Shogo Akiyama	CIN	110
7	Nick Senzel	CIN	109
7	Starling Marte	NYM	109
9	Harrison Bader	STL	108
10	Aaron Hicks	NYY	106
11	Byron Buxton	MIN	105
11	Cody Bellinger	LAD	105
13	Jordan Luplow	ARI	103
14	Chris Taylor	LAD	102
15	Trent Grisham	SD	101

Right Field DRC+

Rank	Name	Team	DRC+
1	Juan Soto	WAS	171
2	Ronald Acuña Jr.	ATL	148
3	Bryce Harper	PHI	145
4	Aaron Judge	NYY	133
5	Kyle Tucker	HOU	124
6	Mookie Betts	LAD	123
7	Brandon Nimmo	NYM	121
8	Michael Conforto	FA	116
9	Charlie Blackmon	COL	115
10	Joey Gallo	NYY	113
11	Jorge Soler	FA	112
11	Nick Castellanos	FA	112
13	Teoscar Hernández	TOR	107
14	Hunter Renfroe	MIL	106
15	Mitch Haniger	SEA	104

Catcher FRAA

Rank	Name	Team	FRAA
1	Austin Hedges	CLE	21.3
2	Max Stassi	LAA	15.1
3	Yasmani Grandal	CHW	10.8
4	Christian Vázquez	BOS	9.1
5	Roberto Pérez	PIT	8.6
6	Tomás Nido	NYM	8.5
7	Kyle Higashioka	NYY	8.0
7	Austin Barnes	LAD	8.0
9	Jose Trevino	TEX	7.2
10	J.T. Realmuto	PHI	6.8
11	Cal Raleigh	SEA	6.5
12	Joey Bart	SF	6.4
13	Jonah Heim	TEX	6.1
14	Reese McGuire	TOR	5.3
15	Travis d'Arnaud	ATL	4.8

First Base FRAA

Rank	Name	Team	FRAA
1	Joey Votto	CIN	3.7
1	Yuli Gurriel	HOU	3.7
3	Pavin Smith	ARI	3.4
4	Christian Walker	ARI	2.8
5	C.J. Cron	COL	2.7
6	Matt Olson	OAK	2.4
7	Max Muncy	LAD	1.7
8	Jesús Aguilar	MIA	1.6
9	Jared Walsh	LAA	1.5
10	Brandon Belt	SF	1.3
11	Alex Kirilloff	MIN	1.2
12	Brad Miller	FA	0.7
13	Matt Vierling	PHI	0.6
14	Darin Ruf	SF	0.4
14	Lewin Díaz	MIA	0.4

Second Base FRAA

Rank	Name	Team	FRAA
1	Kolten Wong	MIL	5.0
2	Jean Segura	PHI	4.5
3	Jonathan India	CIN	3.7
4	Marcus Semien	TEX	3.5
5	David Fletcher	LAA	3.2
6	Whit Merrifield	KC	2.8
6	Jorge Mateo	BAL	2.8
8	Jorge Polanco	MIN	2.6
9	Dylan Moore	SEA	2.2
10	DJ LeMahieu	NYY	1.7
10	Tommy Edman	STL	1.7
12	Ozzie Albies	ATL	1.5
13	Eric Sogard	CHC	1.2
14	Tony Kemp	OAK	0.9
15	Marwin Gonzalez	HOU	0.8

Shortstop FRAA

Rank	Name	Team	FRAA
1	Ha-Seong Kim	SD	7.1
2	Isiah Kiner-Falefa	TEX	4.5
2	Javier Báez	DET	4.5
4	Willy Adames	MIL	4.0
5	Taylor Walls	TB	3.0
6	Andrelton Simmons	FA	2.1
7	Andrés Giménez	CLE	1.4
8	Nicky Lopez	KC	1.2
8	Sergio Alcántara	CHC	1.2
10	Corey Seager	TEX	1.1
10	J.P. Crawford	SEA	1.1
12	Paul DeJong	STL	1.0
13	Oneil Cruz	PIT	0.8
14	Luis Rengifo	LAA	0.6
14	Brandon Crawford	SF	0.6

Third Base FRAA

Rank	Name	Team	FRAA
1	Santiago Espinal	TOR	7.1
2	Brian Anderson	MIA	3.6
3	Brock Holt	FA	3.2
4	Ke'Bryan Hayes	PIT	3.0
5	Luis Urías	MIL	2.9
6	Nolan Arenado	STL	2.8
7	Charlie Culberson	TEX	1.7
8	Evan Longoria	SF	1.5
9	Travis Shaw	BOS	1.4
10	Justin Turner	LAD	1.3
11	Josh Donaldson	MIN	0.9
12	Luis Arraez	MIN	0.8
13	Joey Wendle	MIA	0.7
13	Austin Riley	ATL	0.7
13	Erik González	MIA	0.7

Left Field FRAA

Rank	Name	Team	FRAA
1	David Peralta	ARI	6.0
2	Connor Joe	COL	2.6
3	Mark Canha	NYM	2.2
3	Anthony Alford	PIT	2.2
5	Jo Adell	LAA	2.0
6	AJ Pollock	LAD	1.6
7	Tyler O'Neill	STL	1.5
8	Jesse Winker	CIN	1.4
8	Oscar Mercado	CLE	1.4
8	Randy Arozarena	TB	1.4
11	Tyrone Taylor	MIL	1.1
11	Lourdes Gurriel Jr.	TOR	1.1
13	Kyle Schwarber	FA	1.0
13	Austin Hays	BAL	1.0
15	Trevor Larnach	MIN	0.9

Center Field FRAA

Rank	Name	Team	FRAA
1	Byron Buxton	MIN	8.0
2	Adolis García	TEX	6.4
3	Jake Marisnick	SD	5.1
4	Cedric Mullins	BAL	3.7
5	Luis Robert	CHW	3.6
6	Jarren Duran	BOS	3.3
7	Cody Bellinger	LAD	3.0
8	Harrison Bader	STL	2.9
9	Sam Hilliard	COL	2.8
10	Michael A. Taylor	KC	2.5
10	Jake Meyers	HOU	2.5
10	Ramón Laureano	OAK	2.5
13	Guillermo Heredia	ATL	2.4
14	Luke Williams	PHI	2.3
14	Enrique Hernández	BOS	2.3

Right Field FRAA

Rank	Name	Team	FRAA
1	Manuel Margot	TB	7.0
2	Brandon Nimmo	NYM	6.7
3	Joey Gallo	NYY	6.4
4	Jesús Sánchez	MIA	5.5
5	Mookie Betts	LAD	4.4
6	Juan Soto	WAS	4.3
7	Mike Yastrzemski	SF	3.3
8	Mitch Haniger	SEA	2.7
9	Teoscar Hernández	TOR	2.4
10	Seth Brown	OAK	2.0
11	Taylor Ward	LAA	1.9
11	Kyle Isbel	KC	1.9
13	LaMonte Wade Jr.	SF	1.4
13	Kyle Tucker	HOU	1.4
15	Kole Calhoun	TEX	1.1

Catcher WARP

Rank	Name	Team	WARP
1	Yasmani Grandal	CHW	5.1
2	Will Smith	LAD	3.1
3	J.T. Realmuto	PHI	3.0
4	Max Stassi	LAA	2.5
5	Christian Vázquez	BOS	2.2
6	Sean Murphy	OAK	2.1
7	Gary Sánchez	NYY	2.0
7	Austin Hedges	CLE	2.0
9	Daulton Varsho	ARI	1.9
10	Tyler Stephenson	CIN	1.8
10	Carson Kelly	ARI	1.8
10	Willson Contreras	CHC	1.8
13	Keibert Ruiz	WAS	1.7
14	Jacob Stallings	MIA	1.6
14	Austin Nola	SD	1.6

First Base WARP

Rank	Name	Team	WARP
1	Vladimir Guerrero Jr.	TOR	5.0
2	Matt Olson	OAK	4.6
2	Freddie Freeman	FA	4.6
4	Paul Goldschmidt	STL	3.6
5	Pete Alonso	NYM	3.5
6	Max Muncy	LAD	3.4
7	Joey Votto	CIN	2.8
8	Anthony Rizzo	FA	2.5
9	Rhys Hoskins	PHI	2.3
9	Yuli Gurriel	HOU	2.3
9	José Abreu	CHW	2.3
12	Yandy Díaz	TB	2.2
13	Jesús Aguilar	MIA	2.1
14	C.J. Cron	COL	2.0
15	Yoshi Tsutsugo	PIT	1.8

Second Base WARP

Rank	Name	Team	WARP
1	Jose Altuve	HOU	3.8
2	Jonathan India	CIN	3.1
3	Jean Segura	PHI	3.0
4	DJ LeMahieu	NYY	2.9
4	Ozzie Albies	ATL	2.9
6	Marcus Semien	TEX	2.8
7	Kolten Wong	MIL	2.7
8	Whit Merrifield	KC	2.5
8	Brandon Lowe	TB	2.5
10	Jorge Polanco	MIN	2.3
11	Tony Kemp	OAK	2.1
11	Adam Frazier	SEA	2.1
11	David Fletcher	LAA	2.1
11	Tommy Edman	STL	2.1
11	Jake Cronenworth	SD	2.1

Shortstop WARP

Rank	Name	Team	WARP
1	Fernando Tatis Jr.	SD	5.4
2	Trea Turner	LAD	4.1
3	Corey Seager	TEX	3.9
4	Wander Franco	TB	3.7
5	Trevor Story	FA	3.6
6	Carlos Correa	FA	3.4
6	Xander Bogaerts	BOS	3.4
6	Bo Bichette	TOR	3.4
9	Gleyber Torres	NYY	2.7
9	Francisco Lindor	NYM	2.7
11	Tim Anderson	CHW	2.5
12	J.P. Crawford	SEA	2.4
13	Willy Adames	MIL	2.2
14	Brandon Crawford	SF	1.9
15	Amed Rosario	CLE	1.6

Third Base WARP

Rank	Name	Team	WARP
1	José Ramírez	CLE	4.1
2	Manny Machado	SD	4.0
3	Alex Bregman	HOU	3.7
4	Anthony Rendon	LAA	3.5
5	Nolan Arenado	STL	3.4
6	Josh Donaldson	MIN	3.2
7	Justin Turner	LAD	3.0
7	Austin Riley	ATL	3.0
9	Rafael Devers	BOS	2.8
10	Yoán Moncada	CHW	2.7
11	Luis Arraez	MIN	2.6
12	Jeimer Candelario	DET	2.0
12	Kris Bryant	FA	2.0
14	Luis Urías	MIL	1.9
14	Matt Chapman	OAK	1.9

Designated Hitter WARP

Rank	Name	Team	WARP
1	Shohei Ohtani	LAA	4.2
2	Yordan Alvarez	HOU	3.6
3	Giancarlo Stanton	NYY	3.1
3	J.D. Martinez	BOS	3.1
5	Nelson Cruz	FA	2.1
6	Franmil Reyes	CLE	1.7
7	Khris Davis	FA	0.6
7	Miguel Cabrera	DET	0.6
9	Ryan O'Hearn	KC	0.4
10	Gavin Sheets	CHW	0.3
11	Mitch Moreland	OAK	0.2
11	Yermín Mercedes	CHW	0.2
11	Seth Beer	ARI	0.2
14	Luis Torrens	SEA	-0.5

Left Field WARP

Rank	Name	Team	WARP
1	Christian Yelich	MIL	4.1
2	Jesse Winker	CIN	3.1
2	Mark Canha	NYM	3.1
4	Kyle Schwarber	FA	3.0
5	Tyler O'Neill	STL	2.8
5	Michael Brantley	HOU	2.8
7	Tommy Pham	FA	2.6
8	David Peralta	ARI	2.5
9	Eloy Jiménez	CHW	2.4
10	Randy Arozarena	TB	2.2
11	Lourdes Gurriel Jr.	TOR	1.9
12	Alex Verdugo	BOS	1.8
12	Andrew Benintendi	KC	1.8
14	Justin Upton	LAA	1.7
14	AJ Pollock	LAD	1.7

Center Field WARP

Rank	Name	Team	WARP
1	Mike Trout	LAA	6.5
2	Luis Robert	CHW	4.1
3	Bryan Reynolds	PIT	4.0
4	George Springer	TOR	3.7
5	Byron Buxton	MIN	3.2
6	Starling Marte	NYM	3.1
7	Ketel Marte	ARI	2.8
8	Trent Grisham	SD	2.6
8	Cody Bellinger	LAD	2.6
10	Harrison Bader	STL	2.5
11	Ramón Laureano	OAK	2.2
11	Lorenzo Cain	MIL	2.2
13	Chris Taylor	LAD	2.1
13	Cedric Mullins	BAL	2.1
13	Enrique Hernández	BOS	2.1

Right Field WARP

Rank	Name	Team	WARP
1	Juan Soto	WAS	7.6
2	Ronald Acuña Jr.	ATL	5.3
3	Bryce Harper	PHI	4.9
4	Aaron Judge	NYY	4.1
5	Mookie Betts	LAD	4.0
6	Kyle Tucker	HOU	3.7
6	Brandon Nimmo	NYM	3.7
8	Joey Gallo	NYY	3.6
9	Michael Conforto	FA	2.8
10	Nick Castellanos	FA	2.6
11	Teoscar Hernández	TOR	2.3
11	Charlie Blackmon	COL	2.3
13	Mitch Haniger	SEA	2.2
14	Manuel Margot	TB	2.1
15	Jorge Soler	FA	2.0

Batting Average

Rank	Name	Team	BA
1	Vladimir Guerrero Jr.	TOR	.299
2	Juan Soto	WAS	.297
2	Luis Arraez	MIN	.297
4	Trea Turner	LAD	.294
4	Michael Brantley	HOU	.294
6	Freddie Freeman	FA	.293
7	Nick Madrigal	CHC	.288
8	Paul Goldschmidt	STL	.286
9	Wander Franco	TB	.285
10	Bo Bichette	TOR	.284
11	Tim Anderson	CHW	.282
12	Corey Seager	TEX	.281
12	Jeff McNeil	NYM	.281
12	DJ LeMahieu	NYY	.281
15	Ketel Marte	ARI	.280
15	Yuli Gurriel	HOU	.280
15	David Fletcher	LAA	.280
18	Luis Robert	CHW	.279
19	Mike Trout	LAA	.278
19	Bryan Reynolds	PIT	.278
19	Whit Merrifield	KC	.278
19	Charlie Blackmon	COL	.278
23	Manny Machado	SD	.277
23	Yordan Alvarez	HOU	.277
23	Ronald Acuña Jr.	ATL	.277

On-Base Percentage

Rank	Name	Team	OBP
1	Juan Soto	WAS	.448
2	Mike Trout	LAA	.416
3	Bryce Harper	PHI	.397
4	Freddie Freeman	FA	.394
5	Yasmani Grandal	CHW	.391
6	Ronald Acuña Jr.	ATL	.389
7	Vladimir Guerrero Jr.	TOR	.386
8	Christian Yelich	MIL	.383
9	Brandon Nimmo	NYM	.380
10	Anthony Rendon	LAA	.374
11	Alex Bregman	HOU	.373
12	Jesse Winker	CIN	.372
13	Mark Canha	NYM	.370
14	Matt Olson	OAK	.369
14	Shohei Ohtani	LAA	.369
14	Paul Goldschmidt	STL	.369
17	Max Muncy	LAD	.368
17	Mookie Betts	LAD	.368
19	Yandy Díaz	TB	.366
20	Bryan Reynolds	PIT	.365
20	Aaron Judge	NYY	.365
22	Luis Arraez	MIN	.364
23	Joey Votto	CIN	.363
24	Justin Turner	LAD	.361
24	Fernando Tatis Jr.	SD	.361

Slugging Percentage

Rank	Name	Team	SLG
1	Mike Trout	LAA	.568
2	Ronald Acuña Jr.	ATL	.559
3	Shohei Ohtani	LAA	.550
4	Fernando Tatis Jr.	SD	.547
5	Vladimir Guerrero Jr.	TOR	.540
6	Juan Soto	WAS	.536
7	Yordan Alvarez	HOU	.526
8	Matt Olson	OAK	.524
8	Bryce Harper	PHI	.524
10	Pete Alonso	NYM	.523
11	Giancarlo Stanton	NYY	.513
12	Aaron Judge	NYY	.508
13	Freddie Freeman	FA	.500
14	J.D. Martinez	BOS	.499
14	Manny Machado	SD	.499
16	Austin Riley	ATL	.498
17	Kyle Tucker	HOU	.493
17	José Ramírez	CLE	.493
19	Paul Goldschmidt	STL	.490
20	Rhys Hoskins	PHI	.489
21	Luis Robert	CHW	.488
22	Trevor Story	FA	.485
22	Nelson Cruz	FA	.485
24	Hunter Renfroe	MIL	.484
25	Tyler O'Neill	STL	.483

Isolated Slugging Percentage

Rank	Name	Team	ISO
1	Mike Trout	LAA	.290
2	Shohei Ohtani	LAA	.286
3	Ronald Acuña Jr.	ATL	.282
4	Fernando Tatis Jr.	SD	.274
5	Joey Gallo	NYY	.268
6	Matt Olson	OAK	.257
6	Pete Alonso	NYM	.257
8	Giancarlo Stanton	NYY	.255
8	Bryce Harper	PHI	.255
10	Aristides Aquino	CIN	.251
11	Yordan Alvarez	HOU	.249
12	Rhys Hoskins	PHI	.245
13	Eugenio Suárez	CIN	.241
13	Miguel Sanó	MIN	.241
13	Vladimir Guerrero Jr.	TOR	.241
16	Juan Soto	WAS	.239
17	Hunter Renfroe	MIL	.238
18	Bobby Dalbec	BOS	.237
19	Tyler O'Neill	STL	.236
19	Aaron Judge	NYY	.236
21	Kyle Schwarber	FA	.233
21	Adam Duvall	ATL	.233
23	José Ramírez	CLE	.228
23	Yasmani Grandal	CHW	.228
25	Austin Riley	ATL	.227

OPS

Rank	Name	Team	OPS
1	Juan Soto	WAS	.984
2	Mike Trout	LAA	.983
3	Ronald Acuña Jr.	ATL	.948
4	Vladimir Guerrero Jr.	TOR	.927
5	Bryce Harper	PHI	.921
6	Shohei Ohtani	LAA	.919
7	Fernando Tatis Jr.	SD	.907
8	Freddie Freeman	FA	.894
9	Matt Olson	OAK	.893
10	Yordan Alvarez	HOU	.880
11	Pete Alonso	NYM	.877
12	Aaron Judge	NYY	.872
13	Giancarlo Stanton	NYY	.861
14	Paul Goldschmidt	STL	.860
15	Yasmani Grandal	CHW	.854
16	Christian Yelich	MIL	.852
16	Manny Machado	SD	.852
18	José Ramírez	CLE	.851
19	J.D. Martinez	BOS	.847
20	Mookie Betts	LAD	.846
21	Jesse Winker	CIN	.841
22	Rhys Hoskins	PHI	.840
23	Max Muncy	LAD	.839
24	Kyle Tucker	HOU	.838
25	Austin Riley	ATL	.837

BABIP

Rank	Name	Team	BABIP
1	Keston Hiura	MIL	.349
2	Brandon Marsh	LAA	.343
3	Oneil Cruz	PIT	.342
4	Gabriel Arias	CLE	.340
5	Franchy Cordero	BOS	.339
5	Micker Adolfo	CHW	.339
7	Shohei Ohtani	LAA	.337
7	Travis Demeritte	ATL	.337
7	Tim Anderson	CHW	.337
10	Connor Wong	BOS	.336
10	Nelson Velazquez	CHC	.336
10	Luis Robert	CHW	.336
13	Willy Adames	MIL	.335
14	Trea Turner	LAD	.333
14	Fernando Tatis Jr.	SD	.333
16	J.D. Davis	NYM	.331
16	Anthony Alford	PIT	.331
18	Julio Rodríguez	SEA	.330
18	Bryan Reynolds	PIT	.330
20	Yoán Moncada	CHW	.329
21	Kyle Stowers	BAL	.328
21	Paul Goldschmidt	STL	.328
21	Jarren Duran	BOS	.328
21	Bo Bichette	TOR	.328
25	Heliot Ramos	SF	.326

Runs Scored

Rank	Name	Team	R
1	Bryce Harper	PHI	125
2	Juan Soto	WAS	122
3	Ronald Acuña Jr.	ATL	121
4	Mookie Betts	LAD	119
5	Fernando Tatis Jr.	SD	116
5	José Ramírez	CLE	116
7	Matt Olson	OAK	115
8	Trea Turner	LAD	114
9	DJ LeMahieu	NYY	113
9	Jose Altuve	HOU	113
11	Vladimir Guerrero Jr.	TOR	112
12	Mike Trout	LAA	109
12	Manny Machado	SD	109
12	Aaron Judge	NYY	109
15	Max Muncy	LAD	108
15	Rhys Hoskins	PHI	108
17	Alex Bregman	HOU	106
18	George Springer	TOR	105
19	Yordan Alvarez	HOU	104
20	Christian Yelich	MIL	102
20	Shohei Ohtani	LAA	102
20	Paul Goldschmidt	STL	102
20	Pete Alonso	NYM	102
24	Bo Bichette	TOR	100
25	Joey Votto	CIN	99

Runs Batted In

Rank	Name	Team	RBI
1	Yordan Alvarez	HOU	118
2	Pete Alonso	NYM	111
3	Vladimir Guerrero Jr.	TOR	109
4	Juan Soto	WAS	105
5	Matt Olson	OAK	104
5	Manny Machado	SD	104
5	Bryce Harper	PHI	104
8	Fernando Tatis Jr.	SD	103
8	Franmil Reyes	CLE	103
10	Justin Turner	LAD	100
10	Giancarlo Stanton	NYY	100
10	Max Muncy	LAD	100
13	Kyle Tucker	HOU	98
13	Mike Trout	LAA	98
15	Teoscar Hernández	TOR	96
15	Joey Gallo	NYY	96
17	Aaron Judge	NYY	94
17	Alex Bregman	HOU	94
17	Cody Bellinger	LAD	94
20	Salvador Perez	KC	93
20	Shohei Ohtani	LAA	93
20	Rhys Hoskins	PHI	93
20	Adam Duvall	ATL	93
20	Josh Bell	WAS	93
25	Trea Turner	LAD	92

Home Runs

Rank	Name	Team	HR
1	Matt Olson	OAK	37
2	Fernando Tatis Jr.	SD	36
2	Ronald Acuña Jr.	ATL	36
4	Joey Gallo	NYY	35
5	Mike Trout	LAA	34
5	Shohei Ohtani	LAA	34
7	Franmil Reyes	CLE	33
7	Vladimir Guerrero Jr.	TOR	33
7	Pete Alonso	NYM	33
10	Giancarlo Stanton	NYY	32
11	Manny Machado	SD	31
11	Aaron Judge	NYY	31
11	Adam Duvall	ATL	31
11	Yordan Alvarez	HOU	31
15	Tyler O'Neill	STL	30
15	Rhys Hoskins	PHI	30
15	Bryce Harper	PHI	30
18	Patrick Wisdom	CHC	29
18	Jorge Soler	FA	29
18	Kyle Schwarber	FA	29
18	Miguel Sanó	MIN	29
18	José Ramírez	CLE	29
23	Joey Votto	CIN	28
23	Salvador Perez	KC	28
23	Max Muncy	LAD	28

Stolen Bases

Rank	Name	Team	SB
1	Trea Turner	LAD	34
2	Starling Marte	NYM	32
3	Adalberto Mondesi	KC	30
3	Whit Merrifield	KC	30
5	Myles Straw	CLE	27
5	Ronald Acuña Jr.	ATL	27
7	José Ramírez	CLE	26
8	Jonathan Villar	FA	23
8	Fernando Tatis Jr.	SD	23
8	Vidal Bruján	TB	23
11	Luis Robert	CHW	22
11	Garrett Hampson	COL	22
11	Jarren Duran	BOS	22
14	Bo Bichette	TOR	21
15	Tim Anderson	CHW	20
16	Michael A. Taylor	KC	19
16	Cedric Mullins	BAL	19
18	Trevor Story	FA	18
18	Josh Rojas	ARI	18
18	Shohei Ohtani	LAA	18
18	Manuel Margot	TB	18
18	Tommy Edman	STL	18
18	Lorenzo Cain	MIL	18
18	Randy Arozarena	TB	18
25	Christian Yelich	MIL	17

Walk Rate

Rank	Name	Team	BB%
1	Juan Soto	WAS	21.1
2	Yasmani Grandal	CHW	19.5
3	Mike Trout	LAA	17.4
4	Bryce Harper	PHI	16.8
5	Joey Gallo	NYY	16.6
6	Daniel Vogelbach	FA	16.2
7	Christian Yelich	MIL	15.5
8	Max Muncy	LAD	14.7
8	Matt Joyce	PHI	14.7
8	Aaron Hicks	NYY	14.7
11	Carlos Santana	KC	14.4
12	Matt Carpenter	STL	14.1
12	Brandon Nimmo	NYM	14.1
14	Josh Donaldson	MIN	13.8
14	Robbie Grossman	DET	13.8
14	Ji-Man Choi	TB	13.8
14	Ronald Acuña Jr.	ATL	13.8
18	Jason Castro	HOU	13.7
19	Tommy Pham	FA	13.6
19	Joey Votto	CIN	13.6
21	Cavan Biggio	TOR	13.5
21	Shohei Ohtani	LAA	13.5
21	Zack Collins	CHW	13.5
24	Andrew McCutchen	FA	13.3
24	Brandon Belt	SF	13.3

Strikeout Rate

Rank	Name	Team	K%
1	Nick Madrigal	CHC	6.1
2	David Fletcher	LAA	8.6
3	Luis Arraez	MIN	8.7
4	Tommy La Stella	SF	9.0
5	Steven Kwan	CLE	9.1
6	Kevin Newman	PIT	9.7
7	Michael Brantley	HOU	10.4
7	Yuli Gurriel	HOU	10.4
9	Keibert Ruiz	WAS	11.0
9	Adam Frazier	SEA	11.0
11	Hanser Alberto	KC	11.2
12	Alex Bregman	HOU	11.6
13	Andrelton Simmons	FA	11.7
14	Ronald Torreyes	PHI	11.8
15	Wander Franco	TB	11.9
16	Joe Panik	MIA	12.3
17	Jose Altuve	HOU	12.4
18	Tyler Freeman	CLE	12.6
19	Raimel Tapia	COL	12.8
19	Nicky Lopez	KC	12.8
19	Jeff McNeil	NYM	12.8
22	Nolan Arenado	STL	12.9
22	José Ramírez	CLE	12.9
24	DJ LeMahieu	NYY	13.0
24	Tony Kemp	OAK	13.0

Catcher Defense Added

Rank	Name	Team	Total Runs
1	Austin Hedges	CLE	17.0
2	Max Stassi	LAA	14.8
3	Yasmani Grandal	CHW	10.6
4	Roberto Pérez	PIT	9.3
5	Tomás Nido	NYM	8.7
6	Austin Barnes	LAD	8.1
7	J.T. Realmuto	PHI	7.3
7	Travis d'Arnaud	ATL	7.3
9	Jonah Heim	TEX	7.0
9	Jacob Stallings	MIA	7.0
11	Ryan Jeffers	MIN	6.9
12	Reese McGuire	TOR	6.7
12	Kyle Higashioka	NYY	6.7
14	Martín Maldonado	HOU	6.3
14	Manny Piña	ATL	6.3
16	Danny Jansen	TOR	6.2
17	Cal Raleigh	SEA	5.9
18	Joey Bart	SF	5.7
19	Christian Vázquez	BOS	5.6
20	Will Smith	LAD	4.9
21	Dom Nuñez	COL	4.1
22	Jose Trevino	TEX	4.0
23	Tyler Stephenson	CIN	3.6
24	Carson Kelly	ARI	3.4
25	Mike Zunino	TB	3.2

Framing Runs

Rank	Name	Team	Framing Runs
1	Austin Hedges	CLE	16.3
2	Max Stassi	LAA	13.3
3	Yasmani Grandal	CHW	10.1
4	Austin Barnes	LAD	7.8
5	Travis d'Arnaud	ATL	7.6
6	Roberto Pérez	PIT	7.2
6	Tomás Nido	NYM	7.2
6	Jonah Heim	TEX	7.2
9	Ryan Jeffers	MIN	7.0
10	Kyle Higashioka	NYY	6.4
11	Cal Raleigh	SEA	5.7
12	Christian Vázquez	BOS	5.5
13	Reese McGuire	TOR	5.4
14	Joey Bart	SF	5.2
15	Manny Piña	ATL	4.9
15	Danny Jansen	TOR	4.9
15	J.T. Realmuto	PHI	4.9
15	Martín Maldonado	HOU	4.9
19	Will Smith	LAD	4.7
20	Jose Trevino	TEX	4.2
21	Mike Zunino	TB	3.9
22	Jacob Stallings	MIA	3.8
23	Tyler Stephenson	CIN	3.3
24	Dom Nuñez	COL	3.1
25	Carson Kelly	ARI	2.8

Called Strikes Above Average

Rank	Name	Team	CSAA
1	Austin Hedges	CLE	.015
1	Austin Barnes	LAD	.015
3	Tomás Nido	NYM	.013
4	Max Stassi	LAA	.012
4	Kyle Higashioka	NYY	.012
6	Reese McGuire	TOR	.010
6	Jonah Heim	TEX	.010
6	Ryan Jeffers	MIN	.010
9	Yasmani Grandal	CHW	.009
9	Manny Piña	ATL	.009
9	Ben Rortvedt	MIN	.009
9	Cal Raleigh	SEA	.009
13	Tres Barrera	WAS	.007
13	Patrick Mazeika	NYM	.007
13	Travis d'Arnaud	ATL	.007
13	Roberto Pérez	PIT	.007
13	Jose Trevino	TEX	.007
18	Danny Jansen	TOR	.006
18	Joey Bart	SF	.006
20	Dom Nuñez	COL	.005
20	Christian Vázquez	BOS	.005
22	J.T. Realmuto	PHI	.004
22	Jason Castro	HOU	.004
22	Martín Maldonado	HOU	.004
22	Mike Zunino	TB	.004

Throwing Runs

Rank	Name	Team	Throwing Runs
1	Elias Díaz	COL	2.1
2	Martín Maldonado	HOU	1.0
3	Salvador Perez	KC	0.9
4	Yadier Molina	STL	0.7
5	Tomás Nido	NYM	0.6
5	Christian Vázquez	BOS	0.6
5	J.T. Realmuto	PHI	0.6
5	Reese McGuire	TOR	0.6
9	Yan Gomes	CHC	0.5
9	Manny Piña	ATL	0.5
11	Sean Murphy	OAK	0.4
11	Max Stassi	LAA	0.4
13	Jacob Stallings	MIA	0.3
13	Connor Wong	BOS	0.3
15	Daulton Varsho	ARI	0.2
15	Yasmani Grandal	CHW	0.2
15	Willson Contreras	CHC	0.2
15	Joey Bart	SF	0.2
15	Francisco Mejía	TB	0.2
15	Danny Jansen	TOR	0.2
21	Pedro Severino	MIL	0.1
21	Cal Raleigh	SEA	0.1
21	Ali Sánchez	STL	0.1
21	Will Smith	LAD	0.1
21	Jake Rogers	DET	0.1

Blocking Runs

Rank	Name	Team	Blocking Runs
1	Jacob Stallings	MIA	2.9
2	Roberto Pérez	PIT	2.5
3	Tucker Barnhart	DET	1.9
4	J.T. Realmuto	PHI	1.8
5	Danny Jansen	TOR	1.1
5	Max Stassi	LAA	1.1
7	Tom Murphy	SEA	1.0
7	Dom Nuñez	COL	1.0
9	Tomás Nido	NYM	0.9
9	Manny Piña	ATL	0.9
9	Austin Hedges	CLE	0.9
12	Cam Gallagher	KC	0.8
12	Reese McGuire	TOR	0.8
14	Michael Perez	PIT	0.6
14	Kevin Plawecki	BOS	0.6
14	Carson Kelly	ARI	0.6
14	Yan Gomes	CHC	0.6
14	Tyler Stephenson	CIN	0.6
19	Willson Contreras	CHC	0.5
19	Austin Nola	SD	0.5
19	Martín Maldonado	HOU	0.5
22	Austin Barnes	LAD	0.4
23	Yasmani Grandal	CHW	0.3
23	Victor Caratini	SD	0.3
23	Kyle Higashioka	NYY	0.3

Swipe Rate Above Average

Rank	Name	Team	SRAA
1	Elias Díaz	COL	-.046
2	Connor Wong	BOS	-.043
3	Ali Sánchez	STL	-.036
4	Tomás Nido	NYM	-.031
5	Yan Gomes	CHC	-.030
6	Reese McGuire	TOR	-.028
7	Manny Piña	ATL	-.023
8	Martín Maldonado	HOU	-.021
9	Salvador Perez	KC	-.018
10	Jake Rogers	DET	-.017
11	Yadier Molina	STL	-.013
11	Christian Vázquez	BOS	-.013
13	J.T. Realmuto	PHI	-.012
14	Daulton Varsho	ARI	-.010
15	Max Stassi	LAA	-.009
16	Sean Murphy	OAK	-.008
16	Francisco Mejía	TB	-.008
16	Pedro Severino	MIL	-.008
19	Jacob Stallings	MIA	-.007
19	Alex Jackson	MIA	-.007
19	Ben Rortvedt	MIN	-.007
22	William Contreras	ATL	-.006
22	Sebastian Rivero	KC	-.006
22	Cam Gallagher	KC	-.006
22	Cal Raleigh	SEA	-.006

AL Hitter WARP

Rank	Name	Team	WARP
1	Mike Trout	LAA	6.5
2	Yasmani Grandal	CHW	5.1
3	Vladimir Guerrero Jr.	TOR	5.0
4	Matt Olson	OAK	4.6
5	Shohei Ohtani	LAA	4.2
6	Luis Robert	CHW	4.1
6	José Ramírez	CLE	4.1
6	Aaron Judge	NYY	4.1
9	Corey Seager	TEX	3.9
10	Jose Altuve	HOU	3.8
11	Kyle Tucker	HOU	3.7
11	George Springer	TOR	3.7
11	Wander Franco	TB	3.7
11	Alex Bregman	HOU	3.7
15	Joey Gallo	NYY	3.6
15	Yordan Alvarez	HOU	3.6
17	Anthony Rendon	LAA	3.5
18	Xander Bogaerts	BOS	3.4
18	Bo Bichette	TOR	3.4
20	Josh Donaldson	MIN	3.2
20	Byron Buxton	MIN	3.2
22	Giancarlo Stanton	NYY	3.1
22	J.D. Martinez	BOS	3.1
24	DJ LeMahieu	NYY	2.9
25	Marcus Semien	TEX	2.8

NL Hitter WARP

Rank	Name	Team	WARP
1	Juan Soto	WAS	7.6
2	Fernando Tatis Jr.	SD	5.4
3	Ronald Acuña Jr.	ATL	5.3
4	Bryce Harper	PHI	4.9
5	Christian Yelich	MIL	4.1
5	Trea Turner	LAD	4.1
7	Bryan Reynolds	PIT	4.0
7	Manny Machado	SD	4.0
7	Mookie Betts	LAD	4.0
10	Brandon Nimmo	NYM	3.7
11	Paul Goldschmidt	STL	3.6
12	Pete Alonso	NYM	3.5
13	Max Muncy	LAD	3.4
13	Nolan Arenado	STL	3.4
15	Jesse Winker	CIN	3.1
15	Will Smith	LAD	3.1
15	Starling Marte	NYM	3.1
15	Jonathan India	CIN	3.1
15	Mark Canha	NYM	3.1
20	Justin Turner	LAD	3.0
20	Jean Segura	PHI	3.0
20	Austin Riley	ATL	3.0
20	J.T. Realmuto	PHI	3.0
24	Ozzie Albies	ATL	2.9
25	Joey Votto	CIN	2.8

WARP

Rank	Name	Team	WARP
1	Juan Soto	WAS	7.6
2	Mike Trout	LAA	6.5
3	Fernando Tatis Jr.	SD	5.4
4	Ronald Acuña Jr.	ATL	5.3
5	Yasmani Grandal	CHW	5.1
6	Vladimir Guerrero Jr.	TOR	5.0
7	Bryce Harper	PHI	4.9
8	Matt Olson	OAK	4.6
8	Freddie Freeman	FA	4.6
10	Shohei Ohtani	LAA	4.2
11	Christian Yelich	MIL	4.1
11	Trea Turner	LAD	4.1
11	Luis Robert	CHW	4.1
11	José Ramírez	CLE	4.1
11	Aaron Judge	NYY	4.1
16	Bryan Reynolds	PIT	4.0
16	Manny Machado	SD	4.0
16	Mookie Betts	LAD	4.0
19	Corey Seager	TEX	3.9
20	Jose Altuve	HOU	3.8
21	Kyle Tucker	HOU	3.7
21	George Springer	TOR	3.7
21	Brandon Nimmo	NYM	3.7
21	Wander Franco	TB	3.7
21	Alex Bregman	HOU	3.7
26	Trevor Story	FA	3.6
26	Paul Goldschmidt	STL	3.6
26	Joey Gallo	NYY	3.6
26	Yordan Alvarez	HOU	3.6
30	Anthony Rendon	LAA	3.5
30	Pete Alonso	NYM	3.5
32	Max Muncy	LAD	3.4
32	Carlos Correa	FA	3.4
32	Xander Bogaerts	BOS	3.4
32	Bo Bichette	TOR	3.4
32	Nolan Arenado	STL	3.4
37	Josh Donaldson	MIN	3.2
37	Byron Buxton	MIN	3.2
39	Jesse Winker	CIN	3.1
39	Giancarlo Stanton	NYY	3.1
39	Will Smith	LAD	3.1
39	J.D. Martinez	BOS	3.1
39	Starling Marte	NYM	3.1
39	Jonathan India	CIN	3.1
39	Mark Canha	NYM	3.1
46	Justin Turner	LAD	3.0
46	Jean Segura	PHI	3.0
46	Kyle Schwarber	FA	3.0
46	Austin Riley	ATL	3.0
46	J.T. Realmuto	PHI	3.0

DRC+

Rank	Name	Team	DRC+
1	Juan Soto	WAS	171
2	Mike Trout	LAA	161
3	Vladimir Guerrero Jr.	TOR	148
3	Ronald Acuña Jr.	ATL	148
5	Bryce Harper	PHI	145
6	Freddie Freeman	FA	142
7	Fernando Tatis Jr.	SD	138
8	Matt Olson	OAK	137
9	Shohei Ohtani	LAA	136
10	Aaron Judge	NYY	133
10	Paul Goldschmidt	STL	133
10	Pete Alonso	NYM	133
13	Yasmani Grandal	CHW	131
14	Yordan Alvarez	HOU	130
15	Giancarlo Stanton	NYY	128
15	Anthony Rendon	LAA	128
17	Christian Yelich	MIL	127
17	José Ramírez	CLE	127
17	Max Muncy	LAD	127
17	Manny Machado	SD	127
21	Bryan Reynolds	PIT	125
21	Alex Bregman	HOU	125
23	Kyle Tucker	HOU	124
24	Jesse Winker	CIN	123
24	Corey Seager	TEX	123
24	Josh Donaldson	MIN	123
24	Mookie Betts	LAD	123
28	Austin Riley	ATL	121
28	Brandon Nimmo	NYM	121
28	J.D. Martinez	BOS	121
28	Rhys Hoskins	PHI	121
28	Nolan Arenado	STL	121
33	Trea Turner	LAD	120
34	Luis Robert	CHW	119
34	Carlos Correa	FA	119
36	Joey Votto	CIN	118
36	Justin Turner	LAD	118
36	George Springer	TOR	118
36	Marcell Ozuna	ATL	118
36	Wander Franco	TB	118
36	Nelson Cruz	FA	118
42	Darin Ruf	SF	117
42	Anthony Rizzo	FA	117
42	Mark Canha	NYM	117
42	Xander Bogaerts	BOS	117
42	Jose Altuve	HOU	117
47	Trevor Story	FA	116
47	Rafael Devers	BOS	116
47	Michael Conforto	FA	116
47	José Abreu	CHW	116

Earned Run Average - Starters

Rank	Name	Team	ERA
1	Jacob deGrom	NYM	1.41
2	Shane Bieber	CLE	2.38
2	Corbin Burnes	MIL	2.38
4	Gerrit Cole	NYY	2.52
5	Max Scherzer	NYM	2.65
6	Luis Severino	NYY	2.79
7	Clayton Kershaw	FA	2.87
7	Brandon Woodruff	MIL	2.87
9	Joe Ryan	MIN	2.98
10	Walker Buehler	LAD	3.02
11	Aaron Nola	PHI	3.03
12	Justin Verlander	HOU	3.04
13	Zack Wheeler	PHI	3.05
14	Dustin May	LAD	3.06
15	Chris Sale	BOS	3.07
16	Michael Kopech	CHW	3.15
17	Pablo López	MIA	3.16
18	Carlos Rodón	FA	3.17
19	Charlie Morton	ATL	3.23
20	Kevin Gausman	TOR	3.28
21	Noah Syndergaard	LAA	3.31
21	Alex Wood	SF	3.31
23	Shane Baz	TB	3.32
24	Jack Flaherty	STL	3.34
25	Frankie Montas	OAK	3.36

Strikeout Percentage - Starters

Rank	Name	Team	K%
1	Jacob deGrom	NYM	39.8%
2	Shane Bieber	CLE	35.3%
3	Gerrit Cole	NYY	33.7%
4	Freddy Peralta	MIL	33.3%
5	Corbin Burnes	MIL	33.1%
6	Chris Sale	BOS	32.3%
7	Max Scherzer	NYM	32.0%
8	Luis Severino	NYY	31.2%
9	Carlos Rodón	FA	30.9%
9	Blake Snell	SD	30.9%
11	Grayson Rodriguez	BAL	30.4%
11	Robbie Ray	SEA	30.4%
13	Michael Kopech	CHW	29.8%
13	Shane Baz	TB	29.8%
15	Clayton Kershaw	FA	29.3%
16	Alek Manoah	TOR	29.0%
17	José Quintana	PIT	28.8%
17	Luis Gil	NYY	28.8%
19	Justin Verlander	HOU	28.7%
20	Lucas Giolito	CHW	28.6%
20	Nate Pearson	TOR	28.6%
22	Dylan Cease	CHW	28.5%
22	Triston McKenzie	CLE	28.5%
24	Cristian Javier	HOU	28.4%
25	Aaron Ashby	MIL	28.3%

Walk Percentage - Starters

Rank	Name	Team	BB%
1	Ryan Yarbrough	TB	4.8%
2	Clayton Kershaw	FA	4.9%
2	Zack Greinke	FA	4.9%
4	Miles Mikolas	STL	5.1%
4	Jacob deGrom	NYM	5.1%
6	Daulton Jefferies	OAK	5.2%
6	Kyle Hendricks	CHC	5.2%
6	John Means	BAL	5.2%
9	Ryu Hyun-jin	TOR	5.3%
10	Zach Eflin	PHI	5.4%
10	Nathan Eovaldi	BOS	5.4%
10	José Urquidy	HOU	5.4%
10	Chris Paddack	SD	5.4%
14	Cole Irvin	OAK	5.5%
14	Sean Manaea	OAK	5.5%
16	Michael Pineda	MIN	5.6%
17	Bailey Ober	MIN	5.8%
17	Tyler Alexander	DET	5.8%
19	Zack Wheeler	PHI	5.9%
19	Max Scherzer	NYM	5.9%
19	Justin Verlander	HOU	5.9%
22	Marco Gonzales	SEA	6.0%
23	Gerrit Cole	NYY	6.1%
23	Zach Plesac	CLE	6.1%
25	Thomas Eshelman	BAL	6.3%

Earned Run Average - Relievers

Rank	Name	Team	ERA
1	Josh Hader	MIL	2.44
1	Liam Hendriks	CHW	2.44
3	Taylor Rogers	MIN	2.51
4	Raisel Iglesias	LAA	2.52
5	Ryan Pressly	HOU	2.64
6	Aroldis Chapman	NYY	2.76
7	Giovanny Gallegos	STL	2.83
8	Emmanuel Clase	CLE	2.84
9	Matt Barnes	BOS	2.86
9	Aaron Bummer	CHW	2.86
9	Devin Williams	MIL	2.86
12	Diego Castillo	SEA	2.90
13	Edwin Díaz	NYM	2.97
14	Tommy Kahnle	LAD	3.03
15	Ken Giles	SEA	3.04
16	Jordan Romano	TOR	3.07
17	Andrew Kittredge	TB	3.08
18	Kirby Yates	ATL	3.11
19	Jake Cousins	MIL	3.12
20	Jay Jackson	ATL	3.13
21	Blake Treinen	LAD	3.14
22	Chad Green	NYY	3.18
23	Corey Knebel	PHI	3.19
23	Paul Sewald	SEA	3.19
25	Craig Kimbrel	CHW	3.22

Strikeout Percentage - Relievers

Rank	Name	Team	K%
1	Josh Hader	MIL	45.2%
2	Aroldis Chapman	NYY	39.8%
3	Devin Williams	MIL	39.1%
4	Craig Kimbrel	CHW	39.0%
5	Edwin Díaz	NYM	37.7%
6	Liam Hendriks	CHW	37.6%
7	James Karinchak	CLE	36.2%
8	Austin Adams	SD	35.9%
8	Alex Vesia	LAD	35.9%
10	Jake Cousins	MIL	35.5%
11	Angel Perdomo	MIL	35.1%
12	Raisel Iglesias	LAA	34.4%
13	Ken Giles	SEA	34.3%
14	Art Warren	CIN	33.6%
15	Tanner Rainey	WAS	33.4%
15	Matt Barnes	BOS	33.4%
15	Kirby Yates	ATL	33.4%
18	Brad Wieck	CHC	33.3%
19	Jovani Moran	MIN	33.2%
20	Lucas Sims	CIN	32.8%
21	Paul Sewald	SEA	32.7%
22	Jimmy Nelson	LAD	32.5%
23	Nick Sandlin	CLE	32.4%
24	Cody Stashak	MIN	32.3%
24	Amir Garrett	CIN	32.3%

Walk Percentage - Relievers

Rank	Name	Team	BB%
1	Josh Tomlin	ATL	3.8%
2	Chris Martin	FA	4.1%
3	Richard Bleier	MIA	4.5%
4	Craig Stammen	SD	4.7%
5	Yusmeiro Petit	OAK	4.9%
6	Liam Hendriks	CHW	5.1%
7	Taylor Rogers	MIN	5.4%
8	Jake McGee	SF	5.9%
8	Tyler Rogers	SF	5.9%
10	Hoby Milner	MIL	6.0%
10	Richard Rodríguez	ATL	6.0%
12	Joe Smith	SEA	6.1%
13	Andrew Kittredge	TB	6.2%
14	Chad Green	NYY	6.3%
14	Cooper Criswell	LAA	6.3%
16	Brent Suter	MIL	6.4%
16	Raisel Iglesias	LAA	6.4%
16	John King	TEX	6.4%
19	Bailey Falter	PHI	6.5%
19	Ryan Pressly	HOU	6.5%
19	Adam Cimber	TOR	6.5%
19	Alexander Wells	BAL	6.5%
19	Giovanny Gallegos	STL	6.5%
24	Scott Effross	CHC	6.6%
24	Edgar Santana	ATL	6.6%

Wins

Rank	Name	Team	W
1	Germán Márquez	COL	13
1	Gerrit Cole	NYY	13
3	Brandon Woodruff	MIL	12
3	Zack Wheeler	PHI	12
3	Max Scherzer	NYM	12
3	Lance Lynn	CHW	12
3	Lucas Giolito	CHW	12
3	Luis Castillo	CIN	12
3	Corbin Burnes	MIL	12
3	Walker Buehler	LAD	12
3	Shane Bieber	CLE	12
3	José Berríos	TOR	12
3	Sandy Alcantara	MIA	12
14	Adam Wainwright	STL	11
14	Framber Valdez	HOU	11
14	Julio Urías	LAD	11
14	Antonio Senzatela	COL	11
14	Reiver Sanmartin	CIN	11
14	Ryu Hyun-jin	TOR	11
14	Robbie Ray	SEA	11
14	Aaron Nola	PHI	11
14	Frankie Montas	OAK	11
14	Sean Manaea	OAK	11
14	Kevin Gausman	TOR	11
14	Yu Darvish	SD	11

Strikeouts

Rank	Name	Team	K
1	Gerrit Cole	NYY	251
2	Shane Bieber	CLE	246
3	Corbin Burnes	MIL	231
4	Max Scherzer	NYM	225
5	Robbie Ray	SEA	220
6	Lucas Giolito	CHW	217
7	Brandon Woodruff	MIL	202
7	Freddy Peralta	MIL	202
9	Chris Sale	BOS	197
10	Germán Márquez	COL	195
10	Luis Castillo	CIN	195
12	Kevin Gausman	TOR	192
13	Jacob deGrom	NYM	191
14	Aaron Nola	PHI	190
15	Walker Buehler	LAD	189
16	Zack Wheeler	PHI	185
16	Frankie Montas	OAK	185
16	Yu Darvish	SD	185
19	José Berríos	TOR	184
20	Tyler Mahle	CIN	181
21	Lance Lynn	CHW	178
22	Joe Musgrove	SD	175
23	Stephen Strasburg	WAS	174
24	Justin Verlander	HOU	173
25	Blake Snell	SD	170

WHIP - Starters

Rank	Name	Team	WHIP
1	Jacob deGrom	NYM	0.85
2	Max Scherzer	NYM	1.00
3	Gerrit Cole	NYY	1.02
4	Shane Bieber	CLE	1.04
4	Corbin Burnes	MIL	1.04
6	Clayton Kershaw	FA	1.07
6	Joe Ryan	MIN	1.07
6	Justin Verlander	HOU	1.07
9	Chris Sale	BOS	1.09
9	Brandon Woodruff	MIL	1.09
11	Aaron Nola	PHI	1.10
11	Carlos Rodón	FA	1.10
11	Luis Severino	NYY	1.10
14	Walker Buehler	LAD	1.12
14	Michael Kopech	CHW	1.12
16	Shane Baz	TB	1.14
16	Pablo López	MIA	1.14
16	Zack Wheeler	PHI	1.14
19	Yu Darvish	SD	1.15
19	Kevin Gausman	TOR	1.15
19	Charlie Morton	ATL	1.15
19	Joe Musgrove	SD	1.15
23	Jack Flaherty	STL	1.16
23	Dustin May	LAD	1.16
23	Freddy Peralta	MIL	1.16

Saves

Rank	Name	Team	SV
1	Aroldis Chapman	NYY	39
2	Ryan Pressly	HOU	38
2	Josh Hader	MIL	38
4	Jordan Romano	TOR	36
5	Raisel Iglesias	LAA	35
5	Emmanuel Clase	CLE	35
7	Lou Trivino	OAK	33
7	Blake Treinen	LAD	33
7	Liam Hendriks	CHW	33
7	Kyle Finnegan	WAS	33
7	Edwin Díaz	NYM	33
12	Will Smith	ATL	32
13	Taylor Rogers	MIN	31
14	Lucas Sims	CIN	30
15	Rowan Wick	CHC	27
15	Giovanny Gallegos	STL	27
17	Dylan Floro	MIA	26
17	José Alvarado	PHI	26
19	Scott Barlow	KC	25
20	Joe Barlow	TEX	23
21	J.B. Wendelken	ARI	21
22	Jake McGee	SF	20
23	Carlos Estévez	COL	19
24	Garrett Whitlock	BOS	18
24	Matt Barnes	BOS	18

Holds

Rank	Name	Team	HLD
1	Caleb Thielbar	MIN	23
1	Tanner Scott	BAL	23
1	Spencer Patton	TEX	23
1	Tim Mayza	TOR	23
1	Mike Mayers	LAA	23
1	Seth Lugo	NYM	23
1	Aaron Loup	LAA	23
1	Jonathan Loáisiga	NYY	23
1	James Karinchak	CLE	23
1	Chad Green	NYY	23
1	Tyler Duffey	MIN	23
1	JT Chargois	TB	23
1	Diego Castillo	SEA	23
14	Austin Warren	LAA	22
14	Josh Staumont	KC	22
14	Deolis Guerra	OAK	22
14	J.P. Feyereisen	TB	22
14	José Cisnero	DET	22
14	Jake Brentz	KC	22
20	Brad Wieck	CHC	20
20	J.B. Wendelken	ARI	20
20	Tyler Rogers	SF	20
20	Alex Reyes	STL	20
20	Noé Ramirez	ARI	20
20	Tanner Rainey	WAS	20

WHIP - Relievers

Rank	Name	Team	WHIP
1	Liam Hendriks	CHW	0.95
2	Josh Hader	MIL	0.99
3	Raisel Iglesias	LAA	1.03
3	Taylor Rogers	MIN	1.03
5	Giovanny Gallegos	STL	1.04
6	Edwin Díaz	NYM	1.08
6	Chad Green	NYY	1.08
6	Ryan Pressly	HOU	1.08
9	Kirby Yates	ATL	1.10
10	Paul Sewald	SEA	1.11
11	Craig Kimbrel	CHW	1.12
12	Ken Giles	SEA	1.13
13	Matt Barnes	BOS	1.14
13	Diego Castillo	SEA	1.14
13	Aroldis Chapman	NYY	1.14
13	Hoby Milner	MIL	1.14
13	Cody Stashak	MIN	1.14
18	Jay Jackson	ATL	1.15
18	Devin Williams	MIL	1.15
18	Matt Wisler	TB	1.15
21	John Brebbia	SF	1.16
21	Andrew Kittredge	TB	1.16
21	Emilio Pagán	SD	1.16
21	Jordan Romano	TOR	1.16
21	Will Smith	ATL	1.16

Fastball Velocity - Starters

Rank	Name	Team	FB Velo
1	Jacob deGrom	NYM	98
1	Sixto Sánchez	MIA	98
1	Noah Syndergaard	LAA	98
1	Gerrit Cole	NYY	98
5	Drew Rasmussen	TB	97
5	Michael Kopech	CHW	97
5	Sandy Alcantara	MIA	97
5	Nate Pearson	TOR	97
5	Luis Castillo	CIN	97
5	Dustin May	LAD	97
5	Carlos Hernández	KC	97
5	Shane Baz	TB	97
5	Nathan Eovaldi	BOS	97
5	Zack Wheeler	PHI	97
5	Dylan Cease	CHW	97
5	Michael Lorenzen	LAA	97
5	Shane McClanahan	TB	97
5	Adrian Morejon	SD	97
5	Edward Cabrera	MIA	97
5	Aaron Ashby	MIL	97
5	Roansy Contreras	PIT	97
5	Brandon Woodruff	MIL	97
5	Huascar Ynoa	ATL	97
24	Frankie Montas	OAK	96
24	Luis Gil	NYY	96

Groundball Rate - Starters

Rank	Name	Team	GB%
1	Framber Valdez	HOU	66.0%
2	Logan Webb	SF	57.2%
3	Adrian Houser	MIL	56.7%
4	Aaron Ashby	MIL	56.1%
5	Randy Dobnak	MIN	56.0%
6	Dakota Hudson	STL	55.8%
7	Lance McCullers Jr.	HOU	55.1%
8	Brett Anderson	FA	55.0%
9	Josh Fleming	TB	54.9%
10	Ranger Suárez	PHI	54.5%
10	Sean Hjelle	SF	54.5%
10	Luis Castillo	CIN	54.5%
13	Dallas Keuchel	CHW	53.9%
14	Paul Blackburn	OAK	51.7%
15	Dustin May	LAD	51.5%
16	Max Fried	ATL	51.3%
17	Mike Soroka	ATL	51.1%
17	Dane Dunning	TEX	51.1%
19	Marcus Stroman	CHC	50.7%
19	Antonio Senzatela	COL	50.7%
21	Kyle Gibson	PHI	50.6%
21	Alex Cobb	SF	50.6%
21	Sandy Alcantara	MIA	50.6%
24	Brady Singer	KC	50.4%
24	Sixto Sánchez	MIA	50.4%

Whiff Rate - Starters

Rank	Name	Team	Whiff%
1	Jacob deGrom	NYM	38.0%
2	Corbin Burnes	MIL	36.6%
3	Shane Bieber	CLE	35.7%
4	Shane Baz	TB	35.3%
5	Freddy Peralta	MIL	34.3%
6	Max Scherzer	NYM	34.0%
7	Gerrit Cole	NYY	33.5%
8	Mike Clevinger	SD	33.4%
9	Justin Verlander	HOU	33.3%
9	Blake Snell	SD	33.3%
11	Lucas Giolito	CHW	33.0%
12	Michael Kopech	CHW	32.8%
13	Patrick Sandoval	LAA	32.6%
13	Robbie Ray	SEA	32.6%
15	Carlos Rodón	FA	32.4%
16	Ryan Feltner	COL	32.1%
16	Shane McClanahan	TB	32.1%
16	Dylan Cease	CHW	32.1%
19	Clayton Kershaw	FA	31.7%
20	Kervin Castro	SF	31.6%
21	Kevin Gausman	TOR	31.5%
22	Luis Severino	NYY	31.3%
23	Reiver Sanmartin	CIN	31.1%
23	Dominic Leone	SF	31.1%
25	Luis Gil	NYY	31.0%

Fastball Velocity - Relievers

Rank	Name	Team	FB Velo
1	Jordan Hicks	STL	101
2	Emmanuel Clase	CLE	100
2	Andrés Muñoz	SEA	100
2	Brusdar Graterol	LAD	100
2	Anthony Gose	CLE	100
6	Nick Snyder	TEX	99
6	José Alvarado	PHI	99
6	Camilo Doval	SF	99
9	Aroldis Chapman	NYY	98
9	Edwin Díaz	NYM	98
9	Javy Guerra	SD	98
9	Trevor Rosenthal	OAK	98
9	Miguel Castro	NYM	98
9	Gregory Santos	SF	98
9	Albert Abreu	NYY	98
9	Jonathan Loáisiga	NYY	98
9	Sam Coonrod	PHI	98
9	Luis García	SD	98
9	Spencer Strider	ATL	98
9	Joe Kelly	FA	98
9	Gregory Soto	DET	98
9	Ryan Helsley	STL	98
9	Jonathan Hernández	TEX	98
9	Ryne Stanek	HOU	98
9	Blake Cederlind	PIT	98

Groundball Rate - Relievers

Rank	Name	Team	GB%
1	Aaron Bummer	CHW	67.9%
2	Emmanuel Clase	CLE	62.1%
3	Richard Bleier	MIA	61.0%
4	Clay Holmes	NYY	60.8%
5	T.J. McFarland	STL	60.1%
6	Adam Kolarek	OAK	58.7%
7	Matt Peacock	ARI	58.4%
8	Sam Clay	WAS	58.3%
9	Brusdar Graterol	LAD	57.2%
10	Tyler Rogers	SF	57.1%
11	Jordan Hicks	STL	56.6%
12	Dillon Tate	BAL	56.1%
13	Tim Hill	SD	55.9%
14	Zach Pop	MIA	55.6%
15	Joely Rodríguez	NYY	54.9%
15	Mark Melancon	ARI	54.9%
17	Joe Kelly	FA	54.8%
18	John King	TEX	54.6%
19	Cristopher Sánchez	PHI	53.8%
20	Jonathan Loáisiga	NYY	53.7%
21	Justin Lawrence	COL	53.5%
22	Phillips Valdez	BOS	53.4%
23	T.J. Zeuch	STL	53.3%
24	Brandon Kintzler	PHI	52.9%
25	Brett Martin	TEX	52.6%

Whiff Rate - Relievers

Rank	Name	Team	Whiff%
1	Devin Williams	MIL	43.6%
2	Josh Hader	MIL	43.4%
3	Ken Giles	SEA	42.1%
4	Jake Cousins	MIL	41.3%
5	Craig Kimbrel	CHW	41.0%
6	Art Warren	CIN	40.8%
7	Bryan Baker	BAL	40.0%
8	Raisel Iglesias	LAA	39.1%
9	Tanner Rainey	WAS	38.9%
10	Edwin Díaz	NYM	38.2%
10	Aroldis Chapman	NYY	38.2%
12	Tommy Kahnle	LAD	37.7%
13	Jovani Moran	MIN	37.5%
14	Liam Hendriks	CHW	37.3%
15	Alex Vesia	LAD	37.2%
16	Sam Howard	PIT	37.0%
17	Tanner Scott	BAL	36.6%
18	Darien Núñez	LAD	36.5%
19	Amir Garrett	CIN	36.4%
19	Seth Romero	WAS	36.4%
19	Brailyn Márquez	CHC	36.4%
22	Ryan Tepera	FA	36.1%
23	Jake Diekman	OAK	35.9%
24	Héctor Neris	HOU	35.8%
25	Austin Adams	SD	35.7%

Batting Average Against

Rank	Name	Team	AVG
1	Josh Hader	MIL	.168
2	Aroldis Chapman	NYY	.173
3	Craig Kimbrel	CHW	.182
3	Jacob deGrom	NYM	.182
5	Austin Adams	SD	.183
6	Devin Williams	MIL	.186
7	Angel Perdomo	MIL	.189
8	James Karinchak	CLE	.191
9	Jake Cousins	MIL	.195
10	Matt Barnes	BOS	.196
10	Edwin Díaz	NYM	.196
12	José Alvarado	PHI	.201
12	Darwinzon Hernandez	BOS	.201
12	Alex Vesia	LAD	.201
15	José Leclerc	TEX	.202
15	Brad Wieck	CHC	.202
17	Michael Kopech	CHW	.203
17	Freddy Peralta	MIL	.203
17	Art Warren	CIN	.203
20	Liam Hendriks	CHW	.204
20	José Quijada	LAA	.204
22	Trevor Rosenthal	OAK	.205
23	Shane Bieber	CLE	.206
23	Jay Jackson	ATL	.206
23	Josh James	HOU	.206

AL WARP

Rank	Name	Team	WARP
1	Gerrit Cole	NYY	4.9
2	Shane Bieber	CLE	4.8
3	Chris Sale	BOS	3.1
4	Justin Verlander	HOU	2.9
5	Kevin Gausman	TOR	2.7
6	Joe Ryan	MIN	2.6
6	Lance Lynn	CHW	2.6
8	Frankie Montas	OAK	2.5
9	Ryu Hyun-jin	TOR	2.3
9	Eduardo Rodriguez	DET	2.3
9	Lance McCullers Jr.	HOU	2.3
9	José Berríos	TOR	2.3
13	Lucas Giolito	CHW	2.2
13	Nathan Eovaldi	BOS	2.2
13	Shane Baz	TB	2.2
13	Chris Bassitt	OAK	2.2
17	Noah Syndergaard	LAA	2.1
17	Shohei Ohtani	LAA	2.1
17	Dylan Cease	CHW	2.1
20	Luis Severino	NYY	2.0
20	Robbie Ray	SEA	2.0
20	Shane McClanahan	TB	2.0
23	Framber Valdez	HOU	1.9
24	Jordan Montgomery	NYY	1.8
24	Sean Manaea	OAK	1.8

Slugging Percent Against

Rank	Name	Team	SLG
1	Aaron Bummer	CHW	.302
2	Jacob deGrom	NYM	.312
3	Aroldis Chapman	NYY	.317
4	Tanner Scott	BAL	.332
5	Devin Williams	MIL	.333
6	José Alvarado	PHI	.334
7	Austin Adams	SD	.340
8	Jordan Hicks	STL	.341
9	Corbin Burnes	MIL	.342
9	Emmanuel Clase	CLE	.342
11	Matt Barnes	BOS	.343
11	Diego Castillo	SEA	.343
13	Jake Cousins	MIL	.344
14	Framber Valdez	HOU	.347
15	Clay Holmes	NYY	.348
16	Josh Hader	MIL	.351
17	Camilo Doval	SF	.352
17	Lance McCullers Jr.	HOU	.352
19	Aaron Ashby	MIL	.353
19	Shane Bieber	CLE	.353
21	Luis Severino	NYY	.354
22	Darwinzon Hernandez	BOS	.355
22	Taylor Rogers	MIN	.355
24	Edwin Díaz	NYM	.356
24	Paul Fry	BAL	.356

NL WARP

Rank	Name	Team	WARP
1	Jacob deGrom	NYM	5.2
2	Corbin Burnes	MIL	4.8
3	Max Scherzer	NYM	4.4
4	Brandon Woodruff	MIL	4.0
5	Zack Wheeler	PHI	3.5
6	Aaron Nola	PHI	3.4
6	Walker Buehler	LAD	3.4
8	Luis Castillo	CIN	3.2
9	Germán Márquez	COL	2.7
9	Sandy Alcantara	MIA	2.7
11	Charlie Morton	ATL	2.6
12	Julio Urías	LAD	2.5
12	Freddy Peralta	MIL	2.5
12	Joe Musgrove	SD	2.5
12	Zac Gallen	ARI	2.5
16	Yu Darvish	SD	2.4
17	Blake Snell	SD	2.3
17	Jack Flaherty	STL	2.3
19	Alex Wood	SF	2.2
20	Logan Webb	SF	2.1
20	Pablo López	MIA	2.1
20	Sonny Gray	CIN	2.1
20	Max Fried	ATL	2.1
24	Tyler Mahle	CIN	2.0
25	Trevor Rogers	MIA	1.7

WARP

Rank	Name	Team	WARP
1	Jacob deGrom	NYM	5.2
2	Gerrit Cole	NYY	4.9
3	Corbin Burnes	MIL	4.8
3	Shane Bieber	CLE	4.8
5	Max Scherzer	NYM	4.4
6	Brandon Woodruff	MIL	4.0
7	Zack Wheeler	PHI	3.5
8	Aaron Nola	PHI	3.4
8	Walker Buehler	LAD	3.4
10	Luis Castillo	CIN	3.2
11	Chris Sale	BOS	3.1
12	Justin Verlander	HOU	2.9
13	Clayton Kershaw	FA	2.8
14	Germán Márquez	COL	2.7
14	Kevin Gausman	TOR	2.7
14	Sandy Alcantara	MIA	2.7
17	Joe Ryan	MIN	2.6
17	Charlie Morton	ATL	2.6
17	Lance Lynn	CHW	2.6
20	Julio Urías	LAD	2.5
20	Freddy Peralta	MIL	2.5
20	Joe Musgrove	SD	2.5
20	Frankie Montas	OAK	2.5
20	Zac Gallen	ARI	2.5
25	Carlos Rodón	FA	2.4
25	Yu Darvish	SD	2.4
27	Blake Snell	SD	2.3
27	Ryu Hyun-jin	TOR	2.3
27	Eduardo Rodriguez	DET	2.3
27	Lance McCullers Jr.	HOU	2.3
27	Jack Flaherty	STL	2.3
27	José Berríos	TOR	2.3
33	Alex Wood	SF	2.2
33	Lucas Giolito	CHW	2.2
33	Nathan Eovaldi	BOS	2.2
33	Shane Baz	TB	2.2
33	Chris Bassitt	OAK	2.2
38	Logan Webb	SF	2.1
38	Noah Syndergaard	LAA	2.1
38	Shohei Ohtani	LAA	2.1
38	Pablo López	MIA	2.1
38	Sonny Gray	CIN	2.1
38	Max Fried	ATL	2.1
38	Dylan Cease	CHW	2.1
45	Luis Severino	NYY	2.0
45	Robbie Ray	SEA	2.0
45	Shane McClanahan	TB	2.0
45	Tyler Mahle	CIN	2.0
49	Framber Valdez	HOU	1.9
50	Jordan Montgomery	NYY	1.8

DRA– Starters

Rank	Name	Team	DRA–
1	Jacob deGrom	NYM	37
2	Corbin Burnes	MIL	61
3	Shane Bieber	CLE	64
4	Gerrit Cole	NYY	65
5	Max Scherzer	NYM	68
6	Luis Severino	NYY	72
7	Brandon Woodruff	MIL	73
8	Clayton Kershaw	FA	74
9	Chris Sale	BOS	76
10	Michael Kopech	CHW	77
10	Aaron Nola	PHI	77
12	Dustin May	LAD	78
13	Walker Buehler	LAD	79
13	Carlos Rodón	FA	79
13	Justin Verlander	HOU	79
13	Zack Wheeler	PHI	79
17	Freddy Peralta	MIL	80
18	Luis Castillo	CIN	81
18	Joe Ryan	MIN	81
20	Pablo López	MIA	82
20	Blake Snell	SD	82
22	Charlie Morton	ATL	83
23	Shane Baz	TB	84
23	Zac Gallen	ARI	84
23	Kevin Gausman	TOR	84
23	Joe Musgrove	SD	84
27	Jack Flaherty	STL	85
28	Lance McCullers Jr.	HOU	86
28	Noah Syndergaard	LAA	86
28	Julio Urías	LAD	86
31	Sandy Alcantara	MIA	87
31	Aaron Ashby	MIL	87
31	Dylan Cease	CHW	87
31	Yu Darvish	SD	87
31	Shohei Ohtani	LAA	87
31	Ranger Suárez	PHI	87
31	Alex Wood	SF	87
38	Sonny Gray	CIN	88
38	Tanner Houck	BOS	88
38	Lance Lynn	CHW	88
38	Frankie Montas	OAK	88
38	Eduardo Rodriguez	DET	88
38	Grayson Rodriguez	BAL	88
38	Patrick Sandoval	LAA	88
38	Logan Webb	SF	88
46	Mike Clevinger	SD	89
46	Nathan Eovaldi	BOS	89
46	Max Fried	ATL	89
46	Germán Márquez	COL	89
46	Tylor Megill	NYM	89

DRA– Relievers

Rank	Name	Team	DRA–
1	Josh Hader	MIL	57
2	Liam Hendriks	CHW	62
3	Aroldis Chapman	NYY	66
4	Raisel Iglesias	LAA	67
5	Devin Williams	MIL	68
6	Taylor Rogers	MIN	69
7	Ryan Pressly	HOU	70
8	Matt Barnes	BOS	71
8	Aaron Bummer	CHW	71
8	Edwin Díaz	NYM	71
11	Giovanny Gallegos	STL	74
12	Diego Castillo	SEA	75
12	Jake Cousins	MIL	75
12	Craig Kimbrel	CHW	75
15	Emmanuel Clase	CLE	76
15	Tommy Kahnle	LAD	76
15	Art Warren	CIN	76
18	Jordan Romano	TOR	77
19	Ken Giles	SEA	78
19	Corey Knebel	PHI	78
21	Chad Green	NYY	79
21	Kirby Yates	ATL	79
23	Kenley Jansen	FA	80
23	Andrew Kittredge	TB	80
25	Jay Jackson	ATL	81
25	Blake Treinen	LAD	81
27	Paul Sewald	SEA	82
28	David Bednar	PIT	83
28	James Karinchak	CLE	83
28	Héctor Neris	HOU	83
31	Tanner Scott	BAL	84
32	Joe Kelly	FA	85
32	Seth Lugo	NYM	85
32	Will Smith	ATL	85
35	Caleb Ferguson	LAD	86
35	Dinelson Lamet	SD	86
35	Tim Mayza	TOR	86
35	Wyatt Mills	SEA	86
35	Ryan Tepera	FA	86
35	Brad Wieck	CHC	86
41	Scott Effross	CHC	87
41	Jonathan Loáisiga	NYY	87
41	Phil Maton	HOU	87
41	Hoby Milner	MIL	87
41	Sean Newcomb	ATL	87
41	José Quijada	LAA	87
41	Casey Sadler	SEA	87
41	Lucas Sims	CIN	87
41	Craig Stammen	SD	87
41	Cody Stashak	MIN	87

Team Codes

CODE	TEAM	LG	AFF	NAME
ABD	Aberdeen	A+ E	Orioles	IronBirds
ABQ	Albuquerque	AAA W	Rockies	Isotopes
ADE	Adelaide	ABL	-	Giants
AGS	Aguascalientes	MEX	-	Rieleros
AGU	Aguilas	LIDOM	-	Aguilas
AKL	Auckland	ABL	-	Tuatara
AKR	Akron	AA NE	Guardians	RubberDucks
ALT	Altoona	AA NE	Pirates	Curve
AMA	Amarillo	AA C	D-backs	Sod Poodles
ANG	ACL Angels	ACL	Angels	ACL Angels
ANG	AZL Angels	AZL	Angels	AZL Angels
ARA	Aragua	LVBP	Tigres	Tigres
ARI	Arizona	NL	-	D-backs
ARK	Arkansas	AA C	Mariners	Travelers
ASGO	AZL Athletics Gold	AZL	Athletics	AZL Athletics Gold
ASGR	AZL Athletics Green	AZL	Athletics	AZL Athletics Green
ASH	Asheville	A+ E	Astros	Tourists
AST	FCL Astros	FCL	Astros	FCL Astros
AST	GCL Astros	GCL	Astros	GCL Astros
ATH	ACL Athletics	ACL	Athletics	ACL Athletics
ATL	Atlanta	NL	-	Braves
AUB	Auburn	NYP	Nationals	Doubledays
AUG	Augusta	A E	Braves	GreenJackets
BAL	Baltimore	AL	-	Orioles
BAT	Batavia	NYP	Marlins	Muckdogs
BEL	Beloit	A+ C	Marlins	Snappers
BG	Bowling Green	A+ E	Rays	Hot Rods
BIL	Billings	PIO	Reds	Mustangs
BIR	Birmingham	AA S	White Sox	Barons
BLU	Bluefield	APP	Blue Jays	Blue Jays
BLU	FCL Blue Jays	FCL	Blue Jays	FCL Blue Jays
BLU	GCL Blue Jays	GCL	Blue Jays	GCL Blue Jays
BLX	Biloxi	AA S	Brewers	Shuckers
BNG	Binghamton	AA NE	Mets	Rumble Ponies
BOI	Boise	NWL	Rockies	Hawks
BOS	Boston	AL	-	Red Sox
BOW	Bowie	AA NE	Orioles	Baysox
BRA	FCL Braves	FCL	Braves	FCL Braves
BRA	GCL Braves	GCL	Braves	GCL Braves
BRB	AZL Brewers Blue	AZL	Brewers	AZL Brewers Blue
BRD	Bradenton	A SE	Pirates	Marauders
BRG	AZL Brewers Gold	AZL	Brewers	AZL Brewers Gold
BRI	Brisbane	ABL	Bandits	Bandits
BRK	Brooklyn	A+ E	Mets	Cyclones
BRS	Bristol	APP	Pirates	Pirates
BRWB	ACL Brewers Blue	ACL	Brewers	ACL Brewers Blue
BRWG	ACL Brewers Gold	ACL	Brewers	ACL Brewers Gold
BUF	Buffalo	AAA E	Blue Jays	Bisons

CODE	TEAM	LG	AFF	NAME
BUR	Burlington	MID	Angels	Bees
BUR	Burlington	APP	Royals	Royals
CAG	Caguas	PWL	Caguas	Caguas
CAM	Campeche	MEX	-	Piratas
CAN	Canberra	ABL	Cavalry	Cavalry
CAR	Carolina	A E	Brewers	Mudcats
CAR	FCL Cardinals	FCL	Cardinals	FCL Cardinals
CAR	GCL Cardinals	GCL	Cardinals	GCL Cardinals
CAR	Carolina	PWL	Carolina	Carolina
CAR	Caracas	LVBP	Leones	Leones
CC	Corpus Christi	AA C	Astros	Hooks
CHA	Charlotte	INT	White Sox	Knights
CHA	Charlotte	FSL	Rays	Stone Crabs
CHA	Chattanooga	AA S	Reds	Lookouts
CHC	Chi Cubs	NL	-	Cubs
CIN	Cincinnati	NL	-	Reds
CLE	Cleveland	AL	-	Guardians
CLI	Clinton	MID	Marlins	LumberKings
CLR	Clearwater	A SE	Phillies	Threshers
CLT	Charlotte	AAA E	White Sox	Knights
COL	Colombia	CS	-	Colombia
COL	Colorado	NL	-	Rockies
COL	Columbia	A E	Royals	Fireflies
COL	Columbus	AAA E	Guardians	Clippers
CON	Connecticut	NYP	Tigers	Tigers
CR	Cedar Rapids	A+ C	Twins	Kernels
CSC	Charleston	A E	Rays	RiverDogs
CUB	ACL Cubs	ACL	Cubs	ACL Cubs
CUB1	AZL Cubs 1	AZL	Cubs	AZL Cubs 1
CUB2	AZL Cubs 2	AZL	Cubs	AZL Cubs 2
CUBB	AZL Cubs Blue	AZL	Cubs	AZL Cubs Blue
CUBR	AZL Cubs Red	AZL	Cubs	AZL Cubs Red
CUL	Culiacan	LMP	-	Culiacan
CHW	Chi White Sox	AL	-	White Sox
DAN	Danville	APP	Braves	Braves
DAY	Dayton	A+ C	Reds	Dragons
DBT	Daytona	A SE	Reds	Tortugas
DE	Down East	A E	Rangers	Wood Ducks
DEL	Delmarva	A E	Orioles	Shorebirds
DET	Detroit	AL	-	Tigers
DIA	ACL D-backs	ACL	D-backs	ACL D-backs
DIA	AZL D-backs	AZL	D-backs	AZL D-backs
DOD	ACL Dodgers	ACL	Dodgers	ACL Dodgers
DOD1	AZL Dodgers 1	AZL	Dodgers	AZL Dodgers 1
DOD2	AZL Dodgers 2	AZL	Dodgers	AZL Dodgers 2
DODL	AZL Dodgers Lasorda	AZL	Dodgers	AZL Dodgers Lasorda
DODM	AZL Dodgers Mota	AZL	Dodgers	AZL Dodgers Mota
DR	Dom. Rep.	CS	-	Dom. Rep.
DSL ANG	DSL Angels	DSL	Angels	DSL Angels

CODE	TEAM	LG	AFF	NAME
DSL AST	DSL Astros	DSL	Astros	DSL Astros
DSL ATH	DSL Athletics	DSL	Athletics	DSL Athletics
DSL BAU	DSL Dodgers Bautista	DSL	Dodgers	DSL Dodgers Bautista
DSL BLJ	DSL Blue Jays	DSL	Blue Jays	DSL Blue Jays
DSL BRA	DSL Braves	DSL	Braves	DSL Braves
DSL BRW	DSL Brewers	DSL	Brewers	DSL Brewers
DSL BRW1	DSL Brewers1	DSL	Brewers	DSL Brewers1
DSL BRW2	DSL Brewers2	DSL	Brewers	DSL Brewers2
DSL CARB	DSL Cardinals Blue	DSL	Cardinals	DSL Cardinals Blue
DSL CARR	DSL Cardinals Red	DSL	Cardinals	DSL Cardinals Red
DSL COL	DSL Colorado	DSL	Rockies	DSL Colorado
DSL COOP	DSL MIL/TOR	DSL	DSL MIL/TOR	DSL MIL/TOR
DSL COOP	DSL Guardians/ Brewers	DSL	DSL Guardians/ Brewers	DSL Guardians/ Brewers
DSL CUB1	DSL Cubs1	DSL	Cubs	DSL Cubs1
DSL CUB2	DSL Cubs2	DSL	Cubs	DSL Cubs2
DSL CUBB	DSL Cubs Blue	DSL	Cubs	DSL Cubs Blue
DSL CUBR	DSL Cubs Red	DSL	Cubs	DSL Cubs Red
DSL DB1	DSL D-backs1	DSL	D-backs	DSL D-backs1
DSL DB2	DSL D-backs2	DSL	D-backs	DSL D-backs2
DSL GIA	DSL Giants	DSL	Giants	DSL Giants
DSL GIA	DSL Giants1	DSL	Giants	DSL Giants1
DSL GIB	DSL Giants Black	DSL	Giants	DSL Giants Black
DSL GIO	DSL Giants Orange	DSL	Giants	DSL Giants Orange
DSL GIT	DSL Giants2	DSL	Giants	DSL Giants2
DSL IND	DSL Guardians	DSL	Guardians	DSL Guardians
DSL IND1	DSL Guardians1	DSL	Guardians	DSL Guardians1
DSL IND2	DSL Guardians2	DSL	Guardians	DSL Guardians2
DSL INDB	DSL Guardians Blue	DSL	Guardians	DSL Guardians Blue
DSL INDR	DSL Guardians Red	DSL	Guardians	DSL Guardians Red
DSL MET1	DSL Mets1	DSL	Mets	DSL Mets1
DSL MET2	DSL Mets2	DSL	Mets	DSL Mets2
DSL MIA	DSL Marlins	DSL	Marlins	DSL Marlins
DSL NAT	DSL Nationals	DSL	Nationals	DSL Nationals
DSL NYY	DSL Yankees	DSL	Yankees	DSL Yankees
DSL NYY1	DSL Yankees1	DSL	Yankees	DSL Yankees1
DSL NYY2	DSL Yankees2	DSL	Yankees	DSL Yankees2
DSL OR1	DSL Orioles1	DSL	Orioles	DSL Orioles1
DSL OR2	DSL Orioles2	DSL	Orioles	DSL Orioles2
DSL PAD	DSL Padres	DSL	Padres	DSL Padres
DSL PHR	DSL Phillies Red	DSL	Phillies	DSL Phillies Red
DSL PHW	DSL Phillies White	DSL	Phillies	DSL Phillies White
DSL PIR1	DSL Pirates1	DSL	Pirates	DSL Pirates1
DSL PIR2	DSL Pirates2	DSL	Pirates	DSL Pirates2
DSL PIRB	DSL Pirates Black	DSL	Pirates	DSL Pirates Black
DSL PIRG	DSL Pirates Gold	DSL	Pirates	DSL Pirates Gold
DSL RAN2	DSL Rangers2	DSL	Rangers	DSL Rangers2
DSL REDS	DSL Reds	DSL	Reds	DSL Reds
DSL RGR1	DSL Rangers1	DSL	Rangers	DSL Rangers1
DSL RNG1	DSL Rangers1	DSL	Rangers	DSL Rangers1
DSL RNG2	DSL Rangers2	DSL	Rangers	DSL Rangers2
DSL ROC	DSL Rockies	DSL	Rockies	DSL Rockies
DSL ROY1	DSL Royals1	DSL	Royals	DSL Royals1
DSL ROY2	DSL Royals2	DSL	Royals	DSL Royals2
DSL ROYB	DSL Royals Blue	DSL	Royals	DSL Royals Blue
DSL ROYW	DSL Royals White	DSL	Royals	DSL Royals White
DSL RS1	DSL Red Sox1	DSL	Red Sox	DSL Red Sox1
DSL RS2	DSL Red Sox2	DSL	Red Sox	DSL Red Sox2
DSL RSB	DSL Red Sox Blue	DSL	Red Sox	DSL Red Sox Blue

CODE	TEAM	LG	AFF	NAME
DSL RSR	DSL Red Sox Red	DSL	Red Sox	DSL Red Sox Red
DSL SEA	DSL Mariners	DSL	Mariners	DSL Mariners
DSL SHO	DSL Dodgers Shoemaker	DSL	Dodgers	Dodgers Shoemaker
DSL TB1	DSL Rays1	DSL	Rays	DSL Rays1
DSL TB2	DSL Rays2	DSL	Rays	DSL Rays2
DSL TIG	DSL Tigers	DSL	Tigers	DSL Tigers
DSL TIG1	DSL Tigers1	DSL	Tigers	DSL Tigers1
DSL TIG2	DSL Tigers2	DSL	Tigers	DSL Tigers2
DSL TWI	DSL Twins	DSL	Twins	DSL Twins
DSL WSX	DSL White Sox	DSL	White Sox	DSL White Sox
DUN	Dunedin	A SE	Blue Jays	Blue Jays
DUR	Durham	AAA E	Rays	Bulls
DUR	Durango	MEX	-	Generales
ELP	El Paso	AAA W	Padres	Chihuahuas
ELZ	Elizabethton	APP	Twins	Twins
ERI	Erie	AA NE	Tigers	SeaWolves
ESC	Escogido	LIDOM	-	Leones
EST	Estrellas	LIDOM	-	Estrellas
EUG	Eugene	A+ W	Giants	Emeralds
EVE	Everett	A+ W	Mariners	AquaSox
FAY	Fayetteville	A E	Astros	Woodpeckers
FBG	Fredericksburg	A E	Nationals	Nationals
FLO	Florida	FSL	Braves	Fire Frogs
FRE	Frederick	CAR	Orioles	Keys
FRE	Fresno	A W	Rockies	Grizzlies
FRI	Frisco	AA C	Rangers	RoughRiders
FTM	Fort Myers	A SE	Twins	Mighty Mussels
FTM	Fort Myers	FSL	Twins	Miracle
FW	Fort Wayne	A+ C	Padres	TinCaps
GBO	Greensboro	A+ E	Pirates	Grasshoppers
GDD	Glendale	AFL	-	Desert Dogs
GEE	Geelong-Korea	ABL	-	Geelong-Korea
GIB	AZL Giants Black	AZL	Giants	AZL Giants Black
GIG	Gigantes	LIDOM	-	Gigantes
GIO	AZL Giants Orange	AZL	Giants	AZL Giants Orange
GJ	Grand Junction	PIO	Rockies	Rockies
GL	Great Lakes	A+ C	Dodgers	Loons
GNTB	ACL Giants Black	ACL	Giants	ACL Giants Black
GNTO	ACL Giants Orange	ACL	Giants	ACL Giants Orange
GRN	Greeneville	APP	Reds	Reds
GSV	Guasave	LMP	-	Guasave
GTF	Great Falls	PIO	White Sox	Voyagers
GVL	Greenville	A+ E	Red Sox	Drive
GWN	Gwinnett	AAA E	Braves	Stripers
HAG	Hagerstown	SAL	Nationals	Suns
HBG	Harrisburg	AA NE	Nationals	Senators
HER	Hermosillo	LMP	-	Hermosillo
HFD	Hartford	AA NE	Rockies	Yard Goats
HIC	Hickory	A+ E	Rangers	Crawdads
HIL	Hillsboro	A+ W	D-backs	Hops
HOU	Houston	AL	-	Astros
HV	Hudson Valley	A+ E	Yankees	Renegades
IDF	Idaho Falls	PIO	Royals	Chukars
IE	Inland Empire	A W	Angels	66ers
IND	ACL Guardians	ACL	Guardians	ACL Guardians
IND	Indianapolis	AAA E	Pirates	Indianapolis
INDB	AZL Guardians Blue	AZL	Guardians	AZL Guardians Blue
INDR	AZL Guardians Red	AZL	Guardians	AZL Guardians Red
IOW	Iowa	AAA E	Cubs	Cubs
JAL	Jalisco	LMP	-	Jalisco

CODE	TEAM	LG	AFF	NAME
JAX	Jacksonville	AAA E	Marlins	Jumbo Shrimp
JC	Johnson City	APP	Cardinals	Cardinals
JS	Jersey Shore	A+ E	Phillies	BlueClaws
JUP	Jupiter	A SE	Marlins	Hammerheads
JXN	Jackson	SOU	D-backs	Generals
KAN	Kannapolis	A E	White Sox	Cannon Ballers
KAN	Kannapolis	SAL	White Sox	Intimidators
KC	Kane County	MID	D-backs	Cougars
KC	Kansas City	AL	-	Royals
KNG	Kingsport	APP	Mets	Mets
LAA	LA Angels	AL	-	Angels
LAD	LA Dodgers	NL	-	Dodgers
LAG	Laguna	MEX	-	Algodoneros
LAG	La Guaira	LVBP	Tiburones	Tiburones
LAK	Lakeland	A SE	Tigers	Flying Tigers
LAN	Lancaster	CAL	Rockies	JetHawks
LAN	Lansing	A+ C	Athletics	Lugnuts
LAR	Lara	LVBP	Cardenales	Cardenales
LAR	Dos Laredos	MEX	-	Tecolotes
LC	Lake County	A+ C	Guardians	Captains
LE	Lake Elsinore	A W	Padres	Storm
LEO	Leon	MEX	-	Bravos
LEX	Lexington	SAL	Royals	Legends
LHV	Lehigh Valley	AAA E	Phillies	IronPigs
LIC	Licey	LIDOM	-	Tigres
LOU	Louisville	AAA E	Reds	Bats
LOW	Lowell	NYP	Red Sox	Spinners
LV	Las Vegas	AAA W	Athletics	Aviators
LWD	Lakewood	SAL	Phillies	BlueClaws
LYN	Lynchburg	A E	Guardians	Hillcats
MAG	Magallanes	LVBP	Navegantes	Navegantes
MAN	Manati	PWL	Manati	Manati
MAR	AZL Mariners	AZL	Mariners	AZL Mariners
MAR	Margarita	LVBP	Bravos	Bravos
MAY	Mayaguez	PWL	Mayaguez	Mayaguez
MAZ	Mazatlan	LMP	-	Mazatlan
MB	Myrtle Beach	A E	Cubs	Pelicans
MEL	Melbourne	ABL	Aces	Aces
MEM	Memphis	AAA E	Cardinals	Redbirds
MET	FCL Mets	FCL	Mets	FCL Mets
MEX	Mexico	MEX	-	Diablos Rojos
MEX	Mexico	CS	-	Mexico
MIA	Miami	NL	-	Marlins
MID	Midland	AA C	Athletics	RockHounds
MIL	Milwaukee	NL	-	Brewers
MIN	Minnesota	AL	-	Twins
MIS	Mississippi	AA S	Braves	Braves
MIS	Missoula	PIO	D-backs	Osprey
MOB	Mobile	SOU	Angels	BayBears
MOC	Los Mochis	LMP	-	Los Mochis
MOD	Modesto	A W	Mariners	Nuts
MRL	FCL Marlins	FCL	Marlins	FCL Marlins
MRL	GCL Marlins	GCL	Marlins	GCL Marlins
MRN	ACL Mariners	ACL	Mariners	ACL Mariners
MSS	Mesa	AFL	-	Solar Sox
MTG	Montgomery	AA S	Rays	Biscuits
MTS	GCL Mets	GCL	Mets	GCL Mets
MTY	Monterrey	LMP	-	Sultanes
MV	Mahoning Valley	NYP	Guardians	Scrappers
MVA	Monclova	MEX	-	Acereros
MXC	Mexicali	LMP	-	Mexicali
NAS	Nashville	AAA E	Brewers	Sounds
NAT	FCL Nationals	FCL	Nationals	FCL Nationals
NAT	GCL Nationals	GCL	Nationals	GCL Nationals

CODE	TEAM	LG	AFF	NAME
NAV	Navojoa	LMP	-	Navojoa
NH	New Hampshire	AA NE	Blue Jays	Fisher Cats
NO	New Orleans	PCL	Marlins	Baby Cakes
NOR	Norfolk	AAA E	Orioles	Tides
NWA	NW Arkansas	AA C	Royals	Naturals
NYM	NY Mets	NL	-	Mets
NYY	NY Yankees	AL	-	Yankees
OAK	Oakland	AL	-	Athletics
OAX	Oaxaca	MEX	-	Guerreros
OBR	Obregon	LMP	-	Obregon
OGD	Ogden	PIO	Dodgers	Raptors
OKC	Okla. City	AAA W	Dodgers	Dodgers
OMA	Omaha	AAA E	Royals	Storm Chasers
ORI	Caribes	LVBP	Caribes	Caribes
ORI	GCL Orioles	GCL	Orioles	GCL Orioles
ORIB	FCL Orioles Black	FCL	Orioles	FCL Orioles Black
ORIO	FCL Orioles Orange	FCL	Orioles	FCL Orioles Orange
ORM	Orem	PIO	Angels	Owlz
PAD	ACL Padres	ACL	Padres	ACL Padres
PAN	Panama	CS	-	Panama
PAW	Pawtucket	INT	Red Sox	Red Sox
PEJ	Peoria	AFL	-	Javelinas
PEO	Peoria	A+ C	Cardinals	Chiefs
PER	Perth	ABL	Heat	Heat
PHE	GCL Phillies East	GCL	Phillies	GCL Phillies East
PHI	FCL Phillies	FCL	Phillies	FCL Phillies
PHI	Philadelphia	NL	-	Phillies
PHW	GCL Phillies West	GCL	Phillies	GCL Phillies West
PIR	GCL Pirates	GCL	Pirates	GCL Pirates
PIRB	FCL Pirates Black	FCL	Pirates	FCL Pirates Black
PIRG	FCL Pirates Gold	FCL	Pirates	FCL Pirates Gold
PIT	Pittsburgh	NL	-	Pirates
PMB	Palm Beach	A SE	Cardinals	Cardinals
PNS	Pensacola	AA S	Marlins	Blue Wahoos
POR	Portland	AA NE	Red Sox	Sea Dogs
POT	Potomac	CAR	Nationals	Nationals
PRN	Princeton	APP	Rays	Rays
PUE	Puebla	MEX	-	Pericos
PUL	Pulaski	APP	Yankees	Yankees
PUR	Puerto Rico	CS	-	Puerto Rico
QC	Quad Cities	A+ C	Royals	River Bandits
RA12	RA12	PWL	-	RA12
RAN	ACL Rangers	ACL	Rangers	ACL Rangers
RAN	AZL Rangers	AZL	Rangers	AZL Rangers
RAY	FCL Rays	FCL	Rays	FCL Rays
RAY	GCL Rays	GCL	Rays	GCL Rays
RC	Rancho Cuca.	A W	Dodgers	Quakes
RCK	ACL Rockies	ACL	Rockies	ACL Rockies
RCT	Rocket City	AA S	Angels	Trash Pandas
REA	Reading	AA NE	Phillies	Fightin Phils
RED	ACL Reds	ACL	Reds	ACL Reds
RED	AZL Reds	AZL	Reds	AZL Reds
RIC	Richmond	AA NE	Giants	Flying Squirrels
RMV	Rocky Mountain	PIO	Brewers	Vibes
RNO	Reno	AAA W	D-backs	Aces
ROC	Rochester	AAA E	Nationals	Red Wings
ROM	Rome	A+ E	Braves	Braves
ROY	AZL Royals	AZL	Royals	AZL Royals
ROYB	ACL Royals Blue	ACL	Royals	ACL Royals Blue
ROYG	ACL Royals Gold	ACL	Royals	ACL Royals Gold
RR	Round Rock	AAA W	Rangers	Express
RSX	FCL Red Sox	FCL	Red Sox	FCL Red Sox
RSX	GCL Red Sox	GCL	Red Sox	GCL Red Sox

CODE	TEAM	LG	AFF	NAME
SA	San Antonio	AA C	Padres	Missions
SAC	Sacramento	AAA W	Giants	River Cats
SAL	Salem	A E	Red Sox	Red Sox
SAL	Saltillo	MEX	-	Saraperos
SAN	Santurce	PWL	Santurce	Santurce
SB	South Bend	A+ C	Cubs	Cubs
SC	State College	NYP	Cardinals	Spikes
SCO	Scottsdale	AFL	-	Scorpions
SD	San Diego	NL	-	Padres
SD1	AZL Padres 1	AZL	Padres	AZL Padres 1
SD2	AZL Padres 2	AZL	Padres	AZL Padres 2
SEA	Seattle	AL	-	Mariners
SF	San Francisco	NL	-	Giants
SI	Staten Island	NYP	Yankees	Yankees
SJ	San Jose	A W	Giants	Giants
SK	Salem-Keizer	NWL	Giants	Volcanoes
SL	Salt Lake	AAA W	Angels	Bees
SLU	St. Lucie	A SE	Mets	Mets
SOM	Somerset	AA NE	Yankees	Patriots
SPO	Spokane	A+ W	Rockies	Spokane
SPR	Springfield	AA C	Cardinals	Cardinals
SRR	Salt River	AFL	-	Rafters
STK	Stockton	A W	Athletics	Ports
STL	St. Louis	NL	-	Cardinals
STL	St. Lucie	FSL	Mets	Mets
STP	St. Paul	AAA E	Twins	Saints
SUG	Sugar Land	AAA W	Astros	Skeeters
SUR	Surprise	AFL	-	Saguaros
SWB	Scranton/WB	AAA E	Yankees	RailRiders
SYD	Sydney	ABL	Blue Sox	Blue Sox
SYR	Syracuse	AAA E	Mets	Mets
TAB	Tabasco	MEX	-	Olmecas
TAC	Tacoma	AAA W	Mariners	Rainiers
TAM	Tampa	A SE	Yankees	Tarpons
TB	Tampa Bay	AL	-	Rays
TDN	Tren del Norte		-	Tren del Norte
TEX	Texas	AL	-	Rangers
TIG	GCL Tigers East	GCL	Tigers	GCL Tigers East
TIG	Quintana Roo	MEX	-	Tigres
TIGE	FCL Tigers East	FCL	Tigers	FCL Tigers East
TIGW	FCL Tigers West	FCL	Tigers	FCL Tigers West
TIJ	Tijuana	MEX	-	Toros
TIW	GCL Tigers West	GCL	Tigers	GCL Tigers West
TNS	Tennessee	AA S	Cubs	Smokies
TOL	Toledo	AAA E	Tigers	Mud Hens
TOR	Toronto	AL	-	Blue Jays
TOR	Toros	LIDOM	-	Toros
TRI	Tri-City	A+ W	Angels	Dust Devils
TRI	Tri-City	NYP	Astros	ValleyCats
TRN	Trenton	EAS	Yankees	Thunder
TUL	Tulsa	AA C	Dodgers	Drillers
TWI	FCL Twins	FCL	Twins	FCL Twins
TWI	GCL Twins	GCL	Twins	GCL Twins
VAN	Vancouver	A+ W	Blue Jays	Canadians
VEN	Venezuela	CS	-	Venezuela
VER	Vermont	NYP	Athletics	Lake Monsters
VIS	Visalia	A W	D-backs	Rawhide
WCH	Wichita	AA C	Twins	Wind Surge
WIL	Williamsport	NYP	Phillies	Crosscutters
WIL	Wilmington	A+ E	Nationals	Blue Rocks
WIS	Wisconsin	A+ C	Brewers	Timber Rattlers
WM	West Michigan	A+ C	Tigers	Whitecaps
WOR	Worcester	AAA E	Red Sox	Red Sox
WS	Winston-Salem	A+ E	White Sox	Dash

CODE	TEAM	LG	AFF	NAME
WAS	Washington	NL	-	Nationals
WSX	ACL White Sox	ACL	White Sox	ACL White Sox
WSX	AZL White Sox	AZL	White Sox	AZL White Sox
WV	West Virginia	NYP	Pirates	Black Bears
WV	West Virginia	SAL	Mariners	Power
YAE	GCL Yankees East	GCL	Yankees	GCL Yankees East
YAW	GCL Yankees West	GCL	Yankees	GCL Yankees West
YNK	FCL Yankees	FCL	Yankees	FCL Yankees
YUC	Yucatan	MEX	-	Leones
ZUL	Zulia	LVBP	Aguilas	Aguilas

Contributors

Robert Au is the Director of Operations at Baseball Prospectus. His San Francisco Bay Area household includes three other humans and a heat-seeking cat.

Darius Austin is a fantasy writer and depth-chart administrator at Baseball Prospectus. He'd like to say he's the UK's biggest Tim Lincecum fan, but it's much more likely he's the UK's biggest Ryan Webb fan.

Emma Baccellieri is a staff writer for *Sports Illustrated*, where she writes mostly about baseball. She still has not finished reading *The Power Broker*. She lives in Washington, DC.

Demetrius Bell is a writer whose work has been found on plenty of websites. Some of these websites are established names on the internet. Others came and went within two weeks. Currently, you can find him writing about baseball for SB Nation's Atlanta Braves blog and giving opinions about sports logos and uniforms in general on Forbes Sports.

Sydney Bergman is an educator and writer living in the Washington, DC, area. In her spare time, she collects data about player ejections and writes baseball romance novels under the name KD Casey. Her debut novel, *Unwritten Rules*, is available through Carina Press, a Harlequin imprint.

Daniel Brim was born and raised in L.A. and grew up obsessed with the Dodgers. In 2014, he co-founded *Dodgers Digest*, and his work has also appeared at *The Athletic* and *The Hardball Times*. The third sentence is where the clever thing is supposed to go, but he couldn't think of anything.

Grant Brisbee is a staff writer for *The Athletic*, where he writes about the San Francisco Giants. He lives in an Oakland suburb with his two daughters, two dogs and one wife, and he will tell you that he coaches his daughter's softball team if you talk to him for more than a minute.

Shawn Brody is a former writer for *Beyond the Box Score* and BP Mets. He now works for the BP Stats team on PECOTA and other assorted projects and is happy he gets to do research without the need to write about it. Now that he has finished grad school, he lives with his wife in Austin, Texas.

Russell A. Carleton is actually a respected health policy, program evaluation professional and father of five in Atlanta. Seriously. He writes about baseball at night so that his wife won't bug him.

Ben Carsley is a Senior Author at Baseball Prospectus. When he's not writing about baseball, Ben can be found cooking, drinking wine, thinking about cooking and drinking wine and losing NFL parlays. By day, he manages a team of SEO analysts and content writers who are fairly convinced he's Ron Swanson. By night, he's a personal assistant to his cat.

Alex Chamberlain is a 30-grade econometrician who writes for RotoGraphs, the fantasy baseball arm of FanGraphs. He is an eight-time Fantasy Sports Writers Association award finalist and was 2018's FSWA Baseball Writer of the Year. He tries and largely fails to conduct Statcast research and distill it into something digestible. Mostly, he's the Mike Tauchman guy.

Michael Clair is a writer for MLB.com. He believes in the aesthetic beauty of sacrifice bunts and stirrup socks and would like to know why there aren't more reports of UAP (Unidentified Aerial Phenomena) above baseball stadiums—Bernard Gilkey in *Men in Black* notwithstanding.

Alex Coffey is a Phillies beat writer for *The Philadelphia Inquirer*. She previously covered the Oakland A's for The Athletic Bay Area.

Cliff Corcoran is a national baseball writer and a freelance book editor who has contributed to eight Baseball Prospectus Annuals, five as a writer and now three as an editor. He has also contributed to several other baseball books, including BP's *Mind Game* and *It Ain't Over 'Til It's Over*, and edited Howard Bryant's *Juicing the Game* and Brad Snyder's *A Well-Paid Slave*. Perhaps best known for his past work at SI.com and *The Athletic*, he is the author of the daily *MLBTR Newsletter* and his own baseball newsletter, *The Cycle*.

Zach Crizer is the baseball editor at Yahoo Sports and a former Baseball Prospectus columnist. He lives in New York City.

Patrick Dubuque has served at Baseball Prospectus as writer, editor and guy with ideas that seem like too much work since 2015. He also founded and managed Short Relief, BP's gone-but-not-forgotten literary vertical. He lives in the Pacific Northwest with his wife Kjersten and his two impetuous children.

Mike Duncan is one of the most popular history podcasters in the world and author of the *New York Times*–bestselling books *Hero of Two Worlds: The Marquis de Lafayette in the Age of Revolution* and *The Storm Before the Storm: The Beginning of the End of the Roman Republic*. His award-winning series *The History of Rome* remains a legendary landmark in the history of podcasting. Duncan's ongoing series, *Revolutions*, explores the great political revolutions that have driven the course of modern history. Born and raised in Redmond, Washington, he was assigned to the Seattle Mariners at birth by the gods of baseball geography.

Daniel R. Epstein contributes to Baseball Prospectus, Off the Bench Baseball, and *Bronx Pinstripes*. He also serves as co-director of the Internet Baseball Writers Association of America. Outside of baseball, he is an elementary special-education teacher, president of the Somerset County Education Association, a drummer, a father of two and a husband of one.

Drew Fairservice is the co-host of *The Athletic*'s *Spin Rate* podcast covering the Toronto Blue Jays. He used to write a lot about baseball for *The Score*, FanGraphs and *VICE* Sports, but now he only writes a little.

Connor Farrell is a lifelong Rockies sufferer (or fan, depending how you view it) who has written for SB Nation and various dead blogs. He currently lives in Michigan, where he stays up until 1:00 a.m. over 30 nights a year to watch the Rockies lose by six runs in California. It's a lot of fun, and he wouldn't trade it for anything.

James Fegan is a staff writer for *The Athletic* covering the Chicago White Sox, a team he has written about in some form since 2010, with stops at Baseball Prospectus, FanSided, ESPN Sweetspot Network and others.

Chad Finn is sports media and online columnist at *The Boston Globe* and Boston.com. He lives in Wells, Maine, with his wife, Jen, children, Leah and Alex, and four replacement-level cats. He deeply misses the Maine Guides and remains the internet's foremost Butch Hobson apologist.

Noah Frank is a freelance writer and editor in Washington, DC, and a contributing writer for Baseball Prospectus. Contrary to popular belief, he did not conceive of NATITUDE, but he is at least partially responsible for its widespread use.

Bailey Freeman is the creator of the YouTube channel Foolish Baseball, where he produces a flagship video essay series called *Baseball Bits*. He lives in Atlanta, where he's very proud of his apartment balcony and in-unit washer/dryer.

Ken Funck has contributed to the Baseball Prospectus Annual each year since 2009, during which time saplings became trees, children blossomed into adults, and baseball analytics grew from nerdy outsider subculture to core organizational competency. Ken designs and manages Business Intelligence systems and lives outside Madison, Wisconsin, with his wife, Stephanie (an ideal travel companion and the worst possible choice to participate in any focus group), a van that doubles as a camper but is not a camper van, and an enduring belief that the Oxford comma has its time and place. [*We left this one in for him. –ed.*]

Brendan Gawlowski is a weekly contributor at FanGraphs. He lives in Seattle with his wife, Sierra, and dog, Yukon; she is still part of the family.

Mike Gianella is a senior writer at Baseball Prospectus. He lives in Pennsylvania with his wife, two awesome kids and two annoying cats. He's still a Mets fan for some stupid reason.

Steven Goldman, former BP editor-in-chief and current consulting editor, edited, co-edited and contributed to multiple volumes of this book and was also responsible for BP's books *Mind Game*, *It Ain't Over 'Til It's Over*, and *Extra Innings: More Baseball Between the Numbers*. He's also the author of the Casey Stengel biography *Forging Genius*. His work has appeared in numerous other places ranging from *Deadspin* to *The Daily Beast*. He's the host of the long-running *Infinite Inning* podcast, which sits at the crossroads of baseball, history, politics and culture. All of the above originates from New Jersey, where he resides with his wife, son, occasionally his daughter, three cats and an unmanageable number of books, the mass of which has only grown since the last edition.

Craig Goldstein is the editor-in-chief of Baseball Prospectus. His work has appeared in *Sports Illustrated*, *VICE* Sports, Fox Sports MLB/JABO and SB Nation MLB. He lives in Maryland, where he spends just the right amount of time being Jokerfied.

Bryan Grosnick is an author of Baseball Prospectus and has consulted for both an MLB franchise and a Little League one. This is his eighth consecutive appearance in the Annual, for which he is very thankful. He lives in New England with his vegetable-enthusiast wife, as well as his outstanding son, two dogs, and an increasingly large collection of unconventional Christmas cards.

Jon Hegglund has trick-or-treated at Johnnie LeMaster's house and had his younger siblings share a babysitter with Robby Thompson's kids, earning Jon his stripes as a millennium-spanning Giants fan. He currently lives in Idaho, works in Washington, and still dreams of the glorious refrigerated wind tunnel that was Candlestick Park. On sabbatical from fantasy-baseball writing, most of Jon's wit, wisdom, dog photos, kitchen hacks and beard influencing can currently be found on Twitter.

Jonathan Judge is a lawyer who also designs statistics and models for Baseball Prospectus. He believes in hierarchical (modeling) structures, full paragraph justification, and two spaces between sentences. [*We did not leave this in for him. –ed.*]

Justin Klugh is an award-winning writer and podcaster whose work has appeared in *The Philadelphia Inquirer*, *The Athletic*, *Baltimore Magazine*, Baseball Prospectus, FanGraphs and SB Nation MLB. His thoughtful critiques of baseball stock photos are available on Twitter free of charge.

Patrick Lackey is a biochemistry professor at Westminster College in New Wilmington, Pennsylvania. In a previous lifetime, he chronicled the trials and tribulations of the Pittsburgh Pirates on his blog, *Where Have You Gone, Andy Van Slyke?*.

Rob Mains is a writer at Baseball Prospectus, where his career in finance is distressingly handy in discussing the game today. He lives in a redoubt in upstate New York surrounded by Finger Lakes wine, waging a lonely battle to preserve the *Chicago Manual of Style* usage of the word "only."

Kelsey McKinney is a staff writer and co-owner of Defector Media. Her first novel *God Spare the Girls* came out in 2021, and she still scores all the games she watches with a pen. She never learns.

Dan McQuade is a co-founder of Defector Media and the site's video and multimedia editor. He lives in Philadelphia with his wife and their perfect cat.

Brian Menéndez is a contributor to Baseball Prospectus, *FiveThirtyEight* and *DRaysBay*. He lives in Seattle, Washington, where he fathers two cats, Leonard and Lily, who are also avid baseball fans. At least, they haven't told him otherwise. When they wrestle, he imagines they are arguing over whether xFIP or DRA is a better metric for evaluating pitchers.

Steve Neuman (aka *RandBall*'s Stu) is a St. Paul-based copywriter by day. He writes for *Twins Daily* and co-hosts *The Sportive* podcast on nights and weekends. He keeps Junior Ortiz in his heart forever.

Joan Niesen is an editor at *The Athletic* who still tries to write as much as she can in her free time. She previously reported, wrote and hosted a narrative podcast about the steroid era, *Crushed*, and worked as a staff writer at *Sports Illustrated*, *The Denver Post* and FoxSports.com. She grew up in St. Louis, still watches far too many of that particular baseball team's games (sorry!), and now lives in Washington, DC.

Alva Noë is a philosopher at the University of California, Berkeley. He is the author of *Infinite Baseball: Notes from a Philosopher at the Ballpark* (Oxford, 2019), as well as other writings about perception, consciousness and art.

Marc Normandin currently writes on baseball's labor issues at marcnormandin.com and about retro video games at retroxp.substack.com. He is one of the founding members of *Publication To Be Named Later*, and frequently writes labor-centric features for Baseball Prospectus. His writing has also appeared at SB Nation, *Defector*, *Deadspin*, *Sports Illustrated*, ESPN, *Sports on Earth*, *The Guardian*, *The Nation*, and *TalkPoverty*.

Dustin Nosler is one of the co-founders of *Dodgers Digest*. His work has also appeared at *The Hardball Times* and SB Nation. He resides in Stockton, California, with his wife and their horde of cats and dogs.

Robert O'Connell is a writer and editor whose work has appeared in *Sports Illustrated*, *The Atlantic*, *Defector*, *The New York Times* and other publications.

Jeffrey Paternostro is the Lead Prospect Writer and Multimedia Production Manager for Baseball Prospectus. He does podcasts, prospect lists, has gotten really into fancy coffee, and might try out being a Free Jazz guy and making his own bitters in 2022.

Harry Pavlidis is the director of R&D for Baseball Prospectus.

Mike Piellucci is the sports editor at *D Magazine*. He is a former staffer at *The Athletic*, *Front Office Sports*, and *VICE* Sports, and his freelance work has been featured in *Sports Illustrated*, *The New York Times*, *Los Angeles Magazine*, and *The Ringer*. He lives in Dallas with his wife and rescue dog.

Amy Pircher is a software engineer for NASA JPL by day and Baseball Prospectus by night. Her cats think she should do neither.

Kate Preusser is a contributor at Baseball Prospectus and editor-in-chief at SB Nation's *Lookout Landing*, where she writes about the Mariners and spends too much time considering the hip-size-to-power ratio of Dylan Moore.

Matthew Ritchie is a graduate student at the Medill School of Journalism at Northwestern. His work has appeared in *Pitchfork*, *Hip Hop DX*, and *Audiomack*, as he also freelances as a music writer. He lives in Chicago, where he's continually locked in a battle with the CTA Brown line.

David Roth is a co-founder and co-owner of *Defector* and the co-host of *The Distraction* podcast. He is from New Jersey and lives in New York.

Shaker Samman is a writer based in Los Angeles. His work has previously appeared in *Sports Illustrated*, *The Ringer*, *The Guardian*, *Slate*, and the *Tampa Bay Times*. His time at Baseball Prospectus mostly involved him sending dumb memes to coworkers. Don't follow him on Twitter.

Bret Sayre is the President of Baseball Prospectus. By day, he tells investment professionals what not to do. By night, he is a full-time family man and part-time nurse, cook, dynasty ranker, copy editor, musician and human dog toy. As an eight-year-old boy, he was knocked over by a man in his thirties as he tried to catch a dead ball thrown by Kevin Mitchell at Shea Stadium. Now, he lives in New Jersey with his wife, Carolyn, their two children, Aly and Josh, a big-eyed bear named Hobbes, a fridge full of wine and more baseball and softball training equipment than a mid-range sporting-goods store.

Janice Scurio is an IT professional with degrees in English literature and library science. Her work has appeared in SB Nation (*South Side Sox*), Baseball Prospectus, *Sports Illustrated* and *NBC Sports EDGE*. She lives in the north suburbs of Chicago on a steady diet of hot dogs and pizza.

Ginny Searle is a writer and an associate editor for Baseball Prospectus. Her work has previously appeared in SB Nation, *Deadspin* (RIP), and *Allure*. She lives in Southern California and spends her free time reading dead authors and developing backstories for stuffed animals.

Andrew Seeley is putting his Classics degree to good use as a data scientist for a consulting company that advises water and wastewater utilities, and he promises that this isn't a Mad Lib. He lives in Minnesota, and he appreciates the local weather and sports teams for teaching him that Good Things Aren't Possible.

Jarrett Seidler is the Senior Prospect Writer and Evaluation Coordinator for Baseball Prospectus. He also co-hosts *For All You Kids Out There*, a weekly BP podcast which is occasionally about the Mets. As a lifelong New Jersey resident, he strongly disagrees with MJF that Long Island is the most magical place in the world; it's actually the Jersey Shore.

Jordan Shusterman is one half of Céspedes Family BBQ. His work has appeared on Baseball Prospectus, Cut4, MLB Pipeline and *The Ringer*. He lives in Washington, DC, and is an MLB analyst for FOX Sports Digital. When he's not covering Major or Minor League Baseball, he's podcasting about Division-III baseball. No, seriously.

Susan Slusser covered the Oakland A's for 23 years for the *San Francisco Chronicle* before moving to the Giants beat in 2021. She is the only woman to have served as the president of the BBWAA, and she is glad to no longer have to write about *Moneyball*.

Ben Spanier is a member of BP's prospect team and also a twentysomething North Carolina resident who enjoys moderate hikes and popular indie music when he isn't scouring the biographical details of Low-A baseball players.

Matt Sussman is an IT professional from Toledo, Ohio, the head drawmaster at the Bowling Green Curling Club, and writes about baseball and curling depending on the outdoor temperature.

Michael Tae Sweeney is a film and television editor who lives in San Diego. In his spare time, he is the host of *The Next American Built Environment*, a podcast about urban planning and transportation.

Jon Tayler is an editor at FanGraphs and a former writer at *Sports Illustrated*, where he never did find a football phone. He lives in New York City, where he can get you a good deal if you're looking to buy a bridge, and would like to apologize to Mets fans for the number of times he described the franchise in his player comments as, essentially, a haunted house run by drunks.

Shakeia Taylor is a writer based in Chicago. Her work focuses on the intersection of Black culture and sport in America and has appeared in such places as *FiveThirtyEight*, MLB.com, Yahoo Sports, and *Victory Journal*.

Lauren Theisen is a co-owner and a blog girl at *Defector*, where she writes about hockey prospects, pro-wrestling pay-per-views and everything in between. A New Yorker by way of Livonia, Michigan, she occupies her time by remembering Guys, including but not limited to Brennan Boesch, Adam Everett and Jonathan Broxton.

John Trupin is a former crafty righty and current youth counselor who scouts the minor leagues with a focus on the Pacific Northwest. He lives in Seattle, where he spends his time appreciating retractable roofs and advances in field-turf technology.

Hi, I'm **Levi Weaver**, and I have taken a solemn vow to stop writing bios in the third person. I cover the Texas Rangers for *The Athletic*—not the Athletics, which is a distinction that has caused confusion more often than you might think. I used to drive around and play guitar for people, but now I'm about to start my seventh year of writing about the Rangers and (probably unrelated??) I started therapy this year. Things are going great! My favorite album of 2021 was *Crawler* by IDLES. Okay, this feels long enough. Thanks for reading!

Collin Whitchurch is the MLB editor for The Action Network and a former editor for Baseball Prospectus. He lives in Austin, where he's tired of thinking of something witty to say about the weather, music scene and/or college football.

Tony Wolfe is a writer who has worked for FanGraphs and *Red Reporter*, as well as daily newspapers like the *Times West Virginian* and *The Lima News*. He lives in Columbus, Ohio, where he can be found cooking fried chicken, and also eating it.

Alex Wong is a writer, author and producer based in Toronto. He has written for *The New York Times*, *The Atlantic*, ESPN, *GQ* and other places.

Acknowledgments

Robert Au: Thank you to the human and feline members of my family for bringing me joy and love. To those of you who have departed, I miss you. Thanks again to everyone on the BP stats team for your camaraderie and hard work; to Kathy Woolner and Rob Mains for their patience and diligence; and to Craig Goldstein for inviting me into this crazy world in the first place.

Darius Austin: Rob Mains and the rest of the tireless Depth Charts team: Kaz Yamazaki, Randy Holt, Brian Duricy, Derek Albin and Tim McCullough. J.P. Breen, Mark Barry and the rest of the BP Fantasy crew for another year of excellent content and outstanding advice. The *Bat Flips and Nerds* team, a constant source of daft inspiration and unwavering support: John McGee, Tom Pringle, Ben Carter, Russell Eassom, Rob Noverraz, Rachel Steinberg and Gavin Tramps.

Emma Baccellieri: Every person and group chat who continues to help make writing about baseball such a joy.

Demetrius Bell: Patricia Bell, Garry Bell, Sheretha Bell, Kris Willis, Gaurav Vedak, the Baseball Prospectus editorial staff, anybody who has read and shared anything I've ever written and published and Xavier Wulf.

Sydney Bergman: Thank you to the Bear-pen, Jenn, Dara, Noah and Kay; my publishing buddy Nathalie; my book midwife Laura; my family, who read my books even when I say not to; and to Sam, who cares not for baseball but a lot for me.

Daniel Brim: Thanks to Mom and Dad for putting up with my baseball obsession. To grandpa Dick for making sure I was a Dodger fan before he passed on. To Dustin Nosler, Mike Petriello and Chad Moriyama for taking a chance on an extremely unproven baseball writer. To everybody who has come through *Dodgers Digest* since for making us lifers look better by being closer to your work. And finally, to the Baseball Prospectus team for inviting me to contribute this year.

Grant Brisbee: Thanks to my co-workers, family and friends. No thanks to the editor who removed the serial comma from that last sentence.

Shawn Brody: Thank you to my wife, Grace, for your patience in tolerating my perpetually inconsistent schedule and incoherent rants about the Mets and MLB economics. Thank you to my mom, dad, brother, friends and family for always supporting me and ensuring at least 10 views on anything I wrote/recorded. Thank you to R.J. Anderson, who has helped me continue to push forward more than almost anyone I know, and Harry Pavlidis for allowing me the privilege to work with the amazing folks on the BP Stats team.

Ben Carsley: My Red Sox–crazed family, the ever-patient Allyson Carsley, Bret Sayre, Craig Goldstein, Sam Miller, R.J. Anderson, Patrick Dubuque, Robert O'Connell, Xander Bogaerts, Mary Donovan, Daniel Ohman, anyone who doesn't tweet and the C-4 Content Team. RIP, Jerry Remy.

Alex Chamberlain: Jill, for always supporting me no matter how much longer it takes me to write than I say it will; Remi, for simply being; Dad, for the genesis of a lifetime of love for baseball; Mom, who I know would have been proud of me and read everything I wrote; Eric Longenhagen, for letting me annoy you immensely; Patrick Dubuque, for knowingly wasting a chapter on me; Craig Goldstein, for the reassurances; Eno Sarris, for giving me a shot forever ago; everyone else, for believing in me (or not).

Michael Clair: Thanks much to Marissa Maggs for withstanding hours of spin-rate discussion, Dan Epstein, Mike Petriello and Davy Andrews for a very loud outlet, my amazingly kind and insightful MLB.com colleagues, and every reader who believes in supporting good and weird sportswriting.

Cliff Corcoran: Thank you to Robert Au, Patrick Dubuque, Craig Goldstein and Robert O'Connell for their patience with my incessant queries and nitpicking, to Bret Sayre and Craig Brown for additional support, and to Steven Goldman for his friendship, compassion and constant faith. Thanks also to my wife and daughter for allowing and enabling me to work from home for the last 14 years, and to our pets for keeping me company while I do.

Zach Crizer: Thanks to Craig Goldstein and R.J. Anderson for being an incalculably valuable brain trust, to Hannah Keyser for keeping me honest and engaged, to Patrick Dubuque for the thoughtful guidance, to Nerd Chat 2.0 for keeping things interesting, and to Amy for turning up the volume and showing me a more deeply felt way of loving baseball.

Patrick Dubuque: Thanks to Kjersten, Sylvie and Felix for accepting late afternoons and punctual bedtimes, and for putting up with a sport that only really exists as an obstruction for more interesting television and as faces cut out of 1990 Upper Deck baseball cards. Thanks also to Detroit Tigers reliever Paul Gibson.

Daniel Epstein: Thanks to Heather, Andrew, Sofia, Ronni and Ray, Theresa and Joe, Max Frankel and Sean Morash, the *Banished to the Pen* guys, the North American Strat-O-Matic Association (except for Eric), a very good band called Subway Ghosts (Davy Andrews, Michael Clair and Mike Petriello), Jonathan Becker and the IBWAA, I suppose J Shin, and fifth infielder Tyler Saladino for playing "right field" in 2016. That was cool.

Drew Fairservice: Thanks to Lauren, Maddie, Wilson and Pancakes the dog for affording me space and/or whips, as required. Thanks to my co-host Kaitlyn and former co-host Stoeten. Forever in debt to invaluable resources FanGraphs, Baseball Savant, Baseball-Reference and, of course, Baseball Prospectus—Jeff and the prospect team specifically—for enabling this delightful hidden world. Thanks to Craig and Patrick for the opportunity.

Connor Farrell: My grandfather James and my mother, Leslie, for giving me the talent to write. My 12th grade English teacher Beth Dent for telling me I was good and to stop being a screw up. My wife, Suzy, for not being too worried about me when I stay up late to whine about baseball. My father, Kevin, and my grandmother Carol for showing me that loving sports can be a beautiful thing too.

James Fegan: Almost every player commented upon here has given me a moment of their time to describe their game, their approach, their strengths and struggles. I thank them and apologize in advance.

Chad Finn: Thank you to so many colleagues, friends and family that have been there for me or inspired me during my sports writing career: Mike Pride, Yuri Pride, Steve Mistler, Jeff Novotny, Dave Cummings, Ray Duckler, Sandy Smith, Dana Wormald, Matthew T. Hall, Dave D'Onofrio, CJ Lampman, Hans Schulz, Bob Ryan, Peter Gammons, Dan Shaughnessy, Peter Abraham, Alex Speier, Julian McWilliams, the late, great Nick Cafardo, Scott Thurston, Ken Fratus, Gary Dzen, Matt Pepin, Bob Hohler, Fluto Shinzawa, Greg Lee, Joe Sullivan, Katie McInerney, Greg Lang, Jim Hoban, Jim McBride, Dave Lefort, Eric Wilbur, Steve Silva, Chris Greenberg, Rachel Bowers, Andrew Mahoney, Steve Buckley, Kris Poulin, Tom Poulin, Tim Hopley, Chris Castellano, John Black, Chris DeBeck and Milo Finn.

Noah Frank: To the editors of this massive labor of love and to editors everywhere, who are largely overlooked and vastly underappreciated . . . thanks.

Bailey Freeman: Thank you to my parents for believing in my unorthodox career, my Youtube viewers for indulging me, and Jeff Mathis for still being Jeff Mathis.

Ken Funck: R.J. Anderson, Steph Bee, Patrick Dubuque, Aaron Gleeman, Steven Goldman, Craig Goldstein, Christina Kahrl, King Kaufman, Ben Lindbergh, Sam Miller, Robert O'Connell, John Perrotto, Bret Sayre, Cecilia Tan, Jason Wojciechowski and anyone else who has worked their editorial magic on my behalf.

Brendan Gawlowski: I would like to thank Patrick Dubuque and Craig Goldstein for their patience with my laissez-faire approach to deadlines this year. I would also like to thank Eric Longenhagen and Meg Rowley for helping me write the projects I want to write, and to my wife, Sierra, without whom I'd never get anything done.

Mike Gianella: Colleen, Lucy and Elliot for being there and supporting my love of baseball, even if they don't always understand it. Bret Sayre, Mark Barry, J.P. Breen and everyone else on the awesome fantasy team at Baseball Prospectus. Alex Patton, Steve Gardner, Peter Kreutzer, Jeff Erickson, Eric Karabell, Tristan Cockcroft and so many others in the fantasy industry whose advice and contributions were instrumental along the way. Jon Hegglund and Samuel Hale, who started out as a podcast co-host and producer and ended as friends and two instrumental people in my life.

Steven Goldman: As always, immeasurable gratitude to Stefanie, Sarah, Clemens, Reuven, Eliane, Ilana, Andy, Rick, Cliff, Mickey, Raven and Charity for making the work possible.

Craig Goldstein: Katherine and Charlie Pappas, Laurie Gross, Harvey Goldstein, Alexis Goldstein, Tony Pappas, Patrick Dubuque, Robert O'Connell, R.J. Anderson, Bret Sayre, Sam Miller, Jason Wojchiechowski, Ginny Searle, Marc Normandin, Shaker Samman, Rob McQuown, Ben Carsley, Jacob Raim, Harry Pavlidis, Jeffrey Paternostro, Lucas Apostoleris, Jonathan Judge, Rob Mains, Jason Parks, Ben Lindbergh, the BP Prospect Team, Jarrett Seidler, Zach Mortimer, Tucker Blair, Ethan Purser, Mike Ferrin, Tommy Rancel, Michael Baumann, Meg Rowley, James Fegan, Emma Baccellieri, Shakeia Taylor, Mauricio Rubio, Bradford William Davis, J.P. Breen, Zach Crizer, Amy Pircher, Robert Au.

Bryan Grosnick: Sarah Grosnick, Luke Grosnick, Phil and Debbie Grosnick, Craig Goldstein, Jonathan Judge, Robert Au, Patrick Dubuque, Brendan Gawlowski, Bret Sayre, R.J. Anderson, Jarrett Seidler, Jeffrey Paternostro, Jason Wojciechowski, Sam Miller, bubble tea, Blake Newberry and the staff at Viva el Birdos, the BP Stats team, and the data providers at Baseball Prospectus, FanGraphs, Baseball-Reference, Brooks Baseball, and Baseball Savant.

Jon Hegglund: Thank you to the *Flags* crew, Mike and Samuel, for taking a fantasy podcast and making it into a gloriously whimsical and sustaining group-therapy session during some difficult times. RIP, Weird Flags. Thanks to Duane Kuiper, Mike Krukow, Jon Miller and Dave Fleming for keeping me company last summer. And thanks to Emily and Oscar for everything else.

Justin Klugh: My lovely small wife for her support, my wonderful parents and two sisters for being a loving baseball family, my grandparents for establishing a baseball family, and my friends for never listening to or reading my work but supporting me nonetheless. Also, the BP editors for always thinking of and/or for me while they make my writing better.

Patrick Lackey: Thanks to Patrick Dubuque and Baseball Prospectus for the opportunity to write this essay after close to six years away from baseball writing, and for the patience and thoughtful suggestions that helped me get back on track after spending so long away. One of the great joys of writing my blog for as long as I did is that, through its lifetime, I made a number of internet friends who eventually just became friends. They have been asking me for years when I was going to write about baseball again, and so this is for them. Primarily, though, I want to acknowledge my dad, Gary, for introducing me to baseball and for spending countless spring and summer nights with me on the right field wall at PNC Park; this essay was shaped more by all of our conversations about the Pirates than anything else.

Rob Mains: My mother, Rhoda Mains, for instilling a love of the game and my wife, Amy Durland, for encouraging me to pursue it and often not regretting having done so. Martín Alonso, José Hernández, Marco Gámez, Pepe Latorre, and Carlos Pérez for making BP en español, our daily Spanish-language content, a reality. Craig Goldstein and Ginny Searle for putting up with my overuse of charts and tables. AM and PM for who they are.

Kelsey McKinney: Thank you to Baseball Prospectus for allowing me to file my essay late every single year. To my husband, Trey, who always supports me, and the whole *Defector* staff, who helped build a place where I have enough time to write things for fun.

Dan McQuade: This could not have been done without my wife, Jan Cohen, and my parents, Drew and Denise. Thanks to everyone at *Defector*; to Jason Merrill, the only person I know who will still text about the Phillies with me; and to Dave Hall, my favorite person to watch Phillies games with, in the hopes of better days ahead for us and the Phillies.

Brian Menéndez: Endless thanks to my wonderful and loving partner, Aimee, for supporting my pursuit of a career in baseball since Day One. To my father, who passed down his love of baseball to me, which he also got from his father. To all of the great people who have allowed me to write words on their platform: Danny Russell at *DRaysBay*, Kenny Kelly at *Beyond the Box Score*, Sara Ziegler at *FiveThirtyEight*, and Craig Goldstein at Baseball Prospectus. To everyone who has read and offered constructive criticism about my writings.

Steve Neuman: All the jokes that failed to land are mine. All the smart stuff came from reading smart and capable Twins/MLB content providers like Aaron Gleeman, Dan Hayes, Phil Miller, John Bonnes, Nick Nelson, Parker Hageman, Betsy Helfand and Do-Hyoung Park. My wife, Mandy, and daughters, Celia and Piper, are the finest support system one person could ever have.

Joan Niesen: I'd never written about baseball before I started working on *Crushed* at Religion of Sports, and getting to spend a year and a half immersed in the world of my favorite sport was more fun than I've had in a long time. A bonus podcast episode about sticky stuff inspired this essay, and without speaking at length with James Deffinbaugh, the co-creator of Spider Tack, and Dr. Alan Nathan, a physicist who studies baseball, I would have been downright ill-informed. Most of all, though, I have to thank Jesse: for being my partner in all things life and baseball and for pushing me to pitch stories when I'm certain no one wants to read my writing.

Alva Noë: Thanks to Patrick Dubuque for helpful comments.

Marc Normandin: Thanks to my friends and family for their support both this year and in others. I'd also like to curse my enemies and assume everyone knows which of these groups they belong to.

Dustin Nosler: My wife, my *Dodgers Digest* cohorts past and present—Cody Bashore, Max Bay, Daniel Brim, Alex Campos, Chad Moriyama, Mike Petriello, Sarah Wexler, Stacie Wheeler, Allan Yamashige—as well as Molly Knight, Eric Stephen, Josh Thomas and Jon Weisman.

Robert O'Connell: David Roth, Lenika Cruz, Adam Duerson, Patrick Dubuque and Craig Goldstein.

Jeffrey Paternostro: Jess for taking care of dinner and bedtime for when I have to be at the park for batting practice. Evelyn for being occasionally willing to sit still while I'm watching High-A video. Jarrett, even when he's annoying. Craig, especially when he's annoying. The BP Prospect Team for keeping me mostly on deadline this year.

Harry Pavlidis: Martín Alonso, Robert Au, Jonathan Judge, Sean O'Rourke, Shawn Brody, Amy Pircher.

Mike Piellucci: Thank you to my parents, Joe and Doreen, and my wife, Sarah—the three people without whom none of this would be possible. Thank you to my friends and family both in and out of the business, all of whom have created community in what can be an isolating profession. Lastly, thank you to you, for reading.

Amy Pircher: Thank you to my therapist for telling me to work less, only for me to mostly ignore it. Progress. And my cats, for forcing me to take breaks.

Kate Preusser: I'd like to acknowledge everyone who took a shaky cell-phone video of minor leaguers playing their first professional games on dusty back fields, especially those who cover the Padres' and Cubs' systems. I would also like to express gratitude for the wealth of medical knowledge shared online which helped me navigate the 2021 Padres' injured-list designations.

Matthew Ritchie: Thank you to my parents and brother, the Cedric Mullins Booster Club (Jake Mintz and Connor Newcomb), Chris Herring for reading through my nonsensical first draft, Baseball Reference and FanGraphs, and the 2021 Orioles for briefly restoring the feeling.

David Roth: I am lucky to be joined by so many members of *Defector*'s elite Quit Squad in this book, and grateful to have been asked back to write about a team that the editors suspected would make me upset. They were correct in this case, as they have been for the last eight Annuals. I read useful stuff for this essay in *The Arizona Republic*, FanGraphs, and (naturally) Baseball Prospectus. Thank you again to the editors, and to everyone who puts up with me.

Shaker Samman: Shoutout to Craig Goldstein, Patrick Dubuque, YouTube clips of the 2014 World Series, Baseball-Reference and the two dogs wailing like banshees throughout my attempts to finish writing my essay. Oh, and Lani Kim, who did her best to corral them.

Bret Sayre: Carolyn, for not only being better than me at everything, but not holding it against me. Aly and Josh, for always making me smile. Lynn and Peter Sayre. Team DIY. Craig Goldstein, Ben Carsley, Patrick Dubuque, Sam Miller, R.J. Anderson, Mike Gianella. The Heights Heat. The Jr Highlanders. My BH softball family. Annie Young. Rob McQuown.

Janice Scurio: The fine folks at *South Side Sox* for developing and perpetually encouraging my "wild card" narrative voice, and Shakeia Taylor for being an early set of eyes.

Ginny Searle: Thanks to so many people from BP, including but not limited to: Craig Goldstein, Patrick Dubuque, Shaker Samman, Rob Mains, Steven Goldman. Trans people: You are loved, you are wanted. To Tori: Thank you for you; IOU bones.

Andrew Seeley: Thank you to Haley, the best partner there is. Thank you to Jewel, the best cat there is. And thank you to the entire BP team, the best community there is.

Jarrett Seidler: For once I shall be uncharacteristically brief: Kate, for a little bit of everything, all of the time.

Jordan Shusterman: Bailey Bowers, David Shusterman, Rebecca Shusterman, Gila Shusterman, Alan Shusterman, Jake Mintz, Kinza Baad, Kendall Guillemette, Craig Goldstein, Patrick Dubuque, Zach Mortimer, Meg Rowley, Kiley McDaniel, Eric Longenhagen, Jim Callis, Ryan Divish, Matthew Roberson, Josh Herzenberg, Sarah Langs, Bailey Freeman, Amy Brachmann and Bobby Wagner.

Susan Slusser: Farhan Zaidi spoke with me to discuss the state and shape of the Giants in an interview on November 3, 2021.

Ben Spanier: I would like to thank my family and close friends for accepting that most conversations with me eventually devolve into baseball minutiae, at least briefly.

Matt Sussman: To Michael Sussman Shepard (1949–2021), a zealous Red Sox fan from Eugene, Oregon, who sent me whole sets of late '80s Topps baseball cards. They galvanized my interest in baseball, but I think Uncle Mike did it because he thought they'd be valuable someday.

Michael Tae Sweeney: I'd like to thank my beloved wife, Annie, for helping me find the time to write, and to thank the Orioles' Twitter DM for bringing up the 2016 AL Wild Card Game less than they used to.

Jon Tayler: Thanks to the fine folks at BP for letting me join the Annual party for a third year in a row and for being cool about the definition of "deadline." Thanks to Meg and the folks at FanGraphs for giving me a new baseball home. Thanks to the friends and family who helped keep me sane and upright in 2021. Thanks to Fisher for being Fisher.

Lauren Theisen: David Roth and Barry Petchesky.

John Trupin: My prospect-loathing partner, Isabelle Minasian, my friend and longest-tenured editor, Kate Preusser, Sarah Newgarde and the accommodating staff of the Everett AquaSox, Jeffrey Paternostro, Jarrett Seidler, and the rest of the BP prospect writing team, and, of course, Craig Goldstein, Patrick Dubuque, Shaker Samman, Ginny Searle and the rest of the editors.

Collin Whitchurch: Thanks to my parents for supporting my work, even if they still have only a vague understanding of what I do for a living. Thanks to Craig for letting me continue to contribute to this amazing book despite my joining The Dark Side. Thanks to Vladimir Guerrero Jr. (33/1) for leading the league in home runs in 2021.

Tony Wolfe: I'd like to thank Wick Terrell, Meg Rowley and my fiancée/live-in copy editor, Taylor. I would also like to thank my Aunt Wendy, who probably would not have actually read this book but would have been overjoyed to know I was in it.

Alex Wong: Thanks to anyone who has ever watched a Blue Jays game with me at the SkyDome. They include my parents and friends who I only exclusively have met and hung out with at the ballpark. ■

Index of Names

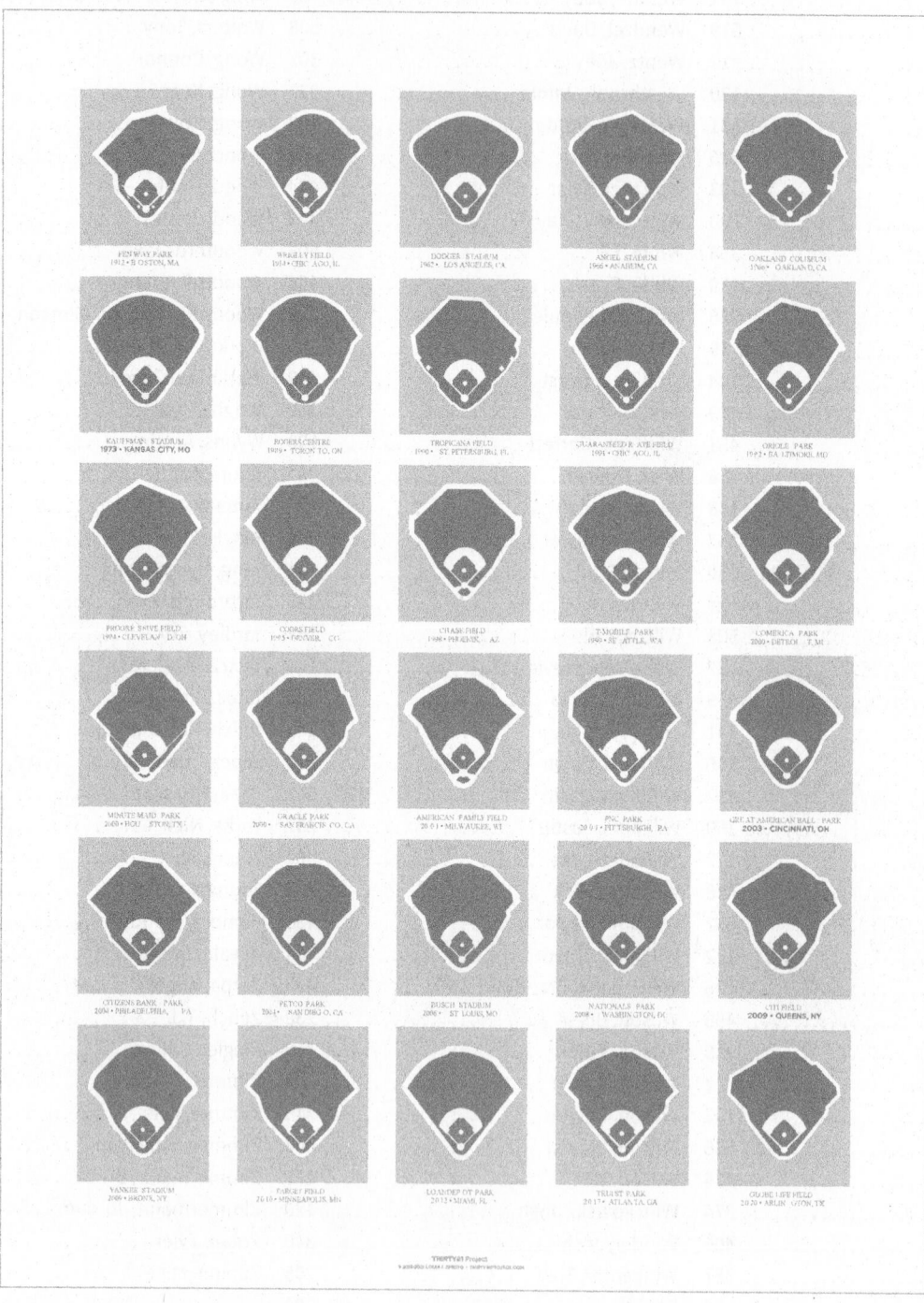